THIRD SUPPLEMENT TO
THE WORLD'S ENCYCLOPÆDIA OF
RECORDED MUSIC

THIRD SUPPLEMENT 1953-1955

TO

THE WORLD'S ENCYCLOPÆDIA OF RECORDED MUSIC

Compiled by

F. F. CLOUGH and G. J. CUMING

Associate Editor : E. A. HUGHES
Research Associate : Angela NOBLE

GREENWOOD PRESS, PUBLISHERS
WESTPORT, CONNECTICUT

The Library of Congress cataloged this book as follows:

Clough, Francis F   comp.
  The world's encyclopaedia of recorded music, by Francis
F. Clough and G. J. Cuming. Westport, Conn., Green-
wood Press [1970, ʿ1966]
    xviii, 890 p.   27 cm.
    First published in 1952.
    "First supplement, April 1950–June 1951" : p. 725–860.
    —— ——Supplement. 2d–3d; 1951/52–1953/55. Westport,
Conn., Greenwood Press [1970, ʿ1966]
    2 v.   27 cm.

	ML156.2.C6 1970 Suppl.	
1. Music—Discography.	I. Cuming, G. J., joint comp. II. Title.	
ML156.2.C6 1970	016.7899ʹ12	71–100214
ISBN 0–8371–3003–4		MARC
Library of Congress	71 [7]	MN

Copyright 1966 by Sidgwick and Jackson Ltd., London

Originally published in 1966 by Sidgwick and Jackson
Limited, London, in association with the Decca Record
Company Limited

Reprinted with the permission of Sidgwick and Jackson Ltd.

Reprinted by Greenwood Press,
a division of Williamhouse-Regency Inc.

First Greenwood Reprinting 1970
Second Greenwood Reprinting 1975

Library of Congress Catalog Card Number 71-100214

ISBN 0-8371-3003-4 (set)
ISBN 0-8371-3002-6 (Vol. 3)

Printed in the United States of America

FOREWORD

THE THIRD SUPPLEMENT to the WORLD'S ENCYCLOPÆDIA OF RECORDED MUSIC covers the new issues which have come to our notice from all countries during the period January 1953 to December 31st 1955, and, in addition, all English issues and re-issues, and certain other important new issues and re-issues, down to March 1956. As before, all possible endeavours have been made towards a proper and intelligible identification of the music recorded.

Our period may be fairly described as that of the greatest and most valuable expansion of the recorded repertory ever known. As we write in mid-1956, a surprising proportion of the listed new issues has had its brief day in the country of origin, and has fallen back into the obscurity of an "unavailable" or even definitely deleted category, while still awaiting or receiving further circulation abroad, or even re-issue at home. (It has not been possible to incorporate any "non-available" markings in this volume, as the situation is so fluid.) It can therefore be reasonably conjectured that within the covers of this Supplement are gathered the details of the recorded classical repertory at the time of its fullest flowering, and that our next volume will see the onset of a period of consolidation or even of retraction: we would expect fewer new issues and relatively more re-issues in the next few years. The number of active small producers, particularly in the U.S.A., has declined sharply within the last few years, though some new makes have appeared, to maintain the reputation of the best of such makers for an intelligent covering of the less hackneyed areas of the repertoire. From certain of these makers we have had valued co-operation in documentation and access to discs which do not circulate in Britain—perhaps invidiously, we must gratefully mention (among others) Unicorn, Opus, Overtone, Music Library, McIntosh and Colosseum in the U.S.A., the Club National du Disque and Erato in France, and Mr. Oord of the Dutch Agents of E.M.I., for their enlightened attitude to discography in the supply of records for research. We have fortunately been able to rely on valuable co-operation from most of the English manufacturers, and we acknowledge gratefully the special assistance received from the Decca Record Co. in the matter of access to discs needing more consideration before entry than is afforded by our usual sources, and from Philips & the E.M.I. combine in connection with copies of certain specially difficult discs. From the major producers in France, Italy, Spain, Germany, etc., we have received much help in the way of printed data, though not enough in the way of actual discs.

At some risk of tedium, we wish to reiterate that the special assistance from the makers acknowledged above only covers a very small part of the total field which we cover, and that the usual sources from which we work are: periodicals and reviews (see list of main sources, *post*); publicity matter issued by the makers (and some, even the largest and most reputable, do not co-operate even to the extent of supplying news of the new issues as made); correspondence with the makers, whose assistance is much appreciated (though some will not even reply to letters, and some lack the knowledge to identify the musical content of their productions); and, above all, local assistance from enthusiastic record-lovers, who make, in the last resort, the fullest and most valuable contributions to the comprehensiveness of this work. If any omissions are found, they may be the fault of the authors, who cannot claim immunity from the usual human failings, but are perhaps more likely to stem from the shortcomings of the publicity matter of the makers, who frequently do not deign to provide detailed descriptions of their productions, while readily advertising recordings which never appear. The efforts of our team of correspondents are directed towards remedying such mis-information and omissions and to identifying contents of insufficiently documented discs. We fear that they must cause much trouble to dealers in their efforts to glean data from the labels or covers of discs on their shelves, and we take this opportunity to send our apologies and thanks to those dealers who have, knowingly or unwittingly, afforded such facilities. We have been particularly grateful to William Lennard Concerts Ltd., E. M. G. Handmade Gramophones Ltd., and The Gramophone

v

Exchange Ltd. of London; Messrs. Sam Goody of New York and their Mr. Levin; La Boîte-à-Musique, Paris; Cado-Radio (M. Polinet) and Music-Bar (Mlle Vanbalberghe) of Brussels; Svensk Belysningskonst of Stockholm; Wm. Hansen of Copenhagen; R. E. Westerlund of Helsinki; and R. Teuchtler of Vienna. But for them, and the help of our volunteer correspondents, among whom we specially thank Messrs. J. London, N. Ferber, A. J. Franck and Wm. Darrah Kelley Jnr. and Father K. Edkins of the U.S.A.; Messrs. Cohn and Gibbs of Buenos Aires; Dr. J. Léon of Brazil; Prof. P. Berri of Rapallo, Italy; Messrs. Feuerstein and Baur of Switzerland; and others (including many of our original team, named in WERM) whose contributions are equally valued, we should never have been able to bring this task to its conclusion. We are still in need of new volunteers to help in gleaning and checking of information, especially in countries not specifically named above; though reinforcements in those countries (other than the U.S.A.) would also be welcome. Our present and future correspondents can be assured that the whole body of record collectors and users—and the more enlightened makers—will be the better informed as a result of their labours. We also wish to acknowledge the help we have received from many music publishers, and from libraries and librarians, in particular Mr. A. Hyatt King, of the British Museum; Mr. C. L. Cudworth, of Cambridge; Mr. K. H. Anderson, of the Liverpool Music Library; Mr. L. Duck, of the Henry Watson Music Library, Manchester; and their helpful staffs.

Our able and assiduous lieutenants, Mr. Eric Hughes and Miss Angela Noble, have also devoted much time and energy towards the completion of the present work, and our indebtedness to them can hardly be measured. We thank also the typists who have worked so well in translating the authors' handwritten script into material intelligible to the printers; and those who have assisted with the dreary task of correcting the proofs. Errors may even now have gone undetected, and readers who discover them are earnestly requested to communicate them, fully documented with authorities, to the authors, as soon as possible.

The layout of this Supplement follows that of Supplement II almost exactly, though a small revision has been made in the method of listing re-issues (marked ☆) in the interests of clarity and conciseness. An effort has been made to break down the contents of all Anthology records and to enter or cross-reference them under the respective composers. The large number of "historical" re-issues covered are shown by **H** in the composer entries and also summarised in the *Anthologies* section under *Vocal Re-issues*. As we explained before, within the confines of this volume it is not always possible to distinguish between different recordings of the same piece by the same artist, nor to specify recording dates or places.

We have compiled a full table of the record makes included in this volume (which may also include a few carried over from previous volumes to demonstrate a particular reason for otherwise inexplicable code letters) and a few tables to assist in the identifying of the various different branch numbering systems of the E.M.I. and Decca combines, and the meanings of Victor and Philips prefixes, etc. These are not exhaustive, being merely intended as a guide to nationality, size, and so on. The development, mentioned in the Foreword to Supplement II, of the transfer of the American Columbia re-issue rights for Europe and other areas from the E.M.I. combine to Philips has duly taken place, and this Supplement lists these issues in detail. Unfortunately, the Philips management has thought fit to endow all their English issues with a special English number, in addition to the International number which is current in other areas of activity, and which is also shown on the English issues. During the currency of this Supplement, the English E.M.I. group has acquired control of the Capitol Company (U.S.A.) and the English distribution rights have passed over from Decca in consequence, though E.M.I. have so far made no new Classical issues, and have adopted the numbers allotted under the Decca *régime* for existing issues taken over. The R.C.A.-Victor rights for most European countries, notably France, Italy, Holland and Spain, have passed from the hands of the E.M.I. group, and these records are now issued under the R.C.A. label, in each case using a different method of numbering. Fortunately, the transfer of the English rights from E.M.I. to Decca does not take place until 1957, so that is a complication for the future. It would be a vast simplification for the work of the discographer if some system could be evolved for the international currency of record numbers, to avoid the proliferation caused by varying national systems. Various makers do attain to a certain degree of international currency—e.g. the use of the original Vox, Capitol and Urania numbers for European re-issues, or the

Philips International system; unfortunately the tendency in England is away from such simplification, as witness the Philips renumberings mentioned above. We have had to steer a careful middle course between the madness induced in the discographer by the attempt to list every possible number for every record, and the madness of the reader in finding his own national number omitted for some recording he wishes to order. In general, we have attempted to be comprehensive with the English, U.S., and French numbers; reasonably so within other main European series; and highly selective in connection with minor European, South American, and similar peripheral series. It should therefore be clearly understood that the non-listing of an additional number for a particular recording does not necessarily imply its non-availability in some particular country—local catalogues should be checked. Where re-issues bear the original number, or mere variants in prefixes, etc., leaving the substantive part of the number unaltered, they are in general (except for a few English cases) not re-entered.

The position regarding Automatic couplings of sets of LP discs (complete Operas, etc.) has become most confused; we have not been able to ascertain in all cases how such sets are coupled and have therefore omitted in our listings any distinguishing marks. In general, it can be taken that sets issued by the Decca group (G.B., Europe, etc.) and London (U.S.A.); by Nixa (G.B.); Philips; Cetra (Italy); and by all U.S. companies (including their branches) are issued in automatic couplings only. The E.M.I. group in England began their LP issues (of sets in 3 or more discs) in automatic couplings only, but since *c.* November 1953, their sets have been issued in manual couplings only. The catalogues of their European branches are mainly silent as to their practice, but they probably follow the same method. Deutsche Grammophon appears to be the only firm issuing operas, etc., in *both* manual and automatic couplings regularly, and where known to us, both numbers are listed. The English issues by Heliodor of their recordings are however in automatic couplings only, and probably German issues are similar where only one set of numbers is quoted, as in the case of the Bruckner symphonies, though this is by no means certain. Certain sets are issued in manual couplings even by those firms usually adopting automatic sequence, where more appropriate to the subject matter—*e.g.* the LOL. sets of Couperin and Rameau harpsichord music.

A further complication has been introduced during the currency of this Supplement by the introduction of pre-recorded tapes. While the position is not yet stable enough to enable us to include such tapes in the body of the work, we include as an Appendix a summary of such tapes as we know to fall within our period. By the time the next Supplement is ready for publication, it may be possible to evolve some way of incorporating tape into the body of the Supplement without undue complication.

We are always happy to hear from our readers, and to assist with queries on any specific points; but queries requiring a reply should be accompanied by a stamped addressed envelope if from the United Kingdom, or by International or Imperial Reply Coupons to cover the reply—surface or air mail, as required—if from abroad.

F. F. CLOUGH
G. J. CUMING
"Kingswood"
Upper Colwyn Bay,
Wales.

July 1956

DIAGRAM OF SETTING OUT OF THE NORMAL ENTRY

COMPOSER (Date of birth & death)
CLASSIFICATION where applicable.
GENRE or TITLE OF OPERA, etc.
Title of the individual item. Voice or
instrumentation, date of composition, etc.
Name of Artist or Orch.—Conductor **Main No.**
(No. of sides, *coupling*, or anthology ref.) (Subsidiary Nos.)

▽ Omission from previous vols., or correction.

☆ Re-issue of recording included in previous vols. in
another country, or with different nos. in the country
of origin.

[The more important of these have extended entries
with nos. in bold type and coupling stated (mainly
British re-issues); others in tabular form.]

Ⱨ Re-issue or dubbing of acoustic recording.

SONGS & ARIAS, etc., are set out:
Title, Op. No. (Author of text) Date
Singer & accompanist **Main No.**
(*Coupling*) (Subsidiary Nos.)

The language is the original unless otherwise shown,
except in certain cases (*e.g.* USSR. issues) where it is not
always possible to ascertain definitely what language is used.
Russian singers have recently shown a tendency to sing in
original languages, however.

Excerpts from a larger work (unless it is divided
into numbered or other sections) are shown:
... **Adagio** only

while an arrangement of such an excerpt is introduced by a double dash, thus:
— — ARR. VLN. & PF. Auer

with the name of the arranger stated; unless there
is only one line for the whole title, when a single
dash suffices. On a line by itself, a single dash
— ARR. BAND Wright

refers back to the complete work, and not to any
preceding excerpts introduced by ...

The symbols Ⱨ, ☆, ▽, etc., prefixed to an artist entry with
no. in **bold type** only refer to that particular entry, and not
to any following entries. The same symbols prefixed to a
number of entries forming a list, refer to all entries forming
that list, until the appearance of a new symbol changes the
description, or a new title intervenes.

It has become customary to record collections of songs, etc., by one composer; these are grouped at the head of the relevant section and the individual contents not re-entered under titles. In certain cases, the symbol □ is added to subsequent mentions of those titles which are contained in these collections, to refer back to them.

Where there are several subsidiary numbers in one bracket, different nos. of the same make are divided by colons (:) and the code reference for the make is not repeated. Different makes and, in some cases, different speeds or versions of the same make, are separated by semi-colons (;). Where the first subsidiary no. quoted is the same make as the main no., the code is usually not repeated where the context is clear. Similarly, where all discs mentioned in one bracket are of the same speed, the symbol ♯ or ♭ is only given once; in brackets of mixed speeds where these are grouped together, each symbol is usually given once only. Where a ♯ set is quoted below a ♯ disc no., the symbol is omitted where the meaning seems clear; so is the indication "in" for collection and anthology entries.

Usually, with 45 and 78 r.p.m. main nos., the coupling applies to all subsidiary nos. *of the same speed,* unless a different coupling is quoted, or the notation "d.c." indicates a different coupling. With ♯ numbers, the same applies, with the reservation that it is not always possible to be certain as to couplings of certain subsidiary nos., and all couplings are here given in summary form, merely to guide to the fuller entries elsewhere, and do not necessarily apply to any numbers of a different speed quoted.

The sign † directs to the Anthology entries at the back of the book; all but a few unimportant composers in these are listed in their alphabetical positions in the body of the work, and to this extent this volume is self-indexing. For indexing purposes, Spanish compound names are placed under the letter of the first component (e.g. MORENO TORROBA under M, not T) and German modified vowels are placed as if they had an added E (thus SCHÜTZ reads SCHUETZ for this purpose). Although not conforming to the usage in these languages, Scandinavian modified vowels are treated similarly. Where a surname commences with a separate article or particle, this is ignored, whatever the national usage of the country of origin (thus: JOIO, Dello, and not DELLO JOIO).

In *Coupling* lines, the composers' names are followed by a colon (:) to separate them from titles of works; where there are several composers, they are usually divided by commas. The name of an opera or other large work is followed by a dash (—) to separate it from the *words* of an aria or other excerpt; but where a descriptive title is used instead of the words, a comma replaces the dash. Where no composer is named in the coupling line, it may be assumed that the work is by the same composer as the obverse, except where the coupling is from some named opera or other well-known work, where the name of a composer would be redundant. In the case of operatic lists, where neither composer nor opera is named, the title quoted for the coupling will be from the same opera as the obverse. The variation in size of type in the couplings has no importance, being dictated by the need in some cases to occupy free space in the artists' name or main no. line.

Dates quoted with titles of Operas and other Stage works are normally those of first performance; with other works, the date of composition is given where possible, except in cases where Opus numbers or other satisfactory systems of reference render this unnecessary. Sometimes, however, dates of first performance or even of publication have to be given (indicated "f.p." or "pub."), and in a few cases this may be done unwittingly in reliance on sources which do not define which date is given. "COMPLETE" Operas are generally only *roughly* complete; where possible, *substantial* omissions are noted.

It has been impossible to secure complete consistency in spelling of artists' names, where these vary from country to country; in some cases the spelling current in the place of first issue has been adopted. Similarly, the same orchestra may appear under different titles according to the practice adopted by different makers, though we have tried to reconcile the worst discrepancies and adopt the original title where possible (*e.g.* the Residentie Orch., called Hague Phil. in G.B. & U.S.A.; F.O.K. Orch., called Prague Sym.; and so on). Where the title of an orch. has been revised by the makers since first issue, our entries in general follow the original version, unless that is known to be erroneous.

In view of the large number of re-issues (largely dubbings) of "Historic" recordings included, it should be emphasised that no attempt is made to separate different recordings of the same item by the same artist, except where origins are obvious. Where the attempt is made, and the lay-out permits, "&" or "also" are frequently used to separate the different versions, though these do appear also in other contexts.

LIST OF RECORD MAKES & ABBREVIATIONS

The Abbreviations precede the record no. and are divided from it by a full point (.)

A.440	A.440 (U.S.A.)	BrzOd.	Brazilian Odeon
Abb.	Abbey (U.S.A.)	BrzV.	Brazilian Victor
ABCD.	Associação Brasileiro dos Colectionadores de Discos (Brazil)	Bulg.	Radioprom & Orfei (Bulgaria)
Acad.	Academy (U.S.A.)	C.	Columbia (G.B., Europe, Australia, etc.)
ACap.	Australian Capitol	CA.	Concert Artist (G.B.; many listed items of
Ace.	Ace Records (U.S.A.)		this make have not appeared)
ACC.	Classic Record Club (U.S.A.) [See note 1]	Cam.	Camden, division of Victor (U.S.A.)
AD.	Artist Direct (U.S.A.)	Camb.	Cambridge (U.S.A.)
AdL.	A. de Lara Limited edn. Recordings; now Orfeo with same nos. (G.B.)	Cant.	Canterbury (U.S.A.)
		CanT.	Canadian Telefunken
AF.	Addison Foster (U.S.A.)	Cap.	Capitol (U.S.A.)
AFest.	Australian Festival	Capri.	Capri (U.S.A.) [the disc entered as *Capri. 1*
Alld. or Ald.	Allied Record Sales (U.S.A.)		in fact has no number on the label.]
Allo.	Allegro-Elite (formerly Allegro) (U.S.A.)	Cdia.	Concordia (U.S.A.)
Ama.	Amadeo (Austria, etc.)	CdM.	Chant du Monde (France)
AmB.	American Brunswick (U.S.A.)	CEd.	Classic Editions (U.S.A.)
Ambra.	Alhambra (Spain)	Cet.	Cetra (Italy; the use of P. as abbreviation
AmC.	American Columbia (U.S.A.)		for this make has been discontinued)
AmD.	American Decca (U.S.A.)	CCet.	Capitol-Cetra (U.S.A.)[including all U.S.A.
AmEsq.	American Esquire (U.S.A.)		pressings of Cetra issues by Capitol—
Amf.	Amfión (Mexico)		these nos. also being valid in Italy in most
Ami.	Amiga (East Germany)		cases. The use of Sor. for such American
AmLum.	American Lumen (U.S.A.)		pressings has been discontinued, in view
Amph.	Amphion (France)		of the transfer of the rights to Capitol]
AmVien.	American Viennola (U.S.A.)	CFD.	Club français du Disque (France)
AmVox.	American Vox (U.S.A.; these numbers also	Chan.	Gloria Chandler Recordings (U.S.A.)
	current in Europe, etc. Where also	Chap.	Chappell (G.B.)
	issued in G.B. with same number, nota-	Chr.	Christschall (Austria)
	tion E. & AmVox. is used)	CHS.	Concert Hall Society (U.S.A.)
Ang.	Angelicum (Italy)	ChOd.	Chilean Odeon
Angel.	Angel (U.S.A.; subsidiary of E.M.I., Hayes, England)	ChV.	Chilean Victor
		CID.	Compagnie industrielle du disque (France)
ANix.	Australian Nixa		[This label has now taken over certain
ANM.	New Music (Australia)		French re-issues of AmD. recordings,
Aphe.	Audiophile (U.S.A.)		which we continue to list as D.—these
APM.	Pro Musica (U.S.A.)		may be recognised by prefixes UMT,
ArgA.	Argentine Angel		UAT, *UA*, etc.]
ArgC.	Argentine Columbia	CIDM.	Conseil International de Musique
ArgD.	Argentine Decca		(U.N.E.S.C.O.)
ArgLon.	Argentine London	CIM.	Cleveland Institute of Music (U.S.A.)
ArgOd.	Argentine Odeon	Clc.	Classic (France)
ArgP.	Argentine Parlophone	CM.	Conciertos Mexicanos (Mexico)
ArgPat.	Argentine Pathé	CMS.	Collectors Music Shop (U.S.A.)
ArgV.	Argentine Victor	CND.	Club national du Disque (France)
Argo.	Argo (G.B.)	Coda.	Coda issues of SMC. (U.S.A.)
Arp.	Arpeggio (Italy)	Copa. or Cop.	Copacabana (Brazil)
AS.	Anthologie Sonore (France; American	Corn.	Cornell University (U.S.A.)
	issues by HS. are shown as HS.AS . . .)	Cpt.	Contrepoint (France)
ARS.	American Recording Society (U.S.A.)	CRG.	Children's Record Guild (U.S.A.)
Arzi.	Hed-Arzi (Israel)	Crl.	Coral (U.S.A., Europe)
ASK.	Aeolian-Skinner Organ Co. (U.S.A.)	CRS.	Collectors Record Society (U.S.A.)
Asty.	Artistry (U.S.A.)	Csm.	Colosseum (U.S.A.)
Atl.	Atlantic (U.S.A.)	CubV.	Cuban Victor
Attn.	Austroton (Austria, Germany, etc.)	Cum.	Concerteum (France)
Atst.	Artist (U.S.A.)	Cty.	Contemporary Records (Los Angeles, U.S.A.)
AudA.	Audio Archives (U.S.A.)		
AudC.	Audio Collectors (U.S.A.)	CtyNY.	Contemporary Records (New York, U.S.A.)
AudR.	Audio Rarities (U.S.A.)	Cup.	Cupol (Sweden)
AusT.	Austrian Telefunken	Cus.	Cantus (Sweden)
		Cwal.	Cwaliton (Qualiton), Swansea (Wales)
B.	Brunswick (G.B.)	D.	Decca (G.B., Europe, Australia, etc.)
BàM.	Boîte-à-Musique, Paris (France)	DCap.	Capitol (G.B.—see note 5)
Ban.	Banner (U.S.A.)	DDP.	Erato [Discophiles de Paris series] (France)
B & B.	B. & B. Productions, N.J. (U.S.A.)	Dely.	Delysé (G.B.)
BB.	Bluebird, division of Victor (U.S.A.)	DFr.	Discophiles français (France)
BC.	Bach Choir (U.S.A.)	Dia.	Diaphon (Australia)
Bea.	Beaver (Canada)	Dial.	Dial (U.S.A.)
BH.	Boosey & Hawkes (G.B., U.S.A.)	Discur.	Discuriosities (U.S.A.)
Bib.	Bibletone (U.S.A.)	DO.	Oiselet (France; all are V♯)
Bne.	Bartone (U.S.A.)	DT.	Telefunken, pressed by Decca (G.B.)
Bo.	Boston Records (U.S.A.)	Dur.	Durium (Italy)
Book.	Book Records (U.S.A.)	DV.	Dutch R.C.A. [Victor]
BRS.	Bartók Recording Studio (U.S.A.)		
BrzA.	Brazilian Angel	EA.	English pressed Allegro
BrzC.	Brazilian Columbia	Edu.	Educo (U.S.A.)
BrzCont.	Brazilian Continental	EFL.	Folkways [Ethnic Folkways Library] (U.S.A.)
BrzEli.	Brazilian Elite		
BrzMGM.	Brazilian MGM		

Eko.	Eko (France)	ItMGM.	Italian MGM [only entered in special cases]
Elec.	Electro (Finland)	ItV.	Italian R.C.A. [Victor]
Elek.	Elektra (U.S.A.)	ItVox.	Italian Vox, special local nos. [mainly issues U.S. numbers]
Eli.	Elite (Europe)		
EMI.	E.M.I. Special Issues (G.B.)	Jay.	Jay Records (U.S.A.)
EMS.	Elaine Music Shop (U.S.A.)	JpC.	Japanese Columbia
EMer.	Mercury, available in G.B. with U.S.A. nos. (Some of these announced, but not issued, in G.B., though apparently on sale in Scandinavia.) [As we go to press, these nos. are obsolete in G.B., though still current in U.S.A.; the English rights have been taken over by Nixa, using new nos., which however do not appear in this volume]	JpPol.	Japanese Polydor-Deutsche Grammophon
		JpPV.	*Idem*, variable microgroove
		JpV.	Japanese Victor
		Jug.	Jugoton (Jugo-Slavia)
		Kan.	Kantorei (Germany)
		Ken.	Kendall (U.S.A.)
		Kings.	Kingsway (U.S.A.)
		Know.	Knowledge (U.S.A.)
EOM.	Enjoyment of Music series, E.M.I. (G.B.)	KR.	Key Records (U.S.A.)
EPhi.	English Philips		
EPP.	Éditions phonographiques parisiennes—Allegro label (France)	Layos.	Layos, Hollywood (U.S.A.)
		Lei.	Leijona (Finland)
Epic.	Epic, division of Columbia Records Inc. (U.S.A.)	LH.	L. Hungerford private rec. (G.B.)
		LI.	London International (G.B., U.S.A., etc.)
ERC.	Epic Record Co., N.Y. (U.S.A.)	Lin.	Linden (U.S.A.)
Era.	Erato (France)	LO.	Louisville Orchestra—subscription series (U.S.A.)
Esc.	Escort (France)		
Eso.	Esoteric (U.S.A.)	Lon.	London (export issues of English Decca—mainly U.S.A., Canada, etc.)
Esq.	Esquire (G.B.) [The U.S.A. label is coded AmEsq.]		
		LOL.	London—Oiseau-Lyre (G.B., U.S.A., etc.)
Eta.	Eterna (East Germany)	LQS. or QS.	Les Quatre Saisons (France)
Ete.	Eterna (U.S.A.)	LT.	London—Ducretet-Thomson (G.B., U.S.A., etc.)
Etu.	Etude (U.S.A.)		
Eur.	Eurochord (France)	Lum.	Lumen (France)
Eut.	Euterpe (U.S.A.)	Lyr.	Lyrichord (U.S.A.)
EVox.	English Vox [Most issues use the U.S. nos. and are entered as E. & AmVox.]		
		MA. or MApp.	Musical Appreciation (U.S.A.) [see note 2]
		Mae.	Maestro (Belgium, etc.)
FCap.	French Capitol [mainly, however, the U.S. nos. are current in France]	Magy.	Magyar Muza (Hungary)
		McInt.	McIntosh Music (U.S.A.)
Fdn.	Fonodan (Denmark)	Mer.	Mercury (U.S.A.)—[nos. common to G.B. also, are entered as EMer.]
Fel.	Felsted (G.B., etc.)		
Felix.	Felix (Denmark)	MF. or MFr.	Mélomanes français (France) [These also bear various other labels, including Disquaires réunis, Galeries Lafayette, etc.]
Fest.	Festival (U.S.A.)		
FestF.	Festival (France)		
FFB.	Friends of Fritz Busch, subscription issue (U.S.A.)	MGM.	Metro-Goldwyn-Mayer (U.S.A., G.B., etc.)
		MH.	Music Hall (U.S.A.)
FGM.	Freunde guter Musik Club (Germany)	MHF.	Microsillon et Haute-Fidelité (France) [Special issues for subscribers]
Flo.	Florilège (France)		
FMer.	French Mercury	Mjr.	Major (U.S.A.)
FMGM.	French M.G.M.	ML.	Music Library Records (U.S.A.)
Fnt.	Fonit (Italy)	MMS.	Musical Masterpiece Society (U.S.A., Europe)
FPV.	French Polydor variable micrograde		
For.	Forum (U.S.A.)	Moll.	Moller Organ Co. (U.S.A.)
Fred.	Fredonia (U.S.A.)	Mon.	Monarch (G.B.)
FRP.	Famous Records of the Past (U.S.A.)	Mono.	Monogram (U.S.A.)
FSM.	Fellowship Recorded Libraries of Sacred Music, Atlanta, Ga. (U.S.A.)	Mont.	Montilla (U.S.A., Spain, etc.)
		MR.	Music Records (U.S.A.)
FSor.	French Cetra-Soria	Mrt.	Merit (U.S.A.)
FT.	French Telefunken (local nos.)	MSB.	Music Sound Books (U.S.A.) [Their 78-r.p.m. discs are all "long-playing"]
FUra.	French Urania [local nos.; usually the U.S.A. numbers are current]		
		MSL.	Masterseal (U.S.A.)
FV.	French R.C.A. [Victor] [The use of this code for Fonodan variable microgroove has been discontinued]	Msq.	Masque (U.S.A.)
		MTR.	Magic-Tone Records (U.S.A.)
		Mtr.	Metronome (Scandinavia, Germany, etc.)
		MTW.	Music Treasures of the World (U.S.A.) [see note 2]
G.	H.M.V., Gramophone Co. (G.B., Europe, etc.) [Including Electrola, Germany]	Mur.	Murlyn (U.S.A.)
		Musette.	Musette (U.S.A.)
GA.	Grand Award (U.S.A.)	MusH.	Music Hall (Argentine)
GAR.	Golden Age Records (U.S.A.)	Muza.	Muza and other labels (Poland)
GID.	Guilde International du Disque (France; mainly issues MMS. items, which are not re-listed)	MV.	Music of the Vatican (France)
		NE.	New Editions (U.S.A.)
GIOA.	Gregorian Institute of America (U.S.A.)	Nera.	Nera & Musica (Norway)
GkOd.	Greek Odeon	Nix.	Nixa (G.B., etc.; including Vanguard label re-issues [PVL prefix])
GNYO.	Guild of New York Opera, members' issues (U.S.A.)		
		NMQR.	New Music Quarterly Review (U.S.A.)
Gram.	Gramophone, division of Record Corpn. of America, N.J. (U.S.A.)	NOC.	Norwegian Government Office of Culture
		NRI.	New Records, Inc. (U.S.A.)
Gramo.	Gramola (Belgium)	NWRS.	North-West Recording Society (U.S.A.)
Hall.	Hallmark (Canada)	Oce.	Oceanic (U.S.A.)
Harv.	Harvard Vocarium (U.S.A.)	Od.	Odeon (Europe, etc.)
HDL.	Handel Society (U.S.A.)	Ofo.	Orfeo (U.S.A.)
Hélios.	Hélios—Joies de la musique (France)	OL.	Oiseau-Lyre (France) [English pressings coded LOL.]
Hel.	Heliodor (G.B.)		
HP.	Heliodor (G.B.) and Pol. (Germany etc.) [see note 3]	Ome.	Omega (Belgium, etc.)
		Opa.	Opera of the Month Club (U.S.A.—members only)
Her.	Herald (G.B.)		
HH.	Hemmets Härold (Sweden)	Ophn.	Orpheon (Poland)
HIFI.	High Fidelity Records (U.S.A.)	Opus.	Opus Records (U.S.A.)
Hispa.	Hispavox (Spain)	Orb.	Orbis (Germany, etc.)
Hma.	Harmona (Austria)	Orf.	Orfeo (Argentine)
HRS.	Historic Record Society (U.S.A.)	Ori.	Oriole (G.B.)
HS. or HSLP.	Haydn Society (U.S.A.)	OTA.	Off-the-air Record Club (U.S.A.—members only)
Ifma.	Ifma (Argentine)		
Imp.	Imperial (Germany, etc.)	Over.	Overtone (U.S.A.)
Inno.	Innovations (U.S.A.)	Ox.	Oxford (U.S.A.)
IPV.	Italian Polydor variable microgroove		
IRCC.	International Record Collectors' Club (U.S.A.)	P.	Parlophone (G.B., Italy, Australia, etc.) [The use of this code for Cetra issues in Italy has been discontinued]
Isis.	Isis Recording Studios, Oxford (G.B.)		
ISR.	International Sacred Recordings, Christian Artists' Record Corpn. (U.S.A.)	Pac.	Pacific (France)
		Pam.	Pampa (Brazil)
		Pan.	Panthéon (France, etc.)

Pat.	Pathé (France)
PaV.	Pathé-Vox (France) [Local nos.—usually uses U.S.A. nos.]
Pax.	Paxton (G.B.)
Pde.	Parade (U.S.A.)
Peer.	Peerless (U.S.A., Mexico)
Per.	Period (U.S.A.)
Persp.	Perspective (U.S.A.)
PFCM.	Pittsburgh Festival of Contemporary Music (U.S.A.) [for distribution to libraries & institutions]
Phi.	Philips (Holland & International) [English issues coded EPhi.]
Phil.	Philharmonia (U.S.A.)
PhM.	Philips Minigroove, 78 r.p.m. 17 cm. discs
Plé.	Pléiade (France)
Ply.	Plymouth (U.S.A.)
Pnt.	Panart (Cuba, U.S.A.)
POc.	Porte-Océane (France)
Pol.	Polydor & Deutsche Grammophon (Germany, Europe, etc.); also Polyphon (Denmark, etc.) [X, Z, HM prefixes]; & Archive series (Germany). The English re-issues of the latter may be recognised by the A in the prefix; the AmD. by the prefix ARC
Polym.	Polymusic (U.S.A.)
Pop.	Populare (Rumania)
PRCC.	Peoria Record Club (U.S.A.)
PV.	Polydor/Deutsche-Grammophon (inc. Archive series) variable microgroove (Germany)
Qual.	Qualiton & MHV. (Hungary) [The Welsh issues of this name are coded under the Welsh spelling: Cwal.]
Queens.	Queensway Studios (G.B.)
QS. or LQS.	Les Quatre Saisons (France)
Rad.	Radiola (Australia)
Radi.	Radium (France)
RadT.	Radiola-Telefunken (Australia)
Rar.	Rare Records (U.S.A.)
RE.	Radio-Eireann (Eire)
REB.	R. E. Blake (U.S.A.)
Reg.	Regal, branch of E.M.I. (Spain)
Rem.	Remington (U.S.A., Europe, etc.)
Ren.	Renaissance (U.S.A.)
Rgt.	Regent (U.S.A.)
Riv.	Riviera (France)
Roc.	Rococo Records (Canada, U.S.A.)
Rom.	Romany Records (U.S.A.)
RR.	Record Rarities (U.S.A.)
RS.	Rachmaninoff Society (U.S.A.)
Roy.	Royale & Allegro-Royale (U.S.A.)
Ryt.	Rytmi (Finland)
RZ.	Regal-Zonophone (G.B.)
Sat.	Saturn (France)
SBDH.	Sociedade Brasileira de Discos Historicos J. Léon (Brazil)
Sca.	Scala (U.S.A.)
Sel.	Ducretet-Thomson [formerly Ducretet Selmer] (France)
SFA.	Symphony Foundation of America (U.S.A.) [The first issue of this organisation, formed by members of the former N.B.C. Sym., is listed in this volume as played by the N.B.C. Sym., without conductor; since the original announcements, the orch. has been named "Symphony of the Air".] Records issued to subscribers only.
Sin.	Sinter (Brazil)
Sir.	Sirius (Sweden)
SM.	Studio S.M. (France)
SMC.	Spanish Music Centre (U.S.A.)
SMP.	St. Mary's Press, N.Y. (U.S.A.)
Son.	Sonora (Sweden)
Sor.	Soria (U.S.A.) [Discs of Cetra origin are now excluded, and the remainder taken over by Angel.]
SOT.	Sounds of our times, Cook Studio (U.S.A.)
SPA.	Society of Participating Artists (U.S.A.)
SPAM.	Society for the Publication of American Music (U.S.A.)
SpC.	Spanish Columbia, San Sebastian (Spain)
SpD.	Spanish Decca, San Sebastian (Spain)
SpOd.	Spanish Odeon, Barcelona (Spain)
SpFest.	Spanish Festival
SpT.	Spanish Telefunken
SpV.	Spanish R.C.A. [Victor]
Spot.	Spotlight (Australia)
SRC.	Sound Recording Co. (U.S.A.)
SRS.	Sound Recordings Specialists (U.S.A.)
SS.	Swedish Society, Discofil (Sweden)
Sti.	Stinson (U.S.A.)
StO.	St. Olaf (U.S.A.)
Strad.	Stradivari (U.S.A.)
Sup.	Supraphon (Czechoslovakia, ♯ export nos.)
Sym.	Symphony Recording Co. (U.S.A.)
Symf.	Symfoni & Artist (Sweden)
T.	Telefunken (Germany, etc.)
Täh.	Tähti (Finland)
Tec.	Technichord (U.S.A.)
Tem.	Tempo (U.S.A.)
Tim.	Timely (U.S.A.)
Tit.	Titan (U.S.A.)
TMS.	Technisonic (U.S.A.)
Tono.	Tono (Denmark)
Top. or TRC.	Topic (G.B.)
Tpo.	Tempo (Germany)
Trla.	Triola (Finland)
Triad.	Triad Records (U.S.A.)
TV.	Telefunken Variable microgroove (Germany)
U.	Ultraphon & Supraphon (Czechoslovakia, ♯ domestic nos. & 78 r.p.m. export nos.)
Uni.	Unicorn (U.S.A.)
UOI.	University of Illinois (U.S.A.)
UOK.	University of Oklahoma (U.S.A.)
UOS.	University of the South (U.S.A.)
Ura.	Urania (U.S.A., Europe, etc.)
USSR.	State Music Trust (Russia)
USSRM.	*Idem*, 78 r.p.m. "long-playing" [see note 7]
Van.	Vanguard (U.S.A.) [Issued in G.B., and coded Nix. here; PVL prefix]
Var.	Varsity (U.S.A.)
VdN.	Voix des Nôtres (France)
Véga. or Vég.	Véga (France)
Ven.	Vendôme (France)
Vic.	Victor (U.S.A., Canada, etc.)
Vien.	Viennola (Austria) [American issues have different nos. coded: AmVien.]
Vill.	Villandry Festival (France)
Vog.	Vogue (France)
VS.	Vocal Students Practice Aid Records (U.S.A.)
Wal.	Waldorf (U.S.A.)
Wald.	Walden (U.S.A.)
WCFM.	WCFM, Washington (U.S.A.)
West.	Westminster (U.S.A.)
WFB.	WFB (U.S.A.)
Word.	Word Records, Waco, Texas (U.S.A.)
X.	X Records, division of R.C.A.-Victor (U.S.A.)
Zod.	Zodiac Records (U.S.A.)

NOTES

1. The artists here are truly anonymous, in that they are not identified on the labels of discs examined. Where they are equated with some other recording, in most cases this is purely inferential.

2. In these cases, where artists are entered as "Anon." this should be taken to indicate merely that they are anonymous in the sources available to us; they may well be identified on the discs or other sources which we have not seen.

3. Heliodor records (G.B.) use the German Pol. nos. in most cases, and where Pol. recordings are available in both countries, the code used is HP. The letter prefix which follows applies to the G.B. issue only, though based on (but not identical with) the similar letter combinations used in Germany as price class indications.

4. In certain cases (e.g. AFest., FestF.; AmLum., Lum.) there is apparently no connection, however remote, between issues of similar name in different countries. In other cases, a connection did once exist but has been broken (AmC., C., SpC.) in others, branches or associates of the same makers are involved (e.g. ArgA., Angel.; Vic., DV., FV., ItV.).

5. DCap. issues are those made by the Capitol division of the Decca Record Co. (G.B.) before the change in control of the mark. E.M.I. have now taken over, and if they make new classical issues, these will be denoted ECap. in our next Supplement. Existing issues retain their DCap. nos. under the new management.

6. Where an adjectival form of the country of origin is used in the above list before a mark (e.g. Australian Festival) it should be understood that in the country of origin, the mark will be used alone, without such notation of nationality.

7. USSR. and USSRM. issues (and a few other minor makes) use one number per side, and not one number per disc. USSRM. discs are 78 r.p.m. "long-playing" (variable microgroove) discs, but they are playable only with LP stylus, in contradistinction to TV., PV., and other similar 78 r.p.m. issues which are designed to be played with the normal 78 r.p.m. stylus.

LIST OF OTHER ABBREVIATIONS

A.	Alto (Contralto)
AAYO.	All-American (Youth) Orchestra
Accord.	Accordion
Auto(s).	Automatic coupling(s)
B or Bar	Baritone
B & H	Breitkopf & Härtel
Bk.	Book
B.M.	British Museum
bsn.	Bassoon
BSO(O)	Berlin State (Opera) Orch.
Bs	Bass
BWV.	Bach Werke-Verzeichnis (Schmieder nos.)
CBs, cbs	Contra-bass
CBS.	Columbia Broadcasting System Sym. Orch.
Cha.	Chamber
Cho.	Chorus, choral or choir
Chu. or Ch.	Church
cl.	clarinet
clav.	clavier
clavi.	clavichord
Cond.	Conductor, or conducted [by]
Cons.	Conservatoire
cont.	continuo
C-T	Counter-tenor
CU.	Clavierübung (Bach)
CUMS.	Cambridge University Madrigal Society
Cz	Czech
D.	Deutsch references (Schubert)
d.c.	different coupling
d.v.	different version
Dan	Danish
DTB.	Denkmäler der Tonkunst in Bayern
DTÖ.	Denkmäler der Tonkunst in Oesterreich
DDT.	Denkmäler Deutscher Tonkunst
E.	Eighteen "Great" Ch.-Preludes (Bach)
Ed.	Edited by, or Edition
Ens.	Ensemble
F.	Falck Nos. (W. F. Bach)
Finn	Finnish
F.O.K.	Prague Film and Concert Orch.
Forte-pf.	Forte-piano (a piano made during period c. 1750-1825, or a modern reproduction of such a piano)
f.p.	First performance
Fr	French
FVB	Fitzwilliam Virginal Book
G.	Grove' No. (Beethoven, etc.)
GA.	Gesamt-Ausgabe
G.B.	Great Britain
Ger	German
guit.	guitar
ℌ	Vocal or other re-issue in "historical" series
hp.	harp
hpsi.	harpsichord
hrn.	horn
Icel	Icelandic
Inc. Mus.	Incidental Music
Ital or It	Italian
K.	Köchel Nos. (Mozart)
Kk.	Kirkpatrick Nos. (D. Scarlatti)
KFUM.	Y.M.C.A., Sweden & Denmark
L.	Longo Nos. (Scarlatti)
Lat	Latin
Latv	Latvian
Lith	Lithuanian
L.P.O.	London Philharmonic Orchestra
L.S.O.	London Symphony Orchestra
M-S or MS	Mezzo-soprano
MS.	Manuscript (of scores)
mbrs.	members
NBG.	Neue Bach-Gesellschaft
n.d.	no data or nos. discoverable
n.n.	new number
No., nod.	Number, Numbered
NSO	National Symphony Orchestra
N.W.D.R.	Nord-West-Deutsche-Rundfunk Orchestra (Hamburg)
N.Y.P.S.O.	N.Y. Phil. Sym. Orch.
n.v.	new version

OB.	Orgelbüchlein (Bach)
o.n.	old number (i.e. same recording has been renumbered in the same country)
Ov.	Overture
o.v.	old version
ob.	oboe
orch.	orchestra or orchestrated
Op.	Opus, or opera
P.	Pincherle references (Vivaldi)
P.	polka (Strauss family)
Perc.	Percussion
pf.	piano
Pte.	Private
prep.	preparation
Q.H.O.	Queen's Hall Orchestra
Qtt.	Quartet
R.A.M.	Royal Academy of Music
RAHO.	Royal Albert Hall Orchestra
RCS	Royal Choral Society
R.I.A.S.	Berlin Radio (American Sector)
RPO	Royal Philharmonic Orchestra
rec.	recorder, recorded, or recording
ROH	Royal Opera House
r.p.m.	revolutions per minute
r.r.	re-recorded
RSCM.	Royal School of Church Music
Rum	Rumanian
Russ	Russian
S or Sop	Soprano
s.c.	same coupling (this is to be understood, however, in usual cases)
Sch.	School
Sch.	Schübler Chorale-Preludes (Bach)
SECM	School of English Church Music (now RSCM)
s, ss.	side(s)
"Siena" pf.	The piano built in the early 1800's by Marchesio of Turin, & presented in 1868 by the City of Siena to Crown Prince Umberto of Italy; restored by A. Carmi after many vicissitudes; see the disc cover notes by J. Lyons, or A. Carmi's promised book.
signs	(see also Foreword)
†	see Anthologies section
▢	see collection of this composer
*	non-electrical recording: or electrical re-recording from acoustic original
¶	pre-1936—re-issued in G.B. with pre-1936 number (in errata only)
§	pre-1936—not available in G.B. (in errata only)
▽	Omission from, or Correction of entry in, WERM and Supplements I & II
☆	Re-issue (re-pressing, or occasionally, dubbing) of recording to be found in WERM or Supplements I & II
♯	record played at 33⅓ r.p.m.
♭	record played at 45 r.p.m.
V♯	7-inch or 8-inch record played at 33⅓ r.p.m. (All records play at 78 r.p.m. unless marked as above.)
♮	Auto. couplings, 78 r.p.m.
Soc., Socy.	Society
Sp.	Special (attributed to pressings)
Sp or Span	Spanish
Swed	Swedish
T or Ten	Tenor
Tr	Treble
trs.	transcribed (of music)
—	translated (of texts)
tpt.	trumpet
unid.	unidentified (= heard, but not identifiable, or not included in standard lists of composers' works)
unspec.	unspecified (= not heard, and insufficient catalogue details to permit identification among several possibilities)
vlc.	violoncello
vln.	violin
v.o.v.	very old version
vla.	viola
vv.	voices
W.	Waltz (Strauss family)
W.	Wotquenne (C.P.E. Bach)

SELECTED LIST

of useful periodical and other sources consulted.

This list excludes general musical periodicals and reference works, unless of some special relevance to discography or of particular interest otherwise (the important works used will be found mentioned in WERM Introduction). In the case of certain periodicals mentioned, only individual copies have been used; the country of publication is stated, or in the case of books, the town or place. We have had much valuable assistance from the editorial staff and contributors of many of the publications listed, which is gratefully acknowledged. Certain periodicals mentioned have ceased publication.

AMERICAN LIBRARY IN LONDON: Catalog of Recordings and Musical Scores
American Record Guide (U.S.A.)
American Record Letter (U.S.A.)
Boletin de Música y Artes Visuales (Pan-American Union, Washington, D.C.)
BARLOW & MORGENSTERN: A Dictionary of Musical Themes (N.Y. & London)
BARLOW & MORGENSTERN: A Dictionary of Vocal Themes (N.Y. & London)
Cado-Radio *Bulletin mensuel* (Belgium)
Cado-Radio *Catalogue général Long-Playing* (Belgium)
Cado-Radio *Officiel du Disque* (Belgium)
Cahiers du Disque, Les (France)
CASSINI, L: Music in Rumania (London)
Catalogue of Finnish Orchestral and Vocal Compositions (TEOSTO, Helsinki)
Cercle musical, Le (France)
Contemporary Music from Holland (DONEMUS, Amsterdam)
Critique (G.B.)
Diapason (France)
Discofilen (Denmark)
Discofilia (Spain)
Disco-Nieuws (Holland)
Discos microsurco, Los (Spain)
Disques (France)
Disques de Longue-Durée (France)
Entré (Sweden)
Forty-Fiver, The (U.S.A.)
Gramophone, The (G.B.)
Gramophone LP Classical Record Catalogue (G.B.)
Gramophone Record Review, The (G.B.)
Gramophone Shop Supplement, The (U.S.A.)
Gramofoonplaten-Nieuws (Holland)
Guide du Concert, Le (France)
HALL & LEVIN: Disc Book (New York)
Harrison *Catalog of Recorded Tapes* (U.S.A.)
Harrison *EP-45* (U.S.A.)
Harrison *Opera Catalog* (U.S.A.)
Harrison *This Month's Records* (U.S.A.)
HI-FI Music at Home (U.S.A.)
High Fidelity (U.S.A.)
HINRICHSEN, M. (*ed.*): Music Books VII, VIII (London)
Langspielplatte, Die (Germany)
Larga Duración (Catalogo de Discos) (Argentine)
Library of Congress Catalog, Music & Phonorecords (Washington, D.C.)
Liens (France)
Long Player, The (U.S.A.)
Luister (Holland)
Microsillon et Haute-Fidelité (France)
Microsurco (Argentine)
MILLER, KOLODIN & SCHONBERG: Guide to Long Playing Records (New York)
Monthly Letter, The (G.B.)
MOOSER, R. A.: Panorama de la Musique contemporaine, 1947-1953 (Geneva & Monaco)
MOTTE, W. DE: Long Playing Record Guide (New York)
Music & Musicians (G.B.)
Music & Recordings, 1954/5 (New York)
Música (Spain)
Musica e Dischi (Italy)
Musik der Zeit: No. 10 [Swiss Composers] (Germany)
MYERS, K. (ed.): Consolidated Index of Record Reviews (Washington, D.C.)
MYERS & HILL (eds.): Record Ratings (This work was only received as the present Supplement was in the press)
New Records, The (G.B.)
New Records, The (U.S.A.)
Notes (U.S.A.)
Nyare Svenska Orkester- och Vokalverk (FST, Stockholm)
Orphée (France)
Pan Pipes (Menaska, Wis., U.S.A.)
QVAMME: Norwegian Music & Composers (London)
Record Guide (Australia)
Record News (G.B.)
Revista Musical 33⅓ (Mexico)
Revue des Disques (Belgium)
SACKVILLE-WEST & SHAWE-TAYLOR: Record Guide, & Supplement (London)
Santandrea *Catalogo generale Dischi Microsolco* (Italy)
Saturday Review of Literature, Record Section (U.S.A.)
Schwann *Digest* (U.S.A.)
Schwann *Long Playing Record Catalogue* (U.S.A.)
Semaine Radiophonique, La (France)
Tempo (G.B.)

SELECTED LISTS OF CURRENT RECORD PREFIXES

Not all these are to be found in this Supplement; and the list is not exhaustive

GENERAL NOTE: Where part of a series prefix is shown below in square brackets [ ], it forms part of the order number, but is in general omitted in our lists—*e.g.* the [33] of the Columbia 33⅓ r.p.m. discs, which represents our symbol ‡.

E.M.I. COMBINE

Country	Label	33⅓ r.p.m. ‡		♭ 45 r.p.m. 7-inch (17 cm.)	
		10-inch (25 cm.)	*12-inch (30 cm.)*	*Extended play*	*Standard*
GREAT BRITAIN & INTERNATIONAL	H.M.V. Columbia	*BLP, DLP* [33] *C, S*	*ALP, CLP* [33] *CX, SX*	*7ER, 7EB, 7EP, 7EG SEL, SEB, SED, SEG*	*7R, 7P, 7M SCB, SCD, SCM*
	Parlophone (& Odeon)	*PMB, PMD*	*PMA, PMC*	*GEP*	*BSP, DSP, MSP*
	M.G.M.	*MGM.D*	*MGM.C*	*MGM.EP*	*MGM.SP*
INTERNATIONAL SPECIAL ISSUES (Made in G.B.)	H.M.V. Columbia Parlophone	*BLPC, DLPC* [33] *CS* *CPMD*	*ALPC* [33] *CCX* —	*7ERC, 7EGF, etc. SEGC, SEGF, etc. CREP, CGEP, CBEP*	*7RC, 7PC, etc. SCMC, SCMF, etc CMSP, QMSP, FMSP, etc.*
FRANCE BELGIUM SWITZERLAND etc.	H.M.V.	*FBLP, FDLP, FFLP, FKLP, FMLP, FOLP*	*FALP, FCLP, FELP, FJLP, FLLP*	*7ERF, 7EBF, 7EGF, 7EMF*	*7RF, 7BF, 7GF, 7MF, etc.*
	Columbia	[33] *FC, FH, FA, FJ, FP, FS*	[33] *FCX, FSX, FHX, FPX*	*ESBF, ESDF, ESRF, ESVF*	*SCBF, SCDF, SCRF, SCVF*
	Odeon	*OD, OS*	*ODX, OSX*	*7MOE, 7AOE, 7SOE*	*7MO, 7AO*
	Pathé	[33] *DT, ST, AT, PC, PAC*	[33] *DTX, ATX, PCX*	[45] *EA, ED, EG*	[45] *A, D, G*
	Pathé-Vox Témoignages	*VPO, VL* *TLP, TLPS*	*VP, PL; DL* (sets) —	*VIP* —	— [45] *T*
	M.G.M.	*F 1-[MGM]*	*F 6-[MGM]*	*EPF-[MGM]*	*SPF-[MGM]*
ITALY	H.M.V.	*QBLP, QDLP, QFLP, QKLP*	*QALP, QCLP, QELP, QJLP*	*7ERQ, 7EPQ, 7EMQ*	*7RQ, 7BQ, 7MQ*
	Columbia	[33] *QC, QS, QP*	[33] *QCX, QSX, QPX*	*SEBQ, SEDQ, SEMQ*	*SCMQ, SCDQ, SCBQ*
	Parlophone Odeon	*PMDQ* *MODQ, VT [Vatican]*	— *MOAQ*	*QDSE DSEQ*	*DSOQ*
	Pathé	[33] *MT, QT, QAT*	[33] *MTX, QTX, QATX*	[45] *EAQ, EDQ, EGQ*	[45] *AQ, DQ, GQ*
	M.G.M.	*QD, QF, QB*	*QA, QC, QE*	*ESPQ, ESCQ*	*SPQ, SCQ*
GERMANY	H.M.V. (Electrola)	*WBLP, WDLP* [1500 series, local	*WALP, WCLP* issues; or as G.B.]	*7ERW [14–], 7EPW [13–], 7EGW [11–]*	*7RW [19–], 7PW [18–], 7MW [17–]*
	Columbia Imperial Odeon	[33] *WS, WC* *ILP* *OLA, OLZ*	[33] *WSX, WCX* *ILPX* *OLZX*	*SEDW* — *BEOW, GEOW*	*SCMW* — *OBL [37–]*
SPAIN	H.M.V. Regal	*LBLP, LDLP* [33] *LC, LS*	*LALP, LCLP* [33] *LCX, LSX*	*7ERL, 7EPL, etc. SEBL, SEML, SEDL*	—
	Odeon	*MOBL, MODL*	*MOAL, MOCL*	*BSOE, DSOE, MSOE*	—
	Pathé	[33] *AM, DM*	[33] *AMX, DMX*	[45] *EMA, EMD, etc.*	—
DENMARK	H.M.V. Columbia Odeon	*KBLP, KDLP* [33] *KC* *MODK*	*KALP, KCLP* [33] *KSX* —	*7ERK, 7EGK, etc. SEGK BEOK*	*7RK, 7MK, etc.* — —
NORWAY	H.M.V.	*NBLP* & as G.B.	—	*7EBN*	*7PN, 7MN*
	Columbia Odeon	— —	— —	— —	*SCDN MSON*
SWEDEN	H.M.V.	as G.B. etc.	—	*7ERS, 7EBS, 7EPS, 7EGS*	—
	Elite Odeon Pathé	— — —	— — —	[45] *EPA* *GEOS* Issued as H.M.V. but with original Pathé (Fr.) Nos.	— —
HOLLAND	H.M.V. Columbia	as G.B. etc. [33] *HS*	— —	*7EPH* —	— —
AUSTRALIA AUSTRIA	All All	ADD extra letter O to English series: OALP, [33] OSX, etc. ADD extra letter V to English series: VALP, [33] VSX, etc.			

DECCA GROUP AND ASSOCIATES

Country	Label	33⅓ r.p.m. ♯		♭ 45 r.p.m. 7-inch (17 cm.)	
		10-inch (25 cm.)	12-inch (30 cm.)	Extended play	Standard
GREAT BRITAIN & INTERNATIONAL	Decca	LX, LF, LM / LW (Medium play)	LXT, LK	DFE	[45–] 10000 / [45–] 71000
GREAT BRITAIN (Series marked* also current in U.S.A. and other areas.)	Brunswick	AXL, LA	AXTL, LAT	OE	[45–] 01000
	Capitol (DCap.)	CCL	CTL	EAP	[45–] KC, CL
	*Telefunken (DT.)	LGM / TM (Medium play)	LGX	—	—
	*London	H-APB, HB, AL, LZ	HA, LTZ	EZ-A, REP, RE-A	[45–] L, HL, CAY
	*Oiseau-Lyre (LOL.)	DL	OL	—	—
	*Ducretet-Thomson (LT.)	EL; D (7-inch) / MEL (Medium play)	DTL, TKL	DEP	—
	*London-International (LI.)	W, WB, WBV, WV	TW, TWB, TWBV, TWV	—	—
	Felsted	EDL, SDL	RL, PDL	ESD	—
	Beltona	ABL	—	SEP	[45–] BL
	Durium	DLU	TLU	U	—
U.S.A., CANADA	London	LS, LB / LD (Medium play)	LL	REP	—
FRANCE	Decca¹	FS 123000 / FM 133000 / FA 143000 / (& AK, AX etc.)	FST 153000 / FMT 163000 / FAT 173000	EFM 455500 / EFS 450500 / (& EFA, etc.; DME, DFE, etc.)	FA 80500 / FS 70500 / FM 75500
	C.I.D.¹	US 223000 / UM 233000, 333000 / UA 243000	UST 253000 / UMT 263000 / UAT 273000	EUS 100000 / EUM 105000	BM 5000 / BM 75500 / MU 95500
		[also some 5-digit series]			

		17 cm.	21 cm.	25 cm.	30 cm.	Extended play	Standard
	Ducretet-Thomson² (Sel.)⁴	190.C / LAP / LPP	230.C / 230.E / 220.C / 255.C / LLA	270.C/CW / 250.V / 260.V / LAC 21000 / LAC 25000 / LA, LP, LM	320.C/CW / 300.V / 310.C/V / LAC 30000 / LPG, LAG / LA 1063	470.C/CW / 460.V / 450.V	500.V
	Telefunken (FT.)	—	—	270.TC / 260.TV	320.TC	470.TC / 460.TV	500.TV / 510.TC

Country	Label	25 cm. (10-inch)	30 cm. (12-inch)	Extended play	Standard
BELGIUM	Decca	LX, BA 133000 and as France	BAT 133000	etc.	—

Country	Label	10-inch	12-inch	Extended play	Standard
GERMANY, and recently, **AUSTRIA** (the individual Austrian nos. are obsolescent)	Decca³	NLM, PLX, NLX; / LX 35000	NLK, NLXT; / LXT 2000	DX, VD	D.DK [45–]
	Telefunken	LA, LS, LB, NBL, / PLB / TW (Medium play)	LE, LSK, LT	UX, UV	U, UE [45–]
	Capitol	LCA, NLCB, LCB, / LAL, LCS / H (with U.S. no.)	LCE, LCSK / P (with U.S. no.)	EAP, EBF, FBF, / FAP (with U.S. no.)	CF
SPAIN	Decca (local)	LF 91000, DFP		SCGE, ECGE, CGE	—
	Columbia (SpC.)⁴	CLP	CCL, CCLP		
	Alhambra (Ambra.)⁴	MC, MCP	MCC, MCCP	SMGE, EMGE, MGE	—

¹ Series listed are as current in 1955. There have been many changes, both in prefixes and no. series, over the previous few years, and most discs have had two nos. at least, but the final three digits have remained mainly constant. At present many series commence at 500.

² The nos. with the numerical prefixes are the most recent; those incorporating W are Westminster re-pressings.

³ A few discs with G.B. series nos. are issued in Germany but not in G.B. Additional local LP series: LF 1500, LW 50000, LK 40000, LXT 15000 [adding 10000 to G.B. no.]

⁴ These labels are only loosely associated with the Decca group through reciprocal issue agreements in export markets.

Type	33⅓ r.p.m.	45 r.p.m.			
	(12-inch unless otherwise stated)	Extended Play		Standard	
		Sets (see note)	Individual discs	Sets	Individual discs
Classical "Red Seal"	LM (see note)	ERA	549–0000	WDM	49–0000
Classical, H.M.V.	LHMV (see note)	EHA	—	WHMV	149–0000
Collectors' "Red Seal"	LCT (see note)	ERAT	949–0000	WCT	{ 17–0000 449–0000
Popular	LPM (3000, 10-in.)	EPA	547–0000	WP	47–2000
Collectors' Popular	LPT (3000, 10-in.)	EPAT	947–0000	WPT	{ 27–0000 447–0000
"Concert Cameo"	LRM (10-inch; obsolete)	—	—	—	—
Collectors' ditto	LRT (ditto)	—	—	—	—
"Original Cast"	LOC (3000, 10-in.)	EOA	519–0000	WOC	19–0000
"Musical Shows"	LK (3000, 10-in.)	EKA	552–0000	WK	52–0000
Collectors' ditto	LKT (3000, 10-in.)	EKAT	952–0000	WKT	452–0000
Special issues	SRL	—	—	—	—
BLUEBIRD Classics	LBC	ERAB	—	WBC	249–0000
Children's	LY, LRY (8000, 10-in.)	EYA	—	WY	47–0000
BLUEBIRD Children's	—	—	—	WBY	—
CAMDEN	CAL (to CFL, 6 discs)	CAE	—	—	—

NOTES: In the Extended play sets, letter A indicates 1 disc set; B, two discs, and so on.
LM sets numbered: 6000 series, 2 discs; 6100, 3 discs; 6400, 4 discs; 6700, 5 discs. (LPT, LCT similarly.) 9000 series is a single disc, coupling "two features".
LM disc numbers under 1000 were 10-inch, but now obsolescent.
LHMV sets numbered: 600 series, 2 discs; 700, 3 discs; 800, 4 discs; 900, 5 discs. Disc numbers under 1000 are 12-inch.
In the 45 r.p.m. columns, various series start at a higher point than 0000.
Camden are mainly re-issues, with artists concealed under pseudonyms; we have tried to identify these, but some names are only our (or others') surmises.

PHILIPS INTERNATIONAL NUMBERING SYSTEM

The PREFIX letter refers to the type and price-class of the disc:

B, P = Popular   S = Favourites (lower-priced classics; perhaps "Medium play")
N = Medium   A = Artistic (Classical)

The SUFFIX letter shows the size and speed of the disc:

H = 10-inch (25 cm.) normal 78 r.p.m.
G = 12-inch (30 cm.) normal 78 r.p.m.
S = 7-inch (17·5 cm.) "minigroove" 78 r.p.m. (obsolete now?)
R = 10-inch (25 cm.) LP 33⅓ r.p.m.
L = 12-inch (30 cm.) LP 33⅓ r.p.m.
E = 7-inch (17 cm.) Extended-play 45 r.p.m.

In certain recent lists, the prefix and suffix letters for the 45 r.p.m. discs are combined as a two-letter suffix. In this Supplement, however, we have adhered to the original scheme in most entries.

The ENGLISH numbering uses a PREFIX only, of three letters; the first being the prefix letter shown above; the second, the constant letter B; the last, the suffix letter shown above. The numbers are, however, entirely different from the international series which are also shown on the discs and covers.

The only 78 r.p.m. discs issued in England are of the Popular series, and these have the prefix PB (and not PBH, as might have been expected).

FRENCH R.C.A. NUMBERING

L.P. (33⅓ r.p.m.):   "Artistic"—630000 series, 12-inch; 330000, 10-inch
                "Medium"—530000 series, 12-inch; 230000, 10-inch
                "Standard"—430000 series, 12-inch; 130000, 10-inch
E.P. (45 r.p.m.):   "Artistic"—95000 series
                "Medium"—85000 series
                "Standard"—75000 series
45 r.p.m.:   "Standard"—45000 series
78 r.p.m.:   "Standard"—18000 series

USSR. NUMBERING

All 12-inch side numbers begin with a zero.
All 10-inch side numbers begin with a digit.
All 7- or 8-inch numbers begin with two zeros.

All numbers with prefix D are microgroove "long-playing" discs. Those with symbol ♯ are the usual LP, 33⅓ r.p.m.: the others are given code USSRM. and may be of all three sizes, but are all 78 r.p.m. [and see NOTE 7, p. xi, above].

CONSOLIDATED LISTS
of
ERRATA, CORRIGENDA & ADDENDA

The Authors are very grateful to those readers who have responded to their appeal for corrections —which is still open— and particularly to Mr. William Darrah Kelley, Junior, of the U.S.A., for his assiduous discoveries.

These lists do not contain *every* item discovered. The following are excluded:

    (i) Purely textual errors of an obvious nature.
    (ii) Minor records, numbers which were obsolete at date of WERM, and similar items which were designedly omitted.
    (iii) Additional numbers, alterations in prefixes and similar developments (including changes in names of Orchestras) since the closing of the relevant volumes for press.
    (iv) Deaths of Composers, new research dates, and similar discoveries since the closing of the relevant volumes.

        [*Important* items in classes iii and iv are, however, either noted in the correction tables or re-entered in Supplement III].

Readers are recommended to transfer these corrections to their copies of the volumes concerned as they will not be repeated in future supplements.

Further reports of corrections (carefully checked, please, with sources stated) will be gratefully received, but it would assist the Authors if the reports could be cast in similar form to the present lists, and the corrections for each volume kept separate.

PART I
For Supplement II

Page	Col.	Entry	Remarks
xv	—	(115–1) Symphony (Chausson)	The added footnote should, according to report, refer to Stock—and not to Coppola.
xvii	—	(415–1) Symphony No. 26	*To read No. 36.*
xix	—	(620–2) Serenade No. 2, Waltz	Mengelberg: AmC. set *to read* M 104.
2	1	In the dance	Number *to read: USSR, 18204.*
2	2	Malagueña, Op. 71, No. 6	*Transfer* Iturbi entry *below* under Malagueña, Op. 165, No. 3.
3	1	TIEFLAND—Excerpts	Some items are stated to be electric.
3	2	ALFVÉN, Folk song arrs.	For Darlarna *read* Dalarna.
3	2	ANDRICU, Mihail	*Add* date: (b. 1894).
4	1	ARENSKY: Fantasia . . ., Grünberg	*Is* (6ss). No. *to read: USSR. 015930/5.*
4	1	Song: The Brilliant Star	Op. No. *to read: Op. 60, No. 8.*
4	2	Suite No. 2, Op. 23	An older recording was ▽ Eastbourne Municipal—Amers (C. 9749).
5	1	AUBER: Domino Noir, Overture	The Federer recording is not this. *Transfer to new entry:* GUSTAVE III, or Le Bal Masqué, 5 Acts 1833: Overture.
6	1	BABADZHANYAN	*Add* name and date: Arno Arutyunovich (b. 1921).
6	1	BACH, C. P. E.: Concerto, A mi.	*Supply* missing letters in: Swoboda.
6	2	BACH, J. S.: Clavier Collection, Browne	*Move* disc no.: Pax.PR 486 down one line.
7	2	Partita No. 1, B flat major	*Add* to Suite E flat: . . . Bourrée only
		(6) Little Preludes etc. . . . Two unspec.	*Insert* omission: . . . . Gigue only ☆ L. Selbiger (C.LX 8915). F. Kramer: *add* (pf.).
8	1	Toccata, D minor (BWV 913)	*Transfer* entry for F. Neumeyer *to new entry:* D major (BWV 912).
8	2	BACH: ORGAN MUSIC, Schweitzer	AmC. set no. *to read:* SL 175.
9	1	Orgelbüchlein—Krarup	Vater unser is OB 37.
9	1	COLLECTION—Heitmann	Allein Gott in der Höh' sei Ehr! *is really* (BWV 662-E12) and not as stated.
12	2	Brandenburg Concerto 4	*For* Anon. orch. *read:* Berlin Sym—Günther.
13	—	Footnote 2	*Add:* . . . and the soloists as T. Nikolayeva, P. Serebriakov, & D. Shostakovich. This work occupies one side only, coupled with *Handel: Concerto Grosso, Op. 6, No. 7,* though there is no mention of any coupling in the Rgt. catalogue.
14	1	CANTATA NO. 4, Prohaska	*Delete* soloists' names (they do not sing on this side).
		. . . No. 19	*For* erhob *read* erhub.
16	2	Mass, F major (BWV 233)	*Add* Couplings: (*Cantata 42, Sinfonia;* & *Cantata 118*).
		Mass, B minor—Balzer	Soloists named on discs: E. Stolle, E. M. Römer, F. Vogel, E. Wagner.
17	1	Johannes-Passion, ABRIDGED	The Rem. Catalogues spell: Preinfalk.
18	2	Islamey—ARR. ORCH.	Gauk recording: no. *to read* USSR. 020154/5.
20	1	BARTÓK: PF. COLLECTION, Bartók	♯ Rem. 199–94 *also includes* Bagatelle, Op. 6, No. 2.
20	1	FOR CHILDREN: Seemann	The 17 pieces are: Vol. I, Nos. 7, 8, 13-15, 17, 19, 21, 26-30, 34-6.
		MIKROKOSMOS, Books V & VI	Laforge: *Add* footnote to COMPLETE: [1] Except for No. 127.
22	1, 2	Piano Sonatas 10, 22, 24	Backhaus, LXT 2754. *Add* in each case, additional coupling: (. . . & *Schumann*).
24	1	Quintet, E♭ major, Op. 16	Pianist in ♯ Pat.DT 1006 is J. Françaix.
25	2	CONTRETÄNZE, (2) unspec.	Goehr in fact plays Nos. 1 to 3 of the 12 Deutsche Tänze, G.140. *Transfer* entry below.
26	1	Pf. Concerto 1, Gieseking	*Add* new footnote: [1] Thought to be cond. by Karajan (Kolodin).
		Pf. Concerto 3, Stein	Conductor named on disc as Rubahn.
		Pf. Concerto 4, Everett	Conductor named on disc as Balzer.
		Pf. Concerto 5, Huttner	Conductor named on disc as Balzer.
26	2	Vln. Concerto, Haendel	♯ BB prefix *to read:* LBC.
		Vln. Concerto, Balachowsky	Conductor named on disc as Rubahn.
26	2	Coriolan Overture—Ormandy	Symbol ♭ *to read:* ♯.
		idem—Singer	Conductor *to read:* H. Wolf (Singer conducts reverse only).
27	1	Romances, Fuchs	Initial *to read* J, not L.
27	1	Symphony, No. 3—Toscanini	This is ☆ of the n.v. listed in Supp. I.
27	1	Symphony No. 3—Schubert	*For* Hamburg *read* Homburg.
27	2	Symphony No. 6—Guenther	Conductor *to read*—Guthan.
28	1	Symphony No. 9—Rubahn	Soloists named as: I. Camphausen, E. M. Römer, W. Horst, G. Eismann.
28	2	Leonore Overture 3—Keilberth	If this is the same recording as that listed in Supp. III, Orch. *to read:* Bamberg Sym. In that case, the Supp. III entry would be ☆.

Page	Col.	Entry	Remarks
29	1	Fantasia, C major, Op. 80	
		Berlin Radio entry	*To read:* H. Schmidt & Berlin Radio—Kerstaad.
		Wührer, Krauss entry	*Delete* the EVox no.; the English issue now bears the U.S. no.: PL 6480 (Note: This applies *passim* to all EVox. issues with 3 digit numbers).
29	1	Mass, D major—Balzer	Anon. Soloists now named E. Stolle, E. M. Römer, F. Vogel, E. Wagner.
29	1, 2	Ich liebe dich	Author: *for* Herrosen *read* Herrosee.
31	1	Lyric Suite	Symbol ♯ *to read* ♮.
		LULU, cast list	*Add:* Maler ... ...W. Kmentt (T). *Delete* St. Op. Cho.
31	2	Carnaval romain, Ov.—Martinon	*For* ♯ Ura. 7043 *read* ♯ Ura. 7048.
31	2	Damn. of Faust, Suite	Van Beinum: ♯ *Lon.* no. to read: *LS 620.*
		Marche hong. & Danse ...	Kubelik: S 10536 *to read* S 10586.
32	1	Danse des Sylphes... ...	Kostelanetz: *Add:* C.DWX 5083; in ♯ *AmC.ML 2161.*
32	1	Roi Lear, Ov.—Ludwig ...	Boston *to read:* Berlin.
32	2	Troyens, Ballet Music	Conductor *to read:* Heger.
32	2	The Triumph of Neptune	*Add* new footnote to Beecham recording: [1] This Suite contains Cloudland and The Frozen Forest not in the earlier recording in WERM.
			Royal Phil. *to read* Philadelphia.
33	1	BILLINGS	Insert omission: SONGS: The Bird; I am the Rose of Sharon M. Truman (S), Cho. & orch. (in ♮ *Vic. set DM/♭WDM 1445:* ♯ *LM 57*).
33	1	L'Arlésienne, Suites 1 & 2	Stokowski—♭ set prefix *to read* WDM.
33	2	Carmen, Set B	The ♭ *WDM* set is 32ss.
35	1	PÊCHEURS DE PERLES ...	*Transfer* heading Act II *above* De mon amie ...
35	2	BLACHER: Variations ...	PV. 56001 is 12-inch.
35	2	Schelomo	♯ *Vic.LCT 14 is 10-inch.*
36	1	Quintet, E major—Minuetto	Basile: *for* 20258 *read* 20528.
37	1	BONONCINI, Marc Antonio	Should read ... Antonio Maria (1675-1726) (see *Grove,* 5th edn., Vol. i, p. 809).
37	1	BONPORTI—Concerto, F major	Opus no. to read: Op. 11, No. 5.
39	1	Symphony 1—Toscanini ...	10ss. applies only to the ♮ set; the ♭ set is 8ss.
41	1	HUNGARIAN DANCES, COLLECTION (Walter)	Key of No. 10 *to read:* E major [the orch. arr. is transposed to F major]
41	2	WALTZES, Op. 39, Chasins, Keene	*Add* new footnote: [1] Nos. 1, 2, 11, 14, 15 are played in Brahms' own 2-pf. arrangement.
		Idem, Schwalb	Omits No. 13.
44	2	BULL, John	Rondo *to read* Round.
		BUSH, Geoffrey	Date of birth *to read* 1920.
45	2	Aperite mihi	*See* correction to WERM p. 104-2, *infra.*
45	2	Jesu, meine Freude	U. No. *to read* 54.
45	2	Nun bitten wir..., Biggs ...	Ref. *to read:* (Pt. 2, No. 24)
47	2	CASTELNUOVO TEDESCO, Concerto	*Add* symbol ☆.
47	2	CAVALLI: Il Giudizio Universale	This work should be entered under CAVALLI, Pietro Francesco; *transfer* entry below, and *add* soloists: N. Panni, L. Rossi, P. Besma, A. Gaggi; B. Nicolai (org.), K. Josi (pf.).
48	1	España—Fiedler	*For* 7BF 1032 *read* 7BF 1034.
48	2	CHAUSSON: Viviane, Op. 5 ...	Rubahn—*add* new footnote: [1] Announced on this disc, but a copy checked did not contain it.
50	2	ÉTUDES, Op. 25: No. 1 ...	Key *to read:* A flat major.
51	1	MAZURKAS	*Add* new entry: No. 1 F sharp minor—ARR. 2 PFS. A. Sandford & C. Vidusso (in ♯ Roy. 1214).
52	1	NOCTURNES	*Add* new entries to Nos. 5 and 9: — ARR. 2 PFS: A. Sandford and C. Vidusso (in ♯ Roy. 1214).
53	2	VALSES: COLLECTION, Cortot ...	*Add* to contents omitted item: No. 3, A minor, Op. 34, No. 2.
		Idem: COLLECTION, Sandford & Vidusso	*Add* to contents, omission: No. 9.
55	1	Les Sylphides, Berlin—List ...	*Delete.* Although announced, this does not appear on the disc or in later editions of the catalogue [see amendment to p. 64—2, *below*]
55	2	Matrimonio Segreto, Overture ...	Serafin—G.C no. *to read* 4185.
55	—	Footnote²	*To read:* ² Prelude No. 7 & Valse No. 7 only.
56	1	CLEMENTI: Gradus ad Parnassum	Schwalb plays: Études Nos. 12, 18, 20, 21.
58	2	CRAMER	Schwalb plays: Études Nos. 8, 17, 42, 55, 29, 21, 36, 26, 27, 47, 53, 56, 57 of the Bülow edn. (in that order). See Supp. III entry, *below*, p. 126.
			Delete École de Vélocité.
59	1	CZERNY: Études	*Add* heading: ÉCOLE DE VÉLOCITÉ, Op. 299. Schwalb plays Nos. 39, 27, 14, 23, 34, 38, 37.
59	1	DANZI: Quintet, Op. 67, No. 1 ...	*Add* key: G major. Number *to read* CE 2010.
61	1	Petite Suite—Reiner	Orchestra *to read :* N.B.C. Sym.
62	2	Nocturnes—Galliera	*For* DX 1780 *read* DX 1782.
64	1	COPPÉLIA: Unspec. excerpts. ...	Braithwaite recording contains Nos. 1 (b) and 7. *Transfer* up under previous heading.
			List recording, coupling *to read:* (*Sylvia*).
64	2	SYLVIA; Ballet Suite	Braithwaite recording contains Nos. 1b and 4 only. *Transfer* down under new heading.
			Add omission: Unspec. excerpts (or may be whole suite) Berlin Sym.—List (♯ Roy. 1338). [See amendment to p. 55-1.]
67	1	Lucia, Highlights	*Add* after Pinza: Vic. Cho. and Sym.—Cellini.
68	1	L'Apprenti Sorcier... ...	André recording: *Add* ☆.
68	2	DVARIONAS	*Add:* Balis Dominikovich (b. 1904). *For* vla. probably read: vln.
69	1	Cello Concerto, Op. 104 ...	Seidler's conductor is named as Rubahn on the label.
69	1	Golden Spinning Wheel ...	*Add* new footnote to LPM 9: [1] This is the coupling as originally announced. Later and current catalogues show the Tchaikowsky Sym. coupled with *Capriccio italien.*
69	1	Noonday Witch	*For* H 23734/5 *read* H 23784/5.
69	1	Slavonic Rhapsody No. 3 ...	*For* Leitner *read* Lehmann.
69	2	Sym. No. 4—Szell... ...	*For* LXT 2461 *read* LXT 2641.
69	2	Sym. No. 5—Singer ...	*Add* new footnote: [1] This recording has probably also been substituted for that by Wöss (see Supp. I, p. 767-1) on later pressings of ♯ Rem. 199-4.
71	2	EGK, Werner	Date of birth *to read* 1901.
77	1	Variations symphoniques, Huttner	Conductor named on disc as Balzer.
77	2	FRIEDRICH II: Sonata, C minor	Rampal is understood to play Sonata No. 2, C minor.
		FROBERGER: Suite & Variations	*Delete* (announced ... issued).
78	1	GALLON, first title	*To read:* Chanson du vieux Canada.
78	2	American in Paris ⎫	The orch. is called Vienna Pro Musica by AmVox, though
79	1	Rhapsody in Blue ⎭	Vienna Sym. by Pathé.
80	1	GIORDANI: Caro mio ben ...	Brückner, no. *to read: Tpo. 3648.*

Page	Col.	Entry	Remarks
81	2	Valse de Concert, No. 1	Golovanov recording; coupling to read: (3ss—*Liadov: Naenia, Op. 67*)—*See* entry in Supp. III, *below*, p. 250.
81	2	Valse (unspec.)	Now identified as Petite Valse, Op. 36.
84	2	GOEB, Roger	Date of birth stated by H. C. Schonberg to be 1914.
		Prairie Songs	Composed 1946.
85	1	GOLDMARK: Symphony ...	Op. No. *to read:* **Op. 26.**
85	2	GOTTSCHALK: Cakewalk ...	Performers *to read:* Philadelphia—Ormandy.
86	1	Faust—Valse, Lehmann	PV. 72014 *to read :* PV. 72104.
89	2	Symphonic Dances—v. Kempen ...	For Dresden Phil. *read* Berlin State.
89	2	PEER GYNT—Digest	For DTX 111 *read* DTX 114.
89	2	PEER GYNT—Orch. Suite ...	The item **Bridal Procession** is ARR. Halvorsen.
		Suite No. 1, Bamberg Sym. ...	For Leitner *read* Suitner.
90	1	SONGS—COLLECTION, Sönnerstedt ...	*Add* omission: (The) First Meeting, Op. 21, No. 1.
90	1	SONGS—COLLECTION, Niemala ...	The name is usually: Niemela.
92	1	HAIEFF, Concerto	Composed 1949-50, first perf. 1952.
		HALFFTER	The item in † HARP MUSIC is by HALFFTER, Rodolfo (b. 1900).
		HALVORSEN—Entry of Boyars ...	Fiedler: for *7RF* read *7BF*.
93	2	PASSION (ST. JOHN)	*Add* new footnote: [2] Ed. E. Hess; includes interpolations from *Brockes-Passion* (1716). [See Supp. III entry, *below*, p. 203.]
95	2	CONCERTOS, Oboe & orch. ...	See Supp. III entries, *below*, for general correction of numbering. *Add* to "No. 4" new footnote: [2] Printed as No. 12 of *XII Concertos in 8 parts* by Robert Woodcock (1735).
96	—	Footnote[1]	*Continue:* . . . and the *Festival* Suite, from the Occasional Oratorio.
97	1	HAUER	Names *should read:* **Joseph Matthias** (b. 1883).
97	2	Mass No. 12	*See* Footnote to Supp. III reissue entry, *below*.
97	2	The CREATION—Krauss ...	The Part III Solos are sung by F. Riegler & A. Pernerstorfer.
100	2	Marches, Haas recording ...	Coupling—for *Divertimento* read *Notturno*.
		Notturni	*See* Supp. III entries, *below*, for general revision of numberings.
101	1	*Add* omission:	
		No. 21, A major }	
		No. 42, D major }	☆ Vienna Cha.—Litschauer (♯ Nix. HLP 1025).
101	1	Symphony 49, Blech	D. number *to read* LXT 2753.
102	—	Footnote [1]	*Continue:* . . . not by Haydn, but probably by A. Zimmermann (1741-1781). Numbered by H. C. Robbins Landon as App. II, No. 27.
103	1	Zampa, Overture—Berlin Sym. ...	Conductor is L. Ludwig *not* Balzer.
103	1	HILL, Alfred	The songs recorded on *DO 3325* and *3330* are by Mirrie Hill (b. 1894) and A. Hill.
105	2	HANSEL AND GRETEL—Suite	Nilius recording is the **Dream Pantomime** only. *Transfer* to entry *below* (p. 106).
106	1	IBERT: Capriccio & Divertissement ...	Are performed by Winterthur—Swoboda.
108	2	The Comedians, Suite	For *U.C 23847/8* read *U.C 23897/8*.
113	1	NAMOUNA—Orch. Suites ...	Sebastian recording: *Add* new footnote: [1] Also includes *Danse de Namouna*, not in the usual suites.
114	2	MASS, Octavi toni ...	The Mass 'Puisque j'ai perdu' though correctly described as a Mass *octavi toni*, is not the one *usually* so described; the excerpts on *Chr. 327A* are probably from the latter. To prevent confusion, insert new line Octavi toni above this entry and transpose the previous heading to make 'Puisque j'ai perdu' the main title.
115	2	Nachledil Marsch	Is from Wiener Frauen. *Transfer below*.
116	2	Lustige Witwe, Waltz	Schönherr—♯ *VNLP 1003* is 10-inch.
120	1	Am Grabe Richard Wagners ...	G. number *to read* G.113.
120	2	Sonetto del Petrarca 104 ...	*For* T.v.d. Pas *read* A. Uninsky.
122	1	Tannhäuser March	*Delete* * from Voc. A 0268.
122	2	LITOLFF, Concerto . . . Scherzo	*Add* omission: ☆ M. Lympany & Philharmonia—Susskind (♭ G. 7P 105).
123	1	LOEILLET	*See* newly arranged complete discography, *below*, pp. 259/60.
123	2	WILDSCHÜTZ, Overture ...	For Pol. 15430 *read* Pol. 15480.
126	1	Symphony No. 2	Current Number is ♯ E. & AmVox set 7012. (The o.n. was ♯ AmVox. set PL 7010 not 7080.)
126	1	Symphony No. 8	Key *to read:* E flat major.
126 / 258	1 / 2 }	MALEINGRAU	Should be spelt: **MALEINGREAU.**
126	2	MANFREDINI: Sinfonia da chiesa	*Correct* title to: Concerto Grosso, C major, Op. 3, No. 12.
126	2	MARCHAND, Louis	*Add* reference: † MÂITRES D'ORGUE.
127	1	MARTINŮ: Concerto, str. qtt. & orch....	Date *to read:* 1931.
127	2	Cavalleria Rusticana, Set F ...	*Add:* (4ss).
130	1	Phèdre, Overture—Federer ...	This disc is 10-inch. No. *to read* ♯ *Rgt. 5050.*
131	1	Organ Sonata 6, Schweitzer ...	Set no. *to read:* SL 175.
131	1	Variations sérieuses—Cortot ...	*Add* new footnote: *G.DA 1994/5* (manual, Italy, etc.).
132	1	Violin Concerto—Stern ...	For C.LX 1445/7 *read* C.LX 1455/7.
132	2	Symphony No. 3	Opus No. *to read:* Op. 56.
132	2	M.S.N.D.—Ov. & Nos. 1, 7, 9—Brown	For No. 9 *read* No. 11.
133	2	Elijah, No. 4 } Saint Paul, No. 2 }	I. Lindholm *is* (S) *not* (T).
134	1	MENGELBERG: Salve Regina ...	*Add* coupling: (3ss—*Andriessen*). *See* Supp. III entry, *below*.
135	1	O Paradis!, R. Schock ...	*Delete* (? Ger): definitely in French.
136	1	Saudades do Brasil	*Correct* spelling. J. Germain *plays* Nos. 1, 5, 12, 7, 3.
137	2	MINKUS, Louis	Date *to read* (1827-1890).
139	1	VESPERS	Title Magnificat does not form part of this work. *Transfer* above VESPERS and add: . . . primo (XV) 1641.
140	1	By the water	Identified as pf. arr. of song: By the river (No. 6 of **Sunless Cycle**). *Transfer* entry *below*, under SONGS.
140	1	Pictures from an Exhibition ...	Berlin Sym: *add* Conductor: H. Hermann.
142	1	CHORUSES (Masonic) ... ... }	COLLECTION on ♯ MR. 101 now fully identified; see revised entry in Supp. III, *below*, p. 299.
147	2	Songs—Gesellenreise, etc. ... ... }	
142	2	Vesperae de Dominica, C ma., K 321	*Add* new footnote to Reinhart: [3] Includes interpolated hymn *In me gratia omnis* and cadenzas, composed by the Conductor.
143	1	COSI FAN TUTTE, Overture ...	Lehmann: *PV* no. to read: *36050.*
143	1	Don Giovanni, No. 4	Schoeffler sings in German.
143	2	Idem, No. 22	Schock sings in Italian on ♯ Roy. 1256.
144	1	ENTFÜHRUNG Overture—Nilius ...	Both the ♯ discs are *10-inch* and the numbers should be in *italics*.
144	1	*Idem*, No. 2	Probable omission: **H** W. Hesch (in ♯ Ete.O-479*) (labelled *Osmin's entrance*).
144	2	IDOMENEO, Overture	*Delete* entry for ♯ Per.SPL 559. The disc does not contain this Overture. Further contents are listed in Supp. III below.

Page	Col.	Entry	Remarks
145	1, 2	NOZZE DI FIGARO, Nos. 9, 10, 11, 19	The arias on ‡ D.LXT 2685 are sung in *German*.
146	1	THAMOS, Entractes—Günther...	‡ *Rem. no. to read:* 199-54.
146	2	ZAUBERFLÖTE, Ov.—Toscanini ...	*For* ♭ *Vic.* 49-1423 *read* ♭ *Vic.* 49-0903. The *WEPR* prefix is now obsolete; *read ERA 14.*
148	1	Wiegenlied—Gerholdt	Number *to read: Tono. K 8082.*
149	2	Oboe Quartet, Tabuteau	⎫
151	2	Divertimento K251, idem	⎪
152	1	Serenade 13, Casals	⎬ *Substitute for* '(& in set SL 170)':
154	1	Vln. Concerto 5, Morini	⎪ (& in set SL 167; also set SL 170, limited edn.).
154	2	Sinfonia Concertante, Casals	⎪
155	1	Sym. 29, Casals	⎭
152	1	Fl. Concerto No. 1, Wummer	⎫
152	2	Pf. Concerto, K 271, Hess	⎪
152	2	Pf. Concerto, K 449, Istomin	⎬ *Substitute for* '(& in set SL 170)':
153	1	Pf. Concerto, K 482, Serkin	⎪ (& in set SL 168; also set SL 170, limited edn.).
153	2	Pf. Concerto, K. 595, Horszowski	⎭
151	1	Cassation No. 2, K 99 / Divertimento, D major K 247 ...	Orch. *to read:* Salzburg Mozarteum.
151	1	Serenade No. 6, Newstone	*For* MWL 301 *read* MWL 302.
152	1	Serenade No. 13, Berlin Sym.	*Add* Conductor:—Balzer.
153	1	Pf. Concerto, K 453, Kirkpatrick	*For Eur. read* Era.
153	2	Pf. Concerto, K 503, Seemann ...	AmD. *no to read* DL 9568.
153	2	Pf. Concertos, K 107, Balsam	Conductor *to read* :—Ackermann.
154	1	Vln. Concerto 4, PL 7240	Conductor *to read:* Seegelken.
154	1	Sinfonia Concertante, K 297b—Wöss	Soloists are: B. Dörrschmidt, O. Drapal, H. Lorch, E. Mühlbacher.
155	1, 2	Symphonies 26, 35	‡ Pol. 18066 also contains Sym. 32 [see Supp. III entry, *below*]. *Add* to coupling.
156	—	Footnote [1]	*Delete* all except first three words. Correctly identified as listed.
157	2	NIN—COMENTARIOS, No. 3...	*For* ANGELÈS *read* ANGLÈS.
158/9	1, 2	OFFENBACH, Overtures—Dupré	*For* LCSK 8012 *read* LCSK 8102.
158	2	Belle Hélène Overture, Nilius	Is now stated to be cond. Schönherr.
159	1	Orphée Overture, Nilius ...	‡ *AmVien.* VNLP 1007 is *10-inch*.
159	1	Contes d'Hoffmann, Complete ...	Soloists in Rubahn recording named as: W. Horst (Hoffmann), H. Schenck (Nicklausse), E. V. Kovatsy (Stella), I. Camphausen (Olympia), E. Niehaus (Giulietta), H. Tock (Antonia), G. Schneider (Coppélius), H. Neuwald (Dapertutto), etc.
161	1	PALESTRINA—COLLECTION	*For* IMPROPERIUM *read* IMPROPERIA.
	1	MASS—Papae Marcelli	Number suffix *to read* R not L.
163	2	PIZZETTI—Concerto dell'Estate...	‡ NRI. 106 is 12-inch.
164	2	POOT—Overture joyeuse ⎱	PhM *no. to read* A 09001S.
206	1	Valse triste ⎰ ...	
165	1	POWELL: Rhapsodie négre	Soloist is L. Davis.
165	2	PRAETORIUS	All the items listed are from *Musae Sioniae*, 1609.
166	2	Peter and the Wolf, first entry	*For* Matetskaya *read* Maretskaya.
167	1	Romeo & Juliet, Suite No. 2	Mravinsky (‡ Van.VRS 6004) is stated to be 4 movts. only.
		On Guard for peace, Op. 124	Date *to read* 1950.
		Winter Holiday	*Add:* Op. 122 (Marshak), 1949.
168	1	MADAMA BUTTERFLY—Set H, Highlights	*For* ‡ Rem. 199-100 *read* 199-101.
169	1	Letter Duet & Con onor—Destinn	*Delete*: (Ger).
171	1	Chacony, G minor; Chaconne	*Delete* footnote [1]. *See* corrected entries in Supp. III *below*, for VRS 419, 420.
171	2	DIDO & AENEAS, No. 37—Adler ...	‡ *CHS.CHS* 1161 is *10-inch*.
171	2	KING ARTHUR, COMPLETE ...	Disc code *to read* MTR.
172	2	Pf. Concerto No. 2—Everett	Conductor named as:—Rubahn; Pianist's initial given as E, not F.
175	2	Minuet (unspec.) — ARR. GUITAR	Identified as *Suite 5 ... No. 4. Transfer up.*
177	1	La Valse, Brussels—André ...	It is doubtful whether this item was in fact issued in ♭ *Cap. set KBM 8083.*
177	2	Chansons madécasses	Author *to read* (Parny) *not* (Paray).
179	1	Boutique fantasque—Braithwaite	*Add* footnote: : Tarantella, Scene (Andante mosso) & Can-can only.
180	1	Scheherazade—Berlin Sym. ...	Later catalogues name the Conductor as K. List.
181	1	MAY NIGHT, COMPLETE ...	Later Vanguard lists agree that conductor is Nebolsin.
182	2	ROSSINI: QUARTETS	*See* footnote to Supp. III entry, *below*, p. 383.
183	2	Barbiere No. 7—Supervia	No. *to read* DL 9533.
184	1	Gazza Ladra, Overture—Haarth	No. *to read* 15532/3.
184	1	Guillaume Tell, Overture—Toscanini	No. *to read* ♭ G. 7RF188/9.
		idem, Berlin Phil.—v. Kempen	*Delete* 'attrib. Fricsay', from AmD. number.
185	1	Tancredi, Overture—Federer	Is *10-inch. No. to read* ‡ Rgt. 5050.
185	1	ROZSA, Quo Vadis Suite	Delete Orchestral from title; *Add* 'Cho. &' *before* artists.
185	2	(The) Red House ...	♭ *Cap. set* CB 48 is *10-inch*.
187	2	Danse Macabre—Malko ...	G.DB number *to read* 10504.
189	1	Messe pour les pauvres ...	Coupling line *to read*: (Schoenberg: *Variations*).
193	2	DEUTSCHE TÄNZE	Goehr on ‡ CHS.F6 is the D.820 set. Moralt on ‡ AmVox.PL 7280 is presumably identical with the ♭ reissue: See Supp. III entry. Stokowski, if the same as the Eng. reissue, is Op. 33, Nos. 1, 3, 4, 5, 7, 10, 13 only; but this may apply to the ♭ issues only.
194	1	ROSAMUNDE—Meylan ...	‡ *Sup.* LPM 23 contains Nos. 2 & 9 only.
195	2	PARTSONGS—COLLECTION ...	Nachthelle: Op. no. *to read:* Op. 134.
195	2	COLLECTION—Mauranne ...	Is sung in *French*. Artist's name now spelt: Maurane.
196	2	Ave Maria	R. Ponselle sings in *Latin*.
198	2	Also hat Gott	Reference *to read* (MC) *not* (GK. 1636).
		Ehre sei dir, Christe	Is final chorus of MATTHÄUS-PASSION. *Transfer* to p. 199 under that title and amalgamate with existing entry.
		Die Worte der Abendmahleinsetzung	Original title *reads* Die Wort der Einsetzung des heiligen Abendmahls; for 4 vv.
		COLLECTION on ‡ BàM.LD 02 ...	*See* Supp. III entry of English reissue, for full references to contents.
198	2	Weihnachts-Historie	The Ghedini edition is used on ‡ Csm.CLPS 1034.
200	1	Études symphoniques	Kolessa omits No. 9, but plays 2 of the Posth. Études
200	2	SONATA No. 2, F minor ...	Goldsand plays the first edition, with cut in Scherzo [Wührer (see Supp. III entry, p. 417) uses the revised edition.]
201	2	CONCERTO, pf. & orch, Haskil	Is *10-inch*; no. *to read: A 00134R.*
201	2	CONCERTO, vlc. & orch., Seidler	Conductor named on disc as Balzer.
203	2	Symphony No. 2—Golovanov ...	No. *to read:* USSR. 018720/31.

Page	Col.	Entry				Remarks
204	2	QUARTET, Strings, No. 2	...		...	*Add* key: A major, and date: 1943.
		The Song of the Forests	...	...	...	*Add.* Op. 81.
205	1	Finlandia—Malko	...		...	*For* 7R101 *read* 7P101.
209	ff.	STRAUSS family	...	...	...	The following Viennola recordings are now said to be conducted by Schönherr, *not* Nilius: Loreley Rheinklänge; Annen-Polka; Tritsch-Tratsch; Märchen aus dem Orient; Lustige Krieg Overture. Feuerfest Polka & Sphärenklänge are now attributed to Nilius.
210	1	COLLECTION: POLKAS, Vol. II				*For* Um *read* Im Sturmschritt.
211	1	An der schönen, blauen Donau	...			Lanner recording is 10-inch: ♯ *MGM.E 133.* C. Krauss conducts Vienna Phil. *not* Sym.
	1	Frühlingsstimmen	...	...	...	Günther conducts Vienna Radio *not* Phil. *Add* no.(*Pht.P 41076H*). Krauss and Szell conduct Vienna Phil. *not* Sym.
	2	G'schichten aus dem Wiener Wald		...		Lanner recording: *delete* reference to zither solo.
	2	Kaiserwalzer—Paulik.			...	The two recordings are different. SL 129 is cond. Anton Paulik, FLD 2 cond. Herbert Paulik. [*Add* initial H. to all other entries of FLD 2, *passim.*]
212	1	Morgenblätter	...	...	...	The recording listed on ♯ Rem. 199-97 is said to be cond. Günther.
213	2	INDIGO—ABRIDGED RECORDING			...	Includes Waltz Seid umschlungen, Millionen, as ballet music.
215	1	Feuerfest Polka—Ormandy			...	*For* A 1013 *read* A 1031.
215	1	Frauenherz Polka, Wöss	...		...	Rem. No. to read: 149-34.
216	1	Don Juan—Balzer			...	♯ Roy. 1370 contains an excerpt only.
216	1	Symphony, F minor, Op. 12			...	This recording is *not* by the Vienna Phil., notwithstanding the original SPA catalogue. The Commercial Court in Vienna granted an injunction in May 1954, restraining SPA from so describing any records, as the Vienna Phil. had never recorded for them.
216	1	Till Eulenspiegel	...	...	...	Berlin Sym.—*add* conductor:—Rubahn.
217	1	ROSENKAVALIER, Highlights...			...	♯ Roy. 1352 is now said to be performed by I. Camphausen, W. Horst, L. Borrmann, F. Jungmann & Berlin Op. Cho. & Orch.—Rubahn.
220	2	Boccaccio, Overture—Graunke	...			*Transfer* entry to Banditenstreiche (with *DL 4021*). [*Delete* Boccaccio as coupling under Schöne Galathée, *below*, p. 227-1.]
220	2	Banditenstreiche, Overture }				
221	1	Schöne Galathée, Overture }		...		Federer recording is 10-inch: ♯ *Rgt. 5050.*
221	1	SWEELINCK: Fantasia No. 11 in echo-style				This is No. 16 in the Seiffert edn. (1943); *see* Supp. III entry *below*, p. 456.
222	1	TARTINI: Sonata, G minor	...		...	*For* Op. 2, No. 7 *read* Op. 3, No. 7.
224	2	Nutcracker Suite	...		...	*Delete* heading: . . . Unspec. excerpts above Braithwaite, and *transfer* entry *above*: this contains No. 3, Valse des Fleurs.
224	2	Sleeping Beauty, No. 6	...		...	*Delete* Malko entry. The nos. quoted are in fact a Suite from the ballet, by Philharmonia—Malko, containing (as far as can be ascertained without hearing) Intro. & Nos. 3 (a & b, part), 4, 8a, 9, 22 (b, c), 29. Most of this recording has since been re-issued: see column N in the table in Supp. III, *below*.
224	2	Swan Lake, Complete	...	...	...	Krombholc has new no.: ♯ Ura. set 605.
225	1	Swan Lake, excerpts			...	Braithwaite ♯ MGM.E 3006 is Nos. 9, 14, 16; List ♯ Roy. 1319 is Intro. & Nos. 4, 13, 14, 17; Rignold ♯ BB.LBC 1016 is Nos. 1, 5, 7, 19, 20, 26.
225	2	Hamlet, Op. 67—Boult	...		...	No. to read LXT 2696.
226	1	Ouverture solennelle, 1812			...	Malko recording may be the n.v. (*see* Supp. III entry, *below*, p.467)
226	1	Romeo & Juliet Ov.—Münch			...	*Delete.* These are the German Nos. for Berlioz: Romeo and Juliet excerpts (see WERM, p. 66).
		—Lehmann	...	...	...	♯ Pol. number *to read* 18036.
		—Wöss	...	...	...	♯ Mrt. 1-3 is 10-inch.
226	2	Serenade—Waltz	...		...	*Delete* Koussevitzky entry. ♭ Vic. WEPR 7 was the Finale only, coupled with *Haydn.* Prefix now is ERA.
227	1	ENCHANTRESS—My fate is strange	...			The tenor is G. Nelepp.
227	1	EUGENE ONIEGIN, No. 9			...	Albanese: coupling is *Bachianas No. 5,* not *8.*
228	2	TCHAIKOVSKY—Songs, *passim*			...	Shaposhnikov is (B), Lavrova is (S), Migai is (B), Orfenov is (T), Gaidai is (S).
	etc.					
230	2	Sonatas, 2 vlns.	...	...	...	The Nos. quoted are those of the Peters edn.; orig. Op. 2, Nos. 3, 2, 4; Op. 5, No. 3, respectively.
231	1	Mignon, Overture—Nilius			...	Vienna Radio, *not* Sym.
231	2	THOMPSON—Sym. No. 2			...	*Delete:* . . . 1st movt. only. The recording is complete.
232	2	TORELLI: Concerto, Op. 8, No. 6			...	Key *to read:* G minor.
		Concerto, Op. 8, No. 3				Key *to read:* E major.
232	2	TOURNIER, Marcel			...	Date to read (1879-1951).
232/3	2/1	TURINA	...	...	...	*Add* Opus nos. and other information from Supp. III entries *below*. Triptico: *Transfer* author's name after Farruca.
234	1	Requiem Mass—Balzer	...		...	Soloists named on discs as E. Stolle, E. M. Römer, F. Vogel, E. Wagner.
234	2	SONGS—COLLECTION	...		...	Author of Il Mistero is Romani.
236	1	Don Carlos	...	...	...	*For* Io t'ho perduto *read* Io l'ho . . .
237	1	Reverenza!	...	...	...	*To read:* Signore, v'assista il ciel! (the Falstaff-Ford duet).
237	1	Forza del Destino, Overture			...	♭ UREP 2, listed under Rother, is really from the complete recording cond. Parodi. *Transfer* above with set, as: Overture only . . .
241	2	Timor di me—Destinn	...		...	*Delete:* (Ger).
241	2	Vêpres Siciliennes—Ballet music	...			*Add:* . . . Autumn only.
242	1	O magnum mysterium	...	...		St. Olaf Cho.—in coupling, for *Schubert* read G. Schumann. The number of this disc should be elaborated to *DLP 5. Add:* (in ♮ set D5: ♭ set D5-45). This applies also to the other entries for this disc. Other StO. recordings also exist on 78 r.p.m. discs—e.g. the contents of ♯ DLP 3 as sets D1 & D2 (see pp. 17, 90, 137, 161).
242	2	Ave Maria No. 20		...	...	Sung in *English.*
244	1	Concerto, Fl. ob. & bsn., (P 402)			...	*Delete.* Although announced, it does not appear on the actual disc as issued.
		Concerto, 2 Trumpets, E flat major			...	*For* P 273 *read* P 320.
		Concertos, Viola d'amore (P 233 & 287)				*Add* conductor:—Peatfield.
		Idem, P 287 (DL 9575 etc.)			...	*Add* soloist: R. Sabatini; & conductor:—Fasano.
		Sinfonia, B minor (P 21)	...		...	The conductor on ♯ Csm.CLPS 1029 is Ephrikian.
244	2	Laudate pueri	...	...	...	*Delete* reference to a Chorus.
		Juditha triumphans	...	...		*Add* missing soloist: M. Cortis, *before* G. Ferrein.
245	1	Siegfried Idyll, Münchinger				Orch. *should read:* Stuttgart Cha. & Suisse Romande Members.
245	2	FLIEGENDE HOLLÄNDER	...		...	Date of first perf. *to read* 1843.

Page	Col.	Entry				Remarks
246	1	LOHENGRIN—Excerpts, Act II			...	♯ Ete. O-472 is said by P. L. Miller to contain an electrical recording of Act II, Scene 1 by Olszewska & Schipper. No trace of an earlier issue of this can be found, but an acoustic version by these artists was on Pol. 72989/90*.
248	2	Götterdämmerung: Trauermusik ...			...	Furtwängler for ♭ G. 7RF 151 read ♭ G. 7RF 149.
		Starke Scheite . . ., Flagstad			...	Vic. no. to read: LHMV 1024.
251	1	Concertino, Clarinet and Orch.			...	Key to read E flat major.
251	2	Wanderers Nachtlied (unid.)			...	Probably the setting by B. A. Weber (1766-1821), wrongly attributed.
252	1	Oberon Overture—v. Kempen			...	PhM. no. to read: N 09017S.
252	2	WEBER—SONGS—Mott			...	Add Op. nos.: Op. 71, No. 3; 47, Nos. 1 & 2; 64, No. 3; 30, No. 3, respectively.
252	2	WEBERN—4 Songs, Op. 12			...	Add Authors: Anon., Bethge, Strindberg, Goethe, respectively.
254	2	SONGS—COLLECTION (Dieskau)			...	Third title: for Ketten read Kutten.
255	2	YARNOLD			...	Add first name: Benjamin.
257	2	AMERICAN MUSIC—J. ANTES: Trios.			...	♯ NRI. 2016 is 12-inch.
258	1	EARLY ENG. KEYBOARD MUSIC ...				Add new footnotes: To BULL: Walsingham Variations: [1] Omitting variations 7, 10, 13, 16-18, 21-24, 27, 29. To FARNABY: Woodycock: [2] Omitting variation 4. Delete * against BULL: In Nomine. This item is not in the ♯ issue.
259	1	HARP MUSIC			...	The item attributed to HALFFTER is by R. Halffter (see correction to p. 92, above). Add footnote to this title: [1] Harp version of 3 movements of Homenaje a Antonio Machado, Op. 13, pf. solo.
259	2	MAÎTRES D'ORGUE DE J. S. Bach ...				Add items omitted: L. MARCHAND: Basse de trompette Fonds d'orgue
—	—	Piano music, passim		...	...	It is now known that the Russian pianist Neuhaus, always previously given the initial G, has the first name Heinrich. We apologise for the error, caused by the confusion in the Russian alphabet of the letters G and H.

PART II

FOR W.E.R.M. AND SUPPLEMENT I

Page	Col.	Entry				Remarks
3	1	Malagueña, Op. 71, No. 6			...	Iturbi is not this, but Op. 165, No. 3. Transfer entry, below.
		Idem — ARR. VLN. & PF. ...			...	Haendel is also Op. 165, No. 3. Transfer. Pianist is N. Mewton-Wood, not as stated.
7	1	ARENSKY—Valse			...	Add omission: § D. T. Sprishevskaya (S) (Vic. 4071) [reverse of this disc already entered—see Rubinstein: Demon].
10	1	Chantons pour passer le temps			...	CdM. 522 later reissued as CdM. 527, d.c.
		Le roi a fait battre tambour			...	CdM. 515 to read CdM. 512.
10	2	Magnificat, D major			...	Add to Vic. 14869/70:, set M 444. This recording includes only: Opening Chorus; Suscepit Israel (A); Et misericordia (Cho.).
13	1	March, D major			...	BWV. ref. to read: Anh. 122.
13	2	Minuets, G major and minor, BWV 841-3				E. Goll should read: BWV 841 only. Disc is 10-inch (AmB. 15210).
14	1	(6) [Little] Preludes for beginners			...	BWV nos. to read: BWV. 933/8.
14	2	English Suite No. 2 . . . Prelude ...			...	J. Dennery: AmD. no. to read 25028.
15	2	Suite, C minor, BWV 997			...	Add omission: ... Double only § E. Goll (AmB. 15210).
24	1	Fugue, G minor — ARR. ...			...	Is for PF. QUINTET not STR. QTT.
24	2	Sonata No. 3 . . . Allegro only			...	E. Goll: No. to read (AmB. 15210).
30	2	Canons à 2 voci, etc.—Weyns			...	The no. U.F 22503 refers to T.E 2296 (Ricercare) and not to E 3082.
33	1	Cantata 106			...	For Sinfonia read: No. 1, Sonatina.
33	2	Cantata 147, No. 10 —ORCH.			...	Add to AmC. set MM 486: & LP: ML 2088.
34	1	Cantata 206, No. 9. Ginster Debička			...	Add: & pf. For orch. read pf.
34	2	Jesu, meine Freude (—Excerpt) ...			...	Shaw recording is sung in English. Pro Musica is No. 7 not No. 1 [also on 37-2].
35	2	Mass, B minor			...	Revise item numbers: 21, Sanctus; 22, Osanna; 23, Benedictus; 24, Agnus Dei.
36	1	Weihnachtsoratorium, No. 17			...	To read: Schaut hin! [The melody is Vom Himmel hoch.]
		Idem, No. 36			...	Dank to read Danken.
37	1	Lass ihn kreuzigen			...	This is part of No. 54, not No. 55.
38	1	Es ist das Heil . . .			...	Stated to be Nun danket alle Gott (BWV 252) and Sei Lob' und Ehr' (BWV 251).
45	2	BAGATELLES, Op. 119: No. 11			...	Key to read: B flat major.
		No. 9 ...			...	Key to read: A minor.
53	1	(12) Contretänze, Barlow			...	Add to AmC. no.: (Set X 184).
55	1	Zur Weihe des Hauses Ov.			...	Weingartner—Add to AmC. no.: set X 140.
56	—	Footnote [4] ...			...	For Vic. 14743/7S read Vic. 14793/7S.
59	1	MASS, D major—Kittel ...			...	Add: (& ♮ AmVox. set 466).
61	2	Mira, o Norma ...			...	Spell Arangi-Lombardi (this error may recur, passim).
63	1	BENJAMIN: Cookie			...	Add new footnote: [1] No. 2 of 2 Jamaican Street Songs, orig. pf. duet.
63	2	Jamaican Rumba— ARR. 2 PFS. ...			...	Delete: Jamaican Street Song No. 1.
		Matty Rag — ARR. 2 PFS....			...	Is: Jamaican Street Song No. 1 (not No. 2).
71	1	Habanera			...	N. Vallin: add Pat. X 90030 & . . .
		Parle-moi de ma mère ...			...	Delete Vallin & Villabella.
71	2	Séguedille			...	Supervia (P.R 20127) has anon. T. [probably G. Micheletti?].
73	2	Mêlons! Coupons! ...			...	Pape no. to read C.LF 197.
76	1	Ouvre ton cœur ...			...	The date 1887 is that of publication as a song. This is from the Ode-symphony Vasco de Gama (1859-60).
78 711	1} 2}	String Quartet, Op. 1, No. 2 ...			...	Key to read: B flat major.
78	1	Quintet, Op. 13, No. 5 . . . Minuet			...	Weingartner—Add: (AmC 70674D, in set M 428).
81	1	MEFISTOFELE—La notte del Sabba classico			...	Artists on Od./AmD. also include M. Castagna and G. Nessi.

Page	Col.	Entry	Remarks
81	1	NERONE—Vivete in pace	*Add* omission: E. de Franceschi Fnt. 35056 (with *Tannhäuser*).
81 748	2} 1}	BONONCINI, Giovanni Battista ...	*Delete* Battista. (See *Grove*, 5th. edn.).
		Deh più a me	Is *not* by this composer, but by BONONCINI, Giovanni Maria (1642-1678). Insert new heading accordingly.
81	2	BONONCINI, Marc Antonio (1677-1726)	Names and date *to read*: Antonio Maria (1675-1726). See *Grove*.
85	2	Symphony No. 1, Philadelphia—Stokowski	*Add* to Vic. 8971/5: set M 301.
86	1	Symphony No. 2—Stokowski ...	*Add* to Vic. 7277/82: set M 82.
		—Damrosch ...	*Add* to AmC. nos.: set M 82.
86	1	Symphony No. 3—Koussevitzky ...	*For* set M 1009 *read* M 1007 (disc nos. already corrected in Supp. II list).
		—Mengelberg ...	*Add* to AmC. nos.: set M 181.
88	1	Trio No. 2, Op. 87 ...	*Add* omission: Court of Belgium Trio (C.DFX 185/8).
91	1	Hungarian Dance No. 2—Furtwängler ...	*Delete* here & transfer to No. 10, E major.
98	1	Vergebliches Ständchen, E. Schumann ...	*Add* omitted no.: *Vic. 1756*.
101	2	Heigh ho! Heigh ho!	Correct reading: Ého! Ého!
		Came ye not	*To read*: Come you not . . .
104	2	Aperite mihi justitiae portas ...	*To read*: . . . portas justitiae. Is for A, T, Bs & orch.; *add* Bs: H. Nergaard.
105	1	Canzonetta, G major	Ref. *to read*: (S. Vol. I, No. 24).
106	2	La Volta	Both recordings are FVB 159. Footnote 6 applies.
109	2	CASADESUS, Henri-Gustave ...	Died 1947.
117	1	ÉTUDES—COLLECTION, Backhaus ...	Vic. set no. *to read* M 43.
134	1	Io sono l'umile ancella} Troppo, Signori } ...	This is the same aria. *Amalgamate* entries.
143	1	Canaries, D minor, v.d. Wiele ...	*Add* reference: [52].
143	2	Sarabande, D minor. v.d. Wiele ...	*Add* reference: [51]
145	2	Darling Girl	*Add* omission: A. Kipnis (Bs) & balalaika orch. (*Vic. 10-1017* in set M 919) [labelled *Maiden of my Heart* but presumably this song].
147	1	Children's Corner Suite—ORCH. ...	Caplet—*add* to Vic. nos.: *set M 280*.
147	1	*Idem*—No. 3 § Horowitz ...	*Add*: *G.DA 1032* [same coupling as *Vic. 1353*].
152	1/2	Gigues—Monteux	*Delete* G.DB 11139 here and *transfer* to No. 3, Rondes . . .
158	2	Naïla Valse—Isserstedt ...	*Add* no.: (U.F 14401).
160	2	On hearing the first cuckoo	Lambert—*add* no.: (*Vic. 4496*).
160	2	Indian love song, etc.	N. Evans—AmD. no. *to read*: *AmD. 20178*.
163	2	Cheti, Cheti, Fregosi	AmD. no. *to read*: AmD. 29019.
179	1	May Song—Elgar	*Add* no.: Vic. 11356 (in set M 145).
179	2	Pomp & Circ. Marches: Nos. 1 & 2 ...	*Add* entry: § Berlin St. Op.—Melichar (*Pol. 25070*).
		No. 1 ...	*Add* entry: § Chicago Sym.—Stock (Vic. 6648).
184	1	Danza ritual } } Levant ...	*Add* no.: (in AmC.ML 2018, LP).
186	1	Danza del molinaro}	
191	1	Clair de lune}	*Add* omission:
192	1	Prison }	§ C. Croïza (M-S), F. Poulenc (pf.) (*C.D 13033*).
194	1	Dreaming Lake	Op. no. *to read*: Op. 36, No. 6.
195	1	JOURNAL DU PRINTEMPS, No. 1 ...	No. *to read*: † AS. 52.
206	1	MERRIE ENGLAND, Abridged ...	Is 12ss *not* 16ss. English Rose is (S9); Who shall say . . . is (S10).
208	2	The Silver Swan—Lee Jones ...	No. *to read*: *Vic. 26782*.
214	2	Life for the Tzar, No. 16 ...	No. *to read*: (G.EK 36*).
215	2	Ruslan and Ludmilla, No. 13 ...	Not in Disc. set 751; *delete* here, & *transfer* no. to No. 12.
221	1	Sym., Ländliche Hochzeit... ...	Op. no. *to read*: Op. 26.
224	1	FAUST, COMPLETE—Busser ...	Vic. nos. *to read*: Vic. 11000/19.
226	1	Salut, demeure	Hislop: DB 944 is o.v. *not* o.n.; this is a studio recording, while DB 1189 is actual performance, Covent Garden.
226	1	Il était un roi de Thulé} Air des bijoux } ...	B. Sayão—*Add* omitted no.: (and in ML 4056, LP).
227	1	Seigneur, daignez permettre	Tirard—*AmD*. no. *to read*: *20512/3*.
		Vous qui faites l'endormie ...	Pasero, o.v.—*add* no.: *C.D 1617*.
229	2	Ange adorable	Noréna, Micheletti: Od. no. *to read* 123604.
231	2	Ave Maria — ARR. VLC.	Piatigorsky—AmD. no. *to read*: 20019.
234	2	El Pelele	Is No. 7 of Goyescas. *Transfer* up.
241	2	Concerto, A minor, De Greef ...	*Add* to Vic. nos.: o.n. 9151/4, set M 24.
242	2	Symphonic Dances—v. Kempen ...	*For* Dresden Phil. *read* Berlin State.
247	2	First entry	*For* Parry *read* Perry.
248	1	GRUENBERG: Vln. Concerto ...	Vic. no. *to read*: 11-9333/6.
251	2	Rachel, quand du Seigneur	Caruso: *Add* no.: G.DB 123*.
254	1	La speranza è giunto	*To read*. . . . è giunta.
254	1	Corali e perle	*To read*: Coralli. . . .
		PASTOR FIDO, 1st Version ...	*Add*: Overture—1, 2, 4, 5, 6th movts. *See* II (c), Faithful Shepherd (Kindler).
		PASTOR FIDO, 2nd Version ...	*Delete* Minuet, G major.
		Musette	*Add*: ARR. Kindler: See II (c), Faithful Shepherd.
254	2	SCIPIONE, March	*Add* omission: § Malvern Girls College, etc. (*G.B 4333*).
255	1	O sleep! why dost thou . . .} ...	*Add* omitted entry:
260	1	THEODORA, No. 17 }	§ C. Rider-Kelsey (AmC. 5071M).
257	2	MESSIAH, Set V. ...	Does *not* omit Nos. 34-5; they are placed out of sequence between Nos. 55 and 56.
261	2	Chaconne, G major	Is no. 3a of 3 Lessons (with 21 variations).
264	2	Concerto Grosso No. 5—Diener ...	Main No. *to read*: G.C 3065/6. Take EH 1202/3 down to next line.
264	2	Concerto Grosso No. 10—Defauw ...	Played in the Kogel edn., reversing order of 4th & 5th movts.
266	2	The Faithful Shepherd (Beecham) ...	*Delete* from 4: (a) Minuet. *Add* new item: 4 (a): Musette (unid., *not* in *Pastor Fido*). *Delete* sub-head: . . . Nos. 1, 3b, 4a, 6, etc. and *substitute* new heading:
		The Faithful Shepherd — ARR. Kindler ...	Pastor Fido (1712): Overture . . . 1, 2, 4, 5, & 6th movts. Pastor Fido (1724): Musette.
270	1	Creation, HS. Recording	The Part III solos are sung by F. Riegler (Eve) and A. Pernerstorfer (Adam) and not by Eipperle and Hann, as stated in various reviews and (by implication) in the Nixa catalogue.
271	2	The Sailor's Song	E. Rogers sings in German.
273	2	Op. 3, No. 5 . . . Serenade — ORCH. ...	Philadelphia—Stokowski, Vic. no. *to read*: 7256.
278	1	Symphony No. 100—Rignold ...	*Add* to AmC. set MM 890: d.c. [has *Schubert: Marche militaire*, *not* Gluck].
281	1	Waiata poi, Dawson	*Add* additional no.: (*Vic. 10-1025*).
285	1	Automne, Croïza	*Add*: A. Honegger (pf.).

Page	Col.	Entry	Remarks
285	2	JUDITH, excerpts	*Add* new footnote: ² D. 15241 exists in two forms:—(a) coupling *Cantique des vierges & Cantique de victoire;* (b) coupling the latter with *Cantique de la bataille.*
290	2	Caucasian Sketches—Fiedler ...	Vic. set M 797 is only 5ss. *Add* coupling: (5ss—*Golden Cockerel, Bridal Procession*).
292	1	General Booth enters heaven ...	R. Pazmor is (A) not (S), despite label.
294	2	Carnet de bal—Valse grise⎱ Le 14 Juillet—Valse ⎰	*Add* new footnote to *C.DF 2333:* ¹ Apparently this coupling was only wartime temporary. Originally, and again later, it has *Romberg* with *Carnet de bal* only.
295	1	Murmelndes Lüftchen — ARR. PF.	R. Ganz—*Add* no.: *G.DA 1205.*
296	1	Et incarnatus est (unspec.) ...	Is from Mass: *Pange Lingua.*
299	2	KILPINEN SONG SOCIETY ...	4th title line *to read:* (5) LIEDER DER LIEBE (Book 2) Op. 61 ... Nos. 1, 2, 4, 5 only. 6th title line *to read:* (8) SPIELMANNSLIEDER, Op. 77 ... Nos. 4, 5, 8 only.
309	1	Once upon a time, Suite, Høeberg	*For* Z 60102 *read* Z 60121.
312	1	Bonjour, et puis quelle nouvelle ...	*Delete* title and *transfer* entry below existing record of Bonjour, mon cœur.
318	2	Rastelbinder duet, Tauber ...	AmD no. *to read:* 25775.
319	2	LEKEU: Adagio, Op. 3 ...	*Add* no. omitted: (C.LBDX 11/12).
320	2	PAGLIACCI, Set A ...	Vic. set no *to read:* M 249.
322	2	No, Pagliaccio non son! ...	Pertile—*add* no.: AmD 25869.
323	1	Zazà, piccola zingara ...	*Add:* § R. d'Alessio *C.GQ 7020.*
326	1	Feux follets & Chasse-neige ...	Grundeis—*Add* no.: (AmD. 25772).
328	2	Grand Galop chromatique, G. 132	The orchestral record (C.DX 1516) is *not* this, but the Galop, A minor, G. 131 (H. Searle).
330	2	MOZART—Serenade	Petri does not play Liszt's version but Busoni's. Amend pp. 104-1, 394-2 accordingly.
331	1	CHOPIN—No. 5, My joys ...	Ansorge is said not to play this; *transfer* to new title, section A. III (4): Glanes de Woronince. G. 162 ... No. 2, Mélodies polonaises.
340	1	Pur dicesti	Could be added: § J. McCormack (T) (*Vic. 10-1435** in set M 1228).
347	1	MARCELLO, A.—Concerto, D mi.	Goossens—add: (3ss—*Fiocco*).
350	1	Son pochi fiori	*Add:* § I. Fuentes *P.P 9319.*
353	1	In pure stille	*Add:* § I. Fuentes (P.P 9319).
354	2	CLÉOPÂTRE—A-t-il dit vrai? ...	Vanni-Marcoux recording is 12-inch, G.DB 4822.
355	2	Il est doux.... Vallin ...	AmD. no. *to read:* 25847.
355	2	Ce breuvage ... Vision fugitive ...	P. Silveri sings in *Italian.*
360	1	Va! laisse-les couler ...	Pape no. *to read: C. LF 197.*
363	1	Spanish Romance	Is sung by Makushina, *not* Slobodskaya.
365	2	Song without words 30 ...	*Add* omission: § R. Ganz (*G.DA 1205; Vic. 1508*).
368/9	2/1	A Midsummer Night's Dream ...	The Wedding March is No. 9, *not* No. 10.
377 714	1⎱ 1⎰	MÍČA, František Václav ...	The Symphony, D major is now attributed to MÍČA, František Antonín (1746- ?).
380	1	BETTELSTUDENT—ABRIDGED, Tauber, etc.	*Add* no.: *AmD. 20429/32.*
383	1	(Le) DÉSERTEUR	Date *to read:* 1769.
386	2	From Foreign Lands ...	*Add:* Hungarian Dance— ARR. BAND Sommer § BBC—O'Donnell (C.DX 46).
387	1	By the water (unid.)	This proves to be an arr. of No. 6 of Sunless cycle. *Transfer* to p. 390-2.
387	2	Pictures from an Exhibition ...	Horowitz plays his own arrangement.
395	1/2	ENTFÜHRUNG, COMPLETE ...	*Add* footnote: No. 17 (Act III) is replaced by No. 15 (Act II).
397 398	2⎱ 1⎰	Figaro, Nos. 6 & 12, E. Schumann	*Delete* (o.v., Ger) relating to *G.EW 34.* ;This disc is in *Ital* and is identical with *DA 844.*
401	2	Moto di gioia ...⎱ Lied der Trennung; Ridente ...⎰	Angelici no. *to read:* † AS. 93.
402	1		
404	1	Sonata No. 7, C major ...	Joyce—Lon. set no. *to read* LA 180.
412	2	Vln. Concerto No. 4, Kreisler ...	*For* Orch. *read* L.P.O.
415	2	Symphony No. 40—Toscanini ... —Stock	Vic. no. *to read:* 15753/5. *Add* before Vic. no.: Vic. 36257/9, set G 3; o.n. ....
417	1	DUBROVSKY ... ... Masha's Romance	*Add* omission: § S. A. Baturina (*Vic. 4064*).
426	2	Belle nuit....	Could be added: § G. Féraldy and G. Cernay (*C.LF 122*).
430	2	Moto perpetuo, Ricci ...	*For* VLP 5490 *read* VLP 6490.
433	2	PALMGREN	Died 1951.
439	2	PFITZNER	*Add* omission:
		Die Rose vom Liebesgarten ...	Opera, 1901.
		Funeral March	§ Berlin State Op.—Pfitzner (Pol. 66557).
445	2	Caprice, C major	*Add* footnote: ⁵ After the finale of *Bal Masqué.*
448	1	Pf. Concerto No. 3, Prokofiev ...	Vic. no. *to read:* 7772/4.
449	1	Alexander Nevsky, excerpts on ...	*C.FB 2758* also issued as *D.M 579.*
452	2	In un coupé ..., Rumbo and Panerai	Coupling *to read:* (*Trovatore—Non m'inganno*).
454	1	MADAMA BUTTERFLY, Set C ...	Vic. nos. *to read:* 9851/66 (nos. printed are autos.).
456	2	RONDINE—Ora dolci e divina ...	*To read:* Ore dolci e divine. This aria is coupled with *Falla: Vida breve, aria* and not as shown.
457	1	TOSCA, Set C	Soprano's name *to read* C. Melis.
459	2	O dolci mani, Tagliavini ...	*Add* omitted d.c. (*Barbiere—Ecco ridente* ... on P.BB 25181).
462	1	Minuet and Jig (unspec.) — ARR. GUITAR	Identified as: Minuet from *Musick's Handmaid* [29] Jig from *Overture, Air and Jig* [57].
462	2	Chacony, G minor (4 viols) ...	DX 1230 is not this, but arr. of *Sonata 6, G minor.* Transfer entry [& see Supp. III, p. 359, for full entry].
463 466	1⎱ 1⎰	ABDELAZOR	*Spell* ABDELAZER [also 101, note].
464	1	GORDIAN KNOT UNTIED ...	Saidenberg—add (& LP: CHS.CHC 22).
467	1/2	QUILTER—Songs	*Add: AmC.* 275M to each entry of *C.DB 1629.*
468	2	Pf. Concerto No. 3, Horowitz ...	Vic. nos. *to read:* 7462/6.
471	2	Do not depart, Rosing ...	AmD. no. *to read:* 25188.
472	1	To the Children	McCormack sings in *English.*
479	2	Bolero—Koussevitzky (o.v.) ...	Vic. set no. *to read:* M 352.
489	1	Golden Cockerel: Bridal Procession	Fiedler: *add* (& Vic. 11-8509 in set M 797).
491	1	The Forest gaily awakens ...	Is for S, *not* T.

Page	Col.	Entry			Remarks
492	2	(& footnote 6): **You will pay**	...	...	*U.S.S.R. 8529/30* is now catalogued as Act I, so this will probably be **It cannot be**; while *8531* will be the Act II aria.
495	1	Barbiere, No. 2, Tagliavini	...	...	*Add* omitted d.c.: (*Tosca—O dolci mani* on P.BB 25181).
496	1	Una voce poco fa ...	...	...	M. Salvi—P. no. *to read* E 10691.
498	1	GUILLAUME TELL, No. 18	...	...	*Add* omission: E. de Franceschi (*Ital*) (Fnt. 35041).
500	1	Jazz dans la nuit, Crolza ...	...	...	*Add:* G. Reeves (pf.).
509 827	2} 2}	SARTI: Lungi dal caro bene	...	...	*Is from* GIULIO SABINO (Opera, 3 Acts, 1781) and not as stated.
513	1	L. 104, C major, Zecchi ...	...	...	No. *to read:* P. CB 20352.
516	1	Sonata, unspec.— ARR. GUITAR	...	...	Is L 352. *Transfer to* 514-1.
516	1	"Pastorale & Capriccio" ... Capriccio	...	...	§ Horowitz. *Add no.: G.DA 1032.*
520	1	Marche militaire No. 1— ARR. ORCH.	...	...	*Add* to Sargent recording: (AmC. 72956D, in set MM 890).
523	2	(12) Ländler, Op. 171	...	...	Meyer omits Nos. 2, 9, 10, 12.
524	2	WALTZES, Op. 50 (Sentimentales)	...	...	Meyer plays only Nos. 1, 2, 3, 12, 13, 18-22, 27, 34.
541	1	Also hat Gott. . . .	...	...	Is MC *not* GK.
541	1	Gott Vater in Ewigkeit (Kyrie)	...	...	*To read:* Kyrie Gott Vater in Ewigkeit.
541	2	Der Pharisäer . . .	...	...	*To read:* Es gingen zween Menschen.
543	2	Carnaval — ORCH. —Goossens ...	...	...	Vic. set no. *to read::* M 513.
548	2	Dichterliebe, Nos. 1, 2, 3 & 13, Tauber ...	...	...	Nos. 1-3 are on *AmD.* 20348; No. 13 on *20347.*
551	2	Der Nussbaum	...	...	E. Schumann is (S) not (T).
552	1	Alte Laute, Lehmann	...	...	Vic. no. *to read:* Vic. 1859.
559	1	Salute to Life (as The United Nations)	...	...	*Add* omission: P. Robeson (Bs) & orch. (Key. 1200).
559	2	SIBELIUS Society—VOL. I	...	...	*Add:* (Vic. 11503/9, set M 333).
574	1	Vltava—Kindler	...	...	Vic. nos. *to read:* 11-8389/90 (nos. printed are autos.).
589	1	INDIGO, Intermezzo—Axholm	...	...	This name *to read:* Axelson.
596	2	Nicht dort, dort . . .	...	...	AmD. no. *to read:* AmD. 25237.
597	1	Bin so viel Finesse . . .	...	...	*For* Merrem-Nikisch *read* Stünzner.
598	1	Blaue Sommer	...	...	*To read:* Blauer Sommer.
		Blinderklage			*To read:* Blindeklage.
602	2	Fire Bird, Revised Orch. Suite	...	...	Philadelphia—Stokowski, o.v.; Vic. nos. *to read:* 6773/5.
603	1	Rite of Spring—Stokowski	...	...	Vic. nos. *to read:* 7227/30 (nos. printed are autos.).
606	2	Princess Ida, COMPLETE ...	...	...	Vic. nos. *to read:* 11596/605.
607	1	Ruddigore, Set B	...	...	Vic. nos. *to read:* 11510/8, set C 19.
620	1	Romeo and Juliet, N.Y.—Stokowski	...	...	Already amended in Supp. II list; amend further *to read:* (5ss—Serenade—Waltz).
620	2	Serenade Op. 48 ... Waltz only ...	...	...	*Add* omissions: N.Y.P.S.O.—Stokowski AmC. 13068D (*Romeo & Juliet*) in set MM 898. § Detroit Sym.—Gabrilowitsch (Vic. 6835).
626	2	Only thou, Op. 57, No. 6	...	...	Aksarova recording is not this, but **Does the day reign, Op. 47, No. 6.** *Transfer to* 625-1.
629	2	HAMLET: Être ou ne pas être ...	...	...	Vanni-Marcoux is 12-inch: G.DB 4822.
630	2	Connais-tu le pays?	...	...	Could be added: ¶ G. Cernay (*C.LF 109*).
633	1, 2	TURINA ...	...	...	*Add* Op. nos. *passim:* see *Grove,* 5th edn., and Supp. III entries, *below.*
635	2	The Invaders, Film music...	...	...	This is the American title of the film **49th Parallel.** Incorporate entry, *above.*
640	2	O terra addio!	...	...	A.-Lombardi & Merli: *add* English o.n.: C.L 2039.
642 849	1} 1}	Don Carlos...	...	...	*For* Io t'ho perduto *read* Io l'ho ...
646	1	Io muojo! ...	...	...	Merli, etc.: no. *to read:* GQX 10213.
662	2	(2) Studies, guitar ...	...	...	Are: No. 1, E minor; No. 8, C ♯ minor, of 12 Studies, 1929.
664	1	Concerto, Vln., A minor	...	...	*For* (P) 12 *read:* (P) 13 [G.DB 5065].
		Concerto, Vln., C major	...	...	*For* (P) 388 *read* (P) 88 [P.BB 25256].
664	2	Sinfonia, B minor...	...	...	Dur.SA 108 is cond. Ephrikian, not Fanna.
666	1	Siegfried Idyll, Vienna—Walter ...	...	...	Vic. set no. *to read:* G 12.
666	1	(5) GEDICHTE	...	...	Orch. accompaniments are by Mottl.
		Nos. 3 & 5, Lehmann	...	...	No. *to read:* AmC. 71469D.
670	1	Höchstes Vertrau'n, Völker	...	...	No. *to read:* T.SKB 2053.
674	1	Nein! Lasst ihn. . . ., Janssen	...	...	Is 2ss—ArgC. 266484.
675	1	Ja, Wehe! ...	...	...	*Add:* H. Janssen (2ss) ArgC. 266483. [Both these discs are acc. by Colón Theatre Orch.—Kinsky; the latter also has a brief choral passage and continues to Parsifal's entrance.]
675	2	RHEINGOLD, Danish excerpts...	...	...	Grimert *to read* Grunert. *Add* more artists: M. Müller, C. Madsen.
678	1	SIEGFRIED, Set C ...	...	...	Vic. nos. *to read:* 7691/6.
		Set D ...			Vic. set *to read:* M 167,
679	1	GÖTTERDÄMMERUNG, Set A	...	...	Vic. nos. *to read:* 9456/9 & 9486/7.
683	1	TRISTAN UND ISOLDE, Set D	...	...	Vic. nos. *to read:* 9265/9.
		Set F			Høeberg is (iv).
690	1	Beherrscher der Geister, Ov.	...	...	Susskind no. *to read:* C.DX 1262.
695	1	Švanda, Polka—Harty	...	...	*For* LX 193 *read* LX 293.
704	1	Schlafendes Jesuskind, McCormack	...	...	*Insert* "with orch." before Vic. *1272.* There are three different recordings.
706	2	SEGRETO—Gioia, la nube	...	...	Title *to commence* with: O, gioia.... This aria is on Vic. **14616** with *Manon.*
707	1	YSAŸE—Sonatas, Op. 27	...	...	*Add* keys: No. 1, G minor; No. 3, D minor.
717	1	T. DAMETT ...	...	...	Date *to read:* (d. 1436).
727	2	ARRIAGA—Str. Qtt. No. 1	...	...	*Add:* ... Allegro only ▽ Rafael Qtt. (G.AB 465).
739	1	BARTOŠ—Bourgeois gentilhomme	...	...	*Add:* Also on U.G 14011. *Delete* this no. under École des femmes. Composer's date *to read:* (b. 1905).
739	1	Beethoven—Bagatelle, Op. 119, No. 11 ...			Key *to read:* B flat major.
739	2	Sonata No. 8, Rubinstein	...	...	No. *to read:* ♯ Vic.LM 1072.
741	1	Sonata No. 7, Schneiderhan	...	...	Is *10-inch.* No. *to read:* ♯ *Rem. 149-35.*
742	2	Symphony No. 7—Walter...	...	...	*Delete* symbol ☆; should be among large type entries.
747	2	TRIO No. 3, Op. 35	...	...	Key *to read:* E flat major.
748	1	BONONCINI—Per la gloria	...	...	Is from GRISELDA, 1718 [& see 81-2, *above*].
748	2	Prince Igor Dances—Stokowski ...	...	...	*Delete* Philadelphia. The orch. is "Sym." only.
748	2	Bowles—Sonata, 2 pfs.	...	...	Is *10-inch:* ♯ *CHS.CHS 1089.*
751	1	WALTZES, Chasins, Keene.	...	...	Nos. 1, 2, 11, 14, 15 are played in Brahms' own arr. for 2 pfs. *Add* footnote accordingly.
		First Pf. Qtt. ...			*Includes* No. 15 *not* No. 14.
751	1	SONGS—COLLECTION, Poell	...	...	Der Gang zum Liebchen is solo arr. of Op. 31, No. 3, *not* the Op. 48 song.
751	2	First title ...	...	...	*To read:* Ach, wende ...
752	2	Rejoice in the Lamb, WCFM. 4 ...	...	...	Stated to have soloists: K. Hansel (S), A. Koerner (A), G. Barritt (T), D. Baker (B).

Page	Col.	Entry	Remarks
755	2	Poème de l'amour	Author *to read* Bouchor.
783	1	NOTTURNI	For renumberings, *see* Supp. III, p. 215.
789	1	COLAS BREUGNON, Overture . . .	The recording on U.H 23720 is not 2ss; it is coupled with **Fête populaire** (No. 2 of the Orch. Suite—based on Act I, Sc. 2 of the Opera).
790	1	Missa brevis.	Stated to have soloists: R. Koerner (A), G. Barritt (T), H. Ronk (B).
794	2	Mephisto Waltz No. 1, Barere . . .	♯ Rem. 199-17 contains the two previous titles (**Faust Waltz** & **Liebestraum**) and *not* this.
796	1	MANFREDINI: Sinfonia da chiesa . . .	Correct title *to read*: Concerto grosso, C major, Op. 3, No. 12.
799	1	Symphony No. 9, C major (Str.) . . .	Date *to read*: 1823.
804	2	Vesperae de Dominica . . .	*See* addendum to Supp. II, 142-2, *above.*
807	1	Fantasia, C minor, K 475, Kitchin . . .	Coupling is K 545, not K 457.
807	1	Sonata No. 14, Kitchin . . .	*Transfer* this entry to K 545, *below.*
807	2	Fantasia, K 608 — ARR. ORCH. . . .	♯ Rem. 199-2 is cond. Fekete *not* Wöss.
822	1	How sad I feel	Is probably Sorrow in Spring, Op. 21, No. 12 (Galina).
822	2	RANGSTRÖM—Songs, Sönnerstedt . . .	No. *to read:* **L 2008**.
825	1	Flight of the Bumble Bee — ARR. PF. . . .	Sukman—*add* symbol: ☆.
826	2	SAINT-SAËNS	
		Fantasia, C major, Op. 95 hp. . . .	This title *to read*: Fantasia, A major, Op. 124 hp. & vln. Artists *to read*: E. Vito & A. Eidus. *Add*: Debussy to coupling.
		Prelude & Fugue . . . . . . (Cherkassky)	This title *to read*: **Études, Op. 52** . . . No. 3, F minor (Prelude & Fugue). *Transfer* above Fantasia.
827	2	Concerto Grosso, Op. 11 No. 4 . . .	*Add* key: **D minor**.
830	1	Quartet, G major D. 96. . .	Order of artists *to read*: Mess, Kirchner, S. Barchet, A. Faiss.
831	2	COLLECTION—Symonette . . .	*Add* coupling: (*Brahms: Ernste Gesänge*).
833	1	SCHÜTZ (b. 1585)	First three titles in PL 6860 are MC *not* GK. Ich sterbe is Madrigal Io moro (1611), sung in German.
836	2	Romance, Op. 24, No. 9 . . .	Is 12-inch: Symf.RT 1011 [also reverse, 837-1].
		King Christian II—Fool's Song . . .	Is 12-inch: Ryt.RK 1001.
838	1	SOLER, Sonatas—COLLECTIONS	Valenti plays: 1. D major (N.I-5). 2. D minor (N.I-4). 3. C minor (N.II-3). 4. D♭ major (N.II-9). 5. D major (N.I-12). Boschi plays: 1. A minor (N.II-2). 2. F♯ minor (N.I-6). 3. G minor (N.I-11). 4. D major (N.I-5). 5. F♯ major (N.I-12). 6. C♯ minor (N.I-2). [N. Refs. to Nin: Classiques espagnols . . .]
842	1	STRAVINSKY	*Add*: 5 Pièces faciles ☆ A. Gold & R. Fizdale (in ♯ CHS.CHS. 1089).
843	1	Song of the Volga Boatmen . . .	For Croft *read* Craft.
845	2	Capriccio italien ⎫ —Fiedler . . .	Apparently is n.v.—move entry up into large type & *add*: n.v.
846	1	1812 Overture ⎭	
847	2	SUITES: E minor	*To read*: A minor (amalgamate with next entry) [Bärenreiter edn. IX-5].
848	1	TURINA: Homenaje a Tárrega . . .	*Add*: Op. 69. This is only pieces 1 and 2. Nos. 3 and 4 are separate pieces, Opp. 29 & 36 respectively.
852	2	VIOTTI	Dates *to read*: (1755-1824).
853	1	Concerti, Violin, G mi. & D mi. . . .	Kaufman: *Delete* ♯ from Cap. set ECL 8076. *Add*: (3ss each).
853	2	Line 1, already corrected in Supp. II to: . . .	Concerto, Vln. & vlc., B♭ major (P.388). The name of the 'cellist is J. Neilz.
853	2	Concerto, vlc., G major [♯ CHS. E 2] . . .	For P.118 *read* P 120.
853	2	Sonata, Op. 1, No. 2 . . .	For Baumann *read* Bochmann.
854	1	Albumblatt; Sonata, Karrer . . .	The works on ♯ Rem. 199-26 are now identified as: **Albumblatt, A flat major** 1875 (?) **Sonata, B flat major** 1831. **Sonata (Album sonata) E flat major** 1853; and not as listed.
858	1	SONGS—Fischer-Dieskau collection . . .	Third title: For Ketten *read* Kutten.
882	1	The ENCHANTRESS	Ref. *to read:* 622a.

NOTE. We have been sent a complete list of omitted numbers from the AmD. classical catalogue of 1938-9 (Odeon-Parlophone repressings) which lack of space compels us to omit. This catalogue was obsolete at the time WERM went to press, and these numbers were omitted of design, to clear the columns. A few of the more interesting were retained, where space permitted; and a couple more are inserted above, for which there *would* have been room in WERM.

CORRIGENDA

PART III

For THIS Volume

Page	Col.	Entry	Remarks
17	1	W.T.C. excerpts, Landowska	*Delete* Nos. 17-24 and *add* ItV. no. to Nos. 41-48.
27	2	Brandenburg Concerto 6, Koussevitzky . .	ItV. no. *to read:* A12R 0090.
30	2	Suite 3, Szell	Said to be a new recording, *not* ☆.
36	2	Weihnachtsoratorium, Parts 1-3	For G. Luhe *read* G. Lutze.
40	2	BANISTER, John	Date *to read*: (1630-1679) [also WERM, 719-2].
52	2	Sonatina, C minor	Is WoO 43-1, *not* WoO 44.
57	2	Symphony No. 6—Wöss	*Delete* reference to ♯ Rem. 2 here, and *transfer* to Symphony 5—Wolf.
65	2	Beatrice & Benedict Ov., Smallens . .	AFest. prefix *to read:* CFR.
81	2	Violin Concerto, Heifetz ☆ . .	*Transfer* FV. & ItV. nos. to Chicago recording.
82	1	Symphony No. 1—Otterloo . .	♯ Phi. no. *to read:* ♯ Phi.S 04006L.
82	2	Symphony No. 4—Toscanini . .	*Transfer:* ♯ FV.A 630228 to Sym. 3, *supra.*
		—Rother . .	*Add* n.n.: ♯ Ura. 7154.
86	2	Hungarian Dances 1, 17, 20, 21 . .	Toscanini: DV. no. *to read:* L 16483.
87	1	Hung. Dance No. 1, Furtwängler . . .	No. *to read:* G.ED 1233.
96	2	ORGAN COLLECTION, Biggs . .	*Add* ø to first title: Chaconne. . . .
97	2	BYRD: COLLECTION, Neumeyer . .	*Add* omitted title: Fortune (Variations), FVB 65

THE
WORLD'S ENCYCLOPÆDIA
OF RECORDED
MUSIC

ABACO, Evaristo Felice dall' (1675–1742)

Sonata, F major, Op. 3 No. 2   2 vlns. & cont.
☆ J. Fournier, J. Pasquier (vlns.), R. Gerlin (hpsi.), E. Pasquier (vlc.) (in †‡ HS.AS 13)

ABACO, Giuseppe Marie Clément dall'
(1710-1805)
Sonata, G major   vln. & cont.
— ED. Moffatt & Salmon as Sonata by G. B. Sammartini, q.v.

ABEL, Karl Friedrich (1723-1787)

Sonata, C major   (*Hortus musicus* edn., No. 1)
H. E. Deckert (gamba) & L. Larsen (virginals)
(*Telemann & Leclair*)   ‡ *Felix.LP 300*

Symphony, E flat major, Op. 7, No. 6[1]
Netherlands Phil.—Ackermann
‡ CHS.CHS 1178
(*Mozart: Symphonies 13, 15, 16, q.v.*)   (‡ Clc. 6253)
O. L. Cha.—Froment   **V‡ DO.LD 20**
(in ‡LOL.OL 50018)

ABSIL, Jean (b. 1893)

Impromptu (unspec.)   pf.
(3) MARINES ... No. 1 only   pf.   1939
▽ S. Cambier   *C.DCB 59*
PEAU D'ÂNE, Op. 26   Opera   1937
... Ballet Music: The three wishes
Petite Suite, Op. 20   Orch.   1935
(Marche; Conte; Carrousel)
Belgian Radio Cha.—Doneux
‡ *Gramo.GLP 2505*
Quartet, saxophones, Op. 31
M. Mule Sax. Qtt.   ‡ *D.LX 3142*
(*Françaix & Rivier*)   (‡ *Lon.LS 1188*)
Rêverie, Op. 35; Tarantelle, Op. 39   Sax. qtt.
M. Mule Sax. Qtt.   ‡ *D.LX 3135*
(*Schmitt & Pierné*)   (‡ *Lon.LS 1076*)

ADAM, Adolphe Charles (1803-1856)

GISELLE   Ballet   2 Acts   1841
L.S.O.—Fistoulari   ‡ DCap.CTL 7097
(‡ Cap.P 8306)
Paris Opéra—Blareau   ‡ **D.LXT 2844**
(‡ Lon.LL 869)

... Excerpts [Giselle's Solo; Danse générale; Mad Scene (Act I); Meeting Prince-Giselle (Act II)]
☆ Orch.—Stokowski (in ‡ G.ALP 1133: FALP 277; in ‡ Vic.LRY 8000: ♭ WRY 8000)
... Grand Valse only   — ARR. ORGAN
R. Foort *sub nom.* M. Cheshire
(in ‡ Nix.SLPY 156; ‡ SOT. 10501)

Noël—Minuit, Chrétiens (Cappeau)
J. Peerce (T) & Columbus Boys' Cho.
—Huffmann (*Eng*)   ♭ *Vic.ERA 132*
(*Praetorius, Yon, etc.*)

A. Deguil (♭ *Pat.EG 144*)
R. Jobin (T) & Cho. (in ‡ *Vic.LM 7014*)
H. Hasslo (B, *Swed*) (♭ *G. 7EPS 1*)
J. Borthayre (B) (*D.MF 36083*: ♭ *EBM 455003*)
F. Clément (*D.8068, Belgium*)
X. Depraz (Bs) & org. (*Sel. 800.C.000*)
J. M. Shea (B), Cho. & Orch. (*Vic.* 20-5408: ♭ 47-5408: in ‡ LPM 3149: ♭ set EPB 3149)
▽ R. Amade (T) (*Pat.PAE 18*)
☆ M. Anderson (A), F. Rupp (pf.) (♭ *Vic.ERA 116*; in ‡ *DV.T 16408*)
G. Thill (in ‡ *C.FH 504*)
T. Rossi (in ‡ *C.FJ 502*)
etc.

OPERAS
(Le) CHALET   1 Act   1834
Arrêtons nous ici   Bs.
Ħ P. Plançon (*AF.AGSA 32**)
Vallons d'Helvétie   Bs.
Ħ M. Journet & pf. (in ‡ *SBDH.LPG 5**)
P. Plançon (in ‡ *SBDH.LLP 6**)

(Le) POSTILLON DE LONGJUMEAU   3 Acts
1836
Mes amis, écoutez l'histoire   T & Cho.   (Act I)
(*Freunde, vernehmet die Geschichte*)
R. Schock (*Ger*) & Ens.   G.EH 1452
(*Mignon—Adieu, Mignon*)   (♭ *PW 532*)
L. Fehenberger (*Ger*)   *PV. 36100*
(*Mignon—Elle ne croyait pas*)   (♭ *Pol.* 34002: 32052)
☆ N. Gedda (*Swed*) (*Od.ZAA 25*)
J. Lohe (*Ger*) (in ‡ *T.LA 6077*)
J. Schmidt (*Ger*) (in ‡ *Od.OLA 1008*)
H. Roswaenge (*Ger*) (o.v.) (in ‡ *CEd.* 7010)

SI J'ÉTAIS ROI   3 Acts   1852
Overture
Vienna Radio—Schönherr   ‡ **Vien.L 6164**
(in ‡ *LPR 1025*; GA. 33-307)
Opera Orch.—Rossi   ‡ *Mae.OA 20005*
(*Nicolai, Suppé*)
R.I.A.S. Sym.—Becker   in ‡ Rem. 199-181
☆ Bournemouth Municipal—Schwarz   ♭ *G.7EP 7004*
(*Mendelssohn: Son & Stranger Overture*)

(*continued on next page*)

---

[1] Recorded as *Mozart: Symphony No. 3*, K. 18 (new K.Anh.109 I).

SI J'ÉTAIS ROI Overture (continued)
☆ Bamberg Sym.—Lehmann (FPV. 5058;
    ‡ AmD.DL 4046; in ‡ Pol. 17033: ♭ 30146)
L.P.O.—Martinon (‡ D.LW 5007: ♭ DX 1778)

(Le) TOREADOR   2 Acts   1849
Ah! Vous dirai-je, maman—based on Mozart's
    Variations for pf.   K 265
M. Gyurkovics (Hung) (Qual.MN 1012)
L. Zubrack (♭ Vic. ERA 261)

ADAM DE LA HALLE (c. 1237-1287)

SEE ALSO: † MUSIC OF THE MIDDLE AGES
          † HISTORY OF MUSIC IN SOUND (14 & 20)
          † ANTHOLOGIE SONORE

(Le) Jeu de Robin et de Marion   Pastorale   c. 1283
Pro Musica Antiqua—Cape   ‡ HP.APM 14018
(below; G. d'Amiens; & Anon: 17 Dances of XIIIth Cent.)[1]
[also PV. 5414 & ♭ Pol. 37076, below] (‡ AmD.ARC 3002)

RONDEAUX
COLLECTION

ø Li dous regars
   Je muir
   A jointes mains
   Dieus soit en cheste maison (Balade)
ø Hé Diex
ø Or est Baiars
ø A Dieu comant amouretes (Motet)
ø Bonne amourete
   Dame or suis trais
   Fi maris
   Trop désir
   Diex comment porroie
ø Fines amouretes (Virelai)

Pro Musica Antiqua—Cape   ‡ HP.APM 14018
(above; & Anon: 17 Dances of XIIIth Cent.)
                               (‡ AmD.ARC 3002)
[items marked ø also on PV. 5414: ♭ Pol. 37076]

ADSON, John (d. c. 1640)
SEE: † GOLDEN AGE OF BRASS

AGAZZARI, Agostino (1578-1640)
SEE: † ANTHOLOGIE SONORE

AGUIRRE, Julián B. (1869-1924)

(2) Aires criollos   vln. & pf.
A. Mus & D. Colacelli   ArgOd. 56022
... No. 1 only   ▽ A. Inzaurraga (ArgV.P 91)

(5) Aires nacionales
E. Jackson (org.)   ArgV.pte.

(3) Canciones Argentinas   pf.
P. Spagnolo   in ‡ D.LXT 2947
                             (in ‡ Lon.LL 1040)

... Nos. 1 & 3
O. Penna   ArgOd. 66032
(Khachaturian: Toccata)   (♭ BSOAE 4504)

... Unspec. — ARR. GUITAR   Segovia
A. Segovia   in ‡ AmD.DL 9734
(† Segovia Plays)   (‡ D.UAT 273573)

Gato
Huella
Sym. Orch.—Gianneo   ♭ Pam.1001
(also on ArgV., pte.)   (in ‡ LRC 15501)

— PF. VERSION
S. Singer   ArgOd. 66062
(Ginastera: Preludios Americanos)

— ARR. ORG.: J. Perceval (ArgOd. 57057)

... Huella — ARR. VLN. & PF.
▽ J. Heifetz (in ‡ AmD.DL 8521; B.LAT 8020)

Triste No. 1
A. Barletta (bandoneon)   in ‡ SMC. 547

Triste No. 4   vln. & orch.
Orch.—Fidanzini   ArgV. 68-8031
(Guastavino: Bailecito, etc.)
Orch.—Vlady (in ‡ Pam.LRN 1001)
Orch.—Artola (in ‡ ArgOd.LDM 302)

— ARR. GUITAR
M. L. Anido   ArgOd. 57026
(Rameau: Gavotte)   (in ‡ LDC 521)

AICHINGER, Gregor (1564-1628)
SEE: † MOTETS OF THE XVTH & XVITH CENTURIES

ALABIEV, Alexander Alexandrovitch
(1787-1851)

(The) ENCHANTED DRUM   Ballet
Orchestral Suite
(Overture; Marche-Nocturne; Allegretto & Finale, Scene 1;
    Prelude, Scene 2; Excerpts, Scenes 3 & 4)
Leningrad Radio—Rabinovich ‡ USSR.D1191/2

Quintet, E flat major   pf. & str.
(in one movement)
E. Gilels & Beethoven Qtt.   ‡ USSR.D 1387
(Taneiev: Quartet, s. 3)

Sonata   vln. & pf.
D. Tziganov & E. Gilels   ‡ USSR.D 1125/6

Song: (The) Nightingale   S
E. Katulskaya (USSR. 18406)
L. Zubrack (♭ Vic.ERA 261)
H. Mickewiczowna (Muza. 2066)
R. Streich (‡ HP.DG 17052, & Ger, ‡ Pol. 17051)
etc.

Trio, A minor, pf., vln., vlc.
☆ E. Gilels, D. Tziganov & S. Shirinsky
                              (USSRM.D 347/8)

ALAIN, Jehan (1911-1940)

ORGAN MUSIC
2 Danses à Agni Yavishta   1934
Le jardin suspendu   1934
Variations sur un thème de Jannequin   1937
Berceuse sur deux notes qui cornent   1929
M-C. Alain   V‡ Era.LDE 1019
[St. Merry organ, Paris]

Litanies, Op. 79   1937
M-C. Alain   ‡ Era.LDE 3024
(below, & Langlais) [Ste. Clotilde org., Paris]
P. Kee   ♭ G.7EPH 1005
(Daquin, F. Couperin senior, with spoken intro. by E.
Lemaire) [Org. of St. Bavo Chu., Haarlem]
Anon. Artist   in ‡ ASK. 2
(Davies, Langlais, etc.) [Org. of Symphony Hall, Boston]
A. Hamme   in ‡ SRS.H 1
(† Organ Recital)

Postlude pour l'Office des Complies   org.   1932
Suite pour orgue   1934
(1. Introduction & varns.; 2. Scherzo; 3. Finale)
M-C. Alain   ‡ Era.LDE 3024
(above) [Postlude, on Ste. Clotilde; Suite, on St. Merry]

ALBANO, Enrique (b. 1910)

Obertura norteña   orch.   1950
Argentine Radio—Bandini   ArgOd. 66031
                             (in ‡ LDC 502)

---

[1] NOTE: Ten of the seventeen anon. dances are also on ♭ Pol. 37002.

ALBENIZ, Isaac (1860-1909)

PIANO MUSIC
(unless otherwise stated)

IBERIA, BOOKS I–IV
COMPLETE RECORDING
Bk. I: 1. Evocación; 2. El Puerto; 3. El Corpus en Sevilla
Bk. II: 4. Rondeña; 5. Almeria; 6. Triana
Bk. III: 7. El Albaicín; 8. El Polo; 9. Lavapiés
Bk. IV: 10. Malaga; 11. Jerez; 12. Eritaña.

I. Kohler   ‡ **CA.LPA 1015/6**
(3½ss—*Navarra*)
[Triana only, with *Navarra*, **V**‡ *MPO 5005*]

J. Falgarona (4ss)   ‡ **AmVox. set PL 9212**

J. Echaniz (*see* COLLECTION, *below*)

☆ L. Querol (3½ss—*Navarra*)   ‡ *LT.DTL 93022/3*

... **Nos. 1, 2, 3, 6, 7** — ARR. ORCH. Arbós
Paris Cons.—Argenta   ‡ **D.LXT 2889**
(*Turina*)   (‡ SpC.CCL 32000; ‡ Lon.LL 921)
L.S.O.—Poulet   in ‡ **P.PMC 1006**
(*Granados, Turina, Falla*)   (‡ Od.ODX 137; MGM.E 3073)
Lamoureux—Toldra (2ss)   ‡ *Phi.N 00699R*
(*Bizet*, on ‡ Epic. LC 3068)
Colonne Sym.—Sebastian   ‡ **Nix.ULP 9085**
(2ss)   (o.n. ‡ Ura. 7085)
(*Debussy: Iberia*, on ‡ Ura. 7130, n.n.; also ‡ *ACC.MP 24*)
(1½ss—*Moussorgsky: Night on bare mountain*,
on ‡ *MTW. 502*)
(Nos. 2 & 6 only also on ♭ *Ura.UREP 68*)

☆ Berlin Radio—Schultz (‡ *AFest.CFR 10-64*)

SEE ALSO: Evocación, El Puerto, Triana

SUITE ESPAÑOLA
1. Granada   2. Cataluña   3. Sevillañas
4. Cádiz   5. Asturias   6. Aragon (Jota)
7. Seguidillas (Castilla)   8. Cubana (Tango)

COMPLETE RECORDING
R. Spivak (2ss)   ‡ **ArgV.ARL 3012**
[Some are ☆; others, *see below*]

... **Nos. 3, 4 & 7** — ARR. ORCH.
Buenos Aires—Cases   ‡ *Tem.TT 2056*
(*Granados*)

COLLECTIONS
IBERIA: COMPLETE, BOOKS I–IV
CANTOS DE ESPAÑA, Op. 232
   1. Prelude, G minor (Leyenda)
   2. Orientale
   3. Sous le palmier
   4. Córdoba
   5. Seguidillas (Castilla)
Navarra (completed by De Séverac)
J. Echaniz (4ss)   ‡ **West. set WAL 219**

Malagueña, Op. 71, No. 6 (Rumores de la Caleta)
   (*Recuerdos de Viaje No. 6*)
Malagueña, Op. 165, No. 3
Tango, A minor, Op. 164, No. 2
Tango, D major, Op. 165, No. 2
SUITE ESPAÑOLA
   1. Granada (Serenata)
   3. Sevillañas (Sevilla)
   4. Cádiz (Saeta)
J. Echaniz   ‡ **West.WL 5382**
(*Mompou*)

CANTOS DE ESPAÑA, Op. 232 . . . Nos. 1, 3, 4, 5
Malagueña, Op. 71, No. 6 (Rumores de la Caleta)
Tango, D major, Op. 165, No. 2
O. Frugoni   ‡ **AmVox.PL 9420**
(*Granados, Turina, Falla*)

CANTOS DE ESPAÑA, Op. 232
   ... No. 1, Prelude, G minor (Leyenda)
   No. 4, Córdoba
   No. 5, Seguidillas (Castilla)
M. Regules   ‡ **Eso.ESP 3002**
(*Turina, Villa-Lobos, Mompou*) ("Siena" pf.)

COLLECTIONS — ARR. ORCH.
Suite Española: 1. Granada   4. Cádiz
           3. Sevillañas   6. Aragon
           7. Seguidillas (Castilla)
Puerta de Tierra, Op. 71, No. 5
Malagueña, Op. 71, No. 6 (Rumores de la Caleta)
Torre bermeja

Madrid Audio Museum—Olmedo
              ‡ *DT.LGM 65029*
           (‡ *T.NLB 6039; FT. 270.TC.023*)

Triana (Iberia 6) (& in ♭ *7EPL 13028*)
Cadiz (S.E.4) (& in *G.AA 778:* ♭ *7EPL 13029*)
Pepita Jiménez—Intermezzo (& in ♭ *7EPL 13028*)
Sevillañas (S.E.3) (& in ♭ *7EPL 13028: AA 778*)
Córdoba, Op. 232, No. 4 (& in ♭ *7EPL 13029*)
Eritaña (Iberia 12) (& in ♭ *7EPL 13029: AA 779*)

P. Lopez (Castanets) & Sym.—Franco
(*Granados, Vivas*)   ‡ *G.LDLP 1011*

(El) **Albaicin** (Iberia, No. 7)
D. Raucea   in ‡ **D.LXT 2969**
(*Casella, Pick-Mangiagalli, Granados,etc.*)
            (in ‡ Lon. LL 1033)

— ARR. CASTANETS & DANCING
P. López, P. de Ronda & A. Montoya
      (in ‡ G.LCLP 102: ♭ *EPL 13041*)

Aragon S.E.6 (Jota)
▽ R. Spivak (*below*)   ArgV. 11-7969

Asturias S.E.5 (Leyenda)
R. Arroyo   in ‡ *CND. 1002*
(*below; & Angles, M. Albeniz, etc.*)
R. Spivak   ArgV. 11-8075
(*Liszt: Hung. Rhapsody No. 1*)
☆ E. Osta (in ‡ *Coda. 1000*)

— ARR. GUITAR
L. Almeida   ‡ **DCap.CTL 7089**
(† *Guitar Music of Spain*)   (‡ Cap.P 8295)
G. Zepoll (in ‡ Nix.SLPY 142; ‡ SOT. 1024)
N. Yepes (in † ‡ D.LXT 2974: FST 153076)
M. D. Cano (in ‡ Dur.AI 506; AI 10150)
M. L. Anido (ArgOd. 57014: in ‡ LDC 52)
J. F. Arguelles (in ‡ SMC. 506)
A. Lagoya (♭ Pat.ED 2)
☆ A. Segovia (in † ‡ D.UAT 273141)

— ARR. ORCH. Madrid Cha.—Lloret   in ‡ **Mont.FM 22**

Berceuse, Op. 201 — ARR. CASTANETS & HARP
S. Agnès & L. Laskine   *Radi. 745*
(*Malagueña, Op. 71, No. 6, & San Sebastian: Onanz Dolor*)

Cádiz S.E.4
☆ C. de Groot   ♭ *Phi.N 402006E*
(*Seguidillas*)   (in ‡ Epic.LC 3175)

— ARR. ORCH.
☆ Decca Concert—Horlick (in ‡ AmD.DL 5070;
                 ArgOd.LTM 8316)

Cataluña S.E.2
▽ R. Spivak (*above & below*)   ArgV. 11-7969

Córdoba, Op. 232, No. 4 (*Cantos de España*, No. 4)
A. Iturbi   in ‡ **Vic.LM 1788**
(*Granada; & Infante, etc.*)   (in ‡ FV.A 630231)
M. Pressler   in ‡ **MGM.E 3129**
(*Bartók, Chabrier, Granados, etc.*)   (♭ set X 254)
☆ G. Copeland   in ‡ **MGM.E 3025**
(*Falla, Granados, Laparra, etc.*)
— ARR. ORCH.
Madrid Cha.—Lloret   in ‡ **Mont.FM 22**
Madrid Theatre Orch.—Machado   in ‡ **B.AXTL 1074**
         (‡ SpC.CCL 35002; AmD.DL 9757)
☆ Decca Concert—Horlick
      (in ‡ AmD.DL 5070; ArgOd.LTM 8316)
— ARR. VLN. & PF.   ☆ A. Campoli & E. Gritton (♭ D. 71065)
— ARR. ORG. J. Perceval (ArgOd. 66018 : in ‡ LDC 508)

(El) **Corpus en Sevilla** (*Iberia*, No. 3)
R. Arroyo   in ‡ *CND.1002*

☆ = Re-issue of a recording to be found in previous volumes.

Cuba S.E.8
R. Spivak   ArgV. 66-6114
(*Granados: Danza No. 5*)

España, Op. 165   6 pieces[1]
1. Prelude   4. Serenata
2. Tango, D major   5. Capricho catalan
3. Malagueña   6. Zortzico

W. Masselos   ♯ MGM.E 3165
(*Nin, Surinach, Turina*)

Evocación (*Iberia*, No. 1)
R. Caamaño   ArgOd. 66023
(*El Puerto*)   (♭ *BSOAE 4520*)
R. Arroyo   in ♯ *CND.1002*

— ARR. ORCH.
☆ Decca Concert—Horlick
    (in ♯ *AmD.DL 5070; ArgOd.LTM 8316*)

Granada S.E.1
A. Iturbi   in ♯ Vic.LM 1788
(*Córdoba; Granados, Turina, etc.*)   (in ♯ *FV.A 630231*)
☆ E. Osta (in ♯ *Coda. 1000*)

— ARR. GUITAR
L. Walker   in ♯ *Phil.N 00640R*
     (♯ Epic.LC 3055)
C. Aubin   in ♯ *Eko.LG 1*
(† Guitar Recital)

☆ A. Segovia (in ♯ *D.UMT 273029;*
     ♭ *AmD.ED 3510;* ♭ *SpC.SCGE 80005*)
— ARR. ORCH.
☆ Decca Concert—Horlick
    (in ♯ *AmD.DL 5070; ArgOd.LTM 8316*)
— ARR. HARP   ▽ N. Zabaleta (*ChOd. 195021*)

Malagueña, Op. 71, No. 6 (Rumores de la Caleta)
(*Recuerdos de viaje No. 6*)
☆ E. Osta (in ♯ *Coda. 1000*)
C. de Groot (in ♯ Epic.LC 3175)

— ARR. VLN. & PF.   Kreisler
D. Erlih & M. Bureau   G.DB 11252
(*Sarasate: Zapateado*)
— ARR. ORCH.
Madrid Theatre—Moreno Torroba   in ♯ *AmD.DL 9789*
Spanish Sym.—Moreno Torroba   in ♯ Angel.SS 70008
     (♯ Pam.LRC 15905)
Sym.—R. Ferrer   in ♯ C.FSX 104
(♯ Angel. 65008 : ♭ *70018;* ♭ *Reg.SEDL 108:* ♯ *LCX 104*)
☆ Decca Concert—Horlick
    (in ♯ *AmD.DL 5070;* ♯ *ArgOd.LTM 8316*)
— ARR. VLC. & PF.
J. Starker & L. Pommers
    (in ♯ Nix.PLP 584; ♯ Per.SPL 584; ♯ Cpt.MC 20054)
— ARR. GUITAR
N. Yepes   in ♯ *D.LXT 2974*
(† Spanish Music)   (♯ FST 153076; Lon.LL 1042)

Malagueña, Op. 165, No. 3
C. de Groot   ♯ *Phi.N 00761R*
(*Falla & Mompou*)   (in ♯ Epic.LC 3175)

K. Baekkelund   G.AL 3286
(*Schuman: Romance, Op. 28, No. 2*)
▽ R. Spivak (*above*)   ArgV. 11-7969

— ARR. VLC. & PF.
A. Navarra & J. Dussol   in ♯ *Od.OD 1014*
— ARR. GUITAR
N. Yepes   in ♯ *D.LXT 2974*
(† Spanish Music)   (♯ FST 153076; Lon.LL 1042)
— ARR. HARP: N. Zabaleta (*ChOd. 195020; ArgOd. 46087*)
— ARR. ORGAN: J. Perceval (ArgOd. 66018: in ♯ *LDC 508*)
— ARR. VLN. & PF.
I. Zilzer & F. Eberson   C.LDX 18
(*Granados: Danza No. 5*)
☆ I. Haendel & pf. (ArgOd. 263772)
— ARR. CASTANETS & HARP
S. Agnès & L. Laskine   Radi. 745
(*Berceuse, Op. 201, etc.*)

Malagueña (unspec.)
— ARR. VLC. & PF.: D. Shafran & pf. (*USSRM.D 363*)

Mallorca, Op. 202 (Barcarolla)
— ARR. ORCH.
Madrid Cha.—Lloret   in ♯ Mont.FM 22

[1] Individual recordings under individual titles.

Navarra (completed by de Séverac)
I. Kohler   ♯ CA.LPA 1016
(*Iberia*)   (& in V♯ *MPO 5005*)
P. Cavazzini   ♯ *Arp.ARC 2*
(*Triana; Debussy, etc.*)
☆ L. Querol   in ♯ *LT.DTL 93022*
☆ E. Osta (in ♯ *Allo. 3151*)

Orientale, Op. 232, No. 2 (*Cantos de España, No. 2*)
— ARR. GUITAR   Segovia
L. Almeida   in ♯ DCap.CTL 7089
(† Guitar Music of Spain)   (♯ Cap.P 8295)

Pavana capricho, Op. 12
— ARR. GUITAR
M. D. Cano   Dur.AI 10152
(*Tarrega: Capricho arabe*)   (in ♯ *AI 506*)

(El) Puerto (Iberia No. 2)
R. Caamaño   ArgOd. 66023
(*Evocación*)   (♭ *BSOAE 4520*)
R. Arroyo   in ♯ *CND.1002*
— ARR. ORCH.   Arbós
☆ Paris Cons.—Jorda (♯ *D.LW 5055; Lon.LD 9042*)

Puerta de Tierra, Op. 71, No. 5 (Bolero)
— ARR. ORCH.
Madrid Cha.—Lloret   in ♯ Mont.FM 22
Colón Theatre—Cases   in ♯ *Od.OD 1018*
(*Granados, Falla, etc.*)   (♯ *ArgOd.LDC 519* & *66052*)

Rapsodia española   — ARR. BAND
▽ Royal Corps of Halbardiers Band (*ArgOd. 132040*)

Seguidillas (Castilla) S.E.7
P. Spagnolo   in ♯ D.LXT 2947
(*Falla, Granados, etc.*)   (♯ Lon.LL 1040)
R. Spivak   ArgV. 66-6003
(*below*)
L. Pennario   in ♯ DCap.CTL 7054
(*below, & Falla, Infante, etc.*) (in ♯ Cap.P 8190: ♭ *FAP 8204*)
☆ C. de Groot   ♭ *Phi.N 402006E*
(*Cádiz*)   (in ♯ Epic.LC 3175)
☆ E. Boynet (in ♭ *AmVox.VIP 45500*)

— ARR. ORCH.
Hollywood Bowl Sym.—Dragon
     (in ♯ Cap.P 8314; ♭ *FAP 8314*)

Sérénade espagnole, Op. 181
☆ R. Viñes (*JpV.NF 4068*)

Sevillañas (Sevilla) S.E.3
L. Pennario   ♯ DCap.CTL 7054
(*above, Falla, etc.*)   (♯ Cap.P 8190 & in ♯ *LAL 9024*)
☆ C. de Groot (in ♯ Epic.LC 3175)
— ARR. ORCH.: Spanish Sym.—Martinez (in ♯ Mont.FM 16)
☆ Decca Concert—Horlick (in ♯ *AmD.DL 5070*)
— ARR. GUITAR   Tárrega
L. Almeida   in ♯ DCap.CTL 7089
(† Guitar Music of Spain)   (♯ Cap.P 8295)
☆ A. Segovia (in ♯ *D.UMT 273029;*
     ♭ *SpC.SCGE 80004; AmD.ED 3503*)
— ARR. VLN. & PF.
☆ A. Campoli & E. Gritton (♭ *D. 71065*)
— ARR. HARMONICA & PF.
L. Adler & L. Colin   in ♯ *CHS.CHS 1168*
     (in ♯ *FMer.MLP 7026*)
— ARR. SAX. QTT.
A. Sax Qtt. (Phi.N 12050G: ♯ *N 00616R*)

SONG: Love comes to all (*Six Songs, No. 6*)
(F. B. Money-Coutts) c. 1892
— ARR. SAX. QTT.   Mule
A. Sax Saxophone Qtt.   Phi.N 12050G
(*Sevillañas*)   (in ♯ *N 00616R*)

— ARR. VLN. & PF.   ("*Chant d'amour*")
D. Oistrakh & V. Yampolsky   ♯ *USSR.D 1201*
(*Brahms, St. Saëns, Sarasate*)
▽ D. Oistrakh & V. Topilin
     (*USSR. 10497;* in ♯ Csm.CRLP 105)

Tango, A minor, Op. 164, No. 2[1]
  ☆ R. Viñes (*JpV.NF 4068*)

Tango, D major, Op. 165, No. 2
  M. Lympany[2]   **C.C 4203**
  (*Debussy: Clair de lune*)   (♭ *Vic.EHA 13*)
  L. Pennario   in ♯ **DCap.CTL 7054**
  (*above; Falla, etc.*)   (in ♯ Cap.P 8190: ♭ *FAP 8235*)
  E. Osta   in ♯ **Allo. 3151**
  A. Semprini   **G.B 10826**
  (*Granados: Danza No. 5*)

  ▽ O. Levant (in AmC. set MM 560: ♭ *A 560*: ♯ *ML 2018*)
  ☆ C. Keene (in ♯ EMer.MG 10113;
            ♭ *FMer.MEP 14502; Mer.EP 1-5011*)
    G. Copeland (in ♯ MGM.E 3025)
    E. Boynet (♭ *AmVox.VIP 45500*)
    A. Foldes (in *PV. 36104*)

— ARR. VLN. & PF.   Kreisler
  T. Magyar & W. Hielkema (in ♯ *Phi.S 06049R*)
  A. Campoli & E. Gritton (♯ *D.LW 5180; Lon.LD 9192*)
  ☆ Z. Francescatti & A. Balsam (in ♯ EPhi.NBL 5010;
            & Phi.N 02101L: *S 06602R*)
— ARR. VLN. & ORCH.
  I. Zilzer & Orch. (in C.DDX 39: ♭ *SCDK 1*)

— ARR. ORCH.
  Hollywood Bowl Sym.—Dragon
            (in ♯ Cap.P 8314: ♭ *FAP 8314*)
  ☆ Decca Concert—Horlick
          (in ♯ *AmD.DL 5070; ArgOd.LTM 8316*)

Torre bermeja (*Piezas carac. 12*)
— ARR. GUITAR   Segovia
  M. A. Funes   **ArgOd. 66067**
  (*Sor: Siciliana*)
  ☆ A. Segovia (in ♯ D.UMT 273029)
— ARR. ORCH.   Moreno Torroba (*et al.*)
  Madrid Theatre—Moreno Torroba   in ♯ AmD.DL 9763
  Spanish Sym.—Ferrer   ♭ *Reg.SEDL 109*
  (*Malats: Serenata*)   (in ♯ Reg.LCX 104; C.FSX 104)
  (in ♯ Angel. 65008: ♭70019)
  Sym.—Moreno Torroba
       (in ♯ Pam.LRC 15905; Angel.SS 70008)

Triana (*Iberia No. 6*)
  P. Cavazzini   ♯ **Arp.ARC 2**
  (*Navarra; & Debussy, Liszt, Ravel*)
  A. de Raco   ♯ **ArgOd.LDC 520**
  (*Mompou & Prokofiev*)   (♭ BSOAE 4522, d.c.)
  E. Osta   in ♯ **Allo. 3151**
  M. Tagliaferro   in **V**♯ *Sel.LAP 1006*
  ☆ C. Keene (♭ *Mer.EP 1-5011; FMer.MEP 14502;*
                 ♯ EMer.MG 10113)
— ARR. ORCH.   Arbós
  Col. Sym.—Kurtz   in ♯ **AmC.CL 773**
  ☆ Boston Pops.—Fiedler (G.DB 4325)
    Paris Cons.—Jorda (♯ *D.LW 5055; Lon.LD 9042*)

ALBENIZ, Mateo (1760-1831)

Sonata, D major   hpsi.   (Nin I-13)
  R. Arroyo (pf.)   in ♯ **CND. 1002**
  (*Granados, Larregla, etc.*)
  F. Blumenthal (pf.)   in ♯ **D.LXT 2805**
  († Spanish Keyboard Music)   (♯ Lon.LL 769)

  J. Falgarona (pf.) (in † ♯ AmVox.PL 8340)
  F. Valenti (hpsi.) (in † ♯ Nix.WLP 5312; West.WL 5312)
  ☆ H. Boschi (pf.) (in † **V**♯ CdM.LD Y 8081)
Sonata (unspec.)   ▽ N. Zabaleta (*ChOd. 195023*)

ALBERO, Sebastian (fl. XVIIIth Century)
  SEE: † CLAVECINISTES ESPAGNOLS . . .

ALBERT, Eugene d' (1864-1932)

Gavotte & Minuet, Op. 1, No. 4   pf.
  E. Burton   in ♯ **CEd.CE 1027**

OPERAS
TIEFLAND   Prologue & 2 Acts   1903
COMPLETE RECORDING
  Marta   ...   .   M. Kenney (S)
  Pepa   ...   .   H. Vopenka (A)
  Nuri   ...   .   E. Riegler (S)
  Pedro   ...   .   W. Kmentt (T)
  Nando   ...   .   K. Equiluz (T)
  Sebastiano ...   .   O. Wiener (B)
  Tommaso ...   .   L. Heppe (Bs)
  etc., Vienna State Op. Cho. & Vienna Phil.[3]
    Orch.—Adler   (6ss)   ♯ **SPA. 40/2**

EXCERPTS
Symphonic Prelude; Szene der Marta; Wolfserzählung;
Erzählung der Marta: Ich weiss nicht, wer mein Vater war S
Tanzlied des Sebastiano; Pedros Abschied
  A. Kupper (S), W. Windgassen (T), H. Uhde (B),
    K. Böhme (Bs), Bavarian Radio Cho. &
    Munich Phil. Orch.—Rother   ♯ *Pol. 17002*

Wolfserzählung
Erzählung der Marta: Ich weiss nicht, wer mein Vater war S
Pedros Abschied von den Bergen: Hast dies gehört T
  From above   **PV. 72378**

Traumerzählung   T (Prologue)
Wolfserzählung   T (Act I)
  ☆ R. Tauber (in ♯ Ete. 712)
Hüll in die Mantille   B   (Act II)
H L. Demuth (in ♯ *HRS. 3003**)

(Die) TOTEN AUGEN   Prologue & 1 Act   1916
Orch. Selection
  Imperial Light Orch.—Koschat   *Imp.ILP 125*
  (*La Bohème, Selection*)

Psyche wandelt durch Säulenhallen   S
  A. Kupper   *Pol. 62926*
  (*Korngold: Tote Stadt—Glück, das mir verblieb*) (♭ 32014)

ALBERT, Henrich (1604-1651)
  SEE: † SEVEN CENTURIES OF SACRED MUSIC

ALBINONI, Tommaso (1671-1750)

Adagio, G minor   Str. & org.[4]
  Sinfonia Ens.—Witold (n.v.)   ♯ **Cpt.MC 20101**
  (*below*)   (in ♯ Per.SPL 723)
  (*Bach: Clavier Fugue, BWV 951 on* ♭ *Cpt.EXTP 1005*)
  [P. Lamacque, vln., D. Gouarne, org.]
  ☆ Milan Angelicum—Gerelli (Ang.SA 3011)

CONCERTOS
COLLECTIONS
(12) CONCERTI a 5, Op. 5   1707
  No. 1, B flat major
  No. 7, D minor
(12) CONCERTI, Op. 7   *c.* 1716
  No. 3, B flat major
  No. 6, D major
  No. 9, F major
  No. 12, C major
  P. Pierlot (ob.) & O. L. Ens.—Froment
                  ♯ **LOL.OL 50041**
                  (♯ OL.LD 92)
Op. 5, No. 7, D minor
Op. 5, No. 11, G minor
Op. 5, No. 12, C major
C major (no Op. No.)[5]
  Sinfonia Ens.—Witold   ♯ *EPP.SLP 3*

(*continued on next page*)

---

[1] A Tango in A minor is also listed as Op. 124. It is not clear if the same work.
[2] ARR. Godowsky.   [3] So catalogued, but apparently incorrectly.
[4] A work by Giazzotto based on a concerto movement by Albinoni, discovered at Dresden.
[5] Not in Giazzotto Thematic catalogue.   Pub. 1718, Amsterdam.

CONCERTOS (*continued*)
Op. 5, No. 9, E minor   ("Sonata")
Op. 5, No. 12, C major
C major (no Op. No.)[1]
  Sinfonia Ens.—Witold   # Cpt.MC 20101
  (*Adagio; & Concerto, Op. 7, No. 1*)
  [*Op. 5, No. 12 & C major, with Adagio, above, &Op. 7, No. 1,
  below; & Vivaldi, on # Per.SPL 723*]

Op. 5, No. 7, D minor
  Italian Cha.—Jenkins   # HS.HSL 74
  (*Corelli & Sammartini*)   (in set HSL-C)

CONCERTOS a 5, Op. 9, COMPLETE
No. 1, B flat major (vln.)   No. 2, D minor (ob.)
No. 3, F major (2 obs.)   No. 4, A major (vln.)
No. 5, C major (ob.)   No. 6, G major (2 obs.)
No. 7, D major (vln.)   No. 8, G minor (ob.)
No. 9, C major (2 obs.)   No. 10, F major (vln.)
No. 11, B flat major (ob.)   No. 12, D major (2 obs.)
  C. Ferraresi (vln.), M. Visai & F. Milanesi (obs.),
  Ital. Baroque Ens.—Bryks
  (6ss)   # AmVox. set DL 193

Op. 7, No. 1, D major   str.   *c.* 1716
Op. 9, No. 2, D minor   ob. & str.   *c.* 1722
  A. Jensen & Salzburg Mozarteum
  —Paumgartner   # CFD. 14
  (*Torelli, Telemann, Caix, etc.*)

Op. 7, No. 1, D major
  Sinfonia Ens.—Witold   # Cpt.MC 20101
  (*above*)   (in # Per.SPL 723)

Op. 9, No. 2, D minor   ob. & str.
  S. Gallesi & Italian Cha.—Jenkins
                                # HS.HSL 137
  (*Durante & Viotti*)   (in set. HSL-N)

Op. 7, No. 3, B flat major   ob. & orch.
  ... 1st movt., Allegro
  ☆ L. Goossens & Philharmonia—Susskind
                              (C.DOX 1023, d.c.)

Op. 9, No. 7, D major   vln. & str. orch.   *c.* 1722
  F. Ayo & I Musici Ens.[2]   # C.CX 1163
  (*G. Gabrieli, B. Marcello & Vivaldi*)
  (# QCX 10039: FCX 305; Angel. 35088)
  ☆ A. Pelliccia & Virtuosi di Roma—Fasano
  (*Cirri, Pergolesi, Marcello*)   # B.AXTL 1023
                          (# Fnt.LP 3003; D.UAT 273581)

No Op. No., A major   vln. & str.[3]
  M. Abbado & Milan Str.—Abbado
                                # C.FCX 370
  (*Pergolesi, Vivaldi*)

SONATAS ("SINFONIAS") a tre, Op. 1   1694
No. 2, F major   No. 3, A major
No. 4, G minor   No. 6, C major
No. 7, G major
  M. L. Girod (org.), Paris Coll. Mus.—Douatte
                                # EPP.SLP 6

No. 3, A major
  O. Kinch & P. Elbaek (vlns.), J. E. Hansen
  (virginals) & B. Anker (vlc.)
  (*Vivaldi*)   ♭ Mtr.MCEP 3021
  (*idem, Stradella & A. Scarlatti, on* # HS.HS 9011)

Sonata (Sinfonia a 5) G minor, Op. 2, No. 6
  str.   pub. 1694   (ed. Fasano)
  ☆ Virtuosi di Roma—Fasano
              (in # D.UAT 273091; Fnt.LP 3006)

Sonata, F major, Op. 2, No. 8   — ARR. ORGAN   Walther, *q.v.*

Sonata, A major, Op. 6, No. 11   vln. & cont.[4]
  O. Kinch, J. E. Hansen (virginals),
  H. G. Petersen (vlc.)   ♭ Mtr.MCEP 3003
  (*A. Scarlatti*)

ALFANO, Franco (1876-1954)

RÉSURRECTION   Opera   4 Acts   1904
Dieu de Grâce   S
  ☆ M. Garden (AF.AGSB 44; in # Vic.LCT 1158)

ALFONSO X (the Wise) (1221-1284)

Cantiga (unspec.)   — ARR. GUITAR
  M. L. Anido   ArgOd. 66035
  (‡s—*Mozart & Tárrega*) (in # LDC 521; ♭ BSOA 4011 &
                                              4516)

ALFVÉN, Hugo (b. 1872)

Gustav II Adolf, Op. 49   1932
  (Suite from Inc. Music to L. Nordström's play *Vi*)
  ... No. 7, Elegy
  Covent Garden Op.—Hollingsworth
                                # P.PMC 1021
  (*below, Sibelius, Svendsen, Nielsen*)   (# MGM.E 3082)
Midsommarvaka, Op. 19   (*Swedish Rhapsody No. 1*)
                                              1904
  Stockholm Royal Op.—Alfvén   # SS. 33100
  (*below*)   (*below, & Rangström, on* # West.WN 18131)
  Covent Garden Op.—Hollingsworth
                                # P.PMC 1021
  (*above & Svendsen, etc.*)   (# MGM.E 3082)
  Philadelphia—Ormandy   # AmC.AL 35
  (*Grieg: Peer Gynt Suite No. 1, excpts.*)   (♭ A 1645)
  ☆ Cincinnati Sym.—Johnson
                      (♭ D.DME 8001; ♭ Lon.REP 8001)

(The) Mountain King, Op. 37   Ballet Pantomime
Orch. Suite   1923
1. Incantation   3. Summer rain
2. Troll-maidens' dance   4. Herd-maidens' dance
  Stockholm Royal Op.—Alfvén   # SS. 33100
  (*above*)   (& 2ss, ♭ 45101)
  (*above, & Rangström, on* # West.WN 18131)

SONGS
Evening   (Sätherberg)
  V. Davidova (S, *Russ*)   USSR. 021814
  (*Alnaes, & Folksong*)

(The) Swedish Flag   (Nilsson)   — ARR. CHO.
  Stockholm Students—Ralf   .in # SS. 33105
  (*Grieg, Sibelius, Folksongs, etc.*)

ALLEGRI, Gregorio (1582-1652)

Miserere mei, Deus
  Harvard Glee Club & Radcliffe Cho. Soc.
  —Woodworth   in # Camb.CRS 202
  († *Chansons & Motets*)
  U.O.S. Cho.—McConnell   in # UOS. 2
  (*Bach, Handel, Victoria, etc.*)   (pte. recording)

ALNAES, Eyvind (1872-1932)

SONGS
I sat by the sea
  C. Hague (T), G. Steele (pf.)   in # ML. 7034
  († *Scandinavian Songs*)

Selma
  V. Davidova (S)   USSR. 021815
  (‡s—*Folksong; & Alfvén*)
  (There have also been many ▽ recordings, including
  G.AL 2613, DA 11900/1, DA 1516, etc., in addition to the
  more recent issues listed in WERM Supp. II.)

---

[1] Not in Giazzotto Thematic catalogue.   Pub. 1718, Amsterdam
[3] Dresden MS 2199/04; Giazzotto No. 116.
[2] Ed. Giazzotto.
[4] From *Trattenimenti armonici per camera*, 1711.

ALONSO, Francisco (1887-1948)

ZARZUELAS & SAINETES
(Abridged listings only. There are many individual recordings in Spanish catalogues from the following and other works.)

(La) CALESERA
Pasacalle Orch.—Delta (in ♭ *Od.MSOE 101: ▽ 188861*)
Vocal Excerpts
  M. Ausensi (in ♯ *LI.W 91028; Ambra.MC 25005*)
  ▽ M. Fleta (*G.DB 918*), etc.

(Las) CORSARIOS
March Spanish Air Force Band—Arriba
  (in ♯ *B.LAT 8075*; AmD.DL 9764)

DOÑA MARIQUITA DE MI CORAZON
▽ R. Rodrigo, E. Goya, C. Páez, etc., Cho. & Orch.—
  Alonso (*SpC.A 9104/8*)

(Las) LEANDRAS   1931
D. Reubens, M. Aznar, T. Moto, Cho. & Madrid
  Orch.—Montorio   ♯ *Mont.FM 32*

Prelude Madrid Cha. Orch.—Navarro in ♯ Mont.FM 39

(La) LINDA TAPADA
Canción del Borrico L. Sagi-Vela (B) (in ♯ *MusH.LP 5006*)

LUNA DE MIEL EN EL CAIRO
▽ A. Ballesta, A. Pérez, R. Cervera, etc., Cho. & Orch.
  —Alonso (*SpC.R 14081/5*)

MANUELITA ROSAS
▽ C. Panadés, C. Leonis, M. Alares, etc., Cho. & Orch.
  —Alonso (*SpC.A 9012/5*)

(La) PARRANDA   3 Acts   1928
L. Rovira, C. Panadés, M. Redondo, B. Bardají,
  Cho. & Orch.—Delta   ♯ *Reg.LC 1007*
          (♯ Angel.SS 70007, d.c.; Pam.LRC 15502)

Prelude in ♭ *Angel. 70011*
Vocal Excerpts in ♭ *Reg.SEDL 19040: SEBL 7016;*
    ♭ *Angel. 70017;* ♯ *LI.W 91028; Ambra.MC 25005;*
    ♭ *SpC.SMGE 80000*, etc.

(La) PERFECTA CASADO
March Spanish Air Force Band—Arriba
  (in ♯ AmD.DL 9792)

ROSA LA PANTALONERA
▽ M. Vázquez, P. Huerta, A. Muelas, etc., Cho. & Orch.
  —Alonso (*SpC.A 6032/6*)

(La) RUMBOSA   f.p. 1951
P. Lorengar (S), M. Ausensi (B), R. Leonis (S),
  & Sym. Orch.—Echevarria   ♯ *Mont.FM 8*

TRES DIAS PARA QUERERTE
▽ C. Olmedo, M. Thipaut, etc., Cho. & Orch.—Alonso
          (*SpC.R 14349/54*)

VEINTCUATRO HORAS MINTIENDO
▽ M. Boldoba, A. Navalón, A. Goda, etc., Cho. & Orch.
  —Alonso (*SpC.R 14595/600*)

(La) ZAPATERITA
▽ A. Medio, T. Pello, Ch. Leonis, C. Panadés, etc.,
  Cho. & Orch.—Alonso (*SpC.A 9021/5 & AG 11000/1*)

ALPAERTS, Florent (b. 1876)

James Ensor Suite orch. 1931
  ☆ Belgian Nat.—Weemaels (*Legley*)   ♯ Lon.LL 874

AMBROSIUS, Hermann (b. 1897)

Suite No. 1 guitar *c.* 1940
  L. Walker   in ♯ *Phi.N 00640R*
                  (in ♯ Epic.LC 3055)

AMIROV, Fikret (b. 1922)

Caucasian Dances (Azerbaijan Mugams)
  Leipzig Radio—Abendroth   ♯ **Ura. 7117**
  (*Arensky & Liadov*)
  U.S.S.R. State—Anosov   ♯ **CEd.CE 3001**
  (*Glier, Glinka, Prokofiev*)   (*USSR. 16545/6*, excerpts)
Folk Song arrangements on ♯ *USSR.D 2030*, etc.

ANCHIETA, Juan de (1462-1523)

Domine Jesu Christe Offertorium
  Vatican Cho.—Bertolucci   ♯ **Per.SPL 706**
  (*Binchois, Victoria, Palestrina*, etc.)

ANDREAS, Carolus (d. 1627)
SEE: † POLYPHONIC MASTERS

ANDREWS, Herbert Kennedy (b. 1904)
SEE: † ENGLISH CHURCH MUSIC, VOL. III

ANDRICU, Mihail (b. 1894)[1]

Symphony No. 2   1947
  Rumanian Sym.—Rogalsky   Pop. 5029/31
  (6ss)

ANDRIESSEN, Hendrik (b. 1892)

Intermezzo fl. & hp.
  H. Barwahser & P. Berghout   ♯ *Phi.N 00695R*
  (*Badings, Roesgen-Champion, Tomasi*)
Magna res est amor
  ▽ J. Vincent (S) & Amsterdam—Mengelberg (*T.SK 3085*)

ANGLEBERT, Jean-Henry d' (1628-1691)
SEE: † CLAVECINISTES FRANÇAIS

ANGLES, (Padre) Rafael (1730-1816)

Aria, D minor hpsi. (Nin II-9)
  R. Arroyo (pf.)   ♯ *CND. 1002*
  (*M. Albeniz, Granados*, etc.)
  & SEE ALSO: † SPANISH KEYBOARD MUSIC
          † OLD SPANISH KEYBOARD MUSIC

ANON.

An increasing amount of music by this prolific composer is being recorded. Examples will be found in many Anthologies and similar collections, including:

  † AIRS À BOIRE
  † ANTHOLOGIE SONORE
  † CARILLON PIECES
  † CHANSONS FROM MUSIC BOOKS OF MARGARET OF AUSTRIA
  † CHANSONS HISTORIQUES
  † CHANSONS DE FRANCE
  † CHANSONS POÉTIQUES
  † CHORAL MUSIC
  † CHORAL MUSIC OF XIIITH–XVITH CENTURIES
  † DANCERIES ET BALLETS
  † ENGLISH MEDIEVAL CAROLS
  † FRENCH CHANSONS
  † GLOGAUER LIEDERBUCH
  † GOLDEN AGE OF BRASS
  † HISTOIRE DE LA MUSIQUE VOCALE
  † HISTORY OF MUSIC IN SOUND
  † HISTORY OF THE DANCE
  † HYMNS OF PRAISE
  † ITALIAN AIRS
  † LUTENIST SONGS
  † MANUSCRIT DE BAYEUX
  † MASTERS OF EARLY ENGLISH KEYBOARD MUSIC
  † MONUMENTA ITALICAE MUSICAE

(continued on next page)

---

[1] b. 1897 according to L. Cassini: *Music in Rumania*, but 1894 confirmed by the Rumanian Institute of Cultural Relations.

† Musical Organ Clock
† Musiciens de la cour de Bourgogne
† Music of the Renaissance
† La Musique et la Poésie
† Parisian Songs of XVIth Century
† Renaissance Music
† Renaissance Music for Lute
† Recorder Music
† Segovia, Art of
† Shakespeare Songs and Lute Solos

ANROOIJ, Peter G. van (1879-1954)

Piet Hein Rhapsody, Orch. 1901
Residentie—Dorati   **♯ Phi.S 06036R**
(*Wagenaar*)   (& Phi.N 12060G, 2ss)

ANTES, John (1740-1811)

TRIOS, Op. 3 2 vlns., vlc. (ed. T. Johnson)
E flat major; D minor; C major   *c. 1790*
▽ I. Cohen, W. Torkanowsky, S. Barab   **♯ NRI. 2016**

Go, Congregation, go!
M. Noster (S) & Cha. Orch.—T. Johnson
                                       ♯ NRI. 2017
(† American Music—Vocal)
▽ M. Truman (S), Cho. & orch. (in *Vic. set DM 1445:*
                       ♭ *WDM 1445:* ♯ *LM 57*)

ANTHEIL, George (b. 1900)

Ballet mécanique[1]   airplane propeller, anvil,
electric bells, 8 pfs. & player-pf. 1925
N.Y. Percussion Group—Surinach
(*Brant*)   **♯ AmC.ML 4956**

Capital of the World Ballet 1953
Ballet Theatre—Levine[2]   **♯ DCap.CTL 7081**
(*Banfield*)   (♯ Cap.P 8278)
[Excerpt in ♯ Cap.SAL 9020]

(8) Fragments from Shelley Cho. 1951
R. Wagner Chorale   **♯ SPA. 36**
(*below*)

McKonkey's Ferry, Overture orch. 1948/50
Vienna State Philharmonia—Adler **♯ SPA. 47**
(*Siegmeister, Jacobi, North, Cowell*)

Sonata No. 2, vln. & pf. 1947
▽ ☆ I. Baker & Yaltah Menuhin   **♯ ML. 7006**
(*Ratner*)

Valentine Waltzes pf.
G. Antheil   **♯ SPA. 36**
(*above*)

ARAKISHVILI, Dmitri Ignatyevich
                                    (b. 1873)

The Calm of the starry night
                (Fet, trs. I. Mchedlishvili)
Georgian State Cho.—Khakhanashvili (*USSR. 17571*)

(The) TALE OF SHOTA RUSTAVELI Opera
(in Georgian)
Overture
Moscow Radio—Dimitriadi   **USSR. 018355/6**

Tsaritsa Tamara's Cavatina
L. Georgadze   **USSR. 23776**
(*Snow Maiden, Aria*)
(also, with *Ballet Music,* on ♯ *USSR.D 2210*)

Ballet Music orch.
Georgian State Orch.   **♯ USSR.D 2210**
(*above*)

ARBEAU, Thoinot (1519-1595)
(Tabourot, Jehan)
SEE: † Chansons historiques
     † Danceries et Ballets
also: Warlock: Capriol Suite

ARCADELT, Jacob (*c.* 1505-*c.* 1567)

SEE: † Chansons & Motets; also under Ortiz, *post.*
Ave Maria[3]
Cho.—R. Wagner   in ♯ Layos.LL 102
— arr. solo: J. Mojica (T) (*BrzC.CB 4019*)
— arr. organ: C. Cronham (*Mjr. 5133*)
☆ C. Courboin (in ♯ Cam.CAL 218)

ARCHANGELSKY, Alexander Andreievitch
                                    (1846-1924)

SEE: † Choral Masterpieces from the Russian Liturgy
(There have been many previous recordings of his Liturgical
music.)

ARDÉVOL, José (b. 1911)

Sonatina, vlc. & pf. 1950
A. Odnoposoff & Berta Huberman **♯ Pnt. 4001**
(*Vega, Roldán, Menendez*)

Sonatina, pf. 1934
▽ H. Brant (NMQR. 1213)

ARENSKY, Antony Stepanovitch
                                    (1861-1906)

Concerto, A minor, Op. 54 vln. & orch.
S. Furer & Moscow Radio—Smirnov
(*below*)   **♯ Mon.MWL 322**

... Tempo di Valse — arr. vln. & pf. Heifetz
☆ J. Heifetz (in ♯ G.ALP 1206: FALP 248; ♭ *Vic. ERA 57*)

(A) DREAM ON THE VOLGA, Op. 16 Opera 1892
Overture
Moscow Radio—Gauk (2ss)   **USSR. 022080/1**

Fantasia on Russian epic themes (Ryabin), Op. 48
▽ M. Grünberg (pf.) & Radio Orch.—Samosud
                        (USSR. 015930/5, 6ss)

(The) Fountain of Bakhchisarai, Op. 46 (Pushkin)
Cantata Solo, Cho., Orch.
... Sarema's Aria (unspec.)
V. Borisenko (S)   **♯ USSR.D 1592**
(*Ponchielli, Meyerbeer, Bizet*)

PIANO MUSIC
Nocturne, D flat major, Op. 36, No. 3
Étude, F sharp minor, Op. 36, No. 13
A. Goldenweiser   **USSRM.D 00626**
(*Grieg*)

Chant triste, Op. 56, No. 3 — arr. vlc. & pf.
S. Knushevitzky & pf.   **USSRM.D 001269**
(*Davidoff*)

SONGS
(The) Brilliant Star, Op. 60, No. 8
V. Borisenko (M-S)   **USSR. 22265**
(*Rimsky: Naughty Girl*)

(The) Day has ended, Op. 49, No. 1
A. Pirogov (B)   **USSR. 20420**
(*Balakirev*)   (& USSRM.D 00978)

Do not ask, Op. 6, No. 2 (A. Tolstoy)
V. Borisenko (M-S)   **USSRM.D 00740**
(*Rimsky, Rubinstein*)

---

[1] Originally written to accompany abstract film by Léger.   [2] Recording supervised by composer.
[3] Arr. P. L. Dietsch (1808-65) from madrigal *Nous voyons que les hommes:* See † Chansons & Motets.

8

SONGS (continued)

Dozing, Op. 60, No. 3 (Minstein)
☆ I. Kozlovsky (T) (*USSRM.D 00697*)

I do not tell you, Op. 6, No. 4 (Sologub)
A. Pirogov (in *USSRM.D 00956*)

In silence & in darkness, Op. 38, No. 1 (Fet)
Weep not, my friend, Op. 38, No. 4
☆ And. Ivanov (B) (*USSRM.D 00737*)

(The) Minstrel, Op. 17, No. 1 (Maikov)
Dear Pages, Op. 60, No. 6 (Fet)
☆ A. Pirogov (B) (*USSRM.D 00977/8*)

Lily of the Valley, Op. 38, No. 2 (P. Tchaikovsky)
N. Kazantseva (S)   *USSR. 20148*
(*Brahms: Mädchenlied*)

SUITES, 2 pianos.
No. 1, G minor, Op. 15
No. 2, C minor, Op. 23 "Silhouettes"
R. Holder & A. Hayward   ♯ **CA.LPA 1031**

No. 1 … 2, Valse, only
E. Bartlett & R. Robertson   in ♯ **MGM.E 3150**
(♭ set X 273)
☆ V. Vronsky & V. Babin
(in ♯ Phi.N 02100L; AmC.ML 4517)

No. 2 — ARR. ORCH
Berlin Radio—Lederer   ♯ **Ura. 7117**
(*Amirov & Liadov*)

Symphony No. 2, A major, Op. 22
Moscow Radio—Kovalev   ♯ **Mon.MWL 322**
(*above*)

Valse de concert (? ARR.) tpt. & pf.
T. Dokshitser & A. Kaplan (*USSR. 21666/7*)

Variations on a theme of Tchaikovsky, Op. 35a
☆ Hirsch Qtt.   ♯ **Argo.RG 3**
(*Debussy, Rawsthorne*)

ARIOSTI, Attilio (1666- ?1740)

Lesson No. 5, E minor 1724
E. Seiler (vla. d'amore), W. Gerwig (lute),
K. E. Glückselig (hpsi.), J. Koch (gamba)
♯ **HP.APM 14024**
(*A. Scarlatti & Corelli*)   (♯ AmD.ARC 3008)
[& 2ss, ♭ *Pol. 37044*]

ARMSTRONG, Thomas Henry Wait (b. 1898)
SEE: † ENGLISH CHURCH MUSIC, VOL. III

ARNE, Michael (1740-1786)

(The) Lass with the delicate air (ARR. Lehmann)
J. McCormack (T), G. Moore (pf.)
(*E. P. Cockram, etc.*)   ♭ **G.7ER 5054**
▽ M. Kurenko (S) (*AmC. 2042M*)

ARNE, Thomas Augustine (1710-1778)

ALFRED Masque 1740 (J. Thomson)
… Rule, Britannia T, Cho., Orch.
P. Pears & Aldeburgh Fest. Cho. & Orch.
—I. Holst   in ♯ **D.LXT 2798**
(*below, Purcell, etc.*)   (♯ Lon.LL 808)
Royal Cho. Soc. & Philharmonia—Sargent[1]
(A. Grier, org.)   **G.C 4213**
(*Parry: Jerusalem*)
— ARR. ORCH.
New Sym.—Harvey (in *D.F 10571*: in ♯ *LF 1218*)
— ARR. BAND
Grenadier Guards—Harris (*D.F 10084*)
also in (♯ *G.DLP 1050*), etc.

AS YOU LIKE IT (Shakespeare) 1740
Blow, blow, thou winter wind
Under the greenwood tree
J. Heddle Nash (B), E. Lush (pf.)   **G.C 4256**
(*below*)

Then is there mirth in heaven (Hymen's Song)
L. Chelsi (B), lute & pf. in ♯ **MTR.MLO 1015**
(† Shakespeare Songs, Vol. III)

COMUS Masque 1738 (Milton, adapted Dalton)
COMPLETE RECORDING (omitting Dialogue: ed.
Herbage)
M. Ritchie & E. Morison (S), W. Herbert (T),
St. Anthony Singers & O.L. Ens.—A. Lewis
♯ **LOL.OL 50070/1**
[R. Gerlin, hpsi.]   (♯ OL.LD 104/5)

Air (unspec.: perhaps *Preach me not …*)
S. Rayner (T), S. Leff (pf.)   in ♯ **Mur.P 107**
(*followed by pf. acc. only*)

(The) FAIRY PRINCE Masque 1771
Now all the air shall ring Duet, 2S
A. Mandikian & G. Whitred, Aldeburgh Fest.
Cho. & Orch.—Holst   ♯ **D.LXT 2798**
(*above, Purcell, etc.*)   (♯ Lon.LL 808)

(The) JUDGMENT OF PARIS (Congreve) 1740
O ravishing delight
M. Ritchie (S), G. Malcolm (hpsi.)
in ♯ **Nix.NLP 921**
(*Mozart, Schubert, Purcell, etc.*)
J. Vyvyan (S), E. Lush (pf.)   in ♯ **D.LXT 2797**
(† Songs of England)   (♯ Lon.LL 806)
(*also on* ♯ *D.LW 5102*)

LOVE'S LABOUR'S LOST (Shakespeare) 1740
When icicles hang by the wall
J. Heddle Nash (B), E. Lush (pf.)   **G.C 4256**
(*above & below*)

Overture, B flat major[2] orch.
Linz Sym.   ♯ **Ply. 12-36**
(*Haydn, Schubert, Gluck*)

SONATAS (or Lessons) hpsi. or org. *c.* 1743
No. 1, F major … Allegro only
T. Dart (hpsi.)   in ♯ **LOL.OL 50075**
(† Masters of Early English Keyboard Music)

No. 7, A major … Finale (Allegro) only ("*Flute
Solo*")
E. White (org.)[3]   ♯ **Moll.E4QP 3443**
(*Bach, Martini, Karg-Elert, etc.*)
E. Hilliar (org.)[4]   in ♯ **ASK. 4**
(*Loeillet, Bach, Dupré, Couperin*)

(The) TEMPEST (Shakespeare) 1746
Where the bee sucks
J. Vyvyan (S), E. Lush (pf.)   in ♯ **D.LXT 2797**
(† Songs of England)   (♯ Lon.LL 806)
(*also on* ♯ *D.LW 5102*)
J. Heddle Nash (B), E. Lush (pf.)   **G.C 4256**
(*above*)

While you here do snoring lie[5]
L. Chelsi (B), lute & pf. in ♯ **MTR.MLO 1015**
(† Shakespeare Songs, Vol. III)

MISCELLANEOUS
Arniana Orch. Suite — ARR. Korn
1. (a) Britannia (Opera, 1755), Ov: Intro. only
(b) Judith (Oratorio, 1761), Choruses:
Who can Jehovah's wrath abide?
To Him the first & last be giv'n
(c) Coda, based on (b)
2. (a) The Tempest: Where the bee sucks Air
(b) Comus: Nor on beds of fading flowers Air
(c) reprise of (a)
(*continued on next page*)

---

[1] ARR. Sargent.
[2] No. 6 of 8 Overtures, pub. *c.* 1751: ed. Herbage.
[3] Organ of St. Mary the Virgin, N.Y.
[4] Organ of St. Mark's Chu., Mt. Kisco, N.Y.
[5] Attrib. Arne; from *Caulfield's Collection*, not in the incidental music.

MISCELLANEOUS: Arniana (continued)
3. Alfred: Dirge
4. (a) Whittington's Feast (Opera, 1776): The Aldermen stun
   their own ears with applause   Cho.
   (b) Alfred: Rule, Britannia
   (c) The Fairy Prince (Masque, 1771): Final Chorus
   (d) Coda, based on (b), (a), & 2 (a).
   Hamburg Philharmonia—Korn   # Allo. 3153
   (Liszt)

ARNOLD, Malcolm (b. 1921)

Beckus the Dandipratt, Op. 5   Comedy Overture
                                          1943
   Royal Phil.—Arnold   # EPhi.NBL 5021
   (Symphony No. 2, etc.)   (# Phi.N 10712L)
   ▽ L.P.O.—v. Beinum (D.K 1844)

English Dances, Sets I & II   (Nos. 1-8) 1950/1
   L.P.O.—Boult   # D.LW 5166
   [Nos. 1-4 on ♭ D. 71096]   (# Lon.LD 9178)
   Philharmonia—Irving   # BB.LBC 1078
   (Chopin: Les Sylphides)

... Set I, No. 3, & Set II, No. 5
   Philharmonia—Arnold (below)   ♭ C.SED 5529

Homage to the Queen   Ballet 1953
   Philharmonia—Irving   # G.CLP 1011

Symphony No. 2, Op. 40   1953
   Royal Phil.—Arnold
Tam o' Shanter, Overture, Op. 52   1955
   Royal Phil.—Hollingsworth   # EPhi.NBL 5021
   (above)   (# Phi.N 10712L)

Tam o' Shanter, Overture, Op. 52
   Philharmonia—Arnold   ♭ C.SED 5529
   (above)

ARRIAGA Y BALZOLA, Juan Crisostomo
Jacobo Antonio (1806-1826)

Symphony, D major
(Los) ESCLAVOS FELICES   Opera   1820
... Overture only
CANTATA: Agar   S & orch.
   M. Ripolles (S), & Madrid Nat. Orch.
   —Arámbarri   # B.AXTL 1075
              (# AmD.DL 9756; SpC.CCL 35010)

Quartet, Strings, No. 3, E flat major
   ☆ Guilet Qtt. (# MMS. 3005)

ARRIETA Y CORERA, Emilio
(1823-1894)

MARINA   Zarzuela, 2 Acts, 1855
COMPLETE RECORDING of the Zarzuela
   M. Caballer (S), F. B. Ferrando (T),
   L. S. Vela (B), J. L. Lobo (B), J. Deus (Bs),
   Madrid Cho. & Cha. Orch.   # Mont.FM 23/4
   (4ss) [Highlights on # FM 30]

COMPLETE RECORDING of the later Opera (1871)
   M. Capsir, J. Mardones, H. Lazaro,
   M. Redondo, etc.   # SpC.CCLP 31000/1
   (▽ o.n. C.GQX 10000/11; AmC. 67769/80D;
                                  ArgC. 264780/91)

Prelude, Act III
   Span. Sym.—Martinez   in # Mont.FM 16

Orch. Selection   Sym.—Argenta (# Ambra.MCP 10007)

Vocal Excerpts
   M. Linares (S) (in # Mont.FM 17)
   R. Lagares (T) & Cho. (ArgV. 68-1181)
   ▽ M. Fleta (T) (G.DB 1026: ♭ 7ERL 1044)
   and many others.
Bolero   S
   ℍ Mme. Moga-Georgescu (in # HRS. 3002*)

ASOLA, Giovanni Matteo (c. 1560-1609)
   SEE: † MOTETS OF THE VENETIAN SCHOOL

ATTAIGNANT, Pierre (d. c. 1522)
   SEE: † ANTHOLOGIE SONORE
        † FRENCH CHANSONS
        † LUTE MUSIC OF XVITH & XVIITH CENTURIES
        † RENAISSANCE MUSIC FOR THE LUTE
        † XVITH & XVIITH CENTURY FRENCH SONGS
        † XVITH & XVIITH CENTURY SONGS

ATTEY, John (d. 1640)
   SEE: † DOWLAND AND HIS CONTEMPORARIES
        † SEVEN CENTURIES OF SACRED MUSIC

AUBER, Daniel François Esprit
(1782-1871)

OPERAS & OPÉRAS-COMIQUES
(Le) CHEVAL DE BRONZE   3 Acts   1835
   (The Bronze Horse)
Overture
   Paris Cons.—Wolff   # D.LXT 5005
   (below)   (# Lon.LL 1157)
   (Diamants de la Couronne on # D.LW 5167; Lon.LD 9172)
   Lamoureux—Fournet   ♭ Phi.N 402023E
   (below)   (in # Epic. LC 3174)
   Moscow Radio—Samosud (USSR. 021577/8)

(Les) DIAMANTS DE LA COURONNE
   (The Crown Diamonds)   3 Acts   1841
Overture
   Paris Cons.—Wolff   # D.LXT 5005
   (above & below)   (# Lon.LL 1157)
   (Cheval de Bronze on # D.LW 5167; Lon.LD 9172)

(Le) DOMINO NOIR   3 Acts   1837
Overture
   Lamoureux—Fournet   ♭ Phi.N 402022E
   (below)   (in # Epic. LC 3174)
   French Nat. Radio—Tzipine   # C.FC 1040
   (Boïeldieu & Cimarosa)
   Moscow Radio—Samosud   # USSR.D 1105
   (Rossini)
   ☆ Munich Phil.—Lehmann (in # Pol. 17033)

Nous allons avoir, grâce à Dieu   Bs
   ℍ R. Mayr (in # Sca. 822*)

FRA DIAVOLO   3 Acts   1830
Overture
   Paris Cons.—Wolff   # D.LXT 5005
   (above & below)   (# Lon.LL 1157)
   (Muette de Portici, overture, on # D.LW 5154; Lon.LD 9173)
   Lamoureux—Fournet   ♭ Phi.N 402022E
   (above)   (in # Epic. LC 3174)
   Berlin Sym.—Rubahn (in # Roy. 1537)
   Moscow Radio—Stalyarov (USSR. 022696/7)
   R.I.A.S.—Becker (in # Rem. 199-181)
   ☆ Munich Phil.—Lehmann
                (♭ AmD.ED 3518; in # Pol. 17033)

Io son, signore, infelice[1]   Act I   B
   ℍ V. Bellatti (Ital) (SBDH.G 3*)

Voyez sur cette roche   Act I   S
   G. Arnaldi (Ital)   Cet.AT 0343
   (Figaro—Voi che sapete)

Quel bonheur   Act II   S
   (Or son sola)
   S. Chissari (Ital)   (2ss)   Cet.AT 0360
   ℍ M. Barrientos (Ital) (in # Sca. 806*)

Oui, c'est demain   Act II   S
   ℍ R. Storchio (Ital) (in # HRS. 3001* & SBDH.G 1*)

Je vois marcher   Act III   T
   W. Ludwig (Ger)   PV. 36059
   (Boïeldieu: Dame Blanche, aria)
   (Faust on ♭ Pol. 30007)

---

[1] Appendix No. 2, not in Fr. score; one of additional nos. for performance, London, 1857.

(Le) LAC DES FÉES　5 Acts　1839
Overture
　Berlin Sym.—Rubahn　　　　　　in ♯ Roy. 1537

(Le) MAÇON　3 Acts　1825
Overture
　Berlin Sym.—Rubahn　　　　　　in ♯ Roy. 1537

(La) MUETTE DE PORTICI (MASANIELLO)
　　5 Acts　1823
Overture
　Paris Cons.—Wolff　　　　　♯ D.LXT 5005
　(above)　　　　　　　　　　　(♯ Lon.LL 1157)
　(Fra Diavolo, Ov. on ♯ D.LW 5154; Lon.LD 9173)
　Lamoureux—Fournet　　　　b Phi.N 402023E
　(above)　　　　　　　　　　(in ♯ Epic. LC 3174)
　Berlin Sym.—Rubahn　　　　　in ♯ Roy. 1537
　　☆ Bournemouth Municipal—Schwarz
　　　　　　　　　　　　(b G.7EP 7015; 7EPQ 534)
　　Bamberg Sym.—Lehmann (FPV. 5058; b Pol. 30146)

Du pauvre seul ami fidèle　Act IV　T
　N. Gedda　　　　　　　　in ♯ C.CX 1130
　(Bizet, Cilea, Donizetti, etc.)　(♯ FCX 302; Angel. 35096)

AUBERT, Louis (b. 1877)

Feuille d'images　orch.　1930
1. Confidence　　　4. Pays lointains
2. Chanson de route　5. Danse de l'ours en peluche
3. Sérénade
　Paris Cha. Assoc.—Oubradous　♯ Pat.DT 1019
　(Honegger)

Habanéra　orch.　1919
　Paris Opéra—Fourestier　　　♯ Angel. 35120
　(Charpentier)

SONGS
(Les) Souliers de l'avocat
　☆ C. Panzéra (B), M. Panzéra (pf.) (in ♯ Clc. 6260)

(Les) Yeux　(Sully Prud'homme)
　G. Moizan (S), M. Barthomieu (pf.)
　(Messager)　　　　　　　　b D.EFM 455550

AUDRAN, Edmond (1840-1901)

(La) MASCOTTE　Operetta　1880
ABRIDGED RECORDING
　N. Renaud, D. Renard, L. Berton, M. Dens,
　Cho. & orch.—Gressier　　　♯ Pat.DTX 143
(Les) Envoyés du Paradis　　B
　M. Dens (b Pat.ED 4)
　J. Lebreque (in ♯ D.LM 4527; ♯ Lon.LS 268)
Ballade　　　　　B
　M. Dens (b Pat.ED 3)
(Le) Secret de Polichinelle　　T
　C. Devos (b Pat.ED 35)
　There have been a number of ▽ recordings of extracts
from this and other operettas.

AULETTA, Domenico (fl. XVIIIth Cent.)

Concerto, G major, hpsi. & str. orch.
　R. Gerlin & O.L. Ens.—Froment
　　　　　　　　　　　　♯ LOL.OL 50009
　(Paisiello, Durante, Mancini)　　(♯ OL.LD 66)

AURIC, Georges (b. 1899)

(La) Fête à Henriette　Film music
... Sur le pavé de Paris
　A. Flore (Pat.PG 684)

(La) Fontaine de Jouvance　Ballet Suite
　☆ Paris Phil.—Leibowitz (♯ Clc. 6137)

Impromptu　ob. & pf.　1954
　P. Pierlot & A. d'Arco　　　　b Pat.G 1051
　(Jolivet, Murgier, Barraud, Planel)

Impromptu No. 2, F major　pf.
　J-M. Damase　　　　　　　♯ D.FST 153527
　(Messiaen, Damase, Françaix, etc.)

Malbrouck s'en va-t-en guerre　Ballet Suite　1924
　☆ Paris Phil.—Leibowitz (♯ Clc. 6137)

Moulin Rouge　Film music
　There are many recordings of excerpts from this, in all
　current catalogues.

Phèdre　Ballet　1950
... Sym. Suite
　Paris Cons.—Tzipine　　　　♯ C.CX 1253
　(Milhaud)　　　(♯ FCX 265; Angel. 35118, in set 3515)

SONGS
(Une) Allée de Luxembourg　(Nerval)　1926
Fantaisie　(Nerval)　1926
(Le) Gloxinia　(Chalupt)　1918
　I. Joachim (S), M. Franck (pf.)　♯CdM.LDA 8079
　(Durey, Honegger, Milhaud, Poulenc, Tailleferre)

Trio　ob., cl. & bsn.　1938
　New Art Wind Trio　　　　in ♯ CEd. set 2006
　(Durey, Poulenc, etc.)

(Une) Valse　2 pfs.
　☆ A. Gold & R. Fizdale (in ♯ Phi.S 06614R)

AVONDANO, Pedro Antonio (d. 1782)
　SEE: † CLAVECINISTES ESPAGNOLS ...

AXMAN, Emil (1887-1949)

(8) Moravian Dances　orch.
　Brno Radio—Plichta (Nos. 1, 2, 7, 8), Hudec
　(Nos. 3 & 6), Deváký (No. 4), Slabý (No. 5)
　　　　　　　　　　　　　♯ Sup.LPM 127
　　　　　　　　　　　　　　(♯ U. 5076C)

BABADZHANYAN, Arno Arutyunovich
　　　　　　　　　　　　　　　(b. 1921)

Heroic Ballad　pf. & orch.
　☆ A. Babadzhanyan & U.S.S.R. State Radio
　(Gomoliaka)　　　　—Rakhlin　♯ CdM.LDA 8072
　(Nikolayeva, on ♯ USSR.D 0263)
　(Tchaikovsky, on ♯ CEd.CE 3007)

Trio, F sharp minor　pf., vln., vlc.　1952
　A. Babadzhanyan, D. Oistrakh, S. Knushevitzky
　　　　　　　　　　　　　♯ Mon.MWL 367
　(Ravel)　　(♯ USSR.D 1372/3; V♯ CdM.LDZA 8103, 2ss)

BACH, Carl Philipp Emanuel (1714-1788)

COLLECTION
　Sonata, D major　fl. & cont.　(W.131)　1747
　Trio, B minor　fl., vln. & cont.　(W.143)　1731
　Duo, E minor　fl. & vln.　(W.140)　1770
　Solfeggio, C minor　hpsi.　(W.117-2)　1770
　Quartet, G major　fl., vla., vlc., hpsi.　(W.95)　1788
　Collegium Pro Arte　　　　♯ LOL.OL 50017
　[K. Redel, fl.; U. Grehling, vln.; I. Lechner hpsi.;
　　G. Schmid, vla.; M. Bochmann, vlc.] (♯ OL.LD 53)

Chromatic Fantasia　(W.117-13)　1770
　☆ D. Pinkham (hpsi.) (in ♯ Lyr.LL 57)

☆ = Re-issue of a recording to be found in previous volumes.

CONCERTOS, Flute & orch.
A minor (W.166) 1750
G major (W.169)[1] 1755
J-P. Rampal & Orch.—Froment   ♯ **OL.LD 85**

CONCERTOS, Piano (or org.) & orch.
A minor (W.1) 1733
☆ F. Holetschek & Vienna Sym.—Swoboda
(*Symphonies*)   ♯ Nix.WLP 5040
(*idem; & J. C. Bach, on* ♯ West.WN 18025)
A minor (W.21) 1747
H. Boschi & Sinfonia—Witold   ♯ **EPP.SLP 5**
(*below*)
D major (W.43-2) 1772
H. Schnabel & Vienna Philharmonia—Adler
(*Trio*)   ♯ **SPA. 37**
E flat major (W.35) 1759
M-C. Alain (org.) & Leclair Ens.—Paillard
(*Soler: Quintet*)   ♯ **DDP.DP 501**
E flat major, 2 pfs. (or hpsi. & pf.) (W.47) 1788
G. Malcolm (hpsi), L. Salter (fortepiano) &
London Baroque Ens.—Haas ♯ **P.PMA 1009**
(*J. S. Bach*)
F major, 2 pfs. or hpsis. (W.46) 1740
H. Boschi & J. Castérède (pfs.) & Sinfonia
—Witold   ♯ **EPP.SLP 5**
(*above*)

CONCERTO, Vlc. & orch.
A minor (W.170) 1751
A. Tusa & Winterthur Sym.—Dahinden
(*Stamitz*)   ♯ **CHS.H 11**

Magnificat, D major S, A, T, B, cho. (W.215) 1749
☆ Soloists, Vienna Academy Cho. & State Op. Orch.
—Prohaska (2ss) (♯ Van.BG 552; Ama.AVRS 6007)
Rondo, G major clavier (W.59-2) 1785
R. Gerlin (pf.)   in ♯ **LOL.OL 50097**
(*below; & J. S. Bach, W. F. Bach*)
Siciliana — ARR. GUITAR
A. Segovia   in ♯ **AmD.DL 9734**
(† *Segovia Plays*)
Solfeggio, C minor W.117-2 (*Spring's awakening*)
— ARR. VLA. & PF. Primrose
☆ W. Primrose & J. Kahn (♭ *Cam.CAE 244*)
SONATA, B minor, harp (W.139) 1762
(*Solo für Harfe*)
N. Zabaleta (hp.)   in ♯ **Eso.ES 524**
(† *18th Century Harp Music*)

SONATAS, Clavier
C minor (W.65-31) 1757
D. Handman (pf.)   ♯ **LOL.OL 50078**
(† *Sonatas of the XVIIth & XVIIIth centuries*)
E minor (W.59-1) 1785
R. Gerlin (pf.)   in ♯ **LOL.OL 50097**
(*Rondo, above*)

SONATAS, Wind instruments (W.184) 1775
1. D major   4. E flat major
2. F major   5. A major
3. G major   6. C major
London Baroque Ens.—Haas ♯ **P.PMB 1004**
(*Telemann*)

SONGS
COLLECTIONS ed. Dørumsgaard
Die Gute Gottes (Gellert) (W.194-34)
Busslied (Gellert) (W.194-46)
Passionslied (W.202-17)
Preis sei dem Gotte (Cramer) (W.196-41)
K. Flagstad (S), G. Moore (pf.)
                        ♯ **Vic.LHMV 1070**
(† *German Songs*)

Jesus in Gethsemane (Sturm) (W.198-29) 1781
Weihnachtslied (*Vom Grab . . .*) (Sturm) (W.197-11) 1785
Über die Finsternis kurz vor dem Tode Jesu (Sturm) (W.197-29) 1780
G. Souzay (B), J. Bonneau (pf.) ♯ **D.LXT 2835**
(† *Canzone Scordate*)   (♯ Lon.LL 731; D.FAT 173072)

Suite, D major ("Concerto"—ed. Casadesus)[2]
Ancient Insts. Ens.—M. Casadesus ♯ **Plé.P 3073**
(*Maschera, Tomasini, G. Gabrieli*)
— ARR. ORCH. Steinberg
M. G. M. Cha.—I. Solomon   ♯ **MGM.E 3109**
(*Haydn*)
☆ Boston Sym.—Koussevitzky (♯ Cam.CAL 174)

SYMPHONIES
No. 2, C major (W.174)
☆ Cha. Orch.—M. v. d. Berg. (♯ MMS. 3003)

No. 11, C major (W.182-3: "No. 3") 1773
Augsburg Cha.—Deyle   †♯ **AS.3005 LD**
(*Telemann, J. S. Bach*)   (♯ HS.AS 35)
☆ Vienna Sym.—Günther   ♯ Nix.BLP 304
(*below; & J. C. Bach*)   (♯ CID.UMT 263022)
(*below; & Mozart, on* ♯ MTW. 556)
☆ Vienna Sym.—Swoboda   ♯ Nix.WLP 5040
(*below*)   (♯ West.WN 18025)

No. 15, D major (W.183-1) 1780
No. 16, E flat major (W.183-2) 1780
No. 17, F major (W.183-3) 1780
Hamburg Cha.—G. L. Jochum ♯ **Pat.DTX 155**

No. 15, D major (W.183-1: "No. 1") 1780
☆Vienna Sym.—Günther
(♯ Nix.BLP 304; CID.UMT 263022; MTW. 556, d.c.).
Vienna Sym.—Swoboda
(♯ Nix.WLP 5040; ♯ West.WN 18025)

No. 16, E flat major (W.183-2) 1780
Paris Sinfonia—Witold   ♯ **EPP.SLP 4**
(*W. F. Bach*)

TRIOS, Fl., vln., cont.
B minor (W.143) 1731
Alma Musica Ens.   ♯ **Sel.LPG 8481**
(*W. F., J. C. F., & J. C. Bach*)   (♯ T.LE 6527)

B flat major (W.161-2) 1751
C. Wanausek, W. Schneiderhan & H. Schnabel
(*Concerto*)   ♯ **SPA. 37**
☆ L. Schaefer, R. Brink, D. Pinkham (hpsi.) (♯ Lyr.LL 57)

(12) Variations on 'Folies d'Espagne' D minor
(W.118-9) clav.
J. Newmark (fortepiano)   ♯ **Hall.RS 4**
(*Clementi, Haydn*)

BACH, Johann Christian (1735-1782)

CHAMBER MUSIC COLLECTION
Quintet, F major ob., vln., vla., vlc., hpsi. (Terry, p. 311
No. 3) c. 1785
QUINTETS, Op. 11 fl., ob., vln., vla., vlc., cont.
...No. 4, E flat major; No. 6, D major
SONATAS, Op. 16 fl. & hpsi. c. 1789
...No. 1, D major; No. 2, G major
Collegium Pro Arte   ♯ **LOL.OL 50046**
[K. Redel, fl.; H. Winschermann, ob.; U. Grehling, vln.;
G. Schmid, vla.; M. Bochmann, vlc.; I. Lechner, hpsi.]
(♯ OL.LD 55)

CONCERTOS, Clavier & orch.
E flat major, Op. 7, No. 5 c. 1780
G. Leonhardt (hpsi.) & Vienna Sym.—Sacher
                        ♯ **EPhi.ABR 4029**
(*Sinfonia concertante*)   (♯ Phi.A 00675R)
(*Sinf. concertante & Symphonies*,
on ♯ AmC.ML 4869; Phi.S 04003L)

G major, Op. 7, No. 6
☆ M. Roesgen-Champion (hpsi.) & Str. Trio
(*JpV.NB 1226/7*)

---

[1] Originally pf. concerto, W.34.   [2] Origin unknown.

F minor Terry, p. 298, No. 2 (MS)
A major Terry, p. 297
(pub. Riga, 1771; perhaps not by J. C. Bach)
R. Veyron-Lacroix (pf.) & Saar Cha.
—Ristenpart **♯ DFr. 156**
[Concerto, F minor, also on ♯ *DFr.EX 25054*]

CONCERTO, C minor, vlc. & orch. (ed., or ? by, Casadesus)
J. Schuster & Los Angeles—Waxman
♯ DCap.CTL 7041
(Bruch; Schumann) *(♯ Cap.P 8232)*

Quintet, E flat major, Op. 11, No. 4 fl., ob., vln., vla. & cont. *c.* 1772-1777
Alma Musica Ens. **♯ Sel.LPG 8481**
(W. F., C. P. E. & J. C. F. Bach) *(♯ T.LE 6527)*
Collegium Pro Arte: see Collection, *above*

Quintet, D major, Op. 22, No. 1 hpsi., fl., ob., vln., bsn.[1]
R. Veyron-Lacroix, J-P. Rampal, P. Pierlot, M. Gendre, P. Hongne **♯ BàM.LD 011**
(Scarlatti, Telemann, Handel, Quantz) *(♯ HS.HSL 117)*

Sinfonia Concertante, A major[2] vln., vlc. & orch.
c. 1770
W. Schneiderhan, N. Hübner & Vienna Sym.—Sacher **♯ EPhi. ABR 4029**
(Concerto, E flat, Op. 7, No. 5) *(♯ Phi.A 00675R)*
(Symphonies, Op. 18, Nos. 1 & 4, & Concerto, on ♯ Phi.S 04003L; AmC.ML 4869)
G. Alès, P. Coddée & Orch.—Froment
♯ LOL.OL 50074
(below; & J. S. Bach: vln. & ob. Concerto) *(♯ OL.LD 96)*

Sinfonia Concertante, E flat major orig. 2 vlns., 2 fl., 2 hrns. & orch. (Terry, p. 284)
☆ Vienna Sym.—Günther
(♯ Nix.BLP 304; CID.UMT 263022)
... **Andante** only
M. Wilk (vln.), M. Miller (ob.) & Little Sym.—Saidenberg **♯ AmC.ML 4916**
(J. S. Bach & Mozart)

Sonata, G major, Op. 15, No. 5 pf. duet *c.* 1779
☆ P. Badura-Skoda & J. Demus **♯ Nix.WLP 5069**
(Mozart) *(C. P. E. Bach, on ♯ West.WN 18025)*

SYMPHONIES

Op. 6, No. 6, G minor ... **Andante** only *c.* 1770
Augsburg Cha. Orch.—Deyle †♯ **AS. 3007 LD**
(♯ HS.AS 39)

Op. 9, No. 2, E flat major
Lamoureux Cha.—Colombo **♯ LOL.OL 50007**
(below, & Haydn: Concerto) *(♯ OL.LD 59)*
Saar Cha.—Ristenpart **V♯ DFr.EX 17039**

Op. 18, No. 1, E flat major
Vienna Sym.—Sacher **♯ EPhi.ABR 4005**
(below) *(♯ Phi.A 00642R)*
(below, & Sinfonia concertante, on ♯ AmC.ML 4869; Phi.S 04003L)

Op. 18, No. 2, B flat major
Bologna Orch.—Jenkins **♯ Cpt.MC 20019**
(Rameau, Vivaldi)
Danish Radio Cha.—Wöldike **♯ D.LXT 5135**
(Haydn, Mozart, Dittersdorf) *(♯ Lon.LL 1308)*

Op. 18, Nos. 2 & 3, B flat major & D major
☆ Cha. Orch.—M. v. d. Berg (♯ MMS. 3003)

Op. 18, No. 4, D major
Vienna Sym.—Sacher **♯ EPhi.ABR 4005**
(above) *(♯ Phi.A 00642R)*
(& on ♯ AmC.ML 4869; Phi.S 04003L)
Lamoureux Cha.—Colombo **♯ LOL.OL 50007**
(above, & Haydn: Concerto) *(♯ OL.LD 59)*

"Sinfonia No. 4", D major[3]
O.L. Orch.—Froment **♯ LOL.OL 50074**
(above) *(♯ OL.LD 96)*

BACH, Johann Christoph (1642-1703)

MOTET: Ich lasse dich nicht[4]
Stuttgart Vocal & Inst. Ens.—Couraud
in **♯ DFr. 149/50**
(J. S. Bach: Motets)
Cho. & Orch.—Goldsbrough **† G.HMS 54**
(J. S. Bach: Mass, F major, excpt.) (in ♯ Vic.setLM 6030)

VARIATIONS on: Hpsi.
Aria of Daniel Eberlin, E flat major (15)
(Aria Eberliniana pro dormiente Camillo, variata)
Ed. Freyse (NBG.XXXIX Vol. 2)
Sarabande, G major (12) ed. Riemann
F. Viderø **♯ HS.HSL 3069**
(Buxtehude)

BACH, Johann Christoph Friedrich
(1732-1795)

Septet, E flat major fl., ob., vln., vla., 2 hrns. & cont. 1794
Trio, C major fl., ob., hpsi. & cont.
Collegium Pro Arte **♯ OL.LD 54**
(W. F. Bach)
[K. Redel, fl.; H. Winschermann, ob.; U. Grehling, vln.; G. Schmid, vla.; I. Lechner, hpsi.; M. Bochmann, vlc.]

Septet, E flat major 1794 (as above)
—ARR. FL., OB., VLN., VLA., VLC., HPSI. Schünemann
Alma Musica Ens. **♯ Sel.LPG 8481**
(W. F., C. P. E. & J. C. Bach) *(♯ T.LE 6527)*

BACH, Johann Sebastian (1685-1750)

CLASSIFIED: I. Instrumental: A. Clavier; B. Organ;
C. Chamber; D. Orchestral;
E. Miscellaneous
II. Choral
III. Chorales & Songs

I. INSTRUMENTAL

A. CLAVIER

"COMPLETE CLAVIER WORKS"
I. Ahlgrimm (hpsi.) **♯ Phi.—in prep.**
For items already issued see:
Suites   Chamber Music
Preludes   Partitas
W.T.C.   Air & 30 Variations (Goldberg)

G. Johansen (double-keyboard pf.)
♯ AD. in prep. (pte. issue)
For items already issued see:
Concerto nach ital. Gusto   Fantasias
Musikalisches Opfer: Ricercari   Partitas
Passacaglia & Fugue (org.)   Variations
Ouvertüre nach französischer Art.
Prelude, Fugue and Allegro

COLLECTIONS
Chromatic Fantasia & Fugue (BWV 903)
Fugue, A minor (BWV 947)
Toccata, E minor (BWV 914)
Fantasia & Fugue, A minor (BWV 904)
Fantasia (Prelude), C minor (BWV 921) (doubtful)
Toccata, D major (BWV 912)
C. Wood (hpsi.) **♯ Ven.CM 9103**
(♯ HS.HSL 9009)

---

[1] Ed. Veyron-Lacroix. [2] No. 3 of set in Royal Music Library, British Museum; Terry, p. 284.
[3] No. 1 of "Op. 18", pub. Schmidt, Amsterdam; Terry, p. 271. The *Allegro assai* is the overture to *La Clemenza di Scipione* (1778); the *Andante* the slow movt. from overture to *Amadis des Gaules* (1779).
[4] BWV.Anh. 159. Has been attributed to J. S. Bach but almost certainly by J. Christoph Bach.

VOL. I   ♯ Van.BG 543
Chromatic Fantasia & Fugue, D minor (BWV 903)
Concerto nach italianischen Gusto, F major (BWV 971)
Capriccio, B flat major (BWV 992) 1704
   (Sopra la lontananza del suo fratello dilettissimo)
Toccata, C minor (BWV 911)
Cantata 106 . . . Sonatina (ARR. Friskin)

VOL. II   ♯ Van.BG 544
French Suites, Nos. 3, 4, 5 & 6

VOL. III   ♯ Van.BG 545
15 Two-part Inventions (BWV 772-786)
Prelude (Fantasia) & Fugue, A minor (BWV 944)
Fantasia, C minor (BWV 906—omitting fugue)
Chorale Prelude: O Mensch, bewein . . . (ARR.)
Fantasia & Fugue, A minor (BWV 904)

J. Friskin (pf.)   ♯ Van.BG 543/5

Chromatic Fantasia & Fugue, D minor (BWV 903)
                                              c. 1720
French Suite No. 3—Sarabande (BWV 814)
English Suite No. 2—Bourrées I & II (BWV 807)
Partita No. 1—Minuets I & II & Gigue (BWV 825)
Fantasia, C minor (BWV 919)

G. Hengeveld (pf.)   ♯ Phi.N 00645R

NOTENBUCH FÜR ANNA MAGDALENA BACH
                    (BWV.Anh. nos. in brackets)
. . . Marches: D major (122), E flat major (127)
     Minuets: G major (114), G major (116)
     Musette, D major (126)
     Polonaises: G minor (119), G minor (123)
LITTLE PRELUDES (BWV. nos. in brackets)
. . . C major (933); C major (939); D minor (940);
     C minor (934); C major (943); C minor (999; orig. lute)
INVENTIONS (Two Part)
. . . F minor (780); F major (779); A minor (784);
     B flat major (785)
Suite, E minor (996, orig. lute) . . . Bourrée only
Suite, G minor (822) . . . Minuet only
French Suite No. 6, E minor (817) . . . Polonaise only
English Suite, No. 3, G minor (808) . . . Gavotte &
     Musette
Capriccio, B flat major (Sopra la lontananza del suo
     fratello dilettissimo) (992)
W.T.C. Book I: Prelude, C major (846)

L. Kraus (pf.)   ♯ Edu.EP 3001

Air & 30 Variations, G major (Goldberg)
SEE: VARIATIONS, infra

Aria variata alla maniera italiana, A minor
SEE: VARIATIONS, infra   (BWV 989)

Capriccio, B flat major (BWV 992)
(Sopra la lontananza del suo fratello dilettissimo)
☆ B. Seidlhofer (pf.) (Variations)   ♯ Sup.LPM 77

Chromatic Fantasia & Fugue, D minor (BWV 903)
                                              c. 1720
G. Malcolm (hpsi.)   ♯ D.LW 5170
(below)   (♯ Lon.LD 9187)
G. Kraus (hpsi.)   ♯ Hall.RS 5
(Variations)
G. Ramin (hpsi.)   ♯ MMS. 72
(Partita No. 4)
D. Matthews (pf.)   ♯ C.S 1004
(Italian Concerto)   (♯ WS 1004)
(3ss—W.T.C. No. 1 on ♮ C.DX 8403/4)
W. Malcuzynski (pf.)   ♯ C.CX 1144
(Brahms & Beethoven)   (♯ FCX 228)
R. Slenczynski (pf.)   ♯ ML. 7030
(Italian Concerto, Sonata, D major, Toccata)
☆ W. Landowska (hpsi.)   ♯ Vic.LCT 1137
(Italian Concerto, Toccata & Partita)
             (also JpV.ND 847/8, set JAS 271)
☆ E. Picht-Axenfeld (hpsi.)   ♯ Pol. 13009
(Fantasias & Fugues)   (&, 2ss, ♭ 37050)
☆ W. Kempff (pf.)   ♯ D.LXT 2820
(Ch. Preludes & Fl. Sonata, excpt.) (♯ Lon.LL 791)
☆ F. Valenti (hpsi.)
     (♯ Nix.LLP 8047; ♯ Lyr.LL 47; Cum.CLL 341)
R. Serkin (pf.) (in ♯ C.CX 1110)

CLAVIERÜBUNG
SEE: DUETTOS
     CONCERTO NACH ITALIENISCHEN GUSTO
     OUVERTÜRE

CONCERTOS
Concerto nach italienischen Gusto, F major
     (Italian Concerto)   (BWV 971) 1735
G. Malcolm (hpsi.)   ♯ D.LW 5170
(above)   (♯ Lon.LD 9187)
E. Picht-Axenfeld (hpsi.)   PV. 2449
(Ouvertüre nach französischer Art on ♯ HP.APM 14008)
S. Kind (hpsi.)   Eta.20-118/9
(3ss—Fantasia, C minor)   (o.n. 25-C 014/5)
D. Matthews (pf.)   ♯ C.S 1004
(Chromatic Fantasia & Fugue)   (♯ WS 1004)
R. Slenczynski (pf.)   ♯ ML. 7030
(Chromatic Fantasia; Sonata)
E. Wollmann (pf.)   ♯ West.WL 5298
(Ouvertüre . . . & Aria variata)
H. Steurer (pf.) (4ss)   Eta. 21-5/6
C. Chailley-Richez (pf.)   ♯ D.FA 143538
(4 Clavier Concerto, A minor)
G. Johansen (double-keyboard pf.) in ♯ AD. set 3
☆ W. Landowska (hpsi.) (♯ Vic.LCT 1137)
  R. Kirkpatrick (hpsi.) (♭ Mtr.MCEP 3039)
  E. Weiss-Mann (hpsi.) (♯ Allo. 3087)
  R. Serkin (pf.) (♯ C.CX 1110)

— ARR. ORCH.   Otto
Belgian Radio—André   ♯ DT.LGM 65016
(Handel: Organ Concerto, Op. 7 No. 4) (♯ T.LS 6027)

(16) Concertos after Vivaldi (et al.) (BWV 972/87)
COLLECTION
No. 3, D minor   (BWV 974) (after Marcello)
No. 5, C major   (BWV 976) (Vivaldi, Op. 3, No. 12)
No. 7, F major   (BWV 978) (Vivaldi, Op. 3, No. 3, G ma.)
No. 9, G major   (BWV 980) (Vivaldi, Op. 4, No. 1)
J. Goldschwartz (hpsi.)[1]   ♯ McInt.MC 1001

No. 1, D major (after Vivaldi's Op. 3, No. 9, q.v.)
☆ W. Landowska (hpsi.)   in ♯ G.ALP 1246
(Scarlatti, Rameau, etc.)
     (in ♯ G.FALP/QALP 218; ♭ Vic.ERA 127)
☆ R. Gerlin (hpsi.) (in †♯ HS.AS 31)

No. 3, D minor (after oboe concerto by A. Marcello)
L. Hungerford (pf.)   in ♯ LH. 101/2 (Pte.)
☆ E. Weiss-Mann (hpsi.) (♯ Allo. 3087)

. . . Adagio only
P. Spagnolo (pf.)   ♯ D.LW 5142
(D. Scarlatti, Rodrigo, etc.)   (♯ Lon.LD 9135)
(Scarlatti only, ♭ D. 71075)

No. 8, B minor (composer unknown)
— ARR. PF. & ORCH.   Tamburini
☆ M. Salerno & EIAR orch.—Parodi (♮ Orf. 54023/4)

DUETTOS (BWV 802-5) (CU) 1739
1. E minor   3. G major
2. F major   4. A minor
H. Steurer (pf.)   ♯ Eta.LPM 1020
(Inventions)
G. Johansen (double-keyboard pf.) in ♯ AD. set 3
☆ H. Walcha (hpsi.) (in ♯ HP.APM 14048: ♭ 37071)
  R. Kirkpatrick (hpsi.) (♭ Mtr.MCEP 3041)
. . . No. 2 only ☆ F. Heitmann (org.)
          (in ♯ T.LSK 7033; FT. 320.TC.073)
. . . No. 4 only ☆ R. Tureck (pf.) (in ♯ Roy. 1901)

FANTASIAS
A minor   (BWV 922)
☆ R. Gianoli (pf.)   in ♯ Nix.WLP 5101

C minor   (BWV 906)
E. Picht-Axenfeld (hpsi.)[2]   ♯ Pol. 13009
(Fantasia & Fugue, & Chromatic Fantasia)
(Fantasia & Fugue, only, on ♭ Pol. 37024)

---

[1] The labels are reversed on the original pressing.
[2] Including the "unfinished" fugue, played here according to the theory of J. Schreyer (the first section repeated).
The fugue is omitted on ♭ Pol. 37024.

FANTASIA, C minor, BWV 906 (*continued*)
S. Kind (hpsi.)   *Eta. 20-119*
(*Ital. Concerto*, s. 3)   (o.n. 25-C 015)
G. Johansen (double-keyboard pf.)[1]
                                                 in # **AD. set 3**

C minor   (BWV 919)
☆ W. Landowska (hpsi.)
                            (in # G.ALP 1246: FALP & QALP 218)

C minor   (BWV.Anh. 86)   doubtful
R. Gerlin (hpsi.)   in # **LOL.OL 50097**
(*Variations, below; C. P. E. & W. F. Bach*)

FANTASIAS & FUGUES
A minor   (BWV 904)
E Picht-Axenfeld (hpsi.)   # *Pol. 13009*
(*Fantasia, & Chromatic Fantasia & Fugue*)
(*Fantasia, C minor, only on* ♭ *Pol. 37024*)
G. Johansen (double-keyboard pf.) in # **AD. set 3**

... Fantasia only
☆ W. Supper (org.) († # Cpt.MC 20029)

D minor: SEE CHROMATIC FANTASIA, *ante.*

Fugue, A minor   (BWV 947)
— ARR. STR. ORCH.   Münchinger
☆ Stuttgart Cha.—Münchinger   ♭ *D.71090*
(*Fantasia & Fugue, G mi.—Fugue*)   (♭ *DK 23357*)

Fugue, B minor   (BWV 951)[2]
C. de Lisle (org.)   ♭ *Cpt.EXTP 1005*
(*Albinoni*)

INVENTIONS
(15) Two-part   (BWV 772-786)
(15) Three-part   (BWV 787-801)
☆ E. Harich-Schneider (clavi.) (4ss)   # *Pol. 13014/5*

(15) Two-part   (BWV 772-786)
H. Steurer (pf.)   # **Eta.LPM 1020**
(*Duettos*)

(15) Three-part   (BWV 787-801)
☆ L. Foss (pf.) (2ss)   # **B.AXTL 1027**
                                     (# **D.UST 253545**)
... No. 11, G minor only
C. Zecchi (pf.) (*Mozart, Chopin, etc.*) in # **West.WN 18139**
... Nos. 12 & 13.   F. Kramer (in # MTR.MLO 1012)
... B flat major & F major (unspec.): M. v. Doren (pf.)
                                 (in # Chan.MVDP 3)

MARCHES
D major   (BWV.Anh. 122: AMB)
H. Unruh (hpsi.)   *MSB. 78039*
(*below; & D. Scarlatti*)

S. Bianca (pf.)   *MSB.MSB 27*
(*below*) [with spoken commentary]

M. v. Doren (pf.)   in # **Chan.MVDP 3**

MINUETS
G major   (BWV.Anh. 114: AMB)
G minor   (BWV.Anh. 115: AMB)
H. Steurer (pf.)   *Eta. 21-4*
(*Little Preludes*)   (# *LPM 1019*)

G major (unspec. but probably the above)
H. Unruh (hpsi.)   *MSB. 78039*
(*March; & D. Scarlatti: Sonatas*)

S. Bianca (pf.)   *MSB.MSB 27*
(*March*) [with spoken commentary]

Musette, D major   (BWV.Anh. 126: AMB 22)
H. Steurer (pf.)   in # **Eta.LPM 1019**
(*Minuets & Little Preludes*)
— ARR. GUITAR: A. Segovia (in # Roy. 1422)

**NOTENBUCH FÜR ANNA MAGDALENA
BACH**   (BWV.Anh.)
... Marches: D major (122), E flat major (127)
Minuets: D minor (132), F major (113), G major (116)
Musette, D major (126)
Polonaises: F major (117a), G major (130), G minor (123)
Prelude, C major (W.T.C.1)
Rondo, B flat major (183)[3]
Solo per il cembalo, E flat major (129)
☆ K. Rapf (hpsi.) (# CID.VXT 33017)

Ouvertüre nach französischer Art   (BWV 831)
(*French Overture—Partita, B minor*)
E. Picht-Axenfeld (hpsi.)   # **HP.APM 14008**
(*Italian Concerto*)
S. Heller (hpsi.) (2ss)   # *Dely.EC 3135*
E. Wollmann (pf.)   # **West.WL 5298**
(*Aria variata ... & Ital. Concerto*)
G. Johansen (double-keyboard pf.) in # **AD. set 3**

(6) PARTITAS, Op. 1   (BWV 825–830)
No. 1, B flat major   No. 2, C minor
No. 3, A minor   No. 4, D major
No. 5, G major   No. 6, E minor

COMPLETE RECORDINGS
I. Ahlgrimm (hpsi.)   # **Phi.A 00172/4L**
(6ss)
G. Johansen (double-keyboard pf.) # **AD. set 2**
☆ P. Badura-Skoda (pf.) (6ss)   # **Nix.WLP 6303-1/3**
☆ R. Tureck (pf.) (# Roy. 1415/8)

No. 1, B flat major
A Kitain ("Siena" pf.)   # **Eso.ESP 3001**
(*Chaconne, etc.*)
C. Eloffe (pf.)   VdN.ML 61/2
(3ss—*Cantata 147, excpt.*)
☆ D. Lipatti (pf.)   # *C.C 1021*
(*Mozart: Sonata*) (# *WC 1021*: *FC 1023*: *QC 5013*)
(*Cantata No. 147, excpt., & Mozart on* # *AmC.ML 4633*)
                                     (& in # *C.FCX 494*)
☆ W. Landowska (hpsi.)   # *Vic.LCT 1137*
(*Chromatic Fantasia, Ital. Concerto, etc.*)
☆ J. Demus (pf.) (# Cum.CR 241)

... Gigue only
☆ J. Demus (in # AFest.CFR 10-106; ▽ # Rem. 149-4)

No. 2, C minor
☆ G. Anda (pf.)   # *DT.TM 68011*
                                     (TV.VE 9023)

No. 3, A minor
H. Steurer (pf.)   # **U. 5177G**
(*Vlc. Suite No. I*)

... **Burlesca** only
I. Ahlgrimm (hpsi., from set) (in # Phi.S 06040R)
H. Steurer (pf., from above) (*Eta. 21-2*: # LPM 1019)

No. 4, D major
G. Ramin (hpsi.)   # *MMS. 72*
(*Chromatic Fantasia & Fugue*)
W. Kapell (pf.)[4]   # **Vic.LM 1791**
(*Schubert & Liszt*)
T. Nikolayeva (pf.) (*USSRM.D 671/4*)

... **Gigue**
I. Ahlgrimm (hpsi., from set) (in # Phi.S 06040R)

No. 5, G major
... **Allemande**
E. Heiller (hpsi.)   in # **Uni.LP 1010**
(† *History of the Dance*)

No. 6, E minor
W. Gieseking (pf.), (? n.v.)   # **AmC.ML 4646**
(*Handel & Scarlatti*)   (# *C.FCX 367*)
☆ J. Demus (# Cum.CR 309, & with commentary by
     S. Spaeth, # Rem. 19)
... Air: I. Ahlgrimm (hpsi., from set) (in # Phi.S 06040R)

---

[1] Includes the unfinished fugue, played as left by Bach, and again as completed by Busoni.
[2] Authenticity doubtful.   Theme is from Albinoni's Op. 1.
[3] This is *Les Moissonneurs* by F. Couperin.   [4] Omitting Gigue.

PRELUDES

COLLECTION

   (9) Little Preludes   (BWV 924-932: unfinished)
   (6) Little Preludes   (BWV 933-938)
   (5) Little Preludes   (BWV 939-943)

   I. Ahlgrimm (hpsi.)   **‡ Phi.A 00155/6L**
   (*French Suites*)

(6) Little Preludes for Beginners[1] (BWV 933-938)
   H. Steurer (pf.)   *Eta. 21-1/2*
   (3ss—*Partita, A minor, excpt.*)   (‡ LPM 1019)

... Nos. 1-3: ☆ W. Landowska (hpsi.) (JpV.ND 848)

(12) Little Preludes (BWV 924-30[1], 939-42, 999)
   H. Steurer (pf.)   *Eta. 21-3/4*
   (3ss—*Minuets*)   (& ‡ LPM 1019)

... No. 1, C major & No. 8, F major
   I. Ahlgrimm (hpsi.)   from set; in *‡ Phi.S 06040R*
... No. 2, C major & No. 7, G minor
   F. Kramer (pf.)   in ‡ MTR.MLO 1012
... No. 3, C minor (orig. lute) (BWV 999)
   —— ARR. GUITAR Segovia
   A. Segovia (n.v.)   in ‡ B.AXTL 1069
   († *Segovia Evening II*)   (‡ AmD.DL 9751)
   M. D. Cano   *Dur.AI 10231*
   (*Vlc. Suite 6—Gavotte, arr.*)   (‡ MSE 2)

   ☆ A. Segovia, o.v. (in ‡ MGM.E 3015 & in ‡ Roy. 1422)

Prelude, Fugue & Allegro, E flat major (BWV 998)[2]
   G. Johansen (double-keyboard pf.) in ‡ AD. set 3

   ☆ W. Landowska (hpsi.)
       (in ‡ G.ALP 1246: FALP & QALP 218)
   F. Valenti (hpsi.) (‡ Nix.LLP 8048; ‡ Lyr.LL 48)

... **Prelude & Fugue** — ARR. GUITAR Segovia
   C. Aubin († *Guitar Recital*)   in ‡ Eko.LG 1

Sarabande con partite, C major (BWV 990)
   P. Aubert (hpsi.)   **‡ CFD. 29**
   (*Musicalisches Opfer—Trio Sonata*)

Sonata, D major (BWV 963)
   R. Slenczynski (pf.)   **‡ ML. 7030**
   (*Chromatic Fantasia & Ital. Concerto*)

SUITES

(6) ENGLISH SUITES (BWV 806-11)

No. 1, A major	No. 2, A minor
No. 3, G minor	No. 4, F major
No. 5, E minor	No. 6, D minor

COMPLETE RECORDINGS

   F. Valenti (hpsi.)   **‡ West.WL 5253/5**
   (6ss)   (set WAL 305)

   I. Ahlgrimm (hpsi.) (6ss)   **‡ Phi.A 00169/71L**

   A. Borowsky (pf.) (4ss) **‡ E. & AmVox.PL 7852**

   R. Gianoli (pf.)   **‡ West.WL 5256/8**
   (6ss)   (set WAL 306)

No. 2, A minor ... Bourrées only
   ☆ A. Ehlers (hpsi.) (in ‡ D.UAT 273084)
   —— ARR. ORCH. Stokowski
   ☆ Sym.—Stokowski
     (in ‡ G.FALP 282; ‡ ItV.A12R 0022; ♭ Vic.ERA 89)

... **Bourrée 2 only**
   B. P. Joseph (pedal hpsi.)   in ‡ *SOT. 1131*

No. 3, G minor
   F. Gulda (pf.)   **‡ D.LXT 2826**
   (*W.T.C. No. 32; & Mozart*)   (‡ Lon.LL 756)

No. 5, E minor
   ☆ A. Ehlers (hpsi.) (‡ Allo. 3094)
   M. Fedorova (pf.) (‡ Sup.LPM 72)

No. 6, D minor
   W. Gieseking (pf.)   **‡ Ura. 7107**
   (*Schumann: Kreisleriana*)

   ☆ A. Ehlers (hpsi.) (‡ Allo. 3094)

... **Gavottes I & II:** I. Ahlgrimm (hpsi., from set)
     (in ‡ *Phi.S 06040R*)
... **Gavottes** — ARR. VLN. & PF. Heifetz
   ☆ J. Heifetz (in ‡ G.ALP 1206: FALP 248;
     ♭ Vic.ERA 214; ♭ FV.A 95225)

(6) FRENCH SUITES (BWV 812-817) 1722

No. 1, D minor	No. 2, C minor
No. 3, B minor	No. 4, E flat major
No. 5, G major	No. 6, E major

COMPLETE RECORDINGS

   F. Valenti (hpsi.)   **‡ West.WN 18157/8**
   (4ss)   (o.n., 6ss, WL 5250/2, set WAL 310)

   I. Ahlgrimm (hpsi.)[3]   **‡ Phi.A 00155/6L**
   (3ss—*Little Preludes*)   (2ss, ‡ AmC.ML 4746)

   R. Gianoli (pf.)   **‡ West.WN 18155/6**
   (4ss)   (o.n., 6ss, WL 5259/61, set WAL 307)

   A. Borowsky (pf.)   **‡ E. & AmVox. set PL 8192**
   (4ss)

   ☆ I. Nef (hpsi.) (now 4ss)   **‡ OL.LD 70/1**

No. 1, D minor
... **Sarabande** only
   ☆ A. Ehlers (hpsi.) (in ‡ D.UAT 273084)

No. 2, C minor
... **Gigue** — ARR. 2 PFS.
   E. Bartlett & R. Robertson (in ‡ MGM.E 3150)

No. 3, B minor
   L. Selbiger (hpsi.) (*below*)   **‡ C.KC 3**
... **Sarabande:** I. Ahlgrimm (hpsi., from set)
     (in ‡ *Phi.S 06040R*)

No. 5, G major
   C. Keene (pf.)   **‡ Mer.MG 10138**
   (*Beethoven & Brahms*) (♭ EP 1-5020; ♭ FMer.MEP 14527)
   ☆ T. Nikolayeva (pf.) (‡ Sup.LPM 72)
   J. Demus (pf.) (‡ Cum.CR 241)

... **Gavotte & Bourrée** only
   W. Schetelich (hpsi.)   *Eta. 320111*
   (*W.T.C. 1*)   (o.n. 25-C 013)

... **Gavotte** only
   ☆ A. Ehlers (hpsi.) (in ‡ D.UAT 273084)

No. 6, E major
   L. Selbiger (hpsi.) (*above*)   **‡ C.KC 3**
   ☆ R. Casadesus (pf.) (‡ *Phi.A 01620R*)

... **Allemande:** I. Ahlgrimm (hpsi., from set) (‡ *Phi.S 06040R*)
   ☆ A. Ehlers (hpsi.) (in ‡ D.UAT 273084)

... **Courante, Sarabande, Gavotte, Bourrée, Minuet & Gigue**
   I. Ahlgrimm (hpsi., from set) (*AmC.J 217:* ♭ *J 4-217*)

MISCELLANEOUS SUITES (orig. for Lute)

COLLECTION

E minor (BWV 996)
G minor (BWV 995), from Vlc. suite 5 (BWV 1011)
Prelude, Fugue & Allegro, E flat major (BWV 998)
... Prelude & Fugue only

   M. Podolski (lute)   **‡ Per.SPL 724**

C minor (Partita) (BWV 997)
   — ARR. FL. & HPSI. Veyron-Lacroix
   ☆ J.-P. Rampal & R. Veyron-Lacroix   **‡ HS.HSL 80**
   (*Vivaldi*)

E minor (BWV 996)
... **Sarabande & Bourrée** — ARR. GUITAR Segovia[4]
   ☆ A. Segovia (in ‡ MGM.E 3015 & in ‡ Roy. 1422)
... **Bourrée only** — ARR. Segovia
   ☆ A. Segovia (in † *Segovia Program*, ‡ B.AXTL 1060)
... **Prelude & Bourrée** — ARR. GUITAR
   S. Behrend   *Eta. 130114*
   (*above; & Sanz*)

TOCCATAS

C minor (BWV 911)
   F. Neumeyer (hpsi.)   **PV. 2443**
     (‡ *Pol. 13033*)

   R. Slenczynski (pf.)   **‡ ML. 7030**
   (*Italian Concerto, etc.*)

   ☆ F. Valenti (hpsi.) (in ‡ Nix. LLP 8047; ‡ Lyr.LL 47;
     Cum.CLL 341)

---

[1] Clavierbüchlein für Wilhelm Friedemann Bach (1720).   [2] For Lute recording see *Suites*, below.
[3] Omits all repeats.
[4] It has not been possible to hear these recordings, and probably the Sarabande is that from BWV 997 *above*, there being no movement so called in BWV 996.

D major (BWV 912)
S. Marlowe (hpsi.)   ♯ **Rem. 199-136**
(Couperin & Scarlatti)   (♯ Cum.CR 207)
A. Bundervoët (pf.)   ♯ **LT.DTL 93051**
(below, & Ch. Prel. & Chaconne arrs.) (♯ Sel. 270.C.048)
☆ W. Landowska (hpsi.)   in ♯ Vic.LCT 1137
▽ F. Neumeyer (hpsi.) (PV. 2436; ♯ Pol. 13033)
☆ F. Valenti (hpsi.)
   (in ♯ Nix.LLP 8047; ♯ Lyr.LL 47; Cum.CLL 341)

D minor (BWV 913)
☆ F. Valenti (hpsi.) (in ♯ Nix.LLP 8048; ♯ Lyr.LL 48)
R. Gianoli (pf.) (in ♯ Nix.WLP 5101)

E minor (BWV 914)
A. Bundervoët (pf.)   ♯ **LT.DTL 93051**
(above; & Busoni arrs.)   (♯ Sel.270.C.048)
☆ E. Istomin (pf.)   in ♯ **C.CX 1109**
(Vln. & Clav. Concertos, etc.)   (♯ FCX 325)
☆ F. Valenti (hpsi.) (in ♯ Nix.LLP 8048;♯ Lyr.LL 48)

VARIATIONS
Aria with 30 Variations, G major (BWV 988) 1742
(Goldberg Variations)
G. Leonhardt (hpsi.)   ♯ **Van.BG 536**
I. Ahlgrimm (hpsi.)   ♯ **Phi.A 00267/8L**
(3½ss—below)
J. Demus (pf.)   ♯ **Nix.WLP 5241**
   (♯ Véga.C30. A 5; West.WL 5241)
G. Gould (pf.)   ♯ **AmC.ML 5060**
☆ W. Landowska (hpsi.)   ♯ **G.ALP 1139**
   (QALP 137)
G. Johansen (pf.)[1]   ♯ **AD. set 1**
(3ss—Passacaglia & Fugue)   (Pte.)

Aria variata alla maniera italiana, A minor
   (BWV 989)
R. Gerlin (hpsi.)   in ♯ **LOL.OL 50097**
(Fantasia, C mi.; & C. P. E. & W. F. Bach)
I. Ahlgrimm (hpsi.)   in ♯ **Phi.A 00267L**
(above & below)
G. Kraus (hpsi.)   ♯ **Hall.RS 5**
(Chromatic Fantasia)
E. Wollmann (pf.)   ♯ **West.WL 5298**
(Italian Concerto & Ouvertüre . . .)
☆ B. Seidlhofer (pf.) *(Capriccio)*   ♯ **Sup.LPM 77**

Air with 2 Variations, C minor[2] (BWV 991)
I. Ahlgrimm (hpsi.)   in ♯ **Phi.A 00267L**
(above)

(DAS) WOHLTEMPERIRTE CLAVIER
   (BWV 846-93)
BOOKS I & II; COMPLETE RECORDINGS
W. Landowska (hpsi.) (12ss) ♯ **Vic.set LM 6800**
(Nos. 1-40 are ☆; for separate issues, see below)
I. Ahlgrimm (hpsi.) Book I   ♯ **Phi.A 00157/9L**
(12ss)   Book II   ♯ **Phi.A 00185/7L**
(Book I also on ♯ AmC.ML 4747/9 in set SL 191)
R. Tureck (pf.) (n.v.)   ♯ **B.AXTL 1036/41**
(12ss)   (♯ D.UST 253530/5; ♯ AmD. sets DX 127/8)
Nos. 17-24 ☆ W. Landowska (hpsi.) (♯ ItV.A12R 0123)
Nos. 25-32 ☆ W. Landowska (hpsi.) (♯ ItV.A12R 0106)
Nos. 33-40 ☆ W. Landowska (hpsi.) (♯ ItV.A12R 0108)
Nos. 41-48   W. Landowska (hpsi.)   ♯ **Vic.LM 1820**
BOOK I: COMPLETE RECORDING
J. Demus (pf.) (4ss)   ♯ **West. set WAL 221**
R. Riefling (pf.) (4ss)   ♯ **HS.HS 9013/4**
BOOK I: Nos. 1, 2, 9, 10
L. Selbiger (hpsi.)   ♭ **C. SELK 1003**
BOOK I
No. 1, C major (4 voice fugue)
L. Selbiger (hpsi.)   **C.LDX 7023**
(Concerto, F minor, s. 1)

W. Schetelich (hpsi.)   *Eta. 320111*
(Fr. Suite 5, excerpts)   (o.n. 25.C 013)
D. Matthews (pf.)   **C.DX 8403**
(Chromatic Fantasia, s. 1)
I. Ahlgrimm (hpsi., from set) (in ♯ Phi.S 06040R)

... **Prelude:** W. Landowska (hpsi.) from set, in ♯ Vic.LM 1877
—— ARR. GUITAR: G. Zepoll (in ♯ Nix.SLPY 142: SOT.1024)

No. 2, C minor . . . Fugue only (ARR.)   (3 v. fugue)
Victor Electronic Music Synthesizer
   (in ♯ Vic.LM 1922: ♭ set ERD 1922)

No. 3, C sharp major   (3 voice fugue)
☆ A. Borowsky (pf.)   (JpV.NF 4222)

No. 5, D major   (4 voice fugue)
T. Nikolayeva (pf.) *(No. 9)*   *USSR. 18853*
I. Ahlgrimm (hpsi., from set) (in ♯ Phi.S 06040R)

... **Prelude only**
No. 7, D minor . . . Fugue only
W. Landowska (hpsi.) from set (in ♯ Vic.LM 1877)

No. 8, E flat minor   (3 voice fugue)
— ARR. STR. TRIO, F major, Mozart (K 404a)
Members of Alma Musica Sextet
   ♯ **LT.DTL 93046**
(Mozart: Adagio, D minor; & Willaert, etc.)
   (♯ Sel.LAG 1019; T.LT 6551)

No. 9, E major   (3 voice fugue)
T. Nikolayeva (pf.) *(No. 5)*   *USSR. 18852*

No. 10, E minor; No. 11, F major
T. Nikolayeva (pf.)   *USSR. 18970/1*

No. 13, F sharp major   (3 voice fugue)
C. Zecchi (pf.)   ♯ **West.WN 18139**
(3-pt. Invention No. 11; Chopin, Scarlatti, etc.)

No. 16, G minor   (4 voice fugue)
D. Swainson (clavi.)   **G.HMS 59**
(† History of Music in Sound)   (in ♯ Vic. set LM 6031)

BOOK II
No. 26, C minor (4 voice fugue)
M. Yudina (pf.)   *USSR. 22573/4*
☆ C. Solomon (pf.) (♭ G.7PW 116)

No. 31, E flat major   — ARR. VOCAL QTT.
▽ G. Carrillo Qtt. *(Span)* (in Orf. 22003)

No. 32, E flat minor (4 voice fugue)
F. Gulda (pf.)   ♯ **D.LXT 2826**
(Eng. Suite 3, & Mozart)   (♯ Lon.LL 756)

No. 39, G major; No. 43, A major (3 voice fugues)
S. Feinberg (pf.)   *USSR. 18854/5*

No. 39; & No. 40, G minor (4 voice fugue)
☆ J. Demus (pf.) (in ♯ Cum.CR 306; & with commentary
   by S. Spaeth, in ♯ Rem. 19)

No. 44, A minor (3 voice fugue)
S. Feinberg (pf.) (2ss)   *USSR. 18984/5*

Unspecified Preludes & Fugues
F major & B flat minor I. Baudo (hpsi.) *USSR. 5609 & 6809*

B. ORGAN
COLLECTIONS (General)
(see below for Chorale-Prelude Collections)

THE COMPLETE ORGAN WORKS (in progress)
A. Heiller

VOL. I.		
Fantasia, C minor	(BWV 562)
Toccata & Fugue, F major	(BWV 540)
Trio, D minor	(BWV 583)
Prelude, A minor	(BWV 569)
Toccata & Fugue, D minor (Dorian)	(BWV 538)
[Thalwil Church organ]	♯Phi.A 00205L

(continued on next page)

---

[1] Double-keyboard pf.   [2] Incomplete.

COMPLETE WORKS: Heiller (*continued*)

VOL. II.   Fugue, G minor ("Little")   (BWV 578)
    Fantasia & Fugue, C minor   (BWV 537)
    Prelude & Fugue, C major   (BWV 545)
    Prelude & Fugue, G major   (BWV 541)
    Toccata, Adagio & Fugue, C major   (BWV 564)
    [Thalwil Church organ]   ♯ Phi.A 00206L

VOL. III. Allabreve, D major   (BWV 589)
    Toccata & Fugue, D minor   (BWV 565)
    Preludes & Fugue, D major   (BWV 532)
    Toccata (or Prelude & Fugue),
      E major   (BWV 566)
    Prelude & Fugue, A minor   (BWV 543)
    [Thalwil Church organ]   ♯ Phi.A 00223L
                       (♯ Epic.LC 3132)

VOL. IV.   Canzone, D minor   (BWV 588)
    Fantasia, G major   (BWV 572)
    Preludes & Fugues, G minor   (BWV 535)
      E minor   (BWV 533)
      A minor   (BWV 543)
      C minor   (BWV 549)
    [Wald Church organ]   ♯ Phi.A 00224L

VOLS. V & VI (in prep.) will contain the complete
Orgelbüchlein (♯ Phi.A 00275/6)

THE COMPLETE ORGAN WORKS (in progress)
C. Weinrich
[Organ of Skänninge Church, Sweden]
This project was only announced shortly before going to
press.
SEE *below* under COLLECTIONS & ORGELBÜCHLEIN.

THE ORGAN WORKS OF J. S. BACH
(in progress)
F. Germani
[Organ of All Souls, Langham Place, London]

VOL. I
Sonatas Nos. 1, 2, 3   (BWV 525/7)   ♯ G.CLP 1025
                      (QCLP 12012)
VOL. II
Sonatas Nos. 4, 5, 6   (BWV 528/30)   ♯ G.CLP 1026
[Vols. I & II, ♯ Vic. set LHMV 601, 4ss]

THE COMPLETE ORGAN WORKS (in progress)
H. Walcha   **Pol. various**

This series was not issued as a whole in Europe, but
relevant items are listed individually below. Just as we
close for press, we learn of the issue by AmD. of these
as a set; some are ☆. The following is a summary of
the available information; it has not been possible to
insert these details under the individual works below.

♯ ARC 3013   Sonatas 1, 3, 6
♯ ARC 3014   Sonatas 2, 4, 5
♯ ARC 3015   Preludes & Fugues
        (BWV 531, 533, 535, 532)
      Fantasia & Fugue, C minor (BWV 537)
♯ ARC 3016   Prelude & Fugue, A major (BWV 536)
      Toccatas & Fugues (BWV 538, 540)
      Fugue, D minor (BWV 539)
♯ ARC 3017   Preludes & Fugues (BWV 541, 543)
      Fantasias & Fugues (BWV 542, 562)
♯ ARC 3018   Preludes & Fugues
        (BWV 544, 550, 545, 546)
♯ ARC 3019   Preludes & Fugues (BWV 548, 551, 547)
      Toccata & Fugue, D minor (BWV 565)
♯ ARC 3020   Toccata, Adagio & Fugue (BWV 564)
      Toccata, C (or E) major (BWV 566)
      Fantasia, G major (BWV 572)
      Prelude & Fugue, F minor (BWV 534)
♯ ARC 3021   Passacaglia & Fugue, C mi. (BWV 582)
      Fugue, G minor (BWV 578)
      Allabreve, D major (BWV 589)
      Canzona, D minor (BWV 588)
♯ ARC 3022/4 CLAVIERÜBUNG & 5 other Choral-
      Preludes
♯ ARC 3025/6 ORGELBÜCHLEIN
♯ ARC 3027/9 Choral-Preludes
      (inc. the 18 "Great" and 6 Schübler)
♯ ARC 3030   Chorale-Variations (BWV 768, 769)
      Fuga sopra il Magnificat (BWV 733)
The complete set is ♯ AmD.ARC 3013/30, 36ss.

COLLECTIONS
Aria, F major[1]   (BWV 587)
Canzona, D minor   (BWV 588)
CHORALE-PRELUDES:
  Erbarm' dich mein, O Herre Gott   (BWV 721)
  In dulci jubilo   (BWV 729)
Concerto, Vivaldi, No. 2, A minor   (BWV 593)
Prelude & Fugue, C minor   (BWV 549)
Prelude & Fugue, G major   (BWV 550)
TRIOS: D minor   (BWV 583)
      C minor   doubtful   (BWV 585)

M-C. Alain   ♯ DDP. 32-1
[St. Merry organ, Paris]   (♯ HS.HSL 104)
(Canzona & Prel. & Fugue, G major
                also on V♯ *Era.LDE 1006*)
[For other recordings by Mme. Alain, *see below*: Sonatas,
Pastorale, Fantasias, Passacaglia, Preludes & Fugues,
Toccatas & Fugues]

Fantasia & Fugue, G minor   (BWV 542)
Prelude & Fugue, E minor   (BWV 548)
CHORALE-PRELUDES: Wachet auf
                  (BWV 645-Sch. 1)
  Kommst du nun, Jesu, vom Himmel herunter
                  (BWV 650-Sch. 6)
  Vom Himmel hoch   (BWV 606-OB 8)
K. Richter   ♯ D.LXT 5029
[Organ of Victoria Hall, Geneva]   (♯ Lon.LL 1175)
(Kommst du nun . . . only, on ♭ D. 71125)

BACH ORGAN MUSIC—A. Schweitzer
☆ VOL. I
Toccata, Adagio & Fugue, C major   (BWV 564)
Prelude & Fugue, A minor . . . Fugue only (BWV 543)
Fantasia & Fugue, G minor (BWV 542)   ♯ C.CX 1074
                  (♯ Phi.A 01109L)
[BWV 543 & 542 on ♭ EPhi.ABE 10000; ♭ Phi.A 40900E]
☆ VOL. II
CHORALE-PRELUDES
O Mensch, bewein' dein' Sünde gross (BWV 622) (2 versions)
Wenn wir in höchsten Nöten sein
        (BWV 668) (*Vor deinen Thron* . . .)
Ich ruf' zu dir, Herr Jesu Christ   (BWV 639)
Gelobet seist du, Jesus Christ   (BWV 604-OB 6)
Herzlich tut mich verlangen   (BWV 727)
Nun komm' der Heiden Heiland (BWV 659) ♯ C.CX 1081
                  (♯ Phi.A 01110L)
☆ VOL. III
Prelude & Fugue, C major . . . Prelude only (BWV 531)
Prelude & Fugue, D major . . . Prelude only (BWV 532)
Canzona, D minor (BWV 588)   ♯ C.CX 1084
(with *Mendelssohn: Sonata No. 6*)   (♯ Phi.A 01111L)
VOL. IV
Toccata & Fugue, D minor (BWV 565) β
Preludes & Fugues: E minor (BWV 533) β
      A minor (BWV 543) β
      C major (BWV 547)
      C minor (BWV 546)   ♯ AmC.ML 5040
VOL. V
Toccata & Fugue, D minor (Dorian) (BWV 538)
Preludes & Fugues: A major (BWV 536)
      F minor (BWV 534)
      B minor (BWV 544) ♯ EPhi.ABL 3092
      (♯ AmC.ML 5041; ♯ Phi.A 01208L)
VOL. VI
Passacaglia & Fugue, C minor   (BWV 582) β
Prelude & Fugue, G major   (BWV 541) β
CHORALE-PRELUDES:
Ein' feste Burg ist unser Gott   (BWV 720) α
Gottes Sohn ist kommen   (BWV 724) α
Liebster Jesu, wir sind hier   (BWV 731)
Sei gegrüsset, Jesu gütig . . . Variation XI only (BWV 768) α
Vater unser im Himmelreich   (BWV 737)
Alle Menschen müssen sterben   (BWV 643-OB 44)
                  ♯ AmC.ML 5042
(Vols. IV-VI form ♯ AmC. set SL 223)
Items marked α also on ♯ & ♭ AmC.PE 15; marked β also
  ♯ Phi.A 01209L
[Recorded on the organ of Gunsbach Church, Alsace, in
September 1952]

Preludes & Fugues: B minor   (BWV 544)
            C minor   (BWV 546)
Fantasias & Fugues: G minor   (BWV 542)
            C minor   (BWV 537)
A. Marchal   ♯ LT.DTL 93056
[Organ of S. Eustache, Paris]   (♯ Sel. 320.C.055)
(See also Fantasias, below)

Fantasia & Fugue, G minor   (BWV 542)
Passacaglia & Fugue, C minor   (BWV 582)
Prelude & Fugue, E flat major   (BWV 552-CU)
P. Cochereau   ♯ Ven.CM 9102
[Organ of St. Roch, Paris]   (♯ HS.HSL 129)

Prelude & Fugue, E minor   (BWV 548)
Christ, der du bist der helle Tag (Variations) (BWV 766)
  ("*Partita, F minor*")
Sonata No. 5, C major   (BWV 529)
CHORALE-PRELUDES:
  Wie schön leuchtet . . .   (BWV 739)
  Wachet auf!   (BWV 645-Sch. 1)
  Wir glauben all' . . .   (BWV 680-CU.12)
G. Litaize   ♯ CFD. 5
[Organ of Notre Dame de Versailles]

---

[1] An org. arr. by Bach of Courante II from *La Françoise* (*Les Nations No. 1*) by F. Couperin.

ORGAN COLLECTIONS (*continued*)

Passacaglia & Fugue, C minor	(BWV 582)
Preludes & Fugues: A major	(BWV 536)
E flat major	(BWV 552-CU)
Toccata & Fugue, D minor	(BWV 565)

G. Litaize   **♯ LT.DTL 93037**
                      (♯ Sel. 320.C.014)
[Organ of Institut national des jeunes aveugles]

Preludes & Fugues: A minor	(BMV 543)
E minor	(BWV 533)
D major	(BWV 532)
Fantasia, G major	(BWV 572)
Toccata, Adagio & Fugue, C major	(BWV 564)

G. Litaize   **♯ Era.LDE 3020**
[St. Merry Organ]

Fugue, G major, à la gigue	(BWV 577)
Prelude & Fugue, A minor	(BWV 543)
Toccata, Adagio & Fugue, C major	(BWV 564)
CHORALE-PRELUDES:	
Jesus Christus, unser Heiland	(BWV 688-CU 20)
Nun komm', der Heiden Heiland	(BWV 659-E 9)
Wenn wir in höchsten Nöten sein	(BWV 641-OB 42)

J. Demessieux   **♯ D.LXT 2915**
[Organ of Victoria Hall, Geneva]   (♯ Lon.LL 946)
(BWV 688 & 659 also on ♭ D. 71120)

Preludes & Fugues: A major	(BWV 536) *a*
B minor	(BWV 544)
Pastorale, F major	(BWV 590) *b*
Fantasia, G major	(BWV 572) *a*

F. Viderø   **♯ HS.HSL 128**
[Organ at Kaerteminde, Denmark]
(marked *a* also on ♭ *Mtr. MCEP 3001*;
              b on ♭ *Mtr.MCEP 3000*)

Passacaglia & Fugue, C minor	(BWV 582)
Prelude & Fugue, E minor	(BWV 533)
Fantasia, G major	(BWV 572)

A. Nowakowski   **♯ DT.LGM 65030**
[Organ of Sorø Church, Denmark]   (♯ *T.LB 6094*)

Toccata & Fugue, D minor	(BWV 565)
Preludes & Fugues: C major	(BWV 545)
B minor	(BWV 544)

A. Nowakowski   **♯ T.NLB 6097**
[Organ of Sorø Church, Denmark]

Passacaglia & Fugue, C minor	(BWV 582)
TOCCATAS & FUGUES: D minor (Dorian)	
	(BWV 538)
F major	(BWV 540)
Ch.-Prelude: Nun komm der Heiden Heiland	
	(BWV 659-E 9)

M. Dupré   **♯ Lum.LD 3-106**
[Organ of St. Sulpice, Paris]

Toccata & Fugue, D minor	(BWV 565)
Vivaldi Concertos:	
No. 2, A minor . . . Adagio	(BWV 593)
No. 5, D minor . . . Adagio	(BWV 596)
Chorale-Prelude: Herzlich tut mich verlangen	
	(BWV 727)

G. de Donà   **♯ AmVox. VL 3100**
(*Handel, Boëllmann*)

Toccata & Fugue, D minor	(BWV 565)
Toccata & Fugue, C major	(BWV 564)
. . . Adagio (A minor) only	
Chorale-Prelude: Wachet auf!	(BWV 645-Sch. 1)

S. Rasjö   **♭ Mtr.MCEP 5007**

Toccatas & Fugues: D minor	(BWV 565)
F major	(BWV 540)
Chorale-Preludes: Dies sind die heil'gen zehn Gebot'	
Three versions: CU 11 (Fughetta—BWV 679)	
The same with different registration	
OB 36 (BWV 635)	

C. Weinrich   **♯ West.LAB 7023**
[Organ of Skänninge Church, Sweden]

Toccata & Fugue, D minor (Dorian)	(BWV 538)
Allabreve, D major	(BWV 589)
Toccata & Fugue, E major	(BWV 566)
Canzona, D minor	(BWV 588)

C. Weinrich   **♯ West.WN 18148**
[Organ of Skänninge Church, Sweden]
This disc forms Vol. II of an intended issue of The
Complete Organ Works.

Allabreve, D major	(BWV 589)
☆ Pastorale, F major	(BWV 590)
☆ Passacaglia & Fugue, C minor	(BWV 582)

H. Walcha   **♯ HP.AP 13028**
[Schnitger organ, Cappel]

Prelude & Fugue, G major	(BWV 541)
Toccata, Adagio & Fugue, C major	(BWV 564)
Prelude & Fugue, E minor	(BWV 548)
Ch.-Prelude: Ach bleib' bei uns	(BWV 649)
Prelude & Fugue, D major . . . Fugue only	(BWV 532)

☆ **J. Eggington**   **♯ LOL.OL 50012**
[Organ of Ste. Radegonde, Poitiers]

Fantasia & Fugue, G minor	(BWV 542)
Prelude & Fugue, B minor	(BWV 544)
Prelude & Fugue, A minor	(BWV 543)
Ch.-Preludes: Nun freut euch . . .	(BWV 734)
Der Tag, der ist so freudenreich	(BWV 605)
Toccata, F major	(BWV 540)

☆ **J. Eggington**[1]   **♯ OL.LD 39**

Toccata, Adagio & Fugue, C major	(BWV 564)
Toccata & Fugue, D minor	(BWV 565)
Toccata, F major	(BWV 540)

A. Schreiner[2]   **♯ MMS. 32**

CHORALE-PRELUDES	
(6) "Schübler" Preludes	(BWV 645/50)
An Wasserflüssen Babylon	(BWV 653-E 3)
Ein' feste Burg ist unser Gott	(BWV 720)
(6) CONCERTOS after Vivaldi	
. . . No. 2, A minor	(BWV 593)
Passacaglia & Fugue, C minor	(BWV 582)

☆ **C. Weinrich**   **♯ MGM.E 3021**

Fantasia, G major	(BWV 572)
Pastorale, F major	(BWV 590)
CHORALE-PRELUDES: In dulci jubilo	
	(BWV 608-OB 10)
Lobt Gott, ihr Christen, allzugleich	
	(BWV 609-OB 11)
Vom Himmel hoch	(BWV 606-OB 8)
Vom Himmel hoch (Canonische Veränderungen)	
	(BWV 769)

☆ **F. Heitmann**   in **♯ DT.LGX 66009**
(† Christmas Organ Music)   (♯ FT. 320.TC.075)

COLLECTION — ARR. PF.

Prelude & Fugue, A minor	(BWV 543) ARR. Liszt
Toccata & Fugue, D minor	(BWV 565) ARR. Sandor
Toccata, C major (Toccata, Adagio & Fugue)	
	(BWV 564) ARR. Busoni
Prelude & Fugue, D major	(BWV 532) ARR. Busoni
Fantasia & Fugue, G minor	(BWV 542) ARR. Liszt

G. Sandor   **♯ AmC.ML 4684**

Allabreve, D major   (BWV 589)
H. Vollenweider   **Phi.N 12059G**
(*Ch. Prel.—O Mensch, bewein'*)

CHORALE-PRELUDES
(inc. Partite, Variations)

COLLECTIONS (Integral)

(18) "GREAT" PRELUDES   (BWV 651-668)

1. Komm, heiliger Geist (Fantasia)
2. Komm, heiliger Geist
3. An Wasserflüssen Babylon
4. Schmücke dich, o liebe Seele
5. Herr Jesu Christ, dich zu uns wend'
6. O Lamm Gottes unschuldig
7. Nun danket alle Gott
8. Von Gott will ich nicht lassen
9. Nun komm', der Heiden Heiland
10. Nun komm', der Heiden Heiland (Trio)
11. Nun komm', der Heiden Heiland
12. Allein Gott in der Höh' sei Ehr'
13. Allein Gott in der Höh' sei Ehr'
14. Allein Gott in der Höh' sei Ehr' (Trio)
15. Jesus Christus, unser Heiland
16. Jesus Christus, unser Heiland
17. Komm, Gott Schöpfer, heiliger Geist
18. Vor deinen Thron tret' ich (or: Wenn wir in höchsten Nöten sein)

COMPLETE RECORDINGS

H. Walcha (5ss—*below*)	**♯ Pol. 14039/41**
[Schnitger Organ, Cappel]	(♯ AmD.ARC 3027/9)
A. Heiller (4ss)	**♯ Lyr. set LL 39**
	(♯ Clc. 6209/10)

---

[1] This recording is finally confirmed in this form.   [2] Salt Lake City Tabernacle organ.

CLAVIERÜBUNG—PART III 1739
(BWV 552, 669/89, & 802/5, clavier)

Prelude, E flat major (Jakobikirche org.)
7 Longer Chorale-Preludes (Jakobikirche org.)
11 Shorter Chorale-Preludes (Cappel organ)
4 Duettos (harpsichord)
Fugue, E flat major (Jakobikirche organ)

☆ H. Walcha   # HP.APM 14047/9
(5ss—Chorale-Preludes, below)   (# AmD.ARC 3022/4)

... Nos. 1, 7, 10, 12, 15, 17, 18, 20
☆ F. Heitmann (# T.LSK 7033; FT. 320.TC.073)

ORGELBÜCHLEIN (BWV 599-644)

1. Nun komm', der Heiden Heiland
2. Gott, durch deine Güte (or: Gottes Sohn ist kommen)
3. Herr Christ, der ein'ge Gottes Sohn
    (or: Herr Gott, nun sei gepreiset)
4. Lob sei dem allmächtigen Gott
5. Puer natus in Bethlehem
6. Gelobet seist du, Jesu Christ
7. Der Tag, der ist so freudenreich
8. Vom Himmel hoch
9. Vom Himmel kam der Engel Schar
10. In dulci jubilo
11. Lobt Gott, ihr Christen, allzugleich
12. Jesu, meine Freude
13. Christum wir sollen loben schon
14. Wir Christenleut'
15. Helft mir Gottes Güte preisen
16. Das alte Jahr vergangen ist
17. In dir ist Freude
18. Mit Fried' und Freud' ich fahr' dahin
19. Herr Gott, nun schleuss den Himmel auf
20. O Lamm Gottes unschuldig
21. Christe, du Lamm Gottes
22. Christus, der uns selig macht
23. Da Jesus an dem Kreuze stund'
24. O Mensch, bewein' dein' Sünde gross
25. Wir danken dir, Herr Jesu Christ
26. Hilf Gott, dass mir's gelinge
27. Christ lag in Todesbanden
28. Jesus Christus unser Heiland
29. Christ ist erstanden
30. Erstanden ist der heil'ge Christ
31. Erschienen ist der herrliche Tag
32. Heut' triumphiret Gottes Sohn
33. Komm, Gott Schöpfer, heiliger Geist
34. Herr Jesu Christ, dich zu uns wend'
35. Liebster Jesu, wir sind hier (2 versions)
36. Dies sind die heil'gen zehn Gebot'
37. Vater unser im Himmelreich
38. Durch Adam's Fall ist ganz verderbt
39. Es ist das Heil uns kommen her
40. Ich ruf' zu dir, Herr Jesu Christ
41. In dich hab' ich gehoffet, Herr
42. Wenn wir in höchsten Nöten sein
43. Wer nun den lieben Gott lässt walten
44. Alle Menschen müssen sterben
45. Ach wie nichtig, ach wie flüchtig

COMPLETE RECORDINGS
C. Weinrich   # West.WN 18110/1
(4ss) [Skänninge Chu. org., Sweden]   (set WN 2203)
[only the second version of No. 35 is played: BWV 634]
[Vol. I of The Complete Organ Works]

E. Power Biggs (6ss)   # AmC. set SL 227
[Org. Symphony Hall, Boston]
[includes also the original Chorales]

H. Walcha (4ss—some ☆)   # HP.APM 14021/2
(Schnitger organ, Cappel)   (# AmD.ARC 3025/6)
(Nos. 2, 6-11, 14, 17, also on ♭ Pol. 37068; Nos. 20, 22, 24, 25
on ♭ 37084; Nos. 28-32 on ♭ 37085)

F. Viderø (4ss)   # HS.HSL 83/4
[Org. of Sorø Chu., Denmark] (set HSL-D; # Ven.LM 8/9)

... Nos. 1 to 19 inclusive ("Christmas" Preludes)
G. Litaize (2ss)   # Sel.LA 1015
[Organ of St. Merry, Paris]   (# T.PLB 6134)

(6) SCHÜBLER PRELUDES (BWV 645-650)
1. Wachet auf, ruft uns die Stimme
2. Wo soll ich fliehen hin
3. Wer nun den lieben Gott lässt walten
4. Meine Seele erhebet den Herren
5. Ach, bleib' bei uns, Herr Jesu Christ
6. Kommst du nun, Jesu, vom Himmel herunter

☆ H. Walcha   # Pol. 14041
(Great Preludes 15-18, above)   (# AmD.ARC 3029)
[St. Jakobikirche organ, Lübeck]

ASSORTED COLLECTIONS OF CHORALE-PRELUDES

Christum wir sollen loben schon	(BWV 696)
Gelobet seist du Jesu Christ	(BWV 697)
Gottes Sohn ist kommen	(BWV 703)
Herr Christ der ein'ge Gottes Sohn	(BWV 698)
Herzlich tut mich verlangen	(BWV 727)
Herr Jesu Christ, dich uns zu wend	(BWV 709)
Liebster Jesu, wir sind hier	(BWV 706)
Lob sei dem allmächtgen Gott	(BWV 704)
Nun komm', der Heiden Heiland	(BWV 699)
O Gott, du frommer Gott (Variations)	(BWV 767)
Vom Himmel hoch da komm' ich her	(BWV 769)
(Canonische Veränderungen)	
Wer nur den lieben Gott lässt walten (2 settings)	
	(BWV 691 & 690)

F. Viderø   # HS.HSL 94
[Sorø and Kaerteminde organs]

Vater unser im Himmelreich	(BWV 737)
Nun komm', der Heiden Heiland	(BWV 659-E 9)
Liebster Jesu, wir sind hier	(BWV 731)
Von Gott will ich nicht lassen	(BWV 658-E 8)
Schmücke dich, o liebe Seele	(BWV 654-E 4)
Sei gegrüsset, Jesu gütig (Variations)	(BWV 768)

F. Viderø   # HS.HSL 3063
[Sorø Church organ, Denmark]

Christum wir sollen loben schon	(BWV 611-OB 13)
Liebster Jesu, wir sind hier	(BWV 731)
Mit Fried und Freud' ich fahr' dahin	(BWV 616-OB 18)
Christus der uns selig macht	(BMV 620-OB 22)
Da Jesus an dem Kreuze stund'	(BMV 621-OB 23)
O Mensch, bewein' dein' Sünde gross	(BWV 622-OB 24)
Sei gegrüsset, Jesu gütig (Variations)	
... Variation XI	(BWV 768)
An Wasserflüssen Babylon	(BWV 653-E 3)
O Lamm Gottes, unschüldig	(BWV 656-E 6)
Schmücke dich, o liebe Seele	(BWV 654-E 4)
Jesus Christus, unser Heiland	(BWV 665-E 15)
Christ lag in Todesbanden	(BWV 625-OB 27)
Erschienen ist der herrliche Tag	(BWV 629-OB 31)

☆ A. Schweitzer   # C.CX 1249
[Organ of Ste. Aurélie, Strasbourg]

Lob sei dem allmächtigen Gott	(BWV 602-OB 4)
Schmücke dich, o liebe Seele	(BWV 654-E 4)
Wir glauben all an einem Gott	(BWV 680-CU 12)
Nun komm', der Heiden Heiland	(BWV 659-E 9)
Aus der Tiefe rufe ich	(BWV 745)
Heut' triumphiret Gottes Sohn	(BWV 630-OB 32)

J. Harms   # Uni.UN 1004
(Karg-Elert, Peeters, Reger, Weinberger, etc.)
[Organ of Community Church, N.Y.]

Meine Seele erhebet den Herren	(BWV 648-Sch. 4)
Wer nur den lieben Gott lässt walten	(BWV 647-Sch. 3)

☆ E. Power Biggs (C.DOX 1042)

Wachet auf!	(BWV 645-Sch. 1)
Wo soll ich fliehen hin?	(BWV 646-Sch. 2)
Wer nur den lieben Gott lässt walten	(BWV 647-Sch. 3)

"Staff Organist," Sym. Hall, Boston in # ASK. 2
(Sonata No. 1; Concerto No. 2, excpt.;
     & Alain, Langlais, etc.)

(18) Great Preludes, Nos. 4, 8, 12
Orgelbüchlein, Nos. 17, 24, 32, 37, 39, 42
☆ F. Heitmann   # DT.LGM 65008
    (# FT. 270.TC.058)

An Wasserflüssen Babylon	(BWV 653b)
Vom Himmel hoch (Fuga)	(BWV 700)
Herzlich tut mich verlangen	(BWV 727)
Nun freut euch, lieben Christen, g'mein (Trio)	(BWV 734)
Valet will ich dich geben	(BWV 736)

☆ H. Walcha   # HP.APM 14049
(Clavierübung, s. 5) [Schnitger organ, Cappel]
    (# AmD.ARC 3024)
[BWV 653b, 727 & 736 also on ♭ Pol. 37086]

Fuga sopra il Magnificat (BWV 733), with BWV 734 &
700, as above   Pol. 1023
    (♭ 37069; in # AmD.ARC 3030)

Fuga sopra il Magnificat	(BWV 733)
Sei gegrüsset, Jesu gütig (Variations)	(BWV 768)
Vom Himmel hoch (Variations)	(BWV 769)

☆ H. Walcha [Schnitger org.] # HP.APM 14030
    (# AmD.ARC 3030)

Nun freut euch, lieben Christen, g'mein	(BWV 734)
Nun komm', der Heiden Heiland	(BWV 659)

R. Owen   in # ASK. 3
(Walther, Daquin, Vierne, etc.)
[Organ of Christ Church, Bronxville, N.Y.]

= Long-playing, 33⅓ r.p.m.   ♭ = 45 r.p.m.   ♮ = Auto. couplings, 78 r.p.m.

Nun komm', der Heiden Heiland (BWV 599-OB 1)	
Wo soll ich fliehen hin (BWV 646-Sch. 2)	
Wachet auf! (BWV 645-Sch. 1)	
Komm' Gott Schöpfer, heil' ger Geist (BWV 667)	

P. Kee ♭ *G. 7EPH 1003*
[Organ of St. Laurens, Alkmaar]

COLLECTIONS OF PF. ARRS.

Nun komm', der Heiden Heiland (BWV 659-E 9)☆
In dulci jubilo (BWV 751)
Nun freut euch, lieben Christen, g'mein (BWV 734)
Wachet auf! (BWV 645-Sch. 1)☆ [& on ♭ D. 71124]
— ARR. PF.

W. Kempff in ♯ **D.LXT 2820**
(*Chromatic Fantasia, etc.*) (in ♯ Lon.LL 791)

Ich ruf zu dir, Herr Jesu Christ (BWV 639-OB 40)
Nun freut euch, lieben Christen, g'mein (BWV 734)
Wachet auf! (BWV 645)
— ARR. PF. Busoni

☆ R. Trouard in ♯ *ArgOd.LDC 7501*

Ich ruf zu dir, Herr Jesu Christ
Wachet auf!
— ARR. PF. Busoni

P. Sancan ♯ *FV. 230004*
(*Cantata 147, excpt.; & Schumann*)

Allein Gott in der Höh' sei Ehr' (Variations)
— ARR. BANDONEON Barletta[1] (BWV 771)
A. Barletta ♯ *SMC. 548*

An Wasserflüssen Babylon (BWV 653b)
☆ H. Walcha Pol. 1024
(*Valet will ich dir geben*) [Schnitger organ, Cappel]
(also on ♯ Pol. 14049)

Christ lag' in Todesbanden (BWV 625-OB 27)
F. Viderø in ♯ **HS.HSL 2073**
(† Masterpieces of Music before 1750)

Durch Adams Fall (BWV 637)
G. Jones in G.HMS 61
(† History of Music in Sound) (in ♯ Vic. set LM 6031)

(Ein') feste Burg (BWV 720)
E. P. Biggs in ♯ **AmC.ML 4635**
(Bach Festival)

Herzlich tut mich verlangen (BWV 727)
P. Isolffson G.DB 30001
(*below; & Pastorale*)
M-L. Girod (in ♯ SM. 33-19)
☆ C. Courboin (in ♯ Cam.CAL 218)
— ARR. VLC. & PF.
P. Fournier & E. Lush in ♯ **D.LXT 2766**
(*Sonata; & Bloch, Nin, etc.*) (in ♯ Lon.LL 700)
— ARR. ORCH. Walton
See: Wise Virgins, Section I.E. below
— ARR ORCH. Anon.
Florence Festival—Gui in ♯ **Tem.TT 2046**

Heut' triumphiret Gottes Sohn (BWV 630-OB 32)
N. Coke-Jephcott in ♯ **ASK. 8**
(*below; & Prel. & Fugue, E minor; & Vierne, Purcell, etc.*)
[Organ of Cath. of S. John the Divine, N.Y.]

Ich ruf' zu dir, Herr Jesu Christ (BWV 639-OB 40)
K. Richter ♯ **D.LXT 5110**
(*Passacaglia; Toccata & Fugue, D minor; & Liszt*)
(♯ Lon.LL 1174)
[Organ of Victoria Hall, Geneva] (& on ♭ D. 71125)
N. Coke-Jephcott (*above*) in ♯ **ASK. 8**
— ARR. PF. Busoni
☆ D. Lipatti in ♯ **AmC.ML 4633**
(♯ C.FCX 494; & ♭ C.ESBF 112)

In dulci jubilo (BWV 608)
G. Jones in G.HMS 61
(† History of Music in Sound) (in ♯ Vic. set LM 6031)
P. Isolfsson G.DB 30004
(*below, & "Short" Prelude No. 2*)

Jesus Christus, unser Heiland (BWV 626)
P. Isolfsson G.DB 30001
(*above, & Pastorale*) [Organ of All Souls, London]

Komm, Gott Schöpfer, Heiliger Geist (BWV 667)
M-L. Girod (in ♯ SM. 33-19)

Kommst du nun, Jesu, vom Himmel herunter
(BWV 650-Sch. 6)
L. Thybo in ♯ **Phi.A 09801L**
(*Sonata No. 1; Thybo & Walther*)
— ARR. ORCH. Gui
☆ Florence Festival—Gui (in ♯ Tem.TT 2046)

Nun freut euch, lieben Christen, g'mein (BWV 734)
P. Kee ♭ *G.7EPH 1001*
(♯s—*Toccata & Fugue, D minor*)

Nun komm', der Heiden Heiland (BWV 659-E 9)
R. Noehren in ♯ **Allo. 3044**
— ARR. PF. Busoni
☆ D. Lipatti in ♯ **AmC.ML 4633**
(♯ C.FCX 494 & ♭ C.ESBF 112)
— ARR. ORCH. Goldschmidt
Champs-Élysées Th.—Goldschmidt
♯ **LT.DTL 93053**
(*Fugue & Concertos*) (♯ Sel. 320.C.012)

O Gott, du frommer Gott (Partite diverse)
(BWV 767)
F. Viderø[2] ♯ *Fdn.FDL 1022*
(*Prelude & Fugue, B minor*)
L. Farnam[3] ♯ *CEd.CE 1040*
(*Handel, Vierne, Sowerby*)
E. White[4] in ♯ **Moll.E4QP 3443**
(*Elmore, Martini, Fiocco, etc.*)
☆ R. Noehren (♯ Pac. LDAD 70)

O Mensch, bewein' dein' Sünde gross
(BWV 622-OB 24)
H. Vollenweider Phi.N 12059G
(*Allabreve, D major*)
E. Hilliar in ♯ **ASK. 4**
(*Sonata 4; & Pachelbel, Loeillet, etc.*)
— ARR. PF.
J. Friskin in ♯ **Van.BG 545**
(see Clavier Collections)
— ARR. ORCH. Gui
☆ Italian Radio—Gui (in ♯ Tem.TT 2046)

Valet will ich dir geben (BWV 736)
☆ H. Walcha Pol. 1024
(*An Wasserflüssen Babylon*) (also on ♯ Pol. 14049)
[Schnitger organ, Cappel]

Vom Himmel hoch (BWV 738)
E. P. Biggs in ♯ **AmC.ML 4635**
(Bach Festival)

Vom Himmel hoch (BWV 769)
(*Canonische Veränderungen*)
☆ H. Walcha (♭ Pol. 37070)
R. Noehren (♯ Pac.LDAD 70)

Vom Himmel hoch (unspec.)
E. Barthe in *PV. 36095*
(*Eccard, Pachelbel, etc.*) (♭ Pol. 32099)

Wachet auf! (BWV 645-Sch. 1)
— ARR. PF. Busoni
A. Bundervoët ♯ **LT.DTL 93051**
(*Chaconne, arr. Busoni; & Toccata*) (♯ Sel. 270.C.048)
M. Schwalb in ♯ **Roy. 1474**

---

[1] This disc has not been heard, but as there are 17 variations it is assumed these are these, probably in a free adaptation by the soloist.
[2] Organ of Sorø Church, Denmark.
[3] Recorded from an organ roll of 1930, with registration by C. Watters; organ of St. John's Church, West Hartford, Conn., U.S.A.   [4] Organ of St. Mary the Virgin, N.Y.

Wenn wir in höchsten Nöthen sein (BWV 668-E 18)
(*Vor deinen Thron . . .*)
☆ F. Heitmann   in ‡ *DT.LGM 65009*
(*Kunst der Fuge, excpts.*)

— ARR. 2 PFS.   Seidlhofer
J. & G. Dichler   in ‡ **West. set WAL 215**
(as final section of *Kunst der Fuge*)

Wer nur den lieben Gott lässt walten
                   (BWV 691-AMB)
P. Isolfsson   **G.DB 30004**
(*above & "Short" Prelude No. 2*)

☆ K. Rapf (hpsi.) (in ‡ *CID.VXT 33017*)

Wie schön leuchtet der Morgenstern (BWV 763)
E. P. Biggs   in ‡ **AmC.ML 4635**
(*Bach Festival*)

Wir glauben all' an einem Gott (BWV 680-CU 12)
— ARR. ORCH.   Stokowski
☆ Orch.—Stokowski   (♭ *G.7ER 5004: 7ERW 5004;*
DV.L 26031; Vic.*ERA 89*; & in ‡ *G.FALP 281*)

CONCERTOS after Vivaldi, et al. (BWV 592-7)
No. 1, G major (after Johann Ernst von Saxe-
   Weimar) (BWV 592)
— ARR. VLC., STR. ORCH. & HPSI.   Fasano
☆ M. Amfitheatrov & Virtuosi di Roma
                (‡ *D.UAT 273091;* Fnt.*LP 3006*)

No. 2, A minor (after Vivaldi's Op. 3, No. 8)
                     (BWV 593)
A. V. Nuñez[1]   ‡ *SOT. 1056*
(*Fantasia & Fugue, & Fugue*) [Morelia (Mex.) Cath. Organ]
B. P. Joseph (pedal hpsi.)   ‡ *SOT. 1131*
(*Eng. Suite 2, excpt.; Prelude, G maj.; & Mozart*)

… **1st movt., Allegro, only**
G. Faxon   in ‡ **ASK. 2**
(*Langlais, Alain, etc.*) [St. Paul's Cath. Boston]
R. Ellsasser (own arr.)   ‡ *CM. 3*
(*Fantasia & Fugue; & Mendelssohn*)
                 (‡ *Eli.LPE/Attn.LPV 106*)

No. 3, C major (after Vivaldi's Op. 7, No. 11)
                     (BWV 594)
… **2nd movt. Recitative** — ARR. VLC. & PF.   Rosanoff
P. Casals & E. Istomin   in ‡ **AmC.ML 4926**

No. 5, D minor (after Vivaldi's Op. 3, No. 1)
                     (BWV 596)
H. Ash   ‡ **McInt.MC 1005**
(*Fantasia & Fugue, G minor; etc.*)   (o.n. ‡ WCFM. 19)

— ARR. PF.   Schneider & Murdoch
A. Brailowsky   ‡ *Vic.LRM 7050*
(*Bach-Busoni: Chaconne*) (♭ set ERB 7050; ‡ *FV. 330205*)

FANTASIAS
C minor (BWV 562)
G major (BWV 572)
M-C. Alain   ‡ *DFr. 120*
(*Sonatas & Pastorale*)   (‡ *HS.HSL 120, in set L*)
[Org. St. Merry, Paris]
H. Walcha   ♭ *Pol. 37037*
[Schnitger organ, Cappel]
A. Marchal   ‡ *Sel. 270.C. 057*
(*Prelude & Fugue, E minor*) [St. Eustache organ]

FANTASIAS & FUGUES
COLLECTION
   G minor (BWV 542)
   A minor (BWV 561)
   C minor (BWV 562)
M.-C. Alain   ‡ *DFr. 147*
(*Toccata & Fugue; & Fugue, G mi.*) [St. Merry organ, Paris]

G minor (BWV 542)
J. Demessieux   ‡ *D.LW 5095*
(*Toccata & Fugue, D minor*)
P. Kee   ♭ *G.7EPH 1002*
(2ss) [Organ St. Laurens, Alkmaar]

H. Ash   ‡ **McInt.MC 1005**
(*Vivaldi Concerto No. 5; Liszt, Bingham, etc.*)
                 (o.n. WCFM. 19)
W. Watkins   ‡ **McInt.MM 106**
(*Dupré, Handel, etc.*)
R. Ellsasser   ‡ *CM. 3*
(*Concerto excpt., & Mendelssohn*)
       (‡ *Attn.LPV 106*; ‡ *Eli.LPE 106*)
[Mexico City Cath. organ]
A. V. Nuñez   ‡ *SOT. 1056*
(*Vivaldi Concerto 2, & Fugue*) [Morelia Cath. Org.]
☆ H. Walcha (Schnitger organ)   ♭ *Pol. 37023*

… **Fugue only** — ARR. STR. ORCH.   Münchinger
☆ Stuttgart Cha.—Münchinger (♭ *D. 71090: DK 23357*)

FUGUES
D minor (BWV 539)
H. Walcha   **PV. 1429**
(*Toccata, E major*) [Schnitger organ, Cappel]
(*Fugue, G minor, on* ♭ *Pol. 37066*)

Fugue, F major, on the Magnificat
     SEE: Chorale-Preludes, Collection (Walcha)

G major, à la gigue (BWV 577)
M. Salvador   in ‡ *TMS. 3/4*
(*Schubert, Franck, etc.*) [St. Louis Cath. organ]

G minor "Little" (BWV 578)
M-C. Alain   ‡ *DFr. 147*
(*Fantaisias & Fugues*)
H. Walcha   ♭ *Pol. 37066*
(*Fugue, D minor*)
A. Marchal   V‡ *Era.LDE 1024*
(*Toccata & Fugue, D mi.*) [St. Eustache organ]
A. V. Nuñez   ‡ *SOT. 1056*
(*Vivaldi Concerto 2, & Fantasia & Fugue*)
☆ E. P. Biggs (♭ *AmC.A 1882*; ♭ *Phil.A 40900E*)

— ARR. ORCH.   Stokowski
☆ Orch.—Stokowski   **G.DB 21570**
(*Cantata 147—Jesu, joy . . .*)   (♭ *7R 170*)
(also in ♭ *G.7ER 5004: 7ERW 5004;* Vic.*ERA 89*;
   & ‡ *G.FALP 281*)
☆ Philadelphia—Stokowski (in ‡ *Cam.CAL 120*)

— ARR. ORCH.   Goldschmidt
Champs-Élysées Th.—Goldschmidt
              ‡ **LT.DTL 93053**
(*Concertos, etc.*)   (‡ *Sel. 320.C.012*)

— ARR. 2 ACCORDEONS & CBS.   (in ‡ *Capri. I*)

Passacaglia & Fugue, C minor (BWV 582)
K. Richter   ‡ **D.LXT 5110**
(*Toccata & Fugue, D mi., etc.; & Liszt*) (‡ *Lon.LL 1174*)
M-C. Alain   ‡ *DFr. 136*
(*Preludes & Fugues*)   (‡ *HS.HSL 154*)
(*Prel. & F. E flat maj. only, on* ‡ *DFr.EX 25016*)
☆ H. Walcha (PV. 1430; ♭ *Pol. 37083*)
   F. Asma (‡ *Epic.LC 3025* & in ‡ *Phi.S 04009L*)

— ARR. PF. (Double keyboard)
G. Johansen   in ‡ **AD. set 1**
(*Variations, Goldberg*)   (pte. issue)
— ARR. ORCH.   Respighi
☆ San Francisco Sym.—Monteux   ‡ *Vic.LM 1799*
(*Berlioz & Beethoven*)   (‡ *ItV.A12R 0158, d.c*)
— ARR. ORCH.   Stokowski
☆ Orch.—Stokowski (in ‡ *G.FALP 282;* ItV.*A12R 0022;*
   & ‡ *Vic.LRM 7033:* ♭ set ERB 7033)
— ARR. ORCH.   Ormandy
☆ Philadelphia—Ormandy (in ‡ *AmC.ML 4797*)
— ARR. ORCH.   Goedike
State Sym.—Rakhlin (‡ *USSR.D 644*)

Pastorale, F major (BWV 590)
M-C. Alain   in ‡ *DFr. 120*
(*Fantasia, & Sonatas*)   (‡ *HS.HSL 120, in set L*)
☆ H. Walcha (♭ *Pol. 37067*)
   E. White (♭ *FMer.MEP 14522*)

---

[1] The final allegro is omitted and replaced by Fugue, G minor.

... **1st & 2nd Movts.** only
P. Isolffson   **G.DB 30001**
(*Chorale Preludes*)

... **Aria** only   — ARR. VLC. & ORCH.
☆ P. Casals & Perpignan Fest. Orch.
     (in ♯ *AmC.ML 4926* & ♭ *A 1922*)

PRELUDES & FUGUES
COLLECTIONS
D major (BWV 532) G major (BWV 541) C major (BWV 545)
B minor (BWV 544) E minor (BWV 548)
   M-C. Alain [St. Merry organ]   ♯ **DFr. 131**
                         (♯ HS.HSL 148)

C major (BWV 531) G minor (BWV 535) D minor (BWV 539)
C minor (BWV 546) E minor (BWV 552) E minor (BWV 533)
   M-C. Alain [St. Merry organ]   ♯ **DFr. 143**
   (E minor BWV 552 also on ♯ *EX 25016*)

F minor (BWV 534) A major (BWV 536)
A minor (BWV 543) C major (BWV 547)
   M-C. Alain [St. Merry organ]   ♯ **DFr. 136**
   (*Passacaglia & Fugue, C minor*)   (♯ HS.HSL 159)

B minor (BWV 544) C major (BWV 547) E minor (BWV 533)
   P. Cochereau   ♯ **OL.LD 119**
   [Organ of Notre Dame, Paris]

A minor (BWV 543) C major (BWV 531) D minor (BWV 533)
D major (BWV 532) B minor (BWV 544)
   ☆ R. Noehren (♯ *Pac.LDAA 31/2*; ♯ *Allo. 3147*)

A major (BWV 536) C major (BWV 531) A minor (BWV 543)
   ☆ C. Weinrich (in ♯ *MGM E 3015*)

---

(8) "Short" Preludes & Fugues (BWV 553-560)
... **Nos. 1, 2, 4, 8**
☆ E. White (♭ *FMer.MEP 14504*; ♭ *Mer.EP 1-5016*)

... **No. 2, D minor**
P. Isolffson   **G.DB 30004**
(*Chorale-Preludes*) [org. of All Souls, Langham Place, London]

INDIVIDUAL PRELUDES & FUGUES
A major (BWV 536)
☆ H. Walcha (*below*)   ♭ *Pol. 37022*

A minor (BWV 551)
H. Walcha   ♭ *Pol. 37047*
(*Prelude & Fugue, G major*) [Schnitger org., Cappel]

. **minor** (BWV 543)
☆ F. Heitmann   ♯ *T.TW 30003*
(*Toccata & Fugue, D minor*) (& in † Organ Music)

— ARR. PF. Liszt
A. Collard   V♯ *Sat.MSAS 5005*
(*Saint-Saëns*)
S. Weissenberg   ♯ *Lum.LD 3-400*
(*Czerny, Haydn, Soler*)

B minor (BWV 544)
F. Viderø   ♯ *Fdn.FDL 1022*
(*Chorale Prelude*) [Org. of Sorø Chu. Denmark]
J. Perceval   ♯ *ArgOd.LDC 501*
(*Reger*) [Organ of Basilica of Mercy, Buenos Aires]
☆ H. Walcha (PV. 1428)

C major (BWV 531)
H. Walcha   **Pol. 1027**
(*Prelude & Fugue, E minor*) [Schnitger Organ, Cappel]
           (♭ 37048)

C major (BWV 545)
E. White   in ♯ **Moll.E4QP 7231**
(*Vierne, Reger, Widor, Dandrieu, etc.*)
[Organ of Washington Shrine, Alexandria, Va.]
G. Ramin (2ss)   *Eta. 320103*
           (o.n. 25.C. 022)
☆ H. Walcha (*above*) [Schnitger organ]   ♭ *Pol. 37022*

C major (BWV 547)
☆ H. Walcha (*below*)   PV. 1408

C major (BWV 553)
— ARR. BANDONEON
A. Barletta   in ♯ *SMC. 549*

C minor (BWV 546)
P. Isolfsson   **G.DB 30005**
[All Soul's Church, Langham Place, London]
R. Noehren   in ♯ *Allo. 3044*
☆ H. Walcha (*E minor, below*)   ♭ *Pol. 37046*

D major (BWV 532)
M. Mason   in ♯ *ASK. 7*
(*Crandell, Copland, etc.*)
☆ H. Walcha (*above*)   PV. 1427
— ARR. PF. Busoni
A. de Raco   ♯ *ArgOd.LDC 514*
(*Chopin & Mozart*)

D minor (BWV 539)
Anon. Artist   in ♯ *FSM. 402*

E minor ("Little") (BWV 533)
H. Walcha   **Pol. 1027**
(*Prelude & Fugue, C major*)   (♭ *37048*)
[Schnitger Organ, Cappel]
R. Noehren   **Aphe.AP 9**
(*Toccata & Fugue, D minor*)
[Organ of Grace Episcopal Chu., Sandusky, Ohio]
N. Coke-Jephcott   in ♯ *ASK. 8*
(*Ch. Prel., Vierne, etc.*) [Org. of Cath. S. John the Divine, N.Y.]
... **Fugue** only   ☆ R. K. Biggs (♭ *Cap.FAP 8236*)

E minor ("Great") (BWV 548)
A. Marchal   ♯ *Sel. 270.C.057*
(*Fantasias*)
☆ F. Germani (♯ *G.WDLP 1002: QDLP 6007: FMLP 1002:*
                        ♭ *7ERL 1031*)
   H. Walcha (♭ *Pol. 37046*)

E flat major ("St. Anne") (BWV 552)
P. Isolfsson (4ss)   **G.DB 30002/3**
☆ F. Heitmann (in ♯ *T.LSK 7033*; FT. 320.TC.073)
— ARR. ORCH.
☆ Chicago Sym.—Stock (in ♯ *Cam.CAL 192*)

G major ("The Great") (BWV 541)
W. Schetelich (2ss)   *Eta. 320106*
[Leipzig Heilandskirche org.]
            (o.n. 25-C.012: & ♯ *LPM 1025*)
☆ H. Walcha (*below*)   ♭ *Pol. 37049*
... **Prelude** only   V. Kuosma (*D.SD 5166*)
B. P. Joseph (pedal hpsi.) (in ♯ *SOT. 1131*)

G major (BWV 550)
H. Walcha   ♭ *Pol. 37047*
(*Prelude & Fugue, A minor*) [Schnitger Organ, Cappel]

G minor (BWV 535)
☆ H. Walcha (*above*)   ♭ *Pol. 37049*
... **Prelude** only   — ARR. PF. Siloti
☆ E. Ballon   in ♯ *D.LX 3070*[1]

SONATAS (BWV 525-530) 1727
No. 1, E flat major   No. 2, C minor
No. 3, D minor   No. 4, E minor
No. 5, C major   No. 6, G major
COMPLETE RECORDINGS
M-C. Alain   ♯ **DFr. 119/20**
(3ss—*Pastorale, Fantasias*)   (♯ HS.HSL 119/20, set L)
F. Germani   ♯ **G.CLP 1025/6**
(See *Organ works*, supra)   (♯ Vic. set LHMV 601)
☆ H. Walcha (4ss)   ♯ **HP.APM 14503/4**
           (in ♯ AmD.ARC 3013/4; also 6ss,
                 ♯ Pol. 13004, 13009, 13014)
☆ R. Noehren (Nos. 1, 3, 4, 6 on ♯ Allo. 3039;
               Nos. 2 & 5 on ♯ *Allo. 4002*)

Nos. 1 to 4
J. Eggington   ♯ **OL.LD 111**
[Organ of Meaux Cathedral]

---

[1] Announced but not issued.

No. 1, E flat major (BWV 525)
L. Thybo   # Phi.A 09801L
(Kommst du nun, Jesu; Walther & Thybo)
[Organ of Christianskirken, Lyngby, Denmark]

G. Faxon   in # ASK. 2
(above) [organ of St. Paul's Cath. Boston, U.S.A.]

No. 4, E minor (BWV 528)
E. Hilliar   # ASK. 4
(Couperin, Dupré, Arne, etc.)
[Organ of St. Mark's, Mt. Kisco, N.Y.]

No. 5, C major (BWV 529)
☆ H. Walcha (3ss)   PV. 1025/6S

Sonatina: See Cantata 106, *post*, & COLLECTIONS, *ante*

TOCCATAS & FUGUES
COLLECTIONS
D minor (Dorian)   (BWV 538)
F major   (BWV 540)
C major (Toccata, Adagio & Fugue)   (BWV 564)
D minor   (BWV 565)
E major   (BWV 566)
M-C. Alain   # DFr. 146/7
(BWV 566 on # DFr. 147 with *Fantasias & Fugues, & Fugue, G minor*)

D minor (Dorian)   (BWV 538)
C major (Toccata, Adagio & Fugue)   (BWV 564)
☆ H. Walcha [St. Jakobikirche org.]   # Pol. 13024

C major (Toccata, Adagio & Fugue) (BWV 564)
☆ F. Asma (in # Epic.LC 3025 & in # Phi.S 04009L)

... **Adagio** — ARR. PF. Hess
A. Kitain (in # Eso.ESP 3001)

D minor (Dorian) (BWV 538)
☆ H. Walcha (♭ *Pol. 37065*)
F. Germani (♭ *G.7PW 114/5*)

... **Toccata** only
A. Wyton   in # ASK. 6
(Stanley, Sowerby, etc.)
[org. Cath. of S. John the Divine, N.Y.]

☆ M. Dupré (JpV.SD 3097)

D minor (BWV 565)
K. Richter[1]   # D.LXT 5110
(Passacaglia, etc.; & Liszt)   (# Lon.LL 1174)

E. Power Biggs[2]   # AmC.ML 5032
[Toccata only, with *Purcell, Sweelinck, Buxtehude,* on
EPhi.ABL 3066; AmC.ML 4971 in set SL 219]

J. Demessieux[1] (n.v.)   # D.LW 5095
(Fantasia & Fugue, C minor)

P. Kee   ♭ G.7EPH 1001
(1½ss—Ch. Prel.—Nun freut' euch . . .) [Alkmaar org.]

A. Marchal   V# Era.LDE 1024
(Fugue, G minor) [St. Sulpice organ]

P. Isolffson   G.DB 30000
[org. of All Souls, Langham Place, London] (ArgA. 266602)
R. Elmore *(Franck, Handel, etc.)*   in # Cant.MRR 270
R. Noehren *(Prel. & Fugue, E mi.)*   Aphe.AP 9
A. E. Floyd [Melbourne Town Hall] in # Spot.SC 1002
(Handel, Wesley, Schumann, etc.)
R. Foort   in # SOT. 1054
                                    (& # SOT. 10545)
G. Ramin (2ss) (o.n. 25-C.023)   Eta. 20-104
W. Schetelich (2ss)   Eta. 320105
[Leipzig Heilandskirche org.]
                           (o.n. 25-C 011; & # LPM 1025)
☆ H. Walcha   # Pol. 13025
(Toccatas & Fugues, F ma. & E ma.) (& 2ss, ♭ 37030)
  ☆ G. Jones (G.C 4214)
  F. Heitmann (# T.TW 30003 & in † Org. Recital)
  R. K. Biggs (♭ Cap.FAP 8236)
  E. P. Biggs (o.v.) (♭ AmC.A 1882; ♭ Phi.A 409001E)
  A. Schreiner (in # MMS. 100W
                        & in # MMS. 54 Spec.)

... **Toccata** only
M. Salvador   in # TMS. 1/2
(Gigout, Gounod, Purcell, etc.)
— ARR. ORCH. Stokowski
  ☆ Orch.—Stokowski (in # Vic.LRM 7033: ♭ set ERB 7033)
— ARR. ORCH. Ormandy
  ☆ Philadelphia—Ormandy (in # AmC.ML 4797)
— ARR. ACCORDEON(s)
  F. Boscaini (in V# FestF.FLD 18)
  Wurthner Accordeon Orch. (Pat. PAT 163)

E major[3] (BWV 566)
H. Walcha   PV. 1429
(Fugue, D minor) [Schnitger Organ, Cappel]
(Toccatas & Fugues, F ma. & D mi. on # Pol. 13025)

F major (BWV 540)
H. Walcha   PV. 1425/6S
(3ss) [Schnitger Organ, Cappel]
(Toccatas & Fugues, E maj. & D min. on # Pol. 13025)

TRIOS (BWV 583, 585)
SEE: COLLECTIONS: Heiller, M-C. Alain, *above*

C. CHAMBER MUSIC

(6) SONATAS, Violin unacc. (BWV 1001-6)
COMPLETE RECORDINGS
J. Martzy   # C.CX 1286/8
(6ss)   (# Angel. 35280/2)
R. Schroeder[4]   # AmC.ML 4743/5
(6ss)   (set SL 189)
E. Telmanyi[5]   # D.LXT 2951/3
(6ss)   (# Lon. set. LLA 20)
J. Heifetz   # Vic. set LM 6105
(6ss) (# ItV.A12R 0051/3)   (♭ set WDM 6105)
H. Szeryng (6ss)   # Od.ODX 122/4
  ☆ A. Schneider (# Clc. 6285 & 6287/9)

No. 1, G minor
N. Milstein   # DCap.CTL 7088
(No. 4)   (# Cap.P 8298)
I. Oistrakh   # CdM.LDA 8092
(Vitali & Mozart) *(idem, Wieniawski, etc.,* on
Van.VRS 461; *Vln. & clav. Sonata 5, & Vitali,*
on # Csm.CRLP 193, prob. d.v.)
J. Olevsky *(No. 4)*   # West.WL 5306
... **Fugue** only
— ARR. GUITAR
  C. Aubin († *Guitar Recital)*   in # Eko.LG 1
  ☆ A. Segovia (in # MGM.E 3015 & n.v., †#AmD.DL 9795;
    D.UAT 273594)
— — ARR. 4 TROMBONES Thilde
  Paris Trombone Qtt.   in # D.LX 3145
... **Siciliano** only
— ARR. GUITAR
  ☆ A. Schneider (in ♭ Mer.EP 1-5059; ♭ FMer.MEP 14519)
  ☆ A. Segovia (in † Segovia Programme, # B.AXTL 1060)
— — ARR. 4 HORNS Thilde
  Paris Horn Qtt.   in # D.LX 3143

No. 2, B minor (Partita No. 1)
... **Sarabande & Bourrée** only
  ☆A. Schneider (in ♭ Mer.EP 1-5061; ♭ FMer.MEP 14514)
— — ARR. GUITAR
  C. Aubin († *Guitar recital)*[6]   in # Eko.LG 1
... **Courante (Double, Presto)** only
  ☆ A. Schneider (in ♭ Mer.EP 1-5059; ♭ FMer.MEP 14519)
... **Sarabande** only
  A. Rácz (cymbalom), A. Rácz (pf.) (Qual.ZN 3001)
... **Bourrée** only — ARR. PF. Saint-Saëns
  E. Burton   in # CEd. 1024
— — ARR. GUITAR Segovia
  M. D. Cano   Dur.AI 10232
  (Cello Suite 3—Courante, arr.)   (in # MSE 2)
  G. Zepoll[7]   in # Nix.SLPY 142
                                        (# SOT. 1024)
  L. Almeida (in # DCap.LC 6669; Cap.H 193)
  M. A. Funes (ArgOd. 57047)[7]
  ☆ A. Segovia (in † # D.UAT 273142)

---

[1] Organ of Victoria Hall, Geneva.
[2] Organ of Royal Festival Hall, London. ML 5032 also contains the Toccata recorded 13 times on 13 different organs.
[3] Also called *Prelude & Fugue.*
[4] Played with "Bach" bow. Recorded Gunsbach, Alsace, September 1952, under supervision of A. Schweitzer.
[5] Played with Vega "Bach" bow.
[6] The Sarabande is listed as from "Suite 4 for Vln." but from information supplied by M. Aubin it would appear to be this.
[7] Double only.

No. 3, A minor (Sonata No. 2)
J. Olevsky (*No. 6*) # **West.WN 18072**
... 1st movt. only: V. Abedjiev *Bulg. 1336*
... 3rd movt. only: ☆ A. Schneider (♭ *Mer.EP 1-5061*)
— — ARR. STR. ORCH. Bachrich
In *Suite for Str. Orch, see* MISC. *below*

No. 4, D minor (Partita No. 2)
N. Milstein # **DCap.CTL 7088**
(*No. 1*) (# *Cap.P 8298*)
(*Chaconne only, with* Milstein: *Paganiniana on*
DCap.CCL 7526; Cap.H 8297)
T. Magyar # **Phi.N 00238L**
(*No. 6*)
Z. Francescatti # **AmC.ML 4935**
(*No. 6*)
J. Olevsky # **West.WL 5306**
(*No. 1*)
W. Schneiderhan (2ss) # **HP.AP 13029**
(*Chaconne only, also* ♭ *Pol. 37051*)
☆ E. Telmanyi, with "Bach bow" (# *Tono.LPA 34002*)
... **Chaconne** only
A. Grumiaux # **Bo.B 202**
(*Mozart, Fiocco*)
R. Odnoposoff # **MMS. 54**
(*Vln. Concerto, E major*)
☆ R. Ricci (♭ *AmVox.VIP 45360*)
A. Schneider (♭ *Mer.EP 1-5060*; ♭ *FMer.MEP 14518*)
— — ARR. PF. Busoni
A. Brailowsky # *Vic.LRM 7050*
(*Vivaldi Concerto, org., D minor, Arr.*) (♭ *set ERB 7050*;
FV. 330205)
A. Bundervoët # **LT.DTL 93051**
(*Wachet aufl, & Toccatas*) (# *Sel. 270.C.048*)
A. Kitain ("Siena" pf.) # *Eso.ESP 3001*
(*Partita 1, Cantata 147 excpt., etc.*)
C. Giraud-Chambeau # *Sat.LDA 7002*
(*Chopin: Fantasie*)
☆ A. B. Michelangeli # *G.FBLP 1044*
(*Brahms*) (# *QBLP 1044*)
☆ R. Gianoli (*Fantasia, Toccata*) in # *Nix.WLP 5101*
— — ARR. GUITAR Segovia
A. Segovia (n.v.) # **B.AXTL 1069**
(† *Segovia Evening II*) (# *AmD.DL 9751*)
☆ A. Segovia (o.v.) (in # *MGM.E 3015* & # *Roy. 1422*;
♭ *MusH.LP 1076/7*)
— — ARR. ORCH. L. Steinberg
Leningrad Phil.—Khaikin (3ss) USSR. 018634/6
— — ARR. ORCH. Stokowski
☆ Orch.—Stokowski (in # *G.FALP 282*; ItV.A12R 0022)

No. 5, C major
... Fuga — ARR. 4 HORNS Thilde
Paris Horn Qtt. (in # *D.LX 3143*)

No. 6, E major (Partita No. 3)
Z. Francescatti (*No. 4*) # **AmC.ML 4935**
T. Magyar (*No. 4*) # **Phi.N 00238L**
J. Olevsky (*No. 3*) # **West.WN 18072**
... Prelude & Gavotte en rondeau, only
☆ A. Schneider (in ♭ *Mer.EP 1-5059*; ♭ *FMer.MEP 14519*)
— — ARR. STR. ORCH. Bachrich
In *Suite for Strings, see* MISC. *below*
... Prelude only. ☆ Y. Menuhin (♭ *G.7RW 120*)
— — ARR. VLN. & PF. ☑ P. de Sarasate (in *AudA.LP 0079*)
... Gavotte only. — ARR. VLN. & PF. Kreisler
☆ F. Kreisler (in # *Vic.LCT 1142*)
— — ARR. GUITAR Segovia
A. Segovia (n.v.) in # **B.AXTL 1069**
(† *Segovia Evening II*) (# *AmD.DL 9751*)
— — ARR. ORCH
L.S.O.—Weldon C.DX 1896
(*Suite No. 3—Air*)
(C.SVX 50: ♭ *SCD 2030: SCDW 114*: in # *SX 1045*)

"SONATA" (Suite), A minor fl. unacc.
(BWV 1013)
P. Birkelund ♭ *Mtr.MCEP 3017*
J-P. Rampal (*below*) # *Sel. 320.C.027*
J. Wummer in # **West. set WAL 216**
(*below*) (# *Véga.C 30.A 20*)
☆ P. Kaplan (# *Allo. 4004*)

SONATAS, Flute & clavier
(1-3, fl. & clavier; 4-6, fl. & cont.)
No. 1, B minor No. 2, E flat major No. 3, A major
No. 4, C major No. 5, E minor No. 6, E major
(BWV 1030/5)
"No. 7", G minor (BWV 1020; BG.IX) orig. vln. & cont.
COMPLETE RECORDING
J. Wummer & F. Valenti (hpsi.)
West. set WAL 216
(3½ss—*Sonata, unacc. fl.*) (# *Véga. C30. A 19/20*)
COLLECTIONS
Nos. 1 to 6, COMPLETE
☆ J. Baker & S. Marlowe (hpsi.) (# *D.UAT 273077/8*)
Nos. 4 to 7
☆ J-P. Rampal, R. Veyron-Lacroix (hpsi.) & vlc.
[Realised by Veyron-Lacroix] # **LT.DTL 93058**
(# *T.LE 6544*; # *Sel. 320.C.021*)
[No. 4 also, ? d.v., on V#*BàM.LD 1001*]
Nos. 1, 2 & 7
P. Birkelund & F. Viderø (hpsi.)
HS.HSL 3067
Nos. 1, 2 & 3
L. v. Pfersmann, I. Ahlgrimm (hpsi.),
J. Herrmann (gamba) # **Phi.A 00265L**
J-P. Rampal & R. Veyron-Lacroix (hpsi.)
(*above*) # **Sel. 320.C.027**

No. 1, B minor (BWV 1030)
G. Scheck & F. Neumeyer (hpsi.) PV. 2447/8S
(3ss)
☆ P. Kaplan & E. Bodky (hpsi.) (# *AFest.CFR 10-575*)

No. 2, E flat major (BWV 1031)
☆ P. Kaplan & E. Bodky (hpsi.) & vlc. (# *Allo. 4003*)
... Siciliana — ARR. PF. Kempff
☆ W. Kempff (in # *D.LXT 2820; Lon.LL 791*)
D. Lipatti (♭ *C.SCBQ 3008: ESBF 112: SCBF 110*;
in # *C.FCX 494*; AmC.ML 4633)

No. 5, E minor (BWV 1034)
K. Redel & I. Lechner (hpsi.) # **LOL.OL 50015**
(*Vln. sonatas, etc., below*) (# *OL.LD 52*)

No. 6, E major (BWV 1035)
P. Birkelund, L. Selbiger (hpsi.) & H. E. Deckert
(gamba) ♭ *G.7EBK 1000*

(3) SONATAS, vla. da gamba & clavier
(BWV 1027/9)
1. G major 2. D major 3. G minor
J. Scholz & E. G. Sartori (hpsi.)
E. & AmVox.PL 9010
A. Wenzinger & F. Neumeyer (hpsi.)
Pol. 14009
[Nos. 1 & 2 are ☆; No. 3 also on PV 2445/6S, 3ss]
(# *AmD. ARC 3009*)

No. 1, G major (BWV 1027) — ARR. VLC. & PF.
P. Fournier & E. Lush in # **D.LXT 2766**
(*Bloch, Kreisler, Debussy, etc.*) (in # *Lon.LL 700*)

No. 2, D major (BWV 1028) — ARR. VLC. & PF.
G. Piatigorsky & R. Berkowitz # *Vic.LM 1792*
(*Prokofiev*) (# *FV.A 630224*; # ItV.A12R 0142)

No. 3, G minor (BWV 1029) — ARR. VLC. & PF.
☆P. Casals & P. Baumgartner # *C.CX 1110*
(*Chromatic Fantasia & Ital. Concerto*).

(6) SONATAS, vln. & clavier (BWV 1014/9)
No. 1, B minor No. 2, A major
☆ Y. Menuhin & L. Kentner (pf.) # *G.BLP 1026*
(*WBLP 1026*)

No. 2, A major (BWV 1015)
Z. Francescatti & R. Casadesus (pf.)
AmC.Pte.Rec.
(*Casadesus & Francescatti*)(For American Library in Paris)

☆ = Re-issue of a recording to be found in previous volumes.

SONATAS, vln. & clavier (*continued*)

No. 3, E major (BWV 1016)
I. Stern & A. Zakin (pf.)   ‡ **EPhi.ABL 3011**
(*below*)   (‡ AmC.ML 4862; ‡ Phi.A 01126L)

☆ Y. Menuhin & W. Landowska (hpsi.) ‡ **Vic.LCT 1120**
(*Concerto, 2 vlns., D minor*) (♭ *set WCT 1120;*
‡ G.FJLP 5018)

No. 4, C minor (BWV 1017)
... Siciliano — ARR. ORCH.   Stokowski
☆ Orch.—Stokowski (in ‡ Vic.LM 1875: ♭ *set ERB 52:*
♭ *ERA 244;* ‡ G.FALP 282; ItV.A12R 0022)

No. 5, F minor (BWV 1018)
D. Oistrakh & L. Oborin (pf.) ‡ **Mon.MWL 311**
(*Schubert*)   (2ss, V‡ CdM.LDYA 8108)
(*Mozart: Trio K564, & Kings. 261*)
(*Unacc. Sonata No. 1, & Vitali, on* ‡ Csm.CRLP 193)

SONATAS, various: accompanied vln.
E minor (BWV 1023) vln. & cont. ("Partita")
I. Stern & A. Zakin (pf.)   ‡ **EPhi.ABL 3011**
(*Sonatas, above & below*)(‡ AmC.ML 4862; Phi.A 01126L)

M. Rostal, F. Pelleg (hpsi.), & A. Tusa (vlc.)
‡ **CHS.CHS 1174**
(*Biber & Tartini*) [Ed. H. Ferguson]   (‡ Clc. 6187)

G major (BWV 1021) vln. & cont.
U. Grehling, I. Lechner (hpsi.), & vlc.
‡ **LOL.OL 50015**
(*above & below*)   (‡ OL.LD 52)

L. Friedemann,[1] F. Viderø (hpsi.) & H. E.
Deckert (gamba)   ‡ **HS.HSL 95**
(*Corelli, Leclair & Handel*)

G minor (BWV 1020) vln. & clavier[2]
I. Stern & A. Zakin (pf.)   ‡ **EPhi.ABL 3011**
(*above*)   (‡ AmC.ML 4862; ‡ Phi.A 01126L)

G. Barinova & S. Richter (pf.)   *USSR. 21412/5*
(4ss)

SONATAS, Two violins & continuo
D minor (BWV 1036) (doubtful)
K. Redel (fl.), H. Winschermann (ob.),
I. Lechner (hpsi.), & vlc.   ‡ **LOL.OL 50015**
(*above & below*)   (‡ OL.LD 52)
G. Barinova, R. Sobolevsky (vlns.), T. Nikolayeva (pf.),
& vlc. (USSRM.D 01302)

C major (BWV 1037)
D. & I. Oistrakh, V. Yampolsky (pf.)
V‡ *CdM.LDY 8138*

C. Monteux (fl.), H. Shulman (ob.), S. Marlowe
(hpsi.), & B. Greenhouse (vlc.) ‡ **Eso.ES 528**
(*Handel*)   (‡ Cpt.MC 20084)

☆ W. Schneiderhan, G. Swoboda, F. Holetschek (hpsi.),
& vlc. (‡ Sel. LPG 8717)

SONATA, Flute, violin & continuo
G major (BWV 1038) (doubtful)
K. Redel (fl.), U. Grehling (vln.), I. Lechner
(hpsi.), & vlc.   ‡ **LOL.OL 50015**
(*above*)   (‡ OL.LD 52)

☆ J. Wummer, I. Stern, E. Istomin (pf.) ‡ **C.CX 1109**
(*Vln. & Clav. Concertos & Toccata & Fugue*) (‡ FCX 325)

☆ P. Kaplan, R. Posselt, E. Bodky (hpsi.), & vlc.
(‡ Allo. 4004)

SONATA, Two flutes & clavier
G major (BWV 1039)
(a version of Gamba Sonata No. 1)
☆ P. Kaplan, L. Schaefer, E. Bodky (hpsi.), & vlc.
(‡ Allo. 4003; AFest.CFR 10-575)

SUITES, Vlc. unacc.
No. 1, G major (BWV 1007)
A. Janigro   ‡ **West.WL 5217**
(*Suite No. 3*)
J. Starker   ‡ **Nix.PLP 582**
(*Suite No. 4*)   (‡ Per.SPL 582; Cpt.MC 20047)
E. Mainardi   ‡ **HP.APM 14029**
(*Suite No. 2*)

H. Honegger (2ss)   ♭ *Mtr.MCEP 3016*
D. Shafran   ‡ **U. 5177G**
(*Clavier Partita No. 3*) (Courante & Minuet also,
USSR. 18919/20)

... Prelude — ARR. GUITAR Segovia
M. L. Anido (ArgOd. 57055)

☆ A. Segovia (in ‡ D.UAT 273141)

No. 2, D minor (BWV 1008)
E. Mainardi   ‡ **HP.APM 14029**
(*Suite No. 1*)
A. Janigro   ‡ **West.WL 5348**
(*Suite No. 6*)
☆ P. Casals   ‡ **Vic.LCT 1104**
(*Suite No. 3*)   (♭ *set WCT 1104*)
— ARR. VLA
☆ L. Fuchs (‡ D.UAT 273074)

No. 3, C major (BWV 1009)
E. Mainardi   ‡ **Pol. 14044**
(*Suite No. 4*)
A. Janigro   ‡ **West.WL 5217**
(*Suite No. 1*)
E. Bayens   ‡ *DT.LGM 65023*
                         (‡ T.LS 6059)
☆ P. Casals   ‡ **Vic.LCT 1104**
(*Suite No. 2*)   (♭ *set WCT 1104*)
☆ J. Starker (‡ Clc. 6164)
... Courante — ARR. GUITAR Segovia
M. D. Cano   *Dur.AI 10232*
(*Vln. Sonata 2—Bourrée, arr.*)   (in ‡ *MSE 2*)
C. Aubin († Guitar Recital)   in ‡ Eko.LG 1
☆ A. Segovia (in ‡ MGM.E 3015; & in † ‡ D.UAT 273142)
... Bourrée — ARR. GUITAR Segovia
A. Segovia (in † Segovia Evening II, ‡ B.AXTL 1069;
AmD.DL 9751)

No. 4, E flat major (BWV 1010)
E. Mainardi   ‡ **Pol. 14044**
(*Suite No. 3*)
J. Starker   ‡ **Nix.PLP 582**
(*Suite No. 1*)   (‡ Per.SPL 582; Cpt.MC 20047)
A. Janigro   ‡ **West.WN 18073**
(*Suite No. 5*)
— ARR. VLA.: L. Fuchs (*No. 5*)   ‡ **AmD.DL 9660**

No. 5, C minor (BWV 1011)
E. Mainardi (2ss)   ‡ *Pol. 13034*
A. Janigro (*No. 4*)   ‡ **West.WN 18073**
— ARR. VIOLA: L. Fuchs (*No. 4*)   ‡ **AmD.DL 9660**
... Prelude & Allemande — ARR. GUITAR
(after Bach's Suite G mi., BWV 995, for lute; see *ante*)
S. Behrend   *Eta. 130114*
(*Lute Suites, & Sanz*)
... Courante & Gigue
M. Rostropovitch (*USSR. 18976/7 & USSRM.D 00325*)

No. 6, D major (BWV 1012)
A. Janigro (*No. 2*)   ‡ **West.WL 5348**
☆ A. Baldovino (vlc. piccolo) (‡ *Sup.SLPM 63*)
J. Starker (‡ Clc. 6164)
— ARR. VIOLA ☆ L. Fuchs (‡ D.UAT 273074)
... Prelude & Gavottes, only — ARR. GUITAR Lagoya
A. Lagoya (*Albeniz: Asturias*)   ｜ *Pat. ED 2*
... Gavotte(s) — ARR. GUITAR Segovia
M. D. Cano   *Dur.AI 1023*
("*Little*" *Prelude, C minor*)   (in ‡ *MSE 2*)
☆ A. Segovia (in † ‡ D.UAT 273141)

=====

D. ORCHESTRAL

BRANDENBURG CONCERTOS
                    (BWV 1046/51) 1721
COMPLETE RECORDINGS
Schola Cantorum Basiliensis—Wenzinger
                         Pol. various
No. 1 on PV.2455/6: ‡ HP.APM 14011; also ‡ Pol. 18148
[R. Felicani (violino piccolo), H. Winschermann
(ob.), & 2 corni di caccia]

---

[1] Contemporary violin.   [2] *See also* Flute Sonata "No. 7", *above*.

No. 2 on PV.2457: ♯ *HP.AP 13016*; also ♯ *Pol. 16079*
& ♭ *37052* [A. Zeyer (tpt. in F), G. Scheck (flauto dolce), H. Winschermann (ob.), W. Kägi (vln.)]
No. 3 on PV.2452: ♯ *HP.AP 13016*; also ♯ *Pol. 16079*
& ♭ *37039*
No. 4 on PV.2453/4S: ♯ *HP.APM 14011*; also ♯ *Pol.* 18148 [W. Kägi (vln.), G. Scheck & V. Kägi (fl.)]
No. 5 on PV.2422/3: ♯ *HP.APM 14012*; also ♯ *Pol.* 18149 [E. Müller (hpsi.), J. Bopp (fl.), R. Felicani (vln.)]
No. 6 on PV.2414/5S: ♯ *HP.APM 14012*; also ♯ *Pol.* 18149 [W. Kägi & M. Majer (viole da braccio), A. Wenzinger (vlc.)]

Saar Cha.—Ristenpart   ♯ **DFr. 110/1**
[L. Vaillant (tpt.), U. Grehling (vln.), P. Pierlot (ob.), J.-P. Rampal (fl.), E. Friedland & C. Hampe (recorders in No. 4), F. Neumeyer (hpsi.)]
(No. 5 also on ♯ *DFr.EX 25005*; Nos. 2 & 3 on ♯ *DFr.EX 25013*)

Soloist Ens.—Horenstein
(4ss)   ♯ **E. & AmVox. set DL 122**
[A. Holler (tpt.), W. Schneiderhan (vln.),[1] F. Wächter (ob.), C. Wanausek (fl.), K. Trötzmüller & P. Angerer (recorders in No. 4), P. Angerer (solo hpsi. & vla.), J. Nebois (hpsi. continuo), etc.]
(Nos. 1-4 on ♯ *Orb.BL 701*)

Vienna St. Op. Cha.—Prohaska ♯ **Van.BG 540/2**
[H. Wobitsch (tpt.), J. Tomasow (vln.),[1] K. Mayrhofer (ob.), H. Rezniček (fl.), K. Trötzmüller (recorder in No. 4), A. Heiller (hpsi.)]
(Nos. 2 & 3 also on ♯ *MTW. 19*: ♭ set *EP 19*; Nos. 3 & 4 on ♯ *Nix.PVL 7016*)

Basle Cha. Orch.—Sacher
    ♯ **Phi.A 00214/5L & A 00719R**
(5ss—*Vln. & Ob. Concerto with No. 6*)
[A. Haneuse (tpt.), R. Felicani (vln.) E. Shann (ob.), J. Bopp (fl.), E. Müller (hpsi.)] (♯ Epic. set SC 6008, 4ss)
[No. 6 also ♯ *EPhi.NBR 6028*]

Cento Soli—Scherchen (6ss)   ♯ **CFD. 34/6**
[R. Delmotte (tpt.), G. Tessier (vln.), R. Casier (ob.), MM. Lavaillotte & Hériché (fls.), R. Gerlin (hpsi.)]

Munich Pro Arte—Redel   ♯ **Era.LDE 3033/4**
[A. Scherbaum (tpt.), R. Barchet (vln.), P. Pierlot (ob.), K. Redel (fl.), H. Priegnitz (hpsi.)]

Hamburg Cha.—Schüchter   ♯ **Pat.DTX 165/6**
[A. Scherbaum (tpt.), B. Hamann (vln.),[1] H. Eggers (ob.), G. Otto (fl.), F. Conrad & H. M. Linde (recorders in No. 4), H. Bernstein (hpsi.)]

☆ London Baroque Ens.—Haas
    ♯ **Nix.WLP 6301-1/3**
[No. 5 with R. Veyron-Lacroix, hpsi.]
(Nos. 1 & 5 on ♯ *Sel.* LAG 1041, Nos. 3 & 6 on ♯ *Sel.LA 1042*, Nos. 2 & 4 on ♯ *Sel. 270.C.001*)

☆ W. Vacchiano (tpt.), H. Holberg (vln.), S. Baker & F. Eyle (fls.), S. Marlowe (hpsi.), & Cha. Ens.—Reiner
    (♯ AmC.RL 3104/6)
Berlin Radio Cha.—Haarth, & (No. 2)—Rucht (4ss) (♯ Cum.CT 263/4)

Nos. 1, 2, 3
Danish State Radio Cha.—Wöldike (n.v.)
    ♯ **G.KALP 10**

No. 1, F major   vln., 3 obs., bsn., 2 hrns., str.
☆ Boston Sym.—Koussevitzky (♯ ItV.A12R 0090)

... Allegro, Andante, Minuet & Trios
— — ARR. Bach as Sinfonia, F major (BWV 1071)
Paris Collegium Musicum—Douatte
    ♯ **EPP.APG 124**
(*Vln. Concerto & Motet—Geist hilft . . .*)

No. 2, F major   tpt., fl., ob., vln., strs.
Philharmonia—Fischer [H. Jackson, tpt.]
    ♯ **G.ALP 1084**
(No. 5)   (♯ WALP 1084: QALP 10037: FALP 308)
       (♯ Vic.LHMV 8; ArgA.LPC 11542)
Berlin Cha.—v. Benda [H. Eichler, tpt.]
    ♯ **DT.LGX 66012**
(No. 5)   (♯ T.LE 6503)
Sonor Sym.—Ledermann   ♯ **Pde. 1016**
(No. 3)
☆ Boston Sym.—Koussevitzky (♯ Cam.CAL 147; Allegro assai only, in ♯ Vic.LM 1877)

No. 3, G major   3 vlns., 3 vlas., 3 vlcs., cbs.
Netherlands Phil.—Goehr   V♯ *MMS. 93*
Sonor Sym.—Ledermann   ♯ *Pde. 1016*
(No. 2)
Berlin Sym.—Balzer   ♯ *Roy. 1438*
(Suite No. 4)
Boston Orch. Soc.—Page   ♯ *SOT. 1062*
(Suite, below; Stravinsky & Villa-Lobos)
Berlin Radio—Rucht   *Eta. 120112/3*
(3ss—Suite 2, Polonaise) (o.n. 25-C 019/20; & ♯ LPM 1002)
☆ Copenhagen Palace Cha.—Wöldike ♯ Vic.LHMV 1048
(Nos. 4 & 5)
☆ Ansbach Fest.—Leitner (PV. 72358: ♯ Pol. 16126)
Boston Sym.—Koussevitsky (♯ Cam.CAL 174)[2]

No. 4, G major   vln., 2 fls., & str.
P. Rybar, P. L. Graf, W. Klemm & Winterthur Sym.—Goehr   ♯ *MMS. 13*
(No. 5)   (♯ ANix.MLPY 13; ♯ Clc. 11009)
Anon. & Leipzig Gewandhaus—Ramin
    Eta. 120114/6
(5ss—Suite 3, Air)   (o.n. 25-C 016/8)
W. Bemdsen, H. Hoefs (fls.), R.I.A.S. Sym.—Sawallisch   ♯ *Rem. 199-194*
☆ L. Hansen (vln.) & Danish Radio Cha.—Wöldike
(Nos. 3 & 5)   ♯ Vic.LHMV 1048
☆ Boston Sym.—Koussevitzky (♯ Cam.CAL 174)

No. 5, D major   clavier, fl., vln., str.
F. Pelleg (hpsi.), P. Graf, P. Rybar & Winterthur Sym.—Goehr   ♯ *MMS. 13*
(No. 4)   (♯ ANix.MLPY 13; ♯ Clc. 11009)
E. Fischer (pf.), G. Morris, M. Parikian & Philharmonia Orch.   ♯ *G.ALP 1084*
(No. 2)   (♯ WALP 1084: QALP 10037: FALP 308)
       (& ♯ ArgA.LPC 11542; ♯ Vic.LHMV 8)
S. Kind (hpsi.), A. Nicolet, V. Brero, & Berlin Cha.—Benda   ♯ *DT.LGX 66012*
(No. 2)   (♯ T.LE 6503)
Emil Gilels (pf.), N. Kharykovsky, Elis. Gilels, U.S.S.R.—Kondrashin   ♯ *USSR.D 1432/3*
C. Chailley-Richez (pf.), J-P. Rampal, C. Ferras & Paris Cha.—Enesco   ♯ *D.FAT 173530*
(Concerto, A minor)
☆ I. Nef (hpsi.), E. Defrancesco, A. Wachsmut-Loew, Lausanne Cha.—Desarzens   ♯ *OL.LD 69*
(Concerto, BWV 1044)
☆ H. D. Koppel (hpsi.), P. Birkelund, L. Hansen & Danish Radio Cha.—Wöldike   ♯ Vic.LHMV 1048
(Nos. 3 & 4)
☆ L. Foss (pf.), G. Laurent, R. Burgin & Boston Sym.—Koussevitzky (♯ Cam.CAL 147)

No. 6, B flat major   2 vlas., 2 gambas, vlc., cbs.
☆ Boston Sym.—Koussevitzky (♯ ItV.A12R 0190)

CONCERTOS, Solo instrument(s) & str. orch.

CLAVIER & ORCH.

COLLECTIONS
A major   (BWV 1055)   D minor   (BWV 1052)
F minor   (BWV 1056)
R. Reinhardt (hpsi.) & Pro Arte Cha.—Redel
    ♯ *Sel. 320.C.061*
[D minor also on ♯ Sel. 320.C.091 with clavier, vln. & fl. concerto, below]
F. Viderø (hpsi.) & Copenhagen Collegium Musicum—Friisholm   ♯ *HS.HSL 92*
    (& in ♯ set HSL-K)

A major   (BWV 1055)
C. Chailley-Richez (pf.) & Paris Cha.—Enesco
    ♯ *D.FAT 173068*
(Concerto, F major, clav. & 2 fls.)
T. Nikolayeva (pf.) & State Sym.—Kondrashin
(6ss)   *USSR. 21105/10*
— ARR. OBOE D'AMORE, STR. & CONT. Tovey
L. Goossens & Philharmonia—Susskind
    ♯ *AmC.ML 4782*
(Ostern-Oratorium, excpts; Cimarosa, Marcello, Handel)

---

[1] Violino piccolo in No. 1.   [2] The *Sinfonia* of Cantata 4 is interpolated as a slow movement.

D major (BWV 1054)
(from Vln. Concerto, E major, BWV 1042)
C. Chailley-Richez (pf.) & Paris Cha.—Enesco
(*Concerto, 3 claviers*)   ♯ **D.FAT 173119**

☆ I. Nef. (hpsi.) & Cha.Ens.—Colombo ♯ **LOL.OL 50042**
(*below*)

☆ M. v. d. Lyck (hpsi.) & Stuttgart Ton-Studio—Michael
(♯ Clc. 6139)

D minor (BWV 1052)
H. Elsner (hpsi.) & Stuttgart Pro Musica
—Reinhardt (*below*)   ♯ **AmVox.PL 9510**
F. Neumeyer (hpsi.) & Saar Cha.—Ristenpart
(2ss)   ♯ **DFr.EX 25027**
(*Concerto, E ma.*, on ♯ DFr. 78)
K. Richter (hpsi.) & Ansbach Fest. Ens.
(*below*)   ♯ **D.NLK 40105**
C. Chailley-Richez (pf.) & Paris Cha.—Enesco
(*below*)   ♯ **D.FAT 173053**

☆ W. Landowska (hpsi.) & orch.—Bigot ♯ **G.FJLP 5056**
(*Handel: Concerto*)

☆ L. Foss (pf.) & Zimbler Sinfonietta (♯ D.UMT 263575)

E major (BWV 1053)
H. Elsner (hpsi.) & Stuttgart Pro Musica
—Reinhardt (*above*)   ♯ **AmVox.PL 9510**
F. Neumeyer (hpsi.) & Saar Cha.—Ristenpart
(*above*)   ♯ **DFr. 78**
C. Chailley-Richez (pf.) & Paris Cha.—Enesco
(*Concerto, G mi.*)   ♯ **D.FAT 173050**

F minor (BWV 1056)
L. Selbiger (hpsi.) & Danish Radio Cha. Orch.
(3ss—*W.T.C. No. 1*)   ♮ **C.LDX 7023/4**
C. Chailley-Richez (pf.) & Paris Cha.—Enesco
(*above*)   ♯ **D.FAT 173053**

☆ I. Nef (hpsi.) & Cha. Ens—Colombo ♯ **LOL.OL 50042**
(*above*)

☆ C. Haskil (pf.) & Prades Fest.—Casals
(*Vln. Concerto, etc.*)   ♯ **C.CX 1109**

☆ L. Foss (pf.) & Zimbler Sinfonietta (♯ D.UMT 263575)

... 2nd movt. — ARR. PF. SOLO Cortot (*"Aria"*)
☆ A. Cortot (in ♯ G.ALP 1197: QALP 10080: FALP 349)

G minor (BWV 1058)
(from Vln. Concerto, BWV 1041)
C. Chailley-Richez (pf.) & Paris Cha.—Enesco
(*Concerto, E major*)   ♯ **D.FAT 173050**

TWO CLAVIERS & ORCHESTRA
C major (BWV 1061)
H. Elsner & R. Reinhardt (hpsis.) & Stuttgart
Pro Musica Orch.   ♯ **AmVox.PL 9580**
(*below, & vln. & ob. concerto*)
F. Viderø & S. Sørensen (hpsis.) & Copenhagen
Coll. Mus.—L. Friisholm   ♯ **HS.HSL 93**
(*below*)   (& in set HSL-K)
K. Richter & E. Müller (hpsis.) & Ansbach Fest.
Ens. (*above*)   ♯ **D.NLK 40105**
V. Appleton & D. Field (pfs.), Castle Hill
Fest. Orch.—Brief   ♯ **Nix.NCL 16007**
(*below*)   (♯ Per.SPL 700)
C. Chailley-Richez & F. le Gonidec (pfs.),
Paris Cha.—Enesco   ♯ **D.FAT 173094**
(*C minor, below*)

☆ H. Andreae, T. Sack (hpsis.) & Winterthur Sym.
—Dahinden (♯ Clc. 6165; ♯ MMS. 77)
R. Gerlin & M. Charbonnier (hpsis.) & Str. Orch.
—Sachs (in † ♯ HS.AS 31)
A. & K. U. Schnabel (pfs.), L.S.O.—Boult
(♯ Vic.LCT 1140)

C minor (BWV 1060)
L. Salter & C. Spinks (hpsis.) & London
Baroque Ens.—Haas   ♯ **P.PMA 1009**
(*C. P. E. Bach*)
H. Elsner & R. Reinhardt (hpsis.) & Stuttgart
Pro Musica Orch.   ♯ **AmVox.PL 9580**
(*above & below*)

F. Viderø & S. Sørensen (hpsis.) & Copenhagen
Coll. Mus.—L. Friisholm   ♯ **HS.HSL 93**
(*above*)   (& in set HSL-K)
V. Appleton & D. Field (pfs.) Castle Hill
Fest. Orch.—Brief   ♯ **Nix.NCL 16007**
(*above*)   (♯ Per.SPL 700)
C. Chailley-Richez & F. le Gonidec (pfs.) &
Paris Cha.—Enesco   ♯ **D.FAT 173094**
(*above*)

C minor (BWV 1062)
(from 2 vln. Concerto, BWV 1043)
F. Viderø, S. Sørensen (hpsis.) & Copenhagen
Coll. Mus.—L. Friisholm   ♯ **HS.HSL 115**
(*below*)   (& in set HSL-K)
C. Chailley-Richez & F. le Gonidec (pfs.),
Paris Cha.—Enesco   ♯ **D.FAT 173119**
(*Clavier Concerto, D major*)

THREE CLAVIERS & ORCHESTRA
C major (BWV 1064)
H. Elsner, R. Noll, F. Goebels (hpsis.) &
Stuttgart Pro Musica—R. Reinhardt
(*below*)   ♯ **E. & AmVox.PL 8670**
K. Richter, E. Müller, G. Aeschbacher, Ansbach
Fest.—Richter (*below*)   ♯ **D.LX 35001**
C. Chailley-Richez, F. le Gonidec, J-J. Painchaud
(pfs.), Paris Cha.—Enesco ♯ **D.FAT 173097**
(*below*)
G. Kuhn, G. Astorg, L. Rev (pfs.) & Champs-
Elysées Th. Orch.—Goldschmidt
                   ♯ **LT.DTL 93053**
(*below, & Ch. Prel. Nun komm ... & Fugue, G minor*)
                   (♯ Sel. 320.C.012)

☆ E. Fischer, D. Matthews, R. Smith (pfs.) & Philharmonia
Orch.   ♯ **G.ALP 1103**
(*Schubert: Moments musicaux*) (♯ QALP 10064:
(*Mozart* on ♯ G.FALP 375)   WALP 1103)

☆ Soloists & Orch.—Heiller (in ♯ HS. set HSL-K &
♯ MTW. 532)
Soloists & Ansbach Fest. Orch.—Rieger (♯ Pol. 14050)

D minor (BWV 1063)
H. Elsner, R. Reinhardt, F. Goebels (hpsis.) &
Stuttgart Pro Musica—R. Reinhardt
(*above & below*)   ♯ **E. & AmVox.PL 8670**
F. Viderø, S. Sørensen, E. Møller (hpsis.) &
Copenhagen Coll. Mus.—L. Friisholm
                   ♯ **HS.HSL 115**
(*above*)   (& in set HSL-K)
C. Chailley-Richez, F. le Gonidec, J-J.
Painchaud (pfs.) & Paris Cha.—Enesco
(*below*)   ♯ **D.FAT 173097**
G. Kuhn, G. Astorg, L. Rev (pfs.) & Champs-
Elysées Th. Orch.—Goldschmidt
                   ♯ **LT.DTL 93053**
(*above, below, etc.*)   (♯ Sel. 320.C.012)
☆ R., G. & J. Casadesus (pfs.) & N.Y.P.S.O.
—Mitropoulos (♯ Phi.A 01620R)
Anon. Pianists & Berlin Radio—Kondrashin
                   (♯ AFest.CFR 10-34)

FOUR CLAVIERS & ORCHESTRA
A minor (BWV 1065)
(after Vivaldi's Op. 3, No. 10, *q.v.*)
K. Richter, E. Müller, G. Aeschbacher,
H. Gurtner (hpsis.), Ansbach Fest.—Richter
(*above*)   ♯ **D.LX 35001**
H. Elsner, R. Noll, F. Goebels & W. Spilling
(hpsis.) & Stuttgart Pro Musica—R.
Reinhardt   ♯ **E. & AmVox.PL 8670**
(*above*)
G. Kuhn, G. Astorg, L. Rev, M. Mercier (pfs.)
& Champs-Elysées Th. Orch.—Goldschmidt
                   ♯ **LT.DTL 93053**
(*above*)   (♯ Sel. 320.C.012)

♯ = Long-playing, 33⅓ r.p.m.   ♭ = 45 r.p.m.   ♮ = Auto. couplings, 78 r.p.m.

28

A minor (BWV 1065) (*continued*)
  C. Chailley-Richez, F. le Gonidec, J-J. Painchaud,
  Y. Grimaud (pfs.) & Paris Cha.—Enesco
  (*Italian Concerto*)   ‡ *D.FA 143538*
  ☆ Soloists & Orch.—Heiller
              (in ‡ HS. set HSL-K & ‡ MTW. 532)

VIOLIN & ORCHESTRA
COLLECTIONS
A minor   (BWV 1041)   E major   (BWV 1042)
D minor   2 vlns. & orch.   (BWV 1043)
  R. Barchet, W. Beh & Stuttgart Pro Musica
  Str. Orch.—Davisson ‡ E. & AmVox.PL 9150
  U. Grehling, —. Hendel & Saar Cha.
  —Ristenpart   ‡ DFr. 127
  [E major only, ‡ *DFr.EX 25017*]

A minor   (BWV 1041)
  D. Erlih & Pro Arte—Redel ‡ *Sel. 270.C. 080*
  (*below*)
  J. Heifetz & Los Angeles Phil.—Wallenstein
                      ‡ *G.BLP 1070*
  (*below*) (‡ Vic.LM 1818; ‡ FV.A 630223;
                     ‡ ItV.A12R 0019; DV.L 16486)
  W. Schneiderhan & Zürich Coll. Mus.—Sacher
                         PV. 2462
                         (♭ Pol. 37025)
  W. Barylli & Vienna St. Op.—Scherchen
  (*below*)   ‡ West.WL 5318
  H. Szeryng & Pasdeloup—Bouillon
  (*below*)   ‡ Od.ODX 114
  ☆ I. Stern & Prades Fest.—Casals   ‡ C.CX 1109
  (*Clav. Concerto, Sonata, etc.*)   (‡ FCX 325)

E major   (BWV 1042)
  H. Merckel & Pro Arte—Redel
  (*above*)   ‡ *Sel. 270.C. 080*
  J. Heifetz & Los Angeles Phil.—Wallenstein
                      ‡ *G.BLP 1070*
  (*above*) (‡ Vic.LM 1818; FV.A 630223;
                ItV.A12R 0019; DV.L 16486)
  W. Barylli & Vienna St. Op.—Scherchen
  (*above*)   ‡ West.WL 5318
  H. Szeryng & Pasdeloup—Bouillon
  (*above*)   ‡ Od.ODX 114
  Z. Francescatti & Col. Sym.—Szell
                       ‡ AmC.ML 4648
  (*Prokofiev: Concerto No. 2*)
  R. Odnoposoff & Netherlands Phil.—Goehr
                       ‡ MMS. 54
  (*Sonata 4—Chaconne*)
  ☆ S. Goldberg & Philharmonia—Süsskind ‡ P.PMA 1007
  (*Haydn: Concerto*)
  ☆ T. Varga & Berlin Phil.—Lehmann (‡ Pol. 14050)
  L. Kaufman & Bach Cha. Group (in ♭ Tem. set 4600)

D minor
  (restored from Clavier Concerto, BWV 1052)
  ☆ J. Szigeti & Prades Fest.—Casals   ‡ C.CX 1113
  (*below*)   (FCX 326)
G minor   (BWV 1056)
  (restored by G. Schreck from Clavier Concerto, F minor)
  J. Szigeti & Col. Sym.—Szell ‡ EPhi.ABL 3058
  (*Handel & Tartini*) (‡ Phi.A 01140L; ‡ AmC.ML 4891)
D major   (BWV 1045)[1]   vln., tpts. & orch.
  G. Alès (vln.), R. Delmotte (tpt.) & Paris
  Coll. Mus.—Douatte   ‡ EPP.APG 124
  (*Brandenburg Concerto 1, arr., & Motet arr.*)

TWO VIOLINS & ORCHESTRA
D minor   (BWV 1043)
  Y. Menuhin, G. de Vito & Philharmonia
  —Bernard   ‡ *G.BLP 1046*
  (*Handel*)   (‡ QBLP 5028: FBLP 1061)
  (*Handel & Vivaldi*, on ‡ Vic.LHMV 16)

  D. Erlih, H. Merckel, & Pro Arte—Redel
  (*Vln. & oboe concerto*)   ‡ *Sel. 270.C.081*
  M. Korn, P. Hoffner & orch.—Disenhaus
  (*Mozart*)   ‡ *MF.2506*
  ☆ Y. Menuhin, G. Enesco & Paris Sym.—Monteux
                      ‡ Vic.LCT 1120
  (*Vln. & Clav. Sonata No. 3*) (♭ set WCT 1120;
                       ‡ G.FJLP 5018)
  ☆ H. Krebbers, T. Olof & Residentie—v. Otterloo
                      (‡ Epic.LC 3036)
  — FOR PRACTICE: Recorded without solo vln. parts
                      (‡ CEd.MMO 307)

VIOLIN & OBOE (OR 2 VLNS.) & ORCH.
C minor   (BWV 1060)
  2 W. Beh, F. Milde, Stuttgart Pro Musica
  —Reinhardt   ‡ AmVox.PL 9580
  (*Concertos, 2 claviers*)
  2 G. Alès, P. Pierlot & orch.—Froment
                     ‡ LOL.OL 50074
  (*J. C. Bach*)   (‡ OL.LD 96)
  2 M. Hendriks, H. Töttcher & Berlin Radio
  —Koch   ‡ Ura.RS 7-31
  (*Haydn*)
  F. Zepparoni, H. Winschermann, Augsburg
  Cha.—Deyle   † ‡ AS. 3005LD
  (*C. P. E. Bach, Telemann*)   (‡ HS.AS 35)
  U. Grehling, P. Pierlot & Saar Cha.
  —Ristenpart   V‡ DFr.EX 17024
  2 R. Felicani, E. Shann & Basle Cha. Orch.
  —Sacher   ‡ EPhi.NBR 6028
  (*Brandenburg Concerto No. 6*)   (‡ Phi.A 00719R)
  R. Barchet, K. Kalmus & Pro Arte—Redel
  (*Concerto, 2 vlns.*)   ‡ *Sel. 270.C.081*
  ☆ 2 P. Rybar, E. Parolari & Winterthur Sym.—Dahinden
                      (‡ MMS. 77)
  ... 2nd movt., Adagio, only
  M. Wilk, M. Miller & Little Sym.—Saidenberg
                      ‡ AmC.ML 4916
  (*Cantata No. 156, excpt.; & J. C. Bach, Mozart*)

CLAVIER, FLUTE, VIOLIN & ORCHESTRA
A minor   (BWV 1044)
  F. Neumeyer (hpsi.), J-P. Rampal, U. Grehling,
  & Saar Cha.—Ristenpart   ‡ *DFr.EX 25025*
  (2ss)
  H. Priegnitz (hpsi.), K. Redel, R. Barchet &
  Orch.—Redel   ‡ Sel. 320.C.091
  (*Clavier Concerto, BWV 1052*)
  C. Chailley-Richez (pf.), J-P. Rampal, C. Ferras
  & Paris Cha.—Enesco   ‡ *D.FAT 173530*
  (*Brandenburg Concerto 5*)
  ☆ I. Nef (hpsi.), E. Defrancesco, A. Wachsmut-Loew,
       Lausanne Cha.—Desarzens[3]   ‡ OL.LD 69
       (*Brandenburg Concerto 5*)
  ☆ M. Horszowski (pf.), J. Wummer, A. Schneider &
       Prades Fest.—Casals   ‡ C.CX 1113
       (*above*)   (FCX 326)

CLAVIER, 2 FLUTES & ORCHESTRA
F major   (BWV 1057)
  (from Brandenburg Concerto No. 4)
  C. Chailley-Richez (pf.), G. Crunelle &
  J-P. Rampal (fls.), Paris Cha.—Enesco
                      ‡ *D.FAT 173068*
  ☆ L. Salter (hpsi.), M. & L. Taylor (recorders) & London
       Baroque Orch.—Haas (‡ Od.O-9185/6)
  M. v. d. Lyck (hpsi.) & Stuttgart Ton-Studio—Michael
                      (‡ Clc. 6139)

—— END OF CONCERTOS

Sinfonia, D major   SEE: Concerto, violin (BWV 1045)
Sinfonia, F major   SEE: Concerto, Brandenburg No. 1 (ARR.

---

[1] One movement only: Sinfonia to a lost Church Cantata.
[2] Ed. Schneider—D minor. Others are probably also this version.
[3] Announced but perhaps not issued.

SUITES (BWV 1066/9)
No. 1, C major   No. 2, B minor
No. 3, D major   No. 4, D major

COMPLETE RECORDINGS (all 4ss; fl. soloist in
   No. 2 named)
Philharmonia—Klemperer   # C.CX 1239/40
[G. Morris, fl.] [# QCX 10137 & 9; Angel. 35234/5,
                                      set 3536]

Munich Pro Arte Cha.—Redel
                        # LT.DTL 93073/4
[K. Redel, fl.]   (# Sel. 270.C.036/7)

English Baroque—Scherchen
                      # West.WN 18012/3
[R. Adeney, fl.]   (set WN 2201)

[1] Vienna State Op.—Prohaska   # Van.BG 530/1
[K. Rezniček, fl.]   (# Ama.AVRS 6005/6)

Victor Sym.—Reiner   # Vic. set LM 6012
[J. Baker, fl.] (# FV.A 630261/2; ItV.B12R 0054/5;
                               DV. set 16462)

☆ Orch.—Hewitt   # HS.HSL 90/1
[J-P. Rampal, fl.]   (set HSL-F)

No. 1, C major   2 obs., bsn., strings
Amsterdam—v. Beinum   # Phi.A 00289L
(Suite No. 2)   (# Epic.LC 3194)

Berlin Cha.—v. Benda   # DT.LGX 66040
(Suite No. 3)   (# T.LE 6525)

Berlin Radio—Haarth   # Ura.RS 7-33
(Mozart: Symphony 25)

Saar Cha.—Ristenpart   # DFr.EX 25034

☆ Prades Festival—Casals[2]   # C.CX 1108
(below)   (FCX 323)
Leningrad Phil.—Sanderling (USSRM.D 893/6)
Berlin Sym.—Balzer (# Roy. 1393)
☆ Winterthur Sym.—Swoboda (# MMS. 74)

... **Bourrées I & II**
Victor Sym.—Reiner, from set (in # Vic.LM 1877)

No. 2, B minor   fl. & str.
G. Scheck & Cha. Ens.—Rieger
(No. 3)   # HP.APM 14033

J-P. Rampal & Saar Cha.—Ristenpart
                      # DFr.EX 25010

Anon. & Amsterdam—v. Beinum
                      # Phi.A 00289L
(No. 1)   (# Epic.LC 3194)
E. Milzkott & Berlin Radio—Haarth
(5ss—Vivaldi)   Eta. 120100/2
P. L. Graf & Winterthur Sym.—Dahinden
(No. 1)   # MMS. 74
C. Larde & Cha. Orch.—Kuentz   # CND. 2
(Mozart & Vivaldi)
☆ J. Wummer & Prades Fest.—Casals   # C.CX 1108
(above)   (FCX 323)
Anon. Orch. (# ACC.MP 14)
☆ A. Pepin & Stuttgart Cha.—Münchinger (# Lon.LL 848)
G. Laurent & Boston Sym.—Koussevitzky
                       (# Cam.CAL 158)
J. Baker & Orch.—Stokowski (# G.FALP 281)

... **Polonaise only**
E. Milzkott & Berlin Radio—Haarth   Eta. 120113
(Brandenburg Concerto 3, s. 3)
               (o.n. 25-C 020; & # LPM 1002)
... **Sarabande** only.   ☆ Orch.—Stokowski
      (in # Vic.LM 1875; ♭ set ERB 521: ♭ ERA 244)
... **Badinerie** only.   ☆ Orch.—Stokowski (in # Vic.LM 1877)

No. 3, D major   2 obs., 3 tpts., strs., timpani
Ansbach Fest. Ens.—Rieger # HP.APM 14033
(No. 2)

Berlin Cha.—Benda   # DT.LGX 66040
(No. 1) [Air only in # T.LB 6124]   (# T.LE 6525)

Berlin Sym.—Balzer   # Roy. 1393
(No. 1)
☆ Paris Cons.—Weingartner (Brahms)   # AmC.ML 4783
☆ Stuttgart Cha.—Münchinger (# Lon.LL 848)
Slovak Phil.—Talich (# Csm.CRLP 229)
Boston Sym.—Koussevitzky (# Cam.CAL 158)
Sym. Orch.—Szell (# MApp. 26)
... **Overture**
Hamburg Philharmonia—H-J. Walther   MSB. 78208
... **Air & Gavotte**
Hamburg Philharmonia—H-J. Walther   MSB. 78040
... **Bourrée & Gigue**
Hamburg Philharmonia—H-J. Walther   MSB. 78041
... **Air, Gavotte, Bourrée & Gigue.** Regent Sym. (in # Rgt. 7005)
... **Air & Gigue**
Victor Sym.—Reiner, from set   in # Vic.LM 1877
... **Air only**
L.S.O.—Weldon   C.DX 1896
(Unacc. Vln. Sonata No. 6—Gavotte)
     (C.SVX 50; ♭ SCD 2030; in # SX 1045)
Berlin Radio—Abendroth   Eta. 120116
(Brandenburg Concerto 4, s. 5)   (o.n. 25-C 018)
Victor Sym.—Reiner   ♭ Vic.ERA 215
(Orphée No. 29)   (♭ G.7ER 5052; FV.A 95226)
☆ F. Akos (vln.) & Berlin Municipal Op. Ens. ♭ T.U 45514
(Gounod: Ave Maria)
N. W. Ger. Phil.—Schüchter
               (# Imp.ILP 132; ♭ Od.OBC 29007)
Polish Radio—Krenz (Muza.X 2381)
Boyd Neel Orch. (♭ Phi.N 402029E)
Belgian Radio-Glière (in # Mae.OAT 25001)
Str. Orch.—Bernard (♭ Pac.EP 90012)
Mantovani Orch. (in # D.LK 4072; Lon.LL 877;
                    D.F 43842; ♭ D 17842, etc.)
Melachrino Str. Orch. (in # Vic.LPM 1003; ♭ set EPB 1003;
             G.C 3775: in # DLP 1083)
Anon. Orch. (in # Roy. 1432), etc. etc.

☆ Pro Arte—Marrow (in # MGM.E 3046)

— — ARR. VLN. & PF.   Wilhelmj
M. Wilk & F. Kramer (in. # MTR.MLP 1012)
☆ J. Dumont & A. Collard (♭ Pat.D 106)
Y. Menuhin & M. Gazelle (♭ G.7RW 120)
— — ARR. VLC. & PF.   ("Aria")
A. Navarra & J. Dussol (in # Od.OD 1014)
— — ARR. 10 VLCS. & ORCH.   U.S.S.R.—Golovanov
                       (USSR. 12414/5)
— — ARR. GUITAR   A. Valenti (in # SMC. 1002)
— — ARR. ORG.   ☆ C. Courboin (in # Cam.CAL 218)

No. 4, D major
Berlin Sym.—Balzer   # Roy. 1438
(Brandenburg Concerto No. 3)
... **Réjouissance:** Vic. Sym.—Reiner, from set
                      (in # Vic.LM 1877)

G minor (Overture)   Str. orch.   (BWV 1070)
                               (doubtful)[3]
Paris Inst. Ens.—Froment   # EPP.APG 117
(Telemann)

E. MISCELLANEOUS

KUNST DER FUGE (Art of Fugue) (BWV 1080)
                                 1749/50
COMPLETE RECORDING (ed. Leonhardt)[4]
    G. Leonhardt (hpsi.)   (4ss)   # Van.BG 532/3

ORCH. VERSION   ed. Redel (complete, with both
    13 & 18)
Munich Pro Arte Cha. Orch.—Redel
                       # Sel. LAG 1075/6
[The Canons are played by hpsi. & org.]
        (# T.LE 6535/6; West. set WAL 220)

2 PFS. VERSION, ARR. Seidlhofer
... **Nos. 1-11, 15, 17, 16, 14, 13, 12, 19**
J. & G. Dichler   # West set WAL 215
(Ch. Prelude—Wenn wir . . .)

UNSPEC. VERSION & EXTRACTS
Berlin Sym.—Rubahn   # Roy. 1560
... **No. 1 only** — ARR. BRASS ENS.   King
Brass Ens.—Voisin   # Uni.UN 1003
(† Golden Age of Brass)

---

[1] Nos. 3 & 4 Overtures played twice, first with dotted notes given XVIIIth Century value, then with their modern value.
[2] Omitting 5th movement, Minuet.   [3] Perhaps by Wilhelm Friedemann Bach.
[4] Uses No. 10a instead of No. 10, and No. 18 instead of No. 13.

... **No. 3** only
F. Viderø (org.) · in ‡ **HS.HSL 2073**
(† Masterpieces of Music before 1750)

... **Nos. 4, 11, 19**
☆ F. Heitmann (org.) ‡ *DT.LGM 65009*
(*Ch. Prel.—Wenn wir in höchsten Nöthen sein*)

(Ein) MUSIKALISCHES OPFER (BWV 1079)
(*A Musical Offering*) 1749
COMPLETE RECORDINGS
Stuttgart Cha. Orch.—Münchinger[1]
‡ **D.LXT 5036**
(‡ Lon.LL 1181)

Naples Scarlatti Orch.—Ghedini[2]
‡ **Csm.CLPS 1044**

Soloists & Berlin Sym.—Balzer[3] ‡ **Roy. 1532**

☆ Ensemble—Scherchen[4] ‡ **Nix.WLP 5070**

☆ Alma Musica Sextet[5] (‡ T.LE 6520)

... **Trio Sonata, C minor** fl., vln. & cont.
L. Lavaillotte, G. Tessier & P. Aubert (hpsi.)
‡ *CFD. 29*

(*Sarabande con partite*)

... **Ricercari** (à 3 & à 6)
G. Johansen (double-keyboard pf.) in ‡ **AD. set 3**

"BACH FESTIVAL"
(Chorale-Preludes and arrts. of Chorales)
SIDE 1
Nun danket alle Gott (Cantata 79, No. 3)
Vom Himmel hoch (a) Christmas Oratorio, No. 23
(b) Chorale-Prelude, BWV 738
(c) Christmas Oratorio, No. 9
Wachet auf! (a) J. L. KREBS: Chorale-Prelude
(b) Cantata 140, No. 7
Wie schön leuchtet . . . (a) Chorale-Prelude, BWV 763
(b) Cantata 1, No. 6
SONGS from AMB (a) Schaff's mit mir, Gott
(b) Dir, dir, Jehova
(3) Wedding Chorales, BWV 250, 251, 252
(a) Was Gott tut . . .
(b) Sei Lob und Ehr' . . .
(c) Nun danket . . .
SIDE 2
Jesu, nun sei gepreiset (Cantata 171, No. 6)
Lobe den Herren (Cantata 137, No. 5)
Herr Gott, dich loben alle wir (Cantata 130, No. 6)
G. A. HOMILIUS: Chorale-Prelude, Durch Adams Fall
Schmücke dich . . . (Cantata 180, No. 7)
Herzlich tut mich . . . (Christmas Oratorio, No. 5)
Valet will ich . . . (St. John Passion, No. 52)
Was Gott tut . . . (unspec. setting)
Nun ruhen alle Wälder (St. Matthew Passion, No. 16)
Ein feste Burg (a) Chorale-Prelude, BWV 270
(b) unid. setting
E. P. Biggs (org.) & Brass Ens.—Mazzeo
‡ **AmC.ML 4635**

"THE SMILING BACH"
EXCERPTS from Bach's Works, including:
    Orch. Suites 1, 2, 3 & 4
    Wohltemperirtes Clavier
    Cantatas 140, 147, 41, 208
    St. John Passion
    Brandenburg Concerto No. 2
performed by various artists ‡ **Vic.LM 1877**

SUITE for String Orch. ARR. Bachrich
Arrangements of Solo Vln. Sonata movements:
No. 3, A minor . . . Andante only
No. 6, E major . . . Prelude & Gavotte only
Boston Orch. Soc.—Page ‡ **SOT. 1062**
(*Brandenburg Concerto 3; & Stravinsky, etc.*)

THE WISE VIRGINS Ballet Suite ARR. Walton
(SEE under Cantata 208 for individual recordings of No. 5)
    1. Cantata 99—Opening Chorus
    2. Chorale-Prelude, Herzlich tut mich . . .
    3. Cantata 85—Tenor aria
    4. Cantata 26—Opening Chorus
    5. Cantata 208—Soprano aria
    6. Cantata 129—Final Chorale
L.P.O.—Boult ‡ *D.LW 5157*
(*Walton, in ‡ D.LXT 5028; Lon.LL 1165*) (‡ *Lon.LD 9179*)

Vienna State Op.—Litschauer ‡ **Nix.PVL 7024**
(*D. Scarlatti*) (‡ Van.VRS 440)

Lecture with pf. demonstrations: Bach's Ornaments
R. Lanning ‡ **B & B. 5**
(Contains excerpts from the Clavier works played as
illustrations; including the Overture from Partita,
G minor, by Stölzel, in the W F B. Clavierbüchlein.)

Bach, his life and his music
D. Randolph (narrator), etc. ‡ *Per.PCS 9*

II. CHORAL
(for Chorales see III)

CHURCH CANTATAS
COLLECTION
Bach Aria Group ‡Vic. set LM 6023
SEE below: Cantatas 60, 127, 155, 99, 47, 79, 132, 110,
41 & 42. (‡ FV.A 630279/80)

No. 1, Wie schön leuchtet der Morgenstern
S, T, Bs. & cho. 1735-44
G. Weber, H. Krebs, H. Schey, Berlin Motet
Cho. & Phil.—Lehmann ♮ **PV. 2437/8**
(4ss) (2ss, on ‡ *Pol. 13018*) (*No. 19* on ‡ AmD.DL 9671)

... **No. 6, Wie bin ich doch so herzlich froh** — ARR.
Brass Ens.—Mazzeo in ‡ AmC.ML 4635
(Bach Festival)

No. 4, Christ lag in Todesbanden
S, T, B, cho., orch. 1724
[6]Columbus Cho. & Str. Quintet ‡ **B.LAT 8070**
(*Choir Recital*) (‡ AmD.DL 8106: ♭ *set ED 831*)
☆ Victor Chorale—Shaw (‡ Vic.LM 9035)

... Sinfonia : *see footnote to Brandenburg Concerto 3, supra*
... Sinfonia; No. 3, Den Tod niemand zwingen kunnt
☆ Cho. & Orch.—Prohaska (♭ Van.VREP 5)
... No. 4, Jesus Christus, Gottes Sohn — ARR. ORCH.
☆ Sym.—Stokowski (♭ *G.7ER 5004*: in ‡ FALP 281)
... No. 5, Es war ein wunderlicher Krieg
No. 8, Wir essen und leben wohl
Danish Radio Cho. & Cha. Orch.—Wöldike
(† Masterpieces of Music before 1750) in ‡ HS.HSL 2073
(also in † Histoire de la Musique vocale)

No. 6, Bleib' bei uns A, T, Bs, cho, orch.
☆ Soloists & Stuttgart Cho. Soc. & Bach Orch.
—Grischkat (‡ Clc. 6136; ‡ Cum.CPR 336)

No. 11, Lobet Gott in seinen Reichen
S, A, T, B, & cho. (*Himmelfahrtsoratorium*)
☆ Soloists & Swabian Cho. Soc. & Stuttgart Bach Orch.
—Grischkat ‡ Nix.LLP 8034; Cum.CLL 337)
E. Mitchell (S), K. Ferrier (A), etc. Cantata Singers
& Jacques Orch. (*Eng*)[7] (in ‡ Lon.LL 845)

No. 12, Weinen, Klagen, Sorgen, Zagen 1724
... No. 4, Kreuz und Krone A
☆ M. Anderson (in ‡ Vic.LCT 1111: ♭ *set WCT 1111*)

No. 19, Es erhub sich ein Streit
S. T, Bs, cho. & orch.
G. Weber, H. Krebs, H. Schey, Berlin Motet
Cho. & Phil.—Lehmann ‡ **AmD.DL 9671**
(*No. 1*) (*No. 79* on ‡ Pol. 14005)
☆ Soloists & Stuttgart Cho. Soc. & Ton-Studio Orch.
—Grischkat (‡ Clc. 6136; ‡ Cum.CPR 336)

No. 21, Ich hatte viel Bekümmernis
S. T, Bs, & cho. 1714
G. Weber, H. Krebs, H. Schey, Berlin Motet
Cho. & Phil. Orch.—Lehmann
‡ **HP.APM 14007**
(‡ AmD.DL 9673)
T. Stich-Randall, W. Kmentt, P. Schoeffler,
Vienna St. Op. Cho. & Orch.—Sternberg
‡ **CFD. 31**

... No. 4, Wie hast du dich, mein Gott T
... No. 5, Bäche von gesalz'nen Zähren T
... No. 10, Erfreue dich, Seele, erfreue dich, Herze T
☆ H. Cuénod (in ‡ Van.BG 526)

---

[1] Arr. Münchinger.   [2] Arr. Ghedini, 2 pfs. & orch. 1946; omits 3e (Canon), 4 (Fugue), & Trio Sonata.
[3] Arr. not known.   [4] Arr. Vuataz.   [5] Arr. David.
[6] The solos are sung by sections of the choir.
[7] ▽ Omits No. 9 (recit.), middle section & *da capo* of No. 10 (Aria) and part of No. 11 (Chorale).

No. 22, Jesus nahm zu sich die Zwölfe
A, T, B, cho. 1723
... **No. 5, Ertöt uns durch dein' Güte** Chorale
All Saints Chu. Male Cho.—Self
in ♯ CEd.CE 1023
(† Five Centuries of Choral Music) (*Eng*)
[with ob., bsn. & hpsi.]

No. 26, Ach wie flüchtig S, A, T, B, cho.
... Opening Chorus — ARR. ORCH. Walton
See: Wise Virgins, Section I.E, *above*
... No. 6, Chorale: in Collection, *post, q.v.*

No. 29, Wir danken dir, Gott
S, A, T, B, cho., orch. 1731
... No. 1, Sinfonia — ARR. PF. Saint-Saëns
☆ R. Trouard (in ♯ ArgOd.LDC 7501)

No. 31, Der Himmel lacht S, T, B, cho., orch. 1715
☆ Soloists, Academy Cho. & Vienna Cha.—Prohaska
(♯ MTW. 517)

No. 32, Liebster Jesu, mein Verlangen
S, B, cho., orch.
☆ M. Laszlo, A. Poell, Vienna Academy Cho. & St. Op.
Orch.—Scherchen (♯ Nix.WLP 5122; Sel. LAC 30008)

No. 38, Aus tiefer Noth S, A, T, B, cho., orch.
... No. 6, Chorale: in Collection, *post, q.v.*

No. 39, Brich dem Hungrigen dein Brot
S, A, Bs, cho. 1732
G. Weber, L. Fischer, H. Schey, Berlin Motet
Cho. & Phil.—Lehmann ♯ *Pol. 13003*
(2ss) (No. 79 on ♯ AmD.DL 9672)

No. 41, Jesu, nun sei gepreiset
S, A, T, B, cho., orch. c. 1735
E. Farrell, C. Smith, J. Peerce, N. Farrow,
Shaw Cho. & Bach Aria Group—Shaw
♯ Vic. set LM 6023
(Cantatas 42, 60; & Arias, etc.) (excpt. in ♯ LM 1877)
(Cantata 42 only on ♯ FV.A 630280)

No. 42, Am Abend aber desselbigen Sabbaths
S, A, T, B, cho., orch. 1731
E. Farrell, C. Smith, J. Peerce, N. Farrow,
Shaw Cho. & Bach Aria Group—Schiede
♯ Vic. set LM 6023
(Cantata 60 & Aria from 127, etc.) (& in ♯ FV.A 630280)
... Sinfonia
▽ Winterthur Sym.—Henking ♯ CHS.F 12
(Mass, F major & Cantata 118)

No. 46, Schauet doch und sehet A, T, B, cho.
... No. 2, So klage du T
☆ H. Cuénod (in ♯ Van.BG 526)

No. 47, Wer sich selbst erhöhet
S, B, cho., orch. 1720
... No. 4, Jesu beuge doch mein Herze
Bs, ob., vln., cont.
N. Farrow, R. Bloom, M. Wilk, pf. & vlc
in ♯ Vic. set LM 6023
(♯ FV.A 630279)

No. 50, Nun ist das Heil Cho. & orch. c. 1740
Cho. & Orch.—Goldsbrough G.HMS 56
(† History of Music in Sound) (in ♯ Vic. set LM 6030)

No. 51, Jauchzet Gott in allen Landen S & orch.
1731-2
S. Danco & Stuttgart Cha. Orch.—Münchinger
(No. 202) ♯ D.LXT 2926
(♯ Lon.LL 993)
L. Marshall & Orch.—MacMillan ♯ Hall.CS 2
(Mozart)
T. Stich-Randall & Vienna St. Op. Orch.
—Heiller ♯ Van.BG 546
(No. 209) (♯ Ama.AVRS 6004)
☆ E. Schwarzkopf & Philharmonia Orch.—Gellhorn
[H. Jackson, tpt.] (No. 82, etc.) ♯ AmC.ML 4792
☆ M. Guilleaume & Stuttgart—Grischkat
(♯ Cum.CPR 334)
... No. 5, Alleluja Aria: B. Troxell & org. (in ♯ Ply. 12-123)

No. 53, Schlage doch, gewünschte Stunde A. & orch.
H. Rössl-Majdan & Vienna St. Op.—Scherchen
♯ Nix.WLP 5197
(Nos. 54 & 170) (♯ West.WL 5197; Sel. 320.CW.086)

H. Glaz (M-S) & Guilet Qtt. ♯ MGM.E 3156
(Cantata 170; & Pergolesi)
☆ H. Hennecke & Basle Cha. Ens.—Wenzinger
(♭ Pol. 37063)

No. 54, Widerstehe doch der Sünde A. & Orch.
c. 1730
H. Rössl-Majdan & Vienna St. Op.—Scherchen
♯ Nix.WLP 5197
(Nos. 53 & 170) (♯ West.WL 5197; Sel. 320.CW.086)
A. Deller (C-T) & Leonhardt Baroque Ens.
♯ Nix.PVL 7028
(No. 170, & Mass, B minor, excpt.) (♯ Van.BG 550)

No. 56, Ich will den Kreuzstab gerne tragen
B, cho. & orch. 1731-2
G. Hüsch & Victor Cha. Orch.—Gurlitt
(4ss) JpV.SD 3079/80
(Schubert, R. Strauss, & Wolf on ♯ LS 2006) (set JAS 251)
☆ D. Fischer-Dieskau, Berlin Motet Cho. & Cha. Orch.
—Ristenpart (No. 82) ♯ HP.APM 14004

No. 60, O Ewigkeit, du Donnerwort
A, T, B, cho., orch. 1732
C. Smith, J. Peerce, N. Farrow, Shaw Cho. &
Bach Aria Group—Brieff
in ♯ Vic. set LM 6023
(Cantata 42 & Arias from 127, etc.) (in ♯ FV.A 630279)

No. 63, Christen, ätzet diesen Tag
S, A, T, B, cho., orch. 1723
... No. 2, O sel'ger Tag!
☆ H. Rössl-Majdan (in ♯ Van.BG 526)

No. 65, Sie werden aus Saba alle kommen
T, Bs, cho., orch. 1724
☆ R. Sands (T), R. Isbell (Bs.), Cho. & Orch.—Wagner
♯ CA.LPA 1027
(No. 106) (♯ Cum.CLL 338; Lyr.LL 50)
... No. 2, Chorale: in Collection, *post, q.v.*
... No. 6, Nimm mich dir T ☆ G. Thill (*Fr*) (in ♯ C.FH 504)

No. 67, Halt im Gedächtnis Jesum Christ
A, T, B, cho.
☆ K. Ferrier, W. Herbert, W. Parsons, Cantata Singers
& Jacques Orch. (*Eng*) (in ♯ Lon.LL 845)

No. 68, Also hat Gott die Welt geliebt 1735
... No. 2, Mein gläubiges Herze S & orch.
(My heart ever faithful; Air de la Pentecôte)
M. Maurene & J. Ullern (org.) (*Fr*) *Sat.S 1141*
(Mozart: Exsultate Jubilate—Alleluia)
T. Fridén (Tr., *Swed*) (Cus. 33)
☆ E. Schwarzkopf, vlc. & org. (in ♯ AmC.ML 4792)

No. 70, Wachet, betet
S, A, T, Bs, cho., orch. 1716, rev. 1723
A. Felbermeyer, E. Wien, H. Meyer-Welfing,
N. Foster, Vienna Cha. Cho. & St. Op. Orch.
—Prohaska ♯ Van.BG 524
... No. 7, Freu' dich sehr. In Chorale Collection, *post, q.v.*

No. 71, Gott ist mein König
S, A, T, B, cho. & orch. 1708
P. Curtin, L. Knowles, D. Lloyd, M. Harrell,
Bethlehem Bach Cho. & Orch.—I. Jones
♯ BC.Pte

No. 76, Die Himmel erzählen die Ehre Gottes
S, A, T, B, cho. 1723
M. Laszlo, H. Rössl-Majdan, P. Munteanu,
R. Standen, Academy Cho. & Vienna St.
Op. Orch.—Scherchen ♯ Nix.WLP 5201
(♯ Sel. 320.CW.060; West.WL 5201)

No. 78, Jesu, der du meine Seele
S, A, T, B, cho., orch.
T. Stich-Randall, D. Hermann, A. Dermota,
H. Braun, Cho. & Orch.—Prohaska
♯ Van.BG 537
(No. 106) (♯ Ama.AVRS 6003)
☆ Soloists, Reinhart & Winterthur Chos. & Orch.
—Reinhart (♯ MMS. 70)
... No. 2, Wir eilen mit schwachen doch emsigen Schritten
Leipzig Thomanerchor—Ramin Eta. 120107
(Singet dem Herrn, excpt.) (o.n. 25-C 021)
Augustana Cho. (*Eng*)—Veld, pf. acc. ♯ BB.LBC 1075
(Cantata No. 104, excpt.; Brahms, Dvořák, etc.)

♯ = Long-playing, 33⅓ r.p.m.   ♭ = 45 r.p.m.   ♮ = Auto. couplings, 78 r.p.m.

No. 79, Gott, der Herr, ist Sonn' und Schild
S, A, Bs, cho., orch. *c.* 1735
G. Weber, L. Fischer, H. Schey, Berlin Motet
Cho. & Phil. Orch.—Lehmann
♯ **AmD.DL 9672**
(*No. 39*)   (*No. 19 on* ♯ Pol. 14005)

... **No. 3, Nun danket alle Gott**   — ARR. ORG. & BRASS
E. P. Biggs & Brass Ens.   in ♯ **AmC.ML 4635**
(Bach Festival)

... **No. 5, Gott, ach Gott, verlass die Deinen nimmermehr!**
S, Bs, Str. & cont.
E. Farrell & N. Farrow   in ♯ **Vic. set LM 6023**
(♯ FV.A 630279)

No. 80, Ein feste Burg   S, A, T, B, cho. & orch.
☆ Soloists, Akademie Cho. & Vienna St. Orch.—Prohaska
(♯ CID.VXT 33013)

No. 81, Jesus schläft   A, T, B, cho. 1724
... **No. 1, Opening aria**   A
☆ M. Anderson (in ♯ Vic.LCT 1111: ♭ *set WCT 1111*)

No. 82, Ich habe genug   B. & orch. 1731-2
R. Titze, Saar Cha.—Ristenpart
♯ *DFr.EX 25033*
(2ss) [P. Pierlot, ob.]
☆ D. Fischer-Dieskau & Cha. Orch.—Ristenpart
(*No. 56*)   ♯ **HP.APM 14004**
☆ H. Hotter & Philharmonia Orch.—Bernard
(*No. 51, etc.*) [S. Sutcliffe, ob.]   ♯ **AmC.ML 4792**

No. 84, Ich bin vergnügt   S & Cho. 1731-2
☆ M. Laszlo, Vienna Academy Cho. & State Op. Orch.
—Scherchen   ♯ **Nix.WLP 5125**
(*No. 106*)   (*No. 140 on* ♯ Sel.LAG 1043)

No. 85, Ich bin ein guter Hirt
S, A, T, B, Cho. 1735
... **No. 5, Seht, was die Liebe tut!**   T
☆ G. Thill (*Fr*) (in ♯ C.FH 504)
Y. Tinayre (*Fr*) (in † Seven Centuries of Sacred Music,
♯ AmD.DL 9654)
— — ARR. ORCH. Walton
See: Wise Virgins, Section I. E, *above*

No. 99, Was Gott tut, das ist wohlgetan   *c.* 1733
... **No. 1, Opening Cho.**   — ARR. ORCH. Walton
See: Wise Virgins, Section I. E, *above*
... **No. 3, Erschüttre dich nur nicht**   T, fl. & cont.
J. Peerce, J. Baker, pf. & vlc.   in ♯ **Vic.LM 6023**
(♯ FV.A 630279)

No. 104, Du Hirte Israel, höre
T, B, cho., orch. *c.* 1725
... **No. 1, Opening Chorus**
Augustana Cho. (*Eng*)—Veld [pf. acc.] in ♯ **BB.LBC 1075**
(*Cantata 78, excpt., etc.*)
... **No. 2, Der höchste Hüter sorgt für mich**   T
... **No. 3, Verbirgt mein Hirte sich zu lange**   T
☆ H. Cuénod (in ♯ Van.BG 526)

No. 105, Herr, gehe nicht ins Gericht
S, A, T, B, cho. & orch. *c.* 1725
G. Weber, L. Fischer, H. Krebs, H. Schey &
Berlin Motet Cho. & Phil. Orch.—Lehmann
(4ss)   ♭ **PV. 2441/2**
(*No. 170 on* ♯ AmD.DL 9682)

No. 106, Gottes Zeit ist die allerbeste Zeit
A, Bs, cho. orch. (*Actus tragicus*) 1711
T. Stich-Randall (S), D. Hermann, A. Dermota
(T), H. Braun, Cho. & Orch.—Prohaska
♯ **Van.BG 537**
(*No. 78*)   (♯ Ama.AVRS 6003)
☆ K. Hilgenberg, R. Sands (T), R. Isbell, Cho. & Orch.
—Wagner   ♯ **CA.LPA 1027**
(*No. 65*)   (♯ Cum. CLL 338; Lyr.LL 50)
☆ H. Rössl-Majdan, A. Poell, Vienna Academy Cho.
& St. Op. Orch.—Scherchen   ♯ **Nix.WLP 5125**
(*No. 84*)   (*No. 198 on* ♯ Sel. LAG 1038)

... **Sonatina**   — ARR. ORG. Guilmant
Anon. Artist   in ♯ **FSM. 403**
— — ARR. PF. Friskin: in Clavier Collection, *q.v. supra.*

No. 110, Unser Mund sei voll Lachens
... **No. 5, Ehre sei Gott**   S, T, & cont.
E. Farrell & C. Smith, pf. & vlc.
in ♯ **Vic.LM 6023**
(♯ FV.A 630279)

No. 112, Der Herr ist mein getreuer Hirt   1731
☆ Soloists & Stuttgart Cho. & Orch.—Grischkat
(♯ Eli.PLPE 5003)

... **No. 2, Zum reinen Wasser**   A
☆ M. Anderson (in ♯ Vic.LCT 1111: ♭ *set WCT 1111*)

No. 118, O Jesu Christ, mein's Lebens Licht
Cho. & orch. 1740
▽ Zürich Bach Cho. & Winterthur Sym.—Henking
(*Mass, F major; & Cantata 42, Sinfonia*)   ♯ **CHS.F 12**

No. 127, Herr Jesu Christ, wahr'r Mensch   *c.* 1740
... **No. 3, Die Seele ruht**   S, ob., 2 fls., str. & cont.
E. Farrell & Ens.—Brieff   in ♯ **Vic. set LM 6023**
(*Cantatas 60, 41, 42; & arias from 155, etc.*) (♯ FV.A 630279)

No. 129, Gelobet sei der Herr
S, A, B, Cho., orch. 1732
... **No. 5, Dem wir das Heilig itzt**   Cho.
See: Wise Virgins, Section I. E, *above*

No. 130, Herr Gott, dich loben alle wir
— — **No. 6, Darum wir billig loben dich**   Final Chorale
— — ARR. ORGAN & BRASS
E. P. Biggs & Brass Ens.   in ♯ **AmC.ML 4635**
(Bach Festival)

No. 131, Aus der Tiefe rufe ich
T, B, cho., orch. 1707
☆ W. Hess, P. Matthen, Shaw Chorale & Victor Sym.
—Shaw (♯ ItV.A12R 0067)

No. 132, Bereitet die Wege
S, A, T, B, orch. 1715
... **No. 5, Christi Glieder**   A, vln. & cont.
C. Smith, M. Wilk, & pf. & vlc.
in ♯ **Vic. set LM 6023**
(♯ FV.A 630279)

No. 133, Ich freue mich in dir
S, A, T, B, cho., orch. 1735-7
... **No. 2, Getrost! es fasst ein heil'ger Leib**   A
☆ H. Rössl-Majdan (in ♯ Van.BG 526)

No. 137, Lobe den Herren   S, A, T, B, cho., orch.
... **No. 5, Lobe den Herren**   Final Chorale   — ARR.
Brass Ens.—Mazzeo   in ♯ **AmC.ML 4635**
(Bach Festival)

No. 140, Wachet auf!   S, T, Bs, cho., orch.
☆ S. Freil, R. Russell, P. Matthen, Shaw Cho. & Vic.
Orch.—Shaw (♯ ItV.A12R 0067; excpt. in
♯ Vic.LM 1877)
M. Laszlo, W. Kmentt, A. Poell, Vienna Academy Cho.
& St. Op. Orch.—Scherchen
(♯ Nix.WLP 5122; ♯ Sel.LAG 1043)

... **No. 1 only in Helios—"Joies de la musique"**
... **No. 4, Zion hört die Wächter**   T
☆ A. Uhl & Orch.—Prohaska (♭ Van.VREP 5)
... **No. 7, Gloria sei dir gesungen (Chorale—Wachet auf!)**
Yale Univ. Divinity Sch. Cho.—Borden in ♯ **Over.LP 2**
(† Hymns of Praise)
— — ARR. BRASS INSTS.
Brass Ens.—Mazzeo (Bach Festival)   in ♯ **AmC.ML 4635**

No. 146, Wir müssen durch viel Trübsal
(*Easter Cantata*)   S, A, T, B, cho., orch. *c.* 1740
A. Felbermeyer, E. Wien, H. Meyer-Welfing,
N. Foster, Vienna State Op. Cha. Cho. &
Orch.—Prohaska   ♯ **Van.BG 525**

... **No. 7, Wie will ich mich freuen**   T, B
— — ARR. CHO.
U.O.S.—McConnell (*Eng*) & org., in ♯ *UOS. 2*
(*Magnificat, excpt.; & Gevaert, A. Scarlatti, etc.*) (Pte.)

No. 147, Herz und Mund und Tat und Leben
S, A, T, B, cho., orch.
... **No. 10, Jesu bleibet meine Freude**   Final Chorale
(*Jesu, joy of man's desiring*)
All Saints Choristers, ob., bsn. & hpsi.—Self ♯ **CEd. 1021**
All Saints Male Cho., ob., bsn. & hpsi.—Self ♯ **CEd. 1023**
☆ Glasgow Orpheus Cho.—Roberton (*Eng*)
(in ♯ *G.DLP 1020*)
Cantata Singers—Jacques (*Eng*) (in ♯ Lon.LL 845)
(continued on next page)

☆ = Re-issue of a recording to be found in previous volumes.

No. 147, Herz und Mund und Tat und Leben...No. 10 (contin.)
— — ARRANGEMENTS
SOLO VOICE
  I. Gorin (B) (*Eng*)   in ♯ *Alld*. 2000
  J. Warren (Tr., *Eng*)   in ♯ *Queens*.LPR 21
ORCH. (Stokowski)
  ☆ Sym.—Stokowski   G.DB 21570
    (*Fugue, G minor*) (♭ *G.7R 170*: ♯ FALP 281;
                                ♭ *Vic.ERA 89*)
    (also ♭ *G.7ER 5004*: 7ERW 5004; in ♯ Vic.LM 1877)
ORCH. (Cailliet)
  ☆ Philadelphia—Ormandy (in ♯ AmC.ML 4797)
ORGAN & ORCH.
  ☆ E. P. Biggs & orch. (in ♭ *AmC.A 1641*)
PIANO (Hess)
  A. Kitain ("Siena" piano)   in ♯ *Eso*.ESP 3001
  (*Partita, etc.*)
  G. Hengeveld   Phi.N 12080G
  (*Beethoven: Für Elise*)   (& in ♭ *N 402018E*)
  ☆D. Lipatti (♭ *C.SCBQ 3008: SCBF 110: ESBF 112*:
                   in ♯ FCX 494; AmC.ML 4633)
PIANO (Kempff)
  W. Kempff   in ♯ D.LXT 2824
  (*Wachet auf!* on ♭ *D. 71124*)   (♯ Lon.LL 791)
PIANO (Bauer)
  E. Burton   in ♯ *CEd*.CE 1026
PIANO (Sancan)
  P. Sancan (*Ch. Prels.; & Schumann*) in ♯*FV.* 230004
PIANO (Anon.)
  Ch. Eloffe (*Partita No. 1, s. 3*)
                              VdN.ML 62
  M. v. Doren (in ♯ Chan. MVDP 3)
TWO PIANOS
  E. Bartlett & R. Robertson   in ♯ MGM.E 3150
                         (♭ set X 273)
  A. Whittemore & J. Lowe   in ♭ *Vic*.ERA 123
ORGAN
  ☆ F. Asma (in ♯ Epic.LC 3029; *Phl*.S 06017R)
  R. K. Biggs (in ♯ DCap.LCT 6011;
                 Cap.H 9013: ♭ *EBF 9013*)
HARMONICA L. Adler (in ♯ *FMer*.MLP 7054)
TWO HARPS (Vito)
  E. & J. Vito (in ♯ SOT. 1031 & in ♯ 10301)

No. 151, Süsser Trost, mein Jesus kommt
... No. 5, Heut' schleusst er Chorale
 [1] Trapp Family Cho. (in ♯ B.LAT 8043; ▽ AmD.DL 9553)

No. 152, Tritt auf die Glaubensbahn S, B, orch. 1715
H. Mack, W. Hauck & E. Seiler Cha. Ens
(3ss—*No. 200*)   ♭ PV. 2458/9
[T. v. Sparr (rec.); H. Töttcher (ob.); E. Seiler (vla. d'am.);
  J. Koch (gamba)]

  ☆ D. Bond, R. Irwin, London Baroque Ens.—Haas
                       (♯ Sel.LAC 30008)

... No. 1, Concerto Recorder, ob., vla. d'am., gamba, cont.
L. Davenport, E. Schuster, J. Tryon (vln.), M. Neal (vlc.)
P. Davenport (hpsi.)   ♯ *CEd*.CE 1051
(*Loeillet, A. Scarlatti, Telemann*)

No. 155, Mein Gott, wie lang', ach lange 1716
... No. 1, Mein Gott, wie lang' S, str. & cont.
E. Farrell & Ens.—Brieff in ♯ Vic. set LM 6023
                        (♯ FV.A 630279)

No. 156, Ich steh' mit einem Fuss im Grabe 1729-30
... Sinfonia ob. & strs.[2]
M. Miller & Little Sym.—Saidenberg
                    ♯ AmC.ML 4916
(*Concerto, vln. & ob., excpt.; J. C. Bach, Mozart*)

— — ARR. FL. & PF. "*Arioso*"
A. Anderson & H. Solum (*G.GN 1505*)

— — ARR. ORG. H. Grace
R. I. Purvis (*Purvis, Purcell, M. Shaw, etc.*) in ♯ HIFI.R 703

No. 158, Der Friede sei mit dir
B, cho., vln., ob. & cont.
H. Günter, Hannover Cha. Cho., U. Grehling,
H. Töttcher, K. E. Glückselig (org. & cond.),
gamba & CBs.   ♭ *Pol*. 37020

No. 161, Komm, du süsse Todesstunde
A, T, cho., orch. 1715
☆ H. Rössl-Majdan, W. Kmentt, Cho. & Orch.—Prohaska
(*No. 202*)   ♯ Nix.PVL 7004
                (also announced as ♯ BLP 313)
... No. 1, Komm du süsse Todesstunde A
... No. 4, Der Schluss ist schon gemacht A
☆ H. Rössl-Majdan (in ♯ Van.BG 526)

No. 170, Vergnügte Ruh', beliebte Seelenlust
A, oboe d'amore & orch. 1731-2
H. Rössl-Majdan & Vienna St. Op. Orch.
  —Scherchen   ♯ Nix.WLP 5197
(*Nos. 53 & 54*)   (♯ West.WL 5197; Sel. 320.CW.086)
H. Glaz (M-S), MGM. Cha. Orch.—I. Solomon
                     ♯ MGM.E 3156
(*No. 53; & Pergolesi*)
A. Deller (C-T) & Leonhardt Baroque Ens.
                     ♯ Nix.PVL 7028
(*No. 54 & Mass, B minor, excpt.*) (♯ Van. BG 550)
  ☆ E. Höngen, S. Hopf & Bavarian State Orch.—Lehmann
(*No. 189*)   ♯ HP.APM 14028
(*No. 105* on ♯ AmD.DL 9682)

No. 171, Gott, wie dein Name
S, A, T, B, cho., orch.
... No. 6, Dein ist allein die Ehre Chorale
— ARR. ORG. & BRASS
E. P. Biggs & Brass Ens.   in ♯ AmC.ML 4635
(Bach Festival)

No. 180, Schmücke dich, O liebe Seele
S, A, T, B, cho., orch.
... No. 7, Jesu, wahres Brot des Lebens — ARR.
Brass Ens.—Mazzeo   in ♯ AmC.ML 4635
(Bach Festival)

No. 185, Barmherziges Herze ...
S, A, T, B, cho., orch. 1715
☆ Soloists & Stuttgart Cho.—Grischkat (♯ Eli.PLPE 5003)

No. 189, Meine Seele rühmt und preist
T, rec., ob., vln., cont.
A. Schiøtz, J. Wummer (fl.), M. Tabuteau (ob.),
  A. Schneider (vln.), R. Veyron-Lacroix
  (hpsi.) & P. Tortelier (vlc.) ♯ AmC.ML 4641
(*Beethoven: An die ferne Geliebte*)
P. Bernac (B) & inst. ens. (n.v.)
                      V♯ *Lum*.LD 1-107
  ☆ W. Ludwig, G. Scheck, H. Töttcher, R. Noll (hpsi.),
    A. Wenzinger (vlc.) (*No. 170*)   ♯ HP.APM 14028
  ☆ C. Stemann & Stuttgart Bach Ens.
                       (♯ *Cum*.CPR 334)

No. 198, Lass, Fürstin, lass noch einen Strahl
(*Trauerode*) S, A, T, B, cho., orch. 1727
  ☆ M. Laszlo, H. Rössl-Majdan, W. Kmentt, A. Poell,
    Vienna Academy Cho. & State Op. Orch.—Scherchen
(2ss)   ♯ Nix.WLP 5123
                (*Cantata 106*, on ♯ Sel.LAG 1038)

No. 200, Bekennen will ich seinen Namen
A, 2 vlns., cont.
  ☆ H. Hennecke & Basle Cha. Ens.—Wenzinger PV. 2458
(*No. 152, s. 1*)   (*No. 53*, on ♭ *Pol*. 37063)

SECULAR CANTATAS
No. 201, Der Streit zwischen Phöbus und Pan
S, A, T, T, B, Bs, cho., & orch. 1731
A. Schlemm, I. Lorenzen, C. Esser, H. Friedrich,
  G. Niese, Berlin Komisches Op. Cho.
(8ss)   Eta. 21-C 024/7
(Attrib. to Leipzig Gewandhaus Cho.—Ramin, perhaps
                  n.v., or. ♯ LPM 1003)

  ☆ Soloists, Swabian Cho. & Orch.—Grischkat
                       (♯ Clc. 6150)

No. 202, Weichet nur, betrübte Schatten S, orch.
("*Wedding Cantata*")
J. Delman & London Baroque Orch.—Haas
(*J. M. Haydn*)   ♯ P.PMA 1023
S. Danco & Stuttgart Cha. Orch.—Münchinger
                      ♯ D.LXT 2926
(*No. 51*)   (♯ Lon.LL 993)
G. Weber & Pro Arte Cha. Orch.—Redel
                      ♯ Sel.LAG 1074
[H. Töttcher (ob.), U. Grehling (vln.)]
  ☆ A. Felbermeyer & Orch.—Prohaska ♯ Nix.PVL 7004
(*No. 161*)   (also announced as BLP 313)

---

[1] Sung to words of first verse: *Lobt Gott, ihr Christen.*
[2] Also found as slow movt. of Clavier Concerto, F minor, *q.v.*

No. 203, Amore traditore (*Ital*) Bs. & cont. *c.* 1735
B. Müller & H. Elsner (hpsi.)
(*Cantata No. 211*)   ♯ **E. & AmVox.PL 8980**

No. 205, Der zufriedengestellte Aeolus
S, A, T, B, cho., orch. 1725
☆ Soloists, Swabian Cho. & Orch.—Grischkat
(♯ Clc. 6134)

No. 208, Was mir behagt, ist nur die munt're Jagd
... **No. 9, Schafe können sicher weiden** S
(*Sheep may safely graze*)
R. Fairhurst (Tr.) & org. (*Eng*)   ♭ *D. 71069*
(*Handel: Semele—Where'er you walk*)
Augustana Cho. (*Eng*)—Veld[1]   ♯ **BB.LBC 1075**
(*Cantatas 78 & 104, excpts., etc.*)
☆E. Schwarzkopf, 2 fls., hpsi., vlc. (in ♯ AmC.ML 4792)
— — ARR. ORCH. Walton
Philharmonia—Weldon   ♯ **C.SX 1032**
(*Suppé, Offenbach, etc.*) ("Haydn" on ♭ *SED 5509*)
Philharmonia—Walton   in ♯ *C.C 1016*
(*Walton*) (& ♭ *C.SEL 1504*)   (in ♯ *Angel. 30000*)
(& in *Wise Virgins*, see Section I. E, *above*)
— — ARR. ORCH. Stokowski
☆ Sym.—Stokowski
(in ♯ Vic.LM 1877; in ♯ G.FALP 281, d.c.)
— — ARR. ORG. Purvis: R. I. Purvis (in ♯ HIFI.R 704)
— — 2 PFS. Howe
E. Bartlett & R. Robertson   in ♯ **MGM.E 3150**
(♭ *set X 273*)

A. Whittemore & J. Lowe   ♭ *Vic.ERA 123*
(*No. 147, excpt.; Gluck, Rachmaninoff*)
— — ARR. PF. Petri
A. Kitain ("Siena" pf.)   in ♯ Eso.ESP 3001
(*Chaconne, Partita, etc.*)

No. 209, Non sa che sia dolore S & Orch.
T. Stich-Randall & Orch.-Heiller ♯ **Van.BG 546**
(*No. 51*)   (♯ Ama.AVRS 6004)
G. Weber & Pro Arte Cha.—Redel
(*No. 202*)   ♯ **Sel.LAG 1074**

No. 210, O holder Tag S & orch. 1734–5
☆ M. Laszlo & Vienna State Op.—Scherchen
♯ **Nix.WLP 5138**

No. 211, Schweigt stille, plaudert nicht
(*Coffee Cantata*) S, T, B, orch. 1732
F. Sailer, J. Feyerabend, B. Müller & Stuttgart
Pro Musica—Reinhardt
(*No. 203*)   ♯ **E. & AmVox.PL 8980**
G. Weber, H. Krebs, W. Hauck, & Berlin
Radio Cha. Ens.—Koch   ♯ *CdM.LDA 8057*
(1½ss—*Quodlibet*)
... **No. 4, Ei! Wie schmeckt der Kaffee süsse** S
... **No. 8, Heute noch**
A. Schlemm (o.n. 25-C 031)   *Eta. 320117*

No. 212, Mer hahn en neue Oberkeet 1742
(*Peasant Cantata*) S, Bs, orch.
ABRIDGED RECORDING[2]
H. Joppink (S), G. Baden-Rühlmann (B),
Leipzig Youth Cho. & Cha. Orch.—Sandig
▼♯ *CdM.LDY 8097*

MAGNIFICAT, D major (BWV 243) 1723
S, M-S, A, T, Bs, cho., orch.
E. McLoughlin, H. Harper, A. Deller (C-T),
W. Brown, M. Bevan, St. Anthony Singers,
Kalmar Cha. Orch.—Colombo
♯ **LOL.OL 50101**
[T. Lofthouse (hpsi.), D. Vaughan (org.)] (♯ OL.LD 127)
J. Delman, G. Vivante, C. Carbi, A. Nobile,
M. Cortis, Scuola di Arzignano Cho. & Orch.
—Pellizzari   ♯ **Fnt. 2002**

[3] F. Sailer, L. Wolf-Matthaeus, H. Plümacher,
J. Feyerabend, B. Müller, Stuttgart Radio
Cho. & Pro Musica Orch.—R. Reinhardt
♯ **E. & AmVox.PL 8890**
[F. Milde (ob. d'amore), E. Hölderlin (org.)]
☆ Soloists, R. Lamy Cho. & Ansbach Fest. Orch.—Leitner
♯ **HP.APM 14001**
☆ Soloists, Reinhart & Winterthur Chos. & Orch.
—W. Reinhart (♯ *MMS. 31*)
... **No. 10, Sicut locutus est** Cho.
U.O.S. Cho.—McConnell (unacc.) in ♯ *UOS. 2*
(*Cantata 146 excerpt; & Allegri, Peeters, etc.*)   pte. issue

MASSES (BWV 233-6 are "Lutheran" Masses)
F major (BWV 233)   **A major** (BWV 234) 1737
☆ Soloists, Swabian Cho. & Ton-Studio Orch.—Grischkat
(*Sanctus* with each Mass)   ♯ **Clc. 6128/9**

A major (BWV 234) ... **Qui tollis** S
☆ Y. Tinayre (T)   in ♯ **AmD.DL 9654**
(† *Seven Centuries of Sacred Music*) (in set DX 120)

F major (BWV 233) ... **Kyrie eleison** Cho.
Chorus & Orch.—Goldsbrough   **G.HMS 54**
(† *History of Music in Sound*) (in ♯ Vic. set LM 6030)

G major (BWV 236) 1737-8
☆ Soloists, Swabian Cho. & Ton-Studio Orch.—Grischkat
(*Sanctus*)   ♯ **Cpt.MC 20025**

G minor (BWV 235) *c,* 1737
☆ Soloists, Swabian Cho. & Orch.—Grischkat
(*Sanctus*)   ♯ **Cpt.MC 20059**

B minor (BWV 232) S, A, T, B, cho., orch. 1733/7
COMPLETE RECORDINGS
Swabian Singers & Stuttgart Pro Musica
Orch.—Grischkat   ♯ **E. & AmVox.PL 8063**
(6ss)   (♯ PaV.PL 7743)
[M. Guillaume, H. Plümacher, W. Hohmann, H. Günter]
Frankfurt Chu. Cho. & Coll. Mus.—K. Thomas
(6ss)   ♯ **LOL.OL 50094/6**
[L. Schwarzweller, L. Fischer, H. Kretschmar, B. Müller]
(♯ OL.LD 112/4)
Vienna Musikfreunde Cho. & Orch.—Karajan
(6ss)   ♯ **C.CX 1121/3**
[E. Schwarzkopf, M. Höffgen, N. Gedda, H. Rehfuss]
(♯ Angel 35015/7, set 3500; ♯ C.FCX 291/3: QCX 10055/7)
Berlin Cha. Cho. & Radio Orch.—Lehmann
(4ss)   ♯ **Ura.RS 2-1**
[G. Weber, M. di Landi, H. Krebs, K. Wolfram]
(also ♯ Van.BG 527/8, Ura. set 236, & MTW. set 38)
Bavarian State Cho. & Orch.—Ramin
(4ss)   ♯ **MMS. set 2021**
[U. Graf, H. Töpper, G. Lutze, M. Pröbstl]
(♯ CHS. set 1234)
☆ Soloists, Academy Cho. & Vienna Sym.—Scherchen
♯ **Nix.WLP 6301-1/3**
[Gloria & Sanctus only on ♭ Sel. 470.CW.006]
Anon. Artists   ♯ **Gram. 20164/6**
☆ Soloists, Victor Cho. & Orch.—Shaw
(♯ DV. set CLC 16319)
... **No. 9, Qui sedes; No. 24, Agnus Dei** A
K. Ferrier (*below, & Handel*)   in ♯ **D.LXT 2757**
(& in ♯ *D.LW 5083; Lon.LD 9096*) (in ♯ Lon.LL 688)
... **No. 21, Sanctus** Cho.
Helsinki Cho. & Orch.—Klemetti   Od.PLDX 4
... **No. 23, Benedictus** T, vln.   ☆G. Thill (in ♯ *C.FH 504*)
... **No. 24, Agnus Dei** A
A. Deller (C-T) & Leonhardt Baroque Ens.
in ♯ **Nix.PVL 7028**
(*Cantatas 54 & 170*)   (♯ Van.BG 550)
... **Nos. 4 & 20** ☆ Vienna Academy Cho. from set
(♭ *Sel. 470.CW.006*)
... **Nos. 22 & 24** ☆ A. Dermota & G. B. Schuster, from set
(♭ *Sel. 470.CW.005*)
... **No. 25, Dona nobis pacem** Finale
Dresden Cath. Cho. & Phil. Orch.—Mauersberger
Eta. 20-108
(*Matthaeus-Passion, No. 78*)(o.n. 25-C 028; & ♯ LPM 1025)

---

[1] ARR. Male Cho. & 2 pfs.
[2] A free arrangement and text is used; Nos. 5-8, 19 and 20 (which is same as Cantata 201, No. 7), are omitted; others ar abridged.
[3] Includes the 4 Supplementary numbers from the original E flat major version: **A. Vom Himmel hoch; B. Freut euch;**
C. Gloria; D. Virga Jesse floruit (in the setting in Cantata 110); here transposed into D major.

MOTETS

COLLECTION

Fürchte dich nicht	(BWV 228)
Der Geist hilft unsrer Schwachheit auf	(BWV 226)
Jesu, meine Freude	(BWV 227)
Komm, Jesu, komm!	(BWV 229)
Lobet den Herrn	(BWV 230) with cont.
Sei Lob und Preis mit Ehren	(BWV 231)[1]
Singet dem Herrn	(BWV 225)

Stuttgart Vocal & Inst. Ens.—Couraud
‡ **DFr. 149/50**
(3ss—*J. Christoph Bach: Ich lasse dich nicht*)
[BWV 227 sung unaccompanied; the others have inst. acc.
arr. Couraud]

Fürchte dich nicht (BWV 228)
Leipzig Thomanerchor—Ramin   ♭ *Pol. 37036*

(Der) Geist hilft unsrer Schwachheit auf (BWV 226)
Berlin Motet Cho.—Arndt   ‡ *T.PLB 6133*
(*below*)

Leipzig Thomanerchor—Ramin   ‡ *Pol. 13008*
(*below*)   (2ss, ♭ *Pol. 37080*)
☆ St. Olaf Cho.—Christiansen (*Eng*)
(in ‡ *Alld. 2005:* ♭ *EP 2005*)

— ARR. ORCH. Bach (BWV 226a)[2]
Paris Coll. Mus.—Douatte   ‡ *EPP.APG 124*
(*Brandenburg Conc. 1 & Vln. Concerto*)

Jesu, meine Freude (BWV 227) 1723
Vienna Academy Cho.—Grossmann
(*below*)   ‡ **West.WL 5289**
Berlin Motet Cho.—Arndt   ‡ *DT.LGM 65032*
(*below*)   (‡ *FT. 270.TC.092; T.NLB 6102*)
Concordia Cho.—P. J. Christiansen (*Eng*)
in ‡ *Cdia.CDLP 3*
(*Kodaly, Palestrina, etc.*)

☆ Leipzig Thomanerchor—Ramin   ‡ *Pol. 13008*
(*Der Geist*)
☆ Victor Cho.—Shaw (*Eng*)   ‡ *Vic.LM 9035*
(*Cantata No. 4*)
... No. 7, Chorale In Collection, *post, q.v.*
Oratoire Cho.—Hornung (*Fr*)   in ‡ *SM. 33-19*

Komm, Jesu, komm! (BWV 229)
Vienna Academy Cho.—Grossmann
(*below & above*)   ‡ **West.WL 5289**
R. Shaw Chorale & str.   ‡ *Vic.LM 1784*
(*Schubert, Brahms*)   (‡ *FV.A 630230*)

Lobet den Herrn (BWV 230)
Berlin Motet Cho.—Arndt   ‡ *T.PLB 6133*
(*above*)

O Jesu Christ, mein's Lebens Licht
SEE: Cantata No. 118, *above*

Singet dem Herrn (BWV 225)
Berlin Motet Cho.—Arndt   ‡ *DT.LGM 65032*
(*above*)   (‡ *FT. 270.TC.092; T.NLB 6102*)
Yale Univ. Music School Cho.—Hindemith
‡ *Over.LP 4*
(† Yale Univ., Vol. I)
Vienna Academy Cho.—Grossmann
(*above*)   ‡ **West.WL 5289**
Concordia Cho.—Christiansen (*Eng*)
in ‡ *Cdia. 4*

... **Alles was Odem hat** (Finale)
Leipzig Thomanerchor—Ramin   *Eta. 120107*
(*Cantata No. 78, excpt.*)   (o.n. 25-C 021)
G. Carrillo Vocal Qtt. (*Span*)   *Orf. 22003*
(‡s—*W.T.C. No. 31 & Chorales*)

ORATORIOS

OSTERN-ORATORIUM

S, A, T, B, cho., orch. (BWV 249) *c.* 1736
L. Dutoit, M. Nussbaumer, F. Gruber,
O. Weiner, Academy Cho. & Vienna Pro
Musica Orch.—Grossmann
‡ **E. & AmVox.PL 8620**
[J. Nebois, org.]
☆ Soloists, Academy Cho. & Vienna Cha. Orch.—Prohaska
(‡ CID. VXT 33012)
... Sinfonia ... Adagio only
☆ L. Goossens (ob.) & Liverpool Phil.—Sargent
(in ‡ AmC.ML 4782)
... No. 9, Saget mir geschwinde A
☆ H. Rössl-Majdan, from set   in ‡ Van.BG 526

WEIHNACHTS-ORATORIUM (BWV 248) 1734
(*Christmas Oratorio*) S, A, T, B, cho., orch.
COMPLETE RECORDING
☆ G. Weber, L. Fischer, H. Marten, H. Günter, Detmold
Acad. Cho. & Orch.—Thomas[3] ‡ LOL.OL 50001/3
(6ss)

COMPLETE RECORDINGS of Parts 1–3
C. Owen, H. Töpper, G. Luhe, H. Günter,
Munich Bach Cho. & Bavarian St. Op. Cha.
—Richter   ‡ *D.LXT 2000/1*
(4ss) [recorded in Chu. of Ascension, Munich]
G. Weber, S. Wagner, H. Krebs, H. Rehfuss,
Berlin Motet & R.I.A.S. Chos. & Phil.
—F. Lehmann (4ss)   ‡ *Pol. 14051/2*
[Nos. 10, Sinfonia, & Nos. 21/3, on ♭ *Pol. 37075*]

HIGHLIGHTS
☆ Soloists, Stuttgart Cho. & Orch.—Grischkat, from set
(‡ Rem. 199-155; excerpt also, ‡ Ply. 12-90)
... No. 4, Bereite dich, Zion A
☆ M. Anderson (in ‡ Vic.LCT 1111: ♭ set WCT 1111)
... No. 5, Wie soll ich dich empfangen Chorale
... No. 9, Ach mein herzliebes Jesulein Chorale
Baldwin-Wallace Bach Fest. Cho. & org.—Poinar
(*Orch. Suite No. 3—Bourrée & Gigue*)   MSB. 78041
... No. 12, Brich an, o schönes Morgenlicht Chorale
Kings College Chapel—Ord[4] (*Eng*) & org. in ‡ Argo.RG 39
(† Festival of Lessons & Carols)
R. Shaw Chorale (*Eng*)   in ♭ Vic.ERA 225
... No. 17, Schaut hin! Chorale
Trapp Family Singers—Wasner[5]   in ‡ B.LAT 8038
(*Christmas Music Vol. 2*) (‡ AmD.DL 9689: ♭ set ED 1200)
(& o.v. ☆ in ‡ Cam.CAL 209)
... Nos. 5, 9, 23 (Chorales) — ARR. ORG. & BRASS
E. P. Biggs & Brass Ens. (Bach Festival) in ‡ AmC.ML 4635

PASSION MUSIC

JOHANNES-PASSION (BWV 245) 1722-3
COMPLETE RECORDINGS
Leipzig Thomanerchor & Gewandhaus Orch.
—Ramin (6ss)   ‡ **HP.APM 14036/8**
(‡ Pol. 501/3 & auto., ‡ 511/3)
[Soloists: A. Giebel (S), M. Höffgen (A), F. Kelch &
H. O. Hudemann (Bs.); uses recorders, lute, gamba]
(‡ Eta. 820012/4)
Excerpts from this set:
Nos. 10-13 on ♭ Pol. 37081
Nos. 47, 48, 67 on ♭ Pol. 37082
Frankfurt Chu. of the Magi Cho. & Collegium
Musicum—K. Thomas   ‡ **LOL.OL 50023/5**
(6ss)   (‡ OL.LD 101/3)
[Soloists: G. Weber (S), S. Plate (T), H. Hess (T),
P. Gümmer (Bs.), H. Drewanz (hpsi.), K. Storck (vlc.)]
Anon. Soloists & Berlin Bach Soc. & Cath. Choirs
—Burckhardt[6] (4ss)   ‡ *Roy. 1522/3*
☆ Soloists, R. Shaw Cho. & Collegiate Cho. & Cha.
Orch.—Shaw (*Eng*)   ‡ G.ALP 1188/90
(‡ DV. set CLC 16319)
ABRIDGED RECORDING
☆ Soloists, Cho. & Austrian Sym.—Preinfalk
(‡ Cum.CR 287; excerpt from No. 1 in ‡ Ply. 12-90)
... Nos. 26-31 T, Bs, Bs, Bs, cho.
E. Greene, D. Franklin, S. Joynt, N. Walker, Cho., Orch.
& org.—Westrup   G.HMS 55
(† History of Music in Sound) (in ‡ Vic. set LM 6030)

---

[1] Chorus by Bach for insertion in Telemann's Motet *Jauchzet dem Herrn* (BWV Anh. 160).
[2] Intended as orch. acc. to a choral performance but here recorded as a separate orch. work.
[3] Abridges *da capos* of Nos. 1, 29, 41, 43 and does not repeat No. 24 at end of Part III.
[4] Including Recit. No. 11: *Und es waren Hirten.*   [5] Sung to words of the Chorale: *Vom Himmel hoch.*
[6] Omissions include Nos. 4, 6, 10, 32, 56, 60, 62, 64-66, 68, and parts of Nos. 11, 12, 13, 63.

... **No. 52, In meines Herzens Grunde**   Chorale   —ARR.
     Brass Ens.—Mazzeo (Bach Festival)   in ♯ AmC.ML 4635
... **No. 58, Es ist vollbracht**   A
     K. Ferrier (*Eng*)   in ♯ D.LXT 2757
     (*above & Handel*)   (in ♯ Lon.LL 688)
          (also in ♯ *D.LW 5083; Lon.LD 9096*)
     P. Schreier (Boy A)   *Eta. 320109*
     (*Songs*)   (o.n. 25-C 029; & ♯ LPM 1025)
     ☆ M. Anderson (*Eng*)
          (in ♯ Vic.LCT 1111: ♭ set WCT 1111)
... **No. 67, Ruht wohl, ihr heiligen Gebeine**   Cho.
     ☆ Salzburg Fest. Cho. & Austrian Sym.—Preinfalk
        (from set, ♭ *Rem.REP 16; ♭ Cum.ECR 50*)
... **No. 68, Ach Herr, lass dein lieb' Engelein**
     ☆ R. Shaw Cho. & Orch. (from set, in ♯ Vic.LM 1877)

MATTHAEUS-PASSION (BWV 244) 1729
(St. Matthew Passion)

COMPLETE RECORDINGS
Vienna Academy Cho. & State Op. Orch.
  —Scherchen[1]   ♯ **Nix.WLP 6401-1/4**
(8ss)   (♯ West. set WAL 401)
[M. Laszlo (S), H. Rössl-Majdan (A), P. Munteanu &
  H. Cuénod (T), R. Standen, H. Rehfuss, E. Wächter,
  P. Lagger, L. Heppe (Bs.)]

Vienna Academy Cho. & Cha. Orch.
  —Grossmann[2]   ♯ **E. & AmVox. set PL 8283**
(6ss)
[L. Dutoit (S), M. Nussbaumer (A), E. Majkut (T),
  H. Buchsbaum & O. Wiener (Bs)]

Anon. Artists (♯ Gram. 20167/70)

☆ Soloists, Berlin Cho. & Orchs.—Lehmann
        (♯ AmVox. set PL 6074, n.n.)

ABRIDGED RECORDINGS
Amsterdam Toonkunst Cho. & Orch.
  —Mengelberg[3] (8ss)   ♯ **EPhi.ABL 3035/8**
          (♯ Phi.A 00150/3L)
[K. Erb (T), J. Vincent (S), I. Durigo (A), L. v. Tulder (T),
  G. Ravelli & H. Schey (Bs)]
[also ♯ Phi.A 00320/2L & ♯ AmC. set SL 179, 6ss, auto.]

Bloor St. Chu. & Toronto Mendelssohn Chos.
   & Sym.—MacMillan[4]   ♯ **BB. set LBC 6101**
(6ss)   (♯ Bea. set LPS 002)
[L. Marshall, M. Morrison, J. Newton (S), M. Stilwell (A),
  E. Johnson & J. Lamond (T), D. Brown, J. Milligan,
  E. Tredwell (B), in *Eng*, G. Kraus (hpsi.) F. S.
  Sylvester (org.)]

☆ T. Lemnitz, K. Erb, etc.; Leipzig Cho.—Ramin
        (▽ ArgV. set DM 1218/9)

SELECTED EXCERPTS
No. 1, Kommt ihr Töchter   Chorus
No. 3, Herzliebster Jesu   Chorale
No. 16, Ich bin's, ich sollte büssen   Chorale
No. 21, Erkenne mich, mein Hüter   Chorale
No. 33b, Sind Blitze, sind Donner   Chorus
No. 35, O Mensch, bewein dein Sünde gross   Chorale a due cori
No. 39, Hat man die Welt trüglich gerichtet   Chorale
No. 44, Wer hat dich so geschlagen   Chorale
No. 48, Bin ich gleich von dir gewichen   Chorale
No. 50, Befiehl du deine Wege   Chorale
No. 78, Wir setzen uns mit Tränen nieder   Chorale a due cori
Danish State Radio Cho. & Orch.—Wöldike
        ♯ **HSL.HSL 2070**

... **Nos. 1 & 78** (from complete recording)
     ☆ Berlin Radio Cho.—Lehmann (▽♯ DFr.EX 17016)
... **No. 1, Kommt, ihr Töchter**   Cho.
     ☆ Rotterdam Toonkunst Cho.—Niels (♭ Phi.N 402026E)
... **No. 3, Herzliebster Jesu**   Chorale
     ☆ Netherlands Cha. Cho.—de Nobel (in ♯ Phi.S 06026R)
... **No. 10, Buss' und Reu'**   A
     K. Ferrier (*Eng*)   in ♯ D.LXT 2757
     (*above & Handel*)   (in ♯ Lon.LL 688)
     (& in ♯ *D.LW 5083; Lon.LD 9096*)
... **No. 16, Ich bin's, ich sollte büssen**   Chorale   —ARR.
     Brass Ens.—Mazzeo (Bach Festival)   in ♯ AmC.ML 4635
... **No. 47, Erbarme dich, mein Gott**
     J. Tourel (M-S) & Perpignan Festival Orch.—Casals
     (*Beethoven, Mozart*)   in ♯ AmC.ML 4640
     ☆ K. Ferrier (*Eng*), D. McCallum (vln.), etc. (♭ D. 71037)
     M. Anderson (in ♯ Vic.LCT 1111: ♭ set WCT 1111)

... **No. 51, Gibt mir meinen Jesum wieder**   Bs
     ☆ N. Cordon (*Eng*) (in ♯ Cam.CAL 269)
... **No. 53, Befiehl du deine Wege**   Chorale   —ARR. PF. Kempff
     ☆ W. Kempff   in ♯ D.LXT 2820
     (also on ▽ K 28226)[5]   (in ♯ Lon.LL 791)
... **No. 58, Aus Liebe will mein Heiland sterben**   S
     ☆ E. Schumann, fl. & obs. (in ♯ Vic.LCT 1158)
... **No. 63, O Haupt voll Blut und Wunden**
     Berlin Motet Cho.—Arndt   *T.A 11421*
     (*Chorale—Jesus, meine Zuversicht*)
     ☆ Netherlands Cha. Cho.—de Nobel   in ♯Phi.S 06026R
     (*Chorales; & Okeghem, Lotti, Lassus, Handl*)
     Cho.—R. Wagner (*Eng*)   in ♯ Layos.LL 102
... **No. 68, Ach Golgotha**   A
... **No. 69, Sehet, Jesus hat die Hand ...**
     E. Brems (M-S) & Ens.   in ♯ HS.HSL 2073
     († *Masterpieces of Music before 1750*)
     (also in † *Histoire de la Musique vocale*)
... **No. 72, Wenn ich einmal soll scheiden**
     In Chorale Collection, *post, q.v.*
... **No. 78, Wir setzen uns mit Tränen nieder**
     Dresden Kreuzchor & Phil. Orch.—Mauersberger
                Eta. 20-108
     (*Mass in B minor, excpt.*)   (o.n. 25-C 028)
     ☆ Rotterdam Toonkunst Cho.—Niels (♭ Phi.N 402026E)

Quodlibet (BWV 524)   S, A, T, B
W. Behrend, C. Behr, C. Esser, H. Rosenberg,
   & Berlin Radio Cha. Ens.—Mielenz
                    Eta. 320110
(2ss)   (o.n. 25-C 030; ♯ LPM 1002)
     ☆ H. Töttcher, E. Manrau, J. Hausmann, G. Raeker &
     Berlin Radio Cha. Ens.—Haarth ♯ *CdM.LDA 8057*
     (¼s—*Cantata No. 211*)

SANCTUS
C major (BWV 237)
D major (BWV 238)
     ☆ Swabian Cho. & Ton-Studio Orch.—Grischkat
                    (♯ Clc. 6128/9)

D minor (BWV 239)
     ☆ Swabian Cho. & Ton-Studio Orch.—Grischkat
                 (♯ Cpt.MC 20059)

G major (BWV 240)
     ☆ Swabian Cho. & Ton-Studio Orch.—Grischkat
                 (♯ Cpt.MC 20025)

III. CHORALES & SONGS

CHORALES

COLLECTIONS
Freu' dich sehr, O meine Seele   (Cantata 70, No. 7)
Nun sich der Tag geendet hat   (BWV 396)
Herzlich tut mich Verlangen   (Matthäus-Passion, No. 72)
Alle Menschen müssen sterben   (BWV 262)
Aus tiefer Noth   (Cantata 38, No. 6)
Christus, der ist mein Leben   (BWV 281)
Welt, ade! ich bin dein müde   (Cantata 27, No. 6)
Liebster Jesu, wir sind hier   (BWV 373)
Puer natus in Bethlehem   (Cantata 65, No. 2)
Jesu, meine Freude   (Motet—No. 7)
Ach wie flüchtig   (Cantata 26, No. 6)
Christ lag in Todesbanden   (BWV 277)
Für Freuden lasst uns springen   (BWV 313)
Ich hab' mein Sach' Gott heimgestellt   (BWV 351)
Gott sei uns gnädig und barmherzig   (BWV 323)
     ☆ Pro Musica Cho. Soc.—Calder   ♯ *Allo. 4005*

Ach Gott, erhör mein Seufzen   (BWV 254)
Christ ist erstanden   (BWV 276)[6]
Es spricht der Unweisen Mund wohl   (BWV 308)
     ▽ G. Carrillo Vocal Qtt. (*Span*)   Orf. 22003
     (*Motet excpt. & W.T.C. No. 31*)

Alle Menschen müssen sterben   (BWV 262)
     ☆ Augustana Cho.—Veld (*Eng*) (in ♯ Word.W 4001)

Jesus, meine Zuversicht   (BWV 365)
Berlin Motet Cho.—Arndt   *T.A 11421*
(*Matthaeus-Passion, No. 63*)

---

[1] Omits second verse in No. 63.   [2] Omits *da capo* in Nos. 10, 29, 61, 75; a few other cuts are made.
[3] Omits Nos. 23, 29, 38, 41, 48, 50-52, 55, 61, 65, 66, 70, 75; cuts occur in Nos. 9, 12, 37, 39, 49, 54, 63, 64, 67, 75, 76, 78.
Recorded at public performance, Palm Sunday, 1939.
[4] Omits Nos. 10, 23, 41, 50, 51, 55, 61, 70, 75 and 76, and the *da capo* of Nos. 12 and 19.
[5] Erroneously listed as Chorale-Prelude in Supplement I.
[6] Or perhaps Cantata No. 66, Alleluia.

Ein' feste Burg (unid. setting)
Brass Ens.—Mazzeo   in ♯ AmC.ML 4635
(Bach Festival)

O Ewigkeit du Donnerwort (BWV 397)
(as: *Hosanna to the living Lord*)
Yale Univ. Sch. Cho.—Borden in ♯ Over.LP 2
(† *Hymns of Praise*)

O Lamm Gottes unschuldig (BWV 401)
☆ Netherlands Cha. Cho.—de Nobel   ♯ Phi.S 06026R
(*Okeghem, Lotti, Lassus, Handl*) [G. Stam, org.]

(3) Wedding Chorales (BWV 250-2) Cho. & orch.
(*Was Gott tut; Sei Lob und Ehr'; Nun danket*)
Brass Ens.—Mazzeo   in ♯ AmC.ML 4635
(Bach Festival)

Nun danket alle Gott (BWV 252)
☆ Trapp Family Cho. (in ♯ Cam.CAL 209)

Was Gott tut, das ist wohlgetan (unspec. setting)
Brass Ens.—Mazzeo   in ♯ AmC.ML 4635
(Bach Festival)

SONGS

GEISTLICHE LIEDER "COMPLETE"

The Schemelli Gesangbuch, Complete; with songs from
the Anna Magdalena Bach Notenbuch, marked AMB.
The numbering used here at the left-hand side of the titles
is that of the *Bach Gesellschaft* (and of the recording).

1.	Ach, dass nicht die letzte Stunde	(BWV 439)
2.	Auf! Auf! die rechte Zeit	(BWV 440)
3.	Auf! Auf! mein Herz *c*	(BWV 441)
4.	Beglückter Stand getreuer Seelen	(BWV 442)
5.	Beschränkt, ihr Weisen dieser Welt *c*	(BWV 443)
6.	Brich entzwei, mein armes Herze	(BWV 444)
7.	Brunnquell aller Güten	(BWV 445)
8.	Der lieben Sonne Licht und Pracht *c*	(BWV 446)
9.	Der Tag ist hin	(BWV 447)
10.	Der Tag mit seinem Lichte	(BWV 448)
11.	Dich bet' ich an, mein höchster Gott *c*	(BWV 449)
12.	Die bittre Leidenszeit beginnet *c*	(BWV 450)
13.	Die goldne Sonne *c*	(BWV 451)
14.	Dir, dir, Jehovah *c*	(BWV 452)
15.	Eins ist Not	(BWV 453)
16.	Ermuntre dich, mein schwacher Geist	(BWV 454)
17.	Erwürgtes Lamm, das die verwahrten Siegel *c*	(BWV 455)
18.	Es glänzet der Christen inwendiges Leben	(BWV 456)
19.	Es ist nun aus mit meinem Leben *c*	(BWV 457)
20.	Es ist vollbracht!	(BWV 458)
21.	Es kostet viel, ein Christ zu sein	(BWV 459)
22.	Gib dich zufrieden *c* (AMB)	(BWV 511)
23.	Gib dich zufrieden *c* (AMB)	(BWV 512)
24.	Gib dich zufrieden *c*	(BWV 460)
25.	Gott lebet noch; Seele,was verzagst du doch? *c*.	(BWV 461)
26.	Gott, wie gross ist dein Güte *c*	(BWV 462)
27.	Herr, nicht schikke deine Rache	(BWV 463)
28.	Ich bin ja, Herr, in deiner Macht	(BWV 464)
29.	Ich freue mich in dir	(BWV 465)
30.	Ich halte treulich still *c*	(BWV 466)
31.	Ich liebe Jesum alle Stund'	(BWV 467)
32.	Ich lass dich nicht	(BWV 468)
33.	Ich steh' an deiner Krippen hier	(BWV 469)
34.	Jesu, Jesu, du bist mein *c*	(BWV 470)
35.	Jesu, deine Liebeswunden	(BWV 471)
36.	Jesu, meines Glaubens Zier	(BWV 472)
37.	Jesu, meines Herzens Freud'	(BWV 473)
38.	Jesus ist das schönste Licht *c*	(BWV 474)
39.	Jesus, unser Trost und Leben	(BWV 475)
40.	Ihr Gestirn', ihr hohen Lüfte *c*	(BWV 476)
41.	Kein Stündlein geht dahin *c*	(BWV 477)
42.	Komm, süsser Tod	(BWV 478)
43.	Kommt, Seelen, dieser Tag *c*	(BWV 479)
44.	Kommt wieder aus der finstern Gruft *c*	(BWV 480)
45.	Lasset uns mit Jesu ziehen	(BWV 481)
46.	Liebes Herz, bedenke doch *c*	(BWV 482)
47.	Liebster Gott, wann werd' ich sterben? *c*	(BWV 483)
48.	Liebster Herr Jesu *c*	(BWV 484)
49.	Liebster Immanuel	(BWV 485)
50.	Mein Jesu, dem die Seraphinen	(BWV 486)
51.	Mein Jesu, was für Seelenweh *c*	(BWV 487)
52.	Meines Lebens letzte Zeit	(BWV 488)
53.	Nicht so traurig, nicht so sehr *c*	(BWV 489)
54.	Nur mein Jesus ist mein Leben	(BWV 490)
55.	O du Liebe meiner Liebe *c*	(BWV 491)
56.	O Ewigkeit, du Donnerwort (AMB)	(BWV 513)
57.	O finstre Nacht, wenn wirst du doch *c*	(BWV 492)
58.	O Jesulein süss	(BWV 493)
59.	O liebe Seele	(BWV 494)
60.	O wie selig seid ihr doch *c*	(BWV 495)
61.	Schaff's mit mir, Gott (AMB)	(BWV 514)
62.	Seelenbräutigam, Jesu, Gottes Lamm! *c*	(BWV 496)
63.	Seelenweide, meine Freude	(BWV 497)
64.	Selig, wer an Jesum denkt *c*	(BWV 498)
65.	Sei gegrüsset, Jesu gütig	(BWV 499)

66.	So gehst du nun, mein Jesu, hin *c*		(BWV 500)
67.	So gibst du nun, mein Jesu, gute Nacht		(BWV 501)
68.	So wünsch' ich mir zu guter Letzt		(BWV 502)
69.	Steh' ich bei meinem Gott *c*		(BWV 503)
70.	Vergiss mein nicht, dass ich dein nicht vergesse *c*		(BWV 504)
71.	Vergiss mein nicht, vergiss mein nicht *c*		(BWV 505)
72.	Warum betrübst du dich? *c* (AMB)		(BWV 516)
73.	Was bist du doch, o Seele, so betrübet *c*.		(BWV 506)
74.	Wie wohl ist mir *c* (AMB)		(BWV 517)
75.	Wo ist mein Schäflein? *c*		(BWV 507)

H. Rössl-Majdan (A), H. Cuénod (T),
F. Holetschek (hpsi.), R. Harand (vlc.)
    ♯ Nix.WLP 6402-1/4
(8ss)   (♯ West. set WAL 402)
(Cuénod sings those marked *c* above; Rössl-Majdan the
remainder).
[Nos. 14, 42 and 71 are admitted by BWV as Bach's
compositions; Wüllner admits Nos. 14, 26, 51 and 71,
and probably others].

SONGS FROM THE NOTENBUCH FÜR A. M. BACH

Bist du bei mir (No. 25)
Gedenke doch, mein Geist (No. 41)
Ich habe genug (Cantata 82)
O Ewigkeit, du Donnerwort (No. 42)
Schlummert ein (Cantata 82)
Willst du dein Herz mir schenken (No. 37)
☆ M. Weis-Osborn (S), K. Rapf (hpsi.), & vlc.
    (♯ CID.VXT 33017)

Bist du bei mir (No. 25) (BWV 508)
E. Schwarzkopf (S), G. Moore (pf.) C.LX 1580
(*Mozart: Abendempfindung*) (in ♯ CX 1044: FCX 182)
    (in ♯ Angel 35023)

S. Danco (S), J. Demessieux (org.)
    in ♯ D.LX 3113
(*below; & Caldara, Caccini, etc.*) (in ♯ Lon.LS 698)

R. Hayes (T), R. Boardman (pf.)
    in ♯ Van.VRS 448
(*Caccini, Caldara, Monteverdi, etc. & Trad.*)

C. Maurane (B, Fr) & str. orch. (in ♭ Pat.ED 15)

— ARR. ORGAN R. Foort (in ♯ SOT. 1054 & in ♯ 10545)

Dir, dir, Jehova (No. 39) (BWV 452)
Schaff's mit mir, Gott (No. 35) (BWV 514)
Brass Ens.—Mazzeo   in ♯ AmC.ML 4635
(Bach Festival)

Liebster Herr Jesu (BWV 484)
— ARR. CHO. Elokas
Finlandia Cho.—Elokas (*Ryt.R 6229*)

— ARR ORG. V. Kuosma (in D.SD 5166)

Warum betrübst du dich? (No. 33) (BWV 516)
S. Danco (S), J. Demessieux (org.)
    in ♯ D.LX 3113
(*Caldara, Schütz, Durante, etc.*) (in ♯ Lon.LS 698)

Willst du dein Herz mir schenken (No. 37)
("*Aria di Giovannini*", copied by Bach) (BWV 518)
S. Schöner (S), H. Hartig (hpsi.) Pol. 62900
(*W. F. Bach: Kein Hälmlein . . .*) (♭ Pol. 32105)

Unspec. collection (probably the same as ♯ Van.BG 510)
☆ M. Weis-Osborn (S), K. Rapf (hpsi.)
    ♯ Van.VRS 5002[1]

SONGS FROM THE SCHEMELLI GESANGBUCH
(numbers refer to BG xxxix)
COLLECTION ed. Dørumsgaard
Vergiss mein nicht (No. 71) JSB
O finstre Nacht (No. 57)
Liebster Herr Jesu (No. 48) JSB?
Komm, süsser Tod (No. 42) JSB
Dir, dir Jehova (No. 14) JSB
K. Flagstad (S), G. Moore (pf.)
    ♯ Vic.LHMV 1070
(† *German Songs*)

Dir, dir, Jehova (No. 14) JSB
D. Bergquist (Tr.), G. Edmundh (pf.) Sir. 119
(*Söderman: Hymn*)

Es ist nun aus mit meinem Leben (No. 19)
G. Pechner (B)   in ♯ Roy. 1557

[1] Announced but not issued.

Es kostet viel, ein Christ zu sein (No. 21)
Was bist du doch, O Seele, so betrübet (No. 73)
  P. Schreier (Boy A.), H. Otto (org.) *Eta.* **320109**
  (*Johannes-Passion, aria*)   (o.n. 25-C 029; & ‡ LPM 1025)

Komm, süsser Tod (No. 42) JSB
  S. Danco (S), J. Demessieux (org.)
                in ‡ *D.LX 3113*
  (*above; & Caldara, Schütz, etc.*)   (in ‡ *Lon.LS 698*)
  M. Powers (A, *Eng*), F. la Forge (pf.)
                in ‡ Atl. 1207
  (*Franz, Haydn, Handel, Brahms, Schubert, etc.*)
  All Saints Chu. Male Cho.—Self (*Eng*)
              in ‡ CEd.CE 1023
  († Five Centuries of Choral Music)
— ARR. VLA. & ORG. de Tar
  W. Primrose & V. de Tar   in ‡ *AmC.AAL 33*
— ARR. ORG. V. Kuosma (*D.SD 5166*)
— ARR. ORCH. Stokowski
  ☆ Sym.—Stokowski (in ‡ *G.FALP 281*;
            in ‡ *Vic.LRM 7033*: ♭ set ERB 7033)
— ARR. ORCH.
  Milan Angelicum—Jones   *Ang.CPA 056*
  (*Mozart: Ave verum corpus*)

Mein Jesu, was für Seelenweh (No. 51) JSB
— ARR. ORCH. Stokowski
  ☆ Orch.—Stokowski (in ‡ Vic.LM 1875: ♭ set ERB 52;
             ‡ G.FALP 282; ‡ ItV.A12R 0022)

O Jesulein süss (No. 58)
  St. Paul's Cath. Cho.—Dykes Bower (*Eng*)
                    C.LB 148
  (*Arr. Pettman: The Infant King*)
        (in ‡ CX 1193; ‡ Angel. 35138 in set 3516)
  Petits Chanteurs—Debat (in ‡ *D.FMT 133159*)

MISC. UNIDENTIFIED, etc.
Bach, his story and his music
  D. Randolph (narr.) etc.   ‡ *Per.PCS 9*
Herre Gud, du er og bliver
  O. Werner (T), R. Holger (org.)   *Od.ND 7221*
  (*Arr. Holger: The Lord is here & calls thee*)
Lob und Ehre und Weisheit und Dank (BWV.Anh. 162)
  (*Blessing, Glory, & Wisdom*; Motet, double Cho., really by
    G. G. Wagner)
  Augustana Cho.—Veld (*Eng*)   in ‡ Word.W 4005
  (*Britten, Rachmaninoff, Kodály, etc.*)
O darkest woe
  Redlands Univ. Cho.—Jones (*Eng*) in ‡ AmC.ML 4866
O Jesus Guds Son G. Stenlund (*HH.F 1073*)

BACH, Wilhelm Friedemann (1710-1784)

Fantasia, D minor ("Capriccio") (F. 19)
  M. Jonas (pf.)   in ‡ AmC.ML 4624
FUGUES, Clavier:
No. 4, D minor; No. 5, E flat major (F 31-4, 5)
Polonaise No. 9, F major (F 12-9)
  R. Gerlin (pf.)   in ‡ LOL.OL 50097
  (*J. S. Bach, C. P. E. Bach*)
Polonaise No. 4, D minor (F. 12) clav.
  ☆ A. Ehlers (hpsi.) (in ‡ *D.UAT 273084*)
Sonata (Trio), F major fl., vln. & cont. (F. p.13)
  Alma Musica Ens.[1]   ‡ Sel.LPG 8481
  (*C. P. E. & J. C. Bach*)   (‡ T.LE 6527)
  ☆ L. Schaefer, R. Brink & D. Pinkham (hpsi.)
                  (‡ Lyr.LL 57)
Sonata, B major vln. & hpsi. (F. p.12; dubious)
Trio, D major fl., ob. & cont. (F. 47)
  Collegium Pro Arte   ‡ OL.LD 54
  (*J. C. F. Bach*) [for soloists, see under J. C. F. Bach]
SONG: Kein Hälmlein wächst auf Erden (doubtful)
  S. Schöner (S), H. Hartig (hpsi.)   *Pol. 62900*
  (*J. S. Bach: Willst du dein Herz*)   (♭ *Pol. 32105*)
SYMPHONIES
D major (F. 64)
  Paris Sinfonia—Witold   ‡ *EPP.SLP 4*
  (*C. P. E. Bach*)

D minor (F. 65)
  ☆ Cha. Orch.—M. v. d. Berg (‡ MMS. 3003)

BACHIXA, Francisco Xavier (fl. XVIIIth Century)
  SEE: † CLAVECINISTES ESPAGNOLS ET PORTUGAIS

BACILLY, Bénigne, Sieur de (1625-1692)
  SEE: †AIRS À BOIRE

BACKER-GRØNDAHL, Agathe Ursula
(1847-1907)
SONGS
At eventide, Op. 42, No. 7 (*Mot Kvæld*) (Jynge)
  E. Berge (S), K. Olssen (pf.)   *Felix Ø 70*
  (*Grieg: Spring*)
At eventide, Op. 42, No. 7
East Wind, Op. 56, No. 2 (Ingemann)
(The) Linden, Op. 23, No. 1 (Bergsøe)
  C. Hague (T), G. Steele (pf.)   in ‡ ML. 7034
  († Scandinavian Songs)

BACON, Ernst (b. 1898)

(The) Enchanted Island orch. suite[2] 1954
  Louisville—Whitney   ‡ LO. 11
  (*Malipiero & Rieti*)
Ford's Theatre (Easter Week, 1865) orch. 1943
  A.R.S. Phil.—Schönherr   in ‡ ARS. set 335
  (*Parker*)
(A) Tree on the plains   1942
  (excerpts from the music-play by P. Horgan)
  ▽ R. Pazmor (A), etc., Spartanburg Op. Cho. & Orch.
      —Bacon (6ss, NMQR. set 1613)

BADINGS, Henk (b. 1907)

Ballade fl. & hp.
  H. Barwahser & P. Berghout   ‡ *Phi.N 00695R*
  (*Roesgen-Champion, Andriessen, Tomasi*)
Sonatina pf. 1936
  ☆ J. Antonietti (♭ *Pol. 32036*)

BAIRSTOW, Edward Cuthbert
(1874-1946)
Let all mortal flesh keep silence Anthem
  St. Paul's Cath. Cho.—Dykes Bower
                in ‡ C.CX 1237
  (*Wesley, Schütz, Stanford, etc.*) (‡ Angel. 35139, in set 3516)

BALAKIREV, Mily Alexeivich
(1836/7-1910)

Concerto No. 1, F sharp major pf. & orch.
  B. Shirinsky & Radio Sym.—Gauk
                 ‡ *USSR.D 1324*
  (*Veligorsky: Theme & Varns.*)
Islamey (Oriental Fantasia) pf. 1869
  S. Barere   in ‡ Rem. 199-141
  (*Liszt, Rachmaninoff, etc.*)   (‡ Cum.CR 328)
  J. Katchen   ‡ *D.LW 5160*
  (*Liszt*)   (‡ *Lon.LD 9175*)
  Y. Boukoff   in ‡ *Phi.A 76700R*
  (*Prokofiev, Khachaturian, Rachmaninoff, Scriabin*)
  E. Bernáthová   ‡ *Sup.LPM 223*
  (*Miaskovsky & Tchaikovsky*)   (‡ *U. 5199C*)
  A. Brendel   ‡ AmVox.PL 9140
  (*Moussorgsky, Stravinsky*)
              (continued on next page)

---

[1] Ob., vln. & cont. The authenticity of the work is dubious.   [2] From Incidental Music for *The Tempest*.

Islamey (*continued*)
N. Yemelyanova   **USSRM.D 642**
(*Rachmaninoff: Humoresque & Valse*)

☆ V. Yankoff (ArgPat.FXC 0015)

— ARR. ORCH.   Casella
Philharmonia—v. Matačić   **‡ C.CX 1280**
(*below*)   (‡ Angel. 35291)

☆ U.S.S.R. Nat.—Gauk
                    (in *USSRM.D 147*; ‡ *CdM.LDA 8056*)
King Lear   Inc. Music   1861
... Procession ☆ Moscow Radio—Ginsburg *USSR. 20101/2*

Nocturne No. 2, B minor   pf.
P. Serebriakov   **USSRM.D 001348**
(*Rachmaninoff: Études tableaux*)

Overture on three Russian themes   orch.   1858
U.S.S.R. State—Anosov   **USSRM.D 923**
(*Borodin: In the Steppes of Central Asia*)

Russia   Sym. Poem   orch.   1862
Philharmonia—v. Matačić   **‡ C.CX 1280**
(*above & below*)   (‡ Angel. 35291)
U.S.S.R. State—Gauk   **‡ U. 5175C**
(*Tchaikovsky*)   (*Glazounov*, on ‡ *USSR.D 518*)
(*Islamey; & Moussorgsky & Glinka* on ‡ *CdM.LDA 8056*)

SONGS
COLLECTION
(The) Bright moon (Yatsevich)   1858
(The) Rock (Lermontov) [also on *USSR. 19693*]
☆ Song (Lermontov)   1903-4
When I hear thy voice (Lermontov)   1863
My heart is torn (Koltsov)
M. Maksakova (S)   (2ss)   **USSRM.D 00610/1**

(The) Bright moon (Yatsevich)   1858
Z. Dolukhanova (A)   **USSR. 22550**
(*Song of the golden fish*)

N. Kazantseva (S)   **USSRM.D 00687**
(*below, & Rimsky-Korsakov: Song*)

Embrace, Kiss (Koltsov)   1858
B. Gmyria (B)   **USSR. 22268**
(*Glinka: Ah Night*)

Georgian Song (Pushkin)   1863
When I hear thy voice (Lermontov)   1863
N. Kazantseva (S)   **USSRM.D 00688**
(*above*)

I loved him (Koltsov)   1895-6
☆ Z. Dolukhanova (A) (*USSRM.D 00605*)

(The) Rosy sunset fades (Kulchinsky)
A. Pirogov (B)   **USSR. 20419**
(*Arensky*)

Selim's Song (Lermontov)   1858
P. Lisitsian (B)   **USSR. 023883**
(*Glier: Eastern Song*)

Song of the golden fish (Lermontov)   1860
Z. Dolukhanova (A)   **USSR. 22549**
(*The bright moon*)

Spanish Song (Mikhailov)   1855
S. Lemeshev (T)   in ‡ **USSR.D 1163**
(*below, & Glinka, Bulakov, Rimsky*)

Thou art so captivating (Golovinsky)   1855
S. Lemeshev (T)   **USSR. 21553**
(*Glinka*)   (& in ‡ *D 1163*)

(The) Wilderness (Zhemchuznikov)   1895-6
A. Pirogov (B)   **USSR. 22824**
(*Tchaikovsky: Again, as before, alone*)

SYMPHONIES
No. 1, C major   1898
☆ Philharmonia—Karajan (‡ C.FCX/QCX 170)

No. 2, D minor   1898
Moscow Radio—Kovalev   **‡ USSR.D 01452/3**
                                  (‡ *CdM.LDA 8058*)

Thamar   Symphonic Poem   orch.   1882
Royal Phil.—Beecham   **‡ EPhi.ABL 3047**
(*Dvořák*)   (‡ AmC.ML 4974; Phi.A 01164L)
Suisse Romande—Ansermet   **‡ D.LXT 2966**
(*Liadov*)   (‡ Lon.LL 1068)
Philharmonia—v. Matačić   **‡ C.CX 1280**
(*above*)   (‡ Angel. 35291)
L.S.O.—Fistoulari   **‡ P.PMC 1009**
(*Rimsky-Korsakov*)   (‡ MGM.E 3076; Od.ODX 142)
Moscow Radio—Golovanov **‡ Mon.MWL 307**
(*Prokofiev*)   (*Ippolitoff-Ivanoff*, on ‡ Kings. 281)
(*Scriabin*, on ‡ USSR.D 0703)

BALBÂTRE, Claude (1729-1799)
SEE: † FRENCH BAROQUE ORGAN MUSIC
        † VIEUX NOËLS DE FRANCE

BALFE, Michael (1808-1870)

(The) BOHEMIAN GIRL   3 Acts   1843
The heart bowed down   B
M. Langdon, J. Lee (pf.)   in ‡ **Queens.LPR 21**
(*below, Britten, Massenet, Bach, etc.*)
KEOLANTHE   Opera   2 Acts   1841
From rushy beds
M. Langdon (Bs), J. Lee (pf.)
(*above*)   in ‡ **Queens.LPR 21**

BANCHIERI, Adriano (1567-1634)

(2) Fantasias[1]
Music Hall Brass Ens.   in ‡ **Mono. 817**
(† *Music for Brass*)

(II) Festino della sera del Giovedì Grasso
Madrigal Comedy   10 Scenes   5 vv.   1608
Vocal & Inst. Ens. of Bologna Madrigalists
—Giani   **‡ CFD. 50**
Primavera Singers—Greenberg   **‡ Eso.ES 516**
[B. Winogron, virginals]
(*below, Dalza, Frescobaldi, Gabrieli*)   (‡ Cpt.MC 20022)
A. Banchieri Ens.—Schapiro   **‡ SPA. 66**
☆ L. Marenzio Ens.—Saraceni (in † ‡ HS.AS 8)
... No. 12, Contraponto bestiale   Madrigal
Sale & District Musical Soc., Minneapolis
Choralaires, & Bologna Nuovo Madrigaletto
Italiano, in turn   in ‡ **Nix.WLP 6209-2**
                                  (‡ West. set WAL 209)
[at International Eisteddfod, Llangollen]
Sonata in aria francese[2]
B. Winogron (virginals)   in ‡ **Eso.ES 516**

BANFIELD, Raffaello de (b. 1922)

(The) Combat   Ballet   1953
Ballet Theatre—Levine[3]   **‡ DCap.CTL 7081**
(*Antheil*)   (‡ Cap.P 8278)

BANISTER, John (d. 1735)
SEE: † SHAKESPEARE SONGS, VOL. III

BANTOCK, Sir Granville (1868-1946)

Fifine at the Fair   Orch. drama   1901
☆ Royal Phil.—Beecham   **‡ G.BLP 1016**
                    (‡ Vic.LHMV 1026; ♭ set WHMV 1026)
SONGS
Lord Rendall (Trad.)
K. Joyce (A), H. Greenslade (pf.)   **P.E 11508**
(*Dunhill: The Cloths of heaven; Thiman: The Silver Swan*)

Songs of the Western Isles   pub. 1930
... No. 6, Song to the Seals   (Boulton)
☆ J. McCormack (T) (V‡ *Rar.M 304*)

---

[1] From *Canzoni alla francese ... a 4 voci*, 1603.   [2] Sonata No. 8 from *L'Organo Suonarino*, Op. 13, 1605.
[3] Recording supervised by composer.

BARAB, Seymour (b. 1921)

(A) Child's Garden of Verses (R. L. Stevenson) 1953

1. Intro. & Marching Song	2. At the Sea-Side
3. The Moon	4. The Swing
5. Windy nights	6. Foreign Lands
7. From a Railway Carriage	8. Where go the boats?
9. A good boy	10. The Land of Nod
11. The Cow	12. Time to rise
13. Pirate Story	14. Autumn Fires
15. The Sun's travels	16. Foreign Children
17. The Wind	18. Young Night-Thought
19. My Shadow	20. Singing
21. Fairy Bread	22. Bed in Summer
23. Picture Books in Winter	24. Farewell to the Farm

R. Oberlin (T), R. Crisara (tpt.), D. Weber (cl.), H. Goltzer (bsn.), B. Melnick (pf.)
      ♯ *Eso.ESJ 5*

BARANOVIĆ, Krešimar (b. 1894)

(The) GINGERBREAD HEART   Ballet   1924
Orchestral Suite
   Belgrade Phil.—Baranović   ♯ **D.LXT 5058**
   (*Lhotka*)   (♯ Lon.LL 1235)

BARATI, George (b. 1913)

Quartet, str.   1944
   California Qtt.   ♯ *Cty.C 2001*

BARBER, Samuel (b. 1910)

Adagio for Strings (from Str. Qtt., Op. 11) 1936
   Philharmonia—Kletzki   **C.LX 1595**
   Eastman-Rochester Sym.—Hanson
   (*below; & Gould*)   ♯ **EMer.MG 40002**
   Concert Arts.—Golschmann ♯ **DCap.CTL 7056**
   (*Diamond, Creston, Copland*)   (♯ Cap.P 8245)
   Boston Orch. Soc.—Page   ♯ *SOT. 1068*
   (*Honegger & Debussy*)   (and in ♯ SOT. 10683)
   (*Honegger only, on ♭ Nix.EP 651*)
   Hamburg Philharmonia—H-J. Walther
           MSB. 78157

Commando March   Band   1943
   Eastman Sym. Ens.—Fennell   ♯ **Mer.MG 40006**
   (*Persichetti, Gould, Piston, etc.*)
   U.S. Military Acad. Band—Resta
          ♯ **PFCM.CB 177**
   (*Still, Ravel, Stravinsky, Milhaud*)
   Concert Band—Harp   ♯ **Fred. 1**
   (*Handel, Hanson, Respighi, etc.*)

Concerto, vln. & orch., Op. 14   1930-9
   ☆ L. Kaufman & Sym.—Goehr (*Copland*) ♯ *MMS. 105*

Dover Beach, Op. 3 (Arnold) B & Str. Qtt. 1931
   ☆ S. Barber & Curtis Qtt. (in ♯ Vic.LCT 1158)

Essay for orchestra, No. 1, Op. 12   1937
   Eastman-Rochester Sym.—Hanson
   (*above & below*)   ♯ **EMer.MG 40002**
   ☆ Philadelphia—Ormandy (in ♯ Cam.CAL 238)

Essay for orchestra, No. 2, Op. 17   1942
   Hamburg Philharmonia—Korn   ♯ **Allo. 3148**
   (*Creston, Gottschalk, etc.*)

Music for a scene from Shelley, Op. 7 orch. 1933
   A.R.S. Orch.—Hendl   ♯ **ARS. 26**
   (*below & Copland*)

Reincarnation, Op. 16 (James Stevens)
   Mixed Cho. unacc.   1936-40
   Hufstader Singers   in ♯ *SOT. 1092*

(The) School for Scandal, Overture, Op. 5   1932
   Eastman-Rochester Sym.—Hanson
          ♯ **EMer.MG 40002**
   (*above; & Gould*)   (♭ *Mer.EP 1-5018*)
   A.R.S. Orch.—Hendl   ♯ **ARS. 26**
   (*above; & Copland*)
   ☆ Janssen Sym. (Los Angeles)—Janssen
          (in ♯ Cam.CAL 205)

SONG CYCLE: Hermit Songs, Op.29 (Anon.) 1953
   L. Price (S), S. Barber (pf.)   ♯ **AmC.ML 4988**
   (*Haieff*)

SONG: The Daisies   (J. Stephens)   1927
   D. Gramm (Bs), R. Cumming (pf.) in ♯ **ML. 7033**
   (*Wolf, Cesti, Bowles, etc.*)

Souvenirs, Op. 28   Suite, pf.   4 hands   1952
   R. Gold & A. Fizdale   ♯ **AmC.ML 4855**
   (*Haieff*)   (in set SL 198)

SYMPHONY No. 1, Op. 9   1936, rev. 1943
   Eastman-Rochester Sym.—Hanson
   (*Hanson*)   ♯ **Mer.MG 40014**

BARBIERI, Francisco Asenjo (1823-1894)

ZARZUELAS   (Abridged listings only)
(EL) BARBERILLO DE LAVAPIÉS 4 Acts 1874
   D. Pérez, S. Ramalle, Cho. & Madrid Cha.
   —Navarro   ♯ **Mont.FM 48**
Prelude   Madrid Cha. Orch.—Argenta
      (in ♯ LI.TW 91004; Ambra.MCCP 29001
          & in ♭ *Ambra.MGE 60002*)
     Madrid Cha.—Navarro (♯ Mont.FM 51)
Tirana   Madrid Th.—Moreno Torroba
    ⦀ (in ♯ B.AXTL 1078; SpC.CCLP 34003; AmD.DL 9736)
Orch. Selection   ▽ Madrid Orch. (G.AF 242)
Vocal Excerpts in ♯ Mont.FM 17, etc.

(Los) DIAMANTES DE LA CORONA 3 Acts 1854
Bolero   orch.
   Spanish Sym.—Martinez   in ♯ **Mont.FM 16**

JUGAR CON FUEGO   3 Acts   1851
   P. Lorengar, M. Ausensi, C. Munguía, A. Campó, etc., Donostiarra Cho. & Sym.
   —Argenta   ♯ **Ambra.MCC 30029**
Vocal excerpts on ♯ LI.TW 91087;
      ♯ Ambra.MCC 30024: *MCC 25008*

BARLOW, Wayne (b. 1912)

(The) Winter's past   ob. & str.   1938
   Eastman-Rochester Sym.—Hanson
          ♯ **EMer.MG 40003**
   (*Rogers, Copland, Kennen, Keller, Hanson*) (♭ *EP 1-5064*)
   (*o.v.*, ▽ Vic. 18101, in set M 802)

BARON, Ernst-Gottlieb (1696-1760)

Concerto, C major   Lute, vln, continuo   1765
   M. Podolski, J. Tryssesoone, F. Terby (vlc.)
          ♯ **Per.SPL 587**
   (*Haydn, Vivaldi, Saint-Luc*)   (♯ Cpt.MC 20058)

BARONVILLE (fl. *c.* 1700)
   SEE: † MUSIQUE DE LA GRANDE ÉCURIE

BARÔZAI, Guy (Bernard de la Monnoye)
             (XVIIth Cent.)
   SEE: † BIBLE DES NOËLS

☆ = Re-issue of a recording to be found in previous volumes.

BARRAUD, Henry (b. 1900)

Nina au matin bleu ob. & pf. 1954
P. Pierlot & A. d'Arco   ♭ *Pat.G 1051*
(*Jolivet, Auric, Murgier, Planel*)

BARRE, Michel de la (1675-1744)

Suite No. 9, G major (Bk. II) flute & cont.   *c.* 1710
G. Scheck, F. Neumeyer (hpsi.), H. Müller
(gamba) (2ss)   ♭ *Pol. 37061*

BARSANTI, Francesco (1690-1760)

(12) CONCERTI GROSSI, Op. 3   *c.* 1743
No. 4, D major; No. 10, D major
Lamoureux Cha.—Colombo   ‡ **LOL.OL 50008**
(*Cimarosa: Concerto*)   (‡ *OL.LD 61*)

BARTLETT, John (fl. 1606-1610)

AYRES 1606
(A) **Pretty duck there was**
What thing is love
When from my love
  ☆ H. Cuénod (T), H. Leeb (lute)   in ‡ **Nix.WLP 5085**
(† XVIth & XVIIth Century Songs)

Of all the birds that I do know
A. Deller (C-T), D. Dupré (lute)
         in ‡ **Van.BG 539**
(† Elizabethan & Jacobean Music)

What thing is love
F. Fuller (B), J. de Azpiazu (lute) in ‡ **EMS. 11**
(† Dowland & his Contemporaries)

Whither runneth my sweetheart
Primavera Singers   in ‡ *Eso.ESJ 6*
(† Elizabethan Songbag for young people)

BARTÓK, Béla (1881-1945)

CLASSIFIED: I. Orchestral
           II. Chamber Music
           III. Piano
           IV. Vocal

I. ORCHESTRAL

Concerto for orchestra 1943
Philharmonia—Karajan   ‡ **C.CX 1054**
     (‡ *C.QCX 10052: FCX 199*; ‡ *Angel. 35003*)
Philadelphia—Ormandy   ‡ **EPhi.ABL 3090**
             (‡ *AmC.ML 4973*)
Minneapolis Sym.—Dorati   ‡ **EMer.MG 50033**
             (‡ *FMer.MLP 7526*)
CONCERTOS, Pf. & orch.
No. 2   1931
E. Farnadi & Vienna St. Op.—Scherchen
              ‡ **Nix.WLP 5249**
(*below*)   (‡ *West.WL 5249; Sel. 320.CW.081*)

  ☆ A. Foldes & Lamoureux—Bigot   ‡ **AmVox.PL 8220**
(*below*)
No. 3   1945
E. Farnadi & Vienna St. Op.—Scherchen
              ‡ **Nix.WLP 5249**
(*above*)   (‡ *West.WL 5249; Sel. 320.CW.081*)
J. Katchen & Suisse Romande—Ansermet
              ‡ **D.LXT 2894**
(*Prokofiev*)   (‡ *Lon.LL 945*)
L. Pennario & St. Louis Sym.—Golschmann
              ‡ **DCap.CTL 7060**
(*Prokofiev*)   (‡ *Cap.P 8253*)

M. Haas & R.I.A.S. Sym.—Fricsay ‡ **Pol. 18223**
(*Kodály*)   (*Martin,* on ‡ *AmD.DL 9774*)
L. Shankson & Berlin Sym.   ‡ **Roy. 1569**
(*Pf. pieces*)   (‡ *MusH.LP 12008*)
E. Silver & "Philharmonic"—Berendt   ‡ **Allo. 3145**
(*Hindemith*)

Concerto, vln. & orch. 1938
Y. Menuhin & Philharmonia—Furtwängler
              ‡ **G.ALP 1121**
   (‡ *G.FALP 313*; ‡ *Vic.LHMV 3*; *ArgA.LPC 11593*)
I. Gitlis & Vienna Pro Musica—Horenstein
(*Sonata*)   ‡ **E & AmVox.PL 9020**
  ☆ T. Varga & Berlin Phil.—Fricsay   ‡ **HP.DGM 18060**

Concerto, viola & orch. (completed Serly)
M. Lemoine & Orch.—Froment   ‡ **CND. 6**
(*Divertimento*)

Dance Suite 1923
L.P.O.—Solti   ‡ **D.LXT 2771**
(*Kodály: Dances of Galanta*)   (‡ *Lon.LL 709*)
R.I.A.S. Sym.—Fricsay   ‡ **HP.DGM 18153**
(*Divertimento*)
Leipzig Phil.—Pflüger   ‡ **Ura. 7161**
(*Wooden Prince*)
  ☆ New Sym.—Autori   ‡ **BRS. 304**
(*Portraits*)   (‡ *Clc. 6244*)

Divertimento for Strings 1939
R.I.A.S. Sym.—Fricsay   ‡ **HP.DGM 18153**
(*Dance Suite*)
(*Portraits,* on ‡ *AmD.DL 9748*)
Zürich Cha.—E. de Stoutz   ‡ **D.LXT 5081**
(*Müller*)   (‡ *Lon.LL 1183*)
Paris Inst. Ens.—Froment   ‡ **CND. 6**
(*Vla. Concerto*)
  ☆ Minneapolis Sym.—Dorati   ‡ **Vic.LM 1750**
     (*Kodály*)   (♭ set *WDM 1750*; ‡ *ItV.A12R 0063*)

Hungarian Sketches Small orch. 1931
   (ARR. of piano pieces)
1. Evening in Transylvania
2. Bear Dance
3. Melody
4. A bit drunk
5. Swineherd's dance
Hungarian Radio—Somogyi   *Qual.B 54*
(*For Children, excerpts*)

(2) Images, Op. 10 1910
  ☆ New Sym.—Serly   ▽ ‡ **BRS. 305**
(*Rhapsodies,* on ‡ *BRS. 307*)

(The) MIRACULOUS MANDARIN Ballet 1919
Orch. Suite
Chicago Sym.—Dorati   ‡ **EMer.MG 50038**
(*Kodály*)   (‡ *FMer.MLP 7525*)
Cento Soli—Husa   ‡ **CFD. 4**
(*below*)

Music for Strings, Percussion & Celesta 1936
R.I.A.S. Sym.—Fricsay (2ss)   ‡ **Pol. 16074**
L.P.O.—Solti   ‡ **D.LXT 5059**
(*Kodály*)   (‡ *Lon.LL 1230*)
London Phil. Prom.—Boult   ‡ **West.LAB 7021**
Pittsburgh Sym.—Steinberg   ‡ **PFCM.CB 155**
(*Britten*)
  ☆ Los Angeles Cha.—Byrns   ‡ **DCap.CTL 7094**
     (*Chavez & Milhaud*)
   (‡ *Cap.P 8299*; & ‡ *T.NLCB 8048*; *ACap.CLC 039*, 2ss)
  ☆ Chicago Sym.—Kubelik (2ss)   ‡ **G.BLP 1032**
     (*Schoenberg,* on ‡ *Mer.MG 50026*)
     (*Bloch,* on ‡ *G.FALP 291*)

(2) Portraits, Op. 5 vln. & orch. 1908
  ☆ J. Pougnet & New Sym.—Autori   ‡ **BRS. 304**
     (*Dance Suite*)   (‡ *Clc. 6244*)
  ☆ R. Schulz & R.I.A.S. Sym.—Fricsay   ‡ **Pol. 16054**
     (*Divertimento,* on ‡ *AmD.DL 9748*)

... No. 1 only
  ☆ J. Szigeti & Philharmonia—Lambert   **C.LOX 815**
     (*Contrasts & Rhapsody No. 1,* on ‡ *AmC.ML 2213*)

---

‡ = Long-playing, 33⅓ r.p.m.   ♭ = 45 r.p.m.   ♮ = Auto. couplings, 78 r.p.m.

Rhapsody, Op. 1 pf. & orch. 1904
  ☆ A. Foldes & Lamoureux—Désormière
   (*above*)   # AmVox.PL 8220

(2) Rhapsodies vln. & orch. 1928
  D. Erlih & Cento Soli—Husa   # CFD. 4
  (*above*)
  ☆ E. Vardi & New Sym. Orch.   # BRS. 307
   (*Images*) [No. 1, cond. Serly; No. 2 by Autori]

Suite No. 1, Op. 3 1905
  ☆ Salzburg Mozarteum—Fekete   # CA.LPA 1019
                         (# Cum.CF 326)

(The) WOODEN PRINCE, Op. 13 Ballet 1917
  New Sym.—Susskind   # BRS. 308 & 308a
  (3ss)

...Orch. Suite
  Leipzig Phil.—Pflüger   # Ura. 7161
  (*Dance Suite*)

II. CHAMBER MUSIC

Contrasts vln., cl., & pf. 1938
  R. Mann, S. Drucker & L. Hambro # BRS. 916
  (*Sonata, vln. unacc.*)
  M. Ritter, R. Kell & J. Rosen # AmD.DL 9740
  (*Milhaud*)
  M. Latchem, G. Dobree & G. Watson
                        # *Argo.TM 9*
  (*Out of Doors Suite*)   (o.n. *ATM 1002*)
  ☆ J. Szigeti, B. Goodman & B. Bartók # AmC.ML 2213
  (*Rhapsody No. 1 & Portrait*)
  ☆ D. Guilet, H. Tichman, R. Budnevich (# *MMS. 89*)

(44) Duets for two violins 1931
  H. Krebbers & T. Olof   # Phi.N 00209L

... 15 duets only
  ☆ G. Lengyel & A. M. Gründer (V# *Sel.LAP 1008*)

QUARTETS, String
COMPLETE RECORDING
No. 1, A minor, Op. 7   1908
No. 2, A minor, Op. 17   1917
No. 3   1927
No. 4   1928
No. 5   1934
No. 6   1939
  Parrenin Qtt. (6ss)   # Véga. C30.A 29/31

Nos. 1 & 2
  ☆ Juilliard Qtt.   # EPhi.ABL 3064
                    (# Phi.A 01153L)

No. 1, A minor, Op. 7 1908
  ☆ Hirsch Qtt.   # *Argo.TM 8*

No. 3 1927
  ☆ New Music Qtt.   # Clc. 6119
  (*Mikrokosmos; & Stravinsky*)

No. 4 1928
  New Music Qtt.   # PFCM.CB 171
  (*Martinů*)
  ☆ Guilet Qtt. (# *MMS. 89*)

No. 6 1939
  Tatrai Qtt. (8ss)   *Qual.set B 53*

Rhapsody No. 1 1928 vln. [or vlc.] & pf.
  ☆ J. Szigeti (vln.) & B. Bartók   # AmC.ML 2213
  (*Contrasts & Portrait No. 1*)
  ☆ J. Starker (vlc.) & O. Herz
       (# Cpt.MC 20031; Per.SPL 602 & SPL 715)

Sonata, two pianos & percussion 1937
  G. Yessin, R. Viola, E. Jones, A. Howard
   —Stokowski   # Vic.LM 1727
  (*Goeb: Symphony No. 3*)   (♭ *set WDM 1727*)
  B. Rubinstein & A. Loesser, C. Duff &
   E. Sholle   # CIM. pte.
  (*B. Rubinstein*)

SONATA, Vln. & pf.
No. 2 1922
  R. Druian & J. Simms   # Mer.MG 80000
  (*Ravel: Sonata*)

Sonata, violin unacc. 1944
  I. Gitlis   # E & AmVox.PL 9020
  (*Concerto*)
  R. Mann   # BRS. 916
  (*Contrasts*)
  A. Gertler   # C.FCX 297
  (*Berg*)   (# Angel. 35091)
  ☆ Y. Menuhin   (*Prokofiev*)   # G.FALP 265
  ☆ W. Tworek   # D.LM 4557
                    (# *Lon.LS 711*)

III. PIANO, ORGAN

COLLECTIONS

VOL. I:
  For Children: Bk. I—Nos. 1-4, 13-15, 18, 21, 22, 25, 26,
   28, 30-32, 40
  Sonatina 1915
  Mikrokosmos—Nos. 97, 100, 102, 108, 113, 115, 122,
   125, 126, 128, 130, 137, 139, 140-3, 146, 148-53
                         # Pol. 18270

VOL. II:
  For Children: Bk. II—Nos. 1-3, 8, 13, 18, 26, 28, 34, 36-7
  2 Elegies, Op. 8b   1908-9
  6 Rumanian Folk Dances   1915
  Fantasia No. 2   (4 *Pf. pieces, 1903*, No. 3)
  7 Sketches, Op. 9   1908-10
  8 Improvisations on Hungarian Folksongs, Op. 20   1920
                        # HP.DGM 18271

VOL. III:
  15 Hungarian Peasant songs   1917
  Sonata   1926
  3 Rondos on Folk-Tunes   1916-27
  (20) Rumanian Christmas Carols   1915
  Suite, Op. 14   1915   # Pol. 18272

VOL. IV:
  Out of Doors Suite   1926
  9 Little pieces   1926
  10 Easy pieces   1908
  3 Burlesques, Op. 8c   1908-11
  Allegro barbaro   1911   # Pol. 18273
  A. Foldes   # Pol. 18270/3
                        (# AmD.DL 9801/4)

  Allegro barbaro   1911
  For Children: Bk. I—Nos. 6, 10, 13-15, 18-19, 21, 25-26,
   30 to 40 (omitting 38)
  (15) Hungarian Peasant Songs   1917
  (6) Rumanian Folk Dances   1915
  Suite, Op. 14   1916
  G. Sandor   # AmC.ML 4868
                        (# Phi.N 02119L)

  (3) Rondos on Folk Tunes   1916-27
  Sonatina   1915
  For Children: Bk. I—Nos. 1, 2, 5, 17, 22, 25, 36, 40
  I. Kabos   # BRS. 917

  Bagatelle, Op. 6, No. 2   1905
  Rondo No. 1   1916
  Petite Suite   1938
  Little Pieces No. 9   1926
  Improvisations 1, 2, 6, 7, 8, Op. 20
  Wallachian Dance
  (3) Hungarian Folk-tunes (for Paderewski)
  Mikrokosmos Nos. 67, 127, 145 — ARR. 2 pfs.
  ☆ B. Bartók (& Mme. Bartók in duets) (# Cum.CR 289)

  Sonatina   1915
  15 Hungarian Peasant Songs   1917
  For Children: Bk. I—Nos. 1-21 inclusive[1]
  L. Kraus   # Edu.EP 3008

  (8) Improvisations on Hungarian Folksongs, Op. 20   1920
  Mikrokosmos, Nos. 142, 146, 151
  Rondo No. 1
  (6) Rumanian Folk Dances   1915
  L. Shankson (2ss)   # *Allo. 4012*
  (also with *Pf. Concerto 3* in # Roy. 1569; MusH.LP 12008)

---

[1] Nos. 1, 4, 6, 10, 14, 15, 17, 18 are played twice, in the original and the revised versions.

Allegro barbaro 1911
R. Caamaño   *ArgOd. 57052*
(*Turina: Cuentos de España, No. 3*)

I. Engel   *Qual.SZK 3553*
(*Mikrokosmos, excerpts*)

B. Webster   in ♯ **Persp.PR 2**
☆ C. de Groot (*Phi.A 11245H:* ♭ *N 402019E*)

(14) Bagatelles, Op. 6   1908
T. Kosma   ♯ **BRS. 918**
(*below*)

(3) Burlesques, Op. 8c   1908-11
... No. 2, A bit drunk
(4) Dirges   1910
... No. 2, Melody
— ARR. SMALL ORCH.   Bartók   *SEE:* Hungarian Sketches

(10) Easy pieces   1908
... No. 5, Evening in Transylvania[1]
M. Pressler   ♯ **MGM.E 3129**
(*Ravel, Respighi, Granados, etc.*)   (in ♭ *set X 254*)

... No. 5; & No. 10, Bear Dance
— ARR. SMALL ORCH.   Bartók.   *SEE:* Hungarian Sketches

En Bateau   organ   1943[2]
R. Ellsasser   in ♯ **MGM.E 3064**
(† Organ Music by Modern Composers)

FOR CHILDREN
1909; revised & re-numbered 1945
VOL. I—Nos. 1-40
VOL. II—Nos. 1-39
COMPLETE RECORDINGS
T. Kozma   (4ss)   ♯ **BRS. 919/20**
[Excerpts, unspec., also on ♯ BRS. 921]
M. Pressler   ♯ **MGM.E 3009 & E 3047**

VOL. I, Nos. 1-40
COMPLETE RECORDING
G. Anda   ♯ **C.CX 1176**
(*Sonatina*)   (♯ FCX 347; Angel. 35126)

Vol. I: Nos. 7, 8, 13, 14, 15, 17, 19, 21, 26, 27, 28, 29, 30, 34, 35, 36
☆ C. Seemann   ♯ *Pol. 16041*
(*Improvisations*)   (♯ AmD.DL 4085)

VOL. I: Nos. 33, 31, 36, 3, 6
VOL: II: Nos. 7, 8, 26
(=Old Version, Vol. I, Nos. 3 & 6; Vol. II, Nos. 35, 33;
Vol. III, Nos. 7, 8; Vol. IV, No. 28)
— ARR. VLN. & PF.   Zathureczky
E. Zathureczky & A. Bálint   *Qual.SZK 3503*
(or *M 275/6*)

VOL. I: Nos. 3 (or 11), 13, 17, 23, 27, 40
VOL. II: Nos. 26, 31
P. Sebok   *Qual.B 52*

VOL. I: Nos. 6, 13, 18, 25, 31, 36, 40
— ARR. VLN. & PF.   Szigeti "*Hungarian Folk Tunes*"
G. Garay & E. Petri   *Qual.SZN 3054*
T. Magyar & W. Hielkema   ♯ *Phi.N 00700R*
(*below; & Dohnányi*)
D. Oistrakh & pf.   *USSRM.D 00905/6*

VOL. II: Nos. 36, 37
P. Kadosa   *Qual.B 54*
(*above*)

VOL. I: No. 40, Swineherd's dance
(=Old version, Vol. II, No. 42)
— ARR. SMALL ORCH.   Bartók: *SEE* Hungarian Sketches

(15) Hungarian Peasant Songs ... Nos. 7 to 15
S. Biro   ♯ **Rem. 199-133**
(*Kabalevsky & Kodály*)

(8) Improvisations on Hungarian Folksongs, Op. 20
                         1920
M. Few   ♯ *Argo.ARL 1008*
(*Sonata*)   [announced but perhaps never on sale]

C. Seemann   ♯ *Pol. 16041*
(*For Children*)   (♯ *AmD.DL 4085*)

MIKROKOSMOS   1926-7
Nos. 97, 128, 113, 125, 130, 138, 100, 139, 116, 109
G. Moore   (4ss)   *G.B 10409/10*

Nos. 140, 144, 146, 147, 148, 149, 151, 153
J. Katchen   ♯ *D.LXT 2812*
(*Rorem: Sonata No. 2*)   (♯ Lon.LL 759)

Nos. 109, 114, 116, 121, 128, 129
P. Kadosa   *Qual.B 51*

Nos. 148-153
J. Rappaport   ♯ **Etu.ER 101**
(*Bloch, Hindemith, Kabalevsky*)

Nos. 102, 108, 116, 139, 142
— ARR. STR. QTT.   Serly
☆ New Music Qtt.   ♯ **Clc.6119**
(*Qtt. No. 3 & Stravinsky*)

Unspec. excerpts
I. Engel   *Qual.SZK 3553*
(*Allegro barbaro*)

Out of Doors Suite   1926
G. Watson   ♯ *Argo.TM 9*
(*Contrasts*)   (o.n. ATM 1002)

Rumanian Christmas Carols   1915
T. Kozma   ♯ **BRS. 918**
(*above & below*)

(2) Rumanian Dances, Op. 8a   1910
K. Zempléni   *Qual.B 55*
(*Sonatina*)
S. Contreras[3]   ♯ **CM. 17**
(*Prokofiev, Kabalevsky, Shostakovich*)

... No. 1 only
M. Schwalb   in ♯ *Acad. 310*
(*Fauré, Liszt, etc.*)

(6) Rumanian Folk Dances   1915
T. Kozma   ♯ **BRS. 918**
(*above*)
G. Kaemper   *Ifma.MA 26000*

— ARR. VLN. & PF.   Székely
T. Magyar & W. Hielkema   ♯ *Phi.N 00700R*
(*above, & Dohnányi*)
I. Haendel & G. Moore   in ♯ *G.CLP 1021*
(*Paganini, Kreisler, etc.*)   (*Paganini only,* ♭ *7EP 7013*)
A. Grumiaux & P. Ulanowsky   ♯ *Bo.B 203*
(*Ravel, Debussy*)

A. Vadas & pf. (*Qual.SZK 3552*)
I. Bezrodny & pf. (*USSRM.D 00624*)
I. Zilzer & F. Schröder (*Eta. 120043*)
... Nos. 4, 5, 6 only
☆ Y. Menuhin & A. Baller
   (in ♯ Vic.LM 1742: ♭ set *WDM 1742*; in ♯ JpV.LS 2006)
— ARR. ORCH.
Varsity Concert Orch. (in ♯ Var. 2055)
— ARR. VLN. & ORCH.
L. Yordanoff & Paris Ens.—Froment   ♯ **EPP.APG 120**
(*Roussel & Shostakovich*)
(originally with *Roussel* only, ♯ EPP.APG 115)
— ARR. HARMONICA & PF.
L. Adler & L. Colin   in ♯ *CHS.CHS 1168*
                               (♯ *FMer.MLP 7026*)
... No. 5 only —ARR. CYMBALOM & PF.
I. Tarjani-Tóth & I. Aitoff   in ♯ *G.FBLP 1067*
(*Purcell, Gluck, Leclair, etc.*)

Sonata   1926
Z. Skolovsky   ♯ **EPhi.NBL 5025**
(*Berg, Hindemith, Scriabin*)
                 (♯ Phi.N 02131L; AmC.ML 4871)
M. Few   ♯ *Argo.ARL 1008*
(*Improvisations*)   [announced but perhaps never on sale]

---

[1] Labelled *Evening in the country* but probably this.
[2] "Written in sketch form and dedicated to Mr. Ellsasser"—unpublished.
[3] Labelled just *Rumanian Dances*, this may be the next set; it has not been possible to check.

Sonatina 1915
G. Anda   ♯ **C.CX 1176**
(*For Children*)   (♯ FCX 347; Angel. 35126)
K. Zempléni   *Qual. B 55*
(*2 Rumanian Dances*)
☆ M. Haas (in ♯ Pol. 18077)

— ARR. VLN. & PP. Gertler
☆ E. Zathureczky & M. Karin (in ♯ *U. 5185C*)

— ARR. CYMBALOM & PF. I. T-Tóth
I. Tarjani-Tóth & I. Altoff   in V♯ *CdM.LDZA 8120*

IV. VOCAL

Cantata profana T, B, double cho., orch. 1930
R. Lewis, M. Rothmüller, New Sym. & Cho.
—Susskind (*Eng*)   ♯ **BRS. 312**
(*Partsongs*)

DUKE BLUEBEARD'S CASTLE, Op. 11
   Opera 1 Act 1918
Judith   ...   .   J. Hellwig (S)
Duke Bluebeard   ...   ...   E. Koreh (Bs)
& New Sym. Orch.—Susskind   ♯ **BRS. 310/1**
(4ss)

SONGS & FOLK SONGS
COLLECTION
(8) Hungarian Folksongs 1907-17
... Nos. 1-5 only
   1. Black is the earth
   2. God, Oh God in heaven
   3. Women, women
   4. All the snow in my heart
   5. When I went looking in the blue hills
(20) Hungarian Folk Songs 1929
... Bk. II, Nos. 5-8 only
   5. This I would like to know
   6. Little Neighbour
   7. What does the swineherd wear
   8. I looked many hours
(5) Songs, Op. 16   (Ady)
M. Laszlo (S), F. Holetschek (pf.)
          ♯ **Nix.WLP 5283**
(*below*)   (♯ West.WL 5283)

PARTSONGS: COLLECTION
4 Slovak Folk Songs 1917
27 Part Songs 2 & 3 pt. cho. unacc. 1935
... Nos. 1, 2, 7, 9, 10, 11, 13, 14
Concert Cho.—Hillis   ♯ **BRS. 312**
(*Cantata profana*)

(20) Hungarian Folksongs 1906-16
... No. 1 M. Székely (Bs), I. Hajdu (pf.) (*Qual.SZK 3564*)

(8) Hungarian Folksongs 1907-17
  ☆ N. Valery (S), R. Goehr (pf.) (♯ *Allo. 4020*)

... Nos. 1-6 only
J. Sándor (S), I. Hajdu (pf.)   *Qual.ZK 3502*
... No. 1 only
M. Székely (Bs), I. Hajdu (pf.) (*Qual.SZK 3564*)

(27) Part Songs 2 & 3 pt. cho. unacc. 1935[1]
   published 1937
... Nos. 1, 17, 24
Women's Cho.—Tóth   *Qual.NB 240*
... Nos. 7, 23
Women's Cho.—Tóth   *Qual.NB 241*
(*Kodály: Evening Song*)
... Nos. 2, 9
Cho.—Vásárhelyi   *Qual.KK 2502*
(*Kodály*)
... Nos. 1, 7, 11, 12
Hung. Pop. State Ens.—Imre   ♭ *Phi.N 402034E*
(*Folk-songs*)

(4) Slovak Folk Songs mixed cho. & pf. 1917
— ARR. ORCH. Szervansky
Hungarian Radio—Lehel   *Qual.B 56*

(5) Songs, Op. 16 (E. Ady)
☆ N. Valery (S), R. Goehr (pf.) (♯ *Allo. 4020*)

---

(5) **Village Scenes** (Trad.) voice & pf. 1924
1. Haymaking   2. At the bridal house
3. The Wedding   4. Cradle Song
5. Peasants' Dance
I. Seefried (S, *Ger*), E. Werba (pf.)   ♯ **Pol. 19050**
(*Wolf, Strauss, Schubert, etc.*)   (♯ AmD.DL 9809)
R. Meinl-Weise (S, *Ger*), J. D. Link (pf.)
(4ss)   *Eta. 120017/8*

FOLK SONG ARRANGEMENTS
NOTE: ▽ EFL. *set 1000*: ♯ P 1000 contains a selection of Bartók's original recordings of Hungarian Folk Music (some in his own transcriptions), and EFL. *set 1419*: ♯ P 419 contains a similar selection of Roumanian Folk Music.

BARTOŠ, Jan Zdeněk (b. 1908)

Quartet No. 5, Op. 66, str.
Hábovo Qtt.   ♯ *U. 5181C*
(*Hába*)
There have probably been a number of other recordings of smaller works in Czech catalogues.

BASSANI, Giovanni Battista (1657-1716)

CANTATAS
(L') **Amante spietata**
M. Cortis (B) & Paris Inst. Ens.—Froment
(*Cimarosa & A. Scarlatti*)   ♯ **C.FCX 386**

Fuor dalle placid' onde
(La) **Serenata ... Posate, dormite**
☆ M. Laszlo (S), F. Holetschek (pf.)
          in ♯ **Nix.WLP 5119**
(† Italian Songs)

(La) **Serenata ... Posate, dormite**
G. Prandelli (T), D. Marzollo (pf.)
          in ♯ **AmVox.PL 7930**
(† Old Italian Airs)
☆ B. Gigli (T) & Orch.   in ♯ **G.ALP 1174**
(† Italian Classic Songs)   (♯ FALP 340: QALP 10073)

BASSANO, Giovanni (fl. XVIth Century)

Fantasia a tre 1585
Musicians Workshop Recorder Consort
          ♯ **CEd.CE 1018**
(† Recorder Music of Six Centuries)

BATAILLE, Gabriel (c. 1574-1630)

SEE: † FRENCH CHANSONS
      † DANCERIES ET BALLETS

BATESON, Thomas (c. 1570-1630)

MADRIGALS (refs. to Vols. of Eng. Madrigal School)
COLLECTION
I heard a noise XXII 5 vv
When to the gloomy woods XXII 4 vv
Camilla fair tripped o'er the plain XXII 5 vv
Come, sorrow, help me to lament XXII 5 vv
Come, follow me XXI 3 vv (S, A, T)
She with a cruel frown XXII 6 vv
Cupid in a bed of roses XXII 6 vv
Cytherea smiling said XXII 6 vv
Randolph Singers   ♯ **West.WL 5361**
(*Weelkes*)

Hark! hear you not XXI 5 vv
When Oriana walked to take the air XXI 6 vv
Randolph Singers—Randolph
          in ♯ **Nix.WLP 6212-2**
(† Triumphs of Oriana)   (♯ West. set WAL 212)

---

[1] Numbered from the list in H. Stevens: *The Life & Music of Béla Bartók.*

BATTEN, Adrian (*c.* 1590-1637)

SEE: † ENGLISH CHURCH MUSIC, Vol. IV

BATTISHILL, Jonathan (1738-1801)

SEE: † ENGLISH CHURCH MUSIC, VOL. IV

BAUSTETTER, Johann Konrad (fl. 1726-1782)

SEE: † CARILLON PIECES

BAX, Sir Arnold Edward Trevor
(1883-1953)

Coronation March orch. 1953
L.S.O.—Sargent   **‡ D.LXT 2793**
(*Walton, Elgar*)   (*‡ Lon.LL 804*)
(*Walton: Orb and Sceptre only,*
in ‡ D.LW 5057; Lon.LD 9046)

(A) GARLAND FOR THE QUEEN
(with Bliss, Ireland, V. Williams, etc.) 1953
... **What is it like to be young and fair** (C. Bax)
Golden Age Singers & Cambridge Univ.
Madrigal Soc.—Ord   in † ‡ **C.CX 1063**

Mediterranean orch. (orig. pf.) 1921
— ARR. VLN. & PF. Heifetz   ☆ J. Heifetz (*G.EC 193*)

Overture to a Picaresque Comedy orch. 1930
N.Y.P.S.O.—Mitropoulos[1]   in ‡ **OTA. set 8**

Quintet, Oboe & strings 1923
E. Schuster & Classic Qtt.   ‡ **CEd.CE 1030**
(*Elgar, McBride*)

Tintagel 1917
L.P.O.—Boult   ‡ **D.LXT 5015**
(*Butterworth, Holst*)   (*‡ Lon.LL 1169*)
L.S.O.—Weldon   ‡ **C.SX 1019**
(*Holst, Vaughan Williams*)

BEAULIEU, Lambert de (fl. *c.* 1587)

SEE: † DANCERIES ET BALLETS

BEETHOVEN, Ludwig van (1770-1827)

CLASSIFIED: A. INSTRUMENTAL
          1. Piano, 2. Chamber Music, 3. Dances
          and Marches, 4. Orchestral

          B. STAGE MUSIC
          C. VOCAL

References for works without Op. Nos. are to Grove's
list [G] and the numbers [WoO] allocated in Kinsky & Halm:
Das Werk Beethovens, Thematisch-Bibliographisches Ver-
zeichnis..., Munich, 1955. Certain works are also referred
to the B & H complete edition.

A. INSTRUMENTAL

1. PIANO

COLLECTIONS OF PIANO PIECES & DANCES
(7) **Ländlertänze**[2] G. 168   (WoO 11) 1798
... **Nos. 1-5, 7 & Coda**
(12) **Deutsche Tänze**[2] (WoO 13) 1796-7
... **Nos. 1, 2, 3, 6, 8, 12 & Coda**
(6) **Minuets**[2] G. 167 (WoO 10) *c.* 1795
Sonatina, G major G. 163-1 (Kinsky Anh. 5-1) (doubtful)
Sonatina, E flat major G. 161-1 (WoO 47-1) 1783
(6) **Variations on a Swiss air** G. 183 (WoO 64) *c.* 1798
                                    hpsi. or harp
P. Zeitlin   ‡ **Opus. 6002**
[to accompany a *Matching Music Book*, pub. Marks, N.Y.]

Allegretto, C minor[3] B & H 299 (WoO 53) *c.* 1796
Allemande, A major B & H 299 (WoO 81) *c.* 1796
(6) **Bagatelles, Op. 126**
Bagatelle: Lustig-traurig, C major & minor B & H 300
                                              (WoO 54)
Waltzes, D major & E flat major B & H 304, 303
                                    (WoO 84/5) 1824/5
R. Dirksen   in ‡ **Eso.ES 525/6**
(*Variations, fl. & pf.*)   (‡ Cpt.MC 20081)

Bagatelles: Op. 119, Nos. 1-4, 9-11
          A minor, "Für Elise"
Minuet, G major G. 167 (WoO 10-2)
SONATAS: 8, 19, 20
L. Kraus   ‡ **Edu.EP 3006**

COLLECTION, PF. 4 HANDS
(3) **Marches, Op. 45** (C ma.; E♭ ma.; D ma.)
(8) **Variations, C major, on a theme of Waldstein** G. 159
                                    (WoO 67) 1791-2
Sonata, D major, Op. 6 *c.* 1796-7
C. Norwood & E. Hancock   ‡ **Lyr.LL 55**
(*Mendelssohn*)

Andante, F major[4] G. 170 (WoO 57)
"*Andante favori*"
G. Puchelt   **G.EH 1451**
(*Rondo, G major, Op. 129*)
B. Vitebsky   ‡ **CA.LPA 1079**
(*Bagatelle & Concerto No. 3*)
(*Variations on* V‡ *MPO 5012*)

BAGATELLES
COLLECTION
(7) Op. 33
(11) Op. 119
(6) Op. 126
(2) **C minor, C major** (WoO 56 & 52) 1797, 1803-4
G. Johannesen   ‡ **Nix.CLP 1199**
[Op. 33 only on V‡ *MMS. 919*] (‡ CHS.CHS 1199;
                                    Clc. 6273)
(11) **Op. 119**
... **No. 1, G minor; No. 2, C major**
▽ H. Priegnitz (*Od.D 5136*)

... **No. 1, G minor**
B. Vitebsky   ‡ **CA.LPA 1079**
(*Andante, & Concerto No. 3*)

... **No. 3, D major; No. 4, A major**
H. Steurer   *Eta. 20–14*
(*Sonata 14, s. 5*)
(6) **Op. 126**
L. Hambro (*Variations*)   ‡ *SOT. 1039*

A minor "Für Elise" G. 173 (WoO 59) 1810
W. Kempff   ♭ *D. 71091*
(*Bagatelle, C minor*)   (♭ DK 23359)
(*idem, & Handel, on ‡ D.LW 5212*)

G. Hengeveld   **Phi.N 12080G**
(*Bach: Cantata 147—Jesu joy*)
                          (♭ N 402018E: in ‡ P 10064R)

G. v. Renesse   ♭ *G. 7EPH 1012*
(*Minuet; & Durand*)
W. MacGregor   in ‡ **Kings.KLP 200**
(*Rondos; & Schubert*)
R. Bergroth   *D.SD 5085*
(*Chopin: Valse No. 14*)

☆ J. Iturbi (♭ G.7EB 6010)
  O. Frugoni (♭ AmVox.VIP 45370)
  P. Kalender (BrzOd.X 3385)
  A. Aeschbacher (♭ Pol. 32031)

— ARR. GUITAR A. Valenti (in ‡ SMC. 1002)

C minor[3] B & H 291-1 (WoO 52)
W. Kempff   ♭ *D. 71091*
(*Für Elise*)   (♭ DK 23359)
(*Für Elise, & Handel, on ‡ D.LW 5212*)

Fantasia, G minor, Op. 77
☆ R. Serkin   in ‡ **C.CX 1043**
(*Sonata 24, & Trio*)   (QCX 10035)

---

[1] Transcription of a broadcast performance.   [2] Originally for orchestra.
[3] Originally intended for Pf. Sonata, Op. 10, No. 1. [4] Originally intended for Pf. Sonata, Op. 53

Polonaise, C major, Op. 89
P. Badura-Skoda   in ♯ Nix.WLP 5277
(Schubert, Brahms, etc.)   (in ♯ West.WL 5277)

RONDOS
C major, Op. 51, No. 1
W. Kempff   PV. 72314
(Sonata No. 32, s. 1)
(Rondo, Op. 51, No. 2 on ♯ AmD.DL 4086; ♭ Pol. 30121)
(Concerto No. 4, on ♯ AmD.DL 9742)

G major, Op. 51, No. 2
W. Kempff   PV. 72423
(Concerto No. 3, s. 1)
(Rondo, Op. 51, No. 1, on ♯ AmD.DL 4086; ♭ Pol. 30121)
B. Vitebsky   ♯ CA.LPA 1007
(Sonatas 8 & 14, & Variations)
W. MacGregor   in ♯ Kings.KLP 200
(Bagatelle, Rondo, Op. 129; & Schubert)

G major, Op. 129 (Rondo a capriccio)
W. MacGregor   in ♯ Kings.KLP 200
(Rondo, Op. 51, No. 2, Bagatelle; & Schubert)
G. Puchelt   G.EH 1451
(Andante, F major)   (in ♯ WDLP 1503)
S. Bianca   MSB. 78144
(Minuet in G)
M. Grünberg   USSRM. 001247
(Minuets)

☆ A. Aeschbacher (in ♯ Pol. 18220)

SONATAS
COMPLETE RECORDING: W. Backhaus
The recordings, issued at various times, are:—

Nos. 1, 26, 27	♯ D.LXT 2902; Lon.LL 949
Nos. 2, 11	♯ D.LXT 2920; Lon.LL 948
Nos. 3, 17	♯ D.LXT 2747; Lon.LL 627
Nos. 4, 7	♯ D.LXT 2809; Lon.LL 950
Nos. 5, 6, 25	♯ D.LXT 2603; Lon.LL 393
Nos. 8, 9, 15	♯ D.LXT 2903; Lon.LL 952
Nos. 10, 22, 24 (& Schumann)	♯ D.LXT 2931; Lon.LL 603
Nos. 12, 21	♯ D.LXT 2532; Lon.LL 265
Nos. 13, 14, 19, 20	♯ D.LXT 2780; Lon.LL 705
Nos. 16, 18	♯ D.LXT 2950; Lon.LL 951
Nos. 23, 28	♯ D.LXT 2715; Lon.LL 597
No. 29	♯ D.LXT 2777; Lon.LL 602
No. 30 (& Chopin)	♯ D.LXT 2535; Lon.LL 266
Nos. 31, 32	♯ D.LXT 2939; Lon.LL 953

COMPLETE RECORDING: Y. Nat

Nos. 1, 12, 13	♯ DFr. 153
Nos. 2, 3	♯ DFr. 154
Nos. 4, 11	♯ DFr. 155
Nos. 5, 6, 7, 24	♯ DFr. 145
☆ Nos. 8, 14, 23	♯ DFr. 57; HS.HSL 109
Nos. 9, 10, 16, 22	♯ DFr. 133; HS.HS 9006
Nos. 15, 18	♯ DFr. 161
Nos. 17, 19, 20, 21	♯ DFr. 126; HS.HSL 144
Nos. 25, 26, 27, 28	♯ DFr. 125; HS.HSL 145
No. 29 (& 32 Variations)	♯ DFr. 144
Nos. 30, 31, 32	♯ DFr. 109; HS.HSL 110

No. 21 also on ♯ DFr.EX 25006;
No. 27 on V♯ EX 17003; No. 26 on V♯ EX 17030;
Nos. 25, 24 on V♯ DFr.EX 17018, o.n. V♯ DFr. 73;
No. 23 on ♯ DFr.EX 25059; No. 27 on V♯ EX 17033;
No. 14 on V♯ DFr.EX 17012

COLLECTION: W. Kempff
☆ The following Sonatas, part of the complete recording, are
reissued :—

Nos. 1, 2	on	♯ Pol. 18105
Nos. 3, 10	on	♯ Pol. 18079
Nos. 4, 9	on	♯ Pol. 18071
Nos. 5, 6	on	♯ Pol. 18106
No. 6 only	also on	PV. 72336
No. 9 only	also on	PV. 72285
Nos. 11, 14	on	♯ HP.DGM 18020
Nos. 8, 14	on	♯ Pol. 17026
Nos. 12, 13	on	♯ Pol. 18067
No. 12 only	also on	♮ PV. 36065/6
No. 14 only	also on	♭ Pol. 30072; IPV.RVR 8202
Nos. 15, 16	on	♯ Pol. 18055
No. 16 only	also on	♮ PV. 72390/1
Nos. 17, 18	on	♯ Pol. 18056
No. 18 only	also on	♮ PV. 72303/4
Nos. 21, 22	on	♯ Pol. 18089
No. 22 only	also on	PV. 72286; FPV. 5055
Nos. 24-27	on	♯ Pol. 18135
No. 26 only	also on	PV. 72322
No. 27 only	also on	JpPV.KVM 20085
Nos. 28, 30	on	♯ Pol. 18145

[1] Carnegie Hall recital, May 30, 1954.

No. 29	on	♯ HP.APM 18146;
		♯ JpPol.LGM 6 & 6ss, ♮ PV. 72392/4
Nos. 31, 32	on	♯ Pol. 18045
No. 32 only	also on	♮ PV. 72314/5, 3ss.

COLLECTIONS
Nos. 8, 17, 25, 26, 32
W. Backhaus[1]   ♯ Lon.LL 1108/9
(Brahms, Liszt, Schubert, Schumann)

Nos. 8, 14, 19, 20, 25
S. Petitgirard   ♯ MFr.MF 3001

Nos. 8, 14, 21   I. Nádas   ♯ Per.SPL 726

Nos. 17, 23, 26   I. Nádas   ♯ Per.SPL 729

No. 1, F minor, Op. 2, No. 1
F. Gulda   ♯ D.LXT 2958
(No. 2)   (♯ Lon.LL 996)
C. Solomon   ♯ Vic.LM 1821
(No. 3)
☆ A. Baller (♯ Allo. 4037)
... **Minuet & Trio** only
E. Heiller (pf.)   in ♯ Uni.LP 1010
(† History of the Dance)
... **1st movt., Allegro,** only
with spoken analysis in EMI.EOM

No. 2, A major, Op. 2, No. 2
F. Gulda   ♯ D.LXT 2958
(No. 1)   (♯ Lon.LL 996)
R. Casadesus   ♯ AmC.ML 4622
(No. 23)   (♯ Phi.A 01618R)
☆ A. Schnabel *(Nos. 14, 26)*   ♯ Vic.LCT 1155
... **Scherzo** only
M. v. Doren (in ♯ Chan.MVDP 1)
L. Oborin (USSR. 020590)

No. 3, C major, Op. 2, No. 3
F. Gulda   ♯ D.LXT 2938
(Nos. 19, 20)   (♯ Lon.LL 999)
E. Gilels   ♯ CHS.CHS 1312
(Mendelssohn: Concerto No. 1)   (USSR. 021621/6)
☆ C. Solomon *(No. 1)*   ♯ Vic.LM 1821

No. 4, E flat major, Op. 7
K. Appelbaum *(No. 28)*   ♯ West.WN 18056

No. 7, D major, Op. 10, No. 3
P. Levi *(No. 28)*   ♯ Mon.MWL 304
☆ K. Appelbaum *(No. 21)*   ♯ Nix.WLP 5044

No. 8, C minor, Op. 13 ("*Pathétique*")
C. Solomon (n.v.)   ♯ G.ALP 1052
(No. 30)
P. Badura-Skoda   ♯ Nix.WLP 5184
(Nos. 14, 23)   (♯ West.WL 5184; Véga C30.A6)
E. Fischer   ♯ G.ALP 1094
(No. 23)   (♯ QALP 10047; FALP 311)
W. Gieseking   ♯ C.CX 1073
(No. 14)   (♯ FC 1024; QCX 10080; Angel. 35025)
A. Rubinstein (n.v.) *(No. 23)*   ♯ Vic.LM 1908
A. van Barentzen *(No. 14)*   ♯ G.FBLP 1032
G. Johannesen *(No. 31)*   ♯ MMS. 52
B. Vitebsky   ♯ CA.LPA 1007
(No. 14, Rondo, & Variations)
H. Steurer *(No. 14)*   ♯ Eta.LPM 1018
(5ss—Écossaises, on Eta. 20-11)
G. Stein *(No. 23)*   ♯ Roy. 1479
M. Grünberg (2ss)   USSRM.D 827/8
            (USSR. 021699/702)
☆ A. Rubinstein (♯ G.FALP 251; ItV.A12R 0084;
                       DV.CL 16067)
T. v. der Pas (♯ AmC.RL 3074; Phi.S 06067R)
O. Frugoni (♯ AFest.CFR 12-85;
                ♭ AmVox. set VIP 45212)
A. Foldes (in ♯ Clc. 6277)
... **2nd movt., Adagio**   M. v. Doren (in ♯ Chan.MVDP 1)

No. 9, E major, Op. 14, No. 1
☆ A. Baller (♯ *Allo. 4037*)

— ARR. STR. QTT.   Beethoven   (F major)
Pascal Qtt.   ♯ CHS.CHS 1216
(*Sextet, Op. 81b*)   (♯ Clc. 6238)

No. 10, G major, Op. 14, No. 2
D. Matthews   (*No. 23*)   ♯ C.SX 1023

No. 12, A flat major, Op. 26
W. Gieseking   (*No. 15*)   ♯ C.FCX 206
M. Karin   ♯ Sup.LPV 209
(*No. 17*)   (♯ U. 5196G)

No. 14, C sharp minor, Op. 27, No. 2 ("*Moonlight*")
C. Solomon   (n.v.)   ♯ G.BLP 1051
(*No. 26*)
P. Badura-Skoda   ♯ Nix.WLP 5184
(*Nos. 8, 23*)   (♯ West.WL 5184; Véga.C30.A6)
G. Anda   ♯ C.CX 1302
(*Concerto No. 1*)   (♯ Angel. 35248)
G. Novães   ♯ AmVox.PL 8530
(*Concerto No. 4*)   (*Mozart*, ♯ MApp.MAR 5953;
    & ♯ Pan.XPV 1011, d.c.)
A. v. Barentzen   (*No. 8*)   ♯ G.FBLP 1032
B. Vitebsky   ♯ CA.LPA 1007
(*No. 8, Rondo, & Variations*)
☆ W. Gieseking   ♯ C.CX 1073
(*No. 8*)   (QCX 10080: *FC 1024*; Angel. 35025)
☆ A. Schnabel   (*Nos. 2, 26*)   ♯ Vic.LCT 1155
☆ V. Horowitz   (*Mozart*)   ♯ G.BLP 1014
(♯ QBLP 5010: VBLP 803: FBLP 1048; ♭ Vic.ERA 144;
    ♯ BrzV.BRL 10)
L. Oborin (*USSR. 22718/23*)
H. Kann (♯ *MMS. 44*)
R. Spivak (ArgV. 66-6000/1)
M. Schwalb (♯ Roy. 1464; 2nd movt. only in ♯ Roy. 1901)
H. Steurer (Eta. 20-12/14 & ♯ LPM 1018)
E. Silver (♯ *Roy. 1825*)
☆ F. Rauch (♯ Sup.LPV 163; U. 5165G)
T. van der Pas (♯ AmC.RL 3074; Phi.S 06067R)
O. Frugoni (♯ AFest.CFR 12-85;
    ♭ AmVox. set VIP 45212)
V. Schiøler (♭ Mer.EP 1-5057;
    Adagio only, ♭ Mer.EP 1-5004; FMer.MEP 14529)
A. Jenner (♯ Cum.CR 250; Adagio only, in Ply. 12-75)

... **1st movt., Adagio** only
☆ W. Kempff, from set (PV. 72321: ♭ Pol. 30063)

— — ARR. ORCH.
Boston Prom.—Fiedler[1]   ♭ G.7EP 7018
(*Massenet, Brahms*) (in ♯ Vic.LM 1910: ♭ ERA 212;
    ♭ FV.A 95218; ItV.A72R 0050)
[excpt. on G.B 10810; Vic. 10-4217: ♭ 49-4217]
☆ Berlin Municipal Op. Orch. Members (in ♯ T.LS 6031)

— — ARR. PF. & ORCH.
L. Pennario & Hollywood Bowl—Dragon (in ♯ Cap.P 8326)

No. 15, D major, Op. 28 ("*Pastorale*")
D. Matthews   ♯ C.SX 1021
(*No. 21*)   (♯ WSX 1021)
O. Frugoni   ♯ E. & AmVox.PL 8650
(*Nos. 21, 25, 26*)
W. Gieseking   (*No. 12*)   ♯ C.FCX 206
☆ A. Schnabel   (*Nos. 19, 31*)   ♯ Vic.LCT 1154

No. 16, G major, Op. 31, No. 1
S. Nordby   ♯ ML. 7055
(*Schubert: Fantasia*)

No. 17, D minor, Op. 31, No. 2
C. de Groot   (*No. 18*)   ♯ Phi.A 00204L
A. Aeschbacher   ♯ Pol. 18220
(*No. 26, & Rondo, Op. 129*)
L. Kraus   ♯ Sel. 320.C.017
(*Variations, Op. 35*)
J. Lateiner   (*No. 21*)   ♯ West.WN 18086
C. Haskil   (*No. 18*)   ♯ Phi.A 00296L
☆ G. Novães   (*No. 26*)   ♯ EVox.PL 6270
☆ M. Fedorova   ♯ Sup.LPV 209
(*No. 12*)   (♯ U. 5196G)
☆ B. Janis (ArgV. 66-6060/2, set AR 8009)
A. Foldes (in ♯ Clc. 6277)

No. 18, E flat major, Op. 31, No. 3
C. de Groot   (*No. 17*)   ♯ Phi.A 00204L
A. v. Barentzen   ♯ G.FALP 192
(*Nos. 24, 26*)
C. Haskil   (*No. 17*)   ♯ Phi.A 00296L
☆ A. Rubinstein (♯ G.FALP 274; ItV.A12R 0103;
    DV.CL 16336)

No. 19, G minor, Op. 49, No. 1
No. 20, G major, Op. 49, No. 2
F. Gulda   ♯ D.LXT 2938
(*No. 3*)   (♯ Lon.LL 999)
W. Backhaus   (from Collection)   ♭ D.VD 510
... **No. 19**
☆ A. Schnabel   (*Nos. 15, 31*)   ♯ Vic.LCT 1154

No. 21, C major, Op. 53 ("*Waldstein*")
C. Solomon   (*No. 32*)   ♯ G.ALP 1160
L. Kraus   (*No. 30*)   ♯ Sel. 320.C.008
W. Gieseking   (n.v.)   ♯ C.CX 1055
(*No. 23*) (FCX 205: QCX 10069; VCX 529; Angel. 35024)
R. Serkin   (*No. 30*)   ♯ AmC.ML 4620
D. Matthews   (*No. 15*)   ♯ C.SX 1021
O. Frugoni   ♯ E. & AmVox.PL 8650
(*Nos. 15, 25, 26*)
S. Gorodnitzki   ♯ DCap.CTL 7067
(*No. 23*)   (♯ Cap.P 8264)
A. van Barentzen   (*No. 23*)   ♯ G.FALP 199
J. Lateiner   (*No. 17*)   ♯ West.WN 18087
A. S. Rasmussen   ♮ Tono.A 186/8
(6ss)   (*No. 23* in ♯ LPA 34004)
H. Reims   (*Gershwin*)   ♯ Roy. 1512
☆ W. Gieseking   (o.v.)   (*No. 23*)   ♯ AmC.ML 4774
☆ E. Kilenyi (♯ Cum.CR 229)
K. Appelbaum (♯ Nix.WLP 5044)
A. Fischer (♯ Sup.LPM 62; U. 5039C)

No. 22, F major, Op. 54
☆ C. Solomon (G.EB 565)

No. 23, F minor, Op. 57 ("*Appassionata*")
C. Solomon   (*No. 28*)   ♯ G.ALP 1272
P. Badura-Skoda   ♯ Nix.WLP 5184
(*Nos. 8, 14*)   (♯ West.WL 5184; Véga. C30.A6)
E. Fischer   (n.v.)   ♯ G.ALP 1094
(*No. 8*)   (QALP 10047: FALP 311)
(*Schubert*, on ♯ Vic.LHMV 1055)
R. Casadesus   ♯ AmC.ML 4622
(*No. 2*)   (♯ Phi.A 01618R)
D. Matthews   (*No. 10*)   ♯ C.SX 1023
S. Gorodnitzki   ♯ DCap.CTL 7067
(*No. 21*)   (♯ Cap.P 8264)
A. Rubinstein   (n.v.)   (*No. 8*)   ♯ Vic.LM 1908
A. van Barentzen   (*No. 21*)   ♯ G.FALP 199
S. Fiorentino   (*Chopin*)   ♯ CA.LPA 1087
H. Kann   (*No. 14*)   ♯ MMS. 44
G. Lasson   (*Chopin*)   ♯ Pac.FDPF 26
G. Stein   (*No. 8*)   ♯ Roy. 1479
☆ W. Gieseking   (*No. 21*)   ♯ C.CX 1055
(*No. 21*) (FCX 205: VCX 529: QCX 10069; Angel. 35024)
☆ W. Gieseking   (o.v.)   (*No. 21*)   ♯ AmC.ML 4774
☆ W. Malcuzynski   ♯ C.CX 1144
(*Bach & Brahms*)   (FCX 228)
☆ A. Rubinstein (♯ G.FALP 274; ItV.A12R 0103;
    ♭ Vic. set ERB 20; ♯ DV.CL 16336)
A. S. Rasmussen (♯ Tono.LPA 34004)
O. Vondrovic (♯ Sup.LPV 163; U. 5165G)
O. Frugoni (♯ AFest.CFR 12-85)
A. Kitchen (♯ Ply. 12-48)

No. 24, F sharp major, Op. 78
A. v. Barentzen   ♯ G.FALP 192
(*Nos. 18, 26*)
G. Johannesen   ♯ MMS. 100W
(*Corelli, Mozart, Moussorgsky*)

[1] ARR. Piston

No. 24, F sharp major, Op. 78 (*continued*)
B. Webster   in ♯ **Persp.PR 2**
☆ R. Serkin   ♯ **C.CX 1043**
(Fantasia, Op. 77 & Trio, Op. 70, No. 1) (QCX 10035)
☆ A. Foldes (♭ *Mer.EP 1-5055; FMer.MEP 14526;*
                                              ♯ *Clc. 6277*)

No. 25, G major, Op. 79
O. Frugoni   ♯ **E. & AmVox.PL 8650**
(Nos. 15, 21, 26)
☆ A. Foldes (♭ *FMerMEP 14526; ♭ Mer.EP 1-5055;*
                                              ♯ *Clc. 6277*)

No. 26, E flat major, Op. 81a (*"Les Adieux"*)
C. Solomon   ♯ *G.BLP 1051*
(No. 14) (No. 29 on ♯ Vic.LM 1733: ♭ set WDM 1733)
O. Frugoni   ♯ **E. & AmVox.PL 8650**
(Nos. 15, 21, 25)
A. v. Barentzen   (*Nos. 18, 24*)   ♯ **G.FALP 192**
☆ A. Schnabel (*Nos. 2, 14*)   ♯ **Vic.LCT 1155**
☆ G. Novães (♯ *EVox.PL 6270*)
  E. Kilenyi (♯ *Cum.CR 229*)
  A. Aeschbacher (in ♯ *Pol. 18220*)

No. 28, A major, Op. 101
C. Solomon   (*No. 23*)   ♯ **G.ALP 1272**
P. Badura-Skoda (*No. 30*)   ♯ **West.WL 5357**
K. Appelbaum   (*No. 4*)   ♯ **West.WN 18056**
P. Levi   (*No. 7*)   ♯ **Mon.MWL 304**
L. Lukas   ♯ **ML. 7050**
(Chopin: Sonata No. 3)

No. 29, B flat major, Op. 106 (*"Hammerklavier"*)
C. Solomon   ♯ **Vic.LM 1733**
(No. 26)   (♭ set WDM 1733)
O. Vondrovic   ♯ **Sup.LPV 169**
                                    (♯ U. 5164G)
I. Nádas (*No. 30*)   ♯ **Per.SPL 718**
☆ K. Appelbaum   ♯ Nix.WLP 5150

— ARR. ORCH.   Weingartner
Bavarian Sym.—Graunke   ♯ **Nix.ULP 9089**
                                    (♯ Ura. 7089)
☆ Royal Phil.—Weingartner (♯ AmC.ML 4675)

No. 30, E major, Op. 109
M. Hess   ♯ **G.ALP 1169**
(No. 31)   (♯ Vic.LHMV 1068)
R. Serkin (*No. 21*)   ♯ **AmC.ML 4620**
V. Schiøler (*No. 32*)   ♯ **G.KALP 2**
P. Badura-Skoda (*No. 28*)   ♯ **West.WL 5357**
E. Petri (*No. 31*)   ♯ **Roy. 1598**
I. Nádas (*No. 29*)   ♯ **Per.SPL 718**
L. Kraus (*No. 21*)   ♯ **Sel. 320.C.008**
☆ C. Solomon (*No. 8*)   ♯ **G.ALP 1062**
☆ J. Demus (♯ Cum.CR 239)

No. 31, A flat major, Op. 110
M. Hess   ♯ **G.ALP 1169**
(No. 30)   (♯ Vic.LHMV 1068)
G. Johannesen (*No. 8*)   ♯ **MMS. 52**
B. Siki[1] (*No. 32*)   ♯ **C.CX 1185**
E. Malinin   V♯ *CdM.LDA 8106*
E. Petri (*No. 30*)   ♯ **Roy. 1598**
☆ A. Schnabel (*Nos. 15, 19*)   ♯ Vic.LCT 1154
☆ J. Demus (♯ Cum.CR 239)

No. 32, C minor, Op. 111
C. Solomon (*No. 21*)   ♯ **G.ALP 1160**
B. Siki[1] (*No. 31*)   ♯ **C.CX 1185**
V. Schiøler (*No. 30*)   ♯ **G.KALP 2**

VARIATIONS
(6), F major, Op. 34
A. Ferber   ♯ *LT.MEL 94006*
(below)   (V♯ *Sel.LLA 1032*)

(15), E flat major, Op. 35 "*Eroica*"
C. Arrau   ♯ **B.AXTL 1024**
(Variations, Op. 120) (♯ D.UAT 273095; & UA 243521, 2ss;
(also ♯ *AmD.DL 4067*)   in AmD. set DX 122)
L. Kraus   ♯ **Sel. 320.C.017**
(Sonata No. 17)
☆ A. Schnabel (in ♯ Vic. set LCT 6700)

(6), D major, on Turkish March, Op. 76
F. Wührer   ♯ **E. & AmVox.PL 9490**
(Concerto No. 5)

(33), on a Waltz by Diabelli, Op. 120
W. Backhaus   ♯ **D.LXT 5016**
                                    (♯ Lon.LL 1182)
C. Arrau   ♯ **B.AXTL 1024/5**
(3ss—above) (♯ D.UAT 273095/6; in ♯ AmD. set DX 122)
J. Katchen   ♯ **D.LXT 2804**
                                    (♯ Lon.LL 745)
P. Baumgartner   ♯ **Pol. 18054**
☆ M. Horszowski (♯ EVox.PL 7730)

(6), on a Swiss Song G. 183 (WoO 64) pf. or hp.
N. Zabaleta (hp.) (n.v.)   in ♯ **Eso.ES 524**
(† XVIIIth Century Harp Music)

(6), G major G. 188 (WoO 77) 1800
B. Vitebsky   V♯ *CA.MPO 5012*
(Andante favori)
(idem & Sonatas Nos. 8, 14 on ♯ LPA 1007)

(10), B flat major, on 'La Stessa, la stessissima'
(Salieri) G. 185 (WoO 73) 1799
A. Ferber   ♯ *LT.MEL 94006*
(above)   (V♯ *Sel.LLA 1032*)

(32), C minor G. 191 (WoO 80) 1806
L. Hambro   ♯ *SOT. 1039*
(Bagatelles)
E. Gilels   ♯ *Sup.LPM 184*
(Brahms: Hungarian Dances)
*(Tchaikovsky: Trio, on ♯ A440.AC 1202; Concerto No. 3
                          & Mozart on ♯ Csm.CRLP 177)*
A. de Lara (*Brahms*)   ♯ **AdL.LP 5**
S. Fiorentino (*Scarlatti*)   V♯ *CA.MPO 5026*
Y. Nat (*Sonata No. 29*)   ♯ **DFr. 144**
C. Keene (*Bach & Brahms*)   ♯ **Mer.MG 10138**
☆ E. Ballon (in ♯ *D.LX 3070*)[1]

───────────

A. 2. CHAMBER MUSIC

Adagio   Mandoline—*see* Sonatina, *post.*

(3) DUOS, Clarinet & bassoon G. 147 (WoO 27)
1. C major   2. F major   3. B flat major
A. Simonelli & T. di Dario   ♯ **CEd.CE 1013**

... No. 3 only
J. Lancelot & P. Hongne   ♯ **LOL.OL 50033**
(Quintet, & Horn Sonata)   (♯ OL.LD 62)

Duo, E flat major vla., vlc.
"and a pair of spectacles" (WoO 32)[2] 1795-8
J. de Pasquale & S. Mayes   ♯ **Bo.B 210**
(Bréval, Haydn, Mozart)

QUARTETS, Pf., vln., vla., vlc.
No. 1, E flat major; 2. D major; 3. C major
                               G. 152 (WoO 36) 1785
☆ A. Balsam & Pascal Trio (♯ Clc. 6208)

No. 4, E flat major, Op. 16
(from Quintet, pf. & wind)
M. Horszowski & New York Str. Qtt. Members
(Mozart: Qtt., K478)   ♯ **AmC.ML 4627**
L. Mittman, L. Eidus, D. Mankowitz &
  G. Ricci   ♯ **Strad.STR 616**
(Wind Quintet, Op. 16)   (♯ Cpt.MC 20062)

---

[1] Announced but not issued.
[2] A second movement (Minuet) was first published 1952. Presumably the recording listed is the usual Allegro only.

QUARTETS, STRING

COMPLETE RECORDINGS (including *Grosse Fuge*)
Hungarian Qtt.

Nos. 1 & 2	on ♯ C.CX 1168
	(FCX 240; Angel. 35106, in set 3512)
Nos. 3 & 4	on ♯ C.CX 1172
	(FCX 241; Angel. 35107, in set 3512)
Nos. 5 & 6	on ♯ C.CX 1191
	(FCX 242; Angel. 35108, in set 3512)
No. 7	on ♯ C.CX 1203
	(FCX 243; Angel. 35109, in set 3513; G.LALP 162)
Nos. 8 & 11	on ♯ C.CX 1236
	(FCX 244; Angel. 35110, in set 3513)
Nos. 9 & 10	on ♯ C.CX 1254
	(FCX 245; Angel. 35111, in set 3513)
Nos. 12 & 16	on ♯ C.CX 1272
	(FCX 246; Angel. 35112, in set 3514)
No. 13 & Grosse Fuge	on ♯ C.CX n.d.
	(FCX 247; Angel. 35113, in set 3514)
No. 14	on ♯ C.CX n.d.
	(FCX 248; Angel. 35114, in set 3514)
No. 15	on ♯ C.CX n.d.
	(FCX 249; Angel. 35115, in set 3514)

Végh Qtt.

[some are ☆; others separately issued, *see below*]

Nos. 1 & 2	on ♯ DFr. 24
Nos. 5 & 6	on ♯ DFr. 25
Nos. 3 & 12	on ♯ DFr. 26
Nos. 7 & 11	on ♯ DFr. 27
Nos. 4 & 14	on ♯ DFr. 28
Nos. 8 & 16	on ♯ DFr. 29
No. 15	on ♯ DFr. 30
Nos. 9 & 10	on ♯ DFr. 39
No. 13 & Grosse Fuge	on ♯ DFr. 40

The American pressings (♯ HS. sets HSQ-N, O, P) are
differently arranged on 10 discs as follows:

Nos. 1 & 2	on ♯ HSQ 43 ⎤
Nos. 3 & 4	♯ HSQ 44 ⎬ Set HSQ-N
Nos. 5 & 6	♯ HSQ 45 ⎦
No. 7	on ♯ HSQ 41 ⎤
Nos. 8 & 11	♯ HSQ 42 ⎬ Set HSQ-O
Nos. 9 & 10	♯ HSQ 40 ⎦
Nos. 12 & 16	on ♯ HSQ 46 ⎤
No. 13	♯ HSQ 47 ⎬
No. 14 & Grosse Fuge	♯ HSQ 48 ⎬ Set HSQ-P
No. 15	♯ HSQ 49 ⎦

☆ Budapest Qtt. (in progress)

Nos. 1 & 2	on ♯ Phi.A 01194L
Nos. 3 & 4	on ♯ *Phi.A 01631R*
Nos. 5 & 6	on ♯ Phi.A 01195L
No. 7	on ♯ *Phi.A 01632R*

---

6 Quartets, Op. 18—COMPLETE
Barylli Qtt.   ♯ West.WN 18121/3
                                          (set WN 3302)

[for individual issues *see below*; No. 5 is ☆]

No. 1, F major, Op. 18, No. 1
Barylli Qtt. (*No. 2*)   ♯ West.WL 5203
Paganini Qtt.   ♯ Vic.LM 1729
(*No. 2*)   (♭ set WDM 1729; ♯ ItV.A12R 0050)
☆ Pascal Qtt. (♯ Clc. 6249)

No. 2, G major, Op. 18, No. 2
Paganini Qtt.   ♯ Vic.LM 1729
(*No. 1*)   (♭ set WDM 1729; ♯ ItV.A12R 0050)
Barylli Qtt. (*No. 1*)   ♯ West.WL 5203
Royale Qtt. (*No. 3*)   ♯ Roy. 1400
Beethoven Qtt. (2ss)   ♯ USSR.D 929/30
☆ Pascal Qtt. (♯ Clc. 6155)

No. 3, D major, Op. 18, No. 3
Barylli Qtt. (*No. 4*)   ♯ West.WL 5211
Royale Qtt. (*No. 2*)   ♯ Roy. 1400
☆ Pascal Qtt. (♯ Clc. 6155)

No. 4, C minor, Op. 18, No. 4
Barylli Qtt. (*No. 3*)   ♯ West.WL 5211
☆ Paganini Qtt. (♯ ItV.A12R 0121)
Pascal Qtt. (♯ Clc. 6250)

No. 5, A major, Op. 18, No. 5
☆ Pascal Qtt. (♯ Clc. 6250)
Paganini Qtt. (♯ ItV.A12R 0121)
Barylli Qtt. (♯ Sel. 320.CW.018)

No. 6, B flat major, Op. 18, No. 6
Barylli Qtt.   ♯ West.WL 5212
(*Quintet, Op. 29*)

Italian Qtt.   ♯ D.LXT 2811
(*Haydn*)
Komitas Qtt. (2ss)   ♯ USSR.D 1738/9
☆ Pascal Qtt. (♯ Clc. 6213)

No. 7, F major, Op. 59, No. 1
Italian Qtt.   ♯ D.LXT 2856
                                          (♯ Lon.LL 673)
Paganini Qtt.   ♯ Vic.LM 7000
                                          (♭ set WDM 7000)
☆ Vienna Konzerthaus Qtt. (♯ Sel. 270.CW.045)

No. 8, E minor, Op. 59, No. 2
Paganini Qtt.   ♯ Vic.LM 7001
                                          (♭ set WDM 7001)
☆ Pascal Qtt. (♯ Clc. 6117)
Vienna Konzerthaus Qtt. (♯ Sel. 320.CW.078)

... 4th movt. only
Bolshoi Theatre Qtt. (2ss)   USSR. 8586/7

No. 9, C major, Op. 59, No. 3
Paganini Qtt.   ♯ Vic.LM 1722
(*No. 10*) (♭ set WDM 1722; ♯ DV.L 16371; ItV.A12R 0095)
☆ Vienna Konzerthaus Qtt. (♯ Sel. 270.C.024)

No. 10, E flat major, Op. 74
Koeckert Qtt. (*No. 11*)   ♯ Pol. 18257
Oistrakh Qtt. (2ss)   ♯ USSR.D 1308/9
(10ss—USSR. 021241/50)
Paganini Qtt.   ♯ Vic.LM 1722
(*No. 9*) (♭ set WDM 1722; ♯ DV.L 16371; ItV.A12R 0095)
American Art Qtt.   ♯ BB.LBC 1073
(*Haydn*)   (♯ FV.A 530204)
☆ Pascal Qtt. (♯ Clc. 6146)
Vienna Konzerthaus Qtt. (♯ Sel.LA 1045)

No. 11, F minor, Op. 95
Koeckert Qtt. (*No. 10*)   ♯ Pol. 18257
Végh Qtt.   ♯ DFr. 75
(*Grosse Fuge*)   (2ss, ♯ EX 25004)
☆ Barylli Qtt. (♯ Sel.LA 1039)

No. 12, E flat major, Op. 127
Koeckert Qtt.   ♯ Pol. 18103
☆ Pascal Qtt. (♯ Clc. 6213)
Vienna Konzerthaus Qtt. (♯ Sel. 270.C.011)

No. 13, B flat major, Op. 130
Italian Qtt.   ♯ C.CX 1103
                    (♯ FCX 260: QCX 10026; Angel. 35064)
Koeckert Qtt.   ♯ Pol. 18168
Erling Bloch Qtt.   ♯ G.KBLP 3
Beethoven Qtt.   ♯ CdM.LDX 8140
☆ Barylli Qtt. (♯ Sel. 270.CW.015)

... 5th movt., Cavatina, only
☆ Berlin Phil.—Furtwängler (♭ T.UV 115)

No. 14, C sharp minor, Op. 131
Paganini Qtt.   ♯ Vic.LM 1736
(♯ ItV.A12R 0072; DV.L 16424)   (♭ set WDM 1736)
Koeckert Qtt.   ♯ Pol. 18187
Beethoven Qtt. (USSR. 20511/22)
☆ Pascal Qtt. (♯ Clc. 6118)
Barylli Qtt. (♯ Sel. 320.C.002)

No. 15, A minor, Op. 132
Koeckert Qtt.   ♯ Pol. 18226
Czechoslovak Qtt.   ♯ Sup.LPV 172
                                          (♯ U. 5126G)
☆ Vienna Konzerthaus Qtt. (♯ Sel.LPG 8675)
Pascal Qtt. (♯ Clc. 6227)
Paganini Qtt. (♯ ItV.A12R 0099)

No. 16, F major, Op. 135
Koeckert Qtt. (*below*)   ♯ HP.DGM 18154
Végh Qtt., from set   ♯ DFr.EX 25020
☆ Barylli Qtt. (♯ Sel. 320.CW.018)

... Adagio & Scherzo only — ARR. ORCH.
☆ N.B.C. Sym.—Toscanini (♭ G.7RQ 222)

♯ = Long-playing, 33⅓ r.p.m.   ♭ = 45 r.p.m.   ♮ = Auto. couplings, 78 r.p.m.

Grosse Fuge, B flat major, Op. 133
Koeckert Qtt. (*above*) ♯ **HP.DGM 18154**
Végh Qtt. (*No. 11*) ♯ **DFr. 75**
☆ Barylli Qtt. (♯ *Sel.LA 1039*)

— STRING ORCH. VERSION
English Baroque—Scherchen ♯ **West.WN 18034**
(*Symphony No. 1*)

C major (from Pf. Sonata, Op. 2, No. 3)
☆ Pascal Qtt. (♯ *Clc. 6249*)

QUINTETS, 2 vlns., 2 vlas., vlc.
E flat major, Op. 4   1795-6
[arrt. & revision of the Wind Octet, Op. 103]
Pascal Qtt. & W. Gerhard ♯ **CHS.CHS. 1217**
(♯ *Clc. 6251*)
C major, Op. 29   1801
Barylli Qtt. & W. Hübner ♯ **West.WL 5212**
(*Str. Qtt. No. 6*)
☆ Pascal Qtt. & W. Gerhard (♯ *Clc. 6202*; ♯ *MMS. 48*)

Quintet, E flat major, Op. 16   pf., ob., cl., hrn., bsn.
[*see also above, Pf. Qtt. No. 4*]   *c.* 1796
W. Gieseking, S. Sutcliffe, B. Walton, D. Brain,
C. James ♯ **C.CX 1322**
(*Mozart*) (♯ *Angel. 35303*)
A. d'Arco, P. Pierlot, J. Lancelot, G. Coursier,
P. Hongne ♯ **LOL.OL 50033**
(*Horn Sonata & Duo*) (♯ *OL.LD 62*)
R. Serkin & Philadelphia Wind Ens.
(*Mozart*) ♯ **AmC.ML 4834**
H. Wingreen & New Art Wind Qtt.
(*Mozart*) ♯ **CEd.CE 2007**
F. Maxian & Czech Phil. Wind Ens. ♯ **U. 5216G**
(*Rossini*)
L. Mittman, H. Schulman, D. Weber, E. Carmen
& F. Klein ♯ **Strad.STR 616**
(*Pf. Quartet No. 4*) (♯ *Cpt.MC 20062*)
Recorded lacking one instrument, in turn, for practice
(from above) (♯ *CEd.MMO 101/5*)

Rondino, E flat major   2 ob., 2 cl., 2 hrns., 2 bsns.
G. 146 (WoO 25)   1792
Vienna Phil. Wind Ens. ♯ **Nix.WLP 5262**
(*Trio & Variations*) (♯ *West.WL 5262*)

Septet, E flat major, Op. 20   *c.* 1799-1800
cl., hrn., bsn., vln., vla., vlc., cbs.
Vienna Octet Members ♯ **D.LXT 5094**
(♯ *Lon.LL 1191*)
N.B.C. Sym.—Toscanini[1] ♯ **G.ALP 1106**
(*Cherubini*)
(♯ *G.FALP 246*; *Vic.LM 1745*: ♭ *set WDM 1745;*
♯ *DV.L 16428*; *ItV.A12R 0046*)
Barylli Str. Ens. & Vienna Phil. Wind Trio
♯ **West.WN 18003**
Cha. Ens.—Lindenberg ♯ **Od.ODX 107**
(♯ *ArgOd.LDC 7905*)
☆ Jilka Septet (♯ *Cum.CR 246*)

SERENADES
D major, Op. 8   vln., vla., vlc.   *c.* 1796-7
J. Pougnet, F. Riddle & A. Pini ♯ **Nix.WLP 5219**
(*Trio, Op. 9, No. 3*) (♯ *West.WL 5219*)
E. Röhn, R. Wolf & A. Troester ♯ **Pol. 16087**
☆ J. Fuchs, L. Fuchs & L. Rose ♯ **B.AXL 2004**
(♯ *D.AK/UA 243075*)

D major, Op. 25   fl., vln. & vla.
J. Bentzon, E. M. Bruun & J. Koppel
(6ss) ♭ **C.LDX 7020/2**
☆ J. Baker, J. & L. Fuchs ♯ **B.AXTL 1033**
(*Str. Trio No. 4*) (♯ *D.UAT 273054*)

Sextet, E flat major, Op. 81b   Str. Qtt. & 2 hrns.
1795
Pascal Qtt., W. Speth & C. Rawyler
♯ **CHS.CHS 1216**
(*Str. Qtt. version of Pf. Sonata 9*) (♯ *Clc. 6238*)

SONATA, F major, Op. 17   hrn. & pf.   1800
G. Coursier & A. d'Arco ♯ **LOL.OL 50033**
(*Duo & Quintet*) (♯ *OL.LD 62*)
☆ M. Stefek & A. Holeček (4ss) Eta. 0029-40/1
(*Dussek: Sonata, on* ♯ *Sup.LPM 47; U. 5068C*)

SONATAS, Vln. & pf.
No. 1, D major, Op. 12, No. 1   No. 2, A major, Op. 12, No. 2
No. 3, E flat major, Op. 12, No. 3   No. 4, A minor, Op. 23
No. 5, F major, Op. 24   No. 6, A major, Op. 30, No. 1
No. 7, C minor, Op. 30, No. 2   No. 8, G major, Op. 30, No. 3
No. 9, A major, Op. 47   No. 10, G major, Op. 96

COMPLETE RECORDINGS
J. Heifetz & E. Bay (pf.) ♯ **Vic. set LM 6701**
(10ss) [B. Moiseiwitsch (pf.) in No. 9]
(Nos. 1, 2, 5, 7, 9 are ☆; for individual reissues see below)

W. Schneiderhan & W. Kempff ♯ **Pol. various**
Nos. 1 & 2 on ♯ HP.DGM 18083
(also ♭ PV. 72339/41)
Nos. 3 & 4 on ♯ Pol. 18138
Nos. 5 & 6 on ♯ Pol. 18082
No. 5 also ♭ PV. 72312/3S
Nos. 7 & 10 on ♯ Pol. 18209
No. 7 also ♭ PV. 72353/4
No. 8 (with *Brahms*) ♯ Pol. 18144
No. 9 (2ss) on ♯ HP.DGM 18092
(also ♭ PV. 72329/31)
No. 10 also ♭ PV. 72376/7

J. Fuchs & A. Balsam ♯ **B & AmD. various**
Nos. 1 & 9 on ♯ B.AXTL 1045; AmD.DL 9640
Nos. 2 & 10 on ♯ B.AXTL 1046; AmD.DL 9641
Nos. 3 & 6 on ♯ B.AXTL 1050; AmD.DL 9643
(♯ AFest.CFR 12-539)
Nos. 4 & 7 on ♯ B.AXTL 1057; AmD.DL 9644
Nos. 5 & 8 on ♯ B.AXTL 1052; AmD.DL 9642

J. Fournier & G. Doyen ♯ **West. various**
[Though not issued as a set, these artists have recorded all
10 Sonatas. For details, see Supp. II and entries below]

No. 1, D major, Op. 12, No. 1
Y. Menuhin & L. Kentner ♯ **G.ALP 1050**
(*No. 3*) (QALP 10026)
(*Walton on* ♯ *Vic.LHMV 1037*: ♭ *set WHMV 1037*)
J. Fournier & G. Doyen ♯ **West.WL 5176**
(*No. 10*)
D. Oistrakh & V. Yampolsky ♯ **Sup. LPV 244**
(*Romance No. 2; & Mozart*)

No. 2, A major, Op. 12, No. 2
Y. Menuhin & L. Kentner ♯ **G.ALP 1338**
(*No. 4*)
J. Fournier & G. Doyen ♯ **West.WL 5272**
(*No. 9*)
W. Schneiderhan & E. Berg ♯ **Rem. 199-95**
(*No. 8*) (♯ *Cum.CR 225*)

No. 3, E flat major, Op. 12, No. 3
Y. Menuhin & L. Kentner ♯ **G.ALP 1050**
(*No. 1*) (♯ *QALP 10026*)
J. Heifetz & E. Bay (n.v.) ♯ **Vic.LM 1912**
(*No. 6*) (*No. 4 on* ♯ *ItV.A12R 0046*)
J. Fournier & G. Doyen ♯ **West.WL 5247**
(*No. 5*)
☆ Z. Francescatti & R. Casadesus ♯**EPhi.ABR4025**
(*No. 4*) (♯ *Phi.A 01611R*)

No. 4, A minor, Op. 23
Y. Menuhin & L. Kentner ♯ **G.ALP 1338**
(*No. 2*)
J. Heifetz & E. Bay ♯ **Vic.LM 1842**
(*No. 7*) (*No. 3 on* ♯ *ItV.A12R 0060*) (*FV.A 630250*)
☆ Z. Francescatti & R. Casadesus
♯ **EPhi.ABR 4025**
(*No. 3*) (♯ *Phi.A 01611R*)
☆ P. Kling & O. Schulhof (♯ *Cum.CR 222*)

No. 5, F major, Op. 24   ("*Spring*")
Y. Menuhin & L. Kentner ♯ **G.ALP 1105**
(*No. 10*)
(*Mozart on* ♯ *Vic.LHMV 1053*)
M. Elman & J. Seiger ♯ **D.LXT 5126**
(*No. 9*) (♯ *Lon.LL 1258*)

(*continued on next page*)

---

[1] Played in an orchestral version.

No. 5, F major, Op. 24 (*continued*)

J. Fournier & G. Doyen (*No. 3*)	♯ **West.WL 5247**
J. Szigeti & M. Horszowski (*No. 6*)	♯ **AmC.ML 4870**
A. Plocek & J. Páleníček	♯ *Sup.LPM 129* (♯ *U. 5114C*)
C. Ferras & P. Barbizet	♯ **DT.LGX 66014**
(*Brahms: Sonata No. 3*) (♯ *T.LE 6501*; & 2ss, ♯ *TW 30011*)	
N. de Klijn & A. Heksch (*No. 6*)	♯ **Phi.A 00234L**
H. Drescher & M. Huttner (*No. 8*) (*Bruch*, on ♯ Roy. 1435)	♯ **Roy. 1511**
☆ D. Oistrakh & L. Oborin	♯ **Per.SPL 573**
(*Tartini & Schubert*) (2ss, **V**♯ *CdM.LDZA 8110*)	
(*Prokofiev* on ♯ *Csm.CRLP 152*)	
☆ P. Kling & H. Kann (♯ *Cum.CR 222*)	

No. 6, A major, Op. 30, No. 1

J. Heifetz & E. Bay (*No. 3*)	♯ **Vic.LM 1912** (*No. 8* on ♯ *ItV.A12R 0058*)
J. Szigeti & M. Horszowski (*No. 5*)	♯ **AmC.ML 4870**
N. de Klijn & A. Heksch (*No. 5*)	♯ **Phi.A 00234L**

No. 7, C major, Op. 30, No. 2

Z. Francescatti & R. Casadesus (*No. 8*)	♯ **AmC.ML 4861**
A. Plocek & J. Páleníček	♯ *Sup.LPM 128* (♯ *U. 5113C*)
J. Fournier & G. Doyen (*No. 8*)	♯ **West.WL 5292**
R. Ricci & F. Gulda (*No. 10*)	♯ **D.LXT 2942** (♯ *Lon.LL 1004*)
L. Kogan & A. Mytnik (2ss)	♯ *CdM.LDA 8129*
☆ J. Heifetz & E. Bay (♯ *Vic.LM 1842*; DV.A 63025; FV.A 630250)	
W. Schneiderhan & E. Berg (♯ *Cum.TCR 270*)	

No. 8, G major, Op. 30, No. 3

J. Heifetz & E. Bay (n.v.) (*No. 10*) (*No. 6* on ♯ *ItV.A12R 0058*)	♯ **Vic.LM 1914**
J. Martzy & J. Antonietti (*Mozart: Sonata K376*)	♯ **Pol. 18075**
H. Aïtoff & C. Chailley-Richez (*No. 2*) (♯ *Cum.CR 225*)	♯ **Rem. 199-95**
Z. Francescatti & R. Casadesus (*No. 7*)	♯ **AmC.ML 4861**
J. Fournier & G. Doyen (*No. 7*)	♯ **West.WL 5292**
H. Drescher & M. Huttner (*No. 5*)	♯ **Roy. 1511**

No. 9, A major, Op. 47 (*Kreutzer*)

G. de Vito & T. Aprea	♯ **G.ALP 1319**
M. Elman & J. Seiger (*No. 5*)	♯ **D.LXT 5126** (♯ *Lon.LL 1258*)
D. Oistrakh & L. Oborin	♯ *CdM.LDA 80771*
(*Leclair & Ysaÿe* on ♯ *Van.VRS 6024*)	
(*Leclair & Vladigerov* on ♯ *Csm.CRLP 153*)	
J. Fournier & G. Doyen (*No. 2*)	♯ **West.WL 5272**
M. Crut & J. C. Englebert	♯ *Sel. 270.C.007* (♯ *T.LB 6123*)
Y. Menuhin & L. Kentner (*Corelli*)	♯ **Vic.LHMV 10**
A. Plocek & J. Páleníček	♯ *Sup.LPM 116* (♯ *U. 5099C*)
H. Drescher & M. Huttner	♯ **Roy. 1526**
O. Colbentson & D. Garvey	♯ *MMS. 18*
M. Polikin & A. Dyakov (*USSR. 6527/30, 8286/90,*	
8349/51)	
☆ J. Heifetz & B. Moiseiwitsch (♯ *G.ALP 1093*:	
FBLP 1023; *ItV.A12R 0062*)	
Z. Francescatti & R. Casadesus (♯ *EPhi.ABR 4007*;	
♯ *Phi.A 01607R*)	
E. & A. Wolf (♯ *Tono.LPA 34001*)	

No. 10, G major, Op. 96

J. Fournier & G. Doyen (*No. 1*)	♯ **West.WL 5176**
J. Szigeti & M. Horszowski (*Schubert: Rondo, Op. 70*)	♯ **AmC.ML 4642**
J. Heifetz & E. Bay (*No. 8*) (*No. 9* on ♯ *ItV.A12R 0062*)	♯ **Vic.LM 1914**
(*Handel & Schubert* on ♯ *ItV.A12R 0159*)	
R. Ricci & F. Gulda (*No. 7*)	♯ **D.LXT 2942** (♯ *Lon.LL 1004*)
Y. Menuhin & L. Kentner (*No. 5*)	♯ **G.ALP 1105**

SONATAS, Vlc. & pf.

No. 1, F major, Op. 5, No. 1 No. 2, G minor, Op. 5, No. 2
No. 3, A major, Op. 69 No. 4, C major, Op. 102, No. 1
No. 5, D major, Op. 102, No. 2

COMPLETE RECORDINGS

P. Casals & R. Serkin	♯ **AmC.ML 4876/8**
(5ss—*Variations*, on ML 4877) (set SL 201)	
[Nos. 1 & 5 on ML 4876; Nos. 3 & 4 on ML 4878; No. 2	
is thought to be ☆]	
☆ J. Starker & A. Bogin	♯ **Nix.PLP 560/1**
(Nos. 1, 4 & 5 on PLP 561, Nos. 2 & 3 on PLP 560;	
also ♯ Cpt.MC 20050/1, differently coupled)	

Nos. 3, 4, 5

☆ P. Fournier & A. Schnabel	♯ **Vic.LCT 1124** (♭ *set WCT 1124*)

No. 2, G minor, Op. 5, No. 2

☆ P. Casals & R. Serkin	♯ **C.CX 1093**
(*Variations*)	(♯ *QCX 10068*)
☆ M. Gendron & J. Françaix	♯ **LT.DTL 93036**
(*No. 3*)	(♯ *T.LE 6521*)

No. 3, A major, Op. 69

E. B. Bengtsson & V. Schiøler (*Brahms*)	♯ **G.KALP 9**
P. Tortelier & K. Engel (*No. 4*)	♯ **G.FALP 259**
☆ M. Gendron & J. Françaix (*No. 2*)	♯ **LT.DTL 93036**
☆ E. Feuermann & M. Hess (*Variations; & Reger*)	♯ **AmC.ML 4678**

No. 4, C major, Op. 102, No. 1

A. Janigro & C. Zecchi (*No. 5*)	♯ **West.WL 5180** (♯ *Véga. C30.A7*)
P. Tortelier & K. Engel (*No. 3*)	♯ **G.FALP 259**

No. 5, D major, Op. 102, No. 2

A. Janigro & C. Zecchi (*No. 4*)	♯ **West.WL 5180** (♯ *Véga. C30.A7*)

Sonatina, C minor mandoline & hpsi.
G. 150 (WoO 44)
Adagio, E flat major (WoO 43-2)
— ARR. MANDOLINES
Caecilia Mandoline Players—Dekker
in ♯ **Phi.N 00686R**
(*Hasse, Mozart, Vivaldi*)

TRIOS, Pf., vln. & vlc.

COLLECTION
Nos. 1-3, Op. 1, Nos. 1-3
Nos. 4 & 5, Op. 70, Nos. 1 & 2
B flat major, Op. 11 pf., cl., vlc. — ARR. pf., vln. & vlc.
For practice—recorded lacking one instrument
in turn ♯ **CEd. sets MMO 91/3**
(18ss) (each set 6ss)

No. 1, E flat major, Op. 1, No. 1

Classic Pf. Trio (*No. 3*)	♯ **CEd.CE 1063**

No. 2, G major, Op. 1, No. 2
☆ Boston Trio (♯ *Pac.LDAD 79*)

---

1 Paris recording, 1953. The Csm. is probably a different recording.

No. 3, C minor, Op. 1, No. 3
P. Badura-Skoda, J. Fournier & A. Janigro
(Trio, Op. 11) ♯ **West.WN 18030**
Bolzano Trio ♯ **Cpt.MC 20018**
(Brahms: Trio)
Classic Pf. Trio *(No. 1)* ♯ **CEd.CE 1063**

No. 4, D major, Op. 70, No. 1 *"Geister"*
Trio di Trieste ♯ **D.LXT 5253**
(Mozart) (♯ Lon.LL 1177)
Albeneri Trio ♯ **Mer.MG 10139**
(No. 5) (♯ Clc. 6268)
☆ Busch-Serkin Trio ♯ **C.CX 1043**
(Fantasia, Op. 77 & Sonata No. 24) (QCX 10035)
☆ Santoliquido Trio (♯ AmD.DL 9691)
Boston Trio (♯ Pac.LDAD 79)

No. 5, E flat major, Op. 70, No. 2
Santoliquido Trio (2ss) ♯ **Pol. 16039**
(& 4ss, ♮ PV. 72283/4) *(No. 4 on* ♯ AmD.DL 9691)
Albeneri Trio ♯ **Mer.MG 10139**
(No. 4) (♯ Clc. 6268)
Gilels Trio *(Haydn)* ♯ **USSR.D 1234**

No. 6, B flat major, Op. 97 *"Archduke"* 1811
Albeneri Trio ♯ **Mer.MG 10140**
(♯ Clc. 6274)
L. Nadelmann, S. Blanc & L. Rostal ♯ **MMS.78**
☆ P. Badura-Skoda, J. Fournier & A. Janigro
♯ **Nix.WLP 20018**
(o.n. WLP 5131)
☆ A. Rubinstein, J. Heifetz & E. Feuermann
♯ **G.ALP 1184**
(♯ DV.L 17041)
☆ Jilka Trio (♯ Cum.CR 240)
A. Jambór, V. Aitay, J. Starker (♯ Cpt.MC 20080)

No. 7, B flat major G. 154 (WoO 39) 1812
☆ J. Mannes, B. Gimpel & L. Silva ♯ **B.AXTL 1019**
(C. Schumann) (♯ D.UAT 273071)

Trio, B flat major, Op. 11 pf., cl. (or vln.), vlc. 1798
P. Badura-Skoda, J. Fournier (vln.), A. Janigro
(Trio No. 3) ♯ **West.WN 18030**
R. Veyron-Lacroix, J. Lancelot & R. Albin
(Trio, C major, Op. 87) † ♯ **AS. 2505LD**
☆ M. Horszowski, R. Kell & F. Miller (♯ D.UAT 273056)
— PF., VLN., VLC. version
For practice: Recorded with each instrument missing in
turn, *see* Trios, *above.*

Trio, C major, Op. 87 2 obs. & cor anglais *c.* 1794
H. Kamesch, M. Kautsky & H. Hadamousky
♯ **Nix.WLP 5262**
(Variations & Rondino) (♯ West.WL 5262)
P. Pierlot (playing all 3 parts) † ♯ **AS. 2505LD**
(Trio, B flat major, Op. 11)

TRIOS, Vln., vla. & vlc.
No. 1, E flat major, Op. 3 1792
J. Pougnet, F. Riddle & A. Pini ♯ **West.WL5226**

No. 2, G major, Op. 9, No. 1
J. Pougnet, F. Riddle & A. Pini ♯ **Nix.WLP5198**
(No. 3) (♯ West.WL 5198)
☆ Bel Arte Trio ♯ **B.AXTL 1056**
(No. 3) (♯ D.UAT 273543)

No. 3, D major, Op. 9, No. 2
J. Pougnet, F. Riddle & A. Pini ♯ **Nix.WLP5198**
(No. 2) (♯ West.WL 5198)
☆ Bel Arte Trio ♯ **B.AXTL 1056**
(No. 2) (♯ D.UAT 273543)

No. 4, C minor, Op. 9, No. 3
J. Pougnet, F. Riddle & A. Pini ♯ **Nix.WLP5219**
(Serenade, Op. 8) (♯ West.WL 5219)
☆ Fuchs Trio ♯ **B.AXTL 1033**
(Serenade, Op. 25) (♯ D.UAT 273054)

VARIATIONS, Fl. & pf. (or vln. & pf.)
(6) Easy themes varied, Op. 105 (½s)
(10) National themes with variations, Op. 107 (2ss)[1]
W. Mann & R. Dirksen ♯ **Eso.ES 525/6**
(Piano Collection) (♯ Cpt.MC 20081/2)
... Op. 105, No. 3; Op. 107, Nos. 1, 6 & 7
☆ J-P. Rampal & R. Veyron-Lacroix **(V**♯ **Sel.LAP 1003)**

VARIATIONS, Vlc. & pf.
(12) on 'Ein Mädchen oder Weibchen', Op. 66
M. Amfiteatrof & O. P. Santoliquido
♯ **ItV.A12R 0162**
(below; Della Ciaja, Handel)
☆ P. Casals & R. Serkin ♯ **C.CX 1093**
(below) (♯ QCX 10068)
(also ♯ AmC.ML 4877, in set SL 201)

(7) on 'Bei Männern' G. 158 (WoO 46) *c.* 1801
M. Amfiteatrof & O. P. Santoliquido
(above) ♯ **ItV.A12R 0162**
A. Schmidt & C. Fannière ♯ **Vill. 1**
(Haydn, Rubino, etc.)
☆ P. Casals & R. Serkin ♯ **C.CX 1093**
(above; & Sonata 2) (QCX 10068)
(also ♯ AmC.ML 4877, in set SL 201)
☆ E. Feuermann & T. van der Pas ♯ **AmC.ML 4678**
(Sonata, Op. 69 & Reger)

(12) on 'See, the Conquering hero comes'
G.157 (WoO 45)
P. Casals & R. Serkin ♯ **AmC.ML 4640**
(Bach & Beethoven Songs)

Variations on 'La ci darem' 2 obs. & cor ang.
(WoO 46) *c.* 1796
H. Kamesch, M. Kautsky & H. Hadamousky
♯ **Nix.WLP 5262**
(Trio & Rondino) (♯ West.WL 5262)

═══════════════

A. 3. DANCES & MARCHES
(see also PIANO COLLECTIONS, *supra)*

(12) Contretänze G. 141 (WoO 14) orch. 1800-1
Vienna State Op.—Litschauer ♯ **Nix.VLP 429**[2]
(Wiener Tänze) (♯ Van.VRS 429)
... No. 1 only Inst. Ens. (in *G.B 10659*)
— — ARR. ACCORDEONS B. Hughes, B. Palmer & L. Manno
(cbs.) in ♯ **Capri. 1**
Unspec. Moscow Radio—Kovalev (2ss) *USSR. 18605/6*
(12) Deutsche Tänze G. 140 (WoO 8) orch.
... Nos. 1, 2, 3 only
☆ Winterthur Sym.—Goehr (♯ ANix.MLP Y 10;
♯ Clc. 11005)
(6) Écossaises B & H 302 (WoO 83) pf. *c.* 1806
H. Steurer *Eta. 20-11*
(Sonata 8, s. 5)
☆ A. Aeschbacher (♭ Pol. 32031)
— ARR. HARP O. Erdeli *(USSRM.D 00477)*
"Folk Dance" — ARR. VLN. & PF.; Heifetz[3]
☆ J. Heifetz (in ♯ G.ALP 1206: FALP 248; ♭ Vic.ERA 184)

MINUETS
Twelve G. 139 (WoO 7) orch. 1795
Frankenland Sym.—Kloss ♯ **CA.LPA 1013**
(Romance, pf. & orch.) (♯ Lyr.LL 45)
(6) Gesellschafts Menuette orig. 2 vlns. & bass
(WoO 9) pub. 1933, Schott[4]
1. E flat major 2. G major
3. C major 4. F major
5. D major 6. G major
London Baroque Orch.—Haas ♮ **P.SW 8149/50**
(3ss—Dvořák: Gavotte) (♯ AmD.DL 4096)
E flat major G. 142 (WoO 3) orch.
(Gratulations-Minuet)
☆ Boston Sym.—Münch *(Figaro, Overture)* ♭ **G.7RF 281**

---

[1] Op. 105-4 on *The last Rose of Summer*; Op. 107-4 on *The Pulse of an Irishman.*
[2] Nix.VLP 429, also ♯ *Van.VRS 5000*, 2ss, were announced but not issued.
[3] Pub. C. Fischer Inc. (N.Y.); from No. 2 of 3 *Deutsche Tänze* arr. (or by ?) I. Seiss, pub. Schirmer, 1915. (Information from *Record Ratings*) [4] And not as labelled.

E flat major G. 165 (WoO 82) pf. *c.* 1803
M. Grünberg   *USSRM.D 001248*
(*below, & Rondo*)

G major G. 167-2 (WoO 10-2) pf. (? orig. orch.)
S. Bianca   *MSB. 78144*
(*Rondo, G major*)

G. v. Renesse   ♭ *G.7EPH 1012*
(*Für Elise; & Durand*)

M. Grünberg (*above*)   *USSRM.D 001248*

E. Silver (hpsi.)   in ♯ *Roy. 1550*

— ARR. VLN. & PF.
W. Tworek & E. Vagning   *Pol. HA 70004*
(*Schubert: Wiegenlied, Op. 98, No. 2*)
☆ M. Elman & W. Rosé (♭ *DV. 26035*)

— ARR. CBS. & PF.
☆ S. Koussevitzky & pf. (in ♯ Vic.LCT 1145)

— ARR. GLASS HARMONICA Hansen
E. Hansen   in ♯ *Ban.BC 2000*
(*Mozart, Gossec & Folksongs*)

— ARR. ORCH. Anon. Orch. (in ♯ *Jay. 3004*)

(11) Wiener Tänze (WoO 17) 1819
("*Viennese*" or "*Mödlinger*" *Dances*) (pub. 1907, B & H)
Vienna State Op.—Litschauer ♯ *Nix.VLP 429*[1]
(*Contretänze*)   (♯ Van.VRS 429)
French Radio Sym.—Leibowitz ♯ *Oce.OCS 34*
(*König Stefan & Wellington's Sieg*)

MARCHES
Marsch für die böhmische Landwehr 1809
("York'scher Marsch", F major)   G. 145-1 (WoO 18)
East Berlin Police Band—Kaufmann
                                        Eta. 110208
(*Anon: Marsch der freiwilligen Jäger*)

Musik für die Grosse Wacht-Parade 1816
(*March No. 4, D major*)   G. 144 (WoO 24)
☆ London Baroque Ens.—Haas   ♭ *P.CREP 1*
(*Cherubini*)

A. 4. ORCHESTRAL

CONCERTOS, Piano & Orch.
COLLECTION of the Five
W. Kempff & Berlin Phil.—v. Kempen[3]
(6ss)   ♯ *AmD.DL 9686/8*
[see below for details]   (set DX 125)
R. Serkin & Philadelphia—Ormandy[2]
                                ♯ *AmC. various*
[see below for details]
☆ A. Schnabel & L.P.O.—Sargent[2]
                                ♯ *Vic. set LCT 6700*
(9ss—*Variations, Op. 35*)   [L.S.O. in Nos. 1 & 5]

No. 1, C major, Op. 15
W. Kempff & Berlin Phil.—v. Kempen[3]
                                ♯ *Pol. 18129*
P. Badura-Skoda & Vienna State Op.
—Scherchen   ♯ *Nix.WLP 5209*
                          (♯ BrzV.SLP 5503; West.WL 5209)
R. Serkin & Philadelphia—Ormandy[2]
                                ♯ *EPhi.ABR 4040*
                          (♯ AmC.ML 4914; ♯ Phi.A 01627R)
F. Wührer & Vienna Pro Musica—Swarowsky
                                ♯ *E. & AmVox.PL 8400*
(*Rondo, B flat, pf. & orch.*)
G. Anda & Philharmonia—Galliera[2]
                                ♯ *C.CX 1302*
(1½ss—*Sonata No. 14*)   (♯ Angel. 35248)
H. Steurer & Leipzig Radio—Pflüger
                                ♯ *Ura.RS 7-23*
(*Mendelssohn*)   (♯ MTW. 518)
F. Egger & Linz Sym.   ♯ *Ply. 12-25*
☆ H. Roloff & Berlin Radio—Rucht
                          (♯ Sel.LA 1035 & ♯ CdM.LDX 8015)

No. 2, B flat major, Op. 19
P. Badura-Skoda & Vienna State Op.—
—Scherchen   ♯ *Nix.WLP 5302*
(*Coriolan & Zur Weihe des Hauses Ovs.*)
                   (♯ West.WL 5302; 2ss, ♯ Sel. 270.CW.069)
R. Serkin & Philadelphia—Ormandy[2]
(*No. 4*)   ♯ *AmC.ML 5037*
C. Solomon & Philharmonia—Cluytens
                                ♯ *G.BLP 1024*
(*Mozart, on ♯ Vic.LHMV 12*) (*FBLP 1055: QBLP 5012*)
W. Kempff & Berlin Phil.—v. Kempen[3]
                                ♯ *Pol. 16071*
A. Balsam & Winterthur Sym.—Goehr
                                ♯ *MMS. 17*
P. Jacobs & Fr. Radio Sym.—Leibowitz[2]
                                ♯ *Oce.OCS 35*
(*Concerto, E flat*)
G. Stein & Berlin Sym.—Balzer   ♯ *Roy. 1397*
("*Jena*" *Sym.*)
☆ W. Kapell & N.B.C. Sym.—Golschmann
                                        (♯ Vic.LM 9026)

No. 3, C minor, Op. 37
W. Kempff & Berlin Phil.—v. Kempen[3]
                                ♯ *HP.DGM 18130*
(5ss—*Rondo, Op. 51, No. 2 on* ♮ PV. 72423/5)
E. Fischer & Philharmonia Orch.[4] ♯ *G.BLP 1063*
                                        (*QBLP 5033*)
E. Gilels & Paris Cons.—Cluytens[2]♯ *C.CX 1188*
                          (♯ FCX 300; Angel. 35131)
R. Serkin & Philadelphia—Ormandy[2]
                                ♯ *AmC.ML 4738*
J. Iturbi & Victor Sym.   ♯ *Vic.LM 1759*
                          (♭ set WDM 1759; ♯ ItV.A12R 0012)
E. Gilels & Moscow Radio—Kondrashin
                                ♯ *Per.SPL 601*
(*Mozart*)   (2ss, ♯ USSR.D 01193/4)
(*32 Variations; & Mozart on* ♯ Csm.CRLP 177)[5]
C. de Groot & Vienna Sym.—v. Otterloo
                                ♯ *Phi.A 00646R*
B. Vitebsky & Orch.—Vicars ♯ *CA.LPA 1079*
(*Andante favori & Bagatelle*)
G. Johannesen & Netherlands Phil.—Goehr
                                ♯ *MMS. 25*
☆ L. Kraus & Vienna Sym.—Moralt ♯ *EVox.PL 7270*
                          (♯ AFest.CFR 12-291)
☆ C. Arrau & Philadelphia—Ormandy[2] ♯ *C.CX 1080*
                          (♯ FCX 142: QCX 10075)
☆ M. Long & Paris Cons.—Weingartner (♯ C.FHX 5007)
E. Erdmann & Berlin Phil.—Rother (Sup. 70000/3)

No. 4, G major, Op. 58
C. Arrau & Philharmonia—Galliera
                                ♯ *C.CX 1333*
                                  (♯ Angel. 35300)
W. Kempff & Berlin Phil.—v. Kempen[3]
                                ♯ *HP.DG 16072*
(5ss—*Fidelio Overture on* ♮ PV. 72450/2)
(*Rondo, Op. 51, No. 1, on* ♯ AmD.DL 9742)
C. Solomon & Philharmonia—Cluytens[2]
                                ♯ *G.BLP 1036*
          (♯ FBLP 1056: QBLP 5016; ♯ Vic.LHMV 1056)
C. Curzon & Vienna Phil.—Knappertsbusch
                                ♯ *D.LXT 2948*
                                  (♯ Lon.LL 1045)
G. Novães & Vienna Pro Musica—Swarowsky
(*Sonata No. 14*)   ♯ *AmVox.PL 8530*
C. de Groot & Vienna Sym.—v. Otterloo[2]
                                ♯ *EPhi.ABR 4038*
                                  (♯ Phi.A 00718R)
R. Serkin & Philadelphia—Ormandy[2]
(*No. 2*)   ♯ *AmC.ML 5037*
[6]A. Rubinstein & New York Phil. Sym.—Mitropoulos
                                in ♯ *OTA. 8*

---

[1] VLP 429 was announced but not issued.
[2] Cadenzas by Beethoven. Others not marked, probably also use his.
[3] Cadenzas by Kempff, based on Beethoven.
[4] Cadenza not by Beethoven.
[5] Csm. catalogue says Gauk conducts.
[6] Transcribed from a broadcast performance.

No. 4, G major, Op. 58 (*continued*)
E. Silver & "Philharmonic"—Berendt ♯ **Allo. 3076**
N. Mewton-Wood & Utrecht Sym.—Goehr ♯ **MMS. 24**
J. Páleníček & Czech Phil.—Ančerl ♯ *Sup. LPM 246*
☆ W. Gieseking & Philharmonia—Karajan[1] ♯ *C.C 1007*
          (♯ *VC 804: QC 1014*)
☆ P. Badura-Skoda & Vienna State Op.—Scherchen[1]
                ♯ **Nix.WLP 5143**
          (♯ *Sel.LA 1036;* BrzV.SPL 5504)
☆ A. Schnabel & Philharmonia—Dobrowen[1]
                (♭ *Vic.LCT 1131*)
G. Novães & Vienna Sym.—Klemperer
                (♯ *Pan.XPV 1017*)

No. 5, E flat major, Op. 73 (*"Emperor"*)
W. Backhaus & Vienna Phil.—Krauss
                ♯ **D.LXT 2839**
                (♯ *Lon.LL 879*)
W. Kempff & Berlin Phil.—v. Kempen
                ♯ **HP.DGM 18131**
(♯ AmD.DL 9741)   (& 6ss, ♮ PV. 72407/9)
C. Solomon & Philharmonia—Menges
                ♯ **G.ALP 1300**
R. Casadesus & N.Y.P.S.O.—Mitropoulos[2]
                ♯ **Phi.A 01215L**
F. Wührer & Vienna Pro Musica—Hollreiser
(*Variations, Op. 76*)   ♯ **E. & AmVox.PL 9490**
E. Ney & Vienna Phil.—Böhm   ♯ **Ura. 7150**
                (also ♯ RS 7-10)
☆ E. Fischer & Philharmonia—Furtwängler
                ♯ **G.ALP 1051**
   (♯ *QALP 10024: FALP 121: VALP 536;* Vic.LHMV 4)
☆ R. Serkin & Philadelphia—Ormandy ♯ *C.CX 1070*
    (♯ *QCX 10041;* ♭ *AmC. set A 1064*)
☆ P. Badura-Skoda & Vienna State Op.—Scherchen
                ♯ **Nix.WLP 5114**
             (♯ *Sel. 270.CW. 072*)
☆ C. de Groot & Residentie—v. Otterloo
                ♯ **EPhi.ABL 3032**
             (♯ *Epic.LC 3014*)
L. Oborin & Moscow Radio—Gauk   ♯ *CdM.LDA 8107*
      (♯ Csm.CRLP 219; USSR.D 01438/9)
Anon. Artists (♯ *ACC.MP 1*—perhaps Ney, *above*)
H. Kann & Netherlands Phil.—Ackermann (♯ *MMS. 45*)
F. Rauch & Czech Phil.—Šejna
        (♯ *Sup.LPV 145;* U. 5152G)
E. Silver & Varsity Sym. (♯ *Var. 2056*)
☆ V. Horowitz & Vic. Sym.—Reiner
   (♯ *G.FALP 240;* ItV.A12R 0039; DV.L 16411)
F. Karrer & Austrian Sym.—Wöss
        (♯ Msq. 10004; Cum.CR 206)
W. Gieseking & Philharmonia—Karajan (♯ *C.VCX 507*)
D. Matthews & Philharmonia—Susskind
             (♯ *AmC.RL 3037*)
V. Schiøler & Danish Radio—Garaguly
             (♯ *Tono.LPX 35006*)
M. Long & Paris Cons.—Münch (♯ *C.FHX 5006*)

E flat major B & H 310 (WoO 4) 1784
Reconstruction by W. Hess
A. Sandford & Orch.—Berendt   ♯ **Allo. 3050**
                (♯ *Pac.LDAD 57*)
P. Jacobs & French Radio Sym.—Leibowitz[3]
(*Concerto No. 2*)   ♯ **Oce.OCS 35**

CONCERTO, D major, Op. 61, vln. & orch.
Y. Menuhin & Philharmonia—Furtwängler[4]
                ♯ **G.ALP 1100**
(♯ *FALP 314: QALP 10056: VALP 537;* Vic.LHMV 1061)
D. Oistrakh & Stockholm Fest.—Ehrling[4]
                ♯ **C.CX 1194**
(♯ *QCX 10120;* FCX 354; Angel. 35162; G.LALP 231)
W. Schneiderhan & Berlin Phil.—v. Kempen
                ♯ **HP.DGM 18099**
(♯ AmD.DL 9784; Eta. 820005) (6ss, ♮ PV. 72366/8)
B. Gimpel & Bamberg Sym.—Hollreiser
(*Romances*)   ♯ **E. & AmVox.PL 9340**
H. Szeryng & Paris Cons.—Thibaud
                ♯ **Od.ODX 109**
                (♯ ArgOd.LDC 7904)
M. Elman & L.P.O.—Solti[5]   ♯ **D.LXT 5068**
                (♯ *Lon.LL 1257*)

A. Spalding & Austrian Sym.—Loibner
                ♯ **Rem. 199-144**
                (♯ Cum.CR 218)
N. Milstein & Pittsburgh Sym.—Steinberg[6]
                ♯ **Cap.P 8313**
☆ G. Kulenkampff & Berlin Phil.—Schmidt-Isserstedt[4]
                ♯ **DT.LGX 66017**
(Sup. 70004/9, 11ss)   (♯ T.LE 6507)
☆ Z. Francescatti & Philadelphia—Ormandy
                (♭ *AmC. set A 1086*)
H. Krebbers & Residentie—v. Otterloo
        (♯ Epic.LC 3023; Phi.S 04000L)
B. Huberman & Vienna Phil.—Szell (♯ AmC.ML 4769)
J. Heifetz & N.B.C. Sym.—Toscanini (♯ G.FJLP 5017)
D. Oistrakh & Moscow Radio—Gauk
  (2ss, ♯ CHS.CHS 1303; MMS. 2017; USSR.D 0498/9;
  also with *Glazounov* on ♯ Per.SPL 598; *Mozart* on
  ♯ Csm.CRLP 155) (Some of these *may* be n.v.)
I. Haendel & Philharmonia—Kubelik (♯ G.FELP 138)

— ARR. PF. & ORCH. Beethoven 1807
H. Schnabel & Vienna Philharmonia—Adler
                ♯ **CA.LPA 1051**
                (♯ SPA. 45)
☆ A. Balsam & Winterthur—Dahinden (♯ CHS.CHS 1239)

CONCERTO, C major, Op. 56 vln., vlc., pf. & orch.
D. Oistrakh, S. Knushevitzky, L. Oborin &
   U.S.S.R. Radio—Golovanov ♯ **Per.SPL 590**
(*Mozart*)   (*Brahms* on ♯ Csm.CRLP 10200)
☆ R. Odnoposoff, S. Auber, A. Morales & Vienna Phil.
   —Weingartner (♯ *AmC.ML 2218*)
J. Corigliano, L. Rose, W. Hendl & N.Y.P.S.O.—
   —Walter (♯ *C.QC 1002*)

OVERTURES (*See also* STAGE WORKS, *below*)
Coriolan, Op. 62
Philharmonia—Karajan   ♯ **C.CX 1227**
(*Sym. No. 2*)   (♯ *QCX 10185;* Angel. 35196)
Philharmonia—Malko   **G.C 4232**
(GB 83: in ♯ *DLP 1061: QDLP 6022: FFLP 1047*)
(also in ♯ BB.LBC 1087, d.c.)
Vienna State Phil.—Horenstein
                ♯ **E. & AmVox.PL 8020**
(*Egmont, Leonore 3, Prometheus*)
Royal Phil.—Beecham   ♯ **AmC.ML 5029**
(*Brahms, Boccherini, Méhul, Grétry*)
Vienna State Op.—Scherchen ♯ **Nix.WLP 5302**
(*Zur Weihe des Hauses & Concerto No. 2*)
(♯ West.WL 5302; & in ♯ Nix.WLP 5335; West.WL 5335;
              ♯ Sel. 320.CW.082)
Minneapolis Sym.—Dorati, in ♯ **Mer.MG 50017**
                (♯ FMer.MLP 7501)
Berlin Phil.—Lehmann   **PV. 72342**
(*Symphony 2,* s. 1)   (in ♯ *AmD.DL 4068*)
(*Alceste Overture* on ♭ *Pol. 30122;*
          also in ♯ HP.DGM 18234)
Leipzig Gewandhaus—Konwitschny   **Eta. 120003**
              (in ♯ LPM 1000)
Netherlands Phil.—Goehr (*Egmont Ov.*) V♯ *MMS.97*
U.S.S.R. State—Gauk   **USSRM.D 001223**
(*Romance, vln. & orch.*)
☆ L.P.O.—v. Beinum (♯ *D.LW 5015;* ♯ Lon.LL 357)
N.B.C. Sym.—Toscanini (♭ *G.7ERF118;* ♭ *Vic.ERA 91;*
                DV. 26033)
Residentie—v. Otterloo (Phi.N 12058G: ♭ *S 06001R*)
Philharmonia—Schüchter (♭ *C.SED 5503: SEDQ 509*)
Orch.—Hewitt (V♯ *DFr.EX 17002* & in ♯ DFr. 90)
Bamberg Sym.—Keilberth (♯ *DT.TM 68002;*
       TV.VSK 9025; ♯ *FT.260.TC.033*)
Philadelphia—Ormandy (♭ *AmC.A 1595*)
Italian Radio—Gui (in ♯ Tem.TT 2046)
Minneapolis Sym.—Mitropoulos (in ♯ AmC.RL 3038)
Austrian Sym.—Singer (or Wolf) (in ♯ Rem. 149-48;
       ♭ Cum.ECR 51; & ♯ Ply. 12-102)

Namensfeier, Op. 115
Vienna State Op.—Scherchen ♯ **Nix.WLP 5335**
(*Zur Weihe des Hauses, Coriolan, etc.*)
      (in ♯ West.WL 5335; Sel. 320.CW.082)
Dresden State—Schreiber   in ♯ **Allo. 3117/8**
(*Symphony No. 9*)

---

[1] Cadenza by Beethoven.   [2] Paris recording, 19 Sept. 1955.
[3] Ed. and Cadenzas by Leibowitz.   [4] Cadenzas by Kreisler.
[5] Cadenzas by Elman.   [6] Cadenzas by Milstein.

Zur Weihe des Hauses, Op. 124
Vienna State Op.—Scherchen ♯ **Nix.WLP 5302**
(*Coriolan & Pf. Concerto 2*) (♯ *West.WL 5302*)
(*Overtures in* ♯ Nix.WLP 5335; West.WL 5335;
Sel. 320.CW.082)

☆ Berlin Phil.—v. Kempen (2ss) **PV. 72470**
(*Bach: Brandenburg Concerto 3, on* ♯ *Pol. 16126*)
(*Coriolan, on* ♯ *AmD.DL 4068*)
☆ N.B.C. Sym.—Toscanini **Vic.LM 9022**
(*Schubert & Schumann*)
(*Leonore Ov. 3, & Schubert, on* ♯ *ItV.A12R 0121*)
☆ L.P.O.—v. Beinum ♯ *D.LW 5016*
(*Leonore 3*) (in ♯ Lon.LL 357)
Leipzig Op.—Rubahn (♯ Allo. 3067)
Berlin Sym. (in ♯ Roy. 1380; in ♯ Gram. 2074)
☆ L.P.O.—Weingartner (in ♯ AmC.ML 4647)
Rhineland Sym.—Federer (in ♯ *AFest.CFR 33*)
Boston Prom.—Fiedler (in ♯ Cam.CAL 250)

ROMANCES, Vln. & orch.
No. 1, G major, Op. 40
No. 2, F major, Op. 50
Y. Menuhin & Philharmonia—Furtwängler
♯ **G.ALP 1135**
(*Mendelssohn*) (♯ FALP 312: QALP 10071;
ArgA.LPC 11582)
C. Ferras & Hamburg State Phil.—Ludwig
♯ *DT.TM 68043*
(TV.VSK 9206: ♭ *T.UV 114*)
B. Gimpel & Bamberg Sym.—Hollreiser
(*Vln. Concerto*) ♯ *E. & AmVox.PL 9340*
A. Plocek & Czech Phil.—Šejna ♯ *U. 5166C*
(*Brahms*)
R. Koeckert & Bamberg Sym.—Leitner
(2ss) **PV. 72432**
(*Spohr on* ♯ *Pol. 19012*)
☆ J. Heifetz & Vic. Sym.—Steinberg ♯ *G.BLP 1022*
(*Saint-Saëns*) (♯ *QBLP 5011: VBLP 808: FALP 270*)
(1s. each, ♭ *G.7ER 5035: 7ERF 102: 7ERQ 103*;
♭ *DV. 26001*)
(No. 1 also on ED 1218; No. 2 also on DB 21600:
ED 1255)
☆ Z. Francescatti & Col. Sym.—Morel ♭ *EPhi.ABE 10003*
(♭ *Phi.A 409009E*)
☆ M. Rostal & Winterthur Sym.—Goehr (V♯ *MMS. 917*)
J. Fuchs & Little Orch.—Scherman (♯ *D.UW 333006*)
T. Olof (No. 1), H. Krebbers (No. 2) & Residentie
—v. Otterloo (♯ *Phi.S 06000R*; in ♯ Epic.LC 3036)

No. 1 only
D. Oistrakh & U.S.S.R. State—Kondrashin
(*Coriolan Overture*) **USSRM.D 001224**

No. 2 only
D. Oistrakh & Czech Phil.—Ančerl ♯ Sup.LPV 244
(*Vln. Sonata No. 1; & Mozart*)
J. Krachmalnick & Philadelphia—Ormandy
(*Handel, Weber, Chabrier, Griffes, etc.*) ♯ AmC.ML 4629
S. Gawriloff & Berlin Radio—Guhl *Eta. 120007*

Romance cantabile, E minor pf. & orch.[1]
ed. W. Hess MS., British Museum c. 1788-90
H. Schultes & Frankenland Sym.—Kloss
♯ **CA.LPA 1013**
(*Minuets*) (♯ Lyr.LL 45)

Rondo, B flat major pf. & orch. G. 151 (WoO 6)
F. Wührer & Vienna Pro Musica—Swarowsky
(*Concerto No. 1*) ♯ **E. & AmVox.PL 8400**

SYMPHONIES
Collections: Nos. 1-9 complete
N.B.C. Sym.—Toscanini ♯ **G.FALP 231/7**
(Nos. 1, 3 & 9 are ☆) (♯ Vic.set LM 6900, limited edn.)
(14ss) [see below for individual issues]
London Phil. Sym. & Vienna State Op. Orchs.
—Scherchen ♯ **West. set WN 7701**
(14ss) [Nos. 1, 6, 7, 9, are ☆; see below for individual
issues]

No. 1, C major, Op. 21
Philharmonia—Karajan ♯ **C.CX 1136**
(*Egmont & Leonore 3*) (♯ QCX 10099: FVX 250;
[& with analysis, ♯ MApp. n.d.] Angel. 35097)
Bamberg Sym.—Perlea ♯ **E. & AmVox.PL 9120**
(*No. 7*)

Vienna Sym.—Pritchard ♯ **Phi.A 00179L**
(*No. 8*) (♯ Epic.LC 3095) (2ss, ♯ *Phi.S 06037R*)
Berlin Phil.—Fricsay ♯ **HP.DGM 18100**
(*No. 8*) (♯ AmD.DL 9626)
Vienna Phil.—Furtwängler ♯ **Vic. set LHMV 700**
(*Fidelio, s. 1*)
Belgian Radio—André ♯ *DT.LGM 65020*
(*Schubert on* ♯ DT.LGX 66042) (♯ *T.LS 6052*)
Austrian Sym.—"Srbny-Holstein"[2]
♯ **Rem. 199-156**
(*Leonore 3*) (♯ Cum.CR 298; & with *Sym. 8*, ♯ CR 350)
Moscow Radio—Golovanov ♯ *USSR.D 1085/6*
Berlin Phil.—Rother ♯ **Ura.RS 7-17**
(*No. 4*) (2ss, ♭ *UREP 65*)
(*No. 9, in* ♯ Ura. set URSP 101; ♯ MTW. set 11)
Leipzig Radio—Abendroth *Eta. 321007/9*
(6ss) (o.n. 26-47/9)
☆ Vienna State Op.—Scherchen ♯ **Nix.WLP 6208**
(*No. 9*) (♯ BrzV.SPL 5518; Sel.LAG 1026)
(*Grosse Fuge on* ♯ West.WN 18034)
☆ Vienna Phil.—Schuricht ♯ **D.LXT 2824**
(*No. 8*) (♯ Lon.LL 825)
☆ N.B.C. Sym.—Toscanini ♯ **G.ALP 1040**
(*No. 9*) (♯ ItV.B12R 0001; DV.LB 16312)
(♯ G.VALP 513: QALP 191)
☆ N.Y.P.S.O.—Walter (*No. 5*) ♯ AmC.ML 4790
Frankfurt Op.—Goehr ♯ **MMS. Set 2034F**
(*No. 9 & Jena*) (also with *Nos. 8 & 9*, MMS. set 2034)
Czech Phil.—Ančerl (♯ *Sup.LPM 147*; ♯ *U. 5155C*)
Dresden State Op.—Schreiber (♯ Allo. 3111)
☆ Philadelphia—Ormandy (♯ Cam.CAL 241)
Cleveland Sym.—Rodzinski (♯ AmC.RL 3047)
Amsterdam—Mengelberg (♯ T.LSK 7013)
B.B.C. Sym.—Toscanini (in ♯ G.FJLP 5058)

No. 2, D major, Op. 36
Philharmonia—Karajan ♯ **C.CX 1227**
(*Coriolan Ov.*) (♯ QCX 10185; Angel. 35196)
N.B.C. Sym.—Toscanini ♯ **G.ALP 1145**
(*No. 4*) (♯ Vic.LM 1723: ♭ *set WDM 1723*;
♯ ItV.A12R 0045; DV.L 16470)
(*No. 8 on* ♯ G.FALP 228)
Berlin Phil.—Lehmann ♯ *Pol. 16059*
(5ss—*Coriolan Overture, on* ♮ PV. 72342/4)
Amsterdam—v. Beinum ♯ *EPhi.ABR 4036*
(♯ *Phi.A 00720R*)
London Phil. Sym.—Scherchen ♯**Nix.WLP5362**
(*No. 8*) (♯ West.WL 5362)
☆ A.B.C. Sydney Sym.—Goossens ♯ **G.ALP 1134**
(OALP 1004)
Cologne Gürzenich Orch.—Wand ♯ **CFD. 40**
Dresden State Op.—Schreiber (♯ Allo. 3112)
Anon. Orch. (♯ Gram. 20129)
☆ San Francisco Sym.—Monteux (♯ G.QALP 114)
Boston Sym.—Koussevitzky (♯ Cam.CAL 157)

No. 3, E flat major, Op. 55 ("Eroica")
Royal Phil.—Beecham ♯ **C.CX 1086**
(♯ QCX 10064; AmC.ML 4698)
Philharmonia—Karajan ♯ **C.CX 1046**
(♯ FCX 204: QCX 10013; Angel. 35000)
Vienna Phil.—Furtwängler (n.v.) ♯ **G.ALP 1060**
(♯ QALP 10030: VALP 530: FALP 287; ♯ Vic.LHMV 1044)
Vienna State Op.—Scherchen ♯ **Nix.WLP 5216**
(♯ Sel.LAG 1061; West.WL 5216)
Berlin Phil.—v. Kempen ♯ **EPhi.ABL 3013**
(♯ Phi.A 00177L; Epic.LC 3016)
N.Y. Stadium Concerts—Bernstein
♯ **B.AXTL 1065**
(♯ AmD.DL 9697; SpC.CCL 35009)
Berlin Phil.—E. Jochum ♯ **Pol. 18179**
Vienna Pro Musica—Horenstein
♯ **E. & AmVox.PL 8070**
☆ N.Y.P.S.O.—Walter ♯ **C.CX 1117**
(♯ FCX 232: QCX 10061; ♭ AmC. set A 1072)
Rochester Phil.—Leinsdorf ♯ AmC.RL 3069

---

[1] Not in Kinsky & Halm *Verzeichnis*.
[2] According to *Luister*, quoting Remington management, the conductor is A. Rodzinski, who had to be pseudonymous for contractual reasons.

No. 3, E flat major, Op. 55 (*continued*)

Vienna Phil.—Kleiber	♯ **D.LXT 5064**[1]
Chicago Sym.—Reiner	♯ **Vic.LM 1899**
Vienna Phil.—Furtwängler[2]	♯ **Ura. 7095**
Utrecht Sym.—Neumark	♯ **MMS. 2031**
U.S.S.R. State—Ivanov	♯ **USSR.D 0532/3**

(12ss, USSR. 020178/89)

Saxon State—Konwitschny (♯ Eta. 820001)
Dresden State Op.—Schreiber (♯ Allo. 3113)
Anon. Orch. (♯ Gram. 2002)
☆ L.P.O.—Koussevitzky (♯ Cam.CAL 102)
  Homburg Sym.—Schubert (♯ Mtr.CLP 511)
  Austrian Sym.—Busch
             (♯ Cum.CR 204; AFest.CFR 12-91)
  N.B.C. Sym.—Toscanini (♯ ItV.A12R 0124)
  Amsterdam—Mengelberg (♯ T.LSK 7006)
  Berlin Sym.—Friedl (♯ MusH.LP 9015)

No. 4, B flat major, Op. 60

N.B.C. Sym.—Toscanini[3]	♯ **G.ALP 1145**

(*No. 2*) (♯ Vic.LM 1723; ♭ set WDM 1723; ♯ ItV.A12R 0045; DV.L 16470)

Amsterdam—Krips	♯ **D.LXT 2874**

(♯ Lon.LL 915)

London Phil. Sym.—Scherchen	♯ **Nix.WLP 20003**

(*No. 5*)   (♯ West.WL 5406; Véga.C30.A17)

Vienna Philharmonia—Perlea	♯ **AmVox.PL8740**

(*No. 8*)   (♯ Orb.BL 707)

Berlin Phil.—E. Jochum	♯ **Pol. 18206**
Vienna Phil.—Furtwängler (n.v.)	♯ **G.ALP 1059**

(♯ FALP 116: VALP 518: QALP 10025; Vic. LHMV 1059)

Belgian Radio—André	♯ **DT.LGX 66010**

(♯ T.LE 6502)

Philharmonia—Karajan	♯ **C.CX 1278**

(1½ss—*Ah, Perfido*)   (♯ QCX 10149; Angel. 35203)

Leningrad Phil.—Mravinsky	♯ **USSR.D 01466/7**
Leipzig Radio—Abendroth	♯ **Ura.RS 7-17**

(*No. 1*)

Dresden State Op.—Schreiber (♯ Allo. 3112)
Anon. Orch. (♯ Gram. 20129)
☆ Hallé—Harty (♯ AmC.RL 3034)
  Austrian Sym.—Singer (♯ Cum.CR 234)
  Austrian Sym.[4] (♯ MHF.3)

No. 5, C minor, Op. 67

Philharmonia—Karajan	♯ **C.CX 1266**

(1½ss—*Fidelio, No. 10*)   (♯ Angel. 35231)

N.B.C. Sym.—Toscanini[5]	♯ **G.ALP 1108**

(*No. 8*) (♯ Vic.LM 1757: ♭ set WDM1757; ♯ ItV.A12R 0003)

Minneapolis Sym.—Dorati	♯ **Mer.MG 50017**

(♯ FMer.MLP 7501)

Amsterdam—Kleiber	♯ **D.LXT 2851**

(♯ Lon.LL 912)

Berlin Phil.—Böhm	♯ **HP.DGM 18097**

(also 5ss—PV. 72346/8S)

Vienna Phil.—Furtwängler	♯ **G.ALP 1195**

(♯ FALP 260: QALP 10086)
(*Fidelio Overture* on ♯ Vic.LHMV 9)

Pittsburgh Sym.—Steinberg	♯ **DCap.CTL 7083**

(*No. 8*)   (♯ Cap.P 8292)

London Phil. Sym.—Scherchen	♯ **Nix.WLP 20003**

(*No. 4*)   (♯ West.WL 5406; Véga. C30.A17)

Hamburg State Phil.—Keilberth	♯ **DT.LGX 66005**

(♯ T.LSK 7021; FT. 320.C.029)

L.S.O.—del Mar	♯ **MApp. 81**

(*Spoken analysis by T. Scherman, with orch.*)

Utrecht Sym.—Hupperts[6]	♯ **MMS. 22**

(♯ Clc. 11007)

Leipzig Radio—Konwitschny	♯ **Ura.RS 7-6**

(*Leonore Ov. No. 3*)
[&, attrib. Gewandhaus orch., ♯ Eta.LPM 1009]

Leningrad Phil.—Mravinsky (2ss)	♯ **USSR.D 0416/7**

☆ N.Y.P.S.O.—Walter (2ss)	♯ **C.CX 1077**

(♯ FCX/QCX 211: VCX 533; ♭ AmC. set A 1065)
(*No. 1* on ♯ AmC.ML 4790)

☆ Berlin Phil.—E. Jochum	♯ **EPhi.NBR 6030**

(♯ Phi.A 00766R; Epic.LC 3002)

Czech Phil.—Ančerl (♯ Sup.LPV 148; U. 5153G)
Orch.—Emmer (♯ MTW. 12)
Dresden State Op.—Schreiber (♯ Allo. 3114)
Sonor Sym.—Ledermann (♯ Pde. 2019)
Anon. Orch. (♯ Gram. 2001; ♯ Roy. 18130)
Boston Orch. Soc.—Page (♯ SOT. 1067; with
            Mozart: Sym. 40, on ♯ SOT. 10657)
American Artists—Leinsdorf (♯ GA. 33-319)
☆ Vienna Phil.—Karajan (♯ C.VCX 506; AmC.RL 3068)
  Vienna Sym.—Klemperer (♯ AFest.CFR 12-122)
  Boston Sym.—Koussevitzky (♭ Vic.set ERB 15)
  L.P.O.—Koussevitzky (♯ Cam.CAL 103)
  Austrian Sym.—Wolf (♯ Cum.TCR 211; Ply. 12-65, etc.)

…1st movt. only, abridged
Boston Prom.—Fiedler
          (in ♯ Vic.LM 1752: ♭ set WDM 1752)
… 2nd movt. only
N.Y.P.S.O.—Walter & Stransky*[7] (♯ & ♭ AmC.PE 21)

— — ARR. ORGAN: C. Cronham (*Mjr. 5135*)

No. 6, F major, Op. 68   (*"Pastoral"*)

N.B.C. Sym.—Toscanini	♯ **G.ALP 1129**

(♯ Vic.LM 1755: ♭ set WDM 1755; ♯ ItV.A12R 0004; DV.L 16464)

Amsterdam—Kleiber	♯ **D.LXT 2872**

(♯ Lon.LL 916)

Royal Phil.—Beecham	♯ **C.CX 1062**

(♯ QCX 10020; AmC.ML 4828)

Philharmonia—Karajan	♯ **C.CX 1124**

(♯ QCX 10093: FCX 234; Angel. 35080)

Vienna Phil.—Furtwängler	♯ **G.ALP 1041**

(♯ QALP 10034: FALP 288: VALP 535; ArgA.LPC 11526; Vic.LHMV 1066)

Vienna Sym.—v. Otterloo	♯ **EPhi.ABL 3043**

(♯ Phi.A 00176L; Epic.LC 3011)

Detroit Sym.—Paray	♯ **Mer.MG 50045**

(♯ FMer.MLP 7529)

Berlin Phil.—E. Jochum	♯ **Pol. 18202**
Netherlands Phil.—Goehr	♯ **MMS. 2001**

(*Prometheus, Overture*)   (& ♯ MMS. 120, 2ss)

Leipzig Gewandhaus—Konwitschny	*Eta. 21-103/8*

N.B.C. Members—Stokowski	♯ **G.ALP 1268**

(*"Sounds of Nature" described by Stokowski*)
                (♯ Vic.LM 1830)
(2nd movt. only in ♯ LM 1875: ♭ set ERB 52)

Cento Soli—Lehmann	♯ **CFD. 22**
☆ Vienna State Op.—Scherchen	♯ **Nix.WLP 5108**

(♯ Sel.LPG 8676)

Leningrad Phil.—Mravinsky (♯ USSR.D 01091/2)
Czech Phil.—Šejna (♯ Sup.LPV 138; U. 5127G)
Dresden State Op.—Schreiber (♯ Allo. 3115;
                      Pac.LDAD 81)
Nat. Op. Orch. (♯ Gram. 2060)
☆ Pittsburgh Sym.—Steinberg (♯ ACap.CLCX 001;
           3rd movt. only in ♯ Cap.LAL 9024)
  Philadelphia—Walter (♭ AmC.set A 1062)
  B.B.C. Sym.—Toscanini (♯ G.FJLP 5060)
  Rome Augusteo—Sabata (∇ ArgV. 12-0543/7,
                       set DM 1257)
  Austrian Sym.—Wöss (♯ Cum.CR 232; & with
           commentary by S. Spaeth, ♯ Rem. 2)
  N.Y. City Sym.—Stokowski (♯ Cam.CAL 187)
  Austrian Sym.[4] (♯ MHF. 2 or 4)

No. 7, A major, Op. 92

N.B.C. Sym.—Toscanini	♯ **G.ALP 1119**

(♯ Vic.LM 1756: ♭ set WDM 1756; ♯ ItV.A12R 0005; DV.L 16477)

Philharmonia—v. Karajan	♯ **C.CX 1035**

(♯ QCX 10007: FCX 160: VCX 519; ♯ Angel. 35005)

Detroit Sym.—Paray	♯ **EMer.MG 50022**

(♯ FMer.MLP 7502)

(*continued on next page*)

---

[1] Announced but may not have been on sale, though reviewed.
[2] According to press reports, Furtwängler repudiated this recording, and obtained injunctions preventing its circulation bearing his name, in certain countries.
[3] From a broadcast performance, Feb. 3, 1951.
[4] The manufacturer requests us to suppress any reference to name of conductor.
[5] From a broadcast performance, March 22, 1952.
[6] So advertised but *labelled* Zürich Tonhalle—Ackermann on ♯ MMS. 22.
[7] 1s. each. The Walter side is a modern recording; the Stransky was recorded 1917.

No. 7, A major, Op. 92 (*continued*)

Belgian Radio—André   ‡ **DT.LGX 66011**
                              (‡ T.LSK 7023)
Berlin Phil.—E. Jochum   ‡ **HP.DGM 18069**
(also, 6ss, ♮ PV. 72294/6)   (‡ AmD.DL 9690)
Berlin Phil.—v. Kempen   ‡ **EPhi.ABL 3017**
                              (‡ Phi.A 00180L; Epic.LC 3026)
Vienna State Phil.—Perlea
(*No. 1*)   ‡ **E. & AmVox.PL 9120**
Rochester Phil.—Leinsdorf   ‡ **AmC.RL 6622**
Zürich Tonhalle—Ackermann   ‡ **MMS. 33**
☆ N.Y.P.S.O.—Walter   ‡ **C.CX 1120**
                              (‡ QCX 10072: FCX 233)
☆ Vienna State Op.—Scherchen ‡ **Nix.WLP 5089**
☆ Orch.—Hewitt   ‡ **DFr. 90**
(*Coriolan & Egmont Overtures*)
Czech Phil.—Georgescu (‡ Sup.LPV 249)
Dresden State Op.—Schreiber (‡ Allo. 3116)
U.S.S.R. State—Ivanov (USSR. 020525/35: ‡ D 0530/1)
Anon. Orch. (‡ Gram. 2086)
☆ Philharmonia—Galliera (‡ AmC.RL 3035)
   Austrian Sym.—Wöss (‡ Msq. 10001; Cum. CR 233)
   Boston Sym.—Münch (‡ G.QALP 106; DV.L 16307)
   Philadelphia—Stokowski (‡ Cam.CAL 212)
... 3rd movt , Presto
Hamburg Philharmonia—H-J. Walther (*MSB. 78143*)

No. 8, F major, Op. 93
N.B.C. Sym.—Toscanini   ‡ **G.ALP 1108**
(*No. 5*) (‡ Vic.LM 1757: ♮ set WDM 1757:
                              ‡ ItV.A12R 0003)
(*No. 2*, on ‡ G.FALP 228)
Royal Phil.—Beecham   ‡ **C.CX 1039**
(*Schubert: Sym. No. 8*) (‡ WCX 1039: VCX 517:
                              QCX 10040)
(*Mendelssohn: Sym. No. 4*, on ‡ AmC.ML 4641)
Vienna Phil.—Böhm   ‡ **D.LXT 2824**
(*Symphony No. 1*)   (‡ Lon.LL 825)
Los Angeles Phil.—Wallenstein ‡ **B.AXTL 1058**
(*Mendelssohn*)   (‡ D.UAT 273546; AmD.DL 9726)
Vienna Philharmonia—Perlea   ‡**AmVox.PL8740**
(*No. 4*)   (‡ Orb.BL 707; 2ss, ‡ Pan.XPV 1008)
[Excerpt in ‡ *AmVox.UHF 1*]
Pittsburgh Sym.—Steinberg   ‡ **DCap.CTL 7083**
(*No. 5*) [Excerpts in ‡ *Cap.LAL 9024*] (‡ Cap.P 8292)
London Phil. Sym.—Scherchen   ‡**Nix.WLP5362**
(*No. 2*)   (‡ West.WL 5362)
Berlin Phil.—v. Kempen   ‡ **EPhi.ABL 3031**
(*Sym. 9*, s. 3)   (‡ Phi.A 00221L)
   (*No. 1*, on ‡ Phi.A 00179L; Epic.LC 3095)
Berlin Phil.—Fricsay   ‡ **HP.DGM 18100**
(*No. 1*)   (& 4ss, ♮ PV. 72364/5)   (AmD.DL 9626)
Cento Soli—F. Lehmann   ‡ **CFD. 28**
☆ San Francisco Sym.—Monteux ‡ **Vic.LM 1799**
(*Berlioz & Bach*)
Dresden State Op.—Schreiber (‡ Allo. 3111)
U.S.S.R. State—Ivanov (‡ USSR.D 1454/5)
Anon. Orch. (‡ Gram. 2048)
☆ Vienna Phil.—Karajan (in ‡ AmC.set EL 51)
   N.Y.P.S.O.—Walter (in ‡ AmC.set SL 186;
             ‡ Phi.S 06625R, o.n. A 01602R)
   Winterthur Sym.—Goehr (‡ Clc. 11005; ANix.MLPY 10;
             ‡ MMS. 2034, d.c.)
   Hastings Sym.—Bath (‡ Pac.LDAD 30)
   Austrian Sym.—Busch (‡ Rem. 199-149;
             Cum.CR 208: & CR 350, d.c.)
   Boston Sym.—Koussevitzky (‡ Cam.CAL 157 &
             in set CFL 104)
   Amsterdam—Mengelberg (‡ T.LSK 7013)

No. 9, D minor, Op. 125 (*"Choral"*) S, A, T, B
Bayreuth Fest. Orch.—Furtwängler[1]
(4ss)   ‡ **G.ALP 1286/7**
                              (‡ FALP 381/2; QALP 10116/7)
[E. Schwarzkopf, E. Höngen, H. Hopf, O. Edelmann &
   Bayreuth Fest. Cho.]
Bavarian Radio—E. Jochum
(4ss)   ‡ **Pol. 18070 & 16070**
[C. Ebers, G. Pitzinger, W. Ludwig, F. Frantz &
   Bavarian Radio Cho.]   (also ♮ PV. 72306/10)

N.Y.P.S.O.—Walter   ‡ **AmC. set SL 186**
(3ss—*No. 8*)   (♮ set A 1067)
[F. Yeend, M. Lipton, D. Lloyd, M. Harrell &
                              Westminster Cho.]
(1st, 2nd & 3rd movts. are ☆; the last was remade)
Netherlands Phil.—Goehr   ‡ **MMS. set 2034F**
(3ss—*Syms. No. 1 & "Jena"*)
(3ss—*Syms. 1 & 8*, also ‡ MMS. set 2034)
[C. Bijster, E. Pritchard, D. Garen, L. Wolovsky]
Cologne Gürzenich—Wand   ‡ **CFD. set 58**
[T. Stich-Randall, L. Fischer, E. Koch, R. Watzke]
☆ N.B.C. Sym.—Toscanini   ‡ **G.ALP 1039/40**
(3ss—*Sym. 1*) [E. Farrell, N. Merriman, J. Peerce,
   N. Scott, R. Shaw Chorale]
(‡ QALP 190/1: VALP 513/4; DV. set LB 16312;
   ItV.B12R 0001/2)
(Finale only, also on ‡ *Vic.LRM 7046*: ♮ set ERB 7046)
☆ Vienna State Op.—Scherchen ‡ **Nix.WLP 6208-1/2**
(3ss—*Sym. 1*)   (‡ BrzV. SLP 5518; Sel.LAG 1025/6)
[M. Laszlo, H. Rössl-Majdan, P. Munteanu, R. Standen,
   Singakademie Cho.]
☆ Residentie—v. Otterloo   ‡ **EPhi.ABL 3030/1**
(3ss—*No. 8*)   (‡ Phi.A 00220/1L)
[E. Spoorenberg, M. v. Ilosvay, F. Vroons, H. Schey,
   Amsterdam Toonkunst Cho.]
Dresden State Op.—Schreiber   ‡ **Allo. 3117/8**
(3ss—*Namensfeier Overture*)
[Anon. soloists & Dresden Cho. Soc.]
☆ Soloists, Musikfreunde Cho. & Vienna Phil.
                  —Karajan (‡ AmC.set EL 51)
   Soloists, Leipzig Radio Cho. & Sym.—Abendroth
   (‡ *Sup.LPM 48/50; U. 5048/50C*; Ura. set URSP 101,
                  4ss; MTW. set 11, 4ss; & 18ss, Eta 26-1/9)

C major G. 257 (*"Jena"*) (Kinsky Anh. 1)
Paris Cons.—Saguer   ‡ **Sel.LPG 8327**
(*Fantasia, pf., cho. & orch.*)
Netherlands Phil.—Goehr   ‡ **CHS.H 1**
(*Musik zu einem Ritterballet*)
(*Syms. 1 & 9*, in ‡ MMS. set 2034F)
Leipzig Radio—Kleinert   ‡ **Ura. 7114**
(*A. & F. Mendelssohn*)   (‡ MTW. 559)
Dresden State Op.—Schreiber   ‡ **Allo. 3114**
(*No. 5*)
Berlin Sym.—Balzer   ‡ **Roy. 1397**
(*Pf. Concerto No. 2*)
☆ Janssen Sym.—Janssen (‡ Cam.CAL 241)

Wellingtons Sieg, Op. 91 (*"Battle Symphony"*)
French Radio Sym.—Leibowitz   ‡ **Oce.OCS 34**
(*Wiener Tänze & König Stefan*)
Berlin Radio—Lederer   **V‡ CdM.LDY 8053**

B. STAGE WORKS

EGMONT, Op. 84   Inc. Music to Goethe's play
                              S, Speaker, Orch. 1809-10

COMPLETE RECORDINGS
   M. Laszlo, F. Liewehr, Vienna State Op. Orch.
   —Scherchen   ‡ **West.WL 5281**
             (‡ T.LE 6548; Sel. 320.C.001)
   E. Grümmer & Berlin Radio Orch.—Gühl &
   Rother (6ss)   *Eta. 120002 & 320019/20*
   (Overture also in ‡ LPM 1000)   (o.n. Eta 25-1/3)
   [no speaker is named, so the relevant passages may be
   omitted]

Overture & Nos. 1, 3, 4, 5, 7, 8, 9
☆ L. Wissmann, P. Hartmann, Württemberg State Orch.
   —Leitner (‡ AmD.DL 7540)

Overture
N.B.C. Sym.—Toscanini   in ‡ **G.ALP 1235**
(*Brahms, Berlioz, Hérold, etc.*) (in ‡ Vic.LM 1834;
   ♮ ItV.A72R 0001; ‡ FV.A 630247; DV.L 16483)
   (*Wagner: Walkürenritt*, on ♮ *Vic.ERA 249*)
Minneapolis Sym.—Dorati in ‡ **Mer.MG 50017**
(*Sym. 5, Leonore, etc.*)   (‡ FMer.MLP 7501)
Vienna Philharmonia—Horenstein
                              ‡ **E. & AmVox.PL 8020**
(*Coriolan, Leonore 3, Prometheus*)

---

[1] Bayreuth Festival performance, Aug. 1951.   4th Movt. only also on ‡ G.WALPS 1508.

Philharmonia—Karajan ♯ **C.CX 1136**
(*Leonore 3 & Sym. 1*) (♯ QCX 10099: FCX 250;
Angel. 35097)
(*Leonore Overture 3, & spoken analysis, in* ♯ MApp., n.d.)

L.S.O.—Collingwood **C.DX 1903**

Netherlands Phil.—Goehr **V♯ MMS. 97**
(*Coriolan*)

Anon. Orch.—Busch ♯ **FFB. n.d.**
(*Schubert & Wagner*)

Hamburg Philharmonia—Walther *MSB. 78142*

☆ L.P.O.—v. Beinum ♯ *D.LW 5015*
(*Coriolan*) (in ♯ *Lon.LL 357*)

Berlin Phil.—Celibidache (in ♯ *Per.SPL 716*)[1]
Moscow Radio—Golovanov (USSR. 020885/6 &
USSRM.D 437)
☆ Berlin Phil.—Keilberth (♯ *DT.TM 68002*: TV.VSK 9025)
Vienna State Op.—Swarowsky (in ♯ *Sup.LPM 48;*
U. 5048C; CdM.LDM 8042)
Danish Radio—Malko (in ♯ *BB.LBC 1048:*
♭ *set WBC 1048*)
Orch.—Hewitt (V♯ *DFr.EX 17002 & in* ♯ *DFr. 90*)
Residentie—Otterloo (in ♯ *Phi.S 06001R*)
Vienna Phil.—Weingartner (in ♯ *AmC.ML 4647*)
Boston Sym.—Koussevitzky (in ♯ *Vic.LRM 7021:*
♭ *set ERB 7021*)
Austrian Sym.—Wolf (in ♯ *Rem. 149-48*; Ply. 12-102;
♭ *Cum.ECR 51*)
Saxon State—Böhm (ArgV. 12161)

No. 4, Freudvoll und leidvoll S
J. Giraudeau (T), J. Dupont (pf.)
(*Songs, Collection*) in ♯ **D.FAT 173600**
H Lilli Lehmann (in ♯ *Ete. 702**)

FIDELIO, Op. 72 Opera 3 Acts 1805; 2 Acts 1806
COMPLETE RECORDINGS

Casts		Set C	Set D
Leonore	...	M. Mödl (S)	R. Bampton (S)
Marzelline	...	S. Jurinac (S)	E. Steber (S)
Florestan	...	W. Windgassen (T)	J. Peerce (T)
Jacquino	...	R. Schock (T)	J. Laderoute (T)
Don Pizarro	...	O. Edelmann (B)	H. Janssen (B)
Rocco	...	G. Frick (Bs)	S. Belarsky (Bs)
etc.			

Set C[2] with Vienna State Op. Cho. & Phil.
—Furtwängler ♯ **G.ALP 1130/2**
(6ss) (♯ FALP 323/5: QALP 10061/3: WALP 1130/2)
(5ss—*Symphony No. 1 in* ♯ Vic. set LHMV 700)

Set D[2] with Cho. & N.B.C. Sym. Orch.
—Toscanini[3] ♯ **Vic.LM 6025**
(4ss) (♯ DV. set LB 16488: ItV.B12R 0127/8)

☆ M. Bäumer (S), H. Sauerbaum (T), etc., Leipzig Radio
Cho. & Orch.—Pflüger ♯ **Nix.OLP 7301-1/3**[4]
(♯ MTW. 529/31)
☆ H. Konetzni (S), I. Seefried (S), T. Ralf, etc.,
Vienna State Op. Cho. & Vienna Phil. Orch.—Böhm
(6ss) ♯ EVox. set PL 7793[4]

Set E. "National Op." Soloists & orch.
♯ **Gram. 20130/1**
(3ss—*Leonore Overtures 1 & 2*)

ABRIDGED RECORDING
I. Camphausen (S), H. Wilhelm (T),
G. Ramms (B), Leipzig Op. House Cho. &
Orch.—Rubahn ♯ **Allo. 3066/7**
(3ss—*Zur Weihe des Hauses*)

Overture
Vienna Phil.—Furtwängler ♭ *G.7ER 5036*
(*Tristan, Prelude*) [from set] (♭ 7ERQ 123)
(*Symphony No. 5 on* ♯ Vic.LHMV 9)

Vienna Phil.—Krauss ♯ *D.LW 5165*
(*Leonore No. 3*) (& in ♯ *Lon.LL 1319*) (♯ *Lon.LL 9186*)

Vienna State Op.—Scherchen ♯ Nix.WLP 5177
(*Leonore Overtures*) (♯ West.WL 5177; Sel. 320.CW.044)

Bamberg Sym.—Leitner **PV. 72396**
(*Cherubini: Medea Overture*)
(*Prometheus & Ruinen von Athen Overtures*
on ♯ *AmD.DL 4047:* ♭ *ED 3536*)
(*No. 11, below, on* ♭ *Pol. 30023*)

Philharmonia—Klemperer ♯ **C.CX 1270**
(*Leonore Overtures*) (♯ Angel. 35258)
☆ L.P.O.—v. Beinum ♯ *D.LW 5018*
(*below*) (♭ *DX 1764*; ♭ *Lon.REP 8020:* in ♯ *LL 357*)
☆ Vienna State Op.—Swarowsky (in ♯ *Sup.LPM 48;*
U. 5048C; CdM.LDM 8042)
L.P.O.—Weingartner (in ♯ *AmC.ML 4647*)
Vienna Phil.—Böhm (♭ *AmVox.VIP 45280, from set*)

ACT I

No. 4, Mir ist so wunderbar Qtt.: S, S, T, B
☆ Soloists, etc. (♭ *AmVox.VIP 45390, from set*)

No. 5, Hat man nicht auch Gold Bs
H P. Knüpfer (in ♯ *SBDH.PL 1**)
R. Mayr (in ♯ *Sca. 822**)

No. 8, Ha! welch ein Augenblick B
P. Schoeffler ♯ **MSL.MW 51**
(*Saxe & Wagner*)
☆ P. Schoeffler (♭ *AmVox.VIP 45390, from set*)

No. 10, Abscheulicher! Wo eilst du hin?
Komm, O Hoffnung S
E. Schwarzkopf ♯ **C.CX 1266**
(*Symphony No. 5*) (♯ Angel. 35231)
M. Mödl ♯ *DT.TM 68003*
(*Tristan—Mild und leise*) (TV.VSK 9021: ♯ *T.TW 30010:*
♭ *UV 102*; ♭ *FT. 470.TC.013*)
C. Goltz (*Goetz*) **PV. 72291**
(& in ♯ *Pol. 19043*)
☆ I. Borkh (♭*G.7ERW 5011*; ♭ *Vic.EHA 2*)

No. 11, Finale . . . O welcher Lust!
(*Prisoners' Cho.*)
Vienna Cha. Cho.—Loibner ♯ *EPhi.NBR 6027*
(*below & Weber*) (♯ *Phi.N 00629R*)
Berlin State Op.—K. Schmidt *Eta. 120008*
☆ Württemberg State Op. Cho.—Leitner (♭ *Pol. 30023;*
in ♯ *AmD.DL 4056 & DL 9797 & Pol. 19033*)
Vienna State Op.—Böhm (♭ *AmVox.VIP 45390, from set*)
Berlin Municipal Op.—Rother (♭ *G.7ERW 5011*)

ACT II

No. 13, Gott, welch' Dunkel hier! (Recit.)
In des Lebens Frühlingstagen (Aria) T
F. Vroons in ♯ *EPhi.NBR 6027*
(*above, & Weber*) (♯ *Phi.N 00629R*)
(*Leonore Ov. 3, on* ♯ *S 06020R*)
☆ P Anders (♭ *G.7RW 517:* in ♯ *WDLP 1513*)

(Die) GESCHÖPFE DES PROMETHEUS, Op. 43
Ballet 1801
Unspecified excpts. ▽ Berlin Sym.—Ludwig (in ♯ *Roy. 1383*)
Overture
Vienna State Phil.—Horenstein
♯ **E. & AmVox.PL 8020**
(*Egmont, Coriolan, Leonore 3*) (♭ *AmVox.VIP 45280*)
Vienna State Op.—Scherchen ♯ **Nix.WLP 5335**
(*König Stefan, Ruinen von Athen, etc.*)
(♯ West.WL 5335: Sel. 320.CW.082)
Philharmonia—Malko ♯ *G.DLP 1061*
(*Coriolan & Leonore 3*) (♯ *QDLP 6022: FFLP 1047;*
& in ♯ *BB.LBC 1087, d.c.*)
☆ L.P.O.—v. Beinum ♯ *D.LW 5018*
(*Fidelio Overture*) (♭ *DX 1764:* ♭ *Lon.REP 8020*)
Linz Sym. (in ♯ *Ply. 12-30*)
☆ N.B.C.—Toscanini (♭ *G.7RQ 222*; ♭ *Vic.ERA 91;*
♭ *DV. 26033*)
Vienna Phil.—Weingartner (in ♯ *AmC.ML 4647*)
Netherlands Phil.—Goehr (♭ *MMS. 2001*)
Munich Phil.—Rieger (♭ *Pol. 32039*)

KÖNIG STEFAN, Op. 117
Inc. Music to Kotzebue's play
Overture
Vienna State Op.—Scherchen ♯ **Nix.WLP 5335**
(*Ruinen von Athen, Namensfeier, etc.*)
(♯ West.WL 5335: Sel. 320.CW.082)
French Radio Sym.—Leibowitz ♯ **Oce.OCS 34**
(*Wellingtons Sieg, & Wiener Tänze*)

[1] From sound-track of film *Symphony*; the label lists *Coriolan*, but this is played, and the conductor is identified by the narrator; other items included, unless entered under individual titles, are excerpts only or by unidentified artists.
[2] Includes *Leonore No. 3 Overture*.
[3] From broadcast performance, December 1944. No. 10 is ☆. [4] Announced but never issued.

LEONORE OVERTURES (orig. for *Fidelio*)
Nos. 1-3, Opp. 138 & 72a
Vienna State Op.—Scherchen ♯ Nix.WLP 5177
(*Fidelio, Overture*)   (♯ West.WL 5177; Sel. 320.CW.044)
Philharmonia—Klemperer   ♯ C.CX 1270
(*Fidelio, Overture*)   (♯ Angel. 35258)
Vienna Phil.—Krauss   ♯ Lon.LL 1319
(*Fidelio Overture*) [See below & above for other issues]

No. 1, Op. 138
Vienna Phil.—Krauss   ♯ D.LW 5164
(*No. 2*)   (♯ Lon. LD 9185)
Nat. Op. Orch. (in ♯ Gram. 2074 & in ♯ Gram. 20130)
☆ B.B.C. Sym.—Toscanini (♭ G.7RQ/RF 275)

No. 2, Op. 72a
Residentie—Otterloo   ♯ Phi.S 06045R
(*Schumann: Manfred, Overture*)
Vienna Phil.—Krauss   ♯ D.LW 5164
(*No. 1*)   (♯ Lon.LD 9185)
Nat. Op. Orch. (in ♯ Gram. 2074 & in ♯ Gram. 20130)
Anon. Orch. (in ♯ ACC.MP 28)
☆ L.S.O.—Weingartner (in ♯ AmC.ML 4647)

No. 3, Op. 72a
Vienna State Phil.—Horenstein
                                ♯ E. & AmVox.PL 8020
(*Egmont, Coriolan, Prometheus*)
Minneapolis Sym.—Dorati in ♯ Mer.MG 50017
(*Sym. 5, Egmont, Coriolan*)   (♯ FMer.MLP 7501)
Philharmonia—Karajan   ♯ C.CX 1136
(*Egmont & Sym. 1*) (♯ FCX 250: QCX 10099; Angel.35097)
(*Egmont Overture* & spoken analysis, on ♯ MApp. n.d.)
Vienna Phil.—Krauss   ♯ D.LW 5165
(*Fidelio Overture*)   (♯ Lon.LD 9186)
Philharmonia—Malko   ♯ G.DLP 1061
(*Coriolan & Prometheus*) (♯ QDLP 6022: FFLP 1047;
                             & in BB.LBC 1087, d.c.)
Berlin Phil.—Lehmann   PV. 72455
(*Coriolan & Fantasia, Op. 80*, on ♯ HP.DGM 18234)
                                (♭ Pol. 30066)
Bamberg Sym.—Keilberth   ♯ DT.TM 68025
(*Smetana*) (♯ T.TW 30005 &, 2ss, TV.VSK 9013;
                             & ♯ FT. 260.TC.033)
N.W. German Phil.—Schüchter ♯ Imp.ILP 104
(*Brahms*)
Austrian Sym.—" Srbrny-Holstein"[1]
                                ♯ Rem. 199-156
(*Sym. 1*)   (♯ Cum.CR 298)
Residentie—Moralt   ♯ Phi.S 06020R
(*Fidelio, No. 13*)
☆ L.P.O.—v. Beinum   ♯ D.LW 5016
(*Zur Weihe des Hauses, Overture*)   (in ♯ Lon.LL 357)
☆ N.B.C. Sym.—Toscanini ♯ G.FALP/QALP 229
(*Mendelssohn*) (♭ 7ERF 122: 7ERQ 111;
                                ♭ ItV.A72R 0035)
(*Wagner*, in ♯ Vic.LRM 7023: ♭ set ERB 7023)
(*Weihe des Hauses; & Schubert*, on ♯ ItV.A12R 0121)
                          (also in ♯ Vic. set LM 6025)
Berlin Radio—Konwitschny (♭Ura.UREP 40:
                                & ♯ Ura.RS 7-6)
Leipzig Gewandhaus—Konwitschny (Eta. 120005/6;
                                & in ♯ LPM 1000)
USSR. Sym.—Ivanov (USSR. 021764/7: ♯ D 645)
☆ Danish Radio—Malko (in ♯ BB.LBC 1048:
                                ♭ set WBC 1048)
Minneapolis Sym.—Mitropoulos (in ♯ AmC.RL 3038)
Vienna Phil.—Böhm (♭ AmVox.VIP 45400)

Musik zu einem Ritterballett G. 149 (WoO 1) 1790
Netherlands Phil.—Goehr   ♯ CHS.H 1
(*Jena Symphony*)
Berlin Radio—Koch   ♯ Ura. 7111
(*Lully & Mozart*)

(Die) RUINEN VON ATHEN, Op. 113
Inc. music to Kotzebue's play
Overture
San Francisco—Monteux   ♭ ItV.B72R 0011
(*Brahms*)   (▽ ♭ Vic. 49-3691 in set WDM 1637)
Vienna State Op.—Scherchen
                          in ♯ Nix.WLP 5335
(in ♯ West.WL 5335; Sel. 320.CW.082)

F.O.K. Sym.—Smetáček   U.H 24431
(*below*)
☆ Munich Phil.—Rieger (♭ AmD.ED 3536; ♭ Pol. 32039)

Nos. 3, Chor der Derwische, & 4
☆ Netherlands Phil. Cho. & orch.—Goehr (in ♯ MMS. 54)

No. 4, Marcia alla turca
Israel Radio—Goehr   Arzi. 769
(*J. Strauss: Pizzicato Polka*)   (in ♯ Bne. 501)
Vienna Radio—Schönherr in ♯ Vien.LPR 1025
F.O.K. Sym.—Smetáček   U.H 24431
(*above*)
— ARR. PF. Liszt: Fantasia, q.v., Sec. A.II.1
— ARR. VLN. & PF. L. Kogan & pf. (*USSR. 15902*)

No. 8, Finale . . . Heil unserm König
— ARR. BAND: Band—Mortimer (*Pax.PR 601*)

═══════════════

C. VOCAL

Ah, perfido! Op. 65 Scena, S. & orch.
E. Schwarzkopf & Philharmonia—Karajan
                                ♯ C.CX 1278
(*Symphony No. 4*)   (♯ QCX 10149; Angel. 35203)
J. Hammond & Philharmonia—Susskind
                                ♯ G.BLP 1073
(*Berlioz & St. Saëns*)
G. Brouwenstijn & Residentie Orch.—
    v. Otterloo   Phi.N 12055G
(*Freischütz—Wie nahte mir . . .* on ♯ S 06019R)
A. Varnay & Bavarian Radio—Weigert
                                PV. 72491
(*Mozart* on ♯ Pol. 19019: 18219)   (♭ Pol. 30091)
E. Bandrowska-Turska (*Russ*) ♯ USSR.D 2145
(*Puccini & Gounod*)

**CANTATA on the death of the Emperor Josef II:
Todt! Todt! Stöhnt es durch . . .** S, A, T, Bs & Cho.
G. 196a (WoO 87) 1790
E. Laux, E. Munzing, A. Kühnert,
    W. Schwerdtfeger, Berlin Radio Cho. & orch.
    —Koch   ♯ CdM.LDX 8059
☆ I. Steingruber (S), A. Poell (Bs), Vienna Sym.—Krauss
                                (♯ MF.DG 010)

CHRISTUS AM ÖLBERGE Op. 85 Oratorio
S, T, Bs, Cho. & orch. 1803
COMPLETE RECORDING
☆ Soloists, Vienna Academy Cho. & State
    Op. Orch.—Swoboda (♯ Clc. 6159; ♯ MMS. 2024)
. . . Halleluja! only Cho.
☆ Mormon Tabernacle Cho. (*Eng*, with org.)
                (C.LHX 11: SVX 42; in ♯ AmC.ML 4789)

Elegischer Gesang, Op. 118 4 vv & str. qtt. 1814
(*Sanft wie du lebtest . . .*)
☆ Randolph Singers & Guilet Qtt. (♯ Clc. 6271)

Fantasia, C major, Op. 80 pf., cho. & orch.
A. Schoen & Berlin Radio Cho. & orch.
    —Ludwig   ♯ Sel.LPG 8327
(*"Jena" Symphony*)
A. Foldes, R.I.A.S. Cha. Cho., Berlin Motet
    Cho. & Berlin Phil.—Lehmann
                                ♯ HP.DGM 18234
(*Coriolan & Leonore 3*)
S. Richter, Moscow Radio Cho. (? *Russ*) &
    Sym.—Sanderling   ♯ USSR.D 0931
(*Tannhäuser Overture*)

MASSES
C major, Op. 86 S, A, T, B, Cho., orch. 1807
☆ G. Rathauscher, E. Hofstätter, A. Planyavsky,
    W. Berry, Academy Cho. & Vienna Sym.—Moralt
                                (♯ EVox. PL 6300)

─────────────────────────────

[1] According to *Luister*, quoting Remington management, the conductor is A. Rodzinski.

D major, Op. 123 ("Missa Solemnis")
S, A, T, B, Cho., Orch.
L. Marshall, N. Merriman, E. Conley, J. Hines,
R. Shaw Chorale & N.B.C. Sym.
—Toscanini   ♯ **G.ALP 1182/3**
(4ss) (♯ Vic. set LM 6013: ♭ set ERG 6013;
     ♯ FV.A 630207/8; ItV.B12R 0056/7)

M. Stader, M. Radev, A. Dermota, J. Greindl,
St. Hedwig's Cath. Cho. & Berlin Phil.
—Böhm   ♯ **Pol. 18224/5**
(4ss)   (auto, 18232/3; ♯ AmD. set DX 135)
Anon. Artists (♯ Gram. 20162/3)

☆ Soloists, Academy Cho. & Vienna Sym.—Klemperer
(♯ AFest. set CFR 12-86)

SONGS

COLLECTIONS
"BEETHOVEN SONGS":
VOL. I.
   Adelaide, Op. 46 (Matthisson) α
   Andenken G. 240 (WoO 136) (Matthisson)
   An die Hoffnung, Op. 94 (Tiedge)
   Es war einmal..., Op. 75, No. 3 (Aus Goethes Faust)
   Ich liebe dich G. 235 (WoO 123) (Herrosee) αβ
   In questa tomba oscura G. 239 (WoO 133) (Carpani) αβ
   (Der) Kuss, Op. 128 (Weisse)
   Mailied, Op. 52, No. 4 (Goethe)
   Marmotte, Op. 52, No. 6 (Goethe)
   Mit einem gemalten Bande, Op. 83, No. 3 (Goethe)
   Neue Liebe, neues Leben, Op. 75, No. 2 (Goethe)
   Sehnsucht, Op. 83, No. 2 (Goethe) (Was zieht mir...)
   Wonne der Wehmut, Op. 83, No. 1 (Goethe)

D. Fischer-Dieskau (B), H. Klust (pf.)
    ♯ **G.WALP 1509**
[Items marked α also on ♭ G.7ERW 5014; marked β also
on G.DA 5527]

VOL. II.
   (6) Lieder von Gellert, Op. 48
   Abendlied unterm gestirnten Himmel G. 253 (WoO 150)
            (Goeble)
   (L') Amante impaziente, Op. 82, Nos. 3 & 4 (Metastasio)
         (Stille Frage; Liebesungeduld; sung in German)
   (Die) Liebe, Op. 52, No. 6 (Lessing)
   Lied aus der Ferne G. 242 (Wo 137) (Reissig)
   (Das) Liedchen von der Ruhe, Op. 52, No. 3 (Veltzen)
   Resignation G. 252 (WoO 149) (v. Haugwitz)
   Sehnsucht G. 246 (WoO 146) (Reissig) (Die stille Nacht...)
   (Der) Wachtelschlag G. 237 (WoO 129)
            (Metastasio-Sauter)
   (Der) Zufriedene, Op. 75, No. 6 (Reissig)

D. Fischer-Dieskau (B), H. Klust (pf.)
    ♯ **G.WALP 1510**

   (L') Amante impaziente, Op. 82[1] (Metastasio)
   An die Geliebte, G. 247 (WoO 140) (Stoll)
   Hoffnung, Op. 82, No. 1 (Metastasio)
   In questa tomba oscura G. 239 (WoO 133) (Carpani)
   Mignon: Kennst du das Land, Op. 75, No. 1 (Goethe)
   Mailied, Op. 52, No. 4 (Goethe)
   Marmotte, Op. 52, No. 7 (Goethe)
   Neue Liebe, neues Leben, Op. 75, No. 2 (Herz, mein Herz;
            Goethe)
   Sehnsucht: Nur wer die Sehnsucht kennt[2] G. 241 (WoO 134)
            (Goethe)
   Wonne der Wehmut, Op. 83, No. 1 (Goethe)

J. Giraudeau (T), J. Dupont (pf.)
    ♯ **D.FAT 173600**
(Egmont—No. 4) [with poems spoken by M. de Rieux (Fr)]

   Andenken G. 240 (WoO 136) (Matthisson)
   Ich liebe dich G. 235 (WoO 123) (Herrosee)
   Mignon: Kennst du das Land, Op. 75, No. 1 (Goethe)
   (Der) Kuss, Op. 128 (Weisse)
   Mailied, Op. 52, No. 4 (Goethe)
   Sehnsucht: Nur wer die Sehnsucht kennt, No. 4 G. 241-4
            (WoO 134-4) (Goethe)
   Wonne der Wehmut, Op. 83, No. 1 (Goethe)

H. Glaz (M-S), L. Müller (pf.)   ♯ **MGM.E 3012**

   Ich liebe dich G. 235 (WoO 123) (Herrosee)
   (Der) Kuss, Op. 128 (Weisse)
   Mailied, Op. 52, No. 4 (Goethe)
   Neue Liebe, neues Leben, Op. 75, No. 2 (Goethe)
   (Der) Zufriedene, Op. 75, No. 6 (Reissig)

M. Lichtegg (T), H. W. Häusslein (pf.)
(Schumann)   ♯ **Lon.LD 9183**

Mignon: Kennst du das Land, Op. 75, No. 1 (Goethe)
Wonne der Wehmut, Op. 83, No. 1 (Goethe)
Neue Liebe, Op. 75, No. 2 (Herz, mein Herz...)
            (Goethe) T
Sehnsucht: Nur wer die Sehnsucht kennt[2] G. 241
            (WoO 134) (Goethe)
Andenken G. 240 (WoO 136) (Matthisson)
Zärtliche Liebe: Ich liebe dich G. 235 (WoO 123)
            (Herrosee)

S. Schöner (S), G. Lutze (T, where marked),
F. Schröder (pf.)   ♯ **Eta.LPM 1001**
(An die ferne Geliebte) [also on Eta. 120004, 320160, etc.]

An die ferne Geliebte, Op. 98 (Jeitteles)
Adelaide, Op. 46 (Matthisson)
Ich liebe dich G. 235 (WoO 123) (Herrosee)
In questa tomba oscura G. 239 (WoO 133) (Carpani)
(Der) Kuss, Op. 128 (Weisse)
Lied aus der Ferne G. 242 (WoO 137) (Reissig)
Mailied, Op. 52, No.4 (Goethe)
(Der) Wachtelschlag G. 237 (WoO 129)
            (Metastasio-Sauter)
Wonne der Wehmut, Op. 83, No. 1 (Goethe)

☆ A. Poell (B), V. Graef (pf.)   ♯ **Nix.WLP 5124**
         (♯ Sel. 270.CW.053)

(6) Gellert-Lieder, Op. 48
Adelaide, Op. 46 (Matthisson)
Mailied, Op. 52, No. 4 (Goethe)
Herz, mein Herz, Op. 75, No. 2 (Goethe)
Wonne der Wehmut, Op. 83, No. 1 (Goethe)

☆ R. Herbert (B), F. Waldman (pf.) (♯ Allo. 4022)

Adelaide, Op. 46 (Matthisson)
Andenken G. 240 (WoO 136) (Matthisson)
Ich liebe dich G. 235 (WoO 123) (Herrosee)
Wonne der Wehmut, Op. 83, No. 1 (Goethe)

A. Koskinen (T), E. Møller (pf.)
    ♭ **Mtr.MCEP 3008**

(Die) Liebe, Op. 52, No. 6 (Lessing)
(Der) Zufriedene, Op. 75, No. 6 (Reissig)
(25) Scotch Songs, Op. 108
... No. 20, Faithful Johnnie (Anon.)

M. Orlowa & E. Busch[3] & pf.   **Eta. 20-13**
[Inst. Trio in Op. 108]   (also listed as 20-5)

Adelaide, Op. 46 (Matthisson)
G. Lutze (T), G. Ramin (pf.)   **Eta. 20-1**
☆ H. Schlusnus (B) (♭ Pol. 30152: ▽ Pol. 67361)

An die ferne Geliebte, Op. 98 (Jeitteles)
A. Schiøtz (T), M. Horszowski (pf.)
(Bach: Cantata No. 189)   ♯ **AmC.ML 4641**
E. Nikolaidi (A), J. Behr (pf.)   ♯ **AmC.ML 4628**
(below, & Schubert)
☆ D. Fischer-Dieskau (B), G. Moore (pf.) ♯ **G.ALP 1066**
(Schubert: Schwanengesang Nos. 8-13)   (FALP 307)
(Schubert & Schumann, in ♯ Vic.LHMV 1046:
         ♭ WHMV 1046; also ♭ Vic.EHA 5)
(also G.DB 21347/8, in Germany)
H. Friedrich (B), F. Schröder (pf.) Eta. 320157/8
(3ss—Neue Liebe, neues Leben)(o.n. 25-9/10; & ♯ LPM 1001)
☆ H. Schlusnus (B), S. Peschko (pf.)   ♯ **AmD.DL 9668**
(Brahms)

Es war einmal... Op. 75, No. 3 (Flohlied; Goethe)
Marmotte, Op. 52, No. 7 (Goethe)
E. Busch (Bs) & Ens.   **Eta. 20-6**
[Marmotte also on 20-008 with Loewe]

(Der) Freie Mann G. 233 (WoO 117) (Pfeffel)
(25) Scotch Songs, Op. 108
... No. 20, Faithful Johnnie (Anon.) (Ger)
W. Eckert & Male Cho.   **Eta. 20-5**

Ich liebe dich G. 235 (WoO 123) (Herrosee)
M. Powers (A), F. la Forge (pf.) in ♯ **Atl. 1207**
(Bach, Brahms, etc.)

In questa tomba oscura G. 239 (WoO 133)
    (Carpani)
R. Ponselle (S), I. Chicagov (pf.)
         in ♯ **Vic.LM 1889**
(Lully, Brahms, Chausson, etc.)   (♯ DV. 16493)
G. Pechner (B, Ger)   in ♯ **Roy. 1557**
H. Pelayo (B)   in ♯ **SMC. 1003**
☆ J. C. Thomas (in ♯ Cam.CAL 208)
⌑ E. Calvé (S) (IRCC. 3141*)

---

[1] It has not been possible to ascertain whether No. 3, Arietta buffa, or No. 4, Arietta assai seriosa; or whether both are sung.
[2] Unspec. setting.   [3] It is not clear which singer sings which song.

(Der) Kuss, Op. 128 (Weisse)
☆ N. Eddy (B) (in ♯ *Phi.S 06613R*)

(6) Lieder von Gellert, Op. 48

No. 1	Bitten	No. 2	Die Liebe des Nächsten
No. 3	Vom Tode	No. 4	Die Ehre Gottes
No. 5	Gottes Macht	No. 6	Busslied

E. Höngen (M-S) & M. Raucheisen (pf.)
(2ss)　　　　　　　　　　　　**PV. 72399**

E. Nikolaidi (A), J. Behr (pf.) ♯ **AmC.ML 4628**
(*above; & Schubert*)

I. Matthews (M-S), L. Farr (pf.) ♯ **Per.SPL 717**
(*Schubert*)

E. Brusasca (S, *Ital*), A. Surbone (org.)
(4ss)　　　　　　　　　**Cet.AB 30040 & *AT 0372***

... **No. 4, Die Ehre Gottes**
K. Borg (Bs), M. Wöldike (org.)　　　*Pol. 62921*
(*Handel: Dank sei dir, Herr*)　　　(♭ *Pol. 32104*)

B. Troxell (S) & org.　　　in ♯ **Ply. 12-123**

H. Hasslo (B, *Swed*) (♭ *G. 7EPS 1*)

☫ J. Schwarz (B) (in ♯ *Ete. 498**)

— ARR. CHO.
Young Vienna—Lehner (in ♯ *AudC. 1093*)
Hague Cha. Cho.—Backers (*C.DHX 74*)
Berlin Liedertafel Cho.—Müller-Lampertz (*T.VE 9044:*
　　　　　　　　　　　　　　　♭ *UX 4590*)
Neeber-Schüler (*T.A 11387:* in ♯ *LA 6086*)
Karlskoga Cho. (*Swed*) (*D.F 44296 & F 44258*)
etc.

Sehnsucht, Op. 83, No. 2
(*Was zieht mir das Herz*—Goethe)
R. Hayes (T), R. Boardman (pf.)
　　　　　　　　　　　in ♯ **Van.VRS 449**
(*Berlioz, Schubert, etc.; & Trad.*)

Wonne der Wehmut, Op. 83, No. 1 (Goethe)
E. Schwarzkopf (S), G. Moore (pf.)
　　　　　　　　　　　in ♯ **C.CX 1044**
(*Bach, Brahms, etc.*)　　(in ♯ *FCX 182;* ♯ *Angel. 35023*)
R. Hayes (T), R. Boardman (pf.) in ♯ **A440.12-3**

FOLK SONG ARRANGEMENT
Come fill, fill, Op. 108, No. 13 (Smyth)
M. Reizen (Bs), N. Walter (pf.)　　in ♯ **Csm.CLPS 10420**

D. MISCELLANEOUS

King Lear Inc. music for Shakespeare
— ARR. from Beethoven's works & included in a performance
of the play, in *Russian* (♯ *USSR.D 02123/32*, 10ss)

Beethoven: his life, his times, his music
D. Randolph (narr.) & illustrations　　　♯ **Per.PCS 3**

Farewell to the piano (J. Öian on ♭ *Nera. EPI-2000* etc.) is not
by Beethoven

BÈGUE, Nicolas Antoine le (*c.* 1630-1702)

SEE: † FRENCH BAROQUE ORGAN MUSIC
　　　† CHACONNE & PASSACAGLIA
　　　† HISTORY OF MUSIC IN SOUND (62)

& SEE ALSO: CHARPENTIER, M-A: Messe de Minuit

BELLE, Jean van (fl. *c.* 1570)

SEE: †FLEMISH CHORAL MUSIC

BELLINI, Vincenzo (1801-1835)

I. SONGS

COLLECTIONS
　L'Abbandono
　Malinconia, ninfa gentile
　Per pietà, bell' idol mio
P. Neway (S), T. Mayer (pf.)　　　♯ **Ete. 101**
(*Mascagni & Verdi*)

Il fervido desiderio
Dolente immagine di Filli mia　(Fumaroli)
Vanne, o rosa fortunata
Vaga luna, che inargenti
S. Danco (S), G. Agosti (pf.)　　♯ *D.LW 5128*
(*Gounod*)　　　　　　　　　(♯ *Lon.LD 9144*)

(Il) Fervido desiderio
I. B. Lucca (S) & orch.　　　in ♯ **Dur. MSE 6**
(*Donizetti, Rossini, Chopin, etc.*)

II. OPERAS

BIANCA E FERNANDO 2 Acts 1826
Sorgi o padre　S
☫ C. Muzio (in ♯ LI.TWV 91053**)[1]

(I) CAPULETI E I MONTECCHI 4 parts 1830
Eccomi in lieta vesta　S
Oh! quante volte　S
L. di Lelio　　　　　　　　　*Cet.AT 0297*

Deh! Tu bell' anima
G. Simionato (M-S)　　　　♯ *D.LW 5139*
(*Barbiere, Don Carlos, Cenerentola*)　(♯ *Lon.LD 9162*)
(*Don Carlos—O don fatale, only on* ♭ *D. 71094*)

NORMA 4 Acts 1831
COMPLETE RECORDINGS

Norma...	...	...	... M. M. Callas (S)
Adalgisa	...	...	E. Stignani (M-S)
Clothilde	...	...	R. Cavallari (S)
Pollione	...	...	M. Filippeschi (T)
Flavio ...	...	...	P. Caroli (T)
Oroveso	...	...	N. Rossi-Lemeni (Bs)

La Scala Cho. & orch.—Serafin ♯ **C.CX 1179/81**
(6ss)　　(♯ *FCX 351/3:* QCX 10088/90; Angel. set 3517)
☆ G. Cigna (S), E. Stignani (M-S), etc., E.I.A.R. Cho. &
Orch.—Gui (♯ *FSor.CS 550/2*)

"Highlights"
G. Martinelli, G. Cigna (S), B. Castagna (A), etc.
(*Verdi: Trovatore*)　　　　　　　♯ **PRCC. 1**
☫ G. Russ (S), V. Guerini (A), G. Zenatello (T),
U. Luppi (Bs), M. Gilion (T), E. Mazzoleni (S),
C. Boninsegna (S), W. Amerighi-Rutili (S), etc.
(Some are ☆; see below)　　　　　♯ **Ete. 706***

Overture
Bamberg Sym.—Lehmann　　　♭ *Pol. 30016*
(*Otello, Ballet Music*) (in ♯ *16062: 17039;* ♯*AmD.DL 4089*)
La Scala—Serafin, from set　　　♭ *C.SEL 1536*
(*Forza, Overture*)

ACT I

Ite sul colle, o Druidi!　　　　Bs
N. Rossi-Lemeni　　　in ♯ **G.ALP 1074**
(*Faust, Sonnambula, Don Giovanni, etc.*)
　　　　　　　　　(QALP 10033: FALP 306)
☫ F. Chaliapin (in ♯ *Sca. 801** & in ♯ *SBDH.LLP 4**)

Meco all' altar di Venere　　T [& T]
G. Penno & A. Mercuriali　　　♯ *D.LW 5111*
(*Trovatore, Simone Boccanegra*)　(♯ *Lon.LD 9117*)
K. Baum　　　　　　　　　in ♯ **Roy. 1582**
(*Rosenkavalier, La Juive, etc.*)

Sediziose voci (Recit); **Casta diva** (Cavatina)　S
L. Malagrida　　　　in ♯ **Mon.MWL 303**
(*below, & Favorita*)
☆ R. Ponselle & cho. (in ♯ *Vic.LCT 1138:* in ♯ *LM 1909:*
　　　　　　　　　　　　　　　♭ *ERAT 19*)
T. dal Monte (in ♯ *G.QALP 10089*)
Z. Milanov (in ♯ *Vic. set LCT 6701*)
☫ Lilli Lehmann (in ♯ *Cum.CE 186**)
R. Ponselle (in ♯ *Sca. 803**)
C. Boninsegna (♯ & ♭ *AmC.PE 23**; in ♯ *Ete. 706**;
　　　　　　　　　　　　　　in ♯ *Sca. 813**)
G. Russ (in ♯ *Sca. 808**)
E. Calvé (IRCC. 3141*)
M. Sembrich (in ♯ *Vic.set LCT 6701**)

Ah si, fa core, abbracciami　　2 Ss
☫ Lilli Lehmann & H. Helbig (in ♯ *Cum.CE 186**)

---

[1] From Edison & Pathé hill & dale recordings. Issued and immediately withdrawn.

ACT II

Mira, o Norma   S & A
L. Malagrida & M. Mandalari
(above, & Favorita)   in # **Mon.MWL 303**
☆ R. Ponselle & M. Selva (in # G.FJLP 5010: QJLP 101;
                 ♭ *Vic.ERAT 19*)

Ah! del Tebro   Bs & cho.
N. Rossi-Lemeni   in # **G.ALP 1074**
(Prince Igor, Faust, Don Giovanni, etc.)
                (QALP 10033: FALP 306)

Qual cor tradisti   S & T
☆ W. Amerighi-Rutili & Oldrati (in # Ete. 706)

Ah troppo tardi   T
◫ G. B. de Negri (in # HRS. 3004*; also IRCC. 3148*)

Deh non volerli vittime   S, T, B, & cho.
☆ W. Amerighi-Rutili, Oldrati, A. Righetti & Cho.
                (in # Ete. 706)

(I) PURITANI   3 Acts   1835

COMPLETE RECORDING

Elvira	M. M. Callas (S)	
Arturo	G. di Stefano (T)	
Riccardo	R. Panerai (B)	
Giorgio	N. Rossi-Lemeni (Bs)	
Bruno	A. Mercuriali (T)	
Gualtiero Valton	C. Forti (Bs)	
Enrichetta	A. Cattelani (S)	

etc., La Scala Cho. & orch.—Serafin
                # **C.CX 1058/60**
(6ss) (# FCX 255/7: QCX 10016/8; # Angel. set 3502;
                     G.LALP 219/21)

March, *see* LISZT: Hexameron, Section A.III (5)

ACT I

A te, o cara, amor talora   T
L. Francardi   *Cet.AT 0324*
(Favorita—Una vergin)
◫ A. Bonci (in # Sca. 811*)
   H. Lazaro (in # Sca. 806*)

Son vergin vezzosa   S
R. Peters   in # **Vic.LM 1786**
◫ F. Toresella (in # HRS. 3004*)

ACT II

Rendetemi la speme ...
Qui la voce ... Vien diletto   S
R. Peters   in # **Vic.LM 1786**
I. F. Gasperoni   **Cet.PE 201**
(Don Pasquale—Quel guardo)
G. Sciutti   in # **Phi.N 00705R**
(Sonnambula; Donizetti, Rossini)
R. Doria   ♭ *Plé.P 45145*
(Linda di Chamounix—O luce ...)
H. Reggiani   in # **Roy. 1603**
☆ M. M. Callas (in # CCet.A 50175)
   M. Carosio (♭ G.7RQ 3006)
◫ S. Kurz (AF.AGSB 47*)
   F. Hempel (in # Vic. set LCT 6701*)

Suoni la tromba   B & Bs.
◫ P. Amato & M. Journet (in # SBDH.LPG 5*)

ACT III

Vieni, vieni fra queste braccia   S & T
... Tenor part only
◫ H. Lazaro (in # Ete. 492*; in # Sca. 806*;
                  in # SBDH.GL 1*)
   A. Giorgini (in # SBDH.JAL 7000*)

A una fonte   T
◫ A. Giorgini (in # SBDH.GL 1*)

(La) SONNAMBULA   3 Acts   1831

COMPLETE RECORDING

Amina ...	...	...	L. Pagliughi (S)
Elvino ...	...	...	F. Tagliavini (T)
Rodolfo	...	...	C. Siepi (Bs)
Teresa ...	...	...	A. Anelli (M-S)
Lisa ...	...	...	W. Ruggeri (S)

etc., Italian Radio Cho. & orch.—Capuana
                # **CCet.set 1240**
(6ss)   (# FSor.CS 553/5)
[*Excerpts on* ♭ *Cap.FAP 7011: Cet.EPO 0315*]

ACT I

Come per me sereno   S
G. Sciutti   in # **Phi.N 00705R**
(Puritani; Donizetti & Rossini)
R. Scotto   **Cet.PE 206**
(Don Pasquale—Quel guardo)
◫ M. Barrientos (in # Sca. 806*)

Prendi l'anel ti dono   S & T
L. Pagliughi & F. Tagliavini in # **CCet.A 50178**
(from set)
☆ T. dal Monte & T. Schipa (in # G.QALP 10089)

... Tenor part only
☆ F. Tagliavini   **G.DB 21579**
(Mascagni: Amico Fritz, aria) (G.ED 1240; &
                in # CCet.A 50155)
◫ T. Schipa (in # Sca. 805*)

Vi ravviso, o luoghi ameni   Bs.
☆ N. Rossi-Lemeni   in # **G.ALP 1074**
(Norma, P. Igor, Faust, etc.) (QALP 10033: FALP 306)
◫ F. Chaliapin (in # Sca.SC 801* & ♭ Per.PEP 12*:
                      Cpt.EXTP 1002)
M. Journet & pf. (in # SBDH.LPG 5*)
P. Plançon (in # SBDH.JAL 7002*)

Son geloso del zefiro   S & T
◫ A. de Angelis & F. de Lucia (in # CEd.set 7002*)

ACT II

Ah, perchè non posso odiarti   T
C. Valletti   in # **Cet.LPC 55002**
(Don Giovanni, Werther, Lucia, etc.)

ACT III

Ah! non credea mirarti   S
M. Dobbs   in # **C.CX 1305**
(Lakmé, Rigoletto, etc.)   (# Angel. 35095)
M. C. Verna   in # **Cet.LPC 55005**
(A. Lecouvreur, Wally, Ernani, etc.)
R. Gigli   **G.DB 21619**
(Forza del Destino—Pace, pace)
M. del Pozo   **G.C 4237**
(Don Pasquale—Quel guardo)   (♭ 7P 146)
R. Peters   in # **Vic.LM 1786**
☆ T. dal Monte (in # G.QALP 10089)
   L. Pagliughi (♭ AmD.ED 3529)

Ah! non giunge   S
◫ L. Tetrazzini (in # G.FJLP 5004*: QJLP 104*:
                  also in # FRP. 3*)

BELLMANN, Carl Michael (1740-1795)

SEE: † CANZONE SCORDATE Vol. II

NOTE: This poet's songs were excluded from WERM
and previous supplements on grounds we still deem sufficient.
There have been many previous recordings, including a
series by A. Schiøtz (T) on G.X 6404, X 6998/9 & X 7200.

BENDA, Jiři (1722-1795)

Symphony, B flat major   str. orch.
Czech Phil.—Talich   *U.C 24383*

BENET, John (fl. XVth Cent.)

SEE: † SEVEN CENTURIES OF SACRED MUSIC

☆ = Re-issue of a recording to be found in previous volumes.

BENEVOLI, Orazio (1602-1672)

MASS, Festival 53 voices 1628 (3ss)[1]
Plaudite, tympana (Hymnus a St. Ruperti) 56 voices[1]
I. Steingruber, M. Gimmi, G. Stieger, L. Leitner
(SS), H. Münch, L. Haager-Gruber, M. Filipp,
T. Sannwald (As), G. Maran, K. Wehofschütz,
G. Schmid, K. Schmidinger (TT), O. Wiener,
E. Siegert, F. Heuschober, J. Lassner (Bss),
Salzburg Cath. Cho., Vienna Sym. Orch.
—Messner   ‡ *EPhi.ABR 4015/6*
[F. Sauer, org.]   (‡ *Phi.A 00622/3R;* Epic.LC 3035)

BEN-HAIM (or Frankenberger), Paul
(b. 1897)

Berceuse vln. & pf.
S. Parnes & J. Páleníček   *U.A 24369*
(*Polyakin: Canary*)

Fanfare to Israel March orch.
Israel Phil.—Kletzki   *C.LX 1620*
(*Trad.: Hatikvah*)

Sonatina, Op. 38 pf. 1946
L. Granetman   in ‡ *Phi.N 00641R*
(*Lavry, Stutschewsky, Boscovich*)

Suite, Op. 34 pf.
D. Bar-Illan   ‡ *Kings.KL 211*
(*Liszt, Chopin, Debussy*)

BENJAMIN, Arthur (b. 1893)

Concerto, harmonica & orch. 1953
L. Adler & L.S.O.—Cameron   ‡ *C.S 1023*
(*Vaughan Williams*)   (‡ *FC 1004*)

Heritage Ceremonial March orch. 1935
New Concert Orch.—F. Curzon   *BH.OT 2213*
(*Duncan: Fanfares*)

Jamaican Rumba (No. 2 of *Two Jamaican Pieces*)
orch. 1940
Orch.—Kostelanetz (in ‡ AmC.ML 4822: ♭ *A 1099*)
Mantovani Orch. (*D.F 10168:* F 43666: ♭ *D 17666*:
in ‡ *LK 4079* & ‡ *LF 1192*; ‡ Lon.LL 979)
☆ Queen's Hall Light Orch.—Torch (♭ *C.SEDQ 523*)
— ARR. 2 PFS.
E. Bartlett & R. Robertson   in ‡ MGM.E 3150
                                     (♭ set *X 273*)
— ARR. VLN. & PF.
☆ J. Heifetz & M. Kaye (in ‡ B.LAT 8066 & ‡ *AXL 2017*;
D.UAT 273572 & *UM 243086*; AmD.DL 5214 & DL 9760)

Overture to an Italian Comedy orch. 1937
☆ Chicago Sym.—Stock (in ‡ Cam.CAL 162)

Scherzino pf. 1936
R. Smith   *D.F 10101*
(*Holst: Toccata*)

BENNET, John (c. 1575-c. 1625)

MADRIGALS (Vol. XXIII in English Madrigal
School)
All creatures now are merry-minded
Randolph Singers—Randolph
in ‡ Nix.WLP 6212-1/2
(† *Triumphs of Oriana*)   (‡ West. set WAL 212)

Thyrsis, sleepest thou?
Danish State Radio Madrigal Cho.—Wöldike
‡ HS.HSL 2072
(† Masterpieces of Music before 1750)
(also in † Histoire de la musique vocale)

Weep, O mine eyes
St. Paul's Cath. Cho.—Dykes Bower
in ‡ *C.CX 1237*
(*Morley, Haydn, Wood, Bairstow, etc.*)
(‡ Angel. 35139 in set 3516)

BENTZON, Niels Viggo (b. 1919)

Sonata, cor anglais & pf., Op. 71
P. T. Hansen & N. V. Bentzon
Woodcut, Op. 65 (*Traesnit*) pf.
N. V. Bentzon   ‡ *G.KBLP 8*

BERCHEM, Jachet van (d. 1580)

CHANSONS: Jehan de Lagny
Que feu craintif
☆ M. Gérar (S) & insts. (in † ‡ HS.AS 6)

O Jesu Christe Motet
Petits Chanteurs à la Croix de bois[5] *C.LZX 277*
(*Palestrina: Sicut cervus*)
N.Y. Primavera Singers   in ‡ Per.SPL 597
(† *Renaissance Music*)   (‡ Cpt.MC 20077)
N.Y. Blessed Sacrament Qtt.   in ‡ *Bib.CL 221*
(† Music of the Church)

BERG, Alban (1885-1935)

Chamber Concerto vln., pf., & 13 wind insts. 1925
I. Gitlis, C. Zelka & Vienna Pro Musica Wind
Ens.—Byrns   ‡ E. & AmVox.PL 8660
(*below*)
☆ R. Charmy, J. Monod & Paris Cha.—Leibowitz
‡ Fel.RL 89004
(‡ Clc. 6098)

Concerto, vln. & orch. 1935
A. Gertler & Philharmonia—Kletzki ‡*C.C1030*
(*Bartók* on ‡ C.FCX 297; ‡ Angel. 35091)
I. Gitlis & Vienna Pro Musica—Strickland
(*above*)   ‡ E. & AmVox.PL 8660
S. Goldberg & Pittsburgh Sym.—Steinberg
‡ PFCM.CB 180
(*Thomson & Schoenberg*)
☆ L. Krasner & Cleveland Sym.—Rodzinski
(*Schoenberg*)   ‡ AmC.ML 4857

Quartet, str., Op. 3 1909/10
Juilliard Qtt.   ‡ AmC.ML 4737
(*Webern*)   (in set SL 188)
(*Schönberg & Webern*, on ‡ Phi.A 01178L)

Sonata, Op. 1 pf. 1906/8
Z. Skolovsky   ‡ EPhi.NBL 5025
(*Scriabin, Hindemith, Bartók*) (‡ Phi.N 02131L;
AmC.ML 4871)
J. Manchon-Theis   ‡ LT.MEL 94008
(*Webern & Schönberg*) (V‡ Sel.LAP 1059; ‡ T.TW 30031)
G. Gould   ‡ Hall.RS 3
(*Prokofiev, Shostakovich, Taneiev*)
T. Ury   ‡ Argo.ATM 1006[2]
(*Prokofiev & Stravinsky*)

SONGS: COLLECTIONS
An Leukon 1908
(2) "Unpublished" Songs[3] (Storm) 1900-25
(7) Early Songs 1905-7
  ☆ B. Beardslee (S), J. L. Monod (pf.)
(4) Songs, Op. 2 (Hebbel & Mombert) 1908-9
  ☆ I. Joachim (S) & orch.—Leibowitz (‡ Clc. 6174)

(4) Stücke, Op. 5 cl. & pf. 1913
  ☆ E. Thomas & J. L. Monod (in ‡ Clc. 6174)

WOZZECK, Op. 7 Opera 3 Acts 1925
COMPLETE RECORDING
  ☆ E. Farrell, M. Harrell, F. Jagel, D. Lloyd, etc. N.Y.P.S.O
  —Mitropoulos[4] (4ss)   ‡ OTA. 5
Excerpts
"Philharmonic" Orch.—Berendt   ‡ Allo. 3144
(*R. Strauss*)

---

[1] DTÖ., Vol. XX. The Mass for the Consecration of Salzburg Cathedral.
[2] If ever on sale, very soon withdrawn.   [3] Now published by Universal Edn., Vienna.
[4] Recording of a 1951 radio performance.   [5] May be ☆ of Pat. PDT 273 in Supp. II.

BERGER, Arthur Victor (b. 1912)

Duo vlc. & pf. 1946
B. Greenhouse & A. Makas
Quartet, C major fl., ob., cl. & bsn. 1941
Fairfield Wind Ens.   ‡ **AmC.ML 4846**
(Hill)

BERGER, Jean (b. 1909)

Brazilian Psalm
St. Olaf Cho.—O. C. Christiansen
                          in ‡ *Ald.LP 2002*
                          (▽ in ‡ *StO.DLP 5*)
▽ Fleet St. Cho.—Lawrence (announced as ‡ Argo.ARS
                                                    1003)
Fandango brasileiro
L. Adler (harmonica) & pf. (in ‡ *CHS.CHS 1168;* in
          ‡ *FMer.MLP 7026;* **V**‡ *MMS.POP 20*)

Vision of peace
▽ St. Olaf Cho.—O. C. Christiansen (in ‡ *StO.DLP 6*)

BERGSMA, William Laurence (b. 1921)

(A) Carol on 12th Night orch. *c.* 1953-4 (f.p. 1954)
Louisville—Whitney   ‡ **LO. 10**
(Ginastera, Sauguet, Ward)

BÉRIOT, Charles Auguste de (1802-1870)

Scène de Ballet, Op. 100 vln. & orch. (orig.
  vln. & pf.)
C. Taschke & Leipzig Phil.—Kegel ‡ **Ura. 7166**
(Bruch & Svendsen)

BERKELEY, Lennox Randal Francis
                                          (b. 1903)

(A) GARLAND FOR THE QUEEN   1953
  (with Ireland, V. Williams, etc.)
... **Spring at this hour** (Dehn)
Cambridge Univ. Madrigal Soc.—Ord
                          in † ‡ **C.CX 1063**

Sonatina, Op. 17 vln. & pf. 1942
Theme & Variations, Op. 33, No. 1 vln. unacc.
                                                    1950
F. Grinke & L. Berkeley   ‡ **D.LXT 2978**
(Rubbra)   (‡ *Lon.LL 1055*)

Trio, Op. 44 vln., hrn. & pf. 1952
M. Parikian, D. Brain & C. Horsley
(Mozart)   ‡ **G.CLP 1029**

Trio, E minor, Op. 19 vln, vla., vlc. 1944
J. Pougnet, F. Riddle & A. Pini
                                    ‡ **Nix.WLP 20017**
(Dohnanyi & Français)   (‡ *West.WL 5316*)

**Variation on an Elizabethan tune (Sellinger's
  Round)**[1] orch.
Aldeburgh Fest.—Britten   in ‡ **D.LXT 2798**
(Britten, Oldham, Searle, Tippett, Walton) (in ‡ *Lon.LL 808*)

BERLIOZ, Hector (1803-1869)

BÉATRICE ET BÉNÉDICT
  Opéra-comique 2 Acts 1862
Overture
Suisse Romande—Denzler   ‡ *D.LW 5125*
(Benvenuto Cellini)   (‡ *Lon.LD 9143*)
Munich Phil.—Ludwig   **PV. 72431**
(Cornelius: Barbier von Bagdad Overture)
Lamoureux—v. Otterloo   ‡ *Phi.S 06043R*
(Francs Juges)

☆ Philharmonia—Kletzki   **C.GQX 11524**
(2ss)   (LOX 818)
(& in ‡ AmC.RL 3071; C.QCX 10027: FCX 173)
(& with *Schubert: Rosamunde* excpt.
                              on ♭ *C.SEL 1502: SEBQ 103*)
☆ Boston Sym.—Münch
              (G.DB 4321: in ‡ ALP 1245; ♭ *Vic.ERA 68*)
Stadium Concerts—Smallens
                          (‡ *AFest.CPR 10-427; D.UW 333004*)
— ARR. BAND Henning
  Band of the Air—Revelli (in ‡ AmD.DL 8157)
☆ Goldman Band (in ‡ Cam.CAL 240)

BENVENUTO CELLINI, Op. 23
  Opera 2 Acts 1838
Overture
Suisse Romande—Denzler   ‡ *D.LW 5125*
(Beatrice & Benedict)   (‡ *Lon.LD 9143*)
Lamoureux—v. Otterloo   ‡ **Phi.A 00191L**
(Carnaval romain, Roméo et Juliette, etc.)(in ‡ Epic.LC 3054)
Czech Phil.—Jiráček   ‡ *Sup.LPM 170*
(Reicha: Overture, C major)   (‡ *U. 5178C*)
San Francisco Sym.—Monteux ‡ **Vic.LM 1799**
(Bach & Beethoven)   (♭ set ERB 5)
(Bach & Chausson on ‡ ItV.A12R 0158)
☆ Paris Cons.—Münch   ‡ *D.LW 5014*
(Corsaire Overture)   (‡ *Lon.LD 9019*)
☆ Opéra-Comique—Wolff   ‡ *D.LW 5042*
(Lalo: Roi d' Ys, Overture)   (‡ *Lon.LD 9040*)
☆ Philharmonia—Kletzki (in ‡ C.FCX 173: QCX 10027;
                                              AmC.RL 3071)
  Concerts Colonne—Paray (♭ *AmVox.VIP 45450*)
  Berlin Phil.—v. Kempen (♭ *Pol. 32037*)

(Le) Carnaval romain, Overture, Op. 9 orch. 1844
Royal Phil.—Beecham   ‡ **EPhi.ABL 3083**
(below)   (‡ *AmC.ML 5064*)
Philharmonia—Kletzki   **C.LX 1574**
                          (GQX 11526; ArgA. 266604)
Amsterdam—v. Beinum   ‡ *D.LW 5176*
(Damnation of Faust, excerpts)
N.B.C.—Toscanini   ‡ **G.ALP 1235**
(Hérold, Ponchielli, Sibelius, etc.) (in ‡ Vic.LM 1834;
                FV.A 630247; DV.L 16483; ♭ *ItV.A72R 0041*)
Lamoureux—v. Otterloo   ‡ **Phi.A 00191L**
(Damnation de Faust, Benvenuto Cellini, etc.)
(also ♭ Phi. N402051E)   (in ‡ Epic.LC 3054)
Philharmonia—Schüchter   ‡ **P.PMC 1022**
(below)   (‡ *MGM.E 3115*)
N.B.C. Sym.   ‡ **SFA. 1**
(Wagner, Tchaikovsky)
Philadelphia "Pops"—Hilsberg ‡ *AmC.AL 34*
(Suppé)
Moscow Radio—Rakhlin (*USSRM.D 148*)
Orch.—Swarowsky (in ‡ MTW. 9; in ‡ *ACC.MP 11*)
Linz Sym. (in ‡ Ply. 12-29)
Anon. Orch. (in ‡ Gram. 2074 & MMS. *100W*)
☆ Boston Sym.—Koussevitzky (G.DB 4324)
  Lamoureux—Martinon (♭ *Nix.EP 709*)
  Lamoureux—Fricsay (♭ *Pol. 32038*)
  Minneapolis Sym.—Dorati
                    (♭ *Mer.EP 1-5051: FMer.MEP 14516*)
  Rhineland Sym.—Federer (‡ *AFest.CFR 10-608*)

(Le) Corsaire, Overture, Op. 21 1831
Royal Phil.—Beecham   ‡ **EPhi.ABL 3083**
(above & below)   (‡ *AmC.ML 5064*)
Philharmonia—Schüchter   ‡ **P.PMC 1022**
(above & below)   (‡ *MGM.E 3115*)
Unspec. Orch.—Münch in ‡ **AmVox.PL 7170**
("This is Paris")
Czech Phil.—Šejna   **U.H 24402**
☆ Paris Cons.—Münch   ‡ *D.LW 5014*
(Benvenuto Cellini)   (‡ *Lon.LD 9019*)
☆ Philharmonia—Kletzki
          (in ‡ C.FCX 173: QCX 10027; in ‡ AmC.RL 3071)

(La) DAMNATION DE FAUST, Op. 24 1846
COMPLETE RECORDINGS in *French*

Marguerite	...	...	...	S. Danco (S)
Faust	...	...	...	D. Poleri (T)
Méphisto	...	...	...	M. Singher (B)
Brander	...	...	...	D. Gramm (Bs)

(continued on next page)

[1] Part of a set of variations, jointly with the other composers named; for Coronation, 1953.

(La) DAMNATION DE FAUST, Op. 24 (*continued*)
Harvard Glee Club, Radcliffe Choral Soc. &
Boston Sym.—Münch   ♯ **G.ALP 1225/7**
(6ss)(♯ Vic.set LM 6114; FV.A 630210/2; ItV.C12R 0133/5)
[usual orch. suite from this, ♭ *Vic.ERA 250*]

☆ M. Lauréna (S), G. Jouatte (T), P. Cabanel (B),
M. Pactat (Bs), Passani Cho. & Radio-Paris Orch.
—Fournet (♯ C.FHX 5003/5)

HIGHLIGHTS
Sans regrets j'ai quitté les riantes campagnes   T   (Act II)
Autrefois un roi de Thulé   S   (Act III)
Grand Dieu! que vois-je? . . . Ange adoré   S & T   (Act III)
D'amour l'ardente flamme   S   (Act IV)
Nature immense   T   (Act IV)
I. Kolassi (M-S), R. Jobin (T) & L.S.O.
—Fistoulari   ♯ **D.LXT 5034**
(*Werther excerpts*)   (♯ Lon.LL 1154)
Entrée de Marguérite
Autrefois un roi de Thulé
Duet: Ange adoré
D'amour l'ardente flamme
N. Vallin (S), G. Fouché (T) & Pasdeloup Orch.
—Cruchon   ♯ **Plé.P 3082**

Orchestral Suite
Marche hongroise; Danse des sylphes; Menuet des follets
Lamoureux—v. Otterloo   ♯ **Phi.A 00191L**
(*Benvenuto Cellini, Carnaval romain, etc.*) (♯ Epic.LC 3054)
Philharmonia—Schüchter   ♯ **P.PMC 1022**
(*Corsaire, Carnaval romain, Troyens—Marche*)
    (♯ MGM.E 3115)
Los Angeles Phil.—Wallenstein ♯ **B.AXTL 1063**
(*Chabrier, Smetana, etc.*) (♯ AmD.DL 9728: ♭ ED 3556;
    ♯ D.UA 243584)

☆ Boston Sym.—Koussevitzky (in ♯ Vic.LCT 1146)
Paris Cons.—Sebastian (in ♯ Nix.ULP 9061: ♭EP 750;
   ♯ Ura. 5000: ♭ UREP50: in ♯ MTW. 511, d.c.)
Amsterdam—v. Beinum (Danse & Menuet on
♯ D.LW 5176 with Carnaval romain; Marche &
      Menuet on ♭ D. 71117)

Marche hongroise   orch.   Act I
N.B.C. Sym.—Toscanini[1] in ♯ **Vic.set LM 6026**
(*Weber, Humperdinck, etc.*) (*Wagner*, on ♭ *ItV.A72R 0058*)
N.W. German Phil.—Schüchter
    in ♯ *Imp.ILP 117*
(*Chabrier, Dvořák, Tchaikovsky*)
Berlin Phil.—Fricsay   **PV. 72297**
(*below, & Borodin*)   (*J. Strauss*, on *Pol. 62894*: ♭ *30005*)
Orch.—Swarowsky (in ♯ *ACC.MP 11*)
Moscow Radio—Orlov (USSR. 09687)

☆ Philharmonia—Weldon (in ♯ AmC.RL 3042)
L.P.O.—Martinon (in ♯ MGM.E 3037)
Concerts Colonne—Paray (♭ AmVox.VIP 45450)
San Francisco—Monteux
   (♭ G.7RF 278: in ♭ Vic. set ERB 5)
Paris Cons.—Lindenberg (♭ Od.7AO 2008)
Italian Radio—Basile (in ♯ Tem.TT 2046)
Vienna Sym.—Stolz (♭ D. 71021)

H Boston Sym. (in ♯ Vic.SRL 12-11)[2]

— ARR. BAND
Garde Républicaine Band (♭ D.EFA 458501)

Chanson de la puce   B   (Act II)
(*Song of the Flea*)
S. Baccaloni (Bs)   in ♯ **Roy. 1547**
H P. Plançon (in ♯ Vic.set LCT 6701*)
M. Journet (Bs) (in ♯ SBDH.LPG 5*)

Voici des roses   B   (Act II)
H M. Battistini (*Ital*) (in ♯ Ete. 709*)

Danse des sylphes   orch. (Act II)
R.I.A.S. Sym.—Fricsay   **PV. 72297**
(*above, & Borodin*)
Philharmonia—Markevitch   ♯ in **C.CX 1273**
(*Stravinsky, Chabrier, Saint-Saëns*) (♭ SEL 1539;
    in ♯ QCX 10172; Angel. 35154)
☆ Orch.—Stokowski (in ♯ Vic.LM 9029)
Florence Fest.—Markevitch (in ♯ Tem.TT 2046)
A. Kostelanetz (♭ C.SED 5511: SEDQ 526: ESDF1027)

Autrefois un roi de Thulé   S   (Act III)
S. Michel   in ♯ **Pat.DTX 137**
(*Orphée, Werther, Samson et Dalila, etc.*)

Menuet des Follets   orch.   (Act III)
U.S.S.R. State—Eliasberg (*USSR. 18962/3*)

Devant la maison   B   (Act IV)
G. London   in ♯ **AmC.ML 4658**
(*Rheingold, Walküre, Faust, etc.*)
H P. Plançon (*AF.AGSA 45**)

D'amour l'ardente flamme   S   (Act IV)
J. Hammond (*Eng*)   ♯ **G.BLP 1073**
(*Beethoven & St. Saëns*)
☆ R. Bampton (in ♯ Vic.set LCT 6701)
... incomplete: G. Farrar[3]   in ♯ *IRCC.L 7001*

Nature immense   T   (Act IV)
H F. Ansseau (AF.AGSB 82*)

(L') ENFANCE DU CHRIST, Op. 25   oratorio
S, T, B, Bs, cho. orch.   1854
M. Davenport (A), L. Simoneau, M. Singher,
D. Gramm, Choral Art & Little Orch. Socs.
—Scherman   ♯ **EPhi.NBL 5022/3**
(4ss)   (♯ AmC.set SL 199)

(Les) Francs-Juges, Overture, Op. 3   orch.   1828
Royal Phil.—Beecham   ♯ **EPhi.ABL 3083**
(*above & below*)   (♯ AmC.ML 5064)
Residentie—v. Otterloo   ♯ *Phi.S 06043R*
(*Béatrice et Bénédict Overture*)
☆ Philharmonia—Kletzki (in ♯ C.FCX 173: QCX 10027;
    AmC.RL 3071)

Grande Messe des Morts, Op. 5   1837   (*Requiem*)
R. de Voll (T), Rochester Oratorio Soc. Cho.
& Orch.—Hollenbach   ♯ **AmC. set EL 53**
(4ss)
☆ G. Jouatte (T), Passani Cho. & Radio-Paris Orch.
—Fournet (♯ C.FHX 5001/2)

Harold en Italie, Op. 16   vla. & orch.   1834
F. Riddle & London Phil. Sym.—Scherchen
    ♯ **Nix.NLP 911**
    (♯ West.WL 5288)
L. Černý & Czech Phil.—Jiraček ♯**Sup.LPV221**
(♯ U.5214H; o.n. ♯ Sup.LPM 83/4; U. 5033/4C, 4ss)
☆ W. Primrose & Boston Sym.—Koussevitzky
(*Damnation de Faust, excpts.*)   ♯ Vic.LCT 1146
"Europa Sym." (♯ Ply. 120–130)
☆ W. Primrose & Royal Phil.—Beecham
(♯ C.QCX 10005: FCX 178; ♭ AmC.set A 1074)

Lélio, or The Return to Life, Op. 14 bis[4]   1827-32
J. Kerol (T), G. Bacquier (B), A. Charpak
(narrator), New Paris Sym. Cho. & orch.
—Leibowitz   ♯ **E. & AmVox.PL 8250**
[K. Humble (pf.); H. Druart (cl.), B. Galais (hp.)]

Marche funèbre, Op. 18, No. 3   orch.   1848
(for the last scene of Hamlet)
☆ Paris Cons.—Sebastian   in ♯ Nix.ULP 9061
    (♯ Ura. 5000)

(Le) Roi Lear, Overture, Op. 4   1831
Royal Phil.—Beecham   ♯ **EPhi.ABL 3083**
(*above & below*)   (♯ AmC.ML 5064)
☆ Rhineland Sym.—Federer (in ♯ AFest.CFR 608)

ROMÉO ET JULIETTE, Op. 17   Dramatic Sym.
                                     1839
COMPLETE RECORDING
M. Roggero (A), L. Chabay (T), Yi-Kwei-Sze
(Bs), Harvard & Radcliffe Chos. & Boston
Sym.—Münch (4ss)   ♯ **G.ALP 1179/80**
(♯ FALP 271/2; ♭ set Vic.set LM 6011: ♭ set WDM 6011;
    ♯ DV. set LB 16461; ♯ ItV.B12R 0111/2)
[Roméo seul, Grande fête, Scène d'amour & Reine Mab
Scherzo, only, in ♯ Vic.set LM 6028]

ORCHESTRAL PART, COMPLETE
1. Introduction   2. Roméo seul & Grande fête chez Capulet
3. Scène d'amour, Part II; 4. La Reine Mab—Scherzo, Part IV;
5. Mort de Roméo, Part V.
N.Y.P.S.O.—Mitropoulos   ♯ **AmC.ML 4632**

---

[1] Broadcast performance.
[2] First part cond. Muck*, second Koussevitzky, third Münch, as illustrations to a history of the orchestra.
[3] Recorded 1935.   [4] "Lyric Monodrama", intended to follow immediately the *Symphonie fantastique.*

ROMÉO ET JULIETTE, Op. 17: ORCH. (*continued*)
... **Nos. 2 & 3** only
Sym. Orch.—Swarowsky   ♯ **MTW. 23**
(1½ss—*Dukas*)   (♭ *set EP 23*)
  ☆ N.B.C. Sym.—Toscanini (♯ ItV.A12R 0078)
... **Nos. 2 & 4** only
Olympia Sym.—Saïke   ♯ **Allo. 3070**
(*Bizet: Jeux d'enfants*)
... **No. 1** only
Anon. Orch. (in ♯ Roy. 1432)
... **No. 2, Roméo seul & Grande fête chez Capulet**
                                       (Part II)
Lamoureux—v. Otterloo   ♯ **Phi.A 00191L**
(*Troyens—Marche, Benvenuto Cellini, etc.*)
                            (in ♯ Epic.LC 3054)
... **No. 4, La Reine Mab, Scherzo** (Part IV)
N.B.C. Sym.—Toscanini[1] in ♯ **Vic.set LM 6026**
(*Damnation de Faust, March; & Bizet, Verdi, etc.*)
SONGS
COLLECTION
(La) Captive, Op. 12 (Hugo) with pf., 1832; orch. 1848
(Le) Jeune Pâtre breton, Op. 13, No. 4 (Gautier) 1831;
                            orch. 1834
Zaïde, Op. 19, No. 1 (Gautier) 1845; orch. 1850.
  E. Steber & Col. Sym. Orch.—Morel
(*below*)   ♯ **AmC.ML 4940**
                          (♯ Phi.N 02115L)
(La) Captive, Op. 12   Rêverie, voice & pf.
    (V. Hugo)
  B. Rawson (S), J. Strasser (pf.)[2]   **Berlioz Soc.**
(2ss)   (pte. issue)
Irlande, Op. 2   9 Songs   (Gounot, after T. Moore)
                                  1829-30
... **No. 1, Le coucher du soleil**
... **No. 4, La belle voyageuse**
  B. Rawson (S), P. Gellhorn (pf.)
              ♯ *Berlioz Soc. BSLP 1*
             (single-sided, pte. issue)
(Les) NUITS D'ÉTÉ, Op. 7 (Gautier) 1834
Song cycle   S & orch.
  V. de los Angeles & Boston Sym.—Münch
(*Debussy*)   ♯ **Vic.LM 1907**
  E. Steber & Col. Sym.—Mitropoulos
(*above*)   ♯ **AmC.ML 4940**
                        (♯ Phi.N 02115L)
... **No. 4, Absence**
  R. Hayes (T), R. Boardman (pf.)
                in ♯ **Van.VRS 449**
(*Beethoven, Schubert, etc.; & Trad.*)
  ⊞ E. Clément (T) (in ♯ *HRS. 3008**)

Premiers transports que nul n'oublie 1838[3]
G. Swarthout (M-S), G. Trovillo (pf.), hp.
& vlc.   ♯ **G.ALP 1269**
(*Chausson, Duparc, etc.*)   (♯ Vic.LM 1793; FV.A 630227)
Symphonie fantastique, Op. 14[4] orch. 1831
Philharmonia—v. Karajan   ♯ **C.CX 1206**
                 (♯ QCX 10136; Angel. 35202)
L.S.O.—Scherchen   ♯ **Nix.NLP 908**
                    (♯ West.WL 5268)
Berlin Phil.—Markevitch   ♯ **HP.DGM 18167**
                    (♯ AmD.DL 9783)
Minneapolis Sym.—Dorati   ♯ **Mer.MG 50034**
                    (♯ FMer.MLP 7522)
R.I.A.S. Sym.—Sebastian   ♯ **Rem. 199-176**
Boston Sym.—Münch   ♯ **Vic.LM 1900**
                    (♯ ItV.A12R 0179)
Moscow Radio—Rakhlin   ♯ **USSR.D 01440/2**
(3ss—*Wagner: Siegfried Idyll*)
  ☆ San Francisco—Monteux   ♯ **G.ALP 1137**
                    (♯ ItV.A12R 0092)
  ☆ Berlin Phil.—Otterloo   ♯ **EPhi.ABL 3019**[5]
            (♯ Phi.A 00254L; ♯ Epic.LC 3005)
Anon. Orch. (♯ Gram. 2091)
  ☆ Cleveland Sym.—Rodzinski (♯ AmC.RL 3059)
  Philadelphia—Ormandy
      (♯ Phi.A 01159L; ♭ *AmC.set A 1069*)

... **2nd movt., Un bal** only
U.S.S.R. State Sym.—Mravinsky (*USSR. 16695/6, 2ss*)
Symphonie funèbre et triomphale, Op. 15 1834-40
Cologne Cho. & Brass & Str. Orchs.—Straub
              ♯ **Nix.LLP 8040**
                  (♯ Lyr.LL 40)
Vienna Cha. Cho., Brass Ens. & Vienna State
Op. Orch.—Gräf   ♯ **Ura.X 100**
Te Deum, Op. 22   T, cho. & orch.   1849-54
A. Young, Dulwich College Boys' Cho.,
London Phil. Cho. & Royal Phil. Orch.
—Beecham[6]   ♯ **EPhi.ABL 3006**
[D. Vaughan, organ] (♯ Phi.A 01127L; ♯ AmC.ML 4897)
(Les) TROYENS À CARTHAGE
Opera   3 or 4 Acts   1859 (f.p. 1863)
(Part II of *Les Troyens*, forming Acts III, IV, V of complete work)
COMPLETE RECORDING
Didon ...   .   A. Mandikian (S)
Ascanius   ...   ...   M. Rolle (S)
Anna ...   .   J. Collard (A)
Aeneas...   ...   ...   J. Giraudeau (T)
Narbal   ...   ...   X. Depraz (Bs)
  ☆ Cho. & Paris Cons. Orch.—Scherchen
              ♯ **LT.DTL 93001/3**
                  (♯ Sel.LPG 8492/4)
Orchestral Suite
(Overture; Chasse royale et orage; Ballet Music; March)
  ☆ Lamoureux—Martinon (2ss)   ♯ *P.PMD 1024*
  (*Glinka on ♯ MGM.E 3053; March only also in*)
                ♯ **MGM.E 3046**
Marche troyenne   Cho. & orch.[7]
(Concert version, ARR. Berlioz)
Lamoureux—v. Otterloo   in ♯ **Phi.A 00191L**
(*Carnaval romain, on ♭ Phi.N 402051E*) (in ♯ Epic.LC 3054)
Philharmonia—Schüchter   in ♯ **P.PMC 1022**
(*above*)   (♯ MGM.E 3115)
Ballet Music   (Act II)
Berlin Sym.—List   in ♯ **Roy. 1398**

Waverley, Overture, Op. 2 bis orch.   c. 1827
Royal Phil.—Beecham   ♯ **EPhi.ABL 3083**
(*Overtures, above*)   (♯ AmC.ML 5064)

Berlioz, his story & his music
A. Robinson (narr.), cho. & orch.
              (♯ *AmVox.VL 2640 & set 264*)

BERNAL JIMENEZ, Miguel (b. 1910)

Quartet, Strings ("*Virreinal*") 1936
Mexican Str. Qtt.
(2) Villancicos
Morelia Boys' Cho.—Picutti   ♯ **CM. 5**

BERNART DE VENTADORN (c. 1125-1195)

SEE: † MUSIC OF THE MIDDLE AGES
     † FRENCH TROUBADOUR SONGS
     † MUSIQUE ET LA POÉSIE

BERNERS, Lord (1883-1950)

Nicholas Nickleby   Film Music   1947
... Excerpts ☆ Philharmonia—E. Irving (in ♯ AmC.RL 3029)
PIANO MUSIC
Fragments psychologiques   1915
   1. La Haine   2. Le Rire   3. Un Soupir
(Le) Poisson d'or   1914
(3) Petites Marches funèbres   1914
   1. Pour un Homme d'État; 2. Pour un canari; 3. Pour une
     tante à héritage
M. Pressler   ♯ **MGM.E 3081**
(*Lambert*)

---

[1] Broadcast performance.   [2] Recorded in an ARRT. by S. Heller, from the 1848 version by Berlioz for voice & orch.
[3] Later interpolated into *Roméo et Juliette*.   [4] See *Lélio, above*.
[5] Two editions; the later one avoids break in 3rd movt. between ss. 1 and 2.
[6] Omits ad lib. movts. (Nos. 3 & 8).   [7] Originally in Act I, Sc. 9, of the complete opera.

BERNIER, Nicolas (1664-1734)

Confitebor tibi Domine Motet
MS. Paris Cons. (Ed. A. Cellier)
M. Angelici (S), J. Archimbaud (C-T), J. Collard
& Y. Melchior (A), J. Giraudeau & P.
Gianotti (T), L. Noguéra (Bs), Jeunesses
Musicales Françaises Cho.—Martini
♯ **Pat.DTX 158**

(Charpentier) [H. Roget, organ]

O triumphantes Jerusalem Motet, T. & insts. 1703
M. Casadesus Ens. ♯ **Plé.P 3083**
(† Musiques à la Chapelle du Roi) (♯ West.WN 18167)
[J. Giraudeau (T)]

BERNIER, René (b. 1905)

Du Coq à l'âne 7 part-songs (Carème)
French Nat. Radio Female Cho.—Besson
Pat.PD 172/3
(4ss) (♭ *ED 11*)

Présages 3 Songs (Marin) 1946-8
L. Devos (T), Y. Étienne (Reciter) & Belgian
Radio Cha. Orch.—Doneux
(Lekeu) ♯ ***Gramo.GLP 2507***

BERNSTEIN, Leonard (b. 1918)

(7) Anniversaries pf. 1948
... **Nos. 1-5**
☆ L. Bernstein *(Copland & Ravel)* ♯ **Cam.CAL 214**

FANCY FREE Ballet 1944
Orch. Suite (with Prologue for Sop.)
☆ B. Holliday & Ballet Theatre Orch.—Bernstein
♯ *AmD.DL 6023*

— **omitting Prologue**
Ballet Theatre—Levine ♯ **DCap.CCL 7517**
(2ss) *(Copland on ♯ Cap.P 8196)* (♯ *Cap.L 8197*)

... **Galop, Waltz & Danzon**
Boston Prom.—Fiedler (n.v.) in ♯ **Vic.LM 1726**
(also ♭ ERA 146) (in ♭ *set WDM 1726*)

ON THE TOWN Operetta 1945
Songs & Ballet Music
☆ Victor Cho. & orch.—Bernstein & Shaw
♯ **Cam.CAL 196**
(below) (♭ *CAE 203*, & in ♯ *set CFL 102*)

Sonata, Clarinet & pf. 1942
H. Tichman & R. Budnevich ♯ **CHS.H 18**
(Bloch & Milhaud)

Symphony, "Jeremiah" M-S & Orch. 1942
☆ N. Merriman & St. Louis Sym.—Bernstein
(♯ *Cam.CAL 196*)

WONDERFUL TOWN Musical Play
R. Russell & Members of original New York
Production ♯ **AmD.DL 9010**
(♮ *set DA 937*: ♭ *set D 9-391*)

Selection Boston "Pops"—Fiedler ♭ *Vic.ERA 131*

MISCELLANEOUS
Piano Medley (ARR. from "On the Town", Fancy Free, etc.)
♯ *Persp. 3*

BERTRAND, Anthoine de (d. 1581)
SEE: † ANTHOLOGIE SONORE

BESARD, Jean-Baptiste (c. 1567-1625)
SEE: † ANTHOLOGIE SONORE (♯ HS.AS 13)
† XVITH & XVIITH CENTURY FRENCH SONGS
† XVITH & XVIITH CENTURY SONGS
& also RESPIGHI: Antiche Danze, Suites 2 & 3

BETTINELLI, Bruno (b. 1913)

(2) Invenzioni str. orch. 1938
Angelicum Str.—Janes ♯ **Ang.LPA 956**
(Debussy, Vivaldi, Bonporti)

Sinfonia da camera str. orch. 1939
Naples Scarlatti Orch.—Lupi ♯**Csm.CLPS1040**
(Catalani: La Wally, Prelude, Act 3)

BEYDTS, Louis (1895-1953)

SONGS
C'est moi (*La Guirlande de Marcelline*)
Le passé qui fila (Le Roy)
C. Devos (T), G. Lecompte (pf.) ♭ *Pat.D 110*
(Hahn)

BIBER, Heinrich Ignaz Johann Franz von (1644-1704)

SEE ALSO: † HISTORY OF MUSIC IN SOUND (62)

Partita No. 7, C minor[1] 2 vlas. d'amore & cont.
E. Seiler & I. Brix-Meinert, J. Koch (gamba),
H. Stöhr (cbs.), W. Gerwig (lute),
K-E. Glückselig (hpsi.) **PV. 8403**

Passacaglia, G minor[2] vln. unacc.
M. Rostal ♯ **CHS.CHS 1174**
(J. S. Bach & Tartini) (♯ *Clc. 6187*)

BILLINGS, William (1746-1800)
SEE: † HYMNS OF PRAISE

BINGHAM, Seth (b. 1882)

Baroques Suite, organ 1943
... **Rhythmic Trumpet**
C. Crozier ♯ **Ken. 2555**
(† American Organ Music)

Roulade, Op. 9, No. 3 organ
H. Ash ♯ **McInt.MC 1005**
(Bach, Liszt, Zechiel, Langlais) (o.n. ♯ *WCFM. 19*)
V. Fox ♭ *AmC.A 1594*
(Dvořák & Humperdinck)

BINKERD, Gordon Ware (b. 1916)

Sun Singer Sym. poem orch.
Student Orch.—Goodman ♯ *UOI.CRS 2*
(Weigel)

BINCHOIS, Gilles (1400-1460)

CHANSONS
Adieu m'amour et ma maistresse
D. Schou (A), recorder & gambas
in ♯ **HS.HSL 2071**
(† Masterpieces of Music before 1750)
(also in † Histoire de la musique vocale)

De plus en plus
E. Metzger-Ulrich (S) & Inst. ens
in ♯ **E. & AmVox.PL 8120**
(† Music of the Renaissance)
M. Rollin Inst. Ensemble in ♯ **CND. 9**
(† La Musique et la poésie ...)
☆ H. Guermant (S), F. Anspach (T) & insts
(in † ♯ HS.AS 4)

Filles à marier
Pro Musica Antiqua Ens.—Cape **G.HMS 26**
(† History of Music in Sound) (in ♯ Vic.set LM 6016)

---

[1] From *Harmonia artificiosa-ariosa*, c. 1700. [2] Sonata No. 16, in DTÖ. vol. XXV.

SACRED MUSIC
Ave, verum corpus　Motet
　Vatican Cho.—Bertolucci　　in ♯ **Per.SPL 706**
　(*Victoria, Palestrina, etc.*)

Kyrie feriale
Virgo prefulgens　Motet
　Cho.—Eekhout　　　　　in ♯ **OL.LD 81**
　(† *Musiciens de la Cour de Bourgogne II*)

Mass No. 2　(MS., Brussels) (doubtful)[1]
　Cho.—Eekhout　　　in ♯ **LOL.OL 50104**
　(† *Musiciens de la Cour de Bourgogne I*)　(♯ OL.LD 80)

BISHOP, Sir Henry (1786-1855)

Bid me discourse　(after Shakespeare)
　M. Ritchie (S), G. Malcolm (hpsi.)
　　　　　　　　　　in ♯ **Nix.NLP 921**
　(*Boyce, Arne, Mozart, etc.*)

(The) Dashing White Sergeant　(Burgoyne)
　R. Wilson (B) & orch.　　　　　**G.B 10521**
　(*M. & W. Webb: The northern lights of Aberdeen*)
　S. MacEwan (T) & orch.　　♭ *EPhi.NBE 11012*
　(*Folk Songs & Carols*)

— ARR. CHO.
　Kirkintilloch Junior Cho. (*P.R 3943*)
　☆ Glasgow Orpheus Cho.—Roberton (in ♯ *G.DLP 1019*)
　　etc.

Home, sweet home　(Payne)
　(from the opera *Clari*, 1823)
　P. Munsel (S) & orch.　　in ♯ *G.BLP 1023*
　(Film version) (♯ *QBLP 5015; Vic.LM 7012:*
　　　　　　　　　　　　♭ *set WDM 7012*)
　G. Fleischer (S, *Dan*)　　　*Phi.P 55037H*
　(*Martini: Plaisir d'amour*)
　J. C. Thomas (B) (in ‡ *ISR. 10023*)
　E. Sigfuss (A, *Dan*) (*Tono.L 28072*)
　⌶ A. Patti (S) (**V♯** *Rar.M 314**)

— ARR. CHO.
　R. Shaw Chorale (Male Cho.) (in ♯ Vic.LM 1815;
　　　　　　　　　　　in ♭ set *ERB 1815*)
— ARR. ORCH.
　Royale Concert Orch. (in ♯ Roy. 1567)

BITTNER, Jacques (fl. c. 1682)

　SEE: † GUITAR RECITAL II

BIZET, Georges (1838-1875)

CLASSIFIED:　I. Stage Works
　　　　　　II. Inst. & Orchestral
　　　　　　III. Songs

I. STAGE WORKS

(L') ARLÉSIENNE　Inc. Music　1872
Incidental Music (Stage Version)
　Cho. & Orch.—Wolff　in ♯ **D.FAT 173679/80**
　(in a performance of Daudet's play)

Marche des rois　— ARR. SOLO VOICE (& pf.?)
　▽ R. Amade (T) (*Pat.PAE 16*)

Suites Nos. 1 & 2, COMPLETE
Suite No. 1　(ARR. Bizet)
　1. Prelude　　　　2. Minuetto No. 1
　3. Adagietto　　　4. Carillon
Suite No. 2　(ARR. Guiraud)
　5. Pastorale　　　6. Intermezzo
　7. Minuetto No. 2[2]　8. Farandole
　French Nat. Radio.—Cluytens　♯ **C.CX 1153**
　(*Jolie Fille de Perth*) (♯ QCX 10081; Pat. DTX 145;
　　　　　　　　　　　　　　　　Angel. 35048]
　[Nos. 1 & 5 on ♭ *C.SEL 1521: SEBQ 117*]
　Lamoureux—Fournet　　　♯ *Phi.A 00635R*
　[Nos. 2 & 4 on ♭ *Phi.N 402003E*]　(♯ Epic.LC 3018)
　Belgian Radio—André　　♯ **DT.LGX 66021**
　　　　　　　　　　　(♯ T.LE 6509; FT. 320.TC.062)

London Phil. Sym.—Rodzinski
　　　　　　　　　　♯ **West.LAB 7006**
　(*Carmen Suite,* on ♯ Véga. C30.A23)
Philadelphia—Ormandy　　♯ **AmC.ML 5035**
　(*Grieg*) [much cut]　　(Excerpts in ♭ *A 2038*)
Paris Opéra—Cloëz[3]　　　♯ **Od.ODX 139**
　[Nos. 1 & 5 on ♭ *AOE 1017*]
Moscow Radio—Rakhlin　♯ *USSR.D 1109/12*
　☆ Sym. Orch.—Stokowski　　　♯ *G.ALP 1181*
　(*Symphony*) (♯ ItV.A12R 0089; ♭ Vic.set ERB 24;
　　FV.A 9522I/2, 4ss; ♯ *G.FBLP 1045:* No. 2, Adagietto,
　　only in ♯ Vic.LM 1875: ♭ set ERB 52 & ♭ ERA 244)
　☆ Bamberg Sym.—Leitner (♯ *AmD.DL 7538;* Pol. 19034)
　Czech Phil.—Désormière (♯ Sup.LPV 61)
　Vienna Radio—Schönherr (♯ GA. 33-309)
　Hallé & Philharmonia—Sargent (♯ AmC.RL 3051)
　Orch.—Kostelanetz (♯ AmC.CL 739)

Nos. 1, 2, 3, 5, 8
Paris Opéra—Le Conte　　♯ **DCap.CTL 7101**
　(*Fauré*)　　　　　　　(♯ Cap.P 8311)

Nos. 1, 2, 5, 7, 8
Belgian Radio—Marinetti　♯ **Mae.OAT 25005**
　(*Jeux d'enfants, Carmen, etc.*)

Nos. 1, 3, 8
Moscow State Phil.—Ginsburg (*USSR.* 7288/9, 91 & 95)

Suite No. 1
Vienna State Op.—Rossi　　♯ **Nix.PVL 7002**
　(*Carmen, Suite*)　　　(♯ Van.VRS 455; Ama.AVRS 6015)
Austrian Sym.—Koslik　　　♯ **Rem. 199-129**
　(*Nicolai, Mendelssohn*)　　　(& ♭ *REP 131*)
Linz Sym.　　　　　　　in ♯ **Ply. 12-31**
　(*below, & Delibes, Offenbach*)
Berlin Sym.—Rubahn　　　♯ *MusH.LP 5007*
　[No. 3 & 4 only, ♯ Roy. 1530 & ‡ *1859*]
　　　　　　　　(also ♯ *MusH.LP 9012,* perhaps excerpts)
　☆ Orch.—Kostelanetz (♭ *AmC.A 1627*)
… Nos. 1 & 3
　☆ Hallé—Barbirolli (in ♯ *G.WBLP 1004: QBLP 5003;*
　　　　　　　　　　　BB.LBC 1047: ♭ set *WBC 1047*)
… No. 2 only　▽ U.S.S.R. State—Fayer (*USSR.* 5368)

Suite No. 2
Orch.—Graunke　　　　　♯ **MTW. 14**
　(*Saint-Saëns, & J. Strauss*) (♭ set *EP 14*; & ‡ *ACC.MP 18*)
Berlin Sym.—Rubahn　　　♯ **Roy. 1530**
　(*above; & Ippolitoff-Ivanoff*) (♯ *MusH.LP 9012,* perhaps
　　　　　　　　　　　　　　　　　　　excerpts)
　☆ Boston Prom.—Fiedler (♯ Cam.CAL 114 &
　　　　　　　　　　　　　　　　in ♯ set CFL 103)
… No. 6　Linz Sym. (in ♯ Ply. 12-31)
… Nos. 7 & 8 — ARR. BAND
　Brass Band—Mortimer (*Pax.PR 598*)
… No. 7, Minuetto No. 2 — ARR. FL. & HP.　Guiraud
　J. Roberts & E. Vito (in ♯ Per.SPL 721)
… No. 8, Farandole only
　☆ Victor Sym.—Reiner (♭ *G.7ER 5020;* ♭ *Vic.ERA 78*)
　Covent Garden—Braithwaite (in ♯ P.PMC 1020)
　Hallé—Barbirolli (in ♯ *G.QBLP 5003*; ♯ BB.LBC 1047:
　　　　　　　　　　　　　　　　　♭ set *WBC 1047*)
　Col. Sym.—Rodzinski (in ♯ Phi.S 04601L)

CARMEN　Opera　4 Acts　1875
COMPLETE RECORDINGS
Set R　(in *Russian*)
　Carmen　　…　　…　　V. Borisenko (M-S)
　Don José　　…　　…　　G. Nelepp (T)
　Escamillo　…　　…　　Al. Ivanov (B)
　Micaëla　　…　　…　　E. Shumskaya (S)
　etc., Bolshoi Th. Cho. & orch.—Nebolsin
　(8ss)　　　　　　　　♯ **USSR.D 01508/15**
　[Excerpts on ♯ *USSR.D 1527;* USSR. 022658/9, 021972,
　022640, etc.]
Set B　☆ R. Stevens (M-S), L. Albanese (S), etc.
　Shaw Chorale & Victor Sym.—Reiner
　　　　　　　　　　　　♯ **G.ALP 1115/7**
　(also ♮ ArgV.set AR 8011/2, 32ss)　(♯ ItV.C12R 0086/8)
　[Excerpts on ♯ *Vic.LRM 7011:* ♭ set *ERB 7011*]
　☆ Soloists, Cho. & orch. of Opéra-Comique—Cluytens
　　　　　　　　　　　　(♯ *C.VCX 512/4*)
　[Cho: La cloche a sonné; Habanera; Flower Song;
　　& Non! tu ne m'aimes pas, on ♭ *C.SEL 1538;* other
　　excerpts in ♭ *AmC.set A 607*]

(*continued on next page*)

---

[1] The attribution to Binchois dates only from the XVIIIth Century and it is suggested that this is an error for BUSNOIS.
[2] From *La Jolie Fille de Perth,* Act III.　　　　　　[3] Much abbreviated.

CARMEN (continued)

Highlights

C. C. Meyer (M-S), L. Larsen (T), C. v. Beckum (S),
G. Holthaus (B), Cho. & Netherlands Phil. Orch.
—Goehr   ‡ MMS. 2009
[Prelude only in **V**‡ *MMS. 920*]   (also ‡ *OP 4*)

S. Wagner (M-S), R. Schock (T), J. Metternich (B),
L. Otto (S), R. Schaffrian (S) & Berlin Municipal
Orch.—Schüchter *(Ger)*   ‡ G.WDLP 1502
[*See below* for individual excerpts from this collection]

☆ N. Vallin (S), M. Villabella (T), A. Baugé (B)
(Bohème)   ‡ Pat.PCX 5001

☆ S. Juyol (M-S), L. de Luca (T), J. Micheau (S), Opéra-
Comique Cho. & orch.—Wolff   ‡ Lon.LL 1115
(from set) [Excerpts, ‡ *D.LW 5137*]

☆ C. Supervia (M-S), G. Micheletti (T), A. Vavon (S), &
A. Bernadet (S) (‡ Od.ODX 116)

E. Wysor (M-S), A. Herbin (S), G. Utley (T), etc. &
Paris Opéra Cho. & Orch.—Allain
(‡ Ply. 12-52; also ♭ Ply. 10-29)

J. Peebles, R. Jobin, etc. Met. Op. Cho. & orch.
—Pelletier
(‡ Cam.CAL 221, set CFL 101; & in ‡ Cam. CAL 249)

Soloists & La Scala Cho. & Orch.—Questa *(Ital)*·
(‡ Roy. 1850: ♭ set EP 110)

COLLECTION OF ARIAS

Habanera Act I
Séguidille [with V. Bonomo (T)] Act I
Chanson bohème Act II
Air des cartes Act III

S. Couderc (M-S)   ♭ *CA.EPO 5029*
               (♭ *Plé.P 45143*)

COLLECTION OF CHORUSES

Avec la garde montante Act I
Dans l'air Act I
Quant au douanier Act III
A deux cuartos Act IV
Les voici! (March & Cho.) Act IV

Paris Opéra-Comique Cho. & Orch.—Wolff
(from set)   ‡ *D.LW 5183*

ORCHESTRAL SUITES (classified below)

1. Prelude, Act I	2. Entr'acte, Act II
3. Entr'acte, Act III	4. Entr'acte, Act IV
5. Avec la garde montante, Act I	6. Habanera, Act I
7. Danse bohème, Act II	8. Marche des contrebandiers, Act III

Nos. 1-8 complete

St. Louis Sym.—Golschmann ‡ DCap.CTL 7078
(Faust)   (‡ Cap.P 8288; ACap. CLCX 052)
[Excerpts on ♭ *Cap.FAP 8288*]

London Phil. Sym.—Rodzinski
               ‡ West.LAB 7005
(Arlesiana, on ♭ Véga. C30.A23)

☆ N.Y. Stadium Sym.—dell' Isola (‡ *D.UW 333012*)

Nos. 1-4, 5 & 7

☆ Col. Sym.—Beecham   ‡ C.CX 1037
(Tchaikovsky) (‡ QCX 10012: VCX 521; *Excerpts*
in ‡ *AmC.AL 27:* ♭ *A 1640* & ♮ *J 211:* ♭ *J 4-211*)

Nos. 1-4, 5, 7, 8

Vienna State Op.—Rossi   ‡ Nix.PVL 7002
(L'Arlésienne)   (‡ Van.VRS 455; Ama.AVRS 6015)

Nos. 1-4 ("Suite No. 1")

(No. 1, Prelude Act I, is usually divided; some suites appear
also to include No. 8)

N.B.C. Sym.—Toscanini   ‡ *Vic.LRM 7013*
(Thomas)
(♭ set ERB 7013; ‡ FV.A 330207; also in ‡ Vic.set LM 6026)
(2ss, ♭ G.7ERF 116; ♭ ItV.A72R 0009)
(& with *Ponchielli* & *Tchaikovsky,* ‡ G.FALP 220)

L.S.O.—Previtali   ‡ *G.DLP 1064*
(Kodály)   (♮ *B 7035/6*)

Lamoureux—Fournet   ‡ *Phi.S 06021R*
(Patrie)   (*idem, & Albeniz* on ‡ Epic.LC 3068)

Berlin Municipal Op.—Rother ‡ *DT.TM 68019*
               (TV.VE 9033: ♭ UX 4534)

Leipzig Radio—Gerdes   *Eta. 120039/40*

Champs-Elysées Th.—Inghelbrecht
(Gounod)   ‡ *Sel. 270.C.065*

Zagreb Radio Sym. *(Jug.P 16043/4)*
Regent Sym. (in ‡ *Rgt. 7000*)

☆ Vienna Radio—Schönherr (or Nilius?) (in ‡ *GA.33-309*)
Vienna Sym.—Singer (‡ Ply. 12-97; Nos. 1 & 4 only, in
‡ Rem. 199-122; Ply. 12-39, etc.)

[1] Sound track of film *Interrupted Melody.*

Nos. 1, 3, 4

☆ Victor Sym.—Reiner, from set B
             (♭ *G.7ER 5020;* ♭ *Vic.ERA 78*)

Paris Cons.—Lindenberg (♭ *Od.7AO 2007*)

Nos. 2 & 4

☆ Philharmonia—Schüchter (in ‡ *P.PMD 1022:*
            ♭ *BrzMGM.SCA 3502; SpOd.BSOE 4006*)

Nos. 3 & 4

☆ Czech Phil.—Désormière
            (in ‡ *Sup.LPM 225;* ‡ *U. 5204C*)

Orch. Suites (unspecified)

Radio City Music Hall—Paige   ♭ *Vic.ERA 175*
(Faust—Suite)

Netherlands Phil.—Goehr   **V**‡ *MMS. 96*

Belgian Radio—Marinetti   ‡ Mae.OAT 25005
(Arlésienne, Jolie Fille, etc.)

Anon. Orch. (‡ *ACC.MP 12*)

Selections, Fantasias, etc.

— ARR. ORCH.   Kostelanetz "Carmen for Orchestra"
Kostelanetz Orch.   ‡ EPhi.NBL 5003
(‡ Phi.N 02105L; AmC.CL 735,o.n. ML 4826: ♭ *set A 1097;*
Excerpts on ♭ *A 1821* : Prelude only in ‡ *KZ 1*)

— ARR. VLN. & ORCH.   SEE Sarasate

— ARR. PF.   Horowitz
☆ V. Horowitz (♭ *Vic.ERA 74; DV. 26010*)

— ARR. 2 PFS.
☆ A. Chasins & C. Keene
            (♭ *Mer.EP 1-5053;* ♭ *FMer.MEP 14520*)

ACT I

Prelude

Lamoureux—Fournet   in ‡ *Phi.N 00707R*
(Massenet, St.-Saëns, etc.)   (in ‡ Epic.LC 3079)

Boston Orch. Soc.—Page   in ‡ *Nix.SLPY 801*
(Rossini, Mendelssohn, etc.)   (‡ *SOT. 2064*)

☆ Württemberg State Op.—Leitner
            (in PV. 58617 & ‡ *Pol. 45047*)

Paris Opéra—Allain (in ‡ *AFest.CFR 26*)

Avec la garde montante Boys' cho. & soli

☆ R. Jobin (T), J. Thirache (B) & Opéra-Comique Cho.,
from set *(C.LB 146)*

— ARR. ORCH. only
Hamburg Philharmonia—H-J. Walther *(MSB. 78136)*

Dans l'air Cho.

Württemberg State Op.—Leitner *(Ger)*
(below)   PV. 36068

☆ Opéra-Comique Cho.—Cluytens, from set *(C.LB 146)*

Habanera: L'amour est un oiseau rebelle   M-S

S. Michel   in ‡ Pat.DTX 137
(Massenet, Gluck, etc.)

E. Stignani *(Ital)*   C.LX 1578
(Mignon—Connais-tu . . .)   (♭ SCB 111: SCBQ 3010)

T. de Igarzabel *(Ital)*   ♭ ArgOd.BSOA 4006
(Samson et Dalila—Mon cœur . . .)   (in ‡ LDC 517)

E. Höngen *(Ger)*   PV. 36038
(above)

S. Wagner *(Ger)*   G.DB 11570
(Card Scene)   (♭ 7RW 521)

E. Farrell & pf.[1]
            (in ‡ MGM.E 3185: ♭ set X 304: EP 527/8)
D. Eustrati *(Ger) (Eta. 120045)*
I. Dimcheva *(Bulg) (Bulg. 1383)*
A. Kawecka *(Pol) (Muza. 2346)*
K. Szczepánska *(Pol) (Muza.X 1773)*
V. Borisenko *(Russ)* (USSR. 021971)
L. Rudenko *(Russ)* (in ‡ USSR.D 2072)

☆ R. Stevens (BrzV. 886-008)
E. Wysor (in ‡ Ply. 12-47)

⊞ E. Calvé (in ‡ G.FJLP 5004*: QJLP 104*:
            in ‡ Vic. set LCT 6701*)

Parle-moi de ma mère   S & T

P. Alarie & L. Simoneau   in ‡ LT.DTL 93018
(Gounod & Massenet) (‡ West.WL 5358; ‡ Sel. 270.C.008)

☆ J. Micheau & L. de Luca (from set)   ‡ *D.LW 5035*
(Act IV—Finale)   (‡ *Lon.LD 9052*)

☆ L. Albanese & J. Peerce (from set)
            (in ‡ Vic. LRM 7020: ♭ set ERB 7020)
A. Schlemm & R. Schock *(Ger)* (♭ G.7RW 531)

⊞ L. Marsh & J. McCormack (in ‡ Vic. set LCT 6701*)
L. Bori & M. Fleta (AF.AGSB 58*)

Séguedille: Près des ramparts de Séville   M-S
K. Meyer   in ♯ **G.ALPC 1**
(Bartered Bride, Barbiere, etc.)
   E. Farrell [& W. Olvis][1]
     (in ♯ *MGM.E 3185*: ♭ *set X 304*: ♭ *EP 527/8*)
   ⧓ M. Gay *(AF.AGSA 17*)*

ACT II

Danse bohème et Chanson bohème
— ARR. ORCH.   Hamburg Philharmonia   *(MSB. 78136)*

Chanson bohème   M-S
V. Borisenko   *(Russ)*   in ♯ *USSR.D 1593*
   ☆ S. Onegin (in ♯ *Sca. 821*)

Chanson du Toreador: Votre toast   B & Cho.
M. Dens   in ♯ *Pat.DT 1020*
(Pagliacci, Tannhäuser, etc.)
J. Metternich, L. Otto (S), R. Schaffrian (S),
   D. Eustrati (A), & Cho. *(Ger)*[2]   **G.DB 11548**
(Pagliacci—Prologue)   *(♭ 7RW 505)*
A. Sved   in ♯ **Sup.LPV 207**
(Handel, Gluck, Verdi, etc.) (♯ *U. 5191G*; also,
               Qual.MN 1017)
F. Valentino   in ♯ **Roy. 1585**
H. Uhde, Ens. & Cho. *(Ger)*[2]   **PV. 36085**
(Rigoletto—Cortigiani)   *(♭ Pol. 32077)*
   H. Thompson (in ♯ *MH. 33-104*)
   L. Jambor *(Hung)* *(Qual.KM 5009)*
   ☆ R. Merrill & Ens., set B   in ♯ *Vic.LM 1847*
   L. Warren   ♭ *Vic.ERA 114*
   L. Tibbett   in ♯ *Cam.CAL 171*
   C. Tagliabue *(Ital)*   Orf. 54003
   P. Silveri *(Ital)*   ♭ *C.SCB 107: SCBQ 3007*
   H M. Sammarco *(Ital)*   ♯ *HRS. 1069**
   J. Mardones *(Ital)*   in ♯ *SBDH.LPP 3**
   G. Campanari   in ♯ *FRP 2**

Nous avons en tête une affaire   M-S, S, S, T, B
   H G. Lejeune, M. Duchêne, S. Dumesnil, M. Leroux &
     C. Gilibert *(AF.AGSB 73*)*

Je vais danser en votre honneur   M-S & T
   H G. Farrar & G. Martinelli *(AF.AGSB 51*)*

Air de la fleur: La fleur que tu m'avais jetée   T
R. Tucker   in ♯ **AmC.ML 4750**
F. Vroons   in ♯ *Phi.N 00706R*
G. Burris   in ♯ **PRCC. 2**
   J. McCracken (in ♯ *Roy. 1595*)
   E. Rösler *(Qual.KM 5013)*
   G. Nelepp *(Russ)* (in ♯ *USSR.D 2074*)
   A. Frinberg *(Latv)* (in ♯ *USSR.D 1900*)
   ☆ J. Björling
     (in ♯ *G.BLP 1055*; ♯ *Vic.LM 1839;FV.A 630259*)
   G. Thill (in ♯ *C.FH 503*)
   M. Lanza (in ♯ *G.ALP 1202*)
   E. Conley (♭ *Lon.REP 8005*)
   R. Schock *(Ger)* (in ♯ *G.WBLP 1501*: ♭ *7RW 509*)
   H. Roswaenge *(Ger)*
     (♭ *D.DK 23188*; also, o.v., in ♯ *CEd. 7010*)
   H C. Vezzani (in ♯ *Od.ODX 126**)
   G. Martinelli (in ♯ *SBDH.LPG 4**)
   (Ital) E. Caruso (♭ *Vic.ERAT 7**; in ♯ *G.FJLP 5009**:
                        *QJLP 105**)
   F. de Lucia (in ♯ *CEd. set 7002**)
   (Eng) J. McCormack (in ♯ *Ete. 496**; ♯ *Cum.CE 185**;
                      & in ♯ *Roy. 1555**)

ACT III

Entr'acte (Prelude)   orch.
Écoute, compagnons   cho.   — ARR. ORCH.
   Hamburg Philharmonia—H-J. Walther
                       MSB. 78137

Notre métier est bon   M-S, S, S, T, T, B
   H M. Duchêne, G. Lejeune, S. Dumesnil, D. Devriès,
     M. Leroux, C. Gilibert *(AF.AGSA 17*)*

Mêlons! Coupons!   M-S, S, S
(Trio des cartes: Card Scene)
S. Wagner (A), L. Otto & R. Schaffrian *(Ger)*
                    G.DB 11570
(Habanera)   *(♭ 7RW 521)*

En vain pour éviter (Air des Cartes)   M-S
M. v. Ilosvay *(Ger)*   ♯ *Phi.N 12079G*
(Mignon—Connais-tu le pays)   (in ♯ *N 00649R*)
Z. Palii   in ♯ **Sup.LPV 207**
(Handel, Gluck, Verdi, etc.)   *(♯ U. 5191G)*
   K. Szczepánska *(Pol)*   Muza.X 1773
   L. Rudenko *(Russ)*   in ♯ *USSR.D 2022*
   ☆ E. Wysor   in ♯ *Ply. 12-47*
   M. Garden   in ♯ *Vic. set LCT 6701*
   H E. Calvé   V♯ *Rar.M 317**; in ♯ *B & B. 3**
                      & *IRCC. 3119**
   Bressler-Gianoli   in ♯ *FRP. 3**

Je dis que rien ne m'épouvante   S
(Micaëla's Aria)
D. Kirsten   in ♯ **AmC.ML 4730**
M. Angelici   in ♯ **G.FBLP 1051**
P. Alarie   in ♯ *Phi.N 00663R*
(Gounod, Delibes, etc.)   *(♭ N 402005E)*
M. Minazzi *(Ital)*   **Cet.PE 173**
(Louise—Depuis le jour)
E. Rizzieri *(Ital)*   **Cet.BB 20545**
(Puccini: La Rondine—Ora dolci)
   D. Seremak *(Pol)* *(Muza.X 2187)*
   ☆ L. Albanese, from set B
             (in ♯ *Vic.LRM 7020*: ♭ *set ERB 7020*)
   S. Danco (D.K 23302: Z 974)
   E. Shumshaya *(Russ)* *(USSRM.D 00848)*
   H E. Eames *(AF.AGSB 60**)*

Je suis Escamillo   T & B
   H M. Dalmores & M. Journet *(AF.AGSB 19**)*

ACT IV

Entr'acte (Prelude)   "Aragonaise"
Philharmonia—Karajan   in ♯ **C.CX 1265**
(Contes d'Hoffmann, Thais, Hary Janos, etc.)
     (in ♯ *Angel. 35207*; *C.QCX 10150: FCX 407*)
Bolshoi Th.—Golovanov *(USSR. 14657)*

Les voici!   Cho.
Berlin Comic Op. Cho.—Lange   *Eta. 120045*
(Habanera) *(Ger)*

Si tu m'aimes   M-S, B, T
… M-S & B parts only
   H M. Matzenauer & P. Amato (in ♯ *Vic. set LCT 6701**)

C'est toi? C'est moi M-S & T   (Final Duet)
P. Alarie & L. Simoneau   ♯ **LT.DTL 93018**
(Gounod & Massenet) (♯ *West.WL 5358*; ♯ *Sel. 270.C.008*)
   ☆ S. Juyol & L. de Luca   ♯ *D.LW 5035*
   (Duet, Act 1) (from set)   *(♯ Lon.LD 9052)*
   V. Borisenko & G. Nelepp *(Russ)* *(USSR. 022826/7)*
   ☆ R. Stevens & J. Peerce, from set B (♭ *Vic.ERA 211*)
   B. Kemp & T. Pattiera *(Ger)* (in ♯ *Ete. 494*)

"Carmen Jones"   Musical play ARR. from Bizet's
   music by Oscar Hammerstein
Film Sound-track   ♯ **G.CLP 1034**
[Excerpts on ♭ *Vic. set ERA 233*] (♯ *Vic.LM 1881*:
                      ♭ *set ERC 1881*)
Broadway Cast   ♯ **B.LAT 8057**
(♯ *AmD.DL 9021 & 8014*)   *(♭ AmD. set ED 904)*

DJAMILEH   Opéra-comique   1 Act   1872
Overture
Linz Sym.   in ♯ **Ply. 12-31**
(Arlésienne; & Delibes, Offenbach)

J'aime l'amour   T
F. Gatto & pf.   ♭ *Plé.P 45135*
(in Song collection, below)

(La) JOLIE FILLE DE PERTH   4 Acts   1867
Orch. Suite
Prelude; Aubade, Sérénade, Marche, Danse bohémienne (Act II)
Paris Cons.—Lindenberg[3]   ♯ **D.LXT 2860**
(Jeux d'enfants; & Chabrier)   *(♯ Lon.LL 871)*
French Nat. Radio—Cluytens[3]   ♯ **C.CX 1153**
(Arlésienne) *(QCX 10081; Pat.DTX 145:* ♭ *ED 50;*
                         ♯ *Angel. 35048)*

(continued on next page)

---

[1] Sound track, *Interrupted Melody*.   [2] A more extended version of the scene.   [3] Omits *Aubade*.

(La) JOLIE FILLE DE PERTH: Suite (*continued*)

... **Danse bohémienne** only
    Belgian Radio—Marinetti (in ♯ Mae.OAT 25005)
    Bolshoi Th.—Nebolsin (*USSR. 9648*)

    ☆ Victor Sym.—Reiner (♭ *G.7ER 5020;* ♭ *Vic.ERA 78*)
    Covent Garden—Braithwaite (in ♯ P.PMC 1020;
                              Od.ODX 146)
    Orch.—Kostelanetz (in ♯ AmC.CL 739)

Sérénade: À la voix ... T Act II
— ARR. CHO. Kirkintilloch Junior Cho. (*Eng*) (*P.R 3992*)
— ARR. BAND. All Star Brass Band (*Pax.PR 634*)

Quand la flamme de l'amour B Act II
    ♮ C. Gilibert (AF.AGSB 73*)

Ah! Écho, viens sur l'air embaumé S Act IV
    ♮ S. Kurz (*Ital*) (in ♯ Sca. 817*)

Rêve de la Bien-aimée[1]   S
    V. Mauret, J. Zayde (pf.)   in ♯ *Asty. 100*

(Les) PÊCHEURS DE PERLES 3 Acts 1863
COMPLETE RECORDINGS

Casts		Set A	Set B
Leila	...	P. Alarie (S)	M. Angelici (S)
Nadir	...	L. Simoneau (T)	H. Legay (T)
Zurga	...	R. Bianco (B)	M. Dens (B)
Nourabad	...	X. Depraz (Bs)	L. Noguéra (Bs)
etc.			

Set A with E. Brasseur Cho. & Lamoureux Orch.
    —Fournet   **♯ Phi.A 00188/9L**
    (4ss)   (♯ Epic. set SC 6002)

Set B with Opéra-Comique Cho. & orch.
    —Cluytens   **♯ C.CX 1232/3**
    (4ss)   (♯ FCX 344/5; Angel. 35174/5, set 3524)

Set R: N. Kazantseva, S. Lemeshev, V. Zacharov,
    T. Antonenko, Bolshoi Theatre Cho. & orch.
    —Bron (*Russ*) (6ss)   **♯ USSR.D 02133/8**
    [Excerpts on *USSRM.D 1342*, USSR. *020593/4, 19593/4,*
                                etc.]

    ☆ Soloists, Paris Phil. Cho. & Orch.—Leibowitz
    (♯ Per. set SX 205, 4ss; Cpt. set MCM 120005;
        Highlights on ♯ *MMS.* set OP 15, 4ss)

EXCERPTS

Au fond du temple saint (Act I) T & B
Me voilà seul ... Comme autrefois (Act I) S
Leila ... Dieu, puissant, le voilà (Act II) S & T
    J. Micheau (S), L. de Luca (T), J. Borthayre (B)
    & Paris Cons. Orch.—Erede   ♯ **D.LXT 2789**
    (*Gounod: Mireille, excerpts*)   (♯ Lon.LL 939)

ACT I

Au fond du temple saint   T & B
    J. van Haagen & G. Genemans   *Phi.P 17478H*
    (*below*)
    ☆ J. Björling & R. Merrill   in ♯ *G.BLP 1053*
                    (♭ *7RQ 3008;* Vic.ERA 134)
    ☆ B. Gigli & G. de Luca (*Ital*) (♭ *Vic.ERAT 10*)
    ♮ B. Gigli & A. Pacini (*Ital*) (in ♯ *SBDH.LPP 3*)

À cette voix ... Je crois entendre encore T
    N. Gedda   **C.LX 1614**
    (*Manon—En fermant les yeux*)   (♭ *SCB 118*)
        (in ♯ CX/WCX 1130: FCX 302; ♯ Angel. 35096)
    H. Legay   **C.LFX 1031**
    (*Manon—En fermant les yeux*)   (♭ *SCBF 111*)
    B. Gigli (*Ital*)[2]   **AF.AGSB 56**
    (*Bohème—O Mimi*)   (in ♯ *G.FJLP 5039*)
    J. van Haagen   *Phi.P 17478H*
    (*above*)
    J. Traxel (*Ger*)   ♭ *Pol. 32030*
    (*Faust—Salut demeure*)
        G. Pishchaev (*Russ*) (USSR. 021804)
        B. Paprocki (*Pol*) (*Muza.* 2457)
    ☆ R. Crooks (*Ital*) (in ♯ Cam.CAL 129)
    ♮ E. Caruso (in ♯ *G.FJLP 5009*: QJLP 105*;
                     ♭ *Vic.ERAT 7*)
    F. de Lucia (*Ital*) (in ♯ Sca. 814* & ♯ CEd. set 7002*)

O dieu Brahma!   S & Cho.
    ☆ T. dal Monte & cho. (*Ital*) (in ♯ G.QALP 10089)

[1] No. 3 of Supplement to the score.

ACT II

Me voilà seule ...
Comme autrefois dans la nuit sombre S
    P. Alarie   in ♯ *Phi.N 00663R*
    (*Gounod, Delibes, etc.*)   (♭ *N 402005E*)
    R. Carteri (*Ital*)   **Cet.CB 20543**
    (*Otello—Ave Maria*)
    G. Arnaldi (*Ital*)   **Cet.PE 192**
    (*Louise—Depuis le jour*)
    I. F. Gasperoni (*Ital*)   **Cet.PE 202**
    (*Proch: Theme & Variations*)
    R. Scotto (*Ital*)   **Cet.PE 205**
    (*Traviata—Addio del passato*)

De mon amie fleur endormie (*Serenade*) T
    C. Zampighi (*Ital*)   in ♯ *G.QALP 10081*
    (*below*)
    F. Gatto & pf.   ♭ *Plé.P 45136*
    (in Song collection, *below*)

Par cet étroit sentier (Love Duet) S & T
    M. Carosio & C. Zampighi (*Ital*)
                    ♯ *G.QALP 10081*
    (*above; Manon, Lucia, Amico Fritz*)

... Ton cœur n'a pas compris
    ♮ G. Huguet & F. de Lucia (*Ital*) (in ♯ Sca. 814* & in
                             ♯ CEd. set 7002*)

ACT III

L'Orage s'est calmé   B
    M. Singher   in ♯ Roy. 1613
    (*Samson & Dalila, Louise, etc.*)

II. INSTRUMENTAL & ORCHESTRAL

JEUX D'ENFANTS, Op. 22 pf. duet
[Orchestral version by Bizet & Kopyloff; numbers vary
as shown in brackets]

1.   L'Escarpolette, rêverie
2.   La Toupie, impromptu
3.   La Poupée, berceuse
4.   Les Chevaux de bois, scherzo
5.   Le Volant, fantaisie
6.   Trompette et Tambour, marche
7.   [—] Les Balles de savon, rondino
8.   [8] Les Quatre Coins, esquisse
9.   [7] Collin-Maillard, nocturne
10. [—] Saute-mouton, caprice
11. [9] Petit mari, petite femme, duo
12. [10] Le Bal, galop

PIANO DUET VERSION
    S. Bianca & F. Takakjian   *MSB. 78008/9*
    (7ss—*Gretchaninoff: Pf. pieces, Op. 198*) & *78209/10*

... **Nos. 2, 6, 9, 11, 12**
    K. U. & H. Schnabel   ♯ *Phi.S 06046R*
    (*Schubert*)

... **Nos. 1-6, 10, 12** (with narration)
    J. Anderson (narrator), J. & K. Wentworth
    (4ss)   *AmC.J 248/9*

ORCH. VERSION (orch. nos.)
... **Nos. 6, 3, 2, 9, 10** (*Petite Suite,* orch. Bizet)
    Paris Cons.—Lindenberg   ♯ **D.LXT 2860**
    (*Jolie Fille Suite; & Chabrier*)   (♯ Lon.LL 871)
    Moscow Radio—Samosud   ♯ *USSR.D 1704*
    (*Debussy: Nocturne*) [Nos. 2, 6, 10 on *USSR.* 22625/6]
    ☆ Covent Garden—Braithwaite   in ♯ P.PMC 1020
                           (♯ Od.ODX 146)
    Olympia—Saike (♯ Allo. 3070)
... **Nos. 2, 6, 10** Moscow Radio—Samosud (*USSR.* 22625/6)
... **Nos. 3, 9, 10**
    Leighton Lucas Orch. (EMI.EPX 16, 76 & EP 21)
... **Nos. 2, 3, 6, 10**
    Belgian Radio—Marinetti (in ♯ Mae.OAT 25005)
... **No. 10** Sym.—Straszynsky (*Muza.* 1744)

Patrie, Overture, Op. 19 (to Sardou's play) orch.
                                      1874
    French Nat. Radio—Cluytens   ♯ **C.CX 1173**
    (*below*)   (♯ QCX 10110: FCX 273; ♯ Angel. 35119)

[2] Recorded 1929.

Patrie, Overture, Op. 19 (*continued*)
Lamoureux—Fournet   ♯ *Phi.S 06021R*
(*Carmen Suite*)
(*idem & Albeniz on* ♯ Epic.LC 3068)

Suisse Romande—Ansermet   ♯ **D.LXT 5030**
(*below*)   (♯ Lon.LL 1186)

Netherlands Phil.—Hausdörfer   ♯ **CHS.H 13**
(*below*)

Roma, Suite orch. 1866-8
Netherlands Phil.—Hausdörfer   ♯ **CHS.H 13**
(*above*)

"Philharmonic"—Berendt   ♯ **Allo. 3051**
     (4ss ♭ *MusH.LP 1080/1*)
Anon. Orch. (♯ Gram. 2082)

... **Nos. 2, Scherzo; 3, Andante; & 4, Carnaval**[1]
N.Y. City Ballet—Barzin
(*Chabrier*)   ♯ **E. & AmVox.PL 9320**

Symphony, C major orch. 1855
Suisse Romande—Ansermet   ♯ **D.LXT 5030**
(*above*) (2ss, ♯ *D.LX 3128*)   (♯ Lon.LL 1186)

French Nat. Radio—Cluytens   ♯ **C.CX 1173**
(*above*) (QCX 10110: FCX 273; Angel. 35119; & MApp.
     n.d.)

French Radio Sym.—Leibowitz ♯ **Oce.OCS 33**
(*Schubert: Symphony No. 1*)   (♯ Nix.OLP 7035)[2]

☆ Sym.—Stokowski   ♯ **G.ALP 1181**
(*Arlésienne*)   (♯ ItV.A12R 0089; ♯ *G.FBLP 1037*, 2ss)

☆ Paris Cons.—Allain (♯ Cum.CR 238)
L.P.O.—Goehr (♯ Cam.CAL 193 & in set CFL 102)
N.Y.P.S.O.—Rodzinski (♯ AmC.RL 6629)

Variations chromatiques pf. 1868
H. Boschi   **V**♯ *CdM.LDY 8069*
(*Emmanuel*)

III. SONGS

COLLECTION
Agnus Dei[3] (in Latin) 1872   (g)
Douce mer (Lamartine) 1866   (c)
Adieu de l'hôtesse arabe, Op. 21, No. 4 (Hugo) (c)
J'aime l'amour[4] (Gallet)   (g) ♭ *Plé.P 45135*

(Le) Matin[3] (unid.)   (g)
(La) Chanson du fou (Hugo) 1868   (c)
Berceuse (Desbordes-Valmore) 1868   (c)
Sérénade[5] (Carré)   (g) ♭ *Plé.P 45136*

Ouvre ton cœur (Boléro) (Delâtre) 1837 (g)
Pastorale (Régnard) 1868   (d)
Chanson d'avril, Op. 21, No. 1 (Bouilhet)(d)
Vieille chanson (Millevoye)   (d) ♭ *Plé.P 45137*

R. Doria (S), S. Couderc (M-S), F. Gatto (T),
H. Cox, G. Grisoli & S. Gouat (pfs.)
[(d) by Doria; (c) by Couderc; (g) by Gatto]

Agnus Dei (to Intermezzo from l'Arlésienne)
H. Pelayo (B)   in ♯ **SMC. 1003**

R. Schock (T), cho. & orch.   **G.EG 8158**
(*Gounod: Ave Maria*)   (♭ *7MW 618*)

M. Maurene (S), J. Ullern (org.)   *Sat.S 1142*
(*Stradella: Ave verum corpus*)
G. Jónsson (B) & cho. (G.DB 30007)
☆ R. Tauber (T) (in ♯ AmD.DL 7535)
G. Thill (T) (in ♯ C.FH 504)
B. Gigli (T) (♭ *G.7EB 6013: 7ERQ 134*)
H. Schlusnus (B) (♭ *Pol. 30151*)

— ARR. DUET
R. Ponselle (S) & C. Ponselle (S)[6]   Pte. rec.
(*Franck & Schubert*)   (& ♯ *Pte.*)

— ARR. ORGAN
J. Perceval (ArgOd. 66027)
C. Cronham (*Mjr. 5140*)

Chanson d'avril, Op. 21, No. 1 (Bouilhet)
M. Sénéchal (T), J. Bonneau (pf.)
     in ♯ *Phi.N 00681R*
(*Lalo, Chausson, Chabrier, etc.*)

C. Devos (T), G. Lecompte (pf.)   **Pat.PDT 283**
(*Lalo, Gounod, Massenet*)   (♭ *D 111*)

Ouvre ton cœur (Boléro) (Delâtre) 1887
N. Merriman (M-S), G. Moore (pf.)
     in ♯ **C.CX 1213**
(*Debussy, Bachelet, Fauré, etc.*)   (♯ Angel. 35217)

— ARR. GUITAR (*Sérénade espagnole*)
L. Almeida (in ♯ Crl. 56049)

Vieille chanson: Dans les bois (Millevoye) *c.* 1865
V. Mauret (S), J. Zayde (pf.)   in ♯ *Asty. 100*

BLACHER, Boris (b. 1903)

Studie in Pianissimo, Op. 45 orch. f.p.1954
Louisville—Whitney   ♯ **LO. 7**
(*Persichetti & Sanders*)

Variations on a theme of Paganini, Op. 26 orch.
☆ R.I.A.S. Sym.—Fricsay   ♯ **AmD.DL 9769**
(*Einem, Fortner, Hartmann, Liebermann*)
(*Bartók on* ♯ *Pol. 16054*)

PARTSONG (unid.)
Justav, erobere nischt in *Eta. 10/55*

BLANCHARD, Esprit Joseph Antoine (1696-1770)

SEE: † MUSIQUES À LA CHAPELLE DU ROY

BLAVET, Michel (1700-1768)

CONCERTO, A minor, fl. & str. orch.
   (MS. State Library, Karlsruhe)
J-P. Rampal & Ens.—Paillard ♯ *Era.LDE 2009*
(*Leclair: Concerto*)

(Le) JALOUX CORRIGÉ Opéra-bouffon, 1 Act
                       1752
COMPLETE RECORDING, ed. Paillard

M. Hazon	A. Vessières (Bs)
Mme. Hazon	D. Monteil (S)
Suzon	H. Prudhon (S)

& J-M. Leclair Inst. Ens.—Paillard
     ♯ **Era.LDE 3021**
[A-M. Beckensteiner, hpsi.]

NOTE: The Overture, recitative, divertissement and vaudeville
only are by Blavet; the Arias are borrowed, 4 from *La
Serva Padrona* (Pergolesi); 4 from *Il Giocatore* (1752),
attributed to Anon., G. M. Orlandini, G. M. Buini and
A. Caroli; & 2 from *Il Maestro di Musica*, attrib. to
Galuppi & Capelli.

BLISS, Sir Arthur (b. 1891)

(7) American Poems 1940
Gone, gone again is summer (E. St. V. Millay)
Siege; Feast (Millay)
Little Elegy (E. Wylie)
Rain comes down (Millay)
Fair Annet's song (Wylie)
Being young and green (Millay)
▽ J. Fraser (A), G. Moore (pf.)   *G.JH 69/70*
     (British Council pte. rec.)

Concerto, piano & orch., B flat major 1939
☆ N. Mewton-Wood & Utrecht Sym.—Goehr
     (♯ Nix.CLP 1167)

(A) GARLAND FOR THE QUEEN 1953
   (with V. Williams, Tippett, etc.)
... **Aubade** (Reed)
E. Suddaby & M. Field-Hyde (SS) & Cambridge
Univ. Madrigal Soc.—Ord in † ♯ **C.CX 1063**

---

[1] ARR. for Balanchine's ballet, 1954.   [2] Announced but not issued.
[3] Melody from *L'Arlésienne*. Probably not Bizet's arr.   [4] From *Djamileh*.
[5] From *Les Pêcheurs de Perles*.
[6] It is not clear whether C. Ponselle does in fact sing, or if she is only accompanying: or possibly two versions may differ.

73

MIRACLE IN THE GORBALS   Ballet   1944
...Orchestral Suite
    Philharmonia—Bliss   # C.CX 1205
    (below)   (# Angel. 35136)

Music for Strings   1935
    Philharmonia—Bliss   # C.CX 1205
    (above)   (# Angel. 35136)

Sonata   pf.   1927
    C. Lythgoe   # CA.LPA 1075
    (Fergusson)

Welcome the Queen[1]   orch.   1954
    Philharmonia—Bliss   C.DX 1912
                   (ArgOd. 266701)

BLITHEMAN, William (d. 1591)
    SEE: † Masters of Early English Keyboard Music

BLOCH, André (b. 1873)

Concerto-ballet   pf. & orch.   1943   (f.p. 1946)
    S. Bianca & Hamburg Philharmonia
    —H-J. Walther   # MGM.E 3178
    (Massenet)

Goguenardises   bsn. & pf.   1954
    M. Allard & F. Gobet   ♭ *Pat.G 1055*
    (Bitsch: Passepied; & Oubradous, Lavagne, etc.)

BLOCH, Ernest (b. 1880)

Baal Shem   vln. & pf.   1923
    (3 Pictures of Chassidic life)
    ☆ J. Szigeti & A. Foldes[2]   # AmC.ML 4679
    (Vln. Concerto)
    ... No. 2, Nigun   *(Improvisation)*
    N. Milstein & C. Bussotti   in # DCap.CTL 7058
                     (in # Cap.P 8259)
    I. Haendel & G. Moore   ♭ *G.7EP 7011*
    (Tartini: Andante & Presto) (♭ 7EPQ 525: in # CLP 1021)
    —— ARR. VLC. & PF.
    P. Fournier & E. Lush   in # D.LXT 2766
    (Bach, Fauré, Debussy, etc.)   (# Lon.LL 700)

Concerto, vln. & orch.   A minor   1938
    ☆ J. Szigeti & Paris Cons.—Münch   # AmC.ML 4679
    (Baal Shem)

Concerto Grosso, Str. Orch. & pf.   1928
    Pittsburgh Sym.—Steinberg   # DCap.CTL 7039
    (Schuman: Symphony for Strings)   [H. Franklin (pf.)]
             (# Cap.S 8212; & PFCM.CB 153)
    [1st movt. only in # Cap.SAL 9020]
    ☆ Chicago Sym.—Kubelik & G. Schick   # Mer.MG 50027
    (Hindemith)   *(Bartók, on # G.FALP 291)*

(10) Enfantines   pf.   1923
    M. Pressler   in # MGM.E 3010

(4) Episodes   pf. & cha. orch.   1926
    W. Masselos & Knickerbocker Cha. Players—
    I. Solomon   # *MGM.E 290*
    (Britten)
    ☆ Zürich Radio—Scherman (# CHS.CHS 1238)

From Jewish Life   vlc. & pf.   1925
    ... No. 1, Prayer
    P. Olevsky & G. Silfies   in # McInt.MM 103
    (Falla, Frescobaldi, etc.)
    A. Janigro & E. Bagnoli   in # West.WN 18004
    (Tartini, Popper, Granados, etc.)

(3) Poems of the sea   pf.   1922-4
    J. Rappaport   # Etu.ER 101
    (Bartók, Kabalevsky, Hindemith)
    M. Tipo   # Cpt.MC 20020
    (Rameau, R. Strauss, Schumann)

(3) Poèmes juifs   orch.   1913
    ☆ A.R.S. Orch.—Hendl   *(Powell & Mason)*   # ARS. 113

QUARTETS, String

No. 1	1916	LXT 5071
No. 2	1945	LXT 5072
No. 3	1951-2	LXT 5073
No. 4	1953	LXT 5073

    Griller Qtt.   # D.LXT 5071/3
    (6ss)   (# Lon. 1125/7, set LLA 23)

No. 2   1945
    Hirsch Qtt.   # Argo.RG 7
    (Wolf: Italian Serenade)   (o.n. ARS 1011)
    Musical Arts Qtt.   # Van.VRS 437

No. 3   1951-2
    Griller Qtt.   (o.v.?)   # D.LM 4558
                   (# Lon.LS 840)

Quintet, pf. & str., C major   1924
    J. Harris & Walden Qtt.   # MGM.E 3239

Schelomo   vlc. & orch.   1915
    Z. Nelsova & L.P.O.—Ansermet # D.LXT 5052
    (below)   (# Lon.LL 1232)
    A. Janigro & London Phil. Sym.—Rodzinski
    (Bruch)   # West.WN 18007
    ☆ T. Machula & Residentie—Otterloo   # Epic.LC 3072
    (Lalo)   (2ss, # Phi.S 06030R)
    ☆ E. Feuermann & Philadelphia—Stokowski
                   (in # Cam.CAL 254)

Sonata, pf.   1935
    ▽ ☆ R. Cumming   *(Cumming)*   # ML. 7015

Sonata, No. 1, vln. & pf.   1920
    J. Heifetz & E. Bay   # Vic.LM 1861
    (Handel & Schubert)
    L. Kaufman & P. Pozzi   # CHS.H 18
    (Bernstein & Milhaud)

Voice in the Wilderness   vlc. & orch. [or pf.]   1936
    Z. Nelsova & L.P.O.—Ansermet   #D.LXT 5062
    (above)   (# Lon.LL 1232)

BLODEK, Vilem František (1834-1874)

Concerto, D major, flute & orch.   1863
    ☆ K. Hanžl, Prague Radio—Smetáček # Csm.CLPS 1047
    (Vivaldi, Leo, Busoni)   (Ševčík on # Sup.LPM 197)

BLOMDAHL, Karl Birger (b. 1916)

Pastoral Suite   Str. orch.   1948
    Stockholm Radio—Frykberg   # LI.TW 91091
    (Fernström & Larsson)

BLONDEL DE NESLES (XIIth Cent.)

    SEE: † Anthologie Sonore
          † French Troubadour Songs

BLOW, John (1649-1708)

(2) Corants   (Egerton MS., British Museum)
    T. Dart (hpsi.)   in # LOL.OL 50075
    († Masters of Early English Keyboard Music)

I'll tell my mother[3]
Ring the bells[4]
    Glee Singers—Bath   in # Allo. 3046
    († More Catches & Glees)

Magnificat, G major[5]   4 vv
    Westminster Abbey Cho.—McKie   C.LX 1607
    (Purcell: O Lord God of Hosts) [† Eng. Chu. Music IV]

Ode on the death of Henry Purcell   (Dryden)   1696
    R. Oberlin & C. Bressler (C-Ts) & N.Y. Pro
       Musica Antiqua Ens.   # Eso.ES 519
    (Purcell)   (# Cpt.MC 20055)

---

[1] From the film of the Commonwealth tour.
[2] *Sub nom.* A. Farkas.
[3] From *New Ayres & Dialogues*, 1678.
[4] From *Pleasant Musical Companion*, Bk. II, 1701.
[5] Transposed to A; ed. H. Watkins Shaw.

O Lord God of my salvation   Anthem 8 vv.
St. Paul's Cath. Cho.—Dykes Bower C.LX 1565
(*Child: Sing we merrily*)
(† English Church Music, Vol. III)

VENUS AND ADONIS   Opera   Prol. & 3 Acts
                                                      c. 1684
COMPLETE RECORDING
☆ M. Ritchie (S), M. Field-Hyde (S), E. Cooper (S),
   G. Clinton (B), cho. & orch.—Lewis
                                                  ♯ LOL.OL 50004

Lesson Scene   M-S, S, cho.
N. Evans, M. Studholme, Mary Datchelor
School Cho., etc.   G.HMS 49
(† History of Music in Sound)   (in ♯ Vic. set LM 6030)

BOCCHERINI, Luigi (1743-1805)

NOTE: The Opus Nos. quoted for the published works
are those used by the *publishers*. In the case of unpublished or recently published works, where the
composer's *own* Op. Nos. are used, these are indicated
(b).

(La) CLEMENTINA   "Opera or Melodrama"
                                                   (f.p. 1786)
Ahimè, cuor mio, Act I   S
E. Rizzieri   Cet.CB 20544
(*Pergolesi: La Contadina Astuta, aria*)

Concerto, B flat major   vlc. & orch.
(A synthetic work, compiled by F. Grützmacher; *see*
WERM, p. 747)
P. Fournier & Stuttgart Cha.—Münchinger
                                                  ♯ D.LXT 2968
(*Haydn: Concerto*)   (♯ Lon.LL 1036)
(*Couperin & Vivaldi* on ♯ D.LXT 2765; ♯ Lon.LL 687)

J. Starker & Castle Hill Fest.—Pilzer
                                                  ♯ Per.SPL 579
(*Mozart: Horn Concerto, K447*, ARR.) (♯ ANix.PLP 579;
                                                  Cpt.MC 20057)

☆ A. Janigro & Vienna State Op.—Prohaska
(*Haydn*)   ♯ Nix.WLP 5126

Concerto, D major, Op. 27   fl. & str. orch.
                                                   (doubtful)
C. Wanausek & Vienna Pro Musica—Adler
                                                  ♯ AmVox.PL 9440
(*Gluck & Pergolesi*)

Overture, D major, Op. 43   1790
Royal Phil.—Beecham   ♯ AmC.ML 5029
(*Beethoven, Brahms, Méhul, Grétry*)

QUARTETS, 2 vlns., vla., vlc.
COLLECTION
B flat major, Op. 1, No. 2   1761
E flat major, Op. 40, No. 2   1796
E flat major, Op. 58, No. 2   1799
B minor, Op. 58, No. 4   1799
New Music Qtt.   ♯ AmC.ML 5047

D major, Op. 6, No. 1   1769
☆ I.C.B.S. Qtt.   (*Corelli & Gambini*)   ♯ MV.VT 51

D minor, Op. 10, No. 2   1770
☆ Guilet Qtt. (♯ Clc. 6205)

G minor, Op. 33, No. 5   1781
Frye Cha. Music Group   ♯ Lind.LP 1007
(*Mozart*)
☆ Guilet Qtt. (♯ Clc. 6205)

A major, Op. 39, No. 8   (Bk. III-2) 1787
E flat major, Op. 58, No. 2   1799
(Labelled Op. 39, No. 3, & Op. 58, No. 3 respectively)
Italian Qtt.   ♯ C.CX 1101
               (♯ C.QCX 10024: FCX 262; Angel. 35062)

QUINTETS, String   2 vlns., vla., 2 vlcs.   1771
D major, Op. 12, No. 4   1771
... Pastorale only
☆ Virtuosi di Roma—Fasano   in ♯ B.AXTL 1032
   (*Torelli, Corelli, etc.*)   (♯ D.UAT 273551; Fnt.LP 3004)

E major, Op. 13, No. 5
... Tempo di Minuetto
Bartels Ens.   MSB. 78019
(*Tchaikovsky: Qtt. No. 1—Andante cantabile*)

— — ARR. STR. QTT.
Pessina Qtt.   in ♯ ArgOd.LDC 510
(& with *Mendelssohn*, ArgOd. 66046)

— — ARR. HPSI.   E. Silver (in ♯ Roy. 1550)

— — STRING ORCH. RECORDINGS
Champs-Élysées Th.—Allain in ♭ Sel. 470.C.002
                                                   (♭ T.UV 118)
Leipzig Radio—Haarth   Ami. 140026
(*Haydn: Qtt., Op. 3, No. 5—Serenade*)

Belgian Radio—P. Glière (in ♯ Mae.OAT 25001)
☆ Philharmonia—Weldon (♭ C.SED 5507: SEBQ 112)
   Philadelphia—Stokowski (in ♯ Cam.CAL 120)

— ARR. ORCH.
N.Y.P.S.O.—Kostelanetz (in ♯ AmC.CL 758: ♭ A 2036)

C minor, Op. 29, No. 1 (b)   1779
G major, Op. 60, No. 5 (b)   1801
Boccherini Quintet   ♯ G.ALP 1144
                                                   (♯ QALP 10055)

C major, Op. 37, No. 7   1779
... Rondo only   — ARR. VLC. & PF.   Bazelaire
E. B. Bengtsson & H. D. Koppel   G.DA 5280
(*Popper-Cassadó: Elves' Dance*)
D. Shafran & pf.   USSR. 21595
("*Couperin*": *Pastorale*)   (& USSRM.D 001215)

C major   (unspec.)
I. Shuk Quintet   ♯ USSR.D 1722/3

Quintet, fl. & str., E flat major   1769
☆ R. Adeney & London Baroque Ens.—Haas
                                            in ♯ Nix.WLP 5080
                       (& in ♯ West.WN 18050, d.c.)

QUINTETS, Pf. & str.
A major, Op. 57, No. 1 (b)
D minor, Op. 57, No. 4 (b)   1799
Chigi Quintet   ♯ D.LXT 2841
                       (♯ D.NLK 40102; Lon.LL 749)

SEXTETS
E flat major, Op. 24, No. 1   2 vlns., 2 vlas., 2 vlcs. 1776
E flat major, Op. 41   ob., hrn., bsn., vln., vla., cbs. 1787
Sinfonia Concertante, G major, Op. 8   ob., hrn.,
                              bsn., str. 1769
☆ London Baroque Ens.—Haas   ♯ Nix.WLP 5077
   [Op. 41 & Sinfonia also on ♯ West.WN 18052;
                       Op. 24, No. 1 on ♯ West.WN 18051

SONATAS, vlc. & continuo   (Picquot p. 141)
No. 5, C minor
M. Amfiteatrof & O.P. Santoliquido (pf.)
                                                  ♯ ItV.A12R 0140
(*Vivaldi, Galuppi, etc.*)

No. 6, A major
... 1st & 2nd movts., Adagio & Allegro
A. Janigro & E. Bagnoli (pf.)   ♯ West.WL 5234
(*Locatelli & Frescobaldi*) (& above & below,
                                            ♯ West.WN 18050)
L. Rose & L. Hambro (pf.)   ♯ AmC.ML 4984
(*Sammartini & Schubert*)

— ARR. VLN. & PF.   Primrose
☆ W. Primrose & J. Kahn (JpV.SD 3090)

SYMPHONIES
C major, Op. 16, No. 3   1771
B flat major, Op. 35, No. 6 (b)   1782   (*Funèbre*)
Vienna Orch. Soc.—Adler   ♯ Uni.LP 1017

A major, Op. 37, No. 4 (b)   1786
Winterthur Sym.—Dahinden   ♯ CHS.H 8
(*Haydn: Sym. 27, & Concerto*)

F major, Op. 35, No. 4 (b)   1782
Italian Cha.—Jenkins   ♯ HS.HSL 79
(*Rosetti*)   (in set HSL-C)
(*Brunetti*, on ♯ Era.LDE 3022)

☆ = Re-issue of a recording to be found in previous volumes.

TRIOS, 2 vlns. & vlc. Op. 35
☆ W. Schneiderhan, G. Swoboda, S. Benesch
reissued with new couplings:
No. 1, F minor, No. 2, G major on ♯ West.WN 18050 (*Quintet*)
No. 3, E flat major; No. 4, D major
on ♯ West.WN 18051 (*Sextet*)
No. 5, C major; No. 6, E major on ♯ West.WN 18052
(*Sextet & Sinfonia concertante*)

Scuola di Ballo Ballet Suite, ARR. Françaix
☆ L.P.O.—Dorati (*Field*)   ♯ AmC.RL 3043

BOECK, Auguste de (1865-1937)

Capriccio pf.
S. Cambier   *C.DCB 56*
(*Poot: Toccata*)

Symphony, G minor 1896
Belgian Nat.—Weemaels   ♯ D.BA 133100

BOËLLMANN, Léon (1862-1897)

Ronde française, Op. 37 org. [or pf.]
E. Linzel   ♯ Discur.BCL 7201
(*Elmore & Roger-Ducasse*)

Suite gothique, Op. 25 organ
1. Introduction & Chorale   2. Menuet
3. Prière à notre Dame   4. Toccata
P. Kee   ♭ G. 7EPH 1004
[org. of St. Bavo's Church, Haarlem]
... Nos. 2 & 3 R. Foort   ♯ SOT. 1054
         (*Bach & Dubois*)   (and in ♯ SOT. 10545)
... No. 3   G. de Donà   in ♯ AmVox.VL 3100
         (*Bach, Handel*)
... No. 4   M.-C. Alain   V♯ Era.LDE 1014
         (*Gigout & Widor*)
         J. Ropek (*Widor*)   U.H 24412

BÖHM, Georg (1661-1733)

KEYBOARD WORKS
(references to the three parts of the Gesamtausgabe
(B & H), Vol. I)

COLLECTION
Preludes & Fugues: C major (i-1)
                   A minor (i-2)
                   D minor (i-4) ø
Capriccio, D major (i-5) ø
Chorale-Partita: Ach wie nichtig (iii-1)
Chorale-Preludes: Aus tiefer Not (iii-4)
                  Vater unser (iii-12 i)
H. Heintze   ♯ Pol. 14043
[org. of St. Johns Church, Lüneburg]
(marked ø also on ♭ Pol. 37060)

CHORALE PRELUDES:
Ach wie nichtig, ach wie flüchtig (Partita) (iii-1)
Auf meinen lieben Gott (iii-3)
Herr Jesu Christ, dich zu uns wend (iii-10)
F. Viderø   ♯ HSL.HSL 3066
(*Walther*) [Jaegersborg organ, Denmark]

Gelobet seist du, Jesu Christ (iii-9 i)
☆ F. Heitmann   in ♯ DT.LGX 66009
(† Christmas Organ Music)

Wer nur den lieben Gott lässt walten (iii-14)
☆ F. Heitmann († Organ Music) in ♯ DT.LGX 66037

Partita on 'Jesu, du bist allzu schöne' (ii-13)
Suite No. 7, F major (ii-7)
H. Heintze (hpsi.)   ♭ Pol. 37034

Praeludium, Fuga, Postludium, G minor (i-6)
E. Bodky (hpsi.)   ♯ Uni.LP 1002
(† Music of the Baroque Era)

SONGS
Bringet meinen Herrn zur Ruh[1]
G. Souzay (B), J. Bonneau (pf.) ♯ D.LXT 2835
(† Canzone Scordate) (♯ Lon.LL 731; D.FAT 173072)

Geh' ein, mein Lieb, in deine Kammer[1]
K. Flagstad (S), G. Moore (pf.)
(† German Songs)   ♯ Vic.LHMV 1070

BOERO, Felipe (b. 1884)

(El) Cielito
(El) Caramba
(La) Media Caña
(La) Huella
State Sym. Orch.—Kinsky   *ArgV.P 1496/8*
(*A. Williams*)

(3) Danzas argentinas
El Escondido; Hueya; La Firmeza
Arg. Radio Cha.—Bandini   ♯ ArgOd.LDC 505
(*Gil, etc.*) (& 2ss, Od. 66001)

BOESSET, Antoine (c. 1585-1643)

SEE: † FRENCH CHANSONS
      † OLD FRENCH AIRS

BOÏELDIEU, François (1775-1834)

OPERAS
(Le) CALIFE DE BAGDAD 1 Act 1800
Overture
Lamoureux—Fournet   ♭ EPhi.NBE 11017
(*Hérold: Zampa Ov.*) (♭ Phi.N 402011E, d.c.)
(*below; Bizet, St.-Saëns, Massenet, etc.*, in ♯ Epic.LC 3079)
French Nat. Radio—Tzipine   ♯ C.FC 1040
(*below; Auber, Cimarosa*)
Pasdeloup—Allain   ♭ Plé.P 45144
(*Barbiere, Overture*)
Vienna Radio—Schönherr   Vien.L 6165
                        (in ♯ LPR 1024)
F.O.K. Sym.—Smetáček   U.H 24432
☆ L.P.O.—Martinon (♯ D.LW 5023: ♭ DX 1777;
                        ♯ Lon.LD 9036)
Bamberg Sym.—Lehmann (PV. 72279: ♭ Pol. 30068:
                      ♯ 17033; ♯ AmD.DL 4046)
Rhineland Sym.—Federer (♯ AFest.CFR 38)
— ARR. BAND
☆ Goldman Band (in ♯ Cam.CAL 240)

(La) DAME BLANCHE 3 Acts 1825
Overture
Bamberg Sym.—Lehmann   PV. 72279
(*above*)   (♭ Pol. 30068)
(*Borodin on* ♯ AmD.DL 4069)
Lamoureux—Fournet   ♭ Phi.N 402011E
(*above*) (*Calife Overture, etc.*, in ♯Epic.LC 3079)
French Nat. Radio—Tzipine   ♯ C.FC 1040
(*above*)
Paris Opéra—Fournet   Phi.N 12064G
☆ L.P.O.—Martinon (♯ D.LW 5023: ♭ DX 1777:
                        ♯ Lon.LD 9036)
Boston Prom.—Fiedler (in ♯ Cam.CAL 250: ♭ CAE 181)
Ah! quel plaisir d'être soldat
Déjà la nuit
Quand la paix
Viens, gentille dame
☆ M. Villabella (in ♯ Od.ODX 136)
Ah! quel plaisir & Viens, gentille dame
Ħ E. Clément (in ♯ Sca. 819*)
Viens, gentille dame T Act II
W. Ludwig (*Ger*)   PV. 36059
(*Fra Diavolo—Je vois marcher*)

JEAN DE PARIS 2 Acts 1812
Overture
Linz Sym.   in ♯ Ply. 12-34
(*Thomas, Rossini, etc.*)

---

[1] Ed. Dørumsgaard.

BOISMORTIER, Joseph Bodin de
(1691-1755)

CANTATA: Diane et Actéon (attrib. to Rameau)
C. Collart (S) & Cha. Orch.—Belai
(*Rameau*)   ♯ *CdM.LDA 8116*
 ☆ H. Cuénod (T), R. Brink (vln.), A. Zighéra (gamba),
    & D. Pinkham (hpsi.)   ♯ Nix.LLP 8044
    (*Rameau*)   (♯ Lyr.LL 44)

Concerto, A minor, Op. 15, No. 2   5 fls. unacc. 1727
 ☆ J-P. Rampal, playing all parts (in † ♯ HS.AS 19)

Concerto à 5, E minor, Op. 37   fl., vln., ob., bsn. &
    cont.   1732
J. Rocheblave, G. Raymond, A. Lardrot,
J. Charpentier, A-M. Beckensteiner (hpsi.),
M-A. Mocquot (gamba)   ♯ **DDP. 21-1**
(*Leclair & Naudot*)   (♯ HS.HSL 103)

DAPHNIS ET CHLOË   Pastorale   3 Acts   1747
Ballet Suite

1. Marche	5. Loure
2. Menuet	6. Bourrée
3. Contre danse	7. Musette
4. Air pour les Zéphires	8. Tambourin

Seiler Cha. Ens.   (2ss)   **PV. 8407**
(*Mouton: Lute pieces, on* ♯ *HP.AP 13027*)   (♭ *Pol. 37079*)

Trio-Sonata, B minor, Op. 4, No. 1   fl., ob., cont.
Lutèce Qtt.   ♯ *Era.LDE 1021*
(*Naudot*)   [fl., ob., hpsi., vlc.]

BOITO, Arrigo (1842-1918)

OPERAS
MEFISTOFELE   Prologue, 4 Acts, Epilogue 1868
COMPLETE RECORDING

Elena...	... ...	S. dall'Argine (S)
Margherita ...	... ...	R. Noli (S)
Marta ⎱	... ...	E. Ticozzi (M-S)
Pantalis ⎰		
Faust...	... ...	G. Poggi (T)
Wagner ⎱	... ...	G. del Signore (T)
Nereo ⎰		
Mefistofele ...	... ...	G. Neri (Bs)

Cho. & orch. of Milan Opera—Capuana
    ♯ **Nix.ULP 9230-1/3**
(6ss)   (♯ Ura. set 230; MTW 541/3)
[L'altra notte; Lontano, lontano & Amore! misterio
    on ♭ *Ura UREP 28*; *Nix.EP 728*;
   Opening of Act I in ♯ Nix.ULP 9084; Ura. 7084]
 ☆ G. Arangi-Lombardi (S), M. Favero (S), N. de Angelis
    (Bs), etc., La Scala Cho. & orch.—Molajoli
        ♯ **AmC. set EL 9**
(6ss)   (♯ C.QCX 10117/9)

PROLOGUE
COMPLETE PROLOGUE
N. Moscona (Bs), Columbus Boys' Cho. &
N.B.C. Sym.—Toscanini[1]   ♯ **Vic.LM 1849**
(*Verdi*)   (♯ ItV.A12R 0145; FV.A 630269)

... Ave Signor   Bs
 ☆ B. Christoff (♭ *G.7RF 263*)
 ⊞ F. Chaliapin (in ♯ *AudA.LPA 1002** & in ♯ Sca. 801*)
    J. Mardones (in ♯ Sca. 810*)

ACT I
Il bel giovanetto   Cho.
— ARR. ORCH.   "*Peasant Waltz*"
 ☆ Cincinnati Summer Op.—Cleva (in ♯ B.AXTL 1035;
    ♯ AmD.DL 8053: ♭ *ED 3525;* in ♯ D.UST 233087;
    ♯ AFest.CFR 12-457: ♭ *SpC.SCGE 80007*)

Dai campi, dai prati   T
 ⊞ G. Zenatello (in ♯ *SBDH.LLP 8** & in ♯ Sca. 818*)
    G. Anselmi (in ♯ Ete. 711*)

Son lo spirito che nega   Bs   (*Ballata*)
 ☆ B. Christoff (♭ *G.7RF 263*)

 ⊞ F. Chaliapin (in ♯ *SBDH.LLP 4**)
    M. Journet (in ♯ *SBDH.PL 1**)
    J. Mardones (in ♯ Sca. 810*)
    E. Pinza (in ♯ SBDH.JAL 7002*)

Se tu mi doni un'ora   T & Bs
 ⊞ B. Gigli & C. Scattola (in ♯ *SBDH.LPP 5**)

ACT II, Scene 2
Ecco il mondo   Bs
    G. London   in ♯ **AmC.ML 4658**
(*Rubinstein, Moussorgsky; & Damnation of Faust,
               Rheingold, etc.*)

 ⊞ J. Mardones (in ♯ Sca. 810* & in ♯ *SBDH.LPP 3**)

ACT III
L'altra notte, in fondo al mare   S
    J. Hammond   **G.DB 21625**
(*Korngold: Die Tote Stadt, aria*)
    V. de los Angeles   in ♯ **G.ALP 1284**
(*Cenerentola, Cavalleria, La Wally, etc.*)   (♯ QALP 10115)
    M. M. Callas   in ♯ **C.CX 1231**
(*Barbiere, Dinorah, Lakmé, etc.*)   (♯ QCX 10129 &
                      Angel. 35233)
    M. Benetti   **Cet.PE 193**
(*Louise—Depuis le jour*)
    M. C. Verna   in ♯ **Cet.LPC 55005**
(*Sonnambula, A. Lecouvreur, La Wally, etc.*)
 ☆ R. Tebaldi (in ♯ *Fnt.LP 301*)
 ⊞ R. Raisa (in ♯ Sca. 808*)
    C. Muzio (in ♯ I.I.TW 91053*)[2]

Lontano, lontano   S & T
 ☆ P. Tassinari & F. Tagliavini (in ♯ *FSor.CS 544*)
 ⊞ G. Farrar & E. Clément (AF.AGSB 25*)

... Sop. part only—incomplete
    G. Farrar   in ♯ *IRCC.L 7001*[3]

Spunta l'aurora pallida   S, T, B, & Cho.
... Sop. part only
 ⊞ C. Boninsegna (*IRCC. 3140**)
    G. Russ (in ♯ Sca. 808*)

ACT IV
Forma ideal   S, T, & Bs
... Tenor part only
 ⊞ F. de Lucia (in ♯ CEd. set 7002*)

Folleto, folleto   T & Bs
 ⊞ G. de Tura & G. Mansueto (*SBDH.P 9**)

EPILOGUE
Giunto sul passo estremo   T
 ☆ A. Pertile   in ♯ Ete. 710
 ⊞ G. Zenatello   in ♯ Sca. 818*
    F. de Lucia   in ♯ CEd. set 7002*
    G. Anselmi & pf.   in ♯ Ete. 711*

NERONE   4 Acts   1924
"HIGHLIGHTS"
 ⊞ M. Journet (Bs), A. Pertile (T), M. Stabile (B), G.
    Arangi-Lombardi (S), etc.   ♯ **Ete. 704***

Queste ad un lido fatal   T   Act I
 ⊞ A. Pertile (in ♯ Od.ODX 127*: MOAQ 301*;
                   & in ♯ *HRS. 3007**)
    S. Pollicino (in ♯ Ete. 492*)

Pensa i reami   Bs   Act I
 ⊞ M. Journet (in ♯ SBDH.LPG 5* & in ♯ JALP 19*)

Ecco il magico specchio   B   Act II
 ⊞ M. Journet (Bs) (in ♯ SBDH.LPG 5* & ♯ ABCD. 1*)

Scendi, scendi sul sognator   T   Act II
... No, nel tuo cor sangue umano
 ⊞ A. Pertile (in ♯Od.ODX 127*: MOAQ 301*
                  & in ♯ *HRS. 3007**)

---

[1] Broadcast performance March 1954.
[2] From Edison & Pathé hill & dale recordings.   Withdrawn immediately on issue.   [3] Recorded 1935.

BONDEVILLE, Emmanuel de (b. 1898)

(L') ÉCOLE DES MARIS Opéra-comique 1935
EXCERPTS
M. Robin (S), L. Musy (B), X. Depraz (Bs),
J. Giraudeau (T), R. Massard (B), A. Disney
(M-S), Opéra-Comique Cho. & Orch.—Wolff
‡ **LI.TW 91024**
(‡ D.FAT 133518)
Gaultier-Garguille Sym. Poem 1953
French Nat. Radio—Cluytens   ‡ **C.FCX 270**
(below)

(Les) Illuminations Orch. Suite (after Rimbaud)
Belgian Nat.—Sebastian   ‡ **LI.TW 91023**
(Madame Bovary, Suite)   (‡ D.BAT 133058)

MADAME BOVARY Opera 3 Acts 1948
Orchestral Suite
Belgian Nat.—Sebastian   ‡ **LI.TW 91023**
(Les Illuminations)   (‡ D.BAT 133058)

Duet, Rodolphe & Emma, Act II
Je souffre, pourquoi mon amour? Act III
(Death of Emma)
J. Brumaire (S), M. Dens (B), L. Riallant (T),
E. Rousseau (B), etc., & Opéra-Comique
Orch.—Cluytens   ‡ **C.FCX 270**
(above)

BONELLI, Aurelio (fl. XVIIth Century)
SEE: † GOLDEN AGE OF BRASS

BONI, Guillaume (c. 1545-1594)
SEE: † PARISIAN SONGS OF XVITH CENTURY

BONNEAU, Paul (b. 1918)

Caprice en forme de valse sax. unacc.
M. Mule   ‡ **D.LX 3130**
(Tomasi, Decruck, Bozza, etc.)   (‡ Lon.LS 986)

BONNET, Pierre (1538-1608)
SEE: † FRENCH RENAISSANCE MUSIC
   † PARISIAN SONGS OF XVITH CENTURY

BONONCINI, Giovanni Maria (1642-1778)
SEE: † ITALIAN AIRS

BONONCINI, Giovanni (1670-c. 1755)
SEE: † ITALIAN CLASSIC SONGS

BONPORTI, Francesco Antonio
(1672-1749)

(12) CONCERTI a 4, Op. 11 str. (ed. Barblan)
No. 1, A major
Milan Angelicum—Janes   ‡ **Ang.LPA 956**
(Debussy, Bettinelli, Vivaldi)
No. 3, B flat major
No. 8, D major
Milan Angelicum—Janes   ‡ **Ang.LPA 957**
(Vivaldi)
(No. 3 only, in ‡ LPA 958)
No. 5, F major
... Adagio (Recitativo) only
G. Mozzato & Virtuosi di Roma—Fasano
‡ **B.AXTL 1042**
(Rossini, Cambini & Marcello) (‡ AmD.DL 9674;
Fnt.LP 3005; D.UAT 273583)
No. 8, D major
Società Corelli   ‡ **Vic.LM 1880**
(Vivaldi, Corelli, Galuppi) (‡ FV.A 630292; ItV.A12R 0146)
Milan Cha.—Abbado   ‡ **C.FCX 369**
(Tartini, Cambini, Vivaldi)

BORLET (fl. XIVth Cent.)
SEE: † FRENCH CHANSONS

BORODIN, Alexander (1834-1887)

In the Steppes of Central Asia orch. 1880
Philharmonia—Collingwood (2ss) C.DX 1879
(Weinberger: Švanda—Polka & Fugue on ♭ SED 5513)
Paris Cons.—Ansermet   ‡ **D.LXT 2833**
(Glinka, Prokofiev, Moussorgsky) (‡ Lon.LL 864)
(Moussorgsky only, on ‡ D.LW 5060; Lon.LD 9086)
N.Y.P.S.O.—Mitropoulos   ‡ **EPhi.NBL 5015**
(Prince Igor—Dances; & Ippolitoff-Ivanoff)
   (‡ AmC.CL 751, o.n. ML 4815; Phi.N 02107L)
Lamoureux—Fournet   ‡ **Phi.S 06022R**
(Moussorgsky: Night on the bare mountain)
Sym.—Stokowski   ‡ **Vic.LRM 7056**
(Prince Igor—Dances)   (♭ set ERB 7056)
(Glier, Moussorgsky, Rimsky, on ‡ LM 1816;
   ‡ ItV.A12R 0141; FV.A 630215; DV.L 16482)
Moscow Radio—Orlov   **USSRM.D 924**
(Balakirev: Overture on Russian Themes)
Linz Sym. (in ‡ Ply. 12-35)
☆ R.I.A.S. Sym.—Fricsay (PV. 72297; ♭ AmD.ED 3521)
Paris Cons.—Cluytens (in ‡ Pat. QTX 116)
French Nat. Radio—Lindenberg (Od.O-3710:
   ♭ 7AOE 1001: DSEQ 426)

MLADA Act IV of unfinished opera 1872
... **Finale** (ARR. Rimsky-Korsakov)
Leningrad Phil.—Khaikin   **USSRM.D 001094**
(Liadov)

PRINCE IGOR Opera 4 Acts 1890
Completed by Rimsky-Korsakov and Glazounov; Act III
   almost entirely composed by the latter.

COMPLETE RECORDINGS

Prince Igor ...	...	...	D. Popovich (B)
Jaroslavna ...	...	...	V. Heybalova (S)
Vladimir ...	...	...	N. Zhunetz (T)
Galitsky }	...	...	Z. Tzveych (Bs)
Konchak }			

etc., Belgrade Nat. Op. Cho. & orch.—Danon
‡ **D.LXT 5049/53**
(10ss)[1]   (‡ Lon. set XLLA 30)
☆ And. Ivanov (B), E. Smolenskaya (S), S. Lemeshev (T),
A. Pirogov (Bs), M. Reizen (Bs), etc. Bolshoi
Theatre Cho. & Orch.—Melik-Pasheyev[2]
‡ **Mon.MWL 326/9**
(8ss)   (‡ USSR.D 0632/9)
[Prologue & Act I on ‡ Csm.CRLP 166, Act II on
‡ CRLP 10220; various excerpts on ‡ USSR.D 1410/1;
USSRM.D 00875, etc.]

Excerpts
A. Pirogov (Bs), I. Kozlovsky (T), M. Mikhailov
(Bs), etc., Bolshoi Theatre Cho. & Orch.
—Golovanov   ‡ **Csm.CRLP 122**
M. Reizen, I. Skobtsov, F. Godovkin, Bolshoi
Theatre—Nebolsin   in ‡ **USSR.D 01368**
(Moussorgsky)

Orchestral Suite
Overture; No. 17—Polovtsi Dances;
No. 18—Prelude Act III (Polovtsi March)
Philharmonia—Susskind   ‡ **P.PMD 1023**
   (‡ MGM.E 3008; Od.MODQ 6245)
Overture
Suisse Romande—Ansermet   ‡ **D.LXT 5022**
(Symphonies Nos. 2 & 3)   (‡ Lon.LL 1178)
Bamberg Sym.—Lehmann   **PV. 36077**
(Boieldieu on ‡ AmD.DL 4069)   (♭ Pol. 32046)
Austrian Sym.—Koslik   ‡ **Rem. 199-130**
(No. 17, & Rimsky-Korsakov) (‡ Cum.CR 293; also listed
   as 296)
☆ Bolshoi Theatre—Melik-Pasheyev, from set
   (‡ Mon.MWL 335)
Hallé—Heward (in ‡ AmC.RL 3072)

---
[1] Excludes Scenes 1 - 3, Act IV.
[2] Act III is omitted. This recording was also announced on ‡ Csm.CS 1/4, but may not have been issued.

PRINCE IGOR (*continued*)

ACT I

No. 2, I hate a dreary life   Bs
(*Galitzky's Song*)
N. Rossi-Lemeni   **G.DB 21559**
(*Life for the Tsar—Sussanin's Aria*)
(in ‡ ALP 1074: FALP 306: QALP 10033; ♭ *Vic.ERA 186*)
R. Arié   ‡ *D.LW 5061*
(*Sadko, Life for the Tsar, E. Oniegin*)   (‡ *Lon.LD 9074*)
S. Belarsky   in ‡ *Vic.LPM 3274*
(*Tchaikovsky, Dargomijsky, etc.*)   (♭ *set EPB 3274*)
   ☆ A. Pirogov, from set (*USSRM.D 887*)
   B. Christoff (in ‡ *G.QBLP 5002*: ♭7RW 134: 7RQ 3033:
                                          7ERQ 107)

   ⌸ F. Chaliapin (in ‡ Sca. 801*; ♭ *Cpt.EXTP 1002**;
                                          ♭ *Per.PEP 12**)

No. 3, For long past (Jaroslavna's Arioso) S
   ☆ N. Koshetz (in ‡ Vic. set LCT 6701)

ACT II

No. 7, The prairie floweret (Girl's Cho.)
No. 8, Dance of the Polovtsi Girls Orch.
(see also No. 17)

— ARR. VLC. & PF. Kozolupov
M. Rostropovich & M. Karandaszhova
                    ‡ **LI.TW 91068**
(*Prokofiev, Shostakovich, etc.*) (*USSR. 17836/7 & ‡ D 1177*)

No. 11, Daylight is fading   T
N. Gedda (*Swed*)   **Od.SD 6080**
(*Zauberflöte, No. 3*)
W. Kmentt (*Ger*)   in ‡ *Phi.S 06075R*
(*Sadko, The Kiss, etc.*)
   ☆ I. Kozlovsky (*USSRM.D 00806*)
   S. Lemeshev (in ‡ *USSR.D 1412*)

No. 13, No sleep, no rest for my afflicted soul B
M. Grishko   in ‡ *USSR.D 1952*
K. Shekerlysky (2ss)   **Bulg. 1384**
   T. Kuuzik (*Est*) (USSR. 023574/5)
   ☆ And. Ivanov (in ‡ *Sup.LPM 186*; in ‡ *U. 5176C*;
                     USSR. 022906/7 & *USSRM.D 001230*)
   P. Silveri (*Ital*) (♭ *C.SCB 107*; *SCBW 105*: *SCBQ 3007*)

No. 15, How goes it, Prince (Konchak's Aria) Bs
M. Popov (*Bulg*) (2ss)   **Bulg. 1387**
                    (& in ‡ *USSR.D 2157*)
   ☆ B. Christoff   ♭ *G.7ER 5007*
   (*Khovanshchina, aria*) (♭ *7ERF 132: 7RW 111*:
                              ‡ *QBLP 5002*)
   ☆ M. Reizen (from set) (in ‡ Csm.CRLP 142
                              & *USSRM.D 00252*)

No. 17, Polovtsian Dances Cho. & Orch.[1]
French Nat. Radio Cho. (*Fr*) & Orch.
   —Markevitch   ‡ **C.CX 1208**
(*Moussorgsky & Tchaikovsky*)   (& ♭ *G.7ERL 1032*)
                    (‡ QCX 10134: FCX 349; ‡ Angel. 35144)
Cho. & Berlin Sym.—Rucht (?*Ger*) ‡ **Ura. 7146**
(*Kabalevsky, Prokofiev, Shostakovich*)   (♭ UREP 34)
(*Symphony No. 2 on* ‡ Ura.RS 7-4)
   ☆ Bolshoi Theatre—Melik-Pasheyev (‡ Csm.CRLP 10110;
                     USSRM.D 146; in ‡ CdM.LDA 8060)

— ARR. ORCH. ONLY Rimsky-Korsakov
Philharmonia—Karajan   ‡ **C.CX 1327**
(*Gioconda, Tannhäuser, etc.*)   (‡ Angel. 35307)
N.Y.P.S.O.—Mitropoulos   ‡ **EPhi.NBL 5015**
(*In the Steppes . . . ; & Ippolitoff-Ivanoff*)
   (‡ AmC.CL 751, o.n. ML 4815: ♭ A 1823; ‡ Phi.N 02107L)
Los Angeles Phil.—Wallenstein ‡ **B.AXTL 1062**
(*Enesco & Ippolitoff-Ivanoff*) (‡ AmD.DL 9727;
                                          D.UAT 273577)
Philharmonia—Malko   ‡ *G.DLP 1092*
(*No. 18; & Liadov*)
London Phil. Sym.—Rodzinski ‡ **West.LAB 7039**
(*Ippolitoff-Ivanoff*)
Florence Fest.—Gui   ‡ **AudC. 502**
(*Debussy, Dukas, Moussorgsky*)

Austrian Sym.—Koslik   ‡ **Rem. 199–130**
(*Overture; & Rimsky*) (‡ Cum.CR 293; also
                          ‡ Rem. 199-186, d.c.)
International Sym.—Schneiderhann (in ‡ *Mae.OA 20007*)
☆ R.I.A.S. Sym.—Fricsay (in ‡ *HP.DG 16006*;
                              ♭ *AmD.ED 3547*)
Philadelphia—Stokowski (‡ Cam.CAL 203 &
                          in ‡ set CFL 102)
— ARR. ORCH. Stokowski
Sym—Stokowski (n.v.)   ‡ *Vic.LRM 7056*
(*above*)   (♭ *set ERB 7056*)
(excerpts, Vic. 10-4212: ♭ 49-4212; G.DA 2073)
— ARR. 2 PFS. Babin
V. Vronsky & V. Babin (in ‡ AmD.DL 9791)
— ARR. ORGAN: R. Ellsasser (in ‡ MGM.E 3127)

ACT III

No. 18, Prelude (Polovtsi March) Cho. & orch.
— ARR. ORCH. only
Philharmonia—Malko   in ‡ *G.DLP 1092*
(*above*)
   ☆ Bolshoi Theatre—Nebolsin (*USSRM.D 00204*)

QUARTETS, String
No. 1, A major 1878
   ☆ Vienna Konzerthaus Qtt.   ‡ Nix.WLP 5035
No. 2, D major 1881
Komitas (Armenian) Qtt.   ‡ **C.CX 1334**
(*Shostakovich*)   (‡ Angel. 35239)
Hollywood Qtt.   ‡ **DCap.CTL 7031**
(*Tchaikovsky*)   (‡ Cap.P 8187; AFest.CLCX 022)
[Notturno only, on ♭ *Cap.FAP 8217*]
Glazounov Qtt. (4ss)   *USSRM. 291/4*
(2ss—‡ *Sup.LPM 173*; ‡ *U. 5072C*)
... 3rd movt., Notturno, only
Pessina Qtt. (2ss)   **ArgOd. 66043**
                              (in ‡ *LDC 510*)
   ☆ Galimir Qtt. (♭ *Cpt.EXTP 1004*; ♭ *Per.PEP 11*;
                                          ‡ Clc. 6148)
— — ARR. STR. ORCH. Sargent
   ☆ Philharmonia—Sargent (in ‡ AmC.RL 3042)

Quartet, D major fl., ob., vla., vlc.
G. Madatov, N. Meshkov, M. Ternan,
   S. Knushevitzky   *USSRM.D 001300/1*

Scherzo, A flat major[2]
   ☆ L. Oborin (in ‡*CdM.LDA 8076* & in ‡Csm.CRLP 224)

SONGS
(The) Sleeping Princess (composer) 1867
Z. Dolukhanova (A)   *USSRM.D 00663*
(*Tchaikovsky*)

Song of the Dark Forest (Borodin)
   ☆ M. Reizen (Bs), N. Walter (pf.) (in ‡ Csm.CLPS 10420
                          & *USSRM.D 00865*)

To distant shores (Pushkin)
   ☆ B. Gmyria (B)   *USSRM.D 00659*
   (*Tchaikovsky: O bless you, forests*)

(The) Tower (unid.)
M. Maksakova (S)   *USSR. 21100*
(*Varlamov: Alas they have gone*)

SYMPHONIES
No. 1, E flat major 1862-7
   ☆ Bavarian Sym.—Graunke   ‡ Nix.ULP 9066
   (*Dohnányi*)   (‡ MTW. 511, d.c.)
   ☆ U.S.S.R. State Sym.—Ivanov ‡ *CdM.LDA 8060*
   (*Prince Igor, Dances*) (2ss, ‡ USSR.D 01159/60;
                              ‡ Sup.LPV 176; U. 5150G)
   (*Ippolitoff-Ivanoff, on* ‡ Csm.CRLP 205)
No. 2, B minor 1869-76
Philharmonia—Kletzki   ‡ **C.CX 1167**
(*Ippolitoff-Ivanoff*)   (‡ Angel. 35145)
Suisse Romande—Ansermet   ‡ **D.LXT 5022**
(*No. 3 & Prince Igor Overture*)   (‡ Lon.LL 1178)
Leipzig Phil.—Pflüger   ‡ **Ura. 7148**
(*Tchaikovsky*)   (‡ MTW. 551)
(*Prince Igor, Dances on* ‡ Ura.RS 7-4)

(*continued on next page*)

---

[1] Recordings usually include No. 8, Dance of the Polovtsian Girls, and some No. 7 (ARR).
[2] Included in some edns. as No. 8 of *Petite Suite*. The CdM. disc may be n.v, not ☆

SYMPHONIES: No. 2, B minor (*continued*)
N.Y.P.S.O.—Mitropoulos   ♯ EPhi.ABL 3079
(*Tchaikovsky: Suite No. 1*) (♯ AmC.ML 4966;
Phi.A 01160L)
French Nat. Radio—Dobrowen ♯ *G.FBLP 1030*
Moscow Radio—Golovanov ♯ *CdM.LDA 8050*
(2ss)   (♯ USSR.D 0383/4)
(*Ippolitoff-Ivanoff, & Nyazi, on ♯ Csm.CRLP 10030*)
☆ Minneapolis Sym.—Dorati   ♯ EMer.MG 50004
(*Stravinsky*)
☆ Chicago Sym.—Defauw (♯ Cam.CAL 172)

No. 3, A minor
(unfinished; orchestrated by Glazounov)
Suisse Romande—Ansermet   ♯ D.LXT 5022
(*above*)   (♯ Lon.LL 1178)

MISCELLANEOUS

KISMET Musical Play 1955
(Score arr. from Borodin's music by R. Wright & G. Forrest)
Broadway Cast (♯ EPhi.BBL 7023; AmC.ML 4850)
T. Osborne Orch. (♯ Rem. 199-186; Ply. 12-118)
etc.
— FILM VERSION, from sound track
H. Keel, A. Blyth, D. Gray, etc. (♯ MGM.E 3281:
♭ set X 3281)

BORTNIANSKY, Dmitri S. (1752-1825)
SEE: † CHORAL MASTERPIECES FROM THE RUSSIAN
LITURGY
(There have been many ▽ recordings)

BOSCOVICH, Alexander Uria (b. 1908)

Semitic Suite orch.
... Excpts. — ARR. PF. SOLO
[Allegretto; Andantino; Vivace; Allegretto non troppo]
L. Granetman   in ♯ *Phi.N 00641R*
(*Stutschewsky, Ben-Haim, Lavry*)

BOTTESINI, Giovanni (1821-1889)

ERO E LEANDRO Opera 1879
Romanza di Ero: Splendi! erma facella S
Ħ A. Pinto (SBDH.G 2*)

Grand Duo Concertante, A minor vln., cbs. & pf.
J. Tryon, M. Anastasio & H. Wingreen
(*Dragonetti*)   ♯ CEd.CE 1035

BOULANGER, Lili (1893-1918)

Nocturne vln. or fl. & pf. 1911
☆ P. Fournier (vlc.), E. Lush (pf.)
(in ♯ Vic.LHMV 1043: ♭ set WHMV 1043)

BOURGUIGNON, Francis de (b. 1890)

Concerto, pf. & str. orch., Op. 99 1952
Berceuse, Op. 64 orch. 1940
(2) Danses, Op. 55 pf. 1937
N. Strycek (pf.) & Belgian Radio Cha. Orch.
—Doneux   ♯ *Gramo.GLP 2506*
Concerto, vln. & orch., Op. 86 1947
Recuerdos, Op. 79, No. 2[1] orch. 1943
C. van Neste (vln.) & Belgian Nat.—Weemaels
♯ *D.BA 133104*
Trio, vln., vla., vlc., Op. 49 1936
▽ E. Bouquet Trio (FT.E 5024/5)

BOUZIGNAC, Guillaume (d. c. 1650)
SEE: † FRENCH SACRED MUSIC
† HISTOIRE DE LA MUSIQUE VOCALE

BOWLES, Paul (b. 1910)

Music for a farce, Suite cl., tpt., percussion & pf.
1938
D. Glazer, H. Mueller, E. Bailey & W. Masselos
Scènes d'Anabase T, ob., & pf. (St. J. Perse) 1932
W. Hess, J. Marx & W. Masselos
(*Joio*)   ♯ AmC.ML 4845
Night Waltz 2 pfs.
☆ A. Gold & R. Fizdale (in ♯ *Phi.S 06614R*)
(A) Picnic Cantata (Schuyler) 4 vv., 2 pfs., timp.
1952
G. Davy (S), M. Flowers (S), M. Gaither (M-S),
G. Wyader (A); A. Gold & R. Fizdale (pfs.),
A. Howard (timp.)   ♯ AmC.ML 5068
(*Poulenc: Sonata*)
SONG CYCLE: (4) Blue Mountain Ballads
(T. Williams)
D. Gramm (Bs), R. Cumming (pf.)
in ♯ ML. 7033
(*Cesti, Martini, Chanler, etc.*)

BOYCE, William (1710-1779)

ANTHEM: O where shall wisdom be found?
York Minster Cho.—Jackson   C.LX 1608
(2ss) († English Church Music, Vol. IV)
'Mongst other roses
Glee Singers—Bath   in ♯ Allo. 3046
(† More Catches & Glees)
Overture, G major (No. 2 of 12 Overtures . . .,1770)[2]
Westminster Light—Bridgewater
in ♯ West.WL 4007
(*Leclair, Jones, Lawes, etc.*)
(The) SHEPHERD'S LOTTERY 1751
Inc. music for "Musical Entertainment" (Mendez)
1. Symphony, Act I
a. Prelude ("Overture")
b. Gavotte
c. Pastoral Dance
2. Symphony, Act II ("Finale") [ARR. Bridgewater]
Allegro String Orch.—Bath   ♯ Allo. 4011
(*Rameau*)   (♯ AFest.CFR 10-577)
(12) SONATAS 2 vlns. & cont. 1747
No. 12, G major
Royale Orch.—Everett   ♯ Roy. 1395
(*Symphonies*)
(8) SYMPHONIES, Op. 2 c. 1750
No. 1, B flat major
No. 5, D major
Royale Orch.—Everett   ♯ Roy. 1395
(*Trio Sonata*)
Nos. 1, 4, 6, 8   ♯ Nix.WLP 5073
Nos. 2, 3, 5, 7   ♯ Nix.WLP 5159
☆ London Baroque Ens.—Haas

BOYDELL, Brian (b. 1917)

Quartet, str., Op. 31 1949
Benthien Qtt.   ♯ RE.DGG 32291/2

---

[1] No. 2 of *Impressions Sud-américaines.*   [2] Originally Overture to *Birthday Ode* 1765.

BOZZA, Eugène (b. 1905)

Improvisation et Caprice sax. unacc.
M. Mule   in ♯ *D.LX 3130*
(*Tomasi, Tcherepnin, etc.*)   (♯ *Lon.LS 986*)

Variations sur un thème libre, Op. 40
fl., ob., cl., hrn., bsn. 1943
Copenhagen Wind Quintet   ♯ **D.LXT 2803**
(*Ibert & Nielsen*)   (♯ *Lon.LL 734*)

BRÆIN, Eduard Fliflet (b. 1924)

Concert Overture, Op. 12 1949
Oslo Phil.—Grüner-Hegge   NOC. **62613/4**
(2ss)   (& in ♯ *Mer.MG 90002*)

BRAHMS, Johannes (1833-1897)

CLASSIFIED: *I. INSTRUMENTAL*
     1. Orchestral   2. Chamber
     3. Piano & Organ
     4. Hungarian Dances & Waltzes
    II. VOCAL
     1. Choral   2. Partsongs
     3. Songs   4. Volkslieder
    III. MISCELLANEOUS

I. INSTRUMENTAL

1. ORCHESTRAL

Akademisches Fest-Ouvertüre, Op. 80
N.Y.P.S.O.—Walter (n.v.)   ♯ **AmC.ML 4908**
(*Tragische Ouvertüre & Sym. No. 1, s. 1*) (in set SL 200)
Bamberg Sym.—Hollreiser
        ♯ **E. & AmVox.PL 9350**
(*Liszt, Sibelius, Wagner*)
Phil. Prom.—Boult   ♯ **West.WN 18035**
(*Tragische Ov., Variations, Rhapsodies, Op. 53*)
        (in ♯ set WN 4401)
Amsterdam—v. Beinum   ♯ **D.LXT 2778**
(*Tragische Ouvertüre & Variations*)   (♯ *Lon.LL 735*)
(*Tragische Ouvertüre only on ♯ D.LW 5041; Lon.LD 9038*)
Utrecht Municipal—Huppertz   ♯ *MMS. 15*
(*Variations on a theme of Haydn*) (& in ♯ *MMS. 100S*)
Philharmonia—Schüchter   ♮ **C.DX 8405/6**
(3ss—*Nozze di Figaro, Overture*)   (♮ *DOX 1016/7*)
Florence Festival—Gui   ♯ **AudC. 501**
(*Schubert & Schumann*)
L.S.O.—Collingwood   ♯ **P.PMC 1024**
(*below, & Schumann*)(♯ MGM.E 3102; & in ♯ E 3177, d.c.)
F.O.K. Sym.—Smetáček   ♯ *Sup.LPM 149*
(*Rimsky*)   (♯ *U. 5171C*)
Residentie—v. Otterloo   ♯ *Phi.S 06008R*
(*below*)
Regent Sym. (in ♯ Rgt. 7004)
Anon. Orch. (in ♯ Gram. 2095)
☆ L.S.O.—Krauss (♭ *D. 71005*)
Liverpool Phil.—Sargent (in ♯ AmC.RL 3060)
Boston Sym.—Koussevitzky (in ♯ *Vic.LRM 7021:*
        ♭ *set ERB 7021*)
Vienna Phil.—Walter (in ♯ *Cam.CAL 242*)
Berlin Phil.—v. Kempen (♯ *Pol. 17056*)

CONCERTOS, Pf. & orch.
No. 1, D minor, Op. 15
F. Wührer & Vienna State Phil.—Swarowsky
        ♯ **E. & AmVox.PL 8000**
        (♯ *Orb.BL 704*)
C. Solomon & Philharmonia—Kubelik
        ♯ **G.ALP 1172**
(♯ *QALP 10103*; Vic.LHMV 1042: ♭ *set WHMV 1042*)

R. Serkin & Cleveland Sym.—Szell
        ♯ **EPhi.ABL 3028**
     (♯ AmC.ML 4829; Phi.A 01124L)
A. Rubinstein & Chicago Sym.—Reiner
        ♯ **G.ALP 1297**
   (♯ Vic.LM 1831; ItV.A12R 0119; FV.A 630244)
C. Curzon & Amsterdam—v. Beinum
        ♯ **D.LXT 2825**
        (♯ *Lon.LL 850*)
W. Malcuzynski & Philharmonia—Rieger
        ♯ **C.CX 1048**
   (♯ QCX 10062: FCX 195; Angel. 35014)
W. Backhaus & Vienna Phil.—Böhm
        ♯ **D.LXT 2866**
        (♯ *Lon.LL 911*)

No. 2, B flat major, Op. 83
A. Rubinstein & Boston Sym.—Münch
        ♯ **G.ALP 1123**
  (♯ G.FALP 250; ItV.A12R 0041; Vic.LM 1728:
        ♭ *set WDM 1728*)
M. de la Bruchollerie & Stuttgart Pro Musica
  —Reinhardt   ♯ **AmVox.PL 7950**
H. Reims & Berlin Sym.—Rubahn   ♯ **Roy. 1481**
E. Kilenyi & R.I.A.S. Sym.—Perlea
        ♯ **Rem. 199-164**
☆ R. Serkin & Philadelphia—Ormandy   ♯ **C.CX 1027**
        (♯ QCX 10010)
☆ V. Horowitz & N.B.C. Sym.—Toscanini
     (♯ G.QJLP 102: FJLP 5001)

Concerto, D major, Op. 77, Vln. & orch.
J. Martzy & Philharmonia—Kletzki[1]
        ♯ **C.CX 1165**
   (♯ QCX 10102; ♯ Angel. 35137)
C. Ferras & Vienna Phil.—Schuricht[2]
        ♯ **D.LXT 2949**
        (♯ *Lon.LL 1046*)
G. de Vito & Philharmonia—Schwarz[1]
        ♯ **G.ALP 1104**
   (♯ QALP 10060; ♯ Vic.LHMV 5)
N. Milstein & Pittsburgh Sym.—Steinberg[3]
        ♯ **DCap.CTL 7070**
   (♯ Cap.P 8271; ACap.CLCX 034)
J. Heifetz & Chicago Sym.—Reiner[4]
        ♯ **G.ALP 1334**
        (♯ Vic.LM 1903)
W. Schneiderhan & Berlin Phil.—v. Kempen
        ♯ **Pol. 18132**
J. Olevsky & Nat. Sym. (Washington)
  —Mitchell[1]   ♯ **Nix.WLP 5273**
        (♯ West.WL 5273)
I. Haendel & L.S.O.—Celibidache[1]
        ♯ **G.CLP 1032**
  (♯ QCLP 12011; ♯ BB.LBC 1051: ♭ *set WBC 1051*)
D. Oistrakh & Saxon State—Konwitschny[1]
        ♯ **HP.DGM 18199**
  (♯ AmD.DL 9754; ♯ Eta. 820003, o.n. LPM 1015)
D. Oistrakh & Moscow Radio—Kondrashin[1]
        ♯ **Mon.MWL 310**
(♯ USSR.D 0857/8; ♯ Van.VRS 6018; & ♯ CdM.LDA 8106)
(& 9ss, USSR. 021869/77) (*Ysaÿe*, on ♯ Csm.CRLP 150)
E. Wolf & L.S.O.—Goehr   ♯ **MApp.MAR 15**
A. Spalding & Austrian Sym.—Loibner   ♯ **Rem. 199-145**
        (♯ Cum.CR 216)
G. Manke & Leipzig Radio—Abendroth   ♯ **Ura.RS 7-24**
        (♯ MTW. 550)
L. Kogan & Paris Cons.—Bruck   ♯ **C.FCX 404**
☆ I. Stern & Royal Phil.—Beecham   ♯ **EPhi.ABL 3023**
        (♯ Phi.A 01106L)
☆ J. Heifetz & Boston Sym.—Koussevitzky
  (♯ DV.L 17093; FV.A 630299; ItV. A12R 0170)
Y. Menuhin & Lucerne Fest.—Furtwängler
        (♯ JpV.LS 2002)
P. Rybar & West Austrian Radio—Moltkau
      (♯ MMS. 2007; ♯ Clc. 6215)
— SPOKEN ANALYSIS by T. K. Scherman with musical
  illustrations
O. Shumsky & orch.—Scherman (♯ *MApp. 1015*)

---

[1] Cadenza by Joachim.
[3] Cadenza by Milstein.
[2] Cadenza by Kreisler.
[4] Cadenza by Heifetz.

Concerto, A minor, Op. 102, Vln., vlc., & orch.
D. Oistrakh, S. Knushevitzky & Leningrad
Radio—Eliasberg   ♯ **Mon.MWL 333**
(*Hungarian Dances*)
G. de Vito, A. Baldovino & Philharmonia
—Schwarz   ♯ *G.BLP 1028*
     (♯ *QBLP 5017;* Vic.LHMV 1057)
☆ J. Fournier, A. Janigro & Vienna State Op.—Scherchen
     ♯ Nix.WLP 20019
     (o.n. WLP 5117)
☆ D. Oistrakh, M. Sadlo & Czech Phil.—Ančerl
     (♯ Csm.CRLP 10200)
N. Milstein, G. Piatigorsky & Robin Hood Dell
     —Reiner (♯ ItV.A12R 0094)
J. Heifetz, E. Feuermann & Philadelphia—Ormandy
     (♯ DV.L 17069)

SERENADES
No. 1, D major, Op. 11
Little Orch. Society—Scherman ♯ **B.AXTL 1026**
     (♯ D.UMT 263580; AmD.DL 9651)
... Minuets 1 & 2
Hamburg Philharmonia—H-J. Walther   *MSB. 78146*
(*Schubert: Moment musical No. 3*)

No. 2, A major, Op. 16
Amsterdam—Zecchi   ♯ *Phi.A 00723R*
(2ss)   (♯ Epic.LC 3116)
Saar Cha.—Ristenpart   ♯ **DFr. 132**
(*Wagner: Siegfried Idyll*)

SYMPHONIES
Nos. 1-4, COMPLETE RECORDINGS
N.B.C. Sym.—Toscanini   ♯ **Vic. set LM 6108**
(6ss)   (♯ ItV.C12R 0069/71)
[Nos. 1, 2 & 4 are ☆; for separate issues see below]
N.Y.P.S.O.—Walter   ♯ **AmC.ML 4908/11**
(6½ss—*Overtures, Haydn Variations, Hung. Dances*)
[No. 4 is ☆; for separate issues see below]   (set SL 200)
Phil. Prom. Orch.—Boult ♯ **West. set WN 4401**
(6ss—*Overtures, Variations, Rhapsody Op. 53*)

No. 1, C minor, Op. 68
Philharmonia—Karajan   ♯ **C.CX 1053**
   (♯ QCX 10044: FCX 162; Angel. 35001; BrzA.CBX 78)
Philharmonia—Cantelli   ♯ *G.ALP 1152*
   (♯ FALP 319: QALP 10074; Vic.LHMV 1054)
Vienna State Op.—Scherchen ♯ Nix.WLP 5189
     (♯ West.WL 5189)
Los Angeles Phil.—Wallenstein ♯ **B.AXTL 1064**
   (♯ D.UAT 273579; AmD.DL 9603; SpC.CCL 35005)
Berlin Phil.—E. Jochum   ♯ **HP.DGM 18182**
N.Y.P.S.O.—Walter   ♯ *EPhi.ABR 4037*
     (♯ *Phi.A 01625R*)
Phil. Prom.—Boult   ♯ **West.WN 18104**
Residentie—Otterloo   ♯ **Phi.A 00198L**
     (also ♯ Phi.S 04601L; ♯ Epic.LC 3155)
Cento Soli—Husa   ♯ **CFD. 13**
Leningrad Phil.—Mravinsky   ♯ **USSR.D 01257/8**
Boston Orch. Soc.—Page   ♯ **SOT. 1060**
Dresden State Op.—Schreiber   ♯ **Allo. 3121**
Anon. Orch.   ♯ **Gram. 2076**
☆ Chicago Sym.—Kubelik   ♯ **EMer.MG 50007**
     (♯ FMer.MLP 7516)
☆ Berlin Phil.—Keilberth   ♯ **DT.LGX 66003**
     (♯ FT. 320.TC.072)
☆ Leipzig Radio—Abendroth (♯ Sup.LPV 69; ♯ U. 5045G;
     Eta 26-10/15, 12ss)
N.B.C. Sym.—Toscanini (♯ G.QALP 10009: FALP 201:
     VALP 519; ItV.A12R 0139)
Philadelphia Sym.—Stokowski (♯ Cam.CAL 105)
Philadelphia—Ormandy (♭ AmC. set A 1089)
Austrian Sym.—Brown (♯ Msq. 10006; & with
     commentary by S. Spaeth, ♯ Rem. 100-1)
N.Y.P.S.O.—Rodzinski (♯ AmC.RL 3117)

No. 2, D major, Op. 73
Amsterdam—v. Beinum   ♯ **EPhi.ABL 3020**
     (♯ Phi.A 00218L; Epic.LC 3098)
Vienna Phil.—Schuricht   ♯ **D.LXT 2859**
     (♯ Lon.LL 867)

Philadelphia—Ormandy (n.v.) ♯ **AmC.ML 4827**
N.Y.P.S.O.—Walter   ♯ **EPhi.ABL 3095**
(*Variations*)   (♯ Phi.A 01163L; also ♯ Phi.A 01184L)
Leningrad Phil.—Sanderling   ♯ **USSR.D 01730/1**
Berlin Phil.—Kempe   ♯ **G.WALP 1507**
Dresden State Op.—Schreiber (♯ Allo. 3122)
Berlin Sym.—Rubahn (♯ Roy. 1414)
Anon. Orch. (♯ Gram. 20135)
☆ N.B.C. Sym.—Toscanini (♯ Vic.LM 1731:
     ♭ set WDM 1731; ♯ G.FALP 202: WALP 1013;
     ♯ ItV.A12R 0138)
Leipzig Radio—Abendroth (♯ Sup.LPV 56; ♯ U. 5043G)
N.Y.P.S.O.—Barbirolli (♯ AmC.RL 3044)
Vienna Phil.—Karajan (♯ Angel. 35007; ♯ C.FCX 285)
Danish Radio—Busch[1] (♯ Cam.CAL 236)

— REHEARSAL RECORDING . . . 1st movt. only
N.Y.P.S.O.—Walter (♯ *AmC. 32785*)

No. 3, F major, Op. 90
N.B.C. Sym.—Toscanini   ♯ *G.ALP 1166*
    (♯ Vic.LM 1836; ♯ ItV.A12R 0074; DV.L 16479)
Vienna Phil.—Böhm   ♯ **D.LXT 2843**
     (♯ Lon.LL 857)
Hallé—Barbirolli   ♯ *G.BLP 1015*
   (♯ BB.LBC 1042: ♭ set WBC 1042; ♯ G.QBLP 5007;
     ArgV.ARL 2)
Hamburg State Phil.—Keilberth
     ♯ **DT.LGX 66035**
     (♯ T.LSK 7020; FT. 320.TC.032)
N.Y.P.S.O.—Walter   ♯ *EPhi.ABR 4031*
(2ss)   (♯ Phi.A 01623R)
(*Tragische Ouvertüre & Haydn Variations*
     on ♯ AmC.ML 4927)[2]
Zürich Tonhalle—Ackermann   ♯ *MMS. 28*
Prague Radio—Abendroth   ♯ **Sup.LPV 57**
     (♯ U. 5044G)
Leipzig Radio—Abendroth   ♯ **Ura.RS 7-5**
     (♯ MTW. 547; ACC.MP 26)
Dresden State Op.—Schreiber   ♯ **Allo. 3123**
Anon. Orch. (♯ Gram. 2083)
☆ Chicago Sym.—Stock (♯ AmC.RL 3013)
Philadelphia—Stokowski (♯ Cam.CAL 164)
Hamburg Phil.—E. Jochum (announced as
     ♯ T.LSK 7014)

— REHEARSAL RECORDING . . . Finale only
N.Y. Phil. Sym.—Walter (♯ *AmC. 32785*)

No. 4, E minor, Op. 98
Berlin Phil.—E. Jochum   ♯ **HP.DGM 18183**
N.Y. Stadium Concerts—Bernstein
     ♯ **B.AXTL 1066**
    (♯ D.UMT 263576; AmD.DL 9717)
Berlin Radio—Rother   ♯ **Ura.RS 7-14**
     (♯ MTW. 520)
Detroit Sym.—Paray   ♯ **Mer.MG 50057**
Cologne Gürzenich—Wand[3]   ♯ **CFD. 49**
☆ N.B.C. Sym.—Toscanini   ♯ **G.ALP 1029**
   (♯ VALP 520: FALP 204; ItV.A12R 0037;
     DV.L 16469; FV.A 630228)
☆ N.Y.P.S.O.—Walter   ♯ **EPhi.ABL 3008**
    (♯ Phi.A.01118L; ♭ AmC. set A 1090)
Leipzig Radio—Abendroth (♯ Eta. 820006)
Dresden State—Schreiber (♯ Allo. 3124)
Anon. Orch. (♯ Gram. 20136)
☆ Boston Sym.—Münch (♯ G.QALP 144)
B.B.C. Sym.—Walter (♯ Cam.CAL 246)

Tragische Ouvertüre, Op. 81
Amsterdam—v. Beinum   ♯ *D.LW 5041*
(*Akademisches Fest-Ouvertüre*)   (♯ *Lon.LD 9038*)
(*idem & Haydn Variations* on ♯ D.LXT 2778;
     ♯ *Lon.LL 735*)
Royal Phil.—Beecham   ♯ **AmC.ML 5029**
(*Beethoven, Boccherini, Méhul, Grétry*)
N.Y.P.S.O.—Walter   ♯ **AmC.ML 4908**
(*Akademisches Fest-Ouvertüre, Hungarian Dances & Sym.*
No. 1, s.l.)   (in set SL 200)
(*Haydn Variations; & Haydn* on ♯ ML 4814)[4]
(*Haydn Variations & Sym. No. 3* on ♯ ML 4927)[4]

---

[1] Called *Claridge Sym.*, this has not been definitely established as this recording.
[2] Announced but apparently not issued with this no.; *see* Collection, *above*.
[3] Recorded from score prepared by Brahms for a performance in Cologne.
[4] These couplings were announced but apparently not issued, at least for general circulation.

Tragische Ouvertüre, Op. 81 (*continued*)

L.S.O.—Collingwood   ♯ **P.PMC 1024**
(*above; & Schumann*)   (♯ MGM.E 3102)

Residentie—Otterloo   ♯ *Phi.S 06008R*
(*above*)

Phil. Prom.—Boult   ♯ **West.WN 18035**
(*Akademisches Fest-Ov., etc.*)   (in set WN 4401)

Anon. Orch. (♯ Gram. 2095)

☆ Philharmonia—Kletzki (in ♯ AmC.RL 3060)
B.B.C. Sym.—Toscanini (in ♯ G.FJLP 5058)

Variations on a theme of Haydn, Op. 56a

N.Y.P.S.O.—Walter   **EPhi.ABL 3095**
(*Symphony No. 2*)   (♯ Phi.A 01163L)
(⅓s—*Symphony No. 4, s. 2 & Symphony No. 3*
    on ♯ AmC.ML 4911 in set SL 200)
(*Tragische Ouvertüre; & Haydn* on ♯ ML 4814)[4]
(*Tragische Ouvertüre & Symphony No. 3* on ♯ ML 4927)[4]

N.B.C. Sym.—Toscanini   ♯ **G.ALP 1204**
(*Elgar*) (♯ FALP 269; Vic.LM 1725: ♭ *set WDM 1725*;
    ♯ ItV.A12R 0036)

Amsterdam—v. Beinum   ♯ **D.LXT 2778**
(*Overtures*)   (♯ Lon.LL 735)

Residentie—v. Otterloo   ♯ *EPhi.ABR 4026*
(*Wagner*)   (♯ Phi.A 00709R)

Phil. Prom.—Boult   ♯ **West.WN 18035**
(*Overtures & Rhapsody, Op. 53*)   (in set WN 4401)

Philharmonia—Klemperer   ♯ **C.CX 1241**
(*Hindemith*)   (♯ Angel. 35221)

N.W. German Phil.—Schüchter   ♯ *Imp.ILP 104*
(*Beethoven: Leonore No. 3*)

Utrecht Sym.—Hupperts   ♯ *MMS. 15*
(*Akademisches Fest-Ouvertüre*)

"Philharmonic"—Berendt   ♯ *Allo.* 3092
(*Liszt*)

Leighton Lucas Orch. (*EMI.EP 25/6* & EPX 34)
Anon. Orch. (♯ Gram. 2095)

☆ Philharmonia—Markevitch
    (♯ *G.QBLP 5035: FBLP 1057*)
Württemberg State—Leitner (in ♯ *Pol. 16105*)
Vienna Phil.—Furtwängler
    (♯ *G.FALP/QALP 188: VALP 505*)
L.P.O.—Weingartner (♯ AmC.ML 4783)
Minneapolis Sym.—Mitropoulos (in ♯ AmC.RL 3038)

I. 2. CHAMBER MUSIC

QUARTETS, Strings
COMPLETE RECORDING
No. 1, C minor, Op. 51, No. 1
No. 2, A minor, Op. 51, No. 2
No. 3, B flat major, Op. 67

Budapest Qtt.   ♯ **AmC.ML 5052/3**
(3½ss—*Haydn*)   (set SL 225)
[No. 1 is probably ☆; *see below*]

No. 1, C minor, Op. 51, No. 1

☆ Budapest Qtt.   ♯ **EPhi.ABL 3073**
(*Dvořák*)   (♯ AmC.ML 4799; Phi.A 01151L)

No. 2, A minor, Op. 51, No. 2

Amadeus Qtt.   ♯ **G.ALP 1337**
(*Schubert: Qtt. No. 10; & Mendelssohn*)

Végh Qtt.   ♯ **D.LXT 5027**
(*No. 3*)   (♯ Lon.LL 1142)

☆ Curtis Qtt. (*No. 3*)   ♯ Nix.WLP 5152

☆ Budapest Qtt., o.v. (JpV. set JAS 315)
Hollywood Qtt. (♯ ACap.CLCX 015)

No. 3, B flat major, Op. 67

Italian Qtt.   ♯ **C.CX 1244**
    (♯ FCX 390: QCX 10113; Angel. 35184)

Végh Qtt.   ♯ **D.LXT 5027**
(*No. 2*)   (♯ Lon.LL 1142)

☆ Curtis Qtt. (*No. 2*)   ♯ Nix.WLP 5152

QUARTETS, Piano & strings
No. 1, G minor, Op. 25

☆ R. Serkin & Members of Busch Qtt. (♯ C.QCX 10053)

... 4th movt., (Rondo alla zingarese)
E. Gilels, D. Tziganov, V. Borisovsky, S. Shirinsky
(2ss)   USSR. 016701/2

No. 2, A major, Op. 26

C. Curzon & Budapest Qtt. Members
    ♯ **AmC.ML 4630**
    (♯ Phi.A 01192L)

No. 3, C minor, Op. 60

M. Hess, J. Szigeti, M. Katims & P. Tortelier
    ♯ **AmC.ML 4712**
[also ♯ ML 4702 in set SL 185]   (in set SL 182)

QUINTETS, Strings
No. 1, F major, Op. 88

☆ Vienna Konzerthaus Quintet (♯ *Sel.LA 1011*; with
    Pf. Trio, A major, on ♯ West.WN 18063)

No. 2, G major, Op. 111

I. Stern & A. Schneider (vlns.), M. Katims &
    M. Thomas (vlas.), P. Tortelier (vlc.)
    ♯ **AmC.ML 4711**
(*Schumann*)   (in set SL 182)
[also ♯ ML 4701, in set SL 185]

Quintet, B minor, cl. & str., Op. 115

A. Boskovsky & Members of Vienna Octet
    ♯ **D.LXT 2858**
    (♯ Lon.LL 858)

C. Paashaus & Classic Qtt.   ♯ **CEd.CE 1061**
(*Mozart*)

A. Burkner & Berlin Phil. Members
    ♯ *Lum.LD 2-403*

☆ L. Wlach & Vienna Konzerthaus Qtt. ♯ Nix.WLP 5155

☆ A. Gallodoro & Stuyvesant Qtt. (♯ Clc. 6204)
R. Kell & Fine Arts Qtt. (♯ D.UAT 273073)

— FOR PRACTICE, without clarinet (♯ CEd.MMO 61)

Quintet, F minor, Op. 34, pf. & strings

V. Aller & Hollywood Qtt.   ♯ **DCap.CTL 7075**
[3rd. movt. excpt. in ♯ Cap.SAL 9020]   (♯ Cap.P 8269)

☆ J. Demus & Vienna Konzerthaus Qtt. ♯ Nix.WLP 5148
    (♯ Sel. 320.CW.009)

— FOR PRACTICE: Recorded without pf., 1st vln., vla. & vlc. in
turn (♯ CEd.MMO 31/4)

SEXTETS, Strings
No. 1, B flat, Op. 18

I. Stern & A. Schneider (vlns.), M. Katims
    & M. Thomas (vlas.), P. Casals & M.
    Foley (vlcs.)   ♯ **EPhi.ABL 3085**
    (♯ AmC.ML 4713, in set SL 182; ♯ Phi.A 01170L)
[also ♯ ML 4703, in set SL 185]

☆ Vienna Konzerthaus Sextet (♯ Sel.LPG 8670)

No. 2, G major, Op. 36

Vienna Konzerthaus Qtt., W. Hübner &
    G. Weiss   ♯ **Nix.WLP 5263**
    (♯ West.WL 5263)

SONATAS, Clarinet [or vla.] & pf.
No. 1, F minor, Op. 120, No. 1
No. 2, E flat major, Op. 120, No. 2

L. Wlach & J. Demus   ♯ **West.WL 5236**

J. Lancelot & A. d'Arco   ♯ **LOL.OL 50030**

A. de Bavier & A. Wasowski   ♯ **Pol. 18227**

R. Kell & J. Rosen   ♯ **AmD.DL 9639**

P. Doktor (vla.) & N. Reisenberg
    ♯ **West.WN 18114**

SONATAS, Vln. & pf.
No. 1, G major, Op. 78

G. de Vito & E. Fischer   ♯ **G.ALP 1282**
(*No. 3*)

S. Goldberg & A. Balsam   ♯ **AmD.DL 9720**
(*No. 2*)

L. Kaufman & H. Pignari (2ss)   ♯ *MMS. 109*

☆ I. Stern & A. Zakin   ♯ **AmC.ML 4912**
(*No. 3*)   (in set SL 202)

No. 2, A major, Op. 100

I. Stern & A. Zakin   ♯ **EPhi.ABL 3068**
(*Sonatensatz; Dietrich & Schumann*)
    (♯ AmC.ML 4913, in set SL 202; ♯ Phi.A 01133L)

(*continued on next page*)

---

[4] These couplings were announced but apparently not issued, at least for general circulation.

No. 2, A major, Op. 100 (*continued*)
S. Goldberg & A. Balsam   **♯ AmD.DL 9720**
(*No. 1*)

R. Druian & J. Simms   **♯ Mer.MG 80002**
(*Schumann*)

☆ A. Eidus & L. Mittman (♯ Cpt.MC 20056)

No. 3, D minor, Op. 108
G. de Vito & E. Fischer   **♯ G.ALP 1282**
(*No. 1*)

I. Stern & A. Zakin   **♯ AmC.ML 4912**
(*No. 1*)   (in set SL 202)

C. Ferras & P. Barbizet   **♯ DT.LGX 66014**
(*Beethoven*)   (♯ T.LE 6501)

W. Schneiderhan & F. Wührer   **♯ Pol. 18144**
(*Beethoven*)

R. & A. Kitain   **♯ MGM.E 3103**
(*Franck*)

S. Wiener & M. Stoesser   **♯ McInt.MM 108**
(*Martinu*)

D. Oistrakh & V. Yampolsky[1]   **♯ JpV.LS 2025**
(*Locatelli, Kreisler, etc.*)

I. Ozim & M. Few   **♯ Argo.ARL 1015[2]**

☆ D. Oistrakh & V. Yampolsky (o.v.)   **♯ Csm.CRLP 148**
(*Tartini*)

☆ J. Heifetz & W. Kapell (♯ ItV.A1OR 0003)
N. Milstein & V. Horowitz (♯ G.QBLP 1026)

Sonatensatz (Scherzo), C minor (Frei aber einsam)
(for joint Sonata with Dietrich & Schumann)   1853
N. Milstein & C. Bussotti in **♯ DCap.CTL 7058**
(*Schumann, Pergolesi, Suk, etc.*)   (in ♯ Cap.P 8259)

I. Stern & A. Zakin   **♯ EPhi.ABL 3068**
(*Sonata No. 2; Dietrich & Schumann*)
(♯ AmC.ML 4913, in set SL 202; ♯ Phi.A 01133L)

SONATAS, Vlc. & pf.
No. 1, E minor, Op. 38
No. 2, F major, Op. 99
P. Fournier & W. Backhaus   **♯ D.LXT 5077**
(♯ Lon.LL 1264)

J. Starker & A. Bogin   **♯ Nix.PLP 593**
(♯ Per.SPL 593; Cpt.MC 20070)

P. Tortelier & K. Engel   **♯ G.ALP 1233**
(FALP 356)

M. Maréchal & J. M. Darré   **♯ Pat.DTX 127**

T. de Machula & T. Mikkilä   **♯ Phi.A 00231L**
(♯ Epic.LC 3133)

No. 1, E minor, Op. 38
L. Hoelscher & H. Richter-Hasser   **♯ Pol. 18178**
(*R. Strauss*)

☆ G. Cassadó & E. Schulhof (♯ Cum.TCR 271)
G. Piatigorsky & A. Rubinstein (♯ Vic.LCT 1119:
♭ set WCT 1119)

No. 2, F major, Op. 99
E. B. Bengtsson & V. Schiøler   **♯ G.KALP 9**
(*Beethoven*)

TRIOS, Pf., vln., vlc.
No. 1, B major, Op. 8
Trio di Trieste   **♯ D.LXT 2901**
(♯ Lon.LL 955)

P. Badura-Skoda, J. Fournier & A. Janigro
♯ Nix.WLP 5237
(♯ West.WL 5237; Véga.C30.A9)

M. Hess, I. Stern & P. Casals   **♯ AmC.ML 4719**
(in set SL 184)
(also ♯ ML 4709, in set SL 185; Phi.A 01207L)

☆ A. Rubinstein, J. Heifetz, E. Feuermann   **♯G.BLP 1056**
(♯ DV.L 17046)

No. 2, C major, Op. 87
Trio di Trieste   **♯ D.LXT 5204**
(*Haydn*)   (♯ Lon.LL 1176)

Trio di Bolzano   **♯ Cpt.MC 20018**
(*Beethoven*)

M. Hess, J. Szigeti, P. Casals   **♯AmC.ML 4720**
(also ♯ ML 4710, in set SL 185)   (in set SL 184)

▽ Court of Belgium Trio, 8ss (C.DFX 185/8)
☆ Alma Trio (♯Allo. 4035)

No. 3, C minor, Op. 101
N. M-Minchin, H. Clebanoff, K. Früh
♯ APM.PMT 201
(*Loeillet & Tcherepnin*)

A major   (discovered 1924; doubtful)
☆ F. Holetschek, W. Hübner & R. Harand
(2ss)   **♯ Nix.WLP 5058**
(*Quintet, Op. 88 on* ♯ West.WN 18063)

Trio, pf., cl., vlc., A minor, Op. 114
☆ F. Holetschek, L. Wlach, F. Kwarda   ♯Nix.WLP 5146
(*below*)
☆ M. Horszowski, R. Kell & F. Miller   ♯ **B.AXL 2011**
(2ss)   (♯ D.UA 243559)
(*Mozart: Cl. Concerto on* ♯ B.AXTL 1071:
AmD.DL 9732)

Trio, pf., vln., hrn., E flat major, Op. 40
M. Horszowski, A. Schneider & M. Jones
(*Schumann*)   **♯ AmC.ML 4892**
E. Gilels, L. Kogan & Y. Shapiro
♯ USSR.D 1746/7

☆ F. Holetschek, W. Barylli & F. Koch ♯ Nix.WLP 5146
(*above*)
☆ A. d'Arco, G. Alès & J. Devemy   **♯ Esq.TN 22-001**

I. 3. PIANO & ORGAN

A. PIANO (*Solo & Duet*)

COLLECTIONS
W. Kempff   **♯ D. & Lon.**
(4) BALLADES, Op. 10
(8) CAPRICCI & INTERMEZZI, Op. 76
on ♯ D.LXT 2914
(♯ Lon.LL 959)
(7) FANTASIAS, Op. 116 (Capricci & Intermezzi)
(4) KLAVIERSTÜCKE, Op. 119
(3 Intermezzi & Rhapsody)   on ♯ D.LXT 2935
(♯ NLK 40104; Lon.LL 960)
(3) INTERMEZZI, Op. 117
(2) RHAPSODIES, Op. 79   on ♯ D.LX 3134
(♯ Lon.LS 961)
(6) KLAVIERSTÜCKE, Op. 118   on ☆ ♯ D.LX 3032
(♯ Lon.LS 204)
[for separate issues, *see below*]

(7) FANTASIAS, Op. 116 (Capricci & Intermezzi)
(7) KLAVIERSTÜCKE, Op. 76
(Capricci & Intermezzi)
W. Gieseking   **♯ C.CX 1255**
(♯ FCX/QCX 200; Angel. 35028)

KLAVIERSTÜCKE, Opp. 79, 118, 119
W. Gieseking   **♯ C.CX 1256**
(♯ FCX/QCX 201; Angel. 35027)
[see below for individual issues]

(4) BALLADES, Op. 10
INTERMEZZI, Op. 76, Nos. 3, 4, 6
RHAPSODIES, Op. 79, Nos. 1 & 2
E. Petri   **♯ Roy. 1630**
[Op. 76, No. 3 only, on ♯ Roy. 1901]

(8) CAPRICCI & INTERMEZZI, Op. 76
(7) FANTASIAS, Op. 116 (Capricci & Intermezzi)
D. Wayenberg   **♯ Sel. 320.C.067**

(7) FANTASIAS, Op. 116 (Capricci & Intermezzi)
(6) KLAVIERSTÜCKE, Op. 118
C. Seemann   **♯ AmD.DL 9667**
[Op. 116 is ☆; Op. 118 only on ♯ Pol. 16040: ♮ PV. 72325/6]

(6) KLAVIERSTÜCKE, Op. 118
T. Battista   **♯ MGM.E 3056**
(*Sonata No. 2*)

Capriccio, D minor, Op. 116, No. 7
Intermezzo, E major, Op. 116, No. 4
Intermezzo, E major, Op. 116, No. 6
Intermezzo, E flat minor, Op. 118, No. 6
Rhapsody, E flat, Op. 119, No. 4
M. van Monnerberg   **♯ Her. 1**
(*Chopin*)

[1] Tokyo recording, 1955.   [2] Announced but not issued.

BALLADES,
D minor, Op. 10, No. 1   ("*Edward*")
☆ C. Seemann (♭ *Pol. 30032*)

G minor, Op. 118, No. 3
G. Kämper   **Ifma.MA 40000**
(*Intermezzo, Op. 118, No. 2*)
☆ W. Kempff   ♭ *D. 71064*
(*Intermezzo, Op. 118, No. 6*)   (♭ *DK 23353*)

Capriccio, B minor, Op. 76, No. 2
A. Rubinstein   in ♯ **G.ALP 1213**
(*Intermezzi & Rhapsodies*)
(in ♯ Vic.LM 1787; ItV.A12R 0113; FV.A 630205;
                  DV.L 16473)
J. Smeterlin   ♯ **BB.LBC 1076**
(*Variations*)
☆ F. Kramer (in ♯ MTR.MLP 1012)

INTERMEZZI
COLLECTION
B flat minor, Op. 117, No. 2
C sharp minor, Op. 117, No. 3
A major, Op. 118, No. 2
E flat minor, Op. 118, No. 6
E minor, Op. 119, No. 2
C major, Op. 119, No. 3
A. Rubinstein   ♯ **G.ALP 1213**
(*Capriccio, Op. 76, No. 2 & Rhapsodies*)
(♯ Vic.LM 1787; FV.A 630205; DV.L 16473;
                   ItV.A12R 0113)

B flat major, Op. 76, No. 4
C. Friedberg   in ♯ **Zod. 1001**

A minor, Op. 116, No. 2
☆ E. Freund (in ♯ Ply. 12-75)

E major, Op. 116, No. 4
W. Gieseking   **C.LX 1586**
(*Rhapsody, Op. 79, No. 2*)   (GQX 11534)

E flat major, Op. 117, No. 1
L. Hungerford   in ♯ **LH. 101/2**
                     (Pte.)
C. Friedberg   in ♯ **Zod. 1001**
G. Scherzer   (*No. 2*)   **P.E 11512**
☆ L. Kolessa (in ♯ Clc. 6252)

B flat minor, Op. 117, No. 2
M. Lympany   **G.C 4209**
(*Chopin: Fantaisie-Impromptu*)   (S 10609: ♭ *7P 141*)
G. Scherzer   **P.E 11512**
(*Intermezzo, Op. 117, No. 1*)
☆ E. Freund (in ♯ Ply. 12-75)

C sharp minor, Op. 117, No. 3
☆ L. Kolessa (in ♯ Clc. 6252)

A minor, Op. 118, No. 1
B. Webster   in ♯ **Persp.PR 2**

A major, Op. 118, No. 2
G. Gorini (2ss)   *Cet.AT 0332*
E. Burton   in ♯ **CEd.CE 1027**
G. Kämper   **Ifma.MA 40000**
(*Ballade, Op. 118, No. 3*)

E flat minor, Op. 118, No. 6
L. Hungerford   in ♯ **LH. 101/2**
                     (Pte.)
☆ W. Kempff   ♭ *D. 71064*
(*Ballade, Op. 118, No. 3*)   (♭ *DK 23353*)
☆ W. Malcuzynski (in ♯ C.CX 1144: FCX 228)
   F. Kramer (in ♯ MTR.MLP 1012)

B minor, Op. 119, No. 1
W. Gieseking   *C.LB 135*
(*Intermezzo, Op. 119, No. 3*)   (*GQ 7255: LO 97*)

E minor, Op. 119, No. 2
W. Gieseking   **C.LX 1581**
(*Rhapsody, Op. 119, No. 4*)   (LOX 823: GQX 11530)
W. Kempff (from set) (♭ *D. 71119*)

C major, Op. 119, No. 3
W. Gieseking   *C.LB 135*
(*Intermezzo, Op. 119, No. 1*)   (*GQ 7255: LO 97*)
W. Backhaus[1]   in ♯ **Lon.LL 1108/9**
(*Beethoven, Liszt, Schubert, etc.*)
D. Barenboim   ♭ *EPhi.NBE 11013*
(*Mendelssohn & Mozart*)   (♭ *Phi.N 425008E*)

RHAPSODIES
B minor, Op. 79, No. 1
G minor, Op. 79, No. 2
E flat major, Op. 119, No. 4
A. Rubinstein   ♯ **G.ALP 1213**
(*Capriccio, Intermezzi*)
(♯ Vic.LM 1787; ItV.A12R 0113; FV.A 630205;
                     DV.L 16473)
☆ A. Chasins (♭ *FMer.MEP 14506;* Op. 79, No. 2 only,
                      in ♭ *Mer.EP 1-5040*)

Op. 79, Nos. 1 & 2
M. Schwalb   ♯ **Roy. 1464**
(*Walzes; & Beethoven*)
W. Kempff (from set)   ♯ *D.LW 5211*
(2ss)   (♯ *Lon.LD 9116*)
      [☆ (o.v.) on ♯ *D.LW 5043; Lon.LD 9048*]
A. de Lara   ♯ **AdL.LP 5**
(*Scherzo; & Beethoven: Variations*)
A. d'Arco   **V♯ DO.LD 28**
L. Gousseau   ♯ *Plé.P 3069*
(*Schumann*)

B minor, Op. 79, No. 1
☆ W. Gieseking (C.GQX 11525)

G minor, Op. 79, No. 2
W. Gieseking   **C.LX 1586**
(*Intermezzo, Op. 116, No. 4*)   (GQX 11534)
P. Badura-Skoda   in ♯ **Nix.WLP 5277**
                 (in ♯ West.WL 5277)

E flat major, Op. 119, No. 4
W. Gieseking   **C.LX 1581**
(*Intermezzo, Op. 119, No. 2*)   (GQX 11530: LOX 823)
W. Kempff (from set) (♭ *D. 71119*)
☆ A. Chasins (♭ *Mer.EP 1-5010*)

Romance, F major, Op. 118, No. 5
M. Schwalb   in ♯ *Acad. 310*
(*Fauré, Liszt, etc.*)

Scherzo, E flat minor, Op. 4
C. Friedberg   ♯ **Zod. 1001**
(*Intermezzi; & Schumann*)
A. de Lara   ♯ **AdL.LP 5**
(*Rhapsodies, Op. 79; & Beethoven: Variations*)

SONATAS
No. 2, F sharp minor, Op. 2
J. Battista   ♯ **MGM.E 3056**
(*Klavierstücke, Op. 118*)

No. 3, F minor, Op. 5
P. Badura-Skoda   ♯ **Nix.WLP 5245**
                 (♯ West.WL 5245)
L. Nadelmann   ♯ *MMS. 79*
☆ E. Fischer   ♯ *G.BLP 1017*
(2ss)   (♯ *QBLP 5023*)
(*Schumann on ♯ Vic.LHMV 1065: ♭ set WHMV 1065*)

F minor, Op. 34a   2 pfs.
T. Whelan & W. Hamilton   ♯ **Edu.ECM 4004**

VARIATIONS
On a theme of Schumann, Op. 9
A. Foldes (*below*)   ♯ *Pol. 17048*
V. Frieda   ♯ *Ply. 12-28*
(*Schumann: Fantasia*)
☆ J. Blancard (♯ CID.UM 63020)

                 (*continued on next page*)

---

[1] Carnegie Hall recital, March, 1954.

VARIATIONS (*continued*)

On an original theme, Op. 21, No. 1
A. Foldes (2ss)   **PV. 72338**
(*Schumann on ♯ AmD.DL 9708; above on ♯ Pol. 17048*)
J. Smeterlin   **♯ BB.LBC 1076**
(*Capriccio, Op. 76, No. 2; & below*)

On a theme of Handel, Op. 24
A. Simon   **♯ Phi.A 00195L**
(*below*)   (♯ Epic.LC 3050)
B. Moiseiwitsch   **♯ G.CLP 1017**
(*Schumann*)
S. Gorodnitzki   **♯ DCap.CTL 7049**
(*below*)   (♯ Cap.P 8227; ACap.CLCX 044)
J. Lateiner (*below*)   **♯ West.WN 18100**
☆ L. Kolessa (♯ Clc. 6252)

On a theme of Paganini, Op. 35
G. Anda[1]   **♯ C.CX 1072**
(*Schumann: Études symphoniques*)
                                        (♯ C.FCX 283; Angel. 35046)
S. Gorodnitzky   **♯ DCap.CTL 7049**
(*above*)   (♯ Cap.P 8227; ACap.CLCX 044)
C. Rosen   **♯ *D.LW 5092***
(2ss) (*Waltzes on* ♯ D.FST 153083)   (♯ *Lon.LD 9104*)
F. Wührer   **♯ E. & AmVox.PL 8850**
(*Liszt & Schumann*)
A. Simon   **♯ Phi.A 00195L**
(*above*)   (♯ Epic.LC 3050)
J. Smeterlin[2]   **♯ BB.LBC 1076**
(*above & Capriccio, Op. 76, No. 2*)
C. Keene[3]   **♯ Mer.MG 10138**
(*Bach & Beethoven*)
A. Foldes (2ss)   **♯ *Pol. 16049***
J. Lateiner   **♯ West.WN 18100**
(*above*)
☆ A. B. Michelangeli   **♯ *G.FBLP/QBLP 1044***
(*Bach-Busoni: Chaconne*)
☆ R. Goldsand (♯ Clc. 6270)

On a theme of Haydn, Op. 56b 2 pfs.
E. Bartlett & R. Robertson   **♯ MGM.E 3027**
(*Waltzes; & Schumann*)
☆ P. Luboshutz & G. Nemenoff (in ♯ Cam.CAL 206)

---

3. B. ORGAN

COMPLETE ORGAN WORKS (in progress)
VOL. I
Prelude & Fugue, G minor 1857
Fugue, A flat minor *c.* 1857
Chorale Prelude & Fugue 'O Traurigkeit, O Herzeleid' *c.* 1857
Prelude & Fugue, A minor 1856
R. Elmore   **♯ Cant.MRR 293**

(11) CHORALE-PRELUDES, Op. 122
COMPLETE RECORDING
V. Fox[4]   **♯ Vic.LM 1853**
(*below*)   (♯ ItV.A12R 0161; FV.A 530206)
[Org. of Hammond Museum, Gloucester, Mass.]

Nos. 1, 2, 4, 8, 11
☆ E. White (♭ *Mer.EP 1-5014;* ♭ *FMer.MEP 14510,*
              omitting No. 1 according to list)

No. 3, O Welt, ich muss dich lassen
☆ C. Snyder[5]   in ♯ Word.W 4003
(*Schumann, Karg-Elert, Franck, etc.*)

No. 5, Schmücke dich, O liebe Seele
A. Hamme   in ♯ SRS.H 1
(† *Organ Recital*)

No. 8, Es ist ein' Ros' entsprungen
W. Watkins   in ♯ McInt.MM 106
R. I. Purvis   in ♯ HIFI.R 705
(*Dupré, Purvis*)

No. 10, Herzlich tut mich verlangen
— ARR. VLA. & ORG. de Tar
W. Primrose & V. de Tar (in ♯ *AmC.AL 33*)

Chorale Prelude & Fugue on 'O Traurigkeit' ...
V. Fox (*above*)   **♯ Vic.LM 1853**

════════════

I. 4. HUNGARIAN DANCES & WALTZES

HUNGARIAN DANCES orig. pf. duet

THE 21, COMPLETE (ORCH. VERSION)
☆ Oklahoma Sym.—Alessandro (♯ Pac.LDAD 35)

COLLECTION: ORIGINAL PF. DUET VERSION
Nos. 1-4, 11-13, 17
K. U. & H. Schnabel   **♯ Phi.N 00255L**
(*Schubert*)   (♯ Epic.LC 3183)

COLLECTIONS — ARR. VLN. & PF. Joachim (*et al.*)
Omitting Nos. 10-13, 16 & 18
☆ A. Spalding & A. Kooiker (♯ *Cum.CR 214;*
       Nos. 1, 4, 5, 6 only on ♭ *ECR 37;* ♭ *Rem.REP 13*)
Nos. 5, 8, 9 & 20
D. Oistrakh & V. Yampolsky   **♯ *Sup.LPM 184***
(*Beethoven*)   (♯ *U. 5166C;* in ♯ *USSR.D 1202, d.c.*)
(Nos. 5, 8 & 9 only on ♯ Van.VRS 6020; ♯ Csm.CRLP 149;
                              ♯ Mon.MWL 333, d.cs.)
Nos. 5, 6, 7 & 17
☆ E. Morini & A. Balsam (♭ *Cam.CAE 129:* in ♯ *CAL 207*)
Nos. 1 & 8
☆ E. Morini & A. Balsam (♭ *Cam.CAE 180:* in ♯ *CAL 207*)

COLLECTIONS — ARR. ORCH.
[USUAL VERSIONS: Nos. 2 & 7, Hallén; 5, 6, 11-16, Parlow;
   17-21, Dvořák]
Nos. 1, 2, 3, 5, 6, 7, 10
N.W.D.R.—Schmidt-Isserstedt   **♯ *D.LW 5066***
(2ss)   (♯ *Lon.LD 9071*)
(*Dvořák on* ♯ D.LXT 2814; ♯ Lon.LL 779)
Nos. 1-6
Pasdeloup—Lindenberg   **♯ *Od.OD 1012***
(*Liszt*) [Nos. 2, 4, 5, 6 on ♭ *7OAE 1015;* Nos. 4 & 5 only
                                        on ♭ *DSOQ 201*]
☆ Boston Prom.—Fiedler   **♯ Vic.LM 9017**
(*Smetana & Dvořák*)
   Separate issues from above set:—
No. 1: G.HN 3248; in ♯ *Vic.LRM 7003;* ♭ *set ERB 7003*
No. 2: G.HN 3248: ♭ *7BF 1063;* in ♯ *Vic.LRM 7002:*
                                      ♭ *set ERB 7002.*
No. 3: in ♯ *Vic.LRM 7002;* ♭ *set ERB 7002;* ♭ *G.7PQ 2005*
No. 4: in ♯ *Vic.LRM 7003;* ♭ *set ERB 7003;* ♭ *G.7PQ 2005*
No. 5: G.B 10631; ♭ *7PQ 2023;* ♭ *DV. 16304*
No. 6: G.B 10631; ♭ *7PQ 2023;* ♭ *DV. 16304*
Nos. 1, 3, 5, 6, 7, 11, 12, 17
Westminster Light—Bridgewater   **♯ West.WL 4009**
(*Tchaikovsky*)   (♭ *AFest.XP 45-453/4*)
(No. 5 only in ♯ *West.WL 3016 & WP 1022*)
Nos. 1, 3, 5, 6, 17, 18, 19, 20, 21
☆ Berlin Phil.—v. Kempen (♯ *AmD.DL 4078;*
       Nos. 1, 6, 17, 20, only on ♭ *Pol. 30028*)
Nos. 1, 4, 5, 6 (may be No. 2 and not No. 1)
N.W. German Phil.—Schüchter   **♯ Imp.ILP 103**
(*Liszt: Rhapsody No. 2*)(♯ *G.QDLP 6028;* ♭ *Od.BEOW 3007*)
Nos. 1-7 & 17
☆ Decca Concert—Horlick
                (♯ *AmD.DL 5210;* AFest.CFR 10-732)
Nos. 3-10, 12-17, 20, 21
Berlin Sym.—Rubahn   **♯ Roy. 1434**
(also Nos. 1-10, ♯ *Var. 69106*)
Nos. 11-21 (*sic*)
Berlin Sym.—Rubahn (♯ *MusH.LP 6004*)
Nos. 1, 17, 20, 21
N.B.C. Sym.—Toscanini   **♯ G.ALP 1235**
(*Beethoven, Berlioz, Hérold, etc.*)
             (♯ Vic.LM 1834; FV.A 630247; DV.L 16843)
(Nos. 1, 20, 21 only on ♭ *ItV.A72R 0018*)
Nos. 2, 5, 6, 7
F.O.K. Sym.—Smetáček   **♯ *Sup.LPM 113***
. (*Glinka & Sibelius*)
(*Glazounov & Rubinstein on* ♯ *U. 5124G*)

---

[1] Omits coda, Bk. I, and Theme, Bk. II.
[2] Omits Bk. I, Variation 14, and Bk. II, Theme and Variations 1, 5, 8, 9.
[3] Omits Bk. I, Nos. 4, 8, 14; Bk. II, Theme and Variations Nos. 7 and 9.
[4] Each chorale-prelude is preceded by the chorale as harmonised by J. S. Bach.
[5] The unid. on KR. 15, now reissued and identified.

HUNGARIAN DANCES (*continued*)

Nos. 1, 3, 10, 17
☆ N.Y.P.S.O.—Walter ♭ *EPhi.ABE 10002*
(also ♯ ML 4908, in set SL 200; Nos. 1, 10, 17 only
on ♭ *A 1577*) (♭ *Phi.N 409513E*)

Nos. 1-3
☆ Philharmonia—Kletzki
(♭ *C.SEL 1510: SEBQ 114: ESBF 115*)
Vienna Phil.—Furtwängler (♭ *Vic.EHA 17*)

Nos. 1, 2, 3, 5, 6, 7, 10
Orch.—Swarowsky ♯ *MTW. 19*
(*Dach & Sibelius*) (♭ *set EP 19*)

Nos. 1, 5, 6, 17
Moscow Radio—Gauk *USSR. 16522/3 & 17673/4*

Nos. 1, 2, 7, 17
Moscow Radio—Gauk *USSRM.D 00648/51*
[So listed, but may well be meant for same selection as
last entry]

Unspec. Dances
Anon. Orch. (*Saint-Saëns*) ♯ *ACC.MP 5*

No. 1, G minor — ARR. ORCH.
Poznán Phil.—Wislocki *Muza. 2361*
(*No. 3*)
☆ Philadelphia—Stokowski (in ♯ Cam.CAL 123:
♭ *CAE 192*)
Vienna Phil.—Furtwängler (G.ED 1234)
L.S.O.—Krauss (♭ *D.DME 8006; Lon.REP 8006*)

— ARR. VLN. & PF. (may be No. 5, trs. to G minor)
I. Oistrakh & pf. (*USSR. 5877*)
☆ I. Bezrodny & pf. (*USSRM.D 00922*)

— (ARR.) Victor Electronic Music Synthesizer
(in ♯ *Vic.LM 1922*: ♭ *set ERD 1922*)

No. 2, D minor — ARR. VLN. & PF.
♨ J. Joachim & pf. (in ♯ *AudA.LP 0079**)

No. 3, F major — ARR. ORCH.
Poznán Phil.—Wislocki *Muza. 2361*
☆ L.S.O.—Krauss (♭ *D.DME 8006; Lon.REP 8006*)
Berlin Phil.—v. Kempen (♭ *Pol. 32010*)

No. 5, F sharp minor — ARR. ORCH.
(Trs. to G minor)
Hollywood Bowl—Dragon in ♯*DCap.CTL7072*
(in ♯ Cap.P 8276: ♭ *FAP 8283*)
International Sym.—Schneiderhann (in ♯ *Mae.OA 20009*)
Hamburg Philharmonia—H-J. Walther
(*MSB. 78110*; in ♯ MGM.E 3195)
Israel Radio—Goehr (*Arzi. 768*; in ♯ *Bne. 501*)
W. Fenske Orch. (in ♯ *Phi.P 10200R*)
A. Sciascia Orch. (*Fnt. 14470*; in ♯ *LP 310*)
Orch.—Robinson (in ♯ Argo.RG 50; West. WP 6002,
o.n. WN 18097)
☆ Philharmonia—Kletzki (in ♯ AmC.RL 3091)
Berlin Phil.—v. Kempen (♭ *Pol. 32010*)
Florence Fest.—Gui (*Orf. 53003*)
Paris Opéra—Cloëz (♭ *Od.7AO 2001*)
Liverpool Phil.—Sargent (in ♯ AmC.RL 3050)
A. Kostelanetz Orch. (in ♯ *C.S 1029*; ♭ *AmC.A 1557*, etc.)
Kingsway Sym.—Olof (♭ *Lon.REP 8007*)

— ARR. VLN. & PF.
☆ J. Szigeti (♭ *AmC.A 1887*; ♭ *Phi.N 409506E*)

No. 6, D flat major — ARR. ORCH. (trs. to D major)
Boston Orch. Soc.—Page in ♯ *Nix.SLPY 802*
(♯ *SOT. 2066*)
International Sym.—Schneiderhann (in ♯ *Mae.OA 20009*)
Hamburg Philharmonia—H-J. Walther
(*MSB. 78110*; in ♯ MGM.E 3195)
Israel Radio—Goehr (*Arzi. 768*; in ♯ *Bne. 501*)
W. Fenske Orch. (in ♯ *Phi.P 10200R*)
☆ Philharmonia—Kletzki (in ♯ AmC.RL 3091)
Paris Opéra—Cloez (♭ *Od.7AO 2001*)
Florence Fest.—Gui (*Orf. 53003*)

No. 7, A major — ARR. VLN. & PF.
☆ J. Heifetz (♭ *AmD.ED 3501* & in ♯ DL 9780;
♭ *D.EUA 108503*)

No. 8, A minor — ORIG. PF. DUET
E. Bartlett & R. Robertson in ♯*MGM.E 3150*

— ARR. CYMBALOM:
D. Marta (in ♯ *Nix.SLPY 149*; ♯ *SOT. 1032*)

No. 9, E minor — ARR. VLN. & PF.
D. Oistrakh & pf. (*USSR. 22332*)

No. 11, C major — ARR. VLN. & PF.
D. Oistrakh & pf. (*USSR. 22333*)

No. 17, F sharp minor — ARR. ORCH.
M.G.M. Orch.—Marrow (in ♯ MGM.E 3136)

No. 18-21 — ARR. ORCH. Dvořák
☆ Minneapolis Sym.—Ormandy
(♯ Cam.CAL 119: ♭ *CAE 215*)

No. 20, E minor
— ARR. VLN. & PF. D. Oistrakh & pf. (*USSR. 10462*)
— ARR. VLC. & PF. D. Shafran & pf. (*USSRM.D 364*)

WALTZES

(16) WALTZES, Op. 39 pf. duet
COMPLETE RECORDINGS — ARR. PF. SOLO
R. Weisz ♯ *D.LW 5109*
(2ss) (♯ *Lon.LD 9129*)
(*Schumann* on ♯ D.LK 4063; ♯ Lon.LL 798)
C. Rosen ♯ *D.FST 153083*
(*Variations on a theme of Paganini*)

Nos. 1-6 & 12-15 (or 16?)
☆ A. Chasins & C. Keene
(♭ *Mer.EP 1-5058*; ♭ *FMer.MEP 14508*)

Nos. 1, 2, 5, 6, 10, 14, 15
☆ N. Boulanger & D. Lipatti (JpV.SD 3095)

Nos. 1, 2, 11, 14, 15 — ARR. 2 PFS. Brahms
E. Bartlett & R. Robertson in ♯ MGM.E 3027

Nos. 1, 2, 4-10, 14-16 — ARR. PF. SOLO
M. Schwalb ♯ *Roy. 1464*
(*Rhapsodies; & Beethoven*)

Nos. 4, 8 & 15 — ARR. PF. SOLO
E. Burton in ♯ *CEd.CE 1025*

No. 2 — ARR. GUITAR Segovia
☆ A. Segovia (in † ♯ *B.AXTL 1060*)

No. 15, A flat major — ARR. PF. SOLO
S. Bianca (*MSB. 25*: in ♯ 60041, with spoken commentary)
E. Silver (hpsi.) (in ♯ *Roy. 1550*)
R. Spivak (ArgV. 66-6001)
P. Palla (*Phi.N 17802H*)

— ARRANGEMENTS
ORCH. Anon. Orch. (in ♯ *Roy. 1432*)
J. Schmied (in ♯ *Vien.LPR 1031*)
☆ Boston Prom.—Fiedler
(♭ *Vic. 49-1434*; in ♯ Cam.CAL 142: ♭ *CAE 135*)
VLN. & PF. I. Haendel & G. Moore in ♯ *G.CLP 1021*
E. Zathureczky & M. Karin (in ♯ *U. 5185C*)
BAND Anon. Band (in ♯ *Jay. 3004*)
ORGAN V. Fox (♭ *AmC. set A 1008*)
HARP O. Erdeli (*USSR. 22731*)
CHO. "Jugend" (*Ger*)
Vienna Boys' Cho.—Kühbacher (pf.)
(in ♯ *EPhi.NBR 6024*; Phi.N 00726R: ♭ *N 402038E*)

Liebeslieder Walzer, Op. 52 (Daumer)
Pf. duet & vocal qtt. ad lib.
E. Roon (S), M. Nussbaumer (A), M. Dickie (T),
N. Foster (Bs) & Academy Cho.
—F. Grossmann[1] ♯ *AmVox.PL 9460*
(*below*) [J. & G. Dichler (pfs.)]
Stuttgart Vocal Qtt.—Couraud ♯ *DFr. 107*
(*below*) [W. Bohle & I. Zucca-Sehlbach, (pfs.)]
S. Bianca & G. Arnoldi *MSB.78105/6*
(4ss) [pfs. only]
Nos. 1, 3, 5, 6, 9, 10, 11, 12, 13, 17, 18
☆ Vienna Academy Cha. Cho.—Grossmann & pf. duet
(V♯ *Sel.LPP 8610*)
Nos. 1, 2, 6, 7, 8, 9 — ARR. ORCH. Hermann
Boyd Neel Orch.—Dumont ♯ *Phi.S 06052R*
(*Elgar*)

Neue Liebeslieder Walzer, Op. 65
Pf. duet & vocal qtt. ad lib. (Daumer & Goethe)
F. Wend (S), N. Wough (M-S), H. Cuénod (T),
D. Conrad (Bs) ♯ *AmD.DL 9650*
(*Part Songs*) [N. Boulanger & J. Françaix (pfs.)]
E. Roon (S), M. Nussbaumer (A), M. Dickie (T),
N. Foster (B), Academy Cha. Cho.
—Grossmann[1] ♯ *AmVox.PL 9460*
(*above*) [J. & G. Dichler (pfs.)]

(*continued on next page*)

---

[1] Some items by soloists, others by choir.

Neue Liebeslieder Walzer, Op. 65 (*continued*)
Stuttgart Vocal Qtt.—Couraud ♯ DFr. 107
(*above*) [W. Bohle & I. Zucca-Sehlbach, pfs.]
... No. 15, Zum Schluss (Goethe) (*Nun, ihr Musen*)
R. Shaw Cho. & 2 pfs. (in Part Song collection, *below*)

II. VOCAL

1. CHORAL (with orchestra)

(Ein) DEUTSCHES REQUIEM, Op. 45
S, B, Cho., Orch. (in *German*)
M. Stader, O. Wiener, St. Hedwig's Cath. Cho.,
Berlin Motet Cho. & Berlin Phil. Orch.
—Lehmann (4ss) ♯ HP.DGM 18258/9
(also manual, ♯ Pol. 18238/9)
E. Grümmer, D. Fischer-Dieskau, St. Hedwig's
Cath. Cho. & Berlin Phil. Orch.—Kempe
♯ G.ALP 1351S/2
(3ss) (♯ WALP 1505/6S)
L. Wissmann, T. Adam, Frankfurt Op. Cho.
Frankfurt Op. & Museum Orchs.—Solti
(4ss) ♯ Cap. set PBR 8300
I. Seefried, G. London, Westminster Cho. &
N.Y.P.S.O.—Walter ♯ AmC. in prep.
☆ E. Steber, J. Pease, R. Shaw Cho. & Victor Sym.
—Shaw (♯ ItV.B12R 0151/2)

No. 4, Wie lieblich sind deine Wohnungen Cho.
(*How lovely is thy dwelling-place*)
Mormon Tabernacle Cho.—Cornwall
(*Eng*) in ♯ EPhi.NBL 5012
(Phi.N 02125L; AmC.ML 5048)

Gesang der Parzen, Op. 89 (Goethe)
Nänie, Op. 82 (Schiller)
☆ Vienna Cha. Cho. & Sym.—Swoboda ♯ Nix.WLP 5081
(*R. Strauss*) (V♯ Sel.LLA 8715)
(*Nänie only, with Gesänge, Op. 17 & Marienlieder,
on ♯ West.WN 18062*)

Rhapsodie, Op. 53 (Goethe) (*"Alto Rhapsody"*)
A, Male Cho., Orch.
M. Sinclair, Croydon Phil. Cho. & Phil. Prom.
Orch.—Boult ♯ West.WN 18035
(*Overtures & Variations*) (in set WN 4401)
☆ K. Ferrier, L.P.O. & Cho.—Krauss ♯ D.LXT 2850
(*Songs*) (♯ Lon.LL 903)
☆ M. Anderson, Shaw Chorale, Victor Sym.—Reiner
(*Mahler*) ♯ G.ALP 1138
(♯ ItV.A12R 0085)
☆ E. Höngen, Berlin Liedertafel Cho., Berlin Phil. Orch.
—Leitner ♯ Pol. 16105
(*Variations on a theme of Haydn*)
(*Zigeunerlieder* on ♯ AmD.DL 4074)

Rinaldo, Op. 50 (Goethe) T, Male Cho. & Orch.
J. Kerol, New Paris Cho. & Pasdeloup Orch.
—Leibowitz ♯ E. & AmVox.PL 8180

Schicksalslied, Op. 54 (Hölderlin) Cho. & Orch.
(*Song of Destiny*)
Berlin Motet Cho. & Berlin Phil. Orch.
—Lehmann ♯ Pol. 19046
(*Schubert & Mendelssohn*)
☆ Stanford Univ. Cho. (*Eng*) & San Francisco Sym.
—Monteux ♭ ItV.B72R 0011/2
(3ss—*Beethoven: Ruinen von Athen, Overture*)

II. 2. PART SONGS & MOTETS
(unacc. unless an instrument is named)

COLLECTIONS
Op. 31, No. 1 Wechsellied zum Tanze (Goethe)
No. 2 Neckereien (Trad.)
No. 3 Der Gang zum Liebchen (Trad.)
Op. 64, No. 1 An die Heimat (Sternau)
No. 2 Der Abend (Schiller)
No. 3 Fragen (Daumer)

Op. 92, No. 1 O schöne Nacht (Daumer)
No. 2 Spätherbst (Allmers)
No. 3 Abendlied (Hebbel)
No. 4 Warum (Goethe)
Op. 112, No. 1 Sehnsucht (Kugler)
No. 2 Nächtens (Kugler)
No. 3 Himmel strahlt so helle
No. 4 Rote Rosenknospen
No. 5 Brennessel steht am Wegesrand
No. 6 Liebe Schwalbe
—Nos. 3-6, Zigeunerlieder (Conrat)
Stuttgart Vocal Qtt.—Couraud ♯ DFr. 106
[W. Bohle (pf.)]

An die Heimat, Op. 64, No. 1 (Sternau)
(Der) Abend, Op. 64, No. 2 (Schiller)
Fragen, Op. 64, No. 3 (Daumer)
O schöne Nacht, Op. 92, No. 1 (Daumer)
Sehnsucht, Op. 112, No. 1 (Kugler)
Nächtens, Op. 112, No. 2 (Kugler)
F. Wend (S), N. Wough (M-S), H. Cuénod (T),
D. Conrad (Bs), N. Boulanger & J. Françaix
(pfs.) ♯ AmD.DL 9650
(*Neue Liebeslieder, Op. 65*)
(Der) Abend, Op. 64, No. 2 (Schiller) cho. & pf.
Nächtens, Op. 112, No. 2 (Kugler) cho. & pf.
Zum Schluss, Op. 65, No. 15 (Goethe) cho. & 2 pfs.
R. Shaw Chorale, J. Wustman &
J. MacInnes (pfs.) ♯ Vic.LM 1784
(*Bach, Schubert*) (♯ FV.A 630230)

(Der) Bücklichte Fiedler, Op. 93a, No. 1 (Trad.)
☆ Augustana Cho.—Veld (in ♯ Word. 4001)

(Der) Gang zum Liebchen, Op. 31, No. 3 (pf. acc.)
— ARR. SOLO VOICE & PF.
A. Poell (B), V. Graef (pf.) in ♯ Nix.WLP 5053
[not Op. 48, No. 1, as previously listed]
(∇ in ♯ West.WL 5053)

(4) Gesänge für Frauenchor, Op. 17
Female Cho., 2 hrns., & hp.
1. Es tönt ein voller Harfenklang
(*Whene'er the sounding Harp*—Ruperti)
2. Komm' herbei, Tod
(*Come away, Death*—after Shakespeare)
3. Der Gärtner
(*The Gardener*—Eichendorff)
4. Gesang aus Fingal
(*The Death of Trenar*—after Ossian)
☆ Vienna Cha. Cho.—Schmid ♯ Nix.WLP 5014
(*below*) (♯ Sel. 270.CW.004)
(*idem, & Nänie on* ♯ West.WN 18062)

Ich aber bin elend, Op. 110, No. 1 Motet
(*Thy servant is downcast*)
Augustana Cho. (*Eng*)—Veld ♯ BB.LBC 1075
(*Bach, Dvořák, Kodály, etc.*)

(7) Marienlieder, Op. 22 Fem. cho.
☆ Vienna Cha. Cho.—Schmid ♯ Nix.WLP 5014
(*above*) (♯ Sel. 270.CW.004)
(*idem & Nänie on* ♯ West.WN 18062)

Psalm 13, Op. 27 Female voices & org. or pf.
Vienna Boys' Cho.—Kühbacher (pf.)
♯ EPhi.NBR 6024
(*Waltz No. 15; Schumann, Reger, Schubert. etc.*)
(♯ Phi.N 00726R)

Zigeunerlieder, Op. 103
See below for solo version recordings

II. 3. SONGS (Lieder)
(for explanation of abbreviations, see II-4 *below*)

COLLECTIONS (including *Volkslieder*)
(Die) Trauernde (Mei Mudder), Op. 7, No. 5 (Trad.)
Volkslied (Die Schwalbe ziehet fort), Op. 7, No. 4
Feinsliebchen, du sollst mir nicht barfuss geh'n DV.12
Schwesterlein DV.15
In stiller Nacht DV.42
Vergebliches Ständchen, Op. 84, No. 4 (Zuccalmaglio)
I. Seefried (S), E. Werba (pf.) PV. 72380
(*Cornelius on* ♯ Pol. 16077)
(*Wolf, on* ♯ AmD.DL 9743)

♯ = Long-playing, 33⅓ r.p.m.   ♭ = 45 r.p.m.   ♮ = Auto. couplings, 78 r.p.m.

Ach, wende diesen Blick, Op. 57, No. 4　(Daumer)
Es träumte mir, Op. 57, No. 3　(Daumer)
Immer leiser wird mein Schlummer, Op. 105, No. 2
　　　　　　　　　　　　　　　　(Lingg)
Liebestreu, Op. 3, No. 1　(Reinick)
Meine Liebe ist grün, Op. 63, No. 5　(F. Schumann)
O wüss' ich doch den Weg zurück, Op. 63, No. 8
　　　　　　　　　　　　　　　　(Groth)
Der Schmied, Op. 19, No. 4　(Uhland)
Der Tod, das ist die kühle Nacht, Op. 96, No. 1　(Heine)
Wiegenlied, Op. 49, No. 4　(Trad.)

C. Smith (A), R. Cellini (pf.)　♯ BB.LBC 1071
(*Schubert*)

Wie rafft ich mich auf in der Nacht, Op. 32, No. 1 (Platen)
Nicht mehr zu dir zu gehen, Op. 32, No. 2　(Daumer)
Ich schleich' umher betrübt und stumm, Op. 32, No. 3
　　　　　　　　　　　　　　　　(Platen)
Der Strom, der neben mir verrauschte, Op. 32, No. 4
　　　　　　　　　　　　　　　　(Platen)
Wehe, so willst du mich wieder, Op. 32, No. 5　(Platen)
Du sprichst, dass ich mich täuschte, Op. 32, No. 6 (Platen)
Wie bist du, meine Königin, Op. 32, No. 9　(Daumer,
　　　　　　　　　　　　　　　　after Hafiz)

D. Fischer-Dieskau (B), H. Klust (pf.)
(*Mahler*)　　　　　　　　　　**♯ G.ALP 1270**

(4) Ernste Gesänge, Op. 121　("Prediger Salomo")
　(*Four Serious Songs*)
Geistliches Wiegenlied, Op. 91, No. 2　(Geibel)
Gestillte Sehnsucht, Op. 91, No. 1　(Rückert)
　[both with C. Cooley (vla.)]
In stiller Nacht　DV. 42
Sandmännchen . VK.4

N. Rankin (M-S), C. v. Bos (pf.)
　　　　　　　　　　　♯ DCap.CTL 7079
　　　　　　　　　　　　(♯ Cap.P 8289)

Ach und du mein kühles Wasser, Op. 85, No. 3
　　　　　　　　　　　　(Kapper, from Serbian)
Dort in den Weiden, Op. 97, No. 4　(Trad.)
Vergebliches Ständchen, Op. 84, No. 4　(Zuccalmaglio)
Wiegenlied, Op. 49, No. 4　(Trad.)
Da unten im Tale　DV.6
Feinsliebchen, du sollst mir nicht barfuss geh'n　DV.12
In stiller Nacht　DV.42
Sandmännchen　VK.4
Schwesterlein　DV.15
Die Sonne scheint nicht mehr　DV.5

A. Felbermayer (S), V. Graef (pf.)
(*Dvořák*)　　　　　　　　　　**♯ Van.VRS 446**

Auf dem Schiffe, Op. 97, No. 2　(Reinhold)
Wiegenlied, Op. 49, No. 4　(Trad.)
Nachtigallen schwingen, Op. 6, No. 6　(v. Fallersleben)
Die Botschaft, Op. 47, No. 1　(Daumer)

M. Dobbs (S), G. Moore (pf.)　　♯ C.CX 1154
(*Schubert, Wolf, Chausson, Fauré, Hahn*)
　　　　　(♯ FCX 299 : QCX 10097 ; Angel. 35094)

Meine Liebe ist grün, Op. 63, No. 5　(F. Schumann)
Der Schmied, Op. 19, No. 4　(Uhland)
Wiegenlied, Op. 49, No. 4　(Trad.)

M. Powers (A), F. la Forge (pf.)　♯ Atl. 1207
(*Beethoven, Franz, Schubert, Wagner, Respighi, etc.*)

(8) Zigeunerlieder, Op. 103　(Conrat)　Solo version
Nicht mehr zu dir zu gehen, Op. 32, No. 2　(Daumer)
Wehe, so willst du mich wieder, Op. 32, No. 5　(Platen)

H. Glaz (M-S), L. Müller (pf.)　♯ MGM.E 3012
(*Beethoven*)

Ach, wende diesen Blick, Op. 57, No. 4　(Daumer)
Komm' bald, Op. 97, No. 5　(Groth)
Die Mainacht, Op. 43, No. 2　(Hölty)
Minnelied, Op. 71, No. 5　(Hölty)
Die Schnur, 'die Perl' an Perle, Op. 57, No. 7　(Daumer)
Wie bist du, meine Königin, Op. 32, No. 9　(Daumer,
　　　　　　　　　　　　　　　　after Hafiz)
Wie Melodien zieht es mir, Op. 105, No. 1　(Groth)
Wir wandelten, Op. 96, No. 2　(Daumer)

☆ **B. Boyce (B), J. Bonneau (pf.)**
　　　　　　　　　　　♯ LOL.OL 50044

(*Ernste Gesänge*)

Am Sonntag Morgen, Op. 49, No. 1　(Heyse)
Auf dem Kirchhofe, Op. 105, No. 4　(Liliencron)
Dein blaues Auge, Op. 59, No. 8　(Groth)
Der Gang zum Liebchen, Op. 48, No. 1　(Wenzig)
Geheimnis, Op. 71, No. 3　(Candidus)
In Waldeseinsamkeit, Op. 85, No. 6　(Lemcke)
Meine Liebe ist grün, Op. 63, No. 5　(F. Schumann)
O kühler Wald, Op. 72, No. 3　(Brentano)
Ruhe Süssliebchen, Op. 33, No. 9　(Tieck)
Der Überläufer, Op. 48, No. 2　(Knaben Wunderhorn)

Vor dem Fenster, Op. 14, No. 1　(Trad.)
Ein Wanderer, Op. 106, No. 5　(Rheinhold)
Wie Melodien zieht es mir, Op. 105, No. 1　(Groth)
Wiegenlied, Op. 49, No. 4　(Trad.)
Wir wandelten, Op. 96, No. 2　(Daumer)
In stiller Nacht　DV.42
Mein Mädel hat 'nen Rosenmund　DV.25
Sandmännchen　VK.4

☆ **A. Kipnis (Bs), E. V. Wolff (pf.)**
　　　　　　　　　　　♯ Vic.LCT 1157

An eine Aeolsharfe, Op. 19, No. 5　(Mörike)
Immer leiser wird mein Schlummer, Op. 105, No. 2
　　　　　　　　　　　　　　　　(Lingg)
Mein wundes Herz verlangt, Op. 59, No. 7　(Groth)
Wiegenlied, Op. 49, No. 4　(Scherer)
Lerchengesang, Op. 70, No. 2　(Candidus)
Der Tod, das ist die kühle Nacht, Op. 96, No. 1　(Heine)
Vorüber, Op. 58, No. 7　(Hebbel)
Wir wandelten, Op. 96, No. 2　(Daumer)

☆ **E. Berger (S), M. Raucheisen (pf.)**
　　　　　　　　　　　♯ AmD.DL 9666
(*R. Strauss*)　　　(*Pfitzner on ♯ Pol. 18081*)

Geistliches Wiegenlied, Op. 91, No. 2　(Geibel)
Gestillte Sehnsucht, Op. 91, No. 1　(Rückert)
Des Liebsten Schwur, Op. 69, No. 4　(Wenzig)
Nachtigall, Op. 97, No. 1　(Reinhold)

☆ **L. Sydney (A), F. Morawetz (vla.) W. Loibner (pf.)**
　　　　　　　　　　　(♯ CID.VXT 33021)

An die Nachtigall, Op. 46, No. 4　(Hölty)
Auf dem Kirchhofe, Op. 105, No. 4　(Liliencron)
Die Botschaft, Op. 47, No. 1　(Daumer)
Dein blaues Auge, Op. 59, No. 8　(Groth)
Feldeinsamkeit, Op. 86, No. 2　(Allmers)
Der Gang zum Liebchen, Op. 31, No. 3 (Trad.), *see* II-2,
　　　　　　　　　　　　　　　　above
Die Mainacht, Op. 43, No. 2　(Hölty)
Minnelied III, Op. 71, No. 5　(Hölty)
Nachtigall, Op. 97, No. 1　(Reinhold)
O liebliche Wangen, Op. 47, No. 4　(Flemming)
O wüss' ich den Weg zurück, Op. 63, No. 8　(Groth)
Sapphische Ode, Op. 94, No. 4　(Schmidt)
Sonntag, Op. 47, No. 3　(Uhland)
Ständchen, Op. 106, No. 1　(Kugler)
Tambourliedchen, Op. 69, No. 5　(Candidus)
Unbewegte laue Luft, Op. 57, No. 8　(Daumer)

☆ **A. Poell (Bs), V. Graef (pf.)　♯ Nix.WLP 5053**

Alte Liebe, Op. 72, No. 1　(Candidus)
Bei dir sind mein Gedanken, Op. 95, No. 2　(Halm)
Beim Abschied, Op. 95, No. 3　(Halm)
Der Gang zum Liebchen, Op. 48, No. 1　(Wenzig)
Nachtwandler, Op. 86, No. 3　(Kalbeck)
Salamander, Op. 107, No. 2　(Lemcke)
Sonntag, Op. 47, No. 3　(Uhland)

☆ **R. Herbert (B), F. Waldman (pf.)** (♯ *Allo. 4021*)

Die Botschaft, Op. 47, No. 1　(Baumer)
Geistliches Wiegenlied, Op. 91, No. 2　(Geibel)
Gestillte Sehnsucht, Op. 91, No. 1　(Rückert)
　[both with M. Gilbert (vla.)]
Sapphische Ode, Op. 94, No. 4　(Schmidt)

☆ **K. Ferrier (A), P. Spurr (pf.)　♯ D.LXT 2850**
(*Alto Rhapsody*)　　　　　　　(♯ Lon.LL 903)

Meine Liebe ist grün, Op. 63, No. 5　(F. Schumann)
Therese, Op. 86, No. 1　(Keller)
Der Tod, das ist die kühle Nacht, Op. 96, No. 1　(Heine)

☆ **L. Lehmann (S), E. Balogh (pf.)** (in ♯ Vic.LCT 1108:
　　　　　　　　　　　　♭ *set WCT 1108*)

An eine Aeolsharfe, Op. 19, No. 5　(Mörike)
Es liebt sich so lieblich im Lenze, Op. 71, No. 1　(Heine)
Ständchen, Op. 106, No. 1　(Kugler)
Der Tod, das ist die kühle Nacht, Op. 96, No. 1　(Heine)
Wiegenlied, Op. 49, No. 4　(Trad.)

S. Schöner (S), F. Schröder (pf.)　*Eta. 120182/3*

Liebestreu, Op. 3, No. 1　(Reinick)
Meine Liebe ist grün, Op. 63, No. 5　(F. Schumann)
Sind es Schmerzen, sind es Freuden, Op. 33, No. 3 (Tieck)

K. Flagstad (S), E. MacArthur (pf.)
　　　　　　　　　　　♯ G.ALP 1309
(*Schubert, R. Strauss, etc.*)　　(♯ Vic.LM 1870)

İNDIVIDUAL SONGS & CYCLES
Am Sonntag Morgen, Op. 49, No. 1　(Heyse)
Z. Milanov (S), B. Kunc (pf.)　in ♯ **Vic.LM 1915**
(*Wiegenlied; Giordano, Schumann, etc.*)

☆ = Re-issue of a recording to be found in previous volumes.

Auf dem Kirchhofe, Op. 105, No. 4 (Liliencron)
D. Eustrati (A), F. Schröder (pf.)   *Eta. 120163*
(*Über die Heide*)

(Die) Botschaft, Op. 47, No. 1 (Daumer)
☆ H. Schlusnus (in ‡ HP.APM 18029)

Dein blaues Auge, Op. 59, No. 8 (Groth)
I. Seefried (S), E. Werba (pf.)   in ‡ **Pol. 19050**
(*Ständchen; Moussorgsky, Bartók, etc.*) (‡ AmD.DL 9809)

(4) Duets, Op. 28 A, B, pf.
No. 1, Die Nonne und der Ritter (Eichendorff)
No. 2, Vor der Tür (Trad.)
No. 3, Es rauscht das Wasser (Goethe)
No. 4, Der Jäger und sein Liebchen (Fallersleben)
☆ S. Liss, R. Herbert, F. Waldman (‡ *Allo. 4021*)

(4) Ernste Gesänge, Op. 121 (*"Prediger Salomo"*)
H. Schey (B), F. de Nobel (pf.)   **Phi.N 12068/9G**
(4ss)   (*Loewe on* ‡ *N 00625R*)
W. Warfield (B), O. Herz (pf.)   ‡ **AmC.ML 4860**
(*Schumann*)

☆ B. Boyce (B), J. Bonneau (pf.)   ‡ LOL.OL 50044
(*Collection, above*)
☆ D. Fischer-Dieskau (B), H. Klust (pf.) ‡ AmD.DL 9668
(*Beethoven*)   (2ss, ‡ *Pol. 17047*)
☆ K. Ferrier (A), J. Newmark (pf.)[1]   ‡ *D.LW 5094*
(2ss)   (‡ *Lon.LD 9097*)

Es hing der Reif, Op. 106, No. 3 (Groth)
J. Harsanyi (S), O. Herz (pf.) in ‡ **Per.SPL 581**

Feldeinsamkeit, Op. 86, No. 2 (Allmers)
S. Schöner (S), F. Schröder (pf.)   *Eta. 120164*
(*Wir wandelten*)

— FOR PRACTICE, pf. acc. only: P. Ulanowsky (in ‡ *Bo.B 502*)

Gestillte Sehnsucht, Op. 91, No. 1 (Rückert)
Geistliches Wiegenlied, Op. 91, No. 2 (Geibel)
☆ K. Flagstad (S), H. Downes (vla.), G. Moore (pf.)
(♭ *G. 7EB 6012; Vic.EHA 18*)

Immer leiser wird mein Schlummer, Op. 105, No. 2
(Lingg)
J. Harsanyi (S), O. Herz (pf.) in ‡ **Per.SPL 581**
D. Eustrati (A), F. Schröder (pf.)   *Eta. 120165*
(*below*)

(Der) Jäger, Op. 95, No. 4 (Halm)
G. Fleischer (S), K. Olsson (pf.)   *Phi.N 56000H*
(*Wiegenlied; & Schubert*)

Liebestreu, Op. 3, No. 1 (Reinick)
D. Eustrati (A), F. Schröder (pf.)   *Eta. 120165*
(*above*)

Mädchenlied (unspec.)
N. Kazantseva (S, *Russ*)   *USSR. 20149*
(*Arensky: Song*)

(Die) Mainacht, Op. 43, No. 2 (Hölty)
A. Konetzni (S), E. Werba (pf.)   *C.LV 20*
(*Wolf: Verborgenheit*)
J. Björling (T), F. Schauwecker (pf.)
in ‡ **G.ALP 1187**
(*Schubert, Liszt, Tosti, etc.*)   (‡ *Vic.LM 1771*)

Meine Liebe ist grün, Op. 63, No. 5 (F. Schumann)
☆ K. Flagstad (S) & pf. (*JpV.SF 724*)

— FOR PRACTICE, pf. acc. only: P. Ulanowsky (in ‡ *Bo.B 502*)

Minnelied III, Op. 71, No. 5 (Hölty)
(*Holder klingt der Vogelsang*)
H. Janssen (B), S. Leff (pf.)   in ‡ **Mur.P 102**
(followed by pf. accomp. only)

O wüsst' ich doch den Weg zurück, Op. 63, No. 8
(Groth)
K. Flagstad (S), E. McArthur (pf.)
‡ **G.ALP 1191**
(*below; & Schumann, etc.*) (in ‡ Vic.LM 1738:
♭ *set WDM 1738*)
D. Gramm (Bs), R. Cumming (pf.)
in ‡ **ML. 7033**

Ruhe, Süssliebchen, Op. 33, No. 9 (Tieck)
E. Schumann (S), L. Rosenek (pf.) **G.DB 21572**
(*Schubert: An die Geliebte & Nachtviolen*) (o.n. DB 3598)[2]

Sapphische Ode, Op. 94, No. 4 (Schmidt)
J. Garda (B, *Pol*), V. Makarov (pf.) *Muza. 2416*
(*Grieg: I love thee*)
— ARR. CHO. Jenkins
Mormon Tabernacle Cho.—Cornwall (*Eng*)
(in ‡ EPhi.NBL 5012; Phi.N 02125L; AmC.ML 5048)

Sonntag, Op. 47, No. 3 (Uhland)
G. Pechner (B)   in ‡ **Roy. 1558**

Ständchen, Op. 106, No. 1 (Kugler)
(*Serenade—Der Mond steht über dem Berge*)
I. Seefried (S), E. Werba (pf.)   in ‡ **Pol. 19050**
(*Dein blaues Auge; Bartók, etc.*)   (‡ AmD.DL 9809)

Über die Heide, Op. 86, No. 4 (Storm)
D. Eustrati (A), F. Schröder (pf.)   ‡ *Eta. 120163*
(*Auf dem Kirchhofe*)

Unüberwindlich, Op. 72, No. 5 (Goethe)
M. Harrell (B), B. Smith (pf.) in ‡ **Rem. 199–140**

Vergebliches Ständchen, Op. 84, No. 4
(*Zuccalmaglio*)
E. Schwarzkopf (S), G. Moore (pf.)
in ‡ **C.CX 1044**
(*Bach, Beethoven, Gluck, etc.*)
(in ‡ FCX 182; in ‡ Angel. 35023)
G. Pechner (B)   in ‡ **Roy. 1558**

Von ewiger Liebe, Op. 43, No. 1 (Wenzig)
K. Flagstad (S), E. McArthur (pf.)
in ‡ **G.ALP 1191**
(*above*)   (in ‡ Vic.LM 1738: ♭ set *WDM 1738*)
T. Duncan (B), W. Allen (pf.)   **Phi.A 56504G**
(*Schubert: Erlkönig*)
R. Ponselle (S), I. Chicagov (pf.)
in ‡ **Vic.LM 1889**
(*Schubert, Lully, Chausson, Persico, etc.*) (‡ DV. 16493)
☆ V. de los Angeles (S) (♭ *G.7RF 276*)
S. Onegin (A) (*JpV.ND 488*)

Vor dem Fenster, Op. 14, No. 1 (Trad.)
☆ E. Gerhardt (M-S) (*JpV.NF 4133*)

Wie bist du, meine Königin, Op. 32, No. 9 (Daumer)
H. Janssen (B), S. Leff (pf.)   in ‡ **Mur.P 102**
(followed by pf. accomp. only)
☆ H. Schlusnus (B) & pf. (in ‡ HP.DGM 18029)

Wie Melodien zieht es mir, Op. 105, No. 1 (Groth)
— FOR PRACTICE, pf. acc. only: P. Ulanowsky (in ‡ *Bo.B 502*)

Wiegenlied, Op. 49, No. 4 (Trad.)
Z. Milanov (S), B. Kunc (pf.) in ‡ **Vic.LM 1915**
(*Am Sonntag Morgen, etc.*)
G. Fleischer (S), K. Olsson (pf.)   *Phi.N 56000H*
(*Der Jäger; & Schubert*)
C. Lynch (T, *Eng*), E. Bossart (pf.)
in ‡ **AmC.RL 3016**
I. B. Lucca (S, *Ital*) (in ‡ *Dur.MSE 6*)
G. Rondinella (T, *Sp*) (in ‡ *MusH.LP 5001*)
M. Santreuil (S, *Fr*) (♭ *POc.A 03*)
☆ R. Stevens (M-S) & Orch. (in ‡ *Vic.ERA 88*)
B. Gigli (T) & Orch. (♭ *G.7EB 6013*)
— ARR. CHO.
Obernkirchen Children's Cho.—Möller
(*Od.O-29006:* ♭ *OBL 29006:* in ‡ *OLA 1011*)
Consolatrix Afflictorum Cho.—Vermeulen
(Phi.N 17908G: in ‡ *P 10064R*)
Montserrat Monastery Cho. (*Span*) (♭ *G.EPL 13026*)
U.S.S.R. State Cho.—Shveshnikov
(*Eta. 730002:* ‡ *LPM 1008*)
☆ R. Shaw Chorale (*Eng*) (in ‡ Vic.LM 1800)
Bielefeld Children's Cho. (‡ *U 45228*)
E. Bender Children's Cho. (♭ *Pol. 32074*)
— ARR. PF.
A. Cortot (in ‡ G.ALP 1197: QALP 10080: FALP 349)
E. Silver (hpsi.) (in ‡ Roy. 1550)
A. Semprini (*G.B 10809*)

[1] The set listed in WERM, p. 95 (AK 1742/3) was apparently never made; certainly never issued, though announced and listed, both in England and U.S.A. [2] This number allocated but not issued.

Wiegenlied, Op. 49, No. 4 (*continued*)
— ARR. ORCH.
  Boston Prom.—Fiedler (♭ *G.7EP 7018;* ♭ *Vic.ERA 66;*
    & ☆ (o.v.) in ♯ *Cam.CAL 142:* ♭ *CAE 135)*
  Mantovani Orch. (in ♯ *D.LK 4072: LF 1161;*
                                    ♯ *Lon.LL 877)*
  W. Tworek (vln.) & orch.—Binge
                    (*Pol. X 51706;* in ♯ *Lon.LB 1121)*
  ☆ A. Kostelanetz (in ♯ *C.S 1029;* ♭ *AmC.A 1571)*
    etc.

— ARR. ORGAN
  V. Fox (in ♭ *AmC.A 1008)*
  J. Perceval (*ArgOd. 57054:* ♭ *BSOAE 4518:* in ♯ *LDC 513)*

Wir wandelten, Op. 96, No. 2 (Daumer)
  S. Schöner (S), F. Schröder (pf.)   ♯ *Eta. 120164*
  (*Feldeinsamkeit*)

(8) Zigeunerlieder, Op. 103 (Conrat) Solo version
  E. Höngen (M-S), G. Weissenborn (pf.)
                                    ♯ *Pol. 17024*
  (*Dvořák: Gipsy Songs*)
  E. Höngen (M-S), M. Raucheisen (pf.)
                                    ♯ *AmD.DL 4074*
  (*Rhapsodie, Op. 53*)
  E. Davis (S), K. Olsson (pf.)   **Phi.A 56500/1G**
  (4ss)
  H. Zadek (S), G. Frid (pf.)   ♯ *Phi.S 06062R*
  (*Dvořák*)

II. 4. VOLKSLIEDER

DV : (49) Deutsche Volkslieder
VK : (14) Volkskinderlieder
CV : (26) Deutsche Volkslieder (cho.)

COLLECTIONS
  Schwesterlein DV.15
  Wach auf, mein Herzenschöne DV.16
  Mein Mädel hat 'nen Rosenmund DV.25
  All mein' Gedanken DV.30
  Dort in den Weiden steht ein Haus DV.31
  Wie komm' ich denn DV.34
  Es steht ein Lind DV.41
  M. Lichtegg (T), H. W. Häusslein (pf.)
                                    ♯ *D.LW 5146*
  (*Dvořák*)   (♯ *Lon.LD 9148)*

  Da unten im Tale DV.6
  Mein Mädel hat 'nen Rosenmund DV.25
  Och Mod'r, ich well en Ding han! DV.33
  Schwesterlein DV.15
  E. Schumann (S), L. Rosenek (pf.) **G.DB 21605**
                                    (o.n.DB 3597)[1]

  Das Schlaraffenland VK.7
  Die Henne VK.3
  Marienwürmchen VK.13
  Sandmännchen VK.4
  Die Nachtigall VK.2
  V. Osborne (S, *Eng*), R. Vetlesen (pf.)
                                    in ♯ *ML. 3000*

Da unten im Tale DV.6
  E. Schwarzkopf (S), G. Moore (pf.) (n v.)
                                    in ♯ *C.CX 1044*
                      (♯ *FCX 182;* Angel. 35023)
  [& o.v. ☆ with *Schumann: Nussbaum* on *C.LD 6*]
— ARR. ZITHER
  R. Welcome (in ♯ *Nix.SLPY 149;* in ♯ *SOT. 1032)*

In stiller Nacht CV.8
  Obernkirchen Children's Cho.   *Od.O-28719*
  (*Pacius: Finnish Song*) (in ♯ *OLA 1007;* Angel. 64012)
  ☆ Bielefeld Children's Cho. (*G.BA 1021*)

Och Mod'r, ich well en Ding han! DV.33
  E. Schwarzkopf (S), G. Moore (pf.)
                                    in ♯ *C.CX 1044*
                      (in ♯ *FCX 182;* Angel. 35023)
Sandmännchen VK.4
— ARR. CHO.
  Regensburg Cath. Cho.—Schrems   *T.A 11602*
  (*Humperdinck: Wiegenlied*) (in ♯ *LA 6087;* ♭ *U 45602)*

III. MISCELLANEOUS

Brahms, his life, his times, his music
  D. Randolph (narrator) with illus. ♯ *Per.PCS 7*
Brahms, his story & his music
  G. Kean (narrator) & orch.
          (♯ *AmVox.VL 2580:* also ♮ *set VOX 258)*

BRANT, Henry Dreyfus (b. 1913)

Concerto saxophone & orch. 1941
  S. Rascher & Cincinnati Sym.—Johnson
                                    ♯ *Rem. 199-188*
  (*Glanville-Hicks & Rudhyar*)

Galaxy No. 2 wind & perc. ens. 1954
Signs & Alarms wind & perc. ens. 1953
  Cha. Ens.—Brant   ♯ *AmC.ML 4956*
  (*Antheil*)

Symphony No. 1, B flat major 1945, rev. 1950
  A.R.S. Sym.—Swarowsky   ♯ *ARS. 38*
  (*Phillips*)

BRASART, Johannes (XVIth Cent.)
  SEE: † ANTHOLOGIE SONORE

BRENTA, Gaston (b. 1902)

Florilège de Valses Ballet Suite, orch. 1940
                                    (f.p. 1947)
  Belgian Radio Cha.—Doneux
  (*Poot*)   ♯ *Gramo.GLP 2502*

BRETON, Tomás (1850-1923)

STAGE WORKS
(Abridged listing only)

(La) DOLORES Opera, 3 Acts 1895
Jota
  P. Civil & J. Marquez (T), Cho. & Sym.
  —Ferrer   ♯ *Angel.SS 70007*
  (*Alonso: La Parranda*) (in ♯ *C.FSX 104;* Reg. LCX 104;
          Pam.LRC 15905, d.c.; & ♭ Angel. 70011)
  (also in ♯ *Reg.LS 1006)*
  C. Munguía, J. Uribe & Cho. in ♯ *LI.TW 91087*
            (in ♯ *Ambra.MCC 30024 & MCC 25008)*
— ORCH. ONLY
  Madrid Cha.—Argenta   in ♯ *LI.TW 91020*
  (& in ♯ *Mont.FM 6;* Ambra.MCC 30002: ♭ *MGE 60002)*
  Colón Theatre—Cases   in ♯ *Od.OD 1018*
                      (ArgOd. 66044: in ♯ *LDC 519)*
Vocal excerpts
  L. Berchman (S) (in ♯ *Mont.FM 28)*
  ▽ M. Fleta (T) (G.DB 1483: Vic. 6392)
  A. Arno (G.AF 385) etc.

(La) VERBENA DE LA PALOMA Sainete, 1 Act
                                              1894
  A. M. Iriarte (S), M. Ausensi (B), T. Rosado (S),
  Madrid Cho. & Cha. Orch.—Argenta
                                    ♯ *LI.TW 91015*
                    (♯ *Mont.FM 2;* Ambra.MCC 30000)
  (Prelude only in ♯ *LI.TW 91004;* Ambra.MCC 30009 &
                            MCCP 29000: ♭ *MGE 60003)*
  M. D. Ripollés, I. Rivadeneyra, A. Rojo,
  T. Pardo, S. Castelló, P. Vidal, Madrid Cho.
  & Sym.—Moreno Torroba   ♯ *Phi.N 00996R*
  (2ss) [L. Maravilla, guitar]
  L. Rovira (S), L. Torrentó (S), R. Gómez (A),
  E. Tarín (B), A. Aguilá (B), etc., Cho. & orch.
  —Ferrer   ♯ *Reg.LCX 102*
  (2ss)   (♯ *Pam.LRC 15901;* Angel.SS 70005)
  ▽ Soloists, Cho. & Orch.—Capdevila (*ArgOd. 203796/803:*
                                              196503/10)

          (*continued on next page*)

-----

[1] This number allocated but not issued.

(La) VERBENA DE LA PALOMA (*continued*)
Prelude
Colón Theatre—Cases   ArgOd. 66059
(*Cases: Léon*)   (♭ *BSOAE 4509:* ‡ *LDC 511*)
Sym.— Ferrer   in ‡ C.FSX 104
(‡ Reg.LCX 104; Angel. 65008; Pam.LRC 15905;
                                  ♭ *Reg.SEDL 105*)
Madrid Theatre—Moreno Torroba   in ‡ AmD.DL 9763

Polo gitano — ARR. DANCING & ORCH.
(from *Escenas Andaluzas*)
P. Tomás & orch.—Cisneros (in ♭ *SpC.ECGE 70167*)

En el cortijo—Zapateado orch.
(from *Escenas Andaluzas*)
Madrid Theatre—Machado in ‡ B.AXTL 1074
(*Moreno Torroba, Sandoval, etc.*) (‡ SpC.CCL 35002;
                                     AmD.DL 9757)

Madrid Theatre—Moreno Torroba
                              ‡ B.AXTL 1077
(*Chueca, Moreno Torroba, etc.*)   (‡ AmD.DL 9735)

▽ Older recordings of other works included:
En la Alhambra (on C.D 41011; AmC. 67819D)
Escenas Andaluzas (on AmC. 67820D; ArgC. 264543)
Garin—Sardana (on *G.AE 2834*)

BRÉVAL, Jean Baptiste (*c.* 1756-1825)

Sonata, G major vlc. & pf. ed. Moffat
J. Starker & L. Pommers   ‡ Nix.PLP 708
(*Debussy, Fauré, Couperin, etc.*)   (‡ Per.SPL 708)
S. Mayes & S. Pearlman   ‡ Bo.B 210
(*Haydn, Beethoven, Mozart*)

BRIDGE, Frank (1879-1941)

(An) Irish Melody (Londonderry Air) Str. Qtt. 1908
American Art Qtt.   in ‡ BB.LBC 1086
(*Grainger, Tchaikovsky, Mendelssohn, etc.*)

(2) Old English Songs Str. Qtt. or Orch. 1916
(*Sally in our Alley & Cherry Ripe*)
New Sym.—Goossens   ♭ D. 71071

SONG
Go not, happy day (Tennyson)   (pub. 1916)
K. Ferrier (A), F. Stone (pf.)[1] in ‡ D.LX 3133
(*Britten, Parry, Stanford, Hughes, etc.*)   (‡ Lon.LS 1032)

BRIDGEWATER, Ernest Leslie (b. 1893)

INCIDENTAL MUSIC for Shakespeare's plays
(for the Stratford Memorial Theatre)
King John   (EMI.EPX 102/5)
The Winter's Tale   (EMI.EPX 111/9)
Troilus and Cressida   (EMI.EPX 106/10 & 120/2)
Much ado about nothing (EMI.EPX 175/82)
All by Orch.—Bridgewater

SONGS FROM SHAKESPEARE'S PLAYS
Brooklet Song (Prelude to a Comedy)
Tell me where is fancy bred (*Merchant of Venice*)
You spotted snakes (*Midsummer Night's Dream*)
Sigh no more, ladies (*Much ado about nothing*)
Under the Greenwood tree
Blow, blow, thou winter wind } (*As you like it*)
It was a lover and his lass
O Mistress mine }
Come away death } (*Twelfth Night*)
When icicles hang by the wall }
When daisies pied } (*Love's labour's lost*)
Come unto these yellow sands }
Full fathom five } (*The Tempest*)
Where the bee sucks }
Who is Sylvia? (*Two Gentlemen of Verona*)
Hark, hark the lark (*Cymbeline*)
Take, O take those lips away (*Measure for Measure*)
M. Dickie (T) & Westminster Light Orch.
—Bridgewater   ‡ West.WL 4010

BRIGNOLI, Giacomo (b. *c.* 1550)

SEE: † OLD ITALIAN MASTERS

---

[1] Broadcast performance, 5 June, 1952.

BRITTEN, Benjamin (b. 1913)

(A) Ceremony of Carols, Op. 28 Tr. Cho. & hp.
                                          1942
Copenhagen Boys' Cho.—Britten ‡ D.LW 5070
[E. Simon (hp.)]   (‡ *Lon.LD 9102*)
(*Simple Symphony*, on ‡ Lon.LL 1336)
Concordia Cho.—Christiansen   in ‡ Cdia. 4
(*Bach, Willan, etc.*)
Augustana Cho.—Veld[2]   in ‡ Word.W 4005
(*Grieg, Kodály, etc.*)
☆ Washington Cath. & Cha. Choirs—Callaway
                                ‡ McInt.MC 1004)
R. Shaw Chorale—Shaw & L. Newell (‡ G.FALP 273)
...No. 3, There is no rose only
Nat. Presbyterian Chu. Cho.—Schaefer, & org.
                              in ‡ McInt.MM 107

Diversions on a theme, Op. 21 pf. (left hand) & orch.
1940, rev. 1950
J. Katchen & L.S.O.—Britten   ‡ D.LXT 2981
(*Sinfonia da Requiem*)   (‡ Lon.LL 1123)
S. Rapp & Berlin Radio—Rother ‡ Ura. 7101
(*R. Strauss: Burleske*)

Fantasy-quartet, Op. 2 ob. & str. 1932
☆ H. Gomberg & Galimir Trio   ‡ LI.TW 91054
(*below*) [deleted immediately after issue]

Hymn to St. Cecilia, Op. 27 (Auden)
☆ Augustana Cho.—Veld (in ‡ Word.W 4001)
Washington Cath. & Cha. Cho.—Callaway
                              (in ‡ McInt.MC 1004)

(Les) Illuminations, Op. 18 (Rimbaud) S & str. orch
                                          1939
P. Pears (T) & New Sym.—Goossens
                              ‡ D.LXT 2941
(*below*)   (‡ Lon.LL 994)
P. Anders (T) & Prussian State—Heger
                              ‡ Ura. 7104
(*Schillings: Glockenlieder*)

(6) Metamorphoses after Ovid, Op. 49 oboe unacc.
                                          1951
E. Parolari   ‡ CHS.H 4
(*below; & Shostakovich*)

PETER GRIMES, Op. 33 Opera 3 Acts 1945
Four Sea Interludes, Op. 33a Orch.
Passacaglia, Op. 33b Orch.
Amsterdam—v. Beinum (n.v.)   ‡ D.LXT 2886
(*below*)   (‡ Lon.LL 917)

Prelude & Fugue on a theme by Vittoria org. 1947
R. Ellsasser   in ‡ MGM.E 3064
(† *Organ Music by Modern Composers*)
A. Wyton   ‡ in ASK. 6
(*Howells, Bach, Sweelinck, etc.*)

QUARTETS, String
No. 1, D major, Op. 25 1941
☆ Galimir Qtt. (*above*)   ‡ LI.TW 91054

Rejoice in the Lamb, Op. 30 (Smart) cho. & org.
☆ Washington Nat. Presbyterian—Schaefer
                              (‡ McInt.MC 1002)

St. Nicolas, Op. 42 Cantata (Crozier) 1948
T, cho., pf. duet, str., perc. & org.
P. Pears, D. Hemmings (Tr.), Aldeburgh Fest.
Cho. & orch.—Britten   ‡ D.LXT 5060
[R. Downes, org.]   (‡ Lon.LL 1254)

Serenade, Op. 31 T, horn & strings 1943
P. Pears, D. Brain & New Sym.—Goossens
                              ‡ D.LXT 2941
(*above*)   (‡ Lon.LL 994)
D. Lloyd, J. Stagliano & Boston Sym. Members
(*Folk Songs*)   ‡ Bo.B 205
L. Chabay, F. Standley & Pittsburgh Sym.
—Steinberg   ‡ PFCM.CB 154
(*Bartók*)

---

[2] Contains only Nos. 2, 3, 5, 6, 10 of the score.

Simple Symphony, Op. 4 str. orch. 1925, rev. 1934
New Sym.—Goossens (2ss)   ‡ *D.LW 5163*
(*Ceremony of Carols, on* ‡ Lon.LL 1336) (‡ *Lon.LD 9184*)
Munich Cha. Orch.—Stepp   ‡ *Pol. 16128*
(*Mozart: Dances*)
Concert Hall Sym.—Ackermann   ‡ CHS.H 4
(*above; & Shostakovich*)
M.G.M. String—Solomon   ‡ MGM.E 3074
(*Ireland*)
(*Sentimental Sarabande only, in* ‡ E 3124)

Sinfonia da Requiem, Op. 20 orch. 1940
Danish Radio—Britten   ‡ D.LXT 2981
(*Diversions on a theme, Op. 21*)   (‡ Lon.LL 1123)

Sinfonietta, Op. 1 cha. orch. 1932
M.G.M. Cha. Ens.—I. Solomon ‡ *MGM.E 290*
(*Bloch*)

SONGS
COLLECTION
On this Island, Cycle, Op. 11 (Auden) 1937
Fish in the unruffled lakes (Auden) 1937
(2) Ballads: Mother comfort 2S (Slater) 1937
          Underneath the abject willow 2S (Auden) 1937
B. Troxell (S),[1] T. Kozma (pf.)
          ‡ McInt.MC 1003
(*Hindemith: English Songs*)   (o.n. ‡ WCFM. 15)

(The) Holy Sonnets of John Donne, Op. 35 1945
A. Young (T), G. Watson (pf.) ‡ Argo.RG 25
(*below*)   (‡ West.WN 18077)

(7) Sonnets of Michelangelo, Op. 22 1940
P. Pears (T), B. Britten (pf.)   ‡ D.LXT 5095
(*below*)   (‡ Lon.LL 1204)
A. Young (T), G. Watson (pf.) ‡ Argo.RG 25
(*above*)   (‡ West.WN 18077)

Winter Words, Op. 52 (Hardy) 1953
P. Pears (T), B. Britten (pf.)   ‡ D.LXT 5095
(*above*)   (‡ Lon.LL 1204)

Te Deum, C major 1935
☆ Washington Cho.—Callaway (in ‡ McInt.MC 1004)

(The) TURN OF THE SCREW, Op. 54 Opera
Prologue & 2 Acts 1954 (M. Piper after Henry James)
COMPLETE RECORDING

The Prologue ⎱	...	...	P. Pears (T)
Quint ⎰		
The Governess	...	...	J. Vyvyan (S)
Miles	...	...	D. Hemmings (Tr.)
Flora	...	...	O. Dyer (S)
Mrs. Goose	...	...	J. Cross (S)
Miss Jessel	...	...	A. Mandikian (S)

& English Op. Group Orch.—Britten
          ‡ D.LXT 5038/9
(4ss)   (‡ Lon.LL 1207/8)

**Variation on an Elizabethan tune (Sellinger's
Round)[2]** orch.
Aldeburgh Fest.—Britten   in ‡ D.LXT 2798
(*Berkeley, Oldham, Searle, Tippett, Walton*)
          (in ‡ Lon.LL 808)

Variations on a theme of Frank Bridge, Op. 10
str. orch. 1937
Philharmonia—Karajan   ‡ C.CX 1159
(*Vaughan Williams*)   (‡ QCX 10109; ‡ Angel. 35142)
Boyd Neel Orch. (n.v.)   ‡ D.LXT 2790
(*Warlock*)   (‡ Lon.LL 801)
Naples Scarlatti Orch.—Caracciolo
(*Martucci*)[3]   ‡ Csm.CLPS 1051

(The) Young Person's Guide to the orchestra, Op. 34
1946 (Variations & Fugue on a theme of Purcell)[4]
Amsterdam—v. Beinum   ‡ D.LXT 2886
(*above*)   (‡ Lon.LL 917)
Minneapolis Sym.—Dorati   ‡ Mer.MG 50047
(*Ginastera*)
Orch.—Wallenstein   ‡ MApp. 711
(*Spoken analysis by T. Scherman; & Prokofiev*)

— WITH NARRATION
P. Pears & Philharmonia—Markevitch
          ‡ C.CX 1175
(*Saint-Saëns*) (‡ Angel. 35135; ‡ C.FCX 376, with *Fr*
          narration by A. Reybaz)
B. de Wilde & Vienna Pro Musica—Swarowsky
(*Prokofiev*)   ‡ AmVox.PL 9280
D. Taylor & Minneapolis Sym.—Dorati
(*Tchaikovsky*)   ‡ Mer.MG 50055

TRANSCRIPTIONS & ARRANGEMENTS

Matinées musicales, Op. 24 after Rossini 1941
New Sym.—Cree   ‡ *LI.W 91075*
(*below*)
          ☆ Covent Garden— Braithwaite   ‡ *P.PMD 1020*
          (*below*)   (*idem; & Rossini on* ‡ MGM.E 3028)

Soirées musicales, Op. 9 after Rossini 1936
New Sym.—Cree   ‡ *LI.W 91075*
(*above*)
Berlin Radio—Kleinert   ‡ Ura. 7136
(*Elgar*)
          ☆ Covent Garden—Braithwaite   ‡ *P.PMD 1020*
          (*above*)   (*idem; & Rossini on* ‡ MGM.E 3028)

BRITISH FOLK SONGS
COLLECTIONS
The Sally Gardens   (Yeats)   ø
Little Sir William   α
The Miller of Dee   α
Sweet Polly Oliver   α
The Bonny Earl o' Moray
The Ash Grove   ø
A brisk young widow
There's none to soothe   ø
Oliver Cromwell
P. Pears (T), B. Britten (pf.)   ‡ *D.LW 5122*
[ø *also on* ♭ D. 71074, α *also* ♭ D. 71109] (‡ *Lon.LD 9136*)

The Sally Gardens   (Yeats)
Little Sir William
The Trees grow so high
The Ash Grove
Oliver Cromwell
D. Lloyd (T), W. Schauzer (pf.)
Come you not from Newcastle
Sweet Polly Oliver
O waly, waly
M. Willauer (S), W. Schauzer (pf.)   ‡ Bo.B 205
(*Serenade*)

Come you not from Newcastle
O waly, waly   (The water is wide)
K. Ferrier (A), F. Stone (pf.)[5]   ‡ in *D.LX 3133*
(*Bridge, Parry, Stanford, V. Williams. etc.*)
          (in ‡ *Lon.LS 1032*)

(The) Foggy Dew
M. Langdon (Bs), J. Lee (pf.)   in ‡ Queens.LPR 21
(*Schubert, Bohm, Massenet, etc.*)

O waly, waly   (The water is wide)
P. Pears (T), B. Britten (pf.)   *G.DA 2032*
(ARR. *Grainger: Six Dukes went a fishin'*)
          ☆ K. Ferrier (A), P. Spurr (pf.) (♭ *D. 71072*)

Sweet Polly Oliver
J. Vyvyan (S), E. Lush (pf.)   in ‡ D.LXT 2797
(† *Songs of England*)   (in ‡ Lon.LL 806)
FRENCH FOLK SONG
(La) Belle est au jardin d'amour
S. Wyss (S), M. Korchinska (hp.)   in ‡ Argo.RG 34

BRUCH, Max (1838–1920)

Canzone, Op. 55 vlc. & orch.
A. Janigro & London Phil. Sym.—Rodzinski
          ‡ West.WN 18007
(*below; & Bloch*)

---

[1] Sings both parts in the duets.   [2] Contributed to joint set of Variations by all the composers named.
[3] Original announcements also had coupling by Vitalini.   [4] Theme from Abdelazer.
[5] Broadcast performance, 5 June, 1952.

CONCERTOS, Vln. & orch.

No. 1, G minor, Op. 26

N. Milstein & Pittsburgh Sym.—Steinberg
         ♯ **DCap.CTL 7059**
(*Mendelssohn*)   (♯ Cap.P 8243; ACap.CLCX 046)

T. Varga & Philharmonia—Susskind
(*Mozart*)   ♯ **C.SX 1017**

I. Gitlis & Vienna Pro Musica—Horenstein
(*Sibelius*)   ♯ **AmVox.PL 9660**

D. Oistrakh & L.S.O.—von Mataćić
                 ♯ **C.CX 1268**
(*Prokofiev*)   (♯ Angel. 35243)

R. Odnoposoff & Netherlands Phil.—Goehr ♯ **MMS. 40**
(*Paganini*)

M. Kayser & N.W. German Phil.—Schüchter
                 ♯ *Imp.ILP 115*
(*Svendsen*) [*Adagio* only, ♭ *Od.BEOW 3003*]

F. Petronio & Belgian Radio—P. Glière ♯ **Mae.OAT 25002**
(*Mendelssohn*)

M. Auclair & Austrian Sym.—Loibner
(*below*)   ♯ **Rem. 199-127**
                   (♯ Cum.CR 219)

H. Drescher & Berlin Sym.—Schreiber   ♯ **Roy. 1435**
(*Beethoven: Vln. Sonata No. 5*)

☆ J. Heifetz & L.S.O.—Sargent   ♯ **G.ALP 1124**
(*Mozart*)

☆ A. Campoli & New Sym.—Kisch   ♯ **D.LXT 2904**
(*Mendelssohn*)   (♯ NLK 40103; Lon.LL 966)
(*Adagio* only on ♭*D.VD 507*)

☆ N. Milstein & N.Y.P.S.O.—Barbirolli ♯ **AmC.RL 6631**
(*Tchaikovsky: Concerto*)

☆ Y. Menuhin & Boston Sym.—Münch   ♯ **Vic.LM 1797**
(*Mendelssohn*)

☆ Z. Francescatti & N.Y.P.S.O.—Mitropoulos
                 ♯ *EPhi.ABR 4011*
(*Wieniawski*)   (♯ Phi.A 01610R)

☆ W. Schneiderhan & Bamberg Sym.—Leitner
       (♯ Pol. 17028; Adagio only on ♭ Pol. 30063)

... 1st movt., ... excerpt
    ♫ F. Drdla & pf. (in ♯ *AudA.LP 0079**)

... Adagio only
    ☆ M. Gardi & Hamburg Phil.—Brückner-Rüggeberg
                     (♭ Pol. 20047)

— FOR PRACTICE: Recorded without vln. part, pf. accomp.
only (♯ CEd.MMO 305)

No. 2, D minor, Op. 44

E. Moris & Berlin Sym.—Kleinert   ♯ **Ura. 7166**
(*Bériot, Svendsen*)

(Das) Feuerkreuz, Op. 52   Cantata   (Scott)
Soloists, cho. & orch.

... Ave Maria   S

J. Hammond   in ♯ **G.ALP 1076**
(*Catalani, Cilea, Massenet, etc.*)

Kol Nidrei, Op. 47   vlc. & orch.

J. Schuster & Los Angeles Orch. Soc.
  —Waxman   ♯ **DCap.CTL 7041**
(*J. C. Bach & Schumann*)   (♯ Cap.P 8232)

A. Janigro & London Phil. Sym.—Rodzinski
(*above*)   ♯ **West.WN 18007**

☆ T. de Machula & Residentie—v. Otterloo
(*Dvořák*)   ♯ **Epic.LC 3083**

☆ M. Auclair (vln.) & Austrian Sym.—Loibner
(*above*)   ♯ **Rem. 199-127**
                 (♯ Cum.CR 219)

Scottish Fantasia, Op. 46   vln., hp. & orch.

☆ J. Heifetz, S. Chaloupka & Victor Sym.—Steinberg
(*Korngold*)   ♯ **G.ALP 1288**
       (*Mendelssohn* on ♯ Vic.LM 9016)

BRUCKNER, Anton (1824-1896)

CHORAL MUSIC

Ave Maria   4 pt. cho. & org.   1856
Ave Regina coelorum   1879
Afferentur tibi   4 pt. cho. (orig. with 4 trombones)
                              1861
    Aachen Cath. Cho.—Rehmann   **Pol. 62892**
Ave Maria
Os justi (Graduale)   unacc. cho.   1879
    St. Hedwig's Cath. Cho.—Forster   **G.EG 8536**
                      (♭ 7MW 17-8536)

MASSES

No. 2, E minor   1866

☆ Hamburg State Op.—Thurn   ♯ **DT.LGX 66033**
                     (♯ T.LSK 7029)

No. 3, F minor   S, A, T, B, cho. & orch.
1867-8, revised

D. Siebert, D. Herrmann, E. Majkut, O. Wiener,
Academy Cha. Cho. & Vienna State
Philharmonia—Grossmann
         ♯ E. & **AmVox.PL 7940**

Psalms 112 & 150   S, cho. & orch.   1863, 1892

☆ H. Čcska, Vienna Cha. Cho. & Vienna Sym.—Swoboda
(*R. Strauss*)   ♯ **West.WL 18075**
(and with original coupling, *below*, ♯ Nix.WLP 6201-1)

Te Deum   S, A, T, B, cho., org., orch.   1881-4

F. Yeend, M. Lipton, D. Lloyd, M. Harrell,
Westminster Cho. & N.Y.P.S.O.—Walter
(*Mahler*)   ♯ **AmC.ML 4980**

☆ M. Cunitz, G. Pitzinger, L. Fehenberger, G. Hann,
Munich Radio Cho. & Orch.—Jochum ♯ **Pol. 18248**
(*Syn. 9, s. 3*)

Um Mitternacht   (Prutz)   1886
male voice qtt., T solo & pf.

— ARR. A. & CHO.

S. Hermann (boy A) & Vienna Boys' Choir
   — Kühbacher (pf.)   in ♯ *EPhi.NBR 6024*
(*Brahms, Reger, Buxtehude, etc.*)   (in ♯ Phi.N 00726R)

Virga Jesse floruit   4-pt. cho.   1885

Berlin Motet Cho.—Arndt   **D.F 43805**
(*Schnabel: Transeamus*)   (in ♯ D.LW 5131: ♭ D 17805)

Overture, G minor   orch.   1862-3

Residentie—Otterloo   ♯ **Phi.A 00249L**
(*Symphony No. 7, s. 1*)   (in ♯ Epic.SC 6006)

Quintet, F major   str.   1879

☆ Koeckert Qtt. & G. Schmid (vla.) (♯ AmD.DL 9796

SYMPHONIES

"No. 0", D minor   1863-4, rev. 1869

☆ Concert Hall Sym.—Spruit (♯ Clc. 6225

No. 1, C minor   1865-6

Vienna Orch. Soc.—Adler   ♯ **Uni.LA 1015**

No. 3, D minor   1873

Vienna Sym.—Andreae   ♯ **Phi. A00273L**
                   (♯ Epic.LC 3218)

Vienna Phil.—Knappertsbusch   ♯ **D.LXT 2967**
                   (♯ Lon.LL 1044)

Vienna Philharmonia—Adler   ♯ **SPA. 30/1**
(3ss—*Mahler*)

Netherlands Phil.—Goehr   ♯ **MMS. 2018**
               (o. n. ♯ CHS.CHS 1195)

Berlin Sym.—Rubahn   ♯ **Roy. 1579**

☆ Salzburg Mozarteum—Fekete (♯ CA.LPA 1018;
           ♯ Rem. 199-138; ♯ Cum.CR 223)

No. 4, E flat major   1874   (Romantic)

Vienna Phil.—Knappertsbusch[1]   ♯ **D.LXT 5065/6**
(3ss—*Wagner: Siegfried Idyll*)   (♯ Lon.LL 1250/1)

Philharmonia—v. Mataćić[1]   ♯ **C.CX 1274S/5**
(3ss—first blank)

Residentie—v. Otterloo   ♯ *Phi.A 00658/9R*
(4ss) (*Mahler: Kindertotenlieder*, in ♯ Epic. set SC 6001)

Hastings Sym.—Tubbs   ♯ **Allo. 3106/7**
(3ss—*Rameau*)

Czech Phil.—Konwitschny   ♯ **Sup.SLPV 122/3**
(4ss)   (♯ U. 5096/7G)

☆ Netherlands Radio Phil.—v. Kempen[2] ♯**T.LGX 66026/7**
(3ss—*Sibelius: Symphony No. 7*)

☆ Vienna Sym.—Klemperer (♯ EVox.PL 6930;
                   AFest.CFR 196)

No. 5, B flat major   1875-6

Leipzig Phil.—Pflüger   ♯ **Ura. set 239**
(3ss—*Weber*)

---

[1] The "Revised" version is played. In Germany, LXT 5066 is single-sided, there being no fill-up.
[2] The *da capo* of the Scherzo is omitted, the user being expected to replay the opening section.

No. 6, A major   1879-81
☆ Vienna Sym.—Swoboda (2ss)   ♯ **West.WN 18074**
(and 3ss, *above*, ♯ Nix.WLP 6201-1/2)

No. 7, E major   1881-3
Amsterdam—v. Beinum (n.v.) ♯ **D.LXT 2829/30**
(3ss—*Franck: Psyché*)   (♯ Lon.LL 852/3)
Vienna Sym.—Otterloo   ♯ **Phi.A 00249/50L**
(3ss—*above*)   (♯ Epic. set SC 6006)
☆ Berlin Phil.—E. Jochum (♯ Pol. 18112/3)

No. 8, C minor   1884-5
Amsterdam—v. Beinum   ♯ **EPhi.ABL 3086/7**
(3ss—*Schubert*)   (♯ Phi.A 00294/5L; Epic. set SC 6011)
☆ Hamburg Phil.—E. Jochum (4ss)   ♯ **Pol. 18124/5**
(& auto. ♯ 18051/2)

No. 9, D minor   1887-94
Vienna Pro Musica—Horenstein
                        ♯ **E. & AmVox.PL 8040**
                        (♯ Orb.BL 703)
Munich Radio—E. Jochum   ♯ **Pol. 18247/8**
(3ss—*Te Deum*)

BRUHNS, Nikolaus (1665-1697)

Prelude & Fugue, No. 3, E minor   org.
☆ W. Supper (in † *Baroque Organ Music*)

BRULÉ, Gace (d. *c.* 1220)

    SEE: † HISTORY OF MUSIC IN SOUND   (14)
         † FRENCH TROUBADOUR SONGS

BRUMEL, Antoine (*c.* 1460-1520)

    SEE: † MUSICIENS DE LA COUR DE BOURGOGNE
         † CHANSONS FROM THE MUSIC BOOKS . . .

BRUNEAU, Alfred (1857-1934)

(L') ATTAQUE DU MOULIN   4 Acts   1893
Adieux à la forêt: Le jour tombe   T
♮ L. Campagnola (in ♯ *Ete. 708**)
▽ G. Thill (C.LFX 38)   etc.

Imprecations   M-S
♮ M. Delna (*HRS. 1075**)
▽ There were several other items from this opera and
from *Messidor, L'Ouragan, Virginie,* and some songs.

BRUNETTI, Gaetano (*c.* 1740-1808)

SYMPHONIES
C minor[1]   ("No. 1")
Italian Cha.—Jenkins   ♯ **HS.HSL 77**
(*Giordani & Valentini*)   (in set HSL-C)
(*below, & Boccherini,* on ♯ Era.LDE 3022)

G minor   ("No. 22")   *c.* 1745
Italian Cha.—Jenkins   ♯ **HS.HSL 78**
(*Viotti*)   (in set HSL-C)
(*above, & Boccherini,* on ♯ Era.LDE 3022)

D minor   ("No. 31")
Italian Cha.—Jenkins   ♯ **HS.HSL 135**
(*Paisiello*)   (in set HSL-N)

C minor   ("Il Maniatico")   (" No. 33")
Italian Cha.—Jenkins   ♯ **HS.HSL 138**
(*Clementi*)   (in set HSL-N)

BRUSLARD, Jacques (fl. XVIIth Cent.)

    SEE: † ANTHOLOGIE SONORE (♯ AS 3004LD)

BUCHNER, Hans (1483-1538)

    SEE: † HISTORY OF MUSIC IN SOUND   (30)

BULL, Dr. John (*c.* 1562-1628)

VIRGINALS PIECES
Corant: The Prince's   (MS., British Museum)
T. Dart (hpsi.)   in ♯ **LOL.OL 50075**
(† *Masters of Early English Keyboard Music*)

Dr. Bull's my selfe   (FVB 189)
(The) Duke of Brunswick's Toye   (Cosyn 38)
B. Winogron (virginals)   in ♯ **Eso.ESJ 6**
(† *Elizabethan Song Bag*)

Dr. Bull's my selfe   (FVB 189)
M. Hodsdon (virginals)   † **G.HMS 42**
(*Farnaby, Gibbons, etc.*)   (in ♯ Vic. set LM 6029)

Fantasia on a Flemish Folk Song[2]
Vexilla regis   (Plainsong Fantasy)[2]
F. Peeters (org.)   in ♯ **Per.SPL 578**
(† *Old English Masters*)   (♯ Cpt.MC 20049)

Galiarda, D minor   (Parthenia 14)
C. J. Chiasson (hpsi.)   in ♯ **Nix.LLP 8037**
(† *Elizabethan Love Songs*)   (♯ Lyr.LL 37)
T. Dart (hpsi.)   in ♯ **LOL.OL 50075**
(† *Masters of Early English Keyboard Music*)

In Nomine   (FVB 37)
Pavan & Galliard   (FVB 34 & 38)
C. Koenig (hpsi.)   in ♯ **EMS. 236**
(† *Elizabethan Keyboard Music*)

(The) King's Hunt   (FVB 135)
— ARR. ORCH.   Barbirolli (in *An Elizabethan Suite*)
Hallé—Barbirolli   ♯ **G.BLP 1065**
(*Byrd, Farnaby, Anon.; & Elgar*)

BULL, Ole (1810-1880)

    SEE: † SCANDINAVIAN SONGS

BULLOCK, Sir Ernest (b. 1890)

    SEE: † CORONATION OF QUEEN ELIZABETH II
         † ENGLISH CHURCH MUSIC, Vol. IV

BUONAMENTE, Giovanni Battista (d. 1643)

    SEE: † GOLDEN AGE OF BRASS

BUSCA, Padre Ludovico (fl. XVIth Cent.)

    SEE: † ANTHOLOGIE SONORE

BUSONI, Ferruccio (1866-1924)

ARLECCHINO, Op. 50   Opera   1 Act   1917
COMPLETE RECORDINGS in *German*

Harlequin	...	K. Gester (narrator)
Ser Matteo del Sarto	...	I. Wallace (B)
Abbate Conspicuo	...	G. Evans (B)
Dottor Bombasto	...	F. Ollendorff (Bs)
Leandro	...	M. Dickie (T)
Columbine	...	E. Malbin (M-S)

& Glyndebourne Fest. Orch.—Pritchard
                        ♯ **G.ALP 1223**
                (♯ FALP 370; ♯ Vic. LM 1944)
Unspec. Artists—Mitropoulos[3]   ♯ **OTA. 12**
(4ss)

Concertino, clarinet & small orch., Op. 48
G. Sisillo & Naples Scarlatti Orch.
—Caracciolo   ♯ **Csm.CLPS 1047**
(*Leo: Vlc. Concerto; & Blodek & Vivaldi*)

Duettino concertante on a theme of Mozart   2 pfs.
J. Zak, E. Gilels (2ss)   USSR. **018683/4**

Fantasia contrappuntistica   pf.   1910
on themes from Bach's *Kunst der Fuge*
A. Brendel   ♯ **SPA. 56**

---

[1] Ed. H. David.   [2] MS., British Museum.   [3] Transcription of a broadcast performance.

Sonata No. 2, E minor, Op. 36a   vln. & pf.
  M. Rostal & N. Mewton-Wood   ♯ **Argo.RG 14**
                                 (o.n. ARS 1014)

Tanzwalzer, Op. 53   orch.
  Philharmonia—Markevitch   in ♯ **C.CX 1273**
  (*Liszt, Berlioz, Stravinsky, etc.*)
                      (♯ QCX 10172; Angel. 35154)

BÜSSER, (Paul) Henri (b. 1872)

Petite Suite   orch.
  French Nat. Radio—Büsser   ♯ *Pat.DT 1014*
  (*Debussy: Petite Suite*)

Pièce de concert   harp & orch.
  ☆ L. Laskine & Sym. Orch.—Büsser (JpV.ND 964)

BUTTERWORTH, George Sainton Kaye (1885-1916)

(The) Banks of Green Willow   orch.   1913
  L.P.O.—Boult   ♯ **D.LXT 5015**
  (*below; Bax & Holst*)   (♯ Lon.LL 1169)

(A) Shropshire Lad   Rhapsody   orch.   1912
  L.P.O.—Boult   ♯ **D.LXT 5015**
  (*above, Bax & Holst*)   (♯ Lon.LL 1169)
  (*Holst only on ♯ D.LW 5175*)
  A.B.C. Sydney Sym.—Goossens ♮ **G.DB 9792/3**
  (3ss—ARR. *Grainger: Londonderry Air*)

BUTTING, Max (b. 1888)

Kleine Kammermusik, Op. 70 fl., cor. ang., vln., vlc.
  E. Milzkott, E. Erthel, M. Michailow, W. Haupt
  (4ss)   *Eta. 120041/2*

BUXTEHUDE, Diederik (Dietrich) (1637-1707)

I. VOCAL

(U = Ugrino edition)

CANTATAS

COLLECTIONS

Herr, auf dich traue ich   (U.5)
Singet dem Herrn   (U.16)   S, vln. & cont.
Jesu, meine Freude   (U.54)
Lauda, Sion, Salvatorem   (U.57)   S, S, B. & cont.
  Helen Boatwright & St. Thomas's Chu. Cho.,
    New Haven—Howard Boatwright ♯ **Over.LP 6**
  [with vlns., vlc., bsn., cbs., hpsi. & org.]

Jubilate Domino   (U.19)   C-T & insts.
In dulci jubilo   (U.52)   S, C-T, Bs., insts.
  E. McLoughlin, A. Deller, M. Bevan, 2 vlns.,
    vlc. & gamba   ♯ **LOL.OL 50102**
  (*Org. fugue, below; & † Lutenist Songs*)

Also hat Gott die Welt geliebt   (U.1)
Herr, wenn ich dich nur habe   (U.6)
Ich sprach in meinem Herzen   (U.8)
O clemens, O mitis, O coelestis Pater   (U.10)
Schaffe in mir, Gott, ein reines Herz   (U.14)
  ☆ M. Guilleaume (S) & Hamburg Festival Ens.—Bechert
                     ♯ **EVox.PL 7330**

Also hat Gott die Welt geliebt   (U.1)   S & cont.
O fröhliche Stunden   (U.12)   2 vlns. & cont.
O Gottes Stadt   (U.13)   S & cont.
Singet dem Herrn   (U.16)   S, vln. & cont.
  ☆ P. Neway & Allegro Cha. Ens.   ♯ **Allo. 3085**

Ich bin die Auferstehung   (U.25)
Ich bin eine Blume zu Saron   (U.26)
Mein Herz ist bereit   (U.27)
  ☆ B. Müller (Bs), Stuttgart Pro Musica Orch.—Grischkat,
    E. Hölderlin (org.)
O Lux beata Trinitas   (U.38)
  ☆ M. Guilleaume & B. Groth (S), Hamburg Bach Fest.
    —Bechert (org. cont.)   ♯ **EVox.PL 7620**

Befiehl dem Engel, dass er kommt   Cho. & orch.
Erbarm' dich mein, O Herre Gott   S, B, cho. & orch.
Fürwahr er trug unsere Krankheit   S, B, cho. orch.
  ☆ M. Guilleaume (S), E. M. Lühr (B), Hamburg
    Musikfreunde Cho. & Orch.—Bechert
                     ♯ **EVox.PL 7430**

Alles was ihr tut   S, A, T, B, cho. orch.   1678
  ☆ Soloists, Stuttgart Cho. & Swabian Sym.—Grischkat
                     (♯ Cpt.MC 20028)

Entreisst euch, meine Sinnen   (U.2)
  M. Svendsen (S), & Copenhagen Music Soc.
  Ens.   ♭ *Mtr.MCEP 3026*
  (*below*)

Ich halte es dafür   (U.32)
... Du gibest mir Ruh   S & Bs
  I. Wolf & S. Joynt   **G.HMS 56**
  († History of Music in Sound)   (in ♯ Vic. set LM 6030)

Jesu, meine Freude   (▽U.54)
  ☆ Soloists, Washington Presbyterian Chu. Cho. (*Eng*)
    —Schaefer (♯ WCFM. 20)

Wachet auf   (U.75)
... Zion hört die Wächter singen   Chorale
  Vienna Boys' Cho.—Kühbacher
                 in ♯ *EPhi.NBR 6024*
  (*Brahms, Bruckner, Schumann, etc.*)   (♯ Phi.N 00726R)

Was mich auf dieser Welt betrübt   (U.17)
  M. Svendsen (S) & Mbrs. Copenhagen Music
  Soc. Orch. (*above*)   ♭ *Mtr.MCEP 3026*

Magnificat   5 voices & orch. (discovered 1931)
  ☆ Stuttgart Cho. & Swabian Sym.—Grischkat
                   (♯ Cpt.MC 20028)

II. INSTRUMENTAL

The references for organ works are: S, to the old Spitta edition, B & H (as in WERM); NS, to the revision of the same by Seiffert, 1952, where the numbering differs. A reference to the Hedar edn. (Novello) is given where a work is not in S or NS.

COLLECTIONS OF ORGAN MUSIC
COMPLETE ORGAN WORKS   (in progress)

VOL. I
Chaconnes: E minor   (S. I-3)
            C minor   (S. I-2)
Chaconne (Passaglia), D minor   (S. I-1)
Chorale-Preludes (Fantasias)   (S. II; NS. III/IV)
  Wie schön leuchtet der Morgenstern   (Pt. 1, No. 10)
  Ich dank der schon durch deinen Sohn   (Pt. 1, No. 4)
  Ich ruf zu dir, Herr Jesu Christ   (Pt. 1, No. 15)
  A. Linder   ♯ **West.WN 18117**
  [Skänninge Church organ, Sweden]

VOL. II
Toccata & Fugue, F major   (S. I-20;NS. II-26)
Canzonettas: G minor   Hedar I-12
             C major   I-5
             E minor   I-9
Canzonas: B flat major   I-11
         G major   I-7
         G major   I-8
         C major   I-4 (NS. II-32)
         D minor   I-10 (NS. II-31)
         G minor   I-6
  A. Linder [same org.]   ♯ **West.WN 18149**

Chaconne (Passaglia), D minor[8]   (S. I-1)
CHORALE-PRELUDES   (S. II-NS. III/IV)
  Auf meinen lieben Gott[3]   (Partita) (Pt. 2, No. 31)
  Wir danken dir, Herr Jesu Christ[6]   (Hedar IV-57)
  Lobt Gott, ihr Christen[6]   (Pt. 2, No. 21) ø
  (or Erschienen ist der herrliche Tag) ø
  Fugue, C major[7]   (S. 1-17; NS. II-22) ø

(continued on next page)

♯ = Long-playing, 33⅓ r.p.m.   ♭ = 45 r.p.m.   ♮ = Auto. couplings, 78 r.p.m.

PRELUDES & FUGUES:
   F major[4]   (S. I-15)
   F major   (Toccata[1] & Fugue[2])   (S.I-20)
   G minor[5]   (S.I-14) ø
Prelude, Fugue & Chaconne, C major[3]   (S.I-4)
  E. P. Biggs   ♯ AmC.ML 4971/2
  (*Pachelbel, etc.*)   (in set SL 219)
  [Items marked ø also in ♯ EPhi.ABL 3066;
         the remainder in ♯ ABL 3110]
  Organs played: [1] St. Jacobikirche, Lübeck
            [2] Danish State Radio, Copenhagen
            [3] Oskarskyrkan, Stockholm
            [4] Monastery Church, Sorø, Denmark
            [5] Trondheim Cathedral
            [6] Frederiksborg Castle Church, Hillerød
            [7] Drottningholm Castle Chapel, Sweden
            [8] Leufsta Bruk, Sweden

Prelude, Fugue & Chaconne, C major   (S. I-4)
PRELUDES & FUGUES
   D major   (S.I-11)   (*La Chasse*)
   G minor   (S.I-14)
   A minor   (S.I-9)
   E minor   (S.I-6)
Canzona, D minor   (S.I-25; NS.II-31)   "*Canzonetta*"
CHORALE-PRELUDES   (S.II; NS. III/IV)
   Nun komm' der Heiden Heiland   (Pt. 2, No. 25)
   Wie schön leuchtet der Morgenstern   (Pt. 1, No. 10)
   Gelobet seist du, Jesu Christ   (Pt. 2, No. 10)
   In dulci jubilo   (Pt. 2, No. 17)
  M-C. Alain   ♯ Era.LDE 3026
  [St. Merry Organ, Paris]

CHORALE PRELUDES:
   Magnificat primi toni   (Pt. 1, No. 5a)
   Nun bitten wir den heiligen Geist   (Pt. 2, No. 23)
   Wie schön leuchtet der Morgenstern   (Pt. 1, No. 10)
PRELUDES & FUGUES: D major   (S.I-11)
                F sharp minor   (S.I-12)
Prelude, Fugue & Chaconne, C major   (S.I-4)
  ☆ R. Noehren (♯ Lyr.LL 56)

Aria Rofilis, D minor[9]   hpsi.
— ARR. HARP   Boye
  H. Boye (hp.)   ♯ D.LW 5177
  (*below; & Handel*)

Canzonetta (unspec.)   — ARR. BANDONEON
  A. Barletta   in ♯ SMC. 549

La Capricciosa, G major   hpsi.
  (partite diverse sopra un aria d'inventione) ed. Bangeot.
  F. Viderø   ♯ HS.HSL 3069
  (*J. Christoph Bach*)
  — ARR. HARP
  H. Boye   in ♯ D.LW 5177
  (*below; & Handel*)

Chaconne, E minor   (S. I-3)
  N. Pierront   in ♯ Lum.LD 2-104
  († Chaconne & Passacaglia) [St.-Merry organ, Paris]
  J. E. Hansen   ♭ Mtr.MCEP 3040
  (*Toccata*) [Christiansborg Palace Chapel org.]

CHORALE-PRELUDES   (S.II; NS.III/IV)
Ich ruf' zu dir   (Pt. 2, No. 15)
  ☆ C. Weinrich (in ♯ Allo. 4029)

In dulci jubilo   (Pt. 2, No. 17)
  G. Jones   in G.HMS 61
  († History of Music in Sound)   (in ♯ Vic. set LM 6031)

Lobt Gott, ihr Christen   (Pt. 2, No. 21)
  ☆ C. Weinrich (in ♯ Allo. 4029)

Wie schön leuchtet der Morgenstern (Pt. 1, No. 10)
  ☆ F. Heitmann (in † ♯ DT.LGX 66009; FT. 320.TC.075)
  C. Weinrich (in ♯ Allo. 4029)

Fugue, C major   ("*Gigue*")   (S.I-17; NS.II-22)
  D. Vaughan   ♯ LOL.OL 50102
  (*Cantatas, above; etc.*)
  ☆ C. Snyder (♯ Word.W 4003)

Magnificat primi toni   (S.II. Pt. 1, No. 5a)
  ☆ C. Weinrich (in ♯ Allo. 4029)

Magnificat noni toni   (NS.II-35)
  ☆ H. Liedecke (in ♯ Cpt.MC 20028)

PRELUDES & FUGUES, Organ
D major   (S.I-11)
  ☆ N. O. Raasted (♭ Mer.EP 1-5050)

E minor   (S.I-6)
  ☆ C. Weinrich (in ♯ Allo. 4029)

F sharp minor   (S.I-12)
  P. Kee   in ♯ G.DLP 1053
  († "Baroque" Organ Music)

G minor   (S.I-14)
  F. Asma   in ♯ Phi.S 06032R
  (*Sweelinck*) [Organ of Old Church, Amsterdam]

SUITES, Clavier
No. 1, C major
  ☆ F. Krakamp (hpsi.)   (*Krieger*)   ♭ Pol. 37013

No. 6, D minor . . . Sarabande
— ARR. HARP: H. Boye (in ♯ D.LW 5177)

Toccata & Fugue, D minor   (NS.II-30)
  J. E. Hansen   ♭ Mtr.MCEP 3040
  (*Chaconne, E minor*)

Toccata & Fugue, F major   (S.I-21; NS.II-27)
  ☆ W. Supper († ♯ Cpt.MC 20029 & ♯ Ren.X 54)
  C. Weinrich (in ♯ Allo. 4029)

BYRD, William (1543-1623)

[References in Roman figs. to the vols. of the collected edn., ed. Fellowes]

I. INSTRUMENTAL

COLLECTIONS OF VIRGINALS MUSIC

Praeludium No. 3	FVB 100
Fantasia No. 4	FVB 52
The Bells	FVB 69
Pavan No. 3	FVB 252
Galliard No. 36	FVB 164
Allemande No. 3	FVB 156
La Volta	FVB 155

  F. Neumeyer (hpsi.)   ♯ HP.AP 13026

Rowland, or Lord Willoby's welcome home	Nevell 33
Pavan & Galliard: No. 1 FVB 167/8	Nevell 10/11
No. 5	Nevell 18/19
The Queen's Alman, FVB 172	
Pavan & Galliard, The Earl of Salisbury	Parthenia 6/7
French Coranto No. 1 FVB 218	

  T. Dart (hpsi.)   (*Tomkins*)   ♯ LOL.OL 50076

(The) Bells   FVB 69
  F. Peeters (org.)   in ♯ Per.SPL 578
  († Old English Masters)   (♯ Cpt.MC 20049)
  ☆ P. Aubert (virginals) (in † ♯ HS.AS 13)
  — ARR. ORCH.   G. Jacob
  Sydney Sym.—Heinze   in ♯ Rad.LXR 5002
  (*below; & Walton, Vaughan Williams*)

(The) Earl of Oxford's March   FVB 259
  — ARR. ORCH.   Jacob
  Sydney Sym.—Heinze   in ♯ Rad.LXR 5002
  (*above; Walton, Vaughan Williams*)

Fantasy à 3, No. 1   (Vol. XXII)
  Musicians' Workshop Recorder Consort
                   in ♯ CEd.CE 1018
  († Recorder Music of Six Centuries)

Fortune (Variations)   FVB 65
  ☆ F. Heitmann (org.)   in ♯ DT.LGX 66037
  († Organ Music Sweelinck to Hindemith)

O Mistress mine (Divisions)   FVB 66
  S. Bloch (virginals)   in ♯ CHS.CHS 1225
  († Music in Shakespeare's Time)

PAVANES & GALLIARDS
No. 19, The Earl of Salisbury   (Parthenia 6 & 7)
  — ARR. ORCH.   Barbirolli (in *An Elizabethan Suite*)
  Hallé—Barbirolli   in ♯ G.BLP 1065
  (*Bull, Farnaby, Anon; & Elgar*)
. . . Pavane only   ☆ A. Ehlers (in ♯ D.UAT 273084)

Based on Shepherd's Song, from Lully: *L'Impatience.*

II. VOCAL

A. CHURCH MUSIC

MASSES
Four Voices
Pro Musica Antiqua—Cape   # EMS. 234
  (*below*)
☆ Fleet Street Cho.—Lawrence   # D.LXT 2919
  (*below*)   (# Lon.LL 888)

Five Voices
Pro Musica Antiqua—Cape   # EMS. 234
  (*above*)
☆ Fleet Street Cho.—Lawrence   # D.LXT 2919
  (*above*)   (# Lon.LL 888)

MOTETS
Ave, verum corpus (V) 4 voices 1605
St. Paul's Cath. Cho.—Dykes Bower
    in # C.CX 1193
  (*Sweelinck, Weelkes, Bach, etc.*)
    (# Angel. 35138 in set 3516)

Beata viscera (IV) 5 voices 1605
Confirma hoc, Deus (VII) 5 voices 1607
Welch Chorale   in # Lyr.LL 52
  († Motets of the XVth & XVIth Centuries)

Ego sum panis vivus (VI) 4 voices 1607
Copenhagen Boys' & Men's Cho.—Møller
    in # HS.HSL 2072
  († Masterpieces of Music before 1750)

Exsurge, quare obdormis, Domine? (III) 5 vv. 1591
Westminster Abbey Cho.—McKie C.LX 1605
  (*below; & Batten*)   [† Eng. Chu. Music]

Haec dies quam fecit Dominus (III) 6 vv. 1591
St. Paul's Cath. Choir—Dykes Bower
    G.HMS 37
  († History of Music in Sound) (in # Vic. set LM 6029)
Welch Chorale   in # Lyr.LL 52
  († Motets of XVth & XVIth Centuries)
Festival Singers—Iseler   # Hall.ChS 3
  (*Willan, Mundy, Lassus, Gibbons*)

Justorum animae (IV) 5 voices 1605
King's College Cho.—Ord   C.LX 1605
  (§s—*Batten & above*)   [† Eng. Chu. Music]
Harvard Glee Club—Woodworth[1]
    in # Camb.CRC 101

Laudibus in sanctis (III) 5 voices 1591
New College Cha. Cho.—Andrews C.LB 132
  († English Church Music, Vol. III)

Senex puerum portabat (V) 4 voices 1605
Kings College Cho.—Ord   C.LX 1604
  (*Morley & Taverner*)   [† Eng. Chu. Music]
Trapp Family Singers—Wasner
    in # B.LAT 8038
  (*Christmas Music Vol. 2*)(# AmD.DL 9689: ♭ set ED 1200)

SERVICE
(The) Great Service (X)
Washington Cha. Cho.—Callaway
    # Van.VRS 453

II. B. SECULAR VOCAL MUSIC

Hey, ho, to the greenwood Round[2]
Primavera Singers   in # Eso.ESJ 6
  († Elizabethan Songbag for young people)

Though Amaryllis dance in green (XII) Madrigal
  5 vv. 1588
Madrigal Singers—Robe   in # Fred. 2
  (*Martinu, Marvel, Persichetti, etc.*)

BYTTERING (*or Gyttering*) (fl. 1420)
    SEE: † HISTORY OF MUSIC IN SOUND (23)

CABANILLES, Juan (1644-1712)
    SEE: † ANTHOLOGIE SONORE (# HS.AS 11)
        † CHACONNE & PASSACAGLIA

CABEZON, Antonio de (1500-1566)
    SEE: † ANTHOLOGIE SONORE (# HS.AS 11)
        † SPANISH RENAISSANCE MUSIC
        † SPANISH KEYBOARD MUSIC

CACCINI, Giulio (*c.* 1545-1618)

(Le) NUOVE MUSICHE 1601/2
Amarilli
S. Danco (S), G. Agosti (pf.) in # D.LX 3113
    (in # Lon.LS 698)
I. Kolassi (M-S), J. Bonneau (pf.)
    in # Lon.LL 747
  († Arie Antiche & German Lieder) (# D.FAT 173160)
R. Hayes (T), R. Boardman (pf.)
    in # Van.VRS 448
  (*Monteverdi, Bach, Telemann, etc.; & Trad.*)
☆ M. Laszlo (S), F. Holetschek (pf.) in # Nix.WLP 5119
  († Italian Songs)
Accompaniment, etc., for practice (in # VS.ML 3004)

Dovrò dunque morire
V. Garde (M-S), T. Nielsen (lute)
    in # HS.HSL 2072
  († Masterpieces of Music before 1750)
  (*also in* † Histoire de la Musique Vocale)

Occh' immortali ed. Dørumsgaard
G. Souzay (B), J. Bonneau (pf.)
    in # D.LXT 2835
  († Canzone Scordate) (# D.FAT 173072; Lon.LL 731)

CAIX d'HERVELOIS, Louis de
           (*c.* 1670-1760)

SUITES[3] gamba & continuo
No. 1, A major (ed. Schröder)
  (La Milanese; Sarabande; Tambourin; Menuet; L'Agréable;
  Gavotte)
No. 2, D minor (ed. Döbereiner & Schröder)
  (Prelude—Grave; Menuets; Plainte; La Napolitaine)
P. Doktor (vla.), F. Valenti (hpsi.)
  (*Marais*)   # West.WN 18088

No. 2, D minor — ARR. GAMBA & ORCH.
K-M. Schwamberger & Mozarteum Cha. Orch.
  —Paumgartner   # CFD. 14
  (*Albinoni, Fesch, Telemann, etc.*)

Suite, G major, Op. 6, No. 3 recorder & cont.
... Prelude; La Tubeuf
C. Dolmetsch & J. Saxby (hpsi.) # D.LXT 2943
  († Recorder & Hpsi. recital) (# Lon.LL 1026)

CALDARA, Antonio (1670-1736)

ARIAS
Alma del core, spirto dell' alma
R. Hayes (T), R. Boardman (pf.)
    in # Van.VRS 448
  (*Caccini, Telemann, Bach, Trad., etc.*)

Come raggio del sol
S. Danco (S), G. Agosti (pf.) in # D.LX 3113
  (*Schütz, Bach, Caccini, etc.*) (in # Lon.LS 698)
F. Barbieri (M-S), D. Marzollo (pf.)
    in # AmVox.PL 7980
  († Old Italian Songs & Airs)

---

[1] ARR. MALE VOICES Davison.
[2] MS., British Museum 31441.
[3] Synthetic suites from the *Premier livre de pièces de viole.*

Come raggio del sol (*continued*)
  B. Christoff (Bs), G. Moore (pf.)   **G.DB 21592**
  (*Lishin: She mocked*)
  M. Laszlo (S), F. Holetschek (pf.)
                            in ♯ **Nix.WLP 5375**
  († Italian Airs)   (♯ West.WL 5375)

Sebben, crudele (from *La Costanza in amor*)
  G. Prandelli (T), D. Marzollo (pf.)
                            in ♯ **AmVox.PL 7930**
  († Old Italian Airs)
  M. Vitale (S), A. Beltrami (pf.)   **Cet.AT 0315**
  (*Handel: Serse—Ombra mai fu*)

Selve amiche
  ☆ B. Gigli (T) & orch.   in ♯ **G.ALP 1174**
  († Italian Classic Songs) (♯ QALP 10073: FALP 340)

CALESTANI, Vincenzo (fl. XVIIth Cent.)
  SEE: † CANZONE SCORDATE

CALVISIUS, Seth (1556-1615)
  SEE: † MOTETS ON LUTHER TEXTS

CAMBINI, Giovanni Giuseppe (1746-1825)

CANTATA in French
Andromaque (MS., Paris Cons. Library)
  M. Tyler (S) & Italian Cha.—Jenkins
                            ♯ **HS.HSL 76**
  (*Pergolesi & Galuppi*)   (in set HSL-C)

Concerto, G major, Op. 15, No. 3 clavier & strings
  O. P. Santoliquido (pf.) & Virtuosi di Roma
  —Fasano   ♯ **B.AXTL 1042**
  (*Rossini, Bonporti & Marcello*)
                  (♯ AmD.DL 9674; Fnt.LP 3005; D.UAT 273583)
  C. Abbado (pf.) & Milan Cha. Orch.
  —M. Abbado[1]   ♯ **C.FCX 369**
  (*Tartini, Vivaldi, Bonporti*)

CAMPIAN, Thomas (1567-1620)

SONGS
COLLECTIONS
**Nos. 1–10 from Philip Rosseter's Book of Ayres,
  Part I** 1601
My sweetest Lesbia
Though you are young
I care not for these ladies
Follow thy fair sun
My love hath vowed
When to her lute Corinna sings
Turn back, you wanton flyer
It fell on a summer's day
The cypress curtain of the night
Follow your saint
  R. Soames (T), W. Gerwig (lute), J. Koch
  (gamba) (2ss)   ♯ **HP.AP 13006**
  (*Dowland & Morley*, in ♯ AmD.ARC 3004)

From Book I of Ayres c. 1613 (Fellowes, VIII)
Never weather-beaten sail
Most sweet and pleasing are thy ways, O God
Author of light
To music bent
  A. Deller (C-T), D. Dupré (lute)
                            ♯ **LOL.OL 50102**
  († Lutenist Songs; & *Buxtehude*)

I care not for these ladies (Rosseter's book)
  A. Deller (C-T), D. Dupré (lute) ♯ **Van.BG 539**
  († Elizabethan & Jacobean Music)

Jack and Joan they think no ill (Book I)
  N.Y. Pro Musica Antiqua Ens.   ♯ *Eso.ESJ 6*
  († Elizabethan Songbag)

(The) Peaceful western wind (Book II) c. 1613
  S. Bloch (S) & lute   ♯ *CHS.CHS 1225*
  († Music in Shakespeare's time)

CAMPION, François (fl. 1703-1719)
  SEE: † GUITAR RECITAL

CAMPRA, André (1660-1744)

MOTETS
Beati omnes T & insts. 1706
  M. Casadesus Ens.   in ♯ **Plé.P 3083**
  († Musiques à la Chapelle du Roy) (♯ West.WN 18167)
  [J. Giraudeau (T)]
Pange lingua 1723[2]
  A. Fontana (S), B. Demigny (B), Versailles
  Cho. & Orch.—Roussel   ♯ **SM. 33-06**
  (*Caurroy, F. Couperin, Lalande*)

OPERAS
(Les) FÊTES VÉNITIENNES 1710
Chanson du papillon
  ☆ M. Laszlo (S), F. Holetschek (pf.) ♯ **Nix.WLP 5119**
  († Italian Songs)

IDOMÉNÉE 1712
Rigaudon, A major — ARR. ORGAN
  W. Watkins   in ♯ **McInt.MM 106**
  (*Handel, Langlais, Dupré, etc.*)

CANTALLOS (b. c. 1760)
  SEE: † SPANISH KEYBOARD MUSIC
        † OLD SPANISH KEYBOARD MUSIC

CANTELOUBE, Marie Joseph (b. 1879)
  (Abridged listing only)

Danse hrn. & pf. 1954
  G. Coursier & A. d'Arco   ♭ *Pat.G 1057*
  (*Passani, Martelli, Françaix, Ameller*)

FOLK SONG SETTINGS
Chants d'Augoumois
  L. Daullène (S), J. Canteloube (pf.) (♯ Sel.LPG 8220)
Chants de France
  D. & J-C. Benoit (S & B), L. Benoit-Granier (pf.)
                            (♯ Sel.LPG 8220)
  L. Daullène (S), J. Canteloube (pf.)
                            (♯ LOL.OL 50047; OL.LD 2)
Chants d'Auvergne
  L. Daullène (S), J. Canteloube (pf.) (♯ Sel.LPG 8220)
  M. Grey (S) & orch. (AmC.ML 4459: o.n. 7328M:
                  7249M: 7262M; C.LCX 151/3: LFX 27/9)
  S. Reed (S) & Cha. Orch. (in ♯ AmC.ML 4368)
  G. Swarthout (S) (♯ Vic.LM 1156: ♭ set WDM 1540)
...Excerpts: G. Souzay (B) in ♯ D.LW 5091: Lon.LD 9109)
Chants Basques
Chants Occitans
  Pamplona Cho.—Morondo
                  (♯ Sel.LA 1070; in ♯ West.WL 5350)
Noëls populaires français
  G. Touraine (S), I. Altoff (pf.) (♭ Lum.LD 1-503)
  Paris Trad. Cho. & Champs-Elysées Orch.—M. Honegger
                  (♯ West.WL 5372; Sel. 270.C.009)
À l'âge de quinze ans
  Vocal Ens.—P. Caillard (in V♯ Era.LDE 1013)
O Houp!; Chaîne de Bourrées: in V♯ Era.LDE 1025
ALSO: *Pat.PD 79, PA 2621, etc.*
  ▽ Other recordings included:
  Bourrée auvergnate
    E. Feuermann (vlc.) & pf. (*Vic. 2166; G.EC 113*)
  Les Canards (*Lum. 33175*)
  etc.

---

[1] Ed. Barblan.   [2] Ed. J. H. de la Montagne.

CAPLET, André (1878-1925)

(Le) Masque de la mort rouge Conte fantastique
(after Poe) 1909 Hp. & Str. Orch., orig. hp. & str. qtt.
A. M. Stockton & Concert Arts—Slatkin
‡ DCap.CTL 7057
(*McDonald*)   (‡ Cap.P 8255)

CARA, Marchetto (d. 1527)

SEE: †RENAISSANCE MUSIC FOR THE LUTE

CARISSIMI, Giacomo (1605-1674)

DUETS—COLLECTION
A piè d'un verde alloro (Benigni)
Detesta la cattiva sorte in amore (Benigni)
Il mio core
Lungi omai
E. Schwarzkopf & I. Seefried (SS),
G. Moore (pf.)   ‡ C.CX 1331
(*Dvořák & Monteverdi*)   (‡ Angel. 35290)

(Il) GIUDIZIO UNIVERSALE Cantata (Benigni)
Suonera l'ultima tromba
L. Ribacchi (M-S) & Società Corelli
‡ Vic.LM 1767
(*Vivaldi, Geminiani, Marcello*)
(in ♭ set WDM 1767; ‡ ItV.A12R 0098)

JEPHTE Oratorio *c.* 1660 (DDT. II)
J. Feyerabend (T), L. Schwarzweller (S), North
German Singers—Wolters ‡ HP.APM 14020
[C. Lipp (hpsi.), J. Koch (gamba), J. Lippert (cbs.)]
(*Monteverdi*)   (‡ AmD.ARC 3005)

... **Plorate, filii Israel**
U.O.S. Cho.—McConnell   in ‡ *UOS.* 2
(*Smit, Handl, Bach, etc.*)   (private rec.)
JONAS Oratorio S, A, T, T, B, B, Cho.
COMPLETE RECORDING
☆ Soloists, Angelicum Cho. & Orch.—Gerelli
(6ss)   CGD.SA 3012/4

... **Justus es, Domine** T
W. Herbert   G.HMS 50
(† History of Music in Sound)   (in ‡ Vic. set LM 6030)

JUDICIUM SALOMONIS Oratorio *c.* 1669
Afferte gladium
E. Simonsen (S), V. Garde (M-S), H. Nørgaard
(Bs), vlc. & org.   in ‡ HS.HSL 2072
(† Masterpieces of Music before 1750)
(also in † Histoire de la Musique Vocale)

SONGS
Piangete, ohimé, piangete (from a Cantata)
F. Barbieri (M-S), D. Marzollo (pf.)
in ‡ AmVox.PL 7980
(† Old Italian Songs & Airs)
M. Laszlo (S), F. Holetschek (pf.)
in ‡ Nix.WLP 5375
(† Italian Airs)   (‡ West.WL 5375)

Sventura, cuor mio
☆ H. Cuénod (T), H. Leeb (lute)   in ‡ Nix.WLP 5059
(† Italian Songs of the XVIth & XVIIth Centuries)

Vittoria, vittoria, mio core
G. Prandelli (T), D. Marzollo (pf.)
(† Old Italian Airs)   in ‡ AmVox.PL 7930
☆ B. Gigli (T) & orch.[1]   in ‡ G.ALP 1173
(† Italian Classic Songs)   (QALP 10073: FALP 340)
☆ M. Laszlo (S), F. Holetschek (pf.) in ‡ Nix.WLP 5119
(† Italian Songs)

CARLTON, Richard (*c.* 1558-*c.* 1638)

SEE: † TRIUMPHS OF ORIANA

---

[1] Ed. Parisotti. The others are probably the same.

CARMEN, Johannes (fl. XIV-XVth Cent.)

SEE: † MUSIC FROM THE MIDDLE AGES TO RENAISSANCE

CAROSO, Fabritio (b. *c.* 1531)

SEE: RESPIGHI—Antiche Danze, Suite 2

CAROUBEL, Pierre Francisque (d. *c.* 1619)

SEE: † ANTHOLOGIE SONORE (‡ AS. 3004LD; HS.AS 36)

CARPENTER, John Alden (1876-1951)

Krazy Kat Ballet 1922
... **Excerpts**
Hamburg Philharmonia—Korn in ‡ Allo. 3150
(*Taylor, Stringfield, Chadwick, etc.*)
Skyscrapers Ballet 1926
A.R.S. Sym.—M. v. Zallinger   ‡ ARS. 37
(*Elwell: The Happy Hypocrite*)
☆ Vic. Sym.—Shilkret (JpV.ND 313/5)

CARRILLO, Julián (b. 1875)

Preludio a Cristóbal Colón 1940
S & "Sonido 13" quintet
▽ Havana Ens.—Reyes (AmC. 7357M, o.nn. 5115M:
50216 D; C.DFX 62)

String Quartet, Atonal, No. 1 1928
Bredo Qtt.   ‡ CM. 12

CARTER, Elliot Cook Jr. (b. 1908)

Quintet fl., ob., cl., bsn. & hrn. 1948
New Art Wind Quintet   in ‡ CEd. set 2003
(*Cowell, Dahl, etc.*)

CASADESUS, Robert Marcel (b. 1899)

Hommage à Chausson, Op. 51 vln. & pf. 1954
Z. Francescatti & R. Casadesus   ‡ AmC.Pte.
(*Bach & Francescatti*) (for American Library in Paris)

PIANO MUSIC
(8) Études
... Sardane & Resonances (sur le nom de Claude Pasquier), only
Toccata, Op. 40
J. Casadesus   ‡ Angel. 35261
(*Rameau, Couperin, Poulenc, etc.*)
Sonata, fl. & pf., Op. 18
(pub. 1948; recorded *c.* 1933)
▽ R. le Roy & R. Casadesus (C.LFX 330 & LF 147)

CASANOVAS, Narciso (1747-1799)

SEE: † SPANISH KEYBOARD MUSIC

CARVALHO, João de Sousa (*c.* 1730-1798)

SEE: † PORTUGUESE KEYBOARD MUSIC

CASCIA, Giovanni de (b. *c.* 1270)

SEE: † HISTORY OF MUSIC IN SOUND (21)
† ANTHOLOGIE SONORE
† MADRIGALS & CACCIE

CASCIOLINI, Claudio (1670- ?)

SEE: † MUSIC OF THE CHURCH

CASELLA, Alfredo (1883-1947)

(La) GIARA, Op. 41 Ballet 1924
Orch. Suite, Op. 41 bis . . . Excerpts
   Hamburg State Phil.—di Bella   ♯ *T.TW 30030*
   (*Marinuzzi*)

Italia, Op. 11 1909
   Berlin Radio—Kleinert   ♯ **Ura. 7118**
   (*below*)

(11) Pezzi infantili, Op. 35 pf. 1920
... No. 4, Bolero, & No. 11, Galop finale
   M. Jonas   in ♯ **AmC.ML 4624**

(5) Pieces, Op. 34 Str. Qtt. 1920
   ☆ New Music Qtt. (♯ BRS. 906)

Scarlattiana, Op. 44 pf. & orch.
   T. de Maria & Naples Scarlatti Orch.
   —Caracciolo   ♯ **Csm.CLPS 1038**
   (*Pizzetti: Danza bassa dello sparviero*)

Serenade, Op. 47 small orch. 1930
   Leipzig Radio—Kegel   ♯ **Ura. 7118**
   (*above*)

Sinfonia, arioso e toccata, Op. 59 pf. 1936
... Toccata only
   D. Raucea   in ♯ **D.LXT 2969**
   (*Granados, Albeniz, Pick-Mangiagalli, Castelnuovo-Tedesco,*
   St.-Saëns)   (in ♯ Lon.LL 1033)

Sonata, Op. 68 harp 1943
   L. Newell   ♯ **Phil.PH 109**
   (*Respighi & Donizetti*)

NOTE:
Dos miniaturas Criollas
   Radio Sym.—Bandini on ♯ *ArgOd.LDC 502;* &
Lloran las Quenas
   Sym.—Gianneo on ♯ Pam.LRC 15501, are by Enrique
   Casella

CASES, Guillermo (b. 1899)

(Los) GITANOS
Buliera del Borracho
Fandango de la Garbosa
   Colón Theatre Orch.—Cases   *ArgOd. 57050*

Rapsodias Españolas
   (*Valencia; Leon*)
   Colón Theatre Orch.—Cases ♯ *Od.OD 1018*
   (*Breton, Granados, Falla, Albeniz*)   (♯ *ArgOd.LDC 519*)
   (*Leon only, on ArgOd. 66059:* ♭ *BSOAE 4527*)

CASSADÓ, Joaquin (1867-1926)

SEE: † Segovia, Art of

CASTELNUOVO-TEDESCO, Mario
(b. 1895)

Capriccio diabolico guitar
   A. Segovia   in ♯ B.AXTL 1070
   († Segovia Evening) (♯ AmD.DL 9733; SpC.CCL 35015;
                                   AFest.CFR 10-729)

Concerto, guitar & orch. 1939
   ☆ A. Segovia & New London—Sherman
                                   (♯ AmC.ML 4732)

(Le) Danze del Re David orch. 1925
   (Hebrew Rhapsody on trad. themes)
— ARR. PF.
   D. Raucea   in ♯ **D.LXT 2969**
   (*Casella, Pick-Mangiagalli, St.-Saëns, etc.*)
                                   (in ♯ Lon.LL 1033)
Études d'ondes pf. 1916/19
— ARR. VLN. & PF. Heifetz as "*Sea Murmurs*"
   ☆ J. Heifetz & E. Bay (*G.DA 2037: EC 208*)

Much ado about nothing Overture, orch. f.p. 1954
   Louisville—Whitney   ♯ **LO. 4**
   (*Hovhaness & Surinach*)

Tarantella, A minor guitar
   A. Carlevaro   **P.PXO 1073**
   (*Villa-Lobos & Barrios*)
   C. Aubin   in ♯ **Eko.LG 1**
   († Guitar recital)
   ☆ A. Segovia (♭ *C.SCB 110: SCBQ 3016*)

Tonadilla on the name of Andrés Segovia guitar
   A. Segovia   in ♯ **AmD.DL 9795**
   († Segovia, Art of)   (♯ D.UAT 273594)

Two maids wooing Song (Shakespeare)
— ARR. VLN. & PF. Heifetz "*Tango*"
   ☆ J. Heifetz (*G.EC 193*)

CASTRO, Jean de (fl. XVIth Cent.)

SEE: † Musiciens de la Cour de Bourgogne

CASTRO, José Maria (b. 1892)

Concerto grosso orch.
   State Sym.—Castro (4ss)   **ArgV.P 1513/4**
                                   (pte. rec.)

CATALANI, Alfredo (1854-1893)

OPERAS
LORELEY 3 Acts 1890
Nel verde maggio T (Act I, Sc. 1)
   M. del Monaco   in ♯ **D.LXT 2928**
   (with *A. Chénier aria,* D.X 578)   (♯ Lon.LL 990)
   (& in ♯ D.LXT 2964; Lon.LL 1025; also ♯ *D.LW 5121;*
   Lon.LD 9132)

Danza delle ondine (Act II)
   N.B.C. Sym.—Toscanini   ♭ **Vic.ERA 101**
   (*Wally—Prelude, Act IV*)
   (♭ *ItV.A72R 0003* & in ♯ Vic. set LM 6026)
   [announced as G.DB 21610: ♭ *7R 177*]

Amor, celeste ebbrezza S (Act II)
   M. Olivero   *Cet.AT 0320*
   (*Traviata—Amami Alfredo*)
   E. Rizzieri   *Cet.AT 0369*
   (*Puccini: La Rondine—Chi il bel sogno*)

DEJANICE 4 Acts 1883
Mio bianco amor T (Act II)
   S. Puma   *Cet.AT 0390*
   (*Pagliacci—Vesti la giubba*)

(La) WALLY 4 Acts 1892
Ebben, ne andró lontana S (Act I)
   V. de los Angeles   in ♯ **G.ALP 1284**
   (*Ernani, Otello, Bohème, etc.*)   (♯ QALP 10115)
   J. Hammond   **G.DB 21580**
   (*Aïda—O Patria mia*)   (♭ 7R 172: in ♯ ALP 1076)
   M. Benetti   *Cet.AT 0359*
   (*Vêpres Siciliennes—Mercè, dilette amiche*)
   M. M. Callas   in ♯ **C.CX 1231**
   (*Mefistofele, Barbiere, Dinorah, etc.*)
                                   (♯ QCX 10129; Angel. 35233)
   D. Rigal   in ♯ *ArgOd.LDC 503*
   (*Traviata, Pagliacci, etc.*) (in ♯ AmD.DL 4060: ♭ ED 3508)
   A. Hownanian   ♭ *Cet.EPO 0322*
   (*Forza, Manon Lescaut, Amico Fritz*)
   M. C. Verna   in ♯ **Cet.LPC 55005**
   (*Ernani, Adriana Lecouvreur, Otello, etc.*)
   ☆ M. Vitale   in ♯ **Cet.LPC 55001**
   (*Gioconda; & Handel, Respighi, etc.*)
   ☆ L. Albanese (in ♯ Vic.LM 1839; FV.A 630253)
   R. Tebaldi (♭ *AmD.ED 3530;* also in ♯ *Fnt.LP 301*)

☆ = Re-issue of a recording to be found in previous volumes.

LA WALLY (*continued*)
Prelude, Act 3 (*A sera*); **Serenatella**
Naples Scarlatti Orch.—Argenta
(*Bettinelli: Sinfonia*)   # Csm.CLPS 1040

Prelude, Act 4
N.B.C. Sym.—Toscanini   ♭ Vic.ERA 101
(*Loreley—Danza*)
(♭ *ItV.A72R 0003*; & in # Vic. set LM 6026)
[announced as G.DB 21610: ♭ 7R 177]

CATURLA: See GARCIA CATURLA

CAURROY, Eustace du (1549-1609)

(Un) Enfant du ciel nous est né
Sors de ton lit paré
Paris Vocal Ens.—Jouve   in V# Sel.LPP 8611
(*Costeley, Praetorius, & Trad.*)

Missa pro defunctis
... **Requiem aeternam** (Introit) (ed. E. Martin)
Versailles Cho. & Orch.—Roussel # SM. 33-06
(*Campra, F. Couperin, Lalande*)
Petits Chanteurs de la Renaissance
    V# Era.LDE 1009
(† French Sacred Music)   (# HS.HS 9007)
(also in † Histoire de la musique vocale)
NOTE: There is a song attrib. Caurroy in † Chansons
historiques françaises.

CAVALIERI, Emilio de (1550-1602)

(La) Rappresentazione di Anima e di Corpo 1600
MS., Vallicelli Library, Rome
Y. Gouverné Vocal Ens. & Inst. Ens.—Chaillé
(*Cesti: Serenata*)   † # AS. 3009 LD

CAVALLI, Pietro Francesco (1602-1676)
SEE: † HISTORY OF MUSIC IN SOUND (45)
† OLD ITALIAN SONGS & AIRS

CAVAZZONI, Girolamo (c. 1500-1560)
SEE: † OLD ITALIAN MASTERS

CAVENDISH, Michael (c. 1565-1628)
SEE: † TRIUMPHS OF ORIANA

ČERNOHORSKÝ, Bohuslav Matej
    (1684-1742)
ORGAN WORKS
Toccata, C major
Fugue, G minor
☆ F. Michálek   # Sup.LPM 71
(*below; & Kuchař*)   (# U.5074C)

Fugue, A minor
☆ J. Ropek (in # Sup.LPM 71:U.5074C)

Fugue, G sharp minor
M. Šlechta   U.H 24406
(*Seger: Prelude & Fugue, C major*)

CERTON, Pierre (c. 1510-1572)
SEE: † PARISIAN SONGS OF XVITH CENTURY
† XVITH & XVIITH CENTURY SONGS
† MADRIGALS & MOTETS

CERVANTES, Ignacio (1847-1905)

(17) Danzas cubanas pf.
F. Godino   # Pnt. 4000
(*Saumell*)

CESTI, Pietro Antonio (1623-1699)

ARIA: Tu mancavi a tormentarmi 1660
— ARR. ORCH. Stokowski
Orch.—Stokowski   in # Vic.LM 1721
(*Lully, Palestrina, Gabrieli, etc*)   (♭ set WDM 1721)
(in # G.FALP 245; ItV.A12R 0040)
(& in # Vic.LM 1875: ♭ set ERB 52)

OPERAS & STAGE WORKS
(I CASTI AMORI D') ORONTEA
Prologue & 3 Acts 1649
Intorno all'idol mio
G. Prandelli (T), D. Marzollo (pf.)
(† Old Italian Airs)   in # AmVox.PL 7930
I. Kolassi (M-S), J. Bonneau (pf.)
    in # Lon.LL 747
(† Arie Antiche & German Lieder)   (# D.FAT 173160)
☆ M. Laszlo (S), F. Holetschek (pf.) in # Nix.WLP 5119
(† Italian Songs)
☆ B. Gigli (T) & orch.   in # G.ALP 1174
(† Italian Classic Songs)   (# QALP 10073: FALP 340)

EGISTO 1643 (Ed. Wellesz from MS., Vienna)
Musici della selva S & T
V. de los Angeles & R. Lewis   G.HMS 45
(† History of Music in Sound)   (in # Vic. set LM 6030)

(Il) POMO D'ORO 1666 or 1667
E dove t'aggiri S (Act I)
A. Mandikian   G.HMS 45
(† History of Music in Sound)   (in # Vic. set LM 6030)
D. Gramm (Bs), R. Cumming (pf.)
    in # ML. 7033

Serenata 1662[1]
Gouverné Vocal Ens. & Inst. Ens.—Chaillé
(*Cavalieri*)   † # AS. 3009LD

CHABRIER, Alexis Emmanuel (1841-1894)

Bourrée fantasque Ballet (Balanchine) 1954
(Contains Bourrée fantasque, GWENDOLINE—Interlude,
ROI MALGRÉ LUI—Fête polonaise; & Joyeuse marche,
q.v.)

Bourrée fantasque pf.   1891
G. Doyen   # Nix.WLP 5294
(*Collection—below*)   (# West.WL 5294)
— ARR. ORCH. Mottl
N.Y. City Ballet—Barzin
(*below; & Bizet*)   # E. & AmVox.PL 9320
☆ Colonne—Fourestier (♭ Pat.D 104)

(Une) EDUCATION MANQUÉE
Operetta 1 Act 1879
COMPLETE RECORDING
Gontran de Boismassif ... C. Castelli (S)
Hélène de la Cerisaie ... C. Collart (S)
Maître Pausanias ... ... X. Depraz (Bs)
& orch.—Bruck   # CdM.LDA 8098
    (# Van.VRS 460)

España Rapsodie orch. 1883
Philharmonia—v. Karajan   ♭ C.SEL 1528
(*Waldteufel: Les Patineurs*)   (♭ SEBQ 129)
Detroit Sym.—Paray   # Mer.MG 50056
(*Ibert & Ravel*)
Suisse Romande—Ansermet   in # D.LXT 2760
(*below & St.-Saëns*)   (# Lon.LL 696)
(& in # D.LW 5033; Lon.LD 9039 & ♭ REP 8022)
Hallé—Barbirolli (2ss)   G.DB 21615
(*Liadov on ♭ G.7ER 5026: 7ERQ 119; ♭ Vic.ERAB 13, d.c.*
also in # G.BLP 1058: QBLP 5032)
Los Angeles Phil.—Wallenstein
    in # B.AXTL 1063
(# D.UA 243584; AmD.DL 9728 & DL 4087: ♭ ED 3557)
Lamoureux—Fournet   in # EPhi.NBL 5000
(*below*)   (# Phi.N 00161L; Epic.LC 3028)
(*Ravel: Menuet antique on ♭ Phi.A 400001E*)

---

[1] 'Fatta in Firenze per la sera della nascita del Serenissimo Principe Sposo Cosmo di Toscana'; may be by Remigio Cesti.

España (*continued*)
Hollywood Bowl—Dragon
　　　　　　　　　in ‡ **DCap.CTL 7074**
　　　(‡ Cap.P 8275: SAL 9020: ♭ *FAP 8286*)
London Phil. Sym.—Quadri　‡ **Nix.WLP 20000**
(*Mossolov & Revueltas*)　　　(‡ West.LAB 7004)
Belgian Radio—André　　　　‡ *DT.TM 68016*
(*Massenet: Phèdre Overture*)
　　　　　　　(‡ *FT. 270.TC.044*; TV.VE 9031)
(*Meyerbeer: Fackeltanz No. 1* on ♭ *T.UX 4529*)
Bamberg Sym.—Lehmann　　　　　**PV. 72352**
(*Saint-Saëns: Danse macabre*)　(in ‡ AmD.DL 9775)
(*Delibes*, on ♭ *Pol. 30004*)
Philadelphia—Ormandy　　　　‡ **AmC.ML 4983**
(*Debussy, Ibert, Ravel*)
N.W. Ger. Phil.—Schüchter　　‡ *Imp.ILP 117*
(*Berlioz, Dvořák, Tchaikovsky*)
Berlin Phil.—Rother　　　　　in ‡ **Ura. 7096**
　　　　　　　　　　　　　　(♭ *UREP 56*)
☆ Royal Phil.—Beecham　　　　　　**C.LX 1592**
(GQX 11539: ♭ *SEL 1509: SEBQ 108*;
　　　　　　　　　　♭ *AmC.A 1640 & 4-4806*)
Concert Orch.—E. Robinson (in ‡ Argo.RG 66)
Hamburg Philharmonia—H-J. Walther (*MSB. 78122*)
Leighton Lucas Orch. (EMI.EPX 77)
☆ Boston Prom.—Fiedler (♭ *G.7EBF 1: 7EPQ 501:
　　　　　　7EG 8009: 7EPK 1001, d.c.; DV.B 26014*)
Colonne—Fourestier (♭ *AmVox.VIP 45230*; ♭ *Pat.ED 8*)

(L') ÉTOILE Opéra-bouffe, 3 acts　1877
Romance: Oh! petite étoile S
R. Doria, T. Janopoulo (pf.) in ‡ **Plé.P 3066**
(*Songs*)

GWENDOLINE Opera 2 Acts　1886
Overture
Lamoureux—Fournet　　　‡ **EPhi.NBL 5000**
(*above & below*)　　　(‡ Phi.N 00161L; Epic.LC 3028)
(*Lalo: Roi d' Ys Ov.* on ‡ *Phi.S 06034R*)
La Fileuse S
C. Castelli, H. Boschi (pf.) in ‡ *CdM.LD 8087*
(*Songs*)
Interlude orch.
N.Y. City Ballet—Barzin
　　　　　　　　　　‡ **E. & AmVox.PL 9320**
(*above, below; & Bizet*)

Habanera (orig. pf. 1885; orch. by Chabrier)
Los Angeles Phil.—Wallenstein
　　　　　　　　　　in ‡ **B.AXTL 1063**
(‡ *D.UA 243584; AmD.DL 4087 & DL 9728: ♭ ED 3557*)
☆ Concerts Colonne—Fourestier
　　　　　　　　(♭ *Pat.ED 8; AmVox.VIP 45230*)

Joyeuse marche orch.　1890
Lamoureux—Fournet　　　in ‡ **EPhi.NBL 5000**
(*above & below*)　　　(‡ Phi.N 00161L; Epic.LC 3028)
Los Angeles Phil.—Wallenstein
　　　　　　　　　　in ‡ **B.AXTL 1063**
(in ‡ *AmD.DL 4087 & DL 9728: ♭ ED 3557:*
　　　　　　　　　　　　　‡ *D.UA 243584*)
N.Y. City Ballet—Barzin[1]
　　　　　　　　　　‡ **E. & AmVox.PL 9320**
(*above, below; & Bizet*)
London Phil. Sym.—Quadri　‡ **West.LAB 7009**
(*Dukas & Saint-Saëns*)　　　(‡ Véga. C30. A 18)
Suisse Romande—Ansermet　　‡ **D.LXT 2760**
(*above; Saint-Saëns, etc.*)　　　(‡ Lon.LL 696)
(*Russlan & Ludmilla Overture* on ♭ *D. 71068*)
　　　　　　　　　　(& in ‡ *D.LW 5033; Lon.LD 9039*)
☆ Concerts Colonne—Fourestier (♭ *Pat.ED 8: D 104;*
　　　　　　　　　　　　　♭ *AmVox.VIP 45230*)
Brussels Radio—André (in ‡ *T.LA 6066;*
　　　　　　　　　　　　　FT.270.TC.044)
— ARR. VLN. & PF.　Dushkin
☆ Z. Francescatti & A. Balsam
　　　　　　(♭ *Phi.N 409514E; EPhi.NBE 11010*)
Larghetto horn & orch.　1874
M. Jones & Philadelphia—Ormandy
　　　　　　　　　　in ‡ **AmC.ML 4629**
(*J. Clarke, Handel, Griffes, Weber, Beethoven, etc.*)

[1] Much abbreviated.

PIANO MUSIC—COLLECTION
Impromptu　1860
(5) **MORCEAUX**　1891
　1. Aubade　　2. Ballabile　　3. Caprice
　4. Feuillet d'album　　5. Ronde champêtre
Bourrée fantasque　1891
G. Doyen　　　　　　　　　‡ **Nix.WLP 5294**
(*Saint-Saëns*) (‡ Véga. C30.A 8; ‡ West.WL 5294;
　　　　　　　　　　　　　Sel.270.CW.078, 2ss)

PIÈCES PITTORESQUES pf.　1880
　1. Paysage　　　　6. Idylle
　2. Mélancolie　　7. Danse villageoise
　3. Tourbillon　　8. Improvisation
　4. Sous bois　　　9. Menuet pompeux
　5. Mauresque　　10. Scherzo-valse
G. Doyen　　　　　　　　　‡ **West.WN 18141**
... Nos. 4-7 & 10
P. Barbizet　　　　　　　　V‡ *CdM.LDY 8080*
... No. 6 only
M. Pressler　　　　　　　　in ‡ **MGM.E 3129**
(*Albeniz, Bartók, Granados, etc.*)　(♭ *set X 254*)
... No. 10 only
C. de Groot　　　　　　　　in ‡ *Phi.N 00632R*
—— ARR. ORCH.　Chabrier
U.R.C. Sym.—Marinetti
(*Offenbach & Messager*)

(Le) ROI MALGRÉ LUI Opera, 3 acts　1887
Chanson de l'alouette (Act I)
C. Castelli (S), H. Boschi (pf.)
(*Songs*)　　　　　　　　in ‡ *CdM.LDA 8087*
Fête polonaise B, Cho. & Orch.
P. Germain, E. Brasseur Cho. & Lamoureux
　Orch.—Fournet　　　　　‡ **EPhi.NBL 5000**
(*above*)　　　(‡ Phi.N 00161L; Epic.LC 3028)
— ORCH. VERSION
N.Y. City Ballet—Barzin
(*above; & Bizet*)　　　　‡ **E. & AmVox.PL 9320**
Philharmonia—Markevitch　in ‡ **C.CX 1273**
(*St.-Saëns, Sibelius, Mozart, etc.*)　(‡ QCX 10172;
(*Liadov: Kikimora*, on ♭ *C.SEL 1544*)　Angel. 35154)
☆ San Francisco Sym.—Monteux (♭ *Vic. 49-0517*)

SONGS
COLLECTIONS
Chanson de l'alouette　SEE ROI MALGRÉ LUI, *above*
Chanson pour Jeanne (Mendès)　1886
L' Ile heureuse (Mikhaël)　1889
La Fileuse　SEE GWENDOLINE, *above*
Ballade des gros dindons (Rostand)　1889
Pastorale des cochons roses (Rostand)　1889
C. Castelli (S), H. Boschi (pf.) ‡ *CdM.LDA 8087*
(*Duparc*)
Lied (Mendès) pub. 1897　(*a*)
Tes yeux bleus (Rollinat)　1885　(*a*)
La Sommation irrespectueuse (Hugo)　(*b*)
Toutes les fleurs (Rostand)　1889　(*a*)
A quoi bon entendre (from *Ruy Blas*) (Hugo)　(*a*)
Credo d'amour (Silvestre)　1883　(*a*)
Romance　SEE L'ÉTOILE, Opera, *above*　(*b*)
Villanelle des petits canards (Gérard)　(*b*)
Les Cigales (Gérard)　1889　(*b*)
Ballade des gros dindons (Rostand)　1889　(*b*)
Pastorale des cochons roses (Rostand)　1889　(*b*)
L'Ile heureuse (Mikhaël)　1889　(*a*)
Chanson pour Jeanne (Mendès)　1886　(*b*)
**Duo de l'ouvreuse de l'Opéra-comique et de l'employé du Bon
　Marché** Duet, S & T (Fuchs & Lyon)　1889
L'Invitation au voyage (Baudelaire), with bsn. *ad lib.*　(*a*)
R. Doria (S), J. Giovannetti (Bs), G. Fouché
　(T), A. Rabot (bsn.), T. Janopoulo (pf.)
　　　　　　　　　　　　‡ **Plé.P 3066**
[(*a*) by Doria, (*b*) by Giovannetti]
Les Cigales (Gérard)
L'Ile heureuse (Mikhaël)
Lied (Mendès)
G. Touraine (S), J. Bonneau (pf.)
　　　　　　　　　　　　‡ **Lum.LD 3-402**
(*Debussy, Fauré, Gounod, etc.*)

(*continued on next page*)

SONGS (continued)
Les Cigales (Gérard)
Ballade des gros dindons (Rostand)
Villanelle des petits canards (Gérard)
L'Ile heureuse (Mikhaël)
    J. Jansen (B), J. Bonneau (pf.) ♯ **D.LXT 2774**
    (*Debussy & Ravel*)   (♯ Lon.LL 644)

L'Ile heureuse (Mikhaël)
    M. Sénéchal (T), J. Bonneau (pf.)
            in ♯ *Phi.N 00681R*

    (*Duparc, Hahn, Saint-Saëns, etc.*)

Souvenirs de Munich pf. duet
    (*Quadrille sur motifs de Tristan*) c. 1887
    F. Petit & A. M. Beckensteiner
    (*Fauré & Messager*)   **V♯ *Era.LDE 1017***

Suite pastorale orch. versions of pf. pieces 1897
  1. Idylle   2. Danse villageoise
  3. Sous bois   4. Scherzo-valse
    Paris Cons.—Lindenberg   ♯ **D.LXT 2860**
    (*Bizet*)   (♯ Lon.LL 871)
    Lamoureux—Fournet   ♯ **EPhi.NBL 5000**
    (*above*)   (♯ Phi.N 00161L; Epic.LC 3028)
    ☆ Covent Garden—Braithwaite   ♯ **P.PMC 1020**
    (*Bizet*)   (♯ Od.ODX 146)
    (No. 1 only in ♯ MGM.E 3124)

CHADWICK, George Whitefield
(1854-1931)

SYMPHONIC SKETCHES orch. 1895-1907
No. 3, Hobgoblin
    Hamburg Philharmonia—Korn in ♯ **Allo. 3150**
    (*Carpenter, Parker, Griffes, etc.*)

Tam o' Shanter Ballad, orch. 1914-15
    A.R.S. Sym.—Schoenherr   ♯ **ARS. 29**
    (*Converse*)

CHAILLEY, Jacques (b. 1910)

Missa Solemnis a cappella 1947
    Psallette Notre-Dame—Chailley
             ♯ **D.FMT 163640**
    (1½ss—*Franck: Prélude, Choral & Fugue*)
    [recorded in Church of St.-Eustache, Paris]

CHALLAN, René (b. 1910)

Concerto pastoral, Op. 20 pf. & orch. 1943
    S. François & Paris Cons.—Tzipine ♯ **C.FCX 229**
    (*François*)

Flirt cl. & pf. 1954
    J. Lancelot & F. Gobet   ♭ *Pat.G 1053*
    (*Loucheur, Gallon, Tomasi*)

Incidental music harp, recorder, viol.
  to accompany readings of poems in Les Blasons du
    Corps féminin   ♯ **Pat.DTX 147**

CHAMBONNIÈRES,
Jacques Champion de (1602-c. 1672)

[Refs. to numbers in Complete edn.]

HARPSICHORD MUSIC 1670
Sarabande, G major [120]
La Drollerie [129]
Allemande (L'Affligée) [124]
Volte, F major [110][1]
    A. van der Wiele   **G.HMS 60**
    († History of Music in Sound) (in ♯ Vic. set LM 6031)

Sarabandes: D minor [88]
           G major [120]
           C major [74]
Allemande (L'Affligée) [124]
Courante, C major [65]
Gigue, C major [76]
Chaconne, F major [116]
Volte, F major[1] [110]
Rondeau, F major [106]
    D. Pinkham   ♯ **CEd.CE 1054**
    (*Couperin*)

Allemande (La Rare) [1]
Courante, A minor [4]
Sarabande, A minor [5]
    I. Nef   in ♯ **LOL.OL 50028**
    († Clavecinistes français)   (♯ OL.LD 64)

Le Moutier[2] [61]
Gigue où il y a un canon [53]
Sarabande (O beau jardin)[3] page 119
Courante (Les Barricades) [16]
Rondeau, F major [106]
    M. Charbonnier   † **AS.169**

Chaconne, G major [123]
    N. Pierront (org.)   in ♯ *Lum.LD 2-104*
    († Chaconne & Passacaglia)

Sarabande, D minor [88]
    ☆ W. Landowska (in ♯ G.ALP 1246: FALP/QALP 218)

CHAMINADE, Cécile (1857-1944)

Automne pf. — ARR. ORCH.
  Orch.—Robinson (in ♯ Argo.RG 40; West.WP 6002,
  Melachrino Orch. (G.C 3570)   [o.n. WN 18097)
Autrefois pf
  ▽ S. Cherkassky   G.DB 21183
    (*Liszt: Consolation No. 3*)
Serenade, D major, Op. 29
  V. Young Orch. (in ♯ B.LA 8642; AmD.DL 5454;
                AFest.CFR 10-533)
Sérénade espagnole — ARR. VLN. & PF. Kreisler
  G. Barinova (USSRM.D 00445)

SONG: Au pays bleu (Fuster)
  ℍ P. Plançon (Bs.) (in ♯ SBDH.LLP 6*)

NOTE: Only a few recent (re)issues listed here;
    there have been many other ▽ recordings.

CHANLER, Theodore Ward (b. 1902)

SONGS

(The) Children (Feeney) Song Cycle 1945
  N. Ornest (S), J. Brown (pf.)   ♯ **NE. 3**
  (*Flanagan: Times long ago*)

(8) Epitaphs (W. de la Mare) 1937
  S. Carter (S), B. Weiser (pf.)   ♯ **NE. 2**
  (*R. Smith, Citkowitz, Flanagan*)

    NOTE: The discs as entered are believed to be in the
    final form; but various conflicting reports as to contents
    and numbers have been received.

I rise when you enter (Feeney) 1942
The Policeman in the park (Feeney) 1946
  D. Gramm (Bs), R. Cumming (pf.) in ♯ **ML. 7033**
  (*Cesti, Schubert, Wolf, Cumming, etc.*)

CHAPI Y TORENTE, Ruperto
(1851-1909)

ZARZUELAS, etc.
               [Abridged listings only]
(El) BARQUILLERO (with Valverde) 1900
  T. Rosado, C. Munguía, etc., Madrid Cho. & Orch.
  —Argenta   ♯ *LI.W 91025*
                (♯ Ambra.MC 25003)

---

[1] On O beau jardin.   [2] Theme by Chambonnières, with variations by L. Couperin.
[3] Theme by Chambonnières, with variations by D'Anglebert. An elaborated version of Volte [110].

ZARZUELAS, etc. (*continued*)

(La) BRUJA   Comic opera, 3 Acts   1887
M. Ripollés, I. Rivadeneyra, M. Sierra, R. Alonso,
  Madrid Cho. & Orch.—Moreno Torroba
            ♯ AmC.ML 4930
            (♯ Phi.N 00593L)
Prelude: Madrid Cha. Orch.—Lloret   in ♯ Mont.FM 22

(Los) HIJAS DEL ZEBEDEO   2 Acts   1889
Aria (unspec.)
L. Berchman (S)   in ♯ Mont.FM 28

(El) PUÑAO DE ROSAS   1 Act   1902
A. M. Iriarte, P. Lorengar, M. Ausensi, etc., Madrid Cho.
  & Cha. Orch.—Argenta   ♯ Ll.TW 91002
            (♯ Ambra.MCC 30006)
L. Berchman, D. Reubens, E. Rincon, F. Hernández, etc.,
  Madrid Radio Cho. & Orch.—Montorio & Navarro
  (*Gimenez & Vives*)   ♯ Mont.FM 56
(Passacalle on ♯ Mont.FM 39)

Pasadoble: Spanish Air Force Band—Arriba
          (in ♯ AmD.DL 9792)

(El) REY QUE RABIÓ   3 Acts   1891
P. Lorengar, T. Rosado, M. Ausensi, C. Munguía,
  A. M. Fernández, etc.; Madrid Cho. & Sym.—Argenta
              ♯ Ll.TW 91111
∇ A. Albiach, M. Isaura, etc.; Barcelona Theatre—Gelabert
            (G.AF 439/46)
Yo que siempre
Madrid Orch.—Moreno Torroba   in ♯ AmD.DL 9788
Intermezzo Madrid Cha. Orch.—Navarro in ♯ Mont.FM 39

(La) REVOLTOSA   Sainete   1 Act   1897
M. Ausensi, A. M. Iriarte, I. Rivadeneyra, etc.; Madrid
  Cho. & Cha. Orch.—Argenta   ♯ Ll.TW 91014
       (♯ Mont.FM 3; Ambra.MCC 30001)
R. Gómez, C. Panadés, M. Redondo, etc.; Cho. & Orch.
  —Ferrer   ♯ Reg.LC 1004
        (♯ Angel.SS 70003; Pam.LRC 15505)
(Excerpts in ♭ Reg. SEBL 7005; ♭ Angel. 70013)
C. Rubio, I. Rivadeneyra, S. Castelló, P. Vidal, etc.,
  Madrid Cho. & Orch.—Moreno Torroba
           ♯ Phi.N 00594L
(*Fernández Caballero: Gigantes*)   (♯ AmC.ML 4931)
Prelude
Colón Theatre—Cases   ArgOd. 66021
  (♭ BSOA 4002: ♭ BSOAE 4514: in ♯ LDC 504)
Sym.—Ferrer   in ♯ Reg.LCX 104
(♯ Pam.LRC 15905; C.FSX 104; Angel. 65008;
          ♭ Reg.SEDL 105)
Madrid Cha.—Argenta   in ♯ Ll.TW 91020
(♯ Ambra.MCC 30002; ♯ Mont.FM 6;
           ♭ Ambra.MGE 60003)
Madrid Theatre—Moreno Torroba   in ♭ B.AXTL 1078
        (♯ SpC.CCLP 34003; AmD.DL 9736)

(El) TAMBOR DE GRANADEROS   1 Act   1894
T. Berganza, T. Rosado, R. Campo, etc.; Madrid Cho. &
  Sym.—Argenta   ♯ Ambra.MC 25013
Prelude
Madrid Cha.—Argenta   in ♯ Ll.TW 91020
(♯ Ambra.MCC 30002; Mont.FM 6; &
       ♯ Ambra.MCCP 29000: ♭ MGE 60001)
Madrid Theatre—Moreno Torroba   in ♭ B.AXTL 1078
        (♯ SpC.CCLP 34003; AmD.DL 9736)
March
Spanish Air Force Band—Arriba   in ♯ B.LAT 8075
          (♯ AmD.DL 9764)

(La) TEMPESTAD   3 Acts   1882
T. Rosado, P. Lorengar, M. Ausensi, C. Munguia, etc.;
  Madrid Singers & Cha. Orch.—Argenta
           ♯ Ll.TW 91029/30
(4ss)   (♯ Ambra.MCC 30012/3)

OTHER WORKS
(El) Sospiro del Moro
◻ H. Lazaro (in ♯ Sca. 806*)
Fantasia morisca . . . Serenata
∇ Madrid Orch. Ibérica (ArgOd. 193591)

CHARDON de Reims   (fl. XIIIth Cent.)

SEE: † FRENCH TROUBADOUR SONGS

CHARPENTIER, Gustave   (1860-1956)

Impressions d'Italie orch.   1887, rev. 1913
Paris Opéra—Fourestier (2ss)   ♯ C.FC 1030
(*Aubert on* ♯ Angel. 35120)

LOUISE   Opera   4 Acts & 5 Tableaux   1900
ABRIDGED VERSION, ARR. Charpentier
☆ N. Vallin (S), G. Thill (T), A. Pernet (Bs), etc.; Raugel
  Cho. & Orch.—Bigot (4ss)   ♯ AmC. set EL 7

Depuis le jour   S   (Act III)
Géori-Boué   in ♯ Ura. 7070
(*Faust, Hérodiade; & Debussy*)   (♭ UREP 72)
J. Brumaire   in ♯ Phi.S 06025R
(*Faust, Contes d'Hoffmann*)
M. Benètti (*Ital*)   Cet.PE 193
(*Mefistofele—L'altra notte*)
M. Minazzi (*Ital*)   Cet.PE 173
(*Carmen—Je dis que rien . . .*)
G. Arnaldi (*Ital*)   Cet.PE 192
(*Pêcheurs de Perles—Comme autre fois . . .*)
L. Castellano, S. Leff (pf.)   in ♯ Mur.P 106
(followed by pf. acc. only)
☆ M. Angelici (in ♯ G.FBLP 1051)
L. Albanese (in ♯ Vic.LM 1839: ♭ ERA 139;
           in ♯ FV.A 630253)
N. Vallin (♭ Od.7AO 2003)
D. Maynor (in ♯ Vic. set LCT 6701)
J. Micheau (♭ D.71086)
M. Garden (AF.AGSB 44)
G. Moore (in ♯ Vic.LCT 7004: ♭ set WCT 7004)
◻ C. Muzio (IRCC. 3134*)

Berceuse: Reste, repose-toi   B   (Act IV)
M. Singher   in ♯ Roy. 1613
(*below*)
☆ Vanni-Marcoux (in ♯ G.FJLP 5035)
M. Journet (in ♯ G.FJLP 5004)

Les pauvres gens peuvent-ils être heureux?
  B   (Act IV)
M. Singher   in ♯ Roy. 1613
(*above; G. Tell, Africaine, etc.*)

CHARPENTIER, Marc-Antoine
(1634-1704)
(Refs. in Roman figures are to the Vols. of MS. in the
  Bibliothèque Nationale, Paris).

COLLECTIONS
Te Deum   2S, A, T, Bs, cho. & orch.[1]   (X)
Marche de triomphe (X) (a); Air de trompette[2] (XXII) (a)
3e Leçon des Ténèbres du Vendredi Saint: Recordare (IV)
  2S, A. & cont.[3]
... Announcement, Verses 1 & 2 & concluding verse only
Oculi omnium   2S, A, cho. & org.[3]   (XXII)   (a)
  (Motet pour le St. Sacrement au Reposoir)
  C. Collart, J. Archimbaud, Y. Melchior,
    P. Gianotti, L. Noguéra, Jeunesses Musicales
    Cho. & Pasdeloup Orch.—L. Martini
               ♯ Era.LDE 3009
              (♯ HS.HSL 2065)
[Items marked (a) also on ∇♯ Era.LDE 1011]
MAGNIFICAT   8vv. & orch.   (XI)
MESSE POUR PLUSIEURS INSTRUMENTS
... Offerte à deux choeurs   Orch.   (I)
Sub tuum praesidium   3vv. a cappella   (XXVIII)
1re Leçon des Ténèbres du Mercredi Saint   (IV)
...BETH: Plorans ploravit   A. & cont.
Regina coeli   2S. & cont.   (XXIII)
Salve regina   3vv. & org.   (III)
  C. Collart (S), J. Archimbaud (C-T), Y. Melchior
    (A), P. Gianotti (T), L. Noguéra (Bs),
    Jeunesses Musicales Cho., Pasdeloup Orch.
    —L. Martini   ♯ Era.LDE 3017
[H. Roget (org.), F. Petit (hpsi.), H. Varron (vlc.)]
              (♯ HS.HSL 102)

DAVID ET JONATHAS   Tragédie spirituelle, Prologue &
  5 Acts   1688
... Prelude, Act IV
Tenebrae factae sunt[4]   Bs. & cho.   (IV)
Symphonie pour un Reposoir   (XV)   Str. orch.
Supplicatio pro Defunctis
  3vv. & insts.   (XVIII)   (ed. G. Lambert)
  X. Depraz (Bs), Paris Vocal Ens. & Paris
    Cha. Orch.—Capdevielle   ♯ Sel.LPG 8683
[also announced as ♯ LA 1073]

De Profundis (XX) (ed. G. Lambert) 7 vv. & 5 insts.
  M. Angelici (S), J. Archimbaud (C-T), J. Collard
    & Y. Melchior (A), J. Giraudeau & P.
    Gianotti (T), L. Noguéra (Bs), Jeunesses
    Musicales Françaises Cho. & orch.—Martini
             ♯ Pat.DTX 158
(*Bernier: Confitebor tibi*) [H. Roget (org.)]

---

[1] With C. H. Barber, organ.   [2] G. Coursier, tpt.; M-L. Girod, organ.   [3] M-L. Girod, organ, with 2 fls. & vlc.
[4] Second Response of 2nd Nocturne for Maundy Thursday.   This item also on ♭ Sel. 470.C.009.

(La) Couronne de Fleurs Pastorale (Molière) (VII)
Anon. Artists & Collegium Pro Musica[1]
MHF. 2001
In Nativitatem Domini
Solo voice, cho., 5 insts. (XV)
... Nuit Str. orch. (ed. G. Lambert)
☆ Paris Cons.—Cluytens (♭ Pat.D 103)
Leçon de Ténèbres du Samedy Saint A, cho., orch.
J. de Faria & R. Alix Cho.
[R. Chaumont, diction]
Magnificat S, A, Bs, org. & orch (XV)
J. Subra, J. de Faria, H. Jullien & Paris Coll.
Musicum Orch.—Douatte # QS.AR 1
[M-L. Girod, org.]
(Le) MALADE IMAGINAIRE
... Epilogue—"Death of Molière" (unspec. works of
Charpentier, Gervais & Lully used)
Orch.—Cadou (in a performance of the play) in
LI.TW 91076/7; D.FMT 163507/8
MÉDÉE Opera: Prol. & 5 Acts 1693
SELECTED EXCERPTS

Créon	D. Conrad (B)
Créuse	N. Sautereau (S)
Médée	I. Kolassi (M-S)
Jason	P. Derenne (T)
Cléone	F. Wend (S)

with M. Férès & V. Jorneaux (A), B. Demigny
(Bs) & Inst. Ens.—N. Boulanger
B.AXTL 1049
(# D.UMT 263544; AmD.DL 9678)
Contents—Prologue: Air de la Victoire: Duet of shepherdesses;
Passepied
Act I: Que je serais heureux (Air de Jason)
Disparaissez, inquiètes alarmes
(S, S, T, B)
Fanfare, Sc. 4
Act III: Noires filles du Styx (M-S)
L'Enfer obéit à ta voix (S, T, B, Bs)
Dieu de Cocyte (M-S)
Non, non, les plus heureux amants (Cho.)
Vous avez servi mon courroux (M-S)
Act IV: Prelude (2 fls., 2 vlns. & cont.)
Ah, que d'attraits (S, T)
D'un amant qui veut plaire (3S & Cho.)
Noires divinités (Air de Créon)
Act V: Prelude (orch.)
Ah, funeste revers (S & Cho.)
Mort de Créuse, Sc. 6
Adieu, Jason (M-S)
MASSES
Assumpta est Maria
6vv. & orch. (XXVII) (ed. G. Lambert)
M. Angelici (S), S. Michel (A), J. Collard (A),
J. Archimbaud (C-T), J. Giraudeau (T),
L. Noguéra (B), Jeunesses Musicales Cho., &
Orch.—Martini # Pat.DTX 140
[L. Martini, org.] (# AmVox.PL 8440)
De minuit (pour Noël)
2 S, A, T, Bs, cho. & orch (XXV)
C. Collart & J. Fort, M-T. Cahn, G. Friedmann.,
G. Abdoun, Paris Vocal Ens. & Cha. Orch.
—Jouve[2] # LT.EL 93006
[A. G. Dechaume, org.] (2ss) (# T.LB 6140; Sel.LA 1060)
(with Vivaldi, on # West.WL 5287; LT.DTL 93080)
[Offertory & Sanctus only, on # Sel. 470.C.009]
Versailles Cath. Cho.—G. Roussel[3] # SM. 33-03
(Couperin, Victoria, Lalande; & Gregorian) (# Per.SPL 712)
MOTETS: COLLECTION
Salve regina (ed. Lambert) T & cont. [IV]
O vos omnes T, 2 fl. cont. ⎱ MS.
Lauda Sion T. & hpsi. ⎰
M. Casadesus Ens. in # Plé.P 3083
(† Musiques à la Chapelle du Roy) (# West.WN 18167)
[J. Giraudeau (T)]

CHAUSSON, Ernest (1855-1899)

Concert, D major, Op. 21 vln., pf., str. qtt.
Y. Menuhin, L. Kentner & Pascal Qtt.
(2ss) # G.ALP 1285
(Vieuxtemps, on # Vic.LHMV 30) (# FALP 353)

Z. Francescatti, R. Casadesus & Guilet Qtt.
AmC.ML 4998
☆ J. Heifetz, J. M. Sanromá & Musical Art Qtt.
Vic.LCT 1113
(Sibelius: Vln. Concerto) (♭ set WCT 1113)
☆ L. Kaufman, A. Balsam & Pascal Qtt. (# Clc. 6217)
Poème, Op. 25 vln. & orch.
J. Heifetz & Victor Sym.—I. Solomon
G.BLP 1072
(Conus) (# Vic.LM 7017; # FV.A 330202)
C. Ferras & Belgian Nat.—Sebastian
D.LXT 2827
(Honegger & Ravel) (# BAT 173071; Lon.LL 762)
E. Lockhart & L.S.O.—Fistoulari
MGM.E 3041
(Honegger, Ravel, Milhaud)
I. Bezrodny & Moscow Radio—Kondrashin
(Sibelius) # USSR.D 2161
G. Neveu & Philharmonia—Dobrowen
Angel. 35128
(Debussy & Ravel)
A. Grumiaux & Lamoureux—Fournet
Phi.A 00228L
(Lalo & Ravel) (# Epic.LC 3082)
☆ Z. Francescatti & Philadelphia—Ormandy # C.C 1029
(Saint-Saëns) (# QC 5012)
☆ J. Thibaud & Lamoureux—Bigot # AmVox.PL 8600
(Mozart) (♭ VIP 45470; # Cum.CVX 358)
(Fauré on # EVox.PL 6450)
(Le) ROI ARTHUS, Op. 23 Opera, 3 Acts, 1903
Pommiers verts
Ne m'interroge plus, ô Roi B (Act II)
☆ A. Endrèze (in # Pat.PCX 5006)

SONGS
COLLECTION
Cantique à l'épouse, Op. 36, No. 1 (Jhouney)
(Le) Charme, Op. 2, No. 2 (Sylvestre)
(Le) Colibri, Op. 2, No. 7 (L. de Lisle)
Nanny, Op. 2, No. 1 (L. de Lisle)
(Les) Papillons, Op. 2, No. 3 (Gautier)
Sérénade italienne, Op. 2, No. 5 (Bourget)
(Les) Temps des lilas (from Op. 19) (Bouchor)
G. Souzay (B), J. Bonneau (pf.) # D.LW 5201
(La) Cigale, Op. 13, No. 4 (Leconte de Lisle)
(Le) Colibri, Op. 2, No. 7 (Leconte de Lisle)
M. Dobbs (S), G. Moore (pf.) # C.CX 1154
(Schubert, Wolf, Brahms, Fauré, Hahn)
(# FCX 299; QCX 10097; Angel. 35094)
Poème de l'amour et de la mer, Op. 19 (Bouchor)
G. Swarthout (M-S) & Victor Sym. Orch.
—Monteux # G.ALP 1269
(J. Clergue: Carmen; & Berlioz, Hahn, Debussy, etc.)
(# Vic.LM 1793; FV.A 630227)
(Bach & Berlioz on # ItV.A12R 0158)
... **Les Temps des lilas**, only
N. Merriman (M-S), G. Moore (pf.)
in # C.CX 1213
(Duparc, Bizet, Debussy, etc.) (# Angel. 35217)
R. Ponselle (S), I. Chicagov (pf.)
in # Vic.LM 1889
(Beethoven, Donaudy, Brahms, Sadero, etc.) (# DV. 16493)
Sérénade italienne, Op. 2, No. 5 (P. Bourget)
M. Sénéchal (T), J. Bonneau (pf.)
in # Phi.N 00681R
(Chabrier, Duparc, Hahn, etc.)
Symphony, B flat major, Op. 20
Pasdeloup—Fournet (2ss) # EPhi.NBR 6018
(Franck on # Epic.LC 3067) (# Phi.N 00701R)
☆ Chicago Sym.—Stock # BB.LBC 1056
(Franck) (♭ set WBC 1056)
☆ San Francisco Sym.—Monteux (# ItV.A12R 0021;
G.FALP 227)

---

[1] This recording was offered to subscribers, but may not actually have reached them.
[2] Three Noëls by N. le Bègue (1630-1702) are inserted where improvisations are called for in the score. Those following the 2 sections of the Kyrie are played by the organist; the other is ARR. STR. ORCH.
[3] ARR. for Cho. and 2 organs, by G. Roussel. A Gregorian chant Alleluia, Dies sanctificatus is interpolated after the Gloria.

Trio, G minor, Op. 3   pf., vln., vlc.
Bolzano Trio   **‡ AmVox.PL 8950**
(Franck)

CHAVCHAVADZE, Georges

(L') AIGRETTE   Ballet   1953
Cuevas Ballet Orch.—Cloëz   **‡ LT.TWV 91048**
(Tchaikovsky)   (‡ Cpt.MC 20041)

Suite on themes from El Amor Brujo (Falla) pf.
SEE entry in Supp. I.   *s.v.* Falla

CHÁVEZ, Carlos (b. 1899)

☆ Republican Overture   1935
Sinfonia India   1936 (▽ ‡ AmD.DL 9527)
☆ (El) Sol, Corrido   Cho. & Orch.   1934
Mexico Sym. & Cons. Cho.—Chávez
(Moncayo)   **‡ B.AXTL 1055**

Toccata for percussion instruments   1942
Concert Arts Ens.—Slatkin   **‡ DCap.CTL 7094**
(Bartók & Milhaud)   (‡ Cap.P 8299)
[3rd movt. only in ‡ Cap.SAL 9020 & SAL 9027]
Ens.—I. Solomon   **‡ MGM.E 3155**
(Revueltas, Surinach, Villa-Lobos)
Gotham Percussion Players   **‡ Ura. 7144**
(Granados & Respighi)
Boston Percussion Group   **‡ Bo.B 207**
(Farberman)
Pittsburgh Sym. Members—Harris
(Ginastera)   **‡ PFCM.CB 186**
Illinois Univ. Perc. Ens.—Price   **‡ UOI.CRS 3**
(Colgrass, Harrison, McKenzie, Varèse)

CHÉDEVILLE, Nicolas (1705-1783)

SEE: † ANTHOLOGIE SONORE

CHERUBINI, Luigi C. Z. S. (1760-1842)

(4) Marches pour la Garde Nationale   wind insts.
(Bellasis 231, 232, 301; & Deux Journées March)
☆ London Baroque Ens.—Haas   ♭ **P.CREP 1**
(Beethoven)

Pater Noster   vln. & str. orch.   1834[1]
J. Pougnet & London Baroque—Haas
                              P.R 20618
                              (in ‡ *AmD.DL 4081*)

OPERAS
ANACREON   2 Acts   1803
Overture
☆ Vienna Phil.—Furtwängler (ArgA. 266601)
Austrian State Sym.—Gui (in ‡ Rem. 199-123)

DÉMOPHON   3 Acts   1788
Ah! Peut-être à mes yeux . . .
(Ahi! che forse . . .)
F. Barbieri (M-S), D. Marzollo (pf.) *(Ital)*
                         in ‡ **AmVox.PL 7980**
(† Old Italian Songs & Airs)

(Les) DEUX JOURNÉES   3 Acts   1800
                    (The Water Carrier)
Overture
☆ Austrian Sym.—Gui (in ‡ Rem. 199-142 & ‡ Ply. 12-65)

MÉDÉE   3 Acts   1797
Overture
Bamberg Sym.—Leitner   **PV. 72396**
(Beethoven: Fidelio Overture)   (in ‡ AmD.DL 8509)
(Mendelssohn: Ruy Blas Overture, on ♭ *Pol. 30129)*

Quartet, Strings, No. 1, E flat major   1814
... Scherzo only   — ARR. ORCH.
Angelicum Orch.—Gerelli   **CGD.SA 3019**

Requiem Mass, C minor   1816
Santa Cecilia Academy Cho. & Orch.—Giulini
                              ‡ C.CX 1075
(‡ C.QCX 10045: FCX 231; Angel. 35042)

Symphony, D major   1815
N.B.C. Sym.—Toscanini   **‡ G.ALP 1106**
(Beethoven) (‡ Vic.LM 1745; ♭ set WDM 1745;
       ‡ G.FALP 246; ItV.A12R 0046; DV. 16428)

CHIARINI, Pietro (1715-?)

SEE: PERGOLESI: IL GELOSO SCHERNITO

CHILD, William (1606-1697)

SEE: † ENGLISH CHURCH MUSIC, VOL. III

CHOPIN, Frédéric François (1810-1849)

CLASSIFIED: I. Piano solo   II. Concerted Works
              III. Songs   IV. Miscellaneous

I. PIANO
(Solo unless specified)

"COMPLETE PIANO WORKS" (in Progress)
VOL. I. (the only one issued)
    (4) BALLADES
    Barcarolle, F sharp minor, Op. 60
    (4) IMPROMPTUS
    (4) SCHERZOS
C. Arrau   **‡ B.AXTL 1043/4**
(4ss)   (‡ D.UAT 273563/4; ‡ AmD. set DX 130)

COLLECTIONS
[The sign □ refers back to these General Collections from the
individual titles, *below*]

    Ballade No. 2
    Impromptu No. 1
    Mazurkas: Nos. 21, 25, 45
    Nocturnes: Nos. 7 & 15
    Scherzo No. 2
    Valses: Nos. 6 & 11
W. Malcuzynski   **‡ C.CX 1338**

    Sonata No. 2, B flat minor, Op. 35
    Études: Op. 10, No. 3; Op. 25, No. 9
    Impromptu No. 2
    Nocturne No. 2
    Prelude No. 15
    Valse No. 6
A. Cortot [Tokyo recording]   **‡ JpV.LS 2001**
(Nocturne & Prelude also ♭ *JpV.EP 3039*)

    Ballade No. 4
    Études: Op. 10, No. 10 & Op. 25, No. 5
    Impromptu No. 1
    Nocturne No. 2
    Prelude No. 1
    Scherzo No. 3
    Valses: Nos. 1 & 11
S. François   **‡ C.FCX 180**

    Berceuse, Op. 57
    Études: Op. 10, Nos. 3, 5, 12; Op. 25, No. 9
    Impromptu No. 4
    Mazurkas: Nos. 13 & 14
    Nocturne No. 5
    Polonaises: Nos. 3 & 6
    Preludes: Nos. 4 & 15
    Scherzo No. 2
    Valse No. 6
I. Nádas   **‡ Per.SPL 722**

    Berceuse, Op. 57
    Mazurka No. 23
    Polonaise No. 6
    Scherzo No. 2
    Valse No. 6
E. Reuchsel   *(Liszt)*   **‡ Phi.A 77404L**

---

[1] ARR. by Cherubini of Pater Noster à 4 with organ and orch.   1816.   B. 341.

Berceuse, Op. 57
Mazurka No. 23
Polonaise No. 6
Scherzo No. 2
Valse No. 1

E. Reuchsel (*Liszt*) **♯ Pol. 545003**

Andante Spianato & Grande Polonaise brillante, E flat
  major, Op. 22
Ballade No. 1
Berceuse, Op. 57
Étude, Op. 25, No. 9
Nocturnes: Nos. 2 & 5
Valses: Nos. 5 & 6

J. Hofmann[1] **♯ AmC.ML 4929**
(*Liszt, Rachmaninoff, Moszkowski, Mendelssohn*)

Barcarolle, F sharp major, Op. 60
Berceuse, Op. 57
Écossaises, Op. 72, No. 3
Étude, Op. 25, No. 9
Mazurkas: Nos. 7 & 41
Nocturne No. 8
Polonaises: Nos. 3 & 6
Prelude No. 26, A flat major (pub. 1918)

R. Trouard **♯ Od.ODX 143**

Études, Op. 25: Nos. 1 & 2
Impromptu No. 4
Nocturne No. 2

R. Trouard (*Mozart*) **♯ Od.ODX 118**

Ballade No. 1
Berceuse, Op. 57
Études, Op. 10: Nos. 5 & 8
Études, Op. 25: Nos. 4 & 20

L. Bertolini **♯ Dur.MSE 3**

Études, Op. 10: Nos. 3, 6, 12
Scherzo No. 2
Valse No. 7

L. Bertolini **♯ Dur.MSE 1**

Barcarolle, Op. 60
Berceuse, Op. 57
Fantaisie, Op. 49
(4) Impromptus
Mazurka No. 17

J. v. Karolyi (most are ☆) **♯ HP.DGM 18068**

Étude, Op. 10, No. 3
Impromptu No. 4
Mazurka No. 23
Nocturne No. 7
Polonaises: Nos. 3 & 6
Valses: Nos. 1, 6, 7, 9

B. Hesse-Bukowska **♯ CdM.LDM 8083**

Ballade No. 1
Impromptu No. 3
Mazurka No. 32
Nocturne No. 4
Polonaise No. 6
Scherzo No. 3
Valse No. 5

P. Entremont **♯ MMS. 80**

Études: Op. 10, No. 11; Op. 25: Nos. 6, 10, 11
Polonaise No. 6
Preludes: Nos. 16 & 17

☆ J. Lhevinne **♯ Cam.CAL 265**
(*Schumann, Debussy, etc.*)

Andante Spianato & Grande Polonaise brillante, E flat
  major, Op. 22
Valse No. 5

M. Tagliaferro
Berceuse, Op. 57
Mazurkas: Nos. 2 & 23
Nocturne No. 7

Z. Dygat **♯ Sel.LP 8737**

Nocturnes: Nos. 5, 12
Polonaise No. 1
Impromptu No. 4

M. v. Monnerberg **♯ Her.RPL 775**
(*Schumann, Schubert*) Pte. rec.

Berceuse, Op. 57
Mazurkas: Nos. 4 & 17
Nocturne No. 4
Polonaise No. 10
Preludes: Nos. 3 & 16

L. Rev **♯ Pat.DT 1013**

Étude, Op. 10, No. 12
Nocturne No. 13
Preludes: Nos. 8 & 20
Scherzo No. 4

M. v. Monnerberg (*Brahms*) **♯ Her. 1**

Ballades, Nos. 3 & 4
Étude, Op. 10, No. 3
Impromptu No. 1
Nocturne No. 15
Scherzo No. 1

☆ V. Horowitz **♯ G.ALP 1111**
(♯ FALP 238)

Allegro de concert, A major, Op. 46 1841
S. Fiorentino **♯ CA.LPA 1092**
(*Rondo, Op. 16, Krakowiak, & Fantasie on Polish Airs*)

Andante Spianato & Grande Polonaise brillante,
E flat ma., Op. 22 ☐ pf. & orch. or pf. solo
O. Frugoni & Vienna Pro Musica—Swarowsky
♯ AmVox.PL 9030
(*Krakowiak, Variations; & Liszt*)

E. Beckmann-Shcherbina & Sym.—Samosud
(*Moniuszko*) **♯ USSR.D 1295**

— PIANO SOLO VERSION
A. Cortot in JpV. set JAS 269
M. Ciampi **♯ Clc. 6177**
(*Polonaises, s.3*)

☆ A. Rubinstein **♯ G.BLP 1027**
(*Polonaise No. 7*)(*FBLP 1034*: QBLP 5013; DV.L 16279)
(& in ♯ FALP 255/7; ♯ Vic. set LM 6109)
☆ B. Siki **♯ P.PMA 1022**
(*Nocturne, Étude; & Schumann*)

☆ V. Horowitz (in ♯ G.FALP 280; in ♯ Vic.LRM 7051:
♭ set ERB 7051; in ♯ DV.B 26040)

(4) BALLADES ☐
COMPLETE RECORDINGS
B. Siki **♯ P.PMA 1008**
P. Levi[2] **♯ Mon.MEL 700**
F. Gulda **♯ D.LW 5156**
(♯ Lon.LD 9177)
S. François **♯ C.FC 1041**
E. Silver **♯ Gram. 2041**
☆ R. Casadesus (*Sonata No. 2*) **♯ AmC.ML 4798**
☆ C. de Groot **♯ EPhi.NBR 6025**
(♯ Phi.A 00739R)
(*Berceuse, Nocturne, etc. on* ♯ Epic.LC 3037)
☆ G. Doyen **♯ Nix.WLP 5169**
(♯ Véga. C30.A 10)

☆ E. Wild (♯ ANix.MLPY 26; ♯ MMS. 26)

... Nos. 1, 3 & 4 only
M. Schwalb **♯ Roy. 1486**
(*Écossaise, Études, Polonaise, Preludes*) (in ♯ Ply. 12-84)

No. 1, G minor, Op. 23
G. Lasson **♯ Pac.LDPF 26**
(*Nocturne 5, Polonaise 3; & Beethoven*)
J. Weingarten **♯ CA.LPA 1046**
(*Études, Op. 10*) [announced but not issued]
S. Fiorentino (*No. 3*) **V♯ CA.MPO 5019**
☆ V. Horowitz (in ♯ G.ALP 1087: FALP 215; &
♯ Vic.LRM 7018: ♭ ERB 7018)
W. Backhaus (in ♯ D.LW 5026; Lon.LD 9047)
H. Stefanska (♭ G.7PW 119)
V. Schiøler (♭ FMer.MEP 14523; ♭ Mer.EP 1-5013)
S. Barere (in ♯ Ply. 12-84; in ♯ Cum.CR 280;
♭ Rem.REP 2)
E. Gilels (USSRM.D 199, & in ♯ Csm.CRLP 210)

No. 2, F major, Op. 38
P. Mildner **♯ DT.LGM 65025**
(*Impromptu No. 2; J. Strauss; Liszt*)
(♯ T.LB 6060; ♭ UV 112)
P. Cavazzini **♯ Arp.ARC 2**
(*Étude, Polonaise; & Liszt*)
L. Gousseau **♭ Plé.P 45149**
(*Étude, Op. 25, No. 1 & Impromptu No. 3*)
☆ J. v. Karolyi (*No. 3*) PV. 72337
(*Barcarolle on* ♭ Pol. 30030)
☆ B. Moiseiwitsch (G.EB 561)

---

[1] Recorded Metropolitan Opera House, Nov. 1937.   [2] Announced but not issued.

No. 3, A flat major, Op. 47

V. Schiøler   **G.DB 10517**
(*Études, Op. 10, Nos. 3 & 12 on* ♭ *7EBK 1002*)

S. Fiorentino   (*No. 2*)   **V♯ CA.MPO 5019**

☆ V. Horowitz (in ♯ G.ALP 1111: FALP 238: ♭ *ERF 109*)
J. v. Karolyi ((PV.72237))
C. Arrau (Od.NR 2)
L. Godowsky (in ♯ Roy. 1402)[1]
J. Demus (♭ *Cum.ECR 38;* in ♯ Ply. 12-84;
                      ♭ *Rem.REP 7*)
   L. Oborin (in ♯ Cam.CRLP 210)

No. 4, F minor, Op. 52

☆ V. Horowitz (♭ *G.7RF 202;* in ♯ *Vic.LRM 7018:*
                      ♭ *set ERB 7018*)
J. Demus (in ♯ Ply. 12-84)

Barcarolle, F sharp minor, Op. 60 □

L. Pennario   **♯ DCap.CCL 7523**
(*Liszt*)   (♯ *Cap.H 8246*)

G. Bachauer   in ♯ **G.CLP 1057**
(*Écossaises; Shostakovitch, Liszt*)

J. Páleníček   **♯ Sup.LPM 167**
(*Berceuse & Fantaisie*)   (♯ *U. 5161C*)

Y. Nat   **♯ DFr. 84**
(*Fantaisie, & Sonata No. 2*)   (♯ *HS.HSL 97*)

M. Schwalb   in ♯ **Roy. 1577**

R. Slenczynski (*Liszt*)   **♯ ML. 7031**

E. Kilenyi   **♯ Rem. 199-165**
(*Berceuse, Prelude 16, Nouvelle Étude 1; & Schumann*)

☆ A. Rubinstein   **G.DB 21613**
                    (♭ *G.7RF/RQ 252*)

☆ D. Lipatti (in ♯ AmC.ML 4721 & ♯ C.FCX 493)
J. v. Karolyi (♭ *Pol. 30030*)
A. Uninsky (in ♯ *Phi.S 06004R;* in ♯ Epic.LC 3122)

Berceuse, D flat major, Op. 57 □

V. Schiøler   **G.DB 10532**
(*Impromptu No. 1*)

N. Magaloff   **♯ D.LXT 5037**
(*Impromptus & Sonata No. 3*)   (♯ *Lon.LL 1189*)

E. Kilenyi   in ♯ **Rem. 199-165**

J. Páleníček   **♯ Sup.LPM 167**
(*Barcarolle & Fantaisie*)   (♯ *U. 5161C*)

A. d'Arco   in *Plé.P 102*

M. Schwalb   in ♯ **Roy. 1474**

☆ A. Cortot (in ♯ G.ALP 1197: QALP 10080: FALP 349)
G. Novães (in ♯ EVox.PL 7810)
A. Rubinstein (♭ *G.7RF 287*)
C. de Groot (in ♯ Epic.LC 3037)
E. Joyce (Od.NLX 21)

Bolero, C major, Op. 19

T. Nikolayeva   **♯ USSR.D 01190**
(‡s—*Polonaise No. 5; & Schumann*)

Écossaises, Op. 72, No. 3 □

G. Bachauer   in ♯ **G.CLP 1057**
(*Barcarolle; & Liszt, Shostakovich*)

R. Spivak   **ArgV. 66-6002**
(*Valse No. 6; & Liszt*)

A. Dorfman   in ♯ **Vic.LM 1758**
         (♭ *set WDM 1758: & ♭ ERA 238*)

B. Vitebsky   **V♯ CA.MPO 5008**
(*Fugue; Marche funèbre; Valse 15*)
(*Valse 11 on* SPO 9002)

☆ J-M. Darré (*ArgPat.FC 0013*)

... No. 1, only: M. Schwalb (in ♯ Roy. 1486)

ÉTUDES

COMPLETE RECORDING (of the 27 Études)
(Op. 10, Op. 25 & 3 Nouvelles Études)

S. Cherkassky (4ss)   **♯ G.ALP 1310/1**

☆ A. Brailowsky   **♯ G.FALP 242/3**
                  (♯ *ItV.B12R 0096/7*)
[Op. 10, Nos. 1, 3, 10, 12 & Op. 25, No. 1 on
            ♭ *Vic.ERA 197; FV.A 95223*]

COMPLETE RECORDINGS (of the 24 Études)

A. Uninsky   **♯ Phi.A 00710/1R**
(4ss)   (♯ *Epic.LC 3065*)

K. Leimer   **♯ Pol. 16047/8**

J-M. Darré   **♯ Pat.DT 1016/7**

☆ A. Cortot, 1942 recording (♯ G.FJLP 5050)

COLLECTIONS
Op. 10: Nos. 2, 5, 8, 10
Op. 25: Nos. 1, 2, 3, 6, 7, 8, 9, 11

W. Backhaus   **♯ D.LX 3091**
[Op. 10, No. 2 only on ♭ *D.VD 505*]   (♯ *Lon.LS 704*)

Op. 10: Nos. 3, 5, 12
Op. 25: Nos. 2, 3, 9, 10, 12
Nouvelle Étude No. 2, A flat major

S. Niedzielski   **♯ Sel. 320.C.024**
(*Sonata No. 2*)   (♯ T.LE 6539; West.WL 5340)

Op. 10: No. 12; Op. 25: Nos. 1, 2, 9
   ☆ R. Turner (in ♯ *T.NLCB 2003*)

(12) ÉTUDES, Op. 10

COMPLETE RECORDINGS

G. Novães   **♯ E. & AmVox.PL 9070**
(*Scherzo No. 1*)

J. Weingarten   **♯ CA.LPA 1046**
(*Ballade No. 1*) [announced but not issued]

☆ E. Kilenyi (♯ Cum.CR 242)
R. Goldsand (♯ Clc. 6216)

No. 2, A minor — ARR. ORCH. Bowden
Philharmonia—Kurtz   in ♯ **G.ALP 1301**

No. 3, E major □

S. Cherkassky   **G.DB 21598**
(*Op. 10, No. 5 & Op. 25, No. 12*)

V. Schiøler   **G.DB 10518**
(*Nos. 4 & 5*)   (♭ *7EBK 1002, d.c.*)

P. Badura-Skoda   in ♯ **Nix.WLP 5277**
                   (♯ *West.WL 5277*)

A. Cortot   in JpV. set **JAS 289**
[See also COLLECTION, *above*]   (in ♯ *LS 103*)

R. Spivak   **ArgV. 11-7972**
(*Rachmaninoff: Prelude, Op. 25, No. 5*)

A. S. Rasmussen   **Tono.A 196**
(*Nocturne No. 2*)   (♭ *EP 45052*)

E. Burton (in ♯ CEd.CE 1024)
X. Prochorova (in ♯ *Imp.ILP 109*)
E. Silver (in ♯ Var. 2055)
Liberace (in ♯ AmC.ML 4900, etc.)

☆ G. Novães (in ♯ EVox.PL 7810)
V. Horowitz (♭ *Vic.ERA 241;* ♭ *ItV.A72R 0062;*
                      FV.A 95230)
W. Backhaus (D.X 353: ♭ *71063:* ♭ *DK 23351:*
                    ♭ *VD 505, d.c.*)
W. Malcuzynski (♭ *C.SCB 104: SCBQ 3003*)
E. Kilenyi (in ♯ Ply. 12-84)

— ARR. ORCH. Mantovani Orch. (*D.F 10183: F 43655:*
          in ♯ D.LK 4021: LF 1161; ♯ Lon.LL 877*)
— ARR. VLC. & PF. ☆ S. Popoff (in ♯ *Vien.LPR 1022*)
— ARR. VOICE ☆ G. Pederzini (M-S) (*ArgOd. 57022*)

No. 4, C sharp minor

V. Schiøler   **G.DB 10518**
(*Nos. 3 & 5*)

B. Webster   in ♯ **Persp.PR 2**

☆ S. Cherkassky   in ♯ **G.BLP 1013**
(*Liszt, etc.*)   (*WBLP 1013: VBLP 805*)
☆ M. Sheyne (in ♯ CID.UM 6301)

No. 5, G flat major

V. Schiøler   **G.DB 10518**
(*Nos. 3 & 4*)   (♭ *7EBK 1001, d.c.*)

A. Cortot   in ♯ **G.ALP 1197**
(*Valses, etc. & Purcell, Schumann, etc.*)   (♯ *FALP 349*)

S. Cherkassky   **G.DB 21598**
(*No. 3 & Op. 25-12*)

E. Burton   in ♯ **CEd.CE 1024**

D. Bar-Illan   in ♯ **Kings.KLP 211**
(*Op. 25-6; Ben-Haim, Liszt, etc.*)

P. Cavazzini   in ♯ **Arp.ARC 1**
(*Ballade No. 2, Polonaise No. 6; Liszt*)

B. Davidovich (*USSR. 17893*)

☆ W. Malcuzynski (♭ *C.SCB 104: SCBQ 3003: SCBW 104*)
M. Sheyne (in ♯ CID.UM 6301)

No. 6, E flat minor

C. Horsley   **G.C 4215**
(*No. 7, & Weber*)   (EB 599: in ♯ CLP 1012)

L. Oborin (*USSR. 17787*)
Anon. Artist (in ♯ Ply. 1284)

---

[1] From a player-pf. roll.

No. 7, C major
C. Horsley   G.C 4215
(No. 6, & Weber)   (EB 599: in ♯ CLP 1012)

No. 8, F major
B. Siki   ♯ P.PMA 1022
(Andante Spianato, etc.; & Schumann)
☆ E. Kilenyi (in ♯ Ply. 12-84)

No. 9, F minor
M. Schwalb (in ♯ Roy. 1464)
Liberace (in ♯ AmC.ML 4900: in ♯ CL 6328;
                                    in ♯ Phi.S 06609R)

No. 10, A flat major   (□ only)

No. 11, E flat major   (□ only)

No. 12, C minor   □
V. Schiøler   G.DA 5281
(Valse No. 7)   (♭ 7RK 3: 7EBK 1002)
K. Leimer (from set)   in ♯ Pol. 19016
E. Burton   in ♯ CEd.CE 1025
X. Prochorova   in ♯ Imp.ILP 109
    F. Schröder (Eta. 120171)
    I. Ungar (Qual.SZN 3052)
☆ W. Malcuzynski (♭ C.SCB/SCBW 104: SCBQ 3003)
    M. Sheyne (in ♯ CID.UM 6301)
    J. Iturbi (♭ Vic.ERA 194; in ♯ DV.T 16069;
                                    ♭ FV.A 95207)
    O. Frugoni (♭ AmVox.VIP 45370)
    A. Semprini (♭ G.7EG 8053)
— ARR. ORCH. Philharmonia—Kurtz   in ♯ G.ALP 1301

(12) ÉTUDES, Op. 25
COMPLETE RECORDINGS
J. Weingarten   ♯ CA.LPA 1047
(Polonaise No. 7)
☆ G. Novães (♯ EVox.PL 7560)
    R. Goldsand (♯ Clc. 6190; MMS. 101)
Nos. 1, 2 & 9   ☆ M. Sheyne (in ♯ CID.UM 6301)
Nos. 1-3 G. Ginsburg (USSR. 22214/5: USSRM.D 001282)
Nos. 1-6   ☆ A. Jenner (in ♯ Ply. 12-20)
Nos. 1, 2 & 7   ☆ A. Jenner (in ♯ AFest.CFR 10-106;
                                    ▽ ♯ Rem. 149-4)

No. 1, A flat major   □
L. Gousseau   ♭ Plé.P 45149
(Ballade 2 & Impromptu 3)
A. Semprini   G.B 10809
(Brahms: Wiegenlied)
Liberace (in ♯ AmC.ML 4900: in ♯ CL 6327;
                            in ♯ Phi.S 06608R, etc.)

No. 2, F minor   □
☆ A. Cortot   in ♯ G.ALP 1197
        (in ♯ QALP 10080: FALP 349; ♭ Vic.EHA 14)

No. 3, F major
B. Davidovich   USSR. 17893
(♯s—Op. 10-5, & Mazurka 20)

No. 5, E minor   □
M. Schwalb (in ♯ Roy. 1486)
L. Oborin (USSR. 17786 & in ♯ Csm.CRLP 210)
S. Richter (USSR. 021052)

No. 6, G sharp minor   □
D. Bar-Illan (Debussy, etc.) in ♯ Kings.KL 211
M. Schwalb (in ♯ Roy. 1486)
G. Ginsburg (USSR. 23048)

No. 7, C sharp minor
P. Badura-Skoda   in ♯ Nix.WLP 5277
                                    (in ♯ West.WL 5277)
G. Werschenska   Tono.A 193
(No. 9, & Mazurka No. 5)
— ARR. VLC. & PF.
D. Shafran & pf. (USSRM.D 00207)

No. 9, G flat major   □
A. Cortot   in ♯ G.ALP 1197
(in ♯ QALP 10080: FALP 349; in ♯ JpV.LS 103, d.c.)
E. Burton   in ♯ CEd.CE 1026
G. Werschenska   Tono.A 193
(No. 7 & Mazurka No. 5)

L. Gousseau   ♭ Plé.P 45150
(Nocturne 8 & Scherzo 3)
M. Schwalb   in ♯ Roy. 1474

No. 10, B minor   □
W. Merzanow   Muza.X 1658
(Scriabin: Study, Op. 8)

No. 11, A minor   □
E. Burton   in ♯ CEd.CE 1027
P. Sebastiani   ArgV. 66-6005
(D. Scarlatti: Sonatas)

No. 12, C minor
S. Cherkassky   G.DB 21598
(Études, Op. 10, 3 & 5)
G. Ginsburg (USSR. 23049)

(3) NOUVELLES ÉTUDES No Op. No.
COMPLETE RECORDINGS
J. MacInnes   ♯ McInt.MM 104
(Polonaise No. 7; Mozart)
☆ G. Novães (in ♯ EVox.PL 7560)
    R. Goldsand (♯ Clc. 6216)

No. 1, F minor
E. Kilenyi   in ♯ Rem. 199-165
A. Goldenweiser (USSR. 17866)

No. 2, A flat major
E. Burton   in ♯ CEd.CE 1025
A. Goldenweiser (USSR. 17867)

F minor (unspec.)
I. Ungár (Qual.SZN 3052)

_____

Fantaisie, F minor, Op. 49   □
Y. Nat   ♯ DFr. 84
(Barcarolle, & Sonata No. 2)   (♯ HS.HSL 97)
A. Cortot (n.v.)   in JpV. set JAS 273
S. Sorin   ♯ SOT. 1038
(Liszt, Scriabin, Granados)
J. Páleníček   ♯ Sup.LPM 167
(Berceuse & Barcarolle)   (♯ U. 5161C)
C. Giraud-Chambeau   ♯ Sat.LDA 7002
(Bach-Busoni: Chaconne)
☆ W. Malcuzynski (in ♯ BB.LBC 1066: ♭ set WBC 1066;
    in ♯ G.BLP 1013: WBLP 1013: VBLP 805)

Fugue, A minor   1841
B. Vitebsky   V♯ CA.MPO 5008
(Marche funèbre, Écossaises, Valse 15)

Hexaméron See LISZT, section A. III (5)

IMPROMPTUS   □
Nos. 1-4, COMPLETE
M. Horszowski   ♯ E. & AmVox.PL 7870
(Pf. Concerto No. 1)
(Polonaises, on ♯ Pan.XPV 1003)
[Nos. 1, 2 & 4 only, ♭ AmVox.VIP 45510]
N. Magaloff   ♯ D.LXT 5037
(Berceuse & Sonata No. 3)   (♯ Lon.LL 1189)
(also, 2ss—♯ D.LW 5190)
J. v. Karolyi   PV. 72430
                                         (♭ Pol. 30127)
(in ♯ HP.DGM 18068; No. 4 only also in ♯ Pol. 19016)

No. 1, A flat major, Op. 29
V. Schiøler   G.DB 10522
(Berceuse)
    M. Schwalb (in ♯ Roy. 1474)
☆ V. Horowitz (♭ G.7RF/RQ 255; ♭ Vic.ERA 241;
                            ♭ ItV.A72R 0062; FV.A 95230)
— ARR. VOICE & PF.
☆ S. Onegin (A) (in ♯ Vic.LCT 1115; ♭ set WCT 1115)

♯ = Long-playing, 33⅓ r.p.m.   ♭ = 45 r.p.m.   ♮ = Auto. couplings, 78 r.p.m.

No. 2, F sharp major, Op. 36
A. Cortot (n.v.)   **in JpV. set JAS 269**
            (in ♯ *LS 103*)
P. Mildner   **♯ DT.LGM 65025**
(*Ballade No. 2; J. Strauss, Liszt*) (♯ *T.LB 6060:* ♭ *UV 112*)
E. Burton   **in ♯ CEd.CE 1026**

☆ G. Novães (in ♯ *EVox.PL 7810*)
I. Friedman (*C.GQX 11521*)

No. 3, G flat major, Op. 51
L. Gousseau   **♭ Plé.P 45149**
(*Ballade 2 & Étude, Op. 25, No. 1*)

No. 4, C sharp minor, Op. 66
(*Fantaisie-Impromptu*)
M. Lympany   **G.C 4209**
(*Brahms: Intermezzo, Op. 117, No. 2*)
      (*G.S 10609:* ♭ *7P 141;* ♭ *Vic.EHA 13*)
R. Goldsand   **♯ MMS. 21**
(*Sonata No. 2*)   (♯ *ANix.MLPY 21*)
[& in ♯ *MMS. 100S & 100W*]
M. T. Garatti   **C.QCX 16668**
(*Debussy: Suite bergamasque—Clair de lune*)
V. Schiøler   **Tono.A 194**
(*Liszt: Liebestraum No. 3*)   (♭ *EP 45025*)
E. Burton   **in ♯ CEd.CE 1024**
S. Bianca (*Valse No. 7*)   **MSB. 78107**

Liberace (in ♯ *AmC.ML 4900:* in ♯ *CL 6327;*
      in ♯ *Phi.S 06608R*)
A. Semprini (*G.B 10472*)
L. Babits (♭ *Tit.TI 7011*)
☆ J. Iturbi (♭ *Vic.ERA 194;* in ♯ *DV.T 16069;*
      ♭ *FV.A 95207*)
A. Jenner (▽ in ♯ *Rem. 149-4;* in ♯ *Ply. 12-84 & 12-20;*
      in ♯ *Cum.CR 250*)
E. Joyce (*Od.NLX 21;* ♭ *AmD.ED 3500*)
F. Ellegaard (*D.K 24014*)

— ARR. HARP. ☆ E. Vito (in ♯ *Nix.SLPY 145* & *SOT. 10301*)
— ARR. ORCH. Schmid (etc.)
Philharmonia—Kurtz   **in ♯ G.ALP 1301**

☆ Kostelanetz Orch. (♭ *C.SCD 2019: SCDQ 2027:*
      SCDW 112)

Largo, E flat major (pub. 1938)
R. Bakst   **Muza. 1712**
(*Polonaise No. 6*)

Marche funèbre, C minor, Op. 72, No. 2
B. Vitebsky   **V♯ CA.MPO 5008**
(*Fugue, Écossaises, Valse No. 15*)

MAZURKAS
Nos. 1-51, COMPLETE
A. Rubinstein (n.v.)   **♯ G.FALP 255/7**
(*5ss—Polonaise No. 7 & Andante spianato*)
      (♯ Vic. set LM 6109)
[Nos. 1-12 only, ♯ *Vic.LRM 7001:* ♭ *set ERB 7001:*
      ♯ *ItV.A10R 0002*]
J. Smeterlin   **♯ Epic.LC 3151/2**
(4ss)   (set SC 6007)
T. Sadlowski (4ss)   **♯ Csm.LAB 5001/2**

COLLECTIONS
Nos. 2, 6, 11, 12, 20, 22, 26, 27, 31, 32, 36, 37, 40, 41, 43,
47, 51 (*Notre temps*)
W. Kapell   **♯ Vic.LM 1865**
[Nos. 26, 27, 36, 37 only on ♭ *Vic.ERA 213;* *FV.A 95224;*
Nos. 6, 32, 41, 47 on ♭ *Vic.ERA 232*]

Nos. 9, 11-14, 16, 18, 21, 22, 27, 29, 35, 36, 41, 45, 48, 50, 51, 53
☆ M. Jonas   **♯ AmC.RL 6624**

Nos. 13, 15, 17, 23, 24, 25, 26, 34, 37, 39, 51
G. Novães   **♯ E. & AmVox.PL 7920**

Nos. 20, 21, 26, 32, 38, 40, 41
☆ V. Horowitz   **♯ G.ALP 1069**
(*Schumann*)   (♯ *FALP 215*)
[Nos. 20, 21, 38, 40, 41 only, on ♭ *G.7ER 5006:*
7ERQ 104: 7ERF 101; DV. 26005; see below for other
re-issues]

Nos. 1, 2, 3, 4, 22, 23, 24, 25
B. Vitebsky   **V♯ CA.MPO 5016**

Nos. 7, 15, 17, 20, 27, 32, 41
W. Malcuzynski   **♯ C.CX 1138**
(*Polonaises*)   (♯ *FCX 197*)

Nos. 13, 17, 23, 27, 40
A. Uninsky (*Nocturnes*)   **♯ Phi.A 00653R**
(*idem, Barcarolle & Fantaisie* on ♯ Epic.LC 3122)

Nos. 9, 35, 45, 48, 49, 52 ☆ W. Kapell (♭ *Vic.ERA 102*)

Nos. 4, 36, 39 H. Neuhaus (*USSR. 17752/3*)

Nos. 7, 31, 41, 42, 43, 47 ☆ M. Sheyne (in ♯ *CID.UM 6301*)

Nos. 17, 20, 24
☆ W. Backhaus   **♯ D.LW 5026**
(*Ballade No. 1*)   (♯ *Lon.LD 9047*)
(Nos. 20 & 24 on D.X 353; No. 24 also on ♭ *D.VD 505*)
No. 13, A minor, Op. 17, No. 4
No. 25, B minor, Op. 33, No. 4
C. Zecchi   **in ♯ West.WN 18139**
(*Schumann, Scarlatti, Bach, etc.*)

No. 2, C sharp minor, Op. 6, No. 2 □
▽ Lazare-Lévy (JpV.SD 55)

No. 5, B flat major, Op. 7, No. 1 □
G. Werschenska   **Tono.A 193**
(*Études, Op. 25, Nos. 7 & 9*)
☆ J. Iturbi (in ♯ *DV.T 16069*)

No. 6, A minor, Op. 7, No. 2
M. Schwalb (in ♯ *Roy. 1474*)
H. Neuhaus (*USSR. 15744*)

No. 7, F minor, Op. 7, No. 3 □
☆ V. Horowitz (in ♯ *G.FALP 280:* ♭ *7RF/RQ 255;*
      ♭ *Vic.ERA 241; FV.A 95230*)

No. 13, A minor, Op. 17, No. 4 □
A. Uninsky   **♭ Phi.A 400000E**
(*Polonaise 6 & Valse 5*)   (from Collection)
F. Ellegaard (*Tarantelle*)   **Pol.HM 80068**
H. Czerny-Stefanska (*Valse 1*)   **U.H 24379**

No. 14, G minor, Op. 24, No. 1
M. Schwalb (in ♯ *Roy. 1474*)
— ARR. ORCH. See Suite, sec. IV, *below*.

No. 15, C major, Op. 24, No. 2
L. Oborin (*USSR. 22195*)

No. 16, A flat major, Op. 24, No. 3
W. Kapell   **in ♭ Vic.ERA 232**

No. 17, B flat minor, Op. 24, No. 4 □
J. v. Karolyi   **in ♯ HP.DGM 18068**
      (& in ♯ Pol. 19016, d.c.)
L. Oborin (*USSR. 22196*)

No. 20, D flat major, Op. 30, No. 3 □
B. Davidovich   **USSR. 17894**
(*Études, Op. 10-5 & 25-3*)

No. 21, C sharp minor, Op. 30, No. 4 □
A. Goldenweiser (*No. 23*)   **USSR. 17212**

No. 23, D major, Op. 33, No. 2 □
A. Goldenweiser (*USSR. 17213*)
☆ S. Cherkassky (in ♯ *G.BLP/WDLP 1013: VBLP 805;*
      in ♯ *Vic.LBC 1066:* ♭ *set WBC 1066*)

— ARR. ORCH. See Suite & Sylphides, *below*

No. 25, B minor, Op. 33, No. 4 □
M. Schwalb   **in ♯ Roy. 1577**

No. 26, C sharp minor, Op. 41, No. 1
H. Neuhaus (*No. 6*)   **USSR. 15745**
V. Sofronitsky (*Valse No. 12*)   **USSR. 18367**
☆ V. Horowitz (in ♯ *Vic.LRM 7018:* ♭ *set ERB 7018*)

No. 29, A flat major, Op. 41, No. 4
N. Yemelyanova   **USSRM.D 00128**
(½s—*Nocturne No. 5 & Prelude No. 25*)

No. 30, G major, Op. 50, No. 1
L. Oborin (*USSR. 21541*)
☆ J. Smeterlin (in ♯ *Roy. 1901*)

No. 31, A flat major, Op. 50, No. 2
▽ Lazare-Lévy (JpV.SD 55)

☆ = Re-issue of a recording to be found in previous volumes.

No. 32, C sharp minor, Op. 50, No. 3 □
V. Sofronitzky (*USSR. 15145/6*)

☆ V. Horowitz (♭ *G.7RF/RQ 243*)
D. Lipatti (in ‡ *AmC.ML 4721* & ‡ *C.FCX 493*)

No. 34, C major, Op. 56, No. 2
☆ W. Landowska (hpsi.) (♭ *Vic.ERA 128*)

— ARR. ORCH. See Suite, Sec. IV, *below*

No. 38, F sharp minor, Op. 59, No. 3
No. 40, F minor, Op. 63, No. 2
No. 41, C sharp minor, Op. 63, No. 3
☆ V. Horowitz   G.DB 21590
[Nos. 40 & 41 also ♭ *7RF/RQ 243*]

No. 41, C sharp minor, Op. 63, No. 3 □
A. Uninsky   in ‡ *Phi.S 06004R*
J. Rein   *Pam.S 19046*
(*Preludes Nos. 4 & 22*)

— ARR. GUITAR   M. A. Funes (*ArgOd. 56544*)

No. 44, C major
— ARR. ORCH. See Sylphides, Sec. IV, *below*

No. 45, A minor, Op. 67, No. 4 □
— ARR. VLN. & PF.   N. Carol & J. Levine in ‡ BB.LBC 1155

No. 46, C major, Op. 68, No. 1
No. 47, A minor, Op. 68, No. 2 □
H. Czerny-Stefanska   **Muza.X 2143**
(*Valse No. 2*)

No. 50, A minor (dedicated to E. Gaillard)
No. 51, A minor (*Notre temps*)
L. Oborin (*USSR. 13248 & 21542*)

No. 51, A minor, No Op. No.   (*Notre temps*)
R. Bakst   (*Valse No. 9*)   **Muza.X 1713**

NOCTURNES
Nos. 1-20: COMPLETE
J. Smeterlin   **‡ Phi.A 00256/7L**
(4ss)   (‡ Epic. set SC 6007)
E. Istomin   **‡ AmC.ML 5054/5**
(4ss)   (set SL 226)

Nos. 1-19
☆ A. Rubinstein   **‡ G.ALP 1157 & 1170**
[1-10 on ALP 1157]   (‡ FALP/QALP 210/1)

COLLECTIONS
Nos. 1-10
P. Katin   **‡ D.LXT 5122**
[Nos. 2 & 5 also ♭ *D. 71098*; Nos. 7 & 8, ♭ *71114*]
Nos. 11-20
S. Askenase   **‡ Pol. 16103/4**
(4ss) [Nos. 1-10 are on ‡ *16033/4*, see Supp. II]
Nos. 2, 5, 10, 12, 13, 20
N. Reisenberg   **‡ West.LAB 7029**
Nos. 1, 8, 13
A. Uninsky   (*Mazurkas*)   **‡ Phi.A 00653R**
(*idem, Barcarolle & Fantaisie* in ‡ Epic.LC 3122)
Nos. 8 & 12   ☆ G. Novães (♭ *AmVox.VIP 45310*)

No. 1, B flat minor, Op. 9, No. 1
M. Schwalb   in ‡ Roy. 1474

No. 2, E flat major, Op. 9, No. 2 □
A. Cortot   in JpV. set JAS 269
(& ☆ ♭ *G.7RF 239*)   (in ‡ LS 103)
E. Møller   (*Preludes*)   ♭ *Mtr.MCEP 3033*
A. S. Rasmussen   **Tono.A 196**
(*Étude, Op. 10, No. 3*)   (♭ EP 45052)
P. Sancan (♭ *FV.A 95001*)
Liberace (in ‡ AmC.ML 4900: ‡ CL. 6327;
                                in ‡ Phi.S 06608R)
☆ E. Joyce (♭ *AmD.ED 3500*)
S. Rachmaninoff (in ‡ Vic.LCT 1136)
S. Askenase (in ‡ Pol. 19016)

— ARR. VLN. & PF.   Sarasate
I. Zilzer & F. Eberson   **C.LDX 17**
(*Dvořák: Slav. Dance No. 2*)   (♭ SCBK 1)
☆ D. Oistrakh (♭ *Mer.EP 1-5008*)

☆ G. Cassadó & O. Schulhof (in ‡ Rem. 199-128)

— ARR. ORCH.
Concert Orch.—E. Robinson (in ‡ Argo.RG 66)
J. Schmied Orch. (in ‡ *Vien.LPR 1031*)

No. 3, B major, Op. 9, No. 3
☆ A. Rubinstein (in ‡ Vic.LRM 7015: ♭ set ERB 7015)

No. 4, F major, Op. 15, No. 1 □
Anon. Artist (in ‡ Roy. 1549)
☆ A. Cortot (♭ *G.7RW 147; 7RF/RQ 265: 7R 162;*
                                    ♭ *Vic.EHA 14*)

— ARR. ORCH. See Suite, Sec. IV, *below*

No. 5, F sharp major, Op. 15, No. 2 □
G. Lasson   **‡ Pac.LDPF 26**
(*Ballade 1, Polonaise 3; & Beethoven*)
A. Cortot (n.v.)   in ‡ G.ALP 1197
                                (in ‡ QALP 10080: FALP 349)
E. Burton   in ‡ CEd.CE 1024
O. Penna   **ArgOd. 66051**
(*Satie: Sonatine bureaucratique*)
F. Schröder (*Eta. 120171*)
L. Oborin (*USSR. 13247*)
N. Yemelyanova (*USSRM.D 001281*)
Liberace (in ‡ AmC.ML 4900: in ‡ CL 6327;
                                in ‡ Phi.S 06608R)
☆ A. Rubinstein (from set) (♭ *G.7ER 5030*; ♭ *Vic.ERA 99*)
G. Novães (in ‡ EVox.PL 7810)
V. Horowitz (in ‡ G.ALP 1087: FALP 215:
    FALP 280, d.c.; in ‡ Vic.LRM 7018: ♭ set ERB 7018)
C. de Groot (in ‡ Epic.LC 3037)
M. Sheyne (in ‡ CID.UM 6301)

— ARR. ORCH.   Hinrichs
☆ Philharmonia—Kurtz   in ‡ G.ALP 1301

No. 6, G minor, Op. 15, No. 3
☆ M. Sheyne (in ‡ CID.UM 6301)

No. 7, C sharp minor, Op. 27, No. 1 □
R. Smendzianka   (2ss)   **Muza.X 1588**
☆ A. Cortot (♭ *G.7R 162: 7RF/RQ 265: 7RW 147;*
                                    ♭ *Vic.EHA 14*)

No. 8, D flat major, Op. 27, No. 2 □
A. Brailowsky   (*Valses*)   **♭ *Vic.ERA 255***
B. Vitebsky   **V‡ CA.MPO 5007**
(*Valses Nos. 9-11*)
L. Gousseau   ♭ *Plé.P 45150*
(*Étude, Op. 25-9 & Scherzo 3*)
X. Prochorova   in ‡ *Imp.ILP 109*
☆ D. Lipatti (in ♭ AmC. set A 1085 & in ‡ ML 4732;
                                    ‡ C.FCX 493)

— ARR. VLN. & ORCH.   Wilhelmj
M. Salpeter & Philharmonia—Kurtz   in ‡ G.ALP 1301
— ARR. VLN. & PF.   Balakirev
L. Kogan & pf.   (*Wieniawski*)   **USSRM.D 001264**

No. 9, B major, Op. 32, No. 1
J. Iturbi   in ‡ Vic.LRM 7057
(*Preludes 9 & 10; Schumann, Granados, etc.*)
                                (♭ set ERB 7057)
E. Burton   in ‡ CEd.CE 1025
☆ B. Siki (in ‡ P.PMA 1022)

No. 10, A flat major, Op. 32, No. 2
— ARR. ORCH. See Sylphides, Sec. IV, *below*

No. 12, G major, Op. 37, No. 2
☆ A. Rubinstein (in ‡ Vic.LRM 7015: ♭ set ERB 7015)
L. Godowsky (in ‡ Roy. 1402)[1]

No. 13, C minor, Op. 48, No. 1 □
— ARR. ORCH. See Suite, Sec. IV, *below*

No. 14, F sharp minor, Op. 48, No. 2
A. d'Arco   in *Plé.P 103*
☆ A. Rubinstein (♭ DV. 26006)

No. 15, F minor, Op. 55, No. 1 □
☆ A. Rubinstein (♭ *Vic.ERA 99*)
V. Horowitz (in ‡ Vic.LRM 7051: ♭ set ERB 7051;
                                in ‡ DV.B 26040)

No. 16, E flat major, Op. 55, No. 2
☆ I. Friedman (C.GQX 11521)

---

[1] From a player-pf. roll.

No. 18, E major, Op. 62, No. 2
☆ A. Rubinstein (♭ *Vic.ERA 216;* ♭ *FV.A 95227*)

No. 19, E minor, Op. 72, No. 1
V. Horowitz   in ♯ **Vic. set LM 6014**
(*Schubert, Scriabin, etc.*)
(♭ *set ERG 6014: ERA 241;* in ♯ *ItV.B12R 0064/5:*
♭ *A72R 0033;* ♭ *FV.A 95230*)
☆ A. Rubinstein, from set (♭*Vic.ERA 216;* ♯ FV.A 630202:
♭ *A 95227*)
S. Cherkassky (in ♯ BB.LBC 1066: ♭ *set WBC 1066*)
— ARR. VLN. & PF.   Auer
D. Oistrakh & pf.   (*No. 20*)   **USSR. 017369**

No. 20, C sharp minor, No Op. No.
— ARR. VLN. & PF.   Rodionov, *et al.*
N. Carol & J. Levine   in ♯ **BB.LBC 1155**
D. Oistrakh & pf.   (*No. 19*)   **USSR. 017370**

— ARR. VLC. & PF.
A. Janigro & E. Bagnoli   in ♯ **West.WN 18004**

POLONAISES
(See also Andante Spianato, *supra*)
Nos. 1-10 & Andante Spianato: COMPLETE
M. Ciampi   (4ss)   ♯ **Clc. 6176/7**

COLLECTIONS
Nos. 1-6
A. Rubinstein   ♯ **G.ALP 1028**
(♯ FALP 212: VALP 529: QALP 10021; DV.L 16274)
[Nos. 1 & 2 only on ♭ *G.7ER 5048;* ♭ *Vic.ERA 121;*
Nos. 3 & 6 ♭ *G.7ER 5005*]
No. 3, A major, Op. 40, No. 1
No. 6, A flat major, Op. 53
No. 14, G sharp minor   1822
No. 15, B flat minor   1826 "*Adieu à Guillaume Kolberg*"
☆ G. Johannesen   (*Impromptus*)   ♯ *Pan.XPV 1003*

Nos. 2, 5, 6
W. Malcuzynski   ♯ **C.CX 1138**
(*Mazurkas*)   (♯ WCX 1138: FCX 197)
[Nos. 2 & 6 only on ♭ *SEL 1514: SEBQ 119*]

No. 1, C sharp minor, Op. 26, No. 1
E. Burton   in ♯ **CEd.CE 1026**
V. Sofronitzky (*USSR. 15533/4*)

No. 2, E flat major, Op. 26, No. 2
G. Ginsburg (*USSR. 12876/7*)
☆ S. Askenase (FPV. 5039)

No. 3, A major, Op. 40, No. 1   ☐
S. Bianca   *MSB. 78044*
E. Burton   in ♯ **CEd.CE 1025**
F. Ellegaard   (*Valse No. 7*)   **Pol.HM 80071**
P. Cavazzini   ♯ *Arp.ARC 4*
(*Scherzo 1, Valse 14; & D. Scarlatti*)
S. Fiorentino   (*No. 6*)   **V♯** *CA.MPO 5001*
G. Lasson   ♯ **Pac.LDPF 26**
(*Ballade 1, Nocturne 5; & Beethoven*)
H. Czerny-Stefanska (*Muza. 2466*)
M. Schwalb (in ♯ Roy. 1486)
Liberace (in ♯ AmC.ML 4900: in ♯ CL 6327;
in ♯ *Phi.S 06608R*)
☆ S. Askenase (♭ *Pol. 30040;* in ♯ 19016 & *17031;*
FPV. 5039)
E. Gilels (*USSR. 13299;* in ♯ Csm.CRLP 159)
N. Magaloff (♭*D.71107*)
A. Rubinstein (♭ *G.7RF 287; Vic.ERA 76*)
G. Johannesen (♭*AmVox.VIP 45240*)
M. Sheyne (in ♯ CID.UM 6301)
A. Jenner (in ♯ Cum.CR 250; in ♯ Ply. 12-20)
— ARR. ORCH.   Glazounov (from Chopiniana, Op. 46)
☆ Boston Prom.—Fiedler
(♭ *Cam.CAE 142* & in ♯ *CAL 142*)
— ARR. ORCH.   See Suite, Section IV.

No. 4, C minor, Op. 40, No. 2
L. Hungerford   in ♯ **LH. 101/2**
(Pte.)
☆ A. Rubinstein (from set)   ♭ *G.7ER 5030*
(*Nocturnes Nos. 5 & 15*)   (♭ *Vic.ERA 99*)

No. 5, F sharp minor, Op. 44
B. Vitebsky   **V♯** *CA.MPO 5015*
(*Variations*)

S. Askenase   *PV. 36067*
(♭ *Pol. 32043*)
T. Nikolayeva (in ♯ USSR.D 01190)

No. 6, A flat major, Op. 53   ☐
P. Cavazzini   ♯ *Arp.ARC 1*
(*Ballade, Étude; & Liszt*)
A. Cortot   in JpV. set **JAS 273**
(*Valse No. 11, on* ♭ *JpV.EP 3042*)
P. Serebriakov   in ♯ **Eta.LPM 1013**
(*Tchaikovsky & Rachmaninoff*)
(*Étude, Op. 10-12 & Nocturne 5, on Eta. 120171*)
L. Margaritis   *GkOd.A 241618*
E. Gilels   *USSRM.D 200*
(*Ballade No. 1*)   (& in ♯ Csm.CRLP 210)
X. Prochorova   in ♯ *Imp.ILP 109*
(*Études, Nocturne; Liszt, Rachmaninoff*)
S. Fiorentino   (*No. 3*)   **V♯** *CA.MPO 5001*
R. Bergroth   (2ss)   *D.SD 5003*
R. Bakst (*Muza. 1712*)
G. Ginsburg (USSR. 019006/7)
Liberace (in ♯ AmC.ML 4900; in ♯ CL 6328;
in ♯ *Phi.S 06609R*)
☆ V. Horowitz (♭ *G.7ERF 109:* in ♯ FALP 280)
L. Pennario (in ♯ DCap.CTL 7102; Cap.P 8312:
♭ *FAP 8204*)
A. Rubinstein (♭ *Vic.EHA 76*)
V. Schiøler (♭ *Mer.EP 1-5013;* ♭ *FMer.MEP 14523*)
G. Johannesen (♭*AmVox.VIP 45240*)
W. Wolf (G.EH 1428)
S. Askenase (FPV. 5057; ♭ *Pol. 30040:* ♯ *17031*)
J. Iturbi (in ♯ *DV.T 16369*)
A. Uninsky (♭ *Phi.A 400000E*)
M. Sheyne (in ♯ CID.UM 6301)
A. Jenner (in ♯ Cum.CR 250; in ♯ Ply. 12-20)

No. 7, A flat major, Op. 61 ("Polonaise-fantaisie")
J. Weingarten   ♯ **CA.LPA 1047**
(*Études, Op. 25*)
J. MacInnes   ♯ **McInt.MM 104**
(*Nouvelles Études; Mozart*)
S. Askenase   *PV. 36037*
(♭ *Pol. 32040*)
☆ A. Rubinstein   ♯ *G.BLP 1027*
(*Andante Spianato & Grande Polonaise*)
(♯ FBLP 1034: QBLP 5013; DV.L 16279)
(& in ♯ FALP 255/7; ♯ Vic. set LM 6109)

No. 8, D minor, Op. 71, No. 1
H. Czerny-Stefanska   *Muza. 2465*

No. 9, B flat major, Op. 71, No. 2
G. Ginsburg   *USSR.D 001283*
(*Études Op. 25, Nos. 1–3*)
☆ S. Askenase (FPV. 5057)

No. 10, F minor, Op. 71, No. 3   ☐

No. 13, A flat major   1821
No. 14, G sharp minor   1822
S. Fiorentino   **V♯** *CA.MPO 5009*

Polonaise (unid.)   M. Schwalb (in ♯ Roy. 1474)

---

(24) PRELUDES, Op. 28
COMPLETE RECORDINGS
F. Gulda   ♯ **D.LXT 2837**
(♯ Lon.LL 755)
S. Askenase   ♯ **HP.DGM 19002**
(♯ Pol. 18214)
J. Weingarten   ♯ **CA.LPA 1041**
[includes Prelude No. 25]
M. Lympany   ♯ **G.CLP 1051**
(♯ QCLP 12018)
☆ C. de Groot   ♯ *EPhi.ABR 4042*
(♯ *Phi.A 00660R;* Epic.LC 3017)
☆ A. Rubinstein   ♯ **G.ALP 1192**
(♯ G.FALP 249)
☆ E. Petri   (*Liszt*)   ♯ **AmC.RL 3040**
☆ G. Novães   ♯ **EVox.PL 6170**
[Nos. 1, 3, 7, 10, 15, 16, 18, 20, 22, 24 on
♯ *AmVox.VIP 45220*]
☆ A. Brailowsky (BrzV. 12-3384/7; ♯ ItV.A12R 0083;
Nos. 1-12 on ♭ *Vic.ERA 69;* ♭ *DV. 26011;*
Nos. 13-15 on ♭ *Vic.ERA 104*)

☆ = Re-issue of a recording to be found in previous volumes.

COLLECTIONS
Nos. 1, 6, 7, 10, 15, 20, 21, 22
  M. Schwalb   **‡ Roy. 1486**
  (*Ballades, Écossaises, etc.*)

Nos. 1-24 (so the catalogue)
  V. Sofronitzky (4ss)   *USSRM.D 953/4 & D 001041/2*

Nos. 11-24
  ☆ B. Moiseiwitsch   **‡ BB.LBC 1038**
  (*Scherzos*)   (♭ set *WBC 1038*)

Nos. 3, 8 & 16   ☆ C. Keene (in ‡ *EMer.MG 10113*)
Nos. 3, 4, 6, 7   Y. Bryushkov (*USSR. 16336/7*)
Nos. 6 & 7   ☆ R. Turner (in ‡ *T.NLCB 2003*)
Nos. 7 & 15   E. Møller (in ♭ *Mtr.MCEP 3033*)

No. 1, C major, Op. 28, No. 1   □

No. 2, A minor, Op. 28, No. 2
  A. d'Arco   in *Plé.P 104*
  L. Oborin (*USSR. 20955*; & in ‡ *Csm.CRLP 210*)

No. 3, G major, Op. 28, No. 3   □
  Anon. Artist (in ‡ *Hélios: Joies de la Musique*)
  L. Oborin (*USSR. 20955*; & in ‡ *Csm.CRLP 210*)

No. 4, E minor, Op. 28, No 4
  B. Webster   in **‡ Persp.PR 2**
  J. Rein (*Pam.S 19046*)
  Liberace (in ‡ *AmC.ML 4900*: in ‡ *CL 6328*;
                     in ‡ *Phi.S 06609R*)

No. 6, B minor   □

No. 7, A major
  Liberace (in ‡ *AmC.ML 4900*: in ‡ *CL 6328*;
                     in ‡ *Phi.S 06609R*)
  Y. Bryushkov (*USSR. 16337*)
  ☆ M. Sheyne (in ‡ *CID.UM 6301*)
  J. Therrien (in ‡ *MH. 33-111*)

— ARR. GUITAR   C. Santias (in ‡ *FestF.FLD 32*;
                          SpFest.HF 3201)
  M. A. Funes (*ArgOd. 56544*)
  ☆ A. Segovia (in † ‡ *B.AXTL 1060*)

— ARR. ORCH. See Sylphides, Sec. IV, *below*

No. 8, F sharp minor   □
  S. Andersen   in **‡ Oce.OCS 38**

No. 9, E major
No. 10, C sharp minor
  J. Iturbi   **‡ Vic.LRM 7057**
  (*Nocturne No. 9; Debussy, Schumann, etc.*)(♭ set *ERB 7057*)

No. 9, E major — ARR. ORGAN: C. Cronham (*Mjr.5120*)

No. 10, C sharp minor
  A. d'Arco   in *Plé.P 105*

No. 15, D flat major
  A. Cortot (n.v.)   in **‡ JpV.LS 103**
                 (& in set *JAS 269*)
  S. Bianca   *MSB. 78044*
  (*Polonaise No. 3*)
  F. Gulda (from set)   ♭ *D. 71084*
  (*Debussy: Clair de lune*)   (♭ *23354*)
  V. Sofronitzky (*USSR. 17061/2*)
  I. Ungár (*Qual. SZN 3052*)

— ARR. ORCH. See Suite, Sec. IV, *below*

No. 16, B flat major   □
  E. Kilenyi   in **‡ Rem. 199-165**

No. 17, A flat major   □

No. 20, C minor   □
  A. Goldenweiser (*USSR. 17867*)
— ARR. ORGAN: C. Cronham (*Mjr. 5121*)

No. 22, G minor
  J. Rein   *Pam.S 19046*
  (½s—*No. 4 & Mazurka 41*)

No. 24, D minor
  ☆ J. Therrien (in ‡ *MH. 33-111*)

No. 25, C sharp minor, Op. 45
  J. Weingarten   **‡ CA.LPA 1041**
  (*Preludes, Op. 28*)
  N. Yemelyanova   *USSRM.D 001280*
  (*Nocturne No. 5 & Mazurka No. 29*)
  ☆ A. Cortot (♭ *G.7RF 239*)

No. 26, A flat major (1834, pub. 1918)   □

Rondo, E flat major, Op. 16
  S. Fiorentino   **‡ CA.LPA 1092**
  (*Allegro de Concert, etc.*)

Rondo, C major, Op. 73 2 pfs.
  P. Luboshutz & G. Nemenoff   **‡ Rem. 199-143**
  (*Reger, Weber, etc.*)

(4) SCHERZOS   □
COMPLETE RECORDINGS
  B. Siki   **‡ P.PMA 1011**
  L. Kentner   **‡ C.SX 1033**
  J. Bolet   **‡ Rem. 199-161**
  ☆ A. Rubinstein   **‡ G.ALP 1136**
                     (*QALP 147*)

No. 1, B minor, Op. 20
  G. Novães   **‡ E. & AmVox.PL 9070**
  (*Études, Op. 10*)
  P. Cavazzini   **‡ Arp.ARC 4**
  (*Polonaise 3, Valse 14; & D. Scarlatti*)
  V. Horowitz (n.v.)[1]   in ‡ **Vic. set LM 6014**
  (*Nocturne; Schubert, Scriabin, etc.*)
  (♭ set *ERG 6014*; in ‡ *ItV.B12R 0064/5*;
                 FV.A 630202; ♭ *ItV.A 72R 0062*)
  ☆ V. Horowitz (in ‡ *G.ALP 1111*: *FALP 233*;
    (o.v.)   in ‡ *Vic.LRM 7051*; ♭ set *ERB 7051*)
  A. Rubinstein (in ‡ *Vic.LRM 7015*: ♭ set *ERB 7015*;
                      in ‡ *DV.B 26040*)
  B. Moiseiwitsch (in ‡ *BB.LBC 1038*: ♭ set *WBC 1038*)

No. 2, B flat minor, Op. 31
  A. Cortot   in *JpV.* set *JAS 273*
  A. de Raco   **‡ ArgOd.LDC 514**
  (*Bach & Mozart*)
  Anon. Artist (in ‡ *Roy. 1549*)
  E. Malinin (*USSR. 022654/5*)
  ☆ A. Rubinstein (in ‡ *Vic.LRM 7015*: ♭ set *ERB 7015*)

No. 3, C sharp minor, Op. 39
  E. Silver   in ‡ *Var. 2052*
  L. Gousseau   ♭ *Plé.P 45150*
  (*Étude, Op. 25, No. 9 & Nocturne 8*)
  R. Tamarkina (*USSR. 20425/6: USSRM.D 00920*)
  ☆ G. Novães (in ‡ *EVox.PL 9070*)
  A. Jenner (in ‡ *Cum.CR 250*; in ‡ *Ply. 12-20*)
  B. Moiseiwitsch (in ‡ *BB.LBC 1038*: ♭ set *WBC 1038*)
  S. Barere (♭ *Rem.REP 2*; in ‡ *Cum.CR 280*)
  L. Godowsky (in ‡ *Roy. 1402*)[2]

SONATAS
No. 1, C minor, Op. 4
  ☆ R. Goldsand (‡ *Clc. 6231*)

No. 2, B flat minor, Op. 35
  A. Cortot   **‡ Vic.LHMV 18**
  (*Schumann*)   (also ‡ *JpV.LS 103* & *LS 2001*, d.c.)
  J. Katchen   **‡ D.LXT 5093**
  (*No. 3*)   (‡ *Lon.LL 1163*)
  V. Schiøler   **‡ G.ALP 1243**
  (*No. 3*)   (‡ *FALP 371*: *KALP 5*)
  A. Brailowsky (*No. 3*)   **‡ Vic.LM 1866**
  S. Fiorentino (*Beethoven*)   **‡ CA.LPA 1087**
  C. Chailley-Richez (*Franck*)[3]   **‡ D.FST 153640**
  Y. Nat   **‡ DFr. 84**
  (*Barcarolle & Fantaisie*)
  S. Niedzielski   **‡ Sel. 320.C.024**
  (*Études*)   (‡ *T.LE 6539*; West.*WL 5340*)

---

[1] Carnegie Hall recital, Feb. 1953. It is not completely certain that all the subsidiary nos. quoted are this version and not the o.v.
[2] From a player-pf. roll.
[3] This recording was announced, but may possibly not exist in this form. See note to Franck: *Prélude, Choral et fugue.*

No. 2, B flat minor, Op. 35 (*continued*)

R. Goldsand ♯ *MMS. 21*
(*Impromptu No. 4*) (♯ *ANix.MLPY 21*)

M. Schwalb (*No. 3*) ♯ **Roy. 1471**

☆ W. Malcuzynski ♯ *C.FCX/QCX 194*
(*No. 3*) (♯ *Angel. 35052*)
☆ V. Horowitz ♯ *G.ALP 1087*
(*Ballade, Nocturne; & Liszt*) (♯ *QALP 195*)
☆ A. Uninsky ♯ *Phi.A 00168L*
(*No. 3*) (♯ *Epic.LC 3056*)
☆ R. Casadesus (*Ballades*) ♯ *AmC.ML 4798*
☆ E. Kilenyi (♯ *Cum.CR 226*)

... 3rd movt., Marche funèbre, only
C. M. Savery (C.DDX 35)

— — ARR. ORCH.: Boston Prom.—Fiedler
(♭ *Vic.ERA 254; ItV.A72R 0060*)
— — ARR. BAND: Garde Républicaine—Borin (Pat.PDT 281)
— — ARR. ORGAN: C. Cronham (*Mjr. 5130*)

No. 3, B minor, Op. 58
J. Katchen ♯ **D.LXT 5093**
(*No. 2*) (♯ *Lon.LL 1163*)

N. Magaloff ♯ **D.LXT 5037**
(*Berceuse & Impromptus*) (♯ *Lon.LL 1189*)

V. Schiøler ♯ **G.ALP 1243**
(*No. 2*) (♯ *KALP 5: FALP 371*)

A. Brailowsky (*No. 2*) ♯ **Vic.LM 1866**

L. Lukas (*Beethoven*) ♯ **ML. 7050**

L. Hungerford ♯ **LH. 101/2**
(*Schubert, Brahms, etc*) (Pte.)

☆ A. Uninsky ♯ *Phi.A 00168L*
(*No. 2*) (♯ *Epic.LC 3056*)
☆ W. Malcuzynski ♯ *C.FCX/QCX 194*
(*No. 2*) (♯ *Angel. 35052*)
(2ss, ♯ *C.QC 5001: VC 802: WC 1005*)
☆ D. Lipatti ♯ *C.CX 1337*
(*Enesco: Sonata*)
(♯ *C.FCX 493 & ♯ AmC.ML 4721, d.c.*)
☆ S. Askenase (♯ *Pol. 16035*)
E. Kilenyi (♯ *Cum.CR 226*)
A. Rubinstein (in ♭ *DV. 26006*)

Tarantelle, A flat major, Op. 43
A. Cortot *G.DA 2071*
(*Valse No. 7*) (in ♯ *ALP 1197: QALP 10080: FALP 349*)

F. Ellegaard **Pol.HM 80068**
(*Mazurka No. 13*)

☆ J-M. Darré (*ArgPat.FC 0013*)

VALSES
COMPLETE RECORDINGS: **Nos. 1-15**
(including No. 15, E major, No Op. No. 1829)
G. Novães E. & AmVox.**PL 8170**
[Nos. 6, 7, 9, 13 only on ♭ *AmVox.VIP 45300*]

L. Rev[1] ♯ **Sel. 320.C.066**

COMPLETE RECORDINGS: **Nos. 1-14**
A. Rubinstein ♯ **G.ALP 1333**
(♯ *Vic.LM 1892; ItV.A12R 0168*)
[Nos. 2, 4, 5, 7, 8, 10, 13, 14 in ♭ *set ERB 1892*
Nos. 1, 6, 9, 11 on ♭ *ERA 204;* ♭ *FV.A 95214;*
♭ *ItV.A72R 0026*
Nos. 2, 4, 10, 13 on ♭ *ItV.A72R 0053;*
Nos. 5, 7, 8, 14 on ♭ *ItV.A72R 0054*]

A. Dorfmann ♯ **BB.LBC 1050**
(♭ *set WBC 1050*)
[Nos. 1, 3, 6, 7 on ♭ *ERAB 10; FV.A 85212*]

S. Petitgirard ♯ **MFr.MF 3002**

☆ D. Lipatti ♯ *C.CX 1032*
(♯ *FCX 492: VCX 531;* ♭ *AmC. set A 1085*)
[Nos. 1, 3, 6, 11 on ♭ *C.SEB 3506: SEBQ 130*]
[Nos. 2, 10, 12, 14 on ♭ *C.SEB 3508; Nos. 4, 5, 7, 9*
on ♭ *SEB 3509*]

☆ A. Brailowsky (♭ *BrzV.* 12-1198/1204, 14ss);
♯ *ItV.A12R* 0109; Nos. 1, 7, 9, 12 on ♭ *DV.* 26044;
Nos. 8, 11 14 on ♭ *Vic.ERA 255*)
R. Trouard (♯ *ArgOd.LDC 7903;* Nos. 4, 7, 9, 14 on
♭ *BSOAE 7501;* Nos. 4, 7, 9, 13 on ♭ *Od.7AOE 1010*)
L. Pennario (♯ *T.LCE 8172;* Nos. 1, 7, 8, 14
on ♭ *Cap.FAP 8262;* Nos. 4 & 11 on ♭ *Cap.FAP 8261*)
E. Kilenyi (♯ *Cum.CR* 227; with commentary by
S. Spaeth on ♯ *Rem.* 15; Nos. 1, 6, 7, 8, 9
on ♭ *Cum.ECR 39;* ♭ *Rem.REP 11*)

COLLECTIONS
Nos. 1, 2, 4, 5, 7-14 E. Freund ♯ Ply. 12-125
Nos. 1-4 & 6-8 L. Shankson in ♯ Roy. 1449
Nos. 2, 6, 7, 14 ☆ S. Askenase ♯ Pol. 17031
Nos. 3, 6, 7, 9, 13 P. Entremont V♯ MMS. 913
Nos. 3, 6, 7, 9, 11
☆ A. Cortot (♭ Vic.EHA 19; & excluding No. 3,
in ♯ G.ALP 1197: QALP 10080: FALP 349)
Nos. 7, 11, 14 ☆ L. Godowsky (in ♯ Roy. 1402)[2]
No. 9-11
B. Vitebsky (Nocturne No. 8) V♯ CA.MPO 5007
(3ss—Écossaises on SPO 9001/2)
Nos. 2, 4, 6 — ARR. ORCH. See Suite, Sec. IV, below
Nos. 1, 7, 9, 11 — ARR. ORCH. See Sylphides, IV, below

No. 1, E flat major, Op. 18 □
H. Czerny-Stefanska **U.H 24379**
(*Mazurka No. 13*)
T. Guseva (*USSR. 21018/9*)
Anon. Artist (in ♯ *Roy. 1549*)

No. 2, A flat major, Op. 34, No. 1
H. Czerny-Stefanska **Muza.X 2143**
(*Mazurkas 46 & 47*)
J. Flier (USSR. 07532)
Y. Muravlev (*USSR. 21380/1*)
☆ W. Backhaus (♭ *D 71063: VD 505,* d.c.: *DK 23351*)
— ARR. ORCH.
☆ Kostelanetz Orch. (♭ *C.SCDW 109: SCDQ 2008*)

No. 3, A minor, Op. 34, No. 2
V. Horowitz in ♯ **Vic. set LM 6014**
(♭ *set ERG 6014;* in ♯ *ItV.B12R 0064/5;* ♭ *ItV.A72R 0033*)
E. Silver in ♯ **Var. 2052**
☆ A. Brailowsky, from set (♭ *Vic.ERA 104*)

No. 4, F major, Op. 34, No. 3
J. Zak (*USSR. 20437*)

No. 5, A flat major, Op. 42 □
Liberace (in ♯ *AmC.ML 4900:* in ♯ *CL 6328;*
in ♯ *Phi.S 06609R*)
☆ A. Brailowsky, from set (♭ *Vic.ERA 224 & ERA 104;*
FV.A 95228)
A. Uninsky (♭ *Phi.A 400000E*)

No. 6, D flat major, Op. 64, No. 1 □
A. Cortot (n.v.) in JpV. **set JAS 269**
(in ♯ *LS 103*)
R. Spivak **ArgV. 66-6002**
(*Écossaises; & Liszt*)
☆ N. Magaloff ♭ **D. 71107**
(*Valse No. 8 & Polonaise No. 3*)
L. Miki (♭ *Rem.REP 74*)
Liberace (in ♯ *AmC.ML 4900*:
in ♯ *CL 6328;* in ♯ *Phi.S 06609R*)
☆ G. Novães (in ♯ *EVox.PL 7810*)
S. Askenase (in ♯ *Pol.* 19016)
J. Iturbi (♭ *Vic.ERA 194;* in ♯ *DV.T 16069;*
♭ *FV.A 95207*)
C. de Groot (in ♯ *Epic.LC 3037*)
E. Kilenyi (in ♯ *Ply.* 12-93)
L. Pennario (♭ *Cap.FAP 8205*)
— ARR. ORCH.
N. W. German Phil.—Schüchter
(in ♯ *Imp.ILP 114; G.QDLP 6026*)
☆ Hollywood Sym.—Newman (in ♯ *FMer.MLP 7052*)
A. Bernard Str. Orch. (♭ *Pat.ED 31*)

No. 7, C sharp minor, Op. 64, No. 2 □
V. Schiøler **G.DA 5281**
(*Étude, Op. 10-12*) (♭ *7RK 3*)
A. Cortot **G.DA 2071**
(*Tarantelle*) (See also COLLECTION, above)
S. Bianca **MSB. 78107**
(*Impromptu No. 4*)
D. Bar-Illan in ♯ **Kings.KLP 211**
(*Études; Debussy, Liszt, Ben-Haim*)
E. Burton in ♯ **CEd.CE 1026**

(*continued on next page*)

---

[1] Includes also "No. 16", A flat major and "No. 17", E flat major, 1827.
[2] From a player-pf. roll. It is stated in *Music & Musicians* that a recording of Chopin Valses labelled as by Godowsky is actually played by J. Abram. This one *may* be meant.

No. 7, C Sharp minor, Op. 64, No. 2 (*continued*)

F. Ellegaard   **Pol.HM 80071**
(*Polonaise No. 3*)

Liberace (in ♯ AmC.ML 4900; in ♯ *CL 6327*;
                in ♯ *Phi.S 06608R*)

☆ C. de Groot (in ♯ Epic.LC 3037)
J. Iturbi (♭ *Vic.ERA 194*; in ♯ *DV.T 16069*;
                     ♭ *FV.A 95207*)
S. Askenase (in ♯ *Pol.* 19016)
J. Therrien (in ♯ *MH. 33-111*)

— ARR. ORCH.
New Prom. Str.—Robertson (in ♯ *Lon.LB 581*)
Melachrino Str. Orch. (*G.B. 10207*; in ♯ *Vic.LPM 1003*)

No. 8, A flat major, Op. 64, No. 3
☆ N. Magaloff   ♭ *D. 71107*
(*Valse No. 6 & Polonaise No. 3*)
V. Sofronitzky (*USSR.* 13076)
☆ M. Sheyne (in ♯ *CID.UM* 6301)

No. 9, A flat major, Op. 69, No. 1 ☐
E. Burton   in ♯ **CEd.CE 1027**
R. Bakst   **Muza.X 1713**
(*Mazurka No. 51*)
V. Sofronitzky (*USSR.* 13077)
P. Sancan (♭ *FV.A 95001*)

— ARR. ORGAN : J. Perceval (ArgOd. 66012)

No. 10, B minor, Op. 69, No. 2
E. Burton   in ♯ **CEd.CE 1027**
☆ A. Brailowsky, from set (♭ *Vic.ERA 224*; ♭ *FV.A 95228*)

No. 11, G flat major, Op. 70, No. 1 ☐
M. Lympany   ♭ *Vic.EHA 13*
(*Impromptu 4; Albeniz, Granados*)
A. Cortot   ♭ *JpV.EP 3042*
(*Polonaise No. 6*) [said to be local recording]
L. Hungerford   in ♯ **LH. 101/2**
                             (Pte.)

No. 12, F minor, Op. 70, No. 2
L. Hungerford   in ♯ **LH. 101/2**
                             (Pte.)
V. Sofronitzky (*USSR.* 18368)
☆ A. Cortot (♭ *Vic.EHA 12*)

No. 14, E minor, No Op. No.
P. Cavazzini   in ♯ *Arp.ARC 4*
(*Polonaise 3, Scherzo 1; & D. Scarlatti*)
R. Bergroth   **D.SD 5085**
(*Beethoven: Für Elise*)
M. Schwalb   in ♯ **Roy. 1474**

No. 15, E major, No Op. No. 1829
B. Vitebsky   **V♯ *CA.MPO 5008***
(*Écossaises, Fugue, Marche funèbre*)

VARIATIONS ON:
A German Theme 1824
B. Vitebsky   **V♯ *CA.MPO 5015***
(*Polonaise No. 5*)
☆ R. Goldsand (♯ Clc. 6231)

Je vends des scapulaires, Op. 12 (Hérold)
T. Nikolayeva   **USSRM.D 400**
(*Rachmaninoff*)
☆ R. Goldsand (♯ Clc. 6190)

Là ci darem, Op. 2 pf., or pf. & orch.
O Frugoni & Vienna Pro Musica—Swarowsky
                 ♯ **AmVox.PL 9030**
(*Andante spianato & Polonaise, Krakowiak; & Liszt*)
E. Beckmann-Shcherbina & Radio Sym.
  —Samosud   ♯ **USSR.D 01196**
(*Schumann*)
☆ R. Goldsand (♯ Clc. 6231)

II. CONCERTED WORKS
A. CHAMBER MUSIC

Introduction & Polonaise, C major, Op. 3 vlc. & pf.
M. Rostropovich & pf.   **USSRM.D 167**
(*Rachmaninoff: Oriental Dance*)

Sonata, G minor, Op. 65 vlc. & pf.
☆ D. Markevitch & A. Collard (♯ *Pol. 540004*)

Trio, G minor, Op. 8 pf., vln. & vlc.
Bolzano Trio   ♯ **E. & AmVox.PL 8480**
(*Schumann*)

B. PF. & ORCHESTRAL
[*See also:* Andante Spianato & Polonaise; Variations on
Là ci darem . . . *supra.*]

CONCERTOS
No. 1, E minor, Op. 11
F. Gulda & L.P.O.—Boult[1]   ♯ **D.LXT 2925**
                           (♯ *Lon.LL* 1001)
P. Badura-Skoda & Vienna State Op.
  —Rodzinski   ♯ **Nix.WLP 5308**
(*No. 2*)   (♯ West.WL 5308; 2ss, ♯ *Sel. 270.CW.070*)
A. Rubinstein & Los Angeles Phil.—Wallenstein
                 ♯ **G.ALP 1250**
(♯ Vic.LM 1810: ♭ set *ERC 1810*; ♯ ItV.A12R 0117;
                          FV.A 630216)
A. Uninsky & Residentie—Otterloo
                 ♯ *Phi.A 00651R*
                       (♯ Epic.LC 3012)
S. François & Paris Cons.—Tzipine ♯ **C.CX 1238**
(*Liszt*)   (♯ FCX 341; ♯ Angel. 35168)
M. Horszowski & Vienna State Phil.
  —Swarowsky   ♯ **E. & AmVox.PL 7870**
(*Impromptus*)
G. Sandor & Philadelphia—Ormandy
                 ♯ **AmC.ML 4651**
B. Musulin & South German Radio—Kray
                 ♯ **Nix.PLP 574**
(*No. 2*)   (♯ Per.SPL 574; Cpt.MC 20071)
H. Neuhaus & Moscow Radio—Gauk
           (USSR. 022732/41: ♭ *D* 01103/4)
☆ E. Kilenyi & Minneapolis Sym.—Mitropoulos
                     (♯ AmC.RL 3028)
N. Mewton-Wood & Netherlands Phil.—Goehr
         (♯ Copa.CLP 4000; Clc. 6214; ♯ *MMS. 35*)
A. Brailowsky & Vic. Sym.—Steinberg (♯ G.VALP 527)
E. Kilenyi & Austrian Sym.—Prohaska (♯ Cum.CR 312)

No. 2, F minor, Op. 21
P. Badura-Skoda & Vienna State Op.
  —Rodzinski   ♯ **Nix.WLP 5308**
(*No. 1*)   (2ss, ♯ *Sel. 270.CW.071*)   (♯ West.WL 5308)
A. Brailowsky & Boston Sym.—Münch
                 ♯ **G.ALP 1321**
(*Saint-Saëns*)
         (♯ Vic.LM 1871: ♭ set *ERB 51*; ♯ FV.A 630242)
B. Musulin & South German Radio—Kray
                 ♯ **Nix.PLP 574**
(*No. 1*)   (♯ Per.SPL 574; Cpt.MC 20071)
A. Rubinstein & Vic. Sym.—Steinberg[2]
                 ♯ **G.FALP 254**
                 (♯ ItV.A12R 0082)
M. Long & Paris Cons.—Cluytens ♯ **C.FCX 193**
B. Davidovich & Moscow Youth Sym.—Kondrashin
                 ♯ *USSR.D 1087/8*
☆ W. Malcuzynski & Philharmonia—Kletzki
                 ♯ **C.CX 1066**
(*Fantaisie*) (♯ FCX 123: QCX 10034: VCX 530;
                        Angel. 35030)
☆ S. Askenase & Berlin Phil.—Lehmann
                 ♯ **HP.DGM 18040**
☆ N. Mewton-Wood & Zürich Radio—Goehr
                 (♯ Clc. 11008; ANix.MLPY 4)
G. Novães & Vienna Sym.—Klemperer
         (♯ EVox.PL 7100; Pan.XPV 1019)
M. Slezarieva & F.O.K. Sym.—Smetáček
                 (♯ Sup.LPV 82)

Krakowiak (Rondo), Op. 14
O. Frugoni & Vienna Pro Musica—Swarowsky
                 ♯ **AmVox.PL 9030**
(*Andante Spianato, Variations; & Liszt*)
S. Fiorentino & Pasdeloup—Russell
(*below*)   ♯ **CA.LPA 1092**

---

[1] Orchestrated by Balakirev.
[2] Thus the French and Swiss catalogues; but it may well be ☆ of N.B.C.—Steinberg (see WERM). This is confirmed by
the Italian entry.

Grande Fantaisie on Polish Airs, A major, Op. 13
(1828)
H. Kann & Netherlands Phil.—Ackermann
(*Dvořák*)　　　　　　　　　　‡ **CHS.H 6**
S. Fiorentino & Pasdeloup—Russell
　　　　　　　　　　‡ **CA.LPA 1092**
(*Krakowiak, Allegro de concert & Rondo, Op. 16*)

III. SONGS

(17) Polish Songs, Op. 74
COMPLETE RECORDING
D. Conrad (Bs), H. Jackson (pf.)
　　　　　　　　　‡ **AmVox.PL 8310**
☆ M. Kurenko (S), R. Hufstader (pf.)　‡ **CA.LPA 1040**

— ARR. PF.　Liszt: *q.v.*

No. 16, Lithuanian Song
I. B. Lucca (S, *Ital*) & Orch.　♭ *Dur.AI 6021*
(*Schubert: Ständchen*)　　　　(& in ‡ *MSE 6*)

IV. MISCELLANEOUS

Suite de danses (ARR. Messager & Vidal)
Polonaise No. 3　(*Militaire*)
Nocturnes Nos. 13, 4
Prelude No. 16
Mazurkas Nos. 34, 14, 23
Valses, Nos. 2, 6, 4

　　Champs-Élysées Th.—Bonneau ‡ *Sel. 270.C.073*

(Les) SYLPHIDES
USUAL CONTENTS: Prelude No. 7
　　　　　　　　Nocturne No. 10
　　　　　　　　Mazurka Nos. 44, 23
　　　　　　　　Valses, Nos. 11, 9, 7, 1 — ARR. ORCH.

　　Covent Garden—Irving[1]　　‡ **G.CLP 1013**
　　(*Schumann*)　　　(‡ QCLP 12007: FELP 118)
　　(*Arnold on* ‡ BB.LBC 1078)　(4ss, ♭ *G.ERL 1049/50*)

　　Philadelphia—Ormandy[2]　‡ **EPhi.NBL 5019**
　　(*Offenbach*) (‡ AmC.CL 741: o.n. ML 4895: ♭ *set A 1919*)
　　　　　　　　　　　(2ss, ‡ *Phi.S 06607R*)

　　Ballet Theatre—Levine[3]　**DCap.CCL 7518**
　　(2ss)　　(‡ T.LCB 8194: ♭ Cap.L 8194: ♭ FAP 8199/200)
　　(*Tchaikovsky on* ‡ Cap.P 8193)

　　☆ N.Y.P.S.O.—Kurtz[2]　　　‡ **C.SX 1011**
　　　(*Villa-Lobos*)　　　　(♭ AmC. set A 874)
　　　[excerpts in ♭ AmC.A 1768]
　　☆ Paris Cons.—Désormière　　‡ **D.LXT 2868**
　　　(*Ibert*)　　　　　　　(‡ Lon.LL 884)

　　Anon. Orchs. (‡ ACC.MP 16 & MTW. 27)

　　☆ Boston Prom.—Fiedler[4] (‡ ItV.A12R 0107;
　　　　　　　　　　　　　　　　　DV.T 16071)
　　　[Mazurka 23, Nocturne 10 & Valse 1 only on
　　　‡ Vic.LM 1752: ♭ set WDM 1752: & in
　　　‡ Vic.LM 9027; Mazurka 23, Prelude 7 & Valse 1
　　　on ♭ Vic.ERA 82]

　　... Prelude No. 7 & Valse No. 1 only
　　　☆ Covent Garden—Braithwaite (in ‡ P.PMC 1008)

　　... Mazurka No. 23 only
　　　Philharmonia—Markevitch　　‡ **C.CX 1198**
　　　(*Tchaikovsky, D. Scarlatti, Falla*)　　(‡ FCX 358)
　　　　　　　　　　　(‡ Angel. 35152 in set 3518)

　　... Prelude 7, Valses 1 & 11, Mazurka 44
　　　☆ Orch.—Stokowski (in ‡ G.ALP 1133: FALP 277;
　　　　in ‡ Vic.LRM 7022: ♭ set ERB 7022: & excluding
　　　　Valse No. 1, on ‡ Vic.LRY 8000: ♭ set WRY 8000)

　　... Prelude 7, Mazurka 23, Nocturne 10, Valses 1 & 11
　　　☆ L.P.O.—Sargent (♭ BB.ERAB 5)

　　... Selection　— ARR.　Douglas
　　　☆ L.P.O.—Goehr (in ‡ AmC.RL 3056)

Une Journée de Chopin à Paris en 1840
　　　　(Dramatic Reconstruction with music)
Music includes (*inter alia*):
Étude, C minor, Op. 10, No. 12
Prelude No. 25, C sharp minor, Op. 45
Prelude No. 1, C major, Op. 28, No. 1
Nocturne No. 7, C sharp minor, Op. 27, No. 1
Mazurka No. 12, A flat, Op. 17, No. 3
(3) Écossaises, Op. 72, No. 3
Ballade No. 2, F major, Op. 38
　　Jacque-Dupont (pf.)
Valse No. 1, E flat, Op. 18
　　R. Munro Orch.　　　　　　‡ **D.FMT 163077**

Chopin: his life, his times, his music
　　D. Randolph (narr.)　　　　　　‡ **Per.PCS 4**

(The) Story & Music of Chopin
　　Narrator & Orch.　(4ss)　　　　*AmC. set J 207*

CHUECA Y DURAN, Federico
(1846-1908)

ZARZUELAS, etc. (abridged listings only)
(Marked V written in collaboration with VALVERDE)

AGUA, AZUCARILLOS Y AGUARDIENTE
　　"Pasillo veraniego"　1 Act　1897
A. M. Iriarte, T. Rosado, T. Berganza, etc.; Madrid Cho.
　& Orch.—Argenta　　　　　　‡ *LI.W 91016*
　　　　　　　　　(‡ Ambra.MC 25000; Mont.FM 7)
M. D. Ripollés, I. Rivadeneyra, etc.; Madrid Cho. &
　Orch.—Moreno Torroba　　　　‡ *Phi.N 00995R*
(*below*)

Orch. excerpts (as Ballet Suite: "Madrid, 1890")
J. Greco Ballet & Madrid Theatre—Machado
　　　　　　　　　　in ‡ **B.AXTL 1074**
　　　　　　　(‡ AmD.DL 9757; SpC.CCL 35002)

Pasacalle
　　Madrid Theatre Orch.—Moreno Torroba
　　　　　　　　　　　in ‡ **B.AXTL 1077**
　　　　　　　　　　　(‡ AmD.DL 9735)

Prelude
　　Sym.—Ferrer (in ‡ Reg.LC 1002: ♭ SEDL 108)

(La) ALEGRÍA DE LA HUERTA　1 Act　1900
T. Rosado, C. Munguía, T. Berganza, Madrid Cho. &
　Sym.—Argenta　　　　　　　　‡ *LI.W 91039*
　　　　　　　　　　　(‡ Ambra.MC 25006)
L. Berchman, V. Simon, E. Rincon, R. Alonso, etc.;
　Madrid Cho. & Orch.　　　　　‡ *Mont.FM 35*
▽ P. Vidal, J. Torró, etc. (G.AB 759/62 & AF 375/8)

Jota
　　Madrid Theatre Orch.—Moreno Torroba
　　　　　　　　　　in B.AXTL 1078
　　　　　　　(‡ SpC.CCLP 34003; AmD.DL 9736)

Prelude
　　Madrid Cha. Orch.—Navarro　in ‡ **Mont.FM 39**

(EL) AÑO PASADO POR AGUA　(V)　1889
Vocal Excerpts　▽ (SpC.A 638, 778, etc.)

(EL) CABALLERO DE GRACIA　(V)
Unspec. excerpt
　　Madrid Theatre Orch.—Moreno Torroba
　　　　　　　　　　in ‡ **AmD.DL 9763**

CÁDIZ　(V)　2 Acts　1886
Sevillanas　— ARR. CASTANETS & ORCH.
J. J. Andrade, etc. (in ‡ Od.MODL 1001)

March　▽ Madrid Cho. & Orch. (SpC.A 1448)

(La) GRAN VIA　(V)　1 Act　1886
I. Rivadeneyra (A), L. Rodrigo (B), Ramaye (T), Madrid
　Cha. Cho. & Orch.—Estela　　　‡ *Mont.FM 12*
A. M. Iriarte, T. Rosado, M. Ausensi, etc.; Cho. &
　Cha.—Argenta　　　　　　　‡ *LI.W 91008*
(*Excerpts*, Ambra.ALG 23000)　(‡ Ambra.MC 25002)
(*Overture* only, in ‡ LI.TW 91004; Ambra.MCC 30009:
　　　　　　　　　　　　　　　　MCCP 29001)
M. D. Ripollés, I. Rivadeneyra, M. Serra, Madrid Zarzuela
　Orch.—Moreno Torroba　　　　‡ *Phi.N 00995R*
(*above*)
▽ Soloists, Cho. & Orch.—Capdevila　*ArgOd. 193665/7*

Overture
　　Madrid Cha. Orch.—Navarro　in ‡ **Mont.FM 52**

CIAJA, Azzolino Bernardino della
(1671-1755)

SONATA, G major, Op. 4 hpsi.　1727
... 2nd & 3rd movts., Toccata & Canzone
— — ARR. VLC. & PF. Silva
　　M. Amfiteatrof & O. P. Santoliquido
　　(*Handel & Beethoven*)　　　‡ **ItV.A12R 0162**

... Toccata, G major
　　R. Gerlin　　　　　in ‡ **LOL.OL 50043**
　　(† *Clavecinistes Italiens*)　　　(‡ OL.LD 67)

---

[1] ARR. Douglas　　　　[2] ARR. Gretchaninoff.
[3] ARR. Britten (Contents: Mazurkas 23 and 44, Nocturne 10, Prelude 7, Waltzes, 1, 7, 11).　　[4] ARR. Anderson and Bodge.

117

CICONIA, Johannes (fl. 1400)
SEE: † HISTORY OF MUSIC IN SOUND (25)

CIKKER, Ján (b. 1911)

Concertino, pf. & orch., Op. 20 1942
R. Macudzinski & Bratislava Radio—Cikker
(*Suk*)   ♯ **U. 5183G**

CILEA, Francesco (1866-1950)

OPERAS in Italian
ADRIANA LECOUVREUR   4 Acts   1902

ACT I
Io sono l'umile ancella   S
M. M. Callas   in ♯ **C.CX 1231**
(*below; Chénier, La Wally, etc.*)
       (♯ QCX 10129; Angel. 35233)
M. C. Verna   in ♯ **Cet.LPC 55005**
(*Ernani, Andrea Chénier, etc.*)
M. Benetti   **Cet.PE 211**
(*Forza—Pace, pace, mio Dio*)

Ecco il monologo   B
A. Poli   **Cet.PE 199**
(*Falstaff—È sogno*)

La dolcissima effigie   T [& S]
M. del Monaco   **G.DA 11349**
(*below*) (♭ 7EB 6006: 7ERF 137: 7ERQ 120:
       in ♯ QBLP 5021: FBLP 1050)
☆ G. Prandelli [& C. Gavazzi] from set (in ♯ CCet.A 50178)
A. Pertile (in ♯ Ete. 710)

ACT II
L'anima ho stanca   T
M. del Monaco   **G.DA 11349**
(*above*) (♭ 7EB 6006: 7ERF 137: 7ERQ 120:
       in ♯ QLBP 5021: FBLP 1050)
☆ A. Pertile (in ♯ Ete.710)
◨ F. de Lucia (in ♯ CEd. set 7002*)

Intermezzo   orch.
☆ Italian Radio—Simonetti, from set (in ♯ CCet.A 50159)

ACT IV
No più nobile   T
◨ E. Caruso & pf. (*SBDH.P 8**)

Poveri fiori   S
M. M. Callas   in ♯ **C.CX 1231**
(*above*)   (♯ QCX 10129; Angel. 35233)
J. Hammond   in ♯ **G.ALP 1076**
(*Bruch, Massenet, Mozart, etc.*)
☆ L. Albanese (in ♯ Vic.LM 1839; ♯ FV.A 630253)

(L') ARLESIANA   3 Acts   1897
COMPLETE RECORDING

Rosa Mamai	... ...	P. Tassinari (M-S)
Federico	... ...	F. Tagliavini (T)
Vivetta	... ...	G. Galli (S)
Baldassarre	... ...	P. Silveri (B)
Metifio	... ...	B. Carmassi (Bs)
Marco	... ...	A. Zerbini (Bs)
L'innocente	... ...	L. di Lelio (S)

& Ital. Radio Cho. & Orch.—Basile
(4ss)   ♯ **Cet. set 1255**

È la solita storia   T   (Act II)
N. Gedda   in ♯ **C.CX 1130**
(*Favorita, Martha, etc.*)   (♯ FCX 302; Angel. 35096)
☆ J. Björling (♭ Vic.ERA 134)
G. di Stefano (♭ G.7RQ 3001: 7RW 130)
F. Tagliavini (o.v.) (in ♯ CCet.A 50155)
B. Gigli (in ♯ Vic.LCT 1138: ♭ ERAT 12:
         ♯ G.FJLP 5039)
R. Crooks (in ♯ Cam.CAL 148)

Esser madre è un inferno   S
☆ E. Stignani (M-S) (in ♯ C.QC 5024)
GLORIA   3 Acts   1907
Pur dolente son io
L. Francardi   **Cet.AT 0323**
(*Mascagni: Lodoletta, aria*)

CIMAROSA, Domenico (1749-1801)

Concerto, G major   2 fls. & orch.   1793
J-P. Rampal, R. Hériché & Lamoureux Cha.
Orch.—Colombo   ♯ **LOL.OL 50008**
(*Barsanti: Concerti grossi*)   (♯ OL.LD 61)
A. Tassinari, P. Esposito, & A. Scarlatti Orch.
—Caracciolo[1]   ♯ **C.CX 1171**
(*A. Scarlatti, Paisiello*)   (♯ QCX 10036; Angel. 35141)
J-P. Rampal, P. Pierlot (ob.) & Saar Cha.
—Ristenpart[2]   V♯ **DFr.EX 17038**

OPERAS
(Il) MAESTRO DI CAPELLA[3]
Intermezzo, 1 Act   Bs. & orch.
C. Maugeri & Milan Cha.—Gerelli
     ♯ **E. & AmVox.PL 8450**
(*Matrimonio Segreto, excpts.*)
F. Corena & Milan Afternoon Concerts
—Arnaducci (2ss)   ♯ **D.LW 5112**
       (♯ Lon.LD 9118 & in LL 1334)
G. Taddei & Italian Radio Orch—Fighera
     ♯ **Cet.N 45001**
M. Cortis & Paris Inst. Ens.—Froment
     ♯ **C.FCX 386**
(*Bassani, A. Scarlatti*)

(Il) MATRIMONIO SEGRETO   2 Acts   1792
Overture & Excerpts:
ACT I: Cara, non dubitar
        Io ti lascio
        Perdonate, signor mio
ACT II: Or sappi; Pria che spunti
E. Ribetti (S), A. Blaffard (T), & Milan Cha.
Orch.—Gerelli   ♯ **E. & AmVox.PL 8450**
(*Il Maestro di Capella*)

Overture
Covent Garden—Braithwaite   ♯ **MGM.E 3013**
(*Malipiero & Respighi*)
French Nat. Radio—Tzipine   ♯ **C.FC 1040**
(*Auber & Boïeldieu*)
☆ Florence Festival—Serafin (G.DB 4326)
Pria che spunti in ciel l'aurora   T (Act II)
L. Francardi   **Cet.PE 185**
(*Favorita—Spirto gentil*)

SONATAS, hpsi, Nos. 23, 24, 29, 31
— ARR. OBOE & STR.   Benjamin—"*Concerto*"
G. Gallesi & Naples Scarlatti Orch.
—Caracciolo   ♯ **C.CX 1277**
(*Tartini & Lully*)   (♯ Angel. 35255)
(*Tartini & Vivaldi on ♯ C.QCX 10138*)
C. Maisonneuve & Inst. Ens.—Froment
     ♯ **CND. 1003**
(*Mozart, Vivaldi*)
H. Schneider & Saar Cha.—Ristenpart
     V♯ **DFr.EX 17013**
☆ L. Goossens & Liverpool Phil.—Sargent
     ♯ **AmC.ML 4782**
   (*Bach, Handel, Marcello*)
☆ P. Pierlot & Paris Cha.—Duvauchelle
   (*Vivaldi*)   ♯ **Lum.LD 2-401**
☆ M. Miller & Little Sym.—Saidenberg
     (♭ FMer. 14503; ♭ Mer.EP 1-5005)

CIPRIANO: SEE: RORE, Cyprien de

---

[1] Ed. Cece.   [2] Labelled *Sinfonia concertante*.   [3] Not an opera, but an *Aria buffa*, ed. Zanon.

CIRRI, Giovanni Battista (1740-d. ?)

Concerto, A minor   vlc., fl., str.   (MS., Bologna)
☆ Virtuosi di Roma—Fasano   ‡ **B.AXTL 1023**
(*Albinoni, Pergolesi, etc.*) (‡ D.UAT 273581;
                              Fnt.LP 3003)

CITKOWITZ, Israel (b. 1909)

(3) Songs from "Chamber Music"   (Joyce)   1930
1. Strings in the earth and air
2. Donkey—Carney
3. Bid Adieu
    S. Carter (S), B. Weiser (pf.)   ‡ **NE. 2**
    (*Chanler, Smith, Flanagan*)

CLARKE, Jeremiah (1673/4-1707)

(The) Duke of Marlborough's March
    Inst. Ens. (in *G.B 10660*)

(The) Prince of Denmark's March[1]   hpsi.
    T. Dart   in ‡ **LOL.OL 50075**
    († *Masters of Early English Keyboard Music*)

— ARR. TPT. [ORG.] & ORCH. H. J. Wood & others
    S. Krauss & Philadelphia—Ormandy
    (arr. Ormandy)   in ‡ **AmC.ML 4629**
    A. Marchal & Belgian Radio Cha.—Doneux
    (*Haydn, Grétry*)   ‡ **Mae.OA 20003**
    ☆ H. Mortimer, R. Foort & London Brass Ens.—Weldon
       (♭ *C.SCD 2005: SCDQ 2002: SCV 1004*)
       H. Mortimer, H. Croudson & Massed Bands
       —F. Mortimer (♭ *C.SEG 7610*)
       Hollywood Bowl—Stokowski[2] (in ‡ *Cam.CAL 153*)

— ARR. ORGAN SOLO[3]
    N. Coke-Jephcott   in ‡ **ASK. 8**
    (*Bach, Vierne, etc.*) [Org. of Cath. of St. John the Divine, N.Y.]

— ARR. BAND
    Massed Bands, Searchlight Tattoo
                in ‡ **G.DLP 1050**

CLAUDE le Jeune (c. 1523-1600)

CHANSONS
Hélas, mon Dieu (*Meslanges* II, 1612)
Revecy venir du printans (*Le Printemps*, I)
Tu ne l'entends pas, c'est latin (*Meslanges* I, 1607)
    Vocal & Inst. Ens.—Boulanger ‡ **B.AXTL 1048**
    († *French Renaissance Music*) (‡ *D.FAT 263102*;
                         AmD.DL 9629)
Qu'est devenu ce bel œil?
Voicy du gay printems (*Le Printemps*, I)
    Paris Vocal Ens.—Jouve   in **V**‡ *Sel.LLA 1079*
    († *French Madrigals*)
Quand la terre (*Octonaires . . .* 1608)
Le chant de l'alouette (Or sus) (*Le Printemps*, I)
                      (after Jannequin)
    R. Blanchard Ensemble   ‡ *Phi.N 00994R*
    († *French Chansons*)
Rossignol mon mignon (*Meslanges* I)
Fière cruelle
Prince, la France te veut
    Vocal Ens.—F. Lamy   ‡ **LOL.OL 50027**
    († *Parisian Songs*)   (‡ *OL.LD 76*)

SACRED MUSIC
Psalm 35
    Dijon Cathedral Cho.—Samson   ‡ **SM 33-05**
    († *Polyphonie sacrée*)

Psalms 42 & 69
    ☆ Vocal Ens.—Expert (in † ‡ *HS.AS 6*)

Psalm 138
    Rennes Cath. Cho.—Orhant   ‡ **SM. 33-23**
    (*A. Gabrieli, Viadana, etc.*)

Te Deum laudamus   (*Psaumes mesurés* I)
    Paris Trad. Singers—M. Honegger
                     † ‡ **AS. 3006LD**
                     (‡ HS.AS 41)

CLEMENS NON PAPA (c. 1500-1556)

(Jacques Clément)

SEE: † AIRS À BOIRE
       † ANTHOLOGIE SONORE
       † FLEMISH CHORAL MUSIC
       † FRENCH CHANSONS
       † MADRIGALS & MOTETS
       † MUSICIENS DE LA COUR DE BOURGOGNE

CLEMENTI, Muzio (1752-1832)

Concerto, pf. & orch., C major
    C. Bussotti & Italian Cha.—Jenkins[4]
                     ‡ **HS.HSL 138**
    (*Brunetti*)   (in set HSL-N)

GRADUS AD PARNASSUM   pf.   1817
Études, Nos. 12, 18, 20, 21
    ☆ M. Schwalb   ‡ **Esq.TW 14-004**
    (*Cramer & Czerny*)

SONATAS   pf. solo
COLLECTION

B minor, Op. 40, No. 2
E flat major, Op. 12, No. 4
G minor, Op. 50, No. 2   (*Didone abbandonata*)
G major, Op. 25, No. 2
    V. Franceschi   ‡ **West.WN 18091**

F minor, Op. 14, No. 3
F sharp minor, Op. 26, No. 2
G major, Op. 34, No. 2
    V. Horowitz   ‡ **Vic.LM 1902**

D major, Op. 26, No. 3
E flat major, Op. 24, No. 3
... 2nd movt., Arietta con variazioni, only
    J. Newmark   (forte-pf.)   ‡ *Hall.RS 4*
    (*C. P. E. Bach, Haydn*)

F sharp minor, Op. 26, No. 2
    L. Bertolini   (*below*)   ‡ *Dur.MSE 5*

B minor, Op. 40, No. 2
    ☆ A. Balsam   ‡ **Nix.CLP 1311**
    (*Hummel*)   (& n.n., ‡ **CHS.CHS 1241**)

B flat major, Op. 47, No. 2
... Rondo
    ☆ V. Horowitz   ♭ *G.7RF 256*
    (*Mozart: Rondo alla turca*)   (♭ 7RQ 256)

SONATINAS   pf.

C major, Op. 36, No. 1
G major, Op. 36, No. 2
F major, Op. 36, No. 4
D major, Op. 36, No. 6
    L. Kraus   (*Kuhlau*)   ‡ **Edu.EP 3003**

F major, Op. 36, No. 4
G major, Op. 36, No. 5
D major, Op. 36, No. 6
    L. Bertolini   (*below*)   ‡ *Dur.MSE 4*

C major, Op. 36, No. 3
D major, Op. 37, No. 2
    P. Zeitlin   ‡ *Opus. 6005*
    (*Diabelli, Dussek, Kuhlau*)
    [with accompanying *Matching Music Book*, pub. Marks, N.Y.]

---

[1] From *Ayres for the harpsichord . . .* 1700; often attributed to Purcell as *Trumpet Voluntary*.
[2] ARR. Stokowski.
[3] The solo Tpt. stop and the accompaniment recorded separately and subsequently amalgamated.
[4] From MS. copy in library of *Gesellschaft der Musikfreunde*, Vienna. The pf. Sonata Op. 36, No. 3, is stated to be taken from the pf. part of this concerto. Cadenza in first movement is original; in the second movement by N. Jenkins.

Symphony, D major, Op. 18, No. 2
Virtuosi di Roma—Fasano ♯ *G.BLP 1041*
(*Corelli*) (♯ *QBLP 5024: FBLP 1053*)
(*Corelli & Vivaldi, on* ♯ *Vic.LHMV 2*)

TRIOS, pf., vln., vlc.
COLLECTION
No. 1, D major
No. 2, G major
No. 3, C major
No. 6, C major ("La Chasse") (pf. version D major, Op. 17)
Op. 32, No. 1, F major
Op. 32, No. 2, D major
Bolzano Trio ♯ **Phi.A 00245L**

WALTZES, No Op. No. pf.
C major (*Allegro*)
A major (*Andantino*)
C major (*del Glissé*)
(said to be from collection published 1824, Ricordi)
M. T. Garatti ♯ *C.QS 6023*
(*A. & D. Scarlatti*)

Nos. 1 & 2, F major
No. 3, G major
No. 4, C major
(said to be from collection pub. 1875, Ricordi)
L. Bertolini ♯ *Dur.MSE 5*
(*Sonata*)
(*Sonatinas, on* ♯ *Dur.MSE 4*)

CLÉRAMBAULT, Louis Nicolas
(1676-1749)

SUITES, Clavier
C major
(Prelude; Allemande; Courante; Sarabandes I & II;
Gavotte; Gigue; Menuet I; Menuet en Rondeau II)
C minor
(Prelude; Allemande; Courante; Sarabande; Gigue)
M. Charbonnier (hpsi.) ♯ **Phi.A 00292L**
(*Marchand*)

SUITES, Organ
No. 1, D minor ('du premier ton')
1. Grand plein jeu 2. Fugue 3. Duo
4. Trio 5. Basse et dessus de trompette
6. Récits de cromorne et de cornet
7. Dialogue sur les grands jeux
No. 2, G minor ('du deuxième ton')
1. Plein jeu 2. Duo 3. Trio
4. Basse de cromorne 5. Flûtes 6. Récit de nazard
7. Caprice sur les grands jeux
COMPLETE RECORDING
M-C. Alain ♯ **DFr. 158**
(*L. Couperin*) [St. Merry org., Paris]

Suite No. 1 . . . Nos. 5 & 7 only
C. Watters in ♯ **CEd. set 1008**
(† *French Baroque Organ Music*)

O mysterium ineffabile motet
☆ C. Maurane (B) & str. orch.—Challan (♭ *Pat.ED 15*)

COBBOLD, William (1560-1639)
SEE: † TRIUMPHS OF ORIANA

COLEMAN, Ellen (b. 1884)
COLLECTIONS
Caprice 1937
Romance 1954
Scherzo 1954
Pastoral Sonata, A major 1945
... 3rd movt., In a cottage, only
Happy Landscape 1953
N. Marriner (vln.) & E. Brook (pf.)
Romances: D minor; E major 1953
The Shepherd & his Reed (from *3 pieces*, orig. hpsi.) 1938
Legend (after Coleridge) 1954
Waltz (from *Pictures of the Mind*) 1939
Caprice 1954
On the road to Damascus (from *36 pieces*) 1953-4
Blow, blow thou winter wind 1954
E. Brook (pf.) ♯ **Her.RPL 607**

SONGS: The Wakeful Nightingale (Campbell) 1944
High among the lonely hills (Kingsley) 1939
The Water lily (Nichols) 1936
Rondel (Winder) 1955
Infant Joy (Blake) 1945)
Über allen Gipfeln (Goethe) revised 1936
We'll go no more to the wood (McEwan) 1943
La joie de rêver (Gerardy) 1935
Piano Sonata No. 5 1954-5
H. Mott (S), E. Brook (pf.) ♯ **Her.HLV 102**
Sonata, vlc. & pf.
▽ J. Serres & A. Leyvastre (4ss) **G.L 1051/2**
NOTE: Some other pte. recordings of songs & pf. pieces
also exist.

COMPÈRE, Loyset (c. 1455-1518)
SEE: † HISTORY OF MUSIC IN SOUND (31)
† ANTHOLOGIE SONORE
† POLYPHONIE SACRÉE
† MUSICIENS DE LA COUR DE BOURGOGNE
† FRENCH CHANSONS

CONUS, Julius Edwardovich (1869-1912)
Concerto, E minor, Op. 1 vln. & orch.
J. Heifetz & Vic. Sym.—I. Solomon
♯ *G.BLP 1072*
(*Chausson*) (♯ *FV.A 330202; Vic.LM 7017*)

CONVERSE, Frederick Shepherd
(1871-1940)
(The) Mystic Trumpeter, Op. 19
Orch. Fantasy 1903-4
A.R.S. Sym.—Schoenherr ♯ **ARS. 29**
(*Chadwick*)

CONVERSI, Girolamo (fl.1570-1584)
Sola, soletta
Youth Academy Cho.—Asmussen *Felix.F 84*
(*Hassler & Purcell*)

COOPER, W. Gaze
Concerto, pf. & orch. Op. 71 1953
J. Hatto & London Classical—Dennington
V♯ *CA.MPO 5034*

COPERARIO, Giovanni (1575-1626)
(COOPER, John)
SEE: † HISTORY OF MUSIC IN SOUND (41)

COPLAND, Aaron (b. 1900)
Appalachian Spring Ballet Suite 1944
Nat. Sym. (Washington)—Mitchell
♯ **Nix.WLP 5286**
(*below*) (♯ *West.WL 5286*)
Vienna State Op.—Litschauer ♯ **Van.VRS 439**
(*El Salon Mexico*)
A.R.S. Orch.—Hendl ♯ **ARS. 26**
(*Barber*) ·
Berlin Radio—Rother ♯ **Ura. 7092**
(*Piston*)
Hastings Sym.—Bath ♯ *Allo. 4056*
Berlin Sym.—Rubahn ♯ **Roy. 1513**
(*below*)
☆ Boston Sym.—Koussevitzky ♯ **Vic.LCT 1134**
(*El Salon Mexico*)
... Simple gifts (Variations)
Hamburg Philharmonia—H-J. Walther
MSB. 78152
(*Gardiner: Shepherd Fennel's Dance*)

♯ = Long-playing, 33⅓ r.p.m. ♭ = 45 r.p.m. ♮ = Auto. couplings, 78 r.p.m.

BILLY THE KID Ballet 1938
Ballet Suite orch.
Ballet Theatre—Levine[1]   ‡ **DCap.CTL 7040**
(*Wm. Schuman: Undertow*)
       (‡ Cap.P 8238; ACap.CLCX 047)
(*Excerpts also in* ‡ *Cap.LAL 9024*)
Nat. Sym. (Washington)—Mitchell[2]
       ‡ **Nix.WLP 5286**
(*above & below*)   (‡ West.WL 5286)

(2) **Children's pieces** pf. 1935-6
   1. Sunday Afternoon Music
   2. The Young Pioneers
M. Richter   in ‡ **MGM.E 3147**
(*Cowell, Diamond, Hovhaness, etc.*)

Concerto, pf. & orch. 1926
☆ L. Smit & Rome Radio—Copland   ‡ *MMS. 105*
(*Barber*)   (*Bloch, on* ‡ *CHS.CHS 1238*)

Episode org. 1941
R. Ellsasser   in ‡ **MGM.E 3064**
(† Organ Music by Modern Composers)
M. Mason   in ‡ **ASK. 7**
(*S. Wright, Walther, Kerll, etc.*)

Fanfare for the Common Man Brass & perc.[3] 1942
Nat. Sym. (Washington)—Mitchell
       ‡ **Nix.WLP 5286**
(*above & below*)   (‡ West.WL 5286)

(An) **Immorality** (E. Pound) Fem. cho. & pf. 1925
Pennsylvania College of Women Cho.
—Wichmann   in ‡ **PFCM.CB 161**
(*Santa Cruz, Malipiero, Rosenberg, etc.*)

(A) **Lincoln Portrait** Narrator & orch. 1942
J. Raglin & Pittsburgh Sym.—Steinberg
(*Honegger*)   ‡ **PFCM.CB 179**
☆ M. Douglas & Boston Sym.—Koussevitzky
(*Fauré, Sibelius, Stravinsky*)   ‡ Vic.LCT 1152

Music for the Theatre 1925
M.G.M. Orch.—I. Solomon   ‡ **MGM.E 3095**
(*Weill*)
☆ A.R.S. Orch.—Hendl   (*Herbert*)   ‡ ARS. 110

(The) **NORTH STAR** Film Music 1943
... **Younger generation**
P. Hope, R. Brynner, M. Martin & pf.
       in ‡ **Wald.W 301**

Our Town Sym. picture, orch.
(based on Film Music, 1940)
☆ Little Orch. Soc.—Scherman   ‡ *B.AXL 2006*
(*Thomson*)

Passacaglia pf. 1922
W. Aitken   ‡ **Wald.W 101**
(*Sonata & Variations*)

(2) **Pieces** Str. orch.
   1. Lento molto   1928
   2. Rondino   1923
M.G.M. Str.—I. Solomon   ‡ **MGM.E 3117**
(*Persichetti, Diamond, Goeb, Porter*)

Quiet City Tpt., cor ang. & str. 1940
(from Incidental music to I. Shaw's Play)
Concert Arts—Golschmann   ‡ **DCap.CTL 7056**
(*Diamond, Barber, Creston*)   (‡ Cap.P 8245)
Eastman-Rochester Sym.—Hanson
       ‡ **EMer.MG 40003**
(*Barber, Hanson, Kennan, etc.*)
Hamburg Philharmonia—Korn   ‡ **Allo. 3149**
(*MacDowell, Harris, etc.*)

(The) **RED PONY** Film Music 1948
Orch. Suite
☆ Little Orch. Soc.—Scherman   ‡ *B.AXTL 1022*
(*Thomson*)

RODEO Ballet 1942
Four Dance Episodes
Ballet Theatre—Levine   ‡ *DCap.CCL 7516*
(2ss)   (‡ Cap.L 8198)
(*Bernstein on* ‡ Cap.P. 8196)
[Excerpt also in ‡ Cap.SAL 9020]
... **Nos. 3 & 4**
Boston Prom.—Fiedler (in ‡ Vic.LM 1726:
       ♭ set WDM 1726: ♭ ERA 251)

(El) **Salon Mexico** orch. 1936
Nat. Sym. (Washington)—Mitchell
       ‡ **Nix.WLP 5286**
(*above*)   (‡ West.WL 5286)
Vienna State Op.—Litschauer   ‡ **Van.VRS 439**
(*Appalachian Spring*)
Boston Prom.—Fiedler   ‡ **Vic.LM 1928**
(*Grofé*)
Berlin Sym.—Balzer   in ‡ **Roy. 1517**
☆ Colombia Sym.—Bernstein   ‡ *EPhi.NBR 6019*
(*Milhaud*)   (‡ Phi.N 02600R)
☆ Boston Sym.—Koussevitzky   ‡ Vic.LCT 1134
(*Appalachian Spring*)   (♭ G.7ERL 1040)
... **Themes from** — ARR. PF. & ORCH.   J. Green
      "*Fantasia Mexicana*"
A. Semprini & Orch. (in ‡ *Fnt.LP 110*)
☆ L. Hambro & Orch.—Marrow (‡ *MGM. 9144:*
       in ‡ *E 3136;* ♭ *ItMGM.ESPQ 502*)

Sonata pf. 1941
W. Aitken   ‡ **Wald.W 101**
(*Passacaglia & Variations*)
☆ L. Bernstein (*Bernstein & Ravel*)   ‡ **Cam.CAL 214**

Sonata vln. & pf. 1943
☆ J. Fuchs & L. Smit   (*Stravinsky*)   ‡ **B.AXTL 1047**

Sunday Traffic[4]
Anon. Orch. (*BH.O 2241*)

Symphony No. 3 1946
Minneapolis Sym.—Dorati   ‡ **EMer.MG 50018**
Berlin Sym.—Rubahn   ‡ **Roy. 1513**
(*above*)

Vitebsk pf., vln., vlc. 1929
(Study on a Jewish theme)
K. Wallingford, R. Gerle, G. Magyar ‡ **UOK. 1**
(*Harris, Kerr*)

Variations pf. 1930
W. Aitken   ‡ **Wald.W 101**
(*Passacaglia & Sonata*)

FOLKSONG ARRANGEMENTS
(5) **Old American Songs** (1st set)
   ▽ R. Symonette (Bs) (in ‡ *Csm.CLPS 1008*)

CORBETT, Francisque (*c.* 1612-1681)
   SEE: † ANTHOLOGIE SONORE (‡ HS.AS 13)

CORELLI, Arcangelo (1653-1713)

Concerto, D major 2 tpts. & str.[5]
R. Delmotte, A. Adriano, & Paris Collegium
Mus.—Douatte   ‡ **Cpt.MC 20115**
(*Sonatas; & Vivaldi*)

(12) **CONCERTI GROSSI, Op. 6**
COMPLETE RECORDING
English Baroque Orch.—Quadri
       ‡ **West.WN 18038/40**
(6ss) [Nos. 8 & 11 also on ‡West.LAB 7015] (set 3301)
☆ Corelli Tri-Centenary Str. Orch.—Eckertsen
(6ss)   ‡ **EVox. set PL 7893**
[No. 8 also, ♭ AmVox.VIP 45270]

---

[1] Supervised by composer; certain minor cuts recommended by him, and material additional to published suite added.
[2] Abbreviated.   [3] Later incorporated in 4th movt. of Sym. 3.
[4] Unid., perhaps from *Music for Movies*, 1942.
[5] Originally "Violino principale, 2 Trombe o violini, violoncello e basso", MS.D'Este No. 120 Vienna State Library; arr. Douatte.

(12) CONCERTI GROSSI, Op. 6 (*continued*)

COLLECTION
No. 1, D major
No. 2, F major
No. 7, D major
No. 8, G minor   (*fatto per la Notte di Natività*)
No. 9, F major
  Società Corelli   ♯ **Vic.LM 1776**
        (♯ *FV.A 630226*; ♯ *ItV.A12R 0038*)

No. 1, D major
  ☆ Bavarian State—F. Lehmann   ♭ *Pol. 37018*
  ☆ E.I.A.R.—Zecchi (Orf. 54015/6)

No. 3, C minor
  Paris Collegium—Douatte   ♯ *LT.EL 93042*
  (*Manfredini & Torelli*)   (♯ *T.LB 6091; Sel.LA 1018*)

No. 4, D major
  Virtuosi di Roma—Fasano   ♯ *G.BLP 1041*
  (*Clementi*)   (♯ *FBLP 1053: QBLP 5024*)
  (*Clementi & Vivaldi*, on ♯ *Vic.LHMV 2*)

No. 8, G minor (*"Christmas Concerto"*)
  Vienna Sym.—Pritchard   ♯ *EPhi.ABR 4014*
  (*Manfredini & Handel*)   (♯ *Phi.A 00668R*)
  Paris Coll. Musicum—Douatte   ♯ *Eko.LM 4*
  (*No. 12*)
  N.W. Ger. Phil.—Schüchter   ♯ *Imp.ILP 132*
  (*Bach & Pachelbel*)
  Cologne Cha.—Wenzinger   ♭ *Pol. 37062*
  [F. Neumeyer, hpsi.]
  Winterthur Sym.—Dahinden   V♯ *MMS. 92*
  [also, omitting *Pastorale*, on ♯ *MMS. 100*]
  ☆ Virtuosi di Roma—Fasano   ♯ *B.AXTL 1032*
    (*Vivaldi, Torelli, etc.*) (♯ *Fnt.LP 3004; D.UAT 273551*)
  ☆ Vienna Sym.—Heiller (♭ *Cpt.EXTP 1001;* ♭ *Per.PEP 9;*
    ♭ *Mtr.MCEP 5004;* ♯ *Cum.CR 317;* ♯ *Eli.PLPE 5004*)

No. 12, F major
  Paris Collegium Musicum—Douatte
  (*No. 8*)   ♯ *Eko.LM 4*
  Saxon State Coll. Musicum—Liersch
                   ♯ *Ura.7113*
  (*Rosenmüller & Telemann*)

SONATAS, Vln. & Cont. Op. 5[1]
No. 1, D major
No. 6, A major
No. 12, D major
  ☆ A. Spalding & A. Kooiker (♯ *Cum.CR 281*)[2]

No. 1, D major
No. 3, C major
  F. Zepparoni & R. Veyron-Lacroix (hpsi.)
            † ♯ *AS. 3008LD*
  (*Tartini & Veracini*)   (♯ *HS.AS 40*)

No. 1, D major
  ... 4th movt., Adagio — ARR. STR. QTT.
  ☆ I.C.B.S. Qtt. (in ♯ *MV.VT 51*)

No. 2, B flat major
  — ARR. STR. ORCH. Geminiani ("Concerto Grosso
    No. 2") 1726
  Italian Cha.—Jenkins   ♯ **HS.HSL 74**
  (*Albinoni & Sammartini*)   (in set HSL-C)

No. 3, C major
  ... 3rd movt., Adagio — ARR. STR. QTT.
  ☆ I.C.B.S. Qtt (in ♯ *MV.VT 51*)

No. 5, G minor
  L. Friedemann,[3] F. Viderø (hpsi.), & H. E.
    Deckert (gamba)   ♯ **HS.HSL 95**
  (*J. S. Bach, Leclair, Handel*)

No. 7, D minor
  ☆ J. Starker (vlc.) & M. Meyer (pf.)
      (in ♯ *Cum.CR 317;* ♯ *Eli.PLPE 5004*)

... 3rd movt., Sarabande
— ARR. ORCH: *in* Suite, ARR. Arbós, *below*

No. 9, A major
  ... Giga only — ARR. ORCH.
  Inc. in *Golden Coach* film music *q.v.* under Vivaldi *post*;
    also in Suite, ARR. Arbós, *below*
  — — ARR. HP. Salzédo: C. Salzédo (in ♯ *Mer.MG 80003*)

No. 10, F major
  ... 3rd & 4th movts., Sarabande & Gavotte
  — — ARR. STR. ORCH
  ☆ Decca Little Sym.—Mendoza
        (in ♯ *AmD.DL 5211; D.US 223524*)

No. 11, E major ... 5th movt., Gavotte
  — ARR. ORCH.: In Suite, ARR. Arbós, *below*

No. 12, D minor (La Follia)
  U. Grehling,[3] F. Neumeyer (hpsi.), A.
    Wenzinger (vlc.)   ♯ **HP.APM 14024**
  (*A. Scarlatti & Ariosti*)   (♯ *AmD.ARC 3008*)
  (2ss, PV. 4414; ♭ *Pol. 37035*)
  Y. Menuhin & G. Moore (pf.) ♯ **Vic.LHMV 10**
  (*Beethoven*)
  — ARR. STR. ORCH.
  Società Corelli[4]   ♯ **Vic.LM 1880**
  (*Bonporti, Galuppi, Vivaldi*)
        (♯ *FV.A 630292; ItV.A12R 0146*)
  Milan Str.—Abbado[4]   ♯ **C.FCX 368**
  (*Vivaldi & Tartini*)
  Argentine Radio—Bandini   ArgOd. 66069

SONATAS, 2 violins & continuo
(12) SONATAS, Op. 3[5]

No. 1, F major	No. 2, D major
No. 3, B flat major	No. 4, B minor
No. 5, D minor	No. 6, G major
No. 7, E minor	No. 8, C major
No. 9, F minor	No. 10, A minor
No. 11, G minor	No. 12, A major

(12) SONATAS, Op. 4[6]

No. 1, C major	No. 2, G major
No. 3, A major	No. 4, D major
No. 5, A minor	No. 6, E major
No. 7, F major	No. 8, D minor
No. 9, B flat minor	No. 10, G major
No. 11, C minor	No. 12, B minor

COMPLETE RECORDING
  Arcadia Ens.   ♯ **E. & AmVox. set DL 163**
  (6ss) [E. G. Sartori, hpsi.; G. Spinelli, org.]

B flat major, Op. 3, No. 3
B minor, Op. 3, No. 4
  Paris Collegium Musicum—Douatte
  (*above; & Vivaldi*)   ♯ **Cpt.MC 20115**
  [ed. Douatte; oboes added to orig. str. parts, played by
  ensemble]

E minor, Op. 3, No. 7
  L. Hansen & C. Senderovitz (vlns.), M. Wöldike
    (org.), V. Norup (vlc.)   in ♯ **HS.HSL 2073**
  († *Masterpieces of Music before 1750*)

F minor, Op. 3, No. 9
  W. Roberts (vln.), N. Marriner (vln.), A.
    Goldsbrough (org.), T. Weil (vlc.) **G.HMS 65**
  († *History of Music in Sound*) (in ♯ Vic. set LM 6031)

MISCELLANEOUS
"Concerto" F major — ARR. OB. & STR. Barbirolli
              from Vln. Sonatas, Op. 5
1. Preludio: 1st movt. of No. 10, F major
2. Vivace: 2nd movt., Allegro, of No. 10
3. Sarabande: 3rd movt. of No. 7, D minor
4. Gavotte: 4th movt. of No. 10
5. Gigue: 5th movt., Giga, of No. 10
  P. Pierlot & Ens.—Froment ♯ *EPP.APG 119*
  (*Handel, Scarlatti, Pergolesi*)

"Suite for Strings" — ARR. Arbós, Pinelli, *et al.*
  (3 movements from Vln. Sonatas, Op. 5)
1. Sarabande (3rd movt. of No. 7, D minor)
2. Giga (2nd movt. of No. 9, A major)
3. Badinerie (5th movt., Gavotte, of No. 11, E major)
  Hamburg State Phil.—di Bella
              ♯ *DT.LGM 65031*
  (*Rossini*)   (♯ *T.NLB 6108*)

---

[1] See also "Concerto", *below*.   [2] Identities now confirmed.   [3] Baroque violin.
[4] ARR. Geminiani, "Concerto Grosso No. 12".
[5] Originally 2 vlns., violone or arciliuto, and cont. for org. 1689.   [6] Originally 2 violins, gamba, and hpsi. continuo.

"Suite for Strings" (*continued*)
Hamburg Philharmonia—H-J. Walther
♯ **MGM.E 3087**
(*Mendelssohn & Prokofiev*)   (also *MSB. 78207 & 78101*)
Philadelphia—Ormandy   in ♯ **AmC.ML 4797**
(*Bach, Handel*)
International Str.—A. Schneiderhann
(*Kreisler, Mozart*)   ♯ *Mae.OA 20002*
... Sarabande & Badinerie only
☆ Czech Phil.—Pedrotti (in ♯ Csm.CLPS 1029 with
    Vivaldi (see Supp. II) & *Krommer*)

CORNELIUS, Peter (1824-1874)

(Der) BARBIER VON BAGDAD   Opera
2 Acts   1858
Overture, D major
Vienna Sym.—Loibner   ♭ *Phi.N 402032E*
(*Martha Overture*)
Munich Phil.—Rother   **PV. 72431**
(*Berlioz: Beatrice & Benedict, Overture*)

Mein Sohn, sei Allah's Frieden
(Entrance of Abdul)   Bs. & T.
Er lebt, er lebt   (Final Scene) Bs, T, B
☆ G. Hann (Bs), L. Fehenberger (T), K. Hoppe (B)
♯ **HP.DGM 18003**
(*Lortzing*)   (& ♭ *Pol. 30117*)
[Mein Sohn ... also in ♯ Pol. 19025]

Weihnachtslieder, Op. 8   Song Cycle (Cornelius)
☆ I. Seefried (S), E. Werba (pf.)   ♯ *Pol. 16077*
(*Brahms*)   (in ♯ *AmD.DL 7545*)

... No. 3, Die Könige   — ARR. CHO.   Atkins
Kings Coll. Chapel—Ord (*Eng*)
in ♯ **Argo.RG 39**
(n.v.) († Festival of Lessons & Carols) (♯ West.WN 18105)

CORNER, David (fl. XVIIth Century)

(Ein) neues andächtiges Kindelwiegen[1]
G. Souzay (B), J. Bonneau (pf.) in ♯ **D.LXT 2835**
(† Canzone Scordate)   (♯ Lon.LL 731; D.FAT 173072)
St. Simon the Apostle Chu. Cho.—Lewis
in ♯ **Hall.J 75**
(*Eng, as A Babe lies in the cradle*)

Who is she ascends so high?   1631
Biggs Family Ens.   in ♯ *GIOA.BF 1*

CORNET, Pieter   (c. 1560-1626)

SEE: † OLD NETHERLANDS MASTERS

CORRETTE, Michel (fl. c. 1720-1758)

SEE ALSO: MILHAUD: Suite d'après Corrette

(Le) MALADE IMAGINAIRE   Inc. Music
— ARR.   Bridgewater[2]
Westminster Light Orch.—Bridgewater
in ♯ **West.WL 4007**
(*Couperin, Jones, Lawes, etc.*)

Marche des gardes françaises
Marche des gardes suisses
Marche du Maréchal de Saxe
Paris Coll. Mus.—Douatte   ♯ **Cpt.MC 20102**
(† Musique de la Grande Écurie)

COSTELEY, Guillaume (1531-1606)

CHANSONS   1570
Allons au vert bocage
Pro Musica Antiqua Ens.—Cape   † **G.HMS 34**
(*Sermisy, Passereau, Victoria*)   (in ♯ Vic. set LM 6029)

Allons, gay, gay, gay, bergères
Paris Vocal Ens.—Jouve   in **V♯** *SEL.LPP 8611*
(& † French Madrigals, in ♯ *Sel.LLA 1079* & ♭ *T.UV 116*)
☆ Motet & Madrigal Cho.—Opienski (in †♯ HS.AS 6)

En ce beau moys
Vocal Ens.—F. Lamy   in ♯ **LOL.OL 50027**
(† Parisian Songs of XVIth Century)   (♯ OL.LD 76)

Hélas! que de mal j'endure
R. Blanchard Ens.   in ♯ *Phi.N 00993R*
(† French Chansons)

Je vois des glissantes eaux
Paris Vocal Ens.—Jouve   in ♯ *LT.MEL 94007*
(*Josquin & Jannequin*)   (**V♯** *Sel. 190.C.002*)
(& † French Madrigals, **V♯** *Sel.LLA 1079*)
Stanford Univ. Cho.—Schmidt   in ♯ **ML. 7022**
(† Madrigals & Motets)

Lautrier priay de danser
Stanford Univ. Cho.—Schmidt   in ♯ **ML. 7022**
(† Madrigals & Motets)

Mignonne, allons voir si la roze
Vocal Ens.—Boulanger   in ♯ **B.AXTL 1048**
(† French Renaissance) (♯ D.FAT 263102; AmD.DL 9629)
Paris Vocal Ens.—Jouve   in ♯ *LT.MEL 94007*
(*Josquin & Jannequin*)   (**V♯** *Sel. 190.C.002*)
☆ Motet & Madrigal Cho.—Opienski (in † ♯ HS.AS 6)

Noblesse gît au cœur
Vocal & Inst. Ens.—Boulanger ♯ **B.AXTL 1048**
(† French Renaissance) (♯ D.FAT 263102; AmD.DL 9629)

(La) Prise du Havre   (6 chansons)
Paris Trad. Singers—M. Honegger
in † ♯ **AS. 3006LD**
(♯ HS.AS 41)

COUPERIN, François (1631-1701)

Domine Deus   (Agnus Dei)
P. Kee   ♭ *G.7EPH 1005*
(*Daquin & Alain*)
[org. of St. Laurens Chu., Alkmaar]

Qui tollis peccata mundi
P. Kee [same org.]   in ♯ *G.DLP 1053*
(† "Baroque" organ music)

COUPERIN, François ("le Grand")
(1668-1733)

CLASSIFIED: I. (a) Harpsichord (b) Organ
II. Chamber Music
III. Vocal Music

I. A. HARPSICHORD

THE COMPLETE WORKS
R. Gerlin   (32ss)   ♯ **LOL.OL 50052/67**
LOL.OL 50052: Ordre I (parts 1 & 2)
50053: Ordres I (part 3) & II (parts 1 & 2)
50054: Ordres II (part 3) & III (part 1)
50055: Ordres III (part 2), IV, & V (part 1)
50056: Ordres V (parts 2 & 3) & VI (part 1)
50057: Ordres VI (part 2) & VII
50058: Ordres VIII & IX (part 1)
50059: Ordres IX (part 2) & X (part 1)
50060: Ordres X (part 2) & XI & XII
50061: Ordres XIII & XIV (part 1)
50062: Ordres XIV (part 2) XV & XVI (part 1)
50063: Ordres XVI (part 2) XVII & XVIII
50064: Ordres XIX, XX, XXI (part 1)
50065: Ordres XXI (part 2), XXII, XXIII, XXIV
(part 1)
50066: Ordres XXIV (part 2), XXV
50067: Ordres XXVI, XXVII
L'Art de Toucher le Clavecin
(8 Preludes & Allemande)

---

[1] ANON. melody, ed. Corner. From *Gesangbuch*, 1625.
[2] For the 1951 London production, from Music of Couperin and Corrette. It has not been possible to identify the music used for the recorded items: Prelude; Ballet Scene; Charade.

COLLECTIONS

Ordre XXVI, complete
Les Fastes de la Grande et Ancienne Ménéstrandise   (XI)
Passacaille   (VIII)
   S. Marlowe   # Rem. 199-202

L'Auguste   (I)
Le Croc en jambe   (XX)
La Lutine   (III)
Les Ombres errantes   (XXV)
Le Réveil-matin   (IV)
Le Rossignol en amour   (XIV)   [with L. Lavaillotte (fl)]
   P. Aubert   (below)   # CFD. 11

Le Dodo, ou l'amour au berceau   (XV)
Les Barricades mystérieuses   (VI)
Les Fauvettes plaintives   (XIV)
Les Ombres errantes   (XXV)
Le Tic-toc-choc ou les maillotins   (XVIII)
   M. Meyer (pf.)   # DFr. 86
   (Rameau, Ravel, Debussy)   (# HS.HSL 98)

Les Vieux Seigneurs   (Sarabande)   (XXIV)
Les Jeunes Seigneurs   (XXIV)
La Forqueray ou la Superbe   (XVII)
Courante, E minor   (XVII)
Musette de Taverni   (XV)
Les Rozeaux   (XIII)
Les Dars homicides   (XXIV)
Le Tic-toc-choc ou les maillotins   (XVIII)
L'Amphibie   (Passacaille)   (XXIV)
Le Rossignol en amour   (XIV)
   R. Wallenborn (pf.)   # DT.LGX 66041
   (Ravel: Tombeau de Couperin) (# T.LE 6530)

La Bandoline   (V)
Le Dodo, ou l'amour au berceau   (XV)
Les Moissonneurs   (VI)
Le Tic-toc-choc ou les maillotins   (XVIII)
Les Tricoteuses   (XXIII)
   J. Casadesus (pf.)   # Angel. 35261
   (Poulenc, Françaix, Tailleferre, etc.)

Allemande   (La Ténébreuse)   (III)
Sarabande   (La Lugubre)   (III)
Courante   (III)
Les Lis-naissans   (XIII)
Les Petits Moulins à vent   (XVII)
Les Barricades mystérieuses   (VI)
Le Bavolet flottant   (IX)
Le Moucheron   (VI)
   H. Boschi (pf.)   # Sup.LPM 224
   (Rameau)   (# U. 5197C)

Air dans le goût polonais   (XX)
   ☆ W. Landowska (♭ Vic.ERA 128)

Allemande   (L'Auguste)   (I)
   E. Heiller   in # Uni.LP 1010
   († History of the Dance)

(L') Arléquine   (XXIII)

(Les) Barricades mystérieuses   (VI)
   ☆ W. Landowska (in # G.ALP 1246:
       FALP/QALP 218; ♭ Vic.ERA 127)

(La) Bandoline   (V)
   A. Rácz (cymbalom), A. Rácz (pf.) (Qual.SZN 3004)
   I. Tarjani-Tóth (cymbalom), I. Altoff (pf.)
       (in # G.FBLP 1067)

(Le) Carillon de Cythère   (XIV)
   W. Kempff (pf.)   ♭ D. 71083
   (Rameau: Rappel des oiseaux) (♭ DK 23358)
   ☆ C. Solomon (pf.) (♭ G.7PW 116)

(Les) Folies françaises ou les Dominos   (XIII)
   S. Marlowe   # Rem. 199-136
   (Scarlatti & Bach)   (# Cum.CR 207)
   L. Selbiger   in # C.KC 2
   (below & Rameau)

(La) Gabriéle   (X)
— ARR. ORCH. See Ballet Suite, post.

(La) Galante   (XII)
   F. Viderø   in # HS.HSL 2073
   († Masterpieces of Music before 1750)

(Les) Graces incomparables   (XVI)
— ARR. ORCH. See Ballet Suite, post

(Les) Graces naturéles   (XI)
   ☆ L. Selbiger (C.DB 3374: DO 3650)

(Les) Lis-Naissans   (XIII)
   ▽ Lazare-Lévy (pf.) (JpV.SD 53)

(La) Passacaille   (VIII)
   L. Selbiger   # C.KC 2
   (above & Rameau)
— ARR. ORCH. See Ballet Suite, post

(Les) Petits moulins à vent   (XVII)
   I. Nef   in # LOL.OL 50028
   († Clavecinistes français) (# OL.LD 64)
   S. Bianca (pf.)   MSB. 26
   (Soeur Monique) (with spoken commentary)

(Le) Rossignol en amour   (XIV)
   ☆ L. Selbiger (C.DB 3374: DO 3650)

(Les) Rozeaux   (XIII)
   I. Nef   in # LOL.OL 50028
   († Clavecinistes français) (# OL.LD 64)
   ▽ Lazare-Lévy (pf.) (JpV.SD 53)

Soeur Monique   (XVIII)
   S. Bianca (pf.)   MSB. 26
   (Petits moulins à vent) (with spoken commentary)

(Les) Vendangeuses   (V)   (Rigaudon)
   ☆ A. Ehlers (in # D.UAT 273084)

I. B. ORGAN

MESSE À L'USAGE DES CONVENTS
COMPLETE RECORDINGS
   A. Marchal   # Era.LDE 3025
   (Titelouze) [La Flèche organ, Paris]
   S. Rasjö   # Cpt.MC 20088
   [organ of Church of Our Lady, Skänninge, Sweden]

... **Nos. 1, 2, 6, 7, 8, 10, 14, 15** only
   X. Guerner   # MFr. 3003
   (below & L. Couperin) [La Flèche organ]

... **No. 1, Premier Couplet du Kyrie**   ("Prelude")
   G. Roussel   in # SM. 33-03
   (M. A. Charpentier, Marchand, Lalande)   (# Per.SPL 712)

... **Nos. 15 & 16, Offertoire & Sanctus**
   ☆ J. Bonnet (in † # HS.AS 11)

... **Gloria: Domine Deus & Amen**, only
   G. Roussel   # SM. 33-06
   (Campra, Cauroy, Lalande) [Versailles Chapel organ]

MESSE À L'USAGE DES PAROISSES   1690
COMPLETE RECORDINGS
   S. Rasjö   # LI.TWV 91110
   [org. of Church of Our Lady, Skänninge, Sweden]
       (# Cpt.MC 20087)
   G. Litaize   # LT.DTL 93039
   [org. of St. Merry, Paris] (# Sel.LAG 1064)

... **No. 1-3, 5-7, 9-11, 16-18, 20, 21**
   X. Guerner   # MFr. 3003
   (above & L. Couperin) [La Flèche organ]

... **No. 15, Offertoire sur les grands jeux**
   E. Hilliar   # ASK. 4
   (Dupré, Arne, J. S. Bach, etc.)
   [Organ of St. Mark's, Mt. Kisco, N.Y.]

... **No. 15; & 16, Sanctus**
   ☆ J. Bonnet (in † HS.AS 11)

... **No. 18, Benedictus (Elevation)—Cromorne en taille**
   C. Watters   in # CEd. set 1008
   († French Baroque Organ Music)

Fugue on the Kyrie   (unspec.)
   Anon. Artist (in # FSM. 403)

II. CHAMBER MUSIC

CONCERTS ROYAUX   fl., vlc., hpsi.   1722
The FOUR CONCERTS, COMPLETE
   ☆ P. Kaplan, S. Mayes, E. Bodky (in # CID.UM 63002;
       # Lyr.LL 54)

= Long-playing, 33⅓ r.p.m.   ♭ = 45 r.p.m.   ♮ = Auto. couplings, 78 r.p.m.

No. 3, A major
I. Nef & R. Gerlin (hpsis.)   ♯ **LOL.OL 50031**
(*La Steinquerque*)   (♯ OL.LD 63)

No. 4, E minor
J-P. Rampal (fl.) & R. Veyron-Lacroix (hpsi.)
     ♯ **D.FST 153139**
(*Telemann*) [ed. Veyron-Lacroix]

(Les) GOÛTS RÉUNIS
No. 5, F major
L. Lavaillotte (fl.), M. Allard (bsn.), P. Aubert
(hpsi.)   ♯ **CFD. 11**
(*above & below*)

No. 6, B flat major
… **Air de diable & Sicilienne** only
— — ARR. Bazelaire *"Pièces en concert"*
P. Fournier (vlc.) & Stuttgart Cha.—Münchinger
     ♯ **D.LXT 2765**
(*below, Boccherini & Vivaldi*)   (♯ Lon.LL 687)
(*Vivaldi, on* ♯ *D.LW 5196*)

No. 8, G major (Concert dans le goût théâtral)
Paris Cha. Concerts Assoc.—Oubradous[1]
     ♯ **Pat.DTX 146**
(*Rameau*)   (♯ ArgA.LPC 11668)

No. 10, A minor *"La Tromba"*
Paris Collegium—Douatte   ♯ **Cpt.MC 20118**
(*Philidor, Lully*)

… **Prelude, La tromba & Plainte** only
— — ARR. Bazelaire *"Pièces en concert"*
P. Fournier (vlc.) & Stuttgart Cha.—Münchinger
     in ♯ **D.LXT 2765**
(*above, Boccherini & Vivaldi*)   (♯ Lon.LL 687)
(*Vivaldi, on* ♯ *D.LW 5196*)

Marche du Régiment de Champagne
Paris Coll. Mus.—Douatte   in ♯ **Cpt.MC 20102**
(† *Musique de la Grande Écurie*)

(Les) NATIONS 1726
No. 1, La Françoise
… **Courante II** — ARR. ORGAN J. S. Bach
See: Aria, F major, *s.v.* Bach, Organ Collections

No. 4, La Piémontoise
G. Alès & G. Tessier (vlns.), D. Gouarne
(hpsi.), G. Schwartz (vlc.)   ♯ **CFD. 11**
(*above & Songs*)

SONATAS
(L') Apothéose de Lully 2 vlns. & cont. 1725
Hewitt Cha. Orch[2] (n.v.)   ♯ **Phi.A 00759R**

(Le) Parnasse, ou l'apothéose de Corelli 1724
C. Monteux (fl.), H. Shulman (ob.), B.
Greenhouse (vlc.), S. Marlowe (hpsi.)
     ♯ **Eso.ES 517**
(*Frescobaldi & Rosenmüller*)   (♯ Cpt.MC 20023)

(La) Steinquerque (Sonade en trio) 1692
I. Nef & R. Gerlin (hpsis.)   ♯ **LOL.OL 50031**
(*Concert Royal No. 3*)   (♯ OL.LD 63)
Paris Cha. Ens.—Douatte[3]   ♯ **LI.TWV 91092**
(*Mouret, Lalande, Lully, Philidor*)   (♯ Cpt.MC 20086)

III. VOCAL
AIRS
Doux liens de mon cœur (Air sérieux) 1701
Qu'on ne me dise plus (Air sérieux) 1697
Zéphyre, modère en ces lieux (Brunète) 1711
C. Mauranne (B), D. Gouarne (hpsi.)
     ♯ **CFD. 11**
(*above*)

LEÇONS DE TÉNÈBRES 1713-7
No. 1, Incipit lamentatio Jeremiae Prophetae S. & cont.
No. 2, Et egressus est filia S. & cont.
No. 3, Manum suam misit hostis 2 S. & cont.
N. Sautereau (S), J. Collard (A), N. Pierront
(org.), & gamba   ♯ **DPP. 23-1**
(*Motets*) [& 2 vlns. in No. 3]   (♯ HS.HSL 105)
H. Cuénod (T), G. Sinimberghi (T), F.
Holetschek (hpsi. & org.), R. Harand (vlc.)
     ♯ **Nix.WLP 5387**
     (♯ West.WL 5387)
P. Alarie & B. Retchitzka (S), A. G. Dechaume
(org.)   ♯ **LT.DTL 93077**
(*below*)   (♯ Sel. 320.C.051)

MOTETS
COLLECTION
Veni, veni, Sponsa Christi S, T, Bs, cho, 3 instr. c. 1698-1702
     (*Motet de Sainte-Suzanne*)
4 Versets d'un motet (from Ps. 119) S, S, cho., & insts. 1703
  1. Tabescere me fecit S, S unacc.
  2. Ignitum eloquium tuum
  3. Adolescentulus sum
  4. Justitia tua in aeternum
5 Versets d'un motet ("*de l'année dernière*") 1702
  … No. 5, Qui dat nivem S & insts.
7 Versets d'un motet (from Ps. 80) 1705
  … No. 7, Deus virtutum, convertere Bs & insts.
Accedo ad te (Dialogus inter Deum et hominem) T, Bs & cont.
E. Morison & J. Vyvyan (S), W. Herbert (T)
G. James (Bs), St. Anthony Singers, Inst.
Ens.—A. Lewis   ♯ **LOL.OL 50079**
[R. Downes (org.); B. Ord (hpsi.)]   (♯ OL.LD 110)

Audite omnes (Élévation) 1 v., 2 vlns., & cont.
Victoria! Christo resurgenti 2 vv. & cont.
     (ed. Boulay)
N. Sautereau (S), J. Collard (A), 2 vlns.,
N. Pierront (org.) & gamba   ♯ **DDP. 23-1**
(*Leçons de Ténèbres*)   (♯ HS.HSL 105)

Veni, veni, Sponsa Christi S, T, Bs, cho., 3 insts.
     c. 1698-1702 (*Motet de Sainte-Suzanne*)
P. Alarie, L. Simoneau, G. Abdoun, Paris
Vocal Ens. & Cartigny Cha. Ens.—Bour
     ♯ **LT.DTL 93077**
(*above*)   (♯ Sel. 320.C.051)
J. Vyvyan, W. Herbert, G. James, St. Anthony
Singers & Inst. Ens.—Lewis   V♯ **DO.LD 32**
(2ss) [R. Downes (org.), B. Ord (hpsi.)] (from Collection)

(7) Versets d'un Motet 1704
     (Psalm 85, Vv. 4-11)
… **Ostende nobis**
M. Casadesus Ens.   in ♯ **Plé.P 3083**
(† *Musiques à la Chapelle du Roy*)   (♯ West.WN 18167)
☆ Y. Tinayre (T) & Strs.   in ♯ **AmD.DL 9654**
(† Seven Centuries of Sacred Music)   (in set DX 120)

MISCELLANEOUS
Ballet Suite, G major — ARR. ORCH.
     (from hpsi. pieces)
1. Prélude: Maestoso (*Les graces incomparables*)
2. Rondeau: Tempo comodo (*Passacaille*)
3. Alla giga: Grazioso (*La Gabriéle*)
Netherlands Phil.—v. d. Berg   ♯ **CHS.H 9**
(*Lully & Leclair*)

(Le) MALADE IMAGINAIRE Incid. Music
— ARR. Bridgewater[4]
Westminster Light Orch.—Bridgewater
     in ♯ **West.WL 4007**
(*Leclair, Boyce, Jones, Lawes, etc.*)

Pastorale — ARR. VLC. & PF. Cassadó[5]
J. Starker & L. Pommers   in ♯ **Nix.PLP 708**
(*Debussy, Bréval, Ravel, Poulenc, etc.*)   (♯ Per.SPL 708)
D. Shafran & pf. (USSR)   (USSR. 21594)

---

[1] Edited Oubradous.   [2] Trs. L. Saguer.   [3] 2 obs., bsn. and str.
[4] For the 1951 London production, from music of Couperin and Corrette. It has not been possible to identify the music used for the items recorded: Prelude; Ballet Scene; Charade.
[5] Unidentified. It is suggested that it was in fact composed by Cassadó.

COUPERIN, Louis (1626-1661)

SEE ALSO: CHAMBONNIÈRES, *supra*

HARPSICHORD MUSIC
[References to Nos. in the complete edn.]

COLLECTIONS

Prelude, A minor	[6]
La Piémontoise, A minor	[103]
Courante, A minor	[104]
Sarabande, A minor	[110]
Sarabande D minor	[51]
Canaries, D minor	[52]
Volte, D minor	[53]
La Pastourelle, D minor	[54]
Chaconne, D minor	[55]
Branle de Basque, F major	[73]
Gaillarde, F major	[77]
Le Tombeau de M. Blancrocher, F major	[81]
Chaconne, G minor	[122]
Passacaille, G minor	[99]

D. Pinkham   ‡ CEd.CE 1054
(*Chambonnières*)

Chaconne, G minor	[122]
Allemande, G minor	[92]
Duo, G minor	[98]
Sarabande ou canon	[47]
Fantasie, G minor	[97]
Chaconne ou Passacaille, G minor	[95]
Les Carillons de Paris	[137] (Receuil Philidor)

M-C. Alain   ‡ DFr. 158
(*Clérambault*) [St. Merry organ, Paris]

CHACONNES

D minor [55]; F major [80]
N. Pierront   in ‡ *Lum.LD 2-104*
(† Chaconne & Passacaglia) [St. Merry org.]

D minor [55]
☆ A. Ehlers (in ‡ D.UAT 273084)

G minor [122]
I. Nef (hpsi.)   in ‡ LOL.OL 50028
(† Les Clavecinistes français)   (‡ OL.LD 64)

X. Guerner (org.)   ‡ MFr. 3003
(*F. Couperin: Masses, excerpts*)

Passacaglia, G minor [99]
— ARR. GUITAR Segovia
A. Segovia   in ‡ AmD.DL 9734
(† Segovia plays)   (‡ D.UAT 273573)

COWELL, Henry Dixon (b. 1897)

Ballad & Dance orch.
Eastman-Rochester Sym.—Hansen
(*Riegger: New Dance*)   ♭ *Mer.EP 1-5063*

... Ballad only
Vienna Orch. Soc.—Adler   ‡ Uni.LP 1011
(*below; & Mendelssohn*)

Fiddler's jig vln. & str. orch. 1952
Vienna Orch. Soc.—Adler   ‡ Uni.LA 1008
(*below; & Schoenberg*)

Hymns & Fuguing Tunes
No. 2   1944   Str. orch.
No. 5   1945   Str. orch.
Vienna Orch. Soc.—Adler   ‡ Uni.LP 1011
(*above*)

(The) Irishman dances pf. 1934
M. Richter   in ‡ MGM.E 3147
(*Diamond, Hovhaness, Laurence, etc.*)

Processional organ
R. Ellsasser   in ‡ MGM.E 3064
(† Organ Music by Modern Composers)

Saturday Night in the Firehouse orch. 1948
Vienna State Philharmonia—Adler   ‡ SPA. 47
(*Jacobi, Antheil, Siegmeister, etc.*)

Sonata No. 1, vln. & pf. 1945
J. Szigeti & C. Bussotti   ‡ AmC.ML 4841
(*Shapero*)

Suite fl., ob., cl., bsn., hrn.
New Art Wind Quartet   in ‡ CEd. set 2003

SYMPHONIES

No. 4 "Short" 1946
Eastman-Rochester Sym.—Hanson
                                   ‡ Mer.MG 40005
(*Riegger & Hovhaness*)

No. 5 1948
☆ A.R.S. Orch.—Dixon   ‡ ARS. 112
(*Piston*)

No. 10 1953
Vienna Orch. Soc.—Adler   ‡ Uni.LA 1008
(*above; & Schönberg*)

No. 11 ("Seven Rituals of Music") f.p. 1954
Louisville Orch.—Whitney   ‡ AmC.ML 5039
(*Creston & Ibert*)
(*Tcherepnin & Wagenaar on ‡ LO. 2*)

Toccanta S, fl., vlc., pf. 1938
H. Boatwright, C. S. Smith, A. Parisot &
J. Kirkpatrick   ‡ AmC.ML 4986
(*Ruggles*)

NOTE : The programme notes in various Folksong recordings (‡ EFL.P 505, P 510, etc.) are by Cowell, and some
of the contents of the former disc are from his collection.

CRAMER, Johann Baptist (1771-1858)

ÉTUDES pf.
[Nos. in brackets refer to the Bülow edn.]

No. 4, C minor	[27]	No. 16, A♭ major	[8]
No. 29, G major	[26]	No. 33, D major	[17]
No. 36, G minor	[21]	No. 37, B♭ major	[42]
No. 41, E major	[56]	No. 61, A major	[47]
No. 63, G minor	[29]	No. 67, F minor	[57]
No. 76, A minor	[36]	No. 77, D major	[53]
No. 80, D♭ major	[55]		

☆ M. Schwalb   ‡ Esq. TW 14-004
(*Clementi & Czerny*)
[contents of ‡ Acad.ALP 303 now identified]

CRANDELL, Robert (b. 1910)

Carnival Suite org.
M. Mason   in ‡ ASK. 7
(*Copland, Wright, Walther, etc.*)

CRÉQUILLON, Thomas (d. 1557)

CHANSONS
Pour ung plaisir
Copenhagen Univ. Cho.—Møller
                                   in ‡ HS.HSL 2071
(† Masterpieces of Music before 1750) (sets HSL B & I)
(also in † Histoire de la musique vocale)

— ARR. HPSI. A. Gabrieli
F. Viderø   in † ‡ HS.HSL 2071

Puisque malheur me tient (*Hortus musarum*, 1553)
A. Doniat (B) & insts.   in ‡ *Phi.A 00994R*
(† French Chansons II)

Quand me souvient
B. de Pauw (T) & insts. in ‡ LOL.OL 50104
(† Musiciens de la cour de Bourgogne I) (‡ OL.LD 80)
☆ H. Cuénod (T), H. Leeb (lute)   in ‡ Nix.WLP 5085
(† XVIth & XVIIth Century Songs)
                                   (& in †V‡ *Sel.LAP 1021*)

CRESTON, Paul (b. 1906)

(2) Choric Dances, Op. 17b Full or Small orch. 1938
Concert Arts—Golschmann ‡ DCap.CTL 7056
(*Diamond, Barber, Copland*)   (‡ Cap.P 8245)

Invocation & Dance, Op. 58 orch. 1953
Louisville Orch.—Whitney   ‡ AmC.ML 5039
(*Cowell & Ibert*)
(*Stevens, Villa-Lobos, on ‡ LO. 1*)

---

‡ = Long-playing, 33⅓ r.p.m.   ♭ = 45 r.p.m.   ♮ = Auto. couplings, 78 r.p.m.

Partita, fl., vln. & str. orch., Op. 12   1937
A.R.S. Sym.—Hendl   ♯ *ARS. 23*
(Taylor)

Quartet, Strings, Op. 8   1936
Hollywood Qtt.   ♯ **DCap.CTL 7063**
(Turina & Wolf)   (♯ Cap.P 8260)

(A) Rumor   orch.   1941
Hamburg Philharmonia—Korn in ♯ **Allo. 3148**
(Hopkinson, Fry, Barber, etc.)

Sonata, Op. 19   sax. & pf.   1939
V. J. Abato & P. Creston   ♯ **AmC.ML 4989**
(Persichetti)

SYMPHONIES
No. 2, Op. 35   1944
No. 3, Op. 48   1950
National Sym. (Washington)—Mitchell
♯ **Nix.WLP 5272**
(♯ West.WL 5272)

CROCE, Giovanni   (*c.* 1557-1609)
SEE: † TRIUMPHS OF ORIANA
      † MOTETS OF THE VENETIAN SCHOOL II

CROFT, William   (1678-1727)
SEE: † OLD ENGLISH MASTERS
      † MASTERS OF EARLY ENGLISH KEYBOARD MUSIC

CRÜGER, Johann   (1598-1662)
SEE: † GERMAN SONGS

CUESTA, Francisco (1889-1921)

Valencian Dance   pf.
A. Iturbi   in ♯ **Vic.LM 1788**
(♭ ERA 198; in ♯ FV.A 630231)

CUI, César Antonovitch (1835-1918)

Berceuse russe, Op. 50, No. 5   vln. & pf.
G. Barinova & pf. (*USSR. 18561*)

Orientale, Op. 50, No. 9   vln. & pf.
G. Barinova & pf. (*USSR. 18560 & USSRM.D 439*)
— ARR. 2 PFS.   Luboshutz
☆ P. Luboshutz & G. Nemenoff (in ♯ Cam.CAL 198)

SONGS
Bolero
E. Chavdar (S)   in ♯ *USSR.D 2089*
(Glinka, Rimsky, etc.)

(The) Burnt Letter   (Pushkin)
E. Belov   *USSR. 22546*
(Glazounov: Song)

Evening Glow
E. Katulskaya (M-S)   *USSR. 20011*
(Grieg: I love thee)

Parting (Mickiewicz) ☆
It grows dark   (A. Tolstoy)
N. Shpiller (S)   *USSRM.D 001265*
(Tchaikovsky)

Suite No. 3, G minor, Op. 43   orch.
    (Petite Suite in modo populari)
Moscow Radio—Gauk   ♯ *USSR.D 1119/20*

CUMMING, Richard (b. 1928)

Sonata   pf.   1951
R. Cumming   ♯ **ML. 7027**
(Bloch)

SONG: Loveliest of trees   (A. E. Housman)
D. Gramm (Bs.), R. Cumming (pf.)
in ♯ **ML. 7033**
(Cesti, Wolf, Diamond, etc.)

CUSHING, Charles (b. 1905)

Hommage à A. Roussel   sax. & pf.   1954
D. Defayet & F. Gobet   ♭ *Pat.G 1052*
(Vuataz, Semenoff, Lacazinière, Herbin)

CUTTING, Francis (or Thomas) (fl. 1596-1611)

SEE: † MUSIC IN SHAKESPEARE'S TIME
      † SHAKESPEARE SONGS & LUTE SOLOS

CZERNY, Carl (1791-1857)

ÉCOLE DE VÉLOCITÉ, Op. 299   pf.
Études, Nos. 39, 27, 14, 23, 34, 38, 37
☆ M. Schwalb (*Cramer & Clementi*)   ♯ **Esq.TW 14-004**
Étude (unspec.)   M. Schwalb   in ♯ **Roy. 1474**
Hexaméron   *See* Liszt, section A. III (5)

Variations on "La Ricordanza", Op. 33   pf.
S. Weissenberg   ♯ **Lum.LD 3-400**
(Bach-Liszt, Haydn, Soler)

DAHL, Ingolf (b. 1912)

Allegro & Arioso   fl., ob., cl., hrn., bsn.
New Art Wind Quintet   in ♯ **CEd. set CE 2003**
(Carter, Cowell, etc.)

DALL'ABACO   SEE: ABACO, dall'

DALLAPICCOLA, Luigi (b. 1904)

Canti di Prigionia[1]   Cho. & orch.   1938-41
Santa Cecilia Cho. & Orch.—Markevitch
♯ *G.FBLP 1029*

Quaderno musicale di Annalibera   pf.   1952
V. Persichetti   ♯ **PFCM.CB 185**
(Persichetti & Schönberg)

Tartiniana   vln. & orch.   1951
R. Posselt & Columbia Sym.—Bernstein
♯ **AmC.ML 4996**
(Hill & Lopatnikoff)

Variazioni per Orchestra   orch.   f.p. 1954
Louisville—Whitney   ♯ **LO. 8**
(Kay, Milhaud, Moncayo)

DALZA, Joanambrosio
(fl. early XVIth Cent.)

Pavana alla Ferrarese[2]   lute
M. Podolsky   in ♯ **Per.SPL 577**
(† Lute Music of XVIth & XVIIth Cent.) (Cpt.MC 20052)

Pavana alla Veneziana[2]   lute
B. Winogron (virginals)   in ♯ **Eso.ES 516**
(Banchieri, Frescobaldi, Gabrieli)

---

[1] Text is composed of sayings of Mary Stuart, Boëthius, and Savonarola.
[2] From Petrucci's *Intablatura de Lauto*, Vol. IV, 1508.

DAMASE, Jean-Michel (b. 1928)

Concerto, hp. & orch. 1951
M. Flour & Radio-Luxembourg—Pensis
(*Donatoni, Ravel*) ‡ FestF.FLD 25

(La) CROQUEUSE DE DIAMANTS
Ballet 1949-50
Valse à cinq temps; Nocturne; Adagio
Rome Radio Light Orch.—Savina
Cet.AT 0308/9
(3ss—*Thiriet: Oeuf à la Coque, s. 5 on AT 0308*)

Sonata, Op. 24 pf.
J-M. Damase ‡ D.FST 153527
(*Auric, Messiaen, Poulenc, etc.*)

SONGS
Mon âme (Colette) (a)
(La) Perle égarée (Colette) (b)
(a) J. Peyron (T), (b) R. Doria (S) & J-M.
Damase (pf.) ‡ FMer.MLP 7073
(*Poulenc & Wolff*)

DANDRIEU, Jean François (1682-1738)

HARPSICHORD MUSIC
Suite No. 2, G major
... Les Tourbillons — ARR. 2 HPS. Salzédo
C. Salzédo & L. Lawrence (in ‡ Mer.MG 10144)
... Le Concert des oiseaux: 1. La ramage; 2. Les
amours; 3. L'hymen
I. Nef in ‡ LOL.OL 50028
(† *Clavecinistes français*) (‡ OL.LD 64)

Suite No. 4, G major
... Les Fifres
R. Ellsasser (org.) ‡ CM. 4
("*Sammartini*" & *Ellsasser*)

ORGAN MUSIC
Basse et dessus de trompette, D major
H. Roget G.HMS 62
(† *History of Music in Sound*) (in ‡ Vic. set LM 6031)

Dialogue et Musette (Guilmant edn., pp. 60/68)
E. Linzel in ‡ Moll.E4QP 7231
(*Karg-Elert, Pachelbel, Schröder, Bach, etc.*)

Musette, A major (Guilmant edn., p. 93)
C. Watters in ‡ CEd. set 1008
(† *French Baroque Organ Music*)

Où s'en vont ces gays bergers Noël
N. Pierront V‡ Lum.LD 1-105
(† *Vieux Noëls de France*)

Fanfares de Chantilly
Paris Collegium Musicum—Douatte
in ‡ Cpt.MC 20102
(† *Musique de la Grande Écurie*)

DANKEVITCH, Konstantin (?)

OPERA in *Ukrainian*
BOGDAN KHMELNITSKY 4 Acts (1951-3)
COMPLETE RECORDING
Bogdan Khmelnitsky ... M. Grishko (B)
Maxim Krivonos ... ... B. Gmyria (Bs)
Bogun ... ... V. Borisenko (S)
Solomija ... ... L. Rudenko (M-S)
etc., Kiev Opera Cho. & Orch.—Piradov
(10ss) ‡ USSR.D 01813/22
Bogdan's Arias, Acts I & II M. Grishko (in ‡ USSR.D 2095)

DANKOWSKI, Wojciech (b. *c.* 1765)

Symphony, D major (ARR. Krenz)
Polish Radio—Krenz Muza.X 2379/80
(4ss)

DANYEL (or Daniel), John
(*c.* 1565-*c.* 1630)

SONGS Voice, lute & viol 1606
Why canst thou not, as others do
Time, cruel time (Samuel Daniel)
I die whenas I do not see
R. Soames (T), W. Gerwig, J. Koch (gamba)
(*Dowland*) ♭ Pol. 37010

DANZI, Franz (1763-1826)

Gypsy Dance — ARR. fl., ob., cl., hrn., bsn., Maganini
Chicago Sym. Woodwind Quintet in ‡ Aphe. 16

QUINTETS fl., ob., cl., hrn., bsn.
B flat major, Op. 56, No. 1
G minor, Op. 56, No. 2
French Wind Quintet ‡ LOL.DL 53005
(‡ OL.LD 43)

SONATAS horn & pf.
E flat major, Op. 28
E major, Op. 44
A. Koch & L. Granetman ‡ SPA. 29

DAQUIN, Louis Claude (1694-1772)

HARPSICHORD PIECES
(*Premier livre de pièces de clavecin*, 1735)
(Les) Bergères
Musette et Tambourin
I. Nef in ‡ LOL.OL 50028
(† *Clavecinistes français*) (‡ OL.LD 64)
Le Coucou
Z. Růžičková U.C 24398
(*Rameau: Tambourin*)
— ARR. ORGAN
R. Ellsasser [Hammond electric organ] in ‡ MGM.E 3031
— ARR. HARP ☆ O. Erdeli (*USSRM.D 00477*)

NOËLS, Op. 2 Organ
No. 1, D minor, sur les jeux d'anches
No. 3, G major, en musette
No. 9, D major, sur les flûtes
No. 10, G major, Grand jeu et duo
No. 12, A major, Noël suisse
C. Watters in ‡ CEd. set 1008
(† *French Baroque Organ Music*)
No. 1, D minor, sur les jeux d'anches
No. 8, G major, Noël étranger
N. Pierront V ‡ Lum.LD 1-105
(† *Vieux Noëls de France*)
No. 10, G major, Grand jeu et duo
R. Owen in ‡ ASK. 3
(*Bach, Messiaen, etc.*)
[Organ of Christ Chu. Bronxville, N.Y.]
No. 12, A major, Noël suisse
P. Kee ♭ G.7EPH 1005
(*F. Couperin senior, & Alain*)
[Organ of St. Laurens Chu. Alkmaar]

DARE, Marie (b. 1902)

(3) Highland Sketches Str. orch
Orch.—Fogell V‡ CA.MPO 5006

---

‡ = Long-playing, 33⅓ r.p.m. ♭ = 45 r.p.m. ♮ = Auto. couplings, 78 r.p.m.

DARGOMIJSKY, Alexander (1813-1869)

Baba-Yaga orch. before 1864
Moscow Radio—Gauk   in ♯ *CdM.LD 8055*
(*Glinka & Tchaikovsky*)   (*Glinka only, USSRM.D 151*)
(*Tchaikovsky: Sym. No. 6 on* ♯ *Csm.CRLP 213*)

Kazachok (Little-Russian fantasia) orch.
☆ Moscow Radio—Gauk   *USSRM.D 00111*
(*Glinka: Polonaise*)

OPERAS

ROUSSALKA 4 Acts 1856
Collected Excerpts
  ☆ A. Pirogov, I. Kozlovsky & Bolshoi Theatre Cho.,
    probably from complete recording ♯ *USSR.D 1524*
  (*Rimsky: Snow Maiden*)

Ah, you young girls (*Miller's Aria*) Bs (Act I)
S. Belarsky   in ♯ *Vic.LPM 3274*
(*Moussorgsky, Glinka, Rimsky, etc.*)   (♭ *set EPB 3274*)
A. Pirogov (*USSRM.D 887*)
N. Chastiy (*Ukranian*) (USSR. 021952)

Roussalka's Aria S (Act I)
K. Dzherzinskaya   in ♯ Csm.CRLP 139

Bridal Chorus (Act II)
  ☆ Bolshoi Theatre Cho.—Nebolsin, from set (*USSR. 6382*)

Some unknown power (*Prince's Cavatina*) T
  (Act III)
  ☆ S. Lemeshev   in ♯ *Mon.MWL 337*
    (in ♯ *Sti. 1000;* in ♯ *Csm.CRLP 139*)
I. Kozlovsky (*USSRM.D 00805* & USSR. 022910/1)
P. Belinnik (*Ukrainian*) (in ♯ *USSR.D 2092*)

What does this mean? Bs & T (Act III)
  (*Mad Scene & Death of Miller*)
  ☆ M. Reizen & G. Nelepp   in ♯ *Mon.MWL 337*
  (in ♯ Csm.CRLP 139; in ♯ CHS.CHS 1302;
   USSRM.D 00831/2: ▽ USSR. 017799/802)

Natasha's Aria S (Act IV)
  ☆ E. Smolenskaya (in ♯ Csm.CRLP 139)

(The) STONE GUEST 3 Acts 1872
Laura's Arias: Fog has descended on Granada;
  Here am I, Inezlia S
V. Davidova   *USSRM.D 00915*
(*Rimsky-Korsakov & Serov*)
  ☆ M. Maksakova (in ♯ *Sti. 1000;* in ♯ *Csm.CRLP 139*)

SONGS
COLLECTIONS

I am sad, because . . . (Lermontov)
I loved you (Pushkin)   ☆
Oriental Ballad (Pushkin)
Curls (Delvig)
  Al. Ivanov (B) (2ss)   *USSR.D 00608/9*

I loved you (Pushkin)
I am in love, my beauty (Yazikov)
The Youth & the maiden (Pushkin)
  I. Kozlovsky (T)   *USSR. 22090/1*

Lonely and sad (Lermontov)
I am in love, my beauty (Yazikov)
  I. Kozlovsky (T)   ♯ *USSR.D 1429*
(*Glinka, Verdi, etc.*)
[*Lonely & sad also in USSRM.D 00695*]

Don't ask me why (Pushkin)
Dreams, dreams (Pushkin)
  M. Maksakova (S)   *USSR. 22330/1*
(*also with Varlamov, in USSRM.D 00696*)

The Worm (Kurotchkin)
The Old Corporal (Kurotchkin)
  ☆ B. Gmyria (B) (*USSRM.D 00665/6*)

How often I hear (Zhadovsky)
  ☆ S. Preobrazhenskaya (*USSRM.D 00743*)

I am grieved (Lermontov)
B. Gmyria (B)   *USSR. 22085*
(*Tchaikovsky: Serenade*)

I'll light the candle (Kolstov)
N. Postavnicheva (S) (*USSR. 21450*)

I love him still (Zhadovsky)
Z. Dolukhanova (A)   *USSR. 22094*
(ARR. *Shaporin: The Field has many roads*)

I shan't tell anyone (Koltsov)
N. Kazantseva (S)   *USSRM.D 00700*
(*Rimsky & Rachmaninoff*)

(The) Night Wind
B. Gmyria (B)   *USSR. 22542*
(*Rimsky: On the hills of Georgia*)

Without sense, without reason (Koltsov)
  (*"The passionate Lover"*)
S. Preobrazhenskaya (S)   *USSRM.D 00743*
(*How often I hear; & Moussorgsky*) (*also USSR. 20566*)

Wandering clouds (Lermontov)
E. Chavdar (S)   in ♯ *USSR.D 2089*
(*Cui, Glinka, etc.*)

We parted proudly (Kurotchkin)
N. Obukhova (M-S)   *USSRM.D 00615*
(*Rimsky & Moussorgsky*)

While soundly slept a silver evening cloud
  (Lermontov) Trio
I. Maslennikova, I. Petrov & A. Orfenov (USSR. 021384)

DASCANIO, Josquin (XVth/XVIth Cent.)

SEE: † SACRED & SECULAR SONGS FROM THE
   RENAISSANCE

DÁVID, Gyula (b. 1913)

Concerto, viola & orch. 1952
P. Lukács & Budapest Phil.—Koródy
(6ss)   **Qual.MN 1064/6**

DAVIES, Sir Henry Walford (1869-1941)

ANTHEMS
Blessed are the pure in heart
York Minster Cho.—Jackson   C.LX 1569
(♯s—*Ouseley & S. S. Wesley*)
(† *English Church Music, Vol. III*)

Confortare ("Be strong") 1937
St. Margaret's Westminster Cho.
     in ♯ Ori.MG-20003

God be in my head
St. Paul's Cath.—Dykes Bower in ♯ C.CX 1193
    (in ♯ Angel. 35138, in set 3516)
Augustana Cho.—Veld   in ♯ BB.LBC 1075
(*Bach, Dvořák, Wagner, etc.*)

CAROLS & HYMNS — ARR. Walford Davies
(The) Holly and the Ivy
S. Forbes & A. Ryan (trebles) & Hampstead Parish Church
  Cho.—Sidwell (*P.R 3498:* ♭ *GEP 8520*)
New Haven Trinity Cho.—Byles (in ♯ *Over.LP 11*)

Love came down at Christmas (unid.—may be by another
  Davies)
St. Mary's Chu. Cho.—Linzel (in ♯ *SMP. n.d.*)

O little town of Bethlehem (Brooks)
Templars Octet (♭ *G.7EP 7021*)

Solemn Melody Str. & organ 1908
  ☆ Philharmonia—Weldon [G. Jones, org.]
       (♭ *C.SED 5507: SEBQ 112*)

— ARR. ORGAN SOLO
R. Perry   in ♯ ASK. 2
(*Bach, Alain, Langlais, Sowerby*)
[org. of 1st Presbyterian Chu., Kilgore, Texas]
C. Smart   *D.F 10466*
(*Easthope Martin: Evensong*)   (♭ *45F 10466*)

— ARR. BAND
Munn and Feltons Works Band—Mortimer (*C.DB 3706*)

☆ = Re-issue of a recording to be found in previous volumes.

DAVY, Richard (*c.* 1467-*c.* 1516)

SEE: † HISTORY OF MUSIC IN SOUND (29)

DEBUSSY, Achille Claude (1862-1918)

CLASSIFIED: I. Instrumental
    A. Piano   B. Chamber Music
    C. Orchestral
    II. Vocal
    A. Cantatas   B. Dramatic Works
    C. Songs & Part Songs

I. INSTRUMENTAL

A. PIANO

COLLECTIONS

Preludes, Book I. Complete
(6) Épigraphes antiques pf. duet
En blanc et noir 2 pfs. ♯ ML 4977; ¹EPhi.ABL 3081
      (♯ Phi.A 01225L)
Preludes, Book II. Complete
(2) Arabesques
Children's Corner Suite   ♯ML 4978
Images, Books I & II
Estampes
Masques
L'Isle joyeuse   ♯ML 4979
R. Casadesus (with G. Casadesus in duets)
    ♯ AmC.ML 4977/9
    (set SL 222)
[It has been stated that Children's Corner & Preludes, Book II are ☆]

Danse (Tarantelle styrienne) 1890
Rêverie 1890
Nocturne, D flat major 1890
(2) Arabesques 1888
Valse romantique 1898
L'Isle joyeuse 1904
Le Petit nègre (from *Boîte à joujoux*)
Masques 1904
Danse bohémienne 1880
Ballade [slave] 1890
Mazurka 1891
La Plus que lente Valse 1910
Berceuse héroïque 1914
Hommage à Haydn ("Sur le nom d'H ...") 1909
W. Gieseking   ♯ C.CX 1149
    (♯ FCX 296: QCX 10096; ♯ Angel. 35026)
[See below for individual issues from this Collection; some items may be ☆]

Suite Bergamasque: No. 3, Clair de lune
Preludes II: 12, Feux d'artifice
Pour le piano: No. 3, Toccata
M. Barthel   ♯ Aphe.AP 25
(*Liszt, Schumann*)

CHILDREN'S CORNER
Preludes: I, 10: La Cathédrale engloutie
    II, 8: Ondine
L'Isle joyeuse
ESTAMPES
Étude No. 11, Pour les arpèges composés
M. Regules ("Siena" pf.)   ♯ Eso.ESP 3003
☆ Arabesques 1 & 2
☆ ESTAMPES
☆ La Plus que lente
    PRELUDES I: 8, La fille aux cheveux de lin Ø
☆ Rêverie Ø
    SUITE BERGAMASQUE (Clair de lune Ø)
M. Pressler   ♯ MGM.E 3054
(those marked Ø also on ♭ X 1085)
Arabesques 1 & 2 (also on ♭Phi.A 400002E)
PRELUDES: I, 5: Les Collines d'Anacapri
    I, 8: La fille aux cheveux de lin
        (also on ♭ Phi.A 400002E)
    II, 3: La Puerta del vino
Images: I, 3: Poissons d'or
La Plus que lente
☆ H.Henkemans   ♯ EPhi.ABR 4023
(&, excluding Prelude I-5, in ♯ Phi.S 04007L)

SUITE BERGAMASQUE: No. 3, Clair de lune
PRELUDES: I,1 & 12
Pour le piano
Images: I, 2: Hommage à Rameau
☆ G. Copeland   ♯ MGM.E 3024
(*L'Après-midi, etc., Rameau, Satie*)

---

(2) Arabesques 1888
A. Sandford   in ♯ Allo. 3079
☆ J. Iturbi (♭ *Vic.ERA 87*)
— ARR. HARP Renié
E. Vito   in ♯ Per.SPL 704
(*Handel, Mozart, Prokofiev, etc.*)
... No. 1, E major: E. Burton   in ♯ CEd.CE 1024
— ARR. VLC. & PF.
A. Vlasov   in♯ USSR.D 1180
(*Ravel, Tchaikovsky*)
— ARR. SAX. QTT. F. Carillon
A. Sax. Qtt. (in ♯ *Phi.N 00616R*)

Ballade [slave] 1890
☆ W. Gieseking (♭ *C.ESBF 102*)

Boîte à joujoux See I.C, *below*

CHILDREN'S CORNER, Suite 1908
A. Ferber   ♯ LT.EL 93078
(*Estampes*)   (♯ *Sel. 270.C.020*)
P. Spagnolo   ♯ D.LW 5187
S. Bianca (4ss)   MSB. 78036/7
H. Henkemans (*Estampes*)   ♯ Phi.A 00627R
[Nos. 1 & 6 only on ♭ *A 400002E*]
☆ W. Gieseking   ♯ C.C 1014
(*Schumann*)   (♯ *FC 1025: QC 5005*)
(*Suite Bergamasque*, on ♯ *C.FCX 306*; Angel. 35067)
(Nos. 1, 3, 6, only on ♭ *C.SEL 1540*)
☆ C. Seemann (♯ *AmD.DL 4053*)
— ARR. ORCH. Caplet
French Nat. Radio—Cluytens   ♯ C.CX 1282
(*Boîte à joujoux*)   (♯ *FCX 307*: Angel. 35172)
Belgian Radio—André   ♯ DT.TM 68013
    (TV.VE 9010)
☆ Orch.—Stokowski   ♯ Vic.LM 9023
(*Tchaikovsky*)   (2ss, ♯ *ItV.A10R 0005*)
(No. 4 only on ♭ *Vic.ERA 119*; No. 5 on ♭ *ERA 244*)
Nos. 3, 5 & 6 only M. v. Doren   in ♯ Chan.MVDP 2
No. 3, Serenade for the doll
☆ V. Horowitz (in ♯ Vic. set LM 6014; ♭ set ERG 6014;
    in ♯ *ItV.B12R 0064/5*; FV.A 630203)
No. 5, The little shepherd ☆ O. Levant (♭ *AmC.A 1856*)
— ARR. CL. & ORCH.
R. Kell & Orch.—Camarata (in ♯ *B.AXL 2016*;
    AmD.DL 7550)
No. 6, Golliwogg's Cake-walk
H. Henkemans, from set (*Estampes No. 3*) Phi.A 11247G
A. Cortot   in ♯ JpV.LS 105
☆ C. Keene (in ♯ EMer.MG 10113; ♭ *Mer.EP 1-5007*)
— ARR. VLN. & PF.
☆ J. Heifetz (♭ *AmD.ED 3502* & in ♯ DL 9780)
— ARR. FL., OB., CL., BSN., HRN.
Chicago Woodwind Quintet (in ♯ Aphe.AP 17)

Danse (Tarantelle styrienne) 1890
☆ W. Gieseking   ♭ C.SCB 105
(*La plus que lente*)   (♭ *SCBF 108: SCBQ 3009*)
— ARR. ORCH. Ravel
Boston Orch. Soc.—Page   ♯ SOT. 1068
(*Honegger & Barber*)   (& in ♯ 10683)

D'un cahier d'esquisses 1903
W. Gieseking   ♯ Angel. 35250
(*Études*)

En blanc et noir 2 pfs. 1915
J. Bonneau & G. Joy   ♯ Pat.DT 1026
(*Fauré*)
☆ J. & A. Iturbi (in ♯ Vic.LM 9018)

(6) Épigraphes antiques pf. duet 1915
R. Gold & A. Fizdale   ♯ AmC.ML 4854
(*Milhaud, Satie, Poulenc*)   (in set SL 198)
... Nos. 1, 2, & 4 only
K. U. & H. Schnabel   ♭ EPhi.NBE 11004
(*Schubert: Polonaises*)   (♭ *Phi.N 402024E*)
— ARR. ORCH. Ansermet
Suisse Romande—Ansermet   ♯ D.LXT 2927
(*Jeux*)   (♯ *Lon.LL 992*)

---

¹ Although reviewed, it is doubtful if ever on sale.

ESTAMPES 1903
1. Pagodes   2. Soirée dans Grenade
3. Jardins sous la pluie

W. Gieseking (n.v.)   # C.CX 1137
(*Images & Pour le piano*) (#FCX 282: QCX 10103;
        # Angel. 35065)

R. Gianoli   in # Nix.WLP 6214-1/2
(#s—*Preludes, Bks. I & II*) (# West. set WAL 214;
        Véga.C 30.A 21)

A. Ferber   # *LT.EL 93078*
(*Children's Corner*)   (# Sel. 270.C.020)

H. Henkemans   # *Phi.A 00627R*
(*Children's Corner Suite*)   (& in # Phi.S 04007L, d.c.)

E. Gilberg   # AmVox.PL 8760
(*Images, Set I, No. 1; & Ravel*)

☆ W. Gieseking (o.v.) (*Images; & Ravel*) # AmC.ML 4773
☆ C. Arrau (*below*)   # AmC.ML 4786

No. 2, Soirée dans Grenade
L. Morel   # *D.LW 5127*
(*Preludes, Bk. I, No. 5; Marescotti, Ravel, etc.*)
        (# Lon.LD 9149)

☆ O. Levant (♭ AmC.A 1856)

No. 3, Jardins sous la pluie
J. Iturbi   in # Vic.LRM 7057
(*Chopin, Granados, Schumann, etc.*) (♭ set ERB 7057)

H. Henkemans   Phi.A 11247G
(*Children's Corner Suite, No. 6*)   (from set)

A. d'Arco   in *Plé.P 104*

A. Sandford   in # Allo. 3079

(12) ÉTUDES 1915
COMPLETE RECORDINGS
W. Gieseking   # Angel. 35250
(*D'un cahier d'esquisses*)

H. Henkemans   # Phi.A 00237L
        (# Epic.LC 3104)

A. Ferber   V# *Sel.LLA 1031 & 230.C.005*
(4ss)

... No. 6, Pour les huits doigts
G. Gorini (*Prelude No. 12; & Scriabin*) Cet.AB 30025
... No. 11, Pour les arpèges composés
E. Gilels (*Prokofiev: Visions fugitives*) *Eta. 120024*
(*Prokofiev, Shostakovich, Tchaikovsky,*
        in # CdM.LDA 8104)
(& in # Csm.CRLP 224)

Hommage à Haydn ("Sur le nom d'H . . .") 1909
☆ E. R. Schmitz (♭ Cam.CAE 198)

IMAGES
SET I (1905) 1. Reflets dans l'eau
        2. Hommage à Rameau
        3. Mouvement
SET II (1907) 1. Cloches à travers les feuilles
        2. Et la lune descend . . .
        3. Poissons d'or

COMPLETE RECORDINGS
A. Ferber   # *LT.EL 93049*
        (# T.LB 6119; V# Sel.LLA 1030)
[Set I also on # Sel.LP 8312; # SpT.TLE 20001 with
Sonata 2]

J-M. Damase   # *D.FS 123606*
☆ W. Gieseking   # C.CX 1137
(*Estampes & Pour le piano*) (# FCX 282: QCX 10103;
        Angel. 35065)
(*Estampes* (o.v.); & Ravel on # AmC.ML 4773)
☆ C. Arrau (*above & below*)   # AmC.ML 4786

SET I
No. 1, Reflets dans l'eau
E. Gilberg   # AmVox.PL 8760
(*Estampes; & Ravel*)
B. Webster   in # Persp.PR 2
W. MacGregor   in # Kings.KLP 201
(*II, No. 2; Preludes; & Schubert*)
P. Cavazzini   # *Arp.ARC 2*
(*Albeniz, Liszt, Ravel*)
☆ A. Benedetti-Michelangeli (♭ G.7R 148: 7RQ 3017:
        7RW 139)
W. Gieseking, from set (♭ C.SEL 1527: SEBQ 125)
O. Levant (♭ AmC.A 1856)
M. Panzéra (in # Clc. 6269)

SET II
No. 2, Hommage à Rameau
M. Meyer   # DFr. 86
(*Couperin, Ravel, Rameau*)   (# HS.HSL 97)
W. MacGregor (*above*)   in # Kings.KLP 201
☆ A. Rubinstein (♭ G.7ER 5040; ♭ Vic.ERA 36)

No. 3, Poissons d'or
☆ A. Rubinstein (♭ G.7RF 228)

(L') Isle joyeuse 1904
W. Gieseking (from Collection)   C.LX 1618
(*Masques*)
G. Joy   JpV.SD 3083
(*Preludes, Bk. I—No. 20*)

Lindajara 2 pfs. 1901
P. Luboshutz & G. Nemenoff in # Rem. 199-147

Masques 1904
W. Gieseking (from Collection)   C.LX 1618
(*L'Isle joyeuse*)
☆ A. Rubinstein   G.DB 21589
(*Preludes, Bk. II-7*) (♭ 7ER 5040: 7RF 228;
        ♭ Vic.ERA 86; ♭ ItV.A72R 0002)

Nocturne, D flat major 1890
☆ W. Gieseking (♭ C.ESBF 102)

Petite Suite four hands 1889
☆ E. Bartlett & R. Robertson   # MGM.E 3114
(*Ravel & Saint-Saëns*)

— ARR. ORCH. H. Büsser
French Nat. Radio—Büsser   # *Pat.DT 1014*
(*Büsser*)   (& ED 18: EDQ 105, 2ss)
Lamoureux—Fournet   # *Phi.N 00737R*
(*Fauré*)
(*idem, & Roussel on # Epic.LC 3165*)
Berlin Str. Orch.   # Roy. 1565
(*Suite Bergamasque & Preludes, etc.*)
☆ N.B.C. Sym.—Reiner (# ItV.A12R 0025)
  Berlin Radio—Celibidache (# ANix.ULPY 9006)

— ARR. ORGAN: R. Ellsasser (in # MGM.E 3125)

(La) Plus que lente Valse 1910
☆ W. Gieseking   ♭ *C.SCB 105*
(*above*)   (♭ SCBF 108: SCBQ 3009)
☆ A. Rubinstein (♭ G.7EB 6009: 7RQ 248)

— ARR. VLN. & PF. Roques
J. Tomasow & F. Holetschek (in # Van.VRS 464)
☆ I. Kawaciuk & F. Vrána (in # Sup.LPM 135; U. 5185C)
  J. Heifetz (in # G.ALP 1206: FALP 248; ♭ Vic.ERA 57)

— ARR. CL. & ORCH.
R. Kell & Orch.—Camarata
     (in # B.AXL 2016; AmD.DL 7550

— ARR. ORCH: Orch—Chevreux (in V# CdM.LDYM 4020)

POUR LE PIANO, Suite 1901
W. Gieseking   # C.CX 1137
(*Images*)   (# FCX 282: QCX 10103; Angel. 35065)
(*Suite Bergamasque on # C.FC/QC 1018*)
G. Bachauer   # *G.CLP 1067*
(*Preludes; & Chopin, Ravel, Mompou*)
☆ C. Arrau (*above*)   # AmC.ML 4786

... No. 3, Toccata, C sharp minor ☆ M. Haas (in # Pol. 18077)

PRELUDES, Books I & II 1910-1913
COMPLETE RECORDINGS
F. Gulda   # *D.LXT 5116/7*
(4ss)   (# Lon.LL 1289/90)
[Bk I-8, 10 on ♭ D. 71104; Bk. I-5 & Bk. II-5 on ♭ D. 71097]
R. Gianoli   # *Nix.WLP 6214-1/2*
(3½ss—*Estampes*) (# West. set WAL 214; Véga. C 30.A21/2)
A. Ferber (4ss)   # *Sel.LA 1066/7*
☆ W. Gieseking   # *C.FCX 185/6*
  [Book I only on # C.CX 1098: QCX 10063;
        Angel. 35066]
☆ M. Barzetti (# Argo.RG 21/22)[1]

COLLECTIONS
Book I: 1, 8; Book II: 5
G. Bachauer   # G.CLP 1067
(*Pour le piano; Ravel & Mompou*)

---

[1] Announced but not issued.

Book I: 8, 12; Book II: 3, 5, 6
P. Sancan   ♯ *FV.F 230003*
(*Ravel*)

BOOK I

COMPLETE RECORDINGS
☆ A. Cortot (♯ *G.FALP 360: QBLP 5020*)
E. Kilenyi (♯ *Cum.CR 236*; ♯ *Rem. 100-17*; & with
   commentary by S. Spaeth on ♯ *Rem. 11*)
E. Robert Schmitz (♯ *Cam.CAL 179: Nos. 8 & 10 only*
   on ♭ *CAE 186: Nos. 3, 5, 6 & 9 on* ♭ *CAE 210*)

COLLECTIONS
Nos. 1, 2, 3 & 12 E. Burton   in ♯ *CEd.CE 1027*

Nos. 6-10   ☆ A. Cortot, from set (♭ *Vic.EHA 3*)

Nos. 8, 11 & 12
L. Shankson   in ♯ *Roy. 1565*
(*Suite Bergamasque, Petite Suite, etc.*)

No. 1, Danseuses de Delphes
D. Bar-Illan   ♯ **Kings.KL 211**
(*BK. II, No. 12; Chopin, Ben-Haim, Liszt*)

No. 5, Les Collines d'Anacapri
L. Morel   ♯ *D.LW 5127*
(*Estampes No. 2; Ravel, Marescotti, etc.*) (♯ *Lon.LD 9149*)

No. 8, La Fille aux cheveux de lin
A. Sandford   in ♯ **Allo. 3079**
☆ C. Keene (in ♯ *EMer.MG 10113*; ♭ *FMer.MEP 14505*;
                                ♭ *Mer.EP 1-5007*)
A. Rubinstein (♭ *G.7RF 228: 7ER 5040*; ♭ *Vic.ERA 86*;
                            ♭ *ItV.A72R 0002*)
W. Gieseking, from set (♭ *C.SEL 1527: SEBQ 125*)
— ARR. VLN. & PF.   Hartmann
☆ Y. Menuhin & G. Moore   ♯ *Vic.LHMV 22*
(*Falla, Nielsen, Ravel*)   (& *ArgA. 292705*)
☆ J. Heifetz & E. Bay   *G.DA 2058*
(*Dinicu: Hora staccato*)   (♭ *Vic.ERA 126*)
☆ Z. Francescatti & M. Lanner (in ♯ *EPhi.NBL 5010*;
                                Phi.N 02101L*)
F. Kreisler (in ♯ *Vic.LCT 1142*)
— ARR. GUITAR Balaguier
C. Santias (in ♯ *FestF.FLD 32; SpFest.HF 3201*)
— ARR. CL. & ORCH.
R. Kell & orch.—Camarata (in ♯ *AmD.DL 7550*;
                         in ♯ *B.AXL 2016*)

No. 10, La Cathédrale engloutie
L. Hungerford   in ♯ **LH. 101/2**
                                    (Pte.)
W. MacGregor   in ♯ **Kings.KLP 201**
(*Bk. II, Nos. 3 & 6; Images; & Schubert*)
R. Spivak   **ArgV. 66-6172**
(*Glinka: The Lark*)
☆ W. Gieseking, from set (♭ *C.SEL 1527: SEBQ 125*)
C. Solomon (*G.EA 4097*)
A. Rubinstein (*G.DA 2053*: ♭ *7RF 227*)
H. Cohen (♭ *C.SCD 2021: SCDQ 3015*)
M Panzéra (in ♯ *Clc. 6269*)
H. Henkemans (in ♯ *Phi.S 04007L*)
— ARR. ORGAN.   R. Ellsasser (in ♯ *MGM.E 3120*)

No. 12, Minstrels
A. Rubinstein   ♭ *G.7ER 5040*
(*No. 8, Images I-2, & Masques*) (♭ *Vic.ERA 86*;
                            ♭ *ItV.A72R 0002*)
G. Gorini   **Cet.AB 30025**
(*Étude; & Scriabin*)
G. Joy   **JpV.SD 3083**
(*L'Isle joyeuse*)
☆ M. Panzéra (in ♯ *Clc. 6269*)
— ARR. VLN. & PF.
J. Tomasow & F. Holetschek (in ♯ *Van.VRS 464*)
☆ Z. Francescatti & M. Lanner
                (in ♯ *EPhi.NBL 5010*; Phi.N 02101L*)

BOOK II

COMPLETE RECORDINGS
W. Gieseking (n.v.)
                         ♯ **C.CX 1304**
                              (♯ *Angel. 35249*)
☆ E. Robert Schmitz (♯ *Cam.CAL 180: No. 8 only*
        on ♭ *CAE 186; No. 12 on* ♭ *CAE 210*)

No. 3, La Puerta del vino
W. MacGregor   in ♯ **Kings.KLP 201**
(*No. 6; Bk. I, No. 10; Images; & Schubert*)
☆ C. Arrau (*C.LOX 819*)

No. 4, Les Fées sont d'exquises danseuses
☆ H. Henkemans (in ♯ *Phi.S 04007L*)

No. 6, General Lavine, Eccentric
W. MacGregor (*above*)   in ♯ **Kings.KLP 201**
☆ O. Levant (♭ *AmC.A 1856*)
H. Henkemans (in ♯ *Phi.S 04007L*)

No. 7, La terrasse des audiences au clair de lune
☆ A. Rubinstein   *G.DB 21589*
(*Masques*) (♭ *7RF 227*; ♭ *Vic.ERA 216*; ♭ *FV.A 95227*,
                                    d.cs.)

No. 8, Ondine
☆ A. Rubinstein (♭ *G.7RF 227*; ♭ *Vic.ERA 216*;
                                ♭ *FV.A 95227*)

No. 12, Feux d'artifice
D. Bar-Illan   ♯ **Kings.KL 211**
(*Bk. I, No. 1; etc.*)
P. Sebastiani   **ArgV. 66-6004**
(*Clair de lune*)

Rêverie 1890
W. Gieseking, from Collection   **C.LX 1598**
(*Valse romantique*)   (♭ *SCB 114: SCBQ 3018*)
A Sandford (in ♯ *Allo. 3079*)
E. Gilels (*USSR. 8241/2*)
☆ J. Iturbi (♭ *G.7EB 6010*)
— ARR. VLC. & PF. Fournier
P. Fournier & E. Lush   *G.DA 2028*
(*Fauré: Berceuse*) (♭ *Vic.EHA 20*: in ♯ *LHMV 1043*:
                         ♭ set *WHMV 1043*)
— ARR. ORCH.   Berlin String Orch. (in ♯ *Roy. 1565*)
— ARR. CL. & ORCH.   R. Kell & Orch.—Camarata
                (in ♯ *B.AXL 2016*; AmD.DL 7550*)

SUITE BERGAMASQUE 1890
F. Gulda   ♯ *D.LXT 2817*
(*Ravel*)   (♯ *Lon.LL 754*)
[*No. 3 only on* ♭ *D. 71084: DK 23354*]
☆ W. Gieseking   ♯ *C.FC/QC 1018*
(*Pour le piano*)
(*Children's Corner* on ♯ *C.FCX 306*; ♯ Angel. 35067)
[*Clair de lune* only on ♭ *C.SEL 1540*]
☆ F. Glazer   ♯ *Nix.QLP 4005*
(*Ravel*)   (♯ *Cum.CPL 200*)
L. Shankson   ♯ *Roy. 1565*
(*Petite Suite, Prelude, etc.*)
☆ E. R. Schmitz (♭ *Cam.CAE 198*)
— ARR. ORCH. Caplet (No. 3) & Cloëz (Nos. 1, 2, 4)[1]
Cuevas Ballet Orch.—Cloëz ♯ *LI.TWV 91049*
(*Serra*)   (♯ *Cpt. MC 20042*)
Sinfonia Orch.—Cloëz   ♭ *Cpt.EXTP 1006*
[probably in fact the same recording]

No. 3, Clair de lune
M. Lympany   *G.C 4203*
(*Albeniz: Tango*)
M. Tagliaferro   in **V♯** *Sel.LAP 1006*
(*Mompou, Albeniz, etc.*)
M. T. Garatti   **C.CQX 16668**
(*Chopin: Impromptu No. 4*)
A. Sandford   in ♯ *Allo. 3079*
S. Bianca (*Herbert: March of the Toys*) *MSB. 78153*
E. Burton   in ♯ *CEd.CE 1024*
P. Sebastiani   **ArgV. 66-6004**
(*Preludes Bk. II, No. 12*)
R. Bergroth   **Ryt.RK 1005**
(*Mozart: Sonata No. 11, Rondo*)
L. Miki (♭ *Rem.REP 74*)
L. Sangiorgi (*Dur.AI 10350*)
☆ C. Keene (in ♯ *EMer.MG 10113*)
H. Cohen (♭ *S.SED 2021: SCDQ 3015*)
L. Pennario (in ♯ *DCap.CTL 7102; Cap.P 8312*:
                                ♭ *FAP 8205*)
O. Frugoni (♭ *AmVox.VIP 45370*)
— ARR. PF. & ORCH.
W. Stech & Hamburg State Phil.—Wal-Berg
                (in ♯ *T.TW 30027*)

[1] For Ballet *L'Ange gris*.

No. 3, Clair de lune (*continued*)

— ARR. ORCH
Hollywood Bowl—Dragon (in ♯ DCap.CTL 7072;
    Cap.P 8276: ♭ *FAP 8281;* ♭ *SpC.SCGE 80001*)
Boston Prom.—Fiedler (in ♯ Vic.LM 1879: ♭ *set ERB 54;*
    ♭ *ERA 212; FV.A 95218; ItV.A72R 0050*)
Philadelphia—Ormandy (in ♯ AmC.ML 4983)
Melachrino Orch (in ♯ *G.DLP 1083*)
A. Kostelanetz Orch. (in ♯ C.SX 1004: QSX 12004;
    AmC.CL 798 & CL 792, o.n. ML 4692)
Frankenland Sym.—Kloss (in ♯ CA.LPA 1025;
                   Lyr.LL 48)
Belgian Radio—P. Glière (in ♯ Mae.OAT 25001)
Berlin Str. Orch. (in ♯ Roy. 1565)
  etc.
☆ Orch.—Stokowski (♭ *G.7ER 5011;* ♭ *ItV.A72R 0017*)
Cincinnati Summer Op.—Cleva (in ♯ B.AXTL 1035;
    D.UST 253087; in ♯ AmD.DL 8053: ♭ *ED 3526;*
                   in ♯ AFest.CFR 12-45)
Philadelphia—Stokowski (in ♯ Cam.CAL 123:
                  ♭ *CAE 188*)
Col. Sym.—Rodzinski (in ♯ AmC.CL 726;
               Phi.S 04601L)

— ARR. PF. & ORCH.
O. Levant & Kostelanetz Orch. (♭ *AmC.A 1831*)

— ARR. VLN. & PF.
D. Oistrakh & V. Yampolsky (in ♯ JpV.LS 2026)
☆ J. Heifetz (♭ *AmD.ED 3502* & in ♯ DL 9780)

— ARR. HARP ☆ E. Vito (in ♯ *Nix.SPLY 145;* SOT. 10301)

— ARR. 2 HARPS   C. Salzédo & L. Lawrence
    (in ♯ Mer.MG 10144: ♭ *EP 1-5006*)

Valse romantique 1898
W. Gieseking (from Collection)   **C.LX 1598**
(*Rêverie*)   (♭ *SCB 114: SCBQ 3018*)

I. B. CHAMBER MUSIC

Quartet, G minor, Op. 10   Strings 1893
Italian Qtt.   ♯ **C.CX 1155**
(*Milhaud*)   (♯ C.QCX 10054: FCX 309; ♯ Angel. 35130)
Parrenin Qtt.   (*Ravel*)   ♯ **Pac.LDPF 48**
Pascal Qtt. (*Sonata No. 1*)   ♯ ***MMS. 53***
Curtis Qtt.   ♯ **West.WN 18049**
(*Ravel*)   (& 2ss, ♯ LAB 7045)
Loewenguth Qtt.   (*Haydn*)   ♯ **Pol. 18137**
G. Tessier, M. Hugon, J. Balout & R. Cordier
(*Sonatas No. 1 & 2*)   ♯ **CFD. 2**
☆ Hirsch Qtt. (*Arensky, Rawsthorne*) ♯ **Argo.RG 3**
☆ Budapest Qtt. (*Ravel*)   ♯ **AmC.ML 4668**

SONATAS
No. 1, D minor, vlc. & pf. 1915
A. Janigro & G. Doyen   ♯ **West.WL 5207**
(*Nos. 2 & 3*)
R. Albin & C. Helffer   ♯ **CFD. 2**
(*Sonata No. 2 & Quartet*)
C. Arnold & L. Schauffler   ♯ **Fred. 2**
(*Morley, Wilbye, Lassus, etc.*)
A. Lévy & G. Gay   ♯ **LT.EL 93045**
(*No. 3*)   (♯ *T.NLB 6101;* V♯ *Sel.LLA 1033*)
J. Starker & L. Pommers   ♯ **Nix.PLP 708**
(*Ravel, Fauré, Poulenc, Bréval, Couperin*) (♯ *Per.SPL 708*)
P. Olefsky & G. Silfies   ♯ **McInt.MM 103**
(*Fauré, Frescobaldi, Senallié, etc.*)
☆ R. Garbusova & A. Balsam (*Str. Qtt.*) ♯ *MMS. 53*

No. 2, flute, vla. & harp 1916
C. Wanausek, E. Weiss, H. Jellinek
(*Nos. 1 & 3*)   ♯ **West.WL 5207**
L. Lavaillotte, P. Ladhuie & B. Galais ♯ **CFD. 2**
(*Sonata No. 1 & Qtt.*)
J. Baker, L. Fuchs, L. Newell ♯ **AmD.DL 9777**
(*Syrinx; & Roussel*)   (♯ *D.UAT 273588*)
☆ J-P. Rampal, P. Pasquier & O. Ledentu ♯ *Sel.LP 8312*
(*Images*)   (♯ *SpT.TLE 2000I*)

No. 3, G minor, vln. & pf. 1917
J. Fournier & G. Doyen   ♯ **West.WL 5207**
(*Nos. 1 & 2*)
O. Colbentson & E. Ulmer   ♯ **CHS.H 12**
(*below; & Dukas, Malipiero, Roussel, etc.*)
(*Franck on* ♯ *MMS. 103*)

J. Tomasow & F. Holetschek   ♯ **Van.VRS 464**
(*Prelude Bk. I, No. 12, etc. & Fauré*)
M-C. & F. Theuveny   ♯ *LT.EL 93045*
(*No. 1*)   (♯ *T.NLB 6101;* V♯ *Sel.LLA 1033*)
A. Grumiaux & P. Ulanowsky   ♯ **Bo.B 203**
(*Bartók, Ravel*)
G. & J. Neveu   ♯ **Angel. 35128**
(*Chausson & Ravel*)
G. Staples & G. Silfies   ♯ **McInt.MM 101**
(*Sarasate, Szymanowski, Prokofiev, etc.*)
☆ Z. Francescatti & R. Casadesus ♯ **C.CX 1111**
(*Franck*)
☆ C. Ferras & P. Barbizet   ♯ **D.LXT 2810**
(*Fauré*)   (♯ Lon.LL 909; D.FAT 173138)
☆ J. Heifetz & E. Bay (♯ *G.QALP 165*)

Syrinx Unacc. fl. (for Inc. music to Psyché, 1912)
J-P. Rampal (n.v.)   in ♯ **Edu.ECM 4001**
(*Mozart & Schubert*)
J. Baker (*above*)   ♯ **AmD.DL 9777**

I. C. ORCHESTRAL

(La) Boîte à joujoux
  (orig. pf. solo, 1913; orch. Caplet for ballet, 1923)
French Nat. Radio—Cluytens   ♯ **C.CX 1282**
(*Children's Corner*)   (♯ FCX 307; Angel. 35172)
R.I.A.S. Sym.—Perlea   ♯ **Rem. 199-159**
                   (♯ Cum.CR 299)
Naples Scarlatti Orch.—Argenta
              ♯ **Csm.CLPS 1045**
(*Saint-Saëns & Zanetti*[1])

— ORIGINAL PF. VERSION
M. Pressler   ♯ **P.PMC 1027**
(*Ibert*)   (♯ MGM.E 3042)
Y. Lefébure   ♯ *Pol. 540005*
[with narration by P. Bertin]
... Ronde only
☆ G. Copeland   in ♯ MGM.E 3024
... Le petit nègre only: See Gieseking, COLLECTION
— — ARR. SAX. QTT.
A. Sax Saxophone Qtt. (in ♯ *Phi.N 00616R*)
— — ARR. FL., OB., CL., BSN. & HRN.
Chicago Sym. Wind Quintet (in ♯ Aphe.AP 14)

(2) Danses   Hp. & strings 1904
1. Danse sacrée   **2. Danse profane**
P. Jamet & Ens.—Capdevielle
               V♯ *Sel.LPP 8608*
(*Ballades de Mallarmé*)
L. Gianuzzi & Angelicum Str.—Janes
              ♯ **Ang.LPA 956**
(*Bettinelli, Vivaldi, Bonporti*)
(*Mozart, Bonporti, Vivaldi, Tchaikovsky, on* ♯ LPA 958)
☆ A. Stockton & Ens.—Slatkin ♯ **DCap.CTL 7096**
(*Ravel & Schoenberg*)   (♯ Cap.P 8304)
☆ E. Vito & Str. Qtt. (♯ Cum.CS 192)
... No. 1, Danse sacrée — ARR. PF. Copeland
☆ G. Copeland (in ♯ MGM.E 3024)

Fantasia pf. & orch. 1889
F. Jacquinot & Westminster Sym.—Fistoulari
              ♯ **P.PMC 1019**
(*Poulenc*)   (♯ MGM.E 3069; Od.ODX 149)
H. Schultes & Frankenland State Sym.—Kloss
              ♯ **CA.LPA 1025**
(*Rhapsody & Clair de lune*)   (♯ Lyr.LL 38)

IMAGES (Set III) 1906-12
1. Gigues   **2. Ibéria**   **3. Rondes de printemps**
COMPLETE RECORDING
Amsterdam—v. Beinum   ♯ *EPhi.ABR 4032*
             (♯ Epic.LC 3147; Phi.A 00722R)
No. 1, Gigues
☆ San Francisco Sym.—Monteux
      (♭ *ItV.A72R 0019;* (o.v.) ♯ Cam.CAL 161)

---

[1] The latest catalogue omits Zanetti from this disc.

No. 2, Ibéria
N.B.C. Sym.—Toscanini   **‡ Vic.LM 1833**
(*La Mer*)   (‡ It*V*.A12R 0154; FV.A 630266)

Champs-Élysées Theatre—Inghelbrecht
    ‡ LT.DTL 93017
(*La Mer*)   (‡ Sel. 320.C.016; West.WL 5327; T.LE 6541)

Prussian State—Schüler   **‡ Ura.RS 7-26**
(*La Mer*)   (*Stravinsky* on ‡ MTW. 537)
(*Albeniz: Ibéria* on ‡ Ura. 7130; *ACC.MP 24*)

☆ Philadelphia—Ormandy (*La Mer*)   **‡ Phi.A 01100L**

No. 3, Rondes de printemps
☆ San Francisco Sym.—Monteux
    (♭ *ItV.A72R 0019*; o.v. ‡ Cam.CAL 161)

Jeux (Poème dansé) 1913
Suisse Romande—Ansermet   **‡ D.LXT 2927**
(*Épigraphes antiques*)   (‡ Lon.LL 992)

☆ Augusteo (St. Cecilia) Sym.—Sabata (‡ G.QALP 178)

Marche écossaise 1908
French Nat. Radio—Inghelbrecht   **‡ C.CX 1229**
(*Prélude à l'après-midi d'un faune, & Nocturnes*)
    (‡ C.FCX 216; Angel. 35103)

(La) Mer 1905
Philharmonia—Cantelli   **‡ G.ALP 1228**
(*Le Martyre de St. Sebastien*) (‡ QALP 10093: FALP 366)

Philharmonia—Karajan   **‡ C.CX 1099**
(*Ravel*)   (‡ QCX 10059: FCX 298; Angel. 35081)
(also, ‡ MApp. n.d.)

Champs-Élysées Theatre—Inghelbrecht
    ‡ LT.DTL 93017
(*Ibéria*)   (‡ T.LE 6541; West.WL 5327; Sel. 320.C.016)

Leipzig Radio—Borsamsky   **‡ Ura.RS 7-26**
(*Ibéria*)   (*Grieg* on ‡ MTW 30; also ‡ ACC.MP 6)

☆ N.B.C. Sym.—Toscanini   **‡ G.ALP 1070**
(*Ravel*)   (‡ FALP 160; ♭ Vic. set ERB 17)
(*Ibéria* on ‡ Vic.LM 1833: ♭ set ERB 48;
    ‡ ItV.A12R 0154;.FV.A 630266)

☆ N.Y.P.S.O.—Mitropoulos (*Ibéria*) **‡ Phi.A 01100L**
☆ Czech Phil.—Désormière   **‡ Sup.LPV 210**
(*Ravel*)   (‡ U. 5198G)
Berlin Sym.—List (‡ Roy. 1401)

☆ Philharmonia—Galliera (‡ AmC.RL 3055)
Cleveland Sym.—Rodzinski (‡ AmC.RL 6628)

(3) NOCTURNES 1893-9
1. Nuages   2. Fêtes   3. Sirènes (with Fem. Cho.)
Paris Vocal Ens. & Paris Cons.—Fournet
    ‡ Phi.A 00160L
(*Ravel*)   (‡ Epic.LC 3048)

M. Briclot Cho. & French Nat. Radio
—Inghelbrecht   **‡ C.CX 1229**
(*Marche écossaise & L'après-midi . . .*)
    (‡ FCX 216; Angel. 35103)

☆ Minneapolis Sym.—Dorati   **‡ EMer.MG 50005**
(*Stravinsky* on ‡ Mer.MG 50025; ‡ FMer.MLP 7505)
☆ Orch.—Stokowski (‡ ItV.A12R 0017) (with Shaw
    Chorale)
Philharmonia—Galliera (‡ C.WS 1002: QS 6003) (with
    Glyndebourne Chorus)
    [Nos. 1 & 2 only on ♭ C.SED 5510: SEBQ 111]
Philadelphia—Stokowski (‡ Cam.CAL 140)

Nos. 1 & 2 only
Boston Orch. Soc.—Page   **‡ Nix.SLPY 803**
(*below*)   (‡ SOT. 1063 & in ‡ 10683)
Leningrad Phil.—Mravinsky   **‡ USSR.D 1705**
(*Bizet*)

No. 2, Fêtes
☆ Orch.—Stokowski   ♭ *G.7ER 5011*
(*Suite bergamasque—Clair de lune*) (♭ It*V*.A72R 0017)
— ARR. 2 PFS. Ravel
☆ J. & R. Lhevinne (*JpV.SF 3*; in ‡ Cam.CAL 265)

Prélude à l'après-midi d'un faune 1894
(Eglogue for orch., after Mallarmé)
Philharmonia—Markevitch   **‡ C.CX 1197**
(*Satie, Weber, Ravel*) (‡ FCX 357; Angel. 35151,
    in set 3518)

Philharmonia—Cantelli   **‡ G.ALP 1207**
(*Dukas, Falla, Ravel*)   (‡ QALP 10097)

Hallé—Barbirolli   **‡ G.BLP 1058**
(*Chabrier & Rimsky*)   (‡ QBLP 5032)

Lamoureux—Martinon   in ‡ **Phi.A 00175L**
(*Dukas, Honegger, etc.*)   (‡ Epic.LC 3058)
(*Dukas only, ‡ Phi.S 06011R*)

French Nat. Radio—Inghelbrecht ‡ **C.CX 1229**
(*Marche écossaise & Nocturnes*) (‡ FCX 216; Angel. 35103)

Westminster Sym.—Collingwood   **C.DX 1899**

Philadelphia—Ormandy (? n.v.)   **‡ AmC.AL 26**
(*Dukas*)

Berlin Phil.—Lehmann   **‡ Pol. 16091**
(*R. Strauss: Don Juan*)

Florence Fest.—Gui   **‡ AudC. 502**
(*Dukas, Borodin, Moussorgsky*)
Sym. Orch—Schönherr   **‡ MTW. 20**
(*R. Strauss, Grieg*)   (♭ set EP 20)
Boston Orch. Soc.—Page   **‡ Nix.SLPY 803**
(*Nocturnes*)   (‡ SOT. 1063 & in ‡ SOT. 10683)
Vienna Artists' Sym. (*Mendelssohn*)   ‡ Ply. 12-26
"Philharmonic"—Berendt   in ‡ Allo. 3079
☆ Suisse Romande—Ansermet   **‡ D.LW 5031**
(*Ravel*)   (‡ Lon.LD 9031)

☆ Danish Radio—Malko (♭ G.7RK 5)
Aarhus Municipal—Jensen (in ‡ Tono.LPX 35005)
Orch.—Stokowski (in ‡ Vic.LRM 7024: ♭ set ERB 7024)
Philharmonia—Galliera (in ‡ AmC.RL 3055)
Austrian Sym.—Moreau (♭ Msq. 10017)
    ‡ Cum.TCR 272; Rem. 100-17; ‡ AFest.CFR 10-88;
    & with commentary by S. Spaeth, ‡ Rem. 11)

— ARR. PF. Copeland ☆ G. Copeland (in ‡ MGM.E 3024)

Printemps 1887
☆ R.P.O.—Beecham   **‡ Vic.LM 9001**
(*Sibelius: Tapiola*)   (♭ set WDM 1293)

Rhapsody, clarinet & orch. 1910
J. D'Hondt & Concert Hall Sym.—Goehr
    ‡ CHS.H 12
(*Sonata, above; & Honegger, Dukas, Goossens, etc.*)
(*Fantasia, pf. & orch.* on ‡ MMS. 81)

☆ R. Kell & C. Rosen (pf.) (♭ AmD.ED 3505)

Rhapsody, saxophone & orch. 1903
J. de Vries & Frankenland State Sym.—Kloss
    ‡ CA.LPA 1025
(*Fantasia, & Clair de lune*)   (‡ Lyr.LL 38)

M. Mule & Paris Phil.—Rosenthal
    ‡ DCap.CCL 7524
(*Ibert*)   (‡ Cap.L 8231)

II. VOCAL

A. CANTATAS

(La) Demoiselle Élue (Rossetti, trs. Sarrazin)
2 S, cho. & orch. 1887
V. de los Angeles, C. Smith, Radcliffe Cho. &
    Boston Sym.—Münch   **‡ Vic.LM 1907**
(*Berlioz*)

M. Gorge, J. Joly (M-S), Cho. & Champs-
    Élysées Theatre Orch.—Inghelbrecht
    ‡ LT.DTL 93009
(*Enfant Prodigue & Noël des enfants...*)
    (‡ West.WL 5336; Sel. 320.C.011)

(L') ENFANT PRODIGUE (Guinand)
Soli, cho. & orch. 1884
COMPLETE RECORDING
M. Gorge (S), H. Legay (T), B. Cottret (Bs),
    Cho. & Champs-Élysées Theatre Orch.
    —Inghelbrecht   **‡ LT.DTL 93009**
(*above & Noël des enfants . . .*)
    (‡ West.WL 5336; Sel. 320.C.011)

Prelude — ARR. ACCORDEONS & CBS.
B. Hughes, B. Palmer & L. Manno (in ‡ Capri. 1)

Azraël! Pourquoi m'as-tu quittée ? (Air de Lia)
☆ E. Wysor (A) (in ‡ Roy. 1589; in ‡ Ply. 12-47)

B. DRAMATIC WORKS

(Le) MARTYRE DE ST. SEBASTIEN 1911
S, S, A, cho. orch. (Inc. Music to play by d'Annunzio)
A. Falcon (speaker), C. Collart, J. Collard,
    C. Gayrand, French Radio Cho. & Champs-
    Élysées Theatre Orch.—Inghelbrecht[1]
    ‡ LT.DTL 93040/1
    (‡ Sel. 270.C.028/9)

---

[1] Text arranged for narrator by Inghelbrecht, in accord with author and composer, for concert performance.

V. Korène, & other speakers; M. Angelici, M. Dobbs, J. Brumaire (S), S. Michel, R. Gohr (A), L. Noguéra (Bs), St. Paul Cho. & Fr. Nat. Orch.—Cluytens (6ss)[1]

‡ C.FCX 338/40

S. Danco, N. Wough, L. de Gontmollin, Tour-de-Peils Cho. & Suisse Romande Orch.—Ansermet[2] ‡ D.LXT 5024
(‡ Lon.LL 1061)

☆ Soloists, Oklahoma City Cha. & Orch.—Alessandro[2]
(‡ CID.AX 33003; MusH.LP 12001)

Symphonic fragments
Philharmonia—Cantelli ‡ G.ALP 1228
(*La Mer*) (‡ QALP 10093: FALP 366)

PELLÉAS ET MÉLISANDE Opera 5 Acts 1902
COMPLETE RECORDINGS

Pelléas	...	...	...	...	C. Maurane (B)
Golaud	...	...	...	...	M. Roux (B)
Arkël	...	...	...	...	X. Depraz (Bs)
Mélisande	...	...	...	...	J. Micheau (S)
Geneviève	...	...	...	...	R. Gorr (M-S)
Yniold	...	...	...	...	A. Simon (S)
A Doctor	...	...	...	...	M. Vigneron (B)

E. Brasseur Cho. & Lamoureux Orch.—Fournet
‡ EPhi.ABL 3076/8
(6ss) (‡ Phi.A 00192/4L; ‡ Epic. set SC 6003)

☆ I. Joachim (S), G. Cernay (M-S), J. Jansen (T), M. Etcheverry (B), etc., Y. Gouverné, Cho. & Sym. Orch.—Désormière ‡ G.FJLP 5030/2
(6ss) (also in ‡ CND. set TM 14)

SELECTED PASSAGES
☆ M. Nespoulous, C. Croiza, etc. & Sym. Orch.—Truc
‡ AmC.RL 3092

C. SONGS & PARTSONGS

COLLECTIONS
(3) CHANSONS DE BILITIS (Louÿs) 1897
Mandoline (Verlaine) 1880
(5) POÈMES DE CHARLES BAUDELAIRE 1887-9
... No. 3, Le Jet d'eau
(3) BALLADES DE FRANÇOIS VILLON 1910
... No. 3, Ballade des femmes de Paris
FÊTES GALANTES, Series I (Verlaine) 1892
N. Merriman (M-S), G. Moore (pf.)
‡ C.CX 1213
(*Bachelet, Fauré, Chausson, Duparc, Bizet*)(‡ Angel.35217)

FÊTES GALANTES, Series I (Verlaine) 1892
... No. 2, Fantoches only
(3) BALLADES DE FRANÇOIS VILLON 1910
LE PROMENOIR DES DEUX AMANTS
(T. Lhermitte) 1910
J. Jansen (B), J. Bonneau (pf.) ‡ D.LXT 2774
(*Chabrier & Ravel*) (‡ Lon.LL 644)

(3) CHANSONS DE BILITIS (Louÿs) 1897
FÊTES GALANTES, Series I & II (Verlaine)
LE PROMENOIR DES DEUX AMANTS
Proses lyriques (Debussy) 1894-5
... No. 2, De grève
(3) BALLADES DE FRANÇOIS VILLON 1910
... No. 3, Ballade des femmes de Paris
☆ M. Teyte (S), A. Cortot (pf.) ‡ Vic.LCT 1133
(*Fauré, Hahn, Duparc, Paladilhe*)

ARIETTES OUBLIÉES (Verlaine) 1888-1903
... No. 2, Il pleure dans mon cœur
... No. 5, Green
Mandoline (Verlaine) 1880
Géori-Boué (S), M. Faure (pf.) ‡ Ura. 7070
(*Gounod, Charpentier, Massenet, etc.*) (♭ UREP 73)

(3) BALLADES DE FRANÇOIS VILLON, No. 2 only
(3) CHANSONS DE FRANCE: No. 2, La Grotte
(Lhermitte)
Mandoline (Verlaine) 1880
☆ G. Souzay (B) & orch. ‡ D.LW 5078
(*Ravel*) (‡ Lon.LD 9091)

(3) CHANSONS DE BILITIS (Louÿs) 1897
FÊTES GALANTES, Series I, Nos. 1 & 2 only
LE PROMENOIR DES DEUX AMANTS
I. Kolassi (M-S), A Collard (pf.) ‡ D.LW 5161
(‡ Lon.LD 9176)

PROSES LYRIQUES (Debussy) 1894-5
(3) CHANSONS DE BILITIS (Louÿs) 1897
(3) BALLADES DE FRANÇOIS VILLON 1910
F. Wend (S), O. Gartenlaub (pf.) ‡ HS.HSL 106
(‡ Ven.CM 9101 & in ‡ CND. set TM 14)

Romance (Bourget)
La Grotte (*Chansons de France*—Lhermitte)
Le Faune; Colloque sentimentale (*Fêtes Galantes*
—Verlaine)
☆ C. Panzéra (B), M. Panzéra (pf.) (in ‡ Clc. 6269)

ARIETTES OUBLIÉES (Verlaine) 1888-1903
1. C'est l'extase   2. Il pleure dans mon cœur
3. L'Ombre des arbres dans la rivière
4. Paysages belges—Chevaux de bois
5. Green (Aquarelle No. 1) 6. Spleen (Aquarelle No. 2)
G. Sciutti (S), J. Bonneau (pf.) ‡ *Phi.A 76705R*
(*Fauré & Ravel*)

G. Touraine (S), F. Poulenc (pf.)
‡ *BàM.LD 012*
(*Poulenc & Roussel*) (‡ HS.HSL 154)
Y. Furusawa (S), A. Collard (pf.)
V‡ *Sel.LPP 8718*
(*Chansons de Bilitis*)
R. Doria (S), S. Gouat (pf.) ♭ *Plé.P 45129*

No. 2, Il pleure dans mon cœur — ARR. VLN. & PF. Hartmann
J. Tomasow & F. Holetschek (in ‡ Van.VRS 464)
☆ J. Heifetz (in ‡ G.ALP 1206: FALP 248)

(3) BALLADES DE FRANÇOIS VILLON 1910
1. Ballade de Villon à s'amye
2. Ballade que fait Villon à la requeste de sa mère
3. Ballade des femmes de Paris
S. Danco (S), G. Agosti (pf.) ‡ *D.LW 5145*
(*Fêtes Galantes, Series I*) (‡ Lon.LD 9146)

... No. 2, only
B. Demigny (?) in ‡ CND. 9
(† *La Musique et la Poésie*)

(3) BALLADES DE MALLARMÉ 1913
1. Soupir 2. Placet futile 3. Éventail
J-C. Benoît (B), J. Stip (pf.) V‡ *Sel.LPP 8608*
(*Danses, sacré et profane*)

Beau Soir (Bourget) 1878
J. Harsanyi (S), O. Herz (pf.) in ‡ Per.SPL 581
R. Hayes (T), R. Boardman (pf.) in ‡ A 440.12-3
E. Sachs (M-S), S. Leff (pf.) in ‡ Mur.P 111
(followed by pf. acc. only)
☆ C. Muzio (S) & orch. (in ‡ AmC.ML 4634)

— ARR. VLN. & PF. Heifetz
☆ J. Heifetz & M. Kaye (in ‡ *B.AXL 2017;*
D.UA 243086; ‡ AmD.DL 9780 & DL 5214)
— ARR. VLC. & PF. P. Fournier & E. Lush
(in ‡ D.LXT 2766; Lon.LL 700)
— ARR. ORCH. Berlin Str. Orch. (in ‡ Roy. 1565)
— FOR PRACTICE: pf. acc. etc., only (in ‡ *VS.ML 3000*)

(3) CHANSONS DE BILITIS (Louÿs) 1897
Y. Furusawa (S), A. Collard (pf.)
V‡ *Sel.LPP 8718*
(*Ariettes oubliées*)
☆ J. Tourel (M-S), G. Reeves (pf.) (‡ *Phi.S 06610R*)

... No. 2, La Chevelure — ARR. VLN. & PF. Heifetz
☆ J. Heifetz & E. Bay (♭ *G.7EB/EBW 6001;* ♭ *Vic.ERA 71*)

(3) CHANSONS DE CHARLES D'ORLÉANS
Part Songs S, A, T, B. 1908
Harvard Glee Club & Radcliffe Cho. Soc.
—Woodworth in ‡ Camb.CRS 202
(† *Chansons & Motets*)
Paris Vocal Ens.—Jouve V‡ *Sel.LAP 1034*
(*Ravel*)

(L') Échelonnement des haies (Verlaine) 1891
G. Touraine (S), J. Bonneau (pf.)
in ‡ Lum.LD 3-402
(*Fêtes Galantes, Series I; Fauré, Gounod, etc.*)

---

[1] In a performance of the play with text revised and adapted by V. Korène. [2] Abridged; no spoken narration.

FÊTES GALANTES (Verlaine)
Series I 1892

1. En sourdine   2. Fantoches   3. Clair de lune
S. Danco (S), G. Agosti (pf.)   ♯ *D.LW 5145*
(*Ballades de Villon*)   (♯ *Lon.LD 9146*)

G. Touraine (S), J. Bonneau (pf.)
♯ **Lum.LD 3-402**
(*above; Poulenc, etc.*)

... **No. 2,** only
M. Sénéchal (T), J. Bonneau (pf.)
in ♯ *Phi.N 00681R*
(*Ravel, Roussel, Gounod, etc.*)

Series II 1904
No. 2, Le Faune
R. Hayes (T), R. Boardman (pf.)
in ♯ *Van.VRS 449*
(*Beethoven, Schumann, etc.; & Trad.*)

Fleur des Blés (Girod)
— ARR. CHO. Darcieux
Venlona Cho.—Vranken   ♭ *G.7EPH 1013*
(*d'Indy, Pierné, Poulenc*)

Mandoline (Verlaine) 1880
G. Swarthout (M-S), G. Trovillo (pf.)
in ♯ *G.ALP 1269*
(*Chausson, Berlioz, Hahn, etc.*) (in ♯ Vic.LM 1793;
FV. 630227)
J. Harsanyi (S), O. Herz (pf.) in ♯ *Per.SPL 581*

Noël des enfants qui n'ont plus de maisons (Debussy)
M. Gorge (S) & orch.—Inghelbrecht[1]
in ♯ *LT.DTL 93009*
(*Cantatas*)   (♯ *West.WL 5336; Sel. 320.C.011*)

PROSES LYRIQUES (Debussy) 1894-5
V. Osborne (S), R. Vetlesen (pf.) ♯ **ML. 7044**
(*Fauré*)

Romance (Bourget) 1887
FOR PRACTICE (in ♯ *VS.ML 3000*)

DEFOSSEZ, René (b. 1905)

Aquarium Impressions for orch. 1934
1. Alcyonium palmatum
2. Évolutions des Mulli barbati
3. Repas des Callapae granulatae
Belgian Radio Cha.—Doneux
♯ *Gramo.GLP 2501*
SEE also: LEKEU

DELALANDE, Michel-Richard

SEE: LALANDE, M-R. de

DELANNOY, Marcel (1898)

Suite à danser

1. Mille et trois—Pasodoble
2. Tangommina—Tango
3. Sambaratino—Samba
4. Bal Mabille—Polka-quadrille
5. Kew Garden—Slow
6. Danse des Négrillons—Rumba[2]
7. Nanou Filhadoué—Beguine[3]
8. Jeunesse—Valse Cho. & Orch.
Hewitt Orch. & Cho.   ♯ *DFr.SD 2*

DELIBES, Clément Philibert Léon
(1836-1891)

I. STAGE WORKS

NOTE: The Ballets are numbered according to the Heugel
contemporary pf. reductions.

COPPÉLIA Ballet, 2 Acts 1870

ACT I
1. (a) Prelude, with Mazurka   1. (b) Valse lente
2. Scène, Swanhilda et Frantz   3. Mazurka
4. Scène, Préparatifs de Fête   5. Ballade de l'Épi
6. Thème slave varié[4]   7. Czardas   8. Finale

ACT II SCENE I
9. (a) Entr'acte, with Valse. 9. (b) Scène, L'Atelier de
Coppélius ("Nocturne"). 10. Scène. 11. Musique des
Automates. 12. Scène. 13. Chanson à boire et scène.
14. Scène et Valse de la Poupée. 15. Scène. 16. Boléro.
17. Gigue. 18. Finale.

ACT II SCENE II
19. Marche de la Cloche. 20. Fête de la Cloche, Divertissement,
(a) Valse des heures; (b) L'Aurore; (c) La Prière;
(d) Le travail (La Fileuse); (e) L'Hymen (Noce
villageoise); (f) La discorde et la guerre; (g) La paix;
(h) Danse de fête; (i) Galop final.

[5] Nos. 3, 4, 5, 6, 7, 9 (a & b), 11, 14, 15, 16, 17, 19, 20 (a-e, h, i)
Covent Garden—Irving   ♯ *G.CLP 1046*

Nos. 1 (a & b), 7, 14, 5, 6
Boston Sym.—Monteux   ♯ *Vic.LM 1913*
(*Sylvia*)   (♯ *ItV.A12R 0131*)
(*Stravinsky,* on ♯ FV.A 630218)
(& in ♯ Vic. set LM 6113; Nos. 1 (b), 6 & 7, on ♭ *ERA 253*)

Nos. 1 (b), 6, 7, 9 (b), 11, 19, 20 (a & h)[6]
Bamberg Sym.—Lehmann   ♯ *Pol. 17040*
(o.n. *16095*)

Nos. 1 (b), 6, 7, 9 (b), 11, 20 (a & h)[6]
Berlin Sym.—Dobrindt   ♯ *Ura. 7165*
(*J. Strauss*) (*Ravel* on ♯ MTW. 536)

Nos. 1 (a), 1 (b), 7
Phil. Prom.—Boult   ♯ *West.LAB 7027*
(*Sylvia*)
Belgian Radio Cha.—Doneux   ♯ *Mae.OAT 25004*

Nos. 1 (a & b), 3, 4 (▽), 5, 6, 7, 14
☆ Paris Cons.—Désormière (*Sylvia*)   ♯ *Lon.LL 846*

Nos. 1, 14, 5 ☆ Paris Opéra—Blot (in ♭ *G.7ERL 1038*)

Nos. 6, 7, 9 (b), 11, 20a ☆ Vienna Radio—Schönherr
(in ♯ *GA. 33-306*)

Nos. 1 (a), 3, 9 (a), 6,[7] 7
Lamoureux—Fournet   ♯ *EPhi.NBR 6005*
(*Sylvia*)   (♯ *Phi.N 00674R*)
(also *Gounod & Rabaud* on ♯ Epic.LC 3030)
(No. 6 only on ♭ *Phi.N 402003E*)
(*Sylvia,* & *Gounod,* on ♯ Phi.S 04013L)

Nos. 1 (b), 3 & 7
☆ Lower Austrian—Schönherr (in ♯ *AFest.CFR 56;*
Rem. 199-126; & No. 1 (b) only, ♭ *Rem.REP 67*)

Nos. 1 (b), 7, 11
☆ Boston Prom.—Fiedler (♭ *Cam.CAE 151:*
in ♯ CAL 151 & in ♯ set CFL 102)

Nos. 3, 6, 7, 9 (a) ☆ L.P.O.—Kurtz (in ♯ AmC.RL 3056)

Nos. 6, 7, 17 ☆ Covent Garden—Irving (♭ *G.7PW 103*)

Nos. 1 (b), 7
☆ Covent Garden—Braithwaite   in ♯ *P.PMC 1008*

Nos. 3 & 9 (a) French Radio—Dervaux   ♭ *Pac. 45041*

Nos. 1 (b) & 9 (a)
☆ Minneapolis Sym.—Ormandy (in ♯ Cam.CAL 119)

No. 1 (b) Warsaw Op.—Tarski (*Muza. 2346*)

No. 1 (b) — ARR. PF. Dohnányi
G. Anda   ♭ *C.SEL 1516*
(*Liszt: Étude de Concert No. 3*) (♭ *SEBQ 118: ESBF 121*)
(in ♯ C.CX 1156: WCX 1156: FCX 295: QCX 10095;
Angel. 35083)

No. 1 (b) — ARR. ORGAN
R. Foort, sub nom. M. Cheshire (in ♯ *Nix.SLPY 156* &
in ♯ *SOT. 1050* & 10501)

---

[1] Orchestrated by Inghelbrecht.   [2] From ballet *La Pantoufle de Vair*, 1935.   [3] From Film *Le Bateau à Soupe*.
[4] The theme is taken from Moniuszko's *Echoes of Poland*.
[5] No. 3 is prefaced with a few bars of No. 2; No. 11 is followed by No. 11 bis, Scène; No. 14 is prefaced by *Très lent* of
No. 13; Nos. 14 and 15 are abbreviated; No. 20 (h) lacks the introduction; parts of this recording are probably ☆.
[6] If, as seems likely, these are the Orch. Suite arr. Weninger, they will also contain extracts from Nos. 10 and 14. It has not
been possible to hear the discs.   [7] Omits 4th variation.

COPPÉLIA (*continued*)

No. 3 — ARR. ACCORDEON: T. Tollefsen (*C.DC 674*)

Unid. excerpts[1] & Nos. 19 & 20 (a)
Bolshoi Theatre—Fayer   ♯ *USSR.D 1145/7*
(3ss—*Drigo: Esmeralda, Ballet Suite*)
(also *USSR. 8536/43* & *16547/8*, probably different excerpts)

LAKMÉ   Opera   3 Acts   1883
COLLECTED EXCERPTS

No. 8, Pourquoi dans les grands bois, Act I   S
No. 10, D'où viens-tu? (Recit.); C'est la Dieu de la jeunesse, Act I   S & T
No. 20, Où va la jeune Hindoue?... Là-bas, dans la forêt, Act II   S
No. 24, Lakmé! c'est toi.. Dans la forêt, Act II   S & T
No. 27, Sous le ciel étoilé, Act III   S

P. Alarie (S), L. Simoneau (T), Lamoureux
—Jouve & Dervaux   ♯ *Phi.N 00638R*
[Nos. 10 & 20 also on ♭ *Phi.N 402007E*]

No. 8, Pourquoi dans les grands bois
No. 20, Où va la jeune hindoue
No. 24, Dans la forêt près de nous
☆ L. Pons (in ♯ *Od.OD 1013*; ♭ *AmD.ED 3513*)

HIGHLIGHTS (from set)

☆ M. Robin (S), L. de Luca (T), etc. Paris Opéra-Comique
Cho. & Orch.—Sebastian   ♯ *D.LXT 5018*
(♯ Lon.LL 1129)

ACT I

No. 6, Fantaisie aux divins mensonges   T
I. Kozlovsky (*Russ*)   *USSRM.D 001220*
☆ C. Friant   in ♯ *Ete. 708*
G. Thill   in ♯ *C.FH 503*
M. Villabella   in ♯ *Od.ODX 136*
♄ J. Mojica   in **V**♯ *IRCC.L 7005**
E. Clément   in ♯ *Sca. 819**

No. 8, Pourquoi dans les grands bois   S
M. Dobbs   in ♯ *C.CX 1305*
(*No. 27; Rigoletto, Golden Cockerel, etc.*) (♯ Angel. 35095)
M. Zvezdina (*Russ*)   *USSRM.D 00903*
(*No. 20*)

No. 10, C'est le Dieu de la jeunesse   S & T
M. Zvezdina & I. Kozlovsky (*Russ*)
(*No. 24; & Moniuszko*)   *USSRM.D 890*

ACT II

No. 16, Ballet Music
... Danse persane & Coda only
Belgian Radio Cha.—Doneux (in ♯ Mae.OAT 25004)

No. 18, Lakmé, ton doux regard se voile   Bs
("Stances")
☆ A. Pernet   in ♯ *Od.ODX 135*
B. Gmyria (*Russ*)   *USSRM.D 00856*
A. Majak (*Pol*)   *Muza.X 1723*
♄ M. Journet   in ♯ *SBDH.LPG 5*
F. Chaliapin in ♯ *SBDH.PL 1** & *LLP 4**

No. 20, Où va la jeune Hindoue?...
Là-bas, dans la forêt...   S   (*Bell Song*)
M. M. Callas (*Ital*)   in ♯ *C.CX 1231*
(*Vêpres siciliennes, A. Lecouvreur, etc.*)
(♯ QCX 10129; Angel. 35233)
G. Galli (*Ital*) (2ss)   *Cet.AT 0400*
H. Reggiani   in ♯ *Roy. 1603*
F. F. Jenkins (in ♯ *Vic.LRT 7030*, ♭ *set ERBT 7000*)
G. Gasparian (*Russ*) (in ♯ *USSR.D 1901*)
☆ L. Pons (in ♯ *Vic.LM 1786*: & *set LCT 6701*)
M. Zvezdina (*Russ*) (*USSRM.D 00904*)
♄ S. Kurz (*Ger*) (in ♯ *Sca. 817**)

No. 24, Lakmé! c'est toi... Dans la forêt   S & T
M. Zvezdina & I. Kozlovsky (*Russ*)
(*No. 10; & Moniuszko*)   *USSRM.D 890*

ACT III

No. 27, Sous le ciel étoilé   S
M. Dobbs   in ♯ *C.CX 1305*
(*above*)   (♯ Angel. 35095)

No. 29, Ah! viens dans la forêt profonde   T
♄ E. Clément (*IRCC. 3118**)

No. 34, Tu m'as donné le plus doux rêve   S
P. Alarie   in ♯ *Phi.N 00663R*
(*Gounod, Bizet, etc.*)

Naïla Valse (Pas des Fleurs) 1867 (for *Le Corsaire*)
Philharmonia—Malko   *G.C 4261*
(*Gounod: Mors et Vita—Judex*)   (♭ *7P 152*)
(in ♯ BB.LBC 1080)
Sym.—Fayer (*USSR. 015508*)
Moscow Radio—Orlov (*USSR. 9698*)
☆ Kingsway Sym.—Olof (ArgD.X 288982)
Lower Austrian—Schönherr (in ♯ *AFest.CFR 56* & *CFR 61*; ♯ Rem. 199-126 & ♭ *REP 67*)

— ARR. PF. SOLO   Dohnányi
L. Pennario   in ♯ *DCap.CTL 7087*
(*Ravel & J. Strauss*)   (in ♯ Cap.P 8295)

(Le) ROI L'A DIT   Opéra-Comique   3 Acts   1873
Overture
Linz Sym.[2]   in ♯ *Ply. 12-31*
(*Bizet, Offenbach*)

(La) SOURCE   Ballet   3 Acts   1876
Orch. Suite (Nos. 1, 2, 3, 6)
☆ Suisse Romande—Olof   ♯ *D.LW 5034*
(♯ *Lon.LD 9049*)
Linz Sym. (listed as being in ♯ Ply. 12-31, but missing from the copy checked)
☆ Minneapolis Sym.—Ormandy (in ♯ Cam.CAL 119:
♭ *CAE 212*)
No. 1, Pas des écharpes, only
☆ R. Munro Orch. (♭ *D.DFE 6066*)
Nos. 1 & 2
Belgian Radio Cha.—Doneux (in ♯ Mae.OAT 25004)
No. 3 ("Variation")
— ARR. FL., OB., CL., BSN. & HRN.
Chicago Sym. Woodwind Quintet (in ♯ *Aphe. 17*)

SYLVIA   Ballet   3 Acts   1876
Prelude   [1 (a)]
ACT I: 1. Faunes et Dryades (Scherzo)   [1 (b)]
2. Le Berger (Pastorale)
3. Les Chasseresses (Fanfare)
4. (a) Intermezzo (b) Valse lente "L'Escarpolette"
5. Scène—Allegro (F major)
6. Cortège rustique
7. Scène—Allegro (E flat major)
8. (a) Entrée du sorcier (b) Final—Maestoso
ACT II: 9. Scène—Moderato (La Grotte d'Orion)
10. Pas des éthiopiens
11. Chant bachique
12. (a) Scène et danse de la Bacchante
(b) Rentrée de Sylvia
13. Scène finale—Allegro (A flat major)
ACT III: 14. (a) Marche—Moderato (b) Cortège de Bacchus
15. (a) Scène—Allegro (b) Barcarolle
16. Divertissement
(a) Pizzicato—Scherzettino
(b) Violin solo—Andante
(c) Pas des esclaves
(d) Variation—Valse
(e) Strette—Galop (Danse générale)
FINALE: 17. Le Temple de Diane—Allegro
18. Apparition d'Endymion—Andante con moto
(Apothéose)

COLLECTION
(Nos. 1b, 2, 3, 4 (a & b), 6, 7, 8 (b), 10, 11, 12 (a & b), 14 (a & b), 15 (a & b), 16 (a & b), 18; Nos. 7, 12, 14 are slightly abbreviated)
Philharmonia—Irving   ♯ *G.CLP 1058*

ORCHESTRAL SUITES
Nos. 1 (a), 3, 4 (a & b), 10, 11, 16 (a), 14 (a & b)
Boston Sym.—Monteux   ♯ *Vic.LM 1913*
(*Coppélia*)   (♯ ItV.A12R 0131)
(*Ravel & Weber* on ♯ FV.A 630219)
(& with *Piston, Roussel, Ravel, etc.* in ♯ Vic. set LM 6113)
[Nos. 10, 4a & b, 16a, 11, 14b, on ♭ *Vic.ERA 252*]
☆ Paris Cons.—Désormière (♯ Lon.LL 846, *above*)

Nos. 1 (a), 3, 4 (a & b), 14 (a & b), 16 (a)
(The usual "Suite")
Lamoureux—Fournet   ♯ *EPhi.NBR 6005*
(*Coppélia*)   (♯ *Phi.N 00674R*)
(& with *Gluck & Rabaud*, ♯ Epic.LC 3030)
[No. 4a only, on ♭ *Phi.N 402003E*]
(*Coppélia, & Gounod*, on ♯ Phi.S 04013L)
(*continued on next page*)

---

[1] Called Nos. 8-13 and Finale, but presumably by some different system of reference.
[2] Labelled *Ballet Music*.

SYLVIA, Suite (*continued*)
Phil. Prom.—Boult ♯ **West.LAB 7027**
(*Coppélia*)
Hamburg Philharmonia—H-J. Walther *MSB. 78154/5*
(4ss)
☆ Covent Garden—Rignold ♯ *P.PMD 1005*
(*Gounod: Faust Ballet*)
☆ Munich Phil.—Lehmann (*Faust Ballet*) ♯ **Pol. 19026**
(& 3ss, PV. 72464/5S)
[Nos. 4a & b, 16a also on ♭ *Pol. 30004*]
☆ Vienna Radio—Schönherr (in ♯ GA. 33-306)
Paris Opéra—Fourestier (♯ *BB.LBC 1025:*
♭ *set WBC 1025*)

Various Selections
Nos. 3 & 16a. Covent Garden—Braithwaite (in ♯ *P.PMC 1008*)
Nos. 3, 4a & b, 16a ☆ L.P.O.—Kurtz (in ♯ *AmC.RL 3056*)
Nos. 3, 4a & b, 14a & b
Belgian Radio Cha.—Doneux (in ♯ *Mae.OAT 25004*)
Nos. 14a & b, & 16a
☆ Paris Opéra—Fourestier ♭ *BB.ERAB 12*
(*Tchaikovsky: Serenade—Finale*)
☆ Minneapolis—Ormandy (♭ *Cam.CAE 212*: in ♯ *CAL119*)
Austrian Sym.—Schönherr (in ♯ *AFest.CFR 61*;
♯ *Rem. 199-126*; *Ply. 12-50*; ♭ *Rem.REP 67*;
14 a & b only, in ♯ *Ply. 12-79*)
Nos. 4b & 16a
Sym.—Stokowski in ♯ *G.ALP 1133*
(♯ *FALP 277*; in ♯ *Vic.LRM 7022*: ♭ *set ERB 7022*)
[No. 16a only, in ♯ *Vic.LRY 8000*: ♭ *set WRY 8000*]
No. 4a & b Sym.—Fayer (USSR. 015474)
No. 4b ☆ R. Munro Orch. (♭ *D.DFE 6066*)
Nos. 14a & b — ARR. BAND
Cities Service Band—Lavalle (in ♯ *Vic.LPM 1133*:
♭ *set EPC 1133*)
Nos. 16a ☆ Palm Court—Jenkins (♭ *G.7P 137*: *7EG 8052*)
Unspec. "Nat. Op. Orch." (in ♯ *Var.6967*), etc.

II. SONGS

Bonjour, Suzon (A. de Musset)
R. Doria (S), S. Gouat (pf.) ♭ *Plé.P 45140*
(*below*)
☆ C. Muzio (S) & Orch. (in ♯ *AmC.ML 4634*)

(Les) Filles de Cadiz (A. de Musset)
R. Doria (S), S. Gouat (pf.) ♭ *Plé.P 45140*
(*above; Hüe & Koechlin*)
R. Streich (S) & Orch. ♯ **HP.DG 17052**
(*Alabiev, Flotow, etc.*) (also ♯ *Pol. 17051*)
L. Zubrack (S) (♭ *Vic.ERA 261*)
L. Cortese (S) & pf.[1] (in ♯ *ERC. 101*)
☆ C. Muzio (S) & Orch. (in ♯ *AmC.ML 4634*)

Regrets (Sylvestre)
Z. Dolukhanova (A, *Russ*) *USSRM.D 00661*
(*Grieg*)

DELIUS, Frederick (1862-1934)

Collections
Dance Rhapsody No. 1 1903 orch.
☆ Summer night on the river 1912 orch.
☆ Summer Evening (Ed. & ARR. Beecham) orch.
HASSAN Inc. Music to Flecker's Play 1920
Entr'acte & Serenade orch.
Twilight fancies (Bjørnson) S & orch.
☆ A Song before sunrise 1918 orch.
☆ On hearing the first cuckoo in spring 1912 orch.
E. Suddaby (S), Royal Phil.—Beecham
♯ **Vic.LHMV 1050**

Brigg Fair, an English Rhapsody orch. 1907
On hearing the first cuckoo in spring (No. 1 of Two Pieces)
orch. 1912
A Song of Summer 1930
A VILLAGE ROMEO & JULIET Opera 1907-10
...Intermezzo: The Walk to the Paradise Garden
L.S.O.—Collins ♯ **D.LXT 2788**
[*On hearing ... & Village Romeo ... also on*
♯ *D.LW 5036*; *Lon.LD 9067*; *Song of Summer also*
on ♯ D.LW 5173]
Appalachia Cho. & orch 1902
Variations on an old slave song
Cho. & Royal Phil.—Beecham ♯ **C.CX 1112**
(2ss) (*Koanga—Closing Scene on* ♯ *AmC.ML 4915*)

Caprice & Elegy Vlc. & orch. (dictated 1930)
A. Pini & W. Parry (pf.) ♯ **Argo.RG 47**
(*below*) (♯ *West.WN 18133*)
Dance Rhapsody No. 1 orch. 1908
Royal Phil.—Beecham ♮ **G.DB 9785/6**
(3ss—*Hassan—Entr'acte & Serenade*) (from collection)
Eventyr Ballade, orch. 1917
☆ Royal Phil.—Beecham ♯ **AmC.ML 4637**
(*North Country Sketches*)
HASSAN Inc. Music to Flecker's Play 1920
Entr'acte & Serenade
Royal Phil.—Beecham **G.DB 9785**
(*Dance Rhapsody No. 1, s. 1*) (from Collection)
Serenade — ARR. VLC. & PF.
A. Pini & W. Parry ♯ **Argo.RG 47**
(*above & below*) (♯ *West.WN 18133*)
In a summer garden orch. 1908
Royal Phil.—Beecham ♯ *C.C 1017*
(*Over the hills and far away*)
L.S.O.—Collins ♯ **D.LXT 2899**
(*Paris & Summer night on the river*) (♯ *Lon.LL 923*)
KOANGA Opera 1895-7
Closing Scene
☆ Cho. & Royal Phil.—Beecham ♯ **AmC.ML 4915**
(*Appalachia*)
(Eine) MESSE DES LEBENS (Nietzsche)
("*A Mass of Life*") S, A, T, B, cho. & orch 1904-5
Complete Recording in *German*
R. Raisbeck, M. Sinclair, C. Craig, B. Boyce,
London Phil. Cho. & Royal Phil. Orch.
—Beecham ♯ *C.CX 1078/9*
(4ss) (♯ *AmC. set SL 197*)
North Country Sketches 1913-14
☆ Royal Phil.—Beecham (*Eventyr*) ♯ **AmC.ML 4637**
On hearing the first cuckoo in spring
(No. 1 of *Two Pieces*, orch. 1912)
Hastings Sym.—Bath ♯ *Allo. 4053*
(*Haydn & Roussel*)
☆ Royal Phil.—Beecham (♭ *Vic.EHA 12*)
Concert Arts—Slatkin (♭ *Cap.FAP 8201*)
Over the hills and far away orch. 1895
☆ Royal Phil.—Beecham ♯ *C.C 1017*
(*In a summer garden*)
Paris (The Song of a great city) orch. 1899
Royal Phil.—Beecham ♯ **EPhi.ABL 3088**
(*Sea Drift*) (♯ *AmC.ML 5079*; *Phi.A 01229L*)
L.S.O.—Collins ♯ **D.LXT 2899**
(*In a summer garden, & Summer night on the river*)
(♯ *Lon.LL 923*)
Sea Drift (Whitman) B. cho. orch. 1903
B. Boyce, B.B.C. Cho. & Royal Phil.—Beecham
♯ **EPhi.ABL 3088**
(*Paris*) (♯ *AmC.ML 5079*; *Phi.A 01229L*)
SONATAS, vln. & pf.
No. 2 1915
M. Rostal & C. Horsley ♯ **Argo.RG 47**
(*above & below*) (♯ *West.WN 18133*)
No. 3 dictated 1930
E. Michaelian & V. L. Hagopian ♯ **ML. 7047**
(*Dohnányi*)
Sonata, vlc. & pf. 1917
A. Pini & W. Parry ♯ **Argo.RG 47**
(*above*) (♯ *West.WN 18133*)
Summer night on the river
(No. 2 of *Two Pieces*, orch. 1912)
L.S.O.—Collins ♯ **D.LXT 2899**
(*Paris & In a summer garden*) (♯ *Lon.LL 923*)
(*Song of Summer on* ♯ *D.LW 5173*)
☆ Concert Arts—Slatkin (♭ *Cap.FAP 8201*)
Royal Phil.—Beecham (♭ *Vic.EHA 12*)
(A) VILLAGE ROMEO & JULIET
Opera Prol. & 3 Acts 1907
Intermezzo: The walk to the Paradise Garden
ARR. Beecham
☆ Cincinnati Sym.—Goossens (in ♯ *Cam.CAL 215*)

---

[1] Sung twice: in *Fr*, and in *Eng* version by L. Cortese.

Dello JOIO, Norman

SEE: JOIO, Norman dello

DELVINCOURT, Claude (1888-1954)

Lavandière cho. *c.* 1948
Petits Chanteurs à la Croix de Bois—Maillet
♭ *Pat.D 116*
(*Ravel: Trois beaux oiseaux de Paradis*)

Quartet, Strings
Parrenin Qtt.

Sonata, pf. & vln. 1922
J-P. Sevilla & L. Garnier ♯ **CND. 3**

SONG: L'Enlèvement en mer
☆ C. Panzéra (B), M. Panzéra (pf.) (in ♯ Clc. 6260)

DEMANTIUS, Christoph (1567-1643)

SEE: † CHORAL SONGS (*c.* 1600)

DÉMOPHON, Alexander (fl. 1507)

SEE: † HISTORY OF MUSIC IN SOUND (32)

DERING, Richard (*c.* 1580-1630)

SEE: † ENGLISH CHURCH MUSIC, VOL. III

DESLANDRES, Adolphe E. Marie (1840-1911)

(3) Pieces fl., ob., cl., hrn., bsn.
1. **Andante** 2. **Scherzo** 3, **Finale**
Garde Républicaine Wind Quintet
♯ *D.FM 143658*
(*Desserre: Suite dans le style ancien; & Rameau*)

DESPARD, Marcel (b. 1912)

Symphony Str. orch.
Paris Inst. Ens.—Froment[1] ♯ **EPP.APG 120**
(*Shostakovitch*)

DESPLANES, Jean Antoine Piani (fl. XVII-XVIIIth Cent.)

Intrada (Adagio, B minor) vln. & pf.
W. Schneiderhan & H. Priegnitz *PV. 36084*
(*Nash: Minuet & S-Saëns: Le Cygne*) (♭ *Pol.* 32047)

DESTOUCHES, André-Cardinal (1672-1749)

(Le) MALADE IMAGINAIRE
Inc. Music to Molière's play
Orch.—Cadou (in a performance of the play,
in ♯ D.FMT 163507/8; ♯ LI.TW 91076/7)

DETT, Robert Nathaniel (1882-1943)

In the bottoms Suite, pf.
... **1. Prelude** (Night) only ▽ P. Grainger (in AmD. set A 586)
... **4. Juba dance** ▽ P. Grainger (in AmD. set A 586)

...No. 4 — ARR ORCH.
Hamburg Philharmonia—H-J. Walther
MSB. 78024
(*Dubensky, Skilton, etc.*) (& in ♯ MGM.E 3195
▽ Vic. Sym. (*Vic. 21750 & E76*)

Listen to the lambs Part-song
Mormon Tabernacle Cho.—Cornwall
♯ **EPhi.NBL 5012**
(*Liszt, Brahms, Elgar, etc.*) (♯ Phi.N 02125L;
AmC.ML 5048)
▽ Older issues include:
Adagio cantabile pf. J. Behrend (Vic. 17912 in set M 764)

DIABELLI, Antonio (1781-1858)

SONATINAS, pf.
A minor, Op. 168, No. 7; B flat major, Op. 168, No. 4
P. Zeitlin ♯ **Opus. 6005**
(*Clementi, Dussek, Kuhlau*)
[accompanying a *Matching Music Book*, pub. E. Marks, N.Y.]

Trio, C major fl., vla. & guitar. *c.* 1807-11
(ed. Schindler)
P. Birkelund, R. D. Eriksen & U. Neumann
♯ **D.LXT 5070**
(*Fürstenau & Schubert*) (♯ Lon.LL 1079)

DIAMOND, David (b. 1915)

(8) Piano pieces 1935
M. Richter in ♯ MGM.E 3147
(*Copland, Cowell, Hovhaness, etc.*)

Rounds Str. Orch. 1944
Concert Arts.—Golschmann ♯ DCap.CTL 7056
(*Creston, Barber, Copland*) (♯ Cap.P 8245)
M.G.M. Str.—I. Solomon ♯ MGM.E 3117
(*Persichetti, Copland, Goeb, Porter*)
☆ A.R.S. Orch.—Hendl ♯ ARS. 116
(*Ives, McBride & Swanson*)

SONG: David weeps for Absalom
D. Gramm (Bs), R. Cumming (pf.)
in ♯ ML. 7033
(*Wolf, Schubert, Cesti, Barber, etc.*)

DIAZ, Eugène Emile (de la Peña) (1837-1901)

OPERAS
BENVENUTO CELLINI 1890
De l'art, splendeur immortelle B
C. Cambon ♭ *Plé.P 45153*
(*Barbiere—Bartolo's aria*)
▽ L. Musy G.W 1176
P. Deldi C.DFX 91
A. Baugé Pat.X 90042
L. Richard C.RFX 10
etc.
H E. de Gogorza AF.AGSB 69*

(La) COUPE DU ROI DE THULÉ 3 Acts 1867
Il est venu ce jour de lutte B
H D. Gilly (*AF.AGSA 29**)

Hélas, il avait vingt ans . . . Il aurait vu son amour
▽ A. Baugé (Pat.PGT 5)

DIBDIN, Charles (1745-1814)

LIBERTY HALL Opera 1785
The Bells of Aberdovey (*Clychau Aberdyfi*)
Hywel Girls' Cho.—Williams (*Cwal.RD 3125*)

---

[1] This disc was so announced, but later lists show APG 120 containing Shostakovich, Roussel and Bartók with no sign of this work. The existence of this recording is therefore suspect.

DIEPENBROCK, Alphons (1862-1921)

Electra Inc. Music to Sophocles' Play 1920
... **Sym. Suite** — ARR. Eduard Reeser
Residentie—v. Otterloo   ♯ *EPhi.NBR 6006*
(Dresden)   *(♯ Phi.N 00662R)*

Marsyas, The Enchanted Spring
Inc. Music to Verhagen's play, 1909-10
... **Prelude & Entr'acte**
Amsterdam—v. Beinum   ♯ *D.LXT 2873*
(Pijper)   *(♯ Lon.LL 851)*

DIETRICH, Albert (1829-1908)

Sonata, vln. & pf. (Frei aber einsam)[1] 1853
... **Allegro, A minor**
I. Stern & A. Zakin   ♯ *EPhi.ABL 3068*
(Brahms & Schumann) *(♯ AmC.ML 4913, in set SL 202;*
                            in ♯ Phi.A 01133L)

DILLON, Henry (b. 1912)

Concerto 2 pfs.
I. Marika & J. Manchon-Theis ♯ *Cpt.MC 20024*
(Harsányi & Spitzmüller)

DIOMEDE, Caton (fl. c. 1600)

SEE: † RECORDER MUSIC OF SIX CENTURIES

DISTLER, Hugo (1908-1942)

Chaconne (Partita) **on Nun komm, der Heiden
Heiland, Op. 8, No. 1** org.
P. Kee   in ♯ *G.DLP 1053*
(† "Baroque" Organ Music)
PARTSONGS
Dors, mon chéri (unid.)
Lyons Psalette—Geoffray   in ♯ *SM. 33-21*
(Hindemith, Poulenc, etc.; & Noëls)

Vorspruch (Mörike)
(from Mörike-Chorliederbuch, Op. 17) 1939
Cologne-Mülheim Cha. Cho.
                            in ♯ *Nix.WLP 6209-2*
[at International Eisteddfod, Llangollen]
                            (in ♯ West. set WAL 209)

(Die) Weihnachtsgeschichte, Op. 10 Cantata 1933
T. v. Raalte (S), E. Lugt (S), W. Drayer (T),
B. v. T. Hoff (T), K. Deenik (B), H. Driessen
(Bs), Netherlands Madrigal & Motet Cho.
—Voorberg (2 ss)   ♯ *Phi.N 00736R*
(Honegger, on ♯ Epic.LC 3153)

DITTERSDORF, Karl Ditters von
(1739-1799)

Concerto, A major hpsi. & orch. 1779
— ARR. HARP & ORCH.
H. Helmis & Berlin Radio Cha.—Haarth
(Hoffmann)   ♯ *Ura. 7110*

Concerto, G major vln., str. & cont. 1767
(Krebs No. 160)
J. Pougnet & London Baroque Orch.—Haas
[L. Salter, hpsi].   ♯ *P.PMA 1004*
(Haydn: Symphony No. 22)

(25) PARTITAS wind insts.
No. 2, F major
No. 4, A major
No. 20, D major
French Wind Quintet   ♯ *OL.OL 50014*
(Pleyel) (ed. G. Rhau)   *(♯ OL.LD 74)*

[1] Joint Sonata with Brahms & Schumann.

Partita, D major 2 ob., 2 hrn., bsn.
(MS. British Museum, ed.Haas)
London Baroque Ens.—Haas   ♯ *P.PMB 1008*
(Mozart: 6 Notturni)

Sinfonia Concertante, D major vla., cbs. & orch.
F. Riddle, J. E. Merrett & London Baroque
—Haas   ♯ *P.PMA 1017*
(Schubert & Haydn)
[Announced in Scandinavia; not issued in England]

SYMPHONIES
No. 1, C major c. 1765-6 (DTÖ LXXXI)
Danish Radio Cha.—Wöldike   ♯ *D.LXT 5135*
(J. C. Bach, Haydn, Mozart)   *(♯ Lon.LL 1308)*

**No. 76, F major: Die Rettung der Andromeda
durch Perseus**
(No. 4 of 12 Programme Symphonies after Ovid, 1786)
E. Parolari (ob.) & Winterthur Sym.—Dahinden
No. 96, E flat major ed. Liebeskind
Zürich Radio—Dahinden   ♯ *CHS.CHS 1227*

No. 95, A minor
☆ Frankenland State Sym.—Kloss   ♯ *Nix.LLP 8026*
(Hohenzollern)

DOBIÁŠ, Václav (b. 1909)

Czechoslovak Polka A Peace Cantata
☆ Czech Singers & Children's Cho., Czech Phil.—Ančerl
                            ♯ *Sup.LPM 76*
                            (♯ U. 5160C)

DOHNÁNYI, Ernö (b. 1877)

QUARTETS, Str.
No. 2, D flat major, Op. 15
Curtis Qtt.   ♯ *Nix.WLP 5301*
(below)   *(♯ West.WL 5301)*
☆ Stradivari Qtt. *(♯ Cpt.MC 20061)*
No. 3, A minor, Op. 33
Hollywood Qtt.   ♯ *DCap.CTL 7098*
(Dvořák)   *(♯ Cap.P 8307)*

QUINTETS, Pf. & str.
No. 2, E flat minor, Op. 26
V. Sokoloff & Curtis Qtt.   ♯ *Nix.WLP 5301*
(above)   *(♯ West.WL 5301)*

(4) RHAPSODIES, Op. 11 pf.
☆ M. Schwalb *(♯ Esq.TW 14-003)*
... **No. 2, F sharp minor**, only
☆ E. Dohnányi *(♭ Rem.REP 11; ♭ Cum.CR 271)*

RURALIA HUNGARICA, Op. 32A pf.
— ORCHESTRAL VERSION, Op. 32B
(Nos. 3, 2, 5, 6, 7 of pf. Suite)
Philharmonia—Schüchter   ♯ *P.PMC 1017*
(Kodály)   *(♯ MGM.E 3019)*

— VIOLIN & PF. VERSION, Op. 32C
(Nos. 2, 6 & 7 of pf. Suite)
A. Campoli & G. Malcolm   ♯ *D.LX 3115*
(Paganini)   *(♯ Lon.LS 793)*
T. Magyar & W. Hielkema   ♯ *Phi.N 00700R*
(Bartók)

Serenade, C major, Op. 10 vln., vla., vlc.
J. Pougnet, F. Riddle & A. Pini
                            ♯ *Nix.WLP 20017*
(Berkeley & Françaix)   *(♯ West.WL 5316)*
☆ J. Heifetz, W. Primrose, E. Feuermann ♯ *Vic.LCT 1160*
(Gruenberg)   *(♯ FV.A 630291)*
☆ Stradivari Trio *(♯ Cpt.MC 20061)*

Sonata, C sharp minor, Op. 21 vln. & pf.
E. Michaelian & V. Hagopian   ♯ *ML. 7047*
(Delius)

Suite, F sharp minor, Op. 19 orch.
　Philharmonia—Irving　　　# **G.CLP 1043**
　(*Tchaikovsky*)　　　　　　(# BB.LBC 1090)
　☆ Los Angeles Phil.—Wallenstein　# *B.AXL 2008*
　　　　　　　　　　　　　　(# *AFest.CFR 10-731*)
　☆ L.S.O.—Sargent (# *C.QC 5007*)

Symphonic Minutes, Op. 36 orch. 1933
　☆ Bavarian Sym.—Graunke　　# Nix.ULP 9066
　　(*Borodin*)
　[Rondo only in # Nix.ULP 9084; Ura. 7084:
　　　　　　　　　　　　　　♭ *UREP 53*]

Variations on a Nursery Song, Op. 25 pf. & orch.
　C. Smith & Philharmonia—Sargent
　(*Mozart*)　　　　　　　　# **C.SX 1018**
　J. Katchen & L.P.O.—Boult　# **D.LXT 2862**
　(*Rachmaninoff*)　　　　　(# Lon.LL 1018)
　☆ F. Jacquinot & Philharmonia—Fistoulari
　　(*R. Strauss*)　　　　　# *P.PMC 1005*
　　(*Liszt & Rimsky* on # *FMGM.F6-101*)

(The) Veil of Pierrette Ballet Suite 1910
　... No. 5, Wedding Waltz
　☆ Bavarian Sym.—Graunke
　　　　　　　　(in # *AmD.DL 4064;* ♭ *Pol. 30029*)

Winterreigen, Op. 13 pf.
　... Marche humoristique
　☆ E. Dohnányi (from a piano roll) (in # Roy. 1402 & 1573)

DOMENICO, Gian (d. 1570)
　　　　　(Il Giovane da Nola)
　　SEE: † ANTHOLOGIE SONORE

DONATONI, Franco (b. 1927)

Concerto, timpani, bass & str. orch. 1952-3
　J-P. Kemmer & Radio-Luxembourg Orch.
　—Pensis　　　　　　　　# FestF.FLD 25
　(*Damase & Ravel*)

DONIZETTI, Gaetano (1797-1848)

I. NON-OPERATIC MUSIC

Quartet No. 1, E flat major Strings 1817
　Parrenin Qtt.　　　　　# **Strad.STR 518**
　(*Lalo & Gounod*)

SONG: Il Sospiro
　I. B. Lucca (S) & Orch.　♭ *Dur.AI 6020*
　(*Rossini: La Danza*)　　(& in # *MSE 6*)

II. OPERAS

BETLY 1 Act 1836
COMPLETE RECORDINGS
　Betly ... ...　A. Tuccari (S)
　Daniele ... ...　G. Gentile (T)
　Max ... ...　N. Catalini (B)
　Rome Opera Comica Cho. & Orch.—Morelli
　　　　　　　　　　　　# Nix.PLP 585
　　　　　(# Per.SPL 585; # Cpt.MC 20038)

DON PASQUALE 3 Acts 1843
COMPLETE RECORDINGS

Casts	Set V	Set X
Norina ...	A. Noni (S)	J. Guido (S)
Ernesto ...	C. Valletti (T)	A. Pirino (T)
Dr. Malatesta	M. Borriello (B)	W. Monachesi (B)
Don Pasquale	S. Bruscantini (Bs)	A. Mongelli (B)
Notary... ...	A. Benzi (T)	R. Stralliari (B)

Set V with Italian Radio Cho. & Orch.—
　Rossi　(4ss)　　　　　# CCet.set 1242
Set X with Rome Op. Cho. & Orch.—
　Ricci　(6ss)　　　　　# Ply.set 45-3
Set W
　☆ Soloists, Vienna Cha. Cho. & State Op. Orch.—Quadri
　　　　　　　　　　# Nix.WLP 6206-1/2
　　　　　　　　　　(# Sel.LAG 1027/8)

Set U
　☆ Soloists, La Scala Cho. & Orch.—Parodi
　　　　　　　　　　　　(# MTW. 506/7)
HIGHLIGHTS in *German*
Overture
Bella siccome un angelo
Un foco insolito
Che interminable andirivieni!
Cheti, cheti
So anchio la virtù magica
Com' è gentil
Tornami a dir
　R. Streich (S), K. Wehofschütz (T), K. Schmitt-
　Walter (B), J. Greindl (Bs), Bavarian Radio
　Cho. & Orch.—Lehmann　　# *Pol. 17053*
Vocal Selection
　Soloists & Berlin Op. Co. Cho. & Orch.　# Roy. 1446
　(*Lucia di Lammermoor*)

Overture
　N.B.C. Sym.—Toscanini　　# *Vic.LRM 7028*
　(*Weber Overtures*) (♭ set ERB 7028: also
　　　　　　　　　　# set LM 6026; FV.A 330201)
　(*Oberon only,* ♭ *G.7ERF 111*)
　(*Beethoven: Egmont* on ♭ *ItV.A72R 0001*)
　Berlin Sym.—Rubahn　　in # Roy. 1537
　☆ New Sym.—Erede (# *D.LW 5006:* ♭ *DX 1765*)
　　Hallé—Barbirolli (*G.EC 197:* ♭ *7ER 5009: 7ERQ 113*)
　　Berlin Municipal Op.—Rother (in # Nix.ULP 9057)
　　La Scala—Parodi (from set U) (♭ *Nix.EP 702*)

ACT I

Un foco insolito Bs
　F. Corena　　　　　in # *D.LX 3019*
　(*Elisir d'amore, Gazza Ladra, etc.*)
　　　　　　　　(# *Lon.LS 701* & in LL 1334)

Bella siccome un angelo B
　F. Valentino　　　　in # Roy. 1585

Sogno soave e casto T
　C. Valletti, from set V　in # CCet.A 50154
　☆ T. Schipa (♭ *Vic.ERAT 22*)
　⊞ G. Anselmi & pf. (in # Ete. 492* & in # Sca. 816*)

Quel guardo il cavaliere
So anch'io la virtù magica S
　M. del Pozo　　　　　G.C 4237
　(*Sonnambula—Ah! non credea*)　(♭ *7P 146*)
　R. Scotto　　　　　Cet.PE 206
　(*Sonnambula—Come per me sereno*)
　I. F. Gasperoni　　　　Cet.PE 201
　(*Puritani—Qui la voce*)
　G. Arnaldi　　　　　Cet.PE 186
　(*Rigoletto—Caro nome*)
　G. Sciutti　　in # *Phi.N 00705R*
　(*Linda di Chamounix; Bellini, Rossini*)
　E. Berger (*Ger*)　　　G.DB 11562
　(*Nozze di Figaro, No. 27*)　　(♭ *7RW 513*)
　☆ D. la Gatta (♭ *Nix.EP 735;* ♭ *Ura.UREP 35,* from set U)
　　M. Carosio (♭ *G.7RQ 3006*)
　　T. dal Monte (in # *G.QALP 10089*)
　⊞ R. Storchio (in # *HRS. 3001**)
　　M. Ivogün (in # Sca. 815*)
　　S. Kurz (in # Sca. 817*)

Pronto io son ... Vado, corro S & B
　☆ D. la Gatta & A. Poli (♭ *Nix.EP 735;* ♭ *Ura. UREP 35,*
　　　　　　　　　　　　　　from set U)
　　L. Schöne & W. Domgraf-Fassbänder (*AF.AGSB 10*)
　⊞ M. Sembrich & A. Scotti (in # Vic. set LCT 6701*)

ACT II

Povero Ernesto!
Cercherò lontana terra T
　C. Valletti, from set V　in # CCet.A 50154
　☆ G. Prandelli　　　　♭ *D.71106*
　(*Gioconda—Cielo e mar*)
　⊞ T. Schipa (in # Sca. 805*)
　　A. Bonci (in # Sca. 811*)
　　F. de Lucia (in # CEd. set 7002*)

☆ = Re-issue of a recording to be found in previous volumes.

ACT III

Che interminabile andirivieni!   Cho.
(Servants' chorus)
Netherlands Op. Cho. & Residentie Orch.
—Moralt   in ‡ *EPhi.NBR 6003*
(Cav., Lombardi, Trovatore, Rigoletto)   (‡ *Phi.N 00634R)*
(Rigoletto only, Phi.N 12081G)
Bavarian Radio Cho. *(Ger)*   in ‡ **Pol. 19048**

Cheti, cheti   B & Bs
♮ G. de Luca & F. Corradetti (in ‡ Sca. 812*)

Com' è gentil (Serenata)   T
G. di Stefano   **G.DA 11340**
(Werther—Pourquoi me réveiller)
C. Valletti, from set V   in ‡ CCet.A 50154
   M. Alexandrovitch *(Russ)* (USSR. 016129)
☆ A. Lazzari (♭ *Nix.EP 735;* ♭ *Ura.UREP 35,* from set U)
♮ F. de Lucia (in ‡ Sca. 814*)

Tornami a dir   S & T
A. Noni & C. Valletti   in ‡ CCet.A 50154
         (from set V)
☆ T. dal Monte & T. Schipa (in ‡ G.QALP 10089)
D. la Gatta & A. Lazzari (♭ *Nix.EP 735;*
        ♭ *Ura.UREP 35,* from set U)
♮ R. Pinkert & A. Bonci (in ‡ Sca. 811*)
M. Ivogün & K. Erb *(Ger)* (in ‡ Sca. 815*)

(Il) DUCA D'ALBA   4 Acts   1882
Angelo casto e bel   T   (Act IV)
♮ F. Constantino (in ‡ SBDH.JAL 7000*)
G. Anselmi (in ‡ SBDH.GL 1*)

(L') ELISIR D'AMORE   2 Acts   1832
COMPLETE RECORDINGS

Casts	Set H	Set D
Adina	M. Carosio (S)	H. Gueden (S)
Nemorino ...	N. Monti (T)	G. di Stefano (T)
Belcore ...	T. Gobbi (B)	R. Capecchi (Bs)
Dulcamara ...	M. Luise (Bs)	F. Corena (Bs)
Giannetta ...	L. de Lelio (S)	L. Mandelli (S)

Set H with Cho. & orch. of Rome Opera—Santini
       ‡ **G.ALP 1067/8**
(4ss)   (‡ QALP 10014/5: FALP 292/3: VALP 531/2)
(‡ Vic. set LM 6024)
Set D with Florence May Fest. Cho. & orch.
—Pradelli (6ss)   ‡ **D.LXT 5155/7**
Set C ☆ Soloists, Italian Radio Cho. & Orch.—Gavazzeni
(‡ FSor.CS 531/3; excerpts on ♭ *Cap.FAP 7014;*
                    Cet.EPO 0316)

ACT I

Prelude & Opening Cho.
Rome Op. Cho. & Orch.—Santini
       ♭ *G.7ERQ 105*
(Barbiere di Siviglia—Overture)   *(from set)*

Quanto è bella!
☆ B. Gigli   ♭ *G.7RW 113*
C. Valletti, from set C   in ‡ CCet.A 50154
♮ A. Bonci   in ‡ Sca. 811*
F. de Lucia   in ‡ CEd. set 7002*

Come paride vezzoso   B
♮ A. Scotti (AF.AGSB 24*)

Udite, udite o rustici   Bs & cho.
F. Corena   in ‡ **D.LX 3109**
      (‡ *Lon.LS 701* & in LL 1334)
(Don Pasquale, Gazza Ladra, etc.)
E. Pinza   in ‡ **PRCC. 5**
☆ L. Neroni (Orf. 54009)

Obbligato, obbligato   T & B
♮ F. de Lucia & E. Badini (AF.AGSA 25* &
            in ‡ CEd. set 7002*)

ACT II

La donna à un animale . . . Venti scudi!   T & B
N. Monti & T. Gobbi   **G.DB 21612**
              (from H set)

Una furtiva lagrima   T
N. Gedda   in ‡ **C.CX 1130**
(Favorita, Martha, Manon, etc.) (‡ FCX 302; Angel. 35096)
R. Tucker   in ‡ **AmC.ML 4750**
A. Hendriksen   in ‡ **G.ALPC 1**
(Tosca, Figaro, Carmen, etc.)
R. Schock   **G.EH 1461**
(Königin von Saba—Magische Töne)   (♭ *7PW 18-543)*
(& Ger, on EH 1462: ♭ *7PW 18-542)*
A. Dermota   ‡ *DT.TM 68037*
(Eugen Oniegin & Tosca)   (♭ *FT. 470.TC.015*)
W. Kmentt *(Ger)*   in ‡ *Phi.S 06076R*
(Gioconda, Manon Lescaut, etc.)
B. Powell   in ‡ *Dely.EC 3136*
(Lucia, A. Chénier, Fedora)
   M. Gafni   in ‡ *For.FLP 1001*
   M. Alexandrovich *(Russ)*   in ‡ *USSR.D 2220*
   B. Paprocki *(Pol)*   *Muza.* 2457
☆ J. Björling   ♭ *Vic.ERA 245*
   B. Gigli   in ‡ *G.FJLP 5039*
   M. Lanza   in ‡ *G.ALP 1202*
        (‡ *FBLP 1043;* ♭ *Vic.ERA 136)*
   P. Munteanu   in ‡ Pol. 18169: ♭ *32049*
   C. Valletti, from set C   in ‡ CCet.A 50154
   T. Schipa   ♭ *Vic.ERAT 22*
   P. Anders *(Ger)*   RadT.E 052T
   R. Crooks   in ‡ Cam.CAL 148
♮ E. Caruso   in ‡ G. FJLP 5009*: QJLP 105*
   A. Bonci   in ‡ Sca. 811*
   F. de Lucia   in ‡ Sca. 814*

Prendi per me   S
G. Arnaldi   *Cet.AT 0392*
(Linda di Chamounix—O luce . . .)
G. Galli   Cet.PE 213
(Fille du Régiment—Il faut partir)

(La) FAVORITA   4 Acts   1840
COMPLETE RECORDINGS

Casts	Set C	Set D
Alfonso XI ...	C. Tagliabue (B)	E. Bastianini (B)
Leonora ...	F. Barbieri (M-S)	G. Simionato (M-S)
Fernando ...	G. Raimondi (T)	G. Poggi (T)
Don Gasparo ...	M. Caruso (T)	P. di Palma (T)
Ines	L. de Lelio (S)	B. Magnani (S)
Baldassare ...	G. Neri (Bs)	J. Hines (Bs)

Set C with Italian Radio Cho. & Orch.—Questa
(6ss)   ‡ **Cet. set 1256**
Set D with Florence Festival Cho. & Orch.
—Erede   ‡ **D.LXT 5146/8**
(6ss)   (‡ Lon.LL 1367/9, set XLLA 39)

COLLECTED EXCERPTS

Introduction
Bell' alba foriera   Cho.
Una vergine, un angel di Dio   T
Ah mio bene   M-S & T   (Act I)
Vien, Leonora   B
Voi tutti che m'udite   Ens.   (Act II)
O mio Fernando   M-S   (Act III)
Spirto gentil   T   (Act IV)
Ah! va, t'invola   (Finale)   M-S & T   (Act IV)
   V. Garofalo (M-S), D. Formichini (T), O.
   Borogonovo (B), P. Washington (Bs), S.
   Zanolli (S), A. Mercuriali (T), Cho. & Orch.
   —Curiel   ‡ **C.QSX 12006**
              (‡ Angel. 35322)

Highlights
   S. Couderc (M-S), G. Fouché (T), C. Cambon
   (B), etc., Pasdeloup Orch.—Allain *(Fr)*
              ‡ **Plé.P 3071**
♮ A. Bonci (T), M. Battistini (B), M. Sammarco (B),
O. Luppi (Bs), A. Parsi-Pettinella (M-S), I. Roselli
(S), L. del Lungo (M-S), E. Colli (T), L. Beyle (T),
M. Brohly (M-S) *(Ital & Fr)*   ‡ Ete. O-489*

Overture
L.S.O.—Ellenberg   in ‡ **Mon.MWL 303**
(below; & Norma)
March (based on the Overture) — ARR. Pares
   Garde Républicaine Band—Brun
      (in ‡ C.FCX 190; ‡ Angel. 35051)

---

‡ = Long-playing, 33⅓ r.p.m.   ♭ = 45 r.p.m.   ♮ = Auto. couplings, 78 r.p.m.

142

ACT I

Una vergine, un angel di Dio (Romanza) T
  L. Francardi   *Cet.AT 0324*
  (*Puritani—A te o cara*)
  G. Poggi   in ♯ SBDH.TOB 2
  (*Trovatore, Ballo in Maschera, Boccanegra, etc.*)
  M. Alexandrovich (*Russ*) (in USSRM.D 00115)
  ☷ G. Anselmi & pf. (in ♯ Ete. 711*; in ♯ Sca. 816*)
    A. Bonci (in ♯ Sca. 811*)

Vien, Leonora B
  A. Manca-Serra   in ♯ Mon.MWL 303
  (*above, below & Norma*)
  M. Dens (*Fr*)   ♭ *Pat.ED 34*
  (*Hérodiade, Roméo et Juliette*)   (in ♯ *DT 1020*)
  ☆ R. Stracciari   in ♯ Sca. 802
    A. Endrèze (*Fr*)   in ♯ Pat.PCX 5006
  ☷ H. Albers (*Fr*)   in ♯ HRS. 3008*
    T. Ruffo   AF.AGSB 91*
    M. Renaud   in ♯ FRP. 2*

ACT II

Quando le soglie paterne S & B
  L. Malagrida & A. Manca-Serra
           in ♯ Mon.MWL 303
  (*above, below; & Norma*)

Ah l'alto ardor M-S & B
  ☷ E. Mantelli & T. Parvis (in ▼♯ IRCC.L 7007*)

Ah paventa del furor d'un Dio vendicator Bs
  ☷ M. Journet (*Fr*) (in ♯ SBDH.LPG 5*)

ACT III

A tanto amor B
  F. Valentino   in ♯ Roy. 1585
  ☆ A. Endrèze   in ♯ Pat.PCX 5006
    R. Stracciari   in ♯ Sca. 802
  ☷ M. Sammarco   in ♯ FRP. 3*
    G. de Luca   in ♯ Sca. 812*

Fia dunque vero . . . O mio Fernando M-S or A
  T. de Igarzabal   ArgOd. 66053
  (*Mignon—Connais-tu le pays*)   (in ♯ *LDC 517*)
  S. Couderc (*Fr*)   ♭ *Plé.P 45132*
  (*Gluck: Orphée, No. 43*)
    V. Borisenko (*Russ*) (USSRM.D 1434)
  ☆ M. Anderson (in ♯ AFest.CFR 10-149; in ♯ Roy. 1589)
    E. Stignani (in ♯ C.QC 5024)
  ☷ E. Mantelli (in ▼♯ IRCC.L 7007*)

ACT IV

Splendon più belle in ciel Bs & cho.
  A. Basso   in ♯ ABCD. 2
  (*Don Carlos, Tosca, Trovatore, etc.*)
  ☷ M. Journet & Cho. (in ♯ SBDH.JALP 19*
                & in ♯ JAL 7002*)
    U. Luppi (in ♯ SBDH.PL 1*)

Spirito gentil T
  N. Gedda   in ♯ C.CX 1130
  (*Arlesiana, Martha, etc.*)   (in ♯ FCX 302; Angel. 35096)
  L. Francardi   Cet.PE 185
  (*Cimarosa: Matrimonio Segreto, aria*)
  P. Ferraro   in ♯ Mon.MWL 303
  (*above; & Norma*)
  B. Landi   in ♯ Roy. 1595
  ☆ G. Poggi   in ♯ Cet.LPC 55003
  ☷ G. Anselmi   in ♯ Ete. 711*
    J. McCormack   in ♯ Roy. 1555*
              & in ♯ Cum.CE 185*)
    A Bonci   in ♯ Sca. 811*
    E. Caruso   in ♯ Vic. set LCT 6701*

Pietoso al par d'un Nume S
  ☷ E. Burzio (in ♯ HRS. 3007*)

Vieni! Ah, vieni! M-S & T
  ☷ E. Casazza & B. Gigli (in ♯ SBDH.LPP 5*)

(La) FILLE DU RÉGIMENT 2 Acts 1840
Overture
  Bamberg Sym.—Leitner   PV. 72498
  (*Alessandro Stradella, Overture*)   (♭ *Pol. 30098*)
  Lamoureux—van Kempen   ♭ *Phi.A 400006E*
  (*Barbiere Overture*)
  ☆ Berlin Municipal Op.—Rother (in ♯ Nix.ULP 9057)

ACT I

Chacun le sait S & Cho.
  P. Munsel & Cho.   in ♯ *G.BLP 1023*
  [Film *Melba*] (in ♯ *G.QBLP 5015*; in ♯ Vic.LM 7012:
                       ♭ set *WDM 7012*)

Eccomi finalmente[1] T
  ☆ C. Valletti, from set (in ♯ CCet.A 50154)

Quel destin, quel favor T
  ☆ C. Valletti (*Ital*), from set (in ♯ CCet.A 50154)

Il faut partir S (*Convien partir*)
  G. Galli (*Ital*)   Cet.PE 213
  (*Elisir d'amore—Prendi per me*)

De cet aveu si tendre S & T
  ☷ M. Sembrich & T. Salignac (in ♯ IRCC.L 7006*)[2]

ACT II

En avant, ra-ta-plan Ens.
  ☷ M. Sembrich, M. van Cauteren, T. Salignac, G. Gilbert
                   (in ♯ IRCC.L 7006*)[3]
Par le rang et par l'opulence S
  ☆ T. dal Monte (*Ital*) (in ♯ G.QALP 10089)

(Il) FURIOSO ALL' ISOLA DI SAN DOMINGO
          2 Acts 1833
Raggio d'amore B
  ☷ G. Bernal-Resky (*SBDH.P 3**)

LINDA DI CHAMOUNIX 3 Acts 1842

ACT I

Ambo nati B
  ☷ G. de Luca (in ♯ Sca. 812*)

O luce di quest' anima S
  R. Peters   ♭ *Vic.ERA 151*
  (*Lucia—Regnava nel silenzio*)
        (♭ *FV.A 95229*; in ♯ Vic.LM 1786 & LM 1847)
  G. Sciutti   in ♯ *Phi.N 00705R*
  (*Don Pasquale; Bellini, Rossini*)
  R. Doria   ♭ *Plé.P 45145*
  (*Puritani—Qui la voce*)
  G. Arnaldi   *Cet.AT 0392*
  (*Elisir d'amore—Prendi per me*)
  ☆ T. dal Monte (in ♯ G.QALP 10089)
  ☷ R. Storchio (in ♯ HRS. 3001*)

LUCIA DI LAMMERMOOR 3 Acts 1885
'COMPLETE' RECORDINGS

Casts	Set A	Set B	Set C
Enrico (B)...	... T. Gobbi	A. Colzani	F. Guarrera
Lucia (S)...	... M. Callas	D. Wilson	L. Pons
Ravenswood (T)	G. di Stefano	G. Poggi	R. Tucker
Bucklaw (T)...	V. Natali	M. Carlin	T. Heyward
Raimondo (Bs)...	R. Arié	S. Maionica	N. Scott
Alisa (M-S)...	A. M. Canali	E. Ticozzi	T. Votipka
Normanno (T)...	G. Sarri	G. Fazzine	J. McCracken

Set A with Florence Fest. Cho. & Orch.—Serafin
                     ♯ C.CX 1131/2
(4ss) (♯ FCX 258/9: QCX 10030/1; ♯ Angel. 35038/9,
                          set 3503)

Set B with Milan Op. Cho. & Orch.—Capuana
                     ♯ Nix.ULP 9232-1/3
(6ss)[4]   (♯ Ura. set 232)
(Highlights on ♯ Ura. 7120; MTW 10; ♭ Nix.EP 766; the
  Sextet also on ♭ Ura.UREP 66)

Set C with Metropolitan Op. Cho. & Orch.
  —Cleva   ♯ AmC.ML 4933/4
(4ss)   (set SL 127; ♯ Phi.A 01161/2L)

---

[1] An equivalent for these words cannot be traced in the French score.   [2] Excerpt only: from Mapleson cylinders.
[3] From Mapleson cylinders.
[4] Includes Act III, scene 1, omitted from set A.

Set Z: Unspec. Artists from La Scala, Milan[1]
(6ss)   # OTA. set 2

Set S
☆ Soloists, E.I.A.R. Cho. & Orch.—Tansini
    (# FSor.CS 516/8; Excerpts on # CCet.A 50139;
    ♭ Cet.EPO 0310 & EPO 0323; ♭ Cap.FAP 7005)

Highlights
F. Valentino, B. Landi, H. Reggiani & Orch.
—H-J. Walther   # Roy. 1617
☆ P. Munsel (S), J. Peerce (T), R. Merrill (B), E. Pinza (Bs)
                              # Vic.LRM 7012 & 7030
                              (♭ sets ERB 7012 & 7030)
☆ L. Rossi (S), C. Valletti (T), etc. (# Roy. 1833:
                                        ♭ set EP 109)

Vocal Selection
Soloists, Berlin Op. Cho. & Orch.   (Ger)
(Don Pasquale selection)   # Roy. 1446

ACT I

Cruda, funesta smania B (Cavatina)
F. Valentino   in # Roy. 1585

Regnava nel silenzio ... Quando rapita S
(Cavatina)
R. Peters   ♭ Vic.ERA 151
(Linda di Chamounix—O luce ...)
                    (& in # LM 1786; ♭ FV.A 95229)
M. M. Callas [& A. M. Canali] ♭ C.SEL 1522
(Tombe degl' avi ... Act III) (from set A) (♭ SEBQ 116)
D. Wilson   ♭ Nix.EP 771
[& E. Ticozzi (M-S)] (from set B)
N. Kazantseva (Russ) (USSRM.D 879)
... **Intro.** (Harp solo only)
L. Newell (Casella & Respighi)   # Phil.PH 109

Lucia, perdona ... Sulla tomba S & T (Love Duet)
M. Robin & L. de Luca   # D.LXT 2898
(below; & Gounod: Mireille) [abridged] (# Lon.LL 922)
M. Carosio & C. Zampighi   # G.QALP 10081
(Pêcheurs de Perles, Manon & Amico Fritz)
D. Wilson, G. Poggi   ♭ Nix.EP 772
[& E. Ticozzi (M-S)] (from set B)
☆ L. Pagliughi & C. Malipiero, from set S (Orf. 54002)

ACT II

Chi mi frena Sextet
☆ Galli-Curci, Homer, Gigli, de Luca, Pinza, Bada
                              (♭ G.7RW 19-539)
H Galli-Curci, Égener, Caruso, de Luca, Journet, Bada
                              (♭ Vic.ERAT 8*)
— ARR. ORCH only
Boston "Pops"—Fiedler (in # Vic.LRM 7045)

Dalla stanze, ove Lucia Bs & Cho.
H M. Journet (IRCC.ABHA 1* & in # SBDH.LPG 5*)

Ardon gl' incensi ... Spargi d'amaro pianto
(Mad Scene) S, T, Bs
... **Sop. part only**
M. Robin (n.v.)[2]   # D.LXT 2898
(above; & Gounod)   (# Lon.LL 922)
M. Robin[2]   # D.LX 3114
(Thomas: Hamlet)   (# FA 133034; # Lon.LS 676)
R. Doria   ♭ Plé.P 45131
(Proch: Variations)
D. Wilson (from set B) & Cho.   ♭ Nix.EP 773
H. Reggiani   in # Roy. 1603
N. Kazantseva (Russ) (USSR. 01856/7: USSRM.D 880)
☆ T. dal Monte (♭ G.7RQ 3038)
H M. Ivogün (in # Sca. 815*)
... **Abridged** (Film version)
P. Munsel & J. Cameron (B) (in # G.BLP 1023: QBLP 5015;
                    # Vic.LRM 7012: ♭ set WDM 7012)
... **Alfin son tua,** only
☆ L. Pagliughi (Orf. 54010, d.c., from set S)
H E. B. Yaw (AF.AGSB 66*)

ACT III

Tombe degli avi ... Fra poco a me ricovero T
G. di Stefano   ♭ C.SEL 1522
(Regnava nel silenzio, Act I) (from set A) (♭ SEBQ 116)
B. Powell   in # Dely.EC 3136
(Lucia, A. Chénier, Fedora)
☆ J. Peerce   in # Vic. set LCT 6701
H A. Bonci   in # Sca. 811*
G. Anselmi & pf.   in # Sca. 816*
J. McCormack   ♭ Vic.ERAT 17*

Tu che a Dio T & Bs
☆ G. Malipiero & L. Neroni, from set S (Orf. 54002)

... **Tenor part** only
B. Powell   in # Dely.EC 3136
(above)
C. Valletti   in # Cet.LPC 55002
(Barbiere, Don Giovanni, Werther, etc.) (in # CCet.A 50176)
G. Prandelli   in # Roy. 1595
E. Lorenzi   Cet.PE 208
(Gioconda—Cielo e mar)
H A. Bonci   in # Sca. 811*
F. Marconi   in # Roc. 1*

LUCREZIA BORGIA Prologue & 2 Acts 1833
Di pescatore ignobile T (Prologue)
H F. Vignes & pf.   in # SBDH.JAL 7002*
C. Albani   AF.AGSB 65*

Come è bello S (Prologue)
H M. de Macchi   IRCC. 3150*

Qualunque sia l'evento Bs (Prologue)
H E. Brancaleoni   SBDH.G 5*

Vieni la mia vendetta Bs (Act I)
H F. Chaliapin (in # SBDH.LLP 4*; in # Sca.SC 801*;
    & ♭ Per.PEP 12*; ♭ Cpt.EXTP 1002*)
J. Mardones (in # SBDH.JAL 7002*)

Il segreto per essere felice (Brindisi) A (Act II)
H C. Butt   AF. AGSB 75* & in # FRP 1*
R. Olitzka   HRS. 1032*

MARIA DI ROHAN 3 Acts 1843
Voce fatal B H M. Battistini in # ABCD. 1*

MARIA DI RUDENZ 3 Acts 1838
Ah! non avea pui lagrime B
H M. Battistini   in # ABCD. 1*

POLIUTO 3 Acts 1840-1
Di quai soavi lagrime S (Act I)
H M. de Macchi   # IRCC. 3150*

(La) ZINGARA 1822
Fra l'erbe cosparse S
L. Cortese & pf.[3]   # ERC.102
(Don Giovanni, No. 19)

DONOVAN, Richard (b. 1891)

Quartet wind insts. 1953
Yale Woodwind Qtt.   # CtyNY.AP 121
(Kraehenbuehl & Gruen)

New England Chronicle Orch. 1946-7
Eastman-Rochester Sym.—Hanson
(Hively & Porter)   # Mer.MG 40013

Suite ob. & str. orch. 1943
A. Genovese & Baltimore Little Sym.—Stewart
(Ives)   # Van.VRS 468

DORNEL, Louis Antoine (c. 1685-1765)
SEE: † VIEUX NOËLS DE FRANCE

---

[1] From a broadcast performance.   [2] Commencing at Il dolce suono.
[3] Sung both in Ital and in an Eng version by L. Cortese.

DØRUMSGAARD, Arne (b. 1921)

SONGS (in Norwegian)
SONGS BELOW THE STARS, Op. 17 (Blomberg)
  1. Be not afraid of darkness
  2. Night envelops the earth
  3. Hide me, you blinding darkness
  4. Be quiet, my heart
Gudrid was standing by the window, Op. 11, No. 2 (Vaage)
Night, Op. 4, No. 1 (Vaage)
Rain, Op. 6, No. 2 (Obstfelder)
Hymn, Op. 5, No. 2 (Obstfelder)
Evening, Op. 1, No. 1, (Garborg)
Blue evening, Op. 16, No. 3 (Vaa)
Corn and gold, Op. 16, No. 1 (Vaa)
There's a fjord 'tween parted kinsfolk, Op. 8, No. 3 (Holm)
The Shepherd-Girl's Call, Op. 8, No. 5 (Holm)
Weave, spirit, Op. 10, No. 1 (Holm)
Wind-flower in the Southern slope, Op. 12, No. 1 (Holm)
White Northern light, Op. 12, No. 5 (Holm)
Sleep, Op. 6, No. 1 (Øverland)
The Child, Op. 7, No. 1 (Øverland)
Motto on the Wall, Op, 5, No. 1 (Øverland)
Lullaby, Op. 11, No. 1 (Sveen)
(2) Norwegian Folk Songs, Op. 21
  1. I went to sleep so late one eve
  2. All men have feet
    K. Flagstad (S), G. Moore (pf.) ♯ **G.ALP 1140**

See also: † Canzone Scordate

DOURIAN, Ohan

Pastorales Nos. 3 & 4 orch. 1951-4
Lamoureux—Martinon ♯ *Phi.A 76707R*
(*Glinka & Smetana*)

DOWLAND, John (1563-1626)

[Roman figur es refer to the Books of Ayres, 1597, 1600
  1603, 1612]

Collections
AYRES Voice & Lute
  Flow not so fast, ye fountains (III)
  Sweet, stay awhile (Donne) (IV)
  Fine knacks for ladies (II)
  Come away, come, sweet love (I)
    F. Fuller (B), J. de Azpiazu (lute)
LUTE MUSIC
  An Unnamed Piece (attrib. Dowland)
  Dowland's Adieu (Ayres, II)
  Melancholy Galliard[1]
  Mrs. Vauxe's Gigge[1]
  My Lady Hunsdon's Puffe[2]
  Forlorne Hope[1]
  Queen Elizabeth's Galliard[3]
  Orlando sleepeth[1]
    J. de Azpiazu (guitar) in ♯ **EMS. 11**
    († Dowland & his Contemporaries)

AYRES
  Can she excuse my wrongs? (I)
  From silent night (IV)
  If my complaints could passions move (I)
LUTE: My Lady Hunsdon's Puffe[2]
    A. Deller (C-T), D. Dupré (lute) ♯ **Van.BG 539**
    († Elizabethan & Jacobean Music) (♯ Ama.AVRS 6001)

Dear, if you change (I)
Sorrow, sorrow, stay (II)
Weep you no more, sad fountains (III)
A shepherd in a shade (II)
Come away, come, sweet love (I)
Who ever thinks or hopes of love (I)
Flow not so fast, ye fountains (III)
    R. Lewis (T), J. Bonneau (pf.)[4] ♯ **LI.TW 91067**
    († Canzone Scordate II) (♯ D.FAT 173102)

Away with these self-loving lads (Brooke) (I)
Now, O now, I needs must part (I)
Sorrow, sorrow, stay (II)
Weep you no more, sad fountains (III)
    H. Cuénod (T), C. J. Chiasson (hpsi.)
      in ♯ **Nix.LLP 8037**
    († Elizabethan Love Songs) (♯ Lyr.LL 37)

Flow, my tears (II)
I saw my lady weep (II)
Fantasia (lute)[3] (Curwen edn. No. 15)
  ☆ H. Cuénod (T), H. Leeb (lute) ♯ **Nix.WLP 5085**
  (XVIth & XVIIth Century Songs)

AYRES for 4 voices: "Vol. I"
  Come again! Sweet love (I)
  Woeful heart (II)
  White as lilies (II)
  If floods of tears (II)
  Disdain me still (IV)
  Sleep, wayward thoughts (I)
  O sweet woods (II)
  Awake, sweet love (I)
  Love, those beams that heed (IV)
  When Phoebus first (III)
  Come away, come, sweet love (I)
  Dear, if you change (I)
  Shall I sue ? (II)
  Come, heavy sleep (I)
  What if I never speed (III)
  O what hath overwrought (III)
  To ask for all thy love (IV)
  Fine knacks for ladies (II)

  Golden Age Singers—Field-Hyde
      ♯ **West.WLE 102**

  (2ss) [Julian Bream, lute]

Come again! Sweet love doth now invite (I)
  H. Traubel (S) & orch. in ♯ *Vic.LM 7013*
    (in ♭ set WDM 7013)
  R. Hayes (T), R. Boardman (pf.) in ♯ **A440.12-3**

I saw my lady weep (II)
Flow, my tears (Lachrymae) (II)
  R. Soames (T), W. Gerwig (lute), J. Koch
    (gamba) (*Danyel*) ♭ *Pol. 37010*
  (*Campion & Morley* in ♯ AmD.ARC 3004)

Flow, my tears (II)
  A. Deller (C-T), D. Dupré (lute) **G.C 4236**
  (*Trad: Callino castore me*)

Go, crystal tears (I)
  ☆ Motet & Madrigal Cho.—Opienski (in † ♯ HS.AS 10)

In darkness let me dwell[5]
  R. Oberlin (C-T), & Pro Musica Ens.
    in ♯ **AmC.ML 5051**
  († Evening of Elizabethan Verse & Music)

Sleep, wayward thoughts (I)
  R. Soames (T), D. Poulton (lute) **G.HMS 40**
  († History of Music in Sound) (in ♯ Vic. set LM 6029)

Weep you no more, sad fountains (III)
  Hufstader Singers in ♯ *SOT. 1092*
  New England Cons. Alumni Cho.—de Varon
    († English Madrigals) in ♯ **HSL.HSL 2068**

Wilt thou unkind thus reave me? (I)
  S. Bloch (S. & lute) in ♯ *CHS.CHS 1225*
  († Music in Shakespeare's Time)

LUTE MUSIC
Pavan—Semper Dowland, semper dolens (*Lachrymae*) 1605
Galliard—The King of Denmark (*Lachrymae*) 1605
Allemande englessa[6] (*Linzer Lautenbuch, c.* 1610)
  M. Podolsky in ♯ **Per.SPL 577**
  († Lute Music of the XVIth & XVIIth Centuries)
    (♯ Cpt.MC 20052)

Fantasia[3] (Curwen edn. No. 15)
Tarleton's riserrection[7]
Toye—The Shoemaker's wife[8]
  D. Dupré in ♯ **G.ALP 1265**
  († Shakespeare Songs & Lute Solos)

Galliards—Captain Digorie Piper (*Lachrymae*) 1605
      The King of Denmark (*Lachrymae*) 1605
  K. Scheit (guitar) in ♯ **Van.BG 548**
  († Renaissance & Baroque)

---

[1] MS., Cambridge University Library, England.   [2] MS., British Museum.
[3] From Robert Dowland: *Varietie of Lute Lessons* (1610).   [4] ARR. Dørumsgaard.
[5] From *A Musical Banquet*, 1610.   [6] *Aliter:* The Lady Laiton's Almayne.
[7] MS. lately in the possession of Mr. E. Marshall-Johnson.   [8] MS., Cambridge University Library, England.

Pavan—Semper Dowland, semper dolens
(*Lachrymae*) 1605
S. Bloch (lute), n.v.   in ♯ *CHS.CHS 1225*
(† *Music in Shakespeare's Time*)
☆ S. Bloch (lute) o.v. (in † *Allo. 4043*)

DRAESEKE, Felix August Bernhard
(1835-1913)

Sinfonia tragica, Op. 40
Berlin Sym.—Desser   ♯ *Ura. 7162*

DRAGONETTI, Domenico (1763-1846)

Concerto, C major CBs. & orch.
M. Anastasio & H. Wingreen (pf.)
(*Bottesini*)   ♯ *CEd.CE 1035*

DRESDEN, Sem (b. 1881)

Dance Flashes for Orch. 1951
Intrada.
1. Alla polacca   2. Siciliano   3. Tempo di valsa
4. Passamezzo   5. Menuetto   6. Marcia funebre
7. Alla tarantella
    Residentie—v. Otterloo   ♯ *EPhi.NBR 6006*
(*Diepenbrock*)   (♯ *Phi.N 00662R*)

DRESE, Adam (1620-1701)

Seelenbräutigam Chorale
("*Round me falls the night*", arr. Ley)
St. Paul's Cath. Cho.—Dykes Bower
          in ♯ *C.CX 1237*
(*Haydn, Gibbons, Morley, C. Wood, etc.*)
          (♯ *Angel. 35139 in set 3516*)

DUBENSKY, Arcady (b. 1890)

Gossips Str. orch. 1930
Hamburg Cha.—H-J. Walther (*MSB. 78024*)

DUBOIS, François Clément Théodore
(1837-1924)

(Les) Sept paroles du Christ Oratorio 1867
M. Stagliano (S), C. Nelson (T), Mac Morgan
(B), Boston Chorale—Page, & R. Foort (org.)
(in *Latin*)   ♯ *SOT. 1094*
L. Storer (S), B. Stern (T), C. Watson (B),
New Jersey Oratorio Cho.—C. Snyder (org.)
(in *English*)   ♯ *Word.W 4002*

Toccata, G major organ
R. Foort   ♯ *SOT. 1054*
(*Bach, Boëllmann*)   (& in ♯ *10545*)
[Symphony Hall org., Boston]

DUFAY, Guillaume (before 1400-1474)
COLLECTION
Adieu m'amour (Rondeau) L. Dauby (A), F. Anspach (T)
Alma redemptoris mater (Motet)
Salve quae fama—Vos nunc—Viri mendaces (Motet)
Mass, 'Se la face ay pale': Kyrie I
☆ Vocal Ens.—Cape & de Van (in † ♯ *HS.AS 3*)

COLLECTION: 5 SACRED SONGS
Vergine bella (Petrarch) Ø
Vexilla regis (Hymn) Ø
O Flos florum (Motet)
Veni creator (Hymn)
Alma Redemptoris Mater (Motet) Ø
    Pro Musica Antiqua—Cape   ♯ **HP.APM 14019**
    († *Madrigals & Caccie*)   (♯ *AmD.ARC 3003*)
    [Ø also on PV. 5415; ♭ *Pol. 37057*]

CHANSONS, etc.
Adieu ces bons vins de Lannoys
    A. Doniat (B), M. Rollin (lute)   ♯ *BàM.LD 019*
    († *Airs à boire*)

Le Belle se siet (Ballade)[1]
Ce Moys de May (Rondeau)[1]
    M. Rollin Ensemble   ♯ *LI.W 91116*
    (†*Music from Middle Ages to Renaissance*) (♯*D.FS 123632*)

Mon chier amy (Ballade)[1]
    Recorder Trio   ♯ *OL.LD 81*
    († *Musiciens de la Cour de Bourgogne II*)

Pour l'amour de ma douce amye
    Pro Musica Antiqua Ens.—Cape   G.HMS 26
    († *History of Music in Sound*)   (in ♯ Vic. set LM 6016)

Se la face ay pale
    E. Metzger-Ulrich (S), K. Metzger (T)
          ♯ **E. & AmVox.PL 8120**
    († *Music of the Renaissance*)

Vergine bella (Petrarch)
    ☆ Y. Tinayre (T) & Strings (in † 7 Centuries of Sacred
    Music)

Gloria (ad modum tubae) (DTÖ VII, No. 145)
    Welch Chorale   in ♯ *Lyr.LL 52*
    († *Motets of the 15th & 16th Centuries*)

MASSES
Ave Regina coelorum *c.* 1464
... Kyrie, only
    Yale Univ. Music School Cho.—Hindemith
          in ♯ *Over.LP 5*
    († *Yale University, Vol. II*)

"Caput" (ed. D. Stevens) *c.* 1440
    Ambrosian Singers—Stevens   ♯ **LOL.OL 50069**
    [J. Whelan, trombone]   (♯ *OL.LD 79*)

"Se la face ay pale" ... Kyrie I   1450
    Copenhagen Men's & Boy's Cho.—Møller
          in ♯ *HS.HSL 2071*
    († *Masterpieces of Music* ...)
    (& in † *Histoire de la Musique vocale*)

Sine nomine *c.* 1440
    Vocal Ens.—Caillard   ♯ *Era.LDE 3023*
    & 3 trombones   (♯ *HS.HSL 9008*)
    (*Langlais*) [Recorded St. Roch, Paris, 7. iii. 55]

Unspec. ... **Kyrie eleison** 3 voices
    N.Y. Primavera Singers—Greenberg
          in ♯ *Per.SPL 597*
    († *Renaissance Music*)   (♯ *Cpt.MC 20077*)

MOTETS
Alma redemptoris mater
    ☆ Y. Tinayre (T) & Strings (in † 7 Centuries of Sacred
    Music)
    F. Peeters (org.) (in † ♯ Cpt.MC 20069)

Ave, regina coelorum
    Schola Polyphonica—Washington   G.HMS 25
    († *History of Music in Sound*)   (in ♯ Vic. set LM 6016)

In festis beatae Mariae Virginis
    Netherlands Cha. Cho.—de Nobel
          in ♯ *Phi.N 00678R*
    († *Sacred & Secular Songs from the Renaissance*)

O Flos Florum
Veni creator spiritus
    E. Metzger-Ulrich (S), K. Metzger (T)
          in ♯ **E. & AmVox.PL 8120**
    († *Music of the Renaissance*)

---

[1] From MSS., Oxford.

DUKAS, Paul (1865-1935)

(L') Apprenti sorcier orch. 1897
(Scherzo after Goethe)
Paris Cons.—Ansermet   ♯ **D.LXT 5004**
(*Ravel & Honegger*)   (♯ Lon.LL 1156)
(*Honegger only*, ♯ *D.LW 5155; Lon.LD 9174*)
Philharmonia—Cantelli   ♯ **G.ALP 1207**
(*Debussy, Falla, Ravel*)   (QALP 10097)
Philharmonia—Markevitch   ♯ **C.CX 1049**
(*Falla, Ravel & Prokofiev*)
              (♯ QCX 10015: FCX 203; ♯ Angel. 35008)
Detroit Sym.—Paray   ♯ **EMer.MG 50035**
(*Fauré & Roussel*)   (♯ FMer.MLP 7519)
Rome Radio—Previtali   ♯ *G.DLP 1038*
(*Rossini & Verdi*)   (♯ *QDLP 6018: FFLP 1038*)
London Phil. Sym.—Quadri   ♯ **West.LAB 7009**
(*Chabrier & Saint-Saëns*)   (♯ Véga. C30.A 18)
Lamoureux—Martinon   ♯ **Phi.A 00175L**
(*Debussy, Fauré, Roussel, etc.*)   (♯ Epic.LC 3058)
(*Debussy only*, ♯ *Phi.S 06011R*)
Philadelphia—Ormandy (? n.v.)   ♯ *AmC.AL 26*
(*Debussy*)
Boston Pops.—Fiedler   ♯ **Vic.LM 1803**
(*Prokofiev, Saint-Saëns, German*)
Florence Fest.—Gui   ♯ **AudC. 502**
(*Debussy, Borodin, Moussorgsky*)
Utrecht Sym.—Hupperts (♯ *MMS. 27*)
Royale Concert Orch. (in ♯ Roy. 1432)
Sym.—Swarowsky (♯ *MTW. 23:* ♭ *set EP 23*)
☆ Minneapolis Sym.—Mitropoulos (in ♯ *AmC.RL 3021*)
    Philadelphia—Stokowski (in ♯ Cam.CAL 118 &
                                in ♯ set CFL 103)
    Belgian Radio—André (♯ *T.TW 30008/; FT.255.TC.008*)
    Moscow Radio—Gauk (♯ *USSR.D 1133*)
— WITH NARRATION: M. Cross & Orch. (♯ Roy. 18145)
           D. Wilson & Brussels Radio
             —André (♮ *Cap. set DBS 3094:*
                                ♭ *CBSF 3094*)

(La) Péri Ballet 1 Act orch. 1910-12
Concerts Colonne—Sebastian[1] ♯ **Nix.ULP 9097**
(*Fauré*)   (♯ Ura. 7097)
Westminster Sym.—Fistoulari   ♯ **P.PMC 1011**
(*Indy*)   (♯ MGM.E 3062; Od.ODX 153)
Paris Cons.—Ansermet   ♯ **D.LXT 5003**
(*Rachmaninoff*)   (♯ Lon.LL 1155)

(La) Plainte, au loin, du faune pf. 1921
(for *Le Tombeau de Debussy*)
E. Ulmer   ♯ **CHS.H 12**
(*Roussel, Goossens, Stravinsky, Malipiero & Debussy*)

Symphony, C major 1896
Concerts Colonne—Sebastian ♯ **Nix.ULP 9102**
                                          (♯ Ura. 7102)

Variations, Interlude, & Finale pf. 1903
(*on a theme of Rameau*)
L. Thyrion   ♯ *Phi.N 00666R*
(*Roussel & Schmit*)
H. Boschi (2ss)   **V**♯ *CdM.LDY 8117*

Villanelle Horn & pf. 1906
D. Brain & G. Moore   (2ss)   *C.DB 3300*
L. Thevet & C. Ambrosini   ♯ *D.LX 3143*
(*Gallay, Bach, Wagner*)

DUMANOIR, Guillaume (1615–1697)
SEE: † ANTHOLOGIE SONORE

DUMONT, Henry (1610-1684)
SEE: † MUSIQUES À LA CHAPELLE DU ROY

DUNSTABLE, John (d. 1453)
SEE: † HISTORY OF MUSIC IN SOUND (24 & 25)
     † MOTETS of the XVTH & XVITH CENTURIES
     † ENGLISH MEDIEVAL CAROLS

DUPARC, M. E. Henri F. (1848-1933)

SONGS
COLLECTIONS
La Vie antérieure (Baudelaire)
Le Manoir de Rosemonde (de Bonnières)
Élégie (T. Moore)
Phidylé (Leconte de Lisle)
Soupir (S. Prudhomme)
Chanson triste (J. Lahor)
Lamento (Gautier)
La Vague et la cloche (Coppée)
Sérénade florentine (Lahor)
Testament (Silvestre)
Extase (J. Lahor)
L'Invitation au voyage (Baudelaire)
G. Souzay (B), J. Bonneau (pf.)   ♯ **D.LXT 2823**
                                          (♯ Lon.LL 813)
C. Maurane (B), L. Bienvenu (pf.)
                                    ♯ **Phi.N 00225L**

La Vie antérieure (Baudelaire)
L'Invitation au voyage (Baudelaire)
Chanson triste (J. Lahor)
Élégie (T. Moore)
Extase (J. Lahor)
C. Castelli (S), H. Boschi (pf.) ♯ *CdM.LDA 8087*
(*Chabrier*)

L'Invitation au voyage (Baudelaire)
Phidylé (L. de Lisle)
Chanson triste (Lahor)
Extase (Lahor)
Le Manoir de Rosemonde (de Bonnières)
G. London (B), P. Ulanowsky (pf.)
                                    ♯ **AmC.ML 4906**
(*Moussorgsky*)   (♯ Phi.N 02117L)

Extase (J. Lahor)
Lamento (T. Gautier)
Sérénade florentine (Lahor)
Testament (Silvestre)
La Vague et la cloche (Coppée)
☆ C. Panzéra (B) (JpV.SD 3087/8)

Chanson triste (J. Lahor) 1868
G. Swarthout (M-S), G. Trovillo (pf.)
                                    in ♯ **G.ALP 1269**
(*Chausson, Debussy, Hahn, etc.*)
                                          (♯ Vic.LM 1793; FV.A 630227)
J. Harsanyi (S), O. Herz (pf.) in ♯ **Per.SPL 581**
Géori-Boué (S), M. Faure (pf.) in ♯ **Ura. 7070**
(*below; Debussy, Fauré, etc.*)   (♭ UREP 73)
L. Castellano (S), S. Leff (pf.) in ♯ **Mur.P 105**
(followed by pf. acc. only)
☆ J. C. Thomas (B) (in ♯ Cam.CAL 208)
    M. Teyte (S) (in ♯ Vic.LCT 1133)

Élégie (T. Moore)
M. Sénéchal (T), J. Bonneau (pf.)
                                    in ♯ *Phi.N 00681R*
(*Hahn, Saint-Saëns, Fauré*)

Extase (J. Lahor)
M. Powers (A), F. la Forge (pf.) in ♯ **Atl. 1207**
(*Handel, Bach, Brahms, Fauré, etc.*)

(Le) Manoir de Rosemonde (de Bonnières)
M. Harrell (B), B. Smith (pf.) in ♯ **Rem. 199-140**

Phidylé (L. de Lisle)
N. Merriman (M-S), G. Moore (pf.)
                                    in ♯ **C.CX 1213**
(*below; Bizet, Debussy, Fauré, etc.*)   (♯ Angel. 35217)
Géori-Boué (S), M. Faure (pf.)   in ♯ **Ura. 7070**
(*above*)   (♭ UREP 73)
M. Harrell (B), B. Smith (pf.) in ♯ **Rem. 199-140**

(La) Vie antérieure (Baudelaire)
N. Merriman (M-S), G. Moore (pf.)
                                    in ♯ **C.CX 1213**
(*above*)   (♯ Angel. 35217)

---

[1] Including *Fanfare pour précéder La Péri*, 1912.

DUPRÉ, Marcel (b. 1886)

ORGAN MUSIC
Cortège et Litanie, Op. 19, No. 2
In dulci jubilo ("*Christmas Cradle Song*")
  R. I. Purvis   in # HIFI.R 705
  (*Purvis, Brahms*) [Org. Grace Cathedral, San Francisco]
  [Cortège et Litanie only, also in # HIFI.R 704, d.c.]

Cortège et Litanie, Op. 19, No. 2
  E. Hilliar   # ASK. 4
  (*Arne, J. S. Bach, Pachelbel, etc.*)
  [Org. of St. Mark's, Mt. Kisco, N.Y.]

In dulci jubilo, Op. 28, No. 41 Chorale-prelude
  A. Hamme   in # SRS. 1
  († Organ Recital)

Intermezzo
  ☆ C. Snyder (in # Word.W 4003)

Symphonie-Passion, Op. 23
  P. Cochereau   # LOL.OL 50112
  [Org. of Notre-Dame, Paris]   (# OL.LD 118)

Variations sur un Noël, Op. 20
  W. Watkins   # McInt.MM 106
  (*Bach, Handel, etc.*)

Vêpres du Commun, Op. 18
... Adagissimo
  R. I. Purvis   in # HIFI.R 704

DURAND, Marie-Auguste (1830-1909)

Valses: No. 1, E flat major, Op. 83
       No. 2, A flat major, Op. 86 pf.
  G. v. Renesse   ♭ G.7EPH 1012
  (*Beethoven: Bagatelle, & Minuet*)

NOTE:
Printemps (Clarinet Sextet on # D.LX 3138; Lon.LS 1096) is by PAUL DURAND.

DURANTE, Francesco (1684-1755)

ARIAS
Danza, danza, fanciulla[1]
  S. Danco (S), G. Agosti (pf.)   in # D.LX 3113
  (*Schütz, Bach, Gluck, etc.*)   (in # Lon.LS 698)
  M. Laszlo (S), F. Holetschek (pf.)
         # Nix.WLP 5375
  († Italian Airs)   (# West.WL 5375)
  G. Gari (T), S. Neff (pf.) followed by pf. acc. only for
  study (in # Mur.P 104)
  Accompaniment etc. for practice (in # VS.MH 1002)

Vergin, tutto amor[2]
  G. Prandelli (T), D. Marzollo (pf.)
         in # AmVox.PL 7930
  († Old Italian Airs)
  ☆ B. Gigli (T) & orch.   in # G.ALP 1174
  († Italian Classic Songs)   (# FALP 340: QALP 10073)

Concerto, B flat major, hpsi. & str. (MS., Naples)
  R. Gerlin & O.L. Ens.—Froment
         # LOL.OL 50009
  (*Paisiello, Auletta, Mancini*)   (# OL.LD 66)

(8) CONCERTI (Quartetti concertanti)
  2 vlns., vla., cont.
No. 1, F minor ("*Divertimento*")
  Cha. Orch.—Cartigny   # LT.DTL 93044
  (*Pergolesi & Vivaldi*)   (# Sel.LA 1079; T.NLB 6096)

No. 4, E minor
  Ital. Cha.—Jenkins   # HS.HSL 137
  (*Albinoni & Viotti*)   (in set HSL-N)

No. 5, A major
No. 6, A major
  Netherlands Phil.—v. den Berg   # CHS.H 16
  (*Vivaldi, Torelli, B. Marcello*)

TOCCATAS hpsi. 1732
D minor; A minor (MS., Naples)
  R. Gerlin   in # LOL.OL 50043
  († Clavecinistes italiens & allemands)   (in # OL.LD 67)

DUREY, Louis (b. 1888)

(3) Poèmes (Petronius) 1918
  1. Boule de Neige   2. La Métempsychose
  3. La Grenade
  I. Joachim (S), M. Franck (pf.)
         in # CdM.LDA 8079
  (*Auric, Honegger, Milhaud, Poulenc, Tailleferre*)

(Le) Printemps au fond de la mer (Cocteau)
  Cantata S & orch. 1920
  D. Duval & Paris Cons.—Tzipine # C.CX 1252
  (*Tailleferre, Honegger, Poulenc*)
      (# FCX 264; Angel. 35117, in set 3515)

Quartet wind insts.
  New Art Wind Qtt.   in # CEd. set 2006

DUSSEK (or DUSÍK), Jan Ladislav
(1760-1812)

(La) Consolation, Op. 62 pf.
  M. Jonas   in # AmC.ML 4624

SONATAS (Sonatinas) pf.
F major, Op. 20, No. 3; E flat major, Op. 20, No. 6
  P. Zeitlin   # Opus. 6005
  (*Kuhlau, Clementi, Diabelli*)
  [Accompanying a *Matching Music Book*, pub. E. Marks, N.Y.]

F sharp minor, Op. 61 "*Élégie harmonique*"
  ☆ O. Vondrovic   # Sup.LPM 47
  (*Beethoven: Sonata, hrn. & pf.*)   (# U. C5068)

DUTILLEUX, Henri (b. 1916)

(Le) Loup Ballet (Anouilh & Neveux) 1952
  J. Anouilh (narrator)[3] & Champs-Elysées
  Theatre Orch.—Bonneau   # Sel.LD 1377
         (also # 270.C.060)

Symphony No. 1 1951
  Paris Opéra—Dervaux   # CIDM. n.d.
  (*Petrassi*) [No. 1 of subscription series: in prep.]

DVOŘÁK, Antonin (1841-1904)

CLASSIFIED I. Orchestral   II. Slavonic Dances
       III. Instrumental
         A. Piano   B. Chamber Music
       IV. Operas   V. Choral
       VI. Songs

I. ORCHESTRAL

CONCERTOS
G minor, Op. 33, pf. & orch
  [4]R. Firkusny & Cleveland—Szell # AmC.ML 4967
         (# Phi.A 01619R)
  ☆ F. Maxián & Czech Phil.—Talich   # Sup.LPV 70
         (# U. 5054G)

A minor, Op. 53, vln. & orch.
  J. Martzy & R.I.A.S. Sym.—Fricsay
         # HP.DGM 18152
  [3rd movt. only in # Pol. 19017]
  T. Magyar & Vienna Sym.—Loibner
         # Phi.A 00751R
  (*Mendelssohn: Concerto, on* # Epic.LC 3173)
  D. Oistrakh & USSR. State—Kondrashin
         # Van.VRS 6016
  (1½ss—*Glier*) (2ss, # CdM.LDA 8111)
  (*Glazounov* on # Csm.CRLP 137)
  ☆ G. Kulenkampff & Berlin Phil.—E. Jochum
         # DT.LGX 66020[5]
         (# FT. 310.TC.008)
  ☆ N. Milstein & Minneapolis Sym.—Dorati
  (*Glazounov*)   # G.FALP/QALP 241

---

[1] A XIXth Cent. adaptation of No. 137 of *Solfèges d'Italie*.   [2] A similar adaptation of No. 150.
[3] Reading the argument of the ballet.   [4] Revised version, ed. Firkusny.   [5] Announced but not issued.

B minor, Op. 104, vlc. & orch.
P. Fournier & Vienna Phil.—Kubelik
♯ **D.LXT 2999**
(♯ Lon.LL 1106)
A. Navarra & New Sym.—Schwarz
♯ **DCap.CTL 7090**
(♯ Cap.P 8301)
P. Tortelier & Philharmonia—Sargent
♯ **G.ALP 1306**
A. Janigro & Vienna State Op.—D. Dixon
♯ **Nix.WLP 5225**
(♯ West.WL 5225)
T. de Machula & Vienna Sym.—Moralt
♯ **Phi.A 00687R**
(*Bruch*, on ♯ Epic.LC 3083)
E. Mainardi & Berlin Phil.—Lehmann
♯ **Pol. 18236**
P. Tortelier & Zürich Tonhalle—Ackermann
♯ **MMS. 2006**
(& ♯ *MMS. 124*)
M. Rostropovich & Czech Phil.—Talich
♯ **Sup.LPM 88/9**
(3ss—*Noonday Witch*)   (♯ U. 5055/6C)
(*Tchaikovsky*, on ♯ Csm.CRLP 231)
M. Rostropovich & Sym.—Rakhlin
(2ss)   ♯ **USSR.D 0566/7**
☆ G. Cassadó & Austrian Sym.—Wöss (♯ Cum.CR 282)

(10) LEGENDS, Op. 59 orig. pf. duet, later orch.
COMPLETE RECORDING
Little Orch. Society—Scherman
♯ **AmC.ML 4920**

Nos. 1, D minor; 2, G major; 3, G minor
Moscow Radio—Anosov   ♯ **USSR.D 552**
(*Smetana*)

No. 10, B flat major
☆ Philharmonia—Kubelik
(♭ G.7RF/RQ 259 & G.DB 4328)

(The) Noonday Witch, Op. 108
☆ Czech Phil.—Talich (♯ Sup.SLPM 88; U. 5055C)

Notturno, B major, Op. 40 Str. orch.
London Cha.—Bernard   **G.C 4249**
Boyd Neel—Dumont   ♭ **EPhi.NBE 11006**
(*Grieg & Tchaikovsky*)   (♭ Phi.N 402030E)
A. Winograd Str. Orch.   ♯ **MGM.E 3295**
(*Mendelssohn & Wolf*)
Leningrad Phil.—Khaikin (*USSRM.D 001096*)
Linz Sym. (in ♯ Ply. 12-37)
☆ Vienna Sym.—Swoboda (in ♯ Clc. 6160)

OVERTURES
COLLECTION "Nature, Life and Love"
Amid Nature, Op. 91
Carnival, Op. 92
Otello, Op. 93
☆ Vienna Sym.—Swoboda (♯ Clc. 6160)
[Carnival only, in ♯ MMS. 42]

Amid Nature, Op. 91
☆ Chicago Sym.—Stock (in ♯ Cam.CAL 162)

Carnival, Op. 92
Philharmonia—Collingwood   **C.DX 1881**
Linz Bruckner Sym.—G. L. Jochum ♯ **Ura. 7094**
(*Jacobin; & Smetana*)
☆ City of Birmingham—Weldon (in ♯ AmC.RL 3091)
    Stadium Concerts—Smallens (♯ D.UW 333004;
        AFest.CFR 10-427)
    Boston Prom.—Fiedler (in ♯ Cam.CAL 122)

(The) Hussites, Op. 67
☆ Czech Phil.—Šejna   ♯ **Sup.LPM 203**
(*Slav. Rhapsody No. 3*)   (♯ U. 5188C)
☆ Boston Prom.—Fiedler   ♯ **Vic.LM 9017**
(*Brahms & Smetana*)

Othello, Op. 93
☆ Czech Phil.—Talich (♯ Csm.CRLP 235)

Scherzo capriccioso, Op. 66
Philharmonia—Sawallisch   ♯ **C.SX 1034**
(*below*)   (♯ Angel. 35214)
Bamberg Sym.—Perlea   ♯ **AmVox.PL 9500**
(*Enesco, Kodály, Smetana*)
☆ Vienna Sym.—Swoboda   ♯ **Nix.WLP 5029**
(*Symphony, E flat major*)
(*idem, & Slav. Rhapsody No. 2 on* ♯ West.WN 18067)

Serenade, E major, Op. 22 Str. orch.
Bamberg Sym.—Lehmann   ♯ **Pol. 17050**
... Moderato only Leningrad Phil.—Khaikin (USSR. 020625)

Serenade, D minor, Op. 44 wind, vlcs. & cbs.
Netherlands Phil. Members—Ackermann
(*Chopin*)   ♯ **CHS.H 6**
☆ London Baroque Ens.—Haas (♯ Od.OD 1009)

SLAVONIC RHAPSODIES, Op. 45
No. 1, D major
No. 2, G minor
Czech Phil.—Šejna   ♯ **Sup.LPM 198**
(♯ U. 5187C)

No. 2, G minor
☆ Vienna Sym.—Swoboda   ♯ **West.WN 18067**
(*above & below*)

No. 3, A flat major
Residentie—Dorati   ♯ **EPhi.NBR 6010**
(*Smetana: My Country—Vltava*)
    (♯ Phi.S 06053R: N 00620R; Epic.LC 3015)
Czech Phil.—Šejna   ♯ **Sup.LPM 203**
(*Hussites Overture*)   (♯ U. 5188C)

Suite, D major, Op. 39 ("*Czech*")
☆ Winterthur Sym.—Swoboda   ♯ Nix.CLP 1157
(*Qtt. No. 6*)   (♯ Clc. 6223)

... Furiant only
Moscow Radio—Gortchakov   ♯ **USSR.D 1150**
(♭s—*Slav. Dances Nos. 2, 3, 6*)

Symphonic Variations, Op. 78
Royal Phil.—Beecham   ♯ **EPhi.ABL 3047**
(*Balakirev*)   (♯ Phi.A 01164L; AmC.ML 4974)
☆ Czech Phil.—Šejna   ♯ Sup.LPV 109
(*Pf. Variations, Op. 36*)   (♯ U. 5088G)

SYMPHONIES
E flat major 1873 (orig. Op. 10)
☆ Vienna Sym.—Swoboda   ♯ Nix.WLP 5029
(*Scherzo Capriccioso*)
(*idem & Slav. Rhapsody No. 2 on* ♯ West.WN 18067)

No. 1, D major, Op. 60 1880
☆ Czech Phil.—Šejna   ♯ **Sup.LPM 45/46**
(4ss) (2ss, ♯ Csm.CRLP 237)   (♯ U. 5062/3C)
☆ Cleveland Sym.—Leinsdorf (♯ Phi.A 01108L;
        AmC.RL 6627)

No. 2, D minor, Op. 70 1885
N.W.D.R.—Schmidt-Isserstedt   ♯ **D.LXT 2807**
(♯ Lon.LL 778)
Philharmonia—Kubelik   ♯ **G.ALP 1075**
(♯ QALP 10042: FALP 244; Vic.LHMV 1029:
         ♭ set WHMV 1029)
☆ Czech Phil.—Šejna (♯ Sup.LPV 27; ♯ U. 5020G)
    Berlin Phil.—Schrader (ANix.ULP 9015)

No. 3, F major, Op. 76 1875
Leipzig Phil.—Schüler   ♯ **Ura. 7153**
(& ♯ Ura. 7-11; MTW. 503)
☆ Netherlands Phil.—Goehr
(♯ CHS.CHS 1240; MMS. 121)

No. 4, G major, Op. 88 1889
Philharmonia—Sawallisch   ♯ **C.SX 1034**
(*Scherzo*)   (♯ Angel. 35214)
Bamberg Sym.—Lehmann   ♯ **HP.DGM 18141**
Leipzig Radio—Pflüger   ♯ **Ura.RS 7-29**
(♯ MTW. 557; n.n. Ura. 7160)
Cincinnati Sym.—Johnson   ♯ **Rem. 199-168**
(♯ Cum.CR 301)
(*continued on next page*)

☆ = Re-issue of a recording to be found in previous volumes.

No. 4, G major, Op. 88 (*continued*)
Leningrad Phil.—N. Rabinovich
⧣ **USSR.D 01728/9**

☆ Philharmonia—Kubelik   ⧣ **G.ALP 1064**
(⧣ QALP 10036: VALP 534)
☆ N.Y.P.S.O.—Walter   (⧣ **C.CX 1036**
(⧣ QCX 10011)
☆ Czech Phil.—Talich   ⧣ **Sup.LPV 44**
(*Othello Overture,* on ⧣ Csm.CRLP 235)

No. 5, E minor, Op. 95 ("*From the New World*")
1895
N.B.C. Sym.—Toscanini   ⧣ **G.ALP 1222**
(⧣ Vic.LM 1778: ♭ set ERC 1; ⧣ ItV.A12R 0049;
FV.A 630209)
Philharmonia—Galliera (n.v.?)   ⧣ **C.SX 1025**
(⧣ FCX 124: QCX 10128; Angel. 35085)
New Sym.—Schwarz   ⧣ **DCap.CTL 7099**
(⧣ Cap.P 8308)
London Phil. Sym.—Rodzinski
⧣ **Nix.WLP 20001**
(⧣ West.WL 5370)
N.W.D.R.—Schmidt-Isserstedt ⧣ **DT.LGX 66007**
(⧣ T.LE 6505; FT. 320.TC.026)
R.I.A.S. Sym.—Fricsay   ⧣ **HP.DGM 18142**
[4th movt. only in ⧣ Pol. 19017]   (6ss, ♭ PV. 72420/2)
Residentie—Dorati   ⧣ **EPhi.ABL 3021**
(⧣ Phi.A 00154L; Epic.LC 3001)
Leipzig Radio—Pflüger   ⧣ **Ura. 7132**
(& ⧣ Ura.RS 7-3)
(*Slav. Dances & Bartered Bride Over.* on ⧣ MTW.22;
3rd movt. only, ♭ Ura.UREP 61)
☆ Vienna State—Horenstein   ⧣ **EVox.PL 7590**
(⧣ AFest.CFR 12-309)
Welsh Nat. Youth Sym.—Raybould[1] (⧣ Cwal.QLP 1000)
Moscow Radio—Rakhlin
(USSR. 020105/15 & ⧣ D 0484/5)
Zürich Tonhalle—Ackermann
(⧣ MMS. 36; ANix.MLPY 36; Copa.CLP 4003)
Olympia Sym.—Saike (⧣ Allo. 3071; Pac.LDAD 46)
Anon. Orchs. (⧣ Gram. 2047 & ⧣ ACC.MP 15)
☆ Czech Phil.—Talich (in ⧣ Csm.CRLP 162/3)
Chicago Sym.—Kubelik (⧣ G.FALP 347:
VALP 517; Largo, on ♭ Mer.EP 1-5026)
Cleveland Sym.—Szell (♭ AmC. set A 1082)
Philadelphia—Stokowski (⧣ Cam.CAL 104 &
in set CFL 104)
Austrian Sym.—Singer (⧣ Cum.CR 245; Msq. 10004 &
with commentary by S. Spaeth, on ⧣ Rem. 3;
2nd movt. only in ⧣ Rem. 199-114)
Philadelphia—Ormandy (⧣ AmC.CL 731)

... **2nd movt. (Largo) only (abridged)**
Boston Prom.—Fielder (in ⧣ Vic.LM 1752:
♭ set WDM 1752)
Melachrino Str. Orch. (in ⧣ Vic.LPM 1004:
♭ set EPB 1004)

— — ARR. VLN. & PF.   Kreisler
("*Negro Spiritual Melody*")
☆ Y. Menuhin & A. Baller[2] (in ⧣ Vic.LM 1742:
♭ set WDM 1742; ♭ JpV.EP 3043: ⧣ JpV.LS 2004)
— ARR. ORGAN   V. Fox (♭ AmC.A 1594)
C. Cronham (Mjr. 5125)

(The) Water Sprite, Op. 107 (*Vodnik*)
Berlin Radio—Wiesenhütter   ⧣ **Ura. 7082**
(*Kabalevsky & Prokofiev*)

II. SLAVONIC DANCES

Opp. 46 & 72, COMPLETE. Orig. pf. duet, later orch.
London Phil. Sym.—Rodzinski
(4ss)   ⧣ **West.WN 18108/9**
(set WN 2204)
Philharmonia—Malko   ⧣ **G.CLP 1019/20**
(3ss—*Grieg: Lyric Suite*) (⧣ QCLP 12008/9: FALP 341/2)
Vienna Phil.—Kubelik   ⧣ **D.LXT 5079/80**
(3ss—*Tchaikovsky: Romeo & Juliet*) (⧣ Lon.LL 1283/4)
[Nos. 1 & 2 also ♭ D.71115]
☆ Czech Phil.—Talich   ⧣ **Csm.CRLP 007/8**
(4ss) (Op. 46 with *Malat; & Op. 72 with *Schneider-
Trnavsky, Weiss, Šebor*) (20ss, Muza.X 1942/51)
(also ♭ Sup.LPV 214/5; U. 5210/11/G)
(Nos. 6 & 7 only on ♭ Ura.UREP 48)

Op. 46   ☆ Czech Phil.—Talich, o.v. (⧣ Cam.CAL 197;
& in ⧣ Cam. set CFL 103)
COLLECTIONS
Nos. 1-8
Munich Phil.—Rieger   ⧣ **Pol. 17038**
[Nos. 5-8 also on PV. 72333; Nos. 1-4 are ☆]
(also ⧣ Pol. 16058)
☆ Austrian Sym.—Singer (⧣ Cum.CR 224; Ply. 12-44;
Nos. 1, 4 & 7 only on ⧣ AFest.CFR 10-338;
♭ Rem.REP 15)
Nos. 1, 2, 3, 16
N.W.D.R.—Schmidt-Isserstedt   ⧣ **D.LW 5048**
(Lon.LD 9063)
(*Brahms: Hungarian Dances* on ⧣ D.LXT 2814;
Lon.LL 779)
Nos. 1, 2, 4 & 8
Indianapolis Sym.—Sevitzky   ⧣ **Cap.H 8211**
(⧣ ACap.CLC 004)
(*Enesco* on ⧣ DCap.CTL 7038; Cap.S 8209)
(Nos. 1, 4, 8 only, on ♭ Cap.FAP 8215)
Nos. 1, 3, 8, 10, 15
☆ Cleveland Sym.—Szell[3] (*Smetana*)   ⧣ **AmC.ML 4785**
Unspec. Nos.   Anon. Orch. (in ⧣ ACC.MP 30; perhaps as
⧣ MTW. 22, *below*)

No. 1, C major, Op. 46, No. 1
Hamburg Philharmonia—H-J. Walther
MSB. 78111
(*No. 3*)   (& in ⧣ MGM.E 3195)
Sym. Orch.—Graunke   in ⧣ **MTW. 22**
Orch.—Gräf (in ⧣ Pan.XPV 1022)
Moscow Radio—Orlov (USSR. 5369)
☆ L.P.O.—Martinon (in ⧣ MGM.E 3037)
St. Louis Sym.—Golschmann (in ⧣ Cam.CAL 178)

No. 2, E minor, Op. 46, No. 2
Sym. Orch.—Graunke   in ⧣ **MTW. 22**
USSR. State Sym.—Khaikin (in ⧣ USSR.D 1149)
Moscow Radio—Orlov (USSR. 5370)
— ARR. VLN. & PF.   Kreisler ("*No. 1, G minor*")
I. Haendel & G. Moore   **G.C 4262**
(*Falla: Vida Breve, Danza*)   (in ⧣ CLP 1021)
I. Stern & A. Zakin   in ⧣ **AmC.AL 23**
(⧣ Phi.S 06617R)
M. Rabin & A. Balsam   in ⧣ **AmC.AL 30**
H. Szeryng & M. Berthelier in ⧣ **Pac.LDPC 50**
(♭ ED 90019)
C. Wicks & pf.   **G.DA 11906**
(*Kroll: Banjo & Fiddle*)
F. Akos & H. Altmann (G.EG 8177)
G. Barinova & pf. (USSRM.D 00445)
☆ J. Szigeti & pf. (♭ AmC.A 1887; ♭ Phi.N 409506E)

No. 3, D major, Op. 46, No. 3
Hamburg Philharmonia—H-J. Walther
MSB. 78111
(*No. 1*)   (& in ⧣ MGM.E 3195)
USSR. State Sym.—Khaikin (in ⧣ USSR.D 1150)

No. 6, A flat major, Op. 46, No. 6   (Orch. "*No. 3*")
International Sym.—Schneiderhann (in ⧣ Mae.OA 20009)
USSR. State Sym.—Khaikin (in ⧣ USSR.D 1149)
☆ L.S.O.—Krauss (♭ D.DME 8006)
St. Louis Sym.—Golschmann (in ⧣ Cam.CAL 178)

No. 8, G minor, Op. 46, No. 8
International Sym.—Schneiderhann (in ⧣ Mae.OA 20009)
Moscow Radio—Rakhlin (USSR. 020116)
USSR. State Sym.—Khaikin (USSR. 020198)
Orch.—Gräf (in ⧣ Pan.XPV 1022)
☆ L.S.O.—Krauss (♭ D.DME 8006)
Boston Prom.—Fiedler (♭ G.7BF 1061; ♭ DV. 16293)
— ARR. BAND   All Star Brass Band (Pax.PR 636)
— ARR. 4 TROMBONES: Paris Trombone Qtt. (in ⧣ D.LX 3145)

No. 10, E minor, Op. 72, No. 2
V. Vronsky & V. Babin   in ⧣ **AmD.DL 9791**
Hamburg Philharmonia—H-J. Walther
MSB. 78112
(*Moussorgsky: Sorotchintsy Fair, Gopak*)
(& in ⧣ MGM.E 3195)

---

[1] Actual performance, Edinburgh International Festival, 1955.
[2] This is the Japanese recording; the Victor issue has also been stated to be acc. G. Moore and recorded in England.   It is not possible to ascertain which is the correct information.
[3] Orch. Szell.

No. 10, E minor, Op. 72, No. 2 (*continued*)
N.W. Ger. Phil.—Schüchter   ♯ *Imp.ILP 117*
(*Chabrier, Berlioz, Tchaikovsky*)
— ARR. VLN. & PF.   Kreisler ("No. 2")
I. Zilzer & F. Eberson[1]   C.LDX 17
(*Chopin: Nocturne No. 2*)   (♭ SCBK 1)
M. Stiglitz & pf.[1]   *Arzi. 700*
  ☆ J. Szigeti & pf. (♭ *AmC.A 1887;* ♭ *Phi.N 469506E*)
    Y. Menuhin & A. Baller[2] (in ♯ JpV.LS 2004;
                      ♭ *JpV.EP 3043*)

No. 11, F major, Op. 72, No. 3
Leningrad Phil.—Sanderling (*USSR. 22648*)
— ARR. VLN. & PF.   S. Furer & pf. (*USSR. 18477*)

No. 13, B flat major, Op. 72, No. 5
Leningrad Phil.—Sanderling (*USSR. 22649*)
— ARR. VLN. & PF.   S. Furer & pf.   (*USSR. 18478*)

III. INSTRUMENTAL & CHAMBER MUSIC
A. PIANO

(8) HUMORESQUES, Op. 101
No. 7, G flat major
—. Maznek   ♯ *Sup.LPV 114*
(*Quintet, Op. 81*)
E. Silver (hpsi.) (in ♯ *Roy. 1550*)
— ARR. ORCH.
   Belgian Radio—P. Glière (in ♯ *Mae.OAT 25001*)
   W. Fenske Orch. (in ♯ *Phi.P 10200R*)
   M. Weber Orch. (in ♯ AmC.CL 519)
  ☆ A. Kostelanetz Orch. (♭ *C.SCD 2014: SCDQ 2008:*
     SCW 109: in ♯ *S 1029: FS 1043,* etc.; ♭ *AmC.A 1557*)
     etc.
— ARR. VLN. & PF.
   F. Akos & H. Altmann (*G.EG 7934*)
   W. Tworek & Orch. (*Pol.X 51704;* in ♯ *Lon.LB 1121*)
   Z. Grach & pf. (*USSR. 021393*)
  ☆ J. Heifetz (in ♯ *B.AXL 2017; D.UA 233086;*
                  ♯ *AmD.DL 9780 & DL 5214*)
   L. Kaufmann (♭ *Cap.FAP 8208; ACap.CEC 004*)
— ARR. VLA. & PF.   ☆ W. Primrose (♭ *Cam.CAE 251*)
— ARR. FL., OB., CL., HRN., & BSN.
   Chicago Sym. Wind Quintet (in ♯ *Aphe.AP 17*)
— ARR. 4 TROMBONES   Paris Trombone Qtt. (in ♯ *D.LX 3145*)
— ARR. VOICE   ☆ R. Tauber (T, *Ger*)(*P.PO 189*)

Variations, A flat major, Op. 36
  ☆ J. Páleníček   ♯ *Sup.LPV 109*
     (*Symphonic Variations*)   (♯ *U. 5088G*)

(8) WALTZES, Op. 54   — ARR. ORCH.   Dvořák
Nos. 1 & 4 only
  ☆ Prague Soloists Orch.—Talich (♭ *Ura.UREP 48*)
Nos. 1 & 2 only
   Leningrad Phil.—Khaikin (*USSRM.D 001095;*
               No. 1 also USSR. 020626)

III. B. CHAMBER MUSIC

Gavotte   3 vlns.   1890
London Baroque Ens.—Haas   **P.SW 8149**
(*Beethoven: Minuets,* s.1)   (in ♯ *AmD.DL 4096*)

QUARTETS, Strings
No. 2, D minor, Op. 34
Bolshoi Theatre Qtt.   ♯ *USSR.D 1131/2*

No. 3, E flat major, Op. 51
Vienna Philharmonia Qtt.   ♯ *DT.LGM 65024*
                     (♯ *T.LB 6061*)

No. 6, F major, Op. 96   ("*American*")
Curtis Qtt.   ♯ **West.WL 5199**
(*Smetana: Qtt., E minor*)
Hollywood Qtt.   ♯ *DCap.CTL 7098*
(*Dohnányi*)   (♯ Cap.P 8307)
Pascal Qtt.   ♯ *MMS. 42*
(*Carnival Overture*)
  ☆ Hungarian Qtt.   ♯ Nix.CLP 1157
     (*Suite*)   (♯ Clc. 6223)
  ☆ Koeckert Qtt.   (2ss)   ♯ *HP.DG 16001*
  ☆ Stradivari Qtt. (♯ Cpt.MC 20068)

No. 7, A flat major, Op. 105
Barchet Qtt. (2ss)   ♯ **E. & AmVox.PL 7570**
Barylli Qtt.   ♯ **Nix.WLP 5337**
(*Quintet, Op. 81*)   (♯ West.WL 5337)
Smetana Qtt.   ♯ *Sup.LPM 227*

No. 8, G major, Op. 106
Barchet Qtt.   ♯ **AmVox.PL 9250**

QUARTETS, Pf. & Strings
No. 2, E flat major, Op. 87
Galimir Pf. Qtt.   ♯ **Strad.STR 619**
(*Janáček*)

QUINTETS
E flat major, Op. 97   2 vlns., 2 vlas., vlc.
  ☆ Budapest Qtt. & M. Katims   ♯ **EPhi.ABL 3073**
     (*Brahms*)   (♯ AmC.ML 4799; Phi.A 01151L)

G major, Op. 77   Str. qtt. & cbs.
  ☆ Vienna Konzerthaus Quintet   ♯ **West.WN 18066**
     (*Romantic Pieces & Sonata*)

A major, Op. 81   pf. & str.
C. Curzon & Budapest Qtt.   (2ss)
                     ♯ **AmC.ML 4825**
E. Farnadi & Barylli Qtt.   ♯ **Nix.WLP 5337**
(*Str. Qtt. No. 7*)   (♯ West.WL 5337)
—. Maznek (?) & Smetana Qtt.   ♯ *Sup.LPV 114*
(*Humoresque*)

(4) Romantic Pieces, Op. 75   vln. & pf.
  ☆ P. Rybar & F. Holetschek   ♯ **West.WN 18066**
     (*Quintet, Op. 77 & Sonata*)
  ☆ L. Kaufman & A. Balsam (♯ *T.LCB 8112*)

Sonata, F major, Op. 57   vln. & pf.
  ☆ P. Rybar & F. Holetschek   ♯ **West.WN 18066**
     (*Romantic Pieces & Quintet, Op. 77*)

Sonatina, G major, Op. 100   vln. & pf.
... 2nd movt., Larghetto   — ARR. VLC. & PF.
A. Vlasov (*Smetana*)   *USSR. 21828*

Terzetto, C major, Op. 74   2 vlns. & vla.
Classic Trio   ♯ **CEd.CE 1033**
(*Kodály: Serenade*)

TRIOS, pf., vln. & vlc.
No. 3, F minor, Op. 65
  ☆ Czech Trio (♯ *Sup.LPV 58;* ♯ *U. 5064G*)
   A. Balsam, L. Kaufman & M. Cervera (♯ Clc. 6248)

No. 4, E minor, Op. 90   ("*Dumky*")
L. Mittman, A. Eidus & G. Ricci
(*Smetana*)   ♯ **Strad.STR 620**
C. Hansen, E. Röhn & A. Troester   ♯ *T.LB 6122*
  ☆ Czech Trio (♯ *Sup.LPM 64; U. 5037C*)
   Budapest Trio (♯ *Tono.LPK 32001*)

IV. OPERAS

(The) DEVIL & KATE, Op. 112
   (*Čert a Káca*)   3 Acts   1899
Prelude, Act III; Devil's dance
Prague Nat. Th.—Folprecht   U.H 24378

(The) JACOBIN, Op. 84   3 Acts   1889
Highlights
  ☆ L. Červinková, M. Fidlerová, V.   ♯ *Sup.LPV 139*
     Bednář, I. Židek, E. Haken, etc.   (♯ *U. 5125G*)
     Cho. & orch. of Prague Nat.
     Theatre—Vogel
Orch. Suite
Berlin Radio—Kretschmar   ♯ **Ura. 7094**
(*Carnival Overture; & Smetana*)
We are foreigners, we have wandered S & B
Oh God, how hopeless S
  ☆ E. Trötschel & H. Günter (*Ger*)(in ♯ *Pol. 19036*)

---

[1] Labelled "No. 2"; not heard.
[2] Entered in Supp. II as No. 2 (Kreisler "No. 1") but now *thought* to be this.

RUSALKA, Op. 114 3 Acts 1901
COMPLETE RECORDING

The Prince ... ... B. Blachut (T)
The Foreign Princess ... M. Podvalová (S)
Rusalka ... ... L. Červinková (S)
The Water Sprite ... ... E. Haken (Bs)
The Witch ... ... M. Krásová (A)
The Gamekeeper ... ... J. Joran (T)
etc., Cho. & orch. of Prague Nat. Theatre
—Krombholc (8ss) *# Sup.SLPV 94/7*
(6ss, # Csm.CRLP 232/4) (# U. 5118/21G)

Opening Chorus
O moon in the deep sky S (Act I)
☆ E. Trötschel, G. Frick (T), Dresden State Op. Cho. &
Orch.—Keilberth, from set (Ger) (♭ Ura.UREP 55)

... O moon in the deep sky, only
☆ J. Hammond (G.ED 1223)
E. Trötschel (Ger) (in # Pol. 18057: 19036: ♭ 34017)
Ⓗ E. Destinn (in # Sca. 804*)

Polonaise Ballet Music (Act II)
Munich Phil.—Hollreiser *PV. 36086*
(Eugen Oniegin, Polonaise) (♭ Pol. 30013)

V. CHORAL

STABAT MATER, Op. 58 Oratorio
S, A, T, B, cho. & orch.
☆ Soloists, Czech Singers & Czech Phil. Orch.—Talich
 # Ura. set 234
(4ss) (# Sup.LPV 228/9; U. 5212/3H)
(3ss—Symphony No. 5 on # Csm.CRLP 162/3)

VI. SONGS

COLLECTIONS
(10) BIBLICAL SONGS, Op. 99
(7) GYPSY SONGS, Op. 55 (Heyduk)
(8) LOVE SONGS, Op. 83 (Pfleger-Moravský)
H. Rössl-Majdan (A, Ger), F. Holetschek (pf.)
 # Nix.WLP 5324
(# West.WL 5324)

(7) GYPSY SONGS, Op. 55 (Heyduk)
(8) LOVE SONGS, Op. 83 (Pfleger-Moravský)
... Nos. 1, 2, 3 & 6 only
D. Warenskjöld (S, Eng), & orch
 # DCap.CTL 7065[1]
(Grieg) (# Cap.P 8247)
[Gypsy Songs No. 3 & 4 only on
♭ Cap.FAP 8250; ACap.CEC 009]

(10) BIBLICAL SONGS, Op. 99
COMPLETE RECORDINGS
M. Krásová (A), P. Kočí (B), M. Kampelsheimer
(org.) *# Sup.LPM 136*
(# U. 5128C)
E. L. Duarte (S, Eng), F. Murphy (pf.)
 # ML. 7024

... Nos. 1-5, only
G. Clinton (B,Eng), P. Oyez (pf.) # CA.LPA 1095
(Handel & Stanford)
... Nos. 1 & 6 — ARR. VLC. & PF.
K. Reher & M. di Tullio (in # Layos.CB 594/5)

Echoes from Moravia, Op. 32 S, A, pf.
E. Schwarzkopf & I. Seefried (SS, Ger),
G. Moore (pf.) *# C.CX 1331*
(Carissimi & Monteverdi) (# Angel. 35290)

Grief, Op. 43, No. 1 (Trad.) Part Song
Augustana Cho. (Eng) & pf.—Veld
in *# BB.LBC 1075*
(Bach, Brahms, etc.)

(7) GYPSY SONGS, Op. 55 (Heyduk)
COMPLETE RECORDINGS in German
A. Felbermayer (S), V. Graef (pf.)
 # Van.VRS 446
(Brahms)
M. Lichtegg (T), H. W. Häusslein (pf.)
 # D.LW 5146
(Brahms) (# Lon.LD 9154)
E. Höngen (M-S), G. Weissenborn (pf.)
(Brahms) *# Pol. 17024*

H. Zadek (S), G. Frid (pf.) *# Phi.S 06062R*
(Brahms)

No. 1, My song tells of my love
N. Kazantseva (S, Russ) (USSR. 21539)

No. 4, Songs my mother taught me
M. Krásová (A) & orch. (U.H 24388)
I. Te Wiata (Bs, Eng), E. Lush (pf.)
(in # Nix.NLPY 915: ♭ EP 901)
E. Katulskaya (M-S, Russ) (USSR. 22826)
R. Crooks (T, Eng) (in # Cam.CAL 251), etc.

— ARR. VLN. & PF.
Y. Menuhin & G. Moore G.DB 21608
(Schubert: Ave Maria) (♭ 7R 176: 7RQ 3035)
M. Auclair & O. Schulhof in # Rem. 199-128
☆ E. & A. Wolf (♭ Mer.EP 1-5040)

— ARR. ORCH. Royale Concert Orch.
(in # Roy. 1567; in # Ply. 12-128)

— ARR. CARILLON Chapman
C. Chapman (Luray Tower Carillon) in # McInt.MM 102
— ARR. ORGAN. V. Fox (in ♭ AmC. set 1008)

LOVE SONGS, Opp. 2 & 83 (Pfleger-Moravský)
Your wonderful eyes
Not meant for me
I bring oft my love (all unid.)
S. Shaposhnikov (B) *USSRM.D 00116*
& *USSR.21452*

Leave me alone, Op. 82, No. 1
(Kej duch můj sam) (Malybrok-Stieler)
M. Krásová (A) & orch. U.H 24389
(Grieg: Solveig's Song)

DYSON, Sir George (b. 1883)

SEE: † CORONATION OF QUEEN ELIZABETH II

▽ O praise God in His holiness
Coronation Cho. (1937) in G.RG 8
(3) Songs of Courage ... Reveillé; Praise
Boys' School Cho. in G.C 3681

EAST, Michael (c. 1580-1648)

SEE: † TRIUMPHS OF ORIANA

EBELING, Johann Georg (1637-1676)

Warum sollt' ich mich denn grämen
— ARR. F. M. Christiansen
▽ St. Olaf Cho.—Christiansen (Eng) in # StO.DLP 6

ECCARD, Johann (1553-1611)

SEE ALSO: † MOTETS ON LUTHER TEXTS
† SONGS OF THE RENAISSANCE

Vom Himmel hoch Chorale setting
St. Michael's Cho. (Hamburg)—Brinkmann
PV. 36099
(Freylinghausen, Bach, Pachelbel) (♭ Pol. 32099)

ECCLES, Henry (c.1670-1742)

Sonata, G minor vln. & cont.
— ARR. VLC. & PF.
A. Schmidt & C. Fannière *# Vill. 1*
(Beethoven, Haydn, etc.)
K. Rehr & M. di Tullio in # Layos.CB 594/5
... Largo — ARR. CBS.
☆ S. Koussevitzky (in # Vic.LCT 1145)

ECCLES, John (c. 1668-1735)

SEE: † MORE CATCHES & GLEES OF THE RESTORATION

---

[1] Announced but not issued in England.

EDMUNDSON, Garth

SEE: † AMERICAN ORGAN MUSIC

EGGE, Klaus (b. 1906)

Concerto No. 2, Op. 21 pf. & orch. 1944
☆ R. Riefling & Oslo Phil—Fjeldstad ‡ Mer.MG 90003
(*Groven*)   (also NOC. 63189/93, 5ss)

Fantasy in Halling style, Op. 12 pf. 1939
☆ R. Riefling (NOC. 68194)

Gukko-Slåtten pf.
K. Baekkelund   *G.AL 3285*
(‡s—*Grieg: Folk Song & Humoreske*)

EGGEN, Arne (1881-1955)

Bøgulv the Fiddler
Oslo Phil.—Grüner-Hegge   **Nera.SK 15530**
(*below*)   (NOC. 63185; in ‡ Mer.MG 10150)

LITTLE KIRSTEN Inc. Music
(to Garborg's play, after H. C. Andersen)
... Rustic Dance (*Vosserull*)
Oslo Phil.—Grüner-Hegge   **Nera.SK 15530**
(*above*)   (NOC. 63177)
(*Svendsen, Halvorsen, etc.* in ‡ Mer.MG 10150)

OLAV LILJENKRANS Opera 1940
Dance Scene
Oslo Phil.—Grüner-Hegge   **NOC. 63182/3**
(2ss)   (& in ‡ Mer.MG 90002)

Olav's Monologue & Aria T
B. Bantz   **NOC. 63184**
                    (& in ‡ Mer.MG 90002)

SONG: Thou land (Hurom)
P. Grønneberg (B)   *G.AL 3024*
(*Olsen: Song*)

EHRHARDT, C. Michael (b. 1914)

Balletti Suite pf. 1954
1. Intrada   4. Volta
2. Marcia   5. Partita
3. Tema   6. Reprisa
C. M. Ehrhardt   ‡ **Edu. 1001**

EINEM, Gottfried von (b. 1918)

Capriccio for Orchestra, Op. 2
☆ R.I.A.S. Sym.—Fricsay   ‡ **AmD.DL 9769**
(*Blacher, Fortner, etc.*)   (♭ *Pol. 32041*)

Meditations, Op. 18 orch. f.p.1954
Louisville—Whitney   ‡ **LO. 9**
(*Perle & Rathaus*)

EISLER, Hanns (b. 1898)

Cantata: Mitte des Jahrhunderts 1950
... Intermezzo & Final Chorus
Cho. & Orch.—Eisler   **Eta. 28-C 033**
(*below*)

(Die) MUTTER Didactic play after Gorky by B. Brecht
COLLECTED EXCERPTS
H. Weigel, C. Braunbock, E. Busch, E. Kahler, Berlin Cho.
& Orch.—Guhl (10ss)   *Eta. 110006/10*

Neue Deutsche Volkslieder (J. R. Becher)
A. Schlemm (S), E. Busch (B), Children's & Youth Chos.
                    Eta. 110069/70
                    110073/74, 144/5

Rhapsodie für grosses Orchester
Leipzig Radio—Abendroth   **Eta. 28-C 032/3**
(3ss—*above*)

OTHER SONGS & PARTSONGS
Lied der Einheitsfront; Lied der Solidarität on *Eta. 10-121*
Ein Pferd klagt an on *Eta. 10-154*
Brüder, seid bereit!; Dank Euch on *Eta. 10-100*
Ami! Go home; In allen Sprachen on *Eta. 110157*
Hymn of the E. German Republic on *Eta. 110220, 110132, etc.*
▽ Older recordings include:
Songs on Timely (n.d.), *CdM. 502, etc.*
Mr. Pickwick's Christmas
Dickens' Story narrated by Charles Laughton, with orig.
music composed & cond. by Eisler
(‡ AmD.DL 8010, o.n. ♮ 29151/2 in set A 379)

ELGAR, Sir Edward (1857-1934)

(3) Bavarian Dances, Op. 27 orch.
(originally Nos. 1, 3 & 6 of the Cho. & orch. version)
L.S.O.—Collingwood   ‡ **C.SX 1030**
(*below*)   (‡ *QSX 12008*)
[Nos. 1 & 2 only, on C.DX 1914: ♭ *SCD 2036: SED 5523*]
L.P.O—Boult   ‡ *D.LW 5174*
(*below*)   (‡ *Lon.LD 9193*)
[Nos. 1 & 2 only on ♭ *D. 71067*]

(La) Capricieuse, Op. 17 vln. & pf.
I. Haendel & G. Moore   in ‡ *G.CLP 1021*
F. Akos & H. Altmann   *G.EG 8177*
(*Dvořák: Slav. Dance No. 2*)
A. Campoli & E. Gritton   ♭ *D. 71085*
(*Drdla: Souvenir*)
— ARR. ORCH J. Schmied Orch. (in ‡ *Vien.LPR 1031*)

Chanson de nuit, Op. 15, No. 1
Chanson de matin, Op. 15, No. 2 Small orch.
L.S.O.—Weldon   **C.DX 1908**
                    (♭ *SCD 2035: in ‡ SX 1045*)
L.P.O.—Boult   **D.X 574**
(*Bavarian Dances on ‡ LW 5174: ‡ Lon.LD 9193*) (♭ *71088*)
☆ A. Sandler Orch. (♭ *C.SEG 7530*)
... Chanson de matin, only
G. Melachrino Orch. (*G.B 10404:* ♭ *7EG 8002: 7EGF 133;*
                    in ‡ Vic.LPM 1004)

Cockaigne, Op. 40 Concert Overture
Philharmonia—Weldon   ‡ **C.SX 1024**
(*Variations; & Pomp & Circumstance Marches*)
Royal Phil.—Beecham   ‡ **EPhi.ABL 3053**
(*Serenade & Variations*) (‡ *Phi.A 01180L; AmC.ML 5031*)
☆ Hallé—Barbirolli   ‡ *G.BLP 1065*
(*Elizabethan Suite*, ARR. *Barbirolli*)

Concerto, B minor, vln. & orch. Op. 61
A. Campoli & L.P.O.—Boult   ‡ *D.LXT 5014*
                    (‡ *Lon.LL 1168*)
☆ J. Heifetz & L.S.O.—Sargent (‡ G.QALP 10019)

Concerto, E minor, vlc. & orch. Op. 85
P. Tortelier & B.B.C. Sym.—Sargent
                    ‡ *G.BLP 1043*
                    (‡ *FBLP 1058*)

CORONATION ODE, Op. 44 (A. C. Benson)
... No. 6, Land of Hope & Glory A, cho. & orch.
South Australian Fest. Cho. & Band
                    in ‡ **EPhi.ABL 3016**

Dream Children, Op. 43 2 pieces, small orch.
... No. 1 only
Hallé—Barbirolli   **G.DB 21594**
(*Grieg: The Secret*)

(The) DREAM OF GERONTIUS, Op. 38
Oratorio (Newman) A, T, B, cho. & orch.
COMPLETE RECORDING
M. Thomas, R. Lewis, J. Cameron, Huddersfield
Cho. & Liverpool Phil. Orch.—Sargent
                    ‡ **C.CX 1247/8**
(4ss)   (‡ *Angel. set 3543*)

Falstaff, Op. 68 Symphonic Study orch.
L.S.O.—Collins   ‡ **D.LXT 2940**
                    (‡ *Lon.LL 1011*)

Froissart, Op. 19 Concert Overture
Leipzig Radio—Pflüger   ‡ **Ura. 7136**
(*In the South; & Britten*)

☆ = Re-issue of a recording to be found in previous volumes.

Imperial March, Op. 32
L.S.O.—Sargent   in ♯ **D.LXT 2793**
(below; Bax & Walton)   (♯ Lon.LL 804)

In the South, Op. 50   Concert Overture
L.S.O.—Weldon   ♯ **C.SX 1028**
(Sea Pictures)

Leipzig Radio—Pflüger   ♯ **Ura. 7136**
(Froissart; & Britten)

Introduction and Allegro, Op. 47   Str. orch.
☆ New Sym.—Collins (♯ *D.LW 5047*; ♯ *Lon.LD 9062*)

KING OLAF, Op. 30   (Longfellow & Acworth)
Cantata
... **As torrents in summer**
Mormon Tabernacle Cho.—Cornwall
    in ♯ **EPhi.ABL 5012**
(Purcell, Brahms, Liszt, etc.)
    (♯ Phi.N 02125L; AmC.ML 5048)

Nursery Suite   1931   orch.
L.S.O.—Collingwood   ♯ **C.SX 1030**
(above & below)   (♯ QSX 12008)
[Nos. 4-8 on ♭ *SED 5527*, Nos. 2, 3, 6 on DX 1916]

PART SONG: The Herald   (Smith)   1925
Rossendale Male Voice Cho.
    in ♯ **Nix.WLP 6209-1**
    (in ♯ West set WAL 209)
[At International Eisteddfod, Llangollen]

POMP & CIRCUMSTANCE MARCHES,
Op. 39
No. 1, D major;   No. 2, A minor   1901
No. 3, C minor;   No. 4, G major   1905-7
No. 5, C major   1930

COLLECTIONS
Nos. 1, 2, 4, 5
Royal Phil.—Pope   ♭ *EPhi.NBE 11002*
    (♭ *Phi.A 400007E*)

Nos. 1 & 4
Philharmonia—Weldon   ♯ **C.SX 1024**
(Cockaigne & Variations) [No. 1 only on ♭ *SED 5520*]
L.S.O.—Sargent   ♯ **D.LXT 2793**
(above; Bax & Walton)   (♯ Lon.LL 804)
    (♭ *D. 71070*; & in ♯ *LW 5058*; *Lon.LD 9057*)
New Concert Orch.—Curzon   **BH.OT 2221**
☆ Philharmonia—Sargent (♭ *C.SCD 2026*: *SCBQ 3014*;
    in ♯ AmC.RL 3042)

No. 1 only
Hollywood Bowl—Dragon in ♯ **DCap.CTL 7072**
(above)   (in ♯ *Cap.P 8276*: ♭ *FAP 8283*)
Hamburg Philharmonia—H-J. Walther
    MSB. 78120
(Sousa: Stars & Stripes)   (& in ♯ MGM.E 3143)
☆ Royal Fest. Hall Orch. & Cho.—Sargent
    (♭ *BB.ERAB 2*)
Chicago Sym.—Stock (in ♯ Cam.CAL 192)
Boston Prom.—Fiedler (in ♯ Vic.LM 1790:
    LPM 3251: ♭ set *ERB 26*; ♭ *DV. 16295*)

No. 3
L.P.O.—Boult   **G.DB 21588**
(Nicolai: Lustigen Weiber Overture on ♭ *7ER 5039:*
          7ERQ 130)

Unspec. Marches
Varsity Concert Orch. (in ♯ Var. 2055)
Regent Sym. (in ♯ Rgt. 7003)

Quartet, strings, E minor, Op. 83
Element Qtt.[1]   ♯ **Argo.RG 49**
(below)
Classic Qtt.   ♯ **CEd.CE 1030**
(Bax & McBride)[2]

Quintet, pf. & strings, A minor, Op. 84
A. di Bonnaventura & Classic Qtt.
    ♯ **CEd.CE 1030**
(above) [This side may not have been issued]

Salut d'amour, Op. 12   orch.
L.S.O.—Weldon   **C.DB 3329**
(German: Nell Gwyn Dance No. 1)
W. Fenske Orch. (in ♯ *Phi.P 10200R*)
M. Weber Orch. (in ♯ AmC.CL 519)
Anon. Orch. (in ♯ Ply. 12-128)
— ARR. VI N. & ORCH.
W. Tworek & R. Binge Orch. (*Pol.X 51703*;
    in ♯ *Lon.LB 1121*)
— ARR. ORGAN
J. Perceval (♭ *ArgOd.BSOAE 4528*: in ♯ LDC 513)

Sea Pictures, Op. 37   Song Cycle   A & Orch.
1. Sea Slumber Song   (R. Noel)
2. In Haven   (A. Elgar)
3. Sabbath morning at sea   (E. B. Browning)
4. Where corals lie   (R. Garnett)
5. The Swimmer   (A. L. Gordon)
G. Ripley & L.S.O.—Weldon   ♯ **C.SX 1028**
(In the South) [Nos. 2, 4 & 5 only, ♭ *SED 5525*]

Serenade, E minor, Op. 20   String orch.
Royal Phil.—Beecham   ♯ **EPhi.ABL 3053**
(above & below)   (♯ Phi.A 01180L; AmC.ML 5031)
L.S.O.—Collingwood   ♯ **C.SX 1030**
(above)   (♯ QSX 12008)
[2nd movt., Larghetto only, ♭ *SED 5523*]
Boyd Neel—Dumont   ♯ *Phi.S 06052R*
(Brahms)
☆ New Sym.—Collins (♯ *D.LW 5047*; ♯ *Lon.LD 9062*)

Sonata, vln. & pf., E minor, Op. 82
M. Rostal & C. Horsley[1]   ♯ **Argo.RG 49**
(above)

SONG: Speak, Music, Op. 41, No. 2
(A. C. Benson)
K. Joyce (A), H. Greenslade (pf.)   *P.R 3804*
(Scott: The Unforeseen)

SYMPHONIES
No. 1, A flat major, Op. 55
☆ L.P.O.—Boult   ♯ **G.ALP 1052**
    (♯ Vic.LHMV 1036: ♭ set WHMV 1036)

No. 2, E flat major, Op. 63
Hallé—Barbirolli   ♯ **BB.LBC 1088**

Variations on an Original Theme, Op. 36
("Enigma")   orch.
N.B.C. Sym.—Toscanini   ♯ **G.ALP 1204**
(Brahms: Haydn Variations) (♯ ItV.A12R 0036;
    G.FALP 269; Vic.LM 1725: ♭ set *WDM 1725*)
L.S.O.—Sargent   ♯ **D.LXT 2786**
(1½ss—Purcell)   (♯ Lon.LL 740)
L.P.O.—Boult   ♯ **G.ALP 1153**
(below)   (♯ QALP 10072; ♯ Vic.LHMV 7)
Royal Phil.—Beecham   ♯ **EPhi.ABL 3053**
(above)   (♯ Phi.A 01180L; AmC.ML 5031)
Philharmonia—Weldon   ♯ **C.SX 1024**
(Cockaigne, Pomp & Circumstance)
[Variations Nos. 8 & 9 only on ♭ *SED 5520*]

WAND OF YOUTH SUITES   Orch.
No. 1, Op. 1a
L.P.O.—Boult   ♯ **G.ALP 1153**
(above)   (♯ QALP 10072; ♯ Vic.LHMV 7)
☆ Liverpool—Sargent   *(Walton)*   ♯ **AmC.ML 4793**

No. 2, Op. 1b
B.B.C. Sym.—Sargent   ♯ *G.BLP 1019*
(Vaughan Williams)
Hamburg Philharmonia—H-J. Walther
(4ss)   *MSB. 78148/9*
(Coates & Quilter on ♯ MGM.E 3142)

MISCELLANEOUS
God save the Queen (ARR. Elgar) S, cho. & orch. 1902
    Royal Choral Soc., Philharmonia—Sargent (*G.B 10484*)

ELIZALDE, Federico (b. 1907)

Concerto, vln. & orch.
C. Ferras & L.S.O.—Poulet   ♯ *D.LX 3116*
(& 6ss, ▽ D.AK 1777/9)   (♯ *Lon.LS 564*)

---

[1] Announced but not issued.   [2] Coupling originally announced as Elgar: Quintet, pf. and strings.

ELLIS, W.   (1620-1674)
SEE: † More Catches & Glees of the Restoration

ELLSASSER, Richard (b. 1926)

ORGAN MUSIC
Collections
Concert Study on a theme of P. Yon, D minor 1942
Improvisation on a theme of M. B. Jiménez[1]
Scherzo on themes of Mendelssohn 1949
   R. Ellsasser   ♯ CM. 4
   ("Sammartini" & Dandrieu)   (♯ Eli.LPE 116)
   [Mexico Cathedral Organ]

Chorale-Prelude on an English lullabye 1950
Concert Study on a theme of P. Yon, D minor
Recreation on "Turkey in the Straw"
Londonderry Air (ARR. Ellsasser)
   R. Ellsasser   in ♯ MGM.E 3031
   (Yon: Humoresque; & Daquin, Nevin, etc.)

Erin, O Erin—A Thomas Moore Suite
   R. Ellsasser   ♯ MGM.E 3205
   [Excerpts in ♭ set X 314]

Icarus Tone Poem 1945
   R. Ellsasser   ♯ MGM.E 3066
   (Vierne & Russell)

Marche fantastique 1948
   ▽ R. Ellsasser (in ♯ MGM.E 3005)

Toward Evening
   R. Ellsasser   in ♯ MGM.E 3127

ELMORE, Robert (b. 1913)

Pavanne organ
   E. White   in ♯ Moll.E4QP 3443
   (Arne, Bach, Karg-Elert, etc.)

Rhumba organ
   E. Linzel   in ♯ Discur. 7201
   (below; Boellmann, Ducasse, etc.)

Rhythmic Suite organ
   R. Elmore   ♯ Cant.MRR 270
   (Bach & Franck)
   E. Linzel   in ♯ Discur. 7201
   (above)

ELWELL, Herbert (b. 1898)

(The) Happy Hypocrite Ballet[2] 1925
... Orch. Suite 1931
   A.R.S. Orch.—Hendl   ♯ ARS. 37
   (Carpenter: Skyscrapers)

Pastorale S & Orch. 1947
   (Song of Songs, Chapters I-III)
   L. Marshall & Toronto Sym.—MacMillan
                        ♯ Hall.CS 1

EMMANUEL, Maurice (1862-1938)

Sonatine bourguignonne pf. 1893
   H. Boschi   V♯ CdM.LDY 8069
   (Bizet: Variations chromatiques)

ENCINA, Juan del (c. 1468-1529)
SEE: † Spanish Music (c. 1500)

ENESCO, Georges (1881-1955)

RUMANIAN RHAPSODIES, Op. 11   orch.
No. 1, A major
No. 2, D major
   Indianapolis Sym.—Sevitzky ♯ DCap.CTL 7038
   (Dvořák)   (♯ Cap.S 8209; 2ss, ♯ Cap.H 8210)
   Orch.—Stokowski (2ss)   ♯ Vic.LRM 7043
        (♭ ERB 7043; ♯ FV.A 330212; ♭ ItV.A72R 0042
   (Liszt on ♯ Vic.LM 1878)   & A72R 0052)
   ☆ Concerts Colonne—Enesco   ♯ Rem. 199-207
   (Villa-Lobos)

No. 1, only
   N.Y.P.S.O.—Kostelanetz   ♯ AmC.CL 809
   (Prokofiev & Weber)   (o.n. ML 4957)
   Bamberg Sym.—Perlea   ♯ AmVox.PL 9500
   (Dvořák, Kodály, Smetana)
   Orch.—Swarowsky   ♯ MTW. 26
   (Rachmaninoff)
   Berlin Sym. (Liszt)   ♯ Roy. 1424
   Orch.—Gräf   ♯ Pan.XPV 1022
   (Dvořák & Liszt)
   ☆ Los Angeles Phil.—Wallenstein   ♯ B.AXTL 1062
   (Borodin & Ippolitov-Ivanov) (♯ AmD.DL 9727;
              D.UAT 273577; UW 333009, d.c.)
   ☆ Concerts Colonne—Enesco (♭ Rem.REP 116;
               Cum.ECR 83; in ♯ AFest. 10-100)
   N.Y.P.S.O.—Rodzinski (in ♯ AmC.RL 6628)
   L.P.O.—Martinon (in ♯ MGM.E 3037)
   Sym.—Stokowski (o.v.) (♭ G.7RF 234; DV. 16248)

— ARR. 2 PFS.
   ☆ A. Whittemore & J. Lowe (in ♯ Vic.LRM 7010:
                  ♭ set ERB 7010

— ARR. HARMONICA & PF.
   L. Adler & L. Colin (in ♯ CHS.CHS 1168;
           FMer.MLP 7026; V♯ MMS.POP 20)

No. 2, only
   ☆ Concerts Colonne—Enesco (♯ Cum.TCR 269)
   Nat. Sym. (U.S.A.)—Kindler (in ♯ Cam.CAL 115)

Sonata No. 3, D major, Op. 24   pf.
   D. Lipatti (Chopin)   ♯ C.CX 1337
   (Ravel, Scarlatti, Liszt, Schubert on ♯ FCX 495)

Sonata No. 3, A minor, Op. 25   vln. & pf.
   (In the popular Rumanian style)
   R. Druian & J. Simms   ♯ Mer.MG 80001
   (Janáček)
   ☆ Y. & H. Menuhin (JpV.SD 3001/3, set JAS 164)

ERBACH, Christian (1573-1635)
SEE: † XVIIth Century Organ Music

ERKEL, Ferenc (1810-1893)
(Abridged listing only)

Festive Overture orch. 1887
   Philharmonia Orch.—Koródy   Qual.MN 1011

Hymn ("Hymnusz") (Kölcsey) Cho. & orch.
   Budapest Cho. & Hungarian State Orch.—Forrai
                      (Qual.MK 2554)
— ARR. ORCH.
   Hungarian State Op.—Ferencsik (Qual.MO 456)
   E. Berlin Police—Kaufmann (Eta. 10-217)

OPERAS
BANK-BÁN 3 Acts 1861
Drinking Song
   L. Jámbor (B)   Qual.KM 5009
   (Carmen—Toreador Song)
   (Hunyadi Laszlo, aria, on MK 1580)
Home, Home ☆ E. Rösler (T) (Qual.KM 5015)
Melinda's Aria S: M. Mátyós (Qual.MK 1505)
My country T
   J. Joviczky   Qual.MN 1077
   (Hunyadi Laszlo—Laszlo's aria)
   J. Simándy (below)   Qual.MK 1590
Riverside scene S J. Osváth   Qual.MN 1002
Romance (unspec.) J. Simándy   Qual.MK 1590

---

[1] A genuine extempore improvisation on a submitted theme.   [2] After Max Beerbohm.

HUNYADI LÁSZLÓ 4 Acts 1844

Overture
Hungarian Radio—Somogyi   Qual.MN 1564/5
(4ss)   (*USSR. 18828/31*)

Folk Dance orch.
Hungarian State Op.—Komor   Qual.MN 1006
(*The plotter is dead*)

Ah, Rebe ... ⌶ L. Nordica (S) (in ♯ *FRP. 2*)

László's Aria J. Joviczky   Qual.MN 1077
(*Bank-Bán—my country*)

Palatine Gara's aria B
L. Jambór (*above*)   *Qual.MK 1580*

La Grange's Aria
J. Osváth (S)   *Qual.MK 1501*

Maria Gara's Aria M. Matyas (*Qual.MK 1505*)

The plotter is dead
L. Nagypál (*Folk Dance*)   Qual.MN 1006

ERLEBACH, Philipp Heinrich (1657-1714)

SEE: † HISTORY OF MUSIC IN SOUND (59)

ESCOBAR, Pedro (d. 1514)

SEE: † MUSIC OF THE RENAISSANCE

NOTE: The recorded item may also be by Andrea Escobar
(fl. middle XVIth century)

ESPLÁ, Oscar (b. 1889)

SEE: † SPANISH MUSIC OF THE XVITH-XXTH CENTURIES

ESTEVE Y GRIMAU, Pablo (fl. XVIIIth Cent.)

SEE: † SPANISH TONADILLAS

EVANS, Lindley (b. 1895)

Vignette pf.
M. Barton   C.DOX 1025
(*R. Agnew: Album Leafe; R. Morgan: Bagatelle; M. Hyde: The Fountain*)

▽ items include
Berceuse for a sleeping sand-baby (*C.DO 3050*)
Idyll, 2 pfs. & orch. (*C.LOX 554*)
Merry Thought (*C.DO 3272*)
Waltz (*C.DO 2567*)

FAIDIT, Gaucelin (fl. *c.* 1199)

SEE: † LA MUSIQUE ET LA POÉSIE

FALCONIERI, Andrea (1586-1656)

SEE: † CANZONE SCORDATE
        † ARIE ANTICHE & GERMAN LIEDER

FALK, Georg Paul (d. 1778)

SEE: † TYROLESE XVIIITH CENT. ORCH. MUSIC

FALLA, Manuel de (1876-1946)

COLLECTIONS
COMPLETE PF. MUSIC
AMOR BRUJO: Nos. 7, 11, 13 — ARR. Falla
Fantasia bética   1919
Homenaje, pour le tombeau de Debussy   orig. guitar
Homenaje, pour le tombeau de Dukas   orig. orch.
Nocturne   pub. 1903
(4) Pièces espagnoles   1907-8
Serenata andaluza   pub. 1903
(EL) SOMBRERO ...: Nos. 2 & 3 — ARR. Falla
Valse capriccio   pub. 1903
J. Echaniz   ♯ West.WL 5218

Fantasia bética   1919
(4) Pièces espagnoles   1907-8
Serenata andaluza   pub. 1903
M. Pressler   ♯ MGM.E 3071
(*Amor Brujo, No. 7*)
[Pièce espagnole No. 4, also on ♭ *X 10718*]

(El) AMOR BRUJO Ballet M-S & orch. 1915

COMPLETE RECORDINGS
D. Eustrati & Berlin Phil.—Lehmann
       ♯ HP.DGM 18177
(*El Sombrero*)   (& ♯ Pol. 19044)
(*idem & Chabrier* on ♯ AmD.DL 9775)
A. Delorie & Netherlands Phil.—Goehr
       ♯ MMS. 76
(*Canciones populares españolas*)
I. de Rivadeneyra & Madrid Sym.—Branco
       ♯ LT.DTL 93010
(*El Retablo ...*)   (♯ Sel.LAG 1047; West.WL 5238)
☆ A. M. Iriarte & Paris Cons.—Argenta
     (♯ C.QC 1010, 2ss; with *El Retablo* ... on
       ♯ C.FCX 217; Reg.LCX 112)
N. Merriman & Hollywood Bowl—Stokowski
       (♯ ItV.A12R 0017)

Orchestral Suite
"Philharmonic"—Tubbs   ♯ Allo. 4051
Berlin Sym.—Balzer   ♯ Roy. 1509
(*El Sombrero*)

No. 7, 11, 13 — ARR. PF. Falla
J. Echaniz (in Collection)

Nos. 7 & 11 — ARR. PF.
☆ J. Iturbi (♭ G.7EB 6010; DV. 16300)

No. 7, Danza ritual del fuego
Hollywood Bowl—Dragon in ♯ DCap.CTL 7074
     (in ♯ Cap.P 8275: ♭ FAP 8286)
Paris Cons.—Lindenberg   ♭ Od.7AO 2012
(*Vida Breve—Danza*)
A. Sciascia Orch. (Fnt. 14320: in ♯ LP 305 & LP 309)
Polish Radio—Krenz (Muza.X 2381)
☆ A. Kostelanetz Orch. (C.DHX 73; ♭ AmC.A 1634)
Boston Prom.—Fiedler (♭ G.7EG 8027: 7EPQ 503:
       in ♯ DLP 1091: FMLP 1005, etc.)

— ARR. PF.
L. Pennario   in ♯ DCap.CTL 7054
(*Granados, Albeniz, etc.*)   (in ♯ Cap.P 8190: ♭ FAP 8204)
O. Frugoni   in ♯ AmVox.PL 9420
·M. Pressler   ♯ MGM.E 3071
(*Piano music*)   (♭ X 1087)
J. M. Sanromá   in ♯ Polym. 1011
     (in ♯ Cum.CPL 202)
L. Sangiorgi (*Dur.AI 10350*)
E. Silver (hpsi) (in ♯ Roy. 1550)
☆ O. Levant (in ♯ AmC.ML 2018)
G. Copeland (in ♯ MGM.E 3025)
C. de Groot (♭ Phi.N 402006E & in ♯ Epic.LC 3175)

— ARR. 2 PFS.
L. Shankson & I. Wright (in ♯ Roy. 1447)
☆ G. Luboshutz & P. Nemenoff (in ♯ Rem. 199-147;
     o.v. in ♯ Cam.CAL 198: ♭ CAE 219)
A. Whittemore & J. Lowe (in ♯ Vic.LRM 7010:
       ♭ set ERB 7010)

— ARR. VLC. & PF. Piatigorsky
J. Starker & L. Pommers (in ♯ Nix.PLP 584; ♯ Per.SPL 584;
       ♯ Cpt.MC 20054)

— ARR. HARMONICA & PF.
L. Adler & L. Colin (in ♯ CHS.CHS 1168;
       FMer.MLP 7026; MMS.POP 20)

No. 9, Canción del fuego fatuo
No. 12, El circulo magico — ARR. GUITAR
L. Almeida   in ♯ DCap.CTL 7089
(† Guitar Music of Spain)   (♯ Cap.P 8295)

No. 11, Danza del terror — ARR. PF. Falla
☆ E. Osta (in ♯ Coda. 1000)

No. 13, Romanza del pescador — ARR. 2 GUITARS
I. Presti & A. Lagoya (♭ FV.F 75017)

No. 14, Pantomime — APR. VLN. & PF. Kochanski
☆ J. Heifetz (in ♯ G.ALP 1206: FALP 248)

(7) CANCIONES POPULARES ESPAÑOLAS
(Blas de Laserna) 1914
1. El paño moruno   2. Seguidilla murciana
3. Asturiana   4. Jota
5. Nana   6. Canción   7. Polo
A. Estanislão (B), H. Salquin (pf.) ♯ D.LW 5192
(*Ravel: Don Quichotte à Dulcinée*)   (♯ Lon.LD 9180)
N. Merriman (M-S), G. Moore (pf.) ♯ C.CX 1243
(† Spanish Songs)   (♯ FCX 392; Angel. 35208)

♯ = Long-playing, 33⅓ r.p.m.   ♭ = 45 r.p.m.   ♮ = Auto. couplings, 78 r.p.m.

(7) CANCIONES POPULARES ESPAÑOLAS (continued)

C. C. Meyer (M-S), L. Ruembe-Hoppen (pf.)
(Amor Brujo)　　　　　　　　　♯ MMS. 76

L. Marshall (S), W. Kilburn (pf.) ♯ Hall.RS 1
(Purcell)

A. P. de Prulière (S), G. T. Valentin (pf.)
　　　　　　　　　　　　　V♯ Sel.LPP 8640

N. Chayres (T), O. Kosches (pf.) ♯ Peer.LPP 015
(Fuste, Obrados, Valverde, etc.)
(Granados & Turina on ♯ Kings. 300)

☆ V. de los Angeles (S), G. Moore (pf.) ♯ G.BLP 1037
(Granados, Guridi, etc.)　　(♯ FBLP 1040: ♭ 7ERL 1030)

☆ A. M. Iriarte (M-S), R. Machado (pf.) (♭ Pat.ED 17)

Nos. 2, 4 & 6 only
M. Plaza (M-S)　　　　　　　in ♯ Roy. 1561
(Granados, Ginastera, Nin, etc.)

Nos. 3 & 5　☆ O. Coelho (S & guitar) (♭ P.CBEP 2)

Nos. 1 & 6　— ARR. PF.　Halffter
☆ C. de Groot (in ♯ Epic.LC 3175)

No. 3　☆ M. Barrientos (S), M. de Falla (pf.) (in ♯ Sca. 806)

No. 5　— ARR. CHO.
Pamplona Cho.—Morondo (in ♯ CFD. 26)

Nos. 1 & 3-7　— ARR. VLN. & PF.　Kochanski
"Suite populaire espagnole"
R. Odnoposoff & J. Antonietti
(Nin & Ysaÿe)　　　　　♯ CHS.CHS 1175

Nos. 1, 3, 5, 6, 7
D. Oistrakh & V. Yampolsky　　♯ USSR.D 2164
(Szymanowski & Wieniawski)

Nos. 1 & 4
H. Szeryng & M. Berthelier (in ♯ Pac.LDPC 50)

No. 4　D. Oistrakh & V. Yampolsky
　　　　　(in ♯ JpV.LS 2025 & in USSRM.D 00544)

Nos. 1 & 3-7　— ARR. VLC. & PF.
J. Starker & L. Pommers　　♯ Nix.PLP 584
(Amor Brujo, No. 7; & Granados, Albeniz, etc.)
　　　　　　　　　(♯ Per.SPL 584; Cpt.MC 20054)

P. Olefsky & G. Silfies　　♯ McInt.MM 103
(Debussy, Fauré, Prokofiev, etc.)

H. Honegger & E. Møller　♭ Mtr.MCEP 3014

No. 2　A. Janigro & E. Bagnoli (in ♯ West.WN 18004)

No. 5　P. Casals & E. Istomin (in ♯ AmC.ML 4926:
　　　　　　♭ A 1937; ♭ EPhi.ABE 10004; ♭ Phi.N 409008E)

Concerto, hpsi., fl., ob., cl., vln. & vlc.　1923-6
S. Marlowe & Concert Arts Players
(Rieti & Surinach)　　　　♯ Cap.P 8309

Fantasia bética　pf. or hpsi.　1919
P. Spagnolo (pf.)　　　　　in ♯ D.LXT 2947
　　　　　　　　　　　　　(in ♯ Lon.LL 1040)

L. Querol (pf.)　　　　　　♯ LT.EL 93011
(Pièces espagnoles)　　(♯ Sel.LP 8678; T.PLB 6135)

Homenaje, pour le Tombeau de Debussy guit.　1921
A. Iglesias　　　　　　　　Od.DK 1234
(Iglesias: Aires regionales)

N. Yepes　　　　　　　in ♯ D.LXT 2974
(† Spanish Music of the XVIth-XXth Centuries)
　　　　　　　　　(♯ D.FST 153076; Lon.LL 1042)

☆ A. Segovia (in † ♯ D.UAT 273142)

Homenajes　Orch. suite　1940
French Nat. Radio—Halffter　♯ C.CX 1221
(below) (♯ QCX 10135: FCX 272; Angel. 35134;
　　　　　　　　　　　　　　　G.LALP 118)

Noches en los jardines de España pf.& or. 1909-15
G. Novães & Vienna Pro Musica—Swarowsky
　　　　　　　　♯ E. & AmVox.PL 8520
(Grieg: Concerto)

A. Ciccolini & French Nat. Radio—Halffter
　　　　　　　　　　　　　♯ C.CX 1221
(above) (♯ FCX 272: QCX 10135; Angel. 35134;
　　　　　　　　　　　　　　　G.LALP 118)

G. Soriano & Madrid Cha.—Argenta
　　　　　　　　　　　　　♯ LI.TW 91019
(Rodrigo)　　　　　　　(♯ Ambra.MCC 30008)

☆ A. Rubinstein & St. Louis Sym.—Golschmann
　　　　　　　　　　　　　♯ G.ALP 1065
(Grieg: Concerto)　　　　　　(♯ WALP 1065)

☆ C. Curzon & New Sym.—Jorda　D.LW 5216

---

(4) Pièces espagnoles　pf.　1907-8
1. Aragonesa　　　　　2. Cubana
3. Montañesa　　　　　4. Andaluza

L. Querol　　　　　　　♯ LT.EL 93011
(Fantasia bética)　　(♯ Sel.LP 8678; T.PLB 6135)

C. de Groot　　　　　　♯ Phi.N 00761R
(Albeniz & Mompou)　　(in ♯ Epic.LC 3175)

J. M. Sanromá　　　　　♯ Polym. 1011
(Amor Brujo; & Turina)　　(♯ Cum.CPL 202)

… Nos. 2 & 4
R. Machado　　　　　　♭ C.SCBF 105
　　　　　　　　　　　　(♭ SCBQ 3006)

… No. 2, Cubana
☆ E. Boynet (♭ AmVox.VIP 45500)

… No. 4, Andaluza
L. Pennario　　　　in ♯ DCap.CTL 7054
(Albeniz, Infante, etc.)　(♯ Cap.P 8190: ♭ FAP 8235)

O. Frugoni　　　　　in ♯ AmVox.PL 9420
(Amor Brujo, No. 7; Granados, Turina, etc.)

☆ A. Rubinstein (♭ G.7RF/RQ 248)

— — ARR. DANCING, PF. & ORCH.
"Antonio", P. Miquel & Sym.—Currás
　　　　　　　　　(in ♭ SpC.SCGE 80016)

(El) RETABLO DE MAESE PEDRO
Opera　1 Act　1923
COMPLETE RECORDINGS

Casts	Set C	Set D
Trujáman …	L. R. de Aragon (S)	B. M. Secana (S)
Maese Pedro …	C. Renom (T)	F. Navarro (T)
Don Quixote …	M. Ausensi (B)	C. Gonzalo (B)

Set C with French Nat. Radio Orch.—Toldra
(2ss)　　　　　　　　　♯ C.FC 1026
(Amor Brujo on ♯ FCX 217; Reg.LCX 112; Angel. 35089)

Set D with Champs-Élysées Theatre Orch.
—Halffter　　　　　　　♯ LT.DTL 93010
(Amor Brujo)　　　(♯ Sel.LAG 1047; West.WL 5328)

Set E: I. Steingruber (S), W. Kmentt (T), O. Wiener
(Bs) & Vienna Philharmonia—Adler
　　　　　　　　　　　♯ CA.LPA 1023
　　　　　　　　　　　　　　(♯ SPA. 43)

Set F: J. Gardino (S), J. Oncina (T), R. Cesari (B),
& Milan Musical Afternoons Orch.—Gracis
　　　　　　　　　　　♯ Fnt.LP 303

(El) SOMBRERO DE TRES PICOS Ballet 1919
COMPLETE RECORDING (including interludes, Sop.)

☆ A. P. de Prulière & Opéra-Comique—Martinon
(♯ MTW. 519)　　　　　♯ Nix.ULP 9034
[Introduction only, in ♯ Nix.ULP 9084;
　Ura. 7084; 3 Dances from Part II on ♭ Nix.EP 711]

COLLECTIONS
Scenes & Dances from Part I
1. Introduction (Afternoon)
2. Danza della Molinera (Dance of the Miller's Wife)
3. El Corregidor

Three Dances from Part II
1. Los vecinos (The Neighbours)
2. Danza del Molinero (Miller's Dance)
3. Danza finale (Final Dance)

Berlin Phil.—Lehmann　　♯ HP.DGM 18177
(Amor Brujo)　　　　　　　(& ♯ Pol. 19044)
(idem; & Chabrier, on ♯ AmD.DL 9775)

Scenes & Dances from Part I
1. Introduction (Afternoon)
2. Danza de la Molinera;
3. El Corregidor;　　　5. Las Uvas
Three Dances from Part II
Spanish Nat.—Argenta　　♯ LI.TW 91013
(Turina)　　　　　　　(♯ Ambra.MCC 30007)

Pt. I, Nos. 2 & 3　— ARR. PF.　Falla
J. Echaniz (in Collection)

Pt. I, No. 2 only　— ARR. PF.
L. Pennario　　　　　in ♯ DCap.CTL 7054
(above)　　　　　　　　　(♯ Cap.P 8190)

(continued on next page)

☆ = Re-issue of a recording to be found in previous volumes.

(El) SOMBRERO DE TRES PICOS (*continued*)
Three Dances from Part II
Philharmonia—Cantelli ♯ **G.ALP 1207**
(*Debussy, Dukas, Ravel*) (♯ QALP 10097)
[No. 3 only on ♭ *G.7ER 5057*]
Philharmonia—Markevitch ♯ **C.CX 1049**
(♯ FCX 203: QCX 10015; Angel. 35008; ♭ *G.7ERL 1039*)
[No. 2 only in ♯ C.CX 1198: FCX 358; Angel. 35152,
in set 3518; No. 3 only on ♭ *C.SEL 1531*]
St. Louis Sym.—Golschmann ♯ **DCap.CTL 7062**
(*Prokofiev*) (♯ Cap.P 8257: ♭ *FAP 8263*)
Madrid Sym.—Argenta ♯ **Mont.FM 18**
(*Gomes*)
N.Y.P.S.O.—Mitropoulos ♯ **AmC.AL 44**
(*Vida Breve*)(♭ *A 1840*; ♭ *Phi.A 409010E*; *EPhi.ABE 10005*)
Boston Prom.—Fiedler (n.v.) in ♯ **Vic.LM 1726**
(o.v., in ♯ Cam.CAL 176: ♭ *CAE 156*) (♭ *set WDM 1726*)
Residentie—v. Otterloo ♯ **Phi.A 00714R**
(*Ravel*)
☆ Vienna Phil.—Krauss ♯ **DT.LGM 65022**
(*Ravel*) (♯ *T.LB 6058*)
☆ Valencia Sym.—Iturbi (in ♯ Vic.LM 1937; DV.L 16221)
Berlin Sym.—Balzer (♯ Roy. 1509)

Unspec. Contents "Philharmonic"—Tubbs ♯ **Allo. 4060**

... No. 2, Danza del molinero (*Farruca*)
— ARR. PF.
A. Rubinstein ♭ **Vic.ERA 200**
(*Granados & Mompou*) (♭ *FV.A 95209*; *ItV.A72R 0024*)
L. Brunelli ArgV. **66-0003**
(*Granados: Danza No. 5*)
R. Spivak ArgV. **66-6091**
(*Vida Breve—Danza*)
E. Silver (hpsi.) (in ♯ Roy. 1550)
☆ O. Levant (in ♯ *AmC.ML 2018*)
E. Osta (in ♯ *Coda. 1000*)
— ARR. GUITAR Tarrago
C. Santias (in ♯ *FestF.FLD 32*; *SpFest.HF 3201*)
— ARR. VLN. & PF. Szigeti: C. Pessina & pf. (*ArgOd. 57016*)

(La) VIDA BREVE Opera 2 Acts 1913
COMPLETE RECORDING
Salud ... ... V. de los Angeles (S)
Abuela ... ... R. Gomez (M-S)
Carmela ... ... J. Puigsech (M-S)
Paco ... ... P. Civil (T)
Uncle Sarvaor ... ... E. Payá (B)
Manuel ... ... F. Cachadina (B)
etc. Cho. & Barcelona Op. Orch.—Halffter
♯ **G.ALP 1150/1**
(3ss—*Nin, Vives, Respighi, Turina, etc.*)
(♯ FALP 326/7: LALP 141/2)
(3ss—*Laserna, Turina, Fuste, Vives, Pla, Basso*
in ♭ Vic. set LM 6017)

Interlude & Danza No. 1 Act I
L.S.O.—Poulet in ♯ **P.PMC 1006**
(*Albeniz, Granados, Turina*)
(♯ MGM.E 3073; Od.ODX 137: ♭ *BSOE 4005*)
N.Y.P.S.O.—Mitropoulos ♯ **AmC.AL 44**
(*Sombrero de Tres Picos*)

Danza No. 1, only
Colón Theatre—Cases ArgOd. **66048**
(*Goyescas—Intermezzo*) (in ♯ *LDC 519*; *Od.OD 1018*)
Hollywood Bowl—Dragon in ♯ **Cap.P 8314**
(*Albeniz, Respighi, etc.*) (♭ *set FAP 8314*)
Pasdeloup—Lindenberg ♭ **Od.7AO 2012**
(*Amor Brujo, No. 7*)
Belgian Radio—P. Glière (in ♯ Mae.OAT 25001)
Orch.—Kostelanetz (in ♯ AmC.CL 763)
☆ MGM. Orch.—Marrow (*MGM. 9173* & in ♯ E 3136)
— ARR. VLN. & PF. Kreisler
I. Haendel & G. Moore G.C **4262**
(*Dvořák: Slav. Dance No. 2*) (in ♯ *CLP 1021*)
Y. Menuhin & G. Moore in ♯ **Vic.LHMV 22**
(*Debussy, Nielsen, Ravel*)
G. Taschner & H. Giesen Od.O-**9184**
(*Kreisler: Caprice viennois*) (in ♯ *OLA 1006*)
G. Staples & G. Silfies in ♯ **McInt.MM 101**

T. Magyar & W. Hielkema ♯ **Phi.Ş 06049R**
(*Albeniz, Sarasate, etc.*)
G. Jarry & A. Collard in ♯ **C.FCX 222**
M. Auclair & O. Schulhof in ♯ **Rem. 199-128**
☆ F. Kreisler & F. Rupp (in ♯ Vic.LCT 1142)
J. Martzy & J. Antonietti (in ♯ *Pol. 16017*)
— ARR. PF. Samazeuilh
E. Osta in ♯ **Allo. 3151**
(& ☆ o.v. in ♯ *Coda. 1000*)
R. Spivak ArgV. **66-6091**
(*El Sombrero—Miller's Dance*)
M. Tagliaferro in ♯ **Sel.LAP 1006**
☆ C. de Groot (♭ *Phi.N 402006E* & in ♯ Epic.LC 3175)
— ARR. HARP E. Vito (in ♯ Per.SPL 704)
— ARR. 2 GUITARS I. Presti & A. Lagoya (♭ *FV.FV 75017*
— ARR. HARMONICA L. Adler (in ♯ *MMS.POP 20*)
etc.

Vivan los que rien! Act I
Alli esta! Act II
☆ V. de los Angeles (S) (o.v.) (ArgV. 11-8054)

FARBERMAN, Harold (b. 1929)

Evolution S, horn & 25 perc. insts.
D. Baldyga, J. Stagliano & Boston Percussion
Group ♯ **Bo.B 207**
(*Chavez*)

FARKAS, Ferenc (b. 1905)

Old Hungarian Dances pf. 1943
G. Sebok (2ss) *Qual.SZK 3551*
On the bank of the Tisza River
Folk Song Ens. & State Orch.—András *Qual.MN 1063*
(2ss)
Two Hungarian Dances Unspec. Orch. (*Qual.KM 5017*)
SONGS
Lullaby; Sleigh Bell
J. Sandor (M-S), G. Sebok (pf.) (*Qual.SZK 3501*)

FARMER, John (c. 1565-c. 1605)

SEE: † ENGLISH MADRIGALS
† TRIUMPHS OF ORIANA

FARNABY, Giles (c. 1565-1640)

VIRGINALS PIECES
His dreame FVB 194
Tower Hill FVB 245
C. J. Chiasson (hpsi.) in ♯ **Nix.LLP 8037**
(† *Elizabethan Love Songs*) (♯ *Lyr.LL 37*)
His dreame FVB 194
— ARR. ORCH. Barbirolli (in *An Elizabethan Suite*)
Hallé—Barbirolli in ♯ **G.BLP 1065**
(*below; Anon., Byrd, Bull, Elgar*)
His humour FVB 196
T. Dart (hpsi.) in ♯ **LOL.OL 50075**
(† *Masters of Early English Keyboard Music*)
M. Hodsdon (virginals) in G.HMS **42**
(† *History of Music in Sound*) (♯ Vic. set LM 6029)
Loth to depart Variations FVB 230
F. Viderø in ♯ **HS.HSL 2072**
(† *Masterpieces of Music before 1750*)
(The) New Sa-Hoo FVB 148
(A) Toye FVB 270
☆ P. Aubert (virginals) (in † ♯ HS.AS 13)

♯ = Long-playing, 33⅓ r.p.m. ♭ = 45 r.p.m. ♮ = Auto. couplings, 78 r.p.m.

(A) Toye FVB 270
— ARR. ORCH. Barbirolli (in *An Elizabethan Suite*)
Hallé—Barbirolli   in # *G.BLP 1065*
(*above*)

Up tails all Variations FVB 242
G. Leonhardt (hpsi.)   in # *Van.BG 539*
(† *Elizabethan & Jacobean Music*)   (# *Ama.AVRS 6001*)
ARRANGEMENT of Pavan (R. Johnson)
SEE: † ELIZABETHAN KEYBOARD MUSIC

FARNABY, Richard (c. 1590- ?)
SEE: † ELIZABETHAN LOVE SONGS
     † ELIZABETHAN KEYBOARD MUSIC

FARNAM, W. Lynwood (1885-1930)
SEE: † ORGAN RECITAL

FARRANT, Richard (d. 1581)
SEE: † ENGLISH CHURCH MUSIC, VOLS. III & IV
     † HYMNS OF PRAISE

FASOLO, ? (fl. 1627)
SEE: † ITALIAN CLASSIC SONGS

FAURÉ, Gabriel Urbain (1845-1924)

CLASSIFIED: I. Piano   II. Instrumental
          III. Chamber Music IV. Orchestral
           V. Stage Works   VI. Vocal

I. PIANO

COLLECTIONS
Nocturne No. 12, E minor, Op. 107
Barcarolle No. 4, A flat major, Op. 44
Valse-Caprice No. 3, G flat major, Op. 59
Impromptu No. 3, A flat major, Op. 34
J-M. Damase   # *LI.TW 91035*
(*Ravel*)   (# *D.FST 133062*)

Impromptus: No. 1, E flat major, Op. 25
          No. 2, F minor, Op. 31
          No. 3, A flat major, Op. 34
          No. 4, D flat major, Op. 91
          No. 5, F sharp minor, Op. 102
Thème et Variations, C sharp minor, Op. 73
Barcarolle No. 6, E flat major, Op. 70
Nocturne No. 6, D flat major, Op. 63
J. Demus   # *West.WN 18118*

Impromptus: Nos. 2 & 5
Nocturne No. 13, B minor, Op. 119
F. Petit   V# *Era.LDE 1016*

Dolly, Op. 56 (with G. Casadesus)
Nocturne No. 7, C sharp minor, Op. 74
Barcarolle No. 5, F sharp minor, Op. 66
Impromptu No. 5, F sharp minor, Op. 102
☆ R. Casadesus (# *Phi.N 02611R*)

BARCAROLLES
No. 1, A minor, Op. 26
☆ K. Long (in # *Lon.LL 887*)

No. 2, G major, Op. 41
☆ K. Long (in # *Lon.LL 887*)
M. Panzéra (in # *Clc. 6269*)

Dolly, Op. 56 Suite pf. duet
I. Marika & G. Smadja   # *Phi.N 00637R*
(*Ravel*)
J. Bonneau & G. Joy   # *Pat.DT 1026*
(*Debussy: En blanc et noir*)

— ARR. PF. SOLO
▽ K. Yasukawa   JpV.NH 2015/6
(3ss—*Nocturne No. 3*)

— ARR. ORCH. Rabaud
L.S.O.—Fistoulari   # *P.PMC 1004*
(*Poulenc: Les Biches*)   (MGM.E 3098)

IMPROMPTUS
No. 2, F minor, Op. 31
▽ K. Yasukawa   JpV.NH 2017
(*No. 3*)
☆ K. Long (in # *Lon.LL 887*)

No. 3, A flat major, Op. 34
G. Johannesen   in # *Nix.CLP 1181*
(*below; & Poulenc*)   (in # *CHS.CHS 1181*)
▽ K. Yasukawa (JpV.NH 2017)

No. 6. *See* Impromptu for harp

NOCTURNES
COLLECTIONS
No. 2, B major, Op. 33, No. 2
No. 5, B flat major, Op. 37
No. 7, C sharp minor, Op. 74
No. 8, D flat major, Op. 84, No. 8
K. Long   # *D.LXT 2963*
(*Ballade; & Français*)   (# *Lon.LL 1058*)
(also, 2ss, # *D.LW 5194*)

No. 4, E flat major, Op. 36
No. 6, D flat major, Op. 63
No. 13, B minor, Op. 119
☆ K. Long (in # *Lon.LL 887*)

No. 3, A flat major, Op. 33, No. 3
M. Schwalb   in # *Acad. 310*
(*Rachmaninoff, Brahms, etc.*)
▽ K. Yasukawa (*Dolly, s.3*)   JpV.NH 2016

No. 6, D flat major, Op. 63
No. 7, C sharp minor, Op. 74
G. Thyssens-Valentin   V# *Sel.LAP 1009*

Romance sans paroles, A flat maj., Op. 17, No. 3
☆ G. Fauré (from a piano roll) (in # *Roy.* 1573 & 1402)

Souvenirs de Bayreuth pf. duet (with Messager)[1]
F. Petit & A. M. Beckensteiner
(*Chabrier*)   V# *Era.LDE 1017*

Thème et variations, C sharp minor, Op. 73
G. Johannesen   in # *Nix.CLP 1181*
(*above; & Ballade; & Poulenc*) (in # *CHS.CHS 1181*)
☆ K. Long (in # *Lon.LL 887*)

II. INSTRUMENTAL

Berceuse, Op. 16 vln. & pf. (or vln. & orch.)
— ARR. VLC. & PF.
P. Fournier & E. Lush   G.DA 2028
(*Debussy: Rêverie*)   (♭ *Vic.EHA 20*)
(& in # *Vic.*LHMV 1043: in ♭ set WHMV 1043)

Élégie, C minor, Op. 24 vlc. & pf.
H. Honegger & E. Møller   ♭ *Mtr.MCEP 3027*
(*Sicilienne, & Après un rêve, arr.*)
M. Rostropovich & pf.   USSRM.D 00326
(*Bach: Suite No. 5, excerpts*)
☆ P. Fournier & E. Lush (in # *Vic.*LHMV 1043:
                         in ♭ set WHMV 1043: & *EHA* 20)

— VLC. & ORCH. VERSION
☆ B. Michelin & Haarlem Sym.—Hupperts (# *Clc.* 6245)

Impromptu, D flat major, Op. 86 harp
☆ E. Vito (in # *Cum.CS* 192)

Papillon, Op. 77 vlc. & pf.
J. Starker & L. Pommers   # *Nix.PLP 708*
(*below, & Debussy, Bréval, Ravel, Poulenc, Couperin*)
                           (# *Per.SPL 708*)

Sicilienne, Op. 78 vlc. & pf.
(See *Pelléas & Mélisande*, below, for orch. arr.)
H. Honegger & E. Møller   ♭ *Mtr.MCEP 3027*
(*Élégie & Après un rêve, arr.*)

III. CHAMBER MUSIC

QUARTETS, pf. & str.
No. 1, C minor, Op. 15
R. Masters Pf. Qtt. (2ss)   # *Argo.RG 55*
                       (with *No. 2*, # *West.WN 18093*)
                       (*continued on next page*)

---

[1] Fantaisie en forme de Quadrille sur les thèmes favoris de l'Anneau du Niebelung … , c. 1880.

No. 1, C minor, Op. 15 (*continued*)
C. Helffer, C. Tessier, P. Ladhuie, R. Albin
(*Vlc. Sonata*)   ♯ CFD. 8
☆ G. Casadesus & Guilet Trio   ♯ Nix.QLP 4007
  (*below*)   (♯ Cum.CPL 198)
☆ Rubinstein & Members of Paganini Qtt. ♯ G.BLP 1040
                                   (♯ ItV.A10R 0004)

o. 2, G minor, Op. 45
R. Masters Pf. Qtt. (2ss)   ♯ Argo.RG 56
  (with *No. 1*, ♯ West.WN 18093)

G. Casadesus & Guilet Trio   ♯ MGM.E 3166
☆ R. Lev & Pascal Trio (♯ Clc. 6232)

QUARTET, strings, E minor, Op. 121
☆ Guilet Qtt.   ♯ Nix.QLP 4008
                                   (♯ Cum.CPL 197)

SONATAS, vln. & pf.
No. 1, A major, Op. 13
Z. Francescatti & R. Casadesus
  (*below*)   ♯ AmC.ML 5049
J. Fuchs & A. Balsam   ♯ AmD.DL 9716
  (*Franck*)
J. Tomasow & F. Holetschek   ♯ Van.VRS 464
  (*Debussy*)
☆ J. Fournier & G. Doyen (♯ Véga. C 30. A 11)

No. 2, E minor, Op. 108
C. Ferras & P. Barbizet   ♯ D.LXT 2810
  (*Debussy*)   (♯ Lon.LL 909; D.FAT 173138)
Z. Francescatti & R. Casadesus ♯ AmC.ML5049
  (*above*)
☆ D. Guilet & G. Casadesus   ♯ Nix.QLP 4008
                                   (♯ Cum.CLP 197)
☆ J. Fournier & G. Doyen (♯ Véga. C 30. A 11)

SONATAS, vlc. & pf.
No. 1, D minor, Op. 109
G. & M. Fallot   ♯ LT.DTL 93050
  (*No. 2*)   (♯ T.TW 30035; Sel. 270.C.025)

No. 2, G minor, Op. 117
G. & M. Fallot   ♯ LT.DTL 93050
  (*No. 1*)   (♯ T.TW 30035; Sel. 270.C.025)
R. Albin & C. Helffer   ♯ CFD. 8
  (*Pf. Qtt. No. 1*)
☆ D. Soyer & L. Mittman   ♯ Nix.QLP 4007
  (*above*)   (♯ Cum.CPL 198)

Trio, D minor, Op. 120 pf. vln. vlc.
☆ Albeneri Trio (♯ Clc. 6259)

IV. ORCHESTRAL

Ballade, F sharp major, Op. 19 pf. & orch.
J. Doyen & Lamoureux—Fournet
                                   ♯ Epic.LC 3057
(*Franck & Saint-Saëns*)
(*Franck only on* ♯ Phi.N 00704R)
K. Long & L.P.O.—Martinon   ♯ D.LXT 2963
(*Nocturnes; & Français*)   (♯ Lon.LL 1058)
G. Johannesen & Netherlands Phil.—Goehr
                                   ♯ Nix.CLP 1181
(*Impromptu; Thème & vars.; & Poulenc*)(♯ CHS.CHS 1181)
(*Masques et Bergamasques, on* ♯ MMS. 102)
☆ G. Casadesus & Lamoureux—Rosenthal
                                   ♯ EVox.PL 6450
  (*Chausson*)   (♭ AmVox.VIP 45480)
☆ M. Long & Paris Cons.—Cluytens   ♯ Angel. 35013

MASQUES ET BERGAMASQUES, Op. 112
Orch. Suite: 1. Overture   2. Minuet
             3. Gavotte   4. Pastorale
☆ Netherlands Phil.—Goehr (♯ MMS. 102)

...No. 1, Overture, only
London Cha.—Bernard   G.B 10562
(*Handel: Solomon—Sinfonia*)
(*Pavane, below; & Handel, on* ♭ G.7EP 7001: 7EPQ 519)

Pavane, Op. 50 orch. (& cho. *ad lib.*)
Detroit Sym.—Paray   ♯ Mer.MG 50029
(*Franck & Ravel*) (no cho.)

Lamoureux—Martinon   in ♯ Phi.A 00175L
(*Debussy, Honegger, Roussel, etc.*)   (♯ Epic.LC 3058)
☆ London Cha. Orch. & Cho.—Bernard ♭ G.7EP 7001
(*Masques et Bergamasques; & Handel: Solomon, excpt.*)
                                   (♭ 7EPQ 519)

V. STAGE WORKS

PELLÉAS ET MÉLISANDE, Op. 80
  (Inc. Music to Maeterlinck's play; orch. by Koechlin)
Orchestral Suite:
  1. Prelude   2. Fileuses
  3. Molto adagio   (with Sicilienne, ARR.)
Hallé—Barbirolli   ♯ G.ALP 1244
(*Ibert: Divertissement*)
Paris Opéra—Le Conte   ♯ DCap.CTL 7101
(*Bizet: Suites*)   (♯ Cap.P 8311)
L.S.O.—Poulet   ♯ P.PMC 1016
(*Ravel*)   (♯ MGM.E 3116; Od.ODX 152)
Detroit Sym.—Paray   ♯ EMer.MG 50035
(*Dukas & Roussel*)   (♯ FMer.MLP 7519)
Concerts Colonne—Sebastian ♯ Nix.ULP 9097
(*Dukas*)   (♯ Ura. 7097)
Champs-Élysées Th.—Inghelbrecht
  (*below*)   ♯ Sel. 270.C.082
Lamoureux—Fournet   ♯ Phi.N 00737R
(*Debussy*)   (♯ Epic.LC 3165)
☆ Boston Sym.—Koussevitzky   ♯ Vic.LCT 1152
(*Copland, Sibelius, Stravinsky*)

No. 2, Fileuses — ARR. VLC. & PF.
P. Fournier & E. Lush   in ♯ D.LXT 2766
(*Bloch, Nin, etc.*)   (in ♯ Lon.LL 700)

SHYLOCK, Op. 57
  Inc. Music to Haraucourt's play
Orch. Suite; & Chanson et Madrigale
H. Legay (T), Champs-Élysées Theatre
  —Inghelbrecht   ♯ Sel. 270.C.082
  (*above*)

VI. VOCAL

REQUIEM, Op. 48 S, B, cho., orch., org.
P. Alarie, C. Maurane, E. Brasseur Cho. &
  Lamoureux orch.—Fournet ♯ EPhi.ABR 4012
[M. Duruflé (org.)]   (♯ Phi.A 00669R; Epic.LC 3044)
F. Ogéas, B. Demigny, French Radio Cho. &
  Champs-Élysées Th. Orch.—Inghelbrecht
                                   ♯ Sel. 270.C.066
[J. Baudry-Godard (org.)]
P. Beems, T. Uppman, R. Wagner Cho. &
  Concert Arts Orch.—Wagner
                                   ♯ DCap.CTL 7050
                         (♯ Cap.P 8241; ACap.CLCX 023)
☆ M. Angelici, L. Noguéra, St. Eustache Singers & Orch.
  —Cluytens   ♯ C.CX 1145
                                   (♯ Angel. 35019)
☆ N. Sautereau, B. Demigny, Paris Phil. Cho. & Orch.
  —Leibowitz   ♯ Nix.OLP 7026
[Nixa was announced but not issued]   (& ♯ MMS. 82)

SONGS
COMPLETE RECORDING (10ss)   ♯ Plé.P 3060/4
R. Doria, B. Monmart (S); P. Derenne (T), J. Dutey (T),
  P. Mollet (B); S. Gouat & T. Janopoulo (pf.)
                                   (♯ West. set XWN 5502)
♯ Plé.P 3060: Opp. 1, 2, 3, 4, 5, 6, 7, 8 (1860-1870)
♯ Plé.P 3061: Opp. 10 (Duets), 18, 21, 23, 27, 39, 43, 46, 51
  Nos. 1 & 3 (1870-1889)
♯ Plé.P 3062: Opp. 61 (La Bonne Chanson), 51 Nos. 2 & 4,
  57 (Shylock: Chanson & Madrigal), 58;
  & En prière (1889-1895)
♯ Plé.P 3063: Opp. 95, 72 (duet), 76, 83, 85, 87, 92, 94;
  & Vocalise (1896-1910)
♯ Plé.P 3064: Opp. 106 (Le Jardin clos), 113 (Mirages),
  114, 118 (L'Horizon chimérique) &
  Hymne à Apollon (Greek Hymn, 2nd
  cent. B.C., harmonised by Fauré)
  (1918-1922)

[For complete list of titles of songs & authors of texts, see
  Grove, 5th edn. 1954]

♯ = Long-playing, 33⅓ r.p.m.   ♭ = 45 r.p.m.   ♮ = Auto. couplings, 78 r.p.m.

SONGS—Complete (*continued*)
R. Doria sings: Opp. 1-1, 2-1, 3-2, 4-2, 7-1, 8-1, 3; 10 (with
   Monmart); 18-1, 23-2, 27-2, 39-1, 39-4, 43-1, 46-2,
   51-3/4, 58-2, 72 (with Mollet), 76-2, 83-2, 92, 94, 95;
   Hymne; & 114; & Vocalise
B. Monmart sings: Opp. 3-1, 5-1, 6-2, 8-2, 10 (with Doria),
   18-3, 23-1, 3, 39-3, 46-1, 51-1, 51-2, 58-1,76-1, 85-1/2,
   106
P. Mollet sings: Opp. 2-2, 4-1, 5-3, 18-2, 21, 27-1, 39-2,
   43-2, En prière, 58-3/4/5, 61, 72, 83-1, 85-3, 118
J. Dutey sings: Opp. 1-2, 5-2, 6-1, 3, 7-2/3, 37, 57, 87
P. Derenne sings: Op. 113

Collections
   Spleen, Op. 31, No. 3
   Green, Op. 58, No. 3
   C'est l'extase, Op. 58, No. 5
   Prison, Op. 83, No. 1
   Mandoline, Op. 58, No. 1 (all Verlaine)
G. Souzay (B), J. Bonneau (pf.)   **♯ D.LX 3149**
(*Ravel*)

   Clair de lune, Op. 46, No. 2 (Verlaine)
   En prière No. Op. No. (Bordèse)
   Fleur jetée, Op. 39, No. 4 (Silvestre)
   La BONNE CHANSON, Nos. 2, 3, 6, 8
V. Osborne (S), R. Cumming (pf.)   **♯ ML. 7044**
(*Debussy*)

   Clair de lune, Op. 46, No. 2 (Verlaine)
   Les Roses d'Ispahan, Op. 39, No. 4 (L. de Lisle)
   Au bord de l'eau, Op. 8, No. 1 (Sully Prud'homme)
Géori-Boué (S), M. Faure (pf.) in **♯ Ura. 7070**
(*Debussy, Duparc, Gounod, Massenet, etc.*)
(*Debussy, Duparc only, in* ♭ *UREP 73*)

   Arpège, Op. 76, No. 2 (Samain)
   Lydia, Op. 4, No. 2 (L. de Lisle)
   Le Ramier, Op. 87, No. 2 (Silvestre)
G. Touraine (S), J. Bonneau (pf.)
               ♯ Lum.LD 3-402
(*Gounod, Leguerney, etc.*)

   Les Berceaux, Op. 23, No. 1 (Sully Prud'homme)
   Le Secret, Op. 23, No. 3 (Silvestre)
   Poème d'un jour, Op. 21 (Grandmougin)
C. Maurane (B), L. Bienvenu (pf.) ♭ *Pat.ED 23*

   Adieu, Op. 21, No. 3 (Grandmougin)
   Chanson du pêcheur, Op. 4, No. 1 (Gautier)
   L'HORIZON CHIMÉRIQUE, Op. 118 (de Mirmont)
   Lydia, Op. 4, No. 2 (Leconte de Lisle)
   ▽ Le Secret, Op. 23, No. 3 (Sylvestre)[1]
☆ C. Panzéra (B), M. Panzéra (pf.) (♯ Clc. 6269)

Après un rêve, Op. 7, No. 1 (Bussine)
  N. Merriman (M-S), G. Moore (pf.)
               in **♯ C.CX 1213**
(*below; & Debussy, Chausson, Bachelet, etc.*)
                  (♯ *Angel. 35217*)
☆ M. Teyte (S), G. Moore (pf.) (in ♯ Vic.LCT 1133)
  G. Thill (T), M. Faure (pf.)
          (in ♯ C.FHX 5012; Angel. C 33001)
— ARR. VLN. & ORCH. Anderson
☆ N. Milstein & Victor Sym.—Fiedler
          (♭ *Vic.ERA 77; DV. 26009*)
— ARR. VLC. & PF. Casals (*et al.*)
J. Starker & L. Pommers   in **♯ Nix.PLP 708**
(*Papillon, above; etc.*)   (♯ *Per.SPL 708*)
P. Olefsky & G. Silfies   in **♯ McInt.MM 103**
(*Debussy, Prokofiev, etc.*)
A. Janigro & E. Bagnoli (in ♯ *West.WN 18004*)
H. Honegger & E. Møller (in ♭ *Mtr.MCEP 3027*)
M. Rostropovich & pf. (*USSR. 23772*)
— ARR. STR. QTT. Jaffee
American Art Qtt. (in ♯ *BB.LBC 1086*)
— PF. ACC. FOR PRACTICE: (in ♯ *VS.ML 3000*)

(Les) Berceaux, Op. 23, No. 1 (Sully Prud'homme)
  A. Mestral (B) & pf.   ♭ *Phi.N 432012E*
(*below; Schubert, Schumann*)
  M. Powers (A), F. la Forge (pf.) in ♯ **Atl. 1207**
(*Beethoven, Schubert, Brahms, Duparc, etc.*)

(La) BONNE CHANSON, Op. 61
  Song Cycle (Verlaine)
  H. Cuénod (T), F. Holetschek (pf.)
              ♯ Nix.WLP 5278
(*Gounod*)   (♯ *West. WL 5278*)

S. Danco (S), G. Agosti (pf.)   **♯ D.LX 3111**
(2ss)   (♯ *Lon.LS 589*)

CHANSON D'ÈVE, Op. 95
  Song Cycle (v. Lerberghe) 1907-10
I. Kolassi (M-S), A. Collard (pf.) ♯ **D.LXT 2897**
(*Milhaud*)   (♯ *Lon.LL 919*)

Clair de lune, Op. 46, No. 2 (Verlaine)
  M. Dobbs (S), G. Moore (pf.)   in ♯ **C.CX 1154**
(*below; & Schubert, Brahms, Wolf, etc.*)
      (in ♯ FCX 299: QCX 10097; ♯ Angel. 35094)
A. Mestral (B) (*above*)   ♭ *Phi.N 432012E*

Fleur jetée, Op. 39, No. 2 (Silvestre)
  M. Harrell (B), B. Smith (pf.) in ♯ **Rem. 199-140**

Ici-bas, Op. 8, No. 3 (Sully Prud'homme)
  N. Merriman (M-S), G. Moore (pf.)
              in ♯ **C.CX 1213**
(*above*)   (♯ *Angel. 35217*)

Nell, Op. 18, No. 1 (Leconte de Lisle)
  J. Harsanyi (S), O. Herz (pf.) in ♯ **Per.SPL 581**

Noël, Op. 43, No. 1 (Wilder)
  ☆ G. Thill (T), M. Faure (pf.) (in ♯ *C.FH 504*)

Notre amour, Op. 23, No. 2 (Silvestre)
  M. Dobbs (S), G. Moore (pf.) in ♯ **C.CX 1154**
(*above*)   (in ♯ QCX 10097: FCX 299; ♯ Angel. 35094)

Poème d'un jour, Op. 21 (Grandmougin)
1. Rencontre   2. Toujours   3. Adieu
  G. Sciutti (S), J. Bonneau (pf.)   **♯ Phi.A 76705R**
(*Debussy & Ravel*)

... Rencontre, only
  J. Harsanyi (S), O. Herz (pf.) in ♯ **Per.SPL 581**

(Les) Roses d'Ispahan, Op. 39, No. 4 (L. de Lisle)
  M. Sénéchal (T), J. Bonneau (pf.)
              in ♯ **Phi.N 00681R**

FAYRFAX, Robert (1464-1521)
   SEE: † History of Music in Sound (29)

FEKETE, Zoltan (b. 1909)

CAUCASUS, Op. 10   Ballet   1948
Suite
  ☆ Vienna State Op.—Fekete   **♯ CA.LPA 1024**
  (*Tchaikovsky: The Tempest*)

FERGUSON, Howard (b. 1908)

Sonata, F minor   pf.   1940
  C. Lythgoe (*Bliss*)   **♯ CA.LPA 1075**

FERNANDEZ, [Padre] Hipolito (b. *c.* 1762)
   SEE: † Spanish Keyboard Music

FERNANDEZ, Oscar Lorenzo
                    (1897-1948)
SONGS
Samaritana da floresta
Noite de jumbo
A velha historia
Canção do mar
  P. Curtin (S), G. Tucker (pf.)   **♯ Camb.CRS 203**
  (*Garcia Caturla, Galindo, Ginastera*)
Madrecita in ♯ Roy. 1561 is attrib. Oswaldo Fernandez

---

[1] This title is listed for the Clc. reissue, though not in the Mer. original. It has not been possible to check.

FERNÁNDEZ CABALLERO, Manuel
(1835-1906)

ZARZUELAS, etc.   (abridged listings only)
(El) CABO PRIMERO
T. Rosado, G. Monreal, A. M. Fernandez, etc., Madrid
  Cho. & Sym.—Argenta   ♯ Ambra.MC 25014
(El) DUO DE LA AFRICANA   1 Act 1893
A. M. Iriarte, C. Munguía, J. Roa, etc. Madrid Cho. &
  Cha. Orch.—Argenta   ♯ LI.TW 91011
                    (♯ Ambra.MCC 30011)
Vocal Excerpts; in Mont.FM 17
  ▽ M. Fleta & M. Ravenga (G.DB 1507), etc.
GIGANTES Y CABEZUDOS
  (Giants & Big Heads) 1 Act 1898
C. Rubio, T. Pardo, Madrid Cho. & Sym.—Moreno
  Torroba   ♯ AmC.ML 4931
(Chapi)   (♯ Phi.N 00594L)
A. M. Iriarte, T. Erdozain, C. Munguía, N. Aldonondo,
  etc., Donostiarra Cho. & Madrid Sym.—Argenta
                             ♯ LI.TW 91021
                    (♯ Ambra.MCC 30009)
M. Espinalt, J. Permanyer, J. Teruel, O. Pol, etc.; Cho.
  & Sym.—Ferrer   ♯ Reg.LCX 117
                    (♯ Angel. 65011; Pam.LRC 15910)
  [Excerpts on ♭ Reg.SEBL 7010 & SEDL 19041]
L. Berchman & Co.—Montorio   ♯ Mont.FM 19
  [Prelude on ♯ FM 22; Excerpts on ♯ FM 17]
(La) VIEJECITA   1 Act 1897
A. M. Iriarte, T. Rosado, C. Munguía, M. Ausensi, etc.
  Cho. & Madrid Cha.—Argenta   ♯ LI.TW 91003
                    (♯ Ambra.MCC 30010)
  [Prelude in ♯ LI.TW 91004; Ambra.MCCP 29001]
L. Berchmann, E. del Campo, S. Ramalle, etc., Madrid
  Radio Cho. & Cha. Orch.—Montorio & Navarro
                             ♯ Mont.LD 37
  [Prelude only in ♯ Mont.FM 51]

FERNSTRÖM, John (b. 1897)

Concertino, Op. 52   fl., fem. cho. & cha. orch.
E. Holmstedt, cho. & Stockholm Radio
  —Frykberg   ♯ LI.TW 91091
(Blomdahl & Larsson)

FERRABOSCO, Alfonso (c. 1575-1628)

SEE: † EVENING OF ELIZABETHAN VERSE & MUSIC

FERRER, Guillermo (fl. XVIIIth Cent.)

SEE: † SPANISH TONADILLAS
     † SPANISH KEYBOARD MUSIC

FESCH, Willem de (1687-1761)

SEE ALSO: † CARILLON PIECES

Sonata, D minor, Op. 8, No. 9
2 gambas & cont.   1736
— ARR. GAMBA & STR.   "Suite"
K-M. Schwamberger & Salzburg Mozarteum
  —Paumgartner   ♯ CFD. 14
(Torelli, Caix, Telemann, Albinoni, etc.)

FEVIN, Antoine de (1474-1512)

SEE: † POLYPHONIE SACRÉE

FIBICH, Zdeněk (1850-1900)

Komensky Festival Overture, Op. 34   1892
F.O.K. Sym.—Smetáček   ♯ Sup.LPM 133
(below)   (♯ U. 5138C)

OPERAS
(The) BRIDE OF MESSINA, Op. 18 3 Acts 1884
              (Nevěsta Messinská)
EXCERPTS
Overture; Isabella's Prayer; Scene of Reconciliation;
Don Manuele's Tale; I love the Almighty; Finale
☆ M. Krásová, I. Žídek, Z. Otava, K. Kalaš, etc. Prague
  Nat. Theatre Cho. & Orch.—Krombholc
                             ♯ Sup.LPM 125
                                (♯ U. 5107C)
(Smetana: Dalibor, s.5, on ♯ Csm.CRLP 183)

(The) FALL OF ARCONA, Op. 55
  Prologue & 3 Acts 1900
Overture
☆ Prague Nat. Th.—Vogel   ♯ Sup.LPM 85
  (Suk: Asrael Symphony, s. 1)

ŠÁRKA, Op. 51 3 Acts 1897
COMPLETE RECORDING
  Prince Premysl ... ...   V. Bednář
  Ctirád   ... ...   L. Harták
  Vitoraz ... ... J. Veverka (Bs)
  Vlasta   ... ...   M. Krásová (A)
  Sarka   ... ...   M. Podvalová (S)
  etc., Prague Nat. Theatre Cho. & Orch.
  —Krombholc   ♯ Sup.SLPV 154/6
(6ss)   (♯ U. 5129/31G)

(The) WOOING OF PELOPS, Op. 31   1889
  (Námluvy Pelopovy; Part I of Trilogy Hippodamia)
HIGHLIGHTS
  M. Glázrová, E. Kohout, V. Švorc, Z. Štěpánek,
  J. Pivec & Prague Nat. Theatre Orch.—
  Krombholc   ♯ U. 5168/9G
(3ss—below)

Poem, Op. 41, No. 14   pf.
— ARR. ORCH.
  Orch.—Voorhees (in ♯ Alld. 3001: ♭ EP 3001;
                             ♯ MTW. 573)
  Light Orch.—Hayden (Ami. 40-22)
  Royale Concert Orch. (in ♯ Roy. 1567)
  Boyd Neel Orch.—Dumont (♭ Phi.N 402028E)
☆ A. Kostelanetz Orch.
         (in ♯ C.SX 1004; AmC.CL 792: ♭ A 1857)
— ARR. VLN. & PF.
  A. Campoli & E. Gritton
         (in ♯ D.LW 5180; Lon.LD 9192; & ♭ D. 71103)

Romance of Spring, Op. 23 Cantata S, Bs, cho., orch
  D. Tikalová, K. Kalaš, Czech Phil. Cho. &
  Orch.—Šejna   ♯ U. 5168G
(above)

SONG: Dreaming Lake, Op. 36, No. 6
  (Snící jezero) (Dolansky, after Mosen)
  P. Koči (B) & orch.   U.H 24388
(Dvořák: Songs my mother taught me)

Spring, Op. 13 (Vesna) orch.
☆ Czech Phil.—Klíma   ♯ Sup.LPM 133
(above)   (♯ U. 5138C)

Symphony No. 2, E flat major, Op. 33
☆ Czech Phil.—Šejna (♯ Sup.LPV 81; U. 5066G)

FIELD, John (1782-1837)

NOCTURNES   pf.
No. 5, B flat major
No. 13, D minor
  N. Yemelyanova   USSR. 22523/4

Rondo, E major[1]   pf.
  M. Schwalb   in ♯ Roy. 1474

Suite — ARR. ORCH.   Harty
☆ Liverpool Phil.—Sargent   ♯ AmC.RL 3043
  (Boccherini-Françaix)

FINCK, Heinrich (1445-1527)

SEE: † ANTHOLOGIE SONORE
     † MUSICIENS DE LA COUR DE BOURGOGNE
     † SONGS OF THE RENAISSANCE

---

[1] "Midi—12 o'clock"—sometimes known as "Nocturne No. 18".

FINE, Irving (b. 1914)

Quartet, Strings 1949-52
Juilliard Qtt.　　　　　♯ AmC.ML 4843
(*Kirchner*)

FINZI, Gerald (1901-1956)

(A) GARLAND FOR THE QUEEN
(with Ireland, Bax, etc.) 1953
... White flowering days (Blunden)
Cambridge Univ. Madrigal Soc. & Golden Age
Singers—Ord.　　in †♯ C.CX 1063

FIOCCO, Gioseffo Hectore (1703-1741)

SEE ALSO: † CARILLON PIECES

Suite No. 1, G major hpsi. 1730
... Allegro — ARR. VLN. & PF. O'Neill
A. Campoli & E. Gritton　　♯ D.LW 5180
(*Fibich, Albeniz, etc.*)　　(♯ Lon.LD 9192)
A. Grumiaux & G. Tucker　in ♯ Bo.B 202
N. Carol & J. Levine　　in ♯ BB.LBC 1155
G. Barinova & pf. (in ♯ USSR.D 1185)
... Adagio only
E. White (org.)　　in ♯ Moll.E4QP 3443
(*Karg-Elert, Bach, Arne, etc.*)

FIORENTINO, Perino (fl. XVIth Cent.)

SEE: † ITALIAN SONGS OF THE XVITH & XVIITH
CENTURIES
† RENAISSANCE MUSIC FOR THE LUTE

FISCHER, Johann Caspar Ferdinand
(c. 1665-1746)

(Le) JOURNAL DU PRINTEMPS, Op. 1
Suites, orch. 1695
No. 1, C major ... Overture, March, Minuet
☆ Orch.—Sachs (in † ♯ HS.AS 12)
MUSICALISCHER PARNASSUS hpsi. 1738
Suite No. 2, Melpomene ... Passepied
☆ A. Ehlers (in ♯ D.UAT 273084)
MUSICALISCHES BLUMENBÜSCHLEIN
hpsi. 1698
Suite No. 8, Prelude & Chaconne, G major
E. Bodky (clavichord)　　in ♯ Uni.LP 1002
(† Music of Baroque Era)
Prelude, D minor (unspec.) (Anon., in ♯ FSM. 403)

FISCHER, Johann-Christian (1733-1800)

Concerto, C major, ob. & orch.
P. Pierlot & Orch.—de Froment V♯ DO.LD 37

FLANAGAN, William (b. 1923)

(5) SONGS 1946-50
1. Heaven haven
2. Valentine to Sherwood Anderson
3. The Dugout
4. Send home my long-strayed eyes
5. Go and catch a falling star
S. Carter (S), B. Weiser (pf.)　　♯ NE. 2
(*Citkowitz, Chamber, R. Smith*)

Times long ago (Melville)
S. Carter (S), B. Weiser (pf.)　　♯ NE. 3[1]
(*Chanler: The Children*)

FLOTOW, Friedrich von (1812-1883)

OPERAS
ALESSANDRO STRADELLA 3 Acts 1844 (*Ger*)
Overture
Bavarian Radio—Leitner　　PV.72498
(*Fille du Régiment, Overture*)　(♭ Pol. 30098)

Jungfrau Maria T Act III
R. Schock　　G.DB 11545
(*Kienzl: Der Evangelimann—Selig sind...*)　(♭ 7RW 530)
Ⅱ L. Slezak (in ♯ ABCD. 1*)

(L') ESCLAVE DE CAMOËNS 1 Act 1843
(later as "Indra", 3 Acts)
Indra March　Berlin Police Band (*T.A 11668:* ♭ *U 45668*)

MARTHA 4 Acts 1847 (*Ger*)
COMPLETE RECORDINGS
Martha ... ... E. Rizzieri (S)
Nancy ... ...P. Tassinari (M-S)
Lionel ... ... F. Tagliavini (T)
Lord Tristram ... ... B. Carmassi (Bs)
Plunket ... ... C. Tagliabue (B)
etc., Italian Radio Cho. & orch.—Pradelli (*Ital*)
(4ss)　　♯ CCet. set 1254
☆ E. Berger (S), P. Anders (T), etc.—Berlin Municipal
Op. Cho. & Radio Orch.—Rother
(♯ ANix.ULP 9217-1/3)

HIGHLIGHTS
Overture
Mädchen brav und treu　Male cho. Ø
Der Markt beginnt! Die Glocke schallt Bs, cho. & ens.
(Act I) Ø
Letzte Rose S (Act II)
Lasst mich euch fragen (Porterlied) Bs & cho. Ø
Ach, so fromm T
Mag der Himmel euch vergeben Quintet & cho. (Act III) Ø
E. Berger (S), L. Wissmann (S), H. Plümacher
(M-S), W. Ludwig (T), G. Grefe (Bs),
G. Neidlinger (Bs), Bamberg Sym. & Berlin
Phil. Orchs., Württemberg State Op. Cho.
& Orch.—Leitner & Rother　　♯ Pol. 17007
(marked Ø also on ♭ Pol. 30036—these with Neidlinger)

Vocal Selection
☆ T. Richter (S), H. Kraus (T), etc.　♯ DT.TM 68028
(*Freischütz Selection*)　(TV.VE 9005: ♭ T.UE 453912)

Overture
Vienna Sym.—Loibner　　♭ Phi.N 402032E
(*Cornelius: Barbier von Bagdad, Overture*)
Bamberg Sym.—Leitner　　PV. 72418
(*Mignon Overture*)　(♭ Pol. 30144; in ♯ AmD.DL 8509)
F.O.K. Sym.—Smetáček　　U.H 24428
☆ Boston Prom.—Fiedler (G.EH 1433)

Ja, seit früher Kindheit Tagen T & Bs. (Act I)
☆ P. Anders & J. Greindl, from set (♭ Ura.UREP 42)

Nancy! Julia! So bleib doch! S & T (Act II)
A. Rothenberger & R. Schock　G.EH 1458
(*below*)　　(♭ 7PW 539: in ♯ WDLP 1517)

Die letzte Rose S (Act II)
A. Rothenberger　　G.EH 1458
(*above*)　　(♭ 7PW 539)
R. Streich (*Eng*)　　in ♯ HP.DG 17052
(in *Ger*, ♯ Pol. 17051)
☆ E. Berger, from set (♭ Ura.UREP 42)
M. Guillaume (in ♯ DT.TM 68025: T.LA 6107:
♭ UE 453923

Lasst mich euch fragen
(Porterlied) Bs & cho. (Act III)
☆ W. Schirp (*AusT.M 5193*)
Ⅱ P. Plançon (*Ital*) (*AF.AGSA 45**)

---

[1]Announced with this no. which was then used for another work. It is not clear whether the present disc was issued or not, and with what no.

MARTHA (*continued*)
Ach, so fromm   T   (Act III)
N. Gedda   **C.LX 1617**
(*Rigoletto—Parmi veder*)
(in ♯ CX 1130: FCX 302; Angel. 35096)
M. del Monaco (*Ital*)   **G.DA 11350**
(*Chénier—Si fui soldato*)   (♭ 7EB 6006)
(♭ 7ERQ 120: 7ERF 137: ♯ FBLP 1050: QBLP 5021)
E. Lorenzi (*Ital*)   **Cet.AT 0367**
(*Luisa Miller—Quando le sere*)
G. Gari (*Ital*), S. Leff (pf.)   in ♯ **Mur.P 108**
(followed by pf. acc. only)
S. Lemeshev (*Russ*) (USSRM.D 00108 & USSR. 10560)
☆ M. Lanza (*Ital*) (G.DB 21571: ♭ 7R 168: 7RW 146:
                          in ♯ ALP 1202; ♭ Vic.ERA 136)
  B. Gigli (*Ital*) (in ♯ Vic. set LCT 6010: ♭ set WCT 6010)
  P. Anders, from set (♭ Ura.UREP 42)
  E. Conley (*Ital*) (♭ Rem.REP 8005)
  ⌶ E. Caruso (*Ital*) (♭ Vic.ERAT 6*)
  A. Bonci (*Ital*) (in ♯ Sca. 811*)
  G. Martinelli (*Ital*) (in ♯ SBDH.LPG 4*)

FOERSTER, Joseph Bohuslav (1859-1951)

Czech Dance   ☆ Film Sym.—Strništé (in ♯ U. 5215H)

FOOTE, Arthur William (1853-1937)

(A) Night Piece   fl. & str.   1918
☆ J. Baker & Cha. Orch.—Saidenberg   ♯ **B.AXL 2015**
(*Griffes*)

FORNEROD, Aloys (b. 1890)

(Le) Voyage de Printemps   Suite, Cha. orch   1941
1. Eglogue   2. Ronde   3. Nocturne
4. Rigaudon   5. Montferrine
Lausanne Cha. Cho.—Desarzens   ♯ **D.LX 3148**
(*Gagnebin*)   (♯ Lon.LD 9224)
▽ Older issues include:
Concerto, 2 vlns. & pf., Op. 16 (C.DZX 11/12)

FORTEA, Daniel (1878-1953)

GUITAR MUSIC
Sonata   2 guitars
Drologuango   (Estuido poetico)
Cuento al Navidad
Danza al Muñecas de Carton
S. Pastor   in ♯ **NRI.NRLP 5005**
(*Sor, Tarrega, Visée, Pastor*)

Andalusa
M. Gangi   ♭ **ItV.A72R 0043**
(*Anon, Purcell, Villa-Lobos*)

Romance   (ARR.)
G. Zepoll (in ♯ Nix.SLPY 142; in ♯ SOT. 1024)

FORTNER, Wolfgang (b. 1907)

Symphony   1947
... Finale
☆ R.I.A.S. Sym.—Fricsay (in ♯ AmD.DL 9769)

FOSS, Lukas (b. 1922)

(A) Parable of Death   (Hecht, after Rilke)   1952
Narrator, Cho. & orch.
V. Zorina,   F. Stevens,   Southern Baptist
Theological Seminary Cho. & Louisville Orch.
—Whitney   ♯ **AmC.ML 4859**
(*Martinů & Milhaud*)
M. Hayes, R. Robinson, Pomona College Glee
Clubs, Cha. Orch. & org.—Foss[1]
                              ♯ **Edu.ECM 4002**

FRANÇAIX, Jean (b. 1912)

Canon à l'octave   hrn. & pf.   1954
G. Coursier & A. d'Arco   ♭ **Pat.G 1057**
(*Canteloube, Arnella, etc.*)
Concertino   pf. & orch.   1932
K. Long & L.P.O.—Martinon   ♯ **D.LXT 2963**
(*Fauré*)   (♯ Lon.LL 1058)
☆ J. Françaix & Berlin Phil.—Borchard
(*below*)   ♯ **DT.LGM 65021**

NAPOLÉON   Music for Guitry's film
La Chanson des Maréchaux
Y. Montand, A. Mestral & C. Duhour
Le Sacre   March
Orch.—Lanjean   ♭ **Od.7MO 1145**

Petite Quartette   sax. qtt.   1939
A. Sax Saxophone Qtt.   in ♯ **Phi.N 00616R**

(5) Portraits de jeunes filles   pf.   1936
... No. 2, La Tendre;   5. La Moderne
J. Casadesus   in ♯ **Angel. 35261**
(*Tailleferre, Casadesus, Rameau, etc.*)

Quintet, fl., ob., cl., bsn., hrn.   1948
Members of French Nat. Orch.   ♯ **Pat.DTX 135**
(*Poulenc*)   (♯ Angel. 35133)

(Le) ROI NU   Ballet   1936
("*The Emperor's New Clothes*"   1938)
Orch. Suite
Saxon State—Striegler   ♯ **Ura. 7122**
(*Nicodé*)

Scherzo   pf.   1932
J-M. Damase   ♯ **D.FST 153527**
(*Auric, Messiaen, Damase, etc.*)

Sérénade BEA   2 vlns., 2 vlas., vlc., cbs.
(*Jeu musical sur trois notes, c.* 1951)
Pasquier Sextet—Françaix   ♯ **Eso.ES 518**
(*Poulenc*)   (♯ Cpt.MC 20004)

Sérénade comique   sax. qtt.
M. Mule Sax. Qtt.   ♯ **D.LX 3142**
(*Absil & Rivier*)   (♯ Lon.LS 1188)

Sérénade pour 12 instruments   1934
☆ Hamburg Cha. Orch.—Schmidt-Isserstedt
(*above*)   ♯ **DT.LGM 65021**

Trio, C major, vln., vla., vlc.   1933
J. Pougnet, F. Riddle, A. Pini ♯ **Nix.WLP 20017**
(*Berkeley & Dohnányi*)   (♯ West.WL 5316)

"FOLK SONG" ARRANGEMENT [2]
Le "Ça ira"   E. Piaf (♭ C.SCRF 135)

FRANCESCATTI, Zino (b. 1905)

(3) Preludes   pf.
(*Cézanne; Dufy; Modigliani*)
R. Casadesus   ♯ **AmC.Pte. Rec.**
(*Casadesus & Bach*)   (for Am. Library, Paris)

FRANCESCO da Milano (1497-1543)

SEE: † LUTENIST SONGS

FRANCISQUE, Antoine (c. 1570-1605)

SEE: † LUTE MUSIC OF THE XVITH & XVIITH CENTURIES

FRANCK, César Auguste (1822-1890)

CLASSIFIED: I. A. Piano & Organ
                  B. Chamber Music
                  C. Orchestral
              II. Songs

---

[1] Performed in a revised, simplified version.   [2] From Film music *Si Versailles m'était conté*.

I. A. PIANO & ORGAN
(for organ unless otherwise stated)

Andantino, G minor 1858
C. Cronham (*Mjr. 5143*)

(3) CHORALS 1890
COMPLETE RECORDINGS
F. Asma   ♯ **EPhi.NBL 5004**
(*Pièce hérotque*)   (♯ Phi.N 00182L; ♯ Epic.LC 3051)
[organ of Old Church, Amsterdam]

E. White (*below*)   ♯ **Discur. 7280**

A. Reboulot   ♯ **Sel. 320.C.022**
(*below*)   (o.n. LAG 1065)

J. Eggington   V♯ **DO.LD 33/5**
(2ss each) [Auteuil Chu. Org.]

... No. 1, E major, only
F. Germani   ♯ **G.DLP 1043**
(*Mozart*)   (*FBLP 1063*)

... No. 3, A minor
☆ F. Germani(♯ *G.WDLP1002: QDLP6007: FMLP1002*)

Cantàbile, B major (No. 2 of *3 Pieces*, 1878)
E. Nies-Berger   ♯ **Clc. 6254**
(*Grande pièce symphonique; & Liszt*) (▽ ♯ CHS.CHS 1145)[1]
☆ C. Snyder (♯ Word.W 4003)

Final, B flat major, Op. 21
Grande pièce symphonique, Op. 17
Prière, Op. 20
J. Langlais   ♯ **LT.DTL 93071**
[organ of Ste. Clothilde, Paris]
                               (♯ T.LE 6519; Sel.LAG 1017)

L'ORGANISTE, VOL. I
7 Pieces, E flat major & minor
... Andantino poco allegretto (*"Allegretto"*)
... Quasi lento; or Molto maestoso (*"Preludio"*)
— ARR. GUITAR Segovia
A. Segovia   in ♯ **AmD.DL 9734**
(† Segovia Plays)   (♯ D.UAT 273573)

Pièce héroïque, B minor (*3 Pieces*, No. 3) 1878
F. Asma   ♯ **EPhi.NBL 5004**
(*Chorals*)   (♯ Phi.N 00182L; ♯ Epic.LC 3051)
(*Bach & Mendelssohn* on ♯ *Phi.S 06017R*)
[Organ of Old Church, Amsterdam]
M. Salvador   in ♯ **TMS. 3/4**
(*Bach, Schubert, etc.*) [St. Louis Cathedral organ]
R. Elmore   in ♯ **Cant.MRR 270**
(*Bach, Handel, etc.*)
R. I. Purvis   in ♯ **HIFI.R 704**
(*Purvis, Dupré, etc.*)
— ARR. ORCH. O'Connell
☆ San Francisco Sym.—Monteux (in ♯ Cam.CAL 215)

Prélude, aria et final pf. 1886-7
J. Eymar (*below*)   ♯ **Phi.N 00597L**
G. Thyssens-Valentin (*below*)   ♯ **Sel.LPG 8716**
☆ J. Demus (♯ Nix.WLP 5163)

Prélude, choral et fugue pf. 1884
J. Katchen   ♯ **D.LXT 2869**
(*Schumann*)   (♯ Lon. LL 823)
A. Rubinstein   ♯ **Vic.LM 1822**
(*Schumann*)   (♯ FV.A 630114; ItV.A12R 0016)
J. Eymar (*above*)   ♯ **Phi.N 00597L**
G. Thyssens-Valentin   ♯ **Sel.LPG 8716**
(*above*)
C. Chailley-Richez   ♯ **D.FST 153640**
(*Chopin: Sonata No. 2*)[2]
                    (*Chailley: Mass*, on ♯ *D.FMT 163640*)
☆ W. Malcuzynski   ♯ *C.C 1031*
(*Liszt*)   (♯ *FC/QC 1028: WC 1031*)
☆ J. Demus (♯ Nix.WLP 5163)

Prélude, fugue et variation, Op. 18
A. Reboulot   ♯ **Sel. 320.C.022**
(*Chorals*)   (o.n. LAG 1065)
E. White   ♯ **Discur. 7280**
(*Chorals*)

I. B. CHAMBER MUSIC

Quartet, D major strings 1889
Parrenin Qtt.   ♯ **West.WN 18136**
Pascal Qtt.   ♯ **Nix.CLP 1182**
                                              (♯ CHS.CHS 1182)
☆ WQXR Qtt. (♯ Nix.QLP 4010; Cum.CPL 199)

Quintet, F minor pf. & strings 1878-9
V. Aller & Hollywood Qtt.   ♯ **DCap.CTL 7045**
                                              (♯ Cap.P 8220)
V. Sokoloff & Curtis Qtt.   ♯ **Nix.WLP 5331**
                                              (♯ West.WL 5331)
J. M. Darré & Pascal Qtt.   ♯ **Pat.DTX 123**

Sonata, A major, vln. & pf. 1886
D. Oistrakh & V. Yampolsky   ♯ **C.CX 1201**
(*Szymanowski*) (♯ FCX 355: QCX 10260; Angel. 35163)
A. Plocek & J. Paleníček   ♯ **Sup.LPM 115**
                                              (♯ *U. 5090C*)
D. Oistrakh & L. Oborin   ♯ **Van.VRS 6019**
(*Prokofiev*)
(*Schubert* on ♯ Csm.CRLP 151)
(10ss, USSR. 20574/83; 2ss, ♯ USSR.D 0349/50;
                                          CdM.LDA 8112)
J. Fuchs & A. Balsam   ♯ **AmD.DL 9716**
(*Fauré*)
R. & A. Kitain   ♯ **MGM.E 3103**
(*Brahms*)
O. Renardy & E. List   ♯ **Rem. 199-148**
(*Ravel*)   (♯ Cum.CR 285)
L. Kaufman & H. Pignari   ♯ **MMS. 103**
(*Debussy: Sonata*)
☆ Z. Francescatti & R. Casadesus   ♯ C.CX 1111
(*Debussy: Sonata*)   (♯ WCX 1111)
☆ J. Heifetz & A. Rubinstein   ♯ Vic.LCT 1122
(*R. Strauss*)
☆ I. Stern & A. Zakin (♯ *Phi.A 01621R*)
— ARR. VLC. & PF.   Franck
L. Rose & L. Hambro   ♯ **AmC.ML 4652**
(*Grieg*)

Trio, F sharp major, Op. 1, No. 1 pf., vln., vlc. 1841
Bolzano Trio   ♯ **AmVox.PL 8950**

I. C. ORCHESTRAL

(Le) Chasseur maudit Sym. Poem 1882
Lamoureux—Fournet   ♯ *Phi.N 00661R*
(*Rédemption*)
Netherlands Phil.—Goehr   ♯ **CHS.H 2**
(*below*)   (♯ CHS.CHS 1243 & ♯ MMS. 3004)
Paris Cons.—Cluytens   ♯ **Angel. 35232**
(*Psyché & Rédemption*)
Vienna State Op.—Rodzinski ♯ **Nix.WLP 5311**
(*below*)   (♯ Sel. 320.CW.094; ♯ West.WL 5311)
☆ Royal Phil.—Beecham   ♯ C.CX 1087
(*Rimsky-Korsakov*)   (♯ QCX 10085)
☆ Chicago Sym.—Defauw   ♯ BB.LBC 1056
(*below; & Chausson*)   (♭ set WBC 1056)

(Les) Djinns pf. & orch. 1884
A. d'Arco & Concerts Colonne—Sebastian
                                              ♯ **Nix.ULP 9099**
(*Saint-Saëns: Carnaval des animaux*)   (♯ Ura. 7099)

(Les) Éolides Sym. Poem 1876
Netherlands Phil.—Goehr   ♯ **CHS.H 2**
(*above & below*)   (♯ CHS.CHS 1243 & ♯ MMS. 3004)

Psyché Sym. Poem Cho. & orch. 1887-8
1. Sommeil de Psyché
2. Psyché enlevée par les zéphyrs
3. Le Jardin d'Éros   4. Psyché et Éros
5. Les Souffrances et plaintes de Psyché
6. Pardon de Psyché
Netherlands Cha. Cho. & Residentie Orch.
—Otterloo   ♯ **Phi.A 00262L**
                                              (♯ Epic.LC 3146)
(*continued on next page*)

---

[1] Also announced but not issued as ♯ Nix.CLP 1145.
[2] It is probable that the *Chopin* coupling has been replaced by the *Chailley* in view of the similarity in numbers.

Psyché (*continued*)
... **Nos. 1-4 only** — ORCH. VERSION

Amsterdam--v. Beinum   **♯ D.LXT 2829**
(*Bruckner: Symphony No. 7, s. 1*)   (♯ Lon.LL 852)
(*2ss, ♯ D.LW 5069; Lon.LD 9081*)

Paris Cons.—Cluytens   **♯ C.FC 1036**
(*Rédemption*) (*idem & Chasseur maudit, in ♯ Angel. 35232*)

Belgian Radio—André   **♯ DT.LGX 66024**
(*de Greef: 4 Old Flemish Folksongs*)   (♯ T.LSK 7022)
(*Saint-Saëns, on ♯ DT.LGX 66028*)

Netherlands Phil.—Goehr   **♯ CHS.H 2**
(*above*)   (♯ CHS.CHS 1243 & ♯ MMS. 3004)

... **Nos. 1, 2 & 4**
Detroit Sym.—Paray   **♯ Mer.MG 50029**
(*Fauré & Ravel*)
☆ Chicago Sym.—Defauw   **♯ BB.LBC 1056**
(*above; & Chausson*)   (♭ set WBC 1056)

... **No. 4 only**
N.B.C. Sym.—Toscanini   **♯ G.ALP 1218**
(*Moussorgsky*) (♯ Vic.LM 1838; ♯ ItV.A12R 0125;
                   FV.A 630249)

Rédemption   Sym. Poem.   S, cho. & orch.   1871-2
... **No. 5, Morceau symphonique**   orch.   1874
Lamoureux—Fournet   **♯ Phi.N 00661R**
(*Chausseur maudit*)
(*Chausson, on ♯ Epic.LC 3067*)

Paris Cons.—Cluytens   **♯ C.FC 1036**
(*Psyché*)   (*Chasseur maudit & Psyché, ♯ Angel. 35232*)
☆ Paris Cons.—Sebastian (in ♯ Nix.ULP 9061; *Ura. 5000*)

Symphony, D minor   1886-8
Vienna Phil.—Furtwängler   **♯ D.LXT 2905**
                 (♯ Lon.LL 967)

N.B.C. Sym.—Cantelli   **♯ G.ALP 1219**
     (♯ QALP 10114; Vic.LM 1852: ♭ set ERC 1852)

French Nat. Radio—Cluytens   **♯ C.CX 1064**
     (♯ FCX 191: QCX 10033; ♯ Angel. 35029)

St. Louis Sym.—Golschmann **♯ DCap.CTL 7044**
     (♯ Cap.P 8221; ACap.CLCX 018)

Detroit Sym.—Paray   **♯ Mer.MG 50023**
            (♯ FMer.MLP 7510)

Belgian Radio—André   **♯ DT.LGX 66030**
            (♯ T.LE 6515)

Vienna State Op.—Rodzinski   **♯ Nix.WLP 5311**
(*above*)   (♯ West.WL 5311; Sel. 320.CW.094)

Bamberg Sym.—F. Lehmann **♯ HP.DGM 18188**

Netherlands Phil.—Goehr   **♯ MMS. 58**

Philadelphia—Ormandy (n.v.) **♯ AmC.ML 4939**

☆ Philadelphia—Ormandy, o.v. (♭ AmC. set A 1092)
San Francisco—Monteux
           (♯ G. WALP 1019; DV.L 16171)
Residentie—v. Otterloo (♯ Epic.LC 3019; Phi.S 04011L)
Paris Phil.—Désormière (♯ Sup.LPV 75; U. 5122G)
Amsterdam—Mengelberg (♯ FT. 310.TC.007)
Austrian Sym.—Wolf (♯ Cum.CR 237; & with
     commentary by S. Spaeth, on ♯ Rem. 100-7)
San Francisco—Monteux (o.v.)
         (♯ Cam.CAL 107 & in set CFL 104)
Anon. Orch. (♯ Gram. 2088)

Variations symphoniques   pf. & orch.   1885
P. Badura-Skoda & London Phil. Sym.
—Rodzinski   **♯ West.LAB 7030**
(*Rimsky-Korsakov: Concerto*)

A. Ciccolini & Paris Cons.—Cluytens
                ♯ C.CX 1190
(*d'Indy: Symphonie*)   (♯ FCX 213; Angel. 35104)
J. Doyen & Lamoureux—Fournet
                ♯ Epic.LC 3057
(*Fauré & Saint-Saëns*)
(*Fauré only on ♯ Phi.N 00704R*)
E. Bernáthová & F.O.K. Sym.—Smetáček
                ♯ Sup.LPV 202
(*Lalo*)   (♯ U. 5186G)
E. Wollman & Orch.—Swarowsky **♯ ACC.MP 11**
(*Berlioz & J. Strauss II*)
☆ R. Casadesus & Philharmonia—Weldon ♯ C.CX 1118
         (♯ C.FCX 119; QCX 119)

☆ M. Lympany & Philharmonia—Susskind
     (♯ G.WCLP 1002: QCLP 12006)
A. Brailowsky & Vic. Sym.—Morel
     (BrzV. 12-3516/7; ♯ G.QALP 172)
W. Gieseking & Philharmonia—v. Karajan
     (with *Grieg*, ♯ AmC.ML 4885)
F. Valenzi & Austrian Sym.—Moreau
     (♯ AFest.CFR 10-88; ♯ Cum.TCR 272)

II. SONGS

(Le) Mariage des roses   (David)   1871
J. Harsanyi (S), O. Herz (pf.) in **♯ Per.SPL 581**
☆ G. Thill (T) (in ♯ C.FHX 5012; Angel.C 33001)
   ♮ E. de Gogorza (B) (AF.AGSB 69*)

Panis angelicus   1872
A. Nicholson (Tr, *Eng*), choir & org.
          in **♯ CEd.CE 1023**
(† *Five Centuries of Choral Music*)
   O. Werner (T, *Norw*), R. Holger (org.) *Od.ND 7191*
   G. Fleischer (S) & org.   *Phi.P 55035H*
   J. Dragonette (S)   in ♭ *AmC.A 1556*
   P. Germain (B)   in *Lum.LD 1-505*
☆ R. Crooks (T)   in ♯ *Cam.CAL 170:* ♭ *CAE 185*
   R. Tauber (T)   in ♯ *AmD.DL 7535*
   C. Lynch (T) & org.   in ♯ *AmC.RL 3016*
— Accompaniment, etc. for practice (in ♯ *VS.MH 1001*)
— ARR. CHO.
Minnestrelen Men's & Boys' Cho.
     (in ♯ *EPhi.BBR 8042;* ♯ *Phi.P 10028R*)
— ARR. ORGAN   V. Fox (in ♯ Vic.LM 1814: ♭ set ERB 34)
— ARR. DUET
R. Ponselle (S), C. Ponselle (S), etc.   **♯ Pte. n.d.**
(*Bizet: Agnus Dei & Schubert: Ave Maria*) (& Pte. 78 rpm.)
— ARR. ORCH.   Angelicum—Janes (*Ang.CPA 055*)
— ARR. VLC. & PF.   K. Reher & M. di Tullio (in ♯ *Layos. 594*)

(La) Procession   (Brizeux)   1888
M. Olivero (S), E. Magnetti (pf.) **Cet.PE 184**
(*Manon—Adieu notre petite table*)
S'il est un charmant gazon (Hugo)   pub. 1922
☆ G. Thill (T) (in ♯ C.FHX 5012; Angel. C 33001)

(Les) BÉATITUDES   Oratorio   1869-79
No. 4, Heureux les cœurs   T
   ☆ G. Thill (in ♯ C.FH 504)

FRANCK, Johann Wolfgang   (c. 1641-c. 1700)
    SEE: † SEVEN CENTURIES OF SACRED MUSIC
          † GERMAN SONGS

FRANCK, Melchior   (c. 1573-1639)
    SEE: † ANTHOLOGIE SONORE (♯ HS.AS 11)
          † FIVE CENTURIES OF CHORAL MUSIC
          † SONGS OF THE RENAISSANCE

FRANCOEUR, François   (1698-1787)

Sonata, E major, vln. & cont.
... **Largo & Allegro vivo**   — ARR. VLC. & PF.
                            Trowell
J. Starker & L. Pommers   in **♯ Nix.PLP 708**
(*Couperin, Debussy, Fauré, etc.*)   (♯ Per.SPL 708)

FRANÇOIS, Samson   (b. 1924)

Concerto, pf. & orch.   1950
S. François & Paris Cons.—Tzipine
                    ♯ C.FCX 229
(*Challan: Concerto pastoral*)

♯ = Long-playing, 33⅓ r.p.m.   ♭ = 45 r.p.m.   ♮ = Auto. couplings, 78 r.p.m.

FRANZ, Robert (1815-1892)

SONGS

COLLECTIONS

Lieber Schatz, sei wieder gut, Op. 26, No. 2 (Osterwald)
Im Herbst, Op. 17, No. 6 (Müller)
Ein Ständlein wohl vor Tag, Op. 28, No. 2 (Mörike)
Ein Friedhof, Op. 13, No. 3 (Waldau)
Auf dem Meere, Op. 36, No. 1 (Heine) (*Das Meer hat seine Perlen*)
Rosmarin, Op. 13, No. 4 (Waldau)
Nebel, Op. 28, No. 4 (Lenau)
Gute Nacht, Op. 5, No. 7 (Eichendorff)
Ach wär es nie geschehen! Op. 23, No. 3 (Trad.)
Stiller Abend, Op. 5, No. 9 (Schröer)
Mutter, O sing' mich zur Ruh', Op. 10, No. 3 (Hemans, trs. Freiligrath)
Es hat die Rose sich beklagt, Op. 42, No. 5 (Bodenstedt & Schaffy)
Er ist gekommen, Op. 4, No. 7 (Rückert)
Stille Sicherheit, Op. 10, No. 2 (Lenau)
Widmung, Op. 14, No. 1 (Müller)
Aus meinen grossen Schmerzen, Op. 5, No. 1 (Heine)
Vergessen, Op. 5, No. 10 (Osterwald)
Ständchen, Op. 17, No. 2 (Osterwald)
Abends, Op. 16, No. 4 (Eichendorff)
Denk' ich dein, Op. 21, No. 2 (M. Jäger)
Für Musik, Op. 10, No. 1 (Geibel)
Genesung, Op. 5, No. 12 (Schröer)
Auf dem Meer, Op. 11, No. 5 (Heine) (*Es träumte mir . . .*)
Da die Stunde kam, Op. 7, No. 3 (Osterwald)
Um Mitternacht, Op. 16, No. 6 (Mörike)

    H. Rössl-Majdan (A), V. Graef (pf.)
                  ♯ **West.WLE 104**

Aus meinen grossen Schmerzen, Op. 5, No. 1 (Heine) Ø
Bitte, Op. 9, No. 3 (Lenau) Ø
Gute Nacht, Op. 5, No. 7 (Eichendorff)
Liebchen ist da, Op. 5, No. 2 (Schröer)
Mutter, O sing mich zur Ruh', Op. 10, No. 3 (Hemans)
Stille Sicherheit, Op. 10, No. 2 (Lenau) Ø
Vöglein, wohin? Op. 1, No. 11 (Geibel) Ø
Widmung, Op. 14, No. 1 (W. Müller)

    ☆ E. Schumann (S), G. Schick (pf.) ♯ **Roy. 1404**
    (*Mendelssohn & Purcell*)
    (*Mendelssohn only*, ♯ *AFest.CFR 10-222*)
    (Songs marked Ø are also on ♭ *Roy.EP 226*)

Sonntag, Op. 1, No. 7 (Eichendorff)
Schlummerlied, Op. 1, No. 10 (*Ruhe Süssliebchen*) (Tieck)
Nebel, Op. 28, No. 4 (*Du trüber Nebel*) (Lenau)
Die Liebe hat gelogen, Op. 6, No. 4 (Platen)

    M. Schloss (S), J. Brice (pf.) ♯ **IRCC.L 7000**
    (*Wolf, Schumann, R. Strauss*)

Es hat die Rose sich beklagt, Op. 42, No. 5
    (Bodenstedt & Schaffy)
    G. Pechner (B)   in ♯ **Roy. 1557**
    E. Sachs (M-S), S. Leff (pf.)   in ♯ **Mur.P 111**
    (followed by pf. acc. only)

Für Musik, Op. 10, No. 1 (Geibel)
    ☆ L. Lehmann (S), P. Ulanowsky (pf.)
         (in ♯ Vic.LCT 1108: in ♭ *set WCT 1108*)

Gute Nacht, Op. 5, No. 7 (Eichendorff)
    ☆ L. Lehmann (S), E. Balogh (pf.)
         (in ♯ Vic.LCT 1108: in ♭ *set WCT 1108*)

Widmung, Op. 14, No. 1 (Müller)
    M. Powers (A), F. la Forge (pf.) in ♯ **Atl. 1207**
    (*Bach, Brahms, Schubert, Wagner, Duparc, etc.*)

— Accompaniment, etc., for practice (in ♯ *VS.MH 1003*)

FREIXANET (b. c. 1730)

SEE: † SPANISH KEYBOARD MUSIC

FRESCOBALDI, Girolamo (1583-1643)

NOTE: The keyboard works are identified (so far as possible) by the date & book no. of the original edns. and [in Roman figs.] the vols. in the Bärenreiter Edn.

COLLECTIONS OF KEYBOARD MUSIC

From Book 2   1637 [IV]
    Toccata 1, 2, 4, 9
    Aria detta Balletto (Variations)
    Gagliarda No. 2 *d*
    Corrente No. 2 *d*
    Canzona No. 1 *d*
    Aria detta la Frescobalda *d*

                          continued)

Fiori Musicali   1635 [V]
   7. Christe *b*
   8. Kyrie *b*
  16. Toccata cromatica per l'elevazione
  31. Toccata per l'elevazione

    G. de Donà (org.)   ♯ E. & **AmVox.PL 8780**
    [Items marked *b* from *Nuptialia*, *d* from *Liber organi*,
      ed. S. della Libera]

Aria detta la Frescobalda (Book 2) [IV]
Gagliarda No. 2 (Book 2) [IV]
Corrente No. 2 (Book 2) [IV]

    B. Winogron (virginals)   in ♯ **Eso.ES 516**

Aria detta la Frescobalda (Book 2) [IV]
Corrente No. 2 (Book 3) [IV]
— ARR. GUITAR Segovia
    A. Segovia   in ♯ **B.AXTL 1070**
    († *Segovia Evening*)   (♯ AmD.DL 9733;
                  SpC.CCL 35015; *AFest.CFR 729*)

AIRS

Se l'aura spira (Book 1)
    ☆ H. Cuénod (T), H. Leeb (lute) in ♯ **Nix.WLP 5059**
    († *Italian Songs of the XVIth & XVIIth Centuri*

Voi partite (Book 1)
    ☆ M. Meili (T), R. Gerlin (hpsi.) (in † ♯ *HS.AS 9*)

Arietta detto balletto (Book 2) 1637 [IV]
— ARR. BANDONEON
    A. Barletta   in ♯ *SMC. 549*

(5) Canzone per sonar
    (Book 1, a due voci, Nos. 1-5, 1628)
    C. Monteux (fl.), H. Shulman (ob.), B. Greenhouse (vlc.), S. Marlowe (hpsi.)
                     ♯ **Eso.ES 517**
    (*Rosenmüller & Couperin*)   (♯ Cpt.MC 20023)

Capriccio sopra un soggetto
    (*Capricci*, Book 1, 1626) [II]
    T. Dart (hpsi.)   † **G.HMS 42**
    († *History of Music in Sound*) (in ♯ Vic. set LM 6029)

Fugue, G minor (attrib. Frescobaldi)[1]
    F. Peeters (org.)   in ♯ **Nix.PLP 586**
    († *Old Italian Masters*) (♯ Cpt.MC 20048; Per.SPL 586)

FIORI MUSICALI 1635 org. [V]
    Nos. 3, 4, 10, 17, 31
  (Messa della Domenica: Kyrie; Christe; Kyrie; Canzon post il Communio
  Messa delli Apostoli . . . Toccata per l'elevazione)
    F. Peeters   in ♯ **Nix.PLP 586**
    († *Old Italian Masters*) (♯ Per.SPL 586; Cpt.MC 20048)
  No. 31, Toccata per l'elevazione ☆ M. Dupré (in † ♯ *HS.AS 11*)

No. 42 (Messa della Madonna: Ricercare dopo il Credo)
    F. Viderø   in ♯ **HS.HSL 2072**
    († *Masterpieces of Music before 1750*)

(5) Gagliarde hpsi. or org. (Book 2, 1637) [IV]
    ... No. 2, only
    A. Ehlers (in ♯ *D.UAT 273084*)
    — ARR. ORCH. Stokowski
    Sym.—Stokowski   in ♯ **Vic.LM 1721**
    (*Vivaldi, Cesti, Lully, etc.*)   (♭ set *WDM 1721*)
    (in ♯ G.FALP 245; ItV.A12R 0040; Vic.LM 1875:
                             ♭ set *ERB 52*)

Pastorale gentile (unid.)
    ☆ E. Zathureczky (vln.) & M. Karin (pf.) (in ♯ *U. 5185C*)

TOCCATAS

Toccata prima (Book 1, 1637) [III]
    G. Leonhardt   in ♯ **Van.BG 529**
    († *XVIIth Century Organ Music*)

Unidentified Toccata[2] — ARR. VLC. & PF. Cassadó
    A. Janigro & E. Bagnoli   ♯ **West.WL 5234**
    (*Boccherini & Locatelli*)
    M. Amfiteatrof & O. P. Santoliquido
                    ♯ **ItV.A12R 0140**
    (*Veracini, Boccherini, etc.*)
    P. Olefsky & G. Silfies   in ♯ **McInt.MM 103**
    (*Debussy, Falla, Senallié, etc.*)
    K. Reher & M. di Tullio (in ♯ *Layos. 594*)

---

[1] From Clementi's *Selection of Practical Harmony*; certainly spurious.
[2] It has been suggested that this is an original composition by Cassadó.

Toccata, B minor, & Fugue, D major   (unid.)
— ARR. ORCH.   Kindler
☆ National Sym. (U.S.A.)—Kindler (in ♯ Cam.CAL 175)

Toccata, E minor, No. 11   (DTÖ. VIII)
G. Leonhardt   in ♯ Van.BG 529
(† XVIIth Century Organ Music)

FREYLINGHAUSEN, Johann Anastasius
(1670-1739)

Es ist vollbracht   1714
K. Flagstad (S), G. Moore (pf.)
                    ♯ Vic.LHMV 1070
(† German Songs) [ed. Dørumsgaard]

Macht hoch die Tür
St. Michael's Cho. (Hamburg)—Brinkmann
                    PV. 36099
(Eccard, Bach, Pachelbel)   (♭ 32099)

FRIEDRICH II (der Grosse) (1712-1786)

Concerto No. 3, C major   fl. & orch.
H. Schneider & Frankenland State Sym.
—Kloss   ♯ Lyr.LL 51
(Wilhelmina, Markgräfin von Bayreuth)

SONATAS, flute & continuo
No. 2, C minor
No. 5, A major
J. Wummer, F. Valenti (hpsi.) ♯ West.WN 18070
(Quantz)

No 2, C minor   (c. 1747)
☆ J-P. Rampal & R. Veyron-Lacroix (hpsi.)
                    (in † ♯ HS.AS 19)

No. 48, E minor
G. Scheck, F. Neumeyer (hpsi.), A. Wenzinger
(gamba)   ♭ Pol. 37041

FRICKER, Peter Racine (b. 1920)

Sonata, Op. 12   vln. & pf.   1950
M. Lidka & M. Kitchen   ♯ Argo.RG 6
(Searle)   (o.n. ATC 1002)

Symphony No. 2, Op. 14   1951
Liverpool Phil.—Pritchard   ♯ G.DLP 1080

FRIDERICI, Daniel   (1584-1638)
SEE: † CHORAL SONGS (c. 1600)
      † SONGS OF THE RENAISSANCE

FROBERGER, Johann Jacob (1616-1667)

SUITES   harpsichord   DTÖ. Vol. XIII
No. 6, G major   (Variations on 'Die Mayerin')
No. 30, A minor
☆ E. Harich-Schneider   PV. 3404

No. 6, G major   (Variations on 'Die Mayerin')
R. Gerlin   in ♯ LOL.OL 50043
(† Clavecinistes allemands)   (♯ OL.LD 67)

No. 12, C major[1] . . . Allemande
E. Heiller   in ♯ Uni.LP 1010
(† History of the Dance)

No. 22, E minor
F. Viderø (clavichord)   in ♯ HS.HSL 2072
(† Masterpieces of Music before 1750)

Toccata & Fugue, A minor, No. 10   (DTÖ. VIII)
W. Supper   in ♯ Ren.X 53
(† Baroque Organ Music)

FROISSART, Jehan   (c. 1337-after 1404)
SEE: † LA MUSIQUE ET LA POÉSIE

FRY, William Henry (1815-1864)

Overture to Macbeth   1862
Hamburg Philharmonia—Korn in ♯ Allo. 3148
(Hopkinson, Gottschalk, Barber, etc.)

FUENLLANA, Miguel de   (fl. XVIth Cent.)
SEE: † ANTHOLOGIE SONORE

FÜRSTENAU, Kaspar (1772-1819)

(12) Pieces, Op. 35   fl. & guitar
. . . 6, Allegro; 5, Andante; 8, Écossaise; 7, Minuet; 2, Allegro[2]
P. Birkelund & U. Neumann   ♯ D.LXT 5070
(Diabelli & Schubert)   (♯ Lon.LL 1079)

FURTWÄNGLER, Wilhelm (1886–1954)

Symphony, No. 2, E minor   1947
☆ Berlin Phil.—Fürtwangler (auto.)   ♯ Pol. 18114/5

FUX, Johann Joseph (1660-1741)

COLLECTION OF KEYBOARD WORKS, VOL. II
(DTÖ. LXXXV)
(12) Minuets
Sonata quarta, E major
Sonata quinta, A minor
Sonata septima, D major
Suite No. 2, F major
K. Rapf (org., pf., & hpsi.)[3]   ♯ SPA. 61

Minuet No. 2, B flat major
E Heiller (hpsi.)   in ♯ Uni.LP 1010
(† History of the Dance)

Sonata a tre, F major   vlns.
(MS. Hesse State Lib.; ed. Haas)
London Baroque Ens.—Haas   ♯ P.PMB 1005
(Mozart)

GABRIELI, Andrea (c. 1520-1586)

INSTRUMENTAL MUSIC
COLLECTION (Organ)
Toccata Xº Tono   1593
Canzon arioso   1596
Fantasia allegra del XIIº Tono   1596
Ricercare del Vº Tono   (a 2 soggetti)
Ricercare del XIIº Tono   (a quattro voci)   1589
G. de Donà   ♯ AmVox.PL 8470
(G. Gabrieli)

Agnus Dei   (a due voci)
De profundis   (a sei voci)   1590
Ricercare del XIIº tono   (a sette voci)   1589
☆ Brass Ens.—Shuman   in ♯ Cpt.MC 20014
Aria della Battaglia   (pub. 1590)
French Navy Band—Maillot V♯ Sel. 190.C.005

[1] Il Lamento sopra la dolorosa perdita . . . de Ferdinando IV . . .
[2] As Suite for fl. and guitar.   [3] It is doubtful if this disc was ever on sale.

Canzon arioso 1596
  F. Peeters (organ)   in ♯ Nix.PLP 586
  († Old Italian Masters)   (♯ Per.PLP 586; Cpt.MC 20048)

Pour ung plaisir[1]
  F. Viderø (hpsi.)   in † ♯ HS.HSL 2071

Ricercar arioso No. 1 1605
  S. Jeans (org.)   **G.HMS 43**
  († History of Music in Sound)   (in ♯ Vic. set LM 6029)

MASSES
"Pater peccavi" 1570
  Treviso Cath. Cho.—d'Alessi
  (*Motets*)   ♯ E. & AmVox.PL 8370

Brevis
  Rennes Cath. Cho.—Orhant   ♯ SM. 33-23
  (*Gregorian—Proper of Whitsunday*)

MOTETS
Cantate Domino
Bor*u*m est confiteri Domino
C sacrum convivium: all 4 vv. 1576
Egredimini et videte 8 vv. 1578
MASS "Pater peccavi" . . . Sanctus & Benedictus
  Treviso Cath. Chapel Cho.—d'Alessi
            ♯ E. & AmVox.PL 8030
  († Motets of the Venetian School)   (♯ BàM.LD 010)[2]

In decachordo psalterio
Sacerdos et pontifex
Filiae Jerusalem: all 4 vv. 1576
Maria Magdalena 7 vv. 1578
Cor meum conturbatum est
Annuntiate inter gentes 5 vv. (1562-1565)
  Treviso Cath. Cho.—d'Alessi
            ♯ E. & AmVox.PL 8790
  († Motets of Venetian School)

Angelus ad pastores
Pater peccavi (preceding the Mass)
  Treviso Cath. Cho.—d'Alessi
            ♯ E. & AmVox.PL 8370

  (*Mass, Pater peccavi*)

GABRIELI, Giovanni (1557-1612)

ORGAN MUSIC—COLLECTION
Intonazione e ricercare
Canzon: La Spiritata 1608
Fantasia del VIº Tono
Fuga del IXº Tono
Fantasia del IVº Tono
Ricercare
Ricercare del VIIº & VIIIº Tono (1593, 1595)
  G. de Donà   ♯ AmVox.PL 8470
  (*A. Gabrieli*)

CANZONAS
Quarti toni a 15 — ARR ORG. & ORCH. Stokowski
  C. Courboin & Orch.—Stokowski
            in ♯ Vic.LM 1721
  (*below*)   (in ♭ *set WDM 1721*)
        (in ♯ G.FALP 245; ItV.A12R 0040)

Primi toni No. 1
Sonata pian' e forte
  — ARR. DOUBLE STRING ORCH.
  Stuttgart Cha.—Münchinger   **♯ D.LX 3102**
  (*Telemann*)   (♯ Lon.LS 686)

A sei voci 1615
Sonata pian' e forte 1597
  ☆ Inst. Ens.—Sachs (in † ♯ HS.AS 12)

A sei voci 1615
Septimi toni No. 1 1597
  ☆ Brass Ens.—Shuman   in ♯ Cpt.MC 20014

Septimi toni No. 1 1597
  Brass Ens.—Voisin   in ♯ Uni.UN 1003
  († Golden Age of Brass)

In echo duodecimi toni ed. Giuranna 1597
  I Musici Ens.   **♯ C.CX 1163**
  (*Albinoni, B. Marcello, Vivaldi*) (♯ QCX 10039: FCX 305; Angel. 35088)

Canzon primi toni a 8 1597
  Ancient Inst. Ens.—M. Casadesus **♯ Plé.P 3073**
  (*Tomasini, Maschera, C.P.E. Bach*)

Fantasia del VIº tono 1593
  B. Winogron (virginals)   in ♯ Eso.ES 516

MOTETS
COLLECTIONS
  [Symphoniae sacrae Vols. I & II, 1597 & 1615]
In ecclesiis benedicite Domino (with S & T) II
Jubilate Deo I
O Jesu, mi dulcissime II
Benedictus 12 voices Unacc. I
  P. Curtin (S), R. Gartside (T), J. Orosz (B),
  Harvard Glee Club & Radcliffe Cho., Brass
  Ens.—Wordworth[3]   **♯ Camb.CRS 201**
  [D. Pinkham, org.]

Magnificat 8 vv. I	Ego dixi, Domine 7 vv. 1587
Benedixisti Domine 7 vv. I	Inclina Domine 6 vv. 1587
O quam suavis 7 vv. I	Miserere mei Deus 6 vv. I
Beata es, Virgo Maria 6 vv. I	O magnum mysterium 8 vv.
Exaudi Deus I	1587
Cantate Domino 6 vv. I	Sancta Maria 7 vv. I
Domine exaudi orationem meam 10 vv. I	

  Treviso Cho.—d'Alessi ♯ E. & AmVox.PL 8830

In ecclesiis benedicite Domino
  Cho. & Orch.—Stokowski   in ♯ Vic.LM 1721
  (*Vivaldi, Cesti, etc.*)   (in ♭ *set WDM 1721*)
        (in ♯ ItV.A12R 0040; G.FALP 245)
  Soloists, Cho. & Orch.—Goldsbrough
               † G.HMS 39
  (2ss)   (& in ♯ Vic. set LM 6029)

Jubilate Deo 8 voices
  ☆ Danish Radio Madrigal Cho.—Wöldike (C.DX 1863)

Nunc dimittis 3 5-pt. Chos. 1597
Virtute magna 2 6-pt. Chos. 1597
  Yale Univ. Music School Cho.—Hindemith
               in ♯ Over.LP 5
  († Yale University, Vol. II)

Sancta Maria 7 vv. 1597
  Treviso Cath. Chapel Cho.—d'Alessi
             ♯ E. & AmVox.PL 8030
  († Motets of the Venetian School)   (♯ BàM.LD 010)[2]

Ricercare del VIIº Tono 1593
  F. Peeters (org.)   in ♯ Nix.PLP 586
  († Old Italian Masters)   (♯ Per.SPL 586; Cpt.MC 20008)

Ricercare del Xº Tono, a due soggetti 1595
  ☆ M. Dupré (org.) (in † ♯ HS.AS 11)

Sonata a tre, G major[4]
  Members of Alma Musica Sextet
            in ♯ LT.DTL 93046
  (*Sweelinck, Vivaldi, Bach, Mozart, etc.*)
          (♯ Sel.LAG 1019; T.LT 6551)

GABRIELLI, Domenico (*c.* 1655-1690)

FLAVIO CUNIBERTO Opera 1688
Voi tu chi esperi, amore Aria
  J-P. Jeannotte (T), pf. & vlc. in ♯ Hall.RS 6
  († Musica Antica e Nuova)

Ricercare vlc. unacc. 1689
  ☆ D. Shuman (tromb.) (in ♯ Cpt.MC 20014)

GABRIELSKI, Johann Wilhelm
(1791-1846)

March & Trio, C major
  (Companion piece to "Haydn's" *Toy Symphony*)
  Vienna Orch. Soc.—Adler   ♯ Uni.LP 1016
  (*L. Mozart & Hoffmann*)

---

[1] Transcription of Créquillon's Chanson. From *Canzoni alla francese …* V, 1605.
[2] The BàM. pressing was announced but apparently not issued.
[3] Ed. Woodworth from Winterfeld edn.
[4] From *Canzoni e Sonate*, 1615; here played by 2 vlns., ob., hpsi., & vlc.

GADE, Niels Vilhelm (1817-1890)

(The) Children's Christmas Eve, Op. 36 1859
  pf. solo, with voice *ad lib.*
  P. Zeitlin (pf. solo)   ♯ *Opus. 6006*
  (*S. Heller: Album for the Young, Op. 138, & Kullak:*
  Scenes from Childhood, Op. 62)
  [with accompanying *Matching Music Book*, pub. Marks,
  N.Y.]

Echoes of Ossian, Overture, Op. 1 orch. 1840
  Danish Radio—Frandsen   ♯ *Phi.S 06060R*
  (*Hartmann: Hakon Jarl, Overture*)

(The) Erlking's Daughter, Op. 30 (*Elverskud*) 1853
  Ballad, Soli, Cho. Orch.
No. 2, Olaf's Song: When through the meadows
  ☆ A. Schiøtz (T)
No. 7, In the East the sun is rising
  ☆ Copenhagen Boys' & Men's Cho.—Wöldike (♭ *G.7PK 3*)

NAPOLI Ballet 1842
  (jointly with Lumbye & Pauli)
In the blue grotto
  ☆ Danish Radio—Grøndahl   *G.Z 365*
  (*Haydn: 6 Deutsche Tänze*)
SONG
April Song: Green are spring's hedges
  (*Aprilvise: Grøn er vårens hoek*) (*Møller*)
  B. Loewenfalk (B), K. Olsson (pf.)   *G.X 8134*
  (*Peterson-Berger: Irmelin Rose*)

GAGLIANO, Marco da (*c.* 1575-1642)

  SEE: † ITALIAN SONGS OF THE XVITH & XVIITH CENTURIES

GAGNEBIN, Henri (b. 1886)

Marche des gais lurons fl. & pf.
  J-P. Rampal & F. Gobet   ♭ *Pat.G 1056*
  (*Honegger & Massis*)

Toccata No. 1 pf. 1944
  L. Morel   ♯ *D.LW 5127*
  (*Debussy, Ravel, Marescotti*)   (♯ *Lon.LD 9149*)

Trio, D major fl., vln., pf. 1941
  G-A. Nicolet, H. Schneeberger, W. Lang
                                ♯ *D.LX 3148*
  (*Fornerod*)   (♯ *Lon.LD 9224*)

GAILLARD, Marius-François (b. 1900)

Minutes du monde vlc. & pf. 1952-3
  M-A. Bloch & M-F. Gaillard   ♯ *Od.OD 1016*
  (2ss)

Sonate baroque vlc. & pf. 1950
Vespérale d'été vlc. & pf.
  M-A. Bloch & M-F. Gaillard   ♯ *Od.OD 1011*

GAITO, Constantino (1878-1945)

Quartet No. 2, Str. ("Incaico")
  Pessina Qtt. (6ss)   *ArgV.P 1530/2*
                              (pte. rec.)

GALILEI, Vincenzo (*c.* 1520-1591)

Gagliarda lute — ARR. ORCH. Respighi, q.v.

GALINDO, Blas (b. 1910)

SONGS: (3) Canciones
  1. Jicarita
  2. Mi querer pasaba el rio
  3. Paloma blanca
  P. Curtin (S), G. Tucker (pf.) ♯ *Camb.CRS 203*
  (*Ginastera, Garcia Caturla, Fernández*)

FOLK-SONG ARRS.: Sones Mariachi
  ▽ Mexican Orch.—Chávez (in ♯ *AmC.ML 2080* :
                      o.n. 70332D in set M 414)

GALLES, Jose (1761-1836)

  SEE: † SPANISH KEYBOARD MUSIC

GALLIARD, Johann Ernst (*c.* 1680-1749)

(6) SONATAS, bsn. or vlc. & cont.
No. 1, A minor; No. 3, F major
  ☆ H. Busch (vlc.) & E. Weiss-Mann (hpsi.) (♯ *Allo. 4036:*
                                            also 3087)

GALLON, Noël (b. 1891)

Cantabile cl. & pf.
  J. Lancelot & F. Gobet   ♭ *Pat.G 1053*
  (*Challan, Loucheur & Tomasi*)

SONG: Chanson du vieux Canada
  (an arrt. of Folksong *À la claire fontaine*)
  ☆ C. Panzéra (B), M. Panzéra (pf.) (in ♯ *Clc. 6260*)

GALLOT, Jacques (d. *c.* 1685)

  SEE: RESPIGHI: GLI UCCELLI

GALUPPI, Baldassare (1706-1785)

Concerto a quattro, "No. 2", B flat major[1]
  ed. Mortari
  I Musici Ens.   ♯ *C.CX 1192*
  (*Rossini, Tartini, B. Marcello*)
                    (♯ QCX 10037: FCX 303; Angel. 35086)

Concerto a quattro, "No. 2", D major[1] ed. Mortari
  Società Corelli   ♯ *Vic.LM 1880*
  (*Corelli, Bonporti, Vivaldi*)(♯ FV.A 630292; ItV.A12R 0146)

Overture No. 2, D major[2]
  Italian Cha.—Jenkins   ♯ *HS.HSL 76*
  (*Pergolesi & Cambini*)   (in set HSL-C)

SONATAS, hpsi.
D major, Op. 1, No. 4
  ... Giga only — ARR. VLC. & PF.
  M. Amfiteatrof & O. P. Santoliquido
                                ♯ *ItV.A12R 0140*
  (*Frescobaldi, Veracini, etc.*)

C minor (Pizzi 2; Benvenuti 18)
  ... 1st & 2nd movts., Larghetto & Allegro, only
  E. Contestabile (pf.)   *G.DB 11356*
  (*Ravel: Sonatina, s. 3*)

B flat major (unspec.)
  ... Presto only ed. Silvestri
  ☆ A. B. Michelangeli (♭ *G.7R 148: 7RQ 3017: 7RW 139*)

GAMBINI, Carlo (1818-1865)

Quartet, G minor Strings
  ☆ I.C.B.S. Qtt. (*Boccherini & Corelli*) ♯ *MV.VT 51*

---

[1] Probably Nos. 6 & 3 of 6 *Concertos.*   [2] From modern MS. score, Brussels Cons. Library, from old MS. parts.

GANNE, G. Louis (1862-1923)

(Les) SALTIMBANQUES   Operetta 1899
COMPLETE RECORDING
J. Micheau (S), M. Roux (B), R. Amade (T) etc.,
Cho. & Orch.—Dervaux   ♯ LI.TW 91044/5
(4ss)   (♯ D.FMT 163080/1)

ABRIDGED RECORDING
Soloists & Ensemble—Gressier ♯ Pat.DTX 136
There are many ▽ recordings, including
   Marche grecque: Garde Républicaine Band(*Pat.PA 2521*)
   Marche lorraine: idem (*C.DF 1725, G.K 5467, etc.*)
   Le Père la Victoire: idem (in ♯ *C.FCX 190*), etc.
and numerous selections from *Les Saltimbanques.*

GARCIA CATURLA, Alejandro
(1906-1940)

(2) Poemas Afro-Cubanos   1929
   1. Mari-Sabel   2. Juego Santo
Bitu Manué 1929
   P. Curtin (S), G. Tucker (pf.) ♯ *Camb.CRS 203*
   (*Ginastera, Galindo, Fernández*)

Primera Suite cubana   pf. & wind octet 1930-2
H. Roget & Members French Radio Orch.
   —Tzipine[1]   ♯ C.FCX 220
   (*Roldán & Porter*)   (♯ Angel. 35105)

Short Prelude pf. 1934
   ▽ E. Best (NMQR. 1213)

GARCIA ESTRADA, Juan A. (b. 1895)

Introduction & Waltz   Cha. orch.
   Argentina Radio—Bandini in ♯*ArgOd.LDC 512*

Quartet No. 2   Strings
   Armonia Qtt.   ♭ *ArgOd.BSOAE 4506*

GARDANE, Antoine (d. c. 1570)
SEE: † PARISIAN SONGS OF XVITH CENTURY

GARDINER, Henry Balfour (1877-1950)

COLLECTION
April (Carpenter) Cho. & orch.   1912-3
Overture to a comedy orch.   1913
Philomela (M. Arnold) T, fem. cho. & orch. 1923
Shepherd Fennel's Dance orch.   1910
   A. Young (T), Goldsmith's Choral Union &
   L.S.O.—Austin   ♯ Argo.RG 69
▽ Other recordings include:
   Shepherd Fennel's Dance (on G.C 1469; C.DX 1393; etc.)
   Str. Qtt., B flat major   Kutcher Qtt. (EB.X 563)
   Evening Hymn   Phil. Cho. (G.D 1304)
   & Songs

GARNIER (fl. 1529-1542)
SEE: † ANTHOLOGIE SONORE

GARSI, Santino [di Parma] (c. 1540-1604)

LUTE PIECES 1600
Aria del Gran Duca
Corenta
Balleto I/II/I
La Cesarine
Gagliarda Manfredina
Balla del Serenissimo Duca di Parma
La Mutia
Le ne mente per la gola
   W. Gerwig   ♭ *Pol. 37005*
   (*Neusiedler*, on ♯ *Pol. 13031*)

[1] U.N.E.S.C.O. Recording.

GARZO (fl. XIIIth Cent.)
SEE: † MONUMENTA ITALICAE MUSICAE

GASPARINI, Francesco (1668-1727)
SEE: † ITALIAN AIRS
    † OLD ITALIAN AIRS

GASTOLDI, Giovanni G. (c. 1566-1622)

BALLETTI   (*per cantare, sonare e ballare*, 1593)
Il Contento
Il Premiato
L'Inamorato
Il Piacere
La Bellezza
Gloria d'amore   ø
L'Accesso
Caccia d'amore   ø
Il Martellato   ø
Il Belhumore   ø
Amor vittorioso   ø
Speme amorosa   ø
   Pro Musica Antiqua—Cape ♯ HP.APM 14042
   (*Jannequin*)   [marked ø also on ♭ *Pol. 37033*]

Musica a due voci
   Recorder Trio   in ♯ OL.LD 81
   († Musiciens de la Cour de Bourgogne II)

GAULTIER, Denis (c. 1597-1672)
SEE: † LUTE MUSIC OF THE XVITH & XVIITH CENTURIES

GAULTIER, Jacques (1600-1670)
SEE: † GUITAR RECITAL II

GAUTIER de COINCY (d. 1236)
SEE: † FRENCH TROUBADOUR SONGS

GEHOT, Joseph (1756-18 ?)

Quartet, Str., D major, Op. 7, No. 6
   ☆ New Music Qtt. (*Moller & Peter*)   ♯ ARS. 33

GEISER, Walther (b. 1897)

Symphony, Op. 44 1953
   Suisse Romande—Ansermet   ♯ D.LXT 5097
   (*Oboussier*)   (♯ Lon.LL 1265)

GEMINIANI, Francesco (1687-1762)

(6) CONCERTI GROSSI, Op. 3
1. D major   2. G minor   3. E minor
4. D minor   5. B flat major 6. E minor
COMPLETE RECORDINGS
   Barchet Qtt., Stuttgart Pro Musica Orch.
   —Reinhardt   ♯ E. & AmVox.PL 8290
   [H. Elsner, hpsi.]
   English Baroque Orch.—Scherchen
                                ♯ West.WN 18002

No. 2, G minor
   Sinfonia Ens.—Witold   ♯ EPP.SLP 2
   (*Vivaldi, Torelli, Sammartini*)

No. 3, E minor
   Società Corelli   ♯ ItV.A12R 0098
   (*Marcello, Vivaldi, Carissimi*)
                       (♯ Vic.LM 1767: ♭ set WDM 1767)
SEE ALSO: CORELLI, SONATAS, OP. 5, NOS. 2 & 12, ARR.

Sonata, B flat major   vln. unacc.   (ed. Corti)
R. Odnoposoff   ‡ CHS.CHS 1170
(*Tartini & Vitali*)

GENIN, Paul Agricole (1829-1904)

Fantaisie sur 'Carnaval de Venise', Op. 14 fl. & pf.
F. Marseau & pf.   ‡ D.LX 3138
(*Ries, Durand, Tchaikovsky*)   (‡ Lon.LS 1096)

GENTIAN (fl. 1539-1556)

SEE: † ANTHOLOGIE SONORE (‡ HS.AS 6)

GERMAN, Sir Edward (1862-1936)

HENRY VIII Inc. Music 1892
3 Dances: Morris; Shepherd's; Torch
L.S.O.—Weldon   C.DB 3217
(2ss)   (♭ SED 5515: & in ‡ S 1022)
New Sym.—Olof   ‡ D.LK 4057
(*below*) (‡ Lon.LL 772) (also ‡ D.LW 5059; Lon.LD 9061)
Boston Pops.—Fiedler   ‡ Vic.LM 1803
(*Prokofiev, Dukas, Saint-Saëns*)
☆ City of Birmingham—Weldon (in ‡ AmC.RL 3041)

MERRIE ENGLAND Light Opera 2 Acts 1902
Vocal selections
P. Baird (S), M. Thomas (A), A. Young (T),
J. Cameron (B), Cho. & New Sym.—Olof
                                 ‡ D.LK 4057
(*above & below*)   (‡ Lon.LL 772)

Dances: Hornpipe; Minuet; Rustic Dance; Jig
L.S.O.—Weldon   C.DX 1877
(2ss)   (♭ SED 5515: in ‡ S 1022)

The Yeomen of England B   Act I
F. Harvey (*below*)   ♭ C.SCD 2020
☆ P. Dawson (♭ G.7EG 8093)

Long live Elizabeth Cho. Act I
— ARR. ORCH.
Chas. Williams Orch. (*above*) ♭ C.SCD 2020

NELL GWYNN Inc. Music 1900
3 Dances: Country; Pastoral; Merrymakers'
New Sym.—Olof   ‡ D.LK 4057
(*above*)   (‡ Lon.LL 772)
                     (also ‡ D.LW 5059; Lon.LD 9061)
L.S.O.—Weldon   C.DB 3329/30
(3ss—*Elgar: Salut d'amour*)   (& in ‡ S 1022)
Hamburg Philharmonia—H-J. Walther
                                 MSB. 78020
(*Elgar, Sullivan, etc.* in ‡ MGM.E 3143)
Queen's Hall Light—Williams   Chap.C 145/7
(3ss)

TOM JONES Light Opera 2 Acts 1907
Three Dances: Morris Dance; Gavotte; Jig
L.S.O.—Weldon   ‡ C.S 1022
(*above*)
Queen's Hall Light—Williams   Chap.C 137/8
(2ss)

Welsh Rhapsody orch. 1904
☆ City of Birmingham—Weldon (in ‡ AmC.RL 3041)

GERSHWIN, George (1898-1937)
(Abridged listing only)
COLLECTION
Rhapsody in Blue
(3) Preludes   pf.
Concerto, F major   pf. & orch.
An American in Paris
PORGY & BESS
… Excerpt, Act I, Sc. 1 — ARR. PF.
… Symphonic Picture
M. Gould (pf.) & orch.   ‡ Vic. set LM 6033

PIANO MUSIC COLLECTION
☆ L. Hambro (‡ Cum.CPL 203)

(An) American in Paris orch. 1928
Hamburg Philharmonia—H-J. Walther
                                 ‡ MGM.E 3253
(*Porgy & Bess—Symphonic Picture*)
☆ N.B.C. Sym.—Toscanini[1]   ‡ G.ALP 1107
(*Prokofiev*)   (‡ ItV.A12R 0101)
☆ N.Y.P.S.O.—Rodzinski   ‡ C.S 1003
(*Rhapsody in Blue*)
(‡ VS 801: FA 1001: QS 6002; AmC.CL 700, o.n.
                                        ML 4879)
A. Semprini (pf.) & orch.   ‡ Fnt.LP 109
(*below*   (‡ Fnt.LP 110, d.c.)
Orch.—Marschner (‡ Allo. 3063; Pac.LDAA 71)
Orch.—Shankson (in ‡ Roy. 1609, also ‡ 1806;
                                    ‡ Ply. 12-140)
☆ P. Whiteman Orch. (‡ D.UMT 263072: ♭ EUM 10551;
                     ♭ DCap.LC 6550; ♭ AmD.ED 2196)
Hollywood Sym.—Newman (‡ FMer.MLP 7068)
Kingsway Sym.—Camarata (♭ AmD.ED 3538;
                                 ‡ D.UMT 263036)
— ARR. 4 PFS.   ☆ First Pf. Qtt. (♭ G.7EP 7005, etc.)

Concerto, F major, pf. & orch. 1925
J. Katchen & Orch.—Mantovani ‡ D.LXT 5069
(*Rhapsody in Blue*)   (‡ D.LK 40108; ‡ Lon.LL 1262)
L. Pennario & Pittsburgh Sym.—Steinberg
                                 ‡ DCap.CTL 7046
(2ss)   (‡ Cap.P 8219; T.LCE 8219; ACap.CLCX 036)
S. Bianca & Hamburg Philharmonia
        —H-J. Walther   ‡ P.PMC 1026
(*Rhapsody in Blue*)   (‡ MGM.E 3237)
A. Templeton & Cincinnati Sym.—Johnson
(2ss)   ‡ Rem. 199-184
H. Reims & "Philharmonic" (‡ Allo. 3096)
Sauter-Finegan Orch.(♭ G.7EG 8152; in ‡ Vic.LPM 1051:
                                   ♭ set EPC 1051)
☆ O. Levant & N.Y.P.S.O.—Kostelanetz (‡ AmC.CL 700:
                            o.n. ML 4879: ♭ set A 1047)
… Excerpt — ARR. PF. SOLO D. Schuyler (ArgOd. 66070)

(A) Cuban Overture orch. 1932
☆ A. Kostelanetz Orch. (in ‡ AmC.CL 783)
R. Linda & Concert Orch.—Whiteman
                (in ‡ D.UMT 263072; Crl. 57021)

PORGY AND BESS Opera 3 Acts 1935
COMPLETE RECORDING
☆ C. Williams, I. Matthews, L. Winters, etc. Cho. &
     orch.—Engel   ‡ EPhi.NBL 5016/8
                                 (‡ Phi.A 01115/7L)
[Excerpts on ‡ AmC.ML 4766: AAL 31: ♭ set A 1045;
                                 ‡ Phi.S 06600R]
COLLECTED EXCERPTS
Bess, you is my woman now
I got plenty o' nuttin'
It ain't necessarily so
Summertime
☆ R. Stevens & R. Merrill (♭ G.7EB 6015)
Woman is a sometime thing, and the above
☆ H. Jepson (S), L. Tibbett (T) (♭ Vic.ERAT 23)
Various Excerpts & Selections
C. Calloway, N. Scott, etc.   ‡ Vic.LPM 3156
(*Gershwin: Girl Crazy*)   (♭ set EPA 3156)
B. Peters (B), M. Tynes (S), M. Burton (A), etc., Op. Orch.
     —Belanger   ‡ CHS.CHS 1247
                                 (‡ MMS. 2035)
B. Sönnerstedt (B), I. Quensel (B), E. Tibell (A), etc.
(*Swed*) (4ss)   Symf.RT 1006/7
☆ A. Brown, T. Duncan, N.Y. Orch.—Smallens
     (‡ D.UM 233028; AmD.DL 8024: ♭ set ED 808;
[orig. cast]   Excerpts on ▽ B. 05045/6)
Symphonic Picture (ARR. R. R. Bennett)
N.Y.P.S.O.—Kostelanetz   ‡ EPhi.NBL 5020
(*Tchaikovsky: Pique Dame*)
(‡ AmC.CL 721, o.n. ML 4904: ♭ A 1921 & in ♭ set A 1102)
Minneapolis Sym.—Dorati   ‡ EMer.MG 50016
(*Gould*) (‡ FMer.MLP 7508 : ♭ MEP 14534/5;
                                 ♭ Mer.EP 2-501)
Hamburg Philharmonia—H-J. Walther MSB. 78163/4
(4ss)   (*American in Paris* on ‡ MGM.E 3253)
M.G.M.—Ashley   ‡ MGM.E 3131
(*Oklahoma & Kiss me Kate*)
Hollywood Bowl Pops—Green   ‡ B.LA 8690
                                 (‡ AmD.DL 4051)
☆ Indianapolis Sym.—Sevitzky   ‡ BB.LBC 1059
(*Grieg*)   (♭ set WBC 1059)

[1] Recorded 1945.

Orchestral Selections
G. Melachrino Orch.   **G.C 4211**
   (EH 1439: ♭ *7GF 170: 7PQ 2015*)
Boston Prom.—Fiedler (in ♯ Vic.LM 1879: ♭ *ERA 179;*
  ♭ *ItV.A72R 0020;* ♭ *FV.A 95201;* Excerpts,
             Vic. 10-4215; ♭ *49-4215;* etc.)
Orch.—Gibbons (in ♯ *AmC.AL 39*)
☆ Orch.—Kostelanetz (in ♯ AmC.CL 783)
  etc.

Six Songs — ARR. VLN. & PF. Heifetz
☆ J. Heifetz & E. Bay (♯ B.LAT 8066; ♯ *D.UM 233070;*
   ♯ *AmD.DL 7003* & DL 9760; D.UAT 273572)

Bess, you is my woman — ARR. VLN. & PF. Heifetz
A. Ferraresi & E. Galdieri   **G.HN 3537**

Medley — ARR. 2 HARPS
E. & J. Vito (in ♯ *SOT. 1031* & 10301)

I got plenty o' nuttin'
It ain't necessarily so
Deep river[1]
L. Tibbett (*Falstaff, Don Giovanni,* etc.)   ♯ **Roy. 1627**
(*Omitting* Deep river, in ♭ *Roy.EP 388*)

Bess, you is my woman now Bs
N. Lawrence & M. Thomson (*below*)   *Dur.AI 10239*
— ARR. HARMONICA L. Adler (♭ *Angel. 70025*)

I got plenty o' nuttin' Bs
K. Spencer   **C.DW 5240**
(*Weill: September Song*)   (♭ *SCMW 506*)
N. Lawrence (*Dur.AI 10239*)
R. Bennett (in ♯ Vic.LM 9002: ♭ *set WDM 1341*)
— ARR. ORCH. Anon. Orch.—Shankson (in ♯ Roy. 1609)

Intro. & Lullaby (Summertime)
My man's gone now Act III
A. Brown (S) & Copenhagen Royal Orch.—Hye-Knudsen
                      FMer.M 4123
               (∇ Tono.X 25112)
... Lullaby, only E. Ray (♭ *Véga.P 1506*)
☆ E. Steber (in ♯ Vic. set LCT 6701)

It ain't necessarily so — ARR. HARMONICA
L. Adler (♭ *Angel. 70025*)
Where's my Bess
R. Bennett (B) (in ♯ *Vic.LM 9002:* in ♭ *set WDM 1341*)

(3) Preludes pf.
L. Pennario   ♭ *Cap.FAP 8206*
(*Rhapsody in Blue, theme*)
☆ O. Levant (♭ *AmC.A 1047*)
— ARR. VLN. & PF. Heifetz
☆ J. Heifetz (in ♯ B.LAT 8066; *D.UM 233070* &
      UAT 273572; in ♯ AmD.DL 9760)
... No. 2 only
D. Schuyler (*Concerto excerpt*)   ArgOd. 66070
... No. 2 only — ARRANGEMENTS
VLN. & PF. H. Szeryng & M. Berthelier (in ♯ Pac.LDPC 50)
VLC. & PF.
P. Fournier & E. Lush (in ♯ D.LXT 2766; Lon.LL 700)
HARMONICA L. Adler (♭ *Angel. 70025:* in ♯ *64014*)
ORCH. Stone:
Philharmonia—Korn (in ♯ Allo. 3149)
Anon. Orch.—Shankson (in ♯ Roy. 1609)

Rhapsody in Blue pf. & orch. 1924
J. Katchen & Orch.—Mantovani ♯ **D.LXT 5069**
(*Concerto*) (♯ *D.LK 40108;* ♯ *Lon.LL 1262:* ♭ *BEP 6289*)
(& 2ss, ♯ *D.LF 1226*)
S. Bianca & Hamburg Philharmonia
  —H-J. Walther   ♯ **P.PMC 1026**
(*Concerto*)   (♯ *MGM.E 3237*)
H. Heinemann & N.W. Ger. Phil.—Schüchter
                    ♯ *Imp.ILP 116*
(*Addinsell & Gould*)   (♯ *G.FFLP 1059*)
B. Janis & Winterhalter Orch.   ♯ **BB.LBC 1045**
(*Grofé*) (♭ *set WBC 1045;* ♯ FV.A 530201; 2ss,
        ♭ *Vic.EPA 565: ItV.A72R 0001*)
A. Semprini & Orch. (*above*)   ♯ *Fnt.LP 109*
☆ O. Levant & Philadelphia—Ormandy   ♯ *C.S 1003*
(*American in Paris*) (♯ *VS 801: FA 1001: QS 6002;*
   AmC.CL 700: o.n.ML 4879: ♭ *set A 1643*)
N. Seguirini & Rome Orch.—Nicelli (♯ Cet.LPC 55004)
J. Panenka & F.O.K.—Smetáček (♭ U.H 24436/7)
G. Stein & Orch.—Marschner (♯ Allo. 3063;
                  Pac.LDAA 71)
Royale Concert Orch.—Everett (♯ Roy. 1421; *Var. 69139*)

☆ H. Kiessling & Orch.—Edelhagen (♭ *Epic.EG 7067*)
E. Wild & Orch.—Whiteman (♭ *Crl.EC 8111:* ♯ *57021*)
A. Templeton & Orch.—Kostelanetz (♯ AmC.CL 795)
V. Rivkin & Pro Musica—Dixon (♭ *AmVox.VIP 30200*)
L. Pennario & Whiteman Orch. (♯ *DCap.LC 6551*)
R. Bargy & Orch.—Whiteman (in ♯ D.UMT 263072;
                   ♭ *AmD.ED 2195*)
A. Sandford & Kingsway Sym.—Camarata
    (♭ *AmD.ED 3539;* ♯ D.UMT 263036)
— ARR. 2 PFS. & ORCH.
☆ J. & A. Iturbi & Vic. Sym.   in ♯ Vic.LM 9018
(*J. C. Chambers: All American Suite;*   (♭ *ERA 145*)
  Debussy, Infante, etc.)
— ARR. 4 PFS. First Pf. Qtt. (♭ *G.EP 7005,* etc.)
— ARR. 2 HARPS E. & J. Vito (in ♯ SOT. 1031 & 10301)

Second Rhapsody pf. & orch. 1931
H. Reims & Berlin Sym.—Rubahn ♯ **Roy. 1512**
(*Beethoven*)
☆ R. Bargy & Whiteman Orch. (in ♯ D.UMT 263072)

Variations on 'I got rhythm' pf. & orch.
∇ E. Wild & Whiteman Orch. (in ♯ *Crl. 57021*)

GERSTER, Ottmar (b. 1897)

Oberhessische Bauerntänze
E. Berlin Police Orch.—Kaufmann
                       Eta. 130216/7
(3½ss—*Höffer: Erntelied und Tanz*)

PARTSONGS
Hymnus der Jugend (Marchwitza)
Leipzig Radio Youth Cho.—Sandig (*Eta. 110228*)
Karl Marx Lied (Stranka)
E. Ger. Folk Cho.—Willberg (*Eta. 110243*)
Träume und Taten (Dohna)
Berlin Radio Youth Cho.—Dressel (*Eta. 110245*)

(5) Pieces for Accordeon
I. Slota-Krieg (4ss)   *Eta. 130112/3*
SONGS
(Die) heilige Familie (Geiger)
S. Schöner (S), F. Schröder (pf.)   *Eta. 120204*
(*Reger: Mariä Wiegenlied*)
Verkündigung (Geiger)
G. Wuestemann (S), Albert Busch (hpsi.)   *Eta. 120203*
(*Folksongs*)

Symphony No. 2 (Thuringian)
Leipzig Gewandhaus—Konwitschny
                   ♯ *Eta. 720013*

GERVAIS, Charles Hubert (1671-1714)

(Le) MALADE IMAGINAIRE
Inc. Music to Molière's play[2]
Orch.—Cadou   ♯ **Ll.TW 91076/7**
(in a performance of the play)   (♯ D.FMT 163507/8)

O sacrum convivium Motet
M. Casadesus Ens.   in ♯ **Plé.P 3083**
(† *Musiques à la Chapelle du Roy*)   (♯ West.WN 18167)

GERVAISE, Claude (fl. *c.* 1550)

SEE: † ANTHOLOGIE SONORE
    † DANCERIES ET BALLETS

GESUALDO, Don Carlo, Prince of Venosa
                  (c. 1560-1613)

MADRIGALS 5 vv.
  (Bk. IV: 1596; Bk. V-VI, 1611)
COLLECTIONS
Luci serene e chiare Bk. IV
Ecco morirò dunque ... Hai già mi discoloro Bk. IV
Io tacerò ... Invan dunque Bk. IV
Dolcissima mia vita Bk. V
Itene ò miei sospiri Bk. V
Moro lasso al mio duolo Bk. VI
R. Lamy Ensemble   ♯ **Pol. 14045**
(*Marenzio*)

(continued on next page)

---

[1] Not from *Porgy & Bess.*
[2] Unspecified items; labelled *Gevrais* (sic) but probably some work by this composer has been adapted here. The recording also contains items by M. A. Charpentier and Lully; all for *Cérémonie du Malade et d'une Évocation de la mort de Molière,* added as Epilogue. The music for the play itself is by Destouches.

MADRIGALS (continued)
O sempre crudo amore   Bk. IV
Sparge la morte   Bk. IV
Hor che in gioia   Bk. IV
Ecco morirò dunque   Bk. IV
Moro, moro, e mentre sospiro   Bk. IV
   Vienna Cha. Cho.—Schmid   # Phi.N 00682R
   (Hindemith)

Dolcissima mia vita   Bk. V
Io pur respiro   Bk. VI
   Yale Univ. Music School Cho.—Hindemith
                  in # Over.LP 4
   († Yale University I)

Moro lasso al mio duolo   Bk. VI
  ☆ E. Passani Cho. (in † # HS.AS 9)

GHEDINI, Giorgio Federico (b. 1892)

(L') Olmeneta   Concerto, 2 vlcs. & orch.   1951
  B. Mazzacurati, M. Gusella & Naples Scarlatti
  Orch.—Ghedini   # Csm.CLPS 1039

Litanie alla Vergine   S, fem. cho. & orch.   1926
  M. Rizzi, Cho. & Orch.—Ghedini
                # Csm.CLPS 1046
  (Piccinni, Traetta, Paisiello, etc.)

SEE ALSO: J. S. BACH: Musicalisches Opfer

GHEORGHIU, Valentin (b. 1928)

Trio, A major   pf., vln., vlc.   1949
  Gheorghiu Trio   # Sup.LPM 206
              (# U. 5192C)

GHEYN, Mathias van den (1721-1788)

SEE: † CARILLON PIECES

GHIRARDELLO da FIRENZE (XIVth Cent.)

SEE: † ANTHOLOGIE SONORE
     † MADRIGALS & CACCIE

GIANNEO, Luis (b. 1897)

Canción
  M. Landi (S) & pf.   ArgV. pte.
Criolla   Strings
  Wagner Assoc. Qtt.   ♭ ArgOd.BSOAE 4501
  (Tchaikovsky: Andante cantabile)
Danza Aymará   orch.
  Argentine Radio Cha.—Bandini   in # ArgOd.LDC 512
Huella; Bailecito   Strings
  Pessina Trio   ArgV.P 1533
             (Pte. rec.)
Zapateado   Quenas
Pericon   Bailecito
  A. Barletta (bandoneon)   in # SMC. 547
(El) Tarco en flor   orch.   1931
  Sym. Orch.—Gianneo   # Pam.LRC 15501
  (E. Casella, Rogatis, Aguirre)

GIANONCELLI, Bernardo (fl. c. 1650)

SEE: † RESPIGHI: Antiche Danze, Suite 2

GIBBONS, Ellis (1573-c. 1650)

SEE: † TRIUMPHS OF ORIANA

GIBBONS, Orlando (1583-1625)

VOCAL
Behold, thou hast made my days   Anthem
  A. Hepworth (T), Hampstead Chu. Cho. &
    Strings—Westrup   G.HMS 38
  († History of Music in Sound)   (in # Vic. set LM 6029)
Great King of Gods . . . Amen   only
  Coronation Choir   in # G.ALP 1058
  († Coronation of Queen Elizabeth II)
O Lord, increase my faith   Anthem   4 vv.
  Festival Singers—Iseler   # Hall.ChS 3
  (Lassus, Byrd, Mundy, Willan)
(The) Silver Swan   Madrigal   5 vv.   1612
  St. Paul's Cath. Cho.—Dykes Bower
               in # C.CX 1237
  (Bennet, Morley, Haydn, Wood, etc.)
               (# Angel. 35139 in set 3516)
  New England Cons. Cho.—de Varon
               in # HS.HSL 2068
  († English Madrigals)
What is our life   (Raleigh)   Madrigal   5 vv.   1612
  N.Y. Pro Musica Ens.—Greenberg
               in # AmC.ML 5051
  († Evening of Elizabethan Verse & Music)
INSTRUMENTAL
Fantasia No. 3
  Basle Schola Viol Ens.   G.HMS 41
  († History of Music in Sound)   (in # Vic. set LM 6029)
Fantasias Nos. 6 & 4   (of set of 9)   orig. viols.
  Musicians' Workshop Recorder Consort
               in # CEd.CE 1018
  († Recorder Music of Six Centuries)
KEYBOARD
(An) Allman: 'The King's Juell'   (Cosyn 78)
  M. Hodsdon (virginals)   G.HMS 42
  († History of Music in Sound)   (in # Vic. set LM 6029)
Fancy in A minor
The Lord of Salisbury—his Pavane & Galliard
    (Parthenia 18/19)
  T. Dart (org. & hpsi.)   in # LOL.OL 50075
  († Masters of Early English Keyboard Music)
. . . Pavan   only
  C. J. Chiasson (hpsi.)   in # Nix.LLP 8037
  († Elizabethan Love Songs)   (# Lyr.LL 37)
Whoope, doe me no harme, good man
    (MS, Ch. Ch., Oxford)
  S. Bloch (virginals)   in # CHS.CHS 1125
  († Music in Shakespeare's Time)

GIGOUT, Eugène (1844-1925)

ORGAN MUSIC
Grand Chœur dialogué
  M. Salvador   in # TMS. 1/2
  (Gounod, Purcell, Bach, etc.)
  ▽ E. P. Biggs (in AmC. set M 802; # ML 4195)
Scherzo   ▽ G. D. Cunningham (G.C 1650)
Toccata, B minor
  F. Germani   G.C 4229
  (Torres: Saeta)
  M-C. Alain   V# Era.LDE 1014
  (Boëllmann & Widor)
  ▽ V. Fox (Vic. 10-1208)
    E. Commette (C.D 11026; AmC. 50125D)

GILARDI, Gilardo (b. 1889)

(El) Gaucho con botas neuvas
  State Sym. Orch.—Kinsky   ArgV.P 1488
              (pte. rec.)

= Long-playing, 33⅓ r.p.m.   ♭ = 45 r.p.m.   ♮ = Auto. couplings, 78 r.p.m.

174

GIMÉNEZ, Gerónimo (1854-1923)

ZARZUELAS, etc. (Abridged listings only)
(El) BAILE DE LUIS ALONSO 1 Act *c.* 1896
Intermezzo
  Madrid Cha.—Argenta   in ♯ **LI.TW 91020**
  (♭ *Ambra.EMGE 70018*: in ♯ MCC 30002;
                      & ♯ Mont.FM 6)
  Madrid Theatre Orch.—Moreno Torroba
           in ♯ **B.AXTL 1077**
           (in ♯ AmD.DL 9735)
  Colón Theatre—Cases   **ArgOd. 66052**
         (♭ *BSOAE 4523*: in ♯ *LDC 511*)
  Sym.—Ferrer   in ♯ *Reg.LC 1002*
     (♯ *Pam.LRC 15507*; & ♭ *Reg.SEDL 107*)
  Madrid Theatre Orch.—Machado
           in ♯ **B.AXTL 1074**
     (♯ SpC.CCL 35002; ♯ AmD.DL 9757)
  ▽ Sym.—Capdevila (ArgOd. 177623)

(El) BARBERO DE SEVILLA
Polonesa A. M. Olaria (S)   in ♯ **Mont.FM 17**

(La) BODA DE LUIS ALONSO 1 Act 1897
Intermezzo
  Colón Theatre—Cases   in ♯ *ArgOd.LDC 504*
                (♭ *BSOAE 4523*)
  Sym.—Ferrer   in ♯ **Pam.LRC 15905**
  (in ♯ Reg.LCX 104; Angel. 65008; C.FSX 104;
                & in ♭ *Angel. 70018*)
  Madrid Cha.—Argenta   in ♯ **LI.TW 91020**
  (in ♯ Mont.FM 6; ♯ Ambra.MCC 30002 & MCCP 29000)

(La) GITANA BLANCA 1 Act (jointly with Vives)
  L. de Cordoba, E. Rincón, etc., Span. Radio
  Cho. & Madrid Cha. Orch.—Navárro
  (*Chapi*)   ♯ **Mont.FM 56**

(La) TORRE DEL ORO 1892
Prelude
  Madrid Theatre—Moreno Torroba
           in ♯ **AmD.DL 9789**
Intermezzo
  Madrid Cha.—Argenta   in ♯ **LI.TW 91020**
  (in ♯ Mont.FM 6; ♯ Ambra.MCC 30002: ♭ *MGE 60001*)

(La) TEMPRANICA 1 Act 1900
  L. Sagi Vela, D. Pérez, T. Silva, etc., Madrid
  Radio Cho. & Cha. Orch.—Navarro
                ♯ **Mont.FM 49**
Introduction & Zapateado
  Madrid Theatre—Moreno Torroba
           in ♯ **AmD.DL 9789**
Intermezzo; Escena
  Sym.—Ferrer   **Reg.M 10046**
         (♭ *SEDL 111*: in ♯ *LC 1003*)
Aria (unspec.) L. Berchman (S)   in ♯ **Mont.FM 28**

(Los) VOLUNTARIOS
March Spanish Air Force Band (in ♯ **B.LAT 8075**;
                     AmD.DL 9764)

GINASTERA, Alberto Evaristo (b. 1916)

Concertantes variaciones orch. 1953
  Minneapolis Sym.—Dorati   ♯ **Mer.MG 50047**
  (*Britten*)

Cuyana (*3 Pieces for piano*, No. 1) 1940
  H. Giordano   *ArgOd. 57051*
  (*E. Calcagno: Tocatta*)

(3) Danzas Argentinas pf. 1937
1. Danza del viejo boyero
2. Danza de la moza donosa
3. Danza del gaucho matrero
  A. de Raco   **ArgOd. 66006**

Estancias Ballet Suite 1941
... **Danza del Trigo; Danza final** (Malambro)
  Colón Theatre—Martin   **ArgOd. 66024**
         (♭ *BSOA 4005: BOSAE 4510*)

(El) Fausto Criollo, Overture Orch. 1943
  Municipal Sym. Orch.   **ArgV. pte.**

Impresiones de la Luna fl. & cha. orch. 1934
  Argentine Radio—Bandini   **ArgOd. 66009**
               (in ♯ *LDC 505*)

Malambo pf. 1940
  P. Sebastiani   **ArgV. 66-6158**
  (*Granados: Goyescas, No. 4*)

Milonga pf.[1]
  L. Brunelli   *ArgV. 66-0012*
  (*López Buchardo: Canción del carretero*)
  A. Barletta (bandoneon) (in ♯ *SMC. 547*)

Pampeana No. 2 Rhapsody vlc. & pf. 1950
  A. Odnoposoff & B. Huberman **ArgV. 68-8047**
  (2ss)

Pampeana No. 3 (A Pastoral Symphony) orch.
  f.p. 1954
  Louisville—Whitney   ♯ **LO. 10**
  (*Bergsma, Sauguet & Ward*)

(10) Preludios Americanos pf. 1944
... Vidula, Homenaje a Roberto Garcia Morillo,
  Triste, & Danza Criolla, only
  S. Singer   **ArgOd. 66062**
  (*Aguirre: Gato & Huella*)

Quartet No. 1, Strings 1948
  Pessina Qtt.   ♯ *ArgOd.LDC 526*

Sonata pf. 1952
  J. Harris   (*Chávez*)   ♯ **PFCM.CB 187**

SONGS: Collection
(5) CANCIONES POPULARES ARGENTINAS (Trad.) 1943
  1. Chacarera
  2. Triste (*see below*)
  3. Zamba
  4. Arrorró
  5. Gato
Canción al árbol del olvido (Valdés) 1938[2]
  P. Curtin (S), G. Tucker (pf.)   ♯ *Camb.CRS 203*
  (*Garcia Caturla, Galindo, Fernández*)

Canción al árbol del olvido[2] (Valdés)
  E. Arizmendi (S) & orch.   *ArgOd. 57024*
  (*Guastavino: La Rosa y el sauce*) (& ArgC. 302001)
  M. Plaza (M-S)   in ♯ **Roy. 1561**

Triste (C.P.5)
  G. Souzay (B), D. Baldwin (pf.)
           ♭ *ArgLon.DLCE 6501*
  (*Guastavino, López Buchardo, Nin*)
  M. Plaza (M-S)   in ♯ **Roy. 1561**

GIORDANI, Giuseppe (*c.* 1753-1768)

Concerto, pf. & orch., C major, Op. 20, No. 2[3]
  C. Bussotti & Italian Cha.—Jenkins
                ♯ **HS.HSL 77**
  (*Valentini & Brunetti*)   (in set HSL-C)

Caro mio ben[4]
  M. Klose (A)   ♭ *Pol. 32027*
  (*Handel: Serse, Largo*)
  Z. Milanov (S), B. Kunc (pf.) in ♯ **Vic.LM 1915**
  (*Brahms, Schumann, etc.*)
  G. Prandelli (T), D. Marzollo (pf.)
              in ♯ **AmVox.PL 7930**
  († Old Italian Airs)   (*continued on next page*)

---

[1] Transcription by composer of song *Canción al árbol del olvido.*
[2] For pf. version, see above: *Milonga.*
[3] It is not certain which of the brothers Giordani composed this work. The edition of Op. 20 in the Library of the *Gesellschaft der Musikfreunde*, Vienna, does not contain the Christian name. Library of Congress catalogue attributes to Giuseppe.
[4] Previously attrib. to Tommaso Giordani (1733-1806), but now thought to be by his brother.

Caro mio ben (*continued*)

M. Vitale (S), A. Beltrami (pf.)   *Cet.AT 0317*
(*Respighi: Nebbie*)   (in ‡ *LPC 55001*)

☆ B. Gigli (T) & orch.   in ‡ *G.ALP 1174*
(† *Italian Classic Songs*) (& ♭ *G.7RF 266:* in ‡ *FALP 340:*
QALP 10073*)

☆ R. Schock (T) & orch. (♭ *G.7PW 507:*
in ‡ *WDLP 1501*)

H. Schlusnus (B) (♭ *Pol. 30151*)

☲ A. Crossley (A) (♭ *Vic.Pte**: o.n. *Vic. 81001**)
J. Schwarz (B) (in ‡ *Ete. 498**)

Accompaniment etc. for practice (in ‡ *VS.MH 1002*)

GIORDANO, Umberto (1867-1948)

OPERAS
ANDREA CHÉNIER 4 Acts 1896
COMPLETE RECORDINGS

Andrea Chénier	J. Soler (T)
Carlo Gerard	U. Savarese (B)
Maddalena di Coigny ...	R. Tebaldi (S)
Contessa di Coigny }	I. Colasanti (M-S)
Madelon }	
Roucher } ...	G. Ferrein (Bs)
Fouquier-Tinville }	

etc. Italian Radio Cho. & Orch.—Basile
‡ **CCet. set 1244**

(6ss) (Excerpts on ‡ *CCet.A 50169*)   (‡ *Pol. 18243/5*)

☆ G. Sarri (T), A. M. Serra (B), F. Sacchi (S), etc.
Rome Op. Cho. & orch.—Paoletti
(6ss)   ‡ *Nix.ULP 9218-1/3*

☆ B. Gigli (T), G. Bechi (B), M. Caniglia (S), etc., La
Scala Cho. & orch.—O. de Fabritiis
‡ *Vic. set LCT 6014*
(4ss)   (‡ *G.FJLP 5040/1: QALP 10069/70*)

☆ L. Marini (T), L. B. Rasa (S), etc. La Scala Cho. &
orch.—Molajoli   (4ss)   ‡ *AmC. set EL 10*

ACT I

Son sessant' anni B
U. Savarese   **Cet.BB 25297**
(*Nemico della patria*)

Un dì all' azzuro spazio (*Improvviso*) T
M. del Monaco   in ‡ *D.LXT 2928*
(& in ‡ *D.LXT 2964: LW 5121;* Lon.LL 990: *LD 9132*
& LL 1025)
(*Loreley—Nel verde . . .* on *D.X 598*)

B. Powell   in ‡ *Dely.EC 3136*
(*below; Fedora, Elisir, etc.*)

M. Filippeschi   *G.S 10602*
(*Aida—Celeste Aida*)

J. Soler   *Cet.PE 187*
(*Si fui soldato*)

W. Kmentt (*Ger*)   in ‡ *Phi.S 06076R*
(*below; Elisir d'amore, Gioconda, etc.*)

☆ M. Lanza (in ‡ *G.ALP 1202:* ♭ *7RQ 3011;* ♭ *Vic.ERA 110*)

☲ A. Bonci (in ‡ *Sca. 811**)
C. Albani (*AF.AGSB 65**)
B. Gigli (in ‡ *Vic. set LCT 6701**)

ACT II

Credo a una possanza
... Io non ho amato   T
☆ A. Cortis   *IRCC.ABHA 2*

☲ B. de Muro   in ‡ *SBDH.GL 1**
G. Zenatello   in ‡ *SBDH.LLP 8**

Udite! sono sola! S & T
R. Tebaldi & J. Soler (from set)
in ‡ *CCet.A 50178*
(*below; Sonnambula, Bohème, etc.*)

ACT III

Nemico della patria   B
G. Valdengo   **Cet.PE 197**
(*Nozze di Figaro—Non più andrai*) (♭ *Cet.EPO 0318;*
♭ *Cap.FAP 7016*)

U. Savarese   **Cet.BB 25297**
(*Son sessant' anni*)

G. Taddei   **Cet.BB 25300**
(*Otello—Credo*)   (in ‡ *LPC 55006*)
A. Hiolski (*Pol*)   *Muza.X 2186*
☆ J. C. Thomas   in ‡ *Cam.CAL 199*
☲ T. Ruffo   in ‡ *G.FJLP 5004**: *QJLP 104**

La mamma morta   S
M. M. Callas   in ‡ *C.CX 1231*
(*La Wally, Mefistofele, Barbiere*) (‡ *QCX 10129;*
Angel. 35223)

R. Tebaldi   **Cet.BB 25298**
(*Traviata—Di Provenza . . .*)   (from set)

D. Kirsten   in ‡ *AmC.ML 4730*

G. Frazzoni   in ‡ *Cet.LPV 45003*
(*Tosca, Cavalleria Rusticana, etc.*)

M. C. Verna   in ‡ *Cet.LPC 55005*
(*Ernani, Adriana Lecouvreur, Otello, etc.*)

V. Petrova   in ‡ *Ace. 1007/8*
(*Tosca, Gioconda, Cavalleria, etc.*)

☆ R. Tebaldi   in ‡ *Fnt.LP 301*
L. B. Raisa   in ‡ *Vic.set LCT 6701*

Si, fui soldato T
M. del Monaco   *G.DA 11350*
(*Martha—Ach, so fromm*) (♭ *7EB 6006: 7ERF 137:*
7ERQ 120: & in ‡ *QBLP 5021: FBLP 1050*)

J. Soler   *Cet.PE 187*
(*Un dì all'azzurro spazio*)

☆ G. Masini (*Orf. 53002*)

ACT IV

Come un bel dì di maggio   T
R. Tucker   in ‡ *AmC.ML 4750*

G. Poggi   in ‡ *D.LX 3127*
(‡ *Lon.LD 9106*)

B. Powell (*above & below*) in ‡ *Dely.EC 3136*

W. Kmentt (*Ger*) (*above*) in ‡ *Phi.S 06076R*

☆ F. Tagliavini   in ‡ *CCet.A 50155*
G. Masini   *Orf. 53002*
M. Lanza   ♭ *G.7ERQ 127;* ♭ *Vic.ERA 110*
☲ C. Albani   *AF.AGSA 13**

Vicino a te . . . La nostra morte S & T
J. Hammond & R. Schock   *G.DB 21260*
(ED 1247)
R. Tebaldi & J. Soler (from set)
(*above*)   in ‡ *CCet.A 50178*
☲ C. Boninsegna & L. Bolis (in ‡ *Sca. 813**)

(La) CENA DELLE BEFFE 4 Acts 1924
Sempre così S Act II
Mi chiama Lisabetta S Act III
☆ F. Alda (*AF.AGSA 9*)

FEDORA 3 Acts 1898

ACT I

O grandi occhi   S
☲ G. Russ (in ‡ *Sca. 808**)

Ed ecco il suo ritratto   S
N. de Rosa   *Cet.AT 0402*
(*Amico Fritz—Son pochi fiori*)

ACT II

La donna russa   B
☲ T. Ruffo (in ‡ *HRS. 3005**)

Amor ti vieta   T
G. Poggi   in ‡ *D.LX 3127*
(in ‡ *Lon.LD 9106*)

B. Powell   in ‡ *Dely.EC 3136*
(*above; Elisir, Lucia, A. Chénier*)

G. Gari, S. Leff (pf.)   in ‡ *Mur.P 104*
(*followed by pf. acc. only*)

☆ A. Pertile   in ‡ *Ete. 492*
S. Islandi   *G.DA 5278,* d.c.
☲ L. Muratore   *HRS. 1058**
G. Anselmi & pf. in ‡ *Ete. 711** & in ‡ *Sca. 816**

---

‡ = Long-playing, 33⅓ r.p.m.   ♭ = 45 r.p.m.   ☲ = Auto. couplings, 78 r.p.m.

Mia madre   S & T
... Tenor part only   ♭ F. de Lucia (in ♯ CEd. set 7002*)

Vedi, io piango   T & S
... Tenor part only   ☆ A. Pertile (in ♯ Ete. 492)

ACT III

Waltz (*"Elite Waltz"*)   orch.
  ☆ Cincinnati Summer Op.—Cleva (in ♯ B.AXTL 1035;
    AmD.DL 8053: ♭ ED 3525; ♯ D.UST 233087;
       AFest.CFR 12-457)

Death Scene   S & T
  ♭ G. Russ & E. Garbin (in ♯ Sca. 808*)

MADAME SANS-GÊNE   3 Acts (*Ital*)   1915
Che me non facchio   ♭ C. Muzio (in ♯ LI.TWV 91053*)[1]

MALA VITA   3 Acts   1892
  (revised as "IL VOTO" 1897)
Tutto e già pronto   T   ♭ F. Corradetti (*IRCC. 3148**)

MARCELLA   3 Acts   1907
O mia Marcella   T   ♭ G. Anselmi (in ♯ Ete. 711*)

SIBERIA   3 Acts   1903
O bella mia   B   Act I   ♭ T. Ruffo (in ♯ SBDH.LLP 7*)
Nel suo amor rianimata   S   Act I
  ♭ E. Carelli (in ♯ HRS. 3004*)
T'incontrai per via   T   Act I
  ♭ G. Zenatello (in ♯ SBDH.LLP 8*)
  A. Bassi & U. Giordano (pf.) (in ♯ FRP. 1*)
Orride steppe!   T   Act II
  ♭ G. Zenatello (in ♯ SBDH.LLP 8*)
È qui con te   S & T   Act II
  ♭ R. Storchio & G. Zenatello (in ♯ SBDH.LLP 8*)
Non odi là il martir   S   Act III
  ♭ E. Carelli (in ♯ HRS. 3004*)

GIULIANI, Mauro (1780-*c*. 1840)

  SEE ALSO: † SEGOVIA CONCERT

Praeludium, A minor, Op. 83, No. 2   guitar
  A. Malukoff   ♯ *Rom.RR 7*
  (*Tárrega & Sor*)

GLANVILLE-HICKS, Peggy (b. 1912)

Choral Suite (Donne) fem. cho., ob. & str.   1937
  ▽ Cho. & Str. Orch.   *OL. 100*

Concertino da Camera   pf., fl., cl., bsn.   1943
  (f.p. 1945)
Sonata   pf. & percussion   f.p. 1952
  C. Bussotti & N.Y. Woodwind & Percussion
    Groups   ♯ *AmC.ML 4990*
  (*Lopatnikoff*)

(3) Gymnopédies   1935, rev. 1954
  R.I.A.S. Sym.—Perlea   ♯ *Rem. 199-188*
  (*Brant & Rudhyar*)

Sonata   harp   1950
  N. Zabaleta   ♯ *Eso.ES 523*
  (*Tailleferre, Tournier, Hindemith, etc.*)

(The) TRANSPOSED HEADS   Opera   6 Scenes
                      1954
COMPLETE RECORDING
    Sita ...   . A. Nossaman (S)
    Shridaman ...   . M. Harlan (T)
    Nanda ...   . W. Pickett (B)
etc.; cho. & Louisville Orch.—Bomhard   ♯ *LO. 6*
(3ss)

GLAZOUNOV, Alexander K. (1865-1936)

Ballade, Op. 78   orch.
  State Sym.—Gauk   ♯ *USSR.D 519*
  (*Balakirev*)

Album leaf   horn & orch.
  ☆ T. Dokshitser & Radio Sym.—Samosud
                    (*USSRM.D 00343*)

Bauernfräulein   Ballet
  Bolshoi Theatre—Fayer   ♯ *USSR.D 683/6*
  (4ss)

Carnival, Overture, Op. 45   orch.
  ☆ Chicago Sym.—Stock (in ♯ AmC.RL 3022)

Chant du ménestrel, Op. 71   vlc. & pf. or orch.
  M. Rostropovich & Youth Sym.—Kondrashin
  (2ss)   *USSR. 17324/5*
                (& *USSRM.D 1407*)

Christmas Singers (from *Festival Day*[2])   str. qtt.   1887
  USSR. Qtt.   *USSR. 20920/1*
  (*Liadov & Rimsky*)
  ☆ Galimir Qtt. (♯ Clc. 6148)

Concerto, A minor, Op. 82   vln. & orch.   1904
  T. Magyar & Residentie—v. Otterloo
                   ♯ *Phi.A 00269L*
  (*Sibelius*)   (♯ Epic.LC 3184)
  M. Rabin & Philharmonia—v. Matačić
                   ♯ *C.CX 1281*
  (*Paganini*)   (♯ Angel. 35259)
  A. Gabriël & R.I.A.S. Sym.—G. L. Jochum
  (*Sibelius*)   ♯ *Rem. 199-191*
  ☆ D. Oistrakh & USSR. State Sym.—Kondrashin
                   ♯ *Per.SPL 598*
  (*Beethoven: Vln. Concerto*)   (♯ *CdM.LDA 8041*)
  (*Dvořák on* ♯ Csm.CRLP 137)
  (*Fantasia, on* ♯ *USSR.D 03*; alternative coupling,
                          Tchaikovsky)
  ☆ H. Girdach & Berlin Radio—Schultz
                 (♯ AFest.CFR 10-603)
  N. Milstein & Victor Sym.—Steinberg
                 (♯ G.FALP/QALP 241)

Concerto No. 1, F minor, Op. 92   pf. & orch.
  S. Richter & Moscow Youth Sym.
    —Kondrashin   ♯ *Mon.MWL 321*
  (*Valses de Concert*) (2ss, ♯ *CdM.LDA 8135*;
                     ♯ *USSR.D 1067/8*)
  (*Rimsky-Korsakov & Prokofiev, on* ♯ CHS.CHS 1316)
  (*Chopin, on* ♯ Csm.CLPS 210)

Fantasia, Op. 53   orch.
  Moscow Radio—Rakhlin   ♯ *USSR.D 04*
  (*Concerto, vln.*)

From the Middle Ages, Op. 79   Suite   orch.
  Moscow Radio—Golovanov   ♯ *USSR.D 640/1*
  (2ss)
  ☆ Indianapolis Sym.—Sevitzky ♯ *BB.LBC 1062*
  (*Haydn*)   (♭ set WBC 1062)

March on a Russian theme, Op. 76   orch.
  Moscow Radio—Golovanov   *USSRM.D 00188*
  (*Khovanshchina—Prelude*)   (& in ♯ *CdM.LDA 8041*)

Meditation, Op. 32   vln. & pf.
  D. Oistrakh & V. Yampolsky
              in ♯ *Van.VRS 6020*
  (*Rachmaninoff, etc. on USSRM.D 1408*)
              (in ♯ Csm.CRLPX 011)
  ☆ N. Milstein & A. Balsam (♭ G.7RF 279)

Mélodie arabe, Op. 20, No. 1   vlc. & pf.
  M. Rostropovich & A. Dedyukhin
                 USSRM.D 451
  (*Tchaikovsky: Pezzo capriccioso*)
  M. Rostropovich & USSR. State—Anosov
              USSR. 022724/5
  (2ss)   (*Chant du ménestrel on USSRM.D 1406*)

(3) Morceaux, Op. 49   pf.
... No. 1, **Prelude**, only
  V. Sofronitzky   *USSR. 21854*
  (*Scriabin: Prelude, Op. 35, No. 2*)

(5) Novellettes, Op. 15   Str. qtt.
  Hungarian Qtt.   ♯ *CHS.CHS 1183*
  (*Tchaikovsky: Qtt. No. 1*)
  Komitas Qtt.   (4ss)   *USSRM.D 1362/5*

---

[1] From Edison & Pathé hill & dale recordings. This disc was withdrawn very soon after issue.
[2] Composed jointly with Liadov & Rimsky-Korsakov.

Polka from "Les Vendredis" Str. qtt.[1]
— ARR. ORCH.
Philharmonia—Malko   ♯ *G.DLP 1092*
(*Liadov & Borodin*)

QUARTETS, Strings
No. 3, G major (*Quatuor slave*)
Glazounov Qtt.   ♯ *USSR.D 1506/7*
(12ss)

No. 4, A major, Op. 64
Bolshoi Theatre Qtt.   (12ss)   *USSR. 19839/50*

Rhapsodie orientale, Op. 29 orch.
Moscow Radio—Gauk   ♯ *USSR.D 01456*
(*Spendiarov: Three palm trees*)

RAYMONDA, Op. 57 Ballet
Complete Orch. Suite
Paris Phil.—Rosenthal   ♯ *DCap.CTL 7036*
                          (♯ *Cap.P 8184; T.LCE 8184*)
☆ Boston Prom.—Fiedler (♯ *Cam.CAL 166*)

Shorter Orch. Suite
Bolshoi Theatre—Fayer   ♯ *Van.VRS 432*
(*Glier: Red Poppy*)   (♯ *USSR.D 490/1*)
(*Scènes de Ballet*, on ♯ *Csm.CRLP 218*)
[Intro. & Romanesca only, in ♯ *CdM.LDA 8041*;
    Variations & Coda, Act II, *USSR. 18492/4*, Adagio,
                                       USSR. 23898/9]

... Valse fantasque
☆ Philharmonia—Malko (in ♯ BB.LBC 1022:
                          ♭ set *WBC 1022*)

... Entr'acte No. 1
Orch.—Voorhees (in ♯ Alld. 3001: ♭ *EP 3001*; ♯ *MTW. 573*)

— — ARR. VLN. & PF.
I. Bezrodny & S. Wakman   ♯ *Phi.S 06048R*
(*Taneiev, Prokofiev, Rachmaninoff*)
L. Kogan & pf. (*USSR. 022761*)

Adagio & Valse — ARR. VLN. & PF.
L. Kogan & pf.   *USSRM.D 00127*
(*Khachaturian: Gayaneh, excpts.*)

(Les) RUSES D'AMOUR, Op. 61 Ballet 1899
COMPLETE RECORDING
Bolshoi Theatre—Fayer   ♯ *Csm.CRLP 165*
(*Valses de concert*)
[Excerpts on *USSR. 22205/6, 21549/50, 23898/9*]

... Excerpts
Moscow Radio—Orlov (*USSR. 13236/9 & 20378/9*)

Scènes de Ballet, Op. 52 orch.
Moscow Radio—Gauk[2]   ♯ *Per.SPL 596*
(*below*)   (♯ *USSR.D 482/3*, 2ss)
(*Raymonda*, on ♯ *Csm.CRLP 218*)

(The) SEASONS, Op. 67 Ballet
No. 13, Bacchanal
Philharmonia—Kurtz   in ♯ *G.ALP 1301*
(*Tchaikovsky, Lincke, Chopin, etc.*)

No. 15, Finale—Apotheosis, Les Bacchantes
☆ French Nat. Sym.—Désormière (in ♯ Cap.SAL 9020)

Orch. Suite: Nos. 1, 2, 3, 4, 5, 9, 13
☆ Philharmonia—Malko (in ♯ BB.LBC 1022:
                          ♭ set *WBC 1022*)

Serenade, A major, Op. 7 orch.
Moscow Radio—Golovanov   *USSRM.D 00705*
(*Rimsky-Korsakov*)

Sérénade espagnole, Op. 20, No. 2 vlc. & pf.
S. Knushevitzky (*USSRM.D 00346*)

Slavonic Festival, Op. 26 orch.
(from the Str. Qtt. Op. 26)
☆ Moscow Radio—Kovalev (♯ *USSR.D 1203*)

Sonata, F minor, Op. 75 pf.
E. Gilels   ♯ *CHS.CHS 1311*
(*Prokofiev & Tchaikovsky*)
(*Saint-Saëns* on ♯ *Csm.CRLP 178*)

SONGS
In my blood the fire of desire burns (Pushkin)
    (*Oriental Romance*)
P. Lisitsian (B)   *USSR. 15824*
(*Rachmaninoff: As fair as day*)
☆ Z. Dolukhanova (A) (*USSRM.D 00605*)
▽ Vanni-Marcoux (B, *Fr*) (*G.DA 990*)

The Muse, Op. 59, No. 1 (Pushkin)
E. Belov   *USSR. 22545*
(*Cui: The burnt letter*)

Romance (Lermontov)
N. Kazantseva (S)   *USSR. 21308*
(*Rimsky-Korsakov: Zuleika's Song*)

Why are the voices silent? (*Drinking Song*) (Pushkin)
M. Reizen (Bs)   *USSRM.D 001347*
(*Tchaikovsky & Rimsky-Korsakov*)

Song of the Volga Boatman, Op. 97 (ARR.)
B. Gmyria (B) & orch. (in **V**♯ *CdM.LDY 4035*)

Stenka Razin, Op. 13 Sym. Poem   orch.
Suisse Romande—Ansermet   ♯ *D.LXT 2982*
(*Rimsky-Korsakov*)   (♯ *Lon.LL 1060*)
Moscow Radio—Golovanov   *USSRM.D 516/7*

SYMPHONIES
No. 1, E major, Op. 5
State Sym.—Ivanov   ♯ *USSR.D 01370/1*

No. 4, E flat major, Op. 48
☆ Leningrad Phil.—Mravinsky (♯ *USSR.D 53/4*;
                      with *Rimsky-K.*, ♯ *Csm.CRLP 206*)

No. 5, B flat major, Op. 55 1895
☆ Moscow Radio—Golovanov   ♯ *CHS.CHS 1302*
(*Dargomijsky*)   (2ss, ♯ *USSR.D 0387/8*)

No. 6, C minor, Op. 58
USSR. State Sym.—Ivanov   ♯ *Sup.LPV 182*
                               (♯ *U. 5163G*)
Moscow Radio—Golovanov ♯ *Mon.MWL 319*
(*Prokofiev* on ♯ *Kings. 291*)   (♯ *USSR.D 0727/8*)
(*Rimsky-Korsakov* on ♯ *Csm.CRLP 207*)

No. 7, F major, Op. 77
Moscow Radio—Golovanov ♯ *Mon.MWL 320*
(*Rimsky-K.* on ♯ *Csm.CRLP 208*) (♯ *USSR.D 0401/2*)
Berlin Radio—Lederer   ♯ *Ura. 7088*
(*Miaskovsky*)

No. 8, E flat major, Op. 83
Leningrad Phil.—Mravinsky ♯ *USSR.D 01460/1*

VALSES DE CONCERT
No. 1, D major, Op. 47
No. 2, F major, Op. 51
Bolshoi Theatre—Gauk   ♯ *Per.SPL 596*
(*above*)   (*Ruses d'amour* on ♯ *Csm.CRLP 165*)[3]
Moscow Radio—Samosud   ♯ *Mon.MWL 321*
(*Pf. Concerto No. 1*)   (2ss, *USSRM.D 137/8*)
☆ Chicago Sym.—Stock (in ♯ *AmC.RL 3022*)

... No. 1, only
Belgian Radio—André   ♯ *DT.TM 68014*
(*Meyerbeer: Fackeltanz No. 1*)   (TV.VE 9036)
F.O.K.—Smetáček   ♯ *Sup.LPM 121*
(*Rubinstein, Suppé, J. Strauss*)   (2ss, U.H 24433)
(*Brahms & Rubinstein* on ♯ *U. 5117G*)

Variations on a Russian theme Str. qtt.
(Varn. 3; others by Rimsky, Scriabin, Blumenfeld, etc.)
Bolshoi Theatre Qtt. (*USSR. 22504*)

GLIER, Reinhold Moritzovitch (1875-1956)

(The) Bronze Horseman Ballet 1948/49
... Orch. Suite
Berlin Radio—Guhl   ♯ *Ura. 7121*
Bolshoi Th.—Glier (in ♯ *Csm.CRLP 10080*; perhaps ☆)

... On the square; Children's Dance; Dance of the three girls;
Waltz; Folk Dance
Bolshoi Theatre—Fayer (*below*)   ♯ *USSR.D 550*

... Vln. solo (unspec.)
☆ D. Oistrakh & orch.—Glier (in ♯ *Csm.CRLP 179*)

---

[1] Composed jointly with Liadov & Sokolov.
[2] The Period list attributes to Bolshoi Theatre Orch. but the USSR list is followed here.   Part is ☆.
[3] Said to be conducted by Golovanov.

Concerto, hp. & orch., Op. 74   1938
J. Zoff & Leipzig Phil.—Kempe   ♯ **Ura. 7164**
(Handel)
V. Dulova & Moscow Radio—Gauk
         ♯ **Per.SPL 567**
(Rimsky-K.: Symphony No. 3)

Concerto, horn & orch., Op. 91
V. Polekh & Bolshoi Theatre—Glier
         ♯ **CEd.CE 3001**
(Prokofiev, Glinka, Amirov)   (2ss, ♯ *USSR.D 753/4*)

GYULSARA
Opera, in collaboration with T. Sadikov
Vocal Excerpts   (in *Uzbek*)
Soloists of Uzbek State Op. (*USSR. 18532/3, 20025/6*)

LEILI & MEDZHNUN Opera, in collab. as above
1940
Vocal Excerpts   (in *Uzbek*)
Soloists of Uzbek State Op. (*USSR. 22804/5, 22790/4*)

(The) Marriage of Figaro   1927
Incidental Music to Beaumarchais' Play
Moscow Arts Theatre Orch.—Isralevsky
(8ss)   ♯ **USSR.D 01694/701**
(in a performance of the play)

Quartet No. 4, Op. 83   Strings
Beethoven Qtt.   ♯ *USSR.D 911/2*

(The) RED POPPY, Op. 70 Ballet   1926-7
Orch. Suites (the contents vary widely)
Vienna State Op.—Scherchen ♯ **Nix.WLP 6210**
(Symphony No. 3, s. 3) (♯ West. set WAL 210: 2ss, LAB 7001)
Bolshoi Theatre—Fayer   ♯ **Van.VRS 432**
(Glazounov)   *(Bronze Horseman on* ♯ *USSR.D 551)*
Berlin Radio—Gahlenbeck   ♯ **Ura. 7078**
(Rimsky-Korsakov)   (♭ *UREP 49;* ♯ *MTW. 546)*
(Waltz only in ♯ Ura. 7096)
Bolshoi Theatre—Glier   ♯ **Csm.CRLP 226**
(Khachaturian)

... No. 14, Sailors' Dance   *(Yablochko)*
Sym.—Stokowski   ♭ *G. 7ER 5060*
(Moussorgsky: Night on Bare Mountain)
(in ♯ Vic.LM 1816: ♭ set ERB 1816; ♯ ItV.A12R 0141;
            FV.A 630215; DV.L 16482)

☆ Philharmonia—Malko (♭ *G.7PW 104)*
   Minneapolis Sym.—Mitropoulos (in ♯ AmC.RL 3021)
   Col. Sym.—Rodzinski (♭ *AmC.A 1560)*

Romance, C minor, Op. 3[1]   vln. & pf.   1902
D. Oistrakh & USSR. State—Kondrashin
         ♯ **Van.VRS 6016**
(Miaskovsky, Brahms & Tchaikovsky on ♯ *Csm.CRLP 149)*
I. Oistrakh & pf.   *USSRM.D 00121*
(Khachaturian)
☆ I. Bezrodny (*USSRM.D 001284*)

SONGS
Eastern Song   (Minsky)
P. Lisitsian (B)   **USSR. 023882**
(Balakirev: Song of Selim)

Sweetly sang the nightingale
W. Nikitin   *Eta. 30-5017*
(Glinka & Tchaikovsky)
W. Werminska (S), J. Lefeld (pf.)   *Muza. 2468*
(Tchaikovsky: Ballroom meeting)

(The) Winds blow   (Koltsov)
A. Ognivtsev   *USSR. 23009*
(Glinka: Autumn night)

SYMPHONIES
No. 1, E flat major, Op. 8   1899-1900
Moscow Radio—Glier   ♯ **USSR.D 01462/3**

No. 3, B minor, Op. 42   *(Ilya Murometz)*   1909-11
Vienna State Op.—Scherchen
         ♯ **Nix.WLP 6210-1/2**
(3ss—Red Poppy)   (♯ West. set WAL 210)
☆ Philadelphia—Stokowski   (2ss)   ♯ **Vic.LCT 1106**
             (♭ *set WCT 1106)*

... 3rd movt., Scherzo, "Chez Vladimir"
☆ Chicago Sym.—Stock (in ♯ AmC.RL 3022)

GLINKA, Michael Ivanovitch (1803-1851)

COLLECTION (partly ☆)   ♯ **Csm.CRLP 10040**
  Jota Aragonesa   Sym.—Orlov
  Sextet, pf. & str.   L. Oborin & Beethoven Qtt., etc.
  Trio pathétique   as below on CHS.
  Variations, F major   L. Oborin

Festival Polonaise, F major   orch.
☆ Moscow Radio—Gauk (*USSRM.D 00109*)

Jota Aragonesa   orch.   *(Capriccio brillante)*   1845
☆ USSR State—Samosud   *USSRM.D 141*
  (Valse fantaisie)   (in ♯ *CEd.CE 3001)*

Kamarinskaya[2]   orch.   1840
N.B.C. Sym.—Toscanini[3] in ♯ **Vic. set LM 6026**
  (Berlioz, Bizet, Donizetti, etc.)
Philharmonia—Susskind   in ♯ **MGM.E 3045**
  (Rimsky-Korsakov)
USSR. State—Ivanov   in ♯ *CdM.LD 8055*
              (& *USSRM.D 152)*
F.O.K. Sym.—Smetáček   ♯ *Sup.LPM 113*
  (Brahms, Sibelius)   (♯ *U. 5071C, d.c.)*
Florence Fest.—Gui   ♯ *AudC. 1163*
  (Massenet & Rossini)
Lamoureux—Dourian   ♯ *Phi.A 76707R*
  (Dourian & Smetana)

OPERAS
(A) LIFE FOR THE TZAR   4 Acts & epilogue
  (or Ivan Sussanin)   1836
COMPLETE RECORDING
☆ Soloists, Bolshoi Theatre Cho. & Orch.
   —Melik-Pasheyev   ♯ **USSR.D 0373/80**
  (8ss) (Excerpts on ♯ *CdM.LDX 8067)*

No. 2, Antonida's Cavatina; & Act IV, COMPLETE
V. Barsova (S), M. Mikhailov (Bs), Bolshoi Theatre Cho.
  & Orch.—Samosud (♯ *Csm.CRLP 10170)*
No. 2 only   E. Shumskaya (in ♯ *USSR.D 1915)*

Nos. 5-7, Ballet Music
☆ Bolshoi Theatre—Melik-Pasheyev (in ♯ *USSR.D 423)*
  Bolshoi Theatre—Samosud (in ♯ *Csm.CRLP 10110)*

No. 8, Entr'acte, Act III
▽ USSR. Orch.—Samosud (*USSR. 07766*)

No. 14, No, that is not my sorrow   (Romance) S
E. Chavdar   in ♯ *USSR.D 2088*
  (Dargomijsky, Rimsky-Korsakov, etc.)

No. 18, Brothers, follow me   (Sobinin's Aria)   T
☆ H. Roswaenge (*Ger*) (in ♯ *CEd.* set 7010)

No. 19, The poor steed fell (Vanya's aria & cho.) A
A. Kleshcheva & Moscow Radio Cho.
         ♯ *USSR.D 1517*
  (Ruslan & Ludmilla, aria, etc.)

No. 20 b/c, Sussanin's Aria   Bs
R. Arié   ♯ *D.LW 5061*
  (Sadko, E. Oniegin, Prince Igor)   (♯ *Lon.LD 9074)*
N. Rossi-Lemeni   **G.DB 21559**
  (Prince Igor—Galitzky's Aria)
  (in ♯ *G.ALP 1074: FALP 306: QALP 10033; &*
               ♭ *Vic.ERA 186)*
S. Belarsky   in ♯ *Vic.LPM 3274*
  (Ruslan & Ludmilla aria, etc.)   (♭ set EPB 3274)
M. Reizen   *USSRM.D 00886*
   (in ♯ *Mon.MEL 710; USSR.D 1951; Csm.CRLP 142)*
  M. Popov *(Bulg. 1388)*
  A. Pankey (in ♯ Top.TRL 2)
☆ B. Gmyria (*USSRM.D 00245*)
🄷 F. Chaliapin (in ♯ Sca. 801* & ♭ Per.PEP 12*;
               Cpt.EXTP 1002*)

— CHORAL VERSION
Don Cossacks—Jaroff (in ♯ C.SX 1008: FSX 109)

---

[1] Some recordings are labelled Op. 45, No. 3. It has not been possible to check.
[2] Revised by Rimsky-Korsakov.   [3] From a broadcast performance.

RUSLAN AND LUDMILLA   5 Acts   1842
COMPLETE RECORDING

Ruslan	I. Petrov (B)
Ludmilla	V. Firsova (S)
Gorislava	N. Pokrovskaya (A)
Ratmir	E. Verbitskaya (A)
Finn	G. Nelepp (T)
Svetozar	V. Gavrushkov (Bs)
Farlaf	A. Krivchenya (Bs)
Naina...	E. Korneyeva (M-S)
Bayan	S. Lemeshev (T)

etc., Bolshoi Theatre Cho. & Orch.
—Kondrashin   ♯ **West.OPW 11003/6**
(8ss)   (set OPW 1401)
(10ss, ♯ USSR.D 02452/61)

Orchestral Suite
☆ L.S.O.—Fistoulari   ♯ **P.PMC 1031**
(*Nicolai, Rezniček, Rimsky, etc.*)
(*Berlioz, on* ♯ *MGM.E 3053*)

Overture
Paris Cons.—Ansermet   in ♯ **D.LXT 2833**
(*Prokofiev, Borodin, Moussorgsky*)   (♯ Lon.LL 864)
(& ♭ *D. 71068 with Chabrier*)

☆ Danish Radio—Dobrowen   ♭ **G.7P 140**
(*Tannhäuser, March*)   (♭ 7PW 126)
(*Mozart: Contretänze, on* G.DB 10516)

Bolshoi Theatre—Melik-Pasheyev (in ♯ Csm.CRLP 159)
International Sym.—A. Schneiderhann
           (in ♯ *Mae.OA 20007*)
"Nat. Op. Orch." (in ♯ Gram. 20142)

☆ Bamberg Sym.—Lehmann (in ♯ *AmD.DL 4063* &
             ♭ *Pol.* 30020)

   Philadelphia—Ormandy (♭ *AmC.A 1595*)
   City of Birmingham—Weldon (in ♯ AmC.RL 3072)
   Philharmonia—Kletzki (C.GQX 8047)
   Boston Prom.—Fiedler (♭ *Cam.CAE 189* & ♯ CAL 250)
   Bolshoi Th.—Samosud (USSR. 05972/3)

ACT I

No. 1, The Bard's Song: There is a desert country T
☆ S. Lemeshev (in ♯ Csm.CRLP 159)

**No. 2, Ludmilla's Cavatina: Soon I must leave
thee** S
E. Chavdar (in ♯ *USSR.D 1951*)
☆ I. Maslennikova & Cho. (in ♯ Csm.CRLP 159)

ACT II

No. 7, Ah, what grief! (Scene, Farlaf-Naina)
Bs & M-S
M. Reizen & E. Korneyeva   **USSRM.D 00885**
(*Life for the Tsar, aria*)

No. 7a, Farlaf's Rondo: The happy day is gone Bs
S. Belarsky   in ♯ **Vic.LPM 3274**
(*Life for the Tsar; Borodin, Moussorgsky, etc.*)
           (♭ set EPB 3274)

No. 8, Ruslan's Aria: O say, ye fields! B
B. Gmyria   in ♯ **CdM.LDM 8070**
           (♯ USSR.D 1594, d.c.)
☆ M. Reizen (in ♯ Csm.CRLP 159)

ACT III

No. 13, Ratmir's Aria: Wondrous dream of love A
A. Kleshcheva   ♯ **USSR.D 1516**
(*Life for the Tsar, aria*)

No. 14, Dances orch.
Bolshoi Theatre—Melik-Pasheyev
          in ♯ **CdM.LDM 8055**
(*Kamarinskaya; Dargomijsky & Tchaikovsky*)
           (♯ USSR.D 422, d.c.)
(& 4ss, USSR. 022076/9)

ACT IV

No. 17, Ludmilla's Aria: Far from my beloved S
☆ I. Maslennikova (in ♯ *CdM.LDM 8070*)

---

[1] From *Farewell to St. Petersburg*, 1840.
[2] Originally, *Always, everywhere together*, 1838; revised to new words, 1839.

PIANO MUSIC—COLLECTION
Valse mélodique ø
Mazurka, F major ø
Tarantella, G minor   1843   ø
Variations on a theme from Cherubini's opera 'Faniska'
Farewell Waltz, G minor   1831
Polka, D minor   1849
   Y. Bryushkov   ♯ **USSRM.D 00779/80**
   (2ss) [Items marked ø also on *USSR. 19464/5*]

Polka No. 1 pf. duet — ARR. ORCH.   Balakirev
   Moscow Radio—Gauk   (2ss)   **USSR. 21020/1**

Prince Kholmsky Inc. Music (Kukolnik)   1840
... Overture   ☆ State Sym.—Gauk (*USSRM.D 001207*)

Sextet, E flat major pf. & str.   1832
P. Serebriakov & Lukashevsky Ens.
           ♯ **USSR.D 961/2**

SONGS
COLLECTIONS

Doubt (Kukolnik) 1838   B. Gmyria (Bs)
Heart's memory (Batushkov)   1827
I remember the moment (Pushkin)   1838
   S. Lemeshev (T)
Had I but known   (Gypsy song)
The pigeons have gone to rest (Barcarolle) (Kukolnik)[1]
   Z. Dolukhanova (A)
Do not sing, my beauty (Pushkin)
O say, why did you come? (Golitsin)   1827
   S. Shaposhnikov (B)   ♯ **USSR.D 2086/7**

I remember the moment (Pushkin)
Don't say love passes (Delvig) 1833   also on USSR. 022037
Fire of longing (Pushkin) 1839   also on USSR. 022038
   I. Kozlovsky (T)   ♯ **USSR.D 1429**
   (*Dargomijsky, Verdi, etc.*)

Adèle (Pushkin)   1849
   S. Lemeshev (T)   **USSR.18860**
   (*Tchaikovsky: Does the day reign?*)   (& in ♯ *D 1163*)

Autumn Night (Rimsky-Korsakov)
   A. Ognivtsev   **USSR. 23010**
   (*Glier: Song*)
   I. Skobtsov (*USSR. 22729*)

Do not sing, my beauty (Pushkin)
   S. Lemeshev (T)   **USSR. 21553**
   (*O wondrous maiden; & Balakirev*)

Do not tempt me (Baratinsky)   1825, rev. 1851
   N. Obukhova (M-S)   **USSRM.D 00859**
   (*Bachmetiev & Bulakhov*)

Doubt (Kukolnik)   1838
   R. Arié (Bs), W. Parry (pf.)   ♯ **D.LW 5087**
   (*below; & Gretchaninoff, Moussorgsky, Lishin*)
           (♯ *Lon.LD 9103*)
   N. Obukhova (M-S)   **USSRM.D 00118**
   (*Tchaikovsky: Not a word ...* &   (& in ♯ *USSR.D 1548*)
   Song of the Gypsy girl)
   M. Reizen (Bs)   **USSRM.D 00620**
   (*Rubinstein: Gold rolls here below*)
   I. Petrov (Bs)   **USSR. 22750/1**

Forgive me, please (Fedorova)   duet
   N. Alexandriskaya (M-S) & S. Lemeshev (T)
           USSR. 023955
   (*Taneiev: How you caress, silvery night*)

Had I but known (Gypsy Song)
   ☆ N. Obukhova (M-S) (in *USSRM.D 001241*)

Heart's memory (Batushkov)   1827
   S. Lemeshev (T)   **USSR. 22544**
   (*I remember the moment*)   (& USSRM.D 00790, d.c.)

I feel so bitter (Rimsky-Korsakov)   1827
   V. Borisenko (M-S)   **USSR. 022748**
   (*Rubinstein: Song*)

I remember the moment (Pushkin)   1838
   S. Lemeshev (T)   **USSR. 22543**
   (*Heart's memory*)   (*The Lark, on Eta. 130009*)

In my blood the fire of desire burns[2] (Pushkin)
   W. Nikitin (T)   *Eta. 30-5017*
   (*Tchaikovsky & Glier*)

I saw in a magic dream (orig. *Ital*, 1828)
E. Katulskaya (M-S)   in *USSRM.D 00778*
(below; & Tchaikovsky)

(The) Lark (Kukolnik)[1]
S. Lemeshev (T), A. Makarov (pf.)   *Eta. 130009*
(above)
☆ N. Shpiller (S) (*USSRM.D 00967*)

— ARR. PF. Balakirev
R. Spivak   **ArgV. 66-6172**
(Debussy: Prelude Book I No. 10)
☆ L. Oborin (in ♯ Csm.CRLP 224)

— ARR. 2 PFS. Luboshutz
☆ P. Luboshutz & G. Nemenoff (in ♯ Cam.CAL 198)

— ARR. GUITAR Orlovsky
N. Orlovsky (in ♯ *Pat.ST 1017*)

(The) Midnight Review (Zhukovsky)
R. Arié (Bs), W. Parry (pf.)   ♯ *D.LW 5087*
(above, Gretchaninoff, etc.)   (♯ *Lon.LD 9103*)
I. Patorzhinsky (Bs)   **USSR. 022551**
(Rimsky: Anchar)
M. Reizen (Bs)   *USSRM.D 00866*
(Borodin & Kalinnikov)

Night (Delvig) (or: *Ah! Night*)   1829
B. Gmyria (B)   **USSR. 22269**
(Balakirev: Embrace, kiss)

Night Zephyr (Pushkin)   1837
I. Kozlovsky (T)   **USSR. 22351**
(Who is she)

(The) Northern Star (Rostopchina)   1837
E. Shumskaya (S)   in ♯ *USSR.D 1916*
I. Kozlovsky (T)   in USSR. 022038

O say, why did you come? (Golitsin)   1827
(or: Tell me why)
N. Shpiller (S)   **USSR. 22266**
(You will quickly forget me)
S. Shaposhnikov (B)   *USSRM.D 00623*
(Why do you weep; & Tchaikovsky)

O wondrous maiden[1] (Kukolnik)
S. Lemeshev (T)   *USSR. 21554*
(Do not sing, my beauty;   (& *USSRM. 00790, d.c.*)
& Balakirev)

Only one instant (Golitsin) (orig. *Fr*, 1827)
E. Katulskaya (M-S)   in *USSRM.D 00778*

(The) Pigeons have gone to rest[1] (Kukolnik)
(Barcarolle)
N. Shpiller (S)   *USSRM.D 00967*
(above; & Rachmaninoff)

Shall I forget (Golitsin)   1829
I. Petrov (Bs)   **USSR. 22266**
(Tchaikovsky: No response or word of greeting)

Spanish Serenade
G. Vinogradov (T)   *Ete. 30-5018*
(Rimsky-Korsakov & Rachmaninoff)

Venetian night (Kozlov)   1832   — ARR. CHO.
Estonian State Male Qtt. (*Estonian*) (*USSR. 22118*)

Wayfarer's Song[1] (Kukolnik) (or: *Travelling Song*)
M. Reizen (Bs)   **USSR. 15433**
(Schubert: Das Wandern)

Who is she and where is she?[1]   (Kukolnik)
I. Kozlovsky (T)   **USSR. 22350**
(Night zephyr)

Why do you weep? (Delvig)
☆ S. Shaposhnikov (B) (*USSRM.D 00623*)

You will quickly forget me (Zhadovsky)   1847
N. Shpiller (S)   **USSR. 17863**
(O say, why did you come?)

Trio pathétique, D minor pf., cl. & bsn.   1826/7
T. Nikolayeva, V. Petrov & Y. Nekhlyudov
(4ss)   *USSRM.D 835/6*

— ARR. PF. VLN. & VLC.   Hrimaly
L. Oborin, D. Oistrakh & S. Knushevitzky
     ♯ **CHS.CHS 1306**
(Rimsky-Korsakov)   (in ♯ Csm.CRLP 10040)

Valse fantaisie orch.   1839, rev. 1856
Moscow Radio—Gauk   *USSRM.D 150*
(Jota Aragonesa)
(Balakirev & Moussorgsky in ♯ CdM.LDM 8056)
Linz Sym.   in ♯ **Ply. 12-35**
(Rimsky, Borodin, etc.)
Leipzig Radio—Pflüger (2ss)   *Eta. 120030*
☆ Philharmonia—Malko (in ♯ BB.LBC 1021:
         ♭ set WBC 1021)

Variations on a theme of Mozart harp (or pf.)
1822, revised
☆ O. Erdeli (*Beethoven & Daquin*)   *USSRM.D 00476*

GLUCK, Christoph Willibald von
(1714-1787)

I. INSTRUMENTAL

Ballet Suite No. 1   — ARR. Mottl
Don Juan: Introduction
Iphigénie en Aulide: Airs gais & Lento
Armide: Musette & Sicilienne
Orphée: Nos. 29, 30
New Sym.—Irving   ♯ **D.LXT 5063**
(Grétry)   (♯ Lon.LL 1234)
Linz Sym.[2]   ♯ **Ply. 12-36**
(Schubert, Haydn, Arne)
"Viennese Sym." (in ♯ Ply. 12-89)
☆ Prague Ger. Phil.—Keilberth[3] (♭ *Ura.UREP 32*;
         in ♯ ANix.ULP 9018)
Boston Prom.—Fiedler (in ♯ Cam.CAL 151: ♭ *CAE 152*)

Concerto, G major, fl. & orch.[4]
H. Barwahser & Vienna Sym.—Paumgartner
       ♯ **Phi.N 00213L**
(below; Mozart & Quantz)   (♯ Epic.LC 3134)
C. Wanausek & Vienna Pro Musica—Gielen
       ♯ **AmVox.PL 9440**
(Boccherini & Pergolesi)

II. OPERAS

ALCESTE   3 Acts   1776
Overture
Berlin Phil.—Lehmann   *PV. 36073*
(Freischütz Overture on ♯ AmD.DL 4075)
(Beethoven: Coriolan Overture, on ♭ Pol. 30122)
Glyndebourne Fest.—Gui   **G.DB 21616**
Suisse Romande—Münchinger   ♯ *D.LW 5144*
(Schumann: Manfred Overture)   (♯ Lon.LD 9145)
Avellaneda Municipal—Fauré ♯*ArgOd.LDC 523*
(Gomes, A. Williams, Ugarte)   (& ArgOd. 66066)
☆ L.S.O.—Kisch (♯ *D.LW 5022*; ♯ *Lon.LD 9035*)
   Berlin Phil.—Furtwängler (♭ *T.UV 115*)
   Prague German Phil.—Keilberth (in ♯ MTW. 501)

No. 12, Où suis-je?... Non, ce n'est point un
     sacrifice S   Act I
C. Goltz   *PV. 36117*
(No. 15) (♭ *Pol. 34011: 32058*: & in *Ger, PV. 36096*:
         ♭ *Pol. 34010*)
☆ S. Balguérie (in ♯ Ete. 495)

No. 15, Divinités du Styx S   or M-S   Act I
C. Goltz   *PV. 36117*
(No. 12) (♭ *Pol. 34011: 32058*: & in *Ger, PV. 36096*:
         ♭ *Pol. 34010*)
(& in ♯ AmD.DL 9778)
☆ S. Danco (*Dido & Aeneas*)   ♭ *D. 71100*
☆ H. Traubel (in ♯ Vic. set LCT 6701)

ARMIDE   5 Acts   (*French*)   1777
Plus j'observe ces lieux T   Act II
☆ J. Rogatchewsky (in ♯ Ete. 495)

---

[1] From *Farewell to St. Petersburg*, 1840.
[2] Omits Don Juan & Orphée excerpts.   [3] Omits Don Juan excerpts.   [4] ARR. Scherchen from MSS. sources.

Ah! si la liberté S Act III
☆ F. Leider (AF.AGSB 26 & in ♯ Ete. 495)

DON JUAN Ballet 1761
☆ Vienna Sym.—Moralt   ♯ Nix.WLP 5028

IPHIGÉNIE EN AULIDE 3 Acts (*French*) 1774
Overture
Philharmonia—Kubelik   ♮ G.DB 9753/4
(3ss—*Entführung Overture*)
Munich Phil.—Rother   *PV. 36090*
(*Orphée*, on ♯ *Pol. 17062*)
☆ L.S.O.—Kisch (♯ *D.LW 5022; Lon.LD 9035*)
Berlin Phil.—Abendroth (in ♯ *MTW. 501*)

No. 28, Ballet . . . Gavotte Act II
— ARR. PF. DUET Doebber
E. Bartlett & R. Robertson (n.v.)
          in ♯ MGM.E 3150

No. 37, O toi, l'objet le plus aimable B Act II
☆ E. Schipper (*Ger*)   in ♯ Ete. 495

No. 44, Calchas d'un trait mortel (*Der Priester wagt*)
Act III
♅ E. Schmedes (*Ger*) (in ♯ *HRS. 3006**)

IPHIGÉNIE EN TAURIDE 4 Acts (*French*) 1779
COMPLETE RECORDING
Iphigénie ... ... P. Neway (S)
Orestes ... ... P. Mollet (B)
Pylade ... ... L. Simoneau (T)
Thoas... ... ... R. Massard (Bs)
etc., Cho. & Paris Cons. Orch.—Giulini[1]
          ♯ Pat.DTX 130/2
(6ss)   (♯ AmVox. set PL 7822, 4ss)

No. 12, Dieux qui me poursuivez B
No. 14, Le calme rentre B Act II
☆ W. Domgraf-Fassbänder (*Ger*) (in ♯ Ete. 495)

No. 17, O malheureuse Iphigénie S Act II
☆ S. Balguérie (in ♯ Ete. 495)

No. 26, Chaste fille de Latone Cho. Act IV
☆ (*Ger*—"*Gebet*") Irmler Cho. (in ♯ Ete. 495)

(L') IVROGNE CORRIGÉ 2 Acts 1760
COMPLETE RECORDING (Ed. Leibowitz & Gradwohl)
☆ Soloists, Paris Phil. Orch.—Leibowitz (♯ Clc. 6145)

ORPHÉE ET EURIDICE 3 Acts
1762 (*It*) & 1774 (*Fr*)
COMPLETE RECORDING (in *Italian*)[2]
☆ M. Klose (A), E. Berger (S), R. Streich (S), etc., Berlin
Municipal Op. Cho. & Orch.—Rother
          ♯ Nix.ULP 9223-1/3

COMPLETE RECORDING (in *Russian*)
Orphée ... ... I. Kozlovsky (T)
Eurydice ... ... E. Shumskaya (S)
L'Amour ... ... G. Sacharova (S)
etc., Moscow Radio Cho. & Orch.—Samosud
(8ss)   ♯ USSR.D 0933/40

ABRIDGED RECORDING (in *Italian*)[3]
Orfeo... ... ... K. Ferrier (A)
Euridice ... ... A. Ayars (S)
Amor... ... ... Z. Vlachopoulos (S)
☆ Glyndebourne Fest. Cho. & Southern Phil.—Stiedry
          ♯ D.LXT 2893
          (♯ Lon.LL 924)

ACT I
No. 7, Objet de mon amour
No. 10, Euridice, de ce doux nom Recit.
No. 11, Pleine de trouble et d'effroi Aria
R. Siewert (*Ger*)   G.EH 1430
(*No. 43*)   (♭ 7PW 525)

No. 7, Objet de mon amour (Orphée)
M. Klose (*Ital*)   *PV. 36114*
(*No. 43*)   (♭ *Pol. 34005: 32054*)
(& *Ger*, on *PV. 36113*: ♭ *Pol. 34004: 32053*)
☆ E. Leisner (*Ger*) (in ♯ Ete. 495)

ACT II
COMPLETE RECORDING[4] (in *Italian*)
B. Gibson (S), N. Merriman (M-S), R. Shaw
Cho. & N.B.C. Sym.—Toscanini
          ♯ Vic.LM 1850
          (♯ FV.A 630267; ItV.A12R 0143)

No. 22 or 24, Orphée's Aria
I. Kozlovsky (T) (*Russ*)   USSR. 21391/2

No. 28, Danse des Furies
Munich Phil.—Rother   *PV. 72397*
(*Nos. 29, 30*)   (& in ♯ *Pol. 17062*)
(*Zauberflöte, No. 15* on ♭ *Pol. 30011*)
Hamburg Philharmonia—H-J. Walther (*MSB. 78046*)
Belgian Radio Cha.—Doneux (in ♯ *Mae.OA 20003*)

Nos. 29, 30, Dance of the Blessed Spirits orch.
Munich Phil.—Rother   *PV. 72397*
(*No. 28*)   (& in ♯ *Pol. 17062*)
Vienna Sym.—Paumgartner in ♯ Phi.N 00213L
(*above*)   (♯ Epic.LC 3134)
Victor Sym.—Reiner   ♭ G.7ER 5052
(*Bach: Suite No. 3—Air*) (♭ *Vic.ERA 215; FV.A 95226*)
Hamburg Philharmonia—H-J. Walther (*MSB. 78046*)
☆ Liverpool Phil.—Rignold (C.DX 8337)

No. 29, "Minuet" — ARR. GUITAR
A. Segovia   in ♯ B.AXTL 1060
(† *Segovia Program*)   (♯ AmD.DL 9467)
— ARR. FL. & ORG. A. Andersen & H. Solum (*C.GN 1505*)

No. 30 — ARR. VLN. & PF. Kreisler—"Mélodie"
I. Stern & A. Zakin (in ♯ *AmC.AAL 23; Phi.S 06617R*)
E. Morini & L. Pommers (in ♯ *West.WN 18087*)
☆ J. Heifetz (in ♭ *D.EUA108503;* ♯ *AmD.DL 9780: ED3501*)
— ARR. 2 PFS. A. Whittemore & J. Lowe (♭ *Vic.ERA 123*)
... No. 29 or 30 — ARR.
I. Tarjani-Tóth (cymbalom), I. Aïtoff (pf.)
          in ♯ G.FBLP 1067
[labelled *Pastorale* but probably this]

ACT III
No. 39, Viens! Suis un époux qui t'adore
No. 42, Quelle épreuve cruelle
☆ M. Klose (A) & T. Lemnitz (S) (*Ger*) (♭ G.7RF 260)

No. 43, J'ai perdu mon Eurydice (Orphée)
S. Michel   in ♯ Pat.DTX 137
S. Couderc   ♭ Plé.P 45132
(*Favorita—O mio Fernando*)
M. Klose (*Ital*)   *PV. 36114*
(*No. 7*)   (♭ *Pol. 34005: 32054*)
(& *Ger* on *PV. 36113*: ♭ *Pol. 34004: 32053*)
Z. Palii   in ♯ Sup.LPV 207
          (♯ U. 5191G: H 24425)
R. Siewert (*Ger*)   G.EH 1430
(*above*)   (♭ 7PW 525)
☆ K. Ferrier (*Eng*)   ♯ D.LW 5072
(*Handel & Mendelssohn*) (♯ *Lon.LD 9066*; & ♭ *D. 71034*)
☆ M. Mödl (S, *Ger*)   in ♯ DT.TM 68009
(♯ *T.TW 30010* & in *LA 6077*: ♭ *UE 453897*;
          & AusT.E 1200)
K. Szczepanski (*Pol*) (*Muza. 1809*, 2ss)
☆ R. Stevens (M-S, *It*) (♭ *Vic.ERA 138*)
E. Wysor (A, *It*) (in ♯ *Ply. 12-47*)
K. Flagstad (*It*) (♭ *G.7R 164*)
♅ S. Onegin (in ♯ *Sca. 821**; or may be ☆)

Ballet Music
Chaconne (53), Menuet (49), Airs, C, D, & A (31, 46, 52)
☆ Paris Cons. Cha.—Cloëz (in † *AS. 2506LD*)

PARIDE ED ELENA 5 Acts (*Italian*) 1770
O del mio dolce ardor T Act I
S. Danco (S), G. Agosti (pf.) in ♯ D.LX 3113
          (♯ *Lon.LS 698*)
G. Prandelli, D. Marzollo (pf.)
          in ♯ AmVox.PL 7930
(† *Old Italian Airs*)
☆ H. v. Debička (S) & pf. in ♯ Ete. 495
♅ A. Bonci in ♯ *Sca. 811** & ♯ Ete. 492*
H. Jadlowker in ♯ *HRS. 3003**

---

[1] Recorded at the Aix-en-Provence Festival 1952.
[2] Nos. 17, 31, 46, 48, 49, 51 are omitted.
[3] Contains Nos. 1, 2, 6, 10-16, 18, 19, 22-27, 33, 34, 38-44, 50, 51, 45. Cuts are made in Nos. 12, 14, 15, 38, 42, 51 & 45.
The following Nos. contained in the 78 r.p.m. version are omitted now: 53, 20, 21, 30, 32, 45 (first time), 53.
[4] From radio broadcast Nov. 22, 1952.

(II) PROLOGO   S, A, orch.   1767
— ARR. as *Frühlingsfeier* (Klopstock)
  ☆ Berlin Boys' Cho. & Orch.—Steffen (♯ ANix.ULP 9018)

(La) RENCONTRE IMPRÉVUE   3 Acts (*French*)
                                                    1764
C'est un torrent impétueux, Act III   B
Un ruisselet bien clair, Act III   B
  G. Souzay   in ♯ *D.LX 3112*
  (*A. Scarlatti, Mozart, Lully, etc.*)   (♯ *Lon.LS 730*)

Un ruisselet . . . only   (*Einem Bach . . .*)
  E. Schwarzkopf (S, *Ger*), G. Moore (pf.)
                              in ♯ **C.CX 1044**
                              (♯ FCX 182; Angel. 35023)

GODARD, Benjamin (1849-1895)

Adagio pathétique, Op. 128, No. 3   vln. & pf.
— ARR. ORGAN   C. Cronham (*Mjr. 5134*)

Concerto, vln. & orch., No. 1, Op. 35 . . . Canzonetta
  E. Morini & L. Pommers (pf.)
                              in ♯ **West.WN 18087**
  (*Kreisler, Mozart, Tchaikovsky*)

OPERAS
(Le) DANTE   4 Acts   1890
Nous allons partir tous deux   S & T   Act IV
  ♄ G. Farrar & E. Clement (*AF.AGSA 5**)

JOCELYN   4 Acts   1888
Cachés dans cet asile   (*Berceuse*)   T
  ☆ R. Crooks (*Eng*) (in ♯ Cam.CAL 128)
    G. Fields (S, *Eng*) (♭ *D.DFE 6313*)
  ♄ S. Kurz (S) (in ♯ Sca. 817*)
— ARRANGEMENTS   (*inter alia*)
ORGAN: J. Perceval (♭ *ArgOd.BSOAE 4518*: in ♯ *LDC 513*)
  ☆ V. Fox (♭ *AmC.A 1559*)
GUITAR: A. Valenti (in ♯ SMC. 1002)
VLN. & ORCH:
  ☆ W. Tworek (*Pol.X 51705*; in ♯ *Lon.LB 1121*)
ORCH: Polish Radio—Krenz (*Muza. 2386*)
  ☆ G. Melachrino Orch.—Gerhardt (♭ *G.7EGF 133: 7EG 8002*)
    Kingsway Sym.—Olof (♭ *Lon.REP 8007*), etc.

(La) VIVANDIÈRE   3 Acts   1895
Viens avec nous, petit   S
  ♄ J. Gerville-Réache (*AF.AGSA 1**)

SONGS
Chanson de juin, Op. 102, No. 6   (Baroucaud)
  ♄ E. Caruso (in ♯ Vic.LCT 1129*)

Embarquez-vous   (U. Guttin)
  ♄ P. Plançon (Bs) (in ♯ *SBDH.LLP 6**)

GODOWSKY, Leopold (1870-1938)

Alt Wien   pf.
— ARR. 2 PFS.
  V. Appleton & M. Field   in ♯ *AmVox.VX 540*

— ARR. VLN. & PF.   Heifetz
  ☆ J. Heifetz & E. Bay (*G.DA 2037: EC 208*: in ♯ *FALP 248*;
                              ♭ *Vic.ERA 57*)
    J. Heifetz & M. Kaye (in ♯ *B.AXL 2017; D.UA 243086*;
                              AmD.DL 5214: DL 9780)
— ARR. ORCH.   M.G.M. Orch.—Marrow (in ♯ MGM.E 3138)

GOEB, Roger (b. 1914)

(3) American Dances   Str. orch.   1952
  M.G.M. Str.—I. Solomon   ♯ **MGM.E 3117**
  (*Copland, Diamond, Porter*)

Quintet   fl., ob., cl., hrn., bsn.
  New Art Wind Quintet   in ♯ **CEd. set 2003**
  (*Carter, Riegger, Persichetti*)

---

[1] Variations 5 & 8 of 1st movement are omitted.
[2] ARR. Jungnickel.

Symphony No. 3   1951
  Orch.—Stokowski   ♯ **Vic.LM 1727**
  (*Bartók*)   (♭ set *WDM 1727*)

GOETZ, Hermann (1840-1876)

(Der) WIDERSPENSTIGEN ZÄHMUNG   Opera
  4 Acts   1874
Die Kraft versagt   S   Act IV
  C. Goltz   **PV. 72291**
  (*Fidelio—Abscheulicher . . .*)   (in ♯ AmD.DL 9778)

GOLDMARK, Karl (1830-1915)

Concerto, A minor, vln. & orch., Op. 28
  ☆ P. Rybar & Vienna Sym.—Swoboda   ♯ Nix.WLP 5010

(Die) KÖNIGIN VON SABA, Op. 27   4 Acts   1875
Lockruf   S   Act II
  ♄ S. Kurz (in ♯ Sca. 817*)

Magische Töne   T   Act II
  R. Schock   **G.EH 1461**
  (*Elisir d'Amore—Una furtiva lagrima*)   (♭ *7PW 18-543*)
  (*idem in Ger, on G.EH 1462*: ♭ *7PW 18-542*)
  ♄ L. Slezak (in ♯ Vic.set LCT 6701*)
    E. Caruso (*Ital*) (♭ *Vic.ERAT 1**)

Ballet Music   Act III
  Berlin Sym.—Rubahn   in ♯ **Roy. 1533**

(Ein) WINTERMÄRCHEN   Opera   4 Acts   1908
O Menschenglück   B   Act I
  ♄ L. Demuth (in ♯ *HRS. 3003**)

Symphony—Die ländliche Hochzeit, Op. 26   1857
  Royal Phil.—Beecham[1]   ♯ **C.CX 1067**
                              (♯ AmC.ML 4626)
  ☆ Vienna State Op.—Swoboda (♯ Clc. 6154; *MMS. 49*)

GOMBERT, Nicolas (c. 1505-c. 1556)

SEE: † SEVEN CENTURIES OF SACRED MUSIC

GOMES, Antonio Carlos (1836-1896)

COLOMBO   Cantata   1892
Preghiera   B
  J. Athos   in ♯ **SBDH.TOB 1**
  (*Maria Tudor, Lo Schiavo, etc.*)

OPERAS   (in *Italian & Portuguese*)
FOSCA   4 Acts   1873
O tu che sei fra gli angeli   T
  A. Colósimo   in ♯ **SBDH.TOB 1**
  (*Colombo, Maria Tudor, etc.*)   (& ♯ ABCD. 2, d.c.)

(Il) GUARANY   4 Acts   1870
Overture
  Avellaneda Municipal—Fauré   **ArgOd. 66061**
                              (& in ♯ *LDC 523*)
  ☆ [2]Boston Prom.—Fiedler (in ♯ Cam.CAL 176: ♭ *CAE 182*)
— ARR. BAND
  Cities Service Band—Lavalle (in ♯ *Vic.LPM 1026*:
                              ♭ set *EPC 1026*)

Ave Maria   Bs   Act I
  J. Perrota   in ♯ **SBDH.TOB 1**
  (*below, Fosca, Colombo, etc.*)

Gentile di cuore   S   Act I
  M. S. Earp   **BrzCont.CA 4017**
  (*Bohème—Si mi chiamano Mimi*)

Sento una forza indomita   S & T   Act I
  ♄ Mazzoleni & G. Zenatello (in ♯ Sca. 818*)
  (?) J. Huguet & F. de Luca (in ♯ CEd.set 7002*)

(II) GUARANY (continued)

Vanto io pur superba cuna   T   Act II
  B. Gigli   **BrzV.B 5042**
  (Lo Schiavo—Quando nascesti tu)   (♭ 85-0000)
  A. Pacheco   in ♯ **SBDH.TOB 1**
  (above)   (& in ♯ ABCD. 2, d.c.)

Senza tetto   B   Act II
  P. Fortes   **BrzV.P 327**
  (Barbiere di Siviglia—Largo al factotum)
  ♅ M. Battistini (AF. & CRC.ABHB 1*;
                        in ♯ SBDH.JAL 7001*)

Regina della tribù   Bs   Act III
  N. Rossi-Lemeni   (above)   in ♯ **SBDH.TOB 1**

Perchè di mesti   S & T   Act III
  ♅ M. Percina & G. Zenatello (in ♯ SBDH.LLP 8*)

MARIA TUDOR   1879
Maria's Aria   S
  C. Gomes   in ♯ **SBDH.TOB 1**
  (Lo Schiavo, Guarany, etc.)

SALVATOR ROSA   4 Acts   1874
Mia piccirella   T   (Serenata, Acts I & IV)
  ♅ R. King (S) (SBDH.G 4*)

Di sposa, di padre   Bs   Act III
  C. Siepi   ♯ **D.LW 5169**
  (S. Boccanegra, Huguenots, etc.)   (♯ Lon.LD 9169)
  (also in ♯ D.LXT 5096; Lon.LL 1240)
  ♅ J. Mardones (in ♯ Sca. 810*)

E quanto   Bs
  ♅ J. Mardones (in ♯ SBDH.LPP 3*)

(Lo) SCHIAVO   4 Acts   1889
Quando nascesti tu   T
  B. Gigli   **BrzV.B 5042**
  (Guarany—Vanto io pur)   (♭ 85-0000)
  D. Cestari   **Cet.PE 212**
  (Zandonai: Giulietta e Romeo, aria)
  A. Pacheco   in ♯ **SBDH.TOB 1**
  (below, Guarany, etc.)

Ciel di Parahyba   S
  M. C. N. de Freita   in ♯ **SBDH.TOB 1**
  (above)
  ♅ R. King (SBDH.G 4*)

SONG
Quem sabe   (Bittencourt Sempaio)
  M. Sá Earp (S) & orch.   **BrzCont.CA 4018**
  (Madama Butterfly—Un bel di) (& F 010, single-sided)

GOMEZ, Julio (b. 1866)

Suite, A major   orch.   1917
  Madrid Sym.—Gomez   ♯ **Mont.FM 18**
  (Sombrero de Tres Picos)
  ... Excerpt   Spanish Sym.—Martinez   in ♯ **Mont.FM 16**

GÓMEZ CARRILLO, Manuel (b. 1883)

PART SONGS
Vida mía; Vidala del regreso
  University Cho.—G. Carrillo   **ArgV.P 1526**

GOMEZ CRESPO, J.
  SEE: † SPANISH GUITAR MUSIC
       † A. SEGOVIA, ART OF

GOMOLIAKA, Vadim (b. 1914)

Subcarpathian Sketches[1]   Suite orch.   1951
  Moscow Radio—Rakhlin   ♯ **CdM.LDX 8072**
  (Babadzhanyan)

GOMOLKA, Mikolaj (c. 1535-1609)
  SEE: † FOUR CENTURIES OF POLISH MUSIC
       † ANTHOLOGIE SONORE

GOOSSENS, Sir Eugene (b. 1893)

Hommage à Debussy, Op. 28   pf.   1920
  (for Le Tombeau de Debussy)
  E. Ulmer   in ♯ **CHS.H 12**
  (Dukas, Roussel, Malipiero, Stravinsky, Debussy)

GORZANIS, Jacomo (fl. mid-XVIIth Cent.)
  SEE: † LUTE MUSIC OF THE XVITH & XVIITH CENTURIES

GOSS, John (1800-1880)
  SEE: † ENGLISH CHURCH MUSIC, VOL. IV

GOSSEC, François Joseph (1734-1829)

Symphony, E flat major, Op. 5, No. 2   1761
  O.L. Cha. Orch.—Froment   **V♯ DO.LD 86**
  (2ss)

Symphony, F major   (à 17 Parties)   1809
Marche lugubre, D minor   1790
  Paris Cons.—Tzipine   in ♯ **C.FCX 383**[2]
  (Vogel, Lesueur)

ROSINE   Opera   1786
Gavotte
  Champs-Élysées Orch.—Allain   ♭ **Sel. 470.C.002**
  (Rameau, Boccherini)   (♭ T.UV 118)

— ARR. GLASS HARMONICA   Hansen
  E. Hansen   in ♯ **Ban.BC 2000**
  (Mozart, Beethoven, etc ; & Folk Songs)

GOTTSCHALK, Louis M. (1829-1869)

Symphony No. 1, 'La Nuit des Tropiques'   c. 1857-9
  ... **Andante only**[3]
  Hamburg Philharmonia—Korn   in ♯ **Allo. 3148**
  (Gram, Fry, Barber, etc.)

GOUDIMEL, Claude (c. 1510-1572)

CHANSON: Amour me tue
  Vocal Ens.—Lamy   in ♯ **LOL.OL 50027**
  († Parisian Songs of XVIth Century)   (♯ OL.LD 76)

PSALMS
Nos. 1, 55, 68, 130
  Paris Trad. Singers—M. Honegger
                      in † ♯ **AS. 3006LD**
                               (♯ HS.AS 41)

Nos. 19, 25
  ☆ Vocal Ens.—Expert (in † ♯ HS.AS 6)

Nos. 22, 24, 95
  Taizé Community   in ♯ **SM. 33-19**

---

[1] From Music for Film L'Aurore sur les Carpathes, 1947.
[2] Available only as part of a limited "Edition de luxe".
[3] Restored by Maganini from a pf. reduction.

No. 133
Petits Chanteurs de la Renaissance
in **V**‡ *Era.LDE 1009*
(† French Sacred Music)   (‡ HS.HS 9007)
(also in † Histoire de la Musique vocale)

GOUNOD, Charles François (1818-1893)

I. INSTRUMENTAL

Marche funèbre d'une marionette orch. (orig. pf.)
Hamburg Philharmonia—H-J. Walther
MSB. 78021
(*J. Strauss: An der schönen, blauen Donau*)
(also *MSB. 78119*, d.c.; & in ‡ MGM.E 3144)
  ☆ Boston Prom.—Fiedler (♭ *G.7EP 7019: 7EBF 4:*
7EPQ 504)
  Columbia Salon Orch. (in ‡ AmC.CL 518)

Marche pontificale pf. — ARR. ORG.
M. Salvador
in ‡ **TMS. 1/2**
(*Bach, Gigout, etc.*)

Quartet No. 3, A minor Strings pub. 1895
Parrenin Qtt.   ‡ **Strad.STR 618**
(*Lalo & Donizetti*)

Symphony, B flat major 9 Wind insts. 1888
French Navy Band—Maillot **V**‡ *Sel. 190.C.004*

II. CHURCH MUSIC, ORATORIO

GALLIA, "Lamentation" S, Cho., orch. 1871
Jérusalem
All Saints Church Male Cho.—Self (*Eng*)
in ‡ **CEd.CE 1023**
(† Five Centuries of Choral Music)

MORS ET VITA Oratorio 1884
Judex — ORCH. ONLY
Philharmonia—Malko   **G.C 4261**
(*Delibes: Naïla*)   (♭ 7P 152; in ‡ BB.LBC 1080)
Odense Municipal—Lundqvist   **C.DDX 37**
(*Cavalleria Rusticana, Intermezzo*)
Orch.—Warny   **G.Z 364**
(*Adams: Jerusalem*)

— ARR. VOICE, ORGAN & ORCH.
F. Andersson (T), org. & orch.   **Pol.Z 60151**
(*Sjöberg: Tonerna*)

III. OPERAS & Inc. Music

FAUST 5 Acts 1859
COMPLETE RECORDINGS

Casts		Set F	Set M
Marguérite (S)	…	V. de los Angeles	E. Shumskaya
Faust (T)	…	N. Gedda	I. Kozlovsky
Mephistophélès (Bs)	…	B. Christoff	A. Pirogov
Valentine (B)	…	J. Borthayre	P. Lisitsian
Siebel (S)	…	M. Angelici	E. Gribova
Wagner (B)	…	R. Jeantet	I. Skobtsov
Martha (M-S)	…	S. Michel	N. Ostroumova

Set F[1] with Paris Opéra Cho. & Orch.—Cluytens
‡ **G.ALP 1162/5**
(8ss) (‡ FALP 261/4: LALP 102/5: QALP 261/4;
Vic. set LM 6400)
[Il se fait tard … & Soldiers' Cho. also on ♭ *G.7ER 5059*]
[Highlights on ‡ Vic.LM 1825: ♭ set ERB 36]

Set M with Bolshoi Theatre Cho. & Orch.
—Nebolsin   ‡ **USSR.D 021/8**
(8ss, in *Russian*) [Excerpts on ‡ *USSR.D 1426*]

Set D
☆ E. Steber (S), E Conley (T), C. Siepi (Bs),
F. Guarrera (B), etc., Met. Op. Cho. & Orch.
—Cleva   ‡ **EPhi.ABL 3096/8**
(‡ Phi.A 01165/7L)

ABRIDGED RECORDING
U. Graf (S), L. Larsen (T), P. Gorin (Bs),
F. v. d. Ven (B), A. v. d. Graaf (S), etc., Cho.
& Netherlands Phil. Orch.—Goehr
‡ **MMS. set M 127**
(4ss)   (also ‡ set OP 11; o.n. ‡ set MMS. 2020)

[1] *Avant de quitter . . . is omitted.*

COLLECTIONS OF EXCERPTS

Mais ce Dieu	T & Bs	Act I
Salut demeure …	T	Act III
Air des bijoux …	S	Act III
Vous qui faites l'endormie	Bs	Act IV

J. Guihard (S), R. Huylbrock (T),
G. Vaillant (Bs) (*Fr*)   ‡ **LI.TW 91131**
(*Otello; & Paladilhe: La Patrie*)   (‡ D.FAT 173666)

Prelude, Act I
Valse, Act II cho.
Le jour va luire . . . Alerte! Alerte (*Prison Scene, Act V*)
M. Linval (S), J. Michel (T), B. Demigny (Bs),
Cho. & Champs-Elysées Th. Orch.
—Inghelbrecht   ‡ *Sel. 270.C.065*
(*Bizet*)

HIGHLIGHTS
A. Marques (S), G. Curtsinger (T), D. Lore (B), A.
Wilcox (Bs), Cho. & orch.—Peluso   ‡ **Opa. 1003/4**
(2ss) [Excerpts in *set 102*: ♭ *4034*]
R. Bonelli, L. Sgarro, A. de Costa & Orch.—H-J. Walther
(*Puccini*)   ‡ **Roy. 1616**
☆ Soloists, Cho. & Orch. of N.Y. City Op. Co —Halasz
(‡ MGM.E 3023)
E. Steber (S), A. Tokatyan (T), etc. (‡ Cam.CAL 221 &
in set CFL 101)
◧ E. Caruso (T), G. Farrar (Bs), A. Scotti (B)
(‡ Vic LCT 1103*: ♭ set WCT 1103*; ‡ DV.L 17094*)
[Il se fait tard . . . Caruso & Farrar, only
in ‡ G.FJLP 5010*: QJLP 101*]
E. Bettendorf (S), A. Bonci (T), G. de Luca (B),
M. Bohnen (B), O. Luppi (Bs), B. Kuirina (S), etc.
(*It, Fr, Ger—*‡ Ete. 487*)

Orchestral Suite
Radio City Music Hall Sym.—Paige   ♭ *Vic.ERA 175*
(*Carmen, Suite*)
Fantasy — ARR. HARP
O. Erdeli   *USSRM.D 481*
(*Salzédo: Variations*)   (& USSR. 20322/3)

ACT I

Prelude
Lamoureux—Fournet   ♭ *Phi.N 402013E*
(*Hérold: Zampa, Overture*) (in ‡ Phi.N 00707R;
Epic.LC 3079)

Salut, ô mon dernier matin! T
☆ I. Zidek (*Cz*) (in ‡ Sup.LPV 150; U. 5104G)

O merveille! T & Bs
◧ C. Dalmores & M. Journet (AF.AGSB 19*)

ACT II

Avant de quitter ces lieux B
R. Merrill   in ‡ **PRCC. 5**
I. P. Alexeiev (*Cz*)   in ‡ **Sup.LPV 150**
(*above & below*)   (‡ U. 5104G)
A. Sved (*Hung*) (*Serenade*)   **Qual.MN 1078**
J. Metternich (*Ger*)   **G.DB 11547**
(*Barbiere—Largo al factotum*) (♭ 7RW 506:
in ‡ WBLP 1504)
H. Prelayo (*Ital*)   in ‡ **SMC. 1003**
  J. Milligan (*Vic. 10-4221*: ♭ *49-4221*)
  L. Jambór (*Hung*) (*Qual.KM 5008*)
  ☆ T. Baylé (in ‡ *Phi.S 06025R*)
  L. Tibbett (in ‡ Cam.CAL 171)
  H. Schlusnus (*Ger*) (in ‡ Pol. 18086: 19039)

Le veau d'or Bs
N. Rossi-Lemeni   **G.DA 2050**
(*Vous qui faites . . .*) (*G.EC 216*: in ‡ ALP 1074:
QALP 10033: FALP 306; & ♭ Vic.ERA 186)
G. London   in ‡ **AmC.ML 4658**
(*Mefistofele, Walküre, etc.*)
  M. Szekely (*Hung*)   *Qual.KM 5012*
  ☆ A. Pernet   in ‡ Od.ODX 135
  J. Greindl (*Ger*)   ♭ Pol. 30007
  B. Gmyria (*Russ*)   USSRM.D 00742
  ◧ J. Mardones (*Ital*)   in ‡ Sca. 810*
     & in ‡ SBDH.LPP 3*

Valse Cho. — ARR. ORCH.
N.W. Ger. Phil.—Schüchter (in ‡ *Imp.ILP 110;*
         G.QDLP 6025; ♭ *Od.BEOW 3006*)
Belgian Radio—Marinetti (in ‡ *Mae.OAT 25007*)
H. Sandauer Orch. (♭ *Phi.KD 154: P 423154E*)

☆ Cincinnati Summer Op.—Cleva (in ‡ *B.AXTL 1035;*
     D.UST 233087; AmD.DL 8053: ♭ *ED 3525*)
Munich Phil.—Lehmann (*PV. 36105:* ♭ *Pol. 30029:*
                      in ‡ 19026)
Tivoli—Felumb (♭ *Mer.EP 1-5041;* FMer.MEP 14515)
Boston Prom.—Fiedler (♭ *G.7EP 7008;* ItV.A72R 0015;
                    in ‡ Vic.LM 1910)

— ARR. VLN. & PF.   Sarasate
E. Morini & L. Pommers (in ‡ *West.WN 18087*)
▽ E. Morini & pf., o.v. (*Vic. 10-1011;* ♭ *Cam.CAE 180:*
                     in ‡ CAL 207)

ACT III

Faites-lui mes aveux M-S (*Flower Song*)
  ℍ R. Fornia (AF.AGSB 61*)

Salut! Demeure chaste et pure T
R. Tucker   in ‡ **AmC.ML 4750**
N. Gedda (from set F)[1]   ♭ *G.7ER 5050*
(*below*)   (♭ *7ERQ 133*)
A. Schiøtz (*Dan*)[2]   **G.DB 10523**
(*Eugene Oniegin, No. 17*)
K. Baum   in ‡ **Roy. 1582**
A. da Costa   in ‡ **Roy. 1599**
J. Traxel (*Ger*)   ♭ *Pol. 32030*
(*Pêcheurs de Perles—Je crois entendre*)
☆ J. Björling   G.DB 21621
(*Africaine—O Paradis*)(in ‡ *BLP 1055*; in ‡ Vic.LM 1841;
                       FV.A 630259)

    A. Ivanov (*Russ*)   *USSR. 13270/1*
☆ G. Poggi (*Ital*)   in ‡ Cet.LPC 55003
    R. Crooks   in ‡ Cam.CAL 148
    S. Lemeshev (*Russ*)   USSRM.D 00107
  ℍ E. Caruso   ♭ *Vic.ERAT 7**
    A. Bonci (*Ital*)   in ‡ CEd. set 7002*
    F. de Lucia (*Ital?*)   in ‡ Ete. 492*
    G. Lauri-Volpi   ‡ AF.AGSB 57*
    G. Martinelli   in ‡ SBDH.LPG 4*
    F. Nuibo   AF.AGSB 79*
    G. Zenatello (*Ital*) in ‡ SBDH.LLP 8*
    T. Schipa (*Ital*)   in ‡ SBDH.GL 1*
    L. Slezak   in ‡ FRP. 2*

Il était un roi de Thulé
Air des bijoux: Ah! je ris . . . S
M. Stader   *PV. 36126*
             (♭ *Pol. 34034: 32068*)
(& in *Ger* on *PV. 36125:* ♭ *Pol. 34023: 32067*)
V. de los Angeles (from set F) ♭ *G.7ER 5050*
(*above*)   (♭ *7ERQ 133*)
Géori-Boué   in ‡ **Ura. 7070**
[also ☆ in ‡ *Od.ODX 117*]
D. Kirsten   in ‡ **AmC.ML 4730**
E. Bandrowska-Turska (*Pol*) (*USSR.20945/8* & in ‡ *D 2146*)
☆ R. Tebaldi (‡ *D.LW 5013:* D.Z 975: ♭ *VD 511*)
  V. de los Angeles (♭ *G.7R 163: RW 149*)
  J. Hammond (*Eng*) (♭ *G.7R 166*)

Il était un roi de Thulé S
E. Grümmer (*Ger*)   **G.EH 1440**
(*Mignon—Connais tu . . .*)   (GB 80: FKX 259)
G. Farrar (incomplete)[3] in ‡ **IRCC.L 7001**
  ℍ G. Bellincioni (*IRCC. 3140**)

Air des bijoux: Ah! je ris . . . S
G. Arnaldi (*Ital*)   **Cet.PE 203**
J. Brumaire   in ‡ **Phi.S 06025R**
(*above; Louise, Contes d'Hoffmann*)
K. Grayson & Cho.[4] in ‡ **Vic.LOC 3000**
              (♭ set EOB 3000)
    E. Shumskaya (*Russ*) USSRM.D 00847
☆ R. Peters   G.DB 21577
    V. de los Angeles in ‡ Vic.LM 1909
  ℍ M. Nevada   *IRCC. 3139*
    P. Donalda & pf.   AF.AGSA 4*
    E. Calvé[5]   in ‡ IRCC.L 7006*

Il était temps (*Garden Scene*) S. T, Bs
. . . **Bs part only**
    B. Gmyria (*Russ*) (*USSRM.D 00742*)
  ℍ F. Chaliapin (*Russ*) (in ‡ Sca. 801* & ‡ *SBDH.LLP 4**)

Il se fait tard S, T. [& Bs]
D. Kirsten & J. Björling   in ‡ **PRCC. 5**
M. Kišoňová-Hubová & J. Blaho [& F. Zvarik] (*Cz*)
          (in ‡ *Sup.LPM 137;* U. 5111C)
I. Szecsódy & T. Udwardy (*Hung*) (*Qual.MK 1567*)
☆ M. Teschemacher & M. Wittrisch (*Ger*) (♭ *G.7RW 534*)
  ℍ M. Zamboni & B. Gigli (*Ital*) (in ‡ *SBDH.LPP 5**)
    C. Boninsegna & F. de Lucia (*Ital*) (in ‡ Sca. 813*)
. . . **Il m'aime,** only ℍ C. Boninsegna (*Ital*) (AF.ABHB 8*)

ACT IV

Seigneur, daignez permettre S, Bs & cho.
    (*Church Scene*)
  ℍ M. Michaelova & F. Chaliapin (‡ *AudA.LPA 1002**)
. . . **Sop. part only** ℍ F. Litvinne (*IRCC. 3117**)
. . . **Souviens-toi du passé** Bs only
  ℍ J. Mardones (*Ital*) (in ‡ Sca. 810*)

Choeur des soldats Cho.
Royal Male Cho. & Maastricht Orch.
  —Koekelkoren   ♭ **EPhi.NBE 11009**
(*Tannhäuser—Pilgerchor*) (in ‡ *Phi.S 06013R: P 10048R:*
            N 12075G: ♭ N 402014E)
Paris Opéra Cho. & Orch.—Cluytens
(from set)   in ‡ **Vic.LM 1847**
Bavarian Radio Cho. (*Ger*) (in ‡ Pol. 19048)

— ARR. ORCH. only
Boston "Pops"—Fiedler (in ‡ *Vic.LRM 7045*)

Qu'attendez vous encore Bs & T
Vous qui faites l'endormie Bs
☆ E. Pinza & J. Peerce (G.DB 21577)
. . . **Vous qui faites . . .** only (*Serenade*)
N. Rossi-Lemeni   *G.DA 2050*
(*Veau d'or*) (EC 216: in ‡ ALP 1074: FALP 306:
             QALP 10033; & ♭ Vic. ERA 186)
C. Siepi   in ‡ **PRCC. 5**
F. Zvarík (*Cz*)   in ‡ **Sup.LPV 150**
(*above & below*)   (‡ U. 5104G)
A. Sved (*Hung*)   **Qual.MN 1078**
(*Avant de quitter . . .*)
    B. Gmyria (*Russ*) (*USSRM.D 00742*)
    A. Majak (*Polish*) (Muza.X 1723)
☆ A. Pernet (in ‡ Od.ODX 135)
    A. Mestral (♭ *G.7RF 290*)
    J. Greindl (*Ger*) (in ‡ Pol. 18147: 19043: ♭ *Pol. 30007*)
  ℍ J. Mardones (*Ital*) (in ‡ Sca. 810*)

Que voulez-vous, messieurs? (*Duel Scene*)
. . . Excerpt ℍ M. Bauermeister, A. Alvarez, Campanari &
    E. de Reszke (in ‡ *IRCC.L 7006**)[6]

Écoute-moi bien B (*Death of Valentine*)
F. Guarrera   in ‡ **PRCC. 5**
  ℍ T. Ruffo (*Ital*) (in ‡ Sca. 812*)

ACT V

Ballet Music
St. Louis Sym.—Golschmann ‡**DCap.CTL 7078**
(*Bizet: Carmen, Suite*) (‡ Cap.P 8288: ACap.CLCX 052)
[Excerpts on ♭ *Cap.FAP 8279*]
F.O.K. Sym.—Smetáček   ‡ **Sup.LPV 150**
(*above*)   (‡ U. 5104G)
Covent Garden—Braithwaite ‡ **P.PMC 1029**
(*Rossini, Verdi, etc.*)
(*Tchaikovsky* on ‡ MGM.E 3052)
Paris Opéra—Fournet   ‡ **EPhi.NBR 6000**
(*Rabaud*)   (‡ *Phi.A 00636R*)
(*idem & Delibes* on ‡ Epic.LC 3030) (also ‡ Phi.S 04013L)
Boston Prom.—Fiedler in ‡ **Vic.LM 9005**
    (♭ *Vic.ERA 64; ItV.A72R 0016; DV. 26013*)

---

[1] Includes following Trio *C'est ici? . . .* S, T, Bs.
[3] Recorded 1935.
[5] From Mapleson cylinders (incomplete).
[2] Recorded 1944.
[4] Sound-track of film *So this is love.*
[6] From Mapleson cylinders.

Ballet Music (*continued*)

N.W. Ger. Phil.—Schüchter   ‡ *Imp.ILP 128*
(*Liszt, Leoncavallo, Mascagni*)

☆ Covent Garden—Rignold   ‡ *P.PMD 1005*
(*Delibes*)

Regent Sym. (‡ Rgt. 7000)

☆ Paris Opéra—Sebastian (in ‡ MTW. 505; *ACC.MP 13*)
Lamoureux—Cloëz (♭ *Od.7AOE 1003*)
Metropolitan Op.—Cleva, omitting No. 3
(in ‡ *AmC.ML 4886*)
Munich Phil.—Lehmann (‡ Pol. 19026)

... Nos. 1, 3, 4, 5, 7
USSR. State—Samosud (*USSR. 15465/6 & 15686/7*)

... Nos. 1, 3, 5, 7
Belgian Radio—Marinetti (in ‡ *Mae.OAT 25007*)

... No. 7 only   ☆ R. Munro Orch. (♭ *D.DFE 6066*)

Alerte! Alerte! S, T, B (*Prison Scene*)
ℍ G. Farrar, E. Caruso, M. Journet (♭ *Vic.ERAT 8**)

Anges purs ... & Apothéose S, T, Bs
C. Pinza, G. Burris & E. Pinza   in ‡*PRCC. 5*
ℍ N. Melba, A. Saleza & E. de Reszke[1] (in ‡*IRCC.L7006**)

MIREILLE 4 Acts (orig. 5) 1864
COMPLETE RECORDING

Mireille	...	...	J. Vivalda (S)
Taven...		...	C. Gayraud (M-S)
Vincenette	...	...	M. Ignal (S)
Clémence	...	...	C. Jacquin (S)
Vincent	...	...	N. Gedda (T)
Ourrias	...	...	M. Dens (B)
Ramon	...	...	A. Vessières (Bs)
Ambroise	...	...	M. Cortis (B)

etc., E. Brasseur Cho. & Paris Cons. Orch.
—Cluytens[2]   ‡ *C.CX 1299/301*
(‡ FCX 363/5; Angel. set 3533)

EXCERPTS

Valse—O légère hirondelle S   Act I
Vincenette, votre âge S & T   Act I
La Brise est douce S & T (*Chanson de Magali*) Act II
(both with M. Malkassian)
Trahir Vincent . . . Mon cœur ne peut changer S   Act II
Heureux petit berger S   Act III
Ah, parlez encore prière 2S   Act III
(with A. Gabriel)

M. Robin (S) & Paris Cons.—Blareau
(2ss)   ‡ *Lon.LD 9140*
(*Donizetti: Lucia* excpts. on ‡ D.LXT 2898; ‡ Lon.LL 922;
Chanson de Magali is not included)

Valse—O légère hirondelle S   Act I
La Brise est douce S & T (*Chanson de Magali*) Act II
(with P. Gianotti)
Trahir Vincent . . . Mon cœur ne peut changer S   Act II
Heureux petit berger S   Act III
Voici la vaste plaine S (*Désert de la crau*) Act IV

J. Micheau   ‡ *D.LXT 2789*
(*Bizet: Pêcheurs de perles*, excpts.)   (‡ Lon.LL 939)

Valse—O légère hirondelle S   Act I
P. Alarie   in ‡ *Phi.N 00663R*
(*below, Roméo et Juliette, Delibes, etc.*)
☆ L. Pons (in ‡ *Od.OD 1013*)
ℍ F. Hempel (*AF.AGSB 29**)

— ARR. ORCH. Polish Radio—Rachonia (*Muza. 2127*)

La brise est douce S & T (*Chanson de Magali*)
Act II
P. Alarie & L. Simoneau   ‡ *LT.DTL 93018*
(*Roméo et Juliette, Carmen, Manon*)
(‡ Sel. 270.C.008; in ‡ West.WL 5358)

Trahir Vincent . . . Mon cœur ne peut changer S
☆ Géori-Boué (in ‡ *Od.ODX 117*)

Si les filles d'Arles (*Couplets d'Ourrias*) B Act II
☆ A. Pernet (in ‡ *Od.ODX 135*)

Heureux petit berger S   Act III
P. Alarie   in ‡ *Phi.N 00663R*
(*above, Roméo et Juliette, Bizet, etc.*)

Anges du Paradis T   Act III
☆ G. Thill (in ‡ *C.FH 503*)
ℍ C. Vezzani (in ‡ *Od.ODX 126**)
F. Nuibo (*AF.AGSB 79**)

Voici, la vaste plaine S (*Désert de la crau*) Act IV
☆ Géori-Boué (in ‡ *Od.ODX 117*)
M. Angelici (in ‡ *G.FBLP 1051*)

PHILÉMON ET BAUCIS 3 Acts 1860

Au bruit des lourds marteaux Bs   Act I
(*Vulcan's Song*)
☆ A. Pernet (in ‡ *Od.ODX 135*)
ℍ H. Belhomme (in ‡ *FRP. 3**)

Que les songes sont heureux (*Berceuse*) Bs   Act I
☆ A. Pernet (in ‡ *Od.ODX 135*)
ℍ M. Journet (in ‡ *SBDH.LPG 5**)

(La) REINE DE SABA 4 Acts 1862
Cortège orch.
Hamburg Philharmonia—H-J. Walther
MSB. 78202
(*Skilton: Suite primeval—Deer Dance*)
(also *MSB. 78116*, d.c.; in ‡ *MGM.E 3144*)

Sous les pieds (*Cavatine de Soliman*) Bs   Act I
ℍ M. Journet (in ‡ *SBDH.JALP 19** & in ‡ *JAL 7002**)

Plus grand dans son obscurité S   Act III
☆ E. Wysor (A) (in ‡ *Ply. 12-47*)

ROMÉO ET JULIETTE 5 Acts 1867
COMPLETE RECORDINGS

Casts	Set A	Set B
Juliet (S)	J. Micheau	I. Maslennikova
Romeo (T)	R. Jobin	S. Lemeshev
Friar Lawrence (B) ...	H. Rehfuss	M. Mikhailov
Gertrude (M-S) ...	O. Ricquier	N. Ostroumova
Capulet (Bs) ...	C. Cambon	I. Petrov
Tybalt (T) ...	L. Rialland	T. Tcheriyakov
Mercutio (B)... ...	P. Mollet	I. Burlak
Gregory (B) }	A. Philippe	I. Sipayev
Prince of Verona }		
Stephano (S)... ...	C. Collart	N. Sokolova

Set A, with Paris Opéra Cho. & Orch.—Erede
   ‡ *D.LXT 2890/2*
(6ss)   (‡ D.LXT 5021; Lon. set LLA 18)
[Highlights on ‡ D.LXT 5021; Lon.LL 1111]

Set B, with Bolshoi Th. Cho. & Orch.—Nebolsin
(in *Russian*) (6ss)   ‡ *USSR.D 01336/41*

ACT I

Allons, jeunes gens Bs (*Air de Capulet*) Act I
ℍ L. Melchissedec (*IRCC. 3149**)
P. Plançon (*AF.AGSA 32**)

Ballade de la reine Mab B   Act I
M. Dens   ♭ *Pat.ED 34*
(*Hérodiade & Favorita*)   (in ‡ *DT 1020*)

Valse: Je veux vivre dans ce rêve S [B & A] Act I
P. Alarie   in ‡ *Phi.N 00663R*
(*Mireille; & Delibes, Thomas, etc.*)

P. Munsel, J. Cameron (B), J. Howe (A)[3]
   in ‡ *G.BLP 1023*
(in ‡ Vic.LM 7012: ♭ set WDM 7012; ‡ G.QBLP 5015)

K. Grayson[4] (in ‡ *Vic.LOC 3000*: ♭ set EOB 3000)
G. Gasparyan (*Russ*) (in ‡ *USSR.D 1901*)
ℍ G. Farrar (*AF.AGSB 55**)

— ARR. ORCH. ☆ Cincinnati Summer Op.—Cleva
(in ‡ B.AXTL 1035; AmD.DL 8053: ♭ ED 3525;
‡ D.UST 233087; AFest.CFR 457; ♭ SpC.SCGE 80007)

Ange adorable S & T   Act I
ℍ L. Bori & B. Gigli (*AF.AGSB 58**)
G. Farrar & E. Clément (*AF.AGSB 25**)

ACT II

Ah! lève-toi, soleil T (*Cavatina*)
N. Gedda   in ‡ *C.CX 1130*
(*Auber, Bizet, Cilea, etc.*)   (‡ FCX 302; Angel. 35096)
☆ R. Crooks (in ‡ *Cam.CAL 148*)
ℍ F. Nuibo (*SBDH.G 9*)*
E. Clément (in ‡ *Sca. 819**)

---

[1] From Mapleson cylinders.
[2] Recorded at Aix-en-Provence Festival, July 1954. *O légère hirondelle* is performed after the end of the opera on side 6.
[3] Sound-track of film *Melba*.   [4] Sound-track of film *So this is love*.

187

O nuit divine S & T
P. Alarie & L. Simoneau   ♯ **LT.DTL 93018**
(*below; Carmen, Manon, Mireille*)
   (in ♯ *Sel. 270.C.008;* West.*WL 5358*)
E. Shumskaya & I. Kozlovsky (*Russ*) (USSR. 020615/6)

ACT III

Dieu, qui fis l'homme . . . Bs
J. Bailly   in ♯ **SBDH.TOB 2**
(*Barbiere, Don Carlos, Favorita, etc.*)

Que fais tu, blanche tourterelle? M-S
 ♮ R. Fornia (AF.AGSB 61*)

ACT IV

Va, je t'ai pardonné . . . Non, ce n'est pas le jour
                      S & T
P. Alarie & L. Simoneau   ♯ **LT.DTL 93018**
(*above; Mireille, Carmen, Manon*) (in ♯ *Sel. 270.C.008;*
                           West.*WL 5358*)
J. Fenn & R. Manton   ♯ **DCap.CTL 7034**
(*Tchaikovsky: Romeo & Juliet, duet*) (♯ Cap.P 8189;
                        ACap.CLCX 012)

Mon père! . . . Bientôt une pâleur livide effacera
                               Bs & S
 ♮ M. Journet & Y. Gall (*IRCC. 3144**)

Salut, tombeau (*Tomb Scene*) S & T   Act V
. . . Tenor part only ♮ P. Franz (in ♯ Ete. 708*)

SAPHO 3 Acts   1857
Chanson du pâtre   M-S ♮ M. de Reszke (*SBDH.P 6**)
O ma lyre immortelle (*Stances*) S ♮ F. Litvinne (*IRCC. 3117**)

SONGS
Collections

Chanson de printemps (Tourneux) 1860   (d)
Au printemps (Barbier) 1865   (d)
Le Premier Jour de Mai (Passerat)   (G)
Le Vallon (Lamartine) *c.* 1841   (G)
L'Absent (Gounod) 1876 (?)   (d)
À la brise: Madrigal (Barbier) 1875   (d)
Au rossignol (Lamartine)   (d)
Ave Maria 1859   (d)
Medjé: Chanson arabe (Barbier) 1865   (G)
Dite, la jeune belle . . : Barcarolle (Gautier)   (d)
Venise (Musset)   (G)
Le Temps des roses (Roy)   (G)
Mignon (Gallet) 1871   (d)
Sérénade (Hugo) (*Quand tu chantes*)   (d)
La Reine du Matin (Barbier & Carré) 1878 (d)

(d) by R. Doria (S) & T. Janopoulo (pf.)
(G) by J. Giovanetti (Bs) & S. Gouat (pf.)
                        ♯ **Plé.P 3068**

Chanson de printemps (E. Tourneux) 1860
Ce que je suis sans toi (de Peyre) 1882
Venise (Musset)
Ma belle amie est morte (Gautier) 1872
O ma belle rebelle (Baïf)
Viens! les gazons verts (Barbier) 1875
Les deux pigeons (La Fontaine) 1883
   G. Souzay (B), J. Bonneau (pf.)   ♯ **D.LW 5097**
                        (♯ *Lon.LD 9110*)

Venise (Musset)
Au rossignol (Lamartine)
Viens! les gazons sonts verts (Barbier)
   S. Danco (S), G. Agosti (pf.)   ♯ **D.LW 5128**
(*Bellini*)   (♯ *Lon.LD 9144*)

L'Absent (Gounod) 1876
Aimons-nous (Barbier) 1874
Viens! les gazons sonts verts (Barbier) 1875
   G. Touraine (S), J. Bonneau (pf.)
                      ♯ **Lum.LD 3-402**
(*Chabrier, Poulenc, etc.*)

Au printemps (Barbier)
 ♮ E. Calvé (S) & pf. (AF.AGSB 46*)

Ave Maria (Meditation on BACH: Prelude, WTC. 1)
R. Schock (T) & Cho.   **G.DA 5521**
(*Liszt: Es muss ein Wunderbares sein*)   (♭ *7PW 517*)
(*Bizet: Agnus Dei on EG 8158;* ♭ *7MW 618*)

P. Munsel (S), Cho. & org.   in ♯ **G.BLP 1023**
[Film *Melba*] (in ♯ *G.QBLP 5015;* Vic.*LM 7012:*
                         ♭ set *WDM 7012*)
   I. Bozzi (S) & cho.   Dur.*AI 10099:* in ♯ *AI 520*
▽ L. Melchior (T) & Orch.   MGM. 3004
☆ B. Gigli (T) & Orch.   ♭ *G.7EB 6013: 7ERQ 134*
R. Tauber (T) & Orch.   in ♯ *AmD.DL 7535*
J. Candel (S), Cho. & Orch.   in ♯ *EPhi.BBR 8042*
                       (♯ *Phi.P 10028R*)
T. Lemnitz (S) & Orch.   ♭ *T.U 45514;*
                       CanT.*GF 63018*
M. Lanza (T) & Orch.   in ♯ *G.ALP 1071*
H. Schlusnus (B)   ♭ *Pol. 30151*
G. Fields (S)   ♭ *G.7EG 8071*
♮ E. Albani (S)   in ♯ *HRS. 3008**
E. Destinn (S)   in ♯ *Sca. 804**
A. Fitziu   IRCC. 3147*

— **ARRANGEMENTS**
CHORUS: Cho.—W. Schumann (*Cap.DAS 381:* ♭ *KASF 381:*
                       in ♯ *L 382*)
ORGAN: R. Ellsasser (in ♯ *MGM.E 198:* ♭ *X 198*)
HPSI.: E. Silver (in ♯ *Roy.* 1550)
MUSIC BOX from Bornand Collection: in ♭ *AmC.A 1865*, etc.

BIONDINA   Song Cycle
Prologue & 11 Songs in *Italian* (Zaffira)
H. Cuénod (T), F. Holetschek (pf.)
                       ♯ **Nix.WLP 5278**
(*Fauré*)   (♯ West WL 5278)

Medjé: Chanson arabe (Barbier)
☆ G. Thill (T) & Orch. (in ♯ *C.FHX 5012;* Angel.*C 33001*)

Où voulez-vous aller? (Gautier) (*Barcarolle*)
C. Devos (T), G. Lecompte (pf.)   Pat.**PDT 283**
(*Bizet, Lalo, Massenet*)   (♭ *45D 111*)

Repentir (*O Divine Redeemer*)
A. Shilling (Tr.) & Columbus Boys' Choir (*Eng*)
(in ♯ *B.LAT 8070;* AmD.*DL 8106:* ♭ set *ED 831*)

Sérénade (Hugo) (*Quand tu chantes . . .*)
☆ E. Noréna (S) & Orch. (JpV. ND 837)

There is a green hill far away (Mrs. Alexander)
R. Fairhurst (Tr.), C. Smart (org.) (*D.F 10336*)

Viens! les gazons sonts verts (Barbier)
M. Sénéchal (T), J. Bonneau (pf.)
                     in ♯ *Phi.N 00681R*
(*Massenet, Bizet, Lalo, etc.*)

GRADWOHL, Pierre (b. 1905)

Divertissement champêtre Ballet Suite
☆ Paris Cons. Students—Gradwohl (♯ Clc. 6137)

GRAINGER, Percy A. (b. 1882)

Collections

Country Gardens
Shepherd's Hey 1922
Irish Tune from County Derry 1911
Spoon River 1922
Children's March (Over the hills and far away) 1918
Mock Morris
Molly on the shore 1921
   Rochester "Pops"—Gould   ♯ **AmC.AL 49**
                       (♭ *A 1912*)

Handel in the Strand (a)
Irish Tune from County Derry (Londonderry Air) (b)
Mock Morris (a)
Molly on the shore (a)
   ☆ (a) Philharmonia—Braithwaite
      (b) Liverpool Phil.—Sargent   in ♯ *AmC.RL 3042*
      (*Mendelssohn, Berlioz, Elgar*)

Molly on the shore
Handel in the Strand [with P. Grainger, pf.]
Mock Morris
Irish Tune from County Derry
   ☆ Sym.—Stokowski   ♭ *G.7ER 5046*
                     (♭ Vic.*ERA 124*)

Country Gardens
Hamburg Philharmonia—H-J. Walther
(*below*)   **MSB. 78113**
Anon. Orch. (in ♯ *Jay.* 3004)

♯ = Long-playing, 33⅓ r.p.m.   ♭ = 45 r.p.m.   ♮ = Auto. couplings, 78 r.p.m.

Irish Tune from County Derry "*Londonderry Air*"
A.B.C. Sydney Sym.—Goossens   **G.DB 9792**
(*Butterworth: Shropshire Lad*, s. 1)
Hamburg Philharmonia—H-J. Walther (*MSB. 78023:*
in ‡ *60041*)

Molly on the shore orig. pf. 1918; or str. orch.
Hamburg Philharmonia—H-J. Walther
(*above & below*)   **MSB. 78113**
American Art Qtt.   in ‡ **BB.LBC 1086**
☆ Decca Little Sym.—Mendoza (in ‡ *AmD.DL 5211;*
D.US 223524)

Shepherd's Hey pf. or orch.
Hamburg Philharmonia—H-J. Walther
(*above*)   **MSB. 78113**

FOLK SONG ARRANGEMENTS
Six Dukes went a-fishin'
P. Pears (T), B. Britten (pf.)   **G.DA 2032**
(*Arr. Britten: O waly, wcly*)

(The) Sprig of Thyme
J. Vyvyan (S), E. Lush (pf.)   in ‡ **D.LXT 2797**
(† *Songs of England*)   (in ‡ Lon.LL 806)

ARRANGEMENT
Beata viscera Conductus, XIIIth Century 3 vv.
Trapp Family Cho.—Wasner   ‡ **B.LAT 8038**
(*Christmas Music*)   (‡ AmD.DL 9489)

GRAM, Hans (1771-1816)

SONG
Death Song of an Indian chief 1791
Anon. Baritone & orch.—Korn in ‡ **Allo. 3148**
(*Gottschalk, Creston, Barber, etc.*)

GRAM, Peder (b. 1881)

Variations on a theme of Weyse, Op. 15 pf.
Romance, Op. 8a pf. (one side)
F. Jensen   ♭ **C.LDX 7018/9**

GRANADOS Y CAMPINA, Enrique
(1867-1916)

Allegro di concierto, C sharp major pf. *c.* 1890
R. Arroyo   in ‡ **CND. 1002**
(*Albeniz, Angles, Larregla, etc.*)
O. Frugoni   in ‡ **AmVox.PL 9420**
(*below; Falla, Albeniz, Turina*)

(12) DANZAS ESPAÑOLAS, Op. 37 pf. 1893
COLLECTIONS
Nos. 1-12, COMPLETE
J. Echaniz   ‡ **Nix.WLP 5181**
(‡ West.WL. 5181; BrzV.SLP 5516)
A. de Larrocha   ‡ **B.AXTL 1072**
(‡ AmD.DL 9762)
G. Soriano   ‡ **Sel. 320.C.064**

Nos. 8, 9, 12
A. Iturbi   in ‡ **Vic.LM 1788**
(*Turina, Infante, etc.*)   (in ‡ FV.A 630231)
[No. 9 only in ♭ ERA 198; ♭ FV.A 95215]

Nos. 2, 5, 6 — ARR. ORCH. Lamote de Grignon
Philharmonia—Schüchter   ‡ **P.PMD 1018**
(*Turina*)   (‡ MGM.E 3018; *Od.OD 1017*)
[No. 2 only in ‡ MGM.E 3046]
Concerts Colonne—Sebastian   ‡ **FUra. 5102**
(*Respighi*)
(Nos. 2 & 5 only with *Chavez* on ‡ Ura. 7144)

Nos. 4, 6, 12 — ARR. ORCH.
Buenos Aires Sym.—Cases   ‡ **Tem.TT 2256**
(*Albeniz*)

No. 2, C minor, Oriental
R. Spivak   **ArgV. 11-7970**
(*No. 7*)
J. Iturbi   in ‡ **Vic.LRM 7057**
(♭ *set ERB 7057*)
— ARR. HARP N. Zabaleta (*ArgOd. 46087*)
— ARR. ORCH.
Madrid Theatre—Moreno Torroba in ‡ **AmD.DL 9788**

No. 5, E minor, Andaluza *or* **Playera**
P. Spagnolo   in ‡ **D.LXT 2947**
(*Albeniz, Casella, etc*)   (‡ Lon.LL 1040)
O. Frugoni   ‡ **AmVox.PL 9420**
(*above; & Albeniz, etc.*)
L. Pennario   in ‡ **DCap.CTL 7054**
(*below; & Falla, Infante, etc.*) (‡ Cap.P 8190)
A. Rubinstein   ♭ **Vic.ERA 200**
(*below; & Falla, Mompou*) (♭ ItV.A72R 0024; FV.A 95209)
R. Spivak   **ArgV. 66-6114**
(*Albeniz: Cuba*)
L. Brunelli (*ArgV. 66-0003*)
A. Semprini (*G.B 10826*)
☆ J. Iturbi (♭ *G.7RF 109: 7RW 140: 7RQ 3005*)
G. Copeland (n.v. in ‡ MGM.E 3025; o.v. JpV.NF 4222)

— ARRANGEMENTS
GUITAR
M. L. Anido (♭ *ArgOd.BSOAE 4503:* in ‡ *LDC 521*)
M. D. Cano (*Dur.AI 10151:* in ‡ *AI 506:* ♭ *AI 6022*)
☆ A. Segovia (in ‡ *D.UMT 273029;* ♭ *SpC.SCGE 80004*)
ORGAN: J. Perceval (in ‡ *ArgOd.LDC 508*)
2 HARPS: C. Salzédo & L. Lawrence (in ‡ Mer.MG 10144:
♭ EP 1-5006)

VLN. & PF. Kreisler
I. Zilzer & F. Eberson   **C.LDX 18**
(*Albeniz: Malagueña, Op. 165, No. 3*)
A. Campoli & E. Gritton   in ‡ **D.LXT 5012**
(‡ D.LK 40110 & in *LW 5218*)   (in ‡ Lon.LL 1171)
R. Odnoposoff & J. Antonietti   in V‡ **MMS. 915**
T. Magyar & W. Hielkema   in ‡ **Phl.S 06049R**
☆ Y. Menuhin & A. Baller[1]   in ‡ **Vic.LM 1742**
(‡ JpV.LS 2004)
VLC. & PF.: J. Starker & L. Pommers (in ‡ Nix.PLP 584:
Per SPL 584; Cpt.MC 20054)
ORCH.
Madrid Theatre—Moreno Torroba in ‡ **AmD.DL 9788**
J. Schmied Orch. (in ‡ *Vien.LPR 1031*)
VOICE in *Spanish*
R. Gigli (S) & Orch.   **G.DA 11353**
(*Sadko: Song of the Indian Guest*)
P. Fleta (T) & Orch. (in ‡ *Pat.DT 1021*)
☆ G. Pederzini (M-S) (*ArgOd. 57022*)
VOICE & CASTANETS
Argentina & Orch. (in ‡ Mont.FM 42)
HARMONICA & PF.[2]
L. Adler & L. Colin (in ‡ CHS.CHS 1168; FMer.MLP 7026)

No. 6, D major, Rondalla Aragonesa (*"Jota"*)
☆ E. Boynet (♭ *AmVox.VIP 45500*)
— ARR. ORCH.
Madrid Theatre—Moreno Torroba in ‡ **AmD.DL 9789**

No. 7, Valenciana
R. Spivak (*No. 2*)   **ArgV. 11-7970**

No. 10, G major (Allegretto) (*"Danza triste"*)
☆ J. Iturbi (♭ *G. 7RF 109: 7RQ 3004: 7RW 140*)
— ARR. GUITAR
N. Yepes   in ‡ **D.LXT 2974**
(‡ FST 153076; Lon.LL 1042)
(† Spanish Music of XVIth-XXth Cent.)
☆ A. Segovia (in ‡ *D.UMT 273029;* ♭ *AmD.ED 3510;*
SpC.SCGE 80005)

No. 11, G minor
— ARR. CASTANETS & ORCH.
P. Lopez & Sym.—Franco   ♭ **G.7EPL 13029**
(*Albeniz*)   (in ‡ LDLP 1011)

Dedicatoria (*Cuentos para la juventud, No. 1*) pf.
— ARR. GUITAR Santias
C. Santias (in ‡ *FestF.FLD 32;* SpFest.HF 3201)

---

[1] This is the Japanese recording. Other lists give LM 1742 accompanist as G. Moore (English recording). It is impossible to finalise the attributions.
[2] Called "*Beguine*", we are assured by Mr. Adler that it is in fact this dance.

GOYESCAS pf. 1912

BOOK I: 1. Los Requiebros   2. Coloquio en la reja
3. El Fandango del candil
4. Quejas, o la Maja y el ruiseñor
BOOK II: 5. El amor y la muerte (Ballad)
6. Epilogo (Serenada de Espectro)
APPENDIX: 7. El Pelele (Esceno Goyesca)

COMPLETE RECORDINGS

J. Echaniz   ♯ Nix.WLP 5322
                                (♯ West.WL 5322)

L. Querol   ♯ Sel.LPG 8681
                                (♯ T.LE 6528; SpT.TLA 20002)
[Nos. 3 & 7 also on ♭ Sel. 470.C.008)

J. Falgarona   ♯ AmVox.PL 8580

A. Iturbi   ♯ Vic.LM 1925
[Nos. 1, 3, 4, 7, also in ♭ Vic.set ERB 62] (♯ ItV.A12R 0178)

... Nos. 1-4 & 7
A. de Larrocha   ♯ AmD.DL 9779
N. Magaloff   ♯ D.LXT 2900
                                (♯ Lon.LL 954)

... Nos. 5 & 6
N. Magaloff   ♯ D.LW 5179
                                (♯ Lon.LD 9181)

BOOK I, COMPLETE (Nos. 1-4)
☆ F. Valenzi   ♯ Rem. 199-116
[No. 2 only in ♯ Ply. 12-92]

No. 4, Quejas, o la Maja y el ruiseñor
M. Lympany   G.B 10531
(2ss)   (G.EA 4145; ♭ Vic.EHA 13)
(Litolff: Scherzo, on ♭ G.7EP 7014: 7EPQ 528)
L. Pennario   in ♯ DCap.CTL 7054
(below; Falla, etc.)   (♯ Cap.P 8190: ♭ FAP 8235)
P. Spagnolo   in ♯ D.LXT 2947
(Albeniz, Falla, etc.)   (♯ Lon.LL 1040)
D. Raucea   in ♯ D.LXT 2969
(Albeniz, Casella, St.-Saëns, etc.)   (♯ Lon.LL 1033)
A. Rubinstein   ♭ Vic.ERA 200
(above; Falla & Mompou) (♭ ItV.A72R 0024; FV.A 95209)
S. Sorin   ♯ SOT. 1038
(Liszt, Scriabin, Chopin)
P. Sebastiani   ArgV. 66-6158
(Ginastera: Malambo)
M. Pressler   in ♯ MGM.E 3129
(Respighi, Chabrier, Albeniz, etc.)
A. de Rcoa   ♭ ArgOd.BSOAE 4522
(Albeniz: Iberia)
E. Osta   in ♯ Allo. 3151
☆ C. Arrau   ♭ C.SEL 1523
(Mendelssohn: Rondo capriccioso)   (C.LOX 819)

— ARR. 2 PFS.
E. Bartlett & R. Robertson in ♯ MGM.E 3150

GOYESCAS Opera 1916
Intermezzo orch.
Philharmonia—Karajan   in ♯ C.CX 1265
(Gioielli della Madonna, Traviata, etc.)
                          (♯ FCX 407: QCX 10150; Angel. 35207)
L.S.O.—Poulet   in ♯ P.PMC 1006
(Albeniz, Turina, Falla)   (♯ MGM.E 3073; Od.ODX 137)
Madrid Cha.—Argenta   in ♯ LI.TW 91020
(Gimenez, Chapi, etc.)(in ♯ Ambra.MCC 30002 &
                                ♯ Mont.FM 6)
Madrid Theatre—Moreno Torroba
                        in ♯ AmD.DL 9789
Hollywood Bowl—Dragon in ♯DCap.CTL 7074
                        (in ♯ Cap.P 8275: ♭ FAP 8284)
Colón Theatre—Cases   ArgOd. 66048
(Vida Breve—Danza)(♭ BSOAE 4523 & in ♯ LDC 519;
                                ♯ Od.OD 1018, d.c.)
Col. Sym.—Kurtz   in ♯ AmC.CL 773

☆ Philharmonia—Weldon (C.SVX 48)
  Boston Prom.—Fiedler (in ♯ Cam.CAL 176)
  Sym.—Stokowski (in ♯ Vic.LM 9029)

— ARR. VLN. & PF.
A. Mus & D. Colacelli (ArgOd. 66033)

— ARR. VLC. & PF.   Cassadó
J. Starker & L. Pommers (in ♯ Per.SPL 584;
                      in ♯ Nix.PLP 584; ♯ Cpt.MC 20054)
A. Odnoposoff & Berta Huberman (ArgV. 68-8046)
A. Janigro & E. Bagnoli (in ♯ West.WN 18004)
D. Shafran & pf. (USSRM.D 363)
M. Rostropovich & pf. (in ♯ USSR.D 1178)

☆ G. Piatigorsky (♭ G.7RQ 229; in ♯ ItV.A12R 0105;
                                & ♭ Vic.ERA 122)

— ARR. SAX. & PF.   M. Mule (in ♯ D.LX 3140; Lon.LS 1187)

La Maja y el Ruiseñor S
♮ A. Fitziu (IRCC. 3147*)

— ARR. CASTANETS, DANCING & 2 PFS.
Rosario & Antonio & 2 pfs.   C.DB 3461

SONGS
(10) TONADILLAS AL ESTILO ANTIGUO
1. La Maja de Goya   2. El Majo discreto
3. El tra la la   4. El Majo timido
5. La Maja dolorosa (3 songs)   6. El Mirar de la Maja
7. Amor y Odio   8. Callejeo
9. Las Currutacas modestas   10. El Majo olvidado
L. R. de Aragon (S), F. Lavilla (pf.)
                                ♯ LT.EL 93016
                      (♯ Sel.LA 1049; Hispa.HH 1204)
[with F. Sola (M-S) in No. 9; with cor anglais in No. 5]

Nos. 2, 5, 6
☆ V. de los Angeles (S), G. Moore (pf.) ♯ G.BLP 1037
(Falla)   (♯ WBLP 1037: FBLP 1040)
[No. 6 only on ♭ Vic.ERA 106]

No. 1, La Maja de Goya
— ARR. GUITAR   Segovia
C. Aubin   in ♯ Eko.LG 1
(† Guitar recital)
☆ A. Segovia (in ♯ D.UMT 273029)

No. 2, El Majo discreto
L. Huarte (S)   ♯ MusH.LP 3004
(Montsalvatge, Garcia Leoz, Rodrigo, Turina)
M. Plaza (S)   in ♯ Roy. 1561

No. 5, La Maja dolorosa
L. Ibarrondo (M-S), M. Sandoval (pf.)
                           in ♯ Rem. 199-139
(Guridi, etc.)   (♯ Cum.CR 297)

No. 7, Amor y Odio
R. Gomez (M-S), P. Vallribera (pf.) Reg.C 10282
(Turina: Anhelos)   (♭ SEDL 19042)

Unspec. Tonadilla
N. Chayres (T) & pf.   ♯ Kings. 300
(Falla: 7 Pop. Songs, & Turina)

GREAVES, Thomas (fl. 1600)
    SEE: † HISTORY OF MUSIC IN SOUND   (33)
          † TRIUMPHS OF ORIANA

GRECO, Gaetano (c. 1657-c. 1728)
    SEE: † CLAVECINISTES ITALIENS

GREEF, Arthur de (1862-1940)

(4) Old Flemish Folksongs orch.
Belgian Radio—André   ♯ DT.LGX 66024
(Franck)   (♯ T.LSK 7022)
There have been ▽ recordings.

GREEN, Ray (b. 1909)

Sunday Sing Symphony fl., cl., bsn. & orch. 1950
A.R.S. Orch.—Schönherr   ♯ ARS. 31
(Mennin & Dello Joio)
▽ Older Recordings include:
Sea calm Cho.—Vriondes (NMQR. 1008)
Holiday for four pf., vla., cl., bsn. (Alco. set AR 102)

GREENE, Maurice (1695-1755)
    SEE: † OLD ENGLISH MASTERS
          † ENGLISH CHURCH MUSIC, VOL. III
          † HISTORY OF MUSIC IN SOUND (52)

♯ = Long-playing, 33⅓ r.p.m.   ♭ = 45 r.p.m.   ♮ = Auto. couplings, 78 r.p.m.

GREGORIAN CHANT

(Selected items only)

SEE ALSO: † HISTORY OF MUSIC IN SOUND (11, 12, 13)
　　　　　† MASTERPIECES OF MUSIC BEFORE 1750
　　　　　† HISTOIRE DE LA MUSIQUE VOCALE

COLLECTIONS: GREGORIAN INSTITUTE ISSUES

Requiem Mass　　　　　　　　　　　♯ GIOA.PX 1
Masses VIII & IX, Credo I & III　　　　♯ GIOA.PX 2
Masses IV & XI, Credo IV, Ambrosian Gloria　♯ GIOA.PX 3
Masses V, XII, XVII, XVIII　　　　　　♯ GIOA.PX 4
　Pius X Cho. of Liturgical Music—Morgan, with org. acc.

Mass I, Te Deum, Sequences, Antiphons　♯ GIOA.BN 1
Mass X, Sequence, Responses, etc.　　　♯ GIOA.BN 2
　St. Joseph Benedictine Convent

Antiphons of B.V.M., Magnificat, etc.　♯ GIOA.SA 1
Christmas Introits, Communions, etc.　♯ GIOA.SA 2
　Stanbrook Abbey Cho.

Kyrie II, Gloria XV, Sanctus XI, Propers, etc.
　Mount Angel Seminary—Nicholson　♯ GIOA.MALP 1

Holy Saturday Exultet
　Darlington Seminary—Murphy　　　♯ GIOA.DS 1

COLLECTIONS (Various)

Solesmes Abbey Cho.—Gajard　　　♯ D.LXT 2704/8
　(Set I, 10ss; Set II, 8ss)　　　& LX 3118/21
　[Set I also on ♯ Lon.LL 547/51, set LLA 14; and 42ss,
　D.GAF 15120/40; also Set II, ♯ D.FA 133111/4:
　Set I, ♯ FAT 173690/3]
　☆ Solesmes Abbey Cho.—Gajard (♯ Vic. set LCT 6011,
　　　　　　　　　　　　　　　　　　　4ss)
St. Meinrad's Abbey Schola　(4ss)　♯ AmLum. 501/2
Moine Trappist Cho. ('Vol. I')　　　♯ Per.SPL 569
Benedictine Abbey Cho. ('Vol. II')　♯ Per.SPL 570
St. Wandrille de Fontenelle Cho. ('Vol. III')♯ Per.SPL 576
Benedictine Abbey Cho. ('Vol. IV')　♯ Per.SPL 707
Angers Cath. Cho.　(Soriano)　　　♯ SM. 33-02
La Schola des Pères du Saint-Esprit—Deiss　♯ C.FCX 221
　　　　　　　　　　　　　　　　　(♯ Angel. 35116)
St. Francis of Assisi Cho.　　　　♯ G.QCLP 12005
Cho.—R. Wagner　　　　♯ Layos. 106, 596 & 111

Easter Sunday Mass
　Beuron Abbey Cho.—Pfaff　　　♯ HP.APM 14017
　[excerpts also on PV. 5411 & ♭ Pol. 37001]

First Vespers of Christmas
　Beuron Abbey Cho.—Pfaff　　　♯ HP.AP 13005
　　　　　　　　　(♯ AmD.DL 7546; & PV. 5405/6)

Requiem Mass
　Beuron Abbey Cho.—Pfaff　　　♯ HP.APM 14002
　　　　　　　　　　　　　　　　(♭ Pol. 37042)

Orationes Solemnes (Good Friday Liturgy) & Adoration
　Beuron Abbey Cho.—Pfaff　　　♯ HP.APM 14034
　[Orationes solemnes only on ♭ Pol. 37032]

Easter Ordinary of the Mass　　　♭ Pol. 37031
　Beuron Abbey Cho.—Pfaff　　　(in ♯ AmD.ARC 3001)

Office for Good Friday: Veneration of the Cross
Officium pro defunctis
Requiem Mass
　En-Calcat Monastery Cho.　　　♯ SM. 33-13/4
　(with Epistles, Gospels, etc.)

Puer Natus; Alleluia dies sanctificatus
　Versailles Cath. Cho.　　　in ♯ SM. 33-03

Proper of Whitsunday
　Rennes Cathedral—Orhant　　　♯ SM. 33-23
　(A. Gabrieli: Missa Brevis)

GRETCHANINOFF, Alexander
(1864-1956)

INSTRUMENTAL

COLLECTION

A Child's Day, Op. 109　10 pieces　pf.　1927
... At work
Grandfather's Album, Op. 119　27 pieces　pf.　1928
... No. 8, Danse de l'hirondelle;
No. 11, Le chatou malade
　S. Bianca　　　　　　　　　　MSB. 22
　(with spoken commentary)　　　(in ♯ 60041)

Op. 119, No. 1, Mama, ma bien aimée
　S. Bianca (with spoken commentary)　MSB. 23
　(Toch: Tanz und Spielstücke, excerpt)　(in ♯ 60041)

Fantasy on Bashkir themes, Op. 125　fl. & hp.
　J. Roberts & E. Vito　　　in ♯ Per.SPL 721
　(Shaposhnikoff, Jongen, Bizet, etc.)

(3) Pieces, Op. 198　pf.　1951
　S. Bianca　　　　　　　　　MSB. 78210
　(Bizet: Jeux d'enfants, s. 7)

VOCAL

LITURGIES

No. 2, Op. 29　(of St. John Chrysostom)　unacc.
... Litany (after the Gospel)　(Augmented Litany)
　☆ Don Cossack Orch.—Jaroff (in ♯ Phi.S 06611R)

... Creed (I believe in one God)　A. & cho.
　Venlona Cho.—Vranken[1]　　♭ G.7EPH 1011
　(Aplescheev, Archangelsky)

　C. Erikson (B, Eng) & Yale Divinity Sch. Cho.
　—Borden　　　　　　　　　♯ Over.LP 2
　(† Hymns of Praise)

　☆ Russian Cath. Cho.—Afonsky (♭ G.7P 142)
　St. Eustache Singers—Martin (Fr) (♭ Pac. 45030)

... Cherubic Hymn
　All SS. Chu. Male Cho.—Self　♯ CEd.CE 1022
　(† Choral Masterpieces)

Liturgia Domestica, Op. 79　Soli., cho., orch.
... Litany　(Glory to Thee, O Lord)
　B. Christoff & F. Potorjinski Russian Cho.
　　　　　　　　　　　in ♯ G.ALP 1266
　(Folk Songs)　　　　　　　　(FALP 351)

　☆ F. Chaliapin & Russian Cath. Cho. (♭ G.7RF 282;
　　　　　　　　　　　　　　　in ♯ Vic.LCT 1158)

UNID. SACRED CHORUSES

Nunc dimittis
　All Saints Church Male Cho.—Self　in ♯ CEd.CE 1022
　(† Choral Masterpieces from the Russian Liturgy)
　Yale Univ. Divinity Sch. Cho.—Borden　in ♯ Over.LP 2
　(† Hymns of Praise)

Our Father　(Holy, holy, holy)
　▽ St. Olaf Cho.—O. C. Christiansen (Eng)
　(Schein, etc.)　　　　　　　in ♯ StO.DLP 6

SONGS

COLLECTION

Little Fairy's song, Op. 47, No. 10　(Trad.)
Lullaby of the Wind, Op. 89, No. 5　(Gorodetzky)
Night, Op. 20, No. 3　(Pushkin)
Rain, Op. 66, No. 2　(Trad.)
The Rainbow, Op. 66, No. 3
Tom Thumb, Op. 47, No. 5　(Trad.)
　M. Kurenko (S), V. Pastukhoff (pf.)
　　　　　　　　　　　　♯ DCap.CTL 7100
　(Moussorgsky, Prokofiev)　　(♯ Cap.P 8310)

SELECTION: containing (inter alia):[2]
Bringing home the bride (No. 2 of Wedding Songs)
Blow, oh blow (No. 1 of Cossack Songs)
　☆ Don Cossack Cho.—Jaroff　in ♯ C.SX 1008
　　　　　　　　　　(in ♯ FSX 109: WSX 1008)

Death, Op. 15, No. 2　(Kowalewsky)
　R. Arié (Bs), W. Parry (pf.)　in ♯ D.LW 5087
　　　　　　　　　　　　　(in ♯ Lon.LD 9103)

Over the steppe, Op. 5, No. 1　(Pleshcheev)
　M. Oliviero (S, Fr), E. Magnetti (pf.)
　(Gerussi: Panteismo)　　　　Cet.AT 0322

FOLK SONG ARR.: Chant de Danse　(unspec.)
　St. Petersburg Vocal Qtt. (Pat.PG 714)

---

[1] ARR. Vranken.
[2] Delete words Augmented Litany in Supp. II. See Liturgy, above.

GRÉTRY, André Ernest Modeste
(1741-1813)

Concerto, C major, flute & orch.
J-P. Rampal & orch.—Oubradous
‡ *Pat.DT 1022*

(*Mozart: Horn Concerto*)
H. Magnée & Belgian Radio Cha.—Doneux
(*Loeillet*)   ‡ *Gramo.GLP 2509*

OPERAS
CÉPHALE ET PROCRIS 3 Acts 1773
Ballet Suite ARR. Mottl
(*Tambourin; Bourrée; Minuet; Gigue*)
Belgian Radio Cha.—Doneux ‡ *Mae.OA 20003*
(*Gluck, Haydn, Clarke*)

— Omitting Bourrée
☆ Chicago Sym.—Defauw (in ‡ *Cam.CAL 162 &*
set CFL 102)
Belgian Radio—André (TV.VE 9026)

SEE ALSO: Ballet Suite — ARR. Lambert, *below*

L'EMBARRAS DES RICHESSES 3 Acts 1782
Contredanse — ARR. BAND
Geneva Nautical Band (in ‡ *D.LF 1181*)

& SEE Ballet Suite — ARR. Lambert, *below*

LUCILLE 1 Act 1769
Où peut-on être mieux . . . — ARR. BAND Mercier
French Navy Band—Maillot   in ‡ *Sel. 270.C.055*

RICHARD COEUR DE LION 3 Acts 1784
Si l'univers entier T Act II
☒ C. Vezzani (in ‡ *Od.ODX 126**)

Danse rustique, Act II — ARR. BAND
Geneva Nautical Band (in ‡ *D.LF 1181*)

(La) ROSIÈRE RÉPUBLICAINE 1 Act 1794
Ballet Suite
1. Danse légère   2. Gavotte gracieuse
3. Contredanse   4. Romance
5. Danse générale   6. Pas de trois
7. Gavotte retenue & Carmagnole
☆ Paris Phil.—Désormière   V‡ *CdM.LDY 8124*

(Le) TABLEAU PARLANT 1 Act 1769
Vous étiez, ce que vous n'êtes plus S
☆ M. Teyte (in ‡ *Vic.* set LCT 6701)

ZÉMIRE ET AZOR 4 Acts 1771
Pantomime (Air de Ballet)
Royal Phil.—Beecham   ‡ *AmC.ML 5029*
(*Beethoven, Brahms, Boccherini, Méhul*)

AND SEE: Ballet Suite, *below*

BALLET SUITE — ARR. C. Lambert
1. Zémire et Azor: Entrée des génies ("Largo-andante")
2. Céphale et Procris: Gigue légère
3/5. Zémire et Azor: Pantomime; Passepied; Entrée des
     heures du matin ("Largo")
6/11. Céphale et Procris: Pantomime de la Nymphe et Amour;
     Tambourin; Loure; Air lent; Passepied; Gavotte
12. L'Embarras des Richesses: Contredanse générale ("Finale")
New Sym.—R. Irving   ‡ *D.LXT 5063*
(*Gluck-Mottl: Ballet Suite*)   (‡ *Lon.LL 1234*)

(Le) Rossignol (unid.) Male cho.
Maastricht Male Cho.—Koekelkoren
in ‡ *Phi.N 00617R*

GRIEG, Edvard Hagerup (1843-1907)

CLASSIFIED: I. Piano   II. Chamber Music
            III. Orchestral   IV. Dramatic
             V. Choral   VI. Songs

I. PIANO
COLLECTIONS
LYRIC PIECES (Marked L.P. below)
BOOKS I & II, Opp. 12 & 38, COMPLETE
Op. 12: 1. Arietta   5. Folk Song
        2. Valse   6. Norwegian Melody 'Norse'
        3. Watchman's Song 7. Album Leaf
        4. Dance of the Elves 8. National Song

Op. 38: 1. Berceuse   5. Spring-Dance
        2. Folk Song   6. Elegy
        3. Melody   7. Waltz
        4. Norwegian Dance 8. Canon
           (*Halling*)
M. Pressler   ‡ *MGM.E 3196*

Op. 12 COMPLETE
H. Roloff   PV. 72395
(*Sinding: Rustle of Spring*)

Op. 38, . . . Nos. 2-5 only
E. Beckmann-Shcherbina (USSR. 20374/5)

Op. 12: 4, Dance of the elves; 5, Folk Song
Op. 38: 1, Berceuse; 2, Folk Song; 5, Spring-Dance
Op. 43: 1, Butterfly; 4, Little Bird
Op. 47: 6, Norwegian Dance
Op. 54: 1, Shepherd's Boy; 3, March of the dwarfs
Op. 68: 5, At the cradle
A. Rubinstein   ‡ *Vic.LM 1872*
(*Album Leaf, Op. 28, No. 4 & Ballade, Op. 24*)
(♭ set ERB 50; ‡ FV.A 630289)
[Opp. 38-1 & 5; 43-1; 47-6; 54-1 & 3 only, on ♭ Vic.ERA 202;
♭ DV.A 95212; ItV.A72R 0023; FV.A 95212]

Op. 12: 1, Arietta
Op. 38: 1, Berceuse
Op. 43: 5, Erotik
Op. 54: 1, Shepherd's Boy; 2, Norwegian Peasants' March;
        3, March of the dwarfs; 4, Nocturne
Op. 57: 1, Vanished days; 5, She dances
Op. 71: 3, Puck; 7, Remembrances
G. Hengeveld   ‡ *Phi.N 00716R*
[Op. 57-1 only on ♭ N 402018E]

Op. 12: 6, Norwegian Melody 'Norse'
Op. 43: 1, Butterfly; 6, To the Spring
A. Goldenweiser   USSRM.D 00627
(*Arensky*)

Evening in the mountains, Op. 68, No. 4
I know a little maiden, Op. 17, No. 16
Stomping Dance, Op. 17, No. 18
F. Nielsen   G.AL 3455

Album Leaf, F major, Op. 28, No. 2
E. Grieg (from a piano roll)   in ‡ Roy. 1573
Album Leaf, A minor, Op. 28, No. 3
— ARR. VLN. & PF. Hartmann
☆ M. Elman & L. Mittman (♭ DV. 26024)
Album Leaf, C sharp minor, Op. 28, No. 4
A. Rubinstein   in ‡ Vic.LM 1872
(*Collection, above*)(♭ set ERB 50 & ERA 202;
ItV.A72R 0037; FV.A 95212)
At the cradle, Op. 68, No. 5 (L.P. IX)
— ARR. STRING ORCH. Grieg
Winograd Str. Orch. in ‡ MGM.E 3221
(*below; & Orch. Collection*)
Ballade, G minor, Op. 24
A. Rubinstein   ‡ *Vic.LM 1872*
(*Collection, above*) (♭ set ERB 50; ItV.A72R 0037)
M. Pressler   ‡ *MGM.E 3057*
(*Sonata*)
S. Anderson   ‡ *Oce.OCS 38*
(*Messiaen, Rachmaninoff, Kabalevsky, Chopin*)
Bridal Procession, Op. 19, No. 2
— ARR. ORCH. Halvorsen
Hamburg Philharmonia—H-J. Walther (MSB. 78031)
& SEE ALSO Peer Gynt, *below*
Butterfly, Op. 43, No. 1 "Papillon" (L.P. III)
V. Schiøler   G.DA 5277
(*Little Bird*)   (♭ 7RK 4: 7EBK 1001)
E. Møller   ♭ Mtr.MCEP 3031
(*Homesickness; & Sinding, Liszt*)
M. v. Doren   in ‡ Chan.MVDP 3
Elegy, Op. 38, No. 6 (L.P. II)
— ARR. VLC. & PF.: A. Vlasov (USSR. 22531)
Erotik, Op. 43, No. 5 (L.P. III)
V. Schiøler   ♭ G.7RK 4
(*above & below*)   (♭ 7EBK 1001)
☆ E. Grieg (from a piano roll) (in ‡ Roy. 1573)
— ARR. ORCH. Berlin Sym.—Rubahn (in Roy. 1475)

---

‡ = Long-playing, 33⅓ r.p.m.   ♭ = 45 r.p.m.   ♮ = Auto. couplings, 78 r.p.m.

Evening in the mountains, Op. 68, No. 4   (L.P. IX)
— ARR. STR. ORCH.   Grieg
Winograd Str. Orch.   in ♯ **MGM.E 3221**
(*above*)

Folk Song, Op. 12, No. 5   (L.P. I)
Humoreske, Op. 6, No. 4
K. Baekkelund   *G.AL 3285*
(1½ss—*Egge: Gukko-Slåtten*)

Little Bird, Op. 43, No. 4   "*Oisillon*"   (L.P. III)
V. Schiøler   *G.DA 5277*
(*Butterfly*)   (♭ *7RK 4*)

Lonely Wanderer, Op. 43, No. 2   (L.P. III)
☆ W. Gieseking (♭ *G.SCB 108: SCBQ 3012*)
— ARR. ORCH.   ☆ Berlin Sym.—Rubahn (in ♯ Roy. 1475)

Homesickness, Op. 57, No. 6   (L.P. VI)
E. Møller   ♭ *Mtr.MCEP 3031*
(*Butterfly; & Sinding, Liszt*)

March of the dwarfs, Op. 54, No. 3   (L.P. V)
M. v. Doren   in ♯ **Chan.MVDP 3**
T. Nikolayeva (*U.S.S.R. 20373*)

Melody, A minor, Op. 47, No. 3   (L.P. IV)
— ARR. GUITAR
A. Segovia   in ♯ **AmD.DL 9734**
(† *Segovia Plays*)   (♯ *D.UAT 273573*)

Nocturne, C major, Op. 54, No. 4   (L.P. V)
E. Burton   in ♯ **CEd.CE 1024**
☆ J. Therrien (in ♯ *MH. 33-111*)

— ARR. ORGAN
R. Ellsasser (in ♯ MGM.E 3120)
R. Foort[1] (in ♯ *SOT. 1051* & in ♯ 10501)

(4) Norwegian Dances, Op. 35   4 hands
(*see aslo* III, *below*)
K. Baekkelund & R. Levin
(4ss)   *G.ZN 617* & *AL 3419*

Norwegian Dance, Op. 38, No. 4   ('*Halling*')
(L.P. II)
— ARR. ORCH.   Berlin Sym.—Rubahn (in ♯ Roy. 1475)

Norwegian Dance, Op. 71, No. 5   ('*Halling*')
(L.P. X)
V. Schiøler   *G.DA 5284*
(*Sinding: Rustle of Spring*)   (♭ *7RK 7*)

Norwegian Peasant Dances, Op. 72   (Slåtter)
☆ A. Foldes (♯ Tono.LPA 34003; 7 Dances only on
♭ *FMer.MEP 14509; Mer.EP 1-5068*)
... Nos. 2 & 14 only   ☆ R. Riefling (NOC. 63004)

Norwegian Peasants' March, Op. 54, No. 2 (L.P. V)
T. Nikolayeva (*U.S.S.R. 20372*)

Scherzo-Impromptu, Op. 73, No. 2   (from *Moods*)
☆ E. Joyce (♭ *AmD.ED 3527*)

(The) Secret, Op. 57, No. 4   (L.P. VI)
— ARR. ORCH.   Barbirolli, etc.
Hallé—Barbirolli   *G.DB 21594*
(*Elgar: Dream Children*)
Berlin Sym.—Rubahn (in ♯ Roy. 1475)

Sonata, E minor, Op. 7
M. Pressler (*Ballade*)   ♯ **MGM.E 3057**

To Spring, Op. 43, No. 6   (L.P. III)
A. S. Rasmussen   Tono.A 195
(*Wedding Day*)   (♭ *EP 43029*)
A. d'Arco   in *Plé.P 101*
M. v. Doren (in ♯ Chan.MVDP 3)
☆ V. Schiøler (♭ *FMer.MEP 14529*)
W. Gieseking (♭ *C.SCB 108: SCBQ 3012*)
— ARR. VLC. & PF.
E. B. Bengtsson & H. D. Koppel   *G.DA 5279*
(*Sibelius: Valse triste*)
— ARR. ORCH.
N.W. German Phil.—Schüchter   in ♯ *Imp.ILP 123*
— ARR. ORGAN. R. Foort (in ♯ *Nix.SLPY 148; SOT. 1053* &
in ♯ 10522)
— ARR. ACCORDIONS. Wurthner Accordeon Orch.
(*Pat.PA 2941*)

Wedding Day at Troldhaugen, Op. 65, No. 6
(L.P. VIII)
J. v. Karolyi   ♭ *Pol. 30044*
(*Rachmaninoff: Preludes*)
A. S. Rasmussen   Tono.A 195
(*To Spring*)   (♭ *EP 43029*)
☆ M. Flipse (in ♯ *Phi.S 06016R*)
W. Gieseking (♭ *C.SCB 108: SCBQ 3012*)
— ARR. ORCH.
Scandinavian Sym.—Johannesen (in ♯ Mae.OAT 25008)
☆ Bavarian Sym.—Graunke (PV. 72469; ♭ *Pol. 30093;
AmD.ED 3519*)

II. CHAMBER MUSIC

Quartet, Strings, G minor, Op. 27
Pascal Qtt.   ♯ **CHS.H 17**
Guilet Qtt.   ♯ **MGM.E 3133**
(*Rachmaninoff*)
Komitas Qtt.   ♯ **USSR.D 0871/2**

SONATAS, vln. & pf.
No. 1, F major, Op. 8
No. 3, C minor, Op. 45
☆ J. Fuchs & F. Sheridan (♯ *D.UAT 273081*)

No. 3, only
☆ F. Kreisler & S. Rachmaninoff   ♯ **Vic.LCT 1128**
(*Schubert*)   (♭ set *WCT 1128*)

Sonata, vlc. & pf., A minor, Op. 36
L. Hoelscher & H. Richter-Hauser ♯ *Pol. 16097*
(& 4ss, ♭ PV. 72388/9)
L. Rose & L. Hambro   ♯ **AmC.ML 4652**
(*Franck*)

III. ORCHESTRAL

COLLECTION
(2) Elegiac Melodies, Op. 34
From Holberg's time, Op. 40   ("Holberg Suite"
(2) Norwegian Melodies, Op. 53
(2) Norwegian Melodies, Op. 63
Winograd Str. Orch.   ♯ **MGM.E 3221**
(*At the cradle & Evening in the mountains*)

Concerto, A minor, Op. 16, pf. & orch.
G. Nováes & Vienna Pro Musica—Swarowsky
(*Falla*)   ♯ **E. & AmVox.PL 8520**
(♯ *Orb.BL 702*)
F. Wührer & Vienna Pro Musica—Hollreiser
♯ **AmVox.PL 9000**
(*Tchaikovsky*)   (2ss, ♯ *Pan.XPV 1000*)
[Excerpt in ♯ AmVox.UHF 1]
M. Lympany & Philharmonia—Menges
♯ **G.CLP 1037**
(*Rachmaninoff*)   (♯ *QCLP 12013: FELP 123*)
(*Mozart* on ♯ *Vic.LHMV 1067*)[2]
B. Moiseiwitsch & Philharmonia—Ackermann
♯ **G.CLP 1008**
(*Schumann*)   (♯ *WCLP 1008: FELP 126*)
A. Aeschbacher & Berlin Phil.—Ludwig
♯ **HP.DG 16075**
(2ss)   (4ss, ♭ *PV. 72410/1*)
A. Simon & Residentie—v. Otterloo
(2ss)   ♯ *EPhi.ABR 4017*
(*Rachmaninoff*, on ♯ Epic.LC 3182)   (♯ *Phi.A 00689R*)
S. Bianca & Hamburg Philharmonia—H-J. Walther
(*Tchaikovsky*)   ♯ **MGM.E 3278**
A. Dorfmann & Robin Hood Dell—Leinsdorf
(*Mendelssohn*)   ♯ **BB.LBC 1043**
(♭ set *WBC 1043*; ♯ *FV.A 630263*; ItV.A12R 0132)
F. Wührer & Vienna Phil.—Böhm   ♯ **Ura.RS 7-15**
(*Rachmaninoff*)
G. Johannesen & Netherlands Phil.—Goehr ♯ **MMS. 2002**
(*Holberg Suite*) (& 1½ss, ♯ *MMS. 123*, with *Mendelssohn*)
☆ A. Rubinstein & Vic. Sym.—Dorati ♯ **G.ALP 1065**
(*Falla*)   (♯ *FALP/QALP 162*; ♭ *Vic.* set *ERB 16*)
☆ D. Lipatti & Philharmonia—Galliera ♯ **C.C 1040**
(2ss)   (♯ *QC 5026*)
(*Schumann*, on ♯ C.FCX/QCX 322: FCX 491)
(also ♭ AmC. set *A 1083*)

(*continued on next page*)

---

[1] Sub nom. "M. Cheshire".
[2] Stated to be with L.S.O.—Schwarz, but probably the same recording.

Concerto, A minor, Op. 16, pf. & orch. (*continued*)
U. Muravlev & State Sym.—Eliasberg (‡ *USSR.D 1322/3*)
W. Atwell & L.P.O.—Robinson (‡ *D.LF 1206*)
A. Sandford & Orch.—Berendt (‡ *Allo. 3073*)
E. Silver & Varsity Orch. (‡ *Gram. 2065*)
M. Mitchell & Orch.—Strickland (‡ *MTW. 30*)
Anon. Artists (‡ *ACC.MP 31*)
☆ W. Gieseking & Philharmonia—Karajan (‡ *C.VC 801*;
  with *Franck* on ‡ AmC.ML 4885; *Schumann* on
                          ‡ *C.FCX 284*)
O. Levant & N.Y.P.S.O.—Kurtz (‡ *AmC.CL 740*,
                         o.n. ML 4883)
F. Karrer & Viennese Sym.—Wöss (‡ Msq. 10005;
                        Cum.CR 314)
R. Riefling & Oslo Phil.—Grüner-Hegge (NOC. 62997/
  63003; ‡ Roy. 1612; 3rd. movt. only, in ‡ Roy. 1901)

... 1st movt., condensed
☆ A. Semprini & Melachrino Orch. (♭ *G.7EG 8023*)

(2) Elegiac Melodies, Op. 34   Str. orch.
   1. Heart's Wounds   2. Spring
Covent Garden—Hollingsworth ‡ *P.PMC 1010*
(*Sigurd Jorsalfar; & Humperdinck*) (‡ MGM.E 3072:
[No. 1 only, also in ‡ MGM.E 3124]   (♭ X 1077)
Danish Radio—Tuxen (2ss)   ♭ *D. 71095*
(*Sibelius: Finlandia*, on ‡ D.LW 5141; Lon.LD 9126)
Copenhagen Royal—Malko   *G.DB 10520*
Hamburg Philharmonia—H-J. Walther
                          MSB. 78123
N.W. German Phil.—Schüchter   *Od.O-29003*
               (♭ OBL 29003; in ‡ Imp.ILP 123)
☆ Residentie—Otterloo (in ‡ Phi.S 06010R)
... No. 2, only
☆ Boston Sym.—Koussevitzky (♭ Vic.ERA 195;
      FV.A 95208; ♭ Cam.CAE 161 & in ‡ CAL 155)
—— ARR.: Wurthner Accordeon Orch. (Pat.PA 2941)

From Holberg's time, Op. 40   ("*Holberg Suite*")
R.I.A.S. Sym.—Sandberg   ‡ *Pol. 17046*
Leipzig Radio—Kleinert   ‡ *Ura.RS 7-30*
(*Norwegian Dances*)   (‡ MTW. 515)
Netherlands Phil.—v. d. Berg   ‡ *MMS. 2002*
(*Concerto, A minor*)
Sym. Orch.—Vicars   ‡ *CA.LPA 1077*
(*Norwegian Melodies; & Tchaikovsky*) (2ss, V‡ MPO 5031)
Berlin Sym.—Rubahn (in ‡ Roy. 1475)
☆ Metropolitan Sym.—Ganz (‡ GA. 33-307)
—— ARR. ORGAN   Ellsasser
R. Ellsasser   ‡ *MGM.E 3182*
(*MacDowell*)

In Autumn, Op. 11   Overture
Berlin Sym.—Rubahn   ‡ *Roy. 1475*
(*Lyric Suite, From Holberg's time, etc.*)

Lyric Suite, Op. 54
Philharmonia—Malko   ‡ *G.CLP 1020*
(*Dvořák: Slav. Dances, s. 3*) (‡ QCLP 12009: FALP 342)
Danish Radio—Tuxen   ‡ *D.LX 3125*
(*E. Reesen*)   (‡ Lon.LS 849)
Berlin Sym.—Rubahn (in ‡ Roy. 1475)
Linz Sym. (‡ Ply. 10-31)
Moscow Radio—Golovanov (USSRM.D 979/80:
         Nos. 2, 3, 4, on USSR. 018870 & 18183/4)
... No. 4, March of the dwarfs
Hamburg Philharmonia—H-J. Walther (MSB. 78032)
M.G.M. Orch.—Marrow (in ‡ MGM.E 3136)

(4) Norwegian Dances, Op. 35   orig. pf. 4 hands
—— ARR. ORCH.   Sitt
Vienna State Op.—Litschauer   ‡ *Nix.VLP 430*
(*Sibelius*)   (‡ Van.VRS 430)
Leipzig Radio—Wiesenhütter   ‡ *Ura.RS 7-30*
(*From Holberg's time*)   (‡ MTW. 515)
Scandinavian Sym.—Johannesen
                     ‡ *Mae.OAT 25008*
(*Peer Gynt Suite 2, Sigurd Jorsalfar, etc.*)
☆ Philharmonia—Fistoulari   ‡ *P.PMD 1025*
(*Peer Gynt No. 1*)

☆ Danish Radio—Tuxen (‡ Tono.LPX 35003; ♭ Nera.SK
  14015/6; Nos. 1 & 2, ♭ Mer.EP 1-5015;FMer.MEP
  14511; Nos. 2 & 3 also, Nera.E 14013)
  City of Birmingham—Weldon (in ‡ AmC.RL 3041)
... Nos. 2, 3, 4:   L.S.O.—Previtali   *G.C 4257*
                                (S 10621)
... Nos. 2 & 3 only
  Bolshoi Th.—Melik-Pasheyev (USSR. 15593/4)
  Krakov Radio—Gert (Muza. 2338; No. 3 also on
                          Muza. 2281)
... No. 2, only
  Berlin Sym.—Rubahn (in ‡ Roy. 1475)
☆ "Nat. Op. Orch." (in ‡ Var. 2055)
  Robin Hood Dell—Gould (‡ AmC.A 1597)

Norwegian Melody, Op. 53, No. 1   Str. orch.
Berlin Sym.—Rubahn   in ‡ *Roy. 1475*

(2) Norwegian Melodies, Op. 63   Str. orch.
Sym.—Vicars   ‡ *CA.LPA 1077*
(*above*)
... No. 1, Popular Song
Boyd Neel—Dumont   ♭ *EPhi.NBE 11006*
(*Dvořák & Tchaikovsky*)   (♭ Phi.N 402030E)

(4) Symphonic Dances, Op. 64
☆Indianapolis Sym.—Sevitzky   ‡ *BB.LBC 1059*
(*Gershwin*)   (♭ set WBC 1059)
☆ Danish Radio—Jensen[1] (‡ Tono.LPX 35003; No. 1
  only, ♭ Mer.EP 1-5015; FMer.MEP 14511)

IV. DRAMATIC WORKS

PEER GYNT
INCIDENTAL MUSIC, Op. 23 (to Ibsen's play)
Solveig's Sunshine Song, Act I   S
Solveig's Cradle Song, Act V   S
  E. Grümmer (*Ger*)   *G.EH 1436*
  (1s each)   (G.FKX 260: ♭ 7PW 509)
  A. M. Løvberg   *G.AL 3336*
  (1s each)
  V. Urbanová (*Cz*) (U.H 24389)
  N. Kazantzeva (*Russ*) (USSRM.D 00568/9)
  E. Spoorenberg (Phi.N 12056G; Sunshine Song is ☆)
Solveig's Sunshine Song, only
  D. Warenskjöld (*Eng*) & Orch.
            in ‡ *DCap.CTL 7065*[2]
                (in ‡ Cap.P 8247; ♭ FAP 8250)
  G. Dolidzhe (*Russ*) (USSR. 22553/4)
  I. B. Lucca (*Ital*) & Cho. (Dur.AI 10463: ‡ MSE 6)
  ☆ N. Vallin (*Fr*) (♭ Od.7AOE 1004)
—— ARR. VLN. & CHA. ORCH.
  I. Zilzer & Orch. (C.DDX 39: ♭ SCDK 1)
  ☆ F. Akos & Berlin Municipal Op. Ens. (♭ T.U 45187)
—— ARR. GUITAR: A. Valenti (in ‡ SMC. 1002)

Solveig's Cradle Song
SEE SONG COLLECTION, Rössl-Majdan, *below*

COLLECTED EXCERPTS
Suites—No. 1, Op. 46; No. 2, Op. 55;
Prelude; Bridal Procession   (orch. Halvorsen);
The Three Huldres   (with diction)
Dance of the Mountain King's Daughter
Solveig's Cradle Song   (all from Op. 23)
  ☆ E. Prytz (S), actors & Oslo Phil.—Grüner-Hegge
                     ‡Mer.MG 10148
               (‡ Clc. 6276; also NOC. 63081/92, 12ss)
  [Prelude also in ♭ Nera.EPM 220; 4 other nos. also
                          ♭ EPM 212]

ORCHESTRAL SUITES
No. 1, Op. 46; No. 2, Op. 55
Dance of the Mountain King's Daughter[3]
  ☆ Boston Prom—Fiedler   ‡ *G.DLP 1033*
                      (‡ ItV.A10R 0001)
  [Suite No. 1 only in ♭ G.7EP 7022; ♭ Vic.ERA 147;
                      ItV.A72R 0014]
  [Suite No. 2 only in ♭ FV.A 330208; ‡ Vic.LRM 7052:
                      ♭ set ERB 7052]

Suites 1 & 2, COMPLETE
London Phil. Sym.—Rodzinski
                     ‡ *West.LAB 7014*
Philadelphia—Ormandy   ‡ *AmC.ML 5035*
(*Bizet*)   (♭ A 2037/8)

---

[1] Now listed as cond. Tuxen; may be a n.v.   [2] Announced but not issued.
[3] From Inc. Music, Op. 23; originally in Suite 2.

Suites 1 & 2 (*continued*)

Champs-Élysées Th.—Inghelbrecht
                   ♯ *Sel. 270.C.063*
[with C. Masmichel (S)]

N.W. German Phil.—Schüchter ♯ *Imp.ILP 102*
               (♯ *G.FFLP 1062: QDLP 6033*)
[Suite 1—Nos. 1, 3, 4; Suite 2—No. 4 on ♭ *Od.BEOW 3005*]

Hamburg Philharmonia—H.-J. Walther
(*Tchaikovsky*)   ♯ **MGM.E 3139**
[Suite No. 1 also on *MSB. 78031, 78203* & *78029;* Suite
No. 2 also on *MSB. 78204* & *78030*]

Orch.—Paulik   ♯ *MTW. 20*
(*Debussy, R. Strauss*)   (♭ set EP 20)

Bamberg Sym.—Suitner   ♯ *Pol. 16055*
(1s each)   (♯ *Pol. 17037*)
[Suite No. 1 is ☆; Suite No. 1 also on PV. 72359/60S, 3 ss;
Nos. 3 & 4 only, on ♭ *Pol. 30002;* Suite No. 2 also on
PV. 72334; Nos. 1 & 3 only, ♭ *Pol. 30002*]

Vienna Pro Musica—Gräf   ♯ *Pan.XPV 1009*
☆ Residentie—Otterloo   ♯ *EPhi.ABR 4027*
               (♯ *Phi.A 00734R;* Epic.LC 3007)
[Solveig's Song sung by E. Spoorenberg]
[Excerpts in ♯ *Phi.S 06010R*]

☆ Vienna State Op.—Scherchen (♯ *Sup.LPM 119;*
                              U. 5083C)
Vienna Radio—Schönherr (♯ *GA. 33-308*)
Austrian Sym.—Brown & Schönherr (♯*Rem. 199-150;*
                             Cum.CR 254)

Suite No. 1
1. Morning Mood   **2. Ase's Death**
3. Anitra's Dance   **4. In the Hall of the Mountain King**

Florence Fest.—Gui   ♯ *AudC. 503*
(*Sibelius & Wagner*)

Netherlands Phil.—Goehr   V♯ *MMS. 95*

Scandinavian Sym.—Johannesen
                   ♯ **Mae.OAT 25008**
(*Suite 2—No. 4; Norwegian Dances, etc.*)

Moscow Radio—Golovanov *USSRM.D 00791/3*
(3ss—*Svendsen*)
☆ Philharmonia—Fistoulari   ♯ *P.PMD 1025*
(*Norwegian Dance*)
Bolshoi Th.—Melik-Pasheyev (USSR. 015541/4)

☆ Lamoureux—Fournet (♭ *Pat.ED 10: EDQ 101*)
Cincinnati Sym.—Goossens (♯ Cam.CAL 117 &
   in ♯ set CFL 103; Nos. 3 & 4 only in ♭ *CAE 191*)
Berlin State Op.—Weissmann (Od.NLX 1/2)
Philadelphia—Ormandy (♯ AmC.CL 722)

... **EXCERPTS**
Nos. 1, 3, 4, only   Regent Sym. (in ♯ *Rgt. 7004*)

Nos. 1 & 3 only   A. Bernard Orch. (♭ *Pac.EP 90001*)

No. 1 only   ☆ Robin Dell (♭ *AmC.A 1597*)
——ARR. ORGAN: R. Ellsasser (in ♯ MGM.E 3120)

No. 2, only —— ARRS.
Raisner Harmonica Trio (in ♯ *FestF.FLD 33*)
R. Ellsasser (org.) (in ♯ MGM.E 3127)

Nos. 3 & 4 only: Philadelphia—Ormandy (♯ *AmC.AL 35*)

No. 3 only:
Israel Radio—Goehr (*Arzi. 767;* in ♯ *Bne. 501*)
☆ Philharmonia—Fistoulari (in ♯ MGM.E 3046)
—— ARR. GUITAR: M. Funes (ArgOd. 56580)

Suite No. 2
1. Ingrid's Lament   **2. Arabian Dance**
3. Peer Gynt's Return   **4. Solveig's Song**

Moscow Radio—Golovanov ♯ *USSR.D 01703*
(*below*)
Anon. Orchs. (♯ *ACC.MP 6* & ♯ Gram. 2087)
☆ City of Birmingham—Weldon (in ♯ AmC.RL 3041)
L.S.O.—Irving (G.DB 4330/1: EB 573/4)
Indianapolis Sym.—Sevitzky (♯ Cam.CAL 117 &
   in set CFL 103; No. 3 & 4 only on ♭ *CAE 191*)

... **No. 4, Solveig's Song**
Israel Radio—Goehr   *Arzi. 767*
(*Suite No. 1-No. 3*)   (in ♯ *Bne. 501*)
Scandinavian Sym.—Johannesen (in ♯ Mae.OAT 25008)
Anon. Orch. (in ♯ Ply. 12-128), etc.
☆ Robin Hood Dell—Gould (♭ *AmC.A 1597*)

SIGURD JORSALFAR
Inc. Music to play by Bjørnson
ORCH. SUITE, Op. 56
1. In the King's Hall (Prelude)

                        (*continued*)

---

2. Borghild's Dream (Intermezzo)
3. Homage March

Covent Garden—Hollingsworth ♯ *P.PMC 1010*
(*Elegiac Melodies & Humperdinck*)   (♯ MGM.E 3072)
[No. 3 only, in ♯ MGM.E 3177]

Moscow Radio—Golovanov   ♯ *USSR.D 01702*
(*Peer Gynt Suite 2*)
☆ Cincinnati Sym.—Johnson   ♯ *D.LW 5124*
                           (♯ *Lon.LD 9138*)

... **No. 3, Homage March**
Hamburg Philharmonia—H-J. Walther (*MSB. 78032*)
Scandinavian Sym.—Johannesen (in ♯ Mae.OAT 25008)
☆ Bavarian Sym.—Graunke (PV. 72469; ♭ *Pol. 30093;*
                        AmD.ED 3519)

V. CHORAL

(The) Great White Host, Op. 30, No. 10 (Brorson)
B & cho.
Augustana Cho.—Veld   in ♯ *Word.W 4005*
(*Eng*) (*Britten, Bach, Rachmaninoff, etc.*)

Landfall, Op. 31   B, Male cho., orch.
(*Landkjenning*) (*Bjørnson*)
E. Sædén & Stockholm Op. Orch. & Students
Cho.—Ralf   ♯ *SS. 33105*
(*Alfvén, Sibelius, Södermann, etc.*)

VI. SONGS
COLLECTIONS

Autumn Storm, Op. 18, No. 4 (Richardt)
Bright Night, Op. 70, No. 3 (Benzon)
Dereinst, gedanke mein, Op. 48, No. 2 (Geibel)
The First Meeting, Op. 21, No. 1 (Bjørnson)
Haugtussa, Op. 67   Cycle (Garborg)
... No. 6, Kidling's Dance
Hidden Love, Op. 39, No. 2 (Bjørnson)
I love thee, Op. 5, No. 3 (H. C. Andersen)
Jägerlied, Op. 4, No. 4 (Uhland)
Margaret's Lullaby, Op. 15, No. 1 (from *The Pretenders,*
   Ibsen)
Parted, Op. 25, No. 5 (Ibsen)
The Princess (Bjørnson) 1871
Return to Rundarne, Op. 33, No. 9 (Vinje) (*Auf der Reise*)
Solveig's Cradle Song (from *Peer Gynt*)
Spring, Op. 33, No. 2 (Vinje)
Sunset, Op. 9, No. 3 (*Solnedgang*) (Munch)
A Swan, Op. 25, No. 2 (Ibsen)
Verse for an Album, Op. 25, No. 3 (Ibsen) ("*Glücksbote*
   mein")
A Vision, Op. 33, No. 6 (Vinje) ("*Was ich sah*")
When I die, Op. 59, No. 1 (Paulsen) ("*Herbststimmung*")
With a primrose, Op. 26, No. 4 (Pardsen)
Zur Rosenzeit, Op. 48, No. 5 (Goethe)

H. Rössl-Majdan (A, *Ger*), V. Graef (pf.)
                   ♯ *West.WN 18089*

A Dream, Op. 43, No. 6 (Bodenstedt) (*a*)
Eros, Op. 70, No. 1 (Benzon)
I love thee, Op. 5, No. 3 (H. C. Andersen) (*a*)
And I will take a sweetheart, Op. 60, No. 5 (Krag)
   (*St. John's Eve*) (*b*)
Solveig's Sunshine Song (from *Peer Gynt*) (*b*)
Spring, Op. 33, No. 2 (Vinje) (*a*)
A Swan, Op. 25, No. 2 (Ibsen) (*b*)
Thanks for thy counsel, Op. 21, No. 4 (Bjørnson)

D. Warenskjöld (S, *Eng*) & orch.—Greeley
                   ♯ *DCap.CTL 7065*[1]
(*Dvořák*)   (♯ Cap.P 8247)
[items marked (*a*) also on ♭ *Cap.FAP 8249;* those marked
(*b*) also on ♭ *FAP 8250;* ACap.CEC 009]
To Norway, Op. 58, No. 2 (Paulsen)
And I will take a sweetheart, Op. 60, No. 5 (Krag)
Return to Rundarne, Op. 33, No. 9 (Vinje)
I love thee, Op. 5, No. 3 (H. C. Andersen)
A Dream, Op. 48, No. 6 (Bodenstedt)

C. Hague (T), G. Steele (pf.)   in ♯ *ML. 7034*
(† Scandinavian Songs)
Autumn Storm, Op. 18, No. 4 (Richardt)
                   (*Efteraarsstormen*)
Along the river, Op. 33, No. 5 (Vinje) (*Langs ei Aa*)
In the boat, Op. 60, No. 3 (Krag) (*Mens jeg venter*)
The Goal, Op. 33, No. 12 (Vinje) (*Fyremaal*)

K. Flagstad (S), G. Moore (pf.)   ♭ *G.7EB 6007*
With a water lily, Op. 25, No. 4 (Ibsen)
The Hut, Op. 18, No. 7 (H. C. Andersen)
I love thee, Op. 5, No. 3 (H. C. Andersen)
With a primrose, Op. 26, No. 4 (Paulsen)
Bilberry slopes, Op. 67, No. 3 (from *Haugtussa*)

E. Prytz (S), I. Johnson (pf.)   ♭ *Nera.EPM 201*

         (*Collections continued on next page*)

---

[1] Announced but not issued in G.B.

SONGS—COLLECTIONS (continued)
   From Monte Pincio, Op. 39, No. 1 (Bjørnson)
   High on the grassy slope, Op. 39, No. 3 (Lie)
   Bright Night, Op. 70, No. 3 (Benzon)
   E. Prytz (S), I. Johnson (pf.) ♭ *Nera.EPM 204*

   The First Meeting, Op. 21, No. 1 (Bjørnson)
   Bird Song, Op. 25, No. 6 (Ibsen)
   A Vision, Op. 33, No. 6 (Vinje)
   M. Maksakova (S, *Russ*)   USSR. 021756/7

Among the roses, Op. 39, No. 4 (Janson)
   Z. Dolukhanova (A, *Russ*)[1] *USSRM.D 00660*
   (*A Swan; & Delibes*)   (*& USSR. 17688*)

(A) Dream, Op. 48, No. 6 (Bodenstedt) (*Ger*)
   J. Björling (T, *Norw*), F. Schauwecker (pf.)
                     G.DB 21620
    (*R. Strauss: Ständchen*) (in ♯ ALP 1187; Vic.LM 1771:
    (♭ *DV. 26045*)   ♭ *ERA 141*)
              (& in ♯ Vic.LM 1802)
    T. Kuuzik (B, *Estonian*) (in ♯ *USSR.D 2091*)
   ☆ R. Crooks (T) (in ♯ Cam.CAL 128: ♭ *CAE 120*)
   R. Tauber (T) (in ♯ ChOd.LDC 36003)

Eros, Op. 70, No. 1 (Benzon)
   ☆ R. Tauber (T, *Ger*) & Orch. (in ♯ ChOd.LDC 36003)

(The) First Meeting, Op. 21, No. 1 (Bjørnson)
   S. Shaposhnikov (B, *Russ*) *USSRM.D 001115*
   (*Dvořák*)

From Monte Pincio, Op. 39, No. 1 (Bjørnson)
   ☆ K. Flagstad (S) & Orch. (*Spring*) ♭ *G.7EB 6011*

I love thee, Op. 5, No. 3 (H. C. Andersen)
   E. Oldrup (S), P. Østerfelt (pf.) *Tono.L 28097*
   (*Swedish Folksong*)   (♭ *EP 45009*)
   H. Prey (B, *Ger*), H. Heinemann (pf.)
                 in ♯ *Imp.ILP 123*
    E. Katulskaya (M-S, *Russ*) (*USSR. 20012*)
    N. Eddy (B, *Eng*) & Orch. (♭ *AmC.A 1644*)
    T. Kuuzik (B, *Estonian*) (in ♯ *USSR.D 2091*)
    J. Garda (B, *Pol*) (*Muza. 2416*)
   ☆ A. Schiøtz (T) (♭ *G.7EBK 1003*)
  — ARR. SOLO & CHO.: O. Gerthel & Karlskoga Cho. (*Swed*)
          (*D.F 44290* : ♭ *D. 75112*)
  — ARR. ORGAN: R. Ellsasser (in ♯ MGM.F 200, etc.)
  — ARR. ORCH.: ☆ Robin Hood Dell—Gould (♭ *AmC.A 1597*)
  — ACCOMPANIMENT, etc. for practice (in ♯ VS.MH 1003;
                 in ♯ *AmEsq. I*)

(A) Poet's Last Song, Op.18, No. 3 (H. C. Andersen)
   ☆ A. Schiøtz (♭ *G.7EBK 1003*)

Spring, Op. 33, No. 2 (Vinje)
   E. Berge (S), K. Olssen (pf.)   *Felix.Ø 70*
   (*Backer-Grøndahl: At eventide*)
   O. Werner (T), R. Holger (org.) *Od.ND 7222*
   (*Groven: In the evening*)
   ☆ K. Flagstad (S) & Orch.   ♭ *G.7EB 6011*
   (*From Monte Pincio*)

Spring Rain, Op. 49, No. 6 (Drachmann)
   S. Lemeshev (T, *Russ*)   USSR. 022291
   (*Schubert: Du bist die Ruh'*)

(A) Swan, Op. 25, No. 2 (Ibsen)
   J. Björling (T), F. Schauwecker (pf.)
               in ♯ G.ALP 1187
   (*above; & Sibelius, Schubert, etc.*) (in ♯ Vic.LM 1771:
          ♭ *ERA 141*; ♭ *DV. 26045*)
   Z. Dolukhanova (A, *Russ*) *USSRM.D 00660*
   (*above; & Delibes*)   (*& USSR. 17687*)
   N. Kazantseva (S, *Russ*) *USSRM.D 00569*
   (⅓s—*Peer Gynt—Solveig's Songs*)

Two brown eyes, Op. 5, No. 1 (H. C. Andersen)
   ☆ A. Schiøtz (♭ *G.7EBK 1003*)

While I wait, Op. 60, No. 3 (Krag)
   (*Im Kahne: In the boat*)
   H. Prey (B, *Ger*), H. Heinemann (pf.)
               in ♯ *Imp.ILP 123*

---

[1] Labelled simply *Roses*, this might well be *Zur Rosenzeit*, Op. 48, No. 5. It has not been possible to check.
[2] Orch. version of Fantasy Piece, Op. 6, No. 3, *below*, orig. pf.
[3] Coupling has also been listed as Křenek and/or Cumming.

With a waterlily, Op. 25, No. 4 (Ibsen)
   E. Sachs (M-S), S. Leff (pf.) in ♯ Mur.P 111
   (followed by pf. acc. only)

GRIFFES, Charles Tomlinson (1884-1920)

COLLECTION OF ORCH. PIECES
Bacchanale, Op. 6, No. 3[2] 1912
The Pleasure Dome of Kubla Khan 1920
(4) ROMAN SKETCHES, Op. 7 pf. 1915-6
... No. 1, The White Peacock
... No. 4, Clouds   — ARR. ORCH. Griffes
   Eastman-Rochester Sym.—Hanson
   (*Loeffler*)   ♯ Mer.MG 40012

COLLECTION OF PIANO MUSIC
Fantasy Pieces, Op. 6
   1. Barcarolle   2. Notturno   3. Scherzo
(4) Roman Sketches, Op. 7
   1. The White Peacock   2. Nightfall
   3. The Fountains at the Acqua Paola   4. Clouds
(3) Tone Pictures, Op. 5
   1. The Lake at evening   2. The night winds
   3. The vale of dreams
   L. Engdahl   ♯ MGM.E 3225

Poem fl. & orch. 1918
   W. Kincaid & Philadelphia—Ormandy
             in ♯ AmC.ML 4629
   ☆ J. Baker & Cha. Orch.—Saidenberg ♯ *B.AXL 2015*
   (*Foote*)

(4) ROMAN SKETCHES, Op. 7 pf. 1915-6
No. 1, The White Peacock
   M. Pressler   in ♯ MGM.E 3129
   (*Chabrier, Albeniz, Granados, etc.*)

(3) Short Pieces (unid.) pf.
   J. Ranck   ♯ Zod. 1002
   (*Poulenc, Tcherepnin, Werle*)

Sonata, pf. 1920
   Del Purves (*Joio*)[3]   ♯ ML. 7021

(3) Tone Pictures, Op. 5 pf. 1910/12
... No. 3, The Vale of Dreams — ARR. ORCH.
   Hamburg Philharmonia—Korn in ♯ Allo. 3150
   (*Hadley, Carpenter, Taylor, etc.*)

GRIGNY, Nicolas de (1671-1703)

SEE: † ANTHOLOGIE SONORE (♯ HS.AS 11)

GROFÉ, Ferde (b. 1892)

Aviation Suite
   Hollywood Studio—Grofé   ♯ *Rem. 2*

(The) Grand Canyon, Suite orch. 1931
   Boston "Pops"—Fiedler   ♯ Vic.LM 1928
   (*Copland*)   (♭ set ERB 66)
   ☆ N.B.C.Sym.—Toscanini(♯ G.ALP 1232;ItV.A12R 0075;
          DV.L 16466; ♭ *Vic. set ERC 3*)
    [No. 3 only on ♭ *G.7ER 5012*; ItV.A72R 0041, d.c.]
   Orch.—Kostelanetz (♭ AmC. set A 1088: ♯ CL 716)
   Capitol Sym.—Grofé (♯ *ACap.CLP 002*)
   ... Nos. 2, Painted desert; 3, On the trail; 5, Cloudburst
   H. Winterhalter Orch.   ♯ BB.LBC 1045
   (*Gershwin*)   (♭ set WBC 1045; ♯ FV.A 530201)
   [No. 3 only in ♯ *Vic.LPM 1020*]
   ... No. 1, Sunrise; & No. 3
   ☆ Capitol Sym.—Grofé (♭ *Cap.FAP 8207*)
   ... No. 3, only
   Anon. Orch.—Shankson (in ♯ Roy. 1609: ♭ *EP 357*)
   ☆ Orch.—Kostelanetz (C.DX 1878: CQX 16669)

Hudson River Suite orch. 1955
   Orch.—Kostelanetz   ♯ AmC.CL 763
   (*King Norodom of Cambodia: Cambodian Suite; & Falla,
     Kay, etc.*)

March for Americans orch.
☆ M. Wilson Orch. (in ‡ AmD.DL 8025)

Mississippi Suite orch.
☆ A. Kostelanetz Orch. (‡ AmC.ML 4625)

... **Huckleberry Finn & Mardi Gras**
Anon. Orch.—Shankson (in ‡ Roy. 1609)

... **Huckleberry Finn,** only
Hamburg Philharmonia—Korn (in ‡ Allo. 3149)

... **Mardi Gras,** only
New Century—Torch (*FDH. 001*)
Anon.—Shankson (♭ *Roy.EP 357*)

GROSSIN de Paris (XVth Cent.)

SEE: † ANTHOLOGIE SONORE

GROTTE, Nicolas de la (fl. XVIth Cent.)

SEE: † ANTHOLOGIE SONORE (‡ HS.AS 6)

GROVEN, Eivind (b. 1901)

Ballade cho. & orch. 1928-31, f.p. 1933
Oslo University Cho. Soc. & Oslo Phil. Orch.
  —Kramm   **‡ Mer.MG 90003**
  (*Egge*)   (also NOC. 63178/81, 4ss)

SONG: In the evening (Øverland)
O. Werner (T), R. Holger (org.)   *Od.ND 7222*
(*Grieg: Spring*)

GRUEN, John (b. 1927)

SONGS: COLLECTION
Tilly; Watching the Needleboats at San Sabba;
A flower given to my daughter; She weeps over Rahoon;
Simples; Alone; Bahnhofstrasse   from *Poems Penyeach*
(J. Joyce)
Thirteen ways of looking at a blackbird (W. Stevens)
P. Neway (S), J. Gruen (pf.)   **‡ CtyNY.AP 121**
(*Donovan & Kraehenbuehl*)

PART SONGS
(The) Birds (Anon.)
Sweet was the song
Concert Cho.   in ‡ **CtyNY.AP 122**
(*Kraehenbuehl, A. Harris, etc.*)

GRUENBERG, Louis (b. 1884)

Concerto, vln. & orch., Op. 47 1944
☆ J. Heifetz & San Francisco Sym.—Monteux
                   ‡ Vic.LCT 1160
  (*Dohnányi*)   (‡ FV.A 630291)

EMPEROR JONES, Op. 36 Opera 1932
Standin' in the need of prayer B
G. London   in ‡ **AmC.ML 4999**
(*Meistersinger, Boris, etc.*)

GRÜNER-HEGGE, Odd (b. 1899)

Elegiac Melody Str. orch. 1950
Oslo Phil.—Grüner-Hegge   **NOC. 63170/1**
(2ss)   (in ‡ Mer.MG 10150)

GUAMI, Gioseffo (1540-1611)

SEE: † OLD ITALIAN MASTERS

GUARNIERI, Camargo (b. 1907)

SONGS
En vou m'embory; Quebra o coco menina
☆ O. Coelho (S & guitar) (♭ *P.CBEP 2*)

---

¹ 1912 according to *Grove*.

GUASTAVINO, Carlos (b. 1914)¹

Bailecito; Gato (Danza a la manera popular) pf.
(or 2 pfs.) 1940-6
H. Giordano & E. Guastavino   *ArgV. 57004*
(2ss)

— ARR. ORCH. Orch.—Fidenzini (ArgV. 68-8031)

Bailecito pf.
L. Brunelli   *ArgV. 66-0020*
(*Brunelli: Zamba, Op. 2, No. 2*)

Pampeano pf. 1952
H. Giordano   *ArgOd. 57015*
(*A. Williams: 2nd Aire de vale*)   (♭ *BSOA 4008*)

(El) Sauce
Tierra linda pf. 1940
C. Guastavino   *ArgV.P 1525*
                    (Pte. rec.)

SONGS
Desde que te conocí
Mi garganta (*4 Canciones argentinas*, Nos. 1 & 4) 1949
Pueblito, mi pueblo (F. Silva) 1941
M. Landi   Pte. rec.

Por los campos verdes (J. de Ibarbouron) 1942
R. Bignardi (S) & orch.   *ArgOd. 57010*
(*d'Esposito: Lin Carel—Ave Maria*)

Pueblito, mi pueblo
E. Arizmendi & orch.   in ‡ *ArgOd.LDC 506*

(La) Rosa y el Sauce (Silva) 1942
E. Arizmendi (S) & orch. (*ArgOd. 57024*)
G. Souzay (B), D. Baldwin (pf.) (♭ *ArgLon.DLCE 6501*)

Suite Argentina S & orch.
M. Gabarini & Argentine Radio—Fidenzini
                   ArgV. 68-8033

GUÉDRON, Pierre (1565-1625)

SEE: † CHANSONS HISTORIQUES
      † OLD FRENCH AIRS

GUÉNIN, Marie-Alexandre (1744-1819)

Symphony No. 2, C major, Op. 4, No. 2
Orch.—de Froment   **V‡ DO.LD 16**

GUERRERO, Francisco (1527-1599)

SEE: † SPANISH RENAISSANCE MUSIC

GUERRERO TORRES, Jacinto
(1895-1951)

ZARZUELAS, etc. (Abridged listings only)
(La) ALSACIANA 1921
P. Lorengar, C. Munguía, M. Ausensi, Cho. & Madrid
Cha. Orch.—Argenta   **‡ LI.W 91037**
                (‡ Ambra.MC 25007)

(El) CANASTILLO DE FRESAS 1951
M. Ausensi, P. Lorengar, L. Berchman, E. de la Vera,
Cho. & Sym. Orch.—Pavon   **‡ Mont.FM 9**
[Excerpts in ♭ SpC.SCGE 80001]

(La) FAMA DEL TARTANERO
Excerpts M. Redondo, etc. (♭ SpC.CGE 60018)
       ▽ E. Sagi-Barba & Cho. (G.DA 4202)

(Los) GAVILANES (*The Sparrow-Hawks*) 3 Acts
                                1923
T. Rosado, M. Berganza, M. Ausensi, C. Munguía,
Cho. & Madrid Cha. Orch.—Argenta ‡ LI.TW 91012
[Prelude on ♭ Ambra.MGE 60005] (‡ Ambra.MCC 30002)
M. Espinalt, L. Torrentó, J. Simorra, J. Vilardell, Cho. &
Sym.—Ferrer   ‡ Reg.LCX 118
           (‡ Angel. 65015; Pam.LRC 15913)
[Excerpts on ♭ Reg.SEBL 7008]
Soloists, Cho. & Orch.—Capdevila   *ArgOd. 196546/9*
M. Ausensi, L. Berchman, E. de la Vera, Madrid Sym.
Orch.—Montorio & Navarro   ‡ Mont.FM 1

(El) HUESPED DEL SEVILLANO 2 Acts 1926
L. Torrentó, E. Aliaga, J. Simorra, D. Monjo, O. Pol, etc.
Cho. & Sym.—Ferrer   ‡ Reg.LCX 127
[Excerpts on ♭ Reg.SEBL 7011 & SEDL 19040]
L. Sagi-Vela, L. Berchman, T. Silva, Madrid Cha. Orch.
            ‡ Mont.FM 27
Vocal Excerpts
L. Sagi-Vela (in ‡ MusH.LP 5006; Mont.FM 53)
M. Ausensi (in ‡ Ambra.MC 25005; ♭ MGE 60000)
♯ H. Lazaro (in ‡ Sca. 806*)

(Las) LAGARTERANAS
Overture Madrid Cha. Orch.—Lloret   in ‡ Mont.FM 22

(La) ROSA DEL AZAFRAN 3 Acts 1930
M. Espinalt, C. Panadés, M. Redondo, etc., Cho. &
Orch.—Delta   ‡ Reg.LCX 101
(also 10ss, ♭ Pam.PC 4-36014/8) (‡ Angel. 65004;
            Pam.LRC 15903)
[Excerpts on ♭ Reg.SEBL 7018 & 7004; SEDL 19040:
            Angel. 70014, etc.]
▽ Soloists, Cho. & Orch.—Guerrero (ArgOd. 193513,
            196101/2)

GUILLAUME d'Amiens (fl. XIIIth Cent.)

DANCES Inst. Ens.
Ainsi doit entrer en Ville (Ronde)
Main se levoit Aëlis (Ronde)
Prendes-y-garde (Rondeau)
Pro Musica Antiqua Ens.—Cape
            ‡ HP.APM 14018
(Raimbaut, Adam de la Halle, & Anon.)

GUILMANT, Alexandre (1837-1911)

Absolution org.
C. Cronham (Mjr. 5127)

Sonata No. 1, D minor, Op. 42 org.
R. Ellsasser   ‡ P.PMC 1025
(Reubke)   (‡ MGM.E 3078)

GUION, David Wendell (b. 1895)

Mother Goose Suite pf.
... Hickory dickory dock; The North Wind doth blow
S. Bianca   MSB. 21
(with spoken commentary)   (in ‡ 60041)
Turkey in the Straw orch.
Hamburg Philharmonia—H-J. Walther (MSB. 78024)

GUIOT de DIJON (XIIIth Cent.)
SEE: † HISTORY OF MUSIC IN SOUND (14)

GUIRAUT DE BORNELH (fl. c. 1165-1200)
SEE: † FRENCH TROUBADOUR SONGS

GUMPELTZHAIMER, Adam
            (c. 1559-1625)
CHORALES
Vater unser im Himmelreich
Netherlands Madrigal & Motet Cho.
—Voorberg   ‡ Phi.N 00692R
(† Motets on Luther Texts)

Vom Himmel hoch c. 1618
Trapp Family Singers—Wasner
            in ‡ B.LAT 8038
(Bach, etc.)   (‡ AmD.DL 9689; ♭ set ED 1200)

GUNG'L, Josef (1810-1889)
            (Selected listing only)
WALTZES
COLLECTIONS
Amorettentänze, Op. 161 ø
Frühlingslieder, Op. 155 ø
Jungherrentänze, Op. 213 ø
Soldatenlieder, Op. 183 ø
Casinotänze, Op. 237 x
Träume auf dem Ozean, Op. 80 x
Immortellen, Op. 82 x
Die Hydropathen, Op. 149 x

London Prom.—Binge   ‡ D.LF 1188
            (‡ Lon.LB 1017)
(marked ø also on ♭ D.DFE 6180; Lon.BEP 6180;
            x on ♭ Lon.BEP 6181)
Soldatenlieder, Op. 183
Amorettentänze, Op. 161
Die Hydropathen, Op. 149
Casinotänze, Op. 237
Westminster Light—Bridgewater
            ‡ Nix.WLP 6804
(Johann Strauss II)   (‡ West.WL 4004)

GURIDI, Jesús (b. 1886)
            (Abridged listings only)
(El) CASERIO Zarzuela, 3 Acts 1926
P. Lorengar, M. Ausensi, C. Munguía, etc., Donostiarra
Cho. & Madrid Sym.—Argenta   ‡ LI.TW 91087/8
(3ss—Breton: Dolores—Jota; &   (‡ Ambra.MC 30023/4)
other Zarzuela excpts.)
C. Rubio, A. Rojo, S. Castelló, etc. & Madrid Sym.
—Moreno Torroba   ‡ Phi.N 00595L
(Serrano: Alma de Dios, excpts.)
Intermezzo
Madrid Theatre.—Moreno Torroba in ‡ AmD.DL 9763
Colón Theatre—Cases   ArgOd. 57049
Spanish Sym.—Martinez   in ‡ Mont.FM 16
Vocal Excerpts ▽ M. Fleta (T) (G.DB 1024)
            P. Romeu (SpC.AG 7044)
SONGS: Canciones castellanas
Jota; Non quiero tus avellanas
☆ V. de los Angeles (S), G. Moore (pf.) in ‡ G.FBLP 1040
(Non quiero ... only on ♭ Vic.ERA 106) (‡ LBLP 1002)
Canción castellana (unspec.)
L. Ibarrondo (M-S), M. Sandoval (pf.)
            in ‡ Rem. 199-139
            (‡ Cum.CR 297)
FOLK SONG ARR.: Maitasun
Pamplona Cho.—Morondo (in ‡ CFD. 26)

HABÁ, Alois (b. 1893)
Mičvrin (Pioneer's Song)
Children's Cho.—Kühn & G. Novák
(below)   ‡ U. 5181C
QUARTETS, Little Strings
No. 9, Op. 79
Hábovo Qtt.   ‡ U. 5181C
(above & Bartoš)

HADJIEV, Parachev
Quartet, Strings, No. 1
Amarov Str. Qtt. (6ss)   Bulg. 1214/6

HADLEY, Henry Kimball (1871-1937)
Scherzo diabolique orch. 1934
Hamburg Philharmonia—Korn in ‡ Allo. 3150
(Carpenter, Taylor, Stringfield, etc.)

‡ = Long-playing, 33⅓ r.p.m.   ♭ = 45 r.p.m.   ♮ = Auto. couplings, 78 r.p.m.

HÄSSLER, Johann Wilhelm (1747-1822)

Grand Gigue, D minor, Op. 31　hpsi.
R. Corbert (pf.)　　　　　　in ♯ **ML. 7017**

HAHN, Reynaldo (1875-1947)

CIBOULETTE　Operetta　1923
Nous avons fait un beau voyage　S & T
N. Vallin & L. Huberty (B)　　in ♯ **Plé.P 3075**
(Messager)
☆ Géori-Boué & R. Bourdin (B) *(Sat.M 1171)*

MOZART　Inc. music to Guitry's play　1925
VOCAL EXCERPTS
Comme c'est facile; Être adoré　Act I
Quand on pense que des gens . . .
Comme elle danse . . . *(Gavotte)*
Depuis ton départ, mon amour . . .　Act II
Alors . . . adieu donc　*(Air des adieux)*　Act III
　　G. Sciutti (S) & Marigny Theatre Orch.
　　—Gitton　(4ss)　　　　**G.DB 11255/6**

Excerpts
J. Dupont (pf.) (in ♯ **LI.TW 91060/1**)
☆ S. Guitry (in ♯ **G.FKLP 7008**)

SONGS
COLLECTIONS
Si mes vers avaient des ailes　(Hugo)　*a.*
Le Cimetière de campagne　(Vicaire)　*b.*
L'Air　(de Banville)　*a.*
La Nuit　(de Banville)　*b.*
En Sourdine　*(Chanson grise 4—Verlaine)*　*a.*
(10) ÉTUDES LATINES　(de Lisle)
… 2. Nèere　*c.*　　　　　3. Salinum　*c.*
　　5. Lydé　*a.*　　　　　6. Vile potabis　*c.*
　　7. Tyndaris　*a.*　　　 8. Pholoé　*a.*
　10. Phyllis　*b.*
Paysage　(Theuriet)　*b.*
La Barcheta　(Herra)　*a.*
Offrande　(Verlaine)　*c.*
L'Enamourée　(de Banville)　*b.*
D'une prison　(Verlaine)　*a.*
Trois jours de vendange　(Daudet)　*b.*
Le Rossignol des lilas　(Coppée)　*a.*
Je me mets en votre mercy　(Charles d'Orléans)　*c.*
Mai　(Coppée)　*a*
Infidélité　(Gautier)　*a.*
L'Heure exquise　*(Chanson grise 5—Verlaine)*　*a.*
　　R. Doria (S), A. Legros (Bs) & S. Gouat (pf.);
　　P. Derenne (T) & H. Cox (pf.)　♯ **CA.LPA 1091**
　[*a.* by Doria; *b.* by Legros, *c.* by Derenne] (♯ **Plé.P 3067**)

(7) CHANSONS GRISES　(Verlaine)
… 1. Chanson d'automne
　2. Tous deux
　3. L'Allée est sans fin
　4. En Sourdine
　5. L'Heure exquise
Quand je fus pris au pavillon　(Charles d'Orléans)　*(Rondel No. 8)*
L'Incrédule　(Verlaine)
Si mes vers avaient des ailes　(Hugo)
Mai　(Coppée)
Paysage　(Theuriet)
Phyllis　(L. de Lisle)　*(Études latines 10)*
　　J. Jensen (B), J. Bonneau (pf.)　♯ **D.FA 143574**
　　　　　　　　　　　　　　　　(♯ **Lon.LS 645**)

Mai　(Coppée)
Paysage　(Theuriet)
Si mes vers avaient des ailes　(Hugo)
　　G. Moizan (S)

Mélodies retrouvées
　1. La Nymphe de la Source　2. Mon amour　(Saix)
　3. Je me souviens　(de Saix)　4. Amitié　(Paté)
　5. Au Rossignol　(Prud'homme) 6. Naïs　(Saix)
　　J. Fourrier in No. 1; R. Bianco in Nos. 2, 5;
　　R. Bourdin (B) in Nos. 3, 4　♯ **D.FM 133678**
　[M. Berthomieu, pf.]

L'Heure exquise　*(Chanson grise 5—Verlaine)*
Offrande　(Verlaine)
Si mes vers avaient des ailes　(Hugo)
　　☆ M. Teyte (S)　　　　in ♯ **Vic.LCT 1133**
　　(Debussy, etc.)

Dernier vœu　(de Banville)
Ⓗ E. Calvé (S) (IRCC. 3141*)

D'une prison　(Verlaine)
☆ T. Rossi (T) (in ♯ *C.FS 1045*)

(L') Heure exquise　(Verlaine)　CG. 5
C. Devos (T), G. Lecompte (pf.)　♭ *Pat.D 110*
(below, & Beydts)
☆ N. Vallin (S) (♭ *Od.7AO 2010*)

Mai　(Coppée)
C. Devos (T), G. Lecompte (pf.)　♭ *Pat.D 110*
(L'Heure exquise; & Beydts)
Ⓗ E. Clément (T) (in ♯ *Sca. 819**)

Paysage　(Theuriet)
M. Santreuil (S), Y. M. Josse (pf.)　V♯ *POc.A 02*
(Massenet & Saint-Saëns)
Ⓗ A. Crossley (A) (♭ *Vic.Pte. re-issue*; o.n. 2186**)

(Le) Printemps　(de Banville)
M. Sénéschal (T), J. Bonneau (pf.)
　　　　　　　　　in ♯ *Phi.N 00681R*
(Saint-Saëns, Fauré, Debussy, etc.)

Si mes vers avaient des ailes　(Hugo)
M. Dobbs (S), G. Moore (pf.)　in ♯ *C.CX 1154*
(Schubert, Brahms, Wolf, etc.) (♯ FCX 299: QCX 10097;
　　　　　　　　　　　　　　　　　　Angel. 35094)
　　G. Swarthout (M-S), B. Greenhouse (vlc.),
　　G. Agostini (hp.)　　in ♯ *G.ALP 1269*
(Chausson, Debussy, etc.) (♯ Vic.LM 1793; FV.A 630227)
T. Rossi (T) (in ♯ *C.FS 1045*)
☆ N. Vallin (S) (♭ *Od.7AO 2010*)

— ACCOMPANIMENT etc. for practice (in ♯ *VS.ML 3000*)
Misc. Excerpts from Operettas
J. Sylvaire, A. Doniat, Orch.—Cariven (in ♯ *Véga.30M 706*)

HAIEFF, Alexei (b. 1914)

Concerto, pf. & orch.　fp. 1952
S. Bianco & Hamburg Philharmonia
　—H-J. Walther　　　　　♯ **MGM.E 3234**
(below)

(4) Juke Box Pieces　pf.
(5) Piano Pieces
L. Smit　　　　　　　　　♯ **MGM.E 3243**
(above)

Quartet, Strings, No. 1　1951
Juilliard Qtt.　　　　　　♯ **AmC.ML 4988**
(Barber)

Sonata　2 pfs.　1945
R. Gold & A. Fizdale　　♯ **AmC.ML 4855**
(Barber)　　　　　　　　(in set SL 198)

HAINDL, Franz Sebastian (1727-1812)
SEE: † TYROLESE XVIIITH CENT. ORCH. MUSIC

HAINES, Edmund
SEE: † AMERICAN ORGAN MUSIC

HALÉVY, Jacques François Fromental Élias
(1799-1862)

OPERAS
(L') ÉCLAIR　3 Acts　1835
Quand de la nuit l'épais nuage couvrait mes yeux
T　Act III
Ⓗ M. Garrison (S, Eng) (AF.AGSB 70*)

☆ = Re-issue of a recording to be found in previous volumes.

(La) JUIVE 5 Acts 1835
Si la rigueur ou la vengeance Bs Act I
C. Siepi ♯ *D.LW 5169*
(Salvator Rosa, S. Boccanegra, etc.) (♯ *Lon.LD 9169*)
(& in ♯ D.LXT 5096; Lon.LL 1240)
G. Frick *(Ger)* **G.DB 11566**
(Eugen Onegin, No. 20c) (♭ *7RW 519:* in ♯ *WBLP 1505*)
♮ W. Hesch *(Ger)* (in ♯ *SBDH.PL 1*)*
J. Mardones *(Ital)* (in ♯ *Sca. 810*° & *SBDH.LPP 3*)*
E. Brancaleoni *(Ital)* *(SBDH.P 7*)*
Rachel, quand du Seigneur . . . T Act IV
M. del Monaco **D.X 573**
(Forza—O tu che in seno)
(in ♯ *D.LXT 2845;* Lon.LL 880; also in ♯ *D.LXT 2964)*
K. Baum in ♯ **Roy. 1582**
(Faust, Trovatore, G. Tell, etc.)
A. da Costa in ♯ **Roy. 1599**
☆ M. Alexandrovich *(Russ)* *(USSRM.D 00116)*
☆ C. Vezzani (in ♯ *Ete. 708)*
♮ E. Caruso (♭ *Vic.ERAT 26*;* in ♯ *G.FJLP 5009*)*
Ta fille en ce moment T & B Act IV
♮ C. Vezzani & P. Payan (in ♯ *Od.ODX 126*)*

HALL, Henry (*c.* 1655-1707)
SEE: † MORE CATCHES & GLEES OF THE RESTORATION

HALLE, Adam de la (*c.* 1240-1287)
SEE: † HISTORY OF MUSIC IN SOUND (14 & 20)
† MUSIC OF THE MIDDLE AGES
† ANTHOLOGIE SONORE
and Collection under ADAM, *ante*

HALFFTER ESCRICHE, Ernesto
(b. 1905)
Sinfonietta, D major 1927
Naples Scarlatti Orch.—Caracciolo
♯ **Csm.CLPS 1041**
(Napoli: Symphony, excpts.)
SONATINA Ballet 1928
Danza della Gitana — ARR. PF.
▽ J. Cortes (in ♯ *SMC. 501)*

HALVORSEN, Johan (1864-1935)

Entry of the Boyars orch.
Hamburg Philharmonia—H-J. Walther
MSB. 78119
(Gounod: Marche funèbre d'une marionette) (also *78203,* d.c.)
Concert Orch.—Petersen (Pol.Z 60131)
☆ Boston Prom.—Fiedler (G.DB 4325)
Oslo Phil.—Fjeldstad (NOC. 63155)
FOSSEGRIMEN Inc. Music to play by Eldegard
Orch. Suite, Op. 21
Oslo Phil.—Fjeldstad ♯ **Mer.MG 90001**
(below) (also NOC. 63158/63, 6ss)
... No. 5, Fanitullen
S.B. Osa(Hardanger fiddle) & orch.—Fjeldstad *(G.GN 1347)*
Norwegian Rhapsody No. 1, A major
☆ Oslo Phil.—Fjeldstad in ♯ **Mer.MG 10150**
(Svendsen, Grüner-Hegge, etc.) (NOC. 62620/2, 3ss)
(Ole Bull, arr. Halvorsen: La Mélancholie, on
▽ Nera.SK 15503/4)
Suite ancienne, Op. 31 orch.
☆ Oslo Phil.—Fjeldstad ♯ **Mer.MG 90001**
(above) (also NOC. 62623/8, 6ss)
ORCHESTRATION
Ole Bull: La Mélancholie
Oslo Phil.—Fjeldstad in ♯ **Mer.MG 10150**
(▽ Nera.SK 15504; NOC. 63169)

HAMMERSCHMIDT, Andreas (1612-1675)
SEE: † SEVEN CENTURIES OF SACRED MUSIC

HANDEL, George Frederick (1685-1759)

CLASSIFIED: I. VOCAL (A) Operas & other stage works
(B) Oratorios
(C) Other
II. INSTRUMENTAL (A) Harpsichord
(B) Chamber Music
(C) Orchestral

I. VOCAL

A. OPERAS, etc.

ACIS & GALATEA Masque 1720, rev. 1732
S, T, T, B, cho., & orch.
COMPLETE RECORDING
☆ M. Ritchie, W. Herbert, etc., Handel Soc. Cho. & Orch.
—Goehr (♯ Clc. 6169/71)
I rage, I melt, I burn . . .
O ruddier than the cherry Bs
N. Walker **C.DX 1909**
(Judas Maccabaeus, No. 10)
♮ D. Bispham (in ♯ *Ete.O-488*;* Cum.CE 184*)*
AGRIPPINA 1709
Overture
Saar Cha.—Ristenpart **V♯** *DFr.EX 17025*
(Concerto No. 3, ob. & orch.)
ALCINA 1735
Overture
Boyd Neel Orch. ♯ *D.LW 5147*
(Berenice, Ov.) (♯ *Lon.LD 9166)*
... **Musette** only — ARR. VLA. & ORCH. Barbirolli
In *Concerto, q.v.*
Il Ballo . . . Minuet only
Inst. Ens. (in *G.B 10658)*
Ah, mio cor
I. Kolassi (M-S), J. Bonneau (pf.)
♯ *D.FAT 173160*
(† *Arie Antiche & German Lieder)* (♯ *Lon.LL 747)*
ATALANTA 1736
Care selve S
A. Pankey (B), E. Wernikova (pf.) *Muza. 1602*
(below)
☆ B. Gigli (T) in ♯ *G.ALP 1174*
(† *Italian Classic Songs)* (♯ *FALP 340:* QALP 10073)
BERENICE 1737
Overture
Boyd Neel Orch. ♯ *D.LW 5147*
(Alcina, Ov.) (♯ *Lon.LD 9166)*
... **Minuet** only
☆ Philharmonia—Weldon (♭ *C.SED 5507: SEBQ 112)*
— — ARR. BAND: Salvation Army—Munn *(RZ.MF 396)*
GIULIO CESARE IN EGITTO 1724
SLIGHTLY ABRIDGED RECORDINGS

	Set A	Set B
Julius Caesar ...	O. Wiener (Bs)	P. Sandoz (B)
Cleopatra ...	E. Roon (S)	S. Gähwiller (S)
Ptolemy ...	P. Curzon (B)	S. Tappolet (Bs)
Cornelia ...	M. Kalin (A)	M. Helbling (S)
Sextus ...	H. Handt (T)	F. Brückner-Rüggeberg
	etc.	etc. (T)

Set A, with Vienna Academy Cho. & Pro Musica
Cha. Orch.—Swarowsky ♯ **E. & AmVox.PL 8012**
(4ss) [omits all secco recitatives]
Set B, with Handel Soc. Cho. & Orch.—Goehr
♯ **HDL. set 18**
(4ss) (♯ Clc. 6235/6)
No. 8, Alma del gran Pompeo Act I
A. Deller (C-T) **G.C 4222**
(Messiah, No. 9) (EB 584)

No. 14, V'adoro, pupille Act II (*Es blaut die Nacht*)
V. de los Angeles (S), R. Lewis (T)   **G.HMS 47**
(† History of Music in Sound)   (in ♯ Vic. set LM 6030)
☆ E. Liebenberg (A, *Ger*) (in ♯ Ete.O-488; Cum.CE 184)

No. 22, Dall' ondoso periglio . . .
Aure, deh, per pietà B Act III
  (*Atem der blauen See*)
H. Uhde   ♭ *Pol.* 30084
(*Rigoletto—Cortigiani*)
(& in *German*, in ♯ Pol. 18147: 19043, with *Fidelio*,
Mignon, etc.)

HERCULES 1744
Overture . . . Maestoso & Fugue only
Paris Cha.—Douatte   in ♯ **EPP.APG 112**
(*below*)

No. 22, My father! ah methinks I see
— ARR. VLA. & ORCH. Barbirolli, in *Concerto, q.v.*

OTTONE, RE IN GERMANIA 1723
Overture   — ARR. ORGAN
A. E. Floyd   in ♯ **Spot.SC 1002**
(*S. S. Wesley, Schumann, etc.*)

La Speranza è giunta in porto ("*Spring is coming*")
Vieni, o figlio ("*Come to me, soothing sleep*")
☆ K. Ferrier (A), G. Moore (pf.) (in ♭ *C.SED 5526*)

(II) PASTOR FIDO 3 Acts   First version, 1712
ABRIDGED RECORDING[1]

Mirtillo	G. Warner (S)
Eurillo	L. Hunt (S)
Amarilli	G. Rowe (S)
Silvio	E. Brown (A)
Dorinda	V. Paris (A)
Firenio	F. Rogier (B)

& Columbia Cha. Orch.—Engel
        ♯ **AmC.ML 4685**

Overture . . . 1st, 2nd, 4th, 5th & 6th movts.
Nat. Sym.—Kindler: See II (c), *below*
... 4th & 6th movts. R.P.O.—Beecham: See II (c), *below*

(II) PASTOR FIDO   Second version, 1734
Overture; Ballo; March; Minuet, G major
R.P.O.—Beecham: *See II (c), below*
Musette   Nat. Sym.—Kindler: *See II (c), below*

RINALDO 1711
Al valor del mio brando Recit. S
Sinfonia   Orch.
Cara sposa   Aria   M-S (Act I)
E. Berge (S), E. Brems (M-S), & Danish Radio
Cha.—Wöldike   in ♯ **HS.HSL 2073**
(† Masterpieces of Music before 1750)
(also in † Histoire de la musique vocale)
[*Cara sposa* also on ♭ *Mtr.MCEP 3009*]

Lascia ch'io pianga (Act II)
F. Barbieri (M-S), D. Marzollo (pf.)
      in ♯ **AmVox.PL 7980**
(† Old Italian Songs & Airs)
☆ S. Onegin (A) (in ♯ Sca. 821)

— ARR. MALE CHO.
Pancratius Male Cho.—Heydendael
      in ♯ **C.HS 1001**

(*Haydn, Lassus, Schubert, etc.*)

Bel piacere (Act III)
— ARR. VLA. & ORCH. Barbirolli, in *Concerto, q.v.*

RODELINDA 1725
ABRIDGED RECORDING in *Italian*

Rodelinda	F. Sailer (S)
Bertarido	R. Titze (B)
Grimoaldo	F. Fehringer (T)
Edwige	H. Lipp (S)
Unulfo	W. Hagner (Bs)
Garibaldo	H. Lips (Bs)

& South German Radio Cho. & orch.
  —Müller-Kray   ♯ **Nix.PLP 589**
(♯ Per.SPL 589; ♯ Cpt.MC 20046)

Overture
Paris Cha.—Douatte   ♯ **EPP.APG 112**
(*Hercules Ov., Concerto Grosso, Op. 3-9; & Mozart*)

Dove sei, amato bene B ("*Art thou troubled*")
☆ K. Ferrier (A, *Eng*)   ♯ *D.LW 5072*
(*Serse; & Gluck, Mendelssohn*) (♯ *Lon.LD 9066*)
(*Gluck: Orphée*, only, ♭ *D. 71034*)
☆ E. Leisner (A, *Ger*) (in ♯ Ete. O-488; Cum.CE 184)

SCIPIONE 1726
March   — ARR. BAND
Grenadier Guards—Harris (*D.F 10083*: in ♯ LK 4058;
            ♯ Lon.LL 757: ♭ *BEP 6078*)

SEMELE   Opera-Oratorio 3 Acts 1743
COMPLETE RECORDING[2]

Semele	J. Vyvyan (S)
Athamas	J. Whitworth (C-T)
Ino	H. Watts (A)
Jupiter	W. Herbert (T)
Juno	A. Pollak (S)
Somnus	G. James (Bs)

etc., St. Anthony Singers & New Sym.—Lewis
        ♯ **LOL.OL 50098/100**
(6ss) [T. Dart, hpsi.]   (♯ OL.LD 124/6)

Leave me, loathsome light Bs.
A. Pankey (B)   in ♯ **Top.TRL 2**

O Sleep! why dost thou leave me? S
☆ D. Maynor (in ♯ Vic.LCT 1115: ♭ set WCT 1115)

Where'er you walk T
A. Pankey (B)   in ♯ **Top.TRL 2**

R. Fairhurst (Tr.) & org.   ♭ *D. 71069*
(*Bach: Cantata 208, excpt.*)

☆ L. Tibbett (B), S. Wille (pf.) (in ♯ Vic.LCT 1115:
                ♭ set WCT 1115)

☒ J. McCormack (T) (in ♯ Vic.LCT 1138*: ♭ ERAT 17*)

SERSE   Comic Opera 1738
Ombra mai fu ("*Largo*") T
Y. Printemps (S) & orch.   **G.DA 5057**
(*Mozart: Wiegenlied*) (in ♯ *FDLP 1029*; *Angel.C 28003*)
M. Klose (A)   ♭ *Pol. 32027*
(*Giordani: Caro mio ben*)
M. Vitale (S), A. Beltrami (pf.)   *Cet.AT 0315*
(*Caldara: Sebben, crudele*)   (♯ *LPC 55001*)
T. Lemnitz (S) & orch.   ♭ *T.U 45515*
(*Schubert: Ave Maria*)
M. Powers (A, *Eng*), F. la Forge (pf.)
            in ♯ *Atl.* 1207
(*Haydn, Schubert, Fauré, etc.*)
A. Heynis (A, *Lat*), P. Palla (org.)
            in ♯ *Phi.P 10048R*
            (& *Phi.N 17906H*)
Z. Palii (in ♯ Sup.LPV 207; U.5191G; & U.H 24425)
☆ R. Schock (♭ G.7PW 507: in ♯ WDLP 1501)
R. Tauber (in ♯ AmD.DL 7535)
K. Ferrier (♯ D.LW 5072; Lon.LD 9066;
           & ♭ D.71039: D 18060)
H. Schlusnus (B) (♭ Pol. 30151)
☒ E. Caruso (♭ Vic.ERAT 6*; in ♯ G.FKLP 7001*:
                      QKLP 501*)
G. Anselmi (in ♯ Ete.O-488*; Cum.CE 184*)
E. Albani (S) (in ♯ HRS. 3008*)

— ARRANGEMENTS
ORCH.
Hamburg Philharmonia—H-J. Walther (*MSB. 78001*)
Mantovani Orch. (*D.M 33652*; in ♯ *D.LK 4072*;
  Lon.LL 877; *D.F 43706*: ♭ D 17706: ♭ DFE 6089
                & ♭ Lon.BEP 6089)

Boyd Neel—Dumont (♭ *Phi.N 402028E*)
A. Bernard Str. Orch. (♭ *Pac. 90012*)
Belgian Radio—P. Glière (in ♯ Mae.OAT 25001)
☆ Philharmonia—Weldon (♭ *C.SED 5507: SEBQ 112*)
Boston Prom.—Fiedler (♭ *G.7PW 105: 7PQ 2024:*
                    Vic.ERA 66)
Rome Santa Cecilia—Molinari (in ♯ *Tem.TT 2046*)
Chicago Sym.—Stock (in ♯ Cam.CAL 192)

(*continued on next page*)

---

[1] The recits. and Scenes 2, 4-6 and 8 to end, Act I; Scenes 3, 4, 6 (part), 8 (part) to end, Act II; Scenes 1-3, 5 (part), 6, 7 (part), 8 (part), 9 (Sinfonia), are omitted.
[2] The following nos. of the Novello edn. score are omitted: 6, 8, 15-20, 25-7, 51, 52, 67, 69, 71-2; cuts are made in Nos. 4, 37 and 54.

SERSE—Largo (*continued*)
ORGAN G. de Donà (in ♯ *AmVox.VL 3100*)
 R. Ellsasser (in ♯ *MGM.E 198*: ♭ *set K 198*)
 R. Elmore (in ♯ *Cant.MRR 270*)
 A. E. Floyd[1] (in ♯ *Spot.SC 1002*)
 J. Perceval (in ♯ *ArgOd.LDC 513*: ♭ *BSOAE 4528*)
HPSI. E. Silver (in ♯ *Roy. 1550*)
BAND Massed Bands—F. Mortimer (♭ *C.SEG 7610*)

Va godendo vezzoso e bello
 H G. Anselmi (T) (in ♯ *Ete. 711**; Cum.CE 184**)

SOSARME, RE DI MEDIA 3 Acts 1732
COMPLETE RECORDING[2]
Elmira	M. Ritchie (S)
Erenice	N. Evans (A)
Melo	H. Watts (A)
Sosarme	A. Deller (C-T)
Haliate	W. Herbert (T)
Argone	J. Kentish (T)
Altomaro	I. Wallace (Bs)

St. Anthony Singers & St. Cecilia Orch.—Lewis
        ♯ **LOL.OL 50091/3**
(6ss)   (♯ OL.LD 121/3)

Rend' il sereno, al ciglio
 H C. Butt (A) (AF.AGSB 75**)

TAMERLANO 1724
Figlia mia, non pianger no
 R. Hayes (T), R. Boardman (pf.) in ♯ *A440.12-3*

II. B. ORATORIOS, etc.

ALEXANDER'S FEAST Ode 1736
 ☆ Soloists, Cornell Univ. Cho. & Handel Soc. Orch.
 —Hull   ♯ **MMS. set 2016**
(4ss)   (♯ Clc. 6256/7)

**(L') ALLEGRO, IL PENSIEROSO, ED IL
 MODERATO** 1740
No. 13, Sweet bird S & fl.
 ☆ (*Fr*) G. Ritter-Ciampi (in *Ete.O-488*; Cum.CE 184)
 H E. Albani (IRCC. 3131*)

BELSHAZZAR 1744
ABRIDGED RECORDINGS in *German*
	Set A	Set B
Nitocris ...	E. Laux (S)	F. Sailer (S)
Cyrus ...	A. Müller (A)	H. Münch (A)
Balthasar	W. Liebling (T)	F. Fehringer (T)
Daniel ...	H. Friedrich (B)	H. Metz (A)
Gobrias ...	H. Alsen (Bs)	R. Titze (B)

Set A, with Berlin Radio Cho. & Orch.—Koch
(6ss)   ♯ **Sel. 320.C.003/5**
   (4ss, ♯ Van.BG 534/5; ♯ MTW. 525/6)
Set B, with Stuttgart State Cons. Cho. & Orch.
 —Grischkat (4ss) ♯ **Per. set SPL 594**

DEBORAH 1733
No. 2, Immortal Lord of earth and skies
— ARR. ORCH. Fekete: *See* Triumph of Time ... Suite,
 II (c), *infra.*

ISRAEL IN EGYPT 1737
 ☆ E. Morison, M. Kalmus, etc. Handel Soc. Cho. & Orch.
 —Goehr (♯ Clc. 6167/8)

JEPHTHA 1751
No. 18, O God behold
No. 14, When his loud voice ... They now contract Cho.
No. 50, How dark O Lord ... Cho.
 All our joys ... No certain bliss ... Cho.
No. 56, Doubtful fear Cho.
— ARR. ORCH. Fekete *See* Triumph of Time ... Suite,
 II (c), *infra.*

JOSHUA 1747
No. 53, Shall I in Mamre's fertile plains Bs.
 ☆ H. Hotter (*Ger*) (C.LOX 833)

No. 61, Oh! had I Jubal's lyre S
 H Lilli Lehmann (*Ger*) (in ♯ *Ete.O-488**; Cum.CE 184**)

JUDAS MACCABAEUS 1746
COMPLETE RECORDING
 Anon. "Prague Opera" Soloists, Cho. & Orch.—Balzer
        ♯ **Roy. 1524/5**

ABRIDGED RECORDING
 ☆ Soloists, Utah Univ. Cho. & Sym.—Abravanel
        ♯ **MMS. 2032**

No. 10, Arm, arm, ye brave! Bs.
 N. Walker   **C.DX 1909**
 (*Acis & Galatea—I rage, I melt* ...)

No. 33, So shall the lute S
 B. Troxell & org.   in ♯ **Ply. 12-123**
 (*Mozart, Bach, Wolf, etc.*)

No. 45, Sound an alarm T
 ☆ R. Crooks (in ♯ Cam.CAL 170)
 H M. Kingston (in ♯ Ete.O-488;* ♯ Cum.CE 184*)

No. 53, Father of heaven S or T
 K. Ferrier (A)[3]   in ♯ **D.LXT 2757**
 (*Messiah & Samson; & Bach*) (♯ Lon.LL 888)
 (*Messiah & Samson*, only, ♯ *D.LW 5076*; *Lon.LD 9098*)

No. 58, See, the conquering hero comes Cho.
 ☆ St. Hedwig's Cath. Cho.—Forster (*Ger*) (♭ *T.U 453816*)

MESSIAH 1742
COMPLETE RECORDINGS
Set W
M. Ritchie (S), C. Shacklock (A), W. Herbert
 (T), R. Standen (Bs), London Phil. Cho. &
 L.S.O.—Scherchen ♯ **Nix.NLP 907-1/3**
(6ss)   (♯ West. set WAL 308)
[Nos. 4, 7, 12, 24, 28, 37, 39, 41, 44, 46-9, 56 also on
        ♯ West.WN 18099]

Set D
J. Vyvyan (S), N. Procter (A), G. Maran (T),
 O. Brannigan (Bs), London Phil. Cho. & Orch.
 —Boult   ♯ **D.LXT 2921/4**
(8ss)   (♯ Lon. set LLA 19)
Excerpts:
Nos. 1 & 13 on ♭ *D. 71101*
Nos. 2, 3, 12, 14-17, 19-20, 23, 38, 40, 44, 45, 50, 51, 56
 on ♯ *D.LXT 2989*; *Lon.LL 1112*
Nos. 22 & 44 on ♭ *D. 71080*
No. 23 (& *Mendelssohn*) on ♭ *D. 71082*

Set C
E. Morison (S), M. Thomas (A), R. Lewis
 (T), N. Walker (Bs), Huddersfield Cho. Soc.
 & Liverpool Phil.—Sargent ♯ **C.CX 1146/8**
(6ss) [E. Cooper, org.] (♯ FCX 276/8: QCX 10082/4;
      Angel. 35123/5, set 3510)
Excerpts:
Nos. 1 & 13 on C.LX 1601: ♭ *SCB 115*
Nos. 4, 7, 12, 17 on ♭ *C.SEL 1519*
Nos. 8, 9, 19 & 20 on ♭ *C.SEL 1520*
Nos. 23 & 45 on ♭ *C.SEL 1513*
Nos. 22, 24, 26, 28 on ♭ *C.SEL 1517*
Nos. 29-32, 40, 50-1 on ♭ *C.SEL 1518*
Nos. 41, 44, 56, 57 on ♭ *C.SEL 1512*: *SELW 1512*
Nos. 44 & 57 on ♭ *C.SCD 2017*: *SCDW 111*

Set B
A. Addison (S), L. Sydney (A), D. Lloyd (T),
 D. Gramm (Bs), Boston Handel & Haydn Soc.
 Cho. & Zimbler Sinfonietta—Stone
(6ss)   ♯ **Uni. set UNS 1**

Set V
 ☆ E. Suddaby (S), M. Thomas (A), H. Nash
 (T), T. Anthony (Bs), Luton Cho. Soc. &
 Special Cho., R.P.O.—Beecham
       ♯ **G.ALP 1077/80**
(8ss—s.1 includes a talk by Sir Thomas Beecham)
Excerpts:
Nos. 1, 3, 4, 12, 13, 20a, 20b, 22, 23, 44, 45, 50,
       on ♯ Vic.LCT 1130
Nos. 13 & 44 on ♭ G.7RF 280; ♭ Vic. 49-0819

Set T
B. Troxell, J. Sanders, W. Fredericks,
 G. Darwin, Cho. & Orch.—J. Cartwright, org.
(6ss)   ♯ **Roy. 1539/41**
Excerpts:
Nos. 4, 6, 17, 20b, 23, 24, 44, & 46 on ♯ *Var. 69153*
Nos. 23 & 44 on ♭ *Roy.EP 707*
Nos. 40 & 45 on ♭ *Roy.EP 708*
Nos. 20a, 20b, 21, 30 on ♭ *Roy.EP 709*
Nos. 4, 6, 50, 51 on ♭ *Roy.EP 710*
Unspec. excerpts on ♯ *Gram. 20171*

---

[1] ARR. Hellmesberger.
[2] The arias *Il mio dolore* and *Due parti* are omitted; middle sections are omitted from *Forte in ciampo*; *Cuor di madre*;
M'opperrò; *Si minaccia*; *Se discordia*; *Vola d'augello*; the recits. are shortened.   [3] Ed. Prout.

Set M

☆ L. Marshall (S), M. Palmateer (A), J. Vickers (T),
J. Milligan (Bs), Toronto Mendelssohn Cho. &
Toronto Sym.—MacMillan ♯ **BB. set LBC 6100**
(6ss)

Excerpts:
Nos. 1, 3, 9, 12, 23, 26, 45, 50, 57
on ♯ BB.LBC 1053: ♭ set WBC 1053
Nos. 3, 4, 9, 12, 13, 18, 26, 44, 45, 50, 51, 57
on ♯ Bea. 1002

Set R (*German*)

☆ A. Kupper (S), R. Anday (A), L. Fehenberger (T),
J. Greindl (Bs), Salzburg Cath. Cho. & Fest. Orch.
—Messner (♯ Cum. set 205, 4ss)
Excerpts: Nos. 25, 44 on ♯Ply, 12-90
No. 44 on ♭ Rem.REP 16; Cum.ECR 50

NOTES on the complete recordings:

Set W. The Coopersmith edn. is used, revised Scherchen
(original accompaniments; with hpsi. continuo,
G. Malcolm). Nos. 5 & 6 are sung by the contralto.
Set D. The J. Herbage edition is used (Foundling Hospital
accompaniments; with hpsi. & organ continuo,
G. Malcolm & R. Downes).
Set C. Omits Nos. 34, 35, 36, 52, 53, 54, 55; omits middle
section & *da capo* of Nos. 23 & 51. (Mozart's
accompaniments, ed. Prout, Franz etc.; trombone parts
by Smithies).
Set B. Omits Nos. 7, 25, 34-7, 39, 41, 46-9, 52-5, and the
middle section & *da capo* of Nos. 23 & 51. Based on
score prepared for Boston Handel & Haydn Soc. by
R. Franz in 1885, with his own & Mozart's additional
parts; some of these now omitted, others from Prout &
Chrysander edns. added; with D. A. Dwyer (hpsi.),
E. Weidner (org.).
Set V. ∇ Transfers Nos. 34 & 35 between Nos. 55 & 56.
(Mozart's accompaniments, ed. Beecham; with
H. Dawson, organ). Omits *da capos* of Nos. 23 & 51.
Set T. Omits Nos. 34-9 & 52-55 inclusive; no information
as to edition.
Set M. The original issue omits Nos. 34-6, 49-52.
(Mozart's accompaniments, ed. Prout & MacMillan).
The BB. reissue is *stated* to omit Nos. 7, 48, 49, 52-5.
Set R. No information as to cuts or edition.

ABRIDGED RECORDINGS

A. Cole (S), W. Krap (A), T. Larsen (T), G. Hoekman (Bs),
Netherlands Handel Soc. Cho. & Phil. Orch.—Goehr
♯ MMS. set 2019
(4ss) (also ♯ MMS. set Op. 14 & ♯ CHS. set CHS 1245)

Excerpts (with commentary by S. Spaeth:
☆ Soloists, Salzburg Cath. Cho. & Mozarteum Orch.
—Messner, from set R (♯ Rem. 18)

PART I

No. 2, Comfort ye my people T
☆ R. Crooks (in ♯ Cam.CAL 170)

No. 4, And the Glory of the Lord Cho.
Dallas Baptist Church Cho.—Souther
(*No. 44*) Word.WR 776

Munich Phil. Cho. & Orch.—Lamy *PV. 36103*
(*No. 44*) (*Ger*) (& *PV. 46001*; ♭ *Pol. 34019: 32063*)

No 9, O thou that tellest good tidings A
A. Deller (C-T) G.C 4222
(*Handel: Giulio Cesare, aria*) (EB 584)
K. Ferrier[1] in ♯ D.LXT 2757
(*Judas Maccabaeus, below; & Bach*) (in ♯ Lon.LL 688)
(also ♯ D.LW 5076; Lon.LD 9098; & ♭ D. 71038)

No. 13, Pastoral Symphony
☆ Philadelphia—Stokowski (in ♯ Cam.CAL 120)
Sym. Orch.—Stokowski (♭ *Vic. 49-0794*: ♭ *ERA 119*)

— ARR. ORGAN C. Cronham (*Mjr. 5144*)

No. 20 (a), He shall feed His flock A
☆ M. Anderson (in ♯ Vic.LCT 1111: ♭ set WCT 1111)

PART II

No. 23, He was despised A
[1]K. Ferrier[2] in ♯ D.LXT 2757
(*above; & Bach*) (in ♯ Lon.LL 688)
(also, without *Bach*, ♯ D.LW 5076; Lon.LD 9098)
A Deller (C-T)[2] G.B 10682
(EA 4231)
☆ M. Anderson (in ♯ Vic.LCT 1111: ♭ set WCT 1111)

No. 29, Thy rebuke . . .; No. 30, Behold and see T
☆ Y. Tinayre (*Fr*) in ♯ AmD.DL 9654
(† Seven Centuries of Sacred Music) (in set DX 120)

No. 33, Lift up your heads Cho.
— ARR. BAND Salvation Army —Munn (*RZ.MF 397*)

No. 40, Why do the nations Bs
☆ N. Cordon (in ♯ Cam.CAL 269)

No. 44, Hallelujah! Cho.
Festival Cho. (Australia)—Chinner
in ♯ EPhi.ABL 3016
Helsinki Univ. Cho.—Turunen (*Finn*)
in ♯ Rem. 199-167
Dallas Baptist Chu. Cho.—Souther (Word.WR 776)
Munich Phil. Cho. & Orch.—Lamy (*Ger*)
(*PV. 36103: 46001*: ♭ *Pol. 34019: 32063*)
☆ Shaw Chorale & Org. (♭ *G.7EP 7012; DV. 26027*)
St. Hedwig's Cath. Cho.—Forster (*Ger*)
etc. (in ♯ *T.LA 6086* & ♭ *UE 453816*)

(The) OCCASIONAL ORATORIO 1746
Overture . . . March only
L.S.O.—Weldon *C.DB 3399*
(*Solomon—No. 42*) (in ♯ *SX 1045*:
♭ *SED 5516: SEDQ 529: ESBF 120*)

PASSION ACCORDING TO ST. JOHN 1704
☆ Soloists, Zürich Bach Cho. & Winterthur Sym.
—Henking (*Ger*)[3] (♯ Clc. 6281/2)

SAMSON 1743
Overture (Ed. Prout)
☆ Philharmonia—Weldon ♭ *C.SED 5501*
(*Suppé: Leichte Cavallerie, Overture*)

No. 14, Total eclipse! T
☆ R. Crooks (in ♯ Cam.CAL 170)

No. 35, Return, O God of hosts A
K. Ferrier[1] in ♯ D.LXT 2757
(*above*) (in ♯ Lon.LL 688)
(with *Messiah, No. 9 only*, ♭ *D. 71038*)
(& in ♯ *D.LW 5076; Lon.LD 9098*)

No. 41, How willing my paternal love Bs
☆ H. Hotter (*Ger*) (C.LOX 833)

SAUL 1738/9
SLIGHTLY ABRIDGED RECORDING
M. W. Smith, A. Harris (S), N. Marchie (M-S),
J. Craner (A), W. Moonan, H. Sullivan,
R. Wakefield (T), P. Rosen, J. Hudson,
R. Griffith, J. la Falce (B), Collegiate Singers
& Crane Dept. of Music Symphonette
—McElerhan ♯ **HDL. set 15**
(4ss) (♯ Clc. 6206/7)

No. 75, Dead March Orch.
— ARR. ORGAN C. Cronham (*Mjr. 5123*)

SOLOMON 1748
No. 42, Sinfonia "*Arrival of the Queen of Sheba*"
London Cha.—Bernard *G.B 10562*
(*Fauré: Masques et Bergamasques, Overture*)
(& ♭ *G.7EP 7001: 7EPQ 519*)
L.S.O.—Weldon *C.DB 3399*
(*Occasional Overture*) (in ♯ *SX 1045*:
♭ *SED 5516: SEDQ 529: ESBF 120*)

No. 49, Draw the tear from hopeless love. Cho.
Danish Radio Co. & Cha. Orch.—Wöldike
in ♯ HS.HSL 2073
(† Masterpieces of Music before 1750)
(also in † Histoire de la Musique vocale)

SUSANNA 1748
How long, O Lord? Cho.
Cho. & Orch.—Goldsbrough *G.HMS 57*
(† History of Music in Sound) (in ♯ Vic. set LM 6031)

I. C. (a) ANTHEMS

A. CHANDOS ANTHEMS c. 1717-20

No. 2, In the Lord put I my trust (Psalm 71)
J. Vickers (T), Toronto Mendelssohn Cho. &
C.B.C. Sym.—MacMillan ♯ **Bea.LP 1002**
(*Coronation Anthem, & Water Music*)

---

[1] Ed. Prout.
[2] Omits middle section and *da capo*.
[3] Ed. E. Hess; includes interpolations from "*Brockes-Passion*" (1716): 1, Sinfonia. 2. Out of chains (Cho.); 79, Haste ye, souls; and some revision of the text.

... **Overture, D minor** — ARR. Elgar
L.S.O.—Weldon   ♭ C.SED 5516
(*Solomon & Occasional Oratorio, excpts.*)
(in ♯ SX 1045: *SEDQ 529: ESBF 120*)

No. 6, As pants the hart (Psalm 42)
No. 11, Let God arise (Psalm 68)
D. v. Doorn (S), A. Woud (A), L. Larsen (T),
D. Hollestelle (Bs), Netherlands Handel
Soc. Cho. & Orch.—Loorij   ♯ HDL. 17
(♯ Clc. 6191)

No. 9, O praise the Lord
... **That God is great** B
G. Clinton & P. Oyez (pf.)   ♯ CA.LPA 1095
(*Dvořák & Stanford*)

B. CORONATION 1727

No. 1, Zadok the Priest
Coronation Cho. & Orch.—McKie
in ♯ G.ALP 1057
(† Coronation of Queen Elizabeth II) (& G.DB 21583)
☆ Royal Festival Cho. & Orch.—Sargent (*G.EC 213*)

... **Introduction** only Org.
Organist of St. Margaret's Church, Westminster
in ♯ Ori.MG 20003

No. 2, The King shall rejoice
Toronto Mendelssohn Cho. & C.B.C. Sym.
—MacMillan   ♯ Bea.LP 1002
(*Chandos Anthem & Water Music*)

No. 4, Let thy hand be strengthened
☆ Danish Radio Cho. & Orch.—Wöldike
P.R 20620
(AR 1147: in ♯ PMA 1005)

(b) OTHER VOCAL WORKS

CANTATAS (Italian)

A. WITH INSTRUMENTS

Apollo e Dafne S, B, orch. (B & H 16) 1707-8
☆ M. Ritchie, B. Boyce & Orch.—Lewis
♯ LOL.OL 50038

Cecilia, volgi un sguardo S, T, str. & cont. (B & H 6)
D. v. Doorn, L. Larsen, Netherlands Handel Soc.
Orch.—Loorij   ♯ HDL. 19
(*below*)   (♯ Clc. 6195)

Delirio amoroso S, fl., ob., str. & cont. (B & H 12)
... **Introduction** — ARR. VLA. & ORCH. Barbirolli
in *Concerto, q.v.*

Nel dolce dell' oblio S, fl. & cont. (B & H 17)
Spande ancor Bs, str. & cont. (B & H 20)
D. v. Doorn, D. Hollestelle, Netherlands
Handel Soc. Ens.—Loorij   ♯ HDL. 20
(*Salve Regina*)   (♯ Clc. 6220)

Nel dolce dell' oblio only
V. Lamoree, B. Krainis (recorder), H. Chessid
(hpsi.), N. Courant (gamba)   ♯ Eso.ES 515
(*Sonatas*)   (♯ Cpt.MC 20021)

B. WITH CONTINUO ONLY

Dalla guerra amorosa Bs & cont. (B & H 8)
D. Hollestelle, hpsi. & vlc.   ♯ HDL. 19
(*above*)   (♯ Clc. 6195)
☆ H. O. Hudemann, F. Neumeyer (hpsi.), A. Wenzinger
(vlc.) (*Telemann*)   ♯ AmD.DL 7542

Dolce pur d'amor A & cont. (B & H 15)
A. Woud, hpsi. & vlc.   ♯ HDL. 20
(♯ Clc. 6220)

CANTATAS, Various
Unid. . . . **Dank sei dir, Herr** ("*Arioso*")[1]
K. Borg (Bs), M. Wöldike (org.)   Pol. 62921
(*Beethoven: Die ehre Gottes*)   (♭ 32104)

J. Kaiser (B), H. Wolff (org.)   T.E 3936
(*Slunicko: Vater unser . . .*)   (♭ UE 453936)
(& in *Latin*, T.E 3935: ♭ UE 453935; ♭ FT. 510.TC.004)
☆ E. Leisner (A) (in ♯ Ete.O-488; Cum.CE 184)

— ARR. ORG. R. Foort (in ♯ SOT. 1055)
— ARR. VLN. & PF. L. Kogan & pf. (USSR. 15901)

Salve Regina S & orch. c. 1707-12
D. v. Doorn & Netherlands Handel Soc.
Orch.—Loorij   ♯ HDL. 20
(*Cantatas*)   (♯ Clc. 6220)

SONGS

DEUTSCHE ARIEN (Brockes) c. 1729
COLLECTION
Künft'ge Zeiten eitler Kummer (with ob.)
Das zitternde Glänzen der spielenden Wellen (with vln.)
Süsser Blumen Ambra-Flocken (with fl.)
Süsse Stille, sanfte Quelle (with fl.)
Singe, Seele, Gott zum Preise (with vln.)
Meine Seele hört im Sehen (with ob.)
Die ihr aus dunkeln Grüften (with vln.)
In den angenehmen Büschen (with fl.)
Flammende Rose, Zierde der Erden (with vln.)
M. Guilleaume (S), vln., fl., ob., hpsi. & vlc.
♯ HP.APM 14031
[Nos. 4 & 6 also on ♭ Pol. 37026]

Meine Seele hört im Sehen
Süsse Stille, sanfte Quelle
M. Ribbing (S), E. M. Bruun (vln.), L. Selbiger
(hpsi.) & J. Hansen (vlc.)   G.DB 10515

TE DEUM, D major (Dettingen)
S, A, T, B, cho. orch. 1743
☆ Soloists, Presbyterian Cho. & Nat. Gallery Orch.—Bales
(♯ McInt.MC 1014)

... **No. 17** — ARR. VLN. & PF. Flesch (*Prayer*)
☆ Y. Menuhin & G. Moore (*ArgA. 292705*)

TE DEUM, D major (Utrecht)
S, S, A, A, T, B, cho. & orch. 1713
Soloists & Berlin Sym. Cho. & Orch.—Kegel
♯ Ura. 71292[2]

☆ Soloists & Danish Radio Cho. & Orch.—Wöldike
(*Let thy hand be strengthened*)   ♯ P.PMA 1005

Unidentified arias
Chi sprezzando il sommo
A. Pankey (B), E. Wermikova (pf.) Muza. 1602
(*Atalanta—Care selve*)

Sento io gioia[3]
A. Pankey (B)   in ♯ Top.TRL 2

=====

II. INSTRUMENTAL

A. HARPSICHORD

[The Lessons and Suites are arranged according to the
B & H edn. In the *Handel Gesellschaft* edn., Lesson 3a is
called Suite 2, Lesson 2 is part of Suite 1 and Suite 11 is
Suite 4, of Book II].

AYLESFORD PIECES
[Pieces for hpsi. in Library of Marquis of Aylesford, now
Royal Music Library at British Museum. Numbered from the
printed edn. in 2 vols.]

No. 15, Chaconne, C major (abbreviated)
No. 19, Arpeggio, G minor ("Gigue")
— ARR. HARP Boye
H. Boye   ♯ D.LW 5177
(*below, & Buxtehude*)

No. 37, Air, B flat major
No. 43, Allemande, A minor
No. 65, Minuet, G minor
R. Gerlin   ♯ LOL.OL 50043
(† Clavecinistes italiens & allemands) (♯ OL.LD 67)

---

[1] Ed. Ochs, as an interpolation in a performance of *Israel in Egypt*. It is suggested that it is actually his own composition.
[2] Announced and then "temporarily" withdrawn (June 1954).
[3] Perhaps *Sei mia gioia* from *Partenope*. It has not been possible to check.

— GUITAR ARRANGEMENTS Segovia

Nos. 3 & 4, Minuets, G minor ("Allegretto grazioso")
No. 6, Gavotte, G major
☆ A. Segovia (in † ♯ D.UAT 273142 = ♯ B.AXTL 1010,
Supp. II)
No. 15, Chaconne, C major ... excerpt ("Sarabande")
Nos. 28 & 18, Minuet, G major & Allegro, A minor
☆ A. Segovia (in † ♯ B.AXTL 1060)
No. 15, excerpt: A. Lagoya (♭ FV. 75018)[1]

Capriccio, A minor   (No. 3 of 7 *Pieces*)
R. Gerlin   in ♯ LOL.OL 50043
(† Clavecinistes italiens & allemands)   (♯ OL.LD 67)

FUGUES
No. 4, D major; No. 5, A minor c. 1720
☆ F. Pelleg (♯ Clc. 6219)

(3) LESSONS
No. 1, Air & Variations, B flat major
☆ W. Landowska (in ♯ G.FJLP 5056)
No. 2, Minuet, G minor
W. Kempff (pf.)[2]   ♯ D.LW 5212
(*Suite No. 5, excpt.; & Beethoven*)
(*Suite No. 5 excpt.* only, ♭ D. 71113)
No. 3a, Chaconne, G major (with 21 varns.)
K. Richter   ♯ HP.AP 13023
(*Suite No. 5*)
G. Ramin [omits repeats]   Eta. 25-C.043
(*Concerto grosso, Op. 3, No. 5, s. 3*)   (also *Eta. 121055*)

SUITES
COLLECTION. ☆ F. Pelleg
No. 1, A major; No. 2, F major; No. 3, D minor (♯ Clc. 6199)
No. 4, E minor; No. 5, E major; No. 6, F sharp minor
(♯ Clc. 6219)
No. 9, G minor; No. 10, D minor; No. 11, D minor; No. 12,
E minor (♯ Clc. 6195)

BOOK I, 1720
No. 2, F major
☆ F. Valenti (♯ Allo. 4001)
No. 3, D minor
... Prelude — ARR. HARP Boye
H. Boye (*above*)   in ♯ D.LW 5177
... Allemande only
E. Heiller   in ♯ Uni.LP 1010
(† History of the Dance)
No. 5, E major
K. Richter   ♯ HP.AP 13023
(*Lesson 3a*)   (also ♭ Pol. 37028, 2ss)
☆ W. Gieseking (pf.)   ♯ AmC.ML 4646
(*Bach & Scarlatti*)
(♯ C.FCX 367: ♭ SCBF 109: SCBQ 3005)
... Air & Variations only "*Harmonious Blacksmith*"
J. Prelli   Orf. 45002
(*Suite 7, excpt.*)
W. Kempff (pf.)   ♯ D.LW 5212
(*Lesson No. 2, & Beethoven*) (*Lesson No. 2* only, ♭ D. 71113)
☆ W. Landowska (in ♯ G.ALP 1246: FALP/QALP 218)
— — ARR. HARP: C. Salzédo (in ♯ Mer.MG 80003)
No. 6, F sharp minor
... Prelude — ARR. ORGAN Keller
▽ E. Hölderlin (in ♯ E. & AmVox.PL 7802, as interpolation
in Organ Concerto 14)
No. 7, G minor
... Passacaille only
J. Prelli   Orf. 45002
(*No. 5, Air & Variations*)
M. Jonas (pf.)   in ♯ AmC.ML 4624
☆ A. Ehlers (in ♯ D.UAT 273084)
— — ARR. VLN. & VLA. Halvorsen
☆ J. Heifetz & W. Primrose (in ♯ Vic.LCT 1150)
— — ARR. HARP: E. Vito   in ♯ Per.SPL 704
No. 8, F minor ... 1st & 2nd movts.
— — ARR. ORGAN Guilmant ("*Prelude & Fugue*")
☆ P. Alsfelt (♭ Mer.EP 1-5050)

BOOK II c. 1733
No. 10 (3) D minor ... Minuet & 2 variations
E. Heiller   in ♯ Uni.LP 1010
(† History of the Dance)
No. 11 (4) D minor
☆ F. Valenti (♯ Allo. 4001)
C major (on ♯ LOL.OL 50043): a synthetic suite
(*see above*)

Toccata, C major Anon. hpsi. (EMI.EPX 92)

II. B. CHAMBER MUSIC

(2) Arias 2 hrns., obs., & bsns.
Gavotte & March tpt., obs., bsns. & side drum
Overture, D major 2 cl. & hrn. 1748
☆ London Baroque Ens.—Haas (♯ AmD.DL 4070)

CONCERTOS à quatre (not in Gesamtausgabe.
Ed. Zobeley, pub. Schott)
No. 1, D minor 1715 orig. fl., vln. (or 2 vlns.)
& cont.
No. 2, D major orig. 2 vlns. & cont.
C. Monteux (fl.), D. Shulman (ob.), B.
Greenhouse (vlc.), S. Marlowe (hpsi.)
♯ Eso.ES 528
(*Sonata; & Bach*)   (♯ Cpt.MC 20084)

SONATAS
A. SOLOS
(15) SONATAS Op. 1
FLUTE & CONTINUO
COLLECTIONS
No. 1, E minor   No. 7, C major
No. 2, G minor   No. 9, B minor
No. 4, A minor   No. 11, F major
No. 5, G major
with
A minor "Halle Sonata" 1: HG 16
E minor "Halle Sonata" 2: HG 17
B minor "Halle Sonata" 3: HG 18
J. Wummer, F. Valenti (hpsi.), A. Parisot (vlc.)
♯ West. set WAL 218
(4ss: Nos. 16, 17 on s. 1; 18, 1, 5, on s. 2; 9, 2 on s. 3;
4, 7, 11 on s. 4)
Nos. 1, 2, 4, 5, 7, 9, 11
☆ J. Baker & S. Marlowe (hpsi.)   ♯ B.AXTL 1028/9
(♯ D.UAT 273548/9)
Nos. 1, 5, 9 & "16" (labelled "Op. 1, No. 4")
☆ J-P. Rampal & I. Nef (hpsi.)   ♯ LOL.OL 50040
Nos. 2, 4, 7 & 11
A. Mann (rec.), H. Elsner (hpsi.), H. Reimann (vlc.)
♯ AmVox.PL 7910

No. 4, A minor ("No. 3")
☆ G. Scheck (rec.), F. Neymeyer (hpsi.), A. Wenzinger
(gamba) (♭ Pol. 37027: ♯ 13035)
No. 5, G major ("No. 4") ... Bourrée only
Inst. Ens. (in G.B 10660)
No. 7, C major ("No. 5")
[3] C. Dolmetsch (rec.) & J. Saxby (hpsi.)
in ♯ D.LXT 2943
(† Recorder & Harpsichord Recital)   (♯ Lon.LL 1026)
B. Krainis (rec.), H. Chessid (hpsi.), N. Courant
(gamba)   ♯ Eso.ES 515
(*below*)   (♯ Cpt. MC 20021)
No. 9, B minor ("No. 6")
[4] B. Krainis (rec.), H. Chessid (hpsi.), N. Courant
(gamba)   ♯ Eso.ES 515
(*Trio Sonata; Cantata*)   (♯ Cpt. MC 20021)

[1] Called *Sarabande variée* but probably this.
[2] Arr. Kempff.
[3] Arr. Dolmetsch
[4] Played in an earlier D minor version for recorder, ed. T. Dart; pub. Schott, 1948: "*Fitzwilliam Sonata No. 3*".

No. 11, F major ("No. 7")
— ARR. FL. STR. & CONT. Veyron-Lacroix
J-P. Rampal & Paris Inst. Ens.—Froment
‡ *EPP.APG 119*
(Scarlatti, Pergolesi, Corelli)

VIOLIN & CONTINUO
COLLECTION

No. 3, A major   No. 13, D major
No. 10, G minor   No. 14, A major
No. 12, F major   No. 15, E major

☆ A. Schneider, R. Kirkpatrick (hpsi.), F. Miller (vlc.)
‡ *AmC.ML 4787*
— ARR. ORCH. M. Casadesus ("in style of Concerti Grossi")
M. Casadesus Ensemble   ‡ *Plé.P 3077*

No. 10, G minor ("No. 2")
☆ I. B. Meinert, lute & gamba (*No. 4*)   ‡ *Pol. 13035*

No. 12, F major ("No. 3")
— FOR PRACTICE: Recorded without violin part
(‡ *CEd.MMO 306*)

No. 13, D major ("No. 4")
J. Szigeti & C. Bussotti (pf.) ‡ *EPhi.ABL 3058*
(Bach & Tartini)   (‡ *AmC.ML 4891*; ‡ *Phi.A 01140L*)
N. Milstein & A. Balsam (pf.)   ‡ *Cap.P 8315*
(Prokofiev & Vitali)

☆ A. Campoli & G. Malcolm (hpsi.)   ‡ *D.LW 5077*
(No. 15)   (‡ *Lon.LD 9090*)

No. 14, A major ("No. 5")
L. Friedemann,[1] F. Viderø (hpsi.), & H. E.
Deckert (gamba)   ‡ *HS.HSL 95*
(Corelli, J. S. Bach & Leclair)

No. 15, E major ("No. 6")
J. Heifetz & E. Bay (pf.)   ‡ *Vic.LM 1861*
(Bloch & Schubert)
☆ A. Campoli & G. Malcolm (hpsi.)   ‡ *D.LW 5077*
(No. 13)   (‡ *Lon.LD 9090*)

— FOR PRACTICE: Recorded without violin part
(‡ *CEd.MMO 306*)

... 1st & 4th movts. only
I. Bezrodny, V. Yampolsky (pf.) (2ss)   *USSR. 18914/5*

Sonata, C major vla. da gamba & hpsi. *c.* 1705
B. Greenhouse (vlc.) & S. Marlowe
‡ *Eso.ES 528*
(Concertos à quatre; & Bach)   (‡ *Cpt.MC 20084*)

Sonata, G minor vlc. & pf. — ARR. Lindner
SEE: Concerto, G minor, oboe & orch., *infra*

B. TRIOS
(6) TRIOS 1696 Set (2 os. or vlns. & cont.)
No. 3, E flat major
P. Pierlot (ob.), R. Gendre (vln.), R. Veyron-
Lacroix (hpsi.), P. Hongne (bsn.)
‡ *BàM.LD 011*
(Scarlatti, Telemann, Quantz, J. C. Bach) (‡ *HS.HSL 117*)

(9) SONATAS, Op. 2 1724
No. 5, F major fl., vln., cont.
R. Adeney, P. Halling, B. Lam (hpsi.), T. Weil
(vlc.)   *G.HMS 66*
(† History of Music in Sound) (in ‡ *Vic. set LM 6031*)
B. Krainis (rec.), A. Black, H. Chessid (hpsi.),
N. Courant (gamba)   ‡ *Eso.ES 515*
(Sonatas & Cantata)   (‡ *Cpt. MC 20021*)

No. 6, G minor . . . 2nd movt., Allegro giusto
— ARR. VLA. & ORCH. Barbirolli, in *Concerto, q.v.*

(7) SONATAS, Op. 5 2 vlns. & cont. 1739
COMPLETE RECORDING
L. Friisholm & H. Kassow, S. Sørensen (hpsi.),
J. Friisholm (vlc.)   ‡ *HS.HSL 85/6*
(4ss)   (set HSL E)
[Nos. 5, 6, 7 also on ♭ *Mtr.MCEP 3010 & 3023/4*]

No. 2, D major
Y. Menuhin & G. de Vito (vlns.), G. Malcolm
(hpsi.), J. Shinebourne (vlc.) ‡ *G.BLP 1046*
(Bach: Concerto, 2 vlns.)   (‡ *FBLP 1061: QBLP 5028*)
(Bach & Vivaldi on ‡ Vic.LHMV 16)

No. 6, F major
☆ W. Schneiderhan, G. Swoboda, F. Holetschek (hpsi.),
& vlc. (‡ *Sel.LPG 8717*)

II. C. ORCHESTRAL

(6) CONCERTI GROSSI, Op. 3 (B & H 1-6) 1759
COMPLETE RECORDINGS
Boyd Neel Orch.   ‡ *D.LXT 5020*
(‡ *Lon.LL 1130*)

☆ Vienna State Op.—Prohaska (‡ *CID.UM 63023/4*)

No. 2, B flat major
Berlin Radio Cha.—Guhl   (4ss)   *Eta. 121050/1*

No. 5, D minor
Berlin Radio Cha.—Guhl   (4ss)   *Eta. 121052/3*
☆ Berlin Cha.—Lange   *Eta. 25.C.042/3*
(3ss—*Lesson 3a, hpsi.*)

(12) CONCERTI GROSSI, Op. 6
2 vlns., vlc., str. orch. (B & H 12-23) 1739
COMPLETE RECORDINGS
Boyd Neel Orch.   ‡ *D.LXT 5041/3*
(6ss) [T. Dart, hpsi.]   (‡ *Lon.LL 1080/2, set LLA 21*)
[Nos. 1-10 are ☆; Nos. 11 & 12 also on ‡ *D.LX 3124;
Lon.LS 870*]

English Baroque Orch.—Scherchen
‡ *West.WN 18082/5*
(8ss)   (Set WAL 403)
Bamberg Sym.—Lehmann ‡ *AmD. set DX 126*
(8ss) [K. Richter, hpsi.]
(12 ss, on ‡ *HP.AP 13010/1 & APM 14013/6*)[2]
[Nos. 1 to 4 also on ‡ *Pol. 16080/1*; Nos. 5 & 6 on
‡ *Pol. 18150*; No. 4 also on *PV. 7409*; No. 5 on
♭ *Pol. 37040*; No. 2 on ♭ *Pol. 37088*; No. 7 on
♭ *Pol. 37053*; Nos. 1 & 12 on ♭ *Pol. 37072*]

Saar Cha.—Ristenpart   ‡ *DFr. various*
Nos. 1, 8, 9, 10   on ‡ *DFr. 89*
Nos. 2, 4, 7, 11   on ‡ *DFr. 157*
Nos. 3, 5, 6, 12   on ‡ *DFr. 112*

COLLECTIONS
No. 1, G major (3ss)   No. 8, C minor (6ss)
No. 5, D major (4ss)   No. 10, D minor (6ss)
No. 6, G minor (6ss)   No. 12, B minor (6ss)
No. 7, B flat major (4ss)
Berlin Radio Cha.—Guhl   *Eta. 121054/71*
(No. 1 with *Chaconne, Lesson 3a, hpsi.*)
[S. Gawriloff & H. Pietsch (vlns.), W. Haupt (vlc.),
E. Erthel & W. Wätzig (obs.)].
(Nos. 8 & 12 on ‡ *FGM. 10022*)

No. 1, G major   No. 2, F major
No. 6, G minor   No. 7, B flat minor
Vienna Sym.—Pritchard   ‡ *EPhi.ABL 3048*
(‡ *Phi.A 00235L*; *Epic.LC 3097*)

Nos. 6 & 12
Winterthur Sym.—Dahinden   ‡ *MMS. 85*

No. 2, F major
... 3rd Movt., Largo — ARR. ORGAN
Interpolated in Organ Concerto No. 13, *q.v.*

No. 4, A minor
... 1st Movt., Larghetto affetuoso — ARR. ORGAN
Interpolated in Organ Concerto No. 16, *q.v.*

No. 5, D major
R.I.A.S. Sym.—Sawallisch   ‡ *Rem. 199-194*
(Bach)
☆ L.S.O.—Weingartner (‡ *AmC.ML 4676*)
Philharmonia—Markevitch
(‡ *G.FBLP 1057: QBLP 5035*)

No. 6, G minor
☆ L.S.O.—Weingartner (‡ *AmC.ML 4676*)

---

[1] Baroque vln.
[2] Only Nos. 1 and 2 on *AP 13010* and Nos. 5 and 6 on *APM 14013* so far issued in England.

No. 7, B flat major
☆ Homburg Sym.—Schubert (‡ *AFest.CFR 34*)[1]

No. 12, B minor
Vienna Sym.—Pritchard   ‡ *EPhi.ABR 4014*
(*Manfredini & Corelli*)   (‡ Phi.A 00668R)
Paris Inst. Ens.—Froment   ‡ *EPP.APG 114*
(*Concerto, Op. 4, No. 6*)

... Larghetto only ("*Aria*")
☆ Florence Festival—Gui (in ‡ Tem.TT 2046)
— — ARR. ORGAN
Interpolated in Organ Concerto, Op. 7, No. 4, *q.v.*

CONCERTOS, Orchestra
C major (Alexander's Feast) 1736
    2 vlns., 2 obs., str. (B & H. 7)
    ☆ Vienna State Op.—Prohaska (‡ CID.UM 63024)
— ARR. 2 VLCS. & ORCH. Ronchini
    ☆ Janssen Sym. Orch. (‡ T.LCE 8137)
... 1st movt. only
Danish Radio Cha.—Wöldike ‡ *HS.HSL 2073*
(† *Masterpieces of Music before 1750*)

B flat major ("Sonata à 5") vln. & str. (B & H 11)
Berlin Radio Cha.—Guhl[2]   *Eta. 21-76/7*
[For details of soloists, *see* Op. 6, *above*]
— ARR. VLA. & ORCH.
E. Vardi & Cha. Ens.   ‡ *Strad.STR 617*
(*below*)   (‡ Cum.CS 279)
— FOR PRACTICE: Recorded without violin part
         (‡ CEd.MMO 306)

B flat major (a due cori)
    2 obs., 3 bsns., str. (B & H 27)
    ☆ Copenhagen Coll. Musicum—Friisholm ‡ P.PMA 1021

F major (a due cori) (B & H 28)[3]
Berlin Cha.—v. Benda   ‡ *DT.LGM 65022*
     (‡ T.NLB 6079; FT. 270.TC.062)
    ☆ Copenhagen Coll. Musicum—Friisholm
         (‡ P.PMA 1021; Od.ODX 130)

CONCERTOS, Oboe & Orchestra
(B & H " *Concerti grossi*")
    NOTE: There is an error in WERM and Supp. II
numbering and identification. For "No. 1" read "No. 2"
and vice versa, to make our order agree with that of
B & H and HG. To recapitulate older entries:
Goossens (G.C 2993; Vic. 12605) is No. 1 (B & H);
in Supp. I, P. Valentin (‡ CHS.E 16) is No. 3 (B & H 10)
and "No. 4". Other recordings reappear, correctly
identified, as reissues below.

No. 1, B flat major (B & H 8)
E. Schuster & Cha. Orch.—Vardi ‡ *CEd.CE 1062*
(*Telemann & Vivaldi*)
    ☆ H. Shulman & Cha. Orch. (‡ Cum.CS 194)
— FOR PRACTICE: Recorded without oboe part
         (‡ CEd.MMO 301)

No. 2, B flat major (B & H 9)
C. Maisonneuve & Paris Cha.—Douatte[4]
         ‡ *EPP.APG 112*
(*Overtures; & Mozart: Sym. 24*)
    ☆ B. Gassmann & Janssen Sym. (‡ T.LCE 8137)

No. 3, G minor (B & H 10)
H. Schmeider & Saar Cha.—Ristenpart
         V‡ *DFr.EX 17025*
(*Agrippina, Overture*)
M. Tabuteau & Philadelphia—Ormandy
         in ‡ AmC.ML 4629
W. Wätzig & Berlin Radio Cha.—Guhl
         Eta.21-74/5
(4ss) (also listed as *21-72/3*)
    ☆ L. Goossens & Liverpool Phil.—Cameron
(*Bach, Cimarosa, Marcello*)   ‡ AmC.ML 4782

☆ H. Shulman & Cha. Orch. (‡ Cum.CS 194)
I. Tappo & EIAR Sym.—Rapp (in ‡ Tem.TT 2072)
— ARR. VLC. & PF. Lindner ("No. 1")
M. Amfitheatrof & O. P. Santoliquido
         ‡ *ItV.A12R 0162*
(*Beethoven & Della Ciaja*)

CONCERTOS, Organ & Orchestra
CONCERTO, D major, Orch. & Org.[5]
    ☆ Philadelphia—Ormandy[6] (in ‡ AmC.ML 4797)

(6) CONCERTOS, Organ & Orch. Op. 4
(B & H 1-6) (c. 1735-6)
No. 1, G minor
J. Demessieux & Suisse Romande—Ansermet
         ‡ *D.LXT 2759*
(*No. 2*)   (‡ Lon.LL 695)

No. 2, B flat major
G. Jones & Philharmonia—Schüchter
         ‡ *G.DLP 1037*
(*No. 4*)   (‡ QBLP 5029; FBLP 1062)
J. Demessieux & Suisse Romande—Ansermet
         ‡ *D.LXT 2759*
(*No. 1*)   (‡ Lon.LL 695)
— ARR. ORGAN SOLO
R. Owen   in ‡ ASK. 3
(*Bach, Vierne, etc.*)

No. 4, F major
G. Jones & Philharmonia—Schüchter
         ‡ *G.DLP 1037*
(*No. 2*)   (‡ QBLP 5029; FBLP 1062)
C. de Lisle & Paris Inst. Ens.—Froment
(*Concerto No. 7*)   ‡ *EPP.APG 122*

No. 5, F major
L. Farnam (solo)[7]   ‡ *CEd.CE 1040*
(*below; & Bach, Vierne, Sowerby*)
W. Watkins (solo)   ‡ *McInt.MM 106*
(*Bach, Dupré, Langlais, etc.*)

No. 6, B flat major
    ☆ W. Landowska (hpsi.) & orch.—Bigot ‡ G.FJLP 5056
(*Lesson No. 1; & Bach*)
— ARR. HARP & ORCH. Handel
E. Vito & Str. Ens.   ‡ *Per.SPL 704*
(*Mozart: Pf. Sonata K545, arr.; Prokofiev, etc.*)
G. Schimmel & Berlin Cha.—Haarth ‡ *Ura. 7164*
(*Glier: Concerto*)
L. Laskine & Paris Inst. Ens.—Froment
         ‡ *EPP.APG 114*
(*Concerto Grosso, Op. 6, No. 12*)

(6) CONCERTOS, Organ & Orch., Op. 7
(B & H 7-12)
No. 7, B flat major, Op. 7, No. 1 1740
C. de Lisle & Paris Inst. Ens.—Froment
(*No. 4*)   ‡ *EPP.APG 122*

No. 9, B flat major, Op. 7, No. 3 1751
... Minuet only
L. Farnam (org. solo)[7]   in ‡ CEd.CE 1040

No. 10, D minor, Op. 7, No. 4
G. Jones & Philharmonia—Schüchter[8]
         ‡ *G.DLP 1052*
(*below*)   (‡ QBLP 5031; FBLP 1064)
R. Tellier & Belgian Radio—André[8]
         ‡ *DT.LGM 65016*
(*Bach: Italian Concerto*)   (‡ T.LS 6027)
... Aria only[8] Anon. artist (solo)   in ‡ FSM. 402

No. 11, G minor, Op. 7, No. 5 1750
... 2nd movt., Basso ostinato, only
    ☆ F. Asma (solo) (in ‡ Epic.LC 3025 & in ‡ Phi.S 04009L)

---

[1] ▽ ‡ *Rgt. 5020* contains this work in addition to Bach (see Supplement II, p. 13, and errata entry), though not mentioned in the Rgt. catalogue.
[2] Announced but perhaps not issued.
[3] In nine movements, of which the last four also exist as Organ Concerto No. 16, *q.v. infra*.
[4] Labelled "Op. 3, No. 9".
[5] An earlier version of the Fireworks Music.
[6] Arr. Ormandy.
[7] Recorded from an Austin organ roll of 1930, with registration and expression by C. Watters.
[8] *Larghetto* from *Concerto Grosso, Op. 6, No. 12* interpolated as 3rd movement, arr. for organ solo.

(4) CONCERTOS, Organ & Orch. (B & H 13-16)

No. 13, F major (based on Sonata, Op. 5, No. 6)

No. 14, A major (based on Concerto grosso, Op. 6, No. 11)

No. 15, D minor

No. 16, F major (see also Concerto, orch., F major —last 4 movts.)

☆ E. Hölderlin & Pro Musica Orch.—Reinhardt
(4ss)   ♯ EVox. set PL 7802
[▽ The following interpolations are made (ARR. ORG.): into No. 13: Largo from Concerto grosso, Op. 6, No. 2 No. 14: Prelude from Hpsi. Suite 6 No. 16: Larghetto from Concerto grosso, Op. 6, No. 4]

Nos. 13, 14 & 15
☆ F. Pelleg (hpsi.) & Zurich Radio—Goehr (♯ Clc. 6158)

No. 14, A major
G. Jones & Philharmonia—Schüchter[1]
                    ♯ **G.DLP 1052**
(Concerto No. 10)   (♯ QBLP 5031: FBLP 1064)

CONCERTO, Viola & Orchestra
B minor ("Discovered" & ARR. Casadesus)[2]
E. Vardi & Stradivari Cha. Ens.
                    ♯ **Strad.STR 617**
(above; & below, misc.)   (♯ Cum.CS 279)
☆ W. Primrose & Victor Sym.—Weissmann
                    (♯ Cam.CAL 262)

— FOR PRACTICE: Recorded with viola part missing
                    (♯ CEd.MMO 303)

G major: see below, *Compilations*

MUSIC FOR THE ROYAL FIREWORKS 1749
(B & H "Concerto" 26)

1. Overture 2. Largo alla siciliana ("La Paix")
3. Allegro ("La Réjouissance")   4. Bourrée
5. Minuets 1 & 2

Berlin Phil.—F. Lehmann   ♯ **HP.AP 13012**
(also 4ss, ♮ PV. 7410/1)   (also ♯ Pol. 16082)
(Schubert: Sym. No. 8 on ♯ AmD.DL 9696)

Suite — ARR. Harty (omits No. 3)
B.B.C. Sym.—Sargent   ♯ **G.BLP 1059**
(Water Music)   (♯ QBLP 5036)

☆ Amsterdam—v. Beinum   ♯ **D.LXT 2792**
(Water Music)   (♯ Lon.LL 760)

Nos. 2, 3, 4 & 5
Hamburg Philharmonia—H-J. Walther
                    MSB. 78002

... Minuet only: Inst. Ens. (in *G.B 10658*)

— ARR. BAND
Fredonia Concert Band—Harp   ♯ **Fred. 1**
(Hanson, Poulenc, etc.)

... Excerpts: Fairey Aviation Works (*Pax.PR 648*)

(The) WATER MUSIC
1st Suite, F major, 1715; 2nd Suite, D major, 1717
(B & H "Concerto" 25)

COMPLETE RECORDINGS
(original version, ed. Chrysander, *et al.*)

Boyd Neel Orch.—Neel   ♯ **D.LXT 2988**
                    (♯ Lon.LL 1128)

Phil. Prom.—Boult   ♯ **West.WN 18115**
[C. Taylor (recorder), R. Downes (hpsi.)]

☆ Berlin Phil.—Lehmann   ♯ **HP.APM 14006**
(also ♯ Pol. 18151; AmD.ARC 3010)

☆ Cha. Orch.—Hewitt (♯ HS.HSL 107;
          excerpts only, V♯ *DFr.EX 17011*)
Nat. Gallery Orch.—Bales (♯ McInt.MC 1013)

Suite — ARR. Harty (Nos. 3, 5, 6, 7, 8, 11)
B.B.C. Sym.—Sargent   ♯ **G.BLP 1059**
(Music for Royal Fireworks)   (♯ QBLP 5036)

Austrian Sym.—Koslik   ♯ **Rem. 199-131**
(Mozart: Vln. Concerto K 216)   (♯ Cum.CR 286)

Berlin Sym.—Rubahn   ♯ **Roy. 1441**

☆ Philharmonia—Karajan   ♯ **C.CX 1033**
(Tchaikovsky: Nutcracker Suite)   (♯ Angel 35004)
(♯ C.FCX/QCX 164: WCX 1033: VCX 528;
     also ♮ C.GQX 8041/2)

☆ L.P.O.—v. Beinum   ♯ **D.LXT 2792**
(Fireworks Music)   (♯ Lon.LL 760)

"Viennese Sym." (♯ Ply. 12-107)

☆ Chicago Sym.—Defauw (♮ Cam.CAE 202)

Suite — ARR. Ormandy
☆ Philadelphia—Ormandy   ♯ **AmC.ML 4797**
(Concerto; & Bach)

Overture & Nos. 2 (Adagio e Staccato), 3 (Allegro)
C.B.C. Sym.—MacMillan (Anthems) ♯ **Bea.LP 1002**

Nos. 7 & 8, Bourrée & Hornpipe
Hamburg Philharmonia—H-J. Walther   **MSB. 78001**
(Serse—Largo)

Nos. 11, 5, 20 (Alla hornpipe, Air, Coro)
— ARR. ORGAN
R. Foort   in ♯ **SOT. 1055**
(Reubke, etc.)   (& in ♯ 10545)

No. 11, Alla hornpipe (Allegro deciso) only
— ARR. ACCORDEON T. Tollefsen (*C.DC 674*)

MISCELLANEOUS SUITES
"Alceste" Suite[3] — ARR. Fekete
"Festival" Suite[3] — ARR. Fekete
☆ Vienna Sym.—Fekete   ♯ **CA.LPA 1005**

COMPILATIONS (VARIOUS)
Concerto, G major, vla. & orch. — ARR. Barbirolli
     1. Larghetto (Hercules, Act I)
     2. Allegro scherzando (Rinaldo, Act III)
     3. Musette (Alcina, Ov.)
     4. Allegro giocoso (Cantata: Delirio amoroso, Intro.)
     5. Allegro giusto (Trio Sonata No. 6)
E. Vardi & Cha. Ens.   ♯ **Strad.STR 617**
(Vla. Concerto & Concerto grosso)   (♯ Cum.CS 279)
— FOR PRACTICE: with viola part missing, ♯ CEd.MMO 303

(The) Faithful Shepherd — ARR. Beecham
     1. Pastor Fido (1734): Overture
     2. Pastor Fido (1712): Overture: 6th movt., Adagio
     3.   4th movt., Allegro
     4. Pastor Fido (1734): In tempo di bourrée
     5. Musette (unid.)
     6. Pastor Fido (1734): Minuet, G major
     7. Triumph of Time: Dryads, Sylvans
     8. Pastor Fido (1734): Ballo & March
☆ Royal Phil.—Beecham (Mozart: Sym. 38) ♯ **C.CX 1105**
[Nos. 3, 4, 5, 6, also on C.LX 1600]

(The) Faithful Shepherd — ARR. Kindler[4]
Pastor Fido (1712): Overture: 1st, 2nd, 4th, 5th & 6th movts.
Pastor Fido (1734): Musette
☆ Nat. Sym. (USA)—Kindler (♮ Cam.CAE 179)

Jephtha Suite — ARR. Fekete
     1. Jephtha, Overture   2. Solomon, No. 40
     3. Judas Maccabaeus, No. 22 4. Athalia, Cho.
☆ Salzburg Mozarteum—Fekete (Haydn) ♯ **CA.LPA 1074**

Triumph of Time and Truth Suite — ARR. Fekete
Side. 1. Jephtha—O God behold
             When his loud voice
             They now contract (Band I)
             How dark O Lord
             All our joys
             No certain bliss (Band II)
Side 2. Concerto Grosso, Op. 6, No. 2 . . . Largo only
             Jephtha—Doubtful fear (Band I)
             Deborah—Immortal Lord of Earth & Skies
☆ Vienna Sym.—Fekete   ♯ **CA.LPA 1012**
                    (♯ Cum.CF 267)

HANDL (Gallus), Jacob (1550-1591)

Numbers refer to items in: OM, Opus musicum (1586), Books i, ii, iii, iv, in DTÖ Vols. XII, XXIV, XXX, XL, XLVIII, LI, LII.

[1] Labelled "Op. 7, No. 2".   [2] The authenticity of this work has been questioned.
[3] It has not been possible to ascertain the exact contents of these suites. The *Alceste* suite is stated by M. Fekete also to contain extracts from *Solomon* and *Deborah*, and the *Festival* suite from the *Occasional Oratorio*. The CA. catalogue attributes this recording to Salzburg Mozarteum Orch. while the Colosseum Catalogue now lists as Vienna State Opera.
[4] This identification corrects the details given in WERM, p. 266b.

GEISTLICHE CHÖRE
COLLECTION

Pater Noster 8 vv. OM i, 69
De Sancto Michaele Archangelo 5 vv. OM iv, 103
Ecce, quomodo moritur 4 vv. OM ii, 13
Diffusa est gratia 5 vv. OM iv, 100
Hodie Christus natus est 6 vv. OM i, 46
Mirabile mysterium 5 vv. OM i, 54
Ascendo ad Patrem 6 vv. OM ii, 41
Adoramus te 6 vv. OM ii, 6
Laetentur coeli 6 vv. OM i, 12
Jerusalem gaude 6 vv. OM i, 8
　　Vienna Academy Cho.—Grossmann
　　(*Isaac*)　　　　　　♯ **West.WL 5347**

Ascendit Deus 5 vv. OM ii, 48
　　Vienna Boys Cho.—Brenn in ♯ *EPhi.NBR 6013*
　　(*Palestrina, Nasco, Verdi, etc.*)
　　　　　　(in ♯ *Phi.N 00624R;* & AmC.ML 4873)

Ecco quomodo moritur justus 4 vv. OM ii, 13
　　☆ Netherlands Cha. Cho.—de Nobel (in ♯ *Phi.S 06026R*)

Mirabile mysterium 5 vv. OM i, 54
　　Brompton Oratory Cho.—Washington
　　　　　　　　　　　　　　G.HMS 36
　　(† History of Music in sound) (in ♯ Vic. set LM 6029)
　　Yale Univ. Music Sch. Cho.—Hindemith
　　　　　　　　　　　　　♯ **Over.LP 5**
　　(† Yale University, Vol. II)

Pueri, concinite 4 vv. OM i, 58
　　U.O.S. Cho.—McConnell　　in ♯ *UOS. 2*
　　(*Victoria, Carissimi, A. Scarlatti, etc.*)　(pte. rec.)

Repleti sunt omnes 5 vv. OM ii, 64
　　Yale Univ. Divinity Sch. Cho—Borden
　　　　　　　　　　　　　♯ **Over.LP 2**
　　(† Hymns of Praise)

HANFF, Johann Nicolaus (1630-1706)
　　SEE: † ORGAN MUSIC—HEITMANN

HANSON, Howard (b. 1896)

Cherubic Hymn cho. & orch. 1949
　　Bach Cho., Carnegie Inst. of Technology Cho.
　　& Orch.—Hanson　　in ♯ **PFCM.CB 162**
　　(*Vaughan Williams, Thomson, etc.*)
　　Eastman-Rochester Sym.—Hanson
　　(*Barber & below*)　　　♯ **Mer.MG 40014**

Chorale & Alleluia 1953
　　Eastman Sym. Wind Ens.—Fennell
　　　　　　　　　　　♯ **Mer.MG 40011**
　　(*Mennin, Persichetti, Thomson, Reed*)

MERRY MOUNT, Op. 31 Opera 3 Acts 1934
'Tis an earth defiled B
　　☆ L. Tibbett (in ♯ Cam.CAL 171)

Pastorale, Op. 38 ob., str. & hp. (orig. pf.) 1949
Serenade fl., str. & hp. 1946
　　R. Sprenkle (ob.), J. Mariano (fl.), Eastman-
　　Rochester Sym.—Hanson ♯ **EMer.MG 40003**
　　(*Barlow, Rogers, Copland, etc.*)
　　[Pastorale only on ♭ *Mer.EP 1-5064;* Serenade only on
　　　　　　　　　　　♭ *Mer.EP 1-5065*]

SYMPHONIES
No. 1, E minor, Op. 21 "Nordic" 1922
　　Hamburg Philharmonia—H-J. Walther
　　(6ss)　　　　　　　　　*MSB. 78160/2*
　　(*Siegmeister & Skelton* on ♯ MGM.E 3141)
... **2nd movt. only** — ARR. BAND
　　Concert Band—Harp (in ♯ Fred. 1)

No. 2, Op. 30 "Romantic" 1930
　　Eastman-Rochester Sym.—Hanson (n.v.)
　　(*MacDowell*)　　　　　♯ **AmC.ML 4638**

No. 3, A minor, Op. 33 1938
　　☆ Boston Sym.—Koussevitzky　　♯ **Vic.LCT 1153**
　　(*Harris*)

No. 4, Op. 34 "Requiem" 1943
　　Eastman-Rochester Sym.—Hanson
　　　　　　　　　　　♯ **EMer.MG 40004**
　　(*Harris: Symphony No. 3*)
　　☆ A.R.S. Orch.—Dixon (*Wagenaar*)　♯ **ARS. 114**

No. 5, Sinfonia sacra 1954
　　Eastman-Rochester Sym.—Hanson
　　(*above & Barber*)　　　♯ **Mer.MG 40014**

(2) Yuletide pieces, Op. 19 pf. 1920
... **No. 2, March carillon** — ARR. BAND
　　Eastman Sym. Wind Ens.—Fennell
　　(*Marches*)　　　　　♯ **EMer.MG 40007**

HARRIS, Roy (b. 1898)

Abraham Lincoln walks at midnight
(*A Cantata of Lamentation*) M-S, vln., vlc. & pf. (Lindsay) 1954
　　N. Tangeman, S. Thaviu, T. Salzman, J. Harris
　　(*below*)　　　　　　♯ **MGM.E 3210**

Fantasy, pf. & orch. f.p. 1954
　　J. Harris & MGM. Orch.—I. Solomon
　　(*above*)　　　　　　♯ **MGM.E 3210**

Quintet, pf., fl., ob., hrn., bsn. 1932
Sextet, pf., fl., ob., cl., hrn., bsn. 1932
　　New Art Wind Quintet/Sextet ♯ **CEd.CE 2005**

Sonata, vln. & pf. 1942
　　J. Gingold & J. Harris　　♯ **AmC.ML 4842**
　　(*Palmer*)

SYMPHONIES
No. 3 orch. 1938
　　Eastman-Rochester Sym.—Hanson
　　(*Hanson*)　　　　　　♯ **EMer.MG 40004**
　　☆ Boston Sym.—Koussevitzky　♯ **Vic.LCT 1153**
　　(*Hanson*)
　　☆ A.R.S. Sym.—Hendl　　　♯ **ARS. 115**
　　(*Schuman & Sessions*)

No. 4 "Folk Song Symphony" cho. & orch. 1939
... **Interlude No. 1** orch.
　　Hamburg Philharmonia—Korn in ♯ **Allo. 3149**
　　(*Copland, MacDowell, etc.*)

No. 5 1942
　　Pittsburgh Sym.—Steinberg　♯ **PFCM.CB 165**
　　(*Stravinsky*)

Symphony for Band 1952
　　West Point Band—Resta　　♯ **PFCM.CB 175**
　　(*Hindemith & Vaughan Williams*)

Trio vln., vlc., pf. 1934
　　R. Gerle, G. Magyar, K. Wallingford ♯ **UOK. 1**
　　(*Copland & Kerr*)

NOTE: The Carols in CONTEMPORARY CHRISTMAS CAROLS
　　(♯ CtyNY.AP 122) are by Arthur Harris.

HARRIS, William Henry (b. 1883)
　　SEE: † CORONATION OF QUEEN ELIZABETH II.

HARRISON, Lou (b. 1917)

Canticle No. 3 percussion orch.
　　Illinois Univ. Ens.—Price　　♯ *UOI.CRS 3*
　　(*McKenzie, Varese, Colgran, Chavez*)

Suite, vln., pf. & small orch. 1951
　　A. & M. Ajemian, Orch.—Stokowski
　　(*B. Weber*)　　　　　♯ **Vic.LM 1785**

☆ = Re-issue of a recording to be found in previous volumes.

HARSÁNYI, Tibor (b. 1898)

(L') Histoire du petit tailleur   Suite 1939
  Narrator, 7 insts. & percussion (for puppet show)
  C. Dauphin & Lamoureux Ens.—Harsányi
                                        ‡ Phi.N 00999R

Pièce pour deux pianos   1927
  I. Marika & J. Manchon-Theis
  (Dillon & Spitzmüller)   ‡ Cpt.MC 20024

▽ Older recordings include:
  Fox-trot 1929: Pf. wind & percussion (G.K 6114)
  5 Préludes brèves 1928: Composer (pf.) (C.DFX 7/8)
  String Quartet No. 1 1925: Roth Qtt. (C.D 15198/201)
  Sonata, vlc. & pf. 1928: H. Kindler & Composer
                                        (C.DFX 5/7)

HARTLEY, Gerald (b. 1921)

Divertissement   fl., ob., cl., hrn. & bsn.
  Chicago Sym. Wind Ens.   in ‡ Aphe.AP 16

HARTMANN, Johan P. E. (1805-1900)

Hakon Jarl, Op. 40, Overture   orch.
  Danish Radio—Frandsen   ‡ Phi.S 06060R
  (Gade)

LITTLE KIRSTEN, Op. 44   Opera
  (orig. 1 Act, later 2) 1846
Sverkel's Romance   T
  ☆ A. Schiøtz & Young Musicians' Orch.—Wöldike
                                        (♭ G.7EBK 1003)

SONGS
Tell me, Star of night, Op. 63a, No. 5 (Richardt)
You, who have sorrow in your heart, Op. 56, No. 3 (Winther)
  (from Folmer the Minstrel's Songs)
  ☆ A. Schiøtz (T) (in ‡ G.KBLP 11)

HARTMANN, Karl Amadeus (b. 1905)

Symphony No. 4   Str. orch. 1950
... Finale: Adagio appassionato
  ☆ R.I.A.S. Sym.—Fricsay (in ‡ AmD.DL 9769)

HARWOOD, Basil (1859-1949)

SEE: † ENGLISH CHURCH MUSIC, VOL. IV

HASSE, Johann Adolph (1699-1783)

INTERMEZZI
(La) CONTADINA   1728
(Il) TUTORE   1730
  SEE: Sub nom. Pergolesi infra, La Contadina astuta,
  attrib. Pergolesi but mainly by Hasse.

Concerto, G major   mandoline & orch.
  (ed. Neemann)
  Caecilia Mandoline Ens.—Dekker
                                        ‡ Phi.N 00686R
  (Beethoven, Mozart, Vivaldi)

Sonata, D minor, Op. 1, No. 11   fl. & hpsi.
  ☆ J-P. Rampal & R. Veyron-Lacroix (in † ‡ HS.AS 19)

HASSLER, Hans Leo (1564-1612)

MADRIGALS: COLLECTIONS (1596, 1601)
Nun fanget an, ein guts Liedlein zu singen
Jungfrau, dein schön Gestalt
Tantzen und Springen
  Vienna Academy Cho.—Gillesberger ‡ SPA. 58
  († Songs of Renaissance)

Nun fanget an, ein guts Liedlein zu singen
Jungfrau, dein schön Gestalt
Feinslieb, du hast mich g'fangen
Das Herz tut mir aufspringen
Ich brinn' und bin entzündt
Fahr hin, guts Liedlein 1596[1]
Ach weh des Leiden
Tantzen und Springen
Ihr Musici, frisch auf!
Im kühlen Maien 1601
  Berlin Motet Cho.—Arndt   ‡ HP.APM 14010
  (Lechner)

Tantzen und Springen   ("Gagliarda")
  Youth Academy Cho.—Asmussen   Felix.F 84
  (Coversi & Purcell)

MOTETS
Aus tiefer Not
Ein' feste Burg
Vater unser im Himmelreich
  Netherlands Madrigal & Motet Cho.
    —Voorberg   ‡ Phi.N 00692R
  († Motets on Luther Texts)

Cantate Domino
  Yale Univ. Divinity Sch. Cho.—Borden
                                        ‡ Over.LP 2
  († Hymns of Praise)
  Stanford Univ. Cho.—Schmidt   ‡ ML. 7022
  († Madrigals & Motets)

Dixit Maria
  Biggs Family Ens.   in ‡ GIOA.BF 1
  (Praetorius, Josquin, etc.)

Et incarnatus est
  Maastricht Male Cho.—Koekelkoren
                                        Phi.N 12061G

Wenn mein Stündlein 1607
  ☆ M. Meili (T), Basle Cha. Cho.—Sacher & 3 tromb.
                                        in V‡ AS. 1802LD
                                        (‡ HS.AS 7)

HAYDN, Franz Josef (1732-1809)

CLASSIFIED: I. VOCAL
             II. INSTRUMENTAL
             A. Piano   B. Chamber Music
             C. Orchestral D. Miscellaneous

I. VOCAL

MASSES
COLLECTION
No. 5, B flat major, S. Joannis de Deo
No. 6, C major "Mariazeller"
No. 7, C major, in tempore belli
No. 8, B flat major, Sti. Bernardi de Offida
No. 9, D minor "Nelson"
  ☆ Various artists (‡ HS. set HSL G, 10ss)

No. 1, F major, Missa brevis a due soprani c. 1750
  (Novello 11)

No. 5, B flat major, S. Joannis de Deo c. 1775
  (Novello 8)
  ☆ Vienna Academy Cha. Cho. & Sym. Cha. Orch.
      —Gillesberger   ‡ Nix.LLP 8030
  [H. Heusser & A. Berger, sops, in No. 1] (‡ Clc. 6175)

No. 2, E flat major, in honorem B. V. Mariae 1766
  (Novello 12) S, A, T, B, cho. & orch.
  ☆ Soloists, Academy Cho. & Vienna Sym.—Grossmann
                                        ‡ EVox.PL 7020

No. 3, C major, Stae. Caeciliae c. 1768
  (Novello 5)
  ☆ Soloists, Academy Cho. & Vienna Sym.—Gillesberger
  (now 3ss—Partsongs)   ‡ DFr. 114/5

No. 5, B flat major, S. Joannis de Deo c. 1775
  (Novello 8)
  K. Frederiksen (Tr.), Copenhagen Boys' &
    Men's Cho. & Palace Cha. Orch.—Wöldike
                                        ‡ HS.HSL 2064
  [S. Sørensen, org.] (Partsongs)

No. 7, C major, in tempore belli 1796
  (Novello 2)
  ☆ Soloists, Academy Cho. & Vienna Opera Orch.
      —Gillesberger   ‡ P.PMA 1015

---

[1] The above 6 titles from Neue Teutsche Gesang, 1596; the following from Lustgarten Neuer Teutschen Gesang, 1601.

No. 8, B flat major, Sti. Bernardi de Offida 1796
(Novello 1)
☆ Copenhagen Boys' & Men's Cho. & Royal Opera
Orch.—Wöldike ♯ **P.PMA 1010**

No. 9, D minor ("Nelson" or "Imperial") 1798
(Novello 3)
T. Stich-Randall (S), E. Höngen (A), A.
Dermota (T), F. Guthrie (Bs), Vienna State
Op. Cho. & orch.—Rossi ♯ **Van.VRS 470**
[A. Heiller, org.] (♯ Ama.AVRS 6021)

T. Stich-Randall (S), M. Paulee (M-S), R.
Schock (T), G. Frick (Bs), Vienna Academy
Cho. & Vienna State Op. Orch.—Sternberg[1]
♯ **CFD. 1**

L. Bonetti (S), C. Carbi (A), N. Adami (T),
G. Ferrein (Bs) & Angelicum Cho. & orch.
—Janes ♯ **Ang.LPA 954**

... **Gloria, Qui tollis & Quoniam**
St. Paul's Cath. Cho. & Philharmonia Orch.
—Dykes Bower ♯ **C.CX 1237**
(*Wood, Bairstow, Wesley, Schütz, etc.*)
(♯ Angel. 35139 in set 3516)

No. 12, B flat major "Harmonie" 1802
☆ Soloists, Vienna Soc. Cho. & orch.—Larsen[2]
(♯ Ren.X 57; ♯ Clc. 6125; ♯ Cpt.MC 20106)

OPERAS

ARMIDA 1783
Overture, Op. 55 (G.A. No. 14)
London Mozart Players—Blech **G.B 10681**
(*JK 2865*)

(L') ISOLA DISABITATA 2 Acts 1779
Overture (G.A. No. 13)
Hastings Sym.—Bath ♯ **Allo. 4053**
(*Delius & Roussel*)
☆ Winterthur Sym.—Goehr (♯ ANix.MLPY 6)

(Il) MONDO DELLA LUNA (Goldoni) 3 Acts
1777
ABRIDGED ADAPTATION in German[3]
Buonafede ... ... W. Hagner (Bs)
Dr. Ecclitico ... ... K. Schwest (B)
Leandro ... ... A. Gassner (T)
Cecco ... ... W. Lindner (T)
Clarissa ... ... F. Schneider (S)
Lisetta ... ... H. Münch (M-S)
etc., Munich Cha. Op. Orch.—Weissenbach
♯ **Per.SPL 703**

ORFEO ED EURIDICE 3 Acts 1791
ABRIDGED RECORDING
☆ J. Hellwig (S), H. Handt (T), etc.; Vienna State Op.
Cho. & orch.—Swarowsky (♯ MMS. 2030 & OP 18)

PHILEMON UND BAUCIS 1 Act 1773
(for Marionettes)
COMPLETE RECORDING
☆ Soloists, Vienna State Op. Cho. & orch.—v. Zallinger
♯ **EVox.PL 7660**

ORATORIOS

(The) CREATION (Die Schöpfung) 1798
COMPLETE RECORDINGS in *German*
I. Seefried (S), R. Holm (T), K. Borg (Bs),
St. Hedwig Cath. Cho. & Berlin Phil.
—Markevitch ♯ **HP.DGM 18254/6**
(6ss) (& ♯ Pol. 561/3; & manual, 551/3)
T. Stich-Randall (S), A. Felbermayer (S),
A. Dermota (T), F. Guthrie (Bs), P. Schoeffler
(B), Vienna State Op. Cho. & orch.
—Wöldike ♯ **Van.VRS 471/2**
(4ss) (♯ Ama.AVRS 6024/5)

V. Korch (S), G. Unger (T), T. Adam (Bs),
Berlin Radio Cho. & orch.—Koch
(4ss) ♯ **Ura. set 235**
☆ Soloists, Vienna State Op. Cho. & Vienna Phil.—Krauss
(♯ MMS. set 2015, 4ss; Nos. 1, 3, 10, 11, 21-23, 33,
in V♯ Era.LDE 1003)

No. 8, And God said ... (Recit.)
No. 9, With verdure clad S
B. Troxell & org. in ♯ **Ply. 12-123**
(*Handel, Beethoven, Mozart, etc.*)

No. 23, Now Heaven in fullest glory Bs
☆ N. Cordon (in ♯ Cam.CAL 269)

No. 25, In native worth T
— ARR. MUSICAL CLOCK. See Anthologies (♯ Van.VRS 7020)

No. 27, Achieved is the glorious work
☆ Mormon Tabernacle Cho. & org.
(C.LHX 16; in ♯ AmC.ML 4789)

(The) SEASONS (Die Jahreszeiten)
S, T, Bs, cho., orch. 1801
COMPLETE RECORDINGS (in *German*)
☆ E. Trötschel, W. Ludwig, J. Greindl, St. Hedwig's
Cath. Cho., R.I.A.S. Cha. Cho. & Sym.—Fricsay
(6ss) ♯ **AmD. set DX 123**
[Nos. 3 & 5 also on *Pol.* 62892; Nos. 9 & 10 on
PV. 36076; Nos. 20 & 21 on PV. 72406]
☆ T. Eipperle, J. Patzak, G. Hann, Vienna State Op. Cho.
& Phil.—Krauss ♯ **P.PMA 1018/20**[4]
(♯ Od.ODX 111/3)

(Die) SIEBEN WORTE B & orch. 1784
— ARR. S, A, T, B, cho. & orch. 1797
☆ H. Gueden, C. Ölschläger, J. Patzak, H. Braun,
Salzburg Cath. Cho. & Mozarteum Orch.—Messner
(♯ Cum. set 284, 4ss)

... **No. 3, Mutter Jesu die du trostlos ...**
from above set (in ♯ Rem. 199-121)

— ARR. STR. QTT. (Op. 51) 1787
☆ Amadeus Qtt. (3ss—*below*) ♯ **Nix.WLP 6202-1/2**
(also now on 2ss, ♯ West.WN 18055)
☆ Guilet Qtt. (♯ Clc. 6271/2)

PARTSONGS: COLLECTION

Aus dem Dankliede zu Gott (Gellert)
(Der) Augenblick (Anon.)
(Die) Harmonie in der Ehe (Goetz)
(Die) Beredsamkeit (Lessing)
(Der) Greis (Gleim)
Abendlied zu Gott (Gellert)
Danish State Radio Cha. Cho.—Wöldike
♯ **HS.HSL 2064**
[B. Linderud, pf.] (*Mass No. 5*) (♯ DFr. 115, d.c.)

(Die) Beredsamkeit (Lessing)
Pancratius Male Cho.—Haedendael
in ♯ **C.HS 1001**
(*Lassus, Schubert, Milhaud, Handel, etc.*)

Salve Regina No. 3, G minor
S, A, T, B, cho., orch. 1771
A. Cantelo, M. Thomas, D. Galliver, T. Hemsley,
Cho. & London Mozart Orch.—H. Blech
(*Mozart: Mass*) ♯ **G.CLP 1031**

SONGS

Liebes Mädchen, hör mir zu (Serenade)[5]
G. Pechner (B) in ♯ **Roy. 1557**

My mother bids me bind my hair (Mrs. Hunter) 1794
E. Söderström (S), S. Westerberg (pf.)
(*Schubert: Lieder*) **D.F 44248**

(The) Spirit Song (Mrs. Hunter)
M. Powers (A), F. la Forge (pf.) in ♯ **Atl. 1207**
(*Bach, Beethoven, Brahms, Respighi, etc.*)

---

[1] Edition specially revised by H. C. Robbins Landon from orig. sources.
[2] It is understood that "Larsen" is a pseudonym for J. Sternberg. Originally the orchestra was also pseudonymous as "Danish Phil."
[3] Text by W. Treichlinger; score ed. M. Lothar which includes interpolations: Chorus from *Orfeo* (*L'Anima del Filosofo*); Terzetto from *L'Incontro improvviso* (1775); Notturno No. 6, G major; Str. Qtt. Op. 1, No. 4. Only the first of these appears to be on the disc; the following nos. in the Lothar score are omitted: 6-10, 14, 16 (Aria), 17, 18, 20, 22, 24. The Finale, No. 25, is abbreviated.
[4] Announced but not issued.
[5] Also attributed to Mozart (K 441c).

FOLK SONG SETTINGS
SCOTTISH AIRS: COLLECTION
Phely & Willy: O Phely, happy was the day Duet (Burns)
Fee him, father: Saw ye Johnie coming, quo' she (Burns)
Logan Water: O Logan, sweetly didst thou glide (Burns)
Oran Gaoil: Behold the hour Duet (Burns)
Mary's Dream: The Moon had climbed the highest hill (Lowe)
Down the burn: When trees did bud Duet (Crawford)
The Lea Rig: When o'er the hill (Burns)
Maggie Lauder: Wha wadna be in love (Anon.)
Highland Mary: Thou ling'ring star (Burns)
De'il tak the wars: Sleep'st thou or wak'st thou (Burns)
    M. Bleiberg (S), E. Charney (M-S) (in duets), &
    pf., vln., vlc.   # MTR.MLO 1014

═══════════════

II. INSTRUMENTAL

A. PIANO
COLLECTIONS
Str. Qtt., F major, Op. 74, No. 2 . . . 2nd movt., Andante
  grazioso; . . . Finale, Allegro (ARR.)
Arietta con variazioni, A major . . . Arietta only
Minuet No. 1, C major (from *12 Minuets*, 1785;
                        Larsen T 4)
SONATAS: No. 19 (22), D major   1767
         No. 35 (5), C major   1780

    L. Kraus   # Edu.EP 3005

Capriccio, G major, Op. 43   1765
Fantasia, C major, Op. 58   pub. 1789
Variations: A major   before 1768
         C major   1790
         E flat major   before 1774
         F minor, Op. 83   1793
    N. Reisenberg   # West.WN 18057

Capriccio, G major, Op. 43
— ARR. WOODWIND QUINTET   Aaron
  Chicago Sym. Quintet   in # Aphe. 17

SONATAS[1]
"COMPLETE PIANO SONATAS" (projected)
  E. Stevens
VOL. I   # CA.LPA 1052
Contents: No. 34 (2), E minor   *c.* 1785
        No. 35 (5), C major   1780
        No. 36 (6), C sharp minor 1780
        No. 37 (7), D major   1780
VOL. II   # CA.LPA 1053
Contents: No. 5 (25), A major   before 1763
        No. 40 (16), G major   before 1784
        No. 46 (38), A flat major *c.* 1770
        No. 50 (23), C major   *c.* 1790
VOL. III   # CA.LPA 1054
Contents: No. 20 (32), C minor   1771
        No. 30 (35), A major   before 1776
        No. 31 (24), E major   before 1776
        No. 32 (36), B minor   before 1776
VOL. IV   # CA.LPA 1055
Contents: No. 14 (11), D major   *c.* 1766
        No. 23 (13), F major   1773
        No. 27 (9), G major   before 1776
        No. 38 (21), E flat major *c.* 1779

───────────────

COLLECTION
        No. 13 (17), E major   *c.* 1765
        No. 19 (22), D major   1767
        No. 31 (24), E major   before 1776
        No. 32 (36), B minor   before 1776
  ☆ S. Stravinsky
      (# Roy. 1562; No. 13 Finale, in # Roy. 1901)

No. 3, C major . . . Minuet only
  ☆ A. Ehlers (hpsi.) (in # D.UAT 273084)

No. 13 (17), E major   *c.* 1765
. . . **Presto** — ARR. WOODWIND QUINTET
  Chicago Sym. Quintet   in # Aphe.AP 16

No. 19 (22), D major   1767
. . . **Adagio** — ARR. VLC. & PF.
  ☆ P. Casals & E. Istomin (in # AmC.ML 4926 & ♭ *A 1922*)

No. 23 (13), F major   1773
  ☆ G. Anda (*Mozart*)   # DT.TM 68023
  ☆ R. Trouard (# ArgOd.LDC 7501)
  G. Puchelt (in # *G.WDLP 1503*)

No. 34 (2), E minor   *c.* 1785
  L. Kraus   # *LT.EL 93021*
  (*No. 49*)   (# *Sel. 270.C.012*)
  D. Handman   in # LOL.OL 50078
  († Sonatas of XVIIth & XVIIIth Centuries)

No. 36 (6), C sharp minor . . . Minuet only
  E. Heiller   in # Uni.LP 1010
  († History of the Dance)

No. 37 (7), D major   1780
  L. Hambro   # Rem. 199-135
  (*No. 52; & Mozart*)
  ☆ A. d'Arco (ArgPat.FXC 0019)

No. 40 (16), G major   before 1784
No. 41 (19), B flat major   before 1784
No. 42 (20), D major   before 1784
— ARR. VLN., VLA., VLC. (Op. 53, Nos. 1, 2, 3)
  J. Pougnet, F. Riddle, A. Pini # West.WL 5296
  (*Wilton*)

No. 40 (16), G major   before 1784
  G. Puchelt   G.EH 1426

No. 49 (3), E flat major   1790
  L. Kraus   # *LT.EL 93021*
  (*No. 34*)   (# *Sel. 270.C.012*)

No. 50 (23), C major   *c.* 1790
. . . **2nd movt., Adagio (F major)** only
  J. Newmark (fortepiano)   # *Hall.RS 4*
  (*C. P. E. Bach, Clementi*)

No. 52 (1), E flat major   1794
  L. Hambro   # Rem. 199-135
  (*No. 37 & Mozart*)
  S. Weissenberg   # Lum.LD 3-400
  (*Bach-Liszt, Soler, Czerny*)

Unspecified Sonatas
C major . . . Finale only M. v. Doren   in # Chan.MVDP 2
D major . . . Finale only A. d'Arco   in *Plê.P 103*
D major A. d'Arco   in *Plê.P 104*

═══════════════

II. B. CHAMBER MUSIC

Cassation, C major   Lute, vln., gamba
  SEE infra: Str. Qtt., Op. 1, No. 6

DIVERTIMENTI
  NOTE: L references are to the *Ergänzende Themenverzeichnis* in Larsen: *Drei Haydn-Kataloge*; the HV. references to the numbers in Elssler's Catalogue of 1806, as quoted in Grove, 5th edn.

(6) DIVERTIMENTI, Op. 38 (also called Op. 100)
  fl., vln., vlc.
No. 1, D major   No. 2, G major
No. 3, C major   No. 4, G major
No. 5, A major   No. 6, D major
COMPLETE RECORDING
  P. Birkelund, A. Karecki, A. Petersen
                  # HS.HSL 9012
  (also 6ss, ♭ *Mtr.MCEP 3028/30*)

(6) DIVERTIMENTI, Op. 31 fl., 2 hrns., str. 1775
No. 1, G major (L: G 10)
  ☆ London Baroque Ens.—Haas   # *AmD.DL 4066*
  (*below*)

No. 2, A minor (L: a 1)
No. 3, G major (L: G 13)
  London Baroque Ens.—Haas # West.WL 5227
  (*Str. Qtt. Op. 2 (orig. version) & Scherzando*)

---

[1] Numbered according to the GA; the numbers in brackets are those of the Augener edition.

DIVERTIMENTI, various

C major (*Feldparthie*) wind sextet (L : C 1 ; HV : 7)
F major wind sextet[1] *c.* 1760
C major 2 cls., 2 hrns., 2 vlns., 2 vlas., & cont.[2]
(L:C 4; HV:17)
    Vienna State Op. Ens.—Landon ♯ **Strad.STR 622**
    (*Mozart: Divertimenti*)   (♯ Cpt.MC 20104)

C major (*Feldparthie*) (L : C 1 ; HV : 7)
    London Baroque Ens.—Haas   ♯ **P.PMA 1013**
    (*Notturno; & Mozart*)

F major 2 vlns., cor ang., hrns., & bsns.
(L:F 4; HV:16) 1760
    ☆ London Baroque Ens.—Haas   ♯ **AmD.DL 4076**
    (*Marches, Trio*)

G major[3] 2 obs., 2 hrns., str. (L : G 7)
    Danish Radio Cha.—Wöldike ♯ **D.LXT 5135**
    (*Mozart, Dittersdorf, J. C. Bach*)   (♯ Lon.LL 1308)

(6) DIVERTIMENTI (doubtful)
    2 obs., 2 cls., 2 hrns., 2 bsns. ? 1780
No. 1, B flat major[4]
    Paris Wind Ens.   ♯ **Phi.A 77403L**
    (*Mozart & Vivaldi*)
    ☆ London Baroque Ens.—Haas (*above*) ♯ *AmD.DL 4066*

"**C major, 1792**" *SEE* : Notturno No. 1

C major clavier & str. (L:Clavier-divertimenti C 1 ; HV:14)
SEE : CONCERTOS, COLLECTION

Divertimenti à 6 2 hrns. & str., qtt.
SEE : Str. Qtt. Op. 2, Nos. 3 & 5

Octet, F major
    2 obs., 2 cls., 2 hrns., 2 bsns. (doubtful: ed. Wunderer)
    ☆ Vienna Phil. Wind Group   ♯ **West.WN 18058**
    (*above; & J. M. Haydn*)

QUARTETS, String
C major, Op. 1, No. 6
— ARR. LUTE, VLN., & VLC. "*Cassation*"
    M. Podolski, J. Tryssesoone, F. Terby
                             ♯ **Per.SPL 587**
    (*Vivaldi, Saint-Luc, Baron*)   (♯ Cpt.MC 20058)
    ☆ W. Gerwig, I. Brix-Meinert, J. Koch (gamba)
                             (♭ Pol. 37090)

Op. 2—COMPLETE RECORDING
No. 1, A major   No. 4, F major
No. 2, E major   No. 5, D major
No. 3, E flat major   No. 6, B flat major
    Schneider Qtt. (6ss)   ♯ **HS.HSQ 4/6**
    [with W. Wilber & K. Wilber (hrns.)]   (set HSQ-B)
    [in orig. versions of Nos. 3 & 5, as Divertimenti]

E flat major, Op. 2, No. 3
— ORIG. VERSION, DIVERTIMENTO 2 hrns. & str. qtt.
    London Baroque Ens.—Haas ♯ **West.WL 5227**
    (*Divertimenti Op. 31, & Scherzando*)

F major, Op. 3, No. 5 *c.* 1769
    Italian Qtt.   ♯ **C.CX 1230**
    (*Op. 76, No. 2, below*) (♯ QCX 10114; ♯ Angel. 35185)
    E. Bloch Qtt. (n.v.) (*below*)   ♯ *G.KBLP 4*
    Végh Qtt.   **PV. 72311**
    Parrenin Qtt.   ♯ *Pac.LDAC 77*
    (*Mozart: Serenade 13*)
    ☆ Kalki Qtt. (*Qtt. Op. 64, No. 5*) ♯ *DT.LGM 65014*
    ☆ Amadeus Qtt.   in ♯ Nix.WLP 6202
... 2nd movt., **Andante Cantabile** (Serenade) only
    Pessina Qtt. (ArgOd. 66060: in ♯ LDC 510
—— ORCH. VERSION
    Boyd Neel Orch.—Dumont   ♭ *Phi.N 402029E*
    (*Bach & Tchaikovsky*)
    Leipzig Radio—Haarth   *Ami. 14026*
    (*Boccherini: Quintet—Minuet*)
    ☆ Copenhagen Royal—Tango   Tono.X 25185
    (*Tchaikovsky: Serenade—Waltz*)
    ☆ Philadelphia—Stokowski (in ♯ Cam.CAL 120)

—— ARR. 3 HARMONICAS
Raisner Trio (in ♯ *FestF.FLD 33*)

Op. 17, COMPLETE
    ☆ Schneider Qtt.
          (♯ *Era.LDEC 1/3*; No. 6 only, **V**♯ *Era.LDE 1008*)

Op. 20, COMPLETE RECORDING
No. 1, E flat ma.   No. 2, C major   (HLP 16)
No. 3, G minor   No. 4, D major   (HLP 17)
No. 5, F minor   No. 6, A major   (HLP 18)
    Schneider Qtt.   ♯ **Nix.HLP 16/18**
    (6ss)   (♯ HS.HSQ 16/18, set HSQ-F)

G minor, Op. 20, No. 3
    Végh Qtt.   ♯ **Pol. 18094**
    (*Qtt. Op. 77, No. 2*)

D major, Op. 20, No. 4
    Michailow Qtt.   ♯ **Eta. 820016**
    (*Mozart*)

F minor, Op. 20, No. 5
    Vienna Phil. Qtt.   ♯ **DT.LGX 66034**
    (*Schubert*)   (♯ T.LE 6514; FT. 320.TC.074)

Op. 33, COMPLETE RECORDING 1781
No. 1, B minor   No. 2, E flat ma.   (HSQ 19)
No. 3, C major   No. 4, B flat ma.   (HSQ 20)
No. 5, G major   No. 6, D major   (HSQ 21)
    Schneider Qtt. (6ss)   ♯ **HS. set HSQ-G**

E flat major, Op. 33, No. 2
    Budapest Qtt.   ♯ **AmC.ML 5052**
    (*Brahms*)   (in set SL 225)
    Pascal Qtt.   ♯ *MMS. 47*
    (*Qtt. Op. 76, No. 2*)

D minor, Op. 42 1785
    E.M.S. Qtt.   ♯ **EMS. 302**
    (*Qtt. Op. 103*)

C major, Op. 54, No. 2
    Amadeus Qtt.   ♯ **G.ALP 1249**
    (*Mozart: Qtt., K 421*)   (♯ Pol. 18201)

C major, Op. 64, No. 1
    Vienna Konzerthaus Qtt.   ♯ **West.WL 5314**
    (*below*)

B minor, Op. 64, No. 2
    Vienna Konzerthaus Qtt.   ♯ **West.WN 18015**
    (*below*)

B flat major, Op. 64, No. 3
    Vienna Konzerthaus Qtt.   ♯ **West.WL 5314**
    (*above*)

D major, Op. 64, No. 4
    Vienna Konzerthaus Qtt.   ♯ **West.WN 18027**
    (*Op. 76, No. 6, below*)

D major, Op. 64, No. 5 "The Lark"
    E. Bloch Qtt. (*above*)   ♯ *G.KBLP 4*
    Vienna Konzerthaus Qtt.   ♯ **West.WN 18015**
    (*above*)
    Loewenguth Qtt.   ♮ *PV. 72413/4*
    (*3ss—Mozart: Adagio, K 540*) (*Debussy on* ♯ *Pol. 18137*)
    M. Kayser Qtt.   ♯ *Imp.ILP 112*
    (*Op. 76, No. 3, below*)
    American Art Qtt.   ♯ **BB.LBC 1073**
    (*Beethoven: Quartet 10*)   (♯ FV.A 530204)
    ☆ Budapest Qtt.   ♯ **C.CX 1061**
    (*Qtt. Op. 76, No. 4*)   (♯ WCX 1061: QCX 10022)
    ☆ Kalki Qtt. (*above*)   ♯ *DT.LGM 65014*

F major, Op. 74, No. 2
... 2nd movt. & finale — ARR. PF. *SEE* : PF. COLLECTION,
    L. Kraus, *supra*

G minor, Op. 74, No. 3
    Quartetto di Roma   ♯ **Ura.RS 7-20**
    (*Verdi*)
    New Music Qtt.   ♯ **BRS. 923**
    (*Mozart*)

---

[1] First 3 movts. restored by H. C. Robbins Landon from MS. Str. Qtt. version (1765) at Melk (L: Str. Qtt. F 1).
[2] Omitting 1st movt. (March), without conductor's consent.
[3] MS., Schlossbibliothek, Berlin; "*Sinfonia, Le Goutte*".
[4] The 2nd movt. contains the "*Chorale Sti. Antonii*" used by Brahms for his Variations, Op. 56. It has been suggested that this work may be by Pleyel.

Op. 76, Complete Recording *c.* 1799

No. 1, G major	No. 2, D minor ("Quinten")
No. 3, C major ("Emperor")	No. 4, B flat ("Sunrise")
No. 5, D major	No. 6, E flat major

Schneider Qtt.   ♯ **Nix.HLP 34/36**
(6ss)   (♯ HS.HSQ 34/6, set HSQ-L)
Budapest Qtt.   ♯ **AmC.ML 4922/4**
                    (set SL 203)

— FOR PRACTICE, without 1st violin part
                    (♯ CEd. set MMO 501/3, 6ss)

G major, Op. 76, No. 1
Vienna Konzerthaus Qtt.   ♯ **West.WL 5342**
(*below*)
☆ Barchet Qtt. (♯ Clc. 6147)

D minor, Op. 76, No. 2
Italian Qtt.   ♯ **C.CX 1230**
(*Op. 3, No. 5, above*)   (♯ QCX 10114; ♯ Angel. 35185)
Vienna Konzerthaus Qtt.   ♯ **West.WL 5342**
(*below*)
Pascal Qtt. (n.v.)   ♯ **MMS. 47**
(*Qtt. Op. 33, No. 2*)
Berlin St. Op. Qtt.   ♯ **Eta. 720005**
(*Mozart: Serenade No. 13*)
                    (& 6ss, Eta. 120032/4, o.n. 20-32/4)
☆ Galimir Qtt. (♯ Clc. 6149; Cum.CPR 349)

C major, Op. 76, No. 3   "Emperor"
Vienna Konzerthaus Qtt.   ♯ **West.WL 5323**
(*Qtt. Op. 76, No. 4*)
M. Kayser Qtt.   ♯ **Imp.ILP 112**
(*Op. 64, No. 5, above*)
☆ Amadeus Qtt.   ♯ Vic.LHMV 1039
(*Mozart*)   (♭ set WHMV 1039)
☆ Galimir Qtt. (♯ Clc. 6149; Cum.CPR 349;
                    2nd movt. only, ♭ Per.PEP 11)

... 2nd movt., Theme & variations
Bartels Ens. (*MSB. 78042*)
☆ Koeckert Qtt. (PV. 72478: ♭ Pol. 30061)
   Galimir Qtt. (♭ Cpt.EXTP 1004)

— — ARR. STR. ORCH.
☆ Berlin Municipal—Otto   TV.VSK 9023
(*Mozart: Serenade No. 10, excpt.*)
— — ARR. PF.   M. v. Doren (in ♯ Chan.MVDP 2)

B flat major, Op. 76, No. 4   "Sunrise"
Vienna Konzerthaus Qtt.   ♯ **West.WL 5323**
(*Qtt. Op. 76, No. 3*)
☆ Budapest Qtt.   ♯ **C.CX 1061**
(*Qtt. Op. 64, No. 5*)   (♯ WCX 1061: QCX 10022)

D major, Op. 76, No. 5
Koppel Qtt. (*Mozart*)   ♯ **G.KBLP 6**

E flat major, Op. 76, No. 6
Vienna Konzerthaus Qtt.   ♯ **West.WN 18027**
(*Op. 64, No. 4, above*)
☆ Barchet Qtt. (♯ Clc. 6147)

G major, Op. 77, No. 1
Italian Qtt.   ♯ **D.LXT 2811**
(*Beethoven*)
— ARR. FL. & PF.   A. E. Müller
☆ R. le Roy & P. Loyonnet (♯ Clc. 6165)

F. major, Op. 77, No. 2
☆ Végh Qtt.   ♯ **Pol. 18094**
(*Qtt. Op. 20, No. 3*)

B flat major, Op. 103   1803
E.M.S. Qtt.   ♯ **EMS. 302**
(*Qtt. Op. 42*)
☆ Amadeus Qtt.   in ♯ Nix.WLP 6202

Scherzando No. 1, F major   before 1757
fl., ob., 2 hrns., vlns., cbs. (Larsen: Divto. F 6)
London Baroque Ens.—Haas ♯ **West.WL 5227**
(*Divertimenti*)

[1] Possibly by Michael Haydn.

SONATAS, Vln. & vla.
No. 1, C major   — ARR. VLC. & PF.   Piatti
S. Mayes & S. Pearlman   ♯ **Bo.B 210**
(*Beethoven, Bréval, Mozart*)
... 3rd movement, Tempo di minuetto & varns.
L. W. Pratesi & D. O. Colacelli
                    in ♯ **ArgOd.LDC 529**
(*Villa-Lobos, Zandonai, etc.*)

TRIO No. 1, Baryton, vln., vlc., A major
... 1st & 2nd movts. (Andante & Allegro)
— — ARR. VLC. & PF.
A. Schmidt & C. Fannière   ♯ **Vill. 1**
(*Rubino, Schumann, Eccles, Beethoven*)

TRIOS, Pf., vln. [or fl.] & vlc.
(in Larsen order. Nos. in brackets are the B & H nos.)
No. 5 (28), G major, Op. 40, No. 3 1784
No. 16 (30), D major, Op. 63   1790
No. 25 (1), G major, Op. 73, No. 2 *c.* 1795
   P. Badura-Skoda, J. Fournier & A. Janigro
                    ♯ **Nix.WLP 5202**
                    (♯ West.WL 5202)
No. 4 (27), F major, Op. 40, No. 2[1] before 1780
No. 10 (17), E flat major, Op. 42, No. 1 *c.* 1793
No. 17 (29), F major, Op. 68   1790/1
No. 28 (4), E major, Op. 75, No. 2 *c.* 1795
   P. Badura-Skoda, J. Fournier & A. Janigro
                    ♯ **Nix.WLP 5293**
                    (♯ West.WL 5293)
No. 1 (16), G minor, Op. 4, No. 5 1766
No. 12 (10), E minor, Op. 57, No. 2 1789
No. 14 (24), A flat major, Op. 61 1790
   P. Badura-Skoda, J. Fournier & A. Janigro
                    ♯ **West.WN 18054**
No. 7 (21), D major, Op. 45, No. 2   1785
No. 20 (13), B flat major, Op. 70, No. 3 1794
... Andante cantabile only
No. 27 (3), C major, Op. 75, No. 1   1795
Salzburg Mozarteum Trio   † ♯ **AS. 3010LD**
[K. Neumüller, J. Schrochsnadel, G. Weigl]
No. 15 (31), G major, Op. 62   1790
No. 16 (30), D major, Op. 63   1790
No. 17 (29), F major, Op. 68   1790/1
☆ R. Veyron-Lacroix, J-P. Rampal (fl.) & J. Huchot
                    ♯ **LOL.OL 50036**
No. 16 (30), D major, Op. 63
E. Gilels, L. Kogan & M. Rostropovich
(6ss)   *USSR. 19102/7*
No. 19 (14), G minor, Op. 70, No. 2 1794
E. Gilels, L. Kogan & M. Rostropovich
(*Beethoven*)   ♯ **USSR.D 1233**
No. 25 (1), G major, Op. 73, No. 2 *c.* 1795
Trio di Trieste   ♯ **D.LXT 5204**
(*Brahms*)   (♯ Lon.LL 1176)
Budapest Trio (4ss)   ♮ **Tono.L 28050/1**
V. Schiøler, C. Senderovitz, E. B. Bengtsson
(*Mozart*)   ♯ **G.KBLP 9**
... Rondo all' ongarese, only — ARR. PF.
M. v. Doren   in ♯ **Chan.MVDP 2**
No. 27 (3), C major, Op. 75, No. 1
... 3rd movement, Finale
L. Oborin, D. Oistrakh, S. Knushevitzky
(2ss)   *USSR. 18005/6*
No. 28 (4), E major, Op. 75, No. 2
L. Oborin, D. Oistrakh, S. Knushevitzky
                    ♯ **USSR.D 1311**
(*Beethoven: Str. Qtt. No. 10*)

TRIOS, vln., vla., vlc.
G major, Op. 53, No. 1
B flat major, Op. 53, No. 2
D major, Op. 53, No. 3
   SEE: Pf. Sonatas, 40, 41 & 42

TRIOS, 2 fls. & vlc. "London Trios"
No. 1, C major   No. 2, G major
No. 3, G major   No. 4, G major
  ☆ P. Kaplan, L. Schaefer, S. Mayes (# Allo. 4044)

No. 4, G major
  ☆ London Baroque Ens.—Haas   # AmD.DL 4076
  (Divertimento, Marches)

II. C. ORCHESTRAL

CONCERTOS, Clavier & orch.
COLLECTION
D major, Op. 37 (later Op. 21; L: D 2)   before 1784
F major, "No. 6" (L:F 4)   before 1771
G major, "No. 2" (L:G 1)   c. 1770
C major (Concertino) (L: Clavier divertimenti, C 1; HV:14)
  R. Veyron-Lacroix (hpsi.) & Vienna State Op.
  —Horvat   # West.WN 18042

D major, Op. 37 (later Op. 21; L: D 2)
  I. Nef (hpsi.) & Lamoureux—Colombo
           # LOL.OL 50007
  (J. C. Bach: Symphonies)   (# OL.LD 59)
  G. Scherzer (pf.) & London Baroque Ens.—Haas
           # P.PMA 1017
  (Dittersdorf & Schubert) [announced but not issued]
  E. Heiller (hpsi.) & Vienna State Op.—Litschauer
           # Van.VRS 454
  (Trumpet Concerto)   (# Ama.AVRS 6008)

G major, "No. 2"   c. 1770   (L: G 1)
  R. Veyron-Lacroix (hpsi.) & Paris Inst. Ens.
  —Froment[1]   # EPP.APG 118
  (Concerto, fl., clavier & orch.)
  ☆ E. Heiller & Vienna Coll. Mus.—A. Heiller
           (# Era.LDE 2005)

CONCERTOS, Clavier, vln. & orch.
F major   (L: F 3)   1765
  R. Veyron-Lacroix (hpsi.), J-P. Rampal (fl.),
  Paris Inst. Ens.—Froment[1]   # EPP.APG 118
  (Clavier Concerto)
  ☆ L. Salter (hpsi.), J. Pougnet & London Baroque
  —K. Haas[2] (Mozart)   # P.PMA 1012
  ☆ H. Andreae, P. Rybar & Orch.—Swoboda (# Clc. 6156)

CONCERTOS, Fl. & orch.
D major (really by L. Hoffmann) (L:VII. 6)
  H. Barwahser & Vienna Sym.—Paumgartner
           # Phi.N 00208L
  (Telemann)   (# Epic.LC 3075)

CONCERTOS, Horn & orch.
No. 2, D major   1770   (doubtful)
  ☆ Alfred Brain & Janssen Sym. Orch. (# T.LCE 8137)

CONCERTO, Ob. & orch., C major   (doubtful)
  P. Pierlot & Saar Cha.—Ristenpart
           # DFr.EX 25026

CONCERTOS, Organ & orch.
No. 1, C major   1756   (L: Clavier C 1)
No. 2, C major   c. 1760   (L: Clavier C 2)
  ☆ A. Heiller & Vienna Sym.—Gillesberger
  [No. 2 on ♭ Mtr.MCEP 3042]   (# Era.LDE 2004)

CONCERTO, Trumpet & orch.
E flat major   1796
  G. Eskdale & Vienna St. Op.—Litschauer
           # Van.VRS 454
  (Clavier Concerto, D major)   (# Ama.AVRS 6008)
  A. Marchal & Belgian Radio—Doneux
           # Mae.OA 20003
  (Clarke, Grétry, Gluck)
  ☆ H. Wobisch & Vienna State Op.—Heiller   # MMS.55
  (Divertimento)   (2ss, ♭ Mtr.MCEP 3038)
... Andante & Rondo only
  ☆ G. Eskdale & Orch.—Goehr (♭ C.SCD 2006)
... Rondo only
  ☆ H. Mortimer & Philharmonia—Weldon
    (♭ C.SCD 2005: SCVF 1004: SCDQ 2002)

CONCERTOS, Vln. & orch.
C major, "No. 1"   1765
  ☆ S. Goldberg & Philharmonia—Susskind # P.PMA 1007
  (Bach)   (♮ ArgOd. 520004/6)

G major, "No. 2"   c. 1768
  J. Skripka & CHS. Sym.—Goehr   # CHS.H 8
  (Sym. 27; & Boccherini)
  ☆ E. Bertschinger & Collegium Musicum—A. Heiller
           (# Era.LDE 2005)

CONCERTOS, Vlc. & orch.
D major, "Op. 101"   1783
— ORIGINAL SCORING
  P. Fournier & Stuttgart Cha.—Münchinger
           # D.LXT 2968
  (Boccherini)   (# Lon.LL 1036)
  ☆ W. Reichardt & Stuttgart Pro Musica—R. Reinhardt
           (# AFest.CFR 12-312)
— ORCH. PART ARR. Gevaert
  L. Hoelscher & Berlin Phil.—Krauss
  (Bach)   # Ura.RS 7-31
  S. Večtomov & F. O. K. Sym.—Smetáček
           # Sup.LPM 166
  (2ss)   (# U. 5156C)
  ☆ A. Janigro & Vienna State Op.—Prohaska
  (Boccherini)   # Nix.WLP 5126
  ☆ E. Mainardi & Berlin Phil.—Lehmann   # Pol. 18222
  (Schumann)   (# AmD.DL 7536, 2ss)
  ☆ P. Fournier & Philharmonia—Kubelik
       (# Vic.LHMV 1043: ♭ set WHMV 1043)
  E. Feuermann & Sym.—Sargent (# AmC.ML 4677)
  G. Cassadó & Austrian Sym.—Wolf (# Cum.CR 329)

(12) Deutsche Tänze   (L: T 7)   1792
  Orch.—Litschauer   # MTW. 508
  (below; & Mozart) [may in fact be ☆ of Gillesberger's
  recording]
... Nos. 1-6
  ☆ Danish Radio Cha.—Wöldike   G.Z 365
  (Gade: Napoli, excpt.)

Divertimento, D major   fl. & str.   (ed. Scherchen)
  ☆ W. Urfer & Winterthur Sym.—Dahinden (# MMS. 55)

MARCHES
B flat major   1794   (Slow March)
C major   1783   (for Armida)
E flat major   1783
E flat major   1794
  ☆ London Baroque Ens.—Haas   in # Nix.WLP 5080
  (Notturno 1, Octet; & M. Haydn, on # West.WN 18058)

E flat major   ("Grenadier")   c. 1784
E flat major   ("Prince of Wales")   1792
  ☆ London Baroque Ens.—Haas   # AmD.DL 4076
  (Divertimento, & Trio)

(12) Minuets   1792   (L: T 6)
  Orch.—Litschauer   # MTW. 508
  (above; & Mozart) [may really be ☆ of Gillesberger's
  recording?]

NOTTURNI[3]   1790
No. 5, C major   (L: Divertimento C 12)
  Philharmonia—Pritchard   # G.CLP 1061
  (Sym. No. 80; & Mozart) [ed. Geiringer]

No. 7, C major   (L: Divertimento C 13)
  Saar Cha.—Ristenpart   V# DFr.EX 17040
  Linz Sym.   in # Ply. 12-36
  (Schubert, Arne, Gluck)
  ☆ London Baroque Ens.—Haas[4]   # Nix.WLP 5080
  (Marches; Boccherini, M. Haydn)
  (Marches, Octet; & M. Haydn, on # West.WN 18058)

No. 8, C major   (L: Divertimento C 6)
  London Baroque Ens.—Haas   # P.PMA 1013
  (above; & Mozart)
  Hamburg Phil.—di Bella   # DT.TM 68049
  (Lully-Mottl: Ballet Suite)   (# T.TW 30023)

---

[1] Cadenzas by Veyron-Lacroix.   [2] Cadenzas by L. Salter.
[3] The numbering has been revised to agree with Pohl's, Larsen's and Grove's lists. Hence "No. 1" of WERM Supp. II is now No. 7; and "No. 7" of Supp. II is now No. 8.
[4] Called Divertimento, 1792. For other Divertimenti, see II.B, Chamber Music, pp. 212, 213, above.

Sinfonia Concertante, B flat major, Op. 84   1792
ob., bsn., vln., vlc. & orch.
☆ Soloists & Stuttgart Pro Musica—R. Reinhardt
(‡ AFest.CFR 12-312)

SYMPHONIES
No. 1, D major   1759
☆ Vienna Sym.—Swarowsky (*No. 45*)   ‡ Sup.LPV 78
(‡ U.5077G)

No. 7, C major ("Le Midi")   1761
Philadelphia—Ormandy   **‡ AmC.ML 4673**
(*No. 45*)   (‡ Phi.A 01171L)

☆ Vienna Cha.—Litschauer (*No. 8*)   ‡ P.PMA 1014
Berlin Sym.—Balzer (*Rachmaninoff*)   ‡ Roy. 1531
☆ Austrian Sym.—Randolph (‡ Cum.CR 313, d.c.; also
    listed as 213 & 314, which seem to be erroneous)

No. 8, G major ("Le Soir")   *c.* 1761
☆ Vienna Cha. Orch.—Litschauer (*above*) ‡ P.PMA 1014
Anon. Orch. (in ‡ ACC.MP n.d.)

No. 21, A major   1764
Saar Cha.—Ristenpart   **V‡ DFr.EX 17014**

No. 22, E flat major ("The Philosopher")   1764
☆ London Baroque—Haas (*Dittersdorf*) ‡ P.PMA 1004

No. 26, D minor ("Lamentatione")   *c.* 1768
☆ Vienna Cha. Orch.—Heiller (*No. 36*) ‡ P.PMA 1016

No. 27, G major   *c.* 1761 ("Bruckenthal")[1]
Concert Hall Sym.—Goehr   **‡ CHS.H 8**
(*Concerto; & Boccherini*)
F.O.K. Sym.—Silvestri   **‡ Sup.LPV 205**
(*Mozart*)   (‡ U. 5189H)

No. 36, E flat major   *c.* 1761
☆ Vienna Cha. Orch.—Heiller (*No. 26*)   ‡ P.PMA 1016

No. 43, E flat major ("Mercury")   before 1772
☆ Danish Radio—Wöldike (‡ Era.LDE 3007)

No. 44, E minor ("Trauer")   *c.* 1771
Danish Radio—Wöldike   **‡ D.LXT 2832**
(*No. 48*)   (‡ Lon.LL 844)
Vienna Sym.—Sacher   **‡ Phi.A 00212L**
(*No. 85*)   (‡ Epic.LC 3059)
Vienna State Op.—Scherchen ‡ West.WL 5206
(*No. 49*)
R.I.A.S. Sym.—Fricsay   **‡ HP.DGM 18180**
(*No. 95*)   (*Mozart: Sym. 35,* on ‡ AmD.DL 9614)
(*Seasons, excpts.,* on ♮ PV. 72405/6)

No. 45 (18), F sharp minor ("Farewell")   1772
Philadelphia—Ormandy   **‡ AmC.ML 4673**
(*No. 7*)   (‡ Phi.A 01171L)
Berlin Phil.—Lehmann   **‡ Pol. 18194**
(*Stravinsky*)

☆ Met. Sym.—Leinsdorf (‡ GA. 33-301 & 33-319, d.c.)
   Paris Cons.—Goldschmidt (‡ ArgPat.ATD 1008)
   Vienna Sym.—Swarowsky (‡ Sup.LPV 78; U. 5077G)
   Stuttgart Pro Musica—Seegelken (‡ Clc. 6181)

No. 46, B major   1772
Netherlands Phil.—Goehr   **‡ MMS. 129**
(*No. 96*) [This is probably ☆ of CHS. Sym. on ‡ CHS. G14]

No. 48 (25), C major ("Maria Theresia")   1772
Danish Radio—Wöldike   **‡ D.LXT 2832**
(*No. 44*)   (‡ Lon.LL 844)
☆ Vienna State Op.—Scherchen   ‡ Sup.LPV 208
(*No. 97*)   (‡ U. 5195H)

No. 49, F minor ("Passione")   1768
Vienna State Op.—Scherchen ‡ West.WL 5206
(*No. 44*)

No. 50, C major   1773
☆ Danish Radio—Wöldike (‡ Era.LDE 3007)

No. 53, D major ("L'Impériale")   *c.* 1775
Vienna Sym.—Sacher   **‡ EPhi.ABL 3075**
(*No. 67*)   (‡ Phi.A 00181L; Epic.LC 3038)

No. 54, G major   1774
☆ Vienna Academy—Swarowsky   ‡ Nix.LLP 8032
(*No. 70; & Mozart*)

No. 60, C major ("Il Distratto")   1775
Glyndebourne Festival—Gui   **‡ G.ALP 1114**
(*Mozart*)   (‡ Vic.LHMV 1064)
(*Sym. No. 95,* on ‡ G.FALP 320)

No. 61, D major   1776
☆ Danish Radio Cha.—Wöldike (‡ HS.HSL 96)

No. 64, A major   *c.* 1773
☆ Vienna Sym.—Swoboda   **‡ Nix.WLP 5023**
(*No. 91*)   (‡ Sel.LPG 8488)

No. 67, F major   *c.* 1778
Vienna Sym.—Sacher   **‡ EPhi.ABL 3075**
(*No. 53*)   (‡ Phi.A 00181L; Epic.LC 3038)

No. 70, D major   1779
☆ Vienna Academy—Swarowsky   **‡ Nix.LLP 8032**
(*No. 54; & Mozart*)

No. 73 (26), D major ("La Chasse")   1781
☆ Indianapolis Sym.—Sevitzky   **‡ BB.LBC 1062**
(*Glazounov*)   (♭ set WBC 1062)

No. 80, D minor   *c.* 1784
Philharmonia—Pritchard   **‡ G.CLP 1061**
(*Notturno; & Mozart*)
☆ Vienna Sym.—Scherchen (*No. 103*) ‡ Nix.WLP 5050

No. 81, G major   *c.* 1784
Saar Cha.—Ristenpart   **‡ DFr. 116**
(*No. 85*)

No. 83 (24), G minor ("La Poule")   1785
☆ Hallé—Barbirolli   **‡ G.ALP 1038**
(*No. 96*)   (‡ QALP 10035)
(*No. 100,* ‡ BB.LBC 1060)

No. 85 (15), B flat major ("La Reine")   1786
Vienna Sym.—Sacher   **‡ Phi.A 00212L**
(*No. 44*)   (‡ Epic.LC 3059)
MGM.Cha—I. Solomon   **‡ MGM.E 3109**
(*C. P. E. Bach*)
Saar Cha.—Ristenpart   **‡ DFr. 116**
(*No. 81*) (also 2ss, ‡ DFr.EX 25036)
☆ Paris Cons.—Goldschmidt (♮ ArgPat.FXC 0020/1:
   ‡ ATD 1008)

No. 86 (10), D major   1786
London Mozart Players—Blech ‡ G.CLP 1009
(*Mozart: Sym. 40*)   (‡ WCLP 1009)
☆ Salzburg Mozarteum—Fekete (*No. 88*) ‡ CA.LPA 1063
☆ Salzburg Mozarteum—P. Walter (‡ Cpt.MC 20085)

No. 87, A major   1785
☆ Vienna State Op.—Swarowsky (‡ MTW. 512)

No. 88 (13), G major   *c.* 1787
Vienna Phil.—Münchinger   **‡ D.LXT 5040**
(*No. 101*)   (‡ D.NLK 40106; Lon.LL 1199)
Vienna State Op.—Scherchen ‡ West.WL 5178
(*No. 93*)
Leningrad Radio—Sanderling ‡ USSR.D 1742/3
☆ Berlin Phil.—Furtwängler   **‡ HP.DGM 18015**
(*Schubert: Sym. No. 9, s. 3*)
(*Schubert: Sym. 8,* on ‡ Pol. 18283)
(*Schumann,* on ‡ AmD.DL 9767)
☆ Salzburg Mozarteum—Fekete (*No. 86*) ‡ CA.LPA 1063
☆ Salzburg Mozarteum—P. Walter (‡ Cum.CR 228;
   Msq. 10007; with commentary by S. Spaeth on
   ‡ Rem. 8)

No. 89 (20), F major   1787
☆ Vienna State Op.—Swarowsky (‡ MTW. 512)

No. 90 (27), C major   1788
Saar Cha.—Ristenpart   **‡ DFr. 113**
(*No. 91*)

No. 91 (28), E flat major   1788
Saar Cha.—Ristenpart   **‡ DFr. 113**
(*No. 90*)
☆ Vienna Sym.—Swoboda   **‡ Nix.WLP 5023**
(*No. 64*)

---

[1] The "Bruckenthal" Sym. was said to have been "discovered" 1946; published 1950, Bucarest. Also known as the "Hermannstadt" Sym.; but now identified as No. 27 of the G.A.

No. 92 (16), G major ("Oxford") 1788
Sydney Sym.—Schmidt-Isserstedt
♯ *DT.LGM 65012*
(♯ *T.LB 6056*)
Copenhagen Op.—Malko   ♯ **G.CLP 1028**
(*No. 100*) (♯ FALP 346: KALP 4: QCLP 12010)
(*Beethoven*, on ♯ BB.LBC 1087)
L.S.O.—Krips   ♯ **D.LXT 2819**
(*Mozart: Sym. 40*) (♯ Lon.LL 780)
☆ Residentie—v. Otterloo (*Mozart*)   ♯ **Phi.S 04008L**
☆ Vienna St. Op.—Scherchen   ♯ Nix.WLP 5137
(*No. 94*) (♯ Sel. 320.CW.087)
☆ Boston Sym.—Koussevitzky   ♯ G.FALP 239
(*Mozart: Sym. 36*) (QALP 239; DV.CL 16207, d.c.)
☆ Vienna State Op.—Scherchen   ♯ *Sup.LPM 117*
(♯ *U. 5084C*)
☆ Cleveland—Szell (♯ C.QCX 10006: VCX 518)
Paris Cons.—Walter (♯ Cam.CAL 257)

Nos. 93–104 ("London" Symphonies)
COMPLETE RECORDING
Vienna [Sym. & State Op.] Orchs.—Scherchen
♯ **West. set WN 6601**
(12ss) [some are ☆; for individual issues, *see below*]

No. 93 (5), D major 1791
Vienna State Op.—Scherchen ♯ **West.WL 5178**
(*No. 88*)
☆ Royal Phil.—Beecham   ♯ C.CX 1038
(*Mozart: Sym. No. 31*) (♯ WCX 1038: QCX 10032)
(*Sym. 94*, on ♯ FCX 328)
☆ Austrian Sym.—Singer (♯ Cum.CR 220)

No. 94 (6), G major ("Surprise"—"Paukenschlag")
N.B.C. Sym.—Toscanini   ♯ **Vic.LM 1789**
(*Mozart: Sym. 40*) (♯ FV.A 630229)
(*Schubert: Sym. 8*, on ♯ ItV.A12R 0010)
Netherlands Phil.—Swoboda   ♯ **MMS. 59**
(*No. 100*)
Rochester Phil.—Leinsdorf   ♯ **AmC.RL 6621**
(*No. 101*)
Olympia Sym.—Saike   ♯ **Allo. 3056**
(*Mozart: Sym. 40*) (♯ Pac.LDAD 72)
☆ Royal Phil.—Beecham   ♯ C.CX 1104
(*No. 103*) (*No. 93*, on ♯ FCX 328) (♯ QCX 10060)
☆ Vienna State Op.—Scherchen   ♯ Nix.WLP 5137
(*No. 92*) (♯ Sel. 320.CW.087)
☆ Boston Sym.—Koussevitzky   ♯ Vic.LM 9034
(*No. 104*) (also, 6ss, G DB 21506/8: not in G.B.)
(also, o.v., ♯ Cam.CAL 146, sub nom. "Centennial")
☆ Berlin Phil.—Lehmann (2ss)   ♯ HP.DG 16012
Dresden Phil.—Bongartz (♯ *Eta. 720004*)
Orch.—Graunke (♯ MTW. 17)
Havana Sym. (♯ *Roy. 18134*)
Anon. "Radio Sym." (♯ *Var. 6973* & ♯ Gram. 2040)
☆ Vienna Phil.—Furtwängler (♯ G.WALP 1011:
QALP/ALP 188: VALP 505)
Also: Narrator & Orch. (in ♯ Esc. 1)
... 2nd movt., Andante
Hamburg Philharmonia—H-J. Walther (*MSB. 78042*)
... 3rd movt., Minuet — ARR. 2 HARPS[1]
E. & J. Vito (in ♯ *SOT. 1031* & ♯ 10301)

No. 95 (5), C minor 1791
Glyndebourne Fest.—Gui   ♯ **G.ALP 1155**
(*Mozart: Sym. 39*) (♯ Vic.LHMV 11)
(*Haydn: Sym. 60*, on ♯ G.FALP 320)
R.I.A.S. Sym.—Fricsay   ♯ **HP.DGM 18180**
(*No. 44*)
☆ Vienna Sym.—Scherchen (*No. 100*)   ♯ Nix.WLP 5045
☆ Salzburg Mozarteum—P. Walter (♯ Cpt.MC 20085)

No. 96 (14), D major ("Miracle") 1791
Hallé—Barbirolli   ♯ **G.ALP 1038**
(*No. 83*) (♯ QALP 10035)
Amsterdam—v. Beinum (n.v.)   ♯ **D.LXT 2847**
(*No. 97*) (♯ Lon.LL 854)
N.Y.P.S.O.—Walter   ♯ **AmC.ML 5059**
(*No. 102*)
☆ Vienna State Op.—Scherchen (*No. 98*) ♯ Nix.WLP 5111

☆ Vienna Phil.—Walter (*Mahler: Sym. 9*) ♯ Vic.LCT 6015
☆ Winterthur Sym.—Goehr
(♯ *ANix.MLPY 6*; ♯ *MMS. 129*, d.c.)[2]
Stuttgart Pro Musica—Reinhardt (♯ Clc. 6181)
... Minuet only — ARR. GUITAR   Segovia
A. Segovia   in ♯ **AmD.DL 9734**
(† Segovia plays) (♯ D.UAT 273573)

No. 97 (7), C major 1792
Amsterdam—v. Beinum   ♯ **D.LXT 2847**
(*No. 96*) (♯ Lon.LL 854)
Vienna State Op.—Swarowsky ♯ **Sup.LPV 208**
(*No. 48*) (♯ U. 5195H)
☆ Vienna Sym.—Scherchen
(♯ Nix.WLP 5062; Sel.LPG 8487)

No. 98 (8), B flat major 1792
R.I.A.S. Sym.—Fricsay   ♯ *Pol. 16124*
☆ Vienna State Op.—Scherchen (*No. 96*) ♯ Nix.WLP 5111

No. 99 (3), E flat major 1793
☆ Vienna State Op.—Scherchen   ♯ Nix.WLP 5102
(*No. 101*) (♯ Sel.LAG 1024)

No. 100 (11), G major ("Military") 1794
L.P.O.—Solti   ♯ **D.LXT 2984**
(*No. 102*) (♯ Lon.LL 1043)
Netherlands Phil.—Swoboda   ♯ **MMS. 59**
(*No. 94*)
Boston Orch. Soc.—Page   ♯ *SOT. 1069*
☆ Vienna Sym.—Scherchen (*No. 95*) ♯ Nix.WLP 5045
☆ Copenhagen—Malko   ♯ G.CLP 1028
(*No. 92*) (♯ KALP 4: FALP 346: QCLP 12010)
(*No. 83*, on ♯ BB.LBC 1060)
☆ Salzburg Mozarteum—Weidlich (♯ Cum.CR 228;
AFest.CFR 63; & with commentary by S. Spaeth,
♯ Rem. 100-8)
Vienna Phil.—Walter (♯ Cam.CAL 257)

No. 101 (14), D major ("Clock") 1794
Vienna Phil.—Münchinger   ♯ **D.LXT 5040**
(*No. 88*) (♯ D.NLK 40106; Lon.LL 1199)
Rochester Phil.—Leinsdorf   ♯ **AmC.RL 6621**
(*No. 94*)
☆ R.I.A.S. Sym.—Fricsay (2ss)   ♯ HP.DG 16013
☆ Vienna State Op.—Scherchen   ♯ Nix.WLP 5102
(*No. 99*) (♯ Sel.LAG 1024)
☆ Philadelphia—Ormandy (♯ C.QCX 10006: VCX 518)
Austrian Sym.—Busch (♯ Rem. 199-149;
Cum.CR 208; AFest.CFR 32)

No. 102 (12), B flat major 1794
L.P.O.—Solti   ♯ **D.LXT 2984**
(*No. 100*) (♯ Lon.LL 1043)
N.Y.P.S.O.—Walter   ♯ **AmC.ML 5059**
(*No. 96*) [also announced as ML 4814, with *Brahms*]
Orch.—Stiedry, with commentary (♯ MApp. 37)
☆ Vienna Sym.—Scherchen
(♯ Nix.WLP 5062; Sel.LPG 8487)

No. 103 (1), E flat major ("Drum-Roll") 1795
London Mozart Players—Blech ♯ **G.CLP 1066**
(*Mozart: Sym. 33*)
☆ Royal Phil.—Beecham   ♯ C.CX 1104
(*No. 94*) (♯ QCX 10060)
(*Mozart: Sym. 31*, on ♯ C.FCX 329)
☆ Vienna State Op.—Scherchen   ♯ Nix.WLP 5050
(*No. 80*) (♯ Sel.LPG 8320)
Anon. Orch. (♯ Gram. 2096)
☆ Boston Sym.—Münch (♯ G.FALP 219)

No. 104 (2), D major ("London") 1795
Berlin Sym.—List   ♯ **Roy. 1401**
(*Debussy*)
☆ L.P.O.—Beecham (*Schubert*)   ♯ AmC.ML 4771
☆ Boston Sym.—Münch   ♯ G.ALP 1061
(*Schubert: Sym. 2*) (♯ QALP 10031)
(*No. 103*, on ♯ G.FALP 219; *No. 94*, on ♯ Vic.LM 9034)

---

[1] Not heard, but the makers suggest that it is this.   [2] ♯ *MMS. 129* perhaps by Netherlands Phil.—Goehr; ? n.v.

"Toy" Symphony, C major[1]   (Pohl 62)
Berlin Sym.—Rubahn   ♯ **Roy. 1530**
(*Bizet & Ippolitoff-Ivanoff*)   (also ♯ *Roy. 1870*)
Hamburg Philharmonia—H-J. Walther
                                     MSB. 78043
☆ British Sym.—Weingartner (*Mozart*) ♯ **AmC.ML 4776**
☆ Philharmonia—Weldon (C.DDX 28: ♭ *SED 5509*)
Boston Sym.—Koussevitzky (♭ *G.7RQ 176; DV. 26017*)

C major   (ed. Fekete)[2]
☆ Salzburg Mozarteum—Fekete (*Handel*) ♯ **CA.LPA 1074**

II. D. MISCELLANEOUS

Haydn, his life, his times, his music
D. Randolph (narr.) & musical illust.   ♯ **Per.PCS 1**
Haydn: His story and his music
G. Kean (narr.) & orch.   ♯ **AmVox.VL 2610**
The Story and Music of Haydn
Anon. Narrator & orch. (4ss)   *AmC. set J 165*
Let's Listen to Haydn
J. Tillman (narrator) & orchs.   ♯ **HS.HSC 1**
(Musical illustrations include *Deutscher Tanz No. 4;
Minuet No. 4*, & excerpts from *Syms. 39, 31, 82, 6, 85*)

HAYDN, Johann Michael (1737-1806)

[Nos. in brackets refer to the index to the Instrumental
Works, ed. Perger, in DTÖ Vol. XXIX]

Adoro te — ARR. C. de Brant
N.Y. Blessed Sacrament Qtt.   in ♯ *Bib.CL 221*
(† *Music of the Church*)

Concerto, D major fl. & orch. *c.* 1760-70 [56]
Symphony, G major 1768 [7]
Vienna Orch. Soc.—Adler[3]   ♯ **Uni.LA 1007**

Divertimento, C major vln., vlc., cbs. [99]
☆ J. Pougnet, J. Whitehead & J. E. Merritt
                                in ♯ **Nix.WLP 5080**
(*Boccherini & J. Haydn*)
(*below; & J. Haydn,* in ♯ *West.WN 18058*)

MASS, B flat major, Sti. Aloysii 1777
J. Delman (S), E. Scheepers (S), K. Joyce (A),
Hampstead Parish Church Boys' Cho. &
London Baroque Orch.—K. Haas
                                ♯ **P.PMA 1023**
(*Bach: Cantata No. 202*) [M. Sidwell, org.]

Stille Nacht[4]
St. Mary's Chu. Cho.—Linzel (*Eng*)
                         in ♯ **SMP. pte** (n.d.)

Symphony, G major 1783 [16]
See: Mozart ("No. 37")—although attrib. Mozart, the
whole work is by J. M. Haydn except the introduction.

ZAÏRE Inc. Music to Voltaire's Play 1777
... **Turkish Suite** ["Symphony", 13]
☆ Vienna Sym.—Swoboda   ♯ **West.WN 18058**
(*above*)

HAYE, De la (fl. XVIIth Cent.)

SEE: † ANTHOLOGIE SONORE (3004 LD)

HEAD, Michael Dewar (b. 1900)

SONGS
Foxgloves (Hardy) 1932
J. Vyvyan (S), E. Lush (pf.) in ♯ **D.LXT 2797**
(† *Songs of England*)   (in ♯ *Lon.LL 806*)

---

(5) SEA SONGS (C. Fox Smith) 1948
... **No. 2, Limehouse Reach**
No. 6, Sweethearts and Wives
R. Standen (B), F. Stone (pf.) in ♯ **West.WLE 103**
(*Stanford, Ireland, etc.*)

HEISE, Peter Arnold (1830-1879)

SONGS
ARNE Song Cycle (Bjørnson)
... **The Eagle rises on mighty wing**
(*Ørnen lofter med staerke Slag*) (Arne's Song)
☆ A. Schiøtz (T) (in ♯ *G.KBLP 11*)

Forest loneliness (*Skoveensomhed*) (Aarestrup)
A. Schiøtz (T), K. Olsson (pf.)   *G.X 8157*
(*below*)
B. Loewenfalk (B), K. Olsson (pf.) *G.X 8150*
(*below*)
G. Fleischer (S), K. Olsson (pf.) *Phi.N 56001H*
(*Nielsen: Vocalise*)

In the woods it is so still (Drachmann)
B. Loewenfalk (B), K. Olsson (pf.) *G.X 8150*
(*above*)

To a lady friend (*Til en Veninde*) (Aarestrup)
A. Schiøtz (T), K. Olsson (pf.)   *G.X 8157*
(*above*)

HELDER, Bartolomeus (d. *c.* 1635)

Alleluia Chorale
Oratoire Cho.—Hornung   in ♯ **SM. 33-19**

Psalm 23: Der Herr ist mein getreuer Hirt
G. Souzay (B), J. Bonneau (pf.) ♯ **D.LXT 2835**
(† *Canzone Scordate*) (♯ *Lon.LL 731; D.FAT 173072*)

HENKEMANS, Hans (b. 1913)

Concerto, vln. & orch. 1948-50
T. Olof & Amsterdam—v. Beinum
                                ♯ **Phi.A 00219L**
(*Pijper*) (♯ *Epic.LC 3093; o.n. AmC.ML 4937*)

HENRIQUES, Fini Valdemar (1867-1940)

Ballerina vln. & pf. 1921
I. Leth & V. Borggard (*Tono.K 8100*)

Melodie, Op. 15, No. 1 pf.
A. Dalring   *Pol.X 51601*
(*Nielsen & Riisager*)

SONGS
Cradle Song, Op. 3 (*Vuggevise*) (Andersen)
E. Sigfuss (A) & orch.   *Tono.L 28135*
(*Horneman: Mother dear*)

There must be two (Rantzau) 1920
E. Sigfuss (A) & orch.   *Tono.K 8070*
(*Reesen: Two who love one another*)

HENSCHEL, Sir George (1850-1934)

Mass, C major (*English Mass*) 8 vv. 1916
St. Mary's Chu. Cho.—White   ♯ **SMP. pte.**
(*Holst, Davies, M. Haydn, etc.*)

---

[1] Now attrib. to Leopold Mozart. For a recording of the original from which this work is taken, SEE: L. MOZART: *Cassation,
G major.* MS, Munich. (H. C. R. Landon, App. II, No. 26)
[2] One of the 78 symphonies attrib. to Haydn by A. Sandberger; not by Haydn, but probably by A. Zimmermann (1741-1781).
(H. C. R. Landon, App. II, No. 27) Re-scored by M. Fekete.
[3] The concerto recorded from MS. parts at Lambach Abbey, Austria; the symphony from MS. score and parts in library
of *Gesellschaft der Musikfreunde*, Vienna. The latter work was compiled by the composer from the overture and inst.
movements to Singspiel *Die Hochzeit auf der Alm*, and was at one time attributed to Joseph Haydn. The soloist in the
concerto is not named.
[4] Perhaps the setting by E. Fr. Gaebler of an unspec. melody of J. M. Haydn as *Christnachtsgesang, Op. 25*, for S, A, T, B,
and org.

HERBECK, Johann Franz von (1831-1877)

Pueri, concinite Cantus pastoralis S
F. Jankowitsch (Tr.), Vienna Boys' Cho. &
Vienna Sym.—Brenn   in ‡ *EPhi.NBR 6011*
(*Mozart, Pergolesi, Schubert*)   (in ‡ *Phi.N 00694R*)

HERBERIGS, Robert (b. 1886)

(Les) Joyeuses Commères de Windsor
Sym. poem after Shakespeare
(Le) Chant de Hiawatha
Sym. poem after Longfellow
... **Kabibonoka** only
☆ Belgian Nat.—L. Weemaels   ‡ *Lon.LS 872*

HERBERT, Victor (1859-1924)

(Abridged listing only)

Concerto, vlc. & orch., Op. 30, No. 2 1894
☆ B. Greenhouse & A.R.S. Orch.—Schönherr ‡ ARS. 110
(*Copland*)
(*MacDowell* on ‡ ARS. 111)

NATOMA Opera 3 Acts 1911
Dagger Dance
Boston Pops—Fiedler   in ‡ *Vic.LM 1790*
(*Tchaikovsky: Sleeping Beauty Waltz* on ♭ *DV. 16062*)
      (▽ ♭ *49-1438*)
Habanera A. Kostelanetz Orch. (in ‡ *C.SX 1036*, etc.)
Paul's address ⊞ J. McCormack (AF.AGSB 3*)

Serenades
Badinage; Fleurette; Yesterthoughts; Al Fresco
Suite of Serenades
Spanish; Chinese; Cuban; Oriental
Rochester "Pops"—Gould   ‡ *AmC.AL 50*
[omitting Fleurette & Al Fresco, but with *Ketelbey*,
      on ‡ AmC.CL 560]
... **Spanish Serenade**
Allegro Concert—Bath   in ‡ *Allo. 4013*

(The) Willow Plate Suite orch.
Allegro Concert Orch.—Bath   ‡ *Allo. 4013*
(above & MacDowell)   (‡ AFest.CFR 10-578)
ORCH. ARRS. OF MUSICAL COMEDY EXCERPTS, etc.
"Victor Herbert Suite"
Mantovani Orch.   ‡ *D.LK 4060*
(‡ Lon.LL 746: ♮ set LA 242: ♭ sets BEP 1074/5)
Naughty Marietta & Fortune-teller, Selections
Philadelphia Pops—Ormandy (‡ *AmC.AAL 29*)
"Music of Victor Herbert"
A. Kostelanetz Orch.   ‡ *C.SX 1036*
(‡ AmC.CL 756, o.n. ▽ ML 4430: ♮ set MM 1012: ♭ A 1012)

HERBST, Johannes (1735-1812)

SEE: † AMERICAN MUSIC

HÉROLD, Louis Joseph Ferdinand
(1791-1833)

OPERAS
(Le) PRÉ AUX CLERCS 3 Acts 1832
Souvenirs du jeune âge
⊞ E. Albani (IRCC. 3131*)

ZAMPA 3 Acts 1831
Overture
N.B.C. Sym.—Toscanini   in ‡ *G.ALP 1235*
(*Beethoven, Brahms, Berlioz, etc.*) (‡ FV.A 630247;
      DV.L 16483)
(in ‡ Vic.LM 1834 & LRM 7014: ♭ set ERB 7014;
      ItV.A72R 0018)
Philharmonia—Kletzki   ♭ *C.SEL 1541*
(*Nicolai: Lustige Weiber, Overture*)

Philharmonia—Malko   **G.C 4227**
      (S 10616: GB 82
(*Tchaikovsky, Weber, on ‡ DLP 1069: QDLP 6024*)
Lamoureux—Fournet   ♭ *EPhi.NBE 11017*
(*Boïeldieu*)   (*Faust, Prelude* on ♭ *Phi.N 402013E*)
Anon. Orch. (in ‡ *Var. 69134*)
"Philharmonic"—Berendt (‡ Allo. 3101)
☆ Boston Prom.—Fiedler (♭ G.7EP 7002; DV. 26019)
L.P.O.—Martinon (‡ D.LW 5007: ♭ DX 1778)
Rhineland Sym.—Federer (in ‡ AFest.CFR 35)
Liverpool Phil.—Sargent (in ‡ AmC.RL 3054)

— ARR. ORGAN
R. Foort, sub nom. M. Cheshire (in ‡ *Nix.SLPY 156*;
      ‡ *SOT. 1050* & in ‡ *10501*)

Pourquoi trembler (Cavatine) B Act III
⊞ M. Battistini (AF.AGSB 52*)

HESDIN, Pierre (fl. XVIth Cent.)

SEE: † PARISIAN SONGS OF XVITH CENTURY

HILL, Edward Burlingame (b. 1872)

Prelude for orchestra 1953
Columbia Sym.—Bernstein   ‡ *AmC.ML 4996*
(*Lopatnikoff & Dallapiccola*)

Sextet, Op. 39 fl., ob., cl., hrn., bsn. & pf. 1934
N.Y. Woodwind Quintet & L. Kallir
(*Berger*)   ‡ *AmC.ML 4846*

HILMAR, František (1803-1881)

Czech Polkas (Selection) orch.
Prague Radio—Klíma   ‡ *Sup.LPM 126*
(*Malát: Slavonic Maidens*)   (‡ *U. 5075C*

HILTON, John Senior (d. 1608)

SEE: † TRIUMPHS OF ORIANA

HILTON, John Junior (c. 1599-1657)

SEE: † ELIZABETHAN SONGBAG FOR YOUNG PEOPLE
      † SHAKESPEARE SONGS, VOL. III

HINDEMITH, Paul (b. 1895)

Apparebit repentina dies Cho. & Brass Insts. 1947
☆ Singakademie Cho. & Vienna Sym.—Hindemith
      ‡ *DT.LGM 65027*
      (‡ *T.NLB 6078*)

(8) Canons, Op. 44, No. 2 vlns. 1927
M. Levine Str. Orch.   ‡ *MGM.E 3161*
(*below*)

Concerto, horn & orch. 1949
☆ F. Koch & Vienna Sym.—Haefner (‡ Clc. 6112)

Concerto, vla. & orch. "Der Schwanendreher"
      1935
W. Primrose & Cha. Orch.—Pritchard
      ‡ *EPhi.ABL 3045*
(*Walton: Concerto*)   (‡ Phi.A 01132L; AmC.ML 4905)

(Der) Dämon, Op. 28 Ballet-Pantomime 1924
Naples Scarlatti Orch.—Caracciolo
(2ss)   ‡ *Csm.CLPS 1036*

KAMMERMUSIK
No. 1, Op. 24, No. 1 cha. orch. 1922
Philharmonic Cha. Ens.—Hindemith
(*No. 3*)   ‡ *CtyNY.AP 101*
☆ Little Orch. Soc.—Scherman (‡ D.UA 243560)
No. 3, Op. 36, No. 2 vlc. & cha. orch. 1925
L. Varga & Philharmonic Cha. Ens.—Hindemith
(*No. 1*)   ‡ *CtyNY.AP 101*

☆ = Re-issue of a recording to be found in previous volumes.

KAMMERMUSIK (*continued*)
No. 4, Op. 36, No. 3   vln. & orch.   1925
☆ P. Rybar & Winterthur Sym.—Swoboda
(*below*)   ♯ Nix.WLP 5074

Kleine Kammermusik, Op. 24, No. 2   1922
    fl., ob., cl., hrn., bsn.
Fine Arts Wind Quintet   ♯ DCap.CTL 7066
(*Poulenc*)   (♯ Cap.P 8258)
French Radio Wind Quintet   ♯ C.FCX 219
(*Ibert & Milhaud*)
Netherlands Phil. Wind Quintet   ♯ CHS.H 15
(*below, & Poulenc*)
Chicago Sym. Wind Quintet   ♯ Aphe.AP 15
(*Ibert & Milhaud*)
☆ French Wind Quintet[1]   ♯ LOL.DL 53007
(*Sonata, below*)
☆ Fairfield Quintet (♯ Cpt.MC 20076)

Kleine Klaviermusik, Op. 45, No. 4   pf.
    (12 easy pieces on 5 notes, 1929)
M. Richter   ♯ MGM.E 3181
(*Satie, Toch, etc.*)

Konzertmusik, Op. 50   brass & strings   1930
Philadelphia—Ormandy   ♯ EPhi.ABL 3051
(*below*)   (♯ AmC.ML 4816; Phi.A 01138L)
☆ Vienna Sym.—Haefner (♯ Clc. 6112)

Ludus Tonalis   pf.   1943
N. Mewton-Wood   ♯ Argo.ARS 1015[2]

Nobilissima Visione   Ballet   1937
... Orch. Suite
1. Intro. & Rondo
2. March & Pastorale   3. Passacaglia
Philharmonia—Klemperer   ♯ C.CX 1241
(*Brahms*)   (♯ Angel. 35221)
Hamburg Phil.—Keilberth   ♯ T.LE 6554
(*Symphonic Metamorphosis*)

PART SONGS
COLLECTION
(6) CHANSONS   (*Fr*)   (Rilke)   1939
    1. La Biche   2. Un Cygne
    3. Puisque tout passe   4. Printemps
    5. En hiver   6. Verger
LIEDERBUCH FÜR MEHRERE SINGSTIMMEN, Op. 33
... No. 2, Frauenklage (Burggraf von Regensburg)   [1923
    No. 6, Landsknechtstrinklied: 'Tummel dich' (Anon.)
Wahre Liebe   (H. v. Veldeke)   1938
Vienna Cha. Cho.—Schmid   ♯ Phi.N 00682R
(*Gesualdo*)

(6) CHANSONS   (Rilke)   1939
... Nos. 1, 2 & 3
Lyons Psalette—Geoffray   in ♯ SM. 33-21
(*Schmitt, Poulenc, etc.; & Noëls*)

Landsknechtstrinklied, Op. 33, No. 6   (Anon.)
☆ Vienna Cha. Cho.—Grossmann (in V♯ Sel.LPP 8714)

———————

(9) Pieces, Op. 44, No. 1   vlns.
(8) Pieces, Op. 44, No. 3   vlns. & vla.
(5) Pieces, Op. 44, No. 4   str. orch. (or str. qtt.)
M. Levine Str. Orch.   ♯ MGM.E 3161
(*above*)

Quartet, B flat major   cl., vln., vlc. & pf.   1938
A. Williams & N.Y. Trio   ♯ Persp. 2004
(*Piston*)

Quartet No. 3, Op. 22   str.   1922
☆ Hollywood Qtt. (♯ T.LCE 8151)

SONATAS
Bassoon & pf.   1939
A. Swillens & H. Duval
Clarinet & pf.   1940
J. d'Hondt & H. Duval   ♯ CHS.CHS 1250
(*below*)

Harp   1939
N. Zabaleta   in ♯ Eso.ES 524
(† Contemporary Harp Music)

Oboe & pf.   1938
☆ P. Pierlot & A. d'Arco   ♯ LOL.DL 53007
(*Kleine Kammermusik*)

Organ
No. 1,   1937   No. 2,   1937   No. 3,   1940
☆ R. Noehren   ♯ CA.LP 1014
                               (♯ Lyr.LL 53)
... No. 1, only
T. W. Ripper   ♯ PFCM.CB 191
(*Křenek & Piston*)
☆ F. Heitmann (in † ♯ DT.LGX 66038)
... No. 2, only
R. Ellsasser   in ♯ MGM.E 3064
(† Organ Music by Modern Composers)

Piano solo   1936
No. 2, G major
Z. Skolovsky   ♯ EPhi.NBL 5025
(*Berg, Bartók, Scriabin*) (♯ Phi.N 02131L; AmC.ML 4871)
J. Rappaport   ♯ Etu.ER 101
(*Bartók, Bloch, Kabalevsky*)

Piano 4-hands   1942
R. Gold & A. Fizdale   ♯ AmC.ML 4853
(*Stravinsky & Rieti*)   (in set SL 198)
G. & J. Dichler   ♯ SOT. 1037
(*Martin: Ballade*)

Trumpet & pf.   1940
H. Sevenstern & H. Duval   ♯ CHS.CHS 1250
(*below & above*)

Violin & pf., No. 3, E major   1935
☆ R. Posselt & A. Sly (in ♯ Esq.TW 14-005)

Violin unacc. Op. 31, No. 1   1924
H. Merckel   ♭ Pat.ED 24

Viola & pf., F major, Op. 11, No. 4   1922
F. Molnar & T. Ury   ♯ Argo.ARL 1007
(*Honegger: Vln. Sonata*)

Violoncello & pf., A minor, Op. 11, No. 3   1919
J. Starker & L. Pommers   ♯ Per.SPL 715
(*Bartók*)

Viola d'amore & pf., Op. 25, No. 2   1929
J. v. Helden & J. Huckriede   ♯ CHS.H 15
(*Kleine Kammermusik; & Poulenc*)
(*3 Sonatas, above on ♯ CHS.CHS 1250*)

SONGS
(9) English Songs   1942-4
    1. On hearing "The last rose of Summer" (Wolfe)
    2. Echo (Moore)
    3. The Whistling Thief (Lover)
    4. The wild flower's song (Blake)
    5. To music, to becalm his fever (Herrick)
    6. The moon (Shelley)
    7. On a fly drinking out of his cup (Oldys)
    8. Sing on there in the swamp (Whitman)
    9. Envoy (F. Thompson)
B. Troxell (S), T. Kosma (pf.) ♯ McInt.MC 1003
(*Britten*)   (o.n. ♯ WCFM. 15)

(3) Geistliche Motetten   S & pf.
    1. Cum natus esset   1941
    2. Pastores loquebantur   1944
    3. Nuptiae factae sunt   1944
I. Seefried (S), E. Werba (pf.)   PV. 72328
(*Mozart on ♯ AmD.DL 9768*)

(Das) Marienleben, Op. 27   (Rilke)   Song-Cycle
    1924, rev. 1948
J. Tourel (M-S), E. I. Kahn (pf.)
(4ss)   ♯ AmC. set SL 196

———————

Symphonic Dances   orch.   1937
Berlin Phil.—Hindemith   ♯ Pol. 16094
(*Mathis der Maler, below, on ♯ AmD.DL 9818*)

———

[1] Incorrectly listed in Supp. II. Kammermusik No. 2 is Op. 36, No. 1, Concerto for pf. & cha. orch, not recorded.
[2] Announced but never issued.

Symphonic Metamorphosis of themes by Weber
  orch. 1943
  Chicago Sym.—Kubelik   **♯ G.ALP 1251**
  (Schoenberg)   (♯ Mer.MG 50024)
  (Bloch on ♯ Mer.MG 50027)
  Hamburg Phil.—Keilberth   **♯ T.LE 6554**
  (Nobilissima Visione)

Symphony, B flat major military band 1951
  French Navy Band—Maillot **♯ Sel. 270.C.052**
  (Schmitt)
  U.S. Military Acad. Band—Resta
                              ♯ PFCM.CB 174
  (Harris & Vaughan Williams)

Symphony, Die Harmonie der Welt 1951
  Berlin Phil.—Hindemith   **♯ Pol. 18181**
                                 (♯ AmD.DL 9765)

Symphony, Mathis der Maler 1934
  Berlin Phil.—Hindemith, n.v. **♯ Pol. 16130**
  (Symphonic Dances, above, on ♯ AmD.DL 9818)
  Philadelphia—Ormandy   **♯ EPhi.ABL 3051**
  (above)   (♯ AmC.ML 4816; Phi.A 01138L)
  "Philharmonic"—Berendt   **♯ Allo. 3145**
  (Bartók)
  ☆ Berlin Phil.—Hindemith (2ss), o.v. **♯ DT.LGM 65018**
  ☆ N.B.C. Sym.—Cantelli (♯ G.QBLP 5005)

Theme and four Variations pf. & str. orch.
  (The Four Temperaments) 1940 (f.p. 1944)
  V. Aller & Concert Arts—Slatkin
  (2ss)   **♯ DCap.CCL 7521**
                                 (♯ Cap.L 8228)
  (Shostakovich on ♯ Cap.P 8230)
  ☆ F. Holetschek & Vienna Sym.—Swoboda
  (above)   **♯ Nix.WLP 5074**
  ☆ L. Foss & Zimbler Sinfonietta (♯ D.UA 243047)

Trauermusik vla. & str. 1936
  ☆ R. Persinger & Cha. Ens. (♯ Cpt.MC 20076)

TRIOS, vln., vla., vlc.
No. 1, Op. 34 1924
No. 2 1933
  J. Pougnet, F. Riddle & A. Pini **♯ Nix.WLP 5299**
                                 (♯ West.WL 5299)

NOTE: **Op. 43** is *Spielmusik*, 1927
      Op. 44 is *Schulwerk*, 1927
      Op. 45 is *Sing- und Spielmusiken für Liebhaber und
         Musikfreunde*, 1928-43

HIVELY, Wells (b. 1902)

(3) Himnos orch. 1946-7
  Eastman-Rochester Sym.—Hanson
  (Donovan & Porter)   **♯ Mer.MG 40013**

HOFFER, Johann Jacob (1673-1737)

Suite, A major lute *c.* 1700
  W. Gerwig   **PV. 9401**

HOFFMANN, Johann (or Giovanni)
                           (fl. XVIIIth Cent.)

Concerto, D major mandolin & orch. (MS, Vienna)
  G. Linder-Bonelli & Leipzig Radio—Pflüger
  (Dittersdorf)   **♯ Ura. 7110**

HOFFMANN, Leopold (c. 1730-1793)

Concerto, D major fl. & orch.
  See under HAYDN, F. J.

Toy Symphony, D major
  (Sinfonia Berchtolgadensis—MS, Kremsmünster)
  Vienna Orch. Soc.—Adler   **♯ Uni.LP 1016**
  (L. Mozart & Gabrielski)

HOHENZOLLERN, Prince Louis
                 Ferdinand von (1772-1806)

Rondo No. 2, C major, pf. & orch.
  ☆ O. A. Graef & Frankenland State Sym.—Kloss
  (Dittersdorf)   **♯ Nix.LLP 8026**

HOLBORNE, Anthony (d. 1602)
  SEE † MUSIC FOR BRASS

HOLMBOE, Vagn (b. 1909)

QUARTETS, Str.
No. 2, Op. 47 1949
  Musica Vitalis Qtt.   **♯ D.LXT 5061**
  (Nielsen)   (♯ Lon.LL 1078)

No. 3, Op. 48 1949
  Koppel Qtt.   **♯ D.LXT 5092**
  (Nielsen)   (♯ Lon.LL 1119)

HOLMES, John (d. 1602)
  SEE: † TRIUMPHS OF ORIANA

HOLST, Gustav Theodore (1874-1934)

Christmas Day[1] Cho. & orch. (or org.) 1910
  Nat. Presbyterian Chu. Cho.—Schaefer (org.)
                          in **♯ McInt.MM 107**

PART SONGS
Lullay, my liking, Op. 34b (Anon.) 1916
  Westminster Abbey Cho.—McKie   in **♯ D.LK 4085**
  (& in ♯ D.LF 1030; Lon.LPS 267) (♯ Lon.LL 1095)
  Holy Trinity Chu. Cho., New Haven—Byles **♯ Over.LP 11**
  (Praetorius, Victoria, etc.; & Carols)

Midwinter (C. Rossetti)
  Canterbury Cho.—Marrow   in **♯ MGM.E 3061**

This have I done for my true love, Op. 34a, No. 1 (Anon.)
  St. Mary's Chu. Cho.—Linzel   in **♯ SMP. pte.**

(The) PERFECT FOOL, Op. 39 Opera 1 Act
  1923
Ballet Music
  L.P.O.—Boult   **♯ D.LXT 5015**
  (Bax & Butterworth)   (♯ Lon.LL 1169)
  (Butterworth: Shropshire Lad only on ♯ D.LW 5175)
  L.S.O.—Weldon   **♯ C.SX 1019**
  (Bax & Vaughan Williams)

(The) Planets, Op. 32 Suite, orch. 1914-6
  Philharmonic Prom. Orch. & London Phil.
    Cho.—Boult   **♯ Nix.NLP 903**
                                 (♯ West.WL 5235)
  L.S.O. & Female Cho.—Sargent **♯ D.LXT 2871**
                                 (♯ Lon.LL 1019)
  ... Nos. 1, 2, 3, 4
  ☆ Toronto Sym.—MacMillan (♯ Cam.CAL 204)

(2) Suites for Military Band, Op. 28
No. 1, E flat major; No. 2, F major
  Eastman Wind Ens.—Fennell **♯ Mer.MG 40015**
  (Vaughan Williams)

No. 1, E flat major
  ... **No. 3, March,** only
  Royal Marine Band—Dunn *(G.B 10676:* in **♯ CLP 1016;**
                                 in **♯ BB.LBC 1072**

---

[1] Choral Fantasy on old carols, with short solo parts.

Toccata on a Northumbrian pipe tune pf. 1924
R. Smith   *D.F 10101*
(*Benjamin: Scherzino*)

ARRANGEMENTS
Abroad as I was walking
Stanford Univ. Cho.—Schmidt   in ♯ **ML. 7022**
(† Madrigals & Motets)

Christmas Song (Personent hodie)
All Saints Choristers—Self   in ♯ **CEd.CE 1021**

Trymder (Welsh Carol)
Coedpoeth Youth Cho.   in ♯ **Nix.WLP 6209-1**
                  (in ♯ **West. set WAL 209**)
[at International Eisteddfod, Llangollen]

HOMILIUS, Gottfried August (1714-1785)
    SEE: BACH FESTIVAL (*s.v.* BACH, Miscellaneous)

HONEGGER, Arthur (1892-1955)

CLASSIFIED: I. Instrumental II. Orchestral
          III. Songs   IV. Stage Works, Cantatas

I. INSTRUMENTAL

Danse de la chèvre fl. unacc.
G. Nicolet   *♯ D.LXT 2849*
(*below; Moeschinger, Regamey*) (♯ Lon.LL 893)

Fugue & Choral organ 1917
M. Bidwell   *♯ PFCM.CB 188*
(*Messiaen & Sessions*)

Petite Suite fl., vln. & pf. 1936
G. A. Nicolet, H. Schneeberger & P. Souvairan
                    ♯ D.LXT 2849
(*above*)   (♯ Lon.LL 893)

Rhapsodie pf., 2 fl. & cl. 1917
New Art Wind Quintet Members
            in ♯ **CEd. set 2006**
(*Auric, Milhaud, Poulenc, etc.*)

— ARR. PF., FL., OB., CL. Honegger[1]
B. Zighéra, J. Pappoutsakis, L. Speyer,
  P. Cardillo   *♯ Uni.UN 1005*
(*Poulenc, Roland-Manuel, etc.*)

Romance fl. & pf. 1954
J-P. Rampal & F. Gobet   ♭ *Pat.G 1056*
(*Gagnebin & Massis*)

Sonata, A major cl. & pf. 1921-22
U. & J. Delécluse   *♯ D.LX 3139*
(*Saint-Saëns & Milhaud*) (♯ Lon.LS 1097)

Sonata, vln. unacc. 1949
C. Ferras   *♯ D.LXT 2827*
(*Ravel & Chausson*) (♯ BAT 133071; Lon.LL 762)
H. Merckel   ♭ *Pat.ED 25*
[2 movts. only in ♯ FestF.FLD 50]

Sonata, vla. & pf. 1920
F. Molnar & T. Ury   *♯ Argo.ARL 1007*
(*Hindemith: Sonata*)

II. ORCHESTRAL

Chant de joie 1923
London Phil. Sym.—Scherchen
                 ♯ West.LAB 7032
(½s—*Stravinsky: Firebird*)

Concertino, pf. & orch. 1924
☆ F. Jacquinot & Philharmonia—Fistoulari
(*Milhaud, Chausson, Ravel*) ♯ **MGM.E 3041**

Concerto da camera fl., cor ang., str. 1948
J-P. Rampal, P. Pierlot & Paris Cha.
  —Oubradous   *♯ Pat.DT 1019*
(*Aubert*)
☆ A. Gleghorn, W. Kosinski & Los Angeles Cha. Sym.
  —Byrns (♯ T.LCE 8115)

[1] Arrangement made specially for this recording.

Mouvement symphonique No. 3 1932-3
London Phil. Sym.—Scherchen
                ♯ **West.LAB 7010**
(*below & Tempête, Prelude*)
French Nat. Radio—Tzipine   ♯ *C.FCX 337*
(*Symphony No. 4*)

Pacific 231 (Mouvement symphonique No. 1) 1923
Paris Cons.—Ansermet   *♯ D.LXT 5004*
(*Ravel & Dukas*)   (♯ Lon.LL 1156)
(*Dukas only, ♯ D.LW 5155; Lon.LD 9174*)
Paris Cons.—Tzipine   *♯ C.FCX 188*
(½s—*Rugby & Nicolas de Flüe, s. 3*)
(*Rugby only, ♯ FC 1038*)
London Phil. Sym.—Scherchen
(*above & below*)   ♯ **West.LAB 7010**
Boston Orch. Soc.—Page   ♭ *Nix.EP 651*
(*Barber: Adagio*)
(*idem; & Debussy in ♯ SOT. 1068, & in ♯ 10683*)
Hamburg Philharmonia—H-J. Walther
                    MSB. 78156
               (& in ♯ MGM.E 3144)
☆ Sym.—Honegger (♭ *Od.7AOE 1005*)

Pastorale d'été 1920
Lamoureux—Martinon   in ♯ **Phi.A 00175L**
(*Debussy, Dukas, Roussel, etc.*) (♯ Epic.LC 3058)
Concert Arts—Golschmann
                in ♯ **DCap.CTL 7055**
(*Milhaud, Ravel, Satie*) (♯ Cap.P 8244: ♭ FAP 8252)
Concert Hall Sym.—Goehr   ♯ **CHS.H 12**
(*Debussy*)

Prélude, Fugue & Postlude
  (from music for *Amphion*, Melodrama by Valéry, 1931)
Paris Cons.—Tzipine   *♯ C.CX 1252*
(*Tailleferre, Poulenc, Durey*)
(♯ FCX 264; Angel. 35117, in set 3515)

Rugby (Mouvement symphonique, No. 2) 1928
London Phil. Sym.—Scherchen ♯**West.LAB 7010**
(*above and below*)
Paris Cons.—Tzipine   *♯ C.FC 1038*
(*Pacific 231*)   (& in ♯ FCX 188)
☆ Sym.—Honegger (♭ *Od.7AOE 1005*)

SYMPHONIES

No. 2 Str. orch. & trumpet ad lib. 1941
M.G.M. String—I. Solomon ♯ **MGM.E 3104**
(*Rivier*)   (♯ FMGM.F 6-102)
Boston Sym.—Münch   ♯ **Vic.LM 1868**
(*Menotti*)   (♯ FV.A 630275; ItV.A12R 0115)
Rochester Cha.—Hull   ♯ **CHS.CHS 1189**
(*H. Johnson*)
☆ Paris Cons.—Münch   ♯ **G.FJLP 5026**
  (*Danse des Morts*) [3rd movt. only in ♯ FestF.FLD 50]

No. 3, Liturgique 1946
Paris Cons.—Tzipine   ♯ **C.FCX 336**
(*Cantate de Noël*)
[Dies Irae only in ♯ FestF.FLD 50]
Dresden Phil.—Stoschek   ♯ **Ura. 7090**

No. 4, Deliciae basilienses 1946
French Nat. Radio—Tzipine   ♯ **C.FCX 337**
(*Mouvement symphonique No. 3*)

No. 5, di tre re 1949
Pittsburgh Sym.—Steinberg ♯ **PFCM.CB 178**
(*Copland*)
Boston Sym.—Münch   ♯ **Vic.LM 1741**
(*Ravel & Roussel*)(♭ *set WDM 1741; ♯ G.FALP 169;*
                      ItV.A12R 0110)

III. SONGS & PART SONGS

Chanson de Ronsard voice, fl. & str. orch. 1924
(*La Terre, l'eau, l'air et le vent*)
I. Joachim (S) & Orch.—M. Franck
              in ♯ **CdM.LDA 8079**
(*below; Auric, Durey, Milhaud, Poulenc, Tailleferre*)

SONGS

Murcie en fleurs (Aguet) 1940
☆ C. Panzéra (B), M. Panzéra (pf.) (in ♯ Clc. 6260)

(6) POÉSIES (Cocteau) 1920-3
1. Le Nègre   4. Ex-voto
2. Locutions   5. Une Danseuse
3. Souvenirs d'enfance 6. Madame
I. Joachim (S), M. Franck(pf.) ♯ *CdM.LDA 8079*
(*above*)

Psaume 130: Mimaamaqim
☆ M. Martinetti (A) & Orch.—Honegger
(in ♯ FestF.FLD 50)
Unid. PARTSONGS
Jugend dieser Zeit in *Eta.* 10-123
Mit uns die Freude in *Eta.* 10-140

IV. STAGE WORKS, CANTATAS

(Les) AVENTURES DU ROI PAUSOLE
Operetta 3 Acts 1930
Le Coupe de Thule ☆ Dorville (T) (in ♯FestF.FLD 50)

(Une) Cantate de Noël 1941-53, f.p. 1953
B, Children's Cho., Cho., organ, orch.
M. Roux, Versailles & E. Brasseur Chos.,
Lamoureux Orch.—Sacher ♯ *EPhi.NBR 6026*
(2ss) [M. Duruflé, org.]   (♯ *Phi.N 00749R*)
(*Distler* on ♯ Epic.LC 3153)
P. Mollet, Versailles & E. Brasseur Chos., Paris
Cons. Orch.—Tzipine   ♯ *C.FCX 336*
(*Sym. No. 3*) [M. Duruflé, org.]

(La) DANSE DES MORTS Oratorio (Claudel)
1939
☆ J-L. Barrault (orator), O. Turba-Rabier (S), E.
Schenneberg (A), C. Panzéra (B), Gouverné Cho.,
Paris Cons. Orch.—Münch ♯ *G.FJLP 5026*
(*Symphony No. 2*)
[Lamento only, in ♯ FestF.FLD 50]

JEANNE D'ARC AU BÛCHER
Oratorio (Claudel) 1938
Jeanne   ...   ...   V. Zorina (Diction)
Frère Dominique ...   R. Gerome (Diction)
La Vierge   ...   ...   F. Yeend (S)
Marguerite   ...   ...   C. Long (S)
Catherine   ...   ...   M. Lipton (A)
& D. Lloyd (T), K. Smith (B), etc., Temple
Univ. Cho., St. Peter's Boys' Cho. &
Philadelphia Orch.—Ormandy
♯ *EPhi.ABL 3033/4*
(4ss)   (♯ AmC. set SL 178; Phi.A 00128/9L)
☆ Soloists, Cureghem Children's Cho., Antwerp Cecilia
Cho., Belgian Nat. Orch.—de Vocht
(4ss)   ♯ *G.FALP 213/4*
[Finale only, in ♯ FestF.FLD 50]

NICOLAS DE FLUË Dramatic Legend 3 Acts
(C. de Rougemont) 1939, f.p. 1941
J. Davy (narr.) Versailles & E. Brasseur Chos.,
Paris Cons. Orch.—Tzipine ♯ *C.FCX 187/8*
(3ss—*Pacific 231 & Rugby*)
[excerpt in ♯ FestF.FLD 50]

(Le) ROI DAVID Opera-Psalm 1923 version
Narrator, S, A, B, org. & orch.
J. Marchat, A. Guiot, C. Gayraud, C. Maurane,
Paris Univ. Cho. & Cento Soli Orch.—Gitton
♯ *CFD. set 46*
(4ss) [recorded in composer's presence]
☆ Soloists, Cho. & French Nat. Orch.—Honegger
♯ *LT.DTL 93004/5*
(♯ Sel.LPG 8342/3; T.LE 6533/4)

(La) TEMPÊTE, Prélude 1923
London Phil.Sym.—Scherchen ♯West.LAB 7010
(*Mouvements symphoniques*)

MISCELLANEOUS
"Arthur Honegger vous parle"
Excerpts from recordings (see above) with commentary by
the composer   ♯ FestF.FLD 50

HOOK, James (1726-1827)
Piece for 3 flutes (ARR. Recorders)
Trapp Family Ens.   in ♯ AmD.DL 9759

HOOPER, Edmund (*c.* 1553-1621)
SEE: † MASTERS OF EARLY ENGLISH KEYBOARD MUSIC

HOPKINS, Anthony (b. 1921)

Carillon Anthem unacc. cho. 1949
Netherlands Cha. Cho.—de Nobel
(*Poulenc & Martin*)   ♯ *Phl.N 00679R*

(A) Melancholy Song (D. Kilham Roberts) *c.* 1950
J. Vyvyan (S), E. Lush (pf.) in ♯ *D.LXT 2797*
(† Songs of England)   (in ♯ Lon.LL 806)

Sonata No. 3, C sharp minor pf.
L. Crowson (*below*)   ♯ *Argo.RG 52*

THREE'S COMPANY Opera 1953
Intimate Opera Company   ♯ *Argo.RG 51/2*
(3ss—*above*) [E. Boyd (S), S. Manton (T), E. Shilling (Bs),
A. Hopkins (pf.)]

FOLK SONG ARRANGEMENT
(Les) Trois rubans
S. Wyss (S), M. Korschinska (hp.)   in ♯ Argo.RG 34

HOPKINSON, Francis (1737-1791)

SONGS
COLLECTION
Beneath a weeping willow's shade
My days have been so wondrous free (Parnell)
My love is gone to sea
O'er the hills far away
▽ M. Truman (S), Shaw Chorale & orch. (in *Vic.* set DM
1445 : ♭ *WDM* 1445 : ♯ *LM* 57)

Beneath a weeping willow's shade
— ARR. ORCH. Bales
▽ Washington National Gallery Orch.—Bales
(in ♯ WCFM. 1)

(A) Toast [to George Washington] 1778
Anon. Tenor & Hamburg Philharmonia
—Korn   in ♯ *Allo.* 3148
(*Creston, Barber, etc.*)

HORN, Charles Edward (1786-1849)
SEE: † SONGS OF ENGLAND

HOTTETERRE, Louis (le Romain)
(d. *c.* 1719-20)

Suite No. 1, D major[1] fl. & cont.
1. Prélude
2. Allemande: La Royalle
3. Sarabande: La d'Ormagnac
4. Rondeau: Le Duc d'Orléans
5. Gavotte: La Meudon
6. Menuet: Le Comte de Brione
7. Gigue: La Folichon
G. Scheck (fl.), F. Neumeyer (hpsi.), H. Müller
(gamba)   ♭ *Pol. 37016*

HOVHANESS, Alan (b. 1911)

COLLECTION
Concerto (Khaldis) pf., 4 tpts. & perc. 1951, rev. 1954
W. Masselos & Ens.—I. Solomon
PIANO MUSIC
Pastorale No. 1   1952, rev. 1954
Fantasy on an Ossetin tune 1951
Orbit No. 2   1952
Jhala   1952
Hymn to a celestial musician 1952
Achtamar   1948
W. Masselos (pf.)   ♯ MGM.E 3160

---

[1] From Book I of *Pièces pour la Flûte traversière et autres instruments avec la basse*, 1708.

Concerto No. 1 for orchestra "Arevakal" 1951
Eastman-Rochester Sym.—Hanson
(Riegger & Cowell)   ♯ **Mer.MG 40005**

Concerto No. 7 for orchestra 1953, f.p. 1954
Louisville—Whitney   ♯ **LO. 4**
(Castelnuovo-Tedesco & Surinach)

(The) Flowering Peach Inc. Music (Odets) 1954
... Orch. Suite
Cha. Ens.—Hovhaness   ♯ **MGM.E 3164**
(below)

Is there Survival Ballet 1950, rev. 1955
... Suite 4 cls., 4 tpts., alto sax. & perc.
Ens.—Hovhaness   ♯ **MGM.E 3164**
(above & below)

Lullaby; Slumber Song; Siris Dance pf.
M. Richter   in ♯ **MGM.E 3147**
(Lawrence, Persichetti, Richter, etc.)

Mountain Idylls pf. 1954
M. Richter   ♯ **MGM.E 3181**
(Hindemith, Satie, Surinach, Toch)

Orbit No. 1 Ballet Scene 1952
Cha. Ens.—Hovhaness   ♯ **MGM.E 3164**
(above)

Quartet fl., ob., vlc. & hpsi. 1952
H. Bennett, H. Shulman, B. Greenhouse &
S. Marlowe   ♯ **NE. 3**
(Lessard: Toccata in 4 movts; Rieti & Thomson)

HOWELLS, Herbert (b. 1892)

Behold, O God our defender Anthem
Coronation Chorus   in ♯ **G.ALP 1057**
(† Coronation of Queen Elizabeth II)

(A) GARLAND FOR THE QUEEN
(with V. Williams, Tippett, Bliss, etc.) 1953
... Inheritance (De la Mare)
Cambridge Univ. Madrigal Soc.—Ord
in ♯ **C.CX 1063**

Gavotte Song (Newbolt)
J. Vyvyan (S), E. Lush (pf.)   ♯ **D.LXT 2797**
(† Songs of England)   *(♯ Lon.LL 806)*

Magnificat "Collegium Regale"
King's College Chapel Cho., G. Benson (org.)
—Ord   **C.LX 1572**
(Vaughan Williams: Come holy Spirit)
(† English Church Music, Vol. III)

Saraband (in modo elegiaco) organ
(from 5 pieces, 1953)
A. Wyton   in ♯ **ASK. 6**
(Sweelinck, Bach, Stanley, etc.)

(A) Spotless rose (mediaeval, Anon.)
M. Bevan (B) & St. Paul's Cath. Cho.
—Dykes Bower   **C.LX 1619**
(Sweelinck: Hodie Christus natus est)
(in ♯ CX 1193; Angel. 35138, in set 3516)

HUBAY, Jenö (1858-1937)

Hungarian Csárda Scenes vln. & pf. (or orch.)
... Nos. 2, Op. 13; 3, Op. 18 (Hungarian Rhapsody)
6, Op. 34; 7, Op. 41
Michel & His Gypsy Ens.   ♯ **Rom.RR 5**

... No. 4, Op. 32 (Hejre Kati)
H. Zacharias & R.I.A.S. Sym.—Fricsay
PV. 72489
(Sarasate)   *(♭ Pol. 30089)*
J. Shermont & O. Schulhof   ♯ **Rem.YV 2**
(Bériot & Raff)

— ARR. ORCH.
Orch.—Voorhees (in ♯ Alld. 3001: ♭ *EP 3001*; ♯ *MTW.* 573)
Berlin Sym.—Liebe (♭ *Od.OBL 1023*)
J. Schmied Orch. (in ♯ *Vien.LPR 1031*)
Royale Concert Orch. (in ♯ Roy. 1566)

(The) Zephyr, Op. 30, No. 5 vln. & pf.
D. Oistrakh & pf. *(USSR. 10501)*
☆ R. Ricci (♭ *AmVox.VIP 45340*)
— ARR. ORCH. J. Schmied Orch. (in ♯ *Vien.LPR 1031*)

HUBEAU, Jean (b. 1918)

Sonata, tpt. & pf.
L. Menardi & M. Lenom   in ♯ *D.LX 3132*
(♯ Lon.LS 988)

HUBER, Hans (1852-1921)

COLLECTION
MUSIK ZU EINEM FESTSPIEL 1892
(Kleinbasler Gedenkfeier—Wackernagel)
Leise rauscht der Strom dahin	S. & orch.
Gesang der Schar der Wächter	Male cho. & orch.
Reigen und Tanzlied	S, T & orch.
Lied der Greif	B & orch.
Hären	Male cho. & orch.
Rebhaus	T, Male cho. & orch.
Wohlauf mit jungem Mute	Boys' cho. & orch.

DER BASLER BUND 1901
(Gedenkfeier zum Eintritt Basels in dem Schweizerbund
—Wackernagel)
March, A minor	orch.
Einzug der Zünfte	orch.

M. Stader (S), F. Gruber (T), D. Olsen (B),
Basle Liedertafel Cho., Basle Gesangverein,
Gymnasium Boys' Cho. & Sym. Orch.
—H. Münch   ♯ *Phi.N 00738R*
(Suter)

HÜE, Georges (1858-1948)

SONGS: COLLECTION
L'Âne blanc (Klingsor)
À des oiseaux (Adenis)
Sonnez les matines (Alexandre)
R. Doria (S), S. Gouat (pf.)   ♭ *Plé.P 45140*
(Delibes & Koechlin)

HUMFREY, Pelham (1647-1674)

SEE: † HISTORY OF MUSIC IN SOUND (52)
† ENGLISH CHURCH MUSIC, III

HUMMEL, Jan Nepomuk (1778-1837)

Concerto, A minor, Op. 85, pf. & orch.
☆ A. Balsam & Winterthur Sym.—Ackermann
♯ Nix.CLP 1311
(Clementi: Sonata)   *(♯ CHS.CHS 1241)*

Quartet, G major, Op. 30, No. 2 strings
Hollywood Qtt.   ♯ **Cap.P 8316**
(Schumann)

Rondo, E flat major, Op. 11 ("Rondo favori") pf.
— ARR. VLN. & PF.
Z. Grach & pf. (USSR. 021394)

Septet, D minor, Op. 74
pf., fl., ob., hrn., vla., vlc., cbs.
☆ F. Holetschek & ensemble   ♯ Nix.WLP 5018

♯ = Long-playing, 33⅓ r.p.m.   ♭ = 45 r.p.m.   ♮ = Auto. couplings, 78 r.p.m.

HUMPERDINCK, Engelbert (1854-1921)

HÄNSEL UND GRETEL Opera 3 Acts 1893
COMPLETE RECORDINGS

Casts		Set B	Set C
Hänsel	...	E. Grümmer (M-S)	G. Litz (M-S)
Gretel	...	E. Schwarzkopf (S)	R. Streich (S)
Father	...	J. Metternich (B)	H. Günter (B)
Mother	...	M. v. Ilosvay (M-S)	M. Schech (M-S)
Witch	...	E. Schürhoff (M-S)	R. Fischer (M-S)
Sandman	}	A. Felbermayer (S)	{E. Lindermeier (S)
Dew Fairy	}		{B. Brückmann (S)

Set B with Loughton High School & Bancrofts' School Chos. & Philharmonia Orch.—
  Karajan   ♯ C.CX 1096/7
(4ss) (♯ FCX 286/7: QCX 10048/9; Angel. 35049/50,
  set 3506; G.LALP 207/8)

Set C with Wittelsbach School Cho., Bavarian Radio Female Cho. & Munich Phil. Orch.
  —Lehmann   ♯ Pol. 18217/8
(4ss) (also ♯ Pol. 19007/8: autos ♯ 18215/6: 19005/6)
[Excerpts on ♭ Pol. 32092, ♭ 32108, ♭ 30138]

Dresden State Op. Co.—Schreiber   ♯ Roy. 1518/9
(4ss)

☆ Soloists, Boys' Cho., Berlin Radio Sym.—Rother
                              (♯ MTW. 554/5)

Excerpts, from film sound track (♯ X.LXA 1013)

Vocal Selection
  R. Koffmane, R. Lande, S. Schöner, M. Aarden,
  E-M. Michels, Berlin Municipal Opera—Martin
                              ♯ T.TW 30033

Orchestral Suite:
Overture, Preludes Acts II & III, Pantomime, Waltz, Finale

Covent Garden—Hollingsworth ♯ P.PMC 1010
(Grieg: Sigurd Jorsalfar)   (♯ MGM.E 3072)
(Dream Pantomime only in ♯ MGM.E 3124; Prelude,
  Act II, only, in ♯ MGM.E 3177)

Overture
B.B.C.—Sargent (2ss)   G.DB 21591
(Sibelius: Finlandia on ♭ 7ER 5029: 7ERQ 115)

N.B.C.—Toscanini   ♯ Vic.LRM 7014
(Hérold & Liadov)   (♭ set ERB 7014; ItV.A72R 0008)
(also in ♯ Vic. set LM 6026 & ♯ FV.A 330210)

Hamburg Philharmonia—H-J. Walther
                              MSB. 78051
☆ Saxon State—Böhm (♭ BB.ERAB 6; ♯ BB.LBC 1048:
                              ♭ set WBC 1048)
Orch.—Stokowski(G.DB4332: ♭ 7ER5016: 7RF/RQ 271)

— ARR. BAND
Colombia Concert Band—Gould (in ♯ AmC.AL 57:
                              ♭ set A 1108)

Suse, liebe Suse . . .
Brüderchen, komm, tanz' mit mir 2 S. Act I
☆ E. Berger & M. L. Schilp (♭ Ura.UREP 47 from set)

— ARR. CHO.
Obernkirchen Children's Cho. (in ♯ Od.OLA 1011)

Der kleine Sandmann bin ich S
Abends will ich schlafen gehen 2 S. Act II
(Abendsegen: Evening Prayer)
☆ E. Berger & H. Erdmann (♭ Ura.UREP 47, from set)

. . . Abendsegen, only
C. Lynch (T, Eng) & pf. (in ♯ AmC.RL 3016)

— — ARR. CHO.
Obernkirchen Children's Cho. (Od.O-29006: ♭ OBL 29006:
                              in ♯ OLA 1011)

— — ARR. ORGAN R. Ellsasser (in ♯ MGM.E 3031)
              V. Fox (♭ AmC.A 1594)

— — ARR. BAND Allentown Band—Meyer(♭ WFB.WH 1204E)

Dream Pantomime orch. Act II
Anon. Orch. (in ♯ Jay. 3004)

☆ L.P.O.—Collins (♯ D.LW 5025)
Philharmonia—Weldon (♭ C.SCDW 105)
Nat. Sym. (Washington)—Kindler (in ♯ Cam.CAL 175:
                              & in ♯ set CFL 103)
Vienna Radio—Nilius (in ♯ MH. 33-118)

— ARR. 4 PFS. Manhattan Pf. Qtt. (in ♯ MGM.E 3130)

[1] Concert version, 1955.

SONGS
Weihnachten (Wette)
☆ E. Schumann-Heink (A) (in ♯ Vic.LCT 1158)
Wiegenlied (Ebeling)
Regensburg Cath. Cho.—Schrems   T.A 11602
(Brahms: Sandmännchen) [pf. acc.]   (♭ U 45602)

HUNT, Thomas (fl. 1600)
SEE: † TRIUMPHS OF ORIANA

IBERT, Jacques (b. 1890)

Capriccio orch. 1938
☆Winterthur Sym.—Swoboda ♯ Nix.WLP 5061
(Divertissement & Suite)

Carignane bsn. & pf. 1954
M. Allard & F. Gobet   ♭ Pat.G 1055
(Bitsch, Oubradous, Bloch, etc.)

(Le) Chevalier errant Ballet 1934 (f.p. 1950)
Epopée chorégraphique after Cervantes (Arnoux)
J. Davy & O. Mallet (speakers), R. Gardes (T),
M. Roux (Bs), French Nat. Radio Cho. &
Orch.—Tzipine[1]   ♯ C.FCX 435

(La) Cirque
Royal Phil.—Hollingsworth   ♯ MGM.E 3207
(Previn: Ring around the rosy)
[From sound-track of film Invitation to the Dance]

CONCERTOS
Flute & orch. 1913
☆ P. L. Graf & Winterthur Sym.—Desarzens (♯ Clc. 6212)

Saxophone & orch. 1934
(Concerto da camera)
M. Mule & Paris Phil.—Rosenthal
                              ♯ DCap.CCL 7524
(Debussy)   (♯ Cap.L 8231)
Anon. Soloist & Allegro Cha. Orch. ♯ Allo. 4058
(Kodály)

Divertissement cha. orch. 1930
Paris Cons.—Désormière   ♯ D.LXT 2868
(Chopin)   (♯ Lon.LL 884)
Hallé—Barbirolli   ♯ G.ALP 1244
(Fauré)
Concert Arts—Slatkin   ♯ DCap.CTL 7069
(Saint-Saëns)   (♯ Cap.P 8270)
☆ Winterthur Sym.—Swoboda   ♯ Nix.WLP 5061
(above & below)

Escales Suite, orch. 1922
Philadelphia—Ormandy   ♯ AmC.ML 4983
(Chabrier, Debussy, Ravel)
Detroit Sym.—Paray   ♯ Mer.MG 50056
(Chabrier & Ravel)
☆ N.Y.P.S.O.—Rodzinski   ♯ C.C 1027
(Milhaud)   (idem & Bizet on ♯ AmC.RL 6629)
☆ Sym.—Stokowski (♯ Vic.LM 9029)

(10) HISTOIRES pf.
1. La Meneuse de tortues d'or
2. Le Petit Âne blanc
3. Le Vieux Mendiant
4. A Giddy Girl
5. Dans la maison triste
6. Le Palais abandonné
7. Bajo la mesa
8. La Cage de cristal
9. La Marchande d'eau fraiche
10. Le Cortège de Balkis
M. Pressler   ♯ P.PMC 1027
(Debussy)   (♯ MGM.E 3042)

Louisville Concerto orch. 1953
Louisville—Whitney   ♯ LO. 5
(Luening & Read)
(Cowell & Creston on ♯ AmC.ML 5039)

(3) Pièces brèves fl., ob., cl., bsn., hrn. 1921
Copenhagen Wind Quintet   ♯ D.LXT 2803
(Bozza & Nielsen)   (♯ Lon.LL 734)
Chicago Sym. Quintet   ♯ Aphe.AP 15
(Hindemith, Milhaud)

(continued on next page)

(3) Pièces brèves (continued)

Fredonia Faculty Quintet   ♯ Fred. 2
(Marvel, Persichetti, Debussy, etc.)

☆ French Radio Quintet   ♯ C.FCX 219
(Hindemith, Milhaud)

Quartet fl., ob., cl. & bsn.[1]
Garde Républicaine Wind Quartet
(Milhaud & Pierné)   ♯ D.FA 143659

Song: Berceuse du petit Zébu (Nino)
Alauda Cho.—Chailley   in ♯ SM. 33-07

Suite Élisabéthaine S, cho., orch. 1942[2]
☆ E. Loose, Akademie Cha. Cho. & Vienna Sym.
—Swoboda (above)   in ♯ Nix.WLP 5061

Symphonie concertante ob. & cha. orch. 1948-9
P. Pierlot & Paris Cha.—Oubradous
Trio vln., vlc., hp. 1944
R. Charmy, Bartsch & Jacqueline Ibert[3]
    ♯ Pat.DTX 167

IMBRIE, Andrew Welsh (b. 1921)

Quartet, B flat major strings 1942
Juilliard Qtt.   ♯ AmC.ML 4844
(Mennin)

INDIA, Sigismondo d' (fl. 1607-1627)

SEE: † Canzone Scordate

INDY, Vincent d' (1851-1931)

FERVAAL, Op. 40 Opera, 3 Acts 1897
Introduction to Act I
Westminster Sym.—Fistoulari ♯ P.PMC 1011
(below & Dukas)   (♯ MGM.E 3062; Od.ODX 153)

Istar, Op. 42 Symph. variations orch. 1896
Westminster Sym.—Fistoulari ♯ P.PMC 1011
(above)   (♯ MGM.E 3062; Od.ODX 153)
Concerts Colonne—Sebastian   ♯ Ura. 7115
(Rimsky)   (♯ MTW. 564)

Poème des montagnes, Op. 15 Suite, pf. 1881
  1. Le Chant des bruyères
  2. Danses rythmiques
  3. Plein-air
Z. Petit   V♯ CdM.LDY 8086

Suite, D major, Op. 24 tpt., 2 fl., str. qtt. 1886
H. Glantz, J. Baker, C. Monteux & Guilet
Qtt.   ♯ MGM.E 3096
(Saint-Saëns: Septet)

Symphonie sur un chant montagnard français, Op. 25
"Symphonie cévenole" orch. & pf. 1886
A. Ciccolini & Paris Cons.—Cluytens
    ♯ C.CX 1190
(Franck)   (♯ FCX 213; Angel. 35104)
J. Doyen & Lamoureux—Fournet
    ♯ Phi.N 00233L
(Saint-Saëns)   (♯ Epic.LC 3096)
H. Boschi & Czech Phil.—Šejna ♯ Sup.LPM 90
(2ss)   (♯ U. 5078C)
F. Jacquinot & Westminster Sym.—Fistoulari
    ♯ P.PMC 1015
(Saint-Saëns)   (♯ MGM.E 3068)
☆ R. Casadesus & N.Y.P.S.O.—Münch ♯ C.CX 1118
(Franck)   (♯ FCX 119)

Symphony No. 2, B flat major, Op. 57 orch. 1902-3
☆ San Francisco Sym.—Monteux   ♯ Vic.LCT 1125
    (♭ set WCT 1125)

(13) Tableaux de voyage, Op. 31 pf. 1888
... Nos. 4, 5, 6, 8
☆ V. d'Indy (from a piano roll) (in ♯ Roy. 1573 & ♯ 1402)

FOLK SONG SETTINGS 1930
Cadet Roussel, Op. 100, No. 5
French Scout Cho.—Gouge   in V♯ Era.LDE 1026
Compère Guillery, Op. 100, No. 6
Velona Cho.—Vranken   ♭ G.7EPH 1013
(Debussy, Pierné, Poulenc)
Le Roi Loÿs, Op. 90, No. 1
Vocal Ens.—P. Caillard   in V♯ Era.LDE 1013

INFANTE, Manuel (b. 1883)

(3) Danzas andaluzas 2 pfs. 1921
... No. 1, Ritmo; No. 2, Gracia
☆ J. & A. Iturbi   in ♯ Vic.LM 9018

Guadalquivir pf. pub. 1925
A. Iturbi   ♯ Vic.LRM 7038
(below; Milhaud & Nepomuceno) (♭ set ERB 7038;
    ItV.A72R 0055)

Pochades Andalouses pf. pub. 1925
  1. Danse gitane   3. Canto flamenco
  2. Âniers sur la route de Séville 4. Tientos
A. Iturbi   ♯ Vic.LM 1788
(Granados, Turina, Albeniz, etc.) (♯ FV.A 630231)
[Nos. 2 & 3 only on ♭ERA 198; FV.A 95215]
... No. 4 ☆ G. Copeland (in ♯ MGM.E 3025)

Sevillanas pf. 1922
J. Iturbi   ♯ Vic.LRM 7038
(above)   (♭ set ERB 7038; ItV.A72 0055)
E. Osta   in ♯ Allo. 3151

(El) Vito pf. 1922
  1. Variations sur un thème populaire
  2. Danse originale
L. Pennario   in ♯ DCap.CTL 7054
(Albeniz, Granados, etc.)   (♯ Cap.P 8190)
R. Spivak (2ss)   ArgV. 11-8619
— ARR. VOICE, CASTANETS & DANCING
P. Lopez, etc. (in ♯ G.LCLP 102)

INGEGNERI, Marc' Antonio (c. 1545-1592)

Ecce quomodo moritur Responsory[4] T, T, B, B.
☆ Gregorian Inst. Cho.—Vitry   in ♯ GIOA.PM-LP 1
(† Polyphonic Masters)

O bone Jesu 4 vv.
Vienna Boys' Cho.—Brenn in ♯ EPhi.NBR 6013
(Palestrina, Victoria, Verdi, A. Scarlatti, etc.)
    (♯ Phi.N 00624R & AmC.ML 4873)

O Domine Jesu Christe
Treviso Cath. Cho.—d'Alessi
    ♯ E. & AmVox.PL 8610
(† Motets of the Venetian School II)

Tenebrae factae sunt 4 vv.
Darlington Seminary Cho.—Flask
    in ♯ GIOA.DS 1

IPPOLITOFF-IVANOFF, Michael Michaelovitch (1859-1935)

Armenian Rhapsody, Op. 48 orch. 1895
Moscow Radio—Nyazi   ♯ Kings. 271
(Rimsky-Korsakov)
(Borodin & Nyazi on ♯ Csm.CRLP 10030)

Caucasian Sketches, Op. 10 orch. 1894
Philharmonia—Kletzki   ♯ C.CX 1167
(Borodin) (Tchaikovsky on ♯ C.FCX 356; Angel. 35145)
Los Angeles Phil.—Wallenstein ♯ B.AXTL 1062
(Borodin & Enesco) (♯ D.UAT 273577; AmD.DL 9727)
N.Y.P.S.O.—Mitropoulos   ♯ EPhi.NBL 5015
(Borodin) (♯ AmC.CL 751: o.n. ML 4815: ♭ A 1824;
    Phi.N 02107L)

---

[1] Perhaps arrangement of the Qtt. for 2 fl., cl., bsn., 1923.
[2] From Inc. Music to a production of Shakespeare's A Midsummer Night's Dream. Four of the 9 movements are based on themes by Blow, Gibbons, J. Bull & Purcell.   [3] Recorded 1944.   [4] Attributed to Palestrina

Caucasian Sketches (*continued*)

Vienna Pro Musica—Gräf   ♯ AmVox.PL 8770
(*Tchaikovsky*) (Nos. 2, 3, 4 only, ♭ *VIP 45540*)

London Phil. Sym.—Rodzinski
(1½ss—*Borodin*)   ♯ West.LAB 7039

☆ Philharmonia—Schüchter   ♯ P.PMC 1003
(*Rimsky & Tchaikovsky*)   (♯ MGM.E 3022)
[No. 4 only, in ♯ MGM.E 3046]

☆ Boston Prom.—Fiedler (♯ Cam.CAL 176)
Austrian Sym.—Wöss (♭ *Cum.ECR 61; Rem.REP 101;*
No. 4 only, in ♯ Ply. 12-89)

... Nos. 2, 3, 4 only
Berlin Sym.—Rubahn   ♯ Roy. 1530
(*Bizet & Haydn*)   (& ♯ Roy. 1870)

... No. 2, In the Village, only
Decca Little Sym.—Mendoza (in ♯ AmD.DL 5211:
▽ in *set A 90*; ♯ D.US 223524)
USSR. State—Orlov (*USSR. 9699/700*)

... No. 4, Procession of the Sardar, only
Regent Sym. (in ♯ Rgt. 7002)
H. René Orch. (♭ *Cam.CAE 170*)

☆ Chicago Sym.—Stock (in ♯ AmC.RL 3022)
Philharmonia—Weldon (in ♯ C.SX 1032; ♭ *SCD 2024*)
Philadelphia—Stokowski (in ♯ Cam.CAL 123)

Song of Ossian, Op. 56   orch.
Moscow Radio—Golovanov   ♯ Kings. 272[1]
(*Balakirev*)   (♯ *USSR.D 1744/5*, 2ss)
(*Borodin*, on ♯ Csm.CRLP 205)

SONG
In the silence of the night   (Maikov)
A. Pirogov (B)   USSRM.D 00956
(*Varlamov & Arensky*)

(The) SPY   Opera   1912
Erekle's Aria
V. Kilchevsky (T)   USSRM.D 001128
(*Tchaikovsky, Rachmaninoff*)

IRELAND, John (b. 1879)

Concertino pastorale   str. orch.   1939
M.G.M. Str. Orch.—I. Solomon
(*Britten*)   ♯ MGM.E 3074

(A) Downland Suite   Band   1932
... Minuet   — ARR. STR. ORCH.
Boyd Neel Str. Orch.   ♯ D.LW 5149
(*Warlock*)   (♯ Lon.LD 9170)

(A) GARLAND FOR THE QUEEN
(with Bliss, Bax, Tippett, etc.)   1953
... The Hills   (Kirkup)
Cambridge Univ. Madrigal Soc. & Golden Age
Singers—Ord   in † ♯ C.CX 1063

PIANO MUSIC COLLECTIONS

Amberley Wild Brooks	1924
Month's Mind	1933
Prelude, E flat major	1924
Rhapsody	1915
Sarnia	1940-41

E. Parkin   ♯ Argo.RG 28

Decorations	1913
London Pieces	1917-20
Sonata, E minor	1920

E. Parkin (? n.v.)   ♯ Argo.RG 4

SONG: Sea fever   (Masefield)   1913
R. Standen (B), F. Stone (pf.)
in ♯ West.WLE 103
(*Mallinson, Davidson, Warlock, etc.*)

ISAAC, Heinrich (c. 1450-1517)

INSTRUMENTAL CHANSONS   [DTÖ XXVIII]
Chanson   [51]
La la hö hö   [23]
Innsbruck, ich muss dich lassen   [22]
Basle Schola Viol Ens.   G.HMS 31
(† History of Music in Sound)   (in ♯ Vic. set LM 6016)

La Martinella   [24]
R. Graindorge (cor ang.) & 2 bsns
♯ LOL.OL 50104
(† Musiciens de la Cour de Bourgogne I)   (♯ OL.LD 80)

Hélas, que deuera mon coeur   [15]
☆ Viol Trio—Cape (in † ♯ HS.AS 4)

VOCAL
COLLECTIONS (CHORAL)
[References to DTÖ XXVIII, except where otherwise stated]
Jubilate
Innsbruck, ich muss dich lassen   [12]
Ich stand an einem Morgen   [10]
Zwischen Berg und tiefem Tal   (Deutsches Lied)   [22]
Mein Freud' allein   [14]
Mein Lieb' war jung   3 vv.
Es wollt' ein Mädlein grasen gahn   [7]
Ami souffré   (Französisches Lied)   [DTÖ XXXII-2]
Greiner, Zanker, Schnöpfitzer   [9]
Vienna Academy Cho.—Grossmann
(*Handl*)   ♯ West.WL 5347

Chant de Pâques: Christus is opgestanden   [3]
Chanson tendre: Tmeiskin was jonck   [DTÖ XXXII-1]
Chant de l'adieu: Innsbruck, ich muss dich lassen   [12]
☆ Vocal Ens.—Raugel (in † ♯ HS.AS 5)

Et qui la dira   4 vv.   [DTÖ XXXII-13]
Pro Musica Antiqua—Cape   ♯ HP.APM 14032
(† Chansons from the Music Books. . . .)

Innsbruck, ich muss dich lassen
Trapp Family Cho.—Wasner in ♯AmD.DL 9759
(as: Herr Gott lass dich erbarmen)

E. Brems (A, *Dan*), P. Alsfelt (org.)[2] G.DA 5285
(*Berggren: Here we'll wait in silence*)
☆ F. Peeters (org.) (in † ♯ Cpt.MC 20069)

Missa Carminum   Folk-song Mass   c. 1500
(pub. 1541)
Vienna Academy Cha. Cho.—Grossmann
♯ West.WL 5215

IVANOV, Mikhael M. (8849-1927)
SEE: † CHORAL MASTERPIECES FROM THE RUSSIAN LITURGY

IVANOV, Yanis Andreyevich (b. 1906)

Symphony No. 6, E minor   1949
Latvian Radio—Vigner   ♯ USSR.D 013/4

IVES, Charles Edward (1874-1954)

SONGS
COLLECTIONS

Abide with me	(Lyte)	1890
Walking	(Ives)	1902
Where the eagle	(M. P. Turnbull)	1900
Disclosure		?1921
The White gulls	(Morris)	?1921
Two little flowers	(H. T. Ives)	1921
The Greatest men	(Collins)	1921
The Children's hour	(Longfellow)	1901
Berceuse	(Ives)	1900
Ann Street	(Morris)	1921
General William Booth enters heaven	(Lindsay)	1914
Autumn	(H. T. Ives)	1908
Swimmers	(Untermeyer)	1915
Evening	(Milton)	1921
Harpalus	(Percy)	1902
Tarrant Moss	(Kipling)	1902
Serenity	(Whittier)	1919
At the river	(Lowry)	1916
The Seer	(Ives) Song version	1920
Maple leaves	(Aldrich)	1920
"1, 2, 3"	(Ives)	1921
Tom sails away	(Ives)	1917
He is there!	(Ives)	1917
In Flanders fields	(McCrae)	1919

H. Boatwright (S), J. Kirkpatrick (pf.)
♯ Over.LP 7

---

[1] Also listed as Kings. 281.   [2] Sung to Danish words (Hammerich), *Now fields and meadows rest*

SONGS (continued)

When stars are in the quiet skies (Bulwer Lytton) 1891
Tolerance (Hadley) 1909
A night thought (Moore) 1895
At the river (Lowry) 1916
At sea (Johnson) 1921
A Christmas carol (Trad.) 1900
Walt Whitman (Whitman) 1921
Mists (H. T. Ives) 1910
I'll not complain (Dwight, after Heine)
In summer fields (Chapman, after Allmer) 1900
At parting (Petersen) 1889
    J. Greissle (S), J. Wolman (pf.)   ♯ **SPA. 9**
    (*Revueltas*)

Charlie Rutlage (Cowboy Song) 1921
    ▽ R. Symonette (Bs) (in ♯ Csm.CLPS 1008)

SYMPHONIES
No. 2 1902
    Vienna Philharmonia—Adler   ♯ **SPA. 39**

No. 3 1901-11
    Baltimore Little Sym.—Stewart ♯ **Van.VRS 468**
    (*Donovan*)

Three Places in New England orch. 1903-14
    A.R.S. Orch.—Hendl   ♯ **ARS. 27**
    (*McBride*)
    (*McBride, Swanson & Diamond on* ♯ ARS. 116)

JACINTO, Frey (fl. XVIIIth Cent.)
    SEE: † PORTUGUESE KEYBOARD MUSIC

JACOBI, Frederick (1891-1952)

Music Hall Overture orch. 1948-9
    Vienna State Philharmonia—Adler ♯ **SPA. 47**
    (*Antheil, North, etc.*)

JACOPO da BOLOGNA (XIVth Cent.)
    SEE: † ANTHOLOGIE SONORE
          † MADRIGALS & CACCIE

JACOPONE da TODI (d. 1306)
    SEE: † MONUMENTA ITALICAE MUSICAE

JÄRNEFELT, Armas (b. 1869)

Berceuse, G minor orch. (*Kehtolaulu*)
    Orch.—Godzinsky   *Ryt.R 6144*
    (*Merikanto: Valse lente*)

— ARR. VLN. & PF.
    G. Barinova & pf.   ♯ *USSR.D 1186*
    (*Chaminade, Wieniawski, etc.*)

Praeludium orch.
    ☆ Suisse Romande—Olof (in ♯ D.LW 5034; Lon.LD 9049)

(The) SONG OF THE FLAME-RED FLOWER
    Film Music
Excerpts
    ☆ Sym. Orch.—Järnefelt (Od.PLDX 2)

SONGS & PART SONGS
(The) Grasshopper (*Sirkka*)
(The) Sun went down into the sea (*Pois meni merehen päivä*)
    Helsinki Acad. Cho.   *Ryt.R 6069*
(The) Wave's lullaby (*Aallon kehtolaulu*) (Asp)
    A. Rautawaara (S) & Orch.   *Ryt.R 6135*
    (*Madetoja: Song*)

JAMES, Philip (b. 1890)

Symphony No. 1 1943
    Vienna Philharmonia—Adler   ♯ **SPA. 38**

JANÁČEK, Leoš (1854-1928)

Concertino pf., 2 vlns., 2 cl.[1], hrn., bsn. 1925
    F. Holetschek, Barylli Ens.   ♯ **West.WL 5333**
    (*below*)
    R. Firkusny, Philadelphia Ens. ♯ **AmC.ML 4995**
    (*below*)

Diary of one who disappeared (Anon.) 1916-19
    E. Häfliger (T), C. C. Meyer (M-S), (*Ger*);
    F. de Nobel (pf.)[2]   ♯ *EPhi.ABR 4041*
    (♯ *Phi.A 00731R; Epic.LC 3121*)

Dumka vln. & pf. 1880
    W. Barylli & F. Holetschek   ♯ **West.WL 5333**
    (*above & below*)

PIANO MUSIC
COLLECTION
By overgrown tracks (10 pieces) 1902-8
Sonata 1-x-1905
In the mist 1912
    R. Firkusny   ♯ **AmC.ML 4740**

By overgrown tracks (10 pieces) 1902-8
    G. Radhuber   ♯ **SPA. 62**
    I. Hurník (6ss)   ♮ **U.H 24470/2**

OPERAS
FROM THE HOUSE OF THE DEAD 3 Acts
1930 (*Z mrtvého domu*)
COMPLETE RECORDING in *German* (ed. Bakala)

A. P. Gorjančikov	S. Jongsma (B)
Aljeja...	C. Scheffer (T)
F. Morozov (alias	
L. Kuzmič)	J. v. Mantgem (T)
Commandant ...	... G. Holthaus (Bs)
Skuratov	Z. Wozniak (T)
Čekunov	G. Genemans (B)
Šapkin	C. Reumer (T)
Šiškov	C. Broecheler (B)
Čerevin	J. Voogt (T)
Kedril	C. Reumer (T)
Prisoners, etc.	S. v. Trirum (T), P. Gorin (B)
	C. Taverne (T), C. v. Woerkom (T)
Prostitute	J. v. d. Meent (A)
Sergeant of Watch ...	G. Smith (T)
Don Juan	P. Gorin (B)

etc., Netherlands Op. Cho. & Orch.
    —Krannhals   ♯ **Phi.A 00229/30L**
    (4ss)   (♯ Epic. set SC 6005)
    [Recorded at Holland Festival, July 1954]

HER FOSTER-DAUGHTER 3 Acts 1904
(*Jeji Pastorkyna: "Jenůfa"*)
COMPLETE RECORDING

Grandmother	
Buryjovka ...	M. Čadikovičková (A)
Laca Klemeň ...	B. Blachut (T)
Steve Buryja... ...	I. Žídek (T)
Kustelnitchka ...	M. Krásová (A)
Jenůfa	S. Jelínková (S)
The Miller ...	K. Kalaš (B)
Miller's wife ...	... M. Veselá (M-S)
Karolka ...	M. Musilová (M-S)
Barena ...	M. Fidlerová (S)

etc., Prague Nat. Theatre Cho. & Orch.—Vogel
    (6ss)   ♯ **Sup.SLPV 160/2**
    (4ss, ♯ Csm.CRLP 239/40)   (♯ U. 5139/41G)

(6) Lashian Dances orch. 1889-90
    Brno Radio—Bakala   ♯ **Sup.LPV 201**
    (*Slavický*)   (♯ U. 5182G)

Quartet, Strings, No. 2 "Intimate pages" 1927-8
    Galimir Qtt.   ♯ **Strad.STR 619**
    (*Dvořák*)
    Smetana Qtt. (2ss)   ♯ *Eta.LPM 1012*

Sinfonietta orch. 1926
    Vienna Phil.—Kubelik   ♯ *D.LW 5213*
    (♯ Lon.LD 9223)

Sonata, vln. & pf. 1914
    W. Barylli & F. Holetschek   ♯ **West.WL 5333**
    (*above*)
    R. Druian & J. Simms   ♯ **Mer.MG 80001**
    (*Enesco*)

---

[1] Or vla. & cl.; this is probably the version recorded.   [2] Recorded at the Holland Festival, 1954.

Suite, Str. Orch. 1877
Taras Bulba Orch. Rhapsody 1918
☆ Vienna Sym.—Swoboda   ♯ Nix.WLP 5071
(& with *Smetana* on ♯ West.WN 18069)

Youth Suite, wind insts. 1924
Philadelphia Wind Quintet   ♯ AmC.ML 4995
(*above*)

JANIEWICZ, Feliks (1762-1848)
SEE: † FOUR CENTURIES OF POLISH MUSIC

JANNEQUIN, Clément (*c.* 1475-1560)

SEE ALSO: † ANTHOLOGIE SONORE

CHANSONS
COLLECTIONS
Il estoit une fillette
Petite nymphe folâtre
La Guerre (La Battaille de Marignan)
Las! pauvre coeur
Le Chant des oyseaulx
Ma peine n'est pas grande
Au joly jeu
Pro Musica Antiqua—Cape   ♯ HP.APM 14042
(*Gastoldi*)

L'Amour, la mort et la vie
Il estoit une fillette
Ma peine n'est pas grande
Vocal Ens.—Lamy   ♯ LOL.OL 50027
(† Parisian Songs)   (♯ OL.LD 76)

Ce sont gallans
Le Chant de l'alouette   (with Claude le jeune)
Le Chant des oyseaulx
Or, viens ça
R. Blanchard Ensemble   ♯ Phi.N 00993/4R
(† French Chansons)

Le Chant des oyseaulx Cho.—Expert
Au joly jeu
Ce moys de May Cho.—Opienski
☆ in † V♯ AS. 1805LD & ♯ HS.AS 6

L'Alouette — ARR. Heydendael
Pancratius Male Cho.—Heydendael
in ♯ C.HS 1001
(*Lassus, Schubert, Milhaud, etc.*)

Ce moys de May
Vocal & Inst. Ens.—Boulanger ♯ B.AXTL 1048
(† French Renaissance Music) (♯ D.FAT 263102;
AmD.DL 9629)
Paris Vocal Ens.—Jouve   ♯ LT.MEL 94007
(† French Madrigals) (V♯ Sel. 190.C.002 & LLA 1079;
♭ T.UV 116)
Hufstader Singers   in ♯ SOT. 1092

Ce sont gallans
Petits Chanteurs de la Renaissance in ♯ CND. 4/5
(† Histoire de la Musique vocale) (& ♯ Era.LDE 3018/9)

(Le) Chant des oyseaulx—Réveillez-vous
Vocal & Inst. Ens.—Boulanger ♯ B.AXTL 1048
(† French Renaissance Music) (♯ D.FAT 263102;
AmD.DL 9629)

Laissez cela
Petite nymphe folâtre
M. Rollin Ens.   ♯ CND. 9
(† La Musique et la Poésie)

JARZEBSKI, Adam (*c.* 1589-1645/9)
SEE: † FOUR CENTURIES OF POLISH MUSIC

JAUBERT, Maurice (1900-1940)

(L') Eau vive Song Cycle (Giono)
... Le Marmitier only ·
☆ J. Jansen (B), L. Laskine (hp.) (♭ D.FA 80501)

JELINEK, Hans (b. 1901)

(4) TOCCATAS, Op. 15, No. 4 pf.
1. T. solenne   3. T. funèbre
2. T. burlesca   4. T. frizzante
A. Jenner   ♯ G.VDLP 301
(*Stravinsky*)

JENKINS, John (1592-1678)

Fancy, G minor 3 viols
B. Lam Ens.   G.HMS 64
(† History of Music in Sound)   (in ♯ Vic. set LM 6031)

Pavane for four viols
Consort of Viols—Leonhardt   ♯ Van.BG 547
(*Locke & Purcell*)

Fancy, C major
Pavane for four viols
Consort of Viols—Leonhardt   ♯ Van.BG 539
(† Elizabethan & Jacobean Music)

JENSEN, Ludwig Irgens (b. 1894)

(The) Drover (*Driftkaren*)
Inc. Music to play by Kinck
Oslo Phil.—Grüner-Hegge   Nera.SK 15539

Partita sinfonica orch. 1937
Oslo Phil.—Grüner-Hegge   NOC. 63150/3
(4ss) (*Braein, Olsen, Eggen, Johansen,* in ♯ Mer.MG 90002)

JEPPESEN, Knud (b. 1892)

Church Bells (Rode) (*Kirkeklokken*)
K.F.U.M. Cho.—G. Jensen   G.X 8168
(*Grundtvig: Give me, Lord, a tongue to sing*)

March Sunshine, Op. 2, No. 10 (Holstein)
K. B. Bruun (S), F. Jensen (pf.)   C.DD 511
(*Nielsen: Summer Song*)

JERSILD, Jørgen (b. 1913)

Music-making in the Forest fl., ob., cl., hrn., bsn.
(At spille i skoven) 1947
E. Thomsen, S. Andreassen, Nehammer,
B. Lüders, A. Bredahl   ♯ C.KC 1
(*Stravinsky: Octet*)

JIMÉNEZ, Jeronimo
SEE: GIMÉNEZ, GERÓNIMO

JOHNSON, Edward (fl. 1600)
SEE: † TRIUMPHS OF ORIANA

JOHNSON, Hunter (b. 1906)

Concerto, pf. & orch. 1935
J. Kirkpatrick & Rochester Cha.—Hull
(*Honegger*)   ♯ CHS.CHS 1189

JOHNSON, Robert (*c.* 1583-1633)

VIRGINALS PIECES
Almain FVB.146
C. J. Chiasson (hpsi.)   ♯ Nix.LLP 8037
(† Elizabethan love songs)   (♯ Lyr.LL 37)
Alman E. Rogers book, 46
T. Dart (hpsi.)   ♯ LOL.OL 50075
(† Masters of Early English Keyboard Music I)

☆ = Re-issue of a recording to be found in previous volumes.

Alman FVB. 147 (ARR. Farnaby)
G. Leonhardt (hpsi.)   # Van.BG 539
(† Elizabethan & Jacobean Music) (# Ama.AVRS 6001)

Alman (unspec.)
C. Aubin   # *Cpt.MC 20111*
(† Guitar Recital II)

Pavan FVB. 39 (ARR. Farnaby)
C. Koenig (hpsi.)   # EMS. 236
(† Elizabethan Keyboard Music)

SONGS
Full fathom five (Shakespeare)
Where the bee sucks (Shakespeare)
A. Deller (C-T), D. Dupré (lute) # G.ALP 1265
(† Shakespeare Songs & Lute Solos)
L. Chelsi (B)   # MTR.MLO 1015
(† Shakespeare Songs, Vol. III)

JOIO, Norman dello (b. 1913)

Epigraph   orch.   1952
A.R.S. Sym.—Swarowsky   # ARS. 31
(*Mennin & Green*)

Serenade for orchestra   1948
A.R.S. Sym.—Swarowsky[1]   # ARS. 36
(*Porter: Vln. Concerto*)

Sonata No. 3   pf.   1947
Del Purves (*Griffes*)   # ML. 7021

Variations and Capriccio vln. & pf. 1943
P. Travers & N. dello Joio   # AmC.ML 4845
(*Bowles*)

JOLIVET, André (b. 1905)

Air de bravoure   tpt. & pf.   1954
R. Delmotte & F. Gobet   ♭ *Pat.G 1054*
(*Pascal, Lesur, Ameleer*)

Chant pour les piroguiers de l'Orénoque
ob. & pf.   1954
P. Pierlot & A. d'Arco   ♭ *Pat.G 1051*
(*Auric, Murgier, Barraud, Planel*)

Concerto, pf. & orch.   1950
[L. Descaves, pf.]
Concertino, tpt., pf. & str. orch.   1948
[R. Delmotte, tpt.; S. Baudo, pf.]
Andante, str. orch.   1934
Champs-Élysées Theatre—Bour
                    # LT.DTL 93014
          (# West.WL 5239; Sel.LAG 1020)

Concerto, harp & orch.   1952
[L. Laskine, hp.]
Concerto, ondes martenot & orch.   1947
[G. Martenot, ondes martenot]
Paris Op. Orch.—Jolivet   # Véga.C30.A3

JONES, Charles (b. 1910)

On the morning of Christ's nativity (Milton)
The Shepherd's Carol (Tate)
Concert Cho.   in # CtyNY.AP 122
(*Carols by Kraehenbuehl, A. Harris, etc.*)

JONES, Richard
          (fl. beginning XVIIIth Cent.)

Allemande, Minuet & Bourrée
Westminster Light—Bridgewater
              in # West.WL 4007

JONES, Robert (c. 1575-1617)

AYRES
(5 books: 1600, 1601, 1608, 1609, 1610)
COLLECTION
Sweet, if you like & love me still (Davison) III
Sweet Kate, of late IV
Though your strangeness (Campian) IV
Pro Musica Antiqua (N.Y.)   # AmC.ML 5051
(† Evening of Elizabethan Verse & Music)

Go to bed, sweet muse III
Sweet Kate, of late IV
H. Cuénod (T) & hpsi.   # Nix.LLP 8037
(† Elizabethan Love Songs)   (# Lyr.LL 37)

Go to bed, sweet muse III
F. Fuller (B) & lute   # EMS. 11
(† Dowland and his contemporaries)
☆ S. Bloch & lute († Renaissance Music) # *Allo. 4043*

Fair Oriana, seeming to wink at folly   1601
Randolph Singers—Randolph
                        in # Nix.WLP 6212-1/2
(† Triumphs of Oriana)   (# West. set WAL 212)

Farewell, dear love   I
S. Bloch (S) & lute   # *CHS.CHS 1225*
(† Music in Shakespeare's time)
L. Chelsi (B)   # MTR.MLO 1015
(† Shakespeare Songs, Vol. III)
☆ Motet & Madrigal Cho.—Opienski (in † # HS.AS 10)

In Sherwood lived stout Robin Hood   III
Primavera Singers, etc.   # *Eso.ESJ 6*
(† Elizabethan Songbag)

JONGEN, Joseph (1873-1953)

Concerto, Op. 127, pf. & orch.   1943
E. del Pueyo & Belgian Nat.—Quinet
                        # *LI.W 91081*
                        (# D.BA 133185)

Danse lente fl. & hp.
J. Roberts & E. Vito   in # Per.SPL 721
(*Bizet, Tournier, Spohr, etc.*)

JORDA, Luis G. (1875-1900) (?)

Danzas nocturnas   pf.
S. Contreras   # *CM. 18*
(*Ponce*)

JOSQUIN DES PRÉS (c. 1450-1521)

Canzona
☆ F. Peeters (org.) (in † # Cpt.MC 20069)

CHANSONS
Bergerette savoysienne   1501
R. Blanchard Ens.   in # *Phi.N 00994R*
(† French Chansons)

Chanson du soldat: Scaramella
☆ Dutch Vocal Qtt.—Raugel   in # HS.AS 5

(El) Grillo   1505
Je ne me puis tenir d'aimer
Pro Musica Antiqua Ens.—Cape   G.HMS 28
(† History of Music in Sound)   (in # Vic. set LM 6016)

Milles regretz
N. Boulanger Ens.   # B.AXTL 1048
(† French Renaissance Music)
          (# D.FAT 263102; AmD.DL 9629)
Ghent Oratorio Soc.—de Pauw   # Eso.ES 514
(† Flemish Choral Music)   (# Cpt.MC 20017)

---

[1] Also stated to be cond. Schönherr.

Se congié prends
☆ Paraphonistes de St. Jean—Van   in # HS.AS 5

Si je perdu mon amy
Recorder Consort of Musicians' Workshop
in # CEd.CE 1018
(† Recorder Music of Six Centuries)
Chapelle de Bourgogne Recorder Trio
in # OL.LD 81
(† Musiciens de la Cour . . .)

Vive le roy
☆ Paraphonistes de St. Jean—Van   in # HS.AS 5

MASSES
Ave Maris Stella
. . . Kyrie & Agnus Dei
☆ Gregorian Inst. Cho.—Vitry   in # GIOA.PMLP 1
(† Polyphonic Masters)

Hercules . . . Kyrie
☆ Paraphonistes de St. Jean—Van   in # HS.AS 5

L'homme armé . . . Sanctus (part)
Schola Polyphonica—Washington   G.HMS 28
(† History of Music in Sound)   (in # Vic. set LM 6016)

Pange lingua
P. Caillard Vocal Ens.   # Era.LDE 2010
[recorded in Church of S. Roch, Paris]

. . . Et incarnatus est
U.S.S.R. State Cho.—Shveshnikov (in # Eta. 730002:
o.n. # LPM 1008 & 1023)

MOTETS
Ave Maria
Paris Vocal Ens.—Jouve   in # LT.MEL 94007
(† French Madrigals) (in V# Sel. 190.C.002 & LLA 1079;
♭ T.UV 116)
Copenhagen Boys' & Men's Cho.—Møller
in # HS.HSL 2071
(† Masterpieces of Music before 1750)
(also in † Histoire de la Musique vocale)
Netherlands Cha. Cho.—de Nobel
in # Phi.N 00678R
(† Sacred & Secular Songs from the Renaissance)
N.Y. Primavera Singers—Greenberg
in # Per.SPL 597
(† Renaissance Music)   (# Cpt.MC 20077)
☆ Dessoff Cho.—Boepple (# Clc. 6203)

. . . Ave vera verginitas
Biggs Family Ens.   in # GIOA.BF 1
(Victoria, Hassler, etc.)
☆ Gregorian Inst. Cho.—Vitry   in # GIOA.PMLP 1
(† Polyphonic Masters)

Ave verum corpus (orig. 3 mixed vv.)
Yale Univ. Divinity School Cho.—Borden
(† Hymns of Praise)   in # Over.LP 2
Welch Chorale   in # Lyr.LL 52
(† Motets of the XVth & XVIth Centuries)

De profundis
☆ Dessoff Cho.—Boepple (# Clc. 6203)

Jesu, tu pauperum refugium
Concordia Cho.—P. J. Christiansen (Eng)
in # Cdia.CDLP 3

Miserere
☆ Paraphonistes de St. Jean—Van   in # HS.AS 5

Quam pulchra es
Cho.—Eckhout   in # OL.LD 81
(† Musiciens de la Cour de Bourgogne II)

Stabat Mater
☆ Paraphonistes de St. Jean—Van   in # HS.AS 5

Tribulatio et angustia
Schola Polyphonica—Washington   G.HMS 28
(† History of Music in Sound)   (in # Vic. set LM 6016)

[1] Thus the Csm. catalogue, not Anosov as in Supp. II.

Tu solus   4 voices
N.Y. Primavera Singers—Greenberg
in # Per.SPL 597
(† Renaissance Music)   (# Cpt.MC 20077)

JOSTEN, Werner (b. 1885)

SONGS: COLLECTION (Songs of 1914-20)
Sumer is icumen in   (Anon.)
Roundelay   (Dryden)
Lied   (Geibel)
The Indian Serenade   (Shelley)
La Partenza delle rondinelle   (Anon.)
Guarda che bianca luna   (Anon.)
W. McGrath (T), W. Josten (pf.)

Die verschwiegend Nachtigall   (Vogelweide)
Die heiligen drei Könige   (Heine)
Hingabe   (Geibel)
Frühlingsnetz   (Eichendorff)
Im Herbst   (Eichendorff)
Weihnachten   (Eichendorff)
S. M. Endich (S), W. Josten (pf.)

Waldeinsamkeit   (Eichendorff)   duet
S. M. Endich (S), W. McGrath (T),
W. Josten (pf.)   # SPA. 34

JULLIEN, Gilles (fl. 1690-1703)
SEE: † FRENCH BAROQUE ORGAN MUSIC

KABALEVSKY, Dmitri (b. 1904)

COLAS BREUGNON, Op. 24   Opera   3 Acts
(The Master of Clamecy)   1938
Orch. Suite
1. Overture   2. Fête populaire
3. Pestilence   4. Insurrection
Philharmonia—Schüchter   # P.PMC 1007
(Prokofiev)   (# MGM.E 3112)
Moscow Radio—Stassevitch   # USSR.D 01158
(Prokofiev)

. . . Nos. 1 & 2 only
Czech Phil.—Kabalevsky   # CdM.LDX 8046
(Prokofiev & Shostakovich) [The Overture is ☆]

. . . No. 1, Overture, only
Bolshoi Theatre—Kabalevsky # Csm.CRLP 173
(Shostakovich: Symphony No. 10)

(The) Comedians, Op. 26   Orch. Suite
(from Inc. Music to Daniel's play)
Berlin Sym.—Guhl   # Ura. 7146
(Borodin, Prokofiev, Shostakovich)
Berlin Radio—Rother   # Ura. 7082
(Dvořák & Prokofiev)   (♭ UREP 36)
[No. 2, Gallop, only in # Ura. 7096]
Dresden Sym.—van Berten   # Roy. 1462
(Stravinsky)   (# Roy. 1829; Var. 69147)
☆ Bolshoi Theatre—Yuriev   # Csm.CRLP 146
(Shostakovich)
. . . No. 2, Gallop
M.G.M. Orch.—Marrow   in # MGM.E 3136
G. Hansen Orch. (G.X 8141)
☆ Prague Variety Theatre—Vlach (in # U. 10001D)
etc.

Concerto No. 2, G minor   pf. & orch.   1936
☆ G. Ginsberg & U.S.S.R. State—Kabalevsky[1]
(Prokofiev)   # Csm.CRLP 186

Concerto, vln. & orch. C major, Op. 48   1948
☆ D. Oistrakh & U.S.S.R. Sym.—Kabalevsky
(2ss)   V# CdM.LDY 8082
(Cello Concerto on # Mon.MWL 330;
Miaskovsky on # USSR.D 489)

Concerto, vlc. & orch. Op. 49
  D. Shafran & Moscow Radio—Kabalevsky
  (2ss)   **V♯ *CdM.LDY 8094***
  (*Vln. Concerto* on ♯ Mon.MWL 330; *Glazounov* on
  ♯ Van.VRS 6005; *Prokofiev* on ♯ USSR.D 0736)
  (& 6ss, *USSR. 21709/14*)

Impromptu, Op. 21, No. 1 vln. & pf.
  I. Oistrakh & I. Kollegorskaya
                          in ♯ Van.VRS 461
  (*Vieuxtemps, Szymanowski, Wieniawski, etc.*)
  D. Oistrakh & pf.   USSR. 022226
  (*Wieniawski: Scherzo tarantelle*)

(24) PRELUDES, Op. 38 pf. *c.* 1946
COMPLETE RECORDING
  N. Reisenberg   ♯ West.WN 18095

... Nos. 6, 8, 13
  J. Haien   ♯ McInt.MC 1006
  (*below*)   (o.n. ♯ WCFM. 18)
... Nos. 1, 2, 4, 14   ☆ J. Flier (in ♯ Csm.CRLP 147)

... No. 6, only
  S. Andersen   in ♯ Oce.OCS 38
  (*Grieg, Messiaen, Rachmaninoff*)

Quartet, Strings, No. 2, G minor, Op. 44
  Naumann Qtt.   ♯ Ura. 7083
  ☆ Beethoven Qtt. (♯ *USSR.D 849/50*)

SONATAS, pf.
No. 2, Op. 45
  J. Haien   ♯ McInt.MC 1006
  (*above & below*)   (o.n. ♯ WCFM. 18)

No. 3, F major, Op. 46
  S. Biro   ♯ Rem. 199-133
  (*Kodály & Bartók*)
  ☆ V. Horowitz (♯ *G.FALP 230*)

Sonatina, C major, Op. 13, No. 1 pf. 1930
  D. Barenboim   ♭ *EPhi.NBE 11014*
  (*Shostakovich*)   (♭ *Phi.N 425009E*)
  J. Haien   ♯ McInt.MC 1006
  (*above*)   (o.n. ♯ WCFM. 18)
  J. Rappaport   ♯ Etu.ER 101
  (*Bartók, Bloch, Hindemith*)
  S. Contreras   ♯ CM. 17
  (*Bartók, Prokofiev, Shostakovich*)

SYMPHONY
No. 2, E minor, Op. 19 1934
  Moscow Radio—Anosov   ♯ Mon.MWL 331
  (*Miaskovsky*)   (2ss, ♯ *USSR.D 1546/7*)

(The) TARAS FAMILY Opera *c.* 1944, rev. 1949
COLLECTED EXCERPTS
  Taras...   ...   ... I. Yashugin (Bs)
  Efrosinia   ... S. Preobrazhenskaya (M-S)
  Stepan   ...   ...   I. Alexiev (B)
  Andrey   ...   ... V. G. Ulyanov (T)
  etc., cho. & orch. of Kirov Theatre, Leningrad
  (4ss)   ♯ CEd. set CE 3004
  [Excerpts on ♯ *USSR.D 1065/6* & *USSR. 019708/9,*
                                     19735/6]

Taras's aria, Sc. 7
  ☆ A. Pirogov (*USSRM.D 00261* also USSR.D 19711)

KALINNIKOV, Basil Sergeivitch
(1866-1901)

Chanson triste pf. (*4 Pieces*, No. 1)
  L. Zyuzin   *USSR. 22302*
  (*Rachmaninoff: Lilacs*)

On the old burial mound (Nikitin)
  M. Reizen (Bs)   *USSR. 20477*
  (*Taneiev: Not the wind*) & *USSRM.D 00865*

SYMPHONIES
No. 1, G minor
  ☆ Moscow Radio—Rakhlin   ♯ USSR.D 0385/6
  (2ss)(♯ Sup.LPV 178; U. 5148G; 10ss, USSR. 022338/47)

No. 2, A major
  Moscow Radio—Rakhlin   ♯ Per.SPL 566
  (2ss)   (4ss, ♯ *USSR.D 526/9*)

KALOMIRIS, Manolis (b. 1883)

Oblivion voice, str. qtt. & pf.
  N. Frangia (M-S), Kolassis Qtt. & E. Nicolaidou
  (*Varvoglis & Skalkottas*) ♯ Phi.N 00247L

SONGS: COLLECTION
The Old Zoë
The Nymph
FOLK SONG ARR.: **Berceuse**
  L. Liotsi (M-S), Z. Vlahopoulou (S),
     E. Nicolaidou (pf.)   ♯ *Phi.N 00744R*
  (*Riadis; & Folk Songs*)

KARAYEV, Kara Abulfaz ogly (b. 1918)

Leili & Medzhnun Sym. Poem, orch.
  U.S.S.R. State—Nyazi   ♯ *USSR.D 1141*
  (*Mazayev*)

(The) Seven Beauties Ballet
... Orch. Suite
  Czech Phil.—Nyazi   ♯ *Sup.LPM 31*
  (*Ravel: Bolero*)   (♯ *U. 5021C*)
  Moscow Radio—Nyazi   ♯ *USSR.D 2233/4*
  (2ss) [Waltz only on USSR. 019356/7]

KARG-ELERT, Sigfrid (1877-1933)

CHORALE-PRELUDES
Herr Jesu Christ, dich zu uns wend, Op. 78, No. 9
  A. Hamme   in ♯ SRS.H 1
  († Organ Recital)
O Gott, du frommer Gott, Op. 65, No. 50
  E. White   in ♯ Moll.E4QP 7231
  (*Pachelbel, Schröder, Bach, Vierne, etc.*)
  J. Harms   in ♯ Uni.UN 1004
  (*Reger, Peeters, Vierne, Raasted, Bach, etc.*)

Landscape in the mist, Op. 96, No. 2
  ☆ C. Snyder (in ♯ Word. W 4003)

(The) Legend of the Mountain, Op. 96, No. 3 org.
  E. White   ♯ Moll.E4QP 3443
  (*Arne, Bach, Fiocco, etc.*)

(The) Mirrored Moon, Op. 96, No. 6 org.
  L. Farnam[1]   in ♯ CEd.CE 1040
  (*Handel, Bach, Vierne, Sowerby*)

KARLOWICZ, Mieczyslaw (1876-1909)

Concerto, A major, Op. 8 vln. & orch. 1902
  G. Barinova & U.S.S.R. State—Kondrashin
                           ♯ Csm.CRLP 190
  (*Szymanowski*)   (2ss, ♯ *USSR.D 500/1*)

Lithuanian Rhapsody, Op. 11 orch. 1906
  Moscow Radio—Stassevitch ♯ USSR.D 01174
  (*Noskowski*)

Serenade, Op. 2 str. orch. 1898
  Warsaw Phil.—Rowicki   *Muza. 2409/12*
  (7ss—*Moniuszko: Verbum Nobile, aria*)

SONGS
From Passion, Op. 3, No. 6 (Wisniewski)
Song to the bright night, Op. 3, No. 4 (Heine, trs. Konopnicka)
Speak to me once more, Op. 3, No. 1 (Tetmajer)
  A. Hiolski (B), J. Lefeld (pf.)   *Muza. 1640*

---

[1] Recorded from an Austin organ roll of 1930; registration & expression by C. Watters.

Beneath the Sycamore
  M. Alexandrovitch (T)   *USSR. 18501*
  (*Smetana: Evening Song*)

My soul is sad, Op. 1, No. 6   (Tetmajer)
  A. Hiolski (B), J. Lefeld (pf.)   *Muza. 1641*
  (*Where the first stars come from*)

Where the first stars come from, Op. 1, No. 2
  (Slowacki)
  A. Hiolski (B), J. Lefeld (pf.)   *Muza. 1641*
  (*My soul is sad*)
  J. Garda (B), V. Makarov (pf.)   *Muza. 2415*
  (*Rachmaninoff*)
  ▽ H. Ottoczko (M-S) (*Muza. 1123*)

Stanislav & Anna Oswięcimowe, Op. 12 orch. 1912
  Warsaw Radio—Rowicki   **Muza. X2406/8**
  (5ss—*Stefani & Fitelberg: Krakowiecyi Gorálo, Over.*)
▽ items include SONGS:
In the snow, Op. 1, No. 3 (Konopnicka) H. Ottoczko (M-S)
  (*Muza. 1123*)
To a sorrowing girl, Op. 1, No. 1 (Glinski)} J. Koplawski (T)
Disappointment, Op. 15, No. 4 (Tetmajer)}   (*Muza. 1037*)
I remember quiet, happy days (Tetmajer) M. Szopski (T)
  (*Muza. 1530*)

KASTALSKY, Alexander D. (1856-1926)

  SEE: † CHORAL MASTERPIECES FROM THE RUSSIAN
      LITURGY

KAY, Hershy (b. 1919)

Western Symphony Ballet 1954
  N.Y. City Ballet Orch.—Barzin
           ♯ AmVox.PL 9050
  (*Thomson: Filling Station*)
... Saturday Night only
  Orch.—Kostelanetz (in ♯ AmC.CL 763 : ♭ set B 763)
ARRANGEMENT: Bergerettes (XVIIIth Cent. Songs)
  L. Pons (S) & Orch.—Kay (♯ *AmC.AL 53*)

KAY, Ulysses Simpson (b. 1917)

Concerto for orchestra 1948
  La Fenice Theatre—Perlea   ♯ **Rem. 199-173**
  (*Lockwood*)

Round Dance & Polka orch.
  New Sym. Cha.—Camarata   ♯ *Lon.LL 1213*
  (*McBride & Mourant*)

Serenade for orchestra f.p. 1954
  Louisville—Whitney   ♯ **LO. 8**
  (*Dallapiccola, Moncayo, Milhaud*)

KEISER, Reinhard (1674-1739)

  SEE: † HISTORY OF MUSIC IN SOUND (49)

KELLER, Homer (b. 1915)

Serenade cl. & str. orch.
  Eastman-Rochester Sym.—Hanson;
  W. Osseck, cl.   ♯ **EMer.MG 40003**
  Barlow, Hanson, Copland, etc.)

KELLY, Robert Emmet (b. 1905)

Patterns S & orch.
  M. J. Paul & Illinois Univ. Sym.—Ansermet
  (*Phillips*)   ♯ **UOI.CRS 4**

KENNAN, Kent (b. 1913)

Night soliloquy fl. & strgs. 1936
  Eastman-Rochester Sym.—Hanson;
  J. Mariano, fl.   ♯ **EMer.MG 40003**
  (*Barlow, Keller, Copland, etc.*)
  ▽ J. Mariano & Eastman-Rochester—Hanson (Vic. 15659)

KERCKHOVEN, Abraham van der (1627-1673)

  SEE: † OLD NETHERLANDS MASTERS

KERLL, Johann Kaspar (1627-1693)

ORGAN MUSIC DT. Bay. II-ii
Capriccio [sul canto del] cúcú (No. 15)
  M. Mason   in ♯ **ASK. 7**
  (*Pachelbel, Bach, etc.*)

Passacaglia (No. 18)
Toccata cromatica (con durezze e ligature) (No. 4)
  G. Leonhardt   in ♯ **Van.BG 529**
  († XVIIth Century Organ Music)

KERR, Harrison (b. 1899)

Overture, arioso & finale vlc. & pf. 1944-51
  E. Fink & C. Billing   ♯ **Rem. 199-211**
  (*Luening*)

Trio, A minor vln., vlc., pf. 1938, rev. 1949
  R. Gerle, G. Magyar, K. Wallingford
  (*Copland, Harris*)   ♯ **UOK. 1**

KHACHATURIAN, Aram (b. 1903)

Armenian Dance 1951
  Orch.—Dumont   *BH.O 2207*
  (*Carruthers: Prelude for Myosotis*)

(The) Battle for Stalingrad Film Music
... Orch. Suite
  Moscow Radio—Khachaturian ♯ **CEd.CE 3009**
  (*Shostakovich*)

Cheerful March; Concert March
  E. German Police Band—Hunger (*Eta. 110233*)

Concerto, D flat major pf. & orch. 1936
  M. Lympany & L.P.O.—Fistoulari[1]
           ♯ **D.LXT 2767**
           (♯ Lon.LL 692)
  Y. Boukoff & Residentie—v. Otterloo
           ♯ *EPhi.ABR 4039*
  (2[00])   (♯ Phi.A 00708R)
  ☆ M. Pinter & Berlin Radio—Rother (♯ Ura. 7086)

Concerto, D major vln. & orch. 1940
  D. Oistrakh & Philharmonia—Khachaturian[2]
           ♯ **C.CX 1303**
           (♯ Angel. 35244)
  I. Oistrakh & Philharmonia—Goossens[2]
           ♯ **C.CX 1141**
           (♯ QCX 10126; Angel. 35100)
  L. Kogan & Moscow Radio—Khachaturian
           ♯ *CdM.LDA 8051*
           (♯ USSR.D 0548/9; CHS.CHS 1300)
  T. Magyar & Vienna Sym.—Moralt
           ♯ *Phi.A 00684R*
           (♯ Epic.LC 3080)
  D. Oistrakh & U.S.S.R. State—Gauk[3]   ♯ **Per.SPL 709**
  (*Rakov*)
  D. Oistrakh & U.S.S.R. State—Khachaturian[3]
           ♯ **Csm.CRLPX 001**

---

[1] Uses original scoring, including the "flexatone". This is replaced by a glockenspiel in the Philips (and probably other) recordings.
[2] Cadenza by D. Oistrakh.
[3] The only recent recording in the U.S.S.R. catalogues is that by Kogan, cond. by the composer. It has not been possible to trace U.S.S.R. equivalents for the Per. and Csm. issues, which are also said to be modern recordings, though the Csm. re-uses the old number (see Supp. II).

Concerto, vlc. & orch.   1946
W. Posegga & Leipzig Radio—Kempe
Ura. 7119
(*Shostakovich*)   (# MTW. 539)
☆ S. Knushevitsky & U.S.S.R. State—Gauk
(# Van.VRS 6009; U. 5206G)

Dance, B flat major, Op. 1   1926
D. Oistrakh & V. Yampolsky # *CdM.LDA 8075*
(*below; Leclair, Ysaÿe, Tchaikovsky*)
D. Oistrakh & L. Oborin   in # *Van.VRS 6020*

GAYANEH   Ballet   4 Acts   1942
COLLECTED EXCERPTS
1. Awakening & Ayesha's Dance
2. Lyrical Duet & Dance of the Rose Maidens
3. Gopak   4. Armen's Variations
5. Fire   6. Old Men's & Women's Dance
7. Uzundara   8. Sabre Dance
9. Harvesting Cotton 10. Dance of the Young Kurds
11. Gayaneh's Adagio 12. Mountaineers' Dance
13. Greeting Dance   14. Russian Dance
15. Nurse's Variations 16. Lullaby
17. Lezghinka

Leningrad Khirov Theatre—Khaikin
(4ss)   # *USSR.D 2410/1 & D 2372/3*
[probably the same excerpts, # CHS.CHS 1317]

Nos. 1, 2, 6, 8, 11, 16, 17
Philharmonia—Khachaturian   # *C.C 1041*
(2ss)   (*Masquerade*, on # Angel. 35277)

Orchestral Suites
Suite I: 1. Sabre Dance; 2. Dance of Ayesha;
        3. Dance of the Rose Maidens;
        4. Dance of the Kurds; 5. Lullaby;
        6. Dance of the Young Kurds;
        7. Armen's Variation; 8. Lezghinka
Suite II: 9. Russian Dance; 10. Introduction (Andante)
        11. Gayaneh's Adagio; 12. Fire.
☆ N.Y.P.S.O.—Kurtz   # C.SX 1012
                    (# AmC.CL 714: b *set A 1046*)
(# G.LALP 222; Suite 1 excpts. only, b *G.7ERL 1046*)

Prelude & Suite No. 1   — ARR. Sevitzky
Indianapolis Sym.—Sevitzky # *DCap.CTL 7043*
(1½ss—*Masquerade*)   (# Cap.P 8223; ACap.CLCX 021)
(Nos. 1, 5 & 8 only, on b *Cap.FAP 8233*; ACap.CEC 002)

Suite No. 1
☆ Berlin Sym.—Hermann (# *MusH.LP 9005*)
... Nos. 1, 3, 4
Polish Radio—Rachon (*Muza. 2069/70*)
... Nos. 1, 2, 3, 5
☆ Chicago Sym.—Rodzinski (b *Cam.CAE 194*:
            in # CAL 215: & in # set CFL 102)
... Nos. 1, 3, 5
☆ Philharmonia—Malko (b *G.7BF 1054: 7PW 123*)
... Nos. 1 & 9
Vienna Sym.—Loibner   # *Phi.S 06056R*
(*Hellmesberger, Liszt*)
... Unspec. excerpts Leningrad Op. Orch.—R. Feldt
                                    (b *JpV.EK 4*)
... Nos. 1 & 11   — ARR. VLN. & PF.
L. Kogan & pf. (*USSRM.D 00128*; in # Csm.CRLP 179)
... Nos. 1 & 3   — ARR. PF.
L. Brunelli (*ArgV. 66-0001*)
... No. 1 & Gopak
Czech Phil.—Chalabala   *U.C 24394*
... No. 1, Sabre Dance, only
Boston Prom.—Fiedler (in # Vic.LM 1726:
            b *set WDM 1726*: b *ERA 251*; *ItV.A72R 0061*)
M.G.M. Orch.—Marrow (in # MGM.E 3136)
International Sym.—Schneiderhann (in # *Mae.AO 20007*)
Helsinki Balalaika Orch. (*G.JO 345: HO 3217*)
Nat. Op. Orch. (in # *Var. 6966*)
☆ Aarhus Municipal—Jensen (b *Mer.EP 1-5009*;
                        in # Tono.LPX 35005)
Kingsway Sym.—Olof (b *Lon.REP 8007*)
Chicago Sym.—Rodzinski (b *DV. 16303*)
Prague Variety Theatre—Vlach (in # *U. 10001D*)
— ARR. PF.
☆ C. de Groot (*Phi.A 11245H*: # N 00632R: b *N 402019E*)
— ARR. VLN. & PF.
J. Heifetz & B. Smith (b *Vic.ERA 240*)
— ARR. 2 PFS.
☆ M. Rawicz & W. Landauer (b *C.SEG 7506*)

— ARR. 4 PFS.
Manhattan Pf. Qtt. (in # MGM.E 3130)
☆ First Pf. Qtt. (b *Vic.ERA 96*)

In Memoriam   orch.
Philharmonia—Khachaturian   # *C.C 1043*
(*below*)

MASQUERADE   Inc. Music to Lermontov's Play
                                            1939
Orch. Suite
Philharmonia—Khachaturian[1]   *C.C 1043*
(*above*) (*Gayaneh* on # Angel. 35277)
Paris Cons.—Blareau   # *D.LW 5088*
                                 (# *Lon.LD 9100*)
Moscow Radio—Samosud V# *CdM.LDY 8126*
(2ss)   (*Shostakovich*, on # USSR.D 01475)
[L. Kogan, vln., in Nocturne]
[Waltz & Mazurka only, USSR. 022638/9 & 22644/5]
N.Y.P.S.O.—Kostelanetz   # *AmC.CL 758*
(*Tchaikovsky, Toch, etc.*)   (2ss, b *Phi.A 409014E*)
[Waltz only, b *AmC.A 2036*]
Indianapolis Sym.—Sevitzky # *DCap.CTL 7043*
(*Gayaneh*)   (# Cap.P 8223; ACap.CLCX 021)
(Excerpts on b *Cap.FAP 8234*)
Bolshoi Theatre—Khachaturian
(*Glier*)   # *Csm.CRLP 226*
☆ Boston Prom.—Fiedler (# G.FLLP 101: QCLP 12002;
    b *BrzV.86-0009/10*; Waltz only, b *DV. 16303*;
                                 ▽ *Vic. 49-0137*)
... Waltz   — ARR. 2 PFS.
M. Rawicz & W. Landauer (b *C.SEG 7506: SEDQ 514*)

SONGS & PART SONGS
Let's clasp hands, Comrade
Cho. & orch.—Gát (*Qual.MO 447*)
Friendship Waltz   (Rublyov)
V. Krasovitskaya   (*Khrennikov*)   *USSR. 21288*
Russian Cavalry Gala March   Band
Band—Pongrácz (*Qual.MO 5051*)
Song Poem, E major   vln. & pf.   1929
D. Oistrakh & V. Yampolsky
(*above*)   in # *CdM.LDA 8075*
D. Oistrakh & L. Oborin   in # *Van.VRS 6020*
I. Oistrakh & pf.   *USSRM.D 001211*
(*Glier*)
[It is more than likely that confusion exists between the
above recordings.]
Song of Stalin   (unspec. excpt.)
M. Kuti & K. Jász, Cho. & orch.—Gát (*Qual.KN 2002*)
Symphony No. 2   1942
U.S.S.R. Nat.—Khachaturian   # *Csm.CRLP 136*
Toccata, E flat minor   pf.
O. Penna   *ArgOd. 66032*
(*Aguirre: Canciones 1 & 3*)   (b *BSOAE 4504*)
Y. Boukoff   in # *Phi.A 76700R*
(*Balakirev, Rachmaninoff, etc.*)
☆ L. Oborin (in # *CdM.LDA 8076*; in # Csm.CRLP 147
                                    & CRLP 224)

KHRENNIKOV, Tikhon (b. 1913)

(The) CAVALIER WITH THE GOLDEN STAR
... Once in the Kuban Steppe; On the Steppe road
☆ Piatnitsky People's Cho. (*USSRM.D 00302 & D 001012*)

MUCH ADO ABOUT NOTHING, Op. 7
Inc. Music   1935
COMPLETE in a radio performance of the play
Vakhtangov Theatre Orch.—Archangelsky
                             # *USSR.D 01684/7*
Orch. Suite ☆ Moscow Radio—Stassevitch (*USSR. 211004/7*)
Song of the Drunkard
K. Käyhkö (Bs, *Finn*) (*Ryt.RK 1004*)

[1] Waltz, Nocturne, Mazurka only.

SONGS

Merry Eyes   (Dolmatovsky)
   V. Nechayev (T) (*USSR. 21615*)

(The) Nightingale and the rose   (Antokolsky)
   ☆ S. Lemeshev (T) (*USSRM.D 00395*)
     M. Alexandrovitch (T) (in ♯ *Sti.SLP 1001*)

Winter, cold winter   (Gusev)
   V. Krasovitskaya   (*Khachaturian*)   **USSR. 21787**

Winter Road   (Pushkin)
   ☆ G. Vinogradov (T) (*USSR. 16595*)

(The) STORM   (or: The Brothers)   Opera   1937
Natasha's aria
   V. Nestyagina   (2ss)   **USSR. 022746/7**

(The) SWINEHERD & THE SHEPHERD
Film   1942
Song about Moscow   S. Lemeshev (T) (*USSR. 021383*)
Glashla's Song   A. Kleshchova (*USSR. 21239*)

KIENZL, Wilhelm (1857-1941)

(Der) EVANGELIMANN, Op. 45   2 Acts   1895
O schöne Jugendtage   A   Act II
   H. Töpper   **PV. 72458**
   (*below*)   (♭ *Pol. 30046: in* ♯ *19015*)
   ☆ R. Siewert (G.FKX 253: ♭ *7PW 526*)

Selig sind, die Verfolgung leiden   T & Cho.   Act II
   R. Schock & Cho.   **G.DB 11545**
   (*Flotow: Alessandro Stradella, aria*)   (♭ *7RW 530*)
   K. Terkal   **D.F 43549**
   (*Zauberflöte—Dies Bildnis . . .*)
            (♭ *DX 1761; in* ♯ *Lon.LB 892*)
   L. Fehenberger & Cho.   **PV. 72458**
   (*above*)   (♭ *Pol. 30046 & in* ♯ *19015*)
     B. Löwenfalk (B, *Dan*) (Felix.P 85)
   ◫ E. Schmedes (in ♯ *HRS. 3006**)

(Die) KUHREIGEN, Op. 85   3 Acts   1911
Lug! Dürsel, lug!   T
Zu Strassburg auf der Schanz   T & cho.   Act I
   R. Schock & Cho.   **G.EH 1463**
   [Zu Strassburg . . . also in ♯ *WBLP 1515*] (♭ *7PW 18-546*)

Lug! Dürsel, lug!   T   Act I
   ☆ R. Tauber (in ♯ *Ete. 701*)

KILPINEN, Yrjö (b. 1892)

SONGS & PART SONGS
Finland's Arms   (*Suomenvaa*)
   Kotka Lyceum Boys' Cho. & Orch.—Vainio
                        Od.PLD 67

(12) FJELDLIEDER, Opp. 52, 53, 54   (Tormanen)
   (*Tunturilauluja*)
On the shore by the Church, Op. 54, No. 10   (*Kirkkorannassa*)
To Song, Op. 52, No. 3   (*Laululle*)
   M. Lehtinen (B), P. Koskimies (pf.)   **G.TJ 53**
   (*below*)
To Song, Op. 52, No. 3 & Fjeldlied, Op. 54, No. 12 (*Tunturilaulu*)
   M. Heidi (M-S)   **Ryt.R 6138**
To Song   — ARR. CHO.
   Helsinki Univ. Cho.—Turunen (in ♯ Rem. 199-167)

In the evening   (Leino)
   (or: *Evening Song: Iltalaulu*)
   M. Lehtinen (B), P. Koskimies (pf.)   **G.TJ 53**
   (*Fjeldlieder*)

KIRBYE, George (c. 1565-1634)

     SEE: † ENGLISH CHURCH MUSIC, VOL. IV
         † EVENING OF ELIZABETHAN VERSE & MUSIC
         † TRIUMPHS OF ORIANA

KIRCHNER, Leon (b. 1919)

Quartet No. 1   Strings   1949
   American Art Qtt.   **♯ AmC.ML 4843**
   (*Fine*)

KLUGHARDT, August Friedrich Martin
                        (1874-1902)

Quintet, C major, Op. 79   fl., ob., cl., bsn. & hrn.
   Chicago Sym. Woodwind Quintet ♯ Aphe.AP 14
   (*Shostakovich, Leclair, etc.*)
   New Art Wind Quintet   **♯ CEd.CE 2020**
   (*Onslow*)

KOCHAN, Günter (b. 1930)

Concerto, D major, Op. 1   vln. & orch.
   E. Morbitzer & Berlin Radio—K. Lange
   (6ss)   ***Eta. 120035/7***

Grüss an Warschau   (Wiens)   1955
   Berlin Radio Youth Cho. & Sym.
   —Wiesenhütter   ***Eta. 110247***
   (*Werzlau: Lied der Arbeiterjugend*)

KODÁLY, Zoltán (b. 1882)

I. INSTRUMENTAL & ORCH.

Adagio   vln. & pf.   1905
   E. Zathureczky & E. Petri   **Qual.SZN 3053**
                      (also MX 586)

Concerto for orchestra   1939
   Dresden Phil.—Bongartz   **♯ Ura. 7138**
   (*Prokofiev*)

Dances from Galanta   orch.   1933
   L.P.O.—Solti   **♯ D.LXT 2771**
   (*Bartók: Dance Suite*)   (♯ *Lon.LL 709*)
   Vienna Sym.—Moralt   **♯ EPhi.NBR 6009**
   (*Dances from Marosszék*)   (♯ *Phi.N 00667R*)
   London Phil. Sym.—Rodzinski
                    ♯ West.LAB 7020
   (*Dances from Marosszék*)
   Budapest Phil.—Somogyi   **Qual.MN 1022/3**
   (4ss)
   Bamberg Sym.—Perlea   **♯ AmVox.PL 9500**
   (*Smetana, Enesco, Dvořák*)
   R.I.A.S. Sym.—Fricsay   **PV. 72448**
   (*below, on* ♯ *Pol. 17060*)
   ☆ L.P.O.—Cameron   (*Sibelius*)   **♯ G.DLP 1100**
   ☆ Boston Prom.—Fiedler (♯ Cam.CAL 150: ♭ *CAE 249*)
     Berlin Radio—L. G. Jochum (♭ *Ura.UREP 10*)

Dances from Marosszék   orch.   1930
   L.S.O.—Previtali   **♯ G.DLP 1064**
   (*Carmen—Preludes*)
   Vienna Sym.—Moralt   **♯ EPhi.NBR 6009**
   (*Dances from Galanta*)   (♯ *Phi.N 00667R*)
   London Phil. Sym.—Rodzinski
                    ♯ West.LAB 7020
   (*Dances from Galanta*)
   R.I.A.S. Sym.—Fricsay   **♯ AmD.DL 9773**
   (*Psalmus Hungaricus*) (*above, on* ♯ *Pol. 17060*)

— PF. VERSION
   S. Biro   **♯ Rem. 199-133**
   (*Kabalevsky & Bartók*)

Honved Gala March   Band (*Qual.MO 5055*)

☆ = Re-issue of a recording to be found in previous volumes.

(3) Hungarian Dances (unspec.) vln. & pf.
D. Oistrakh & N. Walter   ♯ Eta.LPM 1023
(*Leclair, Tchaikovsky, Prokofiev*)   (♯ 2ss, *Eta. 120021*)

Moorish Dance (unspec.)
Allegro Cha. Orch.   ♯ *Allo. 4058*
(*Ibert*)

(7) Piano Pieces, Op. 11   1910-18
I. Kabos   ♯ BRS. 917
(*Bartók*)

QUARTETS, Strings
No. 1, Op. 2   1908-9
Roth Qtt.   ♯ Mer.MG 80004

No. 2, D major, Op. 10   1916-18
Végh Qtt.   ♯ D.LXT 2876
(*Smetana*)   (♯ Lon.LL 865)

Serenade, F major, Op. 12   2 vlns. & vla. 1919-20
Classic Trio   ♯ CEd.CE 1033
(*Dvořák: Terzetto*)

Sonata, C major, vlc. unacc., Op. 8   1915
E. Kurtz (*Prokofiev*)   ♯ AmC.ML 4867
☆ J. Starker (♯ *Pac.LDPF 29*)

Sonata, vlc. & pf., Op. 9   1909-10
☆ J. Starker & O. Herz (♯ *Cpt.MC 20031*; Per.SPL 602:
   & ♯ Per.SPL 720, *below*)

Sonata (Duo), Op. 7   vln. & vlc.   1914
A. Eidus & J. Starker   ♯ Per.SPL 720
(*above*)

Summer Evening   orch.   1906 (rev. 1929-30)
Sym.—Vicars   ♯ CA.LPA 1086
(*Prokofiev*)
Hungarian Phil.—Vaszy   Qual.MN 1083/4
(4ss)   (also ♮ MX 799/802)

Theatre Overture   orch.   1926
☆ Vienna Sym.—Swoboda (*below*)   ♯ Nix.WLP 5001

Variations on a Hungarian Folksong 'The Peacock'
   orch.   1939
L.P.O.—Solti   ♯ D.LXT 2878
(*below*)   (♯ Lon.LL 1020)
Chicago Sym.—Dorati   ♯ EMer.MG 50038
(*Bartók*)   (♯ FMer.MLP 7525)

II. VOCAL

Missa brevis in tempore belli   A, T, B, Cho., Org.
   1945
☆ R. Koerner, G. Parritt, H. Ronk, Washington
Presbyterian Cho.—Schaefer (♯ McInt.MC 1002)

OPERAS
HARY JANOS, Op. 15   Prol., 5 parts & Epilogue
   1926
Orch. Suite
L.P.O.—Solti   ♯ D.LXT 5059
(*Bartók*)   (♯ Lon.LL 1230)
London Phil. Sym.—Rodzinski
(1½ss—*Moussorgsky*)   ♯ West.LAB 7034
Philharmonia—Schüchter   ♯ P.PMC 1017
(*Dohnányi*)   (♯ MGM.E 3019)
R.I.A.S. Sym.—Fricsay   ♯ Pol. 18223
(*Bartók*)
Moscow Radio—Shomodi   ♯ USSR.D 2177/8
(2ss)
Minneapolis Sym.—Dorati   ♯ Vic.LM 1750
(*Bartók*) (♯ ItV.A12R 0063)   (♭ set WDM 1750)
Budapest Phil.—Somogyi   Qual.MN 1115/7
(6ss)
☆ Austrian Sym.—Halasz (♯ *AFest.CFR 10-98*)

No. 10, Intermezzo
Philharmonia—Karajan   in ♯ C.CX 1265
(*Goyescas, Khovanshchina, etc.*)
   (♯ FCX 407: QCX 10150; Angel. 35207)
—— ARR. VLN. & PF.   Szigeti
☆ J. Szigeti & pf. (♭ *AmC.A 1887*; *Phl.N 409506E*)

(The) SPINNING ROOM OF THE SZEKELYS
(*Székely Fonó*) 1 Act 1932
I'm coming from Transylvania   T
E. Rösler
Where I'm going   B
I. Palló   Qual.MN 1112

Psalmus hungaricus, Op. 13   T, cho., orch.   1923
W. McAlpine, London Phil. Cho. & Orch.
Solti (*Eng*)   ♯ D.LXT 2878
(*above*)   (♯ Lon.LL 1020)
E. Häfliger, St. Hedwig's Cath. Cho. & R.I.A.S.
Sym.—Fricsay (*Ger*) in ♯ HP.DGM 18203/4
(*Rossini*)
(*Dances from Marosszék* on ♯ AmD.DL 9773)

SONGS & PARTSONGS
Evening Song   Children's voices   1938
Women's Cho.—Tóth   Qual.NB 241
(*Bartók: Part Song*)

Greeting to John   Boys' voices   1939
Concordia Cho.—P. J. Christiansen[1]
   in ♯ *Cdia.CDLP 3*
(*Bach, Palestrina, Josquin, etc.*)
Womens' Cho.—Tóth[2] (*Qual.MO 428*)

Huszt (Kölcsey)   Male cho.   1936
Cho.—Vásárhelyi   Qual.KK 2502
(*Bartók: Part Songs*)

Hymn to Saint Stephen   Mixed cho.   1938
Augustana Cho.—Veld (*Eng*)
   in ♯ BB.LBC 1075
(*Bach, Dvořák, Davies, etc.*)

Jesus and the traders   unacc. cho.   1934
Augustana Cho.—Veld (*Eng*)
   in ♯ Word.W 4005
(*Grieg, Sjöberg, Britten, etc.*)

Kállai Kettös   1937
(*Kalló Folkdances*)   S, A, T, B & orch.
... **Excerpts** (unspec.)
N. Allami & Orch.   Magy.M 340/1
State Folk Ens.—Csenky (*Qual.KM 2001*;
   in ♯ *CdM.LDY 4038*)

To the Magyars (Berzsenyi)   1936
Artistic Ens.—Kalmár   Qual.KK 2503
(*Liszt: Jubilee Song*)

Te Deum   S, A, T, B, cho. & orch.   1936
☆ S. Jurinac, S. Wagner, R. Christ, A. Poell, Vienna Cho.
& Sym. Orch.—Swoboda   ♯ Nix.WLP 5001
(*above*)

HUNGARIAN FOLKSONGS
Lofty cliff
Lovely is the wood when clad in green
Carriage, Cart
A. Bárthey (S), I. Hadju (pf.)   Qual.SZN 3002
Which ought one to marry?
☆ N. Eddy (B) (in ♯ *Phi.S 06613R*)

KOECHLIN, Charles (1867-1950)

SONG: Si tu le veux (de Marsan)
R. Doria (S), S. Gouat (pf.)   ♭ *Plé.P 45140*
(*Delibes & Hüe*)
T. Rossi (T) (in ♯ *C.FS 1045*)
(also in ♯*CdM.LD 4013, etc.*)
ⓗ E. Eames (S) (AF.AGSB 60*)

---

[1] Labelled *A Birthday Greeting*, probably this.   [2] Labelled *Greeting*.

KOHS, Ellis B. (b. 1916)

Concerto, viola & str. nonet 1949
☆ F. Molnar & Str. Ens. (*Verrall*)[1]   # ML. 7004

KOPYLOFF, Alexander A. (1854-1911)

SEE: † CHORAL MASTERPIECES FROM THE RUSSIAN
LITURGY

KORNGOLD, Erich Wolfgang (b. 1897)

Concerto, D major, Op. 35 vln. & orch. 1946
J. Heifetz & Los Angeles Phil.—Wallenstein
(*Bruch*)   # G.ALP 1288
(*Lalo* on # Vic.LM 1782)

MUCH ADO ABOUT NOTHING, Op. 11 1919
(for Shakespeare's Play)
Suite (Holzapfel und Schlehwein; Mädchen im Brautgemach)
— ARR. PF.
R. Corbert   # ML. 7017
(*Hässler & Paderewski*)

Overture
☆ Austrian State Sym.—Korngold (Hma. 15012)

(Die) TOTE STADT, Op. 12 Opera 1920
Glück, das mir verblieb S & T
A. Kupper & L. Fehenberger   *Pol. 62926*
(*E. d'Albert: Toten Augen—Psyche wandelt*) . . .
(♭ *Pol. 32014* & in # 19015)
☆ L. Lehmann & R. Tauber (♭ *Od.OBL 1073*)
H. Zadek & A. Dermota (in # Rem. 199-123)

. . . Sop. solo only
J. Hammond   G.DB 21625
(*Mefistofele—L'altra notte*)

Ich werde sie nicht wiedersehen T
☆ R. Tauber (♭ *Od.OBL 1073*)

Final Scene: Die Toten, wo lag sie nicht hier
H R. Tauber (in # Éte. 494*)

KOSMA, Joseph (b. 1905)

Ballade de celui qui chanta dans les supplices (Aragon)
Cantata reciter, T, Bs, Cho. & orch.
M. Bouquet, R. Schmidt, X. Depraz, Paris Opéra Cho. &
Orch.—Baudo

Baptiste Orch. Suite[2]
Paris Opéra Orch.—Baudo   # Véga.T35.A.2501

(Les) Chansons de Bilitis Operetta
Soloists, Capucines Th. Cho. & Orch.—Kosma
Pat.DTX 156
▽ There have been many excerpts from earlier operettas,
etc.

KOVAŘOVIČ, Karel (1862-1920)

(The) DOGHEADS Opera 3 Acts 1898
(*Psohlavci*)
Overture & Chodů's Farewell; Kozinu's Departure;
Lomikarova's Death
☆ O. Kovař, V. Bednář, B. Blachut, Z. Otava, D. Tikalová,
M. Dvořákova, etc., Prague Nat. Theatre Cho. &
Orch.—Folprecht   # Sup.LPV 146
(# U. 5089G)

Miners' Polka orch.
☆ Prague Radio—Vipler (in # U. 5081C; Sup. LPM 191)

KOUSSEVITZKY, Serge (1874-1951)

COLLECTION
Chanson triste, Op. 2 cbs. & pf. (▽ Vic. 7159)
Concerto, F minor, Op. 3 . . . Andante only
Valse miniature cbs. & pf. (▽ *Vic. 1476*)
☆ S. Koussevitzky & P. Luboshutz in # Vic.LCT 1145

KRAEHENBUEHL, David (b. 1923)

Canzona 1953
Yale Woodwind Qtt.   # CtyNY.AP 121
(*Donovan & Gruen*)

CAROLS
The Star Song (Herrick)
Ideo Gloria in excelsis (Trad.)
There is no rose (Anon.)
A Song against bores (Richard Hill)
Concert Cho.   # CtyNY.AP 122
(*Carols by A. Harris, J. Gruen, C. Jones, M. Sasonkin*)

KREBS, Johann Ludwig (1713-1780)

SEE: BACH FESTIVAL (*s.v.* BACH, Miscellaneous)

KREISLER, Fritz (b. 1875)

(Abridged listings only)

I. ORIGINAL WORKS

A. INSTRUMENTAL

(vln. & pf. unless otherwise stated)

COLLECTIONS
Liebesleid ø
Liebesfreud ø
Polichinelle (Serenade) ø
Schön Rosmarin ø
Caprice viennois, Op. 2 α
Tambourin chinois, Op. 3 ø
Rondino on a theme of Beethoven ø
La Gitana α
COMPOSITIONS "IN STYLE OF" OTHER COMPOSERS
Praeludium & Allegro (Pugnani) ø
La Chasse (Cartier)
Variations on a theme of Corelli (Tartini) α
A. Campoli & E. Gritton   # D.LXT 5012
(*Paderewski, Wieniawski, Granados*)   (# Lon.LL 1171)
[Liebesleid & Liebesfreud also on ♭ D. 71076; Caprice
viennois & Tambourin chinois on ♭ D. 71092; DK 23360]
[Items marked ø also on # D.LW 5217; marked α also on
D.LW 5218]

Liebesleid
Liebesfreud
Tambourin chinois, Op. 3
Caprice viennois, Op. 2
Schön Rosmarin
Romance, Op. 4
Rondino on a theme by Beethoven
COMPOSITIONS "IN STYLE OF" OTHER COMPOSERS
Chanson Louis XIII & Pavane (L. Couperin)
La Précieuse (L. Couperin)
Praeludium & Allegro (Pugnani)
Sicilienne et Rigaudon (Francœur)
ARRANGEMENT: The Old Refrain (Brandl)
J. Olevsky & W. Rosé   # Nix.WLP 5346
(# West.WL 5346)

Caprice viennois, Op. 2
Liebesfreud
Liebesleid
The Old Refrain (Brandl, ARR. Kreisler)
Schön Rosmarin
Tambourin chinois, Op. 3
☆ G. Alès (vln.) & Orch.—Dupré   # DCap.CTL 7076
(*Tchaikovsky: Familiar Themes*)

Caprice viennois, Op. 2
Liebesfreud
Liebesleid
La Gitana
Schön Rosmarin
Tambourin chinois, Op. 3
Rondino on a theme of Beethoven
The Old Refrain
A. Krips (vln.) & Boston Pops—Fiedler # Vic.LRM 7047
(♭ set ERB 7047)

Liebesfreud
Liebesleid
Schön Rosmarin
Caprice viennois
The Old Refrain
Tambourin chinois
M. Auclair & O. Schulhof   # Rem. 199-126
(*continued on next page*)

---

[1] Not 2ss as formerly listed. The number has also been seen quoted as 7028.
[2] From the music for the 'Pantomime en 6 tableaux' by J. Prévert; part used also in film *Les Enfants du Paradis*.

COLLECTIONS (*continued*)
Caprice viennois
Liebesleid
Liebesfreud
THE KING STEPS OUT . . . Stars in my eyes
Schön Rosmarin
— ARR. CL. & ORCH.
　R. Kell & Camarata Orch.　　　　　♯ *B.LA 8632*
　　　　　　　　(♯ *D.UA 243522; AmD.DL 4077*)

Caprice viennois, Op. 2 *a*
Liebesfreud *a*
Liebesleid
Rondino on a theme of Beethoven *a*
Schön Rosmarin
Syncopation　vln., vlc., pf.
Tambourin chinois, Op. 2 *a*
Toy Soldiers' March *a*
IN STYLE OF OTHERS: Allegretto　(Boccherini)
ARRANGEMENTS:
The Old Refrain　(Brandl) *a*
Tambourin　(unspec.: prob. either by Rameau or Leclair)
— ARR. ORGAN
　R. Ellsasser　　　　　　　　　　♯ MGM.E 3238
　(items marked *a* also in ♭ *set X 325*)

Caprice viennois, Op. 2
　E. Morini & L. Pommers　　　in ♯ West.WN 18087
　G. Taschner & H. Giesen (Od.O-9184: in ♯ *OLA 1006*)
　R. Odnoposoff & J. Antonietti (V♯ *MMS.POP 8*)
　A. Krips & Boston Prom.—Fiedler, from collection
　　　　　　　　　　　　　　　(in ♯ Vic.LM 1910)
　I. Zilzer & F. Schröder (*Eta. 120044*)
　☆ Y. Menuhin & A. Baller[1] (in ♯ Vic.LM 1742:
　　　　　　　　　　　　　♭ *set WDM 1742:* ♭ *ERA 259*)
　T. Magyar (♭ *Phi.N 402001E*)
　L. Stevens (in ♯ *AFest.CFR 10-191*)
— ARR. ORCH.
　N.W. Ger. Phil.—Schüchter (in ♯ *Imp.ILP 114;*
　　　　　　　　　　　　　　　　　　G.QDLP 6026)
　☆ A. Kostelanetz Orch. (in ♯ *C.SX 1041: QSX 12017;*
　　　　　　♭ *AmC.A 1541:* in ♯ *CL 771:* ♭ *set A635*)
— ARR. 2 PFS.　V. Appleton & M. Field (in ♯ *AmVox.VX 540*)
　☆ A. Whittemore & J. Lowe (♭ *Vic.ERA 95*)
　etc.

(La) Gitana　▽ J. Fuchs & orch. (*MGM. 9504*)
　☆ J. Pougnet & Torch Orch. (♭ *P.CGEP 7*)
　L. Stevens (in ♯ *AFest.CFR 10-191*)
— ARR. 2 PFS.　A. Whittemore & J. Lowe (♭ *Vic.ERA 95*)

Liebesfreud; Liebesleid
　N. Carol & J. Levine　　　　　in ♯ BB.LBC 1155
　　　　　　　　　　　　　　　　　　(♭ *ERAB 15*)
　F. Akos & H. Altmann (*G.EG 7937*)
　A. Krips & Boston Prom.—Fiedler, from Collection
　　　　　　　(in ♯ Vic.LM 1910; ♭ *ItV.A72R 0059*)
　R. Odnoposoff & J. Antonietti (V♯ *MMS.POP 8*)
　☆ T. Magyar (♭ *Phi.N 402001E*)
　L. Stevens (in ♯ *AFest.CFR 10-191*)
— ARR. ORCH.
　N.W. Ger. Phil.—Schüchter (in ♯ *Imp.ILP 114;*
　　　　　　G.QDLP 6026; Od. O-29004: ♭ *OBL 29004*)
　☆ Kostelanetz Orch. (in ♯ *C.SX 1041;* ♭ *AmC.A 1600:*
　　　　　　　　　　　　in ♯ *CL 771:* ♭ *set A635*)

Liebesfreud, only
　☆ J. Pougnet (vln.) & Torch Orch. (in ♯ *P.PMD 1008:*
　　　　　　　　　　　　　　　　　　♭ *CGEP 7*)
— ARR. PF.　Rachmaninoff
　☆ S. Rachmaninoff (in ♯ Vic.LCT 1136)

Liebesleid, only
　E. Morini & L. Pommers　　　in ♯ West.WN 18087
　Y. Menuhin & ? (♭ *Vic.ERA 259*)
— ARR. VLA. & PF.　☆ W. Primrose (♭ *Cam.CAE 251*)
— ARR. ORCH.
　M.G.M. Orch.—Marrow (*MGM. 9126:* in ♯ E 3138)
　A. Bernard Str. Orch. (♭ *Pat.EA 20*)
— ARR. PF.　Rachmaninoff
　X. Prochorova (in ♯ *Imp.ILP 109*)
— ARR. 2 PFS.
　V. Appleton & M. Field (in ♯ *AmVox.VX 540*)
— ARR. VOICE　♮ M. Ivogün (in ♯ *Sca. 815**)

Quartet, Strings, A minor　pub. 1922
　Stuyvesant Qtt.　　　　　　　♯ Phil.PH 107
　(*Paganini*)

Recitative & Scherzo-Caprice, Op. 6　Unacc. vln.
　R. Odnoposoff　　　　　　in V♯ *MMS. 915*

Rondino on a theme of Beethoven
　M. Auclair & O. Schulhof　　　in ♯ Rem. 199-128
　D. Oistrakh & pf. (*USSR. 7592*)
　☆ Z. Francescatti & M. Lanner (in ♯ EPhi.NBL 5010;
　　　　　　　　　　　　　　　　　Phi.N 02101L)
　F. Kreisler & F. Rupp (in ♯ Vic.LCT 1142)
　L. Stevens (in ♯ *AFest.CFR 10-191*)

Schön Rosmarin
　I. Haendel & G. Moore　　　　in ♯ G.CLP 1021
　N. Carol & J. Levine　　　　　in ♯ BB.LBC 1155
　E. Morini & L. Pommers　　　in ♯ West.WN 18087
　I. Stern & A. Zakin　　　　　in ♯ AmC.AL 23
　　　　　　　　　　　　　　　　(♯ *Phi.S 06617R*)
　Y. Menuhin & ? (*above*)　　　　　♭ *Vic.ERA 259*
　J. Bleumers & P. Palla (org.) (♭ *Phi.P 42201IE*)
　R. Odnoposoff & J. Antonietti (V♯ *MMS.POP 8*)
　W. Tworek & Orch. (*Pol.X 51706;* in ♯ *Lon.LB 1121*)
　I. Zilzer & F. Schröder (*Eta. 120044*)
　☆ Z. Francescatti & A. Balsam (in ♯ EPhi.NBL 5010;
　　　　　　　　　　　　　　　　　Phi.N 02101L)

Tambourin chinois, Op. 3
　G. Jarry & A. Collard　　　　in ♯ C.FCX 222
　I. Zilzer & F. Eberson　　　　　　C.LD 7
　(*Sibelius: Romance*)
　N. Carol & J. Levine (in ♯ BB.LBC 1155: ♭ *ERAB 15*)
　☆ I. Kawaciuk & F. Vrána (in ♯ *Sup.LPM 135; U. 5185C*)
　T. Magyar (♭ *Phi.N 402010E*)
　L. Stevens (in ♯ *AFest.CFR 10-191*)
— ARR. ORCH.
　Concert Orch.—E. Robinson (in ♯ *Argo.RG 66*)
　☆ A. Kostelanetz Orch. (in ♯ *C.SX 1041:*
　　　　　　♭ *AmC.A 1541:* in ♯ *CL 771:* ♭ *set A635*)
— ARR. 2 PFS.
　☆ A. Whittemore & J. Lowe (♭ *Vic.ERA 95*)
　P. Luboshutz & G. Nemenoff (in ♯ *Cam.CAL 193*)

I. B. STAGE WORKS

(The) KING STEPS OUT　Film
. . . Stars in my eyes
— ARR. ORCH.
　☆ A. Kostelanetz Orch. (in ♯ *C.SX 1041: QSX 12017;*
　　　　　　♭ *AmC.A 1541:* in ♯ *CL 771:* ♭ *set A635*)
— ARR. 2 PFS.
　☆ A. Whittemore & J. Lowe (♭ *Vic.ERA 95*)

SISSY　Operetta　(*Ger*)
Ich war so gern einmal verliebt
　H. Gueden (S)　　　　　　　in ♯ *D.LW 5133*
　(*Lehár, J. Strauss II, O. Straus, etc.*)
　　　　　　(♯ *Lon.LD 9157; D.LXT 5033; Lon.LL 1116*)

II. COMPOSITIONS "IN STYLE OF"
OTHER COMPOSERS

Allegretto　(Boccherini)
— ARR. VLA. & PF.　W. Primrose (♭ *Cam.CAE 244*)

Andantino　(Padre Martini)
　M. Kozolupova & pf. (*USSR. 22276*)

Chanson Louis XIII & Pavane　(L. Couperin)
　P. Fournier (vlc.), E. Lush　　　in ♯ *D.LXT 2766*
　　　　　　　　　　　　　　　　(♯ *Lon.LL 700*)

(La) Chasse　(Cartier)
　M. Robin & A. Balsam　　　in ♯ *AmC.AL 30*

Concerto, C major　(Vivaldi)　vln. & orch.
　☆ F. Kreisler & Vic. String—Voorhees (in ♯ Vic.LCT 1142)

Grave　(W. F. Bach)
　H. Szeryng & T. Janopoulo　　in ♯ *Od.OD 1008*
　(*below; & Vitali, Wieniawski, Paganini*)
　　　　　　　　　　　　　　(in ♯ *ArgOd.LDC 7504*)
— ARR. VLC. & PF.　D. Shafran & pf. (*USSR. 20435/6*)

Minuet　(Porpora)
　☆ Z. Francescatti (♭ *EPhi.NBE 11010: Phi.N 409514E*)

Praeludium & Allegro　(Pugnani)
　G. Taschner & M. Krause　　　　Od.O-9183
　(*below*)　　　　　　　　　　(in ♯ *OLA 1006*)
　M. Auclair & O. Schulhof　　　in ♯ Rem. 199-128
　G. Barinova & pf. (in ♯ *USSR.D 1185*)
　☆ I. Haendel & G. Moore (♭ *G.7RW 118*)
　Z. Francescatti (♭ *Phi.N 409514E; EPhi.NBE 11010;*
　　　　　　　　　　　　　　　in ♭ *AmC. set A 1086*)
— ARR. ORCH.
　Belgian Radio Cha.—Doneux (in ♯ *Mae.OA 20002*)
　J. Schmeid Orch. (in ♯ *Vien.LPR 1031*)

Sicilienne & Rigaudon　(Francœur)
　G. Jarry & A. Collard　　　　in ♯ C.FCX 222
　Elis. Gilels & pf. (*USSRM.D 001221*)

---

[1] This is the Japanese recording, also stated to be acc. G. Moore and recorded in England.

Variations on a theme of Corelli (Tartini)
  H. Szeryng & T. Janopoulo   in ♯ *Od.OD 1008*
  (*above*)   (♯ *ArgOd.LDC 7504*)
  G. Taschner & M. Krause   *Od.O-9183*
  (*above*)   (in ♯ *OLA 1006*)
  G. Jarry & A. Collard   in ♯ *C.FCX 222*
  N. Carol & J. Levine   in ♯ *BB.LBC 1155*
  D. Oistrakh & V. Yampolsky   in ♯ *JpV.LS 2025*
  R. Odnoposoff & J. Antonietti (**V**♯ *MMS. 915*)
  I. Bezrodny & pf. (*USSRM.D 00922*)
  ☆ Z. Francescatti (in ♯ *EPhi.NBL 5010; Phi.N 02101L*)
  R. Ricci (♭ *AmVox.VIP 45340*)
  D. Oistrakh (♭ *Mer.EP 1-5008*)

— ARR. VLC. & PF.
  A. Janigro & E. Bagnoli (in ♯ *West.WN 18004*)

III. ARRANGEMENTS FROM OTHER COMPOSERS

Aloha Oe (Queen Liliuokalani)
  F. Akos & H. Altmann (pf.) (*G.EG 7938*)
Londonderry Air (Trad.)
  N.W. German Phil.—Schüchter (in ♯ *Imp.ILP 114;*
                                   G.QDLP 6026)
Midnight Bells (Heuberger)
  E. Morini & L. Pommers (in ♯ *West.WN 18087*)
(The) Old Folks at home (Foster)
  F. Akos & H. Altmann (*G.EG 7938*)
(The) Old Refrain (Brandl)
  N. Carol & J. Levine (in ♯ *BB.LBC 1155:* ♭ *ERAB 15*)
  R. Rubato & B. Ritorno (in ♯ *Phi.S 06024R*)
  R. Odnoposoff & J. Antonietti (**V**♯ *MMS. 915*)
  Y. Menuhin & pf. (♭ *Vic.ERA 259*)
— ARR. ORCH.   ☆ A. Kostelanetz Orch. (in ♯ *C.SX 1041:*
                QSX 12017; ♭ *AmC.A 1541 :* in ♯ *CL 771 :* ♭ *set A 635*)
— VOCAL ARR.   ☆ G. Moore (S)   in ♯ *Vic.LCT 7004*
                                      (♭ *set WCT 7004*)
Sérénade espagnole (Chaminade)
  G. Taschner (vln.), H. Giesen (pf.)   *Od.O-4673*
  (*Moussorgsky: Gopak*)   (in ♯ *OLA 1006*)
  M. Auclair & O. Schulhof   in ♯ *Rem. 199-128*
  E. Morini & L. Pommers   in ♯ *West.WN 18087*
  G. Barinova & pf.   in ♯ *USSR.D 1186*

KŘENEK, Ernst (b. 1900)

(4) Bagatelles (Sonata), Op. 70 pf. duet 1931
  E. Křenek & M. Ajemian   ♯ **ML. 7014**
  (*Sonata No. 4*)

Concerto No. 4 pf. & orch. 1950
  M. Molin & orch.—Křenek   ♯ **CtyNY.AP 123**
  [Announced but perhaps never issued]

SONATAS, pf.
No. 4 1948
  ▽ ☆ B. Abramowitsch (*above*)   ♯ **ML. 7014**

No. 5 1950
  C. Zelka   ♯ **ML. 7029**

Sonata, Op. 92, No. 1 organ 1941
  M. Andrews   ♯ **UOK. 2**
  (*Lübeck, Piston, Sessions*)
  R. G. Wichmann   ♯ **PFCM.CB 191**
  (*Hindemith & Piston*)

Sonata, vla. & pf. 1948
  ☆ M. Mann & Yaltah Menuhin (♭ *Pol. 32034*)

KREUTZER, Conradin (1780-1849)

Das ist der Tag des Herrn, Op. 23, No. 1
  (*Schäfers Sonntagslied*)
  Berlin Motet Cho. & Wind Ens.—Arndt
                                   T.A 11600
  (*Mendelssohn: Der Jäger Abschied*)
  (*CanT.GF 63049;* ♭ *T.U 45600:* & in ♯ *T.LA 6075 & 6086*)

Jägerlied, Op. 23, No. 3 (Fallersleben) Male cho.
  (*Es lebe, was auf Erden*)
  Berlin State Op. Male Cho.—K. Schmidt (*Eta. 10-210*)

(Das) NACHTLAGER IN GRANADA
  Opera 2 Acts 1834
March Berlin Police Band—Winkel (*G.EG 7870*)

Schön die Abendglocken klangen (*"Gebet"*)
  Berlin Municipal Op. Cho.—Schüchter
                                   G.EH 1455
  (*Lustigen Weiber—O süsser Mond*)(♭ *7PW 537:*
                                   in ♯ *WDLP 1517*)
  Berlin Municipal Op. Cho.—Otto   *T.A 11535*
  (*Freischütz—Jägerchor*)
  (♭ *UE 45535;* in ♯ *DT.TM 68031; T.LA 6086, LA 6077*
                                   & *TW 30004*)

(Der) VERSCHWENDER 1833
  (Inc. Music to play by Raymund)
Hobellied—Da streiten sich die Leut' B
  G. Pechner   in ♯ **Roy. 1557**

KRIEGER, Adam (1634-1666)

NEUE ARIEN 1667
COLLECTION

Der Augen Schein sein Schmerz und Pein ø
Adonis Tod bringt mich in Not
Der Liebe Macht herrscht Tag und Nacht
  (Nun sich der Tag geendet hat) ø
Der Unbestand ist ihr verwandt
Den liebsten Lohn gibt Venus' Sohn
Zusatz ø
Der Liebsten Herz macht Scherz und Schmerz
Frisch, fröhlich, frei ohn' Heuchelei
Es fehlet ihr nur eine Zier
Aurora und Stell' erschienen schnell ø
Ein Freund, ein Trunk, ein Lieb, ein Sprung
Der Rheinsche Wein tanzt gar zu fein ø

  M. Guilleaume (S), H.-P. Egel (A), J.
  Feyerabend (T), F. Harlan (B), Scheck Cha.
  Ens.—Neumeyer (hpsi.)   ♯ **HP.APM 14035**
  [marked ø also on ♭ *Pol. 37043*]

KRIEGER, Johann (1651-1735)

(6) PARTITAS Clavier 1697
No. 5, A major
  ☆ F. Krakamp (hpsi.) (*Buxtehude*)   ♭ *Pol. 37013*

… **Allemande only**
  E. Heiller (hpsi.)   in ♯ **Uni.LP 1010**
  († History of the Dance I)

KRIEGER, Johann Philipp (1649-1725)

CANTATA
(Die) Gerechten werden weggerafft 1686
  cho., gambas, cont.
  ☆ Basle Cha. Cho.—Sacher   in **V**♯ *AS. 1802LD*

KROMMER (KRAMÁŘ), František
(1759-1831)

Concerto, C major ob. & orch.
  ☆ F. Hantak & Brno Radio—Devaty (♯ *Sup.LPM 59;*
                                   U. 5042C; & ♯ *Csm.CLPS 1029*)

Harmonie, E flat major, Op. 71 wind insts.
  ☆ Prague Wind Inst. Ens. (♯ *Sup.LPM 60; U. 5041C*)

KRUMPHOLZ, Johann Baptist (1745-1790)
  SEE: † XVIIIth CENTURY HARP MUSIC

KUCHAŘ, Jan Ch. (1751-1829)

FANTASIAS org.
  D minor ☆ F. Michalek (in ♯ *Sup.LPM 71; U. 5074C*)
  G minor ☆ M. Šlechta (in ♯ *Sup.LPM 71; U. 5074C*)

☆ = Re-issue of a recording to be found in previous volumes.

KUHLAU, Friedrich Daniel Rudolph
(1786-1832)

(The) ELVES' HILL, Op. 100   1828
(*Elverhøj:* Inc. Music to Heiberg's play)
Overture & No. 12, Ballet Music   Act V
Danish Radio—Frandsen   ♯ *Phi.S 06057R*
(2ss)

SONATINAS, pf.
Op. 20, No. 3, F major
Op. 55, No. 1, C major
Op. 55, No. 2, G major
Op. 55, No. 3, C major
L. Kraus   ♯ *Edu.EP 3003*
(*Clementi*)

Op. 59, No. 1, A major
Op. 88, No. 2, G major
P. Zeitlin   ♯ *Opus. 6005*
(*Diabelli, Clementi, Dussek*)
[with accompanying *Matching Music Book*, pub. Marks, N.Y.]

KUHNAU, Johann (1660-1722)

FRISCHE CLAVIERFRÜCHTE   hpsi.   1692
(DDT. IV)
Sonata quarta, C minor
D. Handman (pf.)   in ♯ *LOL.OL 50078*
(† Sonatas of XVIIth & XVIIIth Cent.)

Partita, F major   hpsi. 1689   (DDT. IV)
... **Gigue luthée**
R. Gerlin   in ♯ *LOL.OL 50043*
(† Clavecinistes italiens et allemands)   (♯ OL.LD 67)

SONATAS, Biblical   hpsi.   1700   (DDT. IV)
No. 1, C major: Der Streit zwischen David und Goliath
No. 3, G major: Jacobs Heyrath
No. 4, C minor: Der todtkrancke und wieder gesunde Hiskias
F. Neumeyer   ♯ *Pol. 14026*
[Titles read in *German* by F. Uhlenbruch]
(No. 1 also on ♭ *Pol. 37014*)

KUPFERMAN, Meyer (b. 1926)

Little Symphony   1952
Vienna State Op.—Litschauer   ♯ *Van.VRS 434*
(*Swanson: Short Symphony*)

LALANDE, Michel-Richard de
(1651-1726)
MOTETS
Beatus vir   Ps. 111   S, A, Bs, cho.   1692 (ed. Pagot)
Usquequo, Domine   Ps. 12   S, A, T, Bs, cho.   1692
(ed. Gervais)
D. Monteil, J. Collard, M. Hamel, A. Vessières,
Caillard Cho. & Leclair Inst. Ens.—Fremaux
♯ *Era.LDE 3027*

Christe, redemptor omnium
St. Louis de Versailles Cath. Cho.—Roussel
♯ *SM. 33-03*
(*M.A. Charpentier, Couperin, Victoria, Marchand*)
(♯ *Per.SPL 712*)

De Profundis   Ps. 129   S, S, T, T, B, cho.
F. Sailer & L. Kiefer, B. Michaelis & N. Poeld,
R. Titze, South German Radio Cho. &
Stuttgart Pro Musica Orch.—Couraud
♯ *E. & AmVox.PL 9040*

Deus in adjutorium   Ps. 70 ... **Adjutor meus**
M. Casadesus Ens.   in ♯ *Plé.P 3083*
(† *Musiques à la Chapelle du Roy*)   (♯ *West.WN 18167*)

Quam dilecta   ed. Abbé Roussel
St. Brieuc Cath. Cho. & Cha. Orch.—Le Coat
♭ *SM. 45-02*
[recorded in the cathedral during the Patronal Festival]

Venite exsultemus   Ps. 95   S, cho., orch.
... Venite exsultemus
Venite adoremus
Hodie si vocem ejus
Venite exsultemus
A. Fontana & Versailles Cho. & Orch.—Roussel
(*Campra, Caurroy, etc.*)   ♯ *SM. 33-06*

SINFONIES pour les soupers du roy
SELECTION, ed. Cellier
Suite I: Ouverture; Air No. 3
Ballet de Flore: Air de Diane
Suite V: Grand air
Menuet de Cardenio
Passepied de l'inconnu
Rondeau—Sarabande
Air de l'inconnu   (*Premier ballet du roy, 1720*)
Paris Coll. Mus.—Douatte   ♯ *LI.TWV 91092*
(*Couperin, Lully, Mouret, etc.*)   (♯ Cpt.MC 20086)

SELECTION, ed. Désormière
Chaconne en écho avec les trompettes
Musette de Cardenio
Aria
Musette pour les hautbois
Fanfare du concert pour les trompettes[1]
Sinfonie du Te Deum   (see below)
Lamoureux—Colombo   ♯ *LOL.OL 50106*
(½s—*Rameau: Les Paladins*)   (2ss, V♯ *DO.LD 29*)

Chaconne en écho avec les trompettes
Musette pour les hautbois
Aria, D minor
Sinfonie du Te Deum
Belgian Radio Cha.—Marinetti
(*Clarke & Lully*)   ♯ *Mae.OA 20001*

(4) SYMPHONIES DE NOËLS   1736 (ed. Cellier)
No. 1
Champs-Élysées Th.—Allain   ♭ *Sel. 470.C.001*
[A. Cellier, hpsi.]
No. 2
... 2nd & 3rd Noëls only
Paris Coll. Musicum—Douatte   ♭ *Pat.D 112*
No. 4
Paris Coll. Musicum—Douatte
♭ *Cpt.EXTP 1008*

Te Deum   S, A, T, B, cho. & orch.   1688
A. Fontana, S. Courtin, P. Derenne, L.
Rondeleux, Versailles Cath. Cho. & Cha.
Orch.—G. Roussel[2]   ♯ *SM. 33-20*

LALO, Victor Antoine Édouard (1823-1892)

Concerto, vln. & orch., F major, Op. 20   1872
☆ M. Solovieff & Vienna State Op.—Swoboda
(♯ Clc. 6221)

Concerto, vlc. & orch., D minor   1876
Z. Nelsova & L.P.O.—Boult   ♯ *D.LXT 2906*
(*Saint-Saëns*)   (♯ Lon.LL 964)
A. Navarra & Czech Phil.—Silvestri
♯ *Sup.LPV 202*
(*Franck*)   (♯ U. 5186G)
A. Navarra & Paris Opéra—Young
(*Saint-Saëns*)   ♯ *Cap.P 8318*
☆ T. de Machula & Residentie—Otterloo ♯ *Epic.LC 3072*
(*Bloch*)
☆ B. Michelin & Haarlem Sym.—T. Verheij (♯ Clc. 6245)

NAMOUNA   Ballet   1882
Orch. Suite No. 1
1. Prélude   2. Sérénade   3. Thème variée
4a. Parade de foire   4b. Fête foraine
(*continued on next page*)

---

[1] This title, though listed on the label, is omitted from the LOL. pressing, though included in the DO. original issue.
[2] At a public performance in Versailles Cathedral.

Orch. Suite No. 2
1. Danse marocaine   2. Mazurka
3. La sieste   4. Pas de cymbales   5. Presto
L.P.O.—Martinon   ♯ **D.LXT 5114**
(♯ Lon.LL 1268)

... Suite No. 1 only
Lamoureux—Fournet   ♯ **Phi.N 00196L**
(*below*)   (♯ Epic.LC 3049)

Quartet, Strings, E flat major, Op. 45   1888
Parrenin Qtt.   ♯ **Strad.STR 618**
(*Gounod & Donizetti*)

Rapsodie norvégienne orch.   1881
Lamoureux—Fournet   ♯ **Phi.N 00196L**
(*above & below*)   (♯ Epic.LC 3049)
Concerts Colonne—Sebastian   ♯ **FUra. 5101**
(*Symphony, G minor*)   (♯ Ura. 7142)
(*Symphonie espagnole* on ♯ Ura. 7156)
☆ Concerts Colonne—Fourestier (♭ *Pat.ED 33: EDQ 103*)

(Le) ROY D'YS Opera 3 Acts   1888
Overture
Lamoureux—Fournet   ♯ **Phi.N 00196L**
(*above*)   (♯ Epic.LC 3049)
(*Chabrier* on ♯ *Phi.S 06034R*)
French Nat. Radio—Fourestier   ♯ **Pat.DTX 126**
(*below & St.-Saëns*)   (♯ ArgPat.ADTX 1802;
♭ *AmVox.VIP 45440*)
☆ Boston Sym.—Münch   ♯ **G.ALP 1245**
(*Berlioz; Ravel, etc.*)
☆ Opéra-Comique—Wolff (♯ *D.LW 5042; Lon.LD 9040*)

Le Salut nous est promis   T   Act I
☆ M. Villabella (in ♯ Od.ODX 136)

Vainement, ma bien aimée—Aubade   T   Act III
☆ R. Crooks   in ♯ Cam.CAL 148
   M. Villabella   in ♯ Od.ODX 136
🄷 C. Rousselière   *HRS. 1084**

Scherzo orch.[1]   1884
French Nat. Radio—Fourestier   ♯ **Pat.DTX 126**
(*above*)   (♯ ArgPat.ADTX 1802)
Belgian Radio—Doneux   ♯ **Mae.OAT 25006**
(*Saint-Saëns*)

SONGS
Ballade à la lune (Musset)   *c.* 1860
C. Devos (T), G. Lecompte (pf.)   Pat.PDT 283
(*Bizet, Gounod, Massenet*)   (♭ *D 111*)

Marine (Theuriet)   *c.* 1884
M. Sénéchal (T), J. Bonneau (pf.)
in ♯ *Phi.N 00681R*
(*Chausson, Chabrier, Duparc, Hahn, etc.*)

Symphonie espagnole, Op. 21   vln. & orch.
Original Version (4 movts., without Intermezzo)
N. Milstein & St. Louis Sym.—Golschmann
♯ **DCap.CTL 7095**
(*Prokofiev*)   (♯ Cap.P 8303)
A. Grumiaux & Lamoureux—Fournet
♯ **Phi.A 00228L**
(*Chausson & Ravel*)   (♯ Epic.LC 3082)
☆ J. Heifetz & Vic. Sym.—Steinberg   ♯ **G.BLP 1029**
(2ss)   (*VBLP 809*)
(*Saint-Saëns & Sarasate* on ♯ FALP 252)
(*Korngold* on ♯ Vic.LM 1782)
F. Meisel[2] & Berlin Sym.—Schartner   ♯ **Ura.RS 7-13**
(*Rimsky*)
(*Rapsodie, above,* on ♯ Ura. 7156; *Liszt* on ♯ MTW. 538;
2ss., ♯ *ACC.MP 19*)

Later Version, with 3rd movt., Intermezzo
A. Campoli & L.P.O.—Beinum   ♯ **D.LXT 2801**
(♯ Lon.LL 763)
D. Oistrakh & Philharmonia—Martinon
♯ **C.CX 1246**
(♯ QCX 10151; Angel. 35205)
D. Oistrakh & State Sym.—Kondrashin
♯ **Csm.CRLP 179**
(*Paganini, Wagner, etc.*)   (8ss, USSR. 015565/72)
L. Kogan & Paris Cons.—Bruck   ♯**C.FCX 403**
R. Odnoposoff & Utrecht Sym.—Goehr   ♯ *MMS. 14*
Y. Heurtevant & Vienna Artists—Anon.   ♯ Ply. 12-46

Symphony, G minor   1885-6
Concerts Colonne—Sebastian   ♯ *FUra. 5101*
(*above*)   (♯ Ura. 7142)

LAMBERT, Constant (1905-1951)

Concerto, pf., fl., 3 cls., tpt., trb., vlc., cbs. & perc.
1930-31
G. Watson & Argo Cha. Ens.—Groves
(1½ss—*Songs*)   ♯ **Argo.RG 50**
M. Pressler & Cha. Ens.—Bloomfield
(*Berners*)   ♯ **MGM.E 3081**

HOROSCOPE   Ballet   1938
Orchestral Suite
L.S.O.—Irving   ♯ **D.LXT 2791**
(*Walton*)   (♯ Lon.LL 771)
... No. 2, Sarabande for the followers of Virgo
... No. 4, Bacchanale
☆ Philharmonia—Lambert   ♯ **C.SX 1003**
(*below, & Walton*)

(The) Rio Grande (Sitwell)   A, pf., cho., orch.
1929
☆ G. Ripley, K. Greenbaum, Philharmonia Cho. & Orch.
—Lambert (*above*)   ♯ **C.SX 1003**

SONGS
(8) Chinese Songs (Li-Po, trs. Obata)   1926
A. Young (T), G. Watson (pf.)   ♯ **Argo.RG 50**
(½s—*above*)

LANDI, Stefano (*c.* 1590-*c.* 1655)

SEE: † History of Music in Sound (44)

LANDINI (or LANDINO), Francesco (1325-1397)

SEE: † Anthologie Sonore
     † Histoire de la Musique vocale
     † History of Music in Sound (22)
     † Madrigals & Caccie
     † Masterpieces of Music before 1750
     † Music of the Renaissance
     † Recorder Music ...

LANDOWSKI, Marcel (b. 1915)

(Le) Barbier de Seville Inc. Music to Beaumarchais' play
In Complete Recording of the play (♯ LI.TW 91058/9;
D.FMT 16365/6)

LANGE-MÜLLER, Peter Erasmus
(1850-1926)

ONCE UPON A TIME, Op. 25
(*Der var engang*) 1886 (Inc. Music to Drachman's play)
Midsummer Song: We love our country
(*Midsommervise: Vi elsker vort Land*)
☆ A. Schiøtz (T) (in ♯ *G.KLP 11*: ♭ *7PK 6*)
Serenade   ☆ A. Schiøtz (T) (♭ *G.7PK 6*)

LANGLAIS, Jean (b. 1907)

ORGAN MUSIC
Chant héroïque
(from 9 *Pieces*, 1945; in memory of Jehan Alain)
W. Watkins   in ♯ **McInt.MM 106**
(*Dupré, Brahms, Whitlock, etc.*)
Nativité
(No. 2 of *3 Poèmes évangéliques*, 1931-2)
H. Ash   ♯ **McInt.MC 1005**
(*Bach, Liszt, Bingham, Zechiel*)   (o.n. ♯ *WCFM.19*)

---

[1] Orch. by Lalo from Trio, A minor, Op. 26.   [2] Or Melser, according to the latest catalogue.

(3) Paraphrases grégoriennes 1933-4
... Hymne d'action de Grâce: "Te Deum"
J. Langlais   ♯ Era.LDE 3024
(below; & J. Alain) [Ste. Clotilde org., Paris]

Anon. Artist   in ♯ ASK. 2
(Bach, Alain, Sowerby, etc.)
[org. of First Presbyterian Chu., Kilgore, Texas]

Suite folklorique . . . Canzona only
Suite médiévale en forme de Messe basse
1947   (pub. 1950)
1. Prélude (Entrée)   2. Tiento (Offertoire)
3. Improvisation (Élévation) 4. Méditation (Communion)
5. Acclamations (sur le thème des acclamations Carolingiennes)
J. Langlais & M-C. Alain, respectively
                                ♯ Era.LDE 3024
(above & Alain) [Ste. Clotilde organ]

VOCAL
Ave mundi gloria
  ▽ Fourrière Basilica Singers—Vuaillat (C.LFX 923)

Missa: In simplicitate
  J. Collard (M-S) & J. Langlais (org.)
  (Messiaen)   ♯ Sel. 270.C.003

Missa: Salve Regina
  3 pt. male cho., Congregation, 2 orgs. & brass 1954
  Schola des Pères du St. Esprit, J. Langlais &
  J. Dattas (orgs.)—Deiss[1]   ♯ Era.LDE 3023
  (Dufay)   (♯ HS.HSL 9008)

FOLKSONG ARRANGEMENT: La Ville d'Is
  C. Gagnepain & Caillard Ens.   in V♯ Era.LDE 1012
  (Sea Songs)

LANNER, Joseph Franz Karl (1801-1843)

WALTZES
COLLECTIONS
    Abendsterne, Op. 180
    'S Hoâmweh, Op. 202
    Die Liebeständler, Op. 105
    Die Romantiker, Op. 167
    Die Schönbrunner, Op. 200
  A. Schneider Str. Ens.   ♯ AmC.CL 556
  (Mozart & J. Strauss) (most are ☆)   (♭ set B 417)

    Hofballtänze, Op. 161
    Krönungswalzer, Op. 133
    Lebenspulse, Op. 172
    Mitternachtswalzer, Op. 8
    Viennese Waltz (unid.)
  ☆ Schneider Str. Ens. (in ♯ AmC.CL 530)

Heart Strings (unid.)
  M.G.M. Orch.—Marrow   in ♯ MGM.E 3138

Hofball-Tänze, Op. 161 (Court-Ball Waltzes)
  Strauss Fest. Orch.—Ries-Walter (in ♯ Mae.OA 20014)
  Wiener Bohème Orch. (P.DPH 74)
  Vienna Salon—Kolesa (in ♯ Phi.P 10100R)
  ☆ Vienna Radio—Schönherr (in ♯ Vien.LPR 1035)
  Bavarian Sym.—Nick (PV. 72467: ♭ Pol. 30096;
                                      FPV. 5042)
  etc.

(Die) Mozartisten, Op. 196 (on themes from Mozart Operas)
  ☆ A. Schneider Str. Quintet (in ♯ AmC.CL 530)

Pestherwalzer, Op. 93
  Vienna Light Orch.—Hellmesberger (V♯ MMS.ML 1504)
  Arzi Orch. (Arzi. 711)

(Die) Romantiker, Op. 167
  Vienna State Op.—Paulik   in ♯ Van.VRS 458
                                 (♯ Ama.AVRS 6013)
  M.G.M. Orch.—Marrow   in ♯ MGM.E 3138
                                 (also MGM. 9126)

(Die) Schönbrunner, Op. 200
  Vienna State Op.—Paulik   in ♯ Van.VRS 458
                                 (♯ Ama.AVRS 6013)
  Strauss Fest. Orch.—Ries-Walter (in ♯ Mae.OA 20014)
  Mantovani Orch. (in ♯ D.LK 4064: LF 1191: ♭ DFE 6007;
                                   ♯ Lon.LL 766: ♭ BEP 6008)
  Polish Radio—Rachonis (Muza. 2119)
  ☆ Bavarian Sym.—Nick (PV. 72467: ♭ Pol. 30096;
                                      FPV. 5042)
  etc.

(Die) Werber, Op. 103
  Vienna Radio—Schönherr (in ♯ Vien.LPR 1029)
  A. Lutter Orch. (Od.O-28518; P.DPW 73)

MISCELLANEOUS
Dampfgalopp, Op. 94[2]
  Vienna Radio—Schönherr   in ♯ Vien.LPR 1030
Waltzes and Styrian Dances[3]
  H. Somer (pf.)   in ♯ Rem. 199-124
  (Schubert, etc.)

LANTINS, Arnold de (fl. c. 1431)
  SEE: † ANTHOLOGIE SONORE

LAPARRA, Raoul (1876-1943)

(La) HABANERA 3 Acts 1908
Et c'est à moi . . .
Le sort m'a désigné Act I Bs
  ☆ Vanni-Marcoux (in ♯ G.FJLP 5035)
Murciana pf.
  ☆ G. Copeland (in ♯ MGM.E 3025)

LARSSON, Lars-Erik (b. 1908)

Concerto, Op. 42 vln. & orch. 1952
  A. Gertler & Stockholm Radio—Frykberg
  (Blomdahl & Fernström)   ♯ Ll.TW 91091

Pastoral Suite, Op. 19 orch. 1938
  ☆ Stockholm Radio—Westerberg (♯ Lon.LS 714;
                      Romance only on D.K 24035: ♭ 71032)

Little March: Serenade
  ▽ Orch.—Hahn (Symf.B 5003)

LASERNA, Blas (1751-1816)
  SEE: † SPANISH TONADILLAS
       † SPANISH RENAISSANCE MUSIC
  & NIN: Tonadillas, transcription

LASSUS, Orlando de (c. 1532-1594)
  (Roman figures refer to Volumes of the Complete Edn.)

CHANSONS, SONGS & MADRIGALS
COLLECTION
  Audite nova! (Der Bau'r von Eselskirchen) XX 1573
  Hört zu ein news Gedicht (Moreske: Das grosse Nasenlied)
                          XVIII 1576
  4 VILLANELLE X 1581
      Matona mia cara (Todescha: Landsknechtsständchen)
      S'io ti videss' una sol
      Io ti vorria contar la pena mia
      Ola! o che bon eccho!
  R. Lamy Ensemble   ♭ Pol. 37008

Bonjour, mon cœur (Ronsard) XII 1564
  N. Boulanger Ens.   in ♯ B.AXTL 1048
  († French Renaissance Music)
                          (♯ D.FAT 263102; AmD.DL 9629)
  Harvard Glee Club & Radcliffe Cho. Soc.
  —Woodworth   in ♯ Camb.CRS 202
  († Chansons & Motets)

Ich weiss mir ein Meidlein XX 1583
  Vienna Academy Cho.—Gillesberger
                                in ♯ SPA. 58
  († Songs of the Renaissance)
  Madrigal Singers—Robe (Eng)   in ♯ Fred. 2
  (Byrd, Ibert, Martinů, etc.)

---

[1] Recorded in Notre-Dame Cathedral, Paris, 18-ii-1955.
[2] From Dampf-Walzer und Galopp, Op. 94; consists of the Introduction to Waltz No. 1 and the Galopp, ARR. Schönherr.
[3] ARR. Somer from Hoffnungsstrahlen, Op. 158; Pesther-W, Op. 93; Steyrische Tänze, Op. 165; Die Romantiker, Op. 167

Lagríme di San Pietro
... No. 7, Ogni occhio del Signor
... No. 17, Ah quanti gia felice

Im Lant zu Wirtenberg XVIII 1567
Yale Univ. Music School Cho.—Hindemith
in ♯ Over.LP 5
(† Yale University, Vol. II)

Matona, mia cara 4 voices X 1581
(*Landsknechtsständchen*)
Ghent Oratorio Soc.—de Pauw in ♯ Eso.ES 514
(† Flemish Choral Music) (♯ Cpt.MC 20017)
Netherlands Cha. Cho.—de Nobel
in ♯ Phi.N 00678R
(† Sacred & Secular Songs from the Renaissance)
Obernkirchen Children's Cho.—Möller (*Ger*)
(in ♯ Od.OLA 1007: ♭ OBL 1061) in ♯ Angel. 64012
☆ Vienna Cha. Cho.—Grossmann (in V♯ Sel.LPP 8714)

Mon cœur se recommande à vous 5 voices XIV
1560
Harvard Glee Club & Radcliffe Cho. Soc.
—Woodworth in ♯ Camb.CRS 202
(† Chansons & Motets)

Ola! o che bon eccho! 8 voices X 1581
Ghent Oratorio Soc.—de Pauw in ♯ Eso.ES 514
(† Flemish Choral Music) (♯ Cpt.MC 20017)
Vienna Boys' Cho. (*Ger*)—Kühbacher
♯ Phi.S 06066R
(*Schubert, Schumann, Mozart & Folk Songs*) [ARR. Böhm]
Pancratius Male Cho.—Heydendael
in ♯ C.HS 1001
(*Waelrant, Jannequin, Handel, etc.*)
U.S.S.R. State Cho.—Sveshnikov Ete. 130004
(*Folksongs*)
Estonian State Cho.—Ernesaks (*Estonian*) (*USSR. 23677*)

Quand mon mary vient de dehors XII 1564
N. Boulanger Ens. in ♯ B.AXTL 1048
(† French Renaissance Music)
(♯ D.FAT 263102: AmD.DL 9629)
Paris Vocal Ens.—Jouve in ♯ LT.MEL 94007
(† French Madrigals) (V♯ Sel.LLA 1079)

Qui dort icy? (Marot) XII 1564
M. Rollin Ens. in ♯ CND. 9
(† La Musique et la Poésie)

Soyons joyeux sur la plaisante verdure XII 1564
Hufstader Singers in ♯ SOT. 1092

Wohl kommt der May XX 1583
Vienna Academy Cho.—Gillesberger ♯ SPA. 58
(† Songs of the Renaissance)

---

(3) Fantasias (Nos. 4, 10, 11 of *Bicinia*, 1609)
Musicians' Workshop Recorder Consort
in ♯ CEd.CE 1018
(† Recorder Music of Six Centuries)

MASSES
'Le Bergier et la bergière' 1574
... **Sanctus & Agnus Dei**
☆ Paraphonistes—de Van (in † ♯ HS.AS 6)

'Douce mémoire' 1577
Paris Vocal Ens.—Jouve ♯ Sel.LA 1072

'Puisque j'ay perdu' (VIII toni)
before 1570; pub. 1577
Vienna Cha. Cho.—Gillesberger ♯ Uni.LP 1013
(*Palestrina: Mass*)

... **Benedictus**
Brompton Oratory Choir—Washington
G.HMS 36
(† History of Music in Sound) (in ♯ Vic. set LM 6029)

Quinti toni ('Pillons, pillons l'orge') 1577
... **Sanctus**
Festival Singers—Iseler ♯ Hall.ChS 3
(*Byrd, Gibbons, Mundy, Willan*)

MOTETS, HYMNS, PSALMS, etc.
Adoramus te 4 voices I 1604
N.Y. Primavera Singers—Greenberg
in ♯ Per.SPL 597
(† Renaissance Music) (♯ Cpt.MC 20077)
☆ Netherlands Cha. Cho.—de Nobel (in ♯ Phi.S 06026R)

De lamentatione Hieremiae prophetae
... **Easter Eve, Nos. 1 & 2**
☆ Dessoff Cho.—Boepple (♯ Clc. 6203)

Domine, ne in furore
(No. 1 of *Penitential Psalms*, 5 vv.)
Amsterdam Motet Cho.—Nobel
♯ CHS.CHS 1196
(*Monteverdi*) (♯ Clc. 6280)

Exaudi, Deus 4 vv. III 1585
Regensburg Cath. Cho.—Schrems D.F 43802
(*Victoria: Popule meus*) (♭ D 17802: ♭ DX 1762)

Hodie Christus natus est (unid.)
Verbum caro factum est (unspec.)
Petits Chanteurs de la Sainte-Croix—Debat
in ♯ D.FMT 163159

In pace in idipsum 3 vv. I 1604
☆ Gregorian Inst. Cho.—Vitry in ♯ GIOA.PM-LP 1
(† Polyphonic Masters)

Missa brevis
(ARR. from unspec. Motets by Theo M. Marier)
... **Sanctus & Benedictus**
N.Y. Blessed Sacrament Qtt. in ♯ Bib.CL 221
(† Music of the Church)

Nos qui sumus 4 vv. I 1753
Vatican Cho.—Bertolucci ♯ Per.SPL 706
(*Victoria, Palestrina, etc.*)
Petits Chanteurs de la Renaissance
V♯ Era.LDE 1001
(† Polyphonic Motets of XVIth Cent.) (in ♯ HSLP. 9007)

Omnia tempus habent 8 vv. 1585
☆ Paraphonistes—de Van (in † ♯ HS.AS 6)

Resonet in laudibus 5 vv. III 1569
N.Y. Primavera Singers—Greenberg
in ♯ Per.SPL 597
(† Renaissance Music) (♯ Cpt.MC 20077)

Salve Regina 4 vv. I
N.Y. Primavera Singers—Greenberg
in ♯ Per.SPL 597
(† Renaissance Music) (♯ Cpt.MC 20077)

Scio enim quod Redemptor meus vivit 4 vv. III 1565
Brompton Oratory Choir—Washington
G.HMS 36
(† History of Music in Sound) (in ♯ Vic. set LM 6029)

Tibi laus, tibi gloria 4 vv. III 1568
Harvard Glee Club—Woodworth
in ♯ Camb.CRC 101
(*Byrd, Palestrina, Victoria, etc.*)

Tristis est anima mea 5 vv. V 1568
Copenhagen Boys' & Men's Cho.—Møller
in ♯ HS.HSL 2072
(† Masterpieces of Music before 1750)
(also in † Histoire de la Musique Vocale)

LATRE, Joan de (d. c. 1589)
SEE: † ANTHOLOGIE SONORE

LAVAGNE, André (b. 1914)

Steeple-chase bsn. & pf. 1954
M. Allard & F. Gobet ♭ Pat.G 1055
(*Ibert, Bloch, etc.*)

☆ = Re-issue of a recording to be found in previous volumes.

LAVRY, Marc (b. 1903)

(5) Jewish Dances pf.
… No. 5, Hora
    L. Granetman   in ♯ *Phi.N 00641R*
    (Ben-Haim, Boscovich, Stutschewsky)

LAWES, William (1602-1645)

COURTLY MASQUING AYRES pub. 1662
Alemain; Corant; Saraband; Jigg
    C. Dolmetsch (recorder), J. Saxby (hpsi.)
               in ♯ **D.LXT 2943**
    († Recorder & Hpsi. Recital)   (♯ Lon.LL 1026)

Saraband; Ayre; Jigg — ARR. Bridgewater
    Westminster Light Orch.—Bridgewater
               in ♯ **West.WL 4007**

(The) Wise Men Catch (*Musical Banquet* iii, 1651)
    Glee Singers—Bath   in ♯ **Allo. 3046**
    († More Catches & Glees . . .)

LAZARIN, (d. 1653)

    SEE: † ANTHOLOGIE SONORE (♯ 3004LD)

LE BÈGUE, Nicolas Antoine (c. 1630-1702)

    SEE: BÈGUE, N. A. LE

LECHNER, Leonhard (c. 1553-1606)

GERMAN LIEDER: COLLECTION (1577-1589)
O Lieb, wie süss und bitter
Die Musik ist eine schöne Kunst
Die Musik g'schrieben auf Papier
Mit Tanzen und Springen
Gott b'hüte dich
Grün ist der Mai
Ein edler Jäger wohlgemut
    Berlin Motet Cho.—Arndt   ♯ **HP.APM 14010**
    (Hassler)

Gott b'hüte dich
    Vienna Academy Cho.—Gillesberger
               in ♯ **SPA. 58**
    († Songs of the Renaissance)

LECLAIR, Jean-Marie (1697-1764)

CONCERTOS, Violin & str. orch.
Op. 7, No. 2, D major (*a*) *c.* 1737
Op. 7, No. 5, A minor (*b*)
Op. 10, No. 1, B flat major (*b*) 1743-4
Op. 10, No. 5, E minor (*a*)
    H. Fernandez (*a*), G. Raymond (*b*), & Leclair
    Ens.—Paillard   ♯ **DDP. 21-2**
                        (♯ HS.HSL 140)

Op. 10, No. 2, A major
    H. Fernandez & Leclair Ens.—Paillard
                      ♯ **DDP. 21-1**
    (below; Boismortier, Naudot)   (♯ HS.HSL 103)

Op. 10, No. 3, D major
    H. Fernandez & Leclair Ens.—Paillard
                V♯ *Era.LDE 1010*

CONCERTO, Oboe & str. orch.
Op. 7, No. 3, C major *c.* 1737
    P. Pierlot & Leclair Ens.—Paillard
    (Blavet)   ♯ *Era.LDE 2009*

SONATAS, Vln. or Fl. & Cont.
Book I: Op. 1, 1723; Book II: Op. 2, 1728; Book III:
    Op. 5, 1734; Book IV: Op. 9, 1738; Op. 2, No. 8 is
    a Trio Sonata
COLLECTIONS   (ed. L. Boulay)
Op. 1: No. 8, G major
Op. 2: No. 1, E minor; No. 12, G minor
Op. 5: No. 1, A major; No. 4, B flat major
Op. 9: No. 4, A major
    G. Alès (vln.), I. Nef (hpsi.)   ♯ **LOL.OL 50087/8**
    [with vlc. in certain movts.]   (♯ OL.LD 47/8)
Op. 1: No. 2, C major; No. 6, E minor
Op. 2: No. 1, E minor; No. 3, C major; No. 5, G major
    No. 11, B minor
Op. 9: No. 2, E minor; No. 7, G major[1]
    J-P. Rampal (fl.), R. Veyron-Lacroix (hpsi.)
                   ♯ **LOL.OL 50050/1**

Op. 2, No. 3, C major
    G. Ciompi (vln.), H. Chessid (hpsi.),
    L. Rostal (vlc.)   ♯ **CHS.H 9**
    (Lully, Couperin)

Op. 2, No. 5, G major
    J. Pougnet (vln.), A. Goldsbrough (hpsi.) &
    gamba   **G.HMS 63**
    († History of Music in Sound)   (in ♯ Vic. set LM 6031)

Op. 2, No. 8, D major (à 3)
    B. Detrekoy,[2] H. E. Deckert (gamba), T. R.
    Poulsen (vlc.), L. Larsen (virginals)
    (Abel & Telemann)   ♯ *Felix.LP 300*

Op. 5, No. 9, E major
… Minuet & La Chasse only[3]
— — ARR. WOODWIND QUINTET   Müller
    Chicago Sym. Quintet   in ♯ **Aphe. 14**
    (Stravinsky, Debussy, etc.)

Op. 5, No. 10, C major
… Tambourin — ARR. ORCH.   Bridgewater
    Westminster Light—Bridgewater
    (Boyce, etc.)   in ♯ **West.WL 4007**

Op. 9, No. 3, D major
    L. Friedemann,[2] F. Viderø (hpsi.), H. E.
    Deckert (gamba)   ♯ **HS.HSL 95**
    (J. S. Bach, Handel, Corelli)
    D. Oistrakh & V. Yampolsky (pf.)
                   ♯ **Van.VRS 6024**
    (Ysaÿe, Beethoven) [Paris recording, 1953]
    (Ysaÿe, Khachaturian, Tchaikovsky, on ♯ *CdM.LD 8075)*
    (Beethoven, Vladigerov, on ♯ *Csm.CRLP 153)*[4]
    D. Oistrakh & N. Walter (pf.)   ♯ **Eta.LPM 1023**
    (Kodály, Tchaikovsky, Prokofiev)   (& 4ss, Eta. 120022/3)
    D. Oistrakh & V. Yampolsky (pf.)
                   ♯ **JpV.LS 2026**
    (Debussy, Zarzycki, etc.) [Tokyo recording, 1955]
… Tambourin — ARR. CYMBALOM & PF.
    I. Tarjani-Tóth & I. Aitoff (in ♯ *G.FBLP 1067)*

SONATAS, 2 vlns. & cont. *c.* 1732
Op. 4, No. 3, D minor
    G. Raymond & J. Lacrouts, A-M. Beckensteiner
    (hpsi.), J. Deferrieux (vlc.)   ♯ **DDP. 21-1**
    (above; Boismortier, Naudot)   (♯ HS.HSL 103)

LECOCQ, Charles (1832-1918)

(La) FILLE DE MME. ANGOT Operetta 1872
COMPLETE RECORDING (*Russian*)
    E. Shumskaya, G. Nelepp, etc., Moscow Radio
    Cho. & Orch.—Akyulov ♯ **USSR.D 01604/9**
    (6ss)
Suites ☆ Covent Garden—Rignold[5] (♭ *G.7EP 7020)*
    N.Y. Phil. Sym.—Kurtz[6] (♭ *AmC. set A 1048)*
Overture Italian Radio—Gallino   in ♯ **Tem.MTT 2058**
                         (▽ *Cet.TI 7034)*
    French Nat. Radio—Dervaux   ♭ *Pac. 45040*
    (Ganne: Les Saltimbanques, Overture)

---

[1] This collection includes all the Sonatas originally intended for the flute.
[2] Baroque violin.   [3] Ed. David: *Hohe Schule*, No. 23.   [4] May not be the same recording.
[5] ARR. Jacob for Ballet *Mam'zelle Angot.*   [6] ARR. Mohaupt.

Rondeau: Certainement j'aimais Clairette   B
　　M. Dens (♭ *Pat.ED 4*)

(Le) PETIT DUC   Operetta   3 Acts   1878
ABRIDGED RECORDING (with *Fr* Narration)
　　N. Renaux (S), W. Clément (B), L. Berton (S),
　　F. Betti (M-S), R. Hérent (T), St. Paul Cho.
　　& Lamoureux Orch.—Gressier
　　　　　　　　　　　　　　　♯ Pat.DTX 141

LECUONA, Ernesto (b. 1896)

(Abridged listing only)

(6) Danzas Afro-Cubanas
(6) Danzas Cubanas
Suite espagnole   (or andalusa)
　　J. Echaniz (pf.)　　　　　　　**♯ Nix.WLP 5343**
　　　　　　　　　　　　　　　(♯ West.WL 5343)
Suite espagnole
Zambra gitana; Granada; Siboney
　　P. Flores (pf.)　　　　　　　　**♯ MGM.E 199**

Suite espagnole: Malagueña; Andalucia
Danzas Afro-Cubanas: La Comparsa; Danza negra; Danza
　　Lucomi
　　E. Lecuona　　　　　　　　　♭ *G.7EG 8143*
　　(in ♯ *Vic.LPM 1055:* ♭ *set EPB 1055*, with other Lecuona
　　titles)

▽ & other items include *inter alia*
COLLECTIONS on: ♯ *D.LF 1004;* ♯ *Lon.LPB 165;*
　　♯ *AmC.ML 4361;* & on *C.DB 2453;* ♭ *Vic.ERA 176:*
　　Vic.EPA 276, etc.   Most of these contain his more
　　"popular" compositions, in various arrangements.

LEFEBVRE, Charles Édouard (1843-1917)

Suite, Op. 57   fl., ob., cl., hrn., bsn.
　　Chicago Sym. Woodwind Quintet   in
　　　　　　　　　　　　　　　♯ Aphe.AP 16
　　(Paganini, Ravel, etc.)

LEGLEY, Victor (b. 1915)

Suite pour orchestre   1944
　　☆ Belgian Nat.—Quinet   *(Alpaerts)*　　♯ *Lon.LL 874*

LEGRENZI, Giovanni (1626-1690)

SEE: † HISTORY OF MUSIC IN SOUND (64)
　　　† OLD ITALIAN AIRS

LEGUERNEY, Jacques (b. 1906)

SONGS: COLLECTIONS
Le CARNAVAL   cycle
　　1. La Grotesque　2. La Belle Brune　3. Le Carnaval
La Nuit, I, II, III   (St. Amant)
Mélodies sur des poèmes de la Pléiade   (Ronsard)
　　1. Epipalinodie　2. Ma douce jouvence
　　3. Sonnet pour Hélène　4. À sa maîtresse
　　5. À son page
　　G. Souzay (B), J. Bonneau (pf.)
　　(Roussel)　　　　　　　　　**♯ Lum.LD 3-407**

L'Adieu   (Apollinaire)
Clotilde   (Apollinaire)
À la fontaine   (Ronsard)
Chanson triste   (Bertaut)
Villanelle   (Desportes)
　　G. Touraine (S), J. Bonneau (pf.)
　　　　　　　　　　　　　　　♯ Lum.LD 3-402
　　(Poulenc, Chabrier, Debussy, etc.)

LEHÁR, Franz (1870-1948)

(Abridged listings only)

I. NON-OPERATIC

Chinesische Ballet-Suite
　　Imperial Light Orch.—Koschat　　♯ *Imp.ILP 124*
　　(Eva, Gold und Silber, Land des Lächelns)

MARCHES
106er Marsch   (or: *Piave-Marsch*)   1920
　　Wind Band (in ♯ *Vien.LPR 1042*)

Lyuk-Lyuk-Lyuk, Op. 13, No. 1
　　Military Band—Ahninger (in ♯ *Van.VRS 7007*)

WALTZES
Donaulegenden   (*An der grauen Donau*)   1921
　　Vienna Radio—Schönherr   *(below)*　　Vien.L 6132

Gold und Silber Walzer, Op. 75
　　Philadelphia—Ormandy　　　　♭ *EPhi.NBE 11000*
　　(*Eva, Lustige Witwe*)   (♭ *Phi.N 409511E; AmC.A 1867* &
　　　　　　　　　　　　　　　　　in ♯ *ML 4893*)
　　Vox Sinfonietta—Gräf　　　　♭ *AmVox.VIP 30270*
　　(*Lustige Witwe, Waltz*)　　　(in ♯ *VX 570*)
　　☆ Hallé—Barbirolli　　　　　♭ *G.7ER 5009*
　　(*Don Pasquale, Overture*) (♭ *7ERQ 113;* ♭ *BB.ERAB 13,*
　　　　　　　　　　　　　　　　　　　　d.c.)
　　☆ Zürich Tonhalle—Lehár　　♯ *D.LW 5054*
　　(*Lustige Witwe, Waltz*)
　　M. Lanner (*G.EG 7980*)
　　Vienna Light Orch.—Kolesa (in ♯ *Phi.P 10101R*)
　　Imperial Light Orch.—Koschat (in ♯ *Imp.ILP 124*)
　　Strauss Fest. Orch.—Ries-Walter (in ♯ *Mae.OA 20015*)
　　Film Sym.—Uzelac (U.H 24420)

　　☆ M. Marrow Orch. (in ♯ *MGM.E 3138*)
　　Vienna Radio—Schönherr (♭ *Rem.REP 18*)
　　Orch.—Kostelanetz (in ♯ *C.S 1049: QS 6048: FS 1054;*
　　　　　　　　　　　　　　　♭ *AmC.A 1621*)
　　etc.

Pikanterien-Walzer, Op. 73 (or: *Asklepios-Walzer*)   1908
　　Vienna Radio—Schönherr   *(above)*　　Vien.L 6132

Ungarische Phantasie, Op. 45   vln. & cha. orch.
　　Vienna Radio—Schönherr   (2ss)　　Vien.L 6140
　　　　　　　　　　　　　　　(in ♯ *LPR 1030*)

VARIOUS POTPOURRIS
　　Danish Radio Light—Kolbe　　　　G.Z 370
　　　　　　　　　　　　　　　　　(♭ *PK 2*)
　　Imperial Light Orch.—Müller-Lampertz　♯ *Imp.ILP 107*
　　(*Fischer: Südlich der Alpen*)

II. OPERETTAS

(Die) BLAUE MAZUR   1920
Walzerscene
　　Vienna Radio—Schönherr　　　　*Vien.P 6145*
　　(*Giudetta—Intermezzo No. 1*)　　(in ♯ *LPR 1021*)

EVA   1911
Orch. Selection   Orch.—Gallino (♭ *Cet.EP 0536*)

Prelude   Imperial Light Orch.—Koschat (in ♯ *Imp.ILP 124*)
　　☆ Italian Radio—Gallino (in ♯ *Tem.MTT 2058*)

Wär es auch nichts als ein Augenblick   S
　　(*Waltz Aria*)
— ORCH. VERSIONS   (Eva Waltz)
　　Philadelphia—Ormandy　　　　♭ *EPhi.NBE 11000*
　　(*Gold und Silber, etc.*)　　(♭ *AmC.A 1867;* in ♯ *ML 4893;*
　　　　　　　　　　　　　　　　　♭ *Phi.N 409511E*)
　　Strauss Fest. Orch.—Ries-Walter (in ♯ *Mae.OA 20015*)
　　Italian Radio—Manno (in ♯ *Tem.MTT 2058;*
　　　　　　　　　　　　　　　▽ *Cet.AA 371*)
　　etc.

FRASQUITA   1922
Hab' ein blaues Himmelbett   T
　　P. Anders　　　　　　　　　　*Pol. 49112*
　　(*Ziehrer: Die Landstreicher—Sei gepriesen*)
　　　　　　　　　　　　(♭ *22112: 20121:* in ♯ *45064*)
　　W. A. Dotzer　　　　　　　in ♯ *Phi.S 06038R*
　　R. Christ (in ♭ *Hma.EP 5515:* in ♯ *L 117*)
　　P. Grundén (*Swed*) (♭ *G.7EGS 2*)
　　☆ R. Tauber (in ♯ *P.PMB 1006*)

Frasquita's Air   (unspec.)
　　☒ G. Farrar (S, *Eng*) (IRCC. 1953*)

FRIEDERIKE   1923
VOCAL SELECTION
　　G. Scheyrer, F. Pöltinger, W. A. Dotzer, etc.
　　　　　　　　　　　　　　　♯ Phi.P 10215R
　　(*Schön ist die Welt, Selection*)   (♭ *P 423106E:* ♭ *KD 156*)

O Mädchen, mein Mädchen   T
　　R. Schock　　　　　　　　　　G.EG 8154
　　(*Land des Lächelns—Von Apfelblüten*)　(♭ *7MW 604*)
　　R. Christ (in ♭ *Hma.EP 5515:* in ♯ *L 117*)
　　☆ R. Tauber (♭ *P.CBEP 1:* in ♯ *PMB 1006*)
　　P. Anders (♭ *T.UE 452830*)
　　M. Lichtegg (ArgEli.EXC 102)

Sah ein knab' ein Röslein steh'n   T
　　W. A. Dotzer　　　　　　　in ♯ *Phi.S 06047R*
　　☆ R. Tauber (in ♯ *P.PMB 1006;* ♭ *Od.GEOW 1009*)

☆ = Re-issue of a recording to be found in previous volumes.

GIUDITTA 1934
COLLECTION OF EXCERPTS
Meine Lippen, sie küssen so heiss S
Freunde, das Leben ist lebenswert T
Schönste der Frauen T
Schön, wie die blaue Sommernacht S & T
  ☆ H. Gueden (S), K. Friedrich (T) (♭ *D.DX 1767*)

Intermezzo No. 1
Vienna Radio—Schönherr   *Vien.P 6145*
(*Blaue Mazur—Walzerscene*) (in ♯ *LPR 1021*)

Du bist meine Sonne T
Freunde, das Leben ist lebenswert T
R. Schock   *G.EG 8105*
    (♭ *MW 570*)
  R. Christ (♭ *Hma.EP 5515:* in ♯ *L 117*)

... **Du bist meine Sonne** only
W. A. Dotzer   in ♯ *Phi.S 06038R*

Meine Lippen, sie küssen so heiss S
M. Reining   in ♯ *Vien.LPR 1038*

(Der) GÖTTERGATTE 1904
Overture & Jupitermarsch
Vienna Radio—Schönherr (in ♯ *Vien.LPR 1021;*
                Overture is ☆)

(Der) GRAF VON LUXEMBURG 1909
Waltz-Intermezzo
  ☆ Orch.—Kostelanetz (in ♯ *C.SX 1004: QSX 12004;*
                ♭ *AmC.A 1556:* in ♯ *CL 792*)
  Vienna Waltz—Pauscher (♭ *Rem.REP 46*)

Bist du's, lachendes Glück (Waltz Song) T & S
  ☆ H. E. Groh (*P.B 555*)
— ORCH. VERSION
Strauss Fest. Orch.—Ries-Walter (in ♯ *Mae.OA 20015*)

Lieber Freund, man greift nicht Act II S & T
  ☆ M. Slezak & H. E. Groh (*P.B 555*)

Mädel klein, Mädel fein T
W. A. Dotzer   in ♯ *Phi.S 06047R*

(Das) LAND DES LÄCHELNS 1923
COMPLETE RECORDING (Dialogue cut)

Lisa	E. Schwarzkopf (S)
Sou-chong	N. Gedda (T)
Mi	E. Loose (S)
Gustav	E. Kunz (B)
Tschang	O. Kraus (B)

etc., Cho. & Philharmonia Orch.—Ackermann
                    ♯ *C.CX 1114/5*
    (♯ *FCX 288/9;* Angel. 35052/3, set 3507)

Highlights, Vocal Selections
G. Scheyrer, W. A Dotzer, etc., & Vienna Radio Cho. &
  Orch.—Sandauer   ♯ *Phi.P 10109R*
(*Paganini*)   (♯ Epic.LC 3130)
C. Riedinger, J. Luccioni, etc. Cho. & Orch.
  —Benedetti (*Fr*)   ♯ *D.FMT 163662*
L. Dolène, L. Lupi, etc. (*Fr*) (♯ *Phi.N 76040R*)
M. Loria & F. Lenzi (*Fr*) (*P.DP 141*)
M. Dens (B) & J. Bourges (S) (♭ *Pat.ED 48*)
  ☆ E. Schwarzkopf (S), R. Glawitsch (T), etc.
                (♭ *T.UE 453115*)
T. Eipperle (S), P. Anders (T), etc. (♭ *Pol.* 20061: 22364)

Overture
Imperial Light Orch.—Koschat (in ♯ *Imp.ILP 124*)
  ☆ Zürich Tonhalle—Lehár (♯ *D.LW 5071; Lon.LD 9043*)

Dein ist mein ganzes Herz T
N. Gedda (*O. Straus: Waltz Dream, excpt.*) *Od.SD 6081*
P. Anders   *G.EH 1164*
(*below*)   (♭ *7PW 523:* in ♯ *WDLP 1513*)
[also, in ♯ *Pol. 45064:* ♭ *20121*]
W. A. Dotzer   in ♯ *Phi.S 00638R*
  R. Christ (in ♯ *Hma.L 117:* ♭ *EP 5515*)
M. Lanza (*Eng*) (in ♯ *Vic.LM 1837:* ♭ *set ERB 1837*)
  ☆ R. Tauber (in ♯ *P.PMB 1006:* & (*Eng*) ♭ *P.BSP 3003*)
H. E. Groh (♭ *Od.OBL 1014*)
R. Merrill (B, *Eng*) (♭ *Vic.ERA 75*)

Dein ist mein ganzes Herz — ARR. ORCH.
Philadelphia—Ormandy (in ♯ *AmC.ML 4893:* in ♯ *AL 48:*
                ♭ *A 1832*)

Ich möcht' einmal ☆ H. Gueden (♭ *D.DX 1766*)

Ich trete ins Zimmer ... Immer nur lächeln T
P. Anders (*above*)   *G.EH 1364*
[also, in ♯ *Pol. 45064:* ♭ *20121*] (♭ *7PW 523:* in ♯ *WDLP 513*)
  ☆ R. Tauber (*Eng*) (♭ *P.BSP 3002*)
H. E. Groh (♭ *Od.OBL 1014*)

Von Apfelblüten einen Kranz T
R. Schock   *G.EG 8154*
(*Friederike—O Mädchen, mein Mädchen*) (♭ *7MW 604*)
P. Anders   in ♯ *Pol. 45064*
                (♭ *20121*)
  M. Lichtegg (ArgEli.EXC 102)
R. Hirigoyen (*Fr*) (in ♯ *D.FM 133509*)
  ☆ P. Anders (o.v.) (♭ *T.UE 452830*)

(Die) LUSTIGE WITWE (Merry Widow) 1905
COMPLETE RECORDING (Dialogue cut)

Danilo	E. Kunz (B)
Hanna	E. Schwarzkopf (S)
Camille	N. Gedda (T)
Baron Mirko Zeta ...	A. Niessner (B)
Valencienne	E. Loose (S)
Cascada	O. Kraus (B)
St. Brioche	J. Schmidinger (Bs)

Philharmonia Cho. & Orch.—Ackermann
                    ♯ *C.CX 1051/2*
(4ss)   (♯ QCX 10050/1: VCX 515/6: FCX 237/8;
    Angel. 35033/4, set 3501)
[Heia, Mädel aufgeschaut, Act II & Viljalied only on
C.LX 1597: LVX 210; Heia Mädel & Wie die Weiber
man behandet on ♭ *SCB 113: SCBW 109: SCQB 3019*)

Highlights
D. Duval, J. Jansen, C. Devos, etc., R. St. Paul Cho. &
  Lamoureux—Gressier (*Fr*)   ♯ *Pat.DTX 113*
L. Berchman, L. S. Vela, M. F. Caballer, etc. & Madrid
  Cha. Orch. (*Span*)   ♯ *Mont.FM 25*
M. Gonzalez, H. Pelayo, A. Crespo, F. Naya, Cho. &
  Orch.—Roig (*Span*)   ♯ *Vic.LPM 1039*
E. Shieder, O. d'Arrigo, G. Scarlini, etc., Cho. & Orch.
  —Gallino (*Ital*)   ♯ *Cet. 45002*
P. Grundén, S. Stjernquist, etc. (*Swed*) ♯ *LI.WB 91099*

Vocal Selections
A. Rothenberger, H. E. Groh, Cho. & Orch.—Stephan
(*Fall,* on ♯ *DT.LGX 66043*)   ♯ *T.TW 30013*
G. Scheyrer, H. Fassler, H. Roland, etc., Cho. & Vienna
  Radio Orch.—Sandauer (♭ *Phi.KD 161*)
  ☆ E. Trötschel, V. Bak, W. Ludwig, etc. (♭ *Pol.* 20040)
F. Lamas, T. Erwin, etc. (*Eng*) (*MGM.* 9135/8)
  (Film Version)
M. Merkes, P. Merval, etc. (*Fr*) (♭ *Od.7MOE 2023*)
G. MacRae & L. Norman (*Eng*) (♯ *DCap.LC 6564:*
                Cap.P 437)

Orchestral Suite
R.I.A.S. Sym.—Becker   ♯ *Rem. 199-170*
(*J. Strauss*)   (♯ Cum.CR 302)
Austrian Sym. (in ♯ *Ply. 12-112*)

Orchestral Selections
H. Bund Orch. (*Imp. 19077*)
Polish Radio—Rachon (*Muza. 2307*)
  ☆ Vienna Radio—Sandauer (in ♯ *Phi.P 10301R*)
G. Melachrino Orch. (*G.EH 1348:* ♭ *7PQ 2008: 7PW 109*)

Overture ☆ Zürich Tonhalle—Lehár (♯ *D.LW 5054*)

Sieh' dort im kleinen Pavillon T
C. Devos (*Fr*)   ♭ *Pat.ED 35*
(*Offenbach, Audran, Messager, etc.*)

S' flüstern Geigen ... Lippen schweigen S & T
  (*Waltz Song*)
— SOLO VERSIONS
H. Gueden (S)   ♯ *D.LW 5126*
(*Zarewitsch—Schön ist die Welt, etc.*)
(♯ *Lon.LD 9158:* & ♯ *D.LXT 5033; Lon.LL 1116*)
  ☆ R. Tauber (T) (in ♯ *P.PMB 1006*)
R. Crooks (*Eng*) (in ♯ *Cam.CAL 128*)
  ♮ M. Sembrich (in ♯ *Vic.* set LCT 6701*)
— ORCH. VERSIONS (Ball-sirenenwalzer, etc.)
Philadelphia—Ormandy   ♭ *EPhi.NBE 11000*
(*Eva, Gold und Silber*) (♭ *Phi.N 409511E; AmC.A 1867:*
    A 1832: in ♯ *AL 48* & ♯ *ML 4893*)
Vox Sinfonietta (in ♯ *Vox.VX 570:* ♭ *VIP 30270*)
Strauss Fest. Orch.—Ries-Walter (in ♯ *Mae.OA 20015*)
M. Lanner Orch. (*G.EG 7920:* in ♯ *VFLP 801*)
Concert Orch.—E. Robinson (in ♯ *Argo.RG 66*)
  ☆ Orch.—Kostelanetz (in ♯ *C.SX 1004:* ♭ *AmC.A 1558*)
etc.

Viljalied S
A. Rothenberger (Pol. 57395; ♭ *20058*)
R. Christ (T) (in ♭ *Hma.EP 5515:* in ♯ *L 117*)
  ☆ L. Welitsch (*D.Z 965*)
J. MacDonald (*Eng*) (♭ *G.7EG 8059*)
etc.
— ARR. ORCH. Philadelphia—Ormandy (♭ *AmC.A 1832:*
    in ♯ *AL 48:* ML 4893; ♭ *Phi.N 409511E*)

♯ = Long-playing, 33⅓ r.p.m.   ♭ = 45 r.p.m.   ♮ = Auto. couplings, 78 r.p.m.

PAGANINI 1925
COMPLETE RECORDING   In *French*

Paganini	... ...	R. Massart (B)
Pimpinelli	... ...	R. Carles (?)
Anna Elisa	... ...	C. Riedinger (S)
Bartucci	... ...	H. Bry (?)

etc., cho. & orch.—Dervaux   ♯**D.FMT 163557/8**
(4ss) [Excerpts on ♭ *EFM 455501*]

Vocal Selections
A. Schlemm (S), P. Anders (T), Cho. & Orch.   PV. 58629
                                                    (♭ *Pol. 20067*)
(*J. Strauss: Eine Nacht in Venedig* on ♯ *Pol. 45067*)
G. Scheyrer (S), W. A. Dotzer (T), etc., Vienna Radio
  Cho. & Orch.—Sandauer   ♯ **Phi.P 10109R**
(*Land des Lächelns*)   (♯ *Epic.LC 3130*)

Hexentanz
Introduction & Violin solo   Act I
Vienna Radio—Schönherr   Vien.L 6148
                                    (in ♯ *LPR 1021*)

Gern hab' ich die Frau'n geküsst T
R. Schock   G.EG 8010
(*Marischka—Du bist die Welt für mich*)
                        (*GA 5130: JK 2851:* ♭ *MW 511*)
N. Gedda (*Swed*)   Od.ZAA 203
(*Gräfin Maritza—Grüss mir mein Wien*)
P. Grundén   D.F 40698
(*Gasparone—Dunkelrote Rosen*)
B. Manazza   Tpo. 3686
(*Nacht in Venedig—Komm' in die Gondel*)
☆ R. Tauber (in ♯ *P.PMB 1006*)

Niemand liebt dich so wie ich S & T
I. Steingruber & W. A. Dotzer   in ♯ *Phi.S 06047R*
☆ E. Sack & M. Wittrisch (♭ *T.UE 452222*)

O Signora, O Signorina T
R. Christ   in ♭ *Hma.EP 5515*
                                    (in ♯ *L 117*)
Schönes Italien T
Was ich denke, was ich fühle T & S
☒ R. Tauber & C. Vanconti-Tauber   in ♯ *Ete. 701**

(Der) RASTELBINDER 1902
Wenn zwei sich lieben S & T
☆ C. V. & R. Tauber (♭ *Od.GEOW 1009*)

SCHÖN IST DIE WELT
Vocal Selection
G. Scheyrer, F. Pöltinger, W. A. Dotzer, etc.
                                ♯ **Phi.P 10215R**
(*Friederike, Selection*)   (♭ *P 423155E:KD 155*)

Intro. & Ich bin verliebt S
H. Gueden   ♯ **D.LW 5126**
(*Lustige Witwe, Zarewitsch; J. Strauss II*)
(♯ *Lon.LD 9158;* & ♯ *D.LXT 5033; Lon.LL 1116*)

Liebste glaub' an mich T
Schön ist die Welt
K. Terkal   D.F 43595
                                    (*F 49712*)
... Liebste glaub' an mich
W. A. Dotzer   in ♯ *Phi.S 06038R*

WIENER FRAUEN 1902
Overture Vienna Radio—Schönherr in ♯ *Vien.LPR 1021*

Nechledil Marsch
☆ Vienna Radio—Schönherr (♭ *Hma.EP 4001*)

WO DIE LERCHE SINGT 1918
Wenn du liebst (Waltz)
Vienna Radio—Schönherr (2ss)   Vien.P 6138

(Der) ZAREWITSCH 1911
Vocal Selection
G. Scheyrer, F. Pöllinger, etc.   ♯ **Phi.P 10305R**
(*Kalman: Die Czardasfürtin, Selection*) (♭ *KD 167*)

Orch. Selection
Imperial Light Orch.—Koschat (♯ *Imp.ILP 122*)

Introduction & Kosende Wellen
H. Gueden   ♯ **D.LW 5126**
(*Lustige Witwe, Wiener Blut, etc.*) (♯ *Lon.LD 9158*)
(& in ♯ *D.LXT 5033; Lon.LL 1116*)

Hast du dort oben vergessen auf mich   T
R. Christ   in ♭ *Hma.EP 5515*
                                    (in ♯ *L 117*)
— ARR. ORCH. (Waltz)
Strauss Fest. Orch.—Ries-Walter (in ♯ *Mae.OA 20015*)

Willst du? T
☆ H. E. Groh (*below*)   Od.O-3709
(also *P.DPW 88; Od.O-28594:* ♭ *OBL 1006*)

Wolgalied: Es steht ein Soldat T
☆ H. E. Groh (*above*)   Od.O-3709
(also *P.DPW 88; Od.O-28594:* ♭ *OBL 1006*)
P. Anders   in PV. 58617
(& ☆ ♭ *G.7PW 522:* in ♯ *WDLP 1513*) (♯ *Pol. 45047*)
W. A. Dotzer   in ♯ *Phi.S 06038R*
                          (in ♯ *P 10064R:* also N 41206G)
J. Traxel (♭ *T.U 45505*)
P. Grundén (*Swed*) (♭ *G.7EGS 2*)
☆ R. Tauber (in ♯ *P.PMB 1006*)

ZIGEUNERLIEBE 1910
COMPLETE RECORDING
☆ Soloists, Berlin Radio Cho. & Orch.—Dobrindt
                          (♯ ANix.ULP 9205-1/2)

Overture
Polish Radio—Rachon (Muza.X 2308)
☆ Zürich Tonhalle—Lehár (♯ *D.LW 5071; Lon.LD 9043*)

Hör ich Cymbalklänge S
H. Gueden   in ♯ **D.LW 5133**
(*Kreisler, J. Strauss II, O. Straus, etc.*) (♯ *Lon.LD 9157*)
(& in ♯ *D.LXT 5033: Lon.LL 1116*)

Ich bin ein Zigeunerkind T
☆ J. Schmidt (in ♯ *Od.OLA 1008*)

Lied und Czardas ☆ L. Welitsch (D.Z 965)

Und nenn' ich mein Lieb' dich T (*Waltz Song*)
— ARR. ORCH.
Strauss Fest. Orch.—Ries-Walter (in ♯ *Mae.OA 20015*)
Mantovani Orch. (in ♯ *D.LF 1191:* LK 4064; Lon.LL 766)
☆ A. Kostelanetz Orch. (in ♯ *C.S 1049: QS 6048: FS 1054*)

LEIMER, Kurt (b. 1922)

Capriccio No. 2 pf.
Improvisation pf.
K. Leimer   PV. 72382

Concerto, C minor pf. & orch.
Concerto, pf. (left hand) & orch. 1948
K. Leimer & Philharmonia—Karajan
                              ♯ **C.WCX 1508**

LE JEUNE, Claude

SEE: CLAUDE LE JEUNE

LEKEU, Guillaume (1870-1894)

SONGS voice & pf.
3 POÈMES 1892
Sur une tombe (composer)
Ronde (composer)
Nocturne (V. Hugo)
Y. Poliart (S) & Orch.—Doneux
                          ♯ **Gramo.GLP 2507**
(*R. Bernier*) [orch. by R. Defossez]

LEMLIN (or Lämmlein), Lorenz (b. c. 1485)

SEE: † SONGS OF THE RENAISSANCE (GERMANY &
AUSTRIA)

LEO, Leonardo (1694-1744)

Concerto, D major vlc. & orch.
G. Caramia, Naples Scarlatti Orch.—Caracciolo
(*Vivaldi, Sacchini*)   ♯ **C.CX 1276**
(*Sacchini & Lully* in ♯ *C.QCX 10140*)
G. Caramia, Naples Scarlatti Orch.—Caracciolo
(o.v.)   ♯ **Csm.CLPS 1047**
(*Busoni: Clarinet Concerto; & Blodek, Vivaldi*)

☆ = Re-issue of a recording to be found in previous volumes.

LEONCAVALLO, Ruggiero (1858-1919)

SONG
Mattinata (*Aubade*)
M. del Monaco (T)　　　　　　　　**D.SV 3810**
(*Drigo: Serenata*)(in ‡*LW 5168;* & Lon.P18214: ‡*LD 9167*)

G. Gari (T), S. Leff (pf.)　　　in ‡ **Mur.P 104**
(followed by pf. acc. only)

P. Fleta (T) & Orch.　　　　in ‡ *Pat.DT 1012*

☆ B. Gigli (T)(♭ *G.7EB/EBW 6003: 7ERQ 108: 7ERF 134*)
M. Lanza (T) (in ‡ G.ALP 1071: ♭ *7ER 5051;*
　　　　　　　　　　　　　　　　　Vic.ERA 100)
J. Björling (T) (♭ *G.7RQ 3007: 7RW 131*)
J. Schmidt (T) (♭ *AmD.ED 3506;* ♭ *P.CGEP 2*)
J. Peerce (T) (♭ *Vic.ERA 79*)
J. Peerce (T) (in ‡ *AFest.CRF 10-134:* also ♭ *EPM 247;*
　　　　　　　　　　　　　　in ‡ Roy. 1610)
J. C. Thomas (B) (in ‡ Cam.CAL 244)
Ⓗ E. Caruso (T) (in ‡ Vic.LCT 1129*)

— ARR. ORCH. Anon. Orch. (in ‡ Ply. 12-128)
　　　　　　　　W. Fenske Orch. (in ‡ *Phi.P 10200R*)

— ARR. VLN. & ORCH.
I. Zilzer & Orch. (C.DDX 40: ♭ *SCDK 2*)

Serenade (unspec.)
N. Kazantseva (S, *Russ*) (*USSR. 21540*)

OPERAS
(La) BOHÈME 4 Acts 1897
Mimì Pinson S
　Ⓗ R. Storchio (*SBDH.G 1**)

Schaunard's entrance B Act I
　Ⓗ V. Bellatti (*SBDH.P 1**)

L'Influenza del blu B Act I
　Ⓗ V. Bellatti (*SBDH.P 1** & in ‡ JAL 7001*
　　　　　　　　　　　　in ‡ ABCD. 1*)

Testa adorata T Act IV
　Ⓗ A. Piccaver (in ‡ Ete. 490*)

CHATTERTON 3 Acts 1896
Tu sola a me rimani B
　Ⓗ T. Ruffo (in ‡ Sca. 812*)

(I) MEDICI 4 Acts 1893
Ascolta il canto mio (*Serenata*) B
　Ⓗ G. Kaschmann (*SBDH.P 3* & in ‡ HRS. 3004*)

PAGLIACCI Prologue & 2 Acts 1892
COMPLETE RECORDINGS

Casts	Set H	Set I	Set J
Nedda (S) …	V. de los Angeles	C. Petrella	M. M. Callas
Canio (T) …	J. Björling	M. del Monaco	G. di Stefano
Tonio (B) …	L. Warren	A. Poli	T. Gobbi
Beppe (T) …	P. Franke	P. di Palma	N. Monti
Silvio (B) …	R. Merrill	A. Protti	R. Panerai

Set H, with R. Shaw Chorale & Victor Sym.
　—Cellini　　　　　　　　　‡ **G.ALP 1126/8**
(3ss—*Mascagni : Cavalleria Rusticana*)
(‡ G.FALP 301/3: QALP 10050/2; ‡ Vic. set LM 6106;
　♭ set WDM 6106; Highlights on ‡ Vic.LM 1828:
　♭ set ERB 38)

Set I, with Santa Cecilia Cho. & Orch.—Erede[1]
　　　　　　　　　　　　　　‡ **D.LXT 2845/6**
(3ss—*Operatic Recital*)　　　　　(♭ Lon.LL 880/1)
(Selection on ‡ *D.LW 5188*)

Set J, with La Scala Cho. & Orch.—Serafin
　　　　　　　　　　　　　　‡ **C.CX 1211S/2**
(3ss) (‡ QCX 10132/3, 4ss)　　　(‡ Angel. set 3527)
(*Cavalleria Rusticana* in ‡ Angel. set 3528)

Set K. Anon. Artists　　　　　‡ **Roy. 1520/1**
(4ss) (Highlights on ‡ Roy. 1857)
Set F. ☆ L. Amara (S), R. Tucker, etc., Metropolitan Op.
　Cho. & Orch.—Cleva (4ss)　　‡ **EPhi.ABL 3041/2**
　(‡ Phi.A 01102/3L; ♭ *AmC. set A 1071*)
(3ss—*Cavalleria Rusticana* in AmC. set SL 124)
Set A. ☆ B. Gigli (T), I. Pacetti (S), etc., La Scala Cho. &
　Orch.—Ghione (3ss—in ‡ Vic.LCT 6010:
　　　　　　　♭ set WCT 6010; 3ss—in ‡ G.FJLP 5038/9)
Set G. ☆ G. Gavazzi (S), C. Bergonzi (T), etc., Italian
　Radio Cho. & Orch.—Simonetto (‡ FSor.CS 527/8;
　Excerpts on ‡ CCet.A 50144; & ♭ *Cap.FAP 7007;*
　　　　　　　　　　　　　　♭ *Cet.EPO 0312*)

ABRIDGED RECORDING
N.B.C. Television Opera (*Eng*)[2]　　‡ **OTA. 13**

Highlights
M. del Monaco (T), N. Greco (S), L. Tibbett (B),
P. Silveri (B), F. Valentino (B)　　　‡ **PRCC. 4**
(details below)
R. Bonelli, G. Martinelli, M. Leone, F. Valentino & Orch.
　—H-J. Walther[3]　　　　　　　‡ **Roy. 1614**

‡ Anon. Artists (‡ Cam.CAL 226, in set CFL 101)
　L. Albanese, J. Peerce, etc. (‡ BrzV.BRL 100)

Excerpts from set H : Prologue, Andiam, & Qual fiamma
　　　　　　　　　　　　on ♭ *7ER 5061*
Prologue on G.DB 21614;
　　　　　　　　　　　in ‡ Vic. LM 1847
Ohè! ohè! . . . Pagliaccio mio marito . . .
　　　No! Pagliaccio on ♭ *G.7ER 5062*
Love Duet, etc. on ♭ *G. 7ER 5055* (below)

PROLOGUE
Si può, signori . . . Un nido di memorie B
M. del Monaco (T)　　　　　　**D.X 572**
(*Gioconda—Cielo e mar*)　　　(in ‡ D.LXT 2964)
(in ‡ Lon.LL 880 & LL 1025; & in ‡ *D.LW 5093;*
　　　　　　　　　　　　　　Lon.LD 9032)
(*Vesti la giubba* on ♭ *D. 71077*)

A. Protti　　　　　　　　in ‡ *D.LX 3109*
(*Trovatore, Barbiere, etc.*)　　(in ‡ *Lon.LS 701*)
(*Barbiere, No. 4* on D.F 43964: ♭ *D 17964*)

I. Gorin　　　　　　　　in ‡ **Alld. 3003**
　　　　　　　　　　(♭ *EP 3003;* ‡ MTW. 572)

A. Sved　　　　　　　in ‡ **Sup.LPV 207**
(& in *Hung*, on Qual.MN 1018)　　(‡ U. 5191G)

J. Metternich (*Ger*)　　　　　**G.DB 11548**
(*Carmen—Toreador Song*) (♭ *7RW 505:* in ‡ *WBLP 1504*)

　G. Radnai (*Hung*)　　　　Qual.MN 1158

☆ L. Warren o.v., in ‡ Vic.LM 1801 ;♭ *ERA 207*
　R. Stracciari　　　　in ‡ Sca. 802
　F. Guarrera　　　　　♭ *AmC.A 1646*
　T. Gobbi　　　　　　♭ *G.7R 165*
　R. Merrill　　　in ‡ Vic.LM 1841; FV.A 630255
　L. Tibbett　　　　　in ‡ Cam.CAL 171
　G. Bechi　　　　　in ‡ G.QALP 10087
　R. Tauber (T, *Ger*)　　　in ‡ Ete. 712
　H. Schlusnus (*Ger*)　in ‡ Pol. 18080 : 19039
　M. Dens (*Fr*)　　　in ‡ Pat.DT 1020
Ⓗ M. Battistini　　　　　AF.AGSB 93*
　A. Scotti　　　　in ‡ SBDH.JAL 7001*

ACT I
Un grande spettacolo T & cho.
M. del Monaco　　　　　　in ‡ **PRCC. 4**
☆ A. Pertile (in ‡ Ete. 710; in ‡ Od.ODX 127: MOAQ 301)
Ⓗ A. Scotti & Cho.[4] (in ‡ *IRCC.L 7006**)

Un tal gioco (*Arioso*) T
M. del Monaco　　　　　　in ‡ **PRCC. 4**
S. Rayner, S. Leff (pf.)　　in ‡ **Mur.P 107**
(followed by pf. acc. only)
P. Anders (*Ger*)　　　　　**Pol. 62913**
(*Traviata—De miei bollenti spiriti*)　(♭ Pol. 30012)
　A. Frinberg (*Latvian*) (in ‡ USSR.D 1900)
☆ A. Pertile (in ‡ Ete. 710)
Ⓗ G. Zenatello (in ‡ Ete. 705*; in ‡ *SBDH.LLP 8**)

Andiam! (*Coro delle Campane*) cho.
☆ Württemberg State Op.—Leitner (*Ger*) (♭ *Pol. 30008;*
　　　　　　　　　& in ‡ AmD.DL 9797; Pol. 19033)

Qual fiamma . . . Stridono lassù S
D. Rigal　　　　　　　　**ArgOd. 66017**
(*Cavalleria Rusticana—Voi lo sapete*)　(in ‡ *LDC 503*)
　　　　　　　　　　(in ‡ *AmD.DL 4060:* ♭ *ED 3508*)

N. Greco　　　　　　　in ‡ **PRCC. 4**

A. Rothenberger (*Ger*)　　　**G.EH 1459**
(*Gianni Schicchi—O mio Babbino caro*)　(♭ *7PW 540*)
☆ L. Albanese (from Highlights, in ‡ *Vic.LRM 7020:*
　　　　　　　　　　　　　♭ set ERB 7020)
D. Ilitsch (in ‡ *U. 5109C*)
Ⓗ R. Ponselle (‡ & ♭ *AmC.PE 25**)
　C. Muzio[5] (in ‡ LI.TWV 91053*)
　E. Destinn (in ‡ Sca. 804*)

So ben che difforme S & B
N. Greco & L. Tibbett　　　in ‡ **PRCC. 4**

---

[1] The Prologue is sung by Protti, not Poli.　[2] Transcribed from sound of a television broadcast.
[3] Said to contain Martinelli's unpub. 1929 rec. of *Vesti la giubba* & a 1955 rec. of *Un tal gioco*, etc.
[4] From Mapleson cylinders.
[5] From Edison & Pathé hill and dale recordings. This disc was withdrawn soon after issue.

Decidi il mio destin . . . E allor perchè
(Love Duet) S & B
Recitar! . . . Vesti la giubba . . . Ridi, Pagliaccio T
Intermezzo orch.
V. de los Angeles, R. Merrill, L. Warren,
J. Björling, from set H   ♭ *G.7ER 5055*
(♭ *7ERQ 136*)
Nedda! Silvio! . . . No, più non m'ami
Decidi il mio destin . . . E allor perchè S & B
N. Greco & F. Valentino   in ♯ **PRCC. 4**
A. Rothenberger & H. Prey (*Ger*)   G.EH 1460
(2ss)   (♭ *7PW 541*)
. . . Nedda! Silvio! . . . No, più non m'ami S & B
☆ L. Albanese & R. Merrill, from Highlights
(in ♯ *Vic.LRM 7020*: ♭ *ERM 7020*)
J. Orosz & G. Radnai (*Hung*) (*Qual.MN 1158*)
Ⓗ C. Muzio & M. Laurenti[1] (in ♯ *LI.TWV 91053*)*
. . . Decidi il mio destin . . . E allor perchè
Ⓗ M. Moscisca & M. Battistini (AF. AGSB 94*)

Recitar! . . . Vesti la giubba T
M. del Monaco, from set I   ♯ *D.LW 5118*
(*below; & Mascagni*)   (♯ *Lon.LD 9133*)
(*Prologue* on ♭ *D. 71077*)   (& in ♯ *Lon.LL 1244*)
(also, not from set, in ♯ PRCC. 4)
J. Soler   *Cet.AT 0319*
(*Tosca—Recondita armonia*)
S. Puma   *Cet.AT 0390*
(*Catalani: Dejanice, aria*)
P. Anders   ♭ *Pol. 32025*
(*Traviata—De' miei bollenti spiriti*)
(& in *Ger* on *Pol. 62911*: ♭ *30020*)
M. Gafni   in ♯ *For.FLP 1001*
☆ J. Björling   G.DB 21602
(*Bohème—Che gelida*) (♭ *7ER 5025* & in ♯ *BLP 1055*;
♭ *DV. 26044*; Vic.LM 1801 & 1841: ♭ *ERA 109*;
♭ *G.7R 173*; ♯ *FV.A 630255*)
D. Dame   in ♯ *MH. 33-104*
H. Secombe (*Eng*)   *EPhi.PB 523*
P. Fleta (*Fr*)   ♭ *Pat.D 121*
J. Huttinen (*Finn*)   *D.SD 5116*
☆ B. Gigli   ♭ *G.7R 152: 7RQ 3019*
B. Gigli (from set A)   ♭ *Vic.ERAT 16*
M. del Monaco (o.v.)   ♭ *G.7R 153*
(♭ *7RF/RQ 269: 7RW142*)
M. Lanza   in ♯ *G.ALP 1071*
(in ♯ *FBLP 1043*; ♭ *Vic.ERA 222*; ♭ *FV.A 95202*)
F. Vroons   ♭ *Phi.N 402010E*
R. Tucker   ♭ *AmC.A 1646*; *C.LOX 821*
J. Peerce   in ♯ *AFest.CFR 10-134*
(♭ *EPM 246*; in ♯ *Roy. 1610*)
K. Baum   ♭ *Rem.REP 6*
A. Pertile   in ♯ *Od.ODX 127: MOAQ 301*
Anon. Artist   in ♯ *Cam.CAL 249*
Ⓗ E. Caruso   ♭ *Vic.ERAT 6**
(in ♯ *G.FJLP 5009: QJLP 105**)
H. Lazaro   in ♯ *Sca. 806**
L. Muratore   *HRS. 1058**
J. McCormack   in ♯ *Roy. 1555**
A. Bassi   in ♯ *HRS. 3005**
F. de Lucia   in ♯ *CEd.set 7002**
G. Zenatello   in ♯ *Sca. 818**
C. Vezzani (*Fr*)   in ♯ *Od.ODX 126**

Intermezzo
Philharmonia—Karajan   in ♯ **C.CX 1265**
(*Carmen, Contes d'Hoffmann, etc.*)(♯*FCX 407*: *QCX 10150*;
Angel. 35207)
Bamberg Sym.—Leitner[2]   *PV. 72439*
(*Verdi & Mascagni*) (in ♯ *Pol. 17001*; & ♯ *AmD.DL 8509*)
(*Rezniček & Wolf-Ferrari*, ♭ *Pol. 30027*)
Hamburg State Phil.—Müller-Lampertz
T.A 11682
(*Cavalleria, Intermezzo*)   (♭ *U 45682* & in ♯ *LA 6107*)
Leipzig Radio—Gerdes   *Eta. 120038*
(*Cavalleria, Intermezzo*)
N.W. Ger. Phil.—Schüchter   *Od.O-29000*
(*Cavalleria, Intermezzo*)
(♭ *OBL 37-29000* & in ♯ *Imp.ILP 128*)
☆ Philharmonia—Schüchter (in ♯ *P.PMD 1022*;
♭ *ArgMGM.SCA 3502*)
Dresden State Op.—Böhm (♭ *G.7R 158*)
Covent Garden Op.—Patanè(♭ *C.SED 5512*: *SEDQ 552*:
SCD 2004: *SDCQ 2001*)
Hilversum Radio—v. Kempen (♭ *Phi.N 402010E*)

ACT II
Minuet (Orch. only)
Pagliaccio, mio marito . . . S & T
O Colombina (*Harlequin's Serenade*)
☆ I. Pacetti & B. Gigli (♭ *G.7R 152: 7RQ 3019*)
. . . O Colombina only T
Ⓗ F. de Lucia   in ♯ Sca. 814*
T. Schipa   in ♯ Sca. 805*
G. Anselmi & pf.   in ♯ Sca. 816*
È dessa S & B
D. Rigal & P. Silveri   in ♯ **PRCC. 4**
No, Pagliaccio non son! T (& cho.)
M. del Monaco   ♯ *D.LW 5118*
(*above; & Mascagni*)(from set I)   (♯ *Lon.LD 9133*)
(& in ♯ Lon.LL 1244)
A. da Costa   in ♯ **Roy. 1599**
P. Anders (*Ger*)   *Pol. 62911*
(*above*)   (♭ *Pol. 30012*)
☆ M. del Monaco, o.v. (in ♯ *G.QBLP 5021: FBLP 1050*)
B. Gigli, from set (♭ *Vic.ERAT 16*)
A. Pertile (in ♯ *Od.ODX 127: MOAQ 301*)
Ⓗ F. de Lucia (in ♯ *CEd. set 7002**)
G. Zenatello (in ♯ *Sca. 818**)
E. Caruso (in ♯ *Vic. set LCT 6701**)

(Der) ROLAND VON BERLIN 4 Acts 1904
Preghiera B
Ⓗ V. Bellatti (SBDH.G 3*)
ZAZÀ 5 Acts 1900
È un riso gentil T Act I
G. Martinelli[3]   *AF.AGSA 23*
M. Alexandrovich (*Russ*) (in ♯ *USSR.D 2220*)
Ⓗ E. Garbin (in ♯ *SBDH.GL 1**)
Buona Zazà del mio buon tempo B Act II
Ⓗ M. Sammarco (in ♯ *Ete. 490**)
T. Ruffo (in ♯ *Sca. 812**)
È finita! S Act III
. . . Dir che ci sono al mondo
Ⓗ C. Muzio (*IRCC. 3135**)
Mai piu Zazà T Act III
Ⓗ A. Bonci (in ♯ *SBDH.GL 1** & in ♯ *Ete. 490**)
Zazà, piccola zingara B Act IV
☆ A. Granforte (*AF.AGSA 23*)
J. C. Thomas (in ♯ Cam.CAL 199)
Ⓗ J. Schwarz (in ♯ *Ete. 490**)
T. Ruffo (in ♯ *Sca. 812**)
Ed ora io mi domando T Act IV
Ⓗ T. Schipa (in ♯ Sca. 805*)
Cascart's aria (unspec.)
K. Laptev (in ♯ *USSR.D 2141*)

LÉONIN, Magister (*c.* 1183)
SEE: † Seven Centuries of Sacred Music
† Anthologie Sonore

LEOPOLD I, Emperor (1640-1705)
(L') ADALBERTO, or La Forza dell' astuzia femminile 1697
MUSICA PER LA COMOEDIA . . . dell' anno 1697
. . . Inst. Excerpts (orig. str.) — ARR. RECORDERS Wasner
"*Ritornello*"
Trapp Family Ens.—Wasner   in ♯ *AmD.DL 9793*

LEROUX, Xavier Henry Napoléon
(1863-1919)
OPERAS
ASTARTÉ 4 Acts 1901
Les adieux d'Hercule T
Ⓗ A. Affre (*IRCC. 3149**)
(Le) CHEMINEAU 4 Acts 1907
Chanson de Moissonneur B Act I
Ⓗ H. Albers (in ♯ *HRS. 3008**)
SONG
(Le) Nil (Renaud) (No. 1 of *Solitaire—3 Chansons persanes*)
N. Vallin (S) (♭ *Od. 7AOE 1004*: ▽ *Od. 123664*; & on
Pat.X 93044)

---

[1] From Edison & Pathé hill and dale recordings. This disc was withdrawn soon after issue.
[2] Early announcements attributed to Württemberg State Orch.   [3] Recorded 1927.

LESCUREL, Jehannot de (d. 1303)

SEE: † History of Music in Sound (20)
† La Musique et la Poésie

LESUEUR, Jean-François (1760-1837)

Marche du sacre de Napoléon Ier 1804
Paris Cons.—Tzipine[1]   in ♯ C.FCX 383
(*Gossec, Vogel*)
Garde Républicaine Band—Brun
                                in ♯ C.FCX 190
(*Vidal*)   (♯ Angel. 35051)

LESUR, Daniel (b. 1908)

Aubade tpt. & pf. 1954
R. Delmotte & F. Gobet   ♭ Pat.G 1054
(*Jolivet, Pascal, Ameller*)

(L') ÉTOILE DE SÉVILLE Inc. mus.
Orchestral Suite 1941
... Overture ; Prelude, Act II
▽ Orch.—Désormière (*Flo. HP 1205*)

Sextet fl., ob., vln., vla., vlc. & hpsi.
☆ Alma Musica Sextet (*Milhaud*)   ♯ Sel.LP 8239

FOLK SONG ARRANGEMENT
Voici le Saint-Jean
Vocal Ens.—P. Caillard   in V♯ Era.LDE 1013

LETELIER LLONA, Alfonso (b. 1912)

Vitrales de la Anunciación S, Fem. cho. & orch.
(*In Memory of Consuelo*) 1950-1
Anon. & Chile Sym.—v. Tevah   ♯ ChV.CRL 2
(*Soro*)

LEWKOWITCH, Bernhard (b. 1927)

Sonata No. 3, Op. 4 pf. 1950
A. Blyme   Phi.A 56509/10G
(*3ss—Stravinsky: Etude*)

(5) SONGS, Op. 8 (Jørgensen)
... No. 1, There is a well
No. 2, Walpurgis Night
No. 4, Folk tune
No. 5, Yes, it is spring
A. Schiøtz (T), K. Olssen (pf.)   G.DA 5286/7
(*4ss*)

LHOTKA, Fran (b. 1883)

(The) Devil in the Village Ballet Suite 1924 f.p. 1935
Zagreb Nat. Op.—Lhotka   ♯ D.LXT 5058
(*Baranović*)   (♯ Lon.LL 1235)

LIADOV, Anatol Constantinovich
                              (1855-1914)

Baba Yaga, Op. 56 orch. (orig. pf.)
Suisse Romande—Ansermet   ♯ D.LXT 2966
(*below; & Balakirev*)   (♯ Lon.LL 1068)
Berlin Radio—Schartner   ♯ Ura. 7117
(*Amirov & Arensky*)
F.O.K. Sym.—Smetáček   ♯ Sup.LPM 54
(*below; Glinka, Sibelius*)   (♯ U. 5071C)
Moscow Radio—Gauk   USSRM.D 151
(*Glinka: Kamarinskaya*)

Ballade, From olden days, Op. 21 (unspec.) pf.
— ARR. ORCH.
Leningrad Phil.—Khaikin   USSRM.D 001093
(*Borodin: Mlada, Finale*)

(The) Enchanted Lake, Op. 62 orch.
Hallé—Barbirolli   ♭ G.7ER 5026
(*Chabrier: España*)   (♭ 7ERQ 119)
Hamburg Philharmonia—H-J. Walther
                              MSB. 78017
☆ F.O.K. Sym.—Smetáček (in ♯ Sup.LPM 54 ; U. 5071C)
Boston Sym.—Koussevitzky (in ♯ Cam.CAL 155 :
                              ♭ CAE 157)

Glorifications (from *Jour de Fête*[2]) str. qtt.
Argentine Cha. Orch.—Bandini   ArgOd. 66039
(*Rimsky-Korsakov: Russian Dance*)
U.S.S.R. Qtt.   USSR. 20920/1
(*Rimsky-K. & Glazounov*)
☆ Galimir Qtt. (in ♯ Clc. 6148)

Idylle, Op. 25 pf.
S. Feinberg   USSRM.D 001251
(*Scriabin: Mazurka*)

(The) Inn Mazurka, Op. 19 scena, orch.
Berlin Radio—Bernhardt   ♯ Ura. 7163
(*below*)

Kikimora, Op. 63 orch.
Suisse Romande—Ansermet   ♯ D.LXT 2966
(*above, below; & Balakirev*) (♯ Lon.LL 1068)
Philharmonia—Markevitch   ♯ C.CX 1199
(*Prokofiev, Stravinsky*)
                    (♯ FCX 359; Angel. 35153, in set 3518)
(*Chabrier: Roi malgré lui, excerpt, on ♭ C.SEL 1544*)
N.B.C. Sym.—Toscanini   ♯ Vic.LRM 7014
(*Humperdinck & Hérold*)(♭ set ERB 7014; ItV.A72R 0008;
                              in ♯ FV.A 330210)
☆ F.O.K. Sym.—Smetáček (♯ Sup.LPM 54; U. 5071C)

Mazurka (unspec.) pf. — ARR. VLC. & PF.
Y. Slobodkin & pf.   USSR. 22304
(*Davidov: Song without words, Op. 23*)

(The) Musical Box, Op. 32 pf.
P. Spagnolo   in ♯ D.LXT 2947
(*Granados, Mignone, etc.*)   (♯ Lon.LL 1040)
V. Sofronitsky (*USSR. 17064*)
E. Silver (hpsi.) (in ♯ Roy. 1550)
— ARR. PF. & ORCH.
O. Levant & Orch.—Kostelanetz (in ♯ AmC.CL 798:
                    o.n. ML 4692: ♭ A 1831)
— ARR. HARP ☆ O. Erdeli (in ♯ USSR.D 1213)
— ARR. ORCH.
Hamburg Philharmonia—Walther (*MSB. 78016*)
☆ Boston Prom.—Fiedler (♭ G.7EG 8066)
— VOCAL ARR. Aslanoff
F. F. Jenkins (S) (in ♯ Vic.LRT 7000: ♭ set ERBT 7000)

Nænia, Op. 67 ("*Song of Grief*") orch.
▽ Moscow Radio—Golovanov   USSR. 12596
(*Glazounov: Valse de Concert No. 1, s. 3, see Supp. II*)

Polka, D major str. qtt.[3]
— ARR. ORCH.
Philharmonia—Malko   ♯ G.DLP 1092
(*below; & Borodin*)

Polonaise, C major, Op. 49
Moscow Radio—Golovanov   USSR. 022407
(*Tchaikovsky: Marche solennelle*)

PRELUDES
B minor, Op. 11, No. 1
V. Sofronitsky (*above*)   USSR. 17063
☆ J. Flier (in ♯ Csm.CRLP 147)
D minor, Op. 40, No. 3
D major, Op. 40, No. 4
M. Federova   USSR. 22270
(*Smetana: Czech Dance No. 2*)

---

[1] Available only as part of a *de luxe* Limited Edition: *Musiques Impériales.*
[2] Jointly with Glazounov & Rimsky-Korsakov.
[3] From *Les Vendredis*; see Glazounov.

(8) Russian Folk Dances (or Songs), Op. 58 orch.
Suisse Romande—Ansermet ♯ **D.LXT 2966**
(above; & Balakirev) (♯ Lon.LL 1068)
Philharmonia—Malko ♯ **G.DLP 1092**
(above)
Berlin Sym.—Bernhardt ♯ **Ura. 7163**
(The Inn Mazurka, & Popov)
☆ Youth Sym.—Kondrashin *(USSRM.D 841/2, 2ss)*
 Philadelphia—Stokowski (♭ *Cam.CAE 256)*

... No. 4, Gnat's Dance
Hamburg Philharmonia—Walther *(MSB. 78016)*
... Excerpts (unspec.)
Polish Radio—Rezler *(Muza. 2280)*

Sarabande, G minor pf.
M. Slezareva *USSR. 22527*
(Prokofiev: Gavotte, Op. 12, No. 2)

STUDIES pf.
E flat major, Op. 12
C sharp minor, Op. 40, No. 1
G. Ginsburg *USSR. 20057/8*

FOLK SONG ARR.
(The) Midge (unid.)[1] St. Petersburg Vocal Qtt. *(Pat.PG 715)*

LIAPOUNOV, Sergius M. (1859-1924)

Solemn Overture on Russian themes, Op. 7
U.S.S.R. State—Eliasberg ♯ *USSR.D 1204*
(Glazounov)

LICHFILD, Henry (fl. XVI-XVIIth Cent.)
SEE: † MADRIGALS & MOTETS

LIE, Sigurd (1871-1904)
SEE: † SCANDINAVIAN SONGS

LIEBERMANN, Rolf (b. 1910)

Concerto for jazz band & symphony orchestra 1954
Sauter-Finegan Orch. & Chicago Sym.
—Reiner ♯ **Vic.LM 1888**
(R. Strauss)(♭ set ERB 56; ♯ DV.L 16491; ♯ ItV.A12R 0160)
Furioso for orchestra 1947
R.I.A.S. Sym.—Fricsay ♯ **AmD.DL 9769**
(Blacher, Fortner, Hartmann, etc.)
Suite on Swiss Folk Songs orch. 1947
▽ Beromünster Radio—Burkhard *(D.K 28137)*

LISLEY, John (fl. *c*. 1600)
SEE: † TRIUMPHS OF ORIANA

LISZT, Franz (1811-1886)

CLASSIFICATION:
A. INSTRUMENTAL I. Orchestral
 II. Piano & Orch.
 III. Piano Solo
 1. Studies
 2. Various Original
 3. Dance Forms
 4. On National Themes
 5. Transcriptions
 IV. Piano 4-hands
 V. 2 Pianos
 VI. Organ
B. VOCAL IX. Sacred Choral
 X. Secular Choral Works
 XI. Songs with piano

NOTE: This classification was based on that in *Grove*, 4th Edn. supplement. Though *Grove* 5th Edn. uses a different order, to prevent confusion the order of WERM and previous Supplements is continued. G numbers are those of *Grove IV*, and WERM; NG numbers are the equivalents in *Grove V*.

A. INSTRUMENTAL

1. ORCHESTRAL

Ce qu'on entend sur la montagne
(Sym. Poem No. 1) G.1 (NG. 95) 1849-53
Berlin Radio—Rother ♯ **Ura. 7091**
(below)

(A) Dante Symphony cho. & orch. G. 15 (NG. 109)
1855-6
Cho. & Los Angeles Phil.—Wallenstein
 ♯ **B.AXTL 1034**
 (♯ D.UAT 273565; AmD.DL 9670)
Concerts Colonne Cho. & Orch.—Sebastian
 ♯ **Nix.ULP 9103**
 (♯ Ura. 7103; MTW. 504)
Vienna State Op. Cho. & Vienna State
 Philharmonia—Adler ♯ **SPA. 44**

Festklänge G. 7 (NG. 101) Sym. Poem No. 7
1853-6
Leipzig Radio—Pflüger ♯ **Ura. 7140**
(Hungaria)

(A) Faust Symphony (with T & cho.)
G. 14 (NG. 108)
Moscow Radio—Gauk ♯ *USSR.D 2169/72*
Concerts Colonne—Sebastian[2] ♯ **Ura. set 606**
(3ss—*Mazeppa*) (2ss, ♯ MTW. 565)

Hungaria G. 9 (NG. 103) (Sym. Poem No. 9) 1854
Bamberg Sym.—Leitner **PV. 72287**
(Les Préludes on ♯ *Pol. 16044: 17034)*
(Tchaikovsky on ♯ *AmD.DL 7544)*
Moscow Radio—Golovanov ♯ *USSR.D 1725*
(Hunnenschlacht)
Berlin Radio—Kleinert ♯ **Ura. 7140**
(Festklänge)

Hunnenschlacht G. 11 (NG. 105) 1857
(Sym. Poem No. 11, after Kaulbach)
London Phil. Sym.—Dixon ♯ **Nix.NLP 912**
(Mazeppa, Orpheus, Les Préludes) (♯ West.WL 5269)
Moscow Radio—Golovanov ♯ *USSR.D 1724*
(Hungaria)

Mazeppa G. 6 (NG. 100) 1851
(Sym. Poem No. 6, after V. Hugo)
London Phil. Sym.—Dixon ♯ **Nix.NLP 912**
(Hunnenschlacht, Les Préludes, Orpheus) (♯ West.WL 5269)
Residentie—v. Otterloo ♯ **EPhi.NBR 6014**
(Les Préludes) (♯ Phi.N 00702R)
Philharmonia—Fistoulari ♯ **P.PMD 1019**
(below) (♯ *PMDQ 8009;* ♯ MGM.E 3014)
Bavarian Sym.—Graunke in ♯ **Ura. set 606**
(Faust Symphony, s. 1)
(Lalo, on ♯ *MTW. 538)*
Moscow Radio—Golovanov ♯ *USSR.D 1473*
(Prometheus)

Mephisto Waltz[3] G. 16-2 (NG. 110-2) *c*. 1860
Paris Cons.—Münchinger ♯ **D.LW 5136**
(Prometheus) (♯ Lon.LD 9153)
Philharmonia—Markevitch in ♯ **C.CX 1273**
(Berlioz, Stravinsky, Chabrier, etc.) (♯ Angel. 35154;
 C.QCX 10172)
Hungarian Radio—Somogyi *Qual.MK 1554/5*
(4ss)
Leningrad Phil.—Mravinsky ♯ *USSR.D 1097*
(Hungarian Rhapsody 9)
☆ Boston Sym.—Koussevitzky (in ♯ Cam.CAL 159 &
 set CFL 103)
N.Y.P.S.O.—Rodzinski (in ♯ AmC.RL 6628)

---

[1] Perhaps a vocal version of Op. 58, No. 4, *Gnat's Dance*.
[2] The *Chorus Mysticus* (Coda, T & Cho.) is omitted. This may also apply to the other disc but it has not been possible to check.
[3] *Der Tanz in der Dorfschenke.* For pf. version see A.III, *below*.

Orpheus G. 4 (NG. 98) (Sym. Poem No. 4) 1853-4
London Phil. Sym.—Dixon   ♯ **Nix.NLP 912**
(*Mazeppa, Les Préludes, Hunnenschlacht*)(♯ West.WL 5269)
Moscow Radio—Golovanov   ♯ *USSR.D 1134*
(*Dukas: L'Apprenti Sorcier*)

(Les) Préludes G. 3 (NG. 97) 1848-50
(Sym. Poem No. 3, " after Lamartine")
London Phil. Sym.—Dixon   ♯ **Nix.NLP 912**
(*Mazeppa, Orpheus, Hunnenschlacht*)   (♯ West.WL 5269)
Philharmonia—Galliera   ♯ **C.SX 1013**
(*Tchaikovsky*)   (♯ FCX 239: QCX 10074; Angel. 35047)
Philharmonia—Schwarz   in ♯ **G.CLP 1022**
(*Schubert & Weber*)   (♯ FELP 111)
(*Hungarian Rhapsodies*, on ♯ BB.LBC 1070:
     ♭ *set WBC 1070*)
Philharmonia—Fistoulari   ♯ *P.PMD 1019*
(*Mazeppa*) (♯ *PMDQ 8009;* ♯ MGM.E 3014; &
     E 3060, d.c.)
Vienna Phil.—Furtwängler   ♯ *G.ALP 1220*
(*Wagner*)   (♯ FALP 362: QALP 10088)
N.W. German Phil.—Schüchter   ♯ *Imp.ILP 106*
(*Wagner: Tannhäuser, Overture*)   (♯ *G.QDLP 6036*)
Bamberg Sym.—Hollreiser
     ♯ **E. & AmVox.PL 9350**
(*Brahms, Wagner, Sibelius*)
     (*Wagner only,* ♯ *Pan.XPV 1006*)
Utrecht Sym.—Hupperts   ♯ *MMS. 73*
(*R. Strauss*)
Detroit Sym.—Paray   ♯ **Mer.MG 50036**
(*Schumann*)   (♯ FMer.MLP 7523)
Boston Sym.—Monteux   ♯ **Vic.LM 1775**
(*Scriabin*)   (♯ FV.A 630204; ItV.A12R 0073)
(*Berlioz,* in ♭ *Vic. set ERB 5*)
"Philharmonic"—Berendt   ♯ **Allo. 3092**
(*Brahms*)
☆ Residentie—v. Otterloo   ♯ *EPhi.NBR 6014*
(*Mazeppa*) (& ♮ ArgC. 90027/8, 4ss)   (♯ *Phi.N 00702R*)
(*R. Strauss,* on ♯ Epic.LC 3032)
☆ Belgian Radio—André (2ss)   ♯ *DT.TM 68004*
(*Tchaikovsky: Capriccio italien,* on ♯ *T.TW 30006*)
Anon. Orchs. (♯ *ACC.MP 16* & ♯ Gram. 2092)
☆ Berlin Phil.—Ludwig (♯ *Pol.* 16044: 17034: ♭ *30057;*
     FPV. 5036)
Amsterdam—Mengelberg (♯ AmC.RL 3039)
Philadelphia—Ormandy (♯ Cam.CAL 238 &
     in ♯ set CFL 103)
Leipzig Gewandhaus—Konwitschny Eta. 21-300/2, 5ss)
U.S.S.R. Radio—Rakhlin (♯ USSR.D 0352)
Austrian Sym.—Singer (♯ *AFest.CFR 10-100;*
     ♯ Msq. 10012; & with commentary by S. Spaeth,
         ♯ Rem. 12)

Prometheus G. 5 (NG. 99) 1850-5
(Sym. Poem No. 5)
Paris Cons.—Münchinger   ♯ *D.LW 5136*
(*Mephisto Waltz*)   (♯ *Lon.LD 9153*)
Moscow Radio—Golovanov   ♯ *USSR.D 1472*
(*Mazeppa*)

Tasso G. 2 (NG. 96) 1849-54
(Sym. Poem No. 2, after Byron)
Berlin Phil.—Zaun   ♯ **Ura. 7091**
(*above*)
Moscow Radio—Golovanov   ♯ **USSR.D 01502**
(*Ravel: Bolero*)
☆ Winterthur Sym.—Desarzens   ♯ **Nix.CLP 1301**
(*Sibelius*)
▽ Moscow Radio—Rakhlin (*USSR. 8157/63*)

A. II. PIANO & ORCHESTRA

CONCERTOS
No. 1, E flat major G. 44 (NG. 124)
W. Kempff & L.S.O.—Fistoulari ♯ **D.LXT 5025**
(*No. 2*)   (♯ Lon.LL 1072)
S. François & Paris Cons.—Tzipine
     ♯ **C.CX 1238**
(*Chopin: Concerto*)   (♯ FCX 341; Angel. 35168)
A. Foldes & Berlin Phil.—Ludwig
     ♯ **HP.DGM 18133**
(*No. 2*) (3ss—*Soirée de Vienne,* on ♮ PV. 72384/5)
(*Excerpts* in ♯ Pol. 19016)

C. de Groot & Hilversum Radio—v. Otterloo
(n.v.)   ♯ **EPhi.ABL 3026**
(*No. 2*)   (♯ Phi.A 00200L; Epic.LC 3020, d.c.)
[& o.v. ☆ ♯ Phi. S 04001L]
G. Anda & Philharmonia—Ackermann
     ♯ **C.CX 1366**
(*Hungarian Fantasia*)   (♯ Angel. 35268)
J. Iturbi & Victor Sym.   ♯ **Vic.LM 1734**
(*Mendelssohn: Concerto No. 1*)   (♭ set WDM 1734;
     ♯ ItV.A12R 0044)
C. Arrau & Philadelphia—Ormandy
(*Hungarian Fantasia*)   ♯ **AmC.ML 4665**
P. Mildner & R.I.A.S. Sym.—Rother
     ♯ **DT.LGX 66022**
(*Weber*)   (♯ T.LE 6513)
E. Gilels & Moscow Radio—Kondrashin
     ♯ **Mon.MWL 308**
(*Mendelssohn: Concerto 1*)
(*Les Préludes,* on ♯ USSR.D 0351) (& 5ss, USSR. 01756/60)
(*Hungarian Rhapsody No. 2* on ♯ CdM.LDM 8052)
(*Saint-Saëns: Concerto* on ♯ Van.VRS 6015)
(*Chopin, Rachmaninoff, Tchaikovsky,* on ♯ Csm.CRLP 158)
O. Frugoni & Vienna Pro Musica.—Swarowsky
(*No. 2*)   ♯ **E. & AmVox.PL 8390**
E. Kilenyi & R.I.A.S. Sym.—Perlea   ♯ Rem. 199-166
(*Totentanz*)   (♯ Cum.CR 297)
P. Entremont & Zürich Radio—Goehr (*No. 2*) ♯ *MMS. 68*
S. Bianca & Lamoureux—Martinon   ♯ Ply. 12-38
(*Weber: Concerto, etc.*)
V. Gheorghiu & Czech Phil.—Georgescu   ♮ U.H 24422/3
☆ S. Cherkassky & Philharmonia—Fistoulari
     ♯ *G.BLP 1013*
(*Chopin*)   (♯ *VBLP 805: WBLP 1013*)
(*Consolation No. 3 & Don Juan Fantasy*
     on ♯ BB.LBC 1041: ♭ *set WBC 1041*)
☆ E. Farnadi & Vienna State Op.—Scherchen
     ♯ Nix.WLP 5168
(*No. 2*)   (♯ Sel.LAG 1037; BrzV.SLP 5513)
☆ A. Rubinstein & Dallas Sym.—Dorati ♯ G.FALP 162
(*Grieg*)   (QALP 162)
☆ V. Schiøler & Danish Radio—Dobrowen ♯ G.KALP 1
(*Saint-Saëns: Concerto*)

No. 2, A major G. 45 (NG. 125)
O. Frugoni & Vienna Pro Musica—Swarowsky
     ♯ **E. & AmVox.PL 8390**
(*No. 1*)   [*Excerpt* in ♯ AmVox.UHF 1]
A. Foldes & Berlin Phil.—Ludwig
(*No. 1*)   ♯ **HP.DGM 18133**
(3ss—*Soirées de Vienne No. 4,* on ♮ PV. 72386/7)
C. de Groot & Residentie—v. Otterloo
     ♯ **EPhi.ABL 3026**
(*No. 1*)   (♯ Phi.A 00200L: Epic.LC 3145, d.c.)
[also ♯ Phi.S 04001L]
W. Malcuzynski & Philharmonia—Susskind
(*Sonata*)   ♯ **C.CX 1106**
[probably n.v.]   (♯ FCX 196: QCX 10067; Angel. 35031)
W. Kempff & L.S.O.—Fistoulari   ♯**D.LXT 5025**
(*No. 1*)   (♯ Lon.LL 1072)
P. Entremont & Zürich Radio—Goehr   ♯ *MMS. 68*
(*No. 1*)
I. Antal & Hungarian State Concert—Vaszy
(5ss—*Soirées de Vienne*)   Qual.MN 1055/7
☆ E. Farnadi & Vienna State Op.—Scherchen
     ♯ Nix.WLP 5168
(*No. 1*)   (♯ Sel.LAG 1037; BrzV.SLP 5513)
☆ R. Casadesus & Cleveland Sym.—Szell (♯ *Phi.A 01624R*)

Hungarian Fantasia G. 43 (NG. 123) 1852
(Based on themes from Hungarian Rhapsody No. 1)
G. Anda & Philharmonia—Ackermann
     ♯ **C.CX 1366**
(*Concerto No. 1*)   (♯ Angel. 35268)
J. v. Karolyi & Munich Phil.—Nick
(*Rhapsodies 2 & 12*)   ♯ *Pol. 17010*
(*Rhapsody No. 2* only, on ♯ AmD.DL 4084; & 2ss,
     PV. 72332)
C. Arrau & Philadelphia—Ormandy
(*Concerto No. 1*)   ♯ **AmC.ML 4665**
E. Farnadi & Phil. Prom.—Boult
(*Totentanz*)   ♯ **West.LAB 7018**

♯ = Long-playing, 33⅓ r.p.m.   ♭ = 45 r.p.m.   ♮ = Auto. couplings, 78 r.p.m.

Hungarian Fantasia (continued)

J. Iturbi & Valencia Sym.   in ♯ **Vic.LM 1937**
(Falla, Rodrigo, etc.)

L. Shankson & Hamburg Philharmonia
(Arne)   **♯ Allo. 3153**

S. Bianca & Lamoureux—Martinon ♯ **Ply. 12-37**
(Smetana & Dvořák)

☆ R. Trouard & French Nat.—Cloëz (♭ Od.7AOE 1008)
  E. Kilenyi & Austrian Sym.—Prohaska (♯ Msq. 10012;
    & with Commentary by S. Spaeth, on ♯ Rem. 12)

Totentanz G. 46 (NG. 126)

P. Katin & L.P.O.—Martinon ♯ **D.LXT 2932**
(Mendelssohn)   (♯ Lon.LL 1007)

E. Kilenyi & R.I.A.S. Sym.—Perlea
    ♯ Rem. 199-166
(Concerto No. 1)   (♯ Cum.CR 297)

O. Frugoni & Vienna Pro Musica—Swarowsky
(Chopin)   **♯ AmVox.PL 9030**

E. Farnadi & Phil. Prom.—Boult
(Hungarian Fantasia)   **♯ West.LAB 7018**

M. Bacher & Hungarian State—Georgescu
(4ss)   **Qual.MN 1071 & 1073**

☆ F. Jacquinot & Philharmonia—Fistoulari
  (Rimsky-Korsakov)   **♯ P.PMD 1026**
  (Rimsky & Dohnányi on ♯ FMGM.F6-101)
  (Les Préludes, etc., on ♯ MGM.E 3060)

☆ A. Brailowsky & Vic. Sym.—Morel (♯ G.QALP 172)
  J. M. Sanromá & Boston Prom.—Fiedler
    (♯ Cam.CAL 165 : ♭ CAE 257)

A. III. PIANO SOLO

GENERAL COLLECTIONS

Mephisto Waltz No. 1 G. 286 (NG. 514)
Liebestraum No. 3 G. 326 (NG. 541-3) α
(2) Concert Studies G. 58 (NG. 145)
... No. 2, Gnomenreigen
Hungarian Rhapsodies Nos. 6 & 12 G. 157 (NG. 244)
Valse oubliée No. 1 G. 128 (NG. 215) α
(Les) Années de Pèlerinage: THIRD YEAR G. 76
    (NG. 163) β
... No. 4, Les Jeux d'eaux à la Villa d'Este
Valse impromptu, A flat major G. 126 (NG. 213) α
(2) Légendes G. 88 (NG. 175)
... No. 1, St. François d'Assise ...

A. Brailowsky   **♯ G.ALP 1110**
(2ss) (♯ Vic.LM 1772; FV.A630232; ItV.A12R 0035)
[Items marked α also on ♭ Vic.ERA 142; marked β on
  ♭ FV.A 95228; Vic.ERA 224]

Sonata, B minor G. 91 (NG. 178)
Années de Pèlerinage: SECOND YEAR, ITALY G. 74
    (NG. 161)
... No. 7, Après une lecture du Dante (Fantasia quasi
          Sonata)
(3) Études de Concert G. 57 (NG. 144)
... No. 2, F minor ("La Leggierezza")
(12) Études d'exécution transcendante G. 52 (NG. 139)
... No. 7, Eroica
(2) Concert Studies G. 58 (NG. 145)
... No. 2, Gnomenreigen

O. Frugoni   **♯ E. & AmVox.PL 8800**

Sonata, B minor G. 91 (NG. 178)
Paganini Études ... No. 3 ("La Campanella")
          (ARR. Busoni)
(3) Études de Concert .... No. 3 ("Un Sospiro")
Mephisto Waltz No. 1 G. 286 (NG. 514)

G. Anda   **♯ C.CX 1202**
[Études only, ♭ G.7ERL 1056] (♯ FCX 331; Angel. 35127)

Sonata, B minor G. 91 (NG. 178)
Études d'exécution transcendante d'après Paganini
... No. 3, A flat major G. 53 (NG. 140)
Harmonies poétiques et religieuses G. 86 (NG. 173)
... No. 7, Funérailles
Hungarian Rhapsody No. 6, D flat major G. 157
          (NG. 244)
VERDI: Rigoletto, Paraphrase de Concert G. 219
          (NG. 434)

F. Mannino   **♯ ItV.A12R 0066**

Harmonies Poétiques et Religieuses G. 86 (NG. 173)
... No. 7, Funérailles [also on ♭ Od.7OAE 1009]
Années de Pèlerinage: SECOND YEAR, ITALY G. 74
... No. 1, Sposalizio   (NG. 61)
(2) Légendes G. 88 (NG. 175)
BACH: Prelude & Fugue, A minor G. 247-1 (NG. 462-1)

R. Trouard   ♯ **Od.ODX 125**

Légende No. 2: St. François de Paule ... (a)
(6) Études d'exécution transcendante d'après Paganini
... No. 3, A flat major ("La Campanella") G. 53
          (NG. 140) (b)
(3) Études de Concert G. 57 (NG. 144)
... No. 3, D flat major ("Un Sospiro")
Mélodie hongroise, B flat major G. 156-3 (NG. 243-3)
Années de Pèlerinage: FIRST YEAR, SWITZERLAND
          G. 73 (NG. 160)
... No. 3, Au lac de Wallenstadt
Hungarian Rhapsody No. 11 G. 157 (NG. 244)

E. Reuchsel (Chopin)

o.v. [including b, excluding a]   **♯ Pol. 545003**
n.v. [including a, excluding b]   **♯ Phi.A 77404L**

Années de Pèlerinage: FIRST YEAR, SWITZERLAND
          G. 73 (NG. 160)
... No. 2, Au lac de Wallenstadt
Années de Pèlerinage: SECOND YEAR, ITALY
          G. 74 (NG. 161)
... No. 6, Sonetto del Petrarca No. 123
Valse oubliée No. 1 G. 128 (NG. 215)
SCHUBERT: Soirées de Vienne, Nos. 4 & 7 G. 212
          (NG. 427)

A. Foldes   **♯ AmD.DL 4071**
[Probably omitting Soirée de Vienne No. 7, PV. 72327;
Soirée de Vienne No. 4 only, on PV. 72386, & No. 7 only,
on PV. 72384, also in ♯ Pol. 19016 with Valse oubliée]

Hungarian Rhapsody No. 12 G. 157 (NG. 244)
Années de Pèlerinage: SECOND YEAR, ITALY G. 74
          (NG. 161)
... No. 4, Sonetto del Petrarca 47
... No. 5, Sonetto del Petrarca 104
... No. 6, Sonetto del Petrarca 123
Années de Pèlerinage: THIRD YEAR G. 76 (NG. 163)
... No. 4, Les Jeux d'eaux à la Villa d'Este
(12) Études d'exécution transcendante G. 52 (NG. 139)
... No. 9, Ricordanza
WAGNER: Spinning Chorus G. 225 (NG. 440)

E. Petri   **♯ Roy. 1618**

Liebestraum No. 1 G. 326 (NG. 514)
Études d'exécution transcendante d'après Paganini
... Nos. 3 & 5 only G. 53 (NG. 140)
Études de Concert G. 57 (NG. 144)
... No. 2, F minor ("La Leggierezza")

M. de Valmalète   **V♯ Sel.LAP 1012**

Harmonies Poétiques et Religieuses G. 86 (NG. 173)
... No. 3, Bénédiction de Dieu dans la solitude
(6) Consolations G. 85 (NG. 172)
... No. 1, E major
☆ La Lugubre Gondola G. 112 (NG. 200)

J-M. Damase   **♯ LI.TW 91041**
(Schumann)   (♯ D.FAT 133066)

Sonata, B minor G. 91 (NG. 178)
Harmonies poétiques ...: No. 7, Funérailles G. 86
          (NG. 173)
Valse impromptu, A flat major G. 126 (NG. 213)
Années de Pèlerinage: SECOND YEAR
... (2) Sonetti del Petrarca (unspec.)

S. Weissenberg   **♯ Lum.LD 3-404**

Années de Pèlerinage: SECOND YEAR, ITALY G. 74
... No. 2, Il Pensieroso   (NG. 161)
(6) Consolations G. 85 (NG. 172)
... Nos. 1 & 4
Harmonies Poétiques et Religieuses G. 86 (NG. 173)
... No. 7, Funérailles
Hungarian Rhapsodies G. 157 (NG. 244)
... Nos. 3 & 11

G. Lasson   **♯ Pac.LDPC 92[1]**

(6) Consolations G. 85 (NG. 172)
... No. 1, E major
Hungarian Rhapsody No. 15, A minor G. 157 (NG. 244)
Années de Pèlerinage: G. 75 (NG. 162)
... Venezia e Napoli
(6) Chants Polonais G. 265

R. Slenczynski   **♯ ML. 7031**
(Chopin: Barcarolle)

A. III. 1. STUDIES

(12) **Études d'exécution transcendante**
G. 52 (NG. 139)

1. Preludio	2. A minor
3. Paysage	4. Mazeppa
5. Feux follets	6. Vision
7. Eroica	8. Wilde Jagd
9. Ricordanza	10. F minor
11. Harmonies du Soir	12. Chasse-neige

... Nos. 3, 4, 5, 6, 10, 11
S. Fiorentino   **♯ CA.LPA 1062**
(Concert Studies, Études de Concert, Ab Irato)

---

[1] Originally announced as LDPF 78 and including Mephisto Waltz, G. 286 (NG. 514).

(6) **Études d'exécution transcendante d'après Paganini** G. 53 (NG. 140)

1. G minor ('Tremolo') Paganini Caprice 6
2. E flat major ('Octave') Paganini Caprice 17
3. A flat minor ('La Campanella') Paganini Concerto, B minor, Rondo
4. E major ('Arpeggio') Paganini Caprice 1
5. E major ('La Chasse') Paganini Caprice 9
6. A minor ('Theme & Varns.') Paganini Caprice 24

COMPLETE RECORDINGS

E. Farnadi   ♯ West.WN 18017
(below)

F. Glazer   ♯ SOT. 1036

☆ R. Goldsand (♯ Clc. 6196)

... **Nos. 2, 4 & 6**, only

R. Slenczynski   ♭ BB.ERAB 7

... **Nos. 3, 4 & 5** only

☆ A. Uninsky   ♯ Epic.LC 3066
(Spanish Rhapsody, & Moussorgsky)

No. 2, E flat major

G. Bachauer   ♯ G.CLP 1057
(Années de Pèlerinage; Sonata; & Chopin, etc.)

No. 3, A flat minor, 'La Campanella'

F. Ellegaard   ♯ D.LW 5051
(Liebestraum No. 3; & Nielsen)   (♯ Lon.LD 9065)
(Liebestraum No. 3 only, Pol. HM 80069)

P. Mildner[1]   ♯ DT.LGM 65025
(Chopin & J. Strauss)   (♯ T.LB 6060)
                              (& in ♯ T.LA 6077 & ♭ UV 111)

E. Gilels   USSR. 13232/3
                              (o.v. 5809/10)

G. Ginsburg   USSR. 19784/5

P. Cavazzini   ♯ Arp.ARC 2
(Liebestraum 3; & Debussy, Ravel, Albeniz)

V. Gheorghiu   U.H 24414 & Pop. 5003
L. Gousseau   ♭ Plé.P 45130

☆ C. Horsley   in ♯ G.CLP 1012
S. Barere in ♯ Cum.CR 325 & ♭ Rem.REP 12
J. Battista   in ♯ MGM.E 3060

— ARR. 4 PFS.   ☆ First Pf. Qtt.   ♭ Vic.ERA 70

— ARR. PF. & ORCH.
A. Semprini & Melachrino Orch.   G.B 10784
(Hung. Rhapsody No. 15)

— ARR. ACCORDEON E. Boscaini (in V♯ FestF.FLD 18)

No. 4, E major, 'Arpeggio'

G. Ginsburg   USSR. 18559
(No. 5)   (& USSRM.D 00506)

No. 5, E major, 'La Chasse'

V. Gheorghiu   Pop. 5007
(Mendelssohn: Song without words)

L. Hernádi   Qual.SZN 305
(Gondoliera)

E. Gilels (USSR. 10606)
G. Ginsburg (USSR. 18558: USSRM.D 00506)

No. 6, A minor, 'Theme & Variations'

F. Wührer   ♯ E. & AmVox.PL 8850
(Brahms & Schumann)

(3) **Études de Concert** G. 57 (NG. 144)

1. A flat major   2. F minor   3. D flat major

E. Farnadi   ♯ West.WN 18017
(above)

S. Fiorentino   ♯ CA.LPA 1062
(above & below)

... **Nos. 2 & 3** only

Y. Boukoff   ♯ Phi.A 76706R
(Hung. Rhapsodies Nos. 2 & 12)

No. 2, F minor, 'La Leggierezza'

M. Schwalb   in ♯ Roy. 1470
☆ S. Barere (in ♯ Cum.CR 325)

No. 3, D flat major, 'Un sospiro'

V. Schiøler   G.DB 10521
(Valse impromptu)

G. Anda (from Collection)   ♭ C.SEL 1516
(Delibes: Coppelia—Valse lente) (♭ SEBQ 118: ESBF 121)

A. Dorfman   in ♯ Vic.LM 1758
                              (♭ set WDM 1758)

M. Schwalb   in ♯ Roy. 1470
(also in ♯ Roy. 1577)[2]

E. Burton   in ♯ CEd.CE 1025

R. Spivak   ArgV. 11-7968
(Consolation No. 3)

A. Sandford (EMI.EPX 75)

☆ C. Horsley (in ♯ G.CLP 1012)
E. Ballon (in ♯ D.LX 3070, announced but not issued)

— ARR. PF. & ORCH.
A. Semprini & Melachrino Orch. (G.B 10426: ♭ 7EG 8053)

(2) **Concert Studies** G. 58 (NG. 145)

1. Waldesrauschen   2. Gnomenreigen

S. Fiorentino   ♯ CA.LPA 1062
(above & below)

☆ J. v. Karolyi (♭ Pol. 30009: in ♯ 19016)
C. Keene (in ♯ EMer.MG 10113: ♭ Mer.EP 1-5007; FMer.MEP 14505)

No. 1, Waldesrauschen

M. Schwalb   in ♯ Roy. 1474
☆ S. Grundeis (Eta. 21-302)

No. 2, Gnomenreigen (Ronde des Lutins)

B. Webster   in ♯ Persp.PR 2
M. Barthel   in ♯ Aphe.AP 25
☆ C. Horsley (in ♯ G.CLP 1012)
S. Barere (in ♯ Cum.CR 328; ♭ Rem.REP 12)

Concert Study, Ab Irato, E minor G. 56 (NG. 143)

S. Fiorentino   in ♯ CA.LPA 1062
(above)
_____

A. III. 2. VARIOUS ORIGINAL WORKS

ANNÉES DE PÈLERINAGE

FIRST YEAR, SWITZERLAND G. 73 (NG. 160)
1. Chapelle de Guillaume Tell   2. Au lac de Wallenstadt
3. Pastorale   4. Au bord d'une source
5. Orage   6. Vallée d'Obermann
7. Églogue   8. Le Mal du Pays
9. Les cloches de Genève

SECOND YEAR, ITALY G. 74 (NG. 161)
1. Sposalizio   2. Il Pensieroso
3. Canzonetta del Salvator Rosa
4. Sonetto del Petrarca No. 47
5. Sonetto del Petrarca No. 104
6. Sonetto del Petrarca No. 123
7. Après une lecture du Dante (Fantasia quasi Sonata)

SUPPLEMENT: VENEZIA E NAPOLI G. 75 (NG. 162)
1. Gondoliera   2. Canzona   3. Tarantella

THIRD YEAR G. 76 (NG. 163)
1. Angelus! Prière aux anges gardiens
2. Aux cyprès de la Villa d'Este, thrénodie (3-4)
3. Aux cyprès de la Villa d'Este, thrénodie (4-4)
4. Les Jeux d'eaux à la Villa d'Este
5. Sunt lacrymae rerum, en mode hongrois
6. Marche funèbre   7. Sursum corda

COMPLETE RECORDING (omitting G. 75-2 & 3)
A. Ciccolini (6ss)   ♯ C.FCX 440/2

FIRST YEAR, SWITZERLAND: COMPLETE
J. Weingarten   ♯ CA.LPA 1010
(No. 4 also on V♯ MPO 5004)

... No. 3 ☆ G. Axelrod (in ♯ Sup.LPM 73; U. 5031C)

... No. 4 ☆ V. Horowitz (in ♯ G.ALP 1087: FALP 215;
                              ♯ Vic. LRM 7019: ♭ set ERB 7019)

... No. 5 G. Axelrod, 2ss (USSR. 20176/7; Sup. 70019, d.c.)

SECOND YEAR, ITALY G. 74 (NG. 161)

No. 5, Sonetto del Petrarca No. 104

R. Tamarkina   USSRM.D 00919
(Chopin: Scherzo)

☆ V. Horowitz (in ♯ G.BLP 1048: FBLP/QBLP 1033;
                ♯ Vic.LM 9021 & LRM 7019: ♭ set ERB 7019)
S. Barere (in ♯ Cum.CR 325)
D. Lipatti (♭ C.SEB 3501: SEBQ 106: ESBF 108; &
            in ♯ C.FCX 495; AmC.ML 2216)
A. Uninsky (in ♯ Epic.LC 3027)

---

[1] ARR. Busoni.

[2] Labelled: Chopin: Étude, F minor.

No. 6, Sonetto del Petrarca No. 123
G. Bachauer   ♯ G.CLP 1057
(Sonata, Paganini Étude 2, Chopin, etc.)
J. Weingarten   V♯ CA.MPO 5004
(Au bord d'une source & Valse oubliée No. 1)
V. Sofronitsky   USSRM.D 001225
(Schumann: Arabeske)

No. 7, Après une lecture du Dante
(Fantasia quasi sonata)
P. Katin   ♯ D.LXT 2877
(Consolations, & Polonaise No. 2)   (♯ Lon.LL 934)
M. Schwalb   ♯ Acad. 310
(Fauré, Bartók, Rachmaninoff, etc.)

SUPPLEMENT: VENEZIA E NAPOLI   G. 75 (NG. 162)
No. 1, Gondoliera
L. Oborin   USSR. 21836/7
(2ss)   (& in ♯ D 1235)
E. Bernáthová   U.H 24414
(Paganini Étude No. 3)
L. Hernádi   Qual.SZN 3051
(Paganini Étude No. 5)

No. 2, Canzona
L. Oborin   in ♯ USSR.D 1236
(above & below)
V. Sofronitsky   USSR. 18628
(Wieniawski: Obertass)

No. 3, Tarantella
A. Walker   V♯ CA.MPO 5002
(Faust Valse)
O. P. Santoliquido   in ♯ Fnt.LP 304
(Liebestraum, & Mephisto Waltz)
L. Oborin   in ♯ USSR.D 1236
(above & below)
X. Prochorowa   in ♯ Imp.ILP 128
(Mascagni, Leoncavallo, Gounod)

THIRD YEAR   G. 76 (NG. 163)
COMPLETE RECORDING
J. Weingarten   ♯ CA.LPA 1011

No. 1, Angelus! — ARR. STR.[1]
Concert Artist Sym.—Vicars   V♯ CA.MPO 5013
(Tchaikovsky: Elegy)

No. 4, Les Jeux d'eaux à la Villa d'Este
L. Oborin *(above)*   in ♯ USSR.D 1235

BALLADES
No. 1, D flat major   G. 83 (NG. 170)
No. 2, B minor   G. 84 (NG. 171)
E. Farnadi   ♯ Nix.WLP 5321
(Légendes, & Liebesträume)   (♯ West.WL 5321)

(6) CONSOLATIONS   G. 85 (NG. 172)
COMPLETE RECORDINGS
P. Katin   ♯ D.LXT 2877
(Années de Pèlerinage, & Polonaise)   (♯ Lon.LL 934)
E. Farnadi   ♯ West.WL 5339
(Spanish Rhapsody, & Hungarian Rhapsodies, 16-19)
(Sonata, on ♯ Sel. 320.CW 080)

No. 3, D flat major
R. Spivak   ArgV. 11-7968
(Étude de Concert No. 3)
M. Schwalb   in ♯ Roy. 1464
    A. Semprini *(G.B 10317: ♭ 7EG 8053)*
   ☆ S. Cherkassky (in ♯ BB.LBC 1041 : ♭ *set WBC 1041*)
    J. v. Karolyi *(♭ Pol. 30019)*
— ARR. 4 PFS.
Phil. Pf. Qtt.   ♭ AmC.A 1572
— ARR. VLN. & PF.   Milstein
E. Zathureczky & Endre Petri   Qual.SKZ 3505
(Weiner: Peasant Songs)

En rêve (Nocturne)   G. 120 (NG. 207)   1885
   ☆ L. Kentner   ♭ C.SED 5519
(Richard Wagner, & Csárdás macabre)

HARMONIES POÉTIQUES ET RELIGIEUSES
   G. 86   (NG. 173)
1. Invocation   2. Ave Maria
3. Bénédiction de Dieu dans la solitude
4. Pensée des Morts   5. Pater Noster
6. Hymne de l'enfant à son réveil
7. Funérailles, Oct. 1849   8. Miserere, d'après Palestrina
9. Andante lagrimoso   10. Cantique d'amour

Nos. 1, 3, 4, 7, 10
A. Brendel   ♯ AmVox.PL 9430
Unspec. items
S. Fiorentino   ♯ CA.LPA 1065
[listed in the last catalogue but apparently withdrawn
before issue]

No. 7, Funérailles
J. Katchen   in ♯ D.LXT 2838
(Mephisto Waltz No. 1; & Mendelssohn) (in ♯ Lon.LL 824)
C. de Groot   ♯ Phi.S 06061R
(Mephisto Waltz No. 1)
   ☆ G. Bachauer (in ♯ G.DLP 1009: WDLP 1009)
    V. Horowitz (in ♯ G.BLP 1048: FBLP/QBLP 1033:
    & FJLP 5047; ♯ Vic.LM 9021: & in ♯ LRM 7019:
    ♭ set ERB 7019)

LÉGENDES   G. 83 (NG. 175)
No. 1, St. François d'Assise   *(La Prédication aux oiseaux)*
No. 2, St. François de Paule marchant sur les flots
E. Farnadi   ♯ Nix.WLP 5321
(Ballades, & Liebesträume)   (♯ West.WL 5321)
   ☆ W. Kempff (♯ D.LW 5073; Lon.LD 9087)

Richard Wagner—Venezia   G. 113 (NG. 201) 1883
   ▽ ☆ L. Kentner   ♭ C.SED 5119
(En rêve & Csárdás macabre)

SONATA, B minor   G. 91 (NG. 178)
W. Malcuzynski   ♯ C.CX 1106
(Concerto No. 2) (♯ C.QCX 10067: FCX 196;
                 Angel. 35031)
G. Bachauer   ♯ G.CLP 1057
(Paganini Étude 2, etc.; & Chopin, Shostakovich)
E. Farnadi   ♯ Nix.WLP 5266
(Mephisto Waltz, & Valse impromptu) (♯ West.WL 5266)
(Consolations, on ♯ Sel. 320.CW. 080)
S. Cherkassky   ♯ G.ALP 1154
(Don Juan Fantasy)
   ☆ A. Foldes (♯ HP.DG 16088)
    A. Uninsky (♯Epic.LC 3027)
    V. Horowitz (♯ G.FJLP 5047)
For recordings by O. Frugoni, G. Anda, F .Mannino,
S. Weissenberg, *See:* COLLECTIONS, above.

Variations on a theme of Bach   G. 93 (NG. 180)
('Weinen, Klagen, Sorgen, Zagen')
— ORGAN VERSION G.463 (NG.673)—*& see p. 258*
   ☆ E. Nies-Berger (♯ Clc. 6254)

Weihnachtsbaum   G. 99 (NG. 186)   (12 pieces)
   ☆ A. Brendel   ♯ CA.LPA 1067

A. III. 3. DANCE FORMS

Csárdás macabre   G. 137 (NG. 224)   1881-2
   ☆ L. Kentner   ♭ C.SED 5519
(En rêve & Richard Wagner)

Galop, A minor   G. 131 (NG. 218)
— ARR. ORCH.   G. Jacob (for Ballet *Apparitions*)
   ▽ ☆ Philharmonia—Lambert (in ♯ AmC.RL 3056)

(2) POLONAISES   G. 136 (NG. 223)
P. Katin   (1 side each)   ♯ D.LW 5116
[No. 2 only in ♯ D.LXT 2877; Lon.LL 934] (♯ Lon.LD 9122)

No. 2, E major
L. Bertolini   Dur.F 10183
   ☆ J. M. Darré (ArgPat.FXC 4)

Mephisto Waltz No. 3[2]   G. 129 (NG. 216)
— ARR. ORCH.   G. Jacob (for Ballet *Apparitions*)
   ☆ Philharmonia—Lambert (in ♯ AmC.RL 3056)

---

[1] Probably Liszt's own version (NG. 378), orig. Str. Qtt.
[2] For Mephisto Waltz for orch., see Section I; Mephisto Waltz Nos. 1 & 2 for pf., see Section III-5, *below*.

VALSES

Valse impromptu, A flat major   G. 126   (NG. 213)
E. Farnadi (n.v.)   **♯ Nix.WLP 5266**
(*Sonata & Mephisto Waltz*)   (♯ West.WL 5266:
                                        Sel. 320.CW.079, d.c.)

V. Schiøler   **G.DB 10521**
(*Étude de Concert No. 3*)
☆ A. Rubinstein (♭ G.7ER 5058; Vic.ERA 201;
                       ItV.A72R 0025; FV.A 95213)

(3) Valses oubliées   G. 128   (NG. 215)
... No. 1   only
J. Weingarten   **V♯ CA.MPO 5004**
(*Petrarch Sonnet No. 123, & Au bord d'une source*)
M. Schwalb   in ♯ **Roy. 1474**
☆ A. Rubinstein   **G.DB 21567**
(*Liebstraum No. 3*)   (ED 1241: ♭ 7EB 6009, d.c.)
☆ V. Horowitz (in ♯ G.BLP 1048: FBLP|QBLP 1033:
           in ♯ Vic.LM 9021 & LRM 7019: ♭ set ERB 7019)
S. Barere (♭ Rem.REP 12 & ♯ Cum. CR 325)
E. Joyce (in ♯ AmD.ED 3500)
J. Therrien (in ♯ MH. 33-111)

A. III. *4. WORKS ON NATIONAL THEMES*

(19) HUNGARIAN RHAPSODIES
G. 157   (NG. 244)
COMPLETE RECORDINGS   (Nos. 1-19)
A. Borowsky   **♯ E. & AmVox.**
Nos. 1-7   on   PL 8900
Nos. 8-13 on   PL 8910
Nos. 14-19 on   PL 8920
     (with *Spanish Rhapsody*)

E. Farnadi   **♯ Nix., West., & Sel.**
Nos. 1-15 on ♯ Nix.WLP 6213-1/2
             ♯ West.WL 5230/1, set WAL 213
Nos. 16-19 on ♯ West.WL 5339 (with *Consolations &
                              Spanish Rhapsody*)
             ♯ Sel. 320.CW.049/50
             ♯ Sel. 320.CW.079 (with *Valses &
                              Spanish Rhapsody*)

... Nos. 1-15
S. François   **♯ C.FCX 332/4**
(6ss) [Nos. 6 & 15 on ♭ G.7ERL 1054]   (♯ G.LALP 194/6)

COLLECTIONS
Nos. 2, 6, 12, 15
L. Kentner   **♯ C.SX 1014**
     (♯ QSX 12005: WSX 1014; ArgA.LPC 11592)

No. 2, 6 & 15
P. Katin   **♯ D.LXT 2971**
(*Liebesträume & Rigoletto Paraphrase*)   (♯ Lon.LL 1087)

COLLECTIONS — ORCH. VERSIONS G. 34 (NG. 359)
Nos. 2, 6, 9 & 14   (Orch. Nos. 4, 3, 6, 1)
Philharmonia—Schwarz   **♯ G.CLP 1033**
(*Les Préludes*)   (♯ BB.LBC 1070: ♭ set WBC 1070)
[for individual issues, *see below*]

Nos. 5, 12 & 14   (Orch. Nos. 5, 2, 1)
London Phil. Sym.—Scherchen
                                     ♯ West.LAB 7003

Nos. 2, 6 & 9   (Orch. Nos. 4, 3, 6)
London Phil. Sym.—Scherchen
                                     ♯ West.LAB 7007

Nos. 12, 6 & 14   (Orch. Nos. 2, 3, 1)
N.B.C. Members—Stokowski   **♯ Vic.LM 1878**
(*Enesco*)

Nos. 1, 2 & 15
Berlin Sym.—Rubahn[1]   **♯ Roy. 1424**
(*Enesco*)

No. 2, C sharp minor
P. Badura-Skoda   in ♯ **Nix.WLP 5277**
(*Liebestraum; & Chopin, Brahms, etc.*) (in ♯ West.WL 5277)
L. Pennario   **♯ DCap.CCL 7522**
(*Rachmaninoff*)   (♯ Cap.H 8186; T.NLCB 8186)
(& in ♯ Cap.P 8312; DCap.CTL 7102)
P. Katin   **♯ D.LW 5134**
(*Rigoletto Paraphrase*)   (♯ Lon.LD 9159)

D. Bar-Illan   **♯ Kings. 211**
(*No. 15; & Ben-Haim, Chopin, Debussy*)
Y. Boukoff   **♯ Phi.A 76706R**
(*No. 12 & Études de Concert*)
L. Oborin   **USSR. 016800/1**
(2ss)   (*Tchaikovsky, on USSRM.D 182*)
A. Cortot   in ♯ **JpV. set JAS 270**
                                 (& in ♯ LS 105: ♭ ES 8016)
V. Horowitz   in ♯ **Vic. set LM 6014**
(in ♯ FV.A 630203: ItV.B12R 0064/5: ♭ A72R 0046)
☆ G. Axelrod (in ♯ Sup.LPM 73; U. 5031C;
                               3ss, Sup. 70015/6)
A. Brailowsky (♭ G.7RF 274)
— ARR. 2 PFS.   L. Shankson & I. Wright (in ♯ Roy. 1447)
— ARR. ORG.   R. Foort (*sub nom. M. Cheshire*)
                       (in ♯ SLPY 156; SOT. 1050 & 10501)
— ORCH. VERSION (No. 4, but usually "No. 2")
Belgian Radio—André   **♯ DT.LGM 65017**
(*No. 14*)   (♯ T.LB 6044)
(*Dukas, on ♯ T.TW 30008*)
Philharmonia—Schwarz[2]   **G.C 4230**
Philharmonia—Weldon[2]   **C.DX 1886**
(SVX 46: DOX 1037: in ♯ SX 1032)
Boston Prom.—Fiedler   **♯ Vic.LRM 7002**
(*No. 14, & Brahms*)   (♭ set ERB 7002; ♭ DV. 16292)
Paris Cons.—Wolff[2]   **♯ D.LW 5150**
(*Massenet*)   (♯ Lon.LD 9171)
Hollywood Bowl—Barnett   in ♯ **Cap.P 8296**
(*Ponchielli, Saint-Saëns, etc.*)   (♭ set FAP 8296)
N.W. German Phil.—Schüchter ♯ **Imp.ILP 103**
(*Brahms*)   (♯ G.QDLP 6028)
Vienna Sym.—Loibner   **♯ Phi.S 06056R**
(*Hellmesberger & Khachaturian*)
Vox Sinfonietta-Gräf (♭ AmVox.VIP 45600
                               & in ♯ Pan.XPV 1022)
Tivoli Concert—Hansen (Tono.X 25191: ♭ EP 43001)
Hungarian State Folk—Boros (Qual.MK 1562/3)
Internat. Sym.—Schneiderhann (in ♯ Mae.OA 20004)
Orch.—Swarowsky (in ♯ MTW. 9; ♯ ACC.MP 18)
Regent Sym. (in ♯ Rgt. 7001)
Orch.—Schönherr (Hma. 15014)
etc., etc.
☆ L.P.O.—Martinon (in ♯ MGM.E 3060 & E 3037)
Bavarian Sym.—Nick (♭ AmD.ED 3514; IPV.RVR 8200;
     PV. 72463: ♭ Pol. 30083: in ♯ 17010;
                               in ♯ AmD.DL 4084)
Philadelphia—Ormandy[2] (in ♯ AmC.CL 722)
Col. Sym.—Rodzinski (in ♯ AmC.CL 726; Phi.S 04601L)
Berlin Phil.—Abendroth (Od.NLX 6)
Paris Cons.—Lindenberg (♯ Od.OD 1012: ♭ 7AOE 1002:
                                     DSEQ 425)
Moscow Radio—Rakhlin (♯ CdM.LD 8052;
                       ♯ USSR.D 453; Bulg. 1380/1)
etc., etc.

No. 6, D flat major
P. Cavazzini   **♯ Arp.ARC 1**
(*Chopin*)
☆ V. Horowitz   in ♯ **G.ALP 1087**
(in ♯ G.FALP 215; ♭ 7ERF 117: 7RQ 3015: 7RW 127;
                                 ♭ DV.26002)
E. Gilels (USSR. 17053/4)
☆ S. Cherkassky (♭ AmVox.VIP 45430)
B. Janis (♭ BB.ERAB 8; FV.A 85211)
— ORCH. VERSION (No. 3)
Philharmonia—Schwarz   **♭ G.7EP 7015**
(*Auber: Masaniello Overture*)   (♭ 7EPQ 534)
Boston Pops.—Fiedler   **♯ Vic.LRM 7003**
(*No. 9, & Brahms Dances*)   (♭ set ERB 7003)
(*Liebestraum No. 3* on ♭ G.7BF 1064)
☆ (ARR. Kindler) Nat. Sym.—Kindler (in ♯ Cam.CAL 115
                                     & set CFL 103)

No. 8, F sharp minor
T. Antal   (*No. 11*)   **Qual.KMN 7101**

No. 9, E flat major
E. Gilels   (4ss)   **USSR. 19469/72**
— ORCH. VERSION   (No. 6)
Boston Pops.—Fiedler   **♯ Vic.LRM 7003**
(*No. 6, & Brahms*)   (♭ set ERB 7003)
(*also* ♭ G.7BF 1062)
U.S.S.R. State—Gauk   **♯ USSR.D 1098**
(*Mephisto Waltz*)

---

[1] H. Reims (pf.) is also named; some may be arr. pf. & orch. or even pf. solo.
[2] ARR. Müller-Berghaus.   Others are also probably in this or other revisions.

No. 10, E major
A. Rubinstein   ♭ *G.7ER 5058*
(*Valse impromptu*) (♭ *Vic.ERA 201; FV.A 95213;*
            ♭ *ItV.A72R 0025*)
   G. Ginsburg (*USSR. 12916/7*)

No. 11, A minor
W. Kapell   ♯ **Vic.LM 1791**
(*Mephisto Waltz; Bach & Schubert*)
A. Cortot   **G.DB 21618**
(*Schubert-Liszt: Litaney*)   (♭ *7R 174: 7RQ 3036*)
(*& in JpV. set JAS 270:* ♯ *LS 105*)
R. Spivak   **ArgV. 11-8075**
(*Albeniz: Asturias*)
   G. Ginsburg (*USSR. 16967/8*)
   I. Antal (*Qual.KMN 7101*)
☆ E. Ballon (in ♯ *D.LX 3070*, announced but not issued)

No. 12, C sharp minor
J. Katchen   ♯ *D.LW 5160*
(*Balakirev*)   (♯ *Lon.LD 9175*)
Y. Boukoff   ♯ *Phi.A 76706R*
(*No. 2, & Études de Concert*)
S. Sorin   ♯ *SOT. 1038*
(*Chopin, Granados, Scriabin*)
☆ G. Bachauer   in ♯ *G.DLP 1009*
(*Funérailles, & Spanish Rhapsody*)   (*WDLP 1009*)
— ORCH. VERSION (No. 2)
Danish Radio—Tuxen[1]   ♯ *D.LW 5114*
(*Tchaikovsky*)
☆ Bavarian Sym.—Nick (*PV. 72463:* ♭ *Pol. 30083:*
   in ♯ *17010;* IPV.RVR 8200; ♭ *AmD.ED 3514*)

No. 14, F minor
— ORCH. VERSION (No. 1)
Belgian Radio—André   ♯ *DT.LGM 65017*
(*No. 2*)   (♯ *T.LB 6044*)
(*Smetana, on* ♯ *T.TW 30002*)
Boston Pops.—Fiedler   ♯ *Vic.LRM 7002*
(*No. 2 & Brahms*)   (♭ set *ERB 7002*)
(*Brahms: Hung. Dance 2, on* ♭ *G.7BF 1063*)
Philharmonia—Schwarz   **G.C 4259**
               (S 10622)
Leipzig Radio—Pflüger   in ♯ **Ura. 7096**
             (♭ *UREP 70*)
Moscow Radio—Rakhlin   ♯ *USSR.D 452*
(*No. 2*)   (*USSR. 17304/7*)
☆ Philadelphia—Ormandy (in ♯ *AmC.CL 722*)

No. 15, A minor   (*Rakóczy March*)
D. Bar-Illan   ♯ **Kings. 211**
(*No. 2; & Ben-Haim*)
M. Barthel   in ♯ **Aphe.AP 25**
(*Gnomenreigen; & Debussy, etc.*)
☆ S. Cherkassky (♭ *AmVox.VIP 45430*)
— ARR. Horowitz.
☆ V. Horowitz (♭ *G.7ERF 117;* ♭ *Vic.ERA 74;*
   in ♯ *Vic.LM 9021;* ♭ *DV. 26010;* in ♯ *G.BLP 1048;*
            FBLP/QBLP 1033)
— ARR. PF. & ORCH.
A. Semprini & Melachrino Orch.   **G.B 10784**
(*Paganini Étude No. 3*)

(Le) Rossignol (after Alabiev) G. 163-1 (NG. 250-1)
E. Bernáthová   (*Liebestraum*)   **U.H 24384**
☆ E. Magnetti (*Orf. 54022*)

Spanish Rhapsody   G. 168 (NG. 254)
E. Farnadi   ♯ **West.WL 5339**
(*Consolations Nos. 1-6, Rhapsodies Nos. 16-19*)
            (♯ *Sel. 320.CW.079, d.c.*)
A. Borowsky   ♯ **E. & AmVox.PL 8920**
(*Hungarian Rhapsodies Nos. 14-19*)
S. Barere   in ♯ **Rem. 199-141**
(*Rachmaninoff, Schumann, etc.*)   (♯ *Cum.CR 280*)
M. Schwalb   ♯ **Roy. 1470**
(*Études, etc., & Schubert*)
☆ W. Malcuzynski   ♯ *C.C 1031*
(*Franck*)   (♯ *FC 1028: QC 1028*)
☆ A. Uninsky   ♯ **Epic.LC 3066**
(*Paganini Étude; & Moussorgsky*)

— ARR. PF. & ORCH.   Busoni
☆ G. Bachauer & New London—Sherman ♯ *G.DLP 1009*
(*Funérailles & Rhapsody No. 12*)   (*WDLP 1009*)
☆ E. Petri & Minneapolis—Mitropoulos   ♯ **AmC.RL 3040**
(*Chopin: Preludes*)

A. III. 5. PF. TRANSCRIPTIONS, PARTITIONS, ETC.

BACH
Prelude & Fugue, A minor   G. 247-1 (NG. 462-1)
For recordings, *see* under BACH, Organ

BEETHOVEN
Turkish March from Ruinen von Athen
   G. 173 (NG. 389)
J. Hofmann[2]   in ♯ **AmC.ML 4929**
(*Chopin, Mendelssohn, Rachmaninoff, etc.*)
BELLINI: Hexaméron, morceau de Concert[3]
   G. 177 (NG. 392)
— ARR. 2 PFS.   Liszt   G. 443 (NG. 654)
V. Appleton & M. Field   ♯ **Roy. 1587**
(*Mephisto Waltz; & J. Strauss*)
CHOPIN: (6) Chants Polonais   G. 265 (NG. 480)
No. 1, The Maiden's Wish, Op. 74, No. 1
Anon. Artist   in ♯ **Roy. 1549**
☆ C. Keene   in ♯ **EMer.MG 10113**

No. 5, My Joys, Op. 74, No. 12
R. Spivak   **ArgV. 66-6002**
(*Chopin: Écossaises & Valse 6*)
E. Burton   in ♯ **CEd.CE 1025**
☆ C. Horsley (in ♯ *G.CLP 1012*)
GOUNOD: Valse from Faust   G. 142 (NG. 407)
A. Walker   V♯ *CA.MPO 5002*
(*Années de Pèlerinage—Tarantella*)

LISZT: (3) LIEBESTRÄUME   G. 326 (NG. 541)
COMPLETE RECORDINGS
E. Farnadi   ♯ **Nix.WLP 5321**
(*Ballades & Légendes*)   (♯ *West.WL 5321*)
P. Katin   ♯ *D.LXT 2971*
(*Hungarian Rhapsodies & Rigoletto Paraphrase*)   (♯ *Lon.LL 1087*)

No. 3, A flat major
F. Ellegaard   ♯ *D.LW 5051*
(*Paganini Étude No. 3; & Nielsen*)   (♯ *Lon.LD 9065*)
(*Paganini Étude only, on Pol.HM 80069*)
O. P. Santoliquido   ♯ *Fnt.LP 304*
(*Années de Pèlerinage—Tarantella, & Mephisto Waltz*)
X. Prochorowa   in ♯ *Imp.ILP 109*
P. Badura-Skoda   in ♯ **Nix.WL 5277**
           (in ♯ *West.WL 5277*)
P. Cavazzini   in ♯ *Arp.ARC 2*
(*La Campanella; Debussy, etc.*)
V. Schiøler   (? n.v.)   **Tono.A 194**
(*Chopin: Impromptu No. 4*)   (♭ *EP 45025*)
L. Miki (in ♯ *Rem. 1022:* ♭ *REP 74*)
M. Schwalb (in ♯ *Roy. 1474*)
E. Bernáthová (*U.H 24384*)
E. Møller (♭ *Mtr.MCEP 3031*)
☆ L. Pennario (in ♯ *Cap.P 8312:* ♭ *FAP 8205;*
              ♭ *DCap.CTL 7102*)
   A. Rubinstein (*G.DB 21567: ED 1241*)
   S. Barere (in ♯ *Ply. 12-92;* ♯ *Cum.CR 328;* ♭ *Rem.REP 12*)
   M. Flipse (in ♯ *Phi.S 06016R &* ♯ *P 10048R*)
   J. v. Karolyi (in ♯ *Pol. 19016:* ♭ *30009*)
   V. Schiøler (♭ *FMer.MEP 14529; Mer.EP 1-5004*)
   E. Magnetti (*Orf. 54022*)
   J. Battista (in ♯ *MGM.E 3060*)
— ARR. 2 PFS.   L. Shankson & I. Wright (in ♯ *Roy. 1447*)
— ARR. PF. & ORCH.
W. Stech & Hamburg State Phil.—Wal-Berg
            (in ♯ *T.TW 30027*)
L. Pennario & Hollywood Bowl—Dragon (in ♯ *Cap.P 8326*)
(*continued on next page*)

---

[1] Labelled "No. 4".
[2] Recorded Metropolitan Op. House, Nov. 1937. There is some doubt whether this is in fact Liszt's version, or if by A. Rubinstein.
[3] On March from "Puritani", with Chopin, Czerny, etc.

Liebestraum No. 3, A flat major (*continued*)
— ARR. ORCH.
Boston Prom.—Fiedler (? n.v.)   in ♯ *Vic*.LRM 7052
                                          (♭ *set* ERB 7052)
(♯ *FV.A 330208;* in ♯ Vic.LM 1910; ♭ G.7BF 1064;
                                  ♭ *DV. 16293: ItV.A72R 0059)*
☆ Cincinnati Summer Op.—Cleva   in ♯ B.AXTL 1035
(in ♯ AmD.DL 8053: ♭ ED 3526; in ♯ D.UST 233087)
G. Melachrino Orch. (in ♯ *G.DLP 1083)*
A. Fenske Orch. (in ♯ *Phi.P 10200R)*
Light Orch.—Robinson (in ♯ Argo.RG 40;
                                          West WN 18097)
Belgian Radio—P. Glière (in ♯ *Mae.OAT 25001)*
A. Sciascia Orch. (*Fnt. 14169:* in ♯ *LP 309)*

Mephisto Waltz No. 1   G. 286 (NG. 514)
  J. Katchen   ♯ **D.LXT 2838**
  (*Funérailles; & Mendelssohn*)   (♯ Lon.LL 824)
  O. P. Santoliquido   ♯ *Fnt.LP 304*
  (*Tarantella, & Liebestraum No. 3*)
  C. de Groot   ♯ *Phi.S 06061R*
  (*Funérailles*)
  E. Farnadi   ♯ **Nix.WLP 5266**
  (*Sonata & Valse impromptu*)
                              (♯ West.WL 5266; Sel. 320.CW.079, d.c.)
  L. Pennario   ♯ *DCap.CCL 7523*
  (*Chopin: Barcarolle*)   (♯ Cap.H 8246)
  ☆ W. Kapell   ♯ Vic.LM 1791
  (*Rhapsody 11; & Bach & Schubert*)
  ☆ S. Barere (in ♯ Cum.CR 328)
— ARR. 2 PFS. [from Liszt's 4 hand arr. G. 375-2 (NG. 599-2)]
  V. Appleton & M. Field   in ♯ *Roy.* 1587

Mephisto Waltz No. 2   G. 287 (NG. 515)
  Y. Flier (*Mendelssohn*)   USSRM.D 001262

MENDELSSOHN
Auf Flügeln des Gesanges   G. 332-1 (NG. 547-1)
  J. Katchen   in ♯ **D.LXT 2838**
  (*above*)   (♯ Lon.LL 824)
Wedding March   G. 195 (NG. 410)
  ☆ V. Horowitz[1] (in ♯ Vic.LM 9021; ♯ *G.FALP 280;*
                                          ♭ *DV. 26002)*
MOZART
Fantasia on Le Nozze di Figaro[2]   G. 694 (NG. 697)
  G. Ginsburg (2ss)   USSRM.D 456/7
Reminiscences of Don Juan   G. 203 (NG. 418)
  S. Cherkassky   ♯ *G.ALP 1154*
  (*Sonata, B minor*)
  (*Consolation No. 3 & Concerto No. 1* in ♯ BB.LBC 1041:
                                          ♭ *set* WBC 1041)
  ☆ S. Barere (in ♯ Cum.CR 325)

SCHUBERT
Horch', horch', die Lerch'   G. 343-9 (NG. 558-9)
  E. Burton   in ♯ CEd.CE 1025

Litaney   G. 347-1 (NG. 562-1)
  A. Cortot   G.DB 21618
  (*Rhapsody No. 11*)   (♭ 7R 174: 7RQ 3036)
Ständchen   G. 345-7 (NG. 560-7)
  M. Jonas   in ♯ AmC.ML 4624
  ☆ S. Rachmaninoff (in ♯ Vic.LCT 1136)
Soirées de Vienne   G. 212 (NG. 427)
  ...No. 6, A major
  W. Backhaus[3]   in ♯ Lon.LL 1108/9
  (*Beethoven, Schubert, Schumann, Brahms*)
  A. Kaplan (2ss)   USSR. 17834/5
  M. Schwalb   in ♯ Roy. 1470
  ...Unspec. No.
  I. Antal   Qual.MN 1057
  (*Pf. Concerto No. 2, s. 5*)
SCHUMANN
Frühlingsnacht   G. 353 (NG. 568)
  ☆ J. Lhevinne (in ♯ Cam.CAL 265)
VERDI
Miserere du Trovatore   G. 218 (NG. 433)
  J. Hatto (*below*)   V♯ *CA.MPO 5003*

Rigoletto, Paraphrase de concert   G. 219 (NG. 434)
  P. Katin   ♯ **D.LXT 2971**
  (*Liebesträume & Hung. Rhapsodies*)   (♯ Lon.LL 1087)
  (*Hung. Rhapsody No. 2* only on ♯ *D.LW 5134;*
                                          ♯ Lon.LD 9159)
  J. Hatto (*above*)   V♯ *CA.MPO 5003*
  R. Tamarkina (*USSR. 10582/3*)

A. V. TWO PIANOS

Concerto pathétique, E minor   G. 423 (NG. 258)
  ☆ J. & G. Dichler   ♯ *Sup.LPM 73*
  (*Pastorale & Rhapsody No. 2*)   (♯ U. 5031C)
Hexaméron: SEE *ante,* section A. III. 5
Mephisto Waltz No. 1: SEE *ante,* section A. III. 5

A. VI. ORGAN

COLLECTION
Fantasia & Fugue on 'Ad nos, ad salutarem undam'
                              G. 447 (NG. 259)
Prelude & Fugue on the name B.A.C.H   G. 448 (NG. 260)
Variations on 'Weinen, Klagen, Sorgen, Zagen'
                              G. 463 (NG. 673)
  [org. version of the pf. varns.   G. 93 (NG. 180) *q.v.*]
  J. Costa   ♯ **CFD. 53**
  [organ of St. Vincent-de-Paul, Paris]

Fantasia & Fugue on 'Ad nos, ad salutarem undam'
                              G. 447 (NG. 259)
  J. Demessieux   ♯ **D.LXT 2773**
  (*Widor*)   (♯ Lon.LL 697)
  [Organ of Victoria Hall, Geneva]
  P. Cochereau (2ss)   ♯ *OL.LD 120*
  [Organ of Notre-Dame, Paris]

Missa pro organo . . .   G. 452 (NG. 264)
  ... **Gloria & Credo,** only
  E. P. Biggs   ♯ AmC.ML 4820
  (*below; & Reubke*) [Methuen organ, Mass., U.S.A.]

Prelude & Fugue on the name B.A.C.H
                              G. 448 (NG. 260)
  E. P. Biggs   ♯ AmC.ML 4820
  (*above, & Reubke*)
  H. Ash   ♯ McInt.MC 1005
  (*Bach, Bingham, Langlais, Zechiel*)   (o.n. ♯ WCFM. 19)
  K. Richter   ♯ **D.LXT 5110**
  (*Bach*)   (♯ Lon.LL 1174)
  [Organ of Victoria Hall, Geneva]
  L. de St.-Martin   in ♯ **SM. 33-22**
  (*L. de St.-Martin: Compositions & Improvisation*)
  [Organ of Notre-Dame, Paris, during service]

B. VOCAL

IX. SACRED CHORAL WORKS
(*Orig. Ger or Latin*)

Ave verum corpus   G. 517 (NG. 44) cho. & org.
  Mormon Tabernacle Cho.—Cornwall
                              in ♯ EPhi.NBL 5012
  (*Brahms, Elgar, Purcell, etc.*) (♯ Phi.N 02125L;
                                          AmC.ML 5048)

Missa Choralis, A minor
                    G. 503 (NG. 10) cho. & org.
  Paris Select Cho.—Leibowitz   ♯ Oce.OCS 37
  [G. Englert, org.]

Via Crucis   G. 558 (NG. 53) 1878-9
  (*14 Stations of the Cross*) Soloists, cho. & org.
  Anon. Soloists & Morley College Cho.—Fricker
  [D. Vaughan, org.]   ♯ *CA.LPA 1093*

B. X. SECULAR CHORAL WORKS

Jubilee Song (unid.) (Bossa)
  Vocal Ens.—Kalmár   Qual.KK 2503
  (*Kodály: To the Magyars*)

---

[1] Further ARR. Horowitz.
[3] Carnegie Hall performance, March 30, 1954.

[2] Unfinished. Completed by Busoni. Pub. 1912.

B. XI. SONGS (with pf.)

COLLECTION

Die Loreley (Heine) G. 592 (NG. 273)
Oh! quand je dors (Hugo) G. 601 (NG. 282)
Freudvoll und leidvoll (Goethe) G. 599 (NG. 280)
   Z. Dolukhanova (A, *Russ*)   *USSRM.D 1117/8*
   (Oh! quand je dors also USSR. 21499/500)

Es muss ein Wunderbares sein (Redwitz)
   G. 633 (NG. 314)
   J. Björling (T), F. Schauwecker (pf.)
          in ♯ *G.ALP 1187*
   (*Wolf, Sibelius, etc.*)   (♭ *G.7ERC 1*; in ♯ *Vic.LM 1771*)
   R. Schock (T) & Orch.   *G.DA 5521*
   (*Gounod: Ave Maria*)   (♭ *7PW 517*; in ♯ *WDLP 1507*)
   G. Pechner (B)   in ♯ *Roy. 1558*
   W. Strienz (Bs) & Orch.   in ♯ *Lon.LB 891*

Oh! quand je dors (Hugo) G. 601 (NG. 282)
  ☆ E. Noréna (S) & Orch. (JpV.ND 837)
   H. Schlusnus (B, *Ger*) (in ♯ *AmD.DL 9624*)
  ⊞ J. Schwarz (B, *Ger*) (in ♯ *Ete. 498*•)

O Lieb', so lang du lieben kannst (Freiligrath)
   G. 617 (NG. 298) (*"Liebestraum"*)
   G. Gasparyan (S, *Eng*) (in ♯ *USSR.D 1902*)
  ☆ G. Thill (T, *Fr*) (in ♯ *C.FHX 5012*; Angel. 33001)

MISCELLANEOUS

Franz Liszt, his story & his music
   A. Robinson (narrator) & Orch.
           ♯ *AmVox.VL 2630*
           (& ♮ *set 263*, 6ss)

LITOLFF, Henry Charles (1818-1891)

Concerto symphonique, Op. 102   pf. & orch.
... **Scherzo**
   L. Pennario & Hollywood Bowl—Dragon
          in ♯ *Cap.P 8326*
   (*Liszt, Beethoven, etc.*)
  ☆ M. Lympany & Philharmonia—Susskind ♭ *G.7EP 7014*
   (*Granados: Goyescas, No. 4*) (♭ *7EPQ 528: 7BF 1053:*
             7PQ 2012: o.n. ♭ *G.7P 105*)
  ☆ W. Atwell & Orch.—Mantovani (♭ *Lon.BEP 6188*)

LOCATELLI, Pietro (1695-1764)

Concerto Grosso, F minor, Op. 1, No. 8 1721
Sinfonia funebre, F minor Str. orch. 1725
   Per l'esequie della sua Donna ; "*Trauer-symphonie*"
   MS. Darmstadt
   Saar Cha.—Ristenpart[1]   ♯ *CND. 1005*
  ☆ Vienna Sym.—Swoboda   ♯ *Nix.WLP 5030*
   (& with *Sammartini & Pergolesi*, in ♯ *West.WN 18032*)

Concerto Grosso, D major, Op. 1, No. 9 1721
   Augsburg Cha. Orch.—Deyle † ♯ *AS. 3007LD*
            (♯ *HS.AS 39*)

(12) CONCERTI, vln. & orch., Op. 3 1733
   (*L'Arte del violino*) with 24 Capriccios for vln. unacc.
No. 2, C minor
   H. Fernandez & Leclair Ens.—Paillard
           ♯ *DDP. 31-1*
   (*below*) [recording includes the Capriccios] (♯ *HSL. 147*)

No. 12, D major ... Capriccio only
  —— ARR. VLN. & PF. "Le Labyrinthe"
   H. Szeryng & M. Berthelier in ♯ *Pac.LDPC 50*

(6) CONCERTI A QUATTRO, Op. 7 1741
No. 6, E flat major (*Il pianto d'Arianna*)
   H. Fernandez (vln.) & Leclair Ens.—Paillard
           ♯ *DDP. 31-1*
   (*above*; & *Torelli, Vivaldi*)   (♯ *HS.HSL 147*)
Sinfonia funebre, *see above*

Sonata, F major, Op. 2, No. 8 fl. & cont. 1732
   S. Gazzelloni & R. Raffalt (hpsi.)
          ♯ *ItV.A12R 0027*
   (*Valentino, Veracini, Platti, etc.*)

SONATAS, vln. & cont.
D major: Op. 3, No. 6 (Allegro & Minuetto) &
   No. 12 (Adagio)
  — ARR. VLC. & PF. Piatti
   A. Janigro & E. Bagnoli   ♯ *West.WL 5234*
   (*Frescobaldi & Boccherini*)

F minor, Op. 6, No. 7[2] 1737
   D. Oistrakh & V. Yampolsky ♯ *JpV.LS 2025*
   (*Kreisler, Tchaikovsky, etc.*) [Tokyo recording, 1955]

LOCKE, Matthew (1630-1677)

Consort of four parts No. 4, F major viols
   (Fantasia, Courante, Ayre, Sarabande)
   Consort of Viols—Leonhardt   ♯ *Van.BG 547*
   (*Purcell & Jenkins*)

Pavan—Almand; Ayre
   (from *Musick for the King's Sagbutts and cornetts*, 1661)
   Brass Ens.—Voisin   ♯ *Uni.UN 1003*
   († *Golden Age of Brass*)

LOCKWOOD, Normand (b. 1906)

Concerto org., 2 tpts., 2 tbnes. 1952
Quiet Design org.
   M. Mason (org.), J. Ware & N. Prager (tpts.),
   G. Pulis & L. Haney (tbnes.) ♯ *Rem. 199-173*
   (*Kay*)

LOEFFLER, Charles Martin (1861-1935)

Memories of my Childhood 1923
   Eastman-Rochester Sym.—Hanson
   (*below*; & *Griffes*)   ♯ *Mer.MG 40012*

(A) Pagan Poem, Op. 14 orch. (after Virgil)
   Paris Phil.—Rosenthal   ♯ *DCap.CTL 7033*
   (*Scriabin*)   (♯ *Cap.P 8188*)

Poem for orchestra (after Verlaine) 1901 rev. 1918
   Eastman-Rochester Sym.—Hanson
   (*above*)   ♯ *Mer.MG 40012*

LOEILLET

There has been much confusion between the members of this family. In view of the new classification of the works in the Thematic Catalogue published by B. Priestman in *Revue belge de musicologie*, Vol. VI, fasc. 4 (1952), we present here the complete discography (including items from WERM & Supps. I & II) reorganised according to his classification; these attributions have since been questioned. It is, however, convenient to follow it here, and Priestman's classification numbers are given in Roman figures below; the Opus numbers are those of the original editions.

JACOB (or Jacques) (1685-1746)

CONCERTO, D major
   fl., 2 vlns., vln., ripieno, cont. (XVIII-MS, Brussels)
   H. Magnée & Brussels Radio Cha. Orch.
   —Doneux   ♯ *Gramo.GLP 2509*
   (*Grétry*)

JEAN-BAPTISTE (or John) (1680-1730)

A. Attributed to JEAN-BAPTISTE (of Ghent)

(12) SONATAS, Op. 3 fl. & cont. (III)
No. 2, B flat major
   D. Barnett (rec.), N. Salas (hpsi.) **C.DOX 1004**

---

[1] Omits the *Pastorale* of Op. 1, No. 8.   [2] Ed. & arr. Ysaÿe: "Au tombeau."

No. 5, C minor
L. Davenport (rec.), P. Davenport (hpsi.) &
vlc. ‡ **CEd.CE 1051**
(*J. S. Bach, A. Scarlatti, Telemann*)

... **1st & 3rd movts., Largo & Poco allegro**
C. Dolmetsch (rec.), J. Saxby (hpsi.)
‡ *D.LM 4535*
(*Corelli, Telemann, etc.*) (‡ *Lon.LS 278*)

B. Attributed to JOHN (of London)

CHAMBER MUSIC

(6) SONATAS, Op. 1 (IX)
No. 1, F major fl., ob. & cont.
— ARR. FL. & PF. de Béon ("No. 7")
P. Kaplan, E. Bodky (hpsi.) & vlc. ‡ *Allo. 4018*
(*below*) (o.n. ‡ *Allo. AL 69;* ‡ *Ome. & CID.LX 33009*)
§ J. Nada & J. Hoorenmann (hpsi.) (C. 8866)
H. Breiden & A. Melichar (pf.) (Pol. 27295)

... **Allegro, Gavotte & Aria only**
§ Anon. Fl. & H. G. Kinscella (pf.) (*Vic. 21947*)

... **Gavotte only** Inst. Ens. (in *G.B 10658*)

No. 5, C minor fl., ob. & cont.
Ithaca Ens. (*Telemann*) ‡ *Corn. 1011*

No. 6, E minor 2 fls. & cont.
K. Redel (fl.), H. Winschermann (ob.),
I. Lechner (hpsi.) & vlc. ‡ **OL.LD 11**
(*Vivaldi*)

(12) SONATAS, Op. 2 (X) *alias* Op. 5
COLLECTION
No. 1, B flat major 2 vlns. & cont.
No. 2, F major Fl., ob. & cont.
No. 6, C minor Fl., ob. & cont.
No. 10, E minor 2 fls. & cont.
— ARR. de Béon as follows:—
"No. 10", B flat major fl. & pf.
"No. 13", G major vln., vlc. & pf.
"No. 2", B minor vln., vlc. & pf.
"No. 12, F sharp minor" vlc. & pf.
G. Alès (vln.), P. Coddée (vlc.), R. Gerlin (hpsi.)
‡ **LOL.OL 50018**
(‡ *OL.LD 49*)
No. 4, D minor fl., ob. & cont.
P. Kaplan, J. Holmes, E. Bodky (hpsi.) & vlc.
(*above & below*) ‡ *Allo. 4018*
(o.n. ‡ *Allo.AL 69; Ome & CID.LX 33009*)
A. Mann (rec.), L. Wann, E. Weiss-Mann (hpsi.)
(3ss—*Telemann*) in **Tec. set T 13**

No. 6, C minor fl., ob. & cont.
— ARR. de Béon (B minor)—*see also* Collection
M. Wittgenstein (fl.), M. Hubert (vlc.),
S. Marlowe (hpsi.) ‡ **West.WL 5076**
(*Telemann*)
H. Clebanoff (vln.), K. Früh (vlc.),
N. M.-Minchin (pf.) ‡ **APM.PMT 201**
(*Brahms & Tcherepnin*)

No. 9, G minor 2 vlns. & cont.
P. Kaplan & L. Schaefer (fls.), E. Bodky (hpsi.)
& vlc. ‡ *Allo. 4018*
(*above*) (o.n. ‡ *Allo.AL 69;* ‡ *Ome & CID.LX 33009*)

(12) SONATAS (Solos) Op. 3 fl. & cont. (VIII)
No. 1, C major ... 1st movt. Largo
No. 10, A minor ... 2nd movt. Allegro
No. 4, A minor ... 1st movt. Largo
No. 1, C major ... 2nd movt. Allegro
— ARR. OB. & PF. Rothwell ("*Sonata, C major*")
E. Rothwell & W. Parry *G.B 10291*
(*JK 2795*)

HARPSICHORD MUSIC

(3) LESSONS (XI)
No. 1, E minor ... No. 3, Corant
A. Ehlers *D.F 7726*
(⅓s—*Bach, Byrd, Frescobaldi*)
(*D.Y 5723; AmD.* 23089 in set A 61)
(& in ‡ *AmD.DL 8019; D.UAT 273084*)

... **No. 2, Slow aire; & No. 3, Corant**
— ARR. VIOLS & HPSI. ("*Aire tendre & Courante*")
§ Am. Soc. Ancient Insts.—Stad (*Vic. 1663* in set M 216)

... **No. 2 only** — ARR. ORGAN
E. Hilliar (*Arne, etc.*) in ‡ **ASK. 4**

—— ARR. CYMBALOM & PF.
A. & A. Rácz (Qual.SZK 3504)

(6) SUITES (XII) *c.* 1722-5
No. 1, G minor
... **5th movt., Minuet**
E. Heiller (hpsi.) in ‡ **Uni.LP 1010**
(† History of the Dance)

... **6th movt., Giga,** only
A. Ehlers *D.M 494*
(⅓s—*Bach: Fr. Suite No. 1 excpt. etc.*)
(*AmD.* 23090 in set A 61; & in ‡ *AmD.DL 8019:*
D.UAT 273084)
§ R. Gerlin (Pat.X 9798)
S. Barere (pf.) (*JpV.JE 147*)

No. 2, A major
... **4th movt., Aria; 6th movt., Giga**
—— ARR. ORGAN F. Peeters
C. Watters in ‡ **CEd.CE 1008**
(† French Baroque Organ Music)

No. 5, F major
... **1st movt., Allemande,** only
— ARR. HARP Grandjany ("*Toccata*")
A. Sacchi in ‡ *NRI. 403*
(*Handel, Haydn, Debussy, etc.*)
M. Grandjany *Vic. 2153*
(*Bach: Vln. Sonata 3, Largo*)

Gavotte — ARR. VLC. & PF. Bazelaire
Attrib. Lully, but may well be the Gavotte from Suite
No. 4 of above set. It has not been possible to find
the records (see WERM, p. 341) to check.

LOEWE, Johann Karl Gottfried
(1796-1869)

LIEDER UND BALLADEN
COLLECTIONS
Tom der Reimer, Op. 135 (▽ Fontane)
Heinrich der Vogler, Op. 56, No. 1 (Vogl)
Die Uhr, Op. 123, No. 3 (Seidl)
Der heilige Franziskus, Op. 75, No. 3 (Wessenberg)
Spirito Santo, Op. 143 (E.v.d. Goltz)
Prinz Eugen, der edle Ritter, Op. 92 (Freiligrath)
J. Greindl (Bs), H. Klust (pf.) ‡ *Pol. 16100*
(‡ *17041*)

Der Erlkönig, Op. 1, No. 3 (Goethe) 1818
Kleiner Haushalt, Op. 71 (Rückert)
Herr Oluf, Op. 2, No. 2 (Herder) 1824
Die wandelnde Glocke, Op. 20, No. 3 (Goethe)
H. Schey (B), F. de Nobel (pf.) ‡ *Phi.N 00625R*
(*Brahms*) (♭ N 402053E)
[Erlkönig & Kleiner Haushalt only, on N 12709G)]

(Der) Alte Goethe, Op. 9, Bk. IX, No. 2 (Goethe)
(*Als ich ein junger Geselle war*)
E. Busch (Bs), F. Schröder (pf.) *Eta. 20-008*
(*Beethoven: Marmotte*)

(Das) Erkennen, Op. 65, No. 2 (Vogl)
☆ H. Schlusnus (B) (in ‡ *AmD.DL 9624*)

(Der) Erlkönig, Op. 1, No. 3 (Goethe) 1818
D. Fischer-Dieskau (B), G. Moore (pf.)
G.DA 5524
(*Wolf: Der Tambour*) (♭ 7PW 534)
(*idem, Feuerreiter & Storchenbotschaft* on ♭ 7ER 5044)

Heinrich der Vogler, Op. 56, No. 1 (Vogl) 1836
☆ G. Hüsch (B), Cho. & Orch. (*JpV.NF 4180*)

Hochzeitslied, Op. 20, No. 1 (Goethe)
Kleiner Haushalt, Op. 71 (Rückert)
K. Borg (Bs), M. Raucheisen (pf.)
(*Schubert, Schumann*) in ‡ *Pol. 17004*

---

‡ = Long-playing, 33⅓ r.p.m. ♭ = 45 r.p.m. ♮ = Auto. couplings, 78 r.p.m.

(Der) Nöck, Op. 129, No. 2   (Kopisch)
☆ H. Schlusnus (B) (in ♯ AmD.DL 9624)

Prinz Eugen, der edle Ritter, Op. 92   (Freiligrath)
☆ G. Hüsch (B), Cho. & Orch. (JpV.NF 4180)

Tom der Reimer, Op. 135   (▽ Fontane)
H. Prey (B), M. Raucheisen (pf.)   C.DWX 5085
(Die Uhr)   (♭ SCDW 501)
☆ H. Rosenberg (B) & Orch. (Imp. 014121)

(Die) Uhr, Op. 123, No. 3   (Seidl)
H. Prey (B), M. Raucheisen (pf.)   C.DWX 5085
(Tom der Reimer)   (♭ SCDW 501)
G. Pechner (B)   in ♯ Roy. 1558
☆ H. Rosenberg (B) & Orch. (Imp. 014121)

LOGI, Graf Johann Anton von (1638-1721)
(or LOSI)
    SEE: † RENAISSANCE & BAROQUE

LOGROSCINO, Nicola (1698-c. 1763)
    SEE: † HISTORY OF MUSIC IN SOUND (47)

LOPATNIKOFF, Nikolai Lvovitch
                                    (b. 1903)
Concertino for orchestra, Op. 30   1944
Columbia Sym.—Bernstein   ♯ AmC.ML 4996
(Hill & Dallapiccola)

Variations & Epilogue, Op. 31   vlc. & pf.   1947
N. & J. Graudan   ♯ AmC.ML 4990
(Glanville-Hicks)

Vocalise (in modo russo)   pub. 1953
South Hills High School Cho.—Crawford
                         in ♯ PFCM.CB 161
(Phillips, Poulenc, Copland, etc.)

LÓPEZ-BUCHARDO, Carlos (1881-1948)
Bailecito   pf.
    ☆ R. Viñes (JpV.NF 4131)

Campera
State Sym.—Kinsky   ArgV.P 1486
                                  (pte. rec.)

SONGS
Canción del Carretero   (Caraballo)
    ▽ R. Cesari (B) & Orch.   ArgOd. 57002
    (Ugarte: Songs)
— ARR. PF. Brunelli
    L. Brunelli   ArgV. 66-0012
    (Ginastera: Milonga)
—ARR. ORCH.
    Argentine Radio—Bandini (ArgOd. 57001)

Si lo hallas   (Camino)   1936
G. Souzay (B), D. Baldwin (pf.)
                         ♭ ArgLon.DLCE 6501
(Ginastera, Guastavino, Nin)

Vidala
E. Arizmendi (S)   in ♯ ArgOd.LDC 506

LORTZING, Gustav Albert (1801-1851)
CHORUS
Trauer-Chor   1848
    [Senke dich, du Geist des Friedens]   (C. Haffner)
Berlin State Op. Male Cho.—K. Schmidt
                                    Eta. 110212

Sieg der Freiheit oder Tod   (Herlossohn)   1848
E. Ger. State Folk Cho.—Schmidt-Böhlander
                                    Eta. 110248

OPERAS
UNDINE   4 Acts   1845
HIGHLIGHTS
Overture
Was seh' ich   T & Bs
So wisse, dass in allen Elementen   S   Act II
Vater, Mutter, Schwestern, Brüder   T
Nun ist's vollbracht   B & S   Act III
Ballet Music, Act II
    A. Schlemm (S), W. Ludwig (T), H. Braun (B),
        T. Blankenheim (Bs), Bavarian State Op. Cho.
        & Bamberg Sym.—Reinshagen   ♯ Pol. 19010

Ballet Music, Act II
Vienna Sym.—Loibner   ♯ Phi.S 06005R
(Hellmesberger: Die Perle von Iberien, Ballet Music)
                                  (in ♯ Epic.LC 3102)
Bamberg Sym.—Reinshagen (from Highlights)
                                    Pol. 62928
(Zar und Zimmermann—Holzschuhtanz)   (♭ Pol. 32017)
Berlin Sym.—Rubahn   in ♯ Roy. 1533

So wisse, dass in allen Elementen   S   Act II
A. Schlemm, from Highlights   PV. 72454
(Nun ist's vollbracht)   (♭ Pol. 30042: in ♯ 19015)

Vater, Mutter, Schwestern, Brüder   T   Act III
R. Schock   G.EH 1432
(Zar und Zimmermann—Lebe wohl . . .)   (♭ 7PW 508)
W. Ludwig, from Highlights   PV. 36061
(Zar und Zimmermann—Lebe wohl . . .)   (♭ Pol. 32075)
☆ P. Anders (AusT.M 5194)

Nun ist's vollbracht . . . O kehr' zurück
    B & S   Act III
D. Fischer-Dieskau & R. Streich   G.DB 11550
                                    (♭ 7RW 501)
H. Braun & A. Schlemm, from Highlights
                                    PV. 72454
(So wisse...)   (♭ Pol. 30042: in ♯ 19015)
... B solo only   ☆ H. Schlusnus (♭ Pol. 32152)

(Der) WAFFENSCHMIED   3 Acts   1846
    (The Armourer)
Vocal Selection
    L. Otto, E. Hagemann, G. Frick, H. Prey,
        G. Unger, Cho. & Orch.—Schüchter
                         ♭ Od.BEOW 3001

Er schläft . . . 'S mag freilich   S   Act I
E. Trötschel   PV. 72398
(Bartered Bride—No. 29)   (in ♯ Pol. 18057: in 19036)

Auch ich war ein Jüngling   Bs   Act III
G. Frick & Cho.   G.EH 1444
(Nicolai: Lustigen Weiber—Als Büblein klein)
                    (FKX 261: ♭ 7PW 519: in ♯ WBLP 1505)

(Der) WILDSCHÜTZ   3 Acts   1842
HIGHLIGHTS
Overture
☆ Lass er doch hören   Bs & S   Act I
☆ Ich habe Numero eins   (Billiards Quintet)
☆ Fünftausend Thaler   Bs   Act II
Wie freundlich strahlt . . . Heiterkeit und Fröhlichkeit   B
    (H. Günter)   Act III
    E. Junker-Giesen & L. Wissmann (S), R.
        Fischer (A), W. Windgassen (T), E. Czubok
        (B), H. Günter (B), G. Hann (Bs), Bamberg
        Sym.—Sawallisch   ♯ Pol. 19009

Overture
Bamberg Sym.—Sawallisch   PV. 72453
(Nicolai: Lustigen Weiber, Overture)   (♭ Pol. 30043)
[from Highlights]
Leipzig Radio—Dobrindt (Eta. 120174)

Lass er doch hören   Bs & S   Act I
☆ G. Hann & E. Junker-Giesen   ♯ HP.DGM 18003
(below; Zar und Zimmermann & Cornelius)
                         (♭ Pol. 30074: in ♯ 19025)

Auf des Lebens raschen Wogen   S   Act I
⌘ F. Hempel (AF.AGSB. 59*)

☆ = Re-issue of a recording to be found in previous volumes.

Ich habe Numero eins (Billiards Quintet) Act II
☆ G. Hann, L. Wissmann, W. Windgassen, R. Fischer,
  E. Czubok (♭ *Pol. 30123*)

Fünftausend Thaler (Baculus' Aria) Bs   Act II
E. Kunz   *C.LB 143*
                                              (*LV 18: LO 92*)

☆ G. Hann   **♯ HP.DGM 18003**
   (*above*)   (♭ *Pol. 30018:* in ♯ *19025*)

Wie freundlich strahlt . . .
Heiterkeit und Fröhlichkeit B   Act III
H. Prey   **C.DWX 5091**
(*Zar und Zimmermann—Sonst spielt' ich*)
                                       (*SVX 47:* ♭ *SCDW 502*)
H. Günter, from Highlights   *PV. 36094*
(*Zar und Zimmermann—Sonst spielt' ich*) (♭ *Pol. 30035*)

ZAR UND ZIMMERMANN 3 Acts   1837
   (*Czar and Carpenter*)
COMPLETE RECORDING
Peter I   ...   .   H. Günter (B)
Peter Ivanov...   ...   ...   A. Pfeifle (T)
Van Bett   ...   ...   G. Neidlinger (Bs)
Maria...   ...   ...   E. J-Giesen (S)
Marquis de Chateauneuf ... W. Ludwig (T)
etc. Cho. & Orch. of Württemberg State Op.
—Leitner (6ss)   **♯ HP.DGM 18060/2**
   (♯ *AmD. set DX 129*; manual: ♯ *Pol. 18126/8*)

Highlights
A. Rothenberger, L. Otto, R. Schock, G. Frick
& Berlin Municipal Op. Cho. & Orch.
—Schüchter   **♯ G.WDLP 1517**
(*Kreutzer & Nicolai*)

O Sancta Justitia Bs & cho.   Act I
G. Frick   **G.EH 1445**
(*below on* ♭ *7EPW 13-7001*)   (*FKX 265*)
☆ G. Hann   **♯ HP.DGM 18003**
(*Wildschütz; & Cornelius*) (♭ *Pol. 30018:* in ♯ *19025*)

Lebe wohl, mein flandrisch' Mädchen T & S Act II
R. Schock & L. Otto   **G.EH 1432**
(*Undine—Vater, Mutter . . .*)   (♭ *7PW 508*)
W. Ludwig & E. Junker-Giesen   *PV. 36061*
(*Undine—Vater, Mutter . . .*) (from set) (♭ *Pol. 32075*)
☆ P. Anders (*AusT.M 5194*)

Den hohen Herrscher (Singschule) Bs & cho.
                                            Act III
G. Frick & Berlin Municipal Op.—Schüchter
(2ss)   **G.EH 1456**
(*above on* ♭ *7EPW 13-7001*)   (♭ *7PW 536*)
☆ G. Hann & Cho.   **♯ HP.DGM 18003**
   (*above*)   (♭ *Pol. 30074:* in ♯ *19025*)

Sonst spielt' ich mit Zepter B Act III
H. Günter, from set   *PV. 36094*
(*Wildschütz—Wie freundlich . . .*)   (♭ *Pol. 30035*)
H. Prey   **C.DWX 5091**
(*Wildschütz—Wie freundlich . . .*) (*SVX 27:* ♭ *SCDW 502*)
☆ H. Schlusnus (♭ *Pol. 32152*)
⊞ J. Schwarz (in ♯ *Ete. 498**)

Holzschuhtanz (Clog Dance) orch. Act III
Württemberg State—Leitner   *Pol. 62928*
(*Undine—Ballet music*) [from set]   (♭ *Pol. 32017*)
Vienna Sym.—Loibner   **♯ Phi.N 00693R**
(*Bayer: Die Puppenfee, Ballet Music*)   (in ♯ *Epic.LC 3102*)
Berlin Sym.—Rubahn   in ♯ **Roy. 1533**
Hamburg State Phil.—Martin   *T.A 11405*
(*Cavalleria Rusticana—Intermezzo*)   (♭ *U 45405*)
(in ♯ *LA 6054 & TW 30004;* ♯ *FT. 260.TV.015*)
N.W. Ger. Phil.—Schüchter   *Od.O-29002*
(*Offenbach*)   (♭ *OBL 29002*)

LOTTI, Antonio (*c.* 1667-1740)

Crucifixus Motet 8 voices[1]
Regensburg Cath. Cho.—Schrems *D.F 43063*
(*below*)   (♭ *D 17963: DX 1762*)

Welch Chorale   in ♯ **Lyr.LL 52**
(† Motets of XVth & XVIth Cent.)
☆ Netherlands Cha. Cho.—de Nobel (in ♯ *Phi.S 06026R*)
  St. Eustache Singers—Martin (♭ *Pac. 45030*)

Pur dicesti (Aria from *Arminio*, 1714)
G. Prandelli (T), D. Marzollo (pf.)
                              in ♯ **AmVox.PL 7930**
(† Old Italian Airs)
⊞ A. Patti (in ♯ *AudR.LPA 2340**)

Vere languores nostros Motet
Regensburg Cath. Cho.—Schrems *D.F 43963*
(*above*)
☆ Netherlands Cha. Cho.—de Nobel (in ♯ *Phi.S 06026R*)

LOUCHEUR, Raymond (b. 1899)

En famille Suite   1933
Paris Clarinet Sextet   **♯ D.LX 3136**
(*Schmitt*)   (♯ *Lon.LS 1077*)

Volière cl. & pf. 1954
J. Lancelot & F. Gobet   ♭ *Pat.G 1053*
(*Challan, Gallon, Tomasi*)

LOUIS XIII, King of France (1601-1643)
SEE: † OLD FRENCH AIRS

LOUIS FERDINAND von HOHENZOLLERN,
                                          Prince
SEE: HOHENZOLLERN, *supra.*

LOUIS FERDINAND OF PRUSSIA,
                            Prince (b. 1907)
SONGS: COLLECTION
Stille (Moehring)   (a.i)
Vorgefühl (Zwillinger)   (a.ii)
Russisches Volkslied (Thiess)   (b.i)
Frühling (Mörike)   (b.i)
Abendfrieden (Lange)   (c.i)
Das Währende (Toussell)   (c.i)
Nachts (Eichendorff)   (b.ii)
Der Heimatlose (Kerckhoff)   (a.ii)
Musikantengruss (Eichendorff)   (a.ii)
Gebet (after Poe)   (b.ii)
Kleines Abendlied (Kamossa)   (c.i)
Schönheit (after Pushkin)   (c.ii)
Herz, sei ruhig (Lange)   (b.ii)
An die Leserin (Thiess)   (a.ii)
Der Tote spricht (Thiess)   (a.ii)
In Danzig (Eichendorff)   (c.ii)
Die Wolke (after Pushkin)   (c.ii)
Liebesglück (Chamisso)   (b.ii)
Dank (Michalewski)   (a.i)
Liebesbotschaft (Lange)   (a.ii)
Morgentau (Chamisso)   (b. & c.ii)
(a) P. Anders (T); (b) L. Thomamueller (S);
   (c) C. Broecheler (B); (i) Prince Louis
   Ferdinand (pf.); (ii) C. Koschnick (pf.)
                                       ♯ T.LSK 7028

LUCHAS (fl. *c.* 1500)
SEE: † SPANISH MUSIC

LÜBECK, Vincent (1654-1740)

CANTATAS
Gott, wie dein Name cho. orch.
Hilf deinem Volk, Herr Jesu Christ
        S, A, T, B, cho. & orch.
☆ Soloists, Stuttgart Cho. & Swabian Sym.—Grischkat
                                    (♯ *Cpt.MC 20067*)

PRELUDES & FUGUES organ
COMPLETE COLLECTION[2]
1. D minor   2. E major   3. F major
4. G minor   5. C minor   6. C major
M. Andrews   **♯ UOK. 2**
(*Křenek, Piston, Sessions*)
[org. Kilgore 1st. Presbyterian Chu., Texas]

---

[1] It is not certain that all recordings are this setting, though it appears that Welch and Martin are 8 vv.
[2] The order of keys given here is that on the record. In the complete edn. the order is G mi.—C ma.—E ma.—C mi.—D mi.—F ma.

2. E major   5. C minor
☆ E. Hölderlin († # Cpt.MC 20067; † # Ren.X 53/4)

Suite, G minor hpsi. (*Clavierübung*, 1728)
... Allemande only
E. Heiller   in # Uni.LP 1010
(† History of the Dance)

LUENING, Otto (b. 1900)

Rhapsodic Variations   tape-recorder & orch.[1]
Louisville—Whitney   # LO. 5
(*Ibert & Read*)

Sonata, vln. & pf.
S. Gawriloff & K. P. Pietsch   # Rem. 199-211
(*Kerr*)

Tape Recorder Music[2]   (# Inno.GB 1)

LULLY, Jean-Baptiste (1632-1687)

ACIS ET GALATHÊE Opera, Prol. & 3 Acts 1686
Musette SEE: Symphonies pour les couchers du Roy, *below*

ALCESTE   Opera, Prol. & 5 Acts   1674
Prelude, Act III, Sc. 5 — ARR. Mottl
— SEE: Ballet Suite, *post*

Inst. Excerpts (Marche gay; Chaconne; Marche en rondeau)
— SEE: Symphonies pour les couchers du Roy, *below*

Scène infernale: Il faut passer tôt ou tard
S, Bs., Cho.   Act IV
A. Mandikian, L. Lovano, Farm Street Singers
& New London Orch.—Désormière
G.HMS 48
(† History of Music in Sound)   (in # Vic. set LM 6030)

... **Air de Caron** (Il faut passer . . .) only   Bs
G. Souzay (B)   in # D.LX 3112
(*below, Gluck, Mozart, etc.*)   (# Lon.LS 730)
& SEE: Symphonies pour les couchers du Roy, *below*

AMADIS DE GAULE Opera, Prol. & 5 Acts 1684
Bois épais—Air d'Amadis   Act II
R. Ponselle (S), I. Chicagov (pf.)
in # Vic.LM 1889
(*Chausson, Beethoven, Donaudy, etc.*)   (# DV. 16493)
⊞ E. Caruso (T) (*AF.AGSA 27**)

Amour, que veux-tu de moi   Act II
⊞ E. Calvé (S) (in # HRS. 3008*)

(L') AMOUR MÉDECIN   Inc. Mus.   1665
Scène du marchand d'orvietan   Act II
Ballet   (Diction & orch.)
☆ D. d'Inès & Comédie-Française Orch.—R. Charpentier
(G.SL 183)

ARMIDE ET RENAUD   Opera Prol. & 5 Acts
1686
Overture
Danish Radio Cha.—Wöldike
in # HS.HSL 2072
(† Masterpieces of Music before 1750)

Inst. Excerpts (Air; Sommeil de Renaud; Gavotte)
— SEE: Symphonies pour les couchers du Roy, *below*

ATYS   Opera   Prol. & 5 Acts   1676
Inst. Excerpts (Air pour Flore; Sommeil d'Atys)
SEE: Symphonies pour les couchers du Roy, *below*

(Le) BOURGEOIS GENTILHOMME
Inc. Music 1670
Cérémonie turque   Act IV   Diction & orch.
☆ D. d'Inès & Orch.—R. Charpentier (G.SL 184)

CADMUS ET HERMIONE   Opera 5 Acts 1673
Belle Hermione, hélas, hélas   (Cantilène)
G. Souzay (B)   in # D.LX 3112
(*above; A. Scarlatti, etc.*)   (# Lon.LS 730)

Chaconne
☆ Versailles Concerts Orch.—Cloëz   in † AS. 2506LD

(L') IMPATIENCE   Ballet, 16 Entrées   1661
Shepherd's Song
SEE: BUXTEHUDE: Aria Rofilis, D minor

(Le) MALADE IMAGINAIRE
Inc. Music to Molière's play[3]
Orch.—Cadou (in a performance of the play
in # LI.TW 91076/7; # D.FMT 163507/8

MARCHES, etc.
Fanfares pour le Carrousel de Monseigneur   1686
(Prélude de la Grande Écurie; Menuet; Gavotte; Gigue
Marche des Mousquetaires du Roy
Marche des Mousquetaires gris
Marche du Régiment de Turenne
Paris Coll. Mus.—Douatte   # LI.TWV 91092
(*Mouret, Philidor, Lalande, Couperin*)   (# Cpt.MC 20086)
Marche des Régiments du Roy
Marche royale
Marche des forçats des galères turcs
Paris Coll. Mus.—Douatte   in # Cpt.MC 20102
(† Musique de la Grande Écurie)
Marche des Mousquetaires du Roy
Marche des Dragons du Roy
Marche française   all ed. & ARR. Maillot
French Navy Band—Maillot
in # Sel. 270.C.056

Marche pour le Régiment du Roy
4 obs., 2 cor ang., 2 bsn., 2 side drums 1670 (Ed. Haas)
London Baroque Ens.—Haas   P.R 20619
(*Philidor: Marches*)   (in # AmD.DL 4081)

(Le) MÉDECIN MALGRÉ LUI   Inc. Music[4]
Air à boire: Qu'ils sont doux
Unspec. Artist   in Plé. set 524
(& in # 525)

Miserere   5 soli & cho.   c. 1664
M. Ritchie & E. Morison (S), W. Herbert &
R. Lewis (T), A. Deller (C-T), B. Boyce (B),
St. Anthony Singers & Orch. Ens.—Lewis
LOL.DL 53003
(# OL.LD 95)

PHAËTON   Opera, Prol. & 5 Acts   1683
Overture & Entrée de danse
☆ Versailles Concerts Orch.—Cloëz   in † # AS. 2506LD

Te Deum   S, A, T, B, double cho. & orch.[5]   1677
C. Collart, M-Th. Cahn, G. Friedmann,
G. Abdoun, Paris Vocal Ens., Paris Cha.
Music Soc. Orch.—Capdevielle
LT.DTL 93043
[A. G. Dechaume, org.] (# Sel.LA 1073; T.NLB 6112;
West.WL 5326)

(Le) TEMPLE DE LA PAIX   Ballet   1685
Prologue: Troupe de Nymphes et Bergers
Entrée des Basques
Menuet & Trio
— ARR. Mottl: SEE Ballet Suite, *post*

THÉSÉE   1675
Marche des sacrificateurs
— ARR. Stokowski
Sym. Orch.—Stokowski   in # Vic.LM 1721
(*Cesti, Frescobaldi, Vivaldi, etc.*)   (in ♭ set WDM 1721)
(in # G.FALP 245; ItV.A12N 0040)

— ARR. Mottl[6]: SEE Ballet Suite, *post*

---

[1] With Vladimir Ussachevsky. First perf. 20 March, 1954.
[2] Contents: Fantasy in Space; Invention in 12 notes; Low Speed; Incantation (in collaboration with Ussachevsky); &
Sonic Contours (Ussachevsky alone).
[3] There is no trace of *original* music by Lully for this play and it has not been possible to check exactly what item(s) by him
have been adapted here for the added Epilogue. The inc. music to the play proper is by Destouches; music by M. A.
Charpentier and Gervais (?) is also used for the Epilogue.   [5] Edited Dechaume.
[4] No *original* inc. music by Lully known.
[6] The second couplet is replaced by some other music, unidentified.

(Le) TRIOMPHE DE L'AMOUR Ballet 1618
Nocturne
— ARR. Stokowski
Sym. Orch.—Stokowski   in ♯ **Vic.LM 1721**
(above)   (in ♭ *set WDM 1721*)
(in ♯ *G.FALP 245;* ItV.A12R 0040 & in ♯ Vic.LM 1875:
♭ *set ERB 52*)
— ARR. Mottl: *SEE* Ballet Suite, *post*

SONG: Au clair de la lune (attrib. Lully)
L. Vernay & Male Qtt. *(Phi.P 77728J)*

Symphonies pour les couchers du Roy
(Orch. suite ARR. Lully from instrumental movements from
Operas: *Alceste, Armide, Atys, Acis et Galathée, q.v.*)
Airs pour Madame la Dauphine
Paris Collegium—Douatte   ♯ **Cpt.MC 20118**
(Philidor, Couperin)

Ballet Suite — ARR. Mottl
1. Introduction: Allegretto (*Le Temple de la Paix, q.v.*)
2. Nocturne (*Le Triomphe de l'Amour*)
3. Minuet (*Le Temple de la Paix*)
4. (a) Prélude (*Alceste*, Act III, Sc. 5)
   (b) Marche des sacrificateurs (*Thésée*)
   (c) Les vents (*Alceste*)
Naples Scarlatti Orch.—Caracciolo ♯ **C.CX 1277**
(Cimarosa & Tartini)   (♯ *Angel. 35255)*
(*Leo & Sacchini* on ♯ C.QCX 10140)
Netherlands Phil.—Goehr   ♯ **CHS.H 9**
(Couperin: Ballet Suite; & Leclair)
Leipzig Radio—Pflüger   ♯ **Ura. 7111**
(Beethoven, Mozart)
... Nos. 1, 2, 4 (b), 4 (c) only
Hamburg Phil.—di Bella   ♯ **DT.TM 68049**
(Haydn: Notturno)   (♯ *T.TW 30025)*
... Nos. 1, 2, 4 (a), 4 (b)[1]
Belgian Radio Cha.—Marinetti
(Lalande)   ♯ **Mae.OA 20001**
Suite (unspec.) — ARR. HARP (may be LOEILLET)
V. Dyulova   *(Saint-Saëns)*   **USSRM.D 1388**

LUMBYE, Hans Christian (1810-1874)

(Abridged listing only)

I. WORKS IN DANCE FORMS

COLLECTION
GALOPS
   Bouquet royal
   Salute to August Bournonville
POLKAS
   Britta
   Tivoli-Vauxhall
WALTZES
   Caecilie
   Hesperus
   Krolls Ballklänge
Tivoli—T. Lumbye   ♯ *Tono.LPL 33007*
[excluding Salute to A. Bournonville & with *Dream Pictures*
on ♯ Mer.MG 90000]

GALOPS
Bouquet royal   Tivoli—T. Lumbye   *Tono.L 28078*
Champagne   H. Busch Orch. (in ♯ *G.SDLP 1001*)
     ☆ Tivoli—T. Lumbye (♭ *Mer.EP 1-5003;*
         in ♯ *Tono.LPL 33001)*
Christmas Galop
K. Fogtmann & G. Hansen's Orch.(*G.X 8224:* ♭ *7EGK 1015*)
Lifeguards at Amager, Final Galop
           (from the eponymous ballet)
     ☆ Tivoli—Felumb (♭ *Mer.EP 1-5048*)
Railway   (*Jernbane*)
     ☆ Tivoli—T. Lumbye (♭ *Mer.EP 1-5003;*
         in ♯ *Tono.LPL 33001)*
Salute to August Bournonville
Tivoli—T. Lumbye   *Tono.L 28078*
MARCHES
King Christian IX
   Royal Orch.—Høeberg   *Pol.Z 60136*
   Royal Guards' Band (*Pol.X 51187*)
   ☆ Tivoli—T. Lumbye (♭ *Mer.EP 1-5003;*
         in ♯ *Tono.LPL 33001)*

King Christian X   Royal Guards' Band (*Pol.X 51107*)
King Frederick VII
   ☆ Tivoli—T. Lumbye (in ♯ *Tono.LPL 33002;*
         ♭ *Mer.EP 1-5003*)

POLKAS & POLKA-MAZURKAS
Amager
   ☆ Tivoli—T. Lumbye (in ♯ *Tono.LPL 33001*)
Britta   Tivoli—T. Lumbye   *Tono.L 28080*
Columbine   (P-M)
   ☆ Tivoli—T. Lumbye (in ♯ *Tono.LPL 33001*)
Concert Polka for 2 violins
   V. Allingham, E. Spillemose & Odense Municipal
     —Lundquist   *C.DDX 38*
Tivoli-Vauxhall   Tivoli—T. Lumbye   *Tono.L 28080*
WALTZES
Amelie
   Odense Municipal—Lundquist   *C.DDX 36*
   ☆ Tivoli—T. Lumbye (♭ *Mer.EP 1-5012;*
         in ♯ *Tono.LPL 33001)*
Caecilie   Tivoli—T. Lumbye   *Tono.L 28079*
         (♭ *EP 43003)*
Herperus   Tivoli—T. Lumbye   *Tono.X 21589*
Krolls Ballklänge   Tivoli—T. Lumbye   *Tono.X 25189*
   ☆ Tivoli—Jensen (♭ *Mer.EP 1-5048*)
Queen Louise
   Odense Municipal—Lundquist   *C.DDX 38*
   Copenhagen Op. Orch.—Høeberg   *Pol.Z 60136*
   ☆ Tivoli—T. Lumbye (in ♯ *Tono.LPL 33001*)
Sophie
   ☆ Tivoli—T. Lumbye (♭ *Mer.EP 1-5012;*
         in ♯ *Tono.LPL 33001)*

II. OTHER WORKS

(An) Afternoon at Tivoli Suite — ARR. Felumb
Tivoli—Felumb   ♯ **C.KSX 1**
(Nielsen)

Dream Pictures orch. 1846
Tivoli—T. Lumbye   *Tono.X 21590*
(2ss)   (♭ *EP 43002;* & in ♯ Mer.MG 90000)
   ☆ Tivoli—Felumb (♭ *Mer.EP 1-5048*)

LUNA, Pablo (1880-1948)

ZARZUELAS, etc.   (abridged listings only)
(El) ASOMBRO DE DAMASCO 2 Acts
L. Sagi Vela, D. Pérez, A. Martelo, etc., Madrid Radio
Cho. & Cha. Orch.—Navarro   ♯ **Mont.FM 50**
(Overture in ♯ Mont.FM 51)
BENAMOR 3 Acts
Vocal Excerpts
M. Ausensi (B) (in ♯ *LI.W 91028;* ♯ *Ambra.MC 25005*)
   ▽ M. Redondo (*Od. 184834*)
(Los) CADETES DE LA REINA 1913
P. Lorengar, M. Ausensi, C. Munguía, A. M. Fernández,
   etc., Madrid Cho. & Sym.—Argenta   ♯ **LI.TW 91112**
             (♯ *Ambra.MCC 30027*)
M. Espinalt, E. Aliaga, L. Torrentó, etc., Cho. & Sym.
   —Ferrer   ♯ **Reg.LCX 126**
Vocal Excerpts   ▽ M. Redondo & Cho. (*Od. 184185*)
MOLINOS DE VIENTO Operetta, 1 Act 1910
P. Lorengar, M. Ausensi, C. Munguía, A. Díaz Martos,
   Madrid Singers & Sym.—Argenta   ♯ **LI.TW 91036**
             (♯ *Ambra.MCC 30002*)
L. Torrentó, M. Redondo, C. Renom, O. Pol, J. Teruel,
   Cho. & Sym.—R. Ferrer   ♯ **Angel. 65012**
          (♯ Reg.LCX 116; Pam.LRC 15908)
L. Berchman, L. Sagi-Vela, Madrid Singers & Cha. Orch.
             ♯ **Mont.LD 26**
   ▽ T. Folgar, M. Isaura, etc., Barcelona Theatre
          —Gelabert (*G.AF 387/91*)
C. Panadés, A. Gonzalo, M. Redondo, Cho. & Orch.
     —Capdevila (♯ *Od. 184500/4: 196139/43*)
Vocal Excerpts: L. Sagi-Vela (in ♯ *MusH.LP 5003*)
(El) NIÑO JUDÍO 2 Acts
Vocal Excerpts
L. Berchman (S) (in ♯ Mont.FM 17)
M. de los A. Morales (S) (♭ *Ambra.EMGE 70019*)
Canción española — ARR. Moreno Torroba
Madrid Theatre—Moreno Torroba   in ♯ **AmD.DL 9789**

---

[1] Arrangement not specified.

(La) PICARA MOLINERA
Intermezzo
　　Madrid Cha.—Argenta (in ♯ LI.TW 91020;
　　　Ambra.MCC 30002: MCCP 29000; & ♯ Mont.FM 6)
Vocal Excerpts ▽ E. Vendrell (Od. 121188)

LUTOSLAWSKI, Witold (b. 1913)

(6) Children's Songs S & orch.
　　J. Godewska (M-S) & Polish Radio Orch.
　　　—Lutoslawski
Little Suite cha. orch.
　　Polish Radio—Kolaczkowski　♯ Van.VRS 6013
　　(ARR. *Sygietgynski: Folk Songs*)
(10) Polish Dances cha. orch.
　　Warsaw Phil.—Lutoslawski　　　*Muza. 2242/4*
　　(6ss)

LUZZASCHI, Luzzasco (d. 1607)

　　SEE: † HISTORY OF MUSIC IN SOUND (32)

LYSENKO, Nikolai (1842-1912)

NATALKA POLTAVKA　Opera in *Ukrainian*
3 Acts
COMPLETE RECORDING
　　Natalka　…　…　…　Z. Gaidai (S)
　　Petro …　…　…　I. Kozlovsky (T)
　　Terpelikha　…　M. Litvinenko-Wohlgemut
　　Mikola　…　…　…　M. Grishko (T)
　　etc., Kiev Opera Cho. & Orch.—Tchistyakov
　　　　　　　　　　　　♯ USSR.D 0428/35
　　(8ss)　　　　　　　(10ss, ♯ *Argee. set 702*)
　　(34ss, USSR. 019385/418)
Vocal Excerpts also, in ♯ USSR.D 2095, USSR. 05280, 08667,
　　　　　　　　　　　　　　　　　　　10676/7, etc.
(The) DROWNED WOMAN
Vocal Excerpt: Ukrainian State Cho. (*USSR. 19445/6*)
Gaidamaki (Shevchenko)
Gamaliya (Shevchenko)
　… Excerpts　(*USSR. 8614, 8643/4*)
SONG: The Eternal Revolution　(Franko)
　　Ukrainian State Cho. (in ♯ *USSR.D 1569*)
Folk Song Arrs. on *USSR. 20553, ♯ USSR.D 1567, etc.*

There are other recordings of this composer in the U.S.S.R.
　　catalogues.

McBRIDE, Robert Guyn (b. 1911)

Concerto, vln. & orch.
　　M. Wilk & A.R.S. Orch.—Hendl　♯ *ARS. 27*
　　(*Ives*)
　　(*Ives, Diamond & Swanson* on ♯ ARS. 116)
Pumkin Eaters Little Fugue
　　New Sym.—Camarata　　　♯ Lon.LL 1213
　　(*below; Kay, Mourant*)
Quintet, oboe & strings　1937
　　E. Schuster & Classic Qtt.　♯ CEd.CE 1030
　　(*Bax, Elgar*)
Workout for 15 instruments　1936
　　New Sym. Cha.—Camarata　♯ Lon.LL 1213
　　(*above*)

McDONALD, Harl (1899-1955)

Builders of America　(E. Shenton) Cantata
　　Narrator, mixed cho. & orch.
　　C. Rains, Cho. & Col. Sym. Orch.
　　　—McDonald (*below*)　　♯ *AmC.ML 2220*
From Childhood Suite hp. & orch.　1940
　　A. M. Stockton & Concert Arts—Slatkin
　　　　　　　　　　　♯ DCap.CTL 7057
　　　　　　　　　　　　(♯ Cap.P 8255)
　　(*Caplet*)

Legend of the Arkansas Traveler　orch.　1939
　　☆ Philadelphia—Stokowski (in ♯ Cam.CAL 238)
SYMPHONIES
No. 2 "Rhumba"　1934
　… Rhumba
　　☆ Philadelphia—Stokowski (in ♯ Cam.CAL 238)
No. 3—Choral　1935
　… Cakewalk (Scherzo)
　　☆ Philadelphia—Ormandy (in ♯ Cam.CAL 238)
Children's Symphony　1948　(pub. 1954)
　　☆ Philadelphia—Ormandy (*above*)　♯ *AmC.ML 2220*

MACDOWELL, Edward　(1861-1908)

A.D. 1620, Op. 55, No. 3　pf.　1898
　　S. Bianca　　　　　　　　　　*MSB. 8*
　　[with spoken commentary]　　　(& in ♯ *60040*)
CONCERTOS, pf. & orch.
No. 1, A minor, Op. 15　1885
　　V. Rivkin & Vienna State Op.—Dixon
　　　　　　　　　　　　♯ Nix.WLP 5190
　　(*No. 2*)　　　　　　　(♯ West.WL 5190)
No. 2, D minor, Op. 23　1890
　　V. Rivkin & Vienna State Op.—Dixon
　　　　　　　　　　　　♯ Nix.WLP 5190
　　(*No. 1*)　　　　　　　(♯ West.WL 5190)
　　J. M. Sanromá & Eastman-Rochester Sym.
　　　—Hanson　　　　　♯ AmC.ML 4638
　　(*Hanson: Symphony No. 2*)
　　☆ J. M. Sanromá & Boston Pops—Fiedler ♯ Cam.CAL 145
　　(*Piston*)
Lamia, Op. 29　Sym. poem, after Keats　1886
　　Hamburg Philharmonia—Korn in ♯ Allo. 3149
　　(*Paine, Harris, Copland, etc.*)
Marionettes, Op. 38　pf.　1888
　… Nos. 4, The Witch; & 5, The Clown
　　S. Bianca　　　　　　　　　　*MSB. 7*
　　[with spoken commentary]　　　(& in ♯ *60040*)
Of a Tailor and a Bear, Op. 4, No. 2　pf.　1897
　　S. Bianca　　　　　　　　　　*MSB. 1*
　　[with spoken commentary]　　　(& in ♯ *60040*)
　　M. v. Doren　　　　　in ♯ Chan.MVDP 1
Of Br'er Rabbit, Op. 61, No. 2　1902
　　S. Bianca　　　　　　　　　*MSB. 78018*
　　(*above*) [with spoken commentary on *MSB. 2*]
　　　　　　　　　　　　　　(& in ♯ *60040*)
　　M. v. Doren　　　　　in ♯ Chan.MVDP 1
SONATAS, pf.
No. 1, G minor, Op. 45　(Sonata tragica)　1893
No. 2, G minor, Op. 50　(Sonata eroica)　1895
　　P. O'Neil　　　　　　　　　♯ SPA. 63
Suite No. 2, "Indian" Op. 48　orch.　1897
　　Eastman-Rochester Sym.—Hanson
　　　　　　　　　　　　♯ Mer.MG 40009
　　☆ A.R.S. Orch.—Dixon　(*Herbert*)　♯ ARS. 111
To a hummingbird, Op. 7, No. 2　1898
　　S. Bianca　　　　　　　　　　*MSB. 6*
　　(*below*) [with spoken commentary]　(& in ♯ *60040*)
Witches' Dance, Op. 17, No. 2　1884
　　S. Bianca　　　　　　　　　　*MSB. 6*
　　(*above*) [with spoken commentary]　(in ♯ *60040*)
　　E. Burton　　　　　in ♯ CEd.CE 1026
(10) Woodland Sketches, Op. 51　pf.　1896
　1. To a wild rose　　　　2. Will o' the wisp
　3. At an old trysting-place　4. In autumn
　5. From an Indian lodge　　6. To a water-lily
　7. From Uncle Remus　　8. A deserted farm
　9. By a meadow brook　　10. Told at sunset
　—ARR. ORCH.　Camarata
　　Orch.—Camarata　　　　♯ AmD.DL 4059
　　　　　　　　　　　(*continued on next page*)

☆ = Re-issue of a recording to be found in previous volumes.

Woodland Sketches (continued)
— ARR. ORGAN Ellsasser
R. Ellsasser   ♯ MGM.E 3182
(Grieg)
... No. 2-8 — ARR. ORCH.
Allegro Concert—Bath   ♯ Allo. 4013
(Herbert)   (♯ AFest.CFR 10-578)
... Nos. 1 & 6 only — ARR. ORCH.
☆ Orch.—Kostelanetz (in ♯ C.SX 1004: QSX 12004;
                               ♭ AmC.A 1857: ♯ CL 792)
Chicago Sym.—Stock (in ♯ Cam.CAL 192)
... No. 1
S. Bianca, with spoken commentary (MSB. 5 & in ♯ 60040)
— — ARR. ORCH.
Melachrino Orch. (G.B 10764)
Varsity Orch. (in ♯ Var. 2043)
... No. 2 S. Bianca, with commentary (MSB. 6 & in ♯ 60040)
... No. 5 S. Bianca, with commentary (MSB. 4 & in ♯ 60040)
... No. 6 S. Bianca, with commentary (MSB. 3 & in ♯ 60040)
... Nos. 7 & 8
S. Bianca   MSB. 78018
(Of Br'er Rabbit)

MACHAUT, Guillaume de (c. 1300-1377)

CHANSONS & BALLADES
Douce dame jolie
R. Hayes (T), R. Boardman (pf.)
                            in ♯ Van.VRS 448
(Monteverdi, Caccini, etc.)
J. Douai (T) & guitar   in ♯ BàM.LD 306
(† Chansons poétiques)

Hélas, pour quoy? (Rondeau No. 2)
M. Rollin Ens.   ♯ LI.W 91116
                               (in ♯ D.FS 123632)
(† Music from the Middle Ages to Renaissance)

Je suis aussi com cil qui est ravi
M. Rollin Ens.   ♯ CND. 9
(† Musique et la poésie) [fl. & lute]

Je puis trop bien
De tout sui (Virelai)
Quant Theseus
☆ Pro Musica Antiqua Ens.—Cape (in † ♯ HS.AS 3)

Ma fin est mon commencement
L. Hughes & C. Roberts (T) & Inst. Ens.
                                   G.HMS 21
(† History of Music in Sound) (in ♯ Vic. set LM 6016)

Mes espris
Musicians' Workshop Recorder Consort
                               ♯ CEd.CE 1018
(† Recorder Music of 6 Centuries)

Plus dure qu'un dyamant
R. Blanchard Ens.   ♯ Phi.N 00993R
(† French Chansons)

MASS, Notre Dame
("Sacre de Charles V", 1364)
J. Archimbaud & P. Deniau (C-T), G. Cathelat
(T), E. Bousquet (B), M. Vigneron (Bs),
Vocal & Inst. Ens.—Blanchard
                               ♯ Sel. 270.C.085
☆ Dessoff Cho. & Brass Ens.—Boepple (♯ Clc. 6193)
... Credo, Sanctus, Agnus Dei & Ite, Missa est
☆ Paraphonistes de St. Jean (V♯ AS. 1803LD
                               & in ♯ HS.AS 3)
... Benedictus (ed. Stevens)
Brompton Oratory Cho.—Washington
                               G.HMS 21
(† History of Music in Sound) (in ♯ Vic. set LM 6016)
... Agnus Dei I
Copenhagen Boys' & Men's Cho.—Møller
                               ♯ HS.HSL 2071
(† Masterpieces of Music)
(& in † Histoire de la Musique vocale)

MADLSEDER, Nonnonus (1730-1797)
SEE: † TYROLESE XVIIITH CENT. ORCH. MUSIC

MAGE, Pierre du (fl. 1700-1733)
SEE: † FRENCH BAROQUE ORGAN MUSIC

MAGNARD, Lucien Denis Albéric
                                   (1865-1914)

GUERCOEUR, Op. 12
Opera 3 Acts 1901, f.p. 1931
Le calme rentre dans mon coeur
Où suis-je, quel murmure me charme? B Act II
A. Endrèze (in ♯ Pat.PCX 5006: o.n. ▽ Pat.X 90079)

MAHLER, Gustav (1860-1911)

(Das) Klagende Lied S, A, T, orch. 1880, rev. 1898
☆ Soloists, Vienna Cha. Cho. & State Op. Orch.—Fekete
                               ♯ CA.LPA 1021

(Das) Lied von der Erde A, T, orch. 1908
☆ Soloists, Vienna Sym.—Klemperer (♯ EVox.PL 7000;
                               ♯ AFest.CFR 12-508)

SONGS
Kindertotenlieder (Rückert) 1902
N. Foster (B) & Bamberg Sym.—Horenstein
                               ♯ AmVox.PL 9100
(Lieder eines fahrenden Gesellen)
D. Fischer-Dieskau (B) & Berlin Phil.—Kempe
(2ss)   ♯ G.WBLP 1511
☆ K. Ferrier (A) & Vienna Phil.—Walter ♯ AmC.ML 4980
(Bruckner)   (2ss, ♯ C.FC 1033)
☆ M. Anderson (A) & San Francisco Sym.—Monteux
                               ♯ G.ALP 1138
(Brahms)   (♯ ItV.A12R 0085)
☆ H. Schey (B) & Residentie—v. Otterloo
                               in ♯ Epic. set SC 6001
(Bruckner: Symphony No. 4)   (2ss, ♯ Phi.S 06028R)

(Das) KNABEN WUNDERHORN 2 Bks. 1892-4
Wer hat dies Liedlein erdacht; Rheinlegendchen
☆ A. Felbermeyer (S), A. Poell (B), V. Graef (pf.)
                               in ♯ CID.UM 63018)
Es sungen drei Engel
Included in ♯ CID.UM 63025, below[1]

(14) LIEDER UND GESÄNGE AUS DER
JUGENDZEIT 1885-92
COMPLETE RECORDINGS
☆ I. Steingruber (S), H. Häfner (pf.)   ♯ CA.LPA 1070
(Symphony No. 3, s. 1)
☆ A. Felbermeyer (S), A. Poell (B), V. Graef (pf.)
                               (♯ CID.UM 63018)
VOL. I: Nos. 1 & 3; VOL. II: No. 2; VOL. III: No. 3;
and Es sungen drei Engel (from Knaben Wunderhorn
Songs, VOL. I)
☆ A. Felbermeyer (S), A. Poell (B), & Vienna State Op.
Orch.—Prohaska[1]   (♯ CID.UM 63025)
VOL. I: No. 3, Hans and Grete (Volkslied)
G. Pechner (B)   in ♯ Roy. 1558
(below, R. Strauss, Marx, etc.)

(7) LIEDER AUS LETZTER ZEIT 1902
... 5 Lieder von Rückert
☆ I. Steingruber (S) & Vienna State Op.—Fekete
                               V♯ CA.MPO 5014
☆ A. Felbermeyer (S), A. Poell (B) & Vienna State Op.
Orch.—Prohaska (♯ CID.UM 63025)
... Nos. 1, 4, 5 only
☆ K. Ferrier (A) & Vienna Phil. Orch.—Walter
                               ♯ D.LW 5123
                               (♯ Lon.LD 9137)
... 3, Blicke mir nicht in die Lieder
G. Pechner (B) (above)   in ♯ Roy. 1558
... 6, Revelge (Reveillé) ⎫ from Des Knaben Wunderhorn
... 7, Der Tambourgesell ⎭
☆ A. Poell (B) & Vienna State Op.—Prohaska
                               (♭ Van.VREP 1)

[1] Accompaniments orchestrated by Heger, Windsperger and Wöss.

Lieder eines fahrenden Gesellen (Mahler) 1883
D. Fischer-Dieskau (B) & Philharmonia
—Furtwängler (*Brahms*)   ♯ **G.ALP 1270**

N. Foster (B) & Bamberg Sym.—Horenstein
(*Kindertotenlieder*)   ♯ **AmVox.PL 9100**

M. Krásová (A, *Cz*) & Czech Phil.—Pedrotti
♮ **U.H 24391/2**

SYMPHONIES
No. 1, D major ("Titan") 1888
N.Y.P.S.O.—Walter   ♯ **EPhi.ABL 3044**
(♯ AmC.ML 4958, in set SL 218; Phi.A 01150L)

Vienna Phil.—Kubelik   ♯ **D.LXT 2973**
(♯ Lon.LL 1107)

Israel Phil.—Kletzki   ♯ **C.CX 1207**
(♯ FCX 378; Angel. 35180)

Vienna Pro Musica—Horenstein
♯ **E. & AmVox.PL 8050**

Pittsburgh Sym.—Steinberg   ♯ **DCap.CTL 7042**
(♯ Cap.P 8224)

London Phil. Sym.—Scherchen
♯ **West.WN 18014**

Berlin Radio—Borsamsky   ♯ **Ura. 7080**
(♯ Van.VRS 436; MTW. 533)

Berlin Sym.—Rubahn   ♯ **Roy. 1554**

☆ Minneapolis Sym.—Mitropoulos   ♯ **C.CX 1068**
(♯ QCX 10065; AmC.RL 3120)

No. 2, C minor
("Resurrection") S, A, cho., orch. 1894
☆ Soloists, Academy & Musikfreunde Chos., Vienna
Sym.—Klemperer   ♯ **E. & AmVox.PL 7012**
(♯ AFest. set CFR 12-83)

No. 3, D minor A, cho., orch. 1895
☆ H. Rössl-Majdan, Vienna State Op. Cho. & Vienna
Philharmonia—Adler   ♯ **CA.LPA 1070/2**
(5ss—*Lieder aus der Jugendzeit*)   (4ss, ♯ SPA. 70/1)

No. 4, G major S. & orch. 1900
☆ M. Tauberová & Czech Phil.—Šejna (♯ Sup.LPV 220:
also 4ss, ♯ Sup.LPM 51/2; U. 5026/7C)
D. Halban & N.Y.P.S.O.—Walter (♯ C.FCX 198)

No. 5, C sharp minor 1902
☆ Vienna State Op.—Scherchen   ♯ **Nix.WLP 6207-1/2**

... Adagietto ☆ N.Y.P.S.O.—Walter (C.LHX 5)

No. 6, A minor 1904
Rotterdam Phil.—Flipse[1]   ♯ **Phi.A 00297/8L**
(4ss)   (♯ Epic. set SC 6012)
Vienna Philharmonia—Adler   ♯ **SPA. 59/60**
(4ss)

No. 7, E minor 1905
Vienna State Op.—Scherchen
♯ **Nix.WLP 6211-1/2**
(4ss)   (♯ West. set WAL 211)
Berlin Radio—Rosbaud   ♯ **Ura. set 405**
(4ss)

No. 8, E flat major
Soloists, 3 chos., orch. 1907
A. Kupper, H. Zadek, C. Bijster (S), A. Hermes,
L. Fischer, A. Woud (A), L. Fehenberger,
F. Vroons (T), H. Schey, G. Frick, D.
Hollestelle (B), Rotterdam Cho. & Phil.
Orch.—Flipse[2]   ♯ **EPhi.ABL 3024/5**
(4ss)   (♯ Phi.A 00226/7L; ♯ Epic. set SC 6004)
F. Yeend (S), E. Conley (T), etc., Cho. &
N.Y.P.S.O.—Stokowski[3] (4ss)   ♯ **OTA. set 6**

No. 9, D minor 1909
Israel Phil.—Kletzki[4]   ♯ **C.CX 1250/1**
(3ss—*Schoenberg*) (♯ FCX 379/80; Angel. 35181/2,
set 3526)
☆ Vienna Sym.—Horenstein (4ss)   ♯ **EVox.PL 7602**
☆ Vienna Phil.—Walter   ♯ **Vic. set LCT 6015**
(3ss—*Haydn*)

No. 10, F sharp major
(unfinished: completed by Křenek)
... 1st movt., Adagio only 1910
Vienna Philharmonia—Adler   ♯ **SPA. 31**
(*Bruckner*)
☆ Vienna State Op.—Scherchen in ♯ Nix. set WLP 6207

MAISTRE, Matthäus le (d. *c.* 1577)
SEE: † MOTETS ON LUTHER TEXTS

MALÁT, Jan (1843-1915)
Slavonic Girls orch. suite
☆ F.O.K. Sym.—Smetáček (*Dvořák*) ♯ **Csm.CRLPX 007**
(*Hilmař: Czech Polkas* on ♯ Sup.LPM 126; U. 5075C)

MALATS, Joáquin (1872-1912)
Serenata española
E. Osta (pf.)   in ♯ *Coda. 1000*
— ARR. ORCH
Madrid Theatre—Moreno Torroba   ♯ **B.AXTL 1078**
(*Chapí, Torroba, etc.*)   (♯ AmD.DL 9736)
Sym.—R. Ferrer   in ♯ **C.FSX 102**
(in ♯ Angel. 70008; Reg. LCX 104; Pam LRC 15905)
Madrid Cha.—Navarro   in ♯ **Mont.FM 39**
— ARR. GUITAR
A. Segovia   in ♯ **AmD.DL 9734**
(† *Segovia Plays*)   (♯ D.UAT 2/3573)
▽ F. Arguelles (in ♯ *SMC. 507*)
— ARR. CASTANETS & ORCH.
J. Andrade (in ♯ *Od.MODL 1001*)

MALIPIERO, Gian Francesco (b. 1882)
(La) Cimarosiana orch. 1921
(5 Symphonic Fragments after Cimarosa)
Covent Garden—Braithwaite   ♯ **MGM.E 3013**
(*Respighi, Cimarosa*)

Concerto, vln. & orch. 1932
F. Kirmse & Leipzig Radio—Kleinert
(*Rakov*)   ♯ **Ura. 7112**

Fantasie di ogni giorno orch. f.p. 1954
Louisville—Whitney   ♯ **LO. 11**
(*Bacon, Rieti*)

Omaggio a Claude Debussy pf. 1920
(for *Le Tombeau de Debussy*)
E. Ulmer   ♯ **CHS.H 12**
(*Dukas, Roussel, Goossens, Stravinsky, Debussy*)

Passer mortuus est (Catullus) 1952
Mt. Mercy College Cho.—Brenneman
in ♯ **PFCM.CB 160**
(*Rosenberg, Read, etc.*)

QUARTETS
No. 4 1934
Italian Quartet   ♯ **C.CX 1295**
(*Prokofiev*)   (♯ QCX 10145; Angel. 35296)

No. 7 1949-50
La Scala Qtt.   ♯ **Ura. 7075**
(*Respighi, Pick-Mangiagalli*)

Rispetti e Strambotti Str. Qtt. 1920
Juilliard Qtt.   ♯ **PFCM.CB 156**
(*Piston, Webern*)

MANCINI, Francesco (1679-1739)
Concerto a quattro, E minor fl., 2 vlns., hpsi. 1729
J-P. Rampal, G. Alès, P. Doukan, R. Gerlin
♯ **LOL.OL 50009**
(*Durante, Paisiello, Auletta*)   (♯ OL.LD 66)

---

[1] Performance at Holland Festival, 29.vi.55.   [2] Recorded at Holland Festival, July 1954.
[3] Transcription of broadcast performance 9.iv.50.
[4] Ed. Kletzki, including omission of 115 bars of Scherzo.

MANFREDINI, Francesco   (1688-?)

Sinfonia da chiesa, con una pastorale, C major,
                                        Op. 2, No. 12
("*Christmas Symphony*") 2 vlns. & orch. 1709
Paris Collegium Musicum—Douatte
                                        ♯ *LT.EL 93042*
(*Corelli, Torelli*)   (♯ *Sel.LA 1018; T.LB 6091*)
Milan Angelicum—Gerelli   Ang.SA 3009/10
(4ss)

... **Pastorale** only
Vienna Sym.—Pritchard   ♯ *EPhi.ABR 4014*
(*Corelli, Handel*)   (♯ *Phi.A 00668R*)

MANZOLI, Domenico   (fl. XVIIth Cent.)

SEE: † ANTHOLOGIE SONORE

MARAIS, Marin   (1656-1728)

PIÈCES DE VIOLE   1, 2, or 3 viols & hpsi.
COLLECTIONS
Book III: Suite 1, A minor   ed. Boulay
Book IV: Part i: Suite 5, A major   ed. Boulay
R. & L. Boulay (vla. & hpsi.)   † ♯ *AS. 2507LD*
                                        (♯ HS.AS 37)
Book II: Suite 1, D minor . . . Prelude
Book IV: Part i: Suite 4, A minor
                    (omitting *Caprice & Rondeau Loure*)
                    Suite 5, A major
                    (omitting *Branle de village & Minuets*)
E. Heinitz (gamba), E. V. Wolff (hpsi.) ♯ *EMS. 8*
Book II: Suite 1, D minor . . . Prelude; Couplets des Folies
                    d'Espagne; Sarabande grave
                    Suite 2, D minor . . . Paysane
Book III: Suite 4, D major . . . Charivari
Book IV: Part i: Suite 3, F major . . . La Provençale
                    Suite 4, A minor . . . Musette
                    Suite 5, A major . . . L'Agréable (Rondeau);
                        Le Basque
                    Suite 6, E minor . . . La Matelotte
Book IV: Part ii: Suite d'un goût étranger . . . L'Ameriquaine
P. Doktor (vla.), F. Valenti (hpsi.)
                                        ♯ *West.WN 18088*
(*Caix d'Hervelois*)
Book IV: Suite 5 . . . Le Basque   (ARR.)
Inst. Ens. (in *G.B 10659*)
Book IV: Part iii: Suite 1, D major
                        Suite 2, G major   3 viols
R. Boulay, M. T. Chailley-Guiard (vlas.),
L. Boulay (in No. 1), I. Lechner (in No. 2)
(hpsi.) [ed. Boulay]   ♯ *LOL.OL 50048*
                                        (♯ OL.LD 56)
Suites ("*Pièces en trio*") fls. or vln. & cont. 1692
No. 3, D major;   No. 5, E minor
F. Caratgé (fl.), R. Boulay (treble viol) &
L. Boulay (hpsi.)   † ♯ *AS. 2508LD*
                                        (♯ HS.AS 38)

MARCABRU of Gascony   (d. *c.* 1147)

SEE: † FRENCH TROUBADOUR SONGS
      † MONUMENTA ITALICAE MUSICAE

MARCELLO, Alessandro   (1684-1750)

Concerto, D minor   oboe & str. orch.
R. Zanfini & Virtuosi di Roma—Fasano[1]
                                        ♯ *B.AXTL 1042*
(*Rossini, Cambini, Bonporti*)
                                (♯ AmD.DL 9674; Fnt.LP 3005)
☆ L. Goossens & Philharmonia—Susskind
(*Cimarosa, Bach, Handel*)   ♯ AmC.ML 4782
... **Adagio**   — ARR. CLAVIER Bach
See BACH: Concertos after Vivaldi No. 3

Concerto Grosso, F major, Op. 1, No. 4   Str. orch.[2]
Società Corelli   in ♯ Vic.LM 1767
(*Geminiani, Vivaldi, Carissimi*)   (in ♭ *set WDM 1767*)
                                        (♯ ItV.A12R 0098)
Netherlands Phil.—v. d. Berg   ♯ CHS.H 16
(*Vivaldi, Torelli, Durante*)
I Musici Ensemble[3]   ♯ C.CX 1163
(*Gabrieli, Albinoni, Vivaldi*) (♯ GQX 10039; FCX 305;
                                        Angel. 35088)

MARCELLO, Benedetto   (1686-1739)

(50) PSALMS   1724-7
No. 19, I cieli narrano . . . Excerpt   — ARR. ORG.
Anon. Organist (in ♯ FSM. 403)

(Le) QUATTRO STAGIONI   Oratorio   1731
Dalle cime dell'Alpi   Bs
N. Walker   G.HMS 50
(† *History of Music in Sound*)   (in ♯ Vic. set LM 6030)

Quella fiamma che m'accende   Cantata
F. Barbieri (M-S), D. Marzollo (pf.)
                                        ♯ AmVox.PL 7980
(† *Old Italian Songs*)
☆ M. Laszlo (S), F. Holetschek (pf.) ♯ in Nix.WLP 5119
(† *Italian Songs*)

SONATAS   hpsi.
A minor[4]
... **Introduction, Aria, & Presto**
—— ARR. STR. ORCH.   Bonelli
I Musici Ens.   ♯ C.CX 1192
(*Rossini, Tartini, Galuppi*) (♯ QCX 10037: FCX 303;
                                        Angel. 35086)
... **Aria** only
☆ Virtuosi di Roma   in ♯ B.AXTL 1023
                                (♯ D.UAT 273581; Fnt.LP 3003)
C minor[5]
R. Gerlin   in ♯ LOL.OL 50043
(† *Clavecinistes italiens*)   (♯ OL.LD 67)
Sonata, F major, Op. 3, No. 1 (or "Op. 1")
fl. & cont. 1712
S. Gazzelloni & R. Raffalt (hpsi.)
                                        ♯ ItV.A12R 0027
(*Vivaldi, Locatelli, Valentino, etc.*)

MARCHAND, Louis   (1669-1732)

ORGAN MUSIC
Dialogue, C major   (Bk. I, No. 12)
... **3rd movt., Final,** only
G. Roussel   ♯ SM. 33-03
(*M. A. Charpentier, Couperin, Lalande,*   (♯ Per.SPL 712)
  Victoria & Gregorian)
Tierce en taille   (Bk. I, No. 6)
C. Watters   in ♯ CEd. set 1008
(† *Fr. Baroque Org. Music*)

CLAVIER MUSIC: PIÈCES DE CLAVECIN
BOOKS I & II, COMPLETE
M. Charbonnier   ♯ Phi.A 00292L
(*Clérambault*)

MARENZIO, Luca   (1553-1599)

MADRIGALS
COLLECTION
Vezzosi augelli
Ahi! dispietata morte
Zefiro torna   4 vv. Bk. I 1585
Ecco più che mai bella
Scaldava il sol
O dolc' anima mia   5 vv. Bk. III 1582
R. Lamy Ensemble   ♯ Pol. 14045
(*Gesualdo*) [Nos. 1, 2, 3, also on ♭ *Pol. 37004*]

---

[1] Labelled "Anon."
[2] Frequently attrib. to Benedetto Marcello, but his Op. 1 is a set of Sonatas, while A. Marcello's is Concertos. Further and definite attribution is not possible.
[3] Ed. Bonelli.   [4] No. 7 of a set of 10; MS. at St. Mark's, Venice.   [5] MS. at Naples.

COLLECTION from *Il Pastor Fido* (Guarini)
Quell' augellin che canta
Cruda Amarilli!   5 vv.   Bk. VII   1595
Ah, dolente partita!   5 vv.   Bk. VI   1594
O Mirtillo, Mirtillo   5 vv.   Bk. VII   1595
Deh, Mirtillo[1]—Che se tu sei'l cor mio   5 vv.   Bk. VI
    Golden Age Singers—Field-Hyde
    (*Monteverdi*)   ♯ **West.WLE 105**

Ahi! dispietata morte   4 vv.   1585
A Roma   5 vv.   1584
    ☆ Marenzio Ens.—Saraceni   † ♯ **HS.AS 8**
    [Ahi! . . . only, also **V**♯ *AS. 1804LD*]

O Rex gloriae   4 vv.   1588
    Petits Chanteurs de la Renaissance—Noyre
                    V♯ *Era. LDE 1001*
    († Polyphonic Motets)   (& in ♯ HS.HS 9007)

Scendi dal paradiso, Venere   5 vv.   1584
    London Cha. Singers—Bernard   **G.HMS 32**
    († History of Music in Sound) (in ♯ Vic. set LM 6029)
    Marenzio Ens.—Saraceni   in † **V**♯ *AS 1804LD*
                         († ♯ HS.AS 8)

S'io parto, i' moro   5 vv.   1594
    Danish Radio Madrigal Cho.—Wöldike
                      ♯ **HS.HSL 2072**
    († Masterpieces of Music before 1750)
    (also in † Histoire de la musique vocale)

MARESCOTTI, André-François (b. 1902)

Fantasque   pf.
    L. Morel   ♯ *D.LW 5127*
    (*Debussy, Ravel, Gagnebin*)   (♯ *Lon.LD 9149*)

MARGOLA, Franco   (b. 1908)

(2) Preludes   pf.
    P. Spagnolo   ♯ *D.LW 5142*
    (*Mompou, Rodrigo, D. Scarlatti, etc.*)   (♯ *Lon.LD 9135*)

MARINI, Biagio   (1597-1663)
    SEE: † ANTHOLOGIE SONORE

MARINUZZI, Gino, senior   (1882-1945)

Rito nuziale   Suite, orch.   1935
... Valzer campestre
    Hamburg State Phil.—di Bella   ♯ *T.TW 30030*
    (*Casella: La Giara*)

MARSCHNER, Heinrich August
(1795-1861)

HANS HEILING   Opera, Intro. & 3 Acts   1833
ABRIDGED RECORDING[2]

    Queen of the Spirits of Earth ...   T. Blacker (S)
    Hans Heiling   ...   .   J. Townend (B)
    Anna   ...   .   B. Rawson (S)
    Gertrud   ...   .   I. Holmes (A)
    Konrad   ...   .   A. Wassermann (T)
    Stephan   ...   .   K. Gough (Bs)
    etc. Oxford Univ. Op. Club Cho. & Orch.
    —Westrup   ♯ **Isis.HHLP 1/2**
    (4ss)   (Pte. recording)
    [excerpts also on HH 3/7, 10ss; *HH 4* being *10-inch*]

Overture
    Vienna Sym.—Loibner   ♭ *Phi.N 402033E*
    (*Reissiger: Die Felsenmühle, Overture*)
    Linz Sym.   in ♯ **Ply. 12-32**
    (*Mendelssohn, Wagner*)

MARSICK, Armand   (b. 1877)

LARA   Opera   3 Acts   1929
Prelude, Act II
    Belgian Nat.—Quinet   ♯ *D.BA 133099*
    (*below*)

Tableaux grecs   orch.   1925
1. Mirologue   2. Danse attique
    Belgian Nat.—Quinet   ♯ *D.BA 133099*
    (*above*)

MARSON, George   (c. 1573-1632)
    SEE: † TRIUMPHS OF ORIANA

MARTELLI, Henri   (b. 1895)

Valse   hrn. & pf.   1954
    G. Coursier & A. d'Arco   ♭ *Pat.G 1057*
    (*Passani, Canteloube, etc.*)

MARTIN, Frank   (b. 1890)

Ballade   fl., pf. & str.[3]   1939
    K. Wanausek & Vienna Collegium Musicum
    —Rapf   ♯ *SOT. 1037*
    (*Hindemith*)

Concerto, 7 Wind insts., timp., perc. & str.   1949
    ☆ Winterthur Sym.—Desarzens (♯ Clc. 6212)

Concerto, vln. & orch.   1951
    W. Schneiderhan & Suisse Romande
    —Ansermet   ♯ *D.LX 3146*
                   (♯ *Lon.LD 9213*)

Concerto, hpsi. & cha. orch.   1952
    I. Nef & O.L. Ens.—Froment   ♯ *LOL.DL 53001*
    (2ss)   (♯ *OL.LD 94*)

Petite symphonie concertante
    hp., hpsi., pf. & double str. orch.   1945
    ☆ I. Helmis, S. Kind, G. Herzog & R.I.A.S. Sym.
    —Fricsay   ♯ **Pol. 18035**
    Stravinsky: Sym. of Psalms)
    (*Bartók* on ♯ AmD.DL 9774)

(4) Sonnets à Cassandre
    (Ronsard)   M-S, fl., vla., vlc.   1922
    N. Rankin, D. Goldberg, K. Malno & T.
    Salzmann   ♯ **PFCM.CB 173**
    (*Prokofiev, Walton*)

(Der) STURM   Opera   3 Acts   1950
    (after Shakespeare's *The Tempest*)
(5) Ariel-Chöre
    1. Come unto these yellow sands
    2. Full fathom five
    3. Before you can say "come" and "go"
    4. You are three men of sin
    5. Where the bee sucks, there lurk I
    Netherlands Cha. Cho.—de Nobel (*Eng*)
    (*Hopkins, Poulenc*)   ♯ *Phi.N 00679R*

MARTIN, Nicolas   (fl. XVIth Cent.)
    SEE: † BIBLE DES NOËLS

MARTINI, [Padre] Giovanni Battista
(1706-1784)

(12) SONATAS, Op. 2   hpsi. or organ   1741
No. 5, E minor
... Aria con variazioni
    E. White (org.)   in ♯ **Moll.E4QP 3443**
    (*Bach, Karg-Elert, Fiocco, etc.*)

---

[1] Set by Marenzio as *Deh Tirsi . . .* but original Guarini text used on this disc.
[2] Contains Intro; Overture; & Nos. 5, 6, 7, 8, 9, 14, 16, 18, 19.
[3] Orchestrated by Ansermet.

SONATAS, Op. 2 (*continued*)
No. 7, E minor
... 1st movt., Prelude & Fugue, only
F. Peeters (org.) in ♯ **Nix.PLP 586**
(† *Old Italian Masters*) (♯ *Per.PLP 586; Cpt.MC 20048*)
No. 12, F major
... Gavotte only ("*Les Moutons*")
A. d'Arco (pf.) in *Plé.P 104*

—— ARR. ORCH
In *Golden Coach* film music, *q.v.* under Vivaldi, *post.*
—— ARR. 2 HARPS Salzédo
C. Salzédo & L. Lawrence (in ♯ *Mer.MG 10144*)

MARTINI IL TEDESCO (1741-1816)
(J. P. A. Schwartzendorf)

Plaisir d'amour (Florian)
M. Laszlo (S), F. Holetschek (pf.)
in ♯ **Nix.WLP 5375**
(† *Italian Airs*) (♯ *West.WL 5375*)
G. Fleischer (S), N. Prahl (pf.) *Phi.P 55037H*
(*Bishop: Home, sweet home*)
S. Rayner (T), S. Leff (pf.) in ♯ **Mur.P 103**
(followed by pf. acc. only for study)
D. Gramm (Bs), R. Cumming (pf.)
in ♯ **ML. 7033**
E. Sigfuss (A) & orch. (*Tono.L 28221;* ♭ *EP 45034*)
G. Gasparyan (in ♯ *USSR.D 1902*)
H E. Clément (T) (in ♯ *Sca. 819**)
— ARR. ORCH.
Westminster Light—Bridgewater (in ♯ *West.WL 4007*)
— ARR. VLN. & ORCH.
W. Tworek & orch. (*Pol.X 51704;* in ♯ *Lon.LB 112*)

MARTINŮ, Bohuslav (1891)

Concerto, str. qtt. & orch 1931
☆ Konzerthaus Qtt. & Vienna Sym.—Swoboda
(*below*) ♯ **West.WN 18079**

Concerto Grosso orch. 1938
☆ Vienna Sym.—Swoboda ♯ **Nix.WLP 5004**
(*R. Strauss: Macbeth*)
(*above & below* on ♯ *West.WN 18079*)

(5) Czech Madrigals Mixed cho. unacc. 1949
1. Geese on the water 2. The Dove's message
3. The fickle sweetheart 4. The lover's ride
5. The witch
... Nos. 1-3
Pamplona Cha. Cho.—Morondo
in **V**♯ *Sel.LLA 1007*
(*Stravinsky, Villa-Lobos, etc.*)
... Nos. 3-5
Fredonia Madrigal Singers—Robe ♯ **Fred. 2**
(*Wilbye, Lassus, Byrd, etc.*)

Intermezzo orch. 1950
Louisville Sym.—Whitney ♯ **AmC.ML 4859**
(*Milhaud, Foss*)

(3) Madrigals vln. & vla. 1948
☆ J. & L. Fuchs ♯ **B.AXTL 1030**
(*Mozart*) (♯ *D.UAT 273082*)

Partita (Suite No. 1) Str. orch. 1931
☆ Winterthur Sym.—Swoboda ♯ **West.WN 18079**
(*above & below*)

Quartet, pf., vln., vla., vlc. 1942
H. Franklin & Walden Trio ♯ **PFCM.CB 170**
(*Bartók*)

Quartet No. 6 Str. 1947
Walden Qtt. ♯ **McInt.MM 109**
(*Piston: Pf. Quintet*) (o.n. ♯ *WCFM. 14*)

Serenade cha. orch. 1930
☆ Winterthur Sym.—Swoboda ♯ **West.WN 18079**
(*above*)
Sonata No. 3, vln. & pf. 1950
S. Wiener & M. Stoesser ♯ **McInt.MM 108**
(*Brahms : Sonata*)

MARTUCCI, Giuseppe (1856-1909)

Notturno, G flat major, Op. 70, No. 1 orch.
Rome Qtt. Soc. Cha.—Vitalini
♯ **Csm.CLPS 1051**
(*Britten*)[1]

MARVEL, Robert

Suite pf., fl., ob., cl., bsn., hrn.
Anon. Artist & Faculty Wind Quintet ♯ **Fred. 2**
(*Persichetti, Ibert, Martinů, etc.*)

MARX, Josef (b. 1882)

LIEDER
Japanisches Regenlied (Anon.)
G. Pechner (B) in ♯ **Roy. 1558**
(*Weill, Liszt, Brahms, etc.*)

MASCHERA, Florentino (fl. *c.* 1590)

La Capriola (Canzona No. 1: Allegro) Book I, 1584
Canzona (unid.) (**Lento; Moderato**)
Ancient Inst. Ens.—M. Casadesus ♯ *Plé.P 3073*
(*G. Gabrieli, Tomasini, C. P. E. Bach*)

MASCAGNI, Pietro (1863-1945)

OPERAS
(L') AMICO FRITZ 3 Acts 1891
COMPLETE RECORDING
☆ F. Tagliavini (T), P. Tassinari (S), etc., EIAR. Cho. &
orch.—Mascagni (♯ *FSor.CS 556/7*)

Son pochi fiori S Act I
A. Hownanian ♭ *Cet.EPO 0322*
(*Forza, Manon Lescaut, La Wally*)
N. de Rosa *Cet.AT 0402*
(*Fedora—Ed ecco il suo ritratto*)

Suzel, buon dì (*Cherry duet*) T & S Act II
M. Carosio & C. Zampighi in ♯ **G.QALP 10081**
(*Lucia, Manon, Pêcheurs de Perles*)
☆ F. Tagliavini & P. Tassinari (in ♯ *FSor.CS 544*)
F. Tagliavini & M. Olivero (*Orf.* 54001)
H B. Gigli & N. Baldisseri (in ♯ *SBDH.LPP 5**)

Intermezzo orch. Act III
Philharmonia—Karajan in ♯ **C.CX 1265**
(*Pagliacci, Carmen, Contes d'Hoffmann, etc.*)
(♯ *FCX 407: QCX 10150; Angel. 35207*)
Colón Theatre—Martini *ArgOd. 66036*
(*Cavalleria Rusticana—Intermezzo*)
(♭ *BSOAE 4525:* in ♯ *LDC 509*)
Orch.—Voorhees
(in ♯ *Alld. 3001:* ♭ *EP 3001;* ♯ *MTW. 573*)
A. Sciascia Orch. (*Fnt. 14320:* in ♯ *LP 309*)
☆ Philharmonia—Schüchter (in ♯ *P.PMD 1022;*
♭ *SpOd.BSOE 4006*)
E.I.A.R.—Tansini (*Orf.* 54014)

---

[1] Early announcements also show a work by Vitalini.

Ed anche Beppe amò . . . O Amore T [& B] Act III
M. del Monaco　　　　　　　　*G.DA 11348*
(*Cavalleria Rusticana—Siciliana*)
(♭ *7EB 6006: 7ERQ 120: 7ERF 137:*
　　　　　in ‡ *FBLP 1050: QBLP 5021*)
☆ F. Tagliavini & S. Meletti[1]　　　G.DB 21579
(*Sonnambula—Prendi, l'anel*)
　　　(ED 1240; in ‡ CCet.A 50155)

☆ B. Gigli (♭ *Vlc.ERAT 26*)

Non mi resta S　Act III
G. Arnaldi　　　　　　　　*Cet.AT 0342*
(*Bohème—Quando m'en vo*)

CAVALLERIA RUSTICANA　1 Act　1890
COMPLETE RECORDINGS

Casts	Set G	Set H	Set I
(i) Santuzza (S)	M. M. Callas	E. Nicolai	Z. Milanov
(ii) Lola (M-S)	A. M. Canali	L. Didier	C. Smith
(iii) Turiddu (T)	G. di Stefano	M. del Monaco	J. Björling
(iv) Alfio (B)	R. Panerai	A. Protti	R. Merrill
(v) Lucia (A)	E. Ticozzi	A. M. Anelli	M.Roggero
etc.			

Set G　with La Scala Cho & Orch.—Serafin
　　　　　　　　　　　　‡ C.CX 1182S/3
(3ss)　　　　　　　　(‡ Angel. set 3509)
(4ss, ‡ C.FCX 266/7: QCX 10046/7)
(3ss—*Pagliacci* in ‡ Angel. set 3528)

Set H　with Cho. & Milan Sym. Orch.—Ghione
　　　　　　　　　　　　‡ D.LXT 2928/9
　　　　　　　　　　　　(‡ Lon.LL 990/1)
(3ss—*Operatic recital by M. del Monaco*)

Set I　with Shaw Chorale & Victor Sym. Orch.
—Cellini　　　　　　　‡ G.ALP 1126/8
(3ss—*Pagliacci*) (‡ FALP 301/3: QALP 10050/2;
　　　　　　　　‡ Vic. set LM 6106: ♭ set WDM 6106)
(Highlights on ‡ Vic.LM 1828: ♭ set ERB 38)
(Easter Hymn, Voi lo sapete & Intermezzo
　　　　　　on ♭ G.7ER 5047: ERQ 135)

Set J.　M. Harshaw (i), M. Miller (ii), R. Tucker
(iii), F. Guarrera (iv), T. Votipka (v), etc.
Metropolitan Op. Cho. & Orch.—Cleva
(4ss)　　　　　　　　‡EPhi.ABR 4000/1
　　　　　　　　　　(‡ Phi.A 01612/3R)
(3ss—*Leoncavallo: Pagliacci* in ‡ AmC. set SL 124)
(3ss—*Verdi: Overtures* in ‡ AmC. set SL 123)

Set K.　T. Apolai (i), P. Geri (ii), A. S. Zola (iii), P.
Campolonghi (iv), L. del Ol (v), etc. La Fenice Theatre
Cho. & Orch.—Sebastian　　‡ Rem. 199-175-1/2
(4ss)　　　　　　　　(& ‡ Ply. 12-142)

Set E.　☆ G. Simionato (i), A. Braschi (iii), etc.
Italian Radio Cho. & Orch.—Basile (‡ FSor.CS 558/9;
　　Excerpts on ‡ CCet. 50144 & ♭ Cap.FAP 7003;
　　　　　　　　♭ Cet.EPO 0308 & 0324)

Set B.　☆ G. Arangi-Lombardi (i), M. Castagna (ii), A.
Melandri (iii), etc. La Scala Cho. & Milan Sym.—Molajoli
(‡ AmC. set EL 5, 4ss)

HIGHLIGHTS in *Italian*

Prelude & Siciliana	T
Il cavallo scalpita	B & Cho.
Voi lo sapete	S
Ah! lo vedi che hai tu detto?	S & T
Addio alla madre . . . Mamma quel vino	T

M. Schech (S), L. Fehenberger (T), J. Pease (B),
Munich State Op. Cho.　　　‡ Pol. 17009

HIGHLIGHTS in *German*

Prelude & Siciliana	T
☆ Gli aranci olezzano	Cho. (b)
Il cavallo scalpita	B & Cho. (a)
☆ Regina Coeli . . . Inneggiamo, il Signor	S & Cho. (b)
Voi lo sapete	S
Ah! lo vedi, che hai tu detto?	S & T
Ah! il Signore vi manda	S & B
Intermezzo	orch. (c)
Addio alla madre . . . Mamma quel vino	T

M. Schech (S), L. Fehenberger (T), J. Pease (B),
(a) Munich State Op. Cho.; (b) Württemberg
State Op. Cho.; (c) Württemberg State Op.
Orch.—Leitner　　　　　‡ Pol. 19011

[1] From set.

HIGHLIGHTS (various)
A. da Costa (T), F. Valentino (B), V. Ruggeri (S), orch.
—Mascagni (pf.)　　　　　☆ Roy. 1581
　　　　　　　　　　(‡ MusH.LP 12009)
☆ G. Cernay (S), G. Micheletti (T), A. Endrèze (B), etc.
(*Fr*)　　　　　　　　　‡ Od.ODX 120
☆ Berlin Opera Co. & Orch. (♭ *Roy.EP 244*)
Vocal Selections
M. Schech (S), L. Fehenberger (T), J. Pease (B), Cho. &
Orch. (*Ger*)　　　　　　PV. 72475
　　　　　　　　　　　(♭ *Pol. 30055*)
Orchestral Selection
☆ Salzburg Fest. Orch.—P. Walter (♭ *Cum.ECR 81*)
Prelude　Opera Orch.—Rossi (in ‡ *Mae.OA 20006*)

Siciliana: O Lola! T
M. del Monaco　　　　　　*G.DA 11348*
(*Amico Fritz—Ed anche Beppe amò*)
　　　　　　(in ‡ *QBLP 5021: FBLP 1050*)
M. Gafni　　　　　in ‡ *For.FLP 1001*
A. da Costa　　　　in ‡ *Roy. 1599*
☆ J. Björling, from Highlights (♭ *G.7ER 5025;*
　　　　　　　　　　　　♭ *Vic.ERA 109*)
B. Gigli, from set (♭ *Vlc.ERA 16*)
Ⓗ T. Schipa　　　　in ‡ *Sca. 805**
E. Clément　　　in ‡ *Sca. 819**
F. de Lucia　　　in ‡ *Sca. 814**
J. McCormack (*Eng*)　in ‡ *Roy. 1555**
　　　　　　& in ‡ *Cum.CE 185**

Gli aranci olezzano Cho.
Netherlands Op. Cho. & Residentie Orch.
- —Moralt　　　　in ‡ *EPhi.NBR 6003*
(*Trovatore, Rigoletto, Don Pasquale, etc.*)
　　　　(‡ *Phi.N 00634R: ♭ N 402039E*)
☆ Württemberg State Op.—Leitner (*Ger*)
　　　(♭ *Pol. 30017:* in ‡ *19033;* ‡ *AmD.DL 9797*)

Il cavallo scalpita B & cho.
☆ R. Merrill (in ‡ *Vic.LM 1841:* ♭ *ERA 107;*
　　　　　　　　　　in ‡ *FV.A 630255*)

Regina Coeli . . . Inneggiamo il Signor S & cho.
(*Easter Hymn*)
L. Rysanek & Berlin Municipal Op.—Schüchter
(*Ger*)　　　　　　　　G.DB 11591
(*Brindisi*)　　　　　　(♭ *7RW 19-551*)
Anon. Soloist (Tr.) & Columbus Cho.—Huffman (*Eng*)
(in ‡ *B.LAT 8070;* ‡ *AmD.DL 8106: ♭ set ED 831*)
☆ Württemberg State Op. Cho.—Leitner
　　　　　　(♭ *Pol. 30017:* in ‡ *19033;* ‡ *AmD.DL 9797*)

Voi lo sapete S　(*Als euer Sohn . . .*)
Z. Milanov (from set I)　　in ‡ *G.ALP 1247*
(*Aida, Forza, etc.*) (in ‡ *Vic.LM 1777: ♭ set ERB 19:*
　　　　　　　　　　　　ERA 228)
V. de los Angeles　　in ‡ *G.ALP 1284*
(*La Wally, Ernani, Otello, etc.*)　(‡ *QALP 10115*)
D. Rigal　　　　　　ArgOd. 66017
(*Pagliacci—Ballatella*) (in ‡ *LDC 503;* in ‡ *AmD.DL 4060:*
　　　　　　　　　　　　♭ *D 3508*)
G. Frazzoni　(*Chénier, Aida, etc.*)　in ‡ *Cet.LPV 45003*
V. Petrova　(*Trovatore, Forza, etc.*)　in ‡ *Ace. 1007/8*
N. de Rosa　　　　　　Cet.PE 209
(*Werther—Werther! Qui m'aurait dit*)
G. Ribla　　　　　　in ‡ *MH. 33-104*
M. Schech (*Ger*) (from Highlights)　　Pol. 62925
(*below*)　　　　　　　(♭ *Pol. 32012*)
☆ L. Albanese　　　in ‡ *Vic.LM 1839*
　　　　　(♭ *ERA 139;* ‡ *FV.A 630253*)
G. Brouwenstijn　　　♭ *Phi.N 402010E*
D. Ilitsch　　　　in ‡ *U. 5109C*
E. Stignani　　　in ‡ *C.QC 5024*
Ⓗ E. Eames　　in ‡ *B & B 3*: V‡ Rar.M 310**
M. Calvé　　　　AF.AGSB 6*
C. Boninsegna　　in ‡ *Sca. 812**
R. Raisa　　　in ‡ *Sca. 808**
E. Destinn　　　in ‡ *Sca. 804**

Ah! lo vedi, che hai tu detto? S & T
M. Schech & L. Fehenberger　　♭ *Pol. 34008*
(*Addio alla madre*)　　　　(♭ *32056*)
(& in *Ger* on ♭ *Pol. 34007: 32055; PV. 36116*)

Tu qui Santuzza . . . No, no, Turiddu S & T
☆ D. Giannini & B. Gigli (in ‡ *Vic.LCT 6010:*
　　　　　　　　　　　♭ *set WCT 6010*)
. . . No, no, Turiddu
☆ M. Teschemacher & M. Wittrisch (*Ger*)(♭ *G. 7 RW 534*)

CAVALLERIA RUSTICANA (continued)
Ah Il Signore vi manda S & B
  M. Schech & J. Pease (Ger, from Highlights)
                                           Pol. 62925
  (Voi lo sapete)   (♭ *32012*)

Intermezzo orch.
  Philharmonia—Karajan   in ‡ *C.CX 1265*
  (Amico Fritz, Pagliacci, Carmen, etc.)   [D. Brain, organ]
                               (‡ FCX 407: QCX 10150; Angel. 35207)
  Württemberg State Op.—Leitner   PV. 72439
  (Pagliacci, Aida)   (♭ Pol. 30008: in ‡ 17001)
  N.W. German Phil.—Schüchter   *Od.O-29000*
  (Pagliacci—Intermezzo)(♭ OBL 37-29000; in ‡ Imp.ILP 128)
  Odense Municipal—Lundquist   C.DDX 37
  (Gounod: Mors et Vita—Judex)
  Hamburg State Phil.—Martin   T.A 11405
  (Zar und Zimmermann—Dance) (♭ U 45405: in ‡ TW 30004)
  (Pagliacci—Intermezzo, on T.A 11682: ♭ U 45682)

  Israel Radio—Goehr (Arzi. 770; in ‡ Bne. 501)
  Leipzig Radio—Gerdes (Eta. 120038)
  Colón Theatre—Martini (ArgOd. 66036:
                               ♭ BSOAE 4525: in ‡ LDC 509)
  Mantovani Orch. (in ‡ D.LF 1191: F 43706: ♭ 17706:
                               ♭ DFE 6089; ♭ Lon.BEP 6089)
  Melachrino Orch. (G.B. 9560: ‡ DLP 1083;
                               in ‡ Vic.LPM 1003: ♭ set EPB 1003)
  Opera Orch.—Rossi (in ‡ Mae.AO 20006)
  etc. etc.
  ☆ Vienna Phil.—Karajan (♭ C.SCB 109: SCBQ 3013:
                                           SCBW 108)
    Covent Garden—Patanè (♭ C.SED 5512: SEDQ 522:
                                 SCD 2004: SCDQ 2001: SCDW 103)
    Philharmonia—Weldon (in ‡ C.SX 1032:
                               ♭ SED 5518: SEDQ 543)
    Philharmonia—Schüchter (in ‡ P.PMD 1022)
    Turin Radio—Basile (in ‡ CCet.A 50159, from set E)
    Hilversum Radio—v. Kempen (♭ Phi.N 402010E)
    Dresden State Op.—Böhm (♭ G.7R 158)
    E.I.A.R. Sym.—Tansini (Orf. 54014)
    Boston Prom.—Fiedler (♭ G.7BF 1060;
                               in ‡ Vic. LM 1752: ♭ set WDM 1752)
    Robin Hood Dell—Mitropoulos (♭ AmC.A 1637)
    etc.

—— ARR. PF.
  ☆ P. Mascagni, from a piano roll (in ‡ Roy. 1573:
                               ‡ 1402; ‡ Allo.AL 39)

Brindisi—Viva il vino T [M-S] & cho.
  M. del Monaco, from set   ‡ *D.LW 5118*
  (below; Leoncavallo) (& in ‡ Lon.LL 1244) (‡ Lon.LD 9133)
  A. da Costa   in ‡ *Roy. 1599*
  R. Schock, L. Losch, Berlin Municipal Op. Cho.
    & Orch.—Schüchter (Ger)   G.DB 11591
  (above)   (in ‡ WBLP 1515: ♭ 7RW 19-551)
  ☆ A. Braschi, F. Cadoni & cho. (Od.O-4674)

Scene—Santuzza, Turiddu, Lola, Alfio
  ... Unspec. excerpts
  S. Roman (S), F. Jagel (T), L. Warren (B) (in ‡ PRCC. 3)

Addio alla madre . . . Mamma quel vino T
  M. del Monaco, from set   ‡ *D.LW 5118*
  (above; & Leoncavallo)   (‡ Lon.LD 9133)
  (& in ‡ Lon.LL 1244)
  L. Fehenberger, from Highlights ♭ *Pol. 34008*
  (Ah, lo vedi)   (♭ *32056*)
  (& in Ger on ♭ Pol. 34007: 32055; PV. 36116)
  M. Gafni   in ‡ *Før.FLP 1001*
  ☆ J. Björling   in ‡ G.BLP 1055
  (in ‡ Vic.LM 1841; FV.A 630255; ♭ DV. 26044)
    R. Tucker   ♭ AmC.A 1646
    M. del Monaco   in ‡ G.FBLP 1050
    M. Lanza   ♭ G.7EB 6005
                               (♭ 7RQ 3009: 7RW 102)
    B. Gigli (& G. Simionato, M-S) ♭ Vic.ERAT 16
    R. Schock (Ger) in ‡ G.WBLP 1501: ♭ 7RW 509
    P. Anders (Ger)   RadT.E 052T
  ⊨ F. de Lucia   in ‡ Sca. 814*

GUGLIELMO RATCLIFF 4 Acts 1895
Ombra esecrata T Act III
  ☆ G. Taccani (in ‡ Ete. 490)

IRIS 3 Acts 1898
Apri la tua finestra (Serenata) T Act I
  ⊨ A. Pertile (in ‡ HRS. 3007*: in ‡ Od.ODX 127*:
                                           MOAQ 301*)
  F. de Lucia (in ‡ CEd. set 7002*)
  B. Gigli & pf. (in ‡ SBDH.JAL 7000*)
Son io! Son io la vita! Cho. Act I
  Rome Op. Cho.—Morelli   in ‡ *G.ALP 1277*
  (Nabucco, Lombardi, etc.)   (‡ QALP 10118)
Io pingo S Act II
  ⊨ L. Cannetti (in ‡ Ete. 490*)
Un dì, ero piccina S Act II
  N. de Rosa   Cet.PE 198
  (Forza del Destino—Pace, pace . . .)
  M. Olivero   Cet.AT 0321
  (Gianni Schicchi—O mio babbino caro)
  ⊨ L. Bori (in ‡ B & B.3* & V‡ Rar.M 309*)

LODOLETTA 3 Acts 1917
Ah! ritrovarla T Act III
  L. Francardi   Cet.AT 0323
  (Cilea: Gloria, aria)
  ⊨ B. Gigli (in ‡ SBDH.GL 1*)
Flammen, perdonami S Act III
  G. Arnaldi   Cet.AT 0326
  (Manon—Adieu, notre petite table)
  R. Scotti   Cet.AT 0389
  (Traviata—Amami Alfredo)

(Le) MASCHERE Prologue & 3 Acts 1901
È la bella di Brighella Cho. Act II
  Rome Op. Cho.—Morelli   in‡ *G.ALP 1277*
  (Iris, Lombardi, etc.)   (‡ QALP 10118)

(Il) PICCOLO MARAT 3 Acts 1921
La mamma ritrova la bimba S Act II
  ⊨ G. Baldassare-Tedeschi (in ‡ Ete. 490*)
Si l'amante più bella B
  ⊨ A. Granforte (in ‡ Ete. 490*)
Sei tu? Che cosa vieni a fare S & T Act II
  ⊨ M. Zamboni & E. Bergamaschi (in ‡ Ete. 490*)

SILVANO 2 Acts 1895
S'e spento il sol T ☆ G. Taccani (in ‡ Ete. 490)

SONGS
  Alla luna (Cipollini)
  Ballata
  Rosa (Pagliara)
  Serenata (Stecchetti)
  P. Neway (S), T. Mayer pf.)   ‡ Ete. 101
  (Bellini, Verdi)

M'ama . . . non m'ama
  S. Rayner (T), S. Leff   in ‡ Mur.P 103
  (followed by pf. acc. only)

MASON, Daniel Gregory (1873–1953)

Chanticleer Overture, Op. 27 orch.
  ☆ A.R.S. Orch.—Dixon (Bloch, Powell)   ‡ ARS. 113

MASSENET, Jules Émile Frédéric
(1842–1912)

I. OPERATIC & STAGE WORKS

ARIANE 5 Acts 1906
O Vierge guerrière T Act III
Phèdre! Ariane! Mes amours! T Act V
  ⊨ L. Muratore (in V‡ IRCC.L 7002*)

CHÉRUBIN 3 Acts 1905
Vive l'amour qui rêve (Aubade) S Act III
  ⊨ E. Eames (AF.AGSB 60*)

---

‡ = Long-playing, 33⅓ r.p.m.   ♭ = 45 r.p.m.   ⊨ = Auto. couplings, 78 r.p.m.

272

(Le) CID 4 Acts 1885
Ballet Music Act II
  Covent Garden—Braithwaite   ‡ **P.PMC 1013**
  (below; & Scènes alsaciennes)   (‡ MGM.E 3016)
  ☆ Netherlands Phil.—Spruit   ‡ Nix.NCL 16008
  (Rimsky-Korsakov: Tsar Saltan)
    (‡ Clc. 6188; MMS. 3001; & 2ss, V‡ *MMS.911*)
  ☆ L.S.O.—Irving (‡ *D.LW 5074; Lon.LD 9089*)
  Paris Phil.—Désormière (V‡ *CdM.LDY 8123*)
  ... Nos. 1-4 only
    ☆ Aarhus Municipal—Jensen (♭ *Mer.EP 1-5036;*
                             FMer.MEP 14045)
  ... Nos. 1, 2, 3, 4, 7
    Belgian Radio—Marinetti   ‡ Mae.OAT 25007
    (Phèdre, Thaïs; & Gounod)
  ... No. 1, Castillane, only
    Hollywood Bowl Sym.—Dragon   in ‡ Cap.P 8314
    (Ravel, Albeniz, etc.)   (♭ set FAP 8314)

Rapsodie mauresque Act III
  Covent Garden—Braithwaite   ‡ **P.PMC 1013**
  (above; & Scènes alsaciennes)   (‡ MGM.E 3016)

Ah! tout est bien fini ...
O Souverain! O Juge! O Père *(Prière)* T Act III
  ⊞ J. de Reszke & pf. (in ‡ SBDH.JAL 7000*)

CLÉOPATRE 4 Acts 1914
A-t-il dit vrai? Bs
  ☆ Vanni-Marcoux (in ‡ G.FJLP 5035)

Solitaire dans ma terrace Bs Act II
  ⊞ M. Journet (in ‡ SBDH.LPG 5*)

DON CÉSAR DE BAZAN 3 Acts 1872
Sevillana S
  G. Gasparyan   in ‡ *USSR.D 1901*
  (Lakmé, Romeo & Juliet, etc.)
  ⊞ A. Galli-Curci (in ‡ ABCD. 1*)

DON QUICHOTTE 5 Acts 1910
C'est vers ton amour Bs Act II
Je suis le chevalier errant Bs Act III
  ☆ A. Pernet (in ‡ Od.ODX 135)
La Mort de Don Quichotte Bs, B, S
O mon maître ... Écoute, mon ami Act V
  ☆ F. Chaliapin & O. Kline (S) (in ‡ Vic. set LCT 6701)
  ... Bass part only   ☆ Vanni-Marcoux (in ‡ G.FJLP 5035)

(Les) ERINNYES Inc. Music 1873
  (to Leconte de Lisle's Play)
Orchestral Suite
  Paris Opéra—Cluytens   ‡ Pat.DTX 129
  (2ss)   (‡ ArgPat.ADTX 1803)
  (Saint-Saëns: Suite algérienne on ‡ AmVox.PL 8100)
  ... Divertissement only, on ♭ Pat.ED 49

ESCLARMONDE 4 Acts 1889
Trahir Vincent ⊞ G. Ritter-Ciampi (in ‡ ABCD. 1*)

GRISÉLIDIS Prologue & 3 Acts 1901
Prologue: Ouvrez-vous sur mon front T
  ⊞ C. Dalmores (AF.ABSB 9*)

Voir Grisélidis T (Prologue)
Je suis l'oiseau T Act II
  ☆ M. Villabella (in ‡ Od.ODX 136)

HÉRODIADE 4 Acts 1881
Il est doux, il est bon S Act I
  Géori-Boué   in ‡ Ura. 7070
  (Charpentier, Fauré, etc.)   (♭ UREP 72)
  ☆ N. Vallin (in ‡ Od.ODX 115)
  ⊞ M. Garden (V‡ *Rar. 312* & in ‡ B & B. 3* also
                        ‡ & ♭ AmC.PE 18*)

Vision fugitive B Act II
  G. Taddei *(Ital)*   Cet.BB 25299
  (Figaro, No. 26)   (in ‡ LPC 55006)
  I. Gorin   in ‡ Alld. 3003
                       (‡ MTW. 572)
  ☆ J. C. Thomas (in ‡ Cam.CAL 199: ♭ CAE 246)
  ⊞ M. Renaud (in ‡ Vic. set LCT 6701*)

Dors, o cité ... Astres étincelantes Bs Act III
  ⊞ M. Journet (in ‡ SBDH.JALP 19*)

Salomé! Demande au prisonnier B Act III
  M. Dens   ♭ Pat.ED 34
  (Roméo & Juliette, Favorita)   (in ‡ DT 1020)
  ☆ J. C. Thomas (in ‡ Vic.LCT 1115:
                    ♭ set WCT 1115: ERAT 25)

Ne pouvant reprimer ... Adieu donc T Act IV
  ⊞ S. Campagnola (in ‡ Ete. 708*)

(Le) JONGLEUR DE NOTRE DAME 3 Acts 1902
Scène du marché et Alleluia du vin T & cho. Act I
  F. Vroons, E. Brasseur Cho., Lamoureux Orch.
    —Fournet   ‡ *Phi.N 00706R*
  (Manon, Werther, etc.)

O Liberté T Act I
  ⊞ M. Garden (S) (‡ & ♭ AmC.PE 18*)

La Vierge entend ... Fleurissait une sauge Bs Act II
  M. Singher   in ‡ Roy. 1613
  (Samson & Dalila, Louise, etc.)
  ☆ Vanni-Marcoux (in ‡ G.FJLP 5035)
  ⊞ D. Gilly (AF.AGSB 13*)

(Le) Miracle Act III
  ... Il fait beau voir ces hommes d'armes
  ... Mon beau Seigneur, je reste sage T
  M. Villabella (in ‡ Od.ODX 136: o.n. ▽ Od. 188557)

(Le) MAGE 5 Acts 1891
Soulève l'ombre de ces voiles T
  ⊞ E. Clément (in V‡ *IRCC.L 7005*)

MANON 5 Acts 1884
COMPLETE RECORDINGS
  Manon Lescaut ... ... V. de los Angeles (S)
  Chevalier des Grieux ... ... H. Legay (T)
  Lescaut ... ... M. Dens (B)
  Comte des Grieux ... ... J. Borthayre (B)
  etc., Opéra-Comique Cho. & Orch.—Monteux
  (8ss)   ‡ G.FALP 377/80
  ☆ G. Féraldy (S), J. Rogatchewsky (T), etc., Opéra-
    Comique Cho. & Orch.—Cohen   ‡ AmC. set EL 6
  (6ss)

HIGHLIGHTS
  ☆ N. Vallin (S), M. Villabella (T), A. Baugé (B)
                            ‡ Pat.PCX 5002
    [Contents: Je suis encore tout étourdie; Voyons, Manon,
    Act I; J'écris à mon père.... On l'appelle Manon;
    Adieu notre petite table; En fermant les yeux,
    Act II; Suis-je gentille ... Je marche sur tous les
    chemins; Obéissons ... ; N'est-ce plus ma main;
    Act III; À nous les amours, Act IV]
  ☆ J. Micheau (S), L. de Luca (T), etc. Opéra-Comique
    Cho. & Orch.—Wolff, from set (‡ Lon.LL 1114)

COLLECTED EXCERPTS (from set)
  Je suis encore tout étourdie S Act I
  Restons ici ... Voyons, Manon S
  Adieu notre petite table S Act II
  Je marche sur tous les chemins S Act III
  Toi! Vous! ... n'est-ce plus ma main S & T
  ☆ J. Micheau (S), L. de Luca (T), Opéra-Comique Cho.
    & Orch.—Wolff   ‡ D.LW 5204

ACT I

Je suis encore tout étourdie S
  J. Hammond   in ‡ G.ALP 1076
  (Bruch, Catalani, Cilea, etc.)
  ☆ N. Vallin (in ‡ Od.ODX 115)
  Géori-Boué (in ‡ Od.ODX 117: ♭ 7AO 2011)

Voyons, Manon, plus de chimères S
  ☆ N. Vallin (in ‡ Od.ODX 115)

J'ai marqué l'heure du départ
Non! Je ne veux pas croire S & T
  P. Alarie & L. Simoneau[1] in ‡ LT.DTL 93018
  (Mireille, Roméo & Juliet, Carmen)
               (‡ Sel. 270.C.008; ‡ West.WL 5358)
  M. Carosio & C. Zampighi *(Ital)*[2]
                   in ‡ G.QALP 10081
  (Pêcheurs de Perles, Lucia, Amico Fritz)
  ☆ J. Micheau & L. de Luca, from set (‡ D.LW 5203)

ACT II

J'écris à mon père ... On l'appelle Manon S & T
  (Duo de la lettre)
  I. Maslennikova & S. Lemeshev ‡ *USSR.D 1519*
  (below, & Traviata) *(Russ)*
  ⊞ G. Farrar & E. Caruso (in ‡ Vic. set LCT 6701*)

---

[1] Begins *Et je sais votre nom.*   [2] Begins *Qualcun! mettiamci presto ...*

Adieu, notre petite table S
M. Angelici   in ♯ *G.FBLP 1051*
M. Stader   *PV. 36119*
(below)   (♭ *Pol. 34013: 32060)*
(& in Ger, on PV. 36118: ♭ *Pol. 34012: 32059)*
J. Hammond *(above)*   in ♯ *G.ALP 1076*
M. Olivero *(Ital)*   *Cet.AT 0326*
(Franck: La Procession)
G. Arnaldi *(Ital)*   *Cet.PE 184*
(Mascagni: Lodoletta—Flammen perdonami)
E. Arizmendi   *ArgOd. 57019*
(Elégie)   (♭ *BSOA 4000)*
☆ Géori-Boué (in ♯ Od.ODX 117: ♭ *7AO 2011)*
N. Vallin (in ♯ Od.ODX 115)
L. Bori (♭ *Vic.ERAT 3)*
M. Minazzi *(Ital) (P.AR 403)*

En fermant les yeux (*Le Rêve*) T
N. Gedda   *C.LX 1614*
(Pêcheurs de Perles—Je crois entendre)   (♭ *SCB 118)*
     (& in ♯ *CX 1130: FCX 302; Angel. 35096)*
F. Vroons   in ♯ *Phi.N 00706R*
(Carmen, Werther, etc.)
H. Legay   *C.LFX 1031*
(Pêcheurs de Perles—Je crois entendre)   (♭ *SCBF 111)*
C. Valletti   in ♯ *CCet.A 50176*
(below; Don Giovanni, Werther, etc.)
R. Schock *(Ger)*   *G.DB 11583*
(Ah! fuyez, douce image)   (♭ *7RW 537)*
G. Vinogradov *(Russ)*   *USSR. 10563*
☆ G. Thill   in ♯ *C.FH 503*
A Dermota *(Ger)*   *RadT.E 177T*
S. Lemeshev *(Russ)*   *USSRM.D 00108*
⌑ E. Clément (in ♯ Vic. set LCT 6701*; in ♯ Sca. 819*)
C. Vezzani (in ♯ Od.ODX 126*)
F. de Lucia *(Ital)* & pf. *(AF.AGSA 25*)*
G. Anselmi *(Ital)* & pf. (in ♯ Ete. 711*; in ♯ Sca. 816*)

ACT III

Suis-je gentille . . . Je marche sur tous les chemins S
M. Stader   *PV. 36119*
(above & below)   (♭ *Pol. 34013)*
(Ger on PV. 36118: ♭ *Pol. 34012)*
☆ L. Jourfier *(ArgPat.FCX 0006)*

Obéissons . . . Profitons bien de la jeunesse S
(Gavotte)
M. Dobbs   in ♯ *C.CX 1305*
(Sonnambula, Lakmé, Rigoletto, etc.)   (♯ *Angel. 35093)*
M. Stader   *PV. 36119*
(above)   (♭ *Pol. 34013: 32060)*
(& in Ger, on PV. 36118; ♭ *Pol. 34012: 32059)*
T. Lavrova *(Russ)*   *USSR. 19479/80*
☆ L. Bori   ♭ *Vic.ERAT 3*
N. Vallin   in ♯ Od.ODX 115
⌑ G. Farrar   in ♯ Vic. set LCT 6701*
S. Kurz *(Ger)*   *AF.AGSA 18**

Épouse quelque brave fille Bs
☆ A. Pernet (in ♯ Od.ODX 135)

Je suis seul . . . Ah! fuyez, douce image T
C. Valletti   in ♯ *Cet.LPC 55002*
(Werther, Italiana in Algeri, Lucia, etc.) (in ♯ *CCet.A 50176)*
R. Schock *(Ger)*   *G.DB 11583*
(En fermant les yeux)   (♭ *7RW 537)*
D. Cestari *(Ital)*   *Cet.PE 194*
(Bohème—O soave fanciulla)
☆ R. Crooks   in ♯ Cam.CAL 148
A. Dermota *(Ger)*   *RadT.E 177T*
⌑ E. Clément   in ♯ *HRS. 3008** & ♯ Sca. 819*
C. Vezzani   in ♯ Od.ODX 126*
F. de Lucia *(Ital)*   in ♯ Sca. 814*

Toi! Vous! . . . N'est-ce plus ma main S & T
(Duo de St.-Sulpice)
D. Kirsten & R. Tucker   ♯AmC.ML 4981
(Bohème & Manon Lescaut) (♭ set A 1112; ♯ Phi.N 02126L)
I. Maslennikova & S. Lemeshev *(Russ)* (♯ *USSR.D 1519)*
. . . Sop. part only: Hélas! l'oiseau qui fuit
⌑ S. Arnoldson (in ♯ *FRP. 1)*

ACT V
Ah! Des Grieux! . . . (Death of Manon)
☆ J. Micheau & L. de Luca, from set (♯ *D.LW 5203)*

(Le) ROI DE LAHORE 5 Acts 1877
Promesse de mon avenir B Act IV
M. Singher   in ♯ *Roy. 1613*
(Jongleur de Notre Dame, Pêcheurs de Perles, etc.)

SAPHO 5 Acts 1897
Pendant un an . . . Viens, m'ami S Act IV
⌑ E. Calvé (in V♯ *IRCC.L 7002*)

THAÏS 3 Acts 1894
COMPLETE RECORDING
☆ Géori-Boué (S), J. Giraudeau (T), R. Bourdin (B), etc.
Paris Op. Cho. & Orch.—Sebastian
     ♯ *Nix.ULP 9227-1/3*
Ballet Suite
☆ Paris Opéra—Sebastian (♭ *Ura.UREP 30)*

ACT I
Va mendiant! . . . Voilà donc la terrible cité B
G. London   in ♯ *AmC.ML 4999*
(Gruenberg, Wagner, Verdi, etc.)

ACT II
Ah! je suis seule . . . Dis-moi que je suis belle S
(Air du miroir)
M. Vitale *(Ital)*   in ♯ *Cet.LPC 55001*
(Schubert, Respighi, Paisiello, etc.)
☆ J. Hammond *(G.EC 195)*

Méditation (Intermezzo) orch.
Philharmonia—Karajan   in ♯ *C.CX 1265*
(Hary Janos, Khovanshchina, etc.)
     (♯ *FCX 407: QCX 10150; Angel. 35207)*
[M. Parikian, vln.]
C. Pessina & Orch.   *ArgOd. 66020*
(S-Saëns: Le Déluge, Prelude) (♭ *BSOA 4003: BSOAE 4513)*
M. Kalki & Berlin Municipal—Otto ♭ *T.U 45559*
(Raff: Cavatina)   (in ♯ *LA 6077)*
Boyd Neel—Dumont (♭ *Phi.N 402028E)*
Belgian Radio—Marinetti (in ♯ Mae.OAT 25007)
W. Tworek & orch. (in ♯ *Lon.LB 1121; Pol.X 51705)*
Palm Court—Jenkins (♭ *G.7EG 8052)*
☆ Boston Prom.—Fiedler (♭ *G.7EP 7018: 7PQ 2024;*
     ♭ *Vic.ERA 66:* in ♯ *LRM 7045:* ♭ set ERB 7045)
Paris Opéra—Sebastian (♭ *Ura.UREP 30)*
— ARR. VLN. & PF.
☆ Z. Francescatti (♭ *Phi.N 409514E: EPhi.NBE 11010)*
M. Elman (♭ *DV. 26024)*

L'amour est une vertu rare S
J. Hammond   in ♯ *G.ALP 1076*
(Manon; & Cilea, Mozart, Weber, etc.)

ACT III
Baigne d'eau S & B
☆ G. Holst & C. Formichi *(Ital)* (in ♯ Ete. 494)

THÉRÈSE 2 Acts 1907
Menuet d'amour S & T
— ARR. HARP Salzédo 1920
C. Salzédo (in ♯ Mer.MG 80003)

(La) VIERGE Oratorio 1880
Le Dernier Sommeil de la Vierge Orch.
Royal Phil.—Beecham (n.v.) ♯ & ♭ *AmC.PE 17*
(Tchaikovsky: Nutcracker, excpts.)

WERTHER 4 Acts 1892
COMPLETE RECORDINGS

Casts		Set A	Set B
Charlotte	...	S. Juyol (M-S)	P. Tassinari (MS)
Sophie	...	A. Léger (S)	V. Neviani (S)
Werther	...	C. Richard (T)	F. Tagliavini (T)
Albert	...	R. Bourdin (Bs)	M. Cortis (B)
Le Bailli	...	M. Roux (Bs)	C. Ferrein (Bs)
etc.			

♯ = Long-playing, 33⅓ r.p.m.   ♭ = 45 r.p.m.   ♮ = Auto. couplings, 78 r.p.m.

Set A with Opéra-Comique Cho. & Orch.
—Sebastian (6ss)   ♯ **Nix.ULP 9233-1/3**
(♯ Ura. set 233)
[Highlights on ♯ Nix.ULP 9124; ♯ Ura. 7124: ♭ *UREP 75/7*]

Set B with Italian Radio Cho. & Orch.—Pradelli
(6ss)   ♯ **CCet. set 1245**

☆ N. Vallin (S), G. Féraldy (S), G. Thill (T), etc. Paris
Opéra-Comique Cho. & Orch.—Cohen
(6ss)   ♯ **C.FHX 5009/11**

HIGHLIGHTS

O nature   T   Act I
Lorsque l'enfant revient   T   Act II
Werther! qui m'aurait dit . . . Des cris joyeux   S
Ah! mon courage m'abandonne   S
Oui, c'est moi   S & T
Pourquoi me réveiller   T
N'achevez-pas!   S & T   Act III
   I. Kolassi (M-S), R. Jobin (T) & L.S.O.
—Fistoulari   ♯ **D.LXT 5034**
(*Berlioz: Damnation de Faust, Highlights*) (♯ Lon.LL 1154)

Prelude
   Opéra-Comique—Wolff (n.v.)   ♯ **D.LW 5150**
(*below; & Liszt*)   (♯ Lon.LD 9171)

ACT I

O nature (Invocation)   T
   C. Valletti   in ♯ **CCet.LPC 55002**
(*below; Don Giovanni, Lucia, etc.*)   (in ♯ CCet.A 50176)
   ℍ S. Rayner (in ♯ Ete. 708*)

Il faut nous séparer   S & T
   ☆ P. Tassinari & F. Tagliavini (*Ital*) (in ♯ FSor.CS 544)

ACT II

Un autre est son époux . . . J'aurais sur ma poitrine
(*Désolation de Werther*)   T
   F. Vroons   in ♯ **Phi.N 00706R**
(*Le Jongleur, Manon, Contes d'Hoffmann, Carmen*)

Lorsque l'enfant revient   T
   ℍ C. Vezzani (in ♯ Od.ODX 126*)

ACT III

Werther! Qui m'aurait dit . . . Des cris joyeux   S
(*Air de la lettre*)
   S. Michel   in ♯ **Pat.DTX 137**
(*Thomas, Bizet, etc.*)
   I. Andréani   ♭ *Plé.P 45151*
(*Mignon—Connais tu le pays*)
   N. de Rosa   **Cet.PE 209**
(*Cavalleria—Voi lo sapete*)
   Z. Dolukhanova (*Russ*) (*USSR. 21858*)
   ☆ N. Vallin (in ♯ Od.ODX 115)
   ℍ M. Delna (*IRCC. 3145*)

Va! laisse-les couler   (*Air des larmes*)   S
   ☆ N. Vallin (in ♯ Od.ODX 115)
   ℍ J. Gerville-Réache (*AF.AGSA 1*)

Pourquoi me réveiller   T
   N. Gedda   in ♯ **C.CX 1130**
(*Auber, Bizet, Cilea, Flotow, etc.*)
     (♯ FCX 302; ♯ Angel. 35096)
   C. Valletti   in ♯ **Cet.LPC 55002**
(*above*)   (in ♯ CCet.A 50176)
   G. di Stefano (*Ital*)   **G.DA 11340**
(*Don Pasquale—Com' è gentil*)
   D. Cestari (*Ital*)   *Cet.AT 0398*
(*Africaine—O. Paradis*)
   ☆ G. Thill   in ♯ *C.FH 503*
   I. Kozlovsky (*Russ*)   in ♯ *USSR.D 1428*
   ℍ C. Vezzani   in ♯ Od.ODX 126*

Ah! mon courage m'abandonne   S
   ☆ N. Vallin (in ♯ Od. ODX 115)

ACT IV

Prelude
   Opéra-Comique—Wolff   ♯ **D.LW 5150**
(*above*)   (♯ Lon.LD 9171)

Werther's aria (unspec.)
   M. Alexandrovitch (*Russ*) (in *USSRM.D 00115*)

II. ORCHESTRAL

Concerto, E flat major, pf. & orch.   1903
   S. Bianca & Hamburg Philharmonia
—H.-J. Walther   ♯ **MGM.E 3178**
(*A. Bloch*)

Phèdre, Overture   1873
   Lamoureux—Fournet   in ♯ *Phi.N 00707R*
(*St-Saëns, Gounod, etc.*)   (♯ Epic.LC 3079)
   Opéra-Comique—Cluytens   ♯ **Pat.DTX 159**
(*below*)
   Belgian Radio—André   ♯ *DT.TM 68016*
(*Chabrier: España*)   (TV.VE 9031)
   Belgian Radio—Marinetti   ♯ **Mae.OAT 25007**
(*Le Cid, Thaïs; Gounod*)
   ☆ Opéra-Comique—Wolff (*Saint-Saëns*)   ♯ *D.LW 5028*
   ☆ Rhineland Sym.—Federer (in ♯ *AFest.CFR 10-601*)

Scènes alsaciennes   (Orch. Suite No. 7)   1884
1. Dimanche matin   2. Au cabaret
3. Sous les tilleuls   4. Dimanche soir
   Lamoureux—Fournet   ♯ **Phi.N 00190L**
(*below*) (n.n., ♯ Phi.S 04010L)   (♯ Epic.LC 3053)
   Pasdeloup—Lindenberg   ♯ **Od.ODX 119**
(*below*)
   Covent Garden—Braithwaite   ♯ **P.PMC 1013**
(*Le Cid*)   (♯ MGM.E 3016)
[No. 4 only, in ♯ MGM.E 3046]
   Paris Opéra—Cluytens   ♯ **Pat.DTX 159**
(*above & below*)
   Paris Cons.—Wolff   ♯ **D.LXT 5100**
(*below*)   (♯ Lon.LL 1298)

. . . No. 3, Sous les tilleuls
   Florence Fest.—Gui   in ♯ *AudC. 1163*
(*Glinka & Rossini*)

Scènes napolitaines   (Orch. Suite No. 5)
. . . No. 1, Danse; No. 3, La Fête
   USSR. Radio—Ginsburg (*USSR.* 16462/3)

Scènes pittoresques   (Orch. Suite No. 4)   1874
1. Marche   2. Air de ballet
3. Angelus   4. Fête bohème
   Paris Cons.—Wolff   ♯ **D.LXT 5100**
(*above*)   (♯ Lon.LL 1298)
   Lamoureux—Fournet   ♯ **Phi.N 00190L**
(*above*) (n.n., ♯ Phi.S 04010L)   (♯ Epic.LC 3053)
   Pasdeloup—Lindenberg   ♯ **Od.ODX 119**
(*above*)
   A.B.C. Sydney Sym.—Goossens   ♭ **G.DB 9781/2**
(4ss)   (♭ G.ED 1225/6: in ♯ *OBLP 7501*)
   Paris Opéra-Comique—Cluytens   ♯ **Pat.DTX 159**
(*above*)

. . . No. 3 — ARR. ORGAN
   R. Ellsasser (in ♯ MGM.E 3120)
   J. Perceval (ArgOd. 66027)

III. SONGS

COLLECTION

Pensée d'automne (Silvestre)	(b)	
Élégie (Gallet)	(a)	
Crépuscule (Silvestre)	(c)	
Noël païen (Silvestre)	(a)	
Nuit d'Espagne (Gallet)	(b)	
Souvenir de Venise (de Musset)	(a)	♭ *Plé. P 45138*
Ouvre tes yeux bleus (Poème d'amour, No. 3—Robique)	(b)	
Chant provençal (Carré)	(a)	
Les Alcyons (Autran)	(c)	
Sérénade du passant (Coppée)	(a)	
Sonnet matinal (Silvestre)	(b)	
Si tu veux, Mignon (Boyer)	(a)	♭ *Plé.P 45139*

   R. Doria (S), F. Gatto (T), S. Couderc (M-S),
H. Cox, S. Gouat, J. Allain (pf.)
[(a) by Doria, (b) by Gatto, (c) by Couderc]
(also announced, but not issued, as ♯ Plé.P 3070)

À Colombine   (*Sérénade d'Arlequin*)   (Gallet)
   C. Devos (T), G. Lecompte (pf.)   **Pat.PDT 283**
(*Bizet, Gounod, Lalo*)   (♭ D 111)

(Les) Âmes   (P. Demonth)
   M. Santreuil (S), Y. M. Josse (pf.)   V♯ *POc.A 02*
(*Hahn & Saint-Saëns*)

☆ = Re-issue of a recording to be found in previous volumes.

Crépuscule (Sylvestre)
(No. 5 of *Poème Pastorale, 1874*)
M. Harrell (B), B. Smith (pf.) in ♯ *Rem. 199-140*

Élégie (Gallet)
(based on the *Invocation* from *Les Erinnyes*) (with vlc. obbligato)
E. Arizmendi (S) & orch.   *ArgOd. 57019*
(*Manon—Adieu notre petite table*)   (♭ *BSOA 4000*)
M. Langdon (Bs), J. Lee (pf.)
in ♯ *Queens.LPR 21*
(*Balfe, Britten, etc.*)
L. Pastor (S)   ♭ *Pat.EG 147*
(*Rimsky, d'Hardelot, Ponce*)
☆ R. Stevens (M-S), M. Elman (vln.) & pf.
(BrzV. 886-5011)
G. Thill (T) (in ♯ C.FHX 5012; Angel.C 33001)
R. Crooks (T) & orch. (in ♯ Cam.CAL 128: ♭ CAE 120)
ℍ F. Chaliapin (Bs, *Russ*) (in ♯ Sca. 807*;
in ♯ Cum.CPR 333*)
E. Caruso (T) (in ♯ G.FKLP 7001*: QKLP 501*)
— ARR. VLC. & PF. A. Navarra & J. Dussol (in ♯ Od.OD 1014)
— ARR. ORGAN
R. Ellsasser (in ♯ MGM.E 198: ♭ set X 198)
C. Cronham (*Mjr. 5126*)

Marquise (Sylvestre)
ℍ V. Maurel (B) (in ♯ Sca. 822*)

Pensée d'automne (A. Silvestre)
P. Fleta (T) & orch.   in ♯ *Pat.DT 1012*
(*Paladilhe, Tosti, etc.*)
☆ G. Thill (T) (in ♯ C.FHX 5012; Angel.C 33001)

Sérénade du passant (Fr. Coppée)
S. Onegin (A)   V♯ *IRCC. 7003*
(*Wolf, Schubert, etc.*)

Si tu veux, Mignon (Boyer)
M. Sénéchal (T), J. Bonneau (pf.)
in ♯ *Phi.N 00681R*
(*Bizet, Lalo, Chausson, etc.*)
☆ N. Eddy (B) (in ♯ Phi.S 06613R)

FOLK-SONG ARRANGEMENT
Ma Lisette ℍ E. Calvé (S) (AF.AGSB 46*)

MATCHAVARIANI, Alexei Davidovich
(b. 1912)

Concerto, vln. & orch. 1950
M. Vaiman & Moscow Radio—Matchavariani
♯ *Csm.CRLP 172*
(*Sibelius*)   (2ss, ♯ USSR.D 0536/7)
[Allegro vivo only on USSR. 019211/2]
M. Yashvili & Youth Sym.—Anosov
(2ss)   ♯ *USSR.D 1726/7*

MATIEGKA, M. Wenzel (1773-1820)

Notturno, Op. 21 fl., vla. & guitar 1807
— ARR. FL., VLA., VLC., GUITAR Schubert: *q.v.*
(*Quartet*)

MATTEIS, Nicola (fl. late XVIIth Cent.)

Prelude, D major *c.* 1670 recorder & cont.
C. Dolmetsch & J. Saxby (hpsi.) ♯ *D.LXT 2943*
(† Recorder & hpsi. recital)   (♯ Lon.LL 1026)

Caro volto pallidetto
O. Moscucci (S), V. Vitali (pf.)   ♭ *C.SEDQ 503*
(*Monteverdi, Pergolesi*)

MATTEO da Perugia (fl. XVth Cent.)

SEE: † ANTHOLOGIE SONORE

MAUDUIT, Jacques (1557-1627)

CHANSONS (Baïf) 1586
À la fontaine
Si d'une petite œillade
☆ E. Passani Cho. (in † ♯ HS.AS 6)
En paradis je me pense voir
Stanford Univ. Cho.—Schmidt   ♯ *ML. 7022*
(† Madrigals & Motets)
Vous me tuez si doucement
N. Boulanger Ensemble   ♯ *B.AXTL 1048*
(† Fr. Renaissance Music) (♯ D.FAT 263102;
AmD.DL 9629)
Paris Ens.—Jouve   ♯ *LT. MEL 94007*
(† French Madrigals)   (V♯ Sel.LLA 1079)
M. Rollin Ens.   ♯ *CND. 9*
(† La Musique et la Poésie)
Psalm 42: Juge le droit de ma cause 1586
☆ E. Passani Cho. (in † ♯ HS.AS 6)

MAXWELL, Michael

Intro. & Allegro pf. & orch.
J. Hatto & London Classical—Dennington
V♯ *CA.MPO 5033*

MAZUEL, Michel (*c.* 1625-1676)

SEE: † ANTHOLOGIE SONORE (♯ AS. 3004LD)

MECK, Joseph (fl. *c.* 1730)

SEE: J. G. WALTHER (Concerto)

MÉHUL, Etienne Henri (1763-1817)

(Le) Chant du départ (Chénier) — ARRS.
Garde Républicaine Band—Brun
in ♯ *C.FCX 190*
(also in ♯ Phi.P 76120R)   (♯ Angel. 35051)
French Navy Band—Maillot[1]
in ♯ *Sel. 270.C.056*
March of the Republic (probably the above)
Brass Orch.—Stieger (*Qual.MO 458*)
OPERAS
(Le) JEUNE HENRI 2 Acts 1797
TIMOLÉON 1794
(Le) TRÉSOR SUPPOSÉ 1 Act 1802
Overtures
Royal Phil.—Beecham   ♯ *AmC.ML 5029*
(*Beethoven, Brahms, Boccherini*)
(Le) JEUNE HENRI 2 Acts 1797
Ouverture de chasse — ARR. HORNS
Le Cercle Dampierre et Bien-Allée de Paris
—Morice   ♭ *Od. 7MO 1025*
JOSEPH 3 Acts 1807
Champs paternels T Act I
ℍ F. Ansseau (AF.AGSB 82*; o.n. G.DB 482*)
J. McCormack (in ♯ Vic. set LCT 6701*)
Ouverture pour les Ballets de Paris
(MS., Bibliothèque nationale, Paris)
Paris Cons.—Tzipine[2]   in ♯ *C.FCX 384S*
(*Paisiello*)
Symphony No. 1, G minor *c.* 1809
Berlin Radio Sym.—Kleinert   ♯ *Ura. 7109*
(*Mozart*)   (♯ MTW. 540)

MEISSEN, Heinrich von (d. 1318)

SEE: † HISTORY OF MUSIC IN SOUND (15)

---

[1] Arr. Pillevestre.   [2] Available only as part of a *de luxe* Limited Edition.

MENASCE, Jacques de (b. 1905)

Concerto No. 2   pf. & orch.   1938-9
Divertimento   orch.
Petite Suite   orch.
   J. de Menasce (pf.) & Vienna State Op.—Appia
                    ♯ **Van.VRS 442**

MENDELSSOHN, Alfréd (b. 1910)

(The) Downfall of Doftanea   Sym. poem, orch.
   Berlin Radio—Kleinert   ♯ **Ura. 7114**
   (F. Mendelssohn & Beethoven)   (♯ MTW. 559)

Suite   vlc. & pf.
   ... **Andante**   V. Orloff & M. Fotino (Pop. 5047)

MENDELSSOHN-BARTHOLDY,
Felix von (1809-1847)

CLASSIFIED: I. Piano & Organ   II. Chamber Music
            III. Orchestral   IV. Stage Music
            V. Songs & Partsongs   VI. Choral
            VII. Miscellaneous

I. PIANO & ORGAN
(for pf. solo unless otherwise stated)

COLLECTIONS

   Prelude & Fugue, E minor, Op. 35, No. 1
   Rondo capriccioso, E major, Op. 14 (with Andante)
   (17) Variations sérieuses, D minor, Op. 54
   (3) Études, Op. 104b
     1. B flat minor;   2. F major;   3. A minor
   (2) Clavierstücke, No Op. No.
     1. Andante cantabile, B flat major
     2. Presto agitato, G minor
   Scherzo a capriccio, F sharp minor
   Perpetuum mobile, C major, Op. 119
   R. Gianoli   ♯ **Nix.WLP 5329**
                    (♯ West.WL 5329)

   Rondo capriccioso, E major, Op. 14 (with Andante) (b)
   Songs without Words
     No. 1, E major, Op. 19, No. 1   (a, b)
     No. 2, A minor, Op. 19, No. 2
   (7) Characteristic Pieces, Op. 7
     ... No. 4, A major   (a, b)
   (17) Variations sérieuses, D minor, Op. 54
   C. de Groot   ♯ *Phi.N 00621R*
   [marked (a) also on *N 12063H;* (b) also on ♭ *N 402004E*]

   Prelude & Fugue, E minor, Op. 35, No. 1
   Scherzo, E minor, Op. 16, No. 2
   Rondo capriccioso, E major, Op. 14   (& Andante)
   J. Katchen   ♯ **D.LXT 2838**
   (Auf Flügeln des Gesanges; & Liszt)   (♯ Lon.LL 824)

Allegro brillant, A major, Op. 92   pf. 4 hands
   K. U. & H. Schnabel   ♯ **SPA. 50**
   (below; & Weber)
   C. Norwood & E. Hancock   in ♯ **Lyr.LL 55**
   ☆ P. Luboshutz & G. Nemenoff (in ♯ Cam.CAL 206)

Capriccio, F sharp minor, Op 5
   D. Barenboim   ♭ *EPhi.NBE 11013*
   (Mozart, Brahms)   (♭ *Phi.N 425008E*)

(3) CAPRICES, Op. 33
No. 3, B flat major
   ☆ D. Winand-Mendelssohn (in ♯ *AmD.DL 4080;*
                       ♯ *Pol. 16118)*

(6) CHILDREN'S PIECES, Op. 72
   (Kinderstücke; Christmas Pieces)
COMPLETE RECORDING
   M. Pressler   ♯ **MGM.E 3204**
   (Tchaikovsky)

(6) PRELUDES & FUGUES, Op. 35
No. 1, E minor
... Prelude only
   E. Burton   in ♯ **CEd.CE 1024**

No. 5, F minor
   J. Dacosta   **Pat.PDT 282**
                      (♭ *D 107*)
Prelude (unspec.)   M. Schwalb   in ♯ **Roy. 1447**

(3) PRELUDES & FUGUES, Op. 37   organ
   No. 1, C minor;   No. 2, G major;   No. 3, D minor
COMPLETE RECORDING
   A. Richardson   ♯ **Argo.RG 30**
   (Sonatas) [Royal Festival Hall org., London]

   ... **No. 1, only**
   ☆ J. Eggington   *(below)*   ♯ **LOL.OL 50013**

Rondo capriccioso, E major, Op. 14 (with Andante)
   A. Brailowsky   ♯ **Vic.LM 1918**
   (Schubert, Schumann, Weber)
   A. Dorfmann   in ♯ **Vic.LM 1758**
   (Schumann, etc.)   (in ♭ set *WDM 1758:* ♭ *ERA 238*)
   M. Pressler   ♯ **MGM.E 3029**
   (below & Schumann)

   ☆ C. Arrau (C.LOX 829: ♭ *SEL 1523*)
   V. Schiøler (♭ *Mer.EP 1-5019;* ♭ *FMer.MEP 14524*)
   D. Winand-Mendelssohn (in ♯ *AmD.DL 4080;*
                       ♯ *Pol. 16118)*

— ARR. PF. & ORCH.
   W. Stech & Hamburg State Phil.—Wal-Berg
                      ♯ *DT.TM 68046*
   (Weber: Aufforderung zum Tanz)   (♯ *T.TW 30020*)

— ARR. 2 PFS.   J. Enos[1] (in ♯ **HIFI.R 201**)

Scherzo, E minor, Op. 16, No. 2
   (*"Fantasy"* or *"Capriccio"*)
   B. Webster   in ♯ **Persp.PR 2**
   E. Gilels *(USSR. 10662)*

— ARR.   2 PFS.
   E. Bartlett & R. Robertson   in ♯ **MGM.E 3150**
                      (♭ *set X 273*)

— ARR. ORGAN
   R. Foort (in ♯ *Nix.SLPY 148;* ♯ *SOT. 1053*)

(6) SONATAS, Op. 65   organ
   No. 1, F minor   No. 4, B flat major
   No. 2, C minor   No. 5, D major
   No. 3, A major   No. 6, D minor
COMPLETE RECORDING
   A. Richardson   ♯ **Argo.RG 30/31**
   (3ss—above) [Royal Festival Hall organ, London]

   ... **Nos. 1, 3, 6**
   ☆ J. Eggington   *(above)*   ♯ **LOL.OL 50013**

No. 1, F minor
... 2nd movt., Adagio only
   R. Ellsasser   ♯ *CM. 3*
   (Bach)   (♯ *Attn.LPV 106;* ♯ *Eli.LPE 106*)

No. 2, C minor
   R. Ellsasser   ♯ **MGM.E 3007**
   (Schumann)
   [org. of Hammond Museum, Gloucester, Mass.]
   ☆ F. Asma (in ♯ *Phi.S 04009L*)

No. 6, D minor
   ☆ A. Schweitzer   ♯ **C.CX 1084**
   (Bach)   (♯ *Phi.A 01111L*)
... 1st movt. (Variations on *Vater unser*)
   ☆ F. Asma (in ♯ *Phi.S 06017R*)
... 2nd movt., Andante   Anon. Artist (in ♯ *FSM. 402*)

SONGS WITHOUT WORDS
COMPLETE RECORDING: G. Doyen
VOL. I: Nos. 1-15: Opp. 19, 30, 38 (Nos. 1, 2, 3)
                         ♯ **West.WL 5192**
VOL. II: Nos. 16-30: Opp. 38 (Nos. 4, 5, 6) 53, 62
                         ♯ **West.WL 5246**
VOL. III: Nos. 31-49: Opp. 67, 85, 102   ♯ **West.WL 5279**
                         (♯ *Véga. C30.A 26/8*)
COLLECTIONS
   No. 12, F sharp minor, Op. 30, No. 6
   No. 29, A minor, Op. 62, No. 5
     (Venetian Gondola Songs 2 & 3)[2]
   No. 30, A major, Op. 62, No. 6   *(Spring Song)* ▽
   ☆ G. Puchelt   in ♯ *G.WDLP 1503*
   (Beethoven, Haydn, Schubert, Weber)

(continued on next page)

---

[1] Playing both parts.   [2] Apparently only one of these is in the re-issue; which is not specified.

SONGS WITHOUT WORDS (*continued*)

No. 19, A flat major, Op. 53, No. 1
No. 34, C major, Op. 67, No. 4
No. 36, E major, Op. 67, No. 6

G. Werschenska   Tono.A 192

No. 1, E major, Op. 19, No. 1
No. 3, A major, Op. 19, No. 3
No. 30, A major, Op. 62, No. 6
No. 34, C major, Op. 67, No. 4

I. Loveridge   C.DX 1880

No. 26, B flat major, Op. 72, No. 2
No. 30 & No. 34

M. v. Doren   in ‡ Chan.MVDP 1
(*above*)

Nos. 1, 26 & 34
M. v. Doren   in ‡ MSB. 60040
(This purports to be the same recording as the above, but
listings differ)

Nos. 24, 30; No. 35, B major, Op. 67, Nos. 5 & 40
☆ V. Horowitz (in ‡ G.FALP 280: ♭ 7RF 233;
Nos. 25 & 25 only on ♭ Vic.ERA 59)

Nos. 9, 12, 28, 36, 45 — ARR. ORCH. Irving "*Little Suite*"
Westminster Light—Bridgewater   ‡ Nix.WLP 6805
(*below; & Raff*)   (‡ West.WL 4005)

Nos. 20, 22, 25, 30 — ARR. TPT.
T. Dokshitser (*USSRM.D 001267/8*)

No. 1, E major, Op. 19 (*Sweet Remembrance*)
— ARR. VLN. & PF. Heifetz
☆ J. Heifetz & E. Bay (♭ G.7RF/RQ 267: 7EB/EBW 6001:
in ‡ FALP 248)
J. Dumont (*ArgPat.FC 5*)

No. 2, A minor, Op. 19, No. 2
J. Flier (*below; & Liszt*)   USSRM.D 001261

No. 6, G minor, Op. 19, No. 6
(*Venetian Gondola Song No. 1*)
— ARR. GUITAR Segovia
☆ A. Segovia (in † ‡ D.UAT 273141)

No. 9, E major, Op. 30, No. 3 (*Consolation*)
— ARR. ORGAN: C. Cronham (*Mjr. 5119*)

No. 14, C minor, Op. 38, No. 2 (*Lost Happiness*)
— ARR. VLC. & PF. S. Knushevitzky & pf. (*USSR. 22519*)

No. 18, A flat, Op. 38, No. 6 (*Duetto*)
M. Schwalb   in ‡ Roy. 1474

No. 20, E flat, Op. 53, No. 2 (*The Fleecy Cloud*)
— ARR. VLC. & PF. S. Knushevitzky & pf. (*USSR. 22520*)

No. 25, G major, Op. 62, No. 1 (*May Breezes*)
M. Jonas   in ‡ AmC.ML 4622
A. Dorfmann   in ‡ Vic.LM 1758
(in ♭ set WDM 1758: ♭ ERA 238)

No. 30, A major, Op. 62, No. 6 (*Spring Song*)
W. Gieseking   C.LB 139
(*Sinding: Rustle of Spring*)   (LW 64: GQ 7259)
A. S. Rasmussen   Tono.K 8098
(*Sinding: Rustle of Spring*)   (♭ EP 45052, d.c.)
— ARR. ORCH.
Philharmonia—Malko   G.C 4246
(*No. 34*) (S 10618: ♭ 7P 148; in ‡ BB.LBC 1080)
☆ Paris Opéra—Cloëz (♭ Od.7AO 2006)
— ARR. VLN. & PF. ☆ J. Dumont (*ArgPat.FC 5*)
— ARR. VLC. & PF. A. Vlasov (*USSR. 22532*)

No. 34, C major, Op. 67, No. 4
(*Bee's Wedding or Spinning Song*)
A. Dorfmann   in ‡ Vic.LM 1758
(in ♭ set WDM 1758: ♭ ERA 238)
J. Hofmann[1]   in ‡ AmC.ML 4929
(*Liszt, Moszkowski, Chopin, etc.*)
C. de Groot   in ‡ Phi.N 00632R
(*Pierné, Poulenc, Rachmaninoff, etc.*)
☆ A. Rubinstein (♭ G.7EB 6009: 7RQ 159)
S. Rachmaninoff (in ‡ Vic.LCT 1136)
— ARR. VLC. & PF.
☆ G. Cassadó & O. Schulhof (in ‡ Rem. 199-128)
— ARR. PF. & ORCH.
W. Stech & Hamburg State Phil.—Wal-Berg
(in ‡ T.TW 30027)
— ARR. ORCH.
Philharmonia—Malko   G.C 4246
(*No. 30*)   (S 10618: ♭ 7P 148; in ‡ BB.LBC 1080)

No. 46, G minor, Op. 102, No. 4
M. Jonas   in ‡ AmC.ML 4624
J. Flier   USSRM.D 001261
(*No. 2, & Liszt*)

Barcarolle (unspec.)
A. d'Arco   in Plé.P 105

A flat major (unspec.)
V. Gheorghiu (*Liszt: Paganini Étude No. 5*) Pop. 5003

E major (unspec.)
V. Gheorghiu (*Liszt: Paganini Étude No. 3*) Pop. 5007

Variations, B flat major, Op. 83a pf. 4 hands 1841
K. U. & H. Schnabel   in ‡ SPA. 50
(*above; & Weber*)
C. Norwood & E. Hancock in ‡ Lyr.LL 55
(*above; & Beethoven*)

(17) Variations sérieuses, D minor, Op. 54 1841
A. Cortot (n.v.)   in JpV. set JAS 270
M. Pressler   ‡ MGM.E 3029
(*above & Schumann*)
☆ V. Horowitz   ‡ G.FALP 280
(*Songs without words*) (in ‡ Vic.LM 9021: ♭ ERA 103)
☆ F. Pelleg   ‡ MMS. 30
(*Pf. Concerto No. 1*) (& ‡ Clc. 6157)
☆ D. Winand-Mendelssohn (‡ AmD.DL 4080 &
‡ Pol. 16118)

II. CHAMBER MUSIC

Octet, E flat major, Op. 20 4 vlns., 2 vlas., 2 vlcs.
Vienna Octet   ‡ D.LXT 2870
(2ss)   (‡ Lon.LL 859)
Stradivari Octet   ‡ Strad.STR 615
(*Qtt. No. 3*) [Announced but apparently not issued]
N.B.C. Sym.—Toscanini[2] ‡ Vic.LM 1869
(*Schubert*)

... Scherzo only
☆ Pro Musica Cha. Ens.(♭ AmVox.VIP 45350)
— — ARR. ORCH. Mendelssohn
Westminster Light—Bridgewater
in ‡ Nix.WLP 6805
(*above & below*)   (in ‡ West.WL 4005)
☆ Hallé—Barbirolli (G.DB 4295)

QUARTETS, pf. & str.
No. 2, F minor, Op. 2 1823
☆ A. Balsam & Guilet Trio (‡ Clc. 6230)
No. 3, B minor, Op. 3 1825
F. Pelleg & Winterthur Trio   ‡ CHS.H 5
(*Serenade & Allegro gioioso, pf. & orch.*)

QUARTETS, Strings
No. 1, E flat major, Op. 12 1829
Curtis Qtt.   ‡ Nix.WLP 5220
(*No. 3*)   (‡ West.WL 5220)
☆ Budapest Qtt. (JpV.SD 3084/6, set JAS 259)
Fine Arts Qtt. (‡ Clc. 6284; Canzonetta only on
♭ Mer.EP 1-5066; FMer.MEP 14517
... 2nd movt. (Canzonetta) only
Oistrakh Qtt. (USSR. 018328/9)
— — ARR. GUITAR Segovia
A. Segovia (in † ‡ B.AXTL 1069; AmD.DL 9751)

No. 2, A minor, Op. 13 1827
New Music Qtt. (*No. 5*)   ‡ AmC.ML 4921

No. 3, D major, Op. 44, No. 1 1838
Curtis Qtt.   ‡ Nix.WLP 5220
(*No. 1*)   (‡ West.WL 5220)
Stradivari Qtt.   ‡ Strad.STR 615
(*Octet*) [Announced but apparently not issued]

No. 4, E minor, Op. 44, No. 2 1837
Endres Qtt. (*No. 5*)   ‡ Strad.STR 615
[See note under No. 3 *above*, as to earlier version of this
number]

... Scherzo, only
American Arts Qtt.   ‡ BB.LBC 1086
(*Rachmaninoff, Turina, etc.*)
Pessina Qtt.[3]   ArgOd. 66046
(in ‡ LDC 510)

---

[1] Metropolitan Op. House recital, November 1937.
[2] From broadcast performance March 1947. Played in a String orchestra version.
[3] Listed merely as *Scherzo*; might equally well be from another Quartet, or other work.

No. 5, E flat major, Op. 44, No. 3   1838
    Endres Qtt.   (*No. 4*)   # *Strad.STR 615*
    New Music Qtt.   (*No. 2*)   # *AmC.ML 4921*

4 Pieces, Op. 81   str.
1. Andante, E major   2. Scherzo, A minor
3. Capriccio, E minor   4. Fugue, E flat major
    A. Winograd Str. Orch.   # *MGM.E 3295*
    (*Dvořák & Wolf*)

... No. 3 only
    Amadeus Qtt.   # *G.ALP 1337*
    (*Brahms & Schubert*)

QUINTETS, 2 vlns, 2 vlas., vlc.
No. 1, A major, Op. 18   1831
No. 2, B flat major, Op. 87   1845
    Pascal Qtt. & W. Gerhard (vla.)
                 # *CHS.CHS 1172*
                       (# *Clc. 6239*)

Sextet, D major, Op. 110
    pf., vln., 2 vlas., vlc. & cbs.
    M. Pressler, Members of Guilet Qtt., N.
    Gordon (vla.), P. Sklar (cbs.)   # *P.PMD 1031*
                       (# *MGM.E 3107*)

SONATAS, vln. & pf.
F major   1838
    Y. Menuhin & G. Moore   # *G.ALP 1085*
    (*Vln. Concerto, D minor*) (# FALP 300; # ArgA.LPC 11546)
    (*Saint-Saëns*, on # Vic.LHMV 1071)

F minor, Op. 4   1825
    ☆ D. Guilet & A. Balsam (# Clc. 6230)

SONATAS, vlc. & pf.
No. 1, B flat major, Op. 45   1838
    ☆ N. & J. Graudan   (*No. 2*)   # *AmVox.PL 8500*

No. 2, D major, Op. 58   1843
    R. Albin & C. Helffer   # *DT.LGX 66015*
    (*Schubert*)   (# *T.LE 6510*)
    ☆ N. & J. Graudan   (*No. 1*)   # *AmVox.PL 8500*

Song without words, D major, Op. 109   vlc. & pf.
— ARR. VLA. & PF.
    E. & L. Wallfisch   # *Od.ODX 140*
    (*Schubert & Schumann*)

TRIOS, pf., vln. & vlc.
No. 1, D minor, Op. 49   1839
    Trio di Bolzano   # *E. & AmVox.PL 9160*
    (*No. 2*)
    Classic Trio   (*No. 2*)   # *CEd.CE 1034*
    Santoliquido Trio   # *Pol. 16107*
    ☆ A. Rubinstein, J. Heifetz & G. Piatigorsky
                       (# G.QALP 10029)
    For Practice—recorded with one instrument missing in
    turn   # CEd.MMO 51/3
    (*No. 2—in each case*)

... 1st movt. only
    L. Oborin, D. Oistrakh, S. Knushevitsky *USSR. 18776/8*
    (3ss—*Borodin: Qtt. movt.*)

... 3rd movt., Scherzo — ARR. VLN. & PF.   Heifetz
    ☆ J. Heifetz & E. Bay (in # G.ALP 1206: FALP 248;
               ♭ Vic.ERA 214; FV.A 95225)

No. 2, C minor, Op. 66   1845
    Classic Trio   (*No. 1*)   # *CEd.CE 1034*
    Trio di Bolzano   # *E. & AmVox.PL 9160*
    (*No. 1*)
    Oistrakh Trio   # *USSR.D 01750/1*
    For practice—recorded with one instrument missing in
    turn   # CEd.MMO 51/3
    (*No. 1—in each case*)

III. ORCHESTRAL

Calm Sea and Prosperous Voyage, Overture, Op. 27
    Vienna Phil.—Schuricht   # *D.LXT 2961*
    (*below*)   (# *Lon.LL 1048*)
    Israel Phil.—Kletzki   # *C.CX 1219*
    (*below*)   (# FCX 381; Angel. 35183)

Berlin Phil.—Lehmann   # *Pol. 17044*
(*below*)
☆ Austrian Sym.—Paulmüller (in # Ply. 12-78)

Capriccio brillant, B minor, Op. 22   pf. & orch.
    M. Lympany & Philharmonia—Malko
                       # *G.CLP 1007*
    (*Rachmaninoff: Concerto No. 2*) (# FELP 113: QCLP 12003;
                       # Vic.LHMV 15)
    O. Frugoni & Vienna Pro Musica—Swarowsky
                    # *E. & AmVox.PL 8350*
    (*Concerto, E major, 2 pfs.*)
    P. Katin & L.P.O.—Martinon   # *D.LW 5119*
    (*below*)   (# *Lon.LD 9134*)
    (with *Liszt* on # D.LXT 2932; # Lon.LL 1007)
    T. Nikolayeva & USSR. State—Kondrashin
    (4ss)   *USSR. 21503/6*

CONCERTOS, pf. & orch.
No. 1, G minor, Op. 25   1834
    R. Gianoli & Vienna State Op.—Horvath
    (*No. 2*)   # *West.WN 18043*
    E. Gilels & USSR. State Sym.—Kondrashin
    (*Liszt*)   # *Mon.MWL 308*
    (*Beethoven* on # CHS.CHS 1312;
              Taktakishvili on # Csm.CRLP 191)
    J. Iturbi & Victor Sym.   # *Vic.LM 1734*
    (*Liszt*)   (♭ set WDM 1734; ♭ ItV.A12R 0044)
    A. Dorfmann & Robin Hood Dell—Leinsdorf
                    # *BB.LBC 1043*
    (*Grieg*) (♭ set WBC 1043; ♭ ItV.A12R 0132; FV.A 630263)
    H. Roloff & Berlin Radio—Rucht # *Ura.RS 7-23*
    (*Beethoven*)
    E. Hoff & Berlin Sym.—Rucht   # *Ura. 7149*
    (*Rachmaninoff*)   (# *MTW. 518*)
    Anon. Artists (# Gram. 20122)
    ☆ J. M. Sanromá & Boston Prom.—Fiedler
                    (# Cam.CAL 165)
    F. Pelleg & Winterthur Sym.—Goehr
                  (# Clc. 6157; # MMS. 30)

No. 2, D minor, Op. 40   1837
    R. Gianoli & Vienna State Op.—Horvath
    (*No. 1*)   # *West.WN 18043*
    Anon. Artists (# Gram. 20122)
    ☆ F. Wührer & Vienna Sym.—Moralt (# Clc. 6130)

Concerto, E major, 2 pfs. & orch.   1824
    O. Frugoni & E. Mrazek, Vienna Pro Musica
    —Swarowsky   # *E. & AmVox.PL 8350*
    (*Capriccio brillant*)

Concerto, D minor, vln. & str. orch.   1822
    Y. Menuhin & Philharmonia—Boult
                    # *G.ALP 1085*
    (*Vln. Sonata, F major*) (# FALP 300; # ArgA.LPC 11546)

Concerto, E minor, Op. 64, vln. & orch.   1844
    Z. Francescatti & N.Y.P.S.O.—Mitropoulos
                    # *AmC.ML 4965*
    (*Tchaikovsky*)   (♭ set A 1109)
    N. Milstein & Pittsburgh Sym.—Steinberg
                    # *DCap.CTL 7059*
    (*Bruch*)   (# Cap.P 8243; ACap.CLCX 046)
    A. Campoli & L.P.O.—v. Beinum # *D.LXT 2904*
    (*Bruch*) (n.v.) (# NLK 40103)   (# *Lon.LL 966*)
    G. de Vito & L.S.O.—Sargent   # *G.BLP 1008*
    (2ss)   (# VBLP 807: QBLP 5008: WBLP 1008)
    J. Martzy & Philharmonia—Kletzki
    (*Mozart*)   # *C.CX 1210*
    A. Grumiaux & Vienna Sym.—Moralt
                    # *Phi.A 00750R*
    (2ss)   (*Dvořák: Concerto*, on # Epic.LC 3173)
    I. Gitlis & Vienna Pro Musica—Hollreiser
                    # *E. & AmVox.PL 8840*
    (*Tchaikovsky*)
    H. Wiesbeck & Orch.—Wilhelm   # *MTW. 15*
    (*Tchaikovsky*)   (& 2ss, # ACC.MP 29)
                   (*continued on next page*)

☆ = Re-issue of a recording to be found in previous volumes.

Concerto, E minor, Op. 64, vln. & orch. (*continued*)
F. Lack & N.W. Stadium Concerts—Smallens
‡ **MApp. 92**
(*spoken analysis of the concerto—T. Scherman, J. Tomasow (vln.) & orch.*)

F. Petronio & Belgian Radio—P. Glière
(*Bruch*) ‡ **Mae.OAT 25002**
☆ Y. Menuhin & Berlin Phil.—Furtwängler ‡ G.ALP 1135
(*Beethoven: Romances*) (‡ QALP 10071: FALP 312;
ArgA.LPC 11582)
☆ I. Stern & Philadelphia—Ormandy ‡ C.CX 1071
(*Mozart: Concerto K 216*) (‡ FCX 210: QCX 10042)
☆ F. Kreisler & L.P.O.—Ronald ‡ Vic.LCT 1117
(*Mozart: Concerto, K 218*) (♭ set WCT 1117)
☆ S. Borries & Berlin Phil.—Celibidache ‡ BB.LBC 1049
(*Symphony No. 4*) (o.n. ‡ LBC/♭ WBC 1021)
(♭ set WBC 1049)
☆ J. Heifetz & Royal Phil.—Beecham ‡ Vic.LM 9016
(*Bruch*)
☆ M. Elman & Chicago Sym.—Defauw ‡ Vic.LM 9024
(*Wieniawski*) (‡ ItV.A12R 0116; DV.T 16103)
Anon. Soloist & "Phil"—List (‡ Allo. 3068;
Pac.LDAD 45)
Anon. Soloist & "Nat. Op. Orch." (‡ Gram. 2071)
☆ L. Kaufman & Netherlands Phil.—Ackermann
(‡ Clc. 11001; ‡ ANix.MLPY 7)
W. Schneiderhan & Austrian Sym.—Scherman
(‡ AFest.CFR 30; ‡ Ply. 12-78; ‡ Cum.TCR 259)
J. Szigeti & L.P.O.—Beecham (‡ AmC.ML 2217)
D. Oistrakh & USSR. Sym.—Kondrashin
(‡ USSR.D 1167/8)
... **Andante & Allegro** only — ARR. CORNET & PF.
K. Smith & pf. (*Pax.PR 603*)
— FOR PRACTICE: Recorded with violin part missing, pf. acc.
(‡ CEd.MMO 305)
Lecture by L. Persinger (‡ Per.STR 101)

Fair Melusina, Overture, Op. 32 1833
Vienna Phil.—Schuricht ‡ **D.LXT 2961**
(*above & below*) (‡ Lon.LL 1048)
Linz Sym. in ‡ **Ply. 12-29**
(*Berlioz, Puccini*)
☆ Vienna State Op.—Prohaska (‡ Ama.AVRS 6011)

(The) Hebrides, Overture, Op. 26 1832
Vienna Phil.—Schuricht ‡ **D.LXT 2961**
(*above & below*) (‡ Lon.LL 1048)
(*Ruy Blas* on ‡ D.LW 5193)
N.Y.P.S.O.—Mitropoulos ♭ **EPhi.ABE 10006**
(*Ruy Blas*) (‡ AmC.AL 52: ♭ A 1923; ♭ Phi.A 409012E)
Zürich Tonhalle—Goehr ‡ **MMS. 2005**
(*Midsummer Night's Dream*)
(*Grieg: Pf. Concerto*, ‡ MMS. 123)
Berlin Phil.—v. Kempen ‡ **Phi.S 06054R**
(*Midsummer Night's Dream, Overture*)
Champs-Elysées Theatre—Bour ‡ **Sei. 270.C.064**
(*Midsummer Night's Dream*)
"Philharmonic"—List ‡ **Allo. 3068**
(*Athalie, & Vln. Concerto*) (‡ Pac.LDAD 45)
☆ Boston Pops—Fiedler (in ‡ Vic.LM 9027;
‡ ItV.A12R 0107; G.FMLP 1003;
♭ ItV.A72R 0061, d.c.)
Hallé—Sargent (in ‡ AmC.RL 3072)
Berlin Phil.—Lehmann (‡ Pol. 17044)
Vienna Phil.—Furtwängler (♭ G. 7RQ 102;
ArgV. 66-6024)
L.P.O.—v. Beinum (♭ D. 71019)
R.P.O.—Beecham (♭ AmC. 4-4805)
Philharmonia—Schüchter (C.DWX 5081)
Hallé—Barbirolli (♭ G. 7RQ 3013: 7RW 136)

Rondo brillant, E flat major, Op. 29 pf. & orch.
P. Katin & L.P.O.—Martinon ‡ **D.LW 5119**
(*above*) (‡ Lon.LD 9134)
(*with Liszt* on ‡ D.LXT 2932; ‡ Lon.LL 1007)

Ruy Blas, Overture, Op. 95 1839
Vienna Phil.—Schuricht ‡ **D.LXT 2961**
(*above*) (*Hebrides* on ‡ D.LW 5193) (‡ Lon.LL 1048)
Philharmonia—Kletzki ♭ **C.SEL 1525**
(*Son & Stranger, Overture*) (♭ SEBQ 123; ♭ G. 7ERL1060)
N.Y.P.S.O.—Mitropoulos ♭ **EPhi.ABE 10006**
(*Hebrides*) (‡ AmC.AL 52; ♭ Phi.A 409012E)
B.B.C. Sym.—Sargent **G.DB 21601**
Berlin Phil.—Leitner ♭ **Pol. 30129**
(*Cherubini: Medea, Overture*)

Berlin Radio—Schartner ‡ **Ura. 7114**
(*A. Mendelssohn & Beethoven*) (‡ MTW. 559)
☆ Royal Phil.—Beecham **C.LX 1584**
(2ss) (GQX 11532)
(*J. Strauss: Morgenblätter* on ♭ SEL 1501: SEBQ 105)
☆ San Francisco Sym.—Monteux (G.DB 4323)
Austrian Sym.—Singer (in ‡ Rem. 199-129 &
▽ ‡ 149-48; ‡ Ply. 12-102)
Vienna Radio—Nilius (in ‡ Vien.LPR 1037)
City of Birmingham—Weldon (in ‡ AmC.RL 3091)

Serenade & Allegro gioioso, B minor, Op. 43
pf. & orch.
F. Pelleg & Zürich Tonhalle—Ackermann
‡ **CHS.H 5**
(*Quartet No. 3, pf. & strgs.*)

SYMPHONIES
No. 1, C minor, Op. 11 1824
☆ Stuttgart Phil.—v. Hoogstraten (‡ Clc. 6130)

No. 2, B flat major, Op. 52 1840
SEE Hymn of Praise, Sec. VI, *below*

No. 3, A minor, Op. 56 "Scottish" 1842
L.S.O.—Solti ‡ **D.LXT 2768**
(‡ Lon.LL 708)
Pittsburgh Sym.—Steinberg ‡ **DCap.CTL 7032**
(‡ Cap.P 8192; T.LCE 8192)
A.B.C. Sydney Sym.—Goossens ‡ **G.BLP 1045**
(‡ FBLP 1059: QBLP 5034; BB.LBC 1089)
Israel Phil.—Kletzki ‡ **C.CX 1219**
(*above*) (‡ FCX 381; Angel. 35183)
N.Y.P.S.O.—Mitropoulos ‡ **EPhi.ABL 3082**
(*No. 5*) (‡ AmC.ML 4864; ‡ Phi.A 01174L)
Netherlands Phil.—Goehr ‡ **MMS. 60**
(2ss)
Bamberg Sym.—Leitner (2ss) ‡ **Pol. 18207**
Orch.—Scherman (‡ MApp. n.d.)
USSR. State—Rakhlin (‡ USSR.D 0731/2)
Anon. Orch. (‡ Gram. 2098)
☆ Vienna Sym.—Klemperer (‡ AFest.CFR 12-146)
Saxon State—Kempe (‡ Sup.LPV 213; U. 5209G;
10ss, Eta. 26-C.034/8)

No. 4, A major, Op. 90 "Italian" 1833
N.B.C. Sym.—Toscanini ‡ **G.ALP 1267**
(*No. 5*) (‡ Vic.LM 1851; DV.L 16490;
ItV.A12R 0148; FV.A 630268)
L.S.O.—Krips ‡ **D.LXT 2887**
(*Schumann*) (‡ Lon.LL 930)
Royal Phil.—Beecham ‡ **C.C 1006**
(2ss) (‡ QC 5002)
(*Beethoven: Sym. No. 8* on ‡ AmC.ML 4681;
Schubert: Sym. No. 8 on ‡ C.FCX 236)
Philharmonia—Cantelli ‡ **G.ALP 1325**
(*Schubert: Sym. No. 8*)
Phil. Prom.—Boult ‡ **West.LAB 7008**
Amsterdam—v. Beinum ‡ **Phi.S 06073R**
Rochester Phil.—Leinsdorf ‡ **AmC.RL 3102**
(*Schubert*)
☆ Minneapolis Sym.—Dorati ‡ EMer.MG 50010
(*Mozart*) (‡ FMer.MLP 7507)
☆ Boston Sym.—Koussevitzky ‡ Vic.LM 1797
(*Bruch*) (o.v. ‡ Cam.CAL 146 & in ‡ set CFL 104)
(2ss, ‡ DV.T 16123)
Moscow Radio—Gauk (‡ USSR.D 1560/1)
Orch.—Swarowsky (‡ MTW. 25; ACC.MP 4)
"Philharmonic"—List (‡ Allo. 3069)
"Nat. Op. Orch." (‡ Gram. 2063)
☆ Winterthur Sym.—Dahinden (‡ Clc. 11003)
Hallé—Barbirolli ‡ BB.LBC 1049: ♭ set WBC 1049;
o.n. ‡ LBC/♭ WBC 1021)

No. 5, D major, Op. 107 "Reformation" 1830
N.B.C. Sym.—Toscanini ‡ **G.ALP 1267**
(*No. 4*) (‡ Vic.LM 1851; DV.L 16490;
ItV.A12R 0148; FV.A 630268)
Los Angeles Phil.—Wallenstein ‡ **B.AXTL 1058**
(*Beethoven*) (‡ D.UAT 273546; AmD.DL 9726)
(2ss, ‡ Pol.16110)
N.Y.P.S.O.—Mitropoulos ‡ **EPhi.ABL 3082**
(*No. 3*) (‡ AmC.ML 4864; ‡ Phi.A 01174L)
☆ Vienna State Op.—Prohaska (‡ Ama.AVRS 6011)
C.B.S. Sym.—Barlow (‡ AmC.RL 3024)

---

‡ = Long-playing, 33⅓ r.p.m. ♭ = 45 r.p.m. ♮ = Auto. couplings, 78 r.p.m.

4. STAGE MUSIC

ATHALIE, Op. 74   Inc. Music (Racine)   1834-5
Overture
"Philharmonic"—List   **♯ Allo. 3068**
(Hebrides & Vln. Concerto)   *(♯ Pac.LDAD 45)*
War March of the Priests
Hamburg Philharmonia—H-J. Walther
             MSB. 78116
(Gounod: Reine de Saba, Cortège)
 ☆ Philharmonia—Weldon (in ♯ AmC.RL 3092)
   Boston Prom.—Fiedler (♭ *Cam.CAE 142*)

(A) MIDSUMMER NIGHT'S DREAM,
     Opp. 21 & 61   Inc. Music
COMPLETE RECORDING of the Play with
   Mendelssohn's music
The Old Vic. Company, P. Brockless & P. Howard (S) as
   Fairies, Cho. & B.B.C. Sym.—Sargent   ♯ *G.ALP 1262/4*
                   (♯ Vic. set LM 6115)
[Nos. 3, 5 & 9 also on ♭ Vic.LM 1863; Nos. 7, 9, 11 also
   in ♭ Vic. set ERB 46; No. 9 only on ♭ Vic.ERA 236]

COLLECTIONS
Overture, Op. 21
No. 1, Scherzo   No. 9, Wedding March
No. 3, Ye spotted snakes 2 S & cho. *(Ger)*
No. 5, Intermezzo   No. 11, Dance of the Clowns
No. 7, Nocturne   No. 12, Finale
A. Cole (S), E. McLoughlin (S), Cho. &
   Philharmonia—Kletzki   **♯ C.CX 1174**
(Eng)   (♯ FCX 366; Angel. 35146)
[Nos. 1 & 5 only on C.LX 1615;
         Nos. 7, 9, 11 on ♭ *SEL 1534*]
 ☆ Soloists & Berlin Phil.—Fricsay   **♯ HP.DGM 18001**
   [includes No. 2b, Fairies' March]

Overture & Nos. 1, 7, 9
Hamburg Philharmonia—H-J. Walther
             MSB. 78025/8
(7ss—Bolzoni: Minuet)
(Corelli & Prokofiev on ♯ MGM.E 3087)
Philharmonia—Kubelik   **♯ G.ALP 1049**
(Smetana: Bartered Bride, excpt.) (♯ VALP 516:
(No. 1 is ☆)   QALP 10027: FALP 304)
[Overture & No. 7 only, on DB 21482/3; No. 7 only
   on ♭ *7ER 5015: 7ERQ 116*]

Overture & Nos. 1 & 7
Amsterdam—v. Beinum   **♯ D.LXT 2770**
(Schubert: Rosamunde)   (♯ Lon.LL 622)
[Overture only on ♯ *D.LW 5046; Lon.LD 9059*]
Orch.—Swarowsky   **♯ MTW. 21**
(Tchaikowsky)

Overture & Nos. 1, 5, 7, 9, 12
 ☆ N.B.C. Sym.—Toscanini   **♯ G.FALP 229**
(Beethoven)   (QALP 229)

Overture & Nos. 1, 5, 7, 9
 ☆ Cleveland Sym.—Rodzinski   **♯ AmC.RL 3047**
(Beethoven: Symphony No. 1)
 ☆ N.Y.P.S.O.—Szell (♯ *C.FC 1019*)
   Robin Hood Dell—Reiner (♯ ItV.A12R 0025;
         Nos. 1, 5, & 7 on ♭ DV. 26025)

Overture & Nos. 5, 7, 9, 11[1]
Netherlands Phil.—Goehr   **♯ MMS. 2005**
(Hebrides Overture)   (& 2ss, ♯ *MMS. 125*)

Overture & Nos. 1, 7, 9
Moscow Radio—Golovanov   **♯ USSR.D 987/8**
(2ss)   (Nos. 1 & 9 also on *USSR 21812/3*)
"Philharmonic"—List   **♯ Allo. 3069**
(Symphony No. 4)

Overture & Nos. 1 & 7
Champs-Elysées Theatre—Bour   **♯ Sel. 270.C.064**
(Hebrides Overture)
Berlin Sym.—List   in ♯ *Roy. 1374*

Overture & Nos. 1, 7, 9, 11[2]
 ☆ Austrian Sym.—Brown (♯ Cum.CR 303;
     AFest.CFR 10-338; ♭ Rem.REP 14; & with
       commentary by S. Spaeth on ♯ Rem. 4)

Overture, only
Lamoureux—v. Kempen   **♯ Phi.S 06054R**
(Hebrides)
 ☆ Vienna State Op.—Scherchen (in ♯ Sup.LPV 213)
   Vienna Sym.—Krauss (♭ *AmVox.VIP 45380*)

No. 1, Scherzo
   Boston Orch. Soc.—Page
     (in ♯ Nix.SLPY 801; ♯ SOT. 2064 & in ♯ 10646)
 ☆ Berlin Phil.—Fricsay (♭ *Pol. 30001*)
   Vienna Sym.—Krauss (♭ *AmVox.VIP 45350*)
   Austrian Sym.—Brown (in ♯ Rem. 199-119 &
          ♯ Ply. 12-56, 12-79, 12-40, 12-60)
   Col. Sym.—Rodzinski (♭ AmC.A 1560;
               in ♯ Phi.S 04601L)
   N.Y.P.S.O.—Walter (♭ *AmC.A 1577*)
— ARR. PF.   Schiøler
 ☆ V. Schiøler (♭ *FMer.MEP 14524; ♭ Mer.EP 1-5019*)

No. 2b, Fairies' March
 ▽ Leighton Lucas Orch. (EMI.EPX 24)

No. 3, Ye spotted snakes   2 S & Female cho.
   H. Wallner, H. Gröger & Vienna Boys' Cho.
     —Kühbacher (pf.)   in ♯ *EPhi.NBR 6024*
(Reger, Schubert, Schumann, etc.)   (♯ Phi.N 00726R)

No. 5, Intermezzo
 ☆ Vienna Sym.—Krauss (♭ *AmVox.VIP 45350*)

No. 7, Nocturne
 ☆ Vienna Sym.—Krauss (♭ *AmVox.VIP 45320*)
   Berlin Phil.—Fricsay (♭ *AmD.ED 3520*)
   Austrian Sym.—Brown (in ♯ Ply. 12-89 & 12-91)
 ▽ L. Lucas Orch. (EMI.EPX 24)
— ARR. ORGAN: R. Ellsasser (in ♯ MGM.E 3127)

No. 9, Wedding March
Victor Sym.—Reiner   ♭ *Vic.ERA 185*
(Wagner)   (♭ FV.A 95216)
   Belgian Radio—P. Glière (in ♯ Mae.OAT 25001)
   USSR. State—Melik-Pasheyev (USSR. 6943/4)
   A. Sciascia Orch. (Fnt. 14319: in ♯ LP 310)
 ☆ Vienna Sym.—Krauss (♭ *AmVox.VIP 45320*)
   Berlin Phil.—Fricsay (♭ *AmD.ED 3520: ♭ Pol.30001, d.c.*)
   Austrian Sym.—Brown (in ♯ Ply. 12-78)
— ARR. ORGAN
   R. Ellsasser (in ♭ *MGM. set 200: ♯ E 200: ♭ set K 200*)
   J. Perceval (ArgOd. 57017)
   R. K. Biggs (Cap.CAS 9017)
   C. Smart (D.F 10252)
   C. Cronham (Mjr. 5173), etc.
— ARR. MUSIC BOX: Music Box in the Bornand Collection
                   (in ♭ *AmC.A 1865*)
— ARR. PF.   Liszt, q.v., Section A. III. 5

SON AND STRANGER   Opera   1 Act   1829
(Heimkehr aus der Fremde)
Overture
Philharmonia—Kletzki   ♭ *C.SEL 1525*
(Ruy Blas, Overture)   (♭ SEBQ 123; G.7ERL 1060)
Linz Sym.   in ♯ *Ply. 12-32*
(Marschner & Wagner)
 ☆ Bournemouth Municipal—Schwarz   ♭ *G. 7EP 7004*
(Adam)

5. SONGS & PART SONGS

A. SONGS & DUETS

COLLECTIONS
Auf Flügeln des Gesanges, Op. 34, No. 2 (Heine
Der Mond, Op. 86, No. 5 (Geibel)
Schilflied, Op. 71, No. 4 (Lenau)
Neue Liebe, Op. 19a, No. 4 (Heine)
Venetianisches Gondellied, Op. 57, No. 5 (Moore
Frühlingslied, Op. 47, No. 3 (Lenau)
M. Lichtegg (T), H. W. Häusslein (pf.)
             ♯ D.LM 4556
(Tchaikovsky)   (♯ Lon.LS 799)
   Bei der Wiege, Op. 47, No. 6 (Klingemann)
   Das erste Veilchen, Op. 19a, No. 2 (Ebert)
   Frühlingslied, Op. 47, No. 3 (Lenau)
   Die Liebende schreibt, Op. 86, No. 3 (Goethe)
   Der Mond, Op. 86, No. 5 (Geibel)
 ☆ E. Schumann (S), G. Schick (pf.) ♯ *Roy. 1404*
(Franz & Purcell) (Franz only, on ♯ AFest.CFR 10-222)
   Auf Flügeln des Gesanges, Op. 34, No. 2 (Heine)
   Neue Liebe, Op. 19a, No. 4 (Heine)
   Der Mond, Op. 86, No. 5 (Geibel)
   Es weiss und rät es doch Keiner, Op. 99, No. 6
     (Eichendorff)
E. Berger (S)   in JpV. set JAS 272

(continued on next page)

---

[1] This is the final form as shown on the labels of the ten-inch issue. The twelve-inch has also been listed as containing
Nos. 2b (Fairies' March) and 3, but we have no confirmation.
[2] The Australian and ♭ Rem. issues are now stated to contain Nos. 1, 7 and 11 only. The others are unspecified.

COLLECTIONS (continued)

    Auf Flügeln des Gesanges, Op. 34, No. 2 (Heine)
    Die Liebende schreibt, Op. 86, No. 3 (Goethe)
    Der Mond, Op. 86, No. 5 (Geibel)
    Neue Liebe, Op. 19a, No. 4 (Heine)
    Schilflied, Op. 71, No. 4 (Lenau)
    ☆ V. Graef (S), L. Pommers (pf.) (‡ Clc. 6228)

Abendlied (Heine) (*3 Volkslieder*, No. 2) Duet
    G. Sakarov & Z. Dolukhanova (*Russ*) (*USSR. 21552*)

Auf Flügeln des Gesanges, Op. 34, No. 2 (Heine)
    I. Te Wiata (Bs, *Eng*), E. Lush (pf.)
                               ♭ *Nix.EP 902*
    (*Tchaikovsky: None but the weary heart, etc.*)
                          (in ‡ *NLPY 915*)
    G. Lutze (T), A. Hecker (pf.)   *Eta. 120121*
    (*Schumann*)
    P. Munsel (S, *Eng*) & pf.)   in ‡ *G.BLP 1023*
    (*film Melba*) (in ‡ *G.QALP 5015*; ‡ *Vic.LM 7012*:
                          ♭ set *WDM 7012*)
    I. Nyberg (*Dan*) (*D.F 44299*)
    ☆ H. Schlusnus (B) (in ‡ *AmD.DL 9624*)

— ARR. ORCH.
    Westminster Light—Bridgewater   ‡ *Nix.WLP 6805*
    (*above & Raff*)   (‡ *West.WL 4005*)
    Mantovani Orch. (in ‡ *D.LK 4072*: *LF 1161*; Lon.LL 877)
    Viennese Str. Orch. (♭ *Rem.REP 17*)

— ARR. PF.   Liszt, *q.v.*, Section A. III. 5

— ARR. ORGAN
    J. Perceval (in ‡ *ArgOd.LDC 513*: ♭ *BSOAE 4528*)

— ARR. 2 HARPS
    C. Salzédo & L. Lawrence   ♭ *Mer.EP 1-5006*
                          (in ‡ *MG 10144*)

— ARR. VLN. & PF.   Achron
    ☆ J. Heifetz & E. Bay (in ‡ *G.ALP 1206*: *FALP 248*;
                          ♭ *Vic.ERA 126*)

— ARR. VLC. & PF.
    J. Pacey & F. Kramer (in ‡ *MTR.MLP 1012*)

Bei der Wiege, Op. 47, No. 6 (Klingemann)
    B. Troxell (S) & org.   in ‡ *Ply.* 12-123
    (*Bach, Haydn, Mozart, etc.*)

Es ist bestimmt in Gottes Rat, Op. 47, No. 4
    (*Volkslied*) (*Feuchtersleben*)
    G. Pechner (B)   in ‡ *Roy.* 1557
    (*Mozart, Schumann, etc.*)

Gruss I, Op. 19a, No. 5 (Heine) (*Leise zieht . . .*)
    G. Lutze (T), A. Hecker (pf.)   *Eta. 120120*
    (*Schubert*)
    G. Pechner (B)   in ‡ *Roy.* 1557
    (*above*)

Gruss, Op. 63, No. 3 (Eichendorff)
Ich wollt', meine Liebe ergösse sich, Op. 63, No. 1
    (Heine) Duets
    ☆ I. Baillie (S), K. Ferrier (A), G. Moore (pf.) (*Eng*)
    (*Handel*)   ♭ *C.SED 5526*

Venetianisches Gondellied, Op. 57, No. 5 (Moore)
    ☆ H. Schlusnus (B) (in ‡ *AmD.DL 9624*)

Volkslied, Op. 63, No. 5 (Burns) Duet
    G. Sakarov & Z. Dolukhanova (*Russ*) (*USSR. 21551*)

---

5. B. PART SONGS

Abschied vom Walde, Op. 59, No. 3 (Eichendorff)
    (*O Täler weit . . .*)
    Bavarian Radio Cho.—Kugler   in ‡ **Pol. 19046**
    (*below; Brahms & Schubert*)
    ☆ St. Hedwig's Cath. Cho.—Forster (♭ *D.D 17150*:
                          in ‡ *T.LA 6086*)

(Der) Jäger Abschied, Op. 50, No. 2 (Eichendorff)
    (*Wer hat dich . . .*)
    Berlin Motet Cho. & Wind Insts.—Arndt
                           T.A 11600
    (*Kreutzer: Das ist der Tag des Herrn*)
             (♭ *U 45600*; & CanT.GF 63049)
    Bavarian Radio Cho.—Kugler   in ‡ **Pol. 19046**
    (*above*)

---

6. CHORAL & SACRED WORKS

ELIJAH, Op. 70 Oratorio   1846
COMPLETE RECORDING
    J. Delman (S), N. Procter (A), G. Maran (T),
    B. Boyce (B), M. Cunningham (Tr.)
    Hampstead Parish Chu. Boys' Cho., London
    Phil. Cho. & Orch.—Krips ‡ **D.LXT 5000/2**
    (6ss)   (‡ Lon. set LLA 27)

No. 4, If with all your hearts   T
    ☆ R. Crooks (in ‡ Cam.CAL 170: ♭ *CAE 171*)

No. 14, Lord God of Abraham   B
No. 26, It is enough   B
    ☆ N. Cordon (in ‡ Cam.CAL 269)

No. 28, Lift thine eyes ("*Engeltrio*") unacc.
    ☆ Mormon Tabernacle Cho.—Cornwall
                       (in ‡ AmC.ML 4789)

No. 29, He watching over Israel   cho.
    ☆ R. Shaw Chorale (♭ G. 7EP 7012; ♭ DV. 26027)

No. 31, O rest in the Lord   A
    N. Procter (from set)   ♭ *D.71082*
    (*Handel: Messiah, No. 23*)
    ☆ K. Ferrier   ♭ *D. 71039*
    (*Serse—Ombra mai fu*)   (♭ *D 18060*)
              (in ‡ *LW 5072*; ‡ *Lon.LD 9066*)
    ☆ M. Anderson (in ‡ Vic.LCT 1111: ♭ set WCT 1111)

— ARR. ORGAN: C. Cronham (*Mjr. 5128*)

No. 39, Then shall the righteous   T
    ☆ R. Crooks (in ‡ Cam.CAL 170: ♭ *CAE 171*)

FESTIVAL HYMN   male cho. & orch.   1840
No. 2, Hark, the herald angels sing[1]   cho.
    Royal Cho. Soc.—Sargent   in ‡ **G.ALP 1159**
    (in ‡ *BB.LBC 1044*: ♭ set *WBC 1044*; ♭ *Vic.ERA 227*)
    Bach Cho.—Jacques   in ‡ **D.LK 4085**
                        (‡ *Lon.LL 1095*)
    Nat. Presbyterian Chu. Cho.—Schafer
                    in ‡ **McInt.MC 107**
    (*Christmas Candlelight Service*)
    Gabriel Singers (in ‡ Rem. 199-153 & 199-154)
    St. Paul's Cath. Cho. (in ‡ Roy. 1501)
    Canterbury Cho.—Marrow (in ‡ MGM.E 3061: ♭ X 15)
    Butlin Cho. Soc.—Glyn Jones (♭ Lon.BEP 6217)
    ☆ R. Shaw Chorale (♭ Vic.ERA 1117: in ♭ set ERB 43)
    etc., etc.

— ARR. SOLO
    ☆ M. Anderson (A) (♭ Vic.ERA 116; in ‡ DV.T 16408)

— ARR. ORGAN
    R. K. Biggs (in ‡ DCap.LCT 6011)
    V. Fox (in ‡ Vic.LM 1835)
    C. Cronham (*Mjr. 5175*)
    etc.

— ARR. ORCH.
    Mantovani Orch. (in ‡ D.LF 1149; ‡ Lon. LL 913)
    Melachrino Orch. (♭ G. 7EG 8047)
    etc., etc.

— ARR. CARILLON
    C. Chapman (Luray Tower Carillon) in ‡ McInt.MM 102

(The) First Walpurgis Night, Op. 60 (Goethe)
    ☆ Soloists, Netherlands Phil. Cho. (*Ger*) & Orch.
    —Ackermann (‡ Clc. 6228; ‡ *MMS. 106²*;
                 excerpts in ‡ *MMS. 100S*)

Hear my prayer . . . O for the wings of a dove
    S, cho., orch., org. (*Psalm 55*)   1844
    D. Linter (Tr.) & St. Paul's Cath. Cho.—Dykes
    Bower   in ‡ **C.CX 1237**
    (*Gibbons, Bennet, Morley, Haydn, etc.*)
            (in ‡ Angel. 35139, in set 3516)
    ☆ E. Lough (Tr.) & Temple Chu. Cho. (♭ G. 7PW 111:
                          7PQ 2016)

HYMN OF PRAISE, Op. 52   Symphony-Cantata
    (*Symphony No. 2; Lobgesang*)   1840
COMPLETE RECORDING in *German*
    I. Steingruber (S), F. Hofstäder (S), R.
    Kreuzberger (T), Vienna State Op. Cho. &
    Vienna Orch. Soc.—Adler   ‡ **Uni.LP 1011/2**
    (3ss—*Cowell*, on 1011 with No. 1, the orch. Sinfonia)

---

[1] ARR. Cummings to C. Wesley's words.
[2] Soloists on ‡ *MMS. 106* are however named as C. Hassels (A) & C. Kalkman (T) in place of A. Woud & L. Larsen. This may indicate a re-recording, of at least part; or pseudonymity.

Laudate pueri Dominum, Op. 39, No. 2
Fem. cho. & org.
Montserrat Monastery Cho.
♭ *Ambra.SMGE 80013*
(*Schubert: Gott in der Natur*)

ST. PAUL, Op. 36
Oratorio S, A, T, B, cho., orch.
ABRIDGED RECORDING[1] in *German*
L. Dutoit, M. Nussbaumer, H. Loeffler, O.
Wiener, Vienna Academy Cho. & Pro
Musica Orch.—Grossmann (4ss)
♯ E. & AmVox.PL 8362

No. 13, But the Lord is mindful A
☆ M. Anderson (in ♯ Vic.LCT 1111: in ♭ set WCT 1111)

No. 15, Rise up, arise! Cho.
☆ Mormon Tabernacle Cho. & org. (in ♯ AmC.ML 4789)

No. 18, O God, have mercy upon me B
☆ N. Cordon (in ♯ Cam.CAL 269)

No. 40, Be thou faithful unto death T
☆ R. Crooks (in ♯ Cam.CAL 170: ♭ CAE 171)

7. MISCELLANEOUS

"Mendelssohn, his life and his music"
D. Randolph (narrator) etc.   ♯ Per.PCS 10

MENEGALI (XVIIIth-XIXth Cent.)

SEE ALSO: † MUSIC OF THE CHURCH

Jesu, Salvator mundi Motet
Trapp Family—Wasner   in ♯ CHS.CHS 1100

MENENDEZ, Pedro (b. 1906)

Canto negro vlc. & pf. 1935
A. Odnoposoff & Bertha Huberman ♯ *Pnt. 4001*
(*Ardévol, Vega, Roldán*)

MENNIN, Peter (b. 1923)

Canzona Wind insts.
Eastman Sym. Wind Ens.—Fennell
♯ Mer.MG 40011
(*Reed, Persichetti, Thomson, Hanson*)

Concertato for Orchestra 1952
A.R.S. Orch.—Swarowsky   ♯ ARS. 31
(*Green & Dello Joio*)

Quartet No. 2, strings 1952
Juilliard Qtt.   ♯ AmC.ML 4844
(*Imbrie*)

SYMPHONIES
No. 3 1946
N.Y.P.S.O.—Mitropoulos   ♯ AmC.ML 4902
(*Riegger*)
No. 6 1953
Louisville—Whitney   ♯ LO. 3
(*Riegger & Toch*)

MENOTTI, Gian-Carlo (b. 1911)

Concerto, F major pf. & orch. 1952
☆ Y. Boukoff & Paris Cons.—Cluytens (♯ G.QALP 176)

Concerto, vln. & orch. 1952
T. Spiwakowsky & Boston Sym.—Münch
♯ Vic.LM 1868
(*Honegger*)
(♯ FV.A 630275; ItV.A12R 0115)

OPERAS
AMAHL AND THE NIGHT VISITORS
Television Opera 24. xii. 1951
COMPLETE RECORDING
☆ Original Cast & Orch.—Schippers   ♯ G.ALP 1196
[Highlights on ♭ *Vic.ERA 120*]

AMELIA GOES TO THE BALL 1 Act 1937
(*Amelia al Ballo*)
COMPLETE RECORDING in *Italian*
Amelia   ...   .   M. Carosio (S)
The Husband ...   .   R. Panerai (B)
The Lover ...   .   G. Prandelli (T)
The Friend ...   .   M. Amadini (A)
The Commissioner of Police   E. Campi (Bs)
etc., La Scala Cho. & Orch.—Sanzogno
♯ C.CX 1166
(♯ QCX 10070: FCX 335; Angel. 35140)

Overture
☆ Philadelphia—Ormandy (in ♯ Cam.CAL 238)

(The) CONSUL 3 Acts 1950
Magda's Aria: To this we've come S, M-S, A, B
☆ I. Borkh (*Ger*), etc. (♭ G. 7RW 518)

(The) MEDIUM 2 Acts 1947
COMPLETE RECORDING of the film version
☆ Soloists, Rome Radio Orch.—Schippers (♯ Clc. 6278/9;
Excerpts on ♭ *Mer.EP 1-5054; FMer.MEP 14532*)

(The) SAINT OF BLEECKER STREET
Musical Drama 3 Acts 1954
COMPLETE RECORDING
Michele   ...   .   D. Poleri (T)
Desideria   ...   .   G. Lane (M-S)
Annina   ...   .   G. Ruggiero (S)
Don Marco   ...   .   L. Lishner (Bs)
etc., Cho. & Orch.—Schippers
(4ss)   ♯ Vic. set LM 6032

**Ricercare & Toccata on a theme from "The Old
Maid and the Thief"** pf.
A. Dorfmann   in ♯ Vic.LM 1758
(*Mendelssohn, etc.*)   (in ♭ set WDM 1758)

SEBASTIAN Ballet 1944
Orchestral Suite
N.B.C. Sym. Members—Stokowski
♯ Vic.LM 1858
(*Gould: Dance Variations*)

... Barcarolle
Boston Prom.—Fiedler   in ♯ Vic.LM 1726
(in ♭ set WDM 1726)

MERCADANTE, Giuseppe Saverio
Raffaele (1795-1870)

Salve Maria (*Andante religioso*)
H F. de Lucia (T)   in ♯ CEd. set 7002*
— ARR. ORG. & HP. (in *Vis. VI 5134, 5135, 5136, 5137, d.cs.*)

MERBECKE, John (c. 1510-1585)

Communion Service 1550
N.Y. Theological Seminary Cho. & org.
—Gilbert   in ♯ AmC.ML 4528

MERRICK, Frank (b. 1886)

(4) SONGS (Thèvenin) (*Esperanto*) 1954
1. Tagomezo (Noon)
2. Oktobro (October)
3. La Cisterno (The Reservoir)
4. La Hirundos (The Swallows)
G. Spinney (M-A), F. Merrick (pf.)   **Merling**
(pte. rec.)
▽ An older recording was
Two movements in Symphonic form 1928
(a completion of Schubert: Sym. No. 8)
(Royal Phil. on C. 9562/3)

---

[1] Nos. 5, 8, 11, 20, 23, 29, 31, 35, 36, 38 are omitted or abbreviated.

MERULA, Tarquinio (fl. 1623-1652)
SEE: † XVIITH CENTURY ORGAN MUSIC

MERULO, Claudio (1533-1604)
SEE: † MOTETS OF THE VENETIAN SCHOOL

MESSAGER, André Charles Prosper
(1853-1923)

(Abridged listings only)

Solo de concours cl. & pf. 1899
U. & J. Delécluse   ♯ *D.LX 3129*
(*Widor, Cahuzac, etc.*)   (♯ *Lon.LS 987*)

SONGS
COLLECTION
Chanson de ma vie (Banville)
Quand tu passes (from *Amours d'hiver*, 6 songs, 1910)
(Silvestre)
Dans les arbres blanc de givre (Clerc, after Heine)
Nouveau printemps (Clerc, after Heine)
    G. Moizan (S), M. Berthomieu (pf.)
               ♭ *D.EFM 455550*
(*Aubert: Les Yeux*)

Souvenirs de Bayreuth pf. duet (with Fauré)[1]
F. Petit & A-M. Beckensteiner
(*Chabrier*)   **V**♯ *Era.LDE 1017*

STAGE WORKS

(La) BASOCHE 3 Acts 1890
À ton amour; Quand tu connaîtras . . . T
  ☆ M. Villabella (in ♯ Od.ODX 136)

Elle m'aime   B
  H L. Fugère (in **V**♯ *IRCC.L 7002**)

Je suis aimé de la plus belle
  H E. Clément (T) (in **V**♯ *IRCC.L 7005**)

(Le) CHEVALIER D'HARMENTAL
Op. Comique 1895
COUPS DE ROULIS
Excerpts in Selections, below

DEBUREAU Inc. Music to play by Guitry 1918
Scène de l'interview
S. Guitry (in ♯ *G.FKLP 7008*: o.n. ▽ G.D 1705: W 1044)

(Les) DEUX PIGEONS Ballet 1886
Orchestral Suite
  Champs-Élysées Th.—Bonneau ♯ *Sel. 270.C.033*
(*Isoline*)
(*Isoline; & Véronique, Overture on* ♯ West.WL 5412)
  U.R.C. Sym.—Marinetti   ♯ *Mae.OA 20010*
(*Offenbach & Chabrier*)
  . . . Entrée des tziganes & Thème et Variations, only
  ☆ Paris Opéra—Fourestier (in ♯ Pat.DTX 150)

(La) FIANCÉE EN LOTERIE
FRANÇOIS LES BAS BLEUS 1883
Excerpts in Selection, below

FORTUNIO 5 Acts 1907
Si vous croyez (Chanson de Fortunio)
Je suis très tendre
  M. Villabella (T)
    (in ♯ Od.ODX 136: o.n. ▽ Od. 188598 & 188638)
La maison grise   ☆ G. Thill (in ♯ *C.FH 503*)

ISOLINE 3 Acts 1888
Orchestral Suite
  Champs-Élysées Theatre—Bonneau
  (*Deux Pigeons*)   ♯ *Sel. 270.C.033*
  (*Deux Pigeons; & Véronique, Overture on* ♯ West.WL 5412)
  ☆ Paris Opéra—Fourestier (♭ *Pat.ED 6*; Pavane & Valse
    only in ♯ DTX 150)

MONSIEUR BEAUCAIRE 3 Acts 1919
(orig. *Eng*)
EXCERPTS (from abridged recording)
  ☆ M. Angelici (S), M. Dens (B), etc., cho. & Lamoureux
    Orch.—Gressier   ♯ Pat.DTX 150
  (*Deux Pigeons, Isoline, Véronique*)

La Rose rouge   M. Merkès (♭ Od.MOE 2023)
                ☆ M. Dens (♭ Pat.ED 3)
Sous les étoiles   ☆ M. Dens (♭ Pat.ED 4)
Valse: Le Rossignol   ☆ M. Angelici (♭ Pat.ED 9)

PASSIONÉMENT Operetta 1926
Excerpt in Selections, below

(Les) P'TITS MICHU 3 Acts 1897
ABRIDGED RECORDING
  L. Berton, N. Renaux, C. Maurane, C. Devos,
    etc. R. St. Paul Cho. & Orch.—Gressier
                     ♯ Pat.DTX 157
. . . Comme une girouette   T
  C. Devos (from set) (♭ Pat.ED 35)

SACHA
Excerpts in Selection, below

VÉRONIQUE 3 Acts 1898
COMPLETE RECORDING
  Géori-Boué (S), R. Bourdin (B), etc. Cho. &
    Orch.—Dervaux   ♯ LI.TW 91093/4
  (4ss)   (♯ D.FMT 163630/1)
  [Excerpts on ♭ D.EFM 455559/60]
ABRIDGED RECORDING
  C. Maurane (B), M. Angelici (S), M. Roux (Bs),
    N. Renaux (S), C. Devos (T), A. Doniat (B),
    R. St. Paul Cho. & Lamoureux Orch.
    —Gressier   ♯ Pat.DTX 125
  [Excerpts on ♯ Pat.DTX 150]   (♯ AmVox.PL 21100)
HIGHLIGHTS
  N. Vallin (S), L. Huberty (B), Pasdeloup Orch.
    —Allain   ♯ Plé.P 3075
  (*Hahn*)

COLLECTION OF EXCERPTS
C'est Estelle et Véronique
Couplets de la lettre—Adieu je pars
Duetto de l'âne—De ci, de là
Duo de l'escarpolette—Ah! méchante!
  R. Riffaud (S), M. Markès (B) ♭ Od.7MOE 2036

Overture
  Champs-Elysées Theatre—Bonneau
                   ♯ West.WL 5412
  (*Deux Pigeons & Isoline*)
Duetto de l'âne—De ci, de là   S & B
  ☆ Géori-Boué & R. Bourdin   Sat.M 1171
  (*Hahn: Ciboulette—Nous avons fait . . .*)
Petite Dinde, ah quel outrage   S
  M. Angelici (from set) (♭ Pat.ED 9)

Selections from Messager's Works
  (Excerpts from Véronique, Monsieur Beaucaire,
    Fortunio, Les P'tits Michu, Le Chevalier d'Harmental,
    La Basoche, La Fiancée en loterie, Sacha, etc.)
  Géori-Boué, R. Bourdin, C. Riedinger,   ♯ LI.TW 91125
    L. Musy, etc.   (♯ D.FMT 163645)

  (Excerpts from L'Amour masqué, Coups de Roulis,
    Monsieur Beaucaire, Passionément)
  J. Silvaire, A. Doniat & Orch.—Cariven in ♯ Véga. 30M 706

MESSIAEN, Olivier E. P. C. (b. 1908)

Apparition de l'Église éternelle org. 1932
  J. Langlais   ♯ *Sel. 270.C.003*
  (*Les Bergers, & O sacrum convivium*)

(L') Ascension (4 Meditations) org. 1933
. . . No. 4, Prière du Christ
  R. Owen   ♯ *ASK. 3*
  (*Walther, Bach, Vierne, etc.*)
  [Organ of Christ Church, Bronxville, N.Y.]

---

[1] 'Fantaisie en forme de quadrille sur les thèmes favoris de l'Anneau du Niebelung . . .'

(Le) **Banquet céleste** org. 1928
R. Ellsasser　　in ‡ **MGM.E 3064**
(† Organ Music by Modern Composers)

(La) **Nativité du Seigneur** org. 1935
(9 Meditations)
J. R. Lively　　**‡ PFCM.CB 188**
(Honegger & Sessions)
☆ E. White (‡ Clc. 6258)

... **No. 2, Les Bergers**
J. Langlais　　**‡ Sel. 270.C.003**
(above & below)

(3) **Petites liturgies de la présence divine**
voices, pf., str. orch. & ondes Martenot 1944
Vocal Ens.& Orch.—Couraud ‡ *Sel. 270.C.075*
[Y. Loriod (pf.), J. Loriod (ondes Martenot)]

(8) **Préludes** pf. 1929
... **7, Plainte calme & 8, Un reflet dans le vent**
S. Andersen　　**‡ Oce.OCS 38**
(Grieg, Kabalevsky, Rachmaninoff)

O sacrum convivium S, A, T, B; or S & org. 1937
J. Collard (M-S), J. Langlais (org.)
(above)　　**‡ Sel. 270.C.003**

Rondeau pf. 1943
J–M. Damase　　**‡ D.FST 153527**
(Auric, Damase, Roussel, etc.)

MEULEMANS, Arthur (b. 1884)
SEE: † FLEMISH CHORAL MUSIC

MEYER, Phillip Jakob (1740–1819)
SEE: † XVIIITH CENTURY HARP MUSIC

MEYERBEER, Giacomo (1791-1864)

OPERAS

(L') **AFRICAINE** 5 Acts 1865
Overture
Paris Opéra—Sebastian　　**‡ Nix.ULP 9141**
(below; Huguenots, Pardon de Ploermel, Prophète)
(‡ FUra. 7003; Ura. 7141; MTW. 509)

Fille des rois; Quand l'amour m'entraîne B Act II
J. Metternich (Ger)　　***Pol. 62934***
(Eugene Oniegin, No. 12)　　(♭ 32024)
P. Schoeffler (Ital)　　in ‡ **Van.VRS 469**
(Meistersinger, Walküre, etc.)　　(‡ Ama.AVRS 6022)
Ⓗ M. Battistini (Ital) (IRCC & AF.ABHB 1*;
　　in ‡ Ete. 709*)
R. Stracciari (Ital) (in ‡ Sca. 802*
　　& in ‡ SBDH.JAL 7001*)

Holà! Matelots B Act III
Ⓗ T. Ruffo (Ital) (in ‡ SBDH.LLP 7*)

Adamastor, roi des vagues B Act III
M. Singher　　in ‡ **Roy. 1613**
(Contes d'Hoffmann, Roi de Lahore, etc.)
G. Taddei (Ital)　　in ‡ **Cet.LPC 55006**
(Figaro, Falstaff, Chénier, etc.)

Prelude (Marche indienne) orch.
Paris Opéra—Sebastian　　**‡ Nix.ULP 9141**
(above) (‡ FUra. 7003; Ura. 7141; MTW. 509;
　　♭ Ura.UREP 77)

O Paradis! T Act IV
R. Tucker (Ital)　　in ‡ **AmC.ML 4750**
D. Cestari (Ital)　　***Cet.AT 0398***
(Werther: Pourquoi me reveiller)
K. Terkal (Ger)　　***D.F 46072***
(Bohème—Che gelida manina)　　(♭ D 18072)
☆ J. Björling (Ital)　　***G.DB 21621***
(Faust: Salut! Demeure)　(in ‡ BLP 1055: ♭ 7ER 5025;
　♭ DV. 26044; in ‡ Vic.LM 1841: ♭ ERA 109)
J. Peerce (in ‡ Var. 6983)
☆ R. Schock (♭ Roy.EP 183)
☆ (Ital) B. Gigli (in ‡ Vic.LCT 6010: ♭ set WCT 6010:
　♭ ERAT 12)

M. Lanza (♭ G. 7RQ 3009: 7RW 102: in ‡ ALP 1202;
　　♭ Vic.ERA 136)
G. Poggi (in ‡ Cet.LPC 55003)
S. Rayner (in ‡ Ete. 708)
A. Cortis (IRCC.ABHA 2)
☆ (Russ) S. Lemeshev (USSR. 10559)
Ⓗ C. Vezzani (in ‡ Od.ODX 126*)
L. Muratore (IRCC. 3118*)
Ⓗ (Ital) E. Caruso (in ‡ G.FJLP 5009*: QJLP 105*)
G. Martinelli (in ‡ SBDH.LPG 4*)
Ⓗ (Ger) L. Melchior (in ‡ SBDH.GL 1*)

Conduisez-moi (Deh! ch'lo ritorni) T Act IV
Ⓗ E. Caruso (Ital) (AF.AGSB 18*
　　& in ‡ Vic. set LCT 6701*)

L'avoir tant adorée B Act IV
Ⓗ M. Battistini (Ital) (in ‡ Ete. 709*)

D'ici je vois la mer immense S Act V
(Death Scene of Sélika)
Ⓗ C. Boninsegna (Ital) (in ‡ Sca. 813* & AF.ABHB 8*)
S. Krusceniski (Ital) (IRCC. 3132*)

Erreur fatal S & T Act V
Ⓗ L. Bréval & J. de Reszke (in ‡ IRCC.L 7006*)[1]

DINORAH—SEE LE PARDON DE PLOERMEL

(L') **ÉTOILE DU NORD** 3 Acts 1854
Veille sur eux toujours (Prayer & Barcarolle) S Act I
Ⓗ R. Chalia (Ital) (IRCC. 3143*)
— ARR. Lambert: used in Les Patineurs ballet, q.v. infra.

O jours heureux Bs Act III
Ⓗ P. Plançon (in ‡ SBDH.LLP 6*)
J. Mardones (Ital) (in ‡ SBDH.LPP 3*)

Valse — ARR. Lambert: used in Les Patineurs Ballet,
q.v. infra.

Là, là, là, air chéri S Act III
Ⓗ S. Kurz (Ger) (in ‡ Sca. 817*)

(Les) **HUGUENOTS** 5 Acts 1836
ABRIDGED RECORDING

Marguerite ... ... R. Doria (S)	
Valentine ... ... J. Rinella (S)	
Urbain ... ... S. Couderc (M-S)	
Raoul ... ... G. Fouché (T)	
Saint-Bris ... ... A. Legros (Bs)	
Nevers ... ... C. Cambon (B)	
Marcel ... ... H. Médus (Bs)	

Cho. & Pasdeloup Orch.—Allain ‡ **Plé.P 3085/6**
(4ss)

"Slow March" (Chorale & Stretta, Act III; Conjuration,
Act IV — ARR. BAND)
Scots Guards Band (in ‡ C.SX 1042; Angel. 35271)

Overture
Paris Opéra—Sebastian　　**‡ Nix.ULP 9141**
(Africaine, Pardon de Ploermel, etc.)
(‡ Ura. 7141; FUra. 7003; MTW. 509)

Sous le beau ciel T Act I
Ⓗ E. Caruso (Ital) & pf. (SBDH.P 8* & in ‡ JAL 7000*;
　in ‡ AudR.LPA 234*; in ‡ FRP. 3*; in ‡ Roy. 1595*;
　　　　　　　　　V‡ Rar.M 301*)

Plus blanche que la blanche ermine T Act I
K. Baum　　in ‡ **Roy. 1582**
(Bohème, Rosenkavalier, etc.)
S. Lemeshev (Russ)　　***USSRM.D 00989***
(Lohengrin)　　(also USSRM.D 001217, d.c.)
☆ H. Roswaenge (Ger) (in ‡ CEd. 7010)
Ⓗ (Ital) G. Lauri-Volpi (AF.AGSB 57*)
E. Caruso (in ‡ G.FJLP 5004*; QJLP 104*)

Seigneur, rempart et seul soutien Bs Act I
(Récit. et Choral de Luther)
C. Siepi　　**‡ D.LW 5169**
(below; Boccanegra, Robert le Diable, etc.) (‡ Lon.LD 9169)
(& in ‡ D.LXT 5096; Lon.LL 1240)

Piff, paff, piff, paff Bs Act I
C. Siepi　　**‡ D.LW 5169**
(above) (‡ Lon.LD 9169; & ‡ D.LXT 5096; Lon.LL 1240)
Ⓗ J. Mardones (in ‡ Sca. 810* & in ‡ FRP. 2*)

Une dame noble et sage (Cavatina) S Act I
R. Streich　　***Pol. 62924***
(Ballo in Maschera, arias)　　(♭ 32011 & in ‡ 18169)
(& in Ger, on Pol. 62922: ♭ 32013)
V. Borisenko (Russ)　　in ‡ **USSR.D 1593**
(Gioconda, Carmen & Arensky)
Z. Dolukhanova (Russ) (USSR. 21859)
Ⓗ M. Garrison (Ital) (AF.AGSB 70*)
M. Ivogün (Ital) (in ‡ Sca. 815*)

---

[1] Three fragments from Mapleson cylinders.

(Les) HUGUENOTS (continued)
O beau pays de la Touraine S   Act II
G. Sakharova & Ensemble *USSRM.D 001276/7*
[The complete scene, in *Russian*]
   ♮ F. Hempel (AF.AGSB 59*)
   Lilli Lehman (*Ger*) (in ♯ Ete 702*)
   N. Melba[1] (in ♯ *IRCC.L 7006*)

Excerpts from Act III
   ♮ J. Gadski & E. de Reszke[2] (in ♯ IRCC.L 7006*)
Le Danger presse T   Act IV
   ♮ F. de Lucia (*Ital*) (in ♯ Sca. 813*)
Gloire au Dieu . . . Pt. 2, Dieu le veut, only Bs   Act IV
   ♮ J. Delmas (in ♯ *SBDH.PL 1*)
O ciel! où courez-vous S & T   Act IV
   ♮ E. Toninello & G. Teganini (*Ital*) (in ♯ Ete. 494*)
... Tenor part only
   ♮ F. de Lucia (*Ital*) (in ♯ Sca. 814*)
Ah quel soave vision (unid.) T
   ♮ J. Mojica (in ♥♯ IRCC.L 7005*)

(Le) PARDON DE PLOERMEL 3 Acts 1859
                    (*Dinorah*)
Overture
   Paris Opéra—Sebastian   ♯ Nix.ULP 9141
   (*Africaine, Huguenots, Prophète*)
                (♯ Ura. 7141; FUra. 7003; MTW. 509)

Ombre légère (Shadow Song) S   Act II
   M. M. Callas (*Ital*)   in ♯ C.CX 1231
   (*Lakmé, Vêpres siciliennes, A. Lecouvreur, etc.*)
                (♯ QCX 10129; Angel. 35233)
   R. Doria   ♭ Plé.P 45142
   (*Barbiere di Siviglia, No. 7*)
   H. Reggiani (*Ital*)   in ♯ Roy. 1603
   G. Gasparyan (*Ital*)   in *USSRM.D 1404*
   ☆ E. Spoorenberg (♭ Phi.N 402009E)
   ♮ S. Kurz (*Ital*) (AF.ABHB 5* & in ♯ Sca. 817*)

En chasse Bs   Act III
   ♮ P. Plançon (in ♯ *SBDH.LLP 6*)
Ah! mon remords te venge B   Act III
   ♮ P. Amato (*Ital*) (AF.AGSB 54*)
   T. Ruffo (*Ital*) (AF.AGSB 91*)
   M. Ancona (*Ital*) (in ♯ SBDH.JAL 7001*)
Les blés sont bons T   Act III
   ♮ C. Vezzani (in ♯ Od.ODX 126*)

(Le) PROPHÈTE 5 Acts 1849
Orchestral excerpts
1. **Valse**
2. **Prelude: Quadrille** (Skating Scene—Act III)
3. **Galop**   4. **Marche du couronnement**
   Paris Opéra—Sebastian   ♯ Nix.ULP 9141
   (*Africaine, Huguenots, Pardon de Ploërmel*)
                (♯ Ura. 7141; FUra. 7003; MTW. 509)
   [No. 4 only on ♭ Ura.UREP 77]
... Nos. 1, 2, 3
   Used in *Les Patineurs* ballet, ARR. Lambert, *see below*,
   Miscellaneous
Pour Bertha . . . (*Pastorale*) T   Act II
   A. da Costa   in ♯ Roy. 1599
Ah! mon fils A   Act II
   E. Wysor   in ♯ Roy. 1589
   (*Clemenza di Tito, Samson et Dalila, etc.*)
   ☆ S. Onegin, o.v. (in ♯ Sca. 821)
Marche du couronnement Orch.   Act III
   Belgian Radio—André   in ♯ T.LA 6077
   Bamberg Sym.—Lehmann   ♭ Pol. 32078
   (*Barbiere—Storm Music*) (in ♯ Pol. 16062: 17039: & 18169;
                ♯ AmD.DL 4089)
   Vienna Radio—Schönherr (in ♯ Vien.LPR 1037: ♭ 4044)
   Regent Sym. (in ♯ Rgt. 7001)
   Zagreb Radio (Jugo.P 16121)
   ☆ Boston Prom.—Fiedler (in ♯ Cam.CAL 142)
   Philharmonia—Weldon (C.SVX 48)
— ARR. BAND Grenadier Guards—Harris (D.F 10083)
Roi du ciel (Hymne triomphale) T & cho. Act IV
   A. da Costa   in ♯ Roy. 1599
   ♮ C. Dalmores (AF.AGSA 15*)

O prêtres de Baal A   Act V
   ♮ E. Schumann-Heink (AF.AGSB 17*)
À la voix de ta mère M-S & T   Act V
   ♮ M. Delna & A. Alvarez (*IRCC. 3145*)

ROBERT LE DIABLE 5 Acts 1831
Nonnes qui reposez Bs   Act III
   C. Siepi   ♯ D.LW 5169
   (*La Juive, Salvator Rosa, etc.*)   (♯ Lon.LD 9169 &
                ♯ LL 1240; D.LXT 5096)
   A. Legros   ♭ Plé.P 45147
   (*Barbiere & Don Carlos*)
   ♮ G. Gravina (in ♯ HRS. 3004*)
   J. Mardones (*Ital*) (in ♯ Sca. 810*)
   F. Chaliapin (*Ital*) (in ♯ SBDH.LLP 4*)
Noirs démons (Valse infernale) Bs (orig. cho.) Act III
   ♮ M. Journet (in ♯ SBDH.LPG 5*)
Ballet Music Act III
... Excerpts — ARR. BRASS BAND
   All Star Brass Band—Mortimer (*Pax.PR 633*)
Va! dit-elle S   Act I
Quand je quittai la Normandie S   Act III
   ♮ E. Destinn (*Ger*) (in ♯ Sca. 804*)
Qu'elle est belle (Cavatina) T   Act IV
   ♮ L. Escalais (in ♯ FRP. 1*)
Robert, toi que j'aime S   Act IV (*Gnadenarie*)
   ♮ F. Hempel (AF.AGSB 29*)
   E. Herzog (*Ger*) (in ♯ Roc. 1*)

MISCELLANEOUS

FACKELTÄNZE (Torch Dances) Orig. Band
No. 1, B flat major 1846
   Belgian Radio—André   ♯ DT.TM 68014
   (*Glazounov: Valse de Concert No. 1*)   (TV.VE 9036)
   (*Chabrier: España* on ♭ T.UX 4529)
   Imperial Light Orch.—Koschat (in ♯ Imp.ILP 127)
No. 3, C minor 1853
   French Navy Band—Maillot[3] in ♯ Sel. 270.C.055
   (*Maillot, Moussorgsky, Saint-Saëns, Grétry*)
(Les) PATINEURS Ballet
   (from various operas, ARR. C. Lambert)
   1. Entrée   2. Pas seul
   3. Pas de deux   4. Ensemble
   5. Pas de trois   6. Duet
   7. Pas des Patineurs 8. Finale
   ☆ L.S.O.—Irving   ♯ D.LW 5086
                (♯ Lon.LD 9105)
... Nos. 1-3 & 5-8
   ☆ Covent Garden—Hollingsworth (♭ C.SED 5521)
... Nos. 2, 3, 7 & 5 (or 1)
   Boston Pops—Fiedler   ♯ Vic.LM 1817
   (*Offenbach*)   (♭ set ERB 1817)
   (*Piston, Ravel, Roussel* on ♯ FV.A 630217;
                & in ♯ Vic. set LM 6113)
... Nos. 1, 3, 5, 7
   ☆ Sadler's Wells—Lambert (♭ G. 7PW 121)

MIASKOVSKY, Nicolai (1881-1950)

Concerto, D minor, Op. 44 vln. & orch. 1938
   ☆ D. Oistrakh & U.S.S.R. Sym.—Gauk
   (with *Glier, Brahms & Tchaikovsky*
                on ♯ Csm.CRLP 149; 2ss, ♯ MusH.LP 9014)
Divertimento, Op. 80 orch.
   Moscow Radio—Stassevitch   ♯ CEd.CE 3006
   (*Symphony No. 27*)
Little Overture, G major 1909
   Moscow Radio—Stassevitch   ♯ CEd.CE 3005
   (*Symphony No. 16*)
Lyric Concertino, G major, Op. 32, No. 3 1927
   Berlin Radio—Guhl   ♯ Ura. 7088
   (*Glazounov*)
Quartet No. 13, A minor, Op. 86 Strings
   Beethoven Qtt. (4ss)   ♯ USSR.D 1121/2

----
[1] Cabaletta only, from Mapleson cylinders.   [2] Incomplete; recorded from Mapleson cylinders.
[3] ARR. Wittmann.

Sonata No. 2, F sharp minor, Op. 13 pf. 1912
 T. Guseva　　　# *Sup.LPM 223*
 (*Balakirev & Tchaikovsky*)　　　(# *U. 5199C*)
Sonata No. 2 vlc. & pf.
 M. Rostropovich & A. Dedyukin　# **Kings. 301**
 (*Tchaikovsky*)
SYMPHONIES
No. 5, D major, Op. 18　1918
 U.S.S.R. State—Ivanov　# **USSR.D 01446/7**
 [Some sources give this on # CEd.CE 3005 in place of
 Overture, above]
No. 16, F major, Op. 39　1936
 U.S.S.R. State—Ivanov　　# **CEd.CE 3005**
 (*Overture, G major*)　　　(10ss, USSR. 021261/70)
No. 21, F sharp minor, Op. 51　1940
 U.S.S.R. State—Ivanov　# **Mon.MWL 331**
 (*Kabalevsky: Sym. No. 2*)
 [Andante sostenuto only, on # *USSR.D 488*]
 ☆ U.S.S.R. State—Rakhlin　# **Csm.CRLP 10070**
 (*Prokofiev: Sym. 7*)
No. 27, C minor, Op. 85　1949-50
 ☆ Moscow Radio—Gauk　　# CEd.CE 3006
 (*above*)　　　(2ss, # USSR.D 0496/7)
 (*Novák, on* # *Csm.CRLP 214*)

MICHAEL, David Moritz　(1751-1827)
　　SEE: † AMERICAN MUSIC (VOCAL)

MICHEELSEN, Hans Friedrich　(b. 1902)

Concerto on the melody 'Es sungen drei Engel'
 Org. 1943
 F. Asma　　　# *Phi.S 06033R*
 (*Vivaldi & Pachelbel*)
Prelude & Fugue, D major　1952
 ☆ F. Heitmann　　in # **DT.LGX 66037**
 († *Organ Music*)

MICHEL, Guillaume　(fl. XVIIth Cent.)
　　SEE: † AIRS À BOIRE

MIELCZEWSKI, Marcin　(d. 1651)
　　SEE: † FOUR CENTURIES OF POLISH MUSIC

MIGNONE, Francesco　(b. 1897)

Sonatina No. 4　(Brasileira) pf. 1951
 P. Spagnolo　　　in # **D.LXT 2947**
 (*Granados, Falla, Aguirre, etc.*)　(in # Lon.LL 1040)
Canção das maes pretas
Doña Janaïna
 S. Gloria (S), A. Chanaka (pf.)
 　　　in # **Vic.LM 1737**
 (*Sandi, etc.*)　　　(# FV.A 530202)

MIHALOVICI, Marcel　(b. 1898)

Ricercari, Op. 46　Variations pf. 1941
 M. Haas　　　# **Pol. 18077**
 (*Debussy, Roussel, Bartók*)

MILAN, Luis　(c. 1500-1565)
 Works are numbered from the Collected edn., a reprint of
 Milan's *Libro de música de Vihuela de Mano, 1536.*[1]
Fantasia No. 16　('*Tener de gala*')
 ☆ A. Segovia (in † # D.UAT 273142)
PAVANS
 (Nos. in brackets are those of the Pujol edn.)
Nos. 1, 3, 6　(Nos. 5, 1, 3)
 ☆ E. Pujol (in † # HS.AS 13)

No. 1 only
 ☆ A. Segovia (in † # B.AXTL 1060)
Nos. 4, 5, 6　(Nos. 2, 4, 3)
 ☆ H. Leeb (in # Nix.WLP 5059, *below*)
Nos. 2 & 4　(Nos. 6 & 2)
 N. Yepes　　　in # **D.LXT 2974**
 († *Spanish Music*)　　(# Lon.LL 1042; D.FST 153076)
No. 5　(No. 4)　'*La Belle Francescina*'
 K. Scheit　　　# **Van.BG 548**
 († *Renaissance & Baroque*)
No. 6　(No. 3)
 G. Zepoll (in # *Nix.SLPY 142; SOT. 1024*)
One unspec.　A. Lagoya (in ♭ *Pat.D 113*)
SONGS　voice & vihuela
Durandarte; Perdida tengo la color; Sospiro
 ☆ H. Cuénod (T), H. Leeb (lute)
 　　　in # **Nix.WLP 5059**
 (*Mudarra; above;* & † *Italian Songs*)
Durandarte　☆ M. Cid (A), E. Pujol (in † # HS.AS 10)
Toda mia vida os amé
 F. Fuller (B), D. Poulton (lute)　**G.HMS 40**
 († *History of Music in Sound*)　(in # Vic. set LM 6029)

MILHAUD, Darius　(b. 1892)

CLASSIFIED:　1. Piano & Organ　2. Chamber Music
　　　　　3. Orchestral　4. Theatre, Film, etc.
　　　　　5. Songs　6. Cantatas

1. PIANO & ORGAN

(Le) Bal martiniquais　(Op. Am. 33)　2 pfs.　1944
 G. Smadja & G. Solchany　　# *LT.MEL 94009*
 (*Scaramouche*)　　　(V# *Sel.LPP 8479*)
Pastorale　(Op. Am. 13)　organ　1941
 R. Ellsasser　　　in # **MGM.E 3064**
 († *Organ Music of Modern Composers*)
SAUDADES DO BRASIL　1920-21
 Overture; No. 1, Sorocaba; No. 2, Botofago; No. 3, Leme;
 No. 4, Copacabana; No. 5, Ipanema; No. 6, Gavea; No. 7,
 Corcovado; No. 8, Tijuca; No. 9, Sumaré; No. 10, Paineras;
 No. 11, Laranjeiras; No. 12, Paysandú
COMPLETE RECORDING
 L. Engdahl　　　# **MGM.E 3158**
 (*Villa-Lobos*)
... Nos. 1, 3, 5, 7, 12
 ☆ J. Germain　　　# **Fel.RL 89002**
 (‡s—*Cheminée . . . & Création du Monde*)
... Nos. 4, 5, 6, 7
 G. Gorini　(2ss)　　　*Cet.AT 0381*
... No. 5, Ipanema　— ARR. VLN. & PF.　Lévy
 ☆ J. Martzy & J. Antonietti (in # *Pol. 16017*)
... No. 7, Corcovado　— ARR. VLN. & PF.　Lévy
 ☆ J. Heifetz (in # G.ALP 1206: FALP 248)
Scaramouche　2 pfs.　1937[2]
 G. Smadja & G. Solchany　# *LT.MEL 94009*
 (*Bal Martiniquais*)　　　(V# *Sel.LPP 8479*)
 J. Bonneau & G. Joy　　# *Pat.DT 1027*
 (*Ravel: Ma mère l'oye*)
 J. & A. Iturbi　　　# **Vic.LRM 7038**
 (*Infante & Nepomuceno*) (♭ set ERB 7038; # FV.A 330206)
 G. Joy & K. Yasukawa　(2ss)　JpV.SD 3096
 ☆ P. Luboshutz & G. Nemenoff (in # Cam.CAL 198)
... No. 3, Brasileira, only
 E. Bartlett & R. Robertson　in # **MGM.E 3150**
Touches noires, touches blanches　(Op. Am. 6)
 　　　　　　pf.　1941
 M. Pressler　　　in # **MGM.E 3010**

---

[1] All recordings are played on the guitar except Leeb (lute) and Pujol (vihuela).
[2] From inc. music for Vildrac's *Le Médecin volant*, after Molière.

2. CHAMBER MUSIC

(La) Cheminée du roi René   fl., ob., cl., hrn., bsn.
1939-41

Chicago Sym. Quintet ♯ **Aphe.AP 15**
(Ibert & Hindemith)
Netherlands Phil. Quintet ♯ **MMS. 108**
(Symphonies for small orch.)
Garde Républicaine Quintet ♯ **D.FA 143659**
(Ibert & Pierné)
[3 movts. only in ♯ FMT 163664]
French Radio Orch. Quintet ♯ **C.FCX 219**
(below & Ibert, Hindemith)
☆Conservatoire Quintet—Oubradous ♯ **Fel.RL 89002**
(♯s—*Création du Monde, & Saudades*)
☆ French Wind Quintet ♯ **LOL.DL 53002**
(Suite d'après Corrette)

(2) Esquisses[1]   fl., ob., cl., hrn., bsn.
1. Madrigal   2. Pastorale
French Radio Orch. Quintet ♯ **C.FCX 219**
(above; Ibert, Hindemith)

QUARTETS, String
No. 1   1912
☆ WQXR Qtt. ♯ **Nix.QLP 4004**
(Turina)   (♯ Cum.CLP 311)
No. 12   *(in memory of Fauré)*   (Op. Am. 36)   1945
Italian Qtt. ♯ **C.CX 1155**
(Debussy)   (♯ QCX 10054: FCX 309; Angel. 35130)

QUINTETS
No. 1   pf. & str. qtt.   1951
No. 2   str. qtt. & cbs.   1952
B. Smith (pf.), Stanley Qtt. & C. Thompson
(cbs.) ♯ **CtyNY.AP 103**
SONATAS, Vln. & pf.
No. 2   1917
R. Soëtens & S. Roche ♯ **Sel.LP 8239**
(Lesur: Sextet)
Sonatina, cl. & pf.   1927
U. & J. Delécluse ♯ **D.LX 3139**
(Honegger & Saint-Saëns)   (♯ Lon.LS 1097)
H. Tichman & R. Budnevich ♯ **CHS.H 18**
(Bloch & Bernstein)
Suite, vln., cl. & pf.[2]   1936
M. Ritter, R. Kell, J. Rosen ♯ **AmD.DL 9740**
(Bartók: Contrasts)
☆ J. Parrenin, U. Delécluse, A. Haas-Hamburger
(Poulenc) ♯ **Fel.RL 89006**
Suite d'après Corrette   ob., cl., bsn.   1937
L. Speyer, P. Cardillo, E. Panenka ♯**Uni.LP 1005**
(St-Saëns, Honegger, Poulenc, Roland-Manuel)
New Art Wind Trio   in ♯ **CEd. set 2006**
(Tailleferre, Honegger, Poulenc, etc.)
☆ P. Pierlot, J. Lancelot, P. Hongne ♯ **LOL.DL 53002**
(above)

3. ORCHESTRAL

Concertino d'automne   1951
2 pfs., ob., 3 hrns., 2 vlas., vlc.
R. Gold, A. Fizdale & Cha. Orch.—Saidenberg
♯ **AmC.ML 4854**
(Satie, Debussy, Poulenc)   (in set SL 198)
Concertino d'été   vla., & cha. orch.   1951
R. Courte & Philharmonic Cha. Ens.—Milhaud
♯ **CtyNY.AP 102**
(Amours de Ronsard)
Concerto, pf. & orch. No. 1   1934
☆ F. Jacquinot & Philharmonia—Fistoulari
(Honegger, Chausson, Ravel) ♯ **MGM.E 3041**
Concerto   percussion & small orch.   1929-30
Concert Arts—Slatkin ♯ **DCap.CTL 7094**
(Chavez & Bartók)   (♯ Cap. P 8299)

(5) Études, pf. & orch.   1920
☆ P. Badura-Skoda & Vienna Sym.—Swoboda
(Rag Caprices, etc.)   in ♯ **Nix.WLP 5051**
Kentuckiana   1949
Louisville Sym.—Whitney ♯ **AmC.ML 4859**
(Foss & Martinů)
Ouverture mediterranéenne   1954
Louisville—Whitney ♯ **LO. 8**
(Dallapiccolo, Kay, Moncayo)
(3) Rag-Caprices   1927
Serenade   1920-1
☆ Vienna Sym.—Swoboda ♯ **Nix.WLP 5051**
(Maximilien, Suite, etc.)
Suite   Band   1952
U.S. Military Acad. Band—Resta
♯ **PFCM.CB 176**
(Stravinsky, Ravel, Barber, Still)
Suite française   (Op. Am. 32)   Band or orch. 1945
Berlin Sym.—List ♯ **Roy. 1465**
(Stravinsky)
☆ N.Y.P.S.O.—Milhaud   *(Ibert)* ♯ **C.C 1027**
(Ibert & Bizet on ♯ AmC.RL 6629)
Suite provençale   1937
☆ Sym.—Désormière   (V♯ *CdM.LDY 8118*)
St. Louis Sym.—Golschmann (♯ Cam.CAL 178:
♭ *CAE 243*)

(5) SYMPHONIES   Small orch.
No. 1, Le Printemps   1917
No. 2, Pastorale   1918
No. 3, Sérénade   1921
No. 5, Dixtuor d'instruments à vent   1922
☆ Concert Hall Cha.—Milhaud ♯ **MMS. 108**
(La Cheminée du Roi René)

SYMPHONIES
No. 1   Full orch.   1939
☆ C.B.S. Sym.—Milhaud   *(Sessions)* ♯ **AmC.ML 4784**
No. 2   (Op. Am. 31)   1944
Paris Cons.—Tzipine ♯ **C.CX 1253**
(Auric)   (♯ FCX 265; Angel. 35118, in set 3515)
No. 4   (1848 Revolution)   1947[3]
Vienna Sym.—Adler ♯ **SPA. 57**

4. THEATRE & FILMS

(Le) Bœuf sur le toit   Ballet   1919
Concert Arts Orch.—Golschmann
♯ **DCap.CTL 7055**
(Honegger, Ravel, Satie)   (♯ Cap.P 8244)
CHRISTOPHE COLOMB
Inc. music to Claudel's play[4]   1936
COMPLETE RECORDING of the play[5], with Milhaud's
music
M. Renaud, J-L. Barrault Co. & Orch.
—P. Boulez   (4ss) ♯ **LI.TW 91084/5**
(♯ D.FMT 163501/2)
(La) Création du monde   Ballet nègre   1923
☆ Cha. Ens.—Oubradous ♯ **Fel.RL 89002**
(Cheminée . . . & Saudades)
☆ Columbia Cha.—Bernstein ♯ **EPhi.NBR 6019**
(Copland) (♯ Phi.N 02600R)
MAXIMILIEN   Opera   3 Acts   1932
Orchestral Suite
☆ Vienna Sym.—Swoboda   *(above)*   in ♯ **Nix.WLP 5051**
PROTÉE   Inc. Music to Claudel's play   1913-19[6]
... **Suite symphonique No. 2**   1919-20
Pittsburgh Sym.—Steinberg ♯ **PFCM.CB 167**
(Villa-Lobos)

---

[1] Nos. 2 (Madrigal) and 1 (Eglogue) of *4 Sketches* for Orch. and wind quintet, 1941 (Op. Am. 11)
[2] From inc. music for Anouilh's *Le Voyageur sans bagages*.
[3] First perf. 1948 at concert for centenary of the 1848 revolution.
[4] This score is not drawn from the opera, apart from one theme: *de la Colombe au dessus de la mer*.
[5] As adapted for performance by J-L. Barrault
[6] First performance of the incidental music, 1929.

5. SONGS & PART SONGS

(Les) Amours de Ronsard　3 part songs　1934
A. Bollinger (S), H. Glaz (A), L. Chabay (T),
M. Harrell (Bs), Philharmonic Cho. Ens.
—Milhaud　　　　　　# *CtyNY.AP 102*
(Concertino d'été)

Catalogue des fleurs　(L. Daudet)
voice & 7 insts.　1921
I. Joachim (S) & Cha. Orch.—M. Franck
　　　　　　　　in # *CdM.LDA 8079*
(Auric, Durey, Honegger, Poulenc, Tailleferre)

(6) Chants populaires hébraïques　(Trad.)　1925
... No. 1, La Séparation
　▽ C. Panzéra (B)　*(G.P 804)*
... No. 4, Berceuse
　☆ C. Panzéra (B), M. Panzéra (pf.) (in # Clc. 6260)

SONGS
PETITES LÉGENDES　(Carème)　1954

BOOK I:	1. Sortilège	2. Les Feuilles
	3. L'Amoureux	4. La Prière
	5. La Dormeuse	6. La Peine
BOOK II:	1. La Chance	2. Le Lièvre et le blé
	3. La Bise	4. Destinée
	5. Le Beau Navire	6. Le Charme

J. Giraudeau (T), M. Petit (pf.)　# **D.FMT 163664**
(La Cheminée, excpt.; & Milhaud interviewed by C. Rostand)

(8) Poèmes juifs　(Anon.)　1916
I. Kolassi (M-S), A. Collard (pf.)　# **D.LXT 2897**
(Fauré: Chanson d'Ève)　　　　　　(# Lon.LL 919)

6. CANTATA, etc.

Cantate de la paix (Claudel) 8-pt. cho. unacc. 1937
St. Olaf Cho. *(Eng)*—Christiansen
　　　　　　　(in # *Alld. 2005:* ♭ *EP 2005)*

Psalm 121　male cho.　1921
Pancratius Male Cho.—Heydendael # *C.HS 1001*
(Andreae, Lassus, etc.)

MILLÖCKER, Karl　(1842–1899)
(Abridged listings only)
OPERETTAS
(Der) BETTELSTUDENT　3 Acts　1882
COMPLETE RECORDING
W. Lipp (S), E. Rethy (S), R. Christ (T),
K. Preger (B), E. Wächter (B), R. Anday
(M-S), Vienna State Op. Cho. & Orch.
—Paulik (4ss)　　　　# **Van.VRS 474/5**
Soloists, Moscow Radio Cho. & Orch.
—Kovalev *(Russ)*　　# **USSR.D 01598/602**
(5ss—J. Strauss: Waltzes)

ABRIDGED RECORDINGS
R. Boesch (S), M. Opawsky (S), R. Christ (T), H. Meyer-
Welfing (T), etc., Vienna Operetta Ens.—Stolz
　　　　　　　　　　　　# **MMS. 2303**
(# Per.RL 1901: ♭ PEP 1/2; # Cpt.MC 120004;
[Excerpts on # *MMS. 303*]　　Gramo.GLP 3002)

Vocal Selection
E. Loose, T. Eipperle, K. Terkal, etc.　# *D.LF 1517*
(Zeller: Vogelhändler selection)
　　　　　　　　　(D.VK 9508; ♭ *D.DX 1723)*
A. Schlemm, P. Anders, R. Streich, etc.　# *Pol. 45049*
(Zeller: Vogelhändler selection)　　(Pol. 58615: ♭ 20042)

Orch. Selection Moscow Radio—Samosud (# USSR.D 01533)
Orch. Suite Orch.—Becker　　　# *Rem. 199-192*

Bei diesen Kuss　S & T
I. Beilke & E. Kunz (B) *(Imp. 19197)*

Ach ich hab' sie ja nur auf die Schulter geküsst　Bs
G. Neidlinger (in # *Eli.LPE 107)*

Ich hab' kein Geld
Ich knüpfte manche zarte Bande　T
R. Schock　　　　　　　*G.EG 8053*
　　　　　　　　　　　(♭ *7MW 17-8503)*
J. Katona *(Imp. 19122)*
Ich hab' kein Geld　☆ J. Björling *(Swed) (G.EC 214)*
Ich setz' den Fall　T & S
E. Kunz (B) & I. Beilke *(Imp. 19197)*

GASPARONE　3 Acts　1884
Carlotta Walzer
A. Lutter Orch. *(Od.O-29009:* ♭ *OBL 29009)*

Dunkelrote Rosen
P. Anders (T)　　　　　　　**in PV. 58617**
　　　　　　　　　　　　　(# *Pol. 45047)*
J. Metternich (B)　　　　　　**G.EG 7990**
(Lincke: Im Reiche des Indra, excpt.)
　　　　　　　(GA 5131: JK 2850: ♭ MW 501)
P. Grundén (T)　　　　　　　**D.F 40698**
(Lehár: Paganini—Gern hab' ich . . .)
F. Klarwein (T) *(Tpo. 3571)*

GRÄFIN DUBARRY　1879　(arr. Mackeben)
Ich denk' zurück　*(Without your love)*　S & T
☆ G. Moore & R. Crooks *(Eng)* (in # Vic.LCT 7004:
　♭ set WCT 7004; o.n. G.DA 1306; Vic. 1614)

Ich schenk' mein Herz　S
M. Raskó *(Hung) (Qual.MK 6560)*
☆ E. Sack (in # *DT.LGM 65015)*
H. Gueden (♭ *D.DX 1766)*

Selection from Millöcker's Works
Vienna Radio—Schneider (in # *Phi.S 05903R)*

MILTON, John, senior　(c. 1563-1647)
SEE: † TRIUMPHS OF ORIANA

MINKUS, Léon [Aloisius Ludwig]
　　　　　　　　　　　　　(1827-1890)
DON QUIXOTE　Ballet Prol. & 4 Acts　1869
Introduction, Adagio, Variation I (Valse), Variation II, & Coda
Concerts Colonne—Stirn　　# **LT.DTL 93019**
(Tchaikovsky)　　　　　　　(# *Sel. 270.C.005)*
Pas de deux
New Sym.—Fistoulari　　　　# **D.LW 5084**
(Weber)　　　　　　　　　(# Lon.LD 9108)

MINISCALCHI, Guglielmo　(fl. XVIIth Cent.)
SEE: † ANTHOLOGIE SONORE

MINORET, Guillaume　(d. 1717)
SEE: † MUSIQUES À LA CHAPELLE DU ROY

MOERAN, Ernest John　(1894-1950)
Jubilate Deo, E flat major　1930
St. George's Chapel Cho.—Harris † C.LX 1613
(Wood: Honour and Glory and laud)
[† English Church Music Vol. IV]

MOESCHINGER, Albert　(b. 1897)
Sonata No. 1, Op. 62　vln. & pf.　1944
H. Schneeberger & P. Souvairan # **D.LXT 2849**
(Honegger & Regamey)　　　　(# Lon.LL 893)

MOHAUPT, Richard　(b. 1904)
DOUBLE TROUBLE　Opera, 1 Act　1954
COMPLETE RECORDING

Hocus	R. Dales
Erotia	M. Pulliam
Naggia	A. Beierfield
Cynthia	C. Riesley
Lucia	W. D. Elliott
Pocus	W. Pickett
Dr. Antibioticus	M. Harlan

Kentucky Op. Assoc. Cho. & Louisville Orch.
—Bomhard (2ss)　　　　　　# **LO. 12**

☆ = Re-issue of a recording to be found in previous volumes.

MOLINARO, Simone (b. *c.* 1565)

(II) CONTE ORLANDO
Balletto — ARR. ORCH. Respighi, *q.v.*

MOLINS, Pierre de (XIVth Cent.)

SEE: † ANTHOLOGIE SONORE

MOLLER, John Christopher (*c.* 1750-1803)

Quartet No. 6, E flat major str.
☆ New Music Qtt. (*Gehot & Peter*)   ‡ ARS. 33

MOMPOU, Federico (b. 1893)

COLLECTIONS OF PIANO MUSIC
La Rue, le guitariste et le vieux cheval (*Suburbis*, No. 1) 1916
Scènes d'enfants   1915-18
... No. 5, Jeunes filles au jardin
Preludes, Nos. 9 & 10   1944-5
Cançós i Danza   1921-1946
... Nos. 1, 4, 5, 7, 8
Impresiones íntimas   1911-1914
... No. 5, Pajaro triste; No. 8, Secreto; No. 9, Gitano
La Fuente y la Campana
El Lago
   F. Mompou   ‡ C.FCX 184
                (‡ Angel. 35147)

Cançó i Danza No. 1   1921
(5) Scènes d'Enfants   1915-18
    1. Cris dans la rue
    2. Jeux sur la plage
    3. Jeu   4. Jeu
    5. Jeunes filles au jardin
Charmes   1921
    1. Pour endormir la souffrance
    2. Pour pénétrer les âmes
    3. Pour inspirer l'amour
    4. Pour évoquer l'image du passé
    5. Pour les guérisons
    6. Pour appeler la joie
   J. Echaniz   ‡ West.WL 5382
   (*Albeniz*)

Cançós i Danza ... Nos. 1, 3, 4, 6
L'Home del l'Aristo (from *Suburbis*) (*c*)
Impresiones íntimas   1911-14
   ... No. 9, Gitano (*c*)
Prelude No. 5   (*c*)
   C. de Groot   ‡ Phi.N 00761R
   (*Albeniz & Falla*)
   [marked (*c*), with *Albeniz & Falla*, in ‡ Epic.LC 3175]

(8) Cançós i Danza pf. 1921-46
   G. Soriano   ‡ LT.DTL 93013[1]
   (*Turina*)   (& 2ss, ‡ Sel.LA 1050; Hispa.HF 1205)

... No. 1
   A. de Raco   ‡ ArgOd.LDC 520
   (*Albeniz & Prokofiev*)
   ☆ G. Copeland (in ‡ MGM.E 3025)

... No. 6
   A. Rubinstein   ♭ Vic.ERA 200
   (*Granados & Falla*)   (♭ FV.A 95209; ItV.A72R 0024)

Con magia
Planys (*Impresiones íntimas*, No. 1)
   ☆ G. Copeland (in ‡ MGM.E 3025)

Preludes, Nos. 8 & 9 pf. 1943-4
   P. Spagnolo   ‡ D.LW 5142
   (*D. Scarlatti, Marcello, Rodrigo, etc.*)   (‡ Lon.LD 9153)

(5) Scènes d'Enfants pf. 1915-18
   M. Regules ("Siena" pf.)   ‡ Eso.ESP 3002
   (*Albeniz, Turina, Villa-Lobos*)

... No. 5, Jeunes filles au jardin
   G. Bachauer   in ‡ G.CLP 1067
   (*Debussy & Ravel*)
   M. Tagliaferro   in V‡ Sel.LAP 1006
   (*Debussy, Falla, Albeniz*)

———— ARR. VLN. & PF. Szigeti
   ☆ H. Szeryng & M. Berthelier (in ‡ Pac.LDPC 50)

SONGS (in *Catalan*)
(El) COMBAT DEL SOMNI (Janés) f.p. 1953
1. Damunt de tu només les flors   1942
2. Aquesta nit mateix vent   1946
3. Jo et pressentia com la mar
   N. Merriman (M-S), G. Moore (pf.)
                in ‡ C.CX 1243
   († *Spanish Songs*)   (‡ FCX 392; Angel. 35208)

MONCAYO, José Pablo (b. 1912)

Cumbres orch. f.p. 1954
   Louisville—Whitney   ‡ LO. 8
   (*Dallapiccola, Kay, Milhaud*)

Huapango orch. 1941
   Mexico Sym.—Chávez   ‡ B.AXTL 1055
   (*Chávez*)   (‡ AmD.DL 9527)

MONIUSZKO, Stanislav (1819-1872)

(A) Fairy-tale Overture orch. (*Bajka*) 1848
   Poznán Op.—Bierdiayew   Muza.X 2140/1
   (3ss—*Russian & Polish Nat. Anthems*)
   Moscow Radio—Stassevitch   ‡ USSR.D 1144
   (*Chopin*)

OPERAS
(The) BARGEMEN (*Flis*) 1 Act 1858
Overture
   Polish Radio—Krenz   Muza.X 2332

(The) COUNTESS (*Hrabina*) 3 Acts 1860
Overture
   Polish Radio—Krenz   Muza.X 2184

Countess' Aria (unspec.) S
   H. Dudicz-Latoszewska   Muza.X 2341
   (*Halka excerpts*)

Kazimirz's Aria T Act III
   B. Paprocki   *Muza. 2456*
   (*Nowowiejski: Legend of the Baltic, excpt.*)

HALKA   4 Acts   1854
COMPLETE RECORDINGS

Casts		Set R	Set P
Halka (S)	...	N. Sokolova	A. Kawecka
Janusz (B)	...	P. Lisitsian	M. Woznicko
Zofia (S) ...	...	I. Maslennikova	F. Kurowiak
Jontek (T)	...	G. Nelepp	W. Domieniecki
Stolnik (Bs)	...	M. Soloviev	E. Kossowski

Set R, with Bolshoi Theatre Cho. & Orch.
(*Russ*) —Kondrashin (6ss) ‡ USSR.D 0538/43
   [Mazurka only, *USSR. 21618*]
                (& 4ss, ‡ Csm.CRLP 188/9)

Set P, with Poznán Theatre Cho. & Phil. Orch.
(*Polish*) —Bierdiayew ‡ CdM.LDXA 8095/6
   (4ss)   (‡ Csm.CRLP 188/9P)
   (also 30ss, *Muza. 2441/55*; various excerpts on
   Muza.X 2144, X 2339/41, X 2147/9, etc.)

ACT I
Like a wind-swept flower
   (Duet, Halka & Janusz) S, B, Cho.
   N. Sokolova, P. Lisitsian & Cho. *USSR. 22282/3*
   (4ss—from set)

ACT IV
The wind whistles (Jontek's aria—Dumka) T
   G. Nelepp (from set)[2]   ‡ USSR.D 2182
   (*below & Smetana*)
   I. Kozlovsky (? n.v.)[2]   *USSRM.D 889*
   (*Delibes: Lakmé—excerpts*)
   B. Paprocki   *USSRM.D 00123*
   (*Noskowski & Folk Songs*)
   P. Belinnik (*Ukrainian*) (in ‡ USSR.D 2092)

---

[1] Withdrawn almost immediately on issue; doubtful if ever on sale.
[2] May equally well be the Act II aria.

O my baby (Halka's aria) S
Z. Gaidai (*Ukrainian*)　　# *USSR.D 2182*
(*above; & Smetana*)　　(& in # *USSR.D 1950*, d.c.)

(The) HAUNTED MANOR (or CASTLE)
4 Acts　1865　(*Strazny Dwór*)
Mazurka; Finale Act II
Poznán Op. Cho. & Orch.—Bierdiayew
　　　　　　　Muza.X 2146/7
(*Tchaikovsky & Halka*)
[Mazurka also on Muza.X 1756]

Stefan's aria (unspec.)　T
A. Klonowski　　　　**Muza.X 2142**
(*Seligowski*)

PARIA　3 Acts　1869
Overture
Polish Radio—Fitelberg　　**Muza.X 1755/6**
(3ss—*Haunted Castle—Mazurka*)

VERBUM NOBILE　1 Act　1861
Stanislav's Aria　B
A. Hiolski　　　　*Muza. 2412*
(*Karlowicz: Serenata*, s. 7)

SONGS
(The) Golden fish
E. Bandrowska-Turska (S) (*USSRM.D 00120*)

Grandfather & his wife (Kraszewski)
Counsel
L. Nowosad (B), W. Klimowiczowna (pf.)
　　　　　　　Muza. 2110

Krakowiak (Wasilowski)
M. Woźniczko (B), S. Nadgryzowski (pf.)
　　　　　　　Muza.X 2150
(⅓s—*Tchaikovsky: Enchantress, aria, etc.*)
J. Garda (B), V. Makarov (pf.)　*Muza. 2417*
(*Halka, aria*)
A. Hiolski (B), J. Lefeld (pf.)　*Muza. 1683*
(*below*)

Master & groom (Mickiewicz)
V. Bregy (T), W. Klimowiczowna (pf.)
(*Pankiewicz: Song*)　　**Muza.X 1732**

Soldier's Song (Korzeniewski)
A. Hiolski (B), J. Lefeld (pf.)　*Muza. 1683*
(*above*)

Two Dawns
A. Hiolski (B), J. Lefeld (pf.)　*Muza. 1684*
(*Karlowicz: Song*)

MONRAD-JOHANSEN, David　(b. 1888

Pan, Op. 22　Sym. Poem Orch.　1939
Oslo Phil.—Grüner-Hegge　　**NOC. 62617/9**
(3ss)　　　　(& in # Mer.MG 90002)
PART SONG
Old Norway　▽ Guldberg Acad. Cho. (G.ZN 527)

MONTE, Philippe de　(1521-1603)

SEE: † HISTORY OF MUSIC IN SOUND (35)
　　　† OLD NETHERLANDS MASTERS

MONTEVERDI, Claudio　(1567-1643)

MADRIGALS
COLLECTIONS
Book I　(1587)　COMPLETE　(5 voices)
1. Ch' io ami la vita mia	12. Se nel partir da voi
2. Se per ha/vervi ohimè	13. Tra mille fiamme
3. A che tormi il ben mio	14. Usciam Ninfe homai
4. Amor per tua mercè	15. Questa ordi il laccio (Strozzi)
5. Baci soavi e cari (Guarini)	16. La vaga pastorella
6. Se pur non ti contenti	17. Amor s'il tuo ferire
7. Filli cara e amata	18. Donna, s'io miro voi
8. Poi che del mio dolore	19. Ardo si ma non t'amo
9. Fumia la pastorella ⎰	(Guarini)
10. Almo divino raggio ⎱(Allegretti)	20. Ardi o gela (Tasso)
11. All'hora i pastori ⎰	21. Arsi e alsi (Tasso)

☆ R. Wagner Madrigal Singers　　# Lyr.LL 43

Book IV　(1603)　COMPLETE　(5 voices)
1. Ah, dolente partita!	11. A un giro sol de' bell' occhi
2. Cor mio, mentre vi miro	12. Ohimè, se tanto amate!
3. Cor mio non mori?	13. Io mi son giovinetta
4. Sfogava con le stelle	14. Quell'augellin che canta
5. Volgea l'anima mia	15. Non più guerra, pietate
6. Anima mia, perdona	16. Si ch'io vorrei morire
7. Che se tu se'il cor mio	17. Anima dolorosa
8. Luci seren' e chiare	18. Anima del cor mio
9. La piaga ch'ho nel core	19. Longe da te, cor mio
10. Voi pur da me partite	20. Piang' e sospira

M. Couraud Vocal Ens.　　# HS.HSL 141/2
(4ss)　　　(set HSL-O; # DFr. 102/3)
[Nos. 3, 9, 13, 18 on V# DFr.EX 17036; Nos. 2, 11, 15, 16
　　　　　　　on V# DFr.EX 17037]

Book V—EXCERPTS　(1605)
Cruda Amarilli
O Mirtillo
Era l'anima mia
Ecco Silvio
Ch'io t'ami

M. Couraud Vocal Ens.　　# HS.HS 9004
　　　　　　　(# DFr. 104)

Book VI—EXCERPTS　(1614)
Lagrime d'Amante al Sepolcro dell' Amata
Lamento di Arianna
Zeffiro torna

☆ M. Couraud Vocal Ens.　　# HS.HS 9005
　　　　　　　(# DFr. 105)

ON *Il Pastor Fido* (Guarini)
Quell' augellin che canta　(IV)
Cruda Amarilli!　(V)
Ah, dolente partita!　(IV)
O Mirtillo, Mirtillo　(V)
Deh, Mirtillo[1]—Che se tu sei'l cor mio　(IV)
Golden Age Singers—Field-Hyde
(*Marenzio*)　　# West.WLE 105

O Mirtillo, Mirtillo　(V)	5 voices
Era l'anima mia　(Guarini) (V)	5 voices
Damigella tutta bella　(X)	S, A, Bs.
O come vaghi　(IX)	2 T
Sfogava con le stelle　(Rinuccini)　(IV)	5 voices
Dolcissimo uscignolo　(VIII)	5 voices
Interrotte speranze　(VII)	2 T
A un giro　(Guarini)　(IV)	5 voices
Quel sguardo sdegnosetto　(X)	S
Su, su, pastorelli vezzosi　(IX)	3 voices
Qui rise Tirsi　(VI)	5 voices

N. Boulanger Vocal & Inst. Ens. # B.AXTL 1051
　　　　　(# D.UMT 263101; AmD.DL 9627)

Ardo e scoprir　　(IX)
O bel pastor　　(IX)　(*Dialogo di Ninfa e Pastore*)
Io son pur vezzosetta pastorella　(VII)
Tornate o cari baci　(VII)　all 2 vv.
E. Schwarzkopf & I. Seefried (SS), G. Moore
(pf.)　　　　# C.CX 1331
(*Dvořák & Carissimi*)　　(# Angel. 35290)

Amor che deggio far (VII) Canzonetta 4 vv. & str.
Madrigalisti Milanesi & Insts.—Fait
　　　　　# E. & AmVox.PL 8560
(*Il Ballo in onore Imperatore Ferdinando . . . & Il
　Combattimento . . .*)

(Il) Ballo (delle Ninfe d'Istro) T & 5 vv. (VIII) 1638
(in onore dell' Imperatore Ferdinando III⁰ della casa
　d'Austria)　(*Volgendo il ciel*)
A. Nobiloff & Madrigalisti Milanesi, String
ens.—Fait　　# E. & AmVox.PL 8560
(*Il Combattimento . . . & Amor che deggio far*)
☆ Scuola Veneziana Ens.—Ephrikian (# Clc. 6127 &
　　　　　　　# Cum.CPR 322)

Lagrime d'Amante al Sepolcro dell' Amata
　　(VI)　1614
Yale Music School Cho.—Hindemith
　　　　　　　in # Over.LP 4
(† Yale University, Vol. I)

Maledetto sia l'aspetto (Scherzo musicale, 1632)
R. Hayes (T), R. Boardman (pf.)
　　　　　　　in # Van.VRS 448
(*Machaut, Caccini, Telemann, etc.*)

Mentre vaga angioletta 2 T (VIII) 1638
☆ Scuola Veneziana Ens.—Ephrikian
　　　　　　(# Clc. 6127 & # Cum.CPR 322)

---

[1] Set by Monteverdi as *Anima mea*, but original Guarini text used on this disc.

O bel pastor (*Dialogo di Ninfa e Pastore*) (IX) 2 vv.
Tornate o cari baci (VIII) 2 vv.
M. Meli (S), O. Moscucci (S), V. Vitale (pf.)
(*Pergolesi, Matteis*)   ♭ *C.SEDQ 503*

Ohimé, ch'io cado (IX) 1651
☆ M. Meili (T), R. Gerlin (hpsi.), vlc. (in † ♯ HS.AS 9)

Partenza amorosa (Se pur destino) (VII) 1619
☆ M. Laszlo (S), F. Holetschek (pf.)
(† Italian Songs)   in ♯ Nix.WLP 5119

Questi vaghi 9 vv. & cont. (V) 1605
... Sinfonia — ARR. BRASS QUINTET Beck
Music Hall Brass Ens.   in ♯ *Mono. 817*
(† Music for Brass)

S'andasse amor a caccia (II) 5 vv. 1590
Vattene pur crudel (III) 5 vv. 1592
L. Marenzio Ens.—Saraceni † V♯ *AS. 1804LD*
    (♯ HS.AS 8)

Tempro la cetra 1 v. & cont. (VII) 1619
... Sinfonia — ARR. BRASS QUINTET Beck
Music Hall Brass Ens.   in ♯ *Mono. 817*
(† Music for Brass)

OPERAS, etc.
ARIANNA 8 scenes 1608
Lasciatemi morire (Lamento)
I. Kolassi (M-S), J. Bonneau (pf.)
    in ♯ *D.FAT 173160*
(† Arie Antiche & German Lieder)   (♯ Lon.LL 747)
E. Höngen (A), 2 hpsis, & cbs.[1]   *PV. 8402*
(2ss)   (♭ *Pol. 37011*)
(*below & Carissimi, on* ♯ HP.APM 14020; AmD.ARC 3005)
F. Barbieri (M-S), D. Marzollo (pf.)
    in ♯ *AmVox.PL 7980*
(† Old Italian Songs & Airs)
E. Höngen (A, *Ger*) & Wurttemberg State Op.
—Leitner[1]   *PV. 72379*
☆ B. Gigli (T)   in ♯ *G.ALP 1174*
(† Italian Classic Songs)   (♯ *FALP 340*: ♭ *7RF 266*)
☆ M. Laszlo (S), F. Holetschek (pf.)
    (in † Italian Songs, ♯ *Nix.WLP 5119*)
— FOR PRACTICE: (in ♯ *VS.MH 1002*)

(II) BALLO DELL' INGRATE 1 Act 1608 (VIII)
COMPLETE RECORDING[2]
E. Tegani (S), C. Carbi (M-S), L. Sgarro (Bs),
Milan Cha. Cho. & Orch.—Gerelli
    ♯ E. & AmVox.PL 8090

**(II) COMBATTIMENTO DI TANCREDI E
CLORINDA** (Tasso) (VIII) 1624
C. Carbi (M-S), E. Tegani (S), A. Nobile (T) &
Milan Monteverdi Ens.—Fait[2]
    ♯ E. & AmVox.PL 8560
[A. Soresino, hpsi.]
(*Amor che deggio far, & Ballo delle Ninfe*)
☆ Soloists & Scuola Veneziana Orch.—Ephrikian
    (♯ Clc. 6127 & ♯ Cum.CPR 322)
Soloists, str. & hpsi. (in † ♯ HS.AS 9), including a
Sinfonia

(L') INCORONAZIONE DI POPPEA 3 Acts 1642
SLIGHTLY ABRIDGED RECORDING ed. Goehr

Poppea	... ... S. Gähwiller (S)
Nerone	... F. Brückner-Rüggeberg (T)
Ottone	... ... M. Ott-Penetto (A)
Seneca	... ... F. Kelch (Bs)
Ottavia	... ... M. Helbing (A)
Amalta	... M. Witte-Waldbauer (A)
Drusilla	... ... H. Juon (S)
Amor	... ... A. Gamper (S)

etc., Cho. & Zürich Tonhalle Orch.—Goehr
(6ss)   ♯ CHS. set CHS 1184
    (♯ Clc. 6240/2)
EXCERPTS from this recording on ♯ CHS.CHS 1226;
    MMS. 2028 & OP 5
ACT I: Intro. & excerpts Sc. 1, 3, 7
ACT II: Excerpts Sc. 1, 2, 7
ACT III: Excerpts Sc. 1, 2, 3

ORFEO 3 Acts 1607
COMPLETE RECORDING
☆ G. Lammers (M-S), E. Trötschel & E. Fleischer (S),
    H. Krebs & M. Meili (T), W. Kahl (Bs), Berlin
    Radio Cho. & Orch.—Koch (6ss) ♯ HS. set 30001
Excerpts:
Sinfonie, Ritornelli & Dances on V♯ *DFr.EX 17020*
Dramatic Scenes, Acts II & IV, M. Meili, on V♯ *DFr.EX 17021*
ORCH. EXCERPTS — ARR. BRASS QUINTET Beck
Sinfonia (Finale, Act I)
Ritornelli (Act V)
Moresca (Act V)
Music Hall Brass Ens.   in ♯ *Mono. 817*
(† Music for Brass)
Ritornelli & Sinfonie
☆ Czech Phil.—Pedrotti (in ♯ Csm.CLPS 1046)
Tu sei morta Act II
N. Brincker (T), T. Nielsen (lute), M. Wöldike
(org.)   in ♯ *HS.HSL 2072*
(† Masterpieces of Music before 1750)
(& in † Histoire de la Musique vocale)
Vi ricordo, o bosch' ombrosi Act II
R. Hayes (T), R. Boardman (pf.) in ♯ *A440.12-3*
Act IV, Excerpt[3]
A. Mandikian (S), R. Lewis (T), J. McCarthy
(T), S. Carr (B), Cho. & Orch.—Westrup
    G.HMS 44
(† History of Music in Sound)   (in ♯ Vic. set LM 6029)

SACRED WORKS
Laetatus sum (Psalm 122) Cho., orch. & orch. (XVI)
Rome Qtt. Soc. Cho. & Orch.—Nucci
    in ♯ Csm.CLPS 1050
(*Vivaldi, Frescobaldi*)
Magnificat primo (XV) 8 voices 1641
☆ Venice Schola & Ens.—Ephrikian (♯ Cpt.MC 20033)
MASS (a 4 voci da cappella) 1651 (XVI)
Amsterdam Motet Cho.—de Nobel
    ♯ CHS.CHS 1196
(*Lassus: Domine, ne in furore*)   (♯ Clc. 6280)

VESPERS OF THE BLESSED VIRGIN
    1610 (XIV)
COMPLETE RECORDINGS
M. Ritchie & E. Morison (S), W. Herbert &
R. Lewis (T), B. Boyce (B), London Singers
& O.L. Ens.—Lewis[4]   ♯ LOL.OL 50021/2
(4ss) [G. Jones, org.; R. Gerlin, hpsi.]   (♯ OL.LD 99/100)
M. Guilleaume & F. Sailer (S), L. Wolf-
Matthäus (A), H. Marten & W. Hohmann
(T), F. Kelch (Bs), Swabian Cho. Soc. &
Stuttgart Bach Orch.—Grischkat[5]
    ♯ E. & AmVox. set PL 7902
(4ss) [H. Liedecke, org.; H. Elsner, hpsi.]
... Domine ad adjuvandum; Nigra sum; Ave, Maris
Stella
☆ Venice Schola & Ens.—Ephrikian (♯ Cpt.MC 20033)
... 8 excerpts[6]
Soloists, Univ. of Illinois Oratorio Soc. & Sym.
—Stokowski   ♯ UOI.CRS 1
... Sonata sopra Sancta Maria S & insts.
St. Hedwig Cath. Cho. Trebles, 2 vlns., 2 cornetti,
3 trombs., gamba & org.—Gorvin[7]
    ♯ HP.APM 14020
(*Arianna, Lamento & Carissimi*)   (♯ AmD.ARC 3005)

MONTSALVATGE, Xavier (b. 1912)
(5) Canciones negras 1944-5
... Nana para dormir a un negrito (Valdes)
... Canto negro (Guillen)
N. Merriman (M-S), G. Moore (pf.)
    ♯ C.CX 1243
(† Spanish Songs)   (♯ FCX 392; Angel. 35208)

---

[1] ARR. Orff.   [2] Ed. Mortari.
[3] Beginning at *Pietade oggi* (p. 120 of Malipiero edn.) and continuing to the end of p. 129.   [4] Ed. Schrade.
[5] Ed. Redlich. Omits *Nisi Dominus* and *Lauda Jerusalem* and uses Magnificat I (7 voices).
[6] Contains Nos. 1, 3, 10, 12, 2, 11, 13 in that order, with cuts; and a T solo *O quam pulchra es* which does not appear to
be part of the *Vespers*.
[7] Ed. Malipiero.

(5) Canciones negras (*continued*)

... **Nana para dormir a un negrito**
L. Huarte (S)   ♯ *MusH.LP 3004*
(*Granados, Turina, etc.*)

MOORE, Douglas   (b. 1893)

Symphony No. 2, A major 1946
Californian Sym.—Jomelli   ♯ *ML. 7037*
(*Nixon*)
☆ A.R.S. Orch.—Dixon   (2ss)   (♯ *ARS. 5*)

MORALES, Cristobal   (*c.* 1500-1553)

Inter vestibulum
Pamplona Cho.—Morondo   ♯ *Sel.LPG 8738*
(† *Spanish Renaissance Music*)

Puer natus est nobis 3 vv. 1543
F.A.D. Polyphonic Cho.—Ribó in ♯ *C.CX 1308*
(*Victoria, Vasquez, etc.*)   (♯ *Angel. 35257*)
Petits Chanteurs de la Renaissance
                                   V♯ *Era.LDE 1001*
(† *Polyphonic Motets*)   (♯ *HS.HS 9007*)

MORATA, Gines de   (fl. XVIth Cent.)

SEE: † SPANISH RENAISSANCE MUSIC

MORENO TORROBA, Federico (b. 1891)

(Abridged listings only)

GUITAR PIECES
Arada[1]: **Burgalesca, F sharp major; Albada**
☆ A. Segovia (in ♯ *D.UMT 273029*)
Arada; Fandanguillo[1]
☆ A. Segovia (in ♯ *AmC.ML 4732*)
Fandanguillo castellano[1]
C. Aubin   in ♯ *Eko.LG 1*
(† *Guitar Recital*)
— ARR. VLC. & PF.
J. Starker & L. Pommers   in ♯ *Nix.PLP 584*
                          (♯ *Per.SPL 584; Cpt.MC 20054*)
Madronos
☆ A. Segovia (in †♯ *B.AXTL 1060*)
Melodia
N. Yepes   in ♯ *D.LXT 2974*
(† *Spanish Music*)   (♯ *FST 153076; Lon.LL 1042*)
Nocturno
A. Segovia   in ♯ *B.AXTL 1070*
(† *Segovia Evening*)
          (♯ *SpC.CCL 35015; AmD.DL 9733; AFest. 10-729*)
C. Aubin   in ♯ *Eko.LG 1*
(† *Guitar Recital*)
A. Lagoya   ♭ *FV.F 75018*
(*Handel: Sarabande & Presti: Danse rythmique*)
Punteado
M. A. Funes   *ArgOd. 57058*
— ORCH. VERSION
Madrid Theatre—Moreno Torroba   in ♯ *AmD.DL 9789*
Serenata burlesca
A. Segovia   in ♯ *AmD.DL 9734*
(† *Segovia Plays*)   (♯ *D.UAT 273573*)
M. A. Funes   *ArgOd. 56544*
(*Chopin: Prelude & Mazurka*)
L. Almeida   in ♯ *DCap.CTL 7089*
(† *Guitar Music of Spain*)
Sonatina
☆ A. Segovia (in † ♯ *D.UAT 273141*)

ORCHESTRAL
COLLECTIONS (Probably largely from Stage Works)
ANTEQUERA: Preludio sevillano[2]
MONTE CARMELO: Habanera
Jardines de Granada
Madrid Theatre Orch.—Moreno Torroba
                          in ♯ *B.AXTL 1077*
(*Gimenez, Chueca, etc.*)   (♯ *AmD.DL 9735*)
Madrigal
Folia canaria
Habañera del Panulito
En la reja Sevillana
Madrid Theatre—Moreno Torrobo
                          in ♯ *AmD.DL 9788*

Danzas Asturianas
Moscico Sevillano orch.
Madrid Th.—Moreno Torroba
                          in ♯ *B.AXTL 1078*
(*below & Chapi, Chueca, etc.*)
                          (♯ *AmD.DL 9736; SpC.CCLP 34003*)
Madrilenas Suite
Madrid Theatre—Moreno Torroba
                          in ♯ *AmD.DL 9763*
(*Albeniz, Breton, Guridi, etc.*)
Marcha Granadera
Spanish Air Force Band—d'Arriba (in ♯ *AmD.DL 9792*)
Mosaico Sevillano
Madrid Theatre Orch.—Machado
                          in ♯ *B.AXTL 1074*
                          (♯ *AmD.DL 9757; SpC.CCL 35002*)
Majestic Orch. (in **V**♯ *MusH.LP 1058*)
Taconeo clasico
Madrid Theatre—Moreno Torroba
                          in ♯ *AmD.DL 9789*
ZARZUELAS
ANTEQUERA: Preludio sevillano[2]
Sym. Orch.—Ferrer   in ♯ *C.FSX 104*
(also, Reg.M 10045: ♭ *SEDL 110*)   (in ♯ *Reg.LCX 104*)
Sym.—Moreno Torroba (in ♯ *Angel. 65008, o.n. SS 70008;*
                                     Pam.LRC 15905)
(La) CARAMBA
C. Rubio, I. Rivadeneyra, T. Pardo, P. Vidal,
etc., cho. & orch.—Moreno Torroba
                          ♯ *Phi.N 00593L*
(*Chapi: La Bruja, excpts.*)   (♯ *AmC.ML 4930*)
LUISA FERNANDA Lyric Comedy 3 Acts
R. Gómez, L. Torrentó, M. Redondo, P. Civil,
etc., cho. & orch.—Moreno Torroba
                          ♯ *Reg.LCX 103*
(♯ *Pam.LRC 15904; Angel. 65009; Excerpts in*
♭ *Angel. 70010; ♭ Reg.SEBL 7003 & 7007: ♭ LS 1005*)
A. Morales, C. Munguía, M. Ausensi, etc., cho.
& orch.—Argenta   ♯ *LI.TW 91022*
                          (♯ *Ambra.MCC 30022*)
M. D. Ripollés (S), A. Rojo (S), I. Rivadenyra
(M-S), etc., cho. & orch.—Moreno Torroba
(*Maravilla*)   ♯ *Phi.N 00596L*
Ay! mi morena; Mazurka de las sombrillas; Habañera de
soldadito
Madrid Zarzuela Theatre—Moreno Torroba
                          (in ♯ *B.AXTL 1078; AmD.DL 9736*)
Orch. Selections in **V**♯ *MusH.LP 1058*
Vocal excerpts
L. Sagi-Vela (in ♯ *MusH.LP 5003*)
R. Cesari & Colón Th. Cho. (*ArgOd. 66064*)
MARAVILLA
C. Rubio (S), M. D. Ripollés (S), P. Vidal (B),
& orch.—Moreno Torroba   ♯ *Phi.N 00596L*
(*Luisa Fernanda*)
Vocal excerpts L. Sagi-Vela (B) (in ♯ *MusH.LP 5003*)
(La) MARCHENERA
La Petenera S
L. Berchman   in ♯ *Mont.FM 28*
PART SONG: Camino de Mieres
Pamplona Cho.—Morondo (in ♯ *CFD. 26*)

---

[1] From *Suite Castellana.*
[2] It has not been possible to confirm that this piece is in fact from a Zarzuela; it may be a separate work for orch.

MORIN, Jean-Baptiste (1677-1745)

(La) CHASSE DU CERF
Divertissement 7 Scenes 1708

Diane	M. Gerault (S)
Psécas	A. Hauville (S)
Phiale	J. Roux-Legrain (S)
Néphèle	S. Gazal (A)

Blanchard Cho. & Orch.—Douatte
♯ Cpt.MC 20109

MORLEY, Thomas (1557-c. 1603)

CLASSIFIED: I. Ayres
           II. Madrigals
           III. Church Music
           IV. Instrumental

I. AYRES
Voice & lute 1600

COLLECTION
It was a lover and his lass (Shakespeare)
Mistress mine, well may you fare
Can I forget what reason's force
Fair in a morn (Breton)
  R. Soames (T), W. Gerwig (lute), J. Koch
   (gamba)   PV. 5410
   (Dowland & Campion, on ♯ AmD.ARC 3004)

I saw my lady weeping
  C. Bressler (T) & Pro Musica Ens.
               in ♯ AmC.ML 5051
   († Evening of Elizabethan Verse & Music)

It was a lover and his lass (Shakespeare)
  A. Deller (C-T), D. Dupré (lute)
              in ♯ G.ALP 1265
   († Shakespeare Songs & Lute Solos)
  ☆ H. Cuénod (T), H. Leeb (lute)
             in ♯ Nix.WLP 5085
   († XVIth & XVIIth Century Songs)

O mistress mine (Shakespeare)[1]
  A. Deller (C-T), D. Dupré (lute)
              in ♯ G.ALP 1265
   († Shakespeare Songs)

Thyrsis and Milla arm in arm
  R. Soames (T), D. Poulton (lute) G.HMS 40
   († History of Music in Sound) (in ♯ Vic. set LM 6029)

II. MADRIGALS

(Roman figures refer to Vols. of *English Madrigal School*)

COLLECTION
Sing we and chant it Ballett, 5 vv. IV
Cease, mine eyes Canzonet, 3 vv. I
Now is the month of maying Ballett, 5 vv. IV
Miraculous love's wounding Canzonet, 2 vv. I
Now is the gentle season Madrigal, 4 vv. II
The fields abroad Madrigal, 4 vv. II
I go before, my darling Canzonet, 2 vv. I
Lady, those cherries plenty Ballett, 5 vv. IV
Phyllis, I fain would die now Dialogue, 7 vv. IV
My bonny lass she smileth Ballett, 5 vv. IV
Lo, she flies when I woo her Ballett, 5 vv. IV
Leave alas this tormenting Ballett, 5 vv. IV
Clorinda false, adieu Madrigal, 4 vv. II
Fire! fire! my heart! Ballett, 5 vv. IV
  Primavera Singers—Greenberg ♯ Eso.ES 520
  (Goe from my window & Galiarda; & Anon.: Barafostus'
  dreame; Irish dumpe; Can she, FVB. 18, 178, 188)
                (♯ Cpt.MC 20072)

About the maypole new Ballett, 5 vv. IV
  N.Y. Pro. Musica Antiqua—Greenberg
               in ♯ Eso.ESJ 6
   († Elizabethan Songbag)

April is in my mistress' face 4 vv. II 1594
  Hufstader Singers   in ♯ SOT. 1092
  New England Cons. Alumni Cho.—de Varon
             in ♯ HSL.HSL 2068
   († English Madrigals)

Arise, awake 5 vv.
Hard by a crystal fountain 6 vv.
  (Madrigals from *Triumphs of Oriana* 1601-3)
  Randolph Singers   in ♯ Nix.WLP 6212-1/2
   († Triumphs of Oriana)   (♯ West. set WL 212)

Fire! fire! my heart! Ballett, 5 vv. IV 1595
  New England Cons. Alumni Cho.—de Varon
             in ♯ HS.HSL 2068
   († English Madrigals)

Ho! who comes here 4 vv. II 1594
  Golden Age Singers   G.HMS 33
   († History of Music in Sound) (in ♯ Vic. set LM 6029)

My bonny lass she smileth Ballett, 5 vv. IV 1595
  St. Paul's Cath. Cho.—Dykes Bower
             in ♯ C.CX 1237
  (Haydn, Bairstow, Wood, etc.) (♯ Angel. 35139 in set 3516)
  New England Cons. Cho.—de Varon
             in ♯ HS.HSL 2068
   († English Madrigals)
  Stanford Univ. Cho.—Schmidt   ♯ ML. 7022
   († Madrigals & Motets)

Now is the month of maying Ballett, 5 vv. IV 1595
— ARR. VOICE & PF. Fellowes
  J. Vyvyan (S), E. Lush (pf.) in ♯ D.LXT 2797
   († Songs of England)   (in ♯ Lon.LL 806)
  (also in ♯ D.LW 5102; Lon.LD 9113)

Since my tears and lamenting 4 vv. II 1594
  ☆ Cho.—Opienski   in ♯ HS.AS 10
   († Anthologie Sonore)

Sing we and chant it Ballett, 5 vv. IV 1595
  Madrigal Singers—Robe   in ♯ Fred. 2
  (Byrd, Wilbye, etc.)

Though Philomela lost her love 3 vv. I 1593
— ARR. RECORDERS
  Chapelle de Bourgogne Recorder Trio
              in ♯ OL.LD 81
   († Musiciens de la Cour ... II)

III. CHURCH MUSIC

Agnus Dei 4 vv. 1597
  St. Paul's Cath. Cho.—Dykes Bower
                 G.HMS 37
   († History of Music in Sound) (in ♯ Vic. set LM 6029)
  N.Y. Primavera Singers—Greenberg
             in ♯ Per.SPL 597
   († Renaissance Music)   (♯ Cpt.MC 20077)
  Stanford Univ. Cho.—Schmidt in ♯ ML. 7022
   († Madrigals & Motets)

Domine, fac mecum 4 vv.
Eheu, sustulerunt Dominum 4 vv.
  N.Y. Primavera Singers   in ♯ Per.SPL 597
   († Renaissance Music)   (in ♯ Cpt.MC 20077)

Nolo mortem peccatoris 4 vv.
  St. Paul's Cath. Cho.—Dykes Bower
  (Taverner & Byrd)   † C.LX 1604

IV. INSTRUMENTAL MUSIC

Air 3 viols 1597
  (from *Plain and easy introduction ...*)
  Consort of Viols   in ♯ Van.BG 539
   († Elizabethan & Jacobean Music) (♯ Ama.AVRS 6001)

FANTASIAS[2]
Il Grillo; Il Lamento
  Musician's Workshop Recorder Consort
             in ♯ CEd.CE 1018
   († Recorder Music of Six Centuries)
La Sampogna
  B. Krames & E. Kyburg (recorders) ♯ Eso.ESJ 6
   († Elizabethan Songbag)

VIRGINALS PIECES
Fantasia FVB. 124
  C. Koenig (hpsi.)   in ♯ EMS. 236
   († Elizabethan Keyboard Music)

---

[1] From the *First Book of Consort Lessons*, 1599; ARR. S. Beck.
[2] From *Canzonets to 2 voices*, 1595.

Galiarda FVB. 154
Goe from my window FVB. 9
    B. Winogron (virginals)   in ‡ Eso.ES 520
    (*Anon. pieces; & Madrigals, above, etc.*) (‡ Cpt.MC 20072)

MOSCHELES, Ignaz (1794-1870)

Études (unspec.) pf.
    A. d'Arco   in *Plé.P 102*

MOSSOLOV, Alexander (b. 1900)

Music of the Machines (Steel Foundry) 1927
    London Phil. Sym.—Quadri ‡ Nix.WLP 20000
    (*Chabrier & Revueltas*)   (‡ West.LAB 7004)

MOSZKOWSKI, Moritz (1854-1925)

Caprice espagnole, Op. 37 pf.
    J. Hofmann[1]   in ‡ AmC.ML 4929
    (*Chopin, Rachmaninoff, etc.*)

Concerto, E major, Op. 59 pf. & orch.
    H. Kann & Netherlands Phil.—Goehr
                            ‡ CHS.CHS 1197
                                (‡ Clc. 6255)

En automne, Op. 36, No. 4 pf.
    E. Burton   in ‡ CEd.CE 1024

Guitare, Op. 45, No. 2 pf.
 — ARR. VLN. & PF. ☆ Y. Sitkovetsky & pf. (*USSRM.D 863*)

Spanish Dances pf. 4 hands — ARR. ORCH.
Bolero, Op. 12, No. 5; & 1 unspec.
    Moscow Radio—Orlov (*USSR. 7448/9*)

Valse, E major, Op. 34, No. 1 pf.
 — ARR. HARP. ☆ E. Vito (in ‡ Nix.SLPY 145)

MOULINIÉ, E. (fl. XVIIth Cent.)

    SEE: † AIRS À BOIRE

MOURET, Jean-Joseph (1682-1738)

SUITES DE SYMPHONIES 1729

No. 1: 1. Allegro en Rondeau 2. Gracieusement
    3. Fanfares   4. Gigue-Guay
                            vlns., obs., tpts, drums
No. 2: 1. Overture   2. Allegro   3. Airs I & II
    4. Gavottes I & II 5. Minuets I & II
    6. Fanfare   7. Air & Fanfare (reprise)
                    vlns., obs. & cors de chasse
    Leclair Ens.—Paillard V‡ Era.LDE 1020
    [Omitting Suite 2, No. 5. The viola part "reconstituted"
    by J-F. Paillard]

... **Suite No. 1** only
    Paris Cha. Ens.—Douatte   ‡ LI.TWV 91092
    (*Lalande, Couperin, Lully, Philidor*) (‡ Cpt.MC 20086)
    [No. 3 only, with *Dandrieu*, ♭ *Cpt.EXTP 1014*]

MOUSSORGSKY, Modest Petrovich
(1839-1881)

I. INSTRUMENTAL & ORCHESTRAL

(The) Capture of Kars
    Triumphal March, orch. 1880[2]
    Philharmonia—Susskind   in ‡ P.PMC 1018
    (*below*)   (‡ MGM.E 3030; Od.ODX 148: ♭ BSOE 4003)

 — ARR. BAND Goguillot "*Turkish March*"
    French Navy Band—Maillot (in ‡ Sel. 270.C.055)

Intermezzo symphonique in modo classico, B minor
    (orig. pf.) 1867
Scherzo, B flat major 1858
    Philharmonia—Susskind   ‡ P.PMC 1018
    (*above; & Opera excerpts*) (‡ MGM.E 3030; Od.ODX 148:
                                ♭ BSOE 4002/3)

Night on the bare mountain 1867
 — ED. & ARR. ORCH. Rimsky-Korsakov
    Paris Cons.—Ansermet   in ‡ D.LXT 2833
    (*Prokofiev, Glinka, Borodin*)   (‡ D.LL 864)
    (*Borodin only, on* ‡ D.LW 5060; Lon.LD 9086)
    London Phil. Sym.—Rodzinski
                            ‡ West.LAB 7034
    (*Kodály: Hary János*)
    French Nat. Radio—Markevitch ‡ C.CX 1208
    (*Tchaikovsky & Borodin*)   (‡ FCX 349: QCX 10134; Angel. 35144)
                                (also ♭ G. 7ERL 1029)
    Philharmonia—Susskind   ‡ P.PMC 1018
    (*above & below*)
                (‡ Od.ODX 148; ‡ MGM.E 3030: & in ‡ E 3046)
    Florence Fest.—Gui   ‡ AudC. 502
    (*Borodin, Debussy, Dukas*)
    Lamoureux—Fournet   ‡ *Phi.S 06022R*
    (*Borodin: In the Steppes of Central Asia*)
    Sym.—Stokowski[3]   ‡ Vic.LM 1816
    (*Khovanshchina, excpts.; & Rimsky, Glier, Borodin*)
                                (♭ G. 7ER 5060)
    (♭ Vic. set ERB 1816; ‡ FV.A 630215; ItV.A12R 0141;
                                DV.L 16482)
    Moscow Radio—Golovanov   ‡ *USSR.D 795*
    (*Rachmaninoff*)
    Austrian Sym.—Koslik   in ‡ Rem. 199-130
    (*Borodin & Rimsky-Korsakov*)   (‡ Cum.CR 293)
    Netherlands Phil.—Goehr   ‡ MMS. 27
    (*Dukas: L'Apprenti Sorcier*)   (& in ‡ MMS. 100)
    ☆ Belgian Radio—André   ‡ T.TW 30007
    (*Tchaikovsky: 1812 Overture*)   (TV.VSK 9012 &
                                ‡ FT. 255. TC. 008, d.cs)
    ☆ Philharmonia—Malko (in ‡ BB.LBC 1022:
                                ♭ set WBC 1022)
    Paris Cons.—Cluytens (♭ AmVox.VIP 45520:
                        in ‡ Pat.QTX 116; ArgPat.ADTX 101)
    Philharmonia—Kletzki (♭ C.GQX 8047/8)
    Berlin Phil.—Ludwig (in ‡ ANix.ULP 9035:
                                & in ‡ MTW. 502)
    [3] Philadelphia—Stokowski (in ‡ Cam.CAL 118 &
                                set CFL 103)

 — ARR. 4 PFS. Manhattan Pf. Qtt. (in ‡ MGM.E 3130)

Pictures from an exhibition pf. 1874
    L. Pennario   ‡ DCap.CCL 7525
                                (‡ Cap.LAL 8266)
    A. Uninsky (2ss)   ‡ *Phi.N 00652R*
    (*Liszt, on* ‡ Epic.LC 3066)
    A. Brendel   ‡ AmVox.PL 9140
    (*Balakirev & Stravinsky*)
    A. Boucourechliev   ‡ Sel. 270.C.022
    L. Oborin   ‡ CdM.LD 8038
    A. Baller   JpV.SD 3029/32
    (*7ss—Baller: Suite, excpt.*)   (set JAS 199
    ☆ V. Horowitz[4] (‡ G.FALP/QALP 146; DV.L 16457)
    S. Biro (‡ Cum.CR 230)
... Intro. & Nos. 3, 4, 5 M. v. Doren (in ‡ Chan.MVDP 3)

 — ARR. ORCH. Ravel[4]
    Suisse Romande—Ansermet   ‡ D.LXT 2896
    (*Ravel: La Valse*)   (‡ Lon.LL 956)
    N.B.C. Sym.—Toscanini   ‡ G.ALP 1218
    (*Franck*) (‡ Vic.LM 1838: ♭ set ERB 35:
                        ‡ ItV.A12R 0125; FV.A 630249)
    Czech Phil.—Pedrotti   ‡ Sup.SLPV 200
    (2ss)   (‡ U. 5180G)
    London Phil. Sym.—Rodzinski
                            ‡ West.LAB 7019
    Berlin Phil.—Markevitch   ‡ HP.DG 16061
    (*Wagner, on* ‡ AmD.DL 9782) (also, 4ss, ♮ PV. 72370/1)
                            (*continued on next page*)

---

[1] Recorded at Met. Op. House recital Nov., 1937.
[2] Using material from *Mlada*.
[3] ARR. Stokowski.
[4] Omitting Promenade preceding No. 7.

Pictures from an exhibition (*continued*)

Belgian Radio—André   **♯ DT.LGX 66008**
(2ss)   (♯ T.LE 6506; FT. 320.TC.030)

Philadelphia—Ormandy   **♯ AmC.ML 4700**
(*Stravinsky*)   (♯ Phi.A 01187L)

Leipzig Radio—Abendroth   **♯ Ura.RS 7-18**
(*Stravinsky*)   (♯ Ura. 7157; MTW. 521)

Moscow Radio—Golovanov ♯ **USSR. 01259/60**
(2ss)   (10ss, *USSR. 7600/12*)

☆ Amsterdam—Dorati (2ss)   ♯ *EPhi.ABR 4013*
(*Smetana* on ♯ Epic.LC 3015)

Anon. Orch. (♯ *ACC.MP 22*)

☆ Chicago Sym.—Kubelik (♯ *G.FBLP 1031: WBLP 1002*)
Boston Sym.—Koussevitzky (♯ Cam.CAL 111)
N.Y.P.S.O.—Rodzinski (♯ AmC.RL 3119)
"Nat. Op." Orch. (♯ Gram. 2069)

— ARR. ACCORDEONS Wurthner
Wurthner Accordeon Orch.   **♯ *Pat.ST 1005***
(*Wurthner: Variations*)

... **No. 5, Ballet of chickens in their shells**
— — ARR. FL., OB., CL., HRN. & BSN.
Chicago Sym. Woodwind Ens. (in ♯ Aphe.AP 17)

... **No. 10, The great gate at Kiev** — ARR. 4 PFS.
Manhattan Pf. Quartet (in ♯ MGM.E 3130)

II. OPERAS

BORIS GODOUNOV Prol. & 4 Acts 1874
COMPLETE RECORDINGS
Set C

Boris	M. Changalovich (Bs)
Feodor	S. Janovich (M-S)
Xenia	Z. Sesardich (S)
Prince Shuisky	S. Andrashevich (T)
Pimen	B. Pivnichki (Bs)
Gregory	M. Brajnik (T)
Varlaam	Z. Tzveych (Bs)

etc. & Belgrade Nat. Op. Cho. & Orch.
—Baranović (6ss)[1]   ♯ **D.LXT 5054/6**

SET A. ☆ B. Christoff (Bs), E. Zareska (M-S), etc., Cho.
& French Radio Orch.—Dobrowen
[Highlights on ♯ Vic.LHMV 1052] ♯ *G.WALP 1044/7*
(♯ ArgA.LPC 11549/52)

☆ Soloists, Bolshoi Theatre Cho. & Orch.—Golovanov
(8ss)   ♯ **USSR.D 0304/12**
(also 6ss, ♯ Roy. 1390/2 & ♯ Gram. 20132/4)
[Excerpts also ♯ *MMS.* set M 114 & OP 13;
also ♭ *Roy.EP 204*]

COLLECTED EXCERPTS

Prologue—Sc. 1, Excerpts; Sc. 2: Coronation Scene, COMPLETE
Chanting of the Monks at Tchudov Monastery Act I, Sc. 1
In the Town of Kazan (Varlaam's Song) Act I, Sc. 2
I have attained power (Monologue) Act II
Ah! I am suffocating (Clock Scene) Act II
Polonaise cho. & orch. Act III, Sc. 2
I am dying (Death of Boris) Act IV, Sc. 1
Revolutionary Scene Excerpts Act IV, Sc. 2
N. Rossi-Lemeni (Bs), R. Cauwet (Tr),
L. Mason (T), San Francisco Op. Cho. &
Boys' Cho., San Francisco Sym. Orch.
—Stokowski   **♯ Vic.LM 1764**
(♭ set *WDM 1764*; ♯ ItV.A12R 0068)

"HIGHLIGHTS"
☆ A. Kipnis (Bs), I. Tamarin (T), Victor Cho. & Orch.
—Berezowsky (♯ BB.LBC 1082)
[2] M. Reizen (Bs), soloists, cho & orch. of Marinsky
Theatre—Kabalevsky (♯ Csm.CRLP 10170)
[3] M. Reizen & Bolshoi Theatre (with *Glinka*)
(in ♯ *Mon.MEL 710*)
Soloists, Berlin Op. Cho. & Orch. (? *Ger*) (♯ Roy. 1428)

Symphonic Synthesis
— ARR. & ORCH. Stokowski
☆ Philadelphia—Stokowski (♯ Cam.CAL 140)

PROLOGUE, Scene II

Coronation Scene ... I am oppressed Bs
☆ Vanni-Marcoux (*Fr*) (in ♯ G.FJLP 5035)

— ARR. 2 PFS.
☆ P. Luboshutz & G. Nemenoff (in ♯ Cam.CAL 198)

ACT I, Scene 1

Still one more page (Pimen's Monologue)
▽ M. Mikhailov   **USSR. 12244/5**

ACT I, Scene 2

COMPLETE RECORDING
M. Reizen (Bs), G. Nelepp (T), etc., & Bolshoi
Theatre Orch.—Nebolsin ♯ **USSR.D 959/60**
(2ss) (also on ♯ USSR.D 01369)

In the town of Kazan (Varlaam's Song) Bs
R. Arié[2]   **♯ D.LW 5067**
(*below; & Rubinstein*)   (♯ Lon.LD 9073)

S. Belarsky   in ♯ **Vic.LPM 3274**
(*below; Sadko, Ruslan, etc.*)   (♭ set EPB 3274)

☆ B. Christoff (♯ *G.WBLP 1005: QBLP 5002;*
♭ *Vic.EHA 11*)

B. Gmyria (*USSRM.D 00810*)

ACT II

I have attained to power (*Monologue*) Bs
R. Arié[2]   **♯ D.LW 5067**
(*above & Rubinstein*)   (♯ Lon.LD 9073)

S. Belarsky   in ♯ **Vic.LPM 3274**
(*above*)   (♭ set EPB 3274)

G. London   in ♯ AmC.ML 4999
(*Falstaff, Rigoletto, Otello, etc.*)

I. Petrov & Dresden Op. Orch.—Konwitschny
♯ Eta. 720002
(*Barbiere & Tchaikovsky: Songs*)   (o.n. *LPM 1017*)

E. Kossowski   **Muza.X 2284**
(*below*) (*Halka, aria, on X 2144*)

A. Pirogov   *USSR. 8236/7*

J. Greindl (*Ger*)   ♭ *Pol. 34006*
(*Eugene Oniegin—Aria*)

T. Kuuzik (*Estonian*)(*USSR. 22234/5:* in ♯ *D 2090*)

☆ B. Christoff (♭ *Vic.EHA 11*)
B. Gmyria (*USSRM.D 00246*)
A. Pernet (*Fr*) (in ♯ *Od.ODX 135*)

Ah! I am suffocating (*Clock Scene*)
G. London   in ♯ **AmC.ML 4999**
(*above; & Rigoletto, Falstaff, etc.*)

E. Kossowski   *Muza. 2250*

☆ A. Pernet (*Fr*) (in ♯ Od.ODX 135)

ACT III, Scene 2

Polonaise
☆ Berlin Phil.—Ludwig (in ♯ ANix.ULP 9035)

Fountain Scene S & T
L. Rudenko & V. Kozeratsky (*Ukrainian*)
♯ USSR.D 1949
(*Halka & Eugene Oniegin*)
✠ M. Davidoff & D. Smirnoff (AF.AGSB 72*)

ACT IV, Scene 1

One evening I was alone (Pimen's Monologue) Bs
I. Mikulin   **Muza.X 2284**
(*above*) [& E. Kossowski, Bs]

I am dying (Farewell & Death of Boris) Bs
M. Reizen, B. Zlatogorova, Bolshoi Th. Cho.
& Orch.[4]   *USSRM.D 00249/50*
A. Pirogov   *USSRM.D 00178*
(*Khovanshchina—All is quiet*)
R. Arié[2]   **♯ D.LW 5079**
(*Don Carlos*)   (♯ Lon.LD 9018)
E. Kossowski (*Muza. 2249*)

☆ B. Christoff (♯ *G.WBLP 1008: QBLP 5002;*
[Farewell only, on ♭ *G. 7RW 135*]   ♭ *Vic.EHA 11*)

'Twas not in vain Bs
(*Ein frommer Diener des Herrn; Pimen's tale*)
K. Borg   *PV. 36095*
(*Barbiere No. 8*)   (& in *Ger*, PV. 36088; ♭ Pol. 30019)

---

[1] The Rimsky-Korsakov version is used; Act III, Sc. 1 is omitted, and there are various other cuts.
[2] Orig. version.
[3] Contains: Pimen's Monologue and Varlaam's Song, Act I; Boris' Monologue, Act II, and Death Act IV.
[4] The complete scene including Feodor's part; perhaps ☆.

ACT IV, Scene 2

Revolutionary Scene ... Excerpt   T & Bs
J. Katin & R. Urbanowicz   *Muza. 2250*
(above)

KHOVANSHCHINA   3 Acts   1886
COMPLETE RECORDING

Prince Ivan Khovansky	N. Tzveych (Bs)
Prince Andrew Khovansky ...	A. Marinkovich (T)
Prince Vassily Galitsin	D. Startz (T)
Boyar Shaklovity	D. Popovich (B)
Dositheus	M. Changalovich (Bs)
Martha	M. Bugarinovich (M-S)
The Scrivener	S. Andrashevich (T)
Emma	S. Jankovich (S)

etc., & Belgrade Nat. Op. Cho. & Orch.
—Baranović (8ss)   ♯ **D.LXT 5045/8**
              (♯ Lon. set LLA 29)

HIGHLIGHTS

Prelude; Act I: The Scribe; Act II: Martha's Divination;
Act III: Martha's Aria, Shaklovitov's Aria; Carousing
Scene & Finale
Z. Dolukhanova (A), P. Pontriagin & V. Shevtzov (T),
A. Pirogov, A. Tikhonov & B. Dobrin (Bs), Moscow
Radio Cho. & Orch.—Kovalev   ♯ **Van.VRS 6022**
           (also ♯ Csm.CRLP 227)

Prelude; Act II: Martha's Divination; Act III: Shaklovitov's
Aria; Carousing Scene
M. Maksakova (S), Al. Ivanov (B), Bolshoi Theatre Cho.
& Orch.   ♯ **USSR.D 02084**
(Sadko)   (Parts are ☆)

ORCHESTRAL EXCERPTS

Prelude (Dawn over Moscow)
Dances of the Persian Slaves, Act IV
Entr'acte, Act IV
Philharmonia—Susskind   ♯ **P.PMC 1018**
(Orchestral pieces)   (♯ MGM.E 3030; Od.ODX 148:
                   ♭ *BSOE 4001/2)*

Sym.—Stokowski   ♯ **Vic.LM 1816**
(above; & Glier, Borodin, etc.)   (♭ set ERB 1816;
    ♯ FV.A 630215; DV.L 16482; ItV.A12R 0141)

Prelude (Dawn over Moscow)
☆ Moscow Radio—Golovanov   *USSRM.D 00187*
(Glazounov: March on a Russian theme)
                   (2ss, *USSR. 15751/2)*
   (& in ♯ CdM.LD 8056)
☆ Boston Sym.—Koussevitzky (in ♭ *Cam.CAE 157* &
                        ♯ *CAL 155)*
   Winterthur Sym.—Desarzens (♯ *MMS. 57)*

ACT II

Mysterious powers!   *(Martha's Divination)*
Z. Dolukhanova   in ♯ *USSR.D 1422*
(below & Rimsky)
☆ A. Rudenko (in ♯ *CdM.LD 8070 ; USSRM.D 861)*

ACT III

Martha's aria   (unspec.)
(probably I a thoughtless maiden)
Z. Dolukhanova   in ♯ *CdM.LDM 8134*
(Rachmaninoff, Rimsky, etc.)   (in ♯ *USSR. D 1422,* d.c.)

All is quiet in the camp   *(Shaklovitov's Aria)*   B
A. Pirogov   *USSRM.D 00177*
(Boris Godounov, aria)
A. Ivanov (? n.v.)   *USSR. 23956/7*

ACT IV

Dances of the Persian Slaves
Philharmonia—Karajan   ♯ **C.CX 1327**
(Prince Igor, Gioconda, Tannhäuser, etc.) (♯ Angel. 35307)
Philharmonia—Kletzki   ♭ **C.SEL 1542**
(Suppé: Pique Dame Overture)
Philharmonia—Schüchter   **C.DX 1862**
(2ss)   (CQX 16666: DWX 5084)
(Beethoven: Coriolan Ov. on ♭ *C.SED 5503: SEDQ 509)*
☆ C.B.S.—Barlow (in ♯ AmC.RL 3030)
   Berlin Phil.—Ludwig (in ♯ ANix.ULP 9035)

Entr'acte
Philharmonia—Karajan   in ♯ **C.CX 1265**
(Goyescas, Carmen, etc.) (♯ FCX 407: QCX 10150;
                      Angel. 35207)
☆ Philharmonia—Malko (♭ *G. 7P 143: 7BF 1059:*
    7PQ 2019; & in ♯ BB.LBC 1022: ♭ set *WBC 1022)*
   Berlin Phil.—Ludwig (in ♯ ANix.ULP 9035)

ACT V

Dositheus' Aria: Here on this spot   Bs
☆ B. Christoff   ♭ *G. 7ER 5007*
(Prince Igor—Konchak's aria) (♭ *7ERF 132: 7ERQ 107)*
   (& in ♯ Vic.LHMV 1033: ♭ set *WHMV 1033)*

(The) MARRIAGE   3 Acts[1]   1868
COMPLETE RECORDING

Podkolessin	N. Agrov (Bs)
Fickla	C. Desmazures (A)
Ketchkarev	J. Mollien (T)
Stepan	A. Popovitsky (B)

& French Radio Sym.—Leibowitz
                 ♯ **Oce.OCS 36**

SOROCHINTSY FAIR   3 Acts   1911-23
Introduction   *(A hot day in Little Russia)*
Philharmonia—Susskind   ♯ **P.PMC 1018**
(below)   (♯ Od.ODX 148: ♭ *BSOE 4001;* ♯ MGM.E 3030)
Why, my sad heart   T   Act I
    (Reverie of the young peasant)
⊞ D. Smirnoff *(Fr)* (AF.AGSB 72*)

Gopak   orch.   Act III
Hamburg Philharmonia—H-J. Walther
                 MSB. 78112
(Dvořák: Slav. Dance No. 10)
Philharmonia—Susskind   in ♯ **P.PMC 1018**
(in ♯ MGM.E 3030; Od.ODX 148: ♭ *BSOE 4001;*
              & in ♯ MGM.E 3177, d.c.)
International Sym.—Schneiderhann (in ♯ *Mae.OA 20007)*
Regent Sym. (in ♯ Rgt. 7002)
☆ Philharmonia—Malko (♭ *G. 7PW 104)*

— ARR. VLN. & PF.
I. Stern & A. Zakin   ♯ & ♭ *AmC.PE 21*
(Stravinsky: Fire Bird—Berceuse)
G. Taschner & H. Giesen   *Od.O-4673*
(Chaminade: Sérénade espagnole)   (& in ♯ OLA 1006)

— ARR. VLN. & PF.   Suskin
W. Wikomirska & J. Szamotulska *(Muza. 2062)*

3. SONGS

COLLECTIONS

SONGS & DANCES OF DEATH   Cycle   (Golenishchev-
                           Kutuzov)
... No. 1, Trepak   B. Gmyria (B)
... No. 3, Death's serenade
The Feast (Koltsov) 1867
The He-goat (Composer) 1867
Kalistratushka (Nekrassov) 1864   A. Pirogov (B)
Song of the Flea (Goethe, trs. Strugovshchikov) 1879
    M. Reizen (Bs), etc.   ♯ **Van.VRS 6023**
    (Rachmaninoff)

Song of the Flea (Goethe, trs. Strugovshchikov)
Song of the old man (Goethe, trs. ?)
The He-goat (Composer)
Night (Pushkin)   The Vision (Golenishchev-Kutuzov)
Savishna (Composer)   The Seminarist (Composer)
Softly the spirit flew up to heaven (A. Tolstoy)
The Feast (Koltsov)
    M. Changalovich (Bs), A. Préger (pf.) ♯ *CFD. 38*

The Grave (after Pleshcheev)
Softly the spirit flew up to heaven (Tolstoy)
☆ B. Christoff (Bs), G. Moore (pf.) (in ♯ Vic.LHMV 1033:
                      ♭ set *WHMV 1033)*
    [The Grave also on ♭ *G. 7R 161: 7RF 261: 7RQ 3030]*

(The) Banks of the Don   (Koltsov)
E. Darchuk   *USSR. 23014*
(The He-goat)

(The) He-Goat   (Composer)
E. Darchuk   *USSR. 23013*
(The Banks of the Don)

---

[1] Only Act I is by Moussorgsky, recorded here; Acts II and III were composed by Ippolitoff-Ivanoff. The orchestration is
by A. Duhamel.

Hebrew Song (Mey) ("*Song of Solomon*")
S. Preobrazhenskaya (M-S)   *USSRM.D 00744*
(*Tell me why; & Dargomijsky*)   (also *USSR. 20567*)
R. Hayes (T), R. Boardman (pf.)
     in ♯ Van.VRS 449
(*Schubert, Debussy, etc. & Trad.*)
D. Eustrati (A, *Ger*), F. Schröder (pf.)
(*Nursery, s. 7*)   *Ete. 120181*

Hopak (Shevchenko, trs. Mey)
☆ N. Eddy (B, *Eng*) & orch.(♭ *AmC.A 1576*)

Kalistratushka (Nekrassov)
Yeremushka's Cradle Song (Nekrassov)
A. Pirogov (B)   *USSRM.D 00957/8*

(The) Little Star (Grekov) 1857
☆ N. Obukhova (M-S) (*USSRM.D 00615*)

(The) Nursery Cycle (Moussorgsky)
COMPLETE RECORDING
M. Kurenko (S), V. Pastukhoff (pf.)
     ♯ DCap.CTL 7068
(*Rachmaninoff*)   (♯ Cap.P 8265)
N. Berowska (M-S), J. Vallet (pf.)
     ♯ Sel.LPG 8677
(*Songs & Dances of Death*)
I. Seefried (S, *Ger*), E. Werba (pf.) ♯ Pol. 19050
(*Bartók, Wolf, R. Strauss, etc.*)   (♯ AmD.DL 9809)
D. Eustrati (A, *Ger*), F. Schröder (pf.)
     Eta. 120178/81
(*7ss—Hebrew Song*)
... No. 5 only: **Evening prayer**
☆ N. Eddy (B, *Eng*) & orch. (♭ *AmC.A 1598*)

(The) Seminarist (Composer)
B. Christoff (Bs), G. Moore (pf.) G.DB 21565
(*Koenemann: When the King went forth*)
T. Duncan (B), W. Allen (pf.)   Phi.A 56503G
(*Saint-Saëns: Danse macabre*)
R. Arié (Bs), W. Parry (pf.)   ♯ D.LW 5087
(*below & Glinka, Gretchaninoff*)   (♯ Lon.LD 9103)

Song of the Flea (Goethe, trs. Strugovshchikov)
R. Arié (Bs), W. Parry (pf.)   ♯ D.LW 5087
(*above*)   (♯ Lon.LD 9103)
G. London (B) & orch.   in ♯ AmC.ML 4658
G. Frick (Bs, *Ger*) & orch.   Ete. 225029
(*Zelter: König in Thule*)   (o.n. 25-006)
☆ B. Christoff (Bs), G. Moore (pf.) (♭ *G.7RQ 3010:*
   7RW 133; in ♯ *Vic.LHMV 1033:* ♭ *set WHMV 1033*)
B. Gmyria (Bs) (*USSRM.D 00665*)
N. Eddy (B, *Eng*) & orch. (♭ *AmC.A 1576*)

Songs and Dances of Death
(Golenishchev-Kutuzov) 4 songs
H. Rehfuss (B, *Fr*), H. W. Häusslein (pf.)
     ♯ D.LW 5037
     (♯ Lon.LD 9070)
V. Resnik (Bs), H. Sadoven (pf.) ♯ Sel.LPG 8677
(*The Nursery*)
G. London (Bs), P. Ulanowsky (pf.)
     ♯ AmC.ML 4906
(*Duparc*)   (♯ Phi.N 02117L)
☆ J. Tourel (M-S), L. Bernstein (pf.)   ♯ C.CX 1029
(*Ravel*)   (♯ WCX 1029)
... Nos. 1, 2, 3 only
J. Giraudeau (T, *Fr*), P. Boulez (pf.)
(*Stravinsky*)   ♯ D.FAT 173601
... No. 3, **Death's Serenade**
N. Berowska (M-S), J. Vallet (pf.)
     in V♯ *Sel.LPP 8714*
(*Lassus, Schubert, Hindemith*)
... No. 4, **Field Marshal Death**
☆ B. Christoff (Bs), G. Moore (pf.) (in ♯ Vic.LHMV 1033:
   ♭ *set WHMV 1033*)

Sunless Cycle (Golenishchev-Kutuzov)
M. Kurenko (S), V. Pastukhov (pf.)
     ♯ DCap.CTL 7100
(*Gretchaninoff, Prokofiev*)   (♯ Cap.P 8310)

... No. 6, **By the water** (or: *On the River*)
— — ARR. PF.   Horowitz
  ☆ V. Horowitz (♭ *Vic.ERA 103;* ▽ Note identification
     of this item)
Tell me why (Anon.) 1858
  ☆ S. Preobrazhenskaya (M-S) (*USSRM.D 00744*)

MOUTON, Charles   (1626-1692)

LUTE PIECES—COLLECTION   1680
Le Dialogue des Grâces sur Iris (Allemande)
La Mallassis (Sarabande)
Le Toxin
La Gaubade (Menuett)
La Changeante
L'Heureuse Hymen (Passacaglia)
L'Amant content (Canarie)
W. Gerwig   (2ss)   PV. 8406
(*Boismortier: Daphnis et Chloé,* on ♯ *HP.AP 13027*)

MOUTON, Jean   (1475-1522)
    SEE: † RENAISSANCE MUSIC

MOYZES, Alexander   (b. 1906)

Dances from Pohronia, Op. 43   orch.
☆ **Down the River Vah, Op. 26**   Suite, orch.
Slovak Phil.—Rajter   ♯ *U. 5207H*

MOZART, Leopold   (1719-1787)

Cassation, G major   2 vlns., cbs., 2 horns, toys.
     c. 1760
MS, Bavarian State Library, Munich; of the 7 movements
of this work, No. 3, Allegro; No. 4, Minuet & Trio; and
No. 7, Presto, form the three movements of the "Toy
Symphony", C major, formerly attributed to Haydn.
See under Haydn for recordings of that version.
Vienna Orch. Soc.—Adler   ♯ Uni.LP 1016
(*Gabrielski & Hoffmann*)

MOZART, Wolfgang Amadeus
               (1756-1791)

CLASSIFIED: I.   VOCAL MUSIC
       A. Church Music   B. Opera
       C. Arias & Songs   D. Miscellaneous
     II.   INSTRUMENTAL MUSIC
       A. Piano   B. Chamber Music
       C. Divertimenti & Serenades
       D. Orchestral

I. VOCAL MUSIC

A. CHURCH MUSIC & MASONIC WORKS

Ave Maria K 554   (Canon)
— ARR. 2 S. & B.   Wasner
Trapp Family Singers—Wasner
     in ♯ B.LAT 8038
(*Christmas Music Vol. 2*) (♯ AmD.DL 9689: ♭ *set ED 120*)

Ave verum corpus   K 618   cho.
St. Paul's Cath. Cho. & Philharmonia Str.
   Orch.—Dykes Bower   in ♯ C.CX 1193
(*Bach, Byrd, Sweelinck, Vaughan Williams, etc.*)
     (♯ Angel. 35138 in set 3516)
Harvard Glee Club & Radcliffe Cho. Soc.
 —Woodworth   in ♯ *Camb.CRS 202*
(† *Chansons & Motets*)
Young Vienna—Lehner   in ♯ *AudC. 1093*
(*Beethoven, Schubert, J. Strauss, etc.*)
Royal Cho. Soc.—Sargent (*Eng.*)[1]
     n.v. in ♯ G.ALP 1159
     (♯ BB.LBC 1044: ♭ *set WBC 1044*)

---

[1] As *Jesu, word of God incarnate.*

Ave verum corpus (*continued*)

Bavarian Radio Cho.   *Pol. 62931*
(*J. Schnabel: Transeamus*)   (♭ *Pol. 32021*)
Consolatrix Afflictorum Cho.—Vermeulen (org. acc.)
     (Phi.N 17908G: in ♯ *P10048R*)
Stockholm Boys' Cho.—Algård (Swed.) (*Sir. 118*)
Finlandia Cho.—Elokas (*Ryt.R 6227*)
  ☆ R. Shaw Chorale (♭ *G.7EP 7012*; ♭ *DV.26027*)
St. Hedwig's Cath. Cho.—Forster
     (♭ *G.7PW 515*: in ♯ *WDLP 1501*)
Mormon Tabernacle Cho. (*Eng*)[1]
     (C.SVX 42; in ♯ AmC.ML 4789)
Netherlands Cha. Cho.—Nobel (♭ *Phi.KD 169*)
R.I.A.S. Boys' Cho.—Arndt (♭ *D.DK 23352*)
— ARR. ORCH.   Angelicum—Janes (*Ang.CPA 056, & 054*, d.c.)
— ARR. ORGAN.   C. Cronham (*Mjr. 5153*)
  ☆ C. Courboin (♭ *Cam.CAE 209* & in ♯ *CAL 218*)

CANTATAS, CHORUSES, etc (Masonic)
COLLECTION
▽ Unspec. in Supp. II; now found to contain:
Die Maurerfreude   K 471   *b*, cho., orch.
Die ihr des unermesslichen Weltalls   K 619   *e*, *pf.*
Laut verkünde uns're Freude   K 623   *h*, *b*, cho. orch.
Lasst uns mit geschlung'nen Händen[2] K 623a   *b*, *e*, *pf.*
Ihr unsere neuen Leiter   K 484   *e*, cho. *pf.*
Zerfliesset heut', geliebte Brüder   K 483   *e*, cho. *pf.*
SONGS: O Gottes Lamm   K 343 No. 1
     Als aus Ägypten Israel   K 343 No. 2 } *b* or *t*, pf.
     Gesellenreise   K 468   *e*, pf.
     O heiliges Band   K 148   *h*, org.
Maurerische Trauermusik   K 477 orch.
Die Zauberflöte, excerpts: Nos. 9 (orch.), 10 & 15 *b*, pf.
     No. 21 . . . Der, welcher wandert
         h, *b*, org.
R. Edwards (*e*), R. Hale (*h*), T; R. Thompson (*t*), B;
E Bayless (*b*), Bs.; Indiana Univ. Cho. & Orch.
—Hoffmann (4ss)   ♯ MR. set 101
[Accompaniments shown in *italics* above, where not the
   originals: G. Nettl (pf.), O. Ragatz (org.)]

CANTATAS
Die ihr des unermesslichen Weltalls   K 619   (*540007*)
Dir, Seele des Weltalls   K 429   (*540006*)
Laut verkünde uns're Freude   K 623   (*540006*)
Die Maurerfreude   K 471   (*540007*)
  ☆ H. Cuénod (T), J. Giraudeau (T), G. Souzay (B),
Mulhouse Oratorio Cho. & Pro Musica Orch.—Meyer
     in ♯ *Pol. 540006/7*
Dir, Seele des Weltalls   K 429
Die Maurerfreude   K 471
Laut verkünde uns're Freude   K 623
R. Christ (T) (in K 471 & 623), E. Majkut (T)
(in K 623), W. Berry (Bs.) (in K 623), Vienna
Cha. Cho. & Sym. Orch.—Paumgartner
     ♯ EPhi.ABL 3022
(*Maurerische Trauermusik*) (♯ Phi.A 00121L; Epic.LC 3062)

CHORUSES (Masonic)
Ihr unsere neuen Leiter   K 484   (*540006*)
Lasst uns mit geschlung'nen Händen[2] K 623a   (*540007*)
Zerfliesset heut', geliebte Brüder   K 483   (*540006*)
  ☆ Mulhouse Oratorio Cho.   in ♯ *Pol. 540006/7*

Dixit Dominus & Magnificat, C major K 193   1774
  ☆ Salzburg Mozarteum Cho. & Orch.—H. Schneider
(*Mass No. 8*)   ♯ Nix.LLP 8018

Exsultate, jubilate K 165   S & orch.
H. Gueden & Vienna Phil.—Erede ♯ *D.LX 3103*
(*Mozart: Operatic Arias*)   (♯ *Lon.LS 681*)
P. Alarie & Pro Musica—Jouve   ♯ *Sel.LPG 8556*
(*Vivaldi*)   (♯ *T.LT 7565*)
M. Stader & R.I.A.S.—Fricsay   PV. 72473
(*Rossini*, in ♯ AmD. set DX 132)   (♭ *Pol. 30082*)
(*Entführung*, arias on ♯ *Pol. 17027*)
L. Marshall & Orch.—MacMillan ♯ **Hall.CS 2**
(*Bach: Cantata 51*)
  ☆ E. Schwarzkopf & Philharmonia—Susskind
(*Arias*)   ♯ AmC.ML 4649
  ☆ B. Troxell & Orch.—Bales (in ♯ McInt.MC 1015)
. . . **Alleluja** only
M. Maurene (S), J. Ullern (org.)   *Sat.S 1141*
(*Bach: Cantata 68, aria*)
F. Jankowitsch (Tr.) & Vienna Sym.—Brenn
     ♯ *EPhi.NBR 6011*
(*Pergolesi, etc.*)   (♯ *Phi.N 00694R*)

☆ S. Onegin (A) (in ♯ Sca. 821)
— ARR. CHO.   W. Schumann Cho.
     (in ♯ *Cap.L 382*: ♭ *KASF 342*: *DAS 342*)
— ARR. BAND   Salvation Army Band (*RZ.MF 367*)

Kyrie, D minor K 341
  ☆ Salzburg Mozarteum Cho. & Orch.—Sternberg
(*Offertory; & Schütz*)   ♯ Cpt.MC 20036

Kyrie, F major K 33
Vocal Ens. & Cha. orch.—Oubradous
(*Violin Sonatas, etc.*)   ♯ **Pat.DTX 191**

LITANIES
D major K 195   (Litaniae Lauretanae)
E flat major K 243   (de venerabili)
J. Vyvyan (S), N. Evans (A), W. Herbert (T),
G. James (Bs.), R. Downes (org.), St. Anthony
Singers & Boyd Neel Orch.—Lewis
     ♯ **LOL.OL 50085/6**
(2ss each)   (♯ *OL.LD 108/9*)
E flat major K 243   (de venerabili)
. . . **Dulcissimum convivium** only   S
  ☆ Y. Tinayre (T)   in ♯ **AmD.DL 9654**
(† Seven Centuries of Sacred Music) (in set DX 120)

MASSES
No. 3, C major K 66   ("*Dominicus*")
. . . **Et in Spiritum Sanctum**   S
  ☆ Y. Tinayre (T)   in ♯ **AmD.DL 9654**
(† Seven Centuries of Sacred Music) (in set DX 120)

No. 8, F major K 192   1774
  ☆ Soloists, Mozarteum Cho. & Orch.—H. Schneider
(*above*)   ♯ Nix.LLP 8018

No. 9, D major   K 194   1774
No. 10, C major   K 220   1775
  ☆ Soloists, Academy Cho. & Vienna Sym.—Grossmann
     ♯ EVox.PL 7060

No. 14, C major K 262
SEE No. 18, below, & footnote[3]

No. 16, C major K 317 ("*Coronation*")
S, A, T, B, cho., orch.
A. Cantelo,   M. Thomas,   D. Galliver,
J. Cameron,   Cho. & London Mozart Orch.
—H. Blech   ♯ G.CLP 1031
(*Haydn*)
M. Stader, S. Wagner, H. Krebs, J. Greindl,
St. Hedwig's Cath. Cho. & Berlin Phil.
Orch.—Markevitch   ♯ *Pol. 16096*
     (*Sym. 38*, on ♯ AmD.DL 9805)
J. Brumaire, S. Michel, J. Giraudeau, M. Roux,
Strasbourg Cath. Cho. & Orch.—Hoch
     ♯ *Pat.DT 1015*

No. 18, C minor K 427
T. Stich-Randall (S), H. Rössl-Majdan (M-S),
W. Kmentt (T), W. Ranninger (B), Vienna
Cha. Cho. & Sym. Orch.—Moralt[3]
     ♯ *EPhi.ABR 4043/4*
(4ss)   (♯ *Phi.A 00762/3R*: ♯ Epic. set SC 6009)
  ☆ Soloists, Vienna Academy Cho. & Vienna Sym.
     —v. Zallinger (♯ MMS. 2026; Era.LDE 3010)
. . . **Et incarnatus est**   B. Troxell & org. (in ♭ Ply. 12-123)

No. 19, D minor K 626   ("*Requiem*")
S, A, T, Bs, cho., orch.
E. Grümmer, M. Höffgen, H. Krebs, G. Frick,
St. Hedwig's Cathedral Cho. & Berlin Phil.
—Kempe   ♯ G.WALP 1514
M. Laszlo, H. Rössl-Majdan, P. Munteanu,
R. Standen, Vienna Academy Cho. &
St. Op. Cho.—Scherchen   ♯ LT.DTL 93079
     (♯ Sel 320.C.000; T.LE 6547; West.WL 5233)
  ☆ Soloists, Cho. & Vic. Sym.—Shaw
     (♯ ItV.A12R 0102; DV.L 16389)
Soloists, Salzburg Cath. Cho. & Mozarteum Orch.
   —Messner (♯ Cum.CR 221; Dies Irae & Sanctus
   only, in ♯Ply. 12-90; Rex tremendae only,
     ♭ Rem.REP 16; Cum.ECR 50)
Soloists, Pennsylvania Univ. Cho. & Philadelphia Orch.
   —MacDonald (in ♯ Cam. set CFL 105; also
     ♯ CAL 276)

---

[1] As *Jesu, word of God incarnate.*
[2] This has been adapted as the present Austrian National Anthem.   Recordings are in the Austrian catalogues (*C.DV 1494*
etc.) and also by the Fr. Navy Band (in ♯ *Sel. 270.C.056*), etc.
[3] Score ed. Paumgartner, supplying missing sections from Mass, C major, K 262.

MOTETS & OFFERTORIES

COLLECTION
Misericordias Domini K 222
Sancta Maria, mater Dei K 273
Lacrimosa[1] K 93c
Offertorium K 117 ... Jubilate
Offertorium K 342 (new K.Anh. 240b)
... Benedicite angeli[2]
Alma Dei Creatoris K 277 (new K 272a)
Regina coeli K 276
  ☆ Soloists, cho. & orch.—Raugel († ♯ HS.AS 34)

Offertorium pro festo St. Johannis Baptistae K 72
  ☆ Salzburg Mozarteum Cho. & Orch.—Sternberg
  (*Kyrie; & Schütz*)   ♯ Cpt.MC 20036

Regina coeli, C major K 108
... Ora pro nobis Deum   S
  ☆ Y. Tinayre (T)   in ♯ AmD.DL 9654
  († Seven Centuries of Sacred Music)   (set DX 120)

Sub tuum praesidium K 198 S & T
  F. & E. Jankowitsch (Tr. & A.)
        in ♯ EPhi.NBR 6011
  (*above & below*)   (♯ Phi.N 00694R)

Vesperae Solennes de Confessore, C major K 339
... No. 5, Laudate Dominum S & Cho.
  E. Jankowitsch (A) & Vienna Boys Choir
  —Brenn   in ♯ EPhi.NBR 6011
        (♯ Phi.N 00694R)
  ☆ E. Spoorenberg & Netherlands Cho. (♭ Phi.KD 169)
  A. Schlemm & St. Hedwig's Cath. Cho.
    (♭ G.7PW 515; in ♯ WDLP 1501)
  Y. Tinayre (T) & Cho. (in ♯ AmD.DL 9654, set DX 120)
  R.I.A.S. Boys' Cho.—Arndt (♭ D.DK 23352)

ORATORIO

LA BETULIA LIBERATA K 118 (new K 74c)
(Metastasio) Soli, cho., orch.
No. 5, Del pari infeconda A
No. 7, Parto, inerme A
  M. v. Ilosvay & Vienna Sym.—Paumgartner
        in ♯ Phi.A 00771R
  (*La Finta Semplice, aria, etc.*)

I. B. OPERAS & STAGE WORKS

BASTIEN UND BASTIENNE K 50 1 Act 1768
COMPLETE RECORDINGS in *German* (some dialogue)

CASTS			Set A	Set B
Bastienne (S)	...	...	I. Hollweg	R. Streich
Bastien (T)	...	...	W. Kmentt	R. Holm
Colas (Bs)	...	...	W. Berry	T. Blankenheim

Set A with Vienna Sym. Orch.—Pritchard
        ♯ EPhi.ABL 3010
  (2ss)   (♯ Phi.A 00167L: AmC.ML 4835)
Set B with Munich Cha. Orch.—Stepp ♯ Pol. 18280
  (2ss)
COMPLETE RECORDING in *French*, by cast of children
  B. Roux, P. Maggiora, R. Lemoine, Vincennes Childrens'
  Cho. & Orch.—Gaeti   ♯ Vega. C35.A2

Overture
  Cetra Orch.—Basile   Cet.AT 0330
  (*Paisiello: Molinara, Overture*)
  ☆ Stuttgart Ton-Studio—Reinhardt
    (in ♯ Clc. 6186 & ♯ Cum.CPR 319)

(La) CLEMENZA DI TITO K 621 2 Acts 1791
COMPLETE RECORDING
  ☆ Soloists, Swabian Cho. Soc. & Stuttgart Ton-Studio
  Orch.—Lund (♯ Clc. 6161/3; abridged version, 2ss
  [Nos. 1, 3, 4, 7, 8, 9, 10, 13, 14, 16, 19, 21, 22, 23, 26]
  ♯ Ren.X 56)

Excerpts
  Soloists & Oxford Univ. Opera Club Ens. (Isis.CT 1/4, Pte.)
Overture
  Philharmonia—Kubelik   G.DB 21556
  (*Cosi fan tutte, Ov.*) (♭ 7R 156: 7RQ 3022: 7RW 144)
  (also in ♯ G.ALP 1109: FALP 318: QALP 10076)
  Vienna Sym.—Moralt   in ♯ Phi.A 00780R
  (*Overtures*)

Austrian Sym.—Koslik   ♯ Rem. 199-125
(*Vln. Concerto 4*)
(*Handel & Mozart Overtures*, on ♯ Cum.CR 286)
Berlin Radio—Lange   Eta. 320185
(*Nozze di Figaro, Ov.*)
  ☆ Berlin Phil.—Lehmann   PV. 72426
  (*Pf. Concerto K 537, s 1*)
  (& in ♯ HP.DGM 18091: Pol. 19040: ♭ 34001: 32051)
  ☆ Boston Sym.—Koussevitzky
    (in ♯ Vic.LRM 7021: ♭ set ERB 7021)
  Stuttgart Ton-Studio—Lund
    (in ♯ Clc. 6186 & ♯ Cum.CPR 319)

ACT I

No. 2, Deh se piacer mi vuoi   S
  H. Zadek (*below*)   in ♯ Phi.A 00207L
No. 9, Parto, parto   A
  ⊞ E. Schumann-Heink (AF.AGSB 21*)
No. 8, Ah, se fosse intorno ...   T
  L. Simoneau   in ♯ Phi.A 00740R
  (*Don Giovanni, Cosi, Idomeneo*)
No. 19, Deh per questo istante   A
  M. v. Ilosvay   in ♯ Phi.A 00771R
  (*Io ti lascio, etc.*)
  ☆ E. Wysor (in ♯ Roy. 1589)

ACT II

No. 22, Ecco il punto   S
  H. Zadek   in ♯ Phi.A 00207L
  (*Idomeneo, Figaro, & Arias*)   (♯ Epic.LC 3135)
No. 23, Non più di fiori   A
  ☆ E. Wysor (in ♯ Roy. 1589)
  ⊞ Kirkby Lunn (AF.AGSB 21*)

COSI FAN TUTTE K 588 2 Acts 1790

COMPLETE RECORDINGS

CASTS		Set E	Set D
Fiordiligi	...	E. Schwarzkopf (S)	L. della Casa (S)
Dorabella	...	N. Merriman (M-S)	C. Ludwig (M-S)
Despina	...	L. Otto (S)	E. Loose (S)
Ferrando	...	A. Simoneau (T)	A. Dermota (T)
Guglielmo	...	R. Panerai (B)	E. Kunz (B)
Don Alfonso	...	S. Bruscantini (B)	P. Schoeffler (Bs)

Set E with Cho. & Philharmonia Orch.
  —v. Karajan[3]   ♯ C.CX 1262/4
  (6ss)   (♯ QCX 10146/8; Angel. 35164/6, set 3522)
Set D with Vienna State Op. Cho. & Phil.—Böhm[4]
        ♯ D.LXT 5107/9
  (6ss)   (♯ Lon.LL 1286/8, set XLLA 32)
Set A ☆ I. Souez, L. Helletsgrüber, H. Nash, etc.
  Glyndebourne Fest. Cho. & Orch.—F. Busch
  (6ss) (♯ Vic.LCT 6104; ♭ set WCT 6104)
Set B ☆ Soloists, Stuttgart Ton-Studio Cho. & Orch.
  —Dünnwald (♯ Clc. 6142/4; ♯ Cum. set CR 315)
Set Z (in *English*: from a broadcast)
  Harkness, Guy, Shields, Johnson, Gignae, Canadian
  Op. Co. Cho. & Orch.—Waddington (6ss) (♯ OTA. set 7)

Collected Excerpts
I. Camphausen (S), H. Wilhelm (T), G. Ramms (B),
  Leipzig Opera Cho. & Orch.—Rubahn (*Ger*)
        ♯ Allo. 3058
Soloists, Dresden State Op. Cho. & Orch.—Schreiber (*Ger*)
        ♯ Roy. 1431

Overture
  Columbia Sym.—Walter   in ♯ AmC.ML 5004
        (♯ Phi.A 01237L)
  Philharmonia—Kubelik   G.DB 21556
  (*Clemenza, Overture*) (♭ 7R 156: 7RW 144: 7RQ 3022)
  (also in ♯ G.ALP 1109: FALP 318: QALP 10076)
  Vienna Sym.—Moralt   in ♯ Phi.A 00780R
  (*Overtures*)
  ☆ Berlin Phil.—Lehmann (in ♯ Pol. 19040;
  HP.DGM 18091; ♭ Pol. 30014; also in ♯ Pol. 18169)
  Lamoureux—Goldschmidt
    (♭ Pat.D 101: EDQ 3001, d.c.)
  Stuttgart Ton-Studio—Dünnwald
    (♯ Clc. 6186 & Cum. CPR 319)
  N.Y. Phil. Sym.—Walter (in ♭ AmC. set A 1065)

---

[1] From a Requiem by J. E. Eberlin (1702–62), copied out by Mozart   [2] Perhaps by Leopold Mozart.
[3] Nos. 7 and 24 are omitted; recitatives are abbreviated.
[4] Nos. 7, 24, 27, 28 & the orch. intro. to No. 8 are omitted; Nos. 11, 25, 29, 31 are seriously cut, and there are many other cuts.

ACT I

No. 12, In uomini, in soldati　　　　S
P. Munsel (*Eng*)　　　　　♭ *Vic.ERA 111*
(*No. 19; & J. Strauss*)

No. 14, Come scoglio　　　　　S
T. Stich-Randall　　　in ♯ *LT.DTL 93075*
(*No. 25; & Idomeneo, Nozze di F., Zauberflöte*)
(Sel. 320.C.056)

☆ D. Illitsch (in ♯ *Sup.LPM 132*; ♯ *U. 5108C*)

No. 17, Un' aura amorosa　　　　T
L. Simoneau　　　　in ♯ *Phi.A 00740R*
(*Clemenza, Don Giovanni, Idomeneo*)
A. Dermota (*Ger*)　　　　　♯ *DT.TM 68047*
(*Zauberflöte & Entführung, arias*)
(♯ *T.TW 30023*)
(*Entführung No. 1, on T.S 11579:* ♭ *US 45759:*
& in ♯ *PLB 6124*)

R. Schock (*Ger*)　　　　　G.DB 11546
(*Zauberflöte, No. 3*)　　　　(♭ *7RW 536*)

☆ C. Holland (♭ *Pat.ED 19*)
H H. Jadlowker (*Ger*) (in ♯ HRS. 3003*)

ACT II

No. 19, Una donna a quindici anni　　S
R. Streich　　　　　♭ *Pol. 32029*
(*Figaro, No. 22*)　　(*Ger. on* ♭ *Pol. 32028, d.c.*)
I. F. Gasperoni　　　　*Cet.AT 0325*
(*Pergolesi: La Serva padrona, aria*)
P. Munsel (*Eng*)　　　　♭ *Vic.ERA 111*
(*No. 12; & J. Strauss*)

No. 20, Prenderò quel brunettino　　2 S
H Lilli Lehmann & H. Helbig (in ♯ Ete. 702*)

No. 25, Per pietà, ben mio　　　S
E. Steber　　　in ♯ *AmC.ML 4694*

T. Stich-Randall　　in ♯ *LT.DTL 93075*
(*No. 14, etc.*)　　　　(♯ *Sel. 320.C.056*)

No. 26, Donne mie, la fate a tanti　　B
☆ F. Corena (in ♯ Lon.LL 1334)

DON GIOVANNI K 527 2 Acts, 1787
COMPLETE RECORDINGS

CASTS		Set D	Set P
Don Giovanni	...	C. Siepi (Bs)	G. London (B)
Donna Anna	...	S. Danco (S)	H. Zadek (S)
Donna Elvira	...	L. della Casa (S)	S. Jurinac (S)
Zerlina	...	H. Gueden (S)	G. Sciutti (S)
Don Ottavio	...	A. Dermota (T)	L. Simoneau (T)
Masetto	...	W. Berry (Bs)	E. Wächter (B)
Il Commendatore	...	K. Böhme (Bs)	L. Weber (B)
Leporello	...	F. Corena (Bs)	W. Berry (Bs)

Set D with Vienna St. Op. Cho. & Vienna Phil.
—J. Krips　　　　♯ *D.LXT 5103/6*
(8ss)　　(♯ Lon.LL 1299/1302, set XLLA 34)

Set P with Vienna Cha. Cho. & Vienna Sym.
—Moralt　　　　♯ *EPhi.ABL 3069/71*
(6ss)　　(♯ Phi.A 00280/2L; Epic. set SC 6010)

Set C			
Don Giovanni	...	...	G. Taddei (B)
Donna Anna	...	...	M. C. Verna (S)
Donna Elvira	...	...	C. Gavazzi (S)
Zerlina	...	...	E. Ribetti (S)
Don Ottavio	...	...	C. Valletti (T)
Masetto	...	...	V. Susca (B)
Il Commendatore	...	...	A. Zerbini (Bs)
Leporello	...	...	I. Tajo (Bs)

Set C with Italian Radio Cho. & Orch.—Rudolf
(6ss)　　　　　♯ *CCet. set 1253*

☆ I. Souez & L. Helletsgrüber (S), etc., Glyndebourne Cho.
& orch.—F. Busch　　　♯ *G.ALP 1199/201*
(♯ QALP 10090/2: FJLP 5044/6)
ABRIDGED RECORDING
☆ M. Stabile, H. Konetzni, etc., Vienna State Op. Cho.
& Vienna Sym.—Swarowsky
(♯ MMS set 2013 & ♯ set OP 8, 4ss)[1]
[Nos. 4, 17, 7, 23 also on V♯ Era.LDE 1002]

COLLECTED EXCERPTS (*Ger*)
☆ Overture
No. 4, Madamina! Bs (Act I) [J. Greindl]
No. 7, La ci darem la mano S & B (Act I)
☆ No. 10, Or sai chi l'onore S (Act I)
☆ No. 17, Deh, vieni alla finestra B (Act II)
No. 22, Il mio tesoro T (Act II)
☆ No. 25, Non mi dir S (Act II)

A. Kupper (S) [in Nos. 10 & 25]; E. Trötschel
(S); H. Günter (B) [in No. 7]; W. Ludwig (T)
[in No. 22]; H. Schlusnus (B), [in No. 17];
Berlin Phil. Orch.—Lehmann　♯ *Pol. 17014*

Highlights
(Ov. & Nos. 4, 7, 12, 13, 19, 21, 22, 23, 25)
L. Hunt (S), B. Troxell (S), J. Pease (B), S. Baccaloni (Bs),
etc.　　　　　　　♯ Roy. 1588

Fantasia　　— ARR. Liszt, q.v.

Overture
Philharmonia—Kubelik　　in ♯ *G.ALP 1109*
(♯ FALP 318: QALP 10076)
Zürich Tonhalle—Ackermann　V♯ *MMS. 98*
(*Entführung, Overture*)
Vienna Sym.—Moralt　　in ♯ *Phi.A 00780R*
(*Overtures*)
☆ L.S.O.—Krips　　　　♯ *D.LW 5001*
(*Zauberflöte Overture*)　　　(♭ *VD 501*)
☆ Berlin Phil.—Lehmann　　in ♯ *HP.DGM 18091*
(in ♯ Pol. 19040: ♭ 30022; ♭ AmD.ED 3534; FPV. 5049)
Prague Nat. Th.—Chalabala (U.H 24400)

☆ Austrian Sym.—Koslik
(in ♯ Rem. 199-125; Cum.CR 286)
Berlin Sym.—Rubahn (in ♯ Roy. 1375), etc.

ACT I

No. 1, Notte e giorno faticar　　Bs
H R. Mayr (in ♯ Sca. 822*)

No. 4, Madamina, il catalogo ...　　Bs
B. Christoff (2ss)　　　　G.DA 2080
N. Rossi-Lemeni　　in ♯ *G.ALP 1074*
(*Bellini, Borodin, etc.*)
(in ♯ QALP 10033: FALP 306; ♭ Vic.ERA 7)
J. Greindl　　　　　PV. 72482
(*Don Carlos* (♭ Pol. 30078; & in Ger., PV.72481:
♭ Pol. 30077)
T. Popescu, 2ss (U.C 24429)
B. Gmyria (*Russ*) (USSRM.D 00855)
M. Székely (*Hung*) (Qual.MK 1589)
☆ E. Pinza (in ♯ Vic.LM 1751; DV.L 16240; FV.A 630233;
& in ♯ Vic.LM 1864: ♭ ERA 229)
F. Corena (in ♯ Lon.LL 1334)
P. Schoeffler (*Ger*) (♭ D.VD 504)

No. 7, Là ci darem la mano　　S & B
E. Trötschel & H. Günter (*Ger*)　　PV. 36087
(*Figaro, No. 10*)　　　　(♭ Pol. 32016)
☆ E. Rethberg & E. Pinza (♭ Vic.ERAT 21)
E. Berger & H. Schlusnus (*Ger*) (♭ Pol. 30153)

No. 10, Don Ottavio, son morta　　S & T
　Or sai chi l'onore　　　　S
H. Zadek & L. Simoneau, from set P
(*Idomeneo, No. 12*)　　　♭ *Phi. 400003AE*

... Aria only, Or sai chi l'onore
☆ A. Kupper (*Ger*) (No. 25)　　♭ Pol. 30006
☆ F. Leider (AF.AGSB 26 & in ♯ Vic. set LCT 6701)
H Lilli Lehmann (in ♯ Cum.CE 186*)

No. 11, Dalla sua pace　　　T
W. Ludwig　　　　　PV. 72305
(*No. 22, & Figaro*)　　　(in ♯ AmD.DL 4073)
(also in *Ger*, ♭ Pol. 30033)
C. Valletti　　　　in ♯ *Cet.LPC 55002*
(*No. 22 & Werther, etc.*)　　(♯ CCet. A 50176)
L. Simoneau　　　in ♯ *Phi.A 00740R*
(*No. 22, & Cosi, etc.*)
☆ P. Anders (*Ger*)
(in ♯ DT.LGM 65019; ♯ T.LS 6005; RadT.EO 18T)
T. Schipa (in ♯ G.FJLP 5004)

---

[1] The original issue of this set (HS., Nix., Era.) followed the score for the Prague first performance, the Vienna additions being added on the last side. It has not been possible to check this re-issue.

No. 12, Finch'han del vino   B
N. Rossi-Lemeni   ¹G.DB 21573
(½s—*No. 17; & Figaro, No. 9*)
L. Tibbett   in ‡ Roy. 1627
A. Sved (*Hung*) (*No. 17*)   *Qual.MK 1535*
  ☆ E. Pinza (‡ *DV. 16240*; FV.A 630233; ♭ *Vic.ERA 137*:
    & in ‡ Vic.LM 1751 & set LCT 6701)
  H. Schlusnus (*Ger*) (♭ *Pol. 30153*)
  K. Schmitt-Walter (*Ger*) (*RadT.A 028T*)
  ♑ A. Scotti   AF.AGSB 24* & ‡ *FRP. 3**
  F. d'Andrade   in ‡ Cum.CE 188*
  M. Battistini   AF.AGSA 24*
  M. Sammarco   HRS. 1069*

No. 13, Batti, batti, o bel Masetto   S
E. Schwarzkopf   *C.LB 145*
(*No. 19, below*)   (*GQ 7260*: ♭ *SEL 1511*)
(& in ‡ *C.CX 1069*: FCX 183: QCX 10058; Angel. 35021)
E. Köth (*Ger*)   ‡ *G.WBLP 1513*
(*No. 19, & Zauberflöte & Entführung*)
  ☆ I. Seefried (*C.LO 82*)
  ♑ G. Farrar (V‡ *Rar.M 316** & in ‡ B & B. 3*)
  A. Patti (in ‡ Vic. set LCT 6701*)

No. 14, Finale ... Minuet   orch.
Hamburg Philharmonia—H-J. Walther
    MSB. 78003
— — ARR. BAND (in ‡ Jay. 3004)
— — ARR. PF. M. v. Doren (in ‡ Chan.MVDP 2)
— — ARR. HPSI. E. Silver (in ‡ Roy. 1550)
— — ARR. GUITAR
  M. L. Anido (ArgOd. 66035: ♭ *BSOA 4011*:
    ♭ *BSOAE 4516*: in ‡ *LDC 521*)

ACT II

No. 17, Deh, vieni alla finestra   B
G. Valdengo   *Cet.AT 0368*
(*Guillaume Tell—Sois immobile*)
(*Guillaume Tell, A. Chénier & Figaro,*
    on ♭ *Cap.FAP 7016*; ♭ *Cet.EPO 0318*)
G. Taddei   *Cet.AT 0403*
(*Falstaff—L'Onore*)
N. Rossi-Lemeni   ¹G.DB 21573
(½s—*No. 12 & Figaro, No. 9*)
A. Sved (*Hung*) (*Qual.MK 1535*)
  ☆ K. Schmitt-Walter (*Ger*) (*RadT.A 028T*)
  E. Pinza (‡ Vic.LM 1751: ♭ *ERA 137*; &
    FV.A 630233; ‡ *DV.16240*; & in ‡ Vic. set LCT 6701)
  ♑ M. Renaud (*Fr*) (in ‡ Cum.CE 188*)
  V. Maurel & pf. (in ‡ Sca. 822*)

No. 19, Vedrai, carino   S
E. Schwarzkopf (*No. 13*)   *C.LB 145*
(in ‡ *C.CX 1069*: QCX 10058: FCX 183; Angel. 35031
  & ♭ *C.SEL 1511*: SEBQ 124: ESBF 122) (*GQ 7260*)
E. Köth (*Ger*)   ‡ *G.WBLP 1513*
(*No. 13, & Zauberflöte, etc.*)
L. Cortese & pf.²   ‡ *ERC.102*
(*Donizetti: La Zingara*)

No. 21, Ah, pietà, signori miei   Bs
  ☆ F. Corena (in ‡ Lon.LL 1334)

No. 22, Il mio tesoro   T
W. Ludwig   PV. 72305
(*No. 11, & Figaro*)   (in ‡ AmD.DL 4073)
(& in *Ger*, ♭ *Pol. 30033*)
C. Valletti   in ‡ Cet.LPC 55002
(*No. 11 & Werther, Barbiere, Sonnambula, etc.*)
    (‡ CCet.A 50176)
L. Simoneau   in ‡ *Phi.A 00740R*
(*No. 11, & Cosi, Idomeneo, Clemenza, etc.*)
  ☆ R. Crooks (in ‡ Cam.CAL 148)
  J. Melton (G.ED 1216)
  P. Anders (*Ger*) (in ‡ DT.LGM 65019; ‡ *T.LS 6005*;
    RadT.E 018T)
  H. Roswaenge (*Ger*) (in ‡ CEd. 7010)
  ♑ J. McCormack (in ‡ G.FJLP 5004*: QJLP 104*)

No. 23, In quali eccessi ... Mi tradì   S
E. Steber   in ‡ AmC.ML 4694
  ☆ E. Schwarzkopf (*Nos. 13 & 19*)   ♭ *C. SEL 1511*

No. 25, Crudele! ... Non mi dir   S
E. Steber   in ‡ AmC.ML 4694
E. Schwarzkopf   in ‡ C.CX 1069
(*Nozze di Figaro, Idomeneo*) (‡ *C.FCX 183*; ‡ Angel. 35021
    & ♭ *C.SEL 1515*: ESBF 122)
  ☆ L. Welitsch (*C.LO 89*)
  A Kupper (*Ger*) (♭ *Pol. 30006*)
  ♑ Lilli Lehmann (in ‡ Ete. 702*)

Don Ottavio's aria, unspec: M. Alexandrovich (*Russ*)
    (‡ *USSR.D 2220*)

(Die) ENTFÜHRUNG AUS DEM SERAIL
K 384 (*Il Seraglio*) 3 acts 1782
COMPLETE RECORDINGS
Konstanze	M. Stader (S)
Blonde	R. Streich (S)
Belmonte	E. Häfliger (T)
Pedrillo	M. Vantin (T)
Osmin	J. Greindl (Bs)
Selim	W. Frank (speaking part)

& R.I.A.S. Cha. Cho. & Sym—Fricsay³
    ‡ HP.DGM 18184/5
(4ss)   (‡ AmD. set DX 133)
    (& manual, ‡ Pol. 18197/8)
(Dialogue is included, spoken by a different cast)
Excerpts also on ♭ *Pol. 32093/7* & *30139/40*
M. Tyler, H. Petrich, J. v. Kesteren,
  K. Schiebener, A. Griebel & Cologne Op.
  Cho. & Gürzenich Orch.—Ackermann⁴
    ‡ *MMS.set M 113*
(4ss)   (& set OP 17)

ABRIDGED RECORDINGS
Konstanze	E. Berger (S)
Blonde	Lisa Otto (S)
Belmonte	R. Schock (T)
Pedrillo	G. Unger (T)
Osmin	G. Frick (Bs)

& Anon. Cho. & Orch.—Schüchter⁵
    ‡ G.WALP 1501
I. Camphausen, I. Mehler, W. Horst, G. Ramms, etc.,
  Dresden State Op. Cho. & Orch.—Schreiber
    ‡ Allo. 3090
Anon. Soloists, Berlin Op. Cho. & Orch.—Rubahn
    in ‡ Roy. 1442

COLLECTED EXCERPTS (Nos. 1, 2, 4, 19)
  ♑ L. Slezak, W. Hesch (in ‡ Cum.CE 188*)

Overture
Vienna Sym.—Moralt   ‡ *Phi.A 00780R*
(*Overtures*)
Berlin Municipal Op.—Rother   T.E 3940
(*Nozze Overture*)   (♭ *UE 453940*)
Philharmonia—Kubelik   G.DB 9753
(*Gluck: Iphigénie en Aulide Ov., s. 1*)
    in ‡ *G.ALP 1109*: FALP 318: QALP 10076)
Zürich Tonhalle—Ackermann   V‡ *MMS. 98*
(*Don Giovanni, Overture*)
  ☆ L.S.O.—Krips   ♭ *D.LW 5021*
(*Schauspieldirektor, Ov.*) (‡ *Lon.LD 9033*: ♭ *REP 8021*)
Pasdeloup—Lindenberg (♭ *Od. 7AOE 1006*)
Zagreb Radio Orch. (*Jug.P 16084*)
Austrian Sym.—Koslik
    (in ‡ Rem. 199-125; Cum.CR 286)
Berlin Sym.—Rubahn (or Balzer) (in ‡ Roy. 1375)
  ☆ Berlin Phil.—Lehmann (in ‡ Pol. 19015: 19040 &
    HP.DGM 18091: ♭ *Pol. 30014*)
Lamoureux—Goldschmidt (♭ *Pat.D 102*, d.c.)
Vienna Radio—Nilius (in ‡ GA. 33-301)

ACT I
No. 1, Hier soll ich dich denn sehen   T
W. Ludwig   ♭ *Pol. 30033*
(*Don Giovanni, Nos. 11 & 22*)

---

¹ Announced but not issued.
² Sung both in Ital. and in Eng. version by L. Cortese.
³ Aria No. 17 is omitted, being replaced by No. 15 from Act II.
⁴ Omits Nos. 10 and 17.
⁵ Contains Overture and Nos. 1, 3, 10, 15, 2, 12, 14, 16, 18, 20, 21, in that order; mostly slightly abbreviated.

No. 1, Hier soll ich dich denn sehen (*continued*)
R. Schock (from set)   **G.EH 1447**
(*No. 15*)   (*FKX 266:* ♭ *7PW 518*)
A. Dermota   **♯ DT.TM 68047**
(*Nos. 4 & 15, etc.*)   (♯ *T.TW 30023*)
(*Cosi No. 17 on T.S 11759:* ♭ *US 45759*)

☆ P. Anders (in ♯ *DT.LGM 65019; T.LS 6005*)
   W. Ludwig (♭ *D.VD 503, from set*)

No. 2, Wer ein Liebchen hat gefunden   Bs
G. Frick   **G.EH 1443**
(*Nos. 3 & 14*)   (*FKX 263*) (from set)

No. 3, Solche hergelauf'ne Laffen   Bs.
G. Frick   **G.EH 1443**
(*Nos. 2 & 14*)   (*FKX 263*) (from set)

No. 4, Konstanze! . . . O wie ängstlich T
A. Dermota   **♯ DT.TM 68047**
(*Nos. 1 & 15, Cosi, etc.*)   (♯ *T.TW 30023*)
☆ P. Anders (in ♯ *DT.LGM 65019; T.LS 6005*)
   W. Ludwig (♭ *D.VD 503, from set*)

No. 6, Ach, ich liebte   S
E. Köth   in ♯ *G.WBLP 1513*
(*below*) (also G.DB 11588: ♭ *7RW 19-548*)
☆ W. Lipp (♭ *D.VD 503, from set*)
Ⅱ Lilli Lehmann (in ♯ *Cum.CE 186**)

ACT II

No. 10, Welcher Kummer . . . Traurigkeit S
E. Köth   in ♯ *G.WBLP 1513*
(*Nos. 6 & 11, & Don Giovanni, etc.*)
                               (also G.DB 11588: ♭ *7RW 19-548*)
E. Steber   in ♯ **AmC.ML 4694**
E. Berger, from set   **G.DB 11560**
M. Stader   **♯ Pol. 17027**
(*No. 11, & Exsultate, Jubilate*)   (perhaps from set)
☆ E. Schwarzkopf (in ♯ *AmC.ML 4649*)

No. 11, Martern aller Arten   S
E. Köth   in ♯ *G.WBLP 1513*
(*above*)   (also G.DB 11585: ♭ *7RW 19-545*)
M. Stader   **♯ Pol. 17027**
(*above*)   (perhaps from set)
I. F. Gasperoni (*It*)   **Cet.PE 183**
(*Nozze di Figaro, No. 27*)
☆ M. Perras (in ♯ *Vic.LCT 1158*)
Ⅱ Lilli Lehmann (in ♯ *Cum.CE 186**)
   M. J. Varnay (*IRCC. 3137**)

No. 12, Welche Wonne   S
P. Alarie   in ♯ *Sel. 270.C.087*
(*Figaro, Zauberflöte, etc.*)
☆ E. Loose (♭ *D.VD 503, from set*)

No. 14, Vivat Bacchus   T & Bs
G. Unger & G. Frick   **G.EH 1443**
(*Nos. 2 & 3*)   (*FKX 263*) (from set)

No. 15, Wenn der Freude Tränen fliessen T
R. Schock (from set)   **G.EH 1447**
(*No. 1*)   (*FKX 266:* ♭ *7PW 518*)
A. Dermota   **♯ DT.TM 68047**
(*No. 1; Zauberflöte & Cosi arias*)   (♯ *T.TW 30023*)

ACT III

No. 18, Im Mohrenland gefangen war T
☆ P. Anders (in ♯ *DT.LGM 65019; T.LS 6005*)

No. 20, Welch ein Geschick!   S & T
E. Berger & R. Schock (from set) **G.DB 11559**

Osmin's aria (arias?) unspec.
   M. Székely (*Hung*) (*Qual.MK 1572*)

(La) **FINTA GIARDINIERA** K 196 3 acts 1774
COMPLETE RECORDING in *German*
☆ Soloists & Stuttgart Orch.—Reinhardt
                               (♯ Cpt. set MC 20035)

Overture
Philharmonia—Kubelik   in ♯ **G.ALP 1109**
                               (♯ FALP 318: QALP 10076)
☆ Stuttgart—Reinhardt, from set
   (in ♯ *Per.SPL 559; Clc. 6186; Cum.CPR 319*)

(La) **FINTA SEMPLICE** K 51 3 Acts 1769
Overture (*see also* Sym. No. 7, *infra*)
☆ Nat. Gallery Orch.—Bales (in ♯ *McInt.MC 1015*)

No. 24, Che scompiglio   A
M. v. Ilosvay   in ♯ *Phi.A 00771R*
(*Betulia liberata & Clemenza arias, etc.*)

IDOMENEO, RE DI CRETA K 366 1781
COMPLETE RECORDING[1] including Ballet K 367
☆ Soloists, Vienna Sym. Orch. & Cho.—v. Zallinger
   (6ss, ♯ *Era.LDE 3014/6;* Overture & Nos. 11, 17, 18, 32
   on ▼♯ *Era.LDE 1005;* Nos. 8, 9, 21, 29 on
                               ▼♯ *Era.LDE 1007*)

COLLECTED EXCERPTS: Set C
Overture &
No. 1, Quando avran fine omai (Recit.)   21527
   Padre, Germani, addio! (Aria) S
No. 6, Vedrommi intorno (Aria) T   21529
No. 11, Se il padre perdei (Aria) S   21529
No. 12, Fuor del mar (Aria) T   21529
No. 15, Placido è il mar Cho.   21526
No. 17, Qual nuovo terrore! Cho.   21528
No. 18, Corriamo, fuggiamo Cho.   21528
No. 19, Zeffiretti lusinghieri (Aria)   21525
No. 21, Andrò ramingo e solo Qtt.   21525
No. 24, O voto tremendo Cho.   21526
No. 26, Accogli, o rè del mar 2 T   21528
☆ S. Jurinac & D. McNeil (S), R. Lewis & A. Young (T),
   Glyndebourne Fest. Cho. & Orch.—F. Busch
(*Nos. 1, 6, 11 & 12 on* ♭ *Vic.EHA 15*)   **G.DB 21525/9**
                               (♯ *FALP 359, 2ss*)
Overture
Vienna Sym.—Moralt   in ♯ *Phi.A 00780R*
(*Overtures*)
☆ Philharmonia—Kubelik (in ♯ *G.ALP 1109: FALP 318:
   QALP 10076;* ♭ *7ER 5002: ERQ 112: ERF 130;*
                               ♭ *Vic.EHA 6*)
   Berlin Phil.—Lehmann (in ♯ *Pol. 19040;*
                     HP.DGM 18091: ♭ *Pol. 34001: 32051*)
   Boston Sym.—Koussevitzky (♭ *G.7RF 273;*
                     in ♯ *Vic.LRM 7021:* ♭ set ERB 7021)
   Lamoureux—Goldschmidt
                     (♭ *Pat.D 101: EDQ 3001, d.c.*)
   E.I.A.R.—Parodi (in ♯ *Tem.TT 2072*)

ACT I

No. 4, Tutte nel cor vi sento   S
H. Zadek   in ♯ *Phi.A 00207L*
(*Clemenza di Tito, Figaro, & Arias*)   (♯ *Epic.LC 3135*)

ACT II

No. 11, Se il padre perdei   S
T. Stich-Randall   in ♯ *LT.DTL 93075*
(*below, Cosi, etc.*)   (♯ *Sel. 320.C.056*)

No. 12, Qual mi conturba i sensa (Recit.)
   Fuor del mar (Aria) T
L. Simoneau   in ♯ *Phi.A 00740R*
(*Aria, Non temer amato bene, Don Giovanni, etc.*)
(*Don Giovanni, No. 10 on* ♭ *400003AE*)
Ⅱ (Aria only) H. Jadlowker (*Ger*) (in ♯ *HRS. 3003**)

ACT III

No. 19, Zeffiretti lusinghieri   S
E. Schwarzkopf   in ♯ *C.CX 1069*
(in ♯ *C.QCX 10058: FCX 183;* Angel. 35021; ♭ *C.SEL 1515:
                               SEBQ 124: ESBF 122*)
J. Tourel (M-S)   ♯ in **AmC.ML 4640**
T. Stich-Randall   in ♯ *LT.DTL 93075*
(*above, Figaro, etc.*)   (♯ *Sel. 320.C.056*)

Ballet Music, K 367
Berlin Sym.—Rubahn   in ♯ *Roy. 1533*

LUCIO SILLA K 135 3 Acts 1772
Overture
London Mozart Players—H. Blech   **G.C 4235**
☆ National Gallery Orch.—Bales (in ♯ *McInt. MC 1015*)

[1] Omits No. 22, part of 23, and various secco recits.

MITRIDATE, RE DI PONTO K 87 3 Acts 1770

Overture
  ☆ National Gallery Orch.—Bales (in ♯ McInt.MC 1015)

(Le) NOZZE DI FIGARO K 492 3 Acts 1772

COMPLETE RECORDINGS

CASTS	Set D¹	Set G²
Susanna ...	H. Gueden (S)	G. Sciutti (S)
La Contessa	L. della Casa (S)	S. Jurinac (S)
Cherubino	S. Danco (S)	R. Stevens (M-S)
Marcellina	H. Rössl-Majdan (M-S)	M. Sinclair (A)
Figaro ...	C. Siepi (Bs)	S. Bruscantini (B)
Il Conte ...	A. Poell (B)	F. Calabrese (Bs)
Dr. Bartolo	F. Corena (Bs)	I. Wallace (Bs)
Don Basilio	M. Dickie (T)	H. Cuénod (T)
etc.		

Set D¹ with Vienna State Op. Cho. & Vienna
  Phil.—Kleiber   **♯ D.LXT 5088/91**
  (8ss)   (♯ Lon. set XLLA 35)

Set G² with Glyndebourne Fest. Cho. & Orch.
  —Gui   **♯ G.ALPS 1312, ALP 1313/5**
  (7ss, first blank)   (♯ Vic. set LM 6401, 8ss)

Set B
  ☆ I. Seefried, E. Schwarzkopf, S. Jurinac, E. Höngen,
   E. Kunz, G. London, etc.; Vienna State Op. Cho. &
   Phil.—v. Karajan (♯ C.VCX 503/5: FCX 174/6:
                 QCX 10002/4: WCX 1007/9)

Set L
  Soloists, Cho. & Orch. of Leipzig Opera House
  —v. Herten   **♯ Roy. 1502/4**
  (6ss) (Ger)   (♯ Gram. 20157/9)

COLLECTED EXCERPTS
No. 3, Se vuol ballare, Act I
No. 4, La vendetta, Act I
No. 9, Non più andrai, Act I
No. 17, Vedro mentr'io sospiro, Act III
No. 26, Aprite un po', Act IV
  G. London (B)   **♯ AmC.ML 4699**
  (Arias)

Overture & Nos. 3, 6, 9, 10, 11, 19, 27, 28 from Set C
  ☆ G. Gatti, I. Tajo, S. Bruscantini, etc. Ital. Radio
  —Previtali (♯ Cet.A 50141; also Nos. 6, 11, 19,
             in ♭ Cap.FAP 7006; ♭ Cet.EPO 0311)

Abridged recordings & excerpts
  A. v. d. Graef (S), M. Opawsky (S), C. C. Meyer (M-S),
   S. Jongsma (Bs), Cho. & Netherlands Phil.—Goehr
            ♯ MMS. 2010; also OP 2
  Soloists, Berlin St. Op. Cho. & Orch.—Rubahn (? Ger)
                     (♯ Roy. 1442)
  ☆ Soloists, Rome Op. Cho. & Orch.—Questa
                  (♭ Roy.EP 104)

Fantasia — ARR. Liszt, q.v.

Highlights
  B. Troxell, L. Hunt, L. Sgarro, J. Pease, etc.
                  ♯ Roy. 1636
  ☆ Anon. artists (♯ Cam.CAL 227: in set CFL 101)

Overture
  Columbia Sym.—Walter in ♯ AmC.ML 5004
                  (♯ Phi.A 01237L)
  Philharmonia—Susskind   **C.DX 8405**
  (Brahms: Akad. Fest.-Ouvertüre)   (DOX 1016)
  Pasdeloup—Allain   **♭ CA.EPO 5028**
  (Zauberflöte Overture)   (♭ Plé.P 45148)
  Berlin Municipal Op.—Rother   **T.E 3940**
  (Entführung Ov.) (♭ UE 453940: in ♯ LB 6124)
  ☆ Berlin Phil.—Lehmann in ♯ HP.DGM 18091
          (in ♯ Pol. 19040: ♭ 32018: 34009)
  ☆ Philharmonia—Kubelik in ♯ G.ALP 1109
              (♯ FALP 318: QALP 10076)
  Berlin Radio—Lange (Eta. 320185)
  Moscow Radio—Samosud (USSR. 015464)
  Linz Sym. (in ♯ Ply. 12-30)
  Netherlands Phil.—Krannhals (in V♯ MMS. 920)
  ☆ Lamoureux—Goldschmidt (♭ Pat.D 102, d.c.)
    Boston Sym.—Münch (♭ G.7RF 281; in ♯ DV.T 16401)
    Minneapolis—Ormandy (in ♯ Cam.CAL 121)
    E.I.A.R.—Parodi (in ♯ Tem.TT 2072)
    Vienna Radio—Nilius (in ♯ GA. 33-301)

— ARR. ACCORDIONS & CBS.
  B. Hughes, B. Palmer & L. Manno (in ♯ Capri. 1)

ACT I

No. 3, Se vuol ballare   **B**
  ☆ E. Pinza (in ♯ Vic.LM 1751 & ♭ ERA 137;
        in ♯ FV.A 630233; DV. 16240)
  H. Rehkemper (Ger) (in ♯ Sca. 809)
  Ⓗ G. de Luca (in ♯ Sca. 812*)

No. 4, La vendetta   **Bs**
  G. Frick (Ger)   **G.DB 11563**
  (Barbiere, No. 8)

No. 6, Non so più   **S**
  E. Schwarzkopf   in ♯ C.CX 1069
    (in ♯ Angel. 35021; C.FCX 183: QCX 10058)
  A. Schlemm (Ger)   **G.DA 5519**
  (No. 11)   (♭ 7PW 520)
  P. Alarie (below) in ♯ Sel. 270.C.087
  L. Castellano, S. Leff (pf.) in ♯ Mur.P 105
  (tuition record, with separate pf. acc. also)
  ☆ R. Stevens   in ♯ Vic. set LCT 6701
  E. Wysor   in ♯ Ply. 12-47

No. 9, Non più andrai   **B**
  G. Valdengo   **Cet.PE 197**
  (Andrea Chénier—Nemico della patria)
            (♭ Cap.FAP 7016, d.c.)
  J. Metternich (Ger)   **G.DA 5522**
  (No. 26)
  R. Merrill   in ♯ PRCC. 5
  N. Rossi-Lemeni   **3G.DB 21573**
  (Don Giovanni, Nos. 12 & 17)
  ☆ J. Greindl   in ♯ AmD.DL 4065
    (♭ Pol. 32070: ♯ 18147: Ger, ♯ 19043:
        ♭ 34035 & ♭ 34026: 32069)
  E. Pinza   in ♯ Vic.LM 1751: ♭ ERA 137
       & ♯ FV.A 630233; DV.16240)
  H. Rehkemper (Ger)   in ♯ Sca. 809
  Ⓗ G. Sammarco   in ♯ Cum.CE 188*
  C. Santley   in ♯ Roc.R 1*

ACT II

No. 10, Porgi amor   **S**
  E. Schwarzkopf   in ♯ C.CX 1069
    (in ♯ Angel. 35021; C.QCX 10058: FCX 183)
  T. Stich-Randall   **♯ LT.DTL 93075**
  (Così, Idomeneo, etc.) (♯ Sel. 320.C.056)
  A. Kupper (Ger)   **PV. 36087**
  (Don Giovanni, No. 7) (♭ Pol. 32016; & in ♯ AmD.DL 4065)
  L. Castellano & pf., followed by pf. acc. only
              (in ♯ Mur.P 105)
  ☆ E. Rethberg   ♭ Vic.ERAT 21
  A. Rautavaara   RadT.E 038T
  T. Lemnitz   ♭ G.7R 167
  Ⓗ Lilli Lehmann (Ger) V♯ Rar.M 313* & in ♯ Ete. 702*

No. 11, Voi che sapete   **S**
  E. Schwarzkopf   in ♯ C.CX 1069
    (♯ C.FCX 183: QCX 10058; Angel. 35021)
  P. Alarie   in ♯ Sel. 270.C.087
  (No. 6; Re Pastore, Zauberflöte, etc.)
  G. Arnaldi   **Cet.AT 0343**
  (Fra Diavolo—Quel bonheur)
  A. Schlemm (Ger)   **G.DA 5519**
  (No. 6)   (♭ 7PW 520)
  P. Munsel[4]   in ♯ G.BLP 1023
    (♯ QBLP 5015; in ♯ Vic.LM 7012: ♭ set WDM 7012)
  K. Grayson[5] (in ♯ Vic.LOC 3000: ♭ set EOB 3000)
  E. Farrell[6] (in ♯ MGM.E 3185: ♭ set X 304)
  M. Teyte   in ♯ PRCC. 2
  E. Ray (Fr)   ♭ Véga.P 1506
  ☆ I. Seefried   C.LO 82
  R. Stevens   ♭ Vic.ERA 138
  Géori-Boué (Fr)   in ♯ Od.ODX 117
  Ⓗ S. Kurz (Ger)   AF.ABHB 5*

No. 12, Venite, inginocchiatevi **S**
  H. Gueden   in ♯ D.LX 3103
            (in ♯ Lon.LS 681)
  ☆ E. Trötschel in ♯ AmD.DL 4065; ♭ Pol. 32035
  E. Schumann in ♯ Vic.LCT 1115: ♭ set WCT 1115

---

¹ Includes (for the first time) No. 24, Il capro e la capretta and No. 25, In quegl'anni, for Marcellina and Basilio respectively. The former is sung by H. Gueden instead of Rössl-Majdan.
² Omits No. 24, includes No. 25. Some recits. are abridged.
³ Announced but not issued.
⁴ Sound track, film Melba.   ⁵ Sound track, film So This is Love.   ⁶ Sound track film, Interrupted Melody.

ACT III

No. 16, Crudel, perchè finora   **S & B**
☆ E. Rethberg & E. Pinza (♭ *Vic.ERAT 21*)

No. 19, E Susanna non vien . . . Dove sono S
A. Kupper   **PV. 72305**
(Don Giovanni, Nos. 11 & 22)   (& in ‡ *Pol.* 18169)

E. Schwarzkopf & Philharmonia —Pritchard
    in ‡ **C.CX 1069**
    (in ‡ *Angel.* 35021; C.FCX 183: QCX 10058)

T. Stich-Randall   in ‡ **LT.DTL 93075**
    (‡ *Sel.* 320.C.056)

N. Hofman   **ArgOd. 66056**
(Schubert: Ave Maria)   (♭ *BSOAE 4519*)

E. Steber   in ‡ **AmC.ML 4694**

H. Zadek   in ‡ **Phi.A 00207L**
(Clemenza di Tito, Idomeneo, & Arias)   (‡ Epic.LC 3135)

☆ E. Schwarzkopf   (o.v., from set) C.GQX 11527
   T. Lemnitz   ♭ *G.7R 167*; in ‡ Vic.LCT 6701
   M. Cebotari in ‡ Vic.LCT 1115: ♭ set WCT 1115
   E. Rethberg   in ‡ Vic.LM 1909: ♭ ERAT 21
   M. Guilleaume (Ger)   ♭ T.UE 453927

No. 20, Sull'aria . . . Che soave zeffiretto   2 S
(Letter Duet)
Ħ Lilli Lehmann & H. Helbig (in ‡ Ete. 702*)

No. 22, . . . March & Fandango   Orch.
☆ Bavarian Radio—Jochum (in ‡ *AmD.DL 4064*;
    ♭ *Pol.* 32029)

ACT IV

No. 26, Aprite un po'   B
E. Sædén   in ‡ **G.ALPC 1**
(Carmen, Bartered Bride, etc.)

G. Taddei   **Cet.BB 25299**
(Hérodiade—Vision fugitive)   (in ‡ LPC 55006)

J. Metternich *(Ger)*   **G.DA 5522**
(No. 9)   (♭ *7PW 124*: in ‡ *WBLP 1504*)

☆ J. Greindl (in ‡ *AmD.DL 4065*; ♭ *Pol.* 32070: 34026;
    & *Ger.*, ♭ 34025: 32069)
   E. Pinza (♭ *Vic.ERA 137*)

Ħ G. de Luca (in ‡ Sca. 812*)

No. 27, Giunse alfin il momento . . . (Recit.)
Deh vieni, non tardar (Aria) S
E. Schwarzkopf   in ‡ **C.CX 1069**
    (in ‡ *Angel.* 35021; C.FCX 183: QCX 10058)

E. Berger *(Ger)*   **G.DB 11562**
(Don Pasquale—Quel guardo . . .)

I. F. Gasperoni   **Cet.PE 183**
(Entführung, No. 11)

N. Hofman   **ArgOd. 66045**
(Schubert: Ständchen)   (♭ *BSOAE 4505*)

☆ R. Tebaldi   in ‡ *Fnt.LP 302*
   Géori-Boué (Fr)   in ‡ *Od.ODX 117*
   M. Guilleaume (Ger)   RadT.E 096T &
    in ‡ *DT.TM 68025*
   E. Trötschel   ♭ *Pol.* 32035

Figaro's Aria, unspec.: T. Kuuzik (in ‡ *USSR.D 2090*)

(Les) PETITS RIENS (new) K 299b Ballet 1778
COMPLETE
Cha. Orch.—Oubradous   ‡ **Pat.DTX 194**
(Symphony No. 31)

Covent Gdn. Op.—Braithwaite   ‡ **MGM.E 3034**
(Scarlatti: Good-Humoured Ladies)
☆ Stuttgart Ton-Studio—Lund (‡ Clc. 6186 & 6161;
    ‡ Cum.CPR 319)
   Paris Cons.—Goldschmidt († ‡ HS.AS 33)

Nos. 2, 4, 6, 7, 9, 10, 12
Leipzig Radio—Pflüger   ‡ **Ura. 7111**
(Lully & Beethoven)

Overture & Nos. 1, 2, 3, 6 & 7
Hamburg Philharmonia—Walther   *MSB. 78205*
    (also *MSB.* 78003)

Overture
Bamberg Sym.—Leitner   *Pol. 62927*
(Re Pastore—Overture)   (♭ *Pol.* 32015)

(Il) RE PASTORE   K 208   2 Acts   1775
COMPLETE RECORDING
☆ Soloists, Stuttgart Ton-Studio Cho. & Orch.—Lund
    (‡ Cpt. set MC 20034)

Overture
Vienna Sym.—Leitner   *Pol. 62927*
(Les Petits Riens, Overture)   (♭ *Pol.* 32015)
(Hindemith, on ‡ AmD.DL 9768)
☆ Stuttgart Ton-Studio— Lund
    (in ‡ Clc. 6186 & ‡ Cum.CPR 319)
   National Gallery—Bales (in ‡ McInt.MC 1015)

No. 10, L'amerò, sarò costante   S
H. Gueden, W. Barylli (vln.) & Vienna Phil.
   —Erede   in ‡ **D.LX 3103**
    (in ‡ Lon.LS 681)

P. Alarie   ‡ *Sel. 270.C.087*
(Aria—Popoli di Tessaglia; Figaro, etc.)

I. Seefried, W. Schneiderhan (vln.) &
   Württemberg State—Leitner   **PV. 72351**
(Aria—Non temer amato ben)   (♭ *Pol.* 30045)
(Hindemith, on ‡ AmD.DL 9768)

B. Troxell & org.   in ‡ Ply. 12-123
☆ E. Schwarzkopf   in ‡ AmC.ML 4649
   G. Ritter-Ciampi   in ‡ Cum.CE 188

(Der) SCHAUSPIELDIREKTOR
K 486   1 Act   1778   *(Impresario)*
COMPLETE RECORDING
☆ Soloists, Stuttgart Orch.—Reinhardt (‡ Clc. 6132)

Overture
Columbia Sym.—Walter   in ‡ **AmC.ML 5004**
    (‡ Phi.A 01237L)

Moscow Radio—Samosud   **USSR. 015463**
(Figaro Overture)

Paris Coll. Musicum—Douatte
    in ‡ **EPP.APG 113**
(Symphonies 24 & 28)

☆ Philharmonia—Kubelik   in ‡ **G.ALP 1109**
    (‡ FALP 318: QALP 10076)
☆ L.S.O.—Krips   ‡ **D.LW 5021**
(Entführung Overture) (‡ Lon.LD 9033:
    ♭ REP 8021; ♭ D.DX 1763)
☆ Stuttgart Orch.—Reinhardt (in ‡ Per.SPL 559:
    Cum.CR 319; Clc. 6186)
   Paris Sym.—Gaillard (Od.O-3706)
   Berlin Phil.—Lehmann (♭ Pol. 32018: 34009 &
    in ‡ HP.DGM 18091; Pol. 19040)
   Boston Sym.—Koussevitzky (♭ G.7RF 273)
   Vienna Radio—Nilius (in ‡ GA. 33-301)

No. 2, Bester Jüngling!   S
E. Steber   in ‡ **AmC.ML 4694**

(Lo) SPOSO DELUSO
K 430 (new K 424a) unfinished
Overture
☆ Nat. Gallery Orch.—Bales (in ‡ McInt.MC 1015)

THAMOS, KÖNIG IN ÄGYPTEN K 347   1780
(Incidental Music to play by T. P. v. Gebler)
COMPLETE RECORDING
R. Boesch (speaker), I. Hollweg (S), M.
   Nussbaumer-Knoflach (A), W. Kmentt (T),
   W. Berry (Bs), Vienna Cha. Cho. & Sym.
   Orch.—Paumgartner   ‡ **EPhi.ABL 3089**
    (‡ Phi.A 00260L; Epic.LC 3158)

(5) Entr'actes
☆ Austrian Sym.—Günther (in ‡ Rem. 199-54;
    ‡ Cum.CR 273; ‡ AFest.CFR 40)

ZAÏDE   K 344 (new K 336b)   1780
COMPLETE RECORDING
☆ M. Dobbs (S), H. Cuénod (T), etc., Paris Phil.
   —Leibowitz   ‡ Nix.QLP 4901-1/2
    (‡ Cum. set CPL 195)

No. 3, Ruhe sanft, mein holdes Leben   S
☆ B. Troxell (in ‡ McInt.MC 1015)

☆ = Re-issue of a recording to be found in previous volumes.

(Die) ZAUBERFLÖTE K 620 2 Acts 1791
COMPLETE RECORDINGS

CASTS		Set D	Set E
Pamina (S)	... ...	H. Gueden	M. Stader
Königin der Nacht (S)		W. Lipp	R. Streich
Tamino (T)	... ...	L. Simoneau	E. Häfliger
Papageno (B)	... ...	W. Berry	D. Fischer-Dieskau
Sarastro (Bs)	... ...	K. Böhme	J. Greindl
Monostatos (T)	...	A. Jaresch	M. Vantin
Sprecher (Bs)	...	P. Schoeffler	K. Borg
Papagena (S)	... ...	E. Loose	L. Otto

Set D with Vienna State Op. Cho. & Vienna
  Phil.—K. Böhm   ♯ **D.LXT 5085/7**
(6ss) [Excerpts on ♯ *D.LW 50002*]
                        (♯ Lon.LL 1291/3, set XLLA 33)

Set E with R.I.A.S. Cho. & Sym.—Fricsay
                        ♯ **HP.DGM 18267/9**
(6ss—includes some dialogue, spoken by a separate cast)
                    (& manual, ♯ Pol. 18264/6)
[Nos. 4 & 14 on ♭ *Pol. 32115*]   (♯ AmD. set DX 134)

Set F. C. Bijster, M. Tyler, D. Garen, A. Gschwend,
  G. Hoekman, etc.; Netherlands Phil. Cho. &
  orch.—Krannhals (4ss)   ♯ **MMS. set 2033**
                            (& OP set 21)

Set A
 ☆ T. Lemnitz, E. Berger, H. Roswaenge, G. Hüsch,
  W. Strienz, etc., Cho. & Berlin Phil.—Beecham
                        ♯ **G.ALP 1273/5**

Set B
 ☆ I. Seefried, W. Lipp, A. Dermota, E. Kunz, L. Weber,
  etc., Musikfreunde Cho. & Vienna Phil.—v. Karajan
                    (♯ C.VCX 508/10: WCX 1013/5)

Highlights
  M. Guilleaume (S), P. Anders (T), K. Schmitt-Walter (B),
  etc. (probably ☆)   ♯ *T.TW 30015*

Excerpts
  Anon. Soloists & Berlin Opera Cho. & Orch.—Rubahn
                        in ♯ *Roy. 1442*

Nos. 9, 10, 15 & 21 ... Der, welcher wandert
In Cantata Collection, *supra*.

Overture
Philharmonia—Kubelik   ♭ *G.7ER 5002*
(*Idomeneo, Overture*)(♭ G.ERF 130; ERQ 112; ♭ Vic.EHA 6
  & in ♯ G.ALP 1109: FALP. 318: QALP 10076)

Pasdeloup—Allain   ♭ *CA.EPO 5028*
(*Figaro Overture*)   (♭ Plé.P 45148)

Vienna Sym.—Moralt   in ♯ *Phi.A 00780R*
(*Overtures*)

Columbia Sym.—Walter   in ♯ **AmC.ML 5004**
                        (♯ Phi.A 01237L)

 ☆ L.S.O.—Krips   ♯ *D.LW 5001*
(*Don Giovanni Overture*)   (♭ VD 501)
Berlin Sym.—Rubahn (or Balzer) (in ♯ Roy. 1375)
Berlin Radio—Gerdes (*Eta.* 120049)
"Nat. Op. Orch." (in ♯ Gram. 20142)
Regent Sym. (in ♯ Rgt. 7004)
Orch.—Swarowsky (in ♯ MTW. 9)

 ☆ Berlin Phil.—Lehmann (♭ *AmD.ED 3534*; in
  ♯ HP.DGM 18091; ♯ Pol. 19040: ♭ 30022;
                        FPV. 5049)
Bamberg Sym.—Keilberth (in ♯ T.LSK 7019;
        FT. 320.TC.028 & in ♯ *T.TW 30015*)
French Nat.—Lindenberg (♭ Od.7AOE 1006)
B.B.C.—Toscanini (♭ G.7ERF 118: in ♯ FJLP 5058)

ACT I

No. 2, Der Vogelfänger bin ich ja   B
H. Prey   **C.DW 5358**
(*No. 20*)   (♭ SCMW 538)
 ☆ K. Schmitt-Walter (in ♯ *T.TW 30004* & TW 30015)

— ARR. GLASS HARMONICA Hansen
E. Hansen (in ♯ *Ban.BC 2000*)

No. 3, Dies Bildnis ist bezaubernd schön T
R. Schock   **G.DB 11546**
(*Cosi fan Tutte, No. 17*) (♭ 7RW 536: in ♯ WBLP 1501)
K. Terkal   **D.F 43549**
(*Kienzl: Evangelimann—Selig sind ...*) (♭ DX 1761)
                        (& in ♯ Lon.LB 892)
N. Gedda (*Swed*)   **Od.SD 6080**
(*Prince Igor—Daylight is fading*)

V. Teodorian   **U.H 24396**
(*Ballo in Maschera, aria*)
 ☆ P. Anders (in ♯ *DT.LGM 65019*; *T.LS 6005*;
                        & ♯ *T.TW 30015*, d.c.)
A. Dermota (♭ *D. 71116*)

No. 4, O zittre nicht ... Zum Leiden bin ich
auserkoren   S
E. Mühl (*No. 14*)   **G.DB 30006**
E. Köth & orch.—Schüchter in ♯ *G.WBLP 1513*
(*No. 14; & Don Giovanni, etc.*) (DB 11586: ♭ 7RW19-546)
[o.v. with orch.—Grüber, G.EH 1449: FKX 267:
                        ♭ 7PW 527]
P. Alarie   in ♯ *Sel. 270.C.087*
(*No. 14; & Figaro, etc.*)
 ♄ M. Ivogün (in ♯ Cum.CE 188*)

No. 7, Bei Männern   S & B
 ♄ S. Kurz & H. Schlusnus in ♯ *HRS. 3006**
  S. Kurz & L. Demuth   in ♯ Sca. 817*
  E. Eames & E. de Gogorza (*Ital*) AF.AGSB 15*

No. 8, Finale
... Wie stark ist doch dein Zauberton T
A. Dermota   ♯ *DT.TM 68047*
(*Cosi & Entführung arias*) (♯ T.TW 30023)

ACT II

No. 10, O Isis und Osiris Bs & Cho.
K. Borg & Cho.   *PV. 36089*
(*No. 15*)
G. Frick & Cho.   **G.DB 11567**
(*No. 15*)   (♭ 7RW 520)
O. Edelmann   ♭ *EPhi.NBE 11005*
(*No. 15 & Maurerische Trauermusik*) (♭ Phi. 400004AE)
M. Székely (*Hung*) & Cho. **Qual.MN 1119**
(*No. 15*)
 ☆ J. Greindl   ♭ *Pol. 32071*
  E. Pinza (*Ital*) in ♯ *Vic.LM 1751*; *DV. 16240*
                        (♯ FV.A 630233)
 ♄ P. Plançon (*Ital*)   in ♯ *SBDH.LLP 6**
  M. Journet (*Fr*)   in ♯ *SBDH.LPG 5**

No. 14, Der Hölle Rache   S
E. Mühl (*No. 4*)   **G.DB 30006**
E. Köth & orch.—Schüchter in ♯ *G.WBLP 1513*
(*No. 4, Entführung, etc.*) (DB 11586: ♭ 7RW19-546)
[o.v. with orch.—Grüber, G.EH 1449: FKX 267:
                        ♭ 7PW 527]
P. Alarie   in ♯ *Sel.270.C.087*
(*No. 4, Figaro, etc.*)
G. Arnaldi (*Ital*)   *Cet.AT 0280*
(*Barbiere, No. 7*)
H. Reggiani (*Ital*)   ♯ *Roy. 1603*
(*Puritani, Lucia, Barbiere, etc.*)
 ☆ F. F. Jenkins (*Ital*) & pf. (in ♯ *Vic.LRT 7000*:
                        ♭ set ERBT 7000)
  L. Pons (*Fr*) (in ♯ *Od.OD 1013*)
 ♄ M. Ivogün (in ♯ Cum.CE 188*)
  M. Galvany (in ♯ AudR.LPA 2340*)

No. 15, In diesen heil'gen Hallen   Bs
K. Borg   *PV. 36039*
(*No. 10*)   (♭ Pol. 30011, d.c.)
J. Greindl   in ♯ *Pol. 19015*
                        (♭ Pol. 32071)
G. Frick   **G.DB 11567**
(*No. 10*)   (in ♯ WBLP 1505) (♭ 7RW 520)
O. Edelmann   ♭ *EPhi.NBE 11005*
(*No. 10 & Maurerische Trauermusik*) (♭ Phi. 400004AE)
M. Székely (*Hung*) (*No. 10*) **Qual.MN 1119**
 ☆ E. Pinza (*Ital*) (in ♯ Vic.LM 1751; ♯ FV.A 630233;
                        ♯ DV. 16240)
 ♄ M. Journet (*Fr*) (in ♯ SBDH.JALP 19*)

No. 17, Ach, ich fühl's   S
H. Gueden   in ♯ *D.LX 3103*
(*Figaro, Re Pastore, Exsultate*) (in ♯ Lon.LS 681)
T. Stich-Randall   in ♯ LT.DTL 93075
(*Cosi, Figaro, Idomeneo*) (♯ Sel. 320.C.056)
E. Steber   in ♯ *AmC.ML 4694*
E. Grümmer   **G.DB 11587**
(*No. 21, below*)   (♭ 7RW 19-547)
 ☆ M. Guilleaume (RadT.E 096T); in ♯ *DT.TM 68025*;
        ♯ T.TW 30015, d.c.: & ♭ T.UE 453927)
A. Rautavaara (RadT.E 038T)

♯ = Long-playing, 33⅓ r.p.m.   ♭ = 45 r.p.m.   ♄ = Auto. couplings, 78 r.p.m.

No. 20, Ein Mädchen oder Weibchen　B
H. Prey　　　　　　　　　　　　*C.DW 5358*
(*No. 2*)　　　　　　　　　　　　(♭ *SCMW 538*)

☆ K. Schmitt-Walter (in ♯ *T.TW 30015*)
H. Rehkemper (in ♯ *Sca.* 809)

No. 21, Finale
... Bald prangt den Morgen zu verkünden
E. Grümmer & Regensburg Cath. Cho.
　　　　　　　　　　　　　　G.DB 11587
(*above*)　　　　　　　　　　　(♭ *7RW 19-547*)

... Papagena! Weibchen! Täubchen!　B
☆ H. Rehkemper (in ♯ *Sca.* 809)

Queen of the Night's Aria (unspec.) (No. 4 or 14)
G. Gasparyan (*Fr*)　　　　　*USSRM.D 1405*
(*Meyerber & Proch*)
H Mme. Moga-Georgesco (in ♯ *HRS. 3002**)

I. C. ARIAS & SONGS

1. ARIAS & SCENAS

COLLECTIONS
Va, dal furor portata　K 21 (new K 19c)[1]
Si mostra la sorte　K 209
Con ossequio, con rispetto　K 210
Se al labbro mio non credi... Il cor dolente　K 295[2]
Per pietà, non ricercate　K 420[3]
Misero! O sogno!... Aura, che intorno　K 431 (new K 425b)
W. Kmentt (T) & Vienna Sym.—Paumgartner
　　　　　　　　　　　　♯ *Phi.A 00197L*
　　　　　　　　　　　　(♯ Epic.LC 3076)

Basta, vincesti... Ah, non lasciarmi　K 486a (new K 295a)
　　　　　　　　　　　　　　　(Metastasio)
Alma grande　K 578 (Palomba)[4]
Bella mia fiamma... Resta, o cara　K 528
H. Zadek (S) & Vienna Sym.—Paumgartner
　　　　　　　　　　　　♯ *Phi.A 00207L*
(*Idomeneo, La Clemenza, Figaro*)　(♯ Epic.LC 3135)

Ah, lo previdi... Ah, t'invola　K 272[5]
Chi sà, chi sà, qual sia　K 582　(Da Ponte)[6]
Vado, ma dove?... Oh Dei!　K 583　(Da Ponte)[6]
Ch'io mi scordi di te?... Non temer amato bene　K 505[7]
Bella mia fiamma... Resta, o cara　K 528
M. Laszlo (S) & Vienna State Op. Orch.
—Quadri　　　　　　　♯ *Nix.WLP 5179*
　　　　　　　　　　　　(♯ West.WL 5179)

Popoli di Tessaglia... Io non chiedo　K 316 (new K 300b)[8]
Nehmt meinen Dank　K 383
Vorrei spiegarvi, oh Dio!... Ahi conte partite　K 418[3]
Voi avete un cor fedele　K 217[9]
I. Hollweg (S) & Vienna Sym.—Pritchard
　　　　　　　　　　　　♯ *Phi.A 00657R*
Alma grande　K 578　(Palomba)[4]
Misera, dove son? Ah, non son io　K 369[1]
M. Stader (S) & Bavarian Radio Orch.
—Lehmann
Mentre ti lascio, o figlia　K 513[10]
Per questa bella mano　K 612[11]
K. Borg (Bs) & Bamberg Sym.—Leitner
　　　　　　　　　　　　♯ *Pol. 19019*
(*Beethoven*)　　　　　　　　(& ♯ 18219)

Mentre ti lascio, o figlia　K 513[10]
Per questa bella mano　K 612[11]
Rivolgete a lui lo sguardo　K 584[12]
G. London (B) & Columbia Sym.—Walter
(*Figaro, Arias*)　　　　♯ *AmC.ML 4699*

Chi sà, chi sà, qual sia　K 582[6]
I. Seefried (S) & London Mozart Players
—H. Blech　　　　　　　*C.LX 1596*
(*below*)

Ch'io mi scordi di te?... Non temer, amato bene
K 505[7]
J. Tourel (M-S), M. Horszowski (pf.)
　　　　　　　　　　in ♯ *AmC.ML 4641*

Männer suchen stets zu naschen　K 433　Bs
(*Warnung*)
R. Hayes (T), R. Boardman (pf.) in ♯ *A 440.12-3*
S. Schöner (S)　　　　　　in *Eta. 120172*
G. Pechner (B)　　　　　　in ♯ *Roy. 1557*
☆ E. Schwarzkopf (S), G. Moore (pf.)
　　　　　　　　　　in ♯ *AmC.ML 4649*
I. Seefried (S), G. Moore (pf.)　*C.LOX 817*

Mentre ti lascio, o figlia　K 513[10]　Bs
G. Souzay (B)　　　　　　in ♯ *D.LX 3112*
(*Gluck, Rameau, A. Scarlatti, etc.*)　(in ♯ *Lon.LS 730*)
K. Borg (B)　　　　　　　　*PV. 72492*
(*below*)　　　　　　　　　(♭ *Pol. 30092*)

Misero! O sogno... Aura, che intorno　K 431
(new K 425b)　T
☆ C. Holland (♭ *Pat.ED 19*)

Misera, dove son?... Ah! non son' iò che parlo
K 369[1]
J. Hammond　　　　　　in ♯ *G.ALP 1076*
(*Bruch, Catalani, Cilea, Weber, etc.*)

(Un) Moto di gioia　K 579　S
(*For Nozze di Figaro—Susanna*)
F. Wend & O. Gartenlaub (pf.)　♯ *Ven.BM 8101*
(*Songs, Collection*)
M. Guilleaume, F. Neumeyer (forte-pf.)
　　　　　　　　　　　　♯ *Pol. 13040*
(*Songs, Collection*)　　　　(& ♭ *37093*)
L. Castellano & S. Leff (pf.)　in ♯ *Mur.P 106*
(*followed by pf. acc. only*)

Ombra felice.... Io ti lascio　K 255
M. v. Ilosvay (A)　　　　in ♯ *Phi.A 00771R*

Per pietà, non ricercate　K 420[3]　T
☆ C. Holland & Paris Cons.—Goldschmidt
(*Cosi, No. 17 & above*)　　　♭ *Pat.ED 19*

Non più, tutto ascoltai...
Non temer, amato bene　K 490[7]　S
I. Seefried & Württemberg State—Leitner
　　　　　　　　　　　　PV. 72351
(*Re Pastore—L'Amerò ...*)　　(♭ *Pol. 30045*)
L. Simoneau (T)　　　　in ♯ *Phi.A 00740R*
(*Idomeneo, Clemenza di Tito, etc.*)

Per questa bella mano　K 612 (with cbs. obbligato)
K. Borg (Bs) & vlc.　　　　*PV. 72492*
(*above*)　　　　　　　　　(♭ *Pol. 30092*)

Popoli di Tessaglia... Io non chiedo[8]　K 316　S
Annik Simon　　　　　　♯ *Pat.DTX 195*
(*Variations, K 265, etc.*)
P. Alarie　　　　　　in ♯ *Sel. 270.C.087*
(*Entführung, Figaro, etc.*)

Vado ma dove?... O Dei!　K 583[6]　S
I. Seefried & London Mozart Players—H. Blech
(*above*)　　　　　　　　　*C.LX 1596*

---

[1] Text from Metastasio's *Ezio*.　　　　[2] For Hasse's opera *Artaserse*.　　　[3] For Anfossi's *Il curioso indiscreto*.
[4] For Cimarosa's *I due Baroni*.　　　[5] Text from Paisiello's opera *Andromeda*.
[6] For V. Martin's opera *Il Burbero di buon cuore*.　　　[7] Text from *Idomeneo*.
[8] Text from Gluck's *Alceste*.
[9] For Galuppi's *Le Nozze*.
[10] Text from Paisiello's *La disfatta di Dario*.
[11] Bs. and cbs. obbligato.　London, with G. Neikrug, vlc.
[12] For *Cosi fan tutte*.

I. C. 2. SONGS

COLLECTIONS

Ridente la calma K 152 (new K 210a)
Oiseaux, si tous les ans K 307 (new K 284d)
Dans un bois solitaire K 308 (new K 295b) (De la Motte)
Die kleine Spinnerin K 531 (Jäger & ?)
Als Luise die Briefe . . . K 520 (Baumberg)
Abendempfindung K 523 (Campe)
Das Kinderspiel K 598 (Overbeck)
Die Alte K 517 (Hagedorn)
Das Traumbild K 530 (Hölty)
Das Veilchen K 476 (Goethe)
Der Zauberer K 472 (Weisse)
Im Frühlingsanfange K 597 (Sturm)
Das Lied der Trennung K 519 (Schmidt)
Die Zufriedenheit K 349 (Miller) 'Was frag' ich . . .'
An Chloe K 524 (Jacoby)
Sehnsucht nach dem Frühlinge K 596 (Overbeck)

E. Schwarzkopf (S), W. Gieseking (pf.)
‡ C.CX 1321
(‡ Angel. 35270)

Oiseaux, si tous les ans K 307 (new K 284d) a
Dans un bois solitaire K 308 (new K 295b)
(De la Motte) a
Ridente la calma K 152 (new K 210a)
Un moto di gioia (Aria) (K 579) a
Abendempfindung K 523 (Campe)
Der Zauberer K 472 (Weisse)
Die Verschweigung K 518 (Weisse)
Als Luise die Briefe . . . K 520 (Baumberg)
Das Veilchen K 476 (Goethe) b
Sehnsucht nach dem Frühlinge K 596 (Overbeck) b

M. Guilleaume (S), F. Neumeyer (fortepiano)
‡ Pol. 13040
[titles marked a also on ♭ 37093; marked b, on ♭ 37092]

Als Luise die Briefe . . . ('Unglückliche Liebe') K 520
(Baumberg)
Abendempfindung K 523 (Campe)
An Chloë K 524 (Jacoby)
Dans un bois solitaire K 308 (De la Motte)
Die Zufriedenheit K 473 (Weisse) 'Wie sanft' . . .
Die Alte K 517 (Hagedorn)
Das Veilchen K 476 (Goethe)

F. Wend (S), O. Gartenlaub (pf.) ‡ Ven.BM 8101
(Aria—Un moto di gioia)

Ridente la calma K 152 (new K 210a)
An Chloë K 524 (Jacoby)
Das Veilchen K 476 (Goethe)

M. Ritchie (S), G. Malcolm (pf.)
(Schubert, Purcell, etc.) ‡ Nix.NLP 921

Das Veilchen K 476 (Goethe)
Das Lied der Trennung K 519 (Schmidt)
Abendempfindung K 523 (Campe)
Sehnsucht nach dem Frühlinge K 596 (Overbeck)
Als Luise die Briefe . . . ('Unglückliche Liebe') K 520
(Baumberg)
Die Verschweigung K 518 (Weisse)
Der Zauberer K 472 (Weisse)
An Chloë K 524 (Jacoby)
Dans un bois solitaire K 308 (De la Motte)

☆ E. Margano (S), J. v. Wering (fortepiano)
‡ Phi.S 06035R

Das Veilchen K 476 (Goethe)
Abendempfindung K 523 (Campe)
Dans un bois solitaire K 308 (De la Motte)
An Chloë K 524 (Jacoby)

S. Danco (S), G. Agosti (pf.) ‡ D.LX 3110
(R. Strauss) (‡ Lon.LS 699)

Der Kinderspiel (Overbeck) K 598
Der Zauberer (Weisse) K 472
Die Zufriedenheit (Miller) K 349

☆ I. Seefried (S), G. Moore (pf.) (C.LOX 817)

Abendempfindung (Campe) K 523
E. Schwarzkopf (S), G. Moore (pf.) C.LX 1580
(Bach: Bist du bei mir)
(Bach, Beethoven, Wolf, etc. in ‡ C.CX 1044: FCX 182;
Angel. 35023)

An Chloë (Jacoby) K 524
☆ I. Seefried (S), G. Moore (pf.) (C.LO 84)
L. Lehmann (S), E. Balogh (pf.) (in ‡ Vic.LCT 1108:
♭ set WCT 1108)

Als aus Ägypten Israel K 343 No. 2
O Gottes Lamm K 343 No. 1
See CANTATA COLLECTION, ante

Gesellenreise (Ratschky) K 468
☆ H. Cuénod (T), H. Salomé (pf.) in ‡ Pol. 540007
& See CANTATA COLLECTION, ante

(Das) Kinderspiel (Overbeck) K 598
See ‡ Pol. 19052, s.v. MISCELLANEOUS, infra

Komm! liebe Zither (Anon.) K 351 (new K 367b)
S or T & Mandoline
P. Conrad (T) & mandoline in ‡ Phi.N 00686R
(below; Beethoven, Hasse, Vivaldi)

O heiliges Band (Anon.) K 148 (new K 125h)
☆ H. Cuénod (T), H. Salomé (pf.) in ‡ Pol. 540006
& in CANTATA COLLECTION, ante

Ridente la calma K 152 (new K 210a)
☆ I. Seefried (S), G. Moore (pf.) (C.LO 84)

Sehnsucht nach dem Frühlinge (Overbeck) K 596
S. Schöner (S) (Eta. 120172)
☆ S. Onegin (A) (JpV.NF 4075)
& see also ‡ Pol. 19052, s.v. MISCELLANEOUS, infra

(Das) Veilchen (Goethe) K 476
G. Pechner (B) in ‡ Roy. 1557
(Mendelssohn, Schubert, Schumann, etc.)
S. Schöner (S) (Eta. 120172)
☆ S. Onegin (A) (JpV.NF 4075)

(Die) Verschweigung (Weisse) K 518
☆ L. Lehmann (S), E. Balogh (pf.)
(in ‡ Vic.LCT 1108: ♭ set WCT 1108)

(Der) Zauberer (Weisse) K 472
☆ E. Schwarzkopf (S), G. Moore (pf.) in ‡ C.CX 1044
(above; & Bach, Brahms, Gluck, etc.) [or ? n.v.]
(in ‡ Angel. 35023; ‡ C.FCX 182)

(Die) Zufriedenheit (Miller) K 349 (new K 367a)
('Was frag' ich')
P. Conrad (T) & mandoline in ‡ Phi.N 00686R
(above, Vivaldi, Beethoven, Hasse)
& see also ‡ Pol. 19052, s.v. MISCELLANEOUS, infra

SPURIOUS

Vergiss mein nicht K.Anh. 246: Really by Lorenz Schneider
— ARR. ORGAN CLOCK: in † ‡ Van.VRS 7020
(Other items attrib. to Mozart in this disc are not identified)

Wiegenlied (Gotter) K 350 ("Schlafe mein Prinzchen")
(Really by B. Flies)
Y. Printemps (S, Fr) & Orch. G.DA 5057
(Handel: Serse, Largo) (in ‡ FDLP 1029; Angel.C 28003)
C. Lynch (T, Eng) (Brahms, etc.) in ‡ AmC.RL 3016
I. B. Lucca (S, Ital), Cho. & Orch. (Dur.AI 10462:
in ‡ AI 520)
G. Vinogradov (T, Russ) (USSR. 8043)
M. Santreuil (S, Fr) (♭ POc.A 03)
T. Angelini (Swed) (G.X 7299)
☆ T. Lemnitz (S) & Orch. (in ‡ T.LA 6228)
⊞ S. Onegin (A) (in ‡ Sca. 821*)
— ARR. CHO.
St. Hedwig Cath. Boys Cho.—Forster G.EG 7865
(Reger: Mariä Wiegenlied) (HE 3148)
Regensburg Cath. Cho.—Schrems T.A 11597
(Reger: Mariä Wiegenlied) (♭ U 45597; & FT. 190. TV. 169)

Obernkirchen Children's Cho. (in ‡ Od.OLA 1007;
Angel. 64012, d.c.)
Montserrat Monastery Cho. (Span)
(G.AA 774: ♭ 7EPL 13026)
Petits Chanteurs à la Croix de Bois (Fr)
(♭ Pat.ED 39; in ‡ Angel. 64024)
☆ Bielefeld Children's Cho. (♭ T.U 45228: in ‡ LA 6087)
E. Bender Children's Cho. (♭ Pol. 32074)

I. D. MISCELLANEOUS

CANONS
COLLECTION

Lacrimoso son' io K 555 4 vv.
Caro, bell' idol mio K 562 3 vv.
Nascoso è il mio sol K 557 4 vv.
V'amo di core teneramente K 348 (new K 382g) 4 vv.
Lieber Freistädtler K 232 (new K 509a) 4 vv.
Difficile lectu mihi Mars K 559 3 vv.
O du eselhafter Martin K 560b 4 vv.
G'rechtelt's enk K 556 4 vv.
Gehn ma in 'n Prada K 558 4 vv.
Bona nox K 561 4 vv.

N. German Singers—Wolters ♭ Pol. 37091

---

‡ = Long-playing, 33⅓ r.p.m. ♭ = 45 r.p.m. ♮ = Auto. couplings, 78 r.p.m.

(6) NOTTURNI S, S, Bs & 2 cl. & basset-horn, or 3 basset-horns

Due pupille amabili (Anon.) K 439
Ecco, quel fiero istante (Metastasio) K 436
Luci care, luci belle (Anon.) K 346 (new K 439a)
Mi lagnerò tacendo (Metastasio) K 437
Più non si trovano (Metastasio) K 549
Se lontan, ben mio, tu sei (Metastasio) K 438

  E. Scheepers (S), M. Sinclair (M-S), G. Evans (B)
    & Members of London Baroque Ens.—Haas[1]
    (*Dittersdorf*)   ♯ *P.PMB 1008*
  (*Pf. Concerto, K 449 & Serenade* on ♯ AmD.DL 9776)
  (K 437, 439 & 549 only on P.R 20622: ♭ *BSP 3004*)

TRIO: **Das Bandel** K441
  ☆ Vienna Boys' Cho.—Lacovitch ♯ *EPhI.NBR 6007*
  (*Schubert & J. Strauss*)   (& in ♯ AmC.ML 4873)

SPURIOUS: **Das Alphabet** K.Anh 294d
  (by C. F. Par)
  Vienna Boys Cho.—Kühbacher ♯ *Phi.S 06066R*
  (*Schubert, Lassus, Schumann; & Folk Songs*) (arr. Böhm)

II. INSTRUMENTAL MUSIC

A. PIANO MUSIC

1. PIANO SOLO
(& Glass Harmonica)

PIANO WORKS COMPLETE—W. Gieseking[2]
                    Angel. set 3511

VOL. I   **♯ C.CX 1128**
    (♯ FCX 311: QCX 10121; ♯ Angel. 35068)
Minuet, G major   K 1
Minuet, F major   K 2
Allegro, B flat major   K 3
Minuet, F major   K 4
Minuet, F major   K 5
Minuet, D major   K 94 (new K 73h)
(8) Variations on a Dutch Song K 24
(7) Variations on 'Willem von Nassau' K 25
(6) Variations on a theme of Salieri K 180 (new K 173c)
Sonata No. 16, B flat major   K 570
Andante (Rondo) in F major (orig. Mechanical Org.) K 616
[3] Adagio, C major K 335 (new 617a) (orig. glass harmonica)

VOL. II   **♯ C.CX 1142**
    (♯ FCX 312: QCX 10125; ♯ Angel. 35069)
Sonata No. 11, A major   K 331 (new K 300i)
Minuet, D major   K 355 (new K 594a)
Andantino, E flat major   K 236 (new K 588b)
Fantasia, D minor   K 397 (new K 385g)
Sonata No. 4, E flat major   K 282 (new K 189g)
Suite, C major   K 399 (new K 385i)
(12) Variations on 'Ah, vous dirai-je, maman'
                       K 265 (new K 300e)

VOL. III   **♯ C.CX 1160**
    (♯ FCX 313: QCX 10127; ♯ Angel. 35070)
Sonata No. 8, A minor   K 310 (new K 300d)
(12) Variations on a Minuet by Fischer K 179 (new K 189a)
Sonata No. 2, F major   K 280 (new K 189e)
Adagio, B minor   K 540
Marche funèbre del Maestro Contrapuncto K 453a
(6) Variations on an Allegretto K 54 (new K 547a, last movt.)

VOL. IV   **♯ C.CX 1220**
       (♯ Angel. 35071; C.FCX 314)
Sonata No. 13, B flat major   K 333 (new K 315c)
(12) Variations on 'La belle Françoise' K 353 (new K 300f)
Fantasia, C minor   K 475
Sonata No. 14, C minor   K 457

VOL. V   **♯ C.CX 1242**
       (♯ Angel. 35072; C.FCX 315)
Sonata No. 1, C major   K 279 (new K 189d)
(6) Variations on 'Ein Weib . . .'   K 613
Sonata No. 9, D major   K 311 (new K 284c)
Fantasia & Fugue, C major   K 394 (new K 383a)

VOL. VI   **♯ C.CX 1271**
       (♯ Angel. 35073; C.FCX 316)
Sonata No. 6, D major   K 284 (new K 205b)
Fugue, G minor   K 401 (new K 375e)
Allegro & Andante, F major[4] K 533
Rondo, F major[4]   K 494
Allegro, G minor   K 312 (new K 189i)

VOL. VII   **♯ C.CX 1315**
       (♯ Angel. 35074; C.FCX 317)
Sonata No. 3, B flat major   K 281 (new K 189f)
(9) Variations on a Minuet   K 573
Gigue, G major   K 574
"Sonata No. 19", F major
         K.Anh. 135 (new K 547a, first 2 movts.)
(12) Variations on an Allegretto, B flat major K 500
Rondo, A minor   K 511
(6) Variations on Paisiello's 'Salve tu . . .'
                       K 398 (new K 416e)

VOL. VIII   **♯ C.CX 1345**
       (♯ Angel. 35075; C.FCX 318)
(9) Variations on 'Lison dormait' K 264 (new K 315d)
Sonata No. 5, G major   K 283 (new K 189h)
Sonata No. 17, D major   K 576
(10) Variations on 'Unser dummer Pöbel meint' K 455

VOL. IX   **♯ C.CX 1358**
       (♯ C.FCX 319; ♯ Angel. 35076)
Sonata No. 12, F major   K 332 (new K 300k)
(8) Variations on 'Come un' agnello' K 460 (new K 454a)
Sonata No. 15, C major   K 545
(12) Variations on 'Je suis Lindor' K 354 (new K 299a)
Fantasia, C minor   K 396 (new K 385f)

VOL. X   **♯ C.FCX 320**
            (♯ Angel. 35077)
Sonata No. 10, C major   K 330 (new K 300h)
Rondo, D major   K 485
Sonata No. 7, C major   K 309 (new K 284b)
(8) Variations on a March by Grétry K 352 (new K 374c)
Capriccio, C major   K 395 (new K 300g)

VOL. XI   **♯ C.FCX 321**
            (♯ Angel. 35078)
(8) Minuets with Trios   new K 315a
Allegro, B flat major   K 400 (new K 372a)
Allegro & Minuet, B flat major new K 498a
(6) Deutsche Tänze   K 509 (orig. orch.)

PIANO WORKS COMPLETE (in progress)
  L. Kraus   **♯DFr. & HS. sets**
♯ DFr. 91: Variations on 'Salve tu, Domine' K 398
(HSL 121) Sonatas 4, 5, 10   K 282, 283, 330
♯ DFr. 92: Allegro, G minor   K 312
(HSL 122) Sonatas 13, 15   K 333, 545
            Variations on 'La belle Françoise' K 353
♯ DFr. 93: Fantasia, C minor   K 396
(HSL 123) Sonatas 12, 17   K 332, 576
            Variations on 'Come un' agnello' K 460
♯ DFr. 94: Fantasia, C minor   K 475
(HSL 124) Sonatas 6, 14   K 284, 457
♯ DFr. 95: Adagio, B minor   K 540
(HSL 125) Sonatas 7, 8   K 309, 310
            Gigue, G major   K 574
            Minuet, D major   K 355
♯ DFr. 96: Fantasia, D minor   K 397
(HSL 126) Sonatas, 3, 9, 11   K 281, 311, 331
♯ DFr. 97: Rondo, A minor   K 511
(HSL 127) Sonatas 1, 2, 16   K 279, 280, 570
(the above in ♯ HS. set HSL-M)

COLLECTIONS
Adagio, C major K 356 (new K 617a) orig. glass harmonica
Allegro, B flat major   K 3
Allegro, G minor   K 312 (new K 189i)
Andantino, E flat major   K 236 (new K 588b)
Minuet, F major   K 2
SONATAS: No. 3, B flat major K 281
          No. 15, C major   K 545
Fantasia, D minor   K 397

  L. Kraus   **♯Edu.EP 3004**

24 pieces from "Mozart as 8-year-old composer"[5]
                            1764
SIDE I
Contredanse, G major   K 15e
Minuet, C major   K 15f
Minuet, G major   K 15c
Rondeau, D major   K 15d
Allemande, B flat major   K 15w
Contredanse, F major   K 15h
Contredanse, A major   K 15l
Minuet & Trio, A major   K 15i & k
Andante, D major   K 15o
Sonatensatz, G major   K 15p
Andante, B flat major   K 15q
Andante, G minor   K 15r
Finalsatz (Allegro molto), F major K 15v

                   (*continued on next page*)

---

[1] R. Temple-Savage, B. Bree, M. Whewell (2 cl. and 1 basset-horn).
[2] Issued as individual discs in Great Britain; Vols. X & XI not yet issued.
[3] This item is not on the English pressings; it has not been possible to check the others, where it is listed.
[4] Together forming "Sonata No. 18".
[5] B. & H, 1909. All K Nos. quoted are "New K". For other excerpts from this, see Miscellaneous, *infra*.

'Mozart as 8-year-old composer' (*continued*)

SIDE II

Sonatensatz (Molto allegro), F major	K 15t
Andante, B flat major	K 15ii
Minuet, E flat major	K 15cc
Minuet, A flat major	K 15ff
Gigue, C minor	K 15z
Andante, E flat major	K 15mm
Finalsatz (Presto), B flat major	K 15ll
Minuet, F major	K 15oo
Rondeau, F major	K 15hh
Schluss-Satz (Allegro), D major	K 15bb

L. Epstein   # SPA. 35

COLLECTION, Ed. Zeitlin[1]

Minuet, G major	K 1
Minuet, F major	K 2
Allegro, B flat major	K 3
Minuet, F major	K 4
Minuet, F major	K 5
Allegro, C major	K 5a
Andante, B flat major	K 5b (old K 9a)
Sonata, C major	K 6 (orig. pf. & vln.)
Minuet, G major	K 15c
Rondeau, D major	K 15d
Contredanse, F major	K 15e
Minuet, C major	K 15f
Contredanse, F major	K 15h
Minuet & Trio, A major	K 15i & k
Contredanse, A major	K 15l
Minuet, F major	K 15m
Rondo, C major	K 15s
Minuet, G major	K 15y
Minuet, E flat major	K 15ee
Minuet, A flat major	K 15ff
Contredanse, B flat major	K 15gg
Rondeau, F major	K 15hh
Minuet, F major	K 15oo
Minuet, B flat major	K 15pp
Minuet, E flat major	K 15qq
(8) Variations on a Dutch Song	K 24
(7) Variations on 'Willem van Nassau'	K 25

{K 5b, K 6} see note

P. Zeitlin   # Opus. 6003

Sonata No. 7, C major	K 309
Allegro, G minor	K 312
Minuet, D major	K 355
Adagio, B minor	K 540
Gigue, G major	K 574

E. Silver   # Gram.20128

Adagio, B minor   K 540
C. Seemann   PV. 72414
(*Haydn: Str. Qtt. Op. 64, No. 5, s. 1*)

   ☆ P. Badura-Skoda[2]   in # Nix.WLP 5153/4

Adagio, C major   K 356 (new K 617a)
Orig. glass harmonica
— ARR. ORGAN
R. Ellsasser   # MGM.E 3075
(*Andante; Adagio & Allegro; Fantasia*)

Allegro & Andante, F major   K 533
("Unfinished" Pf. Sonata "18")
C. Seemann   # Pol. 18205
(*Rondo K 494, & Sonata 6*)

M. Meyer   V# DFr.EX 17009[3]
(*Rondo*)

   ☆ P. Badura-Skoda[2]   in # Nix.WLP 5153/4

Andante, F major   K 616
— ARR. ORGAN
R. Ellsasser   # MGM.E 3075
(*Adagio, Fantasia, Adagio & Allegro*)

Capriccio, C major K 395 (new K 300g) "*Prelude*"
J-M. Darré (*Sonata, K 310, etc.*) # Pat.DTX 196

FANTASIAS

C major   K 394   (Prelude & Fugue)
L. de Barberris   V# Sel.LAP 1010
(*below*)

   ☆ P. Badura-Skoda[2]   in # Nix.WLP 5153/4

C minor   K 396   (Adagio)
L. de Barberris   V# Sel.LAP 1010
(*above*)

C minor   K 475
P. Badura-Skoda   # Nix.WLP 5317
(*Sonatas No. 11 & 14*)   (# West.WL 5317)
[& on fortepiano, # West.WN 18028]

C. Seemann   PV. 72480
(in # Pol. 18251)

L. de Barberris   # Sel.LPG 8736
(*Sonatas K 457 & 448*)

H. Henkemans   # Phi.A 00654R
(*Sonata K 457*)

B. Webster   in # Persp.PR 2
L. Kraus, from set (# DFr.EX 25011)
   ☆ A. Kitchin (# Ply. 12-48)
   A. Chasins (♭ Mer.EP 1-5056: ♭ FMer.MEP 14530)

D minor   K 397
H. Somer   in # Rem. 199-124
(*Schubert, Lanner, etc.*)   (& in # Ply. 12-92)
L. Babits   ♭ Tit.Tl 7011
(*Chopin: Impromptu No. 4*)
A. de Raco   # ArgOd.LDC 514
(*Bach & Chopin*)
L. Kraus, from set (V# DFr.EX 17034)
   ☆ C. Seemann (in # Pol. 17005: 16113: ♭ 30032)

Gigue, G major   K 574
J. MacInnes   # McInt.MM 104
(*Minuet; Sonata, D major; & Chopin*)

MINUETS
G major   K 1
C. Seemann (*Sonatas 3 & 5*)   # Pol. 16120
(*Sonata No. 5 only, PV. 72415*)
M. v. Doren[4]   in # Chan.MVDP 2
& in # Pol. 19052, see MISCELLANEOUS, *infra*

D major   K 355 (new K 594a)
J. MacInnes   # McInt.MM 104
(*Sonata, D major, etc.; & Chopin*)
   ☆ C. Seemann (in # Pol. 17005: 16113)
   W. Landowska (hpsi.) (in # G.ALP 1246:
         FALP/QALP 218)

Romanze, A flat maj. K.Anh. 205 (Not by Mozart)
F. Kramer   # MTR.MLO 1011
(*Deutsche Tänze, arr.*)

RONDOS
A minor   K 511
C. Seemann   # Pol. 18251
(*Sonata No. 14 & Fantasia K 475*)
G. Novães   # AmVox.PL 9080
(*Sonatas 5, 11, 15*)
L. Kraus, from set (V# DFr.EX 17034)

D major   K 485
G. Scherzer   P.R 3803
F. Gulda   in # D.LXT 2826
(*Sonata K 310; & Bach*)   (# Lon.LL 756)
H. Henkemans   # Phi.A 00758R
(*Sonata No. 16, & Variations*)
   ☆ P. Badura-Skoda[2]   in # Nix.WLP 5153/4
   ☆ C. Seemann (in # Pol. 17005: 16113)
   W. Landowska (hpsi.) (in # G.ALP 1246:
         FALP/QALP 218)

F major   K 494
C. Seemann   # Pol. 18205
(*Allegro & Andante K 533, & Sonata No. 6*)
M. Meyer   V# DFr.EX 17009
(*Allegro & Andante*)   [also listed as 17008]
   ☆ P. Badura-Skoda[2]   in # Nix.WLP 5153/4

SONATAS
No. 1, C major   K 279
R. Veyron-Lacroix (*Nos. 13 & 14*)   # OL.LD 68

No. 2, F major   K 280
A. Ciccolini (*No. 9*)   # G.FBLP 1028
G. Gylden (*below*)   # Phi.A 09800R

---

[1] The items listed are those on the original issue. Subsequently K 5a, 5b and 6 were omitted, and replaced by K 15a and 15b—Allegro F major, and Andantino, C major—to agree in contents with the *Matching Music Book* (pub. Marks, N.Y.) which now accompanies the disc.
[2] Each item is recorded twice; on 5153 a piano of 1785 is used, on 5154 a modern piano.
[3] Also listed as *17008*.
[4] Labelled merely *Minuet, G major*; assumed to be this.

No. 3, B flat major   K 281
C. Seemann   ♯ *Pol. 16120*
(*below*)   (& 2ss, PV. 72441)

G. Gylden   (*above*)   ♯ *Phi.A 09800R*

No. 4, E flat major   K 282
P. Spagnolo   ♯ *D.LXT 5219*
(*Nos. 7, 12 & "19"*)   (♯ Lon.LL 1212)

No. 5, G major   K 283
C. Seemann   ♯ *Pol. 16120*
(*above, & Minuet, K 1*)   (with *K 1 only*, PV. 72415)
G. Novães   ♯ *AmVox.PL 9080*
(*Nos. 11 & 15; & Rondo, K 511*)

No. 6, D major   K 284
C. Seemann   ♯ *Pol. 18205*
(*Allegro & Andante, K 533; & Rondo K 494*)

No. 7, C major   K 309
C. Seemann (*No. 13*)   ♯ *Pol. 18159*
P. Spagnolo   ♯ *D.LXT 5219*
(*Nos. 4, 12 & "19"*)   (♯ Lon.LL 1212)

No. 8, A minor   K 310
F. Gulda   ♯ *D.LXT 2826*
(*Rondo; & Bach*)   (♯ Lon.LL 756)
C. Seemann (*No. 11*)   ♯ *Pol. 18140*
Lazare-Lévy   ♯ *Pat.DTX 196*
(*Variations, Capriccio, & Vln. Sonata*)
☆ D. Lipatti   ♯ *C.C 1021*
(*Bach: Partita No. 1*)   (♯ FC 1023: QC 5013)
(also in ♯ AmC.ML 4633 & ♯ C.FCX 494)

No. 9, D major   K 311
A. Ciccolini   (*No. 2*)   ♯ *G.FBLP 1028*
C. Seemann (*No. 17*)   ♯ *Pol. 16111*
C. Zecchi   ♯ *West.WN 18139*
(*Bach, Scarlatti, Schumann, etc.*)

No. 10, C major   K 330
C. Haskil   ♯ *Phi.A 00724R*
(*Variations*)
A. v. Barentzen   ♯ *Pat.DTX 197*
(*Nos. 11 & 12, & Variations*)
☆ C. Seemann (in ♯ *Pol. 17005: 16113*)
... **2nd movt., Andante** — ARR. GUITAR Llobet
M. L. Anido (*Villa-Lobos*)   ArgOd. 66058

No. 11, A major   K 331
C. Solomon   ♯ *G.ALP 1194*
(*Pf. Concerto, K 450*)
(*Schubert, on* ♯ Vic.LHMV 21)
W. Backhaus   ♯ *D.LXT 5123*
(*Concerto, K 595*)   (♯ Lon.LL 1282)
P. Badura-Skoda   ♯ *Nix.WLP 5317*
(*Fantasia, K 475, & Sonata 14*)   (♯ West.WL 5317)
[& on fortepiano, ♯ West.WN 18028]
F. Neumeyer (fortepiano)   ♯ *HP.AP 13013*
(*4ss, on PV. 9405/6*)
(*Pf. Concerto, K 414, on* ♯ AmD.ARC 3012)
C. Seemann (*4ss*)   ♮ *PV. 72316/7*
(*No. 8 on* ♯ Pol. 18140)
L. Hambro   ♯ *Rem. 199-135*
(*Haydn: Sonatas*)
G. Novães   ♯ *AmVox.PL 9080*
(*Nos. 5 & 15, & Rondo*)   (*Beethoven, on* ♯ Pan.XPV 1011)
M. Ciampi   ♯ *Pat.DTX 197*
(*Nos. 10 & 12, & Variations, K 354*)
S. Fiorentino   ♯ *CA.LPA 1078*
(*No. 12, & Concerto, K 467*)
K. Engel   ♯ *Phi.A 76703R*
(*No. 17*)   (♯ A 00997R)
R. Trouard (*Chopin*)   ♯ *Od.ODX 118*
A. Ciccolini (*No. 12*)   ♯ *C.FC 1029*
M. Meyer (*2ss*)   V♯ *DFr.EX 17008*
M. Schwalb   ♯ *Roy. 1577*
(*Chopin & J. Strauss*)
H. Leygraf (*2ss*)   ♭ *Mtr.MCEP 5006*
... **1st movt.** — ARR. GLASS HARMONICA
E. Hansen (in ♯ *Ban.BC 2000*)

... **3rd movt., Rondo alla turca**   "Turkish March"
J. Prelli (hpsi.)   *Orf. 45001*
(*Rameau*)
M. Jonas   in ♯ *AmC.ML 4624*
E. Silver (hpsi.) (in ♯ Roy. 1550)
R. Bergroth (D.RK 1005)
☆ V. Horowitz (♭ G.7RQ/RF 256)
W. Landowska (hpsi.)
     (in ♯ G.ALP 1246: FALP/QALP 218)
A. Ehlers (hpsi.) (in ♯ D.UAT 273084)
— — ARR. ORCH.
Belgian Radio—Glière (in ♯ Mae.OAT 25001)
Regent Sym. (in ♯ Rgt. 7005)
☆ Paris Opera—Cloëz (♭ Od.7OA 2006)
Kingsway Sym.—Olof (♭ Lon.REP 8007)
Vienna Radio.—Nilius (*Vien.P 6156*)
— — ARR. 4 PFS.   ☆ First Pf. Qtt (♭ Vic.ERA 70)

No. 12, F major   K 332
P. Spagnolo   ♯ *D.LXT 5219*
(*Nos. 4, 7 & "19"*)   (♯ Lon.LL 1212)
J. Benvenuti   ♯ *Pat.DTX 197*
(*Nos. 10 & 11, & Variations*)
S. Fiorentino   ♯ *CA.LPA 1078*
(*No. 11, & Concerto K 467*)
A. Ciccolini (*No. 11*)   ♯ *C.FC 1029*
I. Haebler (*No. 13*)   ♯ *Phi.N 00656R*
L. Lessona (*No. 17*)   ♯ *Fnt.LP 312*
☆ V. Horowitz (*Beethoven*)   ♯ *G.BLP 1014*
(♯ BrzV.BRL 10; G.FBLP 1048: QBLP 5010: VBLP 803)

No. 13, B flat major   K 333
R. Veyron-Lacroix (*Nos. 1 & 14*)   ♯ *OL.LD 68*
C. Seemann (*No. 7*)   ♯ *Pol. 18159*
I. Haebler (*No. 12*)   ♯ *Phi.N 00656R*
C. Rosen ("Siena" pf.)   ♯ *Eso.ESP 3000*
(*D. Scarlatti*)

No. 14, C minor   K 457
C. Seemann   ♯ *Pol. 18251*
(*Fantasia K 475, & Rondo K 511*)
R. Veyron-Lacroix (*Nos. 1 & 13*)   ♯ *OL.LD 68*
P. Badura-Skoda   ♯ *Nix.WLP 5317*
(*Fantasia, K 475; & Sonata 11*)   (♯ West.WL 5317)
[and on fortepiano, ♯ West.WN 18028]
H. Henkemans (*Fantasia, K 475*) ♯ *Phi.A 00654R*
L. de Barberris   ♯ *Sel.LPG 8736*
(*Fantasia, K 475; & Sonata, 2 pfs.*)
W. Gieseking (o.v.)   ♯ *AmC.ML 4772*
(*Sonata 15; & Schumann*)
L. Kraus, from set (♯ *DFr.EX 25011*)

No. 15, C major   K 545
G. Novães   ♯ *AmVox.PL 9080*
(*Nos. 5 & 11, & Rondo*)
     (*Beethoven: Sonata 14, on* ♯ MApp.MAR 5953)
C. Seemann (*2ss*)   *PV. 36079*
B. P. Joseph (pedal hpsi.)   ♯ *SOT. 1131*
(*Bach*)
☆ W. Gieseking (o.v.)   ♯ *AmC.ML 4772*
(*Sonata No. 14; & Schumann*)
☆ L. Kraus (o.v.) (♯ AFest.CFR 12-310; ♯ EVox.PL 6880)
A. Kitchen (in ♯ Ply. 12-48; Allegro only
     in ♯ Rem. 149-4; AFest.CFR 10-106; ♯ Ply. 12-75)
... **1st movt., Allegro, only**: J. Katchen (D.F 10338)[1]
... **Andante & Rondo**: M. v. Doren (in ♯ Chan.MVDP 2)
— ARR. HARP & STR.
E. Vito & Str. Ens.   ♯ *Per.SPL 704*
(*Handel, Prokofiev, Debussy, etc.*)

No. 16, B flat major   K 570
H. Henkemans   ♯ *Phi.A 00758R*
(*Rondo, D major; & Variations*)
S. Askenase (*2ss*)   *PV. 72288*
E. Gilels   ♯ *C.CX 1217*
(*Saint-Saëns: Concerto*)   (♯ FCX/QCX 301; Angel. 35132)
E. Gilels (*Beethoven*)   ♯ *Csm.CRLP 177*
E. Møller (*2ss*)   ♭ *Mtr.MCEP 3015*

[1] Labelled: *In an Eighteenth-Century Drawing-room.*

No. 17, D major K 576
C. Seemann (*No. 9*)   ♯ *Pol. 16111*
K. Engel   ♯ *Phi.A 76703R*
(*No. 11*)   (♯ *A 00997R*)
J. MacInnes   ♯ **McInt.MM 104**
(*Gigue, K 574, Minuet K 355 & Chopin*)
L. Lessona (*No. 12*)   ♯ *Fnt.LP 312*
☆ G. Anda (*Haydn*)   ♯ *DT.TM 68023*

"No. 18"—SEE Allegro & Andante, & Rondo,
                                         K 494, *ante*

"No. 19", F major new K 547a, first 2 movts.
(K Anh. 135)
P. Spagnolo   ♯ *D.LXT 5219*
(*Nos. 4, 7 & 12*) _____   (♯ *Lon.LL 1212*)

Suite, C major K 399
... Allemande & Courante ☆ E. Joyce (♭ *AmD.ED 3527*)

VARIATIONS
(12) on 'Ah, vous dirai-je, maman' K 265 (new K 300e)
D. Barenboim   ♭ *EPhi.NBE 11013*
(*Mendelssohn, Brahms*)   (♭ *Phi.N 425008E*)
S. François   in ♯ *Pat.DTX 195*
(*Concert Aria, Str. Qtt., etc.*)

(9) on 'Lison dormait' K 264 (new K 315d)
J-M. Darré
(12) on 'La Belle Françoise' K 353 (new K 300f)
J. Doyen   in ♯ *Pat.DTX 196*
(*Sonata No. 8, Capriccio, etc.*)

(12) on 'Je suis Lindor' K 354 (new K 299a)
L. Descaves   in ♯ *Pat.DTX 197*
(*Sonatas 10 & 11, etc.*)

(9) on a Minuet by Duport K 573
C. Haskil   ♯ *Phi.N 00724R*
(*Sonata No. 10*)
G. Kraus (hpsi.)   ♯ *Hall.RS 2*
(*D. Scarlatti*)

(10) on 'Unser dummer Pöbel meint' (Gluck) K 455
H. Henkemans   ♯ *Phi.A 00758R*
(*Rondo, D major; & Sonata 16*)
☆ A. Foldes (in ♯ *MHF. 6*)

2. PIANO DUETS & TWO PIANOS

Adagio & Allegro, F minor K 594 pf. duet[1]
— ARR. ORGAN
R. Ellsasser   ♯ **MGM.E 3075**
(*below; Adagio; Andante, solo; above*)
M-C. Alain (*below*)   ♯ *DFr.EX 25037*

Fantasia, F minor K 608 pf. duet[1]
— ARR. ORGAN
R. Ellsasser   ♯ **MGM.E 3075**
(*above; Adagio, Andante*)
M-C. Alain (*above*)   ♯ *DFr.EX 25037*
☆ F. Germani   ♯ *G.DLP 1043*
(*C. Franck: Chorale No. 1*)   (♯ *FBLP 1063*)
— ARR. ORCH. ☆ Vienna Sym.—Fekete (♯ *Cum.CR 295, d.c.*)

Fugue, C minor K 426 2 pfs.
☆ J. & G. Dichler (in ♯ *U.5184C*)

SONATAS, PF. DUET
COLLECTION
B flat major   K 358 (new K 186c)
D major   K 381 (new K 123a)
G major   K 357 (unfinished) (new K 497a)
☆ J. Demus & P. Badura-Skoda   ♯ **Nix.WLP 5060**
[K 358 & K 381 also on ♯ West.WN 18044, *below*;
 K 357 also on ♯ West.WN 18045, *below*]

D major K 381 (new K 123a)
L. Kraus   ♯ **Edu.EP 3002**
[playing both parts; recorded separately & complete]
V. Vronsky & V. Babin (*below*) ♯ **AmC.ML 4667**

B flat major K 358
V. Vronsky & V. Babin (*above*) ♯ **AmC.ML 4667**

F major K 497; C major K 521
☆ P. Badura-Skoda & J. Demus   ♯ Nix.WLP 5082
(*also with K 357, above, on* ♯ West.WN 18045)

SONATA, TWO PIANOS
D major K 448 (new K 375a)
R. & G. Casadesus   ♯ **AmC.ML 5046**
(*below; & Schubert*)
C. Smith & P. Sellick   ♯ **C.SX 1018**
(*Dohnányi*)   (♯ *WSX 1018*)
P. Luboshutz & G. Nemenoff ♯ **Rem. 199-147**
(*Saint-Saëns, Debussy, Falla*)
(*Haydn: Sym. No. 7 on* ♯ *Cum.CR 313*)[2]
☆ P. Badura-Skoda & J. Demus   ♯ Nix.WLP 5069
(*Variations K 501*)
(*Fantasia K 475 & Sonata K 457 on* ♯ *Sel.LPG 8736*)
(*K 501, & Sonatas K 358 & K 381, on* ♯ West.WN 18044)

Variations, G major K 501 pf. duet
R. & G. Casadesus   ♯ **AmC.ML 5046**
(*Sonata, above; & Schubert*)
☆ P. Badura-Skoda & J. Demus   ♯ Nix.WLP 5069
(*Sonata, above*)   (*also on* ♯ West.WN 18044)
☆ J. & G. Dichler (in ♯ *U.5184C*)

"COMPLETE MUSIC FOR PF. DUET"
FOR PRACTICE: 1 pf. missing
CONTENTS: SONATAS K 358, 381, 497, 521 without
                                    1st pf.
Adagio & Allegro, K 594 ⎱
Fantasia, K 608   ⎰ without 2nd pf.
Fugue, K 401
Variations, K 501
E. Hancock & C. Norwood
(4ss)   ♯ **CEd. set MMO 402**

---

2. B. CHAMBER MUSIC

Adagio, F major K 410 2 basset-horns & bsn.
☆ Pro Musica Ens.—Meyer (in ♯ Pol. 540006)

Adagio, B flat major K 411 2 cl., 3 basset-horns
☆ London Baroque Ens.—Haas (in ♯ *AmD.DL 4055*)
Pro Musica Ens.—Meyer (in ♯ Pol. 540007)

Adagio, C major K 580a cor. ang., 2 vlns. & vlc.
☆ London Baroque Ens.   ♯ *AmD.DL 4055*
(*above, & Contretänze K 609*)

(4) Adagios K 404a Str. Trio
☆ Pasquier Trio (n.v.) (♯ HSL.HSL 108)
... **No. 1, D minor**
Alma Musica Trio   in ♯ **LT.DTL 93046**
(*Bach: W.T.C. Fugue No. 8; Mozart: Quartet K 285b, etc.*)
(♯ Sel.LAG 1019; T.LT 6551)

Adagio & Rondo, C minor & major K 617
Glass harmonica, fl., ob., vla. & vlc.
B. Hoffmann, G. Scheck, H. Winschermann,
E. Seiler, A. Wenzinger   ♭ *Pol. 37029*
(2ss)
K. Swoboda (celeste), C. Wanausek, F. Wächter,
P. Angerer &V. Görlich ♯ **E. & AmVox.PL 8550**
(*Concerto, fl., hp. & orch.; Andante, fl. & orch.*)
Musart Ens. (with hpsi.)   ♯ **Aphe.AP 22**
(*Divertimento, K 205; & Str. Qtt. No. 4*)

DUOS vln. & vla.
No. 2, B flat major K 424
☆ J. & L. Fuchs   ♯ **B.AXTL 1030**
(*Martinů*)   (♯ *D.UAT 273082*)
☆ J. Heifetz & W. Primrose   ♯ **Vic.LCT 1150**
(*Divertimento K 563; & Handel-Halvorsen*)

QUARTETS, Flute, vln., vla., vlc.
COLLECTION
No. 1, D major K 285
No. 4, A major K 298
One unspec. called K 514
M. H. Wummer & Knickerbocker Cha. Players
                                         ♯ **CEd.CE 1064**
(*& for practice, fl. part missing,* ♯ MMO 106)

---

[1] Originally for mechanical organ.
[2] Also listed as 213 and 314. The latter is also said to be Grieg; the former merely a misprint?

No. 1, D major   K 285
P. Birkelund, A. Karecki, H. H. Andersen,
A. Petersen   ♭ *Mtr.MCEP 3034*
☆ H. Rečnicek & Str. Trio   in ♯ **Nix.WLP 5022**

No. 3, C major   K 285b (old K.Anh. 171)
E. v. Royen & Alma Musica Trio
       ♯ **LT.DTL 93046**
(*Willaert, Vivaldi, Gabrieli, etc.*)
       (♯ Sel.LAG 1019; T.LT 6551)

QUARTET, Oboe, vln., vla., vlc.
F major   K 370
M. S. Andreassen, F. M. Bruun, J. Koppel,
J. Hansen   ♯ *G.KBLP 6*
(*Haydn*)
☆ H. Kamesch & Str. Trio   ♯ **Nix.WLP 5022**
   (*Flute Qtt.*)
☆ M. Tabuteau, I. Stern, W. Primrose, P. Tortelier
       ♯ **C.CX 1090**
   (*Divertimento*)   (FCX 227)
☆ H. Gomberg & Galimir Trio   ♯ **B.AXTL 1021**
   (*Telemann*)   (♯ D.UST 253553)

— ARR. HARMONICA & STR.
☆ L. Adler & Winterthur Trio (in ♯ *FMer.MLP 7054*)

QUARTETS, 2 vlns., vla., vlc.
No. 1, G major   K 80   No. 2, D major   K 155
No. 3, G major   K 156   No. 4, C major   K 157
Barchet Qtt.   ♯ **E. & AmVox.PL 8510**

No. 5, F major   K 158   No. 6, B flat major   K 159
No. 7, E flat major   K 160
Barchet Qtt.   ♯ **AmVox.PL 8690**

No. 1, G major   K 80
Barylli Qtt.   ♯ **West.WN 18150**
(*Divertimenti*)

No. 2, D major   K 155   No. 3, G major   K 156
No. 4, C major   K 157   No. 5, F major   K 158
Barylli Quartet   ♯ **West.WN 18053**
New Music Qtt.   ♯ **AmC.ML 5003**

No. 6, B flat major   K 159   No. 7, E flat major   K 160
No. 8, F major   K 168   No. 9, F major   K 169
Barylli Qtt.   ♯ **West.WN 18092**

No 10, C major   K 170   No. 11, E flat major   K 171
No. 12, B flat major   K 172
Barylli Qtt.   ♯ **West.WN 18103**

No. 2, D major   K 155
Italian Qtt.   ♯ **D.LXT 2852**
(*No. 23*)   (♯ Lon.LL 665)

No. 4, C major   K 157
Musart Qtt.   ♯ *Aphe.AP 22*
(*Adagio & Rondo, K 617 & Divertimento, K 205*)

No. 6 . . . Rondo only: Pessina Qtt. (ArgOd. 66057:
       in ♯ *LDC 510*)

The 6 "Haydn" Quartets   (Nos. 14-19)
COMPLETE RECORDINGS
Budapest Qtt.   ♯ **AmC.ML 4726/8**
(6ss)   (set SL 187)
[Nos. 14 & 15 on ♯ EPhi.ABL 3018; Phi.A 01125L;
     Nos. 16-19 on ♯ Phi.A 01202 & 01204L]
☆ Roth Qtt. (♯ Clc. 6264/6)

No. 14, G major   K 387
Haydn Qtt.   ♯ *T.LB 6035*
       (♯ *DT.LGM 65011*)
Italian Qtt.   ♯ **C.CX 1102**
(*No. 15*)   (♯ C.FCX 261: QCX 10025; Angel. 35063)
Barylli Qtt.   ♯ **Nix.WLP 5265**
(*No. 22*)   (♯ West.WL 5265)
☆ Amadeus Qtt. (♯ *G.WDLP 1003*;
       ♯ Vic.LHMV/♭ *WHMV 1039*)

No. 15, D minor   K 421
Vienna Konzerthaus Qtt.   ♯ **Nix.WLP 5175**
(*No. 19*)   (♯ Sel. 320.CW.034; ♯ West.WL 5175)
Italian Qtt.   ♯ **C.CX 1102**
(*No. 14*)   (♯ C.FCX 261: QCX 10025: WCX 1102;
       Angel. 35063)

Amadeus Qtt.   ♯ **G.ALP 1249**
(*Haydn*)   (♯ Pol. 18201)
Musical Arts Qtt.   ♯ **Van.VRS 463**
(*Schubert*)
Schäffer Qtt.   ♯ **CFD. 47**
(*Clarinet Trio*)

No. 16, E flat major   K 428
☆ Amadeus Qtt.   ♯ **Nix.WLP 5099**
(*below*)   (♯ Sel.LAC 30004)

No. 17, B flat major   K 458   "Hunt"
☆ Amadeus Qtt.   ♯ **Nix.WLP 5099**
(*above*)   (♯ Sel.LAC 30004)
☆ Loewenguth Qtt.   ♯ **HP.DG 16004**

No. 18, A major   K 464
Michailow Qtt.   ♯ *Eta. 720011*
☆ Amadeus Qtt. (*No. 23*)   ♯ **Nix.WLP 5092**

No. 19, C major   K 465
Amadeus Qtt.   ♯ **G.ALP 1283**
(*No. 21*)   (♯ Pol. 18242; Vic. LHMV 32)
Italian Qtt.   ♯ **D.LXT 2853**
(1♯ss—*Adagio & Fugue, K 546*)
New Music Qtt.   ♯ **BRS. 923**
(*Haydn*)
Vienna Konzerthaus Qtt.   ♯ **Nix.WLP 5175**
(*No. 15*)   (♯ West.WL 5175; Sel. 320.CW.034)
☆ Guilet Qtt. (♯ *MMS. 122*)

Nos. 20-23, COMPLETE
Budapest Qtt. (4ss)   ♯ **AmC.ML 5007/8**
       (set SL 228)

No. 20, D major   K 499
Juilliard Qtt.   ♯ **AmC.ML 4863**
(*No. 21*)
Netherlands Qtt.   ♯ **EPhi.ABL 3080**
(*No. 22*)   (♯ Phi.A 00232L; Epic.LC 3100)
Barchet Qtt.   ♯ **AmVox.PL 8730**
(*No. 21*)
☆ Roth Qtt. (♯ Clc. 6262)

No. 21, D major   K 575
Amadeus Qtt.   ♯ **G.ALP 1283**
(*No. 19*)   (♯ Pol. 18242; Vic. LHMV 32)
Juilliard Qtt.   ♯ **AmC.ML 4863**
(*No. 20*)
Barchet Qtt.   ♯ **AmVox.PL 8730**
(*No. 20*)
Barylli Qtt.   ♯ **West.WL 5356**
(*Quintet K 593*)
Gewandhaus Qtt.   ♯ **Eta. 820016**
(*Haydn: Qtt. Op. 20, No. 4*)
Aeolian Qtt. (*No. 23*)   ♯ **Roy. 1516**
☆ Roth Qtt.   ♯ Clc. 6262
   Guilet Qtt.   ♯ *MMS. 122*

No. 22, B flat major   K 589
Barchet Qtt.   ♯ **E. & AmVox.PL 8260**
(*No. 23*)
Barylli Qtt.   ♯ **Nix.WLP 5265**
(*No. 14*)   (♯ West.WL 5265)
Netherlands Qtt.   ♯ **EPhi.ABL 3080**
(*No. 20*)   (♯ Phi.A 00232L; Epic.LC 3100)
☆ Roth Qtt. (♯ Clc. 6263)

No. 23, F major   K 590
Italian Qtt.   ♯ **D.LXT 2852**
(*No. 2*)   (♯ Lon.LL 665)
Barchet Qtt.   ♯ **E. & AmVox.PL 8260**
(*No. 22*)
Aeolian Qtt. (*No. 21*)   ♯ **Roy. 1516**
☆ Amadeus Qtt. (*No. 18*)   ♯ **Nix.WLP 5092**
☆ Roth Qtt. (♯ Clc. 6263)

A major   K.Anh. 212 ("Milanese" No. 1, doubtful)
Pascal Qtt.   ♯ **Pat.DTX 195**
(*Concert Arias, Pf. Variations, Vln. Sonata*)

☆ = Re-issue of a recording to be found in previous volumes.

QUARTETS, Pf., vln., vla., vlc.
No. 1, G minor   K 478
C. Curzon & Amadeus Qtt. Mbrs. ‡ D.LXT 2772
(No. 2)   (‡ Lon.LL 679)
M. Horszowski & Members of N.Y. Qtt.
                              ‡ AmC.ML 4627
(Beethoven: Pf. Qtt., E flat)
No. 2, E flat major   K 493
C. Curzon & Members of Amadeus Qtt.
                              ‡ D.LXT 2772
(No. 1)   (‡ Lon.LL 679)

QUINTET, Cl. & Str. Qtt., A major   K 581
A. Boskovsky & Members Vienna Octet
                              ‡ D.LXT 5032
                              (‡ Lon.LL 1167)
F. Étienne & Végh Qtt.   ‡ DFr. 2
(Cl. Concerto K 581)   (‡ HS.HSL 96)
(& 2ss, ‡ DFr.EX 25031)
P. Simenauer & Pascal Qtt.   ‡ MMS. 37
V. Ríha & Smetana Qtt.   ‡ Sup.LPM 112
                              (‡ U. 5073C)
C. Paashaus & Classic Qtt.   ‡ CEd.CE 1061
(Brahms)
J. Michelin & Champeil Qtt. (‡ BàM. 1001, Pte. rec.)
☆ L. Wlach & Vienna Konzerthaus Qtt. (‡ Nix.WLP 5112)
A. Duques & Eidus Qtt. (‡ Cum.CS 268)
R. Kell & Fine Arts Qtt. (‡ Pol. 18195)
— For Practice, with cl. & vla. pts. missing (‡ CEd.MMO 71)

QUINTET, Pf., ob., cl., hrn., bsn. E flat ma. K 452
C. Horsley, L. Brain, S. Waters, D. Brain,
C. James (Berkeley)   ‡ G.CLP 1029
W. Gieseking, S. Sutcliffe, B. Walton, D. Brain
& C. James   ‡ C.CX 1322
(Beethoven)   (‡ Angel. 35303)
R. Serkin & Members of Philadelphia Wind
Quintet   (Beethoven)   ‡ AmC.ML 4834
H. Wingreen & New Art Wind Qtt.
(Beethoven)   ‡ CEd.CE 2007
(also, ‡ CEd.MMO 101/5, with one inst. missing in turn)
☆ R. Veyron-Lacroix, P. Pierlot, J. Lancelot, G. Coursier,
P. Hongne (Cassation)   ‡ LOL.OL 50016
☆ Y. Grimaud & Oubradous Qtt. ‡ Esq.TW 14-002
(Serenade K 185)

QUINTETS: COLLECTION
(K 407, 46, 174, 406, 515, 516, 593, 614)
Pascal Qtt., et al.   ‡ MMS. 3014/7
[for details of individual issues, see below]

QUINTET, Hrn., vln., 2 vlas., vlc. E flat ma. K407
W. Speth, Members of Pascal Qtt. & W. Gerhard
                              ‡ CHS.CHS 1188
(Quintet, K 46)   (‡ Clc. 6237)
J. Stagliano & Ens.   ‡ Bo.B 201
(Rust: Viola Sonata)
☆ O. de Rosa & Strad. Ens (‡ Cum.CS 268)

QUINTETS, 2 vlns., 2 vlas., vlc.
B flat major   K 46[1]
Pascal Qtt. & W. Gerhard   ‡ CHS.CHS 1188
(Quintet K 407)   (‡ Clc. 6237)
B flat major   K 174
Pascal Qtt. & W. Gerhard   ‡ CHS.CHS 1185
(Quintet K 515)   (‡ Clo. 6233)
C minor   K 406
(ARR. Mozart from Serenade K 388)
Pascal Qtt. & W. Gerhard   ‡ CHS.CHS 1186
(Quintet K 516)   (‡ Clc. 6234)
☆ Budapest Quintet (‡ C.WCX 1031: FCX 179:
                              QCX 10043)
C major   K 515
Barylli Qtt. & W. Hübner   ‡ Nix.WLP 5271
                              (‡ West.WL 5271)
Amadeus Qtt. & C. Aronowitz   ‡ G.ALP 1125
                              (‡ Pol. 18240)
Pascal Qtt. & W. Gerhard   ‡ CHS.CHS 1185
(Quintet, K 174)   (‡ Clc. 6233)

G minor   K 516
Pascal Qtt. & W. Gerhard   ‡ CHS.CHS 1186
(Quintet K 406)   (‡ Clc. 6234)
☆ Amadeus Qtt. & C. Aronowitz (2ss) ‡ Nix.WLP 5086
(1s with K 614 on ‡ West.WN 18036)
D major   K 593
Pascal Qtt. & W. Gerhard   ‡ CHS.CHS 1187
(Quintet K 614)   (‡ Clc. 6229)
Barylli Quintet   ‡ West.WL 5356
(Quartet No. 21)
☆ Budapest Quintet (‡ C.FCX 179: WCX 1031:
                              QCX 10043)
E flat major   K 614
Pascal Qtt. & W. Gerhard   ‡ CHS.CHS 1187
(Quintet K 593)   (‡ Clc. 6229)
☆ Vienna Konzerthaus Quintet (‡ Sel. 230.C.006;
&, with K 516, on ‡ West.WN 18036)

SONATAS, Pf. & vln.
COMPLETE RECORDING (in progress)
The records number the Sonatas according to a
different canon from that adopted in our lists. The
alternative numbers are here given in brackets.
L. Kraus & W. Boskovsky   DFr.

VOL. I (4ss)   ‡ DFr. 121/2
‡ DFr. 121: No. 18 (25), G major   K 301 (new K 293a)
(HSL 131)   No. 19 (26), E flat major   K 302 (new K 293b)
            No. 20 (27), C major   K 303 (new K 293c)
            No. 21 (28), E minor   K 304 (new K 300c)
‡ DFr. 122: No. — (19), F major   K 57 (new K.Anh. 209e)[2]
(HSL 132)   No. 22 (29), A major   K 305 (new K 293d)
            No. 32 (40), B flat major   K 454

VOL. II (4ss)   ‡ DFr. 123/4
‡ DFr. 123: No. — (22), E minor   K 60 (new K.Anh. 209h)[2]
(HSL 133)   No. 17 (24), C major   K 296
            No. 26 (34), B flat major   K 378 (new K 317d)
‡ DFr. 124: No. — (23), E flat major K 58 (new K.Anh. 209f)[2]
(HSL 134)   No. 27 (35), G major   K 379 (new K 373a)
            No. 32 (41), E flat major   K 481

COLLECTIONS
No. 1, C major   K 6   No. 2, D major   K 7
No. 3, B flat major   K 8   No. 4, G major   K 9
R. Veyron-Lacroix (hpsi.) & J. Dumont
                              ‡ Pat.DTX 191
(Concerto, pf. & vln.)
No. 2, D major   K 7
No. 12, G major   K 27
C. Eschenbach & W. Melcher   in ‡ Pol. 19052
[See MISCELLANEOUS, infra]
No. 21, E minor   K 304
No. 26, B flat major   K 378
No. 33, E flat major   K 481
M. Jones & B. Langbein   ‡ D.LXT 2944
                              (‡ Lon.LL 1069)
No. 24, F major   K 376
No. 29, A major   K 402
No. 33, E flat major   K 481
P. Badura-Skoda & W. Barylli ‡ West.WL 5394
No. 17, C major   K 296
No. 18, G major   K 301
No. 21, E minor   K 304
☆ P. Badura-Skoda & W. Barylli
                              ‡ Nix.WLP 5130
No. 22, A major   K 305
No. 25, F major   K 377
E flat major   K 58 (new K.Anh. 209f)[2]
☆ P. Badura-Skoda & W. Barylli
                              ‡ Nix.WLP 5145
No. 18, G major   K 301
No. 21, E minor   K 304
No. 26, B flat major   K 378
No. 27, G major   K 379
☆ A. Heksch (fortepiano) & N. de Klijn
                              ‡ Epic.LC 3034
                              (‡ Phi.S 04012L)

[1] First three and last movements of Serenade, B flat major, K 361, ARR. Str. Quintet by an unknown hand, NOT by Mozart.
[2] According to Einstein, not by Mozart, but probably by a pupil.

No. 6, G major K 11
☆ A. Heksch (fortepiano) & N. de Klijn ♯ Epic.LC 3131
(Sonatas 23, 33 & Variations)

No. 18, G major K 301
G. Tucker & A. Grumiaux   ♯ Bo.B 202
(Sonata No. 21; Bach & Fiocco)

No. 21, E minor K 304
G. Tucker & A. Grumiaux   ♯ Bo.B 202
(Sonata No. 18; Bach & Fiocco)
C. Seemann & W. Schneiderhan   ♯ Pol. 16092
(Sonata No. 28)
V. Perlemuter & R. Charmy   ♯ Pat.DTX 196
(Pf. Sonata, K 310; Variations, etc.)

No. 22, A major K 305
P. Barbizet & C. Ferras   ♯ D.LX 3141
(No. 24)

No. 23, D major K 306
A. Heksch (fortepiano) & N. de Klijn
  ♯ EPhi.ABR 4028
(No. 33)   *(♯ Phi.A 00691R)*
(Nos. 33 & 6, & Variations, on ♯ Epic.LC 3131)
V. Perlemuter & R. Benedetti   ♯ Pat.DTX 195
(Concert Aria, K 316; Milanese Qtt., etc.)

No. 24, F major K 376
P. Barbizet & C. Ferras   ♯ D.LX 3141
(No. 22)
J. Antonietti & J. Martzy   ♯ Pol. 18075
(Beethoven: Sonata No. 8)

No. 26, B flat major K 378
A. Heksch (fortepiano) & N. de Klijn
(No. 27)   ♯ Phi.A 00614R
C. Seemann & W. Schneiderhan   ♯ Pol. 18260
(No. 27)

No. 27, G major K 379
A. Heksch (fortepiano) & N. de Klijn
(No. 26)   ♯ Phi.A 00614R
C. Seemann & W. Schneiderhan   ♯ Pol. 18260
(No. 26)
L. Oborin & D. Oistrakh   ♯ Mon.MWL 334
(No. 32) *(No. 32, & Serenade—Rondo, ♯ Csm.CRLP 194)*
☆ P. Badura-Skoda & W. Barylli *(No. 32)* ♯ Nix.WLP 5109

No. 28, E flat major K 380
C. Seemann & W. Schneiderhan   ♯ Pol. 16092
(Sonata 21)

No. 32, B flat major K 454
K. Taylor & F. Grinke   ♯ D.LXT 2802
(No. 34)   *(♯ Lon.LL 739)*
C. Seemann & W. Schneiderhan   ♯ Pol. 18250
(No. 34)
L. Kentner & Y. Menuhin   ♯ Vic.LHMV 1053
(Beethoven)
I. Yampolsky & D. Oistrakh   ♯ Mon.MWL 334
(No. 27)
(No. 27, & Serenade K 250—Rondo, ♯ Csm.CRLP 194)
C. Rosen & R. Peters   ♯ D.FST 153035
(No. 33)   *(♯ Lon.LL 674)*
G. Szell & J. Szigeti   ♯ AmC.ML 5005
(No. 33)
☆ P. Badura-Skoda & W. Barylli *(No. 27)* ♯ Nix.WLP 5109

— ARR. FL. & PF.
J-P. Rampal & L. Kraus   ♯ Edu.ECM 4001
(Schubert, Debussy)

No. 33, E flat major K 481
A. Heksch (fortepiano) & N. de Klijn
  ♯ EPhi.ABR 4028
(No. 23)   *(& in ♯ Epic.LC 3131)*   *(♯ Phi.A 00691R)*
C. Rosen & R. Peters   ♯ D.FST 153035
(No. 32)   *(♯ Lon.LL 674)*
G. Szell & J. Szigeti   ♯ AmC.ML 5005
(No. 32)

No. 34, A major K 526
K. Taylor & F. Grinke   ♯ D.LXT 2802
(No. 32)   *(♯ Lon.LL 739)*
C. Seemann & W. Schneiderhan   ♯ Pol. 18250
(No. 32)

SONATA, Bsn. & vlc., B flat major K 292
S. Walt & S. Mayes   ♯ Bo.B 210
(Beethoven, Bréval, Haydn)
... 3rd movt., Rondo   — ARR. 2 VLCS.
S. Knushevitzky & A. Vlasov   USSR. 19033
(Weber: Aufforderung z. Tanz. s. 3)

TRIOS, Pf., vln., vlc.
No. 1, B flat major   K 254
No. 2, G major   K 496
No. 3, B flat major   K 502
No. 4, E major   K 542
No. 5, C major   K 548
No. 6, G major   K 564

COMPLETE RECORDING: Nos. 1 to 6; with
Trio, D minor K 442 [on DFr. 82]
L. Kraus, W. Boskowsky, N. Hübner ♯ DFr. 81/3
[No. 2 also on ♯ DFr.EX 25032]   *(♯ HS.HSL 9001/3)*

COMPLETE RECORDINGS: Nos. 1 to 6
P. Badura-Skoda, J. Fournier & A. Janigro
  ♯ West.WL various
(Nos. 1 & 6 on WL 5284; 2 & 3 on WL 5242;
  ♯ Véga.C 30.A15; 4 & 5 on WL 5267)
Bolzano Trio   ♯ E. & AmVox. set PL 8493
(5ss—below)
No. 2 ☆ Rubbra, Gruenberg, Pleeth (♯ Argo.RG 5)
Nos. 3 & 4 ☆ Boston Trio (♯ Pac.LDAD 73)
Nos. 3 & 5 ☆ Jambor, Aitay, Starker (♯ Cum.SPR 323)
Nos. 3 & 6: Mozarteum Trio[1]   ♯ Phi.A 00274L

No. 4, E major K 542
Trio di Trieste   ♯ D.LXT 5253
(Beethoven)   *(♯ Lon.LL 1177)*
V. Schiøler, C. Senderovitz, E. B. Bengtsson
(Haydn)   ♯ G.KBLP 9

No. 6, G major K 564
E. Gilels, L. Kogan, M. Rostropovich
(Bach)   ♯ Kings. 261

TRIO, Pf., cl., vla., E flat major K 498
N. Montanari, E. Brunoni, G. Carpi
(above)   in ♯ E. & AmVox. set PL 8493
P. Schilhawsky, A. Heine, P. Doktor ♯ CFD.47
(Str. Qtt., K 421)
Frye Cha. Music Group   ♯ Lin.LP 1007
(Boccherini) [probably played pf., vln., vla.]
☆ M. Horszowski, R. Kell & L. Fuchs
  (♯ D.UAT 273056)

Variations on 'Hélas, j'ai perdu mon amant'
(Albanèse)   K 360   pf. & vln.
☆ A. Heksch (fortepiano) & N. de Klijn ♯ Epic.LC 3131
(Sonatas)

II. C. DIVERTIMENTI, CASSATIONS & SERENADES

CASSATIONS
No. 1, G major K 63
Vienna Sym.—Sacher   ♯ EPhi.ABR 4010
(No. 2)   *(♯ Phi.A 00676R; ♯ Epic.LC 3043)*
Berlin Radio Cha.—Haarth   ♯ Ura.RS 7-32
(Serenade No. 11)
☆ Zimbler Sinfonietta   ♯ B.AXTL 1001
(Serenade No. 1)   *(♯ D.UAT 273088)*

No. 2, B flat major K 99
Vienna Sym.—Sacher   ♯ EPhi.ABR 4010
(No. 1)   *(♯ Phi.A 00676R; ♯ Epic.LC 3043)*
E flat major[2]   ob., cl., hrn. & bsn.
Paris Wind Ens.   ♯ Phi.A 77403L
(Haydn, Vivaldi)
☆ P. Pierlot, J. Lancelot, G. Coursier & P. Hongne
(Quintet)   ♯ LOL.OL 50016

---

[1] With fortepiano.
[2] Pub. 1936; Andraud, Cincinnati. No evidence of origin (said to have been "discovered" 1910); probably spurious.

DIVERTIMENTI, 2 basset-horns & bsn. K 439b
No. 1, B flat major
No. 4, B flat major
No. 5, B flat major
    L. Wlach, F. Bartosek (cl.), K. Öhlberger
               ♯ West.WL 5213

No. 2, B flat major
    ☆ L. Wlach, F. Bartosek (cl.), K. Öhlberger
      (Fl. Qtt. No. 1 & Ob. Qtt.)   ♯ Nix.WLP 5022

No. 3, B flat major
    ☆ L. Wlach, F. Bartosek (cl.), K. Öhlberger
      (⅓—Sinfonia concertante)   ♯ Nix.WLP 5020

DIVERTIMENTO, E flat major, vln., vla. & vlc.
                              K 563
    J. Pougnet, F. Riddle & A. Pini ♯ Nix.WLP 5191
      (♯ West.WL 5101; Véga.C 30.A13)
    Bel Arte Trio   ♯ B.AXTL 1031
      (♯ AmD.DL 9659; D.UAT 273578)
    ☆ J. Heifetz, W. Primrose, E. Feuermann (♯ Vic.LCT 1150)
    Pasquier Trio (n.v.) (♯ HS.HSL 114)

DIVERTIMENTI Orchestra
E flat major K 113 "No. 1"
    Berlin Sym.—Rubahn   ♯ Roy. 1444
    (below, & Contretänze K 609)

D major K 131 "No. 2"
    Berlin Sym.—Rubahn   ♯ Roy. 1444
    (above, & Contretänze)
    Orch.—Haefner   ♯ MTW. 501
    (Gluck)   (also ♯ ACC.MP 23)
    ☆ Cha. Orch.—Goldschmidt († HS.AS 33)

DIVERTIMENTI String orchestra [or quartet]
D major K 136
B flat major K 137
F major K 138
    Munich Pro Arte—Redel   ♯ LOL.OL 50072
      (♯ OL.LD 106)
    Saar Cha.—Ristenpart   ♯ DFr. 16
    London Mozart Ens.—Vicars ♯ CA.LPA 1076
    Barylli Str. Qtt.   ♯ West.WN 18150
    (Str. Qtt. No. 1)

D major K 136; B flat major K 137
    Paris Collegium Musicum—Douatte
                    ♯ Eko.LM 7

**DIVERTIMENTI, 2 obs., 2 cors angl., 2 cls.,
2 hrns., 2 bsns.**
E flat major K 166 "No. 3"
B flat major K 186 "No. 4"
    Vienna Phil. Wind Group   ♯ West.WN 18011
    (below)

2 DIVERTIMENTI, 2 fls., 5 tpts., 4 drums
C major K 187 & 188 "Nos. 5 & 6"
    Inst. Ensemble—Paillard   V♯ Era.LDE 1022
    ☆ Salzburg Ens.—v. Zallinger   ♯ Strad.STR 622
    (Haydn: Divertimenti)   (♯ Cpt.MC 20104)

DIVERTIMENTI, 2 obs., 2 hrns., 2 bsns.
COLLECTIONS
F major   K 213   "No. 8"
B flat   K 240   "No. 9"
    Vienna Sym. Ens.—Paumgartner ♯ Phi.S 06031R

E flat major K 252 "No. 12"
F major   K 253 "No. 13"
B flat major K 270 "No. 14"
E flat major K 289 "No. 16"
    Vienna Sym. Ens.—Paumgartner
                  ♯ Phi.A 00211L
                  (♯ Epic.LC 3081)

F major   K 213   "No. 8"
E flat major K 252   "No. 12"
F major   K 253   "No. 13"
B flat major K 270   "No. 14"
    ☆ Vienna Sextet   ♯ Nix.WLP 5103

B flat major K 240   "No. 9"
E flat major K 289   "No. 16"
    Vienna Phil. Wind Group   ♯ West.WN 18011
    (above)

E flat major K 252   "No. 12"
F major   K 253   "No. 13"
    Danish Radio Ens.   ♭ C.SELK 1002
    [K 252 only, C.DX 1872: LDX 16]

F major   K 213   "No. 8"
B flat major K 270   "No. 14"
— ARR. FL., OB., CL., HRN. & BSN.
    Paris Wind Ens.   ♯ Sel.LLA 1057
    (above)

B flat major K 240   "No. 9"
E flat major K 289   "No. 16"
— ARR. FL., OB., CL., HRN. & BSN. Viacava
    Paris Wind Ens.   ♯ Sel.LLA 1078
    (above)   (♯ T.TW 30039)

DIVERTIMENTI, 2 obs., 2 cls., 2 hrns., 2 bsns.
E flat major K 196e (K.Anh. 226)
B flat major K 196f (K.Anh. 227)
    Vienna Phil. Ens.   ♯ West.WL 5349

DIVERTIMENTI, Str. & 2 hrns.
D major K 205 (with bsn.) "No. 7"
    Musart Ens.   ♯ Aphe.AP 22
    (Adagio & Rondo K 617 & Str. Qtt. No. 4)
    Salzburg Mozarteum—Paumgartner ♯ CFD. 37
    (March; & Symphonies)

F major K 247 "No. 10"
    Vienna Octet Members   ♯ D.LX 3105
                 (♯ Lon.LS 682)
    ☆ Stuttgart Ton-Studio—Lund (♯ Cpt.MC 20032)

D major K 251 (with oboe) "No. 11"
    A. Jensen & Salzburg Mozarteum Cha.
      —Paumgartner (2ss)   ♯ Pol. 16086
    Anon. & Saar Cha.—Ristenpart   ♯ DFr. 134
    (Concerto, flute & harp)
    Anon. & Cha. Orch.—Redel ♯ Sel. 320.C.092
    (Adagio & Fugue, & Serenade 13)
    ☆ M. Tabuteau & Perpignan Fest.—Casals ♯ C.CX 1090
    (Oboe Quartet)   (FCX 227)

B flat major K 287 "No. 15"
    Vienna Octet Members   ♯ D.LXT 5112
    (2ss)   (♯ Lon.LL 1239)
    Vienna State Op. Ens.—Prohaska
                  ♯ Van.VRS 444
    ☆ Cha. Orch.—Hewitt (Serenade 13)   ♯ HS.HSL 93
    ☆ N.B.C. Sym.—Toscanini (♯ G.QBLP 1027)

D major K 334 "No. 17"
    Vienna Konzerthaus Qtt., J. Hermann (cbs.),
      H. & O. Berger (hrns.)   ♯ West.WL 5276
    J. Tomasow (vln.) & Vienna State Op. Orch.
      —Prohaska   ♯ Van.VRS 441
    ☆ Vienna State Op.—Fekete (♯ CA.LPA 1026;
                      ♯ Cum.CF 261)

... 3rd movt., Minuetto, only
    Israel Radio—Goehr   Arzi. 770
    (Cavalleria Rusticana, Intermezzo) (in ♯ Bne. 501)
    Angelicum—Janes   Ang.SA 3034
    (Tchaikovsky: Serenade—Waltz) (in ♯ LPA 958)
    Mantovani Orch.   ♯ D.LK 4072
    (Rachmaninoff, Rubinstein, etc.)
    (♯ Lon.LL 877; & D.F 43842: ♭ 17842: ♯ LF 1161)

—— ARR. VLN. & PF.
    E. Morini & L. Pommers (in ♯ West.WN 18087)
    ☆ Y. Menuhin & G. Moore (♭ G.7R 104: 7RW 121)
    J. Dumont & A. Collard (♭ Pat.D 106)
    J. Heifetz (in ♯ G.FALP 248)

MARCHES
COLLECTION
D major K 189 (for Andretter Serenade, K 185)
D major K 215 (for Serenade, K 204)
D major K 237 (for Serenade, K 203)
D major K 249 (for Haffner Serenade, K 250)
    ☆ Salzburg Mozarteum Orch.—P. Walter (♯ Clc. 6132)

♯ = Long-playing, 33⅓ r.p.m.   ♭ = 45 r.p.m.   ♮ = Auto. couplings, 78 r.p.m.

F major   K 248 (for Divertimento K 247)
☆ Stuttgart Ton-Studio—Lund (in ‡ Cpt.MC 20032)

D major   K 249 (for 'Haffner' Serenade)
Berlin Cha.—v. Benda   **‡ T.LE 6552**
(Serenade No. 7)
☆ Royal Phil.—Beecham   **C.LX 1587**
(Deutscher Tanz K 605, No. 3)
      (GQX 11537: ♭ SCB 106: SCBQ 3011)
☆ Berlin Phil.—Lehmann (in ‡ Phi.S 04008L)

D major   K 290   (new K 173b)[1] str. & 2 horns
Salzburg Mozartcum—Paumgartner   **‡ CFD. 37**
(Divertimento K 205, & Symphonies)

D major; C major   K 408, Nos. 1 & 2
Berlin Radio Cha.—K. Lange   *Eta. 120031*

D major   K 335 No. 2 (new K 320a No. 2)[2]
Salzburg Fest.—Paumgartner   **‡ Sel.LA 1069**
(Serenade K 185)

———————

(Ein) Musikalischer Spass   K 522   str. & 2 hrns.
Vienna Konzerthaus Qtt.   **‡ Nix.WLP 5315**
(Serenade No. 13)   (‡ West.WL 5315)
[H. Berger, J. Koller (hrns)]
Berlin Radio Ens.—M. Lange   **‡ Ura. 7109**
(Méhul: Symphony)   (‡ MTW. 540)

SERENADES   Orch.

No. 1, D major   K 100
☆ Zimbler Sinfonietta   **‡ B.AXTL 1001**
(Cassation No. 1)   (‡ D.UAT 273088)

No. 3, D major   K 185   "Andretter"
Salzburg Fest.—Paumgartner   **‡ Sel.LA 1069**
(March, K 335)
☆ G. Alès (vln.) & Cha. Orch.—Oubradous
(Quintet, K 452)   **‡ Esq.TW 14-002**

No. 4, D major   K 203
New Sym.—P. Maag   **‡ D.LXT 5074**
      (‡ D.NLK 40107; Lon.LL 1206)
... *Allegro* only
☆ Naples Scarlatti Orch.—Paumgartner
      (in ‡ Csm.CRLP 155)

No. 6, D major   K 239   (Serenata Notturna)
Philharmonia—Pritchard   **‡ G.CLP 1061**
(Haydn: Sym. 80; & Notturno)
Vienna Sym.—Moralt   **‡ EPhi.ABR 4018**
(No. 13)   (‡ Phi.A 00696R)
(No. 13, & Clar. Concerto, in ‡ Epic.LC 3069)
London Baroque Orch.—Haas   **‡ P.PMB 1005**
(Fux)   (in ‡ AmD.DL 9776, d.c.)
☆ Zimbler Sinfonietta   **‡ B.AXTL 1009**
(Telemann: Suite)   (‡ D.UAT 273083)

No. 7, D major   K 250   "Haffner"
Berlin Cha.—v. Benda   **‡ T.LE 6552**
(March, K 249)
Cologne Gürzenich—Wand   **‡ CFD. 43**
[G. Gugel (vln.)]
☆ Vienna Sym.—Krauss   **‡ EVox.PL 6850**
... 4th movt., *Rondeau*, only   vln. & orch.
—— ARR. VLN. & PF.   Kreisler
I. Oistrakh & A. Makarov   **‡ CdM.LDA 8092**
(Bach & Vitali)   (& in ‡ Van.VRS 461 & Csm.CRLP 194)
I. Stern & A. Zakin   in ‡ **AmC.AL 23**
(& in ♭ AmC. set A1087)   (‡ Phi.S 06617R)
G. Jarry & A. Collard   in ‡ **C.FCX 222**
I. Bezrodny & pf. (USSR. 017426/7)
☆ J. Thibaud & T. Janopoulo (in ‡ G.FJLP 5015)

No. 9, D major   K 320   "Posthorn"
Barylli Qtt. & Vienna Wind Ens.
       ‡ West.WN 18033

No. 10, B flat major   K 361   13 instruments[3]
Suisse Romande Ens.—Ansermet **‡ D.LXT 5121**
Vienna Phil. Wind Ens.   **‡ Nix.WLP 5229**
      (‡ West.WL 5229)

R.I.A.S. Wind Ens.   **‡ DT.LGX 66006**
      (‡ T.LE 6504; FT. 320.TC.063)
[5th movt., Romanze, only, on TV.VSK 9203;
               ‡ T.TW 30001]
☆ Los Angeles Ens.—Steinberg (‡ ACap.CLCX 037)
... 1st, 3rd, 4th, 6th & 7th movts. only
☆ Cha. Orch.—E. Fischer (♮ JpV. set JAS 314)

No. 11, E flat major   K 375
2 oboes, 2 cls., 2 horns, 2 bsns.
Vienna Sym. Ens.—Paumgartner
(No. 12)   **‡ Phi.A 00291L**
Munich Phil. Ensemble   **‡ Ura.RS 7-32**
(Cassation No. 1)
Ensemble—Winograd   **‡ MGM.E 3159**
(No. 12)
☆ Vienna Phil. Wind Ensemble   **‡ Nix.WLP 5021**
(No. 12)   (‡ Sel.LPG 8345; West.WN 18134, n.n.)
☆ Prague Wind Ensemble   **‡ Sup.LPV 66**
(Bassoon Concerto)
☆ London Baroque Ens.—Haas (‡ Od.OD 1010)
Vienna Sym. Wind Ens. (‡ EVox.PL 7490)
R. Kell Cha. Players (‡ D.UAT 273093)

No. 12, C minor   K 388   2 obs., 2 cls., 2 hrns., 2 bsns.
London Baroque Ens.—Haas   **‡ P.PMA 1013**
(Haydn: Notturno, etc.)
Vienna Sym. Ens.—Paumgartner
(above)   **‡ Phi.A 00291L**
Ens.—Winograd *(above)*   **‡ MGM.E 3159**
☆ Vienna Phil. Wind Ensemble   **‡ Nix.WLP 5021**
(above)   (‡ Sel.LPG 8345; West.WN 18134, n.n.)
☆ Vienna Sym. Wind. Ens. (‡ EVox.PL 7490)
R. Kell Chamber Players (‡ D.UAT 273093)

No. 13, G major   K 525   str. orch.
(Eine kleine Nachtmusik)
Philharmonia—Karajan   **‡ C.CX 1178**
(Sinf. Concertante, K 297b)   (‡ FCX 308: QCX 10101: Angel. 35098)
Columbia Sym.—Walter   **‡ AmC.ML 5004**
(Dances, Overtures, etc.)   (‡ Phi.A 01237L)
Vienna Sym.—Moralt   **‡ EPhi.ABR 4018**
(No. 6)   (‡ Epic.LC 3069; Phi.A 00696R: ♭ A 400005E)
N.W. German Phil.—Schüchter **‡ Imp.ILP 105**
(Smetana)   (‡ G.QDLP 6029)
[Romanze only, ♭ Od.OBL 29007]
Bamberg Sym.—Keilberth   **‡ DT.TM 68010**
(2ss)   *(Sym. No. 30 on ‡ DT.LGX 66025)*
(Serenade 10, excerpts, on **‡ T.TW 30001:** ♭ **UV 106:**
              TV.VE 9028)
Bavarian Radio—E. Jochum   **‡ HP.DG 17020**
(R. Strauss)   (& 2ss, PV. 72440; ♭ Pol. 30053)
London Mozart Ens.—Vicars
         V‡ CA.MPO 5027
Saar Cha.—Ristenpart   **V‡ Era.LDE 1018**
Champs-Élysées Th.—Goldschmidt
         ‡ Sel. 320.C.006
(Adagio & Fugue, & Fl. & Hp. Concerto)
(Adagio & Fugue, & Divertimento, K 251,
             on ‡ Sel. 320.C.092)
Vienna State Op.—Prohaska   **‡ Van.VRS 435**
(Schubert)
(Sym. No. 40, on ‡ Ama.AVRS 6009; Van.SRV 102)
Paris Inst. Ens.—Froment   **‡ CND. 1003**
(Cimarosa, Vivaldi)
Netherlands Phil.—Goehr   **V‡ MMS 94**
Paris Sinfonia Ens.—Witold   ♭ **Cpt.EXTP 1007**
Pasdeloup Cha.—Lindenburg   ♭ **Od.7AOE 1013**
☆ Perpignan Fest.—Casals *(Sym. 29)*   **‡ C.CX 1088**
             (‡ FCX 223)
☆ Chamber Orch.—Hewitt   **‡ HS.HSL 93**
(Divertimento "No. 15")   (& 2ss, **V‡** DFr.EX 17001)
(Minuets, K 585, on HS.HSL 101)
☆ L.S.O.—Weingartner   **‡ AmC.ML 4776**
(Sym. 39, & Haydn)
Hamburg Philharmonia—H-J. Walter *(MSB. 78206*
                      & 78004)
Internat. Str.—Schneiderhahn (‡ Mae.OA 20002)
Berlin State—Lange (‡ Eta. 720005)
Berlin Radio Cha.—Stross (‡ MF. 2506)
Rochester Sym.—Leinsdorf, omitting *Romanze*
          (AmC.J 218: ♭ J4-218)
(continued on next page)

---

[1] For Divertimento, K 205 (new K 173a).
[2] For Serenade, K 320.
[3] See also String Quintet, K 46, *supra*.

SERENADE No. 13, G major (*continued*)
☆ Vienna Phil.—B. Walter (‡ Cam.CAL 253 &
in set CFL 105)
Boston Sym.—Koussevitzky (‡ DV.CL 16207)
Berlin Phil.—Lehmann (♮ Od.O-50013/4)
Homburg Sym.—Schubert (‡ *Esq. 15-004;*
‡ *Mtr.BLP 20:* ♭ *MCEP 5008;* ‡ *AFest.CFR 10-610*)
Vienna Phil.—Furtwängler
(‡ *G.FALP/QALP 117;* ♮ *ArgV. 11-7965/6*)
Sydney Civic—Beck (Dia.PM 101/2, 4ss)
Vienna Phil.—Böhm (♭ *AmVox.VIP 45250*)
Salzburg Fest.—Weidlich (‡ Ply. 12-87; Cum.TCR 273;
& with commentary by S. Spaeth, ‡ Rem. 11)

CHAMBER RECORDINGS
Vienna Konzerthaus Qtt. & J. Hermann (cbs)
‡ **Nix.WLP 5315**
(*Musikalischer Spass*) (‡ West.WL 5315)
Parrenin Qtt. ‡ **Pac.LDPC 77**
(*Haydn: Str. Qtt. Op. 3-5*)

II. D. ORCHESTRAL MUSIC

1. CONCERTOS

BASSOON & ORCH.
B flat major K 191
H. Helaerts & L.S.O.—Collins[1] ‡ **D.LXT 2990**
(*Concerto, cl. & orch., K 622*) (‡ Lon.LL 1135)
K. Öhlberger & Vienna State Op.—Rodzinski
‡ **Nix.WLP 5307**
(*Clarinet Concerto*) (‡ West.WL 5307)
L. Cermak & Vienna Pro Musica—Emmer
(*Clarinet Concerto*) ‡ **E. & AmVox.PL 8870**
M. Allard & Salzburg Mozarteum
—Paumgartner ‡ *CFD. 52*
(*Horn Concerto No. 2*)
☆ K. Bidlo & Czech Phil.—Ančerl ‡ **Sup.LPV 66**
(*Serenade No. 11*)
☆ L. Sharrow & N.B.C.—Toscanini (‡ DV.L 16063)

B flat major K.Anh. 230a (Spurious)
F. Hollard & Winterthur Sym.—Ackermann
‡ **CHS.H 3**
(*Horn Concerto No. 4 & Org. Sonata*)

CLARINET & ORCH.
A major K 622
G. de Peyer & L.S.O.—Collins ‡ **D.LXT 2990**
(*Concerto, bsn. & orch., K 191*) (‡ Lon.LL 1135)
L. Wlach & Vienna State Op.—Rodzinski
‡ **Nix.WLP 5307**
(*Bassoon Concerto*) (‡ West.WL 5307)
R. Schönhofer & Vienna Sym.—Paumgartner
‡ *EPhi.ABR 4033*
(‡ *Phi.A 00698R;* ‡ Epic.LC 3069)
J. Lancelot & O. L. Ens.—Froment
‡ **LOL.OL 50006**
(*Sinf. concertante*) (‡ OL.LD 75)
R. Jettel & Vienna Pro Musica—Emmer
(*Bassoon Concerto*) ‡ **E. & AmVox.PL 8870**
E. Koch & Berlin Radio Cha.—Haarth
(*R. Strauss*) ‡ **Ura. 7108**
J. D'Hondt & Sym. Orch.—Goehr ‡ **MMS. 2003**
(*Vln. Concerto, K 219*)
A. Heine & Salzburg Mozarteum—Paumgartner
‡ *CFD. 7*
(*Oboe Concerto & Masonic Funeral Music*)
☆ R. Kell & Zimbler Sinfonietta ‡ **B.AXTL 1071**
(*Brahms*) (‡ AmD.DL 9732; & 2ss, ‡ *Pol. 16090*)
☆ F. Etienne & Hewitt Cha. Orch. ‡ **DFr. 2**
(*Clarinet Quintet K 581*) (‡ HS.HSL 96)
[apparently again reissued, d.c.]
(& 2ss, ‡ *DFr.EX 25018*)

FLUTE & ORCH.
No. 1, G major K 313
[2]W. Glass & South German Cha.—Reinhardt
‡ **DT.LGX 66019**
(*Fl. & hp. Concerto*) (‡ T.LSK 7032)
(2ss, ‡ *T.LB 6047*)

---

[2] F. Marseau & Lamoureux—Goldschmidt
‡ **Fel.RL 89001**
(*Pf. Concerto, K 467*) (‡ Clc. 6179)
(*Fl. Concerto No. 2, on* ‡ *Per.SPL 564*)
C. Wanausek & Vienna Pro Musica
—Swarowsky ‡ **E. & AmVox.PL 8130**
(*No. 2*)
H. Barwahser & Vienna Sym.—Pritchard
‡ *EPhi.ABL 3059*
(*No. 2*) (‡ Phi.A 00166L; ‡ Epic.LC 3033)
J-P. Rampal & Saar Cha.—Ristenpart
(*No. 2, & Andante*) ‡ *DFr. 130*
G. Tassinari & Salzburg Mozarteum
—Paumgartner ‡ *Pol. 16127*

No. 2, D major K 314
C. Wanausek & Vienna Pro Musica Cha.
—Swarowsky ‡ **E. & AmVox.PL 8130**
(*No. 1*)
H. Barwahser & Vienna Sym.—Pritchard
‡ *EPhi.ABL 3059*
(*No. 1*) (‡ Phi.A 00166L; ‡ Epic.LC 3033)
J-P. Rampal & Saar Cha.—Ristenpart
(*No. 1, & Andante*) ‡ *DFr. 130*
☆ J-P. Rampal & Lamoureux—Goldschmidt
(*No. 1*) ‡ **Per.SPL 564**
☆ A. Nicolet & Winterthur Sym.—Swoboda (‡ *MMS. 87*)

Andante, C major K 315
C. Wanausek & Vienna Pro Musica Cha. Orch.
‡ **E. & AmVox.PL 8550**
(*below, & Adagio & Rondo, K 617*)
H. Barwahser & Vienna Sym.—Paumgartner
‡ **Phi.N 00213L**
(*Quantz & Gluck*) (‡ Epic.LC 3134)
J-P. Rampal & Saar Cha.—Ristenpart
(‡s—*above*) ‡ *DFr. 130*
F-J. Brun & Cha.—Oubradous ‡ **Pat.DTX 193**
(*Flute & Harp Concerto*)

FLUTE, HARP & ORCH.
C major K 299
J-P. Rampal, D. Wagner & Orch.—Ristenpart
(*Divertimento, K 251*) ‡ *DFr. 134*
W. Glass, R. Stein & South German Cha.
—Reinhardt ‡ **DT.LGX 66019**
(*Fl. Concerto No. 1, K 313*) (‡ T.LSK 7032)
(2ss, on ‡ *T.LB 6050*)
C. Wanausek, H. Jellinek & Vienna Pro Musica
Cha. Orch. ‡ **E. & AmVox.PL 8550**
(*above, & Adagio & Rondo, K 617*)
(Excerpt in ‡ *AmVox.UHF 1*)
R. Bourdin, L. Laskine & Champs-Elysées
Theatre—Scherchen ‡ **Sel. 320.C.006**
(*Serenade No. 13 & Adagio & Fugue*)
F-J. Brun & L. Laskine & Cha.—Oubradous
(*above*) ‡ **Pat.DTX 193**
P. Jamet, M. Larde & Cha. Orch.—Kuentz
(*Bach & Vivaldi*) ‡ *CND. 2*
Anon. Soloists & Orch.—Haefner ‡ **MTW. 508**
(*Haydn*)
☆ K. F. Mess, D. Wagner, Stuttgart—Lund
(‡ Eli.PLPE 5002; Clc. 6133)

HORN & ORCH.
Nos. 1-4, COMPLETE
No. 1, D major K 412 No. 2, E flat major K 417
No. 3, E flat major K 447 No. 4, E flat major K 495
D. Brain & Philharmonia—Karajan
‡ **C.CX 1140**
(‡ FCX 251: QCX 10100; Angel. 35092)
[No. 4 only, on ♭ *G.7ERL 1057*]

No. 1, D major K 412
☆ G. Görmer & Stuttgart Ton-Studio—Lund
(‡ Eli.PLPE 5002; Clc. 6133; ♭ *Mtr.MCEP 3035*)

---

[1] Cadenzas by Ibert.   [2] No cadenzas.

No. 2, E flat major   K 417
P. Delvescovo & Orch.—Oubradous
(*Grétry*)   **‡ *Pat.DT 1022***
L. Bernard & Salzburg Mozarteum
  —Paumgartner   **‡ *CFD. 52***
(*Bassoon Concerto*)

No. 3, E flat major   K 447
☆ M. Jones & National Gallery—Bales
          (in ‡ McInt.MC 1016)
— ARR. VLC. & ORCH.   A. S. Fischer
J. Starker & Castle Hill Fest.—Pilzer
         ‡ Per.SPL 579
(*Boccherini*)   (‡ ANix.PLP 579; ‡ Cpt.MC 20057)

No. 4, E flat major   K 495
D. Ceccarossi & Rome Radio—Argento
(4ss)   **Cet.CB 20540/1**
J. Zwagerman & Winterthur Sym.—Ackermann
        ‡ CHS.H 3
(*Bsn. Concerto, B flat major, & Org. Sonata*)
(*Fl. Concerto K 314, on* ‡ *MMS. 87*)

OBOE & ORCH.
C major   K 314a
M. Miller & Little Sym.—Saidenberg
        ‡ AmC.ML 4916
(*J. S. Bach & J. C. Bach*)
M. Briançon & Salzburg Mozarteum
  —Paumgartner   **‡ CFD. 7**
(*Cl. Concerto & Masonic Funeral Music*)
☆ M. Sailliet & Salzburg Mozarteum—Paumgartner
      (‡ Cpt.MC 20027; Eli.PLPE 5005)

PF. & ORCH.
D major   K 175
☆ A. Balsam & Sym.—Gimpel[3]
      (‡ Cpt.MC 20027; Eli.PLPE 5005)

B flat major   K 238
[4] H. Henkemans & Vienna Sym.—Paumgartner
(*K 459, below*)   **‡ Phi.A 00305L**
I. Haebler & Vienna Pro Musica—Hollreiser
(*K 246, below*)   **‡ E. & AmVox.PL 9290**
T. de Maria & Naples Scarlatti Orch.
        ‡ Csm.CLPS 1052
(*Sinfonia Concertante, K 364*)

C major   K 246
I. Haebler & Vienna Pro Musica—Hollreiser
(*K 238, above*)   **‡ E. & AmVox.PL 9290**

E flat major   K 271
G. Novães & Vienna Pro Musica—Swarowsky
(*K 466, below*)   **‡ E. & AmVox.PL 8430**
[5] W. Kempff & Stuttgart Cha. & Suisse Romande
  Members—Münchinger   **‡ D.LXT 2861**
(*K 450, below*)   (‡ Lon.LL 998)
C. Haskil & Vienna Sym.—Sacher
        ‡ Phi.A 00259L
(*Rondo, K 386*)   (‡ Epic.LC 3162)
☆ [5]M. Hess & Perpignan Fest.—Casals ‡ C.CX 1091
  (2ss)   (‡ FCX 225)
☆ G. Casadesus & Lamoureux—Paray ‡ AmVox.PL 8230
  (*K 503, below*)

F major   K 413
V. Rivkin & Vienna State Op.—Dixon
(*K 482, below*)   **‡ Nix.WLP 5244**
  (‡ West.WL 5244; BrzV.SPL 5515, Sel. 320.CW.083)

A major   K 414
C. de Groot & Vienna Sym.—v. Otterloo
        ‡ Phi.A 00290L
(*K 415, below*)   (‡ Epic.LC 3214)
[5] D. Matthews & Philharmonia—Schwarz
(*K 449, below*)   **‡ C.SX 1031**

---

[5] M. Lympany & Philharmonia—Menges
        ‡ G.CLP 1038
(*K 467, below*)   (‡ QCLP 12014)
[5] I. Haebler & Vienna Pro Musica—Hollreiser
(*K 595, below*)   **‡ E. & AmVox.PL 8710**
L. Kraus & Boston Sym.—Monteux
        ‡ Vic.LM 1783
(*K 456, below*)   (‡ FV.A 630225; ‡ ItV.A12R 0100)
H. Scholz (fortepiano)[6] & Salzburg Mozarteum
  Cha.—Paumgartner (2ss) **‡ *HP.AP 13021***
     (*Pf. Sonata No. 11, on* AmD.ARC 3012)
☆ [5] F. Jensen & Danish Radio—Wöldike (‡ Era.LDE 3008)

C major   K 415 (new K 387b)
C. de Groot & Vienna Sym.—v. Otterloo
        ‡ Phi.A 00290L
(*K 414, above*)   (‡ Epic.LC 3214)
J. Katchen & New Sym.—Maag ‡ D.LXT 5145
(*K 466, below*)

E flat major   K 449
[5] F. Gulda & L.S.O.—Collins   ‡ D.LXT 5013
(*R. Strauss: Burleske*)   (‡ Lon.LL 1158)
G. Scherzer & London Baroque—K. Haas
        ‡ P.PMA 1012
(*Haydn*) (*Notturni, & Serenade K 239 on* ‡ AmD.DL 9776)
[5] D. Matthews & Philharmonia—Schwarz
(*K 414, above*)   **‡ C.SX 1031**
C. Horsley & Philharmonia—Cameron
(*Chopin & Liszt*)   **‡ G.CLP 1012**
H. Henkemans & Vienna Sym.—Paumgartner
(*K 238, above*)   **‡ Phi.A 00305L**
☆ P. Badura-Skoda & Vienna Sym.—Sternberg
  (‡ Nix.OLP 7022, announced but not issued)

B flat major   K 450
[5] W. Kempff & Stuttgart Cha. & Suisse
  Romande Members—Münchinger
        ‡ D.LXT 2861
(*K 271, above*)   (‡ Lon.LL 998)
I. Haebler & Vienna Pro Musica—Swarowsky
(*K 456, below*)   **‡ E. & AmVox.PL 8300**
[5] C. Solomon & Philharmonia—Ackermann[7]
(*Sonata 11*)   **‡ G.ALP 1194**
(*Beethoven, on* ‡ Vic.LHMV 12)

D major   K 451
☆ J. Hajen & Nat. Gallery Orch.—Bales
        (in ‡ McInt.MC 1016)

G major   K 453
I. Haebler & Bamberg Sym.—Hollreiser
(*K 537, below*)   **‡ AmVox.PL 9390**
A. Foldes & Berlin Phil.—Lehmann
(2ss)   **‡ *Pol. 16093***
H. Henkemans & Vienna Sym.—Pritchard
        ‡ Phi.A 00239L
(*K 595, below*)   (‡ Epic.LC 3117)
Anon. Soloist & Berlin Sym.—Guthan
(*Symphonies 26 & 30*)   **‡ Roy. 1406**
☆ E. Fischer & Cha. Orch.   ‡ Vic. set LCT 6013
  (*Concertos K 466, 482, 491*)
☆ L. Hambro & Oklahoma Sym.—Alessandro
  (‡ Roy. 1602; *MusH.LP 9016*; excpt., ‡ Roy. 1907)
  G. Casadesus & Vienna Pro Musica—Bigot (‡ MHF. 7)

B flat major   K 456
I. Haebler & Vienna Pro Musica—Swarowsky
(*K 450, above*)   **‡ E. & AmVox.PL 8300**
H. Henkemans & Vienna Sym.—Pritchard
        ‡ Phi.A 00184L
(*K 459, below*)   (‡ Epic.LC 3047)
L. Kraus & Boston Sym.—Monteux
        ‡ Vic.LM 1783
(*K 414, above*)   (‡ FV.A 630225; ‡ ItV.A12R 0100)

---

[3] Cadenzas: 3rd movt. by Balsam, others Mozart.
[5] Cadenza(s) by Mozart.
[7] Stated to be cond. Cluytens on Victor issue.

[4] Cadenzas by Henkemans.
[6] From Mozart Museum, Salzburg.

F major K 459
H. Henkemans & Vienna Sym.—Pritchard
‡ Phi.A 00184L
(*K 456, above*)
Anon. & Berlin Sym.—Guthan   ‡ Roy. 1437
(*Sym. B flat major, & Deutsche Tänze*)
☆ L. Kraus & Vienna Sym.—Moralt   ‡ EVox.PL 6890
(*K 488, below*)
☆ C. Haskil & Winterthur Sym.—Swoboda
(*K 466, below*)   ‡ Nix.WLP 5054
Anon. Artists (‡ Gram. 2036)
☆ L. Hambro & Oklahoma Sym.—Alessandro
(‡ Roy. 1602; *MusH.LP 9017*)

D minor K 466
E. Fischer & Philharmonia   ‡ G.BLP 1066
[cadenzas by Fischer]   (*FBLP 1073*)
8 W. Gieseking & Philharmonia—Rosbaud
‡ C.CX 1235
(*Concerto K 503, below*)   (‡ Angel. 35215)
8J. Katchen & New Sym.—Maag ‡ D.LXT 5145
(*K 415, above*)
M. de la Bruchollerie & Vienna Pro Musica
—Hollreiser   ‡ Pan.XPV 1005
H. Roloff & R.I.A.S. Sym.—Lehmann
(2ss)   ‡ Pol. 16109
G. Novães & Vienna Pro Musica—Swarowsky
(*K 271, above*)   ‡ E. & AmVox.PL 8430
M. Meyer & Hewitt Orch.   ‡ DFr. 37
(*K 488, below*)   (‡ HS.HSL 88)
C. Haskil & Vienna Sym.—Paumgartner
‡ Phi.N 00752R
(2ss)   (*K 488, on* ‡ Epic.LC 3163)
☆ C. Haskil & Winterthur—Swoboda (‡ Nix.WLP 5054)
R. Serkin & Philadelphia—Ormandy8
(‡ EPhi.ABR 4006; ‡ Phi.A 01600R)
E. Fischer & L.P.O.—Sargent9 (‡ in Vic. set LCT 6013)
F. Pelleg & Sym.—Goehr (‡ ANix.MLPY 9)
F. Weidlich & Salzburg Fest. (‡ Cum.CR 235)
J. Iturbi & Vic. Sym. (‡ DV.L 16381)
— FOR PRACTICE: With piano part missing (‡ CEd.MMO 308)
... Excerpt only Anon. & Berlin Sym. (in ‡ Roy. 1375)

C major K 467
10 M. Lympany & Philharmonia—Menges
‡ G.CLP 1038
(*K 414, above*)   (‡ QCLP 12014)
(*Grieg: Pf. Concerto, on* ‡ Vic.LHMV 1067)
11 J. Demus & Vienna State Op.—Horvath
‡ Nix.WLP 5183
(*K 537, below*)   (‡ West.WL 5183)
M. Roesgen-Champion & Lamoureux
—Goldschmidt12   ‡ Fel.RL 89001
(*Fl. Concerto No. 1*)   (‡ Clc. 6179)
(*K 503, below, on* ‡ Per.SPLP 571)
S. Fiorentino & London Mozart Ens.—Vicars
(*Sonatas, pf. 11 & 12*)   ‡ CA.LPA 1078
☆ R. Casadesus & N.Y.P.S.O.—Münch   ‡ C.C 1024
(2ss)   (‡ WC 1024: QC 5016)
(*K 595, on* ‡ AmC.ML 4791)
☆ 13 F. Jensen & Danish Radio—Wöldike
(‡ Era.LDE 3008)

E flat major K 482
V. Rivkin & Vienna State Op.—Dixon
(*K 413, above*)   ‡ Nix.WLP 5244
(‡ West.WL 5244; BrzV.SPL 5515; Sel. 320.CW.083)
H. Boschi & Czech Phil.—Klima ‡ Sup.LPV 205
(*Haydn*)   (‡ U. 5189H)
☆ L. Kraus & Vienna Sym.—Moralt ‡ EVox.PL 7290
(*Rondo K 382*)
☆ R. Serkin & Perpignan Fest.—Casals ‡ C.CX 1092
(‡ FCX 226)
☆ E. Fischer & Cha.—Barbirolli   ‡ Vic. set LCT 6013
(*Concertos, K 453, 466, 491*)
☆ P. Badura-Skoda & Vienna Sym.—Sternberg
(‡ Nix.CLP 7022, announced but not issued)

A major K 488
5 C. Curzon & L.S.O.—Krips   ‡ D.LXT 2867
(*K 491, below*)   (‡ Lon.LL 918)
C. Solomon & Philharmonia—Menges
(*K 491, below*)   ‡ G.ALP 1316
5 G. Thyssens-Valentin & Salzburg Cha.
—Paumgartner   ‡ LT.DTL 93057
(*Sym. No. 29*)   (‡ Sel.LAG 1068; ‡ T.LE 6531)
5 D. Matthews & Philharmonia—Schwarz
‡ C.S 1039
(2ss)   (*QC 5021*)
C. Haskil & Vienna Sym.—Sacher
‡ Phi.A 00753R
(2ss)   (*K 466, above, on* ‡ Epic.LC 3163)
M. Haas & Berlin Phil.—Leitner ‡ Pol. 16056
(4ss, ♮ PV. 72349/50)
M. Meyer & Hewitt Orch.   ‡ DFr. 37
(*K 466, above*)   (‡ HS.HSL 88)
M. de la Bruchollerie & Vienna Pro Musica
—Hollreiser   (2ss)   ‡ Pan.XPV 1016
☆ L. Kraus & Vienna Sym.—Moralt ‡ EVox.PL 6890
(*K 459, above*)
☆ W. Gieseking & Philharmonia—Karajan ‡ C.C 1012
(2ss)   (‡ QC 5009)

C minor K 491
14 C. Curzon & L.S.O.—Krips   ‡ D.LXT 2867
(*K 488 above*)   (‡ Lon.LL 918)
C. Solomon & Philharmonia—Menges
‡ G.ALP 1316
(*K 488, above*) [Cadenza by St. Saëns]
G. Johannesen & Orch.—Ackermann
(2ss)   ‡ MMS. 46
R. Casadesus & Col.Sym.—Szell ‡EPhi.ABL3060
(*K 537, below*)   (‡ AmC.ML 4901; Phi.A 01142L)
☆ E. Fischer & L.P.O.—Collingwood
(*above*)   in ‡ Vic. set LCT 6013
☆ L. Kraus & Vienna Sym.—Moralt   ‡ EVox.PL 6880
(*Sonata, 15*)   (‡ AFest.CFR 12-310)
☆ P. Badura-Skoda & Vienna Sym.—Prohaska
(*K 595, below*)   ‡ Nix.WLP 5097
— FOR PRACTICE: With piano part missing (‡ CEd.MMO 309)

C major K 503
W. Gieseking & Philharmonia—Rosbaud
‡ C.CX 1235
(*K 466*) [Cadenzas by Gieseking]   (‡ Angel. 35215)
F. Gulda & New Sym.—Collins ‡ D.LXT 5138
(*K 537, below*) [Cadenzas by F. Gulda]
M. Roesgen-Champion & Lamoureux
—Goldschmidt   ‡ Per.SPL 571
(*K 467, above*)
☆ G. Casadesus & Lamoureux—Bigot ‡ AmVox.PL 8230
(*K 271*) [Cadenzas by R. Casadesus] (‡ MHF. 7, d.c.)
☆ E. Fischer & Orch.—Krips (*Bach*)   ‡ G.FALP 375
☆ 15C. Seemann & Munich—Lehmann ‡ HP.DG 16014

D major K 537 "Coronation"
F. Gulda & New Sym.—Collins ‡ D.LXT 5138
(*K 503, above*) [Cadenzas by F. Gulda]
I. Haebler & Vienna Pro Musica—Hollreiser
(*K 453, above*)   ‡ AmVox.PL 9390
R. Casadesus & Col. Sym.—Szell
‡ EPhi.ABL 3060
(*K 491, above*)   (‡ AmC.ML 4901; ‡ Phi.A 01142L)
J. Demus & Vienna St. Op.—Horvath
‡ Nix.WLP 5183
(*K 467, above*)   (‡ West.WL 5183)
C. Seemann & Berlin Phil.—Lehmann
‡ HP.DGM 18143
(*Rondo, K 382*)   (‡ AmD.DL 9631)
(5ss—*La Clemenza di Tito, Overture, on* ♮ PV. 72426/8)

8 Cadenzas by Beethoven.
10 Cadenzas by Winding and Klengel.
12 Uses flutes in the Adagio. Most other recordings use oboes.
13 Cadenzas by Jensen.
14 Cadenzas by Milkina and Szell.

9 No conductor named in original G.B. issue.
11 Cadenzas by Busoni.
5 Cadenzas by Mozart.
15 Cadenzas by Hummel

D major   K 537 (*continued*)
   F. Pelleg & Zürich Tonhalle—Ackermann
                         ‡ *MMS. 50*

   ☆ G. Bachauer & New London—Sherman ‡ *G.DLP 1006*

B flat major   K 595
  [5] I. Haebler & Vienna Pro Musica—Hollreiser
  (*K 414, above*)   ‡ *E. & AmVox.PL 8710*
  [5] D. Matthews & Philharmonia—Schwarz
  (2ss)   ‡ *C.S 1032*
  [5] W. Backhaus & Vienna Phil.—Böhm
                      ‡ **D.LXT 5123**
  (*Sonata 11*)   (‡ Lon.LL 1282)
  H. Henkemans & Vienna Sym.—Pritchard
                     ‡ **Phi.A 00239L**
  (*K 453, above*)   (‡ Epic.LC 3117)
  ☆ R. Casadesus & N.Y.P.S.O.—Barbirolli ‡ *C.C 1028*
  (2ss)   (*K 467, above*, on ‡ AmC.ML 4791)
  ☆ P. Badura-Skoda & Vienna Sym.—Prohaska
  (*K 491, above*)   ‡ Nix.WLP 5097
  ☆ A. Foldes & Vienna Pro Musica—Goldschmidt
                       (‡ MHF. 6)

Rondo, D major   K 382
  C. Seemann & Bamberg Sym.—Lehmann
                       PV. 36064
  (*Concerto, K 537* on ‡ HP.DGM 18143; AmD.DL 9631)
  (*Rondo, K 386* on ‡ *AmD.DL 4079*)
  ☆ L. Kraus & Vienna Sym.—Moralt   ‡ *EVox.PL 7290*
  (*K 482, above*)

Rondo, A major   K 386 (orch. Einstein)
  C. Haskil & Vienna Sym.—Paumgartner
                     ‡ **Phi.A 00259L**
  (*Concerto, K 271*)   (‡ Epic.LC 3162)
  C. Seemann & Bamberg Sym.—Lehmann
  (2ss)   *PV. 36075*
  (*Rondo, K 382* on ‡ *AmD.DL 4079*)

CONCERTOS AFTER FRENCH AND OTHER
COMPOSERS
F major   K 373, [3, 4]
B flat major   K 393, [3, 2]
  ☆ A. Balsam & Winterthur Sym.—Goehr (‡ Clc. 6152)

D major   K 404, [4, 6, 7]
G major   K 413, [3, 4]
  ☆ A. Balsam & Winterthur Sym.—Ackermann
                       (‡ Clc. 6283)

CONCERTOS AFTER J. C. BACH
    K 107 (new K 21b)
No. 1, D major   No. 2, G major
No. 3, E flat major
  R. Veyron-Lacroix (hpsi.) & Paris Collegium
  Musicum—Douatte[16]   ‡ *EPP.APG 116*
... No. 2 only
  ☆ A. Balsam & Winterthur Sym.—Ackermann
  (*Corelli, Beethoven, Moussorgsky*)   ‡ *MMS. 100*
  (*Schubert, Beethoven, & Bach* on ‡ *MMS. 54 Spec.*)

CONCERTO, 2 pfs., & orch., E flat major   K 365
  C. Seemann, A. Foldes, & Berlin Phil.—Lehmann
                     ‡ **Pol. 16125**

  E. Gilels, J. Zak & U.S.S.R. State—Kondrashin
  (*Beethoven*)   ‡ **Per.SPL 601**

  ☆ R. Gianoli, P. Badura-Skoda & Vienna State Op.
    —Scherchen   ‡ Nix.WLP 5097
  (*below*)   (‡ Sel.LPG 8674)
  ☆ A. & K. U. Schnabel & L.S.O.—Boult (‡ Vic.LCT 1140)
  J. & A. Iturbi & Vic. Sym. (‡ DV.L 16381)

CONCERTO, 3 pfs. & orch., F major   K 242
  Anon. Soloists & Orch.   ‡ *Allo. 4057*

— ARR. 2 PFS. & ORCH.   Mozart
  ☆ R. Gianoli, P. Badura-Skoda & Vienna State Op.
    —Scherchen   ‡ Nix.WLP 5095
  (*above*)   (‡ Sel.LPG 8674)

——— *END OF PF. CONCERTOS* ———

CONCERTOS, Vln. & orch.
No. 1, B flat major   K 207
  T. Varga & Philharmonia—Susskind
                     ‡ **C.SX 1017**
  (*Bruch*) [cadenzas by Varga]
  W. Boskowsky & Vienna Konzerthaus Cha.
                     ‡ **HS.HSL 9010**
  (*Concerto No. 4*)   (‡ DFr. 85)
  ☆ A. Stücki & Stuttgart—Lund (‡ Clc. 6131)

No. 2, D major   K 211
  A. Grumiaux & Vienna Sym.—Paumgartner
                     ‡ **EPhi.ABL 3099**
  (*No. 5*)   (‡ Phi.A 00258L; Epic.LC 3157)
  ☆ A. Stücki & Stuttgart—Lund (‡ Clc. 6131)

No. 3, G major   K 216
  A. Grumiaux & Vienna Sym.—Paumgartner
                     ‡ **EPhi.ABL 3040**
  (*No. 4*)   (‡ Phi.A 00199L; ‡ Epic.LC 3060)
  C. Ferras & Stuttgart Cha.—Münchinger
                     ‡ **D.LXT 5044**
  (*No. 7*) [cadenza of composite authorship] (‡ Lon.LL 1172)
  J. Martzy & Philharmonia—Kletzki
  (*Mendelssohn*)   ‡ **C.CX 1210**
  Gérard Poulet & Austrian Sym.—Gaston Poulet
                     ‡ **Rem. 199-131**
  (*Handel*)   (‡ Cum.CR 292, d.c.)
  J. Fournier & Vienna State Op.—Horvath
                     ‡ **Nix.WLP 5187**
  (*Concerto No. 5*)   (‡ West.WL 5187)
  D. Oistrakh & Czech Phil—Ančerl
  (*Beethoven*)   ‡ **Sup.LPV 244**
  ☆ I. Stern & Cha. Orch. [cadenza, Franko] ‡ C.CX 1071
  (*Mendelssohn*)   (‡ WCX 1071: FCX 210: QCX 10042)
  ☆ J. Thibaud & Lamoureux—Paray ‡ AmVox.PL 8600
  (*Chausson*)   (‡ Cum.CVX 358)

No. 4, D major   K 218
  A. Grumiaux & Vienna Sym.—Paumgartner
                     ‡ **EPhi.ABL 3040**
  (*No. 3, above*)   (‡ Phi.A 00199L; ‡ Epic.LC 3060)
  M. Elman & New Sym.—Krips   ‡ **D.LXT 5078**
  (*No. 5, below*) [cadenzas by Joachim]   (‡ Lon.LL 1271)
  Y. Menuhin & Philharmonia—Pritchard
  (*No. 5, below*)   ‡ **G.ALP 1281**
  W. Boskowsky & Vienna Konzerthaus Cha.
                     ‡ **HS.HSL 9010**
  (*No. 1, above*) (also ‡ *DFr.EX 25028*)   (‡ DFr. 85)
  Gérard Poulet & Austrian Sym.—Gaston Poulet
                     ‡ **Rem. 199-125**
  (*Overtures*)   (*Concerto 3*, on ‡ Cum.CR 292)
  J. Martzy & Bavarian Radio Cha.—E. Jochum
                     ‡ *Pol. 16119*
                   (4ss, ♮ PV. 72323/4)
  ☆ F. Kreisler & L.P.O.—Sargent   ‡ Vic.LCT 1117
  (*Mendelssohn: Concerto*)   (♭ set WCT 1117)
  ☆ R. Barchet & Stuttgart Pro Musica—Seegelken
                   (‡ AFest.CFR 12-82)

No. 5, A major   K 219
  A. Grumiaux & Vienna Sym.—Paumgartner
                     ‡ **EPhi.ABL 3099**
  (*No. 2*)   (‡ Phi.A 00258L; Epic.LC 3157)
  Y. Menuhin & Philharmonia—Pritchard
  (*No. 4*)   ‡ **G.ALP 1281**
  M. Elman & New Sym.—Krips   ‡ **D.LXT 5078**
  (*No. 4*) [cadenzas by Joachim]   (‡ Lon.LL 1271)
  D. Oistrakh & Saxon State—Konwitschny
                     ‡ **HP.DG 16101**
  (2ss)   (‡ Eta. 820004, o.n. ‡ LPM 1016)
  (*Sym. No. 32*, on ‡ AmD.DL 9766)
  D. Oistrakh & Bolshoi Th.—Golovanov
  (*Beethoven*)   ‡ **Per.SPL 590**
  (2ss, ‡ *MusH.LP 9013*)   (*No. 6* on ‡ Csm.CRLP 154)

(*continued on next page*)

---

[2] After Schobert.   [3] After Raupach.   [4] After Honauer.
[5] Cadenzas by Mozart.   [6] After Eckard.   [7] After C. P. E. Bach.
[16] Cadenzas by Veyron-Lacroix.

No. 5, A major   K 219 (continued)
J. Fournier & Vienna State Op.—Horvath
‡ Nix.WLP 5187
(Concerto No. 3)   (‡ West.WL 5187)
W. Schneiderhan & Vienna Sym.—Leitner
‡ Pol. 16060
T. Olof & Sym.—Goehr   ‡ MMS. 2003
(Clarinet Concerto)
M. Kozolupova & U.S.S.R. State—Anosov
‡ USSR.D 0751/2

☆ J. Heifetz & L.S.O.—Sargent   ‡ G.ALP 1124
(Bruch)   (Beethoven on ‡ G.FALP 270)
☆ J. Thibaud & Orch.—Münch   ‡ G.FJLP 5015
(Haffner Serenade—Rondeau; & Schubert)
☆ E. Hitzker & Salzburg Fest.—Weidlich (‡ Ply. 10-30)

No. 6, D major   K 271a
D. Oistrakh & U.S.S.R. State—Kondrashin
‡ CEd.CE 3002
(Vladigerov, Vainberg)   (‡ USSR.D 1562/3)
(No. 5 on ‡ Csm.CRLP 154)

No. 7, E flat major   K 268 (new K 365b)
C. Ferras & Stuttgart Cha.—Münchinger
‡ D.LXT 5044
(No. 3)   (‡ Lon.LL 1172)

☆ R. Barchet & Stuttgart Pro Musica—R. Reinhardt
(‡ AFest.CFR 12-82)

Adagio, E major   K 261
Rondo Concertante, B flat major   K 269
Rondo, C major   K 373
N. de Klijn & Vienna Sym.—Paumgartner
‡ Phi.A 00299L
(Sinfonia Concertante)   (‡ Epic.LC 3197)

Adagio, E major   K 261
Rondo, C major   K 373
☆ N. Milstein & Victor Sym.—Golschmann
(♭ G.7ERF/ERQ 106)

Concertone, 2 vlns. & orch., C major   K 190
☆ Vienna Sym.—Swoboda   ‡ Nix.WLP 5013
(1½ss—Sym. 23)

CONCERTO, Pf., vln. & orch., D major
new K 315f (unfinished)
R. Veyron-Lacroix (fortepiano), J. Dumont &
Cha. Orch.—Oubradous   ‡ Pat.DTX 191
(Kyrie K 33, & Violin Sonatas)

SINFONIE CONCERTANTI
E flat major   K 297b ob., cl., hrn., bsn., orch.
P. Pierlot, J. Lancelot, G. Coursier, P. Hongne,
O.L. Ens.—Froment   ‡ LOL.OL 50006
(Cl. Concerto)   (‡ OL.LD 75)
Same Soloists & Saar Cha.—Ristenpart
(2ss)   ‡ DFr.EX 25035
S. Sutcliffe, B. Walton, D. Brain, C. James &
Philharmonia—Karajan   ‡ C.CX 1178
(Serenade No 13) (‡ FCX 308: QCX 10101; Angel. 35098)
P. Pierlot, J. Lancelot, P. Delvescovo, P.
Hongne, Cha. Orch.—Oubradous
(Overture, B flat major)   ‡ Pat.DTX 192
C. Maisonneuve, G. Deplus, A. Fournier,
A. Rabot & orch.—Disenhaus   ‡ MFr. 2505
☆ H. Kamesch, L. Wlach, G. v. Freiberg, K. Öhlberger,
Vienna State Op.—Swoboda   ‡ Nix.WLP 5020
(1½ss—Divertimento)   (‡ West.WN 18041, d.c.)
☆ Soloists & Austrian Cha.—Wöss (‡ Cum.CR 235)
Soloists & Philadelphia—Stokowski
(‡ Cam.CAL 213 & in set CFL 105)

E flat major   K 364 vln., vla. & orch.
N. Brainin, P. Schidlof & London Mozart
—H. Blech   ‡ G.CLP 1014
(Sym. No. 35) [cadenzas by Mozart]
N. de Klijn, P. Godwin & Vienna Sym.
—Paumgartner   ‡ Phi.A 00299L
(Rondos & Adagio)   (‡ Epic.LC 3197)
J. Pollak, W. L. v. Rostock & Saxon State Orch.
—Elsner   ‡ Csm.CLPS 1052
(Pf. Concerto K 238)

C. R. Steiner, P. Doktor & Salzburg Mozarteum
—Paumgartner   ‡ CFD. 16
☆ I. Stern, W. Primrose & Perpignan Festival—Casals
‡ C.CX 1089
(‡ FCX 224)
☆ J. & L. Fuchs & Zimbler Sinfonietta ‡ B.AXTL 1018
(2ss)   (‡ Pol. 16122; D.UAT 273050)
☆ W. Barylli, P. Doktor & Vienna State Op.—Prohaska
(2ss)   ‡ Nix.WLP 5107
(above, ‡ West.WN 18041)
☆ A. Spalding, W. Primrose & New Friends of Music
—Stiedry (‡ Cam.CAL 262 & in set CFL 105)

II. D. 2. DANCES
(For Gigues, Minuets, for Pf. Solo, see section II. A. 1)

COLLECTION

Contretänze	K 534	Das Donnerwetter
	K 609	complete
(6) Ländler	K 606	... Nos. 1-5 only
Deutsche Tänze	K 600	... Nos. 1-5 only
	K 602	... No. 3, Der Leiermann
	K 605	complete

☆ Vienna State Op.—Litschauer   ‡ Nix.VLP 426
(K 609, K 602, No. 3, & K 605, No. 3 only[1], also on
♭ Van.VREP 2)

CONTRETÄNZE
(6) K 462
Munich Cha.—Stepp   ‡ Pol. 16128
(Britten: Simple Symphony)

(5) K 609
Berlin Sym.—Guthan   ‡ Roy. 1444
(Divertimenti)
☆ London Baroque Ens.—Haas (Adagios) ‡ AmD.DL4055

... **Nos. 1, 2, 4 only**
☆ Danish Radio—Busch   G.DB 10516
(Ruslan & Ludmilla, Overture)

DEUTSCHE TÄNZE
(6) K 509
☆ Bamberg Sym.—Keilberth   ‡ LOL.OL 50005
(K 571, & Sym. 29)

(6) K 536 ... No. 1 — ARR. HPSI.
☆ A. Ehlers (in ‡ D.UMT 273084)

(6) K 571
☆ Bamberg Sym.—Keilberth   ‡ LOL.OL 50005
(K 509 & Sym. 29)
☆ Orch.—Gaillard (♮ Od.O-3706/7)

(12) K 586
Orch.—Gaillard   ‡ Od.OD 1015

(6) K 600; (4) K 602; (3) K 605 ... Nos. 1 & 3 only
— ARR. PF. ("Waltzes")
F. Kramer   ‡ MTR.MLO 1011
(Romanze)

(6) K 600
Berlin Sym.—Guthan   ‡ Roy. 1437
(Pf. Concerto K 459, & Sym. "No. 55")

... **Nos. 1, 2, 5; & K 602, No. 3**
Linz Sym.   in ‡ Ply. 12-30
(Schubert, Beethoven, J. Strauss, etc.)

... **Nos. 1 & 5**
☆ Winterthur Sym.—Goehr
(‡ Clc. 11002; ‡ ANix.MLPY 1)

(3) K 605
Columbia Sym.—Walter   in ‡ AmC.ML 5004
(Maurerische Trauermusik, Minuets, etc.) (‡ Phi.A 01237L)

... **No. 3, only** "Die Schlittenfahrt"
Royal Phil.—Beecham   C.LX 1587
(March, K 249)   (GQX 11537: ♭ SCB 106: SCBQ 3011)
Philharmonia—Markevitch   in ‡ C.CX 1273
(Busoni, Liszt, Berlioz, etc.) (‡ QCX 10172; Angel. 35154)
☆ Sym. Orch.—Stokowski (♭ Vic.ERA 119)
Florence Festival—Markevitch (in ‡ Tem.TT 2046)
COLLECTION:
K 600, No. 5; K 602, No. 3; K 605, No. 3; & 5 unspec.
Hamburg Philharmonia—H-J. Walther   MSB. 78140/1
(4ss)

---

[1] Also on ‡ Van.VRS 5001, announced but not issued.

(6) LÄNDLER (Ländlerische Tänze)   K 606
A. Schneider Ens.   in ♯ **AmC.CL 556**
(Lanner, J. Strauss, etc.)   *(♭ set B 417)*

MINUETS
(6) K 599; (4) K 601; (2) K 604
Cha. Orch.—Hewitt   ♯ **HS.HSL 101**
(Serenade No. 13)   *(♯ DFr. 67, 2ss)*

(12) K 568 . . . No. 12 only; (6) K 599 . . . No. 5 only
Columbia Sym.—Walter   ♯ **AmC.ML 5004**
(Maurerische Trauermusik, Deutsche Tänze, etc.)
                        (♯ Phi.A 01237L)

II. D. 3. SYMPHONIES

COLLECTIONS of early Symphonies

No. 2, B flat major	K 17 (new K.Anh. 223a)[2]	LD 19
No. 3, E flat major	K 18 (new K.Anh. 109I)[3]	LD 20
No. 4, D major	K 19	LD 21
No. 5, B flat major	K 22	LD 21
No. 7, D major	K 45[4]	LD 22
No. 8, D major	K 48	LD 23
No. 9, C major	K 73	LD 24
No. 10, G major	K 74	LD 22
No. 11, D major	K 84 (new K. 73q)	LD 25

O. L. Cha.—Froment   V♯ *DO.LD 19/25*
[Nos. 2, 3, 4, 5, 7 on ♯ LOL.OL 50118, Nos. 8, 9, 10, 11
on ♯ LOL.OL 50119]

No. 1, E flat major   K 16
No. 6, F major   K 43
   ☆ Lamoureux-Colombo   ♯ *LOL.DL 53008*

No. 1, E flat major	K 16
No. 2, B flat major	K 17 (new K.Anh. 223a)[2]
No. 5, B flat major	K 22
No. 6, F major	K 43

   ☆ Winterthur Sym.—Ackermann (♯ Clc. 6201)

No. 3, E flat major	K 18 (new K.Anh. 109I)[3]
No. 13, F major	K 112
No. 15, G major	K 124
No. 16, C major	K 128

Netherlands Phil.—Ackermann
                 ♯ **CHS.CHS 1178**
                     (♯ Clc. 6253)

No. 4, D major	K 19
No. 10, G major	K 74
No. 11, D major	K 84
No. 14, A major	K 114

   ☆ Winterthur Sym.—Ackermann (♯ Clc. 6218; No. 14
only, on V♯ MMS. 99)

No. 7, D major	K 45[4]
No. 8, D major	K 48
No. 9, C major	K 73 (new K 75a)
No. 12, G major	K 110 (new K 75b)

Netherlands Phil.—Ackermann
                 ♯ **CHS.CHS 1177**
                     (♯ Clc. 6243)

No. 18, F major	K 130
No. 19, E flat major	K 132
No. 20, D major	K 133
No. 21, A major	K 134

Netherlands Phil.—Ackermann
                 ♯ **CHS.CHS 1193**

No. 22, C major	K 162
No. 23, D major	K 181
No. 24, B flat major	K 182
No. 25, G minor	K 183

Netherlands Phil.—Ackermann
                 ♯ **CHS.CHS 1194**

No. 10, G major   K 74
Salzburg Mozarteum—Paumgartner ♯ **CFD. 37**
(C major, below; & March & Divertimento)

No. 14, A major   K 114
Danish Radio Cha.—Wöldike   ♯ **D.LXT 5135**
(J. C. Bach, Haydn, Dittersdorf)   *(♯ Lon.LL 1308)*

No. 17, G major   K 129
Olympia Sym.—Saike   ♯ **Allo. 3055**
(No. 25, below)
   ☆ Netherlands Phil.—Ackermann (♯ MMS. 23)

Nos. 18 & 22   K 130 & 162
   ☆ Vienna Sym.—Swoboda   ♯ **West.WN 18046**
   (Nos. 30 & 37)

No. 23, D major   K 181
   ☆ Vienna Sym.—Swoboda   ♯ **Nix.WLP 5013**
   (♮s—above)

No. 24, B flat major   K 182
Paris Collegium Musicum—Douatte
                 ♯ **EPP.APG 113**
(No. 28, & Schauspieldirektor, Overture)
   ☆ Stuttgart Ton-Studio—Michael (♯ Cpt.MC 20032)

No. 25, G minor   K 183
L.S.O.—Solti   ♯ **D.LXT 2946**
(No. 38)   *(♯ Lon.LL 1034)*
Columbia Sym.—Walter   ♯ **AmC.ML 5002**
(No. 28)
Vienna Pro Musica—Perlea
           ♯ **E. & AmVox.PL 8750**
(Nos. 29 & 33)   *(♯ Orb.BL 705)*
Saar Cha.—Ristenpart   ♯ **DFr. 117**
(Nos. 28 & 29)   *(also V♯ DFr.EX 17017, 2ss)*
Salzburg Mozarteum—Paumgartner
                 ♯ **Phi.A 00283L**
(No. 33)   *(♯ Epic.LC 3172)*
Berlin Radio—Egk   ♯ **Ura.RS 7-33**
(Bach)
Olympia Sym.—Saike   ♯ **Allo. 3055**
(No. 17)
   ☆ Danish Radio—Wöldike (♯ Era.LDE 3011)

No. 26, E flat major   K 184
Saar Cha.—Ristenpart   ♯ **DFr. 135**
(Nos. 35 & 36)
Berlin Sym.—Guthan   ♯ **Roy. 1406**
(No. 30 & Pf. Concerto, K 453
Paris Cha.—Douatte   ♯ **EPP.APG 112**
(Handel)
   ☆ Boston Sym.—Koussevitzky
           (♯ Cam.CAL 160 & in set CFL 105)
Netherlands Phil.—Ackermann (in ♯ MMS. 100W)

No. 27, G major   K 199
   ☆ Bamberg Sym.—L. G. Jochum   ♯ **LOL.OL 50039**
   (No. 30)

No. 28, C major   K 200
Columbia Sym.—Walter   ♯ **AmC.ML 5002**
(No. 25)
Saar Cha.—Ristenpart   ♯ **DFr. 117**
(Nos. 25 & 29)
Salzburg Mozarteum—Paumgartner
                 ♯ **Phi.A 00768R**
(No. 31)   *(♯ Epic.LC 3215)*
Paris Collegium Musicum—Douatte
                 ♯ **EPP.APG 113**
(No. 24, & Schauspieldirektor Overture)
   ☆ Suisse Romande—Maag *(No. 29)*   ♯ **D.LXT 2840**

No. 29, A major   K 201
Philharmonia—Klemperer   ♯ **C.CX 1257**
(No. 41)   *(♯ Angel. 35209)*
Vienna Pro Musica—Perlea
           ♯ **E. & AmVox.PL 8750**
(Nos. 25 & 33)   *(♯ Orb.BL 705)*
Salzburg Cha.—Paumgartner ♯ **LT.DTL 93057**
(Pf. Concerto, K 488) (♯ Sel.LAG 1068; T.LE 6531)
Saar Cha.—Ristenpart   ♯ **DFr. 117**
(Nos. 25 & 28)
Residentie—v. Otterloo   ♯ **Phi.A 00286L**
(No. 34)
Sonor Sym.—Ledermann   ♯ **Pde. 2013**
   ☆ Suisse Romande—Maag *(No. 28)*   ♯ **D.LXT 2840**
   ☆ Perpignan Festival—Casals   ♯ **C.CX 1088**
   (Serenade No. 13)   *(♯ FCX 223)*
   ☆ L.P.O.—Beecham *(No. 34)*   ♯ **AmC.ML 4781**
   ☆ Bamberg Sym.—Keilberth   ♯ **LOL.OL 50005**
   (Deutsche Tänze)
   ☆ Danish Radio—Wöldike (♯ Era.LDE 3011)
   Vienna St. Op.—Swoboda (♯ MMS. 75)
   Boston Sym.—Koussevitzky
           (♯ Cam.CAL 160 & in set CFL 105)

---

[2] Not by Mozart.   [3] Really by C. F. Abel, *q.v.*
[4] This Symphony was used by Mozart as the Overture to *La Finta Semplice, q.v.*

No. 30, D major   K 202
Bamberg Sym.—Keilberth   ♯ DT.LGX 66025
(*Serenade 13*)
(2ss, ♯ DT.TM 68007; TV.VE 9029)
Berlin Sym.—Guthan   ♯ Roy. 1406
(*No. 26 & Pf. Concerto K 453*)
☆ Bamberg Sym.—L. G. Jochum   ♯ LOL.OL 50039
(*No. 27*)
☆ Vienna Sym.—Swoboda   ♯ West.WN 18046
(*Nos. 18, 22, 37*)

No. 31, D major   K 297   "Paris"
Salzburg Mozarteum—Paumgartner
                                              ♯ Phi.A 00768R
(*No. 28*)   (♯ Epic.LC 3215)
Saar Cha.—Ristenpart (2ss) V♯ DFr.EX 17041
Cha.—Oubradous   ♯ Pat.DTX 194
(*Les Petits Riens*)
☆ Royal Phil.—Beecham   ♯ C.CX 1038
(*Haydn: Sym. No. 93*) (♯ WCX 1038: QCX 10032:
                                              & FCX 329, d.c.)
Anon. Orch. (♯ Gram. 2081)
☆ Hastings Sym.—Bath (♯ Pac.LDAD 30)

No. 32, G major   K 318
Bamberg Sym.—Lehmann   PV. 72429
(*Weber: Preciosa, Overture*)   (& ♭ Pol. 30120)
(*No. 26 on* ♯ AmD.DL 4045; Nos. 26 & 35 on ♯ Pol. 18066)
(*Vln. Concerto K 219 on* ♯ AmD.DL 9766)
Berlin Cha.—v. Benda   ♯ DT.TM 68048
(*Pergolesi*)   (♯ T.TW 30021)
☆ Cha. Orch.—Hewitt (♯ DFr. 88: V♯ EX 17015)

No. 33, B flat major   K 319
Vienna Phil.—Münchinger   ♯ D.LXT 5124
(*No. 40*)   (♯ Lon.LL 1285)
London Mozart Players—Blech ♯ G.CLP 1066
(*Haydn: Sym. 103*)
Vienna Pro Musica—Perlea
                                      ♯ E. & AmVox.PL 8750
(*Nos. 29 & 25*)   (♯ Orb. BL 705)
Salzburg Mozarteum—Paumgartner
                                              ♯ Phi.A 00283L
(*No. 25*)   (♯ Epic.LC 3172)
Berlin Phil.—E. Jochum   ♯ Ura.RS 7-27
(*No. 35*)
Bavarian Radio—E. Jochum   ♯ Pol. 18228
(*No. 36*)
☆ Slovak Phil.—Talich   ♯ Sup.LPV 53
(*No. 35*)   (♯ U. 5047G)
☆ Cha. Orch.—Hewitt (♯ DFr. 88)
  Austrian Sym.—Heger (♯ Cum.CR 295, d.c.)

No. 34, C major   K 338
Berlin Phil.—Markevitch[1]   ♯ HP.DGM 18176
(*No. 38*)   (*Schubert*, on ♯ AmD.DL 9810)
Vienna Phil.—Böhm[1]   ♯ D.LXT 5111
(*No. 38*)   (♯ Lon.LL 1198)
Chicago Sym.—Kubelik   ♯ G.ALP 1239
(*No. 38*)   (♯ G.FALP 374; Mer.MG 50015)
Residentie—v. Otterloo   ♯ Phi.A 00286L
(*No. 29*)
London Mozart Players—H. Blech[1]
(*No. 36*)   ♯ G.CLP 1063
☆ L.P.O.—Beecham (*No. 29*)   ♯ AmC.ML 4781
☆ Boston Sym.—Koussevitzky
                      (♯ Cam.CAL 160 & in set CFL 105)
  Cha. Orch.—Hewitt (♯ DFr. 88)
  Vienna State Op.—Swoboda (♯ MMS. 65)

No. 35, D major   K 385   "Haffner"
Royal Phil.—Beecham   ♯ EPhi.ABL 3067
(*No. 36*)   (♯ AmC.ML 5001)
London Mozart—Blech   ♯ G.CLP 1014
(*Sinfonia Concertante, K 364*)
(*No. 40 on* ♯ BB.LBC 1069: ♭ set WBC 1069)
Pittsburgh Sym.—Steinberg ♯ DCap.CTL 7053
(*No. 41*)   (♯ Cap.P 8242; ACap.CLCX 033)
New York Phil. Sym.—Walter ♯ AmC.ML 4693
(*No. 40*)   (♯ Phi.A 01173L)

London Phil. Sym.—Leinsdorf
(*Nos. 36 & 37*)   ♯ West.WN 18146
Rochester Phil.—Leinsdorf   ♯ AmC.RL 3103
(*No. 41*)
Saar Cha.—Ristenpart   ♯ DFr.EX 25007
(& with *Nos. 26 & 36*, ♯ DFr. 135)
Prussian State—Heger   ♯ Ura.RS 7-27
(*No. 33*)   (*C. P. E. Bach*, on ♯ MTW. 556)
Netherlands Phil.—Swoboda   ♯ MMS. 75
(*No. 29*)
☆ L.P.O.—Beecham (*No. 36*)   ♯ AmC.ML 4770
☆ R.I.A.S. Sym.—Fricsay   ♯ AmD.DL 9614
(*Haydn: Sym. No. 44*)
☆ Vienna Sym.—Scherchen   ♯ Sup.LPV 53
(*No. 33*)   (♯ U. 5047G)
☆ Berlin Phil.—Lehmann   ♯ Epic.LC 3006
(*Schubert: Sym. No. 8*)
(*March, K 249; & Haydn*, on ♯ Phi.S 04008L)
☆ Austrian Sym.—Wolf (♯ Cum.TCR 257; ♯ Ply. 12-53;
  & with commentary by S. Spaeth, ♯ Rem. 11)

No. 36, C major   K 425   "Linz"
Royal Phil.—Beecham   ♯ EPhi.ABL 3067
(*No. 35, above*)   (♯ AmC.ML 5001)
London Mozart Players—H. Blech
(*No. 34*)   ♯ G.CLP 1063
Bavarian Radio—Jochum   ♯ Pol. 18228
(*No. 33, above*)
Berlin Cha.—v. Benda   ♯ DT.LGX 66020
(*Schubert: Sym. No. 5*)   (♯ T.LSK 7031)
London Phil. Sym.—Leinsdorf
(*Nos. 35 & 37*)   ♯ West.WN 18146
Saar Cha.—Ristenpart   ♯ DFr. 135
(*Nos. 25 & 35*)
Columbia Sym.—Walter   ♯ AmC. set SL 224
(4ss—including complete rehearsal of the recorded
performance)
☆ L.P.O.—Beecham (*No. 35*)   ♯ AmC.ML 4770
Europa Sym. (♯ Ply. 12-129; also ♯ Gram. 2081 & 2035)
☆ Boston Sym.—Koussevitzky (♯ G. FALP/QALP 239)
  Winterthur Sym.—Goehr (♯ Clc.11002; ANix.MLPY 1)
  Vienna Sym.—Scherchen (♯ Sup.LPM 131; U. 5112C)

No. 37, G major   K 444 (by Michael Haydn)
London Phil. Sym.—Leinsdorf
(*Nos. 35 & 36*)   ♯ West.WN 18146
☆ Vienna Sym.—Swoboda   ♯ West.WN 18046
(*Nos. 18, 22, 30*)

No. 38, D major   K 504 "Prague"
Glyndebourne Festival—Gui   ♯ G.ALP 1114
(*Haydn: Sym. 60*) (♯ Arg A.LPC 11581; ♯ Vic.LHMV 1064)
(*No. 39 on* ♯ G.FALP 328)
L.S.O.—Solti   ♯ D.LXT 2946
(*No. 25*)   (♯ Lon.LL 1034)
Berlin Phil.—Markevitch   ♯ HP.DGM 18176
(*No. 34*)   (*Mass No. 16 on* ♯ AmD.DL 9805)
Vienna Phil.—Böhm   ♯ D.LXT 5111
(*No. 34*)   (♯ Lon.LL 1198)
Saar Cha.—Ristenpart   ♯ DFr. 137
(*No. 39*)
London Phil. Sym.—Leinsdorf
(*No. 39*)   ♯ West.WN 18116
Chicago Sym.—Kubelik   ♯ G.ALP 1239
(*No. 34*)   (♯ G.FALP 374; Mer.MG 50015)
(*Smetana*, on ♯ Mer. MG 50042)
Sonor Sym.—Ledermann   ♯ Pde. 2014
Moscow Radio—Samosud   USSR. 20491/500
(10ss)   (2ss, ♯ D 1748/9)
☆ Royal Phil.—Beecham   ♯ C.CX 1105
(*Handel*)   (*Sym. 41 on* ♯ FCX 235)
☆ St. Louis Sym.—Golschmann   ♯ BB.LBC 1067
(*Sibelius*)   (♭ set WBC 1067)
☆ Chicago Sym.—Stock   ♯ AmC.RL 3026
(*Schumann: Sym. No. 4*)
☆ Vienna Phil.—Walter
                        (♯ Cam.CAL 237 & in set CFL 105)

[1] Includes Minuet K 409 (new K 383f), composed for insertion in this symphony

No. 39, E flat major K 543

Royal Phil.—Beecham	♯ **EPhi.ABL 3094**
(No. 40)	

Glyndebourne Fest.—Gui	♯ **G.ALP 1155**
(Haydn) (No. 38 on ♯ G.FALP 328)	(♯ Vic.LHMV 11)

Amsterdam—Böhm	♯ **Phi.A 00319L**
(No. 40)	

Saar Cha.—Ristenpart	♯ **DFr. 137**
(No. 38)	

London Phil. Sym.—Leinsdorf	
(No. 38)	♯ **West.WN 18116**

Bavarian Radio—E. Jochum   ♯ *Pol.* **16099**
Berlin State—Loibner   ♯ **Eta.LPM 1010**
    (& 6ss, Eta. 120055/7)
N.Y. Phil. Sym.—Mitropoulos[1] in ♯ **OTA set 8**
Leningrad Phil.—Mravinsky ♯ *USSR*.D 851/2
☆ L.P.O.—Weingartner (♯ AmC.ML 4776)
Vienna Phil.—Karajan (♯ AmC.RL 3068)
L.P.O.—Beecham (♯ AmC.ML 4674)
B.B.C. Sym.—Walter
    (♯ Cam.CAL 237 & in set CFL 105)
... 3rd movt. Minuet only — ARR. GUITAR Neumann
U. Neumann (Tarrega: Etude)   *Od.DK 1168*

No. 40, G minor K 550

[2] Royal Phil.—Beecham	♯ **EPhi.ABL 3094**
(No. 39)	

Vienna Phil.—Münchinger	♯ **D.LXT 5124**
(No. 33)	(♯ Lon.LL 1285)

London Mozart Players—Blech	♯ **G.CLP 1009**
(Haydn: Sym. 86)	(♯ WCLP 1009)
(Mozart: Sym. 35 on ♯ BB.LBC 1069: ♭ set WBC 1069)	

L.S.O.—Krips	♯ **D.LXT 2819**
(Haydn: Sym. 92)	(♯ Lon.LL 780)

Bamberg Sym.—Perlea	♯ **AmVox.PL 9450**
(No. 41)	

N.W. Ger. Phil.—Schüchter	♯ *Imp.ILP 133*
(2ss)	

N.Y.P.S.O.—Walter	♯ **AmC.ML 4693**
(No. 35)	(♯ Phi.A 01173L)

N.B.C. Sym.—Toscanini (n.v.)	♯ **Vic.LM 1789**
(Haydn: Sym. 94)	(♯ FV.A 630229)

Vienna Sym.—Lehmann	♮ **PV. 72403/4**
(6ss)	(2ss, ♯ Pol. 17006: 16114)

Champs-Élysées Th.—Scherchen	♯ **LT.DTL 93020**
(No. 41)	(♯ T.LE 6532; Sel. 320.C.007)

[2] Vienna State Op.—Prohaska	♯ **Van.VRS 445**
(Schubert)	
(Serenade No 13, on ♯ Ama.AVRS 6009; Van. SRV 102)	

Saar Cha.—Ristenpart	♯ *DFr.EX 25001*
(& with No. 41, ♯ DFr. 138)	

Amsterdam—Böhm	♯ **Phi.A 00319L**
(No. 39)	

Orch.—Prohaska (Haydn)   ♯ **MTW. 17**
Netherlands Phil.—Swoboda (No. 34) ♯ *MMS.* 65
Olympia Sym.—Saike   ♯ **Allo. 3056**
(Haydn: Sym. No. 94)   (♯ Pac.LDAD 72)
Boston Orch. Socy.—Page   ♯ *SOT.* 2065
(Beethoven No. 5, on ♯ SOT. 10657)
Rochester Phil.—Leinsdorf   ♯ **AmC.RL 3070**
(Schubert: Sym. No. 8)
▽ Moscow Radio—Samosud   USSR. 018272/7
(6ss)   (2ss, ♯ D 0381/2)
☆ Minneapolis Sym.—Dorati ♯ **EMer.MG 50010**
(Stravinsky)   (♯ FMer.MLP 7507)
Amsterdam—E. Jochum (♯ DT.LGX 66036, announced
   but probably never issued)
Anon. orch. & narration (♯ Esc. 1)
☆ L.P.O.—Beecham (♯ AmC.ML 4674)
Vienna Phil.—Furtwangler (♯ G.FALP/QALP 117)
L.P.O.—Koussevitzky (♯ Cam.CAL 188
    & in set CFL 105)
Danish Radio—Tango (♯ Tono.LPL 33004)
Salzburg Fest.—P. Walter
   (♯ AFest.CFR 10-60; Ply. 12-87; also on ♯ Ply. 12-53)
Anon. Orch. (♯ Gram. 2048, ♯ Var. 6972, etc.)

No. 41, C major K 551 "Jupiter"

Philharmonia—Klemperer	♯ **C.CX 1257**
(No. 29)	(♯ Angel. 35209)

Bamberg Sym.—Perlea	♯ **AmVox.PL 9450**
(No. 40)	

Saar Cha.—Ristenpart	♯ **DFr. 138**
(No. 40)	

Champs-Élysées Th.—Scherchen	
	♯ **LT.DTL 93020**
(No. 40)	(♯ T.LE 6532; ♯ Sel. 320.C.007)

Pittsburg Sym.—Steinberg	♯ **DCap.CTL 7053**
(No. 35)	(♯ Cap.P 8242; ACap.CLCX 033)

R.I.A.S. Sym.—Fricsay (2ss)	♯ *HP.DG 16083*
(also, 4ss, ♮ PV. 72442/3)	

Rochester Phil.—Leinsdorf (No. 35) ♯ **AmC.RL 3103**
Winterthur Sym.—Ackermann   ♯ *MMS.* 23
(No. 17)   (♯ Clc. 11006)
Olympia Sym.—Saike   ♯ **Allo. 3075**
Orch.—Gielen (Mendelssohn)   ♯ **MTW. 25**
☆ N.Y. Phil. Sym.—Walter ♯ **C.CX 1082**
(Schubert)   (♯ QCX 10079; ♯ AmC.ML 4880)
"Nat. Op. Orch." (♯ Gram. 2054)
Anon. Orch. (♯ ACC. MP 7)
Saxon State—Konwitschny (♯ Eta. 720012)

☆ N.B.C. Sym.—Toscanini
   (♯ G.QALP 10046, d.c.; DV.L 16063, d.c.)
Royal Phil.—Beecham (♯ C.WC 1002: QC 5006:
             VC 805; & ♯ C.FCX 235, d.c.)
Vienna Phil.—Walter
   (♯ Cam.CAL 253 & ♯ sets CFL 104 & 105)
Austrian Sym.—Wöss (♯ AFest.CFR 10-31;
               Cum.TCR 262)
... Excerpt only: Berlin Sym. (♯ Roy. 1375)

B flat major new K 45b
   (old K.Anh. 214; B & H No. 55)

Berlin Sym.—Rubahn	♯ **Roy. 1437**
(Pf. Concerto K 459 & Deutsche Tänze)	

C major K 96 (new K 111b; B & H No. 46)
Salzburg Mozarteum—Paumgartner ♯ **CFD. 37**
(Sym. No. 10, March and Divertimento)

I. D. *4. OTHER ORCHESTRAL WORKS*

Adagio & Fugue, C minor K 546 str. orch.
Champs-Élysées Th.—Goldschmidt
          ♯ **Sel. 320.C.006**
(Fl. & Hp. Concerto & Serenade 13)
(Divertimento K 251, & Serenade 13, on ♯ Sel. 320.C.092)

— QUARTET RECORDINGS

Italian Qtt.	♯ **D.LXT 2853**
(⅓s—Str. Qtt. No. 19)	

Végh Qtt.	V♯ *DFr.EX 17010*
(Maurerische Trauermusik)	(o.n. V♯ DFr. 68)

Maurerische Trauermusik K 477
Vienna Sym.—Paumgartner in ♯ **EPhi.ABL 3022**
(Cantatas)   (♯ Phi.A 00221L; ♯ Epic.LC 3062)
(Zauberflöte Arias, ♭ Phi.A 400004E; ♭ EPhi.NBE 11005)
Columbia Sym.—Walter   ♯ **AmC.ML 5004**
(Serenade No. 13, Overtures, Dances, etc.) (♯ Phi.A 01237L)
Salzburg Mozarteum—Paumgartner ♯ **CFD. 7**
(Ob. & Cl. Concertos)
☆ Hewitt Cha. Orch.   V♯ *DFr.EX 17010*
(Adagio & Fugue K 546) (o.n. V♯ DFr. 68)
& in CANTATA COLLECTION, ante

Overture, B flat major K 311a	♯ **Pat.DTX 192**
Cha. Orch.—Oubradous	
(Sinfonia Concertante, K 297b)	

☆ Vienna State Acad.—Swarowsky ♯ **Nix.LLP 8032**
(Haydn)
☆ Cha. Orch.—Hewitt (♯ DFr. 88 & V♯ EX 17015)

SONATAS, Organ & orch. (Church Sonatas)
No. 15, C major K 328
K. Matthaei & Winterthur Sym.—Reinhart
                ♯ **CHS.H 3**
(Horn & Bsn. Concertos)

---

[1] From a broadcast performance.   [2] Original scoring, without clarinets.

MISCELLANEOUS

"Mozart in Paris"—An album of 7 # discs containing "all the works composed during his different visits to Paris"   # Pat.DTX 191/7

CONTENTS (full details entered individually above)
DTX 191   Pf. & vln. concerto, K 315f
            Pf. and vln. sonatas, Nos. 1-4
            Kyrie, K 33
DTX 192   Sinfonia Concertante, K 297b
            Overture, B flat major, K 311a
DTX 193   Fl. & Hp. Concerto, K 299
            Andante, fl. & orch., K 315
DTX 194   Symphony No. 31, "Paris"
            Les Petits Riens, K 299b
DTX 195   Popoli di Tessaglia! (Aria) K 316
            "Milanese" Qtt. No. 1
            Piano Variations, K 265
            Pf. & Vln. Sonata, D major, K 306
DTX 196   Pf. Sonata, A minor, K 310
            Variations, K 353 & K 264
            Capriccio, K 395
            Pf. & Vln. Sonata, K 304
DTX 197   Pf. Sonatas K 330, 331, 332
            Variations K 354

"Wolfgang von Gott geliebt"
    A Mozart record for children.   Narration and musical illustrations, which include:
Oragna figata fa[1]
Minuet, G major, K 1; Allegro, B flat major, K 3
Sonata, D major, clavier & vln., K 7
Excerpts (unspec.) from Die Zauberflöte
Song: Das Kinderspiel (Overbeck), K 598
Excerpts from Mozart's 2nd Sketchbook:
    Minuet, G ma., K 15y; Rondeau, F ma., K 15hh; Minuet A♭ ma., K 15ff
Song: Die Zufriedenheit ('Was frag' ich'), K 349 (new K 367a)
Sonata, G major, clavier & vln., K 27
Song: Sehnsucht nach dem Frühlinge, K 596
Symphony No. 5, B flat major K 22
    C. Eschenbach (pf.), W. Melcher (vln.), G. Schefe (lute), B. Junk (S), North Ger. Singers, Children's Cho., Hamburg Music School Cha. Orch.—W. Sternberg (with actors, etc.)   # Pol. 19025

"Mozart Miniature"
    Excerpts from recordings of Nozze di Figaro, Overture; Vln. Concerto, K 218; Mass, C minor; Serenade and duet from Don Giovanni; & Rondo, pf. & orch., K 386; Rondo, pf., K 485   # Phi.S 06100R

The Salzburg Mozart Records
    Illustrated talk by B. Paumgartner (Ger) # Phi.S 05904R
                                      (Eng) # Phi.S 05906R
Mozart: His life, his times, his music
    D. Randolph (narrator)   # Per.PCS 2

The Story & Music of Mozart
    Narrator & Orch. (AmC. set J 166, 4ss)

Minuet   Unspec.: Chicago Sym. Woodwind Quintet
                              (in # Aphe.AP 17)

MUDARRA, Alonso de   (c. 1510-1570)

(all from 3 Libros de Música en Cifra, 1546)

Pavana I; Galliarda; Fantasia X
    M. Podolsky (lute)   in # Per.SPL 577
    († Lute Music, XVI-XVIIth Cent.)   (# Cpt.MC 20052)

Romanesca
    ☆ A. Segovia (in † # D.UAT 273141)

SONGS: Israel; Si me llaman;
        Triste estaba el rey David
Pavana   (lute solo)
    ☆ H. Cuénod (T), H. Leeb (lute)   # Nix.WLP 5059
    (Milan; & † Italian Songs)

MÜLLER, Georg Gottfried   (1762-1821)

SEE: † AMERICAN MUSIC (VOCAL)

MÜLLER, Paul   (b. 1898)

Symphony No. 2 for strings & flute, Op. 53
    Zürich Chamber Orch.—de Stoutz
                              # D.LXT 5081
    (Bartók)   (# Lon.LL 1183)

MUFFAT, Georg   (c. 1645-1704)

Passacaglia, G minor
    (Apparatus Musico-organisticus, 1690)
    N. Pierront (org.)   in # Lum.LD 2-104
    († Chaconne & Passacaglia)

MUFFAT, Gottlieb   (1683-1770)

Suite, B flat major (Componimenti musicali, c. 1739)
... Allemande; Minuets I & II
    E. Heiller (hpsi.)   in # Uni.LP 1010
    († History of the Dance)
Toccata, C minor ... Adagio only [DTÖ. LVIII-9]
    Anon. Artist (in # FSM. 403)

MULET, Henri   (b. 1878)

Carillon-Sortie, D major   organ
    A. Hamme   in # SRS.H 1
    († Organ Recital)
Esquisses byzantines   organ
... Toccata
    E. P. Biggs   in # AmC.ML 4331

MUNDY, John   (c. 1554-1630)

SEE: † TRIUMPHS OF ORIANA
     † MUSIC IN SHAKESPEARE'S TIME

MUNDY, William   (c. 1529-c. 1591)

O Lord, the maker of all thing
    St. George's Chapel Cho.—Harris   C.LX 1564
    († English Church Music, Vol. III)
    Festival Singers—Iseler   # Hall.ChS 3
    (Byrd, Gibbons, Lassus, Willan)

MUÑOZ, Garcia   (fl. XV-XVIth Cent.)

SEE: † SPANISH MUSIC   (c. 1500)

MUREAU, Gilles   (fl. XVth Cent.)

SEE: † FRENCH CHANSONS

MUSET, Colin   (fl. XIIIth Cent.)

SEE: † LA MUSIQUE ET LA POÉSIE

NANINI, Giovanni Maria   (c. 1545-1607)

Stabat Mater   Motet   1586
    Biggs Family Ens.   in # GIOA.BF 1

NAPOLI, Gennaro   (1881-1943)

Symphony, D minor
... Adagio & Scherzo only
    Naples Scarlatti Orch.—Caracciolo
                              # Csm.CLPS 1041
    (Halffter: Sinfonietta)

NÁPRAVNÍK, Edward   (1839-1916)

DUBROVSKY, Op. 58   Opera   4 Acts   1895
Give me oblivion   T
    G. Pishchaev   USSR. 021805
    (Pêcheurs de Perles, aria)
    S. Lemeshev   USSR. 20166/7
                              (USSRM.D 00992)
    P. Belinnik (USSR. 22179/80)
    ☆ I. Kozlovsky (in # Csm.CRLP 139)

NARDIS, Camillo de   (1857-1951)

Scene Abruzzesi   orch.
Suite I: 1. Adunata; 2. Pastorale; 3. Serenata; 4. Temperale
                                              e saltarello
Suite II: 1. Processione notturno del Venerdi Santo
          2. San Clemente a Casauria
          3. Serenata a gli sposi
          4. Festa tragica
    Naples Scarlatti Orch.—P. Argento
                              # Csm.CLPS 1037

[1] A tune composed by Mozart at a tender age and sung by him every night before going to bed.   See Holmes: Life of Mozart (p. 15, Everyman edn.)

NASCO, Giovanni　(d. 1561)

MOTETS　4 voices
Tristis est anima mea
O salutaris hostia
Lamentatio I　　　　　　　in ♯ E. & AmVox.PL 8030
Migravit Judas (Lamentatio)　in ♯ E. & AmVox.PL 8610
Ave Maria
Facti sunt hostes (Lamentatio III) in ♯ E. & AmVox.PL 8790
　Treviso Cath. Cho.—d'Alessi
　(† Motets of Venetian School I, II, III)

O salutaris hostia
　Vienna Boys' Cho.—Brenn in ♯ EPhi.NBR 6013
　(Ingegneri, Handl, Victoria, etc.)
　　　　　　　　　　(♯ Phi.N 00624R; AmC.ML 4873)

NAUDOT, Jean Jacques　(d. 1762)

Concerto, C major, Op. 17, No. 3　ob. & str.[1]
　A. Lardrot & Leclair Ens.—Paillard ♯ DDP. 21-1
　(Leclair & Boismortier)　　　　　(♯ HS.HSL 103)

Sonata, B minor, Op. 4, No. 1　2 fls. unacc.
　☆ J-P. Rampal, playing both parts († ♯ HS.AS 19)

Trio-Sonata, G major, Op. 7, No. 4　fl., ob. & cont.
　Lutèce Qtt.　　　　　　　V♯ Era.LDE 1021
　(Boismortier)　[fl., ob., hpsi., vlc.]

NAUMANN, Johann Gottlieb　(1741-1801)

Andante & Grazioso, C major
　glass-harmonica, fl., vla. & vlc.　1789
　B. Hoffmann, G. Scheck, E. Seiler & A.
　Wenzinger　　　　　　　　　PV. 9403

NEGREA, Martian　(b. 1893)

In the Western Mountains　Sym. Suite, orch. 1953
　Bucharest Radio—Rogalsky　　Pop. 5038/40
　(6ss)

NEGRI, Cesare　(b. c. 1536 or 1546)

　SEE: † LUTE MUSIC OF THE XVITH & XVIITH CENTURIES

NEUPERT, Edmund　(1842-1888)

　SEE: † SCANDINAVIAN SONGS

NEUSIEDLER, Hans　(1508-1563)
　(or: NEWSIDLER)

　SEE ALSO: † LUTE MUSIC OF XVITH & XVIITH
　　　　　　　CENTURIES
　　　　　　† RENAISSANCE MUSIC FOR THE LUTE
　　　　　　† RENAISSANCE & BAROQUE

LUTE PIECES
　(Nos. 1–7 from Ein neugeordnet künstlich Lautenbuch, 1536;
　　No. 8 from Ein neues Lautenbüchlein, 1544)

1. Preambul　　　　2. Zart schöne Frau
3. Der Bethler Tantz　4. Elslein, liebstes Elslein
5. Nach Willen dein　6. Der Künigin Tantz
7. Wol Kumpt der May　8. Wascha mesa

　W. Gerwig　(2ss)　　　　　PV. 5408
　(Garsi da Parma, on ♯ Pol. 13031)

NEWMAN　(fl. XVIth Cent.)

　SEE: † MASTERS OF EARLY ENGLISH KEYBOARD MUSIC

NICHOLSON, Richard　(d. 1639)

　SEE: † TRIUMPHS OF ORIANA

NICODÉ, Jean Louis　(1853-1919)

Faschingsbilder, Op. 24　Orch. Suite
　Leipzig Radio—Weber　　　♯ Ura. 7122
　(Français)

NICOLAI, Carl Otto E.　(1810-1849)

(Die) LUSTIGEN WEIBER VON WINDSOR
　Opera　3 Acts　1849
COMPLETE RECORDING
　☆ I. S. Stein (S), K. Böhme (Bs), etc., Leipzig Radio
　　Orch.—Kleinert (♯ MTW. 534/5)

HIGHLIGHTS
　E. Köth (S), G. Frick (Bs), D. Fischer-Dieskau (B),
　H. Wilhelm (T), Berlin Municipal Cho. & Orch.
　—Schuchter　　　　　　　♯ G.WBLP 1510
　[Excerpts also below]
　A. Schlemm (S), M. Stader (S), M. Klose (A), W. Ludwig
　(T), E. Wächter (B), K. Borg (Bs) & Bavarian Radio
　Cho. & Orch.—Leitner, etc.　　　♯ Pol. 19049

Overture
　Philharmonia—Kletzki　　　　♭ C.SEL 1541
　(Zampa Overture)　　　　　(in ♯ AmC.RL 3054)
　Bamberg Sym.—Sawallisch　　　PV. 72453
　(Lortzing: Wildschütz, Overture)　　(♭ Pol. 30043)
　Hamburg Philharmonia—H-J. Walther
　　　　　　　　　　　　　MSB. 78132
　Austrian Sym.—Schönherr　in ♯ Rem. 199-129
　Berlin Sym.—List (in ♯ Roy. 1394: ♭ EP 186)
　Opera Orch.—Rossi (in ♯ Mae.OA 20005)
　Polish Radio—Krenz (Muza.X 2334)
　☆ L.P.O.—Boult (♭ G. 7ER 5039: 7ERQ 130: 7RW 138)
　Philharmonia—Fistoulari (in ♯ P.PMC 1031)
　Vienna Sym.—Swarowsky (in ♯ Sup.LPM 225:
　　　　　　　　　　　　　　　U. 5204C)
　Suisse Romande—Olof (♯ D.LW 5008: ♭ DX 1779)
　Rhineland Sym.—Federer (in ♯ AFest.CFR 10-602)
　Vienna Phil.—Furtwängler (♭ Vic.EHA 9)

Nun eilt herbei!　S　Act I
　E. Köth　　　　　　　　G.DB 11581
　(Barbiere, No. 7)　　　　　　(♭ 7RW 541)

Als Büblein klein　Bs & cho.　Act II
　G. Frick & Cho.　　　　　G.EH 1444
　(Lortzing: Waffenschmied—Auch ich war . . .)
　　　　　　　　　　(FKX 261: in ♯ WBLP 1505)
　☆ W. Schirp (AusT.M 5193)
　W. Strienz (♭ Ura.UREP 33)

In einem Waschkorb . . . Wie freu' ich mich
　B & Bs　Act II
　D. Fischer-Dieskau & G. Frick　G.DB 11580
　(2ss)　　　　　　　　　（♭ 7PW 535)
　☆ G. Hann & W. Strienz, from set (♭ Ura.UREP 33)

Horch, die Lerche singt im Hain　T　Act II
　☆ W. Ludwig (in ♯ AmD.DL 4073)

O süsser Mond　Cho.　Act III
　Bavarian Radio Cho.—Leitner in ♯ Pol. 19048
　(Bartered Bride, Don Pasquale, etc.)
　Berlin Municipal Op. Cho.—Schüchter
　　　　　　　　　　　　　G.EH 1455
　(Kreutzer: Nachtlager von Granada, excpt.)
　　　　　　(♭ 7PW 537: in ♯ WDLP 1517)

Wohl denn, gefasst ist der Entschluss　Act III
. . . So schweb' ich dir, Geliebter, zu　S
　A. Schlemm　　　　　　　♭ Pol. 30107
　(Contes d'Hoffmann—Elle a fui . . .)

NICOLAS de la Grotte　(fl. XVIth Cent.)

　SEE: † PARISIAN SONGS OF XVITH CENTURY

NICOLAU, Antonio　(1858-1933)

Cançó de la Morenata　Cho.
　Montserrat Monastery—Pujol　♭ G.7ERL 1012
　(Victoria, etc.)

Salve Montserratina　Cho.
　Montserrat Monastery—Pujol　♭ G.7ERL 1013
　(Victoria, etc.)

NIEDHART VON REUENTHAL　(1180-1240)

　SEE: † RECORDER MUSIC OF SIX CENTURIES
　　　† MUSIC OF THE MIDDLE AGES

---

[1] Op. 17 orig. for viols, musettes, flutes, recorders, 2 vlns. and cont. Realisation: J-F. Paillard.

NIELSEN, Carl August (1865-1931)

ALADDIN
Inc. Music to Oehlenschläger's Play 1918
Orchestral Suite
Oriental Festival March; Aladdin's Dream; Dance of Morning
Mists; Prisoners' Dance; Market Place at Ispahan; Hindu
Dance; Negroes' Dance

Tivoli—Felumb   ♯ **C.KSX 1**
(Lumbye)

Chaconne, Op. 32 pf. 1916
F. Ellegaard   ♯ **D.LW 5051**
(Liszt: Liebestraum & Study)   (♯ *Lon.LD 9065)*
(also, 2ss, Pol.HM 80070)
H. D. Koppel (n.v.)   **G.DB 10513**

Commotio, Op. 58 organ 1931
G. Fjelrad   ♯ **D.LXT 2934**
(Motets, Op. 55)   (♯ *Lon.LL 1030)*

Concerto, cl. & orch., Op. 57 1928
I. Erikson & Danish Radio—Wöldike
     ♯ **D.LXT 2979**
(below)   (♯ *Lon.LL 1124)*
☆ L. Cahuzac & Copenhagen Op.—Frandsen
     (♯ *AmC.ML 2219)*

Concerto, fl. & orch. 1926
G. Jesperson & Danish Radio—Jensen
     ♯ **D.LXT 2979**
(above)   (♯ *Lon.LL 1124)*

Concerto, vln. & orch. Op. 33 1911
☆ Y. Menuhin & Danish Radio—Wöldike ♯ **G.BLP 1025**
(2ss)   (♯ *FBLP 1066)*
(Debussy, Falla, Ravel, on ♯ *Vic.LHMV 22)*

Helios, Op. 17 Concert Overture orch. 1904
Danish State Radio—Tuxen   ♯ **D.LX 3101**
(S. Schultz: Serenade)   (♯ *Lon.LS 653)*

(6) Humoreske-Bagatelles, Op. 11 pf. 1894
(5) Piano pieces, Op. 3 pf. 1890
E. Møller   ♭ *Mtr.MCEP 3005*
... **Op. 11, No. 2, The Spinning-top**
A. Dalring   *Pol.X 51601*
(Riisager & Henriques)

MASQUERADE Opera 3 Acts 1906
Overture; Magdelone's Dance Scene, Act I (ARR.)
Prelude, Act II; Dance of the Cockerels, Act III
Danish Radio—Jensen   ♯ **D.LW 5132**
   (♯ *Lon.LD 9156)*
[Overture only, ♯ D.LXT 2980; Lon.LL 1143, with Sym. 5]
[Overture & Dance of the Cockerels only, Pol.HM 80072]

Dance of the Cockerels, Act III
Covent Garden Op.—Hollingsworth
     ♯ **P.PMC 1021**
(Alfvén, Svendsen, Sibelius)   (♯ MGM.E 3082)

(3) MOTETS, Op. 55 1929
   1. Afflictus sum
   2. Dominus regit me
   3. Benedictus Dominus
Danish Radio Madrigal Cho.—Wöldike
     ♯ **D.LXT 2934**
(Commotio)   (♯ *Lon.LL 1030)*

(The) MOTHER, Op. 41 1920
(Moderen) Inc. Music to Rode's play
No. 3, My maid is so fair *(Min Pige er saa lys som Rav)*
No. 8, So bitter was my heart *(Saa bettert var mit Hjerte)*
☆ A. Schiøtz (T), No. 3 with pf., No. 8 with orch.
     (in ♯ *G.KBLP 10)*

No. 13, Song of the Fatherland orch. & cho.
(Like a fleet about to sail: *Som en rejselysten Flaade)*
— ARR. SOLO VOICE
☆ A. Schiøtz (T) & orch.   *G.X 8147*
(The Danish Song)

(3) Piano pieces, Op. 59 1928
☆ A. S. Rasmussen *(below)*   ♯ *Tono.LPK 32002*

QUARTETS, Strings
No. 1, G minor, Op. 13 1888, rev. 1900
Koppel Qtt. *(No. 2)*   ♯ **Tono.LPA 34006**

No. 2, F minor, Op. 5 (orig. Op. 6) 1890
Musica-Vitalis Qtt.   ♯ **D.LXT 5061**
(V. Holmboe)   (♯ *Lon.LL 1078)*
Koppel Qtt. *(No. 1)*   ♯ **Tono.LPA 34006**

No. 4, F major, Op. 44 1906
Koppel Qtt.   ♯ **D.LXT 5092**
(V. Holmboe)   (♯ *Lon. LL 1119)*
E. Bloch Qtt.   ♯ **G.KALP 7**
(Quintet, Op. 43)

Quintet, A major, Op. 43 fl., ob., cl., hrn., bsn. 1922
Copenhagen Wind Quintet (n.v.) ♯ **D.LXT 2803**
(Ibert & Bozza)   (♯ *Lon.LL 734)*
J. Bentzon, W. Wolsing, P. A. Eriksen, I.
   Michelsen, C. Bloch   ♯ **G.KALP 7**
(Quartet No. 4)
☆ Copenhagen Wind Quintet (o.v.)   ♯ Mer.MG 15046
(Schultz)

SONATAS, vln. & pf.
No. 1, A major, Op. 9 1895
E. Telmanyi & V. Schiøler   ♯ **G.KALP 6**
(below)

No. 2, G minor, Op. 35 1912
E. Telmanyi & V. Schiøler   ♯ **G.KALP 6**
(above)
T. Nielsen & C. Christiansen ♮ Tono.X 25186/7
(4ss)   *(Suite, pf. on* ♯ *LPA 34005)*

SONGS
COLLECTION
Green are Spring's hedges (Møller)[1]
In the sun I go behind my plough, Op. 10, No. 4
   (L. Holstein) *(I Solen gaar jeg bag min Plov)*
Irmelin Rose, Op. 4, No. 4 (J. P. Jacobsen)
SPRING IN FUNEN, Op. 42 Cycle (Berntsen)
   ... The mild day is bright and long
     (Den milde Dag er lys og lang)
The Stonebreaker, Op. 21, No. 3 (Aakjaer) *(Jens Vejmand)*
Summer Song, Op. 10 No. 3 (L. Holstein)
This evening, Op. 10, No. 5 *(I Aften)* (L. Holstein)
With a smile I bear my burden (Aakjaer)
   (Jeg baerer med Smil min Byrde)
Wondrous evening breezes (Oehlenschläger)[2]
   (Underlige Aftenlufte)
☆ A. Schiøtz (T) *(The Mother)*   ♯ *G.KBLP 10*

(The) Danish Song (Kai Hoffmann)
   (Den danske Sang)
A. Schiøtz (T) & orch.   *G.X 8147*
(The Mother—No. 13)

God's angels in a host (Grundtvig)[3]
   (Guds engle i flok)
E. Nørby (Bs), P. Alsfelt (org.)   *Tono.K 8079*
(Balle: Christmas Song)

Green are spring's hedges (Møller)[1]
J. Wahl (T), B. Bergreen (pf.)   *Pol.X 51670*
(The mild day ...)

I lay me down to sleep (Chr. Winther)[1]
   (Jeg laegger mig saa trygt til Ro)
E. M. Jeppesen (M-S), K. Olsson (pf.) *Felix.B 78*
(Laub: Song)

I know a lark's nest (H. Bergstedt)
   (Jeg ved en Laerkerede)
R. Teglbærg (M-S) (in Felix.X 80)

Irmelin Rose, Op. 4, No. 4 (J. P. Jacobsen)
P. Torntoft (Tr.), E. Vagning (pf.) *Phi.P 55015H*
(Laub: It is white outside)

My Jesus, take my heart[3] (Grundtvig)
   (Min Jesus, end mit hjerte få)
E. Nørby (Bs), R. Østerfelt (org.) *Tono.K 8096*
(Wonderful to tell)

See you on a summer day[4] (Aakjaer)
E. Nørby (Bs), G. Nørby (pf.)   *Tono.K 8092*
(You are setting out)

---

[1] From 10 Danish Songs *(Danske Smaasange)*.   [2] From *Danske Viser*, Book I.
[3] From *Hymns & Sacred Songs*, 1912-16.
[4] From *Danske Viser*, Book II.

SPRING IN FUNEN, Op. 42
Song Cycle   (Berntsen)
... **The mild day is bright and long**
(*Den milde Dag er lys og lang*)
J. Wahl (T), B. Berggreen (pf.)　　*Pol.X 51670*
(*Green are spring's hedges*)

Vocalise-Étude   1927
G. Fleischer (S), K. Olsson (pf.)   *Phi.N 56001H*
(*Heise: Forest loneliness*)

With a smile I bear my burden   (Aakjaer)
Wondrous evening breezes[2]   (Oehlenschläger)
P. Torntoft (Tr.), E. Vagning (pf.)　*Phi.P 55014H*

Wonderful to tell   (Brorson)
(*Forundlight at sige*)
E. Nørby (Bs), R. Østerfelt (org.)   *Tono.K 8096*
(*My Jesus take my heart,*)

You are setting out on the road of life[2]
(*Ud går du på livets vej*)   (St. Blicher)
E. Nørby (Bs), G. Nørby (pf.)　　*Tono.K 8092*
(*See you on a summer's day*)

Suite, Op. 45   pf.   1919
A. S. Rasmussen　　　　　♯ **Tono.LPA 34005**
(*Vln. Sonata No. 2*)　　(also, 6ss, ♮ Tono.A 189/91)

Suite for Strings, Op. 1   1888
☆ Danish Radio—Tuxen　　　　♮ C.DX 8401/2

Symphonic Suite, Op. 8   pf.   1892
H. D. Koppel   (*below*)　　　　♯ **G.KBLP 5**

SYMPHONIES
No. 5, Op. 50   1922
Danish Radio—Jensen　　　　♯ **D.LXT 2980**
(*Masquerade, Overture*)　　　　(♯ Lon.LL 1143)

No. 6   (Sinfonia semplice)   1924-5
☆ Danish State Radio—Jensen　　♯ Tono.LPX 35004

Theme & Variations, Op. 40   pf.   1916
H. D. Koppel (n.v.)　　　　　♯ **G.KBLP 5**
(*above*)
☆ A. S. Rasmussen   (*above*)　　♯ *Tono.LPK 32002*

NIGRINO, Nicolo   (fl. XVIth Cent.)
SEE: † RENAISSANCE MUSIC FOR THE LUTE

NIKOLAYEVA, Tatiana Petrovna
(b. 1924)
Concerto No. 1, pf. & orch.
☆ T. Nikolayeva & U.S.S.R. State Sym.—Kondrashin
(*Babadzhanyan*)　　　　　♯ USSR.D 0264
(*Prokofiev & Tchaikovsky*, on ♯ Csm.CRLP 221)

NIN Y CASTELLANOS, Joaquin
(1879-1949)
PIANO MUSIC
Homenaje a la jota; Serenata
☆ G. Copeland (in ♯ MGM.E 3025)

Iberian Dance No. 1   1926
W. Masselos　　　　　　♯ **MGM.E 3165**
(*Albeniz, Surinach, Turina*)

Rapsodia ibérica   vln. & pf.   1930
T. Magyar & W. Hielkema　　♯ *Phi.S 06049R*
(*Falla, Albeniz, etc.*)

SONGS: (20) Cantos de España   [CE]   1923
COLLECTIONS
Asturiana　　　[CE. 14]
Paño murciano　　[CE. 15]
El Vito　　　[CE. 18]
Canto andaluz　　[CE. 19]
TRANSCRIPTIONS:
Anon. (*c.* 1786): El amor es come un niño
B. de LASERNA (1740-1799): Las majas madrilenas
I. Kolassi (M-S), A. Collard (pf.)   ♯ *D.LW 5143*
(*arr. Koeckert: Granadina & Serrana*)　(♯ Lon.LD 9142)

El Vito　　　[CE. 18]
Montañesa　　　[CE. 4]
Granadina　　　[CE. 7]
G. Souzay (B), D. Baldwin (pf.)
　　　　　　　♭ *ArgLon.DLCE 6501*
(*Ginastera, Guastavino, López-Buchardo*)

Granadina　　　[CE. 7]
Paño murciano　　[CE. 15]
El Vito　　　[CE. 18]
☆ A. M. Iriarte (M-S), R. Machado (pf.) (♭ *Pat.ED 16*)

Paño murciano　　[CE. 15]
El Vito　　　[CE. 18]
V. de los Angeles (S), G. Moore (pf.) *G.DA 2046*
(*ArgA. 292702;* in ♯ G.ALP 1151: FALP 327: LALP 142)
[Paño murciano only, in ♯ Vic. set LM 6017]
M. Plaza (S) (in ♯ Roy. 1561)

SONGS
Asturiana.   [CE 14]   — ARR. VLN. & PF.   Levy
"*Cantilène asturienne*"
☆ J. Heifetz (in ♯ G.ALP 1206: FALP 248)

Canto andaluz   [CE. 19]
R. Gomez (M-S), P. Vallribera (pf.) *Reg.C 10281*
(*below*)　　　　　　　(♭ *SEDL 19042*)

Granadina   [CE. 7]
L. Ibarrondo (M-S), M. Sandoval (pf.)
　　　　　　　in ♯ **Rem. 199-139**
　　　　　　　(♯ Cum. CR. 297)
— ARR. VLC. & PF.
P. Fournier & E. Lush　　　in ♯ **D.LXT 2766**
　　　　　　　(in ♯ Lon.LL 700)
A. Janigro & E. Bagnoli (in ♯ West.WN 18004)

Malagueña   [CE. 6]
R. Gomez (M-S), P. Vallribera (pf.) *Reg.C 10281*
(*above*)　　　　　　　(♭ *SEDL 19042*)

TRANSCRIPTION of Tonadilla
LASERNA: **(Los) AMANTES CHASQUEADOS**
... **El Jilguera del pico de oro**　　　　1779
V. de los Angeles (S), C. J. Chiasson (hpsi.)
　　　　　　　in ♯ **Vic.LM 1802**
　　　　　　　(& in ♯ Vic. set LM 6017)

Suite espagnole   — ARR. VLN. & PF.   Kochanski
1. **Montañesa**　　　2. **Tonada murciana**
3. **Invocation (Saeta)**　　(*Tonada del Conde Sol*)
4. **Granadina**
R. Odnoposoff & J. Antonietti ♯ CHS.CHS 1175
(*Falla & Ysaye*)

NIXON, Roger   (b. 1921)

Chinese Seasons
L. Bohn (S), F. P. McKnight (pf.)   ♯ **ML. 5005**[5]

Quartet No. 1   str.
▽ ☆ California Qtt.   (*Moore*)　　♯ **ML. 7005**

NORCOME, Daniel   (1576-1625)
SEE: † TRIUMPHS OF ORIANA

NOORDT, Anthony van
SEE: VAN NOORDT

NORTH, Alex   (b. 1910)

Death of a Salesman   Inc. Music[6]
In Complete Recording of play: ♯ B.LAT 8007/8;
　　　　　　　AmD. set DX 102
Holyday Set   orch.   1947
Vienna State Philharmonia—Adler　♯ **SPA. 47**
(*Antheil, Cowell, etc.*)

(The) Rose Tattoo   Film Music[7]
Orch.—North (in ♯ AmC.CL 727)

(A) Streetcar named desire   Film music[7]
▽ Selection from sound-track in ♯ DCap.LC 6542: ♯ Cap.L 289
& P 387: ♭ set FBF 289: ♮ set DDN 289: etc.

---

[2] From *Danske Viser*, Book I.
[6] For the play by Arthur Miller.
[5] Announced but perhaps not issued.
[7] For the film version of play by Tennessee Williams.

NOVÁK, Vitězslav   (1870-1949)

(The) Eternal Longing, Op. 33   Sym. Poem.   1904
☆ Czech Phil.—Šejna   ♯ Sup.LPV 68
   (R. Strauss: Till Eulenspiegel)   (♯ U. 5103G)

In the Tatra, Op. 26   Sym. Poem   1902
☆ Czech Phil.—Ančerl   ♯ Sup.LPV 211
   (below)   (♯ U. 5194H)
   (Miaskovsky, on ♯ Csm.CRLP 214)

Reisl's Polka, Op. 55, No. 21   1920
☆ Film Sym.—Strniště (in ♯ U. 5215H)

Slovak Suite, Op. 32   1903
Czech Phil.—Talich   ♯ Sup.LPV 211
   (above)   (♯ U. 5194H)

Sonata eroica, Op. 24   pf.   1900
☆ F. Rauch (♯ Sup.LPM 55; U. 5046C)

NYAZI, Taki   (b. 1912)

Lezghinka   orch.
   U.S.S.R. State—Nyazi (2ss)   USSR. 19301/2

Rast   Sym. mugam, orch.
▽ Czech Phil.—Nyazi   ♯ Sup.LPM 34
   (Liadov)
   (& in ♯ Csm.CRLP 10070; & 5ss, ♮ U.C 23849/51S)

NYSTROEM, Gösta   (b. 1890)

(The) MERCHANT OF VENICE   Inc. Music
Orchestral Suite   (Theatre suite No. 4)
   Prelude; Burlesque; Nocturne (Frescobaldiana); Masques

SONGS AT THE SEASIDE   1943   (Swedish)
1. Out in the skerries   (Lindquist)
2. Nocturne   (Sodergran)
3. The Song of the Sea   (Gullberg)
4. I have my home at the sea   (Jändel)
5. I await the moon   (Gullberg)
   A. Rautawaara (S, in songs), Stockholm Radio
   Orch.—Mann   ♯ SS. 33103
                                      (♯ West.WN 18147)

OBOUSSIER, Robert   (b. 1900)

Antigone   A. & orch.   1938-9
   (Recit., Aria, Elegy)   (after Sophocles)
   E. Cavelti & Suisse Romande—Ansermet
                                     ♯ D.LXT 5097
   (Geiser)   (♯ Lon.LL 1265)

OBRADORS, Fernando J.   (1897-1945)

SONGS
Corazon porque pasais
El majo celoso   (from Tonadillas, XVIIIth Cent.)
Con amores, la mi madre   (J. Anchieta)
2 Cantares populares   (Trad.)
El Vito   (pop. song, c. 1800)
   N. Merriman (M-S), G. Moore (pf.)
                                     in ♯ C.CX 1243
   († Spanish Songs)   (♯ FCX 392; Angel. 35208)
Del Cabello más sutil
Molondrón
El Vito
   L. Ibarrondo (M-S), M. Sandoval (pf.)
                                     in ♯ Rem. 199-139
   (Granados, Guridi, etc.)   (♯ Cum.CR 297)
(2) Cantares populares
   ▽ B. Sayão (S) (in ♯ AmC.ML 4154)
Coplas de curro dulce
   ▽ J. Tourel (M-S), G. Reeves (pf.) (in ♯ AmC.ML 2198)
Del Cabello más sutil
   M. Plaza (M-S)   in ♯ Roy. 1561
   (Nin, Turina, etc.)
   N. Chayres (T), F. Kramer (pf.)   in ♯ Kings.KL 300
Chiquilla (El Beso)
   M. Powers (A), F. la Forge (pf.) in ♯ Atl. 1207
   (Duparc, Fauré, etc.)

ZARZUELA: LA CAMPANA ROTA
Vocal excerpts ▽ E. Sargi-Barba, etc. (G.AC 139/40)

OBRECHT, Jakob   (c. 1450-1505)

BALLADES & CHANSONS
Den Haghel ende die calde snee   (Ballade)
Ic weinsche all vrowen eere   (Chanson de Nouvel-an)
   ☆ Netherlands Vocal Qtt. (in † ♯ HS.AS 5)
En fröhlich Wesen
   ☆ F. Peeters (org.) (in † ♯ Cpt.MC 20069)
La Tortorella
   Netherlands Cha. Cho. (in † Sacred & Secular Songs ...)
Tsat een meskin
   ☆ Pro Musica Antiqua Ens. (in † ♯ HS.AS 4)

SACRED MUSIC
MASS: Maria zart . . . Credo, excerpts
(Qui propter nos; Et incarnatus est)
   ☆ Paraphonistes—de Van (in † ♯ HS.AS 4)

Parce Domine   motet
   Copenhagen Boys' & Men's Cho.—Møller
                                 in ♯ HS.HSL 2071
   († Masterpieces of Music before 1750)
   (& in † Histoire de la Musique vocale)
   Netherlands Chamber Cho.—Nobel
                                 in ♯ Phi.N 00678R
   († Sacred & Secular Songs)   (in ♯ Epic.LC 3045)

Si oblitus fuero tui
   Schola Polyphonica—Washington   G.HMS 27
   († History of Music in Sound)   (in ♯ Vic. set LM 6106)

OFFENBACH, Jacques   (1819-1880)

CLASSIFIED: I. Operettas
               II. Les Contes d'Hoffmann
               III. Miscellaneous

I. OPERETTAS
(abridged listings only)

BARBE-BLEU   3 Acts   1866
Orchestral Selection
   R.I.A.S. Sym.—Rosenthal (in ♯ Rem. 199-183)

Orch. Suite   — ARR. Dorati (for Fokine's Ballet,
   1941)
   Ballet Theatre—Levine   ♯ DCap.CTL 7082
   (below)   (♯ Cap.P 8277)

Overture
   N.W. German Phil.—Schüchter ♯ Imp.ILP 111
   (Belle Hélène, etc., & J. Strauss)

(La) BELLE HÉLÈNE   3 Acts   1865
COMPLETE RECORDING
   ☆ J. Linda (S), A. Dran (T), etc., Paris Phil. Cho.
      & Orch.—Leibowitz
         (♯ Cpt. set MCM 120006; o.n. ♯ Clc. 6140/1)
   [Abridged version on ♯ Nix.PLP 251; Cpt.MC 120008]
   (also ♯ MMS. set OP 19, 4ss)

ABRIDGED RECORDING in Russian
   Soloists & Moscow Radio Cho. & Orch.—Akulov
                                     ♯ USSR.D 1770/3

Vocal Selection
   M. Hansen, E. Söderström, H. Funck, A. Andersson, etc.
   (Swed—4ss)   T.SK 19854/5

Excerpts   — ARR. Dorati (for Lichine's ballet, 1942)
   SEE Miscellaneous, below

Overture
   Los Angeles Phil.—Wallenstein   ♯ B.AXL 2014
   (Orphée aux Enfers, Overture)   (♯ D.UA 243585;
                                      AmD.DL 4095; AFest.CFR 10-716)
   Belgian Radio—Marinetti   ♯ Mae.OA 20011
   (Contes d'Hoffmann; & J. Strauss II)
   N.W. Ger. Phil.—Schüchter   ♯ Imp.ILP 111
   (Barbe-Bleu, etc.)
   French Nat. Radio—Allain (in ♯ Roy. 1628)
   H. Hagestedt Orch. (♭ Phi.KD 150)
   ☆ L.P.O.—Martinon (♯ D.LW 5027)
   Tivoli—Felumb (♭ Mer.EP 1-5037)
   Boston Prom.—Fiedler (in ♯ Cam.CAL 122: ♭ CAE 102)

Amours divins, ardentes flammes, Act I
Un mari sage, Act II
   ☆ D. Dassy (from set) (♭ Pat.D 109)

Au Mont Ida   (Jugement de Paris)   T
   ☆ C. Devos, from set (♭ Pat.ED 35)
   J. Björling (Swed) (G.EC 214)

♯ = Long-playing, 33⅓ r.p.m.   ♭ = 45 r.p.m.   ♮ = Auto. couplings, 78 r.p.m.

(La) FILLE DU TAMBOUR-MAJOR 3 Acts 1879
Orch. Selection R.I.A.S.—Rosenthal (in ‡ Rem. 199-183)

(La) GRANDE DUCHESSE DE GEROLSTEIN
Orch. Selection R.I.A.S.—Rosenthal (in ‡ Rem. 199-183)

Overture French Nat. Radio—Allain   in ‡ Roy. 1628

GENEVIÈVE DE BRABANT 2 Acts 1859 rev. 1875
Overture ☆ Rhineland—Federer (in ‡ AFest.CFR 37)

ORPHÉE AUX ENFERS 2 Acts 1858-74

COMPLETE RECORDING[1]
 ☆ Soloists, Paris Phil. Cho. & Orch.—Leibowitz
 (‡ Cpt. set MCM 120007; Excerpts on ‡ Nix.PLP 251;
     Cpt.MC 120008)

ABRIDGED RECORDING
 C. Collard (S), C. Devos (T), M. Roux (Bs), etc., R. St. Paul
 Cho. & Lamoureux Orch.—Gressier
                                  ‡ AmVox.PL 21200
                                     (‡ Pat.DTX 142)
Vocal Selections (Danish)
 G. Gilboe, H. Kurt & Orch.—Ase
                           (Od.DK 1354: ♭ GEDK 116)
Overture[2]
 Los Angeles Phil.—Wallenstein **‡ B.AXL 2014**
 (Belle Hélène, Overture)   (‡ D.UA 243585;
                        AmD.DL 4095; AFest.CFR 10-716)

 Hollywood Bowl—Barnett   in ‡ Cap.P 8296
 (Ponchielli, Saint-Saëns, etc.)   (♭ set FAP 8296)

 Brussels Radio—André   ‡ DT.TM 68026
 (Suppé: Dichter und Bauer, Overture)   (TV.VE 9019;
     ♭ UX 4507: in ‡ LSK 7019; ‡ FT. 320.C.028, d.c.)

 U.R.C. Sym.—Marinetti (in ‡ Mae.OA 20010)
 Leipzig Radio—Dobrindt (Eta. 140029)
 H. Hagestedt Orch. (♭ Phi.KD 150)
 ☆ L.P.O.—Martinon (‡ D.LW 5027 & D.KD 2444)
   Boston Prom.—Fiedler (in ‡ G.DLP 1079;
                       ‡ Vic.LRM 7035: ♭ set ERB 7035)
   Philharmonia—Weldon (in ‡ C.SX 1032;
                                  ‡ AmC.RL 3072)
   L.P.O.—Lambert (in ‡ Cam.CAL 242 &
                                in ‡ set CFL 103)
   Strauss Orch.—Lanner (‡ MGM.E 3032: D 123;
              ‡ FMGM.F 6-114; ItMGM.QD 6017)
— ARR. ORGAN
 R. Foort, sub nom. M. Cheshire (in ‡ SOT. 1051 &
                                       in ‡ 10501)
Galop infernal Act IV
 Orch.—Rosenthal   in ‡ AmVox.PL 7170
Quadrille; Scherzo
 French Nat. Radio—Allain (in ‡ Roy. 1628)
 Pasdeloup—Allain (♭ Plé.P 45154)
Can-Can
 M.G.M. Orch.—Marrow (in ‡ MGM.E 3136)
 Concert Orch.—Robinson (in ‡ Argo.RG 40;
                                 West.WP 6002)
 Orch.—Swarowsky (in ‡ MTW. 9)

(La) PÉRICHOLE 2 Acts 1868
Air de la lettre: O mon cher amant S
 ✠ E. Calvé (IRCC. 3119*)

(La) VIE PARISIENNE 5 Acts 1866
ABRIDGED RECORDINGS
Baron Gardefeu	M. Hamel (T)
Baron Gondremarck	M. Roux (Bs)
Gabriella	N. Renaux (S)
Baroness de Quimper ...	L. Dachary (S)
Metella	D. Dassy (S)
A Rich Brazilian	
Frick	W. Clément (B)
Prosper	

 etc. & Lamoureux Orch.—Gressier
                                 ‡ AmVox.PL 21000
 (Highlights on ♭ AmVox.VIP 30080)   (‡ Pat.DTX 128)
 [Vocal excerpts: D. Dassy on ♭ Pat.D 109,
                              & N. Renaux on ♭ Pat.ED 22]

 M. Bach (S), G. Franke (T), H. Wilhelm (B),
 Cho. & Orch.—Berendt (Ger) ‡ Allo. 3078
 [Excerpts on ♭ Roy.EP 227] ‡ AFest.CFR 12-223;
                                   MusH.LP 3005)
Orchestral Selections
 R.I.A.S. Sym.—Rosenthal (in ‡ Rem. 199-183)
 French Nat. Radio—Allain (in ‡ Roy. 1628)
Quadrille
 French Nat. Radio—Allain (in ‡ Roy. 1628)
 Pasdeloup—Allain (♭ Plé.P 45154)

II. OPERA

(Les) CONTES D'HOFFMANN
3 or 4 Acts 1881
COMPLETE RECORDINGS
 ☆ R. Jobin (T), R. Doria (S), V. Bovy (S), Géori-Boué (S),
   etc., Opéra-Comique Cho. & Orch.—Cluytens
                                   ‡ C.CX 1150/2
 ☆ W. Horst (T), H. Schenk (B), E. Kovatsky (S), I.
   Camphausen (S), etc., Dresden State Op. Cho. &
   Orch.—List (or Rubahn) (Ger) (‡ Gram. 20154/6)

ABRIDGED RECORDING in German
 ☆ E. Berger, P. Anders, etc., Berlin Radio Cho. & Orch.
   —Rother (‡ MTW. 548/9)

HIGHLIGHTS in German
 R. Streich (S), R. Schock (T), J. Metternich (B), S. Wagner
 (A), M. Klose (A), Berlin Municipal Op. Cho. & Orch.
 —Schüchter   ‡ G.WBLP 1506
 K. Nentwig (S), A. Schlemm (S), G. Hoffman (S), W.
 Ludwig (T), O. Wiener (B), Bavarian Radio Cho. &
 Württemberg State Op. Cho.   ‡ Pol. 17049
 State Op. Cho. & Orch. (‡ Roy. 6131; Var. 6978;
                          Excerpts on ♭ Roy.EP 150)

COLLECTED EXCERPTS
Je me nomme Coppélius ... J'ai des yeux B Act II
Les oiseaux dans la charmille S Act II
Scintille, diamant B   Act III
Elle a fui, la tourterelle S Act IV
 J. Micheau (S), R. Bianco (B), Opéra-Comique
 Orch.—Wolff   ‡ LI.TW 91132
 (Barbiere & Tosca)   (‡ D.FAT 173665)
Vocal Selections (English)
 ☆ Soloists, Sadler's Wells Cho. & Royal Phil.—Beecham
                            (♮ JpV. set JAS 262: ‡ LF 4)
Orch. Excerpts: Minuet, Intermezzo, Barcarolle
Scintille diamant B
 P. Schœffler (B, Ger) & Orch.—Schönherr
 (‡ AFest.CFR 56: ♭ ECR 99; Intermezzo & Minuet
 only, on ♭ Rem.REP 69; Intermezzo only, ‡ Ply. 12-89;
 Minuet only, in ‡ Ply. 12-82 & 12-94)
Orch. Excerpts: Minuet, Intermezzo & Waltz
French Nat. Radio—Allain   in ‡ Roy. 1628
Orch. Selection C. Dumont Orch. (BrzEli.X 359)

ACT I

Dans les rôles d'amoureux B
 M. Singer (below)   in ‡ Roy. 1613
Il était une fois à la cour d'Eisenach T
 F. Vroons   in ‡ Phi.N 00706R
 (Manon, Werther, etc.)
 I. Kozlovsky (Russ) & Cho. USSRM.D 001219
 [includes N. Postavnitseva as Niklausse]
 R. Schock (Ger, from Highlights)
                             in ‡ G.WBLP 1515
 ☆ G. Lauri-Volpi (AF.AGSA 28)
   J. Patzak (Ger) (D.K 23315)
Intermezzo—Minuet
 ☆ Austrian Sym.—Schönherr (♭ Rem.REP 69)

ACT II

Allons! courage et confiance ... C'est elle
Ah! vivre deux T
 ☆ J. Patzak (Ger) (D.K 23315)
 ✠ C. Dalmores (AF.AGSA 7* & in ‡ SBDH.GL 1*)
Je me nomme Coppélius ... Chacun de ces
 lorgnons ...
J'ai des yeux Bs
 M. Singer   in ‡ Roy. 1613
 (above; Roi de Lahore, Jongleur de Notre-Dame, etc.)
 ☆ A. Pernet (in ‡ OD.ODX 135)
Les oiseaux dans la charmille (Doll Song) S
 P. Alarie   in ‡ Phi.N 00663R
 (Delibes, Gounod, etc.)
 R. Streich (Ger)   ♭ G.7RW 514
 (below)
 A. Hrušovska (Cz)   in ‡ U. 5176C
 ☆ L. Pons   in ‡ Od.OD 1013
 E. Spoorenberg   ♭ Phi.N 402009E
 J. Micheau   ♭ D. 71086
                     (continued on next page)

---

[1] The original prelude is played, not the Carl Binder version.   [2] Actually composed by C. Binder.

HOFFMANN—Doll Song (*continued*)

— ARR. ORCH.
 ☆ Cincinnati Summer Op.—Cleva (in ♯ *B.*AXTL *1035*;
  D.UST *233087*; AmD.DL *8053*: ♭ *ED 3525*, etc.)

Finale: Waltz   Cho. & orch.
 H. Sandauer Orch. (♭ *Phi.KD 154*)

ACT III

Belle nuit, O nuit d'amour
 S, M-S, & wordless Cho. (*Barcarolle*)
 R. Streich, S. Wagner & Berlin Municipal
  Op. Cho.—Schüchter (*Ger*)   **G.DB 11564**
  (*below*) (*above* on ♭ *7RW 514*)   (♭ *7RW 540*)
 M. Ganz, D. Eustrati & Cho. (*Ger*) *Eta. 225025*
 (*Zigeunerbaron—Werberlied*)
 ☆ G. Brouwenstijn, L. v. d. Veen & Netherlands Op. Cho.
  (*below; Faust, Louise*)   ♯ *Phi.S 06025R*

— ARR. SOLO
 L. Cortese (S) & pf. (in ♯ *ERC. 101*)[1]
 ☆ R. Stevens (M-S), M. Elman (vln.) & pf.
            (*BrzV. 886-5011*)
 ⊞ E. Calvé (S) (in ♯ *HRS. 3008**)

— ARR. CHO.
 ☆ Luton Girls' Cho. (*Eng*) (♭ *P.BSP 3002*)

— ARR. ORCH. (*inter alia*)
 Philharmonia—Karajan   in ♯ **C.CX 1265**
 (*Thaïs, Hary János, etc.*) (♯ Angel. 35207; C.QCX 10150:
            FCX 407)
 Boston Prom.—Fiedler   in ♯ *Vic.LRM 7045*
         (♭ set *ERB 7045*)
 Belgian Cha.—Marinetti (in ♯ *Mae.OA 20011*)[2]
 N.W. Ger. Phil.—Schüchter (in ♯ *Imp.ILP 111*;
      Od.O-29002: ♭ *OBL 29002*)
 Linz Sym. (in ♯ *Ply 12-31*)
 Mantovani Orch. (D.F *10183*: F *43655*: in ♯ *LF 1161*;
            ♯ *Lon.LL 877*)
 Orch.—Ase (♭ *Od.GEOK 116*)
 ☆ Austrian Sym.—Schönherr (in ♯ *Rem. 199-115*;
            Ply. 12-58 & 12-60)
  Suisse Romande—Olof (♭ *D.DX 1722*)
  Hollywood Bowl—Stokowski (in ♯ *Cam.CAL 153*)
  Strauss Orch.—Lanner (in ♯ *MGM.D 123*: in ♯ E *3032*;
           ♯ *FMGM.F 6-114*)
— ARR. ORGAN
 R. Ellsasser (in ♯ *MGM.E 198*: ♭ set *X 198*)

Scintille diamant   B
 J. Metternich (*Ger*)   **G.DB 11564**
 (*above*)   (♭ *7RW 540*: in ♯ *WBLP 1504*)
 ☆ T. Baylé   ♯ *Phi.S 06025R*
  (*Barcarolle; Faust & Louise*)
 ☆ A. Pernet   in ♯ *Od.ODX 135*
  L. Warren   in ♯ Vic. set LCT 6701
  R. Merrill   ♭ *Vic.ERA 107*
 ⊞ M. Journet   in ♯ *SBDH.JALP 19**

O Dieu! de quelle ivresse   T
 ▽ J. Peerce (*Ger*) (in ♯ *Roy. 1256 & 1213*)
 ☆ M. Villabella (in ♯ *Od.ODX 136*)
 ⊞ C. Dalmores (*AF.AGSA 7**)

ACT IV

Elle a fui, la tourterelle   S
 A. Schlemm (*Ger*)   ♭ *Pol. 30107*
 (*Lustigen Weiber von Windsor, aria*)

IV. MISCELLANEOUS

Bouffes parisiens (ARR. Mohaupt)
 Orch.—Swarowsky   ♯ **MTW. 28**
 (*Rodgers: Symphonic Suite*)
 (*J. Strauss* on ♯ *ACC.MP 9*)

Can-Can Melodies
 R.I.A.S. Sym.—Rosenthal (in ♯ *Rem. 199-189*)

Gaîté Parisienne   Ballet   — ARR. Rosenthal
 Covent Garden—Susskind   ♯ *G.DLP 1051*
 (2ss)   (♯ *FFLP 1044*)
 (*J. Strauss* on ♯ *BB.LBC 1065*: ♭ set *WBC 1065*)
 Philadelphia—Ormandy   ♯ **EPhi.NBL 5019**
 (*Chopin*)   (♯ AmC.CL *741*, o.n. ML *4895*: ♭ *A 1920*)
 (also, n.v., 2ss, ♯ AmC.KL *5069*)[3] (2ss, ♯ *Phi.S 06606R*)

Boston Prom.—Fiedler (n.v.)   ♯ **Vic.LM 1817**
 (*Meyerbeer*)   (♯ ItV.A12R 0076)
 [Excerpts, *Vic. 20-6028*: ♭ set *ERB 1817*: ♭ 49-6028]
 R.I.A.S. Sym.—Rosenthal   ♯ **Rem. 199-172**
         (♯ Cum.CR 304)
 ☆ Boston Prom.—Fiedler (o.v.)   ♯ **G.CLP 1004**
 [Excerpts in ♭ *Vic.ERA 82* & ♭ set *ERB 13*] (♯ FLLP 102)
 — ABRIDGED ☆ Col. Sym.—Kurtz (♭ *AmC.* set *A 1048*;
       excerpts, ♭ *A 1707*: & *J 216*: ♭ *J 4-216*)

Helen of Troy   Ballet Suite   — ARR. Dorati
 for Lichine's ballet, 1942 (mainly from *La Belle Hélène*)
 Ballet Theatre—Levine   ♯ **DCap.CTL 7082**
 (*above*)   (♯ Cap.P 8277)
 ☆ Minneapolis Sym.—Dorati   ♯ **Vic.LM 9033**
 (*Rosenkavalier, Suite*)   (♯ ItV.A12R 007)

Improvisations on Offenbach   pf. 4 hands
 (ARR. Templeton)
 A. Templeton (duet with himself)   ♯ **Rem. 199-158**
 (*J. Strauss*)

Offenbach Fantasy   — ARR. Stolz
 ☆ Vienna Sym.—Stolz   ♯ **D.LK 4077**
 (*Tchaikovsky*)   (♯ Lon.LL 868)

Offenbachiana
 R.I.A.S. Sym—Rosenthal   ♯ **Rem. 199-183**
 French Nat. Radio—Allain   ♯ **Roy. 1628**

OGINSKI, Michael Cleophas
(1765–1833)

Polonaise, G major
 ☆ W. Landowska (hpsi.) (♭ *Vic.ERA 128*)

OHANA, Maurice   (b. 1914)

Llanto por Ignacio Sanchez Mejias (Lorca) 1950
 Diction, B, cho. & orch.
 M. Molho, B. Cottret & Cento Soli Cho. &
  Orch.—Argenta
Concerto, Guitar & Orch.   1950
 ... Sarabande   — ARR. HPSI. & ORCH.   Ohana
 D. Gouarne & Centi Soli—Argenta ♯ **CFD. 23**

OKEGHEM, Jean de   (c. 1430-1495)

CHANSONS
(Les) Desleaux ont la saison   MS, Dijon
 M. Rollin Ensemble   in ♯ *LI.W 91116*
 († *Music from Middle Ages*)   (♯ *D.FS 123632*)

Ma Maîtresse
 B. de Pauw (T) & insts.   in ♯ *LOL.OL 50104*
 († *Musiciens de la Cour de Bourgogne*) (♯ OL.LD 80)
 ☆ M. Meili (T) & insts. (in † ♯ *HS.AS 4*)

Prenez sur moi
 — ARR. ORG. Peeters "*Fuga trium vocum*"
 F. Peeters († ♯ *Cpt.MC 20069*)

MASSES
"Fors seulement" ... Kyrie only
 Renaissance Singers—Howard   **G.HMS 26**
 († *History of Music in Sound*)   (in ♯ Vic. set LM 6016)

Missa prolationum
 Fleetwood Singers[4]   ♯ **Kings.KL 221**

 ... Sanctus (first section only)
 Copenhagen Boys' & Men's Cho.—Møller
        in ♯ **HS.HSL 2071**
 († *Masterpieces of Music before 1750*)
 (also in † *Histoire de la Musique vocale ...*)

"Sine Nomine" ... Kyrie & Gloria
 Netherlands Cha. Cho.—Nobel
        in ♯ *Phi.N 00678R*
 († *Sacred & Secular Songs*)
 (in ♯ Epic.LC 3045, partly d.c.;
        & also ♯ *Phi.S 06026R*, d.c.)

---

[1] Sung twice, in *Fr* and *Eng*.   [2] Includes Entr'acte.
[3] Said to be the full ballet; the o.v. is a Suite only, as are a number of other recordings.
[4] Recorded from a performing edition prepared by H. Maiben from the complete edn. Vol. II, No. 10, ed. Plamenac.

OLDHAM, Arthur (b. 1926)

Variation on an Elizabethan tune (Sellinger's Round) orch.[1] 1953
Aldeburgh Fest.—Britten   in # **D.LXT 2798**
(*Berkeley, Britten, Searle, Tippett, Walton*) (# Lon.LL 808)

ONSLOW, George (1784-1853)

Quintet, F major, Op. 81 fl., ob., cl., hrn., bsn.
French Wind Quintet   # **LOL.OL 50049**
(*below*)   (# OL.LD 107)
New Art Wind Quintet   # **CEd.CE 2020**
(*Klughardt*)

Septet, B flat major, Op. 79 pf., fl., ob., cl., hrn., bsn. & cbs.[2]
A. d'Arco & French Wind Quintet
     # **LOL.OL 50049**
(*above*)   (# OL.LD 107)

ORBÓN, Julián (b. 1925)

Homenaje a la Tonadilla orch.
Havana Phil.   **Pnt. n.d.**
(*N. Rodriguez: El Son Entero*)

OREFICE, Giacomo (1865-1922)

CHOPIN Opera 1901
Sì, date fiori T
F. Tagliavini   in # **SBDH.TOB 2**
(*Samson et Dalila, Boccanegra, etc.*)

Sera ineffabile S & T
P. Tassinari & F. Tagliavini   in # **ABCD. 2**
(*Guarany, Favorita, Trovatore, etc.*)

ORFF, Carl (b. 1895)

ANTIGONE Opera 1 Act 1949
Scenes IV & V: ALMOST COMPLETE
Antigone	... ...	C. Goltz (S)
Creon	... ...	H. Uhde (B)
Messenger	... ...	J. Greindl (Bs)
Eurydice ...	... ...	H. Rössl-Majdan (A)

Vienna State Op. Cho. & Vienna Sym. members
— Hollreiser   # **AmC.ML 5038**
[recording supervised by the composer]

Carmina burana 1937
Scenic Cantata from the Latin S, T, 2 B, cho. & orch.
E. Trötschel, P. Kuen, K. Hoppe, H. Braun,
Bavarian Radio Cho. & Orch.—E. Jochum
     # **HP.DG 16045/6**
(4ss, auto) (manual # Pol. 16068/9; 2ss, # AmD.DL 9706)

Catulli Carmina (Catullus)
orig. 12 a cappella choruses in *Latin*, 1930; rev. 1943,
S, T, cho., pfs. & perc.
E. Roon, H. Loeffler, Vienna Cha. Cho.
W. Kamper, E. Mrazek, M. Gielen, W. Klein
(pfs), & Percussion Orch.—Hollreiser
     # **E. & AmVox.PL 8640**
[Excerpt on # AmVox.UHF 1]   (# Orb.BL 706)

... **Verses I-XII** (without Prelude & Postlude)[3]
A. Kupper (S), R. Holm (T), Bavarian Radio
Cho.—E. Jochum   # **Pol. 16117**
     (# 17021)

ORREGO SALAS, Juan (b. 1919)

Symphony No. 1 1949
Chile Sym.—Anon.   # **ChV.CRL 1**
(*Santa Cruz: Egloga*)

ORTIZ, Diego (b. c. 1525)

COLLECTION ed. M. Schneider[4]
Recercada quarta por Violon solo
Madrigal à 4: O felici occhi miei,[5] & 2 recercadas
3 Recercadas sobra tenores Italianos
A. Wenzinger (gamba), M. Guilleaume (S),
E. Müller (hpsi.)   ♭ *Pol.* **37009**

Recercada quinta[4]
☆ C. v. L. Boomkamp (gamba), E. Bodky (hpsi.)
     (in † # HS.AS 13)

ORTMANS, René

Concertino No. 1, A minor, Op. 12 vln. & pf.
J. Shermont & O. Shulhof   # **Rem.YV 3**
(*Accolay & Seitz*)

OSWALD von Wolkenstein (c. 1377-1445)

SEE: † MUSIC OF THE MIDDLE AGES
     † MUSICA ANTICA E NUOVA

OTHMAYER, Caspar (1515-1553)

SEE: † SONGS OF THE RENAISSANCE

OUBRADOUS, Fernand (b. 1903)

Cadence et Divertissement cl. & pf.
(sur un air populaire)
▽ P. Lefèbvre & N. Gallon (OL. 9)

Divertissements bsn. & pf. 1954
M. Allard & F. Gobet   ♭ *Pat.G 1055*
(*Ibert, A. Bloch, Duclos, etc.*)

Récit & Variations sur un air populaire bsn. & pf.
▽ A. Rabot & F. Boury (*Pac. 3355*)

OUSELEY, Frederick A. Gore (1825-1889)

SEE: † ENGLISH CHURCH MUSIC, VOL. III

OVALLE, Jayme (b. 1894)

SONGS
Azulao
S. Gloria (S), A. Chaneka (pf.)
     in # **Vic.LM 1737**
(*below; Tavares, Mignone, Sandi, etc.*) (in # FV.A 530202)
Berimbau, Op. 4
(3) Potos de Santo, Op. 10
1. Chario   1. Aruanda   3. Estrella do Mar
E. Houston (S), P. Miguel (pf.)
     in # **Vic.LCT 1143**
(♭ set ERBT 4: ▽ Vic. 13668/9, in set M 798)
... **No. 3 only**
S. Gloria (S), A. Chanaka (pf.)
     in # **Vic.LM 1737**
(*above*)   (in # FV.A 530202)

PACHELBEL, Johann (1653-1706)

A, B, C, D in the references refer respectively to Denkmäler der Tonkunst in Bayern, Vols. II, IV, part 1, and IV, part 2; and Denkmäler der Tonkunst in Oesterreich, Vol. VIII. Where no reference is quoted, it has not been possible to check.

KEYBOARD WORKS
ORGAN MUSIC COLLECTIONS
CHORALE PRELUDES:
Vom Himmel hoch		C 57
Wie schön leuchtet der Morgenstern		C 65
Ricercare, C minor		B 48
TOCCATAS: C minor		B 15
E minor		B 17
F major	(*Pastorale*)	B 18

L. Altman   # **ML. 7054**
(*Reger*) [Org. of Temple Emanuel, San Francisco]

---

[1] Contributed to a joint set of variations with all the composers named.
[2] Performed as a Sextet, omitting the cbs.
[3] A re-recording is promised which will include these sections.
[4] From *Trattado de glosas . . . en la música de violones*, 1553.

[5] The Madrigal is by Arcadelt.

ORGAN COLLECTIONS (*continued*)
CHORALE PRELUDES
Jesus Christus, unser Heiland   C 42
Wie schön leuchtet der Morgenstern   C 65
Warum betrübst du dich, mein Herz?   C 60
Ein' feste Burg ist unser Gott   C 23
Toccata, C major   B 14
Fugue, C major   A 43
Toccata, F major (*Pastorale*)   B 18
  L. Noss   ♯ *Over.LP 8*
  (*J. G. Walther*) [Org. Battel Chapel, Yale.]
  The Chorale-Prels. on the Transept org., the others on
    Apse organ

CHORALE PRELUDES
Durch Adams Fall
Nun lob, mein' Seel', den Herren   C 52
Vater unser im Himmelreich
Vom Himmel hoch
Wie schön leuchtet der Morgenstern   C 65
Toccata, F major (*Pastorale*)   B 18
  C. Watters   ♯ *CEd.CE 1041*
  (*J. G. Walther*)

CHORALE PRELUDES
Vom Himmel hoch[1]   C 57
Wie schön leuchtet der Morgenstern[2] C 65
Was Gott tut, das ist wohlgetan[5]   (Partita No. 4)
TOCCATAS: C major[3]   B 12
           E minor[4]   B 17
Praeludium, D minor[6] ("Toccata")   B 24
  E. P. Biggs   ♯ *AmC.ML 4972*
  (*Buxtehude*)   (in set SL 291)
  [also issued as ♯ EPhi.ABL 3110]
  Organs of: [1] St. Lorenzkirche, Nuremberg.
             [2] Neuenfeld Church.
             [3] Heiliggeist Kirche, Heidelberg.
             [4] Steinkirchen Church.
             [5] Abbey Church, Amorbach. (The work played
                 is No. 4 of 7 *Chorale-Partiten*, not in DTB.)
             [6] Benedictine Abbey, Weingarten, Germany.

Aria Sebaldina & Variations, F minor   A 6
  (*Hexachordum Apollinis*, 1699)
  E. Bodky (clavichord)   in ♯ *Uni.LP 1002*
  († *Music of Baroque Era*)

CHACONNES
D minor   A 17
  F. Asma (org.)   ♯ *Phi.S 06033R*
  (*Micheelsen & Vivaldi*)

F minor   A 19
  N. Pierront (org.)   in ♯ *Lum.LD 2-104*
  († *Chaconne & Passacaglia*)

CHORALE PRELUDES   organ
COLLECTION
Vom Himmel hoch   C 57
Meine Seele erhebt den Herrn (Magnificat) C 48
Gelobet seist du   C 30
O Lamm Gottes   C 53
Ich hab' mein' Sach' Gott heimgestellt C 36
  F. Viderø   ♯ *Mtr.MCEP 3019*
  [Varde organ, Denmark]

Ach, was soll ich Sünder machen?   B 11
  E. White   in ♯ *Moll.E4QP 7231*
  (*Schroeder, Bach, Vierne, Reger, etc.*)
  [Org. of G. Washington Shrine, Alexandria, Va.]

Christus, der ist mein Leben[7]
  M. Mason   in ♯ *ASK. 7*
  (*Bach, Crandell, etc.*)

Durch Adams Fall   C 20
  G. Jones   in *G.HMS 61*
  († *History of Music in Sound*)   (in ♯ Vic. set LM 6031)

Vater unser   C 56
  ▽ M. Dupré (in † ♯ HS.AS 11)

Vom Himmel hoch
  E. Barthe   in *PV. 36099*
  (*Bach, Eccard, Freylinghausen*)   (♭ *Pol. 32099*)

Was Gott tut, das ist wohlgetan[8]
  E. Hilliar   in ♯ *ASK. 4*
  (*Loeillet, Bach, Couperin, etc.*)
  [Org. of St. Mark's, Mt. Kisco, N.Y.]
  ☆ W. Supper (in † ♯ Cpt.MC 20029 & ♯ Ren.X 53)

Fantasia, C major   A 23
  R. Gerlin (hpsi.)   in ♯ *LOL.OL 50043*
  († *Clavecinistes Italiens, Allemands*)   (♯ *OL.LD 67*)

Fantasia, G minor   B 11
  ☆ W. Supper († ♯ Cpt.MC 20029 & ♯ Ren.X 54)

TOCCATAS, organ
E minor   B 17
  F. Viderø   in ♯ *HS.HSL 2073*
  († *Masterpieces of Music before 1750*)

INSTRUMENTAL WORKS
Canon & Gigue, D major   3 vlns. & cont.
Partita No. 6, B flat major   2 vlns. & cont.
  R. Felicani, I. Brix-Meinert, R. Lahrs, H.
    Heintze (hpsi.), J. Koch (gamba) ♭ *Pol. 37056*

... **Canon & Gigue** only (ed. Seiffert)
  N.W. Ger. Phil.—Schüchter
                                  ♭ *Od.BEOW 32-3002*
  (*Bach, Corelli*, in ♯ *Imp.ILP 132*)

PADEREWSKI, Ignace Jan (1860–1941)

Chants du voyageur, Op. 8   5 pieces, pf.   1884
  R. Corbett   in ♯ *ML. 7017*
... No. 3 only
  E. Burton   in ♯ *CEd.CE 1024*
Fantaisie polonaise, Op. 19   pf. & orch.   1893
  F. Blumenthal & L.S.O.—Fistoulari   ♯ *D.LXT 2975*
  (*Tavares: Concerto*)   (♯ *Lon.LL 1104*)
MANRU   Opera 3 Acts   1901
As in the burning sun   T
  ℍ G. Anselmi (*Ital*) & pf. (in ♯ Ete. 711*;
                          in ♯ Sca. 816* & in ♯ ABCD. 1*)
Minuet, G major, Op. 14, No. 1   pf.
  C. Brown (in ♯ *B.LA 8634; AmD.DL 5486*)
  E. Silver (hpsi.) (in ♯ Roy. 1550)
  ☆ M. Flipse (in ♯ *Phi.S 06016R*)
  J. Iturbi (♭ *G. 7RF 288;* ♭ *Vic.ERA 53*)
— ARR. PF. & ORCH.
  W. Stech & Hamburg Phil.—Wal-Berg (in ♯ *T.TW 30027*)
— ARR. VLN. & PF.   Kreisler
  A. Campoli & E. Gritton   in ♯ *D.LXT 5012*
                                  (♯ *Lon.LL 1171*)
Nocturne, B flat major, Op. 16, No. 4   pf.
  E. Burton   in ♯ *CEd.CE 1026*
SONGS
(The) Birch Tree and the maiden, Op. 7, No. 3   (Asnyk)
(The) Day of roses, Op. 7, No. 1   (Asnyk)
  M. Drewniakowna (S), J. Lefeld (pf.)   *Muza. 1681*

PAGANINI, Niccolo (1782-1840)

COLLECTION — VLN. & PF.   (some ARRS.)
Le Streghe, Op. 8 (Witches Dance)   ARR. Kreisler
Variations on 'Dal tuo stellato soglio', from Rossini's *Mosè*
Moto perpetuo, Op. 11   ø
Variations on 'Nel cor più' from Paisiello's *La Molinera*
Variations on God save the Queen, Op. 9
Concerto No. 2, B minor   vln. & orch.
... 3rd movt. ARR. VLN. & PF Kochanski "La Campanella" ø
Sonata No. 12, E minor, Op. 3, No. 6   vln. & guitar
  — ARR. vln. & pf.
I Palpiti, Op. 13   ARR. Kreisler
  R. Ricci & L. Persinger   ♯ *D.LXT 2808*
                                  (♯ *Lon.LL 1005*)
  [items marked ø also on ♭ *D. 71066: 18174*]
Cantabile, Op. 17   vln. & pf.
  L. Kogan & A. Mitnik   ♯ *C.FCX 402*
  (*Concerto No. 1*)

(24) CAPRICES, Op. 1   Unacc. violin
Nos. 1, 5, 9, 11, 13, 14, 16, 17, 18, 21, 24
  ☆ M. Rabin   ♯ *AmC.RL 6633*
                                  (♯ *Phi.S 06616R*)
— ARR. VLN. & PF.
Nos. 1-12 O. Renardy & E. Helmer   ♯ *Rem. 199-146*
Nos. 13-24 O. Renardy & E. Helmer ♯ *Rem. 199-152*

No. 9, E major   "La Chasse"
— ARR. VLN. & PF.
  ☆ Z. Francescatti & A. Balsam (*ArgC. 30000*)
— ARR. FL., OB., CL., HRN., BSN.
  Chicago Sym. Woodwind Quintet (in ♯ Aphe.AP 16)

---

[7] Partita: No. 1 of 7 *Chorale-Partiten*, not in DTB.   [8] Partita: No. 4 of 7 *Chorale-Partiten*, not in DTB

No. 13, B flat major   "Le rire du diable"
— ARR. VLN. & PF.   Kreisler
A. Campoli & G. Malcolm   in ♯ *D.LX 3115*
(*below, & Dohnányi*)   (♯ *Lon.LS 793*)
D. Oistrakh & V. Yampolsky   ♯ *Per.SPL 710*
(*No. 17, & Tchaikovsky: Concerto*)
(*below, & Lalo, on* ♯ *Csm.CRLP 179*)
(*No. 17 only, USSR. 16285*)
M. Wilk & F. Kramer (in ♯ MTR.MLP 1012)
☆ R. Ricci & L. Persinger (♭ *AmVox.VIP 45420*)

No. 14, E flat major
☆ M. Wilk (in ♯ MTR.MLP 1012)

No. 17, E flat major   "Andantino Capriccioso"
D. Oistrakh   ♯ *Per.SPL 710*
(*No. 13, & Tchaikovsky: Concerto*)
      (& in ♯ Csm.CRLP 179 & USSR. 16339)
— ARR. VLN. & PF.   ☆ E. & A. Wolf (♭ *Mer.EP 1-5040*)

No. 20, D major
— ARR. VLN. & PF.   Kreisler
A. Campoli & G. Malcolm   in ♯ *D.LX 3115*
(*above, below, & Dohnányi*)   (in ♯ *Lon.LS 793*)
☆ R. Ricci & L. Persinger (♭ *AmVox.VIP 45420*)

No. 22, F major
— ARR. VLN. & PF.
☆ Z. Francescatti & A. Balsam (*ArgC. 30000*)

No. 24, A minor   ("Tema con variazioni")
— ARR. VLN. & PF.
I. Haendel & G. Moore   ♭ *G.7EP 7013*
(*Bartók: Rumanian Dances*) (♭ *ArgA.SCBAE 6504;*
      in ♯ G.CLP 1021)
H. Szeryng & T. Janopoulo   in ♯ *Od.OD 1008*
(*Vitali, Wieniawski, Kreisler*)   (in ♯ *ArgOd.LDC 7504*)
— ARR. ORCH.   Anon. Orch. (in ♯ Roy. 1432)
— And SEE Paganiniana, *below*

Carnevale di Venezia, Op. 10   vln. & pf.
Z. Francescatti & A. Balsam ♯ & ♭ *AmC.PE 19*

CONCERTOS, Vln. & orch.
No. 1, E flat major, Op. 6
   (often stated to be in D major)
M. Rabin & Philharmonia—v. Matačić
              ♯ *C.CX 1281*
(*Glazounov*) [Cadenza by Flesch]   (♯ Angel. 35259)
R. Ricci & L.S.O.—Collins   ♯ *D.LXT 5075*
(*No. 2*)   (♯ *Lon.LL 1215*)
[ed. Collins; cadenza by Paganini, ed. Sauret]
H. Krebbers & Vienna Sym.—Otterloo
             ♯ *Phi.A 00263L*
(*Vieuxtemps*) [ed. Flesch]
(*below, No. 4, on* ♯ Epic.LC 3143)
L. Kogan & Paris Cons.—Bruck   ♯ *C.FCX 402*
(1½ss—*Cantabile*)
V. Abadjiev & Sofia Phil.   *Bulg. 1355/9*
(9ss—*Sarasate: Intro. & Tarantelle*)
L. Kogan & Moscow Radio—Nebolsin
(8ss)   *USSR. 20199/204 & 20505/6*
J. Novák & F.O.K. Sym.—Smetáček
             ♮ *U.H 24462/4*
(5ss—*Raff*) [Cadenza by Kubelik]
☆ Z. Francescatti & Philadelphia—Ormandy
           (♭ *AmC. set A 1006*)

... 1st movt. only
☆ R. Ricci & Lamoureux—Bigot (♯ EVox.PL 6490;
           AFest.CFR 12-292)
F. Kreisler & Philadelphia—Ormandy[1]
           (in ♯ Vic.LCT 1142)

No. 2, B minor, Op. 7
R. Ricci & L.S.O.—Collins   ♯ *D.LXT 5075*
(*No. 1*)   (♯ *Lon.LL 1215*)
[ed. Collins; cadenza by A. Balsam]
Y. Sitkovetsky & Moscow Radio—Paverman
           ♯ *USSR.D 1089/90*
☆ Y. Menuhin & Philharmonia—Fistoulari ♯ *G.BLP 1018*
           (♯ *VBLP 804: WBLP 1018*)

... 3rd movt., Ronde à la clochette
☆ R. Odnoposoff & Utrecht Sym.—Hupperts
   (*Bruch*)   ♯ *MMS. 40*
☆ Vlns. of Boston Prom.—Fiedler (G.S 10603: ♭ 7PW 110;
         in ♯ Vic.LM 1790: ♭ ERA 243)

— ARR. VLN. & PF.   Kreisler   (*La Campanella*)
A. Campoli & G. Malcolm   in ♯ *D.LX 3115*
(& in ♯ *D.LW 5218*)   (in ♯ *Lon.LS 793;* ♭ *D.VD 507*)
Y. Sitkovetsky & pf.   (2ss)   *USSR. 17200/1*
(*Moszkowski & Saint-Saëns, on USSRM.D 863*)
☆ R. Ricci & L. Persinger (♭ *AmVox.VIP 45420*)

No. 4, D minor   1829
A. Grumiaux & Lamoureux—Gallini[2]
           ♯ *EPhi.ABR 4024*
(*No. 1, on* ♯ Epic.LC 3143)   (♯ *Phi.A 00741R*)
(8ss, ♮ *ArgC. 50004/7*)

Moto perpetuo, Op. 11   vln. & orch.
M. Rabin & Col. Sym.—Voorhees
           ♭ *EPhi.NBE 11003*
(*Sarasate & Novaček*)   (♯ *AmC.AL 38;* ♭ *Phi.A 409007E*)
☆ R. Ricci & L. Persinger (in ♯ EVox.PL 6490;
           ♯ *AmVox.VIP 45340*)
— ARR. ORCH.
Hungarian Radio—Somogyi   *Qual.MN 1075*
(*J. Strauss: Perpetuum mobile*)
☆ Vlns. of Boston Prom.—Fiedler (G.S 10603: ♯ *DLP 1079:*
          ♭ *PW 110;* & in ♯ *Vic.LRM/*♭ *ERB 7035*)
   Chicago Sym.—Stock (in ♯ AmC.RL 3022)
   Decca Little Sym.—Mendoza (in ♯ *AmD.DL 5211;*
          D.US 223524)
   Minneapolis Sym.—Ormandy (in ♯ Cam.CAL 121:
          ♭ *CAE 215*)

Paganiniana   vln. unacc. — ARR. Milstein
   (based on Caprices, Op. 1)
N. Milstein   in ♯ DCap.CTL 7058
(*Brahms, Schumann, Suk, etc.*)   (in ♯ Cap.P 8259)
(*Bach: Sonata 4—Chaconne, on* ♯ *DCap.CCL 7526;*
          Cap.H 8297)

Quartet, String, E major
Stuyvesant Qtt.   ♯ *Phil.PH 107*
(*Kreisler*)
☆ York Qtt. (♯ AFest.CFR 10-605)
   Guilet Qtt. (♯ MMS. 3005)

SONATAS, Violin & guitar
COMPLETE RECORDING

No. 1, A major, Op. 2, No. 1	No. 7, A major, Op. 3, No. 1
No. 2, C major, Op. 2, No. 2	No. 8, G major, Op. 3, No. 2
No. 3, D minor, Op. 2, No. 3	No. 9, D major, Op. 3, No. 3
No. 4, A major, Op. 2, No. 4	No. 10, A minor, Op. 3, No. 4
No. 5, D major, Op. 2, No. 5	No. 11, A major, Op. 3, No. 5
No. 6, A minor, Op. 2, No. 6	No. 12, E minor, Op. 3, No. 6

Michel & A. Malakoff   ♯ *Rom.LP 1501*

Unspec. Sonata . . . Andantino variato
— ARR. GUITAR SOLO   Ponce
A. Segovia   in † ♯ B.AXTL 1060

Sonatina   ("Grande")   Guitar
... Romance
☆ A. Segovia (♭ AmD.ED 3503; ♭ SpC.SCGE 80004)

(Le) Streghe, Op. 8   (Witches' Dance)   vln. & pf.
☆ R. Ricci & L. Persinger   in ♯ EVox.PL 6490

VARIATIONS ON: (for vln. & pf.)
Dal tuo stellato soglio from Rossini's "Mosè"
I. Haendel & G. Moore   in ♯ *G.CLP 1021*
D. Oistrakh & pf.   *USSRM.D 00545*
(*Falla: Jota*)
☆ R. Ricci & L. Persinger (in ♯ EVox.PL 6490)
J. Kawaciuk & F. Vrána (in ♯ *Sup.LPM 135; U. 5185C*)
Di tanti palpiti, Op. 13
☆ Z. Francescatti & A. Balsam (in ♯ EPhi.NBL 5010;
          Phi.N 02101L: *S 06602R*)

---

[1] ARR. Kreisler.   [2] Cadenza by Grumiaux.

PAINE, John Knowles (1839-1906)

As you like it, Op. 28 Overture orch. pub. 1907
Hamburg Philharmonia—Korn in ♯ **Allo. 3149**
(MacDowell, Harris, Copland, etc.)

Oedipus Tyrannus, Op. 35 Inc. music
Overture
▽ Eastman-Rochester Sym.—Hanson
(Vic. 15658 in set M 608)

PAISIELLO, Giovanni (1740-1816)

Concerto, C major hpsi. & cha. orch. 1781
R. Gerlin & O.L. Cha. Orch.—Froment
♯ **LOL.OL 50009**
(Durante, Auletta, Mancini)   (♯ OL.LD 66)
C. Bussotti (pf.) & Italian Cha.—Jenkins
♯ **HS.HSL 135**
(Brunetti)   (in set HSL-N)

Marche du premier Consul 1803
Marche funèbre, pour la mort du Général Hoche
1797
Paris Cons.—Tzipine   ¹in ♯ **C.FCX 384S**
(Méhul)

OPERAS

(Il) DUELLO 1 Act 1774
COMPLETE RECORDING (ed. G. Tintori)

Bettina	... ...	E. de Luca (S)
Clarice	... ...	A. Vercelli
Violetta	... ...	T. Bulgaron (S)
Fortunata	... ...	V. Mastropaolo (M-S)
Leandro	... ...	A. Nobile (T)
Don Policronio	... ...	I. Vinco (Bs)
Topo	... ...	T. Rovetta (Bs)
Don Simone	... ...	G. Viziano (Bs)

& Institute Cha. Orch.—Rapalo
♯ **HS.HSL 130**

(La) MOLINARA 2 Acts 1788
(or: *L'amor contrastato*)
Overture
Cetra Orch.—Basile   *Cet.AT 0330*
(Mozart: Bastien et Bastienne, Overture)

Il mio garzon, il piffero sonabra S & B
G. Sciutti & A. Poli   in ♯ **Csm.CLPS 1046**
(Traetta, Piccinni, etc.)

Nel cor più non mi sento
F. Barbieri (M-S), D. Marzollo (pf.)
in ♯ **AmVox.PL 7980**
(† Old Italian Songs & Airs)
M. Vitale (S), A. Beltrami (pf.)   *Cet.AT 0316*
(A. Scarlatti: Donna Ancora, Aria)   (in ♯ LPC 55001)

NINA 1 Act 1789
Overture ☆ Royal Phil.—Beecham (G.ED 1243)

Il mio ben quando verrà
M. Vitale (S), A. Beltrami (pf.)   *Cet.AB 30024*
(A. Scarlatti: Se tu)

(La) SCUFFIARA 3 Acts 1792
(orig. *La Modista raggiratrice*, 1787)
Overture (ed. Piccioli)
Naples Scarlatti Orch.—Caracciolo ♯ **C.CX 1171**
(A. Scarlatti & Cimarosa) (♯ QCX 10036; Angel. 35141)

(I) ZINGARI IN FIERA 2 Acts 1789
Chi vuol la zingarella
F. Barbieri (M-S), D. Marzollo (pf.)
in ♯ **AmVox.PL 7980**
(† Old Italian Songs & Airs)
I. Kolassi (M-S), J. Bonneau (pf.)
in ♯ **D.FAT 173160**
(† Arie Antiche & German Lieder)   (♯ Lon.LL 747)

PALADILHE, Émile (1844-1926)

PATRIE Opera 5 Acts 1886
Jadis elles chantaient gayement Bs Act I
🎵 H. Belhomme (*SEDH.P 4**)

Pauvre martyr obscur B
E. Blanc   in ♯ **LI.TW 91131**
(Faust & Otello)   (♯ D.FAT 173666)
🎵 T. Ruffo (*Ital*) (in ♯ *SBDH.LLP 7**)

SONGS
(La) fille aux cheveux de lin (L. de Lisle)
Mandolinata (R. Bussine, from the Italian)
P. Fleta (T) & orch.   in ♯ *Pat.DT 1012*
(Massenet, Drigo, etc.)

Mandolinata: 🎵 V. Maurel (B, *Ital*) (in ♯ Sca. 822*)

Psyché (Corneille)
☆ M. Teyte (S), G. Moore (pf.) (in ♯ Vic.LCT 1133)

PALAU-BOIX, Manuel (b. 1893)

Marcha burlesca
Seguidillas (Hommage à Debussy)
☆ Valencia Sym.—Iturbi (in ♯ Vic.LM 1937; DV.L 16221
Marcha only, ▽ G.DB 21456: ♭ 7ERL 1042)

PALESTRINA, Giovanni Pierluigi da
(1525-1594)

(Roman figures refer to the Vols. of the B & H Complete
edn.; dates to the original editions)

COLLECTION
MOTETS: **Dies sanctificatus** VII 8 vv.
Exsultate Deo IV 5 vv. 1570
Hodie Christus natus est III 8 vv
Pueri Hebraeorum V 4 vv. 1581
Super flumina Babylonis V 4 vv. 1581
Tribulationes civitatum—Peccavimus IV 5 vv. 1570
OFFERTORIES: **Bonum est confiteri** IX
Exaltabo te, Domine IX
Laudate Dominum IX all 5 vv. 1593
SONG OF SOLOMON: **Tota pulchra es** IV 5 vv. 1575
Vox dilecti mea IV 5 vv. 1584
IMPROPERIA: **Popule meus** XXXI
☆ Sistine Chapel Cho.—Bartolucci (♯ Cpt.MC 20066)

MOTETS & OFFERTORIES

COLLECTIONS
Super flumina Babylonis V 4 vv. 1581
Tu es Petrus II 6 vv. 1572
Sicut cervus V 4 vv. 1581
Haec dies, quam fecit Dominus III 6 vv. 1575
Welch Chorale   in ♯ **Lyr.LL 52**
(† Motets of the XVth & XVIth Centuries)

Litany: Supplicationes ad Beatam Virginem Mariam XXVI-ii
Confitemini Domino V 4 vv.   [No. 1
Adoramus te, Christe² V 4 vv.
Harvard Glee Club—Woodworth
in ♯ *Camb.CRC 101*
(Anon. Laude: O Maria; & Byrd, Lassus, etc.)

Adoramus te, Christe² V 4 vv.
Confitemini Domino V 4 vv.
Hodie Christus natus est III 8 vv.
Salve Regina IV. 5 vv.
☆ Period Cho.—Strassburg³ (in ♯ Clc. 6138 &
♯ Cum.CPR 318)

Adoramus te, Christe² V 4 vv.
A Capella Cho.—Stokowski in ♯ **Vic.LM 1721**
(below)   (in ♭ set WDM 1721)
(in ♯ ItV.A12R 0040; ♯ G.FALP 245)

Alma Redemptoris Mater V 4 vv.
All Saints Church Male Cho.—Self
in ♯ **CEd.CE 1023**
(† Five Centuries of Choral Music)
Lagon Onak Cho.—Mallea   *ArgOd. 57027*
(Victoria: Ave Maria)
☆ Manécanterie Cho. (*JpV.A 1267*)

Assumpta est Maria VI 6 vv.
N.Y. Primavera Singers—Greenberg
in ♯ **Per.SPL 597**
(† Renaissance Music)   (♯ Cpt.MC 20077)

¹ Only available as part of a *de luxe* Limited Edition.
² By F. Rosselli, attrib. Anerio.   ³ Some are ARR. Female Cho.

Ave Regina
U.S.S.R. State Cho.—Shveshnikov (in ♯ *Eta. 720003:*
            o.n. *LPM 1008* & *1025*)

Ecce quomodo—by Ingegneri, *q.v.*

Ego sum panis vivus (unspec.)[4]
Petits Chanteurs de la Renaissance
           in **V**♯ *Era.LDE 1001*
                    (♯ HS.HS 9007)
(† Polyphonic Motets of the XVIth Century)

Hodie Christus natus est III 8 vv.
Concordia Cho.—P. J. Christiansen
            in ♯ *Cdia.CDLP 3*
Quartetto Polifonico[5]   in ♯ *D.LXT 2945*
(† Choral Music)   (♯ Lon.LL 995)
☆ St. Olaf Cho.—O. C. Christiansen
        (in ♯ *Alld. 2005:* ♭ *EP 2005*)

Improperium exspectavit IX 5 vv.
Vatican Cho.—Bartolucci   ♯ *Per.SPL 706*
(*Victoria, Binchois, Lassus, Anchieta*)

Laudate Dominum II 8 vv.
☆ Gregorian Inst. Cho.—Vitry   in ♯ *GIOA.PM 1*

O bone Jesu (unspec.)
A Capella Cho.—Stokowski in ♯ *Vic.LM 1721*
(*Cesti, Vivaldi, Lully, etc.*)   (in ♭ set *WDM 1721*)
           (in ♯ *G.FALP 245*; *ItV.A12R 0040*)
Darlington Seminary Cho.—Flask
           in ♯ *GIOA.DS 1*

Salvator mundi v 4 vv. 1563
Vienna Boys' Cho.—Brenn in ♯ *EPhi.NBR 6013*
(*Gallus, Ingegneri, Verdi, etc.*) (in ♯ *Phi.N 00624R;*
               AmC.ML 4873)

Sicut cervus v 4 vv. 1581
Hufstader Singers   in ♯ *SOT. 1092*
Vatican Cho.—Bartolucci in ♯ *Per.SPL 706*
(*below*)
☆ International Boys' Cho. (C.LZX 277)

Stabat Mater VI 8 vv. *c.* 1590
Dessoff Choir—Boepple ♯ *CHS.CHS 1231*
(*Assumpta est Maria & Magnificat*)

Super flumina Babylonis v 4 vv. 1581
Vienna Boys' Cho.—Brenn in ♯ *EPhi.NBR 6013*
(*above*)   (in ♯ *Phi.N 00624R;* AmC.ML 4873)
Stanford Univ. Cho.—Schmidt ♯ *ML. 7022*
(† Madrigals & Motets)

Tenebrae factae sunt—by Ingegneri, *q.v.*

MASSES

Aeterna Christi munera XIV 4 vv. 1590
... **Sanctus**
Brompton Oratory Choir—Washington
               G.HMS 35
(† History of Music in Sound) (in ♯ Vic. set LM 6029)
Helsinki Univ. Cho.—Turunen
           in ♯ *Rem. 199-167*
(*Palmgren, Handel, Sibelius, etc.*)

Ascendo ad Patrem XXI 5 vv. 1601
☆ Welch Chorale (♯ Allo. 3097)

Assumpta est Maria XXIII 6 vv.
Dessoff Choir—Boepple ♯ *CHS.CHS 1231*
(*Magnificat & Stabat Mater*)

Brevis XII 4 vv[6] 1570
St. Patrick's Cath. Cho.—P. Jones
             ♯ *Spot.SC 1003*
☆ Welch Chorale (♯ Allo. 3097)

... **Agnus Dei II**[6]
Brompton Oratory Choir—Washington
               G.HMS 35
(† History of Music in Sound) (in ♯ Vic. set LM 6029)

Descendit angelus Domini XX 4 vv. 1600
... **Benedictus**
☆ Period Cho.—Strassburg (in ♯ Clc. 6138 &
                   ♯ Cum.CPR 318)

Iste confessor XIV 4 vv. 1590
☆ Welch Chorale (♯ Lyr.LL 49; Cum.CLL 339)

O admirabile commercium XVII 5 vv. 1599
... **Benedictus**
Harvard Glee Club & Radcliffe Cho. Soc.
—Woodworth   in ♯ *Camb.CRS 202*
(† Chansons & Motets)

O Rex gloriae XXI 4 vv. 1601
... **Crucifixus**
☆ Period Cho.—Strassburg (in ♯ Clc. 6138 &
                   ♯ Cum.CPR 318)

Papae Marcelli IX 6 vv. 1567
☆ Netherlands Cha. Cho.—de Nobel in ♯ *Epic.LC 3045*
(† Sacred & Secular Songs from the Renaissance)
☆ R. Wagner Cho. (♯ T.LCE 8126)

Sacerdotes Domini XVII 6 vv. 1599
... **Pleni sunt coeli**
☆ Period Cho.—Strassburg (in ♯ Clc. 6138 &
                   ♯ Cum.CPR 318)

Sine nomine XV 6 vv. (on *Je suis désheritée*)
☆ Welch Chorale (♯ Lyr.LL 49; Cum.CLL 339)
... **Credo** only
Yale Univ. Music School Cho.—Hindemith
            in ♯ *Over.LP 5*
(† Yale University, Vol. II)

Veni, sponsa Christi XVIII 4 vv. 1599
Vienna Cha. Cho.—Gillesberger ♯ *Uni.LP 1013*
(*Lassus: Mass*)
Copenhagen Boys' & Men's Cho.—Møller
           in ♯ *HS.HSL 2072*
(† Masterpieces of Music before 1750)
(& in † Histoire de la Musique vocale)

VARIOUS SACRED SETTINGS

Hymn: Pange, lingua, gloriosi VIII
Quartetto Polifonico   in ♯ *D.LXT 2945*
(† Choral Music)   (♯ Lon.LL 995)

Improperia—Popule meus XXXI
Aachen Cath. Cho.—Rehmann ♯ *Pol. 37059*
(*with Gregorian Antiphons & O crux ave*)
Quartetto Polifonico   in ♯ *D.LXT 2945*
(† Choral Music)   (♯ Lon.LL 995)

Magnificat on the 3rd tone XXVII 8 vv 1591
Dessoff Choir—Boepple ♯ *CHS.CHS 1231*
(*Mass, Assumpta est Maria & Stabat Mater*)

Magnificat on the 4th tone
Quartetto Polifonico[7]   in ♯ *D.LXT 2945*
(† Choral Music)   (♯ Lon.LL 995)
☆ Period Cho.—Strassburg[8] (in ♯ Clc. 6138 &
                   ♯ Cum.CPR 318)

O vos omnes XXXII Responsorium, 4 vv.
☆ Gregorian Inst. Cho.—Vitry in ♯ *GIOA.PM-LP 1*
(† Polyphonic Masters)

Supplicationes ad B.V.M. XXVI
... **Ave de coelis**
Quartetto Polifonico   in ♯ *D.LXT 2945*
(† Choral Music)   (♯ Lon.LL 995)

Vexilla regis ... O crux, ave! III 1586
Aachen Cath. Cho.—Rehmann in ♭ *Pol. 37059*
(*above*)
☆ Motet & Madrigal Cho.—Opienski (in † ♯ HS.AS 9)

MADRIGAL (XXVIII)

La cruda mia nemica
☆ Motet & Madrigal Cho.—Opienski (in † ♯ HS.AS 9)

INSTRUMENTAL: Organ

Ricercare primi toni XXVII
(Ritter II-6/7; attrib. Palestrina)
F. Peeters   in ♯ *Nix.PLP 586*
(† Old Italian Masters) (♯ Per.SPL 586; Cpt.MC 20048)

---

[4] Probably the 4-part setting in V.
[5] ARR. Casimiri for single 4-pt. cho.
[6] Agnus Dei II is for 5 vv.
[7] Vol. XVI, Appendix.
[8] Vol. XXVII.

PALIASHVILI, Zakharia Petrovich
(1872-1933)

OPERAS In *Georgian*
ABSALOM AND ETERY 1913
Murman's Aria D. Gamrekeli (USSR. 014426)
Duet, Absalom & Murman
  Z. Andzhapariadze & B. Kraveyishvili (in ‡ *USSR.D 2209*)

Dances (unspec.)
  U.S.S.R State —Dimitriadi (*USSR. 14367/8;*
                       in ‡ *Csm.CRLP 102*)
DAICY 1924
Kiazo's Arias D. Gamrekeli (USSR. 014427 & *11991*)
Malkhaz's Aria A. Chakalidi (*USSR. 18754*)
LATAVRA 1930
Dances Tiflis State Opera Orch. (in ‡ *USSR.D 2210*)
Bizir's Song D. Gamrikeli & pf. (*USSR. 14261*)

PALMER, Robert (b. 1915)

Chamber Concerto vln., ob. & cha. orch. 1949
  M. Taylor, R. Sprenkle & Rochester Cha.
  Ch. Orch.—Hull ‡ **CHS.CHS 1190**
  (*below, & Vaughan-Williams*)

Quartet, pf., vln., vla. & vlc. 1947
  J. Kirkpatrick & Walden Trio ‡ **AmC.ML 4842**
  (*Harris*)

Slow, slow, fresh fount 1953
    after Ben Jonson's *Cynthia Revells*
  Cornell a Cappella Cho.—Hull
                ‡ **CHS.CHS 1190**

  (*above; & Vaughan Williams*)

PALMGREN, Selim (1876-1951)

CINDERELLA Music for a fairy play
  (*Tuhkimo: Askungen*)
...**Waltz**
  Orch.—Godzinsky *Ryt.R 6133*
  (*Kuula: The Mutton dance*)

May Night, Op. 27, No. 4 pf.
  E. Burton in ‡ *CEd.CE 1026*
  T. Mikkilä *Ryt.R 6137*
  (*Sibelius: Romance*)
— ARR. ORCH. Concert Orch. (in ‡ *Var. 2043*)

PARTSONGS
Boat Song (*Venelaulu*) (Kanteletar)
  ☆ Finlandia Cho. (Od.PLDX 4)

(An) Idler's Melody, Op. 70, No. 2 (Knape)
  (*En latmansmelodi*)
  Helsinki Acad. Cho.—Fougstedt (*Ryt.R 6067*)

Lullaby (*Tuutulaulu*)
  Helsinki Univ. Cho.—Turunen ‡ in **Rem. 199-167**

SONG: Christmas Song, Op. 34, No. 1 (Nuormaa)
  ☆ S. Saarits (B) & orch. (*G.TJ 123*)

PALUSELLI, Stefan (1748-1805)

  SEE: † TYROLESE XVIIIth CENTURY ORCH. MUSIC

PANIZZA, Ettore (Héctor) (b. 1875)

AURORA Opera 1908
Inno alla bandiera T
  ☒ A. Bassi (in ‡ *HRS. 3005**)

Quartet, C minor str.
  Pessina Qtt. ‡ *ArgOd.LDC 527*

Theme, Variations & Finale Pf. duet
  R. Locatelli & L. la Via ‡ *ArgOd.LDC 530*

PANUFNIK, Andrzej (b. 1914)

  SEE: † FOUR CENTURIES OF POLISH MUSIC

PAPINEAU-COUTURE, Jean (b. 1916)

Eglogues (Baillargeon) 1942
1. Printemps 2. Regards 3. L'ombre
  M. Forrester (A), fl. & pf. in ‡ *Hall.RS 6*
  († Musica Antica e Nuova)

PARADIES, Marie Therese von
(1759-1824)

Sicilienne
— ARR. VLN. & PF. Dushkin
  E. Morini & L. Pommers in ‡ *West.WN 18087*
  (*Tchaikovsky, Godard, Kreisler, etc.*)
  G. Jarry & N. Nova **C.LFX 1036**
  (♭s—*Ries: Mouvement perpétuel; & Wieniawski*)
                        (♭ *SCBF 102*)
  R. & A. d'Arco in *Plé.P 105*

PARADIES, Pietro Domenico (1707-1791)

Quel ruscelletto Aria
  (from Opera *La Forza d'amore*)
  O. Moscucci (S), V. Vitale (pf.) ♭ *C.SEDQ 504*
  (*Sarti, Pergolesi, A. Scarlatti*)

(12) SONATAS, clavier
No. 6, A major . . . 2nd movt., Toccata
  ☆ E. Joyce (pf.) (♭ *AmD.ED 3527*)

No. 10, D major
  D. Handman (pf.) in ‡ **LOL.OL 50078**
  († Sonatas of the XVIIth & XVIIIth Centuries)

PARKER, Horatio (1863-1919)

Hora Novissima S, A, T, Bs, cho. & orch. 1893
  G. Hopf, E. Wien, E. Kent, W. Berry & A.R.S.
  —Strickland ‡ **ARS. set 335**
  (3ss—*Bacon*)
MONA, Op. 71 Opera 1912
Interlude orch.
  Hamburg Philharmonia—Korn in ‡ **Allo. 3150**
  (*Griffes, Hadley, Carpenter, etc.*)

PARRY, Sir Charles Hubert Hastings
(1848-1918)

The Op. Nos. quoted here and in WERM are those of
Grove, 4th edn.

Hear my words, ye people, Op. 121 Anthem
  Cho. & orch.
  St. Paul's Cath. Cho.—Dykes Bower
                      C.LX 1611/2
  [W. H. Gabb, org.] (4ss)
  († English Church Music, Vol. IV)
Jerusalem, Op. 208 (Blake) Unison Song
  Royal Cho. Soc. & Philharmonia—Sargent
  [A. Grier, org.] **G.C 4213**
  (*Arne: Rule Britannia*)
  Royal Festival Cho. (Australia)
                  in ‡ **EPhi.ABL 3016**
— ARR. BAND Jakeway
  Salvation Army—Adams (*RZ.MF 370*)
I was glad, Op. 154 1902
  Coronation Choir in ‡ **G.ALP 1056**
  († Coronation of Queen Elizabeth II) (& G.DB 21581)
  St. Margaret's, Westminster Cho.
                  in ‡ **Ori.MG 20003**
SONGS
Love is a bable, Op. 152, No. 3 (Anon.)
  K. Ferrier (A), F. Stone (pf.)[1] in ‡ *D.LX 3133*
  (*Stanford, V. Williams, Britten, etc.*) (in ‡ *Lon.LS 1032*
Three Aspects, Op. 176, No. 1 (M. Coleridge)
  ☆ J. McCormack (T) (*AF.AGSA 21*, d.c.)

NOTE: Excerpts from the opera Blodwen (1878) by
  J. PARRY (1841-1903) are sung by N. Bateman (S) &
  E. Coslett (T) on *Cwal.RD 3107* & *3102*

---

[1] Broadcast performance, June 5, 1952.

PARSONS, Robert (d. 1570)

SEE: † ELIZABETHAN & JACOBEAN MUSIC

PARTCH, Harry (b. 1901)

SATYR-PLAY MUSIC FOR DANCE THEATRE[0]　1953
Castor & Pollux　Dance for twin rhythms of Gemini
Ring around the moon　Dance for here & now
Even Wild Horses　Dance music for an Absent Drama
(after Rimbaud)
L. Ludlow & A. Louw (Narrators), Gate 5 Ensemble
—H. Schwartz　　　　　　　# Partch.LP 9

OEDIPUS REX Music-drama, after Sophocles 1952, rev. 1954
A. Louw & Ensemble　(4ss)　　　# Partch.LP 2/3

PASCAL, Claude (b. 1921)

Capriccio　tpt. & pf.　1954
R. Delmotte & F. Gobet　　　♭ Pat.G 1054
(*Jolivet, Lesur, Ameller*)

Sonata　sax. & pf.
M. Mule & M. Lenom　　　　# D.LX 3130
(*Bozza, Bonneau, Tomasi, etc.*)　　(# Lon.LS 986)

PASQUINI, Bernardo (1637-1710)

SEE: † SONATAS OF THE XVIITH & XVIIITH CENTURIES
& also: RESPIGHI: Gli Uccelli

PASSEREAU (fl. 1510)

SEE: † FRENCH CHANSONS
† HISTORY OF MUSIC IN SOUND　(34)
† PARISIAN SONGS OF XVITH CENTURY

PAUMANN, Conrad (c. 1410-1473)

SEE: † HISTORY OF MUSIC IN SOUND　(30)
† SEVEN CENTURIES OF SACRED MUSIC

PEDRELL, Carlos (1878-1941)

SEE: † SEGOVIA PLAYS

PEERSON, Martin (c. 1572-1650)

SEE: † ANTHOLOGIE SONORE (# HS.AS 13)
† ELIZABETHAN LOVE SONGS
† ELIZABETHAN KEYBOARD MUSIC
† ELIZABETHAN SONGBAG FOR YOUNG PEOPLE

PEETERS, Flor (b. 1903)

Aria, Op. 51　organ
J. Harms　　　　　in # Uni.UN 1004
(*Bach, Weinberger, Vierne, Reger, etc.*)

Jubilate Deo, Op. 40　cho. & organ
UOS Cho.—McConnell & org.　in # UOS. 2
(*Smit, Handl, Victoria, etc.*)　　(pte. rec.)

PEIKO, Nikolai (b. 1916)

Moldavian Suite　orch.
☆ Moscow Radio—Rakhlin (2ss)　USSRM.D 524/5

PEIROL (fl. c. XIIIth Cent.)

SEE: † MONUMENTA ITALICAE MUSICAE

PEÑALOSA, Francisco (1470-1538)

SEE: † MUSIC OF THE RENAISSANCE

PEPPING, Ernst (b. 1901)

SEE: † ORGAN MUSIC (HEITMANN)

PEPUSCH, John Christopher (1667-1752)

(The) BEGGAR'S OPERA
Ballad Opera　3 Acts　1728
COMPLETE RECORDINGS (version of F. Austin)

CASTS of singers:	Set G	Set A
Polly (S) … … …	E. Morison	C. Prietto
Macheath (B) …	J. Cameron	D. Noble
Lucy (S) … …	M. Sinclair	M. Lipton
Lockit (T) … …	I. Wallace	J. Camburn
Peachum (Bs) …	O. Brannigan	R. Jones
Mrs. Peachum (S) …	C. Shacklock	M. Westbury
Filch (T) … …	A. Young	W. McAlpine
Jenny Diver (A) …	A. Pollak	

Set G with Pro Arte Orch. & Cho.—Sargent
(4ss)　　　　　　　# G.CLP 1052/3

Set A with Cho. & Ens.—R. Austin
(6ss)　　　　　　　# Argo.RG 76/8
(4ss, # West.WO 18119/20, set OPW 1201)
[Dialogue in both sets by separate casts of actors]

Sonata No. 4, F major　fl. & cont.
C. Dolmetsch (recorder) & J. Saxby (hpsi.)
in # D.LXT 2943
(† Recorder & Hpsi. Recital)　(# Lon.LL 1026)

Sonata, F major　ob., fl. & hpsi.
L. Wann, A. Mann (rec.), E. Weiss-Mann
West.WL 5214
(*Telemann & A. Scarlatti*)

PEREZ, Davidde (1711-c. 1779)

SEE: † CLAVECINISTES ESPAGNOLS

PERGOLESI, Giovanni Battista
(1710-1736)

I. INSTRUMENTAL

(6) CONCERTINOS　Str. Orch.[1]

No. 1, G major	No. 2, G major
No. 3, A major	No. 4, F minor
No. 5, E flat major	No. 6, B flat major

COMPLETE RECORDING　(ed. Giuranna)
I Musici Ens.　　　　　# C.CX 1306/7
(3ss—*below*)　　　(# Angel. 35251/2, set 3538)

Nos. 2, 3, 5, 6
Lamoureux Cha. Orch.—Colombo
LOL.OL 50010
(# OL.LD 60)

Nos. 1, 3, 4, 5
☆ Winterthur Sym.—Ephrikian　# Nix.WLP 5295
(# West.WL 5295; Sel. 320.CW.089)

No. 1, G major
Cha. Orch.—Cartigny　　　# LT.DTL 93044
(*Durante & Vivaldi*)　(# Sel.LA 1079; T.NLB 6096)
[M. Tournus, vlc. solo]

Paris Coll. Mus.—Douatte　　# QS.AR 2
(*below*)

Milan Angelicum—Gerelli[2]　Ang.SA 3020/1
(4ss)

No. 2, G major
Berlin Cha. Orch.—v. Benda[3] # DT.TM 68048
(*Mozart: Sym. 32*)　　　　(# T.TW 30021)
Augsburg Cha. Orch.—Deyle in † # AS. 3007LD
(# HS.AS 39)

No. 5, E flat major
☆ Virtuosi di Roma—Fasano　in # B.AXTL 1023
(# D.UAT 273581; Fnt.LP 3003)
☆ Italian Radio—Fighera (Orf. 54017)

No. 6, B flat major … 3rd movt.
— ARR. Stravinsky in *Pulcinella*, q.v.

---

[0] In 43-tone system.　The instruments are: Kithara, Surrogate Kithara, 3 Harmonic Canons, Chromelodeon, Diamond Marimba, Bass Marimba, Cloud Chamber Bowls, Eroica and wood-block, Adapted Viola and Adapted Guitars.
[1] *Concerti armonici*; attrib. to Pergolesi, but true authorship doubtful.　Have also been attrib. to Ricciotti, but this is now discredited.　[2] Ed. Gerelli.　[3] Labelled as by Ricciotti.

Concerto, G major, fl. & orch. "No. 1"
C. Wanausek & Vienna Pro Musica—F. Ch.
Adler # AmVox.PL 9440
(*Boccherini & Gluck*)

☆ R. Meylan & Winterthur Sym.—Dahinden (# Clc. 6165)

Concerto, B flat major, vln. & str. orch.
(*Sonata in stile di Concerto*)
I Musici Ens. # C.CX 1307
(*Sonata & Concertinos 5 & 6*)—ed. Giuranna
M. Abbado & Milan Str.—Abbado # C.FCX 370
(*Albinoni & Vivaldi*)
J. Laurent & Paris Coll. Mus.—Douatte
(*above*) # QS.AR 2

"Concerto", ob. & str. — ARR. Barbirolli
(from 2 Vln. Sonatas 5 & 9; Se tu m'ami; & Stabat
Mater No. 5)
P. Pierlot & Ens.—Froment # EPP.APG 119
(*Corelli, Handel, Scarlatti*)

(14) SONATAS, 2 vlns. & cont.[4]
No. 1, G major . . . 1st movt., Moderato
No. 2, B flat major . . . 1st movt., Presto
3rd movt., Allegro
No. 3, C minor . . . 3rd movt., Allegro assai
No. 7, G minor . . . 3rd movt., Allegro
No. 8, E flat major . . . 1st movt., Andantino
— ARR. Stravinsky in *Pulcinella*, q.v.
No. 5, C major . . . 1st movt., Allegro
No. 9, A major . . . 3rd movt., Allegro
— ARR. Barbirolli in *Concerto*, q.v.

No. 12, E major — ARR. VLN. & PF. Longo
N. Milstein & C. Bussotti in # DCap.CTL 7058
(*Schumann, Bloch, Suk, etc.*) (# Cap.P 8259)

. . . 4th movt., Presto — ARR. Stravinsky in *Pulcinella*, q.v.

No. 13, G minor (*Periodical Trio No. 1*) pub. 1771
☆ Vienna Sym.—Moralt # West.WN 18032
(*Locatelli & Sammartini*)

Sonata, F major vlc. & cont.
I Musici Ens.[5] # C.CX 1307
(*Concerto & Concertinos*)

. . . 4th movt. Presto — ARR. Stravinsky in *Pulcinella*, q.v.

SONATAS, Hpsi.
D major . . . Gavotta; E major . . . Allegro (Toccata)
— ARR. Stravinsky in *Pulcinella*, q.v.

II. VOCAL

CANTATAS
Contrasti crudeli[2] S, T, str. & hpsi.
E. Ribetti, A. Blaffard & Milan Angelicum
Orch.—Gerelli Ang.SA 3022/4
(6ss) (*Il Geloso Schernito, s. 3, on # LPA 953*)

(L') Orfeo: Nel chiuso centro 1735
A. Bianchini (T) & Italian Cha.—Jenkins[6]
HS.HSL 76
(*Cambini & Galuppi*) (in set HSL-C)

OPERAS
ADRIANO IN SIRIA 1734
Contento forse vivere (Aquilo's aria, Act III)
— ARR. Stravinsky in *Pulcinella*, q.v.

(La) CONTADINA ASTUTA 1 Act[7] 1734
COMPLETE RECORDING
Scintilla ... ... A. Tuccari (S)
Don Tabarrano ... ... A. Mineo (B)
& Rome Comic Op. Cho. & Orch.—Morelli
# Per.SPL 592
(# Cpt.MC 20064)

Belle e cocenti lagrime[8] S
E. Rizzieri Cet.CB 20544
(*Boccherini: Clementina, aria*)

(II) FLAMINIO 3 Acts 1735
Mentre l'erbetta pasce ("Serenata—Larghetto") T Act I
Con queste paroline ("Aria—Allegro alla breve") Bs Act I
— ARR. Stravinsky in *Pulcinella*, q.v.
Per te ho io nel core—SEE Contadina astuta, *above*

(Lo) FRATE 'NNAMORATO 3 Acts 1732
Excerpts — ARR. Stravinsky in *Pulcinella*:
Gnora credetemi (Vanella's aria, Act I) — ARR. ORCH.
(only, as "Allegro")
Sento dire; Chi dise ca la femmena (Trio, Act II)
("Largo—Larghetto")
Una te Falanzemprece (T. aria, Act II) ("Presto")
Pupillette fiammette (Don Pietro's aria, Act I)
("Tempo di minuet")

D'ogni pena ("Siciliana") T
M. Laszlo (S), F. Holetschek (pf.)
in # Nix.WLP 5375
(† *Italian Airs*) (# West.WL 5375)

(II) GELOSO SCHERNITO[9] 3 Parts 1746
COMPLETE RECORDING (ed. A. Antonelli)
Dorina ... ... E. Ribetti (S)
Masocco ... ... O. Borgonovo (B)
Cho. & orch of Milan Angelicum—Gerelli
(14ss) Ang.SA 3027/33
(also, 3ss, *above*, on # LPA 952/3)

(II) MAESTRO DI MUSICA[10] 1 Act 1752
E. Söderström (S), A. Ohlson (T), C-A. Hallgren
(B) & orch.—Gandelli # SS. 33117
[1955 Season cast, Drottningholm Theatre, Sweden]

(La) SERVA PADRONA 2 Parts 1733
R. Carteri (S), N. Rossi-Lemeni (B), La Piccola
Scala Orch.—Giulini # C.CX 1340
[E. Cantamessa, hpsi.] (# QCX 10152; Angel. 35279)

Stizzoso, mio stizzoso S
I. F. Gasperoni Cet.AT 0325
(*Cosi fan Tutte, No. 19*)

SONGS
Se tu m'ami (Rolli) (doubtful)
F. Barbieri (M-S), D. Marzollo (pf.)
in # AmVox.PL 7980
(† *Old Italian Songs & Airs*)
O. Moscucci (S), V. Vitale (pf.) ♭ C.SEDQ 504
(*Sarti, A. Scarlatti, Paradisi*)
☆ M. Laszlo (S), F. Holetschek (pf.) # Nix.WLP 5119
(† *Italian Songs*)
☆ C. Muzio (S) & orch. in # AmC.ML 4634
— ARR. Barbirolli as 3rd movt. of *Concerto*, q.v.
— ARR. Stravinsky in *Pulcinella*, q.v.

Tre giorni son che Nina (doubtful)[11]
G. Prandelli (T), D. Marzollo (pf.)
in # AmVox.PL 7930
(† *Old Italian Airs*)
M. Meli (S), V. Vitale (pf.) ♭ C.SEDQ 503
(*Monteverdi, Matteis*)
G. Gari (T), S. Leff (pf.) in # Mur.P 104
(followed by pf. acc. only for practice)
S. Baccaloni (Bs) in # Roy. 1547
ℍ E. Caruso (T) (in # Vic.LCT 1129*)

— ARR. VLC. & PF.
F. Smetana & D. Smetanová U.C 24427
(*Suk*)
J. Pacey & F. Kramer (in # MTR.MLO 1012)

SACRED
Laudate pueri, D major
. . . A solis ortu
☆ Y. Tinayre (T) & orch. in # AmD.DL 9654
(† *Seven Centuries of Sacred Music*) (in set DX 120)

---

[4] Nos. 1-12 published c. 1770; probably not by Pergolesi. [2] Ed. Gerelli.
[5] Ed. Giuranna for vlc. and str.—"*Sinfonia*".
[6] Recorded from MS. in Cherubini Conservatoire, Florence, containing Sinfonia.
[7] Shown by F. Walker (*Music & Letters*, Oct. 1949) to be really Hasse's *La Contadina* (1728) with interpolations from his
Il Tutore (1730); only the finale being by Pergolesi, his *Per te ho io nel core* from *Flaminio* (1735) also used in *La Serva Padrona*.
[8] From Hasse's *Il Tutore*. [9] By Pietro Chiarini.
[10] A pastiche of items from Auletta's opera *Orazio* (1737) with additions for the revivals of 1743, 1747, 1748 and 1752.
No. 9 is by G. M. Capelli; Nos. 3 and 4 may be by Galuppi; and No. 10 by Latilla.
[11] Possibly by V. Ciampi.

Salve Regina No. 4 orig. S & cont. (ed. Gerelli)
I. Bozza Lucca & Milan Angelicum—Gerelli
(4ss)   **Ang.SA 3025/6**

Salve Regina No. 5 S & orch. 1735-6
H. Glaz (M-S), Guilet St. Qtt. & H. Chessid
(hpsi.)[12]   **♯ MGM.E 3156**
(*Bach*)
☆ P. Neway & Allegro Cha. Orch.—Black (♯ *Allo. 4019*)

STABAT MATER S, A, Female Cho., orch. ?1736
COMPLETE RECORDING
T. Stich-Randall, E. Höngen & Vienna Academy
Cho. & St. Op. Orch.—Rossi ♯ **Van.BG 549**
☆ A. M. Augenstein, H. Plümacher, Stuttgart Cho. &
   Orch.—Grischkat (♯ Clc. 6114 & ♯ Cum.CPR 321)
... **Nos. 1, 2, 3, 7, 11, 12**
Regensburg Cath. Choir, Str. Qtt. & Org.
—Schrems   **♯ D.NLM 4560**
... **No. 4, Quae moerebat** A
... **No. 11, Fac ut portem** S & A
F. & E. Jankowitsch   **♯ EPhi.NBR 6011**
(*Mozart, Schubert, Herbeck*)   (♯ *Phi.N 00694R*)
... **No. 5, Quis est homo** — ARR. Barbirolli in *Concerto*

PERI, Jacopo (1561-1633)
SEE: † CANZONE SCORDATE

PERLE, George (b. 1915)
Rhapsody for orchestra, Op. 33 1953
Louisville—Whitney   **♯ LO. 9**
(*Einem & Rathaus*)

PEROSI, Lorenzo (1872-1956)
Missa Pontificalis 3 vv.
Santa Cecilia Acad. Cho. & Orch.—Somma
(*Somma*)   **♯ Csm.CLPS 1048**

PÉROTIN-le-GRAND (Perotinus Magnus)
                                (fl. XIIth Cent.)
COLLECTION (only 2 items actually by Pérotin)
Alle, Psallite Motet (*Anon.*)
Bon vin Motet (*Fr*, Anon.)
Nobilis humilis (Gymel, attrib. Pérotin)
Salvatoris hodie
Vetus abit littera Conductus, 4 voices (attrib. Pérotin)
Viderunt omnes 4 voices
☆ Dessoff Cho. & N.Y. Brass Ens.—Boepple (♯ Clc. 6189)

Alleluya (Nativitas) organum
E. Thorborg & E. Sørensen (T), Copenhagen
Univ. Cho.   **♯ HS.HSL 2071**
(† Masterpieces of Music before 1750)
(also in † Histoire de la Musique vocale)
Yale Univ. Music School Cho.—Hindemith
                                ♯ Over.LP 5
(† Yale University, Vol. II)

Beata viscera Mariae Virginis conductus
☆ Y. Tinayre (T) in † Seven Centuries of Sacred Music
                                (♯ AmD.DL 9653)

Diffusa est gratia organum triplum
☆ F. Anspach (T) & ens.—Cape (in † ♯ HS.AS 1)

PERRIN d'Agincourt (fl. XIIIth Cent.)
SEE: † ANTHOLOGIE SONORE

PERSICHETTI, Vincent (b. 1915)
Concerto, Op. 56 pf. duet & percussion 1952
D. & V. Persichetti & Ensemble
                                ♯ PFCM.CB 184
(*Dallapiccola & Schoenberg*)
(*Creston, in ♯ AmC.ML 4989*)

[12] Ed. Y. Pessl.

Divertimento, Op. 42 Band 1950
Eastman Sym. Wind Ens.—Fennell
                                ♯ Mer.MG 40006
(*Barber, Gould, Piston, etc.*)

(The) Hollow Men, Op. 25 tpt. & str. orch. 1944
S. Baker & M.G.M. Str.—Solomon
                                ♯ MGM.E 3117
(*Copland, Diamond, Goeb, Porter*)

Little Piano Book, Op. 60 14 pieces 1953
M. Richter   in ♯ **MGM.E 3147**
(*Richter, Skelly, Thomson, etc.*)

Pastoral Quintet, Op. 21 fl., ob., cl., hrn., bsn. 1943
New Art Wind Quintet   in ♯ **CEd. set 2003**
(*Goeb, Piston, etc.*)
Fredonia Faculty Wind Quintet   **♯ Fred. 2**
(*Marvel, Barrows, Ibert*)

Psalm, Op. 53 wind insts. 1952
Eastman Wind Ens.—Fennell ♯ **Mer.MG 40011**
(*Hanson, Reed, Mennin, Thomson*)

Symphony for strings, Op. 61 1953
Louisville—Whitney   **♯ LO. 7**
(*Blacher & Sanders*)

PETER, Johann Friedrich (1746-1813)
SEE ALSO: † AMERICAN MUSIC (VOCAL)

Quintet, Str., No. 1, D major
Quintet, Str., No. 6, E flat major 1789
☆ Moravian Quintet (*Moller & Gehot*)   ♯ **ARS. 33**

PETER, Simon
SEE: † AMERICAN MUSIC (VOCAL)

PETERSON-BERGER, Wilhelm
                                (1867-1942)
PIANO MUSIC
FRÖSÖ BLOSSOMS (*Frösöblomster*) pf.
SUITE No. 1
No. 2, Summer Song
C. Tillius   **G.X 7848**
(*Serenade*)
No. 6, At Frösö Church — ARR. VLN. & ORCH.
I. Zilzer (in C.DDX 39 : ♭ SCDK I)

Entry into the Sommerhagen
When the rowan blooms
C. Tillius   **G.X 7849**

Serenade
C. Tillius   **G.X 7848**
(*above*)

SONGS
Böljeby Waltz (Karlfeldt)
T. Hising (T), Y. Flyckt (pf.)   **D.F 44199**
(*Your eyes are like fires*)

Irmelin Rose (Jacobsen)
B. Loewenfalk (B), K. Olsson (pf.) **G.X 8134**
(*Gade: April Song*)

(The) Maiden under the lime-tree (V. d. Recke)
T. Hising (T), Y. Flyckt (pf.)   **D.F 44198**
(*May in Munga*)

May in Munga (Karlfeldt)
T. Hising (T), Y. Flyckt (pf.)   **D.F 44198**
(*Maiden under the lime-tree*)

Your eyes are like fires (Karlfeldt)
T. Hising (T), Y. Flyckt (pf.)   **D.F 44199**
(*Böljeby Waltz*)

PETRASSI, Goffredo (b. 1904)

Coro di Morti (Leopardi) cho. & orch.
Rome Radio Cho. & Sym.—Scaglia
　　　　　　　　　　　　♯ CIDM. n.d.
(*Dutilleux*) [No. 1 of subscription series: in prep.]

(Il) Ritratto di Don Chisciotte Ballet Suite 1945
Vienna State Op.—Litschauer　♯ Van.VRS 447
(*Respighi*)

PETRUCCI, Ottaviano dei (1466-1539)

SEE: † FRENCH CHANSONS

PEUERL, Paul (XVIIth Cent.)

SEE: † HISTORY OF MUSIC IN SOUND (41)

PEZEL (Pezelius), Johann (1639-1694)

COLLECTIONS (Nos. refer to DDT)
SONATAS 5 Brass Insts. (*Hora Decima*, 1670)
　Nos. 4, 6, 12, 30
FÜNF-STIMMIGTE BLASENDE MUSIK 1685
　No. 24. Bal
　No. 25, Sarabande
　No. 29. Bal
　No. 36. Courante
　Nos. 60-64. Allemande, Courante, Bal, Sarabande, Gigue
MUSICA VESPERTINA 5 Brass Insts.
　82. Sarabande

Brass Ens.—Schuller　　　　♯ EMS. 7

FÜNF-STIMMIGTE BLASENDE MUSIK 1685
　No. 29. Bal ("Intrada")
　No. 64. Gigue
MUSICA VESPERTINA
　No. 82. Sarabande
SONATA No. 3 (*Hora Decima*, ed. King)

Music Hall Brass Ens.　　in ♯ Mono. 817
(† Music for Brass)

FÜNF-STIMMIGTE BLASENDE MUSIK
　No. 13. Bal (Intrada)⎫
　No. 62. Bal　　　　 ⎬(ed. King)
　No. 63. Sarabande　⎭
SONATA No. 2 (*Hora Decima*)

Brass Ens.—R. Voisin　　in ♯ Uni.UN 1003
(† Golden Age of Brass)

FÜNF-STIMMIGTE BLASENDE MUSIK
　No. 13. Bal (Intrada)　　No. 17. Allemande
　No. 36. Courante　　　　No. 60. Allemande
　No. 64. Gigue
☆ Brass Ens.—Sachs († HS.AS 12)

PFITZNER, Hans (1869–1949)

PALESTRINA Opera 3 Acts 1917
Preludes, Acts I, II, III
☆ German Phil., Prague—Keilberth (♯ T.LSK 7012)

SONGS
ALTE WEISEN, Op. 33 (Keller) 1923
☆ E. Berger (S), M. Raucheisen (pf.) (*Brahms*)
　　　　　　　　　　　　♯ Pol. 18081

Die Einsame, Op. 9, No. 2 (Eichendorff) 1894-5
☆ Michaelskirchplatz, Op. 19, No. 2 (Busse) 1905
☆ Stimme der Sehnsucht, Op. 19, No. 1 (Busse)

M. Lawrence (S), F. Wolfes (pf.)
　　　　　　　　　　in ♯ Cam.CAL 216
[Op. 19, Nos. 1 & 2, also on ♭ *CAE 195*]

SYMPHONY: Kleine Symphonie, Op. 44 1939
Vienna Coll. Mus.—Rapf　　♯ SOT. 1061

PHILIDOR, André (c. 1647-1730)

MARCHES: COLLECTION ed. Haas
La Marche royale 1679 6 oboes & drums
La Marche pour le Roi de la Chine 1679
　2 cor ang., bsn. & side drums
Marche du Prince d'Orange "Lillibulero"
　4 obs., 2 cor ang., 2 bsn., 2 side drums
London Baroque Ens.—Haas　　P.R 20619
(*Lully: Marche*)　　　(in ♯ AmD.DL 4081)

Ordonnance de la Compagnie des Cannoniers de La Rochelle
　1703
Marche des Boulonnais
Marche des pompes funèbres 1711
Paris Coll. Mus.—Douatte in ♯ Cpt.MC 20102
(† Musique de la Grande Écurie)

Marche pour le carrousel de Monseigneur 1685
　("à quatre timbales")
Paris Coll. Mus.—Douatte　♯ LI.TWV 91092
(*Mouret, Couperin, Lully, Lalande*)　(♯ Cpt.MC 20086)

(Le) MARIAGE DE LA GROSSE CATHOS[1]
　1688 (?)
Orchestral Suite
Paris Coll. Mus.—Douatte　♯ Cpt.MC 20118
(*Lully, Couperin*)

PHILIPPENKO, Arkady Dmitrovich
　　　　　　　　　　　　　　(b. 1912)

Quartet No. 2, Str. 1948
　"Legend of the heroic partisans"
Vilyom Qtt. (2ss)　　USSRM.D 0799/800

PHILIPS, Peter (c. 1560-1634/40, or 1628)

SEE: † ENGLISH CHURCH MUSIC, VOL. IV
　　† OLD ENGLISH MASTERS

PHILLIPS, Burrill (b. 1907)

American Dance bsn. & orch.
▽ V. Pezzi & Eastman-Rochester—Hanson
　　　　　　　　(Vic. 18102, in set M 802)

Concert Piece bsn. & str. orch. 1940
S. Schoenbach & Philadelphia—Ormandy
　　　　　　　　　　in ♯ AmC.ML 4629

Concerto, pf. & orch. 1943
C. Richards & Illinois Univ. Sym.—Ansermet
(*Kelly*)　　　　　　　♯ UOI.CRS 4

PART SONG
(A) Bucket of water
South Hills High Sch. Cho.—Crawford
　　　　　　　　in ♯ PFCM.CB 161
(*Poulenc, Copland, Santa Cruz, etc.*)

Selections from McGuffey's Reader
　Suite, orch. 1934
A.R.S. Sym.—Schönherr[2]　　　♯ ARS. 38
(*Brant*)

Sonata, vlc. & pf.
C. Stern & B. Phillips　　　♯ SPA. 54
(*Swanson*)

PICCINNI, Nicolo (1728-1800)

ATYS Opera 1780
Overture
Naples Scarlatti Orch.—Caracciolo
　　　　　　　　in ♯ Csm.CLPS 1046
(*below, Ghedini, Traetta, etc.*)

Piega l'ale dolce sonno Aria (unid.)
G. Sciutti (S) & Naples Scarlatti Orch.
— Caracciolo　　　in ♯ Csm.CLPS 1046

---

[1] The notes on the record sleeve attribute this work to André-Danican Philidor (1726-1795), and M. Douatte says it was written for Les Divertissements de la Foire de St. Germain, 1754. It has not been possible to reconcile this information with other authorities.
[2] Also stated to be cond. Swarowsky.

PICK-MANGIAGALLI, Riccardo
(1882-1949)

(La) Danza di Olaf, Op. 33, No. 2 pf.
D. Raucea   ‡ **D.LXT 2969**
(*Casella, Granados, Castelnuovo-Tedesco, & Saint-Saëns*)
(‡ Lon.LL 1033)

(3) Fugues str. qtt.
La Scala Qtt.   ‡ **Ura. 7075**
(*Respighi & Malipiero*)

PIERNÉ, Henri Constant Gabriel
(1863-1937)

CYDALISE ET LE CHÈVRE-PIED Ballet 1923
Marche des petits faunes orch.
Hamburg Philharmonia—H-J. Walther
      MSB. 78105
(*Marche des petits soldats de plomb*)
☆ Boston Pops.—Fiedler (in ‡ Vic.LM 1790:
      ♭ set ERB 26)
— ARR. FL., OB., CL., HRN., BSN.
Chicago Sym. Woodwind Quintet (in ‡ Aphe.AP 17)

Étude de concert, Op. 13 pf. 1887
C. de Groot   in ‡ *Phi.N 00632R*
(*Rachmaninoff, Chabrier, etc.*)

FRAGONARD Opérette 1934
Je voudrais plaire S
☆ L. Jourfier (ArgPat.FXC 0006)

Impromptu caprice, Op. 9 hp. 1885
P. Berghout   in ‡ *Phi.N 00633R*
(*J. Thomas, Tournier, Soulage, etc.*)

Introduction & Variations sur une ronde populaire
   sax. qtt. 1936
M. Mule Saxophone Qtt.   ‡ *D.LX 3135*
(*Absil & Schmitt*)   (‡ Lon.LS 1076)
A. Sax Saxophone Qtt.   in ‡ *Phi.N 00616R*
(*Françaix, Debussy, Albeniz*)

Marche des petits soldats de plomb, Op. 14, No. 6
   pf. 1887
— ARR. ORCH.
Hamburg Philharmonia—H-J. Walther
      MSB. 78015
(*Cydalise—Marche*)
Royale Concert Orch. (in ‡ Roy. 1567)
☆ Boston Pops.—Fiedler (♭ G. 7EP 7019; 7EBF 4:
      7EPQ 504; ♭ DV. 16301)
— ARR. FL., OB., CL., BSN., HRN.
Chicago Sym. Woodwind Quintet (in ‡ Aphe.AP 17)

Pastorale, Op. 14, No. 1 pf. 1887
— ARR. FL., OB., CL., BSN., HRN. Pierné
Garde Républicaine Quintet   ‡ *D.FA 143659*
(*Ibert & Milhaud*)

RAMUNTCHO Inc. Music to Loti's play 1894
Overture ☆ Colonne—Pierné (♭ Od. 7AOE 1012)

Serenade, A major, Op. 7 pf.
— ARR. CHO. Darcieux
Venlona Male Cho.—Vranken ♭ *G.7EPH 1013*
(*Debussy, d'Indy, Poulenc*)

SONG: Le Moulin (E. Guinand) 1881
L. Castellano (S), S. Leff (pf.) in ‡ **Mur.P 105**
(followed by pf. acc. only)

PIERO, Maestro (fl. XIVth Century)
SEE: † History of Music in Sound (22)

PIJPER, Willem (1894-1947)

(6) Adagios orch. 1940
Residentie—Flipse   **Phi.N 12051G**

Concerto, pf. & orch. 1927
H. Henkemans & Amsterdam—v. Beinum
(6) Epigrams orch. 1928
Amsterdam—v. Beinum   ‡ **Phi.A 00219L**
(*Henkemans*)   (‡ Epic.LC 3093, o.n. ‡ AmC.ML 4937)
Sonatina No. 2 pf. 1925
☆ J. Antonietti (♭ Pol. 32036)

Symphony No. 3 1926
Amsterdam—v. Beinum   ‡ **D.LXT 2873**
(*Dlepenbrock*)   (‡ Lon.LL 851)

PILKINGTON, Francis (c. 1580-1638)

AYRES 1605
Rest, sweet nymphs
N.Y. Pro Musica Antiqua—Greenberg
      in ‡ *Eso.ESJ 6*
(† Elizabethan Songbag)
Hufstader Singers   in ‡ *SOT. 1092*
☆ H. Cuénod (T), H. Leeb (lute) (in † ‡ Nix.WLP 5085)
Underneath a cypress tree
H. Cuénod (T), C. J. Chiasson (hpsi.)
      in ‡ *Nix.LLP 8037*
(† Elizabethan Love Songs)   (‡ Lyr.LL 37)
MADRIGALS
(The) Messenger of the delightful spring 1613
N.Y. Pro Musica Antiqua—Greenberg
      in ‡ *Eso.ESJ 6*
(† Elizabethan Songbag)
When Oriana walked to take the air
Randolph Singers—Randolph
      in ‡ *Nix.WLP 6212-2*
(† Triumphs of Oriana)   (in ‡ West. set WAL 211)

PISADOR, Diego (1508/9—after 1557)
SEE: † Anthologie Sonore

PISTON, Walter (b. 1894)

Chromatic Study on B.A.C.H. organ 1940
M. Andrews   ‡ **UOK. 2**
(*Lübeck, Křenek, Sessions*)

(The) Incredible Flutist Ballet Suite 1938
Boston Prom.—Fiedler (n.v.)
      in ‡ **Vic. set LM 6113**
(*Meyerbeer, Roussel, Stravinsky, etc.*)   (‡ FV.A 630217)
Berlin Radio—Rother   ‡ **Ura. 7092**
(*Copland*)
☆ Boston Prom.—Fiedler (o.v.)   ‡ **Cam.CAL 145**
(*MacDowell*)

Partita, vln., vla. & org. 1944
S. Thaviu, K. Malno & V. W. Fillinger
      ‡ **PFCM.CB 190**
(*Hindemith & Křenek*)

(3) Pieces fl., cl. & bsn. 1926
Members of New Art Wind Quintet
      in ‡ **CEd. set 2003**
(*Goeb, Persichetti, etc.*)

Quartet No. 1, strings 1933
Juilliard Qtt.   ‡ **PFCM.CB 157**
(*Webern & Malipiero*)

Quintet, pf. & str. 1949
J. Harris & New Music Qtt.   ‡ **PFCM.CB 159**
(*Shostakovich*)
E. Wild & Walden Qtt.   ‡ **McInt.MM 109**
(*Martinů: Qtt. No. 6*)   (o.n. ‡ WCFM. 14)

SYMPHONIES
No. 2 1943
☆ A.R.S. Orch.—Dixon (*Cowell*)   ‡ **ARS. 112**
No. 3 1947
Eastman-Rochester Sym.—Hanson
      ‡ **Mer.MG 40010**

☆ = Re-issue of a recording to be found in previous volumes.

SYMPHONIES (*continued*)
No. 4 1951
  Philadelphia—Ormandy   ♯ AmC.ML 4992
  (*W. Schuman*)

Trio pf., vln., vlc. 1935
  N.Y. Trio   ♯ Persp. 2004
  (*Hindemith*)

Tunbridge Fair Intermezzo, Band 1950
  Eastman Wind Ens.—Fennell ♯ Mer.MG 40006
  (*Persichetti, Barber, Schuman, etc.*)   (♭ EP 1-5062)

PITTALUGA, Gustavo   (b. 1906)

Danza de la Hoguera pf.
  ☆ G. Copeland (in ♯ MGM.E 3025)
(La) ROMERIA DE LOS CORNUDOS
  Ballet with Sop. 1930
... **Romanza de Solita** (C. R. Cherif)
  N. Merriman (M-S), G. Moore (pf.)
           in ♯ C.CX 1243
  († Spanish Songs)   (♯ FCX 392; Angel. 35208)

PIZZETTI, Ildebrando   (b. 1880)

Appassionato (Canto III) vlc. & pf. 1924
  L. W. Pratesi & D. O. Colacelli
           in ♯ ArgOd.LDC 529
  (*Haydn, Saint-Saëns, etc.*)

(La) PISANELLA Inc. Music (D'Annunzio) 1913
Danza bassa dello sparviero Act III
  Naples Scarlatti Orch.—Caracciolo
           ♯ Csm.CLPS 1038
  (*Casella: Scarlattiana*)

PIZZINI, Carlo Alberto   (b. 1905)

(Il) Diavolo scrittore Inc. Music to radio play
... **Scherzando & Valzer nostalgico**
  Cetra Orch.—Kretschmar   Cet.AT 0377

Symphony, C minor ... **Scherzo in classical style**
  ☆ E.I.A.R. Sym.—Tansini (P.DPX 46)

PLANQUETTE, Jean Robert (1848-1903)
         (Abridged listings only)

(Les) CLOCHES DE CORNEVILLE Operetta
COMPLETE RECORDING   [1877
  C. Riedinger, J. Giraudeau, E. Blanc, L. Musy,
  etc. Cho. & Orch.—Dervaux
           ♯ LI.TW 91114/5
  (4ss)   (♯ D.FMT 163641/2)
  [Excerpts on ♭ D.EFM 455563/4]

J'ai fait trois fois le tour du monde Act I B
Non vous le voyez Act II   B & cho.
  ☆ M. Dens & R. St. Paul Cho. (Pat.PA 3007; J'ai fait
    trois fois ... only, ♭ ED 3)

Chanson des cloches
Air: Ne parlez pas de mon courage
  ☆ M. Angelici (S) (from set) (♭ Pat.ED 9)

PLATTI, Giovanni   (c. 1690-1762)

Sonata No. 1, E minor fl. [or vln.] & cont.
  S. Gazzelloni (fl) & R. Raffalt (hpsi.)
           ♯ ItV.A12R 0027
  (*Marcello, Vivaldi, Locatelli, etc.*)

PLEYEL, Ignaz [Joseph]   (1757-1831)

Symphonie concertante No. 5, F major
  fl., ob., hrn., bsn., orch.
  J-P. Rampal, P. Pierlot, G. Coursier, P. Hongne
  & Cha. Ens.—Froment   ♯ LOL.OL 50014
  (*Dittersdorf: Partitas*)   (♯ OL.LD 74)

POLLEDRO, Giovanni Battista   (1781-1853)
  SEE: † MUSICAL ORGAN CLOCK

PONCE, Juan   (fl. XIVth Cent.)
  SEE: † SPANISH MUSIC c. 1500

PONCE, Manuel M.   (1882-1948)

COLLECTIONS
PIANO MUSIC
  Preludio mexicano
  Mazurkas Nos. 1, 6, 17
  Danzas mexicanas 1 to 4
  Cielito lindo ⎫
  La Valentina ⎭ Song Transcriptions
  F. G. Medeles   ♯ Peer.LPP 036

PIANO PIECES:
  Rapsodia mexicana (unspec.)
  Mazurka (unspec.)
  Scherzino mexicana
  Intermezzo
  Gavotte (1900)
  S. Contreras   ♯ CM. 7
           (♯ Eli.LPE 115)

SONGS
  Todo paso; Serenata mexicana
  Perdí un amor; Soño mi mente loca;
  Lejos de tí; A la orilla de un palmar;
  Marchita mi alma; Estrellita
  M. González (S), A. Montiel Olvera (pf.)
           ♯ CM. 9

Amorosamente, Valse; Mayo pf.
  S. Contretras   ♯ CM. 18
  (*J. G. Jorda*)

GUITAR PIECES (Some may be arrs.)
(3) Canciónes mexicanas
  G. Zepoll   in ♯ Nix.SLPY 142
           (♯ SOT. 1024)

... **No. 2 only** (ed. Segovia)
  M. A. Funes   ArgOd. 57058
  (*Moreno Torroba: Punteado*)

... **No. 3, La Valentine** (ed. Segovia)
  A. Segovia   in ♯ AmD.DL 9734
  († Segovia Plays)   (♯ D.UAT 273573)
  M. A. Funes   ArgOd. 57047
  (*Bach: Vln. Sonata, excpt. arr.*)

... **Canción mexicana** (unspec.)
  M. D. Cano   Dur.AI 10154
  (*Yradier: La Paloma*)   (♯ AI 506)

Mazurka (Homage to Tárrega) (No. 1 of 4 *Pieces*)
  A. Segovia   in ♯ AmD.DL 9795
  († Segovia, The Art of)   (♯ D.UAT 273594)

(6) Preludes, Op. posth.
  A. Segovia   ♯ B.AXTL 1070
  († Segovia Evening)   (♯ AmD.DL 9733; SpC.CCL 35015

Sonata No. 3, D minor
  A. Segovia   in ♯ AmD.DL 9795
  († Segovia, The Art of)   (♯ D.UAT 273594)

Sonata No. 5, D major (Meridional)
  ☆ A. Segovia (in † ♯ AmC.ML 4732)

Thème varié et Finale, E minor
  A. Segovia   in ♯ AmD.DL 9734
  († Segovia Plays)   (♯ D.UAT 273573)

♯ = Long-playing, 33⅓ r.p.m.   ♭ = 45 r.p.m.   ♮ = Auto. couplings, 78 r.p.m.

Valse   (No. 2 of 4 *Pieces*)
C. Aubin   ♯ **Eko.LG 1**
(† Guitar Recital)
A. Segovia   in † ♯ **AmD.DL 9795**

Intermezzo pf.
Fausto García Medeles   ♯ **Peer.LPP 036**
(*Villanueva, Rosas, Castro*)
SONGS
A la orilla de un palmar
☆ T. Schipa (T) & orch. (♭ *G. 7EPL 13045*)
Estrellita
L. Pastor (S) (♭ *Pat.EG 147*)
P. Munsel (S, *Eng*) (♭ *G. 7EP 7009; Vic.ERA 80*)
G. Swarthout (M-S, *Eng*) (♭ *Vic.ERA 92*)
E. Sack (S) (in ♯ *D.LM 4531*)
A. M. Alberghetti (in ♯ *Mer.MG 20056*)

— ARR. VLN. & PF.   Heifetz
     A. Campoli & E. Gritton (♭ *D. 71103 & ♯ LW 5180*)
     B. Rubato & B. Ritorno (in ♯ *Phi.S 06024R*)
     ▽ J. Heifetz (*G.DA 1072*)
     and innumerable other versions

PONCHIELLI, Amilcare (1834-1886)

(La) GIOCONDA Opera   4 Acts   1876
COMPLETE RECORDINGS

Gioconda ... ... M. M. Callas (S)
Laura ... ... F. Barbieri (M-S)
La Cieca ... ... M. Amadini (A)
Enzo Grimaldo ... ... G. Poggi (T)
Barnaba ... ... P. Silveri (B)
Alvise ... ... G. Neri (Bs)

Italian Radio Cho. & Orch.—Votto
           ♯ **CCet. set 1241**
(6ss)   (♯ *Pol. 18164/6*)
[Highlights on ♭ *Cap.FAP 7012;* ♭ *Cet.EPO 0320;* Prelude only in ♯ *CCet. 50159*]
☆ A. Corridori, M. Pirazzini, G. Campora, F. Corena, etc.
    La Scala Cho. & Orch.—Parodi
     (♯ *Nix.ULP 9229-1/4:* Ov. & Danza delle ore
     [Other excerpts, ♭ *Nix.EP 718*]   also, ♭ *EP 701*)

ACT I

Assassini!   T & cho.
☆ G. Lauri-Volpi (*AF.AGSA 28*)

Voce di donna . . . A te questo rosario M-S or A
E. Sachs, S. Leff (pf.)   in ♯ **Mur.P 111**
(followed by pf. acc. only)
    V. Borisenko (*Russ*) (in ♯ *USSR.D 1593*)
ℍ S. Onegin (in ♯ *Sca. 821*¹)

Enzo Grimaldo, Principe di Santafior   T & B
☆ B. Gigli & G. de Luca (♭ *Vic.ERAT 10:* in ♯ *LCT 1138*)
ℍ B. Gigli & Zani (in *SBDH.LPP 5**)
    B. Gigli & T. Ruffo¹ (AF.AGSB 49;
               in ♯ *G.FJLP 5010:* QJLP 101)
    E. Caruso & T. Ruffo (in ♯ *SBDH.LLP 7**)
    G. Zenatello, P. Amato & pf. (in ♯ *Ete. 483**)

Maledici? . . . O monumento! (Monologo) B
ℍ T. Ruffo (in ♯ *Vic. set LCT 6701**)

ACT II

Cielo e mar!   T
J. Björling   **G.DB 21563**
(*Aida—Celeste Aida*)   (♭ *7R 160*)
N. Gedda   in ♯ **C.CX 1130**
            (♯ FCX 302; Angel. 35096)
M. del Monaco   **D.X 572**
(*Pagliacci—Prologue*)   (in ♯ *D.LXT 2845;* Lon.LL 880;
           & in ♯ *D.LXT 2964;* Lon.LL 1025)
(also in ♯ *D.LW 5093;* Lon.LD 9082)
J. Soler   **Cet.PE 181**
(*Aida—Celeste Aida*)
R. Tucker   in ♯ **AmC.ML 4750**
A. da Costa   in ♯ **Roy. 1599**

E. Lorenzi   **Cet.PE 208**
(*Lucia—Tu che a Dio*)
W. Kmentt (*Ger*)   in ♯ **Phi.S 06076R**
(*Elisir d'amore, Manon Lescaut, etc.*)
☆ G. Prandelli   ♭ **D. 71106**
(*Don Pasquale—Cercherò lontana*)
M. Alexandrovich (*Russ*) (in ♯ *USSR.D 2219*)
☆ G. Poggi (in ♯ *Cet.LPC 55003*)
    B. Gigli (in ♯ *Vic. set LCT 6010:* ♭ *set WCT 6010:*
                        ♭ *ERAT 12*)
    M. Lanza (in ♯ *G.ALP/WALP 1071:* FBLP 1043:
                        ♭ *7ERQ 127*)
    K. Baum (♭ *Rem.REP 6*)
    J. Löhe (*Ger*) (in ♯ *T.LA 6107*)
ℍ E. Caruso (in ♯ *G.FJLP 5009**: QJLP 105*)
    A. Pertile (in ♯ *Od.ODX 127**: MOAQ 301*)
    G. Anselmi & pf. (in ♯ *Sca. 816**)

Laggiù nelle nebbie remote   M-S & T
F. Barbieri & G. Poggi   in ♯ **CCet.A 50178**
(*Bohème, Chénier, etc.*)   (from set)
ℍ G. Casazzi & B. Gigli (in ♯ *SBDH.LPP 5**)

ACT III

Qui chiamata m'avete?   M-S & Bs
Bella cosi, madonna
W. Heckman & J. Hines   in ♯ **PRCC. 3**

Danza delle ore   (*Dance of the hours*)
Philharmonia—Karajan   in ♯ **C.CX 1327**
(*Tannhäuser, Aida, etc.*)   (♯ Angel. 35307)
N.B.C.—Toscanini   **G.DB 21587**
(in ♯ *ALP 1235:* FALP 220: ♭ *7RF 285;* in ♯ *Vic.LRM 7005:*
     ♭ *set ERB 7005:* ♯ *LM 1834;* ♭ *ItV.A72R 0006;*
           ♯ *FV.A 330211* & A 630247; DV.L 16483)
Belgian Radio—André   ♯ **DT.TM 68020**
(*Scala di Seta, Overture*)   (TV.VE 9037)
(*Rosenkavalier, Waltzes on* ♭ *T.TW 30009*)
N.W. German Phil.—Schüchter ♯ **Imp.ILP 110**
(*Gounod, Schmidt, R. Strauss*)   (♯ *G.QDLP 6025*)
Hollywood Bowl—Barnett   in ♯ **Cap.P 8296**
(*Saint-Saëns, Liszt, etc.*)   (♭ set FAP 8296)
Vienna Radio—Sandauer   ♭ **Phi.KD 160**
(*Schmidt: Notre Dame, Intermezzo*)   (♭ P 423160E)
Sym.—Martini (ArgOd. 66019: ♭ *BSOA 4001:* BSOAE 451)
International Sym.—Schneiderhann (in ♯ *Mae.OAT 25003*)
Berlin Sym.—List (in ♯ *Roy. 1394:* ♭ *EP 186*)
Moscow Radio—Samosud (*USSRM.D 202*)

☆ Hallé—Sargent (♭ *C.SCD 2011:* SCDQ 2003:
                      SCDW 106)
    Paris Cons.—Fistoulari (♯ *D.LW 5010;* Lon.LD 9014)
    Boston Prom.—Fiedler (G.EB 575; ♭ *DV. 16296*)
    Chicago Sym.—Stock (in ♯ *AmC.RL 3022*)
    Covent Gdn.—Braithwaite (in ♯ *P.PMC 1029:*
                        MGM.E 3037)
    Bavarian Sym.—Graunke (FPV. 5041, d.c.; PV. 72466)
    La Scala—Parodi, from set (in ♯ *Nix.ULP 9084;*
       Ura. 7084 & ♯ *RS 5-3;* in ♯ *ACC.MP 13*)
    Col. Sym.—Beecham (♭ *AmC. 4-4801*)
    etc.

ACT IV

Suicidio!   S
Z. Milanov   ♯ **G.ALP 1247**
(*Cavalleria, Trovatore, etc.*)   (in ♯ *Vic.LM 1777:*
                       ♭ *set ERB 19*)
M. M. Callas (from set)   in ♯ **CCet.A 50176**
(*Puritani, Lucia, Tristan*)
M. Vitale   in ♯ **Cet.LPC 55001**
(*Thaïs,, etc.; & Paisiello, Schubert, etc.*)
D. Rigal   **ArgOd. 66013**
(*Traviata—Addio del passato*)   (in ♯ *LDC 503;*
                  in ♯ *AmD.DL 4060*)
V. Petrova   in ♯ **Ace. 1007/8**
(*Cavalleria, Forza, Trovatore, etc.*)
☆ R. Raisa (in ♯ *Vic.LCT 1158*)
ℍ R. Ponselle (in ♯ *Sca. 803**)
    E. Burzio (*IRCC. 3136**; in ♯ *HRS. 3007**)
    C. Boninsegna (in ♯ *Sca. 813**)
    A. Pinto (SBDH.G 2*)

Dal carcere   S & T
ℍ E. Mazzoleni & G. Zenatello (in ♯ *Sca. 818**)

Ecco la barca—addio   S
ℍ E. Burzio (*IRCC. 3136**; in ♯ *HRS. 3007**)

---

¹ 1926 recording, presumably electric.

POOT, Marcel (b. 1901)

Allegro symphonique orch. 1937
☆ Belgian Radio—André (*Grétry*)   **TV.VE 9026**

(3) Danses orch. 1938
1. Sarcastico   2. Erotico   3. Giocoso
Impromptu en forme de rondo pf. 1935
(6) Petites Pièces pf. & orch.
  N. Sluszny & Belgian Radio Cha.—Doneux
       ‡ Gramo.GLP 2504
[*Sarcastico only, with Brenta, on ‡ Gramo.GLP 2502*]

Symphony No. 2 (*Triptyque symphonique*) 1937
Belgian Nat.—Quinet   **‡ D.BA 133101**

Toccata pf.
  ▽ S. Cambier   (*De Boeck: Capriccio*)   **C.DCB 56**

POPOV, Gabriel Nikolaievitch (b. 1904)

Symphony No. 2 (*Patria*)
Leipzig Phil.—Abendroth   **‡ Ura. 7163**
(*Liadov*)

PORTA, Costanzo (c. 1530-1601)

SEE: † MOTETS OF THE VENETIAN SCHOOL

PORTER, Quincy (b. 1897)

Concerto, vla. & orch. 1948
P. Angerer & A.R.S. Orch.—Schönherr
(*Dello Joio: Serenade*)   **‡ ARS. 36[1]**

Concerto concertante 2 pfs. & orch. 1953
Dance in Three time cha. orch. 1937
A. Terrasse, J-L. Cohen & Concerts Colonne
—Porter   **‡ Over.LP 10**
(*below*)

Poem and Dance orch. 1932
Eastman-Rochester Sym.—Hanson
       ‡ Mer.MG 40013
(*Donovan & Hively*)

Quartet, Str. No. 6 1937
Pascal Qtt.[2]   **‡ C.FCX 220**
(*Garcia Caturla & Roldán*)   (**‡ Angel. 35105**)

Music for Strings 1941
M.G.M. Str.—I. Solomon   **‡ MGM.E 3117**
(*Copland, Diamond, Goeb, Persichetti*)

Symphony No. 1 1934
Concerts Colonne—Porter   **‡ Over.LP 10**
(*above*)

POULENC, Francis (b. 1899)

CLASSIFIED: I. Piano   II. Chamber Music
         III. Orchestral   IV. Stage Music
         V. Cantatas   VI. Church Music
         VII. Partsongs   VIII. Songs

I. PIANO
& piano duet, 2 pfs.

COLLECTION

Humoresque 1935
Improvisation No. 5, A flat major 1932
Valse (from *Album des six*) 1926
  ☆ A. Haas-Hamburger   **‡ Fel.RL 89006**
   (*Pf. concerto; & Milhaud*)

(L') Embarquement pour Cythère
(Valse-musette) 2 pfs. 1951
V. Vronsky & V. Babin   in **‡ AmD.DL 9791**
(*Dvořák, Borodin, etc.*)

(12) Improvisations 1932
J-M. Damase   **‡ D.FST 153527**
(*Damase, Messiaen, Roussel, etc.*)

... **No. 5, A flat major** □
J. Casadesus   **‡ Angel. 35261**
(*Français, Tailleferre, Casadesus, etc.*)

(3) Mouvements perpetuels 1918
G. Johannesen   **‡ Nix.CLP 1181**
(*below & Fauré*)   (**‡ CHS.CHS 1181**)
  ☆ O. Levant (in **‡ AmC.ML 2018**)

... **No. 2, only** — ARR.
C. Santias (in **‡ FestF.FLD 32: SpFest.HF 3201**)

Napoli, Suite 1926
... **No. 3, Caprice italien** only
  ☆ M. Panzéra (in **‡ Clc. 6260**)

(8) Nocturnes
(1-7, 1929-35; 8, pour servir du Coda du Cycle, 1938)
G. Johannesen   **‡ Nix.CLP 1181**
(*above & Fauré*)   (**‡ CHS.CHS 1181**)

Pastourelle (*L'Éventail de Jeanne*, No. 8) 1927
M. Pressler   in **‡ MGM.E 3129**
(*Satie, Respighi, Griffes, etc.*)   (♭ set X 254)

Presto, B flat major 1935
C. de Groot   in **‡ Phi.N 00632R**
(*Pierné, Rachmaninoff, Prokofiev, etc.*)

— ARR. VLN. & PF. Heifetz
  ☆ J. Heifetz & E. Bay (♭ Vic.ERA 126)

(Les) Soirées de Nazelles 1936
J. Ranck   **‡ Zod. 1002**
(*Griffes, Tcherepnin, Werle*)

Sonata pf. 4 hands 1918
R. Gold & A. Fizdale   **‡ AmC.ML 4854**
(*Milhaud, Satie, Debussy*)   (in set SL 198)

Sonata 2 pfs. 1953
R. Gold & A. Fizdale   **‡ AmC.ML 5068**
(*Bowles: Picnic*)

II. CHAMBER MUSIC

Sextet pf., fl., ob., cl., hrn., bsn. 1930-2
L. Lurie & Fine Arts Wind Players
       ‡ DCap.CTL 7066
(*Hindemith*)   (‡ Cap.P 8258)
New Art Sextet   in **‡ CEd. set 2006**
(*Tailleferre, Honegger, etc.*)
J. Françaix & French Nat. Orch. Ens.
       ‡ Pat.DTX 135
(*Françaix*)   (‡ Angel. 35133)
H. Krugt & Netherlands Phil. Wind Quintet
(*Hindemith*)   **‡ CHS.H 15**

Sonata hrn., tpt., tbne. 1922
  ☆ A. Barr, H. Glanz, G. Pulis (‡ Cum.CS 191)

Trio pf., ob. & bsn. 1926
B. Zighera, L. Speyer & E. Panenka
       ‡ Uni.UN 1005
(*Roland-Manuel, Milhaud, etc.*)
  ☆ H. D. Koppel, W. Wölsing & C. Bloch
       (♭ Mtr.MCEP 3002)

III. ORCHESTRAL

Aubade
  Concerto chorégraphique, pf. & 18 insts. 1926
F. Jacquinot & Westminster Sym.—Fistoulari
       ‡ P.PMC 1019
(*Debussy*)   (‡ MGM.E 3069; Od.ODX 149)

Concerto, piano & orch. 1948
  ☆ A. Haas-Hamburger & Pasdeloup—Dervaux
  (*Piano pieces; & Milhaud*)   **‡ Fel.RL 89006**

---

[1] Originally announced as ARS. 17 with *McBride*.
[2] U.N.E.S.C.O. recording.
[3] Originally announced as CHS 1176 with *Schubert-Liszt: Wanderer Fantasia*.

IV. STAGE WORKS

(Les) BICHES Ballet Cho. & orch. 1923
Orch. Suite re-orch. 1939-40
L.S.O.—Fistoulari   **♯ P.PMC 1004**
(Fauré)   (♯ MGM.E 3098)

(Les) MAMELLES DE TIRESIAS Opéra-bouffe
Prologue & 2 Acts 1946
COMPLETE RECORDING
R. Jeantet (B), D. Duval (S), J. Giraudeau (T),
S. Rallier (T), E. Rousseau (B), etc., Opéra-
Comique Cho. & Orch.—Cluytens
                             ♯ C.CX 1218
                   (♯ FCX 230; Angel. 35090)

V. CANTATAS

(Le) BAL MASQUÉ 1932 B, Septet & Percussion
☆ W. Galjour & Cha. Orch.—Fendler   ♯ Eso.ES 518
(Français)   (♯ Cpt.MC 20004)

Sécheresses (E. James) Mixed cho. & orch. 1937
E. Brasseur Cho. & Paris Cons. Orch.—Tzipine
                             ♯ C.CX 1252
(Tailleferre, Honegger, Durey)   (♯ FCX 264;
                             Angel. 35117, in set 3515)

VI. CHURCH MUSIC

Ave, verum corpus 1952
Pennsylvania College of Women Cho.
—Wichmann   in **♯ PFCM.CB 161**
(Copland, Santa Cruz, Chajus, etc.)

MASS, G major unacc. cho. 1937
Fredonia Teachers Coll. Cho.—Gunn **♯ Fred. 1**
(Barber, Handel, Petersen, etc.)
☆ R. Shaw Chorale (♯ G.FALP 273)

(4) MOTETS POUR LE TEMPS DE NOËL
1. O magnum mysterium
2. Quem vidistis pastores
3. Videntes stellam magi
4. Hodie Christus natus est
Netherlands Cha. Cho.—de Nobel
                             ♯ Phi.N 00679R
(Salve Regina; Martin, Hopkins)

Salve Regina unacc. cho. 1941
Netherlands Cha. Cho.—de Nobel
                             ♯ Phi.N 00679R
(above; Martin, Hopkins)

Stabat Mater S, cho., orch. 1951
J. Brumaire, Alauda Cho. & Concerts Colonne
Orch.—Frémaux[1]   **♯ Véga.C35 A1**

VII. PART SONGS

(7) Chansons pour chœur mixed vv., unacc.
... No. 1, La Reine de Saba (Legrand)
... No. 2, À peine défigurée (Éluard)
Lyons Psalette—Geoffray   in **♯ SM. 33-21**
(Schmitt, Hindemith, etc.)

Chansons françaises (Trad.) 1945
... No. 4, Clic, clac, dansez, sabots
... No. 6, La belle si nous étions
Venlona Male Cho.—Vrankens ♭ **G.7EPH 1013**
(below; Debussy, d'Indy, Pierné)

(4) Petites prières Male cho. unacc.
(St. Francis of Assisi) 1949
☆ Maastricht Male Cho.—Koekelkoren
                          (in ♯ Phi.N 00617R)

... Seigneur je vous en prie, only
Venlona Cho.—Vranken   ♭ **G.7EPH 1013**
(above, Chansons françaises, excpts.; Pierné, etc.)

Petites voix (Ley) Female cho. unacc. 1936
French Nat. Radio Cho.—Besson   ***Pat.PD 171***

VIII. SONGS

Banalités (Apollinaire) 1940
Chansons villageoises (Fambeure) 1942
☆ P. Bernac (B), F. Poulenc (pf.) *(Ravel)* ♯ **C.CX 1119**
Banalités (Apollinaire) 1940
... Nos. 2, Hôtel; 4, Voyage à Paris
Les Chemins de l'amour (Anouilh) 1940
(for the play *Léocadia*)
G. Swarthout (M-S), G. Trovillo (pf.)
                             in ♯ **G.ALP 1269**
(Chausson, Debussy, Duparc, etc.) (in ♯ Vic.LM 1793;
                             FV.A 630227)

(Le) Bestiaire, ou le cortège d'Orphée
(Apollinaire) Voice, fl., cl., bsn. & str. qtt. 1919
I. Joachim (S) & orch.—M. Franck
                             in ♯ **CdM.LDA 8079**
(below, Auric, Durey, Honegger, Milhaud, Tailleferre)

"C" (L. Aragon) 1943
G. Touraine (S), J. Bonneau (pf.)
                             in ♯ **Lum.LD 3-402**
(below, Chabrier, Debussy, etc.)
☆ P. Bernac (B), F. Poulenc (pf.) (in ♯ Vic.LCT 1158)

(3) CHANSONS (Gattegno, after Lorca) 1947
1. Enfant muet   3. Chanson de l'oranger sec
2. Adalina à la promenade

FIANÇAILLES POUR RIRE (Vilmorin) 1939
1. La Dame d'André   4. Mon cadavre est doux
2. Dans l'herbe   5. Violon
3. Il vole   6. Fleurs
G. Touraine (S), F. Poulenc (pf.)
                             ♯ ***BdM.LD 012***
(Debussy, Roussel)   (♯ HS.HSL 154)

Chansons gaillardes (Anon. XVIIth Cent.) 1926
... No. 8, Sérénade — ARR. VLC. & PF. Gendron
J. Starker & L. Pommers   in ♯ **Nix.PLP 708**
(Debussy, Bréval, Ravel, Couperin, etc.) (♯ Per.SPL 708)

Cimetière (M. Jacob)
D. Darrieux & orch. (*D.MF 36012:* ♯ *LF 1100: FM 133030*)

Métamorphoses (de Vilmorin) 1943
1. Reine des mouettes   2. C'est ainsi...
3. Paganini
G. Touraine (S), J. Bonneau (pf.)
(above)   in ♯ **Lum.LD 3-402**

Plume d'eau claire (Éluard)
(No. 5 of *5 Poèmes*, 1935)
I. Joachim (S) & Orch.—M. Franck
(above)   in ♯ **CdM.LDA 8079**

(Le) Portrait (Colette)
J. Peyron (T), J. Allain (pf.) ♯ ***FMer.MLP 7073***
(Damase, Wolff)

Priez pour paix (Charles d'Orléans) 1938
☆ C. Panzéra (B), M. Panzéra (pf.) (in ♯ Clc. 6260)

POWELL, John (b. 1882)

Overture, In old Virginia, Op. 28 Orch. 1912
Hamburg Philharmonia—H-J. Walther
(4ss)   ***MSB. 78158/9***

Rapsodie nègre pf. & orch. 1918
☆ Anon. soloist & A.R.S. Orch.—Dixon ♯ ARS. 113
(Bloch, Mason)

POWER, Leonel (fl. early XVth Cent.)

SEE: † ENGLISH MEDIEVAL CAROLS

PRAETORIUS, Michael (1571-1621)

(Roman figures refer to volumes of the Complete edn.)

INSTRUMENTAL PIECES
(from *Terpsichore*) XV
Umzug; Springtanz
Musicians' Workshop Ens. in ♯ **CEd.CE 1018**
(† Recorder Music)

---
[1] Recorded under the supervision of the composer.

Ballet de coqs
Ballet des Grenouilles
Paris Ancient Inst. Group—Cotte ♭ *Pat.ED 43*
(† Danceries et Ballets)

Gaillarde avec diminution
Courante
Sarabande
Les Passepieds de Bretagne
Str. Orch.—Raugel   in ♯ *AS. 3004LD*
(† Anthologie Sonore—French Dances)   (♯ HS.AS 36)

ORGAN MUSIC: Hymns XII
A solis ortus cardine
Alvus tumescit virginis
G. Leonhardt   in ♯ *Van.BG 529*
(† XVIIth Cent. Organ Music)

MUSAE SIONIAE
Book VI 4-pt cho. 1609
Wie schön leuchtet der Morgenstern
Geboren ist Immanuel
Trinity Chu. Cho.—Byles   in ♯ *Over.LP 11*
(*Victoria, Holst; Carols, etc.*) (in Eng)

Book IX 3-pt cho. 1610 *Tricinien*
Nun komm, der Heiden Heiland
Christ lag in Todesbanden   ø
Jesus Christus, unser Heiland
Nun freut euch, lieben Christen g'mein   ø
Ich ruf' zu dir, Herr Jesu Christ   ø
Ein' feste Burg ist unser Gott   ø
Mit Fried und Freud ich fahr dahin   ø
Wie schön leuchtet der Morgenstern   ø
Children's Cho.—E. Bender ♯ *HP.APM 14003*
(*Rhaw*)   [marked ø also on ♭ *Pol. 37058*]

MOTETS & HYMNS (various)
Beati omnes X
☆ M. Meili (T), Cho. & trombones
(in † V♯ *AS. 1802LD*; ♯ HS.AS 7)

Es ist ein Rös' entsprungen (*Musae Sioniae*)
H. Gueden (S), Vienna State Op. Cho. & Orch.
—Rossmayer   in ♯ *D.LX 3117*
(♯ *Lon.LS 860*; also *D.F 43608, etc.*)

R. Streich (S), R.I.A.S. Cho. & Orch.—Gaebel
(in *PV. 72447*; ♭ *Pol. 30062*)
J. Peerce (T, *Eng*) & Columbus Boys' Cho.
(in ♭ *Vic.ERA 132*)
G. Fleischer (*Dan*) & org. (*Phi.P 55044H*)
Maastricht Male Cho.—Koekelkoren
(in ♯ *Phi.N 00618R* & ♯ N 00619R: ♭ N 402040E;
♭ *Epic.EG 7147*)
E. Bender Children's Cho. (*Pol. 48827*: ♭ 22097: 20015:
in ♯ 45023)
St. Hedwig's Cath. Cho.—Forster (in ♯ *G.WDLP 1501*)
Berlin Motet Cho.—Arndt (*T.A 11596*:
♭ 45596; *FT. 790.TV.167*)
All Saints Cho.—Self (*Eng*) (in ♯ *CEd.CE 1021*)
Biggs Family Ens. (*Eng*) (in ♯ *GIOA.BF 1*)
Paris Vocal Ens.—Jouve (*Fr*) (in V♯ *Sel.LPP 8611*)
Stockholm Town & Country Housewives Cho.
—Fleetwood (*Swed*) (*G.X 8522*: ♭ 7EGS 21)
☆ Trapp Family Cho. (n.v. in ♯ *B.LAT 8043*;
o.v. in ♯ *CamCAL 209*)

— ARR. INST. ENS. (in *G.C 4252*)
etc. etc.

(Ein') Feste Burg
Vater unser in Himmelreich
Netherlands Madrigal & Motet Cho.—Voorberg
in ♯ *Phi.N 00692R*
(† Motets on Luther Texts)

Mitten wir im Leben sind (*Musae Sioniae*)
Berlin Motet Cho. & Brass Cho.—Arndt
T.VE 9046
(*Schütz: Psalm 84*)   (♭ UV 117)

Wach auf, mit heller Stimm' (*Musae Sioniae*)
Vienna Acad. Cho.—Gillesberger ♯ *SPA. 58*
(† Songs of the Rennaissance)

Wie schön leuchtet der Morgenstern
(*Polyhymnia*, No. 10, 1619) Cho. & insts.
London Cha. Singers & Orch.—Bernard
† *G.HMS 38*
(*O. Gibbons*)   (in ♯ Vic. set LM 6029)

PRÉGER, Leo (b. 1907)
(4) MOTETS 1937
1. Laetentur coeli   3. Exsurge, Domine
2. Verbum caro factum est 4. Dextera Domini
Harvard Glee Club & Radcliffe Cho. Soc.
—Woodworth, D. Pinkham (org.)
in ♯ *Camb.CRS 202*
(† Chansons & Motets)

PRESTON, Thomas (fl. XVIth Cent.)
SEE: † MASTERS OF EARLY ENGLISH KEYBOARD MUSIC

PROKOFIEV, Serge (1891-1953)
CLASSIFIED: I. Piano
II. Chamber Music
III. Orchestral
IV. Ballet, Film, Opera
V. Choral & Songs

I. PIANO
COLLECTIONS
Contes de la vieille grand'mère, Op. 31 . . . Nos. 2 & 3
Étude, Op. 52, No. 3
Gavotta, Op. 32, No. 3
Paysage, Op. 59, No. 2
Sonata No. 4, C minor, Op. 29 . . . Andante only
Sonatine pastorale, C major, Op. 59, No. 3
Suggestion diabolique, Op. 4, No. 4
Symphony No. 1 . . . Gavotte (ARR.)
Visions fugitives, Op. 22 . . . Nos. 3, 5, 6, 9, 10, 11, 16, 17, 18
☆ S. Prokofiev   ♯ *G.FJLP 5048*

Gavotta, F minor, Op. 32, No. 3
Prelude, C major, Op. 12, No. 7
Toccata, D minor, Op. 11
H. Roloff   *PV. 36072*
(1½ss—*Love for Three Oranges, March*) (♭ *Pol. 32044*)

Gavotte, Op. 12, No. 2
M. Slezareva   *USSR. 22528*
(*Liadov: Sarabande*)

March, Op. 12, No. 1 — ARR. VLC. & PF.
P. Olefsky & G. Silfies   ♯ *McInt.MM 103*
(*Debussy, Fauré, Falla, etc.*)

Pieces for Children, Op. 65 1935
M. Pressler   in ♯ *MGM.E 3010*
(*Bloch, Milhaud, Shostakovich*)

— ORCH. VERSION: **"Summer Day Suite"**
Berlin Radio—Guhl   ♯ *Ura. 7082*
(*Kabalevsky, Dvořák*)
Sym.—Vicars (2ss)   V♯ *CA.MPO 5024*
(*Kodály on ♯ LPA 1086*)
Champs-Élysées—Jouve   ♯ *Sel. 270.C.076*
(*Overture on Hebrew Themes & The Ugly Duckling*)

. . . **Waltz, Regrets & March** only — ARR. BAND
Cities Service Band—Lavalle (in ♯ *Vic.LPM 1133*:
♭ set EPC 1133)

Prelude, C major, Op. 12, No. 7
C. de Groot   in ♯ *Phi.N 00632R*
(*Pierné, Mendelssohn, etc.*)   (♭ N 402019E)
Y. Boukoff   ♯ *Phi.A 76700R*
(*below; Balakirev, etc.*)

— HARP VERSION
N. Zabaleta   in ♯ *Eso.ES 523*
(*Hindemith, Roussel, etc.*)
E. Vito   in ♯ *Per.SPL 704*
(*Handel, Debussy, etc.*)

SONATAS
No. 1, F minor, Op. 1 1909
R. Cornman   ♯ *D.FST 153515*
(*Shostakovich*)

No. 2, D minor, Op. 14 1912
E. Gilels   ♯ *CHS.CHS 1311*
(*Glazounov, Tchaikovsky*)   (2ss, V♯ *CdM.LDY 8121;*
USSRM.D 492/3)
(*Concerto No. 1; & Kabalevsky on ♯ Csm.CRLP 186*)

♯ = Long-playing, 33⅓ r.p.m.   ♭ = 45 r.p.m.   ♮ = Auto. couplings, 78 r.p.m.

No. 3, A minor, Op. 28   1917
R. Cornman   ♯ **D.LXT 2836**
(*No. 4 & No. 8*)   (♯ D.FST 153120; Lon.LL 748)
T. Ury   ♯ *Argo.ATM 1006*
(*Berg, Stravinsky*)
S. Contreras   ♯ **CM. 17**
(*Bartók, Kabalevsky, Shostakovich*)
☆ S. Weissenberg (ArgC. 266565)

No. 4, C minor, Op. 29   1917
R. Cornman   ♯ **D.LXT 2836**
(*No. 3 & No. 8*)   (♯ D.FST 153120; Lon.LL 748)
A. de Raco   ♯ *ArgOd.LDC 520*
(*Albeniz, Mompou*)

No. 5, C major, Op. 38   1925
☆ H. Graf (in ♯ Per.SPL 599; ♯ Cpt.MC 20075)

No. 6, A major, Op. 82   1940
S. Prokofiev   ♯ **Csm.CRLPX 1011**
(*Shostakovich*)
R. Cornman   ♯ **D.FST 153087**
(*No. 7*)   (♯ Lon.LL 902)

No. 7, B flat major, Op. 83   1942
R. Cornman   ♯ **D.FST 153087**
(*No. 6*)   (♯ Lon.LL 902)
☆ V. Horowitz (♯ G.FALP 230)
[4th movt. also, n.v., in ♯ Vic. set LM 6014;
ItV.B12R 0064/5; FV.A 630203]

No. 8, B flat major, Op. 84   1945
R. Cornman   ♯ **D.LXT 2836**
(*Nos. 3 & 4*)   (♯ D.FST 153120; Lon.LL 748)

No. 9, C major, Op. 103   1945-7
M. Pressler   ♯ **MGM.E 3192**
(*Cinderella*)

Toccata, D minor, Op. 11   1912
S. François   ♯ **C.CX 1135**
(*Visions fugitives & Concerto No. 3*)   (♯ C.FCX 218:
QCX 10087; Angel. 35045)
(*Schumann: Toccata on* ♭ *C.ESBF 113*)
Y. Boukoff   in ♯ *Phi.A 76700R*
(*above*)
☆ V. Horowitz (♭ G. 7RQ 200; ♭ Vic.ERA 103)

Visions fugitives, Op. 22   1915-17
… Nos. 1, 3, 4, 6, 17, 18
S. François   ♯ **C.CX 1135**
(*Toccata & Concerto No 3*)   (♯ FCX 218: QCX 10087;
Angel. 35045)
… Nos. 3, 5, 7, 10, 11, 17
E. Gilels   ♯ *CdM.LDA 8104*
(*Debussy, Shostakovich, etc.*)
[5 unspec. also on *Eta. 120024*]

… Unspec.   — ARR. WIND INSTS.
New Art Wind Quintet   in ♯ **CEd.CE 2004**

II. CHAMBER MUSIC

(5) Melodies, Op. 35a   vln. & pf.   1925
☆ R. Posselt & A. Sly   in ♯ *Esq.TW 14-005*
… No. 3 only   ☆ D. Oistrakh & pf. (♭ *Mer.EP 1-5008*)

Overture on Hebrew themes, Op. 34
cl., pf., & str. qtt.
Champs-Élysées Th. Orch.—Jouve[1]
     ♯ *Sel. 270.C.076*
(*Summer Day Suite & Ugly Duckling*)
☆ N.Y. Ens.—Mitropoulos   ♯ **B.AXTL 1054**
(*below*)   (♯ D.UAT 273045)
☆ Mbrs. of Paris Cha. Orch.
     (♭ *Per.PEP 10; Cpt.EXTP 1003*)

QUARTETS, Str.
No. 1, B major, Op. 50   1930
Guilet Qtt.   ♯ **MGM.E 3113**
(*Shostakovich*)

No. 2, F major, Op. 92   1941
Italian Quartet   ♯ **C.CX 1295**
(*Malipiero*)   (♯ QCX 10145; Angel. 35296)
Loewenguth Qtt.   ♯ **Pol. 18249**
(*Roussel*)
☆ Hollywood Qtt. (♯ T.LCE 8151)

Quintet, G minor, Op. 39
ob., cl., vln., vla., cbs.   1924
☆ N.Y. Ens.—Mitropoulos   ♯ **B.AXTL 1054**
(*above & Swanson*)   (♯ D.UAT 273045)

SONATAS, Vln. & pf.
No. 1, F minor, Op. 80   1938-46
D. Oistrakh & L. Oborin (n.v.)[2]
     ♯ *CdM.LDA 8078*
(*Franck on* ♯ *Van.VRS 6019;*
     Beethoven on ♯ *Csm.CRLP 152*)
I. Stern & A. Zakin   ♯ **AmC.ML 4734**
(*No. 2*)
☆ Y. Menuhin & M. Gazelle (*Bartók*) ♯ **G.FALP 265**

No. 2, D major, Op. 94a[3]
R. Ricci & C. Bussotti   ♯ **D.LXT 2818**
(*R. Strauss: Vln. Sonata*)   (♯ Lon.LL 770)
I. Stern & A. Zakin   ♯ **AmC.ML 4734**
(*No. 1*)
N. Milstein & A. Balsam   ♯ **Cap.P 8315**
(*Handel, Vitali*)
D. Oistrakh & V. Yampolsky[4]   ♯ **JpV.LS 2026**
(*Leclair, Debussy, etc.*)

Sonata, D major, Op. 94   fl. & pf.   1942-4
D. A. Dwyer & J. M. Sanromá   ♯ **Bo.B 208**
(*Roussel*)
B. Z. Goldberg & J. Harris   ♯ **PFCM.CB 172**
(*Martin*)

Sonata No. 2, C major, Op. 119   vlc. & pf.   1948
E. Kurtz & A. Balsam   ♯ **AmC.ML 4867**
(*Kodály*)
G. Piatigorsky & R. Berkowitz ♯ **Vic.LM 1792**
(*Bach*)   (♯ ItV.A12R 0142; FV.A 630224)

III. ORCHESTRAL

CONCERTOS, pf. & orch.
No. 1, D flat major, Op. 10   1912
S. Richter & Moscow Youth Sym.—Kondrashin
(2ss)   V♯ *CdM.LDY 8122*
(*Kabalevsky on* ♯ *USSR.D 0735; 4ss, USSR. 021670/3*)
(*Vln. Concerto No. 1 on* ♯ *MMS. 61*)
(*Rimsky-Korsakov & Glazounov on* ♯ *CHS.CHS 1316*)
(*Concerto No. 5 on* ♯ *Per.SPL 599*)
(*Kabalevsky & Pf. Sonata 2, on* ♯ *Csm.CRLP 186*)
S. Richter & F.O.K. Sym.—Ančerl U.H **24410/1**
(4ss)

No. 2, G minor, Op. 16   1913
J. Bolet & Cincinnati Sym.—Johnson
     ♯ **Rem. 199-182**

No. 3, C major, Op. 26   1917
J. Katchen & Suisse Romande—Ansermet
     ♯ **D.LXT 2894**
(*Bartók*)   (♯ Lon.LL 945)
L. Pennario & St. Louis Sym.—Golschmann
     ♯ **DCap.CTL 7060**
(*Bartók*)   (♯ Cap.P 8253)
S. François & Paris Cons.—Cluytens
     ♯ **C.CX 1135**
(*Visions fugitives & Toccata*)   (♯ FCX 218: QCX 10087;
Angel. 35045)
A. Uninsky & Residentie—v. Otterloo
(2ss)   ♯ *EPhi.ABR 4022*
   (♯ Phi.A 00650R)
(*Love for Three Oranges on* ♯ *Epic.LC 3042*)

No. 5, G major, Op. 55   1932
☆ A. Brendel & Vienna State Op.—Sternberg
     ♯ **Per.SPL 599**
(*No. 1 & Sonata No. 5*)   (♯ Cpt.MC 20075)

---

[1] The Orchestral version by the Composer is played.
[2] The entry of USSR. 014963/70 in WERM should be here, not under No. 2. It is assumed that all these issues are new recordings, but we have no evidence. *CdM.* is stated to be a Paris recording.
[3] Orig. Op. 94 for fl. and pf., *see below.*
[4] Tokyo recording, 1955.

CONCERTOS, vln. & orch.
No. 1, D major, Op. 19 1914
D. Oistrakh & L.S.O.—v. Matačić ♯ **C.CX 1268**
(*Bruch*)   (Angel. 35243)
N. Milstein & St. Louis Sym.—Golschmann
                                       ♯ **DCap.CTL 7095**
(*Lalo*)   (♯ Cap.P 8303)
H. Drescher & Berlin Sym.—Schreiber
(*No. 2*)   ♯ **Roy. 1483**
☆ D. Oistrakh & Orch.—Gauk (♯ Cpt.MC 20078)
   R. Odnoposoff & Zürich Radio—Hollreiser
                           (♯ MMS. 61; Clc. 6151, d.c.)
No. 2, G minor, Op. 63 1935
Z. Francescatti & N.Y.P.S.O.—Mitropoulos
                                       ♯ **AmC.ML 4648**
(*Bach: Vln. Concerto, E major*)
H. Drescher & Berlin Sym.—Schreiber
(*No. 1*)   ♯ **Roy. 1483**

Concerto, E minor, Op. 58, vlc. & orch. 1935-8
R. Albin & Cento Soli.—R. Albert ♯ **CFD. 25**

Divertimento, C major, Op. 43 1929
☆ Vienna Sym.—Swoboda   ♯ **West.WN 18081**
(*Sinfonietta & Winter Holiday*)

Lyrical Waltzes, Nos. 1 & 2 (? from Suite, Op. 110)
☆ Moscow Radio—Samosud   ♯ **Kings. 291**
(*Glazounov*)

Peter and the Wolf, Op. 67 Narrator & orch.[1]
WITH ENGLISH NARRATION
A. Guinness & Boston Prom.—Fiedler   ♯ **Vic.LM 1761**
(*Saint-Saëns*)   (♭ set WDM 1761)
G. Harding & London Classical—Dennington
(2ss)   **V♯ CA.MPO 8025**
A. Godfrey & Orch.—Kostelanetz   ♯ **AmC.CL 720**
(*Saint-Saëns*) (o.n. ♯ ML 4907: 2ss, ♯ Phi.N 02604R)
(*Grofé & Kern* on ♯ AmC.ML 4625)
                                (also in ♭ AmC. set A 1034)
R. Hale & Boston Prom.—Fiedler   ♯ **Vic.LM 1803**
(*Dukas, German, Saint-Saëns*)   (♭ set ERB 39)
B. de Wilde & Vienna Pro Musica—Swarowsky
                                   AmVox.PL 9280
(*Britten*)   (2ss, ♯ AmVox. 810)
H. Morgan & Sym.—Ackermann (♯ CHS.CHS 1246)
Anon. Narrator & orch.—(♯ Var. 6975)
Actors, Singers, narr. & orch (♯ Gram. 20121)
☆ R. Hale & Boston Sym.—Koussevitzky
                                   (♯ Cam.CAL 101)
   B. D. Walker & orch.—Leopold (♯ AFest.CFR 10-197)
   B. Rathbone & All-American—Stokowski
                                   (♯ AmC.CL 671)
WITH FRENCH NARRATION
Y. Furet & Vienna Pro Musica—Swarowsky
                                   ♯ **Pan.XPV 5000**
                                   (♭ SEP 405)
J. P. Aumont & orch.—Kostelanetz   ♯ **Phi.N 02606R**
C. Duhamel & Concerts Colonne—Disenhaus
                                   ♯ **Cum.TCCX 342**
☆ C. Dauphin & Berlin Phil.—Lehmann (♯ Pol. 16098)
   R. Bertin & Netherlands Phil.—Ackermann
                                   (♯ MMS. 88F)
   A. Reybaz & Philharmonia—Markevitch
                                   (♯ G.FALP 315)
WITH GERMAN NARRATION
H. Jaray & Vienna Pro Musica—Swarowsky
                                   ♯ **Pan.BP 1300**
G. Thielemann & Orch.—Kostelanetz ♯ **Phi.B 02607R**
☆ M. Wiemann & Berlin Phil.—Lehmann (♯ Eta. 720009)
   G. Mosheim & Netherlands Phil.—Ackermann
                                   (♯ MMS. 88G)
WITH ITALIAN NARRATION
I. Colnaghi & Vienna Pro Musica—Swarowsky
                                   ♯ **ItVox.VOF 252**
☆ S. Tofano & Philharmonia—Markevitch
                                   (♯ G.QDLP 6034)
MISCELLANEOUS LANGUAGES
N. I. Menta (*Sp*) & Buenos Aires Sym.—Andreani
                                   (♭ ArgV. set DM 1103, 6ss)
M. Willemsen (*Dutch*) & orch.—Kostelanetz
                                   (♯ Phi.N 02605R)
☆ M. Wieth (*Dan*) & Philharmonia—Markevitch
                                   (♯ G.KDLP 1)

... **Theme & March** — ARR. VLN. & PF. Grunes
I. Bezrodny & S. Wakman (in ♯ Phi.S 06048R)

Russian Overture, Op. 72 1936
☆ Berlin Phil.—Steinkopf (♯ ANix.ULPY 9005)

Scythian Suite, Op. 20 1914 (*Ala & Lolly*)
Fr. Nat.—Markevitch   ♯ **C.FC 1043**
(*Love for 3 Oranges*)
Berlin Radio—Kleinert   ♯ **Ura. 7138**
(*Kodály*)
☆ Vienna Sym.—Scherchen   ♯ **Nix.WLP 5091**
(*Lieut. Kije Suite*)
☆ Chicago Sym.—Defauw   ♯ **BB.LBC 1057**
(*Respighi*)   (♭ set WBC 1057)

Sinfonietta, A major, Op. 48 (orig. Op. 5)
☆ Vienna Sym.—Swoboda (*above*) ♯ **West.WN 18081**

Summer Day Suite, *see* Pieces for Children, Section I

SYMPHONIES
No. 1, D major, Op. 25 "Classical" 1916-17
Philharmonia—Malko   ♯ **G.CLP 1044**
(*No. 7*)   (QCLP 12016)
Concerts Colonne—Horenstein
(*No. 5*)   ♯ **E. & AmVox.PL 9170**
Pittsburgh Sym.—Steinberg ♯ **DCap.CTL 7084**
(*Tchaikovsky*)   (♯ Cap.P 8290)
London Phil. Sym.—Rodzinski
                                   ♯ **West.LAB 7017**
(*Love for three Oranges*)
Paris Cons.—Ansermet   ♯ **D.LW 5096**
(2ss)   (♯ Lon.LD 9114)
(*Borodin, Glinka, etc.,* on ♯ D.LXT 2833; Lon.LL 864)
Philharmonia—Markevitch   ♯ **C.CX 1049**
(*Dukas, Falla, Ravel*)   (♯ FCX 203: QCX 10015;
                                   Angel. 35008)
R.I.A.S. Sym.—Fricsay   **PV. 72457**
(*Tchaikovsky* on ♯ AmD.DL 9737)
Lamoureux—Martinon   ♯ **Phi.A 00670R**
(*Love for three Oranges*)
           (*idem & Pf. Concerto No. 3* on ♯ Epic.LC 3042)
U.S.S.R. State—Stassevich **V♯ CdM.LDY 8125**
(2ss) (*No. 7* on ♯ Kings. 251)   (♯ USSR.D 478/9:
                                   4ss, USSR. 022920/3)
Bolshoi Theatre—Prokofiev   ♯ **Csm.CRLP 209**
(*Romeo & Juliet, Suite 2*)
Hamburg Philharmonia—H-J. Walther
                                   ♯ **MGM.E 3087**
(*Corelli, Mendelssohn*)
(3ss—*Bolzoni: Minuet* on MSB. 78102/3)
Orch.—Wallenstein   ♯ **MApp. 71**
(*Spoken analysis by T. Scherman; & Britten*)
☆ N.B.C. Sym.—Toscanini   ♯ **G.ALP 1107**
(*Gershwin*)   (♯ ItV.A12R 0101)
☆ Philadelphia—Ormandy   ♯ **C.C 1025**
(*Rimsky-Korsakov*)   (♯QC 5015; ♭ AmC.A 1638)
Leipzig Radio—Pflüger (♭ Ura.UREP 52; ♯ ACC.MP 27)
Leipzig Sym.—Forster (♯ Roy. 1420)
☆ St. Louis Sym.—Golschmann (♭ Cam.CAE 155:
                     in ♯ CAL 215 & in ♯ set CFL 102)
   Minneapolis Sym.—Mitropoulos (in ♯ AmC.RL 3021)

... **3rd movt., Gavotte**
Polish Radio—Krenz (Muza. 2439)

— — ARR. PF. Prokofiev
☆ S. Prokofiev (in ♯ G.FJLP 5048, pf. collection)

— — ARR. ACCORDION
C. Magnante (in ♯ SOT. 1013; Nix.SLPY 170)

No. 4, Op. 47 1924-30
Concerts Colonne—Sebastian   ♯ **Ura. 7139**
(*The Prodigal Son, Suite*)   (♯ FUra. 7002)

No. 5, B flat major, Op. 100 1944
Concerts Colonne—Horenstein
(*No. 1*)   ♯ **E. & AmVox.PL 9170**
Danish Radio—Tuxen   ♯ **D.LXT 2764**
(2ss)   (♯ Lon.LL 672)
☆ N.Y.P.S.O.—Rodzinski (♯ Phi.A 01105L)
   Boston Sym.—Koussevitzky (♯ G.QALP 139)

---

[1] The original narration is, of course, in *Russian*. Many of the recordings listed here are of dubbed narration in the languages shown, added to the same orchestral parts (*e.g.* Kostelanetz, Markevitch, etc.)

No. 7, C sharp minor, Op. 131 1951
Philharmonia—Malko   ‡ **G.CLP 1044**
(No. 1)   *(QCLP 12016)*
Philadelphia—Ormandy (2ss) ‡ **EPhl.ABR 4034**
(Lieut. Kije on ‡ AmC.ML 4683)   *(‡ Phi.A 01614R)*
Moscow Radio—Samosud   ‡ **CdM.LDA 8093**
(2ss)[1]
(No. 1 on ‡ Kings. 251)   *(‡ USSR.D 01476/7)*
(Miaskovsky: Sym. 21, on ‡ Csm.CRLP 10070)

(The) Ugly Duckling, Op. 18 voice & orch.
F. Ogéas (S) & Champs-Élysées Theatre
—Jouve *(Fr)*   ‡ *Sel. 270.C.076*
(Summer Day Suite, & Overture on Hebrew themes)

IV. BALLET, FILM, OPERA

ALEXANDER NEVSKY Film Music 1938
(Cantata, Op. 78   1939)
COMPLETE RECORDINGS (of the Cantata, Op. 78)
A. M. Iriarte (M-S), Vienna State Op. Cho. &
Orch.—Rossi   ‡ **Nix.PVL 7001**
                    (‡ Van.VRS 451; Ama.AVRS 6017)
L. Legostayeva (A), Cho. & Moscow Radio
Orch.—Samosud   ‡ **CdM.LDXA 8133**
        (‡ USSR.D 02173/4; West.WN 18144)

(The) BUFFOON, Op. 21 (Chout) Ballet 1921
Suite No. 1, Op. 21a
St. Louis Sym.—Golschmann ‡ **DCap.CTL 7062**
(Falla) (slightly cut)   *(‡ Cap.P 8257)*
Paris Phil.—Horenstein ‡ **E. & AmVox.PL 9180**
(Lt. Kije Suite)

CINDERELLA, Op. 87 1941-4
Gavotte, Act I; The Winter Fairy, Act I: Passepied, Act II;
Mazurka, Act III; Grand Waltz — ARR. VLN. & PF. Fichtenholz
D. Oistrakh & V. Yampolsky ‡ **Mon.MEL 707**
(Szymanowski & Wieniawski)
(Brahms, Khachaturian, etc. on ‡ Van.VRS 6020;
Shostakovich, Rachmaninoff, etc., on ‡ Csm.CRLPX 011;
Excerpts also on USSR. 22517/8; Ete. 20-25
                              & in ‡ Eta.LPM 1023)
... **The Winter Fairy** only — ARR. VLN. & PF.
A. Pratz & G. Gould (in ‡ Hall.RS 3)
... **Gavotte & Winter fairy** — ARR. VLN. & PF.
D. Oistrakh & N. Walter   *Eta. 120025*
... **Waltz** only — ARR. VLN. & PF.
M. Vaiman & M. Karandazhova
                        in ‡ **LI.TW 91068**
                      (in ‡ Lon.LD 9154)
... **Adagio** only (No. 36) — ARR. VLC. & PF., Op. 97a
M. Rostropovich & M. Karandazhova
                        in ‡ **LI.TW 91068**
(Shaporin: Elégie & Romance on USSRM.D 00367)

Orchestral Suite No. 2, Op. 108
Bolshoi Theatre—Stassevitch ‡ **CHS.CHS 1304**
(Romeo & Juliet)

Orchestral Suite No. 3, Op. 109
Bolshoi Theatre—Rozhdestvensky
(2ss)   ‡ *USSR.D 2580/1*

10 Dances — ARR. PF. Prokofiev (Op. 97)
M. Pressler   ‡ **MGM.E 3192**
(Sonata No. 9)

(The) GAMBLER, Op. 24
Opera 4 Acts 1916-28 f.p. 1929
Four Portraits, Op. 49 orch. 1930-31
1. Alexis   2. The General & the Grandmother
3. Pauline   4. Dénouement
Philharmonia—Schüchter   ‡ **P.PMC 1007**
(Kabalevsky)   *(‡ MGM.E 3112)*

LIEUTENANT KIJE Film Music 1935
Suite, Op. 60
Paris Phil.—Horenstein ‡ **E. & AmVox.PL 9180**
(Buffoon)
☆ Vienna Sym.—Scherchen   ‡ **Nix.WLP 5091**
(Scythian Suite)
(Kije's Wedding, Troika & Burial of Kije only,
                      ♭ *Sel. 470.CW.010)*

☆ Boston Sym.—Koussevitzky *(below)* ‡ **Vic.LCT 1144**
☆ Royal Phil.—Kurtz   ‡ **AmC.ML 4683**
(Symphony No. 7)   (2ss, ‡ **Phl.S 06601R**)
☆ French Nat.—Désormière (‡ T.LCSK 8149)

(The) LOVE FOR THREE ORANGES, Op. 33
Opera 4 Acts 1919 (f.p. 1921)
Orch. Suite, Op. 33a
Lamoureux—Martinon   ‡ **Phi.A 00670R**
(Symphony No. 1)
(Pf. Concerto No. 3 on ‡ Epic.LC 3042)
Fr. Nat.—Markevitch   ‡ **C.FC 1043**
(above)
London Phil. Sym.—Rodzinski
(Symphony No. 1)   ‡ **West.LAB 7017**
Berlin Sym.—Rother[2]   ‡ **Ura. 7146**
(Shostakovich, Kabalevsky, Borodin)
Leipzig Sym.—Forster   ‡ **Roy. 1420**
(Symphony No. 1)
Philharmonia—Malko[3]   ‡ **G.CLP 1060**
(Tchaikovsky)
☆ Berlin Radio—Rother (‡ *ANix.ULPY 9005;*
                                    ACC.MP 27)
Copenhagen Opera—Malko (in ‡ **BB.LBC 1022**:
                              ♭ set *WBC 1022*)
French Nat.—Désormière (‡ T.LSK 8149)
... **Nos. 3 & 4, Marche & Scherzo**
☆ Col. Sym.—Rodzinski (♭ AmC.A 1560)
Boston Sym.—Koussevitzky (in ‡ Vic.LCT 1144)
... **No. 3,** only
N.Y.P.S.O.—Kostelanetz (in ‡ *AmC,CL 758*:
                              in ‡ *KZ 1: ♭ A 2036*)
— — ARR. PF.
E. Gilels   in ‡ *CdM.LDA 8104*
                        (& ‡ Csm.CRLP 224, q.v.)
H. Roloff   *PV. 36072*
(♭♭—Piano pieces)   *(♭ Pol. 32044)*
— — ARR. VLN. & PF.
G. Staples & G. Silfies   in ‡ **McInt.MM 101**

(Le) PAS D'ACIER, Op. 41 Ballet 1925 (f.p. 1927)
Orchestral Suite, Op. 41a
Philharmonia—Markevitch   ‡ **C.CX 1199**
(Liadov, Stravinsky) (‡ FCX 359; Angel. 35153, in set 3518)

(The) PRODIGAL SON, Op. 46 Ballet, etc.
COMPLETE RECORDING   [1928-9
N.Y. City Ballet—Barzin   ‡ **AmVox.PL 9310**

Orchestral Suite, Op. 46a
Concerts Colonne—Sebastian   ‡ **Ura. 7139**
(Symphony No. 4)   (‡ FUra. 7002)

ROMEO & JULIET, Op. 64
Orchestral Suites Nos. 1-3, Opp. 64a, 64b & 101
SUITE I: Bolshoi Theatre—Fayer[4]
SUITE II: Leningrad Phil.—Mravinsky
SUITE III: Bolshoi Theatre—Stassevitch
(Suites I & II are ☆)   ‡ **Strad.STR 623**

Orchestral Suites, Nos. 1 & 2, Op. 64a & b
Bolshoi Theatre—Prokofiev ‡ **Csm.CRLP 134**
[Suite No. 2 also on ‡ Csm.CRLP 209 with *Sym. No. 1*]
[Suite No. 2 is ☆; Suite 1 may be]

Orchestral Suite No. 1, Op. 64a
U.S.S.R. Nat.—Stassevitch ‡ **CdM.LDX 8046**
(Shostakovich, Kabalevsky)

Orchestral Suite No. 2, Op. 64b
U.S.S.R. Nat.—Gauk   ‡ **CdM.LDX 8073**
(Suite 3 & Stone Flower, excpt.)
☆ Leningrad Phil.—Mravinsky   ‡ *Mon.MEL 701*
                      (USSR. 22455/67: ‡ D 522/3)
... **Nos. 1, 2, 4, 7,** only
☆ Boston Sym.—Koussevitzky (in ‡ Vic.LCT 1144)

Orchestral Suite No. 3, Op. 101
U.S.S.R. Nat.—Stassevitch ‡ **CdM.LDX 8073**
(No 2 & Stone Flower, excpt.)
(Cinderella, Suite No. 2, on ‡ CHS.CHS 1304;
            Balakirev: Thamar on ‡ Mon.MWL 307)

---

[1] Suppresses the closing bars of the Finale, said to be at express wish of the composer. Malko also abbreviates the Finale.
[2] Possibly ☆ of Berlin Radio, *below.*   [3] Omitting final movt., *La Fuite.*
[4] Omits No. 3, Madrigal; No. 6, Romeo and Juliet.

Romeo at the Fountain, Juliet, Romeo & Juliet,
   Romeo at the Tomb of Juliet, Death of Juliet
N.B.C. Sym. Members—Stokowski
                           ♯ Vic. set LM 6028

(*Berlioz, Tchaikovsky*)

Piano Suite, Op. 75
... Masques — ARR. VLN. & PF. Heifetz
   ☆ J. Heifetz & E. Bay (in ♯ AmD.DL 9780)

SIMEON KOTKO, Op. 81 Opera 5 Acts 1940
Orch. Suite, Op. 81a 1943
   Berlin Radio—Kleinert   ♯ Ura. 7135

(The) STONE FLOWER Ballet 1949-50
... Wedding Suite, Op. 126 orch.
1. Amorous Dance   4. Ceremonial Dance
2. Dance of the fiancée's girl-friends
3. Maidens' Dance   5. Wedding Dance
N.Y.P.S.O.—Kostelanetz   ♯ AmC.CL 809
(*Enesco, Weber*)   (o.n. ML 4957)

... Gypsy Fantasy, Op. 118   1950
   Moscow Radio—Samosud   ♯ CdM.LDX 8073
(*Romeo & Juliet Suites*)
(*Amirov, Glier, Glinka* in ♯ CEd.CE 3001)[1]

V. CHORAL & SONGS

On Guard for Peace, Op. 124
   Oratorio (Marshak) 1951 soli, cho. & orch.
   ☆ Z. Dolukhanova (A), E. Talanov (T), etc., U.S.S.R. State
     Cho. & Orch.—Samosud   ♯ CdM.LDA 8066
(Berceuse only, in ♯ *CdM.LDM 8134*)

(5) SONGS, Op. 27 (Akhmatova) 1916
     1. Sunlight in my room
     2. Tenderness of love
     3. Thoughts of the sunlight
     4. Greeting
     5. The grey-eyed king
   M. Kurenko (S), V. Pastukhoff (pf.)
                           ♯ DCap.CTL 7100
(*Gretchaninoff, Moussorgsky*)   (♯ Cap.P 8310)

Winter Holiday, Op. 122 (Marshak) 1949
   Children's Cho. & U.S.S.R. Radio—Samosud
                           ♯ West.WN 18081
(*Divertimento & Sinfonietta*)
(Excerpts on *USSRM.D 00195*)

PUCCINI, Giacomo A. D. M. S. M.
                           (1858-1924)

NON-OPERATIC

MASS: Messa di Gloria, A major 1876-1880[2]
   N. Petroff (T), E. d'Onofrio (B) & Naples
     Scarlatti Cho. & Orch.—Rapalo
   (2ss)   ♯ Csm.CLPS 1053

SONG: E l'uccellino 1899
   L. Albanese (S) & orch.   in ♯ Vic.LM 1857
                           (♯ FV.A 530211)

OPERAS

(La) BOHÈME 4 Acts 1896
COMPLETE RECORDINGS
Set Q. B. Sayão (S), G. di Stefano (T), Metropolitan Op.
   Cho. & Orch.[3] (4ss)   ♯ OTA. set 1
Set R. (*Russ*) I. Maslennikova, G. Sakharova, S.
   Lemeshev, P. Lisitsian, etc., Moscow Radio Cho. & Orch.
   —S. Samosud (6ss)   ♯ USSR.D 0416/22
Set K. ☆ L. Albanese (S), J. Peerce (T), etc., Cho. & N.B.C.
   Sym.—Toscanini   ♯ G.ALP 1081/2
(♯ QALP 10053/4: WALP 1081/2: FALP 216/7)
[Highlights on ♯ Vic.LM 1844: ♭ *set ERB 41*]
Set L. ☆ R. Carteri (S), F. Tagliavini (T), etc., Italian Radio
   Cho. & Orch.—Santini (♯ FSor.CS 525/6; ♯ Pol. 18107/8)
[Excerpts on ♯ CCet.A 50143; ♭ Cet.FAP 7002 &
   FAP 7010; ♭ Cet.EPO 0307 & 0319; ♯ Pol. 16106]

Set A. ☆ L. Albanese (S), B. Gigli (T), etc., La Scala Cho. &
   Orch.—Berrettoni (♯ G.QALP 10077/8: FJLP 5027/8)
Set M. ☆ D. Ilitsch, R. Boesch, etc., Austrian Sym.
   —Loibner (♯ Ply. set 42-3, 6ss;
                           Excerpts on ♯ *Ply.10-25*; ♭ *Rem.REP 9*)
Set N. ☆ Soloists & Rome Op. Cho. & Orch.—Paoletti
   (♯ Roy. 1542/3; MusH.LP 12003/4;
                           Highlights on ♯ Roy. 1546)

EXCERPTS
ACT I: Che gelida manina   T
          Si, mi chiamano Mimi   S
          O soave fanciulla   S & T
ACT II: Quando m'en vo   S
ACT III: Donde lieta usci   S
   D. Kirsten (S), R. Tucker (T), Metropolitan
   Op. Orch.—Cleva   ♯ AmC.ML 4981
   (*Manon & Manon Lescaut*) (♭ set A 1112; ♯ Phi.N 02126L)

ACT I: Prelude
          Non sono in vena   S & T
          Che gelida manina   T
          Si, mi chiamano Mimi   S
          O soave fanciulla   S & T
ACT II: Quando m'en vo   S
          Finale
ACT III: Donde lieta usci   S
ACT IV: In un coupé ... O Mimi, tu più non torni   T & B
          Sono andati?   Ens.
   E. Berger (S), E. Köth (S), R. Schock (T),
   H. Prey (B), D. Fischer-Dieskau (B), G.
   Frick (Bs), W. Hauck (Bs), Berlin Municipal
   Op. Cha. & Orch.—Schüchter (*Ger*)
                           ♯ G.WALP 1502

HIGHLIGHTS
   ☆ N. Vallin (S), M. Villabella (T), A. Baugé (B), M.
     Sibille (S) (in *French*)   ♯ Pat.PCX 5001
   (*Carmen—Excerpts*)
   [Contents: Che gelida manina; Si, mi chiamano Mimi;
     Donde lieta usci; Addio, dolce svegliare; O Mimi,
     tu più non torni; Sono andati?]

   ☆ R. Tebaldi (S), H. Gueden (S), etc. Santa Cecilia Cho.
     & Orch.—Erede   ♯ D.LW 5158)
   (from set J, ♯ Lon.LL 649; Excerpts on ♯ *D.LW 5158*)
   Anon. Artists[4] (♯ Cam.CAL 222, in set CFL 101)

"Orchestral Scenario"
   Orch.—Kostelanetz   ♯ AmC.CL 707
                           (o.n. ML 4655: ♭ *set A 1044*)

Orchestral Selection
   Imperial Light Orch.—Koschat   ♯ Imp.ILP 125
   (*d'Albert: Toten Augen, selection*)
   "Golden" Sym. (♭ *Cam.CAE 204*)

ACT I

Nei cieli bigi   T & B
   🔲 G. Zenatello & M. Sammarco (in ♯ Ete. 705*)

Che gelida manina
Si, mi chiamano Mimi
O soave fanciulla   S & T
   M. Cebotari & P. Anders (*Ger*)[5] ♯ Ura. 7105
   (*below & Madama Butterfly*)

Che gelida manina   T
   M. del Monaco   ♭ D. 71061
   (*Manon Lescaut—No! pazzo son!*)   (♭ DK 23350)
   (*Fanciulla del West, aria,* on D.X 579)
   (& in ♯ D.LXT 2928, LXT 2964, *LW 5121*;
                           in ♯ Lon.LL 990, LL 1025, *LW 9132*)
   R. Tucker   in ♯ AmC.ML 4750
   R. Schock (*Ger*)   G.DB 11575
   (*O Mimi, Act IV; from set*) (♭ 7RW 525: in *WBLP 1515*)
   W. Kmentt (*Ger*)   in ♯ Phi.S 06076R
   ☆ J. Björling   G.DB 21602
   (*Pagliacci—Vesti la giubba*)   (♭ *G.7R 173*)
   (in ♯ BLP 1055; ♯ FV.A 630259; Vic.LM 1841:
                           ♭ ERA 245)
   N. Nikolov (in ♯ *USSR.D 2158*)
   K. Baum (in ♯ Roy. 1582)
   G. Prandelli (in ♯ Roy. 1592)
   G. Lauri-Volpi (in ♯ Roy. 1595)
   A. da Costa (in ♯ Roy. 1599)
   K. Terkal (*Ger*) (*D.F 46072*; ♭ *D 18072*)
   G. Fouché (*Fr*) (♭ *Plé.P 45152*)

---

[1] Attributed to Bolshoi Theatre orch.
[3] Transcription of a 1951 broadcast performance.
[5] Complete, from departure of Marcello to end of Act I.

[2] Published Mills Music, N.Y., c. 1952.
[4] Perhaps including E. Steber, A. Dickey, L. Warren.

Che gelida manina (*continued*)

☆ G. di Stefano (♭ *G. 7ER 5028*)
I. Kozlovsky (*Russ*) (*USSRM.D 00983*)
G. Thill (*Fr*) (in ♯ *C.FH 503*)
Anon. artist (in ♯ Cam.CAL 249)

H F. de Lucia (in ♯ CEd. set 7002*)
E. Caruso (in ♯ G.FJLP 5009*; QJLP 105*;
♭ *Vic.ERAT 5*)
A. Bonci (in ♯ Sca. 811*)
G. Martinelli (in ♯ SBDH.LPG 4*; in ♯ *FRP. 2*)
T. Schipa (in ♯ Sca. 805*)
A. Pertile (in ♯ Od.ODX 127*: MOAQ 301*)
J. McCormack (in ♯ Roy. 1555*)
G. Anselmi & pf. (in ♯ Sca. 816*)
R. Tauber (*Ger*) (in ♯ Cum.CE 187*)

Si, mi chiamano Mimì S
V. de los Angeles   in ♯ **G.ALP 1284**
(*Donde lieta, Act III; Mefistofele, Cenerentola, etc.*)
(♯ QALP 10115)
M. M. Callas   in ♯ **C.CX 1204**
(*below; Butterfly, Turandot, M. Lescaut, etc.*)
(♯ QCX 10108: FCX 377; Angel. 35195)
L. di Lelio (*below*)   **Cet.PE 180**
(*below*)
E. Berger (*Ger*)   **G.DB 11574**
(*O soave fanciulla*) from set   (♭ *7RW 524*)
M. Sà Earp   **BrzCont.CA 4017**
(*Gomes: Guarany—Gentile di cuori*)
E. Arizmendi   in ♯ *ArgOd.LDC 506*
(o.n. ArgC. 307001)
F. Schimenti (*below*)   in ♯ **Roy. 1611**
K. Grayson[1] (in ♯ *Vic.LOC*/♭ *EOB 3000*)
L. Maslennikova (*Russ*) (*USSRM.D 00902*)
I. Szecsódy (*Hung*) (Qual.MN 1052)

☆ R. Tebaldi (n.v.) (from set J)
(♯ *D.LW 5044: Lon.LD 9053* & in ♯ D.LXT 5076)
R. Tebaldi (o.v.) (♭ *AmD.ED 3530*; in ♯ *Fnt.LP 301*)
M. Carosio (♭ *G. 7R 115: 7RQ 3018: 7RW 143*)
L. Bori (in ♯ *G.FJLP 5004*: in QJLP 104;
& in ♯ Vic.LM 1909)
L. Albanese (♭ *Vic.ERA 105: ERA 210*: & in ♯ LM 1801)
D. Ilitsch (in ♯ *U. 5109C*)
M. Olivero (Orf. 54004)
G. Moore (in ♯ *Vic.LCT*/♭ *WCT 7004*)
Géori-Boué (*Fr*) (in ♯ Od.ODX 117)
N. Vallin (*Fr*) (♭ *Od. 7AO 2003*)
J. Hammond (*Eng*) (♭ *C.SED 5514*)

H C. Muzio (AF.AGSB 14*; in ♯ Vic. set LCT 6701*)
R. Ponselle (in ♯ Sca. 803*)

— ACCOMPANIMENT, etc., for practice (in ♯ *VS.SA 5000*)

O soave fanciulla S & T
M. L. Gemelli & D. Cestari   **Cet.PE 194**
(*Manon—Ah! fuyez douce image*)
E. Berger & R. Schock (*Ger*)   **G.DB 11574**
(*Si mi chiamano Mimi*) from set
(♭ *7RW 524*: in ♯ *WBLP 1514*)
☆ R. Carteri & F. Tagliavini, from set
(in ♯ CCet.A 50178)
J. Hammond & D. Lloyd (*Eng*)
(♭ *C.SCD 2002: SCDW 102*)

H N. Melba & E. Caruso (in ♯ Vic. set LCT 6701*)
M. Zamboni & B. Gigli (in ♯ *SBDH.LPP 5*)
L. Bori & J. McCormack (in ♯ G.FJLP 5010*;
♭ *Vic.ERAT 17*)
G. Farrar & E. Caruso (AF.AGSB 50*)
F. Alda & G. Martinelli (in ♯ ABDH.LPG 4*)

ACT II

Quando m'en vo S
G. Arnaldi   **Cet.AT 0342**
(*Amico Fritz—Non mi resta*)
D. Kirsten   in ♯ **AmC.ML 4730**
L. Hunt   in ♯ **Roy. 1611**
(*above & below*)
E. Farrell [& H. Blankenberg & R. Petrak][2]
(in ♯ MGM.E 3185: ♭ *set X 304*: EP 527/8)
☆ P. Munsel (♭ *G. 7ER 5028*)
R. Boesch, from set (in ♯ Rem. 199-122 & ♯ Ply. 12-51)
A. M. Alberghetti (in ♯ Mer.MG 20056)
I. Maslennikova (*Russ*) (*USSR. 18387*)

H E. Cavalieri (SBDH.P 6*)
— ACCOMPANIMENT only, for practice
(in ♯ AmEsq. 1 & in ♯ *VS.SA 5000*)

ACT III

Mimi? Son io S & B
A. Bolechowska & A. Hiolski (*Pol*) (*Muza. 1768*)

Donde lieta uscì S [& T]
V. de los Angeles   in ♯ **G.ALP 1284**
(*above*)   (♯ QALP 10115)
M. M. Callas   in ♯ **C.CX 1204**
(*above*)   (in ♯ FCX 377: QCX 10108; Angel. 35195)
L. di Lelio (*above*)   **Cet.PE 180**
D. Kirsten   in ♯ **AmC.ML 4730**
M. Cebotari & P. Anders (*Ger*)[3]   ♯ **Ura. 7105**
(*above, & Madama Butterfly*)
E. Arizmendi   **ArgOd. 66028**
(*Turandot—Tu che di gel*)
(in ♯ *LDC 506*; o.n. ArgC. 307002)
F. Schimenti   in ♯ **Roy. 1611**
(*above, Turandot, Rondine, etc.*)
J. Merrill   in ♯ *MH. 33-104*
☆ R. Tebaldi, from set J (♯ *D.LW 5044: Lon.LD 9053*
& in ♯ D.LXT 5076)
L. Albanese (♭ *G. 7ER 5028*; in ♯ Vic.LM 1839;
♯ FV.A 630253)
R. Tebaldi (o.v.) (♭ *AmD.ED 3530*; in ♯ *Fnt.LP 301*)
L. Welitsch (C.*LO 90*)
E. Schwarzkopf (C.*LN 5*: ♭ SCBQ 3001: SCBF 103:
SCBW 101)
J. Hammond (*Eng*) (♭ C.SCD 2002: SCDW 102)
M. Angelici (*Fr*) (in ♯ G.FBLP 1051)

H F. Alda (AF.AGSA 14*)

— ACCOMPANIMENT for practice (in ♯ *VS.SA 5000*)

Addio, dolce svegliare Qtt.
☆ E. Trötschel & R. Streich (S), L. Fehenberger (T),
D. Fischer-Dieskau (*Ger*) (♭ *Pol. 32048*)

ACT IV

In un coupé . . . O Mimi, tu più non torni T & B
R. Schock & D. Fischer-Dieskau (*Ger*)
G.DB 11575
(*Che gelida manina*, from set) (♭ *7RW 525*: ♯ *WBLP 1514*)
B. Gigli & T. Ruffo   **AF.AGSB 56**
(*Pêcheurs des Perles—Au fond du temple*)
(in ♯ SBDH.LPG 4)
☆ J. Björling & R. Merrill (in ♯ *G.BLP 1053*: ♭ *7RQ 3008*:
7RW 110; ♭ *Vic.ERA 134*)
G. di Stefano & L. Warren (♭ *G. 7ER 5028*)
B. Gigli & G. de Luca (♭ *Vic.ERAT 10*)
A. Dermota & G. Oeggl (*Ger*) (RadT.E 178T)
I. Kozlovsky & And. Ivanov (*Russ*) (*USSRM.D 00984*)
K. v. Pataky & H. Schlusnus (*Ger*) (∇ *Pol. 67357*)

H A. Bassi & T. Ruffo (in ♯ Sca. 812*)

Vecchia zimarra Bs
A. Majak (*Pol*) (*Muza. 1725*)
☆ I. Tajo (Orf. 54006, d.c.)

H J. Mardones (in ♯ Sca. 810*)

Sono andati? S & T
☆ L. Albanese & G. di Stefano (in ♯ Vic.LM 1864)
E. Trötschel & L. Fehenberger (*Ger*) (♭ *Pol. 32048*)

(La) FANCIULLA DEL WEST 3 Acts 1910
(*Girl of the Golden West*)
Minnie, della mia casa B   Act I
G. Taddei   **Cet.AT 0404**
(*Guillaume Tell, No. 18*)   (in ♯ LPC 55006)

Una parola sola! . . .
Or son sei mesi T   Act II
M. del Monaco   in ♯ **D.LXT 2928**
(& in ♯ D.LXT 2964; Lon.LL 1025)   (♯ Lon.LL 990)
(*Bohème—Che gelida . . . on D.X 579*)
(& in ♯ D.LW 5121; ♯ Lon.LD 9132)

H B. de Muro (AF.AGSB 63*)
E. Johnson (AF.AGSB 63*)
C. Albani (IRCC. 3138*)

---

[1] From film sound-track *So this is love*.   [2] Sound track of film *Interrupted Melody*.
[3] Continues to the end of Act III, omitting Marcello's and Musetta's parts.

Ch'ella mi creda libero   T   Act III
W. Kmentt (*Ger*)   in ‡ *Phi.S 06076R*
(*Turandot, A. Chénier, Gioconda, etc.*)

L. Bodurov   **U.H 24399**
(*Zauberflöte*)

☆ M. del Monaco   **D.XP 6150**
(*Luisa Miller—Quando le sere*)
                          (& ♭ *Lon.REP 8002:* in ‡ **LL 1244**)

GIANNI SCHICCHI   1 Act   1918
COMPLETE RECORDING
Soloists, Berlin Sym.—Balzer (‡ Roy. 1527;
                                              MusH.LP 12012)
Firenze è come un albero fiorito   T
G. Poggi   in ‡ *D.LX 3127*
(*Luisa Miller, Fedora, etc.*)   (‡ *Lon.LD 9106*)

O mio babbino caro   S
M. M. Callas   in ‡ **C.CX 1204**
(*Bohème, Butterfly, Turandot, etc.*)
                          (QCX 10108: FCX 377; Angel. 35195)

H. Gueden   ‡ *D.LW 5178*
(*Turandot, Traviata, Falstaff*)   (‡ *Lon.LD 9165*)

M. Olivero   *Cet.AT 0321*
(*Mascagni: Iris, aria*)

M. Henderson   in ‡ **Roy. 1611**
(*Turandot, Butterfly, Bohème, etc.*)

L. Castellani, S. Leff (pf.)   in ‡ **Mur.P 105**
(*followed by pf. acc. only*)

A. Rothenberger (*Ger*)   **G.EH 1459**
(*Pagliacci—Ballatella*)   (♭ *7PW 540*)

☆ L. Albanese   **G.DB 21603**
(*Tosca—Vissi d'arte*)   (♭ *Vic.ERA 139*)

☆ D. Kirsten (♭ *AmC.A 1639*)
E. Schwarzkopf (*C.LN 4*)
J. Hammond (*Eng*) (♭ *C.SCD 2001: SCDW 101:
                                          SED 5514*)
G. Fields (*Eng*) (in ‡ *D.LF 1140;* ‡ *Lon.LB 751*)

ℍ C. Muzio (in ‡ *FRP. 1**)
F. Alda (*AF.AGSA 14**)

MADAMA BUTTERFLY   2 Acts   1904
COMPLETE RECORDINGS

Casts	Set I	Set J	Set K
Butterfly (S)	C. Petrella	V. de los Angeles	M. M. Callas
Suzuki (M-S)	M. Masini	A. M. Canali	L. Danieli
Kate (S)	...	M. C. Foscali	M. Huder	L. Villa
Pinkerton(T)	F. Tagliavini	G. di Stefano	N. Gedda
Sharpless (B)	G. Taddei	T. Gobbi	M. Borriello
etc.			

Set I with Italian Radio Cho. & Orch.—Questa
                                          ‡ **CCet. set 1248**
(6ss)   [Highlights on ♭ *Cap.FAP 7010;* ‡ CCet.A 50179]

Set J with Rome Op. Cho. & Orch.—Gavazzeni
                                          ‡ **G.ALP 1215/7**
(6ss)   (QALP 10082/4; Vic. set LM 6121)

Set K with La Scala Op. Cho. & Orch.—Karajan
                                          ‡ **C.CX 1296/8**
(6ss)   (‡ Angel. 35225/7, set 3523)   (‡ QCX 10156/8)

Set L. Soloists, Florence Op. Cho. & Orch.   ‡ **Rŏy. 1495/7**
(6ss)   (‡ Gram. 20145/7)

Set M. E. Shumskaya, I. Kozlovsky, etc. Bolshoi Theatre
Cho. & Moscow Radio Orch.—Bron (*Russ*)
(8ss)   ‡ **USSR.D 0675/82**

Set A.   ☆ T. dal Monte (S), B. Gigli (T), M. Huder (M-S),
etc. Rome Op. Cho. & Orch.—O. de Fabritiis
(4ss)   ‡ **G.FJLP 5020/1**
(‡ QALP 10048/9; Vic. set LCT 6006: ♭ set WCT 6006)

Set S.   ☆ E. Steber (S), R. Tucker (T), G. Valdengo (B), etc.
Metropolitan Op. Cho. & Orch.—Rudolf
(6ss)   ‡ **Phi.A 01119/21L**)

HIGHLIGHTS
M. Stader (S), H. Töpper (M-S), C. van Dijk (T),
Munich State Op. Cho. & Munich Phil.
Orch.—Hollreiser   ‡ *Pol. 17017*
[see *below* for separate issues] (& in *Ger* on ‡ *Pol. 17016*)

E. Berger (S), S. Wagner (A), R. Schock (T),
D. Fischer-Dieskau (B), E. Zimmermann
(T), Berlin Municipal Op. Cho. & Orch.
—Schüchter   ‡ *G.WBLP 1507*
(*Ger*) [see *below* for separate issues]

G. Bardi, M. Leone, B. Lewis, etc. ‡ **Roy. 1616**
(*Faust*)
Vienna Op. Cho. (‡ *Ply.* 10-26: 12-29: 12-103)

☆ R. Tebaldi, I. Campora, etc. Santa Cecilia Cho. & Orch.
—Erede, from set G (‡ Lon.LL 650;
                          excerpts on ♭ *D.LW 5189*)
L. Albanese (S), L. Browning (M-S), J. Melton, Victor
Orch.—Weissmann (‡ FV.A 630253; *DV.T 16049*)
Soloists, Austrian Sym.—Loibner, from set H
(‡ AFest.CFR 12-281; excpts. on ♭ *Rem.REP 4*)
Anon. Artists[1] (‡ Cam.CAL 222: in set CFL 101)
Soloists, Berlin Op. Cho. & Orch. (♭ *Roy.EP 192*)

Orchestral Suite
Rome Sym.—Argento   ‡ **Kings.KL 231**

ACT I

Dovunque al mondo ... Amore o grillo   T & B
(*Im weiten Weltall ... Ob echte Liebe ...*)
R. Schock & D. Fischer-Dieskau **G.DB 11578**
(*below*)   (*Ger*)   (♭ *RW 528*)

Ancora un passo ... Spira sul mar   S
M. Stader   *Pol. 62930*
(*Un bel dì*)   (♭ *Pol. 32020*)
(*Ger, on Pol. 62929:* ♭ *32019*)

I. Szecsódy (*Hung*)   *Qual.MK 1567*
(*Faust—Duet*)

E. Berger (*Ger*)   **G.DA 5523**
(*Un bel dì*)   (♭ *7PW 533*)

☆ L. Albanese (♭ *G. 7ER 5008;* in ‡ Vic.LM 1839)

ℍ C. Muzio[2] (in ‡ *LI.TWV 91053**)

Love Duet: Viene la sera ... Bimba dagli occhi
                                          S & T
FAIRLY COMPLETE RECORDINGS
M. Stader & C. v. Dijk   **PV. 72484**
(*Ger on PV. 72483;* ♭ *Pol. 30079*)   (♭ *Pol. 30080*)

M. Cebotari & H. Roswaenge   ‡ **Ura. 7105**
(*below; Bohème*)   (*Ger*)

M. Kišoňová-Hubová & J. Blaho (*Cz*)
                              in ‡ *Sup.LPM 137*
(*below; & Gounod*)   (‡ *U.* 5111C)

LESS COMPLETE RECORDINGS
V. de los Angeles & G. di Stefano ♭ **G.7ER 5045**
(*Un bel dì, Act II*) (from set J)   (♭ *ERQ 132*)

E. Berger & R. Schock (*Ger*)   **G.DB 11577**
(2ss)   (♭ *7RW 527:* in ‡ **WBLP 1514**)

☆ E. Malbin & M. Lanza (in ‡ *G.ALP 1202*)
R. Peters & J. Peerce (*G.DB 21575*)
L. Albanese & J. Melton (in ‡ Vic.LM 1839)

ACT II, Sc. 1

Un bel dì, vedremo   S
V. de los Angeles, from set J   ♭ **G.7ER 5045**
(*Love Duet*)   (*ERQ 132*)

M. M. Callas   in ‡ **C.CX 1204**
(*below; Bohème, G. Schicchi, Turandot, etc.*)
                          (‡ QCX 10108: FCX 377; Angel. 35195)

M. Stader   *Pol. 62930*
(*Ancora un passo*)   (♭ *Pol. 32020*)
(*Ger, on Pol. 62929:* ♭ *32019*)

M. Minazzi   **Cet.PE 182**
(*Suor Angelica—Senza Mamma*)

M. Cebotari (*Ger*)   ‡ **Ura. 7105**
(*above & Bohème*)

M. Benetti   **Cet.PE 200**
(*Falstaff—Sul fil d'un soffio*)

M. Sá Earp   **BrzCont.A 4018**
(*Gomes: Quem sabe*)   (also single sided F 006)

M. Angelici (*Fr*)   in ‡ *G.FBLP 1051*

L. Castellano, S. Leff (pf.)   in ‡ **Mur.P 106**
(*followed by pf. acc. only*)

M. Leone   in ‡ **Roy. 1611**
(*below, Turandot, Bohème, etc.*)

G. Frazzoni   in ‡ *Cet.LPV 45003*
(*Aida, Chénier, etc.*)

---

[1] Perhaps including E. Steber, A. Dickey, L. Warren.
[2] From Edison and Pathé hill and dale recordings. **This disc was withdrawn almost immediately on issue.**

Un bel dì, vedremo (continued)
  E. Farrell[1] (in ♯ MGM.E 3185: ♭ *set X 304:*
                                ♭ *set EP 527/8)*
  N. Shpiller (*Russ*) (*USSRM.D 001278*)
  E. Bandrowska-Turska (*Polish*)
        (in ♯ *USSR.D 2146 & USSRM.D 00119*)

  ☆ R. Tebaldi (♭ *D. 71062: DK 23356:* in ♯ *LW 5044;*
                            ♯ *Lon.LD 9053)*
  T. dal Monte (in ♯ *G.QALP 10089*)
  L. Albanese (♭ *G.7R 159: 7ER 5008;*
      in ♯ Vic.LM 1801 & LM 1839: ♭ *ERA 210*)
  D. Kirsten (♭ *AmC.A 1639*)
  D. Ilitsch (Hma. 15011)
  E. Arizmendi (in ♯ *ArgOd.LDC 506*)
  E. Schwarzkopf (♭ *C.SCB 102: SCBQ 3004: SCBW 102*)
  G. Moore (in ♯ *B.LAT 8025: ♭ AmD.ED 3504*)
  N. Vallin (*Fr*) (♭ *Od. 7AO 2004*)
  Géori-Boué (*Fr*) (in ♯ *Od.ODX 117*)
  J. Hammond (*Eng*) (♭ *C.SED 5514*)
  Anon. artist (in ♯ *Cam.CAL 249*)
  ▫ R. Raisa (in ♯ *Sca. 808**)
  R. Ponselle (in ♯ *Sca. 803**)

— PF. ACC. only for practice (in ♯ *AmEsq. 1*)

Ora a noi . . . (Letter Duet) S & B
. . . Sop. part only: È questo . . . Che tua madre
  B. Lewis   in ♯ *Roy. 1611*
  (*above & below*)

Il cannone del porto! . . .
Una nave da guerra! . . .
Scuoti quella fronda S & M-S (*Flower Duet*)
  M. Stader & H. Töpper   ♭ *Pol. 32073*
  (*Manon Lescaut—Donna non vidi mai*)
  (*Ger on ♭ Pol. 32072*)

  M. Kišoňová-Hubová & M. Hazuchová (*Cz*)
                    ♯ *Sup.LPM 137*
  (*Love duet & Faust*)   (♯ *U. 5111C*)

  E. Berger & S. Wagner (*Ger*)   **G.DB 11576**
  (*Tu, tu, piccolo iddio, Act III*)   (♭ *7RW 526*)

  E. Shumskaya & E. Gribova (*Russ*) (*USSRM.D 1048*)
  ☆ L. Albanese & L. Browning (in ♯ *Vic.LM 1839*)
  ▫ G. Farrar & J. Jacoby (*AF.AGSB 50**)

Humming Chorus . . . Nello shosi S & Cho.
  Italian Radio Cho., from set I (♭ *Cet.EPO 0324*)
  ☆ Verdi Cho. (*Od. 220098*)

ACT II, Sc. 2

Io so che alle sue pene . . . Trio
Non ve l'avevo detto . . . Addio fiorito asil
  ☆ W. Demmer (S), A. Dermota (T), G. Oeggl (Bs) (*Ger*)
  (RadT.A 176T)

. . . Duet only T & B
  R. Schock & D. Fischer-Dieskau (*Ger*)
                    G.DB 11578
  (*Duet, Act I*)   (♭ *7RW 528:* in ♯ *WBLP 1514*)

  ☆ J. Peerce & E. Dunning (G.DB 21575)
  A. Pertile & G. Fregosi (in ♯ *Ete. 710*)

. . . Tenor pt. only: Addio fiorito asil
  D. Cestari   ***Cet.AT 0399***
  (*Vittadini: Anima Allegra—aria*)

  G. Gari, S. Leff (pf.)   in ♯ ***Mur.P 108***
  (*followed by pf. acc. only*)

  ☆ H. Roswaenge (*Ger*) (in ♯ *CEd. 7010*)
  ▫ R. Tauber (*Ger*) (in ♯ *Cum.CE 187**)

Con onor . . . Tu, tu, piccolo iddio! S
  M. M. Callas   in ♯ **C.CX 1204**
  (*above*)   (in ♯ QCX 10108: FCX 377; Angel. 35195)

  E. Berger (*Ger*)   **G.DB 11576**
  (*Duet, Act II, Sc. 1*)   (♭ *7RW 526*)

  M. Leone   in ♯ **Roy. 1611**
  (*above*)

  ☆ R. Tebaldi, from set (♯ *D.LW 5044; Lon.LD 9053;*
                     & in ♯ *D.LXT 5076*)
  D. Ilitsch (Hma. 15011; in ♯ *U. 5109C*)
  L. Albanese (in ♯ *Vic.LM 1839*)

MANON LESCAUT 4 Acts 1893
COMPLETE RECORDINGS

Casts	Set A	Set B	Set C
Manon (S)	R. Tebaldi	C. Petrella	L. Albanese
Des Grieux (T)	M.del Monaco	V. Campagnano	J. Björling
Lescaut (B)	M. Borriello	S. Meletti	R. Merrill
Geronte (Bs)	F. Corena	P. L. Latinucci	F. Calabrese
Edmondo (T)	P. di Palma	T. Panel	M. Carlin

Set A, with Santa Cecilia Acad. Cho. & Orch.
  —Molinari Pradelli   ♯ **D.LXT 2995/7**
  (6ss)   (♯ Lon. set XLLA 28)
  [Announced as 4ss, ♯ Lon.LL 1131/2, but not issued]

Set B, with Italian Radio Cho. & Orch.
  —del Cupolo (6ss)   ♯ **CCet. set 1243**
  [Highlights on ♭ *Cap.FAP 7013: Cet. EPO0321;* Intermezzo,
                Act III only, in ♯ *CCet.A 50159*]

Set C, with Rome Op. Cho. & Orch.—Perlea
                  ♯ **G.ALP 1326/8**
  (6ss)   (♯ Vic. set LM 6116; ♯ ItV.C12R 0164/6)

  ☆ Soloists, La Scala Cho. & Orch.—Molajoli
                  ♯ **C.QCX 10076/7**

EXCERPTS
L'Ora, o Tirsi S Act II
Tu, tu amore? . . . O tentatrice S & T Act II
Sola, perduta, abbandonata S & T Act IV
  D. Kirsten (S), R. Tucker (T) & Met. Op.
  Orch.—Cleva   ♯ **AmC.ML 4981**
  (*Bohème & Manon*)

Orchestral Selections
  Rome Sym.—Rossellini   ♯ **Kings. 703**
  Linz Sym. (in ♯ *Ply. 12-29*)

ACT I

Tra voi belle . . . T
  ▫ A. Bassi (in ♯ *IIRS. 3005**)

Donna non vidi mai T
  G. Poggi   in ♯ ***D.LX 3127***
  (*Fedora, Luisa Miller, Gianni Schicchi, etc.*)
                  (♯ *Lon. LD 9106*)

  W. Ludwig   ♭ *Pol. 32073*
  (*Butterfly—Flower Duet*)
  (*Ger, on ♭ Pol. 62897, d.c.* also on *Pol. 62897, d.c.*
             & in ♯ *18147 & 19043*)

  W. Kmentt (*Ger*)   in ♯ ***Phi.S 06076R***
  (*below, Tosca, Bohème, etc.*)
  ☆ J. Björling (♭ *G. 7ER 5025; Vic.ERA 109; DV. 26044*)
  ▫ F. de Lucia (in ♯ *CEd. set 7002**)
  G. Anselmi & pf. (in ♯ *Sca. 816**)
  A. Bassi (in ♯ *HRS. 3005**)
  E. Caruso (♭ *Vic.ERAT 5*;* in ♯ *LCT 1138* &*
                  in ♯ *set LCT 6701**)

ACT II

In quelle trine morbide S
  M. M. Callas   in ♯ **C.CX 1204**
  (*below, Bohème, Butterfly, etc.*)
        (in ♯ QCX 10108: FCX 377; Angel. 35195)

  A. Hownanian   ♭ *Cet.EPO 0322*
  (*Forza, La Wally, Amico Fritz*)

  E. Arizmendi   **ArgOd. 66022**
  (*Otello—Ave Maria*)   (in ♯ *LDC 506*)

  F. Alda (*below*)   **AF.AGSA 8**
  ☆ R. Tebaldi   ♭ *D. 71073*
  (*Trovatore—Tacea la notte*)
      (♭ *X 102,* & in ♯ *LW 5065; Lon.LD 9054*)
  ☆ L. Albanese (♭ *Vic.ERA 105:* in ♯ *LM 1839 &*
          in ♯ *LM 1847;* ♯ *FV.A 630253*)
  ▫ C. Muzio (*IRCC. 3135**)
  C. Boninsegna & pf. (in ♯ *Sca. 813**)
  F. Alda (in ♯ *Vic. set LCT 6701**)
  R. Ponselle (in ♯ *Sca. 803**)

L'Ora, o Tirsi (Minuetto) S
  F. Alda (*above*)   **AF.AGSA 8**
  R. Tebaldi, from set A   in ♯ *D.LXT 5076*
  (*below, Bohème, Butterfly, etc.*)
  (*below; & Traviata on ♯ D.LW 5210*)

---

[1] Sound track of film *Interrupted Melody.*

Tu, tu, amore? . . . O tentatrice S & T
R. Tebaldi & M. del Monaco   ‡ *D.LW 5198*
(*Otello—Willow Song & Ave Maria*)   (‡ *Lon.LD 9195*)
(*Aida & Otello duets on* ‡ D.LXT 5067; Lon.LL 1256)
C. Petrella & V. Campagnano, from set B
in ‡ CCet.A 50178
(*Rigoletto, Gioconda, etc.*)

Ah! Manon, mi tradisce T
W. Kmentt (*Ger*)   in ‡ *Phi.S 06076R*
(*above*)
☆ A. Pertile (in ‡ Ete. 710)
☒ G. Anselmi & pf. (in ‡ Sca. 816*)

Intermezzo orch.
Philharmonia—Karajan   in ‡ *C.CX 1265*
(*Carmen, Thaïs, etc.*)
(‡ FCX 407: QCX 10150; Angel. 35207)
☆ Vienna Phil.—Karajan (♭ *C.SCB 109: SCBW 108: SCBQ 3013*)
Robin Hood Dell—Mitropoulos (♭ *AmC.A 1637*)
Covent Garden—Patanè (♭ *C.SED 5512: SEDQ 522*)

ACT III

Ah! non v'avvicinate . . . No! pazzo son! T & B
☆ M. del Monaco   ♭ *D. 71061*
(*Bohème: Che gelida manina*)   (♭ *DK 23350:*
XP 6152, d.c. & ♭ *Lon.REP 8002:* in ‡ *LL 1244*)
☆ A. Pertile (in ‡ Ete. 710)
B. Gigli & G. Noto (in ‡ G.FJLP 5039)
☒ G. Zenatello & pf. (in ‡ Ete. 705*)

ACT IV

Sola, perduta, abbandonata S
M. M. Callas   in ‡ *C.CX 1204*
(*above*)   (in ‡ QCX 10108: FCX 377; Angel. 35195)
R. Tebaldi, from set A   in ‡ *D.LXT 5076*
(*above*)   (also ‡ *D.LW 5210*)
L. Albanese, from set C   in ‡ *Vic.LM 1909*
(*Forza, Tristan, Walküre, etc.*)

(La) RONDINE 2 Acts 1917
COMPLETE RECORDING
Magda ... ... E. de Luca (S)
Lisette ... ... O. Rovero (S)
Ruggiero ... ... G. Prandelli (T)
Prunier ... ... L. della Pergola (T)
Rambaldo ... ... V. Pagano (B)
etc. & Milan Antonio Guarnieri Orch.
—Nabeglio (4ss)   ‡ AmC. set EL 12

Chi il bel sogno di Doretta S Act I
E. Rizzieri   *Cet.AT 0369*
(*Catalani: Loreley—Amor, celeste ebbrezza*)
☆ M. Minazzi (*P.AR 403*)

Ore dolci e divine S Act I
L. Hunt   in ‡ *Roy. 1611*
(*Bohème, Butterfly, etc.*)
E. Rizzieri   *Cet.CB 20545*
(*Carmen—Je dis que rien ...*)

SUOR ANGELICA 1 Act 1918
Senza mamma, o bimbo S
M. M. Callas   in ‡ *C.CX 1204*
(*G. Schicchi, Butterfly, Turandot, etc.*)
(in ‡ QCX 10108: FCX 377; Angel. 35195)
M. Minazzi   *Cet.PE 182*
(*Butterfly—Un bel di ...*)
☆ L. Albanese (♭ *Vic.ERA 105*)

(II) TABARRO 1 Act 1918
Hai ben ragione T
M. del Monaco   in ‡ *D.LXT 2928*
(♭ Lon.LL 990)
(& in ‡ D.LXT 2964: *LW 5121;* Lon.LL 1025: *LD 9132*)

TOSCA 3 Acts 1900
COMPLETE RECORDINGS
Set K
Cavaradossi ... ... G. di Stefano (T)
Tosca ... ... M. M. Callas (S)
Baron Scarpia ... ... T. Gobbi (B)
Angelotti ... ... F. Calabrese (Bs)
Sacristan ... ... M. Luise (Bs)
Spoletta ... ... A. Mercuriali (T)
Sciarrone ... ... D. Caselli (Bs)
Shepherd Boy ... ... A. Cordova (treble)
La Scala Cho. & Orch.—Sabata ‡ *C.CX 1094/5*
(4ss) (‡ FCX 253/4: QCX 10028/9;
Angel. 35060/1, set 3508)
Set C. ☆ B. Scacciati (S), A. Granda (T), E. Molinari (B),
etc., La Scala Cho. & Milan Sym.—Molajoli
(4ss)   ‡ AmC.set EL 4
Set A. ☆ B. Gigli, M. Caniglia, etc., Rome Op.—de Fabritiis
(‡ G.QALP 10004/5: FJLP 5011/2: VALP 506/7)
Set F. ☆ G. Poggi, A. Guerrini, etc., Italian Radio—Pradelli
(‡ Pol. 18095/6)
[Highlights on ‡ CCet.A 50152; ♭ *Cap.FAP 7008;*
♭ *Cet.EPO 0313;* ‡ *Pol. 16106*]
Set G. ☆ Soloists, Cho. & Vienna State Op. Orch.—Quadri
(4ss, ‡ West.WL 5351/2, set WAL 222;
Highlights on ‡ WL 5208; *Sel.LA 1023*)
Set L. "Nat. Opera" Soloists & orch.
(5ss, ‡ Gram. 20142/2)

HIGHLIGHTS
L. Malagrida (S), C. Franzini (T), A. Salsedo
(B), & Milan Antonio Guarnieri Orch.
—Arrigo Guarnieri   ‡ EPhi.NBL 5001
(‡ Phi.S 04004L, o.n. N 00201L)
☆ N. Vallin (S), E. di Mazzei (T), A. Endrèze (B), G.
Payen (T) (*Fr*)   ‡ Od.ODX 121

COLLECTED EXCERPTS (in *French*)
Recondita armonia T Act I
Non la sospira S Act I
Tosca divina S & B Act I
Mi dicon venal ... Se la giurata fede B & S Act II
Vissi d'arte S Act II
E lucevan le stelle T Act III
S. Sarroca (S), J. Luccioni (T), E. Blanc (B),
Opéra-Comique Orch.—Wolff
‡ LI.TW 91132
(*Contes d'Hoffmann & Barbiere*)   (‡ *D.FAT 173665*)

Orchestral Selections
Rome Sym.—Argento   ‡ Kings. 702
Opera Orch.—Rossi (in ‡ *Mae.OA 20006*)

ACT I

Recondita armonia T
J. Soler   *Cet.AT 0319*
(*Pagliacci—Vesti la giubba*)
M. Gafni   in ‡ *For.FLP 1001*
A. Dermota   ‡ *DT.TM 68037*
(*Elisir d'Amore, Eugene Oniegin, etc.*) (♭ *FT. 470.TC.015*)
(in *Ger*, T.A 11599: ♭ U 45599 & ♭ UV 110)
G. Björling   in ‡ *G.ALPC 1*
(*Samson & Dalila, Rigoletto, etc.*)
G. di Stefano [& M. Luise (B)] ♭ *C.SEL 1526*
(*Vissi d'arte*)   from set K   (♭ *SEBQ 122*)
W. Kmentt (*Ger*)   in ‡ *Phi.S 06076R*
(*Turandot, Fanciulla del West, etc.*)
K. Terkal (*Ger*)   *D.F 43569*
(*E lucevan ...*)   (♭ *DX 1761*)
☆ G. Poggi [& C. Badiola (B)]   *P.RO 30007*
(*E lucevan le stelle*)
H. Secombe (*Eng*) (*EPhi.PB 523*)
A. Frinberg (*Latvian*) (in ‡ *USSR.D 1900 &
USSR. 20894*)
☆ M. Lanza (in ‡ *G.ALP 1202: FBLP 1043:* ♭ *7RW 114*)
L. Melchior (MGM. 9133)
M. del Monaco (D.XP 6151: ♭ *Lon.REP 8002:*
in ‡ *LL 1244*)
B. Gigli [& G. Tomei (B)] from set A (♭ *Vic.ERAT 13*)
N. Scattolini, from set G (♭ *Sel. 470.C.007*)
A. Pertile (in ‡ Od.ODX 127: MOAQ 301)
R. Tauber (*Ger*) (in ‡ Ete. 712)
E. di Mazzei (*Fr*) (♭ Od. 7AO 2009)
☒ J. McCormack (in ‡ Cum.CE 185*)
T. Schipa (in ‡ Ete. 492*; in ‡ Sca. 805*; in ‡ FRP. 1*)
C. Albani (AF.AGSA 13*)
E. Caruso (♭ Vic.ERAT 5*)

Mario! Mario!　S & T
(Duet—Tosca & Cavaradossi)
M. M. Callas & G. di Stefano, from set K (♭*C.SEL 1543*, 2ss)
☆ M. Caniglia & B. Gigli, from set A (♭ *G. 7ER 5037:*
7ERQ 122: ♭ *Vic.ERAT 135)* [abridged, 1s.]
P. Tassinari & F. Tagliavini (in ♯ *FSor.CS 544)*

... **Sop. part** only: **Non la sospiri**
☆ D. Ilitsch (in ♯ *U. 5109C)*

Ora stammi a sentir　S
♋ G. Farrar (AF.AGSB 55*)

Tre sbirri, una carrozza (Te Deum)　B & Cho.
☆ L. Tibbett (in ♯ *Cam.CAL 171)*
C. Formichi (in ♯ Ete. 494)
♋ P. Amato (AF.AGSB 54*)
T. Ruffo (in ♯ Vic. set LCT 6701*)

ACT II

Ella verrà　B
A. Sved　　　　　　　　　　　in ♯ **PRCC. 3**

La povera mia cena　S, B & T
☆ M. Caniglia, A. Borgioli, N. Mazziotti, from set A
(in ♯ Vic.LM 1864)

Mi dicon venal . . . Se la giurata fede　B
♋ T. Ruffo (in ♯ Vic. set LCT 6701*)

Vissi d'arte　S
M. M. Callas [& T. Gobbi (B)]　♭ *C.SEL 1526*
(*Recondita armonia*) from set K　　　(♭ *SEBQ 122)*
P. Munsel　　　　　　　　　　in ♯ **G.BLP 1023**
(Film *Melba*)　　(in ♯ *QBLP 5015;* in ♯ *Vic.LM 7012:*
♭ *set WDM 7012)*
D. Rigal　　　　　　　　　　　ArgOd. 66025
(*Catalani: La Wally—Ebben . . .*)　(♭ *BSOAE 4508:*
in ♯ *LDC 503;* in ♯ *AmD.DL 4060:* ♭ *ED 3508)*
V. Petrova　　　　　　　　　in ♯ **Ace.1007/8**
(*Gioconda, Cavalleria, Trovatore, etc.*)
E. Doria　　　　　　　　　　in ♯ **PRCC. 3**
M. C. Verna　　　　　　　in ♯ **Cet.LPC 55005**
(*Mefistofele, Sonnambula, etc.*)
A. Nordmo-Lovberg　　　in ♯ **G.ALPC 1**
(*Figaro, Carmen, Bartered Bride, etc.*)
G. Ribla　　　　　　　　　　in ♯ **MH. 33-104**
G. Frazzoni　　　　　　　in ♯ **Cet.LPV 45003**
(*Cavalleria, Butterfly, etc.*)
☆ R. Tebaldi (♭ *D. 71062; DK 23356:*
in ♯ *LW 5065;* ♯ *Lon.LD 9054)*
D. Kirsten (♭ *AmC.A 1639)*
L. Welitsch (in ♯ *AmC.ML 4795; C.LO 90)*
S. dall' Argine, from set G (♭ *Sel. 470.C.007)*
L. Albanese (*G.DB 21603:* ♭ *7R 159,* d.c.)
G. Moore (in ♯ *B.LAT 8026;* ♭ *AmD.ED 3504)*
J. Hammond (*Eng*) (♭ *C.SCD 2001: SCDW 101:*
SED 5514)
N. Vallin (*Fr*) (♭ *Od. 7AO 2004)*
P. Takács (*Hung*) (*Qual.MK 1582)*
♋ G. Farrar (in ♯ *G.FJLP 5004*: QJLP 104*)*
R. Ponselle (in ♯ Sca. 803*)
E. Destinn (in ♯Sca. 804*)
C. Muzio (in ♯ LI.TW 91053*)[1]

ACT III

O dolci baci . . . E lucevan le stelle　T
G. di Stefano, from set K　　　♭ *C.SEL 1530*
(*below*)　　　　　　　　　　　(♭ *SEBQ 126)*
A. Dermota　　　　　　　　in ♯ **T.TM 68037**
(*above*)　　(& in *Ger, T.A 11599:* ♭ *U 45599: TW 30004)*
M. Gafni　　　　　　　　　in ♯ **For.FLP 1001**
K. Terkal (*Ger*)　　　　　　　　D.F 43569
(*Recondita armonia*)　　　　　　　(♭ *DX 1761)*
S. Rayner, S. Leff (pf.)　　　in ♯ **Mur.P 107**
(followed by pf. acc. only)
P. Fleta (*Fr*)　　　　　　　　♭ *Pat.D 121*
(*Pagliacci—Vesti la giubba*)
J. Huttunen (*Finn*) (*D.SD 5114)*
B. Poprotski (*Russ*) (USSR. 020958)
E. Rösler (*Hung*) (*Qual.KM 5014)*
T. Udvardy (*Hung*) (*Qual.MK 1582)*
☆ G. di Stefano (♭ *G. 7RQ 3001: 7RW 130)*
G. Poggi (*P.RO 30007)*
B. Gigli, from set A (♭ *Vic.ERAT 13)*
N. Scattolini, from set G (♭ *Sel. 470.C.007)*
M. Lanza (in ♯ *G.ALP/WALP 1071: FBLP 1043:*
♭ *7ERQ 127)*

G. Masini (Orf. 54013, d.c.)
M. del Monaco (D.XP 6151; ♭ *Lon.REP 3002:*
in ♯ LL 1244)
L. Melchior (*MGM. 9133)*
M. Fleta (♭ *G. 7ERL 1014)*
A. Pertile (in ♯ *Od.ODX 127:* MOAQ 301)
R. Tauber (*Ger*) (in ♯ Ete. 712)
G. Thill (*Fr*) (in ♯ *C.FH 503)*
E. di Mazzei (*Fr*) (♭ *Od. 7AO 2009)*
♋ J. McCormack (in ♯ Cum.CE 185*; in ♯ Roy. 1555*
& in ♯ 1593*; in ♯ AudR. 2340*)
T. Schipa (in ♯ Sca. 805*)
H. Lazaro (in ♯ Sca. 806*)
E. Caruso (♭ *Vic.ERAT 5*)*

Ah! franchigia . . . O dolci mani　S & T
E. Doria & J. Peerce　　　　in ♯ **PRCC. 3**

... **Tenor part** only
☆ F. Tagliavini (in ♯ CCet.A 50155)
♋ T. Schipa (in ♯ Sca. 805*)

Amaro sol per te　S & T
M. M. Callas & G. di Stefano, from set K
♭ *C.SEL 1530*
(*E lucevan, above*)　　　　　　　(♭ *SEBQ 126)*
♋ N. Baldassari & T. Schipa (in ♯ Sca. 805*)

TURANDOT　3 Acts　1926
COMPLETE RECORDINGS

Turandot　...	I. Borkh (S)
Timur　...	N. Zaccaria (Bs)
Calaf　...	M. del Monaco (T)
Liù　...	R. Tebaldi (S)
Ping　...	F. Corena (Bs)
Pang　...	M. Carlin (T)
Pong　...	R. Ercolani (T)

etc., Santa Cecilia Acad. Cho. & Orch.—Erede
(6ss)　　　　　　　　　　　♯ **D.LXT 5128/30**
(♯ Lon.LL 1347/9, set XLLA 36)

G. Grob-Prandl (S), N. Scott (Bs), A. S. Zola (T)
R. F. Ongara (S), etc., La Fenice Theatre Cho. &
Orch.—Capuana　(6ss)　　　　♯ **Rem. set 199-169**

ACT I

Gira la cote! . . .
Invocazione alla luna . . .
O giovinetto　Cho.
Rome Op. Cho.—Morelli　　　in ♯ **G.ALP 1277**
(*Maschere, Iris, etc.*)　　　　　　(♯ QALP 10118)

Signore, ascolta!　S
M. M. Callas　　　　　　　in ♯ **C.CX 1204**
(*below, Bohème, M. Lescaut, etc.*) (♭ *SEL 1533: SEBQ 127)*
(in ♯ QCX 10108: FCX 377; Angel. 35195)
H. Gueden　　　　　　　　　♯ **D.LW 5178**
(*below, Traviata, Falstaff, Gianni Schicchi*) (♯ *Lon.LD 9165)*
R. Carteri　　　　　　　　　Cet.AT 0291
(*Tu che di gel . . .*)
L. di Lelio　　　　　　　　　Cet.AT 0296
(*Tu che di gel . . .*)
L. Hunt　　　　　　　　　　in ♯ **Roy. 1611**
(*below; Gianni Schicchi, Rondine, etc.*)
☆ E. Schwarzkopf (*C.LN 5:* ♭ *SCBW 101: SCBQ 3001:*
SCBF 108)

Non piangere, Liù　T
I. Tudoran　　　　　　　　U.C 24426
(*below*)
E. Rösler (*Hung*) (*Qual.KM 5014)*
☆ A. Valente (*G.DA 2033: EC 209)*
M. del Monaco (♭ *Lon.REP 8002:*
in ♯ LL 1244; D.X 577)
A. Pertile (in ♯ Ete. 710)
G. Malipiero (Orf. 54019)
R. Tauber (*Ger*) (in ♯ Ete. 712)
H. Roswaenge (*Ger*) (in ♯ CEd. 7010)

ACT II

In questa reggia　S
M. M. Callas　　　　　　　in ♯ **C.CX 1204**
(*above & below*) (in ♯ QCX 10108: FCX 377; Angel. 35195)
(♭ *C.SEL 1533: SEBQ 127)*
W. Stewart　　　　　　　　in ♯ **Roy. 1611**
(*above & below*)
☆ D. Ilitsch (in ♯ *U. 5109C)*

---

[1] From Edison and Pathé hill and dale recordings. This disc was withdrawn almost immediately on issue.

ACT III
Nessun dorma T
M. del Monaco   in ♯ *D.LXT 2928*
(*Non piangere*, on D.X 577)   (♯ Lon.LL 990)
(in ♯ D.LXT 2964; ♯ Lon.LL 1025; & in ♯ *D.LW 5121;*
                                        ♯ *Lon.LD 9132*)
M. Gafni   in ♯ *For.FLP 1001*
I. Tudoran (*above*)   *U.C 24426*
A. da Costa   in ♯ *Roy. 1599*
W. Kmentt (*Ger*)   in ♯ *Phi.S 06076R*
(*Fanciulla del West, A. Chénier, etc.*)
☆ J. Björling (♭ G. 7RQ 3007: 7RW 131;
              in ♯ Vic. set LCT 6701: ♭ ERA 245)
  B. Gigli (♭ G. 7RW 113)
  A. Valente (G.DA 2033: EC 209)
  A. Salvarezza (Orf. 53004)
  K. Baum (in ♯ Rem. 199-123)
  H. Roswaenge (*Ger*) (in ♯ CEd. 7010)
  R. Tauber (*Ger*) (in ♯ Ete. 712)

Tu che di gel sei cinta S
(*Death of Liù*)
M. M. Callas   in ♯ *C.CX 1204*
(*above*)   (♭ SEL 1533: SEBQ 127)
(in ♯ QCX 10108: FCX 377; Angel. 35195)
H. Gueden   ♯ *D.LW 5178*
(*above*)   (♯ Lon.LD 9165)
R. Carteri   *Cet.AT 0291*
(*Signore ascolta*)
E. Arizmendi   **ArgOd. 66028**
(*Bohème—Donde lieta*) (in ♯ LDC 506: o.n. ArgC. 307002)
L. di Lelio   *Cet.AT 0296*
(*Signore ascolta*)
M. Leone   in ♯ *Roy. 1611*
(*above & below*)
☆ E. Schwarzkopf (*C.LN 4*)

Del primo pianto S
W. Stewart (*above*)   in ♯ *Roy. 1611*

(Le) VILLI 2 Acts 1884
COMPLETE RECORDING
  Anna ... ...   E. Fusco (S)
  Guglielmo Wulf ... ...   S. Verlinghieri (B)
  Roberto ... ...   G. dal Ferro (T)
  etc., & Italian Radio Cho. & Orch.—Basile
  (2ss)   ♯ *Cet.N 1251*

PUGNANI, Gaetano (1731-1798)

Symphony No. 5, A major
Ital. Cha.—Jenkins   ♯ *HS.HSL 136*
(*Sammartini & Sarti*)   (in set HSL-N)

PURCELL, Daniel (*c.* 1660–1717)

Sarabande (unspec.) — ARR. CYMBALOM & PF.
I. Tarjani-Tóth & I. Aïtoff (in ♯ *G.FBLP 1067*)

PURCELL, Henry (1658-1695)

COLLECTION (for others, see below, *s.v.* Vocal)
VOCAL MUSIC
DIOCLESIAN: Since from my dear Astrea's sight
THE FAIRY QUEEN: No. 15, I come to lock all fast
                      (Mystery's Song)
                No. 16, One charming night
                      (Secrecie's Song)
                No. 43, Oh! let me forever weep
                      (The Plaint)
If ever I more riches did desire Secular Cantata
... Here let my life
Welcome to all the pleasures Ode for St. Cecilia's Day, 1683
... Here the Deities approve
HARPSICHORD PIECES:
Prelude [53]; Air [37]; Hornpipe [47]
Suite No. 7, D minor: Allemande, Courante, Hornpipe
VIOLS: Fantasia, D major 1680
  A. Deller (C-T), G. Leonhardt (hpsi.) & Inst.
  Ensemble   ♯ *Van.BG 547*
  (*Locke & Jenkins*)

I. INSTRUMENTAL
A. HARPSICHORD
[Page references to the Purcell Society edn.]

COLLECTIONS
Overture; Air; Jig   [56-8]
Trumpet Tune, D major   [37]
Air, D minor   [41]
Rondo, D minor   [38]
  P. Maynard   in ♯ *Eso.ES 535*
  (*Vocal Collection, below*)
A New Irish tune [31] (Lillibulero)
Minuet [29] (both from *Musick's Handmaid*)
Jig [57] (from Overture, Air & Jig)
— ARR. GUITAR Segovia ("*Petite Suite*")
  M. Gangi   ♭ *ItV.A72R 0043*
  (*Anon., Fortea, Villa-Lobos*)
See also G. Leonhardt, in COLLECTION, *above* (♯ Van.BG 547)

Air, D minor [41] SEE Trumpet Tune & Air, *below*

Chaconne, F major [24]
☆ F. Heitmann (org.)   in ♯ *DT.LGX 66037*
  († Organ music, Sweelinck to Hindemith)

Fanfare, C major (Voluntary) [68]
E. P. Biggs (org.)[1]   in ♯ *EPhi.ABL 3066*
  (*Sweelinck, Buxtehude, Bach*)
                                (♯ AmC.ML 4971, in set SL 219)

Ground, C minor [39]
☆ W. Landowska   in ♯ *G.ALP 1246*
  (*Bach, Scarlatti, etc.*)   (in ♯ FALP/QALP 218)

Ground, E minor [30] ('*A new ground*')
F. Viderø   in ♯ *HS.HSL 2073*
  († Masterpieces of Music before 1750)

March, C major [23]
F. Peeters (org.)   in ♯ *Per.SPL 578*
  († Old English Masters)   (♯ Cpt.MC 20049)

Minuet, D minor[2] [32]
E. Heiller   in ♯ *Uni.LP 1010*
  († History of the Dance)

SUITES
COMPLETE RECORDING
☆ I. Nef   ♯ *LOL.OL 50011*

No. 1, G major ... Minuet
☆ A. Cortot (pf.) (in ♯ G.ALP 1197: FALP 349:
                                        QALP 10080)

No. 2, G minor ... Almand only
E. Heiller   in ♯ *Uni.LP 1010*
  († History of the Dance)

No. 5, C major ... Prelude
F. Peeters (org.)   ♯ *Per.SPL 578*
  († Old English Masters)   (♯ Cpt.MC 20049)

No. 7, D minor
G. Leonhardt (in COLLECTION, *above*)
                                ♯ *Van.BG 547*
☆ I. Nef (*Sonata No. 6*)   V♯ *DO.LD 10*
... Hornpipe ☆ A. Ehlers (in ♯ D.UAT 273084)

No. 8, F major ... Minuet
☆ A. Cortot (pf.) (in ♯ G.ALP 1197: FALP 349:
                                        QALP 10080)

Trumpet Tune, C major [27] (The Cebell)
F. Peeters (org.)   in ♯ *Per.SPL 578*
  († Old English Masters)   (♯ Cpt.MC 20049)

Trumpet Tune, D major [37]
Inst. Ens. (in *G.B 10660*)
AND SEE Trumpet Tune & Air, *below*

---

[1] Organ of Westminster Abbey. A version of the *Trumpet Tune* from *The Indian Queen*.
[2] *Musick's Handmaid*, Part II.

"Trumpet Tune & Air" (unspec.)
— ARR. ORGAN
M. Salvador   in ‡ TMS. 1/2
(Gounod, Bach, Gigout, etc.)

R. I. Purvis[3]   in ‡ HIFI.R 705
(Purvis, Bach, Shaw, etc.) [ARR. Purvis]

N. Coke-Jephcott   in ‡ ASK. 8
(J. Clarke, Bach, Vierne, etc.)
[Tpt. solo & accompaniment recorded on different
    occasions & subsequently amalgamated]

"Trumpet Voluntary" SEE: Clarke, Jeremiah

I. B. CHAMBER MUSIC

Chacony, G minor[4] orig. 4 viols
  ☆ New Music Str. Qtt. (‡ BRS. 913)
     Am. Soc. of Ancient Insts.—Stad (G.DB 2146;
                                            Vic. 7873)
  ▽ Vienna Cha. Orch.—Litschauer[5] (‡ Van.VRS 419)

FANTASIAS Viols c. 1680
COLLECTION
THREE-PART: No. 1, D minor
            No. 2, F major
            No. 3, G minor
FOUR-PART: No. 1, G minor   No. 6, A minor
            No. 2, B flat major No. 7, E minor
            No. 3, F major   No. 8, G major
            No. 4, C minor   No. 9, E minor
            No. 5, D minor
FIVE-PART: on one note, F major
SIX-PART: In Nomine, G minor
SEVEN-PART: In Nomine, G minor

A. Wenzinger Gamba Ens.   ‡ HP.APM 14027
                                (‡ AmD.ARC 3007)

(9) FOUR-PART
FIVE-PART: on one note (▽)
  ☆ Vienna Cha. Orch.—Litschauer (‡ Van.VRS 420;
                                       CID.UM 63026)
D major 1680
Inst. Ens. (in Collection, above)   ‡ Van.BG 547

March (Dirge); Canzona[6] Wind Qtt.
Brass Ens.—Voisin   in ‡ Uni.UN 1003
(† Golden Age of Brass)

(10) SONATAS of Four Parts, 2 vlns. & cont. 1697
COLLECTION
No. 1. B minor   2. E flat major   4. D minor
7. C major   8. G minor   9. F major ("Golden")
10. D major
  G. Ciompi & W. Torkanowsky (vlns.), H.
  Chessid (hpsi.), & G. Koutzen (vlc.)
                                ‡ Per.SPL 572
                                (‡ Cpt.MC 20053)

No. 6, G minor "Chacony"
  A. Schwarz (vln.), R. Bas (vln.), A. Navarra
  (vlc.) & I. Nef (hpsi.)   V‡ DO.LD 10
(Hpsi. Suite 7)

— ARR. STR. ORCH. Whittaker
  ▽ Vienna Cha.—Litschauer (‡ Van.VRS 420;
                                  CID.UM 63026)
  ▽ Philharmonia—Lambert (C.DX 1230)

No. 9, F major "Golden Sonata"
  ☆ J. Pasquier, P. Ferret, hpsi. & vlc. (in † ‡ HS.AS 13)

II. VOCAL MUSIC

[References in roman figures to volumes of the Complete
edn.]

COLLECTIONS
DIOCLESIAN (1690): Chaconne (2 in 1 upon a ground),
  Prel. Act III (2 recorders, hpsi. & vlc.)
THE INDIAN QUEEN (1695): Why should men quarrel
  (S, 2 recorders, cont.)
THE SPANISH FRIAR (1694): Whilst I with grief (C-T,
  hpsi. & vlc.)
How pleasant is this flowery plain (Cowley) c. 1688
XXII (S, T, 2 recorders & cont.)   (continued)

What a sad fate is mine (2nd Setting) XXV (C-T, hpsi., vlc.)
What can we poor females do 1694 XXV (S, hpsi., vlc.)
When the cock begins to crow XXII (S, C-T, T, hpsi., vlc.)
  V. Lamoree (S), R. Oberlin (C-T), A. Squires
  (T), N.Y. Pro Musica Antiqua Ens.
                                ‡ Eso.ES 519
  (Blow)   (‡ Cpt.MC 20055)
THE FAIRY QUEEN: No. 24, Ye gentle spirits of the air
  (1692)   No. 51, Hark! the ech'ing air
DIOCLESIAN (1690): Let us dance
TYRANNIC LOVE (1694): Ah! how sweet it is to love (Dryden)
OEDIPUS (1692): Music for awhile (Dryden)
PAUSANIAS (1690): Sweeter than roses
Love, thou canst hear (Howard) XXV 1695
Sylvia, now your scorn give over XXV 1688
I love and I must (Barr) XXV
Fly swift, ye hours XXV 1692
Turn then thine eyes[7] XXV
O how happy's he (Mumford) XXV c. 1694
Lovely Albina's come ashore XXV c. 1695
Evening Hymn: Now that the sun ... (Fuller) 1688
  R. Oberlin (C-T), P. Maynard (hpsi.), S.
  Barab (gamba)   ‡ Eso.ES 535
  (Hpsi. pieces, above)
A FOOL'S PREFERMENT (1688): I'll sail upon the
  dog-star ø
THE INDIAN QUEEN (1695): I attempt from love's sickness
                                   to fly
                              They tell us that you mighty
                                   powers[8]
THE MOCK MARRIAGE (1695): Man is for woman made ø
RULE A WIFE AND HAVE A WIFE (1693): There's not a
  swain of the plain ø
THE TEMPEST (1695): Arise, ye subterranean winds
                    Come unto these yellow sands
  ☆ J. Brownlee (B), V. Harper (pf.) in ‡ Roy. 1404
  [those marked ø also in ♭ Roy.EP 214]

II. A. DRAMATIC MUSIC

ABDELAZER 1695
Nos. 2, 6, 8 SEE: Suite, below

BONDUCA 1695
Overture
... Airs Nos. 4 & 6 — ARR. ORG. Floyd
  A. E. Floyd   in ‡ Spot.SC 1002
  (Handel, S. S. Wesley, Bach, etc.)
... excerpt SEE: Suite, below

O lead me to some peaceful gloom
  M. Ritchie (S), hpsi. & vlc.   G.B 10726
  (Fairy Queen & Indian Queen)

DIDO AND AENEAS Opera, Prol. & 3 Acts 1689
COMPLETE RECORDINGS
Set C ☆ K. Flagstad (S), E. Schwarzkopf (S), etc., Mermaid
  Theatre Singers & Orch.—G. Jones (‡ G.WALP 1026:
                                        FALP 200)
  The following re-issued on ♭ Vic.EHA 16:
  Overture
  No. 2, Ah! Belinda, I am prest
  No. 11, To the hills & vales (Act I)
  No. 24, Oft she visits this lone mountain
  No. 27 (pt), Jove's command shall be obeyed (Act II)
  No. 37, When I am laid in earth (Act III)
Set D ☆ Soloists & Ens.—Gregory (‡ Cum.CPR 324)
Orchestral Suite — ARR. Cailliet
  ☆ Philadelphia—Ormandy (‡ Cam.CAL 213: ♭ CAE 238)

No. 37, When I am laid in earth
  ☆ K. Flagstad (S) (Gluck: Orphée, Aria) ♭ G. 7R 164
  ☆ S. Danco (Alceste—Divinités du Styx) ♭ D. 71100
  ☆ E. Wysor (A) (in ‡ Ply. 12-47)
  B. Marchesi (S) & pf. (in ‡ AudR.LPA 2340)
— ARR. HARMONICA ☆ L. Adler (in ‡ FMer.MLP 7054)
— ARR. ORCH. Stokowski
  ☆ Orch.—Stokowski (in ‡ Vic.LM 1875: ♭ set ERB 52)

DIOCLESIAN 1690
The Masque
  L. Cass (B), P. Gavert (T), M. Mitton (S),
  L. Avery (T), W. Lloyd (M-S), F. Kramer (pf.)
                                ‡ MTR.MLO 1013
SEE also COLLECTIONS, above (‡ Van.BG 547, Eso.ES 519
                                & ES 535)

---

[3] Plays Trumpet Tune, D major; Air, D minor [37, 41].
[4] See also Sonatas of 4 parts, below. Confusion has arisen between the two works, and earlier entries are repeated to clarify
and correct.
[5] Labelled "London Chaconne". [6] For the funeral of Queen Mary II, 1694. Ed. King.
[7] Solo version of the 2-pt. setting, Fairy Queen, No. 53.
[8] ARR. Moffatt as The Message with new words: Ye birds that sing sweetly.

DISTRESSED INNOCENCE 1690
No. 3, Slow Air: *SEE* Suite, *below*

(The) FAIRY QUEEN Opera, Prol. & 5 Acts 1692
Nos. 1-6, 10, 14, 17, 20, 30, 31, 35, 37, 39, 43, 45, 51, 53
☆ P. Curtin (S), E. Davis (M-S), P. Tibbitts (Bs), &
    Cambridge (U.S.A.) Cho. & Orch.—Pinkham
                                              ♯ Allo. 3077
Nos. 4, 22, 23, 43, 49, 51, 54
☆ M. Ritchie (S) & Ens.—Lewis   ♯ LOL.OL 50029
    (Timon of Athens)
Nos. 15, 16, 43
    A. Deller (C-T), in Collection, *above*
                                              ♯ Van.BG 547
Nos. 24, 51   R. Oberlin (C-T), in Collection, *above*
                                              ♯ Eso.ES 535
No. 15, Mystery's Song: I come to lock all fast
    M. Ritchie (S), hpsi. & vlc.   *G.B 10726*
    (Bonduca & Indian Queen)

No. 43, The Plaint: Oh! let me forever weep
    M. Ritchie (S), vln., hpsi. & vlc.   *G.B 10725*
    (2ss)

No. 50, Hark how all things with one sound rejoice
    A. Deller (C-T), B. Lam (hpsi.), T. Weil (vlc.)
                                              G.C 4247

    (Old Bachelor & King Richard II)

(A) FOOL'S PREFERMENT
SEE above, ♯ Roy. 1404

(The) INDIAN QUEEN 1695
Trumpet Overture   Act III
    Orch.—Goldsbrough   *G.HMS 67*
    († History of Music in Sound) (in ♯ Vic. set LM 6031)

I attempt from love's sickness to fly A Act III
    M. Ritchie, hpsi. & vlc.   *G.B 10726*
    (Bonduca & Fairy Queen)

    Accompaniment etc., for practice (in ♯ VS.ML 3002)
    See also COLLECTIONS, *above* (♯ Eso.ES 519; ♯ Roy. 1404)

KING ARTHUR Opera Prol. & 5 Acts 1691
Orchestral Suite
    1. Overture   4. Song tune (Fairest Isle, Act V)
    2. Slow Air   5. Quick Air
    3. Hornpipe   6. Chaconne
    Saar Cha.—Ristenpart   *V♯ DFr.EX 17027*

Harvest Home B Act V
— ARR. ORCH. Bridgewater *"Gigue"*
    Westminster Light—Bridgewater
                                    in ♯ West.WL 4007
Fairest Isle S Act V
    J. Vyvyan, E. Lush (pf.)   in ♯ D.LXT 2797
    († Songs of England)   (in ♯ Lon.LL 806)
    (also in ♯ D.LW 5102)

KING RICHARD II 1681
Retired from any mortal's sight
    A. Deller (C-T), B. Lam (hpsi.), T. Weil (vlc.)
                                              G.C 4247

    (Fairy Queen & Old Bachelor)

(The) LIBERTINE 1692
Nymphs & Shepherds S Act IV
    J. Vyvyan, E. Lush (pf.)   in ♯ D.LXT 2797
    († Songs of England)   (in ♯ Lon.LL 806)
    (also in ♯ D.LW 5102)

— ARR. CHO. Jenkins
    Mormon Tabernacle Cho.—Cornwall
    (in ♯ EPhi.NBL 5012; Phi.N 02125L; AmC.ML 5048)

In these delightful pleasant groves Cho. Act IV
    Youth Acad.Cho.—Asmussen   *Felix.F 84*
    (Conversi & Hassler)

(The) MOCK MARRIAGE
SEE above, ♯ Roy. 1404

OEDIPUS (Dryden) 1692
PAUSANIAS 1690
SEE above, ♯ Eso.ES 535

(The) OLD BACHELOR 1693
Thus to a ripe, consenting maid
    A. Deller (C-T), B. Lam (hpsi.), T. Weil (vlc.)
                                              G.C 4247

    (Fairy Queen & King Richard II)

RULE A WIFE... 1693
SEE above, ♯ Roy. 1404

(The) SPANISH FRIAR 1694
SEE above, ♯ Eso.ES 519

(The) TEMPEST 1695
Flout 'em and scout 'em
    L. Chelsi (B), lute & pf. in ♯ MTR.MLO 1015
    († Shakespeare Songs, Vol. III)
    SEE also ♯ Roy. 1404, *above*

TIMON OF ATHENS 1694
Nos. 1, 7, 10 & Curtain tune on a ground
☆ M. Ritchie (S) & Ensemble—Lewis   ♯ LOL.OL 50029
    (Fairy Queen)

TYRANNIC LOVE 1694
SEE above, ♯ Eso.ES 535

II. B. OTHER VOCAL MUSIC

I. ODES

Arise, my Muse (Durfey) 1690
... Crown the Altar
    M. Ritchie (S), G. Malcolm (hpsi.) in COLLECTION, *below*

Come ye sons of art, away 1694
    M. Ritchie (S), A. Deller & J. Whitworth
    (C-T), B. Boyce (B), St. Anthony Singers &
    Cha. Orch.—A. Lewis   *♯ LOL.DL 53004*
    [R. Gerlin, hpsi.]   *(♯ OL.LD 91; CFD.D)*

... Strike the viol, only
    R. Oberlin (C-T), 2 recorders, hpsi. & vlc.
                                    in ♯ Eso.ES 519
Welcome to all the pleasures 1683
... Here the Deities approve
    A. Deller (C-T)   in ♯ Van.BG 547

What, what shall be done 1682
... Nos. 1, 2, 3, only A, T, B, cho.
    A. Deller, R. Lewis, N. Walker, London
    Chamber Singers & Orch.—Bernard
                                    G.HMS 57
    († History of Music in Sound) (in ♯ Vic. set LM 6031)

II. ANTHEMS & SACRED SONGS

COLLECTIONS
The Blessed Virgin's Expostulation (Tate)
Crown the Altar (from *Ode, above*)
Evening Hymn (Fuller)
    M. Ritchie (S), G. Malcolm (hpsi.)
                                    ♯ Nix.NLP 921
    (Bishop, Boyce, Arne, etc.)

Lord, what is man... Oh! for a quill (Fuller)
We sing to him (Ingelo)
Evening Hymn (Fuller)[9]
    L. Marshall (S), W. Kilburn (pf.) *♯ Hall.RS 1*
    (Falla: Spanish Songs)

Evening Hymn (Fuller)
    M. Harrell (B), B. Smith (pf.) in ♯ Rem. 199-140
    (Schubert, Schumann, Wolf, Duparc, etc.)
    R. Oberlin (C-T), hpsi. & gamba, in ♯ Eso.ES 535

Let my prayer come up into thy presence
    St. Margaret's, Westminster, Cho.
                                    in ♯ Ori.MG 20003
O Lord, grant the [Queen] a long life
    A, T, Bs, cho. & str. 1685
    A. Deller (C-T), P. Pears (T), N. Lumsden (Bs),
    & Aldeburgh Fest. Cho. & Orch.—I. Holst
                                    in ♯ D.LXT 2798
    (Arne, Britten, Berkeley, etc.) (in ♯ Lon.LL 808)

O Lord God of hosts 8 voices c. 1680-2
    Westminster Abbey Cho.—McKie † C.LX 1607
    (Blow: Magnificat)

Thy word is a lantern 3 vv. cho. org. (ARR. Bridge)
    Mormon Tabernacle Cho. & Org.—Cornwall
                                    in ♯ EPhi.NBL 5012
    (Nymphs & Shepherds; Brahms, Liszt, etc.)
                                    (♯ Phi.N 02125L; AmC.ML 5048)

---

[9] All realised Britten: "3 Divine Hymns".

III. SONGS

Ah, how pleasant 'tis to love (Anon.)
Cease, O my sad soul (Webbe)
More love or more disdain I crave (Webbe)
On the brow of Richmond Hill (Durfey)
The Owl is abroad really by J. C. Smith

  ☆ J. Brownlee (B), V. Hayer (pf.) in ♯ **Roy. 1404**
  (*above; Franz, Mendelssohn*)
  [On the brow . . . only, on ♭ *EP 214*]

(The) Fatal hour comes on apace
  J. Alexander (S), A. Goldsbrough (hpsi.) & vlc.
                            G.HMS 58
  († History of Music in Sound) (in ♯ Vic. set LM 6031)
SEE ALSO ♯ Eso.ES 519 & ES 535, above

IV. CATCHES

COLLECTION (all XXII except where stated)
The Macedon Youth 4 vv. 1686
The Miller's Daughter (*Pleasant Musical Companion*
  ii, 1686)
If all be true that I do think 3 vv. 1689
My Lady's Coachman John 3 vv. 1687
Of all the instruments that are 3 vv. 1693
Once, twice, thrice I Julia tried 3 vv.
As Roger last night 3 vv.
One, two, three (unid.)
Wine in a morning (T. Brown) 3 vv. 1686
Young John the gard'ner 4 vv. 1683
Sir Walter enjoying his damsel 3 vv.
Who comes there? 3 vv. 1685
Since time so kind to us doth prove 3 vv.
Prithee be n't so sad (Browne) 3 vv.
Tom making a manteau[10]

  Glee Singers—Bath   ♯ **Allo. 3046**
  († More Catches & Glees of the Restoration)

III. MISCELLANEOUS

Suite for Strings ARR. Coates
1. Abdelazer, No. 2—Rondeau
2. Distressed Innocence, No. 3—Slow air
3. Abdelazer, No. 6—Air
4. Abdelazer, No. 8—Minuet
5. Bonduca, Overture—Allegro quasi assai

  L.S.O.—Sargent   ♯ **D.LXT 2786**
  (*Elgar*)   (♯ Lon.LL 740)

Bourrée, Gigue & Hornpipe (unspec.)
  I. Tarjani-Tóth (cymbalom), I. Aïtoff (pf.)
                  (in ♯ *G.FBLP 1067*)

PURVIS, Richard Irven (b. 1915)

ORGAN MUSIC

COLLECTIONS
Partita on Christ ist erstanden 1953
Pastorale: Forest Green 1945
Adoration (from *Four Prayers in tone*, 1952)
Divinum Mysterium (from *5 Pieces on Gregorian themes*, 1940)
Capriccio on the notes of the cuckoo 1953
Introit; Elevation (from *American Organ Mass*, 1954)

  R. I. Purvis   ♯ **ASK. 5**
  [Organ of Grace Cathedral, San Francisco]

Virgin's Slumber Song 1954
Carol Rhapsody 1939

  R. I. Purvis   in ♯ **HIFI.R 705**
  (*Dupré, Brahms*)

Supplication (from *Four Prayers in tone*, 1952)
Carol Prelude on "Greensleeves" (from *4 Carol-Preludes*, 1945)
Capriccio on the notes of the cuckoo 1953
PURCELL: Trumpet Tune & Air (ARR. Purvis)

  R. I. Purvis   in ♯ **HIFI.R 703**
  (*Bach, M. Shaw, Elmore, Widor*)

4 Dubious Conceits 1953
... Marche grotesque; Nocturne; Les Petites Cloches
Toccata festiva (from *7 Chorale-Preludes*, 1945)
BACH: Sheep may safely graze (ARR. Purvis)

  R. I. Purvis   in ♯ **HIFI.R 704**
  (*Franck, Dupré*)

In Babilone ▽ C. Snyder (in ♯ Word.W 4003, o.n. ♯ KR. 15)

CAROL ARRANGEMENT
What strangers are these
  Nat. Presbyterian Chu. Cho.—Schaefer
            in ♯ **McInt.MC 107**
  (*Christmas Candlelight Service*)

[10] Really by H. Hall: from *Pleasant Musical Companion*, ii, Supp.

QUAGLIATI, Paolo (c. 1555–1628)

  SEE: † CANZONE SCORDATE

QUANTZ, Johann Joachim (1697-1773)

Concerto, G major fl. & strings
  H. Barwahser & Vienna Sym.—Paumgartner
  (*Gluck & Mozart*)   ♯ **Phi.N 00213L**

SONATAS, Fl. & cont.
No. 1, A minor . . . Adagio only
  A. Andersen & H. Solum (org.)   *C.GN 1504*
  (*Gounod: Ave Maria*)

No. 2, B flat major
No. 4, D major
No. 5, E minor
  J. Wummer, F. Valenti (hpsi.) ♯ **West.WN 18070**
  (*Friedrich der Grosse*)

No. 6, G major
  ☆ J-P. Rampal, R. Veyron-Lacroix (hpsi.)(in † ♯ HS.AS 19)

Trio-Sonata, C minor fl., ob., cont. (Schwerin MS)
  J-P. Rampal, P. Pierlot, R. Veyron-Lacroix
  (hpsi.)   ♯ **BàM.LD 011**
  (*J. C. Bach, A. Scarlatti, Telemann, Handel*)(♯ HS.HSL 117)

QUILTER, Roger (1877-1953)

Children's Overture, Op. 17 orch. 1914
  L.S.O.—Weldon   **C.DX 1869**
                    (DOX 1013)
  Hamburg Philharmonia—H-J. Walther
                      MSB. 78022
  (*Coates & Elgar* on ♯ MGM.E 3142; also in ♯ E 3177)

SONGS
COLLECTIONS
TO JULIA, Op. 8 Cycle (Herrick) 1906
  1. Prelude   5. The Night piece
  2. The Bracelet   6. Julia's hair
  3. The Maiden blush 7. Interlude
  4. To Daisies   8. Cherry-ripe
(7) ELIZABETHAN LYRICS, Op. 12 1908
  1. Weep you no more (Anon.)
  2. Come, O come, my life's delight (Campian)
  3. Damask Roses (Anon.)
  4. The faithless shepherdess (Anon.)
  5. Brown is my love (Anon.)
  6. Slow, slow, fresh fount (Jonson)
  7. Fair house of joy (Anon.)
Dream valley, Op. 20, No. 1 (Blake)
The Wild-flower's song, Op. 20, No. 2 (Blake)
Daybreak, Op. 20, No. 3 (Blake)
Arab love song, Op. 25, No. 4 (Shelley)
Love's philosophy, Op. 3, No. 1 (Shelley)
Music when soft voices die, Op. 25, No. 6 (Shelley)

  A. Young (T), G. Watson (pf.)   ♯ **Argo.RG 36**
                  (♯ West.WN 18152)

O mistress mine, Op. 6, No. 2
Come away, Death, Op. 6, No. 1
It was a lover and his lass, Op. 23, No. 3
Heigh, ho, the wind and the rain, Op. 23, No. 5
  (all by Shakespeare)

  J. Heddle Nash (B), E. Lush (pf.) **G.C 4255**

Dream valley, Op. 20, No. 1 (Blake)
  W. Midgley (T), G. Moore (pf.)   *G.DA 2036*
  (*O mistress mine*)

Love's philosophy, Op. 3, No. 1 (Shelley)
  J. Vyvyan (S), E. Lush (pf.) in ♯ **D.LXT 2797**
  († Songs of England)   (♯ Lon.LL 806)

O mistress mine, Op. 6, No. 2 (Shakespeare)
  W. Midgley (T), G. Moore (pf.)   *G.DA 2036*
  (*Dream valley*)

FOLK SONG ARRANGEMENTS

Drink to me only with thine eyes (Jonson)
Ye banks and braes of bonnie Doon (Burns)
  ☆ K. Ferrier (A), P. Spurr (pf.)   ♭ *D. 70135*

RAASTED, Niels Otto (b. 1888)

Chorale-Prelude: An Wasserflüssen Babylon, Op. 46, No. 6
J. Harms   in ♯ Uni.UN 1004
(*Peeters, Weinberger, Vierne, Bach, etc.*)

RABAUD, Henri Benjamin (1873-1949)

MAROUF   Opera   5 Acts   1914
Ballet   Act III
Lamoureux—Fournet   ♯ EPhi.NBR 6000
(*Faust—Ballet*)   (♯ Phi.A 00636R)
(*Delibes & Gounod,* on ♯ Epic.LC 3030)

(La) Procession nocturne, Op. 6   orch.
☆ N.Y.P.S.O.—Mitropoulos (in ♯ Phi.A 01604R)

RACHMANINOFF, Sergei Vassilievitch (1873-1943)

(The) Bells, Op. 35   (Poe, trs. Balmont)
        (sometimes called "Symphony No. 3") Soli, cho. & orch.
F. Yeend (S), D. Lloyd (T), M. Harrell (B), Temple Univ. Cho. & Philadelphia Orch. —Ormandy   (*Eng*)   ♯ AmC.ML 5043
(*Isle of the Dead*)

Caprice bohémienne, Op. 12   orch.
Moscow Radio—Gauk   ♯ USSR.D 01451
(*Scriabin: Sym. No. 1, s. 3*)

COLLECTIONS OF PIANO PIECES

        Études Tableaux, Op. 33:
            No. 2, C major
            No. 7, E flat major (a)
            Op. 39, No. 6, A minor
        Humoresque, Op. 10, No. 5
        Mélodie, E major, Op. 3, No. 3 (a)
        Moment musical, E flat minor, Op. 16, No. 2 (a)
        Oriental Sketch (? ARR. of *Danse orientale*, Op. 2, No. 2)
        Polka de W.R.
        PRELUDES:
            Op. 3, No. 2, C sharp minor (a)
            Op. 23, No. 10, G flat major
            Op. 32: No. 3, E major
                No. 6, F minor (a)
                No. 7, F major (a)
        SONG: Daisies, Op. 38, No. 3 — ARR. PF.
☆ S. Rachmaninoff   ♯ Vic.LCT 1136
(*Chopin, Mendelssohn, etc.*)
[Items marked (a) also on ♭ ERAT 30]

        Barcarolle, G minor, Op. 10, No. 3
        Élégie, Op. 3, No. 1 ø
        Mélodie, E major, Op. 3, No. 3 ø
        Polichinelle, Op. 3, No. 4
        Polka de W.R. ø
        Prelude, C sharp minor, Op. 3, No. 2 ø
        Prelude, G minor, Op. 23, No. 5
S. Rachmaninoff[1]   ♯ Roy. 1549
(*Chopin & Liszt*)
[Marked ø also on ♭ EP 341]

        (5) PIECES, Op. 3
            1. Élégie, E flat minor   4. Polichinelle, F sharp
            2. Prelude, C sharp minor   minor
            3. Mélodie, E major   5. Serenade, B flat minor
        (7) PIECES, Op. 10
            1. Nocturne, A minor   5. Humoresque, G major
            2. Valse, A major   6. Romance, F minor
            3. Barcarolle, G minor   7. Mazurka, D flat major
            4. Mélodie, E minor
        Polka de W.R.
N. Reisenberg   ♯ Nix.WLP 5344
                        (♯ West.WN 18209, o.n. WL 5344)

CONCERTOS, pf. & orch.
Nos. 1-4: COLLECTION
    ☆ S. Rachmaninoff & Philadelphia—Ormandy [in Nos. 1, 3, 4] & Stokowski [No. 2] in ♯ Vic. set LM 6123
    (5ss—*Rhapsody*)

No. 1, F sharp minor, Op. 1   1890, rev. 1917
    M. Lympany & Philharmonia—Malko
                                ♯ G.CLP 1037
    (*Grieg*)   (♯ QCLP 12013: FELP 123)
    C. de Groot & Residentie—v. Otterloo
                                ♯ Phi.N 00756R
    (2ss)   (*Liszt* on ♯ Epic.LC 3145)
    ☆ S. Rachmaninoff & Philadelphia—Ormandy
                        (♯ Vic.LCT 1118; ♭ set WCT 1118)
    B. Moiseiwitsch & Philharmonia—Sargent
                        (♯ Vic.LCT 1127: ♭ set WCT 1127)

No. 2, C minor, Op. 18   1901
    G. Anda & Philharmonia—Galliera ♯C.CX 1143
    (*2 Preludes*)   (♯ FCX 281; Angel. 35093)
    L. Pennario & St. Louis Sym.
        —Golschmann   ♯ DCap.CTL 7093
    (2ss)   (♯ Cap.P 8302)
    O. Frugoni & Vienna Pro Musica—Byrns
    (*below*)   ♯ E. & AmVox.PL 9650
    A. Foldes & Berlin Phil.—Ludwig ♯ Pol. 18190
    M. Mitchell & Orch.—Strickland   ♯ MTW. 26
    (*Enesco*)   (& ♯ ACC.MP 8)
    M. Lympany & Philharmonia—Malko
                                ♯ G.CLP 1007
    (*Mendelssohn*) (♯ FELP 113: QCLP 12003; Vic.LHMV 15)
    C. de Groot & Residentie—v. Otterloo
                                ♯ EPhi.ABL 3014
    (*Mélodie & Prelude*)   (♯ Phi.A 00162L; Epic.LC 3009)
    E. Farnadi & Vienna State Op.—Scherchen
                                ♯ Nix.WLP 5193
    (2ss)   (♯ West.WL 5193; Sel. 270.CW.074)
    L. Oborin & Moscow Radio—Gauk
    (2ss)   ♯ USSR.D 07/8
    (9ss—*Étude Tableau, Op. 39, No. 8* on USSR. 022846/54)
    F. Blumenthal & Concerts Colonne—Giardino
                                ♯ Pat.DTX 134
    (2ss)   (♯ ArgPat.ADTX 1804)
    E. Silver & "Philharmonic"—Berendt (♯ Allo. 3082;
                        Pac.LDAD 47; Gram. 2062)
    ☆ G. Sandor & N.Y.P.S.O.—Rodzinski (♯ AmC.RL 3052)
    A. Rubinstein & N.B.C. Sym.—Golschmann
                        (♯ G.QALP 161; ♭ Vic. set ERB 12)
    F. Karrer & Austrian Sym.—Wöss (♯ Cum.CR 212;
                        1st movt. only in Rem. 199-115; Ply. 12-58)
    T. Nikolayeva & Czech Phil.—Ivanov (♯ Dia.DCM 1;
                        Shostakovich on ♯ Csm.CRLP 223)
    S. Rachmaninoff & Philadelphia—Stokowski
                        (♯ DV.L 17085)
... 1st movt. only
    ☆ L. Pennario & Col. Sym.—Rodzinski (in ♯ Phi.S 04601L)
... 3rd movt. only, abridged
    J. M. Sanromá & Boston "Pops"—Fiedler
                        (in ♯ Vic.LM 1752: ♭ set WDM 1752)

No. 3, D minor, Op. 30   1909
    E. Gilels & Paris Cons.—Cluytens ♯ C.CX 1323
                        (♯ FCX 432; Angel. 35230)
    W. Malcuzynski & Philharmonia—Kletzki
    (? n.v.)   ♯ C.CX 1161
    L. Oborin & State Sym.—Ivanov
                                ♯ USSR.D 1197/8
    (3ss—*Str. Qtt. movts.*)
    H. Reims & Dresden State Sym.—Schreiber (♯ Roy. 1487)
    ☆ V. Horowitz & Victor Sym.—Reiner (♯ G.QALP 10022)

No. 4, G minor, Op. 40   1927, rev. 1938
    J. Zak & Youth Sym.—Kondrashin
                                ♯ Mon.MEL 704

Danse hongroise, Op. 6, No. 2   vln. & pf.
    — ARR. ORCH. J. Schmied Orch. (*Vien.P 6152*)

Danse orientale, Op. 2, No. 2   vlc. & pf.
    M. Rostropovich & pf.   USSRM.D 168
    (*Chopin: Intro. & Polonaise, Op. 3*)

Élégie, Op. 3, No. 1   pf.
    P. Serebriakov   USSRM.D 00925
    (*below*)
    J. Flier (*USSR. 16699*)

---

[1] The origin of these recordings is not known; said to be from player-pf. rolls.

ÉTUDES-TABLEAUX pf.
(8), Op. 33 1911
☆ B. Weiser (♯ MGM.E 3248)

... Nos. 1-4: L. Oborin (4ss) *USSR. 21703/4 & 22529/30*

C minor, Op. 39, No. 1
☆ E. Gilels (in ♯ Csm.CRLP 158 & CRLP 147)

A minor, Op. 39, No. 2
H. Neuhaus   *USSRM.D 001249*
(Scriabin)

F sharp minor, Op. 39, No. 3
A minor, Op. 39, No. 6
P. Serebriakov   *USSRM.D 00926*
(Élégie, above)

B minor, Op. 39, No. 4
D minor, Op. 39, No. 8
P. Serebriakov   *USSRM.D 001349*
(Balakirev) (also, 2ss, *USSR. 19539/40)*

D minor, Op. 39, No. 8
L. Oborin   **USSR. 022855**
(Concerto No. 2, s. 9)

Humoresque, Op. 10, No. 5 pf.
C. de Groot   in ♯ *Phi.N 00632R*
                                            (♭ *N 402050E)*
N. Yemelyanova   *USSRM.D 643*
(Valse; & Balakirev)   *(USSR. 21820)*

— ARR. BAND   Band—Urbanec (*U.C 24393)*

(The) Isle of the Dead, Op. 29 orch. 1907
Paris Cons.—Ansermet   ♯ **D.LXT 5003**
(Dukas)   (♯ *Lon.LL 1155)*
Philadelphia—Ormandy   ♯ **AmC.ML 5043**
(The Bells)

Mélodie, E major, Op. 3, No. 3
C. de Groot   in ♯ **EPhi.ABL 3014**
(Concerto No. 2 & Prelude, Op. 32, No. 10) (♯ Phi.A 00162L;
                                            ♭ *N 402050E)*

(6) MOMENTS MUSICAUX, Op. 16 pf. 1896
No. 3, B minor
No. 5, D flat major
P. Serebriakov   in ♯ *Eta.LPM 1013*
(Prelude, Op. 3, No. 2 & Chopin, Tchaikovsky)
[No. 5 only on *Eta. 120026]*

No. 4, E minor
No. 5, D flat major
T. Nikolayeva   *USSRM.D 399*
(Chopin: Variations) [*No. 4 only also on USSR. 20171]*

OPERAS
ALEKO 1 Act 1893
COMPLETE RECORDING

Aleko...	...	...	...	I. Petrov (B)
Zemfira	...	...	N. Pokrovskaya (S)
The Young Gypsy	...	...	A. Orfenov (T)
The Old Man	...	...	A. Ognivtzev (Bs)
An old gypsy	...	...	V. Zlatogorova (A)

& Bolshoi Theatre Cho. & Orch.—
Golovanov (4ss)   ♯ **USSR.D 015/8**
                                   (2ss, ♯ CHS.CHS 1309)

No. 10, The Moon is high in the sky B
I. Petrov   *USSRM.D 001318*
(Tchaikovsky)
M. Grishko   ♯ *USSR.D 2094*
(Tsar's Bride; & Lysenko & Dankievitch)
☆ B. Gmyria (in *USSRM.D 00113)*

No. 12, Romance of the young gypsy T
V. Kilichevsky   *USSRM.D 001127*
(Tchaikovsky, Ippolitoff-Ivanoff)

FRANCESCA DA RIMINI Prol., 2 Sc. & Epil.
1906
Here is my answer Malatesta's Aria, Sc. 1 Bs
A. Pirogov   *USSRM.D 888*
(Rimsky, Borodin, Dargomijsky)

Polichinelle, Op. 3, No. 4 pf.
C. de Groot   in ♯ *Phi.N 00632R*
(Prokofiev, Bartók, etc.)   (♭ Phi.N 402019E)

Polka de W.R pf.
S. Barere   in ♯ **Rem. 199-141**
                                            (♯ *Cum.CR 328)*

Polka italienne pf. duet
V. Vronsky & V. Babin   in ♯ **AmD.DL 9791**
(Poulenc, Dvořák, Borodin, etc.)

(24) PRELUDES, Op. 3, No. 2; Op. 23; Op. 32.
COMPLETE RECORDING
S. Fiorentino (4ss)   ♯ **CA.LPA 1060/1**
COLLECTIONS
Op. 3, No. 2, C sharp minor
Op. 23: Nos. 2, 4, 5, 6, 8, 9
Op. 32: Nos. 5, 12
D. Wayenberg   ♯ *LT.EL 93038*
                                            (♯ *Sel. 270.C.010)*

Op. 3, No. 2, C sharp minor
Op. 23: Nos. 2, 3, 5, 6, 7, 9
Op. 32: Nos. 1-3, 5, 8, 10-12
R. Goldsand   ♯ **CHS.CHS 1249**

Op. 3, No. 2, C sharp minor
L. Pennario   ♯ *DCap.CCL 7522*
(Prelude, Op. 23, No. 5; & Liszt) (♯ *Cap.H 8186:* ♭ *FAP 8261)*
(also in ♯ DCap.CTL 7102; Cap.P 8312)
J. Rein   *Pam.S 19042*
(Scriabin: Study)
Y. Boukoff   in ♯ *Phi.A 76700R*
(Khachaturian, Prokofiev, etc.)
X. Prochorova   in ♯ *Imp.ILP 109*
B. Böttner (in ♯ *T.LA 6077)*
☆ A. Rubinstein (♭ *G.7EB 6009: 7RQ 159)*
J. v. Karolyi (♭ *Pol. 30044)*
M. Flipse (in ♯ Phi.S 06016R)
J. Iturbi (♭ *G.7RF 288)*
V. Schiøler (♭ *Mer.EP 1-5019; FMer.MEP 14524)*
P. Serebriakov (*Eta. 120026* & in ♯ *LPM 1013)*
— ARR. ORCH.
N.W. German Phil.—Schüchter (in ♯ *Imp.ILP 114;*
                                            G.QDLP 6026)
Belgian Radio—P. Glière (in ♯ Mae.OAT 25001)
Mantovani Orch. (in ♯ *D.LF 1161:* LK 4072; Lon.LL 877)
☆ Philadelphia—Ormandy[1] (♭ *AmC.A 1826)*
Boston Pops.—Fiedler (in ♯ Vic.LM 1879: ♭ *set ERB 54;*
                                   ♭ *ItV.A72R 0049;* ♭ *Vic.ERA 254)*
— ARR. PF. & ORCH.
L. Pennario & Hollywood Bowl—Dragon (in ♯ Cap.P 8326)
W. Stech & Hamburg State Phil.—Wal-Berg
                                            (in ♯ *T.TW 30027)*

Op. 23
No. 4, D major; No. 6, E flat major; No. 9, E flat minor
☆ C. Keene (in ♯ EMer.MG 10113; Nos. 4 & 6 only
                                   ♭ *EP 1-5011; FMer.MEP 14502)*

No. 4, — ARR. VLN. & PF. Yerdenko
I. Bezrodny & pf.   *USSRM.D 001284*
(Romance; & Glier)

No. 5, G minor
G. Anda   **C.LX 1603**
(below) (♭ *SCB 117:* in ♯ CX 1143: FCX 281; Angel. 35093)
L. Pennario   in ♯ *DCap.CCL 7522*
(Prelude, Op. 3, No. 3, & Liszt) (♯ *Cap.H 8186:* ♭ *FAP 8261)*
(also in ♯ DCap.CTL 7102; Cap.P 8312)
R. Spivak   **ArgV. 11-7972**
(Chopin: Étude, Op. 10, No. 3)
S. Andersen   in ♯ **Oce.OCS 38**
S. Barere   in ♯ **Rem. 199-141**
                                            (♯ *Cum.CR 328)*
E. Burton   in ♯ **CEd.CE 1026**
J. Flier (USSR. 022681)
☆ J. v. Karolyi (♭ *Pol. 30044)*
— ARR. ORCH.
☆ Philadelphia—Ormandy (♭ *AmC.A 1826)*
Carnegie Pops—O'Connell (in ♯ AmC.A 1573)

No. 6, E flat major; **No. 7, C minor**
M. Schwalb   in ♯ *Acad. 310*
(Liszt, Brahms, etc.)
No. 6, only: L. Oborin   in ♯ *CdM.LDA 8076*

---

[1] ARR. Cailliet.

Op. 32
No. 2, B flat major; No. 3, E major
T. Nikolayeva (2ss)   *USSR. 23050/1*

No. 5, G major
G. Anda   **C.LX 1603**
(*above*)(♭ *SCB 117:* in ♯ *CX 1143; FCX 281; Angel. 35093*)
S. Andersen   in ♯ **Oce.OCS 38**
☆ J. Therrien (in ♯ *MH. 33-111*)
— ARR. ORCH. Cailliet
☆ Philadelphia—Ormandy (♭ *AmC.A 1826*)

No. 10, B minor
C. de Groot   in ♯ **EPhi.ABL 3014**
(*above*)   (♯ *Phi.A 00162L:* ♭ *N 402050E*)

No. 12, G sharp minor
L. Oborin   in ♯ *CdM.LDA 8076*
H. Giordano   *ArgOd. 57028*
(*Scriabin: Study, Op. 8, No. 12*)
E. Burton   in ♯ **CEd.CE 1024**
S. Barere   in ♯ **Rem. 199-141**
                                       (♯ *Cum.CR 328*)

Prelude (unspec.): A. d'Arco   in *Plé.P 101*

Quartet No. 1, Str., G minor (unfinished)
(Romance & Scherzo)   pub. 1947
Guilet Qtt. (*Grieg*)   ♯ **MGM.E 3133**
Beethoven Qtt.   ♯ *USSR.D 1200*
(*Pf. Concerto No. 3, s. 3*) (& 4ss, *USSR. 16230/1 & 16314/5*)

Rhapsody on a theme of Paganini, Op. 43 pf. & orch.
J. Katchen & L.P.O.—Boult   ♯ **D.LXT 2862**
(*Dohnányi*)   (♯ *Lon.LL 1018*)
[18th Variation only on *D.F 10338*]
O. Frugoni & Vienna Pro Musica—Byrns
(*above*)   ♯ **E. & AmVox.PL 9650**
S. Cherkassky & L.S.O.—Menges
                                       ♯ **BB.LBC 1066**
(*Chopin*)   (♭ *set WBC 1066*)
A. Simon & Residentie—v. Otterloo
(*Grieg: Concerto*)   ♯ **Epic.LC 3182**
J. v. Karolyi & Berlin Radio—Rother
                                       ♯ **Ura.RS 7-15**
(*Grieg*) (*Gounod,* on ♯ *MTW. 505*) (2ss, ♯ *ACC.MP 21*)
(*Mendelssohn* on ♯ *Ura. 7149*)
J. Zak & State—Kondrashin   ♯ *USSR.D 797/8*
(2ss) (*Debussy, Khachaturian, Glinka, etc.*, on
                                       ♯ *Csm.CRLP 224*)
H. Reims & Berlin Sym.—Rubahn   ♯ **Roy. 1531**
(*Haydn*)
V. Georghiu & Czech Phil.—Georgescu
(2ss)   ♯ *Sup.SLPM 120*
☆ A. Rubinstein & Philharmonia—Susskind
      (♯ *Vic.LM 1744;* G.FALP 253; ♭ *Vic. set ERB 1*)
W. Kapell & Robin Hood Dell—Reiner (♯ *Vic.LM 9026;*
      excerpts on *Vic. 10-4210:* ♭ *49-4210;* G.DA 2057*)
S. Rachmaninoff & Philadelphia—Stokowski
      (♯ *Vic.LCT 1118:* ♭ *set WCT 1118* & in ♯ *set LM 6123*)

(The) Rock, Op. 7 Sym. Poem orch.
Moscow Radio—Golovanov   ♯ *USSR.D 796*
(*Moussorgsky: Khovanshchina, excpt.*)

Romance, D minor, Op. 6, No. 1 vln. & pf.
D. Oistrakh & pf.   *USSR. 17367/8*
(2ss)   (*USSRM.D 1409*)
I. Bezrodny & S. Wakman   ♯ *Phi.S 06048R*
(*Glazounov, Prokofiev, Taneiev*)
[also with anon. pf. in *USSRM.D 001284*]
W. Wilkomirsk & J. Szamotulska **Muza.X 2145**
(*Wieniawski: Mazurka, Op. 19, No. 1*) (also X 2061)

Romance, E flat major, Op. 8, No. 2 pf.
E. Burton   in ♯ **CEd.CE 1025**

Serenade, Op. 3, No. 5 pf.
— ARR. STR. QTT.
American Art Qtt.   in ♯ **BB.LBC 1086**
(*Turina, Shostakovich, etc.*)

SONATAS, pf.
No. 1, D minor, Op. 28
☆ W. P. Thew (♯ *MGM.E 3247*)

No. 2, B flat minor, Op. 36 1913, rev. 1931
☆ B. Weiser (♯ *MGM.E 3248*)

Sonata, G minor, Op. 19 vlc. & pf.
J. Schuster & L. Pennario   ♯ *DCap.CTL 7052*
                                       (♯ *Cap.P 8248*)
☆ E. Kurtz & W. Kapell (♯ *ItV.A12R 0018*)

SONGS
COLLECTIONS
     In the silent night, Op. 4, No. 3 (Fet)
     Lilacs, Op. 21, No. 5 (Beketova)
     Summer nights, Op. 14, No. 5 (Rathaus)
     Before my window, Op. 26, No. 10 (Galina)
         (or: *The Cherry Tree*)
     O cease thy singing, maiden fair, Op. 4, No. 4 (Pushkin)
     Sorrow in Spring, Op. 21, No. 12 (Galina)
     The Soldier's wife, Op. 8, No. 4 (Shevchenko, trs.
         Pleshcheev)
     Vocalise, Op. 34, No. 14
M. Kurenko (S), V. Pastukhoff (pf.)
                                       ♯ *DCap.CTL 7068*
(*Moussorgsky*)   (♯ *Cap.P 8265*)
☆ The Soldier's Wife, Op. 8, No. 4 (Shevchenko, trs.
         Pleshcheev)
     O thou billowy harvest field, Op. 4, No. 5 (Tolstoy)
     Like a vision the day-dreams have vanished (Rathaus)
N. Obukhova (M-S)
☆ Floods of Spring, Op. 14, No. 11 (Tyutchev)
     I came to her, Op. 14, No. 4 (Koltsov)
     The Pied Piper, Op. 38, No. 4 (Bryousov)
S. Lemeshev (T)
     O cease thy singing, maiden fair, Op. 4, No. 4 (Pushkin)
     Do not depart, Op. 4, No. 1 (Merezhkovsky)
B. Gmyria (Bs)   ♯ **Van.VRS 6023**
(*Moussorgsky*)
[Individual issues of some of these, *see below*]
     Before my window, Op. 26, No. 10 (Galina)
     Lilacs, Op. 21, No. 5 (Beketova)
V. Firsova (S)
     April (unid.)
     Love's flame, Op. 14, No. 10 (Minsky)
         (or: *In my heart*)
     Sorrow in Spring, Op. 21, No. 12 (Galina)
P. Lisitsian (B)
     All things depart, Op. 26, No. 15 (Rathaus)
     How few the joys, Op. 14, No. 3 (Fet)
V. Borisenko (M-S)
     In the silent night, Op. 4, No. 3 (Fet)
     Night is mournful, Op. 26, No. 12 (Bunin)
     All once I gladly owned, Op. 26, No. 2 (Tyutchev)
A. Pirogov (B)   ♯ *USSR.D 2199/200*
     O cease thy singing, maiden fair, Op. 4, No. 4 (Pushkin)
☆ Before my window, Op. 26, No. 10 (Galina)
     So dread a fate, Op. 34, No. 7[1] (Maikov)
I. Kozlovsky (T)   *USSRM.D 00646/7*
     All once I gladly owned, Op. 26, No. 2 (Tyutchev)
     I came to her, Op. 14, No. 4 (Koltsov)
     The Heart's secret, Op. 26, No. 1 (A. K. Tolstoy)
         (or: *There are many sounds*)
P. Lisitsian (B)   *USSR. 14114/5*
     Child, how like a flower, Op. 8, No. 2 (Heine, trs.
         Pleshcheev)   (also on *USSR. 19037*)
     The Poet, Op. 34, No. 9 (Tyutchev)
     All things pass away, Op. 26, No. 15 (Rathaus)
And. Ivanov (B)   *USSRM.D 00715/6*
(*Tchaikovsky*)
     How fair this spot, Op. 21, No. 7 (Galina)
     What wealth, what rapture, Op. 34, No. 12 (Fet)
     Sorrow in Spring, Op. 21, No. 12 (Galina)
I. Bolotin   *USSR. 12888/9*
     O do not grieve, Op. 14, No. 8 (Apukhtin)
     O thou billowy harvest field, Op. 4, No. 5 (A. K. Tolstoy)
     The Soldier's wife, Op. 8, No. 4 (Shevchenko, trs.
         Pleshcheev)
N. Obukhova (M-S)   *USSRM.D 00689/90*
(2ss)

---

[1] Listed as *It cannot be;* assumed to be this.

All things pass away, Op. 26, No. 15 (Rathaus)
B. Gmyria (Bs) in ♯ *USSR.D 1595*
(*below; & Glinka, Rimsky, etc.*)

Again I am alone (unid.)[1]
As fair as day, Op. 14, No. 9 (Minsky)
B. Gmyria (Bs) *USSRM.D 001210*
(*Tchaikovsky*)

(The) Answer, Op. 21, No. 4 (Hugo, trs. Mey)
☆ Z. Dolukhanova (A), B. Kozel (pf.) *USSRM.D 00606*
(*Water Lily, & Rubinstein*) (in ♯ *CdM.LDM 8134*)

As fair as day, Op. 14, No. 9 (Minsky)
P. Lisitsian (B) *USSR. 15823*
(*Glazounov: Oriental Romance*)

Before my window, Op. 26, No. 10 (Galina)
V. Firsova (S) *USSR. 17290*
(*Rimsky: Of what I dream*)

Beloved, let us fly, Op. 26, No. 5
(Golenishchev-Kutuzov)
A. Ivanov (B) *USSR. 23012*
(*Tchaikovsky: Accept just once*)
☆ G. Vinogradov (T) (*Eta. 30-5018*)

Daisies, Op. 38, No. 3 (Severyanin)
— ARR. PF. Rachmaninoff
☆ E. Gilels (in ♯ *Csm.CRLP 147*)

— ARR. VLN. & PF. Kreisler
☆ F. Kreisler (in ♯ *Vic.LCT 1142*)
D. Oistrakh (*USSR.D 1409*)

Do not depart, Op. 4, No. 1 (Merezhkovsky)
B. Gmyria (Bs) *USSR. 21866*
(*I wait for thee*) (& in ♯ *USSR.D 1595*)

(A) Dream, Op. 8, No. 5[2]
(Shevchenko, trs. Pleshcheev)
N. Shpiller (S) *USSRM.D 00968*
(*To her; & Glinka*)

Fate, Op. 21, No. 1 (Apukhtin)
R. Arié (Bs), W. Parry (pf.) ♯ *D.LW 5104*
(*Rimsky, Koenemann; & Trad.: Song of the Volga Boatmen*)
(♯ *Lon.LD 9101*)

Floods of Spring, Op. 14, No. 11 (Tyutchev)
V. Borisenko (M-S) *USSR. 14006*
(*Tchaikovsky: Only thou*)
J. Garda (B), V. Makarov (pf.) *Muza. 2415*
(*Karlowicz: Whence come the first stars*)
☆ S. Lemeshev (T) (*USSRM.D 00928*)

(The) Fountains, Op. 26, No. 11 (Tyutchev)
⊞ G. Farrar (S, *Eng*) (*IRCC. 1952**)

How fair this spot, Op. 21, No. 7 (Galina)
☆ N. Kazantseva (S) (*USSRM.D 00699*)
⊞ G. Farrar (S, *Eng*) (*IRCC. 1952**)

I came to her, Op. 14, No. 4 (Koltsov)
S. Lemeshev (T) *USSRM.D 00928*
(*Floods of Spring; & Rimsky*)

I wait for thee, Op. 14, No. 1 (Davidova)
☆ B. Gmyria (Bs) (*USSR. 21867*)

In my garden at night, Op. 38, No. 1
(Isaakian, trs. Bloch)
N. Kazantseva (S) *USSRM.D 00699*
(*above; Rimsky & Dargomijsky*)

In the silent night, Op. 4, No. 3 (Fet)
A. Pirogov (B) *USSR. 22548*
(*Tchaikovsky*)

Like a vision the day-dreams have vanished
(Rathaus) (from *Unpublished Songs, 1887-93*)
N. Obukhova (M-S) (*USSR. 22647*)

Lilacs, Op. 21, No. 5 (Beketova)
J. Björling (T, *Eng*), F. Schauwecker (pf.)
in ♯ *G.ALP 1187*
(*Schubert, Brahms, etc.*) (♯ *Vic.LM 1771*)

— ARR. PF.: L. Zyugin (*USSR. 22303*)

(The) Little island, Op. 14, No. 2
(Shelley, trs. Balmont)
S. Lemeshev (T) *USSR. 21306*
(*Rimsky: It was in early spring*)

Love's flame, Op. 14, No. 10 (Minsky)
V. Borisenko (M-S) *USSRM.D 00613*
(*Tchaikovsky*)

Midsummer Nights, Op. 14, No. 5 (Rathaus)
Z. Dolukhanova (A) *USSR. 20392*
(*Tchaikovsky: Do not ask*)

Morning, Op. 4, No. 2 (Yanov)
☆ Z. Dolukhanova (A), B. Kozel (pf.)
(in ♯ *CdM.LDM 8134*)

O do not grieve, Op. 14, No. 8 (Apukhtin)
Z. Dolukhanova (A) *USSRM.D 00668*
(*Tchaikovsky*)

O cease thy singing, maiden fair, Op. 4, No. 4
(Pushkin) (*Chanson géorgienne*)
B. Gmyria (Bs) *USSRM.D 00788*
(*Rubinstein: Ballade*)
⊞ J. McCormack (T, *Eng*), F. Kreisler (vln.) & pf.
(in ♯ *Vic.LCT 1158**)

Oh! stay my love, Op. 4, No. 1 (Merezhkovsky)
M. Reizen (Bs) (*USSR. 21565*)

To her, Op. 38, No. 3 (Belyi)
N. Shpiller (S) *USSRM.D 00968*
(*A Dream; & Glinka*)

Vocalise, Op. 34, No. 14
— ARR. VLN. & PF.
D. Oistrakh & I. Kollegorskaya
in ♯ *Van.VRS 6020*
(*Glazounov, Tchaikovsky, etc.*)
(*Glazounov, Shostakovich, etc.* on ♯ *Csm.CRLPX 011*)
☆ J. Heifetz & E. Bay (♭ *Vic.ERA 94; DV. 26034*)

— ARR. VLC. & PF.
D. Shafran & pf. (*USSR. 22710/1*)
M. Rostropovich & pf. (in ♯ *USSR.D 1177*)

— ARR. ORCH. Stokowski, etc.
Orch.—Stokowski ♭ *Vic.ERA 182*
(*Tchaikovsky*) (♭ *FV.A 95217*)
Philadelphia—Ormandy ♯ *AmC.ML 4961*
(*Symphony No. 3*) (♯ *Phi.A 01156L*)
N.Y.P.S.O.—Kostelanetz (in ♯ *AmC.CL 758:* ♭ *A 2035*)

(The) Water Lily, Op. 8, No. 1
(Heine, trs. Pleshcheev)
☆ Z. Dolukhanova (A) (*USSR.D 00606*)

SUITES, 2 pianos
No. 1, G minor, Op. 5 Fantasie (Tableaux)
No. 2, C major, Op. 17
A. Ferrante & L. Teicher ♯ *West.WN 18059*

No. 1, G minor, only
A. Goldenweiser & H. Neuhaus ♯ *USSR.D 815/6*

... 3rd movt., Tears, only
E. Bartlett & R. Robertson (in ♯ *MGM.E 3150:* ♭ *set X 273*)
A. Whittemore & J. Lowe (♭ *Vic.ERA 123*)

Symphonic Dances, Op. 45 1940
Rochester Phil.—Leinsdorf ♯ *AmC.ML 4621*

SYMPHONIES
No. 1, D minor, Op. 13 (1895, reconstructed 1945)
Dresden Phil.—Bongartz ♯ *Ura. 7131*
(♯ *MTW. 524*)
Moscow Radio—Kovalev[3] ♯ *USSR.D 1184*
(*Rimsky-Korsakov: Overture*)
☆ Stockholm Radio—Rachmilovich (♯ *AFest.CFR 12-176*)

No. 2, E minor, Op. 27 1907
Pittsburgh Sym.—Steinberg ♯ *DCap.CTL 7085*
(♯ *Cap.P 8293*)
☆ Minneapolis Sym.—Ormandy (♯ *Cam.CAL 247*)
N.Y.P.S.O.—Rodzinski (♯ *AmC.RL 3049*)
Minneapolis Sym.—Mitropoulos (♯ *ItV.A12R 0026*)

---

[1] Might be *Loneliness*, Op. 21, No. 6.
[2] Or might be *Dreams*, Op. 38, No. 5 (Sologub).
[3] Listed as "Youthful Symphony"; probably this.

No. 3, A minor, Op. 44 1936
B.B.C. Sym.—Sargent ♯ **G.ALP 1118**
(♯ QALP 10059; Vic.LHMV 20; ArgA.LPC 11562)
Philadelphia—Ormandy ♯ **AmC.ML 4961**
(*Vocalise*) (♯ Phi.A 01156L)
☆ State Sym.—Golovanov (♯ USSR.D 0105/6; ♯ RS.7)

To thee O Lord cho. 1915
All Saints Church Male Cho.—Self
in ♯ **CEd.CE 1022**
(† Choral Masterpieces from the Russian Liturgy)

Trio élégiaque, D minor, Op. 9 pf., vln., vlc. 1893
L. Oborin, I. Oistrakh, S. Knushevitzky
(12ss) **USSR. 019794/805**

Valse, Op. 10, No. 2 pf.
N. Yemelyanova *USSRM.D 643*
(*Humoresque:* & *Balakirev*) (*USSR. 21821*)

Variations on a theme of Chopin, Op. 22 pf.
☆ R. Goldsand (♯ Clc. 6196)

VESPER MASS, Op. 37
… 9 Anthems (unspec.)
Rome Russian Collegium—Butkevitch ♯ **RS. 10**
[It is doubtful whether this was ever on sale]

No. 3, Blessed is the man
Augustana Cho.—Veld in ♯ **Word.W 4005**
(*Kodály, Sjöberg, Grieg, etc.*) (*Eng*)

No. 6, Ave Maria
☆Don Cossack Cho. in ♯ *Phi.S 06611R*

No. 7, Glory be to God
Yale Univ. Divinity School Cho.—Borden
in ♯ **Over.LP 2**
(† Hymns of Praise)

RAFF, Josef Joachim (1822-1882)

COLLECTION
Scherzino, Op. 85, No. 4 vln. & pf. ARR. ORCH. Saunders
Cavatina, A flat, Op. 85, No. 3 vln. & pf. ARR. ORCH. Saunders
Quartet, Str., No. 7, D major, Op. 192, No. 2 ("*Die schöne Müllerin*") … The Mill only
Aria (unspec.) (perhaps from Suite, Op. 204)
Suite, C major, Op. 101 … No. 5, Scherzo orch.
Westminster Light Orch.—Bridgewater
♯ **Nix.WLP 6805**
(*Mendelssohn*) (♯ West.WL 4005)

Cavatina, A flat major, Op. 85, No. 3 vln. & pf.
J. Shermont & O. Schulhof ♯ **Rem.YV 2**
(*Beriot & Hubay*)
M. Kalki & Berlin Municipal—Otto ♭*T.U 45559*
(*Thais—Méditation*) (in ♯ *LA 6066; FT. 270.TC. 044*)
J. Suk & J. Hála **U.H 24462**
(*Paganini: Concerto No. 1, s. 1*)

— ARR. ORCH.
G. Melachrino Orch. (G.C 4250: S 10619)
R. Crean Orch. (in ♯ *D.LF 1082; Lon.LPB 424*)
etc.

— ARR. GUITAR A. Valenti (in ♯ SMC. 1002)

Quartet, Str., No. 7, D major, Op. 192, No. 2
… The Mill only: Pessina Qtt. (ArgOd. 66060: in ♯ *LDC 510*)

RAIMBAUT DE VAQUEIRAS
(1180-1208)

Kalenda maya (Estampie)
Pro Musica Antiqua—Cape
in ♯ **HP.APM 14018**
(*Guillaume d'Amiens, Adam de la Halle* & *Anon.*)
Krefeld Coll. Mus.—R. Haas
in ♯ **E.** & **AmVox.PL 8110**
(† Music of the Middle Ages) (♯ BàM.LD 08)
Y. Tessier (T), M. Clary (lute) in ♯ *Elek.EKL 31*
(† French Troubadour Songs)

RAISON, André (*c.* 1655-*c.* 1720)
SEE: † FRENCH BAROQUE ORGAN MUSIC
† HISTORY OF MUSIC IN SOUND (62)

RAKOV, Nicolai (b. 1908)

Concerto, vln. & orch., E minor 1944
S. Gavrilov & Berlin Radio—Rother
(*Malipiero*) ♯ **Ura. 7112**
D. Oistrakh & USSR. State—Gauk
(*Khachaturian*) (? n.v.) ♯ **Per.SPL 709**

SONG: The Cliff (Garnakerian)
B. Gmyria (Bs) *USSRM.D 00571*
(*Shaporin* & *Rubinstein*) (also *USSR. 21498*)

RAMEAU, Jean Philippe (1683-1764)

I. VOCAL

CANTATAS
Diane et Actéon: by Boismortier, *q.v.*

L'Impatience T & cont. 1728
☆ H. Cuénod, R. Brink (vln.), A. Zighéra (gamba),
D. Pinkham (hpsi.) ♯ **Nix.LLP 8044**
(*Boismortier*) (♯ Lyr.LL 44)

MOTETS
Laboravi 5-pt. cho. & org. 1722
Vocal Ens.—Blanchard in ♯ *CdM.LDA 8116*
(*Boismortier;* & *Concert* & *Hpsi. pieces*)

Quam dilecta 4-pt. cho.
… Cor meum et caro mea cho.
London Cha. Singers & Orch.—Bernard
G.HMS 51
(† History of Music in Sound) (in ♯ Vic. set LM 6030)

OPERAS
COLLECTED EXCERPTS
ACANTHE ET CÉPHISE; CASTOR ET POLLUX;
DARDANUS; LES FÊTES D'HÉBÉ; HIPPOLYTE ET
ARICIE; LES INDES GALANTES; PLATÉE; ZAÏS
Vocal & Inst. Ens.—Boulanger ♯ **B.AXTL 1053**
[*see below* for details] (♯ AmD.DL 9683; D.UMT 263566)

ACANTHE ET CÉPHISE 3 Acts 1751
Suite — ARR. Désormière
1. Musette gracieuse en rondeau
2. Air vif pour les esprits aériens
3. Menuet 4. Musette tendre 5. Rigaudon
Garde Républicaine Wind Quintet
♯ *D.FM 143658*
(*Desserre* & *Deslandres*)

Overture & Fanfare (Act I); **Entr'acte**
Inst. Ensemble—Boulanger in ♯ **B.AXTL 1053**
(♯ D.UMT 263566; AmD.DL 9683)

CASTOR ET POLLUX 5 Acts 1737
Menuet chanté
Naissez, dons de Flore (Prol. Sc. 2) S, S, T, T
N. Sautereau & F. Wend, P. Derenne &
J. Maciet in ♯ **B.AXTL 1053**
(♯ D.UMT 263566; AmD.DL 9683)

Menuet, Act I
Included in: Suite, Str. Orch. *below*

Nature, amour Act II
G. Souzay (B) in ♯ *D.LX 3112*
(*Mozart, A. Scarlatti, etc.*) (♯ Lon.LS 730)

Séjour de l'eternelle paix Act IV T
N. Brincker in ♯ **HS.HSL 2073**
(† Masterpieces of Music before 1750)
(also in † Histoire de la Musique vocale)
P. Derenne in ♯ **B.AXTL 1053**
(♯ D.UMT 263566; AmD.DL 9683)

♯ = Long-playing, 33⅓ r.p.m.   ♭ = 45 r.p.m.   ♮ = Auto. couplings, 78 r.p.m.

366

DARDANUS 5 Acts 1739
Introduction
Tout l'avenir Bs
Suspends ta brillante carrière, soleil Bs
Hâtons-nous Ens.
Nos cris ont pénétré Act II Bs
O jour affreux Act III
   I. Kolassi (M-S), D. Conrad (Bs), Vocal & Ens.
   —Boulanger   in ♯ **B.AXTL 1053**
      (♯ D.UMT 263566; AmD.DL 9683)

O jour affreux S Act III
   A. Mandikian   **G.HMS 48**
   († History of Music in Sound) (in ♯ Vic. set LM 6030)

Air gai en Rondeau Act III
   ☆ Orch.—Gerlin (in † ♯ AS. 2506LD)

Rigaudon, Act I; Rondeau, Act IV
Included in Suite, Str. Orch., *below*

(Les) FÊTES D'HÉBÉ Prol. & 3 Entrées 1739
DANCE SUITE
Air vif ("Danses des Lacédémoniens") (Entrée 2, Sc. VIII)
Gavotte; Rigaudons 1 & 2;
  Tambourins 1 & 2 (Entrée 1, Sc. VIII)
Bourrée (Prol., Sc. IV)
Loure grave ("Entrée") (Entrée 3, Sc. VII)
Contredanse (Entrée 3, Sc. VII)
   Champs-Élysées Theatre—Allain
      ♭ *Sel. 470.C.000*

Chaconne: "Pas de cinq" (Entrée 2, Sc. V)
Passepieds 1 & 2 (Entrée 3, Sc. VII)
   Champs Élysées Theatre—Allain
      ♭ *Sel. 470.C.002*
   (*Platée—Tambourin; Gossec, Boccherini*) (♭ *T.UV 118*)

Volons sur les bords de la Seine (Prol.) 2S.
   N. Sautereau & F. Wend
Je vous revois (Entrée 1) S & T
   F. Wend & P. Derenne   in ♯ **B.AXTL 1053**
      (♯ D.UMT 263566; AmD.DL 9683)

Tambourin en rondeau
Musette en rondeau, E major (Entrée 3)
— ARR. Mottl
   ☆ Boston Prom.—Fiedler (*JpV.SF 709/10*)

Tambourin en rondeau
— ARR. VLA. & PF. Kreisler
   ☆ W. Primrose (♭ *Cam.CAE 244*)

HIPPOLYTE ET ARICIE Prol. & 5 Acts 1733
SELECTED PASSAGES [Acts III, IV, V (Sc. 2 & 3)]
   ☆ C. Verneuil (S), G. Moizan, F. Wend (S), R. Amade (T)
   Cho. & Orch.—Désormière ♯ **LOL.OL 50034**

O disgrâce cruelle Act IV M-S & cho.
Rossignols amoureux Act V S
   F. Wend (S), I. Kolassi, Vocal & Inst. Ens.
   —Boulanger   in ♯ **B.AXTL 1053**
      (♯ D.UMT 263566; AmD.DL 9683)

March (Prologue)
   ☆ Orch.—Gerlin (in † ♯ AS. 2506LD)

(Les) INDES GALANTES Prol. & 4 Entrées 1735
Symphonies & Dances — ARR. Oubradous
Overture
Air tendre; Gavotte (3rd Entrée)
Air polonais (Prologue)
Tambourins (1st Entrée)
Ritournelle; Air vif (3rd Entrée)
Ritournelle (2nd Entrée)
Minuets; Chaconne (4th Entrée)
   Paris Cha. Concerts Assoc.—Oubradous
      ♯ **Pat.DTX 146**
   (*Couperin*) (♯ ArgA.LPC 11668)

Air grave pour deux polonais (Prol.)
   ☆ W. Landowska (hpsi.) (♭ *Vic.ERA 128*)

Tambourins I & II (from 1st Entrée)
Danse du grand calumet de la paix (4th Entrée)
   ☆ Orch.—Gerlin   in † ♯ *AS. 2506LD*

Clair flambeau du monde (2nd Entrée) B. & cho.
   B. Demigny & Ens.   in ♯ **B.AXTL 1053**
      (♯ D.UMT 263566; AmD.DL 9683)

(Les) PALADINS 3 Acts 1760
Orchestral Suites — ARR. Désormière
SUITE I: 1. Entrée très gaye des troubadours
       2. Air pour les pagodas
       3. Gavotte gaye
       4. Gavotte un peu lente
SUITE II: 1. Air vif   4. Menuet en rondeau
       2. Sarabande   5. Très vif
       3. Gaiement
   Lamoureux Cha.—Colombo ♯ **LOL.OL 50106**
   (1½ss—*Lalande*) (4ss, V♯ *DO.LD 30/1*)

PLATÉE Prol. & 3 Acts 1745
Ballet Suites 1 & 2
   ☆ Lausanne Cha.—Desarzens (in ♯ *MMS. 86*)

Chantons Bacchus (Prol.) T & cho.
   P. Derenne & Ens.   in ♯ **B.AXTL 1053**
      (♯ D.UMT 263566; AmD.DL 9683)

Tambourin (Act I)
   Champs-Élysées Theatre—Allain
      in ♭ *Sel. 470.C.002*
      (♭ *T.UV 118*)

Air vif (Act II)
   ☆ Orch.—Gerlin (in † ♯ AS. 2506LD)

Menuet dans le goût de vièle Act II
   ☆ Orch.—Gerlin (in † ♯ AS. 2506LD)
— ARR. Mottl
   ☆ Boston Prom.—Fiedler (*JpV.SF 709*)
— ARR. GUITAR Segovia
   A. Segovia   in ♯ **B.AXTL 1070**
   († Segovia Evening) (♯ SpC.CCL 35015; AmD.DL 9733;
                     AFest.CFR 10-729)

ZAÏS 4 Acts & Prol. 1748 (or: *Zaïre*)
Overture
   Bologna Orch.—Jenkins   ♯ **Cpt.MC 20019**
   (*J. C. Bach & Vivaldi*)

Ballet figuré
   Ens.—Boulanger   in ♯ **B.AXTL 1053**
      (♯ D.UMT 263566; AmD.DL 9683)

II.A. CHAMBER MUSIC

(6) CONCERTS EN SEXTUOR Str. & hpsi.
   1. La Coulicam; La Livri; Le Vézinet
   2. La Laborde; La Boucon; L'Agaçante; Menuets I & II
   3. La La Poplinière; La Timide; Tambourins I & II
   4. La Pantomime; L'Indiscrète; La Rameau
   5. La Forqueray; La Cupis; La Marais
   6. La Poule; Menuets I & II; L'Enharmonique; L'Égyptienne
COMPLETE RECORDINGS
   O.L. Ens.—de Froment   ♯ **LOL.OL 50084**
   ☆ Cha. Orch.—Hewitt (♯ HS.HSL 99)
No. 6, COMPLETE
   Cha. Orch.—Belai   ♯ *CdM.LDA 8116*
   (*Laboravi, Diane et Actéon, & Hpsi. pieces*)
No. 1 . . . La Livri; No. 2 . . . La Boucon
No. 4 . . . La Rameau; No. 5 . . . La Cupis
No. 6 . . . L'Égyptienne
   ☆ Cha. Orch.—Hewitt (V♯ *DFr.EX 17028*)

PIÈCES DE CLAVECIN EN CONCERT 1741
Concert—
   1, C minor: La Coulicam; La Livri; Le Vézinet
   2, G major: La Laborde; La Boucon; L'Agaçante;
                Menuets I & II
   3, A major: La La Poplinière; La Timide; Tambourins
                I & II
   4, B flat major: La Pantomime; L'Indiscrète; La Rameau
   5. D minor: La Forqueray; La Cupis; La Marais
   R. Gerlin (hpsi.), J-P. Rampal (fl.), R. Albin(vlc.)
      ♯ **LOL.OL 50083**

II.B. HARPSICHORD MUSIC

COMPLETE RECORDINGS
   (of complete edition, pub. Durand)
Book I, 1706; Pièces, 1724; Book II, 1727-31;
La Dauphine, 1747; 5 Pièces extraites des Pièces en Concert
   R. Gerlin (6ss)   ♯ **LOL.OL 50080/2**
   R. Veyron-Lacroix   ♯ **West.WN 18124/6**
   (6ss)   (set WN 3303)
   M. Charbonnier[1]   ♯ **Phi.A 77400/1L**
   (4ss)   (♯ Epic.LC 3185)[2]
   M. Meyer (pf.) (4ss)   ♯ **DFr. 98/99**

---

[1] Excluding the 5 *Pièces extraites* . . .
[2] Stated to contain *Suites 1 & 2, E minor & D major; & Pièces.* Probably equivalent to A 77400L only.

SUITES (as arranged by Riemann)
COLLECTIONS
No. 2, E minor; No. 4, A minor
☆ F. Valenti (♯ Nix.WLP 5128)

No. 4, A minor; No. 5, G major
C. Wood   ♯ MF.DG 005

No. 3: 4, La Joyeuse
No. 14: 6, La Triomphante
No. 5: 1, Les Tricotets; 4, La Poule;
     7, L'Enharmonique; 8, L'Égyptienne
J. Casadesus (pf.)   ♯ Angel. 35261
(Couperin, Poulenc, Françaix, etc.)

No. 1: 1, Prelude; 2, Allemande; 3, Courante; 4, Gigue
No. 4: 3, Sarabande; 4, Les Trois Mains;
     5, Fanfarinette; 6, La Triomphante
H. Boschi (pf.)   ♯ Sup.LPM 224
(Couperin)   (♯ U. 5197C)

SUITES: INDIVIDUAL RECORDINGS
No. 1, A minor
... No. 1, Prelude
D. Gouarne   in ♯ CdM.LDA 8116

... No. 6, La Vénitienne   (as Trio to No. 7)
... No. 7, Gavotte
G. Copeland (pf.)[1]   in ♯ MGM.E 3024
(Suite 4, below; & Debussy, Satie)

No. 2, E minor

1. Allemande	2. Courante
3. Gigues en rondeau	4. Le Rappel des oiseaux
5. Rigaudons I & II	6. Musette en rondeau
7. Tambourin	8. La Villageoise

... Nos. 1-7
L. Selbiger (Couperin)   ♯ C.KC 2
(also 4ss, ♮ C.LDX 7025/6)
... Nos. 1, 3, 6-8   ☆ T. Sack (in ♯ MMS. 86)
... No. 3, Gigues en rondeau
— — ARR. STR. ORCH.; See Suite, below
... Nos. 4, 6   E. Gilels (pf.)   USSR.19533/4

... No. 4, Le Rappel des oiseaux
J. Prelli   Orf. 45001
(below & Mozart)
D. Gouarne   in ♯ CdM.LDA 8116
W. Kempff (pf.)   ♭ D. 71083
(Couperin: Le Carillon de Cythère)
R. Casadesus (pf.)   in ♯ AmC.ML 4695
☆ M. Meyer (pf.) (in ♯ DFr. 86; ♯ HS.HSL 98)

... No. 6, Musette en rondeau only
☆ A. Ehlers (in ♯ D.UAT 273084)

... No. 7, Tambourin
Z. Růžičková   U.C 24398
(Daquin: Le coucou & Scarlatti: Sonata, E minor)

— — ARR. CYMBALOM & PF.
I. Tarjani-Tóth & pf. (in ♯ G.FBLP 1067)

No. 3, D minor
... Nos. 1, 6, 8
☆ M. Meyer (pf.)   in ♯ DFr. 86
     (in ♯ HS.HSL 98)

... No. 1, Les Tendres Plaintes   — ARR.
A. Rácz (cymbalom), A. Rácz (pf.) (Qual.SZK 3554)

... No. 2, Les Niais de Sologne
R. Casadesus (pf.)   in ♯ AmC.ML 4695

... No. 4, La Joyeuse
J. Prelli   Orf. 45001
(Suite No. 2, excpt. & Mozart)

— — ARR. 2 HARPS   Salzédo
C. Salzédo & L. Lawrence (in ♯ Mer.MG 10144)

... No. 6, L'Entretien des muses
I. Nef   in ♯ LOL.OL 50028
(† Clavecinistes français)   (♯ OL.LD 64)

No. 4, A minor
... No. 3, Sarabande
G. Copeland (pf.)[1]   in ♯ MGM.E 3024
(Suite 1, above & Debussy, Satie)

[1] Labelled: Suite—Les Grands Seigneurs.

... No. 3, Sarabande
... No. 6, La Triomphante
D. Gouarne   in ♯ CdM.LDA 8116

... No. 7, Gavotte & 5 doubles
R. Casadesus (pf.)   in ♯ AmC.ML 4695
M. Tipo (pf.)   ♯ Cpt.MC 20020
(Bloch, Schumann, R. Strauss)

No. 5, G major
... No. 3, La Poule
— — ARR. ORCH.   Respighi, in Gli Uccelli, q.v.

... No. 4, Minuets I & II
E. Heiller   in ♯ Uni.LP 1010
(† History of the Dance)
— — ARR. GUITAR   M. L. Anido (ArgOd. 57026)

... No. 6, Les Sauvages
R. Casadesus (pf.)   in ♯ AmC.ML 4695
☆ M. Meyer (pf.) (in ♯ DFr. 86; ♯ HS.HSL 98)

... No. 8, L'Égyptienne — ARR. STR. ORCH. in Suite, below

II.C. MISCELLANEOUS

(La) Dauphine   1747
☆ W. Landowska (hpsi.) (in ♯ G.ALP 1246: FALP/QALP
     218; ♭ Vic.ERA 127)

Suite for String Orch.

1. L'Égyptienne	2. Menuet (Castor & Pollux)
3. Rondeau (Dardanus)	4. Rigaudon (Dardanus)
5. Gigues en Rondeau I & II	(Hpsi. Suite 2)

Allegro Str. Orch.—Bath   ♯ Allo. 4011
(Boyce)   (♯ AFest.CFR 10-577)
[Also apparently on ♯ Allo. 3107 with Bruckner. Performed
    sub nom. Hastings Sym.—Tubbs]

RANGSTRÖM, Ture (1884-1947)

Divertimento elegiaco   str. orch.   1918
King Erik's Songs   Song Cycle   (Fröding)   1918
    1. Drink, Welam Welamson! (Drinking Song)
    2. Ballad of myself & Hercules the Fool
    3. Song to Karin when she had been dancing
    4. Song to Karin from Prison
    5. King Erik's last Song
E. Sædén (B, in Songs) & Stockholm Royal
    Orch.—Westerberg   ♯ SS. 33102
(Alfvén, on ♯ West.WN 18131)

... Drink, Welam Welamson!
B. Løwenfalk (B) & Orch.   G.X 8095
(Sibelius: King Christian II, song)

RASSE, François (b. 1873)

Concerto, C major, vln. & orch.
R. Hosselet & Belgian Nat. Orch.—Defossez
            ♯ LI.W 91063
            (♯ D.BA 133183)

RATHAUS, Karol (1895-1954)

Prelude, Op. 71   orch.   f.p. 1954
Louisville—Whitney   ♯ LO. 9
(Perle & v. Einem)

RATHGEBER, Johann Valentin (1682-1750)

SEE: † MUSIC OF BAROQUE ERA

RATNER, Leonard (b. 1916)

Serenade, ob., hrn., str. qtt.
▽ ☆ Cha. Music Ens.—Salgo (Antheil)   ♯ ML. 7023

RAVEL, Maurice (1875-1937)

CLASSIFIED: I. Piano
II. Chamber Music
III. Orchestral
IV. Stage Works
V. Songs

I. PIANO

COLLECTIONS

COMPLETE RECORDING OF THE PIANO WORKS

À la manière de . . .	1913	ABL 3012
GASPARD DE LA NUIT	1908	ABL 3046
Habanera (pf. duet)	1895	ABL 3046
Jeux d'eau	1901	ABL 3046
MA MÈRE L'OYE (pf. duet)	1908	ABL 3046
Menuet antique	1895	ABL 3046
Menuet sur le nom d'Haydn	1909	ABL 3062
MIROIRS	1905	ABL 3012
Pavane pour une infante défunte	1899	ABL 3012
Prelude, A minor	1913	ABL 3062
Sonatina, F sharp minor	1905	ABL 3012
(Le) TOMBEAU DE COUPERIN	1914-7	ABL 3062
Valses nobles et sentimentales	1911	ABL 3062

☆ R. Casadesus (with G. Casadesus in the duets)
(6ss)　　♯ EPhi.ABL 3012, 3046 & 3062
(♯ Phi.A 01112/4L)

"COMPLETE" RECORDING (excluding Duets & À la
manière de . . .)
V. Perlemuter　　♯ AmVox. set DL 153
(Menuet antique on s. 3 of set, with Concerto, G major;
Pavane . . . on s. 4 with Concerto, left hand)

"COMPLETE" RECORDING (excluding Duets, À la
manière de . . . & Prelude, A minor)
M. Meyer　　♯ DFr.DF 100/101
(4ss)　　(♯ HS.HSL 111/2, set HSL-J)

COLLECTIONS

Prelude, A minor
Menuet sur le nom d'Haydn
Valses nobles et sentimentales
Le Tombeau de Couperin
... No. 6, Toccata, only
J-M. Damase　　♯ LI.TW 91035
(Fauré)　　(♯ D.FST 133062)

Gaspard de la Nuit
Jeux d'eau
Menuet sur le nom d'Haydn
Pavane pour une infante défunte
Sonatina, F sharp minor
D. Wayenberg　　♯ LT.DTL 93068
(♯ Sel. 320.C.068)

Jeux d'eau
MIROIRS
... No. 2, Oiseaux tristes
... No. 4, Alborada del gracioso
Valses nobles et sentimentales
Th. Bruins　　♯ Phi.N 00648R

GASPARD DE LA NUIT 1908

1. Ondine　2. Le Gibet　3. Scarbo

G. Bachauer　　♯ G.CLP 1067
(Debussy & Mompou)
H. Faure　　♯ D.FS 123639
(Jeux d'eau & Prelude, A minor)
F. Gulda　　♯ D.LXT 2817
(Debussy: Suite bergamasque)　(♯ Lon.LL 754)
R. Gianoli　　♯ West.WN 18008
(Jeux d'eau, Miroirs & Pavane)
☆ G. Scherzer (Schubert)　　♯ P.PMC 1002
☆ W. Gieseking (Debussy)　　♯ AmC.ML 4773
☆ F. Glazer　　♯ Nix.QLP 4005
(Debussy)　　(♯ Cum.CLP 200)
☆ L. Pennario (♯ T.LCSK 8152)

Jeux d'eau 1901

H. Faure　　♯ D.FS 123639
(Gaspard de la Nuit & Prelude, A minor)
P. Cavazzini　　♯ Arp.ARC 2
(Liszt, Debussy, Albeniz)
R. Gianoli　　♯ West.WN 18008
(above & below)
M. Meyer, from Collection　V♯ DFr.EX 17029
(Sonatine)
☆ M. Panzéra (in ♯ Clc. 6260)

Ma Mère l'Oye

— PF. DUET VERSION 1908
I. Marika & G. Smadja　　♯ Phi.N 00637R
(Fauré)
J. Bonneau & G. Joy　　♯ Pat.DT 1027
(Milhaud: Scaramouche)
☆ E. Bartlett & R. Robertson　　♯ MGM.E 3114
(Debussy & Saint-Saëns)

— ARR. PF. SOLO S. Bianca (4ss)　　MSB. 78013/4

— ORCH. (Ballet) VERSION 1912
French Nat. Radio—Cluytens[1]　　♯ C.FCX 343
(Menuet antique, Pavane, Valses nobles . . .)
Champs-Élysées Theatre—Inghelbrecht[1]
　　♯ Sel. 320.C.088
(Rapsodie espagnole & Barque sur l'océan)
Dresden State Sym.—Schreiber　　♯ Roy. 1468
(Daphnis et Chloe Suite 2)
"Philharmonic"—Tubbs　　♯ Allo. 4052
☆ Boston Sym.—Koussevitzky (♯ G.QALP 10020:
VALP 528; & o.v., ♯ Cam.CAL 161)
Italian Radio—Erede (♭ Tem. set 4500)

MIROIRS 1905

1. Noctuelles　　4. Alborada del gracioso
2. Oiseaux tristes　　5. La vallée des cloches
3. Une barque sur l'océan

COMPLETE RECORDINGS
E. Gilberg　　♯ AmVox.PL 8760
(Debussy: Reflets dans l'eau)
R. Gianoli　　♯ West.WN 18008
(above & below)
☆ L. Pennario (♯ T.LCSK 8152)

No. 2, Oiseaux tristes
L. Morel　　♯ D.LW 5127
(Debussy, Gagnebin, Marescotti)　(♯ Lon.LD 9149)

No. 3, Une barque sur l'océan
— ORCH. VERSION Ravel
L.S.O.—Poulet　　♯ P.PMC 1016
(No. 4, & Fauré)　(♯Od.ODX 152; MGM.E 3116)
Champs-Élysées Th.—Inghelbrecht
　　♯ Sel. 320.C.088
(Ma Mère l'Oye & Rapsodie espagnole)

No. 4, Alborada del gracioso
M. Meyer, from Collection　V♯ DFr.EX 17035
(Pavane pour une infante défunte)
☆ D. Lipatti (♭ C.SEB 3501: SEBQ 106: ESBF 108:
in ♯ FCX 495; in ♯ AmC.ML 2216)

— ORCH. VERSION Ravel
French Radio Sym.—Leibowitz
in ♯ E. & AmVox.PL 8150
(Pavane pour une infante . . . etc.)　(♯ AFest.CFR 12-509)
French Nat. Radio—Cluytens　　♯ C.CX 1134
(Daphnis & Chloë)　(♯ FCX 215; Angel. 35054)
(Pavane pour une infante . . . on ♭ C.SEL 1524: SEBQ 121)
L.S.O.—Poulet　　♯ P.PMC 1016
(No. 3, etc.)　(♯ Od.ODX 152; MGM.E 3116)
Champs-Élysées Th.—Branco　　♯ LT.EL 93008
(Pavane . . . & La Valse)
(Pavane . . . & Valses nobles . . . on ♯ Sel.LA 1055)
(idem & Boléro, La Valse, on ♯ West.WL 5297)
Hastings Sym.—Tubbs　　♯ Allo. 3109
(Concerto for left hand)
☆ Suisse Romande—Ansermet　　♯ D.LW 5031
(Debussy)　　(♯ Lon.LD 9031)
☆ Minneapolis Sym.—Dorati (in ♯ EMer.MG 50005:
♭ Mer.EP I-5000; ♭ FMer.MEP 14501)

Pavane pour une infante défunte 1899

M. Pressler　　in ♯ MGM.E 3129
(Bartók, Granados, Respighi, etc.)　(♭ set X 254)
R. Gianoli (above)　　♯ West.WN 18008
M. Meyer, from Collection　V♯ DFr.EX 17035
(Miroirs, No. 4)

(continued on next page)

[1] Includes Prelude & Danse du rouet (added for the ballet), as does Ansermet (♯ D.LXT 2632, see Supp. I). The other new
recordings have not been heard; Koussevitzky does not include.

Pavane pour une infante défunte (continued)

— ORCH. VERSION Ravel 1912

Suisse Romande—Ansermet ♯ **D.LXT 2760**
(Chabrier & Saint-Saëns) (♯ Lon.LL 696)
(Chabrier only on ♯ D.LW 5033; Lon.LD 9039)

Philharmonia—Cantelli (2ss) G.**DB 21553**
(Dukas, Falla, Debussy on ♯ ALP 1207: QALP 10097)
(Falla only, on ♭ G.7ER 5057)

French Nat.—Cluytens ♭ **C.SEL 1524**
(Alborada del gracioso) (♭ *SEBQ 121*)
(Valses nobles . . . etc., on ♯ C.FCX 343)
(Bolero & Tombeau de Couperin, ♯ C.QCX 10107;
                                       Angel. 35102)

Philadelphia—Ormandy ♯ **AmC.ML 4983**
(Boléro, La Valse; & Chabrier, Debussy, etc.)

Champs-Élysées Th.—Branco ♯ **LT.EL 93008**
(La Valse & Miroirs, 4)
(Valses nobles . . . & Miroirs 4, on ♯ Sel.LA 1055)
(idem, & La Valse, Boléro, on ♯ West.WL 5297)

French Radio Sym.—Leibowitz
                    in ♯ **E. & AmVox.PL 8150**
(above & below) (in ♯ AFest.CFR 12-509)

Boston Sym.—Münch ♯ **Vic.LRM 7016**
(Rapsodie espagnole & La Valse) (♭ set ERB 7016)
(Roussel & Honegger, on ♯ Vic.LM 1741; ItV.A12R 0110)

L.S.O.—Poulet ♯ **P.PMC 1016**
(above & Fauré) (♯ Od.ODX 152; MGM.E 3116 &
                                       in ♯ E 3124)

Residentie—v. Otterloo ♯ **Phi.A 00714R**
(Valses nobles . . .; & Falla)

Polish Radio—Krenz *(Muza. 2439)*

☆ Minneapolis Sym.—Dorati (in ♯ EMer.MG 50005;
       ♭ FMer.MEP 14501; Mer.EP 1-5000)
   Orch.—Kostelanetz (in ♯ C.SX 1004: QSX 12004;
       AmC.CL 798, o.n.ML 4692; & in ♯ AmC.CL 792:
                                       ♭ A 1857)
   Paris Cons.—Cluytens (ArgPat.FC 6)
   Victor Sym.—Anon. (♭ Cam.CAE 204)

— ARR. PF. & ORCH.
   O. Levant & Kostelanetz Orch. (♭ AmC.A 1831)

— ARR. VLN. & ORCH.
   F. Zaback & Orch. (in ♯ AmD.DL 8086: ♭ ED 2173)

— ARR. VLC. & PF.
   A. Vlasov & pf. (in ♯ USSR.D 1180)

Prelude, A minor 1913

H. Faure ♯ **D.FS 123639**
(Gaspard de la nuit & Jeux d'eau)

Sonatina, F sharp minor 1905

A. Dorfman in ♯ **Vic.LM 1758**
(Schumann, Mendelssohn, etc.) (in ♭ set WDM 1758)

E. Contestabile G.**DB 11355/6**
(3ss—Galuppi: Larghetto & Allegro)

E. Møller ♭ **Mtr.MCEP 3012**

P. Sancan *(Debussy)* ♯ **FV.F 230003**

M. Meyer, from Collection V♯ **DFr.EX 17029**
(Jeux d'eau)

(Le) TOMBEAU DE COUPERIN 1914-17
1. Prélude   2. Fugue   3. Forlane
4. Rigaudon   5. Menuet   6. Toccata

Y. Nat ♯ **HS.HSL 98**
(Rameau, Couperin, Debussy) (♯ DFr. 86)

L. Lessona (2ss) ♯ **Fnt.LP 311**

L. Descaves (2ss) ♯ **D.FA 133031**

R. Wallenborn ♯ **DT.LGX 66041**
(F. Couperin) (♯ T.LE 6530)

☆ F. Valenzi (in ♯ Ply. 12-75; ♯ Cum.TCR 304)

... **No. 6, Toccata**
P. Badura-Skoda in ♯ **Nix.WLP 5277**
(Schubert, Liszt, etc.) (♯ West.WL 5277)

— ORCH. VERSION 1918
1. Prelude 2. Forlane 3. Menuet 4. Rigaudon

Suisse Romande—Ansermet ♯ **D.LXT 2821**
(Valses nobles . . .) (& ♯ D.LW 5130) (♯ Lon.LL 795)

Concert Arts—Golschmann ♯ **DCap.CTL 7055**
(Honegger, Milhaud, Satie) (♯ Cap.P 8244: ♭ FAP 8251)

French Nat. Radio—Cluytens ♯ **C.C 1034**
(Boléro) (♯ QC 5022: FCX 214)
(idem & Pavane . . . on ♯ QCX 10107; Angel. 35102)

Janssen Sym.—Janssen ♭ **Cam.CAE 267**
(2ss)

☆ N.B.C. Sym.—Reiner (♯ ItV.A12R 0025)

Valses nobles et sentimentales 1911

L. Pennario ♯ **DCap.CTL 7087**
(La Valse; & Delibes & J. Strauss) (♯ Cap.P 8294)

— ORCH. VERSION 1912 (for *Adelaide* ballet)

Suisse Romande—Ansermet ♯ **D.LXT 2821**
(Tombeau de Couperin) (♯ Lon.LL 795)

Champs-Élysées Th.—Branco ♯ **LT.DTL 93007**
(Boléro)
(Alborada del gracioso & Pavane . . . on ♯ Sel.LA 1055)
(idem, & La Valse, Boléro, on ♯ West.WL 5297)

Residentie—v. Otterloo ♯ **Phi.A 00714R**
(Pavane, & Falla)

French Nat.—Cluytens ♯ **C.FCX 343**
(Ma Mère l'Oye, Menuet antique & Pavane)

☆ San Francisco Sym.—Monteux (♯ Cam.CAL 156:
                                       ♭ CAE 216)

II. CHAMBER MUSIC

Berceuse sur le nom de Fauré vln. & pf. 1922

Z. Francescatti & A. Balsam ♯ **AmC.ML 5058**
(below)

☆ J. Martzy & J. Antonietti (in ♯ Pol. 16017)

Introduction & Allegro, G flat major 1906
(Septet) hp., fl., cl. & str. qtt.

M. Flour & Inst. Ens.—Pensis ♯ **FestF.FLD 25**
(Damase & Donatoni)

☆ A. Stockton, etc. & Hollywood Qtt. ♯ DCap.CTL 7096
(Debussy, Schoenberg) (♯ Cap.P 8304)
(Debussy only on ♯ ACap.CLL 038)

☆ P. Jamet & Fr. Radio Ens.—Capdevielle
                                 ♯ LT.MEL 94002
(Poèmes de Mallarmé) (V♯ Sel.LPP 8632)

☆ J. Cockerill, A. Gleghorn, R. Kell, J. Pougnet, D. Martin,
   F. Riddle, J. Whitehead ♯ AmC.RL 3055
(Debussy)

☆ E. Vito & Ens. (♯ Cum.CS 192)

Pièce en forme de habanera 1907

— ARR. VLN. & PF. Catherine

A. Grumiaux & P. Ulanowsky ♯ **Bo.B 203**
(below, Debussy, Bartók)

G. Jarry & A. Collard in ♯ **C.FCX 222**
(Kreisler, Falla, Mozart, etc.)

J. Heifetz & M. Kaye in ♯ **B.AXL 2017**
(in ▽ ♯ AmD.DL 5214 & ♯ DL 9780; ArgOd.LTC 8503;
                                       D.AU 243086)

Z. Francescatti & A. Balsam ♯ **AmC.ML 5058**
(above & below)

☆ Y. Menuhin & A. Baller[1] (in ♯ Vic.LM 1742)
   J. Martzy & J. Antonietti (in ♯ Pol. 16017)
   E. Morini (♭ Cam.CAE 180: in ♯ CAL 207)

— ARR. 2 PFS.
   E. Bartlett & R. Robertson (in ♯ MGM.E 3150)

— ARR. VLC. & PF.
J. Starker & L. Pommers ♯ **Nix.PLP 708**
(Debussy, Fauré, etc.) (♯ Per.SPL 708)

A. Janigro & E. Bagnoli in ♯ **West.WN 18004**
(Popper, Chopin, Falla, etc.)

☆ P. Fournier & E. Lush (in ♯ Vic.LHMV 1043:
                                       ♭ set WHMV 1043)

— ARR. FL., OB., CL., HRN. & BSN.
   Chicago Sym. Wind Ens. (in ♯ Aphe.AP 16)

Quartet, Strings, F major 1903

Loewenguth Qtt. ♯ **HP.DG 16073**

Curtis Qtt. *(Debussy)* ♯ **West.WN 18049**

Champeil Qtt. *(Trio)* (? n.v.) ♯ **CFD. 32**

Wagner Assoc. Qtt. ♯ **ArgOd.LDC 516**

Parrenin Qtt. ♯ **Eko.LM 2**
(Debussy on ♯ Pac.LDPF 48)

☆ Budapest Qtt. (2ss) ♯ EPhi.ABR 4002
(Debussy on ♯ AmC.ML 4668) (♯ Phi.A 01606R)

☆ Pascal Qtt. (Clc. 6192)
   Paganini Qtt. (♯ ItV.A10R 0008)

— FOR PRACTICE: recorded with one instrument missing in
   turn ♯ **CEd.MMO 41/4**

---

[1] This is the Tokyo recording. This pressing also stated to be acc. G. Moore & recorded in England .

Sonata, vln. & pf. 1927
Z. Francescatti & A. Balsam   **♯ AmC.ML 5058**
(*above & below*)
O. Renardy & E. List   **♯ Rem. 199-148**
(*Franck*)   (♯ *Cum.CR 285*)
R-G. Montbrun & G. Joy   **JpV.SD 3081/2**
(4ss)   (set JAS 250)
J. Gauthier & Y. Lefébure   (n.v.)
     V♯ CdM.LDY 8115
R. Druian & J. Simms   **♯ Mer.MG 80000**
(*Bartók*)

Sonata, vln. & vlc. 1920-2
(*Pour le Tombeau de Debussy*)
☆ O. Shumsky & B. Greenhouse (♯ Clc. 6192)

Trio, A minor   pf., vln., vlc.   1914
L. Descaves, J. & E. Pasquier   **♯ DDP.DP 43-1**
(*Roussel*)   (♯ HS.HSL 149)
L. Oborin, D. Oistrakh, S. Knushevitsky
     ♯ Mon.MWL 367
(*Babadzhanyan*)   (2ss, ♯ *USSR.D 2165/6*)
C. Helffer, D. Erlih & R. Albin   **♯ CFD. 32**
(*Quartet*)
☆ Alma Trio   (*Stravinsky*)   ♯ Allo. 3091
☆ Albeneri Trio (♯ Clc. 6259)
   A. Rubinstein, J. Heifetz, G. Piatigorsky
     (♯ G.QALP 10029)

Tzigane   vln. & pf. or orch.   1924
C. Ferras & Belgian Nat.—Sebastian
     ♯ D.LXT 2827
(*Honegger & Chausson*) (♯ *D.BAT 133071*; ♯ *Lon.LL 762*)
J. Heifetz & Los Angeles Phil.—Wallenstein
     ♯ Vic.LM 1832
(*Sinding & Tchaikovsky*)   (♯ *ItV.A12R 0153*)
I. Bezrodny & S. Wakman   ♭ *Phi.N 402049E*
(*Smetana*)
Z. Francescatti & A. Balsam (pf.)
(*above*)   **♯ AmC.ML 5058**
A. Grumiaux & P. Ulanowsky (pf.)   **♯ Bo.B 203**
(*above, Bartók, Debussy*)
A. Grumiaux & Lamoureux—Fournet
     ♯ Phi.A 00228L
(*Chausson & Lalo*)   (♯ Epic.LC 3082)
B. Gimpel & A. Kotowska (pf.) ♮ *G.JOX 7036/7*
(3ss—*Sibelius: Romance, Op. 78, No. 2*)   (TK 5/6)
E. Lockhart & L.S.O.—Fistoulari
     ♯ MGM.E 3041
(*Chausson, Milhaud, Honegger*)
E. Röhn & Hamburg State Phil.—Martin
(*Schubert*)   **♯ T.TW 30032**
☆ G. & J. Neveu   (*Chausson & Debussy*) ♯ Angel. 35128
Anon. Soloist & Berlin Sym.—Rubahn (♯ Roy. 1458)

III. ORCHESTRAL

Boléro   1927
Philharmonia—Kletzki   **♯ C.CX 1164**
(*Tchaikovsky & Smetana*)
Paris Cons.—Ansermet   **♯ D.LXT 5004**
(*La Valse, Dukas, Honegger*)   (♯ Lon.LL 1156)
French Nat.—Cluytens   **♯ C.C 1034**
(*Tombeau de Couperin*)   (♯ QC 5022: FCX 214)
(*idem & Pavane . . .*, on ♯ C.QCX 10107; Angel. 35102)
     (also on ♭ G.7ERL 1035)
Champs-Élysées Th.—Branco   **♯ LT.DTL 93007**
(*Valses nobles et sentimentales*)
(*idem, La Valse, Alborada, Pavane*, on ♯ West.WL 5297)
(*La Valse* on ♯ Sel.LA 1054)
French Radio Sym.—Leibowitz
     ♯ E. & AmVox.PL 8150
(*Rapsodie espagnole, La Valse, etc.*) (♭ *AmVox.VIP 45530*;
     in ♯ *AFest.CFR 12-509*)
Detroit Sym.—Paray   **♯ Mer.MG 50020**
(*Rimsky*)   (♯ FMer.MLP 7509)
Philadelphia—Ormandy   **♯ AmC.AL 51**
(*La Valse*) (& in ♯ AmC.ML 4983: ♭ A 1869;
     ♯ Phi.S 06604R)

Berlin Radio—Rother   **♯ Ura.RS 5-1**
(*La Valse*)   (♭ *UREP 57 & UREP set 59*)
(*Daphnis & Chloë Suite 2, & La Valse* on ♯ RS 7-28,
     & ♯ 7151)
☆ Belgian Radio—André   **♯ DT.LGM 65022**
(*Falla*)   (♯ T.LB 6058)
☆ French Nat. Radio—Kletzki   **♯ AmC.RL 3058**
(*Daphnis & Chloë Suite 2*)
☆ Lamoureux—Ravel   **♯ Pol. 540008**
(*Chansons madécasses*)
Orch.—Bauer (♯ MTW. 16; ACC.MP 25)
Leningrad Phil.—Mravinsky (USSR. 022864/7:
     ♯ D 01503)
A. Sciascia Orch. (in ♯ Fnt.LP 305)
☆ Boston Sym.—Koussevitzky (♯ G.WALP 1003:
   QALP 10020: VALP 528; ♭ BrzV. 86-0007/8; also,
     o.v., ♯ Cam.CAL 161)
Robin Hood Dell—Kostelanetz (♭ AmC.A 1642)
Nat. Op. Orch. (♯ Var. 6966; ♭ Roy.EP 151)
E.I.A.R. Sym.—Ferrero (♭ Cet. EPO 0304)
... **Abridged**
Boston Pops—Fiedler (in ♯ Vic.LM 1879; ♭ ERA 179;
   ♭ ItV.A72R 0020; ♭ FV.A 95201; excerpt only
     G.B 10810; Vic. 10-4217; ♭ 49-4217)
— **ARR. 2 PFS.**
☆ A. Whittemore & J. Lowe   **♯ Vic.LRM 7009**
(*La Valse*)   (♭ set ERB 7009)
— **ARR. BAND**
U.S Military Acad. Band—Resta (in ♯ PFCM.CB 177)

CONCERTOS

G major, pf. & orch.   1931
J. Blancard & Suisse Romande—Ansermet
     ♯ D.LXT 2816
(*below*)   (♯ Lon.LL 797)
J. Doyen & Lamoureux—Fournet
     ♯ Phi.A 00246L
(*below*)   (♯ Epic.LC 3123)
V. Perlemuter & Concerts Colonne
   —Horenstein   in ♯ **AmVox. set DL 153**
(on s. 3 of Pf. Collection set with *Menuet antique & below*)
(*Concerto, left-hand*, only on ♯ PaV.PL 9220)
N. Henriot & Orch.—Scherman
     ♯ MApp.MAR 5424
(*Analysis of Concerto*)
☆ M. Long & Paris Cons.—Tzipine   ♯ Angel. 35013
(*Fauré: Ballade*)
☆ L. Bernstein & Philharmonia   **♯ Cam.CAL 214**
(*Bernstein & Copland*)

D major, pf. (left hand) & orch.   1931
J. Blancard & Suisse Romande—Ansermet
     ♯ D.LXT 2816
(*above*) (n.v.)   (♯ Lon.LL 797)
J. Doyen & Lamoureux—Fournet
     ♯ Phi.A 00246L
(*above*)   (♯ Epic.LC 3123)
V. Perlemuter & Concerts Colonne—Horenstein
     in ♯ **AmVox. set DL 153**
(on s. 4 of Pf. Collection set with *Pavane . . . & above*)
(*Concerto, G major* only, on PaV.PL 9220)
☆ R. Casadesus & Philadelphia—Ormandy   ♯ C.C 1023
(*Rapsodie espagnole*)   (♯ QC 5011: FC 1032)
   A. Sandford & Hastings Sym.—Tubbs   ♯ Allo. 3109
(*Alborada del gracioso*)

Ma Mère L'Oye: SEE Section I, Piano

Menuet antique (orig. pf.)[1]   orch.   1895
Paris Cons.—Fournet   in ♯ **Phi.A 00160L**
(*below & Debussy*)   (♯ Epic.LC 3048)
(*Chabrier: España* on ♭ Phi.A 400001E)
French Nat. Radio—Cluytens   **♯ C.FCX 343**
(*Ma Mère l'Oye, Pavane, Valses nobles . . .*)
Pavane pour une infante défunte: SEE Section I, Piano

Rapsodie espagnole   1907
Philharmonia—Karajan   **♯ C.CX 1099**
(*Debussy*)   (♯ FCX 298: QCX 10059; Angel. 35081)
Champs-Élysées Th.—Inghelbrecht
     ♯ Sel. 320.C.088
(*Barque sur l'océan & Ma Mère l'Oye*)
Detroit Sym.—Paray   **♯ Mer.MG 50056**
(*Chabrier & Ibert*)

           (*continued on next page*)

---

[1] For orig. pf. version *see* Collections, *above.*

Rapsodie espagnole (*continued*)

Paris Cons.—Fournet ♯ **Phi.A 00160L**
(*above & Debussy*) (♯ Epic.LC 3048)
French Radio Sym.—Leibowitz
♯ **E. & AmVox.PL 8150**
(*Boléro, La Valse, etc.*) (♯ AFest.CFR 12-509)
Czech Phil.—Silvestri ♯ **Sup.LPV 210**
(*Debussy: La Mer*) (♯ U. 5198G)
Berlin Sym.—Rubahn ♯ **Roy. 1458**
(*Tzigane & La Valse*)
☆ Boston Sym.—Münch ♯ **G.ALP 1245**
(*below*) (in ♯ *Vic.LRM 7016:* ♭ set *ERB 7016*)
☆ Philadelphia—Ormandy ♯ *C.C 1023*
(*Concerto, pf. left hand*) (♯ QC 5011: FC 1032)
☆ Cleveland Sym.—Rodzinski ♯ **AmC.ML 4884**
(*Daphnis et Chloë; & R. Strauss*)
☆ Philadelphia—Stokowski (in ♯ Cam.CAL 118)

... **Habanera** only
Hollywood Bowl—Dragon (in ♯ Cap.P 8314:
♭ set *FAP 8314*)

(**La**) **Valse** Poème chorégraphique 1920
Philharmonia—Markevitch ♯ **C.CX 1049**
(*Dukas, Falla, Prokofiev*) (♯ FCX 203: QCX 1015;
Angel. 35008)
French Radio Sym.—Leibowitz
♯ **E. & AmVox.PL 8150**
(*Boléro, Rapsodie espagnole, etc.*) (♭ AmVox.VIP 45460;
♯ AFest.CFR 12-509)
Boston Sym.—Münch ♯ **G.ALP 1245**
(*Rapsodie espagnole, Berlioz, Lalo, Saint-Saëns*)
(in ♯ *Vic.LRM 7016:* ♭ set *ERB 7016* & in ♯ set LM 6113;
♯ ItV.A12R 0130; ♯ FV.A 630217)
Champs-Élysées Th.—Branco ♯ *LT.EL 93008*
(*Alborada & Pavane . . .*) (*Boléro* in ♯ *Sel.LA 1054*)
(*and with same items & Valse nobles,* ♯ West.WL 5297)
Detroit Sym.—Paray ♯ **Mer.MG 50029**
(*Fauré & Franck*)
Philadelphia—Ormandy ♯ *AmC.AL 51*
(*Boléro*) (& in ♯ AmC.ML 4983) (♯ Phi.S 06604R)
Leipzig Radio—Borsamsky ♯ *Ura.RS 5-1*
(*Boléro*) (♭ UREP 58 & ♭ set 59)
(*Daphnis & Chloë Suite 2 & Boléro* on ♯ RS 7-28 & ♯ 7151)
Berlin Sym.—Rubahn ♯ **Roy. 1458**
(*Tzigane & Rapsodie espagnole*)
☆ Paris Cons.—Ansermet ♯ **D.LXT 2896**
(*Moussorgsky*) (♯ Lon.LL 956)
(*Boléro; & Dukas & Honegger* on ♯ D.LXT 5004;
♯ Lon.LL 1156)
☆ N.Y.P.S.O.—Barbirolli (in ♯ AmC.RL 3046)
San Francisco—Monteux (♭ Cam.CAE 130 & in
♯ set CFL 102)

— ARR. PF. Ravel
L. Pennario ♯ **DCap.CTL 7087**
(*Valses nobles et sentimentales, Delibes, & J. Strauss*)
(♯ Cap.P 8294)
— ARR. 2 PFS.
☆ A. Whittemore & J. Lowe (♯ Vic.LRM 7009:
♭ set *ERB 7009*)

IV. STAGE WORKS

DAPHNIS ET CHLOË Ballet 1909-12
orch. & cho.
COMPLETE RECORDINGS
Geneva Motet Cho. & Suisse Romande
—Ansermet ♯ **D.LXT 2775**
(♯ Lon.LL 693)
French Nat. Radio Cho. & Champs-Élysées
Th. Orch.—Inghelbrecht ♯ **LT.DTL 93048**
(♯ Sel. 320.C.015)
Macalester College Cho. & Minneapolis Sym.
—Dorati ♯ **Mer.MG 50048**
New England Cons. Cho. & Boston Sym.
—Münch ♯ **Vic.LM 1893**
(♯ FV.A 630294)
Symphonic Suites Nos. 1 & 2
M. Briclot Cho. & French Nat. Radio Orch.
—Cluytens ♯ **C.CX 1134**
(*Alborada del gracioso*) (♯ C.FCX 215; Angel. 35054)
Netherlands Cha. Cho. & Residentie
Orch.—Otterloo ♯ *EPhi.ABR 4019*
(♯ Phi.A 00665R)

Suite No. 1
☆ San Francisco Sym. & Cho.—Monteux (♯ Cam.CAL 156)
Suite No. 2
Philharmonia—Markevitch ♯ **C.CX 1197**
(*Satie, Debussy, Weber*) (♯ FCX 357; Angel. 35151,
in set 3518)
Leipzig Radio—Borsamsky ♯ **Ura.RS 7-28**
(*La Valse & Boléro*) (♯ Ura. 7151)
(*Delibes on* ♯ *MTW.* 536)
Dresden State Sym.—Schreiber ♯ **Roy. 1468**
(*Ma Mère l'Oye*)
☆ N.B.C. Sym.—Toscanini ♯ **G.ALP 1070**
(*Debussy*) (♯ FALP 160: QALP 10046; ♯ FV.A 630219;
ItV.A12R 0150, d.c.; & in ♯ Vic. set LM 6113)
☆ Cleveland Sym.—Rodzinski ♯ **AmC.ML 4884**
(*Rapsodie espagnole; & R. Strauss*)
☆ Boston Sym.—Koussevitzky (♯ Cam.CAL 156 &
in ♯ set CFL 102)
French Nat. Radio—Kletzki (♯ AmC.RL 3058)

(**L'**) **ENFANT ET LES SORTILÈGES**
Opera-Ballet 2 Acts 1925
COMPLETE RECORDINGS
F. Wend (S), S. Danco (S), P. Mollet (B),
M. L. de Montmollin (M-S), G. Touraine (S),
A. Migliette (S), J. Bise (S), G. Bobillier (S),
L. Lovano (Bs), H. Cuénod (T), Geneva Motet
Cho. & Suisse Romande Orch.—Ansermet
♯ **D.LXT 5019**
(♯ Lon.LL 1180)
☆ Soloists & French Radio Cho. & Nat. Orch.
(♯ C.FCX 189)

(**L'**) **HEURE ESPAGNOLE** Opera 1 Act 1911
COMPLETE RECORDINGS

Casts		Set D	Set C
Concepción	...	S. Danco (S)	D. Duval (S)
Gonzalve	...	P. Derenne (T)	J. Giraudeau (T)
Torquemada	...	M. Hamel (T)	R. Hérent (T)
Ramiro	...	H. Rehfuss (B)	J. Vieuille (B)
Don Gomez	...	A. Vessières (Bs)	C. Clavensy (Bs)

Set D with Suisse Romande Orch.—Ansermet
♯ **D.LXT 2828**
(♯ Lon.LL 796)
Set C with Opéra-Comique Orch.—Cluytens
♯ **C.CX 1076**
(♯ FCX/QCX 172; Angel. 35018)
☆ J. Linda (S), A. Dran (T), etc. Paris Radio Sym.
—Leibowitz (♯ AFest.CFR 12-629)

V. SONGS & PART SONGS

(**3**) **Chansons** (Ravel) S, A, T, B 1915
Paris Vocal Ens.—Jouve **V**♯ *Sel.LAP 1034*
(*Debussy*)
☆ Couraud Ens. (**V**♯ *DFr.EX 17004*)
... **No. 2, Ronde** — SOLO VOICE & PF. VERSION
M. Sénéchal (T), J. Bonneau (pf.)
in ♯ *Phi.N 00681R*
(*Roussel, Gounod, Massenet, etc.*)
... **No. 3, Trois beaux oiseaux de Paradis**
Petits Chanteurs à la Croix de Bois—Maillet
(*Delvincourt: Lavandière*) ♭ *Pat.D 116*
M. Flowers (S) & Hufstader Singers
in ♯ *SOT. 1092*

(**3**) **Chansons madécasses** (Parny) voice, fl., vlc. pf.
1926
J. Jansen (B), J-P. Rampal, M. Gendron,
J. Bonneau ♯ **D.LXT 2774**
(*Debussy & Chabrier*) (♯ Lon.LL 644)
J-C. Benoît (B), F. Dufrène, R. Rochut (fls.),
G. & M. Fallot ♯ *Sel. 270.C.042*
(*Histoires naturelles*)
☆ M. Grey (S) & Ens.—Ravel (*Boléro*) ♭ *Pol. 540008*
☆ J. Tourel (M-S) & Ens. (♯ Phi.S 06610R)

(**4**) **Chants populaires** 1910
☆ C. Panzéra (B), M. Panzéra (pf.) (in ♯ Clc. 6260)
M. Singher (B), P. Ulanowsky (pf.) (in ♯ Clc. 6180)
... **No. 4, Hébraïque** (**Méjerke**) only
☆ P. Bernac (B), F. Poulenc (pf.) in ♯ C.CX 1119

♯ = Long-playing, 33⅓ r.p.m.   ♭ = 45 r.p.m.   ♮ = Auto. couplings, 78 r.p.m.

Don Quichotte à Dulcinée (Morand) 1932
　A. Schiøtz (T), H. D. Koppel (pf.) **G.DB 10511**
　(1½ss—*Jeanneton*)
　A. Estanislao (B), H. Salquin (pf.) ‡ *D.LW 5192*
　(*Falla*)　　　　　　　　　　　　　(‡ *Lon.LD 9180*)
　☆ G. Souzay (B) & Paris Cons.—Lindenberg
　　　　　　　　　　　　　　　　　‡ *D.LW 5078*
　(*Debussy*)　　　　　　　　　　　(‡ *Lon.LD 9091*)

(2) Épigrammes (Marot) 1898
1. D'Anne, jouant de l'épinette
2. D'Anne, qui me jecta de la neige
　▽ M. Singher (B), P. Ulanowsky (pf.)　‡ **CHS.CHS 1124**
　(*above & below*)　　　　　　　　　　(‡ Clc. 6180)

... **No. 1,** only
　Y. Tessier (T) & pf.　　　　　in ‡ **CND. 9**
　(† La Musique et la Poésie)

Histoires naturelles (Renard) 1906
　J-C. Benoît (B), J. Lemaire (pf.)
　(2ss)　　　　　　　　　　　V‡ *Sel.LAP 1016*
　(*Chansons madécasses on* ‡ *270.C.042*)
　☆ G. Souzay (B), J. Bonneau (pf.) ‡ *D.LX 3149*
　(*Fauré*)　　　　　　　　　　　　(‡ *Lon.LD 9203*)
　☆ P. Bernac (B), F. Poulenc (pf.)　in ‡ *C.CX 1119*
　☆ M. Singher (B), P. Ulanowsky (pf.) (‡ Clc. 6180)

(2) Mélodies hébraïques voice & pf. or orch. 1914
1. Kaddisch　　　　　　2. L'énigme éternelle
　S. Danco (S) & Suisse Romande—Ansermet
　　　　　　　　　　　　　　　　‡ *D.LXT 5031*
　(*below*)　　　　　　　　　　　　(‡ *Lon.LL 1196*)
　☆ P. Bernac (B), F. Poulenc (pf.)　in ‡ *C.CX 1119*

... **No. 1** only — ARR. VLN. & PF.
　Y. Menuhin & G. Moore　in ‡ **Vic.LHMV 22**
　Z. Francescatti & A. Balsam in ‡ **AmC.ML 5058**

(5) Mélodies populaires grecques (Calvocoressi)
　　　　　　　　　　　　　　　　　　　1907
　G. Sciutti (S), J. Bonneau (pf.)　‡ *Phi.A 76705R*
　(*Debussy, Fauré*)
　☆ C. Panzéra (B), M. Panzéra (pf.) (in ‡ Clc. 6260)

(3) Poèmes de Mallarmé S. & cha. ens. 1913
1. Soupir　　　　　　2. Placet futile
3. Surgi de la croupe et du bond
　S. Danco & Suisse Romande—Ansermet
　　　　　　　　　　　　　　　　‡ *D.LXT 5031*
　(*above & below*)　　　　　　　　(‡ *Lon.LL 1196*)
　☆ I. Kolassi (M-S) & Ens.　　　　‡ *LT.MEL 94002*
　(*Intro. & Allegro*)　　　　　　　(V‡ *Sel.LPP 8632*)

Ronsard à son âme 1924
　(?) Y. Tessier (T) & pf.　　　　in ‡ **CND. 9**
　(† La Musique et la Poésie)

Sainte (Mallarmé) 1896
　J. Harsanyi (S), O. Herz (pf.)　in ‡ **Per.SPL 581**

Shéhérazade (Klingsor) with orch. 1903
　S. Danco (S) & Suisse Romande—Ansermet
　　　　　　　　　　　　　　　　‡ **D.LXT 5031**
　(*above*)　　　　　　　　　　　　(‡ *Lon.LL 1196*)
　☆ J. Tourel (M-S) & C.B.S. Orch.—Bernstein
　(*Moussorgsky*)　　　　　　　　　‡ *C.CX 1029*

Jeanneton (Folk Song arr.)
　A. Schiøtz (T), H. D. Koppel (pf.)　**G.DB 10511**
　(½s—*Don Quichotte à Dulcinée*)

RAVENSCROFT, Thomas (*c.* 1590-*c.* 1633)

　　SEE: † ENGLISH MADRIGALS
　　　　　† ELIZABETHAN SONGBAG FOR YOUNG PEOPLE

RAWSTHORNE, Alan (b. 1905)

(A) GARLAND FOR THE QUEEN
　(with Bliss, Bax, etc.) 1953
... **Canzonet** (MacNeice)
　Cambridge Univ. Madrigal Soc.—Ord
　　　　　　　　　　　　in † ‡ **C.CX 1063**

Practical Cats narr. & orch. (Eliot) 1954
　R. Donat & Philharmonia—Rawsthorne
　　　　　　　　　　　　　　‡ *C.C 1044*[1]
　(2ss)　　　　　　　　　　　(‡ *Angel.* 30002)

Symphonic Studies orch. 1938
　☆ Philharmonia—Lambert (*Tippett*)　‡ **G.CLP 1056**

Theme and Variations Str. qtt. 1939
　☆ Hirsch Qtt. (‡ Argo.RG 3)

READ, Gardner (b. 1913)

(The) Golden Harp, Op. 93 1952
　Peabody High School Cho.—Shute
　　　　　　　　　　　　in ‡ **PFCM.CB 160**
　(*Saeverud, Willan, Villa-Lobos, etc.*)

Toccata giocosa orch. f.p. 1954
　Louisville—Whitney　　　　　　‡ **LO. 5**
　(*Ibert & Luening*)

REDFORD, John (1485-1547)

　　SEE: † CORONATION OF QUEEN ELIZABETH II
　　　　　† ENGLISH CHURCH MUSIC, VOL. III
　　　　　† HISTORY OF MUSIC IN SOUND (30)

REED, H. Owen (b. 1910)

(La) Fiesta Mexicana 1948
　Eastmann Sym. Wind Ens.—Fennell
　　　　　　　　　　　　　　‡ **Mer.MG 40011**
　(*Mennin, Persichetti, Hanson, Thomson*)

REESEN, Emil (b. 1887)

Himmerland—Danish Rhapsody orch.
　Danish Radio—Reesen　　　　　‡ *D.LX 3125*
　(*Grieg*)　　　　　　　　　　　　(‡ *Lon.LS 849*)

SONG: Two who love one another (Stuckenberg)
　(*To, som elsker hinanden*)
　E. Sigfuss (A) & Orch.　　　　　*Tono.K 8070*
　(*Henriques: There must be two*)
　▽ There have been other songs in the Danish catalogues.

REFICE, Licinio (1885-1955)

Ave Maria
　☆ C. Muzio (S) & Orch. (in ‡ AmC.ML 4634)

Lilium Crucis Oratorio
　Narrator, 2 Female voices, cho., orch. & org. (Mucci)
　L. Vincenti, M. T. Ferrero, E. da Venezia (Narr.)
　Naples Scarlatti Cho. & Orch.—Refice
　(3ss—*below*)　　　　　　　　‡ **Csm.CLPS 1042/3**

Ombra di nube (Mucci)
　☆ C. Muzio (S) & Orch. (in ‡ AmC.ML 4634)

(La) SAMARITANA Oratorio 1928
... **Prelude**
TRITTICO FRANCESCANO Sym. poem
　cho. & orch. 1926
... Le Stimmate (Sym. Interlude) orch.
　Naples Scarlatti—Refice　‡ **Csm.CLPS 1042/3**
　(*above*)

REGAMEY, Constantin (b. 1907)

Quartet No. 1, strings 1948
　Winterthur Qtt.　　　　　　　‡ **D.LXT 2849**
　(*Honegger & Moeschinger*)　　(‡ *Lon.LL 893*)

---

[1] Announced but not yet issued.

REGER, Max (1873-1916)

(53) CHORALE PRELUDES, Op. 67 organ
COLLECTION
No. 12, Gott des Himmels
No. 14, Herzlich tut mich verlangen
No. 24, Lobe den Herren
No. 33, O Welt, ich muss dich lassen
No. 35, Seelenbräutigam
No. 39, Vater unser im Himmelreich
No. 44, Was Gott tut, das ist wohlgetan
No. 45, Wer nur den lieben Gott lässt walten
No. 51, Jesus ist kommen
    L. Altman   # ML. 7054
  (Pachelbel) [Org. of Temple Emmanuel, San Francisco]

Ein' feste Burg, Op. 67, No. 6
Ave Maria, Op. 80b, No. 5   org.
    J. Harms   in # Uni.UN 1004
  (Karg-Elert, Bach, Raasted, Vierne, etc.)

Fantasia and Fugue, D minor, Op. 135b   org.
    R. Noehren (Bach)   # Allo. 3044

Fantasia & Fugue on B.A.C.H., Op. 46
Introduction & Passacaglia, D minor no Op. no. org.
    G. Ramin   # Pol. 16089
  [Beckerath org., Hamburg]

Introduction, Passacaglia & Fugue, B minor, Op. 96
  2 pfs.
    P. Luboshutz & G. Nemenoff   # Rem. 199-143
  (Weber, Chopin, etc.)

Introduction, Passacaglia & Fugue, E minor, Op.127   org.
    J. Perceval   # ArgOd.LDC 501
  (Bach: Prelude & Fugue, B minor) (ArgOd. 66043:
                      ♭ BSOAE 4507)

Prelude, D minor, Op. 65, No. 7   org.
    P. Kee   in # G.DLP 1053
  († "Baroque" Organ Music)

Quintet, A major, Op. 146   cl. & str.
    G. Coutelen & Winterthur Qtt.
  (2ss)   # CHS.CHS 1244
                 (o.n. # CHS.H 7)

(4) Sonatinas, Op. 89   pf.
1. E minor   3. F major
2. D major   4. A minor
    C. de Groot   # Phi.N 00264L

SONGS & PART SONGS
Abendgang im Lenz, Op. 111b, No. 2 (L. Rafael)
  4-pt. song
  Vienna Boys' Cho.—Kühbacher
              in # EPhi.NBR 6024
  (Mendelssohn, Buxtehude, Brahms, etc.) (# Phi.N 00726R)

Im Himmelreich ein Haus steht, Op. 111b, No. 1
  (W. Vesper) 4-pt. song
  Vienna Boys' Cho.—Kühbacher
              in # EPhi.NBR 6024
  (above)   (# Phi.N 00726R)

Mariä Wiegenlied, Op. 76, No. 52 (Boelitz)
  R. Hayes (T), R. Boardman (pf.)
              in # Van.VRS 7016
  S. Schöner (S), F. Schröder (pf.)   Eta. 120204
  .(Gerster: Die heilige Familie)
    T. Fridén (Tr, Swed) (Cus. 32)
  ☆ I. Seefried (S), E. Werba (pf.) (in # AmD.DL 7545)
  E. Grümmer (S), H. Diez (pf.) (♭ G.7RW 507)
  C. Muzio (S, Ital) (in # AmC.ML 4634)

— ARR. CHO.
  Regensburg Cath.—Schrems   T.A 11597
  (Mozart: Wiegenlied)   (FV.790.TV. 169; ♭ T.U 45597)
  Stockholm Folk School Children's Cho.
    —Hammerström   Symf.B 5621
  (Sibelius: Christmas Song)
  St. Hedwig's Cath. Boys' Cho.—Forster
                       G.EG 7865
  (Mozart: Wiegenlied)   (HE 3148)
  S. Saaby Cho. (in # AmD.DL 8204)

— ARR. VLC. & PF.
  K. Reher & M. di Tullio (in # Layos.CB 594/5)

Schelmenliedchen, Op. 76, No. 36 (Schellenberg)
Waldeinsamkeit, Op. 76, No. 3 (Trad.)
  G. Pechner (B)   in # Roy. 1558
  (Liszt, Brahms, Marx, etc.)

Zum Schlafen, Op. 76, No. 59 (Schellenberg)
  ☆ E. Grümmer (S), H. Diez (pf.) (♭ G.7RW 507)

SUITES, Unacc. vlc., Op. 131c
No. 1, G major
  ☆ E. Feuermann (Beethoven)   # AmC.ML 4678

Weihnachten, Op. 145, No. 3 org. 1914
  E. Linzel   in # Moll.E4QP 7231
  (Vierne, Reger, Widor, Dandrieu, etc.)
  [Org. of George Washington Shrine, Alexandria, Va.]

Variations & Fugue on a theme of Hiller, Op. 100
  orch.
  Vienna Philharmonia—Adler   # CA.LPA 1039
                      (# SPA. 51)
  Hamburg State Phil.—Keilberth
                     # DT.LGX 66049
                    (# T.LE 6540)
  ☆ Berlin Phil.—v. Kempen   # Pol. 18074

REGNARD, Franciscus (fl. XVIth Cent.)
SEE: † CHANSONS & MOTETS

REICHA, Antonín (1770-1836)

Overture, C major, Op. 24
  Prague Cha. Orch.—Klíma   # Sup.LPM 170
  (Berlioz)   (# U. 5178C)

QUINTETS, fl., ob., cl., hrn., bsn.
E flat major, Op. 88, No. 2 ("No. 2")
D major, Op. 91, No. 3 ("No. 9")
  French Wind Quintet   # LOL.OL 50019
                    (# OL.LD 65)

REICHE, Johann Gottfried (1667-1734)
SEE: † GOLDEN AGE OF BRASS

RENÉ, N. (fl. XVIth Cent.)
SEE: † ANTHOLOGIE SONORE

RESINARIUS, Balthasar (fl. XVIth Cent.)
SEE: † MOTETS ON LUTHER TEXTS

RESPIGHI, Ottorino (1879-1936)

Concerto gregoriano vln. & orch. 1922
  K. Stiehler & Leipzig Radio—Borsamsky
                     # Ura. 7100

Feste Romane Sym. poem orch. 1929
  Minneapolis Sym.—Dorati   # Mer.MG 50046
  (below)   (# FMer.MLP 7534)
  Phil. Prom.—Boult   (2ss)   # West.LAB 7012

Fontane di Roma Sym. poem. orch. 1917
  N.B.C. Sym.—Toscanini   # G.ALP 1101
  (Pini di Roma) (# Vic.LM 1768: ♭ set WDM 1768;
             # ItV.A12R 0006; G.FALP 266)
  Vienna State Op.—Quadri   # Nix.WLP 5167
  (Pini di Roma)   (# West.WL 5167; Sel.LA 1063)
  Minneapolis Sym.—Dorati   # EMer.MG 50011
  (Pini di Roma)   (# FMer.MLP 7513)
  Berlin Sym.—Rubahn   # Roy. 1477
  (below)
  ☆ Augusteo (St. Cecilia)—Sabata (# G.QALP 178:
                      ♭ 7ERL 1048)

= Long-playing, 33⅓ r.p.m.   ♭ = 45 r.p.m.   ♮ = Auto. couplings, 78 r.p.m.

Impressioni Brasiliane orch. 1927
Concerts Colonne—Sebastian ♯ *FUra. 5102*
(*Granados*)
(*idem & Chávez on* ♯ Ura. 7144)

Notturno, D flat major pf. 1905
M. Pressler in ♯ **MGM.E 3129**
(*Bartók, Poulenc, Satie, etc.*) (♭ *set X 254*)

(I) Pini di Roma Sym. Poem orch. 1924
N.B.C. Sym.—Toscanini ♯ **G.ALP 1101**
(*Fontane di Roma*) (♯ Vic.LM 1768: ♭ *set WDM 1768:*
♭ *set ERB 58;* ♯ ItV.A12R 0006; ♯ G.FALP 266)
Vienna State Op.—Quadri ♯ **Nix.WLP 5167**
(*Fontane di Roma*) (♯ West.WL 5167; Sel.LA 1063)
Minneapolis Sym.—Dorati ♯ **EMer.MG 50011**
(*Fontane di Roma*) (♯ FMer.MLP 7513)
Berlin Sym.—Rubahn ♯ **Roy. 1477**
(*above*)
Hamburg Philharmonia—H-J. Walther
(4ss) *MSB. 78127/8*
☆ Cincinnati Sym.—Goossens (♯ BB.LBC 1057:
♭ *set WBC 1057*)
... No. 4, I Pini della Via Appia, only — ARR. BAND
Concert Band—Harp (in ♯ Fred. 1)

QUARTETS, Strings
No. 2, 'Quartetto dorico' 1924
La Scala Qtt. ♯ **Ura. 7075**
(*Malipiero & Pick-Mangiagalli*)
Barylli Qtt. ♯ **West.WLE 101**
(*below*)

RE ENZO Opera 3 Acts 1905
Stornellatrice S (ARR. Respighi as song)
☆ V. de los Angeles, G. Moore (pf.) (in ♯ G.ALP 1151:
FALP 327; *ArgV.* 66-0016)
SONGS
E se un giorno tornasse (Pompilj)
☆ V. de los Angeles (S) (*ArgV.* 66-0016)

Nebbie (Negri)
M. Powers (A), F. la Forge (pf.) in ♯ **Atl. 1207**
(*Bach, Handel, Haydn, Wagner, etc.*)
M. Vitale (S), A. Beltrami (pf.) *Cet.AT 0317*
(*Giordani: Caro mio ben*) (in ♯ LPC 55001)

(Il) Tramonto (Shelley) M-S. & Str. qtt. 1918
S. Jurinac (S) & Barylli Qtt. ♯ **West.WLE 101**
(*Quartet*)

Trittico Botticelliano small orch. 1927
Naples Scarlatti Orch.—Caracciolo
(*Gli Uccelli*) ♯ **C.CX 1354**
Berlin Sym.—Rubahn ♯ **Roy. 1485**
(*R. Strauss*)

Vetrate di chiesa orch. 1926
Minneapolis Sym.—Dorati ♯ **Mer.MG 50046**
(*above*) (♯ FMer.MLP 7534)

ARRANGEMENTS FOR ORCHESTRA, etc.
ANTICHE DANZE ED ARIE
SUITE No. 1
1. Molinaro: Il Conte Orlando (Balletto)
2. Galilei: Gagliarda
3. Anon.: Villanella
4. Anon.: Passamezzo e Mascherada
Vienna State Op.—Litschauer ♯ **Van.VRS 447**
(*Petrassi*) (*Gli Uccelli on* ♯ Ama.AVRS 6016)
... No. 3 — ARR. HARP
L. Newell in ♯ **Phi.PH 109**
(*below, Casella & Donizetti*)
SUITE No. 2
1. Caroso: Laura soave (Balletto)
2. Besard: Danza rustica
3. Anon.: Campanae parisienses; & Mersenne: Aria
4. Gianoncelli: Bergamasca
Vienna State Op.—Litschauer ♯ **Nix.PVL 7025**
(*below*) (♯ Van.VRS 433)

SUITE No. 3
1. Anon.: Italiana
2. Besard: Arie di corte
3. Anon.: Siciliana
4. Roncalli: Passacaglia
Berlin Radio Cha.—Lange ♯ **Ura. 7093**
(*Stravinsky*)
... Nos. 1 & 3 only — ARR. HARP
L. Newell (*above*) ♯ **Phi.PH 109**

(La) Boutique fantasque 1919
(Ballet Suite, after Rossini)
Philharmonia—Galliera ♯ **C.S 1009**
(2ss) (♯ FC 1031: QC 5010; Angel. 30001)
Philharmonia—Irving ♯ **G.DLP 1032**
(2ss) (♯ QDLP 6014: FFLP 1045)
(*Gounod, etc. on* ♯ BB.LBC 1080)
R.I.A.S. Sym.—Fricsay ♯ **HP.DG 17054**
☆ Covent Garden—Rignold (♯ Od.MODQ 6237)
L.P.O.—Goossens (♯ Cam.CAL 211 & in set CFL 102)
... Excerpts
International Sym.—Schneiderhahn (in ♯ Mae.OAT 25003)
☆ Royal Phil.—Kurtz (♭ AmC.A 1592)
... Tarantella, Scene (Andante mosso) & Can-Can, only
☆ Covent Garden—Braithwaite (in ♯ P.PMC 1008)
... Tarantella only
Hollywood Bowl—Dragon (in ♯ Cap.P 8314:
♭ *set FAP 8314*)
... abridged, with narration
D. Kaye & Covent Garden Op. Orch. (AmD.K 119:
♭ *1-257*)

Rossiniana orch. 1925 (after Rossini's *Riens*)
Covent Garden—Braithwaite ♯ **MGM.E 3013**
(*Malipiero & Cimarosa*)

(Gli) Uccelli (*The Birds*) 1927
1. Pasquini: Arietta ("Preludio")
2. Gallot: La Colombe ("La colomba")
3. Rameau: La Poule ("La gallina")
4. Anon.: The Nightingale ("L'usignuolo")
5. Pasquini: Toccata ("Il cucù")
Vienna State Op.—Litschauer ♯ **Nix.PVL 7025**
(*Antiche Danze Suite 2*) (♯ Van.VRS 433)
(*Antiche Danze Suite 1 on* ♯ Ama.AVRS 6016)
Naples Scarlatti Orch.—Caracciolo
(*Trittico Botticelliano*) ♯ **C.CX 1354**
☆ Chicago Sym.—Defauw (♯ Cam.CAL 172)

REUBKE, Julius (1834-1858)

Sonata, C minor (on Psalm 94) org.
R. Ellsasser ♯ **P.PMC 1025**
(*Guilmant*) (♯ MGM.E 3078)
[Org. J. H. Hammond Museum, Gloucester, Mass.]
E. P. Biggs[1] ♯ **AmC.ML 4820**
(*Liszt*) [Methuen organ, Methuen, Mass.]
... Finale only
R. Foort ♯ **SOT. 1055**
(*Handel*) (& in ♯ 10545)

REVUELTAS, Silvestre (1899-1940)

Cuauhnahuac orch. 1930
Sensemayá orch. 1938
London Phil. Sym.—Quadri ♯ **Nix.WLP 20000**
(*Chabrier & Mossolov*) (♯ West.LAB 7004)

Janitzio Sym. poem, orch. 1933
Col. Sym.—Kurtz in ♯ **AmC.CL 773**

Ocho por radio cha. ens. c. 1933
Ens.—I. Solomon ♯ **MGM.E 3155**
(*Chavez, Surinach, Villa-Lobos*)

Sensemayá orch. 1938
▽ Sym.—Stokowski **G.DB 6915**
(*Granados*) (Vic. 12-0470: ♭ 49-0882)

[1] Ed. C. Koch.

SONGS
COLLECTIONS
Five Songs of Childhood (Lorca) 1938
Two Songs: Serenade; It is true (Lorca) 1938
The Owl (*El Tecolote*) (Castañeda) 1931
Bull Frogs (*Ranas*) (Castañeda) 1931
    J. Greissle (S, *Eng*), J. Wolman (pf.)   ♯ **SPA. 9**
    (*Ives*)

Five Songs of Childhood (Lorca)
Two Songs (Serenade; It is true) (Lorca)
    C. Puig (T), G. Frid (pf.)   in ♯ *Phi.N 00643R*
    (*Mexican Songs*)

REVUTSKY, Lev Nikolayevich (b. 1889)

Symphony No. 2, E minor, Op. 12   1939
    Ukraine State Sym.—Rakhlin
    (2ss)   ♯ **USSR.D 02193/4**

REYER, Ernest (1823-1909)

SIGURD   Opera, 4 Acts   1884
Et, toi, Freia B Act II
  ☆ A. Endrèze (in ♯ Pat.PCX 5006)
Moi, j'ai gardé mon âme T Act II
  ☆ C. Vezzani (in ♯ Ete. 708)
(Le) Bruit des chants . . . Hilda, Vièrge T Act II
  ☆ P. Franz (in ♯ Ete. 708)
  ⯃ C. Rousselière (*HRS. 1084**)

Au nom du Roi Bs. Act III
  ⯃ M. Journet (in ♯ SBDH.JALP 19*)

REZNIČEK, Emil Nikolaus v. (1860-1945)

DONNA DIANA   Opera 3 Acts   1894
Overture
    Württemberg State—Leitner   ♭ *Pol. 30027*
    (*Pagliacci & Gioielli della Madonna*)   (in ♯ *17001*)
    Leipzig Radio—Dobrindt   *Eta. 120176*
    (*Abu Hassan, Overture*)
    International Sym.—Schneiderhann (in ♯ *Mae.OA 20009*)
    ☆ Belgian Radio—André (in ♯ *T.LS 6031*: ♭ *UE 453922*)
    Philharmonia—Fistoulari (in ♯ *P.PMC 1031*)
    Vienna Phil.—Karajan (♭ *C.SCB 112: SCBQ 3017:*
    SCBW 107)
    Boston Prom.—Fiedler (♭ *Vic.ERA 135*)
    Vienna Radio—Nilius (in ♯ *Vien.LPR 1025*)

RHAW, Georg (1448-1548)

BICINIA   (2-pt. cho. & insts.)[1]
Der Mai tritt herein ø
Herzlich tut mich erfreuen ø
Erfreu sich alles, was da lebt ø
Ich habe heimlich ergeben mich ø
Appenzeller Kuhreien
Hildebrandslied
Ich stund an einem Morgen
Für all ich krön ø
Fröhlichen will ich singen ø
Entlaubet ist der Walde ø
Ach Elselein
    I. Brix-Meinert (descant vla.), F. Conrad (fl.),
    Children's Cho.—E. Bender ♯ **HP.APM 14003**
    (*Praetorius*) [items marked ø also on ♭ *Pol. 37077*]

RHUDYAR, Dane (b. 1895)

Sinfonietta   orch.   1931
    R.I.A.S. Sym.—Perlea   ♯ **Rem. 199-188**
    (*Brant & Glanville-Hicks*)

RHYS-WILLIAMS, Elspeth (b. 1938)

(4) Impressions pf. 1954
    J. Hatto
SONGS: Make much of time (Herrick)
    A morning song (Herrick) 1954
    G. Walls (B), J. Hatto (pf.) V♯ *CA.MPO 5023*

RIADIS, Emilios (1890-1935)

SONGS   (or Folk Song Arrs.)
The Old Bey's Song
The Question
The Gypsy
The Maid and the Hunter
    L. Liotsi (M-S), Z. Vlahopoulou (S), E.
    Nicolaidou (pf.)   ♯ *Phi.N 00744R*
    (*Kalomiris & Folk-Songs*)

RIBERA, Antonius de (fl. 1514-22)
    SEE: † SPANISH MUSIC (*c.* 1500)

RICHARD Coeur de Lion (d. 1199)
    SEE: † ANTHOLOGIE SONORE

RICHMOND, Legh (1772-1827)
    SEE: † SHAKESPEARE SONGS, VOL. III

RICHTER, Ferdinand Tobias (1649-1711)
    SEE: † CLAVECINISTES ALLEMANDS

RICHTER, Franz Xaver (1709-1789)

Quartet, Strings, C major, Op. 5, No. 1
    New Music Qtt.   ♯ **BRS. 915**
    (*Stamitz: Quartet*)

RIEGGER, Wallingford (b. 1885)

New Dance   orch.[2] 1934
    Eastman-Rochester Sym.—Hanson
    ♯ **Mer.MG 40005**
    (*Hovhaness & Cowell*)   (♭ EP 1-5063)
Quintet, Op. 51 fl., ob., cl., bsn., hrn.
    New Art Wind Quintet   in ♯ **CEd. set 2003**
    (*Auric, Tailleferre, etc.*)
Symphony No. 3, Op. 24 1947-8
    Eastman-Rochester Sym.—Hanson
    (*Mennin*)   ♯ **AmC.ML 4902**
Variations, Op. 54 pf. & orch. f.p. 1954
    N. Owen & Louisville—Whitney   ♯ **LO. 3**
    (*Mennin & Toch*)

RIETI, Vittorio (b. 1898)

L'ÉCOLE DES FEMMES Inc. music to Molière
    1936
    In a performance of the play, by Louis Jouvet
    & Company   ♯ **Pat.PCX 5003/5**
    (6ss)   (♯ Harv. RL-F-D1/6)
Introduzione e gioco delle ore orch. f.p. 1954
    Louisville—Whitney   ♯ **LO. 11**
    (*Baron & Malipiero*)
Partita fl., ob., str. qtt. & hpsi. 1945
    Concert Arts Players & S. Marlowe ♯ **Cap.P 8309**
    (*Falla & Surinach*)

---

[1] From *Bicinia ex praestantissimis musicorum monumenta collecta*, 1545.
[2] Originally the finale of Dance Suite, pf. duet & percussion.

2nd Avenue Waltzes 2 pfs. 1942
☆ A. Gold & R. Fizdale (in ♯ *Phi.S 06614R*)

Sonata all' antica hpsi. 1946
S. Marlowe   ♯ **NE. 3**
(*Hovhaness, Lessard, Thomson*)

Suite champêtre 2 pfs. 1948
R. Gold & A. Fizdale ♯ **AmC.ML 4853**
(*Hindemith & Stravinsky*) (in set SL 198)

RIISAGER, Knudåge (b. 1897)

The Coxcomb
A Funny Trumpet
(Nos. 4 & 6 of *6 Pf. pieces*)
At dancing class
A. Dalring   *Pol.X 51601*
(*Henriques & Nielsen*)

DARDUSE Inc. Music to Jensen's play 1937
... Excerpts
I. Schønberg (diction) & E. Nielsen (pf.)
        Pol.HA 70041

Final-Galop orch.
☆ Tivoli—Felumb (♭ *Mer.EP 1-5042*)

FOOLS' PARADISE, Op. 33 Orig. orch. 1936
Ballet, 1942 (*Slaraffenland*)
... **No. 4, Lazy Dog's Polka**
☆ Tivoli—Felumb (♭ *Mer.EP 1-5042*)

Little Overture Str. orch.
☆ Danish Radio—Jensen (♭ *Mer.EP 1-5046*)

Sonata, vln., vlc. & pf., Op. 55a 1951
W. Tworek, J. Hye-Knudsen & E. Vagning
Sonata, 2 vlns., Op. 55b 1951
W. Tworek & C. Senderowitz ♯ *D.LM 4555*
        (♯ *Lon.LS 785*)

SONGS
COLLECTION
The Letter
Lullaby (*Sovesang*) (Lorentzen)
North, south, east, west
R. Teglbjærg (M-S), & org. **Felix.X 80**
(*Nielsen, Schierbeck, etc.*)

Mother Denmark (Lorentzen)
☆ A. Schiøtz (T) (in ♯ *G.KBLP 11*)

RIMSKY-KORSAKOV, Nicholas
Andreyevitch (1844-1908)

1. ORCHESTRAL & INSTRUMENTAL

Antar, Op. 9 (Symphony No. 2) 1868
Suisse Romande—Ansermet ♯ **D.LXT 2982**
(*Glazounov*)   (♯ Lon.LL 1060)
L.S.O.—Scherchen   ♯ **Nix.NLP 910**
(*Easter Overture*)   (♯ West.WL 5280)
Detroit Sym.—Paray ♯ **EMer.MG 50028**
(*Easter Overture*)   (♯ FMer.MLP 7517)
U.S.S.R. State—Ivanov ♯ **Sup.LPV 175**
(2ss)   (♯ U. 5124G; USSR.D 0701/2)
(*Glazounov* on ♯ Csm.CRLP 206)

Capriccio espagnol, Op. 34 1887
Suisse Romande—Ansermet ♯ **D.LXT 2769**
(*Golden Cockerel Suite*) (♯ Lon.LL 694)
Hallé—Barbirolli   ♯ **G.BLP 1058**
(*Chabrier & Debussy*) (♯ QBLP 5032)
Detroit Sym.—Paray ♯ **Mer.MG 50020**
(*Ravel*)   (♯ FMer.MLP 7509)
(*Easter Overture* on ♯ Mer.MG 50039)
L.S.O.—Scherchen   ♯ **Nix.NLP 914**
(*Tchaikovsky*)   (♯ West.LAB 7002)
Philadelphia—Ormandy ♯ **AmC.CL 707**
(*Snow Maiden, Tsar Saltan, etc.*) (o.n. ML 4856)

Leipzig Radio—Kleinert ♯ **Ura. 7133**
(*below*)   (♭ *UREP 64*; ♯ *ACC.MP 3*)
(*Lalo* on ♯ Ura.RS 7-13)
Vienna State Op.—Rossi ♯ **Van.VRS 484**
(*Easter Overture*; & *Tchaikovsky*) (o.n. ♯ SRV 101;
        Ama.AVRS 6020)
Youth Sym.—Kondrashin **V**♯ *CdM.LDY 8091*[1]
(2ss) (*Tsar Saltan & Ippolitoff-Ivanoff* on ♯ Kings. 271)
(*Overture on Russian themes* on ♯ Sup.LPM 179; *U. 5158C*)
(*Concerto* on ♯ USSR.D 391)
(*Glazounov* on ♯ Csm.CRLP 208)
☆ Philharmonia—Schüchter ♯ **P.PMC 1003**
(*Ippolitoff-Ivanoff & Tchaikovsky*) (♯ MGM.E 3022)
Regent Sym.—(in ♯ Rgt. 7002)
Anon. Orch. (in ♯ Gram. 2089)
☆ Boston Prom.—Fiedler (n.v.) (in ♯ Vic.LM 9027;
  G.FMLP 1003; ItV.A12R 0107 & (o.v.) in
  ♯ Cam.CAL 150 & ♯ set CFL 103: ♭ *CAE 213*)
Winterthur Sym.—Desarzens (♯ *MMS. 57*)
N.Y.P.S.O.—Barbirolli (♯ AmC.RL 3046)
Paris Cons.—Cluytens (in ♯ *AmVox.* set VIP 45292;
    ♭ *Pat.EMD 10006*: in ♯ QTX 116)
Austrian Sym.—Mehlich (in ♯ Rem. 199-130; Ply. 12-50;
  AFest.CFR 61; Cum.CR 293: ♭ *ECR 98* & with
  Commentary by S. Spaeth on ♯ Rem. 10; Nos. 1, 4, 5,
  only in ♯ Rem. 199-122; Ply. 12-39)
French Nat.—Désormière (♯ *T.LCSK 8155*)
Danish Radio—Malko (G.S 10604/5)
Hallé—Harty (C.CQX 16608/9)

... **Alborada & Fandango** only
☆ Cincinnati Summer Op.—Cleva (in ♯ B.AXTL 1035;
  in ♯ AmD.DL 8053: ♭ *ED 3526*; in ♯ D.UST 253087)

Concerto, pf. & orch., C sharp minor, Op. 30
(on a Russian theme) 1882-3
P. Badura-Skoda & London Phil. Sym.
 —Rodzinski   ♯ **West.LAB 7030**
(*Franck*)
☆ P. Badura-Skoda & Vienna Sym.—Swoboda
        ♯ **Nix.WLP 5068**
(½s—*Scriabin*)   (♯ Sel.LPG 8326, d.c.)
☆ F. Jacquinot & Philharmonia—Fistoulari
        ♯ *P.PMD 1026*
(*Liszt*)   (♯ MGM.E 3045)
(*Golden Cockerel, Mlada, etc.* on ♯ MGM.E 3045)
(*Liszt & Dohnányi*, on ♯ FMGM.F 6-101)
☆ S. Richter & Youth Sym.—Kondrashin
       V♯ *CdM.LDY 8127*
(2ss) (*Tsar Saltan* on ♯ MMS. 67; *Capriccio espagnol*
 on ♯ USSR.D 392; *Glazounov & Prokofiev* on
 ♯ CHS.CHS 1316; *Tchaikovsky: Pf. Concerto*, on
 ♯ Csm.CRLP 158, alternative coupling)

Easter Overture, Op. 36 ("*Grande Pâque Russe*")
Detroit Sym.—Paray ♯ **EMer.MG 50028**
(*Symphony No. 2*)   (♯ FMer.MLP 7517)
(*Capriccio espagnol* on ♯ Mer.MG 50039)
L.S.O.—Scherchen   ♯ **Nix.NLP 910**
(*Symphony No. 2*)   (♯ West.WL 5280)
(*Tchaikovsky* on ♯ West.LAB 7043)
Vienna State Op.—Rossi ♯ **Van.VRS 484**
(*Capriccio espagnol & Tchaikovsky*) (o.n. ♯ SRV 101;
        Ama.AVRS 6020)
Orch.—Stokowski[2]   ♯ **Vic.LM 1816**
(*Borodin, Glier, Moussorgsky*)
(♭ set ERB 1816; ♯ ItV.A12R 0141; DV.L 16482;
        FV.A 630215)
Bavarian Sym.—Graunke ♯ **Ura. 7115**
(*Tale of the Invisible City; & d'Indy*) (♯ MTW. 564)
F.O.K. Sym.—Smetáček ♯ *Sup.LPM 149*
(*Brahms*)   (♯ U. 5171C)
☆ Philadelphia—Ormandy ♯ **C.C 1025**
(*Prokofiev*)   (♯ QC 5015)
Berlin Sym.—Rubahn (in ♯ Roy. 1413)
☆ Philadelphia—Stokowski (♯ Cam.CAL 163)
Paris Cons.—Cluytens (in ♯ Pat.QTX 116;
      ♭ *AmVox.VIP 45292*)
Philharmonia—Dobrowen (♮ G.S 7000/1)

Fairy Tale, Op. 29 (*Skazka*) orch. 1879-80
Philharmonia—Fistoulari ♯ *P.PMD 1028*
(*Snow Maiden, Suite*) (♯ MGM.E 3017)

Fantasia on Serbian themes, Op. 6 orch. 1867
Linz Sym.   in ♯ **Ply. 12-35**
(*Glinka, Borodin, Tchaikovsky*)

---

[1] This is stated to be a new recording, using original catalogue no. It is not clear how many of the other repressings are also of the n.v.
[2] With N. Moscona (Bs).

Khorovod (from *Jour de fête*)[1]   str. qtt.   1887
U.S.S.R. State Qtt   ***USSR. 20920***
(*Glazounov & Liadov*)
☆ Galimir Qtt. (‡ Clc. 6148)

Overture on Russian themes, Op. 28   orch.
Moscow Radio—Kovalev   ‡ ***USSR.D 1183***
(*Rachmaninoff; Symphony*)
(*Capriccio espagnol on* ‡ *Sup.LPM 179; U. 5158C*)
(*Taneiev on* ‡ A 440.AC 1208)
(*Glazounov on* ‡ Csm.CRLP 207)

Quintet, B flat major   pf., fl., cl., hrn., bsn.   1876
☆ R. Raupenstrauch & Vienna Phil. Wind Group
(*below*)   ‡ **West.WN 18071**

Russian Dance   (unspec.)
Argentine Radio—Bandini   **ArgOd. 66039**
(*Liadov: Glorifications*)

Scheherazade, Op. 35
Paris Cons.—Ansermet   ‡ **D.LXT 5082**
(n.v.)   (‡ Lon.LL 1162)
Philadelphia—Ormandy   ‡ **EPhi.NBL 5013**
(n.v.)   (‡ Phi.N 02112L; AmC.ML 4888)
Vienna State Op.—Quadri   ‡ **Nix.WLP 5234**
                                             (‡ West.WL 5234)

Philharmonia—Dobrowen   ‡ **C.SX 1007**
(‡ FCX 268: QCX 10021: VSX 501; Angel. 35009:
                                             G.LALP 234)
Paris Phil.—Ladis   ‡ **AmVox.PL 9380**
Belgian Radio—André   ‡ **DT.LGX 66018**
                              (‡ T.LSK 7018; FT. 320.TC.071)

Philharmonia—Stokowski   ‡ **G.ALP 1339**
(‡ Vic.LM 1732: ♭ *set WDM 1732;* ‡ DV.L 16489)
Berlin Radio—Rucht (n.v.)[2]   ‡ **CdM.LDX 8016**
(*Capriccio espagnol on* ‡ Ura. 7133)   (‡ Ura.RS 7-19)
☆ Minneapolis Sym.—Dorati   ‡ **EMer.MG 50009**
(♭ *Mer. set EP-4-500;* ‡ FMer.MLP 7503: ♭ *MEP 14536/9*)
Moscow Radio—Rakhlin   ‡ USSR.D 0510/1
Bolshoi Theatre—Golovanov   ‡ **Csm.CRLP 135**
Netherlands Phil.—Goehr   ‡ MMS. 2004
                                    (also ‡ *MMS. 126*)
Olympia Sym.—Saike (‡ Allo. 3072; Pac.LDAD 56)
Orch.—Schönherr (‡ MTW. 18)
Vienna State Op.—Gielen (‡ GA. 33-302)
Anon. Orchs. (‡ Gram. 2050 & ‡ Pde. 2021)
☆ San Francisco Sym.—Monteux (♭ *Vic. set ERC 2;*
                                    ‡ ItV.A12R 0077)
   Cleveland Sym.—Rodzinski (‡ AmC.RL 3001)
   Philadelphia—Ormandy, o.v. (♭ *AmC. set A 772*)
... Excerpts
"Nat. Op. Orch." (in ‡ Var. 6967; ♭ Roy.EP 247)
☆ Austrian Sym.—Brown (in ‡ Rem. 199-119; Ply. 12-40,
   56, 60, 91, etc.)

Sinfonietta on Russian themes, A minor, Op. 31
☆ Vienna Sym.—Swoboda (*above*)   ‡ **West.WN 18071**
(*Concerto on* ‡ Sel.LPG 8326)

SYMPHONIES
No. 2, *SEE* Antar, *above*

No. 3, C minor, Op. 32   1873, rev. 1884
Bolshoi Sym.—Gauk   ‡ **Per.SPL 567**
(*Glier*)

Trio, C minor   pf., vln., vlc.   *c.* 1897[3]
L. Oborin, D. Oistrakh, S. Knushevitzky
                                     ‡ **Mon.MWL 317**
(2ss)   (*Glinka on* ‡ CHS.CHS 1306)

Variation No. 4, on a Russian theme[4]   str. qtt. 1899
U.S.S.R. Qtt.   ***USSR. 22504***

III. OPERAS
(The) GOLDEN COCKEREL   3 Acts   1909
(*Coq d'or*)
COMPLETE RECORDING
"National Opera" soloists & orch.
                                     ‡ **Gram. 20148/50**
(5ss—*Ippolitoff-Ivanoff: Caucasian Sketches*)

Orchestral Suite
Suisse Romande—Ansermet   ‡ **D.LXT 2769**
(1⅓ss—*Capriccio espagnol*)   (‡ Lon.LL 694)
Philharmonia—Dobrowen   ‡ **C.SX 1010**
(*Tale of Tsar Saltan, Suite*) (‡ FCX/QCX 207; Angel. 35010)
☆ Royal Phil.—Beecham   ‡ **C.CX 1087**
(*Franck: Chasseur maudit*)   (‡ QCX 10085)
☆ French Nat.—Désormière (‡ T.LCSK 8155)
   Austrian Sym.—Singer (‡ Msq. 10000; Ply. 12-53;
   Cum.TCR 266; & with commentary by S. Spaeth,
   ‡ Rem. 10; Bridal Procession only, in ‡ Rem. 199-114)
   Moscow Radio—Golovanov (‡ *USSR.D 554/5*)
... Intro. & Bridal Procession, only
☆ Winterthur—Desarzens (in ‡ *MMS. 57*)
... Bridal Procession, only
☆ L.S.O.—Weldon (in ‡ MGM.E 3045)
   San Francisco—Monteux (in ‡ Cam.CAL 215)
   Boston Prom.—Fiedler (in ‡ Cam.CAL 176)
... Dance of King Dodon, only
☆ Cincinnati Summer Op.—Cleva (in ‡ B.AXTL 1035;
   AmD.DL 8053: ♭ ED 3526; ‡ D.UST 253087)

Hail to thee, sun!   (Hymn to the Sun) S   Act II
M. Dobbs (*Eng*)   in ‡ **C.CX 1305**
(*Manon, Sonnambula, etc.*)   (‡ Angel. 35095)
— ARR. VLN. & PF.   **Kreisler**
☆ J. Heifetz (♭ *D.EUA 108503;* in ‡ AmD.DL 9780:
                                         ♭ *ED 3501*)
   F. Kreisler (in ‡ Vic.LCT 1142)

Fantasy on a theme from the opera   — ARR. VLN. & PF.
I. Bezrodny & pf. (*USSRM.D 00921*)

(The) IMMORTAL KASHCHEY   1 Act   1902
Kashcheyevna's Aria   (unspec.)
Z. Dolukhanova (A)   in ‡ **CdM.LDM 8134**
(*Tchaikovsky, Prokofiev, etc.*) (in ‡ *USSR.D 1423*, d.c.)
☆ S. Probrazhenshaya (M-S) (*USSRM.D 001205*)

Duet, Kashcheyevna & Ivan   M-S & B
A. Styupaliskaya & S. Shaposhnikov
(2ss)   ***USSRM.D 1344/5***

(The) MAID OF PSKOV   4 Acts   1873, rev. 1898
(*Ivan the Terrible*)
Orchestral Suite
Overture; Intermezzi I & II; Prelude Act III: Hunt & Storm
L.S.O.—Fistoulari   ‡ **P.PMC 1009**
(*Balakirev*)   (‡ MGM.E 3076; Od.ODX 142)

(A) MAY NIGHT   3 Acts   1880
COMPLETE RECORDING in *Russian*
☆ S. Lemeshev (T), S. Krasovsky (B), I. Maslennikova (S),
   V. Borisenko (M-S), etc., Bolshoi Theatre Cho. &
   Orch.—Nebolsin   (6ss)   ‡ **Mon.MWL 338/40**
(4ss, ‡ CdM.LDX 8062/3)   (‡ USSR.D 0592/7)
[*Trio, Act I* on USSR. 17892; Hopak, opening cho. &
two of Levko's Songs on ♭ *Van.VREP 3*]

Overture
☆ Philharmonia—Fistoulari   in ‡ **P.PMC 1031**
                                    (‡ in MGM.E 3045)

Duet, Hanna & Levko: Does she sleep?
                                     S & T   Act I
M. Maksakova & G. Bolshakov   ***USSR. 17891***
(*Trio, Act I*)

Sleep, my beauty   T   Act III
(*Levko's second song*)
S. Lemeshev (? n.v.—2ss)   ***USSR. 021152/3***
[includes recit.]   (& *USSRM.D 00193*)
Ⓗ L. Sobinoff (AF. & CRC.ABHB 7*)

MLADA   Opera-Ballet   4 Acts   1892
Procession of the Nobles   orig. cho. & orch.
☆ L.S.O.—Weldon (in ‡ MGM.E 3045)
— ARR. BAND   **Leidzen**
American Sym. Band—Revelli (in ‡ AmD.DL 8157)

---

[1] Joint work with Liadov & Glazounov,
[2] The CdM. issue is said to be a new recording using the original number. The latest Rem. catalogue now lists on
‡ Rem. 199-11 a recording attributed to R.I.A.S.—Rucht, but probably this refers to this recording, replacing with the same
no. the recording previously listed (*see* Supp. I).
[3] Left unfinished.   Completed by another hand.
[4] The other Variations, also recorded, are by Artsibuchev, Scriabin, Glazounov, Ewald, Winkler, Vitol, Blumenfeld
Sokolov.   The complete set occupies 4ss (*USSR. 22503/6*).

MOZART AND SALIERI, Op. 48 1898
COMPLETE RECORDINGS

Mozart ... ... I. Kozlovsky (T)
Salieri ... ... M. Reizen (Bs)
G. Goldfarb (pf.), Moscow Radio Cho. & Orch.
—Samosud (2ss) ♯ USSR.D 0588/9
(♯ CHS.CHS 1315)
(1½ss—*Borodin, Beethoven, etc.* on ♯ Csm.CLPS 10420)

Mozart ... ... J. Mollien (T)
Salieri ... ... J. Linsolas (B)
P. Jacobs (pf.), French Radio Cho. & Sym.
Orch.—Leibowitz (*Fr*) ♯ Oce.OCS 32

SADKO 7 Scenes 1898
COMPLETE RECORDING

Sadko ... ... G. Nelepp (T)
Liubava ... ... V. Davidova (M-S)
Volkhova ... ... E. Shumskaya (S)
Niezhata ... ... E. Antonova (A)
King of the Sea ... S. Krasovsky (Bs)
Viking Guest ... M. Reizen (Bs)
Hindu Guest... ... I. Kozlovsky (T)
Venetian Guest ... P. Lisitsian (B)
etc., Bolshoi Theatre Cho. & Orch.—Golovanov
(8ss) ♯ Mon.MWL 313/6
(♯ USSR.D 01480/7)
(6ss, ♯ CHS. set CHS 1307; CdM.LDX 8100/2)
[Introduction on *USSR.* 23958; excerpts on ♯ *USSR.D* 02085]

Had I thy pearls and gold T Sc. 1
W. Kmentt (*Ger*) in ♯ *Phi.S 06075R*
(*below; Schwanda, Prince Igor, etc.*)

O you dark forest T (*Sadko's aria*) Sc. 1
G. Nelepp, from set in ♯ *Mon.MWL 337*

Ah! now I know (Liubava's Aria) Sc. 3
Z. Dolukhanova (A) in ♯ *USSR.D 1423*
(*Immortal Kashchey; & Khovanshchina*)

Song of the Viking Guest Bs Sc. 4
R. Arié ♯ *D.LW 5061*
(*Glinka, Tchaikovsky, Borodin*) (♯ *Lon.LD 9074*)
M. Reizen, from set in ♯ *Mon.MWL 337*
(in ♯ Csm.CLRP 159)
S. Belarsky in ♯ *Vic.LPM 3274*
(*Glinka, Borodin, etc.*) (♭ set EPB 3274)
☆ B. Christoff (♭ *G.7RW 134: 7RQ 3033*)
B. Gmyria (*USSRM.D 00810: USSR.* 022289)
ℍ F. Chaliapin (in ♯ *Sca. 801**)

Song of the Indian Guest T Sc. 4
I. Kozlovsky, from set in ♯ *Mon.MWL 337*
(in ♯ Csm.CLRP 159)
W. Kmentt (*Ger*) in ♯ *Phi.S 06075R*
M. Lanza (*Eng*) & cho. *G.DA 2048*
(*Merrill: If you were mine*)
R. Gigli (S, *Fr*) *G.DA 11353*
(*Granados: Danza No. 5*)
L. Pastor (S, *Fr*) ♭ *Pat.EG 147*
(*Massenet, etc.*)
T. Rossi (*Fr*) (in ♯ *C.FS 1045*)
☆ P. Anders (*Ger*) (♭ *T.UE 45232I*)
R. Crooks (*Fr*) (♭ *Cam.CAE 120*)

— ARR. ORCH.
Vox Sinfonietta—Gräf (♭ *AmVox.VIP 45410*)
Hamburg Philharmonia—H-J. Walther (in *MSB. 78050*)
Orch.—Kostelanetz (C.CQX 16672; in ♯ AmC.ML 4822:
KZ 1: ♭ *A 1099*)
A. Sciascia Orch. (Fnt. 14449 & in ♯ *LP 310*)
G. Boulanger (vln.) & Bucharest Gypsy Orch.
(in ♯ Csm.CLRP 200)
☆ Boston Prom.—Fiedler (♭ *G.7BF 1060*; (o.v.)
♭ *Cam.CAE 141*)

Song of the Venetian Guest B Sc. 4
P. Lisitsian, from set in ♯ *Mon.MWL 337*
(in ♯ Csm.CLRP 159)

Sadko's Song: O vast heaven! T. & cho. (unacc.)
Sc. 4
G. Nelepp, Bolshoi Th. Cho., from set
(*above*) [with Davidova] *USSR. 23959*
I. Kuznetsov & Red Army Cho. (*USSR.* 18176)

Farewell, my friends (Sadko's aria) T Sc. 5
G. Nelepp, from set *USSR. 22292*
(*below*)

Dark is the chasm (Song of Praise) T, S, Bs Sc. 6
G. Nelepp, E. Shumskaya, S. Krasovsky
(*above*) [from set] *USSR. 22293*

Sleep went along the river (Lullaby, Sc. 7) S
— ARR. 2 PFS. Babin "*Cradle Song*"
☆ V. Vronsky & V. Babin (in ♯ Phi.N 02100L;
▽♯ AmC.ML 4157)

(The) SNOW MAIDEN Prol. & 4 Acts 1882
(*Snegourochka*)
COLLECTED EXCERPTS: ♯ *USSR.D 1525*
Mizgir's Arioso P. Lisitsian
Snow Maiden's Aria E. Shumskaya
Clouds plotted with thunder S. Preobrazhenskaya
Dance of the Tumblers Unspec. orch.

Orchestral Suite
1a. Introduction 1b. Dance of the Birds 2. Cortège
3. Whitsun Festival 4. Dance of the Tumblers
Philharmonia—Fistoulari ♯ *P.PMD 1028*
(*Fairy Tale*) (♯ MGM.E 3017)
(Nos. 1a/b & 3 also in ♯ E 3045)
☆ Moscow Radio—Gauk *USSRM.D 00520/1*
[Omitting No. 3]
(No. 1b only, *USSR.* 18495 & in ♯ Csm.CRLP 159;
No. 2 only, *USSR.* 22930/1)

Aria, Act I, Sc. 1; Berendey's Aria
B. Kostrzenska & E. Klonowski *Muza.X 2185*

Full of wonders (*Berendey's Cavatina*) T
☆ S. Lemeshev (*USSRM.D 00991*)

Joyous day departs T Act III
ℍ L. Sobinoff (IRCC.ABHB 7*)

Ballet Music (including *Dance of the Tumblers*)
☆ Berlin Radio—Ludwig (♯ ANix.ULP 9035)

Dance of the Tumblers Act III
Philadelphia—Ormandy in ♯ AmC.CL 707
(*Capriccio espagnol, etc.*) (o.n. ♯ ML 4856: ♭ A 1828)
Boston Orch. Soc.—Page ♯ *Nix.SLPY 802*
(*Brahms, Saint-Saëns, J. Strauss*) (♯ SOT. 2066 & in ♯ 10646)
Hamburg Philharmonia—H-J. Walther (*MSB. 78050*)
International Sym.—Schneiderhan (in ♯ *Mae.OA 20007*)
☆ Boston Prom.—Fiedler (♭ *ItV.A72R 0049*; ♭ *G.7BF 1061*;
in ♯ Vic.LM 9005)
Sadler's Wells—Collingwood (in ♯ AmC.RL 3056)
— ARR. 2 PFS. Babin
☆ V. Vronsky & V. Babin (in ♯ Phi.N 02100L)
— ARR. ACCORDEONS & CBS.
B. Hughes, B. Palmer & L. Manno (in ♯ *Capri. 1*)

Clouds plotted with thunder S or M-S Act III
(*Shepherd Lehl's 3rd Song*)
L. Georgadze (*Georgian*) (*USSR.* 23777)
☆ M. Maksakova (in ♯ Csm.CRLP 159)

Spring flowers cho. Act IV
Bolshoi Theatre—Nebolsin *USSR. 6383*
(*Dargomijsky: Roussalka, excpt.*)

And yet I faint (*Death of Snow-Maiden*) S Act IV
E. Chavdar *USSRM.D 00844*
(*Tsar's Bride—Martha's aria*) (also *USSR.* 19904/5)
☆ I. Maslennikova (in ♯ Csm.CRLP 159)

(The) TALE OF THE INVISIBLE CITY OF KITEZH 4 Acts 1907
Orchestral Suite
Bavarian Sym.—Graunke ♯ *Ura. 7115*
(*Easter Overture & d'Indy*) (♯ MTW. 564)

Entr'acte, Act III (*The Battle of Kerzhenetz*)
U.S.S.R. State—Orlov *USSR. 010752*
(*Life for the Tzar: Entr'acte, Act III*)

Oh vain illusion of glory Bs Act III
(*Prince Yuri's aria*)
B. Christoff *G.DB 21626*
(*Eugene Oniegin, No. 20c*) (in ♯ Vic.LHMV 1033:
♭ set WHMV 1033)

☆ = Re-issue of a recording to be found in previous volumes.

(The) TALE OF TSAR SALTAN   Prol. & 4 Acts
1900
Orchestral Suite
Philharmonia—Dobrowen   ♯ **C.SX 1010**
(*Golden Cuckerel*)   (♯ FCX/QCX 207; Angel. 35010)
Berlin Radio—Dobrindt   ♯ **Ura. 7078**
(*Glier*)   (♯ MTW. 546)
Moscow Radio—Golovanov   ♯ **Kings. 271**
(*Capriccio espagnol, & I-Ivanoff*)
[Intro. Act III & ☆ Intro. Act IV, Sc. 2 on *USSRM.D 287/8*;
Intro. Act I also, *USSR. 21590/1: USSRM.D 00705*]
☆ Netherlands Phil.—Spruit   ♯ **Nix.NCL 16008**
(*Massenet: Le Cid, Ballet*)   (♯ Clc. 6188; MMS. 3001)
(*Pf. Concerto, on* ♯ *MMS. 67*)

Introduction (March)   Act I
☆ San Francisco Sym.—Monteux (♭ *G.7RF 278*)

Swan Princess' Aria   S   Act II
I. Maslennikova   **USSRM.D 00901**
(*Bohème—Si, mi chiamano Mimi*)

Flight of the Bumble Bee   orch.   Act III
Philadelphia—Ormandy   in ♯ **AmC.CL 707**
(o.n. ♯ ML 4856: ♭ *A 1828*)
Hollywood Bowl—Dragon in ♯**DCap.CTL 7022**
(*Debussy, Brahms, etc.*)   (in ♯ Cap.P 8276: ♭ *FAP 8285*)
Orch.—Swarowsky (in ♯ MTW. 9)
Hamburg Philharmonia—H-J. Walther (*MSB. 78050*)
Vox Sinfonietta—Gräf (♭ *AmVox.VIP 45410*)
Royale Concert Orch. (in ♯ Roy. 1432)
Belgian Radio—P. Glière (in ♯ Mae.OAT 25001)
Concert Orch.—E. Robinson (in ♯ Argo.RG 66)
☆ Cincinnati Summer Op.—Cleva (in ♯ B.AXTL 1035;
AmD.DL 8053: ♭ *ED 3526*)
Philharmonia—Malko (♭ *G.7PW 104*)
A. Kostelanetz (♭ *C.SED 5511: SEDQ 526:* in ♯ *S 1029*)

— ARR. VLN. & PF.   Heifetz
☆ J. Heifetz & E. Bay (*G.DA 2037: EC 208:* ♭ *Vic.ERA 184*)
— ARR. VLN. & PF.   Hartmann (*et al.*)
H. Szeryng & M. Berthelier (in ♯ *Pac.LDPC 50:* ♭ *EP 90019*)
A. Scholz & D. Colacelli (ArgOd. 66030)
☆ E. & A. Wolf (♭ *Mer.EP 1-5040*)
— ARR. VLC. & PF.
A. Janigro & E. Bagnoli (in ♯ West.WN 18004)
☆ S. Popoff (in ♯ *Vien.LPR 1022*)
— ARR. PF.   G. Cziffra (*Qual.SZK 3576*)
☆ L. Oborin (in ♯ *Csm.CRLP 147*)
— ARR. 2 PFS.   J. Enos[1] (in ♯ HIFI.R 201)
— ARR. ORGAN   R. Foort, *sub nom.* M. Cheshire
(in ♯ *SOT. 1051* & in ♯ 10501)
R. Ellsasser (in ♯ MGM.E 3031)
— ARR. 4 PFS.   Manhattan Pf. Qtt. (in ♯ MGM.E 3130)
— ARR. FL., OB., CL., HRN. & BSN.
Chicago Sym. Woodwind Quintet (in ♯ Aphe.AP 14)
— ARR. TPT. & PF.   R. Mendez (♭ *AmD.ED 2153*)
T. Dokshitser (*USSRM.D 00344*)

Introduction to Act IV, Scene 2
("*The Three Wonders*")
☆ Moscow Radio—Golovanov (*USSRM.D 288*)

(The) TSAR'S BRIDE   3 Acts   1899
COMPLETE RECORDING
Vasili Sobakin   ...   ... B. Gmyria (Bs)
Martha   ...   . E. Chavdar (S)
Lyubasha   ...   ... L. Rudenko (M-S)
Grigori Gryaznoy ...   ... M. Grishko (B)
Dyunasha   ...   . A. Sopova (S)
Ivan Lykov ...   . P. Belinnik (T)
Bomely   ...   . I. Ivanov (T)
Petrovna   ...   ... E. Kuchnareva (A)
etc., Kiev Opera Cho. & Orch.—Piradov
♯ **USSR.D 02307/14**
(8ss)   (6ss, ♯ West OPW 11007/9, set OPW 1301)
COLLECTED EXCERPTS   ♯ **USSR.D 1520/1**
Trio, Act I And. Ivanov, N. Obukhova, V. Shevtsov
☆ **Gryaznoy's Aria** And. Ivanov (also, *USSRM.D 00876*)
Martha's Aria E. Shumskaya
Gryaznoy's Aria   B   Act I
P. Karmalyuk (*Ukrainian*) (*USSR. 21947/8*)
☆ M. Grishko (in ♯ *USSR.D 2094*)

Scene & Duet: Lyubasha & Gryaznoy S & B. Act I
☆ L. Rudenko & M. Grishko (*USSRM.D 862*)
Scene: Lyubasha & Bomely   Act II
S. Preobrazhenskaya, N. Chesnokov,
F. Rosenkranz, L. Grudina, etc., Kiev Op.
Cho. & Orch.—Pokhitonov *USSRM.D 877/8*
(2ss)
L. Rudenko, P. Ivanov & Cho.
(4ss)   *USSR. 021967/70*
In Novgorod (Martha's Aria)   S   Act II
E. Shumskaya   (2ss)   *USSR. 22039/40*
☆ I. Maslennikova (in ♯ *CdM.LDM 8070;*
USSRM.D 00785)
E. Chavdar (*USSRM.D 00841:* in ♯ *D 2088*)
You will pay (Lyubasha's Aria)   S or M-S   Act II
V. Davidova   *USSRM.D 00916*
(*Dargomijsky & Serov*)
N. Goncharenko   *USSR. 19920*
(*Tchaikovsky: Iolanthe, aria*)
L. Rudenko   *USSRM.D 861*
(*above & Khovanshchina*)
☆ M. Maksakova (in ♯ *Sti. 1000*)
S. Preobrazhenskaya (in ♯ *USSR.D 1424*)
She lay asleep (Sobakin's Aria)   Bs   Act III
A. Pirogov   *USSRM.D 888*
(*Rachmaninoff, Borodin, Dargomijsky*)
Martha's Aria, unspec. (prob. Mad Scene) Act III
E. Shumskaya   in ♯ *USSR.D 1915*
☆ I. Maslennikova (*USSRM.D 01786*)

SONGS
COLLECTION
The Sigh, Op. 50, No. 2 (Maikov, from the Greek)
(also on *USSR. 20066*)
It was in early Spring, Op. 43, No. 4 (Tolstoy) (also
on *USSR. 21305*)
☆ ▽ My spoilt darling, Op. 42, No. 4 (Mickiewicz, trs. Mey)
Where thou art, my thought flies to thee, Op. 8, No. 1
(Pushkin)
The Clouds begin to scatter, Op. 42, No. 3 (Pushkin)
S. Lemeshev (T)   ♯ *USSR.D 1164*
(*Balakirev, Glinka, etc.*)
Anchar, Op. 49, No. 1 (Pushkin) (*The Upas-Tree*)
M. Reizen (Bs)   *USSRM.D 00713*
(*The gloomy day has faded*)
I. Patorzhinsky (Bs)   *USSR. 022552*
(*Glinka: Midnight Review*)
(The) Beauty, Op. 51, No. 4 (Pushkin)
S. Lemeshev (T)   *USSRM.D 00927*
(*Come to the kingdom . . .; & Rachmaninoff*)
(also *USSR. 20065*)
Canon (unid.)
Pamplona Cha. Cho.—Morondo
in **V♯** *Sel.LPP 8600*
Come to the kingdom of roses and wine, Op. 8,
No. 4 (Fet, after Hafiz)
☆ S. Lemeshev (T)   *USSRM.D 00927*
(*The Beauty, & Rachmaninoff*)
(The) Gloomy day has faded, Op. 51, No. 5
(Pushkin)
M. Reizen (Bs)   (*Anchar*)   *USSRM.D 00714*
I believe I love, Op. 8, No. 6 (Pushkin)
I. Kozlovsky (T)   *USSR. 22069*
(½s—It was in early Spring; & Tchaikovsky)
In the silence of the night, Op. 56, No. 2 (Maikov)
☆ N. Obukhova (M-S) (in *USSRM.D 00614*)
It is not the wind, Op. 43, No. 2 (A. K. Tolstoy)
S. Preobrazhenskaya (M-S)   in ♯ *USSR.D 1166*
(*below*)
G. Vinogradov (T) (*Eta. 30-5018*)

---

[1] Playing both parts.

It was in early Spring, Op. 43, No. 4 (A. K. Tolstoy)
V. Borisenko (M-S) *USSRM.D 00739*
(*On the yellow cornfields; Rubinstein, Arensky*)
(& *USSR.* 20475)
I. Kozlovsky (T) *USSR.* 22069
(½s—*I believe I love; Tchaikovsky*)
S. Lemeshev (T) *USSR.* 21306
(*Rachmaninoff: The little island*)

(A) Midsummer Night's Dream, Op. 56, No. 2
(Maikov)
N. Kazantseva (S) *USSRM.D 00700*
(*Dargomijsky & Rachmaninoff*)

My spoilt Darling, Op. 42, No. 4
(Mickiewicz, trs. Mey)
S. Shaposhnikov (B) *USSRM.D 00622*
(*Tchaikovsky, Glinka*)

(The) Nymph, Op. 56, No. 1 (Maikov)
N. Kazantseva (S) *USSRM.D 00687*
(*Balakirev*)
E. Chavdar (S) in ♯ *USSR.D 2089*

Of what I dream in the quiet night, Op. 40, No. 3
(Maikov)
V. Firsova (S) *USSR.* 17289
(*Rachmaninoff: Before my window*)

On the hills of Georgia, Op. 3, No. 4 (Pushkin)
B. Gmyria (Bs) *USSR.* 22541
(*Dargomijsky: The night wind*)
I. Kozlovsky (T) *USSR.* 20382
(*Tchaikovsky: I'll tell thee nothing*)
(*Tchaikovsky & Dargomijsky, USSRM.D 00696*)
L. Rudenko (M-S) in ♯ *USSR.D 2073*
(*Carmen & Samson & Delila, arias; & Songs*)

(The) Prophet, Op. 49, No. 2 (Pushkin)
R. Arié (Bs) & Orch. ♯ *D.LW 5104*
(*Rachmaninoff, Koenemann & Trad.*) (♯ *Lon.LD 9101*)
B. Christoff (Bs), G. Moore (pf.)
in ♯ *Vic.LHMV 1033*
(*above; Moussorgsky, etc.*) (♭ *set WHMV 1033*)
B. Gmyria (Bs) in ♯ *USSR.D 1594*
(*Glinka, Rachmaninoff, Tchaikovsky*)

(The) Rose and the Nightingale, Op. 2, No. 2
(*Eastern Romance*) (Koltsov)
S. Lemeshev (T) *USSR.* 21547
(*Withered flowers*)
(*idem, & Glinka, on USSRM.D 00789*)
E. Chavdar (S) in ♯ *USSR.D 2089*
(*Tsar's Bride Aria; & Songs*)

Silence descends on the golden cornfields, Op. 39,
No. 3 (A. K. Tolstoy)
V. Borisenko (M-S) *USSRM.D 00739*
(*It was in early Spring; Rubinstein, Arensky*)

(The) Siren, Op. 7, No. 3 (Mickiewicz, trs. Mey)
V. Borisenko (M-S) *USSR.* 22264
(*Arensky: One star watches over everyone*)
N. Obukhova (M-S) *USSRM.D 00614*
(*In the silence . . .; & Dargomijsky, Moussorgsky*)

So slowly pass my days, Op. 51, No. 1 (Pushkin)
☆ M. Reizen (Bs) (*USSRM.D 001347*)

Thy glance is radiant, Op. 7, No. 4 (Lermontov)
S. Shaposhnikov (B) *USSR.* 22281
(*Tchaikovsky: I opened the window*)

(The) West dies out in pallid rose, Op. 39, No. 2
(A. K. Tolstoy)
S. Preobrazhenskaya (M-S) in ♯ *USSR.D 1166*
(*above; & Sokolov, Tchaikovsky*)

When the yellowing cornfield blows, Op. 40, No. 1
(Lermontov)
☆ Z. Dolukhanova (A) (*USSRM.D 00604*)

Withered flower, Op. 51, No. 3 (Pushkin)
S. Lemeshev (T) *USSR.* 21548
(*The rose & the nightingale*)

Zuleika's Song, Op. 26, No. 4 (after Byron)
Z. Dolukhanova (A) *USSRM.D 00604*
(*When the yellowing . . ., Glazounov, Balakirev*)
N. Kazantseva (S) *USSR.* 21307
(*Glazounov: Nina's Romance*)

Folk Song arr.: Easter Eggs 1877
Trapp Family Cho. (*Eng*) in ♯ *AmD.DL 9793*

———

RIQUIER, Guiraut (*c.* 1230-1293)

SEE: † FRENCH TROUBADOUR SONGS

———

RIVIER, Jean (b. 1896)

Grave et presto Sax. qtt. 1938
M. Mule Saxophone Qtt. ♯ *D.LX 3142*
(*Absil & Françaix*) (♯ *Lon.LS 1188*)
Symphony No. 2, C major Str. orch. 1938
M.G.M. Str. Orch.—Solomon ♯ *MGM.E 3104*
(*Honegger*) (♯ *FMGM. 6-102*)

———

RODRIGO, Joaquín (b. 1902)

Concerto guitar & orch. 1939
(*Concierto de Aranjuez*)
N. Yepes & Madrid Cha.—Argenta
♯ *LI.TW 91019*
(*Falla: Noches . . .*) (♯ *Ambra.MCC 30008*)

(La) Enamorado junto al pequeño surtidor
(from *2 Esbozas, Op. 1*) vln. & pf. 1923
A. Muz & J. Rodrigo *ArgOd.* 66033
(*Granados: Goyescas, Intermezzo*)

En los trigales guitar 1938
N. Yepes in ♯ *D.LXT 2974*
(† *Spanish Music of the XVIth-XXth Centuries*)
(♯ *D.FST 153076; Lon.LL 1042*)
M. L. Anido (*Sanz: Pavana*) *ArgOd.* 57046

Homenaje a la Tempranica orch. 1939
☆ Valencia Sym.—Iturbi ♭ *G.7RF/RQ 272*
(*Iturbi: Seguidillas*) (♭ *G.7ERL 1042*, d.c.)
(*Liszt, Falla, Palau Boix, etc.* in ♯ *Vic.LM 1937; DV.L 16221*)

Musica para un Codice Salmantino Cantata
Bs, cho. & Inst. ens. (Unamuno) 1953
(2) Canciones Sefardies (Anon. XVth Cent.) 1951
1. Malato estaba el Lijo del Rey (unacc. cho.)
2. El Rey que muncho madruga
J. Deus & Nat. Radio Cho.—O. Alonso
(*Victoria*) ♯ *Mont.FM 41*

Pastoral pf. 1926
P. Spagnolo ♯ *D.LW 5142*
(*Mompou, Marcello, etc.*) (♯ *Lon.LD 9135*)

Sarabanda lejana guitar 1926
A. Segovia in ♯ *B.AXTL 1069*
(† *Segovia Evening II*) (♯ *AmD.DL 9751*)

SONGS
(4) Madrigals amatorios (Anon)
S & pf. 1947; orch. 1948
1. Con qué la lavaré?
2. Vos me matasteis
3. De dónde venís, amore?
4. De los álamos vengo, madre
M. del Pozo & Philharmonia—Braithwaite
♭ *G.7BF 1056*
L. Huarte ♯ *MusH.LP 3004*
(*Turina, Montsalvatge, etc,*)

———

RODRIGUEZ, Felipe (1759-1814)
RODRIGUEZ, Vincente (1685-1761)

SEE: † SPANISH KEYBOARD MUSIC

☆ = Re-issue of a recording to be found in previous volumes.

RÖNTGEN, Julius (1855-1932)

Peasant Song (unspec.)[1]
Biggs Family Ens.   in ‡ *GIOA.BF 1*
(*Josquin, Victoria, etc.*)

ROESGEN-CHAMPION, Marguerite
(b. 1894)

Suite française fl. & hp.
... **Complainte & Rondeau**
H. Barwahser & P. Berghout   ‡ *Phi.N 00695R*
(*Badings, Andriessen, Tomasi*)

RÖSSLER, Franz Anton (1746-1792)
(or ROSETTI, Francesco Antonio)

Concerto, E flat major, horn & orch.[2] 1779
P. Rossi & Italian Cha.—Jenkins ‡ **HS.HSL 79**
(*Boccherini*)   (in set HSL-C)

Sonata, E flat major, Op. 2, No. 2 *c.* 1780
orig. hp., hpsi., or pf. with vln.
N. Zabaleta (harp)   in ‡ **Eso.ES 524**
(† XVIIIth Cent. Harp Music)

ROGERS, Bernard (b. 1893)

Leaves from the tale of Pinocchio Suite orch. 1950
A.R.S. Sym.—Schönherr   ‡ *ARS. 30*
(*Tuthill & Sanders*)

Soliloquy fl. & str. 1922
J. Mariano & Eastman-Rochester Sym.
—Hanson   ‡ **EMer.MG 40003**
(*Copland, Barlow, Kennan, etc.*)   (♭ *Mer.EP 1-5065*)
[o.v. ▽ Vic. 18101, in set M 802]

ROLAND-MANUEL, Alexis (b. 1891)

Suite dans le goût espagnol ob., bsn., tpt., hpsi.
pub. 1938
1. Entradilla; 2. Villancico; 3. Melodrama; 4. Final
L. Speyer, F. Panenka, R. Voisin, D. Pinkham
‡ **Uni.UN 1005**
(*Milhaud, S-Saëns, Honegger, Poulenc*)

ROLDÁN, Amadeo (1900-1939)

(2) Canciones populares cubanas vlc. & pf. 1928
A. Odnoposoff & Bertha Huberman ‡ *Pnt. 4001*
(*Ardévol, A. de la Veja, Menéndez*)

Ritmica No. 1 pf. & wind quintet 1930
H. Roget & French Radio Quintet ‡ **C.FCX 220**
(*García Caturla & Porter*)   (‡ *Angel. 35105*)
[U.N.E.S.C.O. recording]
SONG CYCLE: Motivos del Son (Guillén) 1934
... Ayé me dijeron negro; Sigue; Mulata
▽ J. Litante (S), H. Brant (pf.) (NMQR. 1213)

RONCALLI (or RONCELLI), **Ludovico**
(fl. XVII Cent.)
SEE: RESPIGHI: Antiche Danze, Suite 3

RONTANI, Raffaelo (fl. 1610-1622)
SEE: † CANZONE SC ORDATE

ROPARTZ, Joseph Gu y (1864-1955)

Rondo pf.
☆ M. Panzéra (in ‡ Clc. 6260)

RORE, Cyprien de (1516-1565)
SEE: † FLEMISH CHORAL MUSIC
      † PARISIAN SONGS OF XVIth CENTURY

ROREM, Ned (b. 1923)

Sonata No. 2   pf.
J. Katchen   ‡ **D.LXT 2812**
(*Bartók*)   (‡ Lon.LL 759)

ROSA, Salvator (1615-1673)

Selve, voi che le speranze[3] Canzona
C. Sparks   in ‡ *Bib.CL 221*
(† Music of the Church)

ROSEINGRAVE, Thomas (1690-1766)
SEE: † MASTERS OF EARLY ENGLISH KEYBOARD MUSIC

ROSENBERG, Hilding (b. 1892)

Swedish Folksongs (arrs., unspec.)
Peabody High School Cho.—Shute
(*Read, Saeverud, etc.*)   in ‡ **PFCM.CB 160**

Symphony No. 3 "The Four Ages of Man" 1939
Stockholm Concerts Soc.—Mann ‡ **D.LXT 2885**
(2ss)   (‡ Lon.LL 944)

ROSENMÜLLER, Johann (1619-1684)

CANTATAS
Nunc dimittis
In te, Domine, speravi trs. Boatwright
H. Boatwright (S), 2 vlns., hpsi., vlc.
Confitebor tibi, Domine ed. Hamel
Die Augen des Herrn ed. E. F. Schmid
St. Thomas's Chu. Cho. New Haven
—Boatwright; 2 vlns., org., vlc. & cbs.
‡ **Over.LP 9**

Sonata No. 8, E minor 2 vlns. & cont.
(DDT. XVIII)
C. Monteux (fl.), H. Shulman (ob.), S.
Marlowe (hpsi.), B. Greenhouse (vlc.)
‡ **Eso.ES 517**
(*Frescobaldi, Couperin*)   (‡ Cpt.MC 20023)

Suite No. 3, C major str. (*Sonate da camera*, 1670)
☆ Str. Orch.—Sachs (in † HS.AS 12)

Suite No. 9, C minor (from *Studentenmusik*, 1654)
Saxon State Coll. Musicum—Liersch ‡ **Ura. 7113**
(*Telemann, Corelli*)

ROSETTI, Francesco Antonio, SEE **RÖSSLER**

ROSIER, André de (fl. XVIIth Cent.)
SEE: † AIRS À BOIRE

ROSSELLI, Francesco (b. 1520-d. ?)
(Roussel)
SEE: † FIVE CENTURIES OF CHURCH MUSIC
      † MOTETS OF XVIth & XVIIth CENTURIES

ROSSELLINI, Renzo (b. 1908)

Vangelo Minimo Suite orch.
Santa Cecilia Acad.—Rossellini ‡ItV.A12R 0011

---

[1] May be *Der allersüsseste Jesus*, Op. 44, No. 3.   [2] Ed. S. Beck.
[3] See entry in *Grove* 5th edn., as to falsity of this attribution.

ROSSETER, Philip (*c.* 1568-1623)
> SEE: † DOWLAND & HIS CONTEMPORARIES
> † ELIZABETHAN LOVE SONGS
> † RENAISSANCE MUSIC FOR THE LUTE

ROSSI, Luigi (*c.* 1598-1653)
> SEE: † HISTORY OF MUSIC IN SOUND (58)
> † CHACONNE & PASSACAGLIA
> † ANTHOLOGIE SONORE (3004 LD: HS.AS 36)

ROSSINI, Gioacchino (1792-1868)

I. INSTRUMENTAL

Boutique fantasque & Rossiniana : *See* Respighi
Matinées & Soirées musicales: *See* Britten

PIANO PIECES
COLLECTION (from the *Péchés de vieillesse*)

Prélude pretentieux	Regret
Espoir	Savoie aimante
Un Sauté	Ouf! les petits pois!

M. Meyer ♯ *DFr.EX 25008*

(6) QUARTETS fl., cl., hrn., bsn.[1]
No. 1, F major
No. 4, B flat major
French Wind Qtt. ♯ *OL.LD 57*

No. 4, B flat major
E. Thomsen, P. Nehammer, B. Lüders &
A. Bredahl ♭ *C.SELK 1001*

No. 6, F major
Czech Phil. Wind Qtt. ♯ *U. 5216C*
(*Beethoven*)

Riens pf. pieces (*Péchés de vieillesse*)
— Excerpts in Respighi: Rossiniana, *q.v.*

Sonata, C major 2 vlns., vlc., cbs.[2] (ed. Casella)
Virtuosi di Roma—Fasano ♯ *B.AXTL 1042*
(*Cambini, Bonporti, Marcello*) (♯ *D.UAT 273583;*
AmD.DL 9674; Fnt.LP 3005)
I Musici Ens. ♯ *C.CX 1192*
(*Galuppi, Marcello, Tartini*) (♯ *QCX 10037: FCX 303;*
Angel. 35086)
Hamburg State Phil.—di Bella ♯ *DT.LGM 65031*
(*Corelli*) (♯ *T.NLB 6108*)

II. SONGS

SOIRÉES MUSICALES
No. 8, La Danza (Pepoli)
L. Infantino (T) & Orch. *C.LB 137*
(*Infantino: Serenata*)
P. Fleta (T) & Orch. in ♯ *Pat.DT 1018*
I. B. Lucca (S) & Orch. ♭ *Dur.AI 6021*
(*Donizetti: Il Sospiro*) (in ♯ *MSE 6*)
E. Holmstrom (T) & Orch. *Od.O-28492*
(*Tosti: Ideale*)
A. Mickiewiczówna (S) & Orch. (*Muza. 2347*)
☆ B. Gigli (T) (♭ *G.7EB 6003: 7ERQ 108: 7ERF 134*)
J. Schmidt (T) (♭ *P.CGEP 2*)
R. Tucker (T) (*C.LC 38; ♭ AmC.A 1540*)
J. Peerce (T) (♭ *Vic.ERA 79*)
J. Peerce (T), o.v. (in ♯ *Roy. 1610: 1830: ♭ EP 169;*
in ♯ *Var. 6933; in ♯ AFest.CFR 10-134: ♭ EPM 246*)

No. 9, Regata Veneziana
No. 10, Pesca (Duets)
N. Kazantseva (S), Z. Dolukhanova (A) (*Russ*)
USSR. 022175/6

III. SACRED WORKS

MASS: Petite Messe solennelle 1864
S, A, T, Bs, cho., 2 pfs. & harmonium
COMPLETE RECORDING
C. Mancini, O. Dominguez, G. Berdini,
M. Petri, Santa Cecilia Acad. Cho., G. Gorini
& C. Vidusso (pfs.), F. Vignanelli (org.)
—Fasano ♯ *G.ALP 1278/9*
(4ss) (♯ *QALP 10107/8*)

— ORCHESTRAL VERSION pub. 1869
A. Tuccari, G. Salvi, P. Besma, N. Catalani,
Rome Qtt. Soc. Cho. & Orch.—Vitalini[3]
♯ **Nix.PLP 588**
(♯ *Per.SPL 588; Cpt.MC 20065*)

Pietà, Signore (attrib. Stradella)
S. Baccaloni (Bs) in ♯ **Roy. 1547**
L. Castellani (S), S. Leff (pf.) in ♯ **Mur.P 105**
(followed by pf. acc. only)
☆ B. Gigli (♭ *G.7ERQ 134*)

— ARR. ORCH. "*Aria di Chiesa*"
Milan Angelicum—Janes (2ss) *Ang.CPA 057*

STABAT MATER S, A, T, B, Cho., orch. 1842
COMPLETE RECORDING
M. Stader, M. Radev, E. Häfliger, K. Borg, St.
Hedwig's Cath. Cho. & R.I.A.S. Sym.
—Fricsay ♯ **HP.DGM 18203/4**
(3ss—*Kodály*)
(3ss—*Mozart* on ♯ *AmD.DL 9771/2, set DX 132*)
[No. 2 only on ♭ *Pol. 30139;* No. 8 on ♭ *Pol. 32097*]
☆ Soloists, Salzburg Cath. Cho. & Mozarteum Orch.
—Messner (♯ *Cum. set CR 291*[4])
Excerpts from Messner set:
... Cujus animam; Inflammatus et accensus (in ♯ *Rem. 191-121*)
... Amen (♭ *Rem.REP 16; ♭ Cum.ECR 50;* in ♯ *Ply. 12-90*)
No. 2, Cujus animam T
K. Baum in ♯ **Roy. 1582**
No. 4, Pro peccatis Bs
◨ J. Mardones (in Sca. 810*)
P. Plançon (AF.AGSB 74*)
No. 8, Inflammatus S
◨ A. de Montalant (in ♯ *Ete. 707**)

IV. OPERAS

(II) BARBIERE DI SIVIGLIA 2 Acts 1816
(*The Barber of Seville*)
COMPLETE RECORDING (in *Russian*)

Figaro		I. Burlak (B)
Rosina		V. Firsova (S)
Il Conte Almaviva ...		I. Kozlovsky (T)
Don Basilio		M. Reizen (Bs)
Dr. Bartolo		V. Malyishev (B)

etc. Moscow Radio Cho. & Orch.—Samosud
(6ss) ♯ **USSR.D 01550/5**
[Excerpts also on ♯ *USSR.D 1526, USSR. 22668/9, etc.*]
COMPLETE RECORDINGS in *Italian*
☆ V. de los Angeles (S), G. Bechi (B), N. Monti (T),
N. Rossi-Lemeni (Bs), etc., Milan Sym. Cho. &
Orch.—Serafin ♯ **G.FALP 196/8**
(♯ *VALP 508/10*)
(Highlights on ♯ *Vic.LM 1826: ♭ set ERB 37*)
☆ M. Capsir (S), D. Borgioli (T), R. Stracciari (B), etc.
La Scala Cho. & Orch.—Molajoli ♯ **AmC. set EL1**
(6ss) (4ss, ♯ *C.QCX 10115/6*)
☆ Soloists, Italian Radio Cho. & Orch.—Previtali
(♯ *Pol. 18170/1;* Highlights on ♯ *CCet.A 50140;* Nos.
4, 5, 8, only on ♭ *Cap.FAP 7001; ♭ Cet.EPO 0306*)
ABRIDGED RECORDING ("Concert Version")
C. Meyer (M-S), N. Duval (M-S), P. Conrad (T),
P. Gorin (B), etc., Cho. & Netherlands Phil.
—Krannhals ♯ **MMS. set OP 6**
(4ss) (& ♯ *MMS. set 112*)
[Overture only in V♯ *MMS. 920*]
HIGHLIGHTS
Overture & Nos. 2, 4, 5, 6, 7, 8, 12
H. Reggiani (S), B. Landi (T), F. Valentino (B), S.
Baccaloni (Bs) & Orch. ♯ **Roy. 1597**
(♯ *MusH.LP 12010*)
Overture & Nos. 2, 4, 5, 6, 7, 8, 9, 10, 13, 18
R. Doria (S), C. Baroni (T), L. Huberty (B), A. Legros (Bs),
C. Cambon & Pasdeloup Orch.—Allain (*Fr;* No. 5
in *Italian*) ♯ **CA.LPA 1088**
(♯ *Plé.P 3070*)

(*continued on next page*)

---

[1] According to N. Strauss (of N.Y. *Times*), Nos. 1-5 are ARR. by F. Berr (*c.* 1829) for these insts. from the Str. Qtts. of *c.*
1808; these were originally Sonatas for 2 vlns., vlc., cbs.
[2] Orig. No. 3 of 6 Sonatas, *c.* 1808.
[3] Frequent cuts in performance.
[4] Announced, but not issued, as ♯ Nix.OLP 7024.

HIGHLIGHTS (various)

☆ C. Ramirez (B), H. Reggiani (S), B. Landi (T), etc.,
Victor Cho. & Orch.—Bamboschek **‡ BB.LBC 1083**

Florence Op. Co. (‡ *Ply. 10-28* & ‡ *12-57*)

☆ Soloists, Rome Op. Cho. & Orch.—Questa (‡ *Roy. 1841*)
Soloists, Berlin Op. Cho. & Orch.—Rubahn
(‡ *Roy. 1411*)

Overture

R.I.A.S. Sym.—Fricsay **PV. 72490**
(*Viaggio a Reims, Overture*) (♭ *Pol. 30090*)

Belgian Radio—André **‡ DT.TM 68024**
(*Tancredi Overture*) (in ‡ T.LSK 7019 & LS 6026;
in ‡ FT. 320.TC.028 & 270.C.039)

L.P.O.—Solti **‡ D.LW 5207**
(*Italiana Overture*)

Lamoureux—v. Kempen ♭ **Phi.A 400006E**
(*Fille du Régiment, Overture*)

Pasdeloup—Allain ♭ **Plé.P 45144**
(*Boieldieu: Calife de Bagdad, Overture*) [from Highlights]

French Nat. Radio—Mirouze in ‡ **Pat.ST 1069**

Czech Phil.—Šejna **U.H 24377**

Colón Theatre—Martini **ArgOd. 66042**
(in ‡ *LDC 509*)

Bolshoi Th.—Samosud (USSR. 017974/5:
USSRM.D 201)

Linz Sym. (in ‡ Ply. 12-34)
Leipzig Radio—Haarth (*Eta. 120017*)
Orch.—Swarowsky (in ‡ MTW. 9; *ACC.MP 13*)
Orch.—Kostelanetz (in ‡ AmC.CL 798: o.n. ML 4692;
♭ *Phi.N 409512E;* ♭ *EPhi.NBE 11001*)
Sym.—Straszynski (*Muza. 1743/4,* 3ss)
Vienna Op. Orch. (in ‡ Ply. 12-97)
Viennese Sym. (in ‡ Ply. 12-73)

☆ Philharmonia—Galliera (♭ *C.SED 5517: SEBQ 120:
ESBF 123: SCD 2012: SCDW 104: SCDQ 2004*)
Milan Sym.—Serafin, from set (♭ *G.7ERQ 105*)
N.B.C. Sym.—Toscanini (♭ *G.7R 126: 7ERQ 101:
7ERF 103:* ♭ *DV. 16299*)
Suisse Romande—Olof (‡ *D.LW 5008:* ♭ *DX 1779*)
Berlin Municipal—Rother (‡ *Nix.ULP 9057*)
Florence Fest.—Serafin (in ‡ BB.LBC 1039:
♭ *set WBC 1039:* ♭ *ERAB 1*)
Florence Fest.—Ghiglia (in ‡ Rem. 199-114;
AFest.CFR 10-26)
C.B.S. Sym.—Barlow (in ‡ AmC.RL 3030: ♭ *A 1554*)
etc.

— ARR. HARMONICAS
Raisner Harmonica Trio (♭ *FestF.FX 1006M*)

ACT I

No. 2, Ecco ridente in cielo T
C. Valletti in ‡ **Cet.LPC 55002**
(*Italiana in Algieri, Sonnambula, Manon, etc.*)

G. Vinogradov (*Russ*) (*USSR. 13998*)

☆ P. Munteanu (Pol. 8204: ♭ *32049*)
F. Tagliavini (in ‡ CCet.A 50155)
T. Schipa (♭ *Vic.ERAT 26:* in ‡ LCT 1138)
M. Villabella (*Fr*) (in ‡ Od.ODX 136)

ℍ T. Schipa (in ‡ Sca. 805*)
E. Clement (in ‡ Sca. 819*)
F. de Lucia (in ‡ Sca. 814*; in ‡ CEd. set 7002*)

No. 4, Largo al factotum B
A. Protti in ‡ **D.LX 3109**
(*Pagliacci, Trovatore, etc.*) (in ‡ *Lon.LS 701*)
(*Pagliacci—Prologue* on *D.F 43964*)

R. Cesari **ArgOd. 66047**
(*Traviata—Di Provenza*) (in ‡ *LDC 515*)

N. Herlea **U.H 24395**
(*Traviata—Un di felice*)

J. Metternich (*Ger*) **G.DB 11547**
(*Faust—Avant de quitter*) (in ‡ WBLP 1504)

F. Valentino in ‡ **Roy. 1585**

L. Huberty (*Fr*), from Highlights ♭ **Plé.P 45156**
(*Massé—Les Noces de Jeannette, excpt.*)

R. Massard (*Fr*) in ‡ **LI.TW 91132**
(*Contes d'Hoffmann & Tosca*) (‡ *D.FAT 173665*)

I. Gorin (in ‡ Alld. 3003; MTW. 572)
P. Fortes (BrzV.P 327)
L. S. Vela (in ‡ *MusH.LP 5004*)
A. Sved (*Hung*) (Qual.MN 1062)

☆ T. Gobbi (♭ *G.7RW 129*)
G. Bechi (♭ *G.7RQ 3040:* in ‡ QALP 10087)
L. Tibbett (in ‡ Cam.CAL 171)
J. C. Thomas (♭ *Vic.ERAT 25:* in ‡ LCT 1138)
H. Schlusnus (*Ger*) (in ‡ Pol. 18080 & ‡ 19039)
M. Dens (*Fr*) (in ‡ *Pat.DT 1020*)

ℍ R. Stracciari (in ‡ Sca. 802*)
T. Ruffo (**V** ♭ *RR.M 311*;* in ‡ B & B. 3*; in ‡ Sca. 812*)
M. Battistini (*AF.AGSA 24**)
E. de Gogorza (in ‡ SBDH.JAL 7001*)

— ARR. PF. Ginsburg: G. Ginsburg (*USSR. 18269/70*)

— ARR. 2 PFS. Kovacs
P. Luboshutz & G. Nemenoff (in ‡ Rem. 199-143)

— ARR. VLN. & PF. Castelnuovo-Tedesco
☆ J. Heifetz (in ‡ B.LAT 8066; D.UAT 273572;
♭ *AmD.ED 3502:* in ‡ DL 9760)

— ARR. ORCH.
Boston Pops—Fiedler (in ‡ *Vic.LRM 7045;* ♭ *set ERB 7045*)

No. 5, Se il mio nome T

No. 6, All' idea . . . Numero quindici T & B
☆ N. Monti, G. Bechi & V. de los Angeles (S)
[from set] **G.DB 21576**

ℍ F. de Lucia & A. Pini-Corsi (in ‡ CEd. 7002*)

No. 5, only
G. Vinogradov (*Russ*) (*USSR. 13999*)

☆ T. Schipa (in ‡ Vic. set LCT 6701)
M. Villabella (*Fr*) (in ‡ Od.ODX 137)

No. 6, only
☆ L. Infantino & P. Silveri (♭ *C.SCB 103: SCBQ 3002:
SCBW 103*)

ℍ B. Carpi & R. Stracciari (in ‡ Sca. 802*)

No. 7, Una voce poco fa S (or M-S)
M. M. Callas in ‡ **C.CX 1231**
(*Dinorah, Lakmé, etc.*) (‡ QCX 10129; Angel. 35233)

G. Simionato (M-S) **‡ D.LW 5139**
(*Cenerentola, Don Carlos, etc.*) (‡ *Lon.LD 9162*)

E. Mühl (2ss) **G.DA 30001**

G. Arnaldi **Cet.AT 0280**
(*Zauberflöte, No. 14*)

M. Hallin-Boström in ‡ **G.ALPC 1**
(*Tannhäuser, Tosca, etc.*)

R. Streich **PV. 72446**
(*Rigoletto—Caro nome*) (♭ *Pol. 30052*)
(& Ger, on PV. 72445; ♭ *Pol. 30051*)

H. Reggiani, from Highlights in ‡ **Roy. 1603**

D. Pieranti in ‡ **SBDH.TOB 2**
(*Don Carlos, Favorita, etc.*)
(*Trovatore, Fosca, Don Carlos, etc.* in ‡ ABCD. 2)

E. Köth (*Ger*) **G.DB 11581**
(*Lustige Weiber—Nun eilt herbei*) (♭ *7RW 541*)

R. Doria (*Fr*) ♭ **Plé.P 45142**
(*Pardon de Ploërmel—Valse*)

☆ V. de los Angeles, from set **G.DA 2030**
(*EC 204;* ArgV. 66-6178; & in ‡ Vic.LM 1847)
(*No. 13* on ♭ *G.7ER 5038: 7ERQ 129*)
M. Dyurkovich (*Hung*) (in ‡ USSR.D 2139)
V. Firsova (*Russ,* from set) (*USSRM.D 00907*)

☆ A. Galli-Curci (♭ *Vic.ERAT 11:* in ‡ LM 1786)
C. Supervia (in ‡ Od.ODX 138)
T. dal Monte (♭ *G.7RQ 3039*)
E. Sack (♭ *Mer.EP 1-5022*)
G. Ritter-Ciampi (*Fr*) (in ‡ Ete. 707)
H. Maximova (*Russ*) (in ‡ Sup.LPM 186; U. 5106C)

ℍ Mme. Moga-Georgesco (in ‡ HRS. 3002*)
M. Ivogün (*Ger*) (*IRCC. 3133*;* in ‡ Sca. 815*)
M. Galvany (in ‡ AudR.LPA 2340*)
E. Mantelli (in **V**‡ *IRCC.L 7007**)

. . . Part 1, only
P. Munsel in ‡ **G.BLP 1023**
[Film *Melba*] (in ‡ QBLP 5015; in ‡ Vic.LM 7012:
♭ *set WDM 7012*]

No. 8, La calunnia è un venticello Bs
K. Borg **PV. 36095**
(*Boris Godounov—Pimen's narr. Act I*) (♭ *Pol. 30075*)
(& in Ger, PV 36088: ♭ *Pol. 30009*)

N. Rossi-Lemeni **G.DB 11357**
(*Guillaume Tell, No. 18*) (& from set, ♭ *Vic.ERA 229*)

G. Frick (*Ger*) **G.DB 11563**
(*Nozze di Figaro, No. 4*) (in ‡ WBLP 1505)

---

‡ = Long-playing, 33⅓ r.p.m.   ♭ = 45 r.p.m.   ℍ = Auto. couplings, 78 r.p.m.

No. 8, La calunnia è un venticello (*continued*)
I. Petrov (? *Russ*) & Saxon State Orch.
—Konwitschny (n.v.)   ♯ *Eta. 720002*
(*Boris, & Tchaikovsky*)   (o.n. *LPM 1017*)
A. Legros (*Fr*), from Highlights   ♭ *Plé.P 45147*
(*Don Carlos & Robert le Diable*)
☆ T. Pasero (Orf. 54006, d.c.)
  F. Chaliapin (in ♯ G.FJLP 5004: QJLP 104)
  E. Haken (*Cz*) (in ♯ *Sup.LPM 186;* in ♯ *U. 5106C*)
  A. Pernet (*Fr*) (in ♯ *Od.ODX 135*)
  A. Mestral (*Fr*) (♭ *G.7RF 290*)
  H F. Chaliapin (in ♯ *SBDH.LLP 4***)
  J. Mardones (in ♯ *SBDH.LPP 3***)
  A. Didur (in ♯ *Ete. 707***)

No. 9, Dunque io son   S & B
H. Marino & C. Galeffi   *Orf. 29002*
(*Trovatore—Il balen*)
☆ M. Tauberova & Z. Otava (*Cz*) (in ♯ *Sup.LPM 186;*
    in ♯ *U. 5106C*)

No. 10, A un dottor della mia sorte   Bs
C. Cambon (*Fr*)   ♭ *Plé.P 45153*
(*Diaz: Benvenuto Cellini, aria*)
☆ F. Corena (*Gazza Ladra, aria*)   ♭ *D. 71093*
    (& in ♯ Lon.LL 1334)

ACT II

No. 13, Contro un cor . . . Cara immagine   S & T
☆ V. de los Angeles & N. Monti   ♭ *G.7ER 5038*
    (*No. 7*) [from set]   (♭ *7ERQ 129*)
☆ C. Supervia & G. Manuritta (in ♯ *Od.ODX 138*)

No. 17, Storm Music   orch.
Bamberg Sym.—Leitner   ♭ *Pol. 32078*
(*Prophète—March*) (in ♯ *Pol. 17001;* in ♯ *AmD.DL 8509*)
Vienna State Op.—Swarowsky   in ♯ *U. 5106C*

No. 18, Ah! qual colpo inaspettato   S, T, Bs
V. Firsova, I. Kozlovsky & I. Burlak (*Russ*, from set)
    (*USSR. 22668/9*)

(La) **CAMBIALE DI MATRIMONIO**   1 Act
    1810
COMPLETE RECORDING
Fanny ... ... A. Tuccari (S)
E. Milfort ... ... G. Gentile (T)
Slook ... ... N. Catalani (B)
Sir T. Mill ... ... G. Onesti (B)
Clarina ... ... G. Ciferi (S)
Norton ... ... T. Dolciotti (B)
Rome Comic Opera Cho. & Rome Sym. Orch.
—Morelli   ♯ Nix.PLP 583
    (♯ Per.SPL 583; Cpt.MC 20039)
Overture
☆ Royal Phil.—Beecham (♭ *C.SEL 1509: SEBQ 108;*
    ♭ *AmC.4-4807*)

(Il) **CAMBIO DELLA VALIGIA**   1 Act   1812
(*Orig.: L'Occasione fa il ladro*)
COMPLETE RECORDING
Don Eusebius ... ... P. Besma (T)
Berenice ... ... G. Russo (S)
Count Albert ... ... F. Sacchi (T)
Don Parmenio ... ... N. Catalani (B)
Ernestine ... ... G. Salvi (M-S)
Martino ... ... T. Dolciotti (B)
Rome Comic Opera Co. & Orch.—Morelli
    ♯ Nix.PLP 595
    (♯ Per.SPL 595; Cpt.MC 20060)

(La) **CENERENTOLA**   2 Acts   1817
COMPLETE RECORDINGS

Casts	Set A	Set B
Clorinde (S)	A. Noni	K. Konstantinova
Tisbe (M-S)	F. Cadoni	N. Postavincheva
Angelina (Cenerentola)	M. de Gabarain	Z. Dolukhanova
Alidoro (Bs)	H. Alan	G. Troitsky
Don Magnifico (Bs)...	I. Wallace	K. Polyev
Don Ramiro (T) ...	J. Oncina	A. Orfenov
Dandini (B)	S. Bruscantini	E. Belov

Set A with Glyndebourne Fest. Cho. & Orch.
    —Gui   (6ss)   ♯ G.ALP 1147/9
    (♯ QALP 10066/8: FALP 331/3)
(4ss, ♯ Vic. set LHMV 600)

Set B (in *Russian*) with Moscow Radio Cho. &
    Orch.—Bron   (6ss)   ♯ USSR.D 0572/7
☆ O. Rovero, G. Simionato, C. Valletti, etc., Ital. Radio
    Cho. & Orch.—Rossi (♯ FSor.CS 541/2)
Overture
Vienna State Op.—Rossi   in ♯ Nix.PVL 7013
(*Viaggio a Reims, Tancredi, etc.*) (♯ Ama.AVRS 6012;
    Van.VRS 456)
L.S.O.—Gamba   in ♯ D.LXT 5137
(*Siège de Corinth, Guillaume Tell, etc.*)
(*Siège de Corinth, only* ♯ *D.LW 5223*)
Philharmonia—Galliera   in ♯ C.SX 1006
    (♯ FCX/QCX 208; Angel. 35011)
Glyndebourne—Gui   ♭ G.7ER 5024
(*Tancredi, Overture*) [from set]   (♭ *7ERQ 118: 7ERF 136*)
☆ N.B.C. Sym.—Toscanini (♭ *G.7ERF 103: 7ERQ 101*)
Italian Radio—Rossi, from set (in ♯ CCet.A 50151)
Miei rampolli (*Cavatina*)   B   Act I
☆ E. Badini (in ♯ Ete. 707)
Signore, una parola   M-S & Bs
☆ C. Supervia & V. Bettoni (in ♯ Od.ODX 138)
Nacqui all' affanno . . . Non più mesta   M-S
(*Aria & Rondo finale*)   Act II
G. Simionato   ♯ D.LW 5139
(*Barbiere, Capuleti, Don Carlos*)   (♯ *Lon.LD 9162*)
V. de los Angeles (S)   in ♯ G.ALP 1284
(*Cavalleria, La Wally, Ernani, etc.*)   (♯ *QALP 10155*)
☆ C. Supervia (in ♯ Od.ODX 138)

(La) **GAZZA LADRA**   2 Acts   1817
Overture
French Nat. Radio—Mirouze in ♯ Pat.ST 1069
R.I.A.S. Sym.—Fricsay   (2ss)   *PV. 36080*
    (in ♯ Pol. 18093: 19041)
Boston Orch. Soc.—Page   in ♯ Nix.SLPY 801
(*Bizet, Mendelssohn, Weber*)   (♯ *SOT. 2064* & in ♯ *10646*)
Vienna Radio—Schönherr   in ♯ Vien.LPR 1025
☆ Amsterdam—v. Beinum (♫ *D.LW 5017; Lon.LD 9023*)
    Boston Prom.—Fiedler (in ♯ Cam.CAL 122 & in
    ♯ set CFL 103)
— ARR. BAND
Cities Service Band—Lavalle (in ♯ Vic.LPM 1133:
    ♭ *set EPC 1133*)
Il mio piano è preparato   Bs   Act I
F. Corena   in ♯ D.LX 3109
(*Elisir d'Amore, Don Pasquale*)   (in ♯ *Lon.LS 701*)
(*Barbiere, No. 10* on ♭ *D. 71093*)   (also in ♯ Lon.LL 1334)

GUILLAUME TELL   4 Acts   1829   (*French*)
COMPLETE RECORDING (in *Italian*)
☆ R. Carteri (S), G. Taddei (B), M. Filippeschi (T) etc.,
    Italian Radio Cho. & Orch.—Rossi
    (♯ FSor.CS 537/40)
Excerpts
Soloists, Berlin Op. Cho. & Orch.—Rubahn (? *Ger*)
    (♯ Roy. 1411: ♭ *EP 245*)
Overture
N.B.C. Sym.—Toscanini (n.v.)   ♯ Vic.LRM 7054
(*Semiramide, Overture*) (♯ *FV.A 330203;* ♭ *ItV.A72R 0032;*
    in ♭ *Vic. set ERB 7054*)
(& ♯ *Vic.LRY 9000:* ♭ *set WRY 9000;* ♯ *ItV.A12R 0009*)
(also, ? o.v., ♯ *G.FBLP/QBLP 1035*)
Rome Sym.—Previtali   ♯ G.DLP 1038
(*Dukas & Verdi*)   (♯ *FFLP 1038: QDLP 6018*)
(*Ballet Music; & Weber, Verdi, etc. on* ♯ *BB.LBC 1092*)
Philharmonia—Galliera   in ♯ C.SX 1006
    (in ♯ FCX/QCX 208; in ♯ Angel. 35011)
L.S.O.—Gamba   ♯ D.LXT 5137
(*Tancredi, Signor Bruschino, etc.*)
Belgian Radio—André   ♯ T.LS 6026
(*Barbiere & Tancredi Overtures*)   (♯ *FT. 270.TC.039*)
Florence Fest.—Gui   ♯ AudC. 1163
(*Glinka & Massenet*)
☆ Covent Garden—Braithwaite   in ♯ P.PMC 1029
    (in ♯ MGM.E 3028: ♭ *X 1048*)
Hamburg Philharmonia—H-J. Walther (*MSB. 78047/8*)
Regent Sym. (in ♯ Rgt. 7002)
Berlin Sym.—Rubahn (in ♯ Roy. 1413)
Bolshoi Th.—Fayer (*USSR. 21596/9;* ♯ *D 1106*)
(*continued on next page*)

☆ = Re-issue of a recording to be found in previous volumes.

GUILLAUME TELL—Overture (*continued*)

☆ Amsterdam—v. Beinum (‡ *D.LW 5039; Lon.LD 9032*)
Berlin Phil.—v. Kempen (‡ *Pol. 17056:* ♭ *30099*)
Berlin Municipal Op.—Rother (in ‡ Nix.ULP 9057:
    ♭ *EP 739;* in ‡ *Ura.RS 5-4:* ♭ *UREP 39;* ‡ *ACC.MP 28*)
Vienna Sym.—Swarowsky (in ‡ *Sup.LPM 225;*
       U. 5204C; CdM.LDM 8042)
Col. Sym.—Rodzinski (♭ *AmC.A 1591:* in ‡ CL 726;
       Phi.S 04601L)

☆ Italian Radio—Rossi, from set (in ‡ CCet.A 50151)
Boston Prom.—Fiedler (in ‡ Cam.CAL 116 &
       in ‡ set CFL 103)
Austrian Sym.—Wöss (in ‡ Ply. 12-103; in
       ‡ *AFest.CFR 26*)

ACT I

No. 2, Ah! Mathilde   T & B
   ᴴ L. Slezak & L. Demuth (*Ger*) (in ‡ Ete. 707*)

Ballet Music
No. 3, Ciel, qui du monde
... Orch. Intro. only   (Bridal Procession—"Little March")
No. 4, Hymenée, ta journée — ᴀʀʀ. ᴏʀᴄʜ.   ("*Dance*")
No. 5, Pas de six   (*Passo a sei*—"*Ballet*" Act I)
☆ Santa Cecilia—Serafin (in ‡ BB.LBC 1039:
       ♭ *set WBC 1039*)

No. 5, Pas de six   (Ballet)
L.S.O.—Previtali   **G.C 4243**
(*No. 16*)   (in ‡ BB.LBC 1092)

☆ Orch.—Kostelanetz (C.DOX 1024: ♭ *SED 5511:*
       SEDQ 526: ESDF 1027)
N.B.C. Sym.—Toscanini (in ‡ Vic.LRM 7005:
      ♭ *set ERB 7005;* ♭ ItV.A72R 0007; ‡ *FV.A 33021*l)

Unspecified Dances
Bamberg Sym.—Lehmann   ♭ *Pol. 30038*
(*Rosamunde Ballet II*)(in ‡ *Pol. 16062: 17039*; No. 5 only
       in ‡ *AmD.DL 4089*)

ACT II

No. 9, Sombre forêt   S
M. Benetti   (*Ital*, 2ss)   **Cet.PE 210**

N. Shpiller (*Russ*) (*USSRM.D 001279*)
☆ J. Hammond (G.ED 1224)
ᴴ R. Ponselle (*Ital*) (in ‡ Sca. 803*)
C. Muzio (*Ital*) (in ‡ LI.TWV 91053*)[1]

No. 11, Quand l'Helvétie   T, B, Bs
(*Allor che scorre ... Troncar suoi*)
   ᴴ L. Escalais, A. Mengini-Colleti & U. Luppi
       (in ‡ Ete. 707*)

ACT III

No. 15, Pas de trois (orch.);
A nos chants   (cho.—Tyrolienne);
Allegretto & Maestoso   (orch.)[2]
L.P.O.—Martinon   **D.LXT 5149**
(½s—*J. Strauss: Beau Danube*)   (‡ Lon.LL 1383)
☆ Covent Garden Op.—Braithwaite (in ‡ P.PMC 1029;
       MGM.E 3028)

No. 16, Soldiers' March   orch.
L.S.O.—Previtali   **G.C 4243**
(*No. 5*)   (in ‡ BB.LBC 1092)

No. 18, Je te bénis ... Sois immobile   B
N. Rossi-Lemeni (*Ital*)   **G.DB 11357**
(*Barbiere, No. 8*)(in ‡G.ALP 1074: FALP 306: QALP 10033)
G. Valdengo (*Ital*)   ***Cet.AT 0368***
(*Don Giovanni, No. 17*)   (♭ *EPO 0318; Cap. FAP 7016*)
M. Singher (*Ital*)   in ‡ **Roy. 1613**
(*Africaine, Contes d'Hoffmann, etc.*)
G. Taddei (*Ital*)   ***Cet.AT 0404***
(*Fanciulla del West—Minnie della mia casa*)
       (in ‡ LPC 55006)
☆ A. Endrèze (in ‡ Pat.PCX 5006)
G. Bechi (*Ital*) (in ‡ G.QALP 10087)
ᴴ M. Battistini (*Ital*) (in ‡ Ete. 707*)
J. Schwarz (*Ital*) (in ‡ Ete. 498*)

ACT IV

No. 19, Asile héreditaire   T
K. Baum (*Ital*)   in ‡ **Roy. 1582**
   ᴴ M. Gilion (*Ital ?*) (in ‡ Ete. 707*)
G. Martinelli (*Ital*) (in ‡ Vic. set LCT 6701*;
   in ‡ SBDH.GLI 1*; in LPG 4*; & in ‡ JAL 7000*)

(L') INGANNO FELICE   1 Act   1812
Overture
☆ Austrian Sym.—Gui (in ‡ Rem. 199-123 & 199-142;
       & in ‡ Ply. 12-65)

(L') ITALIANA IN ALGERI   2 Acts   1813
Cᴏᴍᴘʟᴇᴛᴇ Rᴇᴄᴏʀᴅɪɴɢ

Zulma	...	...	... M. Masini (M-S)
Elvira...	...	...	G. Sciutti (S)
Lindoro	...	...	C. Valletti (T)
Mustafa	...	...	M. Petri (B)
Haly ...	...	...	E. Campi (Bs)
Isabella	...	...	G. Simionato (M-S)
Taddeo	...	...	M. Cortis (B)

La Scala Cho. & Orch.—Giulini   ‡ **C.CX 1215/6**
(4ss)   (‡ FCX 388/9: QCX 10111/2; Angel. set 3529)

Overture
Philharmonia—Galliera   **C.DX 1910**
(in ‡ SX/WSX 1006: FCX/QCX 208; in ‡ Angel. 35011)
(also on ♭ *C.SED 5502: ESBF 110: SEBQ 104*)
Vienna State Op.—Rossi   in ‡ **Nix.PVL 7013**
(*Semiramide, Cenerentola, etc.*) (in ‡ Ama.AVRS 6012;
       Van.VRS 456)
L.P.O.—Solti   ‡ **D.LW 5207**
(*Barbiere Overture*)
French Nat. Radio—Mirouze in ‡ ***Pat.ST 1069***
Czech Phil.—Šejna   **U.H 24413**
☆ New Sym.—Erede (‡ *D.LW 5006:* ♭ *DX 1765*)
Berlin Phil.—Fricsay (in ‡ *AmD.ED 3543;* ♭ *Pol. 30064:*
   in ‡ Pol. 18093: 19041; IPV. 8190 & 8201, d.c.)
Santa Cecilia—Serafin (♭ *G.7BF 1051: 7PQ 2011;*
     in ‡ BB.LBC 1039: ♭ set WBC 1039)
C. B. S. Sym.—Barlow (in ‡ AmC.RL 3030: ♭ *A 1554*)
E.I.A.R.—Previtali (Orf. 54021)

— ᴀʀʀ. BAND
Col. Concert Band—Gould (‡ *AmC.AL 41*)

Languir per una bella   T   Act I
C. Valletti   in ‡ **Cet.LPC 55002**
(*Barbiere, Werther, Lucia, etc.*)

O che muso   M-S & Bs
Per lui che adoro   M-S, T, B, Bs   Act II
☆ C. Supervia, N. Ederle, C. Scattola, V. Bettoni
       (in ‡ Od.ODX 138)

MOSÈ IN EGITTO   3 Acts   1818
Dal tuo stellato soglio   Bs, A, S, T, Cho.   (*Preghiera*)
... S & Bs parts only
   ᴴ M. Alexina & G. Mansueto (*SBDH.P 9*)

March on themes from the opera — ᴀʀʀ. Vessella
☆ Italian Navy Band—Aghemo (in ‡ *G.QFLP 4010*)

OTELLO   3 Acts   1816
Assisa a piè d'un salice   S   Act III
M. L. Gemelli   (2ss)   **Cet.PE 195**

(La) SCALA DI SETA   1 Act   1812
Cᴏᴍᴘʟᴇᴛᴇ Rᴇᴄᴏʀᴅɪɴɢ

Giulia	...	...	... A. Tuccari (S)
Lucilla	...	...	G. Salvi (M-S)
Dorvil	...	...	G. Gentile (T)
Dormont	...	...	P. Besma (T)
Blansac	...	...	N. Catalani (B)
Germano	...	...	T. Dolciotti (B)

& Rome Qtt. Soc. Cho. & Orch.—Morelli
       ‡ **Nix.PLP 591**
       (‡ Per.SPL 591; Cpt.MC 20063)

Overture
Philharmonia—Galliera   in ‡ **C.SX 1006**
(‡ FCX/QCX 208; Angel. 35011; also ♭ *C.SED 5502:*
       ESBF 110: SEBQ 104)
Belgian Radio—André   ‡ **DT.TM 68020**
(*Ponchielli*)   (TV.VE 9037)
☆ Amsterdam—v. Beinum   ‡ **D.LW 5017**
(*Gazza Ladra*)   (‡ Lon.LD 9023)
☆ Berlin Phil.—Fricsay (in ‡ Pol. 18093: 19041: ♭ *30064;*
     ♭ *AmD.ED 3543;* IPV. 8201)

---

[1] From Edison & Pathé hill & dale recordings. This disc was withdrawn almost immediately on issue.
[2] Excerpts may also be in the Lehmann recording *supra*. There is no cho. in the recordings listed.

SEMIRAMIDE 2 Acts 1823
Overture
  N.B.C. Sym.—Toscanini   **♯ *Vic.LRM 7054***
  (Guillaume Tell, Overture)(♭ set ERB 7054; ♯ FV.A 330203)
  Philadelphia—Beecham   **♯ *AmC.AAL 27***
  (Carmen Suite)
  Philharmonia—Galliera   in ♯ **C.SX 1006**
  (in ♯ Angel. 35011; ♯ C.WSX 1006: FCX/QCX 208)
  Vienna State Op.—Rossi   in ♯ **Nix.PVL 7013**
  (Cenerentola, Viaggio a Reims, etc.) (♯ Ama.AVRS 6012;
                  Van.VRS 456)
  Vienna State Op.—Swarowsky   **♯ *U. 5106C***
  (Barbiere, excerpts)
  French Nat. Radio—Mirouze in ♯ *Pat.ST 1069*
  Colón Theatre—Martini   in ♯ *ArgOd.LDC 509*
                    (♭ BSOAE 4529)
  ☆ Amsterdam—v. Beinum (♯ *D.LW 5039; Lon.LD 9032;*
                & in ♯ ArgLon.LL 17513)
  R.I.A.S. Sym.—Fricsay (in ♯ *Pol. 18093: 19041)*

Bel raggio lusinghier S Act I
  G. Sciutti   in ♯ *Phi.N 00705R*
  (Sonnambula, Puritani, Don Pasquale, Linda, etc.)
  ☆ L. Alessandrini (in ♯ *Ete. 707*)
  H C. Boninsegna (in ♯ *Sca. 813**)
    M. Sembrich (in ♯ *Vic. set LCT 6701**)

(Le) SIÈGE DE CORINTHE 3 Acts 1826
Overture
  Vienna State Op.—Rossi   in ♯ **Nix.PVL 7013**
  (Turco in Italia, Italiana, etc.) (♯ Ama.AVRS 6012;
                    Van.VRS 456)
  L.S.O.—Gamba   in ♯ **D.LXT 5137**
  (Cenerentola, Guillaume Tell, Tancredi, etc.)
  (Cenerentola Overture only, on ♯ D.LW 5223)
  ☆ Austrian Sym.—Gui (in ♯ *Rem. 199-142*)

(II) SIGNOR BRUSCHINO 1 Act 1813
COMPLETE RECORDING
  Gaudenzio ... ... R. Capecchi (B)
  Sofia ... ... E. Ribetti (S)
  Bruschino ... ... C. Maugeri (Bs)
  His son ... ... C. Rossi (T)
  Florville ... ... L. Pontiggia (T)
  etc., & Milan Phil.—Gerelli
               ♯ *E. & AmVox.PL 8460*
Overture
  Philharmonia—Galliera   in ♯ **C.SX 1006**
      (in ♯ Angel. 35011; ♯ C.FCX/QCX 208)
  L.S.O.—Gamba   in ♯ **D.LXT 5137**
  (Cenerentola, Guillaume Tell, etc.)
  (Tancredi Overture on ♭ D. 71111)
  ☆ R.I.A.S. Sym.—Fricsay (in ♯ *Pol. 18093: 19041*
                        ♭ AmD.ED 3544)
  N.B.C. Sym.—Toscanini (♭ *G.7ER 5017*)

TANCREDI 2 Acts 1813
Overture
  Glyndebourne Fest.—Gui   **G.DB 21607**
  (Cenerentola Overture on ♭ 7ER 5024: 7ERQ 118: 7ERF 136)
  Vienna State Op.—Rossi   in ♯ **Nix.PVL 7013**
  (Siège de Corinthe, Turco in Italia, etc.)
          (♯ Ama.AVRS 6012; Van.VRS 456)
  L.S.O.—Gamba   in ♯ **D.LXT 5137**
  (Signor Bruschino, Cenerentola, etc.)
  (Signor Bruschino Overture only, on ♭ D. 71111)
  Belgian Radio—André   **♯ *DT.TM 68024***
  (Barbiere, Overture; in ♯ T.LS 6026; in ♯ FT. 270.TC. 039)
  Vienna State Op.—Swarowsky ♯ *Sup.LPM 226*
  (Weber, Verdi, Wagner)   *(♯ U. 5203C)*
  Linz Sym. (in ♯ Ply. 12-34)
  ☆ Rhineland Sym.—Federer (in ♯ *AFest.CFR 10-601*)
  R.I.A.S. Sym.—Fricsay (in ♯ *Pol. 18093: 19041;*
               ♭ AmD.ED 3544: ♭ DL 4063)

(II) TURCO IN ITALIA 2 Acts 1814
COMPLETE RECORDING
  Fiorilla ... ... M. M. Callas (S)
  Narciso ... ... N. Gedda (T)
  Zaida... ... ... J. Gardino (M-S)
  The Turk ... ... N. Rossi-Lemeni (Bs)
  The Poet ... ... M. Stabile (B)
  & La Scala Cho. & Orch.—Gavazzeni
               ♯ *C.CX 1289S/91*
  (5ss) (♯ QCX 10153S/5; Angel. 35176/8, set 3535)

Overture
  Vienna State Op.—Rossi   in ♯ **Nix.PVL 7013**
  (Italiana, Semiramide, Cenerentola, etc.)
          (♯ Van.VRS 456; Ama.AVRS 6012)

(II) VIAGGIO A REIMS 2 Acts 1825
Overture
  Vienna State Op.—Rossi   in ♯ **Nix.PVL 7013**
  (Tancredi, Siège de Corinthe, etc.) (♯ Ama.AVRS 6012:
                     Van.VRS 456)
  R.I.A.S. Sym.—Fricsay   **PV. 72490**
  (Barbiere, Overture)   *(♭ Pol. 30090)*
  Polish Radio—Krenz   **Muza.X 2301**

ROUSSEL, Albert (1869-1937)

(L') Accueil des Muses pf. 1920
  (for Le Tombeau de Debussy)
  E. Ulmer   **♯ CHS.H 12**
  (Dukas, Goossens, Malipiero, Stravinsky, Debussy)

BACCHUS ET ARIANE, Op. 43 Ballet 1930
Symphonic Suites Nos. 1 & 2
  Lamoureux—Martinon (2ss) **♯ *EPhi.NBR 6031***
  (Debussy & Fauré on ♯ Epic.LC 3165) *(♯ Phi.A 00748R)*
Suite No. 2 only
  Boston Sym.—Münch   **♯ Vic.LM 1741**
  (Honegger & Ravel)(♭ set WDM 1741; ♯ ItV.A12R 0110; &
             ♯ Vic. set LM 6113, d.c.)
  (Ravel, Meyerbeer, Piston, on ♯ FV.A 630217)
  (Honegger only on ♯ G.FALP 169)
  (Ravel & Stravinsky on ♯ ItV.A12R 0130)

Concerto, C major, pf. & orch., Op. 36 1927
  L. Gousseau & Lamoureux—Sacher
              ♯ Phi.A 00251L
  (below)   *(♯ Epic.LC 3129)*

Concerto for small orchestra, Op. 34 1927
  Lamoureux—Sacher   **♯ Phi.A 00251L**
  (above & below)   *(♯ Epic.LC 3129)*
  Saar Cha.—Ristenpart   **♯ DFr. 148**
  (below)

Divertissement, Op. 6 fl., ob., cl., bsn., hrn. & pf.
                        1906
  French Wind Quintet & R. Veyron-Lacroix
              ♯ DFr. 148
  (above & below)

(Le) Festin de l'Araignée, Op. 17 Ballet 1912
  Suisse Romande—Ansermet   **♯ D.LXT 5035**
  (below)   *(♯ Lon.LL 1179)*
  Detroit Sym.—Paray   **♯ EMer.MG 50035**
  (Dukas & Fauré)   *(♯ FMer.MLP 50035)*
  Lamoureux—Martinon   **♯ Phi.A 00175L**
  (Debussy, Honegger, etc.)   *(♯ Epic.LC 3058)*
  ☆ French Radio Sym.—Leibowitz   **♯ Ll.TWV 91055**
  (below)

Impromptu, Op. 21 harp 1919
  N. Zabaleta   in ♯ **Eso.ES 523**
  († Contemporary Harp Music)

(Le) Marchand de sable qui passe, Op. 13 Ballet
                        1908
  Paris Ens.—Froment   **♯ EPP.APG 115**
  (Sinfonietta; & Bartók)
  ☆ French Radio Sym.—Leibowitz   **♯ Ll.TWV 91055**
  (above)

PART SONG: Le Bardit des Francs 1926
  (Chateaubriand) Male Cho. (with brass & perc. ad lib.)
  Paris Univ. Cho. & Paris Cons.—Tzipine
  (below)   **♯ C.FCX 413**

Petite Suite, Op. 39 orch. 1929
  Lamoureux—Sacher   **♯ Phi.A 00251L**
  (above & below)   *(♯ Epic.LC 3129)*
  Suisse Romande—Ansermet   **♯ D.LXT 5035**
  (above)   *(♯ Lon.LL 1179)*
  Paris Cons.—Tzipine   **♯ C.FCX 413**
  (above & below)
  ☆ Berlin Radio—Celibidache (♯ *ANix.ULPY 9006*)

☆ = Re-issue of a recording to be found in **previous** volumes.

(3) Petites pièces, Op. 49 pf. 1933
L. Gousseau ♯ *Plé.P 3072*
(below)
☆ M. Haas (in ♯ Pol. 18077)

Psalm LXXX, Op. 37[1] T, cho., orch. 1928
M. Sénéchal, Paris Univ. Cho. & Paris Cons.
—Tzipine *(Fr)* ♯ *C.FCX 413*
(above & below)

Quartet, D major, Op. 45 Strings 1931-2
☆ Lowenguth Qtt. *(Prokofiev)* ♯ Pol. 18249

Serenade, Op. 30 fl., vln., vla., vlc. & hp. 1925
J-P. Rampal, Pasquier Trio & L. Laskine
(above & below) ♯ *DFr.* 148

Sinfonietta, Op. 52 str. orch. 1934
Lamoureux—Sacher ♯ *Phi.A 00251L*
(above) (♯ Epic.LC 3129)
Paris Cons.—Tzipine ♯ *C.FCX 413*
(above)
Saar Cha.—Ristenpart ♯ *DFr.* 148
(above)
Hastings Sym.—Bath ♯ *Allo.* 4053
(Delius & Haydn)
Paris Str. Orch.—Froment ♯ *EPP.APG 115*
(Le Marchand de sable . . . & Bartók)
(Shostakovich & Bartók on ♯ EPP.APG 120, *replacing the
above coupling)*

Sonatina, Op. 16 pf. 1912
L. Gousseau *(above & below)* ♯ *Plé.P 3072*
L. Thyrion ♯ *Phi.N 00666R*
(Schmitt & Dukas)

SONGS
COLLECTION
Amoureux separés, Op. 12 (No. 2 of *2 Poèmes chinois*)
(Roché, after Fu-Mi)
Le Bachelier de Salamanque, Op. 20, No. 2 (Chalupt)
Cœur en péril, Op. 50, No. 1 (Chalupt)
Le Jardin mouillé, Op. 3, No. 3 (de Régnier)
Light, Op. 19, No. 1 (Jean-Aubry)
Sarabande, Op. 20, No. 1 (Chalupt)
G. Souzay (B), J. Bonneau (pf.) ♯ *Lum.LD 3-407*
(Leguerney)

(Le) Bachelier de Salamanque, Op. 20, No. 2
(Chalupt) (No. 1 of *2 Songs*, 1919)
M. Sénéchal (T), J. Bonneau (pf.)
in ♯ *Phi.N 00681R*
(Gounod, Massenet, Bizet, etc.)

Cœur en péril, Op. 50, No. 1 (Chalupt)
G. Touraine (S), F. Poulenc (pf.) ♯ *BàM.LD 012*
(below; & Debussy, Poulenc) (♯ HS.HSL 154)

(2) Poèmes chinois, Op. 12 (Roché)
1. Ode à un jeune gentilhomme (after Giles)
2. Amoureux separés (after Fu-Mi)
G. Touraine (S), F. Poulenc (pf.) ♯ *BàM.LD 012*
(above) (♯ HS.HSL 154)

Suite, Op. 14 pf. 1910
L. Gousseau *(above)* ♯ *Plé.P 3072*

...No. 4, Ronde, only
J-M. Damase ♯ *D.FST 153527*
(Françaix, Messiaen, Poulenc, etc.)

Suite, F major, Op. 33 orch. 1926
☆ Lamoureux—Tzipine (♯ T.LCE 8104)

Symphony No. 4, A major, Op. 53 1930
☆ Lamoureux—Tzipine (♯ T.LCE 8104)
Philharmonia—v. Karajan (♯ C.FCX 163: QCX 163)

Trio, Op. 40 fl., vla., vlc. 1929
D. A. Dwyer, J. de Pasquale & S. Mayes
(Poulenc) ♯ *Bo.B 208*
J-P. Rampal, P. & E. Pasquier ♯ *DDP.DP 43-1*
(below; & Ravel) (♯ HS.HSL 149)
J. Baker, L. Fuchs & H. Fuchs ♯ *AmD.DL 9777*
(Debussy) (♯ D.UAT 273588)

Trio, Op. 58 vln., vla., vlc. 1937
Pasquier Trio ♯ *DDP.DP 43-1*
(above; & Ravel) (♯ HS.HSL 149)

ROUSSEL, François (fl. XVIth Cent.)
SEE: ROSSELLI, F.

ROY, Adrian le (d. c. 1589)
SEE: † FRENCH CHANSONS
† XVTH & XVITH CENTURY FRENCH SONGS
† XVITH & XVIITH CENTURY SONGS

ROZSA, Miklos (b. 1907)

FILM MUSIC (Abridged listing)
IVANHOE (1952) Sym.—Rozsa (♯ *MGM.E 179*)
JULIUS CAESAR (1952-3)
From Sound Track (in ♯ MGM.E 3033: ♭ *set K 204:* ♯ *C 751*)
PLYMOUTH ADVENTURE (1952-3)
Sym.—Rozsa (♯ *MGM.E 179*)
QUO VADIS (1951)
Frankenland State—Kloss (♯ *DCap.LC 6636;* ♯ *Cap.H 454:*
♭ *set FBF 454 & in* ♯ *T 456*)
(The) RED HOUSE (1947)
☆ Orch.—Rozsa (♯ *DCap.CCL 7505; Cap.H 453:*
& T 456: ♭ *set FAP 2-453*)
SPELLBOUND (1946)
Frankenland State—Kloss (♯ *DCap.CCL 7505:*
Cap.H 453: ♭ *FAP 1-453 & in* ♯ *T 456*)

RUBBRA, Edmund Duncan (b. 1901)

(A) GARLAND FOR THE QUEEN
(with Tippett, Bax, Ireland, etc.)
... Salutation (Hassall) 1953
Cambridge Univ. Madrigal Cho.—Ord
in † ♯ *C.CX 1063*

Missa in honorem Sancti Dominici, Op. 66
unacc. cho. 1949
Fleet Street Cho.—Lawrence[2] ♯ *D.LXT 2794*
(Vaughan Williams) (♯ Lon.LL 805)
Sonata No. 2, Op. 31 vln. & pf. 1931
F. Grinke & E. Rubbra ♯ *D.LXT 2978*
(Berkeley) (♯ Lon.LL 1055)
Symphony No. 5, B flat major, Op. 63 1947-8
☆ Hallé—Barbirolli ♯ *G.BLP 1021*
Trio, Op. 68 pf., vln., vlc. 1950
☆ E. Rubbra, E. Gruenberg, W. Pleeth (♯ Argo.RG 5)

RUBINO, Cesare (fl. XVIIth Cent.)

Adagio, A minor — ARR. VLC. & PF.
A. Schmidt & C. Fannière ♯ *Vill. 1*
(Schumann, Eccles, etc.)

RUBINSTEIN, Anton (1830-1894)

CLASSIFIED: I. Instrumental & Orchestral
II. Operas
III. Songs

I. INSTRUMENTAL & ORCHESTRAL

Bal costumé, Op. 103 20 pieces, pf. duet
... 1. Introduction
3. Berger et bergère
5. Pêcheur napolitain et Napolitaine
7. Toréador et Andalouse
18. Tambour-majeur et vivandière
— ARR. ORCH. Erdmannsdörfer
Bolshoi Theatre—Fayer ♯ *USSR.D 1107/8*
(2ss)
... No. 7 — ARR. ORCH.
Colón Theatre—Fauré in ♯ *ArgOd.LDC 507*

---

[1] Originally to English words.
[2] The *Kyrie* and *Gloria* were cond. by Rubbra.

Barcarolle, G minor, Op. 50, No. 3 pf.
Barcarolle, G major ("No. 4")
A. Rubinstein   ♭ *Vic.ERA 205*
(*Valse caprice*)   (♭ *FV.A 95211;* ♭ *ItV.A72R 0027*)
Concerto No. 4, D minor, Op. 70 pf. & orch. 1864
G. Ginsburg, State Sym.—Shereshevsky
                                           ♯ *USSR.D 1151/3*
(3ss—*National Dances*)
G. Stein & Berlin Sym.—Rubahn ♯ *Roy.* 1556
☆ F. Wührer & Vienna Philharmonia—Moralt
                                           (♯ EVox.PL 7780)

Kamennoi Ostrov, Op. 10 24 pieces, pf.
... **No. 22, Rêve angélique** — ARR. ORCH.
Boston Prom.—Fiedler   in ♯ *Vic.LM 1910*
(*Liszt, Kreisler, Gounod, etc.*)   (♭ *ItV.A72R 0049*)
Decca Sym.—Mendoza (in ♯ *AmD.DL 5211; D.US 223524;*
                                           ▽ *AmD. set A 190*)
Nat. Op. Orch. (in ♯ *Roy.* 1829)
Melody, F major, Op. 3, No. 1 pf.
— ARR. ORCH.
N.W. Ger. Phil.—Schüchter (in ♯ *Imp.ILP 114;*
                                           G.QDLP 6026)
Concert Orch.—E. Robinson (in ♯ *Argo.RG 40;*
                                           West.WP 6002)
New Prom.—Robertson (in ♯ *Lon.LB 581*)
A. Bernard Str. Orch. (*Pat.PT 1005* & ♭ *G 1025*)
Royale Concert Orch. (in ♯ *Roy.* 1567; in ♯ *Ply.* 12-128)
— ARR. ORG.
J. Perceval (*ArgOd. 57054:* in ♯ *LDC 513:* ♭ *BSOAE 4528*)
— ARR. VLC. & PF.
☆ G. Cassadó & O. Schulhof (in ♯ *Rem.* 199-128)
— ARR. GUITAR: A. Valenti (in ♯ *SMC.* 1002)

(7) National Dances, Op. 82 pf.
... **No. 1, Russian Dance : Trepak** — ARR. ORCH.
Bolshoi Th.—Fayer   ♯ *USSR.D 1154*
(*Concerto, s. 3*)
    ▽ Moscow Radio—Orlov (*USSR. 12316/7*)
... **No. 7, Bohemian Polka** J. Flier (in ♯ *Csm.CRLP 147*)

Romance, E flat major, Op. 44, No. 1 pf.
— VOCAL ARR. "Night" (to words by Pushkin)
Z. Dolukhanova (A)   *USSRM.D 00607*
(*The Bard; & Rachmaninoff*)
L. Rudenko (M-S)   in ♯ *USSRM.D 2073*
(*Bizet, St-Saëns, Rimsky, etc.*)
Estonian State Male Qtt. (*Estonian*) (*USSR.* 22117)
— ARR. VLN. & PF.
I. Bezrodny & pf.   *USSRM.D 00342*
(*Wagner: Albumblatt*)
— ARR. VLC. & PF.
E. B. Bengtsson & H. D. Koppel   *G.DA 5283*
(*Saint-Saëns: Le Cygne*)
☆ G. Piatigorsky & R. Berkowitz (*G.DA 2052;*
          ♭ *Vic.ERA 122;* in ♯ *ItV.A12R 0105*)
— ARR. ORCH.
Concert Orch.—E. Robinson (in ♯ *Argo.RG 66*)
Mantovani Orch. (in ♯ *D.LK 4072;* Lon.LL 872)
G. Melachrino Orch. (in ♯ *G.DLP 1083;* Vic.LPM 1003:
                                           ♭ *set EPB 1003*)

Valse caprice, E flat major pf.
A. Rubinstein (n.v.)   ♭ *Vic.ERA 205*
(*Barcarolle*) (♭ *FV.A 95211;* ♭ *ItV.A72R 0027*)
— ARR. ORCH.
Moscow Radio—Samosud   *USSRM.D 00110*
(*Feramors excpt.*)

II. OPERAS

(The) DEMON 3 Acts 1875
Ballet Music
Linz Sym.   ♯ *Ply.* 12-27
(*Tchaikovsky*)
Accursed world! Bs Act I
☆ A. Ivanov (in ♯ *Csm.CRLP 139*)
Invocation to the night Male Cho.
Bolshoi Theatre Cho. (in ♯ *USSR.D 1523*)
    ▽ Red Banner Ens. (*USSR.* 9033)

On desire's soft fleeting wing T Act I
☆ I. Kozlovsky (in ♯ *Sti. 1000;* in ♯ *Csm.CRLP 139*)
S. Lemeshev (*USSRM.D 00194*)
Do not weep, my child Bs Act II
☆ G. London (in ♯ *AmC.ML 4658*)
❏ F. Chaliapin (*AF.AGSB 8*;* ♯ *Sca.* 801*; &
                              in ♯ *SBDH.JAL 7002**)
    G. de Luca (*Ital*) (in ♯ *SBDH.JSL 7001**)
    T. Ruffo (*Ital*) (in ♯ *SBDH.LLP 7**)
    J. Schwarz (*Ger*) (in ♯ *Ete.* 498*)
On the airy ocean Bs Act III
❏ F. Chaliapin (*AF.AGSB 8**)
COMPLETE RECORDING OF CONVENT SC. & FINALE
    (ACT III)
M. Lobanova-Rogacheva (S), M. Grishko (B),
A. Sopova (S), etc., Kiev Op. Cho. & Orch.
    —Piradov (2ss)   ♯ *USSR.D 1137/8*
Calm and clear is the night S Act III
☆ E. Katulskaya (in ♯ *USSR.D 1523*)
❏ A. Neshdanova (*AF.AGSB 71**)
I am he whom you called Bs Act III
R. Arié   ♯ *D.LW 5067*
(*Boris Godounov*)   (♯ *Lon.LD 9073;* ♭ *DX 1776*)
☆ A. Ivanov (in ♯ *Csm.CRLP 139;* in ♯ *USSR.D 1523*)

FERAMORS 2 Acts 1863
Dance of the Kashmir Brides orch.
(*Lichtertanz der Bräute*)
U.S.S.R. State Sym.—Gauk   *USSRM.D 00112*
(*below*)
F.O.K. Sym.—Smetáček   ♯ *Sup.LPM 121*
(*Glazounov, Suppé, J. Strauss*)   (♯ *U. 5117C,* d.c.)

NERO 4 Acts 1879
Epithalamium, Act I Bs
☆ A. Ivanov (in ♯ *Csm.CRLP 139*)

III. SONGS

Ballade (Turgenev)
B. Gmyria (Bs)   *USSRM.D 00787*
(*Rachmaninoff: O cease thy singing*)
    ▽ A. Pirogov (B) (*USSR.* 08269)
(The) Bard, Op. 115, No. 10 (Pushkin)
Z. Dolukhanova (A)   *USSRM.D 00607*
(*above; & Rachmaninoff*)
Had I but known, Op. 101, No. 1 (A. K. Tolstoy)
V. Borisenko (M-S)   *USSR.* 022749
(*Glinka: I feel so bitter*)
(12) Persian Songs, Op. 34 (Mirza-Schaffy)
... No. 1, Zuleika
No. 4, The Rose
No. 6, I feel thy breath
No. 9, Gold rolls here below me
No. 10, The bright sun shines
B. Gmyria (Bs)[1]   *USSRM.D 00570*
(& in ♯ *Sup.LPM 185;* U. *5100C*)   & *001239/40*
... **No. 9, Gold rolls here below me**
    (or: *Persian Love Song*)
M. Reizen (Bs)   *USSRM.D 00621*
(*Glinka: Doubt*)
❏ F. Chaliapin (Bs) (in ♯ *Sca.* 807*; in *Cum.CPR 333**)
(Die) Träne, Op. 83, No. 8 (after T. Moore)
V. Borisenko (M-S, *Russ*)   *USSRM.D 00740*
(*Rimsky, Arensky*)

RUBINSTEIN, Beryl (b. 1898)

Sonata, flute & pf.
M. Sharp & M. M. Mastics   ♯ *CIM.* pte.
(*Bartók : Sonata*)

RUBINUS (fl. XVth Cent.)
SEE: † HISTORY OF MUSIC IN SOUND (31)

---

[1] These identities have been deduced from the USSR listings. The Czech disc is labelled as acc. by L. Ostrin, and may differ; a copy checked has Nos. 1, 4, 9; 8, *Bend, opening blossom;* and one unid.

RUDEL, Jaufré (fl. 1130-1141)

SEE: † FRENCH TROUBADOUR SONGS
     † MONUMENTA ITALICAE MUSICAE
     † POLYPHONIE SACRÉE

RUE, Pierre de la (*c.* 1450-1518)

CHANSONS
Pourquoy non 4 vv.
Autant en emporté le vent insts.
Pro Musica Antiqua Ens.—Cape
     in ‡ HP.APM 14032
(† Chansons from Music Books)
[Pourquoy non, also on PV. 5407]

Autant en emporté le vent
☆ Inst. Ens.—Cape (in † ‡ HS.AS 4)

MASS: Requiem . . . Introit only
Schola Polyphonica—Washington   † G.HMS 27
(*Obrecht*)   (in ‡ Vic. set LM 6016)

MOTETS
O salutaris hostia
Welch Cho.—J. B. Welch   in ‡ Lyr.LL 52
(† Motets of XVth & XVIth Centuries)

Petits Chanteurs—Pagot   in V‡ *Era.LDE 1001*
(† Polyphonic Motets)   (in ‡ HS.HS 9007)

Salve Regina
Cho.—Eeckhout   in ‡ OL.LD 81
(† Musiciens de la Cour de Bourgogne II)

RUFFO, Vincenzo (*c.* 1510-1587)

SEE: † MOTETS OF THE VENETIAN SCHOOL, VOL. II

RUGGIERI, Giovanni Martino
         (fl. 1690-1712)

(10) Sonate di chiesa, Op. 3   2 vlns. & cont.   1693

1. E minor	6. A major
2. B minor	7. A minor
3. B flat major	8. G major
4. F major	9. D minor
5. G minor	10. D major

E. Steinbauer & E. Melkus (vlns.), E. Knava
(gamba & vlc.), A. Planyavsky (cbs.),
K. Scheit (lute & guitar), K. Rapf (org., hpsi.
& pf.)   (4ss)   ‡ SPA. 18/19

RUGGLES, Carl (b. 1876)

Evocations   4 chants for pf.   1937-43, rev. 1954
J. Kirkpatrick
Men and Mountains   Str. orch.   1924
. . . 2nd movt., Lilacs
Portals   Str. orch.   1926, rev. 1952-3
Juilliard Str. Orch.—Prausnitz   ‡ AmC.ML 4986
(*Cowell*)

Men & Mountains . . . Lilacs; SONG: Toys
▽ J. Litante (S) & pf.; Pan-American Orch.—Slonimsky
(NMQR. 1013)

RUMELANT (fl. XIIIth Cent.)

SEE: † ANTHOLOGIE SONORE

RUSSELL, Alexander George (b. 1880)

St. Lawrence Sketches   org.   1916
1. Citadel at Québec   3. Song of the Basket weaver
2. Bells of St. Anne de Beaupré   4. Up the Argnenay
R. Ellsasser   ‡ MGM.E 3066
(*Vierne & Ellsasser*)

RUST, Friedrich Wilhelm (1739-1796)

Sonata, C major   vla., vlc. & 2 hrns.
J. de Pasquale, S. Mayes, J. Stagliano &
   H. Shapiro   ‡ Bo.B 201
    (*Mozart: Quintet, K 407*)

SABARICH, Raymond (contemp.)

Aubade   tpt. & pf.
Lamento   tpt. & pf.
R. Sabarich & M. Lenom (pf.)   ‡ *D.LX 3132*
   (*Thilde & Hubeau*)   (‡ Lon.LS 988)

(10) Études   tpt. unacc.
L. Menardi   ‡ *D.LXT 2976*
     (‡ Lon.LL 1103)

SABOLY, Nicolas (1615-1675)

SEE: † BIBLE DES NOËLS

SACCHINI, Antonio Maria Gasparo
         (1730-1786)

OEDIPE À COLONE   Opera (*Fr*)   3 Acts   1786
Overture
A. Scarlatti Orch.—Caracciolo   ‡ C.CX 1276
(*Vivaldi & Leo*)   (*Leo & Lully* in ‡ QCX 10140)

SAEVERUD, Harald (b. 1897)

Galdreslåtten, Op. 20
(Enchanter's Ballad; Danza sinfonica con Passacaglia)
         (also NOC. 62615/6, 2ss)
Rondo amoroso, Op. 14, No. 7   pf.
— ARR. ORCH.   Saeverud   (also NOC. 63154)
Symphony No. 6, Op. 16   "Sinfonia dolorosa"
         (also NOC. 63174/6, 3ss)
☆ Oslo Phil.—Fjeldstad   ‡ Mer.MG 10149
(*Valen*)

PART SONG: The Shepherd's Farewell, Op. 35
Schenley High School Cho.—Keister (*Eng*)
     in ‡ PFCM.CB 161
(*Willan, Villa-Lobos, Lopatnikoff, etc.*)

SAINT-LUC, Jacques de (1663-*c.* 1720)

"Partita"[1]   lute, vln. & cont.
L'Arrivée du Prince Eugène
. . . 1. Allemande; 2. Air; 6. Bransle: Gillotin dansant au bal
La Feste du nom de S.A.Mgr. le Prince de Lobkowitz
. . . Marche, C major
La Reyne de Prusse
. . . Sarabande, C minor
La Cocq . . . Gigue, C major
M. Podolski, J. Tryssesoone, F. Terby (vlc.)
     ‡ Per.SPL 587
(*Haydn, Vivaldi, Baron*)   (‡ Cpt.MC 20058)

SAINT-SAËNS, Charles Camille
         (1835-1921)

CLASSIFIED: I. Piano, Organ, Harp.   II. Chamber Music
         III. Orchestral   IV. Songs
         V. Church Music   VI. Operas

I. PIANO, ORGAN, HARP

COLLECTION—PIANO
ÉTUDES:
   Op. 52, No. 6, D flat major (*Étude en forme de valse*)
   Op. 111, No. 6, F major   (*Toccata d'après le 5e Concerto*)
Toccata, Op. 72, No. 3
Thème varié, Op. 97
Allegro appassionato, Op. 70   orig. pf. & orch.
   G. Doyen   ‡ Nix.WLP 5294
   (*Chabrier*)(‡Véga.C30.A8;West.WL 5294;*Sel.270.CW.077*)

[1] Compiled from pieces in *Denkmäler der Tonkunst in Österreich*, Vol. L.

ÉTUDES

Op. 52, No. 6, D flat major (*Étude en forme de valse*)
— ARR. VLN. & PF.　Ysaÿe
D. Oistrakh & V. Yampolsky　♯ *USSR.D 1201*
(*Albeniz, Brahms, Sarasate*)　(also ♯ USSR. 021961/2)
Y. Sitkovetsky & pf. (*USSRM.D 864*)

Op. 111, No. 6, F major　pf.
(*Toccata d'après le 5ᵉ Concerto*)
D. Raucea　　　　　　♯ *D.LXT 2969*
(*Casella, Granados, Albeniz, etc.*)　(♯ Lon.LL 1033)

Op. 135, No. 4, G minor　left hand
A. Cortot　　　　in ♯ *JpV.LS 105*
(*Liszt, Debussy, Schubert*)

Fantasia, C major, Op. 95　harp
V. Dyulova　　　　　♯ *USSR.D 1389*
(*Lully: Suite*)

Valse de Mignonne, Op. 104　pf.
☆ C. Saint-Saëns (from a piano roll) (in ♯ Roy. 1573)

Variations on a theme of Beethoven, Op. 35　2 pfs.
P. Luboshutz & G. Nemenoff (n.v.)
　　　　　　　♯ *Rem. 199-147*
(*Mozart, Debussy, Falla*) (☆ o.v. in ♯ Cam.CAL 206)

II. CHAMBER MUSIC

Allegro appassionato, Op. 43　vlc. & pf.
A. Odnoposoff & Bertha Huberman
　　　　　　　ArgV. 68-8046
(*Granados: Goyescas—Intermezzo*)
☆ J. Pacey & F. Kramer (in ♯ MTR.MLO 1012)

Caprice sur des airs danois et russes, Op. 79
fl., ob., cl. & pf.　1887
J. Pappoutsakis, L. Speyer, P. Cardillo,
B. Zighera　　　　　♯ **Uni.UN 1005**
(*Honegger, Poulenc, etc.*)

Fantasia, A major, Op. 124　hp. & vln.
▽ ☆ E. Vito & A. Eidus (in ♯ Cum.CS 192)

Septet, E flat major, Op. 65　pf., tpt., str.qtt., cbs.
M. Pressler, H. Glantz, Guilet Qtt. & P. Sklar
(*Indy*)　　　　　♯ **MGM.E 3096**
J-M. Darré, R. Delmotte, Pascal Qtt. &
G. Logerot　(4ss)　　♭ *Pat.D 8001/2*
☆ B. Smith, H. Glantz, Stradivarius Qtt. & P. Sklar
　　　　　　　(♯ Cum.CS 191)

Sonata, E flat major, Op. 167　cl. & pf.　1920
U. & J. Délécluse　　　♯ *D.LX 3139*
(*Honegger & Milhaud*)　　(♯ Lon.LS 1097)

III. ORCHESTRAL

(Le) Carnaval des animaux　orch. & 2 pfs.
G. Anda, B. Siki & Philharmonia—Markevitch
　　　　　　　♯ **C.CX 1175**
(*Britten*)　　　(♯ FCX 376; Angel. 35135)
V. Aller, H. Sukman & Concert Arts—Slatkin
　　　　　　　♯ **DCap.CTL 7069**
(*Ibert*)　　　(♯ Cap.P 8270: ♭ FAP 8270)
A. d'Arco, R. Boutry & Concerts Colonne
—Sebastian　　　　♯ **Nix.ULP 9099**
(*Franck*)　　　(♯ Ura. 7099; MTW. 27, d.c.)
M. Rawicz, W. Landauer & Hallé—Barbirolli[1]
　　　　　　　♯ **G.ALP 1224**
(*J. Strauss Fantasy, & Friedmann*)　(♯ QALP 10094)
J. Visèle, F. Vanbulck & Brussels Radio—André
(2ss)　　　　　　♯ *DT.LGM 65013*
(*Franck: Psyché* on ♯ DT.LGX 66028)　(♯ T.LB 6034)
A. Whittemore, J. Lowe & Boston Pops—Fiedler
　　　　　　　♯ Vic.LM 1761
(2ss, ♯ *ItV.A10R 0010*)　(♭ set WDM 1761)
J. Antonietti, I. Rossican & Netherlands Phil.—Goehr
(*Pf. Concerto No. 3*)　　♯ **CHS.CHS 1179**
E. Gilels, J. Zak & State Sym.—Eliasberg
(& 6ss, 021323/8)　　　♯ *USSR.D 1101/2*
F. Lazzetti, P. Buonomo & Naples Scarlatti Orch.
—P. Argento　　　　♯ Csm.CLPS 1045
(*Debussy & Zanetti*)[2]

E. Bartlett, R. Robertson & Cha. Ens.—I. Solomon
(*Ravel & Debussy*)　　　♯ MGM.E 3114
Anon. Pianists & R.I.A.S. Sym.—Perlea　♯ Rem. 199-160
(*Tchaikovsky*)
R. Trouard, Mlle. Devèze & Inst. Ens.—Lindenberg
　　　　　　　♯ *Od.OD 1003*
S. Bianca, G. Arnoldi & Hamburg Philharmonia
—H-J. Walther　(6ss)　　　*MSB. 78010/2*
(*Symphony No. 2* in ♯ Roy. 1631)　(♯ 2ss, Roy. 18137)
Anon. Orch. (♯ *ACC.MP 5;* perhaps Sebastian, *above*)
☆ Philadelphia— Stokowski (♯ Cam.CAL 100)

— ARR. with poems by Ogden Nash
☆ N. Coward, L. Hambro, J. Zayde (pfs.) & Orch.
—Kostelanetz　　　♯ *EPhi.NBR 6001*
　　　　　　　(♯ *Phi.N 02602R*)
(*Prokofiev* on ♯ AmC.CL 720: o.n. ML 4907)
[& with *Fr* narration by C. Dauphin, ♯ *Phi.N 02601R*]
… **L'Éléphant**　cbs.
L. Manno & accordeons (in ♯ *Capri. 1*)
… **Le Cygne**　vlc. & pf.
E. B. Bengtsson & H. D. Koppel　　*G.DA 5283*
(*Rubinstein: Romance*)
R. Clark & R. Scheffel-Stein (hp.)　in ♯ *G.ALP 1301*
J. Simandl & A. Holeček　　　*U.C 24390*
(*Schumann: Träumerei*)
L. W. Pratesi & Cha. Ens.—Fauré (in ♯ *ArgOd.LDC 529*)
☆ G. Piatigorsky (♭ *G.7RQ 229;* in ♯ *ItV.A12R 0105;*
　　　　　　　♭ *Vic. ERA 122*)
S. Popoff (in ♯ *Vien.LPR 1022*)
— — ARR. VLN. & ORCH.
G. Boulanger & Bucharest Gypsy Orch.
　　　　　　(in ♯ *Csm.CRLP 200*)
— — ARR. VLN. & PF.
W. Schneiderhan & H. Priegnitz (*PV.* 36084; ♭ *Pol.* 32047)
R. & A. d'Arco (in *Plé.P 105*)
— — ARR. VLA. & PF.　☆ W. Primrose (♭ *Cam.CAE 251*)
— — ORCH. VERSIONS　(perhaps with vlc. solo)
Decca Little Sym.—Mendoza (in ♯ *D.US 223524;*
　　　　　　　♯ *AmD.DL 5211;* ▽ set A 90)
Belgian Radio—Doneux (in ♯ Mae.OAT 25006)
☆ A. Kostelanetz Orch. (♭ *AmC.A 1600*)
etc.
— — ARR. VOICE　☆ R. Tauber (T, *Ger*) (*P.PO 189*)

CONCERTOS, pf. & orch.

No. 2, G minor, Op. 22
E. Gilels & Paris Cons.—Cluytens ♯ **C.CX 1217**
(*Mozart: Sonata No. 16*) (♯ FCX/QCX 301; Angel. 35132)
V. Schiøler & Danish Radio—Malko
(*Liszt*)　　　　　♯ **G.KALP 1**
O. Frugoni & Vienna Pro Musica—Swarowsky
(*Concerto No. 5*)　　　♯ **AmVox.PL 8410**
J. Doyen & Lamoureux—Fournet
　　　　　　　♯ **Phi.N 00233L**
(*d'Indy*)　　　　(♯ Epic.LC 3096)
E. Gilels & U.S.S.R. State—Kondrashin
(2ss)　　　　　♯ *USSR.D 1478/9*
(*Liszt* on ♯ ·Van.VRS 6015)　(6ss, USSR. 016649/54)
[&, stated to be cond. Gauk, ♯ Csm.CRLP 178]

… **Finale**, only
☆ A. Sandford & Hastings Sym.—Bath (in ♯ Roy. 1901)

No. 3, B flat major, Op. 29
P. Pozzi & Winterthur Sym.—Desarzens
(*Carnaval des animaux*)　　♯ **CHS.CHS 1179**

No. 4, C minor, Op. 44
A. Brailowsky & Boston Sym.—Münch
　　　　　　　♯ **G.ALP 1321**
(*Chopin: Concerto No. 2*) (♯ Vic.LM 1871; FV.A 630242)

No. 5, F major, Op. 103
F. Jacquinot & Westminster Sym.—Fistoulari
　　　　　　　♯ **P.PMC 1015**
(*d'Indy*)　　　　(♯ MGM.E 3068)
O. Frugoni & Vienna Pro Musica—Swarowsky
(*Concerto No.2*)　　　♯ **AmVox.PL 8410**
M. Tagliaferro & Lamoureux—Fournet
　　　　　　　♯ **Phi.N 00664R**
(*Fauré & Franck* on ♯ Epic.LC 3057)
S. Richter & Youth Sym.—Kondrashin
　　　　　　　♯ **CdM.LDA 8128**
(2ss)　　　　　(♯ *USSR.D 833/4*)

---

[1] *Le Cygne* is played by vlc. ensemble, not solo.　　　　[2] The latest catalogue does not show a Zanetti coupling.

CONCERTOS, violin & orch.

No. 1, A major, Op. 20
... 1st movt. — ARR. VLN. & PF. (*Concertstück*)
Y. Sitkovetsky & pf. ‡ *USSR.D 1187*
(*Sarasate*)

No. 3, B minor, Op. 61
Y. Menuhin & Philharmonia—Poulet
(*Mendelssohn*) ‡ *Vic.LHMV 1071*
L. Kaufman & Netherlands Phil.—v. d. Berg
(*Havanaise*) ‡ *MMS. 62*

CONCERTO, vlc. & orch.

No. 1, A minor, Op. 33
Z. Nelsova & L.P.O.—Boult ‡ *D.LXT 2906*
(*Lalo*) (‡ Lon.LL 964)
F. Danyi & Berlin Sym.—Kleinert ‡ *Ura. 7143*
(*Symphony No. 2*) (‡ MTW. 516)
P. Tortelier & Zürich Tonhalle—Goehr
(*Symphony No. 2*) ‡ *CHS.CHS 1180*
A. Navarra & Paris Opéra—Young
(*Lalo: Concerto*) ‡ *Cap.P 8318*
C. Bartse & Belgian Radio Cho.—Doneux
 (‡ *Gramo.GLP 2511*; may never have been issued)
☆ G. Piatigorsky & Victor Sym.—Reiner
 (‡ ItV.A12R 0105)

Danse macabre, Op. 40
Philharmonia—Markevitch ‡ *C.CX 1273*
(*Sibelius, Mozart, Busoni, etc.*)
 (‡ QCX 10172; Angel. 35154)
(*Sibelius & Berlioz on* ♭ *C.SEL 1539*)
Suisse Romande—Ansermet ‡ *D.LW 5030*
(*Rouet d'Omphale*) (‡ Lon.LD 9028)
(*idem & Chabrier, Ravel on* ‡ D.LXT 2760; Lon.LL 696)
Concerts Colonne—Fourestier ‡ *C.CX 1158*
(*below*) (‡ FCX 165; Angel. 35058)
Bamberg Sym.—Lehmann PV. 72352
(*Chabrier: España*) (♭ Pol. 30054, d.c.)
Champs-Élysées Th.—Branco ♭ *Sel. 470.C.011*
(*Samson et Dalila—Bacchanale*)
German Sym.—Ludwig in ‡ *Ura. 7096*
 (♭ UREP 56)
London Phil. Sym.—Quadri ‡ *West.LAB 7009*
(*Samson et Dalila, Chabrier, Dukas*) (‡ Véga. C30.A18)
Boston Orch. Soc.—Page in ‡ *Nix.SLPY 802*
(*J. Strauss, Brahms, Rimsky-K.*)(‡ SOT. 2066 & in ‡ 10646)
Sym. Orch.—Schönherr ‡ *MTW. 14*
(*Bizet & J. Strauss*) (♭ set EP 14)
Hamburg Philharmonia—H-J. Walther
 MSB. 78124
Hollywood Bowl—Barnett ‡ *Cap.P 8296*
(*Liszt, Ponchielli, etc.*) (♭ set FAP 8296)
Belgian Radio—Doneux ‡ *Mae.OAT 25006*
(*Havanaise, Intro. & Rondo capriccioso, etc.*)
☆ A.B.C. Sydney Sym.—Goossens G.DB 21617
 (in ‡ OBLP 7501)
Regent Sym. (in ‡ Rgt. 7003)
☆ N.B.C.—Toscanini (♭ G.7ER 5012: ERF 105:
 ERQ 109, d.cs.)
Belgian Radio—André (TV.VSK 9012)
N.Y.P.S.O.—Mitropoulos (in ‡ Phi.A 01604R:
 ♭ A 409013E; ♭ AmC. 4-4788)
French Nat. Radio—Lindenberg (Od. O-3708:
 ♭ 7AOE 1001: ♭ DSEQ 426)
Tivoli—Jensen (♭ Mer.EP 1-5041; ♭ FMer.MEP 14515)
L.S.O.—Weldon (in ‡ MGM.E 3037)
Chicago Sym.—Stock (in ‡ AmC.RL 3022)
Italian Radio—Basile (Orf. 53006)
Philadelphia—Stokowski (in ‡ Cam.CAL 254;
 & in ‡ set CFL 103)
— ARR. 2 PFS. Saint-Saëns
☆ A. Whittemore & J. Lowe (in ‡ Vic.LRM 7010:
 ♭ set ERB 7010)
P. Luboshutz & G. Nemenoff (in ‡ Cam.CAL 198:
 ♭ CAE 219)

Havanaise, Op. 83 vln. & orch.
A. Campoli & L.S.O.—Fistoulari ‡ *D.LW 5085*
(*below*)
L. Kaufman & Netherlands Phil.—v. d. Berg
(*Vln. Concerto No. 3*) ‡ *MMS.62*
F. Pétronio & Belgian Radio—Doneux ‡ Mae.OAT 25006
(*Danse macabre, Suite algérienne—Marche, etc.; & Lalo*)
H. Szeryng & Fr. Radio—Lindenberg ‡ Od.OD 1007
(*below*) (‡ ArgOd.LDC 7502)
☆ J. Heifetz & Vic. Sym.—Steinberg ‡ G.BLP 1022
(*Beethoven*) (‡ VBLP 808; QBLP 5011: FALP 252, d.c.)

Introduction & Rondo capriccioso, Op. 28
vln. & orch.
A. Campoli & L.S.O.—Fistoulari ‡ *D.LW 5085*
(*above*)
F. Pétronio & Belgian Radio—Doneux ‡ Mae.OAT 25006
(*above & below*)
L. Kogan & Moscow Radio—Gauk ‡ *USSR.D 149*
(*Berlioz: Carnaval romain*)
H. Szeryng & Fr. Radio—Lindenberg ‡ Od.OD 1007
(*Havanaise*) (‡ ArgOd.LDC 7502)
I. Oistrakh & I. Kollegorskaya (pf.) Muza.X 2059
☆ Z. Francescatti & Philadelphia—Ormandy ‡ C.C 1029
(*Chausson*) (‡ QC 5012)
☆ J. Heifetz & Vic. Sym.—Steinberg ‡ G.BLP 1022
(*Havanaise & Beethoven*) (also, 2ss, G.ED 1236)
(& in ‡ G.FALP 252, d.c.: VBLP 808: QBLP 5011:
 WBLP 1022; in ‡ Vic.LRM 7055: ♭ set ERB 7055)
J. Schmied & Orch. (in ‡ Vien.LPR 1031)
☆ H. Temianka & pf. (Od.NLX 20)

(La) Jeunesse d'Hercule, Op. 50 Sym. poem
Concerts Colonne—Fourestier ‡ *C.CX 1158*
(*above & below*) (‡ FCX 165; Angel. 35058)

Marche héroïque, Op. 34 — ARR. BAND Mastio
French Navy Band—Maillot (in ‡ Sel. 270.C. 055)

Phaëton, Op. 39
Concerts Colonne—Fourestier ‡ *C.CX 1158*
(*above & below*) (‡ FCX 165; Angel. 35058)
Hamburg Philharmonia—H-J. Walther
 MSB. 78201
 (also 78125; & in ‡ MGM.E 3144)

Rhapsodie d'Auvergne, Op. 73 pf. & orch.
— ARR. PF. & BAND
A. Collard & Miners' Band—Dupont
 V‡ *Sat.MSAS 5005*
(*Bach-Liszt: Prelude & Fugue, A minor*)

(Le) Rouet d'Omphale, Op. 31 Sym. poem
Suisse Romande—Ansermet ‡ *D.LW 5030*
(*Danse macabre*) (‡ Lon.LD 9028)
(*idem., & Chabrier, Ravel, in* ‡ D.LXT 2760; Lon.LL 696)
Concerts Colonne—Fourestier ‡ *C.CX 1158*
(*above*) (‡ FCX 165; Angel. 35058)
Hamburg Philharmonia—H-J. Walther
 MSB. 78126
☆ N.Y.P.S.O.—Mitropoulos (in ‡ Phi.A 01604R:
 ♭ A 409013E)
Liverpool Phil.—Sargent (in ‡ AmC.RL 3050)
Nat. Sym. (U.S.A.)—Kindler (in ‡ Cam.CAL 175)

Suite algérienne, Op. 60
1. Prélude 2. Rapsodie mauresque
3. Rêverie du soir 4. Marche militaire française
Lamoureux—Fournet ‡ *Phi.N 00703R*
(*Luigini: Ballet égyptien*)
French Radio—Fourestier ‡ *Pat.DTX 126*
(*Lalo*) (‡ ArgPat.ADTX 1802)
(*Massenet: Les Erinnyes on* ‡ AmVox.PL 8100)
... No. 4 Belgian Radio—Doneux (in ‡ Mae.OAT 25006)

SYMPHONIES

No. 2, A minor, Op. 55
Netherlands Phil.—Goehr ‡ *CHS.CHS 1180*
(*Cello Concerto*)
Berlin Sym.—Kleinert ‡ *Ura. 7143*
(*Cello Concerto*) (‡ MTW. 516)
Hamburg Philharmonia—H-J. Walther
(*Carnaval des Animaux*) ‡ *Roy. 1631*

---

‡ = Long-playing, 33⅓ r.p.m. ♭ = 45 r.p.m. ♮ = Auto. couplings, 78 r.p.m.

No. 3, C minor, Op. 78 with org. & 2 pfs.
N.B.C. Sym.—Toscanini[1] ♯ **Vic.LM 1874**
[G. Crook, org.] (♯ ItV.A12R 0144)
Residentie—v. Otterloo ♯ *EPhi.NBR 6021*
[F. Asma, org.] (♯ *Phi.A 00715R*; ᵊpic.LC 3077)
Paris Cons.—Cluytens ♯ **C.FCX 447**
[H. Roget, org.]
Champs-Élysées Theatre—Bour
♯ **LT.DTL 93072**
[M. Duruflé, org.] (♯ *Sel. 270.C.054*)
☆ N.Y.P.S.O.—Münch ♯ **C.CX 1116**
[E. Nies-Berger, org.] (♯ FCX/QCX 166)
(also ♮ C.LHX 8003/6)

IV. SONGS

Aimons-nous (Banville) 1891
M. Santreuil (S), Y. M. Josse (pf.) **V**♯ *POc.A 02*
(*Hahn & Massenet*)

(L') Attente (V. Hugo) *c.* 1855
P. Lisitsian (B, *Russ*) *USSR. 23016*
(*Tchaikovsky: Don Juan's Serenade*)

Au cimetière, Op. 26, No. 5 (Renaud) 1870
M. Sénéchal (T), J. Bonneau (pf.)
in ♯ *Phi.N 00681R*
(*Fauré, Debussy, Ravel, etc.*)
M. Santreuil (S), Y. M. Josse (pf.) **V**♯ *POc.A 02*
(*above*)

(Le) Bonheur est chose légère (Barbier)
SEE Opera: Le Timbre d'Argent, below

Danse macabre[2] (Casalis) 1873
T. Duncan (B), W. Allen (pf.) **Phi.A 56503G**
(*Moussorgsky: The Seminarist*)
☆ N. Eddy (B) & Orch. (♭ *AmC.A 1576*)

Guitares et mandolines (Saint-Saëns) 1890
R. Ponselle (S), I. Chicagov (pf.)
in ♯ **Vic.LM 1889**
(*Chausson, Tosti, Donaudy, etc.*) (♯ DV. 16493)

V. CHURCH MUSIC

(Le) DÉLUGE, Op. 45 Oratorio 1876
Prélude vln. & orch.
C. Pessina & Colón Theatre—Martini
ArgOd. 66020
(*Thaïs—Méditation*) (♭ *BSOA 4008: BSOAE 4513*)

ORATORIO DE NOËL, Op. 12 1863
No. 10, Tollite hostias cho.
Cho.—R. Wagner in ♯ **Layos.CB 600/1**

VI. OPERAS

(Les) BARBARES Prol. & 3 Acts 1901
N'oublions-pas les sacrifices T Act III
♯ C. Rousselière (in **V**♯ *IRCC.L 7002**)

DÉJANIRE 4 Acts 1898
Viens, o toi, dont le clair visage Act V
♯ A. Paoli (*AF.AGSA 22**)

ÉTIENNE MARCEL 4 Acts 1879
O beaux rêves évanouis S Act II
J. Hammond ♯ *G.BLP 1073*
(*Beethoven & Berlioz*)

HENRI VIII 4 Acts 1879
Ballet divertissement Act II
Moscow Radio—Samosud ♯ **USSR.D 01583**
(*Aida, s. 7*)

... Gypsy Dance, only
Boston Pops—Fiedler in ♯ **Vic.LM 1803**
(*Prokofiev, Dukas, German*)

(La) PRINCESSE JAUNE, Op. 30 1 Act 1872
Overture
Lamoureux—Fournet in ♯ *Phi.N 00707R*
(*Massenet, Thomas, etc.*) (in ♯ Epic.LC 3079)
☆ Boston Sym.—Münch (in ♯ *G.ALP 1245*; ♭ *Vic.ERA 68*)
Opéra-Comique—Wolff (♯ *D.LW 5028*)

SAMSON ET DALILA, Op. 47 3 Acts 1877
COMPLETE RECORDING
☆ H. Bouvier (A), J. Luccioni (T), etc., Paris Opéra Cho.
& Orch.—Fourestier (6ss) ♯ **AmVox. set PL 8323**

HIGHLIGHTS
Arrêtez, O mes frères T & cho. Act I
Printemps qui commence A Act I
Amour, viens aider ma faiblesse A Act II
La Victoire facile A & Bs Act II (a)
Se pourrait-il? . . . C'est toi . . . Mon cœur s'ouvre à ta voix
A & T Act II
Vois ma misère, hélas! T & cho. Act III
Bacchanale; Gloire à Dagon (Finale) Act III
R. Stevens (M-S), J. Peerce (T), R. Merrill (B),
Shaw Chorale & N.B.C. Sym. Orch.
—Stokowski ♯ **G.ALP 1308**
(♯ Vic.LM 1848)
[excerpts in ♭ *set ERB 49*; item marked (a) in ♭ set only]

ACT I

Arrêtez, O mes frères T & cho.
R. Vinay & Cho. in ♯ **SBDH.TOB 2**
(*Boccanegra, Roméo et Juliette, etc.*)

... Tenor part only
♯ C. Dalmores (*AF.AGSA 15**)
F. Tamagno (*Ital*) & pf. (in ♯ SBDH.JAL 7000**)
A. Paoli (*Ital*) (*AF.AGSA 22**)

Maudite à jamais soit la race Bs
M. Singher in ♯ **Roy. 1613**
(*Louise, G. Tell, Africaine, etc.*)

Printemps qui commence A (or M-S)
S. Michel in ♯ **Pat.DTX 137**
(*Bizet, Massenet, Thomas, etc.*)
S. Couderc (*below*) ♭ *Plé.P 45141*
L. Rudenko (*Russ*) (in ♯ *USSR.D 2072*)
☆ R. Siewert (*Ger*) (G.FKX 253: ♭ *7PW 526*)

Finale — ARR. PF.
☆ C. Saint-Saëns, from a piano roll (in ♯ Roy. 1573)

ACT II

Amour, viens aider ma faiblesse A (or M-S)
M. v. Ilosvay in ♯ *Phi.N 00649R*
(*below; Mignon, Carmen, etc.*)
S. Couderc ♭ *Plé.P 45141*
(*above & below*)
Bette Björling in ♯ **G.ALPC 1**
(*Rigoletto, Traviata, etc.*)
I. Dimcheva (in ♯ *USSR.D 2158*)
☆ E. Wysor (in ♯ Ply. 12-47)
S. Onegin (in ♯ Sca. 821)
E. Stignani (*Ital*) (in ♯ *C.QC 5024*)
M. Anderson (*Eng*) (in ♯ *Var. 6986*; ♯ Roy. 1589:
♭ *EP 113*; ♯ *AFest.CFR 10-149*)

Mon cœur s'ouvre à ta voix A (or M-S)
S. Couderc ♭ *Plé.P 45141*
(*above*)
M. v. Ilosvay in ♯ *Phi.N 00649R*
(*above*)
Z. Palii in ♯ **Sup.LPV 207**
(*Pagliacci, Traviata, etc.*) (♯ U. 5191G)
T. de Igarzabal (*Ital*) ♭ *ArgOd.BSOA 4006*
(*Carmen—Habanera*) (in ♯ LDC 517)
I. Dimcheva (in ♯ *USSR.D 2158*)
K. Szczepánska (*Pol*) (*Muza. 2303*)
Z. Dolukhanova (*Russ*) (USSR. 21856/7)
E. Farrell (*Eng*)[3] (in ♯ *MGM.E 3185*: ♭ *set X 304*)
☆ E. Wysor (in ♯ Ply. 12-47)
S. Onegin (in ♯ Sca. 821)
E. Stignani (*Ital*) (in ♯ *C.QC 5024*)
♯ F. Litvinne (in ♯ *Roc. 1**)
— ARR. ORGAN: V. Fox (in ♭ *AmC. set A 1008*)

---

[1] From a broadcast performance, Nov. 1952.
[2] The original of the Sym. Poem, *supra*.
[3] Sound-track of film *Interrupted Melody*.

SAMSON ET DALILA, Op. 47 (*continued*)
ACT III
Bacchanale - orch.
Philharmonia—Dobrowen   **C.DX 1898**
         (GQX 11544)

Lamoureux—Fournet   ♭ *Phi.N 40202IE*
(*Thomas: Raymond—Overture*)   (in ♯ Epic.LC 3174)
Champs-Élysées Th.—Branco   ♭ *Sel. 470.C.011*
(*Danse macabre*)
Bamberg Sym.—Lehmann   in ♯ *Pol. 16062*
(*Danse macabre*, on ♭ *Pol. 30054*)   (& ♯ *Pol. 17039*)
London Phil. Sym.—Quadri   ♯ **West.LAB 7009**
(*Danse macabre*, etc.)   (♯ Véga.C30.A 18)
Orch.—Swarowsky (in ♯ *MTW. 9; ACC.MP 13*)
☆ Carnegie Pops—O'Connell (♭ *AmC.A 1573*)
   Florence Fest.—Serafin (G.EB 566;
      in ♯ BB.LBC/♭*WBC 1039:* ♭ *ERAB 1*)
   A. Kostelanetz Orch. (C.DOX 1024: ♭ *SED 5511:*
                   ♭ *SEDQ 526*)
   Boston Prom.—Fiedler (in ♯ Cam.CAL 166: ♭ *CAE 182:*
                    & in ♯ set CFL 102)
— ARR. ORGAN: R. Ellsasser (in ♯ MGM.E 3125)

(Le) TIMBRE D'ARGENT   4 Acts   1877
No. 8, Romance: Le Bonheur est chose légère
   V. Mauret (S), J. Zayde (pf.)   in ♯ *Asty. 100*
   ☐ E. Beach-Yaw (AF.AGSB 202*)

SALMON, Maître Jacques (fl. *c.* 1587)
   SEE: † DANCERIES ET BALLETS

SALZÉDO, Carlos (b. 1885)

HARP MUSIC—COLLECTION
Ballade
La Désirade (from *15 Preludes for beginners,* 1927)
Petite valse   1943
Scintillation   1936
Traipsin' thru Arkansaw
   C. Salzédo   ♯ **Mer.MG 80003**
   (*Handel, Corelli, Massenet*)
(8) Dances
   C. Salzédo   ♯ **Mer.MG 10144**
   (*Granados, Mendelssohn, Debussy, etc.*)
Jeux d'eau   1920
   E. Vito   in ♯ **Per.SPL 704**
Steel — ARR. 2 HARPS   Salzédo
   C. Salzédo & L. Lawrence (in ♯ Mer.MG 10144)
Variations (unspec.)
   ☆ O. Erdeli   (*Gounod: Faust Fantasy*)   **USSRM. D 480**

SAMMARTINI, Giovanni Battista
(1698-1775)
CANTATA: Giunta sei pur   *c.* 1745
   (Cantata No. 5 for Fridays in Lent)
   (MS, Einsiedeln & Bavarian State Libraries)[1]
   M. Tyler (S), M. Amadini (A), A. Bianchini (T),
    & Italian Cha. Orch.—Jenkins ♯ HS.HSL 75
   (2ss)   (in set HSL-C)
Concerto No. 2, C major, vln. & orch.[2]
   A. Abussi & Italian Cha.—Jenkins
                    ♯ HS.HSL 74
   (*below; Albinoni & Corelli*)   (in set HSL-C)
Symphony, G major, Op. 3
   (Fonds Blancheton No. 150; MS, Paris Conservatoire)
   Italian Cha.—Jenkins   ♯ HS.HSL 74
   (*above, Albinoni & Corelli*)   (in set HSL-C)
   Inst. Ens.—Witold   ♯ EPP.SLP 2
   (*Geminiani, Torelli, Vivaldi*)

Sonata, G major, vlc. & cont.[3]   (ed. Salmon, *et al.*)
   L. Rose & L. Hambro (pf.)   ♯ **AmC.ML 4984**
   (*Boccherini & Schubert*)
... 1st & 3rd movts., Allegro & Vivace, only
  — — ARR. ORGAN[4]
   R. Ellsasser   ♯ *CM. 4*
   (*Dandrieu & Ellsasser*)   (♯ *Eli.LPE 116*)

SAMMARTINI, Giuseppe (1693-*c.* 1750)

Concerto, F major, ob. & orch.[5]
   S. Gallesi & Italian Cha.—Jenkins
                    ♯ **HS.HSL 136**
   (*Pugnani & Sarti*)   (in set HSL-N)
Concerto Grosso, D minor, Op. 11, No. 4
   ☆ Vienna Sym.—Moralt   ♯ **West.WN 18032**
   (*Locatelli & Pergolesi*)
Sonata, A minor, Op. 1, No. 4   vln. & cont.
... Andante   — ARR. Elman   (*"Canto amoroso"*)
   M. Kozolupova (vln.) & pf. (*USSR. 22277*)
Synthetic Sonata, F major[6]   ed. Wasner
   Trapp Family Recorder Ens.
                 in ♯ **AmD.DL 9793**

SAMSON, Joseph (b. 1889)
   SEE: † POLYPHONIE SACRÉE

SANCTA MARIA, Tomás de (d. 1570)
   SEE: † ANTHOLOGIE SONORE

SANDERS, Robert (b. 1906)

Little Symphony No. 2, B flat major   f.p. 1954
   Louisville—Whitney   ♯ **LO. 7**
   (*Blacher & Persichetti*)
Saturday night   orch.   1933
   A.R.S. Sym.—Schönherr   ♯ *ARS. 30*
   (*Rogers & Tuthill*)

SANDI, Luis (b. 1905)

Ballet: Bonampak   orch.
   Mexico Nat. Sym.—Sandi   ♯ **Vic.LM 1737**
   (*Mignone, Ovalle, Tavares, etc.*)   (♯ FV.A 530202)
Yaqui Indian music   (ARR.)
   ▽ Orch.—Chávez (AmC. 70335D in set M 414: ♯ *ML2080*)

SANDRIN, Pierre Regnault (fl. XVIth Cent.)
   SEE: † PARISIAN SONGS OF XVITH CENTURY

SANTA CRUZ WILSON, Domingo
(b. 1899)

Alabanzas del Adviento, Op. 30   1952
   Pittsburgh Schools Boys' Cho.—Brenneman
                in ♯ **PFCM.CB 160**
   (*Chajes, Ahl, Malipiero, etc.*)
Egloga, Op. 26 (L. de Vega) S, cho. & orch. 1949
   Anon. artists & Chile Sym.   ♯ **ChV.CRL 1**
   (*J. Orrego Salas: Symphony*)

SANTORO, Claudio (b. 1919)

Symphony No. 4
   Sym.—Santoro   ♯ **Sin.SLP 1502**

---

[1] Ed. Jenkins.   [2] Originally for vlc. piccolo and orch.   MS, Marburg.
[3] 1st and 3rd movements actually by G. dall'Abaco, from a MS. Sonata, British Museum. The 2nd movement is not identified.
[4] Listed as Allegro vivace from Sonata G major; assumed to be this.
[5] No. 1 of a collection of concerti by various composers in Gemeenter Museum Library, The Hague.
[6] 1st and 3rd movts. are from Sonata, Op. 6, No. 2, and the 2nd movt. from Sonata, Op. 6, No. 4, original 2 recorders and cont. The Tenor recorder part added by Dr. Wasner after the original figured bass.

SANTORSOLA, Guido (b. 1904)

Concertino　guitar & orch.　1942
L. Walker & Vienna Sym.—Sacher
　　　　　　　　　　　　　　　　　‡ *Phi.N 00626R*
(Sor, Tárrega, etc.)　　　　　　　(‡ Epic.LC 3055)
Praeludium a la antiqua　guitar　1940
L. Walker　　　　　　　in ‡ **Epic.LC 3055**
(also ▽ Phi.N 11225G)　　　(in ‡ *Phi.N 00640R*)

SANTOS, Jozé Joaquin dos (fl. XVIIIth Cent.)

SEE: † Clavecinistes espagnols

SANZ, Gaspard (fl. XVIIth Cent.)

Capriccio arpeado　guitar (orig. vihuela)
S. Behrend　　　　　　　　　　*Eta. 130114*
(Bach: Items from Lute Suites)
Folía　(unspec.)
N. Yepes (in † ‡ D.LXT 2974; Lon.LL 1042)
Pavane　guitar (orig. vihuela)
G. Zepoll　　　　　　in ‡ *Nix.SLPY 142*
　　　　　　　　　　　　　　　(in ‡ *SOT. 1024*)
M. L. Anido　　　　　　　　　*ArgOd. 57046*
(Rodrigo: En los trigales)

SARASATE Y NAVASCUES, Pablo M. M. de (1844-1908)

(All for vln. & pf. unless otherwise stated)

Caprice basque, Op. 24
R. Ricci & L. Persinger　　　‡ **D.LXT 2930**
(below)　　　　　　　　　　(‡ Lon.LL 962)
L. Kogan & pf.　　　　　　*USSR. 22868/9*
Ⓗ P. M. M. de Sarasate & pf. (in ‡ *AudA.LP 0079**)
Carmen Fantasia, Op. 25　— ARR. VLN. & ORCH.
☆ L. Kogan & Moscow Radio—Nebolsin
　　　　　　　　　　　　　　　USSRM.D 839/40
(2ss)　　　　　　　　　(4ss, *USSR. 17980/3*)
☆ J. Heifetz & Vic. Sym.—Voorhees (‡ *DV. 16285*)
… Finale: M. Rabin & A. Balsam (in ‡ *AmC.AL 30*)
DANZAS ESPAÑOLAS
COMPLETE RECORDING of 8: **Opp. 21, 22, 23, 26**
R. Ricci & L. Persinger　　　‡ **D.LXT 2930**
(above & below)　　　　　　(‡ Lon.LL 962)
COLLECTION : **Nos. 1-3**
☆ Y. Menuhin & A. Baller (in ‡ JpV.LS 2004;
　　　　　in ‡ Vic.LM 1742; ♭ *set WDM 1742*)[1]
No. 1, Malagueña, Op. 21, No. 1
Y. Menuhin & G. Moore　　　　**G.DB 21595**
(No. 2)
D. Oistrakh & V. Yampolsky　　**USSR. 021759**
(No. 2)　　　*(No. 2 & Saint-Saëns, in ‡ USSR.D 1188)*
T. Magyar & W. Hielkema　　‡ *Phi.S 06049R*
(Granados, Nin, etc.)
G. Staples & G. Silfies　　　‡ **McInt.MM 101**
(Szymanowski, Falla, Debussy, etc.)
No. 2, Habañera, Op. 21, No. 2
Y. Menuhin & G. Moore　　　　**G.DB 21595**
(No. 1)
D. Oistrakh & V. Yampolsky　　**USSR. 021758**
(No. 1)　　　*(No. 1 & Saint-Saëns, in ‡ USSR.D 1188)*
Ⓗ P. de Sarasate & pf. (in ‡ *AudA.LP 0079**)
— ARR. PF.　Osta
☆ E. Osta (in ‡ *Coda. 1000*)
No. 3, Romanza andaluza, Op. 22, No. 1
☆ J. Heifetz & E. Bay (♭ *Vic.ERA 94*; *DV. 26034*)
No. 6, Zapateado, Op. 23, No. 2
D. Erlih & M. Bureau (pf.)　　**G.DB 11252**
(Albeniz: Malagueña)
☆ J. Heifetz & E. Bay (♭ *G.7EB 6001: 7EBW 6001*)
— ARR. PF.　E. Osta (in ‡ *Allo. 3152*)

No. 12, Zortzico (d'Iparaguirre), Op. 39
D. Oistrakh & V. Yampolsky　‡ *USSR.D 1201*
(Albeniz, Brahms, Saint-Saëns)
(Vieuxtemps: Souvenir, Op. 7 on USSR. 19538)
Introduction & Tarantella, Op. 43
R. Ricci & L. Persinger　　　‡ **D.LXT 2930**
(above & below)　　　　　　(‡ Lon.LL 962)
V. Abadjiev & P. Vladigerov　　*Bulg. 1359*
(Paganini: Concerto No. 1, s. 9)
Ⓗ P. M. M. de Sarasate & pf. (in ‡ *AudA.LP 0079**)
Zigeunerweisen, Op. 20, No. 1　vln. & orch.
R. Ricci & L. Persinger (pf.)　‡ **D.LXT 2930**
(above)　　　　　　　　　　(‡ Lon.LL 962)
M. Rabin & Col. Sym.—Voorhees
　　　　　　　　　　　　　　♭ *EPhi.NBE 11003*
(Paganini: Moto perpetuo; & Novaček)
　　　　　　　(♭ *Phi.A 409007E*; ‡ *AmC.AAL 38*)
N. Carol & J. Levine　　in ‡ **BB.LBC 1155**
H. Zacharias & R.I.A.S. Sym.—Fricsay
　　　　　　　　　　　　　　　PV. 72489
(Hubay)　　　　　　　　　　(♭ *Pol. 30089*)
☆ J. Heifetz & Vic. Sym.—Steinberg (in ‡ *Vic.LRM 7055*:
　　in ♭ *set ERB 7055*; ArgV. 12-3782; in ‡ *G.FALP 252*:
　　　　　　　　　　　　　　♭ *7RF/RQ 225*)
I. Stern & Sym.—Waxman (♭ *AmC.A 1647*)
J. Schmied & Orch. (in ‡ *Vien.LPR 1031*)
W. Tworek & R. Binge Orch. (*Pol. X 51703*;
　　　　　　　　　　　　　in ‡ *Lon.LB 1121*)
Ⓗ P. de Sarasate & pf. (in ‡ *AudA.LP 0079**)

SARRI, Domenico (1679-1744)

SEE: † Italian Airs

SARTI, Giuseppe (1729-1802)

Concertone per più strumenti obbligati, E flat major[2]
(2 cls., 2 hrns. & str. *concertino*; str. & cont. *ripieno*)
Italian Cha.—Jenkins　　　　‡ **HS.HSL 137**
(Pugnani & Sammartini)　　　(in set HSL-N)
GIULIO SABINO　Opera　3 Acts　1781
Lungi dal caro bene
M. Meli (S), V. Vitale (pf.)　　♭ *C.SEDQ 504*
(A. Scarlatti, Pergolesi, Paradies)

SASONKIN, Manus

The Virgin's Lullaby　(Composer)
Three Kings went to call　(Composer)
Rejoice greatly　(Composer)
A King is born　(Composer)
Concert Cho.　　　　　　　　‡ **CtyNY.AP 122**
(Gruen, Kraehenbuehl, etc.: Carols)

SATIE, Erik A. Leslie (1866-1925)

COLLECTIONS OF Pf. MUSIC

Nocturne No. 5	1919
(3) [Véritables] Préludes flasques pour un chien	1912
(3) Gnossiennes	1890
Chapitres tournés en tous sens	1913
Embryons desséchés	1913
Sports et divertissements	1914
(3) Gymnopédies	1888
SONG: La Diva de l'Empire	c. 1909 — ARR. PF. 1919

W. Masselos　　　　　　　　‡ **MGM.E 3155**

Prélude de la Porte héroïque du ciel[3]	1894
Prélude posthume[4]	1893 (pub. 1929)
Gymnopédie No. 1	1888
Sarabande No. 2	1887
Gnossienne No. 3	1890
Avant-dernières pensées	1915
Descriptions automatiques	1912-13
Tyrolienne turque[5]	
Danse maigre[5]	

F. Poulenc　(2ss)　　　　　　‡ *BàM.LD 023*

---

[1] The Victor pressing is also stated to be acc. G. Moore, recorded in England. It has not been possible to ascertain, beyond doubt, which it is.
[2] From MS. parts in Cherubini Conservatoire library, Florence; ed. G. Guerrini.
[3] For a play by Jules Bois.
[4] For *Fête donnée par des Chevaliers Normands en l'honneur d'une jeune Demoiselle.*
[5] Nos. 1 and 2 of *Croquis et Agaceries d'un gros Bonhomme en bois,* 1913.

En habit de cheval 2 pfs. 1911
R. Gold & A. Fizdale ♯ AmC.ML 4858
(*Milhaud, Debussy, Poulenc*) (in set SL 198)

(3) Enfantines 1913
1. Menus propos enfantins
2. Enfantillages pittoresques
3. Peccadilles importunes
M. Richter ♯ MGM.E 3181
(*Hindemith, Hovhaness, Surinach, Toch*)

(3) Gnossiennes pf. 1890
H. Boschi ♯ CdM.LDA 4003
(*Morceaux en forme de poire, & Songs*)

(3) Gymnopédies pf. 1888
— ARR. ORCH.
Debussy (Nos. 1 & 3), R. Jones (No. 2)
Concert Arts—Golschmann ♯ DCap.CTL 7055
(*Honegger, Milhaud, Ravel*) (♯ Cap.P 8244)
(Nos. 1 & 2 only, on ♭ *Cap.FAP 8252*)
... Nos. 1 & 3, only
☆ Boston Sym.—Koussevitzky (♭ *Vic.ERA 195;*
FV.A 95208)
... No. 3, only
M. Pressler in ♯ MGM.E 3129
(*Granados, Bartók*) (♭ *set X 254*)
☆ G. Copeland (in ♯ MGM.E 3024)

(3) Morceaux en forme de poire pf. duet 1903
H. Boschi & S. Nigg ♯ CdM.LDA 4003
(*above, & Songs*)

Parade Ballet 1917
... Orchestral Suite
Philharmonia—Markevitch ♯ C.CX 1197
(*Debussy, Ravel, Weber*)(♯ FCX 357; Angel. 35151, in
set 3518)

Sonatine bureaucratique pf. 1917
O. Penna ArgOd. 66051
(*Chopin: Nocturne, Op. 15, No. 2*)

SONGS
(3) Chansons de Music-Hall 1903-4
1. La Diva de l'Empire (Bonaud et Blès) ☆
2. Je te veux (Pacory)
3. Tendrement (Hyspa)
"Colinette" & self pf. acc.

(3) Mélodies 1916
1. Daphénéo (Godebski)
2. La Statue de Bronze (Fargue)
3. Le Chapelier (Chalupt)
C. Castelli (S), H. Boschi (pf.)
♯ CdM.LDA 4003
(*Gnossiennes & Morceaux*)

Je te veux (Valse) (Pacory)
— ARR. ORCH. Orch.—Chevreux (in V♯ CdM.LD YM 4020)

SAUGUET, Henri (b. 1901)

(Les) Forains Ballet 1945
... Suite
Lamoureux—Sauguet ♯ Phi.S 05800R
(o.v., ☆ ♯ Pol. 540003)

(Les) Trois Lys orch. c. 1953
Louisville—Whitney ♯ LO. 10
(*Bergsma, Ginastera, Ward*)

Valse brève 2 pfs. 1949
☆ A. Gold & R. Fizdale (in ♯ Phi.S 06614R)

SAUMELL, Manuel (1817-1870)

(18) Contradanzas pf.
F. Godino ♯ Pnt. 4000
(*Cervantes*)

SAUVEPLANE, Henri (b. 1892)

Habanéra vln. & pf.
— ARR. ORCH. Orch.—Chevreux (in V♯ CdM.LD YM 4020)

SCANDELLI (SCANDELLO), Antonio
(1517-1580)

Ein Hennlein weiss
Obernkirchen Children's Cho.—Möller
in ♯ Od.OLA 1007
(♯ Angel. 64012; ♭ Od.OBL 1078)
Vienna Acad. Cho.—Gillesberger in ♯ SPA. 58
(† Songs of the Renaissance)

SCARLATTI, Pietro Alessandro Gasparo
(1660-1725)

I. INSTRUMENTAL

CONCERTI GROSSI Strings
No. 1, F minor
Parrenin Str. Qtt. & Paris Coll. Musicum
—Douatte (*below*) ♯ Eko.LM 5
(*below & Vivaldi, on* ♯ Cum.CCX 277, probably n.v.)
☆ Winterthur Sym.—Dahinden (♯ MMS. 3006)

No. 3, F major
A. Scarlatti Orch.—Caracciolo ♯ C.CX 1171
(*below, Cimarosa & Paisiello*)(♯ QCX 10036; Angel. 35141)
☆ Virtuosi di Roma—Fasano[1] (♯ D.UAT 273091;
Fnt.LP 3006)
Winterthur Sym.—Dahinden (♯ MMS. 3006)

Gavotte & Sarabande — ARR. GUITAR
☆ A. Segovia (♭ AmD.ED 3510; SpC.SCGE 80005)

SINFONIAS
No. 4, E minor fl., ob., str.
F. Marseau, P. Pierlot & Paris Coll. Mus.
—Douatte ♯ Eko.LM 5
(*Concerto Grosso, F minor*)
(*above & Vivaldi, on* ♯ Cum.CCX 277, probably n.v.)
☆ Winterthur Sym.—Dahinden (♯ MMS. 3006)

No. 5, D minor fl. & str. orch.
A. Scarlatti Orch.—Caracciolo ♯ C.CX 1171
(*above, Paisiello & Cimarosa*)(♯ QCX 10036; Angel. 35141)
☆ Winterthur Sym.—Dahinden (♯ MMS. 3006)

Sonata, F major fl., 2 vlns. & cont.[2]
A. Mann (rec.), L. Wann (ob.), A. Meli (vln.),
E. Weiss-Mann (hpsi.) ♯ West.WL 5214
(*Pepusch & Telemann*)
M. Svendsen (rec.), O. Kinch & L. Fagerlund
(vlns.), J. E. Hansen (virginals) & vlc.
(*Albinoni*) ♭ Mtr.MCEP 3003
(*Albinoni, Vivaldi & Stradella, on* ♯ HS.HS 9011)

— ARR. FL. & STR. ORCH.
J-P. Rampal & Ens.—Froment ♯ EPP.APG 119
(*Handel, Pergolesi, Corelli*)

Sonata, F major 3 recorders & cont.[2]
L. Davenport (recorder), E. Schuster (ob.),
J. Tryon (vln.), P. Davenport (hpsi.)
M. Neal (vlc.)[3] ♯ CEd.CE 1051
(*J. S. Bach, Loeillet, Telemann*)
J-P. Rampal (fl.), P. Pierlot (ob.), M. Gendre
(vln.), R. Veyron-Lacroix (hpsi.), P. Hongne
(bsn.)[4] ♯ BàM.LD 011
(*J. C. Bach, Telemann, Handel, Quantz*) (♯ HS.HSL 117)

Toccata No. 2, A minor hpsi.
... 5th & 6th movts., Partita alla Lombarda; Fuga
— — ARR. BANDONEON
A. Barletta in ♯ SMC. 549

Toccata No. 7, D minor hpsi.
(with Fugue, & Partitas on *La Folia*—ed. Gerlin)
R. Gerlin in ♯ LOL.OL 50032
(† *Clavecinistes espagnols* ...) (♯ OL.LD 88)
M. T. Garatti (pf.) ♯ C.QS 6023
(*Clementi & D. Scarlatti*)

[1] Ed. Fasano. Labelled "No. 6". Fnt. catalogue attributes to D. Scarlatti.
[2] From the Santini collection. [3] Labelled "*Quartettino*". [4] Labelled "*Quintet*"; ed. Veyron-Lacroix.

II. VOCAL

A. CANTATAS

Pensieri, pensieri, ah Dio
N. Brincker (T), hpsi. & vlc. ♭ *Mtr.MCEP 3011*
(*Stradella: Ombre voi che celate*)
(*idem, & Albinoni & Vivaldi,* ‡ HS.HS 9011)

Per un vago desire S & cont.
M. Cortis (B) & Paris Inst. Ens.—Froment
(*Bassani & Cimarosa*)   ‡ **C.FCX 386**

Sento nel core . . . Opening Aria
G. Prandelli (T), D. Marzollo (pf.)
in ‡ **AmVox.PL 7930**
(† Old Italian Airs)

Su le sponde del Tebro S, tpt, str. *c.* 1705
T. Stich-Randall, H. Wobitsch & Salzburg
Mozarteum Cha. Orch.—Paumgartner[1]
(3ss)   **PV. 8404/5S**
(*Ariosti & Corelli on* ‡ HP.APM 14024; AmD.ARC 3008)

B. OPERAS & ARIAS

COLLECTION: 5 ARIAS
SEE: † CANZONE SCORDATE VOL. I; entered individually
below

(La) DONNA ANCORA È FEDELE 3 Acts 1698
Se Florindo è fedele
S. Danco (S), G. Agosti (pf.)   in ‡ **D.LX 3113**
(*Bach, Schütz, etc.*)   (‡ Lon.LS 698)

I. Kolassi (M-S), J. Bonneau (pf.)
in ‡ **Lon.LL 747**
(† Arie Antiche & German Lieder)   (‡ D.FAT 173160)

E. Brems (M-S) & Orch.   ♭ *Mtr.MCEP 3009*
(*Pirro, aria; & Handel*)

M. Meli (S), V. Vitale (pf.)   ♭ *C.SEDQ 504*
(*Sarti, Pergolesi, Paradies*)

O. Coelho (S) & guitar   in ‡ *Esq. 15-006*
(*Falla, etc.*)   (& in ‡ Van.VRS 7021)

Son tutta duolo
M. Vitale (S), A. Beltrami (pf.)   *Cet.AT 0316*
(*Paisiello: La Molinara—aria*)

FLAVIO 3 Acts 1688
Chi vuole innamorarsi
G. Souzay (B), J. Bonneau (pf.)
in ‡ **D.LXT 2835**
(† Canzone scordate, Vol. I)   (‡ Lon.LL 731)

(L') HONESTÀ NEGLI AMORI 3 Acts 1680
Già il sole del Gange
I. Kolassi (M-S), J. Bonneau (pf.)
in ‡ **Lon.LL 747**
(† Arie Antiche & German Lieder)   (‡ D.FAT 173160)

M. Laszlo (S), F. Holetschek (pf.)
in ‡ **Nix.WLP 5375**
(† Italian Airs)   (‡ West.WL 5375)

☆ B. Gigli (T)   in ‡ **G.ALP 1174**
(† Italian Classic Songs)   (‡ FALP 340: QALP 10073)

— ACCOMPANIMENT, etc., for practice (in ‡ *VS.ML 3004*)

(II) PIRRO E DEMETRIO 3 Acts 1694
Rugiadose, odorose, violette graziose
E. Brems (M-S) & Orch.   ♭ *Mtr.MCEP 3009*
(*La Donna—aria; & Handel*)

F. Barbieri (M-S), D. Marzollo (pf.)
in ‡ **AmVox.PL 7980**
(† Old Italian Songs & Airs)
☆ T. Schipa (T) (in ‡ Vic.LCT 1115; ♭ set WCT 1115)

(II) POMPEO 1683
Bellezza che s'ama
Toglietemi la vita ancor
G. Souzay (B), J. Bonneau (pf.)
in ‡ **D.LXT 2835**
(† Canzone scordate, Vol. I)   (‡ Lon.LL 731)

O cessate di piagarmi
☆ B. Gigli (T)   in ‡ **G.ALP 1174**
(† Italian Classic Songs)   (‡ FALP 340: QALP 10073)

TITO SEMPRONIO GRACCO 1702
Idolo mio, ti chiamo S, S, M-S, T
M. Ritchie, D. Bond, N. Evans, A. Young
G.HMS 46
(† History of Music in Sound)   (in ‡ Vic. set LM 6030)

(II) TRIONFO DELL' ONORE 3 Acts 1718
COMPLETE RECORDING   (ed. Mortari)
☆ Soloists, Italian Radio Cho. & Orch.—Giulini
(‡ FSor.CS 529/30)

UNIDENTIFIED ARIAS
Cara e dolce
G. Souzay (B), J. Bonneau (pf.)
in ‡ **D.LXT 2835**
(† Canzone Scordate, Vol. I)   (‡ Lon.LL 731)
☆ H. Cuénod (T), H. Leeb (lute)   in ‡ **Nix.WLP 5059**
(† Italian Songs of XVIth & XVIIth Centuries & *Milan, Mudarra*)

O dolcissima speranza
G. Souzay (B), J. Bonneau (pf.)
in ‡ **D.LXT 2835**
(† Canzone Scordate, Vol. I)   (‡ Lon.LL 731)

Se tu della mia morte
M. Vitale (S), A. Beltrami (pf.)   **Cet.AB 30024**
(*Paisiello: Nina, aria*)

Su, venite a consiglio, o pensieri ("*Dialoghetto*")
G. Prandelli (T), D. Marzollo (pf.)
in ‡ **AmVox.PL 7930**
(† Old Italian Airs)

Tutto acceso a quai rai
☆ M. Laszlo (S), F. Holetschek (pf) in ‡ **Nix.WLP 5119**
(† Italian Songs)

II. C. SACRED MUSIC

MOTETS
Est dies trophaei (Concerti sacri, No. 14)
. . . Miraculis in coelo fulget cho.
London Chamber Singers & Orch.—Bernard
G.HMS 51
(† History of Music in Sound)   (in ‡ Vic. set LM 6030)

Exsultate Deo 4 vv.
Vienna Boys' Cho.—Brenn in ‡ **EPhi.NBR 6013**
(*Verdi, Victoria, Nasco, Handl, etc.*)
(in ‡ Phi.N 00624R; AmC.ML 4873)

U.O.S. Cho.—McConnell   in ‡ **UOS. 2**
(*Bach, Allegri, Gevaert, etc.*)   (pte. rec.)

PASSION MUSIC: St. John Passion[2] *c.* 1680-5
B. Stern (T), D. Laurent (Bs), J. Borden (T),
St. Thomas's Chu. Cho., New Haven, & Yale
Orch.—Boatwright   ‡ **Over.LP 1**
[G. George, organ]

(II) SEDECIA, RÈ DI GERUSALEMME
Oratorio 1706
. . . Caldo sangue[3]
G. Souzay (B) & Orch.   in ‡ **D.LX 3112**
(*Lully, Gluck, Mozart, etc.*)   (in ‡ Lon.LS 730)

STABAT MATER, D minor S, A, orch.
R. Giancola, M. Truccato-Pace & Venice Cha.
Orch.—Ephrikian   ‡ **E. & AmVox.PL 7970**

SCARLATTI, Domenico (1685-1757)

L. numbers are those of the Longo edn. [Supp. from 501];
numbers in brackets are those of Kirkpatrick's chronological
arrangement in his *Domenico Scarlatti*, 1953, known as **Kk**
numbers.

SONATAS, Harpsichord
COLLECTION: "Sixty Sonatas"[4]

Side 1			
I:	L.378, A mi. [3]	II:	L.379, A mi. [7]
III:	L.397, B♭ ma. [16]	IV:	L.416, D mi. [18]
V:	L.373, E ma. [28]	VI:	L.461, D ma. [29]
VII:	L.432, F ma. [44]		
Side 2			
VIII:	L.25, E ma. [46]	IX:	L.241, A mi. [54]
X:	L.538, B♭ ma. [57]	XI:	L.10, C mi. [84]
XII:	L.267, D mi. [52]	XIII:	L.465, D ma. [96]

(*continued on next page*)

---

[1] MS. Cherubini Conservatoire, Florence.
[2] From MS., Naples Cons., trs. E. Hanley; ed. Boatwright and others.   [3] ARR. Dørumsgaard and Cornman.
[4] Roman figures refer to nos. in the published collection of 60 Sonatas, ed. Kirkpatrick (Schirmer, N.Y.).

SONATAS, Harpsichord (*continued*)

Side 3
XIV: L.204, G ma. [105]   XV: L.407, C mi. [115]
XVI: L.452, C mi. [116]   XVII: L.415, D ma. [119]
XVIII: L.215, D mi. [120]   XIX: L.457, C ma. [132]
XX: L.282, C ma. [133]   XXI: L.429, A mi. [175]

Side 4
XXII: L.107, D ma. [140]   XXIII: L.238, A ma. [208]
XXIV: L.428, A ma. [209]   XXV: L.323, E ma. [215]
XXVI: L.273, E ma. [216]   XXVII: L.27, F mi. [238]
XXVIII: L.281, F mi. [239]   XXIX: L.103, G ma. [259]
XXX: L.124, G ma. [260]

Side 5
XXXI: L.321, E mi. [263]   XXXII: L.466, E ma. [264]
XXXIII: L.359, C ma. [308]   XXXIV: L.454, C ma. [309]
XXXV: L.119, F ma. [366]   XXXVI: L.172, F ma. [367]
XXXVII: L.275, E mi. [394]   XXXVIII: L. 65, E ma. [395]

Side 6
XXXIX: L.427, E mi. [402]   XL: L.470, E ma. [403]
XLI: L.502, C ma. [420]   XLII: L.252, C ma. [421]
XLIII: L.128, C mi. [426]   XLIV: L.286, G ma. [427]
XLV: L.324, C ma. [460]   XLVI: L.8, C ma. [461]

Side 7
XLVII: L.304, G ma. [470]   XLVIII: L.82, G ma. [471]
XLIX: L.206, D ma. [490]   L: L.164, D ma. [491]
LI: L.14, D ma. [492]   LII: L.524, G ma. [493]
LIII: L.287, G ma. [494]

Side 8
LIV: L.503, C ma. [513]   LV: L.512, D mi. [516]
LVI: L.266, D mi. [517]   LVII: L.116, F ma. [518]
LVIII: L.475, F mi. [519]   LIX: L.497, Bb ma. [544]
LX: L.500, Bb ma. [545]

R. Kirkpatrick   # AmC.ML 5025/8
(set SL 221)

COLLECTION: F. Valenti[1]
VOL. I
L.37, G ma. [325] L.204, G ma. [105] L.252, C ma. [421]
L.262, D ma. [535] L.279, F ma. [419] L.345, A ma. [113]
L.395, A ma. [533] L.415, D ma. [119] L.429, A mi. [175]
L.430, E ma. [531] L.449, B mi. [27] L.500, Bb ma. [545]

☆ F. Valenti   # Nix.WLP 5106

VOL. II
L.8, C ma.   [461] L.14, D ma. [492] L.23, E ma. [380]
L.104, C ma. [159] L.127, G ma. [348] L.126, G mi. [347]
L.232, G ma. [124] L.263, B mi. [377] L.413, D ma.   [9]
L.422, D mi. [141] L.465, C ma. [96] L.486, G ma. [13]

☆ F. Valenti   # Nix.WLP 5116

VOL. III
L.10, C mi.   [84] L.25, E ma.   [46] L.33, B mi.   [87]
L.58, D mi.   [64] L.165, D ma. [124] L.241, A mi. [54]
L.352, C mi. [11] L.365, D ma. [401] L.419, D ma. [484]
L.420, D mi. [444] L.432, F ma. [44] L.433, F ma. [446]

☆ F. Valenti   # Nix.WLP 5139

VOL. IV
L.103, G ma. [259] L.136, A mi. [61] L.205, C ma. [487]
L.209, G ma. [455] L.321, E mi. [263] L.323, E ma. [215]
L.381, F ma. [438] L.386, G mi. [35] L.388, F ma.   [2]
L.418, D ma. [443] L.463, D ma. [430] L.475, F mi. [519]

F. Valenti   # Nix.WLP 5186
(# West.WL 5186)

VOL. V
L.86, G ma.   [520] L.84, G ma.   [63] L.129, G ma. [201]
L.155, C ma. [271] L.218, C ma. [398] L.325, E mi. [98]
L.327, Bb ma. [529] L.375, E ma.   [20] L.376, E mi. [147]
L.407, C mi. [115] L.457, C ma. [132] L.487, G ma. [125]

F. Valenti   # Nix.WLP 5205
(# West.WL 5205)

VOL. VI
L.135, A ma. [212] L.163, D mi. [176] L.173, F mi. [185]
L.274, C ma. [399] L.281, F mi. [239] L.282, C ma. [133]
L.286, G ma. [427] L.324, C ma. [460] L.379, A mi.   [7]
L.452, C mi. [116] L.466, E ma. [264] L.497, Bb ma. [544]

F. Valenti   # Nix.WLP 20015
(# West.WL 5325)

VOL. VII
L.179, G ma. [152] L.238, A ma. [208] L.301, C ma. [49]
L.304, G ma. [470] L.378, A mi.   [3] L.385, F ma. [445]
L.428, A ma. [209] L.434, Bb ma. [267] L.470, E ma. [403]
L.479, F ma.   [6] L.511 (Supp. 11), D major [415]
L.539 (Supp. 39), Bb major [441]

F. Valenti   # West.WL 5359

VOL. VIII
L.162, D ma. [178] L.268, D ma. [224] L.273, E ma. [216]
L.357, C mi. [40] L.359, C ma. [308] L.427, E mi. [404]
L.493, A ma. [301] L.510 (Supp. 10) D ma. [335]
L.515 (Supp. 15) D ma. [278] L.519 (Supp. 19) F ma. [297]
L.520 (Supp. 20) F ma. [276] L.527 (Supp. 27) G ma. [328]

F. Valenti   # West.WN 18009

VOL. IX
L.257, E ma. [206] L.302, G ma. [372] L.322, G ma. [305]
L.335, G ma. [55] L.382, F mi. [69] L.423, D ma. [32]
L.458, C ma. [527] L.502 (Supp. 2) C ma. [420]
L.504 (Supp. 4) C ma. [407] L.512 (Supp. 12) D mi. [516]
L.531 (Supp. 31) A ma. [83] L.536 (Supp. 36) Bb ma. [42]

F. Valenti   # West.WN 18029

VOL. X
L.5, C ma.   [406] L.13, G mi.   [60] L.21, E ma. [162]
L.22, E mi.   [198] L.109, D ma. [436] L.140, A mi. [341]
L.255, C ma. [515] L.266, D ma. [517] L.288, G ma. [432]
L.308, D ma. [237] L.349, G ma. [146] L.356, C mi. [56]

F. Valenti   # West.WN 18068

VOL. XI
L.7, C ma.   [302] L.116, F ma. [518] L.24, E mi. [292]
L.206, D ma. [490] L.213, D ma. [400] L.224, E ma. [135]
L.243, A mi. [451] L.265, D ma. [45] L.270, D mi. [295]
L.317, C mi.   [99] L.373, E ma. [28] L.454, C ma. [309]

F. Valenti   # West.WN 18094

VOL. XII
L.56, D ma.   [281] L.134, A mi. [383] L.151, C ma. [464]
L.152, C ma. [327] L.153, C ma. [485] L.172, F ma. [367]
L.175, F ma. [387] L.184, D ma. [454] L.287, C ma. [494]
L.408, G ma. [521] L.439, C ma. [255] L.538 (Supp. 38),
                                          Bb ma. [57]

F. Valenti   # West.WN 18102

VOL. XIII
L.54, C ma.   [200] L.65, E ma. [395] L.107, D ma. [140]
L.125, G ma. [413] L.164, D ma. [491] L.253, C ma. [199]
L.269, D ma. [333] L.311, D ma. [509] L.354, C mi. [230]
L.369, D ma. [145] L.445, G ma. [153] L.503 (Supp. 3),
                                          C ma. [513]

F. Valenti   # West.WN 18112

VOL. XIV
L.55, C ma.   [330] L.57, D ma. [288] L.67, D mi. [294]
L.75, F ma.   [78] L.79, G ma. [391] L.81, G ma.   [71]
L.93, A mi.   [149] L.211, D mi. [89] L.222, A ma. [404]
L.297, F ma. [274] L.364, D ma. [177] L.392, A mi. [218]

F. Valenti   # West.WN 18153

OTHER COLLECTIONS
L.23, E ma. [380] L.33, B mi. [87] L.326, F ma. [505]
L.331, G ma. [169] L.349, G ma. [146] L.413, D mi.   [9]
L.424, D ma. [33] L.450, B ma. [245] L.457, C ma. [132]
L.461, D ma. [29] L.475, F mi. [519] L.483, A ma. [322]
L.487, G ma. [125] L.495, A ma. [24] L.497, Bb ma. [544]
L.498, Bb ma. [202]

G. Malcolm   # D.LXT 2918
(# Lon.LL 963)

L.14, D ma. [492] L.206, D ma. [490] L.232, G ma. [124]
L.257, E ma. [206] L.345, A ma. [113] L.433, F ma. [446]
L.474, F ma. [107]

S. Marlowe   # Rem. 199-136
(*Bach & Couperin*)   (# Cum.CR 207)

L.14, D ma. [492] L.23, E ma. [380] L.58, D mi.   [64]
L.132, A ma. [429] L.189, F mi. [184] L.194, A ma. [181]
L.202, C ma. [242] L.257, E ma. [206] L.338, G mi. [450]
L.499, G mi. [30]

R. Gerlin   # CFD. 44

L.58, D mi. ("Gavotte") [64] (a) L.104, C ma. [159]
L.401, C ma.   [72] L.415, D ma. [119]
L.433, F ma. ("Pastorale") [446] L.461, D ma. [29] (a)
L.488, G mi.   [8] L.503 (Supp. 3) C ma.
                                   ("Pastorale") [513]

E. Hansen   # HP.AP 13001
(Those marked (a) also on b *Pol. 37019*)

L.135, A ma. [212] L.263, B mi. [377]
L.429, A mi. [175] L.432, F ma. [44]

G. Kraus   (*Mozart*)   # Hall.RS 2

---

[1] Vols. I–VII lately re-issued as # West.WN 18328/34.

SONATAS (continued)

L.14, D ma. [492]	L.49, G mi. [234]	L.56, D ma. [281]
L.97, B♭ ma. [440]	L.102, C ma. [423]	L.103, G ma. [259]
L.138, A mi. [109]	L.187, F mi. [481]	L.206, D ma. [490]
L.213, D ma. [400]	L.228, F ma. [256]	L.255, C ma. [515]
L.382, F mi. [69]	L.422, D mi. [141]	L.418, D ma. [443]
L.423, D mi. [32]	L.449, B mi. [27]	L.461, D ma. [29]
L.497, B♭ ma. [544]	L.520 (Supp. 20), D ma. [276]	

    ☆ W. Landowska   ♯ **G.FJLP 5055**

L.12, D ma. [478]	L.14, D ma. [492]	L.23, E ma. [380]
L.33, B mi. [87]	L.58, D mi. [64]	L.288, G ma. [432]
L.338, G mi. [450]	L.344, A ma. [114]	L.382, F mi. [69]
L.413, D ma. [9]	L.415, D ma. [119]	L.423, D mi. [32]
L.429, A mi. [175]	L.449, B mi. [27]	L.450, B ma. [245]
L.468, A ma. [279]		

    M. Meyer (pf.)   ♯ **DFr. 139**

L.107, D ma. [140]	L.202, C ma. [242]	L.221, E ma. [134]
L.256, C♯ mi. [247]	L.432, F ma. [44]	L.487, G ma. [125]

    C. Rosen ("Siena" pf.)   ♯ **Eso.ESP 3000**
    (Mozart)

L.23, E ma. [380]	L.387, G ma. [14]	L.395, A ma. [533]
L.411, D ma. [23]	L.449, B mi. [27]	L.463, D ma. [430]

    R. Casadesus (pf.)   ♯ **AmC.ML 4695**
    (Rameau)
    (L.23, 395, 411, 449, 463, also on ♭ EPhi.ABE 10001;
                     Phi.A 409006E)

L.23, E ma. [380]	L.275, E mi. [394]	L.413, D mi. [9]
L.424, D ma. [33]	L.443, C ma. [356]	

    W. Gieseking (pf.)   ♯ **AmC.ML 4646**
    (Handel & Bach)   (♯ C.FCX 367)
    (L. 275 & 413 also on C.LB 136: GQ 7256; L.23 & 424 also
    on C.LB 144)

L.33, B mi. [87]	L.142, E♭ ma. [193]	L.171, F mi. [386]
L.255, C ma. [515]	L.256, C♯ mi. [247]	L.386, G mi. [35]
L.388, G ma. [2]	L.457, C ma. [132]	L.475, F mi. [519]
L.479, F ma. [6]	L.483, A ma. [322]	

    ☆ C. Haskil (pf.)   (♯ Sel. 270.C.006)

L.381, F ma. [438]	L.422, D mi. [141]	L.430, E ma. [531]

    P. Cavazzini (pf.)   (Chopin)   ♯ *Arp.ARC 4*

SONATAS
L.5, C major [406]
L.30, F major [82]
    P. Spagnolo (pf.)   ♯ *D.LW 5142*
    (Bach, Mompou, Margola, Rodrigo)   (♯ Lon.LD 5135)
    (Bach only, ♭ D.71075)

L.22, E minor [198]
L.104, C major [159]
    P. Sebastiani (pf.)   **ArgV. 66-6005**
    (Chopin: Étude, Op. 25, No. 11)

L.23, E major [380]
    ☆ L. Selbiger (C.LB 134: LW 63)
    D. Lipatti (pf.) (in ♯ AmC.ML 2216 & ♯ C.FCX 495)

L.103, G major [259]
L.104, C major [159]
    C. Zecchi (pf.)   in ♯ **West.WN 18139**
    (Bach, Mozart, Schumann, etc.)

L.104, C major [159]
    ☆ J. Therrien (pf.) (in ♯ MH. 33-111)

L.106, D minor [90] ... Minuet only
    E. Heiller   in ♯ **Uni.LP 1010**
    († History of the Dance)

L.239, A minor [188]
    ☆ V. Horowitz (pf.) (G.7R 155: 7RW 3023)

L.352, C minor [11]
    F. Viderø   in ♯ **HS.HSL 2073**
    († Masterpieces of Music before 1750)

— ARR. GUITAR   Segovia
    ☆ A. Segovia (♭ AmD.ED 3503; ♭ SpC.SCGE 80004)

L.383, F minor [19]
L.396, B flat major [551]
    M. T. Garatti (pf.)   ♯ *C.QS 6023*
    (Clementi & A. Scarlatti)

L.384, F major [17]
    D. Handman (pf.)   in ♯ **LOL.OL 50078**
    († Sonatas of the XVIIth & XVIIIth Centuries)

L.413, D minor [9]   ("Pastorale")
    H. Unruh   *MSB. 78039*
    (L.499; & Bach: March & Minuet)
    ☆ D. Lipatti (pf.) (in ♯ AmC.ML 2216 & ♯ C.FCX 495)

L.418, D major [443]
    ☆ W. Landowska (in ♯ G.ALP 1246 : FALP/QALP 218)

L.422, D minor [141]
    ☆ L. Selbiger (C.LB 134: LW 63)

L.423, D minor [32]
    ☆ W. Landowska (in ♯ G.ALP 1246 : FALP/QALP 218)

L.483, A major [322]
    ☆ V. Horowitz (pf.) (♭ G.7R 155: 7RQ 3023)

L.498, B flat major [202]
    A. van der Wiele   **G.HMS 60**
    († History of Music in Sound)   (in ♯ Vic. set LM 6031)

L.499, G minor [30]
    H. Unruh   *MSB. 78039*
    (L.413; & Bach: March & Minuet)

L.503 (Supp. 3) C major [513]   ("Pastorale")
    ☆ O. P. Santoliquido (pf.)   in ♯ B.AXTL 1032
    (Boccherini, Vivaldi, etc.)   (♯ D.UAT 273551;
                              Fnt.LP 3004)

(8) SONATAS, Violin & hpsi.   ed. Salter
    (Restored from hpsi. Sonatas, which are now held to
    have originally been for violin & cont.)

1. C minor	L.217 [73]	2. D minor L.168 [77]
3. F major	L.75 [78]	4. E minor L.271 [81]
5. G minor	L.36 [88]	6. D minor L.211 [89]
7. D minor	L.106 [90]	8. G major L.176 [91]

    J. Olevsky & F. Valenti   ♯ **West.WN 18113**

TRANSCRIPTIONS
(Le) Donne di buon umore   ARR. Tommasini
(Sonatas L.388, 361, 33, 463, 385) (The Good-humoured Ladies)
    Philharmonia—Markevitch   ♯ **C.CX 1198**
    (Chopin, Falla, Tchaikovsky) (♯ FCX 358; Angel. 35152 in
                                   set 3518)

    Covent Garden Op.—Braithwaite
                              ♯ **MGM.E 3034**
    (Mozart: Les Petits Riens)

    Vienna State Op.—Litschauer   ♯ **Nix.PVL 7024**
    (Bach-Walton: Wise Virgins)   (♯ Van.VRS 440)

(4) SONATAS   — ARR. STR. ORCH.

L.106, D minor	[90]
L.103, C major	[259]
L.263, B minor	[377]
L.499, G minor	[30]

    Allegro Cha. Orch.—Tubbs   ♯ **Allo. 3146**
    (Telemann & Vivaldi)

UNSPECIFIED
    (It has not been possible to check these discs.)
3 Sonatas
    S. Fiorentino (pf.)   V♯ *CA.MPO 5026*
    (Beethoven)

A major
    A. Rácz (cymbalom), A. Rácz (pf.) (Qual.SZK 3554
                                  & SZN 3004)

D minor
    A. d'Arco (pf.)   in Plé.P 101
    A. Rácz (cymbalom), A. Rácz (pf.) (Qual.ZN 3001)

E major
    L. Hernádi   U.H 24430
    (Vinci: Largo)

E minor
    Z. Růžičková   U.C 24398
    (Daquin & Rameau)

F minor   — ARR. CYMBALOM & PF.
    I. Tarjani-Tóth & I. Altoff (in ♯ G.FBLP 1067)

☆ = Re-issue of a recording to be found in previous volumes.

SCHEIDT, Samuel (1587-1654)

MOTET: Ein' feste Burg
Netherlands Madrigal & Motet Cho.—Voorberg
in ♯ *Phi.N 00692R*
(† Motets on Luther Texts)

PADUANA, GALLIARDA, etc.
4 gambas & hpsi. 1621
No. 4, Paduana
No. 7, Galliard, C major
No. 14, Alamande, C major
☆ Schola Cantorum Basiliensis Ens.   ♭ *Pol. 37015*
(*Schein*)

TABULATURA NOVA (3 Books)
org. or clavier 1624
COLLECTION (Book I items are variations)
I. 5. Warum betrübst du dich, mein Herz (*Cantio sacra*)[1]
I. 12. Da Jesus an dem Kreuze stund (*Psalmus*)[2]
III. 9. Magnificat noni toni[3]
III. 19. Modus ludendi pleno organo pedaliter, No. 1
I. 11. Est-ce Mars? (*Cantio gallica*)[4]
Luther Noss   ♯ *Over.LP 3*
[Holtkamp org., Battell Chapel, Yale]

I. 10. Ach du feiner Reiter (*Cantio belgica*)[5]
E. Bodky (hpsi.)   in ♯ *Uni.LP 1002*
(† Music of the Baroque Era)

III. 17. Credo in unum Deum
☆ M. Dupré (in † ♯ HS.AS 11)

SCHEIN, Johann Hermann (1586-1630)

BANCHETTO MUSICALE Insts. 1617
Suite No. 2, D minor   4 & 5 gambas
1. Paduana   2. Gagliarda
3. Courante   4. Allemande   5. Tripla
☆ Schola Cantorum Basiliensis Ens.   ♭ *Pol. 37015*
(*Scheidt*)

Suite No. 14, G major
☆ Brass Ens.—Sachs (in † ♯ HS.AS 12)

Intrada; Paduana (not in Suites)
Music Hall Brass Ens.   in ♯ *Mono. 817*
(† Music for Brass)

(Der) kühle Maien   Chanson
Chapelle de Bourgogne Recorder Trio
in ♯ *OL.LD 81*
(† Musiciens de la Cour)

MOTETS
Die mit Tränen säen
St. Olaf Cho.—O. C. Christiansen
(*Gretchaninoff, etc.*)   in ♯ *StO.DLP 6*

Nun komm' der Heiden Heiland
Netherlands Madrigal & Motet Cho.—Voorberg
in ♯ *Phi.N 00692R*
(† Motets on Luther Texts)

SCHEMELLI, Georg Christian (c. 1678-1762)

SEE: † GERMAN SONGS

SCHEPERS, Geleyn (fl. c. 1660)

SEE: † CARILLON PIECES

SCHERER, Sebastian Anton (1631-1712)

SEE: † XVIITH CENTURY ORGAN MUSIC

SCHIERBECK, Poul (1888-1949)

FÊTE GALANTE, Op. 25   Opera
Overture
☆ Danish Radio—Grøndahl(♭ *Mer.EP 1-5018 & EP 1-5046*)

SONGS
Denmark's Boy (*Danmarks dreng*) (Garff)
F. Andersson (T) & Orch.   *Tono.L 28065*
(*Rygaard: The Flag*)

Farewell to summer   (Woel)
(*Afsked med Sommeren*)
R. Teglbjærg (M-S), K. Olsson (pf.)   *Felix.B 79*
(*T. Laub: It is white outside; & Folksong*)

In Denmark I was born   (H. C. Andersen)
Mercantile Class Cho.—Mortensen
Tono.K 8090
(*Mortensen: Migration Song*)

(The) Starling
R. Teglbjærg (M-S) & self pf. (in Felix.X 80)

SCHILLINGS, Max von (1868-1943)

Glockenlieder, Op. 22 (Spitteler) T & orch.
H. Krebs & Berlin Radio—Rother ♯ *Ura. 7104*
(*Britten*)

SCHMIDT, Franz (1874-1939)

NOTRE DAME   Opera   2 Acts   1914
Intermezzo (*Czardas*)
N.W. Ger. Phil.—Schüchter   ♯ *Imp.ILP 110*
(*Gounod, Ponchielli, R. Strauss*)   (♯ *G.QDLP 6025*)
Vienna Radio—Sandauer   ♭ *Phi.KD 160*
(*Gioconda—Danza*)
Leipzig Radio—Gerdes   Eta. 225024
(*Aida—Ballabili*)
☆ Württemberg State Op.—Leitner (*PV. 36102;*
♭ *Pol. 30037: in ♯ 17001*)
Belgian Radio—André (♭ *T.UE 453915: in ♯ LS 6031*)

Quintet, G major   pf. (left hand) & str. qtt. 1927
— ARR. PF. (two hands) & STR. QTT.   Wührer
☆ J. Demus & Barylli Qtt.   ♯ *Nix.WLP 5158*

Symphony No. 4, C major   1934
Vienna Sym.—Moralt   ♯ *Phi.A 00261L*
(♯ *Epic.LC 3164*)

SCHMITT, Florent (b. 1870)

(Le) Camp de Pompée, Op. 69   1920
(From Inc. Music to Shakespeare's "Anthony & Cleopatra")
— ARR. BAND
French Navy Band—Maillot   ♯ *Sel. 270.C.052*
(*below; & Hindemith*)

(3) Danses, Op. 86   pf.   1936
... No. 2, Bocane
L. Thyrion   ♯ *Phi.N 00666R*
(*Roussel & Dukas*)

(Les) Dionysiaques, Op. 62   Band
1913-14, f.p. 1925
French Navy Band—Maillot   ♯ *Sel. 270.C.052*
(*above*)

PART SONG: Si mes poches, Op. 104, No. 2 (Yks)
Lyons Psalette—Geoffray   in ♯ *SM. 33-21*
(*Hindemith, Distler, etc.*)

Psalm 46, Op. 38   S, cho., org. & orch.   (Mathot)
1904
D. Duval, E. Brasseur Cho., G. Tessier (vln.),
M. Duruflé (org.) & Paris Cons.—Tzipine
♯ *C.FCX 171*
(♯ *Angel. 35020*)

Quatuor de saxophones, Op. 102   1943
M. Mule Sax. Qtt.   ♯ *D.LX 3135*
(*Absil & Pierné*)   (♯ *Lon.LS 1076*)

Sextuor de Clarinettes   1953
Paris Clarinet Sextet   ♯ *D.LX 3136*
(*Loucheur: En famille*)   (♯ *Lon.LS 1077*)

---

[1] 12 Variations.   [2] 6 Variations.
[3] Ed. Crocker.   Recorded with alternating verses of Plain-song by an unspec. cho.   [4] 10 Variations.
[5] 7 Variations.

SCHNABEL, Artur (1882-1951)

Concerto, pf. & orch. 1901
H. Schnabel & Vienna Philharmonia—Adler
♯ CA.LPA 1068
(Songs) *(♯ SPA. 55)*

SONGS 1900-2
COLLECTION
Op. 11: No. 2, **Dann** (Dehmel)
No. 4, **Marienlied** (Novalis)
No. 5, **Dieses ist der rechte Morgen** (George)
No. 7, **Sieh', mein Kind, ich gehe** (George)
No. 8, **Waldnacht** (Dehmel)
No. 9, **Das Veilchen an den Spanischen Flieder** (Sachs)
No. 10, **Tanzlied** (Bierbaum)
Op. 14: No. 1, **Frühlingsdämmerung**[1] (Sachs)
No. 5, **Hyazinthen**
No. 7, **Die Sperlinge**
E. Francoulon (S), H. Schnabel (pf.)
♯ CA.LPA 1068
(Concerto, above) *(♯ SPA. 55)*

SCHNEIDER-TRNAVSKÝ, Mikuláš
(b. 1881)

Dumka & Dance orch.
Bratislava Sym.—Babusek **♯ Csm.CRLPX 008**
(Dvořák, Weis; & Šebor: Goldhead, polka) *(▽ U.H 23682)*

Slovak Sonatina, Op. 75 pf.
▽ M. Karin (2ss) **U.H 23683**

SCHNYDER ZU WARTENSEE, Franz Xavier Joseph Peter (1786-1868)

Der durch Musik überwundene Wüterich, C major
Glass-harmonica & pf. *c.* 1830
B. Hoffmann & F. Neumeyer **PV. 9402**
(♭ Pol. 37055)

SCHÖFFER, Peter (fl. 1510-40)

SEE: † MUSIC OF THE RENAISSANCE

SCHOENBERG, Arnold (1874-1951)

Begleitmusik zu einer Lichtspielszene, Op. 34 orch.
1930
Vienna Orch. Soc.—Adler **♯ Uni.LA 1008**
(Cowell: Symphony 10, etc.)

Concerto, Op. 42 pf. & orch. 1942
☆ C. Helffer & French Radio Sym.—Leibowitz
♯ Per.SPL 568
(Piano works) *(♯ Cpt.MC 20044)*

Concerto, Op. 36 vln. & orch. 1936
L. Krasner & N.Y.P.S.O.—Mitropoulos
(Berg) **♯ AmC.ML 4857**

GURRELIEDER (Jacobsen) 1900-1
S, A, T, T, Bs, Diction, cho. & orch.
E. Semser, N. Tangeman, R. Lewis, F. Gruber,
J. Riley, M. Gesell, Paris New Sym. Cho.
& Orch.—Leibowitz (6ss) **♯ Nix.HLP 3100-1/3**
(excerpts on V♯ Era.LDE 1064) *(4ss, ♯ Era.LDE 3012/3;*
6ss, HS.HSL set 100)
☆ Soloists, Cho. & Philadelphia Orch.—Stokowski
(4ss) **♯ Vic. set LCT 6012**
[with spoken intro. by Stokowski]

Kammersymphonie, Op. 9b[2] 1935
Vienna Sym.—Häfner **♯ AmC.ML 4664**
(Kol Nidrei, & Survivor from Warsaw)

(3) Klavierstücke, Op. 11 pf. 1908
M. Field **♯ Per.SPL 568**
(Suite, Op. 25, & Concerto) *(♯ Cpt.MC 20044)*

(5) Klavierstücke, Op. 23 pf. 1923
... **No. 5, Walzer**
J. Manchon-Theis **♯ LT.MEL 94008**
(Berg & Webern) *(V♯ Sel.LAP 1059; ♯ T.TW 30031)*

(6) Klavierstücklein, Op. 19 pf. 1911
J. Harris **♯ PFCM.CB 185**
(½s—Persichetti & Dallapiccola)

Kol Nidrei, Op. 39 Diction, cho. & orch. 1939
H. Jaray *(Eng)*, Vienna Acad. Cha. Cho. &
Sym.—Swarowsky **♯ AmC.ML 4664**
(Kammersymphonie & Survivor from Warsaw)

Ode to Napoleon Bonaparte, Op. 41 (Byron)
Diction, Str. Qtt. & pf. 1943
☆ E. Adler, Villers Qtt. & J. Monod—Leibowitz
(♯ Clc. 6172)

(5) Pieces for orch., Op. 16 1908
Chicago Sym.—Kubelik **♯ G.ALP 1251**
(Hindemith: Sym. Metamorphosis) *(♯ Mer.MG 50024)*
(Bartók on ♯ Mer.MG 50026)

Pierrot Lunaire, Op. 21 Speaker & Inst. Ens.
1912
E. Semser & Virtuoso Cha. Ens.—Leibowitz
♯ Argo.RG 54
(♯ BàM.LD 016; West.WN 18143)
A. Howland & Cha. Ens.—Winograd
♯ MGM.E 3202

QUARTETS, Strings
COMPLETE (except for D major, 1897)
No. 1, D minor, Op. 7　　　1905
No. 2, F sharp minor, Op. 10　1908　with U. Graf (S)
No. 3, Op. 30　　　　　　　1926
No. 4, Op. 37　　　　　　　1936
Juilliard Qtt. **♯ AmC.ML 4735/7**
(5ss—Berg & Webern) *(set SL 188)*
(Nos. 2 & 3 also on ♯ Phi.A 01177L; No. 4, with Berg &
Webern, ♯ Phi.A 01178L)

No. 3, Op. 30 1926
☆ New Pro Arte Qtt. *(♯ Mtr.CLP 502)*

SONGS
(Das) Buch der hängenden Gärten, Op. 15
(George) 1908
COMPLETE RECORDINGS, 15 Songs
L. Dauby (S), P. Collaer (pf.) **♯ LOL.DL 53006**
M. Hinneberg-Lefèbre (S), H. Roloff (pf.)
♯ Pol. 16129
B. Kibler (M-S), G. Albersheim (pf.)
♯ Lyr.LL 42

Suite, Op. 25 pf. 1925
M. Field **♯ Per.SPL 568**
(Klavierstücke, Op. 11; & Concerto) *(♯ Cpt.MC 20044)*

Suite, Op. 29 pf., 2 cl., bs., cl. & str. trio 1926
R. Sherman & Ens.—Schuller **♯ Per.SPL 705**
(2ss)

(The) Survivor from Warsaw, Op. 46 (Schoenberg)
1947
H. Jaray (diction, *Eng*), Vienna Acad. Male
Cho. & Sym.—Swarowsky **♯ AmC.ML 4664**
(Kol Nidrei & Kammersymphonie No. 2)

Trio, Op. 45 vln., vla., vlc. 1946
New Music Qtt. Members **♯ PFCM.CB 181**
(Thomson & Berg)
☆ Koldofsky Trio *(♯ Clc. 6172)*

Verklärte Nacht, Op. 4 Strings 1899
Israel Phil.—Kletzki **♯ C.CX 1251**
(Mahler: Symphony No. 9, s. 3) *(♯ FCX 380; Angel. 35182*
in set 3526)
☆ Hollywood Str. Qtt., etc. **♯ DCap.CTL 7096**
(Debussy & Ravel) *(♯ Cap.P 8304)*
☆ Orch.—Stokowski **♯ G.ALP 1205**
(Vaughan Williams) *(♯ Vic.LM 1739; ♭ set WDM 1739;*
♯ FV.A 630278)
☆ St. Louis Sym.—Golschmann *(♯ Cam.CAL 178)*

---

[1] Labelled *Frühlingslied*, but probably this.
[2] Originally Op. 9, for 15 instruments, 1908.

SCHRÖDER, Hermann (1843-1909)

Schönster Herr Jesu, Op. 11, No. 6
Chorale-Prelude, org.
E. White   in ♯ Moll.E4QP 7231
(Bach, Vierne, Reger, Widor, etc.)

SCHUBERT, Franz Peter (1797-1828)

CLASSIFIED: I. INSTRUMENTAL
       A. Piano   B. Chamber Music
       C. Dances   D. Orchestral
       II. VOCAL
       A. Stage Works   B. Church Music
       C. Part Songs   D. Songs (Lieder)

I. INSTRUMENTAL

A. PIANO & PIANO DUET
(for solo piano unless otherwise stated)

Adagio, C major
SEE: Sonata No. 3, *below*

Adagio, E major   D.612   1818
F. Pelleg   ♯ CHS.H 14
(Scherzo, below; Adagio & Rondo; & Vln. Sonata)

Allegretto, C minor   D.915   1827
L. Hungerford   in ♯ LH. 101/2
                    (Pte.)

Allegro, A minor, Op. 144   D.947   pf. duet   1828
(Lebensstürme)
☆ P. Badura-Skoda & J. Demus   ♯ Nix.WLP 5147
(Variations)

Andantino varié, B minor, Op. 84, No. 1   D.823
pf. duet   1825
R. & G. Casadesus   ♯ AmC.ML 5046
(below; & Mozart)

Fantasia, C major, Op. 15 *(Wanderer)* D.760 1822
A. Aeschbacher   ♯ HP.DGM 19001
(Moments musicaux)   (♯ Pol. 18213)
(3ss—Impromptu on ♮ PV. 72372/3)
I. Nádas   ♯ Per.SPL 719
(Moments musicaux)
K. U. Schnabel   ♯ McInt.MM 110
(Dances)   (o.n. ♯ WCFM. 17)
S. Nordby *(Beethoven)*   ♯ ML. 7055
W. Hautzig   ♯ HS.HS 9000
(Moments musicaux)
☆ O. Frugoni (♯ EVox.PL 6690)

— ARR. PF. & ORCH.   Liszt
G. Johannesen & Netherlands Phil.—Goehr
(Ländler & Rondo)[1]   ♯ CHS.CHS 1176

Fantasia, F minor, Op. 103   D.940   pf. duet   1828
K. U. & H. Schnabel   ♯ Phi.N 00255L
(Brahms)   (♯ Epic.LC 3183)
R. & G. Casadesus   ♯ AmC.ML 5046
(above)
☆ P. Badura-Skoda & J. Demus   ♯ Nix.WLP 5047
(Rondos & March)
☆ J. & G. Dichler (in ♯ U. 5184C; Sup.LPM 67)

Fantasia   *See also* Sonata No. 18, *below*

IMPROMPTUS
(4) Op. 90   D.899
(4) Op. 142   D.935   1827

COMPLETE RECORDINGS
P. Badura-Skoda (n.v.)   ♯ West.WN 18060
I. Haebler   ♯ E. & AmVox.PL 8940
A. Aeschbacher   ♯ Pol. 16115/6
(4ss) [Op. 90 only on ♮ PV. 72416/7] (& ♯ Pol. 17012/3)
☆ P. Badura-Skoda (o.v.)   ♯ Nix.WLP 6205-1/2
(3ss—Sonata 13)
☆ R. Firkusny   ♯ EPhi.NBL 5014
                   (♯ Phi.A 01157L)
☆ A. Schnabel (♯ G.FALP 295)
R. Goldsand (♯ Clc. 6200)

(4) Impromptus, Op. 90   D.899
K. Engel   (2ss)   ♯ *Phi.S 06069R*
H. Steurer   (2ss)   ♯ *Eta.LPM 1021*
W. MacGregor   ♯ Kings.KLP 201
(Debussy)
☆ O. Frugoni *(Fantasia)*   ♯ EVox.PL 6690
☆ A. Schnabel (♯ G.QBLP 5001: VBLP 806;
                      ArgA.LPC 10506)
P. Badura-Skoda (o.v.) (♯ Sel. 270.C.017)

Nos. 1 & 3   L. Kraus   in ♯ Edu.EP 3007
         (below, Moments musicaux, Scherzo, Ländler)
Nos. 2 & 3   D. Lipatti   ♯ C.FCX 495
         (Enesco, Ravel, D. Scarlatti, etc.)
Nos. 2 & 4   M. Schwalb (in ♯ Roy. 1470)
         E. Silver (in ♯ Roy. 1825)
         ☆ R. Firkusny (♭ Phi.A 409003E)
Nos. 3 & 4   A. Brailowsky   ♯ Vic.LM 1918
         (Mendelssohn, Schumann, Weber)
No. 2, E flat major
        B. Janis   ArgV. 66-6062
        (Beethoven: Sonata No. 17, s. 1)   (in set AR 8009)
        S. Richter *(USSRM.D 00369: USSR. 021051)*
No. 3, G major
        E. Møller   ♭ Mtr.MCEP 3007
        (Moment musical, Op. 94, No. 6)
        ☆ G. Scherzer (in ♯ P.PMC 1002)
No. 4, A flat major
        G. Scherzer (in ♯ P.PMC 1002: also on R 3673)
        M. v. Monnerberg (in ♯ Her.RPL 774, Pte. rec.)

(4) Impromptus, Op. 142   D.935
C. Curzon   ♯ D.LXT 2781
[Nos. 1 & 2 on ♯ D.LW 5135; Lon.LD 9160] (♯ Lon.LL 720)
[Nos. 3 & 4 on ♯ D.LW 5108; Lon.LD 9127]
☆ A. Schnabel   ♯ *G.BLP 1030*
                      (♯ QBLP 5026)
☆ M. Schwalb (♯ Esq.TN 22-002)
P. Badura-Skoda (o.v.) (♯ Sel.LAC 25001)
Nos. 2 & 3   ☆ R. Goldsand (in V♯ MMS. 912)
Nos. 2 & 4
      ☆ A. Schnabel (♭ G.7ER 5042: 7ERQ 131; Vic.EHA 4)
No. 2, A flat major
    W. Kapell   ♯ Vic.LM 1791
    (Dances; Bach & Liszt)   (♭ ERA 199)
    W. Backhaus[2]   in ♯ Lon.LL 1108/9
    (Schumann, Liszt, Brahms, Beethoven)
    L. Kraus *(above)*   in ♯ Edu.EP 3007
    S. Richter *(USSRM.D 00370)*
    ▽ Lazare-Lévy (JpV.SD 53)
    ☆ G. Scherzer (in ♯ P.PMC 1002)
    R. Firkusny (♭ Phi.A 409003E)
No. 3, B flat major
    A. S. Rasmussen   Tono.A 197
    (Schumann: Romance, Op. 28, No. 2)   (♭ EP 43030, d.c.)
    ☆ A. Schnabel (G.DB 21611)
    E. Ballon[3] (in ♯ D.LX 3070)
No. 4, F minor
    L. Gousseau   ♭ *Plé.P 45130*
    (Liszt: La Campanella)
    ☆ A. Schnabel (G.ED 1232)
Unspecified: A. d'Arco   in Plé.P 102

(3) Impromptus *(Klavierstücke)*   D.946   1828
H. Jolles   ♯ BàM.LD 05
(Sonata No. 13)   (♯ HS.HSL 81)

... Nos. 1 & 2 only
E. Darsky   V♯ *Sel.LAP 1004*

Klavierstücke   *SEE:* Impromptus, Sonata No. 3

Lebensstürme   *SEE:* Allegro, A minor

MARCHES   pf. duet
Op. 51, No. 1, D major (Marche militaire) D.733-1
A. S. & I. Rasmussen   Tono.A 198
(Moment musical No. 1)   (♭ EP 43030)

---

[1] Coupling originally announced was *Poulenc: Nocturnes.*
[2] Carnegie Hall recital, March, 1954.   [3] Announced but not issued.

Op. 51, No. 1, D major (Marche militaire) (*continued*)
— ARR. ORCH.
N.Y.P.S.O.—Kostelanetz   in ♯ **AmC.CL 769**
(*J. Strauss, R. Strauss*)
Hamburg Philharmonia—H-J. Walther
         MSB. 78005
(*Ghys: Amaryllis—Gavotte*)
Westminster Light—Bridgewater[1]
     in ♯ **Nix.WLP 6806**
        (♯ West.WL 4006)
Moscow Radio—Orlov (*USSR. 09688*)
International Sym.—Schneiderhann (in ♯ *Mae.OA 20004*)
☆ Amsterdam—v. Kempen (in ♯ *Phi.S 06015R*)
Boston Prom.—Fiedler (♭ *G.7EP 7019: 7EBF 4:*
        7EPQ 504: DV. 16301)
A. Bernard Str. Orch. (*Dur.A 30029*)
— ARR. ACCORDION: E. Rentner (*Eta. 130108*)

Op. 121, No. 1, C major (Marche caractéristique)
☆ P. Badura-Skoda & J. Demus   ♯ **Nix.WLP 5047**
(*Fantasia & Rondos*)
— ARR. ORCH.   Gerhard
Westminster Light Orch.—Bridgewater
     in ♯ **Nix.WLP 6806**
        (♯ West.WL 4006)

MOMENTS MUSICAUX, Op. 94 D.780 1823-7
COMPLETE RECORDINGS
A. Aeschbacher (? n.v.)   ♯ **HP.DGM 19001**
(*Fantasia, Wanderer*)   (& ♯ Pol. 18213)
(& 4ss, ♮ *PV. 72374/5*)
E. Fischer   ♯ **G.ALP 1103**
(*Bach: Concerto, 3 claviers*)   (♯ QALP 10064)
(*Beethoven*, on ♯ Vic LHMV 1055)
[Nos. 1 & 4 on G.DB 21551
Nos. 2 & 3 on G.DB 21568
Nos. 5 & 6 on G.DB 21578]
W. Gieseking   ♯ **C.FCX 373**
(*Schumann*)
[Nos. 1 & 4 on C.LX 1588: GQX 11535
Nos. 2 & 3 on C.LX 1589: GQX 11542
Nos. 5 & 6 on C.LX 1591: LOX 830: GQX 11546]
W. Hautzig   ♯ **HS.HSL 9000**
(*Fantasia, Op. 15*)
L. Hungerford   ♯ **LH. 101/2**
(*Chopin, Debussy, Brahms, etc.*)   (Pte.)
I. Nádas   ♯ **Per.SPL 719**
(*Fantasia, Op. 15*)
☆ Y. Nat (♯ *DFr.EX 25003*)
J. Demus (♯ Msq. 10002; & with commentary by
S. Spaeth, ♯ Rem. 12; Nos. 3 & 4 only, ♭ *Rem.REP 7;*
        Cum.ECR 38)
Nos. 1-3: L. Kraus   ♯ **Edu.EP 3007**
(*Impromptus, Scherzo, Ländler*)
Nos. 1, 3, 5: R. Serkin   ♯ & ♭ **AmC.PE 16**
Nos. 2 & 3: ☆ R. Goldsand (**V♯** *MMS. 912*)
Nos. 2 & 4: ☆ G. Scherzer (in ♯ *P.PMC 1002*)

No. 1, C major
S. Richter   (2ss)   **USSR. 20857/8**
No. 2, A flat major
A. S. Rasmussen   **Tono.A 198**
(*Marche militaire No. 1*)
No. 3, F minor   (Air russe)
A. Cortot   in ♯ **G.ALP 1197**
(♯ QALP 10080: FALP 349; & in JpV. set JAS 270:
        ♯ *LS 105*)
P. Badura-Skoda   in ♯ **Nix.WLP 5277**
        (♯ West.WL 5277)
S. Bianca   **MSB. 78146**
(*Brahms: Serenade, Op. 11-Minuets*)
M. Schwalb (in ♯ Roy. 1470)
E. Silver (in ♯ *Roy. 1825*)
— ARR. VLC. & PF.
A. Navarra & J. Dussol   in ♯ **Od.OD 1014**
☆ G. Piatigorsky & R. Berkowitz   **G.DA 2052**
(*Rubinstein: Romance*)   (♭ *Vic.ERA 122;*
        in ♯ *ItV.A12R 0105*)
— ARR. ORCH.
Regent Sym. (in ♯ Rgt. 7005)
Argentine Radio—Bandini (ArgOd. 66050)
Belgian Radio—P. Glière (in ♯ *Mae.OAT 25001*)
☆ Philadelphia—Stokowski (in ♯ Cam.CAL 123:
        ♭ *CAE 188*)
A. Bernard Str. Orch. (*Dur.A 30029*)

[1] ARR. R. Gerhard.

No. 4, C sharp minor
B. Webster   in ♯ **Persp.PR 2**
No. 6, A flat major
E. Møller   ♭ *Mtr.MCEP 3007*
(*Impromptu, Op. 90, No. 3*)

RONDOS   pf. duet
A major, Op. 107   D.951
D major, Op. 138   D.608
☆ P. Badura-Skoda & J. Demus   ♯ **Nix.WLP 5047**
(*Fantasia & March*)
SCHERZOS
B flat major   D.593, No. 1   1817
L. Kraus   in ♯ *Edu.EP 3007*
☆ G. Puchelt (in ♯ *G.WDLP 1503*)
D flat major   D.593, No. 2   1817
G. Puchelt   **G.EH 1441**
(*Waltzes, Op. 50*)
SONATAS
No. 3, E major   ('*Klavierstücke*')   D.459   1816
... 2nd movt., Scherzo, E major, only
F. Pelleg   ♯ **CHS.H 14**
(*Adagio, above; Vln. Sonata, etc.*)
... 3rd movt., Adagio, C major, only
A. Aeschbacher   **PV. 72372**
(*Fantasia, Op. 15, s. 1*)
No. 4, A minor, Op. 164   D.537   1817
F. Wührer   (*No. 20*)   ♯ **AmVox.PL 9130**
No. 6, E flat major, Op. 122   D.568   1817
F. Wührer   (*No. 17*)   ♯ **AmVox.PL 8820**
K. Appelbaum   (*No. 16*)   ♯ **West.WL 5313**
No. 8, B major, Op. 147   D.575   1817
F. Wührer   (*No. 19*)   ♯ E. & **AmVox.PL 8420**
No. 13, A major, Op. 120   D.664   1819
F. Wührer   (*No. 18*)   ♯ E. & **AmVox.PL 8590**
H. Boschi   ♯ *CFD. 20*
(*Waltzes, Op. 50*)
☆ P. Badura-Skoda   ♯ **Nix.WLP 6205-1**
(*Impromptus*)   (2ss, ♯ *Sel.LAC 21001*)
(*Sonata No. 21* on ♯ West.WN 18154)
No. 14, A minor, Op. 143   D.784   1823
F. Wührer   (*No. 21*)   ♯ E. & **AmVox.PL 8210**
C. Solomon   (*Mozart*)   ♯ **Vic.LHMV 21**
H. Somer   ♯ **Rem. 199-124**
(*Mozart, Lanner, etc.*)
No. 16, A minor, Op. 42   D.845   1825
W. Kempff   ♯ **D.LXT 2834**
(2ss)   (♯ Lon.LL 792)
K. Appelbaum   (*No. 6*)   ♯ **West.WL 5313**
No. 17, D major, Op. 53   D.850   1825
F. Wührer   (*No. 6*)   ♯ **AmVox.PL 8820**
W. Aitken   (2ss)   ♯ **EMS. 108**
... 4th movt. Rondo, only
— — ARR. VLN. & PF.   Friedberg
☆ J. Heifetz (♭ *Vic.ERA 240*)
— — ARR. ORCH.   Gerhard
Westminster Light—Bridgewater (in ♯ Nix.WLP 6806;
        ♯ West.WL 4006)
No. 18, G major, Op. 78 ("Fantasia") D.894 1826
F. Wührer   (*No. 13*)   ♯ E. & **AmVox.PL 8590**
H. Jolles   ♯ **BàM.LD 05**
(*Impromptus*)   (♯ HS.HSL 81)
W. Aitken   ♯ **EMS. 109**
... 3rd movt. Minuet, only
M. v. Doren   in ♯ **Chan.MVDP 2**
— — ARR. GUITAR   Segovia
☆ A. Segovia (in ♯ *D.UMT 273141*)

No. 19, C minor　D.958　1828
F. Wührer　(*No. 8*)　♯ E. & AmVox.PL 8420

No. 20, A major　D.959　1828
F. Wührer　(*No. 4*)　♯ AmVox.PL 9130

No. 21, B flat major　D.960　1828
A. Aeschbacher　♯ Pol. 18139
V. Horowitz　in ♯ Vic. set LM 6014
(*Chopin, Scriabin, etc.*)　(♭ *set ERG 6014*)
(*Chopin, only* ♯ FV.A 630202; ItV.B12R 0064)
F. Wührer　♯ E. & AmVox.PL 8210
(*Sonata No. 14*)
P. Badura-Skoda　♯ West.WN 18154
(1½ss—*Sonata No. 13*)
L. Fleisher　(*Ländler*)　♯ AmC.ML 5061
W. MacGregor　(*Beethoven*)　♯ Kings.KLP 200
☆ C. Haskil　♯ EPhi.ABL 3029
(*Schumann*)　(♯ Epic.LC 3031)
☆ J. Demus (♯ Cum.CR 310)

SONATAS, pf. duet
B flat major, Op. 30　D.617　*c.* 1818
K.U. & H. Schnabel　♯ SPA. 49
(*Polonaises*)

C major, Op. 140　D.812　"Grand Duo"　1824
☆ P. Badura-Skoda & J. Demus　♯ Nix.WLP 5093

— ARR. ORCH.　Oeser　"*Gastein Symphony*"
☆ Salzburg Mozarteum—Fekete　♯ CA.LPA 1022
(♯ Cum.CR 327)

— ARR. ORCH.　Joachim
☆ Vienna State Op.—Prohaska (♯ CID.UM 63019)

VARIATIONS, pf. duet
(8), A flat major, Op. 35　D.813　1824
(4), B flat major, Op. 82, No. 2　D.603　*c.* 1818
☆ P. Badura-Skoda & J. Demus　♯ Nix.WLP 5147
(*Allegro, A minor*)

(8), C major, Op. 82, No. 1　D.908　1827
(On a theme from Hérold's *Marie*)
K.U. & H. Schnabel　♯ *Phi.S 06046R*
(*Bizet*)

I. B. CHAMBER MUSIC

Adagio & Rondo concertante, F major　D.487
pf., vln., vla., vlc. ("*Klavier-Konzert*")　1816
F. Pelleg & Winterthur Orch.—Dahinden
♯ CHS.H 14
(*Pf. Adagio & Scherzo; & Vln. Sonata*)
(*Sym. 3 on* ♯ *MMS. 63*)

Fantasia, C major, Op. 159　vln. & pf.　D.934　1827
M. Rostal & C. Horsley　♯ G.OCLP 7501
(*Stravinsky*)

Nocturne, E flat major, Op. 148　pf., vln., vlc.　D.897
F. Wührer, R. Barchet & H. Reimann
♯ AmVox.PL 8970
(*Quintet, Op. 114*)
☆ L. Mannes, B. Gimpel & L. Silva (♯ D.UST 253547)

Octet, F major, Op. 166　cl., hrn., bsn., str. qtt. cbs.
D.803　1824
Vienna Octet (n.v.)　♯ D.LXT 2983
(♯ Lon.LL 1049)
☆ L. Wlach, G. von Freiberg, K. Öhlberger, Vienna
Konzerthaus Qtt. & J. Hermann　♯ Nix.WLP 5094
☆ Stradivari Octet (♯ Cpt.MC 20073)
Berlin Phil. Cha. Ens. (♯ AmD.DL 9669;
♯ Pol. 16066/7; & 16030/1, auto)
... Scherzo only
D. Oistrakh (vln.) & Ens.　USSR. 18661/2
(2ss)

QUARTETS, String
No. 1, B flat major　D.18　1812
No. 2, C major　D.32　1812
No. 3, B flat major　D.36　1812
Vienna Konzerthaus Qtt.　♯ West.WL 5204

No 4, C major　D.46　1813
No. 5, B flat major　D.68　1813
Vienna Konzerthaus Qtt.　♯ West.WL 5210
(*No. 12*)
No. 6, D major　D.74　1813
Vienna Konzerthaus Qtt.　♯ West.WL 5224
(*No. 9*)
No. 8, B flat major, Op. 168　D.112　1814
Italian Qtt.　♯ D.LXT 2855
(2ss)　(♯ Lon.LL 669)
No. 9, G minor　D.173　1815
Vienna Konzerthaus Qtt.　♯ West.WL 5224
(*No. 6*)
No. 10, E flat major, Op. 125, No. 1　D.87　1813
Amadeus Qtt.　♯ G.ALP 1337
(*Brahms & Mendelssohn*)
Vienna Phil. Qtt.　♯ DT.LGX 66034
(*Haydn*)　(♯ FT.320.TC.074; T.LE 6514)
Vienna Konzerthaus Qtt.　♯ West.WL 5222
(*No. 11*)
No. 11, E major, Op. 125, No. 2　D.353　1816
Vienna Konzerthaus Qtt.　♯ West.WL 5222
(*No. 10*)
Parrenin Qtt.　♯ Pac.LDPF 76
(*Schumann*)
No. 12, C minor　(one movt.)　D.703　1820
('*Quartettsatz*')
Barchet Qtt.　♯ E. & AmVox.PL 8810
(*No. 14*)
Vienna Konzerthaus Qtt.　♯ West.WL 5210
(*Nos. 4 & 5*)
☆ Fine Arts Qtt. (♭ FMer.MEP 14517; ♭ Mer.EP 1-5066)
Barchet Qtt. (♭ Per.PEP 10)
Galimir Qtt. (♭ Cpt.EXTP 1003)
No. 13, A minor, Op. 29, No. 1　D.804　1824
Italian Qtt.　♯ D.LXT 2854
(♯ Lon.LL 668)
Budapest Qtt.　♯ AmC.ML 4831
(& in set SL 194)
Amadeus Qtt.　♯ G.BLP 1069
Pascal Qtt.　♯ MMS. 83
☆ Vienna Konzerthaus Qtt.　♯ Nix.WLP 5115
☆ Fine Arts Qtt. (♯ Clc. 6284)
No. 14, D minor　('*Tod und das Mädchen*')
D.810　1824-6
Amadeus Qtt.　♯ G.ALP 1088
(♯ Pol. 18191; Vic.LHMV 1058)
Vienna Philharmonia Qtt.　♯ DT.LGX 66016
(♯ T.LE 6058)
Budapest Qtt.　♯ AmC.ML 4832
(& in set SL 194)
Barchet Qtt.　♯ E. & AmVox.PL 8810
(*No. 12*)
Musical Arts Qtt.　♯ Van.VRS 463
(*Mozart*)
Komitas (Armenian) Qtt.　♯ C.CX 1284
☆ Koeckert Qtt.　♯ HP.DGM 18043
☆ Hungarian Qtt. (♯ Clc. 6178; MMS. 128)
... Andante only
Oistrakh Qtt.　USSRM.D 00205/6
(3ss—*Mendelssohn: Canzonetta, on* ♯ *USSR.* 018326/7/9)
No. 15, G major, Op. 161　D.887　1826
Budapest Qtt.　♯ AmC.ML 4833
(♯ Phi.A 01172L)　(& in set SL 194)
☆ Vienna Konzerthaus Qtt.　♯ Nix.WLP 5041
☆ Fine Arts Qtt. (♯ Clc. 6286)
Quartet, G major, fl., vla., vlc., guitar　D.96　1814
(A trio by M. W. Matiegka, 1773-1820, to which
Schubert added a vlc. part & Trio II to the minuet)
P. Birkelund, R. D. Eriksen, J. Friisholm &
U. Neumann　♯ D.LXT 5070
(*Diabelli & Fürstenau*)　(♯ Lon.LL 1079)
C. Wanausek, R. Nitsch, V. Goerlich, K. Scheit
(*Variations, Op. 160*)　♯ SPA. 53

♯ = Long-playing, 33⅓ r.p.m.　　♭ = 45 r.p.m.　　♮ = Auto. couplings, 78 r.p.m.

QUINTETS

A major, Op. 114 pf., vln., vla., vlc. & cbs. D.667
(The Trout—Forellen)
F. Wührer & Barchet Qtt. ♯ **AmVox.PL 8970**
(Nocturne, Op. 148)
A. Aeschbacher, R. Koeckert, O. Riedl, J. Merz
  & F. Ortner ♯ **Pol. 18072**
(6ss, ♮ PV. 72300/2) (♯ AmD.DL 9707)
[4th movt. also on PV. 72478: ♭ *Pol. 30061*]
A. Heksch & Amsterdam Qtt. ♯ *Phi.A 00690R*
  (♯ Epic.LC 3046)
M. Pressler, Guilet Trio & P. Sklar ♯ **MGM.E 3128**
P. Pozzi, Winterthur Trio & F. Jacquillard ♯ *MMS. 39*
M. Karin & Bratislava Cha. Ens. ♯ **Sup.LPV 165**
  (♯ U. 5146G)
M. Mercier, J. Dumont, L. Pascal, R. Salles, H. Moreau
  ♯ **Pat.DTX 139**
  (♯ ArgPat.ADTX 1806)
☆ P. Badura-Skoda & Vienna Konzerthaus Qtt.
  ♯ **Nix.WLP 5025**
  (♯ Véga.C30.A12; BrzV.SLP 5511)

C major, Op. 163 2 vlns., vla., & 2 vlcs. D.956
  1828
I. Stern, A. Schneider, M. Katims, P. Casals &
  P. Tortelier ♯ **EPhi.ABL 3100**
  (♯ Phi.A 01188L; AmC.ML 4714 in set SL 183)
(also ♯ AmC.ML 4704 in set SL 185)
Amadeus Qtt. & W. Pleeth ♯ **G.CLP 1006**
  (♯ WCLP 1006)
☆ Vienna Konzerthaus Qtt. & G. Weiss ♯ Nix.WLP 5033

RONDOS

A major vln. & str. qtt. D.438 1816
A. Kamper & Vienna Konzerthaus Qtt.
(Trios) ♯ **West.WL 5223**
E. Röhn & Hamburg State Phil.—Martin
(Ravel) ♯ *T.TW 30032*
☆ M. Solovieff & Vienna State Op.—Swoboda
  (♯ CHS.CHS 1176, d.c.; ♯ Clc. 6221)

B minor, Op. 70 vln. & pf. D.895 1826
("Rondo brilliant")
J. Szigeti & C. Bussotti ♯ **AmC.ML 4642**
(Beethoven: Vln. Sonata No. 10)

Sonata, A minor, Arpeggione & pf. D.821 1824
— ARR. VLA. & PF.
E. & L. Wallfisch ♯ **Od.ODX 140**
(Schumann & Mendelssohn)
— ARR. VLC. & PF.
M. Gendron & J. Françaix ♯ **D.LXT 2857**
(Schumann) (♯ D.FAT 173073; Lon.LL 654)
R. Albin & C. Helffer ♯ **DT.LGX 66015**
(Mendelssohn) (♯ T.LE 6510)
L. Rose & L. Hambro ♯ **AmC.ML 4984**
(Boccherini & Sammartini)
A. Janigro & E. Bagnoli ♯ **West.WN 18016**
(Schumann)
☆ E. Feuermann & G. Moore ♯ **AmC.ML 4767**
  (Haydn)
☆ P. Fournier & L. Hubeau (JpV.SD 3015/6, set JAS 186)
  G. Ricci & L. Mittman (♯ Cum.CS 193)
  E. Mainardi & A. Borciani (♯ *Pol. 16043; AmD.DL 7539*)

Sonata, A major, Op. 162, vln. & pf. ("Duo")
  D.574 1817
D. Oistrakh & L. Oborin ♯ **Mon.MWL 311**
(Bach) (2ss, ∇ ♯ CdM.LDYA 8108)
(Tartini & Beethoven on ♯ Per.SPL 573;
  Franck on ♯ Csm.CRLP 151)
J. Szigeti & M. Hess ♯ **AmC.ML 4717**
(Variations, Op. 160) (in set SL 183)
(2ss, ♯ Phi.S 06624R; & d.c., in ♯ AmC.ML 4707,
  set SL 185)
W. Schneiderhan & C. Seemann ♯ **Pol. 18241**
(Sonatina, Op. 137, No. 2)
L. Kaufman & P. Pozzi ♯ **CHS.H 14**
(Adagio & Rondo, above; Pf. Adagio, etc.)
☆ F. Kreisler & S. Rachmaninoff ♯ **Vic.LCT 1128**
  (Grieg) (♭ set WCT 1128)
☆ F. Lack & L. Hambro (♯ *Allo. 4042*)

SONATINAS, Op. 137, vln. & pf. 1816
No. 1, D major D.384
W. Schneiderhan & C. Seemann ♯ *Pol. 16085*
(No. 3)
No. 2, A minor D.385
W. Schneiderhan & C. Seemann ♯ **Pol. 18241**
(Sonata, A major, Op. 162)
No. 3, G minor D.408
J. Heifetz & E. Bay ♯ **Vic.LM 1861**
(Bloch & Handel)(Beethoven & Handel on ♯ ItV.A12R 0159)
W. Schneiderhan & C. Seemann ♯ *Pol. 16085*
(No. 1)
☆ J. Thibaud & T. Janopoulo ♭ **G.FJLP 5015**
  (Mozart)
— ARR. FL. & PF.
J-P. Rampal & L. Kraus ♯ **Edu.ECM 4001**
(Debussy & Mozart)

TRIOS, pf., vln., vlc.
No. 1, B flat major, Op. 99 D.898 c. 1827
V. Schiøler, H. Holst, E. B. Bengtsson
  ♯ *G.BLP 1077*
P. Badura-Skoda, J. Fournier, A. Janigro
  ♯ **Nix.WLP 5188**
  (♯ Véga.C30.A24; West.WL 5188)
Santoliquido Trio ♯ **Pol. 18261**
E. Istomin, A. Schneider, P. Casals
  ♯ **AmC.ML 4715**
(also ♯ ML 4705, in set SL 185) (in set SL 183)
L. Nadelmann, S. Blanc, L. Rostal
  ♯ *MMS. 119*
Immaculate Heart Trio ♯ **Layos.CB 569/70**
☆ A. Cortot, J. Thibaud, P. Casals ♯ **Vic.LCT 1141**
  (Schumann: Trio No. 1)
☆ Carnegie Trio (♯ Cpt.MC 20079)
  Albeneri Trio (♯ Clc. 6275)
  A. Rubinstein, J. Heifetz, E. Feuermann (♯ DV.I. 17037)
— FOR PRACTICE: recorded with each part omitted in turn
  (in ♯ CEd. sets MMO. 81/3, 12ss)

No. 2, E flat major, Op. 100 D.929 1827
C. Hansen, E. Röhn, A. Troester
  ♯ **DT.LGX 66039**
  (♯ T.LE 6523)
M. Horszowski, A. Schneider, P. Casals
  ♯ **EPhi.ABL 3009**
(♯ AmC.ML 4716, in set SL 183) (♯ Phi.A 01107L)
R. Serkin, A. & H. Busch ♯ **AmC.ML 4654**
☆ P. Badura-Skoda, J. Fournier, A. Janigro
  ♯ **Nix.WLP 5121**
  (♯ Véga.C30.A25; Sel.LAG 1046)
☆ Albeneri Trio (♯ Clc. 6290)
— FOR PRACTICE: recorded with each part omitted in turn
  (in ♯ CEd. sets MMO. 81/3, 12ss)

TRIOS, vln., vla. & vlc.
B flat major (in 4 movements) D.581 1817
A. Kamper, E. Weiss, F. Kwarda
(below & Rondo) ♯ **West.WL 5223**
B flat major ("Sonata", in 1 movt.) D.471 1816
A. Kamper, E. Weiss, F. Kwarda
(above & Rondo) ♯ **West.WL 5223**

Variations on 'Trock'ne Blumen', Op. 160 fl. & pf.
  D.802 1824
C. Wanausek & G. Radhuber ♯ **SPA. 53**
(Quartet, G major)
J. Wummer & L. Mannes ♯ **AmC.ML 4717**
(Sonata, vln. & pf. Op. 162) (in set SL 183)
  (also ♯ ML 4707, in set SL 185)

I. *C DANCES*

DEUTSCHE TÄNZE
  (See also Liszt, Section A. III.5—"Soirées de Vienne")
1. *ORCHESTRAL*
(5) Deutsche Tänze (Minuets) **& 6 Trios** Strings
  D.89 1813
Linz Sym. in ♯ **Ply. 12-36**
(Arne, Haydn, etc.)

☆ = Re-issue of a recording to be found in previous volumes.

(5) Deutsche Tänze & 7 Trios Str. D.90 1813
Vienna State Op.—Litschauer   **♯ Van.VRS 435**
(Mozart)
(Symphony No. 8 on ♯ Ama.AVRS 6010)

Deutsche Tänze (unspec.)
Orch.—F. Busch   **♯ FFB. Pte.**
(Beethoven & Wagner)

(2) Deutsche Tänze (C major; G major) Unspec.
Berlin Sym.—Hildebrandt   *Eta. 120015*

2. *PIANO*
COLLECTION ed. K. U. Schnabel
Deutsche Tänze, Op. 33, Nos. 1, 2, 7 D.783
Deutsche Tänze (Ländler), Nos. 3, 4, 5, 17 D.366
Ländler, Op. 18a, No. 7 D.145
Ländler, Op. 171, Nos. 5 & 6 D.790
Valses sentimentales, Op. 50, Nos. 8, 13, 28 D.779
Waltz, Op. 18, No. 9 D.145
Waltz (Grazer Walzer), Op. 91, No. 2 D.924
Waltzes (Letzte Walzer), Op. 127, Nos. 16, 18 D.146
Waltzes (Original Tänze), Op. 9, Nos. 2, 32, 36 D.365
   K. U. Schnabel   **♯ McInt.MM 110**
   (Fantasia, C major)   (o.n. ♯ WCFM. 17)

COLLECTION
Deutsche Tänze, Op. 33, Nos. 6 & 7 D.783
Ländler, Op. 18a, Nos. 2 & 5 D.145
Waltzes, Op. 9b, Nos. 8, 14, 16 D.365
Waltz, Op. 67, No. 1, G major D.734
   W. Kapell   **♯ Vic.LM 1791**
   (Impromptu, Op. 142, No. 2; Bach & Liszt)   (♭ ERA 199)

(16) Deutsche Tänze, Op. 33 (with 2 Écossaises)
D.783 1824
— ARR. PF. DUET Liszt
   V. Vronsky & V. Babin   **♯ AmD.DL 9791**
   (R. Strauss, Rachmaninoff, etc.)
... Nos. 1, 2, 3, 7
   G. Scherzer *(Waltzes)*   *P.R 3717*
... Nos. 1, 3, 4, 5, 7, 10, 13, 14 — ARR. ORCH. Stokowski
   ☆ Sym.—Stokowski (♭ *G.7ER 5043: 7ERF 120: 7RF 245;*
                     ♭ *Vic.ERA 67)*
... Nos. 1 & 7 — ARR. ORCH. Bridgewater
   "Valse caprice"
   Westminster Light—Bridgewater
           in **♯ Nix.WLP 6806**
                   (♯ West.WL 4006)

COLLECTIONS — ARR. ORCH.
Deutsche Tänze, Op. 33, Nos. 2, 3, 5, 7, 8, 10, 12 D.783
Ländler, Op. 171, Nos. 1, 3, 12 D.790
Valses nobles, Op. 77, Nos. 2 & 4 D.969
Waltz, Op. 67, No. 1 D.734
2 unident. [one being a version of Op. 33, Nos. 14, 15 & 4]
   ☆ Vienna Sym.—Moralt (♭ *AmVox.VIP 45260*)[1]
Deutsche Tänze D.420 ... Coda only
Ländler, Op. 171, Nos. 1, 5-8 D.790
Ländler, Nos. 3-5 D.366
Minuet & Trio, No. 9 D.41
   Berlin Sym.—Rubahn   in **♯ Roy. 1534**
   (Overture, C major; Smetana)

Écossaise, D major ("Galop") D.781, No. 11
Galop, G major, Op. 49, No. 1 D.735
— ARR. ORCH. Bridgewater
   Westminster Light Orch.—Bridgewater
           in **♯ Nix.WLP 6806**
                   (♯ West.WL 4006)

(17) Ländler, Op. 18a D.145 1815-24
... Nos. 1-9 & 11
   L. Kraus   **♯ Edu.EP 3007**
   (Impromptus, Moments musicaux, Scherzo)

(12) Ländler, Op. 171 D.790 1823
   G. Johannesen   **♯ CHS.CHS 1176**
   (Fantasia, C major & Rondo)
   L. Fleisher   **♯ AmC.ML 5061**
   (Sonata No. 21)

(20) Minuets with trios D.41 1813
... No. 12, D major
   ("No. 11" of "*12 Minuets, Op. posth.*")
   E. Heiller (pf.)   in **♯ Uni.LP 1010**
   († *History of the Dance*)

POLONAISES pf. duet
Op. 61, No. 1, D minor D.824 1825
Op. 75, No. 2, B flat major D.599 *c*. 1818
   K. U. & H. Schnabel   ♭ **EPhi.NBE 11004**
   (Debussy: Épigraphes antiques)   (*Phi.N 402024E*)
Op. 61, Nos. 3, B flat major; 4, D major; 6, E major D.824
Op. 75, No. 3, E major D.599 *c*. 1818
   K. U. & H. Schnabel   **♯ SPA. 49**
   (Sonata, B flat major, Op. 30)
Op. 61, No. 4, D major D.824
   ☆ J. & G. Dichler (in ♯ *U. 5184C; Sup.LPM 67*)

WALTZES
Op. 9 D.365
... Nos. 1, 2, 3, 14, 12 & 10
   G. Scherzer   *P.R 3717*
   (Deutsche Tänze)
... No. 14 — ARR. VLN. & PF. Franko "*Valse sentimentale*"
   (with Op. 33-3)
   C. Pessina & pf.   *ArgOd. 57016*
   (Falla: El Sombrero, Danza)

Op. 50 D.779 Valses sentimentales[2]
   M. Meyer (n.v.)   **V♯ DFr.EX 17044**
   (below)   (o.n. **V♯** *DFr. 31*)
   G. Puchelt   **G.EH 1441**
   (Scherzo)
   H. Boschi   **♯ CFD. 20**
   (Sonata No. 13)
   F. Karrer   **♯ Msq. 10002**
   (Waltzes, Op. 77 & Moments musicaux)

Op. 77 D.969 Valses nobles—complete
   M. Meyer (n.v.)   **V♯ DFr.EX 17044**
   (above)   (o.n. **V♯** *DFr. 31*)
   F. Karrer   in ▽ **♯ Rem. 149-4**
   (♯ *AFest.CFR 10-106*; on Msq. 10002; in ♯ *Ply. 12-92*)
   (ARR. Dohnányi: E. Dohnányi[3] (in ♯ *Roy. 1573*)
Unspecified Waltzes
   M. v. Doren   in ♯ **Chan.MVDP 2**

I. *D. ORCHESTRAL*
Konzertstück, D major vln. & orch. D.345 1816
   M. Eitler & orch.[4]   **♯ P.PMA 1017**
   (Dittersdorf & Haydn)

Overture in the Italian style, C major, Op. 170
     D.591 1817
   Berlin Sym.—Rubahn   **♯ Roy. 1534**
   (Dances; & Smetana)
   ☆Sym.—Goehr   **V♯ MMS. 91**
   (Rosamunde, Overture)

SYMPHONIES
No. 1, D major D.82 1813
   Royal Phil.—Beecham   **♯ EPhi.ABL 3001**
   (No. 2)   (♯ *Phi.A 01136L; AmC.ML 4903*)
   French Radio Sym.—Leibowitz   **♯ Oce.OCS 33**
   (Bizet)   (♯ *Nix.OLP 70335*)
   ☆ Austrian Sym.[6] (♯ *MHF. 1*)

No. 2, B flat major D.125 1815
   Royal Phil.—Beecham[7]   **♯ EPhi.ABL 3001**
   (No. 1)   (♯ *Phi.A 01136L; AmC.ML 4903*)
   Saar Orch.—Ristenpart   **♯ DFr. 118**
   (No. 6)
   Berlin Sym.—Balzer   **♯ Roy. 1410**
   (No. 6)
   ☆ Boston Sym.—Münch   **♯ G.ALP 1061**
   (Haydn: Symphony No. 104)   (♯ *QALP 10031*)
   (Symphony No. 8 on ♯ Vic.LM 9032)
   ☆ Salzburg Mozarteum—Sternberg *(No. 5)* ♯ OL.LD 73
   ☆ Pittsburgh Sym.—Steinberg (♯ *T.LCSK 8160*)

---

[1] Probably this serves also to identify ♯ AmVox.PL 7280, see Supp. II.
[2] Each recording probably omits certain dances. Meyer is thought to include only Nos. 1, 2, 3, 12, 13, 18-22, 27, 34.
[3] From a piano roll.
[4] Announced in Scandinavia, but probably not issued; at the time of going to press, it has certainly not appeared in England.
[5] Announced, but never issued.
[6] The manufacturer requests us to suppress any reference to name of the conductor.
[7] Slightly cut.

No. 3, D major D.200 1815
Amsterdam—v. Beinum   ♯ **EPhi.ABL 3086**
(*Bruckner*)   (♯ Phi.A 00294L; in ♯ Epic. set SC 6011)
Berlin Phil.—Markevitch   ♯ **HP.DGM 18221**
(*No. 4*)
     (*Mozart: Sym. 34, with Minuet*, on ♯ AmD.DL 9810)
Concerts Colonne—Sebastian   ♯ **Ura. 7137**
(*No. 6*)   (♯ FUra. 7001; ♯ MTW. 510)
Utrecht Sym.—Hupperts   ♯ *MMS. 63*
(*Adagio & Rondo Concertante*)
Hamburg Cha.—G. L. Jochum ♯ **Pat.DTX 154**
(*No. 5*)
☆ Austrian Sym.—Singer (♯ Cum.CR 220)
   Austrian Sym.[6] (♯ MHF. 1)

No. 4, C minor D.417 "Tragic" 1816
Amsterdam—v. Beinum   ♯ **D.LXT 2779**
(*2ss*)   (♯ Lon.LL 736)
Berlin Phil.—Markevitch   ♯ **HP.DGM 18221**
(*No. 3*)
London Phil. Sym.—Dixon   ♯ **Nix.NLP 913**
(*No. 5*)   (♯ West.WL 5274)
London Mozart Players—Blech ♯ **G.CLP 1010**
(*No. 5*)   (♯ BB.LBC 1091; ArgA.LPC 11532)
Los Angeles Phil.—Wallenstein ♯ **B.AXTL 1059**
(*No. 5*)   (♯ AmD.DL 9725; SpC.CCL 35007)
Vienna Sym.—Sacher   ♯ **FestF.FLD 27**
(*Rosamunde*)   [perhaps n.v.]
Bamberg Sym.—Hollreiser   ♯ **AmVox.PL 9370**
(*No. 8*)   (2ss, ♯ Pan.XPV 1021)
☆ Orch.—Hewitt (♯ HS.HSL 89)
... 2nd movt.   ☆ Austrian Sym.—Wöss (in ♯ Ply. 12-96)

No. 5, B flat major D.485 1816
London Mozart Players—Blech ♯ **G.CLP 1010**
(*No. 4*)   (♯ BB.LBC 1091; ArgA.LPC 11532)
London Phil. Sym.—Dixon   ♯ **Nix.NLP 913**
(*No. 4*)   (♯ West.WL 5274)
Los Angeles Phil.—Wallenstein ♯ **B.AXTL 1059**
(*No. 4*)   (♯ AmD.DL 9725; SpC.CCL 35007)
Berlin Cha.—v. Benda   ♯ **DT.LGX 66020**
(*Mozart: Symphony No. 36*)   (♯ T.LSK 7031)
Vienna Phil.—Böhm   ♯ **D.LXT 2998**
(*No. 8*)   (♯ Lon.LL 1105)
N.B.C. Sym.—Toscanini   ♯ **Vic.LM 1869**
(*Mendelssohn*)   (*Beethoven* on ♯ ItV.A12R 0121)
Saar Cha.—Ristenpart   ♯ *DFr.EX 25009*
(*2ss*)
Hamburg Cha.—G. L. Jochum ♯ **Pat.DTX 154**
(*No. 3*)
Moscow Radio—Rakhlin   ♯ USSR.D 01350/1
☆ L.P.O.—Beecham (*Haydn*)   ♯ AmC.ML 4771
☆ Vienna Sym.—Scherchen   ♯ *Sup.LPM 118*
(*2ss*)   (♯ U, 5098C)
☆ Salzburg Mozarteum—Sternberg (*No. 2*) ♯ OL.LD 73
☆ Boston Sym.—Koussevitzky (♯ Cam.CAL 106)
   Winterthur Sym.—F. Busch (♯ MMS. 20)
... 2nd movt.
   ☆ Austrian Sym.—Paulmüller (in ♯ Ply. 12-96)

No. 6, C major D.589 1818
Bamberg Sym.—Keilberth   ♯ *DT.LGM 65026*
   (♯ T.NLB 6082)
Saar Orch.—Ristenpart   ♯ **DFr. 118**
(*No. 2*)
Concerts Colonne—Sebastian   ♯ **Ura. 7137**
(*No. 3*)   (♯ FUra. 7001; MTW. 510)
Berlin Sym.—Balzer (*No. 2*)   ♯ **Roy. 1410**
☆ Vienna State Op.—Scherchen   ♯ **Sup.LPV 196**
(*2ss*)   (♯ U. 5170G)

No. 8, B minor D.759 "Unfinished" 1822
Philharmonia—Cantelli   ♯ **G.ALP 1325**
(*Mendelssohn*)
Vienna Phil.—Böhm (n.v.)   ♯ **D.LXT 2998**
(*No. 5*)   (♯ Lon.LL 1105)

Berlin Phil.—Lehmann   ♯ *HP.DG 16051*
(2ss) (*Handel* on ♯ AmD.DL 9696)   (♯ Pol. 17035)
(4ss, ♮ PV. 72292/3)   (*Haydn*, on ♯ Pol. 18283)
Philharmonia—Schwarz   ♯ **G.CLP 1022**
(*Liszt & Weber*)   (♯ FELP 111)
(*Rosamunde*; & *Bizet* in ♯ BB.LBC 1047: ♭ set WBC 1047)
Chicago Sym.—Dorati   ♯ **Mer.MG 50037**
(*Tchaikovsky*)   (♯ FMer.MLP 7524)
Bamberg Sym.—Keilberth   ♯ **DT.LGX 66042**
(*Beethoven*) (*Mozart* on ♯ LGX 66036) (2ss, ♯ T.LB 6072)
Vienna State Op.—Prohaska   ♯ **Van.VRS 445**
(*Beethoven*)   (*Dances* on ♯ Ama.AVRS 6010)
Vienna Phil.—Böhm (o.v.)   ♯ **Ura.RS 7-9**
(*Schumann*)
Rochester Phil.—Leinsdorf   ♯ **AmC.RL 3070**
(*Mozart*)
Bamberg Sym.—Hollreiser   ♯ **AmVox.PL 9370**
(*No. 4*)   (2ss, ♯ Pan.XPV 1014)
Florence Fest.—Gui   ♯ **AudC. 501**
(*Brahms & Schumann*)
Covent Garden Op.—Irving   ♯ **Od.MOAQ 302**
(*Tchaikovsky*)
N.W. Ger. Phil.—Schüchter   ♯ *Imp.ILP 101*
   (♯ G.QDLP 6031)
Zürich Tonhalle—Ackermann   ♯ *MMS. 51*
(*Beethoven, Mozart, Bach*, on ♯ MMS. 100S*)
Stadium Concerts—Rudolf   ♯ **MApp.** n.d.
(*Spoken analysis*)
☆ Royal Phil.—Beecham   ♯ **C.CX 1039**
(*Beethoven*) (♯ VCX 517: QCX 10040; ♭ AmC. set A 1070)
(*Mendelssohn* on ♯ C.FCX 236)
☆ N.B.C. Sym.—Toscanini (2ss)   ♯ *G.BLP 1038*
(*Schumann & Beethoven*)   (♯ VBLP 811)
   on ♯ Vic.LM 9022; *Haydn* on ♯ Vic.A12R 0011)
☆ Amsterdam—E. Jochum (2ss)   ♯ *EPhi.ABR 4021*
(*Mozart* on ♯ Epic.LC 3006)
☆ Philadelphia—Walter   ♯ **C.CX 1082**
(*Mozart*)   (♯ QCX 10079; AmC.ML 4880)
Orch.—Emmer (♯ MTW. 12)
Moscow Radio—Rakhlin (USSR. 017960/3
     & 020597/600: ♯ D 454/5)
Havana Sym.—(♯ Roy. 18132)
Sonor Sym.—Ledermann (♯ Pde. 1017)
Anon. Orch. (♯ Gram. 2040; Var. 6971)
☆ Boston Sym.—Koussevitzky (♯ Vic.LM 9032:
   ♭ set ERB 11; ♯ ItV.A10R 0006; o.v., ♯ Cam.CAL 106
     & in set CFL 104)
Vienna Sym.—Scherchen (♯ Sup.LPV 42; U. 5030C)
Orch.—Hewitt (♯ HS.HSL 89; DFr.EX 25002)
Salzburg Fest.—Brown (♯ Msq. 10000; AFest.CFR 10-29
   Rem. 100-13; Cum.TCR 256; Ply. 12-58, etc.)
... 1st movt. (abridged) Boston Pops—Fiedler
     (in ♯ Vic.LM 1752: ♭ set WDM 1752)
Berlin Phil.—Furtwängler (in ♯ Per.SPL 716)[8]
—— ARR. PF.: M. v. Doren (in ♯ Chan.MVDP 2)

No. 9, C major (old No. 7) D.944 1828
N.B.C. Sym.—Toscanini (n.v.)   ♯ **Vic.LM 1835**
   (♯ ItV.A12R 0126; FV.A 630248)
(o.v. ☆ ♯ G.ALP 1120: QALP 170)
Hallé—Barbirolli   ♯ **G.ALP 1178**
   (♯ FALP 350; QALP 10075; BB.LBC 1085)
Phil. Prom.—Boult   ♯ **West.WN 18026**
Berlin Radio—Rother   ♯ **Ura. 7152**
   (also ♯ RS 7-1)
Utrecht Sym.—Neumark   ♯ **MMS. 2023**
   (& ♯ CHS.CHS 1237)
☆ N.Y.P.S.O.—Walter   ♯ **EPhi.ABL 3074**
   (♯ Phi.A 00152L)
☆ Berlin Phil.—Furtwängler   ♯ **HP.DGM 18015/6**
(3ss—*Haydn*)   (2ss, ♯ AmD.DL 9746)
☆ Vienna Phil.—Karajan (♯ AmC.ML 4631)
   L.S.O.—Walter (♯ Cam.CAL 195)
... 4th movt. ☆ Austrian Sym.—Wöss (in ♯ Ply. 12-96)

II. VOCAL

A. STAGE WORKS

ALFONSO UND ESTRELLA, Op. 19
   Opera 3 Acts 1821-2 (f.p. 1854) D.732
Overture: *See below*, Rosamunde.
This is the overture used at the performances of that
   play, subsequently replaced by the *Zauberharfe*
   Overture.

---

[6] The manufacturer requests us to suppress any reference to name of the conductor.
[8] An excerpt recorded at rehearsal, with the voice of Furtwängler, from sound-track of film *Symphony*.

ROSAMUNDE VON CYPERN, Op. 26 D.797
(*Incidental Music to play by von Chezy*) 1823
Overture (orig. *Alfonso und Estrella*) D.732
1. Entracte I, B minor (after Act I)
2. Ballet Music I, B minor
3a. Entracte II, D major (after Act II)
3b. Romanze: Der Vollmond strahlt A
4. Geisterchor: In der Tiefe
5. Entracte III, B flat major (after Act III)
6. Hirtenmelodie
7. Hirtenchor: Hier auf den Fluren
8. Jägerchor: Wie lebt sich's
9. Ballet Music II, G major

COMPLETE RECORDINGS
[2]D. Eustrati (A), Berlin Motet Cho. & Berlin
   Phil.—Lehmann   # *Pol. 18101/2*
(3ss—*Ständchen, Op. 135; Psalm 23*)
[Overtures only on # *AmD.DL 4094;* No. 9 only, also
♭ *Pol. 30038;* Nos. 5 & 9, on PV. 72369; Nos. 3b & 7
on *PV. 36082*]

[3]H. Rössl-Majdan (A) & Vienna Acad. Cho. &
   State Op. Orch.—Dixon   # *Nix.WLP 5182*
                              (# West.WL 5182)

[4]E. Fahsl (A), Vienna Cha. Cho. & Sym.
   —Loibner   # *EPhi.NBL 5007*
              (# Phi.N 00203L; Epic.LC 3063)

COLLECTIONS (all overtures are the *Zauberharfe*)
Overture & Nos. 1, 2, 5, 9
Philharmonia—Kletzki   # *C.CX 1157*
[*see below* for individual issues] (# QCX 10086: FCX 279)
☆ Covent Garden—Braithwaite   # *P.PMD 1027*

Overture & Nos. 5 & 9
Amsterdam—v. Beinum   # *D.LXT 2770*
(*Mendelssohn*)   (# *Lon.LL 622*)
(Overture only on # *D.LW 5046;* Lon.LD 9059)
Sym.—Stokowski[5]   # *G.ALP 1193*
(*Tchaikovsky: Nutcracker Suite 1*)
(*Wagner: Parsifal,* excerpts in # Vic.LM 1730:
                    ♭ set WDM 1730; # ItV.A12R 0042)
[No. 9 also on ♭ *G.7ER 5043*]

Nos. 3b, 5 & 9
H. Prey (B), N.W. Ger. Phil.—Schüchter # *Imp.ILP 123*
(*Grieg*)   [H. Heinemann (pf.) in No. 3b]
[Nos. 5 & 9 only, ♭ *Od.BEOW 3004*]

Overture & Nos. 3a & 9
Rochester Phil.—Leinsdorf   # *AmC.RL 3102*
(*Mendelssohn*)

Overture & No. 2
Orch.—Swarowsky   # *ACC.MP 10*
(*R. Strauss*)

Nos. 2, 5 & 9
☆ Czech Phil.—Meylan   # *Sup.LPV 42*
(*Symphony No. 8*)

Nos. 2 & 9
Berlin Radio—Schartner   ♭ *Ura.UREP 38*

Nos. 5 & 9
L.P.O.—Cameron   *G.C 4217*
                      (♭ 7P 144: 7PW 125)
Westminster Light—Bridgewater in # *Nix.WLP 6806*
                        (# West.WL 4006)
Sonor Sym.—Hagermann   # *FestF.FLD 27*
(*Symphony No. 4*) [labelled *Entracte & Ballet,* but probably
this]
☆ Vienna Phil.—Furtwängler (♭ *G.7RQ 3012: 7RW 122*)
Residentie—v. Otterloo (♭ *Phi.N 402012E*)

Unspecified contents Anon. orch. (# MTW. 552)

Overture (orig. *Die Zauberharfe*)[6] D.644 1819
Berlin Sym.—Hermann   in # *Roy. 1371*
Moscow Radio—Sanderling in # *USSR.D 1100*
(*Schumann: Manfred, Overture*)
☆Sym.—Goehr   V# *MMS. 91*
(*Overture, C major*)
☆ Hallé—Barbirolli   # *BB.LBC 1047*
(*Sym. 8 & Bizet*) (also G.DB 4294/5) (♭ set WBC 1047)
☆ Residentie—v. Otterloo (in # Phi.N 00149L: # S 06002R)
French Nat. Radio—Lindenberg (♭ *Od. 7AOE 1007*)

No. 1, Entr'acte I, B minor
Philharmonia—Kletzki   *C.LX 1576*
                         (GQX 11529)

No. 2, Ballet, B minor
Philharmonia—Kletzki   *C.LX 1582*
                         (GQX 11541)
☆ French Nat. Radio—Lindenberg (♭ *Od.7AOE 1007*)

No. 3b, Romanze: Der Vollmond strahlt
I. Seefried (S), E. Werba (pf.)   *PV. 36109*
(*Ave Maria & Seligkeit*) (o.n. 46007: ♭ *Pol. 30128*)
(& with *Cornelius, Reger & Wolf,* in # *AmD.DL 7545*)
☆ E. Schumann (S) (in # Vic.LCT 1126)

No. 5, Entracte III, B flat major
Philharmonia—Kletzki   *C.LX 1579*
                         (GQX 11531)

No. 9, Ballet, G major
Philharmonia—Kletzki (2ss)   *C.LX 1585*
(*Berlioz: Béatrice & Bénédict, Overture*) (GQX 11533)
on ♭ *C.SEL 1502: SEBQ 103;* Brahms on ♭ *ESBF 115*)
Hamburg Philharmonia—H-J. Walther
                         MSB. 78145
[7]Linz Sym. (in # Ply. 12-30)
[7]Berlin Sym.—List (in # Roy. 1398)
[8]Liverpool Phil.—Sargent (in # AmC.RL 3050)
☆ Philadelphia—Stokowski (in # Cam.CAL 123)
Ballet, unspec. Regent Sym. (in # Rgt. 7005)

(Die) VERSCHWOREN D.787 1 Act 1823
(*Der häusliche Krieg*) (f.p. 1861)
COMPLETE RECORDING

Der Graf	... ...	W. Berry (Bs)
Die Gräfin	... ...	I. Steingruber (S)
Isilla	... ...	L. Dutoit (S)
Udolin	... ...	W. Anton (T)
Helene	... ...	E. Roon (S)
Astolf	...	R. Kreutzberger (T)

Vienna Acad. Cha. Cho. & Pro Musica Orch.
   —Grossmann (2ss)   # E. & AmVox.PL 8160

STAGE WORKS BASED ON SCHUBERT'S WORKS
(Das) DREIMÄDERLHAUS — ARR. Berté
Excerpts (*inter alia*)
Soloists, Acad. Cha. Cho. & Vienna Radio
   Orch.—Sandauer   *Phi.P 41300G*
                          (♭ P 428002E)
Soloists, Cho. & Orch.—Pauspertl
                       # *AmVox.PL 20800*
                          (♭ VIP 30030)

SCHNEEWITTCHEN 1941
(compiled Weingartner)
Ballet Music (ARR. Fekete)
☆ Salzburg Mozarteum—Fekete (2ss) V# *CA.MPO 5032*

II. B. CHURCH MUSIC

MASSES
No. 2, G major S, T, B, cho., orch. D.167 1815
Y. Ciannelli, W. Carringer, R. Keast, Shaw
   Chorale & Victor Sym.—Shaw
                         # *Vic.LM 1784*
(*Bach, Brahms*)   (# FV.A 630230)

No. 6, E flat major S, A, T, B, cho., orch.
       D.950 1828-9
☆ Soloists, Cho. & Vienna Sym.—Moralt
                       # *EVox.PL 7840*

Deutsche Messe, F major D.872 1827
— MALE VOICE VERSION, A flat major
... **Sanctus** (Heilig, heilig . . .)
Male Cho.—Scherzberg   *Eta. 120167*
(*Die Nacht*)

Offertory: Salve Regina, F major, Op. 47 D.223
       S, cho., orch.
F. Jankowitsch (Tr.), Vienna Boys' Cho. &
   Vienna Sym. Orch.—Brenn #*EPhi.NBR 6011*
(*Pergolesi, Mozart, Herbeck*)   (# Phi.N 00694R)

-----

[2] Including both the *Alfonso und Estrella* and *Zauberharfe* Overtures.
[3] Includes *Alfonso & Estrella* Ov. only.
[4] Includes *Zauberharfe* Ov. only.
[6] Also in Complete recordings & collections, above.
[7] Unspec. but doubtless this.
[5] ARR. Stokowski.
This is the usual "Rosamunde Overture".
[8] Stated to be this, but in fact may well be No. 5 ☆.

Psalm 23, Op. 132 D.706 1820
Berlin Motet Cho.—Lehmann **PV. 72345**
(Ständchen, Op. 135) (in ‡ Pol. 18101/2)
[M. Raucheisen, pf.]
Birkenhead Male Cho. *(Eng)* in ‡ **Nix. 6209-2**
(‡ West. set WAL 209)

II. C. PART SONGS

COLLECTIONS
Geist der Liebe, Op. 11, No. 3 (Matthisson) D.747 *(b)* 1822
Gesang der Geister über den Wassern, Op. 167 (Goethe) D.714
(s)
Der Gondelfahrer, Op. 28 (Mayrhofer) D.809 *(b)* 1824
Im gegenwärtigen Vergangenes (Goethe) D.710 T *(b) c.* 1821
Nachtgesang im Walde, Op. 139 (Seidl) D.913 1827
Nachthelle, Op. 134 (Seidl) D.892 T *(b)* 1826
Nachtigall, Op. 11, No. 2 (Unger) D.724 *(b)* 1821
Nachtmusik, Op. 156 (Seckendorf) D.848 1825
N. Pöld (T, where marked); Stuttgart Vocal
Ens.—Couraud **‡ DFr. 141**
[W. Boehle (pf.), in those marked *(b)* above; Stuttgart Str.
Ens., marked *(s)*; 4 horns in *Nachtgesang*]
An den Frühling (Schiller) D.338 *c.* 1816
La Pastorella (Goldoni) D.513 *c.* 1817
Sehnsucht (Goethe) D.656 1819 *(Nur wer die Sehnsucht kennt)*
Ständchen, Op. 135 (Grillparzer) D.921 A & cho., pf. 1827
Widerspruch, Op. 105, No. 1 (Seidl) D.865 *c.* 1827
☆ Victor Men's Cho.—Shaw in ‡ **Vic.LM 1800**
[with B. Krebs (A) & F. Glazer (pf.)]

(Der) Gondelfahrer, Op. 28 (Mayrhofer) D.809
Bavarian Radio Cho.—Kugler in ‡ **Pol. 19046**
(Die Nacht; Mendelssohn & Brahms)

Gott in der Natur, Op. 133 (Kleist) D.757
S, S, A, A, & pf.
Montserrat Monastery Cho. *(Span.)*
♭ **Ambra.SMGE 80013**
(Mendelssohn: Laudate pueri dominum)

(Die) Nacht, Op. 17, No. 4 (Krummacher)
D.983 Male cho.
Nachthelle, Op. 134 (Seidl) D.892 T, Male vv. & pf.
H. Wallner (Tr.) & Vienna Boys' Cho.—
Kühbacher (pf.) in ‡ **EPhi.NBR 6024**
(Brahms, Reger, etc.) (‡ Phi.N 00726R)
[Nachthelle only, in ♭ Phi.N 402038E]

(Die) Nacht, Op. 17, No. 4 Male Cho. D.983
Berlin State Op. Cho.—K. Schmidt **Eta. 20-130**
(Ständchen)
Bavarian Radio Cho.—Kugler in ‡ **Pol. 19046**
(Der Gondelfahrer, etc.)
Male Cho.—Scherzberg **Eta. 120167**
(Deutsche Messe—Sanctus)
Montserrat Cho.—Segerra *(Catalan)* (G.AA 774:
♭ 7EPL 13026)

(La) Pastorella (Goldoni) D.513
Pancratius Male Cho.—Heydendael
(Milhaud, Handel, etc.) in ‡ **C.HS 1001**
☆ Vienna Boys' Cho.—Lacovitch[1] (in ‡ EPhi.NBR 6007:
BBR 8045; AmC.ML 4873; ♭ Phi.N 402000E)

Ständchen, F major, Op. 135 (Grillparzer) D.921
(Zögernd leise) A, Female Cho., pf. 1827
D. Eustrati, Berlin Motet Cho.—Lehmann
[M. Raucheisen, pf.] **PV. 72345**
(Psalm 23) (in ‡ Pol. 18101/2)
H. Friedrich (B) & Male Cho. **Eta. 20-130**
(Die Nacht)
☆ M. Nussbaumer & Vienna Acad. Cha. Cho.—Grossmann
(in V‡ Sel.LPP 8714)
Vienna Boys' Cho.—Lacovitch[1] (in ‡ EPhi.NBR 6007:
AmC.ML 4873; ♭ Phi.N 402000E & ♭ N 402038E)

II. D. SONGS (LIEDER)
(for pf. transcriptions, see LISZT)

CYCLES
(Die) SCHÖNE MÜLLERIN, Op. 25 (Müller)
D.795 1823

1. Das Wandern	2. Wohin?
3. Halt!	4. Danksagung an den Bach
5. Am Feierabend	6. Der Neugierige
7. Ungeduld	8. Morgengruss
9. Des Müllers Blumen	10. Thränenregen
11. Mein!	12. Pause
13. Mit dem grünen	14. Der Jäger
Lautenbande	15. Eifersucht und Stolz
16. Die liebe Farbe	17. Die böse Farbe
18. Trock'ne Blumen	19. Der Müller und der Bach
20. Des Baches Wiegenlied	

[1] ARR. Keldorfer.

COMPLETE RECORDINGS
P. Munteanu (T), F. Holetschek (pf.)
‡ West.WL 5291
A. Dermota (T), H. Dermota (pf.) ‡ **Lon.LL 971**
I. Matthews (M-S), L. Farr (pf.) ‡ **Per.SPL 713**
(later pressings in a set with *Winterreise*)
☆ D. Fischer-Dieskau (B), G. Moore (pf.) ‡ G.ALP 1036/7
(4ss) (‡ FALP 334/5: VALP 511/2; 2ss, Vic.LHMV 6)
G. Vinogradov (T, *Russ*), G. Orentlicher (pf.)
‡ USSR.D 2205/8
☆ A. Schiøtz (T), G. Moore (pf.) (‡ G.KALP 11)
M. Singher (B), P. Ulanowsky (pf.) (‡ Clc. 6247:
MMS. 3013)
Nos. 1, 2, 3, 4, 6, 7, 8, 9, 13, 14, 15, 16, 17, 20
G. Lutze (T), E. Michel (pf.) **Eta. 20-132/6**
(10ss) (‡ LPM 1005)

SCHWANENGESANG D.957 1828

1. Liebesbotschaft	2. Kriegers Ahnung
3. Frühlingssehnsucht	4. Ständchen
5. Aufenthalt	6. In der Ferne
7. Abschied	8. Der Atlas
9. Ihr Bild	10. Das Fischermädchen
11. Die Stadt	12. Am Meer
13. Der Doppelgänger	14. Die Taubenpost

[Though not strictly a Cycle, this set is included
here for convenience of reference]

COMPLETE RECORDINGS
B. Sönnerstedt (B), F. Jensen (pf.) ‡ **G.KALP 3**
I. Matthews (M-S), L. Farr (pf.) ‡ **Per.SPL 717**
(Beethoven)
H. Hotter (B), G. Moore (pf.) ‡ **C.CX 1269**
☆ P. Munteanu (T), F. Holetschek (pf.) ‡ Nix.WLP 5165
☆ G. Hüsch (B), M. Gurlitt (pf.) (‡ JpV.LS 103/4, 4ss;
Nos. 4 & 13 only, ♭ ES 8013)
R. Herbert (B), F. Waldman (pf.) (‡ Allo. 3089)
... **Nos. 8-13 inclusive** (Nos. 12 & 13 are ☆)
D. Fischer-Dieskau (B), G. Moore (pf.)
‡ **G.ALP 1066**
(Beethoven: An die ferne Geliebte) (‡ WALP 1066:
RE-ISSUES: FALP 307)
Nos. 8, 10, 12, 13 on ‡ Vic.LHMV 1046: ♭ WHMV 1046
Nos. 8 & 9 on G.DA 2049
Nos. 10 & 11 on G.DA 2045
Nos. 12 & 13 on G.DB 21586
No. 10 on ♭ Vic.EHA 8
... Nos. 10-14
☆ M. Lichtegg (T), H. W. Häusslein (pf.) ‡ Lon.LD 9093

WINTERREISE, Op. 89 D.911 1827

1. Gute Nacht	2. Die Wetterfahne
3. Gefror'ne Thränen	4. Erstarrung
5. Der Lindenbaum	6. Wasserfluth
7. Auf dem Flusse	8. Rückblick
9. Irrlicht	10. Rast
11. Frühlingstraum	12. Einsamkeit
13. Die Post	14. Der greise Kopf
15. Die Krähe	16. Letzte Hoffnung
17. Im Dorfe	18. Der stürmische Morgen
19. Täuschung	20. Der Wegweiser
21. Das Wirthshaus	22. Muth!
23. Die Nebensonnen	24. Der Leyermann

COMPLETE RECORDINGS
D. Fischer-Dieskau (B), G. Moore (pf.)
‡ **G.ALP 1298S/9**
(3ss) (4ss, ‡ WALP 1503/4)
(3ss—*Schumann*, in ‡ Vic. set LM 6036)
[Nos. 5 & 11 on G.DB 11593: ♭ 7RW 19-553; Nos. 13 &
24 on G.DA 5528: Nos. 1, 13, 24 on ♭ G.7ERW 5013]
H. Hotter (B), G. Moore (pf.) ‡ **C.CX 1222S/3**
(3ss) (Angel. 35160S/1, set 3521)
K. Schmitt-Walter (B), H. Giesen (pf.)
‡ **D.LXT 2799/800**
(4ss) (‡ Lon.LL 702/3)
I. Matthews (M-S), L. Farr (pf.)
‡ **Per. set SPL 714**
(4ss—2 12-in. & 2 7-in.) (also as a set with *Schöne Müllerin*)
L. Bogtman (Bs), F. de Nobel (pf.)
‡ **Phi.N 00746/7R**
(4ss) (2ss, ‡ Epic.LC 3154)
M. Bonilla (S), I. M. Kotkowska (pf.) ‡ **CM. 1/2**
S. Shaposhnikov (B, *Russ*) (USSRM.D 01895/8)
☆ G. Hüsch (B), H. U. Müller (pf.) (‡ JpV.LF 1/2)
Nos. 1, 2, 5, 6, 11, 13, 15, 17, 20, 23, 24
A. Schellenberg (B), K. Striegler (pf.) **Eta. 20-137/41**
(10ss)

COLLECTIONS: New Issues
in Alphabetical order of artist
SCHWANENGESANG: Nos. 5 & 13
WINTERREISE: Nos. 15 & 20
Erlkönig, Op. 1 (Goethe) D.328

C. Akos (A), P. Mosonyi (pf.) V♯ Sel.LAP 1005

Die SCHÖNE MÜLLERIN: No. 17 (b)
SCHWANENGESANG: No. 4 (a)
Die Allmacht, Op. 79, No. 2 (Pyrker) D.382 (b)
Die Forelle, Op. 82 (Schubart) D.550 (a)
Wanderers Nachtlied II, Op. 96, No. 3 (Goethe)
D.768 (b)

J. Björling (T), F. Schauwecker (pf.)
♯ G.ALP 1187
(*Brahms, Wolf, Sibelius, etc.*)   (♯ Vic.LM 1771)
[Marked (a) also on G.DB 21593; (b) on ♭ 7ERC 2]

An die Leyer, Op. 56, No. 2 (Bruchmann) D.737
An eine Quelle, Op. 109, No. 3 (Claudius) D.530
An Schwager Kronos, Op. 19, No. 1 (Goethe) D.369
Fischerweise, Op. 96, No. 4 (Schlechta) D.881
Frühlingsglaube, Op. 20, No. 2 (Uhland) D.686
Geheimes, Op. 14, No. 2 (Goethe) D.719
Der Jüngling am Bache (Schiller) D.30[1]
Der liebliche Stern (Schulze) D.861
Litaney (Jacobi) D.343
Der Musensohn, Op. 92, No. 1 (Goethe) D.764
Nachtviolen (Mayrhofer) D.752
Sei mir gegrüsst, Op. 20, No. 1 (Rückert) D.741
Dem Unendlichen (Klopstock) D.291
Verklärung (Herder, after Pope) D.59
Widerschein (Schlechta) D.949

B. Boyce (B), D. Handman (pf.)
♯ LOL.OL 50045

An Laura, als sie Klopstocks Auferstehungslied sang
   (Matthisson) D.115
Heidenröslein, Op. 3, No. 3 (Goethe) D.257 ø
Liebhaber in allen Gestalten (Goethe) D.558 ø
Nacht und Träume, Op. 43, No. 2 (Collin) D.827 ø
La Pastorella (*Die junge Schäferin*) (Goldoni) D.528

M. Dobbs (S), G. Moore (pf.) in ♯ C.CX 1154
(*Brahms, Wolf, Fauré, etc.*) (in ♯ FCX 299: QCX 10097;
Angel. 35094)
[Items marked ø also on C.LX 1618]

SCHWANENGESANG: Nos. 1, 3, 7
Auflösung (Mayrhofer) D.807
Der Einsame, Op. 41 (Lappe) D.800
Geheimes, Op. 14, No. 2 (Goethe) D.719
Im Abendroth (Lappe) D.799
Der Kreuzzug (Leitner) D.932
Nachtviolen (Mayrhofer) D.752
Rastlose Liebe, Op. 5, No. 6 (Goethe) D.138
Todtengräbers Heimwehe (Craigher) D.842
Über Wildemann, Op. 108, No. 1 (Schulze) D.884
Der Wanderer an den Mond, Op. 80, No. 1 (Seidl)
D.870

D. Fischer-Dieskau (B), G. Moore (pf.)
♯ G.ALP 1295

SCHWANENGESANG: Nos. 4, 8, 10, 12, 13
☆ Du bist die Ruh', Op. 59, No. 3 (Rückert) D.776
☆ Der Erlkönig, Op. 1 (Goethe) D.328
☆ Nacht und Träume, Op. 43, No. 2 (Collin) D.827

D. Fischer-Dieskau (B), G. Moore (pf.)
♯ Vic.LHMV 1046
(*Beethoven, Schumann*)   (♭ set WHMV 1046)
[SG. 4 & 10, Nacht & T., and Du bist . . . also ♭ Vic.EHA 8]

WINTERREISE: Nos. 13 & 20
Die junge Nonne, Op. 43, No. 1 (Craigher) D.828
Die Liebe hat gelogen, Op. 23, No. 1 (Platen) D.751

K. Flagstad (S), E. McArthur (pf.)
♯ G.ALP 1309
(*Brahms, R. Strauss, D. Taylor, etc.*)   (♯ Vic.LM 1870)

SCHÖNE MÜLLERIN: No. 2
SCHWANENGESANG: Nos. 4, 13
WINTERREISE: No. 5
Ave Maria, Op. 52, No. 6 (Storck, after Scott) D.839
Du bist die Ruh', Op. 59, No. 3 (Rückert) D.776
Erlkönig, Op. 1 (Goethe) D.328
Die Forelle, Op. 32 (Schubart) D.550
Heidenröslein, Op. 3, No. 3 (Goethe) D.257
Der Wanderer, Op. 4, No. 1 (Schmidt) D.493

J. Giraudeau (T, *Fr*), J. Dupont (pf.)
♯ D.FAT 173512

Ellens Gesang II: Jäger, ruhe, Op. 52, No. 2 (Scott
trs. Storck) D.838
Erlafsee, Op. 8, No. 3 (Mayrhofer) D.586
Im Walde, Op. 93, No. 1 (Schulze) D.834
Die Liebe hat gelogen, Op. 23, No. 1 (Platen) D.751
Das Lied im Grünen, Op. 115, No. 1 (Reil) D.917
Meeres Stille, Op. 3, No. 2 (Goethe) D.216
Dem Unendlichen (Klopstock) D.291
Der Wachtelschlag, Op. 68 (Sauter) D.742

H. Glaz (S), L. Müller (pf.)   ♯ MGM.E 3055
(*Schumann*)

Der Jüngling an der Quelle (Salis) D.300
Die Liebe hat gelogen, Op. 23, No. 1 (Platen) D.751
Der Musensohn, Op. 92, No. 1 (Goethe) D.764

R. Hayes (T), R. Boardman (pf.)
in ♯ Van.VRS 449
(*Debussy, Schumann, Berlioz, etc.*)

An Sylvia, Op. 106, No. 4 (Shakespeare) D.891
Heimliches Lieben, Op. 106, No. 1 (Klenke) D.922
Nacht und Träume, Op. 43, No. 2 (Collin) D.827
Stimme der Liebe (Stollberg) D.412

A. Koskinen (T), E. Møller (pf.)
♭ Mtr.MCEP 3022

Auf dem Wasser zu singen, Op. 72 (Stolberg) D.774
Fischerweise, Op. 96, No. 4 (Schlechta) D.881
Die Forelle, Op. 32 (Schubart) D.550
Im Abendroth (Lappe) D.799
Die junge Nonne, Op. 43, No. 1 (Craigher) D.828
Nacht und Träume, Op. 43, No. 2 (Collin) D.827

E. Nikolaidi (A), J. Behr (pf.) ♯ AmC.ML 4628
(*Beethoven*)

An die Musik, Op. 88, No. 4 (Schober) D.547
Gretchen am Spinnrade, Op. 2 (Goethe) D.118
Die junge Nonne, Op. 43, No. 1 (Craigher) D.828
Der Knabe (Schlegel) D.692
Die Vögel, Op. 172, No. 6 (Schlegel) D.691

M. Ritchie (S), G. Malcolm (pf.) ♯ Nix.NLP 921
(*Purcell, Boyce, Arne, etc.*)

Auf dem Wasser zu singen, Op. 72 (Stolberg) 120144
Ave Maria, Op. 52, No. 6 (Scott, trs. Storck) 120145
Du bist die Ruh', Op. 59, No. 3 (Rückert) 120146
Die Forelle, Op. 32 (Schubart) 120147
Heidenröslein, Op. 3, No. 3 (Goethe) 120147[2]
Der Hirt auf dem Felsen, Op. 129 120131
   (Müller & Chezy)
        (with E. Koch, cl.; also on ♭ LPM 1011)
Lachen und Weinen, Op. 59, No. 4 (Rückert) 120147
Das Mädchen (Schlegel) 120147[2]

S. Schöner (S), F. Schröder (pf.) ♯ Eta.LPM 1006
(also on 78 r.p.m. as shown)

An die Musik, Op. 89, No. 4 (Schober) D.547
An Sylvia, Op. 106, No. 4 (after Shakespeare) D.891
Auf dem Wasser zu singen, Op. 73 (Stolberg) D.774
Ganymed, Op. 19, No. 3 (Goethe) D.544
Gretchen am Spinnrade, Op. 2 (Goethe) D.118
Im Frühling (Schulze) D.882
Die junge Nonne, Op. 43, No. 1 (Craigher) D.828
Das Lied im Grünen, Op. 115, No. 1 (Reil) D.917
Der Musensohn, Op. 92, No. 1 (Goethe) D.764
Nachtviolen (Mayrhofer) D.752
Nähe des Geliebten, Op. 5, No. 2 (Goethe) D.162
Wehmuth, Op. 22, No. 2 (Collin) D.772

E. Schwarzkopf (S), E. Fischer (pf.) ♯ C.CX 1040
                              (♯ FCX 181; Angel. 35022)

SCHWANENGESANG: No. 4
Auf dem Wasser zu singen, Op. 72 (Stolberg) D.774
Gretchen am Spinnrade, Op. 2 (Goethe) D.118
Im Abendroth (Lappe) D.799
Im Frühling (Schulze) D.882
Nacht und Träume, Op. 43, No. 2 (Collin) D.827
Rastlose Liebe, Op. 5, No. 6 (Goethe) D.138

C. Smith (A), R. Cellini (pf.)   ♯ BB.LBC 1071
(*Brahms*)

SCHWANENGESANG: Nos. 4, 7, 8
An die Leyer, Op. 56, No. 2 (Bruchmann) D.737
Du bist die Ruh', Op. 59, No. 3 (Rückert) D.776
Geheimes, Op. 14, No. 2 (Goethe) D.719
Gruppe aus dem Tartarus, Op. 24, No. 1 (Schiller) D.583
Horch! Horch! die Lerch' (after Shakespeare) D.889
Litaney (Jacobi) D.343
Der Musensohn, Op. 92, No. 1 (Goethe) D.764
Nachtviolen (Mayrhofer) D.752
Das Rosenband (Klopstock) D.280
Der Schmetterling, Op. 51, No. 1 (Schlegel) D.633
Seligkeit (Hölty) D.433

G. Souzay (B), D. Baldwin (pf.) ♯ D.LXT 5023
                              (♯ Lon.LL 1148)

---

[1] First setting, 1812.
[2] 20-148 in the 1953 cat. but see *An Schwager Kronos/Gretchen*.

COLLECTIONS (*continued*)
SCHWANENGESANG: Nos. 1 & 9   (No. 1,   *ø*)
Erster Verlust, Op. 5, No. 4   (Goethe)   D.226   ø
Die Forelle, Op. 32   (Schubart)   D.550   ø
Ganymed, Op. 19, No. 3   (Goethe)   D.544   ø
Der Jüngling an der Quelle   (Salis)   D.300
Der Jüngling und der Tod   (Spaun)   D.545
Nacht und Träume, Op. 43, No. 2   (Collin)   D.827   ø
Der Schiffer, Op. 21, No. 2   (Mayrhofer)   D.536
Der Wanderer an den Mond, Op. 80, No. 1 (Seidl) D.870
G. Souzay (B), J. Bonneau (pf.)   *♯ D.LX 3104*
[Items marked ø also on ♭ *D.VD 508*]   (*♯ Lon.LS 655*)

Die SCHÖNE MÜLLERIN: No. 7
SCHWANENGESANG: No. 4
WINTERREISE: No. 24
Du bist die Ruh', Op. 59, No. 3   (Rückert)   D.776
T. Šrubař (T, *Cz.*) & F.O.K. Sym.—Smetáček
                      ♯ U. 5100C
(*Rubinstein*)   [orch. Smetáček]

An die Musik, Op. 88, No. 4   (Schober)   D.547
Fischerweise, Op. 96, No. 4   (Schlechta)   D.881
Geistertanz   (Matthisson)   D.116
Im Abendroth   (Lappe)   D.799
Die Liebe hat gelogen, Op. 23, No. 1   (Platen)   D.751
Nacht und Träume, Op. 43, No. 2   (Collin)   D.827
Rastlose Liebe, Op. 5, No. 1   (Goethe)   D.138
Schlaflied, Op. 24, No. 2   (Mayrhofer)   D.527
Seligkeit   (Hölty)   D.433
Der Tod und das Mädchen, Op. 7, No. 3 (Claudius) D.531
Dem Unendlichen   (Klopstock)   D.291
Wanderers Nachtlied II, Op. 96, No. 3   (Goethe)   D.768
Wehmuth, Op. 22, No. 2   (Collin)   D.772
Widerschein   (Schlechta)   D.949
Wiegenlied, Op. 98, No. 2   (Claudius)   D.498
L. West (M-S), L. Taubman (pf.)
                   ♯ West.WN 18090

COLLECTIONS: RE-ISSUES
Die SCHÖNE MÜLLERIN: No. 2 (*a*)
SCHWANENGESANG: Nos. 1 & 4
Ave Maria, Op. 52, No. 6 (Starck, after Scott) (*a*, *b*)
Erlkönig, Op. 1   (Goethe)   D.328   (*a*)
Die Forelle, Op. 32   (Schubart)   D.550   (*a*, *b*)
Gretchen am Spinnrade, Op. 2   (Goethe)   D.118
Der Tod und das Mädchen, Op. 7, No. 3   (Claudius)
   D.531   (*b*)
☆ M. Anderson (A), F. Rupp (pf.)   *♯ G.FBLP 1038*
[Items marked (*a*) also on ♭ *7ERF 104; DV. 26022;*
  marked (*b*) also on ♭ *7RC 1*]

An die Musik, Op. 88, No. 4 (Schober) D.547   1817 (*a*)
Gretchen am Spinnrade, Op. 2 (Goethe) D.118   1814
Die junge Nonne, Op. 43, No. 1 (Craigher) D.828   1825
Der Musensohn, Op. 92, No. 1 (Goethe) D.764   1822 (*a*)
☆ K. Ferrier (A), P. Spurr (pf.)   *♯ D.LW 5098*
(*Schumann*)   (*♯ Lon.LD 9099*)
[Titles marked (*a*) also on *D.M 32974*]

WINTERREISE: Nos. 5, 15, 19, 20, 22, 23
Im Abendroth   (Lappe)   D.799
☆ L. Lehmann (S), P. Ulanowsky (pf.)   *♯ Vic.LCT 1108*
(*Brahms & Schumann*)   (♭ set *WCT 1108*)

Die SCHÖNE MÜLLERIN: No. 16
SCHWANENGESANG: No. 13
Auf dem Wasser zu singen, Op. 72 (Stolberg) D.774
Heidenröslein, Op. 3, No. 3   (Goethe)   D.257
☆ C. Maurane (B, *Fr*), L. Bienvenue (pf.)   ♭ *Pat.ED 20*

Die SCHÖNE MÜLLERIN: No. 11
SCHWANENGESANG: No. 1
WINTERREISE: No. 5
Nacht und Träume, Op. 43, No. 2   (Collin)   D.827
☆ C. Maurane (B, *Fr*), L. Bienvenue (pf.)   ♭ *Pat.ED 21*

SCHWANENGESANG: No. 4
An die Musik, Op. 88, No. 4   (Schober)   D.547
Der Blumenbrief   (Schreiber)   D.622
☆ H. Schlusnus (B)   in *♯ AmD.DL 9624*

WINTERREISE: No. 5
An Schwager Kronos, Op. 19, No. 1   (Goethe)   D.369
Im Abendroth   (Lappe)   D.799
Der Jüngling an der Quelle   (Salis)   D.300
☆ H. Schlusnus (B) & pf.   *♯ HP.DGM 18029*
(*Brahms, R. Strauss, Wolf*)

Ave Maria, Op. 52, No. 6   (Scott, trs. Storck)   D.839
Du bist die Ruh', Op. 59, No. 3   (Rückert)   D.776
Die Forelle, Op. 32   (Schubart)   D.550
Heidenröslein, Op. 3, No. 3   (Goethe)   D.257
Horch! Horch! die Lerch' (after Shakespeare) D.889
Das Lied im Grünen, Op. 115, No. 1 (Reil) D.917
ROSAMUNDE, Op. 26   D.797   Inc. Music
 ... No. 3b, Romanze: Der Vollmond strahlt
☆ E. Schumann (S)   *♯ Vic.LCT 1126*
(*Schumann: Frauenliebe und -Leben*)

Die SCHÖNE MÜLLERIN: Nos. 1, 7, 15
WINTERREISE: Nos. 4, 8, 11, 13, 15
Gott im Frühlinge   (Uz)   D.448
Im Frühling   (Schulze)   D.882
Der Kreuzzug   (Leitner)   D.932
Das Lied im Grünen, Op. 115, No. 1   (Reil)   D.917
Der Musensohn, Op. 92, No. 1   (Goethe)   D.764
Todtengräber-Weise   (Schlechta)   D.869
Der Wanderer an den Mond, Op. 80, No. 1 (Seidl) D.870
☆ H. Schey (Bs), M. Reymers (pf.)   *♯ Cum.CPL 201*

Die SCHÖNE MÜLLERIN: Nos. 2 & 18
SCHWANENGESANG: No. 4
An die Musik, Op. 88, No. 4   (Schober)   D.547
Im Abendroth   (Lappe)   D.799
Nacht und Träume, Op. 43, No. 2   (Collin)   D.827
☆ L. Slezak (T) (some with pf., some orch.)   *♯ Ete. 493*
(*Schumann, R. Strauss*)   [S.M. 18 appears not to be ☆]

Die SCHÖNE MÜLLERIN: No. 7
Frühlingsglaube, Op. 20, No. 2   (Uhland)   D.686
Heidenröslein, Op. 3, No. 3   (Goethe)   D.257
☆ R. Tauber (T)   *♯ ChOd.LDC 36003*
(*Schumann, R. Strauss, Grieg, etc.*)

INDIVIDUAL SONGS

Adieu (spurious—by Weyrauch)   D.App.I
I. Petrov (Bs, *Russ*)   **USSR. 022050**
(*Aufenthalt*)

(**Die**) **Allmacht, Op. 79, No. 2** (Pyrker) D.852   □
K. Flagstad (S), G. Moore (pf.)   **G.DB 21596**
(*Du bist die Ruh'*)
K. T. Petersen (M-S), K. Olsson (pf.)
                               C.DDX 41
(*Ave Maria*)
B. Smith (B, *Eng*), G. W. Briggs (pf.)
                         in *♯ Bo.B 501*

Am Meer (SG.12—Heine)   □
K. Schmitt-Walter (B), M. Raucheisen (pf.)
                           T.A 11292
(*Doppelgänger*)

An den Mond, Op. 57, No. 3 (Hölty) D.193
S. Schöner (S), F. Schröder (pf.)   *Eta. 120144*
(*Auf dem Wasser . . .*)   (in *♯ LPM 1011*)

An die Geliebte (Stoll) D.303
E. Schumann (S), L. Rosenek (pf.)   **G.DB 21572**
(½s—*Nachtviolen & Brahms: Ruhe, Süssliebchen*)
                               (o.n. DB 3598)[1]

An die Leyer, Op. 56, No. 2 (Bruchmann) D.737 □
K. Borg (Bs), M. Raucheisen (pf.)   *Pol. 62914*
(*Der König in Thule*)   (in *♯ 17004*)
M. Harrell (B), B. Smith (pf.)   in *♯ Rem. 199-140*
H. H. Wunderlich (B), M. Görgen (pf.)
(*Der Wanderer*)   *Eta. 20-142*
H. Janssen (B), S. Leff (pf.)   in *♯ Mur.P 110*
(followed by pf. acc. only)

An die Musik, Op. 88, No. 4 (Schober) D.547
K. Flagstad (S), E. MacArthur (pf.)
                       in *♯ G.ALP 1191*
(*R. Strauss, Brahms, etc.*) (*♯*Vic.LM 1738: ♭ set *WDM 1738*)
B. Loewenfalk (B), K. Olssen (pf.)   **G.X 8149**
(*Litaney*)
M. Reizen (Bs, *Russ*) (USSR. 15432: USSRM.D 00952)
☆ G. Hüsch (B) (in *♯ JpV.LS 2006*)

An die Nachtigall, Op. 78, No. 1 (Claudius) D.497
E. Söderström (S), S. Westerberg (pf.) *D.F 44248*
(*Heidenröslein; & Haydn: My mother bids me . . .*)
S. Schöner (S), F. Schröder (pf.)   *Eta. 120146*
(*Nacht und Träume & Du bist die Ruh'*)

An Schwager Kronos, Op. 19, No. 1 (Goethe) D.369
H. Rosenberg (B), F. Schröder (pf.)   *Eta. 20-148*
(*Gretchen am Spinnrade*)   (o.n. 25-005)

(**Der**) **Atlas** (SG. 8—Heine)   □
H. H. Wunderlich (B), A. F. Guhl (pf.)
(*Doppelgänger*)   *Eta. 20-12015*
☆ K. Schmitt-Walter (B) (*RadT. A195T*)

---

[1] This number was allocated at time of recording (*c.* 1938) but not issued.

Auf dem Wasser zu singen, Op. 72 (Stolberg) D.774
I. Seefried (S), E. Werba (pf.) in ♯ **Pol. 19050**
(*Lachen und Weinen; Brahms, Moussorgsky, etc.*) (♯ AmD.DL 9809)
☆ E. Gerhardt (M-S) (JpV.ND 196)

Aufenthalt (SG. 5—Rellstab) □
I. Petrov (Bs, *Russ*) **USSR. 022049**
(*Adieu*)
☆ M. Anderson (A) (♭ *DV.L 16288*)

Ave Maria, Op. 52, No. 6 (*Ger*, Storck after Scott)
(*Ellens dritter Gesang*) D.839 □
I. Seefried (S), E. Werba (pf.) ***PV. 36109***
(*Seligkeit & Rosamunde, excpt*)
(o.n. *46007;* ♭ *Pol. 30128;* in ♯ *AmD.DL 7545*)
K. T. Petersen (M-S), K. Olsson (pf.)
(*Die Allmacht*) **C.DDX 41**
N. Hofman (S) & Orch. **ArgOd. 66056**
(*Figaro, No. 19*) (♭ *BSOAE 4519*)
R. Ponselle (S, *Lat*) & vln. **Pte.** n.d.
(*Bizet & Franck*)
G. Bechi (B, *Ital*) & Orch. ***G.DA 11354***
(*Denza: Occhi di fata*)
A. Heynis (A) & org. (Phi.N 17906G)
J. Dragonette (S) & org. (in ♭ *AmC.A 1556*)
J. Warren (Tr.), J. Lee (pf.) (in ♯ Queens.LPR 21)
I. B. Lucca (S, *Ital*) & Cho. (*Dur.AI 10099:* in ♯ *AI 520*)
D. Harrison (Tr.) & Cho. (in ♯ B.LAT 8070; AmD.DL 8106: ♭ *set ED 831*)
☆ E. Grümmer (S) (♭ *G.7RW 507*)
T. Lemnitz (S) & orch. (*CanT.GF 63018;* in ♯ *T.LA 6028:* ♭ *U 45515*)
R. Crooks (T, *Lat*) (in ♯ Cam.CAL 170)
T. Schipa (T, *Ital*) (in ♯ *G.QBLP 5030: FKLP 7009:* ♭ *7ERQ 117: RQ 3037*)
M. Anderson (A) (♭ *DV.D 16288*)
R. Tauber (T) (in ♯ *AmD.DL 7535*)
C. Lynch (T) & org. (in ♯ AmC.RL 3016), etc.

[Many of the above are no doubt sung in *Latin* to liturgical words.]

— ARRANGEMENTS
CHO.: R. Shaw Chorale (in ♯ Vic.LM 1800)

ORCHESTRA: Boston Prom.—Fiedler (♭ *Vic.ERA 66*)
Berlin Sym.—Hermann (in ♯ Roy. 1371)
Westminster Light—Bridgewater (in ♯ Nix.WLP 6806; West.WL 4006)
Mantovani Orch. (in ♯ D.LK 4072: *M 33652;* in ♯ Lon.LL 877: ♭ *BEP 6089*, etc.)
Angelicum—Janes (*Ang.CPA 054*)
etc.

VLN. & ORCH.: ☆ N. Milstein & Vic. Sym.—Fiedler (♭ *Vic.ERA 77; DV. 26009*)

VLN. & PF. Wilhelmj
Y. Menuhin & G. Moore **G.DB 21608**
(*Dvořák: Songs my mother taught me*) (♭ *7R 176: 7RQ 3055*)
E. Morini & L. Pommers in ♯ **West.WN 18087**
☆ J. Heifetz (in ♯ G.ALP 1206: FALP 248: ♭*7RF/RQ 267;* ♭ *Vic.ERA 184*)

VLA. & ORG.: W. Primrose & V. de Tar (in ♯ *AmC.AL 33*)

VLC. & PF.: K. Reher & M. di Tullio (in ♯ *Layos.CB 594/5*)
☆ E. Mainardi (*PV. 36110;* ♭ *Pol. 32103*)
S. Popoff (in ♯ *Vien.LPR 1022*)

ORGAN: R. Ellsasser (in ♯ *MGM.E 200*, etc.)
M. Salvador (in ♯ TMS. 3/4)
J. Perceval (in ♯ *ArgOd.LDC 513:* ♭ *BSOAE 9518*)
☆ C. Courboin (♭ *Cam.CAE 209;* in ♯ CAL 218)

GUITAR: A. Valenti (in ♯ SMC. 1002)

ACCOMPANIMENT, etc., for practice (in ♯ AmEsq. 1; in ♯ *VS.ML 1001*)

(Der) Doppelgänger (SG.13—Heine) □
K. Schmitt-Walter (B), M. Raucheisen (pf.)
(*Am Meer*) ***T.A 11292***
M. Vitale (S, *Ital*), A. Beltrami (pf.)
(*Die Stadt*) ***Cet.AT 0327***
H. H. Wunderlich (B), A. F. Guhl (pf.)
(*Der Atlas*) ***Eta. 20-12015***

Du bist die Ruh', Op. 59, No. 3 (Rückert) D.776 □
I. Kolassi (M-S), J. Bonneau (pf.) in ♯ **Lon.LL 747**
(† Arie Antiche & German Lieder) (♯ D.FAT 173160)
K. Flagstad (S), G. Moore (pf.) **G.DB 21596**
(*Die Allmacht*)

R. Hayes (T), R. Boardman (pf.) in ♯ **A440. 12-3**
S. Lemeshev (T, *Russ*) (USSR. 022290)
☆ S. Onegin (A) (*JpV.NF 4075*)
— ACCOMPANIMENT, etc., for practice, in ♯ *VS.ML 3001*

Erlkönig, Op. 1 (Goethe) D.328 □
T. Duncan (B), W. Allen (pf.) **Phi.A 56504G**
(*Brahms: Von ewiger Liebe*)
I. Kolassi (M-S), J. Bonneau (pf.) in ♯ **Lon.LL 747**
(† Arie Antiche & German Lieder) (♯ D.FAT 173160)
R. Ponselle (S), I. Chicagov (pf.) in ♯ **Vic.LM 1889**
(*Lully, Chausson, Beethoven, etc.*) (♯ DV. 16493)
M. Powers (A), F. la Forge (pf.) in ♯ **Atl. 1207**
(*Tod und das Mädchen; Brahms, etc.*)
A. Mestral (B, *Fr*) ♭ ***Phi.N 432012E***
(*Fauré & Schumann*)
T. Kuuzik (B, *Estonian*) (in ♯ *USSR.D 2090*)
☆ A. Kipnis (Bs), C. Dougherty (pf.) (in ♯ Vic.LCT 1158)
D. Fischer-Dieskau (B) (♭ *G.7RF 240*)
H H. Rehkemper (B) (in ♯ Sca. 809*)

(Das) Fischermädchen (SG.10—Heine) □
G. Lutze (T), A. Hecker (pf.) ***Eta. 120120***
(½s—*Ihr Bild; & Mendelssohn*)
M. Vitale (S, *Ital*), A. Beltrami (pf.)
(*Ihr Bild*) ***Cet.AT 0328***

(Die) Forelle, Op. 32 (Schubart) D.550 □
☆ E. Schwarzkopf (*C.LN 9*)
K. Flagstad (S) (*JpV.SF 724*)
E. Gerhardt (M-S) (*JpV.NT 4133*)
G. Thill (T, *Fr*) (in ♯ C.FHX 5012; Angel. C 33001)
— ARR. CHO.
Vienna Boys' Cho.—Kühbacher (in ♯ *Phi.S 06066R*)
— ACCOMPANIMENT, etc., for practice in (♯ *VS.ML 3001*)
P. Ulanowsky (in ♯ *Bo.B 502*)

Freiwilliges Versinken (Mayrhofer) D.700
H S. Onegin (A) (in **V**♯ *IRCC.L 7003**)

Frühlingsglaube, Op. 20, No. 2 (Uhland) D.686 □
K. Flagstad (S), G. Moore (pf.) **G.DB 21554**
(*Im Abendroth*)

Frühlingstraum (W.11) □
☆ E. Gerhardt (M-S) (JpV.ND 321)
H H. Rehkemper (in ♯ Sca. 809*)

Ganymed, Op. 19, No. 3 (Goethe) D.544 □
K. Flagstad (S), E. McArthur (pf.) in ♯ **G.ALP 1191**
(*An die Musik, etc.*) (♯ Vic.LM 1738: ♭ *set WDM 1738*)
H. Janssen (B), S. Leff (pf.) in ♯ **Mur.P 102**
(followed by pf. acc. only)

Grenzen der Menschheit (Goethe) D.716
K. Borg (Bs), M. Raucheisen (pf.) **PV. 72381**
(*Prometheus*) (in ♯ *Pol. 17004*)
G. Frick (Bs), M. Görgen (pf.) **Eta. 225030**
(2ss) (o.n. *20-149* & 25-010)
H R. Mayr (Bs) (in ♯ Sca. 822*)

Gretchen am Spinnrade, Op. 2 (Goethe) D.118 □
M. Vitale (S, *Ital*), A. Beltrami (pf.) ***Cet.AT 0329***
(*Heidenröslein*) (in ♯ LPC 55001)
E. Grümmer (S), F. Schröder (pf.) ***Eta. 20-148***
(*An Schwager Kronos*) (o.n. Eta 25-005)
G. Farrar (S & pf.) (in ♯ *IRCC.L 7001*)[1]
☆ E. Gerhardt (M-S) (JpV.ND 196)
H E. Eames (AF.AGSB 22*)

Gute Nacht (W.1) □
☆ E. Gerhardt (M-S) (JpV.ND 461)

Heidenröslein, Op. 3, No. 3 (Goethe) D.257 □
E. Söderström (S), S. Westerberg (pf.) ***D.F 44248***
(*An die Nachtigall; & Haydn*)
H. Prey (B), M. Raucheisen (pf.) ***C.DW 5271***
(*Horch! Horch! die Lerch'*)
M. Vitale (S, *Ital*), A. Beltrami (pf.)
(*Gretchen am Spinnrade*) ***Cet.AT 0329***
☆ I. Seefried (S) (*C.LO 81*)
— ARR. VLN. & PF. R. & A. d'Arco (in *Plé.P 101*)
— FOR PRACTICE, pf. acc. P. Ulanowsky (in ♯ *Bo.B 502*)

[1] Incomplete; recorded 1935.

(Der) Hirt auf dem Felsen, Op. 129   D.965
(Müller & Chezy) S, cl. pf. ☐
(The Shepherd on the Rock)
E. Berger, H. Geuser, E-G. Scherzer
G.DB 11569
(♭ *7RW 522*)
E. Spoorenberg, J. Huckriede & Residentie
Orch.—v. Otterloo   **Phi.N 12053G**
(2ss)   (*Weber; & Rosamunde* in ♯ *N 00149L*)

Horch! Horch! die Lerch' D.889
(Shakespeare, trs. Schlegel) *(Ständchen)*
H. Prey (B), M. Raucheisen (pf.)   *C.DW 5271*
(Heidenröslein)
N. Kazantseva (S, *Russ*) (*USSR. 21079*)
☆ K. Schmitt-Walter (B) (*AusT.M 5213*)
— FOR PRACTICE, pf. acc.   P. Ulanowsky (in ♯ *Bo.B 502*)
— ARR. PF.   Liszt, *q.v.*, Section A.III.6

Ihr Bild (SG.9—Heine)   ☐
G. Lutze (T), A. Hecker (pf.)   *Eta. 120120*
(½s—*Fischermädchen; & Mendelssohn*) (o.n. *20-12013*)
M. Vitale (S, *Ital*), A. Beltrami (pf.)
(Fischermädchen)   *Cet.AT 0328*
☆ K. Schmitt-Walter (B) (*RadT.A195T*)

Im Abendroth (Lappe) D.799   ☐
K. Flagstad (S), G. Moore (pf.)   **G.DB 21554**
(Frühlingsglaube)
☆ W. Ludwig (T), M. Raucheisen (pf.) (♭ *Pol. 32033*)

(Der) Jüngling und der Tod (Spaun) D.545 ☐
☆ W. Ludwig (T), M. Raucheisen (pf.) (♭ *Pol. 32033*)

(Der) König in Thule, Op. 5, No. 5 (Goethe) D.367
K. Borg (Bs), M. Raucheisen (pf.)   *Pol. 62914*
(An die Leyer)   (in ♯ *17004*)

(Der) Kreuzzug (Leitner) D.932   ☐
♄ S. Onegin (A) (in ♯ *Sca. 821**)

Lachen und Weinen, Op. 59, No. 4 (Rückert)
D.777 ☐
I. Seefried (S), E. Werba (pf.)   in ♯ **Pol. 19050**
(Auf dem Wasser zu singen, etc.)   (♯ AmD.DL 9809)
☆ K. Flagstad (S) (*JpV.SF 724*)

(Der) Leyermann (W.24)   ☐
☆ E. Gerhardt (M-S) (*JpV.ND 535*)

(Der) Lindenbaum (W.5)   ☐
G. Pechner (B)   in ♯ **Roy. 1557**
T. Kuuzik (B, *Estonian*) (in ♯ *USSR.D 2091*)
☆ E. Gerhardt (*JpV.ND 461*)

— ARR. CHORUS
Obernkirchen Children's Cho.—Möller (in ♯ *Od.OLA 1007;*
Angel. 64008, d.c.; ♭ *Od.OBL 1060*)
Hamburg Liedertafel Cho.—Müller-Lampertz
(*TV.VE 9044*: ♭ *D.UX 4590*)
Young Vienna—Lehner (in ♯ *AudC. 1093*)
— ARR. FL., CL., HRN., VLC. & PF.: in G.C 4252

Litaney (Jacobi) D.343   ☐
(Auf das Fest Aller Seelen)
E. Schwarzkopf (S), G. Moore (pf.)
in ♯ **C.CX 1044**
(Wolf, Brahms, etc.)   (in ♯ FCX 182; Angel. 35023)
B. Loewenfalk (B), K. Olssen (pf.)   *G.X 8149*
(An die Musik)
G. Fleischer (S), N. Prahl (pf.)   *Phi.P 55038H*
(Weyse: The night is so still & Now all God's birds...)
— ARR. PF.   Cortot
A. Cortot (in JpV. set JAS 270 & in ♯ *LS 105*)
— ARR. PF.[1]   Liszt, *q.v.*, Section A.III.6
— ARR. ORGAN: C. Cronham (*Mjr. 5118*)
— ARR. VLA. & ORG.   Primrose
W. Primrose & V. de Tar (in ♯ *AmC.AL 33*)

(Des) Mädchens Klage, Op. 58, No. 3 (Schiller)
D.191
J. Atty (A, *Fr*), C. Verzieux (pf.)   ♭ *Pat.D 119*
(Tod und das Mädchen)

(Der) Musensohn, Op. 92, No. 1 (Goethe) D.764 ☐
I. Kolassi (M-S), J. Bonneau (pf.)
in ♯ **Lon.LL 747**
(† *Arie Antiche & German Lieder*)   (♯ D.FAT 173160)
D. Gramm (Bs), R. Cumming (pf.)
in ♯ **ML. 7033**
(*Cesti, Martini, Wolf, etc.*)

Nacht und Träume, Op. 43, No. 2 (Collin) D.827 ☐
G. Fleischer (S), K. Olssen (pf.)   *Phi.N 56000H*
(*Brahms: Jäger & Wiegenlied*)
R. Hayes (T), R. Boardman (pf.) in ♯ **A440. 12-3**
S. Schöner (S), F. Schröder (pf.)   *Eta. 120146*
(*An die Nachtigall & Du bist die Ruh'*) (in ♯ LPM 1011)

Nachtviolen (Mayrhofer) D.752   ☐
E. Schumann (S), L. Rosenek (pf.)   **G.DB 21571**
(½s—*An die Geliebte; & Brahms: Ruhe, Süssliebchen*)
(o.n. *DB 3598*)[2]

(Der) Neugierige (SM.6)   ☐
G. Vinogradov (T, *Russ*) (*USSR. 18973*)

Orpheus (Jacobi) D.474 1816
♄ H. Rehkemper (B) (in ♯ *Sca. 809**)

(Die) Post (W.13)   ☐
— FOR PRACTICE, pf. acc. P. Ulanowsky (in ♯ *Bo.B 502*)

Prometheus (Goethe) D.674
K. Borg (Bs), M. Raucheisen (pf.)   **PV. 72381**
(*Grenzen der Menschheit*)
H. H. Wunderlich (B), M. Görgen (pf.)
(Schatzgräber)   *Eta. 20-143*

(Das) Rosenband (Klopstock) D.280   ☐
☆ G. Hüsch (B) (in ♯ *JpV.LS 2006*)

(Der) Schatzgräber (Goethe) D.256 1815
H. H. Wunderlich (B), M. Görgen (pf.)
(Prometheus)   *Eta. 20-143*

Sehnsucht (unspec.)
N. Kazantseva (*Russ*) (*USSR. 21080*)

Seligkeit (Hölty) D.433   ☐
I. Seefried (S), E. Werba (pf.)   *PV. 36109*
(*Ave Maria & Rosamunde, excpt.*)(o.n. 46007: ♭ Pol. 30128)
(with *Reger, Wolf & Cornelius* in ♯ AmD.DL 7545)
☆ E. Schwarzkopf (S) (*C.LN 9*)

(Die) Stadt (SG.11—Heine)   ☐
M. Vitale (S, *Ital*), A. Beltrami (pf.)
(Doppelgänger)   *Cet.AT 0327*

Ständchen (SG.4)   ☐
N. Hofman (S) & orch.   **ArgOd. 66045**
(*Nozze di Figaro, No. 27*)   (♭ *BSOAE 4505*)
I. B. Lucca (S, *Ital*), Cho. & orch. (*Dur.AI 10463:*
♭ *AI 6021* & in ♯ *MSE 6*)
L. S. Vela (B, *Sp*) (in ♯ *MusH.LP 5003*)
☆ R. Tauber (in ♯ *P.PMB 1006*)
K. Schmitt-Walter (B) (*AusT.M 5213*)
B. Gigli (T) & orch. (♭ *G.7EB 6013*)
T. Schipa (T, *Ital*) (in ♯ *G.QBLP 5030: FKLP 7009:*
♭ *7ERQ 117: 7RQ 3037*)
G. Thill (T, *Fr*) (in ♯ *C.FHX 5012;* Angel.C 33001)
C. Kullman (T, *Eng*) (in ♯ *C.SED 5524:* SEDQ 607)
G. Moore (S, *Eng*) (in ♯ *B.LAT 8025;* ♭ AmD.ED 3504)
J. Peerce (T, *Eng*) (♭ *Vic.ERA 196*)
♄ C. Vezzani (in ♯ *Od.ODX 126**)
H. Rehkemper (in ♯ *Sca. 809**)

ARRANGEMENTS
CHORUS: Vienna Boys' Cho.—Kühbacher (pf.)
(in ♯ *Phi.S 06066R*)
VLN. & ORCH.   Anderson
N. Milstein & Vic. Sym.—Fiedler (♭ *DV. 26009;*
Vic.ERA 77)
PF. Liszt, *q.v.*, Section A.III.6
ORCH.:   Argentine Radio—Bandini (ArgOd. 66045)
▽ Melachrino Strings (*G.B 9580:* in ♯ *DLP 1083;*
in ♯ *Vic.LPM 1003*)
GUITAR: L. Almeida (in ♯ *Crl. 56049*)

(Der) Tod und das Mädchen, Op. 7, No. 3
(Claudius) D.531   ☐
M. Powers (A), F. la Forge (pf.) in ♯ **Atl. 1207**
(*Erlkönig; Bach, Haydn, Handel, etc.*)
J. Atty (A, *Fr*), C. Verzieux (pf.)   ♭ *Pat.D 119*
(*Des Mädchens Klage*)

---

[1] The Cortot recording (n.v.) on G.DB 21618, etc., is listed as this arrangement, although the o.v. was ARR. Cortot.   It is not clear how they differ.   The recent Japanese recording is said to be Cortot's arr.
[2] Projected but not issued.

Ungeduld (SM.7) □
E. Schwarzkopf (S), G. Moore (pf.)
in ♯ **C.CX 1044**
(above, Wolf, etc.)   (in ♯ PCX 182; Angel. 35023)
— FOR PRACTICE, pf. acc.   P. Ulanowsky (in ♯ *Bo.B 502*)

(Der) Wanderer, Op. 4, No. 1 (Schmidt)
D.493 □
H. H. Wunderlich (B), M. Görgen (pf.)
(An die Leyer)   ***Eta. 20-142***
M. Reizen (Bs, *Russ*) (*USSRM.D 00951*)

(Das) Wandern (SM.1) □
G. Vinogradov (T *Russ*) (*USSR. 18972*)
M. Reizen (Bs, *Russ*) (*USSR. 20568: USSRM.D 00952*)
— ARR. CHO.
Hamburg Liedertafel & Orch.—Müller-Lampertz
(T.VE 9044: ♭ UX 4590)
Vienna Boys' Cho.—Kühbacher (in ♯ *Phi.S 06606R*)
... Excerpt — ARR. FL., CL., HRN., VLC. & PF. in G.C 4252

Wasserfluth (W.6) □
☆ E. Gerhardt (JpV.NS 321)

(Der) Wegweiser (W.20) □
☆ E. Gerhardt (M-S) (JpV.ND 535)

Wiegenlied, Op. 98, No. 2 (Claudius) D.498
(Schlafe, Schlafe ...)
J. Warren (Tr.), J. Lee (pf.) in ♯ **Queens.LPR 21**
(Ave Maria, Balfe, Massenet, etc.)
C. Lynch (T, *Eng*), E. Bossart (pf.) (in ♯ AmC.RL 3016)
M. Santreuil (S, *Fr*) (♭ *POc.A 03*)
☆ I. Seefried (S) (*C.LO 81*)
— ARR. VLN. & PF.
W. Tworek & E. Vagning   *Pol.HA 70044*
(Beethoven: Minuet)

Wohin? (SM.2)
R. Hayes (T), R. Boardman (pf.) in ♯ **A440. 12-3**
Soloist of Vienna Boys' Cho. in ♯ *Phi.S 06066R*
— ACCOMPANIMENT, etc., for practice (in ♯ *VS.ML 3001*)

Excerpts of accompaniments (various)
G. Moore (pf.) as illustrations to lecture
The Unashamed Accompanist (♯ C.SX 1043; Angel. 35262)

MISCELLANEOUS
Schubert, his life, his time, his music
D. Randolph (narr.)   ♯ *Per.PCS 5*

SCHÜTKY, Franz Joseph (1817–1893.)
SEE: † FIVE CENTURIES OF CHORAL MUSIC

SCHÜTZ, Heinrich (1585–1672)
REFERENCES TO:
GK=Geistliche Konzerte, 1636 & 1639
GG=Geistliche Gesänge, 1657
CS=Cantiones Sacrae, 1625
MC=Musicalia ad Chorum Sacrum (Geistliche Chormusik), 1648
SS=Symphoniae Sacrae, 1629, 1647, 1650

COLLECTIONS
MADRIGAL: Io moro *(Ich sterbe)* Bk. I, 1611, No. 13
(Vol. IX, GA)
MOTETS: Also hat Gott die Welt geliebt (MC.12)
Das ist je gewisslich wahr (MC.20)
Der Engel sprach (MC.27)
Selig sind die Toten (MC.23)
DIE SIEBEN LETZTEN WORTE 1645
☆ Soloists, Vienna Acad. Cho. & Sym. Orch.
—Grossmann   ♯ EVox.PL 6860

Eile mich, Gott, zu erretten (GK.I.1)
Was hast du verwirket (GK.II.2)
O Jesu, nomen dulce (GK.II.3)
Ich danke dem Herrn (GK.I.3)
O süsser, O freundlicher, O gütiger Herr (GK.I.4)
Ich liege und schlafe (GK.II.5)
O misericordissime Jesu (GK.II.4)
Die Furcht des Herrn (GK.II.13)
W. Hess (T), P. Matthen (Bs), J. Beaven (org.)
[ed. Mendel]   ♯ REB. 10

Bringt her dem Herren (GK.I.2)
Eile mich, Gott, zu erretten (GK.I.1)
Herr, unser Herrscher! (SS.II.3)
Ich danke dir, Herr (SS.II.7)
Ich werde nicht sterben (SS.II.6)
Ich will den Herren loben allezeit (GK.II.1)
Mein Herz ist bereit (SS.II.1)
O süsser, O freundlicher (GK.I.4)
☆ H. Cuénod (T) & Ens.—Pinkham   ♯ Nix.WLP 5043

Ich weiss, dass mein Erlöser lebet (MC) 7 vv.
Die Worte der Einsetzung des heiligen Abendmahls:
Unser Herr Jesus Christus (GG) 4 vv.
☆ Stuttgart Cho. Soc.—Grischkat   ♯ Cpt.MC 20036
(Mozart: Kyrie & Offertory)

Attendite, popule meus (SS.I.14)
Fili mi, Absolon (SS.I.13)
J. Greindl (Bs), 4 trombones & org. ♭ *Pol. 37012*

(Die) Auferstehungs-Historie Oratorio 1623
E. Majkut (T), K. Greisel (B), G. Schuster-Burgstaller (A), G. Maran (T),
K. Schmidinger (Bs), Salzburg Mozarteum Cha. Cho. & Inst. Ens.—Hinreiner ♯ **CFD. 10**

Eile mich, Gott, zu erretten (GK.I.1)
S. Danco (S), J. Demessieux (org.)
in ♯ **D.LX 3113**
(Bach, Durante, Caccini, etc.)   (♯ Lon.LS 698)
☆ M. Meili (T) & org. (in † ♯ HS.AS 7)

(Die) Furcht des Herrn (GK.II.13)
☆ M. Meili (T), Y. le Marc' Hadour (B) & org.
(in † ♯ HS.AS 7)

Herr, unser Herrscher! (SS.II.3)
☆ Y. Tinayre (T), org. & str. orch.   in ♯ AmD.DL 9653
(† Seven Centuries of Sacred Music) (in set DX 120)

MUSIKALISCHE EXEQUIEN 1636
1. Concert in Form einer deutschen Begräbnis-Missa
(a) Nacket bin ich ...   (b) Also hat Gott ...
2. Motet: Herr, wenn ich nur dich habe
3. Nunc Dimittis
E. Lindermeier & A. Seitz (S), R. Michaelis (A),
F. Brückner-Rüggeberg & R. Gautner (T),
B. Hanson & M. Proebstl (Bs), Munich
Schütz Cho.—Richter   ♯ **HP.APM 14023**
(♯ AmD.ARC 3006)
[H. Wiesmeier (org.), O. Uhl (gamba) F. Ortner (cbs)]

O Herr, hilf (SS.III.5)
E. Brems (S), V. Garde (M-S), A. Schiøtz (T),
2 vlns., vlc. & org.   in ♯ **HS.HSL 2072**
(† Masterpieces of Music before 1750)
(& in † Histoire de la Musique vocale)

PASSION MUSIC
JOHANNES-PASSION T, T, B, Cho. 1665
☆ Soloists & Stuttgart Cho.—Grischkat (♯ Eli.PLPE 5001)

MARCUS-PASSION c. 1623
EXCERPTS in *French*
R. Nargys (T), A. Doniat (B), E. Bousquet (Bs),
J. Hochart (B), Alauda Cho.—Chailley
♯ ***SM. 33-07***
(Anon. XVth Cent.: Réveillez-vous, Picards; & Ibert, Daunais, etc.)

MATTHÄUS-PASSION
... Final Chorus: Ehre sei dir, Christe
St. Paul's Cath. Cho. (*Eng*)—Dykes Bower
in ♯ **C.CX 1237**
(Stanford, Mendelssohn, Gibbons, etc.)
(♯ Angel 35139, in set 3516)

Saul, Saul, was verfolgst du mich? (SS.III.Pt.ii.9)
S, A, T, T, B, B
E. McLoughlin, A. Pearman, H. Krebs, A.
Hepworth, S. Joynt, N. Walker, Cho., Orch.
& Org.—Goldsbrough   **G.HMS 53**
(† History of Music in Sound) (in ♯ Vic. set LM 6030)

Schaffe in mir, Gott, ein reines Herz (GK.I.10)
☆ Mme. Suter-Moser (S), M. Meili (T) & org.
(in † ♯ HS.AS 7)

♯ = Long-playing, 33⅓ r.p.m.   ♭ = 45 r.p.m.   ♮ = Auto. couplings, 78 r.p.m.

Selig sind die Toten (MC.24)
☆ Basle Cha. Cho.—Sacher   in † V♯ AS. 1802LD
                                      (& in ♯ HS.AS 7)

(Die) SIEBEN WORTE c. 1645 (Vol.I.GA)
Darnach als Jesus wusste A, T, T, B
J. Whitworth, H. Krebs, A. Hepworth, S. Joynt,
  Orch. & Org.—Westrup   G.HMS 53
(† History of Music in Sound) (in ♯ Vic. set LM 6030)

WEIHNACHTSHISTORIE Oratorio 1664
G. Weber (S), H. Hess (T), P. Gümmer (Bs),
  Frankfurt Church of the Magi Cho. &
  Detmold Coll. Mus. Ens.—K. Thomas
                                ♯ LOL.OL 50020
[H. Drewanz (hpsi.), K. Storck (vlc.)]   (♯ OL.LD 98)

Wie lieblich sind deine Wohnungen (Psalm 84)
2 4-pt. chos. c. 1619
Berlin Motet Cho. & Brass Ens.—Arndt
                                T.VE 9046
(Praetorius: Mitten wir im Leben sind)   (♭ UV 117)

SCHULTZ, Svend Simon (b. 1913)

(Une) Amourette. fl., ob., cl., bsn., hrn.
☆ Copenhagen Wind Quintet   ♯ Mer.MG 15046
(Nielsen)

Serenade for strings 1940
Danish State Radio Str.—Tuxen   ♯ D.LX 3101
(Nielsen: Helios Overture)   (♯ Lon.LS 653)

SCHUMAN, William Howard (b. 1910)

American Festival Overture orch. 1939
☆ A.R.S. Sym.—Hendl   ♯ ARS. 115
(Sessions & Harris)

George Washington Bridge Impression, Band 1950
Eastman Wind Ens.—Fennell ♯ Mer.MG 40006
(Persichetti, Gould, Bennett, Piston, Barber) (♭ EP 1-5062)

SYMPHONIES
No. 5 Str. orch. 1943
Pittsburgh Sym.—Steinberg[1] ♯ DCap.CTL 7039
(Bloch)   (♯ Cap.S 8212; T.LCE 8212; PFCM.CB 152)

No. 6 (in one movement) 1948
Philadelphia—Ormandy   ♯ AmC.ML 4992
(Piston)

Undertow: Choreographic Episodes from the Ballet
  1945
Ballet Theatre—Levine   ♯ DCap.CTL 7040
(Copland)   (♯ Cap.P 8238; ACap.CLCX 047)

Voyage 5 pieces pf. [or cha. orch.] 1953
B. Webster (Thomson)   ♯ AmC.ML 4987

SCHUMANN, Clara (1819-1896)

Trio, G minor, Op. 17 pf., vln., vlc.
☆ J. Mannes, B. Gimpel, L. Silva   ♯ B.AXTL 1019
(Beethoven)   (♯ D.UAT 273071)

SCHUMANN, Robert (1810-1856)

CLASSIFIED: I. Piano
             II. Chamber Music
            III. Orchestral
             IV. Songs

I. PIANO
(including Pedal piano, pf. duet, 2 pfs.)

Abendlied, Op. 85, No. 12 pf. duet
— ARR. VLC. & PF.
☆ S. Popoff (in ♯ Vien.LPR 1022)
E. Mainardi (PV. 36110: ♭ Pol. 32103)
— ARR. ORCH.
F.F.B. Orch.—Dobrindt (C.DW 5265: DV 1644)
Regent Sym. (in ♯ Rgt. 7005)

ALBUM FÜR DIE JUGEND, Op. 68
COMPLETE RECORDING
P. Zeitlin   ♯ Opus. 6004
[with Matching Music Book, pub. E. Marks Co., N.Y.]

COLLECTIONS
No. 8, Wilder Reiter   No. 9, Volksliedchen
No. 10, Fröhlicher Landmann   No. 11, Sicilianisch
No. 12, Knecht Ruprecht   No. 14, Kleine Studie
No. 15, Frühlingsgesang   No. 16, Erster Verlust
No. 17, Kleiner   No. 18, Schnitterliedchen
     Morgenwanderer   No. 19, Kleine Romanze
No. 20, Ländliches Lied   No. 23, Reiterstück
No. 25, Nachklänge aus dem   No. 28, Erinnerung
         Theater   No. 29, Fremder Mann
No. 31, Kriegslied   No. 32, Sheherazade
No. 33, Weinlesezeit-Fröhliche No. 35, Mignon
         Zeit!   No. 36, Lied italienischer
No. 37, Matrosenlied   Marinari
No. 39, Winterszeit I   No. 40, Winterszeit II
H. Boschi   ♯ Cpt.MC 20074
No. 2, Soldatenmarsch   No. 6, Armes Waisenkind
No. 7, Jägerliedchen   No. 8, Wilder Reiter
No. 10, Fröhlicher Landmann   No. 12, Knecht Ruprecht
No. 16, Erster Verlust
A. Dorfmann   ♯ Vic.LM 1856
(Tchaikovsky)
No. 10, Fröhlicher Landmann J. Öian (♭ Nera.EP 12000)
No. 16, Erster Verlust A. d'Arco   in Plè.P 102
No. 28, Erinnerung E. Burton   in ♯ CEd.CE 1025

ALBUMBLÄTTER, Op. 124
... No 1, Impromptu; 2, Leides Ahnung; 3, Scherzino;
  4, Walzer; 5, Fantasietanz
L. Lessona   ♯ Fnt.LP 313
(Allegro & Romances)

Allegro, B minor, Op. 8
L. Lessona   ♯ Fnt.LP 313
(Albumblätter & Romances)

Andante & Variations, B flat major, Op. 46 2 pfs.
E. Bartlett & R. Robertson   ♯ MGM.E 3027
(Brahms)
☆ P. Luboshutz & G. Nemenoff (in ♯ Cam.CAL 206)

Arabeske, C major, Op. 18
Y. Nat   ♯ DFr. 128
(Kinderszenen, Papillons, Romance, Toccata)(♯ HS.HSL 143)
(Romances & Toccata only, ♯ DFr. 58)
J. Demus   ♯ West.WN 18061[2]
(Blumenstück, Faschingsschwank & Variations)
G. Puchelt   ♯ Imp.ILP 129
(Kinderszenen, Fantasiestücke excpts., etc.)
V. Sofronitsky   USSRM.D 001226
(Liszt: Sonetto del Petrarca 123)
O. Willumsen (2ss)   Eta. 20-16
☆ A. Rubinstein (♭ G.7RQ 3015)
  J. Iturbi (♭ Vic.ERA 87)

Blumenstück, D flat major, Op. 19
J. Demus   ♯ West.WN 18061[2]
(Faschingsschwank, etc.)
M. Pressler   ♯ MGM.E 3029
(Romances; & Mendelssohn)

BUNTE BLÄTTER, Op. 99 ... Nos. 1-8
☆ C. Haskil   ♯ EPhi.ABL 3029
(Schubert: Sonata No. 21)   (♯ Epic.LC 3031)

Carnaval, Op. 9
A. Cortot   ♯ G.ALP 1142
(Études symphoniques)   (♯ QALP 10065: FALP 321)
(Chopin on ♯ Vic.LHMV 18)
G. Anda   ♯ C.CX 1283
(Kreisleriana)   (♯ Angel. 35247)
A. Rubinstein   ♯ Vic.LM 1822
(Franck)   (♯ FV.A 630214; ItV.A12R 0016)
B. Siki (Chopin)   ♯ P.PMA 1022
A. Foldes (2ss)   ♯ HP.DG 16108
A. de Lara   ♯ AdL.LP 2
(Faschingsschwank aus Wien)

(continued on next page)

[1] Performance at Pittsburgh Contemporary Music Festival, 1952.   [2] Announced, but not issued, as WL 5410.

Carnaval, Op. 9 (*continued*)

E. Kilenyi (*Chopin*)	♯ **Rem. 199-165**
M. Tagliaferro (2ss)	♯ *Phi.N 00647R*
M. Barthel	♯ **Aphe.AP 25**
(*Debussy & Liszt*)	
☆ P. Badura-Skoda (*Sonata No. 1*)	♯ **Nix.WLP 5105**
☆ W. Gieseking	♯ **AmC.ML 4772**
(*Mozart*)	(*Schubert* on ♯ C.FCX 373)
☆ G. Anda (*Études symphoniques*)	♯ **DT.LGX 66029**
☆ A. Brailowsky	♯ **G.ALP 1168**
(*Fantasia*)	(4ss, BrzV. 12-3830/1)
☆ G. Novâes (♯ EVox.PL 7830)	
... Unspec. excerpt(s) A. d'Arco	in *Plé.P 102*

— ARR. ORCH. Glazounov

Philharmonia—Irving	♯ **G.CLP 1013**
(*Chopin*)	(♯ QCLP 12007: FELP 118)
(*Delibes* on ♯ BB.LBC 1025: ♭ *set WBC 1025*)	
☆ L.P.O.—Goossens (♯ Cam.CAL 193 & in ♯ *set CFL 102*)	
... Nos. 1,[1] 14, 15	
☆ Covent Garden—Braithwaite (in ♯ P.PMC 1008)	
... Excerpts ☆ Royal Phil.—Kurtz (♭ *AmC.A 1579*)	

Davidsbündlertänze, Op. 6

J. Demus	♯ **Nix.WLP 5232**
(*Papillons*)	(♯ West.WL 5232)
A. de Lara (*below*)	♯ **AdL.LP 1**
J. Battista (2ss)	♯ **MGM.E 3011**
W. Gieseking[2] (2ss)	♯ **Ura. 7106**
M. Tipo	♯ **Cpt.MC 20020**
(*Bloch, Rameau, R. Strauss*)	
F. Wührer	♯ **AmVox.PL 8860**
(*Sonata No. 2*)	

(12) Études symphoniques, Op. 13

J. Katchen	♯ **D.LXT 2869**
(*Franck*)	(♯ Lon.LL 823)
Y. Boukoff[3]	♯ *EPhi.NBR 6015*
(2ss) (*Fantasia* on ♯ Epic.LC 3094)	(♯ *Phi.N 00673R*)
A. Cortot[3]	♯ **G.ALP 1142**
(*Carnaval*)	(♯ QALP 10065: FALP 321)
A. da Lara[4]	♯ **AdL.LP 3**
(*Sonata No. 3*)	
M. Hess (2ss)	♯ *G.BLP 1061*
G. Anda[5] (n.v.)	♯ **C.CX 1072**
(*Brahms*)	(♯ FCX 283; Angel. 35046)
G. Anda[5] (o.v.) (*Carnaval*)	♯ **DT.LGX 66029**
P. Badura-Skoda[6]	♯ **West.WN 18138**
(*Kinderszenen*)	
☆ M. Lympany (♯ G.QCLP 12006)	
Y. Nat (♯ HS.HSL 87)	
A. Brailowsky (♯ G.FALP 243; ItV.B12R 0096)	
... unspec. excpts. A. d'Arco (in *Plé.P 103*)	

Fantasia, C major, Op. 17

C. Curzon	♯ **D.LXT 2933**
(*Kinderszenen*)	(♯ Lon.LL 1009)
B. Moiseiwitsch	♯ **G.CLP 1017**
(*Brahms*)	
A. Foldes (2ss)	♯ *HP.DG 16076*
(*Brahms* on ♯ AmD.DL 9708)	
A. de Lara (*Romances*)	♯ **AdL.LP 6**
G. Scherzer (2ss)	♯ *P.PMD 1010*
V. Perlemuter	♯ **AmVox.PL 9190**
(*Kreisleriana*)	
☆ J. Demus (*Fantasiestücke*)	♯ **Nix.WLP 5157**
☆ A. Brailowsky (*Carnaval*)	♯ **G.ALP 1168**
☆ E. Fischer	♯ **G.FALP 267**
(*Brahms*)	(♯ Vic.LHMV 1065: ♭ *set WHMV 1065*)
G. Johannesen (2ss)	♯ *MMS. 19*
M. Schwalb (2ss)	♯ *Acad.ALP 309*
V. Freida (*Brahms*)	♯ **Ply. 12-28**
A. Fischer (*USSR. 20935/44*)	
☆ Y. Nat (♯ HS.HSL 87)	

FANTASIESTÜCKE, Op. 12
COMPLETE RECORDINGS

B. Moiseiwitsch	♯ **BB.LBC 1081**
(*Concerto, pf. & orch.*)	
K. Engel	♯ **Phi.N 00592L**
(*Faschingsschwank aus Wien*)	(♯ Epic.LC 3070)
M. Haas (2ss)	♯ *Pol. 16123*
☆ J. Demus (*Fantasia*)	♯ **Nix.WLP 5157**
☆ A. Rubinstein (♯ DV.CL 16067; G.FALP 251; ItV.A12R 0084)	
Nos. 1 & 2	
G. Puchelt	in ♯ *Imp.ILP 129*
(*Kinderszenen, etc.*)	
Nos. 2 & 3	
G. Gorini	*Cet.AT 0333*
Nos. 2 & 5	
M. v. Monnerberg	in ♯ **Her.RPL 774**
(*below; & Schubert, Chopin*)	(pte. rec.)
No. 1, Des Abends	
▽ Lazare-Lévy (JpV.SD 55)	
No. 2, Aufschwung	
E. Burton	in ♯ **CEd.CE 1025**
D. Zechlin	*Eta. 120170*
(*Kinderszenen, No. 7*)	
No. 3, Warum	
W. Backhaus[7]	in ♯ **D.LXT 2931**
(*Beethoven: Sonatas*)	
W. Backhaus[8]	in ♯ **Lon.LL 1108/9**
E. Burton	in ♯ **CEd.CE 1027**
No. 7, Traumeswirren	
S. Barere	in ♯ **Rem. 199-141**
▽ Lazare-Lévy (JpV.SD 55)	

(3) Fantasiestücke, Op. 111

A. de Lara	♯ **AdL.LP 1**
(*Davidsbündlertänze*)	

Faschingsschwank aus Wien, Op. 26

G. Thyssens-Valentin	♯ **Sel.LPG 8276**
(*Andante & Variations*)	
R. Weisz	♯ **D.LK 4063**
(*Brahms: Waltzes, Op. 39*)	(♯ Lon.LL 798)
A. de Lara (*Carnaval*)	♯ **AdL.LP 2**
K. Engel	♯ **Phi.N 00592L**
(*Fantasiestücke, Op. 12*)	(♯ Epic.LC 3070)
J. Demus	♯ **West.WN 18061[9]**
(*Arabeske, Blumenstück, Variations*)	
☆ J. Blancard (♯ CID.UM 63020)	

Humoreske, B flat major, Op. 20

J-M. Damase	♯ **LI.TWV 91041**
(*Liszt*)	(♯ D.FAT 133066)
J. Demus	♯ **Nix.WLP 5264**
(*Sonata No. 2*)	(♯ West.WL 5264)

Impromptus, C major, on a theme of Clara Wieck, Op. 5

A. Foldes	in ♯ **Mer.MG 10122**
(*Papillons, etc.*)	(♯ Clc. 6261)

(6) Intermezzi, Op. 4

G. Johannesen	♯ **Nix.CLP 1173**
(*Sonata No. 3*)	(♯ CHS.CHS 1173)
T. Nikolayeva	♯ **USSR.D 01189**
(*Chopin: Polonaise & Bolero*)	

KINDERSZENEN, Op. 15

C. Curzon	♯ **D.LXT 2933**
(*Fantasia*)	(♯ Lon.LL 1009)
G. Puchelt	♯ *Imp.ILP 129*
(*Arabeske, Vogel als Prophets, etc.*)	
G. Novâes	♯ **AmVox.PL 8540**
(*Concerto, A minor*)	
C. Haskil (*Waldszenen*)	♯ *Phi.A 00775R*

[1] Orch. Arensky.
[2] Repudiated by the artist, who took legal action restraining its circulation (in certain countries).
[3] Includes the five posthumous Études.
[4] Omits Étude No. 8.   [5] Includes Posth. Études Nos. 4 & 5.   [6] Omits No. 3.
[7] Studio recording; apparently a re-make of D.LXT 2754; Lon.LL 603 probably now contains this newer version.
[8] Carnegie Hall recital, March 30, 1954.
[9] Announced, but not issued, as WL 5410.

KINDERSZENEN, Op. 15 (*continued*)
A. Aeschbacher   (*Romances*)   ♯ *Pol. 16121*
A. de Lara   (*Kreisleriana*)   ♯ **AdL.LP 4**
C. Zecchi   ♯ **West.WN 18139**
(*Scarlatti, Bach, Mozart, Chopin*)
P. Badura-Skoda   ♯ **West.WN 18138**
(*Études symphoniques*)
S. Fiorentino   (2ss)   **V♯ *CA.MPO 5022***
J. Blancard   (*Sonata No. 3*)   ♯ **CID.UM 63021**
C. Friedberg   (*below & Brahms*)   ♯ *Zod. 1001*
S. Bianca   (4ss)   *MSB. 78006/7*
☆ W. Gieseking   ♯ *C.C 1014*
   (*Debussy*)   (♯ *FC 1025: QC 5005;* 4ss, ♮ *GQX 8045/6*)
☆ V. Horowitz   ♯ *G.ALP 1069*
   (*Chopin*)   (♯ *QALP 195*)
☆ Y. Nat (**V♯** *DFr.EX 17003* & in ♯ *DFr.* 128:
   in ♯ **HS.HSL 143**)
... Nos. 1, 3, 5, 6, 7, 9
M. v. Doren   in ♯ *Chan.MVDP 3*
... No⁻. 7, 8, 9, 13
☆ E. Dohnányi (♭ *Cum.ECR 71; Rem.REP 10;* No. 7 only,
   in ♯ *Ply.* 12-92)
... Nos. 7, 13 — ARR. ORCH.   Regent Sym. (in ♯ *Rgt.7005*)

... No. 7, Träumerei
R. Spivak   **ArgV. 66-6001**
(♯s—*Brahms: Waltz No. 15; Beethoven: Sonata 14*)
D. Zechlin   *Eta. 120170*
(*Fantasiestück, Op. 12, No. 2*)
☆ O. Frugoni (♭ *AmVox.VIP 45370*)

—— ARRANGEMENTS
VLN. & PF.:   ☆ M. Elman (♭ *DV. 26024*)
   L. Kaufmann (♭ *ACap.CEC 004*)

VLN. & ORCH.:
☆ F. Akos & Berlin Municipal Op. (♭ *T.U 45187*)

VLC. & PF.:   A. Navarra & J. Dussol (in ♯ *Od.OD 1014*)
   F. Smetana & D. Smetanova (*U.C 24390*)

ORGAN: C. Cronham (*Mjr. 5122*)
   J. Perceval (in ♯ *ArgOd.LDC 513:* ♭ *BSOAE 4518*)

CHO.: Russian State Cho.—Sveshnikov (*Eta. 130005*)

ORCH.: F.F.B. Orch.—Dobrindt (*C.DW 5265; DV 1644*)
   Orch.—Kostelanetz (♭ *AmC.A 1571;* in ♯ *C.S 1029:*
      QS 6028: FS 1043)
   Orch.—Swarowsky (in ♯ *MTW. 9*)
   International Sym.—Schneiderhann
      (in ♯ *Mae.OA 20004*)

KREISLERIANA, Op. 16
G. Anda   ♯ **C.CX 1283**
(*Carnaval*)   (♯ *Angel. 35247*)
A. de Lara   (*Kinderszenen*)   ♯ **AdL.LP 4**
V. Perlemuter   (*Fantasia*)   ♯ **AmVox.PL 9190**
W. Gieseking²   ♯ **Ura. 7107**
(*Bach: English Suite No. 6*)
☆ J. Demus   ♯ **Nix.WLP 5142**
(*Romance & Toccata*)   (♯ *Vega.C30.A 16*)

Nachtstück, F major, Op. 23, No. 4
A. Rubinstein   ♭ *Vic.ERA 203*
(*Novelette No. 1 & Romance No. 2*)
   (♭ *ItV.A72R 0022; FV.A 45210*)
E. Burton   in ♯ **CEd.CE 1025**

NOVELETTEN, Op. 21
COMPLETE RECORDING
J. Blancard   ♯ **D.LXT 5120**
   (♯ *Lon.LL 1266*)

No. 1, F major
A. Rubinstein   ♭ *Vic.ERA 203*
(*Nachtstück & Romance*)   (♭ *FV.A 95210; ItV.A72R 0022*)
E. Burton   in ♯ **CEd.CE 1027**

No. 4, D major
C. Friedberg   ♯ *Zod. 1001*
(*above & Brahms*)

Papillons, Op. 2
J. Demus   ♯ **Nix.WLP 5232**
(*Davidsbündlertänze*)   (♯ *West.WL 5232*)
A. Foldes   in ♯ **Mer.MG 10122**
(*Impromptu, Op. 5, etc.*)   (♯ *Clc. 6261*)

A. Dorfmann   ♯ **Vic.LM 1758**
(*Ravel, Mendelssohn, etc.*)   (♭ *set WDM 1758*)
P. Sancan   (*Bach*)   ♯ *FV.F 230004*
L. Gousseau   (*Brahms*)   ♯ *Plé.P 3069*
Y. Nat   ♯ **DFr. 128**
(*Arabeske, Kinderszenen, Romances, Toccata*)
   (♯ *HS.HSL 143;* 2ss, **V♯** *DFr.EX 17022*)
F. Schröder   (2ss)   *Eta. 120168/9*
☆ G. Novães (♯ *EVox.PL 7830*)
... unspec. excerpt(s)   A. d'Arco (in ♯ *Plé.P 102*)

(3) ROMANCES, Op. 28
A. de Lara   (*Fantasia, Op. 17*)   ♯ **AdL.LP 6**
Y. Nat   ♯ **DFr. 128**
(*Arabeske, Kinderszenen, Papillons, Toccata*)(♯ *HS.HSL 143*)
(*Arabeske & Toccata only,* ♯ *DFr. 58*)
A. Aeschbacher   ♯ *Pol. 16121*
(*Kinderszenen*)
L. Lessona   ♯ *Fnt.LP 313*
(*Allegro & Albumblätter*)
M. Pressler   ♯ **MGM.E 3029**
(*Blumenstück; & Mendelssohn*)

... No. 2, F sharp major
A. Rubinstein   ♭ *Vic.ERA 203*
(*Nachtstück & Novelette No. 1*) (♭ *ItV.A72R 0022;*
   FV.A 95210)
J. Iturbi   in ♯ *Vic.LRM 7057*
(*Granados, Debussy, Chopin, etc.*)   (♭ *set ERB 7057*)
A. S. Rasmussen   *Tono.A 197*
(*Schubert: Impromptu, Op. 142, No. 3*) (♭ *EP 45052, d.c.*)
M. v. Monnerberg   ♯ *Her.RPL 774*
(*Fantasiestücke, Waldszene; & Schubert, Chopin*)   (pte.)
K. Baekkelund   *G.AL 3286*
(*Albeniz: Malagueña*)
☆ J. Demus   (*below*)   in ♯ *Nix.WLP 5142*
   (♯ *Véga.C30.A 16*)

(4) Sketches, Op. 58   pedal pf.
— ARR. ORGAN
R. Ellsasser   ♯ **MGM.E 3007**
(*Mendelssohn: Sonata No. 2*)

... No. 2, C major
A. E. Floyd (org.)   ♯ **Spot.SC 1002**
(*Handel, Bach, Purcell, Wesley*)

SONATAS
No. 1, F sharp minor, Op. 11
M. Tagliaferro   ♯ *Sel.LA 1001*
A. Brailowsky   ♯ **Vic.LM 1918**
(*Schubert, Weber, Mendelssohn*)
☆ P. Badura-Skoda   (*Carnaval*)   ♯ **Nix.WLP 5105**

No. 2, F minor, Op. 14   "*Concert sans orchestre*"
F. Wührer   ♯ **AmVox.PL 8860**
(*Davidsbündlertänze*)
☆ R. Goldsand (♯ *Clc. 6270*)

No. 3, G minor, Op. 22
J. Demus   ♯ **Nix.WLP 5264**
(*Humoreske*)   (♯ *West.WL 5264*)
A. de Lara   ♯ **AdL.LP 3**
(*Études symphoniques*)
G. Johannesen   ♯ **Nix.CLP 1173**
(*Intermezzo*)   (♯ *CHS.CHS 1173*)
J. Blancard   ♯ **CID.UM 63021**
(*Kinderszenen*)

... Presto passionato (original finale)
A. Vederenikov (*USSR. 22714/5*)

STUDIES
(6) STUDIES, Op. 3   (after Paganini)
   1. A minor   4. B flat major
   2. E major   5. E flat major
   3. C major   6. G minor
F. Wührer   ♯ **E. & AmVox.PL 8850**
(*Brahms & Liszt*)

---

² Repudiated by the artist, who took legal action restraining its circulation (in certain countries).

(6) In Canon-form, Op. 56 (for pedal-piano)
... No. 4, A flat major
  L. Hungerford   in ♯ **LH. 101/2**
                             (Pte.)
... No. 5, B minor — ARR. ORGAN
  R. Ellsasser   ♯ **MGM.E 3007**
  (above & Mendelssohn)
  ☆ C. Snyder (in ♯ Word.W 4003)

Toccata, C major, Op. 7
  Y. Nat   ♯ **DFr. 128**
  (Arabeske, Kinderszenen, Papillons, Romances)
  (Arabeske & Romances only, ♯ DFr. 58) (♯ HS.HSL 143)
  S. Barere   in ♯ **Rem. 199-141**
                      (♯ Cum.CR 280)
  S. François   ♭ **C.ESBF 113**
  (Prokofiev: Toccata)
  ☆ J. Demus   in ♯ **Nix.WLP 5142**
  (above)   (♯ Véga.C30.A 16)
  ☆ A. Foldes (in ♯ Clc. 6261; ♭ FMer.MP 14513;
                Mer.EP 1-5017; Nera.KA 7501)
  J. Lhevinne (in ♯ Cam.CAL 265)
  G. Sandor (ArgC. 266537, d.c.)

Variations on the name "Abegg", Op. 1
  H. Roloff   **PV. 36115**
  J. Demus   ♯ **West.WN 18061[9]**
  (Arabeske, Blumenstück, Faschingsschwank)
  ☆ A. Foldes (in ♯ Clc. 6261; ♭ FMer.MEP 14513;
                Mer.EP 1-5017)

WALDSZENEN, Op. 82
COMPLETE RECORDING
  C. Haskil (Kinderszenen)   ♯ **Phi.A 00775R**

No. 7, Vogel als Prophet
  E. Burton   in ♯ **CEd.CE 1027**
  G. Puchelt   in ♯ **Imp.ILP 129**
  M. v. Monnerberg (pte.)   in ♯ **Her.RPL 774**
  ☆ A. Cortot (in ♯ G.ALP 1197: QALP 10080)
  G. Sandor (ArgC. 266537)
  — ARR. VLN. & PF. Heifetz
  I. Stern & A. Zakin (in ♯ AmC.AL 23; Phi.S 06617R)
  ☆ Z. Francescatti & M. Lanner (in ♯ EPhi.NBL 5010;
                      Phi.N 02101L)

II. CHAMBER MUSIC

Adagio & Allegro, A flat major, Op. 70
  horn (or vlc.) & pf.
  D. Brain (hrn.) & G. Moore   **C.DX 1867**
  A. Janigro (vlc.) & E. Bagnoli ♯ **West.WN 18016**
  (below & Schubert)
  A. Schmidt (vlc.) & C. Fannière   ♯ **Vill. 1**
  (Eccles, Beethoven, etc.)

Andante & Variations, B flat major, Op. 46
  2 pfs., 2 vlcs., hrn.
  J-M. Damase & R. Boutry, J. Hugot &
    M. Recasens, P. Delvescovo ♯ **Sel.LPG 8276**
  (Faschingsschwank aus Wien)

(3) Fantasiestücke, Op. 73 cl. or vlc. & pf.
  A. v. Bavier (cl.), A. Wasowsky ♯ **Pol. 16102**
  (below)
  J. Lancelot (cl.) & A. d'Arco **V♯ DO.LD 27**
  (Weber: Variations, Op. 33)
  M. Gendron (vlc.) & J. Françaix ♯ **D.LXT 2857**
  (below & Schubert)   (♯ D.FAT 173073; Lon.LL 654)
  A. Janigro (vlc.) & E. Bagnoli ♯ **West.WN 18016**
  (above, below & Schubert)

Märchenbilder, Op. 113 vla. & pf.
  E. & L. Wallfisch   ♯ **Od.ODX 140**
  (Mendelssohn & Schubert)
  ... No. 4, only
  W. Müller & A. Wasowski   ♯ **Pol. 16102**
  (above & below)

Marchenerzählungen, Op. 132 cl., vla., pf.
  A. v. Bavier, W. Müller, A. Wasowski
  (above)   ♯ **Pol. 16102**

QUARTETS, Strings, Op. 41
No. 1, A minor
No. 3, A major
  ☆ Curtis Qtt.   ♯ **Nix.WLP 5166**
No. 2, F major
No. 3, A major
  New Music Qtt.   ♯ **AmC.ML 4982**

QUARTET, E flat major, pf. & str., Op. 47
  M. Horszowski, A. Schneider, M. Katims &
    F. Miller   ♯ **AmC.ML 4892**
  (Brahms)
  W. Bohle & Barchet Qtt. Members
  (Pf. Quintet)   ♯ **E. & AmVox.PL 8960**

QUINTET, E flat major, pf. & str., Op. 44
  M. Hess, I. Stern, A. Schneider, M. Thomas &
    P. Tortelier   ♯ **AmC.ML 4711**
  (Brahms)   (in set SL 182)
  (also ♯ AmC.ML 4701 in set SL 185)
  V. Aller & Hollywood Qtt.   ♯ **Cap.P 8316**
  (Hummel)
  W. Bohle & Barchet Qtt. ♯ **E. & AmVox.PL 8960**
  (Pf. Quartet, Op. 47)
  ☆ A. Rubinstein & Paganini Qtt.   ♯ **G.BLP 1031**
                    (♯ QBLP 10034)
  ☆ C. Curzon & Budapest Qtt.   ♯ **C.CX 1050**
                    (♯ QCX 10023)
  ☆ H. Kann & Pascal Qtt.   ♯ **MMS. 41**
  ☆ R. Serkin & Busch Qtt. (♯ Phi.A 01622R)
  — FOR PRACTICE: recorded lacking one inst., in turn
                    (♯ CEd.MMO 21/4)

(3) Romances, Op. 94 ob. or vlc. & pf.
  M. Gendron (vlc.) & J. Françaix ♯ **D.LXT 2857**
  (above, & Schubert) (♯ FAT 173073; Lon.LL 654)

SONATAS, vln. & pf.
No. 1, A minor, Op. 105
  R. Druian & J. Simms   ♯ **Mer.MG 80002**
  (Brahms)
  ☆ L. Kaufman & A. Balsam (♯ T.NLSB 8112)
A minor (Frei aber einsam) 1853
... **Intermezzo & Finale**[1]
  N. Milstein & C. Bussotti ♯ **DCap.CTL 7058**
  (Brahms, Pergolesi, Suk)   (♯ Cap.P 8259)
  I. Stern & A. Zakin   ♯ **EPhi.ABL 3068**
  (Brahms & Dietrich) (♯ Phi.A 01133L; AmC.ML 4913,
                      in set SL 202)

(5) Stücke im Volkston, Op. 102 vlc. & pf.
  P. Casals & L. Mannes   ♯ **AmC.ML 4718**
  (below) (also ♯ ML 4708, in set SL 185) (in set SL 184)
  A. Janigro & E. Bagnoli   ♯ **West.WN 18016**
  (above)
  ... Nos. 1, 3, 4, only
  M. Rostropovich & M. Karandazhova
                   ♯ **LI.TW 91068**
  (Tchaikovsky, Borodin, Prokofiev)

TRIOS, pf., vln., vlc.
No. 1, D minor, Op. 63
  M. Horszowski, A. Schneider, P. Casals
  (above)   ♯ **AmC.ML 4718**
  (also in ♯ ML 4708, in set SL 185) (in set SL 184)
  ☆ A. Cortot, J. Thibaud, P. Casals ♯ **Vic.LCT 1141**
  (Schubert: Trio No. 1, Op. 99)
  ☆ L. Mannes, B. Gimpel & L. Silva (♯ D.UST 253547)
No. 2, F major, Op. 80
  Bolzano Trio   ♯ **E. & AmVox.PL 8480**
  (Chopin)

III. ORCHESTRAL

CONCERTO, A minor, Op. 54, pf. & orch.
  W. Gieseking & Philharmonia—Karajan
  (2ss)   ♯ **C.C 1033**
  (Grieg on ♯ FCX 284)   (♯ QC 5020)
  J. Demus & Vienna State Op.—Rodzinski
                   ♯ **Nix.WLP 5310**
  (below) (♯ West.WL 5310; 2ss, Sel. 270.CW.079)
  W. Kempff & L.S.O.—Krips   ♯ **D.LXT 2806**
  (2ss)   (♯ Lon.LL 781)

---

[9] Announced, but not issued, as WL 5410.
[1] 2nd & 4th movts. only by Schumann; others by Brahms & Dietrich.

CONCERTO, A minor, Op. 54, pf. & orch. (*continued*)
M. Hess & Philharmonia—Schwarz
♯ *G.BLP 1039*
(2ss) (♯ *QBLP 5022;* Vic.LHMV 1062)
B. Moiseiwitsch & Philharmonia—Ackermann
♯ *G.CLP 1008*
(*Grieg*) (♯ FELP 126)
(*Fantasiestücke* on ♯ BB.LBC 1081)
G. Novães & Vienna Pro Musica—Swarowsky
(*Kinderszenen*) ♯ **AmVox.PL 8540**
N. Mewton-Wood & Netherlands Phil.—Goehr
(2ss) ♯ *MMS. 43*
E. Flissler & Little Orch. Soc.—Scherman ♯ MApp. 3
(*Analysis of the concerto—T. Scherman & Orch.*)
☆ C. Haskil & Residentie—v. Otterloo
(2ss) ♯ *EPhi.ABR 4008*
(*Liszt* on ♯ Epic.LC 3020)
☆ D. Lipatti & Philharmonia—Karajan (2ss, ♯ *C.VC 803;*
Grieg on ♯ C.FCX/QCX 322; also FCX 491)
Y. Nat & Sym.—Bigot (♯ *C.FH 506*)
C. Chailley-Richez & Austrian Sym.—Heger
(♯ Cum.CR 234; with commentary by S. Spaeth
on ♯ Rem.14)
G. Novães & Vienna Sym.—Klemperer
(♯ *Pan.XPV 1010,* 2ss)
A. Rubinstein & Vic. Sym.—Steinberg (♯ DV.L 16094)

CONCERTO, A minor, vlc. & orch., Op. 129
[1]P. Casals & Prades Fest. Orch.
♯ *EPhi.ABR 4035*
(2ss) (♯ *Phi.A 01617R*)
(*Bach, Falla, Haydn, etc.,* on ♯ AmC.ML 4926)
[2]M. Gendron & Suisse Romande—Ansermet
♯ *D.LXT 2895*
(*Tchaikovsky*) (♯ Lon.LL 947)
[2]J. Schuster & Los Angeles Orch. Soc.
—Waxman ♯ *DCap.CTL 7041*
(*J. C. Bach & Bruch*) (♯ Cap.P 8232)
E. Mainardi & R.I.A.S. Sym.—Lehmann
(*Haydn: Concerto*) ♯ **Pol. 18222**
T. Machula & Vienna Sym.—Moralt
(2ss) ♯ *Phi.S 06042R*
B. Heran & F.O.K. Sym.—Smetáček ♯ *Sup.LPM 164*
(2ss) (♯ *U. 5154C*)
D. Shafran & State Sym.—Kondrashin ♯ USSR.D 01195
(*Chopin : Variations*)
☆ G. Piatigorsky & L.P.O.—Barbirolli ♯ Vic.LCT 1119
(*Brahms*) (♭ set WCT 1119)
☆ G. Ricci & Rome Sym.—Vittori (♯ Cum.CS 193;
MTW. 528, d.c.)
M. Dorner & Stuttgart Pro Musica—R. Reinhardt[2]
(♯ EVox.PL 7680)
— FOR PRACTICE: recorded without violoncello part
(♯ CEd.MMO 304)

CONCERTO, vln. & orch., D minor ("Op. 134")
☆ P. Rybar & Lausanne Sym.—Desarzens (♯ Clc. 6224)

Fantasia, C major, Op. 131 vln. & orch.
☆ A. Stücki & Stuttgart Pro Musica—R. Reinhardt
(♯ EVox.PL 7680)

Introduction & Allegro, G major, Op. 92 pf. & orch.
J. Demus & Vienna State Op.—Rodzinski
♯ **Nix.WLP 5310**
(*above & below*) (♯ West.WL 5310)

Introduction & Allegro, D minor, Op. 134 pf. & orch
J. Demus & Vienna State Op.—Rodzinski
♯ **Nix.WLP 5310**
(*above*) (♯ West.WL 5310)
☆ W. Bohle & Stuttgart Pro Musica—R. Reinhardt
(♯ EVox.PL 7680)

MANFRED, Op. 115 Inc. Music to Byron's Play
Overture
Suisse Romande—Münchinger ♯ *D.LW 5144*
(*Gluck: Alceste Overture*) (♯ *Lon.LD 9145*)
Florence Festival—Gui ♯ **AudC. 501**
(*Brahms & Schubert*)
Residentie—Otterloo ♯ *Phi.S 06045R*
(*Beethoven*)

Leipzig Gewandhaus—Abendroth ♯ **Ura.RS 7-9**
(*Schubert: Symphony No. 8*) (♭ UREP 45)
☆ Vienna Phil.—Furtwängler ♯ *G.BLP 1009*
(*Smetana: Vltava*) (3ss—♮ G.DB 9787/9)
(♯ *FBLP 1046: QBLP 5006: VBLP 802*)
Leningrad Phil.—Eliasberg (♯ *USSR.D 1099*)
☆ N.B.C. Sym.—Toscanini (in ♯ Vic.LM 9022)

Overture, Scherzo & Finale, Op. 52 1841-5
L.S.O.—Collingwood ♯ *P.PMC 1024*
(*Brahms*) (♯ MGM.E 3102)
Paris Cons.—Schuricht ♯ *D.LXT 2985*
(*Symphony No. 3*) (♯ Lon.LL 1037)

SYMPHONIES

No. 1, B flat major, Op. 38 "Spring"
Bamberg Sym.—Keilberth ♯ *DT.LGM 65010*
(♯ *T.LS 6041*)
R.I.A.S. Sym.—Fricsay ♯ **HP.DGM 18235**
R.I.A.S. Sym.—Matzerath ♯ **Rem. 199-180**
Berlin Phil.—Kempe ♯ *G.WBLP 1512*
☆ Boston Sym.—Münch ♯ G.ALP 1203
Nat. Op. Orch. (♯ Gram. 2066)
☆ Cleveland Sym.—Leinsdorf (♯ *Phi.A 01605R; Sym.No. 4*
on ♯ AmC.ML 4794; Phi.S 04602L)

No. 2, C major, Op. 61
Cleveland Sym.—Szell ♯ **AmC.ML 4817**
(♯ *Phi.A 01616R*)
N.Y. Stadium Concerts—Bernstein
♯ *B.AXTL 1067*
(♯ AmD.DL 9715; SpC.CCL 35003; D.UMT 263582;
Pol. 18246)
☆ Minneapolis Sym.—Mitropoulos (♯ AmC.RL 3025)
Orch.—Stokowski (♯ G.FALP 206)

No. 3, E flat major, Op. 97 "Rhenish"
Paris Cons.—Schuricht[3] ♯ *D.LXT 2985*
(*Overture, Scherzo & Finale*) (♯ Lon.LL 1037)
Berlin Phil.—Leitner ♯ *HP.DG 16084*
(2ss)
Amsterdam—Zecchi ♯ *Phi.N 00721R*
(2ss) (♯ Epic.LC 3092)[4]
Vienna State Op.—Dixon ♯ **West.WL 5285**
(*No. 4*) (♯ Sel.320.CW.085)
☆ N.Y.P.S.O.—Walter ♯ *C.CX 1045*
(♯ QCX 10014)
Moscow Radio—Gauk (♯ *ACC.MP 12*)
Orch.—Swarowsky (♯ *ACC.MP 12*)
Anon. Orch. (♯ Gram. 2085)
☆ Minneapolis Sym.—Mitropoulos (♯ BB.LBC 1058;
♭ set WBC 1058)

No. 4, D minor, Op. 120
Royal Phil.—Pope[5] (2ss) ♯ *EPhi.NBR 6004*
Philharmonia—Cantelli ♯ *G.BLP 1044*
(2ss) (♯ *QBLP 5025; ArgA.LPC 10508*)
(*Wagner* on ♯ Vic.LHMV 13)
L.S.O.—Krips ♯ *D.LXT 2887*
(*Mendelssohn*) (♯ Lon.LL 930)
Berlin Phil.—Furtwängler ♯ *HP.DG 16063*
(2ss) (*Haydn: Sym. No. 88* on ♯ AmD.DL 9767)
(5ss, ♮ PV. 72361/3S)
Detroit Sym.—Paray ♯ *Mer.MG 50036*
(*Liszt*) (♯ FMer.MLP 7523)
Vienna State Op.—Dixon ♯ **West.WL 5285**
(*No. 3*) (♯ Sel.320.CW.085)
☆ Chicago Sym.—Stock (♯ AmC.RL 3026)
Cleveland Sym.—Szell (♯ *Phi.A 01603R; No. 1* on
♯ AmC.ML 4794; Phi.S 04602L)
Cincinnati Sym.—Goossens (♯ Cam.CAL 188)
French Nat. Radio—Cluytens (♯ *C.QC 1001*)
San Francisco—Monteux (♯ DV.L 16393)

---

[1] Cadenza by Casals.
[3] Mahler's re-orchestration is used.
[2] Cadenza by Schumann. The others are probably also his.
[4] Originally announced as AmC.ML 4936. [5] Original 1841 version.

IV. SONGS (LIEDER)

SONG CYCLES

DICHTERLIEBE, Op. 48 (Heine)
G. Souzay (B), J. Bonneau (pf.) (n.v.)
‡ D.LXT 2875
(*Songs—Collection*)   (‡ Lon.LL 940)
A. Dermota (T), H. Dermota (pf.)
‡ DT.LGX 66023
(*Songs—Collection*) (‡ T.LE 6522; FT.320.TC.065)
P. Munteanu (T), F. Holetschek (pf.)
(*below*)   **‡ West.WN 18010**
W. Horne (T) & pf. (2ss)   **‡ Allo. 3152**
M. Meili (T), F. de Nobel (pf.)   **‡ DFr. 47**
(2ss)
I. Kozlovsky (T, *Russ*) & pf. (2ss) ‡ *USSR*.D 1169/07
[Nos. 1, 5, 6, 7, 10, 12, 13, on *USSR*. 22670/1, 22678/9,
23058/9]
☆ W. Ludwig (T), M. Raucheisen (pf.) ‡ *HP.DG 16029*
(2ss)
☆ A. Schiøtz (T), G. Moore (pf.)   ‡ *G.BLP 1064*
(2ss)   (‡ *KBLP 7: FBLP 1074*)
  (& with *performance by* C. Panzera on ‡ Vic.LCT 1132)
☆ L. Lehmann (S), B. Walter (pf.)   ‡ *C.C 1020*
                   (‡ *FC 1034*)
  (*Frauenliebe und -Leben* on ‡ AmC.ML 4788)
☆ C. Panzera (B), A. Cortot (pf.) (‡ Vic.LCT 1132)

FRAUENLIEBE UND -LEBEN, Op. 42
(Chamisso)
S. Jurinac (S), W. Rosé (pf.) ‡ West.WL 5345
(*Liederkreis*)
K. Flagstad (S), E. McArthur (pf.) ‡ *G.ALP 1191*
(*R. Strauss, Schubert, etc.*)
             (‡ Vic.LM 1738: ♭ set *WDM 1738*)
▽ E. Gerhardt (M-S), G. Moore (pf.)   G.GS 37/9
(6ss)
☆ K. Ferrier (A), J. Newmark (pf.) ‡ *D.LW 5089*
                  (‡ *Lon.LD 9098*)
☆ E. Schumann (S), G. Moore (pf.) ‡ Vic.LCT 1126
(*Schubert*)
Z. Dolukhanova (A, *Russ*), B. Kozel (pf.)
               (‡ *USSR*.D 2143/4)
☆ L. Lehmann (S), B. Walter (pf.) (‡ AmC.ML 4788)
U. Graf (S), J. Newmark (pf.) (‡ *Allo. 4034*)

(6) GEDICHTE, Op. 90 (Lenau)
   1. Lied eines Schmiedes
   2. Meine Rose
   3. Kommen und Scheiden
   4. Die Sennerin
   5. Einsamkeit
   6. Der schwere Abend
M. Schloss (S), J. Brice (pf.)   **‡ IRCC.L 7000**
(*Wolf, Franz, R. Strauss*)

LIEDERKREIS, Op. 39 (Eichendorff)
D. Fischer-Dieskau (B), G. Moore (pf.)
‡ G.BLP 1068
(2ss) (*Schubert* in ‡ Vic. set LM 6036) (‡ *FBLP 1072*)
S. Danco (S), G. Agosti (pf.)   **‡ D.LX 3107**
[Nos. 2 & 12 only on ♭ *DV 112*] (‡ *Lon.LS 590*)
S. Jurinac (S), W. Rosé (pf.) **‡ West.WL 5345**
(*Frauenliebe und -Leben*)
P. Munteanu (T), F. Holetschek (pf.)
(*Dichterliebe*)   **‡ West.WN 18010**
W. Warfield (B), O. Herz (pf.) ‡ AmC.ML 4860
(*Brahms: 4 Ernste Gesänge*)
☆ L. Sydney (A), W. Loibner (pf.) (‡ CID.VXT 33021)
[& see note below under *Myrthen*, Boyce]

MYRTHEN, Op. 25
COMPLETE RECORDING
1. Widmung (Rückert)	**2. Freisinn** (Goethe)
3. Der Nussbaum (Mosen)	**4. Jemand** (Burns)
5. Sitz' ich allein (Goethe)	**6. Setze mir nicht** (Goethe)
7. Die Lotosblume (Heine)	**8. Talisman** (Goethe)
9. Lieder der Suleika (Goethe)	**10. Die Hochländer-Witwe**
11. Mutter, Mutter	
12. Lass mich ihm am Busen	**13. Hochländers Abschied**
hangen (Zwei Lieder	(Burns)
der Braut—Rückert)	**14. Hochländisches Wiegenlied**
15. Mein Herz ist schwer	(Burns)
(Byron)	**16. Rätsel** (Burns)

17. Leis' rudern hin (Moore)	**18. Wenn durch die Piazza**
19. Hauptmanns Weib (Burns)	(Moore)
20. Weit, weit (Burns)	**21. Was will die einsame Träne**
22. Niemand (Burns)	(Heine)
23. Im Westen (Burns)	**24. Du bist wie eine Blume**
25. Aus den östlichen Rosen	(Heine)
(Rückert)	**26. Zum Schluss** (Rückert)

P. Munteanu (T), F. Holetschek (pf.)
‡ West.WN 18006

A recording of these cycles by B. Boyce on ‡ OL.LD 26/7
has been continually listed in France for years, but apparently
does not in fact exist.

COLLECTIONS

Aufträge, Op. 77, No. 5 (L'Égru)
Erstes Grün, Op. 35, No. 4 (Kerner)
Ich wand're nicht, Op. 51, No. 3 (Christern)
Im Wald, Op. 107, No. 5 (Müller)
Die letzten Blumen starben, Op. 104, No. 6 (Kulmann)
Melancholie, Op. 74, No. 6 (Mörike)
Die Soldatenbraut, Op. 64, No. 1 (Mörike)
Die Spinnerin, Op. 107, No. 4 (Heine)
(2) Zigeunerliedchen, Op. 79, No. 7 (Geibel)
H. Glaz (S), L. Müller (pf.)   **‡ MGM.E 3055**
(*Schubert*)

An den Sonnenschein, Op. 36, No. 4 (Reinick)
Aufträge, Op. 77, No. 5 (L'Égru)
Märzveilchen, Op. 40, No. 1 (Andersen)
Stille Tränen, Op. 35, No. 10 (Kerner)
Vom Schlaraffenland, Op. 79, No. 5 (Anon.)
M. Lichtegg (T), H. W. Häusslein (pf.)
(*Beethoven*)   **‡ *Lon.LD 9183***

In der Fremde I (*Aus der Heimat*) (Eichendorff)
   (*Liederkreis*, No. 1)
Die Lotosblume, Op. 25, No. 7 (Heine)
Widmung, Op. 25, No. 1 (Rückert)
I. Kolassi (M-S), J. Bonneau (pf.)
                  in **‡ Lon.LL 747**
(† Arie Antiche & German Lieder) (‡ D.FAT 173160)

Mondnacht (Eichendorff) (*Liederkreis*, No. 5)
Der Nussbaum, Op. 25, No. 3 (Mosen)
Volksliedchen, Op. 51, No. 2 (Rückert)
E. Berger (S)   in JpV. set JAS 272

Du bist wie eine Blume, Op. 25, No. 24 (Heine)
Geständnis, Op. 74, No. 7 (Geibel, from the Spanish)
Der Nussbaum, Op. 25, No. 3 (Mosen)
Der Sandmann, Op. 79, No. 12 (Kletke)
G. Souzay (B), J. Bonneau (pf.) **‡ D.LXT 2875**
(*Dichterliebe*)   (‡ Lon.LL 940)

Widmung, Op. 25, No. 1 (Rückert)
Der Nussbaum, Op. 25, No. 3 (Mosen)
Mondnacht (Eichendorff) (*Liederkreis*, No. 5)
Die Lotosblume, Op. 25, No. 7 (Heine)
Schöne Fremde (*Liederkreis* No. 6)
A. Dermota (T), H. Dermota (pf.)
‡ DT.LGX 66023
(*Dichterliebe*)   (‡ T.LE 6522; FT.320.TC.065)
[also, except *Widmung*, on ♭ D.VD 512]

Mondnacht (Eichendorff) (*Liederkreis*, No. 5)
Schöne Wiege meiner Leiden, Op. 24, No. 5 (Heine)
Stille Tränen, Op. 35, No. 10 (Kerner)
J. Harsanyi (S), O. Herz (pf.) in **‡ Per.SPL 581**
(*Debussy, Duparc, etc.*)

DICHTERLIEBE: Nos. 1, 2, 3, 13
Der Nussbaum, Op. 25, No. 3 (Mosen)
Mondnacht (Eichendorff) (*Liederkreis*, No. 5)
Die Lotosblume, Op. 25, No. 7 (Heine)
☆ R. Tauber (T)   ‡ ChOd.LDC 36003
(*Grieg, Schubert, etc.*)

Alte Laute, Op. 35, No. 12 (Kerner)
Du bist wie eine Blume, Op. 25, No. 24 (Heine)
Frühlingsnacht (Eichendorff) (*Liederkreis*, No. 12)
Die Kartenlegerin, Op. 31, No. 2 (Chamisso)
Waldesgespräch (Eichendorff) (*Liederkreis*, No. 3)
☆ L. Lehmann (S), E. Balogh (pf.) ‡ Vic.LCT 1108
(*Brahms & Schubert*)   (♭ set WCT 1108)

Die beiden Grenadiere, Op. 49, No. 1 (Heine)
Flutenreicher Ebro, Op. 138, No. 5 (Geibel)
Talisman, Op. 25, No. 8 (Goethe)
☆ H. Schlusnus (B) (in ‡ AmD.DL 9624)

---

‡ = Long-playing, 33⅓ r.p.m.   ♭ = 45 r.p.m.   ♮ = Auto. couplings, 78 r.p.m.

(Der) Arme Peter, Op. 53, No. 3 (Heine)
1. Der Hans und die Grete: 2. In meiner Brust
3. Der arme Peter wankt vorbei
   H. H. Wunderlich (B), A. F. Guhl (pf.)
   (Ich grolle nicht)   **Eta. 20-12016**

Aufträge, Op. 77, No. 5 (L'Égru) □
   E. Schwarzkopf (S), G. Moore (pf.)
   (n.v.)   in ♯ **C.CX 1044**
   (Der Nussbaum; R. Strauss, Wolf, etc.)
                (♯ FCX 182; Angel. 35023)

Aus meinen Thränen (*Dichterliebe* 2)
   B. Gmyria (*Russ*) (*USSR. 20881*)

(Die) Beiden Grenadiere, Op. 49, No. 1 (Heine) □
   K. Borg (Bs), M. Raucheisen (pf.)
               in ♯ *Pol.* **17004**

   H. Janssen (B), S. Leff (pf.) in ♯ **Mur.P 102**
   (followed by pf. acc. only)
   A. Mestral (B, *Fr*)   ♭ *Phi.N 432012E*
   (Fauré & Schubert)
   ☆ D. Fischer-Dieskau (B) (in ♯ Vic.LHMV 1046:
           ♭ set *WHMV 1046*; ♭ *G.7RF 240*)

Du bist wie eine Blume, Op. 25, No. 24 (Heine) □
   G. Lutze (T), A. Hecker (pf.)   *Eta.* **120121**
   (Lotosblume; & Mendelssohn)   (o.n. 20-12014)
— FOR PRACTICE, pf. acc. P. Ulanowsky (in ♯ *Bo.B 502*)

Flutenreicher Ebro, Op. 138, No. 5 (Geibel) □
— ARR. GUITAR Segovia (*"Romanza"*)
   ☆ A. Segovia (in † ♯ *B.AXTL* 1060)

Frühlingsfahrt, Op. 45, No. 2 (Eichendorff)
   G. Pechner (B)   in ♯ **Roy. 1557**
   H. Prey (B), H. Heinemann (pf.) *C.DW 5369*
   (Wanderlust)   (♭ *SCMW 549*)

Frühlingsnacht (Eichendorff)
   (Liederkreis, No. 12) □
— ARR. PF. Liszt, *q.v.,* Section A.III.6

Ich grolle nicht (*Dichterliebe,* No. 7) □
   H. H. Wunderlich (B), A. F. Guhl (pf.)
   (Der arme Peter)   **Eta. 20-12016**
— FOR PRACTICE, pf. acc. P. Ulanowsky (in ♯ *Bo.B 502*)

Kinderwacht, Op. 79, No. 21 (Anon.)
— ARR. CHO. Urbanek
   H. Wallner (Tr.) & Vienna Boys' Cho.
   —Kühbacher   in ♯ **EPhi.NBR 6024**
   (Schubert, Bruckner, Mendelssohn, etc.) (♯ *Phi.N 00726R:*
              ♭ *N 402038E*)

(Die) Lotosblume, Op. 25, No. 7 (Heine) □
   G. Lutze (T), A. Hecker (pf.)   *Eta.* **120121**
   (Du bist wie eine Blume; & Mendelssohn) (o.n. 20-12014)
   H. Janssen (B), S. Leff (pf.) in ♯ **Mur.P 110**
   (followed by pf. acc. only)

Meine Rose, Op. 90, No. 2 (Lenau)
   ⚏ H. Rehkemper (B) (in ♯ *Sca.* 809*)

Mit Myrten und Rosen, Op. 24, No. 9 (Heine)
   M. Harrell (B), B. Smith (pf.) in ♯ **Rem. 199-140**

Mondnacht (Eichendorff) (*Liederkreis,* No. 5) □
   Z. Milanov (S), B. Kunc (pf.) in ♯ **Vic.LM 1915**
   (Widmung; Brahms, R. Strauss, etc.)
   ☆ D. Fischer-Dieskau (B) (in ♯ Vic.LHMV 1046:
             ♭ set *WHMV 1046*)
   L. Slezak (T) (in ♯ Ete. 493)
   ⚏ Lilli Lehmann (in ♯ Ete. 702*)
— FOR PRACTICE, pf. acc. P. Ulanowsky (in ♯ *Bo.B 502*)

(Der) Nussbaum, Op. 25, No. 3 (Mosen) □
   E. Schwarzkopf (S), G. Moore (pf.)
   (n.v.)   in ♯ **C.CX 1044**
   (Aufträge, etc.)   (♯ FCX 182; Angel. 35023)
   (Brahms: Da unten im Tale on *C.LD 6,* o.v.)
   R. Hayes (T), R. Boardman (pf.)
           in ♯ **Van.VRS 449**
   (Debussy, Moussorgsky, etc.; & Trad.)

   G. Pechner (B)   in ♯ **Roy. 1557**
   (Frühlingsfahrt; Schubert, etc.)
   G. Vinogradov (T, *Russ*) (*USSR. 8044*)
   ☆ V. de los Angeles (S) (♭ *G.7RF 276*)
   A. Dermota (T) (♭ *D.VD 512*)
   L. Slezak (T) (in ♯ Ete. 493)

Unter'm Fenster, Op. 34, No. 3 (Burns) duet
   ⚏ G. Farrar & E. Clément (*AF.AGSA 5**)

Volksliedchen, Op. 51, No. 2 (Rückert) □
   ☆ K. Ferrier (A), P. Spurr (pf.)   in ♯ *D.LW 5098*
   (Widmung; & Schubert)   (♯ *Lon.LD 9099*)

Wanderlust, Op. 35, No. 3 (Kerner)
   (*"Wanderlied"*)
   H. Prey (B), H. Heinemann (pf.) *C.DW 5369*
   (Frühlingsfahrt)   (♭ *SCMW 549*)

Widmung, Op. 25, No. 1 (Rückert) □
   Z. Milanov (S), B. Kunc (pf.) in ♯ **Vic.LM 1915**
   (Mondnacht, etc.)
   H. Janssen (B), S. Leff (pf.)   in ♯ **Mur.P 110**
   (followed by pf. acc. only)
   ☆ K. Ferrier (A), P. Spurr (pf.)   in ♯ *D.LW 5098*
   (Volksliedchen; & Schubert)   (♯ *Lon.LD 9099*)
— FOR PRACTICE, pf. acc. P. Ulanowsky (in ♯ *Bo.B 502*)

V. CHORAL

PART SONGS: COLLECTION (unacc.)

Am Bodensee, Op. 59, No. 2 (Platen)
An die Sterne, Op. 141, No. 1 (Rückert)
Brautgesang, Op. 146, No. 1 (Uhland)
Gute Nacht, Op. 59, No. 4 (Rückert)
Heidenröslein, Op. 67, No. 3 (Goethe)
Mich zieht es, Op. 55, No. 3 (Burns)
Schön Rohtraut, Op. 67, No. 2 (Mörike)
Der Schmidt, Op. 145, No. 1 (Uhland)
Talisman, Op. 141, No. 4 (Goethe)
Ungewisses Licht, Op. 141, No. 2 (Zedlitz)
Ungewitter, Op. 67, No. 4 (Chamisso)
Vom verwundeten Knaben, Op. 75, No. 5 (Trad.)
Zuversicht, Op. 141, No. 3 (Zedlitz)
   M. Couraud Cho.   ♯ **DFr. 80**
   [Op. 141 is for double Cho., the others for S, A, T, B.]

Zigeunerleben, Op. 29, No. 3 (Geibel)
   S, A, T, B & pf.
   4 soloists of Vienna Boys' Cho.—Kühbacher
   (pf.)[1]   in ♯ *Phi.S 06066R*
   (Schubert, Mozart, Lassus; & Folk Songs)

MISCELLANEOUS
Schumann, his story and his music
   D. Randolph (narr.)   ♯ *Per.PCS 8*

NOTE: Psalm 23 on ♯ Alld.LP 2002 is by Georg Schumann

SCHUYT, Cornelis (or: Scutius) (fl. 1616)
   SEE: † SACRED & SECULAR SONGS FROM THE
       RENAISSANCE

SCOTT, Cyril Meir (b. 1879)

Lotus Land, Op. 47, No. 1 pf.
   ☆ C. Scott (from a piano roll) (in ♯ Roy. 1402)
— ARR. ORGAN: R. Ellsasser (in ♯ MGM.E 3120)
— ARR. ORCH.
   Orch.—Kostelanetz (in ♯ AmC.ML 4822)
   Camarata Orch. (in ♯ AmD.DL 8112)

SONG:
(The) Unforeseen, Op. 74, No. 3 (Watson)
   K. Joyce (A), H. Greenslade (pf.)   *P.R 3804*
   (Elgar: Speak, Music)

Think on me in ♯ Mur.P 109 is by Lady John Douglas Scott
(1810-1900), composer of *Annie Laurie*

---

[1] ARR. Gomboz.

SCRIABIN, Alexander Nicolaevitch
(1872-1915)

I. PIANO SOLO

Impromptu, F sharp minor, Op. 14, No. 2
V. Sofronitsky   *USSR.D 001256*
(Mazurka, Polonaise)

MAZURKAS
Op. 3, No. 6, C sharp minor
Op. 3, No. 9, G sharp minor
S. Feinberg   *USSR. 21860/1*

Op. 25, No. 3, E minor   [called G minor]
V. Sofronitsky   *USSRM.D 001256*
(Polonaise, Impromptu)

Op. 25, No. 7, F sharp minor
S. Feinberg   *USSRM.D 001252*
(Liadov: Idylle)

Nocturne, F sharp minor, Op. 5, No. 1
— ARR. VLN. & PF.
☆ D. Oistrakh & pf. (♭ *Mer.EP 1-5008*)

Nocturne for the left hand alone, D flat major, Op. 9, No. 2
S. Sorin   ♯ *SOT. 1038*
(Chopin, Granados, Liszt)
☆ S. Weissenberg (ArgC. 266566)

Polonaise, B flat minor, Op. 21
V. Sofronitsky   *USSRM.D 001255*
(Impromptu, Mazurka)

PRELUDES
(24) PRELUDES, Op. 11
COMPLETE RECORDING of Nos. 1-12

No. 1, C major	No. 2, A minor	No. 3, G major
No. 4, E minor	No. 5, D major	No. 6, B minor
No. 7, A major	No. 8, F ♯ minor	No. 9, E major
No. 10, C ♯ minor	No. 11, B major	No. 12, G ♯ minor

V. Sofronitsky (2ss)   *USSRM.D 867/8*
[Nos. 2, 4, 5, 7 & 8 are ☆]

Nos. 5, 8, 11, 12
H. Neuhaus   *USSRM.D 001250*
(Rachmaninoff: Étude-tableau)

No. 13, G flat major
No. 14, E flat minor
☒ A. Scriabin (*USSR. 21435**)

(6) PRELUDES, Op. 13

No. 1, C major	No. 2, A minor
No. 3, G major	No. 4, E minor
No. 5, D major	No. 6, B minor ▽

COMPLETE RECORDING
H. Neuhaus (2ss)   *USSR. 022525/6*

Op. 35, No. 2, B flat major
V. Sofronitsky   *USSR. 21855*
(Glazounov: Morceau, Op. 49, No. 1)

SONATAS
No. 2, G sharp minor, Op. 19
L. Oborin   ♯ *CdM.LDA 8076*
(Tchaikovsky, Rachmaninoff, Borodin, Khachaturian)
         (& in ♯ *Csm.CRLP 224, ? d.v.*)

No. 4, F sharp major, Op. 30
Z. Skolovsky   ♯ *EPhi.NBL 5025*
(Berg, Hindemith, Bartók)
        (♯ *Phi.N 02131L; AmC.ML 4871*)

No. 9, F major, Op. 68
V. Horowitz   ♯ *Vic. set LM 6014*
(Studies; & Schubert, Debussy, etc.)   (♭ *set ERG 6014*)
   (♯ ItV.A12R 0065: ♭ *A72R 0034; ♯ FV.A 630203*)

STUDIES
Op. 2, No. 1, C sharp minor   *(Mélancholique)*
J. Rein   *Pam.S 19042*
(Rachmaninoff: Prelude, C sharp minor)
☆ V. Horowitz (♭ *G.7RQ 200*)

Op. 8, No. 5, E major
Y. Boukoff   in ♯ *Phi.A 76700R*
(below, Balakirev, etc.)
W. Merzanow   *Muza.X 1658*
(Chopin: Étude, Op. 25, No. 10)

Op. 8, No. 7, B flat minor
V. Horowitz   in ♯ *Vic. set LM 6014*
(below, & Sonata No. 9; Schubert, etc.) (♭ *set ERG 6014*)
   (♯ ItV.A12R 0065: ♭ *A72R 0034; ♯ FV.A 630203*)

Op. 8, No. 9, C sharp minor
Op. 8, No. 11, B flat minor
L. Zyuzin   *USSRM.D 001253/4*

Op. 8, No. 11, B flat minor
☆ V. Sofronitsky (in ♯ Csm.CRLP 147)

Op. 8, No. 12, D sharp minor
Y. Boukoff   in ♯ *Phi.A 76700R*
(above)
H. Giordano   *ArgOd. 57028*
(Rachmaninoff: Prelude, Op. 32, No. 12)
☒ A. Scriabin (*USSR. 21436**)

Op. 42, No. 5, C sharp minor
V. Horowitz   in ♯ *Vic. set LM 6014*
(above)(♭ *set ERG 6014; ♯ ItV.A12R 0065; ♯ FV.A 630203*)

B flat major (unspec.)
— ARR. VLN. & PF.
I. Oistrakh & I. Kollegorskaya (Muza.X 2060)

Vers la flamme, Op. 72 (Poem)
G. Gorini   *Cet.AB 30025*
(Debussy: Étude & Prelude)

II. ORCHESTRAL & INSTRUMENTAL

Concerto, F sharp major, Op. 20   pf. & orch.   1894
F. Wührer & Vienna Pro Musica—Swarowsky
(Tchaikovsky)   ♯ *AmVox.PL 9200*
☆ P. Badura-Skoda & Vienna Sym.—Swoboda
(Rimsky)   ♯ *Nix.WLP 5068*
☆ S. Feinberg & Moscow Radio—Gauk (♯ *USSR.D 418/9*)

Poème d'extase, Op. 54   1908
Paris Phil.—Rosenthal   ♯ *DCap.CTL 7033*
(Loeffler)   (♯ *Cap.P 8188*)
N.Y.P.S.O.—Mitropoulos   ♯ *AmC.ML 4731*
(below)
Boston Sym.—Monteux   ♯ *Vic.LM 1775*
(Liszt)   (♯ ItV.A12R 0073; FV.A 630204)
Moscow Radio—Golovanov   ♯ *USSR.D 0704*
(Balakirev: Tamar)

Prometheus, Op. 60   pf., cho. & orch.   1910
     (The Poem of Fire)
L. Hambro, Cho. & N.Y.P.S.O.—Mitropoulos
(above)   ♯ *AmC.ML 4731*

SYMPHONIES
No. 1, E major   with M-S, T, cho.   c. 1895
Moscow Radio Cho. & Sym.—Golovanov
         ♯ *USSR.D 01448/50*
(3ss—Rachmaninoff)

No. 2, C minor & major, Op. 29   1897-1903
☆ Moscow Radio—Golovanov (4ss) ♯ *USSR.D 584/7*
(Tchaikovsky: The Months, No. 10 on ♯ Csm.CRLP 157)

No. 3, C minor & major, Op. 43   1903
U.S.S.R. State—Ivanov   ♯ *CEd.CE 3003*
☆ Moscow Radio—Golovanov   ♯ *USSR.D 0321/2*
  (2ss)   (♯ *Sup.LPV 183; U.5162G*)

Variation No. 2 on a Russian theme[1] str. qtt.   1899
U.S.S.R. Qtt.   *USSR. 22503*

SEARLE, Humphrey (b. 1915)
Sonata, Op. 21   pf.   1951
G. Watson   ♯ *Argo.RG 6*
(Fricker)   (o.n. ATC 1002)

Variation on an Elizabethan tune (Sellinger's Round)[2]   orch.   1953
Aldeburgh Fest.—Britten   in ♯ *D.LXT 2798*
(Berkeley, Britten, Oldham, Tippett, Walton) (♯Lon.LL 808)

---

[1] The other variations, also recorded, are by Artsibuchev, Glazounov, Rimsky-Korsakov, Ewald, Winkler, Vitol, Blumenfeld, Sokolov. The complete set occupies 4ss (*USSR. 22503/6*).
[2] From a joint work with the composers named for the coupling.

SECCHI, Antonio (1761-1823)

Lungi dal caro bene　Arietta
G. Gari (T), S. Leff (S)　　　in ♯ **Mur.P 104**
(followed by pf. acc. only)

SEGER [SEEGR], Joseph F. N.
　　　　　　　　　　　　　(1716-1782)

Prelude & Fugue, C major　org.
M. Šlechta　　　　　　**U.H 24406**
(*Černohorsky: Fugue, G sharp minor*)

SEGOVIA, Andrés (b. 1893)

Anecdote No. 2; Neblina　guitar
L. Almeida　　　in ♯ **DCap.CTL 7089**
(† Guitar Music of Spain)　　(♯ Cap.P 8295)

SONG: Canción andalusa
▽ O. Coelho (S & guitar) (*P.RO 20580:* ♭ *CBEP 2*)
ALSO: Many various guitar arrangements.

SEIBER, Matyas (b. 1905)

Quartet No. 3, str.　(Quartetto lirico) 1948-51
Amadeus Qtt.　(*Tippett*)　　♯ **G.ALP 1302**

FOLK SONG ARRANGEMENTS
J'ai descendu dans mon jardin
Le Rossignol
Marguerite, elle est malade
S. Wyss (pf.), M. Korchinska (hp.)
　　　　　　　　in ♯ **Argo.RG 34**

SEIDEL, Jan (b. 1908)

ANNA PROLETÁŘKA　Film Music . . . **Prelude**
Prague—Moscow—Mír　Part Song
Czech Male Cho. & F.O.K. Sym.—Smetáček
　　　　　　　　　　♯ **U. 5147C**

People behold!　Cantata
☆ Singers & Children's Cho., Czech Phil.—Šejna
　　　　　　　　(♯ U. 5079/80G)

There are other recordings in Czech catalogues, including
SONG: Lola (Lorca) on ♯ *U. 10010D.*

SEITZ, Friedrich (1848-1918)

Concertino No. 5, D major, Op. 22　vln. & pf.
J. Shermont & O. Schulhof (pf.)　♯ **Rem.YV 3**
(*Accolay & Ortmans*)

SEIXAS, José Antonio Carlos de (1704-1742)

　　SEE: † Portuguese Keyboard Music

SELF, William (b. 1906)

　　SEE: † Five Centuries of Choral Music

SEMENOFF, Ivan (b. 1917)

(Le) Compagnon de Voyage　1954
(Tale for recording, after Andersen)
A. Reybaz (narrator), etc., Inst. Ens.—Froment
　　　　　　　　　♯ **Phi.N 00992R**

Gin-Fizz　sax. & pf.　1955
D. Defayet & F. Gobet　　♭ **Pat.G 1052**
(*Vuataz, Cushing, etc.*)

SENALLIÉ, Jean-Baptiste (1687-1730)

SONATAS, vln. or fl. & cont.
G minor　Bk. I, No. 5　1710
C. Dolmetsch (recorder), J. Saxby (hpsi)
　　　　　　in ♯ **D.LXT 2943**
(† Recorder & Hpsi. Recital 3)　(♯ Lon.LL 1026)

D minor　Bk. II, No. 5
. . . **4th movt., Allegro**　— ARR. VLC. & PF.
("*Allegro spiritoso*")
P. Olefsky & G. Silfies　in ♯ **McInt.MM 103**
(*Debussy, Fauré, etc.*)

SENFL, Ludwig (*c.* 1490-1543)

Collections[1]
Wenn ich des Morgens früh aufsteh
Entlaubet ist der Walde
Es taget vor dem Walde
J. Feyerabend (T), recorders, viols & lute
　　　　　　　　　♭ *Pol. 37007*

Ach Elslein liebes Elslein
Kling, klang (Das Geläut' zu Speyer)
Vienna Acad. Cho.—Gillesberger　♯ **SPA. 58**
(† Songs of the Renaissance)

Also heilig ist der Tag
Kling, klang (Das Geläut' zu Speyer)
☆ Basel Kammerchor—Sacher
Es taget vor dem Walde
☆ M. Meili (T) & insts. (in † ♯ HS.AS 7)

SERMISY, Claudin de (*c.* 1490-1562)

CHANSONS
Au joly boys
Hau hau le boys　1529
Vocal Ens.—Boulanger　in ♯ **B.AXTL 1048**
(† Fr. Renaissance Music)
　　　　　　(♯ D.FAT 263102; AmD.DL 9629)

Hau hau le boys
Petits Chanteurs de la Renaissance　♯ **CND. 4/5**
(† Histoire de la Musique vocale)　(& ♯ Era.LDE 3018/9)

Dictes sans peur
Las, je m'y plains
Vocal Ens.—F. Lamy　　in ♯ **LOL.OL 50027**
(† Parisian Songs, XVIth Cent.)　(♯ OL.LD 76)

En entrant en ung jardin　1529
☆ M. Gerar (S), viols., fl. & guitar (in † ♯ HS.AS 6)

Secourez-moi　(Marot)
Y. Tessier (T) & lute　　in ♯ **CND. 9**
(† Musique et la Poésie)

Tant que vivray en âge florissant　(Marot)　1529
Pro Musica Antiqua Ens.—Cape　**G.HMS 34**
(† History of Music in Sound)　(in ♯ Vic. set LM 6029)
R. Blanchard Ens.　　in ♯ *Phi.N 00993R*
(† French Chansons)

Vivray-je toujours en soucy?
F. Fuller (B), D. Poulton (lute)　**G.HMS 34**
(† History of Music in Sound)　(in ♯ Vic. set LM 6029)

SEROV, Alexander Nikolayevich
　　　　　　　　　　　　(1820-1871)

OPERAS (in *Russian*)
JUDITH　5 Acts　1863
Holofernes' aria　("*Martial Song*")　Bs
▽ M. Reizen　　　　**USSR. 15685**
(*Ruslan & Ludmilla—Farlaf's Rondo*)

(The) POWER OF EVIL　5 Acts　1871
Highlights in ♯ *USSR.D 1597*
Happy Shrovetide (Yeremka's song)
Grunya's Song, Act II
V. Borisenko, N. Shchegolkov, A. Turchina &
Cho.　　　　　　**USSR. 15985/6**
(*continued on next page*)

---

[1] From the Ott & Forster collections.

(The) POWER OF EVIL (*continued*)
Happy Shrovetide (or: *Merry Butterweek*)   Bs
B. Christoff, Cho. & balalaikas
                              in ♯ **G.ALP 1266**
(*Gretchaninoff, etc.*)   (♯ *FALP 351*)
▽ F. Chaliapin (G.DB 1511; USSR. 012292)

ROGNEDA   5 Acts   1865
Rogneda's Ballad   (Variations)   S
V. Davidova   **USSRM.D 00916**
(*Rimsky, Dargomijsky*)
▽ E. Antonova (*USSR. 9004*)

Russian Dance
Orch.—Samosud   **USSR. 11638/9**

Zaporozhye Cossack Dance   orch.
State Sym.—Gauk   **USSR. 17105/6**

SERRA, Joaquín (b. 1907)

Doña Iñes de Castro   Ballet
Cuevas Ballets Orch.—Cloëz   ♯ **LI.TWV 91049**
(*Debussy*)   (♯ *Cpt.MC 20042*)

SARDANAS
El Gegants de Vilanova
El petit Albert
Cobla Girona (in ♯ *Reg.LS 1011*)

SERRANO, Blas (c. 1770- ?)

SEE: † SPANISH KEYBOARD MUSIC

SERRANO SIMEÓN, José (1873-1941)

ZARZUELAS, etc.   (abridged listings only)
(La) ALEGRÍA DLL BATALLÓN
Vocal excerpts
L. Sagi-Vela (B) (in ♯ *MusH.LP 5004*)
▽ A. Cortis (T) (*G.DA 762*)
M. Redondo (B) (*Od. 184177*), etc.

ALMA DE DIOS   1 Act   1907
A. M. Iriarte, M. Ausensi, etc., Madrid Cho. & Cha. Orch.
—Argenta   ♯ *LI.W 91007*
                              (♯ *Ambra.MC 25001*)
I. Rivadeneyra, T. Pardo, S. Castelló, etc., Madrid Cho. &
Sym.—Moreno Torroba   ♯ **AmC.ML 4932**
L. Berchman, V. Simon, T. Montes, etc., Madrid Radio
Cho. & Cha. Orch.—Montorio & Navarro
[*Prelude* only in ♯ Mont.FM 39]   ♯ *Mont.FM 33*
Vocal Excerpts
L. Sagi-Vela (B) (in ♯ *MusH.LP 5006*)
▽ T. Schipa (G.DB 1029; Vic. 6632)
M. Redondo (Od. 121014 & *184810*), etc.

(La) CANCIÓN DEL OLVIDO   1 Act
P. Lorengar, J. Beláustegui, C. Munguía, M. Ausensi, etc.,
Madrid Cho. & Sym.—Argenta   ♯ *LI.TW 91026*
                              (♯ *Ambra.MCC 30020*)
C. Panadés, J. Gual, J. Meseguer, etc., Cho. & Sym.
—Ferrer   ♯ **Reg.LCX 109**
                   (♯ *Pam.LRC 15906*; Angel. 65002)
(8ss, ♮ ArgP.PC 36036/9, set PC 8)
[Excerpts on ♭ *Reg.SEBL 7015 & SEDL 1904*]
L. Sagi-Vela, L. Berchman, etc., Madrid Cha. Orch.
—Navarro, etc.   ♯ *Mont.FM 20*
▽ A. Ottein, M. Castro, M. Redondo, etc., Cho. & Orch.
—Capdevila (*Od.184484/7: 196535/8; AmD.20667/70*)
Vocal excerpts
▽ M. Redondo (Od. 121014: 177140)
N. Martini (*Vic. 4255*)
Marinella — ARR. VLN. & PF.   Persinger
▽ Y. Menuhin & pf. (G.DB 1301; Vic. 7317)
(El) CARRO DEL SOL
Vocal excerpts in ▽ Od. 153345 & *184125*
(Los) CLAVELES   Sainete   1 Act   1929
L. Berchman, J. Picaso, Cho. & Madrid Cha. Orch.
—Montorio & Navarro   ♯ *Mont.FM 13*
A. M. Iriarte, C. Munguía, A. M. Fernández, etc., Cho. &
Sym.—Argenta   ♯ *Ambra.MC 25010*
M. Espinalt, P. Civil, J. Puigsech, etc., Cho. & Sym.
—Ferrer   ♯ **Reg.LC 1001**
                      (♯ *Angel. 64003; Pam.LRC 15506*)
(6ss, ♮ ArgP.PC 36032/4, set PC 7)
[Excerpts on ♭ *Reg.SEBL 7009*]
▽ A. Romo, V. Simón, A. Albiach, etc. (*G.AE 3689/92*)

(Los) DE ARAGÓN   1 Act   *c.* 1927
T. Rosado, C. Munguía, Cho. & Madrid Sym.—Argenta
                                 ♯ *LI.W 91027*
                              (♯ *Ambra.MC 25004*)
M. Espinalt, J. Permanyer, C. Renom, Cho. & Sym.
—Ferrer   ♯ **Reg.LC 1008**
(*La Reina Mora*, on ♯ Angel. 65010)
L. Berchman, V. Simón, S. Ramalle, Madrid Radio Cho.
& Cha. Orch.—Montorio & Navarro ♯ *Mont.FM 34*

(La) DOLOROSA   2 Acts   1931
L. Berchman, J. Picaso, J. Deus, etc., Cho. & Madrid Cha.
Orch.—Montorio & Navarro   ♯ **Mont.FM 14**
A. M. Iriarte, M. Ausensi, C. Munguía, J. Barmejo,
C. Gil, etc., Cho. & Sym.—Argenta
                                 ♯ *Ambra.MC 25009*
M. Espinalt, E. Aliaga, C. Renom, M. Redondo, etc.,
Cho. & Sym.—Ferrer   ♯ **Reg.LCX 120**
[Excerpts on ♭ *Reg.SEBL 7006*]   (♯ Angel. 65013)
L. Sagi-Vela, Miret, Marín, etc., Colón Theatre Cho. &
Orch.   ♯ *MusH.LP 8001*
Vocal excerpts
L. Sagi-Vela (B) (in ♯ *MusH.LP 5006*)
M. Cubas (T) (in ♯ *ArgOd.LDC 528*)
▽ M. Redondo (B) (*Od. 184243/4*), etc.

(La) REINA MORA   1903
A. M. Iriarte, P. Lorengar, M. Ausensi, etc., Madrid
Cho. & Cha. Orch.—Argenta   ♯ *LI.TW 91001*
                              (♯ *Ambra.MCC 30005*)
M. Espinalt, L. Torrentó, P. Martín, C. Renom, etc.,
Sym.—Ferrer   ♯ **Reg.LC 1009**
(*Los de Aragon*, on ♯ Angel. 65010)   (♯ *Pam.LRC 15509*)
Vocal excerpts   ▽ C. Supervia & M. Redondo (*Od. 184480*)

(La) TRIUNFADORA
Vocal excerpt   ▽ M. Fleta (G.DB 920)

(El) TRUST DE LOS TENORIOS   1 Act   1910
Vocal excerpts
P. Fleta (T) (in ♯ *Pat.DT 1021; ArgPat.ADT 1009*)
M. Cubas (T) (in ♯ *ArgOd.LDC 528*)
▽ M. Fleta (T) (*G.DA 1087*)

Te quiero (Jota)   orch. version
Madrid Theatre—Moreno Torroba (in ♯ *AmD.DL 9789*)

SESSIONS, Roger [Huntington] (b. 1896)

(The) BLACK MASKERS   1923
Inc. Music to Andreyev's play
Orchestral Suite
A.R.S. Orch.—Hendl   ♯ **ARS. 115**
(*Harris & Schuman*)

Chorale No. 1   organ   1926
M. Andrews   ♯ **UOK. 2**
(*Lübeck, Křenek, Piston*)
M. Mason   ♯ **Eso.ES 522**
(*below; & V. Thomson*)

(3) Chorale Preludes   organ   1924-26
V. W. Fillinger   ♯ **PFCM.CB 189**
(*Honegger & Messiaen*)
M. Mason   ♯ **Eso.ES 522**
(*above; & Thomson*)

Symphony No. 2   1946
☆ N.Y.P.S.O.—Mitropoulos   ♯ **AmC.ML 4784**
(*Milhaud*)

ŠEVČÍK, Otakar (1852-1934)

(6) BOHEMIAN DANCES, Op. 10
vln. unacc. (also vln. & pf.)
1. Puzzled girl (Holka modrooká)   2. Dance, G major
3. Dance, F sharp minor   4. Fantasie, G major
5. Břetislav   6. Furiant

COMPLETE RECORDING (vln. & pf.)
I. Kawuciak & F. Vrána (Nos. 1 & 5), B. Bělčík & J.
Maštalíř (Nos. 2 & 4), K. Šroubek & F. Maxian (Nos.
3 & 6)   ♯ *U. 5115C*
[Nos. 2, 3, 4, also in ♯ *Sup.LPM 197*; No. 6 also in
Sup.LPM 135; Nos. 2 & 4 also ▽ *U.H 24214*]

♯ = Long-playing, 33⅓ r.p.m.   ♭ = 45 r.p.m.   ♮ = Auto. couplings, 78 r.p.m.

SÉVERAC, Joseph Marie Déodat de
(1873-1921)

COLLECTION OF PIANO MUSIC
EN LANGUEDOC 1904
... No. 3, À Cheval dans la prairie
CERDANA Suite 1910
... No. 3, Ménétriers et glaneuses
... No. 4, Les Muletiers devant le Christ de Llivia
EN VACANCES Suite 1910
... No. 6, Où l'on entend une vieille boîte à musique
　H. Boschi　　　　　　**V♯ CdM.LDY 8037**

EN VACANCES ... No. 7, Valse romantique
Pippermint-Get Valse pf. 1907
— ARR. ORCH.
　Orch.—Chevreux (in **V♯ CdM.LDYM 4020**)
SONGS
Chanson de Blaisine (Magre) 1900
　J. Douai (T)　　　　in ♯ *BàM.LD 312*
　(Recital No. 2)
Ma poupée chérie (D. de Séverac)
　L. Lamercier (S) (*Pat.PAE 14*)

SHAPERO, Harold (b. 1920)

Sonata pf.-4 hands 1941
　H. Shapero & L. Smit　　　♯ **AmC.ML 4841**
　(Cowell)

Symphony for classical orchestra 1948
　Columbia Sym.—Bernstein　♯ **AmC.ML 4889**
　　　　　　　　　　　(♯ *Phi.N 02118L*)

SHAPORIN, Yuri Alexandrovitch (b. 1889)

Élégie; Romance (? ARR.) vlc. & pf.
　M. Rostropovich & pf.　　**USSRM.D 00368**
　(*Prokofiev: Cinderella, Adagio*)
SONGS
Elegy (Yuzikov)
　S. Shaposhnikov (B)　　　**USSRM.D 00746**
　(*Kotchurov: Songs*)
(The) Field has many paths (Folksong Arr.)
　Z. Dolukhanova (A)　　　　**USSR. 22095**
　(*Dargomijsky: I love him still*)
Invocation (Pushkin)
　B. Gmyria (Bs)　　　　　**USSRM.D 00571**
　(*Rakov & Rubinstein*)　　(also *USSR. 20882*, d.c.)
(The) Noise of battle subsided at eventide (Surikov)
　B. Gmyria (Bs)　　　　　**USSR. 21497**
　(*Rakov: The Cliff*)

SHAPOSHNIKOV, Adrian (b. 1888)

Sonata, D minor, fl. & harp 1925
　J. Roberts & E. Vito　　in ♯ *Per.SPL 721*
　(*Jongen, Bizet, Tournier, etc.*)

SHOSTAKOVICH, Dmitri (b. 1906)

(The) AGE OF GOLD, Op. 22 Ballet 1930
Orchestral Suite
1. Introduction　　　2. Adagio
3. Polka　　　　　　4. Russian Dance
　Nat. Sym. (U.S.A.)—Mitchell ♯ **Nix.WLP 5319**
　(*Symphony No. 1*)　　　　(♯ *West.WL 5319*)
... No. 3, Polka
　Hamburg Philharmonia—H-J. Walther
　　　　　　　　　　　　　MSB. 78104
　(*J. Strauss: Frühlingsstimmen*)
　Boston Prom.—Fiedler　in ♯ **Vic.LM 1726**
　　　　　　　　　　　　(♭ *set WDM 1726*)
　☆ Tivoli—Felumb (♭ *Mer.EP 1-5042*)

— —ARRANGEMENTS
PIANO
　V. Schiøler　　　　　　　　　**G.DA 5282**
　(*Tchaikovsky: Chants sans paroles*) (♭ *7RK 2: 7EBK 1001*)
　☆ D. Shostakovich (in ♯ *Csm.CRLP 167*)
2 PFS.
　☆ P. Luboshutz & G. Nemenoff (in ♯ *Cam.CAL 198:*
　　　　　　　　　　　　　　　　　♭ *CAE 219*)
STR. QTT. American Art Qtt. (in ♯ *BB.LBC 1086*)
FL., OB., CL., HRN., BSN.
　Chicago Sym. Wind Quintet (in ♯ *Aphe.AP 14*)
VLN. & PF. Grunes
　☆ Z. Francescatti & M. Lanner (♯ *EPhi.NBL 5010:*
　　　　　　　　　　　　　　　♯ *Phi.N 02101L*)

Ballet russe Suite 1950
　Col. Sym.—Kurtz　　　　　♯ **AmC.ML 4671**
　(*Tchaikovsky*)

BALLET SUITES orch.
No. 1, Op. 84
No. 2,
No. 3,
　U.S.S.R. Orchs.—Gauk (in No. 1), Stassevich
　　(in Nos. 2 & 3)　　　　♯ **CEd.CE 3012**
　[No. 1 is ☆] (for separate issues see below)

No. 1, Op. 84
　Berlin Sym.—Guhl　　　　♯ **Ura. 7146**
　(*Borodin, Kabalevsky, Prokofiev*)
　☆ U.S.S.R. State—Gauk　　♯ **CdM.LDX 8046**
　(*Kabalevsky & Prokofiev*)　(2ss, *USSR.D 00803/4*)
　(*Kabalevsky on ♯ Csm.CRLP 146*)
No. 3
　Moscow Radio—Stassevitch　♯ **USSR.D 01474**
　(*Khachaturian*)
　[Waltz & Dance only with *Prokofiev: Winter Holiday*,
　　excerpts on USSRM.D 00196]

... Galop
　Polish Radio—Rachon　　　　*Muza. 2386*
　(*Godard: Jocelyn—Berceuse*)

(15) Children's pieces, Op. 27 pf.
... 6 unspec.[1]
　M. Pressler　　　　in ♯ **MGM.E 3010**

CHORAL POEMS
No. 1, Let us advance more boldly, friends (Radin)
No. 4, The meeting in a train for exiles (Gmirev)
No. 5, To those who have fallen (Gmirev)
No. 7, The volleys have ceased (Tarasov)
No. 9, May Song (Katz)
No. 10, Song (Tan-Bogoraz, after Whitman)
　Russian State Cho. (& in Nos. 9 & 10, Moscow
　　Choral School Boys' Cho.)—Sveshnikov
　(2ss)　　　　　　　　　♯ **USSR.D 913/4**

Concerto, C minor, pf., tpt. & str. orch., Op. 35
　　1933
　M. Pressler, H. Glantz & M.G.M. Orch.
　　—Bloomfield　　　　　♯ **P.PMC 1023**
　(*Sonata No. 2*)　　　　　(♯ *MGM.E 3079*)
　M. Pinter & Berlin Radio—Wand ♯ **Ura. 7119**
　(*Khachaturian*)　　　　　(♯ *MTW. 539*)
　V. Aller, M. Klein & Concert Arts—Slatkin
　　　　　　　　　　　　♯ **DCap.CCL 7520**
　(*Hindemith on ♯ Cap.P 8230*)　(♯ *Cap.L 8229*)
　[4th movt. only in ♯ *Cap.SAL 9020*]
　N. Mewton-Wood, H. Sevenstern & Concert
　　Hall Sym.—Goehr　　　♯ **CHS.H 4**
　(*Britten*)
　N. Sluszny, A. Marchal & Belgian Radio Cha.
　　—Doneux　　　　　　♯ **Gramo.GLP 2512**
　G. Joye, R. Delmotte & Paris Inst. Cha.
　　—Froment　　　　　　♯ **EPP.APG 120**
　(*Bartók & Roussel*)[2]

Concerto, A major, vln. & orch., Op. 99 1955
　D. Oistrakh & N.Y.P.S.O.—Mitropoulos
　　　　　　　　　　　　♯ **EPhi.ABL 3101**
　　　　　　　　　　　　(♯ *AmC.ML 5077*)

---

[1] Probably the set of 6 pieces, pub. 1946: March; Valse; The Bear; Gay Story; Sad Story; Clockwork Doll.
[2] Originally announced as having *Despard: Symphony* on reverse.

(The) FALL OF BERLIN   Film Music
Orch. Suite
   Moscow Radio—Gauk   # **CEd.CE 3009**
   (*Khachaturian*) [part probably ☆]

(3) Fantastic Dances, Op. 5   pf.   1922
   G. Bachauer   in # **G.CLP 1057**
   (*Liszt, Chopin*)
   S. Contreras   # **CM. 17**
   (*below, Bartók, Kabalevsky, etc.*)
   E. Burton   in # **CEd.CE 1026**

— ARR. VLN. & PF.   Glickman
   A. Pratz & G. Gould   # **Hall.RS 3**
   (*Berg, Prokofiev, Taneiev*)

(The) GOLDEN MOUNTAINS, Op. 30
   Film Music
... Waltz
   Polish Radio—Cajmer   (2ss)   *Muza. 2075*
   ☆ Orch.—Uriev (in # Csm.CRLP 167)

March   Band   1942
   Moscow Radio Band—Katz in # **USSR.D 1556**

MEETING ON THE ELBE   Film Music
Song of peace   (Dolmatovsky)
   Cho. & Radio Orch.—Tóth (*Hung*) (*Qual.MO 443*)
   Berlin State Op. Cho. (*Ger*) (*Eta. 30-28*)
   ☆ Red Banner Ens. (*USSRM.D 00303*)

Longing for home   (Dolmatovsky)
   E. Busch, F. Lapkin & Cho. (*Ger*) (*Eta. 10-99*)
   Red Banner Ens. (*USSRM.D 001058*)

PART SONGS
Towards the future   on *Ete. 10-138*
Oath to Stalin   (Sazhanov)   on *Ete. 30-28*

PIROGOV   Film Music
... Waltz   Polish Radio—Rachon (*Muza. 2017*)

(24) PRELUDES, Op. 34   pf.   1932-3
   R. Cornman   # **D.FST 153515**
   (*Prokofiev*)
   M. Pressler   # **MGM.E 3070**

... Nos. 2, 3, 5, 10, 12, 21, 24
   D. Barenboim   ♭ *EPhi.NBE 11014*
   (*Kabalevsky: Sonatina*)   (♭ *Phi.N 425009E*)
... Nos. 10 & 15 only   — ARR. VLN. & PF.[1]
   ☆ J. Heifetz (in # AmD.DL 9780)
... Nos. 10 & 24 only   — ARR. VLN. & PF.
   M. Wilk & F. Kramer   in # **MTR.MLO 1012**
   (*Wieniawski, Bach, Brahms, etc.*)
... 3 unspec. (or "No. 3"?)   — ARR. VLN. & PF.
   J. Sitkowiecki & I. Kollegorskaya   *Muza.X 2063*
   (*Wieniawski: Polonaise, D major*)
... No. 16 only   S. Contreras (*above*)   in # **CM. 17**

(24) PRELUDES & FUGUES, Op. 87   pf.   1951
COLLECTIONS
No. 1, C major   No. 5, D minor
No. 6, A major   No. 7, F major
No. 8, D major
   D. Shostakovich   *USSRM.D 873/4*

No. 2, A minor   No. 3, G major
No. 4, E minor   No. 5, D minor
No. 12, G sharp minor   No. 14, E flat minor
No. 16, B flat minor
   D. Shostakovich   # **CHS.CHS 1314**

No. 1, C major; No. 24, D minor
   E. Gilels   # **CdM.LDA 8104**
   (*Debussy, Prokofiev, Tchaikovsky*)
   (*Rachmaninoff* on # Csm.CRLP 223, d.v.)

No. 7, F major
   D. Shostakovich   *USSR. 21388/9*

QUARTETS, Strings
No. 1, C major, Op. 49   1938
   Komitas (Armenian) Qtt.   # **C.CX 1334**
   (*Borodin*)   (# Angel. 35239)
   Guilet Qtt.   # **MGM.E 3113**
   (*Prokofiev*)

No. 3, F major, Op. 73
   Tchaikovsky Qtt.   (2ss)   # *USSR.D 2534/5*

No. 4, Op. 83   1949
   Tchaikovsky Qtt.   (2ss)   # *USSR D 2291/2*
   (*No. 5* on # Van.VRS 6021)

No. 5, B flat major, Op. 92   1954
   Beethoven Qtt.   (2ss)   # *USSR.D 2400/1*
   (# *CdM.LDA 8130;* with No. 4 on # Van.VRS 6021)

QUINTET, G minor, Op. 57   pf. & str.   1940
   E. Norton & Juilliard Qtt.   # **PFCM.CB 158**
   (*Piston*)
   ☆ V. Aller & Hollywood Qtt.   # **T.LCE 8171**
   [3rd movt. only in # *Cap.LAL 9024*]
   ☆ D. Shostakovich & Beethoven Qtt. (# *USSR.D 2620/1*)

SONATA No. 2, B minor, Op. 64   pf.   1943
   M. Pressler   # **P.PMC 1023**
   (*Concerto*)   (# *MGM.E 3079*)

SONATA, D minor, Op. 40   vlc. & pf.   1934
   E. Brabec & F. Holetschek   # **D.LW 5068**
   (# *Lon.LD 9075*)

(The) Song of the Forests (Dolmatovsky) T, Bs, cho.
   1951
   I. Petrov, A. Kilichevsky, Cho. & U.S.S.R.
   State Sym.—Mravinsky   # **CdM.LDA 8000**
   [perhaps a new recording, same artists]
   (# Sup.SLPV 177; U. 5149G; Dia.DCM 1;
                     USSR.D 0486/7)

... Excerpt   (unspec.)
   Leningrad Op. Orch.—Feldt   ♭ *JpV.EK 4*
   (*Khachaturian: Gayaneh, excerpts*)

SYMPHONIES
No. 1, F major, Op. 10   1924-5
   Nat. Sym. (U.S.A.)—Mitchell # **Nix.WLP 5319**
   (*Age of Gold, Suite*)   (# West.WL 5319)
   French Nat. Radio—Markevitch   # *C.FC 1042*
   (2ss)
   Leipzig Radio—Pflüger   # **Ura. 7128**
   (*No. 9*)   (# MTW. 562)
   ☆ Bolshoi Theatre—Kondrashin   # **Mon.MWL 318**
   (# Van.VRS 6014; # Sup.LPV 174; U. 5123G;
                CdM.LDA 8044; USSR.D 408/9)
   ☆ Cleveland Sym.—Rodzinski   # **AmC.ML 4881**
   (*Sibelius*)   (# Phi.A 01179L)

No. 5, D major, Op. 47   1937
   St. Louis Sym.—Golschmann   # **DCap.CTL 7077**
                          (# Cap.P 8268)
   London Phil. Sym.—Rodzinski
                      # **Nix.WLP 20004**
                      (# West.WN 18001)
   N.Y.P.S.O.—Mitropoulos   # **AmC.ML 4739**
   Berlin Radio—Borsamsky   # **Ura. 7098**
   ☆ Vienna Sym.—Horenstein   # **EVox.PL 7610**
   ☆ Cleveland Sym.—Rodzi nski (# AmC.RL 6625)
   Leningrad Phil.—Mravi nsky (# USSR.D 02283/4)

No. 7, C major, Op. 60   "Leningrad"   1942
   Leningrad Phil.—Mravinsky # **USSR.D 01380/3**

No. 9, E flat major, Op. 70   1945/6
   Berlin Radio—Kleinert   # **Ura. 7128**
   (*No. 1*)   (# MTW. 562)
   ☆ N.Y.P.S.O.—Kurtz (# Phi.A 01607R)

No. 10, E minor, Op. 93   1953
   Philharmonia—Kurtz   # **G.ALP 1322**
   N.Y.P.S.O.—Mitropoulos   # **EPhi.ABL 3052**
               (# AmC.ML 4959; Phi.A 01175L)
   Leningrad Phil.—Mravinsky # **CHS.CHS 1313**
        (# USSR.D 02243/4; CdM.LDXA 8113)
   U.S.S.R. Nat.—Shostakovich # **Csm.CRLP 173**
   (*Kabalevsky: Colas Breugnon, Overture*)
   Leipzig Gewandhaus—Konwitschny
   (4ss)   # *Eta. 720006/7*

---

[1] Labelled Nos. 1 & 2.

Tahiti Trot, Op. 16   1928
☆ Orch.—Uriev (in ‡ Csm.CRLP 167)

TRIO, E minor, Op. 67   pf., vln., vlc.   1944
☆ D. Shostakovich, D. Oistrakh, M. Sadlo
           ‡ **Csm.CRLPX 1011**
(*Prokofiev, Rachmaninov, Vainberg, etc.*)

———————

SIBELIUS, Jean J. C. (b. 1865)

Belshazzar['s Feast] Op. 51   1906
Inc. Music to Procopé's play
... **Night Music & Khadra's Dance**
Helsinki Municipal Orch.—Schnéevoight
           Od.PLDX 1
▽ Sym.—Jalas (*Ryt.R 6142*)

Concerto, D minor, Op. 47   vln. & orch.
D. Oistrakh & Stockholm Fest.—Ehrling
           ‡ **C.C 1036**
(2ss)   (‡ *QC 5025: FC 1035*)
J. Damen & L.P.O.—v. Beinum   ‡ **D.LXT 2813**
(2ss)   (‡ *Lon.LL 777*)
T. Magyar & Residentie—Otterloo
           ‡ **Phi.A 00269L**
(*Glazounov*)   (‡ *Epic.LC 3184*)
I. Gitlis & Vienna Pro Musica—Horenstein
(*Bruch*)   ‡ **AmVox.PL 9660**
D. Oistrakh & U.S.S.R. Nat.—Kondrashin
(*Matchavariani*)   ‡ **Csm.CRLP 172**
☆ G. Neveu & Philharmonia—Susskind   ‡ **Angel.35129**
(*Suk*)   (‡ *ArgA.LPC 11575*)
☆ J. Heifetz & L.P.O.—Beecham   ‡ **Vic.LCT 1113**
(*Chausson: Concerto*)   (♭ *set WCT 1113*)
☆ I. Stern & Royal Phil.—Beecham (‡ *C.FC 1022:*
                       QC 5003)
C. Wicks & Stockholm Phil.—Ehrling (‡ *Mtr.CLP 510:*
         T.LCSK 8175; with *Legends*, ‡ *Cap.P 8327*)
E. Telmanyi & Danish Radio—Jensen
         (‡ *Tono.LPX 35002*; ♮ *Nera.KE 17518/21*)
A. Eidus & Vienna Orch. Soc.—Hummel
         (‡ *Cpt.MC 20056; MTW. 528, d.c.*)
— FOR PRACTICE: Recorded without violin part
                 (‡ *CEd.MMO 302*)

Finlandia, Op. 26   (Tableau)
Philharmonia—Karajan   **C.LX 1593**
(2ss)   (GQX 11536: LOX 831)
(*Symphony No. 5, s. 2* on ‡ *C.CX 1047: VCX 520:*
       QCX 10019: FCX 192; Angel.35002)
N.B.C. Sym.—Toscanini   in ‡ **G.ALP 1235**
(*Beethoven, Ponchielli, etc.*)
(in ‡ *Vic.LM 1834: LRM 7005:* ♭ *set ERB 7005* &
‡ *ItV.A12R 0007; FV.A 330211* & *A 630247; DV.L 16483*)
Danish Radio—Tuxen   ‡ **D.LW 5141**
(*Grieg: Elegiac Melodies*)   (‡ *Lon.LD 9126*)
Hollywood Bowl—Dragon in ‡ **DCap.CTL 7072**
         (in ‡ *Cap.P 8276:* ♭ *FAP 8282*)
Florence Fest.—Gui   ‡ **AudC. 503**
(*Grieg & Wagner*)
Berlin Phil.—Rosbaud   **PV. 72497**
(*Valse triste*)   (♭ *Pol. 30097:* in ‡ *17025*)
Bamberg Sym.—Hollreiser   ‡ **AmVox.PL 9350**
(*Brahms, Liszt, Wagner*)
Orch.—Swarowsky   ‡ **MTW. 19**
(*Bach & Brahms*)   (♭ *set EP 19*)
Berlin Sym.—Rubahn (in ‡ *Roy. 1459, etc.*)
Regent Sym. (in ‡ *Rgt. 7003*)
☆ Philharmonia—Malko (♭ *G.7PW 117:* ♭ *BB.ERAB 2*)
   Boston Prom.—Fiedler (♭ *G.7EP 7006: 7EPQ 501:*
     7EBF 1: EPK 1001; ♭ *DV. 26014;* in ‡ *Vic.LM 1752:*
     ♭ *set WDM 1752*)
   B.B.C. Sym.—Sargent (♭ *G.7ER 5029: 7ERQ 115*)
   Philadelphia—Ormandy (♭ *EPhi.NBE 11011;*
                ♭ *Phi.A 409011E*)
   Austrian Sym.—Wöss (in ‡ *Rem. 199-115:* ♭ *REP 8;*
     ‡ *AFest.CFR 40;* in ‡ *Ply. 12-58, 12-79* & *12-60*)
   L.S.O.—Fistoulari (in ‡ *MGM.E 3046*)
   Philadelphia—Stokowski (in ‡ *Cam.CFL 103* &
                CAL 120: ♭ *CAE 101*)
— ARR. BAND
   Grenadier Guards—Harris   ‡ **D.LW 5117**
(*Sullivan*)   (‡ *Lon.LD 9131*)

— ARR. ORGAN: R. Ellsasser (in ‡ MGM.E 3125)
... Excerpt, only   — ARR. CHO.
   Helsinki Univ. Cho.—Turunen (in ‡ Rem. 199-167)
   Scottish Massed Male Voice Cho. (*Eng*) (P.E 11515)

(4) Humoresques, Op. 89   vln. & pf. (orig. orch.)
   1917
... **No. 4**
   B. Gimpel & C. Szalkiewicz   *G.JO 351*
   (*Mazurka*)   (*TJ 21*)

Karelia, Overture, Op. 10   orch.   1893
L.S.O.—Collins   ‡ ***D.LW 5209***
(*Pelléas & Mélisande*)

KARELIA, Suite, Op. 11   (Tableaux)   1893
1. Intermezzo   2. Ballade   3, Alla marcia
Olympia Sym.—Saike   ‡ **Allo. 3103**
(*Symphony No. 7*)
... **Nos. 1 & 3**
L.P.O.—Cameron   **G.C 4221**
           (in ‡ *DLP 1100*)
☆ Danish State Radio—Jensen (♭ *D. 71089*)

KING CHRISTIAN II, Op. 27
   (Inc. Music to play by H. Paul)
Orchestral Suite
(Nocturne; Elegy; Musette; Serenade; Ballad)
Stockholm Radio—Westerberg   ‡ **SS. 33104**

Fool's Song (The Spider)   (*Ristilukki*)
B. Loewenfalk (B) & Orch.   *G.X 8095*
(*Rangström: Drinking Song*)
A. Rautawaara (S) & Orch.   ♭ *Mtr.MCEP 3025*
(*Songs, below*)

Musette
L.P.O.—Cameron   **G.C 4242**
(*Valse triste*)   (♭ *7P 147:* in ‡ *DLP 1100*)

KUOLEMA, Op. 44
   Inc. Music to play by Arvid Järnefelt
Scene with cranes   ob., str. & timp.
Finnish Radio Orch.—Fougstedt   **G.TN 2**
(*Madetoja: Laulema*)

Valse triste
L.P.O.—Cameron   **G.C 4242**
(*King Christian II—Musette*)   (♭ *7P 147:* in ‡ *DLP 1100*)
Vienna State Op.—Litschauer   ‡ **Nix.VLP 430**
(*The Lover; & Grieg*)   (‡ *Van.VRS 430*)
(*Grieg: Norwegian Dance 1* on ♭ *Van.VREP 6*)
Hollywood Bowl—Dragon in ‡ **DCap.CTL 7072**
         (in ‡ *Cap.P 8276:* ♭ *FAP 8282*)
Berlin Phil.—Rosbaud   **PV. 72497**
(*Finlandia, Festivo, etc.*)   (♭ *Pol. 30097:* in ‡ *17025*)
Philharmonia—Markevitch   in ‡ **C.CX 1273**
(*Mozart, Busoni, Liszt, etc.*)   (‡ *QCX 10172;* Angel.35154
               & ♭ *C.SEL 1539*)
Hamburg Philharmonia—H-J. Walther
                   MSB. 78108
(*Tchaikovsky: Sleeping Beauty, No. 6*)
F.O.K. Sym.—Smetáček (U.H 24404: in ‡ *5200C*)
Scandinavian Sym.—Johannesen (in ‡ Mae.OAT 25008)
☆ Suisse Romande—Olof (‡ *D.LW 5034;* ‡ *Lon.LD 9049*)
   Liverpool Phil.—Sargent (in ‡ AmC.RL 3050)
   C. B. S.—Barlow (in ‡ AmC.RL 3030)
   Orch.—Stokowski (♭ *G.7RW 137;* in ‡ *Vic.LRM 7024:*
                 ♭ *set ERB 7024*)
   L.S.O.—Fistoulari (in ‡ MGM.E 3124)
   Philharmonia—Kletzki (in ‡ AmC.RL 3091)
   Philadelphia—Stokowski (in ‡ Cam.CAL 123:
                   ♭ *CAE 188*)
   Belgian Radio—André (♭ *T.UE 453915;* ‡ *TW 30010*)
— ARR. VLC. & PF.
E. B. Bengtsson & H. D. Koppel   *G.DA 5279*
(*Grieg: To Spring*)
— ARR. VLN. & ORCH.
I. Zilzer & Orch. (C.DDX 39: ♭ *SCDK 1*)
— ARR. ORGAN: R. Ellsasser (in ‡ MGM.E 3120)
— ARR. ACCORDEONS & CBS.
B. Hughes, B. Palmer & L. Manno (in ‡ *Capri. 1*)

———————

☆ = Re-issue of a recording to be found in previous volumes.

(4) LEGENDS, Op. 22   orch.
1. **Lemminkäinen and the Maidens**
2. **The Swan of Tuonela**
3. **Lemminkäinen in Tuonela**
4. **The Return of Lemminkäinen**

Danish Radio—Jensen   **‡ D.LXT 2831**
(‡ Lon.LL 843)
[Nos. 2 & 4 only on ‡ D.LW 5105; ‡ Lon.LD 9125]

Stockholm Radio—Ehrling   **‡ DCap.CTL 7064**
(‡ Cap.P 8226; ‡ Mtr.CLP 519; ACap.CLCX 048)
[Nos. 2 & 4, with Concerto, ‡ Cap.P 8327]

Philadelphia—Ormandy   **‡ AmC.ML 4672**
[Nos. 1 & 2 only, ‡ Phi.S 06603R]

No. 2, only
Berlin Phil.—Rosbaud   **‡ Pol. 17025**
(Finlandia, Festivo, Valse triste)
(Festivo only on ♭ Pol. 30126)

F.O.K. Sym.—Smetáček   **‡ Sup.LPM 113**
(Brahms, Glinka)   (& U.H 24435)   (in ‡ U. 5071C, d.c.)
Berlin Sym.—Rubahn (in ‡ Roy. 1459)

☆ Orch.—Stokowski (in ‡ Vic.LRM 7024: ♭ set ERB 7024:
& in ‡ LM 9029)
Philadelphia—Ormandy (? o.v.) (♭ AmC. 4-4786)

(The) Lover, Op. 14 (Rakastava) Suite, str. orch.
Vienna State Op.—Litschauer   **‡ Nix.VLP 430**
(Valse triste, & Grieg)   (‡ Van.VRS 430)

Mazurka, Op. 81, No. 1   vln. & pf.
B. Gimpel & C. Szalkiewicz   **G.JO 351**
(Humoresque No. 4)   (TJ 21)
A. Ignatius & J. Jalas   **Ryt. 6146**
(Romance)

Night Ride & Sunrise, Op. 55   Sym. poem
L.S.O.—Collins   **‡ D.LXT 5083**
(½s—Symphony No. 5)   (‡ Lon.LL 1276)

(The) Origin of Fire, Op. 32   Sym. Poem
B, cho., orch.
S. Saarits, Helsinki Univ. Cho. & Cincinnati
Sym.—Johnson   **‡ Rem. 199-191**
(below, & Glazounov)

PART SONGS
(A) Broken voice, Op. 13, No. 1
(Sortunut ääni—Kalevala)
Stockholm Students' Cho.—Ralf   in ‡ SS. 33105
☆ Helsinki Univ. Cho.—Turunen (G.TJ 119)

Boat-journey, Op. 18, No. 3 (Venematka)
☆ Finlandia Cho.—Klemetti (Od.PLDX 4)

Song of my heart, Op. 18, No. 6 (Kivi)
(Sydämeni laulu)
Helsinki Univ. Cho.—Turunen
in ‡ Rem. 199-167
▽ Male Cho. (Ryt.R 6132)

There burns on the island, Op. 18, No. 4
(Saarella palaa—Kanteletar)
Helsinki Acad. Cho.—Bergmann   **G.TJ 12**
(Palmgren & Folksong)

PELLÉAS AND MÉLISANDE, Op. 46
(Inc. music to Maeterlinck's play)
1. At the Castle gate   2. Mélisande
3. On the sea shore   4. A Spring in the park
5. The Three Blind Sisters   6. Pastorale
7. Mélisande at the spinning-wheel   8. Entr'acte
9. Death of Mélisande

COMPLETE RECORDING
☆ Winterthur Sym.—Desarzens   **‡ Nix.CLP 1301**
(Liszt)

... Nos. 2, 7, 8, 9
L.S.O.—Collins   **‡ D.LXT 5084**
(½s—Symphony No. 6)   (‡ Lon.LL 1277)
(Karelia Overture on ‡ D.LW 5209)[1]

... Nos. 1, 2, 4, 5, 6, 7, 9
☆ Berlin Radio—Blomstedt (‡ ANix.ULP 9038)
... No. 5 ▽ A. Rautawaara (S) & Orch.—Jalas (Ryt.R 6140)

---

[1] The LW issue also includes No. 6 in addition.

Pohjola's Daughter, Op. 49   orch.
L.S.O.—Collins   **‡ D.LXT 2962**
(½s—Symphony No. 4)   (‡ Lon.LL 1059)
Cincinnati Sym.—Johnson   **‡ Rem. 199-191**
(above)
☆ Boston Sym.—Koussevitzky   **‡ Vic.LCT 1152**
(Copland, Fauré, Stravinsky)

Romance, C major, Op. 42   str. orch.
Covent Garden Op.—Hollingsworth
‡ P.PMC 1021
(Alfvén, Nielsen, Svendsen)   (‡ MGM.E 3082: ♭ X 1077, &
in ‡ E 3177)
Berlin Sym.—Rubahn   **‡ Roy. 1459**
(Finlandia, Saga, Swan of Tuonela)

Romance, D flat major, Op. 24, No. 9   pf.
▽ T. Mikkilä (Ryt.R 6137)

Romance, F major, Op. 78, No. 2   vln. & pf.
I. Zilzer & F. Eberson   **C.LD 7**
(Kreisler: Tambourin chinois)
B. Gimpel & A. Kotowska   **G.JOX 7036**
(Ravel: Tzigane, s. 1)   (TK 6)
A. Ignatius & J. Jalas   **Ryt. 6146**
(Mazurka)

(A) Saga, Op. 9 (En Saga: Satu)   orch.
Amsterdam—v. Beinum   **‡ D.LXT 2776**
(Tapiola)   (‡ Lon.LL 737)
Berlin Sym.—Rubahn   **‡ Roy. 1459**
(above)

SCÈNES HISTORIQUES   orch.
Op. 25: No. 3, Festivo
Op. 66: No. 1, The Chase
No. 2, Love Song
No. 3, At the drawbridge
☆ Royal Phil.—Beecham   **‡ C.C 1018**
(2ss)   (‡ QC 5014)
[Op. 25, No. 3 & Op. 66, No. 3 also on ♭ C.SEB 3504:
SEBQ 115]

Op. 25, No. 3, Festivo, only
Berlin Phil.—Rosbaud   **‡ Pol. 17025**
(Finlandia, Swan of Tuonela, Valse triste)
(Swan of Tuonela only, ♭ Pol. 30126)

(2) Serenades, Op. 69   vln. & orch.   1912-13
I. Bezrodny & Moscow Radio—Kondrashin
(Chausson: Poème)   **‡ USSR.D 2162**

SONGS
COLLECTION
To evening, Op. 17, No. 6   (Forsman)
A. Rautawaara (S) & Orch.—Jalas
In the fields a maiden sings, Op. 50, No. 3
(Im Feld ein Mädchen singt)   (Susman)
From an anxious heart, Op. 50, No. 4
(Aus banger Brust)   (Dehmel)
A. Koskinen (T), E. Møller (pf.)
(King Christian II)   ♭ Mtr.MCEP 3025

Black Roses, Op. 36, No. 1   (Josephson)
J. Björling (T), F. Schauwecker (pf.)
in ‡ G.ALP 1187
(Schubert, R. Strauss, Wolf, etc.)   (‡ Vic.LM 1771)
(Sjöberg, Liszt & Wolf in ♭ G.7ERC 1;
♭ Vic.ERA 141, d.c.; ♭ DV. 26045)

Christmas Hymn (Topelius, trs. Malmsten)
(En etsi valtaa loistoa—Joulouvirsi)
S. Saarits (B, Finn) & Orch.   **Lei.A 201**
(below)
☆ S. Saarits (o.v.) (G.TJ 122)

— ARR. CHO.
Stockholm Folk School Children's Cho.
—Hammarström (Swed)   **Symf.B 5621**
(Reger: Mariä Wiegenlied)
Soloists, Cho. & Orch.—Christianin (in G.TJ 17)

Christmas Song, Op. 1, No. 4 (Joukahainen)
(Joulu: On hangen korkeat)
S. Saarits (B) & Orch.   **Lei.A 201**
(above)
Vocal & Inst. Ens. (in G.TJ 17)
There is also an unid. Christmas Song (Joululaulu) sung by
E. Värä on ▽ Ryt.R 6006.

Diamonds on the March snow, Op. 36, No. 6
(Wecksell)
☆ A. Rautawaara & Orch.—Jalas (*Ryt.R 6140*)

Driftwood, Op. 17, No. 7 (Calamnius)
Sigh, sigh, sedges, Op. 36, No. 4 (Fröding)
A. Rautawaara (S, *Finn*) & Orch.   *Ryt. 6148*
(*Marvia: Song*)

On a balcony, Op. 38, No. 2 (Rydberg)
A. Rautawaara (S, *Finn*) & Orch.   *Ryt. 6151*
(*Marvia: Song*)

Suite champêtre, Op. 98b   Str. orch.   1921
Finnish Radio—Jalas   ♭ *Mtr.MCEP 3013*
(*Tempest, No. 4*)

(The) Swan of Tuonela SEE: Legends, Op. 22

SYMPHONIES
COLLECTIONS: the 7, COMPLETE
L.S.O.—Collins   ♯ **D. & Lon., various**
[for Nos. 2-7, see below; No. 1 on ♯ D.LXT 2694;
Lon.LL 574]
Stockholm—Ehrling   ♯ **Mer. & Mtr., various**
[for details, see below & Supp. II]

No. 1, E minor, Op. 39
Royal Phil.—Beecham   ♯ **C.CX 1085**
(♯ QCX 10071; ♯ AmC.ML 4653)
Philharmonia—Kletzki   ♯ **C.CX 1311**
☆ Orch.—Stokowski   ♯ **G.ALP 1210**
(♯ ItV.A12R 0129)
☆ Stockholm Radio—Ehrling (♯ Mtr.CLP 514)

No. 2, D major, Op. 43
L.S.O.—Collins   ♯ **D.LXT 2815**
(♯ Lon.LL 822)
Hallé—Barbirolli   ♯ **G.ALP 1122**
(♯ WALP 1122: FALP 338; ♯ BB.LBC 1084)
Stockholm Radio—Ehrling   ♯ **Mer.MG 10141**
(♯ Mtr.CLP 515; AFest.CFR 12-177)
N.B.C. Sym. Members—Stokowski
     ♯ **Vic.LM 1854**
(♭ set ERC 1854; ♯ ItV.A12R 0147; FV.A 630287)
Leipzig Phil.—Abendroth   ♯ **Ura. 7145**
(also ♯ MTW. 514; we are told this *sounds* like a different
recording)
☆ Boston Sym.—Koussevitzky, o.v. (♯ Cam.CAL 108)
Philadelphia—Ormandy (♭ AmC. set A 1094)
N.Y.P.S.O.—Barbirolli (♯ AmC.RL 3045)
Stockholm Concert Soc.—Mann (♯ T.LSK 7007)

No. 3, C major, Op. 52
L.S.O.—Collins   ♯ **D.LXT 2960**
(*No. 7*)   (♯ Lon.LL 1008)
☆ Stockholm Radio—Ehrling (♯ Mtr.CLP 516)

No. 4, A minor, Op. 63
L.S.O.—Collins   ♯ **D.LXT 2962**
(1½ss—*Pohjola's Daughter*)   (♯ Lon.LL 1059)
Philharmonia—Karajan   ♯ **C.CX 1125**
(*Tapiola*)   (♯ QCX 10078: FCX 280: WCX 1125;
♯ Angel. 35082)
Philadelphia—Ormandy   ♯ **EPhi.ABL 3084**
(*No. 5*)   (♯ Phi.A 01226L; AmC.ML 5045)
Stockholm Radio—Ehrling   ♯ **Mer.MG 10143**
(♯ Mtr.CLP 517)
Berlin Sym.—Rubahn   ♯ **Roy. 1492**

No. 5, E flat major, Op. 82
L.S.O.—Collins   ♯ **D.LXT 5083**
(1½ss—*Night ride & sunrise*)   (♯ Lon.LL 1276)
Philadelphia—Ormandy   ♯ **EPhi.ABL 3084**
(*No. 4*)   (♯ Phi.A 01226L; AmC.ML 5045)
Philharmonia—v. Karajan   ♯ **C.CX 1047**
(*Finlandia*) (♯ QCX 10019: VCX 520: FCX 192;
♯ Angel. 35002)
Stockholm Phil.—Ehrling   ♯ **Mtr.CLP 518**
(*No. 6*)   (♯ Mer.MG 10142)
☆ Cleveland Sym.—Rodzinski   ♯ **AmC.ML 4881**
(*Shostakovich*)   (♯ Phi.A 01179L)
☆ Boston Sym.—Koussevitzky (*No. 7*) ♯ Vic.LCT 1151

No. 6, D minor, Op. 104
L.S.O.—Collins   ♯ **D.LXT 5084**
(1½ss—*Pelléas & Mélisande*)   (♯ Lon.LL 1277)
Stockholm Phil.—Ehrling   ♯ **Mtr.CLP 518**
(*No. 5*)   (♯ Mer.MG 10142)

No. 7, C major, Op. 105
L.S.O.—Collins   ♯ **D.LXT 2960**
(*No. 3*)   (♯ Lon.LL 1008)
Olympia Sym.—Saike   ♯ **Allo. 3103**
(*Karelia*)
☆ Hilversum Radio—v. Kempen   ♯ *DT.TM 68005*
(TV.VSK 9200)
(*Bruckner: Sym. No. 4* on ♯ DT.LGX 66026)
☆ B.B.C. Sym.—Koussevitzky   ♯ Vic.LCT 1151
(*No. 5*)
☆ St. Louis Sym.—Golschmann   ♯ **BB.LBC 1067**
(*Mozart*)   (♭ set WBC 1067)
☆ Stockholm Radio—Ehrling (♯ Mtr.CLP 516)

Tapiola, Op. 112   orch.
Philharmonia—Karajan   ♯ **C.CX 1125**
(*Symphony No. 4*)(♯ QCX 10078: FCX 280; ♯ Angel. 35082)
Amsterdam—v. Beinum   ♯ **D.LXT 2776**
(*A Saga*)   (♯ Lon.LL 737)
☆ Royal Phil.—Beecham (♯ Vic.LM 9001: ♭ set WDM 1311)
Boston Sym.—Koussevitzky (♯ Cam.CAL 159)

(The) TEMPEST, Op. 109
Inc. Music to Shakespeare's Play
COLLECTION from the Orch. Suites

Suite I: 1. The Oak Tree   2. Humoresque
(Op. 109, 3. Caliban's Song   4. Canon
No. 2)   6. Scene   7. Berceuse
           9. The Storm
Suite II: 1. Chorus of the Winds   2. Intermezzo
(Op. 109, 3. Dance of the Nymphs   4. Prospero's first song
No. 3)   5. Prospero's 2nd Song   6. Miranda
           7. The Naiads

Royal Phil.—Beecham   ♯ *EPhi.ABR 4045*
(♯ Phi.A 01639R)
... **Suite I, No. 7, Berceuse**
☆ Orch.—Stokowski (♭ G.7RW 137; in ♯ Vic.LRM 7024:
♭ set ERB 7024)
Philadelphia—Stokowski (♭ Cam.CAE 188)
... **Suite II, No. 4** only
Finnish Radio—Jalas   ♭ *Mtr.MCEP 3013*
(*Suite champêtre*)

Valse triste: SEE: Kuolema *above*

SICILIANI, José (b. 1910)

(3) Danzas Argentinas   pf.
1. Danza norteña   1940
2. Danza del gaucho triste 1940
3. Bailecito   1943
P. Spagnolo   in ♯ **D.LXT 2947**
(*Granados, Aguirre, etc.*)   (♯ Lon.LL 1040)

SIEGMEISTER, Elie (b. 1909)

Ozark Set   orch. suite   1943
Hamburg Philharmonia—H-J. Walther
(4ss)   *MSB. 78129/30*
(*Hanson & Skilton* on ♯ MGM.E 3141)

Sunday in Brooklyn   orch.   1946
Vienna Philharmonia—Adler   ♯ **SPA. 47**
(*Antheil, Cowell, etc.*)

SILVA, João Cordeiro da (b. c. 1750)

SEE: † CLAVECINISTES ESPAGNOLS ...

SIMON, Johann Kaspar (fl. c. 1750)

SEE: † BAROQUE ORGAN MUSIC

SIMONDS, Bruce (contemp.)

SEE: † AMERICAN ORGAN MUSIC

☆ = Re-issue of a recording to be found in previous volumes.

SINDING, Christian (1856-1941)

Rustle of Spring, Op. 32, No. 3   pf.
W. Gieseking   **C.LB 139**
(*Mendelssohn: Song without Words, No. 30*)
(*LW 64: GQ 7259*)
H. Roloff   **PV. 72395**
(*Grieg: Lyric Pieces*)
V. Schiøler   **G.DA 5284**
(*Grieg: Halling, Op. 71, No. 5*)   (♭ *7RK 7: 7EBK 1001*)
A. S. Rasmussen   **Tono.K 8098**
(*Mendelssohn: Spring Song*)   (♭ *EP 43029, d.c.*)
E. Møller   ♭ *Mtr.MCEP 3031*
(*Grieg & Liszt*)
A. Semprini (*G.B 10742*)
☆ E. Joyce (♭ *AmD.ED 3500*)

— ARR. 2 PFS.
M. Rawicz & W. Landauer (♭ *C.SEG 7506: SEDQ 514*)
L. Shankson & I. Wright (in ♯ *Roy. 1447*)

— ARR. ORCH
Scandinavian Sym.—Johannesen (in ♯ *Mae.OAT 25008*)
Concert Orch.—E. Robinson (in ♯ *Argo.RG 66*)

Serenade, D flat major, Op. 33, No. 4   pf.
E. Burton   in ♯ **CEd.CE 1027**

SONGS
COLLECTION
Faith, Op. 13, No. 4[1]
Sylvelin, Op. 55, No. 1   (V. Veslie)
There cried a bird, Op. 18, No. 5   (Krag)
We will have our land, Op. 38, No. 1   (Sivle)
C. Hague (T), G. Steele (pf.)   in ♯ **ML. 7034**
(† *Scandinavian Songs*)

Sylvelin, Op. 55, No. 1   (V. Veslie)
Ⴁ G. Farrar (S, *Eng*) (IRCC. 1953*)

Suite, A minor, Op. 10   vln. & orch.
J. Heifetz & Los Angeles Phil.—Wallenstein
♯ **Vic.LM 1832**
(*Tchaikovsky & Ravel*)   (♯ *ItV.A12R 0153*)

SINIGAGLIA, Leone (1868-1944)

Piedmontese Folk Song Arrangements
La Pastora fedele
Il Maritino
Ninna Nanna di Gesu' Bambino
Invito respinto
La bella al mulino
Il cacciatore del bosco
Il pellegrino di S. Giacomo
S. Calcina (S), M. Lessona (pf.)   *Fnt. 14092/3*
(4ss)

SIQUEIRA, José (b. 1907)

(5) Xangos 'Negro Cantata'
A. Ribeiro, Brazilian Cho. & Percussion Ens.
Orch.—Siqueira   **V♯ CdM.LDYA 8114**
(in ♯ *Van.VRS 465*)
Voce
A. Ribeiro (S) & orch.—Siqueira
V♯ CdM.LDY 8119
(in ♯ *Van.VRS 465*)
(*Ovalle & Villa-Lobos*)

SIRET, Nicolas (d. 1754)

SEE: † FRENCH BAROQUE ORGAN MUSIC

SKALKOTTAS, Nikos (1904-1949)

Passacaglia (No. 15 of *32 pf. pieces*, 1941)
Suite No. 4   pf.   1936
Short Variations on a theme of Southern character
pf. 1941
M. Papaioannou
(4) Greek Dances   vln. & pf.   1936
B. Kolassis & Y. Papadopoulos   ♯ **Phi.N 00247L**
(*Kalomiris & Varvoglis*)

SKILTON, Charles Sanford (1868-1941)

Shawnee Indian Hunting dance[2]
▽ Vic. Sym.—Cornwell (*Vic. 45-5075* in set E 89:
& set ♭ *WE 89*)

Suite primeval orig. str. qtt., 1915; orch., 1916
... **Part I: Two Indian Dances**
No. 1, Deer Dance; No. 2, War Dance of Cheyennes
Hamburg Philharmonia—H-J. Walther   *MSB. 78024*
(*Dett, Dubensky, Guion*) (&in ♯ *MGM.E 3141*)   & *78202*
... No. 1 only ▽ Vic. Sym.—Bourdon (*Vic. 22174*)
... No. 2 only ▽ Eastman-Rochester Sym.—Hanson
(*Vic. 11-8302*)
Vic. Sym. (*Vic. 45-5075* in set E 89; & set ♭ *WE 89*)
... **Part II:** No. 1, Sunrise Dance (▽ *Vic. 11-8302, above*)

SLAVENSKI, Josip (b. 1896)

Sinfonia Orienta A, T, B, Bs, cho. orch. 1933-4
M. Bugarinovich, D. Tzveych, D. Popovich,
X. Tzveych, cho. & Belgrade Phil.
—Zdravkovich   ♯ **D.LXT 5057**
(♯ *Lon.LL 1216*)

SLAVICKÝ, Klement (b. 1910)

(3) Moravian Dance Fantasies   1951
Czech Phil.—Ančerl   ♯ **Sup.LPV 201**
(*Janáček*)   (♯ *U. 5182G*)

SMETANA, Bedřich (1824-1884)

I. OPERAS

(The) BARTERED BRIDE   3 Acts   1866
COMPLETE RECORDINGS

Mařenka	... ...	M. Musilová (S)
Kruščina	... ...	V. Bednař (B)
Vašek	... ...	O. Kovář (T)
Jeník	... ...	I. Žídek (T)
Micha	... ...	Z. Otava (B)
Kečal	... ...	K. Kalaš (Bs)

Cho. & orch. of National Theatre, Prague
—Vogel   ♯ **Sup.SLPV 91/3**
(6ss)   (♯ *Ura. set 231; ♯ U. 5093/5G*)
(also ♯ *Csm.CRLP 160/1, 4ss*)
[*Ov. & Nos. 13, 24 also ♭ Ura.UREP 29;*
Highlights, ♯ Ura. 7171]

E. Shumilova, M. Skazin, A. Orfenov, G.
Nelepp, M. Soloviev, etc.; Bolshoi Theatre
Cho. & Orch.—Kondrashin (*Russ*)
(6ss)   ♯ **USSR.D 045/50**
(♯ *CHS. set 1318, 4ss*)
☆ T. Richter (S), S. Hauser (T), etc., Berlin Municipal
Op. Cho. & Orch.—Lenzer (*Ger*)
♯ **Nix.ULP 9210-1/3**

HIGHLIGHTS in *German*
Overture
No. 3, If such a thing   S   Act I
No. 5, As my mother blessed me ... Faithful love   S & T   Act I
No. 9, Polka   cho., ARR. orch.   Act I
No. 13, Furiant   orch.   Act II
No. 17, Each man praises his own darling   T & Bs   Act II
No. 24, Dance of the Comedians   orch.   Act III
No. 29, O what sorrow ... The dream of love   S   Act III
No. 30, Stop it, girl ... What an obstinate girl   S, T, B   Act III
H. Zadek (S), H. Hopf (T), O. Edelmann (Bs)
& Vienna Sym. Orch.—Loibner
♯ **EPhi.NBL 5024**
(2ss)   (♯ *Phi.N 00266L; Epic.LC 3181*)
[*Overture, & Nos. 9 & 24 on ♭ Phi.N 402027E*]

---

[1] This title has disappeared from current lists, though included in the original announcement.
[2] Orig. 3rd movt. of Vln. Sonata 2, G minor, 1922. Later for small orch. 1922; full orch., c. 1929.

No. 1, Why should we not be gay?   Cho.   Act I
No. 5, As my mother blessed me   S & T   Act I
No. 9, Polka   cho.   Act I
No. 15, I know a little girl   S & T   Act II
No. 17, Each man praises his own darling . . .
     I know a girl   T & Bs   Act II
No. 29, O what sorrow . . . The dream of love   S   Act III
No. 30, Stop it, girl . . . What an obstinate girl   S & T

A. Schlemm (S), W. Ludwig (T), P. Kuen (T)
[in No. 15], J. Greindl (Bs), Bavarian Radio
Cho & Orch.—Lehmann   ♯ Pol. 19014
[No. 9 also in ♯ Pol. 19048; Nos. 1 & 9, ♭ Pol. 30145]

Nos. 1, 3, 5, 17, 20, 9, 28, 29, 30, 33 (Finale), 24, 34 (Final Scene)

E. Berger (S), C. Ludwig (M-S), R. Schock (T),
G. Frick (Bs), H. H. Nissen (B), etc., Hanover
Landesstheater Cho. & N.W. Ger. Phil.
Orch.—Schüchter   ♯ G.WBLP 1508
[Excerpts from this are entered individually below]

HIGHLIGHTS in *Russian*
Jenik's aria, Marenka's aria & Polka
  G. Nelepp, I. Maslennikova, Bolshoi Th. Cho.
                  (♯ *USSR.D 2181*)

ORCHESTRAL SUITES
Overture & Nos. 9, 13 & 24
Philharmonia—Kubelik   ♯ G.ALP 1049
(*Mendelssohn*) (♯ QALP 10027: VALP 516: FALP 304)
[Overture & Nos. 13 & 24 are ☆; No. 9 also on
G.DB 4328: ♭ 7RF/RQ 259; Overture, Nos. 13 & 24
also on ♭ Vic.EHA 10; Nos. 9, 13 & 24 ♭ G. 7ER 5010:
7ERF 135: 7ERQ 114; Overture on ♭ 7ERQ 116:
7ER 5015]

☆ Los Angeles Phil.—Wallenstein   ♯ B.AXTL 1063
(*Chabrier & Berlioz*)   (♯ AmD.DL 9728)
(♯ AFest.CFR 10-1122; & 2ss, ♯ ArgOd.LTC 8506;
                         D.UW 333010)

Overture & No. 9
Berlin Sym.—Rubahn   in ♯ Roy. 1534

Overture & Nos. 13 & 24
☆ Berlin Municipal Op.—Lenzer   ♯ Ura.RS 5-3
(*Ponchielli*)   (from set)

Nos. 9, 13, 24
Hamburg Philharmonia—H-J. Walther   *MSB. 78109*
           (in ♯ MGM.E 3195: ♭ set X 307)
Bolshoi Theatre—Kondrashin   ♯ USSR.D 553
(*Dvořák: Legends*)

☆ C.B.S.—Barlow (in ♯ AmC.RL 3030)

Overture
Lamoureux—Dourian   ♯ *Phil.A 76707R*
(*Dourian & Glinka*)

Philharmonia—Kletzki   ♭ *C.SEL 1510*
(*Brahms: Hungarian Dances*)   (♭ *SEBQ 114*)
(*Tchaikovsky & Ravel*, on ♯ *C.CX 1164*)
(also *C.LX 1594*: GQX 11540)

Orch.—Swarowsky   (*Dvořák*)   ♯ *MTW. 22*

Berlin Radio—Kleinert (*Eta. 120048*)
Berlin Sym.—Balzer (in ♯ Roy. 1403)
Philharmonia—Berendt (in ♯ Allo. 3081)
International Sym.—Schneiderhan (in ♯*Mae.OA 20009*)
☆ L.S.O.—Kisch (D.K 23265: ♭ 71022)
    Boston Prom.—Fiedler (♭ *Cam.CAE 105*
                        & in ♯ CAL 122)

ACT I
No. 3, If such a thing . . .   S
(*Gerne will ich dir vertrauen*)
A. Kawecka (*Polish*)   Muza.X 2345
(*No. 29*)
☆ E. Trötschel (*Ger*) (♭ *Pol. 34017*)

No. 9, Polka   Cho.
— ARR. ORCH.   Riesenfeld & others
Philharmonia—Kubelik   G.DB 4328
(*Dvořák: Legend, Op. 59, No 10*)   (♭ 7RQ/RF 259)

Philadelphia—Ormandy   ♯ & ♭ *AmC.PE 20*
(*No. 24*)
☆ Royal Phil.—Beecham (♭ *G. 7RQ 3031*)
    Minneapolis Sym.—Ormandy (in ♯ Cam.CAL 121)

ACT II
No. 15, I know a little girl   S & T
A. Schlemm & P. Kuen (*Ger*)   PV. 72479
(*No. 29*) [from Highlights]   (♭ *Pol. 30065*)
Ⓗ J. Gadski & A. Reiss (*Ger*) (AF.AGSB 12*)

No. 17, Each man praises his own darling . . .
     I know a girl   T & Bs
R. Schock & G. Frick (*Ger*)   G.DB 11582
(*No. 28*) [from Highlights] (♭ *7RW 542:* in ♯ *WBLP 1514*)

... Bass solo only
J. Berglund (*Ger*)   in ♯ G.ALPC 1
(*Barbiere, Tannhäuser, etc.*)

No. 20, How could he believe   T
R. Schock (*Ger*)   in ♯ *G.WBLP 1515*
(*Mignon, Kuhreigen, etc.*)
☆ W. Ludwig (*Ger*) (in ♯ *AmD.DL 4073*)
Ⓗ R. Tauber (*Ger*) (in ♯ Cum.CE 187*)

ACT III
No. 23, March of the Comedians
Berlin Sym.—Rubahn   in ♯ Roy. 1534
Zagreb Radio Sym. (*Jug.P 16121*)

No. 24, Dance of the Comedians
Berlin Sym.—Rubahn   in ♯ Roy. 1534
☆ Royal Phil.—Beecham (♭ *G.7RQ 3031*)
    Aarhus Municipal—Jensen (in ♯ Tono.LPX 35005;
                      ♭ *Mer.EP 1-5009*)
☆ Vienna Radio—Schönherr (in ♯ *Vien.LPR 1037*)
    Philadelphia—Ormandy (♯ & ♭ *AmC.PE 20*: in ♭ *A 1620*)
    Minneapolis Sym.—Ormandy (in ♯ Cam.CAL 121)
    A. Newman Orch. (in ♯ FMer.MLP 7052)

No. 28, Think it over, Mařenka   S, A, A, B, B, Bs.
E. Berger, C. Ludwig, M. Höffgen, H. H.
Nissen, T. Schlott, G. Frick (*Ger*)
                         G.DB 11582
(*No. 17*) [from Highlights]   (♭ *7RW 542*)
☆ Soloists of Berlin Municipal Op.   ♭ *Nix.EP 766*
(*Lucia—Sextet*) [from set]   (♭ *Ura.UREP 66*)

No. 29, O what sorrow . . . The dream of love   S
A. Schlemm (*Ger*)   PV. 72479
(*No. 15*) [from Highlights]   (♭ *Pol. 30065*)
E. Trötschel (*Ger*)   PV. 72398
(*Lortzing: Der Waffenschmied—Er schläft*)
A. Kawecka (*Pol*) (Muza.X 2345)

DALIBOR   3 Acts   1868
COMPLETE RECORDING

Vladislav	V. Bednář (B)
Dalibor	B. Blachut (T)
Budivoj	T. Šrubař (Bs)
Beneš	K. Kalaš (B)
Vitek	A. Votava (T)
Milada	M. Podvalová (S)
Vitka	Š. Petrová (S)

☆ Cho. & Orch. of Prague Nat. Op.—Krombholc
                     ♯ Sup.SLPV 98/100
(6ss)   (♯ U. 5085/7G)
(5ss—*Fibich: Bride from Messina*, on ♯ Csm.CRLP 181/3)

Didst thou hear it, friend?   T   Act I
(*Slyšel's to, příteli*)
Ⓗ E. Schmedes (*Ger*) (in ♯ HRS. 3006*)

How do I feel?   (*Jak je mi?*)   S   Act II
Ⓗ E. Destinn (*Ger*) (AF.AGSB 12*)

(The) KISS   2 Acts   1876   (*Hubička*)
COMPLETE RECORDING

Vendulka	L. Cervinková (S)
Martinka	M. Krásová (A)
Barče	Š. Petrová (S)
Lukáš	B. Blachut (T)
Tomes	P. Kočí (B)
Father Paloucký	K. Kalaš (B)
Matouš	V. Jedenáctik (Bs)

& Prague Nat. Theatre Orch.—Chalabala
                     ♯ Sup.SLPV 142/4
(6ss)   (♯ U. 5132/4G; 4ss, ♯ Csm.CRLP 184/5)

Cradle Song   (*Ukolebavky*)   S   Act I
    A. Kawecka (*Pol*) (Muza.X 2282)
☆ J. Novotná (in ♯ Vic. set LCT 6701)

If I knew how to wash away the guilt   T   Act II
W. Kmentt (*Ger*)   in ♯ *Phi.S 06075R*
(*Švanda, Eugene Oniegin, Prince Igor, etc.*)

☆ = Re-issue of a recording to be found in previous volumes.

LIBUŠE 3 Acts 1872, f.p. 1881
Overture
Berlin Radio—Rother   **♯ Ura. 7094**
(*Dvořák*)

(The) SECRET 3 Acts 1878
(*Tajemství*)
COMPLETE RECORDING

Malina	K. Kalaš (Bs)
Kalina	P. Kočí (B)
Rose	Š. Štěpánová (S)
Bloženka	Š. Petrová (S)
Vít	I. Žídek (T)
Skřivánek	O. Kovář (T)

etc., & Prague, Nat. Theatre Cho. & Orch
—Krombholc (6ss)   **♯ Sup.SLPV 157/9**
(6ss)   (♯ U. 5142/4G)

II. SONGS

Evening Song (unspec.)
M. Alexandrovich (T)   **USSR. 18500**
(*Karlowicz: Song*)

Spring (unspec.)
E. Katulskaya (S)   **USSR. 22827**
(*Dvořák: Songs my mother taught me*)

III. INSTRUMENTAL & CHAMBER MUSIC

From my homeland vln. & pf. 1878
... **No. 2,** only
I. Bezrodny & S. Wakman **♭ Phi.N 402049E**
(*Ravel: Tzigane*)

... **Unspec.**
V. Pickeisen, I. Kollegorskaya **USSR. 17144/5**
(2ss)

Memory, Op. 4, No. 3 (from *Sketches*) pf. 1858
— ARR. VLC. & PF.
M. Rostropovich & pf.   **USSRM.D 00208**
(*Tchaikovsky & Chopin*)

QUARTETS, Strings
No. 1, E minor (From my life) 1876
Végh Qtt.   **♯ D.LXT 2876**
(*Kodály*)   (♯ Lon.LL 865)
Netherlands Qtt.   **♯ Phi.N 00615R**
Curtis Qtt.   **♯ West.WL 5199**
(*Dvořák: Qtt. No. 6*)
Bolshoi Theatre Qtt.   **♯ USSR.D 1298/9**
☆ Stradivari Qtt. (♯ Cpt.MC 20068)

No. 2, D minor 1882
☆ Smetana Qtt. (♯ Sup.LPM 74; U. 5032C)

Trio, G minor, Op. 15 pf., vln., vlc. 1855
L. Mittman, A. Eidus & G. Ricci
(*Dvořák*)   **♯ Strad.STR 620**

Wedding Scenes pf. 1849
— ARR. ORCH.
Leipzig Radio—Pflüger   **♯ Ura. 7132**
(*Dvořák*)
Linz Sym.   **♯ Ply. 12-37**
(*Dvořák & Liszt*)
☆ F.O.K. Sym.—Vostřák (in ♯ U.5215H)

IV. CZECH DANCES

POLKAS (Bohemian Dances) Book I pf.
No. 2, A minor
E. Gilels[1] (*below*)   **USSR. 18784**

No. 3, F major
E. Gilels   **USSR. 18785**
(*Polka, A minor*)

Bohemian Dances, Book II pf.
... **No. 2, The little hen** (*Slepička*)
M. Fedorova   **USSR. 22271**
(*Liadov: Preludes*)

[1] Or perhaps Op. 12, No. 1.

V. ORCHESTRAL

MY COUNTRY (*Ma Vlast*) 1874-9
COMPLETE
Chicago Sym.—Kubelik   **♯ Mer.OL-2-100**
(4ss)   (♯ FMer.MLP 7527/8)
[Nos. 1 & 2, with *Mozart: Sym.* 38, on ♯ Mer.MG 50042]
☆ Prague Radio—Jeremiáš (4ss) ♯ Csm.CRLPX 009/10

No. 1, Vyšehrad
Berlin Sym.—Rubahn   **♯ Roy. 1534**
(*Bartered Bride; & Schubert*)

No. 2, Vltava (*Moldau*)
Philharmonia—Ackermann   **♯ C.C 1042**
(*No. 4, below*)
Berlin Phil.—Fricsay   **♯ HP.DG 17018**
(*No. 4*) (also PV. 72320; IPV. 8203; ♭ Pol. 30049)
Amsterdam—Dorati   **♯ EPhi.NBR 6010**
(*Dvořák*) (♯ Phi.S 06053R, o.n. N. 00620R;
    in ♯ Epic.LC 3015)
Czech Phil.—Šejna   **♯ Sup.LPM 235**
(*No. 4*)
N.W. Ger. Phil.—Schüchter **♯ Imp.ILP 105**
(*Mozart: Serenade No. 13*) (♯ G.QDLP 6029)
Bamberg Sym.—Perlea **♯ AmVox.PL 9500**
(*Dvořák, Enesco, Kodály*)
"Philharmonic"—Berendt   **♯ Allo. 3081**
(*No. 4; & Bartered Bride, Overture*)
Chicago Sym.—Kubelik [from set] ♭ Mer.EP 1-5027
☆ Vienna Phil.—Furtwängler   **♯ G.BLP 1009**
(*Schumann: Manfred Over.*) (♯ QBLP 5006: FBLP 1046:
    VBLP 802 & ♮ G.DB 9787/9)
☆ Bamberg Sym.—Keilberth   **♯ DT.TM 68025**
(*Beethoven: Leonore Ov. 3*)
    (also T.VSK 9201: ♭ UV 101)
(*Liszt: Hung. Rhaps.* on ♯ T.TW 30002)
(*No. 4* on ♯ FT. 270.TC.038)
☆ Los Angeles Phil.—Wallenstein   **♯ B.AXTL 1063**
(*Bartered Bride, excpts. & Chabrier, Berlioz*)
    (♯ AmD.DL 9728)
(*Enesco: Rumanian Rhaps. No. 1*, ♯ D.UW 333009)
☆ N.Y.P.S.O.—Szell   **♯ C.C 1019**
(*No. 4*) (*No. 4, & Dvořák*, ♯ AmC.ML 4785) (♯ QC 5019)
Sym.—Szell (♯ MApp. 610)
Sym.—Swarowsky (♯ ACC.MP 20)
Anon. Orch. (♯ Gram. 2087), etc.
☆ Boston Prom.—Fiedler (♯ Vic.LM 9017)
Nat. Sym. (U.S.A.)—Kindler (in ♯ Cam.CAL 115 &
    set CFL 103)
Austrian Sym.—Singer (♯ Cum.TCR 269; Ply. 12-79)
Rhineland Sym.—Federer (♯ AFest.CFR 33)
Berlin State Op.—Mörike (Od.NLX 3/4)

No. 4, From Bohemia's meadows and forests
Berlin Phil.—Fricsay   **♯ HP.DG 17018**
(*No. 2*) (in ♯ AmD.DL 9738; & 2ss, PV. 72383)
Philharmonia—Ackermann   **♯ C.C 1042**
(*No. 2*)
Czech Phil.—Šejna   **♯ Sup.LPM 235**
(*No. 2*)
☆ N.Y.P.S.O.—Szell (*No. 2*) ♯ C.C 1019
(*No. 2, & Dvořák: Slavonic Dances*, on ♯ AmC.ML 4785)
    (♯ QC 5019)
Berlin Sym.—Balzer (in ♯ Roy. 1403)
"Philharmonic"—Berendt (in ♯ Allo. 3081)
Sym.—Swarowsky (in ♯ ACC.MP 20)
☆ Bamberg Sym.—Keilberth (♯ FT.270.TC. 038)

Wallenstein's Camp, Op. 14 1858
☆ Vienna Sym.—Swarowsky   **♯ West.WN 18069**
(*Janáček*)   (V♯ Sel.LAP 1029, 2ss)

SMITH, Russel (b.1927)

(6) Songs of Innocence (Blake) 1950
S. Carter (S), B. Weiser (pf.) **♯ NE. 2**
(*Flanagan, Citkowitz, Chanler*)

SÖDERMAN, Johan August (1832-1876)

(A) PEASANT WEDDING (Gustafsson)
cho. 1869
... **No. 1, Wedding March** — ARR. ORGAN
H. Lindroth (♭ D.SDE 7015)

... No. 3, Song of wishing
No. 4, In the Bridal house
Stockholm Students—E. Ralf   ♯ *SS. 33105*
(*Sibelius, Grieg, Alfvén, etc.*)

SONGS
Hymn   (Wallmark)   (*Fjärran ack fjärran*)
D. Bergquist (Tr.), G. Edmundh (pf.)   *Sir. 119*
(*Bach: Dir, dir, Jehova*)

(The) WEDDING AT ULFÅSA
Inc. Music to Hedberg's play
Wedding March   ARR. ORGAN
H. Lindroth (♭ *D.SDE 7015*)

SOLER, Padre Antonio (1729-1783)

Quintet, G minor, "Op. 1", No. 6 Org. & str. 1776
M-C. Alain & Ens.—Paillard   ♯ **DDP.DP 501**
(*C. P. E. Bach*)

SONATAS, Hpsi.
COLLECTIONS
(numbered from the NIN edition; Vol. I unless marked)

No. 1, D minor	No. 5, D major	No. 11, G minor
No. 3, C minor	No. 7, D major	No. 12, F♯ major
No. 4, D minor	No. 9, D♭ major	
No. 10, F major	No. 2, A minor (Vol. II)	

F. Valenti   ♯ **West.WL 5196**

No. 2, C♯ minor	No. 11, G minor
No. 5, D major	No. 12, F♯ major
No. 6, F♯ minor	

☆ H. Boschi (pf.)   in **V**♯ *CdM.LDY 8081*
(† *Old Spanish Keyboard Music*)

No. 2, C♯ minor	No. 5, D major

F. Blumenthal (pf.)   ♯ **D.LXT 2805**
(† *Spanish Keyboard Music*)   (♯ *Lon.LL 769*)

No. 4, D minor	No. 8, G minor
No. 5, D major	No. 12, F♯ major
No. 6, F♯ minor	

J. Falgarona (pf.)   in ♯ **AmVox.PL 8340**
(† *Spanish Keyboard Music*)

No. 1, D minor	No. 4, D minor
No. 2, C♯ minor	

S. Weissenberg (pf.)   ♯ **Lum.LD 3-400**
(*Bach-Liszt, Haydn, Czerny*)

No. 5, D major
E. Osta (pf.)   in ♯ **Allo. 3151**
(*Infante, Albeniz, Falla, etc.*)

No. 11, G minor
F. Blumenthal (pf.)   in ♯ **D.LXT 5218**
(† *Spanish Keyboard Music II*)   (♯ *Lon.LL 1194*)

No. 5, D major	No. 6, F♯ minor
No. 7, D major	No. 8, G minor
No. 9, D♭ major	No. 10, F major
No. 11, G minor	No. 12, F♯ major

— ARR. DANCING & ORCH. Currás
"Antonio" & R. Segovia; Sym. Orch.—Currás
                                    ♭ *SpC.SCGE 80014/5*
(4ss)   (♯ *CL 26000*)

SOMIS, Giovanni Battista (1686-1763)

Sonata, D minor vln. & cont.
... Adagio & Allegro — ARR. FL., OB., CL., HRN.
& BSN. Hernried
Chicago Sym. Woodwind Quintet
                    in ♯ **Aphe.AP 16**

SONNINEN, Ahti (b. 1914)

PART SONG: Rippling Water (*Solivesa vesi*)
Helsinki Univ. Cho.—Turunen
                    in ♯ **Rem. 199-167**

PESSI & ILLUSIA Ballet Suite, orch.
Finnish Radio—Sonninen (6ss)   **G.TN 3/5**

SOR, Fernando (*c.* 1778-1839)

GUITAR PIECES
COLLECTIONS
Introduction & Allegro
Minuets: A major; E major
Studies: A major; G major
            B minor; A major
(all unspec.; it has not been possible to check)
A. Segovia   ♯ **AmD.DL 9794**
(*Tárrega*)

Minuets: D major; A major, Op. 11, Nos. 5 & 6
Sonata (Grande), Op. 22
Studies: A minor, Op. 6, No. 6
            B flat major, Op. 29, No. 1
            B minor, Op. 35, No. 22
Variations on a theme of Mozart, Op. 9
☆ R. de la Torre   (*Bach*)   ♯ **Roy. 1422**

Andantino, Op. 24, No. 1
Minuet, D major, Op. 11, No. 5
Sonata, C major, Op. 22 ... Minuet
A. Segovia   in ♯ **B.AXTL 1069**
(† *Segovia Evening II*)   (♯ *AmD.DL 9751*)

Andante largo, Op. 5, No. 5
I. Presti   ♭ *FV.F 75022*
(*Pujol: Évocation cubaine*)

Andantino, Op. 24, No. 1
M. D. Cano   *Dur.AI 10230*
(*below, Bach & Visée, in* ♯ *MSE 2*)

(3) Little Dances (unspec.)
L. Walker   in ♯ *Phi.N 00626R*

Minuets, G major; G minor (unspec.)
S. Pastor   ♯ **NRI.NRLP 5005**
(*Fortea, Visée, Tárrega, Pastor*)

Minuets, G major, Op. 11, No. 1
            D major, Op. 11, No. 5
Rondo (unspec.)
N. Yepes   in ♯ **D.LXT 2974**
(† *Spanish Music*)   (♯ *FST 153076; Lon.LL 1042*)

Minuet (unspec.)
M. D. Cano   *Dur.AI 10230*
(*Andantino*)   (in ♯ *MSE 2*)
A. Iglesias   *Od.DK 1233*
(*Iglesias: Arabesques*)

Preludio (unspec.) ☆ V. Gómez (in ♭ *AmD. set ED 809*)

Siciliana, Op. 33, No. 3
M. A. Funes   *ArgOd. 66067*
(*Albeniz: Torre bermeja*)

Sonata (Grande), C major, Op. 22
R. V. Blain   ♯ *SMC. 546*
(*Miscellaneous unspec. pieces*)

Sonata No. 2, C major, Op. 25
... Minuet only ☆ A. Segovia (in † ♯ *B.AXTL 1060*)
... Allegro only ☆ A. Segovia (in † ♯ *D.UAT 273141*)

Study, A major, Op. 6, No. 6
L. Almeida   ♯ **DCap.CTL 7089**
(† *Guitar Music of Spain*)   (♯ *Cap.P 8295*)
Study (unspec.): F. Casseus (in ♯ *EFL.FP 822*)

Variations on a theme of Mozart, Op. 9[1]
L. Walker   in ♯ *Phi.N 00626R*
                    (♯ *Epic.LC 3055*)
A. Malukoff   ♯ *Rom.RR 7*
(*Giuliani & Tárrega*)
☆ A. Segovia (in † ♭ *D.UAT 273142*)

Variations (petites) sur un air français
☆ L. Walker   in ♯ *Phi.N. 00640R*
                    (in ♯ *Epic.LC 3055*)

SORIANO, Francesco (1549-*c.* 1622)

PASSION MUSIC: St. Matthew Passion 1619
(as part of *Office for Palm Sunday*)
Angers Cath. Cho.—Poirier   ♯ **SM. 33-02**
(*Vespers for All Saints Day; Victoria, etc.*)

---

[1] Theme from *Die Zauberflöte*.

SORO, Enrique (1884-1954)

Andante Appassionato
Danzas Fantásticas
(3) Aires Chilenos orch.
    Chile Sym.—V. Tevah   ♯ ChV.CRL 2
   (A. Letelier: Vitrales de la Annunciaclón)

SOUTULLO, Reveriano (1884-1932)
(with VERT, Juan—1890-1931)

ZARZUELAS (abridged listings only)
(La) DEL SOTO DEL PARRAL 3 Acts 1927
   T. Rosado, T. Berganza, M. Ausensi, C. Munguía, etc.,
   Madrid Cho. & Orch.—Argenta   ♯ LI.TW 91128
                    (♯ Ambra.MCC 30025)
   [Excerpts in ♭ SpC.SMGE 80000; ♯ LI.W 91028;
                  ♯ Ambra.MC 25005]
   M. Espinalt, C. Panadés, M. Redondo, etc., Cho. & Orch.
   —Ferrer   ♯ Reg.LCX 108
                  (♯ Angel. 65000)
   [Excerpts in ♭ Reg.SEDL 19040 & SEBL 7014]
   Vocal excerpts L. Sagi-Vela (B) (in ♯ MusH.LP 5004)
(La) LEYENDA DEL BESO 2 Acts
Intermezzo orch.
   Madrid Cha.—Argenta   in ♯ LI.TW 91004
   (& ♭ Ambra.EMGE 70018)   (♯ Ambra.MCC 30009 &
                         MCCP 29001)
   Madrid Theatre—Moreno Torroba in ♯ B.AXTL 1077
                    (♯ AmD.DL 9735)
   Sym.—Ferrer   ♭ Reg.SEDL 108
   (Chueca & Albeniz)   (♭ Angel. 70018, d.c.)
   (& in ♯ Reg.LCX 104; C.FSX 104; Pam.LRC 15905;
           Angel. 65008; also ♯ Reg.LS 1005)
   Sym.—Martinez   in ♯ Mont.FM 16
   Colón Theatre—Cases   ArgOd. 66021
        (♭ BSOAE 4514: BSOA 4002: in ♯ LDC 504)

SOWERBY, Leo (b. 1895)

ORGAN MUSIC
Canon, Chacony & Fugue pub. 1951
   T. Schaefer   ♯ Den.DR 3
   (below; & Widor)

Carillon, A flat major 1917
   L. Farnam[1]   ♯ CEd.CE 1040
   (Bach, Handel, Vierne)
   "Staff organist"   in ♯ ASK. 2
   (Bach, Langlais, Alain, etc.) [Kilgore organ, Texas]
   T. Schaefer *(above)*   ♯ Den.DR 3

Prelude on 'Deus tuorum militum' 1955
   A. Wyton   in ♯ ASK. 6
   (Whitlock, Britten, etc.)

Requiescat in pace 1920
Suite 1933-4
... 2nd movt., Fantasy for Flute Stops
   C. Crozier   in ♯ Ken. 2555
   († American Organ Music)

Symphony, G major 1930
   C. Crozier   ♯ Ken. 2554
   [Organ of Baptist Church, Longview, Texas]

SPELMAN, Timothy Mather (b. 1891)

Pervigilium Veneris S, B, cho. & orch. 1929
   I. Steingruber, O. Wiener, Vienna Acad. Cho.
   & State Op. Orch.—Fekete ♯ MGM.E 3085

SPITZMÜLLER-HARMERSBACH,
Alexander (b. 1894)

Concerto, Op. 39 2 pfs. 1951
   I. Marika & J. Manchon-Theis ♯ Cpt.MC 20024
   (Dillon & Harsányi)

Beati mortui
   ▽ Vienna Cha. Cho.—Grossmann (Sel. GZ 8024)

SPOHR, Louis (1784-1859)

Concerto No. 8, A minor, vln. & orch. Op. 47 1816
   ("Gesangsscene")
   R. Koeckert & Bavarian Radio—Lehmann
   (Beethoven: Romances)   ♯ Pol. 19012

Fantasia, A flat major, Op. 35 harp
   E. Vito   in ♯ Per.SPL 721
   (Grandjany, Tournier, etc.)

Nonet, F major, Op. 31
   fl., ob., cl., hrn., bsn., vln., vla., vlc., cbs.
   J. Niedmayer (fl.), K. Mayrhofer (ob.) & Vienna
   Octet members   ♯ D.LXT 2782
                  (♯ Lon.LL 710)

SPONTINI, Gasparo Luigi Pacifico
(1774-1851)

(La) VESTALE 3 Acts 1807 *(orig. French)*
Overture
   ☆ L.S.O.—Previtali (in ♯ BB.LBC 1039: ♭ set WBC 1039)

STAINER, Sir John (1840-1901)

(The) CRUCIFIXION Oratorio 1887
COMPLETE RECORDING
   ▽ R. Crooks (T), L. Tibbett (B), Trinity Cho., M. Andrews
   (org.)   ♯ Cam.CAL 235
   (o.n. G.D 1817/22; Vic. 9424/9 in set M. 64)
... God so loved the world ... Cho.
   Protestant Fellowship Cho.   in ♯ FSM. 305
   ☆ Shaw Chorale (♭ G.7EP 7012; ♭ DV. 26027)

STALLAERT, Alphonse (b. 1920)

Concerto, pf. & orch. 1950
   D. Wayenberg & Lamoureux—Stallaert
                 ♯ Phi.N 00688R

STAMITZ, Carl (1746-1801)

Concertos, fl. & orch. : D major ; G major
   ☆ K. Redel & O.L. Ens.   ♯ LOL.OL 50035
Concerto, D major, hpsi. & orch.
   MS., Brussels Cons.
   F. Pelleg & Winterthur Sym.—Dahinden
   (C. P. E. Bach)   ♯ CHS.H 11
Quartet, Strings, A major, Op. 14, No. 6
   New Music Qtt.   ♯ BRS. 915
   (Richter)
Sonata, D major, vla. d'amore & vla.[2] c. 1780
   E. Seiler & I. Brix-Meinert   PV. 9404
   [ed. Seiler]   (♭ Pol. 37074)
Symphony ('Concerto'), F major, Op. 4, No. 4 str.
   Saar Cha.—Ristenpart   V♯ DFr.EX 17026

STANFORD, Sir Charles Villiers
(1852-1924)

ANTHEMS
Coelos ascendit hodie, Op. 38, No. 2[3]
   St. Paul's Cath. Cho.—Dykes Bower
                 in ♯ C.CX 1237
   (Mendelssohn, Gibbons, Bennet, etc.)
           (in ♯ Angel. 35139, in set 3516)
(The) Lord is my shepherd, Op. 38[4] 1886
   Canterbury Cath. Cho., W. T. Harvey (org.)
   —Knight   C.LX 1570
   († English Church Music, Vol. III)
Festal Communion Service, B flat major, Op. 128
... Gloria in excelsis
   Coronation Chorus & Orch.—McKie
               in ♯ G.ALP 1058
   († Coronation of Queen Elizabeth II)

---

[1] Recorded from an Austin player roll of 1930.
[2] The 5th movt. consists of variations on *Malbrouck s'en va-t-en guerre.*
[3] Published as Op. 38 (Boosey & Hawkes); Op. 51 in *Grove*; also known as Op. 47.
[4] Op. no. as given in *Grove.*

PART SONG: The Blue Bird, Op. 119, No. 3
(M. E. Coleridge)
☆ Glasgow Orpheus Cho.—Roberton (in ♯ *G.DLP 1020*)

Sonata, F major, Op. 129 cl. & pf.
... Caoine only
J. Stowell & D. Mayer　　　　　　♯ **Aphe.AP 26**
(*Jean Jean, Verdi, Weber*)

SONGS
(The) Fairy Lough, Op. 77, No. 2 (O'Neill)
(A) Soft day, Op. 141, No. 3 (Letts)
K. Ferrier (A), F. Stone (pf.)[1]　in ♯ *D.LX 3133*
(*Bridge, Britten, Parry, etc.*)　　　(♯ *Lon.LS 1032*)

(6) Songs from 'The Glens of Antrim', Op. 174
(M. O'Neill)

1. Benny's daughter	2. The sailor man
3. Lookin' back	4. At sea
5. I mind the day	6. The boy from Ballytearim

G. Clinton (B), P. Oyez (pf.)　♯ **CA.LPA 1095**
(*Dvořák & Handel*)

SONGS OF THE SEA, Op. 91 (Newbolt)
... No. 1, Drake's Drum; No. 3, The "Old Superb"
R. Standen (B), F. Stone (pf.) in ♯ **West.WLE 103**
(*Warlock, Ireland, etc.*)

STANLEY, John (1713-1786)

Suite, D major, Op. 6, No. 6 organ *c.* 1755
F. Peeters　　　　　　in ♯ **Per.SPL 578**
(† Old English Masters)　　　(♯ *Cpt.MC 20049*)

Toccata for the flutes, Op. 7, No. 7 organ *c.* 1755
A. Wyton　　　　　　　in ♯ **ASK. 6**
(*Sowerby, Whitlock, etc.*)

STARER, Robert (b. 1924)

Lullaby for Amittai pf.
M. Pressler　　　　　in ♯ **MGM.E 3010**

STARK, Richard (b. 1923)
SEE: † HYMNS OF PRAISE

STEFFANI, Agostino (1654-1728)
SEE: † ANTHOLOGIE SONORE

STEHMAN, Jacques (b. 1914)

Chant funèbre
Symphonie de Poche 1952
Belgian Nat.—v. Remoortel　　　♯ *LI.W 91082*
(♯ *D.BA 133184*)

Matins pf. 1938
▽ P. de Clerck　　　　　　*C.BF 5008*
(*Huybrechts: Sicilienne*)

STEIGLEDER, Hans Ulrich (1593-1635)
SEE :† BAROQUE ORGAN MUSIC

STEIN, Leon (b. 1910)

(3) Hassidic Dances 1940-1
Cincinnati Sym.—Johnson　　♯ **Rem. 199-185**
(*Ward*)

STENHAMMAR, Vilhelm Eugen
(1871-1927)

(A) PEOPLE Cantata 1905 (Heidenstam)
No. 5, Sweden (*Sverige*) Cho.
— ARR. SOLO VOICE　☆ J. Björling (T) (♭ *G.7EBS 1*)

STERKEL, Johann Francis Xavier (1750-1817)
SEE: † MUSICAL ORGAN CLOCK

STEVENS, Bernard (b. 1916)

Sonata, Op. 25 pf.
C. Lythgoe　　　　　♯ **CA.LPA 1075**[2]
(*Bliss*)

STEVENS, Halsey (b. 1908)

Triskelion orch. 1954
Louisville—Whitney　　　　♯ **LO. 1**
(*Creston & Villa-Lobos*)

STILL, William Grant (b. 1895)

To you, America Band 1952
U.S. Military Acad.—Resta　　♯ **PFCM.CB 177**
(*Ravel, Milhaud, etc.*)

STÖLZEL, Gottfried Heinrich (1690-1749)

Partita, G minor (in W. F. Bach *Clavierbüchlein*)
... Overture
R. Lenning (pf.)　　　　　♯ **B & B. 5**
(as illustration to lecture on Bach's ornaments)

STOIA, Achim (b. 1910)

(3) Dances from Ardeal orch. 1947
Bucharest Sym.—Elenescu (2ss)　　**Pop. 5036**

STRADELLA, Alessandro (1642-1682)

"Aria da Chiesa" See ROSSINI: Pietà Signore

Ave verum corpus
M. Maurene (S), J. Ullern (org.)　　*Sat.S 1142*
(*Bizet: Agnus Dei*)

FLORIDORO (or MORO PER AMORE)
Opera *c.* 1675
Stelle ingrate, che sarà? Act II
M. Ritchie (S), D. Bond (S)　　**G.HMS 46**
(† History of Music in Sound) (in ♯ Vic. set LM 6030)

Ombre, voi che celate Cantata (MS., Venice)
N. Brincker (T), vlc. & hpsi.　♭ *Mtr.MCEP 3011*
(*A. Scarlatti: Pensieri*)
(idem, & Albinoni & Vivaldi, on ♯ HS.HS 9011)

SUSANNA Oratorio 1681 (ed. Piccioli)
L. Bonetti (S), C. Carbi (A), N. Adami &
A. Ferrario (T), G. Ferrein (Bs), Angelicum
Cho. & Orch.—Janes　　　♯ **Ang.LPA 955**

(6) TRIO SONATAS
(Sinfonie stromentali a 2 & 3)

1. D minor	2. B flat major	3. A minor
4. D major	5. F major	6. D major

— ARR. VLN. VLC. & PF.　Montanari
Bolzano Trio　　　　♯ **E. & AmVox.PL 8380**
(♯ *BàM.LD 09*)

STRAUSS, Eduard (1835-1916)

Bahn frei! Op. 45 (Polka schnell)
☆ Philadelphia—Ormandy (AmC.J 244)
Boston Prom.—Fiedler[3] (in ♯ Cam.CAL 126:
♭ *CAE 214*)

Doctrinen Waltz, Op. 79
☆ Vienna Radio—Schönherr (in ♯ *Vien.LPR 1026*)

---

[1] Broadcast performance, 5 June, 1952.
[2] Announced, but not issued containing this music; *see* BLISS & FERGUSON.　　　　　　[3] ARR. Bodge.

STRAUSS, Johann I (the father)
(1804-1849)

COLLECTION

Donaulieder, Op. 127 Waltz
Loreley-Rheinklänge, Op. 154 Waltz
Radetzky-Marsch, Op. 228
Sperl-Galop, Op. 42
Sperl-Polka, Op. 133

Vienna State Op.—Paulik   ♯ Van.VRS 458
(*Lanner*)   (♯ Ama.VRS 6013)

Loreley-Rheinklänge, Op. 154 Waltz
Strauss Fest. Orch.—Ries-Walter (in ♯ *Mae.OA 20012*)
Orch.—B. Stanley (in ♯ *Var. 6984*)
☆ Vienna Radio—Schönherr (in ♯ Vien.LPR 1026)

POLKAS

COLLECTION

Sperl-Polka, Op. 133
Fortuna Polka, Op. 219
Damen-Souvenir, Op. 236
Piefke und Pufke, Op. 235

Schneider Str. Ens.   ♯ AmC.CL 556
(*J. Strauss II, Jos. Strauss, Mozart, Lanner*) (♭ *set B 417*)

Piefke und Pufke, Op. 235
☆ L.S.O.—Krips (♭ *Lon.REP 8008*)

Radetzky March, Op. 228
Vienna Phil.—Krauss   in ♯ D.LXT 2913
                               (♯ NLK 40100; Lon.LL 970)
R.I.A.S. Sym.—Fricsay   *Pol. 62894*
                               (♭ *30005;* in ♯ AmD.DL 9733)
Vienna Sym.—Salmhofer   in ♯ *Phi.N 00685R*
N.W. Ger. Phil.—Schüchter   in ♯ *Imp.ILP 111*
Philadelphia "Pops"—Ormandy
                         in ♯ AmC.ML 4686
                         (♭ *A 1697;* ♯ *Phi.S 06618R*)
Orch.—Neusser (in ♯ *Hma.LM 811*)
Strauss Fest. Orch.—Ries-Walter (in ♯ *Mae.OA 20012*)
A. Bernard Str. Orch. (*Dur.A 30028*)
☆ Amsterdam—v. Kempen (in ♯ *Phi.S 06015R*)
  Boston Prom.—Fiedler (in ♯ Vic.LM 1790:
                                 ♭ *set ERB 26*)
  Austrian Sym.—Wöss (in ♯ Ply. 12-103;
                                 ♭ *Rem.REP 71*)
  Aarhus Municipal—Jensen (in ♯ Tono.LPX 35005 &
                         LPL 33002; ♭ *Mer.EP 1-5009*)
  Liverpool Phil.—Sargent (in ♯ AmC.RL 3050)
— ARR. BAND
Vienna Deutschmeister Band—Hermann
  (in ♯ *Nix.WLPY 6703; West.WL 3003* & *WP 6004:*
                                 ♭ *WP 1003*)
Berlin Police Band—Winkel (*T.A 11573;* ♭ *U 45573*)
Vox Concert Band (in ♯ *AmVox.VX 590; Orb.BL 601*)
Vanguard Military Band—Ahringer (in ♯ *Van.VRS 7036*)
Band—Kothe (♭ *Pol. 20001*)
☆ Lower Austrian Police—Neusser (in ♯ *D.LF 1518*)

STRAUSS, Johann II (1825-1899)

CLASSIFIED: A. INSTRUMENTAL
        1. Marches
        2. Polkas, Mazurkas, etc.
        3. Waltzes
        4. Other Inst. Works

    B. OPERETTAS & STAGE WORKS
    C. MISCELLANEOUS

[A large number of minor recordings and renumberings has
been eliminated. It has not been possible always to
distinguish between o.v. re-issues and n.v. re-makes,
where several versions by the same conductor are
involved.]

GENERAL COLLECTIONS
    Only important and recent mixed discs are entered here.
    Less interesting or recent items are split up under the
    individual titles.
    ☐ references are added only to the uncommon titles.

'MUSIC OF JOHANN & JOSEPH STRAUSS'
VOL. I
    An der schönen, blauen Donau, Op. 314
    ☆ G'schichten aus dem Wiener Wald, Op. 325
    ☆ Die FLEDERMAUS—Overture
    ☆ Frühlingsstimmen, Op. 410
    ☆ Künstlerleben, Op. 316

Vienna Phil.—Krauss   ♯ D.LXT 2965
                               (♯ Lon.LL 1028)

VOL. II
    ☆ Der ZIGEUNERBARON—Overture
    ☆ Morgenblätter, Op. 279
    Bei uns z'Haus, Op. 361

Vienna Phil.—Krauss   ♯ D.LXT 2991
(*Jos. Strauss*)   (♯ Lon.LL 1029)

Perpetuum mobile, Op. 257   (a)
POLKAS: Annen-Polka, Op. 117
        Champagner-Polka, Op. 211   (a)
        Pizzicato Polka
        Tritsch-Tratsch, Op. 214   (a)
        Unter Donner und Blitz, Op. 324 (P. schnell) (a)
WALTZES: Accelerationen, Op. 234   (b)
        Adelenwalzer, Op. 424   (b)
        Kaiser Walzer, Op. 437

Pittsburgh Sym.—Steinberg ♯ DCap.CTL 7051
                         (♯ Cap.P 8222; ACap.CLCX 024)
[(a) also on ♭ *FAP 8240;* (b) on ♭ *Cap.FAP 8239*]

MARCHES: Indigo Marsch, Op. 349 (on motives from the
            operetta)
         Spanischer Marsch, Op. 433
         Es war wunderschön, Op. 467 (on motives from
            Waldmeister)
POLKAS: Aus der Heimat, Op. 347 (P. Mazurka)
        Rasch in der Tat, Op. 409 (P. schnell)
        Pizzicato Polka
        Liebchen, schwing dich, Op. 394
Perpetuum mobile, Op. 257
Gunstwerber Walzer, Op. 4

Vienna Sym.—Salmhofer   ♯ *Phi.N 00754R*

Egyptischer Marsch, Op. 335   (a) (b)
POLKAS: Annen-Polka, Op. 117   (a)
        Explosions-Polka, Op. 43 (a) (b)
        Fledermaus-Polka, Op. 362
        Pizzicato Polka   (a) (b)
        Tritsch-Tratsch, Op. 214 (a) (b)
        Unter Donner und Blitz, Op. 324 (P. schnell) (a)
Philadelphia "Pops"—Ormandy
                         ♯ AmC.ML 4686
(*Overture, below; & J. Strauss I*)
[items marked (a) on ♯ *Phi.S 06618R;* (b) on ♭*AmC.A 1697*]

Persischer Marsch, Op. 289
POLKAS: Auf der Jagd, Op. 373 (P. schnell—from
            Cagliostro)
        I Tipferl Op. 377 (P. française—from *Prinz
            Methusalem*)
WALTZES: Frühlingsstimmen, Op. 410
        G'schichten aus dem Wiener Wald, Op. 325
        Kaiserwalzer, Op. 437

Vienna State Op.—Paulik   ♯ Nix.PVL 7007
(*Zigeunerbaron, No. 17 & Jos. Strauss*) (♯ Van.VRS 443)

WALTZES: Wein, Weib und Gesang, Op. 333
        Künstlerleben, Op. 316
        Morgenblätter, Op. 279
Frisch ins Feld Marsch, Op. 398 (from *Lustige Krieg*)

Vienna State Op.—Paulik   ♯ Van.VRS 457
(*Ritter Pázmán; & Jos. Strauss*) (♯ Ama.AVRS 6014)

Banditen Galop, Op. 378
Egyptischer Marsch, Op. 335
L'Enfantilage, Op. 202 (P. française)
Tik-tak, Op. 365 (P. schnell—from *Die Fledermaus*)
WALTZES: Rosen aus dem Süden, Op. 388
        Wiener Bonbons, Op. 307

Vienna State Op.—Paulik   ♯ Van.VRS 459
(*Jos. Strauss*)

Egyptischer Marsch, Op. 335
POLKAS: Tritsch-Tratsch, Op. 214 (P. schnell)
        Vergnügungszug, Op. 281 (P. schnell)
        Die Zeitlose, Op. 302 (P. française)
WALTZES: Rosen aus dem Süden, Op. 388
        Wiener Bonbons, Op. 307

Vienna Sym.—E. Strauss   ♯ *EPhi.NBR 6012*
(2ss)   (♯ *Phi.N 00697R:* in ♯ Epic.LC 3064)[1]

Banditengalopp. Op. 378
Gavotte der Königin, Op. 391 (from *Das Spitzentuch der
    Königin*)
Persischer Marsch, Op. 289
POLKAS: Annen-Polka, Op. 117
        Im Krapfenwald'l, Op. 336
        Leichtes Blut, Op. 319 (P. schnell)
        Neue Pizzicato Polka, Op. 449 (from *Fürstin
            Ninetta*)
        Tik-Tak Polka, Op. 365 (P. schnell, from *Die
            Fledermaus*)

Vienna Sym.—Salmhofer   ♯ *Phi.N 00685R*
(*J. Strauss I: Radetzky Marsch*) (in ♯ Epic.LC 3064)

---

[1] The Epic catalogue does not list *Die Zeitlose*.

POLKAS: 's gibt ein Kaiserstadt, Op. 291   (*a*)
  Freikugeln, Op. 326 (P. schnell)   (*b, d*)
  Kreuz Fidel, Op. 301 (P. française)   (*a, b*)
  Pizzicato Polka (with Jos. Strauss)   (*c*)
QUADRILLES: Bijouterie Quadrille, Op. 169   (*b, d*)
  Bouquet Quadrille, Op. 135   (*b*)
WALTZES: An der schönen, blauen Donau, Op. 314   (*d*)
  G'schichten aus dem Wiener Wald, Op. 325 (*c, d*)
  [with R. Karol, zither]
  Jubilee Waltz[1]   (*d*)
  Morgenblätter, Op. 279
Boston Prom.—Fiedler   **‡ G.CLP 1040**
                       (‡ Vic.LM 1809)
[(*a*) also on ♭ *Vic.ERA 237;* (*b*) also on ♭ *It V.A72R 0038;*
(*c*) also on ♭ *It V.A72R 00317;* (*d*) in ♭ set ERB 33]

POLKAS: I Tipferl, Op. 377[2] (P. française)
  Im Sturmschritt, Op. 348 (P. schnell)
  Spleen, Op. 197 (P. Mazurka)
  Unter Donner und Blitz, Op. 324 (P. schnell)
WALTZES: Myrthenblüten, Op. 395
  Nordseebilder, Op. 390
Vienna Sym.—Salmhofer   **‡ EPhi.NBR 6022**
                      (‡ Phi.N 00733R)

Festival Quadrille, Op. 341 (on English themes)
POLKAS: Champagner-Polka, Op. 211
  Electrophor, Op. 297 (P. schnell)
  Explosions-Polka, Op. 43
  Schnellpost-Polka, Op. 159
WALTZES: Ballg'schichten, Op. 150
  Motoren-Walzer, Op. 265
  Paroxysmen, Op. 189
  Serail-Tänze, Op. 5
  Telegraphische Depeschen, Op. 195
☆ C.B.S. Sym.—Barlow   **‡ AmC.RL 3020**

A. 1. MARCHES

Egyptischer Marsch, Op. 335
Vienna Radio—Schönherr   *Vien.P 6134*
(*below*)
Moscow Radio—L. Steinberg (*USSR. 10926*)
☆ Boston Prom.—Fiedler (in ‡ Cam.CAL 127: ♭ *CAE 138*)

Frisch ins Feld, Op. 398
  (on themes from *Lustige Krieg*)
Vienna State Op.—Paulik   in **‡ Van.VRS 457**
[in Collection]   (‡ Ama.AVRS 6014)

Indigo Marsch, Op. 319
  (on themes from the operetta)
☆ Boston Prom.—Fiedler (in ‡ Cam.CAL 126: ♭ *CAE 104*)

Persischer Marsch, Op. 289 □
Vienna Radio—Schönherr   *Vien.P 6134*
(*above*)   (& in ‡ *LPR 1030*)
☆ Boston Prom.—Fiedler (♭ *Cam.CAE 214:* in ‡ *CAL 127*)
Austrian Sym.—Wöss (in ‡ Ply. 12-103)

A. 2. POLKAS, MAZURKAS, ETC.

COLLECTIONS
Annen-Polka, Op. 117
Eljen a Magyar, Op. 332 (P. schnell)
Freikugeln, Op. 326 (P. schnell)
Leichtes Blut, Op. 319 (P. schnell)
Pizzicato-Polka (also on ♭ *VIP 30100*)
Tritsch-Tratsch, Op. 214
Unter Donner und Blitz, Op. 324 (P. schnell)
Vergnügungszug, Op. 281
Vienna State Op.—Paulik   **‡ Nix.PVL 7003**
(*Jos. Strauss*)   (‡ Van.VRS 438)

Auf der Jagd, Op. 373 (P. schnell, from *Cagliostro*)
Im Krapfenwald'l, Op. 336 (also in ‡ *D.LF 1518:* ♭ *71079*)
Pizzicato (also in ‡ *D.LF 1518*)
Stadt und Land, Op. 322 (P. Mazurka)
Vergnügungszug, Op. 281 (P. schnell)
☆ Vienna Phil.—Krauss   **‡ D.LW 5052**
(2ss)   (‡ Lon.LD 9044)

Eljen a Magyar, Op. 332
Stadt und Land, Op. 322
Vergnügungszug, Op. 281
☆ Vienna Phil.—Krauss ♭ *AmVox.VIP 30040*
(*Jos. Strauss*)

"POLKAS, Vol. II"
Brautschau, Op. 417 (from *Zigeunerbaron*)
Furioso, Op. 260 (Polka quasi Galop)
Ritter Pázmán, Op. 441 (themes from Operetta)
Fledermaus-Polka, Op. 362 (themes from Operetta)
Im Krapfenwald'l, Op. 336
Im Sturmschritt, Op. 348 (P. schnell, from *Indigo*)
  ☆ Boston Prom.—Fiedler   **‡ G.CLP 1065**
    (*Waldteufel*)
  [Fledermaus-P., Im Krapfenwald'l & Ritter Pázmán
    with *Unter Donner und Blitz* also on ♭ *G.7EG 8016;*
    for other re-issues, see below]

Annen-Polka, Op. 117
Vienna Phil.—Krauss   in **‡ D.LXT 2913**
             (in ‡ D.NLK 40100; Lon.LL 970)
R.I.A.S. Sym.—Fricsay   **Pv. 72335**
(*Tritsch-Tratsch & Zigeunerbaron, Overture*)
(in ‡ HP.DGM 18050; ‡ Pol. 19085 &
                ‡ AmD.DL 4043: ♭ ED 3535)
Vienna Orch.—Hübener (in ‡ Hma.LM 820)
☆ New Sym.—Krips (♭ Lon.REP 8008)
  Boston Prom.—Fiedler (in ‡ Cam.CAL 126:
                      ♭ *CAE 214*)
— ARR. BAND; Band—Neusser (in ‡ Hma.LM 819)
— ARR. 2 PFS.
M: Rawicz & W. Landauer (♭ D. 71078: in ‡ LK 4094;
                      Lon.LL 1210)
L. Shankson & I. Wright (in ‡ Roy. 1447)

Bitte schön, Op. 372 □
☆ Württemberg State—Leitner   in ‡ HP.DG 16003
              (‡ Pol. 17029; ‡ AmD.DL 4043)
— ARR. 2 PFS.
M. Rawicz & W. Landauer (♭ D. 71078: ‡ LK 4094;
                     Lon.LL 1210)

Brautschau, Op. 417 (themes from *Zigeunerbaron*) □
☆ Boston Prom.—Fiedler (in ‡ *Vic.LRM 7017:*
                    ♭ set ERB 7017)

Freikugeln, Op. 326 (P. schnell) □
☆ Vienna Radio—Schönherr (*Vien.P 6025*)

Furioso, Op. 260 (Polka quasi Galop) □
☆ Boston Pops—Fiedler (♭ *Vic.ERA 237*)

Im Krapfenwald'l, Op. 336 (P. française) □
☆ Boston Prom.—Fiedler (*G.EA 4217;* in ‡ *Vic.LRM 7017*
                    ♭ set ERB 7017)

Im Sturmschritt, Op. 348
    (P. schnell, from *Indigo*) □
☆ Boston Pops—Fiedler (♭ *Vic.ERA 237*)

Leichtes Blut, Op. 319 (P. schnell)
Berlin Municipal—Lenzer (♭ *Ura.UREP 31*)
Vienna Light—Kolesa (in ‡ *Phi.P 10101R*)
Vienna State Op.—Rossmayer (in ‡ *Lon.LS 863*)
Vienna Orch.—Hübener (in ‡ Hma.LM 820)
☆ Württemberg State—Leitner (in ‡ HP.DG 16003;
             ‡ AmD.DL 4043; ‡ Pol. 17029)
Vienna Radio—Schönherr (*Vien.P 6036:* ♭ *4009*)
Boston Prom.—Fiedler (in ‡ *Vic.LRM/*♭ *set ERB 7041;*
      ♭ *DV. 26038;* in ‡ Cam.CAL 127:
                  ♭ *CAE 106*, probably o.v.)
— ARR. BAND
Deutschmeister Band—Hermann (in ‡ Nix.WLPY 6707;
             ‡ West.WL 3007: WP 6004: ♭ WP 1003)

Lob der Frauen, Op. 315 (P. Mazurka)
Vienna Radio—Schönherr   *Vien.P 6144*
(*Sängerlust*)

Neue Pizzicato Polka, Op. 449
  (themes from *Fürstin Ninetta*)
— ARR. PF.   Schulhoff
P. Badura-Skoda (in ‡ Nix.WLP 5277; West.WL 5277)
E. Farnadi (in ‡ West.WN 18064)

Pizzicato-Polka Str. orch. (with Jos. Strauss)
N.Y.P.S.O.—Kostelanetz   in **‡ AmC.CL 769**
Tivoli Concert—Hansen   *Tono.L 28081*
(*Hellmesberger: Ballszene*)   (♭ *EP 45031*)

(*continued on next page*)

---

[1] Thought to have been specially composed for Strauss's 1872 visit to Boston; includes quotation of *The Star Spangled Banner;* orchestrated for this recording by R. R. Bennett from pf. score pub. Springfield, Mass. [Information supplied by Mr. A. Fiedler.]
[2] From *Prinz Methusalem.*

Pizzicato-Polka (*continued*)

Israel Radio—Goehr   *Arzi.* **769**
(*Beethoven: Ruinen von Athen, March*)   (in ♯ *Bne. 501*)
Strauss Orch.—Ries-Walter (in ♯ *Mae.OA 20012*)
Czech Phil. Members—Křenowský (in ♯ U. 5202H)
Westminster Light—Bridgewater (in ♯ Nix.WLP 6804;
           West.WL 4004: ♭ *WP 1022*)
Leipzig Radio—Dobrindt (*Ami. 140045*)
Vienna Orch.—Sandauer (♭ *Phi.N 430000E*:
                ♭ *KD 134: P 44493H*)
☆ Philharmonia—Krips (in ♯ AmC.RL 3056)
   Vienna Sym.—Paulik (♭ *AmVox.VIP 30100*)
   Berlin Phil.—Fricsay (in ♯ *AmD.DL 4043*: ♭ *ED 3535*)
   Vienna Phil.—Furtwängler (♭ *G.7ER 5001: 7ERF 131:
           7ERQ 110: 7RW 101: 7RQ 3032*)
   Stockholm Phil.—Ehrling (in ♯ Mtr.CLP 513:
       ♭ *MCEP 3036;* in ♯ AFest.CFR 12-173;
              ♯ FMer.MLP 7020)
   Minneapolis Sym.—Ormandy (in ♯ Cam.CAL 121:
                ♭ *CAE 215*)
   Boston Prom.—Fiedler (in ♯ Cam.CAL 127: ♭ *CAE 106*)

Ritter Pázmán, Op. 441   (themes from Operetta)
☆ Boston Prom.—Fiedler (*G.EA 4217;* ♭ *Vic.ERA 237*)

Sängerlust, Op. 328   (P. française)
Vienna Radio—Schönherr   *Vien.P* **6144**
(*Lob der Frauen*)   (in ♯ *LPR 1041*)

Sans-Souci, Op. 178
☆ Boston   Prom.—Fiedler   (in   ♯ *Vic.LRM 7041:*
   ♭ *set ERB 7041;* ♭ *DV. set 26038;*
         in ♯ Cam.CAL 126, perhaps o.v.)

Sylphen, Op. 309   (P. française)
Schneider Str. Ens.   in ♯ **AmC.CL 556**
               (in ♭ *set B 417*)

Tik-Tak, Op. 365   (P. schnell)
(on motives from *Die Fledermaus*)
☆ Boston Prom.—Fiedler (in ♯ Vic.LM 1790: ♭ *set ERB 26;*
         in ♯ Cam.CAL 126, perhaps o.v.)
— ARR. 2 PFS.
M. Rawicz & W. Landauer (in ♯ D.LK 4094:
            LW 5205; Lon.LL 1210)

Tritsch-Tratsch, Op. 214
N.Y.P.S.O.—Kostelanetz   in ♯ **AmC.CL 769**
R.I.A.S. Sym.—Fricsay   **PV. 72335**
(*Annen-Polka & Zigeunerbaron Overture*)   (♭ *Pol. 30005*)
(♭ *AmD.ED 3535;* in ♯ HP.DGM 18050;
          ♯ *AmD.DL 4043;* Pol. 19035)
Leipzig Radio—Dobrindt (*Ami. 140045*)
Vienna Orch.—Hübener (in ♯ *Hma.LM 820*)
Leighton Lucas Orch. (EMI.EPX 73)
Concert Orch.—E. Robinson (in ♯ Argo.RG 40;
            West.WN 18097)
☆ N.B.C. Sym.—Toscanini (♭ *G.7RQ 127;* ♭ *DV. 16298*)
   Aarhus Municipal—Jensen (in ♯ Tono.LPX 35005;
            ♭ *Mer.EP 1-5009*)
   Boston Prom.—Fiedler (in ♯ Cam.CAL 127: ♭ *CAE 138*)
   L.S.O.—Krips (in ♯ *Lon.REP 8008*)
▽ Austrian Sym.—Wöss (in ♯ *Rem. 149-8*)

— ARR. 2 PFS.
M. Rawicz & W. Landauer (in ♯ D.LK 4094; Lon.LL 1210)

Unter Donner und Blitz, Op. 324   (P. schnell)
☆ Boston Prom.—Fiedler (♭ *G.7BF 1058;*
   in ♯ Vic.LM 1790; o.v. in ♯ Cam.CAL 126: ♭ *CAE 214*)
S. Torch Orch. (in ♯ *P.PMD 1008*)

WALTZES
COLLECTIONS

An der schönen, blauen Donau, Op. 314
Frühlingsstimmen, Op. 410
Kaiserwalzer, Op. 437
Rosen aus dem Süden, Op. 388
London Phil. Sym.—Rodzinski
               ♯ **West.LAB 7026**

Wiener Blut, Op. 354
Wein, Weib und Gesang, Op. 333
G'schichten aus dem Wiener Wald, Op. 325
[with J. C. Scherer, zither]
Kaiserwalzer, Op. 437
Minneapolis Sym.—Dorati   ♯ **EMer.MG 50019**
               (♯ FMer.MLP 7506)

An der schönen, blauen Donau, Op. 314
G'schichten aus dem Wiener Wald, Op. 325
Schatz-Walzer, Op. 418
Rosen aus dem Süden, Op. 388
Du und du, Op. 367
Künstlerleben, Op. 316
Frühlingsstimmen, Op. 410
Kaiser-Walzer, Op. 437
Wiener Blut, Op. 354
Tausend und eine Nacht, Op. 346

A. Kostelanetz Orch.   ♯ **AmC.CL 805**
               (o.n. ♯ ML 4993)

Accelerationen, Op. 234
Vienna Sym.—Salmhofer   in ♯ *EPhi.NBR* **6008**
(*Kuss, Wo die Zitronen, etc.*)   (♯ *Phi.S 06079R,*
          o.n. *N 00628R; & S 06007R*)
Bamberg Sym.—Leitner   **PV. 72476**
(*Frühlingsstimmen*)   (♭ *Pol. 30059*)
Strauss Fest.—Ries-Walter (in ♯ *Mae.OA 20013*)
Vox Sinfonietta—Gräf (in ♯ *AmVox.VX 570*)
Mantovani Orch. (in ♯ D.LK 4054: ♭ *DFE 6003;*
   ♯ Lon.LL 685: ♭ *set LSF 109:* ♭ *BEP 6003*)
☆ Vienna State Op.—Schönherr (in ♯ *EPhi.BBR 8049;*
          ♯ *AmC.CL 6250* & RL 3073)
   New Sym.—Krips (♯ *D.LW 5012;* Lon.LD 9016)
   Minneapolis Sym.—Ormandy (♭ *Vic.* set ERB 6;
            ♯ *ItV.A12R 0093*)
   Philadelphia—Ormandy (♭ *AmC.A 1763*)
   Austrian Sym.—Wöss (in ♯ *Ply. 12-55;* ♭ *Rem.REP 66*)

An der schönen, blauen Donau, Op. 314
Vienna Phil.—Krauss   in ♯ **D.LXT 2913**
         (♯ D.NLK 40100; Lon.LL 970)
F.O.K. Sym.—Smetáček   in ♯ **Sup.LPV 130**
               (♯ U. 5105G)
Berne Sym.—Ackermann   V♯ *MMS.POP* **9**
(*Kaiserwalzer*)
N.B.C. Sym. Members—Stokowski
               ♭ *Vic.ERA 259*

(*G'schichten aus dem Wienerwald*)
☆ Vienna Sym.—Moralt   ♯ **EPhi.ABL 3002**
   (*below*)   (♯ Epic.LC 3004)
Strauss Orch.—Ries-Walter (in ♯ *Mae.OA 20014*)
Leipzig Radio—Dobrindt (*Ami. 140032*)
Leipzig Radio—Abendroth (in ♯ Ura. 7155:
        RS 5-2 & RS 7-21: ♭ *UREP 54*)
Polish Radio—Krenz (*Muza.* 2440)
Hamburg Philharmonia—H.-J. Walther (*MSB.* 78021)
Bolshoi Theatre—Samosud (USSR. 8431/3 & 8448)
U.S.S.R. State—Rakhlin (♯ *USSR.D 534* & in ♯ 01603)
Vienna Bohemian Orch.—F. Walter (in ♯ G.CLP 1047:
   FELP 140: QCLP 12015; Vic.LM 1876:
          ♭ *set ERB 53; Imp.ILP 119*)
Concert Orch.—Robinson (in ♯ Argo.RG 66)
Orch.—Kostelanetz (in ♯ *AmC.A 1558*)
Vienna Radio—Schönherr (n.v.) (*Eli. 8739;*
   in ♯ Rem. 149-38: ♭ *REP 34;* ♯ AFest.CFR 10-62;
          ♯ *Cum.TCR 213,* may be o.v.)
Vienna Sym.—Paulik (in ♯ *AmVox.VX 510:*
   ♭ *VIP 30170;* & probably ♭ MTW. 14: ♭ *set EP 14;*
          & ♯ *ACC.MP 9*)
Mantovani Orch. (*D.F 10051;* in ♯ LK 4054: *LF 1193;*
       ♭ *DFE 6001;* ♯ Lon.LL 685, etc.)
Hungarian Radio—Somogyi (Qual.MN 1154)
☆ Nat. Sym.—Krips (♯ *D.LW 5011;* Lon.LD 9015)
   Boston Prom.—Fiedler (G.C 4233: S 10615:
     in ♯ *DLP 1005: QDLP 6006;* ♯ *Vic.LRM 7017:*
       ♭ *set ERB 7017;* ♭ *ItV.A72R 0030*)
   Orch.—Stokowski (♭ *G.7R 169: 7RF 182: 7RW 145;*
           ♭ *DV. 16297*)
   Vienna Radio—Günther (in ♯ AmC.RL 3073;
     ♯ *EPhi.BBR 8049;* ♭ *Phi.KD 163: P 428003E:*
           Phi.P 41076H)
   Philadelphia—Ormandy (♭ *AmC.A 2094*)
   Minneapolis Sym.—Ormandy (♭ *Vic.* set ERB 6;
          in ♯ ItV.A12R 0093)
   Royal Phil.—Weingartner (in ♯ AmC.ML 4777)
   Berlin Phil.—Fricsay (in ♯ *AmD.ED 3545;* ♭ *Pol. 30073*)
   Strauss Orch.—F. Lanner (in ♯ MGM.E 3032:
          D 122; ItMGM.QD 6012)
   etc.

— ARR. PF.   Schulz-Evler, etc.
   K. Leimer (*PV.* 36098)
   G. Ginsburg (*USSRM.D 00507*)
☆ J. Lhevinne (in ♯ Cam.CAL 265)
   L. Pennario (in ♯ DCap.CTL 7102; Cap.P 8312)
   B. Janis (♭ *BB.ERAB 8;* ♭ *FV.A 85211*)

♯ = Long-playing, 33⅓ r.p.m.   ♭ = 45 r.p.m.   ♭ = Auto. couplings, 78 r.p.m.

An der schönen, blauen Donau, Op. 314 (continued)
— ARR. 2 PFS.
  ¹ V. Appleton & M. Field (in ♯ Roy. 1587 & 1901;
      also AmVox.VX 540)
  ² M. Rawicz & W. Landauer (in ♯ D.LK 4094:
      Lon.LL 1210)
  ☆ ¹ A. Chasins & C. Keene (♭ FMer.MEP 14512;
      Mer.EP 1-5052)
— ARR. ORGAN. R. Ellsasser (in ♯ MGM.E 3110)
— ARR. VLC. & PF. "Improvisations" Cassadó
  ☆ G. Cassadó & O. Schulhof (in ♯ Rem. 199-128)
— ARR. SOLO VOICE
  M. Gyarkorics (S, Hung) (Qual.B 2002)
  ☆ M. Korjus (S, Eng) (♭ Vic.ERAT 14)
  E. Sack (S, Ger) (♭ Mer.EP 1-5020)
  M. Ivogün (S, Ger) (JpV.ND 404)
— ARR. CHO.
  Young Vienna—Lehner (in ♯ AudC. 1093)
  Vienna Acad. Cho.—Grossmann (V♯ Sel.LPP 8610)
  Vienna Boys' Cho. (♭ C.SEG 7601)

Bei uns z'Haus, Op. 361 □
Vienna Phil.—Krauss   in ♯ D.LXT 2913
            (♯ NLK 40100; Lon.LL 970)
  (& in ♯ D.LXT 2991; Lon.LL 1029)
  ☆ Vienna Sym.—Krauss (o.v.) (in ♯ Sup.LPV 130;
      U. 5105G; TV.VE 9004)

Cagliostro, Op. 370
(on motives from Cagliostro in Wien)
☆ Boston Prom.—Fiedler (in ♯ Cam.CAL 127)

Donauweibchen, Op. 427 (from Simplicius)
Concert Ens.—Krish (USSR. 10694/5)
— VOCAL (Film) ARR.
  ☆ J. Schmidt (T) (in ♯ Od.OLA 1008: ♭ GEOW 1006)

Du und du, Op. 367
Westminster Light—Bridgewater (in ♯ Nix.WLP 6804;
      West.WL 4004)
Vienna Bohemian Orch.—F. Walter (in ♯ G.CLP 1047:
    FELP 140: QCLP 12015; ♯ Imp.ILP 108;
      ♯ Vic.LM 1876: ♭ set ERB 53)
Mantovani Orch. (in ♯ D.LK 4054: LF 1193:
    ♭ DFE 6002: ♭ DX 1728; ♭ Lon.LL 685) etc.
▽ Austrian Sym.—Wöss (in ♯ Rem. 149-8)
☆ Hollywood Bowl—Stokowski (♭ Vic.ERA 67;
      ♭ G.7ERF 120)
Vienna Radio—Schönherr (in ♯ GA. 33-312;
      Vien.LPR 1035: ♭ 4018)
Chicago Sym.—Stock (♭ Cam.CAE 158)
Concert Orch.—Seidler-Winkler (in ♯ BB.LBC 1065:
      ♭ set WBC 1065)
M. Marrow Orch. (in ♯ MGM.E 3138), etc.
— ARR. PF.: H. Seiter (in ♯ Nix.WLPY 6731; West.WL 3031)
— ARR. 4 PFS.: Phil. Pf. Qtt. (♭ AmC.A 1572)

Freut euch des Lebens, Op. 340
Schneider Str. Ens. (in ♯ AmC.CL 556: ♭ set B 417)
☆ Vienna Radio—Schönherr (in ♯ Vien.LPR 1035 &
      ♯ GA. 33-312)

Frühlingsstimmen, Op. 410
Bamberg Sym.—Leitner   PV. 72476
(Accelerationen)   (♭ Pol. 30059)
Leipzig Radio—Kegel in ♯ Ura. 7155
    (♯ RS 5-2 & RS 7-21: ♭ UREP 62)
Moscow Radio—Gauk (USSR. 21545/6:
      USSRM.D 505: & 01645, d.c.)
Orch.—Bonneau (♭ Pat.ED 52)
Belgian Radio—Marinetti (in ♯ Mae.OA 20011)
Hamburg Philharmonia—H-J. Walther (MSB. 78104)
Vienna Bohemian—F. Walter (in ♯ G.CLP 1047:
    FELP 140: QCLP 12015; ♯ Imp.ILP 119;
      ♯ Vic.LM 1876: ♭ set ERB 53)
Mantovani Orch. (in ♯ D.LK 4054: ♭ DFE 6003:
      ♯ Lon.LL 685, etc.)
☆ Vienna Sym.—Moralt (in ♯ EPhi.ABL 3002;
    ♭ Phi.N 402002E; ♯ Epic.LC 3004)
R.I.A.S. Sym.—Fricsay (in ♯ HP.DGM 18050;
    ♭ Pol. 30039 & in ♯ 19035)
Vienna Phil.—Krauss (♭ D.DX 1722)
Boston Prom.—Fiedler (in ♭ Cam.CAE 137)
British Sym.—Weingartner (in ♯ AmC.ML 4777)
Strauss Orch.—Lanner (in ♯ MGM.D 122: E 3032;
    FMGM.F 1-109; ItMGM.QD 6012), etc.
— VOCAL VERSION (orig. Ger. text by Genée) S
W. Lipp & Berlin Phil.—Fricsay ♯ AmD.DL 4041
(G'schichten . . .)   (♭ ED 3524)
  ☆ E. Sack (in ♯ DT.LGM 65015)
  E. Sack (♭ Mer.EP 1-5020)
— ARR. 2 PFS.
  M. Rawicz & W. Landauer (in ♯ D.LK 4094: ♭ DFE 6301;
      ♯ Lon.LL 1210)

G'schichten aus dem Wiener Wald, Op. 325
COMPLETE, with zither solo
☆ Vienna Sym.—Moralt   ♯ EPhi.ABL 3002
(Blue Danube, Frühlingsstimmen, Wiener Blut)
      (♯ Phi.S 06006R; ♯ Epic.LC 3004)
J. C. Scherer & Minneapolis Sym.—Dorati, from
    Collection (♭ FMer.MEP 14507: ♭ Mer.EP 1-5023)
☆ R. Knabl & Bamberg Sym.—Leitner (♯ AmD.DL 4041:
      DL 8509; ♯ Pol. 17057, d.c.)
A. Karas & Vienna Phil.—Krauss (♯ D.LW 5020;
      Lon.LD 9030)
SHORTER VERSIONS, or unknown
N.Y.P.S.O.—Kostelanetz in ♯ AmC.CL 769
N.B.C. Members—Stokowski ♭ Vic.ERA 257
(An der schönen, blauen Donau)
Hamburg Philharmonia—H-J. Walther (MSB. 78151)
Moscow Radio—Samosud (in ♯ USSR.D 01651)
Bolshoi Th.—Samosud (USSR. 8451/4)
Strauss Fest.—Ries-Walter (in ♯ Mae.OA 20014)
Orch.—Kostelanetz (in ♯ AmC.KZ 1)
Vienna Bohemian—F. Walter (in ♯ G.CLP 1047:
    FELP 140: QCLP 12015; Imp.ILP 108;
      ♯ Vic.LM 1876: ♭ set ERB 53)
Vienna Radio—Schönherr (n.v.) (Eli. 8736;
    in ♯ Rem. 149-38: ♭ REP 34; ♯ Cum.TCR 213)
Mantovani Orch. (in ♯ D.LK 4054: LF 1193:
      ♭ DFE 6002; ♯ Lon.LL 685, etc.)
☆ Orch.—Stokowski (♭ G.7R 169: 7RF 182:
      7RW 145; DV. 16297)
Vienna Radio—Günther (in ♯ EPhi.BBR 8049;
    ♯ AmC.RL 3073; ♭ Phi.KD 163:P 428003E)
Austrian Sym.—Wöss (in ♯ Rem. 149-8;
      Ply. 12-61, 100, 110, etc.)
Strauss Orch.—Lanner (in ♯ MGM.D 123 &
      E 3032) etc.
Boston Prom.—Fiedler (in ♯ G.QDLP 6006,
    ♯ Vic.LRM 7017: ♭ set ERB 7017)
Philadelphia—Stokowski (in ♯ Cam. set CFL 103), etc.
— VOCAL ARRANGEMENTS
Vienna Boys' Cho. (Ger.) (♭ C.SEG 7601)
☆ E. Sack (S, Ger) (in ♯ DT.LGM 65015)
R. Tauber (T, Ger) (in ♯ P.PMB 1007:
      ♭ CBEP 1; AmD.ED 3507)
E. Roon (S, Ger) (in ♯ AmVox.VIP 30050)
P. Munsel (S, Eng) (♭ Vic.ERA 111)
— ARR. PF. H. Seiter (in ♯ Nix.WLPY 6731; West.WL 3031)
— ARR. 2 PFS. M. Rawicz & W. Landauer (♯ D.LW 5205:
    LK 4094; ♯ Lon.LL 1210)
— ARR. ORGAN R. Ellsasser (in ♯ MGM.E 3110)

Jubilee Waltz (see footnote, ante) □
Boston Pops—Fiedler   ♭ ItV.A72R 0029
(Kaiserwalzer)   [from Collection]

Juristenballtänze, Op. 177
Moscow Phil. Ens.—L. Steinberg
                USSR. 10923/4

Kaiserwalzer, Op. 437
Boston Pops—Fiedler (n.v.) in ♯ Vic.LRM 7041
    (♭ set ERB 7041 & ERB 7; DV. set B 26038)
F.O.K. Sym.—Smetáček in ♯ Sup.LPV 130
            (♯ U. 5105G)
Berne Sym.—Ackermann V♯ MMS.POP 9
(An der schönen, blauen Donau)
Bamberg Sym.—Leitner   PV. 36093
(Morgenblätter on ♯ AmD.DL 4062) (♭ Pol. 30059)
      (G'schichten on ♯ Pol. 17057)
Berlin Municipal—Lenzer ♭ Ura.UREP 31
Boston Orch. Soc.—Page in ♯ Nix.SLPY 802
    (♯ SOT. 2066 & in ♯ 10646)
Strauss Fest.—Ries-Walter (in ♯ Mae.OA 20013)
Mantovani Orch. (in ♯ D.LK 4054: LF. 1193:
    ♭ DFE 6003; ♯ Lon.LL 658, etc.)
A. Bernard Str. Orch. (in ♯ Nix.SLPY 128;
    Per. 1008; Pac.LDPA 27, etc.)
☆ New Sym.—Krips (♯ D.LW 5011; Lon.LD 9014)
Vienna Phil.—Karajan (AmC.AL 28)
Vienna Sym.—Paulik (in ♯ AmVox.VX 510:
      ♭ VIP 30170)
Concert Orch.—S-Winkler (in ♯ BB.LBC 1065:
      ♭ set WBC 1065)
Vienna Radio—Schönherr (in ♯ EPhi.BBR 8049;
      ♯ AmC.RL 3073)
Strauss Orch.—Lanner (in ♯ MGM.E 3082 & D 122;
    FMGM.F 1-109; ItMGM.QD 6012; etc.)
Orch.—Kostelanetz (in ♯ C.S 1049: FS 1054: QS 6048)
Boston Prom.—Fiedler (o.v., in ♯ ItV.A12R 0093:
    ♭ A72R 0029, perhaps the n.v.)
Philadelphia—Ormandy (♭ AmC.A 2095)
etc.

             (continued on next page)

---

¹ ARR. Chasins.   ² ARR. Rawicz.

Kaiserwalzer, Op. 437 *(continued)*
— ARR. BAND Deutschmeister Band—Hermann
(in ♯ *Nix.WLP Y 6705;* ♯ *West.WL 3005* & in ♯ WP 6004)
— ARR. PF. L. Pennario (♯ T.LCB 8167)
— ARR. ORGAN R. Ellsasser (in ♯ MGM.E 3110)
— ARR. VOICE
☆ E. Sack (S, *Ger*) (♭ *Mer.EP 1-5020*)
M. Korjus (S, *Ger*) (♭ *Vic.ERAT 14*)
P. Munsel (S, *Eng*) (♭ *G.7EP 7016*)

Künstlerleben, Op. 316
Boston Prom.—Fiedler (n.v.) in ♭ *Vic. set ERB 7*
(perhaps o.v., ♯ ItV.A12R 0093: ? n.v., ♭ *A72R 0028*)
☆ Vienna Phil.—Karajan   ♭ *C.SEL 1503*
(*Wiener Blut*) (♭ *SEBQ 101: ERBF 109;*
♯ *AmC.AL 28,* d.c.)
Leipzig Radio—Kegel (in ♯ Ura. 7155: RS 7-21:
♭ *UREP 62*)
Leipzig Radio—Dobrindt (*Ami. 140030*)
Vienna State Op.—Paulik (♯ MTW. 14: ♭ set EP 14;
♯ *ACC.MP 9*)
Strauss Fest.—Ries-Walter (in ♯ *Mae.OA 20013*)
Moscow Radio—Gauk (*USSRM.D 504* &
in ♯ USSR.D 1603)
Bolshoi Theatre—L. Steinberg (*USSR. 10569/70*)
Vienna Radio—Schönherr (in ♯ *Rem. 149-38;*
♭ *REP 54;* ♯ *Cum.TCR 213*)
Vienna Bohemian—F. Walter (in ♯ G.CLP 1047:
FELP 140: QCLP 12015; Vic.LM 1876:
♭ set *ERB 53;* ♯ *Imp.ILP 108*)
A. Bernard Str. Orch. (in ♯ *Nix.SLP Y 128;*
Pac.LDP A 27, etc.)
Westminster Light—Bridgewater (in ♯ Nix.WLP 6804;
West.WL 4004)
Mantovani Orch. (♭ *D.DFE 6003; Lon.BEP 6003,* etc.)
☆ Vienna State Op.—Schönherr (in ♯ *EPhi.BBR 8049;*
♭ *Phi.P 428006E: KD 143;* in ♯ AmC.RL 3073)
Boston Prom.—Fiedler (o.v.) (G.Z 373)
Orch.—Schönherr (♯ GA. 33-312)
etc.
— ARR. PF. Godowsky, etc.
E. Farnadi (in ♯ West.WN 18064)
H. Seiter (in ♯ *Nix.WLP Y 6731; West.WL 3031*)
— ARR. 2 PFS.
V. Appleton & M. Field (in ♯ *AmVox.VX 540;*
also ♯ *Roy. 1587*)
☆ A. Chasins & C. Keene (♭ *Mer.EP 1-5052;*
FMer.MEP 14512)
— ARR. VOICE ☆ P. Munsel (S, *Eng*) (♭ *G.7EP 7016*)

Kuss-Walzer, Op. 400 (from *Lustige Krieg*)
Vienna Sym.—Salmhofer in ♯ *EPhi.NBR 6008*
(*Jos. Strauss; & Accelerationen,* etc.)
(♯ *Phi.S 06079R,* o.n. N 00628R: ♭ N 402002E)
Moscow Phil. Ens.—L. Steinberg *USSR. 10584/5*

Lagunen-Walzer, Op. 411 (from *Nacht in Venedig*)
U.S.S.R. State—Rakhlin (♯ *USSR.D 535* & D 01645, d.c.)
Concert Ens.—Krish (*USSR. 15288/9*)
☆ Boston Prom.—Fiedler (♭ *Cam.CAE 162:* ♯ CAL 126)
H. Horlick Orch. (♭ *MGM.X 1072*)

Liebeslieder, Op. 114
Moscow Radio—Orlov (*USSR. 12512/3*)[1]

Man lebt nur einmal, Op. 167
— ARR. PF. Tausig
C. de Groot   in ♯ *Phi.A 00632R*

Märchen aus dem Orient, Op. 444
☆ Vienna Radio—Schönherr (in ♯ *Vien.LPR 1024*)

Morgenblätter, Op. 279
Boston "Pops"—Fiedler   ♭ *ItV.A72R 0030*
(*An der schönen, blauen Donau*) [from Collection]
R.I.A.S. Sym.—Fricsay   *PV. 36062*
(in ♯ HP.DGM 18050; ♯ Pol. 19035; AmD.DL 4062)
☆ Royal Phil.—Beecham   ♭ *C.SEL 1501*
(*Mendelssohn*) (♭ *SEBQ 105;* ♭ AmC. 4-4802)
Vienna Bohemian—F. Walter (in ♯ G.CLP 1047:
QCLP 12015: FELP 140; *Imp.ILP 119*)
Mantovani Orch. (in ♯ D.LK 4054: ♭ *DFE 6002;*
♯ Lon.LL 685, etc.)
☆ Vienna Phil.—Krauss (♯ *D.LW 5020; Lon.LD 9030*)
Austrian Sym.—Wöss (in ♯ *Rem. 149-8*)
Vienna Radio—Schönherr (in ♯ *Vien.LPR 1035* &
GA. 33-312)
etc.

Neu Wien, Op. 342
Schneider Str. Ens (in ♯ AmC.CL 530)
☆ Boston Prom.—Fiedler (in ♯ Cam.CAL 126)

Nordseebilder, Op. 390 □
Moscow Radio—Orlov   USSR. 05919/20

O schöner Mai, Op. 375
Moscow Phil. Ens.—L. Steinberg *USSR.10937/8*
☆ Vienna Sym.—Krauss (TV.VE 9004)
Schneider Str. Ens. (in ♯ AmC.CL 530)

Orakelsprüche, Op. 90
Schneider Str. Ens.   in ♯ AmC.CL 556
(in ♭ set B 417)

Rosen aus dem Süden, Op. 388
Vienna Phil.—Böhm   in ♯ *AmVox.VX 510*
(♭ *VIP 30250*)
Film Sym.—Urbanec   ♮ U.H 24467/8
(3ss—*Leopold: Tarantelle*)
Vienna Sym.—E. Strauss   ♯ *Phi.S 06006R*
(*G'schichten*)
☆ New Sym.—Krips   ♯ *D.LW 5012*
(*Accelerationen*)   (♯ *Lon.LD 9016*)
Strauss Fest.—Ries-Walter (in ♯ *Mae.OA 20012*)
Leipzig Radio—Dobrindt (*Ami. 140033*)
Berlin Sym.—List (in ♯ Roy. 1394)
Mantovani Orch. (in ♯ D.LK 4054: ♭ *DFE 6001;*
♯ Lon.LL 685, etc.)
☆ R.I.A.S. Sym.—Fricsay (in ♯ HP.DGM 18050;
Pol. 19035: ♭ *30039;* ♯ AmD.DL 4042)
Vienna Radio—Schönherr (in ♯ *Rem. 149-38;*
Cum.TCR 213; in ♯ GA. 33-312)
Berlin State—Lehmann (P.DPX 45)
Chicago Sym.—Stock (♭ *Cam.CAE 158*)
Boston Prom.—Fiedler (in ♯ Cam.CAL 127: ♭ *CAE 138*)
Vienna State Op.—Schönherr (in ♯ *EPhi.BBR 8049;*
AmC.RL 3073; ♭ *Phi.KD 143,* etc.)
Vienna Phil.—Böhm (in ♯ BB.LBC 1008:
♭ set WBC 1008)
— ARR. PF.: H. Seiter (in ♯ *Nix.WLP Y 6731; West.WL 3031*)
— ARR. CYMBALOM: L. Balogh (in ♯ *Per.SPL 1014*)
— VOCAL ARRS.
Vienna Boys' Cho.—Brenn (*Ger*) (in ♯ *EPhi.NBR 6007;*
♭ *Phi.N 402038E;* ♯ AmC.ML 4873)
☆ R. Tauber (T, *Ger*) (♭ *AmD.ED 3507*)

Schatz-Walzer, Op. 418 (from *Zigeunerbaron*)
Vienna Bohemian Orch.—F. Walter (in ♯ G.CLP 1047:
FELP 140: QCLP 12015; *Imp.ILP 108;*
♯ Vic.LM 1876: ♭ set *ERB 53*)
Mantovani Orch. (in ♯ D.LK 4054: *LF 1143;*
Lon.LL 685, etc.)
☆ Orch.—Kostelanetz (in ♯ *C.S 1049: QS 6048:*
FS 1054; ♭ AmC.A 1558)
Boston Prom.—Fiedler (G.S 10607 &
in ♯ QDLP 6006: ♭ 7EP 7006)
Aarhus Municipal—Jensen (in ♯ Tono.LPX 35005)
Vienna Radio—Schönherr (in ♯ GA. 33-312)
— ARR. BAND
Deutschmeister Band—Herrmann (in ♯ *Nix.WLP Y 6705;*
♯ *West.WL 3005* & WP 6004)
— ARR. PF. Dohnányi, etc.
E. Farnadi (in ♯ West.WN 18064)
L. Pennario (in ♯ DCap.CTL 7087; Cap.P 8294)
H. Seiter (in ♯ *Nix.WLP Y 6736; West.WL 3036*)
M. Schwalb (in ♯ Roy. 1577)
— VOCAL ARRS.
☆ M. Korjus (S, *Ger*) (G.EB 560)
P. Munsel (S, *Eng*) (♭ *G.7EP 7016*)
R. Tauber (T, *Ger*) (in ♯ *P.PMB 1007*)

Seid umschlungen, Millionen, Op. 443
Leipzig Radio—Dobrindt   *Ami. 140031*
☆ Vienna Sym.—Krauss (in ♯ Sup.LPV 130; U. 5105G)
▽ Berlin Radio—Dobrindt (in *Indigo,* q.v.)

Solonsprüche, Op. 128
Schneider Str. Ens. (in ♯ AmC.CL 530)

Tausend und eine Nacht, Op. 346
(*1001 Nights*—"*Indigo*")
U.S.S.R. State—Gauk   USSR. 10344/5
Mantovani Orch. (in ♯ D.LK 4054: *LF 1193:*
♭ *DX 1728;* ♯ Lon.LL 685)
Orch.—B. Stanley (in ♯ *Var. 6984*)
☆ British Sym.—Weingartner (in ♯ AmC.ML 4777)
— VOCAL ARR. ☆ M. Korjus (S, *Eng*) (♭ *Vic.ERAT 14*)

(Die) Unzertrennlichen, Op. 108
☆ Schneider Str. Ens. (in ♯ AmC.CL 530)

---

[1] Labelled *Joys of Love*; this seems a fair approximation.

Wein, Weib und Gesang, Op. 333

Boston Prom.—Fiedler (n.v.) in ♭ *Vic. set ERB 7*

F.O.K. Sym.—Smetáček ♮ **U.H 24465/6**
(3ss—*Leopold: Butterflies, Intermezzo*) (in ♯ 5202H)
Vienna State Op.—Paulik (♯ MTW. 14: ♭ *set EP 14*)
Strauss Fest.—Ries-Walter (in ♯ *Mae.OA 20013*)
Vienna Radio—Schönherr (*Eli. 8738;* in ♯ *Rem. 149-38:*
♭ *REP 34;* in ♯ *Cum.TCR 213*)
Mantovani Orch. (in ♯ D.LK 4054: LF 1193: ♭ DX 1728:
♭ DFE 6001; ♯ Lon.LL 685, etc.)
G. Dervaux Orch.(**V**♯ *Sat.MSV 9007*)
▽ Austrian Sym.—Wöss (in ♯ *Rem. 149-8*)

☆ Württemberg State—Leitner (in ♯ *HP.DG 16003;*
Pol. 17029; ♯ *AmD.DL 4042:* ♭ *ED 3524*)
L.S.O.—Krips (♯ *D.LW 5009*)
Vienna Phil.—Karajan (♭ *C.SCB 112: SCBQ 3017*)
Philadelphia—Ormandy (♭ *AmC.A 1763 & A 2094*)
Boston Prom.—Fiedler (? o.v., in ♯ ItV.A12R 0093:
♭ *A72R 0028*)
Paris Cons.—Weingartner (in ♯ *AmC.ML 4777*)
Vienna State Op.—Schönherr (in ♯ *EPhi.BBR 8049:*
♭ *Phi.KD 143:* ♭ *N 428006E;* ♯ *AmC.RL 3073*)
Vienna Radio—Schönherr (in ♯ *Vien.LPR 1028;*
GA. 33-312)
Chicago Sym.—Stock (♭ *Cam.CAE 158*)

— VOCAL ARR.
☆ P. Munsel (S, *Eng*) (♭ *G.7EP 7016*)
M. Korjus (S, *Eng*) (♭ *Vic.ERAT 14*)

— ARR. PF. Godowsky, etc.
E. Farnadi (in ♯ *West.WN 18064*)
H. Seiter (in ♯ *Nix.WLPY 6130; West.WL 3130*)

— ARR. 2 PFS M. Rawicz & W. Landauer (in ♯ *D.LK 4094:*
♭ *DFE 6301;* ♯ *Lon.LL 1210*)

— ARR. ORGAN R. Ellsasser (in ♯ *MGM.E 3110*)
R. Foort (in ♯ *Nix.SLPY 148;* SOT. 10523,
etc.)

Wiener Blut, Op. 354

Boston Pops—Fiedler (n.v.) in ♭ *Vic. set ERB 7*

Vienna Phil.—Böhm in ♯ *AmVox.VX 510*

Berlin Sym.—List (in ♯ *Roy.* 1394)
Film Sym.—Kincl (U.H 24407)
Leighton Lucas Orch.(EMI.EPX 74)
Mantovani Orch. (♭ *D.DFE 6002: DX 1728;* etc.)
Vienna Bohemian—F. Walter (in ♯ *G.CLP 1047:*
FELP 140: QCLP 12015; ♯ Imp.ILP 119;
Vic.LM 1876: ♭ *set ERB 53*)
U.S.S.R. State—Gauk (*USSR. 10346/7*)
☆ Vienna Sym.—Moralt (in ♯ *EPhi.ABL 3002;*
Epic.LC 3004; Phi.S 06007R)
Vienna Phil.—Karajan (♭ *C.SEL 1503: SEBQ 101:*
ESBF 109)
L.S.O.—Krips (♯ *D.LW 5009*)
Berlin Phil.—Fricsay (♭ *Pol. 30073*)
Vienna State Op.—Schönherr (in ♯ *EPhi.BBR 8049;*
♭ *Phi.N 428006E;* in ♯ *AmC.RL 3073*)
Orch.—Kostelanetz (♭ *AmC.A 1621*)
Vienna Radio—Schönherr (*Eli. 8739;*
in ♯ *Rem. 149-38;* ♯ *Cum.TCR 213*)
etc.

— ARR. PF. H. Seiter (in ♯ *Nix.WLPY 6731; West.WL 3031*)

— VOCAL ARRS.
Vienna State Op. Cho. & Orch.—Rossmayer
(*D.F 49646:* in ♯ *LM 4559*)

☆ M. Korjus (S) (G.EB 560)

Wiener Bonbons, Op. 307

Vienna Radio—Schönherr, ? n.v. (*Eli. 8738;*
in ♯ *Rem. 148-38:* ♭ *REP 54;* ♯ *Cum.TCR 213*)
Vienna Light Orch. (**V**♯ *MMS.ML 1505*)
Viennese Sym. (in ♯ *Ply.* 12-100)
H. Bund (*Pol. 47590*)
etc.

— VOCAL ARR. J. Schmidt (T, *Ger*) (♭ *Od.GEOW 1008*)

Wo die Zitronen blüh'n, Op. 364

Vienna Sym.—Salmhofer in ♯ *EPhi.NBR 6008*
(*Accelerationen, etc.*) (♯ *Phi.S 06079R, o.n. N 00628R:*
♭ *N 402045E;* in ♯ *Epic.LC 3022*)
Moscow Radio—Samosud (*USSR. 17780/1*)
A. Lutter Orch. (*P.DPW 73; Od. O-28518*)
H. Hagestadt Orch. (*Pol. 48885*)
☆ Stockholm Phil.—Ehrling (in ♯ *Mtr.CLP 513:*
♭ *MCEP 3036;* ♯ *FMer.MLP 7020;*
♯ *AFest.CFR 12-173*)
Boston Prom.—Fiedler (in ♯ *Cam.CAL 126:* ♭ *CAE 104*)
etc.

I. 4. OTHER INST. WORKS

Perpetuum mobile, Op. 257

Tivoli Concert—Hansen **Pol.L 28081**
(*Helmesberger: Ballszene*) (♭ EP 45031)
Strauss Fest. Orch.—Ries-Walter (in ♯ *Mae.OA 20012*)
Czech Phil. Members—Křenovsky (in ♯ U. 5202H)
Hungarian Radio—Somogyi (Qual.MN 1075)
Moscow Radio—L. Steinberg (*USSR. 10925*)

☆ Boston Prom.—Fiedler (♭ *G7BF 1058; Vic.ERA 243;*
& perhaps o.v., ♯ *Cam.CAL 142:* ♭ *CAE 134*)
Stockholm Phil.—Ehrling (♭ *Mtr.MCEP 3037:*
in ♯ *CLP 513;* ♯ *AFest.CFR 12-173;* FMer.MLP 7020)
Vienna Radio—Schönherr (*Vien.P 6156*)
New Sym.—Krips (♭ *Lon.REP 8008*)

— ARR. 4 PFS.: Phil. Pf. Qtt. (♭ *AmC.A 1572*)

QUADRILLES

Fledermaus Quadrille, Op. 363

☆ Württemberg State—Leitner in ♯ *HP.DG 16003*
(♯ *Pol. 17029*)
Vienna Waltz Orch.—Hübener (in ♯ *Hma.LM 3000 &*
LM 820)

Ziegeunerbaron-Quadrille, Op. 422

W. Stephan Orch. (*Pol. 49170;* ♭ 22170)

B. OPERETTAS & STAGE WORKS

CAGLIOSTRO IN WIEN Operetta 1875

Overture

Vienna Radio—Schönherr **Vien.P 6143**

Die Rose erblüht

R. Schock (T) **G.EH 1457**
(*Nicolas: Alle Sterne dieser Welt*) (♭ 7PW 538)

CARNEVAL IN ROM Operetta 1873

Overture

Vienna Radio—Schönherr **Vien.P 6141**
(in ♯ LPR 1026)

Ballet Music

Vienna Radio—Schönherr **Vien.P 6142**

(Die) FLEDERMAUS Operetta 1874

COMPLETE RECORDINGS (inc. some dialogue)

Set C

Adele … … … …	R. Streich (S)
Rosalinde … … … …	E. Schwarzkopf (S)
Orlovsky … … … …	R. Christ (T)
Alfred … … … …	H. Krebs (T)
Eisenstein … … … …	N. Gedda (T)
Falke … … … …	E. Kunz (B)
Frank … … … …	K. Dönch (B)

etc., Cho. & Philharmonia Orch.—Karajan
♯ **C.CX 1309/10**
(4ss) (♯ QCX 10183/4; Angel. 35263/4, set 3539)
H. Sakharova (S), L. Neverov (T), M. Shchavinsky (T)
K. Rachevskaya (S), V. Zakharov (B), etc., Moscow
Radio Cho. & Orch.—Samosud ♯ **USSR.D 1774/7**
(4ss) (*Russ*)

HIGHLIGHTS
S. Barabas (S), A. Rothenberger (S), R. Schock (T),
H. Günter (B), H. Prey (B), G. Neidlinger (Bs), Hanover
Landestheater Cho. & N.W. Ger. Phil.—Schüchter[1]
♯ **G.DLP 1120**
(♯ WDLP 1518)

U. Graf (S), H. Heusser (S), A. Kunz (T), J. Bartsch (T),
M. Schmid (B), etc., Zürich Radio Cho. & Orch.—Goehr
♯ **MMS. 2022**
(also ♯ OP 3)

M. Janz (S), U. Richter (S), W. Liebing (T), G. Lutze (T)
etc., Leipzig Radio Cho. & Orch.—Dobrindt
♯ **Eta. 740002**

FILM VERSION (*Eng*) modernised as "*O Rosalinda*"
A. Quayle (actor), M. Redgrave (B), A. Rothenberger (S),
S. Barabas (S), A. Young (T), etc., Vienna Sym. Cho. &
Orch.—Melichar ♯ **Nix.NPL 18001**

Vocal Selections
"State Op." Soloists, cho. & orch.
(♯ Roy. 6130; Var. 6979; excerpts ♭ Roy.EP 196)

☆ A. Dermota, J. Patzak, H. Gueden, etc., Vienna Sym. Cho.
& Orch.—Reiner (♯ D.LW 5138)

Soloists, cho. & Vic. Orch.—Reiner
(♯ Vic.LRM 7026: ♭ set ERB 7026)
E. Berger, E. Friedrich, etc. (in ♯ FT. 320.TC.043)
R. Streich, E. Trötschel, P. Anders, etc. (♭ Pol. 20038)

(continued on next page)

---

[1] The Czárdás is sung in Hungarian; the part of Orlofsky is sung by baritone.

(Die) FLEDERMAUS (continued)

Piano Selections — ARR. Dohnányi
("Du und Du Paraphrase"), etc.
E. Farnadi (in ♯ West.WN 18064)
M. Schwalb (in ♯ Roy. 1577)

—ARR. 2 PFS.
V. Appleton & M. Field (in ♯ Roy. 1587;
                    also AmVox.VX 540)

Overture
Vienna Sym.—Moralt   ♯ Phi.N 00631R
(Zigeunerbaron Overture; & Suppé)   (♯ Epic.LC 3022)
(Zigeunerbaron, only ♯ Phi.S 06012R)

Philadelphia "Pops"—Ormandy
                    in ♯ AmC.ML 4686

Zürich Radio—Goehr   V♯ MMS. 910
(Zigeunerbaron Overture)

Vienna Phil.—Böhm   in ♯ Ura. 7155
(♯ Ura. 7096: RS 5-2: RS 7-21: ♭ UREP 60)

N.Y.P.S.O.—Kostelanetz   in ♯ AmC.CL 769
☆ Vienna Phil.—Krauss   ♯ D.LW 5005
(Zigeunerbaron, Overture)
                    (& in ♯ D.LXT 2965; Lon.LL 1028)
Leipzig Radio—Dobrindt (Ami. 245003)
Stalinograd Radio—Krenz (Muza.X 2348)
Belgian Radio—Marinetti (in ♯ Mae.OA 20011)
Moscow Radio—Samosud (USSRM.D 139)
☆ R.I.A.S. Sym.—Fricsay (in ♯ HP.DGM 18050;
          in ♭ Pol. 19035: ♭ 30095; ♯ AmD.DL 4052)
Vienna Sym.—Swarowsky (in ♯ Sup.LPM 121;
                    U. 5116C, d.c.)
Vienna Sym.—Paulik (♭ AmVox.PL 30090)
Hallé—Heward (in ♯ AmC.RL 3072)
Saxon State—Böhm (in ♯ BB.LBC 1048:
                    ♭ set WBC 1048 & ERAB 6)
Vic. Sym.—Reiner (in ♯ Vic.LRM/♭ ERB 7026)
Minneapolis Sym.—Ormandy (in ♭ Vic. set ERB 6;
                    ♯ ItV.A12R 0093)
Stockholm Phil.—Ehrling (in ♯ Mtr.CLP 513:
          ♭ MCEP 3037; in ♯ AFest.CFR 173; FMer.MLP 7020)
Austrian Sym.—Schönherr (in ♯ Rem. 199-119:
          ♭ REP 5; in ♯ Ply. 12-40; & with commentary by
          S. Spaeth, in ♯ Rem. 6)
Strauss Orch.—Lanner (in ♯ MGM.E 3022: in ♯ D 122;
          FMGM.F 1-109: ItMGM.QD 6012)
Berlin Phil.—Karajan (Pol. 57425)

ACT I

No. 5A, Trinke Liebchen...; Glücklich ist...
    T & S
... Tenor solo only
W. A. Dotzer   in ♯ Phi.S 06047R

ACT II

No. 8B, Mein Herr Marquis S
A. Rothenberger   G.EH 1454
(No. 14)   (♭ 7PW 535)
M. Dyurkovich (Hung) (in ♯ USSR.D 2139)
☆ E. Sack (in ♯ DT.LGM 65015)
F. F. Jenkins & pf. (Eng) (in ♯ Vic.LRT 7000:
                    ♭ set ERBT 7000)

No. 11B, Klänge der Heimat (Czárdás) S
K. Bodalska (Pol) (Muza. 2309)
☆ L. Welitsch (in ♯ AmC.ML 4795)
M. Ivogün (JpV.ND 404)

ACT III

No. 12, Entr'acte orch.
Vienna State Op.—Schönherr in ♯ D.LW 5133
(Lehár, O. Straus, Kreisler, etc.)   (♯ Lon.LD 9157)
                    (& ♯ D.LXT 5033; Lon.LL 1116)

No. 14, Spiel' ich die Unschuld vom Lande S
A. Rothenberger   G.EH 1454
(No. 8B)   (♭ 7PW 535)

INDIGO UND DIE 40 RÄUBER 1871
ABRIDGED RECORDING[1]
(in the Reiterer version of 1906—Tausend und eine Nacht)
☆ Soloists, Berlin Radio Cho. & Orch.—Dobrindt
                    (♯ ANix.ULP 9203-1/2)
Overture
Vienna Phil.—Krauss   ♭ AmVox.VIP 30100
(Polkas)

[1] Includes Seid umschlungen... Waltz.

Intermezzo
Leipzig Radio—Dobrindt   Ami. 140034
N.W. Ger. Phil.—Schüchter ♭ Od.BEOW 32008
(Zigeunerbaron Overture)   (in ♯ Imp.ILP 111)
Hamburg State Phil.—Müller-Lampertz
                    T.A 11681
(Hellmesberger: Teufelstanz)   (♭ U 45681)
Czech Phil. Members—Křenovsky in ♯ U.5202H
H. Hagestadt Orch. (PV. 58623)

Launisches Glück
(a song by Julius Bürger, based on a Strauss melody,
    interpolated)
☆ J. Schmidt (T) (Od.O-28583)
— ARR. ORCH. O. Heyden Str. Orch. (Ami. 40-28)

(Der) LUSTIGE KRIEG 1881
HIGHLIGHTS
☆ E. Roon (S), W. Kmentt (T), etc., Cho. & Vienna Sym.
    —v. Pauspertl (from set) (V♯ MMS.ML 1501)

No. 11, Nur für Natur T
☆ E. Kunz (B) (C.LOX 816: ♭ SEB 3507)

(Eine) NACHT IN VENEDIG Operetta 1883
COMPLETE RECORDING
Annina   ...   .   E. Schwarzkopf (S)
Duke of Urbino   ...   .   N. Gedda (T)
Pappacoda ...   .   P. Klein (T)
Caramello   ...   .   E. Kunz (B)
Delaqua   ...   .   K. Dönch (B)
Barbara   ...   .   H. Ludwig (S)

etc., cho. & Philharmonia Orch.—Ackermann
                    ♯ C.CX 1224/5
(4ss)   (♯ Angel. 35197/8, set 3530)

HIGHLIGHTS
☆ E. Rethy (S), K. Friedrich (T), etc., Bregenz Fest.
    Cho. & Vienna Sym.—Paulik (from set)
                    (V♯ MMS.ML 1509; ♯ Orb.BL 602)

HIGHLIGHTS — ARR. ORCH.
R.I.A.S. Sym.—Becker   ♯ Rem. 199-170
(Lehár)   (♯ Cum.CR 302)
Austrian Sym. (♯ Ply. 12-110)

Vocal Selections
R. Streich, R. Weigelt, P. Anders, etc., Cho. & Orch.
    —Marszalek   ♯ Pol. 45067
(also PV. 58626: ♭ 20052)
☆ F. E. Engels (T), Ger. Op. House Orch. & Cho.
    —Schüler (in ♯ FT.320.TC.043)

Overture
Berlin Sym.—List   in ♯ Roy. 1394
☆ "Nat. Op. Orch." (in ♯ Var. 6966: 6999;
                    ♭ Roy.EP 209: & in ♯ 1860)

Ach! wie so herrlich (Lagunen Waltz) T
☆ E. Kunz (B) (♭ C.SEB 3507)
J. Patzak (Pol. 48011)

Komm' in die Gondel T
B. Manazza   Tpo. 3686
(Lehar: Paganini—Gern hab' ich)
P. Anders   in ♯ Pol. 45064
☆ E. Kunz (B) (C.LOX 816: ♭ SEB 3507)
R. Schock (in ♯ G.WDLP 1502: ♭ 7PW 502)
J. Patzak (Pol. 48011)

Sei mir gegrüsst, du mein holdes Venetia T
W. A. Dotzer (Lehár)   ♯ Phi.S 06038R

Treu sein, das liegt mir nicht T
B. Manazza   Tpo. 3696
(Rigoletto—La donna è mobile)
☆ K. Friedrich (in ♯ Od.DX 1766)
H. E. Groh (P.B 556)

RITTER PÁZMÁN Comic opera, 3 Acts 1892
Ballet Music
Berlin Sym.—Guhl (Delibes)   ♯ Ura. 7165
... Csárdás only
Vienna State Op.—Paulik   in ♯ Van.VRS 457
                    (♯ Am.AVRS 6014)
International Sym.—Schneiderhann (in ♯ Mae.OA 20009)
Westminster Light Orch.—Bridgewater
                    (in ♯ Nix.WLP 6804; West.WL 4004)

SIMPLIZIUS Operetta 1887
SEE Donauweibchen Waltz, *above*

(Das) SPITZENTUCH DER KÖNIGIN
Operetta 1880
Overture
Philadelphia "Pops"—Ormandy
in ‡ AmC.ML 4686

WALDMEISTER Operetta 1895
Overture
Philadelphia "Pops"—Ormandy
in ‡ AmC.ML 4686
(‡ Phi.S 06618R)
Leipzig Radio—Abendroth in ‡ Ura. 7155
(& in ‡ RS 7-21: ♭ UREP 60)
Vienna Radio—Schönherr **Vien.L 6149**
(in ‡ LPR 1036)
Leipzig Radio—Dobrindt **Ami. 245004**
☆ German Op. House—Lutze (in ‡ FT.320.TC.043)

(Der) ZIGEUNERBARON Operetta 1885
ABRIDGED RECORDINGS
S. Barabas (S), D. Siebert (S), G. v. Milinkovic (A),
R. Christ (T), H. Braun (B), O. Edelmann (Bs), K.
Preger (Bs), etc., Vienna Cha. Cho. & Sym. Orch.
—Moralt [with narration] ‡ Phi.A 00178L
(‡ Epic.LC 3041)
U. Graf (S), H. Heusser (S), A. Kunz (T), etc., Cho. &
Zürich Radio Orch.—Goehr ‡ MMS. set 130
(4ss) (Overture only, V‡ MMS. 910)
(also ‡ MMS. 2025: OP 12, 2ss)

HIGHLIGHTS
M. Janz (S), G. Stilo (A), E. Witte (T), G. Frei (Bs),
Leipzig Radio Cho. & Orch.—Dobrindt Eta. 340047/8
(4ss) (Kalmán: Gräfin Mariza on ‡ Eta. 740001)
G. Guétary & Orch.—Méthéen (Fr)
(‡ Pat.AT 1048 : QAT 6007)
☆ H. Zadek (S), J. Patzak (T), etc., Vienna State Op. Cho.
& Orch.—Krauss, from set (‡ Lon.LL 648)
Anon. Soloists & Cho. (‡ Var. 6998; excerpts on
on ♭ Roy.EP 222)

Vocal Selection
C. Spletter (S), H. Tolksdorf (T), etc. **Hma. 15013**
☆ A. Gura, P. Anders, etc. (in ‡ FT. 320.TC.043)
Soloists, Austrian Sym. Cho. & Orch.—Schönherr
(‡ Ply. 12-55)
E. Trötschel (S), P. Anders (T), etc. (♭ Pol. 20050)

Overture
R.I.A.S. Sym.—Fricsay ‡ AmD.DL 4052
(Fledermaus, Overture) (♭ ED 3545)
(Polkas on PV. 72335; ♭ Pol. 30095)
Vienna Sym.—Moralt ‡ Phi.N 00631R
(above; & Suppé) (‡ Epic.LC 3022)
(Fledermaus only, ‡ Phi.S 06012R)
Leipzig Radio—Abendroth in ‡ Ura. 7155
(& in ‡ RS 7-21 & 5-2) (♭ UREP 54)
Vienna Sym.—Swarowsky ‡ Sup.LPM 225
(Nicolai, Rossini, Bizet) (‡ U. 5204C)
N.W. Ger. Phil.—Schüchter ♭ Od.BEOW 3008
(Indigo—Intermezzo) (in ‡ Imp.ILP 111)
Moscow Radio—Samosud **USSRM.D 140**
(Fledermaus Overture)
Hungarian Radio—Somogyi **Qual.ON 6582**
☆ Vienna Phil.—Krauss ‡ D.LW 5005
(Fledermaus Overture) (& in ‡ LXT 2991; Lon.LL 1029)
☆ Boston Prom.—Fiedler (♭ G.7EP 7003)
Minneapolis Sym.—Ormandy (in ‡ ItV.A12R 0093;
♭ Vic.ERB 6)
Stockholm Phil.—Ehrling (in ‡ Mtr.CLP 513:
♭ MCEP 3037; ‡ AFest.CFR 12-173;
FMer.MLP 7020)
Vienna Sym.—Paulik (♭ AmVox.VIP 30090)
Austrian Sym.—Schönherr (♭ Rem.REP 5; ‡ Ply. 12-103;
& with commentary, in ‡ Rem. 6)
Anon. Orch. (in ‡ Roy. 1860)

ACT I

No. 2, Als flotter Geist; Ja, das Alles auf Ehr' T
P. Anders in ‡ Pol. 45064
☆ J. Schmidt (Od.O-28583: ♭ GEOW 1066: in ‡ OLA 1008)
R. Schock (♭ G.7PW 502: in ‡ WDLP 1502)

No. 3, Ja, das Schreiben... Mein idealer
Lebenszweck Bs
G. Neidlinger in ‡ Eli.LPE 107
O. Maleczky (Hung) (Qual.ON 6062)
☆ E. Kunz (♭ C.SEB 3507)

No. 6, So elend und treu (Zigeunerlied) S
☆ L. Welitsch (in ‡ AmC.ML 4795)

ACT II

No. 8, Mein Aug' bewacht
No. 9, Ha, seht, es winkt S, A, T
A. Schlemm, G. Stilo & R. Schock **G.EH 1437**
(below) (in ‡ WDLP 1502) (FKX 257)
No. 11, Wer uns getraut? S & T
R. Streich & P. Anders **Pol. 49260**
(Heuberger: Opernball—Im Chambre separée) (♭ 22260)
A. Schlemm & R. Schock **G.EH 1437**
(above) (FKX 257: in ‡ WDLP 1502)
☆ C. V-Tauber & R. Tauber (♭ Od.GEOW 1009)
No. 12b, Her die Hand! (Werberlied) B
H. Wocke **Eta. 225025**
(Contes d'Hoffmann—Barcarolle)

ACT III

No. 17, Hurrah! Die Schlacht... cho. & orch.
— ORCH. ONLY ("Entry March")
Vienna State Op.—Paulik in ‡ Nix.PVL 7007
(Jos. Strauss, & Collection above) (in ‡ Van.VRS 443
☆ Austrian Sym.—Wöss or ? Schönherr
(in ‡ Ply. 12-104; ♭ Rem.REP 71)
Berlin State Op.—Otto (in ‡ T.LA 6054;
in ‡ FT. 260.TV.015)
Boston Prom.—Fiedler (in ‡ Cam.CAL 126: ♭ CAE 104)
— ARR. BAND Vox Concert Band (in ‡ AmVox.VX 590;
Orb.BL 601)

C. MISCELLANEOUS

BALLET COMPILATIONS
(Le) Beau Danube (ARR. Désormière)
L.P.O.—Martinon ‡ D.LXT 5149
(1½ss—Rossini: Guillaume Tell, Ballet) (‡ Lon.LL 1383)
Graduation Ball (ARR. Dorati)
New Sym.—Fistoulari ‡ D.LXT 2848
(‡ Lon.LL 883)

OPERETTA PASTICHES
CASANOVA (ARR. Benatzky)
Nuns' Chorus S, cho., orch.
G. Fields (Eng) (in ‡ D.LF 1140: ♭ DFE 6313;
in ‡ Lon.LB 751)
☆ A. Frind & Cho. (♭ G.7PW 108)
J. Candel (Dutch) & Cho. (in ‡ EPhi.BBR 8042;
Phi.P 10028R)

(Die) TÄNZERIN FANNY ELSSLER
(ARR. Weninger & Stalla)
Draussen in Sievering S
R. Streich in ‡ HP.DG 17052
(also in ‡ Pol. 17051)
H. Gueden in ‡ D.LW 5126
(Wiener Blut, Lustige Witwe, etc.) (‡ Lon.LD 9158)
(also in ‡ D.LXT 5033; Lon.LL 1116)
L. Rehs (Vien.P 6168: in ‡ LPR 1043)
☆ E. Roon (♭ AmVox.VIP 30500)
E. Sack (in ‡ DT.LGM 65015)

WIENER BLUT (ARR. Müller) 1899
COMPLETE RECORDINGS

Prime Minister	...	...	...	K. Dönch (B)
Graf Zedlan	...	...	...	N. Gedda (T)
Gabriele	...	...	...	E. Schwarzkopf (S)
Franzi	...	...	...	E. Köth (S)
Kagler	...	...	...	A. Pernerstorfer (B)
Joseph	...	...	...	E. Kunz (B)
Pepi Pleininger	...	...	...	E. Loose (S)

etc., Cho. & Philharmonia Orch.—Ackermann
‡ C.CX 1186S/7
(3ss) (‡ BrzA.CBX 129/30; ‡ Angel. 35156S/7, set 3519)
☆ I. Beilke (S), T. Richter (S), R. Streich (S), S. Hauser (T),
Berlin Municipal Op. Cho. & Orch.—Lenzer
‡ Nix.ULP 9209-1/2
(4ss) [Highlights on ‡ ULP 9129; ‡ Ura. 7129; Excerpts
on ♭ Nix.EP 705 & EP 751; Ura.UREP 51]

☆ = Re-issue of a recording to be found in previous volumes.

WIENER BLUT (*continued*)

Vocal Selection
E. Lindermeier, G. Schörg, L. de Luca, etc. (♭ *Pol. 20073*)

Overture . . . Introduction only
Vienna State Op.—Schönherr (in *D.LW 5126;*
   ♯ *Lon.LD 9158;* & in ♯ D.LXT 5033; Lon.LL 1116)

Grüss dich Gott, du liebes Nesterl
Wiener Blut muss was eigenes sein
H. Gueden (S)   in ♯ *D.LW 5133*
   (*Fledermaus; O. Straus, Lehár, etc.*)   (♯ *Lon.LD 9157*)
   (& in ♯ D.LXT 5033; Lon.LL 1116)
... Wiener Blut muss . . . only, also in ♯ *D.LW 5126;*
                                        Lon.LD 9158

Cotillon
Vienna Radio—Schönherr   *Vien.P 6130*
   (*Jos. Strauss: Moulinet-Polka*)   (in ♯ *LPR 1026*)

Improvisations on Johann Strauss melodies
A. Templeton (playing duet with himself) ♯ **Rem. 199-158**
(*Offenbach*)

Selection from Strauss Operettas
   (inc. Das Spitzentuch, Tausend und eine Nacht, Lustige
   Krieg, Wiener Blut, Nacht in Venedig, Fledermaus,
   Blindekuh, Zigeunerbaron, Waldmeister, Prinz
   Methusalem)
S. Schöner (S), H. E. Groh (T), Cho. & Orch.—Otto
                                 ♯ *DT.TM 68051*
                                 (♯ *T.TW 30026*)
Soirée de Vienne — ARR. Grünfeld
H. Somer (pf.)   in ♯ **Rem. 199-124**
                                 (♯ Ply. 12-92)
Strauss Fantasy — ARR. Landauer
M. Rawicz & W. Landauer (pfs.)   ♯ *G.ALP 1224*
   (*Saint-Saëns & Friedmann*)   (♯ *QALP 10094*)
Wiener Karneval — ARR. PF. Rosenthal
P. Mildner   ♯ *DT.LGM 65025*
   (*Chopin & Liszt*)   (♯ *T.LB 6060:* ♭ *UV 111*)
J. Strauss & his music
☆ Narration & orch. (♭ *AmVox. set VIP 30132*)

STRAUSS, Josef (1827-1870)

POLKAS
COLLECTION
Aus der Ferne, Op. 270   P.-schnell
Feuerfest, Op. 269   P.-schnell
Frauenherz, Op. 166   P.-Mazurka
Ohne Sorgen, Op. 271   P.-schnell
Vienna State Op.—Paulik   ♯ **Nix.PVL 7003**
   (*J. Strauss II*)   (♯ *Van.VRS 438*)

Feuerfest, Op. 269   P.-schnell
Jockey, Op. 278   ('Gallop')
Die Libelle, Op. 204   P.-Mazurka
Moulinet, Op. 59   P.-française
Ohne Sorgen, Op. 271   P.-schnell
☆ Vienna Phil.—Krauss   ♯ *D.LW 5053*
[Die Libelle also on ♭ *D.71079*]   (♯ *Lon.LD 9045*)

Auf Ferienreisen, Op. 133 P.-schnell
Vienna Phil.—Krauss   in ♯ **D.LXT 2913**
                       (in ♯ D.NLK 40100; Lon.LL 970)

(La) Chevaleresque, Op. 42 P.-Mazurka
Vienna Radio—Schönherr   *Vien.P 6137*
(*below*)   (in ♯ *LPR 1026*)

Eingesendet, Op. 240
Vienna State Op.—Paulik in ♯ **Nix.PVL 7007**
(*Dorfschwalben, below, etc.*)   (♯ *Van.VRS 443*)

Feuerfest, Op. 269 P.-schnell
Vienna Light Orch. (V♯ *MMS.ML 1505*)
   ☆ Philadelphia—Ormandy (AmC.J 244: ♭ *4-244*)

— ARR. BAND   Viennese Band—Hermann
   (in ♯ *Nix.WLPY 6707; West.WL 3007* & *WP 6004*)

Jockey, Op. 278 ('Gallop')
Vienna State Op.—Paulik   in ♯ **Van.VRS 457**
                                (♯ *Ama.AVRS 6014*)
Juckerpolka, Op. 27
Vienna Radio—Schönherr   *Vien.P 6137*
(*above*)   (in ♯ *LPR 1036*)

Moulinet, Op. 57 P.-française
Vienna Radio—Schönherr   *Vien.P 6130*
   (*J. Strauss II: Wiener Blut—Cotillon*) (in ♯ *LPR 1030*)
Strauss Fest. Orch.—Ries-Walter (in ♯ *Mae.OA 20012*)

Ohne Sorgen, Op. 271 P.-schnell
   ☆ Vienna Phil.—Krauss (in ♭ *AmVox.VIP 30040*)

Plappermäulchen, Op. 245 P.-schnell
Vienna Phil.—Krauss   in ♯ **D.LXT 2913**
                       (in ♯ D.NLK 40100; Lon.LL 970)
   ☆ Vienna Radio—Nilius (*Vien.P 6025*)

WALTZES
COLLECTION
   ☆ Dorfschwalben aus Österreich, Op. 164
   ☆ Mein Lebenslauf ist Lieb' und Lust, Op. 263
   Sphärenklänge, Op. 235
Vienna Phil.—Krauss   ♯ **D.LXT 2991**
(*J. Strauss II*)   (♯ *Lon.LL 1029*)

Aquarellen, Op. 258
Vienna State Op.—Paulik in ♯ **Van.VRS 457**
                                (♯ *Ama.AVRS 6014*)
Vienna Sym.—Salmhofer   ♭ *Phi.N 402045E*
   (*J. Strauss II: Wo die Zitronen blüh'n*) (♯ Epic.LC 3022)
(♯ *Phi.S 06079R, o.n. N 00628R;* in ♯ *EPhi.NBR 6008*)
Vienna Radio—Schönherr   *Vien.P 6159*
Linz Sym. (in ♯ Ply. 12-30)
Moscow Radio—Gauk (*USSR. 15258/9*)
   ☆ Vienna Sym.—Baltzer (♭ *Rem.REP 65*)

Delirien, Op. 212
   ☆ Vienna Radio—Schönherr (♭ *Phi.KD 163: P 428003E*)

Dorfschwalben aus Österreich, Op. 164
Vienna State Op.—Paulik in ♯ **Nix.PVL 7007**
(*above; & Joh. Strauss*)   (♯ *Van.VRS 443*)
Mantovani Orch. (*D.F 10051:* in ♯ LK 4054:
   ♭ *DFE 6001;* ♯ *Lon.LL 685:* ♭ *set LSF 108: BEP 6001*)
Concert Orch.—Krish (*USSR. 10577/8*)
Orch.—v. Schmeling (*Bulg. 1001*)
   ☆ Vienna Phil.—Krauss (♯ *D.LW 5019:* ♭ *DX 1737;*
                                    ♯ *Lon.LD 9029*)
   Boston Prom.—Fiedler (in ♯ *Vic.LRM 7041:*
      ♭ *set ERB 7041;* ♭ *DV. 26038;* ♭ *Cam.CAE 137,*
      possibly o.v.)
   H. Zacharias Orch. (♭ *Pol. 22205;* in ♯ AmD.DL 8089:
                                    ♭ *set ED 699*)
— VOCAL ARR. (*Ger*)
   R. Streich (S) & orch. (in ♯ *HP.DG 17052* & *Pol. 17051*)
   ☆ E. Loose (S) & Vienna Radio Orch. (AusT.E 1192)

Dynamiden (Geheime Anziehungskräfte), Op. 173
Schneider Str. Ens.   in ♯ **AmC.CL 556**
                                 (♭ *set B 417*)
Viennese Sym. (in ♯ Ply. 12-69, 61, etc.)

(Die) Ersten und Letzten, Op. 1[1]
   ☆ Schneider Str. Ens. (in ♯ AmC.CL 530)

Mein Lebenslauf ist Lieb' und Lust, Op. 263
   ☆ Vienna Phil.—Krauss (♯ *D.LW 5019;* *Lon.LD 9029*)
   A. Schneider Str. Ens. (in ♯ AmC.CL 530)

Sphärenklänge, Op. 235
Vienna Phil.—Krauss   in ♯ **D.LXT 2913**
                       (in ♯ D.NLK 40100; ♯ Lon.LL 970)
Vienna State Op.—Paulik   ♯ **Van.VRS 459**
(*J. Strauss II*)
Philharmonia—Kletzki   ♭ *C.SEL 1535*
   (*Tchaikovsky: Serenade, Finale*)
   ☆ Vienna Phil.—Karajan   ♭ *C.SEL 1505*
   (*Transaktionen*)   (♭ *SEBQ 107: SELW 24-1505*)
   H. Busch Orch. (Ami. 40-12)
— ARR. CHO. & PF.
   ☆ Vienna Boys' Cho.—Brenner in ♯ *EPhi.NBR 6007*
                       (in ♯ AmC.ML 4873; ♭ *Phi.N 402000E*)

Transaktionen, Op. 184
   ☆ Vienna Phil.—Karajan   ♭ *C.SEL 1505*
   (*Sphärenklänge*)   (♭ *SEBQ 107: SELW 24-1505*)
Strauss Fest. Orch.—Ries-Walter (in ♯ *Mae.OA 20012*)

---

[1] Or possibly *Die Ersten nach die Letzten, Op. 12.* It has not been possible to check.

STRAUSS, Richard (1864-1949)

CLASSIFIED: I. ORCHESTRAL
         II. INSTRUMENTAL & CHAMBER
             MUSIC
       III. STAGE WORKS
       IV. LIEDER
       V. MISCELLANEOUS

I. ORCHESTRAL

(Eine) Alpensinfonie, Op. 64 1915
   ☆ Munich State Op.—Konwitschny   ♯ Nix.ULP 9064
                               (♯ MTW. 545)

Also sprach Zarathustra, Op. 30 1896
   Chicago Sym.—Reiner   ♯ G.ALP 1214
   (*Salome—Tanz*) (♯ Vic.LM 1806; ♭ *set ERD 1806;*
            ♯ ItV.A12R 0120; FV.A 630213; DV.L 16481)
   Berlin Sym.—List   ♯ Roy. 1460
   ☆ Boston Sym.—Koussevitzky (♯ Cam.CAL 173)

Aus Italien, Op. 16 1886
   Vienna Phil.—Krauss   ♯ D.LXT 2917
                            (♯ Lon.LL 969)
   Berlin Radio—Rother   ♯ Ura. 7087
   ☆ Vienna Sym.—Swoboda (*Macbeth*) ♯ West.WN 18078
   ... 3rd movt., Am Strande von Sorrent
   ☆ Chicago Sym.—Stock (in ♯ Cam.CAL 162)

Burleske, D minor pf. & orch. 1885
   F. Gulda & L.S.O.—Collins   ♯ D.LXT 5013
   (*Mozart*)   (♯ Lon.LL 1158)
   E. Ney & Berlin Radio—Rother   ♯ Ura. 7101
   (*Britten*)
   Anon. soloist & "Philharmonic"—Berendt
   (*Serenade; & Berg*)   ♯ Allo. 3144
   ☆ F. Jacquinot & Philharmonia—Fistoulari
   (*Dohnányi*)   ♯ P.PMC 1005
   ☆ C. Arrau & Chicago Sym.—Defauw (♯ Cam.CAL 191)

Concerto No. 1, E flat major, Op. 11 hrn. & orch.
                                 1882-3
   H. Lohan & Leipzig Radio—Wiesenhütter
   (*Mozart*)   ♯ Ura. 7108
   F. Huth & Frankenland State—Kloss
   (*below*)   ♯ Lyr.LL 58
   ☆ D. Brain & Philharmonia—Galliera ♯ AmC.ML 4775
   (*Oboe Concerto*)

Concerto, oboe & orch. 1945
   ☆ L. Goossens & Philharmonia—Galliera ♯ AmC.ML 4775
   (*Horn Concerto*)

Don Juan, Op. 20 1888
   Vienna Phil.—Furtwängler   ♯ G.ALP 1208
   (*Till Eulenspiegel*)   (♯ QALP 10085)
   (*idem & Weber* in ♯ Vic.LHMV 19)
   Bamberg Sym.—Horenstein
                    ♯ E. & AmVox.PL 9060
   (*Till Eulenspiegel, Tod und Verklärung*)
   (*Till only, on* ♯ Pan.XPV 1001)
   Berlin Phil.—Lehmann   ♯ Pol. 16091
   (*Debussy: Prélude à l'après-midi . . .*)
   Chicago Sym.—Reiner   ♯ Vic.LM 1888
   (*Liebermann*)   (♭ Vic.ERB 56; ♯ ItV.A12R 0160;
                                 DV.L 16491)
   N.Y.P.S.O.—Walter   ♯ AmC.ML 4650
   (*Tod und Verklärung*)
   London Phil. Sym.—Rodzinski
                    ♯ West.LAB 7016
   (*Till Eulenspiegel*)
   ☆ Amsterdam—E. Jochum   ♯ EPhi.ABR 4009
   (*below*)
   (*below; & Liszt on* ♯ Epic.LC 3032)
   ☆ N.B.C.—Toscanini   ♯ G.ALP 1173
   (*Wagner*)   (♯ QALP 157)
   ☆ Pittsburgh Sym.—Reiner   ♯ AmC.ML 4800
   (*below; & Bürger als Edelmann*)
   Anon. Orch. (♯ ACC.MP 20)
   ☆ Philharmonia—Karajan (♯ C.VCX 532)
   Austrian Sym.—Wöss (with commentary by S. Spaeth,
     ♯ Rem. 100-20)

Don Quixote, Op. 35 vlc. & orch. 1897
   P. Fournier & Vienna Phil.—Krauss
                          ♯ D.LXT 2842
                          (♯ Lon.LL 855)
   G. Piatigorsky & Boston Sym.—Münch
                          ♯ G.ALP 1211
     (♯ Vic.LM 1781; ♯ ItV.A12R 0047; ♯ FV.A 630206)
   ☆ E. Feuermann & Philadelphia—Ormandy
                         (♯ Cam.CAL 202)
   G. Piatigorsky & Pittsburgh—Reiner (♯ AmC.RL 3027)

Duet-Concertino cl., bsn., str., hp. 1947
   ☆ G. Caylor, D. Christlieb & Los Angeles Cha. Sym.
     —Byrns (♯ T.LCE 8115)

Festmarsch, E flat major, Op. 1 1876
   ☆ Bavarian Sym.—Graunke   in ♯ Nix.ULP 9602-1/2

(Ein) Heldenleben, Op. 40 1898
   Minneapolis Sym.—Dorati   ♯ EMer.MG 50012
   Chicago Sym.—Reiner   ♯ G.ALP 1209
   (♯ Vic.LM 1807; ♭ *set ERD 1807;* ♯ ItV.A12R 0118;
                               ♯ DV.L 16478)
   Philadelphia—Ormandy (n.v.) ♯ EPhi.ABL 3061
             (♯ AmC.ML 4887; Phi.A 01148L)
   "Philharmonic"—Berendt   ♯ Allo. 3088
   ☆ Cleveland Sym.—Rodzinski (♯ AmC.RL 3048)
   Philadelphia—Ormandy (o.v.) (♯ Cam.CAL 194)

Macbeth, Op. 23 1887
   ☆ Vienna Sym.—Swoboda   ♯ Nix.WLP 5004
   (*Martinů: Concerto Grosso*)
   (*Aus Italien on* ♯ West.WN 18078)

Metamorphosen 23 str. insts. 1945
   French Nat.—Horenstein   ♯ Pat.DTX 138
   (*Stravinsky: Sym.*)   (♯ Angel. 35101)

Serenade, E flat major, Op. 7 13 wind insts. 1881
   Vienna Phil. Wind Ens.   ♯ West.WL 5185
   (*Suite, Op. 4*)
   "Philharmonic" Ens.—Berendt   ♯ Allo. 3144
   (*Burleske; & Berg*)

Sinfonia domestica, Op. 53 1903
   ☆ Philadelphia—Ormandy (♯ Cam.CAL 248)

Sonatina No. 2, E flat major 16 wind insts. 1944-5
   ("*Symphony No. 1*": Fröhliche Werkstatt; *Cheerful*
    Workshop)
   London Baroque Ens.—Haas   ♯ P.PMA 1006
                          (♯ AmD.DL 9761)
   M.G.M. Orch.—I. Solomon   ♯ MGM.E 3097

Suite No. 1, B flat major, Op. 4 13 wind insts. 1884
   Vienna Phil. Wind Ens.   ♯ West.WL 5185
   (*Serenade, Op. 7*)

Suite of Dances after Couperin 1923
   Frankenland State—Kloss   ♯ Lyr.LL 58
   (*above*)

Symphony, F minor, Op. 12 1884
   ☆ Vienna Sym.—Haefner   ♯ CA.LPA 1028

Till Eulenspiegels lustige Streiche, Op. 28 1895
   N.B.C. Sym.—Toscanini[1]   ♯ Vic.LM 1891
   (*Tod und Verklärung*)   (♯ FV.A630313; ItV.A12R 0181)
   Vienna Phil.—Furtwängler   ♯ G.ALP 1208
   (*Don Juan*)   (♯ QALP 10085)
   (*idem; & Weber on* ♯ Vic.LHMV 19)
   Berlin Phil.—Furtwängler[2]   ♯ Per.SPL 716
   (*Wagner: Meistersinger Prelude, etc.*)
   Pittsburgh Sym.—Steinberg ♯ DCap.CTL 7086
   (*Tod und Verklärung*)   (♯ Cap.P 8291)
   Bamberg Sym.—Horenstein
                    ♯ E. & AmVox.PL 9060
   (*Don Juan & Tod und Verklärung*)
   ((*Don Juan only, on* ♯ Pan.XPV 1001)
   London Phil. Sym.—Rodzinski
   (*Don Juan*)   ♯ West.LAB 7016
   Philadelphia—Ormandy   ♯ AmC.AL 46
   (*Rosenkavalier Waltzes*)   (♯ Phi.S 06623R)
                          (continued on next page)

---

[1] From a broadcast performance 1952.   [2] From sound-track of film *Symphony*.

Till Eulenspiegels lustige Streiche, Op. 28 (*continued*)

Orch.—Szell   ♯ **MApp. 610**
(*Spoken analysis by T. Scherman; & Smetana*)

Czech Phil.—Konwitschny   ♯ **Sup.LPV 68**
(*Novák*)   (♯ U. 5104G)

☆ Amsterdam—E. Jochum   ♯ **EPhi.ABR 4009**
(*above*)
(*above; & Liszt on* ♯ Epic.LC 3032)

☆ Cleveland Sym.—Rodzinski   ♯ **AmC.ML 4884**
(*Rosenkavalier, Salome; & Ravel*)

☆ Vienna Phil.—Krauss   ♯ **DT.LGX 66032**
(*Tod und Verklärung*)   (♯ T.LE 6517)
(4ss, AusT.E 1184/5)

☆ Cleveland Sym.—Szell   ♯ **AmC.ML 4800**
(*above, & Bürger als Edelmann*)

☆ Berlin Phil.—Fricsay   ♯ **HP.DG 16006**
(*Borodin*)   (♭ Pol. 30067)

Orch.—Schönherr (♯ MTW.20: ♭set EP20;
           ACC.MP 10, d.c.)

Anon. Orch. (♯ Gram. 2097)

☆ Victor Sym.—Reiner (♯ ItV.A12R 0079)
Florence Fest.—Gui (♭ Tem. set 4500)
Boston Sym.—Koussevitzky (♯ Cam.CAL 101 &
           in ♯ set CFL 102)
Philharmonia—Karajan (♯ C.VCX 532)

Tod und Verklärung, Op. 24   1889
N.Y.P.S.O.—Walter   ♯ **AmC.ML 4650**
(*Don Juan*)

N.B.C. Sym.—Toscanini[1]   ♯ **Vic.LM 1891**
(*Till Eulenspiegel*)   (♯ FV.A 630313; ItV.A12R 0181)

Bamberg Sym.—Horenstein
           ♯ **E. & AmVox.PL 9060**
(*Don Juan & Till Eulenspiegel*)

Pittsburgh Sym.—Steinberg   ♯ **DCap.CTL 7086**
(*Till Eulenspiegel*)   (♯ Cap.P 8291)

Utrecht Sym.—Neumark   ♯ **MMS. 73**
(*Liszt*)

Berlin Sym.—Rubahn   ♯ **Roy. 1485**
(*Respighi*)

☆ Concertgebouw—Mengelberg   ♯ **DT.LGX 66032**
(*Till Eulenspiegel*)   (♯ T.LE 6517)

☆ Victor Sym.—Reiner (♯ ItV.A12R 0079)
N.Y. City Sym.—Stokowski (♯ Cam.CAL 189)

II. INSTRUMENTAL & CHAMBER MUSIC

(5) Klavierstücke, Op. 3   pf.   1881
A. Brendel   ♯ **SPA. 48**
(*above*)

SONATA, E flat major, Op. 18   vln. & pf.   1887
R. Ricci & C. Bussotti   ♯ **D.LXT 2818**
(*Prokofiev*)   (♯ Lon.LL 770)

☆ J. Heifetz & A. Sandor (*Franck*)   ♯ **Vic.LCT 1122**

SONATA, F major, Op. 6   vlc. & pf.
L. Hoelscher & H. Richter-Haaser   ♯ **Pol. 18178**
(*Brahms*)

SONATA, B minor, Op. 5   pf.   1880-1
A. Brendel (*above*)   ♯ **SPA. 48**

(5) Stimmungsbilder, Op. 9   pf.   1882
... No. 2, An einsamer Quelle   — ARR. VLC. & PF.
M. Rostropovich & pf.   **USSR. 21827**
(*Popper: Elfentanz*)   (& in ♯ USSR.D 1178)

III. STAGE WORKS

ARABELLA, Op. 79   Opera   3 Acts   1933
HIGHLIGHTS

Ich danke, Fräulein . . . Aber der Richtige   2 S
Finale: Welko, das Bild! . . . Mein Elemer   Act I
Sie woll'n mich heiraten   S & B
Ballroom Scene: Und jetzt sag' ich adieu   Act II
Finale: Das war sehr gut . . . Und diesen unbeührten Trunk
    Act III
E. Schwarzkopf (S), A. Felbermayer (S),
N. Gedda (T), J. Metternich (Bs), W. Berry
(Bs), etc., Philharmonia—v. Matačić
           ♯ **C.CX 1226**
           (♯ FCX 385; Angel. 35094)

ACT I

Er ist der Richtige nicht . . . Ich weiss nicht   2 S
H. Gueden & L. della Casa   ♯ **D.LW 5029**
(*below*)   (♯ Lon.LD 9027)
(& with *Letzte Lieder*, ♯ D.LXT 2865; Lon.LL 856)

☆ M. Fuchs & E. Wieber (♭ T.UE 451477)

ACT II

Der Richtige so hab' ich still zu mir gesagt[2]   S & B
L. della Casa & P. Schoeffler   ♯ **D.LXT 5017**
(*Capriccio & Ariadne auf Naxos*)   (♯ Lon.LL 1047)

Und du wirst mein Gebieter sein   S & B
☆ M. Fuchs & P. Schoeffler (♭ T.UE 451477)

ACT III

Das war sehr gut, Mandryka   S & B
L. della Casa & A. Poell   ♯ **D.LW 5029**
(*above*)   (♯ Lon.LD 9027)
(& with *Letzte Lieder*, ♯ D.LXT 2865; Lon.LL 856)

ARIADNE AUF NAXOS, Op. 60
A. ORIGINAL VERSION, 1912
    (to follow Molière's *Bourgeois Gentilhomme*)
Overture
☆ Württemberg State—Leitner (in ♯ AmD.DL 4063;
           ♭ Pol. 30119)

B. SECOND VERSION, 1916
    (Opera only)   1 Act
COMPLETE RECORDING

Ariadne	E. Schwarzkopf (S)
Zerbinetta	R. Streich (S)
The Composer	I. Seefried (S)
Bacchus	R. Schock (T)
The Major Domo (speaking part)	A. Neugebauer
Music Master	K. Dönch (B)
An Officer	G. Unger (T)
The Dancing Master	H. Cuénod (T)

etc., Philharmonia Orch.—Karajan
           ♯ **C.CX 1292/4**
(6ss)   (♯ QCX 10168/70; Angel. 35222/4, set 3532)

Es gibt ein Reich (Ariadne's aria)   S
L. della Casa   ♯ **D.LXT 5017**
(*Arabella & Capriccio*)   (♯ Lon.LL 1047)

H. Zadek[3]   ♯ **EPhi.ABR 4004**
(*Elektra; & Wagner*)   (♯ Phi.N 00655R)

☆ A. Kupper (♭ Pol. 30119)

Recit. & Aria of Zerbinetta   S
... So war es mit Pagliazzo
☆ M. Ivogün (in ♯ Vic.LCT 1115: ♭ set WCT 1115)

(Der) BÜRGER ALS EDELMANN, Op. 60
    (inc. music for Molière's *Bourgeois Gentilhomme*) 1912-17
Orchestral Suite   1918
Vienna Phil.—Krauss   ♯ **D.LXT 2756**
           (♯ Lon.LL 684)

Berlin Phil.—Leitner   ♯ **HP.DGM 18237**

"Philharmonic"—Berendt   ♯ **Allo. 3101**
(*Hérold*)

☆ Pittsburgh Sym.—Reiner   ♯ **AmC.ML 4800**
(*Don Juan & Till Eulenspiegel*)

☆ Vienna Phil.—R. Strauss (♯ Ura.RS 7-8)

... No. 5   ☆ Royal Phil.—Beecham (♭ G.7ER 5014)

CAPRICCIO   Opera   1 Act   1942
Kein andres, das mir so im Herzen loht   T (Sonnet)
☆ A. Dermota (*Zauberflöte, No. 4*)   ♭ D. 71116

Intermezzo & Closing Scene: Wo ist mein Bruder
L. della Casa (S), F. Bierbach (Bs) & Vienna
    Phil.—Hollreiser   ♯ **D.LXT 5017**
(*Arabella & Adriadne auf Naxos*)   (♯ Lon.LL 1047)

... Closing Scene only: Morgen mittag um elf
E. Schwarzkopf (S) & Philharmonia
    —Ackermann   ♯ **C.CX 1107**
(*Letzte Lieder*)   (♯ FCX 294; Angel. 35084)

---

[1] From a broadcast performance 1952.   [3] Begins somewhat earlier at *Sie lebt hier ganz allein*.
[2] The same duet as *Sie woll'n mich heiraten* in Highlights, but begins somewhat later.

DAPHNE Opera 1 Act 1938
O bleib', geliebter Tag (Monologue) S
☆ Ich komme, grünende Brüder (Closing Scene)
A. Kupper   in ♯ **Pol. 18090**
(*Elektra & Salome*)

ELEKTRA Op. 58 Opera 1 Act 1909
COMPLETE RECORDING in Concert Form
A. Varnay (S), E. Nikolaidi (A), F. Jagel (T),
etc., N.Y.P.S.O.—Mitropoulos[1]   ♯ **OTA. 4**
(6ss)

Allein! Weh, ganz allein S (Elektra)
☆ C. Goltz   ♯ **Pol. 18090**
(*Salome, Daphne*)   (in ♯ AmD.DL 9723)

Ich kann nicht sitzen und ins Dunkel starren
S (Chrysothemis)
H. Zadek   ♯ **EPhi.ABR 4004**
(*Ariadne auf Naxos; & Wagner*)   (♯ *Phi.N 00655R*)

Ich will nichts hören S & A (Elektra-Clytemnestra)
C. Goltz, E. Höngen, & Bavarian State Orch.
—Solti   ♯ **Pol. 18078**
(*below*)   (in ♯ AmD.DL 9723; Pol. 19038)

Was willst du, fremder Mensch (Final scene)
☆ E. Schlüter (S), P. Schoeffler (B), L. Welitsch (S),
W. Widdop (T), etc., Royal Phil.—Beecham
♯ **Vic.LCT 1135**

... S & B part (Elektra & Orestes only)
C. Goltz, F. Frantz & Bavarian State Orch.
—Solti   ♯ **Pol. 18078**
(*above*)   (in ♯ AmD.DL 9723; Pol. 19038)

FEUERSNOT, Op. 50 Opera 1 Act 1901
Love Scene
☆ Royal Phil.—Beecham   ♭ *G.7ER 5014*
(*Bürger als Edelmann, & Intermezzo*)

INTERMEZZO, Op. 72 Opera 2 Acts 1924
Interlude orch.
☆ Royal Phil.—Beecham   ♭ *G.7ER 5014*
(*Bürger als Edelmann, & Feuersnot*)

JOSEPHSLEGENDE, Op. 63 Ballet 1914
☆ Munich State Op.—Eichhorn in ♯ Nix.ULP 9602-1/2

(Der) ROSENKAVALIER, Op. 59
Opera 3 Acts 1911
COMPLETE RECORDINGS
Feldmarschallin   ...   .   M. Reining (S)
Oktavian   ...   .   S. Jurinac (S)
Baron Ochs   ...   .   L. Weber (Bs)
Sophie   ...   .   H. Gueden (S)
Faninal   ...   .   A. Poell (Bs)
Marianne   ...   .   J. Hellwig (S)
Valzacchi   ...   .   P. Klein (T)
Annina   ...   ...   H. Rössl-Majdan (A)
Italian Singer   ...   ...   A. Dermota (T)
Vienna State Op. Cho. & Vienna Phil. Orch.
—Kleiber   ♯ **D.LXT 2954/7**
(8ss)   (♯ Lon. set LLA 22)
[Selection on ♯ *D.NLM 4562*]
☆ U. Richter (S), T. Lemnitz (S), M. Bäumer (S), K.
Böhme (Bs), etc., Saxon State Op. Cho. & Orch.
—Kempe   ♯ **Nix.ULP 9201-1/4**
(8ss)   [Highlights on ♯ ULP 9062 & ♯ MTW. 702]

ABRIDGED RECORDING
☆ L. Lehmann (S), E. Schumann (S), M. Olszewska
(M-S), R. Mayr (Bs), etc., Vienna State Op. Cho &
Vienna Phil. Orch.—Heger (4ss, ♯ Vic.LCT 6005:
♭ *set WCT 6005*)

HIGHLIGHTS
☆ V. Ursuleac (S), A. Kern (S), L. Weber (Bs), etc.,
Munich State Op. Cho. & Orch.—Krauss
♯ **AmVox.PL 8200**
(Excerpts[2] on ♭ *VIP 45330*) [from set]
☆ Anon. soloists, Berlin State Op. (♭ *Roy.EP 241*)

Orchestral Suite — ARR. Dorati
☆ Robin Hood Dell—Dorati   ♯ Vic.LM 9033
(*Offenbach*)   (♯ ItV.A12R 0007)
☆ Cincinnati Sym.—Goossens (♯ Cam.CAL 155 &
in ♯ set CFL 103)

Waltzes, Act II (or unspec.)
Philadelphia—Ormandy   ♯ *AmC.AL 46*
(*Till Eulenspiegel*)   (♯ *Phi.S 06623R*)
N.W. Ger. Phil.—Schüchter   ♯ *Imp.ILP 110*
(*Schmidt, Gounod, Ponchielli*)   (♯ *G.QDLP 6025*)
Vienna State Op.—Swarowsky   ♯ **U. 5202H**
(*J. Strauss II*)
N.Y.P.S.O.,—Kostelanetz   ♯ **AmC.CL 769**
(*J. Strauss II, etc.*)
Orch. Kostelanetz (in ♯ AmC.CL 798, o.n. ML 4692:
♭ *A 1847*; ♭ *EPhi.NBE 11001*; ♭ *Phi.N 409512E*, d.c.)
Tivoli Orch.—Hansen (in ♯ *Tono.LPL 33006*: ♭ EP 43026)
☆ L.P.O.—Collins (♯ *D.LW 5025*)
Boston Prom.—Fiedler (♭ *G7EP 7008*; It *V.A72R 0015*;
in ♯ Vic.LM 1752: ♭ *set WDM 1752*)
Stadium Concerts—Smallens (♯ *D.UW 333001*)
Brussels Radio—André (♯ *T.TW 30009*: in LSK 7019;
FT. 320.TC.028)
Minneapolis Sym.—Ormandy (in ♯ Cam.CAL 121)
Cleveland Sym.—Rodzinski (in ♯ AmC.ML 4884)
Austrian Sym.—Brown, with commentary by S.
Spaeth (in ♯ Rem. 100-20)
M. Marrow Orch. (MGM. 9173: in ♯ E 3138)

— ARR. 2 PFS. Babin
P. Luboshutz & G. Nemenoff (in ♯ Cam.CAL 198)
V. Vronsky & V. Babin (in ♯ AmD.DL 9791)

Waltzes, Act III (*Walzerfolge*)
Berlin Phil.—E. Jochum   ♯ *HP.DG 17020*
(*Schlagobers—Waltz; & Mozart: Serenade 13*)
(*Schlagobers only, on PV. 72474*; ♭ *Pol. 30056*;
& in ♯ 19015, d.c.)

Preludes, Acts I & II
☆ Saxon State Orch.—Kempe   in ♯ Nix.ULP 9601-1/2

ACT I

Di rigori armato (*Arie des Sängers*) T (*Ital*)
K. Baum   in ♯ **Roy. 1582**
G. Gari, S. Leff (pf.)   in ♯ **Mur.P 104**
(followed by pf. acc. only)
☆ P. Anders (♭ *T.U 452321*)
◪ R. Tauber (in ♯ Cum.CE 187*)

ACT II

Herr Gott im Himmel! S & A or M-S
Mir ist die Ehre (Presentation of the Rose)
☆ U. Richter & T. Lemnitz, from set (♭ *Nix.EP 714*)
E. Trötschel & G. v. Milinković (♯ *Pol. 17403*)

Da lieg' ich ... Herr Kavalier Bs & A
☆ K. Böhme & E. Walther-Sachs, from set (♭ *Nix.EP 714*;
▽ ♭ *Ura.UREP 14*)
E. List & E. Schürhoff (in ♯ *Rem. 199-123*)
K. Böhme & R. Michaelis (♯ *Pol. 17043*)

... Herr Kavalier only
☆ A. Kipnis & E. Ruziczka (in ♯ Vic. set LCT 6701)

ACT III

Hab' mir's gelobt Trio
Ist ein Traum 2 S (Final Scene)
☆ T. Lemnitz, E. Trötschel & G. v. Milinković
(♭ *Pol. 30141*)
... Ist ein Traum, only
☆ E. Berger & R. Stevens (in ♯ Vic.LM 1847: ♭ *ERA 138*)

SALOME, Op. 54 1 Act 1905
COMPLETE RECORDINGS

Casts	Set B	Set C
Salome	C. Goltz (S)	W. Wegner (S)
Herodias	M. Kenney (A)	G. v. Milinković (M-S)
Herod ...	J. Patzak (T)	L. Szemere (T)
Jokanaan ...	H. Braun (B)	J. Metternich (B)
Narraboth ...	A. Dermota (T)	W. Kmentt (T)
etc.		

Set B with Vienna Phil.—Krauss   ♯ **D.LXT 2863/4**
(4ss)   (♯ Lon.LL 1038/9)
Set C with Vienna Sym.—Moralt
♯ **EPhi.ABL 3003/4**
(4ss)   (♯ Phi.A 00163/4L; AmC. set SL 126)
Set A ☆ C. Goltz (S), I. Karen (A), B. Aldenhoff (T),
J. Hermann (B), Dresden State Op. Cho. & Orch.
—Keilberth (4ss, ♯ MMS. set 2027; ♯ MTW. 522/3)
(*continued on next page*)

---

[1] Transcription of a broadcast performance.
[2] Prel. Act I, Ital. Serenade, Letter Scene, Finale Act III.

SALOME, Op. 54 (continued)
Excerpts (unspec.)
E. von Kovatsky (S), H. Wilhelm (T), H.
Schenck (A), G. Ramms (B), Leipzig Op.
Cho. & Orch.—Rubahn   ♯ **Allo. 3057**

Salomes Tanz (*Dance of the Seven Veils*) orch. Sc.4
Chicago Sym.—Reiner   ♯ **G.ALP 1214**
(*Also sprach Zarathustra*) (♯ Vic.LM 1806: ♭ set *ERD 1806*)
          (♯ DV.L 16481; ItV.A12R 0120; FV.A 630213)
[Excerpt only, in ♯ Vic.SRL 12-1]
  ☆ Royal Phil.—Beecham (♭ G.7RF 122: 7RW 128)
    Cleveland Sym.—Rodzinski (in ♯ AmC.ML 4884)
    Stadium Concerts—Smallens (♯ D.UW 333001)
    Philadelphia—Stokowski (in ♯ Cam.CAL 254 &
          ♯ set CFL 103)

Ah, du wolltest mich (Finale) S, M-S, T
  ☆ C. Goltz, H. Plümacher & W. Windgassen
    (in ♯ Pol. 18090; in ♯ AmD.DL 9778, d.c.)

... **Sop. part** only
  ☆ L. Welitsch & Met. Op. Orch.—Reiner   ♯ *C.C 1011*
    (*Eugene Oniegin*)   (♯ VC 806; in ♯ AmC.ML 4795)
  ☆ M. Lawrence (*Fr*) & Pasdeloup Orch.—Coppola
          ♯ *Cam.CAL 216*
    (*Songs; Pfitzner, Wolf*)   (♭ *CAE 232*)

SCHLAGOBERS, Op. 70 Ballet-Pantomime 1924
COMPLETE RECORDING
Frankenland State Sym.—Kloss
(4ss)   ♯ **Lyr. set LL 41**

Schlagoberswalzer
Berlin Phil.—E. Jochum   ♯ **HP.DG 17020**
(*Rosenkavalier—Walzerfolge; & Mozart*)
(*Rosenkavalier only, on PV. 72474; ♭ Pol. 30056*)

IV. SONGS (LIEDER)
COLLECTIONS
(4) Lieder, Op. 31
    1. Blauer Sommer (Busse)
    2. Wenn! (Busse)
    3. Weisser Jasmin (Busse)
    4. Stiller Gang (Dehmel)
M. Schloss (S), J. Brice (pf.)   ♯ **IRCC.L 7000**
(*Franz, Wolf, Schumann*)

(6) Lieder des Unmuts, Op. 68 (after Brentano) 1918
    1. An die Nacht
    2. Ich wollt' ein Sträusslein binden
    3. Säusle, liebe Myrte
    4. Als mir dein Lied erklang
    5. Amor (An dem Feuer sass das Kind)
    6. Lied der Frauen (Wenn es stürmt . . .)
E. Berger (S), M. Raucheisen (pf.)
          ♯ **HP.DG 16042**
(*Brahms, on ♯ AmD.DL 9666*)   (4ss, ♭ PV. 72277/8)

(4) Letzte Lieder 1946-8
1. Beim Schlafengehen (Hesse)   2. September (Hesse)
3. Frühling (Hesse)   4. Im Abendroth (Eichendorff)
L. della Casa (S), & Vienna Phil.—Böhm
          ♯ **D.LW 5056**
          (♯ Lon.LD 9072)
(& with *Arabella*, ♯ D.LXT 2865; Lon.LL 856)
E. Schwarzkopf & Philharmonia—Ackermann
          ♯ **C.CX 1107**
(*Capriccio*)   (♯ FCX 294; WCX 1107; Angel. 35084)

Ach Lieb', ich muss nun scheiden, Op. 21, No. 3 (Dahn)
Einerlei, Op. 69, No. 3 (von Arnim)
Hat gesagt . . . Op. 36, No. 3 (Knaben Wunderhorn)
Heimkehr, Op. 15, No. 5 (A. v. Schack)
Morgen, Op. 27, No. 4 (Mackay)
Die Nacht, Op. 10, No. 3 (von Gilm)
Schlagende Herzen, Op. 29, No. 2 (Bierbaum)
Schlechtes Wetter, Op. 69, No. 5 (Heine)
A. Felbermeyer (S), V. Graef (pf.)

Im Spätboot, Op. 56, No. 3 (C. F. Meyer)
Mein Herz ist stumm, Op. 19, No. 6 (A. v. Schack)
Nichts, Op. 10, No. 2 (v. Gilm)
Das Rosenband, Op. 36, No. 1 (Klopstock)
Ruhe, meine Seele, Op. 27, No. 1 (Henckell)
Traum durch die Dämmerung, Op. 29, No. 1 (Bierbaum)
Waldseligkeit, Op. 49, No. 1 (Dehmel)
Winterliebe, Op. 48, No. 5 (Henckell)
A. Poell (B), V. Graef (pf.)   ♯ **Van.VRS 431**

All' mein Gedanken, Op. 21, No. 1 (Dahn)
Allerseelen, Op. 10, No. 8 (v. Gilm)
Aus den Liedern der Trauer: Dem Herzen ähnlich,
    Op. 15, No. 4 (v. Schack)
Befreit, Op. 39, No. 4 (Dehmel)
Cäcilie, Op. 27, No. 2 (Hart)
Du meines Herzens Krönelein, Op. 21, No. 2 (Dahn)
Hat gesagt . . . , Op. 36, No. 3 (Knaben Wunderhorn)
Ich trage meine Minne, Op. 32, No. 1 (Henckell)
Meinem Kinde, Op. 37, No. 3 (Falke)
Sehnsucht, Op. 32, No. 2 (Liliencron)
Von dunklen Schleier umsponnen, Op. 17, No. 4
          (v. Schack)
Wiegenlied, Op. 41, No. 1 (Dehmel)
Die Zeitlose, Op. 10, No. 7 (v. Gilm)
M. Bothwell (S) & pf.   ♯ *Allo. 4059*

Ach Lieb', ich muss nun scheiden, Op. 21, No. 3 (Dahn)
Ach weh mir unglückhafem Mann, Op. 21, No. 4 (Dahn)
Allerseelen, Op. 10, No. 8 (von Gilm)
Heimkehr, Op. 15, No. 5 (v. Schack)
Heimliche Aufforderung, Op. 27, No. 3 (Mackay)
Im Spätboot, Op. 56, No. 3 (Meyer)
Leise Lieder, Op. 41, No. 5 (Morgenstern)
Das Lied des Steinklopfers, Op. 49, No. 4 (Anon.)
Mit deinen blauen Augen, Op. 56, No. 4 (Heine)
Morgen, Op. 27, No. 4 (Mackay)
Die Nacht, Op. 10, No. 3 (von Gilm)
Nachtgang, Op. 29, No. 3 (Bierbaum)
Nichts, Op. 10, No. 2 (von Gilm)
Das Rosenband, Op. 36, No. 1 (Klopstock)
Ruhe, meine Seele, Op. 27, No. 1 (Henckell)
Traum durch die Dämmerung, Op. 29, No. 1 (Bierbaum)
Waldseligkeit, Op. 49, No. 1 (Dehmel)
Zueignung, Op. 10, No. 1 (von Gilm)
N. Foster (B), H. Schmidt (pf.)
          ♯ **AmVox.PL 9610**

Allerseelen, Op. 10, No. 8 (a) (von Gilm)
Breit über mein Haupt, Op. 19, No. 2 (Schack) (a)
Cäcilie, Op. 27, No. 2 (Hart) (b)
Liebeshymnus, Op. 32, No. 3 (Henckell) (b)
Pilgers Morgenlied, Op. 33, No. 4 (Goethe) (b)
Zueignung, Op. 10, No. 1 (von Gilm) (a)
H. Janssen (B) & (a) pf., (b) orch ♯ *Ete. 491*

Freundliche Vision, Op. 48, No. 1 (Bierbaum)
Morgen, Op. 27, No. 4 (Mackay)
Ständchen, Op. 17, No. 2 (v. Schack)
Traum durch die Dämmerung, Op. 29, No. 1 (Bierbaum)
Zueignung, Op. 10, No. 1 (von Gilm)
S. Danco (S), G. Agosti (pf.)   ♯ **D.LX 3110**
(*Mozart*)   (♯ Lon.LS 698)

Cäcilie, Op. 27, No. 2 (Hart)
Heimliche Aufforderung, Op. 27, No. 3 (MacKay)
Ich trage meine Minne, Op. 32, No. 1 (Henckell)
Zueignung, Op. 10, No. 1 (von Gilm)
P. Anders (T) & Munich Phil.—Lehmann
          PV. 36122
          (♭ Pol. 34016: 30103)
Ach, Lieb', ich muss nun scheiden, Op. 21, No. 3 (Dahn)
Allerseelen, Op. 10, No. 8 (von Gilm)
Du meines Herzens Krönelein, Op. 21, No. 2 (Dahn)
Wiegenlied, Op. 41, No. 1 (Dehmel)
Zueignung, Op. 10, No. 1 (von Gilm)
K. Flagstad (S), E. McArthur (pf.)
          ♯ **G.ALP 1309**
(*Brahms, Schubert, McArthur, etc.*)   (♯ Vic.LM 1870)

Allerseelen, Op. 10, No. 8 (von Gilm)
Cäcilie, Op. 27, No. 2 (Hart)
Freundliche Vision, Op. 48, No. 1 (Bierbaum)
Zueignung, Op. 10, No. 1 (von Gilm)
Z. Milanov (S), B. Kunc (pf.)   ♯ **Vic.LM 1915**
(*Kunc, Hagemann, Brahms, etc.*)

Allerseelen, Op. 10, No. 8 (von Gilm)
Morgen, Op. 27, No. 4 (Mackay)
Traum durch die Dämmerung, Op. 29, No. 1 (Bierbaum)
Zueignung, Op. 10, No. 1 (von Gilm)
A. Koskinen (T), E. Møller (pf.)

          ♭ *Mtr.MCEP 3020*
  ☆ Du meines Herzens Krönelein, Op. 21, No. 2 (Dahn)
    Traum durch die Dämmerung, Op. 29, No. 1 (Bierbaum)
    Zueignung, Op. 10, No. 1 (von Gilm)
G. Hüsch (B), M. Gurlitt (pf.) ♯ **JpV.LS 2006**
(*Wolf, Schubert, Bach*)
[Traum . . . & Zueignung also *SF 725*]

Heimkehr, Op. 15, No. 5 (v. Schack)
Heimliche Aufforderung, Op. 27, No. 3 (Mackay)
Ich liebe dich, Op. 37, No. 2 (Liliencron)
Ständchen, Op. 17, No. 2 (v. Schack)
  ☆ H. Schlusnus (B)   ♯ **HP.DGM 18029**
    (*Brahms, Schubert, Wolf*)

♯ = Long-playing, 33⅓ r.p.m.   ♭ = 45 r.p.m.   ♮ = Auto. couplings, 78 r.p.m.

Ach, weh mir unglückhaftem Mann, Op. 21, No. 4
(Dahn)
G. Pechner (B)　　　　　　in # Roy. 1558
(*below; Reger, Marx, Mahler, etc.*)

Amor, Op. 68, No. 5　(Brentano)
R. Peters (S), L. Rosenek (pf.) in # Vic.LM 1802

(Des) Dichters Abendgang, Op. 47, No. 2　(Uhland)
☆ M. Lawrence (S) (♭ Cam.CAE 195: in # CAL 216)

Du meines Herzens Krönelein, Op. 21, No. 1 (Dahn)
H. Janssen (B), S. Leff (pf.)　in # Mur.P 110
(followed by pf. acc. only)

Freundliche Vision, Op. 48, No. 1　(Bierbaum)
☆ H. Schlusnus (B), O. Braun (pf.) (♭ Pol. 30152)

Hat gesagt . . . Op. 36, No. 3
(Knaben Wunderhorn)
E. Schwarzkopf (S), G. Moore (pf.)
in # C.CX 1044
(*below; Bach, etc.*)　　　　(# FCX 132; Angel. 35023)
(o.v., ½s—*Schlechtes Wetter; & Wolf,* on C.LX 1577)

Ich liebe dich, Op. 37, No. 2　(Liliencron)
K. Flagstad (S), E. McArthur (pf.)
in # G.ALP 1191
(*below; Schumann, Schubert, etc.*) (in # Vic.LM 1738:
♭ set WDM 1738)

Lied an meinen Sohn, Op. 39, No. 5　(Dehmel)
☆ M. Lawrence (S) (♭ Cam.CAE 195: in # CAL 216)

Morgen, Op. 27, No. 4　(Mackay)
J. Björling (T), F. Schauwecker (pf.)
in # G.ALP 1187
(*Schubert, Wolf, Grieg, etc.*) (# Vic.LM 1771:
♭ ERA 141; ♭ DV. 26045)

(Die) Nacht, Op. 10, No. 3　(von Gilm)
E. Berger (S)　　　　in JpV. set JAS 272
J. Harsanyi (S), O. Herz (pf.) in # Per.SPL 581

Ruhe, meine Seele, Op. 27, No. 1　(Henckell)
K. Flagstad (S), E. McArthur (pf.)
in # G.ALP 1191
(*above*)　　　　(in # Vic.LM 1738: ♭ set WDM 1738)

Schlagende Herzen, Op. 29, No. 2　(Bierbaum)
E. Berger (S)　　　　in JpV. set JAS 272

Schlechtes Wetter, Op. 69, No. 5　(Heine)
E. Schwarzkopf (S), G. Moore (pf.)
in # C.CX 1044
(*above; Mozart. etc.*)　　　(# FCX 132; Angel. 35023)
(o.v., ½s—*Hat gesagt; & Wolf,* on C.LX 1577)

Ständchen, Op. 17, No. 2　(v. Schack)　(*Serenade*)
J. Björling (T), F. Schauwecker (pf.)
in # G.ALP 1187
(*Schubert, etc.*)　　　　　　(# Vic.LM 1771)
(*Grieg: A Swan & A Dream,* G.DB 21620)
I. Seefried (S), E. Werba (pf.) in # Pol. 19050
(*Schubert, Brahms, Moussorgsky, etc.*) (# AmD.DL 9809)
☆ L. Slezak (T) (in # Ete. 493)
A. Dermota (T) (♭ D.VD 502)
R. Tauber (T) (in # ChOd.LDC 36003)
— ARR. PF.
M. Tipo　　　　　　　　# Cpt.MC 20020
(*Bloch, Rameau, Schumann*)
— FOR PRACTICE: Vln. & pf. acc. (in # VS.MHL 6000)

Traum durch die Dämmerung, Op. 29, No. 1
(Bierbaum)
A. Konetzni (S), E. Werba (pf.)　　C.LV 19
(*Zueignung*)

Zueignung, Op. 10, No. 1　(von Gilm)
J. Harsanyi (S), O. Herz (pf.) in # Per.SPL 581
A. Konetzni (S), E. Werba (pf.)　　C.LV 19
(*Traum durch die Dämmerung*)
H. Janssen (B), S. Leff (pf.)　in # Mur.P 112
(followed by pf. acc. only)
G. Pechner (B)　　　　　in # Roy. 1558
☆ A. Dermota (T) (♭ D.VD 502)
H. Schlusnus (B) (♭ Pol. 30152)
— FOR PRACTICE: Vln. & pf. acc. (in # VS.MHL 6000)

V. MISCELLANEOUS

Wanderers Sturmlied, Op. 14　(Goethe)
6 pt. cho. & orch.
☆ Vienna Cha. Cho. & Sym.—Swoboda # Nix.WLP 5081
(*Bruckner on* # West.WN 18075)

STRAVINSKY, Igor (b. 1882)

CLASSIFIED: I. PIANO
　　　　　II. CHAMBER MUSIC
　　　　　III. ORCHESTRAL
　　　　　IV. BALLET
　　　　　V. VOCAL
　　　　　VI. MISCELLANEOUS

I. PIANO
(and pf. duet & 2 pfs.)

COLLECTION
Concerto, 2 pfs.　　　　1935
Sonata, 2 pfs.　　　　　1943-4
(3) Pièces faciles　　4 hands　1915
(5) Pièces faciles　　4 hands　1917
　E. Bartlett & R. Robertson　　　# MGM.E 3038

Concerto, 2 pianos　1935
R. Gold & A. Fizdale　　　　# AmC.ML 4853
(*Hindemith & Rieti*)　　　　(in set SL 198)
☆ V. Vronsky & V. Babin (# Phi.N 02100L)

(4) Études, Op. 7　1908
... No. 3, only
A. Blyme　　　　　　　　Phi.A 56510G
(*Lewkowitch: Sonata No. 3, s. 3*)

Pastorale　orig. a Vocalise　1908
— ARR. VLN & WIND QTT. Dushkin & Stravinsky
　　1933
Chicago Sym. Woodwind Quintet
in # Aphe.AP 14

Piano Rag-Music　1920
M. Meyer[1]　　　　　　　# DFr. 48
(*Serenade & Pétrouchka, excerpts*)　(# HS.HSL 113)

Serenade, A major　1925
M. Meyer[1]　　　　　　　# DFr. 48
(*Piano Rag-music & Pétrouchka*)　(# HS.HSL 113)
☆ S. Stravinsky (# Allo. 3091)

Sonata　1922
☆ S. Stravinsky　(*above & Ravel: Trio*)　# Allo. 3091

Tango　1940　— ARR. 2 PFS.
☆ V. Vronsky & V. Babin (in # Phi.N 02100L)

II. CHAMBER MUSIC

Concertino, Str. Qtt.　1920
Erling Bloch Qtt.　(2ss)　　　G.DA 5275

Duo Concertant　vln. & pf.　1932
L. Kaufman & H. Pignari　　　# MMS. 107
(*Suite italienne*)
M. Rostal & C. Horsley　　　G.OCLP 7501
(*Schubert*)
☆ J. Fuchs & L. Smit　(*Copland*)　# B.AXTL 1047

Élégie　unacc. vla. (or vln.)　1946
☆ B. Milofsky (in # Clc. 6173)

Octet　Wind insts.　1923
Copenhagen Op. Orch. Ens.　　　# C.KC 1
(*Jersild*)
Col. Cha. Ens.—Stravinsky　# AmC.ML 4964
(*Histoire du soldat & Symphonies for Wind*)
☆ Boston Sym. Ens.—Bernstein　# ItV.A12R 0091
(*Histoire du soldat*)

(3) Pieces for Clarinet solo　1919
☆ R. Kell (♭ AmD.ED 3505)

(3) Pieces for String Qtt.　1914
☆ Gordon Qtt.　　　　# CHS.CHS 1229
(*Concerto, E flat major & Danses concertantes*)
☆ New Music Qtt. (# Clc. 6119)

---

[1] This entry corrects that for the same number in Supp. I—apparently never issued in the form there described.

Russian Maiden's Song
(Parasha's aria from the opera *Mavra*)
— ARR. VLN. & PF. Dushkin & Stravinsky 1920-1
  ☆ J. Szigeti & I. Stravinsky (in ♯ C.CX 1100:
FCX/QCX 212; ♭ *Reg.SEBL 7022*)

III. ORCHESTRAL

Capriccio pf. & orch. 1929
  ☆ J. M. Sanromá & Boston Sym.—Koussevitzky
  (*Copland, Fauré, Sibelius*)   ♯ Vic.LCT 1152

(Le) Chant du Rossignol Suite 1919
  ☆ Cincinnati Sym.—Goossens (♯ Cam.CAL 189)

Circus Polka (after Schubert)[1] 1942
  ☆ N.Y.P.S.O.—Stravinsky   in ♯ C.CX 1100
  (*Fireworks, Ode, etc.*)
(♯ FCX/QCX 212; ♭ *Reg.SEBL 7021*)
— ARR. PF.
  T. Ury   ♯ *Argo.ATM 1006*
  (*Berg & Prokofiev*)
  ☆ A. Foldes (♯ *PV. 36104*)
— ARR. 2 PFS.
  ☆ V. Vronsky & V. Babin (in ♯ Phi.N 02100L)

CONCERTOS
D major Str. orch. 1946
  Boston Orch. Soc.—Page   ♯ SOT. 1062
  (*Villa-Lobos & Bach*)
  ☆ Victor Sym.—Stravinsky (♯ G.QALP 132)

E flat major 16 insts. 1938 ("*Dumbarton Oaks*")
  Rochester Cha. Orch.—Hull ♯ CHS.CHS 1229
  (*below; & 3 Pieces, Str. qtt.*)

Piano & Wind Insts. 1923-4
  S. Stravinsky & Vic. Sym.—I. Stravinsky
    ♯ *Vic.LM 7010*
  (*Scherzo à la russe, Pater Noster, Ave Maria*)
(♭ set *WDM 7010*; ♯ *ItV.A10R 0007*)
  ☆ N. Mewton-Wood & Residentie Soloists—Goehr
(♯ Clc. 6151; ♯ *MMS. 64A*, d.c.)

Danses concertantes 1942
  Rochester Cha. Orch.—Hull ♯ CHS.CHS 1229
  (*above; & 3 Pieces, Str. qtt.*)
  (*Firebird on ♯ MMS. 64*)
  ☆ Victor Sym.—Stravinsky (♯ ItV.A12R 0114)

Ebony Concerto Jazz orch. 1946
  ☆ Woody Herman Orch. (in ♯ C.CX 1100: FCX/QCX 212;
♭ *Reg.SEBL 7020*)

Fireworks, Op. 4 1908 (*Feux d'artifice*)
  ☆ N.Y.P.S.O.—Stravinsky   ♯ C.CX 1100
  (*Norwegian Moods, Concerto, etc.*)
(♯ FCX/QCX 212; ♭ *Reg.SEBL 7020*)
  ☆ Chicago Sym.—Defauw (in ♯ Cam.CAL 162)

(4) Norwegian Moods 1942
  ☆ N.Y.P.S.O.—Stravinsky   in ♯ C.CX 1100
  (*above*)   (♯ FCX/QCX 212; ♭ *Reg.SEBL 7022*)

Ode 1943
  ☆ N.Y.P.S.O.—Stravinsky   in ♯ C.CX 1100
  (*above*)   (♯ FCX/QCX 212; ♭ *Reg.SEBL 7021*)

Scènes de Ballet 1944-5
  ☆ N.Y.P.S.O.—Stravinsky   ♯ *C.C 1015*
  (*Pétrouchka*)   (♯ *QC 5008*)

Scherzo à la russe 1944
  ☆ Victor Sym.—Stravinsky (in ♯ *Vic.LM 7010*:
♭ set *WDM 7010*; ♯ *ItV.A10R 1007*)

SUITES Small orch. (orig. *Pièces faciles*, pf.)
Nos. 1 & 2
  ☆ Cha. Orch.—Oubradous (♭ *Pat.ED 37*)
  Little Orch. Soc.—Scherman (♯ *D.UA 343560*)

No. 1 ☆ N.Y. Cha.—Craft (in ♯ Clc. 6173)

No. 2, ... Valse only 1921
  Philharmonia—Markevitch   in ♯ C.CX 1273
  (*Chabrier, St.-Saëns, Sibelius, etc.*)
(♯ QCX 10172; Angel. 35154)

SYMPHONIES
No. 1, E flat major, Op. 1 1906-7
  Vienna Orch. Soc.—Adler   ♯ Uni.UN 1006

[No. 2], Symphony in C 1940
  Cleveland Sym.—Stravinsky ♯ EPhi.ABL 3108
  (*Cantata*)   (♯ AmC.ML 4899; Phi.A 01149L)
  Berlin Sym.—Rubahn   ♯ Roy. 1489
  (*Card Party*)

No. 3 (in 3 movements) 1945
  Cento Soli—Albert   ♯ CFD. 19
  (*Firebird*)

Symphonies for Wind Instruments 1920, rev. 1946
  N.W. Ger. Radio Orch. Members—Stravinsky
    ♯ AmC.ML 4964
  (*Histoire du Soldat; & Octet*)
  U.S. Military Acad. Band—Resta
    ♯ PFCM.CB 176
  (*Barber, Still, Ravel, etc.*)

... Finale — ARR. PF. Stravinsky[2]
  E. Ulmer   ♯ CHS.H 12
  (*Dukas, Roussel, Goossens, Malipiero & Debussy*)

IV. BALLETS

APOLLON MUSAGÈTE 2 Tableaux 1927
  Vienna Cha.—Hollreiser ♯ E. & AmVox.PL 8270
  (*Pulcinella*)
  ☆ Victor Sym.—Stravinsky (♯ G.QALP 132)

(Le) BAISER DE LA FÉE 4 Scenes 1928
  French Nat. Radio—Markevitch ♯ C.CX 1228
  (*Pulcinella*)   (♯ FCX 350; Angel. 35143)
  ☆ Victor Sym.—Stravinsky (♯ ItV.A12R 0114)

(The) CARD PARTY 1937 (*Jeu de cartes*)
  Philharmonia—Karajan   ♯ C.FCX 163
  (*Roussel*)   (♯ QCX 163)
  Berlin Sym.—Rubahn   ♯ Roy. 1489
  (*Symphony*)

(The) FIRE BIRD 2 Tableaux 1910
  (*Oiseau de feu*)
COMPLETE RECORDING
  Suisse Romande—Ansermet   ♯ D.LXT 5115
    (♯ Lon.LL 1272)
REVISED ORCHESTRAL SUITE 1919
  Philadelphia—Ormandy   ♯ AmC.ML 4700
  (*Moussorgsky*)   (♯ Phi.A 01187L)
  Leipzig Radio—Borsamsky   ♯ Ura. 7157
  (*Moussorgsky*) (& ♯ Ura.RS 7-18; MTW. 521; *ACC.MP 25*)
  (*Valse infernale . . . only in ♯ Ura. 7096*)
  London Phil. Sym.—Scherchen ♯West.LAB 7032
  (1½ss—*Honegger*)
  Netherlands Phil.—Goehr   ♯ *MMS. 64*
  (*Danses concertantes*)
  (*Concerto, pf. & wind on ♯ MMS. 64A*)
  Cento Soli—Albert   ♯ CFD. 19
  (*Symphony No. 3*)
  Dresden Sym.—v. Berten   ♯ Roy. 1462
  (*Kabalevsky*)   (♯ *Var. 69128, 2ss*)
  ☆ Suisse Romande—Ansermet   ♯ D.LXT 2916
  (*Symphonie des Psaumes*)   (♯ Lon.LL 889)
  ☆ Minneapolis Sym.—Dorati   ♯ EMer.MG 50004
  (*Borodin*)
  (*Debussy on ♯ Mer.MG 50025; ♯ FMer.MLP 7505*)
  ☆ Sym. Orch.—Stokowski (♯ Vic.LM 9029 &
  in ♯ set LM 6113; ♯ ItV.A12R 0130; ♯ FV.A 630218)
  Danish Radio—Tuxen (♯ *Tono.LPL 33003*)

... Berceuse — ARR. VLN. & PF.
    Dushkin & Stravinsky
  I. Stern & A. Zakin   ♯ &♭ *AmC.PE 21*
  (*Moussorgsky: Sorochintsy Fair—Gopak*)
  ☆ J. Heifetz & E. Bay (♭ Vic.ERA 94; ♭ *DV. 26034*)

New Orchestral Suite 1945
  ☆ N.Y.P.S.O.—Stravinsky   ♯ *C.C 1010*
    (♯ QC 5004; & ♯ AmC.ML 4882)

(L') HISTOIRE DU SOLDAT (Ramuz)
Narrators & 7 insts. 1918
  M. Auclair, M. Herrand, J. Marchat & Ens..
  —Oubradous   ♯ Pat.DTX 124
    (♯ AmVox.PL 7960)
  F. Weaver, J. Harkins, F. Warriner & Inst.
  Ens.—Vardi (*Eng*)[3] ♯ E. & AmVox.PL 8990

---

[1] 'For a young elephant.'   [2] For *Le Tombeau de Debussy*.
[3] English text by S. Tillim after Newmarch.

(L') HISTOIRE DU SOLDAT (continued)
... **Concert Suite**
Vienna Ens.—Rossi　　**♯ Nix.PVL 7009**
(Les Noces)　　(♯ Van.VRS 452: Ama.AVRS 6018)
Col. Cha. Ens.—Stravinsky　　**♯ EPhi.ABL 3065**
(Symphonie des Psaumes)　　(Phi.A 01193L)
(Octet & Syms. for Wind on ♯ AmC.ML 4964)
☆ Boston Sym. Members—Bernstein (♯ ItV.A12R 0091)

(Les) NOCES　Ballet with song　1923
I. Steingruber (S), M. Kenney (M-S), K.
Wagner (T), E. Wächter (Bs), Vienna Cha.
Cho. & Inst. Ens.—Rossi (Russ)
　　♯ Nix.PVL 7009
(L'Histoire du soldat) (♯ Van.VRS 452; Ama.AVRS 6018)
A. Addison (S), D. Okerson (M-S), R. Price
(T), A. Burrows (B), N.Y. Concert Cho. &
Orch.—Hillis (Eng)　　**♯ E. & AmVox.PL 8630**
(Mass, Ave Maria, Pater Noster)
　　[Excerpt in ♯ AmVox.UHF 1]
C. Bijster (S), C. C. Meyer (M-S), E. Häfliger
(T), H. Schey (Bs), Netherlands Cha. Cho. &
Ens.—Nobel (Fr)　　**♯ Phi.A 00312L**
(Mass & Church Choruses)
H. Luz (S), F. Meesen (B), Dresden State Op.
Cho. & Ens.—Schreiber (Ger)　　**♯ Allo. 4010**
(♯ AFest.CFR 10-576; ♯ Pac.LDA 75)

PÉTROUCHKA　4 Tableaux　1911
COMPLETE RECORDINGS
Minneapolis Sym.—Dorati　　**♯ Mer.MG 50058**
☆ N.Y.P.S.O.—Mitropoulos　　**♯ EPhi.ABL 3027**
　　(♯ Phi.A 01104L)
☆ Sym.—Stokowski　　**♯ G.ALP 1240**
　　(♯ DV.L 16253; ItV.A12R 0030)
☆ Philadelphia—Stokowski (♯ Cam.CAL 203 &
　　in ♯ set CFL 102)
— 1947 VERSION (omitting Final Scene)
R.I.A.S. Sym.—Fricsay　　**♯ HP.DG 17003**
　　(♯ Pol. 16112)
— ORCHESTRAL SUITE
　　(Tableau I (part), & Tableaux II & IV)
Philadelphia—Ormandy　　**♯ AmC.ML 5030**
(Rite of Spring)
Philharmonia—Markevitch　　**♯ C.CX 1199**
(Liadov & Prokofiev) (♯ FCX 359; Angel. 35153, in set 3518)
[Danse Russe & Chez Pétrouchka only, ♭ C.SEL 1531]
London Phil. Sym.—Scherchen　**♯West.LAB 7011**
☆ N.Y.P.S.O.—Stravinsky　　**♯ C.C 1015**
(Scènes de Ballet)　　(♯ QC 5008)
... **Ballerina's dance & Danse russe** (Tableau I)
Boston Prom.—Fiedler　　in ♯ Vic.LM 1726
　　(in ♭ set WDM 1726 & ERA 1251; ♭ ItV.A72R 0061)
... **Excerpts** (unspec.) Berlin Sym.　in ♯ Roy. 1398
... **Danse russe; Chez Pétrouchka; La Semaine Grasse**
— — ARR. PF.　Stravinsky　1921
M. Meyer[1]　　**♯ DFr. 48**
(Piano Rag-music & Serenade)　　(♯ HS.HSL 113)
A. Brendel　　**♯ AmVox.PL 9140**
(Balakirev & Moussorgsky)
... **Danse russe** — ARR. VLN. & PF. Dushkin & Stravinsky
I. Haendel & G. Moore　　in ♯ G.CLP 1021
— — ARR. 2 PFS.　Luboshutz
☆ P. Luboshutz & G. Nemenoff (in ♯ Cam.CAL 198)

PULCINELLA　Ballet with song, 1 Act　1920
(after Pergolesi: original sources quoted)
COMPLETE RECORDING
　　[The voices stated are those used by Stravinsky]
1. **Overture:** Trio-sonata No. 1, 1st movt.
2. **Serenata** (Larghetto): Il Flaminio—Polidoro's aria:
　　Mentre l'erbetta, Act I　(T)
3. **Scherzino:** Trio-sonata No. 2, 1st movt., Presto.
4. **Allegro:** idem, 3rd movt.
5. **Andantino:** Trio-sonata No. 8, 1st movt.
6. **Allegro:** Lo Frate 'nnamorato—Vannella's aria: Gnora
　　credetemi, Act I (arr. orch.)
7. **Allegretto:** Adriano in Siria—Aquilo's aria: Contento forse,
　　Act III　(S)
8. **Allegro assai:** Trio-sonata No. 3, 3rd movt.
9. **Allegro alla breve:** Il Flaminio—Bastiano's aria: Con
　　queste paroline, Act I　(Bs)
10. **Andante** (Largo): Lo Frate . . .—Sento dire, Act II (Trio)
11. **Allegro:** idem—Chi dise ca la femmena, Act II　(T, S)

12. **Presto:** idem—Una te Falanzemprece, Act II　(T)
13. **Allegro alla breve:** Trio-Sonata No. 7, 3rd movt.,
　　Allegro
14. **Tarantella** (Allegro moderato): Concertino No. 6, 3rd
　　movt.
15. **Andantino:** Song, Se tu m'ami　(S)
16. **Allegro** (Toccata): Hpsi. Sonata, E major
17. **Gavotta** (with varns.): Hpsi. Sonata, D major
18. **Vivo:** Sonata, F major, vlc. & cont., 4th movt., Presto.
19. **Tempo di minuet:** Lo Frate . . .—Pupillette fiammette,
　　Act I　(S, T, Bs)
20. **Allegro assai** (Finale): Trio-sonata No. 12, 4th movt.,
　　Presto.
M. Simmons (S), G. Schnittke (T), P.
MacGregor (Bs), Cleveland Sym.
—Stravinsky　　**♯ EPhi.ABL 3091**
(2ss)　　(♯ AmC.ML 4830; Phi.A 01139L)

SUITE FOR ORCH.　— ARR. Stravinsky　1924
　(Nos. 1–5, 14, 16–20)
Bamberg Sym.—Lehmann　　**♯ Pol. 18194**
(Haydn)
French Nat. Radio—Markevitch　**♯ C.CX 1228**
(Baiser de la Fée)　　(♯ FCX 350; Angel. 35143)
Vienna Cha.—Hollreiser　**♯ E. & AmVox.PL 8270**
(Apollon Musagète)
Berlin Radio—Rother　　**♯ Ura. 7093**
(Respighi) (Debussy on ♯ MTW. 537)

SUITE ITALIENNE, VLC. & PF.　1934
☆ R. Garbusova & E. I. Kahn　　**♯ MMS. 107**
(Duo concertante)

(The) RITE OF SPRING　1913 (Sacre du printemps)
Pittsburg Sym.—Steinberg　**♯ DCap.CTL 7061**
[Excerpt in ♯ Cap.SAL 9020]　(♯ Cap.P 8254)
Minneapolis Sym.—Dorati　**♯ EMer.MG 50030**
　　(♯ FMer.MLP 7520)
R.I.A.S. Sym.—Fricsay　　**♯ HP.DGM 18189**
　　(♯ AmD.DL 9781)
Philadelphia—Ormandy　　**♯ AmC.ML 5030**
(Pétrouchka)
Berlin Sym.—List　　**♯ Roy. 1465**
(Milhaud)
☆ N.Y.P.S.O.—Stravinsky　　**♯ C.CX 1083**
(2ss)　　(♯ C.WCX 1083: QCX 10066)
(Firebird, in ♯ AmC.ML 4882)
☆ Boston Sym.—Monteux (♯ G.FALP 294;
　　ItV.A12R 0080)
Philharmonia—Markevitch (♯ G.QCLP 12001;
　　Vic.LHMV 1)
San Francisco Sym.—Monteux (♯ Cam.CAL 110)

V. VOCAL

Cantata S, T, female cho., 2 fls., 2 obs. & vlc. 1952
(Anon. XVth & XVIth Cent. Eng. texts)
1. Lyke-wake Dirge　　2. The maidens came
3. Tomorrow will be my dancing day　4. Westron Wind
J. Tourel (M-S), H. Cuénod (T), N.Y. Concert
Cho. & Philharmonic Cha. Ens.—Stravinsky
　　♯ EPhi.ABL 3108
(Symphony in C)　　(♯ AmC.ML 4899; Phi.A 01149L)

CHURCH CHORUSES[2]
Ave Maria　1934
Pater Noster　1926
N.Y. Concert Cho.—Hillis
　　♯ E. & AmVox.PL 8630
(below, & Les Noces)
Netherlands Cha. Cho.—Nobel　**♯ Phi.A 00312L**
(Mass & Les Noces) [Holland Festival, 1954]
☆ N.Y. Church of Blessed Sacrament Cho.—Stravinsky
　　(in ♯ Vic.LM 7010: ♭ set WDM 7010; ♯ItV.A10R 0007)

MASS
　Cho. of men & boys & Double Wind Quintet　1948
N.Y. Concert Cho. & Inst. Ens.—Hillis
　　♯ E. & AmVox.PL 8630
(above; & Les Noces)
Netherlands Cha. Cho.—Nobel ♯ Phi.A 00312L
(above; & Les Noces) [Holland Festival, 1954]

[1] This entry corrects that for the same number in Supp. I—apparently never issued in the form there described.
[2] All recordings probably sung to the Latin texts of 1949.

PERSÉPHONE Melodrama
Reciter, T, cho. & orch 1933-4 (Gide)
C. Nollier, N. Gedda, Paris Univ. & French
Nat. Radio Chos., Paris Cons. Orch.
—Cluytens   ‡ C.FCX 412

OPERAS
OEDIPUS REX Opera-Oratorio (Cocteau) 1926-7
COMPLETE RECORDINGS

Casts	Set A	Set B
Narrator (Fr) ...	J. Cocteau	P. Pasquier
Oedipus	P. Pears (T)	E. Häfliger (T)
Jocasta ...	M. Mödl (M-S)	H. Bouvier (M-S)
Messenger ⎱ ...	H. Rehfuss (B)	J. Loomis (B)
Creon ⎰		
Tiresias	O. v. Rohr (Bs)	A. Vessières (Bs)
Shepherd	H. Krebs (T)	H. Cuénod (T)

Set A with Cologne Radio Cho. & Orch.
—Stravinsky   ‡ EPhi.ABL 3054
(Latin)   (‡ Phi.A 01137L; AmC.ML 4644)

Set B with E. Brasseur Cho. & Suisse Romande
Orch.—Ansermet   ‡ D.LXT 5098
(Latin)   (‡ Lon.LL 1273)

(The) RAKE'S PROGRESS 3 Acts & Epilogue
(Auden & Kallman) 1951
COMPLETE RECORDING

Anne Trulove	H. Gueden (S)
Tom Rakewell	E. Conley (T)
Baba the Turk	B. Thebom (M-S)
Nick Shadow	M. Harrell (B)
Trulove	N. Scott (Bs)
Mother Goose	M. Lipton (M-S)
Sellem	P. Franke (T)
Keeper of Madhouse ...	L. Davidson (Bs)

Metropolitan Op. Cho. & Orch.—Stravinsky
                         ‡ EPhi.ABL 3055/7
(6ss)   (‡ AmC. set SL 125; Phi.A 01181/3L)

RENARD Opera-Ballet 1 Act 1920
☆ Soloists & N.Y. Cha. Orch.—Craft (Eng) (in ‡ Clc. 6173)

(Le) ROSSIGNOL 3 Acts 1914
COMPLETE RECORDING in French

The Fisherman	J. Giraudeau (T)
The Nightingale	J. Micheau (S)
The Emperor of China	L. Lovano (T)
The Cook	G. Moizan (S)
The Chamberlain	M. Roux (Bs)
The Bonze	B. Cottret (Bs)
Death	C. Gayraud (A)

etc., French Nat. Radio Cho. & Orch.—Cluytens
                         ‡ C.FCX 439
                         (‡ Angel. 35204)

PART SONGS
(4) Russian Peasant Songs[1] 1913
1. On Saints' Days   3. The Pike
2. Ovsen   4. Master Portly
Pamplona Cha. Cho.—Morondo
                  in V‡ Sel.LLA 1007
(Martinů, Bartók, etc.)

SONGS: COLLECTION
(3) Petites chansons
   1. The Magpie; 2. The Rook; 3. Caw caw jackdaw
(3) Stories for children (1917)
   1. Tilim-bom; 2. Ducks, Swans & Geese; 3. The Bear
The Cat's Lullabies (Ramuz, from the Russian—1917)
   1. On the stove; 2. Interior; 3. Dodo; 4. What the cat
   has
Pribaoutki (Peasant songs)—orig. voice & 8 insts. (1914)
   1. Uncle Armand; 2. The Oven; 3. The Colonel; 4. The
   old man & the hare
(4) Russian Songs (1918-9)
   ... No. 3, The Sparrow; No. 4, The Dissident
J. Giraudeau (T, Fr), P. Boulez (pf.)
(Moussorgsky)   ‡ D.FAT 173601

(The) Cat's Lullabies (Ramuz) 1917
☆ A. Carmin (A) & 3 clar. (in ‡ Clc. 6173)

Symphonie de Psaumes cho. & orch. 1930
St. Hedwig's Cath. Cho., R.I.A.S. Cha. & Boys'
Cho., R.I.A.S. Sym. Orch.—Fricsay
                         ‡ Pol. 18035
(Martin: Petite symphonie concertante)
   (2ss, ‡ AmD.DL 7526; & 4ss, ♮ PV. 72318/9)

[1] Labelled Pièces Kirghises.
[2] From Slumber Songs, Op. 33 (Ukolébavky).

French Nat. Radio Cho. & Orch.—Horenstein
                         ‡ Pat.DTX 138
(R. Strauss: Metamorphosen)   (‡ Angel. 35101)
Downtown Cho. & Pittsburgh Sym.—Steinberg
(Harris)   ‡ PFCM.CB 164
☆ Col. Sym. & Cho.—Stravinsky   ‡ EPhi.ABL 3065
(Histoire du Soldat)   (‡ Phi.A 01193L)
☆ London Phil. Cho. & Orch.—Ansermet ‡ D.LXT 2916
(Fire Bird Suite)   (‡ Lon.LL 889)

VI. MISCELLANEOUS

Song of the Volga Boatmen
— ARR. ORCH. Stravinsky 1917
☆ N.Y. Cha. Orch.—Craft (in ‡ Clc. 6173)

STRINGFIELD, Lamar (b. 1897)

From the Southern Mountains, Op. 41
Suite, orch. 1927
... No. 4, Cripple Creek
Hamburg Philharmonia—Korn in ‡ Allo. 3150
(Chadwick, Hadley, Parker, etc.)

STUTSCHEWSKY, Joachim (b. 1891)

Palästinensische Skizzen pf.
... Springtanz, Jüdisches Lied, Ruhiger Tanz, Extase &
Intermezzo
L. Granetman   in ‡ Phi.N 00641R
(Ben-Haim, Lavry, Boscovich)

SUCHOŇ, Evžen (b. 1908)

Fantasy and Burlesque vln. & orch.
☆ T. Gašparek & Slovak Phil.—Rajter (‡ Sup.LPM 79)

(The) WHIRLPOOL Opera 6 Scenes 1949
(Krútňava)
COMPLETE RECORDING
F. Zvarík, Š. Hoza, L. Havlák, M. Česányová,
Z. Frešová, etc., Bratislava Nat. Theatre Cho.
& Orch.—Chalabala   ‡ Sup.SPLV 151/3
(6ss)   (‡ U. 5135/7G)

SUK, Josef (1874-1935)

Christmas dream, Op. 33, No. 5[2] — ARR. VLC. & PF.
F. Smetana & D. Smetanová   U.C 24427
(Pergolesi: Nina)

Fantasia, G minor, Op. 24 vln. & orch. 1903
A. Plocék & Czech Phil.—Ančerl   ‡ U. 5183G
(Cikker)

Love Song, Op. 7, No. 1 pf.
— ARR. VLN. & PF.
G. Barinova & pf.[3]   USSRM.D 00358
(Wieniawski: Mazurka & Trad: Polish Song)
D. Oistrakh & V. Yampolsky[4]   U.C 24409
(2ss)

(4) Pieces, Op. 17 vln. & pf. 1900
☆ G. & J. Neveu   ‡ Angel. 35129
(Sibelius)   (‡ ArgA.LPC 11575)
... No. 4, Burlesque
N. Milstein & C. Bussotti in ‡ DCap.CTL 7058
(Schumann, Brahms, etc.)   (‡ Cap.P 8259)

Quartet, No. 2, Str., Op. 31 1911
Ondriček Qtt.   ‡ Sup.LPM 231
                          (‡ U. 5157C)

Rustic Serenade pf. 1897 — ARR. ORCH.
☆ ▽ Film Sym.—Vostřák (in ‡ U. 5200C)

Symphony, C minor, Op. 27 "Asrael"
Czech Phil.—Talich   ‡ Sup.SLPM 85/87
(5ss—Fibich)   (‡ U. 5051/3C)
(2ss—‡ Csm.CRLP 215)

[3] ARR. Mařák.   [4] ARR. Kocián.

SULLIVAN, Sir Arthur Seymour
(1842-1900)

CLASSIFIED: I. Non Stage Works
II. Stage Works (a) with W. S. Gilbert
(b) with others
(Abridged listings only)

I. NON STAGE WORKS

Onward, Christian soldiers (Baring-Gould)
Cho.—W. Schumann   in ‡ *Cap.L 382*
(*DAS 342:* ♭ *SKASF 342*)

Overture di ballo, E major   1870
L.S.O.—Weldon   ‡ **C.SX 1045**
(*Tchaikovsky, Elgar, Handel, etc.*)

— ARR. BAND
Grenadier Guards—Harris   ‡ *D.LW 5117*
(*Sibelius: Finlandia*)   (‡ *Lon.LD 9131*)

SONG: The Lost Chord (Proctor)
W. Midgley (T) & orch.   G.DB 21604
(*Adams: The Holy City*)

☆ R. Crooks (T) (in ‡ *Cam.CAL 128*)
☰ E. Caruso (in ‡ *G.QKLP 501*)
— ARR. ORGAN   R. Ellsasser (in ‡ *MGM.E 3031*)

II. STAGE WORKS

A. With W. S. GILBERT

COLLECTIONS OF EXCERPTS
" Martyn Green's Gilbert and Sullivan "

Pirates of Penzance: Major-General's Song *a*
H.M.S. Pinafore: When I was a lad
The Yeomen of the Guard: I've jibe and joke
The Mikado: The flowers that bloom in the spring
    There is beauty in the bellow of the blast
      [with E. Halman]
    I've got a little list *a*
    Willow, Tit willow
Princess Ida: If you give me your attention
    When e'er I spoke
The Yeomen of the Guard: I have a song to sing
Patience: Am I alone
Iolanthe: When I went to the Bar
    The Lass is true
Trial by Jury: The Judge's Song *a*
The Yeomen of the Guard: Oh! a private buffoon
Iolanthe: The Nightmare Song *a*
   M. Green (B), Cho. & Orch.—Engel
             ‡ **AmC.ML 4643**
[marked *a* also on ♭ *A 1769*]   (♭ *set A 1042*)

Trial by Jury: The Judge's Song
    When first my old, old love I knew
Gondoliers: In enterprise of martial kind
Pirates of Penzance: The Policeman's Song
Patience: If you're anxious to shine
Iolanthe: The Nightmare Song
The Mikado: The Moon and I
Sorcerer: My name is John Wellington Wells
H.M.S. Pinafore: When I was a lad
   D. Kaye (B) & cho.   ‡ *AmD.DL 5094*
             (4ss, ♭ *set ED 540*)

Various Excerpts
Soloists, Radio City Music Hall Cho. & Orch. (‡*MH. 33-40*)

COLLECTION   — ARR. ORCH.
Iolanthe: March (Finale, Act I)
The Mikado: Entrance of Mikado & Katisha
Yeoman of the Guard: Ye Tower Warders
The Gondoliers: With ducal pomp
H.M.S. Pinafore: We sail the ocean blue
Princess Ida: From the distant panorama
Utopia Limited: Drawing Room music
Ruddigore: Hornpipe
The Gondoliers: Gavotte
The Sorcerer: Minuet
Trial by Jury: Hark! the hour of ten is sounding
The Mikado: Behold the Lord High Executioner
The Gondoliers: Dance a Cuchucha
Utopia Limited: Entrance of Court
Patience: The soldiers of our Queen
The Mikado: Three little maids from school
The Pirates of Penzance: With cat-like tread
The Grand Duke: Dance   ø
The Pirates of Penzance: When the foeman bares his steel   ø
Ruddigore: Dance (Finale, Act I)   ø
Iolanthe: Entrance & March of Peers   ø
   New Sym.—S. Robinson (10ss)   *D.F 10585/9*
[items marked ø in ‡ only]   (‡ *LK 4099; Lon.LL 1263*)

(The) GONDOLIERS   2 Acts   1889
"Highlights"
  ☆ D'Oyly Carte Co.—Godfrey   ‡ *D.LK 4073*
   (*Iolanthe—Highlights*)   (‡ *Lon.LL 784:* ♭ *REP 8017*)
   [from set]

Orchestral Selection
  H. Davidson Orch.   C.DX 1921
                      (♭ *SCD 2042*)

Overture   ☆ Sym.—Godfrey (‡ *D.LW 5226*)

(The) GRAND DUKE   1896
SEE Collections, *above*

H.M.S. PINAFORE   2 Acts   1878
COMPLETE RECORDING
  ☆ B. Lewis, D. Fancourt, G. Baker, Sir Henry Lytton,
    etc., orch.—Sargent   ‡ *G.ALP 1293/4*
  (3ss—*Trial by Jury*) (‡ *Vic.LCT set 6008:* ♭ *set WCT 6008*)

Highlights
  ☆ D'Oyly Carte Op. Co.—I. Godfrey   ‡ *D.LK 4078*
   (*Sorcerer—Highlights*)   (‡ *Lon.LL 809:* ♭ *REP 8016*)
   [from set]

Highlights   — ARR. ORCH.
  Hamburg Philharmonia—Shankson (‡ *Roy. 1596*)

Orchestral Selection
  H. Davidson Orchestra   C.DX 1923
                 (♭ *SCD 2044:* in ‡ *S 1070*)

Overture
  ☆ Boston Prom.—Fiedler (in ‡ *G.CLP 1030;*
              in ‡ *Vic.LM 1798; DV.T 16415*)
  Sym. Orch.—Godfrey (‡ *D.LW 5024; Lon.LD 9007*)

IOLANTHE   2 Acts   1882
Highlights
  ☆ D'Oyly Carte Op. Co.—Godfrey   ‡ *D.LK 4073*
   (*Gondoliers—Highlights*) [from set]   (‡ *Lon.LL 784*)
   (*Overture* only on ‡ *D.LW 5172*)

Orchestral Selection
  H. Davidson Orchestra   C.DX 1924
                      (♭ *SCD 2046*)

Overture
  Hamburg Philharmonia—H-J. Walther   *MSB. 78138*
                 (in ‡ *MGM.E 3143*)
  "Nat. Op. Orch." (in ‡ *Roy. 1396;* ‡ *Var. 6992*)
  ☆ Boston Prom.—Fiedler (in ‡ *G.CLP 1030;*
       ♭ *Vic.ERA 135* & in ‡ *LM 1798; DV.T 16415*)

(The) MIKADO   2 Acts   1885
COMPLETE RECORDINGS
  B. Troxell (S), M. Green (B), J. Pease (B), etc. N.W.
    Ger. Radio Cho. & Hamburg Philharmonia—
    Korn[1] (4ss)   ‡ *Roy. 1574/5*
  ☆ D. Fancourt, M. Green, D. Oldham, etc. Cho. & Orch.
    I. Godfrey   (4ss)   ‡ *G.ALP 1255/6*
          (‡ *Vic. set LCT 6009:* ♭ *set WCT 6009*)

Highlights
  ☆ D'Oyly Carte Op. Co.—Godfrey   ‡ *D.LK 4068*
   (*Patience—Highlights*) (‡ *Lon.LL 782;*
   [from set]   ♭ *REP 8010/2, 6ss*)

Highlights   — ARR. ORCH.
  Hamburg Philharmonia—Korn   ‡ *Roy. 1584*
                    (‡ *Ply. 12-120*)

Orchestral Selection
  H. Davidson Orchestra   C.DX 1920
                (♭ *SCD 2041:* in ‡ *S 1070*)

Overture
  ☆ Sym. Orch.—Godfrey (‡ *D.LW 5024; Lon.LD 9007*)
  Boston Prom.—Fiedler (*G.B 10586:* ♭ *7EG 8001:*
    in ‡ *CLP 1030;* ♭ *Vic.ERA 73:* in ‡ *LM 1798;*
                       DV.T 16415)

A Wandering Minstrel I   T   Act I
The Sun, whose rays . . .   S   Act II
  ☆ K. Baker (T), film version (♭ *G.7EG 8089*)

Madrigal: Brightly dawns our wedding day
  Alistair Cooke (singing all 4 parts)   ‡ *EPhi.BBL 7028*
  (in *An Evening with A. Cooke*)

PATIENCE   2 Acts   1881
Highlights
  ☆ D'Oyly Carte Op. Co.—Godfrey   ‡ *D.LK 4068*
   (*Mikado—Highlights*) [from set]   (‡ *Lon.LL 782*)
   (Excerpts also on ♭ *Lon.REP 8013*)

Orchestral Selection
  H. Davidson Orch. (*C.DX 1927:* ♭ *SCD 2046:* in ‡ *S 1070*)

Quadrille
  Camerons Band (‡ *D.LF 1153; Lon.LB 900*)

Overture
  ☆ Liverpool Phil.—Sargent (♭ *C.SCD 2003;*
                in ‡ *AmC.RL 3050*)
  Sym.—Godfrey (‡ *D.LW 5226*)

---

[1] The orch. recorded in Germany, the voices in U.S.A.

(The) PIRATES OF PENZANCE 2 Acts 1880
Highlights
☆ D'Oyly Carte Op. Co.—Godfrey   # D.LK 4128
(*Princess Ida—Highlights*) [from set]   (# Lon.LL 1243)
(Excerpts on ♭ *Lon.REP 8014*)

Orchestral Selection
H. Davidson Orch. (C.DX 1922: ♭ *SCD 2043:* in # *S 1070*)

Overture
☆ Sym. Orch.—Godfrey, from set (# *D.LW 5172*)
Boston Prom.—Fiedler (*G.B 10574: EB 4182:*
♭ *7EG 8001:* in # *CLP 1030;* ♭ *Vic.ERA 73:*
in # *LM 1798; DV.T 16415*)

PRINCESS IDA 3 Acts 1884
COMPLETE RECORDING

King Hildebrand	F. Morgan (Bs)
Hilarion	T. Round (T)
Cyril	L. Osborn (T)
Florian	J. Skitch (B)
King Gama	P. Pratt (B)
Arac	D. Adams (Bs)
Guron	J. Banks (Bs)
Scynthius	T. Hills (Bs)
Princess Ida	V. Sladen (S)
Lady Blanche	A. Drummond-Grant (A)
Melissa	B. Dixon (M-S)
Sacharissa	C. Morey (S)

D'Oyly Carte Op. Co. & New Sym.—Godfrey
D.LK 4092/3
(4ss)   (# Lon.LL 1200/1)
[Highlights on # D.LK 4128; Lon.LL 1243; Overture
only, ♭ *D. 71118* & in # *LW 5227*]

RUDDIGORE 2 Acts 1887
Highlights
☆ D'Oyly Carte Op. Co.—Godfrey   # D.LK 4069
(*Yeomen of the Guard—Highlights*)   (# Lon.LL 783)
[from set]   (Overture only, in # *D.LW 5226*)

Orchestral Selection
H. Davidson Orch. (C.DX 1929: ♭ *SCD 2049*)

(The) SORCERER 2 Acts 1877
COMPLETE RECORDING

Sir Marmaduke Poindextre	F. Morgan (Bs)
John Wellington Wells	P. Pratt (B)
Lady Sangazure	A. Drummond-Grant (A)
Aline	M. Harding (S)
Mrs. Partlett	B. Dixon (M-S)
Alexis	N. Griffiths (T)
Dr. Daly	J. Skitch (B)
Constance	Y. Dean (M-S)

etc. D'Oyly Carte Op. Co. Cho. & Orch.
—I. Godfrey (4ss)   # D.LK 4070/1
(# Lon.LL 885/6)
[Highlights on # D.LK 4078; Lon.LL 809; Overture
only, # *D.LW 5227*]

TRIAL BY JURY 1 Act 1875
COMPLETE RECORDINGS
☆ W. Lawson, L. Sheffield, G. Baker, D. Oldham, Cho.
& Orch.   # G.ALP 1294
(*H.M.S. Pinafore, s. 3*) (# Vic. set LCT 6008:
♭ *set WCT 6008*)
☆ Regent Light Opera Co. (# *AFest.CFR 10-606*)

Excerpts
☆ D'Oyly Carte Op. Co.—Godfrey
(♭ *Lon.REP 8018*, from set)

UTOPIA LTD. 2 Acts 1893
SEE Collections of Excerpts, *above*

(The) YEOMEN OF THE GUARD 2 Acts 1888
Highlights
☆ D'Oyly Carte Op. Co.—Godfrey   # D.LK 4069
(*Ruddigore—Highlights*) [from set]   (# Lon.LL 783)
(Excerpts also on ♭ *Lon.REP 8015*)

Orchestral Selection
H. Davidson Orch. (C.DX 1928: ♭ *SCD 2047*)

Overture
☆ Liverpool Phil.—Sargent (♭ *C.SCD 2003;*
in # *AmC.RL 3050*)
Sym.—Godfrey (♭ *D. 71118* & in # *LW 5227*)

II. B. WITH OTHER LIBRETTISTS, ETC.

HENRY VIII Inc. Music (Shakespeare) 1878
... **March; Graceful Dance; Water Music**
Vienna Orch. Soc.—Adler   # Uni.LP 1014
(*below*)

(The) TEMPEST, Op. 1 Inc. Music (Shakespeare)
1862
COMPLETE RECORDING[1]
P. Brinton (S) & Vienna Orch. Soc.—Adler
(1½ss—*above*)   # Uni.LP 1014

PINEAPPLE POLL Ballet ARR. Mackerras 1951
EXCERPTS with narration
S. Holloway & Covent Garden Op. Orch.
AmD.K 101

SUPPÉ, Franz von (1819-1895)

OPERETTAS, etc.
BANDITENSTREICHE 1867
Overture
Sym.—Straszynski   Muza.X 1662
☆ Rhineland Sym.—Federer (in # *AFest.CFR 10-601*)
Bavarian Sym.—Graunke (♭ *AmD.ED 3517;*
♭ *Pol. 20051*)

BOCCACCIO 3 Acts 1879
HIGHLIGHTS

Fiammetta	E. Roon (S)
Boccaccio	W. Kmentt (T)
Lambertuccio	K. Preger (B)
Scalza	W. Berry (Bs)

etc., Vienna Volksoper Cho. & State Op.
Orch.—Paulik   # EPhi.NBL 5026
(# AmC.ML 4818; Phi.N 02104L)

Overture
Phil. Prom.—Boult   # West.LAB 7033
(*below*)
Vienna Sym.—Moralt   in # *Phi.N 00631R*
(*below & J. Strauss*)   (# Epic.LC 3022)
Film Sym.—Strništé   # Sup.LPM 121
(*Rubinstein, Glazounov, J. Strauss*) (in # *U. 5116C*, d.c.)
☆ Italian Radio—Gallino (in # *Tem.MTT 2058*)

Hab' ich nur deine Liebe T Act I
R. Schock   G.EH 1453
(*below*)   (♭ *7PW 531*)

Florenz hat schöne Frauen orig. B Act I
G. Rothenberger (S) & R. Schock (T) G.EH 1453
(*above*)   (♭ *7PW 531*)

March
☆ Austrian Sym.—Wöss (in # Ply. 12-103)
Berlin State Op.—Otto (in # *T.LA 6054;*
in # *FT.260.TV.015*)

DICHTER UND BAUER (*Poet & Peasant*)
Inc. Music to Elmar's play
Overture
N.B.C. Sym.—Toscanini[2] in # Vic. set LM 6026
(*Berlioz, Glinka, Bizet, etc.*)
Brussels Radio—André   # DT.TM 68026
(*Orphée aux Enfers, Ov.*)
(TV.VE 9019: in # *T.LSK 7019; FT.320.TC.028;*
♭ *T.UX 4507*, & 2ss, *A 11486*)
Vienna Sym.—Moralt   in # *Phi.N 00631R*
(*J. Strauss*)   (# Epic.LC 3022)
Phil. Prom.—Boult   # West.LAB 7033
(*above & below*)
R.I.A.S. Sym.—Becker   in # Rem. 199-181
Philadelphia—Ormandy   ♭ AmC. 4-4789
Opera Orch.—Rossi (in # *Mae.OA 20005*)
Anon. Orch. (# *Var. 69134*)
☆ L.P.O.—Solti (# *D.LW 5004:* ♭ *DX 1736*)
Boston Prom.—Fiedler (in # *G.DLP 1079:* ♭ *7PQ 2025;*
♭ *DV. 16302;* in # *Vic.LRM 7035:* ♭ *set ERB 7035*)
Vienna State Op.—Reichwein (Od.NLX 7)
E.I.A.R.—Gallino (*Orf. 53007*)
— ARR. HARMONICAS
Raisner Harmonica Trio (in # *FestF.FLD 33*)

---

[1] Omits Melodrama preceding *Come unto these yellow sands* but includes that preceding *While you here do snoring lie;*
omits No. 5 (Act III, Sc. 2); Melodrama following Nos. 6 and 9; and part of No. 11 (Act V, Sc. 1); there is no cho. in
Full fathom five; in No. 9 the soloist sings both parts.
[2] Broadcast performance.

FATINITZA 3 Acts 1876
Overture
Phil. Prom.—Boult   ♯ West.LAB 7033
(*above & below*)
☆ Boston Pops—Fiedler (♭ *Cam.CAE 189:* in ♯ CAL 250)
March   Vienna Light Orch. (**V**♯ *MMS.ML 1505*)

LEICHTE KAVALLERIE 1886
Overture
Philharmonia—Kletzki   ♭ *C.SEL 1529*
(*Ein Morgen, Ein Mittag . . . , Ov.*)   (♭ *SEBQ 128*)
Philadelphia "Pops"—Hilsberg   ♯ *AmC.AL 34*
(*Berlioz*)
Brussels Radio—André   ♯ *DT.TM 68018*
(*Schöne Galathee, Overture*)
(TV.VE 9020: ♯ T.LSK 7019: ♭ UX 4509;
     ♯ FT.320.TC.028: ♭ 460.TV.010)
Phil. Prom.—Boult   ♯ West.LAB 7033
(*above*)
☆ Philharmonia—Weldon   ♭ *C.SED 5501*
(*Handel: Samson Overture*)
     (also DWX 5088 & in ♯ SX 1032)
Opera Orch.—Rossi (in ♯ Mae.OA 20005)
Berlin Sym.—Rubahn (in ♯ Roy.1413)
☆ Boston Prom.—Fiedler (♭ G.7EP 7002: 7EPK 1006:
     7EBF 6: 7EPQ 506; ♭ DV. 26016)
L.P.O.—Solti (♯ D.LW 5003; ♭ Lon.REP 8019)
Bavarian Sym.—Graunke (PV.58616; ♭ Pol. 20019, d.c.)
Berlin State Op.—F. Walter (♭ G.7PW 511)
Rhineland Sym.—Federer (♯ AFest.CFR 39)
etc.
— ARR. ORGAN.   R. Foort (♯ Nix.SLPY 148; SOT. 1053
       & ♯ 10523)
— ARR. HARMONICAS
Raisner Harmonica Trio (♭ FestF.FX 1006)

**(Ein) MORGEN, EIN MITTAG, EIN ABEND
IN WIEN**
Overture
Philharmonia—Kletzki   ♭ *C.SEL 1529*
(*Leichte Kavallerie Overture*)   (♭ *SEBQ 128*)
R.I.A.S. Sym.—Becker   in ♯ **Rem. 199-181**
(*Adam, Auber, Maillart*)
☆ Philharmonia—Lambert   ♭ *C.SED 5504*
(*Waldteufel: Sur le plage*)   (♭ *SEDQ 512*)
     (in ♯ AmC.RL 3054)
☆ L.P.O.—Solti (♯ D.LW 5003; ♭ Lon.REP 8019)

PIQUE DAME 1864
Overture
Philharmonia—Kletzki   ♭ *C.SEL 1542*
(*Moussorgsky*)
Cologne Concert—Hagestedt   PV. 58616
(*Leichte Kavallerie, Overture*)
Vienna Radio—Schönherr   Vien.P 6133
☆ Philharmonia—Lambert (♭ C.SED 5506: SEDQ 113)
L.P.O.—Solti (♯ D.LW 5004: ♭ DX 1736)

(Die) SCHÖNE GALATHEE 1 Act 1865
HIGHLIGHTS
E. Roon (S), W. Kmentt & K. Preger (T), O. Wiener (B),
   & Vienna State Op. Cho. & Orch.—Paulik ♯ Ura. 7167
☆ E. Roon (S), W. Kmentt (T), etc., Vienna Acad. Cho.
   & Philharmonia—Hagen, from set
     (♯ MMS.MEL 1510: Excerpt on **V**♯ ML 1521)

Overture
Hallé—Barbirolli   ♭ *G.7ER 5034*
(*Traviata, Preludes*)
Brussels Radio—André   ♯ *DT.TM 68018*
(*Leichte Kavallerie, Over.*) (TV.VE 9020: in ♯ T.LS 6031:
     ♭ UX 4509; ♭ FT. 460.TV.010)
Leipzig Radio—Dobrindt   Eta. 340046
R.I.A.S. Sym.—Becker   in ♯ Rem. 199-181
☆ Boston Prom.—Fiedler (♭ G.7EP 7003: 7EPK 1006:
     7EBF 6: 7EPQ 506; ♭ DV. 26016;
     in ♯ Cam.CAL 122: ♭ CAE 102, ? o.v.)
Bavarian Sym.—Graunke (♭ Pol. 20019;
       ♭ AmD.ED 3517)
C.B.S.—Barlow (in ♯ AmC.RL 3030)
Rhineland Sym.—Federer (in ♯ AFest.CFR 10-601)

Einmal möcht' ich so verliebt sein S
☆ R. Seegers (P.BX 613)

TEUFEL AUF ERDEN 3 Acts 1878
Teufelsmarsch
Vienna Radio—Schönherr (*Vien.A 6128*)
Selection from Suppé's Works
Vienna Radio—Schneider (in ♯ *Phi.S 05903R:* ♭ *A 430000R*)

SURINACH, Carlos (b. 1915)

Ritmo Jondo   Ballet   1953[1] orch.
(3) Cantos Bereberes   fl., ob., cl., vla., vlc., hp.   f.p. 1952
(3) Tientos   hp. (or hpsi.), cor ang., & timpani   f.p. 1953
   (1. De Queja; 2. De Pena; 3. De Alegría)
Cha. Ens.—Surinach   ♯ MGM.E 3268
[E. Vito (hp.) in *Tientos*]

Ritmo Jondo, Suite   f.p. 1952
1. Bulerias;   2. Saeta;   3. Garrotín
Ens.—I. Solomon   ♯ MGM.E 3155
(*Chavez, Revueltas, Villa-Lobos*)

(3) Spanish Songs & Dances   pf.   1950-1
W. Masselos   ♯ MGM.E 3165
(*Albeniz, Nin, Turina*)

Sinfonietta flamenca   orch.   f.p. 1954
Louisville—Whitney   ♯ LO. 4
(*Castelnuovo-Tedesco & Hovhaness*)

Tales from the flamenco kingdom   pf.   1954
M. Richter   ♯ MGM.E 3181
(*Toch, Hindemith, etc.*)

(3) Tientos   hp. or hpsi., cor ang. & timp.
S. Marlow (hpsi.) & Concert Arts Players
(*Falla & Rieti*)   ♯ Cap.P 8309

SUSATO, Tielman (c. 1500-c. 1564)

Danserye
   (from the *3rd Music Book*, 1551, ed. Cape)
1. Ronde IV   2. Allemande V
3. Salterelle   4. Bransle: De Post
5. Ronde: Il étoit une fillette 6. Allemande IV
7. Basse Danse II   8. Reprise aliud
9. Passe et medio   10. Reprise le pigne
11. Allemande VI: La Paix 12. Ronde IX
13. Pavane I: Mille regrets 14. Bransle I
15. Pavane la dona   16. Gaillarde la dona
Pro Musica Antiqua—Cape ♯ HP.APM 14032
(† *Chansons from Music Books . . .*)
[Nos. 1, 2, 3, 5, 7, 8, 9, 10, 11, 14, 15, 16, also on PV. 5409]

Danseryes (unspec.)   (*Music Books*, 1543-51)
Musicians' Workshop Ens. (Suite)
     in ♯ CEd.CE 1018
(† *Recorder Music*)
Trapp Family Ens. (one)   in ♯ AmD.DL 9759

Int Midden van den Meye
   (Book I, 1551—*Chanson de mai*)
☆ Dutch Vocal Qtt. (in † ♯ HS.AS 5)

SUTER, Hermann (1870-1926)

COLLECTION
FESTSPIEL: SANKT JAKOB AN DER BIRS (Bernoulli)
   1912
   Lied der Pflanser   Male cho. & orch.
   Wir sind das junge Leben   Boys' cho & orch.
RIEHENER FESTSPIEL (Oeri) 1923
   Prelude   orch.
   Hexenlied der Riehener Frauen   Fem. cho. & orch.
   Aufzug der Ratsdeputation   (Gavotte)   orch.
   Aufzug der Basler Stadtreiterei   Male cho. & orch.
Basler Liedertafel (male), Gesangverein (fem.)
   & Gymnasium (boys') Chos. & Orch. Soc.
   —H. Münch   ♯ *Phi.N 00738R*
(*Huber*)

---

[1] An expansion of the work on E 3155, which is for cl., tpt., timpani, sax., and 3 hand-clappers; the ballet is scored for 18 insts. and 3 hand-clappers.

SUTERMEISTER, Heinrich (b. 1910)

Max und Moritz Kleine Hausmusik (Busch)
S, A, T, B & pf. duet 1951
E. Lechner, W. Demmer, J. Brombacher, G.
Fehr, H. Datyner & A. Perret—N.
Aeschbacher ♮ **PV. 72433/4**
(3ss—Poem by Wilhelm Busch—recited by E. Ponto)

SVENDSEN, Johan Severin (1840-1911)

Carnival in Paris, Op. 9 orch.
Covent Garden—Hollingsworth ♯ **P.PMC 1021**
(Alfvén, Nielsen, Sibelius) (♯ MGM.E 3082)

Festival Polonaise, Op. 12 orch.
Danish Radio—Tuxen ♯ **D.LW 5113**
(below) (♯ Lon.LD 9123)
☆ Danish Radio—Malko (G.EH 1431)

Norwegian Artists' Carnival, Op. 16 orch.
Danish Radio—Tuxen ♯ **D.LW 5113**
(above) (♯ Lon.LD 9123)
☆ Oslo Phil.—Fjeldstad (in ♯ Mer.MG 10150;
NOC. 63172/3, 2ss)

Norwegian Folksong Suite orch.
Moscow Radio—Golovanov *USSRM.D 00794*
(Grieg: Peer Gynt Suite No. 1, s. 3)

NORWEGIAN RHAPSODIES
No. 2, Op. 19
Oslo Phil.—Fjeldstad NOC. **63164/6**
(3ss) *(No. 3, & Sym. No. 2 in ♯ Mer.MG 90004)*

No. 3, Op. 21
Oslo Phil.—Fjeldstad NOC. **63195/7**
(3ss) (in ♯ Mer.MG 90004)

No. 4, D minor, Op. 22 orch.
Linz Sym. ♯ **Ply. 10-31**
(Grieg: Lyric Suite)

Romance, G major, Op. 26 vln. & orch.
—. Meisel & Berlin Sym.—Guhl ♯ **Ura. 7166**
(Bériot & Bruch)
M. Kayser & N.W. Ger. Phil.—Schüchter
♯ **Imp.ILP 115**
(Bruch) (♭ Od.BEOW 3003)
H. Hekking & Scandinavian Sym.—Johannesen
♯ **Mae.OAT 25008**
(Grieg, Sinding, Sibelius)
☆ M. Gardi & Hamburg Phil.—Brückner-Rüggeberg
(♭ Pol. 20047)

Serenade: Kom, Karina, Op. 24, No. 3
C. Hague (T), G. Steele (pf.) in ♯ **ML. 7034**
(† Scandinavian Songs)

Symphony No. 2, B flat major, Op. 15
☆ Oslo Phil.—Grüner-Hegge ♯ Mer.MG 90004
(Norwegian Rhapsodies) (8ss, NOC. 62929/36)

Zorahayda, Op. 11 Legend, orch.
Moscow Radio—Golovanov ♯ *USSR.D 1143*
(Tchaikovsky: 1812 Overture)

ORCHESTRATION
Ole Bull: Säterjentens Søndag
Oslo Phil.—Fjeldstad in ♯ **Mer.MG 10150**
(♭ Nera.EPM 210; NOC. 63167)

SWANSON, Howard (b. 1909)

Night Music Cha. orch 1950
☆ N.Y. Ens.—Mitropoulos ♯ **B.AXTL 1054**
(Prokofiev) (♯ D.UAT 273045)

(A) Short Symphony (Symphony No. 2) 1948
Vienna State Op.—Litschauer ♯ **Van.VRS 434**
(Kupferman: Little Symphony)
☆ A.R.S. Orch.—Dixon ♯ **ARS. 116**
(Ives, McBride, Diamond)

Suite vlc. & pf. 1949
C. Stern & A. Bogin ♯ **SPA. 54**
(Phillips)

SWEELINCK, Jan Pieterszoon
(1562-1621)

KEYBOARD WORKS
(numbers refer to the Seiffert edition, 1943)
COLLECTION OF HARPSICHORD WORKS
Fantasias: No. 1, Chromatica
No. 14, Echo-style
Toccatas: No. 23, A minor
No. 24, A minor
Variations: No. 58, Est-ce Mars
No. 60, Mein junges Leben hat ein' End'
No. 64, Von der Fortuna
No. 65, Balletto del Granduca
H. Elsner ♯ **E. & AmVox.PL 9270**

COLLECTION OF ORGAN WORKS
Toccata No. 29, A minor (Aeolian)[1]
Variations:
No. 60, Mein junges Leben hat ein' End'[2]
No. 63, Under der Linden grüne[3]
No. 65, Balletto del Granduca[4]
E. P. Biggs ♯ **EPhi.ABL 3066**
(Buxtehude, Bach, Purcell) (in ♯ AmC. set SL 219)

Canzon on 'O Mensch, bewein dein Sünde gross'
☆ A. Marchal (in † ♯ HS.AS 11) [MS., Hamburg]

Fantasia No. 16, in echo style org.
☆ F. Peeters (in † ♯ Cpt.MC 20069)

Toccata No. 22, A minor
☆ F. Heitmann (in † ♯ DT.LGX 66037)

Toccata No. 29, A minor
P. Kee ♯ *G.DLP 1053*
(† "Baroque" Organ Music)

VARIATIONS
No. 34, Ach Gott, von Himmel sieh' darein
S. Jeans (org.) † **G.HMS 43**
(Gabrieli) (in ♯ Vic. set LM 6029)

No. 60, Mein junges Leben hat ein' End'
G. v. Royen (hpsi.) in ♯ **LT.DTL 93046**
(Willaert, Vivaldi, Gabrieli, Mozart, Bach)
(♯ Sel.LAG 1019; T.LT 6551)
F. Asma ♯ *Phi.S 06032R*
(Buxtehude) [org. of Old Church, Amsterdam]
A. Wyton in ♯ **ASK. 6**
(Bach, Stanley, etc.)
[org. of Cath. of S. John the Divine, N.Y.]
☆ W. Supper († Baroque Organ Music)
A. Marchal († ♯ HS.AS 11)

VOCAL MUSIC
CHANSONS
Madonna, con quest' occhi
Netherlands Cha. Cho.—de Nobel
in ♯ *Phi.N 00678R*
(† Sacred & Secular Songs from the Renaissance)

Rozette pour un peu d'absence 4 vv. 1612
☆ Dutch Vocal Qtt.—Raugel († ♯ HS.AS 5)

MOTETS
Angelus ad pastores (*Cantiones Sacrae* No. 35)
Trapp Family Singers—Wasner in ♯ **B.LAT 8038**
(Christmas Music, Vol. 2) (♯ AmD.DL 9689: ♭ set ED 1200)

Hodie Christus natus est
St. Paul's Cath. Cho.—Dykes Bower C.**LX 1619**
(Howells: A Spotless Rose)
(in ♯ CX 1193; Angel. 35138 in set 3516)

SYLVA, Johann Elias de (1716-1797)
SEE: † TYROLESE XVIIITH CENT. ORCH. MUSIC

SZABÓ, Ferencz (b. 1902)

Ludas Matyi Suite orch.
Hungarian Radio—Somogyi Qual.**MN 1013/6**
(8ss)

---

[1] Grote or St. Jacobskerk, The Hague.   [2] Old Church, Amsterdam (1726).
[3] Kruiskerk, Amstelveen, Holland.   [4] Grote or St. Pieterskerk, Leiden (1639).

Quartet, Strings, Op. 1   1926
Tátrai Qtt. (4ss)   *Qual.MK 1551/2*

Tunes (unid.)
Hungarian Radio Cho. & Orch.—Lehel
(4ss)   **Qual.MN 1009/10**

SZAMOTULSKI
SEE: Waclaw of Szamotul, *post*

SZARZYNSKI, Stanislaw Sylwester (*c.* 1650-1720)
SEE: † Four Centuries of Polish Music

SZELIGOWSKI, Tadeusz (b. 1896)

Lublin Suite   Cha. orch   1945
Polish Radio—Krenz   **Muza.X 2335/7**
(6ss)

(The) STUDENTS' REVOLT   Opera
(*Bunt Zaków*)
Students' Song   T & cho.   Act III
J. Przado & Cho.
Duet, Anny & Konopni   S & T
M. Sowmski & J. Przado   **Muza.X 2283**
The King's Aria   Bs
E. Kossowski
Konopni's Aria   T
J. Pryada   *Muza. 2235*

PART SONGS
Little Watchmaker
(The) Young Hare
Breslau Radio Cho.—Kajdasz   *Muza. 2299*

Under snowy eaves (ARR. Szeligowsky)
Breslau Radio Cho.—Kajdasz   *Muza. 2183*
(*Szymanowski*)

SONG: The Grey Stone
J. Garda (B), V. Makarov (pf.)   *Muza. 2471*
(*Tchaikovsky: Why?*)

SZYMANOWSKI, Karol (1883-1937)

(La) Berceuse d'Aitacho Enia, Op. 52   vln. & pf.
▽ W. Miemczyk & L. Urstein (*C.DM 1721*)

Étude, B flat minor, Op. 4, No. 3   pf.
▽ L. Muenzer (*C.DM 1775*)
W. Malcuzynski (G.JG 340, Pte)

(The) Fountain of Arethusa, Op. 30, No. 1   vln. & pf.
G. Staples & G. Silfies   **♯ McInt.MM 101**
(*Prokofiev, Sarasate, Debussy, etc.*)
D. Oistrakh & I. Yampolsky   **♯ Mon.MEL 707**
(*Prokofiev, Wieniawski*)   (in ♯ *USSR.D 2163*, d.c.)
I. Oistrakh & I. Kollegorskaya in ♯ **Van.VRS 461**
(*Bach, Mozart, Wieniawsky, Kabalevsky, etc.*)
▽ E. Uminska & Z. Guddat (*Ophn. 141*)

HARNASIE, Op. 55   Ballet   1926
Orchestral Suite
▽ L.S.O.—Sargent (G.JG 342/4, Pte.)

Highland Melody — ARR. VLN. & PF. Kochanski
▽ E. Uminska & Z. Dygat (*Ophn. 143*)

KING ROGER, Op. 46   Opera   3 Acts   1926
Roxane's Song   S
▽ E. Bandrowska-Turska (*Od. 217812*)

— ARR. VLN & PF. Kochanski
▽ E. Uminska & Z. Dygat (*C.DM 1846*)

(20) Mazurkas, Op. 50   pf.
... 2 unspec. ▽ W. Malcuzynski (G.JG 340, Pte)
... No. 13   ▽ K. Szymanowski (*C.DM 1785*)

(2) Mazurkas, Op. 62
No. 1   ▽ K. Szymanowski (*C.DM 1785*)

Métopes, Op. 29   (3 pieces)   pf.
R. Collet (*below*)   **♯ CA.LPA 1030**

Narcissus, Op. 30, No. 2   vln. & pf.
▽ E. Uminska & Z. Dygat (*Ophn. 139*)

Nocturne and Tarantella, Op. 28   vln. & pf.
☆ J. Martzy & J. Antonietti (in ♯ *Pol. 16017*)

Pan and the Dryads, Op. 30, No. 3   vln. & pf.
▽ E. Uminska & Z. Dygat (*Ophn. 142*)

PART SONGS
Play, musicians (from "6 Songs from Kurpie")
Breslau Radio Cho.—Kajdasz   *Muza. 2183*
(*arr. Szeligowski: Under snowy eaves*)

Mad Marten, Op. 58, No. 6 (*Bzicem Kunia*)
Breslau Radio Cho.—Kajdasz (*Muza. 2300*)

(12) Songs from Kurpie, Op. 58 (Skierkowski)
... **The cranes' flight**
▽ A. Szleminska (S) & pf. (*Ophn. 137*)
... **One, unspec.** — ARR. VLN. & PF. Kochanski
▽ I. Dutiska & L. Urstein (*C.DM 1931*)
... **Unspec.** — ARR. VLN. & PF. Kochanski
▽ E. Uminska & Z. Dygat (*Ophn. 143*)

Preludes, Op. 1   pf.
No. 1, B minor — ARR. VLN. & PF.
G. Barinova & pf.   *USSR. 22053*

No. 4, B flat minor
▽ J. Sulikowski (G.JG 441, Pte.)

Romance, D major, Op. 23   vln. & pf.
▽ E. Uminska & Z. Dygat (*Ophn. 138*)

Sonata No. 3, D minor, Op. 36   pf.
R. Collet (*above*)   **♯ CA.LPA 1030**

Sonata, D minor, Op. 9   vln. & pf.   1911
D. Oistrakh & V. Yampolsky   **♯ C.CX 1201**
(*Franck*)   (♯ QCX 10160: FCX 355; Angel. 35163)
D. Oistrakh & V. Yampolsky ♯ **Csm.CRLP 190**
(*Karlowicz*)

SONGS
Zuleika Songs, Op. 13
▽ S. Korwin-Szymanowska (S) (*P. 44163*)

Symphonie Concertante, Op. 60, pf. & orch.   1931-2
A. Rubinstein & Los Angeles Phil.—Wallenstein
                                         ♯ Vic.LM 1744
(*Rachmaninoff*)   (♭ set WDM 1744; ♯ G.FALP 253)

Theme & Variations, B flat major, Op. 3   pf.
☆ W. Malcuzynski (G.JG 339, Pte.; also *Ophn. 129*)

TABOUROT, Jehan   (1519-1595)
(ARBEAU, Thoinot)
SEE: † Chansons historiques
     † Danceries et Ballets
(also: Warlock: Capriol Suite)

TAILLEFERRE, Germaine (b. 1892)

(6) Chansons françaises   1929
... No. 2, Souvent un air de vérité (Voltaire)
No. 4, Vrai Dieu qui m'y confortera (Anon. XVth cent.)
No. 6, Les Trois Présents (Sarasin, XVIIth Cent.)
I. Joachim (S), M. Franck (pf.)
                                         in ♯ *CdM.LDA 8079*
(*Auric, Durey, Honegger, Milhaud, Poulenc*)

Larghetto; Valse lente   pf.
J. Casadesus   **♯ Angel. 35261**
(*R. Casadesus, Rameau, etc.*)

Ouverture   orch.   1935[1]
Paris Ens.—Tzipine   **♯ C.CX 1252**
(*Honegger, Poulenc, Durey*)
                  (♯ FCX 264; Angel. 35117, in set 3515)

[1] Now used as Overture to opéra-bouffe *Il était un petit navire*, 1951.

Sonata harp
N. Zabaleta   in ♯ Eso.ES 523
(† Contemporary Harp Music)

Trio wind insts.
New Art Wind Trio   in ♯ CEd. set 2006
(Auric, Durey, Honegger, etc.)

Valses Nos. 1 & 2 2 pfs.
☆ A. Gold & R. Fizdale (in ♯ Phi.S 06614R)

SEE ALSO: † OLD FRENCH AIRS, for an arrangement by
Tailleferre

TAKTAKISHVILI, Otar (b. 1924)

Concerto, C minor, pf. & orch. 1951
A. Yokheles & USSR. Nat. Phil.—Stassevich
♯ Csm.CRLP 191
(Mendelssohn)   (2ss, ♯ USSR.D 0420/1)

Symphony No. 1, A minor
Moscow Radio—Dimitriadi ♯ USSR.D 02348/9

TALLIS, Thomas (c. 1505-1585)

Natus est nobis virginals (Mulliner Bk. No. 9)
T. Dart (hpsi.)   in ♯ LOL.OL 50075
(† Masters of Early English Keyboard Music)

SACRED VOCAL MUSIC
COLLECTION
HYMNS: Jesu salvator saeculi (Tu fabricator)
Deus tuorum militum (Hic nempe mundi)
Jam Christus astra ascenderat (Solemnis urgebat)
Salvator mundi, Domine (Adesto nunc propitius)
(with alternating plainsong) 6 vv.
O nata lux de lumine[1]
Lamentations, sets I & II 5 vv.
A. Deller Vocal Consort   ♯ Van.BG 551

Adesto nunc propitius[2] 5 vv.
St. Paul's Cath. Cho.—Dykes Bower G.HMS 37
(† History of Music in Sound)   (in ♯ Vic. set LM 6029)

Audivi vocem de coelo Motet 4 vv.
Stanford Univ. Cho.—Schmidt in ♯ ML. 7022
(† Madrigals & Motets)

If ye love me Anthem
All Saints Church Male Cho.—Self
in ♯ CEd.CE 1023
(† Five Centuries of Choral Music)

Salvator mundi, salva nos[1] Motet
Canterbury Cath. Cho.—Knight   C.LB 133
(Redford: Reioice in the Lord alway)
(† English Church Music, Vol. III)

Te Deum laudamus 5 vv.
King's College Chapel Cho.—Ord   C.LX 1563
(† English Church Music, Vol. III)

TANEIEV, Sergei Ivanovitch (1856-1915)

Canzona[3]
M. Rostropovich (vlc.) & pf.   USSR. 019607/8

ORESTEIA Opera 3 Acts 1895
Overture
☆ Bolshoi Theatre—Samosud (♯ USSR.D 244)

Clytemnestra's Aria: O hear my prayer S
S. Preobrazhenshaya   USSRM.D 001206
(Rimsky: Immortal Kashchey, aria)

QUARTET No. 6, B flat major, Op. 19, Strings
Beethoven Qtt.   ♯ USSR.D 1384/6
(3ss—Alabiev: Quintet)

QUARTET, E major, Op. 20, pf. & str.
M. Yudina & Beethoven Trio ♯ USSR.D 01736/7

SONGS
(The) Birth of the Harp, Op. 26, No. 1 (after Moore)
E. Shumskaya (S)   USSR. 16069
(Music)

— ARR. VLN. & PF. A. Hartmann
A. Pratz & G. Gould   ♯ Hall.RS 3
(Berg, Prokofiev, Shostakovich)

How you caress, silvery night, Op. 18, No. 1 (Fet)
duet with orch.
N. Alexandryiskaya (M-S), S. Lemeshev (T)
USSR. 023954
(Glinka: Forgive me, please)

Music, Op. 26, No. 4 (after Maeterlinck)
E. Shumskaya (S)   USSR. 16070
(Birth of the Harp)

O wind from the height, Op. 17, No. 5
(A. K. Tolstoy)
M. Reizen (Bs)   USSR. 20478
(Kalinnikov: Song)
☆ A. Pirogov (B) (USSRM.D 001245)

Serenade, Op. 9, No. 2 (Fet)
Venetian Night, Op. 9, No. 1 (Fet)
A. Orfenov (T)   USSR. 22672/3

Suite de Concert, Op. 28 vln. & orch. 1911
I. Bezrodny & State Sym.—Kondrashin
♯ USSR.D 0361/2
[Prelude & Gavotte only, on USSR. 021535/6 & 21420/1;
Fairy Tale only, on USSRM.D 571]

... **Fairy Tale**, only
I. Bezrodny & S. Wakman (pf.) ♯ Phi.S 06048R
(Glazounov, Prokofiev, Rachmaninoff)

... **Gavotte**, only
L. Kogan & USSR. Sym.   USSR. 21420/1

Symphony No. 1, C minor, Op. 12 1901
Moscow Radio—Gauk (2ss)   ♯ Sup.LPV 181
(♯ U. 5145G)
(Rimsky-Korsakov on ♯ A440.AC 1208; 3ss—Oresteia
Overture, on ♯ USSR.D 241/3)

Trio, D major, Op. 22 pf., vln., vlc.
L. Oborin, D. Oistrakh, S. Knushevitzky
♯ USSR.D 10458/9

TANSMAN, Alexander (b. 1897)

Cavatina, Suite guitar 1951
1. Preludio; 2. Sarabande; 3. Scherzino; 4. Barcarola;
5. Danza pomposo
A. Segovia   in ♯ B.AXTL 1070
(† Segovia Evening) (♯ SpC.CCL 35015; AmD.DL 9733;
AFest.CFR 10-729)

Scherzo (from Film Flesh and Fantasy) 1945
☆ Janssen Sym. (in ♯ Cam.CAL 205: ♭ CAE 266)

TARP, Svend Erik (b. 1908)

Duo, fl. & vla., Op. 37
J. Bentzon & J. Koppel   C.LDX 15

TÁRREGA EIXEA, Francisco (1854-1909)

GUITAR PIECES
COLLECTION
Estudios: Brillante
Tremolo (Recuerdos de la Alhambra)
Mazurkas: Marieta
G major
Adelita
Preludes, Nos. 2 & 5
Gavotte: Maria
Capricho arabe
A. Segovia (Sor)   ♯ AmD.DL 9794

---

[1] From Cantiones Sacrae, 1575   [2] From Hymn Salvator mundi, Domine, see collection above.
[3] Perhaps arr. of Song "Canzone XXXII", Op. 26, No. 2.

Alborada
N. Yepes　　　　　in ♯ **D.LXT 2974**
(† Spanish Music)　　　(♯ FST 153076; Lon.LL 1042)

Canción de Cuna
Pavana, E major
S. Pastor　　　　　in ♯ **NRI.NRLP 5005**
(*Visée, Fortea, Pastor, Sor*)

Capricho árabe (*Serenata*)
L. Almeida　　　　in ♯ **DCap.CTL 7089**
(† Guitar Music of Spain)　　　(♯ Cap.P 8295)
M. D. Cano　　　　　　　　　*Dur.AI 10152*
(*Albeniz: Pavana capricho*)
(*Granados: Danza No. 5*, on ♭ *Dur.AI 6022*)

Danza mora; Minueto
☆ A. Segovia (in ♯ *D.UMT 273029*)

ESTUDIOS (Studies)
Tremolo (*Recuerdos de la Alhambra*)
L. Almeida　　　　in ♯ **DCap.CTL 7089**
(† Guitar Music of Spain)　　　(♯ Cap.P 8295)
N. Yepes　　　　　in ♯ **D.LXT 2974**
(† Spanish Music)　　　(♯ FST 153076; Lon.LL 1042)
U. Neumann　　　　　　　　*Od.DK 1168*
(*Mozart: Symphony 39—Minuet*)
L. Walker　　　　　in ♯ **Phi.N 00626R**
(♯ Epic.LC 3055)
M. L. Anido　　　　　　　　*ArgOd. 66063*
(*Arr. Llobet: 2 Catalan Folk Songs*)
A. Malukoff　　　　　　　　♯ *Rom.RR 7*
(*Guiliani & Sor*)
M. D. Cano　　　　　　　　*Dur.AI 10153*
(*Cano: Lamentos de Andalucía*)　　(in ♯ *AI 506*)
L. Maravilla (in **V**♯ *Sel.LPP 8602*)

(2) **Mazurkas** (Marieta; Adelita)
☆ V. Gomez (in ♭ *AmD.* set *ED 809*)

Mazurka (unspec.)
Prelude No. 5, E major
C. Santias　　　　　in ♯ **FestF.FLD 32**
(♯ SpFest.HF 3201)

Sueño
M. L. Anido　　　　　　　　*ArgOd. 66035*
(*Alfonso il Sabio, & Mozart*)(♭ *BSOA 4011:*
BSOAE 4516: in ♯ *LDC 521*)

TARTINI, Guiseppe (1692-1770)

Concerto Grosso, F major ("No. 58")[1]
Naples Scarlatti Orch.—Caracciolo ♯ **C.CX 1277**
(*Cimarosa & Lully*)　　　(♯ Angel. 35255)
(*Cimarosa & Vivaldi*, on ♯ *C.QCX 10138*)

CONCERTOS, vln. & orch. [Dounias nos.]
A minor (Capri No. 76) [115]
F major (ed. Ross) [67]
W. Schneiderhan & Vienna Orch.—Adler
♯ **SPA. 46**

D major (Capri No. 79) [15] (ed. Abbado)
M. Abbado & Milan Str.—Abbado ♯ **C.FCX 368**
(*Vivaldi & Corelli*)

D minor (Capri No. 61) [45]
J. Szigeti & Col. Sym.—Szell[2] ♯ **EPhi.ABL 3058**
(*Sonata, G major; & Bach, Handel*)
(♯ AmC.ML 4891; Phi.A 01140L)

E major (Capri No. 84) [53]
☆ L. Ferro & Virtuosi di Roma (♯ *D.UAT 273091;*
Fnt.LP 1006)

G minor (Capri No. 6) [86]
M. Rostal & Winterthur Sym.—Goehr
♯ **CHS.CHS 1174**
(*Bach & Biber*)　　　　　(♯ Clc. 6187)

CONCERTO, A major, vlc. & str. orch.
(Capri No. 87) (ed. Ravanello)
E. Altobelli & I Musici Ens.　♯ **C.CX 1192**
(*B. Marcello, Rossini, Galuppi*) (♯ QCX 10037:
FCX 303; Angel. 35086)

SONATAS, vln. & cont.
A minor　　　　　B minor[3]
D major　　　　　G minor, Op. 3, No. 7 (▽)
☆ P. Rybar & F. Holetschek (hpsi.)　♯ **Nix.WLP 5141**
A major, Op. 1, No. 13 pub. Amsterdam, 1734
— ARR. VLN. & STR. ORCH. Respighi "*Pastorale*"
M. Abbado & Milan Str.—Abbado ♯ **C.FCX 369**
(*Cambini, Bonporti, Vivaldi*)
B flat major, Op. 5, No. 3—SEE below
G major, Op. 3, No. 12
J. Szigeti & C. Bussotti (pf.)　♯ **EPhi.ABL 3058**
(*Concerto; Bach & Handel*)(♯ AmC.ML 4891; Phi.A01140L)
... **Adagio** — ARR. VLC. & PF.
D. Shafran & pf. (*USSRM.D 364 & D 001216*)[4]
G minor, Op. 1, No. 10 (Didone abbandonata)
A. Campoli & G. Malcolm (pf.)[5] ♯ **D.LX 3137**
(*below*)
F. Zepparoni & R. Veyron-Lacroix (hpsi.)
†♯ **AS. 3008LD**
(*Corelli & Veracini*)　　　(♯ HS.AS 40)
G minor, Op. 7, No. 5 ... **Andante**
B flat major, Op. 5, No. 3 ... **Presto**
— ARR. VLN. & PF. Bridgewater[6]
I. Haendel & G. Moore　　♭ *G. 7EP 7011*
(*Bloch: Baal Shem—Nigun*) (in ♯ CLP 1021: ♭ 7EPQ 525)
... **Presto**, only
N. Carol & J. Levine　　　in ♯ **BB.LBC 1155**
G minor "Il trillo del diavolo"
R. Odnoposoff & H. Wehrle (hpsi.)
♯ **CHS.CHS 1170**
(*Geminiani & Vitali*)
A. Campoli & G. Malcolm (pf.)[7] ♯ **D.LX 3137**
(*above*)
Y. Menuhin & G. Moore (pf.)[8] ♯ **Vic.LM 1742**
(*Bartók, Ravel, etc.*)　　　(♭ set *WDM 1742*)
☆ D. Oistrakh & V. Yampolsky (pf.) **V**♯ *CdM.LDY 8068*
(*Beethoven & Schubert* on ♯ *Per.SPL 573*)
(2ss, ♯ *USSRM.D 508/9*)
(*Brahms: Sonata No. 3*, on ♯ *Csm.CRLP 148, ? d.v.*)
☆ E. & A. Wolf (♭ *Mer.EP 1-5039*)
A. Spalding & A. Kooiker (♯ *Cum.CR 281*)

Sonata a quattro, A major[9] strs. & cont.
London Baroque Orch.—Haas　　**P.R 20621**
[L. Salter, hpsi.]　　　　(in ♯ *AmD.DL 4081*)

TAVARES, Hekel (b. 1896).

Andre de Leae and the Red-haired Demon orch.
▽ Orch.—Tavares (BrzOd. set, 6ss, n.d.)

Anhangüera, Op. 11, No. 7
Sym. Poem. Bs, cho., orch.
J. Bailly, Petropolis Boys' & Monks' Choirs
& Brazilian Concert—Tavares　♯ **Radio**
[in *Latin & Arití*]　　　　(no number)

Concerto in Brazilian forms, Op. 105, No. 2
pf. & orch.
F. Blumenthal & L.S.O.—Fistoulari
♯ **D.LXT 2975**
(*Paderewski*)　　　　(♯ Lon.LL 1104)

FOLK SONG SETTINGS
Bahia
Dansa de Caboclo
Benedicto Pretinho
Bia-ta-tá (*Côco*)
E. Houston (S), P. Miguel (pf.) in ♯ **Vic.LCT 1143**
(*Villa-Lobos, Ovalle, etc.*)(♭ set *ERBT 4;* ▽ in set M 798)
... **Dansa de Caboclo**, only
S. Gloria (S), A. Chanaka (pf.) in ♯ **Vic.LM 1737**
(in ♯ *FV.A 530202*)
▽ O. Coelho (S) & self-acc. guitar (*P.RO 20599*)

---

[1] No. 1 of *Due Concerti con strumenti a fiato*, Capri p. 539.
[2] Cadenza by Szigeti.　　　[3] Padua, No. 14.
[4] One of these is listed as *Adagio*, the other as *Adagio cantabile*; it is possible that one is an (unspec.) different piece.
[5] Contains interpolated *Largo*.　　　[6] Information as to source supplied by Mr. Bridgewater.
[7] Cadenza by Campoli.　　　[8] Also announced as acc. A. Baller (Japanese recording ☆).
[9] Capri, p. 538; ed. Pente; labelled *Sinfonia*.

TAVERNER, John (c. 1495-1545)

SEE: † ANTHOLOGIE SONORE (♯ HS.AS 10)
     † ENGLISH CHURCH MUSIC, VOL. IV
     † HISTORY OF MUSIC IN SOUND (30)

TAYLOR, Joseph Deems (b. 1885)

CASANOVA 1937
Inc. Music to play by De Azertís
Ballet Music
Hamburg Philharmonia—Korn   in ♯ Allo. 3150
(Stringfield, Chadwick, Parker, etc.)

(The) KING'S HENCHMAN Opera 3 Acts 1927
Nay, Maccus, lay him down   Act III   B
☆ L. Tibbett (in ♯ Cam.CAL 171)

Through the Looking Glass, Op. 12
(orig. Cha. orch. 1919-21)
Suite orch.   1922
1a. Dedication;   1b. The Garden of live flowers
2. Jabberwocky   3. Looking glass insects
4. The White Knight
Eastman-Rochester Sym.—Hanson
                                   ♯ EMer.MG 40008

(The) Portrait of a Lady, Op. 14   Rhapsody
Str., wind, & pf.   1917, rev. 1924
A.R.S. Sym.—Hendl   ♯ ARS. 23
(Creston)

SONGS
Captain Stratton's Fancy   (Masefield)
▽ R. Symonette (B) (in ♯ Csm.CLPS 1008)

(A) Song for lovers, Op. 13, No. 2   (Stephens)
K. Flagstad (S), E. McArthur (pf.)
                                   in ♯ G.ALP 1309
(Schubert, Brahms, R. Strauss, etc.)   (♭ Vic.LM 1870)

TCHAIKOVSKY, Peter Ilich (1840-1893)

CLASSIFIED: I. INSTRUMENTAL
              A. Piano   B. Chamber   C. Orchestral
              II. VOCAL
              A. Opera   B. Songs   C. Choral

I. INSTRUMENTAL

A. PIANO

CHANTS SANS PAROLES
A minor, Op. 40, No. 6   See 12 Pieces, below
F major, Op. 2, No. 3   See Souvenir de Hapsal, below

CHILDREN'S ALBUM, Op. 39   1877
COMPLETE RECORDINGS
M. Pressler   ♯ MGM.E 3204
(Mendelssohn)
A. Dorfmann   ♯ Vic.LM 1856
(The Months; & Schumann)   (♭ set ERB 57)
P. Zeitlin   ♯ Opus. 6001
[to accompany Matching Music Book, pub. Marks, N.Y.]

No. 18, Neapolitan Song   — ARR. VLN. & PF.   Burmester
E. Morini & L. Pommers (in ♯ West.WN 18087)

No. 24, In the Church   — ARR. MALE CHO. Jaroff
☆ Don Cossack Cho.—Jaroff (in ♯ Phi.S 006611R)

Dumka, Op. 59, No. 1
☆ L. Oborin (in ♯ CdM.LDA 8076; USSRM.D 181;
                                 & ♯ Csm.CRLP 220)

Humoresque, G major, Op. 10, No. 2
N. Reisenberg   ♯ Nix.WLP 5330
(below)   (♯ West.WL 5330)
S. Fiorentino   V♯ CA.MPO 5033
(Chanson triste & The Months, excpts.)

— ARR. ORCH.   Stokowski, et al.
Orch.—Stokowski   ♭ Vic.ERA 182
(Song, Again as before . . . ; & Rachmaninoff)
(& in ♯ Vic.LM 1774; ♯ ItV.A12R 0008;
                                 FV.A 630264: ♭ A 95217)
Sym.—Rybicka (Muza. 1634)
☆ Hollywood Bowl—Stokowski (in ♯ Cam.CAL 153)

— ARR. VLN. & PF.   ☆ F. Kreisler (in ♯ Vic.LCT 1142)

— ARR. FL., OB., CL., HRN., BSN.
Chicago Sym. Woodwind Quintet (in ♯ Aphe.AP 17)

Impromptu - Capriccio, G major No Op. No.   1884
T. Nikolayeva   USSR. 20170
(Rachmaninoff: Moment musical No. 4)

Mazurka de salon, D minor, Op. 9, No. 3
— ARR. VLN. & PF.   ("Valse créole")
I. Leth & V. Borggaard   Tono.K 8099
(Mortensen: Humoresque)

Mazurka (unspec.)   M. v. Doren (in ♯ Chan.MVDP 1)

(The) MONTHS, Op. 37a
COMPLETE RECORDING
E. Wollmann   ♯ Nix.WLP 5290
                              (♯ West.WL 5290)
☆ L. Oborin   (Dumka)   ♯ Csm.CRLP 220
[Nos. 6, 11, 12 also on USSRM.D 00460/1]

— ARR. PF. & ORCH.   Gould
☆ M. Gould & orch. (♭ AmC. set A 1025)

... Nos. 4, 6, 10, 11, 12
A. Dorfmann   ♯ Vic.LM 1856
(Children's Album; & Schumann)

... Nos. 4, 6, 8, 12:   H. Osieck   ♭ Phi.N 402025E
... Nos. 6, 11   S. Fiorentino   (below)   V♯ CA.MPO 5033
... No. 3, The Song of the Lark
M. v. Doren   in ♯ Chan.MVDP 1
— — ARR. ORCH.
Film Sym.—Neumann   (No. 11)   U.C 24380
... No. 6, Barcarolle
— — ARR. ORCH.:   Sym.—Rybicka (Muza. 1634)
Westminster Light—Bridgewater (in ♯ West.WL 4009;
                                 ♭ AFest.XP 45-455)
☆ Robin Hood Dell—Kostelanetz (in ♯ AmC.CL 730)
— — ARR. ORGAN.   J. Crawford (in ♯ B.LAT 8039;
                                 ♭ AmD.ED 2129)
... No. 10, Autumn Song
— — ARR. VLN. & ORCH.
J. Fuchs & Camarata Orch. (in ♯ B.AXL 2010;
                                 AmD.DL 4082)
— — ARR. ORCH.
Bolshoi Theatre—L. Steinberg (in ♯ Csm.CRLP 157;
                                 also USSR. 010279)
☆ Orch.—Kostelanetz (in ♭ AmC. set A 1041)
... No. 11, Troïka en traîneaux
M. v. Doren   in ♯ Chan.MVDP 1
— — ARR. ORCH.
Film Sym.—Neumann   (No. 3)   U.C 24380

Nocturne, B flat major, Op. 10, No. 1
N. Reisenberg   ♯ Nix.WLP 5330
(above & below)   (♯ West.WL 5330)

(6) Pieces, Op. 19   1873
... No. 2, Scherzo humoristique
No. 4, Nocturne, C sharp minor
No. 5, Capriccioso
E. Gilels   ♯ CHS.CHS 1311
(Glazounov & Prokofiev)
(Concerto No. 2, on ♯ Csm.CRLP 222)

... No. 4, Nocturne, C sharp minor
E. Gilels   in ♯ CdM.LDA 8104
— — ARR. ORGAN: J. Crawford (in ♯ B.LAT 8039;
                                 ♭ AmD.ED 2129)

(12) PIECES, Op. 40
1. Étude   7. In the village
2. Chanson triste   8. Valse, A flat major
3. Funeral March   9. Valse II, F sharp minor
4. Mazurka, C major   10. Russian Dance
5. Mazurka II, D major 11. Scherzo
6. Chant sans paroles 12. Rêverie interrompue
N. Reisenberg   ♯ West.WN 18005[1]
... No. 2, Chanson triste
S. Fiorentino   V♯ CA.MPO 5033
(Humoresque, etc.)
— — ARR. ORCH.
Bavarian Sym.—Graunke   ♭ Pol. 32110
(Chant sans paroles)
☆ Boston Prom.—Fiedler (in ♯ Cam.CAL 142: ♭ CAE 134)

---

[1] Announced, but not issued, as WL 5330, with Pf. Sonata, Op. 37.

— — ARR. VLC. & PF.   ☆ S. Popoff (in ♯ *Vien.LPR 1022*)
— — ARR. ORGAN   J. Crawford (in ♯ B.LAT 8039, etc.)
... No. 9   — ARR. HARP: O. Erdeli (in ♯ *USSR.D 1213*)
... No. 10   — ARR. VLN. & PF.
M. Elman & J. Seiger (in ♯ Vic.LM 1740: ♭ *set WDM 1740;*
                                   ♯ *FV.A 630277*)
G. Barinova & A. Dedyukin (*USSRM.D 439*)
— ARR. ORCH. Schmidt, *et al.*
Philharmonia—Kurtz (in ♯ G.ALP 1301)
Westminster Light—Bridgewater (in ♯ West.WL 4009;
                                   ♭ *AFest.XP 45-455*)
... No. 12   — ARR. ORGAN
J. Crawford (in ♯ B.LAT 8039, etc.)

(6) Pieces on a single theme, Op. 21
... No. 1, Prelude & No. 3, Impromptu
L. Oborin   *USSR. 20055/6*

(18) Pieces, Op. 72
... No. 3, Gentle reproaches; No. 16, Valse à 5/8
M. Fedorova   *USSR. 20172/3*
Polka, unspec.: M. v. Doren (in ♯ Chan.MVDP 1)

Romance, F minor, Op. 5
N. Reisenberg   ♯ **Nix.WLP 5330**
(*above & below*)   (♯ West.WL 5330)
P. Serebriakov   ♯ **Eta.LPM 1013**
(*below; Chopin & Rachmaninoff*)
— ARR. VLC. & PF.
A. Vlasov & pf.   in ♯ *USSR.D 1179*
(*Orch. Suite No. 1, excpt.; & Ravel, Debussy*)
— ARR. ORGAN   J. Crawford (in ♯ B.LAT 8039;
                                   ♭ *AmD.ED 2129*)

(50) Russian Folksongs — ARR. PF. DUET   1868-9
— FOR PRACTICE: One pf. missing (♯ CEd.MMO 401)
SONATA, G major, Op. 37   1878
N. Reisenberg   ♯ **Nix.WLP 5330**
(*above & below*)   (♯ West.WL 5330)

SOUVENIR DE HAPSAL, Op. 2
1. The Castle ruins   1867
2. Scherzo   1865
3. Chant sans paroles, F major   1867
N. Reisenberg   ♯ **Nix.WLP 5330**
(*above*)   (♯ West.WL 5330)
... No. 3, Chant sans paroles, F major
E. Gilels   *USSR. 18101*
(*Suite No. 2, s 13*)
V. Schiøler   *G.DA 5282*
(*Shostakovich: Age of Gold, Polka*) (♭ *7RK 2: 7EBK 1001*)
— — ARR. VLN. & PF.
M. Elman & J. Seiger (in ♯ Vic.LM 1740: ♭ *set WDM 1740;*
                                   ♯ *FV.A 630277*)
E. Morini & L. Pommers (in ♯ West.WN 18077)
B. & G. Goldstein (USSR. 05834)
— — ARR. VLN & ORCH.
J. Fuchs & Camarata Orch. (in ♯ *B.AXL 2010;*
                                   AmD.DL 4082)
J. Corigliano & Decca Sym.—Mendoza (in ♯*D.US 223524;*
                                   AmD.DL 5211; ▽ in *set A 90*)
— — ARR. ORCH.
Bavarian Sym.—Graunke (♭ *Pol. 32110*)
N.W. Ger. Phil—Schüchter (in ♯ *Imp.ILP 114;*
                                   G.QDLP 6026)
A. Bernard Orch. (♭ *Pat.G 1025*)
Anon. Orch. (in ♯ Ply. 12-128)
— — ARR. ORGAN   J. Crawford (in ♯ B.LAT 8039, etc.)

WALTZES
A flat major, Op. 51, No. 1   (*Valse de salon*)
E. Bernáthová   ♯ *Sup.LPM 223*
(*Miaskovsky & Balakirev*)   (♯ *U. 5199C*)
F sharp minor (Nata Valse), Op. 51, No. 4
— ARR. HARP
O. Erdeli (*USSR. 22730*)
F minor (Valse sentimentale), Op. 51, No. 6
P. Serebriakov   in ♯ **Eta.LPM 1013**
(*Chopin & Rachmaninoff*)
— ARR. VLN. & PF.   Grunes
I. Stern & A. Zakin (in ♯ *AmC.AL 23; Phi.S 06617R*)
M. Elman & J. Seiger (in ♯ Vic.LM 1740;
                       ♭ *set WDM 1740;* ♭ ERA 97)
A. Scholz & pf. (ArgOd. 66030)
☆ H. Szeryng & pf. (in ♯ *Pac.LDPC 50:* ♭ EP 90019)

— ARR. VLC. & PF.
M. Rostropovich & pf.[1]
                       (*USSR. 23773 & USSRM.D 00208*)
☆ G. Piatigorsky (♭ Vic.ERA 122; in ♯ ItV.A12R 0105)
G. Cassadó (in ♯ Rem. 199-128)

I. B. CHAMBER MUSIC

QUARTETS, String
No. 1, D major, Op. 11
Hungarian Qtt.   ♯ **CHS.CHS 1183**
(*Glazounov*)
Hollywood Qtt.   ♯ **DCap.CTL 7031**
(*Borodin: Qtt. No. 2*)   (♯ Cap.P 8187; ACap.CLCX 022)
[*Andante cantabile* only on ♭ *Cap.FAP 8217;* 3rd movt.,
abridged, on ♯ Cap.SAL 9020]
☆ Oistrakh Qtt. (*USSRM.D 295/8; with Serenade, Op. 48*
on ♯ Csm.CRLP 10190; 2nd movt.,
                                   on ♯ *USSR.D 1054*)
Beethoven Qtt. (♯ Sup.LPV 180; ♯ U. 5151G)
... 2nd movt., **Andante cantabile**, only
Wagner Assoc. Qtt.   ♭ *ArgOd.BSOAE 4501*
(*Gianneo: Criolla*)
Bartels Ens.   *MSB. 78019*
(*Boccherini: Quintet, E major—Minuet*)
American Art Qtt.   in ♯ **BB.LBC 1086**
— — STR. ORCH. VERSION
L.S.O.—Weldon   **C.DX 1900**
(*Sleeping Beauty—Waltz; & Mascagni,*
                       on ♭ *SED 5518: SEDQ 543*)
Philadelphia—Ormandy   ♭ *EPhi.NBE 11011*
(*Sibelius: Finlandia*) (♭ Phi.N 409011E; AmC.A 1828:
                       in ♯ CL 707, o.n. ML 4856)
Boyd Neel Orch.—Dumont   ♭ *Phi.N 402029E*
(*Bach & Haydn*)
Danish Radio—Malko   **G.DB 10519**
Hollywood Bowl—Barnett   in ♯ **Cap.P 8296**
(*Liszt, Saint-Saëns, etc.*)   (♭ *FAP 8296*)
☆ Minneapolis Sym.—Ormandy (in ♯ Cam.CAL 121:
                                   ♭ *CAE 161*)
Robin Hood Dell—Kostelanetz (in ♯ AmC.CL 730)
Stadium Concerts—Smallens (♯ D.UW 333002)
Salzburg Festival—Weidlich (♭ Rem.REP 70;
                                   in ♯ Ply. 12-76)
Royale Orch. (♭ Roy.EP 102)
— ARR. VLN. & PF.   Kreisler
M. Elman & J. Seiger (in ♯ Vic.LM 1740:
                       in ♭ *set WDM 1740;* ♯ *FV.A 630277*)
☆ W. Primrose (♭ *Cam.CAE 244*)
— ARR. ORGAN   J. Crawford (in ♯ B.LAT 8039, etc.)
R. Ellsasser (in ♯ MGM.E 3127)

No. 2, F major, Op. 22
Komitas (Armenian) Qtt.   ♯ **C.CX 1279**
(also, o.v., ♯ Eta.LPM 1022)   (♯ Angel. 35238)
Bolshoi Theatre Qtt.   ♯ *USSR.D 1314/5*
No. 3, E flat minor, Op. 30
R. Burgin, L. Panasevich, J. de Pasquale &
S. Mayes   ♯ **Bo.B 206**
Pascal Qtt.   ♯ **CHS.H 10**
Leningrad Phil. Qtt.   ♯ **USSR.D 01464/5**
SEXTET, D minor, Op. 70   2 vlns., 2 vlas., 2 vlcs.
                       (Souvenir of Florence)
A. Winograd Str. Ens[2]   ♯ **MGM.E 3173**
☆ Vienna State Op. Strings—Swoboda   ♯ **Nix.WLP 5083**
Souvenir d'un lieu cher, Op. 42   vln. & pf.
1. Meditation   2. Scherzo   3. Melody
— ARR. VLN. & ORCH.
G. Barinova & Moscow Radio—Anosov
                                   USSRM.D 1390/1
[No. 2 also USSR. 022322; No. 3 also USSR. 022323 &
USSRM.D 00444]
... **No. 1, Meditation**
D. Oistrakh & N. Walter (n.v.) ♯ **Eta.LPM 1023**
(*Prokofiev, Leclair, Kodály*)
D. Oistrakh & V. Yampolsky[3] in ♯ **JpV.LS 2025**
(also o.v. ☆, in ♯ Van.VRS 6020; Csm.CRLP 10010;
                                   USSRM.D 393)
... **No. 2, Scherzo**
M. Elman & J. Seiger   in ♯ **Vic.LM 1740**
                       (♭ *set WDM 1740;* ♯ *FV.A 630277*)
                       (*continued on next page*)

---

[1] The same Nos. also attributed to D. Shafran.
[2] edited Winograd.   [3] Tokyo recording, 1955.

Souvenir d'un lieu cher, Op. 42 (*continued*)

... No. 3, Melody, E flat major
  D. Oistrakh & pf.   **USSR. 5876**
  (*Brahms: Hungarian Dance No. 1*)
—— ARR. VLN. & ORCH.
  J. Fuchs & Camarata Orch. (in ♯ *B.AXL 2010;*
                         AmD.DL 4082)
—— ARR. ORCH.
  Westminster Light—Bridgewater (in ♯ West.WL 4009;
                   ♭ *AFest.XP 45-455*)
  ☆ Robin Hood Dell—Kostelanetz (in ♯ AmC.CL 730)

TRIO, A minor, Op. 50 pf., vln., vlc.
  E. Gilels, L. Kogan & M. Rostropovich
                       ♯ Mon.MWL 332
  (♯ CdM.LDX 8040; USSR.D 0289/90;
            Beethoven on ♯ A 440.AC 1202)
  Budapest Trio   **♯ Pol. 18067**
  ☆ A. Rubinstein, J. Heifetz & G. Piatigorsky
          (♯ *DV.L 16212; G.FALP/QALP 166*)

Valse-Scherzo, Op. 34 vln. & pf. or orch.
  M. Vaiman & Karandazhova ♯ **LI.TW 91068**
  (*Sérénade mélancolique; Borodin, Prokofiev, etc.*)
  (*Sérénade & Prokofiev only in ♯ Lon.LD 9154*)
  L. Kogan & USSR. Radio—Gauk
  (*Vln. Concerto*)   **♯ Kings.KL 241**
  ☆ D. Oistrakh & V. Yampolsky (♯ *CdM.LDA 8075;*
    Van.VRS 6020; Csm.CRLP 149; also *USSRM.D 394*
                   & *USSR. 9881/2*)

I. C. ORCHESTRAL
(including Ballet)

BALLETS

Aurora's Wedding—Sleeping Beauty Excerpts, *q.v.*

(The) NUTCRACKER, Op. 71
COMPLETE RECORDINGS of the Original Ballet
Overture
1. Lighting of the Christmas Tree
2. March
3. Children's Galop & Dance of the Parents
4. Dance Scene: Presents for the Children
5. Scene & Grandfather's Dance
6. Scene: Departure of Guests; Bedtime; Magic Spell begins
7. Scene: Battle & Transformation of Nutcracker
8. Scene: Journey through the snow [with Cho., offstage]
9. Waltz of the snowflakes
10. Scene: The Magic Castle
11. Scene: Festival
12. Divertissement: (a) Chocolate (Spanish dance)
              (b) Coffee (Arabian dance)
              (c) Tea (Chinese dance)
              (d) Trepak (Russian dance)
              (e) Danse des Mirlitons
              (f) Mère Gigogne & the Clowns
13. Waltz of the flowers
14. (a) Pas de deux
    (b) Prince Charming's Solo
    (c) Dance of the Sugar-Plum Fairy
    (d) Coda
15. Waltz finale & Apotheosis
  Minnesota Univ. Cha. Singers & Minneapolis
    Sym.—Dorati (4ss)   **♯ EMer.OL 2-101**
                (♯ FMer.MLP 7511/2)
  Berlin Radio Cho. & Sym.—Dobrindt
                  ♯ Ura. set 237
  (4ss)   (& ♯ Ura. 7178/9)

VARIOUS EXCERPTS
... Nos. 14 (a-d) with 15 ... Waltz only, interpolated
  Concerts Colonne—Stirn   ♯ **LT.DTL 93019**
  (*Sleeping Beauty, Swan Lake; & Minkus*) (♯ *Sel. 270.C.005*)
... Nos. 8, 9, 12 (a), 14, 15
  ☆ Boston Prom.—Fiedler (♯ G.FFLP 1001: QCLP 12002)
... Nos. 2, 12 (c), 13, 14 (a), 15
  Leningrad Phil.—Mravinsky   *USSRM.D 00512/5*
  [No. 13 also *USSRM.D 00197,* d.c.; this & No. 2 are ☆]
... Nos. 2, 12 (b), 12 (e), 13, 14 (c)
  Leningrad Phil.—Mravinsky
            USSR. 20423/4, 20370/1,20421/2
... Nos. 12 (b), 12 (c), 14 (c), 15
  Bolshoi Theatre—Fayer *USSR. 9218/9 & 14844/5*
... Nos. 9, 12 (a), 14 (c)
  Westminster Light—Bridgewater in ♯ West.WL 4009
  [No. 12a, also in ♭ *AFest.XP 45-455*]
... No. 14—*See* Suite, Op. 71a (Markevitch)
... No. 15: Orch.—Kostelanetz (in ♯ AmC.CL 747)
... Nos. 8, 14 — ARR. 4 PFS.: Manhattan Qtt.
                 (in ♯ MGM.E 3130)

ORCHESTRAL SUITE, OP. 71A
      [Nos. in brackets refer to Op. 71]
1. Ouverture miniature
2. Danses caractéristiques
  (a) March [2]   (b) Dance of the Sugar-plum
  (c) Danse russe, Trepak   fairy [14 (c)]
      [12 (d)]   (d) Danse arabe [12 (b)]
  (e) Danse chinoise [12(c)] (f) Danse des mirlitons
                      [12 (e)]
3. Valse des fleurs [13]
  Philharmonia—Karajan   **♯ C.CX 1033**
  (*Handel*) (♯ VCX 528: FCX/QCX 164; Angel. 35004)
  [Nos. 1, 2 (a, b) also C.LX 1599: ♭ SCB 116;
                 No. 3, C.LX 1602]
  N.B.C. Sym.—Toscanini   **♯ Vic.LRY 9000**
  (*Rossini & Waldteufel*)(♭ set WRY 9000; ♯ ItV.A12R 0009)
  (*Bizet & Ponchielli on ♯ G.FALP 220*)
            (*Ravel & Weber,* ♯ ItV.A12R 0150)
  Philadelphia—Ormandy (n.v.) **♯ AmC.ML 4729**
  (*Sleeping Beauty*)   (♭ set A 1059)
  Vienna Sym.—Moralt   **♯ EPhi.NBL 5005**
  (*Sleeping Beauty*)   (♯ Phi.A 00210L; Epic.LC 3078)
  (& 2ss, ♯ Phi.S 06050R; No. 3 only, ♭ Phi.N 402016E)
  Bolshoi Theatre—Fayer   **♯ Csm.CRLP 10080**
  (*Glier*) [parts probably ☆]
  N.B.C. Sym. (*Berlioz & Wagner*) (Pte.)   **♯ SFA.1**
  ☆ Philharmonia—Markevitch[1]   **♯ G.FALP 315**
  (*Prokofiev*)
  [Nos. 2 (b, c, d, f) & 3 only on ♭ BB.ERAB 3]
  ☆ Philharmonia—Malko   **♯ G.CLP 1060**
  (*Prokofiev*)
  ☆ Sym.—Stokowski   **♯ G.ALP 1193**
  (*Schubert: Rosamunde*) (*Debussy,* on ♯ Vic.LM 9023)
  [No. 3 only, in ♯ G.ALP 1133: FALP 277: ♭ 7ER 5016:
    DB 21547; No. 2 (c, d, f), ♭ Vic.ERA 247; Nos. 1,
    2 (a, b), 3 only, ♭ G.7ERF 108: 7ERQ 102:
                     ♭ DV. 26028]
  Sym.—Graunke (♯ MTW. 16, & 116, d.c.)
  Hamburg Philharmonia—H-J. Walther
            (MSB. 78033/5 & ♯ MGM.E 3139)
  International Sym.—Schneiderhahn (♯ Mae.OAT 25005;
          Nos. 2 (a, c) also in ♯ OA 20007)
  Berlin Sym.—List (♯ Allo. 3064)
  Concert—Everett (♯ Roy. 1421)
  Anon. Orchs. (♯ ACC.MP 102, ♯ Gram. 2007, etc.)
  ☆ Paris Cons.—Fistoulari (2ss, ♯ D.LW 5110;
                      Lon.LD 9130)
  Orch.—Kostelanetz (♯ AmC.CL 730)
  Munich Phil.—Lehmann (♯ Pol. 19028;
          Nos. 1, 2 (a) & 3 also, ♭ 30003)
  Covent Garden Op.—Irving (♯ Od.MOAQ 302, d.c.;
    Nos. 1, 2 (a) & 3 only, ♭ ArgOd.BSOAE 7502)
  Sym.—Désormière (♯ ACap.CLCX 006; T.LCS 8141;
    Nos. 2 (b, c, e, f) & 3 on ♭ Cap.FAP 8202)
  Philadelphia—Ormandy (o.v.) (♭ Vic. set ERB 8)
  Philadelphia—Stokowski (♯ Cam.CAL 100 &
    in set CFL 102; Nos. 2 (c, d, e, f) & 3 also
             on ♯ Cam.CAE 187)
  Vienna Sym.—Wöss (♯ Ply. 12-56; Cum.TCR 255;
    AFest.CFR 25; Msq. 10003; sundry excerpts
    in ♯ Ply. 12-76, 79, 89; Rem. 199-120: ♭ REP 3, etc.)
  Homburg Sym.—Schubert (♯ Esq. 15-003; Clc. 6185;
                Mtr.BLP 17, etc.)

WITH NARRATION
  D. Taylor & Minneapolis—Dorati
                 ♯ Mer.MG 50055
  (*Britten*) [from complete recording]
  S. Spaeth & Vienna Sym.—Wöss (♯ Rem. 5)
  M. Cross & Anon. Orch. (♯ Roy. 18140)

VARIOUS EXCERPTS
No. 2 (b, c, e) Royal Phil.—Beecham (♯ & ♭ AmC.PE 17)
No. 2 (b, c, e) & 3 Regent Sym. (in ♯ Rgt. 7004)
No. 2 (b, c, d) & 3 Orch.—Kostelanetz (♭ AmC.A 1764;
                 No. 3 only in ♭ KZ 1)
Nos. 2 (a, b, e, f) Orch.—Kostelanetz (AmC. set J 211:
                  ♭ J 4-211)
Nos. 1, 2 (a), 2 ☆ Paris Cons.—Fistoulari (♭ D.DX 1721)

No. 3, Valse des fleurs
  Royal Phil.—Beecham   **♯ AmC.ML 4872**
  (*Symphony No. 2*)
  Prague Radio—Košlík (U.C 24403)
  ☆ Victor Sym.—Reiner (♭ G.7ER 5022; ♭ Vic.ERA 83)
  Covent Garden—Braithwaite (in ♯ P.PMC 1008;
                  MGM.E 3124, d.c.)
  Los Angeles—Wallenstein (in ♯ B.AXL 2012)
  Paris Opéra—Cloëz (♭ Od.7AO 2002: DSOQ 200)
  Robin Hood Dell—Kostelanetz (♭ C.SCD 2019:
                SCDW 112: SCDQ 2007)

ARRANGEMENTS
Nos. 2 (c, f) Paris Clarinet Sextet (in ♯ D.LX 3138;
                  Lon.LS 1096)
No. 3 Manhattan Pf. Qtt. (in ♯ MGM.E 3100:
                  ♭ set X 245)

---

[1] Includes *Pas de deux* from Op. 71.

(The) SLEEPING BEAUTY, Op. 66

Items are numbered from the piano reduction, arr. Siloti, ed. March (N.Y. 1950)

Item Nos.	Items	A	G	H	J	K	L	M	N	P	Q
—	Introduction	X	●	●	..	X	..	●	XA♭	X	X
	Prologue										
1	March: Entrance of King and Court	●	●	●	..	..	●	..	..	..	●
2	Dance Scene: Entrance of Fairies	..	●	●	..	Ẋ	..	..	..	..	●
3	Pas de Six: Fairies present gifts										
a	Intrada	X	●	●	X	●	●	●	..	..	●
b	Adagio; Allegro vivo	X	●	●	X	●	●	●	..	..	●
	Variation I—Candite	●	●	●	●	..	..	●	..	..	●
	II—Coulante	..	●	●	●	..	●	●	..	..	●
	III—Falling crumbs	..	●	●	●	..	..	..	..	..	●
	IV—Song-bird Fairy	●	●	●	●	●	●	..	..	..	●
	V—Violente	..	●	●	●	●	●	..	..	..	●
	VI—Lilac Fairy (Valse)	●	●	●	●	..	..	●	..	..	●
	Coda	..	●	●	●	..	..	●	..	..	●
4	Finale: La Fée des lilas sort	Ẋ	●	●	..	..	..	Ẋ	..	..	●
	ACT 1										
5	Scene: The Palace Garden	..	●	●	..	..	..	..	..	..	X
6	Valse	..	●	●	..	..	..	..	..	..	..
7	Scene: The Four Princes	●	●	●	..	●	..	..	..	●	..
8	Pas d'action:										
a	Intro. (Andante) and Adagio ("Rose Adagio")	●	●	●	..	X	●	..	B♭	●	●
b	Dance of Maids of Honour and Pages	..	●	●	..	..	..	..	C	..	●
c	Variation d'Aurore (with vln. solo)	..	●	●	..	..	..	..	..	..	X
d	Coda	..	●	●	..	..	..	..	..	..	●
9	Finale: La Fée des lilas paraît	Ẋ	●	●	..	..	..	..	XA♭	Ẋ	X
	ACT II, Scene 1										
10	Entracte and Scene	..	●	●	..	..	..	..	..	..	●
11	Colin-Maillard—Allegro vivo	..	●	●	..	..	..	..	..	..	●
12 a	Scene; Moderato	..	●	●	..	..	..	..	..	..	●
b	Danse des duchesses—Minuet	..	●	●	..	..	..	..	..	..	●
c	Danse des baronnes—Gavotte	..	●	●	●	..	..	..	..	..	●
d	Danse des comtesses	●	●	●	..	..	..	..	..	..	●
e	Danse des marquises	..	●	●	..	..	..	..	..	..	●
13 a	Farandole	..	●	●	●	..	..	..	..	..	●
b	Danse—Tempo di Mazurka	●	●	●	●	..	..	..	..	..	●
14	Scene—Arrival of Huntsmen	..	●	●	..	..	..	..	..	..	..
15	Pas d'Action ("Vision") with vlc. solo	X	●	●	..	..	..	..	..	..	●
b	Variation d'Aurore—Allegro commodo	..	●	●	..	..	..	..	..	..	●
c	Coda	..	●	●	..	..	..	..	..	..	●
16	Scene: Allegro agitato	●	●	●	..	..	..	..	..	..	●
17	Panorama: Andantino	●	●	●	..	..	●	..	..	●	●
18	Entr'acte: Andante sostenuto	..	●	●	..	..	..	..	..	..	..
	ACT II, Scene 2										
19 a	Entr'acte and Scene: Aurora's sleep	..	●	..	..	..	..	..	..	..	●
b	Finale: Allegro agitato—breaking of spell	..	●	..	..	..	..	..	..	..	●
	ACT III										
20	Marche	..	●	●	●	..	..	..	..	..	X
21	Polacca: Allegro moderato	●	●	●	●	●	..	●	..	..	●
22	Pas de quatre										
a	Intrada: Allegro non tanto	●	●	●	●	..	●	●	..	..	●
b	Variation I: Valse	..	●	●	●	●	●	..	..	..	●
c	II: Polka—Silver Fairy	..	●	●	●	●	●	..	..	..	●
d	III: Saphir	..	●	●	●	..	..	..	..	..	●
e	IV: Diamant	●	●	●	●	..	●	..	..	..	●
f	Coda	●	●	●	●	..	●	..	..	..	●
23	Pas de caractère—Puss in Boots	●	●	●	..	..	..	..	B	●	●
24	Pas de quatre										
a	Adagio with flute solo	●	●	●	●	●	●	●	..	..	●
b	Variation I: Cinderella and Prince (Valse)	●	●	●	●	●	●	..	A	..	●
c	II: Bluebird and Florisse	●	●	●	●	●	●	..	A	..	●
d	Coda	●	●	●	●	●	●	..	..	..	X
25	Pas de caractère (Red Riding Hood)	..	●	●	●	..	..	●	C	..	●
26	Pas berrichon (Hop o' my thumb)	..	●	●	..	..	..	..	..	..	..
26 a	Cinderella and Prince Fortune (Allegro and Valse)	X	●	●	..	..	..	..	..	..	..
27	Pas de deux										
a	Intrada	..	●	●	..	..	●	..	..	..	..
b	Adagio	..	●	●	●	..	X	..	..	..	●
c	Variation I (Prince)	..	●	●	●	..	..	..	..	..	●
d	II (Aurora)	..	●	●	..	..	..	..	C♭	..	●
e	Coda: Allegro vivace "The Three Ivans"	..	●	●	●	●	●	..	..	..	●
28	Sarabande	●	●	●	●	●	●	..	..	..	●
29	Finale										
a	Allegro brillante (Mazurka)	..	X	●	●	X	●	X	C♭	..	X
b	Apotheosis—Andante molto maestoso	●	●	●	●	●	X	..	..	..	●

Where an item is marked ● in the recordings column, it is included, more or less complete; marked X it is considerably abbreviated, or part only recorded.

FOR ENTRIES SEE PAGE 465

(The) SWAN LAKE, Op. 20

Items	I	II	III	IV	A	C	F	G	H	J	K	L	M	N	P	Q	R
Introduction					●	..	●	●	..	..	..	..	..	..	..	..	●
Act I																	
Opening Scene: Allegro	1	1	1		..	●	●	●	..	..	..	..	..	..	..	..	●
Pas de trois	2	2	4														
Intrada: Allegro moderato					..	..	..	●	..								●
Variations i-iv					X	..	..	X	X	..	..	..	..	..	..	..	●
Coda: Allegro vivace					..	..	..	●	..	..	..	..	..	..	..	..	●
Scene: Entrance of pages	3	3	3		..	..	..	●	..	..	..	..	..	..	..	..	●
Valse (Corps de ballet), A major	4	4	2	2	●	..	●	●	●	●	●	..	..	..	..	●	●
Pas d'action: Andantino																	
quasi moderato	5	5	6		●	●	..	●	..	..	..	..	..	..	..	●	●
Scene (Dusk falls)	6	6	7		..	..	●	●	..	..	..	..	..	..	..	●	●
Danse des coupes (Polonaise)	7	7	8		..	●	●	●	..	..	..	..	..	●	..	..	●
Final Scene: Andante ("Swan theme")	8	8	9		..	..	..	..	..	..	..	..	..	..	..	..	●
ACT II																	
Scene ("Swan theme"): Moderato	9	9	10	1	..	..	●	●	●	●	●	..	●	●	..	●	●
Scene (Benno's entry): Allegro moderato	10	10	11		..	..	..	●	..	..	..	..	..	●	..	..	●
Scene: Allegro	11	11	12		..	..	..	●	..	..	..	..	..	..	..	..	●
Danses des cygnes (Valse, A major)	12	12	13a		..	..	..	●	..	..	..	..	●	..	..	..	●
Scene, with vln. solo: Andante ("Second Dance of the Queen")	13	13	13e	4	●	..	●	●	●	●	●	●	..	..	..	..	●
Danses des [petits] cygnes: Allegro moderato	14	14	13d	3	●	..	●	●	●	●	..	●	..	..	..	..	●
Danse Générale: Valse, A flat major	15	15	13c		..	..	..	●	..	..	..	..	..	..	..	..	●
Scene: Moderato assai ("First Dance of the Queen")	16	16	13b		●	..	..	●	..	..	..	..	..	..	..	..	●
Coda: Allegro vivace	17	17	13f		●	..	..	●	..	..	..	..	..	●	..	..	●
Final scene ("Swan theme")	18	18	14		●	..	..	●	..	..	..	..	..	..	..	..	●
ACT III																	
Scene (Danse de fiançailles)	19	19	15		..	●	..	●	●	..	..	..	..	..	..	X	●
Danses du corps de ballet et des nains	[19a]	20	16		..	..	..	..	..	..	..	..	..	..	..	..	●
Scene (Fanfares) and Valse, A flat major	20	21	17		X	●	..	●	●	..	..	..	..	..	●	●	●
Scene: Allegro	21	22	18		..	●	..	●	..	..	..	..	..	..	●	●	●
Pas de six	—	23	19														
Intrada (Moderato assai)					..	..	..	..	..	..	..	..	..	..	..	..	●
Variation i: Andante con moto					..	..	..	..	..	..	..	..	..	X	..	..	●
Variations ii-iv					..	..	..	..	..	..	..	..	..	..	..	..	●
Coda: Allegro molto					..	..	..	..	..	..	..	..	..	..	..	..	●
Danse russe	—	24	Supp.		..	..	..	..	..	..	..	..	..	..	●	..	●
Danse espagnole	22	25	21		●	..	●	●	●	..	..	..	..	..	..	●	●
Danse napolitaine	23	26	22		●	..	●	●	●	..	..	..	..	..	..	●	●
Danse hongroise (Czardas)	24	27	20	5	●	..	●	●	●	●	●	..	..	..	..	●	●
Mazurka	25	28	23		●	..	●	●	●	..	..	..	..	..	..	●	●
Pas de deux	26	29	5														
Intrada (Valse, D major)					..	●	●	●	..	..	..	..	..	..	●	..	●
Variation i (Andante or Adagio)					..	●	●	●	..	..	..	..	..	●	●	..	●
Variation ii (Valse, B flat ma.)					..	..	..	..	..	..	..	..	..	●	●.	..	●
Interpolation I (Op. 72, No. 12)	—	29a	—		..	..	..	..	..	..	..	..	..	..	●	..	..
Interpolation IV (Polka: by Drigo?)	—	29b	—		..	..	..	●	..	..	..	..	..	●	●	..	..
Coda: Allegro molto vivace	27	30	5		..	..	..	..	..	..	..	..	..	●	●	..	..
Scene: Allegro	28	31	24		..	..	●	●	..	..	..	..	..	..	..	..	●
ACT IV																	
Entracte: Moderato	29	32	25		..	..	X	..	..	..	..	..	..	..	..	..	●
Interpolation II (Op. 72, No. 11)	—	32a	—		..	..	..	●	..	..	..	..	..	..	..	..	..
Scene: Allegro ma non troppo	30	33	26		..	..	X	..	..	..	..	..	..	..	..	..	●
Danses des petits cygnes: Moderato	31	34	27		●	..	●	●	●	..	..	●	..	..	..	●	●
Scene: Allegro agitato	32	35	28	6a	●	..	●	●	..	..	..	..	..	..	..	..	●
Final Scene: Andante; Allegro agitato	33	36	29	6b	●	..	●	X	●	..	..	..	..	..	..	●	●
Interpolation III (Op. 72, No. 15)	—	36a	—		..	..	..	●	..	..	..	..	..	..	..	..	..

The Scores referred to are:
    I: 1896 Piano reduction, ed. Langer [WERM numbers];
    II: 1949 Piano reduction, ed. P. March;
    III: Complete Orchestral score, pub. Jurgenson (the recent Broude score is very similar);
    IV: The "Orchestral Suite", pub. Boosey & Hawkes.

It appears that in some cases the English pressings differ from the American, of issues which purport to be the same. Where English issues exist, they have been checked; Column C by catalogue only.

FOR ENTRIES SEE PAGES 465–6

(The) SLEEPING BEAUTY, Op. 66

THE RECORDINGS TABULATED ARE:

Column A¹ ☆ Sym.—Stokowski   **♯ G.ALP 1002**
(2ss)   (♯ QALP/FALP 133)

Column G¹ ☆ Paris Cons.—Fistoulari   **♯ D.LXT 2762/3**
(4ss)   (♯ Lon.LL 336/7)

Column H Minneapolis Sym.—Dorati   **♯ Mer.MG 50064/7**
(8ss—one disc, Prol. & each act)
(& 6ss, ♯ Mer.MG 50061/3, set OL-3-103)

Column J Orch.—Stokowski   **♯ Vic.LM 1774**
(*Humoresque, "Solitude"*) (♯ ItV.A12R 0008;
                          DV.L 16460; FV.A 630264)
[Intro. & Nos. 21, 3 (a, b), 13 (b), 22 (a), 27 (e), 29
(Labelled *Aurora's Wedding*)   on ♭ *Vic. set ERB 4*]

Column K ¹Orch.—Kostelanetz   **♯EPhi.NBL 5027**
(AmC.CL 804, o.n. ♯ ML 4960: ♭ set A 1106;
                               ♯ Phi.N 02121L)

Column L ¹Ballet Theatre—Levine   **♯ DCap.CCL 7519**
                                          (♯ Cap.L 8195; T.NLCB 8195)
(*Chopin: Sylphides*, on ♯ Cap.P 8193; excerpts
(Labelled *Princess Aurora*)   on ♭ Cap.FAP 8214)

Column M ☆ L.P.O.—Kurtz   **♯ Cam.CAL 211**
(labelled *Aurora's Wedding*)   (& in set CFL 102)
[listed from contents of the original issue]

Column N Philharmonia—Malko
Items marked A on G.C 4205:   S 10612
     ,,   ,, B ,, G.C 4212:   S 10608
     ,,   ,, C ,, G.C 4258:   S 10620
     ,,   ♭ ,,   ♭ G.7EP 7017: 7EPQ 533

Column P "Orchestral Suite, Op. 66A" (Kalmus)
¹Philharmonia—Karajan   **♯ C.CX 1065**
(*Swan Lake*)   (♯ FCX/QCX 202; Angel. 35006)
[Nos. 1 & 9, abridged; & 8a, on ♯ C.SEL 1532]
¹Vienna Sym.—Otterloo   **♯EPhi.NBL 5005**
(*Nutcracker*) (♯ Phi.A 00210L; Epic.LC 3078;
                              2ss, *Phi.S 06051R*)
Philadelphia—Ormandy   **♯ AmC.ML 4729**
(*Nutcracker*) [No. 8a only, in ♭ set A 1063]
☆ ¹Paris Cons.—Désormière (♯ D.LXT 2610; Lon.LL 440)
Linz Sym. (Ply. 12-27)
Berlin Sym.—List (♯ Allo. 3064)
Berlin Sym.—Balzer (♯ Roy. 1407)
Anon. Orch. (♯ Gram. 20100), etc.

Column Q ¹Covent Garden Op.—Irving **♯ G.CLP 1073/4**
(4ss)   (♯ Vic. set LM 6034)

OTHER RECORDINGS ("Complete" or substantial)
Berlin Sym.—Guhl²   **♯ Ura. 7127**
                          (♯ MTW. 527; *ACC.MP 17*)
Bolshoi Theatre—Fayer (4ss) **♯ Csm.CRLP 10081/2**

VARIOUS EXCERPTS
Intro. & Nos. 1 (or 20), 6, 8 (a, b), 17, 21, 29b
Bamberg Sym.—Lehmann   **♯ HP.DG 17045**
Nos. 2, 3a, 3b (part), 6, 8a, 22a, 23 & unspec. Variations &
                                       Adagio, Act III
Leningrad Phil.—Mravinsky   **USSRM.D 00707/12**
(Part is ☆)   (also *USSR. 18607/8: 18523/5*, etc.)
Nos. 21, 22 (a, c, e, f), 23, 24, 25, 27b (part), 27(d, e), 29 (cut)
☆ Covent Garden—Braithwaite   **♯ MGM.E 3052**
(*Gounod: Faust Ballet*)
Intro. & No. 2 Orch.—Kostelanetz (♯ & ♭ *AmC.PE 22*)
Nos. 3a & 6   ☆ Orch.—Stokowski (♭ *Vic.ERA 247*)
Nos. 6 & 23 Vienna Sym.—Otterloo (♭ *Phi.N 402016E*)
No. 6, Valse
Hamburg Philharmonia—H.-J. Walther (*MSB. 78108*)
Orch.—Schneiderhahn (in ♯ *Mae.OA 20008*)
☆ Philharmonia—Weldon (♭ *C.SCD 2024*:
                       SED 5518: SEDQ 543: in ♯ *SX 1032*)
Danish Radio—Malko (G.S 10614: ♭ *7P 145*:
            7PW 124: 7PQ 2014: 7RK 1: 7BF 1049)
Hallé—Sargent (C.DX 1889: *GQX 11538*)
Los Angeles—Wallenstein (♯ *B.AXL 2012*)
Paris Opéra—Cloëz (♭ *Od.7AO 2002: DSOQ 200*)
Orch.—Stokowski (in ♯ *Vic.WR 8000*: ♭ *set WRY 8000*)
Boston "Pops"—Fiedler (in ♯ Vic.LM 1790 & LM 1752:
                ♭ set WDM 1752; ♭ DV. 16062)
Robin Hood Dell—Kostelanetz (in ♯ AmC.CL 730)
Orch.—Kostelanetz (in ♯ AmC.CL 747)
Vienna Radio—Nilius (in ♯ *MII. 33-118*)
etc. etc.

— ARRANGEMENTS
ORGAN: R. Foort, *sub nom.* M. Cheshire (in ♯ *SOT. 1051*)
2 PFS.: L. Shankson & I. Wright (in ♯ *Roy. 1447*)
4 PFS.: Manhattan Pf. Qtt. (in ♯ MGM.E 3100: ♭ set X 245)
No. 8a Philharmonia—Kurtz   in ♯ *G.ALP 1301*
☆ Philadelphia—Ormandy (in ♭ *AmC. set A 1063*)
Nos. 15a & 17 ☆ Covent Garden—Lambert (C.DHX 71)
No. 24 (Adagio—Variations I & II—Coda)
Concerts Colonne—Stirn   **♯ LT.DTL 93019**
(*Nutcracker, Swan Lake; & Minkus*)   (♯ *Sel. 270.C.005*)
Cuevas Ballet—Cloëz   **♯ LI.TWV 91048**
(*Chavchavadze*)   (♯ *Cpt.MC 20041*)

(The) SWAN LAKE, Op. 20

THE RECORDINGS TABULATED ARE:

Column A ☆ St. Louis Sym.—Golschmann ♮ G.DB 9365/9
(♯ Vic.LM 1003: ♭ set ERB 9; ♯ DV.L 16028)

Column C ☆ Covent Garden—Rignold   G.C 3822/3
[Excerpts, ♭ *BB.ERAB 4*]   (♯ BB.LBC 1016:
                                   ♭ set WBC 1016)

Column F Philharmonia—Irving   **♯ G.CLP 1018**
(♯ G.FELP 112; BB.LBC 1064: ♭ set WBC 1064)

Column G ☆ L.S.O.—Fistoulari   **♯ D.LXT 2681/2**
                                          (♯ Lon.LL 565/6)

Column H ☆ French Sym.—Désormière   **♯ DCap.CTL 7015**
                                          (♯ Cap.P 8142; T.LCS 8142)

Column J ☆ Hallé—Barbirolli   **♯ G.BLP 1004**
(*Bizet: L'Arlesienne Suite*) (♯ QBLP 5003: ♮ DB 9549/50)

Column K Philharmonia—Karajan   **♯ C.CX 1065**
(*Sleeping Beauty*) (♯ WCX 1065: QCX/FCX 202;
                                        Angel. 35006)

Column L ☆ Sym.—Stokowski   in ♯ G.ALP 1133
(in "*Heart of the Ballet*")   (♯ FALP 277)
(also ♯ Vic.LM 7022: ♭ set ERB 7022)

Column M ☆ Covent Garden—Braithwaite
                                 in ♯ P.PMC 1008
("*Nights at the Ballet*")   (♯ MGM.E 3006)

Column N Philharmonia—Markevitch   **♯ C.CX 1198**
(*Chopin, Scarlatti, Falla*) (♯ FCX 358; Angel. 35152,
                                       in set 3518)

Column P Concerts Colonne—Stirn   **♯ LT.DTL 93019**
(*Nutcracker, Sleeping Beauty & Minkus*) (♯ *Sel. 270.C.005*)

Column Q ☆ A. Kostelanetz Orch.³   **♯ Phi.N 02122L**
(♯ AmC.CL 715: ♭ set A 1091; excpts., J 215: ♭ 4-215)

Column R Minneapolis Sym.—Dorati **♯ Mer.MG 50068/70**
(6ss)(♯ Mer.MG 50050/2, set OL-3-102; FMer.MLP 7530/2)
[the order is that of Column III]

OTHER RECORDINGS

COMPLETE (or so listed)
Bolshoi Theatre—Fayer   **♯ Csm.CRLP 10090/1**
(4ss) [some are ☆; & see below] (o.n. ♯ CRLPX 004/6, 6ss)
☆ Prague Nat. Theatre—Škvor   **♯ Sup.LPV 110/2**
(4ss)   (♯ U. 5091/2G)

ACTS II & III, "COMPLETE"⁴
N.B.C. Sym. Members—Stokowski
                                   ♯ Vic.LM 1894
                                   (♯ ItV.A12R 0172)

VARIOUS EXCERPTS
Intro. & Nos. 4, 13, 14, 32, 33 (part)
Rome Op.—Questa   **♯ Var. 6997**
Intro. & Nos. 4, 13, 14, 17, 24
▽ Berlin Sym.—List (♯ Roy. 1319, 2ss)
Nos. 2, 4, 19, 19a, 23, 24, 26, 20, 25, 32, 33
Bolshoi Theatre—Fayer
[some are ☆]   **USSRM.D 1005/6, 999/1000, 1392/3**
Nos. 4, 10 Philharmonia—Karajan   ♭ *C.SEL 1537*
No. 4 ☆ Los Angeles—Wallenstein (♯ B.AXL 2012)
No. 13 J. Fuchs (vln.) & Camarata Orch.
                   (in ♯ *B.AXL 2010; AmD.DL 4082*)
Nos. 22, 26 Prague Nat. Theatre—Krombholc
                                   (in ♯ Ura. 7084)
Unspecified (some are probably as Column IV)
"Philharmonic"—List   **♯ Allo. 3059**
(*Eugene Oniegin*, etc.)   (♯ Pac.LDAD 52)
R.I.A.S. Sym.—Perlea (*Saint-Saëns*) **♯ Rem. 199-160**
Leningrad Op.—Dubousky   **♯ JpV.LH 2**
Orch.—Swarowsky (♯ MTW. 21)
"Nat. Op. Orch." (♯ *Gram. 2068*)
Valse (unspec.) Orch.—Schneiderhahn (in ♯ *Mae.OA 20008*)

(*continued on next page*)

---

¹ These discs have been heard and checked.   The others are entered from reviews, labels, or catalogues, and are probably substantially accurate only.   Column H is stated to be absolutely accurate.
² From the cover notes, this appears to contain: Nos. 1, 3 (part), 6, 8 (a-c), 11, 12 (b-d), 13 (b), 15 (a), 17, 21, 22 (a), 23, 27 (a, d), 26, 29.   It has not been possible to compare the disc with the score.
³ It is not possible to reconcile different sources for exact identification of this recording: the most probable of alternatives are shown.
⁴ Contains [WERM] Nos. 9 to 28 inclusive, and Interpolation I. Nos. 13, 18, 20 & 26 are somewhat cut; there are other minor abbreviations and arrangements.

465

(The) SWAN LAKE (*continued*)

Repressings from SET H:
Nos. 4, 9, 14, 16, 24, 33   on ♯ *ACap.CLCX 006*
Nos. 9, 16, 36   on ♭ *Cap.FAP 8203*
Nos. 12, 13, 19, 22, 31   on ♭ *Cap.FAP 8213*
Nos. 14, 20, 24, 25   on ♭ *Cap.FAP 8237*

Nos. 4, 20, 31   — ARR. 4 PFS.
Manhattan Pf. Qtt. (in ♯ *MGM.E 3100*: ♭ *set X 245*)

Capriccio italien, Op. 45
Paris Cons.—Schuricht   ♯ **D.LXT 2761**
(*Suite 3—Theme & Variations*)   (♯ *Lon.LL 640*)

L.S.O.—Scherchen   ♯ **Nix.NLP 914**
(*Rimsky*)   (♯ *West.LAB 7002*)

Philharmonia—Galliera   ♯ **C.SX 1013**
(*Liszt*) (♯ *FCX 239: QCX 10074*; Angel. 35047)

Brussels Radio—André   ♯ **DT.LGM 65005**
(*Romeo & Juliet*)   (2ss, TV.VSK 9014: ♭ *T.UV 108*)
(*Liszt* on ♯ *T.TW 30006*)

Vienna State Phil.—Perlea
(*below*)   ♯ **E. & AmVox.PL 8700**

Philadelphia—Ormandy   ♯ **AmC.CL 707**
(*Str. Qtt. No. 1—Andante; & Rimsky*)   (o.n. ♯ *ML 4856*)

N.W. Ger. Phil.—Schüchter   ♯ **Imp.ILP 117**
(*Berlioz, Chabrier, Dvořak*)

Vienna State Op.—Rossi   ♯ **Van.VRS 484**
(*Ouverture solennelle; & Rimsky*)
              (o.n. ♯ *SRV 101*; Ama.AVRS 6020)

Leipzig Phil.—Pflüger   ♯ **Ura. 7148**
(*Ouverture solennelle; & Borodin*) (♯ *Ura.RS 7-16*;
              MTW. 551; *ACC.MP 32*)

Vienna Pro Musica—Ladis ♭*AmVox.VIP 45550*

Leningrad Phil.—Mravinsky   ♯ **USSR.D 0239**
(*Romeo & Juliet*)

☆ Col. Sym.—Beecham   ♯ **C.CX 1037**
(*Bizet*)   (♯ *VCX 521: QCX 10012*)
☆ Amsterdam—v. Kempen   ♯ **EPhi.ABR 4003**
(*Ouverture solennelle*)   (♯ *Phi.S 06078R*)
(*idem & Romeo & Juliet* on ♯ *Epic.LC 3008*)
Berlin Sym.—Günther (in ♯ *Roy. 1448*)
Rhineland Sym.—Federer (♯ *Rgt. 5058*)
Olympia Sym.—Saike (♯ *Allo. 3052*)
Anon. Orch. (♯ *Gram. 2089*)
☆ Czech Phil.—Šejna (♯ *Sup.LPM 54*)
Boston Prom.—Fiedler (♯ *Cam.CAL 114* & in set
   CFL 103, o.v.; n.v., ♯ *DV.L 16346*; ItV.A12R 0081)
Munich Phil.—Lehmann (♭ *Pol. 30069* & in ♯ *19028*)

CONCERTOS, pf. & orch.
No. 1, B flat minor, Op. 23
G. Anda & Philharmonia—Galliera
              ♯ **C.CX 1156**
(*Delibes: Coppélia*)(♯ *FCX 295: QCX 10095*; Angel. 35083)

G. Bachauer & New London—Sherman
              ♯ **G.CLP 1049**
              (♯ *Vic.LM 1890*)

E. Farnadi & Vienna State Op.—Scherchen
              ♯ **Nix.WLP 5309**
(*No. 2*)   (♯ *West.WL 5309*; & 2ss, ♯ *Sel. 270.CW.067*)

F. Wührer & Vienna Pro Musica—Hollreiser
              ♯ **AmVox.PL 9000**
(*Grieg*) (♯ *Orb.BL 702*) (*Concerto No. 2* on ♯ *PaV.VP 360*)

E. Gilels & Chicago Sym.—Reiner
              ♯ **Vic.LM 1969**
              (♭ *set ERC 1969*)

P. Serebriakov & Leningrad Phil.—Mravinsky
              ♯ **USSR.D 01400/1**

X. Prochorowa & N.W. Ger. Phil.—Schüchter
(2ss)   ♯ **G.FFLP 1058**
              (♯ *Imp.ILP 113*)

C. Hansen & R.I.A.S. Sym.—Sawallisch
              ♯ **Rem. 199-197**

S. Bianca & Hamburg Philharmonia
—H-J. Walther   ♯ **MGM.E 3278**
(*Grieg*)

S. Richter & Czech Phil.—Ančerl
(8ss)   ♮ **U.H 24415/8**

☆ S. Cherkassky & Berlin Phil.—Ludwig
              ♯ **HP.DGM 18013**
              (♯ *AmD.DL 9605*)
☆ A. Uninsky & Residentie—v. Otterloo
              ♯ **EPhi.ABR 4020**
              (♯ *Phi.A 00672R*: Epic.LC 3010)
☆ E. Gilels & USSR. Sym.—Samosud ♯ **Csm.CRLP 158**
(*Chopin, Liszt, Rachmaninoff*)
[also listed with *Rimsky-K: Concerto*, same No.]
A. de Vries & Berlin Radio—Rother (♯ *Ura.RS 7-2*)
A. Sandford & "Philharmonic"—Berendt (♯ *Allo. 3053*)
H. Kessler & Vienna Artists (♯ *Ply. 12-43*)
G. Louegk & Sym.—Wilhelm (♯ *MTW. 15*)
Anon. Artists (♯ *Gram. 2007*)
☆ A. Rubinstein & Minneapolis Sym.—Mitropoulos
              (♯ *G.FALP/QALP 275*)
C. Solomon & Philharmonia—Dobrowen
              (♯ *G.QCLP 12004*)
E. Gilels & Stockholm Phil.—Ehrling (♮ *Nera.B 600/3*;
              ♯ *Mtr.CLP 512*; AFest.CFR 12-175)
O. Levant & Philadelphia—Ormandy (♯ *AmC.CL 740*:
              o.n. ML 4883: ♭ *set A 1063*)
N. Mewton-Wood & Sym.—Goehr (♯ *ANix.MLPY 12*)
V. Schiøler & Danish Radio—Tuxen
              (♯ *Tono.LPX 35001*)
V. Horowitz & N.B.C. Sym.—Toscanini
   (♯*G.CSLP505: QJLP103: FJLP5013*; ♭*Vic. set ERBT3*)
M. Schwertmann & Austrian Sym.—Paulmüller
              (♯ *Cum.CR 231*)
M. de la Bruchollerie & Vienna State Phil.—Moralt
              (♯ *Pan.XPV 1004*)
... 1st movt. only (abridged)
J. M. Sanromá & Boston "Pops"—Fiedler
              (in ♯ *Vic.LM 1752*: ♭ *set WDM 1752*)
... 1st movt. only, Opening theme
☆ A. Semprini & Melachrino Orch. (♯ *G.7EG 8023*)

No. 2, G major, Op. 44
E. Farnadi & Vienna State Op.—Scherchen
              ♯ **Nix.WLP 5309**
(*No. 1*)   (♯ *West.WL 5309*; 2ss, ♯ *Sel. 270.CW.068*)

T. Nikolayeva & State Sym.—Anosov
              ♯ **Mon.MWL 312**
(2ss) (♯*USSR.D 0749/50*; CEd.CE3008; CdM.LDXA 8085)
(*6 Pieces, pf., Op. 19*, on ♯ *Csm.CRLP 222*)

F. Wührer & Vienna Pro Musica—Hollreiser
              ♯ **AmVox.PL 9200**
(*Scriabin*)   (*Concerto No. 1* on ♯ *PaV.VP 360*)

M. Pinter & Berlin Radio—Rother ♯ **Ura. 7081**
(*Andante only*, ♭ *UREP 69*)

☆ B. Moiseiwitsch & Liverpool Phil.—Weldon
              (♭ *set WCT 1127*)
(*Rachmaninoff*)   ♭ **Vic.LCT 1127**
☆ N. Mewton-Wood & Winterthur Sym.—Goehr
              (♯ *Clc. 6211*)

No. 3, E flat major, Op. 75
☆ N. Mewton-Wood & Winterthur Sym.—Goehr
              (♯ *Clc. 6226*)

Concert Fantasia, G major, Op. 56
☆ T. Nikolayeva & State Sym.—Kondrashin
              ♯ **CEd.CE 3007**
(*Babadzhanyan*)   (2ss, *USSR.D 403/4*)
(*Prokofiev & Nikolayeva*, on ♯ *Csm.CRLP 221*)
☆ N. Mewton-Wood & Winterthur—Goehr ♯ (♯ *Clc. 6226*)

CONCERTO, D major, Op. 35, vln. & orch.
M. Elman & L.P.O.—Boult   ♯ **D.LXT 2970**
              (♯ *Lon.LL 1073*)
D. Oistrakh & Saxon State—Konwitschny
              ♯ **HP.DGM 18196**
              (♯ *Eta. 820002*, o.n. LPM 1014; AmD.DL 9755)
N. Milstein & Boston Sym.—Münch
              ♯ **Vic.LM 1760**
              (♯ *FV.A 630243*; G.FBLP 1047)
I. Gitlis & Vienna Pro Musica—Hollreiser
(*Mendelssohn*)   ♯ **E. & AmVox.PL 8840**
Z. Francescatti & N.Y.P.S.O.—Mitropoulos
              ♯ **AmC.ML 4965**
(*Mendelssohn*)   (2ss, ♯ *Phi.A 01615R*)
R. Odnoposoff & Netherlands Phil.—Goehr
              ♯ **MMS. 34**
              (♯ *ANix.MLPY 34*)
L. Kogan & Moscow Radio—Nebolsin
              ♯ **Kings.KL 241**
(*Valse-scherzo*)   (2ss, ♯ *USSR.D 01237/8*)
(*Glazounov: Raymonda—Entr'acte* on USSR. 022752/60)

♯ = Long-playing, 33⅓ r.p.m.   ♭ = 45 r.p.m.   ♮ = Auto. couplings, 78 r.p.m.

CONCERTO, D major, Op. 35, vln. & orch. (*continued*)

N. Shkolnikova & Moscow Radio—Kondrashin
     ‡ **USSR.D 02175/6**

R. Schulz & Leipzig Radio—Abendroth
     ‡ **Ura.RS 7-17**

E. List & " Phil ".—Berendt   ‡ **Allo. 3054**
                   (‡ Pac.LDAD 53)

☆ J. Heifetz & Philharmonia—Susskind   ‡ *G.BLP 1012*
                (‡ *VBLP 801*; ♭ *FV. set A 95205/6*)
   (*Sinding & Ravel on* ‡ Vic.LM 1832: ♭ *set ERB 21;*
                        ‡ *ItV.A12R 0153*)

☆ I. Stern & Philadelphia—Hilsberg   ‡ *C.C 1022*
                  (‡ *VC 807: FCX 167*; ♭ *AmC. set A 1087*)
☆ D. Oistrakh & Moscow Phil.—Gauk   ‡ **Per.SPL 710**
   (*Paganini: Caprices 13 & 17*)   (2ss, ‡ Roy. 1640)
   (*Souvenir d'un lieu cher, No. 1 on* ‡ Csm.CRLP 10010)[1]
R. Marcel & Europa Sym.   (‡ Ply. 12-121; Gram. 2058)

☆ E. Morini & Chicago Sym.—Defauw
                (‡ *BB.LBC 1061*: ♭ *set WBC 1061*)
N. Milstein & Chicago Sym.—Stock (‡ AmC.RL 3023;
                 with *Bruch* on ‡ *RL 6631*)
G. Kulenkampff & German Op.—Rother   (‡ T.LE 6512)
J. Heifetz & L.P.O.—Barbirolli (‡ JpV.LH 1)
M. Auclair & Austrian Sym.—Wöss (‡ Cum.CR 247;
   Canzonetta & Finale only ‡ Rem. 199-120; Ply. 12-54)

… 2nd movt. (Canzonetta) only
M. Kozolupova & pf. (*USSR. 16816/7*)

Elegy str. orch. 1884
Concert Artist Sym.—Vicars **V**‡ *CA.MPO 5013*
(*Liszt*)
☆ Netherlands Phil.—Goehr (in ‡ *MMS. 66*, d.c.)

Francesca da Rimini, Op. 32
St. Louis Sym.—Golschmann ‡ **DCap.CTL 7048**
(*Romeo & Juliet*)   (‡ Cap.P 8225)
Olympia Sym.—Saike   ‡ **Allo. 3052**
(*Capriccio italien*)
Leipzig Radio—Borsamsky   ‡ **Ura. 7158**
(*Romeo & Juliet*)   (o.n. RS 7-22)
Berlin Sym.—Günther[2]   in ‡ **Roy. 1448**
Anon. Orch. (‡ Gram. 20100)
☆ N.Y.P.S.O.—Stokowski (‡ C.QCX 10001: VCX 522:
                          FCX 177)
Boston Sym.—Koussevitzky (‡ Cam.CAL 159)

Hamlet, Overture-Fantasia, Op. 67
Philharmonia—Irving   ‡ **G.CLP 1043**
(*Dohnányi*)   (‡ BB.LBC 1090)
☆ Philharmonia—Fistoulari   ‡ **P.PMC 1014**
(*Romeo & Juliet*)

Manfred, Op. 58 "Symphony"
Philharmonia—Kletzki   ‡ **C.CX 1189**
              (‡ FCX 348; Angel. 35167)
☆ USSR. State Sym.—Gauk   ‡ **Mon.MWL 336**
           (‡ CHS.CHS 1308; 4ss, *USSR.D 2287/90*)
☆ Indianapolis Sym.—Sevitzky (‡ Cam.CAL 184)

Marche slave, Op. 31
L.S.O.—Scherchen   ‡ **Nix.NLP 909**
(*below*)   (‡ West.WL 5282)
Danish Radio—Tuxen   ‡ *D.LW 5114*
(*Liszt: Hung. Rhapsody No. 12*)
Vienna State Phil.—Perlea
           ‡ **E. & AmVox.PL 8700**
(*above & below*)
Hollywood Bowl—Barnett   ‡ **Cap.P 8296**
(*Ponchielli, Saint-Saëns, etc.*)   (♭ set FAP 8296)
Philadelphia—Ormandy   ‡ **AmC.ML 4997**
(*Ouverture solennelle & Romeo & Juliet*)
(*Ouverture only on* ‡ AL 24)
B.B.C. Sym.—Sargent   **G.DB 21569**
L.S.O.—Weldon   **C.DX 1894**
(*Bach, Elgar, Handel, etc. on* ‡ SX 1045)
Berlin Sym.—Rubahn (in ‡ Roy. 1413)
☆ Boston Prom.—Fiedler   (G.DB 4327: ♭ 7EBF 2:
   7EP 7010: 7EPQ 502: 7EPK 1002: in ‡ FMLP 1003;
   ♭ DV. 26015; ‡ ItV.A12R 0107: ♭ A72R 0060;
                   in ‡ Vic.LM 9027)

☆ Philharmonia—Schüchter (in ‡ P.PMC 1003;
               MGM.E 3177 & E 3022)
   Amsterdam—v. Kempen (‡ *Phi.S 06015R*)
   Philharmonia—Sargent (in ‡ AmC.RL 3091)
   Aarhus Municipal—Jensen (in ‡ Tono.LPX 35005)
   N.Y. Stadium—Smallens (‡ *D.UW 333003*)
   Hollywood Bowl—Stokowski (in ‡ Cam.CAL 153 &
                   in ‡ set CFL 103)

Marche solennelle, D major 1885
Moscow Radio—Golovanov   **USSR. 022406**
(*Liadcv: Polonaise*)
☆ Sym. Orch.—Tergowski (in ‡*ANix.MLP Y 5; Clc.11004*)

Ouverture solennelle, 1812, Op. 49
Vienna State Op.—Rossi   ‡ **Van.VRS 484**
(*Capriccio italien; & Rimsky*) (o.n. ‡ SRV 101;
                     ‡ Ama.AVRS 6020)
Cho. & R.I.A.S. Sym.—Fricsay ‡ *HP.DG 17022*
(*Wagner*)   (2ss, PV. 72412; & in ‡ AmD.DL 9738)
Philharmonia—Malko (n.v.)   ‡ *G.DLP 1069*
(*Hérold & Weber*)   (‡ *QDLP 6024*)
L.S.O.—Scherchen   ‡ **Nix.NLP 909**
(*above & below*)   (‡ West.WL 5282)
(*Rimsky* on ‡ West.LAB 7043)
Vienna State Phil.—Perlea   ‡**E.& AmVox.PL8700**
(*above & below*)
Philadelphia—Ormandy   ‡ **AmC.ML 4997**
(*Marche slave & Romeo & Juliet*)   (*Marche only,* ‡ *AL 24*)
Berlin Sym.—Wiesenhütter   ‡ **Ura. 7148**
(*Capriccio italien, & Borodin*) (♭ *UREP 67;*
                 ‡ *ACC.MP 32;* MTW. 551)
(*Capriccio italien, only,* ‡ *Ura.RS 7-16*)
Brussels Radio—André   **TV.VSK 9018**
(*Moussorgsky,* on ‡*T.TW 30007*)   (♭ *UV 107*)
F.O.K. Sym. & Army Band—Stupka ‡ *U. 5175C*
(*Balakirev*)
☆ Amsterdam—v. Kempen   ‡ *EPhi.ABR 4003*
   (*Capriccio italien*)   (‡ *Phi.S 06078R*)
   (*idem & Romeo & Juliet* on ‡ Epic.LC 3008)
☆ Moscow Radio—Golovanov   ‡ *USSR.D 1294*
   (*Svendsen*)
Anon. Orch. (‡ Roy. 1874)
☆ Boston Prom.—Fiedler (‡ ItV.A12R 0081;
     DV.L 16346, n.v.; ‡ Cam.CAL 116, o.v.)
   N.Y. Stadium—Smallens (‡ *D.UW 333003;*
                   ▽ *AmD.DL 4031*)
   Cleveland Sym.—Rodzinski (‡ AmC.RL 6626)
   Sym.—Tergowski (in ‡ *ANix.MLPY 5; Clc. 11004*)
   Austrian Sym.—Wöss (‡ Ply. 12-54; Msq. 10003; &
                 with commentary, ‡ Rem. 5)

Pezzo capriccioso, Op. 62 vlc. & orch. 1887
☆ M. Rostropovich & Youth Sym.—Kondrashin
(*Glazounov: Mélodie*)   *USSRM.D 450*

Romeo & Juliet, Fantasy Overture 1870
French Nat. Radio—Markevitch   ‡ **C.CX 1208**
(*Borodin & Moussorgsky*) (‡ FCX 349: QCX 10134;
                      Angel. 35144)
Vienna Phil.—Kubelik   ‡ *D.LXT 5079*
(*Dvořák*)   (‡ Lon.LL 1283)
L.S.O.—Scherchen   ‡ **Nix.NLP 909**
(*above*)   (‡ West.WL 5282)
Vienna State Phil.—Perlea
          ‡ **E. & AmVox.PL 8700**
(*above*)
St. Louis Sym.—Golschmann ‡ **DCap.CTL 7048**
(*Francesca da Rimini*)   (‡ Cap.P 8225)
Brussels Radio—André   ‡ *DT.LGM 65005*
(*Capriccio italien*)   (2ss, TV.VSK 9202)
Philadelphia—Ormandy   ‡ **AmC.ML 4997**
(*Marche slave & Ouverture solennelle*)
Chicago Sym.—Dorati   ‡ **Mer.MG 50037**
(*Schubert*)   (‡ FMer.MLP 7524)
Netherlands Phil.—Goehr   ‡ *MMS. 66*
(*Elegy & Voyevoda*)
Leipzig Radio—Eibenschütz   ‡ **Ura. 7158**
(*Francesca da Rimini*)   (o.n. RS 7-22)
"Philharmonic"—List   ‡ **Allo. 3059**
(*also, Concert orch.,* ‡ Roy. 1432)
USSR. State—Ivanov   ‡ *USSR.D 0240*
(*Capriccio italien*)   (*Sym. No. 1 on* ‡ Csm.CRLP 211)
(*Serenade, Op. 48—Waltz* on USSR. 022071/5)

                 (*continued on next page*)

---

[1] The Csm. issue is said to be a new version, not a re-issue of the 78 r.p.m. issue. Probably the other Nos. listed here also are new.
[2] Abridged version.

Romeo & Juliet, Fantasy Overture (*continued*)

Rome Op.—Questa (*Swan Lake*)   ♯ *Var. 6997*
Boston Orch. Soc.—Page   ♯ SOT. 1169
(*Serenade, Op. 48*)
Berlin Sym.—Günther   in ♯ Roy. 1448
(*Eugene Oniegin & Swan Lake*)   (♯ Pac.LDAD 52)

☆ Philharmonia—Cantelli   ♯ G.ALP 1086
(*Wagner*)   (♯ QALP 10043; in ♯ Vic. set LM 6028)
☆ Philharmonia—Fistoulari   ♯ P.PMC 1014
(*Hamlet*)

☆ Boston Sym.—Koussevitzky (♯ Vic.LCT 1145)
Amsterdam—Mengelberg (♯ AmC.RL 3039)
N.Y.P.S.O.—Stokowski (♯ C.FCX 177: WCX 1030:
                      VCX 522: QCX 10001)
Bamberg Sym.—Lehmann (with *Liszt: Hungaria,*
                      ♯ *AmD.DL 7544*)
Amsterdam—v. Kempen (♯ Epic.LC 3008;
                      Phi.S 06029R)
Berlin Sym.—Ludwig (♭ *Roy.EP 236*)
N.B.C. Sym.—Toscanini (♯ ItV.A12R 0078;
    ♭ *Vic. set ERB 22;* ♭ *FV.A 95219/20*)
Cleveland Sym.—Rodzinski (in ♯ AmC.RL 6626)
A. Kostelanetz Orch. (♭ *AmC. set A 1041*: ♯ CL 747)
Austrian Sym.—Wöss (♯ Ply. 12-51; ♯ *AFest.CFR 58*)

Serenade, C major, Op. 48   Str. orch.
Philharmonia—Kletzki   ♯ C.CX 1164
(*Ravel & Smetana*)
(*Ippolitoff-Ivanoff* on ♯ FCX 356; Finale only, ♭ *SEL 1535*)
Pittsburgh Sym.—W. Steinberg ♯DCap.CTL 7084
(*Prokofiev*)   (♯ Cap.P 8290)
Lamoureux—v. Kempen   ♯ Phi.N 00271L
(*Suite No. 4*)   (♯ Epic.LC 3213)
R.I.A.S. Sym.—Fricsay   ♯ *Pol. 17036*
           (also ♯ *16052*; 4ss, ♭ PV. 72280/1)
(*Prokofiev* on ♯ AmD.DL 9737)
Vienna Pro Musica—Gräf   ♯ AmVox.PL 8770
(*Ippolitoff-Ivanoff*)   (2ss, ♯ *Pan.XPV 1012*)
[Waltz only on ♭ *AmVox.VIP 45410*]
Leningrad Phil.—Mravinsky   ♯ USSR.D 389/90
(2ss)
Sym. Orch.—Vicars   ♯ CA.LPA 1077
(*Grieg*)
Boston Orch. Soc.—Page   ♯ SOT. 1169
(*Romeo & Juliet*)
Bolshoi Theatre—L. Steinberg   ♯ Csm.CRLP 10190
(*Str. Qtt. No. 1*) (7ss—*Months, No. 10, arr.,*
[Waltz only also on USSR. 08270]   USSR. 010280/6)
Berlin Sym.—Balzer   ♯ Roy. 1407
(*Sleeping Beauty*)
☆ Boston Sym.—Koussevitzky (♯ ItV.A12R 0031)
B.B.C. Sym.—Boult (♯ Cam.CAL 242)
Philharmonia—Dobrowen (♯ BB.LBC 1021:
    ♭ *set WBC 1021;* 4th movt. only, on ♭ *ERAB 12*)

... **2nd movt., Waltz,** only
Boyd Neel—Dumont   ♭ *EPhi.NBE 11006*
(*Dvořák & Grieg*)   (♭ *Phi. 402030E*)
Angelicum Str.—Janes   Ang.SA 3034
(*Mozart: Divertimento 17—Minuet*)   (in ♯ LPA 958)
New Prom.—Robertson (in ♯ *Lon.LB 581*)
Orch.—Schneiderhann (in ♯ *Mae.OA 20008*)
Decca Little Sym.—Mendoza (in ♯ *D.US 223524;*
               AmD.DL 5211; ▽ *in set A 90*)
Rhineland Sym. (in V♯ *Rgt.MG 1000*)
Mantovani Orch. (in ♯ *D.LK 4072 & LF 1161;*
                      Lon.LL 877)
☆ N.W. Ger. Radio—Schmidt-Isserstedt (*PV. 36105*)
Vienna Phil.—Furtwängler (♭ *G.7ER 5001: 7ERF 131:*
           7ERQ 110: 7RW 101: 7RQ 3032)
Danish Radio—Malko (G.S 10614: ♭ *7P 145:*
        7BF 1049: 7PW 124: 7PQ 2014: 7RK 1)
Col. Sym.—Rodzinski (in ♯ Phi.S 04601L)
Philadelphia—Ormandy (in ♭ *AmC. set A 1073*)
Orch.—Kostelanetz (in ♯ AmC.CL 747: ♭ *A 1847*)
Salzburg Fest.—Weidlich (in ♯ Ply. 12-76)
Boston Sym.—Koussevitzky (♭ *DV. 26017;*
         o.v., ♭ *Cam.CAE 161:* in ♯ CAL 155)
Copenhagen Op.—T. Jensen (Tono.X 28185, d.c.)
MGM. Orch.—Marrow (in ♯ MGM.E 3138)
Los Angeles Phil.—Wallenstein (♯ *B.AXL 2012;*
                      D. 15036)

— — ARRANGEMENTS
VLN. & PF.   Auer
M. Elman & J. Seiger   in ♯ Vic.LM 1740
(♭ *set WDM 1740 & ERA 97;* ♭ *DV. 26035;* ♯ *FV.A 630277*)
GUITAR   L. Almeida (in ♯ *Crl. 56049*)
4 PFS.   First Pf. Qtt. (♭ *Vic.ERA 96*)
Manhattan Pf. Qtt. (in ♯ MGM.E 3100:
                      ♭ *in set X 245*)

... **3rd & 4th movts.** only
Boyd Neel Orch.—Dumont   ♭ *Phi.N 402031E*

... **4th movt., Finale,** only
☆ Vienna Phil.—Furtwängler (G.ED 1227: ♭ *7ER 5001:*
    7ERF 131: 7ERQ 110: 7RQ 3002: 7RW 123;
                      ♭ *Vic.EHA 9*)

Sérénade mélancolique, B flat minor, Op. 26
vln. & orch.
Anon. & Col. Sym.—Kurtz   ♯ AmC.ML 4671
(*Symphony No. 1—Andante; & Shostakovich*)
L. Kogan & A. Mitnik (pf.)   ♯ Eta.LPM 1011
(*Wieniawski & Schubert*)
M. Vaiman & M. Karandaszhova (pf.)
                      ♯ Ll.TW 91068
(*Valse-scherzo, Op. 34; Borodin, etc.*)
(*Valse-scherzo* only on ♯ *Lon.LD 9154*)
J. Fuchs & Camarata Orch.   in ♯ *B.AXL 2010*
                     (♯ *AmD.DL 4082*)
V. Abadjiev & pf. (*Bulg. 1337*)

SUITES
No. 1, D minor, Op. 43
N.Y.P.S.O.—Mitropoulos[1]   ♯ EPhi.ABL 3079
(*Borodin*)   (♯ AmC.ML 4966; Phi.A 01160L)
Moscow Radio—Gauk   ♯ USSR.D 01/2
☆ Winterthur Sym.—Goehr (♯ Clc. 6246)
... **Marche miniature,** only
N.Y.P.S.O.—Kostelanetz   in ♯ AmC.CL 758
... **Intermezzo** — ARR. VLC. & PF.
A. Vlasov & Anon.   in ♯ *USSR.D 1179*
(*Romance, above; & Ravel, Debussy*)

No. 2, C major, Op. 53
Moscow Radio—Gauk   ♯ USSR.D 01127/8
(2ss) (13ss—*Chant sans paroles* on USSR. 19771/83)
☆ Winterthur Sym.—Goehr (♯ Clc. 6222)

No. 3, G major, Op. 55
Paris Cons.—Boult   ♯ D.LXT 5099
(2ss)   (♯ Lon.LL 1295)
Moscow Radio—Samosud   ♯ USSR.D 0494/5
(2ss)
☆ Winterthur Sym.—Goehr (♯ Clc. 6126)
... **2nd movt., Valse mélancolique**
☆ Sym. Orch.—Tergowski (in ♯ *ANix.MLPY 5*)
Orch.—Kostelanetz (in ♯ AmC.CL 747)
... **4th movt., Theme & Variations,** only
Paris Cons.—Schuricht   ♯ D.LXT 2761
(*Capriccio italien*)   (♯ Lon.LL 640)

No. 4, G major, Op. 61—Mozartiana
1. Gigue, G major, K 574   (orig. pf.)
2. Minuet, D major, K355   (orig. pf.)
3. Ave verum corpus, K618   (orig. Motet—ARR. PF. Liszt)
4. Variations on 'Unser dummer Pöbel meint', K455 (orig. pf.)
Philharmonia—Fistoulari   ♯ P.PMC 1028
(*The Little Slippers, Suite*)   (♯ MGM.E 3026)
Lamoureux—v. Kempen   ♯ Phi.N 00271L
(*Serenade, Op. 48*)   (♯ Epic.LC 3213)
Moscow Radio—Gauk   ♯ *USSR.D 2285/6*
[1st & 4th movts. probably ☆]
☆ Slovak Phil.—Talich (♯ *Sup.LPM 65; U. 5038C;*
         with *Bach* on ♯ Csm.CRLP 229)

SYMPHONIES
No. 1, G minor, Op. 13   ("Winter rêveries")
Moscow Radio—Golovanov   ♯ Mon.MWL 309
(2ss)   (♯ USSR.D 0650/1)
(*Romeo & Juliet,* on ♯ Csm.CRLP 211)
☆ Vienna Philharmonia—Haefner   ♯ CA.LPA 1017
☆ Indianapolis Sym.—Sevitzky (♯ Cam.CAL 183 &
                     in set CFL 100)
... **Andante,** only
Col. Sym.—Kurtz   ♯ AmC.ML 4671
(*above & Shostakovich*)

---

[1] Omitting 3rd movt., Intermezzo.

No. 2, C minor, Op. 17 ("Little Russian")
Royal Phil.—Beecham   **♯ EPhi.ABL 3015**
(2ss)   (♯ Phi.A 01130L)
(*Nutcracker Suite—Valse*, on ♯ AmC.ML 4872)
Moscow Radio—Rakhlin   **♯ Mon.MWL 335**
(*Prince Igor, Overture*)
(*Liadov* on ♯ A440.AC 1204; *Rimsky-K.*
     on ♯ Csm.CRLP 212)
(3ss—*Str. Qtt.—Andante cantabile*, on ♯ USSR.D 1051/3)
Cincinnati Sym.—Johnson   **♯ Rem. 199-187**
Berlin Sym.—Rubahn   **♯ Roy. 1454**
☆ Minneapolis Sym.—Mitropoulos (♯ AmC.RL 6623)
Cincinnati Sym.—Goossens (♯ Cam.CAL 185 &
     in ♯ set CFL 100)

No. 3, D major, Op. 29 ("Polish")
Moscow Radio—Gauk   **♯ *USSR.D 1069/71***
(3ss—*Voyevoda*)
Berlin Sym.—Balzer   **♯ Roy. 1456**
Anon. Orch. (♯ Gram. 2079)
☆ Nat. Sym. (USA)—Kindler (♯ Cam.CAL 182 &
     in ♯ set CFL 100)
Vienna State Op.—Swoboda (♯ Clc. 6166)

No. 4, F minor, Op. 36
Philharmonia—Malko   **♯ G.CLP 1045**
(♯ FELP 129; BB.LBC 1052: ♭ set WBC 1052)
Philharmonia—Karajan   **♯ C.CX 1139**
(♯ QCX 10106: FCX 274; Angel. 35099)
Philadelphia—Ormandy (n.v.) **♯ AmC.ML 5074**
Moscow Radio—Gauk   **♯ USSR.D 01171/2**
(2ss)   (10ss, USSR. 022396/405)
Netherlands Phil.—Goehr   **♯ MMS. 16**
Leipzig Radio—Abendroth   **♯ Ura. 7159**
[Scherzo only, ♭ UREP 61]   (o.n. RS 7-25)
☆ R.I.A.S. Sym.—Fricsay   **♯ HP.DGM 18039**
     (♯ AmD.DL 9680)
(also 6ss, ♭ PV. 72355/7; 4th movt. only, in ♯ Pol. 19017)
☆ Chicago Sym.—Kubelik   **♯ G.ALP 1083**
     (♯ FALP 336)
[Scherzo only, ♭ Mer.EP-1-5001: FMer. 14533]
☆ Vienna State Op.—Scherchen   **♯ Nix.WLP 5096**
     (♯ Sel.LPG 8587)

☆ Residentie—v. Otterloo (♯ Epic.LC 3029)
Vienna Phil.—Furtwängler (♯ G.FALP 120:
     VALP 515: QALP 10095)
Philadelphia—Ormandy (o.v.) (♯ AmC.CL 766:
     ♭ set A 1093)
Czech Phil.—Nyazi (♯ Sup.LPV 212; U. 5208H)
Boston Sym.—Koussevitzky (♯ G.QALP 138; &
     (o.v.) ♯ Cam.CAL 109 & in ♯ set CFL 100)
Austrian Sym.—Brown (♯ Cum.CR 215; 3rd movt. only,
     ♯ Rem. 199-120; Ply. 12-54, etc.)
… 4th movt. excpt. **H** Boston Sym.—Muck (in ♯Vic.SRL12-11*)

No. 5, E minor, Op. 64
Philharmonia—Karajan   **♯ C.CX 1133**
(♯ QCX 10098: FCX 161; Angel. 35055)
B.B.C. Sym.—Sargent   **♯ G.ALP 1236**
     (♯ Vic.LM 1947)
Hamburg Radio—Schmidt-Isserstedt
     ♯ D.LXT 2758
     (♯ Lon.LL 691)
London Phil. Sym.—Rodzinski
(3ss)   **♯ West.LAB 8001**
Pittsburgh Sym.—Steinberg   **♯ Cap.P 8325**
Orch.—Stokowski   **♯ Vic.LM 1780**
     (♯ FV.A 630201; ItV.A12R 0048)
N.Y.P.S.O.—Mitropoulos   **♯ AmC.ML 5075**
(♯ Phi.S 04605L; also listed as ♯ AmC.CL 764)
Sonor Sym.—Ledermann   **♯ Pde. 2020**
Stadium Concerts—Rudolf   **♯ MApp. 59**
Berlin Radio—Konwitschny   **♯ Ura. 7134**
     (♯ MTW. 558)
Toronto Sym.—MacMillan   **♯ BB.LBC 1093[1]**
     (♯ Bea.LP 1001)
☆ Berlin Phil.—Fricsay   **♯ HP.DGM 18012**
(3rd movt. only, in ♯ Pol. 19017) (IPV.RVR 8187/90)
☆ Minneapolis Sym.—Dorati   **♯ EMer.MG 50008**
     (♯ FMer.MLP 7515)
(3rd movt. only, ♭ Mer.EP 1-5001; FMer.MEP 14533)

☆ Amsterdam—v. Kempen   **♯ EPhi.ABL 3007**
     (♯ Phi.A 00252L[2]; Epic.LC 3013)
Anon Orch. (♯ Gram. 2094)
☆ Philharmonia—Kletzki (♯ AmC.RL 3036)
Boston Sym.—Koussevitzky (♯ G.QALP 134)
La Scala—Cantelli (♯ G.FALP 329: QALP 10018)
Austrian Sym.—Wöss (♯ Msq. 10007; Cum.CR 249)
Philadelphia—Stokowski (♯ Cam.CAL 201 &
     in ♯ set CFL 100)
… 3rd movt., Waltz, only
☆ Victor Sym.—Reiner (♭ G.7ER 5022; ♭ Vic.ERA 83;
     ♭ DV. 26007)
Los Angeles Phil.—Wallenstein (D. 15036;
     ♯ B.AXL 2012)

No. 6, B minor, Op. 74 ("Pathétique")
Berlin Phil.—Markevitch   **♯ Pol. 18193**
     (♯ AmD.DL 9811)
Paris Cons.—Kleiber   **♯ D.LXT 2888**
     (♯ Lon.LL 920)
N.W. Ger. Radio—Schmidt-Isserstedt
     ♯ DT.LGX 66031
     (♯ FT. 320.TC.099; T.LSK 7030)
Pittsburgh Sym.—Steinberg   **♯ DCap.CTL 7071**
     (♯ Cap.P 8272)
London Phil. Sym.—Rodzinski
     ♯ West.WN 18048
Boston Sym.—Monteux   **♯ Vic.LM 1901**
     (♯ FV.A 630297; ItV.A12R 0173)
Berlin Phil.—Fricsay   **♯ HP. DGM 18104**
(6ss, ♭ PV. 72400/2; 3rd movt. only, in ♯ Pol. 19017)
Philharmonia—Cantelli   **♯ G.ALP 1042**
     (♯ FALP 330; Vic.LHMV 1047)
N.Y Stadium Concerts—Bernstein
     ♯ B.AXTL 1068
     (♯ AmD.DL 9718; SpC.CCL 35001)
Leipzig Phil.—Abendroth   **♯ Ura. 7147**
     (♯ Ura. RS 7-12; MTW. 29)
Czech Phil.—Talich   **♯ Sup.LPV 204**
     (♯ U. 5193H)
Zürich Tonhalle—Ackermann   **♯ MMS. 2014**
Leningrad Phil.—Mravinsky   **♯ Kings. 302**
(2ss)   (♯ USSR.D 0237/8)
(*Dargomijsky* on ♯ Csm.CRLP 213)
☆ Amsterdam—v. Kempen   **♯ EPhi.ABL 3000**
     (♯ Epic.LC 3003; Phi.A 00253L[3])
Anon. Orch. (♯ Gram. 2046)
☆ N.B.C. Sym.—Toscanini (♯ G.FALP/QALP 205;
     DV.L 16132)
Chicago Sym.—Kubelik (♯ FMer.MLP 7518)
Philadelphia—Ormandy (♭ AmC. set A 1073)
N.Y.P.S.O—Rodzinski (♯ AmC.RL 3118)
Austrian Sym.—Brown (♯ Cum.CR 248; Msq. 10009)
Hollywood Bowl—Stokowski (♯ Cam.CAL 152 &
     in ♯ sets CFL 100 & 104)
Philharmonia—Malko (♯ G.FELP 139)

… 3rd movt. only
Hamburg Philharmonia—H-J. Walther (*MSB. 78118*)

(The) Tempest, Op. 18
Moscow Radio—Golovanov **♯ *USSR.D 1139/40***
☆ Vienna Sym.—Fekete (*Fekete*)   **♯ CA.LPA 1024**

Valse mélancolique, E minor
☆ Sym. Orch.—Tergowski (in ♯ Clc. 11004)

Variations on a rococo theme, Op. 33 vlc. & orch.
M. Gendron & Suisse Romande—Ansermet
     ♯ D.LXT 2895
(*Schumann*)   (♯ Lon.LL 947)
S. Knushevitzky & Moscow Radio—Gauk
     ♯ USSR.D 0407
(*Glazounov*)   (*Miaskovsky* on ♯ Kings. 301)
(*Dvořák: Concerto*, on ♯ Csm.CRLP 231)
D. Shafran & Moscow Youth Sym.—Kondrashin
     (USSR. 021522/6)

(The) Voyevoda, Op. 78 sym. ballad
☆ State Sym.—Ivanov   **♯ *USSR.D 1071***
(*Sym. No. 3, s. 3*)
☆ Netherlands Phil.—Goehr (in ♯ MMS. 66, d.c.)

---

[1] Originally announced as LBC 1068: ♭ set WBC 1068.
[2] A new edition, restoring cut made in Finale, and avoiding turnover in 2nd movement.
[3] New edition from the original tapes.

II. VOCAL

A. OPERAS

(The) ENCHANTRESS 4 Acts 1887
The Prince's Aria B   Act II
P. Lisitsian   in ♯ Csm.CRLP 138

The Gossip's aria (unspec.) S
M. Foltyn   **Muza.X 2150**
(*Moniuszko: Krakowiak, etc.*)
L. Lobanova-Rogachova   *USSR. 19911*
(*Guardsman, aria*)
A. Yurovskaya (*Ukrainian*) (USSR. 021951)

Where are you (Kuma) S   Act IV
☆ E. Smolenskaya (in ♯ Sti. 1000; in ♯ Csm.CRLP 138)

EUGENE ONIEGIN, Op. 24 3 Acts 1879
COMPLETE RECORDINGS

Casts		Set D	Set R
Oniegin (B)	... ...	D. Popovich	And. Ivanov
Tatiana (S)	... ...	V. Heybalova	E. Kruglikova
Olga (M-S)	... ...	B. Tzveych	M. Maksakova
Lenski (T)	... ...	D. Startz	I. Kozlovsky
Prince Gremin (Bs)	...	M. Changalovich	M. Reizen

Set D with Belgrade Op. Cho. & Orch.—Danon
       ♯ **D.LXT 5159/61**
(6ss)   (♯ Lon.LL 1375/7, set XLLA 41)

Set R with Bolshoi Theatre Cho. & Orch.—Orlov
       ♯ **CdM.LDX 8088/90**
(6ss)   (♯ Csm.CRLP 10270, 80 & 90)

☆ HIGHLIGHTS in *Russian*
No. 12, Written words   And. Ivanov
No. 17, Faint echo of my youth   I. Kozlovsky
No. 20c, Everyone knows love on earth   M. Reizen
No. 19, Polonaise   Bolshoi Th. Orch.
  (*Pique Dame, below*)
       ♯ USSR.D 01402

HIGHLIGHTS in *German*
  Prelude   (*a*)
☆ No. 9, Tatiana's letter scene   S
No. 12, Written words   (Oniegin's aria)   B
No. 13, Waltz   (*a*)
☆ No. 17, Faint echo of my youth   (Lenski's aria)   T
No. 19, Polonaise   (*b*)
No. 20c, Everyone knows love on earth   (Bs)
  E. Trötschel (S), W. Ludwig (T), J. Metternich (B),
   J. Greindl (Bs), (*a*) Bavarian Radio—Lehmann,
   (*b*) Munich Phil.—Hollreiser   ♯ Pol. 19023

HIGHLIGHTS in *German*
I. Camphausen (S), G. Ramms (B), W. Horst (T), I. Mehler
(A), Dresden State Op. Cho. & Orch.—Schreiber
       ♯ Allo. 3098

Selection   — ARR HARP.
O. Erdeli (in ♯ USSR.D 1214)

ACT I

No. 6, I love you, Olga   T   (*Lenski's Arioso*)
☆ I. Kozlovsky (? from set) (USSR. 020895)
S. Lemeshev (in ♯ Csm.CRLP 138 & USSRM.D 00991)
♭ L. Sobinoff (AF.AGSB 86*)

No. 9, Tatiana's Letter Scene   S
☆ L. Welitsch   (*Ger*)   ♯ *C.C 1011*
  (*Salome*) (in ♯ AmC.ML 4795)   (♯ *VC 806*)
☆ L. Albanese   ♯ *G.BLP 1075*
  (*Villa-Lobos*)   (♯ *G.QBLP 1025*)
M. Matyas (Qual.MN 1051)
☆ E. Trötschel (*Ger*) (in ♯ Pol. 19036)

No. 12, Written words   (Oniegin's aria)   B
E. Belov   **USSR. 022320/1**
[with A. Yakovenko (S)]
J. Adamczewski   **Muza.X 2342**
(*Aida—Celeste Aida*)
J. Metternich (*Ger*)   *Pol. 62934*
(*Africaine, aria*)   (♭ *32024*)
B. Puzin (*Ukrainian*) (USSR. 21931/2: in ♯ D 1950)

ACT II

No. 13, Waltz   orch.
Berlin Municipal—Rother   ♭ *T.US 45723*
(*No. 19*)
Westminster Sym.—Collingwood   **C.DX 1893**
(*No. 19*)   (♭ *SCD 2029: SCDW 113*)

Bavarian State—Lehmann   ♭ *Pol. 30020*
(*Ruslan & Ludmilla Overture*)   (♭ *AmD.ED 3521*)
Berlin Sym.—Günther   in ♯ *Roy.* 1448
"Philharmonic"—List   in ♯ *Allo.* 3059
       (♯ *Pac.*LDAD 52)
Orch.—Schneiderhann (in ♯ *Mae.OA 20008*)
U.S.S.R. State—Samosud (*USSR. 16812/3*)
☆ Stadium Concerts—Smallens (♯ *D.UW 333002;*
       D. 15037)
  Boston Prom.—Fiedler (♭ *Cam.CAE 135*)
  Bolshoi Theatre—Melik-Pasheyev (in ♯ Csm.CRLP 145)[1]
  Los Angeles—Wallenstein (in ♯ *B.AXL 2012*)
— ARR. 2 PFS.
  M. Rawicz & W. Landauer (♭ *C.SEG 7506: SEDQ 514*)
— ARR. 4 PFS.   Manhattan Pf. Qtt. (in ♯ MGM.E 3100:
       in ♭ *set X 245*)

No. 17, Faint echo of my youth   T   (*Lenski's Aria*)
N. Gedda   in ♯ *C.CX* 1130
(*Rigoletto, Muette de Portici, etc.*)
       (♯ *FCX* 302; Angel. 35096)
A. Schiøtz (*Dan*)[2]   **G.DB 10523**
(*Faust—Salut, demeure*)
A. Dermota (*Ger*)   ♭ *T.UV 110*
(*Tosca—Recondita armonia*) (in ♯ *DT.TM* 68037;
       ♭ *FT. 470.TC.015*)
W. Kmentt (*Ger*)   in ♯ *Phi.S 06075R*
(*Prince Igor, Sadko, etc.*)
J. Simándy (*Hung*)   **Qual.MN 1007**
(*Trovatore—Di quella pira*)
  S. Lemeshev (? n.v.) (USSR. 022286/7:
     in ♯ *USSR.D 1412;* in ♯ *CdM.LDM 8070;*
       Csm.CRLP 138, d.cs.)
  B. Paprocki (2ss, Muza.X 1716)
  P. Belinnik (in ♯ *USSR.D 1952*)
☆ I. Kozlovsky (in ♯ *USSR.D 1428*)
♭ L. Sobinoff (AF.AGSB 86*)
  G. Martinelli (*Ital*) (in ♯ SBDH.LPG 4*)
  R. Tauber (*Ger*) (in ♯ Ete. 701*)
  E. Caruso (*Fr*) (AF.AGSB 18*)

ACT III

No. 19, Polonaise
Munich Phil.—Hollreiser   *PV. 36086*
(*Dvořák: Rusalka, Polonaise*)   (♭ *Pol. 30013*)
Westminster Sym.—Collingwood   **C.DX 1893**
(*No. 13*)   (♭ *SCD 2029: SCDW 113*)
Berlin Municipal—Rother   ♭ *T.US 45723*
(*No. 13*)   (in ♯ *LB 6124*)
"Philharmonic"—List (in ♯ Allo. 3059; Pac.LDAD 52)
Berlin Sym.—Günther (in ♯ Roy. 1448)
☆ Stadium Concerts—Smallens (♯ *D.UW 333002*)
  Boston Prom.—Fiedler (♭ *Cam.CAE 142* &
       in ♯ CAL 142)
  Bolshoi Theatre—Melik-Pasheyev (in ♯Csm.CRLP 145)[1]

No. 20c, Everyone knows love on earth   Bs
  (*Gremin's aria*)
B. Christoff   **G.DB 21626**
(*Rimsky: Kitezh—aria*)   (in ♯ Vic.LHMV 1033:
       ♭ *set WHMV 1033*)
R. Arié   ♯ *D.LW 5061*
(*Prince Igor, Sadko, Life for the Tsar*) (♯ *Lon.LD 9074*)
G. Frick (*Ger*)   **G.DB 11566**
(*Halévy: La Juive, aria*)   (♭ *7RW 519*: in ♯ *WBLP 1505*)
J. Greindl (*Ger*)   ♭ *Pol. 34006*
(*Boris Godounov—Monologue*)   (♭ *30102*)
S. Belarsky   in ♯ *Vic.LPM 3274*
(*Roussalka, Boris, etc.*)   (♭ *set EPB 3274*)
B. Gmyria   *USSRM.D 00741*
(*Faust, aria*)
B. Sönnerstedt (*Swed*)   *Symf.R 1004*
☆ M. Reizen (USSRM.D 00251)
♭ R. Mayr (in ♯ Sca. 822*)

No. 21, Alas there is no doubt   (*Arioso*)   B
B. Puzin (*Ukrainian*)   in ♯ *USSR.D 1950*
(*above; & Halka, Boris*)   (& USSR. 21918)

(The) GUARDSMAN (*Oprichnik*) 4 Acts 1874
Overture & Ballet Music
Linz Sym.   in ♯ *Ply.* 12-35
(*Rimsky, Glinka, Borodin*)

---

[1] Later lists quote Orlov as conductor (i.e. from set)   [2] Recorded 1944.

(The) GUARDSMAN (*continued*)
Ballet Music
Viennese Sym. (in ♯ Ply. 12-89)

Natasha's Arioso S Act I
L. Lobanova-Rogachova *USSR. 19910*
(*Enchantress, aria*)
E. Kruglikova in ♯ **Csm.CRLP 138**

Morozova's aria: I thought I heard voices Act II
☆ V. Davidova (M-S) *USSRM.D 247*
(*Trovatore—Mal reggendo, etc.*)

IOLANTHE, Op. 69 1 Act 1891
HIGHLIGHTS
  Iolanthe's aria   S   Sc. 1
☆ King René's arioso   Bs   Sc. 4
  Duke Robert's aria   B   Sc. 6
T. Lavrova, B. Gmyria, S. Shaposhnikov
                ♯ *USSR.D 1522*
(*Rubinstein: Demon, excerpts*)

Iolanthe's aria S Sc. 1
☆ G. Zhukovskaya (in ♯ Csm.CRLP 138)

What can compare? Bs (King René) Sc. 4
I. Petrov *USSRM.D 001319*
(*Aleko, aria*)
  ☆ A. Pirogov (in ♯ Csm.CRLP 138)
  B. Gmyria (*USSRM.D 00809*)

Duke Robert's aria: Haste not! B Sc. 6
B. Puzin *USSR. 19854*
(*Tsar's Bride, aria*)
  ☆ Al. Ivanov (in ♯ Csm.CRLP 138)

Duet, Iolanthe & Vaudemont: We are alone
S & T Sc. 7
☆ E. Shumskaya & V. Kilchevsky (*USSRM.D 869/70*)

Vaudemont's Romance: You're weeping T
V. Kilchevsky *USSRM.D 001127*
(*Ippolitoff-Ivanoff & Rachmaninoff*)

JOAN OF ARC 4 Acts 1879
(or: *The Maid of Orleans*)
EXCERPTS
Hymn & Joan's Aria Act I
Scene & Duet, Joan & Lionel Act III
S. Preobrazhenskaya (S), L. Solomyak (T), etc. Leningrad
Kirov Op. & Orch.—Khaikin ♯ *USSR.D 1312/3*

Farewell, forests S or M-S Act I
☆ V. A. Davidova (in ♯ Csm.CRLP 138)
M. Anderson (*Fr*) (in ♯ Roy. 1589; *Var. 6986*)

(The) LITTLE SLIPPERS 3 Acts 1887
(*Cherevitchki*)
See below, VAKULA THE SMITH

MAZEPPA 3 Acts 1883
COMPLETE RECORDING
  Mazeppa ... ... Al. Ivanov (B)
  Maria ... ... N. Pokrovskaya (S)
  Kochubey ... ... I. Petrov (Bs)
  Liubov ... ... V. Davidova (M-S)
  Andrei ... ... G. Bolshakov (T)
  Orlik ... ... V. Tyutunnik (Bs)
  Iskra ... ... T. Cherniakov (T)
  Cossack ... ... F. Godovkin (T)
& Bolshoi Theatre Cho. & Orch.—Nebolsin
(6ss) ♯ **CHS. set CHS 1310**
            (8ss, ♯ USSR.D 01286/93)
(also, 40ss, USSR. 019525/6 & 019633/70)

HIGHLIGHTS
Act II, Sc. 1
I. Yashugin (Bs), I. Shashkov (Bs) & Leningrad Kirov
Op. Orch.—Khaikin
Act II, Sc. 2, Pt. 1
Al. Ivanov (B) & Bolshoi Theatre Orch.—K. Ivanov
Act II, Sc. 2, Pt. 2
I. Alexiev (B), S. Preobrazhenskaya (M-S) & Leningrad
Op. Orch.—Khaikin ♯ **Mon.MWL 353**

Cossack Dance (Gopak) Act I
☆ Philharmonia—Malko ♭ *G.7P 143*
(*Khovanshchina—Entr'acte*) (♭ 7PQ 2019: 7BF 1059)

The Battle of Poltava orch.
Bolshoi Theatre—Nebolsin *USSRM.D 00203*
(*Prince Igor, March*)

Complaint of the mother Act II
V. Davidova (M-S) in ♯ **Csm.CRLP 138**

Duet, María & Liubov S & M-S
N. Serval & S. Preobrazhenskaya
              in ♯ *USSR.D 1424*
(*Aida, Tsar's Bride*)

The Three Treasures B
A. Ivanov in ♯ **Csm.CRLP 138**

O Maria (Arioso) Bs Act III
I. Petrov in ♯ **Csm.CRLP 138**
            (♯ USSR.D 2606)
  T. Kuuzik (*Estonian*) (in ♯ USSR.D 2090)
  B. Puzin (*Ukrainian*) (*USSR. 21931/2*)

PIQUE DAME, Op. 68 3 Acts 1890
(*The Queen of Spades*)
COMPLETE RECORDING
  Herman ... ... G. Nelepp (T)
  Tomsky ... ... Al. Ivanov (B)
  Prince Yeletsky ... ... P. Lisitsian (B)
  Chekalinsky ... ... A. Peregudov (T)
  Lisa ... ... E. Smolenskaya (S)
  Sourin ... ... V. Tyutunnik (Bs)
  Countess ... ... E. Verbitzkaya (M-S)
etc., Bolshoi Theatre Cho. & Orch.—Melik-
Pasheyev ♯ **Mon.MWL 323/5**
(6ss) (♯ CHS. set CHS 1305)
(8ss, ♯ USSR.D 05558/65)
[Highlights on ♯ MMS. 2012: also ♯ OP 7]

HIGHLIGHTS
Tomski's ballad; Liza's arioso; Yeletzky's aria; Hermann's
Arioso & Aria (mainly probably ☆)
B. Gmyria, E. Smolenskaya, S. Shaposhnikov,
G. Nelepp ♯ **USSR.D 01403**

HIGHLIGHTS — ARR. ORCH. Kostelanetz
Orch.—Kostelanetz ♯ **EPhi.NBL 5020**
(*Gershwin*) (♯ AmC.CL 721: o.n. ML 4904;
              ♯ Phi.S 06621R, 2ss)
Orchestral Selection Sym.—Rybicka (*Muza. 1676/7*)
Ballet Music (unspec.)
☆ Bolshoi Theatre—Samosud (in ♯ Csm.CRLP 145)

ACT I

No. 2, Her name is unknown to me ...
  Once I knew happiness (Hermann) T
G. Nelepp (from set) in ♯ **Csm.CRLP 138**
              (USSRM.D 00801)
  V. Kozeratzky (*Ukrainian*) (*USSR. 21718*)
  A. Frinberg (*Latvian*) (*USSR. 22244*: in ♯ *D 1899*)

No. 5, It chanced at Versailles (Tomsky) B
J. Adamczewski **Muza.X 2282**
(*Smetana: The Kiss—Cradle Song*)
B. Gmyria *USSRM.D 00114*
(*Aleko, aria*)

No. 7, Already shades of night 2 S
E. Smolenskaya & V. Borisenko *USSR. 22092*
(*No. 14*)
  T. Ponomarenko & A. Sopova (*Ukrainian*) (*USSR. 21845*)

No. 8, Dear Friends (*Pauline's romance*) S or M-S
Z. Dolukhanova in ♯ **CdM.LDM 8134**
(*Snow Maiden; Glinka, Prokofiev, etc.*)
  A. Sopova (*Ukrainian*) (*USSR. 21844*)

ACT II

No. 10a, O burning tears S
☆ L. Welitsch (*Ger*) ♯ *D.LW 5050*
(*below & Ballo in Maschera*) (♯ Lon.LD 9041)

No. 10b, Forgive me, bright celestial visions T
A. Frinberg (*Latvian*) in ♯ **USSR.D 1899**
(*above, below; Otello, etc.*) (also USSR. 19958)
  V. Kozeratzky (*Ukrainian*) (*USSR. 21917*)

No. 12, I love you, dear Bs (Yeletsky)
A. Hiolski **Muza.X 2146**
(*Moniuszko: The Haunted Castle—Finale, Act II*)
P. Lisitsian (from set) **USSR. 022288**
(*Sadko*)
  B. Puzin (*Ukrainian*) (*USSR. 21928/30*)
  ☆ A. Ivanov (in ♯ Csm.CRLP 138)

(*continued on next page*)

☆ = Re-issue of a recording to be found in previous volumes.

PIQUE DAME, Act II (*continued*)

No. 14, Alas, my darling swain S & M-S
V. Firsova & V. Borisenko *USSR. 22093*
(*No. 7*)

No. 16, Scene & Countess' aria: How stale the world M-S
A. Ludin (*Latvian*) USSR. 021537/8

ACT III

No. 20, 'Twill soon be midnight S
R. Konforti (*Bulgarian*) ♯ *USSR.D 2157*
(*Borodin, Saint-Saëns, etc.*)
☆ L. Welitsch (*Ger*) ♯ *D.LW 5050*
(*above*) (♯ *Lon.LD 9041*)
☆ J. Hammond (*Eng*) (G.ED 1223)

No. 23, Darling maidens B (Tomsky)
☆ A. Ivanov (in ♯ Csm.CRLP 138)

No. 24, What is our life? T
G. Nelepp (from set) *USSRM.D 00801*
(*No. 2; & Vakula the Smith*)
A. Frinberg (*Latvian*) (*USSR. 22245*: & in ♯ *D 1899*)
V. Kozeratzky (*Ukrainian*) (*USSR. 21719*)

SNOW MAIDEN, Op. 12
Inc. Music to Ostrovsky's play 1873

COMPLETE RECORDING
Z. Dolukhanova (A), A. Orfenov (T), Moscow
Radio Cho. & Orch.—Gauk
  ♯ *Mon.MEL 702/3*
(4ss) (2ss, ♯ CHS.CHS 1301; ♯ CdM.LDXA 8054)
Shepherd Lehl's Songs (3)
☆ Z. Dolukhanova (A) (*USSRM.D 00669/70*, 2ss;
Nos. 1 & 2 only, in ♯ *CdM.LDM 8070*; No. 3
in ♯ *CdM.LDM 8134*)

VAKULA THE SMITH 4 Acts 1876
COMPLETE RECORDING of the revised version:
The Little Slippers, 3 Acts 1887
G. Nelepp (T), A. Ivanov (B), etc., Bolshoi
Theatre Cho. & Orch.—Melik-Pasheyev
  ♯ *Csm.CRLP 243/5*
(6ss) (8ss, ♯ USSR.D 089/96)
Orchestral Suite
(Intro.; Minuet; Intro., Act III; Russian Dance; Cossack
Dance; Finale)
Philharmonia—Fistoulari ♯ *P.PMC 1028*
(*Suite No. 4—"Mozartiana"*) (♯ MGM.E 3026)
Vakula's aria, Act I
Vakula's song, Act III T
G. Nelepp (from set) *USSRM.D 00802*
(*Pique Dame, arias*)
☆ S. Lemeshev (in ♯ Csm.CRLP 138)

Dance of the Zaporogues (Cossack Dance)
Bolshoi Theatre—Melik-Pashayev
  in ♯ *CdM.LD 8055*

II. B. SONGS

COLLECTIONS
Does the day reign, Op. 47, No. 6 (Apukhtin) *120.150*
Tell me, what in the shade, Op. 57, No. 1 (Sologub)
  120.150
Serenade, Op. 63, No. 6 (Gd. Duke Constantine)
  120.151
At the open window, Op. 63, No. 2 (idem) *120.151*
A Ballroom meeting, Op. 38, No. 3 (A. K. Tolstoy)
  120.151
I. Maslennikova (S), A. Makarov (pf.)
Mignon's Song, Op. 25, No. 3 (Goethe, trs. Tyutchev)
  120.152
Why? Op. 6, No. 5 (Heine, trs. Mey) *120.152*
O thou moonlight night, Op. 73, No. 3 (Rathaus)
  120.153
Love's beginning, Op. 6, No. 3 (Rathaus) *120.153*
None but the weary heart, Op. 6, No. 6 (Goethe, trs. Mey)
  120.154
So soon forgotten (Apukhtin) 1870 *120.154*
L. Adveyeva (M-S), A. Makarov (pf.)
[above also on ♯ 720003]
Ø Again, as before, alone, Op. 73, No. 6 (Rathaus) *120.155*
Ø The Fearful minute, Op. 28, No. 6 (Tchaikovsky) *120.155*
Don Juan's Serenade, Op. 38, No. 1 (A. K. Tolstoy)
  120.156
Ø A Tear trembles, Op. 6, No. 4 (A. K. Tolstoy) *120.156*
I. Petrov (Bs), N. Walter (pf.) *Eta. 120150/6*

The Maslennikova & Adveyeva songs also on
♯ *LPM 1024* with: Was I not a little blade of grass,
Op. 47, No. 7 (Surikov). The Petrov songs marked
Ø also on ♯ *720002*, o.n. *LPM 1011*, with O bless
you, forests, Op. 47, No. 5 (A. K. Tolstoy), and
Boris and *Barbiere* arias.

The Mild stars shone for us, Op. 60, No. 12 (Polonsky)
Why? Op. 6, No. 5 (Heine, trs. Mey)
N. Obukhova (M-S)

A Ballroom meeting, Op. 38, No. 3 (A. K. Tolstoy)
O thou moonlit night, Op. 73, No. 3 (Rathaus)
Pimpinella, Op. 38, No. 6 (*Florentine Song*)
I. Kozlovsky (T)

Tell me, what in the shade, Op. 57, No. 1 (Sologub)
He loved me so, Op. 28, No. 4 (Anon.)
I. Maslennikova (S)

Silence descends on the golden cornfields, Op. 57, No. 2
  (A. K. Tolstoy)
Don Juan's Serenade, Op. 38, No. 1 (A. K. Tolstoy)
M. Reizen (Bs) ♯ *USSR.D 2008/9*

"Tchaikovsky Romances"
S. Lemeshev (T), I. Kozlovsky (T), N. Obukhova
(M-S), etc. ♯ Csm.CRLP 10040/1
(4ss) [for contents, see below]

Love's beginning, Op. 6, No. 3
  (Gombert, trs. Rostopchina)
☆ The fires in the rooms were already extinguished,
  Op. 63, No. 5 (Gd. Duke Constantine)
Zemfira's song (Pushkin—*The Gypsies*)
Z. Dolukhanova (A) *USSR.D 00667/8*
(1½ss—*Rachmaninoff*)

Reconciliation, Op. 25, No. 1 (Shcherbina)
☆ A Ballroom meeting, Op. 38, No. 3 (A. K. Tolstoy)
☆ The First meeting, Op. 63, No. 4 (Gd. Duke Constantine)
B. Gmyria (Bs) ♯ *USSR.D 1595*
(*Rachmaninoff, Glinka & Rimsky*)

The Fearful minute, Op. 28, No. 6 (Tchaikovsky)
If I could express in one word (Heine, trs. Mey)
☆ The First meeting, Op. 63, No. 4 (Gd. Duke Constantine)
B. Gmyria (Bs) (2ss) *USSRM.D 00602/3*

A Ballroom meeting, Op. 38, No. 3 (A. K. Tolstoy)
Does the day reign, Op. 47, No. 6 (Apukhtin)
Lullaby, Op. 16, No. 1 (Maikov)
Why? Op. 6, No. 5 (Heine, trs. Mey)
Why did I dream of you? Op. 28, No. 3 (Mey)
M. Lichtegg (T, *Ger*), H. W. Häusslein (pf.)
  ♯ *D.LM 4556*
(*Mendelssohn*) (♯ *Lon.LS 799*)

☆ Again as before, alone, Op. 73, No. 6 (Rathaus)
A Ballroom meeting, Op. 38, No. 3 (A. K. Tolstoy)
I'll tell thee nothing, Op. 60, No. 2 (Fet)
A Tear trembles, Op. 6, No. 4 (A. K. Tolstoy)
I. Kozlovsky (T) (2ss) *USSRM.D 00121/2*

At the open window, Op. 63, No. 2
  (Gd. Duke Constantine)
☆ Evening, Op. 27, No. 4 (Shevchenko, trs. Mey)
No, I shall never name her, Op. 28, No. 1
  (A. de Musset, trs. Grekov)
☆ None but the weary heart, Op. 6, No. 6 (Goethe, trs. Mey)
S. Lemeshev (T) (2ss) *USSRM.D 00747/8*

Does the day reign, Op. 47, No. 6 (Apukhtin)
It was in early spring, Op. 38, No. 2 (A. K. Tolstoy)
☆ No response or word of greeting, Op. 28, No. 5
  (Apukhtin)
☆ Serenade, Op. 63, No. 6 (*O Child . . .*)
  (Gd. Duke Constantine)
S. Lemeshev (T) (2ss) *USSRM.D 00693/4*

The Nightingale, Op. 60, No. 4 (Pushkin)
It was in early spring, Op. 38, No. 2 (A. K. Tolstoy)
☆ Serenade, Op. 63, No. 6 (*O Child . . .*)
  (Gd. Duke Constantine)
Does the day reign, Op. 47, No. 6 (Apukhtin)
S. Lemeshev (T) ♯ *USSR.D 1413*
(*Eugen Oniegin; & Borodin*)

The Nightingale, Op. 60, No. 4 (Pushkin)
The Sun has set, Op. 73, No. 4 (Rathaus)
Tell me, what in the shade of the branches, Op. 57, No. 1
  (Sologub)
Mid sombre days, Op. 73, No. 5 (Rathaus)
S. Lemeshev (T) (2ss) *USSRM.D 00691/2*

♯ = Long-playing, 33⅓ r.p.m. ♭ = 45 r.p.m. ♮ = Auto. couplings, 78 r.p.m.

SONGS—COLLECTIONS (*continued*)

    Child's Song: My little Lisa, Op. 54, No. 16 (Aksakov)
    My little garden, Op. 54, No. 4 (Pleshcheev)
    Tell me, what in the shade of the branches, Op. 57, No. 1
        (Sologub)
I. Maslennikova (S)   *USSR. 021627/8*

    The Fearful minute, Op. 28, No. 6 (Tchaikovsky)
    Frenzied nights, Op. 60, No. 6 (Apukhtin)
    None but the weary heart, Op. 6, No. 6 (Goethe, trs. Mey)
    Why did I dream of you, Op. 28, No. 3 (Mey)
G. Nelepp (T)   ♯ *USSR.D 2075*
(*Wagner, Bizet, Verdi*)

  ☆ The Fearful minute, Op. 28, No. 6 (Tchaikovsky)
  ☆ The Fires in the rooms were already extinguished,
    Op. 63, No. 5 (Gd. Duke Constantine)
  ☆ It was in early spring, Op. 38, No. 2 (A. K. Tolstoy)
    The Mild stars shone for us, Op. 60, No. 12 (Polonsky)
    Night, Op. 73, No. 2 (Rathaus)
    None but the weary heart, Op. 6, No. 6 (Goethe, trs. Mey)
  ☆ Serenade, Op. 63, No. 6 (Gd. Duke Constantine)
    Was I not a little blade of grass, Op. 47, No. 7 (Surikov)
N. Obukhova (M-S) (2ss)   ♯ *USSR.D 2464/5*

  ☆ Song of the Gypsy girl, Op. 60, No. 7 (Polonsky)
  ☆ We sat together, Op. 73, No. 1 (Rathaus)
  ☆ Why? Op. 6, No. 5 (Heine, trs. Mey)
N. Obukhova (M-S)   ♯ *USSR.D 1548*
(*Glinka & Folksongs*)

    Forgive & forget, Op. 60, No. 8 (Nekrassov)
    Night, Op. 60, No. 9 (Polonsky)
    O if thou couldst, Op. 38, No. 4 (A. K. Tolstoy)
A. Pirogov (B)   *USSRM.D 00783/4*

  ☆ Dusk fell on the earth, Op. 47, No. 3
      (Mickiewicz, trs. Berg)
    I do not please you, Op. 63, No. 3
      (Gd. Duke Constantine)
    Silence descends on the golden cornfields, Op. 57, No. 2
      (A. K. Tolstoy)
M. Reizen (Bs)   *USSRM.D 00618/9*

    I'll tell thee nothing, Op. 60, No. 2 (Fet)
    The mild stars shone for us, Op. 60, No. 12 (Polonsky)
    Night, Op. 60, No. 9 (Polonsky)
    So soon forgotten (Apukhtin)
    (16) CHILDREN'S SONGS, Op. 54 (Pleshcheev)
    … No. 3, Spring (The grass grows green)
    … No. 4, My little garden
    … No. 9, Spring (The snow's already melting)
    … No. 10, Lullaby in a storm
    … No. 13, Spring Song
G. Vinogradov (T), G. Orentlicher (pf.)
        ♯ *USSR.D 2590/1*

Accept just once, Op. 16, No. 3 (Fet)
And. Ivanov (B)   *USSR. 23011*
(*Rachmaninoff: Beloved let us fly*)

Again, as before, alone, Op. 73, No. 6 (Rathaus) ☐
A. Pirogov (B)   *USSR. 22825*
(*Balakirev: The wilderness*)
  ☆ S. Lemeshev (T) (in ♯ Csm.CRLP 10041)

— ARR. ORCH. Stokowski ("*Solitude*")
Orch.—Stokowski   ♭ *Vic.ERA 182*
(*Humoresque & Rachmaninoff*)
(& in ♯ LM 1774; ♯ FV.A 630264; ItV.A12R 0008;
                  ♭ *FV.A 95217*)
  ☆ Hollywood Bowl—Stokowski (in ♯ Cam.CAL 153)

As o'er the burning ashes, Op. 25, No. 2 (Tyutchev)
  ☆ S. Lemeshev (T) (in ♯ Csm.CRLP 10400)

At the open window, Op. 63, No. 2 ☐
  (Gd. Duke Constantine)
W. Nikitin   *Ete. 30-5017*
(*Glinka & Glier*)

Autumn, Op. 54, No. 14 (Pleshcheev)
M. Reizen (Bs)   *USSRM.D 00617*
(*A Tear trembles*)

(A) Ballroom meeting, Op. 38, No. 3 ☐
(A. K. Tolstoy) (*At the ball; or, The tapers were flashing*)
I. Kozlovsky (T)   in ♯ **Csm.CRLP 10400**
[see collection; also on *USSR.* 20229 & *Eta.* 30-5005]
W. Wermińska (S), S. Nadgryzowski (pf.) (*Muza.* 2467)
  ☆ G. Vinogradov (T) (*Eta.* 30-5019)

Behind the window in the shadow, Op. 60, No. 10
  (Polonsky)
  ☆ S. Shaposhnikov (B) (in ♯ Csm.CRLP 10041)

Disappointment, Op. 65, No. 2 (Collin) (*Déception*)
  ☆ I. Kozlovsky (T) (in ♯ Csm.CRLP 10041)

Do not ask, Op. 57, No. 3 (Strugovshnikov)
Z. Dolukhanova (A)   *USSRM.D 00664*
(*Serenade & Borodin*) (*Rachmaninoff*, on *USSR.* 20417)

Do not doubt me, dear, Op. 6, No. 1 (A. K. Tolstoy)
  (or: *Do not believe . . .*)
E. Kruglikova (S)   *USSR. 9883*
(*Wait*)

Does the day reign? Op. 47, No. 6 (Apukhtin) ☐
S. Lemeshev (T)   *USSR. 18861*
(*Glinka: Adele*)   (in ♯ Csm.CRLP 10040)
[& see collection, above]

Don Juan's Serenade, Op. 38, No. 1 ☐
(A. K. Tolstoy)
P. Lisitsian (B)   *USSR. 22913*
(*Saint-Saëns: L'Attente*)
  ☆ S. Lemeshev (in ♯ Csm.CRLP 10400)
    N. Eddy (B, *Eng*) & orch. (♭ AmC.A 1576)
  Ⓗ E. Caruso (T) (in ♯ Vic.LCT 1129*)

Evening, Op. 27, No. 4 (Shevchenko, trs. Mey) ☐
S. Preobrazhenskaya (M-S) in ♯ *USSR.D 1166*
(*I did not love thee; & Rimsky, Varlamov, etc.*)

(The) Fearful minute, Op. 28, No. 6 ☐
  (Tchaikovsky)
  (or: *One small word*, or: *Sweet maid, give answer*)
  ☆ N. Obukhova (M-S) (in ♯ Csm.CRLP 10400)

(The) Fires in the rooms were already extinguished,
  Op. 63, No. 5 (Gd. Duke Constantine) ☐
  ☆ N. Obukhova (M-S) (in ♯ Csm.CRLP 10041)

Frenzied nights, Op. 60, No. 6 (Apukhtin) ☐
G. Nelepp (T)   *USSR. 22055*
(*Why?*) [see collection]
N. Postavnicheva[1]   *USSR. 17182*
(*So soon forgotten*)
L. Rudenko (M-S)   in ♯ *USSR.D 2073*
(*below; & Rimsky, Bizet, Saint-Saëns*)

Granny and Grandson, Op. 54, No. 1 (Pleshcheev)
  ☆ S. Lemeshev (T) (in ♯ Csm.CRLP 10041)

He loved me, Op. 28, No. 4 (Anon.)
  ☆ T. Lavrova (S) (in ♯ Csm.CRLP 10400)

I did not love thee at first, Op. 63, No. 1
  (Gd. Duke Constantine)
S. Preobrazhenskaya (M-S) in ♯ *USSR.D 1166*
(*Evening; & Rimsky, Sokolov, etc.*)

I do not please you, Op. 63, No. 3 ☐
  (Gd. Duke Constantine)
A. Pirogov (B)   *USSR. 22547*
(*Rachmaninoff: In the silent night*)
E. Katulskaya (S)   *USSRM.D 00777*
(*Lullaby in a storm; & Glinka*)
S. Migai (B)   *USSR. 9890*
(*I'll tell thee nothing*)
  ☆ S. Preobrazhenskaya (M-S) (in ♯ Csm.CRLP 10041)

I opened the window, Op. 63, No. 2
  (Gd. Duke Constantine)
S. Shaposhnikov (B)   *USSR. 22280*
(*Rimsky: Thy glance is radiant*)

If I could express in one word (Heine, trs. Mey) ☐
  ☆ I. Kozlovsky (T) (*Ete.* 30-5005)

I'll tell thee nothing, Op. 60, No. 2 (Fet) ☐
I. Kozlovsky (T)   *USSR. 20383*
(*Rimsky: In the hills of Georgia*) (in ♯ Csm.CRLP 10041)
S. Migai (B)   *USSR. 9889*
(*I do not please you*)

It was in early spring, Op. 38, No. 2 (Fet) ☐
  (A. K. Tolstoy)
N. Chubenko   *USSR. 13234*
(*The sun has set*)
  ☆ N. Obukhova (M-S) (in ♯ Csm.CRLP 10400)

---

[1] This number also attributed to Preobrazhenskaya.

(A) Legend, Op. 54, No. 5 (Pleshcheev)
(Christ in his garden)
☆ N. Eddy (B, *Eng*) & orch. (♭ *AmC.A 1598*)

— ARR. CHO
Columbus Cho.—Huffman (*Eng*) (in ♯ *B.LAT 8070*;
AmD.DL 8106: ♭ *set ED 831*)

Love's beginning, Op. 6, No. 3 □
(Gombert, trs. Rostopchina)
(or: *What torment*, or: *Painfully & sweetly*)
☆ S. Lemeshev (T) (in ♯ *Csm.CRLP 10400*)

Lullaby in a storm, Op. 54, No. 10 (Pleshcheev) □
E. Katulskaya (S)   *USSRM.D 00777*
(I do not please you; & Glinka)
☆ S. Lemeshev (T) (in ♯ *Csm.CRLP 10041*)

(The) Mild stars shone for us, Op. 60, No. 12 □
(Polonsky)
Z. Gaidai (S)   *USSR.12408*
(Only thou)
☆ S. Lemeshev (T) (in ♯ *Csm.CRLP 10041*)

My genius, my angel, my friend (Fet)
☆ M. Maksakova (M-S) (in ♯ *Csm.CRLP 10040*)

My naughty girl, Op. 27, No. 6
(or: *My spoilt darling*) (Mickiewicz, trs. Mey)
☆ S. Shaposhnikov (B) (in ♯ *Csm.CRLP 10400*)

(The) Nightingale, Op. 60, No. 4 (Pushkin) □
S. Lemeshev (T)   *USSR. 019609*
(Shishov: My Grandmother) [see collection]
☒ F. Chaliapin (Bs) (in ♯ *Sca. 807**; in ♯ *Roc. 1**;
*AudM.LPA 1002**)

No response or word of greeting, Op. 28, No. 5 □
(or: *No word from you*; or *No tidings*) (Apukhtin)
I. Petrov (Bs)   *USSR. 22267*
(Glinka: Shall I forget)
☆ S. Lemeshev (T) (in ♯ *Csm.CRLP 10400*)

None but the weary heart, Op. 6, No. 6 □
(Goethe, trs. Mey)
B. Gmyria (Bs)   *USSRM.D 001209*
(We sat together; & Rachmaninoff)
I. Te Wiata (Bs, *Eng*), E. Lush (pf.)
♭ *Nix.EP 902*

(Mendelssohn, etc.)   (in ♯ *NLPY 915*)
M. Bothwell (S)   in ♯ *Roy. 1538*
E. Sachs (M-S), S. Leff (pf.)   in ♯ *Mur.P 111*
(followed by pf. acc. only)
☆ N. Obukhova (M-S) (in ♯ *Sti.SLP 1001*;
Csm.CRLP 10400)
L. Tibbett (B, *Eng*) (♭ *Cam.CAE 217*)
M. Lipton (A) & orch.—Rodzinski (in ♯ *Phi.S 04601L*)

— ARR. CHO.
R. Shaw Chorale (in ♯ *Vic.LM 1800*)

— ARR. ORCH.
Hollywood Bowl—Dragon (in ♯ *DCap.CTL 7072*;
Cap.P 8276: ♭ *FAP 8283*)
N.Y.P.S.O.—Kostelanetz (in ♯ *AmC.CL 758*)
Westminster Light—Bridgewater (in ♯ *West.WL 4009*)
Viennese Str. Orch. (♭ *Rem.REP 17*)
☆ Boston Prom.—Fiedler (in ♯ *Vic.LM 1790*: ♭ *set ERB 26*)
Robin Hood Dell—Kostelanetz (in ♯ *AmC.CL 730*)

— ARR. VLN. & PF.
M. Elman & J. Seiger (in ♯ *Vic.LM 1740*:
♭ *set WDM 1740*; ♯ *FV. 630277*)

— ARR. GUITAR: A. Valenti (in ♯ *SMC. 1002*)

— ARR. ORGAN: J. Crawford (in ♯ *B.LAT 8039*, etc.)
☆ V. Fox (♭ *AmC.A 1559*)

— ARR. 4 PFS.: First Pf. Qtt. (♭ *Vic.ERA 96*)

— PF. ACC. only. R. MacMunn (in ♯ *AmEsq. 1*)

Not a word, O my friend, Op. 6, No. 2 (Pleshcheev)
V. Borisenko (M-S)   *USSRM.D 00612*
(O thou moonlit night, Rondel; & Rachmaninoff)
N. Obukhova (M-S)   *USSRM.D 00117*
(Song of the gypsy girl; & Glinka)
T. Kuuzik (B, *Estonian*), B. Lukk (pf.) (*USSR. 22232*)

O bless you, forests, Op. 47, No. 5 (A. K. Tolstoy)
("Pilgrim's Song" or "To the forest")
B. Gmyria (Bs)   *USSRM.D 00658*
(Borodin)

O if you knew, Op. 60, No. 3 (Pleshcheev)
☆ I. Kozlovsky (T) (in ♯ *Csm.CRLP 10041*)

O sing that song, Op. 16, No. 4
(Pleshcheev, after Mrs. Hemans)
N. Shpiller (S)   *USSRM.D 001266*
(below, & Cui)

O thou moonlit night, Op. 73, No. 3 (Rathaus) □
(or: *In this summer night*)
I. Kozlovsky (T)   *USSR. 22070*
(Rimsky: Early spring & I believe I love)
V. Borisenko (M-S)   *USSRM.D 00612*
(Not a word, Rondel; & Rachmaninoff)
☆ S. Lemeshev (T) (in ♯ *Csm.CRLP 10041*)
A. Pirogov (*USSRM.D 001245*)

Only thou, Op. 57, No. 6 (Pleshcheev)
V. Borisenko (M-S)   *USSR. 14005*
(Rachmaninoff: Spring waters)
Z. Gaidai (S)   *USSR. 12409*
(The mild stars shone for us)
☆ G. Moore (S, *Fr*) & orch. (in ♯ *Vic.LCT 7004*:
♭ *set WCT 7004*)

Pimpinella, Op. 38, No. 6 (Tchaikovsky)
(Florentine Song)
☆ G. Vinogradov (T) (in ♯ *Ete. 30-5019*)
S. Lemeshev (T) (in ♯ *Csm.CRLP 10400*)

Reconciliation, Op. 25, No. 1 (Shcherbina) □
(or: *Sleep of Sorrow*)
M. Reizen (Bs)   *USSRM.D 001346*
(Rimsky-Korsakov, Glazounov)

Rondel, Op. 65, No. 6 (Collin, trs. Gorchakov)
('The Charmer')
V. Borisenko (M-S)   *USSRM.D 00613*
(Not a word; O thou moonlit night; & Rachmaninoff)

Romeo and Juliet "Duet", S, T, A, & orch.[1]
J. Fenn, R. Manton, K. Hilgenberg & Los
Angeles Orch. Soc. (*Fr*)—Waxman
♯ *DCap.CTL 7034*
(Gounod: Romeo et Juliette, duet)   (♯ *Cap.P 8189*:
ACap.CLCX 012)
T. Lavrova, S. Lemeshev, A. Matyurshina
(Bizet, Puccini)   ♯ *USSR.D 2366*

Serenade, Op. 65, No. 3 (Collin, trs. Gorchakov)
(In the bright light of dawn)
S. Shaposhnikov (B)   *USSRM.D 00622*
(Rimsky-Korsakov & Glinka)

Serenade, Op. 63, No. 6 (Gd. Duke Constantine) □
(O child, beneath thy window)
B. Gmyria (Bs)   *USSR. 22086*
(Dargomijsky: I am grieved)
J. Siimon (*Estonian*) (*USSR. 22218*)
☆ S. Lemeshev (T) (in ♯ *Csm.CRLP 10041*)
Z. Dolukhanova (A) (*USSRM.D 00664*)

Sleep! Op. 57, No. 4 (Merezhkovsky)
(or: *I would sleep for ever*)
I. Kozlovsky (T)   *USSRM.D 00695*
(Dargomijsky)

So soon forgotten (Apukhtin)[2] 1870 □
N. Postavnicheva[3]   *USSR. 17183*
(Frenzied Nights)

Song of the gypsy girl, Op. 60, No. 7 (Polonsky) □
L. Rudenko (M-S)   in ♯ *USSR.D 2073*
(above; & Rimsky, Rubinstein, etc.)
☆ N. Obukhova (M-S)   *USSRM.D 00117*
(Not a word . . .; & Glinka) [& see collection]
(in ♯ *Csm.CRLP 10041*)
J. Siimon (*Estonian*) (*USSR. 22219*)

Spring, Op. 54, No. 3 (Pleshcheev) □
(The grass grows green)
N. Shpiller (S)[4]   *USSRM.D 001266*
(above, & Cui)
☆ S. Lemeshev (T) (in ♯ *Csm.CRLP 10041*)

(The) Sun has set, Op. 73, No. 4 (Rathaus) □
N. Chubenko   *USSR. 13235*
(It was in the early spring)

---

[1] Completed and orch. by Taneiev.
[2] No. 19 in Jurgenson edn. of the Songs.
[3] This number also attributed to Preobrazhenskaya.
[4] This is just listed as *Spring*; could equally well be Op. 54, No. 9.

(A) **Tear trembles, Op. 6, No. 4** (A. K. Tolstoy) ☐
I. Kozlovsky (T)   **USSR. 020570**
(*Vilboa: Sailors*)
M. Reizen (Bs)   ***USSRM.D 00616***
(*Autumn*)

Tears, Op. 65, No. 5 (Blanchecotte) (*Les Larmes*)
M. Teyte (S)   in ♯ **PRCC. 2**
☆ S. Shaposhnikov (B) (in ♯ Csm.CRLP 10041)

To Sleep, Op. 27, No. 1 (Ogarev) ("*Invocation*")
A. Pankey (B) & orch.   in ♯ **Top.TRL 2**
(*Glinka, Handel; & Negro songs*)

Wait, Op. 16, No. 2 (Grekov)
E. Kruglikova (S)   **USSR. 9884**
(*Do not believe, my friend*)
☆ S. Lemeshev (T) (in ♯ Csm.CRLP 10040)

Was I not a little blade of grass, Op. 47, No. 7 ☐
(or: *The Bride's complaint—La nouvelle mariée*) (Surikov)
N. Obukhova (M-S, from collection)
in ♯ **Csm.CRLP 10040**

We sat together, Op. 73, No. 1 (Rathaus) ☐
(or: *Side by side*)
S. Lemeshev (T), A. Makarov (pf.) ***Eta. 30-5007***
(*Why?*) (? ☆ or n.v.)
T. Kuuzik (B), B. Lukk (pf.) (*Estonian*) (*USSR. 22233*)
☆ N. Obukhova (M-S) (in ♯ Csm.CRLP 10041)
B. Gmyria (Bs) (*USSR. 21668 & USSRM.D 001209*)

Why? Op. 6, No. 5 (Heine, trs. Mey) ☐
B. Gmyria (Bs)   **USSR. 21669**
(*We sat together*)
S. Lemeshev (T), A. Makarov (pf.) ***Eta. 30-5007***
(*We sat together*) (? ☆ or n.v.)
J. Garda (B), V. Makarov (pf.) (*Muza. 2471*)
☆ N. Obukhova (M-S) (in ♯ Csm.CRLP 10400)
☒ E. Caruso (T, *Fr*) (in ♯ Vic.LCT 1129*)

Why did I dream of you, Op. 28, No. 3 (Mey) ☐
G. Nelepp (T)   **USSR. 22056**
(*Frenzied Nights*) (see collection)
And. Ivanov (B)   ***USSRM.D 00715***
(♯s—*Rachmaninoff*)
▽ G. Vinogradov (T) (*USSR. 13241*)—not Op. 6, No. 5

Winter, Op. 54, No. 12 (Pleshcheev)
☆ S. Lemeshev (T) (in ♯ Csm.CRLP 10040)

II. C. CHORAL

Holy God (Unspec.)
☆ Don Cossack Cho. (C.DCX 107)

LITURGY OF ST. JOHN CHRYSOSTOM, Op. 41
... Nos. 1, 2, 3, 6, 8, 10, 11, 13, 14
Paris Russian Cath. Cho.—Afonsky
♯ *Argee. 716*

MISCELLANEOUS

Familiar Themes from Tchaikovsky
☆ Lamoureux—Tzipine (*Kreisler*)   ♯ **DCap.CTL 7076**
Great Melodies of Tchaikovsky
Philadelphia—Ormandy   ♯ **AmC.ML 4955**
                                   (8ss, ♭ *A 1974/7*)
Tchaikovsky Fantasy — ARR. Stolz
☆ Vienna Sym.—Stolz   ♯ **D.LK 4077**
(*Offenbach*)   (♯ Lon.LL 868)
Tchaikovsky, his life, his times, his music
D. Randolph (narr.)   ♯ **Per.PCS 6**

TCHEREPNIN, Alexander Nikolaievitch
(b. 1899)

COLLECTION
(4) Arabesques, Op. 11 1918-20
(10) Bagatelles, Op. 5
1. C minor   6. D flat major
2. F major   7. E flat major
3. D major   8. A flat major
4. B minor   9. E minor
5. A major   10. C minor
Nocturne, G sharp minor, Op. 2, No. 1
Sonatine romantique, Op. 4 1918
A. N. Tcherepnin (pf.)   ♯ **ML. 7043**

---

(10) Bagatelles, Op. 5 pf.
J. Rauck   ♯ **Zod. 1002**
(*Griffes, Poulenc, Werle*)

Sonatine sportive sax. & pf.
M. Mule & M. Lenom   ♯ ***D.LX 3130***
(*Bozza, Tomasi, etc.*)   (♯ *Lon.LS 986*)

Suite, Op. 87 orch. f.p. 1954
Louisville—Whitney   ♯ **LO. 2**
(*Cowell & Wagenaar*)

Trio, D major, Op. 34 pf., vln., vlc. 1925
N. M.-Minchin, H. Clebanoff & K. Früh
♯ **APM.PMT 201**
(*Brahms & Loeillet*)

TCHEREPNIN, Nikolai Nikolaievitch
(1873-1945)

SONG: Autumn, Op. 7, No. 1 (Lialetchtin)
I. Maslennikova (B)   **USSR. 20476**
(*Rimsky: It was early in spring*)

TCHESNOKOFF, Paul G. (b. 1877)

SEE: † HYMNS OF PRAISE
† CHORAL MASTERPIECES FROM THE RUSSIAN
LITURGY

(There have been many other ▽ recordings of similar items)

TELEMANN, Georg Philipp (1681-1767)

[TM—Tafelmusik; GM—Getreuer Musikmeister]

CANTATAS

Der Schulmeister (Comic Cantata)[1]
H. Günter (B), Lübeck Boys' Cho. & Cha.
Orch.—Stein [G. Goebel, hpsi.]

Das Glück (Moralische Kantaten Bk. I, No. 1)
Die Landlust (Moralische Kantaten, Bk. III, No. 5)
B. Brückmann (Tr.), G. Goebel (hpsi.), H.
Haferland (vlc.)   ♯ **HP.APM 14025**
[& in *Die Landlust*, R. Ermeler (fl.)] (♯ AmD.ARC 3011)
(*Die Landlust* only, ♭ *Pol. 37089*)

Cantata: Ihr Völker, hört A, recorder, cont.
Harmonischer Gottesdienst, 1725-6
☆ H. Hennecke, G. Scheck, F. Neumayer (org), A.
Wenzinger (gamba)   ♯ *AmD.DL 7542*
(*Handel*)   (2ss, ♭ *Pol. 37073*)

CONCERTOS

B flat major, 2 fl. & orch.
J.-P. Rampal, R. Heriché & Paris Inst. Ens.
—Froment   ♯ *EPP.APG 117*
(*Fantasia; & J. S. Bach*)

E major, fl., ob. d'amore, viola d'amore & str.
☆ H. P. Schmitz, H. Töttcher, E. Seiler, Cha. Ens. & hpsi.
(*Vivaldi*)   ♯ *AmD.DL 7537*

G major, vla. & str. orch. (Hortus musicus edn.)
H. Kirchner & Stuttgart Cha.—Münchinger
♯ *D.LX 3102*
(*Gabrieli*)   (♯ *Lon.LS 686*)
P. Doktor & Salzburg Mozarteum
—Paumgartner   ♯ *CFD. 14*
(*Torelli, Caix, Albinoni, etc.*)

G minor, 3 vlns. & orch. (TM. II-3)
Allegro Cha. Orch.—Tubbs   ♯ *Allo. 3146*
(*Scarlatti & Vivaldi*)

D major, strings (à 4)
D major, 4 vlns. (Bärenreiter edn., VI-3)
J. Dejean, J. Pasquier, G. Gaunet, F. Geyr,
Paris Coll. Mus.—Douatte ♯ *EPP.APG 125*
(*Suite*)

F minor, ob. & str. orch. (ed. Stein)
E. Schuster & Cha. Orch.—Vardi
(*Handel & Vivaldi*)   ♯ *CEd.CE 1062*

---

[1] Ed. F. Stein. Text by composer.

Concerto, ob. & orch. (unspec.)
— FOR PRACTICE: recorded with oboe part missing
(♯ CEd.MMO 301)

Fantasia, D minor fl. unacc.
(Bärenreiter edn. VI-6)
J-P. Rampal   ♯ *EPP.APG 117*
(*Concerto & J. S. Bach*)

FANTASIAS hpsi.
BOOK I (in German style): COMPLETE

1. D major	2. D minor
3. E major	4. E minor
5. F major	6. F minor
7. G major	8. G minor
9. A major	10. A minor
11. B flat major	12. E flat major

H. Elsner   ♯ *AmVox.PL 8680*

Heldenmusik 12 pieces, ed. Pätzold
J-P. Rampal (fl.), R. Veyron-Lacroix (hpsi.)
     V♯ *DO.LD 17*

QUARTETS
D minor 3 fl. & cont. (TM. II-2) 1733
E. Seiler Cha. Music Circle[2] (2ss) *PV. 9407*
(*Sonata, D major on* ♯ *HP.AP 13020*)
☆ M. Wittgenstein & Ens. (in ♯ West.WN 18031)

E minor fl., vln., gamba, hpsi. (TM. III-2)
J-P. Rampal, vln., vlc., hpsi.   ♯ *Cpt.MC 20100*
(*Suite, B flat major*)

G major fl., vln., ob. & cont.
L. Davenport (recorder), J. Tryon (vln.),
E. Schuster (ob.), P. Davenport (hpsi.), &
M. Neal (vlc.)   ♯ *CEd.CE 1051*
(*J. S. Bach, Loeillet, A. Scarlatti*)

J-P. Rampal, M. Gendre, P. Pierlot, R. Veyron-
Lacroix (hpsi.), P. Hongne (bsn.)
     ♯ *BàM.LD 011*
(*J. C. Bach, A. Scarlatti, Handel*)   (♯ HS.HSL 117)

SONATAS: Solo
C minor (B & H. 13); **E minor** (Partita No. 5)[3]
ob. & cont.
☆ H. Gomberg & C. Chiasson (hpsi.)   ♯ *B.AXTL 1021*
(*Mozart*)   (♯ D.UST 253553)

F minor vlc. (gamba) & cont. (GM. I-3)
☆ H. Busch & E. Weiss-Mann (hpsi.)
     (♯ Allo. 4036: also ♯ Allo. 3087)

G major (Partita No. 2)[3] fl. & cont.
C. Dolmetsch (recorder), J. Saxby (hpsi.)
     in ♯ *D.LXT 2943*
(† Recorder & hpsi. recital)   (♯ Lon.LL 1026)

C minor fl. & cont. 1732
(*Methodische Sonate*, No. 2)
J-P. Rampal & R. Veyron-Lacroix (hpsi)
     ♯ *D.FST 153139*
(*below; & Couperin*)

SONATAS: Trios
A minor (Sonata Polonaise No. 2) 2 vlns. & cont.
F major recorder, vln. & cont. (pub. Schott)
M. Svendsen (rec.), O. Kinch & L. Fagerlund
(vlns.), J. E. Hansen (virginals) & vlc.
     ♭ *Mtr.MCEP 3004*

A minor (Sonata Polonaise No. 2)
E major 2 vlns. & cont. (*No. 9*)[4]
☆ W. Schneiderhan, G. Swoboda & F. Holetschek
(hpsi.) & vlc. (in ♯ West.WN 18031 & Sel.LPG 8717)

B flat major ("Trio") fl., hpsi., cont.[5]
T. Deckert (rec.), H. E. Deckert (gamba), T.
Nielsen (lute), L. Larsen (virginals)
     ♯ *Felix.LP 300*
(*Abel & Leclair*)

J-P. Rampal & R. V-Lacroix (hpsi.)
     ♯ *D.FST 153139*
(*above & Couperin*)

C minor fl., ob. & cont. (*No. I*)[4]
A. Mann (recorder), L. Wann, E. Weiss-Mann
(hpsi.)   ♯ *West.WL 5214*
(*below; Pepusch & Scarlatti*)

L. Davenport (recorder), E. Schuster, P.
Davenport (hpsi.), M. Neal (vlc.)
     ♯ *CEd.CE 1051*
(*above; J. S. Bach, Loeillet, A. Scarlatti*)
Ithaca Baroque Ens.   ♯ *Corn. 1011*
(*Loeillet*) [with recorder]

D major fl., vla. d'amore & cont. (MS, Dresden)
☆ G. Scheck, E. Seiler, F. Neumeyer (hpsi.) & A.
Wenzinger (gamba) (♯ *HP.AP 13020*)

E major (*No. 9*)[4]
M. Duschenes (fl.), M. Goodman (vln.), pf. &
vlc.   in ♯ *Hall.RS 6*
(† Musica antica e nuova)

E minor fl., ob., vln. & cont.[5]
A. Mann (rec.), L. Mann (ob.), A. Mell (vln.),
E. Weiss-Mann (hpsi.)   ♯ *West.WL 5214*
(*above; Pepusch & A. Scarlatti*)

F major 2 recorders & cont. (GM. I-1)
... 1st & 3rd movts., Vivace & Allegro, only
Trapp Family Ens.   in ♯ *AmD.DL 9759*

SONG: Die rechte Stimmung (GM) 1728
R. Hayes (T), R. Boardman (pf.)
     in ♯ *Van.VRS 448*
(*Bach, Machaut, Caccini, etc., & Trad.*)
C. Bizony (S), B. Diamant (B) & Clements (pf.)
     in ♯ *Hall.RS 6*
(† Musica antica e nuova)

SUITES ('Overtures')
[Nos. in brackets refer to the classification in Büttner:
Das Konzert in den Orchestersuiten . . . Telemanns,
Berlin, 1935]

A minor fl. & str. orch. [B 12]
H. Barwahser & Vienna Sym.—Paumgartner
     ♯ *Phi.N 00208L*
(*Haydn*)   (♯ Epic.LC 3075)
J. Pappoutsakis & Zimbler Sinfonietta[6]
     ♯ *B.AXTL 1009*
(*Mozart: Serenade No. 6*)   (♯ D.UAT 273083)

A minor orch. [H 4] (pub. Hamburg, *c.* 1725)
Augsburg Cha.—Deyle   † ♯ *AS. 3005LD*
(*J. S. & C. P. E. Bach*)   (♯ HS.AS 35)

B flat major 2 ob. & str. (TM. III-1)
P. Pierlot & C. Maisonneuve, Sinfonia Ens.
—Witold   ♯ *Cpt.MC 20100*
(*Quartet, E minor*)

D major str. [B 11]
Saxon State Coll. Mus.—Liersch[7]   ♯ *Ura. 7113*
(*Rosenmüller & Corelli*)

D major Wind insts. *c.* 1733
London Baroque Ens.—Haas   ♯ *P.PMB 1004*
(*C. P. E. Bach*)

E minor 2 fls. & str. (TM. I-1)
... No. 6, Air, only
Orch.—Goldsbrough   *G.HMS 67*
(† History of Music in Sound)   (in ♯ Vic. set LM 6031)

G minor
(Ouverture burlesque: "L'Harlequinade") [A 31]
Paris Collegium Mus.—Douatte ♯ *EPP.APG 125*
(*Concertos*)

TAFELMUSIK
SEE *above*: Suite, Quartets; *below*, Trio

TRIO, E minor (TM. II-4) fl., ob., cont.
☆ M. Wittgenstein, E. Brenner, S. Marlowe (hpsi.) &
vlc. (in ♯ West.WN 18031)

---

[2] Recorder, fl., ob., bsn., lute, hpsi. and gamba.
[3] From *Kleine Kammermusik*, 1716.
[4] From *Essercizi musici, c.* 1720.
[5] *Hortus musicus* edn., Nos. 36 & 25 respectively.
[6] Omitting 6th movt.: *Badinerie*.
[7] This recording has 7 movts.: Overture, La Trompette (Allegro); Sarabande; Rondeau; Bourrée; Courante; Double;
Gigue; while ♯ Ura. 7031 (see Supp. II) omits Rondeau.

TEMPLETON, Alec (b. 1905)

Quartet No. 1 str.
Phoenix Qtt.
Trio fl., vln. & pf.
J. Baker, A. Goltzer & A. Templeton
♯ **Eso.ES 533**

Previous recordings of his works have been of lighter works, particularly **Bach goes to town**. See also *supra*, J. Strauss, Improvisations

---

TERTRE, Etienne de (fl. 1540-60)

SEE: † DANCERIES ET BALLETS

THIBAUT IV de Navarre (1201-1253)

SEE ALSO: † HISTORY OF MUSIC IN SOUND (14)
　　　　　† LA MUSIQUE ET LA POÉSIE
　　　　　† FRENCH TROUBADOUR SONGS

Pour mal temps et pour gelée
J. Douai (T) & orch.　　　♯ *BàM.LD 312*
(in *Recital No. 2*)

THIRIET, Maurice (b. 1906)

Histoire de la 2ᵉ D.B.
(Incid. Music to Documentary recording)
Radio Luxembourg Orch.—Pensis
♯ **FestF.FLD 28**

(L') ŒUF À LA COQUE Ballet pub. 1949
Excerpts
Rome Radio Light Orch.—Savina
Cet.AT 0306/8
(5ss—*Damase: Croqueuse de diamants—Valse*)
... **Valse séduction**
J. Faustin Str. Orch. (*Od.O-28705*: ♭ *7MO 1019*)

SONG: Si j'allais vous voir (No. 3 of *Fleurs*)
G. Guillamat (S), A. Collard (pf.) (*C.GF 1040*)

Suite de danses, No. 6 orch.
Orch.—Hewitt　　　　♯ *DFr.SD 6*

(Les) VISITEURS DU SOIR Film Music
Complainte de Gilles (Prévert)
Démons et merveilles
Le tendre et dangereux visage de l'Amour
☆ J. Jansen (B), L. Laskine (hp.) (♭ *D.FA 80501*)

THOMAS, Charles Louis Ambroise
(1811-1896)

OPERAS

(Le) CAÏD 2 Acts 1849
Air du Tambour-Majeur Bs
Ħ P. Plançon (in ♯ *AudR.LPA 2340**;
　　　in ♯ *SBDH.LLP 6** & *JAL 7002**)

HAMLET 5 Acts 1868
Sa main ... Adieu, dit-il (Air d'Ophélie) S Act II
☆ E. Noréna (*AF.AGSB 83*)

O vin, dissipe la tristesse B Act II
P. Silveri (*Ital*)　　　**C.GQX 11523**
(*below*)
☆ J. C. Thomas (in ♯ *Cam.CAL 199*: ♭ *CAE 246*)
　C. Guichandut (*Ital*) (*Orf. 54012*, d.c.)
Ħ T. Ruffo (*Ital*) (in ♯ *Sca. 812**)

Être ou ne pas être B Act III
P. Silveri (*Ital*)　　　**C.GQX 11523**
(*above*)
☆ Vanni-Marcoux (in ♯ *G.FJLP 5035*)
Scène de la folie S Act IV
A vos jeux ... Partagez-vous mes fleurs!
M. Robin　　　　♯ *D.LX 3114*
(*Lucia di Lammermoor—Mad Scene*)
(♯ *D.FA 133034*; *Lon.LS 676*)
☆ A. Galli-Curci (*Ital*) (in ♯ *Vic. set LCT 6701*)
Ħ N. Melba[8] (*AF.AGSB 7**; V♯ *Rar.M 306**;
　　in ♯ *B & B. 3**; in ♯ *Vic. set LCT 6701**)

---

[8] With interpolated cadenza by the artist.

Comme une pâle fleur B Act V
Ħ M. Battistini (*Ital*) (in ♯ *Ete. 709**)
　G. de Luca & pf. (in ♯ *SBDH.JAL 7001**)

MIGNON 3 Acts 1866
COMPLETE RECORDING

Mignon	G. Moizan (S)
Pauline	J. Micheau (S)
Wilhelm	L. de Luca (T)
Lothario	R. Bianco (B)
Laërtes	R. Destain (B)
Jarno	N. Pierotte (Bs)
Frederick	F. L. Deschamps (T)

Théâtre de la Monnaie Cho. & Belgian Nat.
Orch.—Sebastian　　　♯ **D.LXT 2783/5**
(6ss)　　　　　　　　(♯ Lon. set XLLA 15)

ABRIDGED RECORDING
☆ G. Cernay (M-S), L. Tragin (S), etc., Cho & Orch. of
　Théâtre de la Monnaie—Bastin　♯ *AmC.RL 3093*

COLLECTED EXCERPTS in *German*

Overture
Connais-tu le pays? Act I M-S
Entr'acte Act II Orch.
Adieu, Mignon, courage Act II T
Elle est là ... Elle est aimée Act II S
Je suis Titania Act II S
De son cœur j'ai calmé Act III Bs.
Elle ne croyait pas Act III T

A. Schlemm (S), R. Streich (S), L. Fehenberger (T), T. Blankenheim (Bs), & Bamberg Sym.
—Leitner　　　　♯ **Pol. 19004**
[for individual re-issues from this set, *see below*]

Overture
Lamoureux—Fournet　　　in ♯ *Phi.N 00707R*
　　　　　　　　　　(in ♯ Epic.LC 3079)

Württemberg State Op.—Leitner　　**PV. 72418**
(*Flotow: Martha, Overture*)　　　(♭ Po . 30144)

N.B.C. Sym.—Toscanini (n.v.) in ♯*Vic.LRM7013*
(♭ set *WRM 7013* & in set ♯ *LM 6026*; ♯ *FV. A330207*;
　♭ *ItV.A72R 0010*; announced as ♭ *G.7RF 283*, but
　probably not issued)
☆ Paris Cons.—Fistoulari (♯ *D.LW 5010*; *Lon.LD 9014*)
Rhineland Sym.—Federer (♯ *AFest.CFR 10-35*)
Boston Prom.—Fiedler (in ♯ *Cam.CAL 250*: ♭ *CAE 181*)
Vienna Radio—Nilius (in ♯ *GA. 33-307*; *MH. 33-118*)

ACT I

Connais-tu le pays? M-S
S. Michel　　　　in ♯ *Pat.DTX 137*
(*below*; *Orphée, Damnation de Faust, etc.*)

I. Andréani　　　　♭ *Plé.P 45151*
(*Werther—Air des lettres*)

E. Stignani (*Ital*)　　　**C.LX 1578**
(*Carmen—Habanera*)　　(GQX 11528: ♭ *SCB 111*:
　　　　　　　　　　　　　　SCBQ 3010)

E. Grümmer (*Ger*)　　　**G.EH 1440**
(*Faust—Roi de Thulé*)　　(GB 80: FKX 259)

M. v. Ilosvay (*Ger*)　　　**Phi.N 12079 G**
(*Carmen—Air des Cartes*)　　(in ♯ *N 00649R*)

A. Schlemm (*Ger*)　　　*PV. 36091*
(*Elle est aimée*)　　　(♭ *Pol. 32009*)

T. de Igarzabal (*Ital*)　　**ArgOd. 66053**
(*Favorita—O mio Fernando*)　　(in ♯ *LDC 517*)
　　M. Hazuchová (*Cz*) (in ♯ *U. 5176C*)
　　V. Borisenko (*Russ*) (USSR. 022041/2:
　　　　　　　　　　　　　　　USSRM.D 1435)
☆ M. Guilleaume (*Ger*) (in ♯ *DT.TM 68025*:
　　♭ *T.UE 453923* & in ♯ *LA 6107*)
　L. Bori (in ♯ *Vic.LCT 1138*: ♭ *ERAT 3*)

Légères hirondelles S & Bs
(*Schwalbenduett*)
A. Schlemm & T. Blankenheim (*Ger*)
　　　　　　　　in ♯ **Pol. 18147**
　　　　　　　　(& ♯ 19043)

ACT II

Entr'acte (Gavotte) orch.
Bamberg Sym.—Leitner　　　*Pol. 62897*
(*Manon Lescaut—Donna non vidi mai*)
　　　(in ♯ *Pol. 17001* & *18169*; in ♯ *AmD.DL 8509*)
Anon. Orch. (in ♯ *Jay. 3004*)

MIGNON, Act II (*continued*)

Je connais un pauvre enfant M-S or S (*Styrienne*)
S. Michel (*above*) in # **Pat.DTX 137**
  ☳ S. Kurz (*Ger*) (in # Sca. 817*)

Me voici dans son boudoir M-S
(*Rondo Gavotte*—interpolated by Thomas)
J. Merrill in # *MH. 33-104*
  ☆ L. Bori (S) (♭ *Vic.ERAT 3*)

Adieu, Mignon, courage T
R. Schock (*Ger*) G.EH 1452
(*Adam: Postillon de Longjumeau, aria*)
    (♭ *7PW 532:* in # *WBLP 1515*)
  ☳ G. Anselmi (*Ital*) & pf. (in # Sca. 816*)
  R. Tauber (*Ger*) (in # Cum.CE 187*)

Elle est là . . . Elle est aimée S
A. Schlemm (*Ger*) *PV. 36091*
(*Connais-tu le pays?*) (♭ *Pol. 32009*)

Je suis Titania (*Polonaise*) S
P. Alarie in # *Phi.N 00663R*
(*Gounod, Delibes, etc.*)
R. Streich[1] in # *Pol. 18169*
(*Prophète, Aida, Figaro, etc.*)
  ☆ T. dal Monte (*Ital*) (in # *G.QALP 10089*)
  ☳ L. Tetrazzini (*Ital*) (in # Vic.LM 1786*)
  G. Forst (*Ger*) (in # *HRS. 3003**)

ACT III

De son cœur j'ai calmé Bs
(*Berceuse: Wiegenlied*)
  ☆ Vanni-Marcoux (in # *G.FJLP 5035*)
  ☳ P. Plançon (*AF.AGSB 74**)

Elle ne croyait pas T
L. Fehenberger (*Ger*) *PV. 36100*
(*Adam: Postillon—Mes amis, écoutez . . .*) (♭ *Pol. 34002*)
  G. Vinogradov (*Russ*) (*USSR. 10564*)
  ☳ F. de Lucia (*Ital*) (in # Sca 814*; in # CEd. set 7002*)

RAYMOND 3 Acts 1851
Overture
Lamoureux—Fournet ♭ *Phi.N 402021E*
(*Saint-Saëns*) (in # Epic.LC 3174)
Vienna Radio—Schönherr *Vien.L 6146*
    (in # *LPR 1037* & in # *GA. 33-307*)
Linz Sym. in # *Ply. 12-34*
(*Boïeldieu, Rossini, etc.*)
  ☆ Rhineland Sym.—Federer (in # *AFest.CFR 39*)

(Le) SONGE D'UNE NUIT D'ÉTÉ 3 Acts 1856
Falstaff's Aria (unspec.) Bs
  ☳ H. Belhomme (*SBDH.P 4**)

NOTE: **Cambria** and **Grand Study No. 6** (harp solo)
in # *Phi.N 00633R* are by John Thomas, "Pencerdd
Gwalia", 1826-1913.

THOMPSON, Randall (b. 1899)

Felices ter et amplius (Horace) Motet 1953
Stanford Univ. Cho.—Schmidt in # **ML. 7022**
(† Madrigals & Motets)

Symphony No. 2, E minor 1931
A.R.S. Orch.—Dixon # *ARS. 4*

Tarantella Male cho. & pf. 1937
▽ Princeton Univ. Glee Club—Knapp; K. Moser (pf.)
    (2ss—in *Vic. set Z 1*, pte. rec.)

(The) Testament of Freedom (Jefferson)
Cho. & orch. 1943
... **We fight not for glory**
Pittsburgh Univ. Men's Glee Club—Weiss
    in # **PFCM.CB 162**
(*Thomson, Finney, Hanson, etc.*)

THOMSON, Virgil (b. 1896)

(3) Antiphonal Psalms 1924 (orig. female cho.)
... **No. 1, Psalm 123; No. 3, Psalm 136**
Yale Univ. Divinity School Cho.—Borden
    in # *Over.LP 2*
(† Hymns of Praise)

(10) Études pf. 1943
1. Fanfare; 2. Spinning Song; 3. Canon; 4. Aeolian Harp;
5. Waltz; 6. Tango; 7. Music-box lullaby; 8. Madrigal;
9. Portrait of Briggs Buchanan; 10. Ragtime bass
M. Schapiro # *B.AXL 2009*
(2ss) (# *AmD.DL 4083*)
... **No. 7, Music-box lullaby**, only
M. Jonas in # *AmC.ML 4624*
(*Casella, Handel, Mozart, etc.*)
... **No. 10, Ragtime bass, C sharp major**
  ☆ A. Foldes (in *PV. 36104*)

Eccentric Dance pf. 1940
M. Richter in # *MGM.E 3147*
(*Wolfe, Copland, Cowell, etc.*)

Filling Station Ballet 1937
N.Y. City Ballet Orch.—Barzin
    # *AmVox.PL 9050*
(*H. Kay: Western Symphony*)

FOUR SAINTS IN THREE ACTS Opera 1934
(Text by Gertrude Stein)
ABRIDGED RECORDING (ARR. Thomson)
  ☆ Soloists, Cho. & orch.—Thomson # *Vic.LCT 1139*

Louisiana Story Film Music
... **Acadian Songs & dances** (Orch. Suite No. 2)
  ☆ Little Orch. Soc.—Scherman # *B.AXTL 1022*
(*Copland*)

Pastorale on a Christmas plainsong organ 1921
R. Ellsasser in # *MGM.E 3064*
(† Organ Music by modern composers)

(3) Pictures for orchestra
1. The Seine at night 1947
2. Wheat field at noon 1948
3. Sea Piece with birds 1952
Philadelphia—Ormandy # *AmC.ML 4919*
(*below*)

(The) Plow that broke the Plains Film Music
... **Orch. Suite** 1937
  ☆ Little Orch. Soc.—Scherman # *B.AXL 2006*
(*Copland*)

Psalm XXIII—My Shepherd will supply my need
mixed vv. unacc. 1938[2]
Heinz Chapel Cho.—Finney in # *PFCM.CB 162*
(*Finney, Hanson, Vaughan Williams, etc.*)
Stanford Univ. Cho.—Schmidt in # *ML. 7022*
(† Madrigals & Motets)

QUARTETS, Str.
No. 1 1931
New Music Qtt. # *PFCM.CB 181*
(*Schoenberg & Berg*) (*Walton on # CB 169*)

No. 2 1932
Juilliard Qtt. # *AmC.ML 4987*
(*W. Schuman*)

(A) Solemn Music Band 1949
Eastman Sym. Wind Ens.—Fennell
    # *Mer.MG 40011*
(*Persichetti, Hanson, Read, Mennin*)

Sonata No. 4 (Guggenheim Jeune) pf. 1940
S. Marlowe (hpsi.) # *NE. 3*
(*Rieti, Lessard, Hovhaness*)

(5) SONGS (William Blake) B & orch.
1. The Divine Image 4. The little black boy
2. The Tiger 1926 5. Jerusalem
3. The Land of Dreams
M. Harrell & Philadelphia Orch.—Ormandy
(*above*) # *AmC.ML 4919*

---

[1] Commences earlier with *Oui, pour ce soir, je suis Reine des fées.*
[2] Stated to be a Folksong setting.

Synthetic Waltzes 2 pfs. 1925
☆ A. Gold & R. Fizdale (in ♯ *Phi.S 06614R*)

Variations & Fugues on Sunday School Tunes org.
1. Come ye disconsolate 1927
2. There's not a friend like the lowly Jesus 1927
3. Will there be any stars in my crown 1927
4. Shall we gather at the river? 1930
　M. Mason　　　　　　　　　♯ **Eso.ES 522**
　(Sessions)
　[Organ of St. Paul's Cathedral, Columbia Univ.]

THORPE DAVIE, Cedric (b. 1913)

(The) JOLLY BEGGARS 'Cantata' (Burns) 1952-3
Soldier's Song B & Cho.
Quodlibet Cho.
　F. Westcott, Saltire Music Group Cho., Zorian
　Str. Qtt., H. Oppenheim (pf.) in ♯ **C.CX 1317**
　　　　　　　　　　　　　　(♯ Angel. 35256)
ARRANGEMENT
Auld lang syne—ARR. MASSED CHOS.
　Campbeltown, Falkirk & Newhaven Chos., at Edinburgh
　Fest., 1954 *(C.DB 3565)*

THYBO, Leif (b. 1922)

Preludio, Pastorale & Fugato, Op. 11 organ
　L. Thybo　　　　　　　　♯ **Phi.A 09801L**
　(J. S. Bach & Walther)

TINEL, Jef

SEE: † FLEMISH CHORAL MUSIC

TIPPETT, Michael Kemp (b. 1905)

Boyhood's End Cantata T & pf. (W. H. Hudson)
　　　　　　　　　　　　　　　　　1945
　P. Pears & N. Mewton-Wood　♯ **Argo.RG 15**
　(The heart's Assurance)　　　(o.n. ATC 1008)

Concerto, C major Double str. orch. 1939
☆ Philharmonia—Goehr *(Rawsthorne)* ♯ **G.CLP 1056**

(A) GARLAND FOR THE QUEEN
　(with Bax, Bliss, Berkeley, etc.) 1953
... **Dance, clarion air** (Fry)
　Golden Age Singers & Cambridge Univ.
　Madrigal Soc.—Ord　in † ♯ **C.CX 1063**

(The) Heart's Assurance Song-cycle 1951
　　1. Oh journeyman (A. Lewis)
　　2. The heart's assurance (S. Keyes)
　　3. Compassion (A. Lewis)
　　4. The dancer (A. Lewis)
　　5. Remember your lovers (S. Keyes)
　P. Pears (T), N. Mewton-Wood (pf.)
　　　　　　　　　　　　♯ **Argo.RG 15**
　(Boyhood's End)　　　(o.n. ATC 1005)

Quartet No. 2, F sharp minor str. 1942
　Amadeus Qtt.　　　　　　♯ **G.ALP 1302**
　(Seiber: Str. Qtt.)

Variation on an Elizabethan tune (Sellinger's
Round)[1] orch. 1953
　Aldeburgh Fest.—Britten　in ♯ **D.LXT 2798**
　(Berkeley, Britten, Oldham, Searle, Walton)
　　　　　　　　　　　　(in ♯ Lon.LL 808)

TITCOMB, H. Everett (b. 1884)

SEE: † FIVE CENTURIES OF CHORAL MUSIC

TITELOUZE, Jean (1563-1633)

[refs. to pages in Guilmant edn.]

Ave Maris Stella 4 versets org. 1623 [38]
　A. Marchal　　　　　　　♯ **Era.LDE 3025**
　(Couperin: Messe pour les Paroisses)
Veni Creator org. [16]
　A. Legrand　　　　　　　♯ **SM. 33-23**
　(A. Gabrieli, Viadana, Claude . . .)

TOLLIUS, Jan (c. 1550-c. 1603)

SEE: † SACRED & SECULAR SONGS FROM THE
　RENAISSANCE

TOMASINI, Luigi Aloysius (1741-1808)

Suite pour violetta ed. M. Casadesus
　(Tempo di Gavotte; Rigaudon; Lento amabile;
　　Tambourin)
　M. Casadesus (violetta) & Ens.　♯ *Plé.P 3073*
　(Maschera, G. Gabrieli, C. P. E. Bach)

TOCH, Ernest (b. 1887)

(3) Burlesques, Op. 31 pf.
... **No. 2,** only
　P. Spagnolo　　　　　　in ♯ **D.LXT 2947**
　(Granados, Albeniz, Aguirre, etc.)　(in ♯ Lon.LL 1040)

Circus Overture 1954
　N.Y.P.S.O.—Kostelanetz　　♯ **AmC.CL 758**
　(Prokofiev, Tchaikovsky, etc.)　　(♭ A 2035)

Notturno orch. f.p. 1954
　Louisville—Whitney　　　　　♯ **LO. 3**
　(Mennin & Riegger)

(10) Pieces for beginners, Op. 59 pf.
　M. Richter　　　　　　　♯ **MGM.E 3181**
　(Hindemith, Satie, etc.)

Pinocchio, 'A Merry Overture' orch. 1936
　Hamburg Philharmonia—H-J. Walther
　　　　　　　　　　　　　　MSB. 78045
　　　　　　　　　　　　(in ♯ MGM.E 3144)

Tanz und Spielstücke, Op. 40 pf.
... **Sunbeam Play**
　S. Bianca　　　　　　　　　*MSB. 23*
　(with spoken commentary)　　(& in ♯ 60041)

TOMASI, Henri (b. 1901)

Giration sax. & pf.
　M. Mule & M. Lenom　　　♯ *D.LX 3130*
　(Bozza, Tcherepnin, etc.)　　(♯ Lon.LS 986)

Nocturne cl & pf. 1954
　J. Lancelot & F. Gobet　　　♭ *Pat.G 1053*
　(Challon, Loucheur, Gallon)

(Le) Petit chèvrier corse fl. & hp.
　H. Barwahser & P. Berghout　♯ *Phi.N 00695R*
　(Andriessen, Badings, Roesgen-Champion)

TOMKINS, Thomas (1572-1656)

COLLECTION of Virginals Music
　(MB refs. are to *Musica Brittanica*, Vol. V)
Worster Brawles (FVB. 207; MB. 65)
Pavan & Galliard, Earl Strafford (MB. 41, 42)
Clarifica me, Pater (o) (MB. 4)
Pavan & Galliard, A minor (MB. 47, 48)
Toy: made at Poole Court (MB. 67)
Fancy: Voluntary (o) (MB. 30)
Pavan & Galliard, G major (MB. 49, 50)
Variations on 'What if a day' (MB. 64)
　T. Dart (hpsi., or organ where marked (o))
　(Byrd)　　　　　　　♯ **LOL.OL 50076**

(The) Fauns & satyrs tripping Madrigal 1601 5 vv.
　Randolph Singers　in ♯ **Nix.WLP 6212-1/2**
　(† Triumphs of Oriana)　(♯ West. set WAL 212)

When David heard that Absalom was slain
　Madrigal 6 vv. 1622
　N.Y. Pro Musica Antiqua—Greenberg
　　　　　　　　　　in ♯ **AmC.ML 5051**
　(† Evening of Elizabethan Verse & Music)

---

[1] Contributed to joint work by composers named for coupling.

TORELLI, Giuseppe (c. 1658-1708)

CONCERTOS
A minor (Sonata à 4; Giegling 46)
Salzburg Mozarteum—Paumgartner ♯ **CFD. 14**
(*Caix d'H, Albinoni, Telemann, etc.*)

D major tpt. & orch. (Roger No. 188: MS., Leyden)
M. André & Leclair Ens.—Paillard ♯ **DDP. 31-1**
(*Vivaldi & Locatelli*) (♯ HS.HSL 147)

G major, Op. 6, No. 1 (Concerto à 4) 1698
Sinfonia Inst. Ens.—Witold ♯ **EPP.SLP 2**
(*Vivaldi, Geminiani, Sammartini*)

(12) CONCERTI, Op. 8 1709
(1-6, 2 vlns., str. & cont.; 7-12, solo vln., str. & cont.)

1. C major	2. A minor
3. E major	4. B flat major
5. G major	6. G minor
7. D minor	8. C minor
9. E minor	10. A major
11. F minor	12. D major

COMPLETE RECORDINGS
R. Barchet & W. Beh, & Stuttgart Pro Musica
Str.—Reinhardt ♯ **E. & AmVox. set DL 113**
(6ss) [H. Elsner, hpsi.]

L. Kaufman & G. Alès, O. L. Ens.—Kaufman
(4ss) ♯ **LOL.OL 50089/90**
[R. Albin, vlc.; R. Gerlin, hpsi.; ed. Kaufman]
(♯ OL.LD 115/6)

No. 6, G minor (*in forma di Pastorale*)
Paris Collegium Musicum—Douatte
♯ **LT.EL 93042**
(*Corelli, Manfredini*) (♯ Sel.LA 1018; T.LB 6091)

Netherlands Phil.—v. d. Berg ♯ **CHS.H 16**
(*Vivaldi, Marcello, Durante*)

☆ Virtuosi di Roma—Fasano ♯ **B.AXTL 1032**
(♯ Fnt.LP 3004; D.UAT 273551)

Tu lo sai aria
— FOR PRACTICE (in ♯ **VS.ML 3004**)

TORRE, Francisco de la (fl. 1483-1494)

SEE: † HISTORY OF MUSIC IN SOUND (31)
† MUSIC OF THE RENAISSANCE
† SEVEN CENTURIES OF SACRED MUSIC

TOURNHOUT, Gérard (1520-1580)

SEE: † MUSICIENS DE LA COUR DE BOURGOGNE

TOURNIER, Marcel (1879-1951)

Fresque marine, Op. 46 harp unacc.
H. Boye **G.DA 5276**

Féerie Prelude & Dance hp.
Vers la source dans le bois hp.
E. Vito in ♯ **Per.SPL 721**
(*Spohr, Grandjany, Gretchaninoff*)

... **Féerie Prelude & Dance**, only
— ARR. 2 HPS. E. & J. Vito (in ♯ SOT. 1031 & ♯ 10301)

... **Vers la source**, only
N. Zabaleta in ♯ **Eso.ES 523**
(*Prokofiev, Tailleferre, Roussel, etc.*) (o.v. ▽ ChOd. 195023)

(3) Images, Op. 29 harp
... **No. 1, Au seuil du temple; No. 2, Lolita la danseuse**
P. Berghout **Phi.N 12073G**
(*Soulage: Choral*) (No. 2 only in ♯ N 00633R)

TRAETTA, Tommaso (1727-1779)

Minuetto cantato (unid.)
G. Sciutti (S) & Naples Scarlatti Orch.
—Caracciolo ♯ **Csm.CLPS 1046**
(*Paisiello, Piccinni, Monteverdi, etc.*)

TROMBONCINO, Bartolomeo (fl. c. 1500)

SEE: † MUSIC OF THE RENAISSANCE
† MUSIC FROM MIDDLE AGES TO RENAISSANCE
† RENAISSANCE MUSIC FOR THE LUTE

TRUNK, Richard (b. 1879)

SONG: **Mir träumte von einem Königskind, Op. 4, No. 5**
R. Ponselle (S), I. Chicagov (pf.)
in ♯ **Vic.LM 1889**
(*Wolf-Ferrari, Saint-Saëns, etc.*)

CAROL: **Idyll** (Falke)
K. Hansel (S), T. Schaefer (org.) (*Eng*)
in ♯ **McInt.MM 107**
(*Christmas Candlelight Service*)

TSINTSADZE, Sulkhan Fyodorovich (b. 1925)

QUARTETS, Strings
No. 2
Georgian State Qtt. (2ss) ♯ **USSR.D 313/4**

No. 3, C major
Georgian State Qtt. (2ss) ♯ **USSR.D 1720/1**

Suite for vlc. & pf.
D. Shafran & N. Musinyan **USSRM.D 001376/7**
[excerpts on USSR. 20972/3]

SONGS & FOLK SONG ARRANGEMENTS
Indi-Mindi; Sachidao
Georgian State Vocal Qtt. **USSR. 17607/8**

Fly, my swallow
Shepherd's Song
Georgian State Vocal Qtt. **USSR. 21233/4**

Song: Moment musical; Dance
Georgian State Qtt. **USSR. 21101/2**

TURINA, Joaquín (1882-1949)

COLLECTION OF PIANO MUSIC
Danzas fantásticas, Op. 22 (ARR.)
Preludios Nos. 1-5, Op. 80
Recuerdos de la antigua España, Op. 48
  1. La Eterna Carmen 2. Habañera
  3. Don Juan 4. Estudiantina
Partita, C major, Op. 57 (*Ciclo pianistico*, No. 2)
  1. Preludio 2. Zarabanda
  3. Capricho 4. Introducción y Giga
A. de Larrocha ♯ **B.AXTL 1076**
(♯ D.UAT 273555; SpC.CCL 35011; AmD.DL 9750)

Cuentos de España (Set I), Op. 20 pf.
... **No. 3, Miramar**
R. Caamaño **ArgOd. 57052**
(*Bartók: Allegro barbaro*)

(3) Danzas fantásticas, Op. 22 orch. 1926
Paris Cons.—Argenta ♯ **D.LXT 2889**
(*Albeniz*) (♯ SpC.CCL 32000; Lon.LL 921)
Madrid Sym.—Branco ♯ **LT.DTL 93015**
(*above & below*) (♯ West.WL 5320[1]; Sel.LAG 1048)
Philharmonia—Schüchter ♯ **P.PMD 1018**
(*Granados*) (♯ Od.OD 1017; ♯ MGM.E 3018)

— ARR. PF Turina
G. Soriano ♯ **LT.DTL 93013[2]**
(*below; & Mompou*) (*below only*, ♯ Sel. 270.C.043)

... **No. 1, Exaltación** — ARR. PF.
O. Frugoni ♯ **AmVox.PL 9420**
(*Albeniz, Granados, Falla*)

... **No. 3, Orgia** — ARR. PF.
E. Osta in ♯ **Allo. 3151**
(also in ♯ Roy. 1901)

[1] Announced, but not issued, as WL 5272.
[2] This record was withdrawn immediately after issue, and may never have actually been on sale.

(5) Danzas Gitanas, Op. 55 (Set I) pf.

1. Zambra   2. Danza de la Seducción
3. Danza ritual   4. Generalife
5. Sacro-Monte

M. Regules ("Siena" pf.)   ♯ **Eso.ESP 3002**
(*Albeniz, Villa-Lobos, Mompou*)

... **No. 5, Sacro-Monte**
☆ G. Copeland (in ♯ MGM.E 3025)
   N. Zabaleta (hp.) (♭ Od.BSOAE 4521)

— ARR. DANCING & ORCH.
"Antonio" & Sym.—Currás (in ♭ SpC.SCGE 80016)

En el cortijo, Op. 92 pf. 1936-40

1. La noche en el campo
2. A la sombra de caserio
3. Horizontes y llanuras
4. Caballistas

G. Soriano   ♯ **LT.DTL 93013**[2]
(*above; & Mompou*)   (*above only*, ♯ *Sel. 270.C.043*)

Fandanguillo, Op. 36 guitar
N. Yepes   in ♯ **D.LXT 2974**
(† Spanish Music of XVIth-XXth Centuries)
                            (♯ D.FST 153076; Lon.LL 1042)
A. Lagoya (in ♭ Pat.D 113)
☆ A. Segovia (♭ C.SCB 110: SCBQ 3016;
                            in † ♯ AmC.ML 4732)

Homenaje a Tárrega, Op. 69 guitar
(No. 1, Soleares;   No. 2, Garrotin)
L. Almeida   in ♯ **DCap.CTL 7089**
(† Guitar Music of Spain)   (♯ Cap.P 8295)

MUJERES ESPAÑOLAS, Op. 17 pf. 1917
... No. 2, La Andaluza sentimentale
No. 3, La Bruna coquette
A. Iturbi   ♯ **Vic.LM 1788**
(*Granados, Infante, Cuesta*)   (♯ FV.A 630231)

Niñerias, Op. 21 Suite, 8 pieces pf.
J. M. Sanromá   ♯ **Polym. 1011**
(*Falla*)   (♯ Cum.CLP 202)

(La) Oracion del Torero, Op. 34 orig. Lute Qtt.
(ARR. STR. ORCH. or QTT. by Turina)
Madrid Sym.—Branco   ♯ **LT.DTL 93015**
(*above & below*) (♯ Sel. LAG 1048; West.WL 5320)[1]
Hollywood Qtt.   ♯ **DCap.CTL 7063**
(*Wolf & Creston*)   (♯ Cap.P 8260)
American Art Qtt.   ♯ **BB.LBC 1086**
(*Shostakovich, Wolf, etc.*)
Monteceneri Qtt.   G.S 10623
Madrid Theatre Orch.   in ♯ **AmD.DL 9763**
☆ WQXR Qtt. (♯ Nix.QLP 4004; Cum.CPL 311)

Poema fantastico, Op. 98 pf.
W. Masselos   ♯ **MGM.E 3165**
(*Albeniz, Surinach, Nin*)

(La) Procesión del rocio, Op. 9 orch.
L.S.O.—Poulet   in ♯ **P.PMC 1006**
(*Albeniz, Granados, Falla*) (♯ MGM.E 3073;
                            Od.ODX 137: ♭ BSOE 4005)
Madrid Sym.—Branco   ♯ **LT.DTL 93015**
(*above*)   (♯ Sel. LAG 1048; West.WL 5320)[1]
☆ Paris Cons.—Jorda   ♯ **D.LW 5055**
(*Albeniz*)   (♯ Lon.LD 9042)

Sinfonia sevillana, Op. 23 orch. 1920
Spanish Nat.—Argenta   ♯ **LI.TW 91013**
(*Falla: Sombrero*)   (♯ Ambra.MCC 30007)

SONGS: CYCLES
CANTO A SEVILLA, Op. 37 (J. M. San Román)
1. Preludio orch. only   5. El Fantasma
2. Semana Santa   6. La Giralda
3. Las Fuentecitas del Parque 7. Ofrenda orch. only
4. Noche de Feria orch. only
V. de los Angeles (S) & L.S.O.—Fistoulari
                            ♯ **G.ALP 1185**
(♯ FALP 345: LALP 152; ArgA.LPC 11617)

... Nos. 2, 3, 5, 6, only
L. R. de Aragon (S) & Madrid Sym.—Branco
                            ♯ **LT.DTL 93015**
(*below*) (♯ Sel.LAG 1048; SpT.TLA 20008;
                            West.WL 5320)[1]
... **No. 6, La Giralda**
N. Merriman (M-S), G. Moore (pf.)
                            in ♯ **C.CX 1243**
(† Spanish Songs)   (♯ FCX 392; Angel. 35208)

POEMA EN FORMA DE CANCIONES, Op. 19
(Campoamor)
1. Dedicatoria (pf. only)   4. Los dos miedos
2. Nunca olvida . . .   5. Las locas por amor
3. Cantares
L. Huarte (S)   ♯ *MusH.P 3004*
(*Granados, Rodrigo, etc.*)
... **No. 3, Cantares**
L. Ibarrondo (M-S), M. Sandoval (pf.)
                            in ♯ **Rem. 199-139**
                            (♯ Cum.CR 297)
L. Berchman (S) & orch.   in ♯ **Mont.FM 28**
N. Chayres (T), F. Kramer (pf.) ♯ **Kings.KL 300**
(*Falla, Valverde, etc.*)
M. Cubas (T) & orch.   ArgOd. **57056**
(*Fuste: Pandereta andaluza*)   (in ♯ LDC 528)
... **No. 4, Los dos miedos**
L. Castellano (S), S. Leff (pf.) in ♯ **Mur.P 106**
(followed by pf. acc. only)

SONGS
Anhelos, Op. 54, No. 1 (from *3 Sonetos*) (Marin)
R. Gómez (M-S), P. Vallrebera (pf.) *Reg.C10282*
(*Granados: Tonadillas, No. 7*)   (♭ SEDL 19042)
Farruca, Op. 45, No. 1 (Campoamor)
N. Merriman (M-S), G. Moore (pf.)
                            in ♯ **C.CX 1243**
(† Spanish Songs)   (♯ FCX 392; Angel. 35208)
L. Berchman (S) & orch.   in ♯ **Mont.FM 28**
☆ V. de los Angeles (S), G. Moore (pf.) (in ♯ G.ALP 1151:
            LALP 142: FALP 327; & in ♯ Vic. set LM 6017)

Tango pf. (No. 2 from *3 Danzas Andaluzas, Op. 8*)
— ARR. DANCING, CASTANETS & ORCH.
P. López (in ♯ G.LCLP 102: ♭ 7EPL 13040)

TURNER, William (1651-1740)
SEE: † MORE CATCHES & GLEES OF THE RESTORATION

TUTHILL, Burnet (b. 1888)

Come Seven Rhapsody orch.
A.R.S. Sym.—Schönherr   ♯ *ARS. 30*
(*Rogers & Sanders*)

UGARTE, Floro M. (b. 1884)

De mi tierra No. 1 Suite, orch. 1923
Colón Theatre—J. R. Fauré   ArgOd. **67001**
                            (♯ LDC 507)

De mi tierra No. 2 Suite, orch. 1934
... **No. 1, Voces del pajonal**, only[3]
State Sym.—Kinsky   ArgV.P **1489**
                            (pte. rec.)

Prelude, G minor orch. 1949
Avellaneda College Sym.—Fauré
                            ♭ *ArgOd.BSOAE 4524*
(*A. Williams: El Rancho abandonado*)
(*idem, & Gluck, Gomes in ♯ LDC 523*)

SONGS
Caballito criollo (Roldán); La Shulca (Sánchez)
▽ R. Cesari (B) & orch. (*ArgOd. 57002*)

---

[1] Announced, but not issued, as WL 5272.
[2] This record was withdrawn immediately after issue, and may never have actually been on sale.
[3] Or possibly it may be complete.

USANDIZAGA, Jose Maria (1887-1915)
(Abridged listings only)

(Los) GOLONDRINAS Opera, 3 Acts 1914
  P. Lorengar, A. M. Iriarte, C. Munguía, R. Torres, etc.,
  Donostiarra Cho. & Madrid Sym.—Argenta
                                        ♯ LI.TW 91031/3
(6ss)   (♯ Ambra.MCC 30016/8)
  [Prelude & Pantomime in ♯ LI.TW 91004;
                        Ambra.MCCP 29001: ♭ MGE 60006/7]

Pantomime Sym. Orch.—Ferrer (2ss) ♭ Reg.SEDL 112
                          (in ♯ LC 1003; Pam.LRC 15508)

Vocal Excerpts ▽ M. Redondo (Od. 121137)

USSACHEVSKY, Vladimir (b. 1911)
SEE: LUENING, Otto

VAINBERG, Moisse (b. 1919)

Moldavian Rhapsody, Op. 47 vln. & pf.
  D. Oistrakh & M. Vainberg ♯ CEd.CE 3002
  (Mozart, Vladigerov)
  (Shostakovich, Prokofiev, etc. in ♯ Csm.CRLPX 011)

VALEN, Fartein (1887-1952)

(Le) Cimetière marin, Op. 20 1934 (also NOC. 63156/7, 2ss)
(La) Isla de las Calmas, Op. 21 1934 (also NOC. 63187/8, 2ss)
Sonetto di Michelangelo, Op. 17, No. 1 1932
                        (also NOC. 63199/200, 2ss)
  ☆ Oslo Phil. Orch.—Fjeldstad ♯ Mer.MG 10149
  (Saeverud)

VALENTINI, Giuseppe (1681-c. 1740)

Concerto, C major, oboe & orch. c. 1701
  S. Prestini & Italian Cha.—Jenkins
                                ♯ HS.HSL 77
  (Giordani & Brunetti)   (in set HSL-C)

VALENTINO, Roberto (fl. XVIIIth Cent.)

Sonata No. 9, A minor fl. & cont. 1714
  S. Gazzelloni & R. Raffalt (hpsi.)
                                ♯ ItV.A12R 0027
  (Veracini, Platti, Marcello, etc.)

VALVERDE DURÁN, Joaquin
                                      (1846-1910)

SEE ALSO: CHUECA, FEDERICO; CHAPÍ, R.

SONG: Clavelitos (Cadenas)
  V. de los Angeles (S), G. Moore (pf.)
                        in ♯ G.BLP 1037
                            (▽ DA 1926)
  N. Chayres (T), F. Kramer (pf.) (in ♯ Kings.KL 300)
  ▽ L. Bori (S) (G.DA 1043)
    A. Galli-Curci (S) (G.DA 1095)
    C. Supervia (M-S) (P.RO 20154; AmD. 20461)

VAN NOORDT, Anthony (c. 1610-1675)
SEE: † "BAROQUE" ORGAN MUSIC

VAQUEIRAS, Raimbautz de (c. 1155-c. 1207)
SEE: † MONUMENTA ITALICAE MUSICAE
       † FRENCH TROUBADOUR SONGS

VARÈSE, Edgar (b. 1885)

Ionisation percussion 1931
  Illinois Univ. Ens.—Price ♯ UOI. CRS 3
  (Chavez, Colgran, Harrison, McKenzie)

VARVOGLIS, Marios (b. 1885)

Pastoral Suite str. qtt. 1912
  Kolassis Qtt.   ♯ Phi.N 00247L
  (Kalomiris & Skalkottas)

VASQUEZ, Juán (fl. XVIth Cent.)

VILLANCICOS
D'aquel pastor de la Sierra
De los álamos vengo, madre
Morenica, dame un beso
Ya florencen los árboles, Juan
  F.A.D. Polyphonic Cho.—Ribó in ♯ C.CX 1308
  (Victoria, Morales, etc. & Spanish Trad.) (♯ Angel. 35257)

Vos me mataseis
  M. Cid (S), E. Pujol (vihuela) (in † ♯ HS.AS 10)

Zagaleje
  Pamplona Cho.—Morondo in ♯ Sel.LPG 8738
  († Spanish Renaissance Music)

VAUGHAN WILLIAMS, Ralph (b. 1872)

CHURCH MUSIC
Come, Holy Spirit, most blessed Lord
  St. George's Chapel—Harris   C.LX 1572
  († English Church Music, Vol. III) [L. Dakers, org.]

HYMN TUNE: At the name of Jesus
  (King's Weston)
  Redlands Univ. Cho.—J. W. Jones
                        in ♯ AmC.ML 4866

Lord, thou hast been our refuge
  2 chos. & org. (or orch.)
  ☆ Augustana Cho.—Veld (in ♯ Word.W 4001)

Mass, G minor unacc. cho. 1922
  Fleet Street Cho.—Lawrence (n.v.)
                                ♯ D.LXT 2794
  (Rubbra)   (♯ Lon.LL 805)

... Credo & Sanctus (ARR. Jacobson)
  Coronation Chorus (Eng) in ♯ G.ALP 1056 & 8
  († Coronation of Queen Elizabeth II)

O how amiable Cho. & org. c. 1934
  ☆ Washington Presbyterian Chu. Cho.—Schaefer (org.)
                                    (in ♯ WCFM. 20)

O taste and see Motet 1953[1]
  Coronation Chorus—McKie in ♯ G.ALP 1058
  († Coronation of Queen Elizabeth II)
  D. Linter (Tr.), St. Paul's Cath. Cho.—Dykes
    Bower [H. Gabb, org.]   in ♯ C.CX 1193
  (below)   (in ♯ Angel. 35138, set 3516)

Te Deum laudamus[2] Cho.
... Excerpts
  St. Margaret's, Westminster (in ♯ Ori.MG 20003,
                                Coronation Souvenir)

Concerto, Bass tuba & orch. 1954
  P. Catelinet & L.S.O.—Barbirolli ♯ G.BLP 1078
  (below)

Concerto, Oboe & str. orch. 1944
  E. Rothwell & L.S.O.—Barbirolli ♯ G.BLP 1078
  (above)

Fantasia on 'Greensleeves'[3] orch. 1929
  Philharmonic Prom.—Boult   ♯ Nix.NLP 905
  (below)   (♯ West.WL 5270)
  Sydney Sym.—Heinze   ♯ Rad.LXR 5002
  (Byrd, Walton)
  Hamburg Philharmonia—H-J. Walther
                                MSB. 78151
  (J. Strauss: G'schichten aus dem Wiener Wald)
                                (& in ♯ MGM.E 3143)
  ☆ Hallé—Sargent   C.DX 1889
  (Tchaikovsky: Sleeping Beauty—Waltz) (GQX 11538)

[1] Written for the Coronation of H.M. Queen Elizabeth II.   [2] Unspec. but probably the Festival Te Deum 1937.
[3] ARR. Graves from Sir John in Love.

Fantasia on a theme by Tallis str. orch. 1910
Philharmonic Prom.—Boult   **♯ Nix.NLP 905**
(*above & below*)   (♯ West.WL 5270)
Philharmonia—Karajan   **♯ C.CX 1159**
(*Britten*)   (♯ QCX 10109; Angel. 35142)
B.B.C. Sym.—Sargent   **♯ G.BLP 1019**
(*Elgar: Wand of Youth Suite No. 2*)
(4ss, on ♮ G.DB 9783/4)
Orch.—Stokowski   **♯ G.ALP 1205**
(*Schoenberg*) (♯ Vic.LM 1739; ♭ set WDM 1739;
                                           ♯ FV.A 630278)

Fantasia on the 'Old 104th' Psalm Tune
1950 pf., cho., orch.
J. Hunt (pf.), Cornell a Cappella Cho. &
Rochester Cha. Orch.—Hull **♯CHS.CHS 1190**
(*Folk Song Settings; & Palmer*)

Folk Song Suite Military Band
Cities Service Band—Lavalle **♯ Vic.LPM 1133**
(*Delibes, Rossini, Prokofiev, etc.*) (♭ set EPC 1133)
Eastman Wind Ens.—Fennell **♯ Mer.MG 40015**
(*below, & Holst*)

— ARR. ORCH. Jacob
Philharmonic Prom.—Boult   **♯ Nix.NLP 905**
(*above & below*)   (♯ WestWL 5270)
☆ C.B.S.—Barlow (♯ AmC.RL 3023, with *Beethoven*)

(A) GARLAND FOR THE QUEEN
(with Bliss, Bax, Ireland, etc.) 1953
... **Silence and music** (Wood)
Cambridge Univ. Madrigal Soc.—Ord.
in † ♯ **C.CX 1063**

JOB "A Masque for Dancing" 1930-1
L.P.O.—Boult   **♯ D.LXT 2937**
(♯ Lon.LL 1003)

(The) Lark Ascending vln. & cha. orch. 1914
J. Pougnet & L.P.O.—Boult **♯ P.PMB 1003**
(*Song of Thanksgiving*)

(The) LOVES OF JOANNA GODDEN Film 1947
... Orch. excerpts
☆ Philharmonia—Irving (in ♯ AmC.RL 3029)

Norfolk Rhapsody No. 1, E minor orch. 1906
Philharmonic Prom.—Boult   **♯ Nix.NLP 905**
(*above*)   (♯ West.WL 5270)

OLD KING COLE Ballet 1923
Orch. Suite
Philharmonic Prom.—Boult **♯ West.WL 5228**
(*The Wasps*)
L.P.O.—Boult   **♯ D.LW 5151**

PILGRIM'S PROGRESS Opera 1951
— SONG ARRANGEMENTS by the composer
Watchful's Song: Into thy hands B
Song of the Pilgrims: Who would true valour see B
The Pilgrim's Psalm: I will put on the whole armour B
The Song of the leaves of life & of the water of life: Unto him
  that overcometh 2 S
The Song of Vanity Fair: Come and buy S
The Woodcutter's Song: He that is down S
The Birds' Song: The Lord is my shepherd S
J. Cameron (B), I. Kells (S), P. Bartlett (S),
G. Watson (pf.)   **♯ Argo.RG 20**
(*On Wenlock Edge*)

(3) Preludes on Welsh Hymn tunes org. 1920
1. On 'Bryn Calfaria'
2. On 'Rhosymedre'
3. On 'Hyfrydol'
— ARR. BANDS
Massed Bands—Adams   **♮ RZ.MF 390/2**
(3ss—*Leidzen: Concerto for band & trombone*)
... **No. 2, On 'Rhosymedre'**
H. Mueller   **♯ ML. 7049**
(*Sancta Civitas*)

... **No. 3, On 'Hyfrydol'**
R. Ellsasser   in ♯ **MGM.E 3064**
(† *Organ Music by Modern Composers*)

Romance
"harmonica" [i.e. mouth organ] & str. orch. 1952
☆L. Adler & Str. Orch. & pf.—Sargent   **♯ C.S 1023**
(*Benjamin: Concerto*) (C.DOX 1006: CQX 16667:
                                            ♯ FC 1004)

Sancta Civitas Oratorio T, B, cho. & orch. 1926
C. Harmon (B) & San Francisco Bach Cho.
—Jacobsen[1]   **♯ ML. 7049**
[H. Mueller, org.—actual performance]
(1½ss—*Prelude on 'Rhosymedre'*)

SIR JOHN IN LOVE Opera 4 Acts 1929
Drinking Song
Pittsburgh Univ. Men's Glee Club—Weiss
in ♯ **PFCM.CB 162**
(*Thomson, Thompson, etc.*)

Greensleeves, see Fantasia, *above*

Song of Thanksgiving S, speaker, cho, & orch. 1945
☆ B. Dolemore, R. Speaight, Luton Cho. Soc., Section of
Luton Girls' Cho., L.P.O.—Boult ♯ **P.PMB 1003**
(*Lark Ascending*)

SONGS
COLLECTION
SONGS OF TRAVEL (R. L. Stevenson)
SET I. 1905
No. 1, The Vagabond   No. 2, Bright is the ring of words
No. 3, The Roadside Fire
SET II. 1907
No. 1, Let beauty awake   No. 2, Youth and love
No. 3, In dreams unhappy   No. 4, The infinite shining heavens
Whither must I wander (R. L. Stevenson) c. 1894
Linden Lea (Barnes) 1902
Silent Noon (Rossetti) 1918
The Water Mill (Shove) 1925
R. Standen (B), F. Stone (pf.) ♯ **West.WLE 103**
(*Head, Stanford, etc.*)

ON WENLOCK EDGE Song cycle (Housman)
T, str. qtt. & pf. ad lib. 1908
A. Young, Sebastian Qtt., G. Watson
♯ Argo.RG 20
(*Pilgrim's Progress, excerpts*)

Linden Lea (Barnes) 1902
— ARR. CHO. Morriston Orpheus Cho.—Sims (*C.DB 3228*)

(5) Mystical Songs (Herbert) B & cho. 1911
☆ H. Ronk & Washington Presbyterian Cho.—Schaefer
(in ♯ WCFM. 20)
... **No. 1, Easter; No. 2, I got me flowers;**
No. 4, The Call
M. Bevan & St. Paul's Cath. Cho.—Dykes
Bower [H. Gabb, pf.]   in ♯ **C.CX 1193**
(*above, Sweelinck, Bach, Weelkes, etc.*)
(in ♯ Angel. 35138, set 3516)

(The) New Ghost (Shove) 1925
J. Vyvyan (S), E. Lush (pf.) in ♯ **D.LXT 2797**
(† *Songs of England*)   (♯ Lon.LL 806)

Silent Noon (Rossetti)
K. Ferrier (A), F. Stone (pf.)[2] in ♯ **D.LX 3133**
(*Parry, Stanford, Warlock, etc.*)   (in ♯ Lon.LS 1032)
H. Nash (T), G. Moore (pf.)   **G.C 4210**
(*Songs of Travel, No. 1*)
K. Joyce (A), H. Greenslade (pf.)   **P.E 11511**
(*Peel: Early morning & Gypsies*)

SONGS OF TRAVEL (R. L. Stevenson)
SET I: No. 1, The Vagabond 1905
H. Nash (T), G. Moore (pf.)   **G.C 4210**
(*Silent Noon*)

SYMPHONIES
COMPLETE RECORDING
L.P.O.—Boult   **♯ D. & Lon. various**
[Details, see below, & Supp. II for No. 2
                            (♯ D.LXT 2693; Lon.LL 569)]

No. 1, A Sea Symphony c. 1905-10
S, B, cho. & orch. (Whitman)
I. Baillie, J. Cameron, London Phil. Cho. &
Orch.—Boult   **♯ D.LXT 2907/8**
(3ss—*The Wasps*)   (♯ Lon.LL 972/3)

---

[1] The brief T part is sung by anon. S; the accompaniment is org. and tpts. only.
[2] Broadcast performance, 5 June 1952.

SYMPHONIES (continued)

No. 2, A London Symphony, G major 1914-20
☆ Cincinnati Sym.—Goossens (♯ Cam.CAL 186)

No. 3, A Pastoral Symphony S & Orch. 1922
M. Ritchie, L.P.O.—Boult   ♯ D.LXT 2787
(♯ Lon.LL 721)

No. 4, F minor 1934
L.P.O.—Boult   ♯ D.LXT 2909
(♯ Lon.LL 974)

No. 5, D major 1943
L.P.O.—Boult   ♯ D.LXT 2910
(♯ Lon.LL 975)

No. 6, E minor 1945-7
L.P.O.—Boult   ♯ D.LXT 2911
(with speech by the composer)   (♯ Lon.LL 976)
☆ L.S.O.—Boult (♯ Vic.LHMV 1040: ♭ set WHMV 1040)

No. 7, Sinfonia Antartica 1951-2 S, cho. & orch.
M. Ritchie, Hallé Cho. & Orch.—Barbirolli
♯ G.ALP 1102
(♯ FALP 339)
M. Ritchie, London Phil. Cho. & L.P.O.
—Boult   ♯ D.LXT 2912
[with superscriptions spoken by Sir John Gielgud]
(♯ Lon.LL 977)

Toccata marziale Military Band 1924
West Point Band—Resta   ♯ PFCM.CB 174
(Harris & Hindemith)

Eastman Wind Ens.—Fennell ♯ Mer.MG 40015
(above & Holst)

(5) Tudor Portraits A, B, cho. & orch. 1936
(after Skelton)
N. Rankin, R. Anderson, Pittsburgh
Mendelssohn Cho. & Pittsburgh Sym.
—Steinberg   ♯ DCap.CTL 7047
(♯ Cap.P 8218; ACap.CLC 017; PFCM.CB 182/3)

(The) WASPS Inc. Music to Aristophanes 1909
1. Overture   2. Entr'acte
3. March past of the kitchen utensils
4. Entr'acte   5. Ballet & Finale
Philharmonic Prom.—Boult   ♯ West.WL 5228
(Old King Cole)
L.P.O.—Boult   ♯ D.LXT 2908
(Symphony No. 1, s. 3)   (♯ Lon.LL 972)
L.S.O.—Weldon   ♯ C.SX 1019
(Bax & Holst)
[Nos. 2 & 3 also on DX 1918: ♭ SCD 2039:
Nos 2, 3, 5 on ♭ C.SED 5522: SEDQ 614]

... **No. 1, Overture,** only
Hallé—Barbirolli   G.DB 21623
☆ L.S.O.—Menges (G.EB 586)

FOLK SONG SETTINGS
The Dark-eyed sailor
John Dory Cho.
The Turtle Dove B & Cho.
Cornell a Cappella Cho.—Hull ♯CHS.CHS 1190
(Fantasia on 'Old 104th'; & Palmer)

I will give my love an apple
J. Vyvyan (S), E. Lush (pf.) in ♯ D.LXT 2797
(† Songs of England)   (in ♯ Lon.LL 806)
(also in ♯ D.LW 5102)

On Christmas night
▽ P. Shuldham Shaw & pf. (G.B 9776)

(Le) Paradis
S. Wyss (S), M. Korchinska (hp.)
in ♯ Argo.RG 34

(The) Turtle Dove B & Cho.
W. Imig & Stanford Univ. Cho.—Schmidt
in ♯ ML. 7022
(† Madrigals & Motets)
ARRANGEMENTS
Away in a manger (Carol)
St. Simon-the-Apostle Chu. Cho.—Lewis
in ♯ Hall.J 75

(The) Old 100th
Coronation Chorus, Congregation & Orch.
in ♯ G.ALP 1058
(† Coronation of Queen Elizabeth II)

VAUTOR, Thomas (fl. c. 1620)
SEE: † TRIUMPHS OF ORIANA
    † SHAKESPEARE SONGS & LUTE SOLOS

VECCHI, Orazio (1550-1605)

L'AMFIPARNASO Madrigal Comedy 1594
COMPLETE RECORDING
Bologna Madrigalists—Giani[1]   ♯ CFD. 17
Pampelona Cho.—Morondo[2] ♯ Lum.LD 3-405

Salutis humanae sator Motet
Treviso Cath. Cho.—d'Alessi
♯ E. & AmVox.PL 8610
(† Motets of Venetian School)

VEGA, Aurelio de la (b. 1925)

Leyenda del Ariel Criollo vlc. & pf. 1953
A. Odnoposoff & Bertha Huberman ♯ Pnt. 4001
(Ardevol, Roldán, Menendez)

VENTADORN, Bernart de (d. 1195)
SEE: † HISTORY OF MUSIC IN SOUND (14)
    † MONUMENTA ITALICAE MUSICAE
    † MUSIQUE ET POÉSIE FRANÇAISE
    † FRENCH TROUBADOUR SONGS

VERACINI, Francesco (1690-c. 1750)

SONATAS, Op. 1, vln. & cont. 1721
No. 6, E minor
F. Zepparoni & R. Veyron-Lacroix (hpsi.)
† ♯ AS. 3008LD
(Corelli & Tartini)   (♯ HS.AS 40)

SONATAS, Op. 2, vln. & cont.
(Sonate accademiche) 1744
No. 6, A major ... Largo ed. Corti
— ARR. VLC. & PF.
M. Amfiteatrof & O. P. Santoliquido
♯ ItV.A12R 0140
(Vivaldi, Galuppi, Frescobaldi, etc.)

No. 11, E major ... Minuet & Gavotte
☆ R. Ricci & L. Persinger (♭ AmVox.VIP 45420)

Sonata No. 2, G major[3] fl. & cont.
S. Gazzelloni & R. Raffalt (hpsi.)
♯ ItV.A12R 0027
(Platti, Marcello, Vivaldi, etc.)

VERDELOT, Philippe (d. c. 1567)
SEE: WILLAERT for arrangements of Madrigals

VERDI, Giuseppe Fortunio Francesco
(1813-1901)
I. NON-OPERATIC

(4) Pezzi Sacri 1898
1. Ave Maria (unacc.) 2. Stabat Mater (with orch.)
3. Te Deum (with orch.) 4. Laudi alla Vergine (unacc.)
☆ Aachen Cath. Cho. & Municipal Orch.—Rehmann
♯ HP.DGM 18038
☆ Vienna Acad. Cha. Cho. & State Op. Orch.—Swoboda
(♯ Clc. 6153)

---

[1] Edited Somma.   [2] Announced but not issued.
[3] From 12 Sonatas, no Op. No. (Venice, 1716).

(4) Pezzi Sacri (*continued*)

... No. 3
R. Shaw Chorale & N.B.C. Sym.—Toscanini[1]
    ‡ **Vic.LM 1849**
(*Boito*)   (‡ ItV.A12R 0145; FV.A 630269)

... No. 4
Vienna Boys' Cho.—Brenn in ‡ *EPhi.NBR 6013*
(*Victoria, Handl, A. Scarlatti, etc.*)
     (in ‡ *Phi.N 00624R;* ‡ AmC.ML 4873)

Quartet, Strings, E minor   1873
Quartetto di Roma   ‡ **Ura.RS 7-20**
(*Haydn*)
☆ Paganini Qtt. (‡ *ItV.A10R 0009*)

REQUIEM MASS S, A, T, B, cho. & orch.   1873
COMPLETE RECORDINGS
M. Stader, M. Radev, H. Krebs, K. Borg,
St. Hedwig's Cath. Cho., R.I.A.S. Cha. Cho.
& Sym. Orch.—Fricsay ‡ **HP.DGM 18155/6**[2]
(4ss)   (‡ AmD. set DX 118)
H. Nelli, F. Barbieri, G. di Stefano, C. Siepi,
R. Shaw Chorale & N.B.C. Sym.—Toscanini[3]
    ‡ **Vic. set LM 6018**
(4ss)   (‡ ItV.B12R 0028/9; FV.A 630237/8)
E. Schwarzkopf, O. Dominguez, G. di Stefano,
C. Siepi, La Scala Cho. & Orch.—de Sabata
    ‡ **C.CX 1195/6**
(4ss) (‡ QCX 10104/5; FCX 361/2; Angel. 35158/9,
                  set 3520)
G. Brouwenstijn, M. v. Ilosvay, P. Munteanu,
O. Czerwenka, Rome Santa Cecilia Acad.
Cho. & Orch.—v. Kempen ‡ **Phi.A 00284/5L**
(4ss)

☆ M. Caniglia, B. Gigli, etc. Rome Op. Cho. & Orch.
—Serafin (‡ G.FJLP 5002/3: QALP 10016/7)
[Excerpts on ♭ Vic.ERAT 27]
Soloists, Cho. & Austrian Sym.—Koslik
(‡ Cum. set CR 290; Excerpts in ‡ Rem. 199-121 &
                        ‡ Ply. 12-90)
Soloists, Berlin Cho. & Sym.—Balzer (‡ Gram. 20160/1)
... Ingemisco tamquam reus   T
☆ A. Piccaver (in ‡ Ete. 703)

SONGS
Brindisi (Maffei)
Non t'accostar all' urna (Vittorelli)
Perduta ho la pace (after Goethe's *Gretchen am Spinnrade*)
La Seduzione (Balestri)
P. Neway (S), T. Mayer (pf.)   ‡ **Ete. 101**
(*Bellini & Mascagni*)

More, Elisa, lo stanco poeta (Bianchi)
Stornello: Tu dici che non m'ami (Anon.)
L. Albanese (S) & pf.   in ‡ **Vic.LM 1857**
                    (‡ FV.A 530211)

(Il) Tramonto (Maffei)
I. B. Lucca (S) & Orch.   in ‡ *Dur.MSE 6*
(*Bellini, Donizetti, Rossini, etc.*)

II. OPERAS

AIDA   4 Acts   1871
COMPLETE RECORDINGS

Casts	Set M	Set O	Set R
Aida (S)	Z. Milanov	M. M. Callas	N. Sokolova
Amneris (S)	F. Barbieri	F. Barbieri	V. Davidova
Radames (T)	J. Björling	R. Tucker	G. Nelepp
Amonasro (B)	L. Warren	T. Gobbi	P. Lisitsian
Ramfis (Bs)	B. Christoff	G. Modesti	I. Petrov

Set M with Rome Op. Cho. & Orch.—Perlea
                   ‡ **Vic. set LM 6122**
(6ss)   (‡ ItV.C12R 0175/7)
Set O with La Scala Cho. & Orch.—Serafin ‡ **C.CX 1318/20**
(6ss)   (‡ QCX 10165/7; ‡ Angel. 35287/9, set 3525)
Set R (in *Russ*) with Bolshoi Th. Cho. & Orch.—Melik-
Pashayev   ‡ **USSR.D 01576/82**
(7ss—*St.-Saëns: Henry VIII, Ballet Music*)
Set Q   M. Curtis (S), O. Dominguez (M-S), U. Borsó (T),
E. Bastianini (B), N. Scott (Bs), etc., La Fenice Theatre
Cho. & Orch.—Capuana (6ss)   ‡ **Rem. set 199-178**
Set H   ☆ C. Mancini (S), G. Simionato (M-S), M.
Filippeschi (T), etc. Italian Radio Cho. & Orch.—Gui
               (‡ Pol. 18173/5; FSor.CS 510/2)
[Excerpts on ‡ CCet.A 50142 & ♭ Cap.FAP 7000;
                   ♭ Cet.EPO 0305]

Set A ☆ M. Caniglia (S), B. Gigli (T), etc. Rome Op. Cho.
  & Orch.—Serafin (‡ G.FJLP 5005/8: QALP 10010/3)
[Highlights on ‡ Vic.LCT 1101: ♭ *set WCT 1101*]
Set C ☆ G. Arangi-Lombardi (S), A. Lindi (T), M.
Capuana (M-S), etc. La Scala Cho. & Milan Sym.
  —Molajoli (‡ AmC. set EL 3, 6ss)

ABRIDGED RECORDING
V. Petrova (M-S), E. Wysor (S), G. Sari (T),
Florence Fest. Cho. & Orch.—Tieri (4ss)
               ‡ **Ace. 1009**

HIGHLIGHTS
☆ Soloists, cho. & orch. of N.Y. City Op. Co.—Halasz
                    ‡ **MGM.E 3023**
(*Faust*)   (2ss, ‡ *ItMGM.QD 6015*)
A. da Costa, M. Moll, V. Ruggeri, F. Valentino, etc.
 & orch. (‡ Roy. 1583; MTW. 701; excerpts
                      in ‡ Roy. 18148)
Italian Op. Co. (‡ Ply. 12-114)
☆ Anon. Artists (‡ Cam.CAL 225 & in ‡ set CFL 101;
                    also ‡ CAL 249)
Soloists & Rome Op. Cho. & Orch.—Paoletti, from
              set L (‡ ACap.CLCX 042)

— ARR. ORCH.
Orch.—Kostelanetz   ‡ *EPhi.NBR 6020*
[Celeste Aida only, in ‡ KZ 1] (‡ AmC.CL 755:
                       ♭ *set A 1114*)
Rome Sym.—Morelli   ‡ **Kings. 701**

"Aida of Yesterday"
☆ B. Gigli, E. Rethberg, G. Martinelli, E. Pinza, R.
Ponselle, J. Gadski, P. Amato, L. Homer, E. Caruso
                        (‡ DV.L 17057)

ACT I

Prelude
Philharmonia—Galliera   in ‡ **C.SX 1009**
(*Forza, Nabucco, Traviata, Vêpres siciliennes*)
         (in ‡ FCX 209: QCX 10094; Angel. 35012)
Radio Luxembourg Orch.—Pensis
              in ‡ **FestF.FLD 15**
Philharmonia—Markevitch   **G.C 7937**
(*Macbeth—Ballet Music, s. 1*)
☆ Berlin Municipal Op.—Rother (in ‡ Nix.ULP 9057;
                  in ‡ *Ura.RS 5-4*)
Italian Radio—Gui (in ‡ CCet.A 50159; from set H)
Metropolitan Op.—Cleva (in ‡ AmC.ML 4886:
                       ♭ *A 1551*)

Celeste Aida   T
J. Björling   **G.DB 21563**
(*Gioconda—Cielo e mar*) (♭ 7R 160; ♭ Vic.ERA 209:
                    in ‡ LM 1801)
M. Filippeschi   **G.S 10602**
(*Chénier—Un di . . .*)
J. Soler   **Cet.PE 181**
(*Gioconda—Cielo e mar*)
M. del Monaco [from set K]   in ‡ *D.LW 5064*
(*Luisa Miller, Macbeth, Traviata*) (♭ VD 509;
             ‡ Lon.LD 9051 & in LL 1244)
R. Schock (*Ger*)   **G.DB 11561**
(*Ballo in Maschera—Ma se m'è forza*) (♭ 7RW 511:
                  in ‡ WBLP 1501)
   N. Nikolov (in ‡ USSR.D 2158)
   A. da Costa (in ‡ Roy. 1599)
   G. Nelepp (? from set—*Russ*) (in ‡ USSR.D 2074)
   W. Domeniecki (*Pol*) (Muza.X 2342)
   Anon. Artist (in ‡ Cam.CAL 249)
  ☆ M. Lanza (♭ Vic.ERA 136)
   R. Schock (in ‡ Roy. 1256: ♭ EP 183)
   K. Baum (♭ Rem.REP 6)
   J. Peerce (in ‡ Var. 6981)
   H. Roswaenge (*Ger*) (in ‡ D.DK 23188)
   B. Blachut (*Cz*) (in ‡ U. 5205H)
  🅗 G. Martinelli (in ‡ SBDH.LPG 4* & Roy. 1595*)
   E. Caruso (in ‡ G.FJLP 5009*: QJLP 105*;
                    ♭ Vic.ERAT 6*)
   J. McCormack (in ‡ Cum.CE 185*; in ‡ Roy. 1555*:
    & in ‡ 1595*: ♭ EP 324*; in ‡ AudR.LPA 2340*)

Iside venerata . . . Sul del Nilo   Ens.
R. Tebaldi (S), E. Stignani (M-S), M. del
Monaco (T), D. Caselli (Bs), F. Corena (Bs)
               ‡ *D.LW 5184*
(*Gloria all'Egitto, Act II*)   [☆ from set K][4]

---

[1] Broadcast performance, March 1954.   [2] Auto.; also normal coupling ‡ Pol. 18157/8.
[3] Carnegie Hall performance, Jan. 1951.   [4] Includes also *Nume, custode e vindice* (with recit.).

AIDA, Act I (*continued*)
Ritorna vincitor!   S
Z. Milanov   ♭ *G. 7ER 5041*
(*below*) (in ♯ ALP 1247; Vic.LM 1777: ♭ *ERA 206:*
                                              set ERB 19)
V. Petrova   in ♯ *Ace. 1007/8*
(*Forza, Tosca, Cavalleria, etc.*)
A. Stella   in ♯ *G.QALP 10096*
(*Otello, Ernani, Ballo, etc.*)
M. Cunitz (*Ger*)   *TV.VSK 9015*
(*below*)   (♭ *T.UV 103; FT. 470.TC.012*)
   Anon. Artist (in ♯ Cam.CAL 249)
☆ R. Tebaldi (♯ *D.LW 5013:* ♭ *VD 511, d.c*)
   C. Goltz (♭ *Pol. 30026:* in ♯ *18169; Ger on* ♭ *Pol. 30118*)
H R. Ponselle (♯ & ♭ *AmC.PE 25**)
   C. Boninsegna (in ♯ Sca. 813*)

Immenso Fthà   Cho.   (Temple Scene)
Dance of the Priestesses   orch.
Nume, custode e vindice   T, Bs, cho.
G. Martinelli, E. Pinza, G. Anthony (S) & Cho.
                                  (♭ *Vic.ERAT 15*)

Dance of the Priestesses
☆ Metropolitan Op.—Cleva (in ♯ AmC.ML 4886:
                                        ♭ *A 1551*)
   Boston Prom.—Fiedler (♭ *Cam.CAE 151:*
        in ♯ CAL 151 & in ♯ set CFL 102)

ACT II. Sc. 1
Dance of the Moorish Slave-boys
☆ Metropolitan Op.—Cleva (in ♯ AmC.ML 4886:
                                        ♭ *A 1551*)
   Boston Prom.—Fiedler (♭ *Cam.CAE 151:*
        in ♯ CAL 151 & in ♯ set CFL 102)

Chi mai fra gli inni . . .
Fu la sorte dell' armi . . .   S, M-S, cho.
M. Serval & S. Preobrazhenskaya (*Russ*)
                                  (in ♯ *USSR.D 1425*)
☆ A. Kupper, E. Höngen, Württemberg State Op.
   —Leitner (*Ger*) (in ♯ Pol. 19027)

ACT II. Sc. 2
Gloria all' Egitto!
(March & Cho.)   Cho., Band, orch.
☆ Rome St. Cecilia Acad. Cho.—Erede   ♯ *D.LW 5184*
   (*Iside venerata, Act I*) [☆ from set K]¹
☆ Hilversum Radio Cho. & Orch.—v. Kempen
                                  ♭ *EPhi.NBE 11009*
   (*Faust & Tannhäuser*) (in ♯ *Phi.S 06018R: N 00649R:*
                                  ♭ *N 402014E*)
— ORCH. ONLY
Munich Phil.—Ludwig   *PV. 72439*
(*Pagliacci & Cavalleria Excerpts*) (♭ Pol. 30008:
                                  in ♯ 18169)
Hamburg Philharmonia—H-J. Walther
                                        MSB. 78048
(*G. Tell, Overture,* s. 3)
Orch.—Swarowsky (in ♯ MTW. 9; *ACC.MP 13*)
Regent Sym. (in ♯ Rgt. 7001)
☆ Boston Prom.—Fiedler (♭ *G.7EP 7019: 7EBF 4:*
   7EPQ 504; in ♯ *Vic.LM 1752:* ♭ *set WDM 1752* &
   in ♯ *LRM 7045:* ♭ *set ERB 7045;* in ♭ *DV. 16295;*
                           o.v. in ♭ *Cam.CAE 142*)
   Metropolitan Op.—Cleva (in ♯ AmC.ML 4886)

Ballabili (Ballet Music) orch.
Philharmonia—Karajan   ♯ *C.CX 1327*
(*Khovanshchina, Prince Igor, etc.*)   (♯ Angel. 35307)
Berlin Radio—Gerdes   *Eta. 225024*
(*Schmidt: Notre Dame—Intermezzo*)
Regent Sym. (in ♯ Rgt. 7000)
☆ Metropolitan Op.—Cleva (in ♯ AmC.ML 4886:
                                        ♭ *A 1551*)
   Covent Garden—Braithwaite (in ♯ P.PMC 1029)
   Boston Prom.—Fiedler (♭ *Cam.CAE 151:* in ♯ CAL 151
                           & in ♯ set CFL 102)

ACT III
O Patria mia . . . O cieli azzuri   S
Z. Milanov   ♭ *G.7ER 5041*
(*above*)   (in ♯ ALP 1247; Vic.LM 1777: ♭ *set ERB 19*)
J. Hammond   *G.DB 21580*
(*Wally—Ebben . . .*)   (♭ *7R 172*)

G. Brouwenstijn   ♯ *Phi.N 00712R*
(*Ballo & Otello*)   (♭ *N 402017E*)
G. Frazzoni   in ♯ *Cet.LPV 45003*
(*A. Chénier, Tosca, etc.*)
M. Cunitz (*Ger*)   *TV.VSK 9015*
(*above*)   (♭ *UV 103; FT. 470.TC.012*)
L. Rysanek (*Ger*)   *G.DB 11584*
(*Forza—Pace, pace*)   (♭ *7RW 19-538*)
☆ R. Tebaldi [from set K]   in ♯ *D.LW 5065*
   (*Traviata, Tosca, etc.*) (♯ *Lon.LD 9054;*
                                  in ♯ *D.LXT 5076*)
☆ R. Tebaldi (o.v.) (in ♯ Fnt.LP 302)
   E. Rethberg (in ♯ *G.FJLP 5000: QJLP 104*)
   C. Goltz (♭ *Pol. 30026; Ger on* ♭ *Pol. 30118*)
   D. Ilitsch (in ♯ *Sup.LPM 132; U. 5108C*)
H E. Destinn (in ♯ Vic. set LCT 6701* & in ♯ Sca. 804*)
   C. Boninsegna & pf. (in ♯ Sca. 813*)

Nile Scene, beginning Ciel! mio padre!
S, A, T, Bs & cho.
L. Rysanek, S. Wagner, R. Schock, J. Metternich, P. Roth
   & orch.—Schüchter (*Ger*)²   ♯ *G.WBLP 1509*
☆ R. Tebaldi, E. Stignani, M. del Monaco & A. Protti
   [from set K]   ♯ *D.LW 5045*
                                  (♯ *Lon.LD 9055*)
☆ A. Kupper, L. Fehenberger & H. Reinmar (*Ger*)
                                  (in ♯ Pol. 19027)

. . . Sop. & B. part only
N. Sokolova & P. Lisitsian (*Russ*) (USSR. 022726/7)
☆ M. Nemeth & E. Schipper (*Ger*) (AF.AGSB 45)

. . . Pur ti riveggo, only (*Nile Duet*) S & T
R. Tebaldi & M. del Monaco   ♯ *D.LXT 5067*
(*below; Manon Lescaut, Otello*) [from set K]
                                  (♯ *Lon.LL 1256*)

ACT IV
Già i sacerdoti . . . Di mia discolpa   M-S & T
La fatal pietra . . . O terra addio . . .
(*Finale—Tomb Scene*)   S & T   [& M-S]
☆ R. Tebaldi (S), E. Stignani (M-S), M. del Monaco (T)
   [from set K]   ♯ *D.LW 5080*
                                  (♯ *Lon.LD 9077*)
N. Sokolova, V. Davidova, G. Nelepp, P. Lisitsian
   (*Russ, from set R*) (USSR. 022742/5)
☆ E. Leisner & H. Roswaenge (*Ger*) (in ♯ CEd.CE 7010)
H S. Kalter & R. Tauber (*Ger*) (in ♯ Cum.CE 187*)

**. . . La fatal pietra . . . Morir! Si pura . . . O terra
addio** (*Tomb Scene*)
R. Tebaldi & M. del Monaco   ♯ *D.LXT 5067*
(*above; Otello, Manon Lescaut*)   (♯ *Lon.LL 1256*)
[from set K]
L. Rysanek, S. Wagner, R. Schock, Berlin
   Municipal Op. Cho. & Orch.—Schüchter
   (*Ger*)   ♯ *G.WDLP 1516*
(*Forza del Destino*)
— SHORTER VERSIONS
☆ M. Caniglia, B. Gigli, E. Stignani   ♭ *G. 7ER 5037*
   (*Tosca—Duet, Act I*) [from set A]   (♭ *7ERQ 122*)
☆ R. Ponselle & G. Martinelli (♭ *Vic.ERAT 15;*
                           in ♯ *G.FJLP 5010: QJLP 101*)
H R. Ponselle & C. Hackett (in ♯ Sca. 803*)
   R. Ponselle & G. Martinelli (o.v.) (AF.ABHB 3*)
   R. Raisa & G. Crimi (in ♯ Sca. 808*)
   Mazzoleni & G. Zenatello (in ♯ Sca. 818*)

ALZIRA   2 Acts   1845
Excerpt included in ballet *Lady & the Fool, q.v. post*

AROLDO
4 Acts (originally STIFFELIO 3 Acts) 1850
Excerpt included in ballet *Lady & the Fool, q.v. post*

ATTILA   Prol. & 3 Acts   1846
Excerpt included in ballet *Lady & the Fool, q.v. post*

(Un) BALLO IN MASCHERA   3 Acts   1859
COMPLETE RECORDINGS

Casts	Set D	Set E	Set F
Riccardo (T)	F. Tagliavini	J. Peerce	G. Bardi
Renato (B)	G. Valdengo	R. Merrill	G. Mazzini
Amelia (S)	M. C. Verna	H. Nelli	G. Dezi
Ulrica	P.Tassinari(M-S)	C. Turner (A)	S. Sawyer (A)
Oscar (S)	M. Erato	V. Haskins	J. Guido
etc.			

¹ Contains *Ballabili* also.   ² Begins at *O cieli azzuri*, above.

(Un) BALLO IN MASCHERA (continued)

Set D with Italian Radio Cho. & Orch.—Questa
(4ss)   ♯ CCet. set 1249

Set E with R. Shaw Chorale & N.B.C. Sym.
Orch.—Toscanini[1]   ♯ G.ALP 1252/4
(6ss) (♯ Vic. set LM 6112; ItV.C12R 0155/7;
                                              FV.A 630234/6)

Set F with Rome Teatro Eliseo Cho. & Orch.
—Marini   ♯ Ply. set 101
(6ss)   (♯ Gram. 20151/3)

☆ B. Gigli (T), M. Caniglia (S), G. Bechi (B), F. Barbieri
    (A), etc. Rome Op. Cho. & Orch.—Serafin
                                              ♯ G.FJLP 5033/4
    (4ss) (♯ G.QALP 10057/8; Vic.LCT 6007:
                                              ♭ set WCT 6007)

☆ Soloists, Paris Phil. Cho. & French Radio Sym.
    —Leibowitz (♯ Clc. 6182/4; abridged on
                                    ♯ Ren.X 52, 2ss, & ♯ MMS. set 116, 4ss)

HIGHLIGHTS
    Z. Milanov (S), M. Anderson (A), R. Peters (S), J. Peerce
        (T), L. Warren (B), Metropolitan Op. Cho. & Orch.
        —Mitropoulos   ♯ Vic.LM 1911
                                              (♯ ItV.A12R 0184)
    G. Brouwenstijn (S), F. Vroons (T), Vienna State Op. Cho.
        & Orch.—Loibner   ♯ EPhi.NBR 6023
                                              (♯ Phi.N 00713R)
    S. Roman (S), B. Castagna (A), J. Antoine (S), R. Bonelli
        (B)   ♯ PRCC. 6
    C. Martinis (S), H. Roswaenge (T), T. Baylé (B), Vienna
        Volksoper Cho. & Orch.—Loibner (Ger) ♯ D.LX 3126
                                              (♯ Lon.LS 861)
    ℍ C. Boninsegna (S), S. Kurz (S), M. Gilion (T), A.
        Pertile (T), G. de Luca (B), etc.   ♯ Ete. 497*

Prelude
Radio-Luxembourg Orch.—Pensis
                                    in ♯ FestF.FLD 15
Berlin Sym.—Rubahn   in ♯ Roy. 1537
    ☆ Rhineland Sym.—Federer (in ♯ AFest.CFR 10-602)

ACT I

La rivedrà nell' estasi Ens.
    ℍ A. Pertile & Ens. (in ♯ Od.ODX 127*: MOAQ 301*)

... Tenor part only
    ☆ G. Poggi (in ♯ Cet.LPC 55003)
    ℍ G. Zenatello (in ♯ Sca. 818*)

Alla vita che t'arride B
    L. Warren [from Highlights] in ♯ Vic.LM 1932
    J. Metternich (Ger)   G.DB 11558
    (Eri tu)   (♭ 7RW 510: in ♯ WBLP 1504)
    ℍ M. Battistini (in ♯ Vic. set LCT 6701*)

Volta la terra S
    R. Streich   Pol. 62924
    (below; & Huguenots)   (♭ Pol. 32011 & Ger, ♭ 32013)

Re dell' abisso A
    A. Anneli   U.H 24396
    (Zauberflöte, No. 3)

Di tu se fedele T [& cho.]
    G. Zenatello & Apollo Cho.   AF.AGSB 20
    (below)   (Ltd. edn.)
    G. Poggi (? n.v.)   in ♯ ABCD. 2
    (Guarany, Favorita, Trovatore, etc.)
    A. Frinberg (Latvian) (USSR.19956: in ♯ D 1900)
    ☆ G. Poggi (in ♯ Cet.LPC 55003)
    ℍ G. Martinelli (in ♯ SBDH.LPG 4*)
       G. Zenatello (in ♯ Sca. 808*)

È scherzo od è follia Quintet
    ℍ E. Caruso, F. Hempel, E. Duchêne, L. Rothier, P. de
        Segurola (♭ Vic.ERAT 8*)

ACT II

Ecco l'orrido campo ... Ma dall' arido stelo S
    G. Brouwenstijn   ♯ Phi.N 00712R
    (Aida & Otello)
    E. Barbato   in ♯ SBDH.TOB 2
    (S. Boccanegra, Samson et Dalila, Roméo et Juliette, etc.)
    A. Stella   in ♯ G.QALP 10096
    (below; Trovatore, Aida, etc.)
    ☆ L. Welitsch (♯ D.LW 5050; Lon.LD 9041)

Teco io sto ... O qual soave S & T
    ℍ C. Boninsegna & L. Bolis (in ♯ Sca. 813*)
       E. Burzio, G. Zenatello & pf. (in ♯ Sca. 818*)

ACT III

Morrò, ma prima in grazia S
    A. Varnay   PV. 36121
    (Forza—Pace, pace ...)   (♭ Pol. 34015: 32062)
    (& Ger, on PV. 36129; ♭ Pol. 34014: 32061)
    G. Brouwenstijn   ♭ Phi.N 402017E
    (Aida—O patria mia) [from Highlights]
    A. Stella   in ♯ G.QALP 10096
    (above)
    ☆ L. Welitsch (♯ D.LW 5050; Lon.LD 9041)
       E. Rethberg (in ♯ Vic. set LCT. 6701)
       D. Ilitsch (in ♯ Sup.LPM 132; U. 5108C)

Eri tu, che macchiavi B
    L. Warren [from Highlights] in ♯ Vic.LM 1932
    T. Gobbi   (2ss)   G.DB 21606
    R. Weede   in ♯ DCap.CTL 7080
    (Falstaff, Trovatore, Rigoletto, etc.)
                                      (in ♯ Cap.P 8290: ♭ FAP 8279)
    A. Sved   Qual.MN 1053
    (Rigoletto—Cortigiani)
    I. Gorin   in ♯ Alld. 3003
                                      (♭ EP 3003; & ♯ MTW. 572)
    J. Metternich (Ger)   G.DB 11558
    (Alla vita che t'arride)   (♭ 7RW 510)
    P. Lisitsian (Russ) (USSR. 22246/7)
    A. Hiolski (Pol) (Muza.X 2186)
    ☆ G. Bechi (in ♯ G.QALP 10087)
       R. Stracciari (in ♯ Sca. 802)
       R. Merrill (in ♯ Vic.LM 1841; FV.A 630255)
       L. Warren (G.ED 1215)
       C. Guichandut (Orf. 54012, d.c.)
       L. Tibbett (in ♯ Cam.CAL 171)
       H. Schlusnus (Ger) (in ♯ Pol. 18080 & in ♯ 19039)
    ℍ H. Rehkemper (Ger) (in ♯ Sca. 809*)

Forse la soglia attinse
... Ma se m'è forza perderti T
    R. Schock (Ger)   G.DB 11561
    (Aida—Celeste Aida)   (♭ 7RW 511; in ♯ WBLP 1501)
    R. Tucker   in ♯ AmC.ML 4750
    ℍ F. Vignas (in ♯ Ete. 703*)

Saper vorreste S   (Page's aria)
    R. Streich   Pol. 62924
    (above; & Huguenots)   (♭ 32011; & Ger, ♭ 32013)
    ℍ S. Kurz (in ♯ Sca. 817*; in ♯ FRP. 1*)

Ah! morte, infamia
    (Death of Riccardo) T, B, S, & cho.
    G. Zenatello, G. Marion, A. Boemi & cho.
                                              AF.AGSB 20
    (Di tu se fedele)   (Ltd. edn.)

(La) BATTAGLIA DI LEGNANO 3 Acts 1849
Overture
    ☆ Philharmonia—Markevitch (G.DB 4329)
       Italian Radio—Previtali (in ♯ CCet.A 50151, from set)

DON CARLOS 5 Acts 1867 (later 4 Acts)
COMPLETE RECORDINGS
    Elisabetta di Valois ... ...   A. Stella (S)
    Principessa d'Eboli ... ...   E. Nicolai (M-S)
    Don Carlos... ... ...   M. Filippeschi (T)
    Rodrigo ... ..., ...   T. Gobbi (B)
    Filippo II ... ...   B. Christoff (Bs)
    Inquisitor ... ...   G. Neri (Bs)
    etc. Rome Op. Cho. & Orch.—Santini
                                              ♯ G.ALP 1289/92
    (8ss) (6ss, ♯ Vic. set LM 6124)   (♯ QALP 10109/12)
    ☆ M. Caniglia (S), E. Stignani (M-S), P. Silveri (B),
        N. Rossi-Lemeni (Bs), etc. Italian Radio Cho. &
        Orch.—Previtali (♯ Pol. 18160/3)
    [Highlights on ♯ CCet.A 50168]

ACT II
(Act I in some versions)

Io l'ho perduto ... Quale pallor T, B, Bs
    ☆ J. Björling, R. Merrill & E. Markow   G.DB 21622
        (in ♯ BLP 1053; in ♯ Vic.LRM 7027: ♭ set ERB 7027)
    ℍ (T part only) S. Pollicino (in ♯ Ete. 492*)
        B. de Muro (in ♯ SBDH.JAL 7000*)

[1] Recorded at two broadcast performances, March, 1954.

DON CARLOS, Act II (*continued*)

Carlo, ch'è solo è il nostro amore B
  H G. Kaschmann (in ‡ *HRS. 3004**)

Dio, che nell' alma infondere T & Bs
  R. Schock & J. Metternich (*Ger*) **G.DB 11572**
  (*Forza—Solenne in quest'ora*) (♭ *7RW 532*)
  H G. Martinelli & G. de Luca (in ‡ *SBDH.LPG 4**)

ACT IV
(Act III in some versions)

Ella giammai m'amo . . . Dormirò sol Bs
  C. Siepi (n.v.) ‡ *D.LW 5148*
  (*Nabucco & Ernani*) (‡ *Lon.LD 9168;*
    in ‡ *D.LXT 5096; Lon.LL 1240*)
  J. Greindl **PV. 72482**
  (*Don Giovanni—Madamina*) (♭ *Pol. 30078*)
  (& in *Ger* on PV. 72481; ♭ *Pol. 30077*)
  G. Frick (*Ger*) (2ss) **G.DB 11555**
    (♭ *7RW 502:* in ‡ *WBLP 1505*)
  A. Legros (*Fr*) ♭ *Plé.P 45147*
  (*Rossini & Meyerbeer*)
  ☆ R. Arié ‡ *D.LW 5079*
  (*Moussorgsky*) (‡ *Lon.LD 9018*)
  ☆ B. Christoff (♭ *G.7RF 262*)
  E. Pinza (in ‡ *Vic.LM 1751;* in ‡ *FV.A 630233*)
  Vanni-Marcoux (*Fr*) (in ‡ *G.FJLP 5035*)
  M. Reizen (*Russ*) (*USSRM.D 001274/5*)
  H F. Chaliapin (in ‡ *SBDH.JAL 7002**)
  L. Nicoletti-Korman (in ‡ *HRS. 3002**)
  M. Journet (in ‡ *SBDH.LPG 5**)
  P. Plançon (*Fr*) (in ‡ *Vic. set LCT 6701**)

Son io dinnanti al Re 2 Bs
  B. Christoff & G. Neri in ‡ **SBDH.TOB 2**
  (*Favorita, Trovatore, Ballo, etc.*) (& in ‡ *ABCD. 2*)

O don fatale M-S or A
  M. v. Ilosvay in ‡ *Phi.N 00649R*
  G. Simionato ‡ *D.LW 5139*
  (*Barbiere, Capuleti, Cenerentola*) (‡ *Lon.LD 9162*)
  (*Bellini: Capuleti, aria only,* ♭ *D. 71094*)
  ☆ S. Onegin (in ‡ *Vic. set LCT 6701*)
  M. Mödl (*Ger*) (‡ *DT.TM 68009; T.TW 30010:*
    ♭ *UE 453897; AusT.E 1200*)

Per me giunto . . . O Carlo, ascolta B
  R. Weede in ‡ **DCap.CTL 7080**
  (*Falstaff, Otello, Trovatore, etc.*) (‡ Cap.P 8290:
    ♭ *FAP 8279*)
  ☆ G. Bechi (in ‡ *G.QALP 10087*)
  H. Schlusnus (*Ger*) (in ‡ *Pol. 18080* & ‡ *19039*)
  R. Merrill (♭ *Vic.ERA 107*)
  H M. Battistini (AF & CRC.ABHB 2*)
  R. Stracciari (in ‡ *Sca. 802**)
  T. Ruffo (in ‡ *Sca. 812**; in ‡ *HRS. 3005**)

ACT V

Tu che la vanità S
  ☆ M. Vitale (in ‡ *Cet.LPC 55001*)
  E. Steber (in ‡ *Phi.N 02609R*)
  H G. Russ (in ‡ *Sca. 808**)

Excerpts — ARR. Mackerras
  included in ballet *Lady & the Fool, q.v.*

(I) DUE FOSCARI 3 Acts 1844
O vecchio cor che batti B
  H R. Stracciari (in ‡ *Sca. 802**)
  P. Amato (in ‡ *SBDH.JAL 7001**)

Excerpt in *Lady & the Fool* ballet, *q.v. post*

ERNANI 4 Acts 1844

ACT I

Come rugiada al cespite T
  H F. de Lucia (in ‡ *CEd. set 7002**)
  G. Martinelli (in ‡ *SBDH.LPG 1**)

Ernani, Ernani, involami S
  V. de los Angeles in ‡ **G.ALP 1284**
  (*Otello, Bohème, Mefistofele, etc.*) (‡ *QALP 10155*)

  A. Stella in ‡ **G.QALP 10096**
  (*Ballo, Vêpres sicilennes, etc.*)
  M. C. Verna in ‡ **Cet.LPC 55005**
  ☆ R. Ponselle (in ‡ *G.FJLP 5004: QJLP 104*)
  I. Souez (in ‡ *Vic. set LCT 6701*)
  E. Steber (in ‡ *Phi.N 02609R*)
  H C. Boninsegna (in ‡ *Sca. 813**)
  S. Kurz (in ‡ *Sca. 817**)
  C. Muzio[1] (in ‡ *LI.TW 91053**)

Chi mai vegg'io . . . Infelice! e tuo credevi Bs
  N. Rossi-Lemeni in ‡ **G.ALP 1099**
  (*below; Forza, Nabucco, etc.*) (‡ *QALP 10028: FALP 305*)
  E. Pinza in ‡ **Vic.LM 1751**
  (*Boccanegra, Nabucco, etc.*) (♭ *ERA 140;* in ‡ *FV.A 630233*)
  C. Siepi (n.v.) ‡ *D.LW 5148*
  (*Don Carlos, Nabucco*) (‡ *Lon.LD 9168;* &
    in *D.LXT 5096; Lon.LL 1240*)
  I. Petrov (*Russ*) (in ‡ *USSR.D 2607*)
  ☆ B. Christoff (♭ *G.7RF/RQ 264*)
  H F. Chaliapin (in ‡ *Sca. 801**; in ‡ *SBDH.LLP 4**)
  J. Mardones (in ‡ *Sca. 810**)

L'offeso onor, signori Bs
  N. Rossi-Lemeni in ‡ **G.ALP 1099**
  (*above; Forza, Nabucco, etc.*) (‡ *QALP 10028*)
  ☆ B. Christoff (♭ *G.7RF/RQ 264; Vic.EHA 7*)

ACT II

Lo vedremo B & Bs
  H R. Stracciari & Anon. (in ‡ *Sca. 802**)

ACT III

Oh! de' verd' anni miei B
  ☆ G. Bechi (in ‡ *G.QALP 10087*)
  R. Stracciari (in ‡ *Sca. 802*)
  H T. Ruffo (in ‡ *SBDH.LLP 7**)

March on themes from the opera ARR. Vessella
Italian Navy Band—Aghemo (in ‡ *G.QFLP 4010*)

Excerpts ARR. Mackerras
included in ballet *Lady & the Fool, q.v.*

FALSTAFF 3 Acts 1893
COMPLETE RECORDINGS

John Falstaff	... G. Valdengo (B)
Alice Ford	... H. Nelli (S)
Nannetta	... T. Stich-Randall (S)
Dame Quickly	... C. Elmo (M-S)
Meg Page	... N. Merriman (M-S)
Fenton	... A. Madasi (T)
Ford	... F. Guarrera (B)
Pistol	... N. Scott (Bs)
Bardolph	... J. C. Rossi (T)
Dr. Caius	... G. Carelli (T)

  Robert Shaw Chorale & N.B.C. Sym. Orch.
    —Toscanini[2] ‡ **G.ALP 1229/31**
  (6ss) (‡ *Vic. set LM 6111; FV.A 630220/2;*
    ItV.C12R 0013/5; also, ‡ *OTA. set 3*)
  ☆ G. Rimini (B), P. Tassinari (S), I. Alfani-Tellini (S),
    etc., La Scala Cho. & Orch.—Molajoli (6ss)
    ‡ *AmC. set EL 8*
    (‡ *C.QCX 10141/2*)

ACT I, Sc. 1

L'Onore! Ladri! B
  G. Taddei *Cet.AT 0403*
  (*Don Giovanni, No. 17*) (in ‡ *LPC 55006*)
  L. Tibbett in ‡ **Roy. 1627**
  H A. Scotti (in ‡ *Vic. set LCT 6701**)

ACT II, Sc. 1

Signore, v'assista il ciel! Bs & B
  ☆ J. Metternich & D. Fischer-Dieskau (*Ger*)
    (in ‡ *Pol. 19029*)[3]

È sogno? B (*Ford's Monologue*)
  R. Weede in ‡ **DCap.CTL 7080**
  (*Don Carlos, Otello, etc.*) (in ‡ *Cap.P 8290*)
  L. Warren (n.v.) in ‡ **Vic.LM 1932**
  (*Ballo, Forza, etc.*)

---

[1] From Edison and Pathé hill and dale recordings. This disc was withdrawn immediately after issue.
[2] Broadcast performance, April 1950.
[3] Not *Reverenza!* as in Supp. II. Labelled *Brav, alter Hans!* and will therefore begin at *Va, vecchio John* and contain the Falstaff-Ford duet.

FALSTAFF, Act II, Sc. 1—È sogno? (*continued*)

A. Poli   **Cet.PE 199**
(*Adriana Lecouvreur—Ecco il monologo*)

L. Tibbett   in ♯ **Roy. 1627**

G. London   in ♯ **AmC.ML 4999**
(*Rigoletto, Otello, Thaïs, etc.*)

☆ L. Warren, o.v. (in ♯ Vic.LCT 1115: ♭ set WCT 1115)

ACT II, Sc. 2

Quand' ero paggio   B
  ◫ V. Maurel & pf. (in ♯ HRS. 3001* & ♯ Sca. 822*)
     G. de Luca (in ♯ FRP. 1*)

ACT III, Sc. 1

Ehi! Taverniere   B
   G. Malaspina   **Cet.PE 179**
   (*Missiroli: Songs*)

ACT IV, Sc. 2

Dal labbro il canto   T
  ☆ F. Tagliavini (in ♯ CCap.A 50155)
  ◫ T. Schipa (in ♯ Sca. 805*; in ♯ SBDH.JAL 7000*)

Sul fil d'un soffio etesio   S
   H. Gueden   ♯ **D.LW 5178**
   (*Traviata & Puccini*)   (♯ Lon.LD 9165)

   M. Benetti   **Cet.PE 200**
   (*Madama Butterfly—Un bel di*)

  ☆ T. dal Monte (in ♯ G.QALP 10089;
              in ♯ Vic.LCT 1158, d.c.)

  ◫ F. Alda (AF.AGSB 16*)

(Il) FINTO STANISLAO
     SEE: UN GIORNO DI REGNO

(La) FORZA DEL DESTINO   4 Acts   1862
COMPLETE RECORDINGS

Casts	Set C	Set D
Il Marchese di Calatrava	P. Clabassi (Bs)	S. Maionica (Bs)
Donna Leonora ...	M. M. Callas (S)	R. Tebaldi (S)
Don Carlo di Vargas	C. Tagliabue (B)	E. Bastianini (B)
Don Alvaro ...	R. Tucker (T)	M. del Monaco (T)
Preziosilla	E. Nicolai (M-S)	G. Simionato (M-S)
Padre Guardiano ...	N. Rossi-Lemeni (Bs)	C. Siepi (Bs)
Fra Melitone	R. Capecchi (Bs)	F. Corena (Bs)
Curra	R. Cavallari (S)	G. Carturan (M-S)
Maestro Trabuco...	G. del Signore (T)	P. di Palma (T)

Set C with La Scala Cho. & Orch.—Serafin[1]
                      ♯ **C.CX 1258/60**
(6ss) (♯ FCX 393/5: QCX 10122/4;
               Angel. 35199/201, set 3531)

Set D with Santa Cecilia Acad. Cho. & Orch.
  —Molinari Pradelli   ♯ **D.LXT 5131/4**
(8ss)   (♯ Lon.LL 1350/3, set XLLA 37)

  ☆ M. Caniglia (S), G. Masini (T), etc. Cho. & Orch.
    —Marinuzzi (♯ FSor.CS 534/6; Excerpts
             on ♭ Cap.FAP 7004; Cet.EPO 0309)

HIGHLIGHTS

Me pellegrina ed orfana	S	Act I
Son giunta! ... Madre pietosa Vergine	S	
La Vergine degli Angeli	S	Act II
O tu che in seno	T	
Solenne in quest' ora	T & B	(a)
Morir! tremenda cosa! Urna fatale	2 B	Act III (a)
Invano, Alvaro ... Una suora	T & B	(a)
Pace, pace, mio Dio	S	Act IV
Io muojo! ... Non imprecare	T, Bs, S	

Z. Milanov (S), J. Peerce (T), L. Warren (B),
   R. Keast (B), N. Moscona (Bs) ♯ **Vic.LM 1916**
[items marked (a) are probably ☆]

Me pellegrina, Act I
Madre pietosa Vergine, Act II
Or siam soli, Act II
Pace, pace, mio Dio, Act III

N. Jean (S), J. Salvador (Bs), W. Spada (pf.)
                          ♯ **GNYO. 101**

Overture

Philharmonia—Galliera   ♯ **C.SX 1009**
(*Aida, Nabucco, Traviata, etc.*)
   (♯ FCX 209: QCX 10094; Angel. 35012)
(*Nabucco* only, on ♭ SED 5505: SEBQ 109: ESBF 119)

Rome Radio—Previtali   **G.C 4231**
(in ♯ DLP 1038: FFLP 1038: QDLP 6018:
                   in ♯ BB.LBC 1092)

Metropolitan Op.—Cleva in ♯ AmC. set **SL 123**
(*Cavalleria Rusticana, etc.*)
(*Aida, Traviata, etc.* in ♯ AmC.ML 4886)

R.I.A.S.—Fricsay   in ♯ **Pol. 17015**
(*Nabucco, Traviata, etc.*)(♭ Pol. 30031; in ♯ AmD.DL 9738)

N.B.C. Sym.—Toscanini (n.v.)   ♭ **G.7ER 5021**
(*Weber: Aufforderung zum Tanz*)(♭ 7RF 284 (? o.v.);
     ♭ ItV.A72R 0013; ♭ Vic.ERA 125, &
                 in ♯ Vic. set LM 6026)

La Scala—Serafin, from set C   ♭ **C.SEL 1536**
(*Norma Overture*)

Radio-Luxemburg—Pensis   in ♯ **FestF.FLD 15**

Leipzig Radio—Gerdes   **Eta. 120046**

  ☆ Philharmonia—Markevitch (♭ G.7EP 7007: 7EPQ 522:
                          7PW 101)
     Vienna Sym.—Swarowsky (in ♯ Sup.LPM 226;
                 U. 5203C; ♯ CdM.LDM 8042)
     Berlin Municipal Op.—Rother (in ♯ Nix.ULP 9057;
                       in ♯ Ura.RS 5-4)
     Italian Radio—Marinuzzi(in ♯ CCap.A 50151, from set)
     Bamberg Sym.—Leitner (PV. 72468; ♭ AmD.ED 3516)
     Rhineland Sym.—Federer (in ♯ AFest.CFR 37)
     La Scala—Parodi, from set (♭ Nix.EP 702; Ura.UREP 2)

ACT II

Son Pereda, son ricco d'onore   B & Cho.
   J. Metternich & Cho. (*Ger*)   **G.DB 11579**
   (*Urna fatale, Act III*)   (♭ 7RW 529)

Scenes 5-7 COMPLETE
  ☆ A. Kupper, G. Neidlinger, J. Greindl (*Ger*)(♯ Pol. 17030)

Son giunta! ... Madre pietosa Vergine   S
   Z. Milanov   ♭ **G.7ER 5032**
   (*Pace, pace, Act IV*) (in ♯ G.ALP 1247; ♯ Vic.LM 1777:
                       ♭ set ERB 19)

   T. Richter (*Ger*)   ♯ **DT.TM 68006**
   (*Pace, pace, Act IV*)(TV.VSK 9015:
               ♭ T.UV 104; FT. 470.TC.014

Il santo nome di Dio ...   Bs & cho.
Alzatevi, e partite   Bs
La Vergine degli Angeli   S
   L. Vichegonov (Bs), Z. Milanov (S) & cho.
                 in ♯ **G.ALP 1247**
   (*above, below, Trovatore, etc.*) (♯ Vic.LM 1777:
                   ♭ set ERB 19)

   L. Malagrida, P. Clabassi & cho. in ♯ **G.ALP 1277**
   (*Traviata, Turandot, etc.*)   (♯ QALP 10118)

  ☆ N. Rossi-Lemeni & J. Hammond & cho. ♯ **G.ALP 1099**
   (*Ernani, Nabucco, etc.*)   (♯ QALP 10028: FALP 305)

Alzatevi, e partite   Bs
La Vergine degli Angeli   S
  ☆ E. Pinza & R. Ponselle (♭ Vic.ERAT 20)

... La Vergine degli Angeli, only
  ◫ R. Ponselle (in ♯ Sca. 803*)
     C. Boninsegna (in ♯ Sca. 813*)
     G. Russ & pf. (in ♯ Sca. 808*)

ACT III

La vita è inferno ... O tu che in seno   T
   M. del Monaco   **D.X 573**
   (*Halévy: La Juive, aria*) (in ♯ D.LXT 2845; Lon.LL 880)
   (also in ♯ D.LW 5093; Lon.LD 9082; &
               ♯ D.LXT 2964; Lon.LL 1025)

O tu che in seno   T
  ☆ B. Gigli (in ♯ G.FJLP 5039)

  ◫ G. Zenatello (in ♯ SBDH.LLP 8*)
     E. Caruso (♭ Vic.ERAT 4*)

---

[1] Scenes 1–3 of Act IV are omitted.

(La) FORZA DEL DESTINO, Act III (continued)

Solenne in quest' ora   T & B
B. Gigli & T. Ruffo   **AF.AGSB 49**
(Gioconda—Enzo Grimaldo) [1925 recording]
R. Schock & J. Metternich (Ger)   **G.DB 11572**
(Don Carlos—Duet, Act II)   (♭ 7RW 532)
☆ J. Björling & R. Merrill (in ‡ G.BLP 1053;
                 in ‡ Vic.LRM 7027: ♭ set ERB 7027)
G. Campora & A. Colzani, from set
                 (♭ Nix.EP 717; Ura.UREP 7)
A. Dermota & G. Oeggl (Ger) (RadT.E 178T)
K. v. Pataky & H. Schlusnus (Ger) (▽ Pol. 67357)
♮ E. Caruso & A. Scotti (♭ Vic.ERAT 9*;
                 in ‡ G.FJLP 5010*: QLJP 101*)

Morir! . . . Urna fatale del mio destino   2 B
F. Valentino   in ‡ **Roy. 1585**
J. Metternich (Ger)   **G.DB 11579**
(Son Pereda, Act I)   (♭ 7RW 529)
☆ L. Warren & R. Keast (♭ Vic.ERA 65 & in ‡ LM 1932)
T. Gobbi (♭ G.7R 171: 7RF/RQ 270: 7RW 148)
H. Schlusnus (Ger) (in ‡ Pol. 18080)
♮ T. Ruffo (AF.AGSA 10*)
M. Battistini (AF.ABHB 4*)

ACT IV

Invano, Alvaro . . . Una suora   T & B
R. Schock & J. Metternich (Ger)
(below; & Aida)   ‡ **G.WDLP 1516**
. . . Sulla terra   ☆ G. Masini & C. Tagliabue (Orf. 54018)

Pace, pace, mio Dio   S
Z. Milanov   ♭ **G.7ER 5032**
(Madre, pietosa . . . , Act II)
(in ‡ G.ALP 1247; Vic.LM 1777: ♭ ERB 19;
                 & in ‡ LM 1909 & LM 1847)
A. Hownanian   ♭ **Cet.EPO 0322**
(Manon Lescaut, La Wally, Amico Fritz)
M. Benetti   **Cet.PE 211**
(Adriana Lecouvreur—Io sono l'umile)
A. Stella   in ‡ **G.QALP 10096**
(Ballo, Trovatore, etc.)
R. Gigli   **G.DB 21619**
(Sonnambula—Ah, non credea)
N. de Rosa   **Cet.PE 198**
(Mascagni: Iris—Un di . . .)
A. Varnay   **PV. 36121**
(Ballo—Morrò, ma prima)   (♭ Pol. 34015: 32062)
(Ger, on PV. 36120; ♭ Pol. 34014: 32061)
V. Petrova   in ‡ **Ace. 1007/8**
(Trovatore, Aida, Gioconda, etc.)
T. Richter (Ger)   ‡ **DT.TM 68006**
(Madre pietosa Vergine) (TV.VSK 9205; ♭ T.UV 104;
                 ♭ FT. 470.TC.014)
L. Rysanek (Ger)   **G.DB 11584**
(Aida—O patria mia) (♭ 7RW 19-538: in ‡ WDLP 1516)
M. Foltyn (Pol) (Muza.X 2149)
☆ D. Ilitsch (in ‡ Sup.LPM 132; U. 5108C)
A. Guerrini, from set (♭ Nix.EP 717; Ura.UREP 7)
R. Ponselle (♭ Vic.ERAT 20)
E. Steber (in ‡ Phi.N 02609R)
♮ R. Raisa (in ‡ Sca. 808*)
R. Ponselle (in ‡ Sca. 803*)

Io muojo! . . . Non imprecare   T, Bs, S
☆ G. Martinelli, E. Pinza, R. Ponselle
                 (in ‡ Vic. set LCT 6701)

GERUSALEMME 1850 rev. version of I Lombardi
(orig. Fr as Jérusalem, 1847)
Excerpts included in ballet Lady & the Fool, q.v. post

(Un) GIORNO DI REGNO   2 Acts   1840
(or: Il Finto Stanislao)
Overture
☆ Italian Radio—Simonetto (in ‡ CCap.A 50151, from set)
Excerpts included in Lady & the Fool ballet, q.v. post

GIOVANNA D'ARCO   4 Acts   1845
Overture
Radio-Luxemburg—Pensis   in ‡ **FestF.FLD 15**
☆ Philharmonia—Markevitch (ArgV. 11-7959)
Excerpts included in Lady & the Fool ballet, q.v. post

(I) LOMBARDI ALLA PRIMA CROCIATA
   4 Acts   1843
Gerusalemme . . . La grande   Cho.   Act III
Netherlands Op. Cho. & Residentie Orch.
—Moralt   in ‡ **EPhi.NBR 6003**
                 (Phi.N 12082G: ‡ N 00634R: S 06018R)

O Signore, dal tetto natio   Cho.   Act IV
St. Cecilia Acad. Cho.—Erede   **D.KX 28615**
(Nabucco—Va pensiero) (K 23316: ♭ DK 23316)
Netherlands Op. Cho. & Residentie Orch.
—Moralt   in ‡ **EPhi.NBR 6003**
                 (‡ Phi.N 00634R & N 12082G)
Rome Op. Cho.—Morelli   in ‡ **G.ALP 1277**
(Traviata, Otello, etc.)   (‡ QALP 10118)
☆ Italian Radio Cho.—Wolf-Ferrari (♭ Cet.EPO 0324)
Excerpts included in Lady & the Fool ballet, q.v. post

LUISA MILLER   3 Acts   1849
Overture
Radio-Luxemburg—Pensis   in ‡ **FestF.FLD 15**
☆ Philharmonia—Markevitch (♭ G.7EP 7007:
                 7EPQ 522: 7PW 120; ArgV. 11-7961)

Quando le sere al placido   T   Act II
G. Poggi   in ‡ **D.LX 3127**
(Trovatore, Manon Lescaut, etc.)   (‡ Lon.LD 9106)
E. Lorenzi   **Cet.AT 0367**
(Martha—Ach, so fromm)
G. Gari, S. Leff (pf.)   in ‡ **Mur.P 108**
(followed by pf. acc. only)
☆ M. del Monaco   ‡ **D.LW 5064**
(Aida, Macbeth, Traviata) (♭ VD 509; ‡ Lon.LD 9051
                 & LL 1244)
(Fanciulla del West, aria on D.XP 6150)
M. Alexandrovich (Russ) (in ‡ USSR.D 2219)
♮ F. de Lucia (in ‡ Sca. 814*)
A. Giorgini (IRCC. 3138*)
G. Anselmi & pf. (in ‡ Ete. 711* & in 492*,
                 in ‡ Sca. 816*)
Excerpt in Lady & the Fool ballet, q.v. post

MACBETH   4 Acts   1847
Excerpts (unspec.)
Soloists, Berlin Op. Cho. & Orch.   ‡ **Roy. 1409**
Studia il passo . . . Come dal ciel precipita   Bs   Act II
♮ L. Nicoletti-Korman (in ‡ HRS. 3002*)
La luce langue   S   Act II
(Nun sinkt der Abend: Sleep-walking scene)
☆ M. Mödl (Ger)   ‡ **DT.TM 68006**
(below, Don Carlos & Gluck) (♭ T.UE 453891:
                 ♭ FT. 510.TC.100)
Ballet Music   Act III
Philharmonia—Markevitch   ♮ **G.C 7937/8**
(3ss—Aida—Prelude, Act I)
Ah! la paterna mano   T   Act IV
☆ M. del Monaco   in ‡ **D.LW 5064**
(above)   (♭ VD 509; ‡ Lon.LD 9051 & in LL 1244)
♮ E. Caruso (in ‡ SBDH.GL 1*; in ‡ Vic. set LCT 6701*)
Vegliammo invan due notti
Una macchia è qui tutt' ora M-S or S, B, S Act IV
☆ E. Höngen, G. Grefe, H. Plümacher (Ger)
                 (in ‡ Pol. 19029)
. . . Una macchia . . . only
☆ M. Mödl (Ger) (in ‡ DT.TM 68009; T.TW 30004:
                 ♭ UE 453891; ♭ FT. 510.TC.010)
Pietà, rispetto amore   B   Act IV
♮ M. Battistini (IRCC.ABHB 4*)
Excerpt in Lady & the Fool ballet, q.v. post

(I) MASNADIERI   4 Acts   1847
Come il bacio   T & Bs   Act IV
♮ O. Mieli & E. Brancaleoni (SBDH.G 5*
Excerpt included in Lady & the Fool, q.v. post

---

‡ = Long-playing, 33⅓ r.p.m.   ♭ = 45 r.p.m.   ♮ = Auto. couplings, 78 r.p.m.

NABUCODONOSOR (*Nabucco*) 4 Acts 1842
COLLECTED EXCERPTS

Sperate, o figli! . . . D'Egitto là sui lidi . . .
Come notte Act I Bs & cho. ø
Vieni, o Levita! . . . Tu sul labbro Act II Bs
Oh chi piange? . . . Del futuro nel bujo Act III Bs & cho. ø

N. Rossi-Lemeni   in ‡ G.ALP 1099
(*Ernani, Vêpres Siciliennes, Forza*) (‡ QALP 10028:
FALP 305)
[items marked ø also on G.DB 21610: ♭ 7R 177]

Overture
Philharmonia—Galliera   C.DX 1904
(2ss)   (GQX 11547)
(*Aida, Traviata, Forza, etc.* in ‡ SX 1009:
FCX 209: QCX 10094; Angel. 35012)
(*Forza Overture* only, ♭ C.SED5505: SEBQ109: ESBF119)

R.I.A.S.—Fricsay   in ‡ Pol. 17015
(*Forza, Traviata, Vêpres Siciliennes*)
(♭ 30081; in ‡ AmD.DL 4063)

☆ New Sym.—Erede   ‡ D.LW 5040
(*Vêpres Siciliennes Overture*)   (‡ Lon.LD 9037)

Gli arredi festivi Cho. Act I
☆ Dutch Op. Cho. & Hilversum Radio Orch.—v. Kempen
(in ‡ EPhi.BBR 8042; ‡ Phi.S 06018R: ♭ N 402039E)

Tremin gl'insani Bs Act I
⊞ T. Ruffo (*AF.AGSA 10**)

Tu sul labbro dei veggenti Bs Act II
C. Siepi (n.v.)   ♭ D. 71099
(*Simone Boccanegra—Il lacerato spirito*)
(in ‡ D.LW 5148; Lon.LD 9168; & in ‡ D.LXT 5096;
Lon.LL 1240)

E. Pinza   in ‡ Vic.LM 1751
(*Boccanegra, Ernani, etc.*)   (‡ FV.A 630233)

⊞ J. Mardones (*AF.AGSB 27**; in ‡ SBDH.JAL 7002*)

Va pensiero (Cho.) . . . Oh chi piange (Recit) . . .
Del futuro Bs Act III
G. Frick & Cho. (*Ger*)   G.EH 1450
(FKX 262: ♭ 7PW 528)

☆ G. Hann & Württemberg State Op. Cho.
(♭ Pol. 34018: 30105)

⊞ J. Mardones (no cho.) (in ‡ SBDH.LPP 3*)

. . . Chorus only
Rome Op. Cho.—Morelli   in ‡ G.ALP 1277
(*Lombardi, Traviata, etc.*)   (‡ QALP 10118)

Santa Cecilia Acad.—Erede   D.K 23316
(*Lombardi—O signore*)   (KX 28615: ♭ DK 23316)

Berlin Municipal Op.—Otto (*Ger*)   T.S 11722
(*Meistersinger—Wach' auf!*) (♭ US 45722: in ‡ LA 6107)

☆ Dutch Op. Cho. & Hilversum Radio Orch.—v. Kempen
(in ‡ Phi.S 06018R: in ‡ P 10028R: ♭ N 402039E)
Italian Radio—Previtali (♭ Cet.EPO 0324)
Verdi Cho. (*Od.* 220098)

OBERTO 2 Acts 1839
Excerpt in *Lady & the Fool Ballet, q.v. post*

OTELLO 4 Acts 1887
COMPLETE RECORDINGS

Casts	Set D	Set E
Otello (T)	M. del Monaco	R. Vinay
Iago (B)	A. Protti	G. Valdengo
Desdemona (S)	R. Tebaldi	H. Nelli
Cassio (T)	P. de Palma	V. Assandri
Emilia (M-S)	L. Ribacci	N. Merriman
Ludovico (Bs)	F. Corena	N. Moscona
etc.		

Set D, with Santa Cecilia Cho. & Orch.—Erede
‡ D.LXT 5009/11
(6ss)   (‡ Lon. set LLA 24)

Set E, with Wilhousky Cho. & N.B.C. Sym. Orch.
—Toscanini[1]   ‡ G.ALP 1090/2
(6ss) (‡ VALP 1090/2: FALP 283/5; ‡ Vic. set LM 6107:
♭ set WDM 6107; ‡ ItV.C12R 0032/4)

EXCERPTS FROM SET D

Una vela! . . . Esultate	Act I	
Ora e per sempre addio	Act III	
Dio mi potevi scagliar	Act III	
Niun mi tema	Act IV	‡ D.LW 5199

(‡ Lon.LD 9194)

Dio mi potevi . . . & Niun mi tema, also ♭ D. 71087:
DK 23355

Già nella notte densa	Act I	
Dio ti giocondi	Act III	‡ D.LW 5186

(‡ Lon.LD 9196 & in ‡ LL 1256) (& in ‡ D.LXT 5067)

Mia madre aveva una povera ancella (*Willow Song*)
Ave Maria Act IV   ‡ D.LW 5198
(with *Manon Lescaut—Tu, tu, amore*) (‡ Lon.LD 9195)
(& in ‡ D.LXT 5076)

Ave Maria also on ♭ D. 71105 (with *Traviata—Addio del passato*)

EXCERPTS FROM SET E
Brindisi, Act I; Era la notte; & Credo, Act II
(♭ Vic.ERA 260)

COLLECTED EXCERPTS (SET C)
☆ R. Vinay (T), F. Guarrera (B), E. Steber (S) & Met.
Op. Orch.—Cleva   ‡ EPhi.ABL 3005
(‡ Phi.N 02102L: S 04600L)

COLLECTED EXCERPTS
H. Nelli, R. Vinay, G. Valdengo (in ‡ PRCC. 2)[2]

HIGHLIGHTS
M. Moll (S), A. da Costa (T), F. Valentino (B), cho. &
orch.—H-J. Walther   ‡ Roy. 1629

COLLECTION OF TENOR ARIAS
☆ Una vela! . . . (Esultate!) Act I
Ora e per sempre addio Act II
☆ Si, pel ciel marmoreo giuro Act III [with A. Granforte (B)]
Dio! mi potevi scagliar Act III
Niun mi tema Act IV
⊞ G. Zenatello [some are electric]   in ‡ Ete. 705*

ACT I

Una vela! Ens. & Cho.
. . . **Tenor part** only (*Esultate!*)
A. da Costa   in ‡ Roy. 1599
⊞ J. O'Sullivan (in ‡ FRP. 1*)
F. Tamagno (V‡ Rar.M 315*)

Fuoco di gioia! Cho.
Rome Op. Cho.—Morelli   in ‡ G.ALP 1277
(*Le Maschere, Iris, etc.*)   (‡ QALP 10118)

Inaffia l'ugola! (Brindisi) B & cho.
☆ L. Warren, N. Sprinzena (T), T. Motto (T) & Cho.
(♭ Vic.ERA 65 & in ‡ LM 1932)

Già nella notte densa . . . Ed io vedea T & S
A. Kawecka & W. Domieniecki (*Pol*) (*Muza.* 2234)
☆ B. & R. Gigli (BrzV. 886-5009)

ACT II

Credo in un Dio crudel B
G. London   in ‡ AmC.ML 4999
(*Thais, Emperor Jones, Meistersinger, etc.*)

L. Warren (n.v.)   in ‡ Vic.LM 1932
(*above, below, Ballo, etc.*)

R. Weede   in ‡ DCap.CTL 7080
(*Falstaff, Rigoletto, etc.*)   (in ‡ Cap.P 8290)

G. Taddei   Cet.BB 25300
(*A. Chénier—Nemico della patria*)   (in ‡ LPC 55006)

O. Enigarescu   U.H 24395
(*Rigoletto—Cortigiani*)

R. Merrill (in ‡ PRCC. 5)
R. Bianco (*Fr*) (in ‡ LI.TW 91131; D.FAT 173666)
☆ T. Gobbi (♭ G.7R171: 7RF/RQ 270: 7RW 148)
R. Merrill (o.v.) (in ‡ Vic.LM 1841: in ‡ LRM 7027:
♭ set ERB 7027; in ‡ FV.A 630255)
P. Schoeffler (♭ D.VD 504)
L. Tibbett (♭ Vic.ERAT 24: in ‡ LCT 1138, from set X)
G. Bechi (in ‡ G.QALP 10087)
L. Warren (G.ED 1215)
A. M. Serra (♭ Nix.EP 744; ♭ Ura.UREP 44, from set B)
C. Guichandut (*Orf.* 54013, d.c.)
C. Tagliabue (*Orf.* 54003)
J. C. Thomas (in ‡ Cam.CAL 199: ♭ CAE 246)

---

[1] From broadcast performances, Dec. 1947.
[2] Probably from Set E.

OTELLO, Act II (continued)
Ora e per sempre addio T
A. da Costa   in ♯ Roy. 1599
S. Puma   Cet.PE 204
(Niun mi tema, Act IV)
☆ S. Rayner (in ♯ Ete. 703)
♨ E. Caruso (♭ Vic.ERAT 1*)
  G. Zenatello & pf. (in ♯ SBDH.GL 1*; in ♯ Ete. 492*)
  G. B. de Negri (in ♯ HRS. 3004*)
  J. O'Sullivan (in ♯ FRP. 1*)
  E. Schmedes (Ger) (in ♯ HRS. 3006*)

Era la notte B
L. Warren (n.v.)   in ♯ Vic.LM 1932
(above)
☆ T. Gobbi (♭ G.7RW 129)
  A. M. Serra, from set B (♭ Nix.EP 744; ♭ Ura.UREP 44)
  P. Schoeffler (♭ D.VD 504)
♨ M. Battistini (in ♯ Ete. 709*; in ♯ FRP. 1*)
  M. Sammarco (in ♯ SBDH.JAL 7001*)
  V. Maurel & pf. (in ♯ Sca. 822*)

Si, pel ciel marmoreo giuro! T & B
☆ J. Björling & R. Merrill (in ♯ G.BLP 1053;
                            ♯ Vic.LRM/♭ set ERB 7027)
  G. Sarri & A. M. Serra, from set B
                     (♭ Nix.EP 744; ♭ Ura.UREP 44)
♨ E. Caruso & T. Ruffo (in ♯ G.FJLP 5010*: QJLP 101*)
  G. Zenatello & P. Amato (in ♯ Sca. 818*)
  T. Pattiera & M. Bohnen (Ger) (in ♯ Ete. 494*)

ACT III

Dio! mi potevi scagliar T
A. da Costa   in ♯ Roy. 1595
E. Witte (Ger)   Eta. 320184
(Niun mi tema)
A. Frinberg (Latvian) (USSR. 19957: in ♯ D 1899)
♨ A. Pertile (in ♯ Ete. 703*)
  G. Zenatello (in ♯ Sca. 818*)

Ballabili (Ballet)
Bamberg Sym.—Lehmann   ♭ Pol. 30016
(Norma, Overture) (in ♯ 17039: 16062; in ♯ AmD.DL 4089)

ACT IV

Era più calma . . . S & A (or M-S)
Mia madre aveva una povera ancella . . .
Ave Maria
COMPLETE RECORDING (to end of Ave Maria)
V. de los Angeles & G. Borelli   ♯ G.ALP 1284
(Bohème, Mefistofele, Cenerentola, etc.) (♯ QALP 10155)

Mia madre aveva una povera ancella
(Canzone del Salce—Willow Song)
Ave Maria
J. Hammond   G.DB 21558
                                (ED 1235)
R. Carteri   Cet.CB 20537 & 20543
(Pêcheurs de Perles—Comme autrefois . . .)
R. Tebaldi   in ♯ Fnt.LP 302
[Ave Maria, only in ♯ LP 301]
☆ Géori-Boué (Fr) (in ♯ Od.ODX 117)
  A. la Pollo, from set B (♭ Ura.UREP 25)
  E. Steber (in ♯ Phi.N 02609R)

. . . Mia madre aveva una povera ancella, only
G. Brouwenstijn   ♯ Phi.N 00712R
(Aida & Ballo in Maschera)
B. Montmart (Fr) (in ♯ LI.TW 91131; D.FAT 173666)

. . . Ave Maria, only S
M. C. Verna   in ♯ Cet.LPC 55005
(La Wally, Tosca, Mefistofele, etc.)
A. Stella   in ♯ G.QALP 10096
(Ernani, Ballo, etc.)
E. Arizmendi   ArgOd. 66022
(Manon Lescaut—In quelle trine . . .) (in ♯ LDC 506)
B. Troxell (S) & org.   in ♯ Ply. 12-123
☆ D. Ilitsch (in ♯ Sup.LPM 132; U. 5108C)
♨ R. Raisa (in ♯ Sca. 808*)

[1] Probably the same as in ♯ Roy. 1619, below.
[2] Includes also Solo per me . . .

Niun mi tema T
S. Puma   Cet.PE 205
(Ora e per sempre addio, Act II)
E. Witte (Ger)   Eta. 320184
(Dio mi potevi scagliar)
☆ M. del Monaco (o.v.) (in ♯ G.FBLP 1050: QBLP 5021:
                       ♭ 7R 153: 7RQ/RF 269: 7RW 142)
♨ A. Pertile (in ♯ Ete. 703*)
  G. Borgatti (in ♯ HRS. 3002*)
  G. Zenatello (in ♯ Sca. 818*)
  C. Vezzani (Fr) (in ♯ Od.ODX 126*)

RIGOLETTO 3 Acts 1851
COMPLETE RECORDINGS

Casts		Set F	Set G
Gilda (S)	... ...	L.·Pagliughi	H. Gueden
Maddalena (M-S)	...	I. Colasanti	G. Simionato
Duca di Mantova (T)	...	F. Tagliavini	M. del Monaco
Rigoletto (B)	...	G. Taddei	A. Protti
Monterone (Bs)	...	H. Zerbini	F. Corena
Sparafucile (Bs)	...	G. Neri	C. Siepi
etc.			

Set F, with Italian Radio Cho. & Orch.—Questa
(6ss)   ♯ CCet. set 1247
[Highlights on ♯ CCet.A 50166; Excerpts
on ♭ Cap.FAP 7019; ♭ Cet.EPO 0301]

Set G, with Santa Cecilia Acad. Cho. & Orch.
—Erede   ♯ D.LXT 5006/8
(6ss)   (♯ Lon. set LLA 25)
[Highlights on ♯ D.LW 5206: LW 50001; Lon.LD 9197;
Questa o quella, Donna è mobile & Bella figlia . . .
                                on ♭ D.71081]

Set H

Gilda	... ...	...	M. M. Callas (S)
Maddalena	... ...	...	A. Lazzarini (A)
Duca di Mantova	...	...	G. di Stefano (T)
Rigoletto	... ...	...	T. Gobbi (B)
Monterone	... ...	...	P. Clabassi (Bs)
Sparafucile	... ...	...	N. Zaccaria (Bs)

etc., La Scala Cho. & Orch.—Serafin
(5ss)   ♯ C.CX 1324S/6
                                (♯ Angel. 35318/20, set 3537)
Set I. Soloists[1] & Rome Eliseo Cho. & Orch.—Manrico
(4ss)   ♯ Know. set
Set C. ☆ E. Berger (S), J. Peerce (T), etc., Cho. & Vic. Sym.
—Cellini (6ss—♯ G.FALP 207/9: VALP 501/3:
QALP 10006/8; 4ss—♯ Vic.LM 6021; FV.A 630258/9)
[Excerpts on ♯ Vic.LRM 7000: ♭ set ERB 7000]
Set B. ☆ M. Capsir (S), D. Borgioli (T), R. Stracciari (B),
La Scala Cho. & Milan Sym.—Molajoli (♯ AmC. set EL 2;
                           ♯ C.GQX 10091/2, 4ss)

ABRIDGED RECORDING
H. Heusser (S), A. de Lorie (A), P. Conrad (T), P. Gorin
(B), etc., Cho. & Netherlands Phil. Orch.—Goehr
(4ss)   ♯ MMS. set OP 9
                                (also ♯ MMS. set M 111)

HIGHLIGHTS
R. Streich (S), P. Munteanu (T), H. Uhde (B), K.
Böhme (Bs)   ♯ Pol. 17011
[for individual issues see below]
E. Köth (S), S. Wagner (A), R. Schock (T), J.
Metternich (B), G. Frick (Bs), Berlin Municipal
Op. Cho. & Orch.—Schüchter (Ger) ♯ G.WBLP 1503
[for individual issues see below]
H. Reggiani (S), B. Landi (T), F. Valentino (B), etc.
Rome Teatro Eliseo Cho. & Orch.—Manrico
                                   ♯ Roy. 1619
                                (♯ MTW. 704)
- R. Doria (S), D. Scharley (M-S), G. Fouché (T),
E. Blanc (B), etc. (Fr)   ♯ CA.LPA 1090
                                (♯ Plé.P 3076)
☆ (from set E) Soloists, Florence Fest. Cho. & Orch.
—Ghiglia (♯ Ply. 12-102: 10-27; & with commentary
by S. Spaeth ♯ Rem. 100-16)
Soloists, Berlin State Op. Cho. & Orch. (♭ Roy.EP 189)
Anon. Artists (♯ Cam.CAL 226, in set CFL 101)

COLLECTED EXCERPTS
Pari siamo, Act I; Figlia! mio padre! Act I;
Gualtier Maldè . . . Caro nome, Act I;
Chi è mai . . . Lassù in cielo, Act III
M. Dobbs (S), R. Panerai (B) & Philharmonia
—Galliera   ♯ C.CX 1305
(Golden Cockerel, Manon, etc.)   (♯ Angel. 35095)
☆ L. Pagliughi (S) & A. Sved (B) (♯ FSor.CS 545)[2]

RIGOLETTO (continued)

ACT I

Questa o quella T
M. del Monaco   **D.M 682**
(La donna è mobile, Act III)   (SV 3808: Y 6641)
(in ‡ D.LXT 2845; ‡ Lon.LL 880; also in ‡ D.LW 5093;
‡ Lon.LD 9082 & ‡ D.LXT 2964; ‡ Lon.LL 1025)

K. Terkal   **D.F 43566**
(La donna è mobile, Act III)

R. Schock (Ger)   **G.DA 5520**
(La donna è mobile)   (♭ 7PW 512)

G. Fouché (Fr)   ♭ **Plé.P 45152**
(La donna è mobile; & Bohème)

  J. Simándy (Hung) (Qual.MK 1053)
  B. Paprocki (Pol) (Muza. 1724)
  ☆ P. Munteanu (Pol. 3021: ♭ 30076)
  J. Peerce (♭ G.7ER 5023: Vic.ERA 84, from set)
  J. Björling (♭ Vic.ERA 134)
  M. Lanza (in ‡ G.ALP 1071: FBLP 1043;
                   ♭ Vic.ERA 111)

  E. Conley (♭ Lon.REP 8005)
  R. Tauber (Ger) (in ‡ Ete. 701)
  ⊞ E. Caruso (♭ Vic.ERAT 4*; in ‡ G.FJLP 5004*;
                           QJLP 104*)

  H. Lazaro (in ‡ Sca. 806*)
  G. Lauri-Volpi (in ‡ Ete. 703*)

Pari siamo! B
Figlia! Mio Padre! S & B
Ah! veglia, o donna
[to end of duet, with interjections from M-S & T]
  ☆ E. Berger, L. Warren, J. Peerce, M. Kreste (M-S),
       from set (♭ G.7ER 5056: ERQ 144)

Pari siamo B
G. Taddei   in ‡ **Cet.LPC 55006**
(Africaine, Figaro, Falstaff, etc.)

G. London   in ‡ **AmC.ML 4999**
(Otello, Thaïs, Emperor Jones, etc.)

R. Weede   in ‡ **DCap.CTL 7080**
(below, Otello, Traviata, etc.)   (in ‡ Cap.P 8290)

F. Valentino   in ‡ **Roy. 1585**

  A. Hiolski (Pol) (Muza.X 2362)
  ☆ T. Gobbi (♭ G.7R 154: 7RQ 3021)
  L. Warren (♭ Vic.ERA 65 & in ‡ LM 1932)
  G. Bechi (in ‡ G.QALP 10087)
  ⊞ H. Rehkemper (Ger) (in ‡ Sca. 809*)
  A. Scotti (AF.AGSB 24*)
  G. de Luca (in ‡ Sca. 813*)

Figlia! Mio Padre! S & B
... Deh non parlate al misero, only
  ⊞ S. Kurz & H. Schlusnus (Ger) (in ‡ HRS. 3006*)

Ah! veglia, o donna S & B
  ☆ M. Tauberová & Z. Otava (Cz) (in ‡ U. 5205H)

Giovanna, ho dei rimorsi ... T'amo!
È il sol dell' anima S, T, & A
E. Köth, R. Schock & S. Wagner (Ger)
(Caro nome)   **G.DB 11571**

È il sol dell' anima S & T
L. Pagliughi & F. Tagliavini   in ‡ **CCet.A 50178**
(A. Lecouvreur, Chénier, etc.) (from set F)
  I. Maslennikova & I. Kozlovsky (Russ) (USSR. 20207/8)
  ⊞ G. Huguet & F. de Lucia (AF.ABHB 6*)

Gualtier Maldè ... Caro nome S
G. Arnaldi   **Cet.PE 186**
(Don Pasquale—Quel guardo)

R. Streich   **PV. 72446**
(Barbiere—Una voce poco fa)   (♭ Pol. 30052)

E. Köth (Ger)   **G.DB 11571**
(above)

  Anon. Artist (in ‡ Cam.CAL 249)
  N. Stokowacka (Pol) (Muza. 2362)
  V. Firsova (Russ) (USSR. 16551/2)
  M. Gyurkovics (Hung) (Qual.MN 1131)
  ☆ E. Berger, from set C (♭ G.7ER 5023; ♭ Vic.ERA 84;
  A. Galli-Curci (in ‡ G.FJLP 5004: QJLP 104;
                   ♭ Vic.ERAT 11)

  T. dal Monte (♭ G.7RQ 3039)
  L. Pagliughi (AmD.ED 3529; Orf. 54020, d.c.)
  E. Berger (Ger), from set D (♭ Ura.UREP 41)
  E. Sack (Ger) (♭ Mer.EP 1-5022)
  L. Pons (Fr) (in ‡ Od.OD 1013)
  ⊞ M. Barrientos (in ‡ Sca. 806*)

Zitti, zitti Ens.
Netherlands Op. Cho. & Residentie Orch.
—Moralt   ‡ **EPhi.NBR 6003**
          (‡ Phi.N 00634R: & Phi.N 12081G)

ACT II

Parmi veder le lagrime T
N. Gedda   **C.LX 1617**
(Martha—Ach, so fromm)   (in ‡ CX 1130: FCX 302;
                   in ‡ Angel. 35096)

P. Munteanu   ♭ **Pol. 30076**
(above & below)

A. Dermota (Ger)   **T.E 3356**
(Trovatore—Ah si ben mio)   (♭ UE 453356)

  ☆ F. Tagliavini (in ‡ CCet.A 50155)
  R. Tauber (C.LOX 821)
  J. Peerce, from set C (♭ G.7ER 5053; in ‡ Vic.LM 1847)
  M. Lanza (in ‡ G.ALP 1202: FBLP 1043)
  ⊞ F. de Lucia (in ‡ CEd. set 7002*)
  A. Pertile (in ‡ Ete. 703*; in ‡ Od.ODX 127*:
                      ♭ MOAQ 301*)

  A. Bonci (in ‡ Sca. 811*)

Scorrendo uniti remota via Cho.
Netherlands Op. Cho. & Residentie Orch.
—Moralt   in ‡ **EPhi.NBR 6003**
          (‡ Phi.N 00634R & Phi.N 12081G)

Cortigiani, vil razza dannata B
R. Weede   in ‡ **DCap.CTL 7080**
(above)   (‡ Cap.P 8290)

H. Uhde   ♭ **Pol. 30084**
(Handel: Giulio Cesare, aria)
(& in Ger, Carmen—Toreador Song on PV. 36085;
                       ♭ Pol. 32077)

F. Valentino   in ‡ **Roy. 1585**

L. Tibbett   in ‡ **Roy. 1627**

H. Hasslo   in ‡ **G.ALPC 1**
(Traviata, Elisir, Tosca, etc.)

G. Molis   **U.H 24395**
(Otello—Credo)

J. Metternich (Ger)   **G.DB 11549**
(Traviata—Di Provenza)   (♭ 7RW 503)

  A. Sved (Qual.MN 1053)
  A. Ivanov (Russ) (USSR. 20459/60)
  K. Shekarlysky (Bulg) (Bulg. 1383)
  ☆ R. Merrill (in ‡ Vic.LM 1841; FV.A 630255)
  L. Warren, from set C (♭ G.7ER 5053; ♭ Vic.ERA 114:
             ERA 207: in ‡ LM 1801 & LM 1932)
  R. Stracciari (in ‡ Ete. 802)
  G. Bechi (in ‡ G.QALP 10087)
  Z. Otava (Cz) (in ‡ U.5205H)
  H. Schlusnus (Ger) (in ‡ Pol. 18080 & in ‡ 19039)
  M. Dens (Fr) (in ‡ Pat.DT 1020)

Tutte le feste al tempio S
Solo per me ... Piangi, piangi, fanciulla S & B
R. Streich, H. Uhde & K. Böhme (Bs) (Ger)
               in ‡ **Pol. 18147**
                   (& ♭ Pol. 19043)

  M. Zvezdina & K. Laptev (Russ) (in ‡ USSR.D 2142)
  ⊞ M. Barrientos & R. Stracciari (in ‡ Sca. 806*)

Tutte le feste, only S
H. Reggiano   in ‡ **Roy. 1603**
  ☆ L. Pagliughi (Orf. 54010, d.c.)

Solo per me ... Piangi! piangi, fanciulla only S & B
E. Spoorenberg & T. Baylé   **Phi.N 12065G**
(Meyerbeer & Offenbach on ♭ N 402009E)
  N. Stokowacka & A. Hiolski (Pol) (Muza.X 2344)
  I. Maslennikova & A. Ivanov (Russ) (USSR. 20209/10)

Si vendetta, tremenda vendetta S & B
  ⊞ H. Francillo-Kaufmann & J. Schwarz (in ‡ Ete. 498*)

ACT III

La donna è mobile T
M. del Monaco   **D.M 682**
(Questa o quella, Act I)   (SV 3808: Y 6641)
(in ‡ D.LXT 2845; ‡ Lon.LL 880; also in ‡ D.LW 5093;
‡ Lon.LD 9082 & ‡ D.LXT 2964; ‡ Lon.LL 1025)

(continued on next page)

☆ = Re-issue of a recording to be found in previous volumes.

RIGOLETTO, Act III: La donna è mobile (*continued*)

P. Munteanu ♭ *Pol. 30078*
(*above*) [from Highlights]

R. Schock (*Ger*) *G.DB 11565*
(*below*) (♭ *G.7RW 19-552: also o.n. G.DA 5520: 7PW 512*)

G. Fouché (*Fr*) ♭ *Plé.P 45152*
(*Questa o quella; & Bohème*)

K. Terkal (*Ger*) *D.F 43566*
(*Questa o quella*)

B. Manazza (*Ger*) *Tpo. 3696*
(*Nacht in Venedig—Treu sein*)

　D. Dame (in ‡ *MH. 33-104*)
　J. Simándy (*Hung*) (*Qual.MK 1053*)
　S. Lemeshev (*Russ*) (*USSR. 17968|9: USSRM.D 001218*)
　I. Kozlovsky (*Russ*) (*USSR. 10721|2: in ‡ D 1428*)
　☆ M. Lanza (♭ *G.7EB|EBW 6004: 7ERQ 127:*
　　　in ‡ *ALP 1071: ‡ FBLP 1043; ♭ Vic.ERA 111*)
　B. Gigli (in ‡ *FJLP 3039*)
　M. Fleta (♭ *G.7ERL 1044*)
　J. Peerce, from set C (♭ *G.7ER 5023; ♭ Vic.ERA 84*)
　　(also ☆ o.v. in ‡ *Var. 6983; ♭ Roy.EP 169* &
　　in ‡ *1595 & 1610; in ‡ AFest.CFR 10-134:*
　G. Poggi (in ‡ *Cet.LPC 55003*) ♭ *EPM 246*)
　R. Schock (o.v.) (in ‡ *Roy. 1256: ♭ EP 169*)
　G. Malipiero (*Cet. 54018*)
　E. Conley (♭ *Lon.REP 8005*)
　R. Tauber (*Ger*) (in ‡ *Ete. 701*)
　H T. Schipa (in ‡ *Sca. 805*; in ‡ Ete. 492*)
　F. Giannini (*SBDH.P 5**)
　E. Caruso (♭ *Vic.ERAT 4*; in ‡ G.FJLP 5009*:*
　　　　　　　　　　　　　QJLP 105*)
　J. McCormack (in ‡ *Roy. 1555*: ♭ EP 324*;*
　　　　　　　in ‡ *Cum.CE 185*; in ‡ FRP 1**)
　F. de Lucia (in ‡ *SBDH.JAL 7000**)

Bella figlia dell' amore S, A, T, B
E. Köth, S. Wagner, R. Schock, J. Metternich[1]
G.DB 11565
(*above*) [from Highlights] (*Ger*) (♭ *G.7RW 19-552*)

　☆ E. Berger, N. Merriman, J. Peerce, L. Warren from
　　set C (♭ *G.7ER 5023; ♭ Vic.ERA 84*)
　E. Berger, M. Klose, H. Roswaenge, H. Schlusnus
　　(*Ger*), from set D (♭ *Ura.UREP 41*)
　F. Hüni-Mihacsek, E. Leisner, H. Roswaenge,
　　T. Scheidl (▽ *Pol. 67363*)
　H Galli-Curci, Perini, Caruso, De Luca
　　　　　　　　(♭ *Vic.ERAT 8*; ♭ G.7RW 19-539**)
— ARR. ORCH. only
　Boston "Pops"—Fiedler (in ‡ *Vic.LRM 7045*)
— ARR. PF. Liszt, *q.v.* Section A. III (5)

Chi è mai . . . Lassù in cielo S & B
　M. Zvezdina & K. Laptev (*Russ*) (*USSR. 18677|8:*
　　　　　　　　　　　　　in ‡ *D 2142*)
Melodies — ARR. HARP
　O. Erdeli (*USSR. 20449|50: in ‡ D 1214*)
Fantasia — ARR. CL. & PF. Bassi
　J. Stowell & D. Mayer (in ‡ *Aphe.AP 26*)

SIMONE BOCCANEGRA Prol. & 3 Acts 1857
A te l'estremo addio . . . Il lacerato spirito Bs (Prol.)
E. Pinza in ‡ *Vic.LM 1751*
(*Nabucco, Don Carlos, etc.*) (♭ *ERA 140; in ‡ FV.A 630233*)

C. Siepi ♭ *D. 71099*
(*Nabucco—Tu sul labbro*)
(in ‡ *D.LW 5169; Lon.LD 9169; & in D.LXT 5096;*
　　　　　　　　　　　　　Lon.LL 1240)

M. Petri in ‡ *SBDH.TOB 2*
(*Roméo et Juliette, Barbiere, etc.*)

M. Reizen (*Russ*) ‡ *USSR.D 1317*
(*Vêpres Siciliennes, Walküre*)

　H J. Mardones (in ‡ *Sca. 810**)

Dinne alcun . . . Figlia! a tal nome palpito
S & B　Act I
　☆ R. Bampton & L. Tibbett (♭ *Vic.ERAT 24*)
　A. Varnay & L. Warren (*BrzV. 886-5008*)

Plebe! Patrizi . . . Piangi su voi Ens.
　☆ R. Bampton, G. Martinelli, R. Nicholson, L. Tibbett,
　　L. Warren & Cho. (in ‡ *Vic. set LCT 6701*)

O inferno! . . . Sento avvampar nell' anima T Act II
G. Penno ‡ *D.LW 5111*
(*Norma, Trovatore*) (‡ *Lon.LD 9117*)

M'ardon le tempia B Act III
P. Schoeffler in ‡ *Van.VRS 469*
(*Vêpres siciliennes, Africaine, etc.*) (‡ *Ama.AVRS 6022*)

(**La**) **TRAVIATA** 3 Acts 1853
COMPLETE RECORDINGS

Casts	Set H	Set I
Violetta (S)	M. M. Callas	R. Tebaldi
Flora (M-S)	E. G. Marietti	A. Vercelli
Alfredo (T)	F. Albanese	G. Poggi
Germont (B) ...	U. Savarese	A. Protti
etc.		

Set H, with Italian Radio Cho. & Orch.—Santini
(6ss) **‡ CCet. set 1246**
[Highlights on ‡ A 50167; Excerpts on ♭ *Cap.FAP 7015;*
　　　　　　　　　　　♭ *Cet.EPO 0303 & 0317*]

Set I, with Santa Cecilia Acad. Cho. & Orch.
—Molinari Pradelli **‡ D.LXT 2992/4**
(6ss) [Selection on ‡ *D.LW 5197*] (‡ Lon. set LLA 26)

Set K Soloists & Bolshoi Theatre Cho. & Orch.—Orlov
(*Russ*—6ss) **‡ USSR.D 057/62**

Set A ☆ L. Albanese (S), J. Peerce (T), R. Merrill (B), etc.,
Cho. & N.B.C. Sym. Orch.—Toscanini ‡ *G.ALP 1072/3*
　　　　　　　　　　　(‡ QALP 10044/5)
[Highlights, ‡ *Vic.LM 1843:* ♭ *set ERB 40*]

Set C ☆ A. Guerrini (S), M. Huder (M-S), L. Infantino (T),
P. Silveri (B), etc., Rome Op. Cho. & Orch.—Bellezza
(4ss) (‡ *C.GQX 10008/9*)

Set Y ☆ R. Noli, G. Olini, G. Campora, C. Tagliabue, etc.,
Cho. & Orch.—Berrettoni (6ss—‡ Ply. set 41-3)

Set X ☆ F. Schimenti, L. di Lelio, A. Pola, etc., Rome Op.
Cho. & Orch.—Ricci (4ss, ♭ *Roy. 1544/5;*
　　MusH.LP 12005/6; Highlights on ‡ *Roy. 1552*)

EXCERPTS FROM SET I
　on ‡ *D.LW 5200; Lon.LD 9198*
Dell' invito trascorsa (Opening Scene, Act I)
Libiamo, libiamo (Brindisi, Act I)
Un di felice (Act I); Parigi o cara (Act III)
[Un di . . . & Parigi . . . also on ♭ *D.71129*]

HIGHLIGHTS
　M. Opawsky (S), L. Larsen (T), H. Dreissen (Bs), S.
　Jongsma (Bs), cho. & Netherlands Phil. Orch.—Goehr
　　　　　　　　　　　　‡ MMS. 2011
　[Prelude only in **V‡** *MMS. 920*] (also ‡ OP 1)
　M. Moralès (S), L. Simoneau (T) & Lamoureux Orch.
　—Dervaux **‡ Phi.N 00639R**
　E. Hardy (S), C. Schultz (T), A. Sebaroli (B), etc., cho &
　orch.—Peluso **‡ Opa. 1001/2**
　[Excerpts on *set 101* (6ss): ♭ *102*]
　☆ Anon. Artists (‡ *Cam.CAL 227*, in set CFL 101)

HIGHLIGHTS — ARR. ORCH. Kostelanetz
　A. Kostelanetz Orch. **‡ EPhi.NBL 5006**
　(‡ *AmC.CL 799*: o.n. *ML 4896*; ‡ *Phi.N 02108L*)

Preludes, Acts I & III
Philharmonia—Galliera **C.DX 1890**
(*GQX 11545*: in ‡ *SX 1009: FCX 209: QCX 10094*;
　　　　　　　　　　　　　Angel. 35012)
(& with *Barbiere Overture*, ♭ *C.SED 5517:*
　　　　　　　　　　　SEBQ 120: ESBF 123)

Hallé—Barbirolli ♭ *G.7ER 5034*
(*Suppé: Schöne Galathee, Overture*)

R.I.A.S. Sym.—Fricsay *Pol. 62923*
(♭ *Pol. 32007: in ‡ 17015; in ‡ AmD.DL 9738*)

Berlin Municipal Op.—Rother *T.E 3928*
(♭ *UE 453928; ♭ FT. 510.TC.003*)

Metropolitan Op.—Cleva in ‡ *AmC. set SL 123*
(& in ‡ *ML 4886*)

Linz Sym. (in ‡ Ply. 12-34)
　☆ Bamberg Sym.—Leitner (*PV. 72468; FPV. 5041;*
　　　　　　　　　　　　　♭ *AmD.ED 3516*)
　E.I.A.R.—Parodi (*Orf. 54008*)
　N.B.C. Sym.—Toscanini (♭ *G.7RF 223*)
　Ital. Radio—Santini, from set H (in ‡ *CCet.A 50159*)

ACT I

Prelude
Radio-Luxembourg—Pensis in ‡ *FestF.FLD 15*
Vienna Radio—Schönherr in ‡ *Vien.LPR 1037*
　　　　　　　　　　　　　(♭ 4044)
Nat. Op. Orch. (in ‡ *Gram. 20142*)
Opera Orch.—Rossi (in ‡ *Mae.OA 20006*)

Libiamo, nei lieti calici (*Brindisi*) T & S
P. Munsel, C. Craig & Cho. in ‡ *G.BLP 1023*
[Film *Melba*] (‡ *G.QBLP 5015: Vic.LM 7012:*
　　　　　　　　　　　♭ *set WDM 7012*)
　S. Lemeshev & E. Shumskaya (*Russ*) (in ‡ *USSR.D 1427*)
　☆ L. Albanese & J. Peerce (♭ *G.7ER 5008*)
　E. Malbin & M. Lanza (*G.DB 21571:* ♭ *7R 168:*
　　　　　　　　　7RW 146: in ‡ *ALP 1202*)
　M. Cebotari & H. Roswaenge (*Ger*) (in ‡ *Attn.LPE 114*)
　H E. Caruso & A. Gluck (♭ *Vic.ERAT 9**)

---

[1] Includes G. Frick (Bs), so probably continues into *Venti scudi*.

(La) TRAVIATA, Act I (continued)
Waltz Orch. [& Ens.]
☆ Cincinnati Summer Op.—Cleva (in ‡ B.AXTL 1035;
in ‡ AmD.DL 8053; ♭ ED 3525; in ‡ D.UST 233087)

Un di felice, eterea S & T
M. Janulescu & V. Teodorian **U.H 24397**
(Barbiere—Largo al factotum)
☆ L. Albanese & J. Peerce (G.ED 1216: ♭ 7ER 5019;
♭ Vic.ERA 72)
A. Galli-Curci & T. Schipa (♭ Vic.ERAT 11:
in ‡ LCT 1138)
M. Cebotari & H. Roswaenge (Ger) (in ‡ Attn.LPE 114)
⌶ N. Melba & A. Dippel (in ‡ IRCC.L 7006*)¹

... **Tenor part** only
⌶ F. de Lucia & pf. (in ‡ Sca. 814*)
G. Zenatello (in ‡ SBDH.LLP 8*)

È strano . . . Ah! fors' è lui . . .
Follie! Follie! . . . Sempre libera S [& T]
R. Tebaldi & G. Poggi **‡ D.LXT 5076**
(Addio del passato, Act III; Otello, etc.) [from set I]
(Addio del passato & Manon Lescaut, ‡ D.LW 5210)
H. Gueden **‡ D.LW 5178**
(Falstaff & Puccini) (‡ Lon.LD 9165)
H. Schymberg in ‡ G.ALPC 1
(Elisir, Tosca, Figaro, etc.)
D. Kirsten in ‡ AmCML 4730
M. Sá Earp BrzCont.CA 4016
M. M. Callas [from set H] in ‡ CCet.A 50175
N. Jean (S), W. Spada (pf.) (in ‡ GNYO. 201)
M. Mátyás (Hung) (Qual.MK 1504)
E. Shumskaya (Russ in ‡ USSR.D 1427)
☆ L. Albanese (♭ G.7ER 5008; in ‡ Vic.LM 1864:
♭ ERA 231)
E. Steber (in ‡ Phi.N 02609R)
A. Galli-Curci (♭ Vic.ERAT 11 & in ‡ LM 1909)
M. Cebotari (Ger) (in ‡ Attn.LPE 114)
V. Firsova (Russ) (in ‡ USSRM.D 00908)
⌶ M. Ivogün (in ‡ Sca. 815*)

È strano . . . Ah! fors' è lui, only
☆ T. dal Monte (in ‡ G.QALP 10089)

Sempre libera, only
☆ R. Peters (G.DB 21577)
Lilli Lehmann (in ‡ Cum.CE 186*; in ‡ B & B. 3*²)
⌶ M. Sembrich [& C. Dani (T)] (in ‡ IRCC.L 7006*³)

ACT II

De' miei bollenti spiriti T
R. Tucker in ‡ AmC.ML 4750
P. Anders ♭ Pol. 32025
(Pagliacci—Vesti la giubba) (in Ger on Pol. 62913:
♭ 30012)
☆ M. del Monaco D.XP 6152
(Manon Lescaut—Donna non vidi)
(Aida, etc., on ‡ LW 5064: ♭ VD 509;
‡ Lon.LD 9051: in ‡ LL 1244)
I. Kozlovsky (Russ) (in ‡ USSR.D 1427)
☆ P. Munteanu (Pol. 3021: in ‡ 18169)
H. Roswaenge (Ger, o.v.) (in ‡ CEd. 7010)
R. Schock (? Ger) (in ‡ Roy. 1256: ♭ EP 183)
⌶ J. McCormack (AF.AGSB 3*; ♭ Vic.ERAT 26*:
in ‡ LCT 1138*)
G. Martinelli (in ‡ SBDH.LPG 4*)
T. Schipa (in ‡ Sca. 805*)
G. Zenatello (in ‡ Ete. 705*)
R. Tauber (Ger) (in ‡ Cum.CE 187*)

Madamigella Valéry?
Pura siccome un angelo . . .
Dite alla giovine . . . Imponete S & B
COMPLETE DUET
E. Shumskaya & P. Lisitsian (Russ)
(6ss) **USSR. 21032/7**
... **Dite alla giovine . . . Imponete** S & B
I. Szecsödy & A. Sved (Hung) **Qual.MN 1052**
(Bohème—Si mi chiamano, Mimi)
N. Stokowacka & A. Hiolski (Pol) (Muza.X 2343)
N. Jean, J. de Merchant & W. Spade (pf.)
(in ‡ GNYO. 201)
☆ L. Albanese & R. Merrill (♭ G.7ER 5019;
in ‡ Vic.LM 1801: ♭ ERA 208 & ERA 72;
also in ‡ set LCT 6701)
⌶ F. Hempel & P. Amato (in ‡ Vic. set LCT 6701*)

Amami Alfredo S
M. Olivero Cet.AT 0320
(Catalani: Loreley, aria)
R. Scotto Cet.AT 0389
(Mascagni: Lodoletta, aria)

Di Provenza il mar B
L. Warren (n.v.) in ‡ Vic.LM 1932
(Falstaff, Otello, etc.)
R. Weede in ‡ DCap.CTL 7080
(Otello, Trovatore, etc.) (in ‡ Cap.P 8290)
A. Sved in ‡ Sup.LPV 207
(Trovatore, Carmen, etc.) (‡ U. 5191G)
I. Gorin in ‡ Alld. 3003
(♭ EP 3003; ‡ MTW. 572)
U. Savarese Cet.BB 25298
(Andrea Chénier—La mamma morta)
R. Cesari ArgOd. 66047
(Barbiere—Largo al factotum) (in ‡ LDC 515)
J. Metternich (Ger) G.DB 11549
(Rigoletto—Cortigiani) (♭ 7RW 503: in ‡ WBLP 1504)
H. Pelayo (in ‡ SMC. 1003)
I. P. Alexeyev (Russ, in ‡ U. 5176C; Sup.LPM 186)
A. Sved (Hung) (Qual.MN 1062)
L. Jambór (Hung) (Qual.KM 5009)
P. Lisitsian (Russ) (in ‡ USSR.D 1427)
S. Shaposhnikov (Russ) (USSR. 19477/8)
☆ T. Gobbi (♭ G.7R 154: 7RQ 3021)
R. Merrill (♭ G.7ER 5019; ♭ Vic.ERA 72)
J. C. Thomas (in ‡ Cam.CAL 199)
H. Schlusnus (Ger) (♭ Pol. 30153)
I. Zidek (Cz) (in ‡ U. 5205H)
⌶ G. de Luca (in ‡ Sca. 812*)
T. Ruffo (in ‡ Sca. 812*; in ‡ HRS. 3005*)

Noi siamo zingarelle Gypsy Cho.
Di Madride Matadors' Cho.
A. Marcangeli (S), A. la Porta (B) & Rome Op.
Cho.—Morelli in ‡ G.ALP 1277
(Forza, Otello, Turandot, etc.) (‡ QALP 10118)

Ogni suo aver tal femmina T [& ens.]
(Scena della borsa)
⌶ G. Zenatello (in ‡ Ete. 703*)

Alfredo, Alfredo (Finale, Act II) S
⌶ Lilli Lehmann (in ‡ Ete. 702*)

ACT III

Prelude [& see above]
Philharmonia—Karajan in ‡ C.CX 1265
(Cav. Rusticana, Amico Fritz, etc.) (‡ FCX 407:
QCX 10150; Angel. 35207)

Addio del passato S
D. Rigal ArgOd. 66013
(Gioconda—Suicidio) (♭ BSOAE 4500: in ‡ LDC 503;
AmD.DL 4060)
D. Kirsten in ‡ AmC.ML 4730
R. Scotto Cet.PE 205
(Pêcheurs de Perles—Comme autrefois)
M. M. Callas in ‡ CCet.A 50175
(above, Tristan, Puritani, etc.)
R. Tebaldi, from set I ‡ D.LXT 5076
(Ah fors è lui, Act I, etc.)
(idem & Manon Lescaut only, ‡ D.LW 5210)⁴
(Otello—Ave Maria on ♭ D.71105)
N. Jean, W. Spada (pf.) (in ‡ GNYO. 201)
☆ L. Albanese (in ‡ Vic.ERA 139: ERA 231)
R. Tebaldi, o.v. (in ‡ Fnt.LP 302)
M. Carosio (♭ G.7R 115: 7RQ 3018: 7RW 143)
E. Schwarzkopf (♭ C.SCBW 102: SCBF 107:
SCBQ 3004)
M. Tauberová (Cz) (in ‡ U. 5205H)
⌶ G. Russ (in ‡ Sca. 808*)

Parigi o cara . . . S & T
☆ P. Tassinari & F. Tagliavini (in ‡ FSor.CS 544)
I. Maslennikova & S. Lemeshev (Russ)
(in ‡ USSR.D 1518, see below)
E. Shumskaya & I. Kozlovsky (Russ) (USSRM.D 1048)
⌶ A. de Angelis & F. de Lucia (in ‡ CEd. set 7002*)
M. Barrientos & H. Lazaro (in ‡ Sca. 806*)
G. Huguet & F. de Lucia (IRCC.ABHB 6*)
L. Bori & J. McCormack (♭ Vic.ERAT 17*)

---

¹ Excerpt only, from Mapleson cylinder.
³ From Mapleson cylinder.
² Labelled Mozart: Nozze di Figaro.
⁴ Begins Teneste la promessa, not included on LXT 5076 or 71105.

(La) TRAVIATA (continued)

ACT IV

Prendi, quest'è l'immagine S, T, B (*Finale*)
I. Maslennikova, S. Lemeshev, E. Belov
♯ USSR.D 1518

(*above, & Manon*) (*Russ*)

(II) TROVATORE 4 Acts 1853
COMPLETE RECORDINGS

Set F. V. Petrova (M-S), Nicolai (T), I. Petrov (B), etc.,
Florence Fest. Cho. & Orch.—Tieri   **♯ Ace. set 1001**
(6ss)

Set A. ☆ Z. Milanov (S), F. Barbieri (M-S), J. Björling (T),
etc. Shaw Chorale & Vic. Sym.—Cellini **♯ G.ALP 1112/3**
(♯ DV. set LB 16480; ItV.B12R 0023/4)
[Highlights on ♯ Vic.LM 1827]

Set B. ☆ C. Mancini (S), G. Lauri-Volpi (T), etc., Italian
Radio Cho. & Orch.—Previtali (♯ Pol. 18109/11)
[excerpts on ♯ CCet.A 50153; ♭ Cap.FAP 7009 & 7018;
♭ Cet.EPO 0302 & 0314

HIGHLIGHTS
M. Opawsky (S), L. Larsen (T), G. Swift (B), S.
Jongsma (Bs), cho. & Netherlands Phil.—Goehr
♯ MMS. 2008
(also ♯ OP 16)
A. da Costa (T), F. Valentino (B), V. Ruggeri (S), etc.,
Cho. & Orch.   **♯ Roy. 1601**
[*From set E*]

☆ S. Roman (S), G. Garri (T), etc., Rome Op. Cho. &
Orch.—Ricci   **♯ T.LCSK 8178**
[excerpts also in ♭ Cap.FAP 7009]

ACT I

Di due figli . . . Abbietta zingara Bs & cho
. . . **Bs part only**
☙ M. Journet (in ♯ SBDH.JAL 7002*)

Che più t'arresti . . . Tacea la notte S & M-S
C. Goltz & S. Menz   **PV. 72456**
(*below*)   (♭ Pol. 30047)
(in *Ger* on PV. 72449; ♭ Pol. 30041)

Tacea la notte placida only S
V. Petrova   in ♯ **Ace. 1007/8**
(*below, Aida, Gioconda, etc.*)
A. Stella   in ♯ **G.QALP 10096**
(*Aida, Otello, etc.*)
☆ R. Tebaldi   ♭ **D. 71073**
(*Manon Lescaut—In quelle trine . . .*)   (♭ X 102)
(in ♯ D.LW 5065; ♯ Lon.LD 9054)
☆ Z. Milanov   in ♯ **G.ALP 1247**
(♭ Vic.ERA 108 & ERA 228: in ♯ LM 1777:
♭ set ERB 19: also ♯ LM 1864)
☙ A. Galli-Curci (AF.AGSB 80*)[1]
C. Muzio (in ♯ LI.TWV 91053*)[1]
C. Boninsegna (in ♯ Sca. 813*)
R. Ponselle (in ♯ FRP. 2*)

Deserto sulla terra T
M. Gafni   in ♯ **For.FLP 1001**
☙ H. Winkelmann (*Ger*) (in ♯ HRS. 3003*)
F. Giannini (SBDH.P 5*)

Non m'inganno . . . Di geloso amor S, T, B
E. Farrell, H. Blankenburg & R. Petrak[2]
in ♯ **MGM.E 3185**
(♭ set X 304: EP 527/8)
☆ F. Hüni-Mihacsek, H. Roswaenge, T. Scheidl (*Ger*)
(▽ Pol. 67363)

ACT II

Vedi le fosche . . .   Cho. (*Anvil Chorus*)
Stride la vampa!   M-S
Mal reggendo . . . O giusto cielo   M-S & T
☆ F. Barbieri (M-S), J. Björling (T), N. Sprinzena (T),
G. Cehanovsky & Vic. Cho., from set A
(♭ Vic.ERA 113)

Vedi! le fosche . . . (*Anvil Chorus*) only
Netherlands Op. Cho. & Residentie Orch.
—Moralt   in ♯ **EPhi.NBR 6003**
(♯ Phi.N 00634R & S 06018R)
☆ Württemberg State Op.—Leitner (in ♯ AmD.DL 9797;
in ♯ Pol. 19033)

— ARR. ORCH. only
Boston "Pops"—Fiedler (in ♯ Vic.LRM 7045)

— ARR. ORGAN
R. Foort *sub nom.* M. Cheshire (in ♯ Nix.SLPY 148:
SOT 1053 & in ♯ 10523)

Stride la vampa!   M-S or A
M. v. Ilosvay   in ♯ **Phi.N 00649R**
M. Pirazzini   (2ss)   ♭ **Pol. 32091**
M. Henriques   in ♯ **ABCD. 2**
(*below, Barbieri, Don Carlos, etc.*)
Z. Palii   in ♯ **Sup.LPV 207**
(*Carmen, Samson et Dalila, etc.*)   (♯ U. 5191G)
K. Szczepánska (*Pol*) (*Muza. 2347*)
V. Davidova (*Russ*) (*USSRM.D 248*)
☆ M. Krásová (*Cz*) (in ♯ U. 5205H)
☙ R. Olitzka (HRS. 1032*)

Condotta ell' era in ceppi   M-S or A
☆ E. Höngen (*Ger*) (in ♯ Pol. 19029)
☙ C. Boninsegna (S) (in ♯ Sca. 813*)

Mal reggendo . . . O giusto cielo   M-S & T
V. Davidova & G. Nelepp (*Russ*) (*USSRM.D 248*)
I. Dimcheva & D. Uzunov (*Bulg*) (*USSR. 23950/3*)

Il balen del suo sorriso   B
R. Weede   in ♯ **DCap.CTL 7080**
(*Don Carlos, Falstaff, etc.*)   (in ♯ Cap.P 8290)
A. Sved   ♯ **Sup.LPV 207**
(*Carmen, Serse, Orphée, etc.*)   (♯ U.5191G)
A. Protti   in ♯ **D.LX 3109**
(*Pagliacci, Barbieri, etc.*)   (in ♯ Lon.LS 701)
F. Valentino   in ♯ **Roy. 1585**
J. Metternich (*Ger*)   in ♯ **G.WBLP 1504**
(G.DB 11568: ♭ 7RW 523)
A. Sved (*Hung*) (Qual.MN 1017)
K. Laptev (*Russ*) (in ♯ USSR.D 2141)
☆ L. Warren (♭ Vic.ERA 114: in ♯ LM 1932)
R. Merrill (in ♯ Vic.LM 1841; FV.A 630255)
C. Galeffi (Orf. 29002)
R. Stracciari (in ♯ Sca. 802)
H. Schlusnus (*Ger*) (♭ Pol. 30153: ▽ Pol. 67362)
☙ H. Rehkemper (in ♯ Sca. 803*)
R. Stracciari (in ♯ FRP. 3*)
T. Ruffo (in ♯ HRS. 3005*)

Qual suono . . . Per me ora fatale   B, Bs, cho.
J. Metternich, W. Lang, & Berlin Municipal
Op. Cho. (*Ger*)   **G.DB 11568**
(*above*)   (♭ 7RW 523)
☆ L. Warren, N. Moscona & Cho., from set A
(♭ Vic.ERA 114: in ♯ LM 1932)

ACT III

Or co' dadi . . . (*Soldiers' Chorus*)
Cho.—Alexandrov (*Russ*) (*USSR. 18038*)

Amor, sublime amor . . . Ah! si ben mio . . .   T
G. Poggi   in ♯ **D.LX 3127**
(*Manon Lescaut, Fedora, etc.*)   (in ♯ Lon.LD 9106)
G. Martinelli   in ♯ **PRCC. 1**
M. del Monaco   in ♯ **ABCD. 2**
(*Fosca, Don Carlos, Ballo, etc.*)
J. Soler   **Cet.AT 0318**
(*Di quella pira*)
R. Schock (*Ger*) (n.v.)   **G.DA 5518**
(*Di quella pira*)   (♭ 7RW 513)
A. Dermota (*Ger*)   **T.E 3356**
(*Rigoletto—Ella mi fu rapita*)   (♭ UE 453356)
J. Simándy (*Hung*)   **Qual.MK 1572**
(*below*)
☆ H. Roswaenge (*Ger*) (in ♯ CEd. 7010)
J. Björling (in ♯ Vic. set LCT 6701)
R. Schock (o.v.) (in ♯ Roy. 1256)
☙ G. Lauri-Volpi (in ♯ Ete. 703*)
C. Dalmores (AF.AGSB 9*)
G. Martinelli (in ♯ SBDH.LPG 4*)
E. Caruso (♭ Vic.ERAT 4*)

---

[1] From Edison and Pathé hill and dale recordings. This disc was withdrawn almost immediately.
[2] Sound-track of film *Interrupted Melody*.

(II) TROVATORE, Act III (*continued*)

Di quella pira!   T

G. Poggi   in ‡ *D.LX 3127*
(*above, Luisa Miller, etc.*)   (in ‡ *Lon.LD 9106*)

G. Penno   ‡ *D.LW 5111*
(*Norma, Simone Boccanegra*)   (‡ *Lon.LD 9117*)

J. Soler   *Cet.AT 0318*
(*above*)

M. del Monaco & Cho.   in ‡ **SBDH.TOB 2**
(*Orefice: Chopin; Samson et Dalila, Boccanegra, etc.*)

R. Schock & Cho. (*Ger, n.v.*)   *G.DA 5518*
(*above*)   (♭ *7PW 513:* in ‡ *WBLP 1501*)

J. Simándy (*Hung*)   *Qual.MK 1578*
(*above*)
(*Eugene Oniegin, No. 17 on MN 1007*)

☆ J. Björling & P. Franke, from set A
     (in ‡ *Vic.LM 1847* & *LRM 7027:* ♭ set *ERB 7027*)
     B. Gigli (in ‡ *G.FJLP 5039*)
     K. Baum (♭ *Rem.REP 6;* in ‡ *Roy.* 1582 & 1595)
     A. Salvarezza (*Orf.* 53004)
     R. Schock (o.v.) (in ‡ *Roy.* 1256)
     H. Roswaenge (*Ger*) (in ‡ *CEd.* 7010)
   ⌘ V. Lois (in ‡ *Ete.* 703*)
     H. Lazaro (in ‡ *Sca.* 806*)
     A. Pertile (in ‡ *Ete.* 710*; in ‡ *SBDH.GL* 1*;
                      in ‡ *FRP. 3*)
     G. Martinelli (in ‡ *SBDH.LPG 4*)
     F. Tamagno (in ‡ *Vic.* set *LCT 6701*)
     G. Zenatello (in ‡ *SBDH.JAL 7000*)
     E. Caruso (♭ *Vic.ERAT 4*)
     L. Escalais (*Fr*) (in ‡ *Ete.* 708*)

ACT IV

Timor di me . . . D'amor sull' ali rosee   S

C. Goltz   *PV. 72456*
(*above*)   (♭ *Pol.* 30047)
(in *Ger* on *PV.* 72449; ♭ *Pol.* 30041)

V. Petrova (*above*)   in ‡ *Ace.* 1007/8

☆ Z. Milanov [& P. Franke (T)] from set A
                in ‡ *G.ALP 1247*
   (♭ *Vic.ERA 108:* in ‡ *LM 1777;* ♭ set *ERB 19*)

   ⌘ A. Galli-Curci (*AF.AGSB 80*)
     R. Ponselle (in ‡ *Sca.* 803*)
     C. Boninsegna (in ‡ *Sca.* 813*)

Miserere—Ah! che la morte . . .   S, T, Cho.

☆ Z. Milanov & J. Peerce (*BrzV.* 886-5011)
     Mme. G. Martinelli & R. Verdière (*Fr*)
                (♭ *Od.* 7AOE 1004)

   ⌘ E. Destinn & G. Martinelli (in ‡ *SBDH.LPG 4*)

— ARR. PF.   Liszt, q.v., Section A III (5)

Udiste? . . . Mira d'acerbe lagrime   S & B
Si, la stanchezza m'opprime, o figlio
Ai nostri monti   M-S & T

☆ Z. Milanov, F. Barbieri, J. Björling, L. Warren, from
     set A (♭ *Vic.ERA 112*)

. . . Excerpts   (unspec.)
     Z. Milanov, R. Bonelli, B. Castagna, G. Martinelli
                (in ‡ *PRCC.* 1)

. . . Udisti? . . . Mira, d'acerbe lagrime only   S & B
   ⌘ E. Eames & E. de Gogorza (*AF.AGSB 15*)
     E. Corsi & M. Battistini (in ‡ *Ete.* 709*)
     S. Kurz & H. Schlusnus (*Ger*) (in ‡ *HRS.* 3006*)

. . . Ai nostri monti   M-S & T
   ☆ C. Elmo & B. Gigli (in ‡ *Vic.* set *LCT 6701*)
     K. Thorborg & J. Peerce (*BrzV.* 886-5011)
     E. Höngen & W. Ludwig (*Ger*) (in ‡ *Pol.* 19029)

   ⌘ E. Schumann-Heink & E. Caruso (in ‡ *Vic.LCT 1138*;
                        ♭ *ERAT 9**)
     L. Kirkby-Lunn & B. Davies (*Eng*) (*IRCC.* 3146*)

(Les) VÊPRES SICILIENNES   5 Acts   1855
Overture

Philharmonia—Galliera   in ‡ *C.SX 1009*
(*Aida, Nabucco, etc.*)   (‡ *FCX 209: QCX 10094;*
                      Angel. 35012)

Metropolitan Op.—Cleva in ‡ **AmC. set SL 123**
                    (& ‡ *ML 4886*)

Radio Luxemburg—Pensis   in ‡ **FestF.FLD 15**

☆ New Sym.—Erede   ‡ *D.LW 5040*
(*Nabucco*)   (‡ *Lon.LD 9037*)

☆ R.I.A.S. Sym.—Fricsay (in ‡ *Pol.* 17015; *AmD.DL 4046*)
     Austrian Sym.—Gui (in ‡ *Rem.* 199-123)

O tu Palermo . . .   Bs   Act II

N. Rossi-Lemeni   in ‡ *G.ALP 1099*
(*Forza, Ernani, Nabucco*)   (‡ *QALP 10028: FALP 305*)

P. Schoeffler   in ‡ **Van.VRS 469**
(*Africaine, Meistersinger, etc.*)   (‡ *Ama.AVRS 6022*)

E. Pinza   in ‡ *Vic.LM 1751*
(*Don Carlos, Ernani, etc.*) (♭ *ERA 140;* in ‡ *FV.A 630233*)
     M. Reizen (*Russ*) (in ‡ *USSR.D 1317*)
     I. Petrov (*Russ*) (*USSR. 21458/9:* in ‡ *D 2607*)
   ⌘ J. Mardones (*AF.AGSB 27**)

In braccio alle dovizie   B   Act III
   ☆ H. Schlusnus (*Ger*) (in ‡ *Pol.* 18080 & 19039)
   ⌘ R. Stracciari (in ‡ *Sca.* 802*)

Sogno, o son desto? . . . Quando al mio sen
     T & B   Act III
   ☆ H. Roswaenge & H. Schlusnus (*Ger*) (in ‡ *CEd.* 7010)

Ballet Music   Act III
. . . L'Autunno only
   ☆ Covent Garden—Braithwaite (in ‡ *P.PMC 1008*)

Giorno di pianto   T   Act IV
   ☆ H. Roswaenge (*Ger*) (in ‡ *CEd.* 7010)

Mercè, dilette amiche   (Bolero)   S   Act V

M. Benetti   *Cet.AT 0359*
(*Catalani: La Wally—Ebben . . .*)

M. M. Callas   in ‡ *C.CX 1231*
(*A. Lecouvreur, Chénier, La Wally, etc.*)
             (‡ *QCX 10129;* Angel. 35233)

M. L. Gemelli   *Cet.AT 0401*
(*Zandonai: Giulietta e Romeo, aria*)

A. Stella   in ‡ *G.QALP 10096*
(*Forza, Ballo, etc.*)
   ⌘ R. Raisa (in ‡ *FRP. 3**)
     L. Blauvelt (*AF.AGSA 4**)

Excerpts included in *Lady & the Fool* Ballet, q.v. post

MISCELLANEOUS

(The) LADY & THE FOOL
Ballet — ARR. Mackerras   1954
COMPLETE RECORDING
     (The music is taken from the operas named)
1. **Prelude**   (Alzira)
2. **Adagio**   (Gerusalemme, Alzira)
3. **Divertissement**   (Vêpres siciliennes, Duet Act V)
4. **Tarantella**   (Un Giorno di regno, Giovanna d'Arco,
     Aroldo, Vêpres siciliennes (Tarantella, Act II), Due
     Foscari)
5. **Commedia**   (Un Giorno di regno, Aroldo)
5a. **Allegro vivace**   (Ernani)
6. **Grand Adage**   (Due Foscari, Ernani, Masnadieri, Macbeth,
     Attila)
7. **Scene**   (Attila)
     Entrée (Ernani, Vêpres siciliennes, Alzira)
8. **Midas' Solo**   (Un Giorno di regno, Gerusalemme)
8a. **Entrée & Prince's Solo**
9. **Dance (Girls' variation)** (Un Giorno di regno, Don Carlos
     Ballet excpts.)
10. **Captain's variation**   (Un Giorno di regno, Oberto)
11. **Coda. Pas de cinq** (Gerusalemme Ballet music, Attila
     Finale, Act II)
12. **Scene**   (Vêpres siciliennes)
     Pas de deux (Aroldo Finale, Masnadieri Duet)
13. **Finale**   (Ernani, Lombardi, Vêpres siciliennes, Aroldo,
     Luisa Miller, Gerusalemme)
14. **Epilogue—Adagio molto calmo** (Gerusalemme, Aroldo)

Philharmonia—Mackerras   ‡ *G.CLP 1059*

BALLET SUITE
     [Nos. in brackets refer to complete ballet, *above*]
1. **Tarantella** [4]   2. **Pas seul** [9]   3. **Pas de trois** (Galop) [11]
4. **Romantic pas de deux** [12, part]   5. **Divertissement** [3]
6. **Finale** [13, with concert ending]

New Sym.—R. Irving   ‡ *D.LW 5208*

VERGER, P. Maillard   (Contemp.)

SEE: † LA MUSIQUE ET LA POÉSIE

VERNON, Joseph   (1738-82)

SEE: † SHAKESPEARE SONGS, VOL. III

☆ = Re-issue of a recording to be found in previous volumes.

VERRALL, John (b. 1908)

(The) COWHERD AND THE SKY MAIDEN
Opera
COMPLETE RECORDING
Unspec. Artists   # ML. 7038/40
[announced but probably not issued]

Quartet, No. 4, strings
Washington Univ. Qtt.   # ML. 7028
(*Kohs: Vla. Concerto*)   [or # ML. 7004]

Quintet, pf. & str.
S. Balogh & Seattle Qtt.   # NWRS. 1

VERT, Juan: SEE: SOUTULLO & VERT

VETTER, Daniel (d. 1721)
SEE: † CANZONE SCORDATE

VIADANA, Ludovico Grossi[1]
(*c.* 1564-1645)

Cantate Domino
☆ Gregorian Institute Cho.—Vitry (in † # *GIOA.PM-LPI*)

Magnificat
Rennes Cath. Cho.—Orhant   # SM. 33-23
(*A. Gabrieli, Titelouze, Claude, etc.*)

O sacrum convivium
Treviso Cath. Cho.—d'Alessi
in # E. & AmVox.PL 8790
(† Motets of the Venetian School III)

VICTORIA, Tomás Luis de (*c.* 1548-1611)

[Roman figures refer to Vols. of the Complete edn.]

COLLECTIONS
Ave verum corpus (not in complete edn.)
Tenebrae factae sunt (Responsory, Good Friday) V
Caligaverunt oculi mei (idem)   V
Animam meam (idem)   V
Vere languores nostros   I
Vexilla regis . . . O Crux, ave   V
Popule meus   V
Vatican Cho.—Bartolucci   # Per.SPL 706
(*Anchieta, Binchois, Lassus, Palestrina*)

Ave Maria   VIII
Caligaverunt oculi mei (Responsory)   V
Duo Seraphim   I
Spanish Radio Cho.—Alonso   # *Mont.FM 41*
(*Rodrigo*)

Ave Maria   VIII
Jesu, dulcis memoria   VIII
O magnum mysterium   I
Polyphonic Cho.—Ribó   in # C.CX 1308
(*Morales, Brudieu, etc., & Spanish Trad.*) (# Angel. 35257)

MASS 'Vidi speciosam' 6 vv.   IV
Magnificat (VIII toni)   III
Pange lingua (Hymn)   V
O sacrum convivium 6 vv.   I
Salve regina (Antiphon) 5 vv.   VII 1576
Montserrat Abbey Cho.   # SM. 33-17
(*Gregorian Chant & Catalan Virelai*)

Magnificat IV toni   III
Lecco Acad. Cho.—Camillucci
E. & AmVox.PL 8930
(*Officium defunctorum*)

MASSES
Dominicalis VIII
... **Kyrie 'Orbis Factor'**
Stanford Univ. Cho.—Schmidt   in # ML. 7022
(† Madrigals & Motets)

Officium defunctorum VI Requiem, 6 vv. 1605-10
Pamplona Cha. Cho.—Morondo
in # Sel.LPG 8738
(† Spanish Renaissance Music)
Lecco Acad. Cho.—Camillucci
(*Magnificat*)   # E. & AmVox.PL 8930

O magnum mysterium   II 1592
O quam gloriosum   II 1583
☆ Welch Chorale   # Lyr.LL 46

MOTETS
Ave Maria 4 vv. VIII[2]
N.Y. Primavera Singers—Greenberg
in # Per.SPL 597
(† Renaissance Music)   (# Cpt.MC 20077)
Darlington Seminary Scola Cho.—Flusk
in # GIOA.DS 1
Lagun Onak Cho.—Mallea   *ArgOd. 57027*
(*Palestrina: Alma redemptoris Mater*) (also ArgOd. 67003)
Petits Chanteurs de la Renaissance
in # HSLP. 9007
(also in † Histoire de la Musique vocale)
☆ Manécanterie Cho. (*JpV.A 1267*)
... Excerpt (ed. L. Biggs) Biggs Family Ens. (in # *GIOA.BF I*)

Domine, non sum dignus 4 vv. I
... **Miserere mei** only
Harvard Glee Club—Woodworth
in # *Camb.CRC 101*
(*Palestrina, Lassus, etc.*)

Nigra sum sed formosa I 6 vv. 1576
Montserrat Monastery Cho.—Pujol
(*Nicolau, etc.*)   ♭ *G.7ERL 1012*

O Domine Jesu Christe V 6 vv. 1576
Montserrat Monastery Cho.—Pujol G.HMS 34
(† History of Music in Sound)   (in # Vic set LM 6029)

O magnum mysterium   I
Versailles Cath. Cho.—Roussel   # SM. 33-03
(*M. A. Charpentier, Couperin, Lalande, Marchand*)
(# Per.SPL 712)
Trinity Chu. Cho., New Haven—Byles
in # Over.LP 11
(*Praetorius, Holst & Carols, etc.*)
☆ St. Olaf Cho.—Christiansen (in # *Alld. 2002:*
♭ EP 2002)

O quam gloriosum   I
Angers Cath. Cho.—Poirier   # SM. 33-02
(*Soriano, etc.*)

O vos omnes   I
Quartetto Polifonico   in # D.LXT 2945
(† Choral Music)   (# Lon.LL 995)
N.Y. Primavera Singers—Greenberg
in # Per.SPL 597
(† Renaissance Music)   (# Cpt.MC 20077)
Helsinki Univ. Cho.—Turunen
in # Rem. 199-167
(*Sibelius, Palestrina, Palmgren, etc.*)
Montserrat Cho.—Pujol   ♭ *G.7ERL 1013*
(*Nicolau, etc.*)
U.O.S. Cho.—McConnell   in # UOS. 2
(*Carissimi, A. Scarlatti, Bach, etc.*)   (pte. rec.)

Pastores loquebantur ad invicem I 6 vv.
(labelled: *In Nativitate Domini*)
Trapp Family Singers—Wasner in # B.LAT 8038
(*Christmas Music*)   (# AmD.DL 9689: ♭ set ED 1200)

Popule meus   V
Regensburg Cath. Cho.—Schrems   *D.F 43802*
(*Lassus: Exaudi, Deus*)   (♭ D 17802: ♭ DX 1762)

---

[1] The recorded works are from *Concerti Ecclesiastici*, 1602.
[2] Presumed to be this setting, and not that for 8 vv. (I). SPL 597 definitely is for 4 vv.

Tantum ergo　V
　Welch Chorale　　　　　in ♯ **Lyr.LL 52**
　　(† Motets of the XVth & XVIth Centuries)

Vere languores nostros　I
　Welch Chorale　　　　　in ♯ **Lyr.LL 52**
　　(† Motets of the XVth & XVIth Centuries)

OFFICIUM HEBDOMADAE SANCTAE　V

MAUNDY THURSDAY
Incipit lamentatio Jeremiae Prophetae　4 vv.
Vau: Et egressus est　　　　　　　　4 vv.
Jod: Manum suam　　　　　　　　　5 vv.
Responsories 4 & 7　　　　　　　　　4 vv.
Benedictus ("*Cantique de Zacharie*")　4 vv
　Pamplona Cho.—Morondo　　♯ *Sel.LA 1071*

GOOD FRIDAY
Improperia: Popule meus　4 vv.
Heth: Cogitavit Dominus　(1st. verset)

EASTER EVE
Heth: Misericordiae Domini　(2 versets)
Aleph: Quomodo obscuratum　(2 versets)
　Pamplona Cho.—Morondo[1]　♯ *Lum.LD 2-108*

RESPONSORIES　4 vv.　V
COMPLETE RECORDING
　　(Nos. 1-3 are *Lectiones* in each case & not included)
MAUNDY THURSDAY

4. Amicus meus	5. Judas mercator
6. Unus ex discipulis	7. Eram quasi agnus
8. Una hora	9. Seniores populi

GOOD FRIDAY

4. Tamquam ad latronem	5. Tenebrae factae sunt
6. Animam meam dilectam	7. Tradiderunt me
8. Jesum tradidit impius	9. Caligaverunt oculi mei

EASTER EVE

4. Recessit pastor noster	5. O vos omnes
6. Ecce quomodo moritur	7. Astiterunt reges
8. Aestimatus sum	9. Sepulto Domino

　Montserrat Monastery Cho.—Segarra
　(4ss)　　　　　　　　　♯ **SM. 33-15/16**

GOOD FRIDAY
5. Tenebrae factae sunt
　Vienna Boys' Cho.—Brenn　in ♯ *EPhi.NBR 6013*
　(*Palestrina, Handl, etc.*)　(♯ *Phi.N 00624R*;
　　　　　　　　　　　　　in ♯ *AmC.ML 4873*)
　Elizondo Agrupación Coral
　　　　　　　　　　　　in ♯ **Nix.WLP 6209-1**
　[at Llangollen Eisteddfod]　(♯ *West.* set *WAL 209*)
　Quartetto Polifonico　　in ♯ **D.LXT 2945**
　(† Choral Music)　　　　　(♯ *Lon.LL 995*)

VIDAL, Peire (d. *c.* 1215)

SEE: † MONUMENTA ITALICAE MUSICAE

VIERNE, Louis (1870-1937)

ORGAN MUSIC
Carillon de Westminster, Op. 54, No. 6
　(No. 18 of *24 Pièces de Fantaisie, Opp. 51, 53, 54, 56*)
　R. Ellsasser　　　　　　♯ **MGM.E 3066**
　(*Ellsasser & Russell*)

　A. Hamme　　　　　　　in ♯ **SRS.H 1**
　(† Organ Recital)

　L. Farnam[2]　　　　　　♯ **CEd.CE 1040**
　(*Bach, Handel, Sowerby, Karg-Elert*)

　R. Owen　　　　　　　in ♯ **ASK. 3**
　(*Bach, Handel, Walther, etc.*)
　[organ of Christ Church, Bronxville, N.Y.]

Carillon de Longpont, Op. 31, No. 21
　J. Harms　　　　　　　in ♯ **Uni.UN 1004**
　(*Weinberger, Raasted, Peeters, Bach, etc.*)

SYMPHONIES
No. 1, D minor, Op. 14
　... No. 6, Finale
　M-C. Alain　　　　　　V♯ *Era.LDE 1015*
　(*below*)

　☆ E. P. Biggs (♭ *AmC.A 1883*; ♭ *Phi.N 409505E*;
　　　　　　　　　　　　　♭ *EPhi.NBE 11030*)

No. 2, E major, Op. 20
　P. Cochereau　　　　　♯ **LOL.OL 50103**
　[organ of Notre-Dame, Paris]　　(♯ *OL.LD 117*)

... **Scherzo**
　E. Linzel　　　　　　in ♯ **Moll.E4QP 7231**
　(*Reger, Widor, Dandrieu, etc.*)
　[organ of Washington Shrine, Alexandria, Va.]
　M-C. Alain　　　　　　V♯ *Era.LDE 1015*
　(*above & below*)
　[organ of Ste. Clotilde, Paris]

Prelude; Canzona, Op. 31, Nos. 5 & 12
　(from *24 pieces in free style*)
　N. Coke-Jephcott　　　　in ♯ **ASK. 8**
　(*Purcell, Bach, etc.*)

Toccata, Op. 53, No. 6
　(*Pièces de Fantaisie, No. 12*)
　M-C. Alain　(*above*)　　V♯ *Era.LDE 1015*

VIEUXTEMPS, Henri (1820-1881)

Ballade et Polonaise, G major, Op. 38
　vln. & pf. or orch.
　G. Octors & Belgium Radio Cha. Orch.
　—Doneux　　　　　　♯ *Gramo.GLP 2510*
　(*Ysaÿe*)

CONCERTOS, vln. & orch.
No. 4, D minor, Op. 31
　H. Krebbers & Residentie—v. Otterloo
　(*Paganini*)　　　　　　♯ *Phi.A 00263L*
　☆ Y. Menuhin & Philharmonia—Susskind
　　　　　　　　　　　　(♯ *G.FBLP/QBLP 1036*)

No. 5, A minor, Op. 37
　Y. Menuhin & Philharmonia—Pritchard
　(*Chausson*)　　　　　　♯ *Vic.LHMV 30*
　L. Kogan & State Sym.—Kondrashin
　　　　　　　　　　　　♯*USSR.D 01445*
　(*Wieniawski: Faust Fantasia*)

Suite, D major, Op. 43　vln. & pf.
　... 1, Prelude; 2, Minuet; 4, Gavotte
　Y. Sitkovetzky & B. Davidovich ♯ *USSR.D 2167*
　(*Paganini & Bazzini*)
　[No. 4 only with *Bazzini*, on *USSRM.D 00502*]

Souvenir, Op. 7, No. 3　vln. & pf.
　D. Oistrakh & pf.　　　　*USSR. 19537*
　(*Sarasate: Zortzico*)

Tarantelle, A minor, Op. 22, No. 4　vln. & pf.
　I. Oistrakh & I. Kollegorskaya in ♯*Van.VRS 461*
　(*Szymanowski, Wieniawski, Vitali, etc.*)

VILCHES　(fl. XV-XVIth Cent.)

SEE: † SPANISH MUSIC (*c.* 1500)

VILLA-LOBOS, Heitor (b. 1887)

COLLECTION OF PIANO MUSIC　[No. 2]
Chôros No. 5, Alma Brasileira　1926
CICLO BRASILEIRO
... No. 2, Impressões seresteiras
CIRANDAS　1926
... No. 5, Pobre Céga
... No. 6, Passa, passa, gavião
... No. 10, O pintor de Cannahy
GUIA PRATICO
... No. 76, A maré encheu
　☆ E. Ballon　　　　　　♯ *D.LW 5081*
　　　　　　　　　　　　(♯ *Lon.LD 9095*)

BACHIANAS BRASILEIRAS
No. 1　8 vlcs.　1930　f.p. 1932
　Pittsburgh Sym. Members—Steinberg
　(*Milhaud*)　　　　　　♯ **PFCM.CB 166**
　Ens.—Bloomfield　　　　♯ **MGM.E 3105**
　(*No. 4*)
　☆ Brazilian Fest. Orch. Members—Marx
　　　　　　　　　　　　(♯ *Vic.LCT 1143*)
　(*continued on next page*)

---

[1] The contents of this disc have been deduced from the cover notes; full titles are not given, and it has not been possible to hear the disc.
[2] Recorded from an Austin organ roll of 1930.　Registration by C. Watters.

BACHIANAS BRASILEIRAS (*continued*)
No. 2 orch. 1930
... 4th movt. Toccata (The little train of Caipira) only
Orch.—Kostelanetz   in ♯ AmC.CL 798
(*Liadov, R. Strauss, etc.*)   (o.n. ML 4692)

No. 4 pf. 1930-36
M. Pressler (*No. 1*)   ♯ MGM.E 3105

No. 5 S, 8 vlcs. & cbs. 1938-45
P. Curtin & Members of Boston Orch. Soc.
—Page   ♭ Nix.EP 652
(*Bach & Stravinsky in ♯ SOT. 1062*)
A. Ribeiro & Ens.—Siqueira **V♯CdM.LDY 8119**
(*Ovalle & Siqueira*)
☆ L. Albanese & Ens.—Stokowski   ♯ G.BLP 1075
(*Tchaikovsky*)   (G.DB 4322: ♯ QBLP 1025)
... 1st movt., **Aria**, only 1938
▽ R. V. Correa & Ens.—Villa-Lobos (Od. 104/5)

No. 6 fl. & bsn. 1938
New Art Wind Duo.[1]   ♯ CEd.CE 2002
(*Chôros No. 2 & Quintet for Wind*)
S. Baron & B. Garfield   ♯ Phil.PH 110
(*Chôros No. 2, Quintette, & Wilder*)

No. 8 orch. 1944
French Nat.—Villa-Lobos   ♯ C.FCX 346
(*Momo precoce*)   (♯ Angel. 35179; ArgA.CBX 140)

(O) Canto do cisne negro vlc. (or vln.) & pf. 1917
L. W. Pratesi (vlc.), M. Samek (hp.)
in ♯ *ArgOd.LDC 529*
(*Pizzetti, Haydn, Zandonai, etc.*)

CHÔROS
No. 2 fl. & clarinet 1924
New Art Wind Duo[1]   ♯ CEd.CE 2002
(*above & below*)
S. Baron & D. Glazer   ♯ Phil.PH 110
(*above, below, & Wilder*)

No. 5, Alma brasileira pf. solo 1925
L. Engdahl   ♯ MGM.E 3158
(*below; & Milhaud*)
☆ E. Ballon (*BrzD.B 288983*)
▽ T. Terán (BrzCont. 30101)

No. 6 orch. 1926
R.I.A.S. Sym.—Villa-Lobos   ♯ Rem. 199-207
(*Enesco*)

No. 7 vln., vlc., sax., cl., ob., fl. & perc. 1924
Ens.—I. Solomon   ♯ MGM.E 3155
(*Chavez, Revueltas, Surinach*)

CIRANDAS 16 pieces pf. 1926
1. Therezinha de Jesus. 2. A Condessa. 3. Senhora Dona
Sancha. 4. O cravo brigou com a Rosa. 5. Pobre Céga.
6. Passa, passa, gavião. 7. Xô, xô, passarinho. 8. Vamos
atraz... 9. Fui no tóróró. 10. O pintor de Cannahy.
11. N'esta rua. 12. Olha o passarinho. 13. A Procura de
uma Agulha. 14. A Conôa Virou. 15. Que lindos olhos.
16. Có, có, có.
COMPLETE RECORDING
J. Battista   ♯ MGM.E 3020

Dawn in a tropical forest Overture orch. f.p. 1954
Louisville—Whitney   ♯ LO. 1
(*Creston & H. Stevens*)

Duo, violin & viola 1946
☆ L. & R. Persinger (♯ Cpt.MC 20076)

Momo precoce Fantasia, pf. & orch. 1929
M. Tagliaferro & French Nat.—Villa-Lobos
♯ C.FCX 346
(*above*)   (♯ Angel. 35179; BrzA.CBX 140)

Nonet: Impressão rapidá de todo o Brasil 1923
fl., ob., cl., sax., bsn., celeste, hp., perc. & mixed cho.
Concert Arts Ens. & R. Wagner Cho.—Wagner
♯ DCap.CTL 7037
(*Quatuor*) (T.LCE 8191)   (♯ Cap.P 8191)
(Finale only in ♯ Cap.SAL 9020)
☆ Schola Cantorum—Ross   ♯ Vic.LCT 1143
(*Bachianas Brasileiras, etc.*)

Poema singelo pf. 1942
L. Engdahl   ♯ MGM.E 3158
(*above, below & Milhaud*)

PART SONGS
Lendas Amerindias 1952
1. O lurupari o menino   2. O lurupari e o caeador
5th Ave. High School Cho.—Lowe
in ♯ PFCM.CB 161
(*Phillips, Poulenc, Copland, etc.*)

Prece sem palavras male cho. 1931
Pamplona Cha. Cho.—Morondo
in **V♯** *Sel.LLA 1007*
(*Stravinsky, Bartók, etc.*)

(6) PRELUDES guitar 1940
No. 1, E minor
M. A. Funes[2]   *ArgOd.* 56580
(*Grieg: Anitra's Dance*)
☆ A. Segovia (in † ♯ B.AXTL 1060)

No. 4, E minor
M. Gangi   ♭ *ItV.A72R 0043*
(*Anon., Fortea, Purcell*)
A. Segovia   in ♯ B.AXTL 1069
(† Segovia Evening II)   (♯ AmD.DL 9751)

(A) PRÓLE DO BÉBÉ pf.
(8 pieces, Book I, 1918; 9 pieces, Book II, 1921)
COMPLETE RECORDING of Books I & II
J. Echániz   ♯ West.WN 18065
BOOK I, COMPLETE
J. Abrams   ♯ EMS. 10
(*Tres Marias & Rudepôema*)
M. Regules ("Siena" pf.)   ♯ Eso.ESP 3002
(*Albeniz, Turina, Mompou*)

Quartet, fl., oboe, cl., & bsn. 1928
New Art Wind Qtt.   ♯ Nix.WLP 5360
(*below*)   (♯ West.WL 5360)

Quatuor fl., hp., celesta, sax., & fem. cho. 1921
Concert Arts Ens. & R. Wagner Chorale
♯ DCap.CTL 7037
(*Nonet*)   (♯ Cap.P 8191)
(excerpt also in ♯ Cap.LAL 9024)

Quintet fl., ob., cor ang., cl., bsn. 1928
New Art Wind Quintet (n.v.) ♯ Nix.WLP 5360
(*Quartet & Trio*)   (♯ West.WL 5360)
New Art Wind Quintet[3]   ♯ CEd.CE 2002
(*Chôros No. 2 & Bachiana Brasileira, No. 6*)
—REVISED VERSION 1953, horn replacing cor anglais
"Quintette en forme de Chôros"
N.Y. Wind Quintet   ♯ Phil.PH 110
(*above*)

Rudepôema pf. 1921-6
J. Abrams   ♯ EMS. 10
(*Próle do Bébé & Tres Marias*)

Saudades das Selvas Brasileiras pf. 1927
L. Engdahl   ♯ MGM.E 3158
(*above, below & Milhaud*)

SONATAS, vln. & pf. (Fantasias)
No. 1 1912
☆ R. Posselt & A. Sly (in ♯ Esq.TW 14-005)

SONGS
(12) Serestas
... **No. 8, Canção do carreiro**
☆ E. Houston (S) (in ♯ Vic.LCT 1143: ♭ set ERBT 4)

(12) STUDIES guitar 1929
No. 1, E minor
A. Carlevaro   P.PXO 1073
(♯s—*Barrico: Study; & Castelnuovo-Tedesco*)
C. Aubin   in ♯ Eko.LG 1
(† Guitar Recital)
No. 7, E major
☆ A. Segovia (in † ♯ D.UAT 273142)

---
[1] This disc was announced but perhaps not issued. The recordings may have been transferred to PH 110.
[2] It is possible that this is the Study No. 1. Confusion frequently arises.
[3] Announced but may never have been issued; possibly identical with PH 110, below.

No. 11, A major
M. L. Anido　　　　　　　　　　**ArgOd. 66058**
(Mozart: Andante)

Suite floral, Op. 97 pf. 1917
L. Engdahl　　　　　　　　　　♯ **MGM.E 3158**
(above & Milhaud)

(As) Tres Marias pf. 1939
　　　(Alnitah; Alnilam; Mintika)
J. Abrams　　　　　　　　　　♯ **EMS. 10**
(Próle do Bébé & Rudepôema)

TRIO, vln., vla., vlc. 1945
Members of New York Qtt.　　♯ *AmC.ML 2214*

TRIO, oboe, clar., bsn. 1921
M. Kaplan, I. Neidrich, T. di Dario
　　　　　　　　　　　♯ **Nix.WLP 5360**
(Quatuor & Quintet)　　　　(♯ West.WL 5360)

Uirapúrú (Ballet) orch. 1917
☆ N.Y.P.S.O.—Kurtz　　　　♯ *C.SX 1011*
　(Chopin: Les Sylphides) [& 2ss, ♭ *C.SEBL 7045*]

VINCENT, John (b. 1902)

Quartet, No. 1, G major str.
American Art Qtt.　　　　　　♯ *Cty.C 2002*

VINCENZO d'ARIMINI (fl. XIVth Cent.)

SEE: † ANTHOLOGIE SONORE

VINCI, Leonardo (1690-1730)

(12) SONATAS, flute & continuo
No. 1, D major
S. Gazzelloni & J. Panenka (pf.)　　**U.H 24386**
(2ss)

Unid. Largo — ARR. PF.
L. Hernádi　　　　　　　　　　**U.H 24430**
(D. Scarlatti: Sonata, E major)

VIOTTI, Giovanni Battista (1755-1824)

CONCERTOS, vln. & orch.
No. 4, D major ("Bk. II, No. 2")
A. Abussi & Italian Cha.—Jenkins
　　　　　　　　　　　♯ **HS.HSL 137**
(Albinoni & Durante)　　　(in set HSL-N)

No. 23, G major
J. Shermont & O. Schulhof (pf.) ♯ **Rem.YV 1**
(with teaching material)

Concerto, E flat major, pf., vln. & orch.[1] c. 1787
C. Bussotti, A. Abussi & Italian Cha.—Jenkins
　　　　　　　　　　　♯ **HS.HSL 78**
(Brunetti)　　　　　　　　(in set HSL-C)

VISÉE, Robert de (c. 1650-1725)

GUITAR MUSIC (Book I, 1682; Book II, 1686)
Suite, D minor (ed. Pujol, from Book II)
(Prelude, Allemande, Courante, Sarabande, Gavotte, Minuets I
& II, Bourrée, Gigue)
K. Scheit　　　　　　　in ♯ **Van.BG 548**
(† Renaissance & Baroque)
☆ H. Leeb (in † ♯ *Nix.WLP 5085* & **V**♯ *Sel.LAP 1021*)

... Prelude, Allemande, Sarabande, Gigue
M. D. Cano　　　　　　　　*Dur.AI 10229*
(with *Bach & Sor*, ♯ *MSE 2)*
A. Lagoya (in ♭ *Pat.D 113*)

... Sarabande, Gavotte, Bourrée, Gigue
☆ A. Segovia (in † ♯ *D.UAT 273142* ‒ B.AXTL 1010,
　　Supp. II)

... Sarabande, Minuet II, Bourrée
☆ J. Lafon (in † ♯ *HS.AS 13* ‒ AS. 89, WERM)

Prelude & Allemande, D major (Book I)
☆ A. Segovia, as above

Prelude (unid.)　☆ J. Lafon, as above

Entrada, Giga, Minuet, Bourrée
☆ A. Segovia (in ♯ *D.UMT 273029* = AmD.DL 8022,
　　WERM)

Gavotte, Minuet, Bourrée
S. Pastor　　　　　　in ♯ **NRI.NRLP 5005**
(Fortea, Sor, Tarrega, Pastor)

Prelude, Sarabande, Gavotte, Menuet, Bourrée,
　Andante, Gigue
J. Borredon　　　　　　　　♭ *Pat.EG 148*
(Borredon: Suite)

VITALI, Giovanni Battista (c. 1644-1692)

Sonata, Op. 2, No. 3, E minor 2 vlns. & cont.
Basil Lam Ensemble　　　　　**G.HMS 64**
(† History of Music in Sound)　(in ♯ Vic. set LM 6031)

VITALI, Tommaso Antonio
　　　　　　　　　　　　　　(c. 1665-c. 1735)

Ciaccona, G minor vln. & continuo (ed. David)
N. Milstein & A. Balsam (pf.)　♯ **Cap.P 8315**
(Handel & Prokofiev)

H. Szeryng & T. Janopoulo (pf.)　♯ *Od.OD 1008*
(Kreisler, Wieniawski, Paganini)　(in ♯ *ArgOd.LDC 7504*)

I. Oistrakh & A. Makarov (pf.)♯*CdM.LDA 8092*
(Bach, Mozart)(in ♯*Van.VRS 461*; & ♯ *Csm.CRLP 193, d.v.)*

R. Odnoposoff & H. Wehrle (org.)
(Tartini, Geminiani)　　　　♯ **CHS.CHS 1170**

VITALINI, Alberico (b. 1921)

Meditation on the first 'Mistero Doloroso' str. orch.
Vatican Radio Orch.—Vitalini[2]
　　　　　　　　　　in ♯ **Csm.CLPS 1050**

Rinascita orch.
Rome Qtt. Soc. Cha.—Vitalini[3]
　　　　　　　　　　　♯ **Csm.CLPS 1051**
(below, Britten & Martucci)

Terra siciliana pf. & organ
A. Ruggieri & A. Vitalini[3]　♯ **Csm.CLPS 1051**
(above, Britten & Martucci)

VITTADINI, Franco (1884-1948)

ANIMA ALLEGRA Opera 3 Acts 1921
Ancora non so bene
D. Cestari (T)　　　　　　　*Cet.AT 0399*
(Butterfly—Addio fiorito asil)

VIVALDI, Antonio (c. 1675-1741)

(P. = Classification in Pincherle's Thematic Index)

I. CONCERTOS

A. *WITH* (original) *OPUS NUMBERS*
CONCERTOS, Op. 3 (L'Estro Armonico)
No. 1, D major　　　4 vlns.
No. 7, F major　　　4 vlns. & vlc. obb.
Pro Musica—Saguer　　　　♯ **Sel.LAG 1014**
(Concertos, P. 227 & 349)
[J. Champeil, L. Yordanoff, L. Gali & R. Gendre, vlns.;
G. Marchesini, vlc.]

---

[1] From edition in Bibliothèque nationale, Paris.
[2] This work was included on this disc in the first listings and was reviewed in N.Y. Times (see *Notes*, Sept. 1953); but it has
vanished from later catalogues. See *Vivaldi: Stabat Mater.*
[3] Announced but apparently not issued.

No. 2, G minor   2 vlns. vlc. & str.
No. 12, E major   vln. & str.
L. Ferro & G. Mozzato (vlns.), B. Mazzacurati
(vlc.) & Virtuosi di Roma—Fasano
♯ **AmD.DL 9729**
(*No. 8, below; & Vln. Concerto C mi., P 419*)
(♯ *D.UAT 273589*)

No. 2 . . . 2nd movt. only, in *Golden Coach* film music

No. 6, A minor   vln. & orch.[1]
No. 11, D minor   2 vlns. vlc. & str.
J. Tomasow, W. Hübner & Vienna State Op.
Cha. Orch.—Leonhardt   ♯ **Nix.PVL 7018**
(*Concertos, Op. 10, No. 3 & Op. 12, No. 1*)
[R. Harand, vlc.]   (♯ *Van.BG 538; Ama.AVRS 6002*)

No. 6, A minor   — ARR. HARMONICA & ORCH.
☆ L. Adler & Winterthur Sym.—Goehr
(in ♯ *FMer.MLP 7504*)

No. 8, A minor   2 vlns.
No. 10, B minor   4 vlns.
No. 11, D minor   2 vlns.
Saar Cha.—Ristenpart   ♯ *DFr.EX 25014/5*
(*Ob. Concerto, F major*)

No. 8, A minor   2 vlns.
Società Corelli   in ♯ **Vic.LM 1767**
(*Sinfonia, Cantata; & Geminiani, Marcello, Carissimi*)
(in ♭ *set WDM 1767; ♯ ItV.A12R 0098*)

G. Mozzato, E. Malanotte & Virtuosi di Roma
—Fasano   ♯ **AmD.DL 9729**
(*Concerti, above, & Vln., C mi., P 419*) (♯ *D.UAT 273589*)

R. Gendre, P. Doukan & Ens.—Froment
(*Cimarosa, Mozart*)   ♯ *CND. 1003*
☆ R. Gendre, J. Dejean, Paris Cha.—Duvauchelle
(♯ *Lum.LD 2-401*)

No. 9, D major   vln. & str.
M. Cervera & I Musici Ens.   ♯ **C.CX 1170**
(*Concertos, Str. Orch. P 86, 235; Vla d'amore P 288*)
(♯ *QCX 10038: FCX 304; Angel. 35087*)
☆ J. Fournier & Str. Orch. (in † ♯ *HS.AS 31*)

— ARR. VLC & PF.   Maréchal
☆ J. Starker & M. Meyer (♯ *Eli.PLPE 5004;*
Cum.CPR 317)

No. 10, B minor   4 vlns.
Allegro Cha. Orch.—Tubbs   ♯ **Allo. 3146**
(*Sonata; D. Scarlatti & Telemann*)
☆ Eidus, Shulman, Buldrini, Graeler & Ens.
(♯ *Cum.CS 194*)

No. 11, D minor   2 vlns.
Augsburg Cha. Orch.—Deyle   † ♯ **AS. 3007LD**
(*J. C. Bach, Locatelli, Pergolesi*)   (♯ *HS.AS 39*)
☆ Dumbarton Oaks Cha.—Schneider (♭ *Mer.EP 1-5049:*
♭ *FMer.MEP 14521*)

— ARR. Stokowski
Sym. Orch.—Stokowski   in ♯ **Vic.LM 1721**
(*Cesti, Frescobaldi, Palestrina, etc.*)   (in ♭ *set WDM 1721*)
(in ♯ *G.FALP 245; ItV.A12R 0040*)

. . . 2nd movt., Largo, only
Berlin Radio Cha.—Haarth   *Eta. 120102*
(*Bach: Suite 2, s. 5*)

— — ARR. VLC. & PF.
☆ S. Popoff (in ♯ *Vien.LPR 1022*)

— — ARR. ORGAN   Asma[2]
F. Asma   ♯ *Phi.S 06033R*
(*Pachelbel & Micheelsen*)

(12) CONCERTOS, Op. 4, vln. & str.
(La Stravaganza)
COMPLETE RECORDING
R. Barchet & Stuttgart Pro Musica Orch.
—Reinhardt   ♯ **E. & AmVox. set DL 103**
(6ss) [H. Elsner, hpsi.]

No. 1, B flat major
Paris Collegium Mus.—Douatte[3]   ♯ *Eko.LM 3*
(*Concertos, C minor & G major, P 427 & 143*)

(12) CONCERTOS, Op. 8, vln. & str.   1725
(Il Cimento dell' Armonia e dell' Invenzione)
COMPLETE RECORDING
R. Barchet & Stuttgart Pro Musica—R.
Reinhardt   ♯ **E. & AmVox. set DL 173**
(6ss)   [Nos. 1-4 only, ♯ *Orb.BL 708; PaV.VP 390*]
COLLECTIONS
Nos. 1-4: 'Le quattro Stagioni'
Virtuosi di Roma—Fasano   ♯ **G.ALP 1234**
(♯ *FALP 373: QALP 10032; No. 5 on Vic.LHMV 26*)

G. Alès & Paris Collegium Musicum—Douatte
♯ **Cum.CCX 227P**
[also listed as ♯ *QS.LQS 102 & ♯ Cum.CCX 227 & 278;*
the latter had spoken narration]

F. Ayo & I Musici Ens.[4]   ♯ **Phi.A 00301L**
(♯ *Epic.LC 3216*)

J. Corigliano & N.Y.P.S.O.—Cantelli
♯ **EPhi.ABL 3063**[5]
(♯ *AmC.ML 5044*)

T. Bacchetta & Sinfonia Ens.—Witold
♯ *Cpt.MC 20108*

G. Zazofsky & Zimbler Sinfonietta   ♯ *Bo.B 400*

☆ Santa Cecilia Acad.—Molinari (♯ *FSor.CS 543*)
L. Kaufman & Str. Orch.—Swoboda (♯ *MMS. 56*)

Nos. 5-12
5. E flat major (La Tempesta di mare)
6. C major (Il Piacere)
7. D minor   8. G minor   9. D minor
10. B flat major (La Caccia)   11. D major
12. C major
G. Alès & Paris Coll. Mus.—Douatte
♯ *QS.LQS 103/4*
[M-L. Girod, org.; J. Wiederker, vlc.]
(*Nos. 5, 6, 11, 12, on 103; 7-10 on 104*)

Nos. 6, 7, 9, 11
☆ L. Kaufman & orch.—Dahinden (♯ *MMS. 104*)

No. 1, E major (Primavera)
. . . 3rd movt., Allegro only (*Danza pastorale*)
☆ Virtuosi di Roma—Fasano   in ♯ *B.AXTL 1032*
(*Torelli, Boccherini, etc.*) (♯ *D.UAT 273551;*
Fnt.LP 3004)

No. 5, E flat major (La Tempesta di mare)
E. Malanotte & Virtuosi di Roma—Fasano
♯ **G.QALP 10113**
(*G ma, 2 Mandolines; C mi., str. orch., P 427;*
A ma., vln. & vlc. P 238)
(*Nos. 1-4, on ♯ Vic.LHMV 26*)

No. 6, C major (Il Piacere)
Y. Menuhin & Philharmonia—Boult
(*Bach & Handel*)   ♯ **Vic.LHMV 16**

No. 9, D minor   vln. or ob. (=P 259)
C. Maisonneuve (ob.) & O.L. Ens.—Froment
♯ **LOL.OL 50073**
(♯ *OL.LD 73*)[6]
(*Concertos—Ob., F ma.; Ob. & vln., B♭; Str. Orch. F ma. &*
A ma.)

P. Pierlot (ob.) & Ens.—Witold
♯ **LI.TWV 91052**
(♯ *Cpt.MC 20043*)
(*Concertos—2 vlns. & 2 vlcs.; Bsn., E mi.; 2 vlns., B♭ ma.*)
(*Bsn., E mi.; & Albinoni, on ♯ Per.SPL 723*)

R. Zanfini (ob.) & Virtuosi di Roma—Fasano
♯ **B.AXTL 1061**
(*Concertos—Vla. d'am., P 288; str. orch., P 410; Vln. &*
2 vlcs., P 58)   (♯ *AmD.DL 9679; Fnt.LP 3002*)

R. Casier (ob.) & Paris Cha.—Jouve
♯ **LT.MEL 94005**
(*Concerto, ob. & bsn., P 129*) (♯ *T.TW 30016;*
V♯ *Sel.LLA 1081*)
(*Concertos—P 383, 72 & Op. 10, No. 5, on ♯ Sel.LP 8702;*
T.NLB 6081; ♯ West.WL 5341*)

E. Schuster & Cha. Orch.—Vardi   ♯CEd.CE 1062
(*Handel & Telemann*)
[& for practice, without oboe, ♯ *MMO 301*]
☆ E. Parolari (ob.) & Winterthur Sym.—Dahinden
(♯ *MMS. 84 & CHS.CHS 1242*)

---

[1] Ed. Nachez.   [2] For Bach's version *see* Bach: Concertos.   [3] Labelled "No. 2."
[4] Ed. Bryks. This is part of Monumenta Italicae Musicae series.   [5] Announced but not issued.
[6] LD 73 is announced as containing 6 concerti, not 5 as OL 50073; but we have failed in attempts to confirm contents. It
may even be entirely different, or non-existent.

(12) CONCERTOS, Op. 9 (La Cetra) 1728
COMPLETE
☆ L. Kaufman & Fr. Nat. Radio Str. (♯ Clc 6197/8)

(6) CONCERTOS, Op. 10, flute & orch. 1729-30
COMPLETE

No. 1, F major (La tempesta di mare)
No. 2, G minor (La notte)
No. 3, D major (Il gardellino)
No. 4, G major
No. 5, F major (con sordini)
No. 6, G major

J-P. Rampal & Saar Cha.—Ristenpart
                                    ♯ DFr. 129
[R. Veyron-Lacroix, hpsi.]

☆ J-P. Rampal & Cha. Orch.—Froment ♯ Fel.RL 89003
[R. Veyron-Lacroix, hpsi.]   (♯ Clc. 6070)

No. 2, G minor (La notte)
G. Tassinari & Milan Angelicum—Gerelli
                                    Ang.SA 3016
(2ss) (ed. W. Fortner)
E. v. Royen & Alma Musica Quintet[1]
                                    ♯ LT.DTL 93046
(Gabrieli, Willaert, Sweelinck, Bach, Mozart)
                        (♯ Sel.LAG 1019; T.LT 6551)
G. Novello & Venice Cha.—Ephrikian
                                    ♯ Strad.STR 621
(below)   (♯ Cpt.MC 20078)
G. Pellegrini & Virtuosi di Roma—Fasano
                                    ♯ AmD.DL 9684
(Concertos—2 vlcs., P 411; Vln. & vlc., P 388; & Ob. & vln.,
P 406)   (♯ D.UAT 273574; SpC.CCL 35012)

No. 3, D major (Il gardellino)
L. Pfersmann & Vienna State Op. Cha. Orch.
  —Leonhardt   ♯ Nix.PVL 7018
(Concertos, Op. 12, No. 1 & Op. 3, Nos. 6 & 11)
                        (♯ Van.BG 538; Ama.AVRS 6002)
... Excerpt in Golden Coach film music, q.v.

No. 5, F major
J. Castagnier & Paris Cha.—Jouve ♯ Sel.LP 8702
(Concertos, Op. 8, No. 9; P 72 & P 383) (♯ T.NLB 6081)

CONCERTOS, Op. 12, Violin & Strings
No. 1, G minor (ed. Nachez)
J. Tomasow & Vienna State Op. Cha. Orch.
  —Leonhardt   ♯ Nix.PVL 7018
(Concerto, Op. 3, Nos. 6 & 11 & Op. 10, No. 3)
                        (♯ Van.BG 538; Ama.AVRS 6002)

B. CONCERTOS, without Opus number
[Concertos marked (O) are listed by Fanna in Vol. XII as
Orch. Concertos, but by Pincherle as solo, etc., concertos,
and mainly so performed.]

BASSOON
C major   P. 69
A. Montanari & Milan Angelicum—Gerelli
(2ss)   Ang.SA 3015
A minor   P. 72
G. Faisandier & Paris Cha.—Jouve
                                    ♯ Sel.LP 8702
(Concertos—P 383, Op. 8, No. 9 & Op. 10, No. 5)
                        (♯ T.NLB 6081; West.WL 5341)
E minor   P. 137
P. Hongne & Ens.—Witold ♯ LI.TWV 91052
(Concertos—Op. 8, No. 9; 2 vlns., Bb major; 2 vlns. &
2 vlcs. D ma.)   (♯ Cpt.MC 20043)
(Concerto, Op. 8, No. 9 & Albinoni, on ♯ Per.SPL 723)
B flat major   P. 386
G. Faisandier & Cha. Orch.—Cartigny
                                    ♯ Sel.LA 1080
(Concertos, 2 obs. & 2 cl., C ma.; Fl., A mi.)
B flat major   P. 401 (La Notte)
... Excerpts in Golden Coach film music

2 CORNI DA CACCIA
F major   P. 273   (with 2 ob. & bsn.) (O)
Anon. Horns & Venice Cha.—Ephrikian
                                    ♯ Strad.STR 621
(Op. 10, No. 2 & oboe, P 385)   (♯ Cpt.MC 20078)
F major   P. 320   (trs. to E flat major)
☆ F. Hausdörfer & H. Sevenstern (tpts.) & Sym.
  —Ackermann (♯ CHS.CHS 1242)[2]

FLUTE
A minor   P. 77
J. Castagnier & Cha. Orch.—Cartigny
                                    ♯ Sel.LA 1080
(Concerto, Bsn., B flat ma.; 2 obs. & 2 cl., C ma.)

FLUTE, OBOE, VIOLIN, BASSOON
D major   (La Pastorella) P. 204 fl., ob., vln., bsn. & cont.[3]
G minor   P. 402 fl., ob., bsn.[4]
F major   P. 322 fl., vln., bsn., cont.[5]
J-P. Rampal (fl.), P. Pierlot (ob.), P. Hongne
  (bsn.), R. Gendre (vln.), R. Veyron-Lacroix
  (hpsi.)   ♯ HS.HSL 82
(Sonatas) [P 402 also on V ♯ BàM.LD 1003] (♯ BàM.LD 06
F major, fl., ob., vln., bsn. & cont.   P. 323
D major, fl., ob., bsn.   P. 198
D major, fl., ob., vln., bsn. & cont.   P. 207
J-P. Rampal, P. Pierlot, R. Gendre, P. Hongne,
  R. Veyron-Lacroix   ♯ BàM.LD 013
(Sonatas)   (♯ HS.HSL 116)
G minor   P. 402 fl., ob., bsn.[6]
Paris Wind Ens.   ♯ Phi.A 77403L
(Mozart, Haydn)
G. Peloso, F. Ranzani, E. Mucetti
                                    ♯ Csm.CLPS 1047
(Leo, Blodek, Busoni) (originally announced on CLPS 1015)
G minor   P. 360   (ed. Veyron-Lacroix)[7]
☆ J-P. Rampal, P. Pierlot, R. Gendre, P. Hongne,
  R. Veyron-Lacroix   ♯ HS.HSL 80

MANDOLINE
C major[8]   P. 134
S. Postma & Caecilia Mandoline Ens.—Dekker[9]
                                    ♯ Phi.N 00686R
(Beethoven, Hasse, Mozart)
N. Catania & Angelicum—Janes ♯ Ang.LPA 956
(Bonporti, Bettinelli, Debussy)
(Concerto, Str. orch., G minor & Bonporti on ♯ LPA 957)

TWO MANDOLINES
G major   P. 133
G. Anedda, F. Cornacchia, Virtuosi di Roma
  —Fasano   ♯ G.QALP 10113
(C mi., str. orch., P 427; Op. 8, No. 5; A ma., vln. vlc., P 238)

OBOE
F major   P. 306
H. Schneider & Saar Cha.—Ristenpart
                                    ♯ DFr.EX 25014
(Concerto, Op. 3, No. 10)
C. Maisonneuve & O.L. Ens.—Froment
                                    ♯ LOL.OL 50073
                                    (♯ OL.LD 73)[10]
(Concertos—ob. & vln., P 406; Ob., Op. 8, No. 9; & Str.
orch. P 292 & 235)
R. Zanfini & Virtuosi di Roma—Fasano
                                    ♯ G.BLP 1042
(Vln. Concerto, C major)   (♯ FBLP 1054: QBLP 5019)
(Clementi & Corelli, ♯ Vic.LHMV 14)
☆ E. Parolari & Winterthur Sym.—Dahinden
                                    (♯ CHS.CHS 1242)
B flat major   P.385 (O) (with cor ang.—"Funebre")
Anon. soloist & Venice Cha.—Ephrikian
[R. Fantuzzi (vln.)]   ♯ Strad.STR 621
(Op. 10, No. 2; 2 corni, P 273; etc.) (♯ Cpt.MC 20078)

TWO OBOES
C major   P. 85   ... 3rd movt. only
Included in Golden Coach film music, see below

---

[1] 1st Vln. part played by Oboe; ed. van Royen.
[2] This is ☆ of ♯ CHS.G 6 which is not P. 273; it was wrongly entered in Supp. II on faith of erroneous information.
[3] Orig. 2 fl., violetta, bsn. and cont. Recording follows Malipiero edn.
[4] Played without cont. inst. following Fanna edn.   [5] Orig. fl. and str. orch. Recording follows Malipiero edn.
[6] No continuo in Fanna edn.; P. regards rather as a Sonata a 3.   [7] Orig. fl., ob., violetta, bsn. and cont.
[8] Listed by Pincherle as G major.   [9] Acc. ARR. 2 mandolines, mandola, guitar, hpsi. and cbs.
[10] LD 73 is announced as containing 6 concerti, not 5, as OL 50073, but we have failed in attempts to confirm contents.

OBOE & BASSOON
G major   P. 129
  R. Casier, G. Faisandier & Orch.—Cartigny
                                    ♯ *LT.MEL 94005*
  (*Concerto, Op. 8, No. 9*) (♯ *T.TW 30016;* **V**♯ *Sel.LLA 1081*)

OBOE & VIOLIN
B flat major   P. 406
  C. Maisonneuve, G. Alès & O.L. Ens.—Froment
                                    ♯ *LOL.OL 50073*
                                    (♯ OL.LD 73)[1]
  (*Ob. Concertos P 306 & Op. 8, No. 9; Str. Orch. P 292 &
  P 235*)

  L. Brain, W. Roberts & orch.—Goldsbrough
                                    G.HMS 68
  († *History of Music in Sound*)   (in ♯ Vic. set LM 6031)

  R. Zanfini, A. Pelliccia & Virtuosi di Roma
  —Fasano   ♯ *AmD.DL 9684*
  (*Concertos, 2 vlcs., P 411; Vln. & vlc., P 388; Op. 10-2*)
                                    (♯ *D.UAT 273574;* SpC.CCL 35012)

TWO OBOES, TWO CLARINETS
C major   P. 74 (O)
  R. Casier, A. François, A. Boutard & H.
  Druart; Cha. Orch.—Cartigny ♯ *Sel.LA 1080*
  (*Concerto, Bsn., B flat ma.; fl. A mi.*)

TWO TRUMPETS (see also Corni da Caccia, *ante*)
C major   P. 75
  R. Delmotte & M. André, Paris Coll. Musicum
  —Douatte   ♯ *Cum.CCX 277*
  (*Concertos, Str. Orch.; & A. Scarlatti*)

  R. Tournesac, P. Piton & Cha. Orch.—Kuentz
  (*Mozart & Bach*)   ♯ *CND. 2*

  R. Delmotte, A. Adriano & Paris. Coll. Mus.
  —Douatte   ♯ *Cpt.MC 20115*
  Alla rustica; & Corelli)
  ☆ F. Hausdörfer, H. Sevenstern & Sym.—Ackermann
                        (♯ CHS.CHS 1242 & ♯ MMS. 100W)

VIOLIN
C major   P. 14
  L. Ferro & Virtuosi di Roma—Fasano[2]
                                    ♯ *G.BLP 1042*
  (*Oboe Concerto, F major*)   (♯ *FBLP 1054:* QBLP 5019)

C major   P. 88
  ☆ E. Magaziner & Paris Sym.—Bruck (♯ Cum.CPL 196)

A major   P. 227
  L. Yordanoff & Pro Musica Orch.—Saguer
                                    ♯ *Sel.LAG 1014*
  (*Concertos—P. 349 & Op. 3, Nos. 1 & 7*)

E major   P. 248   (*Il Riposo*)
  Società Corelli   ♯ *Vic.LM 1880*
  (*Bonporti, Corelli*)   (♯ ItV.A12R 0146; FV.A 630292)
  ☆ C. Glenn & Pro Musica—Goldschmidt (in ♯ Clc. 6116)

D minor   P. 311   (with organ) (O)
  Anon. soloist & Naples Scarlatti Orch.
  —Caracciolo   ♯ *C.CX 1276*
  (*Str. Orch. P 235; & Leo, Sacchini*)   (♯ Angel. 35254)
  (*P 235; & Tartini, Cimarosa* on ♯ C.GQX 10138)

F major   P. 325
  G. Alès & Paris Coll. Mus.—Douatte
                                    ♯ *QS.LQS 101*
  (*Concerto, vln., B flat major*)   [also called *LQS 1*]

B flat major   P. 349
  J. Champeil & Pro Musica—Saguer
                                    ♯ *Sel.LAG 1014*
  (*Concerti, P 227 & Op. 3, Nos. 1 & 7*)

B flat major   P. 373
  G. Alès & Paris Coll. Mus.—Douatte
                                    ♯ *QS.LQS 101*
  (*Concerto, vln., F major*)   [also called *LQS 1*]

G minor   P.383 (*"per l'orchestra di Dresda"*)[3] (O)
  Anon. soloist & Paris Cha.—Jouve
                                    ♯ *Sel.LP 8702*
  (*Op. 8, No. 9; Op. 10, No. 5, & P 72*)   (♯ *T.NLB 6081;*
                                              West.WL 5341)

  H. Fernandez & Leclair Ens.—Paillard
                                    ♯ *DDP. 31-1*
  (*Locatelli & Torelli*)
  ☆ C. Glenn & Pro Musica—Goldschmidt (♯ Clc. 6116)

B flat major   P. 405
  ☆ E. Magaziner & Paris Sym.—Bruck (♯ Cum.CPL 196)

G minor   P. 407
  G. Alès & O.L. Ens.—Froment ♯ *LOL.OL 50124*
  (*Concertos—Vln. & vlc., vlc., etc., below*)   (♯ OL.LD 84)

C minor   P. 419   (*Il Sospetto*)
  A. Pelliccia & Virtuosi di Roma—Fasano
                                    ♯ *AmD.DL 9729*
  (*Concertos, Op. 3, Nos. 2, 8, 12*)   (♯ D.UAT 273589)
  ☆ C. Glenn & Pro Musica—Goldschmidt (♯ Clc. 6116)

G minor   (unspec.)
  A. Gertler & Hungarian State—Vaszy
  (4ss)   *Qual.MK 1556/7*

VIOLA D'AMORE
D major   P. 166
  ☆ R. Sabatini & Rome Coll. Mus.—Fasano
                                    (in ♯ FSor.CS 546)

D minor   P. 266
  ☆ E. Sailer, W. Gerwig (lute) & Cha. Ens.   PV. 4413
  (*Telemann* on ♯ AmD.DL 7537)

D minor   P. 287
  ☆ R. Sabatini & Virtuosi di Roma (♯ Fnt.LP 3001)

D minor   P. 288
  R. Sabatini & Virtuosi di Roma—Fasano
                                    ♯ *B.AXTL 1061*
  (*Concertos—str. orch. P 410; vln. & 2 vlcs. P 58; Op. 8,
  No. 9*)   (AmD.DL 9679; Fnt.LP 3002)

  B. Giuranna & I Musici Ens.[4]   ♯ *C.CX 1170*
  (*Concertos—Op. 3, No. 9 & Str. Orch. P 86 & 235*)
                                    (♯ QCX 10038: FCX 304; Angel. 35087)

  J. v. Helden & Netherlands Phil.—v. d. Berg
                                    ♯ *CHS.H 16*
  (*Torelli, Marcello, Durante*)   (& on ♯ MMS. 84)

VIOLONCELLO
C minor   P. 434
  R. Caruana & Milan Str.—Abbado
  (*P. 278, below; Pergolesi, Albinoni*) ♯ *C.FCX 370*
  R. Albin & O.L.Ens.—Froment ♯*LOL.OL50124*
  (*Concertos—Vln., P 407; vln. & vlc. P 388; 2 vlns.,
  2 vlcs., P 135*)   (♯ OL.LD 84)

G major—See Bach: Org. Concerto No. 1

TWO VIOLINS
A major   P. 222   (*L'Eco in lontano*)
  ☆ Italian Radio—Ferrero   ♭ *Tem. set 4600*
  (*Bach: Vln. Concerto, E major*)

A minor[5]   P. 28
  ☆ E. Malanotte & F. Scaglia, Rome Coll. Mus.—Fasano
                                    (in ♯ FSor.CS 546)

C minor   P. 435
  ☆ Vienna Cha. Orch.—Ephrikian (in ♯ Clc. 6116)

B flat major   P. 391
  P. Lamacque, F. Oguse & orch.—Witold
                                    ♯ *LI.TWV 91052*
                                    (♯ Cpt.MC 20043)
  (*Concertos—Op. 8, No. 9; Bsn., E min.; 2 vlns. & 2 vlcs.,
  D ma.*)

D major   P. 159
  ☆ L. Kaufman, P. Rybar & Winterthur—Dahinden
                                    (♯ MMS. 84)

---

[1] LD 73 is announced as containing 6 concerti, not 5, as OL 50073, but we have failed in attempts to confirm contents.
[2] Witvogel collection, Amsterdam; has Grave, C major, in place of Largo, A minor.
[3] For Vln., str. qtt., 2 obs., 2 fls., bsn.   [4] Ed. Giuranna.   [5] ARR. Casella.

THREE VIOLINS
F major   P. 278   (ed. Malipiero)
F. Tamponi, F. Ayo, W. Gallozzi & I Musici
Ens.   ♯ **C.CX 1163**
(*G. Gabrieli, Albinoni, B. Marcello*)
(♯ QCX 10039: FCX 305; Angel. 35088)

M. Abbado, M. Borgo, L. d'Annibale & Milan
Str.—Abbado   ♯ **C.FCX 370**
(*Vlc. Concerto; & Pergolesi & Albinoni*)

FOUR VIOLINS
B flat major   P. 367
Milan Str.—Abbado   ♯ **C.FCX 369**
(*Cambini, Tartini, Bonporti*)

VIOLIN & VIOLONCELLO
A major   P. 238
M. Abbado, R. Caruana & Milan Str.—Abbado
                                ♯ **C.FCX 368**
(*Corelli & Tartini*)
F. Gulli, B. Mazzacurati & Virtuosi di Roma
—Fasano   ♯ **G.QALP 10113**
(*G ma., 2 mandolines; Op. 8, No. 5; C mi., str. orch. P 427*)
B flat major   P. 388
G. Alès, R. Albin & Ens.—Froment
                             ♯ **LOL.OL 50124**
(*Concertos—vln., P 407; vlc., P 434; 2 vlns. & 2 vlcs., P 135*)   (♯ OL.LD 84)
A. Pelliccia, M. Amfitheatrof & Virtuosi di
Roma—Fasano   ♯ **AmD.DL 9684**
(*Concerti, Vln. & ob., P 406; 2 vlcs. P 411 & Op. 10-2*)
                 (♯ D.UAT 273574; SpC.CCL 35012)

VIOLIN & TWO VLCS.
C major   P. 58
A. Pelliccia, M. Amfitheatrof, B. Mazzacurati
& Virtuosi di Roma—Fasano ♯ **B.AXTL 1061**
(*Concertos—vla. d'amore, P 288; str. orch. P 410; & Op. 8, No. 9*)   (♯ AmD.DL 9679; Fnt.LP 3002)

TWO VIOLINS & TWO VLCS.
D major   P. 188
P. Lamacque & F. Oguse (vlns.), C. Brion &
P. Degenne (vlcs.) & Ens.—Witold[1]
                             ♯ **LI.TWV 91052**
(*Concertos, Op. 8, No. 9; bsn. E minor; 2 vlns., B flat major*)
                                (♯ Cpt.MC 20043)
G major   P. 135
G. Alès & R. Gendre (vlns.), R. Albin & A.
Remond (vlcs.) & Ens.—Froment
                             ♯ **LOL.OL 50124**
(*Concertos—Vln., P 407; vlc., P 434; vln. & vlc., P 388*)
                                (♯ OL.LD 84)
Sinfonia Inst. Ens.—Witold   ♯ **EPP.SLP 2**
(*Sammartini, Geminiani, Torelli*)

TWO VIOLONCELLOS
G minor   P. 411
M. Tournus, G. Fleury & orch.—Cartigny
                             ♯ **LT.DTL 93044**
(*Durante & Pergolesi*)   (♯ T.NLB 6096; ♯ Sel.LA 1079)
M. Amfitheatrof & B. Mazzacurati & Virtuosi
di Roma—Fasano   in ♯ **AmD.DL 9684**
(*Concertos—Vln. & vlc., ob. & vln. & Op.10 No. 2*)
                 (♯ D.UAT 273574; SpC.CCL 35012)

ORCHESTRA
C major   P. 87
Venice Cha.—Ephrikian   ♯ **Strad.STR 621**
                                (♯ Cpt.MC 20078)
(*Concertos—Op. 10-2; 2 tpts., P 273; ob., P 385*)

C major   P. 84   "per la solennità di S. Lorenzo"
A. Vivaldi Scuola Cha.—Pellizzari
(*Gloria*)   ♯ **AmC.RL 6632**

STRING ORCHESTRA
Collection
A major   P. 231
G minor   P. 407
G major   P. 143   (*Alla rustica*)
☆ Virtuosi di Roma—Fasano (♯ Fnt.LP 3001)

D minor   P. 86   (*Madrigalesco*)
I Musici Ens.   ♯ **C.CX 1170**
(*Concertos—vla. d'amore, D mi.; Vln. Op. 3-9; & P 235*)
                 (♯ QCX 10038: FCX 304; Angel. 35087)
... Excerpts in *Golden Coach* film music

E minor   P. 127
F major   P. 279
☆ Paris Sym.—Bruck (♯ Cum.CPL 196)

G major   P. 143   (*Alla rustica*)
Paris Coll. Mus.—Douatte   V♯ *Eko.LP 2*
(*Concerto, B flat major, below*)
(*Concerto, C minor & Concerto Op. 4, No. 1, on ♯ LM 3*)
Paris Coll. Mus.—Douatte   ♯ **Cum.CCX 277**
(*Concerto, 2 tpts, C ma.; & A. Scarlatti*)
Paris Coll. Mus.—Douatte   ♯ **Cpt.MC 20115**
(*Concerto, 2 tpts. C ma.; & Corelli*)
[M. Douatte informs us these are all different recordings]

A major   P. 235
Naples Scarlatti—Caracciolo   ♯ **C.CX 1276**
(*Vln. Concerto, P 311; & Leo, Sacchini*) (♯ Angel. 35254)
(*P 311 & Tartini, Cimarosa, on ♯ C.QCX 10138*)
O. L. Ens.—Froment   ♯ **LOL.OL 50073**
(*Oboe Concertos, Op. 8-9 & F ma.; Vln. & ob.; & below*)
                                (♯ OL.LD 73)[2]
I Musici Ens.   ♯ **C.CX 1170**
(*P 86, etc.*)   (♯ QCX 10038: FCX 304; Angel. 35087)
Bologna Orch.—Jenkins   ♯ **Cpt.MC 20019**
(*J. C. Bach & Rameau*)
☆ Rome Coll. Musicum—Fasano (in ♯ FSor.CS 546;
                                Orf. 53008/9)

F major   P. 292
O. L. Ens.—Froment[3]   ♯ **LOL.OL 50073**
(*Oboe Concertos, P 306 & Op. 8, No. 9; Ob. & vln. P 406; & above*)   (♯ OL.LD 73)[2]

B flat major   P. 363
Paris Coll. Mus.—Douatte   V♯ *Eko.LP 2*
(*Concerto, G major*)

G minor   P. 371
Angelicum Orch.—Janes   ♯ **Ang.LPA 957**
(*Concerto, mandoline, C major; & Bonporti*)
(*Debussy, Mozart, Tchaikovsky, Bonporti on ♯ LPA 958*)

G minor   P. 407
☆ Vienna Cha. Orch.—Ephrikian (in ♯ Clc. 6116)
Virtuosi di Roma (in ♯ Fnt.LP 3001)

B flat major   P. 409
... 2nd movt. included in *Golden Coach* film music, *see below*

B flat major   P. 410
Virtuosi di Roma—Fasano   ♯ **B.AXTL 1061**
(*Concertos—Op. 8, No. 9; vla. d'amore P 288; vln. & 2 vlcs., P 58*)   (♯ AmD.DL 9679; Fnt.LP 3002)

C minor   P. 427
Paris Coll. Mus.—Douatte   ♯ *Eko.LM 3*
(*Concerto, Op. 4, No. 1 & Concerto, G major, P 143*)
Virtuosi di Roma—Fasano   ♯ **G.QALP 10113**
(*Op. 8, No. 5; C ma., 2 mandolines, P 133; A major, vln. & vlc., P 238*)

C minor   P. 438
Paris Collegium Musicum—Douatte
(*Sinfonia, C major*)   V♯ *Eko.LP 3*

II. SINFONIE

C major   (P. page 8, No. 9—ed. Landshoff)
Paris Coll. Mus.—Douatte   V♯ *Eko.LP 3*
(*Concerto, C minor*)
Paris Coll. Mus.—Douatte   ♯ **Cum.CCX 277**
(*above, & A. Scarlatti*)

G major   (P. page 8, No. 8—ed. Landshoff)
Società Corelli   in ♯ **Vic.LM 1767**
(*below & Op. 3, No. 8; & Marcello, Carissimi, Geminiani*)
                 (♭ set WDM 1767; ItV.A12R 0098)

---
[1] Labelled Op. 4, No. 4.
[2] OL.LD 73 is announced as containing 6 concerti, not 5 as OL 50073; confirmation of contents has not been possible.
[3] The first movement is abbreviated by omission of opening section, at least in original pressings.

III. SONATAS

SONATAS
Op. 1, No. 2, E minor 2 vlns. & cont.
Allegro Cha. Orch.—Tubbs ♯ **Allo. 3146**
(Concerto, Op. 3, No. 10; Scarlatti & Telemann)
P. Pierlot (ob.), R. Gendre (vln.), R. Veyron-
Lacroix (hpsi.) & P. Hongne (bsn.)[1]
♯ **BàM.LD 013**
(Sonata, C major, & Concertos) (♯ HS.HSL 116)

Op. 2, No. 9, E minor vln. & cont.
O. Kinch, J. E. Hansen (virginals), B. Anker
(vlc.) ♭ **Mtr.MCEP 3021**
(Albinoni)
(Albinoni, Stradella, A. Scarlatti, on ♯ HS.HSL 9011)

SONATAS, Op. 13 vln. & cont. *(Il Pastor Fido)*
No. 4, A major
... **Pastorale** only — ARR. RECORDERS
Members Trapp Ens. in ♯ **B.LAT 8038**
(♯ AmD.DL 9689: ♭ *set ED 1200*)
No. 6, G minor
S. Gazzelloni (fl.), R. Raffalt (hpsi.)
♯ **ItV.A12R 0027**
(Locatelli, Valentino, Veracini, etc.)

SONATAS, Op. 14 vlc. & cont.
No. 5, E minor
M. Amfitheatrof & O. P. Santoliquido (pf.)
♯ **ItV.A12R 0140**
(Galuppi, Frescobaldi, Veracini, Boccherini)

— ARR. VLC. & STRINGS D'Indy ("Concerto")
P. Fournier & Stuttgart Cha.—Münchinger
♯ **D.LXT 2765**
(Couperin & Boccherini) (♯ Lon.LL 687)
(Couperin only, on ♯ D.LW 5196)
☆ M. Amfitheatrof & Rome Coll. Mus.—Fasano
(in ♯ FSor.CS 546; Largo only on *Orf. 53008*)
J. Neilz & Pascal Qtt. (♭ *Pat.ED 13: EMD 10009*)

SONATAS, no Op. no.
A minor P.p. 7 fl., bsn. & hpsi.
C minor P.p. 6 ob. & hpsi.
(Dresden MS.Cx 1106)
J-P. Rampal (fl.), P. Pierlot (ob.), P. Hongne
(bsn.), R.Veyron-Lacroix (hpsi.) ♯ **HS.HSL 82**
(Concertos) (♭ BàM.LD 06)
(Sonata, C minor also on V♯ BàM.LD 1003)

C major fl. & cont.[2]
J-P. Rampal & R.Veyron-Lacroix ♯BàM.LD 013
(above) (♯ HS.HSL 116)

C major lute, vln. & cont. (P.p. 7; Rinaldi, Op. 55-2)
M. Podolski, J. Tryssesoone, & F. Terby (vlc.)
♯ **Per.SPL 587**
(Haydn, Saint-Luc, Baron) (♯ Cpt.MC 20058)

D major (ARR. Respighi; Dresden MS.Cx 1103)
☆ E. Morini & M. Lanner (in ♯ Cam.CAL 207)

D minor fl. & cont. (P.p. 7) (Upsala MS.)
☆ J-P. Rampal & R. Veyron-Lacroix (hpsi.) (♯ HS.HSL. 80)

IV. VOCAL MUSIC

A. SECULAR

(Un) Certo non so che ("Arietta", ed. Parisotti)
M. Laszlo (S), F. Holetschek (pf.)
in ♯ **Nix.WLP 5375**
(† Italian Airs) (♯ West.WL 5375)
F. Barbieri (M-S), D. Marzollo (pf.)
in ♯ **AmVox.PL 7980**
(† Old Italian Songs & Airs)

Cessate omai Cantata
L. Ribacchi (M-S) & Società Corelli
in ♯ **Vlc.LM 1767**
(above & Geminiani, Marcello, Carissimi)
(in ♭ *set WDM 1767; ♯ ItV.A12R 0098)*

Ombra nere voi cadete Cantata 1726
(in honour of Landgrave of Hesse-Darmstadt)
Salve Regina No. 2
A, 2 corni da caccia, vln., vla. & cont.
G. Borelli (A) & Venice Cha. Orch.—Ephrikian
♯ **Ren.X 58**
(♯ Cpt.MC 20105)

Serenata a tre ("La Ninfa e il pastore") ed. V. Frazzi
(Foà Vol. II; Rinaldi 304-1)
Eurilla ... ... G. Rapisardi-Savio (S)
Nice ... ... S. Zanolli (S)
Alcindo ... ... A. Blaffard (T)[3]
& Milan Cha. Orch.—Loehrer
♯ **E. & AmVox.PL 7990**

IV. B. SACRED

Dixit Dominus (Psalm 109) S, S, A, T, B, Bs, cho.
☆ Soloists, Venice Cho. & Orch.—Ephrikian
(announced as ♯ MMS. 2029 but probably not issued)

Gloria 4 voices (ed. Casella)
P. Alarie (S), M-T. Cahn (A), Paris Vocal Ens.
& Paris Cons. Orch.—Jouve ♯ **LT.DTL 93080**
(M-A. Charpentier) (♯ West.WL 5287)
(Mozart, on ♯ Sel.LPG 8556; T.LT 6565)
G. Vivante (S), C. Carbi (M-S) & A. Vivaldi
Scuola Cho. & Cha. Orch.—Pellizzari
♯ **AmC.RL 6632**
(Concerto, C major) (2ss, ♯ Fnt.LP 2003)

Juditha triumphans Oratorio 1716
☆ Soloists, Venice Cho. & Orch.—Ephrikian
(♯ Cum.CR 352/4)

Laudate pueri, Nos. 1 & 2 (Psalm 112) S & orch.
☆ R. Giancola & Orch.—Ephrikian (♯ Cpt.MC 20030)

Salve Regina No. 2
SEE above, with *Ombra nere*

Stabat Mater A & str. (ed. Casella)
G. Simionato (M-S), Rome Qtt. Soc. Cha. Orch.
—Nucci ♯ **Csm.CLPS 1050**
(Monteverdi, Frescobaldi)
☆ M. Amadini & Milan Angelicum—Gerelli
(Ang.SA 3017/8)

MISCELLANEOUS

(The) GOLDEN COACH film music[4]
Includes—
OVERTURE: Concerto, Op. 10, No. 3 ... 1st movt. (abridged)
Concerto, B flat major (P. 409) ... 2nd movt.
Concerto, Bsn. & orch. (P. 401) ... excerpts
Concerto, Str. Orch. (P. 86) ... 1st & 3rd sections
Concerto, G minor, Op. 3, No. 2 ... 2nd movt.
Concerto, Str. Orch. (P. 55) ... 3rd movt.
Rome Sym.—G. Marinuzzi Jnr. ♯ **MGM.E 3111**
(Trad.: Commedia dell'Arte dances) (from sound track)

VIVES, Amadeo (1871-1932)
ZARZUELAS, etc. (Abridged listings only)
BOHEMIOS 1 Act 1904
T. Rosado, A. M. Fernandez, A. Cano, M. Ausensi,
C. Munguía, A. Diaz Martos, G. Gil, Madrid Singers &
Sym. Orch.—Argenta ♯ **LI.TW 91038**
(♯ Ambra.MCC 30019)
L. Torrentó, P. Gómez, A. Serva, T. Sánchez, J. Vilardell,
D. Monjo, M. Redondo, O. Pol, F. Cashadina Cho. &
Sym.—Ferrer ♯ **Angel. 65014**
[Excerpts in ♭ *Reg.SEDL 19041]* (♯ Reg.LCX 119)

Intermezzo
Madrid Cha. Orch.—Argenta in ♯ **LI.TW 91004**
(in ♯ Ambra.MCC 30009 & MCCP 29001)
Colón Theatre Orch.—Cases ArgOd. 66041
(Marques: Anillo de Hierro, Prelude) (♭ BSOAE 4515:
BSOA 4010: in ♯ LDC 511)
Spanish Sym.—Martinez in ♯ **Mont.FM 16**
Madrid Theatre—Moreno Torroba in ♯ **AmD.DL 9789**
Orch.—Ferrer (? from set) Reg.C 10198
(♭ SEDL 106)
Romanza de Casette S
A. M. Olaria in ♯ **Mont.FM 17**

---

[1] Ed. Veyron-Lacroix.
[2] Published 1952, J. & W. Chester Ltd., London, from MS., Cambridge University Library.
[3] And not A. Bianchini, as on the envelope.
[4] Also contains items by Corelli and Martini, *q.v.*, ED. & ARR. G. Marinuzzi Jnr.

DOÑA FRANCISQUITA　3 Acts　1923
A. Morales, A. M. Iriarte, C. Munguía, etc., Donostiarra
Cho. & Sym.—Argenta　　　　　# **LI.TW 91005/6**
　　　　　　　　　　　　(# Ambra.MCC 30014/5)
L. Torrentó, R. Gómez, P. Civil, etc., Cho. & Orch.
—Ferrer　　　　　　　　　　# **Reg.LCX 129**
　　　　　　　　　　(# Angel. 65006; Pam.LRC 15503/4, 4ss)
[Excerpts on ♭ Angel. 70018; ♭ Reg.SEDL 107 & 19041;
Fandango in # Reg.LCX 104; C.FSX 104;
　　　　　　　　　　　　Angel. 65008; Pam.LRC 15905]

▽ Soloists, Cho. & orch.—Montorio (C.DCX 29/36;
　　　　　　　　　　SpC.RG 16012/9; ArgC. 264503/10)

Orch. Excerpts　Orch.—Delta (♭ Od.MSOE 101; ▽ 184861)
　　　　　　Sym.—Argenta (# Ambra.MCP 10007)

Vocal Excerpts　R. Lagares (T) (ArgV. 68-1181)
　　　　　　　M. Cubas (T) (in # ArgOd.LDC 528)
▽ A. Ottein, C. Galeffi (Od. 122014/7 & 121139/41;
　　　　　　　　　　　　　　　　177229)
A. Cortis (G.DB 901)
M. Fleta (Vic. 6549; G.DB 850), etc.

(La) GENERALA
M. Espinalt, L. Torrentó, J. Vilardell, etc.; Barcelona Cho.
& Orch.—Ferrer　　　　　　# **Reg.LCX 128**
[Excerpts in ♭ Reg.SEBL 7002 & 7017]

(La) GITANA BLANCA　　See Gimenez

JUEGOS MALABARES
Prelude
Madrid Cha. Orch.—Navarro in # **Mont.FM 39**

MARUXA　2 Acts　1913
T. Rosado, P. Lorengar, M. Ausensi, E. de la Vara, etc.;
Cho. & Madrid Cha. Orch.—Argenta # **LI.TW 91017/8**
　　　　　　　　　　(# Ambra.MCC 30003/4)
A. M. Iriarte, P. Lorengar, M. Ausensi, etc., Madrid Cho.
& Cha. Orch.—Argenta　　　　# **Mont.FM 4/5**

Intermezzo (Prelude Act 2)
Colón Theatre Orch.—Cases　　　in # **ArgOd.LDC 504**
　　　　　　　　　　(♭ BSOAE 4509)

Orch.—Ferrer　　　　　　　**Reg.C 10197**
(♭ SEDL 106; & in # LC 1002; # Pam.LRC 15507)
Majestic Orch. (in V# MusH.LP 1071)

SONGS
(3) Canciones epigramaticas　1915-16
1. El retrato de Isabela
2. El amor y los ojos
3. La presumida　(Salgado)
A. M. Iriarte (S), R. Machado (pf.)
　　　　　　　　　　　# **Pat.DT 1007**
(Nin, Falla)　(# ArgPat.ADT 1005; ♭ SpPat.EMD 10001)

... Nos. 1 & 2 only
V. de los Angeles (S), G. Moore (pf.) **G.DA 2059**
(G.EC 227: in # ALP 1151: FALP 327: LALP 142;
　　　　　　　　　　　　Vic. set LM 6017)

... No. 3 only
M. de los Angeles Morales (S) & orch.
　　　　　　(Ambra.AL 20015: ♭ EMGE 70019)

L'Émigrant　(Verdaguer)
La Balenguera　(Alcover)
E. Vendrell (T) & orch. (♭ SpC.ECGE 70002)

VLADIGEROV, Panchu (b. 1899)

(2) Bulgarian Dances, Op. 23
☆ Czech Phil.—Popoff (in # U. 5200C)

**Fantasy on the Bulgarian Dance theme 'Khora',
Op. 18**　vln. & pf.
D. Oistrakh & V. Yampolsky # **CEd.CE 3002**
(Mozart, Vainberg)
(Beethoven & Leclair on # Csm.CRLP 153)

Vardar, Op. 16 (Bulgarian Rhapsody) Orch.
Moscow Radio—Vladigerov　　# **USSR.D 557**
(Weiner)
— ARR. VLN. & PF.
I. Bezrodny & pf.　　　　　**USSRM.D 372**
(Taneiev: Fairy Tale)
G. Garay & I. Hajdu (Qual.SZN 3005)

VOGEL, Johann Christoph (1756-1788)

DÉMOPHON
Opera　3 Acts　　(after Metastasio)　1789
Overture
Paris Cons.—Tzipine　　　# **C.FCX 383**[1]
(Gossec, Lesueur)

VOORMOLEN, Alexander (b. 1895)

Concerto, 2 oboes & orch.
... **Arioso** only
▽ Jaap & H. Stotijn & Amsterdam—E. Jochum
　　　　　　　　　　　　(T.SK 3355)

(Le) Livre des Enfants (Bk. I) 24 pieces pf.
... **First Swallow; Mazurka of the Mice; The fox**
S. Bianca　　　　　　　**MSB. 24**
(with spoken commentary)　　(in # 60041)

VOYS, de la　(fl. XVIIth Cent.)
SEE: † # AS. 3004LD; HS.AS 36

VUATAZ, Roger (b. 1898)

Incantation　sax. & pf.　1954
D. Defayet & F. Gobet　　　♭ **Pat.G 1052**
(Herbin, Semenoff, Lacazinière, etc.)
SEE ALSO: BACH: Musicalisches Opfer (arr.)

VULPIUS, Melchior　(1560-1615)
SEE: † SONGS OF RENAISSANCE (GERMANY & AUSTRIA)

WACLAW of SZAMOTUL (c. 1533-34—1567-8)
SEE: † FIVE CENTURIES OF POLISH MUSIC
† ANTHOLOGIE SONORE

WAELRANT, Huibrecht (Hubert)
　　　　　　　　　　(c. 1517-1595)

Musiciens qui chantez　Chanson
Pancratius Male Cho.—Heydendael
　　　　　　　　　　in # **C.HS 1001**
(Lassus, Jannequin, Haydn, etc.)
▽ Antwerp Cho. (C.DF 144)

WAGENAAR, Bernard (b. 1894)

(A) Concert Overture　orch.　f.p. 1954
Louisville—Whitney　　　　# **LO. 2**
(Tcherepnin & Cowell)

Symphony No. 4　1949
☆ A.R.S. Orch.—Haefner　(Hanson)　# **ARS. 114**

WAGENAAR, Johan (1862-1941)

Cyrano de Bergerac, Overture, Op. 23　1905
The Taming of the Shrew, Overture, Op. 25　1909
Residentie—Otterloo　　　# **Phi.S 06036R**
(Anrooij)

WAGNER, Richard (1813-1883)

I. NON-OPERATIC

(Ein) Albumblatt, C major　pf.　1861
— ARR. VLN. & PF.　Wilhelmj
I. Bezrodny & pf.　　　　**USSRM.D 00341**
(Rubinstein: Romance)
D. Oistrakh & V. Yampolsky[2] in # **JpV.LS 2026**
☆ M. & I. Kozolupova (in # Csm.CRLP 179)

---

[1] Only available as part of a de luxe Limited Edition.　　[2] Tokyo recording, 1955.

(Eine) Faust - Ouvertüre   orch.   1840, rev. 1885
Munich Phil.—Rieger   PV. 56018
(*Tannhäuser Overture*, on ♯ *AmD.DL 4061*) (also PV. 72472)
☆ N.B.C. Sym.—Toscanini   ♯ *Vic.LRM 7023*
    (*Beethoven*)   (♭ set ERB 7023; ♭ *ItV.A72R 0021*)

Polonia, Overture, C major   1832
Berlin Radio—Guhl   ♯ Ura. 7116
(*below*)

Siegfried Idyll   orch.   1870
N.B.C. Sym.—Toscanini (n.v.)
                       in ♯ Vic. set LM 6020
(*Tristan, Lohengrin, Meistersinger, etc.*)
            (in ♯ *ItV.A12R 0137; FV.A 630252*)
Vienna Phil.—Knappertsbusch   ♯ D.LXT 5065
(*Bruckner: Symphony No. 4, s. 1*)   (♯ Lon.LL 1250)
Bamberg Sym.—Hollreiser
                       ♯ E. & AmVox.PL 9350
(*Brahms, Liszt, Sibelius*) (Liszt only, on ♯ *Pan.XPV 1006*)
Berlin Phil.—v. Otterloo   ♯ *EPhi.ABR 4026*
(*Brahms*)   (♯ *Phi.A 00709R*)
Berlin Phil.—Markevitch   ♯ Pol. 19024
(*Tannhäuser & Walküre*)
(*Moussorgsky* on ♯ *AmD.DL 9782*)
Saar Cha.—Ristenpart   ♯ DFr. 132
(*Brahms*)
☆ Philharmonia—Cantelli   ♯ G.ALP 1086
(*Tchaikovsky: Romeo & Juliet*)   (♯ QALP 10043)
(*Schumann* on ♯ *Vic.LHMV 13*)
Linz Sym. (in ♯ *Ply. 12-23*)
Moscow Radio—Golovanov (♯ *USSR.D 01443*)
☆ Munich State Op.—Konwitschny (in ♯ *Nix.ULP 9063*)
Vienna Phil.—Furtwängler (in ♯ *Vic.LHMV 1049*)
L.P.O.—Weingartner (in ♯ *AmC.ML 4860*)

— ARR. ORGAN
R. Ellsasser   (*Tristan*)   ♯ MGM.E 3216

Symphony, C major   1832
Leipzig Radio—Pflüger   ♯ Ura. 7116
(*above*)

SONGS
(5) GEDICHTE   (Wesendonck Lieder)
... No. 3, Im Treibhaus; No. 5, Träume
E. Höngen (A), G. Moore (pf.)   C.LX 1590
... No. 5, Träume
M. Powers (A), F. la Forge (pf.) in ♯ Atl. 1207
(*Bach, Brahms, Respighi, Franz, etc.*)

—— ARR. CHO.
Augustana Cho.—Veld   in ♯ BB.LBC 1075
(*Brahms, Dvořák, etc.*)

II. OPERATIC

(Die) FEEN   3 Acts   comp. 1833 [f. p. 1888]
Overture
☆ Munich State Op.—Konwitschny in ♯ Nix.ULP 9069
                                      (♯ MTW. 553)

(Der) FLIEGENDE HOLLÄNDER   3 Acts   1843
COMPLETE RECORDINGS

Casts		Set D	Set G
Der Holländer (B)	...	H. Uhde	J. Metternich
Senta (S)	... ...	A. Varnay	A. Kupper
Daland (Bs)	... ...	L. Weber	J. Greindl
Erik (T)	... ...	R. Lustig	W. Windgassen
Steuermann (T)	...	J. Traxel	E. Häfliger
Mary ...	... ...	E. Schärtel (M-S)	S. Wagner (A)

Set D, with Bayreuth Fest. Cho. & Orch.
    —Keilberth (6ss)   ♯ D.LXT 5150/2
                               (♯ Lon.LL 1389/91)
Set G, with R.I.A.S. Cha. Cho. & Sym.—Fricsay
                               ♯ HP.DGM 18063/5
(6ss) (also ♯ Pol. 18116/8, manual; & ♯AmD. set DX 124)
HIGHLIGHTS in *Czech*
Die Frist ist um ... Wie oft in Meeres tiefsten Schlund B
                                       Act I
Jo-ho-hoe! ... Traft ihr das Schiff S   Act II
Mögst du, mein Kind   M-S   Act II
Versank ich jetzt   S, B, Bs   Act III
Z. Hrnčířová (S), P. Kočí (B), K. Kalaš (Bs) &
    orch.—Šíp   ♯ U. 5190H

Overture
Royal Phil.—Beecham   ♯ EPhi.ABL 3039
(*Meistersinger, Parsifal, Götterdämmerung*)
                       (♯ AmC.ML 4962; Phi.N 02113L)
Vienna Phil.—Knappertsbusch   ♯ D.LXT 2822
(*Walküre & Tannhäuser*)   (♯ Lon.LL 800)
(*Walküre only*, ♯ *D.LW 5106; Lon.LD 9064*)
N.Y. Phil. Sym.—Szell   ♯ AmC.AL 55
(*Tannhäuser, Overture*)   (& in ♯ ML 4918)
R.I.A.S. Sym.—Fricsay   ♯ *HP.DG 17022*
(*Tchaikovsky: Ouverture solennelle*)
Vienna Sym.—Moralt   ♯ Phi.N 00183L
(*Tannhäuser, Overture, etc.*)
(*Tristan, Prelude* only in ♯ *S 06009R*)
Berlin Municipal Op.—Rother ♯ *DT.TM 68050*
(*Tristan*)   (♯ *T.TW 30028*)
Detroit Sym.—Paray   ♯ Mer.MG 50044
(*Parsifal, Tristan, Siegfried*)
Florence Fest.—Gui   ♯ AudC. 503
(*Tannhäuser Overture; Grieg, Sibelius*)
Hamburg Philharmonia—H-J. Walther
                                       MSB. 78147
☆ Vienna Phil.—Furtwängler   ♯ G.FALP 289
(*Meistersinger & Tannhäuser*)   (♯ VALP 538;
                                        G.ED 1233/4)
Austrian Sym.—Koslik (in ♯ Rem. 199-137)
"Nat. Op. Orch." (in ♯ Var. 6990)
☆ Philharmonia—Kletzki (in ♯ AmC.RL 3060)
Munich State Op.—Konwitschny (♭ *Nix.EP 737:*
                       ♯ ULP 9069; ♭ *Ura.UREP 37;* ♯ MTW. 553)
Philharmonia—Malko (in ♯ BB.LBC 1048:
                                       ♭ set WBC 1048)
Rhineland Sym.—Federer (in ♯ *AFest.CFR 37*)
Vienna State Op.—Swarowsky (in ♯ *Sup.LPM 226;*
                                       ♯ U. 5203C)

ACT I

Durch Gewitter und Sturm   T & cho.
... Tenor only
E. Häfliger   PV. 36078
(*Mögst du mein Kind*)   (& in ♯ Pol. 19015)
K. Terkal   ♭ D.VD 513
(*Rienzi—Allmächt'ger Vater*)

Die Frist ist um   B
O. Edelmann   in ♯ *EPhi.ABR 4030*
(*below*)   (♯ *Phi.N 00630R;* ♯ Epic.LC 3052)
P. Schoeffler   in ♯ Rem. 199-137
(in ♯ *MSL.MW 51*; & with commentary by S. Spaeth,
                                       ♯ Rem. 9)
J. Metternich (from set)   ♭ Pol. 32098
☆ S. Björling   ♯ *C.C 1035*
(*below*)   (♯ QC 5023: FC 1039)
☆ A. Endrèze (*Fr*) (in ♯ Pat.PCX 5006)

ACT II

Summ' und brumm' (*Spinning Cho.*)   A & cho.
S. Zimmer & Berlin Municipal Op.—Otto
                               ♯ *DT.TM 68042*
(*below, & Lohengrin*) (& ♯ *T.TW 30014:* ♭ *UE 453938*)
Berlin Comic Op. Cho.—Lange   Eta. 120047
(*below*)
☆ Württemberg State Op.—Leitner (*PV. 36107;*
    ♭ *Pol. 32076:* in ♯ 19033; & in ♯ AmD.DL 9797)
Jo-ho-hoe! Traft ihr das Schiff   S & cho.
(*Senta's Ballad*)
L. Rysanek & Cho.   in ♯ *C.C 1035*
(*above & below*)   (♯ QC 5023: FC 1039;
                               & 2ss, C.LX 1573: LOX 820)
M. Cunitz & Cho.   ♯ *DT.TM 68001*
(*Tannhäuser—Dich, teure Halle*)
(in ♯ *T.TW 30014:* TV.VSK 9022: ♭ *T.UV 109*)
H. Zadek   in ♯ *EPhi.ABR 4004*
(*Lohengrin, Tannhäuser, etc.*)   (♯ *Phi.N 00655R*)
☆ A. Varnay (in ♯ Rem. 199-137 & with commentary by
                              S. Spaeth on ♯ Rem. 9)
F. Austral (*Eng*) (in ♯ Vic. set LCT 6701)
Ⴀ E. Destinn (in ♯ Sca. 804*)

♯ = Long-playing, 33⅓ r.p.m.   ♭ = 45 r.p.m.   ♮ = Auto. couplings, 78 r.p.m.

(Der) FLIEGENDE HOLLÄNDER, Act II (*continued*)
Fühlst du den Schmerz? S & T (*Traumerzählung*)
  A. Kupper & W. Windgassen   **PV. 72419**
  (*Freischütz—Durch die Wälder*) [from set] (♭ *Pol. 30024*, d.c.)

Mögst du, mein Kind Bs   (*Daland's Aria*)
  J. Greindl [from set]   ***PV. 36078***
  (*Durch Gewitter und Sturm*)   (♭ *Pol. 30024*, d.c.)
  ⊞ R. Mayr (in ♯ *Sca. 822**)

Wie aus der Ferne   B
Versank ich jetzt   S & B   (*Love Duet*)
  L. Rysanek & S. Björling   ♯ ***C.C 1035***
  (*above*)   (♯ *QC 5023: FC 1039*)
  A. Kupper & J. Metternich   ♭ ***Pol. 30142***
  [from set]

ACT III

Steuermann, lass' die Wacht (*Sailors' Cho.*)
  Berlin Municipal Op.—Otto   ♯ ***DT.TM 68042***
  (*above*)   (& ♯ *T.TW 30036:* ♭ *UE 543938*)
  Berlin Comic Op.—Lange   ***Eta. 120047***
  (*above*)
  ☆ Württemberg State Op.—Leitner (*PV. 36107;*
     ♭ *Pol. 32076:* in ♯ *19033;* ♯ *AmD.DL 9797*)

Willst jenes Tag's du nicht . . . T   (*Cavatina*)
  H. Hopf   in ♯ ***Phi.N 00732R***
  (*Lohengrin, Meistersinger, Rienzi, Walküre*)
       (in ♯ *Epic.LC 3103*)

(Das) LIEBESVERBOT   2 Acts   1836
Overture
  ☆ Munich State Op.—Konwitschny   in ♯ ***Nix.ULP 9069***
       (♯ *MTW. 553*)

LOHENGRIN   3 Acts   1850
COMPLETE RECORDINGS

Casts				Set D	Set E
Elsa (S)	...	...	...	E. Steber	A. Kupper
Ortrud (S or A)	...	...	A. Varnay	Helena Braun
Lohengrin (T)	...	...	W. Windgassen	L. Fehenberger
Friedrich (B)	...	...	H. Uhde	F. Frantz
König Heinrich (Bs)	...	J. Greindl	O. v. Rohr
Herald (B)	...	...	H. Braun	H. Braun

Cast					Set G
Elsa (S)	...	...	...	...	M. Cunitz
Ortrud (S or A)	...	...	...	M. Klose
Lohengrin (T)	...	...	...	R. Schock
Friedrich (B)	...	...	...	J. Metternich
König Heinrich (Bs)	...	...	G. Frick
Herald (B)	...	...	...	H. Günter
etc.					

Set D, with Bayreuth Fest. Cho. & Orch.
  —Keilberth (10ss)   ♯ **D.LXT 2880/4**
       (♯ Lon. set LLA 16)

Set E, with Bavarian Radio Cho. & Orch.
  —E. Jochum (10ss)   ♯ **Pol. 18119/23**
  (& auto., ♯ *Pol. 18084/8; AmD. set DX 131;*   Eta. 820007/11)

Set G, with North-West Ger. Radio Cho. & Orch.
  —Schüchter (8ss)   ♯ **G.ALP 1095/8**
  (♯ *QALP 10038/41; FALP 296/9; ArgA.LPC 11536/9;*
       Vic. set LHMV 800)

Set U.   ☆ M. Klose, A. Böhm, K. Böhme, etc., Munich
  State Op. Cho. & Orch.—Kempe   ♯ **Nix.ULP 9225-1/5**
  [Highlights on ♯ Ura. 7123]

ABRIDGED RECORDING
U. Graf(S), K. Libl(T), L. Wolovsky(Bs), A. Schlosshauer
  (A), R. Kunz (B), Frankfurt Op. Cho. & Orch.
  —Bamburger (4ss)   ♯ **MMS. set OP 20**
       (also ♯ MMS. set 2029)

COLLECTED EXCERPTS
Preludes, Acts I & III
Treulich geführt, Act III   (*Bridal Cho.*)
In fernem Land, Act III   T
  W. Geisler & Hamburg Op. Cho. & Orch.
  —Ludwig   ♯ **Sel. 320.C.093**
  (*Meistersinger*)

Nun sei bedankt, Act I
Höchstes Vertrau'n, Act III
In fernem Land, Act III
Mein lieber Schwan! Act III
  ⊞ L. Slezak (T)   ♯ **Ete. 499***
  (*Tannhäuser & Meistersinger*)

¹ From Mapleson cylinders.

Preludes, Acts I & III
Treulich geführt   (*Bridal Cho.*)
  ☆ Netherlands Op. Cho. & Hilversum Radio Orch.
     —v. Kempen (♭ *Phi.N 402035E; EPhi.NBE 11028*)

HIGHLIGHTS
  Soloists, Dresden State Op. Cho. & Orch.—Schreiber
       ♯ **Roy. 1412**
  Anon. Artists   ♯ **Var. 69145**
  ☆ R. Bampton, A. Carron, etc. (♯ *Cam.CAL 223;*
       in set CFL 101)

ACT I

Prelude
  N.B.C. Sym.—Toscanini (n.v.)   **G.DB 21574**
  (♭ *7ERF 115;* in ♯ *Vic.LRM 7029:* ♭ set *ERB 7029:* &
     ♯ set *LM 6020;* ♯ *ItV.A12R 0137:* ♭ *A72R 0004;*
       ♯ *FV.A 330209 & A 630252*)

  Vienna Phil.—Furtwängler   ♯ **G.ALP 1220**
  (*Tannhäuser; & Liszt*)   (♯ *QALP 10088: FALP 362*)

  Detroit Sym.—Paray   in ♯ **Mer.MG 50021**
       (♯ *FMer.MLP 7504:* ♭ *Mer.EP 1-5045*)

  Bamberg Sym.—Horenstein   ♯ **AmVox.PL 9110**
  (*Meistersinger, Tannhäuser, Tristan*)

  R.I.A.S. Sym.—Sebastian   ♯ **Rem. 199-177**
  (*Meistersinger & Tannhäuser*)
  Berlin Sym.—List (in ♯ *Roy. 1399*)
  Orch.—Swarowsky (in ♯ *MTW. 24:* ♭ set *EP 24*)
  Rhineland Sym.—Federer (in ♯ *Rgt. 5058*)
  ☆ Philadelphia—Stokowski (in ♯ *Cam.CAL 120*)
     Philharmonia—Kletzki (in ♯ *AmC.RL 3060*)
     Paris Opéra—Fourestier (ArgPat.FCX 10)
     Munich State Op.—Kempe, from set U (♯ *Ura. 7077*)

Einsam in trüben Tagen (*Elsa's Dream*) S   (Sc. 2)
  H. Zadek   in ♯ **EPhi.ABR 4004**
  (*Fliegende Holländer, Tannhäuser; & R. Strauss*)
       (♯ *Phi.N 00655R*)
  ☆ H. Traubel   (*Parsifal*)   ♯ **G.7ER 5027**
  (*Tristan, Walküre,* in ♯ *Vic.LRM 7031:* ♭ set *ERB 7031*)
  ☆ V. de los Angeles   (♭ *G.7RW 115: 7RQ 3024*)

Nun höret mich . . . Mein Herr und Gott
  (*Königs Gebet*)   Bs & Ens. Sc. 3
  O. von Rohr, Ens. & Cho.   **PV. 72444**
  (*below*) [from set E]   (♭ *Pol. 30048*)
  ... Bs part only   ⊞ R. Mayr (in ♯ *Sca. 822**)

ACT II

Prelude & Procession to the Minster
Gesegnet soll sie schreiten Cho.   (Sc. 4)
  Berlin Municipal Op. Cho.—Otto
       in ♯ **DT.TM 68042**
  (*below, & Fliegende Holländer*)
       (♯ *T.TW 30036 &* ♭ *UE 453939*)

Finale . . . Mein Held S & T   (Sc. 4)
  ⊞ J. Gadski & G. Anthes¹ (in ♯ *IRCC.L 7006**)

ACT III

Prelude
  N.W. Ger. Radio—Schüchter   **G.DB 21609**
  (*below*) [from set G]   (♭ *7R 175: 7RQ 3034*)
  N.B.C. Sym.—Toscanini   in ♯ **Vic.LRM 7029**
  (♭ set *ERB 7029 &* in ♯ set *LM 6020;* in ♯ *ItV.A12R 0137:*
     ♭ *A72R 0004;* ♯ *FV.A 330209 & A 630252;*
       ♭ *G.7ERF 115*)
  Philadelphia—Ormandy   in ♯ **AmC.ML 4865**
       (& in ♯ *AL 43:* ♭ *A 1839;* in ♯ *Phi.S 06619R*)
  Detroit Sym.—Paray   in ♯ **Mer.MG 50021**
       (♯ *FMer.MLP 7504*)
  Victor Sym.—Reiner   ♭ **Vic.ERA 185**
  (*Tannhäuser; & Mendelssohn*)   (♭ *FV.A 95216*)
  R.I.A.S. Sym.—Sebastian   in ♯ **Rem. 199-174**
  (*Meistersinger, Tannhäuser*)
  Hamburg Philharmonia—H-J. Walther
       MSB. 78133
  (*below*)
  ☆ Munich State Op.—Kempe   ♯ **Ura. 7077**
  (*above*) from set U
  Orch.—Swarowsky (in ♯ *MTW. 24:* ♭ set *EP 24*)
  Regent Sym. (in ♯ *Rgt.MG 7001*)
  ☆ Philharmonia—Kletzki (in ♯ *AmC.RL 3060*)
     Berlin Phil.—E. Jochum (♭ *AmD.ED 3523*)
     E.I.A.R. Sym.—Failoni (in ♯ *Tem.TT 2046*)
     Boston Pops.—Fiedler (in ♯ *Cam.CAL 142:* ♭ *CAE 134*)
 — ARR. ORGAN   R. Foort (in ♯ *Nix.SLPY 148;* ♯ *SOT. 1053*)

LOHENGRIN, Act III (continued)

Treulich geführt (Bridal Chorus) (Sc. 1)
N.W. Ger. Radio Cho.—Schüchter **G.DB 21609**
(above)   (♭ 7R 175: 7RQ 3034; ♭ Vic.ERA 236, d.c.)
[from set G]

Bavarian Radio Cho.—E. Jochum PV. **72485**
(Tannhäuser—Pilgerchor)   (♭ Pol. 30085 & in ♯ 19048)
[from set E]

Berlin Municipal Op. Cho.—Otto
                              in ♯ DT.TM 68042
(above; & Fl. Holländer)   (♯ T.TW 30036: ♭ UE 453939:
                                             in ♯ LB 6124, d.cs.)
Karlskoga Cha. Cho.—Testtinen (Swed)
          (D.F 44290 & F 44291: ♭ 75112 & 75113, d.c.)

— ARR. ORCH.
Hamburg Philharmonia—H-J. Walther   MSB. 78133
(above)

— ARR. ORGAN
R. Ellsasser (in MGM. set 200: ♯ E 200: ♭ K 200)
C. Smart (D.F 10252)
C. Cronham (Mjr. 5173)
J. Perceval (ArgOd. 57017)
R. K. Biggs (Cap.CAS 9017) etc.

Das süsse Lied verhallt S & T (Sc. 2)
(Bridal Chamber Scene)
☆ K. Flagstad & L. Melchoir   ♯ G.ALP 1276
(Parsifal)   (♯ Vic.LCT 1105: ♭ set WCT 1105)
E. Shumskaya & I. Kozlovsky (Russ)
          (USSRM.D 1175/6; excerpt, T solo, USSR. 21575/6)

... Atmest du nicht ... Höchstes Vertrau'n T
R. Schock (2ss) [from set G]   **G.DB 11556**
H. Hopf   in ♯ Phi.N 00732R
(above & below)   (in ♯ Epic.LC 3103)

In fernem Land (Gralserzählung) T (Sc. 3)
L. Fehenberger [from set E]   PV. **72444**
(above)   (in ♯ Pol. 19043: ♭ 30048: ♯ 18147, d.c. &
                                        Eta. 225021, d.c.)

R. Schock [from set G]   **G.DB 11557**
(below)   (♭ 7ER 5031: 7RW 19-508: 7ERF 139:
                                             in ♯ WBLP 1501)

H. Hopf   in ♯ Phi.N 00732R
(above)   (in ♯ Epic.LC 3103)

L. Havlák (Cz)   in ♯ U. 5205H
(Tannhäuser, Tristan; & Verdi)
I. Kozlovsky (Russ) (USSRM.D 00845 & USSR. 022908/9)
S. Lemeshev (Russ) (USSRM.D 00990)
☆ A. Pertile (Ital) (in ♯ Ete. 710)

Mein lieber Schwan! T (Lohengrin's Abschied)
R. Schock [from set G]   **G.DB 11557**
(In fernem Land)   (♭ 7ER 5031: 7RW 19-508: 7ERF 139)

H. Hopf [1]   in ♯ Phi.N 00732R
(below, Rienzi, Walküre, etc.)   (in ♯ Epic.LC 3013)
I. Kozlovsky (Russ) (USSRM.D 00846, also
                                        USSR. 21575/6)
L. Havlák (Cz) (in ♯ U. 5205H)

(Die) MEISTERSINGER VON NÜRNBERG
                    3 Acts   1868
COMPLETE RECORDING
☆ E. Schwarzkopf, O. Edelmann, E. Kunz, H. Hopf, etc.,
    Bayreuth Fest Cho. & Orch.—Karajan (♯ C.VCX 523/7)
COLLECTED EXCERPTS
Prelude
Fanget an! T Act I (a)
Was duftet doch der Flieder B Act II
Wahn! Wahn! Überall Wahn! B
Selig wie die Sonne S, Bs, T, T, A (b)
Silentium ... Wach' auf! Cho.
Morgenlich leuchtend T (a)
Verachtet mir die Meister nicht B Act III (b)
   A. Kupper (S), H. Töpper (A), W. Windgassen
    (T), R. Holm (T), J. Hermann (B), Bavarian
    Radio Cho., Munich Phil. & Württemberg
    State Orchs.—Leitner   ♯ Pol. 19047
[Wach' auf! only, in ♯ Pol. 19048; marked (a) also
♭ Pol. 32114; (b) on ♭ Pol. 30112. Prelude is ☆; also
on ♭ Pol. 30111: ♯ 17032]

Prelude, Act III
Wahn! Wahn! Überall Wahn! Bs
Morgenlich leuchtend T Act III
  W. Giesler (T), J. Pease (Bs) & Hamburg Op.
   Orch.—Ludwig   ♯ Sel. 320.C.093
  (Lohengrin)

"Sachs Fragments"
Fliedermonolog; Jerum! Jerum! Act II
Wahnmonolog; Euch mahnt ihr's leicht;
Verachtet mir die Meister nicht Act III
  O. Edelmann & Vienna Sym. Orch.—Loibner
                              ♯ Phi.N 00680R
  (Parsifal, Tannhäuser, etc., in ♯ Epic.N 3052)
HIGHLIGHTS
E. von Kovatsky (S), L. Hansen (T), F. Grossman (B),
   Prague Op. House Cho. & Orch.—Wentzel[2]
(4ss)   ♯ Allo. 3061/2
I. Camphausen (S), E. Nachtigall (T), G. Ramms (B),
   Dresden State Op. Cho. & Orch.—Schreiber[3]
                                  ♯ Roy. 1429

ACT I
Prelude
N.B.C. Sym.—Toscanini (n.v.)
                  in ♯ Vic. set LM 6020
(Prelude, Act III, Siegfried Idyll, Lohengrin, etc.)
              (in ♯ ItV.A12R 0137; FV.A 630252)
Bamberg Sym.—Horenstein ♯ AmVox.PL 9110
(Lohengrin, Tannhäuser, Tristan)
Vienna Sym.—Moralt   ♯ Phi.N 00183L
(Fliegende Holländer, Tannhäuser, Tristan)
(Tannhäuser only, on ♯ S 06063R)
N.Y.P.S.O.—Szell   ♯ AmC.AL 54
(Rienzi, Overture)   (& in ♯ ML 4918)
Vienna Phil.—Knappertsbusch (n.v.)
                              ♯ D.LW 5038
(Prelude, Act III)   (♯ Lon.LD 9026)
Detroit Sym.—Paray   in ♯ Mer.MG 50021
(Lohengrin, Tannhäuser, etc.)   (♯ FMer.MLP 7504)
Westminster Sym.—Collingwood C.DX 1887
Zürich Tonhalle—Ackermann   ♯ MMS. 29
(Prelude, Act III & Tannhäuser)   (& in ♯ MMS. 100S)
L.S.O.—del Mar   ♯ MApp. 4
(Tannhäuser Prelude; & Talk by T. Scherman)
R.I.A.S. Sym.—Sebastian   ♯ Rem. 199-177
(Lohengrin & Tannhäuser)
N.W. Ger. Phil.—Schüchter   ♯ Imp.ILP 130
(below & Tannhäuser)
Berlin Phil.—Furtwängler[4]   ♯ Per.SPL 716
(R. Strauss, etc.)
Leipzig Radio—Gerdes   Eta. 225026
N.B.C. Sym.   ♯ SFA. 1
(Berlioz & Tchaikovsky)
Moscow Radio—Golovanov (USSRM.D 436)
Berlin Sym.—List (in ♯ Roy. 1399)
Orch.—Swarowsky (in ♯ MTW. 24: ♭ EP 24)
☆ Vienna Phil.—Furtwängler (in ♯ G.VALP 538:
                    FALP 289; ♯ Vic.LHMV 1049)
Philharmonia—Dobrowen (in ♯ BB.LBC 1048:
                                ♭ set WBC 1048)
Württemberg St. Op.—Leitner (in ♯ Pol. 17032: ♭ 30111)
Rome Sym.—Questa (♭ Roy.EP 219)

Am stillen Herd Ens. (Sc. 3)
— CONCERT VERSION (Tenor part only)
P. Anders   Pol. 62896
(Preislied)   (♭ Pol. 32101)
H. Hopf   in ♯ Phi.N 00732R
(Lohengrin, Rienzi, etc.)   (in ♯ Epic.LC 3103)
☆ L. Slezak (in ♯ Ete. 499)
  R. Tauber (in ♯ Ete. 712)

Fanget an! T (Sc. 3)
H. Hopf   in ♯ Phi.N 00732R
(above & below)   (in ♯ Epic.LC 3103)

ACT II
Was duftet doch der Flieder Bs (Sc. 3)
G. London   in ♯ AmC.ML 4999
(below; Boris, Falstaff, Rigoletto, etc.)
J. Hermann   ♭ Pol. 30109
(Wahnmonolog)

---

[1] This was originally announced and catalogued as the Act I 'Farewell': Nun sei bedankt, but this has been corrected by
Philips. The Epic is labelled Act I, but in fact contains this aria.
[2] Contains Act I, Sc. 1; Act II; Act III, Sc. 3 & 5 excerpts.
[3] Contains Act I, Sc. 1; Act II, Sc. 5; Act III, Sc. 3 & 5 excerpts.
[4] Incomplete; from sound-track of film Symphony.

(Die) MEISTERSINGER—Fliedermonolog (*continued*)
P. Schoeffler & Vienna State Op.—Prohaska
in ‡ **Van.VRS 469**
(*Africaine, Vêpres Siciliennes, etc.*) (‡ Ama.AVRS 6022)
☆ P. Schoeffler [from Decca set] ‡ **D.LW 5082**
(*below*) (♭ *VD 506;* ‡ *Lon.LD 9078*)
☆ P. Schoeffler (in ‡ Rem. 199-137 & with commentary
by S. Spaeth, on ‡ Rem. 9)

Gut'n Abend, Meister S, Bs [& A] (Sc. 4)
H. Gueden, P. Schoeffler & E. Schürhoff
‡ **D.LW 5103**
(*below*) [from Decca set] (‡ *Lon.LD 9079*)
☆ M. Reining & P. Schoeffler (D.Z 966)

ACT III
Prelude
Philadelphia—Ormandy ‡ **AmC.ML 4865**
(*below, Walküre, Tannhäuser, Meistersinger*)
(& in ‡ *AL 43;* in ‡ *Phi.S 06619R*)
Royal Phil.—Beecham ‡ **EPhi.ABL 3039**
(*below, Gotterdämmerung, Fl. Holländer*)
(‡ AmC.ML 4962; Phi.N 02113L)
N.B.C. Sym.—Toscanini G.DB 21564
(ED 1242: ♭ *7ERF 114;* in ‡ *Vic.LRM 7029:*
♭ set ERB 7029 & in ‡ set LM 6020; ‡ItV.A12R 0137:
♭ *A72R 0005;* ‡ *FV.A 330209* & A 630252)
Vienna Phil.—Knappertsbusch (n.v.)
‡ **D.LW 5038**
(*Prelude Act I*) (‡ *Lon.LD 9026*)
Zürich Tonhalle—Ackermann ‡ **MMS. 29**
(*Prel. Act I, & Tannhäuser*)
R.I.A.S. Sym.—Sebastian ‡ **Rem. 199-174**
(*below, Lohengrin, Tannhäuser*)

Wahn! Wahn! Überall Wahn! Bs (Sc. 1)
(*Sachs' Wahnmonolog*)
G. London (*above*) in ‡ **AmC.ML 4999**
J. Herrmann (*above*) ♭ **Pol. 30109**
☆ P. Schoeffler [from Decca set] ‡ **D.LW 5082**
(*above*) (‡ *Lon.LD 9078*)

Grüss Gott, mein Ev'chen S, T, Bs (Sc. 3)
☆ H. Gueden, G. Treptow, P. Schoeffler ‡ **D.LW 5103**
(*above*) [from set] (‡ *Lon.LD 9079*)

SCENE 5
Tanz der Lehrbuben Cho. & orch.
Aufzug der Meistersinger Orch.
Silentium . . . Wach' auf! Cho.
Euch macht ihr's leicht B
☆ P. Schoeffler (B), A. Dermota (T), Vienna State Op.
Cho. & Vienna Phil.—Knappertsbusch
[from set] ‡ **D.LW 5101**
(*below*) (‡ *Lon.LD 9080*)

. . . Tanz der Lehrbuben & Aufzug der Meistersinger
☆ Württemberg State Op. Cho. & Orch.—Leitner
(♭ *Pol. 30015*)
— — ORCH. only
Royal Phil.—Beecham ‡ **EPhi.ABL 3039**
(*above*) (‡ AmC.ML 4962; Phi.N 02113L)
Philadelphia—Ormandy ‡ **AmC.ML 4865**
(*above*) (In ‡ *AL 43:* ♭ *A 1839;* ‡ *Phi.S 06619R*)
N.W. Ger. Phil.—Schüchter ‡ **Imp.ILP 130**
(*above*) (♭ *Od.BEOW 32-3006*)

. . . Tanz der Lehrbuben, only
Hamburg Philharmonia—H-J. Walther
MSB. 78135
(*Wolf-Ferrari: Segreto di Susanna, Overture*)
R.I.A.S. Sym.—Sebastian ‡ **Rem. 199-174**
(*above*)
☆ Vienna Phil.—Furtwängler ♭ **G. 7R 141**
(*Walküre*) (♭ *7RQ 3004: 7RW 125;*
in ‡ *Vic.LHMV 1049:* ♭ *EHA 17*)

Silentium . . . Wach' auf! Cho.
Berlin Municipal Op.—Otto **T.S 11722**
(*Nabucco—Va pensiero*) (& ‡ *T.TW 30036:*
♭ *US 45722:* in ‡ *LB 6124*)
Bavarian Radio—Leitner ♭ **Pol. 32111**
(*Parsifal—Zum letzten Liebesmahle*) (in ‡ AmD.DL 9797)

Morgenlich leuchtend T (Concert version)
H. Hopf in ‡ **Phi.N 00732R**
(*above*) (in ‡ Epic.LC 3103)
P. Anders **Pol. 62896**
(*Am stillen Herd*) (♭ *Pol. 32101*)
☆ L. Slezak (in ‡ Ete. 499)
R. Tauber (in ‡ Ete. 712)
G. Nelepp (*Russ*) (in ‡ USSR. D 2074)

Verachtet mir die Meister nicht Bs
☆ P. Schoeffler [from Decca set] ‡ **D.LW 5101**
(*above*) (‡ *Lon.LD 9080*)

PARSIFAL 3 Acts 1882
EXCERPTS
Prelude, Act II, Sc. 1 & 2 excerpts
H. Neumeyer (T), F. Meesen (B), G. Ramms (Bs), Dresden
State Op. Cho. & Orch.—Schreiber ‡ Allo. 3095

ACT I
Prelude
Orch.—Stokowski ‡ **Vic.LM 1730**
(*below; & Schubert*) (♭ set WDM 1730; ‡ItV.A12R 0042)
☆ N.B.C. Sym.—Toscanini ‡ **G.BLP 1033**
(*below*) (‡ *FBLP 1007* & in ‡ Vic. set LM 6020;
ItV.A12R 0136; FV.A 630251)
☆ Vienna State Op.—Swarowsky ‡**Sup.LPM 134**
(*Tristan, Prelude*) (‡ *U. 5110C*)
☆ Munich State Op.—Konwitschny (in ‡ Nix.ULP 9065)
Philadelphia—Stokowski (in ‡ Cam.CAL 163)

Titurel, der fromme Held Bs
J. Greindl **PV. 36074**
(♭ *Pol. 32045*)

Transformation Music Cho. & orch.
Zum letzten Liebesmahle (*Grail Scene*)
Württemberg State Op.—Leitner ♭ **Pol. 32111**
(*Meistersinger—Wach auf!*)

Nein! Lasst ihn unenthüllt! B [& Bs]
(*Amfortas' Lament*)
O. Edelmann in ‡ **EPhi.ABR 4030**
(*above & below*) (‡ *Phi.N 00630R;* ‡ Epic.LC 3052)
P. Schoeffler [& Anon. Bs] in ‡ **Van.VRS 469**
(*Simone Boccanegra, Vêpres siciliennes, etc.*)
(‡ Ama.AVRS 6022)

ACT II
Dies alles . . . Ich sah' das Kind S, T, Bs
(*Kundry—Parsifal Scene, complete*)
☆ K. Flagstad, L. Melchior & G. Dilworth ‡**G.ALP 1276**
(*Lohengrin—Bridal Chamber Scene*)
(‡ Vic.LCT 1105: ♭ set WCT 1105)
. . . Sop. part only (commences *Nein, Parsifal, du thör'ger
Reiner*)
☆ H. Traubel (2ss) **G.DB 21562**
(*Lohengrin, on* ♭ *7ER 5027*)

ACT III
Symphonic synthesis — ARR. Stokowski
Orch.—Stokowski ‡ **Vic.LM 1730**
(*above; & Schubert*) (♭ set WDM 1730; ‡ItV.A12R 0042)
So ward es uns verhiessen Bs & T
(*Scene I—Good Friday Music*)
. . . Das ist Karfreitagszauber Bs only
☆ J. Greindl (♭ *Pol. 30025*)
Karfreitagszauber — ORCH. ONLY
(Concert version)
Royal Phil.—Beecham ‡ **EPhi.ABL 3039**
(*Fliegende Holländer, Meistersinger, Götterdämmerung*)
(‡ AmC.ML 4962; Phi.N 02113L)
Detroit Sym.—Paray ‡ **Mer.MG 50044**
(*Fliegende Holländer, Tristan, Siegfried*)
☆ N.B.C. Sym.—Toscanini ‡ **G.BLP 1033**
(*Prelude*) (‡ *FBLP 1007;* in ‡ Vic. set LM 6020;
ItV.A12R 0136; ♭ *A72R 0039;* FV.A 630251, d.cs.)
☆ Munich State Op.—Konwitschny (in ‡ Nix.ULP 9065:
♭ *EP 727;* ♭ *Ura.UREP 46*)
Philadelphia—Stokowski (in ‡ Cam.CAL 163)

☆ = Re-issue of a recording to be found in previous volumes.

[COLA] RIENZI, DER LETZTE DER
    TRIBUNEN 5 Acts 1842
Overture
N.Y.P.S.O.—Szell   # *AmC.AL 54*
(*Meistersinger, Prelude*)   (& in # *ML 4918*)
Berlin Municipal Op.—Rother   # *T.NLB 6116*
(*Tannhäuser, Overture*)
Moscow Radio—Golovanov   # *USSR.D 1732*
(*Tristan—Prelude & Liebestod*)
☆ N.Y.P.S.O.—Stokowski   # *C.C 1026*
  (*Walküre*)   (# *FC 1027: QC 1027*)
☆ Vienna Sym.—Swarowsky   # *Sup.LPM 80*
  (*Tannhäuser, Overture*)   (*U. 5067C*)
☆ Munich State Op.—Konwitschny (in # Nix.ULP 9069;
           MTW. 553; ♭ Ura.UREP 26)
Boston Prom.—Fiedler (in # Cam.CAL 250)
Ihr Römer, hört die Kunde Cho. Act II
☆ Württemberg State Op. Cho. & Orch.—Leitner
           (in # *AmD.DL 4056*)
Gerechter Gott! . . . **In seiner Blüthe** . . A Act III
  ◨ E. Schumann-Heink (AF.AGSB 81* &
       V‡ *RR.M 307** & in ‡ *B & B.* 3*)
Allmächt'ger Vater, blick herab T Act V
  (*Rienzi's Prayer*)
H. Hopf   in # *Phi.N 00732R*
(*Walküre, Fliegende Holländer, etc.*) (in # Epic.LC 3103)
K. Terkal   ♭ *D.VD 513*
(*Fliegende Holländer—Mit Gewitter* . . .)
  ◨ H. Jadlowker (AF.AGSB 81*)

(Der) RING DES NIBELUNGEN Cycle, f.p. 1876
1. Das Rheingold   ('Vorabend')
2. Die Walküre   ('Erster Tag')
3. Siegfried   ('Zweiter Tag')
4. Götterdämmerung   ('Dritter Tag')
COMPLETE RECORDING by Dresden State Op. Co.[1]
  SEE individual operas, below

(Das) RHEINGOLD 1 Act (4 Scenes) 1869
COMPLETE RECORDING
  Soloists & Dresden State Op. Cho. & Orch.
    —Schreiber (6ss)   # *Allo. 3125/7*
    [Excerpts from Sc. 1 (almost complete), Scs. 3 & 4,
    on # Allo. 3086—soloists named as H. Lux (S), F.
    Meesen (B), G. Ramms (Bs). This disc has also been
    stated to be a recording of a Frankfurt broadcast]

Weiche, Wotan, weiche! A & B
  (*Erda's Warning*) (Sc. 4)
  . . . **Erda's part** only   (Concert version)
M. Klose   *Pol. 62935*
(*Tristan—Einsam wachend*)   (♭ *32026*)
☆ E. Schumann-Heink (AF.AGSB 1)[2]
   E. Wysor (in ‡ Rem. 9, with commentary by S. Spaeth)
  ◨ S. Onegin (in ‡ Sca. 821*)
Einzug der Götter in Walhall Ens. (Sc. 4)
 — ORCH. ONLY
☆ Munich State Op.—Konwitschny
          in # *Nix.ULP 9063*
      (♭ *Nix.EP 727*; # *Ura. 7084*: ♭ *UREP 27*)
  . . . **Abendlich strahlt der Sonne Auge** B
  (*Wotan's part only*)
G. London   in # *AmC.ML 4658*
  ◨ J. Schwarz (in ‡ Ete. 498*)
   M. Journet (in # SBDH.JALP 19*)

(Die) WALKÜRE 3 Acts 1870
COMPLETE RECORDINGS
  Sieglinde ... ... L. Rysanek (S)
  Siegmund ... ... L. Suthaus (T)
  Hunding ... ... G. Frick (Bs)
  Brünnhilde ... ... M. Mödl (S)
  Fricka ... ... M. Klose (A)
  Wotan ... ... F. Frantz (B)
  Walküre ... Frl. Schreyer, Hellwig, Schmedes,
           Siewert, Köth, Töpper, Blatter &
           Hermann
  & Vienna Phil. Orch.—Furtwängler
          # *G.ALP 1257/61*
  (10ss)   (# *QALP 10098/102*; # Vic. set LHMV 900)
  Soloists & Dresden State Op. Cho. & Orch.
    —Schreiber (10ss)   # *Allo. 3128/32*

ACT I

Trägst du Sorge, mir zu vertrauen
Die sie leidig Los dir beschied . . . **Ein trauriges**
  Kind S, T, Bs (Sc. 2)
☆ M. Müller, W. Windgassen, J. Greindl, from Pol. Act I
  set (*PV. 36053*; first part only on ♭ *Pol. 30031*)
Love Duet—Finale, Act I S & T (Sc. 3)
  . . . **Der Männer Sippe** S only
☆ L. Lehmann (in # Vic.LM 1909)
   A. Varnay (in # Rem. 199-137, & with commentary by
             S. Spaeth, # Rem. 9)
  . . . **Ein Greis in grauen Gewand** S only
  ◨ G. Lubin (IRCC. 3116*)
  . . . **Winterstürme wichen dem Wonnemond** to end
  of Act
☆ M. Müller & W. Windgassen (FPV. 5040)
  . . . **Tenor part** only
  H. Hopf   in # *Phi.N 00732R*
  (*Fliegende Holländer, Meistersinger, etc.*)
☆ L. Melchior (from *G.DA 1664*, see WERM)
           (in # Vic. set LCT 6701)
  ◨ R. Tauber (in # Ete. 701*)
   G. Borgetti (*Ital*) (in # *HRS. 3002**)
  . . . **Du bist der Lenz** S only
☆ H. Traubel (in # Vic.LRM 7031: ♭ set ERB 7031:
               & in # LM 1909)
  ◨ Lilli Lehmann (in # Ete. 702*)
   O. Fremstad (in # AudR.LPA 2340*)
  . . . **Siegmund heiss'ich** T & S   . . . T solo only
  ◨ E. Schmedes (in # *HRS. 3006**)

ACT II

Ho-jo-to-ho! S (Sc. 1)
  ◨ O. Fremstad (in # AudR.LPA 2340*; in # *FRP 3**)

ACT III

COMPLETE RECORDING
☆ A. Varnay (S), L. Rysanek (S), S. Björling (B), etc.,
  Bayreuth Fest. Orch.—v. Karajan (# C.WCX 1506/7:
         auto, # WCX 1005/6: # VCX 501/2)
Prelude: Walkürenritt — ORCH. ONLY
  (Concert Version)
Vienna Phil.—Knappertsbusch # *D.LXT 2822*
(*Fl. Holländer & Tannhäuser*)   (# *Lon.LL 800*)
(*F. Holländer only, # D.LW 5106; Lon.LD 9064*)
Philadelphia—Ormandy   in # *AmC.ML 4865*
(*below; Tannhäuser, Meistersinger*)
           (& in # *AL 43; Phi.S 06619R*)
Berlin Phil.—Markevitch   # *Pol. 19024*
(*Tannhäuser & Siegfried Idyll*)
London Phil. Sym.—Rodzinski
          # *West.LAB 7013*
(*below, & Götterdämmerung*)
Detroit Sym.—Paray   in # *Mer.MG 50021*
(# *FMer.MLP 7504*; ♭ *Mer.EP 1-5045; FMer.MEP 14510*)
Hamburg Philharmonia—H-J. Walther
(*Feuerzauber*)   *MSB. 78049*
☆ N.B.C. Sym.—Toscanini   ♭ *G.7ER 5003*
  (*Tristan—Liebestod*) (*Beethoven*, on ♭ *Vic.ERA 249*)
  (*Damnation de Faust, March* on ♭ *ItV.A72R 0058*)
Orch.—Swarowsky (in # MTW. 24: ♭ set EP 24)
Regent Sym. (in # *Rgt.MG 7001*)
☆ Munich State Op.—Konwitschny (in # Nix.ULP 9063
           & 9084; Ura. 7084: ♭ UREP 27)
  Württemberg State—Leitner (*PV. 36071*;
            ♭ Pol. 30031; ♭ AmD.ED 3523)
  Philharmonia—Sargent (in # AmC.RL 3091)
  Vienna Phil.—Furtwängler (♭ *G.7RQ 3004: 7RW 125*;
          in # Vic.LHMV 1049: ♭ *EHA 17*)
  Paris Cons.—Lindenberg (♭ *Od.7AO 2008*)
  — ARR. 4 PFS.:   Manhattan Pf. Qtt. (in # MGM.E 3130)
Fort denn eile S (Sc. 1)
H. Traubel   in # *Vic.LRM 7031*
(*above; Tristan & Lohengrin*)   (♭ set *ERB 7031*)

---

  [1] Stated in *Review of Recorded Music* (May 1954) by Mr. Hans Hotter to be actually a recording of a radio broadcast from
Bayreuth during the 1953 Festival, cond. Keilberth, with Hotter, Mödl, Windgassen, Greindl, Vinay, etc.
  [2] 1929 recording.

(Die) WALKÜRE (*continued*)

Herrlichstes Mädchen Ens. (Sc. 1)
♬ J. Gadski (S), L. Nordica (S), E. Schumann-Heink (A),
etc.[1] (in ‡ *IRCC.L 7006**)

Leb' wohl . . . (Wotans Abschied)
Feuerzauber Orch. (Sc. 3)
G. London & Vienna Sym.—Moralt
in ‡ **AmC.ML 4658**
P. Schoeffler & Vienna State Op.—Prohaska
‡ **Van.VRS 469**
(*Meistersinger, Parsifal, Africaine, etc.*)
(‡ Ama.AVRS 6022)
M. Reizen (*Russ*) & orch ‡ **USSR.D 1316**
(*Verdi: S. Boccanegra, etc.*)

— ARR. ORCH. only
☆ N.Y.P.S.O.—Stokowski ‡ **C.C 1026**
(*Rienzi Overture*) (‡ *FC/QC 1027*)

. . . Feuerzauber only Orch.
Philadelphia—Ormandy ‡ **AmC.ML 4865**
(*above, Tannhäuser, Meistersinger*)
(& in ‡ *AL 43:* ♭ *A 1839;* in ‡ *Phi.S 06619R*)
Hamburg Philharmonia—H-J. Walther
MSB. 78049
(*Walkürenritt*)
Württemberg State—Leitner **PV. 36071**
(*Walkürenritt*)
(*Götterdämmerung excpts. on* ‡ *AmD.DL 4072*)
London Phil. Sym.—Rodzinski ‡**West.LAB7013**
(*above, & Götterdämmerung*)
Orch.—Swarowsky (in ‡ *MTW.* 24: ♭ *set EP 24*)
☆ Munich State Op.—Konwitschny (in ‡ *Nix.ULP 9063*)
Philadelphia—Stokowski (in ‡ *Cam.CAL 120:*
♭ *CAE 101*)

SIEGFRIED 3 Acts 1876
COMPLETE RECORDING
Soloists & Dresden State Op. Cho. & Orch.
—Schreiber (10ss) ‡ **Allo. 3133/7**

ACT I
Ho-ho! Ho-hei! 2 T
♬ J. de Reszke & A. v. Hübbenet[1] (in ‡ *IRCC.L 7006**)

ACT II
Dass der mein Vater nicht ist T (*Waldweben*)
W. Windgassen[2] ‡ **Pol. 17059**
(*Tannhäuser*)
Waldweben — ORCH. only (Concert Version)
N.B.C. Sym.—Toscanini **G.DB 21599**
(in ‡ *Vic.LRM 7029:* ♭ *set ERB 7029;*
‡ *FV.A 330209;* ♭ *ItV.A72R 0005; G.7ERF 114*)
Detroit Sym.—Paray ‡ **Mer.MG 50044**
(*Fliegende Holländer, Parsifal, Tristan*)
Hamburg Philharmonia—H-J. Walther
MSB. 78134
☆ Paris Opéra—Fourestier (ArgPat.FXC 001)
Hollywood Bowl—Stokowski (in ‡ *Cam.CAL 153*)

Siegfried's Horn-call Horn unacc.
("Sonnerie de Siegfried")
L. Thevet (in ‡ *D.LX 3143*)

ACT III
Wache, Wala! B (Wotan only)
♬ R. Mayr (in ‡ *Sca. 822**)

Interlude (Sc. 3) (*Fire Music*)
☆ Munich State Op.—Konwitschny (in ‡ *Nix.ULP 9065;*
♭ *Ura.UREP 46*)

Heil dir, Sonne! Finale S & T
A. Varnay, W. Windgassen & Bavarian Radio
—Weigert ‡ **Pol. 19045**
(*Götterdämmerung—Immolation*) (& ‡ *Pol. 18200*)
☆ K. Flagstad, S. Svanholm & Philharmonia—Sebastian
(2ss) ‡ *G.BLP 1035*
(‡ *FBLP 1052*)

. . . Ewig war ich (Brünnhilde, solo)
♬ G. Lubin (IRCC. 3116*)
L. Nordica [& G. Anthes (T)][1] (in ‡ *IRCC.L 7006**)

(Die) GÖTTERDÄMMERUNG
(*The Twilight of the Gods*) Prologue & 3 Acts 1876
COMPLETE RECORDING
Soloists, Dresden State Op. Cho. & Orch.
—Schreiber (12ss) ‡ **Allo. 3138/43**

COLLECTED EXCERPTS ‡ **Pol. 19042**
Siegfried's Rheinfahrt orch. (& ‡ *18098*)
Württemberg State—Leitner (also on ‡ *AmD.DL 4072*)
Seit er von dir geschieden (*Waltraute's Narrative*) Act I A
E. Höngen (also on *PV.* 36081)
Hoi-ho! (Hagen's Call) Act III Bs & cho.
☆ J. Greindl & Bavarian State Op. Cho.
Trauermarsch Act III orch.
Württemberg State—Leitner (also on ‡ *AmD.DL 4072*)

EXCERPTS
E. v. Kovatsky (S), L. Hansen (T), G. Ramms (B), Prague
Op. Cho. & Orch.—Wentzel ‡ **Allo. 3065**
(‡ *Pac.LDAD 49*)
♬ F. Leider (S), E. Marherr (S), R. Schubert (T), E.
Schmedes (T), L. Hoffmann (Bs) ‡ **Ete. 488***
[Some are ☆, see below]

PROLOGUE
Prelude
Berlin Sym.—List in ‡ **Roy. 1399**

Zu neuen Thaten S & T . . . Sop. part only
♬ J. Gadski (AF.AGSB 36*)

Siegfrieds Rheinfahrt (Finale) orch.
(Concert versions, usually inc. the interlude—Daybreak)
Paris Cons.—Schuricht[3] ‡ **D.LXT 5026**
(*below; & Tristan*) (‡ *Lon.LL 1074*)
Royal Phil.—Beecham ‡ **EPhi.ABL 3039**
(*below, Meistersinger, etc.*) (‡ *AmC.ML 4962;*
Phi.N 02113L)
Pittsburgh Sym.—Steinberg ‡ **DCap.CTL 7035**
(*Trauermusik; & Tristan*) (‡ *Cap.S 8185; ACap.CLCX 009*)
Berlin Municipal—Rother ‡ **DT.TM 68044**
(*below*) (‡ *T.TW 30018*)
London Phil. Sym.—Rodzinski
(*below, & Die Walküre*) ‡ **West.LAB 7013**
☆ N.B.C. Sym.—Toscanini[4] ‡ **G.ALP 1173**
(*R. Strauss: Don Juan*) (‡ *FALP/QALP 157; Vic.LM 1157*)
(& in ‡ Vic. set LM 6020; ItV.A12R 0136: ♭ *A72R 0040;*
♭ *FV.A 630251*)
☆ Vienna Phil.—Furtwängler ‡ **G.ALP 1016**
(*Trauermusik & Immolation*) (‡ *QALP 10079;*
in ‡ *Vic.LHMV 1049*)
Orch.—Swarowsky (in ‡ *MTW.* 24: ♭ *set EP 24*)
☆ Paris Cons.—Weingartner (in ‡ *AmC.ML 4680*)
Munich State Op.—Konwitschny (in ‡ *Nix.ULP 9065:*
♭ *EP 743;* ♭ *Ura.UREP 43*)

ACT I
Hier sitz' ich zur Wacht Bs
☆ L. Hoffmann (in ‡ *Ete.* 480)
♬ M. Journet (in ‡ *SBDH.JALP 19**)

Höre mit Sinn . . . (*Waltraute's Narrative*) A
Seit er von dir geschieden . . .
☆ E. Schumann-Heink (AF.AGSB 1)
E. Wysor (in ‡ *Ply.* 12-47)

ACT II
Hoi-Ho! (*Hagen's Call*) Bs, B & cho.
☆ L. Hoffmann (in ‡ *Ete.* 480)

Betrug! Schändlichster Betrug!
Schwurszene: Helle Wehr! Heilige Waffe!
. . . Sop. parts only
♬ J. Gadski (AF.AGSA 36*)

---

[1] From Mapleson cylinders. [2] Probably the complete scene—T solo only.
[3] Concert version by Schuricht.
[4] Concert version by Toscanini. Notwithstanding statement by R. C. Marsh in his *Toscanini Discography*, the recording
listed in Supp. II is a n.v., being the 1949 recording and not a reissue of the 1941 recording. We are informed by H.M.V.
that ALP 1173 is definitely the 1949 recording (as no doubt all the other reissues mentioned here are), being taken from
Vic.LM 1157.

(Die) GÖTTERDÄMMERUNG (continued)
ACT III

Brünnhilde, heilige Braut T
(Siegfried's Death)
W. Windgassen   *PV. 36083*
(Tristan—Wie sie selig)

Trauermusik orch. (*"Funeral March"*)
Royal Phil.—Beecham   ♯ EPhi.ABL 3039
(above)   (♯ AmC.ML 4962; Phi.N 02113L)
Paris Cons.—Schuricht[1]   ♯ D.LXT 5026
(above)   (♯ Lon.LL 1074)
Berlin Municipal—Rother   ♯ DT.TM 68044
(above)   (♯ T.TW 30018)
N.B.C. Sym.—Toscanini (n.v.)
in ♯ Vic. set LM 6020
(above, Siegfried Idyll, Meistersinger, etc.)
(♯ FV.A 630252; ♯ ItV.A12R 0137: ♭ A72R 0036)
Pittsburgh Sym.—Steinberg ♯ DCap.CTL 7035
(Rheinfahrt & Tristan)   (♯ Cap.S 8185; ACap.CLX 009)
Philadelphia—Ormandy   ♯ AmC.ML 4742
(Immolation & Tristan)
London Phil. Sym.—Rodzinski
♯ West.LAB 7013
(above; Die Walküre)
☆ Vienna Phil.—Furtwängler   ♯ G.ALP 1016
(Rheinfahrt & Immolation) (♯ QALP 10079: ♭ 7RW 124:
7R 151: RF 149: 7RQ 3011; in ♯ Vic.LHMV 1049:
♭ EHB 2)
☆ Munich State—Konwitschny[2] (in ♯ Nix.ULP 9065:
♭ EP 743; ♭ Ura.UREP 43)
Paris Cons.—Weingartner (in ♯ AmC.ML 4680)

Schweigt eures Jammers S & A
☆ F. Leider & E. Marherr (in ♯ Ete. 480)

Starke Scheite schichtet mir dort S
(Brünnhilde's Immolation—Finale)
K. Flagstad & Philharmonia—Furtwängler
(n.v.)   ♯ G.ALP 1016
(Rheinfahrt & Trauermusik)   (♯ QALP 10079)
(Tristan—Prelude & Liebestod on ♯ Vic.LHMV 1072)
[it is possible that ♯ G.FALP 194 is now the n.v. also]
A. Varnay & Bavarian Radio—Weigert
♯ Pol. 19045
(Siegfried—Heil dir, Sonne!)   (& ♯ Pol. 18200)
M. Mödl & Berlin Municipal Op.—Rother
♯ DT.LGX 66036
(Tristan und Isolde)   (♯ FT.320.TC.095; T.LE 6526)
M. Harshaw & Philadelphia—Ormandy
♯ AmC.ML 4742
(above; & Tristan, excerpts)
☆ F. Leider (in ♯ Ete. 480)

... Fliegt heim ihr Raben! S
E. Farrell[3] (in ♯ MGM.E 3185: ♭ set X 304: EP 527/8)
☒ J. Gadski (AF.AGSB 36*)

... Orch. finale only
☆ Munich State Op.—Konwitschny in ♯ Nix.ULP 9065
(in ♯ Nix.ULP 9084 & in ♯ Ura. 7084)

TANNHÄUSER 3 Acts 1845
COMPLETE RECORDING
☆ M. Schech (S), M. Bäumer (S), A. Seider (T), etc.,
Munich State Op. Cho. & Orch.—Heger
♯ Nix.ULP 9211-1/4
[Overture only on ♭ EP 719; Highlights on ♯ Ura. 7176]
HIGHLIGHTS
☆ Anon Artists (♯ Cam.CAL 233, in set CFL 101)

ACT I
Overture & Venusberg Music (Paris Version)
Vienna Phil.—Knappertsbusch   ♯ D.LXT 2822
(Fliegende Holländer & Walküre)   (♯ Lon.LL 800)
Philharmonia—Kletzki   ♯ C.CX 1129
(Tristan)   (♯ FCX 275: QCX 10073; Angel. 35059)
Philadelphia—Ormandy   ♯ AmC.ML 4865
(Lohengrin, Meistersinger, Walküre)
R.I.A.S. Sym.—Sebastian   ♯ Rem. 199-177
(Lohengrin & Meistersinger)
Anon. Orch. (*Rimsky*)   ♯ ACC.MP 3

... **Venusberg** only [orig. with Fem. cho.]
Berlin Phil.—Markevitch   ♯ Pol. 19024
(Walküre, excpt. & Siegfried Idyll)
Philharmonia—Karajan   ♯ C.CX 1327
(Aida, Khovanshchina, Prince Igor, etc.) (♯ Angel. 35307)

Overture (Concert version)
Vienna Phil.—Furtwängler   ♯ G.ALP 1220
(Lohengrin; & Liszt)   (♯ QALP 10088: FALP 362)
(Fliegende Holländer & Meistersinger)
on ♯ FALP 289: VALP 538)
Bamberg Sym.—Horenstein ♯ AmVox.PL 9110
(Lohengrin, Meistersinger, Tristan)
Vienna Sym.—Moralt   ♯ Phi.N 00183L
(Fliegende Holländer, Tristan, Meistersinger)
(Meistersinger Prelude only on ♯ S 06063R)
N.Y.P.S.O.—Szell   ♯ AmC.AL 55
(Fliegende Holländer, Overture) (♭ A 1876 & in ♯ ML 4918)
Florence Festival—Gui   ♯ AudC. 503
(Fliegende Holländer Overture, Grieg, Sibelius)
L.S.O.—del Mar   ♯ MApp. 4
(Meistersinger, Lohengrin; & talk by T. Scherman)
N.W. Ger. Phil.—Schüchter   ♯ Imp.ILP 130
(Meistersinger)   (Liszt on ♯ ILP 106; G.QDLP 6036)
Berlin Municipal Op.—Rother   ♯ T.NLB 6116
(Rienzi Overture)
London Phil. Sym.—Rodzinski
(Tristan)   ♯ West.LAB 7035
Detroit Sym.—Paray   in ♯ Mer.MG 50021
(♯ FMer.MLP 7504)
Zürich Tonhalle—Ackermann   ♯ MMS. 29
(Meistersinger, Preludes)
Berlin Sym.—List   in ♯ Roy. 1399
Leipzig Gewandhaus—Konwitschny
Eta. 225020/1
(3ss—Lohengrin—Gralserzählung)   (& in ♯ 720010)
Rhineland Sym.—Federer (in ♯ Rgt.MG 5058)
Moscow Radio—Golovanov (♯ USSR.D 0932)
☆ Munich State Op.—Heger   ♯ Ura. 7077
(Prelude Act III, & Lohengrin)   (from set)
(♭ UREP 19; ♭ Nix.EP 719)
☆ Württemberg State—Leitner (♭ Pol. 30071;
in ♯ Pol. 17032 & ♯ AmD.DL 4061)
Vienna Sym.—Swarowsky (in ♯ Sup.LPM 80; U. 5067C)

ACT I
Dir töne Lob! T
☒ L. Slezak (in ♯ Ete. 499*)

Als du in kühnem Sange ... B
D. Fischer-Dieskau   ♭ G. 7ER 5033
(below)   (♭ 7ERW 5033)
☒ M. Battistini (*Ital*) (in ♯ Ete. 709*)

ACT II
Dich, teure Halle S
M. Cunitz   ♯ DT.TM 68001
(Fl. Holländer—Senta's Ballad)
(♯ T.TW 30014; TV.VSK 9022: ♭ T.UV 109)
H. Zadek   ♯ EPhi.ABR 4004
(Lohengrin, Fl. Holländer; & R. Strauss) (♯ Phi.N 00655R)
L. Rysanek   ♭ Pol. 32102
(Elisabeths Gebet)
B. Nilsson   in ♯ G.ALPC 1
(Tosca, Samson & Dalila, etc.)
M. Janz   Eta. 225022
(Elisabeths Gebet)   (& in ♯ 720010)
L. Dvořáková (*Cz*)   in ♯ U. 5205H
(Tristan, etc. & Verdi)
Anon. Artist (in ♯ Roy. 1399)
☆ V. de los Angeles (♭ G.7RW 115: 7RQ 3024)

Fest-Marsch & Einzug der Gäste Cho. & orch.
Berlin Municipal Op.—Otto   T.E 3932
(Pilgerchor)   (♭ UE 453932 & in ♯ TW 30014;
♭ FT. 510.TC.002)
(idem; Kreutzer & Weber on ♯ DT.TM 68031)
☆ Württemberg State Op. —Leitner   ♭ Pol. 30015
(Meistersinger, excpts. Act III)

---

[1] Concert version by Schuricht.   [2] Includes *Finale.*
[3] From film *Interrupted Melody.*

TANNHÄUSER, Act II—Fest-Marsch (*continued*)
— ORCH. ONLY (Grand March)
Victor Sym.—Reiner   ♭ *Vic.ERA 185*
(*Lohengrin & Mendelssohn*)   (♭ *FV.A 95216*)
R.I.A.S. Sym.—Sebastian   in ‡ **Rem. 199-174**

Hamburg Philharmonia—H-J. Walther (*MSB. 78117*)
Moscow Radio—Samosud (USSR. 018679/80)
☆ Philharmonia—Dobrowen (♭ *G.7P 140: 7PW 126, d.c.*)
Chicago Sym.—Stock (in ‡ Cam.CAL 192)

Blick ich umher B
D. Fischer-Dieskau   ♭ *G. 7ER 5033*
(*above & below*)   (♭ *7ERW 5033*)
O. Edelmann   in ‡ *EPhi.ABR 4030*
(*above*)   (‡ *Phi.N 00630R;* Epic.LC 3052)

☆ H. Schlusnus (♭ *Pol. 32151:* ▽ 67353)
M. Dens (*Fr*) (♭ *Pat.D 105*)
A. Endrèze (*Fr*) (in ‡ Pat.PCX 5006)

ACT III

Prelude (*Tannhäuser's Pilgrimage*)
R.I.A.S. Sym.—Sebastian   ‡ **Rem. 199-174**
(*above*)
Württemberg State Op.—Elmendorff
(*below*)   ♭ *AmVox.VIP 45480*

☆ Munich State Op.—Heger   ‡ Ura. 7077
(*Overture & Lohengrin*)   (from set)
☆ Paris Cons.—Weingartner (in ‡ AmC.ML 4680)

Wohl wusst' ich hier sie im Gebet zu finden B
K. Gester   ♭ *AmVox.VIP 45480*
(*above & below*)

Pilgerchor—Beglückt darf nun (*Pilgrims' Chorus*)
Württemberg State Op.—Elmendorff
(*above*)   ♭ *AmVox.VIP 45480*
Berlin Municipal Op.—Otto   T.E 3932
(*above*)   (♭ *UE 453932;* ♭ *FT.510.TC.002*)
(*idem, Kreutzer & Weber on* ‡ *DT.TM 68031*)
   (& ‡ *T.TW 30036*)
Bavarian Radio Cho.   *PV. 72485*
(*Lohengrin—Brautchor*)   (♭ *Pol. 30085* & in ‡ 19048)
Royal Male Cho. & Maastricht Orch.
—Koekelkoren   ♭ *EPhi.NBE 11009*
(*Faust & Aida*) (Phi.N 12075G: in ‡ *S 06013R & P 10048R*)
Mormon Tabernacle Cho. & Org.—Cornwall (*Eng*)
   (C.LHX 15; ▽ ‡ AmC.ML 4789)

O du mein holder Abendstern B
D. Fischer-Dieskau   ♭ *G.7ER 5033*
(*above*)   (♭ *7ERW 5033*)
O. Edelmann   ‡ *EPhi.ABR 4030*
(*above*)   (‡ *Phi.N 00630R;* Epic.LC 3052)
I. Gorin   in ‡ **Alld. 3003**
   (♭ *EP 3003;* ‡ *MTW. 572*)

H. Thompson (in ‡ *MH. 33-104*)
S. Migai (*Russ*) (*USSR. 10109 & 19, sic*)
☆ H. Schlusnus (♭ *Pol. 32151:* ▽ Pol. 67353)
L. Tibbett (in ‡ Cam.CAL 171)
J. C. Thomas (in ‡ Cam.CAL 199: ♭ *CAE 246*)
Anon.—probably one of these (‡ in Cam.CAL 249)
A. Ivanov (*Russ*) (in ‡ *Sup.LPM 186;* U. 5176C)
M. Dens (*Fr*) (♭ *Pat.D 105:* in ‡ *DT 1020*)
A. Endrèze (*Fr*) (in ‡ Pat.PCX 5006)

— ARR. ORGAN: C. Cronham (*Mjr. 5146*)
☆ C. Courboin (in ‡ Cam.CAL 218)

— ARR. GUITAR: A. Valenti (in ‡ SMC. 1002)

Allmächt'ge Jungfrau, hör' mein Flehen S
(*Elisabeths Gebet*)
L. Rysanek   ♭ *Pol. 32102*
(*Dich teure Halle*)
M. Janz   Eta. 225022
(*Dich teure Halle*)   (& in ‡ *720010*)
Anon. artist (in ‡ Roy. 1399)

Inbrunst im Herzen T (*Rome Narration*)
W. Windgassen   *PV. 36101*
(*Siegfried on* ‡ *Pol. 17059*)   (♭ *Pol. 34003: 30101*)
☆ A. Seider (♭ *Ura.UREP 63*)
Ⓗ L. Slezak (in ‡ Ete. 499*)

TRISTAN UND ISOLDE 3 Acts 1865

COMPLETE RECORDING

Isolde	K. Flagstad (S)
Tristan	L. Suthaus (T)
Brangäne	B. Thebom (M-S)
Kurwenal	D. Fischer-Dieskau (B)
König Marke	J. Greindl (Bs)
Sailor ⎫	R. Schock (T)
Shepherd ⎭	
Melot	E. Evans (T)
Steersman	R. Davies (B)

Covent Garden Op. Cho. & Philharmonia
Orch.—Furtwängler   ‡ **G.ALP 1030/5**
(12ss) (‡ FALP 221/6: VALP 521/6;
   10ss, ‡ Vic. set LM 6700)
[Prelude, Act III, only on G.DB 21585:
   ♭ *7ERQ 123: 7ER 5036*]
[[1] Highlights on ‡ Vic.LM 1829]

ABRIDGED RECORDING

☆ N. Larsen-Todsen (S), I. Andrésen (Bs), etc., Bayreuth
Fest. Cho. & Orch.—Elmendorff
(6ss)   ‡ AmC. set EL 11

HIGHLIGHTS

Prelude, Act I	orch.	
Doch nun von Tristan	S & A₁	Act I
Einsam, wachend ...	A₂	Act II
Tatest du's wirklich?	Bs	Act II
Wie sie selig	T	Act III
Mild und leise	S	Act III

A. Varnay (S), H. Töpper (A_1), M. Klose (A_2),
W. Windgassen (T), K. Borg (Bs),
Württemberg State Orch.—Leitner
   ‡ **Pol. 19018**
☆ R. Bampton (S), A. Carron (T), etc. (‡ Cam.CAL 224)

EXCERPTS

Prelude, Narrative, Prelude Act III, Liebestod
☆ H. Traubel (S) & N.Y.P.S.O.—Rodzinski
   ‡ AmC.RL 3057
Act I: Westwärts schweift der Blick
Act II: Doch uns're Liebe
Act III: In mich dringt ... (Liebestod)
E. Farrell (S), H. Blankenberg (T), R. Petrak
   in ‡ MGM.E 3185
[film sound-track, *Interrupted Melody*]   (♭ *set X 304*)

Prelude, Liebesnacht, Liebestod — ARR. ORCH. only
Philadelphia—Ormandy   ‡ **AmC.ML 4742**
(*Götterdämmerung*)

Prelude & Liebestod — ARR. ORCH. only
Pittsburgh Sym.—Steinberg   ‡ **DCap.CTL 7035**
(*Götterdämmerung*)   (‡ Cap.S 8185; ACap.CLCX 009)
(*Liebestod only on* ♭ *Cap.FAP 8216*)
Philharmonia—Kletzki   ‡ **C.CX 1129**
(*Tannhäuser—Overture & Venusberg Music*)(‡Angel.35059)
   (‡ WCX 1129: QCX 10073: FCX 275)
Paris Cons.—Schuricht   ‡ **D.LXT 5026**
(*Götterdämmerung*)   (‡ Lon.LL 1074)
N.B.C. Sym.—Toscanini in ‡ **Vic. set LM 6020**
(*Götterdämmerung, Meistersinger, Siegfried*)
   (in ‡ ItV.A12R 0136; FV.A 630251)
Orch.—F. Busch   ‡ **FFB. pte.**
(*Beethoven & Schubert*)
Bamberg Sym.—Horenstein ‡ **AmVox.PL 9110**
(*Lohengrin, Meistersinger, Tannhäuser*)
Detroit Sym.—Paray   ‡ **Mer.MG 50044**
(*Fliegende Holländer, Parsifal, Siegfried*)
London Phil. Sym—Rodzinski
(*Tannhäuser*)   ‡ **West.LAB 7035**
Moscow Radio—Golovanov (‡ *USSR.D 1733*)
Israel Sym.—Riskin (‡ *Rem. 6*)

— ARR. ORGAN
R. Ellsasser   ‡ **MGM.E 3126**
(*Siegfried Idyll*)

ACT I

Prelude
Philharmonia—Furtwängler
   in ‡ **Vic.LHMV 1072**
(*Liebestod, & Götterdämmerung*)   [from set]
Vienna Sym.—Moralt   ‡ *Phi.S 06009R*
(*Fliegende Holländer Overture*)   (& in ‡ N 00183L)

(*continued on next page*)

---

[1] Contains Narration and Curse, Act I; Liebesnacht, Act II; Liebestod, Act III.

TRISTAN UND ISOLDE, Prelude Act I (*continued*)
Berlin Municipal Op.—Rother ♯ *DT.TM 68050*
(*Fliegende Holländer, Overture*) (♯ *T.TW 30028*)
Berlin Sym.—List in ♯ **Roy. 1399**
☆ Vienna State Op.—Swarowsky (♯ *Sup.LPM 134;*
U. 5110C; CdM.LD 8043)

Doch nun von Tristan? 2 S (or S & A) (Sc. 3)
M. Mödl & J. Blatter[1] ♯ **DT.LGX 66036**
(*Götterdämmerung*) (♯ FT. 320.TC.095; T.LE 6526)
☆ H. Traubel in ♯ *Vic.LRM 7031*
(*Lohengrin & Walküre*) (♭ set ERB 7031)

ACT II

Isolde!... Tristan! Geliebter!
S, T & A (*Love Duet*) (Sc. 2)
M. Mödl, W. Windgassen, J. Blatter & Berlin
Municipal Op.—Rother[2] ♯ **DT.LGX 66004**
(♯ T.LSK 7017; FT. 320.TC.031)

... Excerpt only
⎍ L. Nordica, G. Anthes & E. Schumann-Heink
(in ♯ *IRCC.L 7006**)[3]

... Einsam, wachend ... S or A
(*Brangäne's Warning*)
M. Klose *Pol. 62935*
(*Rheingold—Weiche, Wotan*) (♭ 32026)
☆ E. Wysor (in ♯ Rem. 9, with commentary by S. Spaeth)
⎍ S. Onegin (in ♯ Sca. 821*)

ACT III

Prelude
☆ Paris Cons.—Weingartner (in ♯ AmC.ML 4680)

Wie sie selig, hehr und milde T
(*Death of Tristan*) (Sc. 1)
W. Windgassen *PV. 36083*
(*Götterdämmerung: Brünnhilde, heil'ge Braut*)
(*Parsifal on* ♭ *Pol. 30025*)

Liebestod: Mild und leise S
K. Flagstad [from set] in ♯ *Vic.LHMV 1072*
(*Prelude, Act I & Götterdämmerung*)
(also in ♯ Vic.LM 1909, may be o.v.)
M. Mödl ♯ *DT.TM 68003*
(*Fidelio—Abscheulicher*)
(TV.VSK 9021: ♯ T.TW 30010: ♭ UV 102;
♭ FT. 470.TC.013)
L. Dvořáková (*Cz*) in ♯ **U. 5205H**
(*Lohengrin, Tannhäuser; & Verdi*)
☆ M. M. Callas (*Ital*) (in ♯ CCet.A 50175)

— ARR. ORCH.
☆ N.B.C. Sym.—Toscanini ♭ *G.7ER 5003*
(*Walküre—Walkürenritt*) (♭ 7ERW 5003)
☆ Württemberg State—Leitner (♭ AmD.ED 3522)

WAILLY, Paul de (1854–1933)

Aubade fl., ob. & cl.
Chicago Sym. Wind Trio in ♯ **Aphe.AP 14**

WAISSEL, Mattheus (fl. c. 1564-1592)

SEE: † RENAISSANCE MUSIC FOR THE LUTE
† RENAISSANCE & BAROQUE

WALCHA, Helmut (b. 1907)

Improvisations organ[4]
H. Walcha *Pol. 1028*
[Schnitger organ, Cappel]

WALDTEUFEL, Emil (1837-1915)

(Abridged listing only)

WALTZES
Acclamations, Op. 223
☆ A. Sandler Orch. (♭ *C.SEG 7530:*
in ♯ *QS 1020: S 1033*)

(La) Barcarolle, Op. 178
A. Lutter Orch.(*P.DPW 83:* ♭ *WMSP 50001; Od. O-28581*)

Dolores, Op. 170
M. Weber Orch. (in ♯ *C.S 1055; AmC.CL 6034*)

España, Op. 236
Philadelphia—Ormandy in ♯ **AmC.ML 4893**
(♯ *Phi.S 06612R*)
☆ Boston Prom.—Fiedler (n.v.) *G.B 10563*
(*Estudiantina* on ♭ *G.7EG 8015:* in ♯ *CLP 1065;*
♯ *Vic.LM 1910:* ♭ *ERA 242; ItV.A72R 0048*)
Strauss Orch.—Ries-Walter (in ♯ *Mae.OA 20016*)
Vienna Light—Hellmesberger (V♯ *MMS.ML 1504*)
☆ Munich Phil.—Nick (in ♯ *AmD.DL 4064*)
Vienna Radio—Schönherr (in ♯ *Vien.LPR 1030;*
GA. 33-312)
Berlin Municipal—Otto (♭ *T.U 45278*)
R. Munro (♭ *D/Lon.DFE/BPE 6018*)

Estudiantina, Op. 191
Philadelphia—Ormandy ♭ *AmC.A 1866*
(*Les Patineurs*) (in ♯ *AL 48* & ML 4893; *Phi.S 06612R*)
F.O.K. Sym.—Urbanec *U.C 24408*
☆ Boston Prom.—Fiedler *G.B 10603*
(*España* on ♭ *G.7EG 8015*) (& in ♯ *CLP 1065*)
(o.v. ♭ *Cam.CAE 162*)
"Viennese Sym." (in ♯ Ply. 12-100)
M. Weber Orch. (in ♯ *C.S 1055; AmC.CL 6034*)
Strauss Orch.—Ries-Walter (in ♯ *Mae.OA 20016*)
☆ Philharmonia—Lambert (in ♯ *C.S 1006: QS 6007:*
♭ *SED 5506: SEBQ 113;* in ♯ *AmC.RL 3054*
Vienna Radio—Schönherr (in ♯ *AFest.CFR 62;*
GA. 33-312)
A. Bernard Str. Orch. (in ♯ *Nix.SLPY 128;*
Pac.LDPA 28, etc.)
R. Munro Orch. (♭ *Lon.BEP 6019*)

(L') Étoile polaire, Op. 238
Bolshoi Theatre—Sakharov (*USSR. 10737/8*)

(Les) Grenadiers
Grenadier Guards Band (*D.F 10265*)
☆ R. Munro Orch. (♭ *Lon.BEP 6019*)

Je t'aime, Op. 177
P. Bonneau Orch. (♭ *Pat.ED 26*)

Mon Rêve, Op. 151
☆ Vienna Sym.—Stolz (D.KD 2435)
R. Munro Orch. (♭ *D.DFE 6018; Lon.BEP 6018*)
Vienna Radio—Schönherr (in ♯ GA. 33-312)

(Les) Patineurs, Op. 183 (*The Skaters*)
Philharmonia—Karajan ♭ *C.SEL 1528*
(*Chabrier: España*) (♭ *SEBQ 129*)
Philadelphia—Ormandy ♭ *AmC.A 1866*
(*Estudiantina*) (in ♯ *AL 48* & ML 4893; in ♯ *Phi.S 06612R*)
F.O.K. Sym.—Smetáček ♮ *U.H 24404/5*
(3ss—*Sibelius: Valse triste*)
Strauss Fest.—Ries-Walter (in ♯ *Mae.OA 20016*)
Vox Sinfonietta—Gräf (in ♯ *AmVox.VX 570*)
H. Hagestedt Orch. (*Pol. 49113:* ♭ 22113)
M. Weber Orch. (in ♯ *C.S 1055; AmC.CL 6034*)
Mantovani Orch. (*D.F 10210: F 43700:* ♭ *D 17700:* &
in ♯ *LF 1525;* Lon.LL 913)
Light Orch.—E. Robinson (in ♯ Argo.RG 40;
West.WP 6002)
"Viennese Sym." (in ♯ Ply. 12-100)
☆ Philharmonia—Lambert (in ♯ *C.S 1006: QS 6007;*
in ♯ *AmC.RL 3054*)
N.B.C. Sym.—Toscanini (♭ *G.7ER 5017:* 7ERQ 109:
7ERF 105; ♭ *DV.* 16286; ♯ *G.FBLP/QBLP 1035;*
ItV.A12R 0009; *Vic.LRY 9000, etc.*)
Carnegie Pops—Brockman (♯ *AmC.A 1573*)
Boston Prom.—Fiedler (♭ *Cam.CAE 141*)
Vienna Radio—Schönherr (in ♯ *Vien.LPR 1035*)
Orch.—Marrow (in ♯ MGM.E 3138)
R. Munro Orch. (♭ *D.DFE 6018; Lon.BEP 6018*)
Suisse Romande Orch.—Stolz (D.KD 2435)
— ARR. PF
H. Seiter (in ♯ *Nix.WLPY 6736; West.WL 3036*)
— ARR. 2 PFS. L. Shankson & I. Wright (in ♯ Roy. 1447)

---

[1] Begins *Weh' ach Wehe! Dies zu dulden.*
[2] Commences with Interlude before Sc. 2 and continues to end of scene with cut of 321 bars on side 1.
[3] From Mapleson cylinder.
[4] To demonstrate the registers of the **Schnitger Organ, Cappel,** dating from 1695 (or perhaps 1688), as introduction to his series of Bach recordings.

Pluie de diamants, Op. 160   (or: *Pluie d'or*)
Philadelphia—Ormandy   in ‡ **AmC.ML 4893**
                        (in ‡ *Phi.S 06612R*)
☆ Vienna Radio—Schönherr (in ‡ *GA. 33-312*)

Pomone, Op. 155
Strauss Fest.—Ries-Walter (in ‡ *Mae.OA 20016*)
M. Pagnoul Orch. (♭ *Riv.REP 13045*)
☆ Philharmonia—Lambert (in ‡ *C.S 1006: QS 6007;*
                                     AmC.RL 3054, d.c.)
A. Sandler Orch. (in ‡ *C.S 1033: QS 6020*)

(Les) Sirènes, Op. 154
A. Lutter Orch.(*P.DPW 83:* ♭ *WMSP 50001; Od.O-28581*)
M. Pagnoul Orch. (♭ *Riv.REP 13045*)
☆ R. Munro Orch. (♭ *Lon.BEP 6019*)

Sous la voûte étoilée, Op. 253
Strauss Fest. Orch.—Ries-Walter   in ‡ *Mae.OA 20016*

Souviens-toi, Op. 173
P. Bonneau Orch. (♭ *Pat.ED 27*)

Sur la plage, Op. 234
☆ Philharmonia—Lambert (in ‡ *C.S 1006: QS 6007:*
                              ♭ *SED 5504, d.c.: SEDQ 512*)

Tendresse, Op. 217
P. Bonneau Orch. (♭ *Pat.ED 27*)

Toujours ou jamais, Op. 156
☆ Orch. Mascotte (*P.MP 125*)

Très jolie, Op. 159 (alias: *Ganz allerliebst*)
Strauss Fest.—Ries-Walter   in ‡ *Mae.OA 20016*
☆ Boston Prom.—Fiedler (*G.EG 7891: EA 4102:*
   ♭ *7EG 8009; ItV.A72R 0048;* in ‡ *Vic.LM 1910:*
                ♭ *ERA 242;* in ‡ *G.CLP 1065*)
R. Munro Orch. (♭ *D/Lon.DFE/BEP 6018*)
Vienna Radio—Schönherr (in ‡ *Vien.LPR 1029*)

Violettes, Op. 148
Orch.—B. Stanley (in ‡ *Var. 6984*)
P. Bonneau Orch. (♭ *Pat.ED 26*)

WALLACE, William Vincent (1812-1865)

MARITANA   Opera 3 Acts 1845
Scenes that are brightest S
  ♀ R. Ponselle (in ‡ *Sca. 803**)

WALMISLEY, Thomas Attwood (1814-1856)

SEE: ENGLISH CHURCH MUSIC, VOL. III

WALTHER von der Vogelweide (c. 1165-c. 1230)

SEE: † MUSIC OF THE MIDDLE AGES
     † ANTHOLOGIE SONORE

WALTHER, Johann (1496-1570)

SEE: † MOTETS ON LUTHER TEXTS

WALTHER, Johann Gottfried (1684-1748)

ORGAN MUSIC (Refs. to DTÖ, XXVI, XXVII)
COLLECTIONS
Concerto del Sigr. Meck, G major
   (an organ transcription of a Concerto Grosso for str. by
   Jos. Meck)
CHORALE VARIATIONS on:
  Ach, schönster Jesu, mein Verlangen   [6]
  Aus meines Herzens Grunde   [12]
  Warum betrübst du dich, mein Herz?   [89]
  Allein Gott in der Höh' sei Ehr'   [8]
L. Noss   ‡ **Over.LP 8**
(*Pachelbel*) [Transept org. Battell Chapel, Yale]
CHORALE VARIATIONS on:
  Freu dich sehr, O meine Seele   [33]
  Nun ruhen alle Wälder (or: In allen meinen Thaten) [50]
  Meinen Jesum lass ich nicht   [68]
  Prelude & Fugue, A major   [5]
C. Watters   ‡ **CEd.CE 1041**
(*Pachelbel*)

CHORALE VARIATIONS on:
Jesu, meine Freude   [54]
☆ W. Supper († Baroque Organ Music)   in ‡ **Ren.X 54**
Lobt Gott, ihr Christen, allzugleich   [64]
☆ F. Heitmann   in ‡ **DT.LGX 66009**
   († Christmas Organ Music)   (‡ *FT.320.TC.075*)
Meinen Jesum lass' ich nicht   [68]
Jesu meine Freude   [54]
F. Viderø   **‡ HSL.HSL 3066**
(*Böhm*)   [organ at Jaegersborg, Denmark]
Meinen Jesum lass' ich nicht   [68]
R. Owen   **‡ ASK. 3**
(*Bach, Vierne, Messiaen, etc.*)
[Organ of Christ Chu., Bronxville, N.Y.]

Concerto del Signor Torelli
(an organ transcription of Concerto Grosso (unspec.) by
   Torelli)
M. Mason   in ‡ **ASK. 7**
(*Kerll, Pachelbel, etc.*)
[St. John's Chapel org., Groton, Mass.]

Concerto, F major organ
(an organ transcription of Albinoni's Concerto, Op. 2,
   No. 8)
L. Thybo   **‡ Phi.A 09801L**
(*J. S. Bach & Thybo*)
[Organ of Christianskyrken, Lyngby, Sweden]

WALTON, Sir William Turner (b. 1902)

BELSHAZZAR'S FEAST Oratorio 1931
D. Noble (B), London Phil. Cho. & Phil.
   Prom. Orch.—Boult   **‡ Nix.NLP 904**
                              (‡ West.WL 5248)
☆ D. Noble (B), Huddersfield Cho. Soc., Brass Bands &
   Liverpool Phil.—Walton   **‡ G.ALP 1089**
                                 (‡ FALP 337)

Concerto, Viola & orchestra, A minor 1929
W. Primrose & Royal Phil.—Sargent
                          ‡ EPhi.ABL 3045
(*Hindemith*)   (‡ AmC.ML 4905; ‡ Phi.A 00132L)

Concerto, Violin & orchestra, B minor
1939, rev. 1950
☆ J. Heifetz & Philharmonia—Walton   **‡ G.BLP 1047**
                                        (‡ QBLP 5027)

Crown Imperial Coronation March 1937
Philharmonia—Walton   in ‡ **C.C 1016**
(*above, below & Bach-Walton*)   (in ‡ *Angel. 30000*)
(*Bach-Walton: Wise Virgins excpt. only,* ‡ *C.SEL 1504*)

FAÇADE Recitation with Cha. Orch. 1923
(Poems of E. Sitwell)
E. Sitwell, P. Pears & English Opera Group
   Ens.—Collins   **‡ D.LXT 2977**
                             (‡ Lon.LL 1133)
K. McBeath & New Music Ens.—Hutchens
                             ‡ ANM.NMLP 1
— ORCH. VERSION
Orch. Suites 1 & 2
L.S.O.—Irving   **‡ D.LXT 2791**
(*Lambert*)   (‡ Lon.LL 771)
(2ss, ‡ *D.LW 5107; Lon.LD 9128*)
☆ Philharmonia—Lambert   **‡ C.SX 1003**
(*Lambert*)   (*Elgar* on ‡ *AmC.ML 4793*)

HAMLET Film music 1948
HENRY V Film music 1945
... Excerpts ☆ Philharmonia Orch. (‡ *Vic.LM 1926*)

Orb and Sceptre Coronation March 1953
Philharmonia—Walton   **C.LX 1583**
(2ss)   (LOX 822; in ‡ *C 1016; Angel. 30000*)
(*Portsmouth Point* on ♭ *C.SEL 1506*)
L.S.O.—Sargent   **‡ D.LXT 2793**
(*Bax & Elgar*)   (‡ Lon.LL 804)
(*Bax* only on ‡ *D.LW 5057; Lon.LD 9046*)
Sydney Sym.—Heinze   **‡ Rad.LXR 5002**
(*Byrd, Vaughan Williams*)

☆ = Re-issue of a recording to be found in previous volumes.

Portsmouth Point, Overture orch. 1926
Philharmonia—Walton   in ‡ *C.C 1016*
(*above & Bach-Walton*)   (in ‡ *Angel. 30000*)
(*Orb & Sceptre only,* ♭ *C.SEL 1506*)   •
L.P.O.—Boult   ‡ *D.LXT 5028*
(*below & Bach-Walton: The Wise Virgins*) (‡ *Lon.LL 1165*)
(*Scapino & Siesta on* ‡ *D.LW 5195*)

Quartet, strings, A minor 1947
Walden Qtt.   ‡ **PFCM.CB 168**
(*V. Thomson*)
(*Martin & Prokofiev on* ‡ *CB 172*)

Quartet, pf. & str., D minor 1917
R. Masters Pf. Qtt.   ‡ **Argo.RG 48**
(*below*)   (‡ *West.WN 18024*)

RICHARD III Film music 1955
(for a film version of Shakespeare)
Royal Phil.—Mathieson   ‡ *G.ALP 1341/3*
[In a complete recording of the sound-track]
(‡ *Vic. set LM 6126; excerpts only,* ‡ *Vic.LM 1940*)

Scapino, Overture orch. 1940
L.P.O.—Boult   ‡ *D.LXT 5028*
(*above & below*)   (‡ *Lon.LL 1165*)
(*below, & Portsmouth Point on* ‡ *D.LW 5195*)

Siesta orch. 1927
L.P.O.—Boult   ‡ *D.LXT 5028*
(*above*)   [& in ‡ *D.LW 5195*]   (‡ *Lon.LL 1165*)

Sonata, vln. & pf., A minor 1950
M. Rostal & C. Horsley   ‡ **Argo.RG 48**
(*above*)   (‡ *West.WN 18024*)
☆ Y. Menuhin & L. Kentner   ‡ *Vic.LHMV 1037*
(*Beethoven: Vln. Sonata No. 1*)   (♭ *set WHMV 1037*)

Symphony, B flat minor 1935
Philharmonia—Walton   ‡ *G.ALP 1027*
(‡ *Vic.LHMV 1041:* ♭ *set WHMV 1041*)

Te Deum laudamus 1953
Coronation Chorus & Orch.—McKie
in ‡ *G.ALP 1058*
(† Coronation of Queen Elizabeth II)

TROILUS AND CRESSIDA Opera 3 Acts 1954
EXCERPTS   [(Hassall)
Is Cressida a slave?   Act I
Slowly it all comes back   Act I
How can I sleep?   Act II
If one last doubt   Act II
Now close your arms   Act II
All's well!   Act III
Diomede! Father!   Act III
E. Schwarzkopf (S), R. Lewis (T), M. Sinclair
(A), etc., & Philharmonia Orch.—Walton
‡ *C.CX 1313*
(‡ *QCX 10173; Angel. 35278*)

Variation on an Elizabethan tune (Sellinger's
Round)[1] orch. 1953
Aldeburgh Fest.—Britten   in ‡ *D.LXT 2798*
(*Berkeley, Britten, Oldham, Searle, Tippett*) (‡ *Lon.LL 808*)

(The) Wise Virgins Ballet
SEE: BACH, J.S.

WARD, John (d. before 1641)
SEE: † EVENING OF ELIZABETHAN VERSE & MUSIC

WARD, Robert (b. 1917)
Euphony for orchestra f.p. 19 June 1954
Louisville—Whitney   ‡ **LO. 10**
(*Bergsma, Ginastera, Sauguet*)

Symphony No. 3, D minor 1953
Cincinnati Sym.—Johnson   ‡ **Rem. 199-185**
(*Stein*)

WARLOCK, Peter (1894-1930)
Capriol Suite Str. orch. (after Arbeau) 1926
Boyd Neel Orch.   ‡ *D.LXT 2790*
(*Britten*) (2ss, ♭ *D. 71102*)   (‡ *Lon.LL 801*)
(*below & Ireland on* ‡ *D.LW 5149; Lon.LD 9170*)
London Cha.—Bernard   *G.C 4218*

(The) Curlew (Yeats) 1920-2
voice, fl., cor anglais & str. qtt.
A. Young (T), L. Solomon, P. Graeme &
Sebastian Qtt.   ‡ **Argo.RG 26**
(*Songs*)   (‡ *West.WN 18022*)

Serenade for Frederick Delius Str. orch. 1921-2
(on his sixtieth birthday)
Boyd Neel Str. Orch.   ‡ *D.LW 5149*
(*above*)   (‡ *Lon.LD 9170*)

SONGS (& PART SONGS)
COLLECTION OF SONGS
And wilt thou leave me thus (Wyatt)   1928
Away to Twiver (Anon., XVIth Cent.)   1926
The Fox (Blunt)   1930
Jillian of Berry (Beaumont & Fletcher)   1926
The lover's maze (attrib. Campian)   1927
Mockery (Shakespeare)   1927
Pretty ring time (Shakespeare)   1925
Rest, sweet nymphs (Anon., XVIIth Cent.)   1922
Sigh no more, ladies (Shakespeare)   1927
Sleep (Fletcher)   1922
Sweet and twenty (Shakespeare)   c. 1923
Yarmouth fair (Collins) (Folksong arr.)   1924
A. Young (T), G. Watson (pf.)   ‡ **Argo.RG 26**
(*The Curlew*)   (‡ *West.WN 18022*)

Bethlehem Down (Blunt) Cho. 1927-30
St. Simon-the-Apostle Chu. Cho.—Lewis
in ‡ **Hall.J 75**

Captain Stratton's fancy (Masefield) 1920
R. Standen (B), F. Stone (pf.)
in ‡ **West.WLE 103**
(*Keel, Head, Stanford, etc.*)

Pretty ring-time (Shakespeare) 1925
Sleep (Fletcher) 1922
K. Ferrier (A), F. Stone (pf.)[2] in ‡ *D.LX 3133*
(*Britten, Hughes, Stanford, etc.*)   (‡ *Lon.LS 1032*)

Tyrley Tyrlow (Anon. XVIth Cent.) 1922
— CHORAL VERSION (orig. with orch.) 1923
Nat. Presbyterian Chu. Cho.—Schaefer
in ‡ **McInt.MM 107**
(*Christmas Candlelight Service*) [org. acc.]

For Transcriptions, see † FRENCH CHANSONS

WEBER, Ben (b. 1916)
Symphony on Poems of William Blake, Op. 33
B & orch. 1950
W. Galjour & orch.—Stokowski ‡ **Vic.LM 1785**
(*Harrison*)

WEBER, Carl Maria F. E. von (1786-1826)
Adagio, Op. 10, No. 5 pf. duet J.81, No. 5 1809
K. U. & H. Schnabel   ‡ **SPA. 50**
(*below & Mendelssohn*)

Aufforderung zum Tanz, Op. 65 J.260 1819
(Rondo brillante, D flat major) pf.
A. Brailowsky (n.v. or ☆ ?)   ‡ **Vic.LM 1918**
(*Mendelssohn, Schubert, Schumann*)
G. Puchelt   **G.EH 1442**
(in ‡ *WDLP 1503*)
P. Baldwin   in ‡ *Var. 6982*

— ARR. ORCH. Berlioz[3] 1841
N.B.C. Sym.—Toscanini   ♭ *G.7ER 5021*
(*Verdi: Forza, Overture*) (♭ *Vic.ERA 125:* in ‡ *LM 6113;*
ItV.A12R 0150: ♭ *A72R 0013;* ‡ *FV.A 630219*)
New Sym.—Fistoulari   ‡ *D.LW 5084*
(*Minkus: Don Quixote*)   (‡ *Lon.LD 9108*)
Philharmonia—Markevitch (n.v.)   ‡ *C.CX 1197*
(*Debussy, Satie, Ravel*)   (‡ *FCX 357; Angel. 35151*)
Hollywood Bowl—Dragon in ‡ **DCap.CTL 7072**
(in ‡ *Cap.P 8276:* ♭ *FAP 8284*)
Hamburg Philharmonia—H-J. Walther
MSB. 78121

---

[1] Contributed to a joint set of variations by the other composers named.
[2] Broadcast performance, 5 June 1952.   [3] Certain recordings do not specify the version used.

Aufforderung zum Tanz, Op. 65 —ORCH. (*continued*)
N.Y.P.S.O.—Kostelanetz   ♯ **AmC.CL 809**
(*Enesco & Prokofiev*)   (o.n. ML 4957: ♭ *set A 1102*)
Leipzig Radio—Pflüger   *Eta.* **120029**
Leningrad Phil.—Mravinsky (*USSR. 19030/2:*
        USSRM.D 145)
International Sym.—Schneiderhann (in ♯ *Mae.OA 20004*)
☆ Residentie—v. Otterloo (in ♯ *Phi.S 06002R*)
Bamberg Sym.—Leitner (in ♯ AmD.DL 8509;
          ♭ *Pol. 30058*)
Philharmonia—Markevitch (o.v.)
    (*ArgV. 11-7690; ♭ G.7PQ 2009: 7PW 102*)
French Nat. Radio—Lindenberg (♭ *Od.7AOE 1002:*
               DSEQ 425)
Orch.—Stokowski[1] (in ♯ *G.ALP 1133: FALP 277;*
      in ♯ *Vic.LRM 7022: ♭ ERB 7022*)

— ARR. ORCH. Stokowski (?)
☆ Philadelphia—Stokowski (♭ *Cam.CAE 192:*
       in ♯ CAL 123 & in ♯ *set CFL 102*)

— ARR. ORCH. Johnstone
☆ Liverpool Phil.—Sargent (in ♯ AmC.RL 3091)

— ARR. PF. & ORCH.
W. Stech & Hamburg State Phil.—Wal-Berg
              ♯ *DT.TM 68046*
(*Mendelssohn*)   (♯ *T.TW 30020*)

CONCERTOS
BASSOON & ORCH.
F major, Op. 75   J.127   1811
P. Hongne & O.L. Orch.—Froment
            ♯ **LOL.OL 50105**
(*below*)   (♯ *OL.LD 69*)

PIANO & ORCH.
No. 1, C major, Op. 11   J.98   1810
F. Wührer & Vienna Pro Musica—Swarowsky
(*No. 2*)   ♯ **E. & AmVox.PL 8140**
F. Egger & Linz Sym (*Liszt*)   ♯ *Ply.* **12-38**

No. 2, E flat major, Op. 32   J.155   1812
F. Wührer & Vienna Pro Musica—Swarowsky
(*No. 1*)   ♯ **E. & AmVox.PL 8140**

Konzertstück, F minor, Op. 79   J.282   1821
P. Mildner & R.I.A.S. Sym.—Rother
            ♯ **DT.LGX 66022**
(*Liszt*)   (♯ *T.LE 6513*)
☆ C. Arrau & Chicago Sym.—Defauw (♯ *Cam.CAL 191*)
R. Casadesus & Cleveland Sym.—Szell (♯ *Phi. A01624R*)

CLARINET & ORCH.
No. 1, F minor, Op. 73   J.114   1811
No. 2, E flat major, Op. 74   J.118   1811
☆ A. Heine & Salzburg Mozarteum—P. Walter
           (♯ *Cpt.MC 20026*)
No. 1 only
J. Lancelot & O.L. Orch.—Froment
            ♯ **LOL.OL 50105**
(*above*)   (♯ *OL.LD 69*)
No. 2 only
J. Stowell, & D. Mayer (pf.)   ♯ **Aphe.AP 26**
(*Stanford, Jean Jean, Verdi*)

Concertino, E flat major, Op. 26   J.109   1811
A. Gigliotti & Philadelphia—Ormandy
         in ♯ **AmC.ML 4629**
(*J. Clarke, Griffes, B. Phillips, Chabrier, etc.*)
☆ A. Bürkner & Berlin Phil.—Schrader
          (in ♯ *ANix.ULP 9012*)

Duo concertant, E flat major, Op. 48   cl. & pf.
   J.204   1816
☆ S. Forrest & L. Hambro (♯ *McInt.MM 111*)

Jubel-Ouvertüre, E major, Op. 59   J.245   1818
☆ Bamberg Sym.—Leitner (♭ *Pol.* 30058: in ♯ 18058 &
          ♯ 19037; ♯ *AmD.DL 4054*)
Minneapolis—Mitropoulos (in ♯ *AmC.RL 3038*)

KAMPF UND SIEG, Op. 44 Cantata (Wohlbrück)
   S, A, T, B, cho. & orch   J.190   1815
L. Schmidt-Glazel, E. Fleischer, G. Lutze,
H. Kramer, Cho. & Berlin Sym.—Kegel
          ♯ **Ura. 7126**

LEYER UND SCHWERT, Op. 42   (Körner)
No. 2, Lützows wilde Jagd   J.168   Male cho.
E. Ger. State Cho.—Schmeider   *Eta.* **130103**
(*Folksongs*)

Momento capriccioso, B flat major, Op. 12   pf.
   J.56   1808
C. Horsley   **G.C 4213**
(*Chopin: Études, Op. 10, Nos. 6 & 7*)   (EB 599)

OPERAS & STAGE WORKS
ABU HASSAN   Opera   1 Act   1811   J.106
Overture
Bamberg Sym.—Lehmann   in ♯ **Pol. 18058**
(*Oberon, Freischütz, etc.*)(& ♯ Pol. 19037; ♯ *AmD.DL 4057*)
Leipzig Radio—Kegel   *Eta.* **120176**
(*Donna Diana, Overture*)
Zagreb Radio Orch. (*Jug.P 16029*)
☆ Vienna Radio—Schönherr (or Nilius)
      (in ♯ *GA. 33-307; ♭ Vien. 4014*)
Boston "Pops"—Fiedler (♭ *Vic.ERA 135*)

(Der) BEHERRSCHER DER GEISTER
   ("Rübezahl": *The Ruler of the Spirits*) Opera 2 Acts 1805
Overture, Op. 27   J.122   1811
Berlin Sym.—Balzer   in ♯ **Roy. 1403**

EURYANTHE   Opera   3 Acts   1823   J.291
Overture
Vienna Phil.—Furtwängler   in ♯ **Vic.LHMV 19**
(*Freischütz Overture; & R. Strauss*)
N.B.C. Sym.—Toscanini in ♯ **Vic. set LM 6026**
(*Freischütz, Oberon Overtures; Humperdinck, etc.*)
Philharmonia—Schwarz   in ♯ **G.CLP 1022**
(*Schubert & Liszt*) (2ss, G.C 4208)   (♯ *FELP 111*)
Bamberg Sym.—Keilberth   ♯ **DT.TM 68015**
(*Freischütz Overture*)   (TV.VE 9027)
Bamberg Sym.—Leitner   in ♯ **Pol. 18058**
(*Jubel, Abu Hassan, etc.*) (& ♯ 19037; in ♯ *AmD.DL 4057*)
Boston Orch. Soc.—Page   ♯ *Nix.SLPY 801*
(*Bizet, Rossini, Mendelssohn*)   (♯ *SOT. 2064*)
☆ Vienna Phil.—Böhm   ♯ *D.LW 5002*
   (*Oberon Overture*)
☆ Berlin Radio—Rother (in ♯ *ANix.ULP 9012*)
Berlin Sym.—Balzer (in ♯ *Roy. 1403*)

No. 12, Wehen wir Lüfte Ruh'   T   Act II
F. Vroons   in ♯ **EPhi.NBR 6027**
(*Freischütz & Fidelio*)   (♯ *Phi.N 00629R*)

(Der) FREISCHÜTZ, Op. 77
   Opera   3 Acts   1821   J.277
HIGHLIGHTS

Overture
Durch die Wälder   T   Act I
Hier im ird'schen Jammertal   Bs   Act I
Schweig, schweig, damit niemand wacht   Bs   Act I
Kommt ein schlanker Bursch'   S   Act II
Wie nahte mir der Schlummer . . . Leise, leise   S   Act II
Intermezzo   orch.   Act III
Und ob die Wolke sie verhülle   S   Act III
Einst träumte meiner sel'gen Base   S   Act III
☆ **Was gleicht wohl auf Erden**   Male cho.   Act III
A. Schlemm (S), R. Streich (S), W. Windgassen (T),
H. Uhde (Bs), Württemberg State Op. Cho. & orch.
—Leitner; Overture, (?) Berlin Phil. Orch.—Lehmann
          ♯ **HP.DGM 19013**

HIGHLIGHTS & VOCAL SELECTIONS
I. Camphausen (S), E. Nachtigall (T), G. Ramms (B),
Dresden State Op. Cho. & Orch.—Schreiber ♯ **Roy. 1430**
☆ H. Hopf (T), M. Cunitz (S), E. Loose (S), etc., Vienna
State Op. Cho. & Vienna Phil. Orch.—Ackermann,
from set (♯ *Lon.LL 646*)
T. Richter, S. Schöner, S. Hauser, G. Frei, Berlin
Municipal Op. Cho. & Orch.—Lutze
        (♯ *DT.TM 68028; TV.VE 9005*)

Overture
N.B.C. Sym.—Toscanini (n.v.) ♯ *Vic.LRM 7028*
(*Oberon Overture; & Donizetti*)   (♭ *set ERB 7028*)
      (in ♯ *set LM 6026; in ♯ FV.A 330201*)
Bamberg Sym.—Keilberth   ♯ *DT.TM 68015*
(*Euryanthe, Overture*)   (♯ *T.TW 30037; TV.VE 9027*)
Berlin Phil.—Lehmann, from Highlights
              PV. **36070**
(in ♯ *Pol. 18058: ♯ 19013 & ♯ 19037 & ♯ AmD.DL 4075*)
(*continued on next page*)

---

[1] From *Heart of the Ballet.*

(Der) FREISCHÜTZ, Overture (continued)

Vienna Phil.—Furtwängler ♯ Vic.LHMV 19
(Euryanthe Overture; & R. Strauss)

Residentie—v. Otterloo in ♯ Phi.N 00149L
(Aria, below; & Schubert) (Oberon Ov., ♯ S 06003R)

Berlin Radio—Gerdes (Eta. 225023, o.n. 28-23)
Linz Sym. (in ♯ Ply. 12-33)

☆ Vienna State Op.—Swarowsky (in ♯ Sup.LPM 226;
U. 5203C)
Boston Prom.—Fiedler (in ♯ Cam.CAL 122: ♭ CAE 105)

ACT I

Nein, länger trag' ich nicht . . .
Durch die Wälder, durch die Auen T
F. Vroons in ♯ EPhi.NBR 6027
(below, Euryanthe & Fidelio) (♯ Phi.N 00629R)

W. Windgassen [from Highlights] PV. 72419
(Fliegende Holländer—Fühlst du den Schmerz)

☆ P. Anders (♭ Vic.EHA 2; ♭ G.7PW 521:
in ♯ WDLP 1513)

Hier im ird'schen Jammertal Bs
(Kaspar's Drinking Song)
♮ M. Journet (Fr) (in ♯ SBDH.JALP 19*)
A. Didur (Ital) (in ♯ FRP 2*)

ACT II

Kommt ein schlanker Bursch' gegangen S
R. Streich [from Highlights] ♭ Pol. 32028
(Così fan tutte, No. 19)

Wie nahte mir die Schlummer . . .
Leise, leise, fromme Weise S
T. Richter ♯ DT.TM 68017
(below) (TV.VSK 9204: ♭ T.UV 105; ♭ FT.470.TC.016;
♯ T.TW 30037)

G. Brouwenstijn (2ss) Phi.N 12054G
(in ♯ N 00149L & S 06019R, d.c.)

A. Schlemm [from Highlights] PV. 72477
(below) (♭ Pol. 30060)

E. Shumilova (Russ) (USSR. 22102/3: USSRM.D 1272)
♮ E. Destinn (AF.AGSB 48*; in ♯ Sca. 804*)

ACT III

Und ob die Wolke sie verhülle S (Cavatina)
J. Hammond in ♯ G.ALP 1076
(La Wally, Manon, Thaïs, etc.)

T. Richter ♯ DT.TM 68017
(above) (TV.VSK 9204: ♭ T.UV 105; ♭ FT. 470.TC.016;
♯ T.TW 30037)

A. Schlemm [from Highlights] PV. 72477
(above) (♭ Pol. 30060)
♮ E. Destinn (AF.AGSB 48*)

Einst träumte meiner sel'gen Base
Trübe Augen, Liebchen, taugen S
R. Streich [from Highlights] in ♯ Pol. 19015

Wir winden dir den Jungfernkranz Fem. cho.
(Bridesmaids' Cho.)
☆ Württemberg State Op. Cho. & Orch.—Leitner
(in ♯ AmD.DL 4056; & in ♯ DL 9797;
♭ Pol. 32100: in ♯ 19033)

Was gleicht wohl auf Erden Male Cho.
(Huntsmen's Chorus)
Vienna Cha. Cho. & Sym.—Loibner
in ♯ EPhi.NBR 6027
(above, Euryanthe & Fidelio) (♯ Phi.N 00629R)

Berlin Municipal Op.—Otto T.A 11535
(Kreutzer: Nachtlager, excpt.) (♭ U 45535)
(idem & Wagner on ♯ DT.TM 68031)
(& in ♯ LA 6075 & 6086: TW 30037)

Berlin Comic Op.—Lange Eta. 120175
(Preciosa—Zigeunerchor)

Estonian State Male Cho. (Est) (USSR. 23678)
☆ Württemberg State Op.—Leitner (in ♯ AmD.DL 4056
& in ♯ DL 9797; ♭ Pol. 32100 & in ♯ 19033)

OBERON Opera 3 Acts 1826 J. 306 Eng
COMPLETE RECORDING (in German) (no dialogue)

Oberon	F. Fehringer (T)
Puck	P. Bauer (A)
Rezia	H. Bader (S)
Fatima	H. Münch (M-S)
Huon	K. Liebel (T)
Sherasmin	R. Titze (B)
Mermaid	F. Sailer (S)

South Ger. Radio Cho. & Orch.—Müller-Kray
(4ss) ♯ Per. set SPL 575
(♯ Cpt. set MC 20037)
[Slightly abridged, in ♯ MMS. set OP 10, 4ss]

Overture
N.B.C. Sym.—Toscanini ♭ G.7ERF 111
(Don Pasquale, Overture)
(idem & Freischütz in ♯ Vic.LRM 7028: ♭ set ERB 7028;
also in ♯ Vic. set LM 6026; ♯ FV.A 330201)

Philharmonia—Malko (2ss) G.C 4240
(Hérold & Tchaikovsky on ♯ DLP 1069: QDLP 6024)

Rome Radio—Previtali ♯ BB.LBC 1092
(Segreto di Susanna, Forza, etc.)

Hamburg Philharmonia—H-J. Walther (MSB. 78131)
Dresden Phil.—Bongartz (Eta. n.d.)
Leningrad Phil.—Mravinsky (USSR. 018988/9:
USSRM.D 144)
Regent Sym. (in ♯ Rgt. 7002)
Berlin Sym.—Balzer (in ♯ Roy. 1403)
Linz Sym. (in ♯ Ply. 12-33)

☆ Vienna Phil.—Böhm (♯ D.LW 5002)
Vienna Phil.—Furtwängler (G.ED 1246: ♭ 7RF/RQ 258)
Hilversum Radio—v. Kempen (in ♯ Phi.S 06003R)
Berlin Phil.—E. Jochum (in ♯ Pol. 18058: 19037)
Berlin Radio—Rother (in ♯ ANix.ULP 9012)

No. 13, Ocean, thou mighty monster! S Act II
(Ozean, du Ungeheuer)
E. Shumilova (Russ) USSRM.D 1273
(Freischütz, aria)
☆ K. Flagstad (Ger) (in ♯ Vic. set LCT 6701)
C. Goltz (Ger) (♭ Pol. 32042; ♯ AmD.DL 4058)

PETER SCHMOLL UND SEINE
NACHBARN Opera 2 Acts 1801
Overture, Op. 8 J. 54 1807
Bamberg Sym.—Leitner ♯ AmD.DL 4054
(Jubel Ouvertüre)
Berlin Sym.—Balzer in ♯ Roy. 1403
☆ Vienna Phil.—Böhm (♯ D.LW 5032; Lon.LD 9034)

PRECIOSA, Op. 78 Inc. Music J.279 1821
Overture
Bamberg Sym.—Leitner PV. 72429
(Mozart: Symphony No. 32) (♭ Pol. 30120;
♯ AmD.DL 4057)
Linz Sym. in ♯ Ply. 12-33
☆ Vienna Phil.—Böhm (♯ D.LW 5032; ♯ Lon.LD 9034)

Zigeunerchor: Im Wald . . .
Berlin Comic Op. Cho.—Lange Eta. 120175
(Freischütz—Jägerchor)

SILVANA Opera 3 Acts 1810 J.87
Overture
Linz Sym. in ♯ Ply. 12-33

TURANDOT, Op. 37 J.75 1809
Inc. music to play by Schiller, after Gozzi
Overture
Berlin Sym.—Balzer in ♯ Roy. 1403
☆ Rhineland Sym.—Federer (♯ AFest.CFR 38)

---

(6) PIECES, Op. 3 pf. duet J. 9-14

1. Sonatine	4. Andante con variazioni
2. Romanze	5. Marcia
3. Menuetto	6. Rondo

(8) PIECES, Op. 60 pf. duet

1. Moderato J. 248	5. Alla siciliana J. 236
2. Allegro J. 264	6. Tema variato J. 265
3. Adagio J. 253	7. Marcia J. 266
4. Allegro, tutto ben marcato J. 242	8. Rondo J. 254

A. Gold & R. Fizdale ♯ AmC.ML 4968

. . . Op. 60, Nos. 5-8, only
K. U. & H. Schnabel ♯ SPA. 50
(Adagio, Op. 10, No. 5; & Mendelssohn)

♯ = Long-playing, 33⅓ r.p.m. ♭ = 45 r.p.m. ♮ = Auto. couplings, 78 r.p.m.

Rondo brillante, E flat major, Op. 62 pf. 1819
(*La Gaîté*) J. 252
B. Webster   in ♯ **Persp.PR 2**
— ARR. PF. & ORCH.
W. Stech & Hamburg State Phil.—Wal-Berg
(in ♯ *T.TW 30027*)

SONATAS, Piano
No. 1, C major, Op. 24 J.138 1812
H. Roloff   ♮ **PV. 72289/90**
(4ss)   (♯ *AmD.DL 7543*; ♯ *Pol. 16057*)
A. d'Arco (*below*)   ♯ **LOL.OL 50068**

... 4th movt. Rondo ("*Perpetuum Mobile*")
— — ARR. ORCH.
☆ Rhineland Sym.—Federer (in ♯ *AFest.CFR 35*)

No. 2, A flat major, Op. 39 J.199 1816
A. d'Arco (*above*)   ♯ **LOL.OL 50068**

(6) SONATAS, Vln. & pf., Op. 17[1] 1810
No. 1, F major   J. 99   No. 2, G major   J. 100
No. 3, D minor   J. 101   No. 4, E flat major J. 102
No. 5, A major   J. 103   No. 6, C major   J. 104
COMPLETE RECORDING
R. Ricci & C. Bussotti   ♯ **D.LXT 2959**
                                         (♯ *Lon.LL 1006*)

No. 1, F major ... 2nd movt., Romanze
— ARR. VLN. & PF. Kreisler "*Larghetto*"
R. & A. d'Arco   in *Plé.P 208*

No. 2, G major ... 2nd movt., Adagio
— ARR. VLC. & PF. Piatigorsky
D. Shafran & pf. (*below*)   **USSR. 13948**

No. 3, D minor (*Thème russe & Rondo*)
... 2nd movt., Rondo
— — ARR. VLC. & ORCH. Piatigorsky
L. Monroe & Philadelphia—Ormandy
                               in ♯ **AmC.ML 4629**
(*Concertino, above; & Handel, etc.*)
D. Shafran & pf. (*above*)   **USSR. 13949**
☆ G. Piatigorsky & pf. (in ♯ *ItV.A12R 0105*)
— — ARR. 2 PFS. Luboshutz
P. Luboshutz & G. Nemenoff   ♯ **Rem. 199-143**
(*Reger, Chopin, etc.*)

SONG
Ich sah' ein Röschen, Op. 15, No. 5 (Müchler)
J. 67 1809
G. Pechner (B)   in ♯ **Roy. 1557**

SYMPHONIES
No. 1, C major, Op. 19 J.50
Leipzig Phil.—Pflüger   in ♯ **Ura. set 239**
(*Bruckner: Symphony No. 5*)

No. 2, C major J.51 1807
☆ Berlin Radio—Heger (♯ *ANix.ULP 9012*)

(7) Variations, B flat major, Op. 33 cl. & pf. 1811
J. 128 (*on a theme from Silvana*)
J. Lancelot & A. d'Arco   **V♯ *DO.LD 27***
(*Schumann: Fantasiestücke, Op. 73*)
☆ S. Forrest & L. Hambro (♯ *McInt.MM 111*)

WEBERN, Anton von (1883-1945)

(6) Bagatelles, Op. 9   Str. qtt.   1913
(5) Movements, Op. 5   Str. qtt.   1909
(4) Songs, Op. 12[2]   1915
Quartet, ten. sax., cl., vln., & pf., Op. 22 1930
☆ (New) Pro Arte Qtt., B. Beardslee (S), J. Monod (pf.),
J. C. Williams (sax.), E. Thomas (cl.), F. Chaplin
(vln.)   ♯ **Mtr.CLP 507**
▽ NOTE: ♯ Dial 7 contains the Symphony, Op. 21 & the
first two items above; ♯ Dial 17 the remaining items
above and Concerto Op. 24 & Variations for pf.,
Op. 27.

(5) Movements, Op. 5 Str. qtt. 1909
Juilliard Qtt.   ♯ **AmC.ML 4737**
(½s—*Berg & Schoenberg*) (in set SL 188; Phi.A 01178L)
(*Piston & Malipiero* in ♯ *PFCM. 157, perhaps a different
recording*)

(4) Pieces, Op. 7 vln. & pf. 1910
A. & M. Ajemian   ♯ **MGM.E 3179**
(*Weill: Concerto*)

Variations, Op. 27 pf.
J. Manchon-Theis   ♯ *LT.MEL 94008*
(*Berg & Schoenberg*) (**V♯** *Sel.LAP 1059*; ♯ *T.TW 30031*)

WECKMANN, Matthias (1619-1674)
SEE: † MUSIC OF BAROQUE ERA

WEELKES, Thomas (c. 1575-1623)

ANTHEM: Hosanna to the Son of David 6 vv.
St. Paul's Cath. Cho.—Dykes Bower
                               in ♯ **C.CX 1193**
(*Sweelinck, Howells, V. Williams, Byrd, etc.*)
                               (♯ Angel. 35138 in set 3516)

MADRIGALS
[The Roman figs. refer to the Vols. in the *English Madrigal
School*: IX, 1597; X, 1598; XI, 1600; XII, 1600;
XIII, 1608]
COLLECTION

Death has deprived me   XIII 6 vv.
As wanton birds   XI   5 vv.
O care, thou wilt despatch me;
  Hence, care, thou art too cruel XI 5 vv.
Lord, when I think   XIII 3 vv. (T, B, Bs)
Cease, sorrows, now   XIII 3 vv. (S, A, T)
Thule, the period of cosmography;
  The Andalusian merchant   XII   6 vv.
Randolph Singers   ♯ **West.WL 5361**
(*Bateson*)

As Vesta was from Latmos Hill descending[3]
XXXIII 6 vv.
Randolph Singers   in ♯ **Nix.WLP 6212-1/2**
(† *Triumphs of Oriana*)   (♯ West. set WL 212)
New England Cons. Alumni Cho.—de Varon
                               in ♯ **HS.HSL 2068**
(† *English Madrigals*)

Hark, all ye lovely saints X 5 vv.
Stanford Univ. Cho.—Schmidt   in ♯ **ML. 7022**
(† *Madrigals & Motets*)

O care, thou wilt despatch me;
  Hence, care, thou art too cruel XI 5 vv.
Yale Univ. Music School—Hindemith
                               in ♯ **Over.LP 4**
(† Yale University, Vol. I)
Golden Age Singers[4]   **G.HMS 33**
(† *History of Music in Sound*) (in ♯ Vic. set LM 6029)

(A) Sparrow-hawk proud XI 6 vv.
Yale University Sch. Cho.—Hindemith
                               in ♯ **Over.LP 4**
(† Yale University, Vol. I)

Tan ta ra cries Mars XIII 3 vv.
Pro Musica Ens. (N.Y.)—Greenberg
                               in ♯ **AmC.ML 5051**
(† *Evening of Elizabethan Verse & Music*)

WEERBECKE, Gaspard van (c. 1440-1514)
SEE: † FRENCH SACRED MUSIC

WEIGEL, Eugene John (b. 1894)

Prairie Symphony
Illinois Univ. Orch.—Goodman ♯ *UOI.CRS 2*
(*Binkerd*)

---

[1] Usually known and published as Op. 10, and so labelled here.
[2] Texts by Anon.; Bethge; Strindberg; Goethe.
[3] From *The Triumphs of Oriana*, 1601.   [4] Contains Part 1, *O care ...* , only.

WEIGL, Karl (1881-1949)

Quartet, No. 6, C major, Op. 37   str.
  Loewenguth Qtt.
Sonata, B flat major, Op. 38   vla. & pf.   1940
  P. Doktor & N. Reisenberg
(3) Songs, Op. 36   M-S & Str. Qtt.   (*Eng*)
  1. O cricket, sing   (Dauthendey)
  2. O blessed darkness   (List)
  3. Woe to eyes   (Huch)
  A. Howland & Woodstock Qtt.   ♯ **Triad.TRI 1**

WEILL, Kurt (1900-1950)

Concerto, Op. 12, Vln. & wind orch.   1925
  A. Ajemian & M.G.M. Wind Orch.—I. Solomon
  (*Webern*)   ♯ **MGM.E 3179**
Kleine Dreigroschenmusik   Orch. Suite
  (on themes from *Die Dreigroschenoper*)
  M.G.M. Orch.—Solomon   ♯ **MGM.E 3095**
  (*Copland*)

OPERAS & STAGE WORKS
(Abridged listing only)
COLLECTION OF EXCERPTS
AUFSTIEG UND FALL DER STADT MAHAGONNY
  Opera   3 Acts   1930
    Havanna-Lied; Alabama-Song; Wie man sich bettet
BERLINER REQUIEM   Cantata, 3 male vv. & cha. orch.
    Vom ertrunkenen Mädchen
DIE DREIGROSCHENOPER   Opera, Prol. & 8 scenes
    Barbara-Song; Morität; Seeräuber Jenny
HAPPY END   (Brecht)
    Bilbao Song; Surabaya-Johnny;
    Was die Herren Matrosen sagen   (Sailor Tango)
DAS SILBERSEE   (G. Kaiser)
    Caesars Tod; Lied der Fennimore (I am a poor relative)
  L. Lenya (S)   ♯ **AmC.KL 5056**
      (♭ set AX 5056)

(Die) DREIGROSCHENOPER   Opera   1928
  Prol. & 8 scenes   (Brecht, after 'The Beggar's Opera')
COMPLETE RECORDING (in *German*)
  "Liane", H. Roswaenge, A. Jerger, K. Preger, H. Fassler,
  R. Anday, A. Felbermayer, F. Guthrie, Vienna St. Op.
  Cho. & Orch.—Adler   ♯ **Van.VRS 9002**
  [no dialogue]   (♯ Ama.AVRS 6023)
ABRIDGED RECORDING in *English*[1]
  L. Lenya, S. Merrill, M. Wolfson, J. Sullivan, C. Rae,
  G. Brice, B. Arthur, G. Tyne & Orch.—Matlowsky
  [Excerpts on ♭ EP 559 & 571]   ♯ **MGM.E 3121**
ABRIDGED RECORDING in *German*
  ☆ L. Lenya, K. Gerron, etc., with Band—Mackeben
  [orig. cast]   ♯ **DT.LGM 65028**
    (also ♯ DT.LGX 66053; T.LA 6045)
Vocal Excerpts   G. Keller (S), etc.   ♯ **Atl.ALS 405**
Morität   G. Pechner   in ♯ **Roy. 1558**

(The) FIREBRAND OF FLORENCE   1945
Sing me not a ballad
  L. Carlyle & pf.   in ♯ **Wald. 301**

KNICKERBOCKER HOLIDAY   Mus. Play 1938
September Song
  K. Spencer (Bs) (C.DW 5240; ♭ SCMV 506)
  E. Borieno (Span)   (in ♯ Pnt.LP 301)
— ARR. ORCH.
  Melachrino Orch. (♭ G.7EG 8050)
  D. Rose Orch. (MGM. 30802; ♭ K 30802)
  Pittsburg Sym.—Jones (in ♯ Cap.L 534)
— ARR. ZITHER
  R. Welcome (in ♯ Nix.SLPY 149; in ♯ SOT. 1032)

LADY IN THE DARK   1940
Vocal excerpts
  G. Lawrence (S) & orch.   ♯ **G.DLP 1099**
  (C. Porter: Nymph Errant)   (♯ Vic.LRT 7001)
  A. Sothern, C. Carpenter, Cho. & Orch.
      ♯ **Vic.LM 1882**
      (♭ set ERB 1882)
  N. Walker & pf. (in ♯ Wald. 301)
My ship   — ARR. PF. & ORCH.   Gould   "Rhapsody"
  M. Gould & orch.   in ♯ **AmC.ML 4657**
SONG: Speak low   (O. Nash)[2]   — ARR. ORCH.
  Pittsburgh Sym.—Jones (in ♯ Cap.L 534)

WEINBERGER, Jaromir (b. 1896)

(6) Bible Poems   Suite, org.   1939
... No. 5, The Last Supper   (ed. Harms)
  J. Harms   in ♯ **Uni.UN 1004**
  (Reger, Karg-Elert, Raasted, Bach, etc.)
Czech Rhapsody   orch.
  ☆ Nat. Sym. (U.S.A.)—Kindler (in ♯ Cam.CAL 175)

ŠVANDA THE BAGPIPER   Opera 2 Acts   1927
Polka & Fugue   orch.
  A.B.C. Sydney Sym.—Goossens ♯**G.OBLP 7501**
  (Saint-Saëns & Massenet)   (2ss, ED 1221)
  Philharmonia—Collingwood   **C.DX 1885**
  (Borodin on ♭ SED 5513)
  ☆ Philadelphia—Ormandy (♭ AmC. 4-4785)
... Polka only   MGM. Orch.—Marrow   in ♯ **MGM.E 3136**
Selection   — ARR. 2 PFS.   Chasins
  ☆ A. Chasins & C. Keene (♭ Mer.EP 1-5053)
In the beginning you prosper   T
Dorota, do not weep   T
  W. Kmentt (Ger)   ♯ **Phi.S 06075R**
  (Prince Igor, Sadko, The Kiss, etc.)

WEINER, Leó (b. 1885)

Concertino, Op. 15, pf. & orch.   1928
  L. Hernádi & Hungarian State—Polgár
  (4ss)   **Qual.MN 1098/9**
Divertimento No. 1, Op. 20   str. orch.
  (after Hungarian Dances)
  Hungarian Radio—Somogyi   **Qual.MN 1005**
  Moscow Radio—Shomodi   ♯ **USSR.D 556**
  (Vladigerov)
... Dances Nos. 2 & 5 also on   **USSR. 18078/9**
... Lakodalmas   — ARR. VLC. & PF.
  ☆ J. Starker & O. Herz (♯ Cpt.MC 20031)
Divertimento No. 3, A major, Op. 25
  (Hungarian Impressions)
  Hungarian Radio—Lehel   **Qual.MN 1058/9**
Hungarian Peasant Songs, Op. 22   (▽) pf.
  ☆ M. Schwalb   ♯ **Esq.TW 14-003**
  (Dohnányi)
Hungarian Suite   orch.
... 2nd movt. only
  U.S.S.R. State—Shomodi   **USSR. 18486/7**
Peasant Songs   (? ARR.)   vln. & pf.
  E. Zathureczky & Endre Petri   **Qual.SZK 3505**
  (Liszt: Consolation No. 3)

WEINGARTNER, P. Felix von
(1863-1942)

SONG: Liebesfeier, Op. 16, No. 2   (Lenau)
  W. Langel (T), Cho. & Orch.   **T.A 11553**
  (Hildach: Lenz) (♭ U 45553: in ♯ LA 6066; FT. 270.C.044)
  H R. Tauber (T) & orch. (in ♯ Ete. 701*)
— ARR. ORCH.   W. Fenske Orch. (in ♯ Phi.P 10200R)

WEIS, Karel (1862-1944)

Bohemian Dance No. 3
  F.O.K. Sym.—Smetáček   ♯ **Csm.CRLP 008**
  (Dvořák & Schneider-Trnavsky)   (▽ U.C 23219)
Galop   orch.
  Film Sym.—Pařík (in ♯ U. 5200C & 10021C)
Třasák   Czech dance, orch.
  S.B.S. Orch.—Blažek   in ♯ **U. 5081C**
      (♯ Sup.LPM 191)
▽ Other recordings in Czech catalogues include
  Viola (or The Twins) Overture   U.H 23807
  Revisor Overture   U.E 23199

---

[1] ARR. M. Blitzstein; cast of New York production, 1954.   [2] From *One Touch of Venus*, 1943.

WEISS, Sylvius Leopold (1686-1750)

SEE: † SEGOVIA PLAYS
† SEGOVIA RECITAL
† GUITAR RECITAL II
† RENAISSANCE & BAROQUE MUSIC

WERLÉ, Heinrich (b. 1887)

Sonata brevis No. 2 pf.
J. Ranck   ♯ Zod.Z 1002
(*Griffes, Poulenc, Tcherepnin*)

WESLEY, Charles (1757-1834)

Christ the Lord is risen today[1]
Cho.—W. Schumann   in ♯ Cap.L 282
(♮ *DAS 314:* ♭ *KASF 314*)

WESLEY, Samuel (1766-1837)

(An) Old English Melody (unspec.)
— ARR. ORG. Floyd
A. E. Floyd   in ♯ Spot.SC 1002
(*S. S. Wesley, etc.*) [Melbourne Town Hall Org.]

WESLEY, Samuel Sebastian (1810-1876)

ANTHEMS
Cast me not away from thy presence 6 vv.
St. Paul's Cath. Cho.—Dykes Bower
in ♯ C.CX 1237
(*Schütz, Stanford, Mendelssohn, etc.*)
(in ♯ Angel. 35139, set 3516)
King's College Cho.—Ord   C.LX 1609
(*Battishill*; in † English Church Music, Vol. IV)

Thou wilt keep him in perfect peace 5 vv.
Coronation Cho.—McKie   in ♯ G.ALP 1058
(† Coronation of Queen Elizabeth II)

(The) Wilderness 4 vv.
St. Paul's Cath. Cho.—Dykes Bower
C.LX 1568/9
(† English Church Music, Vol. III)

Larghetto, F sharp minor org.
A. E. Floyd   in ♯ Spot.SC 1002
(*Bach, Handel, Schumann, Purcell, etc.*)

WEYSE, Christoph Ernst Friedrich
(1774-1842)

OPERAS & STAGE WORKS
(The) FEAST AT KENILWORTH 1836
(H. C. Andersen, after Scott)
The Shepherd grazes his flock
(*Hyrden graesser sine Faar*)
A. Schiøtz (T), K. Olsson (pf.) ♭ G.7EBK 1004
(*Gebauer, Paulli, etc.*)

(The) SCHOOL FOR SCANDAL (after Sheridan)
Here's to the maiden . . . (*En Skaal for den Mø*)
☆ A. Schiøtz (T) (in ♯ G.KBLP 12)

(The) SLEEPING DRAUGHT
(*Sovedrykken*) 2 Acts 1809
(The) Clear waves rolled (*De klare Bølger . . .*)
E. Oldrup (S)   Tono.L 28148
(*Telka's Song*)

Fair lady, open your window
(*Skøn Jomfru, luk dit Vindu op*)
☆ A. Schiøtz (T) (in ♯ G.KBLP 12)
— ARR. VOCAL QTT. & PF. (*Phi.P 55050H*)

SONGS & PART SONGS
COLLECTION
Angel of light, go in splendour[2]
(*Lysets Engel, gaar med Glans*)
In distant steeples (List)[3]
(*I ferjne Kirketaarne*)
☆ A. Schiøtz (T), F. Jensen (pf.)
A Castle stands in Vesterled[3]
(*Der staer er Slot i Vesterled*)
Come here, little girls (Grundtvig)[4]
(*Kommer hid, I Piger Smaa*)
Fragrant meadows (Jetsmark)
(*Duftende Enge*)
Give thanks and praise to God[2]
(*Gud ske Tak og Lov*)
The Night is so still (Heiberg)[5]
Now all God's birds awake[2]
(*Nu vaagne alle Guds Fugle smaa*)
Stay with us when day is ending[3]
(*Bliv hos os, naar Dagen haelder*)
☆ A. Schiøtz (T), H. D. Koppel (pf.) ♯ G.KBLP 12
(*above*)

(The) Blessed Day (Grundtvig) (*Den signede Dag*)
Students Cho.—Friisholm   Tono.K 8047
(*Berggren: Partsong*)

(The) Blue sky is beautiful (Grundtvig)
(*Delig er den Himmel blaa*)
— ARR. ORCH. G. Hansens Orch. (in G.X 8223: ♭ 7EGK 1015)

Christmas has brought a blessed message
(Ingemann)[5] (*Julen har bragt velsigned Bud*)
— ARR. SOLO VOICE
O. Svendsen (T) & orch.   Tono.K 8094
(*Happy Christmas*)
G. Fleischer (S), L. Thybo (org.) Phi.P 55036H
(*Carol*)
— ARR. ORCH.
G. Hansens Orch. (in ♯ G.X 8223: ♭ 7EGK 1015)

Happy Christmas, beautiful Christmas (Ingemann)
M. Lundquist (T), P. Alsfelt (org.) Tono.SP 4068
(*Grundtvig: A Child was born*)
O. Svendsen (T) & orch.   Tono.K 8094
(*Christmas has brought a blessed message*)

(The) Night is so still (Heiberg)[5]
(*Natten er så stille*)
G. Fleischer (S), N. Prahl (pf.) Phi.P 55038N
(*below; & Schubert*)

Now all the bells ring[2] (*Nu ringer alle Klokker*)
F. Jena (S), M. Wöldike (org.) Pol.X 51619
(*Folksong*)

Now all God's birds awake[2]
(*Nu vaagne alle Guds Fugle smaa*)
G. Fleischer (S), N. Prahl (pf.) Phi.P 55038H
(*above*)
G. Fleischer (S), L. Thybo (org.) Phi.P 55044H
(*Praetorius: Es ist ein' Ros*)

Tekla's Song (Schiller, trs. Oehlenschläger) 1801
(*Dybt Skovan bruser*)
E. Oldrup (S) & orch.   Tono.L 28148
(*Sleeping Draught, excpt.*)

Welcome again are God's little Angels (Grundtvig)[6]
(*Velkommen igen Guds Engle smaa*)
E. Brems (M-S) & Koppel Str. Qtt. G.X 8229
(*Balle: Christmas bells are pealing*)

WHITE, Robert (c. 1530-1574)

SEE: † MASTERS OF EARLY ENGLISH KEYBOARD MUSIC

WHITLOCK, Percy William (1903-1946)

ORGAN MUSIC
Carol (A tribute to F. Delius)
A. Wyton   in ♯ ASK. 6
(*Britten, Howells, Bach, etc.*)
Paean (from 5 short pieces, 1930)
W. Watkins   in ♯ McInt.MM 106
Ye Holy Angels bright Chorale-Prelude
▽ W. M. Coulthard (*St. Bees. 4, pte.*)

---

[1] Attrib. to Charles Wesley, but he is probably author of words only—the source of the tune not identified.
[2] From *8 Morning Songs for Children* (Ingemann), 1837.   [3] From *7 Evening Songs* (Ingemann), 1838.
[4] From *9 Danish Songs*, 1837.   [5] From *3 Part-Songs for Schools*, 1841-2.   [6] From *2 Books of School Songs*, 1834-8.

WIDMANN, Erasmus (1572-1634)

  SEE: † CHORAL SONGS (*c.* 1600)

WIDOR, Charles Marie (1845-1937)

Introduction et Rondo cl. & pf.
U. & J. Delécluse   **♯ D.LX 3129**
(*Messager, Cahuzac, etc.*)   (♯ *Lon.LS 987*)

SONG: **Le Plongeur,** Op. 43, No. 4
Ħ E. de Gogorza (B) (AF.AGSB 69*)

SYMPHONIES, Organ
No. 5, F minor, Op. 42, No. 1
F. Asma   **♯ Phi.N 00241L**
[organ of Old Church, Amsterdam]   (♯ Epic.LC 3156)

... 5th movt., Toccata: Allegro
R. I. Purvis   in ♯ **HIFI.R 703**
(*Elmore, Purcell, Purvis, etc.*)
[organ of Grace Cathedral, San Francisco]
M-C. Alain   **V♯ Era.LDE 1014**
(*Gigout & Boëllmann*) [Ste. Clotilde organ]
A. Hamme   in ♯ **SRS.H 1**
(† Organ Recital)
J. Ropek   **U.H 24412**
(*Boëllmann: Suite gothique—Toccata*)
☆ E. P. Biggs (♭ *AmC.A 1883;* ♭ *Phi.N 409505E;*
                                ♭ *EPhi.NBE 11030*)
  F. Germani (♭ *G.7PW 106*)

No. 6, G minor, Op. 42, No. 2
R. Ellsasser (2ss)   **♯ P.PMC 1030**
                                     (♯ MGM.E 3065)

No. 9, C minor, Symphonie gothique, Op. 70
C. Watters   in ♯ **CEd. set 1012**
(2ss—*No. 10*)

... 2nd movt., Andante, only
E. Linzel   in ♯ **Moll.E4QP 7231**
(*Dandrieu, Karg-Elert, Pachelbel, etc.*)

... 4th movt., Variations (Moderato), only
J. Demessieux   **♯ D.LXT 2773**
(*Liszt*) [org. of Victoria Hall, Geneva]   (♯ Lon.LL 697)

No. 10, D major, Symphonie romaine, Op. 73
T. Schaefer (*Sowerby*)   **♯ Den.DR 3**
W. Self (2ss—*No. 9*)   **♯ CEd. set 1012**

WIENER, Jean (b. 1896)

Suite à danser sur un thème pf. & orch.
1. Slow   2. Biguine   3. Valse musette
4. Tango   5. Polka   6. Valse
J. Weiner & Hewitt Orch.   **V♯ DFr.SD 3**

WIENIAWSKI, Henryk (1835-1880)

COLLECTION
    Étude-Caprice, E flat major, Op. 10, No. 5
    Étude-Caprice, A minor, Op. 18, No. 4
    Polonaise brillante, D major, Op. 4
    Polonaise brillante, A major, Op. 21
    Scherzo-Tarantelle, Op. 16
    Souvenir de Moscou, Op. 6
☆ A. Eidus (vln.), E. Flissler (pf.) (♯ Cum.CS 275)

Adagio élégiaque, A major, Op. 5 vln. & pf.
L. Kogan & pf.   **USSRM.D 001263**
(*Chopin*)

Capriccio-valse, Op. 7 vln. & pf.
J. Sitkovetzky (unacc.)   **Muza.X 2064**
(*Andrzejewski: Burleska*)
Elis. Gilels & pf.   **USSRM.D 001222**
(*Kreisler*)
☆ E. Morini & pf. (in ♯ Cam.CAL 207)

CONCERTOS, Vln. & orch.
No. 2, D minor, Op. 22
☆ I. Stern & N.Y.P.S.O.—Kurtz   **♯ C.C 1013**
[3rd movt. only on ♭ *AmC.A 1647*]
☆ M. Elman & Robin Hood Dell—Hilsberg
                                 ♯ Vic.LM 9024
(*Mendelssohn*)   (♯ ItV.A12R 0116)
... 2nd movt. Romance, only — ARR. ORCH.
Orch.—Voorhees (in ♯ Alld. 3001: ♭ EP 3001; ♯ MTW. 573)

Étude-caprice, E flat major, Op. 10, No. 5[1]
Étude-caprice, A minor, Op. 18, No. 4
A. Campoli & E. Gritton   in ♯ **D.LXT 5012**
(*Kreisler, Granados, Paderewski*)   (♯ Lon.LL 1171)
                            (♯ D.LK 40110 & *LW 5218:* ♭ 71136)

... Op. 10, No. 5, only
G. Barinova & pf.   in ♯ **USSR.D 1186**
                                    (& USSR. 21817)

... Op. 18, No. 4, only
M. Rabin & A. Balsam   in ♯ **AmC.AL 30**
☆ Z. Francescatti & M. Lanner (in ♯ EPhi.NBL 5010;
                         ♯ Phi.S 06602R & N 02101L)

Étude, E major (unspec.)
D. Oistrakh & V. Yampolsky   **USSR.D 2163**

Fantaisie brillante, Op. 20 vln. & orch. (or pf.)
  (on themes from *Faust*)
L. Kogan & State Sym.—Degtarenko
(*Vieuxtemps*)   **♯ USSR.D 0144**

Légende, Op 17 vln. & pf. (or orch.)
M. Elman & J. Seiger   in ♯ **Vic.LM 1740**
              (♭ set WDM 1740; ♯ FV.A 630277)
G. Barinova & State Sym.—Kondrashin
                                 USSRM.D 438
(*Cui & Tchaikovsky*)   (also USSR. 020061/2)
D. Oistrakh & V. Yampolsky   **♯ Mon.MEL 707**
(*Prokofiev & Szymanowski*)   (♯ USSR.D 2163, d.c.)
L. Kogan & A. Mitnik   **♯ Eta.LPM 1011**
(*below*)

MAZURKAS, Vln. & pf.
A minor, Op. 3—Kuýawiak (also in ♭ *ERA 97*)
G minor, Op. 12, No. 2 (also in ♭ *ERA 97*)
D major, Op. 19, No. 2—Dudziarz
M. Elman & J. Seiger   in ♯ **Vic.LM 1740**
(in ♭ set WDM 1740; ♯ FV.A 630277)
        Opp. 3 & 12, No. 2, also on ♭ DV.26035)

A minor, Op. 3—Kuýawiak
G. Barinova & pf. (*USSRM.D 00445*)
J. Schmied & orch. (in ♯ Vien.LPR 1031)

D major, Op. 12, No. 1—Sielanka[2]
G major, Op. 12, No. 2—Polish Song
G. Barinova & pf.   **USSRM.D 00357**
(*Suk*)   (& USSR. 18685)

G major, Op. 19, No. 1—Obertass
W. Wilkomirska & J. Szamotulska **Muza.X 2145**
(½s—*Rachmaninoff: Romance*)   (also X 2061)
L. Kogan & A. Mitnik   in ♯ **Eta.LPM 1011**
(*above; & Tchaikovsky, Schubert*)

D major, Op. 19, No. 2—Dudziarz (*The Minstrel*)
G. Barinova & pf.   in ♯ **USSR.D 1186**
                                    (& USSR. 21817)
☆ N. Milstein & A. Balsam (♭ G.7RF 279)

POLONAISES BRILLANTES Vln. & pf.
No. 1, D major, Op. 4
J. Heifetz & E. Bay (? n.v.)   ♭ **Vic.ERA 57**
(*Arensky, Debussy, Godowsky*)
M. Elman & J. Seiger   in ♯ **Vic.LM 1740**
                                    (♯ FV.A 630277)
M. Wilk & F. Kramer   in ♯ **MTR.MLO 1012**
(*Bach, Brahms, Pergolesi, etc.*)
J. Sitkowiecki & I. Kollegorskaya **Muza.X 2063**
(*Shostakovich: Preludes*)

No. 2, A major, Op. 21
G. Jarry & A. Collard   in ♯ **C.FCX 222**

---
[1] ARR. Kreisler—*Caprice alla Saltarella.*
[2] Listed as *Mazurka;* may be any of the others. On *18685* the coupled Mazurka is by Mlinarsky, so perhaps the re-issue is wrongly attributed.

Scherzo-Tarantelle, Op. 16　vln. & pf.
　H. Szeryng & T. Janopoulo　　in ♯ *Od.OD 1008*
　G. Jarry & N. Nora　　　　　　**C.LFX 1086**
　(*Ries & Paradies*)　　　　(♭ *SCBF 102:* in ♯ *FCX 222*)
　J. Heifetz & E. Bay (n.v.)　　♭ *Vic.ERA 94*
　(*Rachmaninoff, Sarasate, Stravinsky*)　(♭ *DV. 26034*)
　I. Oistrakh & I. Kollegorskaya　in ♯**Van.VRS 461**
　(*Vitali, Bach, Mozart, etc.*)　　(also Muza.X 2060)
　D. Oistrakh & pf.　　　　　　**USSR. 022227**
　(*Kabalevsky: Impromptu*)
　N. Shkolnikova & pf. (*USSR. 22627/8*)
　☆ Y. Menuhin & A. Baller (in ♯ Vic.LM 1742:
　　　　　　　　　　　　♭ set *WDM 1742*)[1]
　　H. Szeryng & Berthelier (in ♯*Pac.LDPC 50:* ♭ *EP 90019*)

Souvenir de Moscou, Op. 6　vln. & pf. [or orch.]
　G. Barinova & Moscow Radio Sym.
　　—Kondrashin (2ss)　*USSRM.D 00829/30*
　☆ Z. Francescatti & A. Balsam　♯ *EPhi.ABR 4011*
　　(*Bruch*)　　　　　　　　(♯ *Phi.A 01610R*)
　　(also ♯ *EPhi.NBL 5010; Phi.S 06602R* & N 02101L)

WILBYE, John (1574–1638)

MADRIGALS

[Roman figures refer to vols. of *English Madrigal School;*
　Vol. VI, 1598; Vol. VII, 1609]

COLLECTION

Flora gave me fairest flowers	5 vv.	VI
Adieu, sweet Amaryllis	4 vv.	VI
And though my love abounding	5 vv.	VI
As fair as morn	3 vv.	VII
I fall, I fall, O stay me	5 vv.	VI
Weep, O mine eyes	3 vv.	VII
Hard destinies are done	5 vv.	VII
Fly not so swift	4 vv.	VII
Oft have I vowed	5 vv.	VII
Sweet honey-sucking bees;		
Yet sweet, take heed	5 vv.	VII
Happy, O happy he	4 vv.	VII
Ye that do live in pleasures	5 vv.	VII
O what shall I do?	3 vv.	VI
Thus saith my Cloris	4 vv.	VII
All pleasure is of this condition	5 vv.	VII
Weep, weep, mine eyes	5 vv.	VII

　Randolph Singers　　　　♯ **West.WL 5221**

Flora gave me fairest flowers　VI　5 vv.
　N.Y. Pro Musica Antiqua—Greenberg
　　　　　　　　　　　　in ♯ **AmC.ML 5051**
　(† *Evening of Elizabethan Verse & Music*)

(The) Lady Oriana (from 'Triumphs of Oriana')
　Randolph Singers　　in ♯ **Nix.WLP 6212-1/2**
　(† *Triumphs of Oriana*)　　(♯ West. set WAL 212)

Sweet honey-sucking bees　VII　5 vv.
　Madrigal Singers—Robe　　in ♯ **Fred. 2**
　(*Lassus, Martinů, etc.*)
　N.Y. Pro Musica Antiqua—Greenberg
　　　　　　　　　　　　in ♯ **AmC.ML 5051**
　(† *Evening of Elizabethan Verse & Music*)

Ye that do live in pleasures plenty　VII　5 vv.
　Golden Age Singers　　　　**G.HMS 33**
　(† *History of Music in Sound*)　(in ♯ Vic. set LM 6029)

WILDER, Alec (b. 1907)

Quintet　wind insts.
　N.Y. Wind Quintet　　　♯ **Phil.PH 110**
　(*Villa-Lobos*)

WILHELMINE, Markgräfin von Bayreuth
(1709–1758)

Concerto, C major, hpsi. & orch. (MS., Wolfenbüttel)
　W. Spilling & Frankenland State Sym.—Kloss
　(*Friedrich II*)　　　　　　♯ **Lyr.LL 51**

WILLAERT, Adrian (*c.* 1490–1562)

Ego dormivi　Motet
　Treviso Cath. Cho.—d'Alessi
　　　　　　　　　　♯ **E. & AmVox.PL 8610**
　(† *Motets of Venetian School II*)

Ricercar No. 7 (*Ricercari e Fantasie . . . 1549*)
　Basle Schola Viol Ens.　　　**G.HMS 41**
　(† *History of Music in Sound*)　(in ♯ Vic. set LM 6029)

Ricercar No. 10 (*Ricercari e Fantasie . . . 1549*)
　Alma Musica Trio (vln., vla., vlc.)
　　　　　　　　　　　in ♯ **LT.DTL 93046**
　(*Vivaldi, Gabrieli, Mozart, etc.*)　(♯ Sel. LAG 1019;
　　　　　　　　　　　　　　　T.LT 6551)
　Musicians' Workshop Recorder Consort
　　　　　　　　　　　　♯ **CEd.CE 1018**
　(† *Recorder Music*)
　☆ F. Peeters (in † *Old Netherland Masters,*
　　　　　　　　　　　♯ Cpt.MC 20069)

Villotte: Un giorno mi prego
Villanesca: Madonn' io non lo so
Madrigal: O bene mio[2]
　☆ Vocal Qtt.—Raugel (in † ♯ HS.AS 5)

ARRANGEMENTS of Madrigals by P. Verdelot
Con lagrime e con sospir
Fuggi, fuggi, cuor mio
　☆ H. Cuénod (T) & lute (in †Ital. Songs, ♯Nix.WLP 5059)

WILLAN, Healey (b. 1880)

Father of Heaven whose love profound
　Redlands Univ. Cho.—J. W. Jones
　　　　　　　　　in ♯ **AmC.ML ML 4866**

(2) French Canadian Folk-Songs　pub. 1937
1. Ste. Marguerite　　2. Le Navire de Bayonne
　5th Ave. High School Cho.—Lowe
　　　　　　　　　　　in ♯ **PFCM.CB 161**
　(*Lopatnikoff, Phillips, Poulenc, etc.*)

Hodie Christus natus est (Liturgical Motet No. 10)
　Concordia Cho.—Christiansen　　♯ **Cdia. 4**
　(*Bach, Britten; Folksongs & Carols*)

Make we merry　Carol (Hill)　pub. 1949
　St. Simon-the-Apostle Chu. Cho.—Lewis
　　　　　　　　　　　　in ♯ **Hall.J 75**

O Lord our Governor
　Coronation Cho.　　　　in ♯ **G.ALP 1058**
　(† *Coronation of Queen Elizabeth II*)

Rise up my love
Behold the tabernacle of God
　(Liturgical Motets, Nos. 5 & 9)

Missa brevis No. 10, C minor　pub. 1948
　Festival Singers—Iseler　　♯ *Hall.ChS 3*
　(*Mundy, Byrd, Lassus, Gibbons*)

WILLIAMS, Alberto (1862–1952)

En la sierra, Op. 32　pf.
... No. 4, El Rancho abandonado
— ARR. ORCH.　R. Fauré
　Avellaneda Municipal—R. Fauré
　　　　　　　　　　　♯ *ArgOd.LDC 523*
　(*Gluck, Gomez, Ugarte*)　　(♭ *BSOAE 4524*)

Sonata No. 2, D minor, Op. 51, vln. & pf.
... 2nd movt., Andante sostenuto (Vidalita)
　C. Pessina & A. Fasoli　　**ArgOd. 66045**

Vidalita (unspec.), perhaps the song, ARR.
　State Sym.—Kinsky　　　*ArgV.P 1498*
　(*Boero: El Caramba*)　　　(pte. rec.)

---

[1] Acc. Baller is the Japanese recording; this issue is also stated to be acc. G. Moore and recorded in England.
[2] All from *Canzone, Villanesche alla Napolitana,* 1545.

Suite Argentina No. 3 . . . Milonga
   State Radio Cha.—Bandini   ♯ *ArgOd.LDC 512*
   (*Forte: Vidalita*)

   ▽ Older recordings include:
   Vidalita, Op. 45, No. 3: I. Marengo (S) (*ArgV. 4221*)
                 B. Gigli (T) (*G.DA 1891*)
                  T. dal Monte (S) (*Vic. 1202*)
   Aire de Vals No. 2: H. Giordano (pf.)
                (*ArgOd. 57001:* ♭ *BSOA 4008*)

WILSON, John (1595-1674)
   SEE: † SHAKESPEARE SONGS & LUTE SOLOS

WILTON, Charles Henry (fl. 1780-1827)

TRIOS, vln., vla. & vlc.   1783
No. 1, A major   No. 3, C major   No. 6, F major
   J. Pougnet, F. Riddle & A. Pini ♯ *West.WL 5296*

WIRÉN, Dag (b. 1905)

Serenade, Op. 11   Str. orch.
   ☆ Stockholm Radio—Westerberg   ♯ *Lon.LS 714*
   (*Larsson*)
   [Marcia only, D.K 24035: ♭ *71032*]

WITZLAW VON RÜGEN (d. 1325)
   SEE: † MUSIC OF THE MIDDLE AGES

WOLF, Hugo (1860-1903)

(Der) CORREGIDOR   Opera   4 Acts   1896
COMPLETE RECORDING
   ☆ M. Fuchs (S), M. Teschemacher (S), K. Erb (T), etc.,
       Dresden Op. Cho. & orch.—Elmendorff
                 (♯ ANix.ULP 9208-1/3)

Italienische Serenade, G major   (*Italian Serenade*)
— STRING QUARTET VERSION   1887
   Hollywood Qtt.   ♯ *DCap.CTL 7063*
   (*Turina & Creston*)   (♯ *Cap.P 8260*)
   Hirsch Qtt.   ♯ *Argo.RG 7*
   (*Bloch*)   (o.n. ARS 1011)
   New Music Qtt.   ♯ *AmC.ML 4821*
   (*Quartet*)   (♯ *Phi.A 01158L*)
   American Art Qtt.   in ♯ *BB.LBC 1086*
   (*Fauré, Bridge, Grainger, etc.*)
   A. Winograd Str. Orch.   ♯ *MGM.E 3295*
   (*Mendelssohn & Dvořák*)
   ☆ Koeckert Qtt. (♭ *Pol. 30010*)

Quartet, D minor   str.   1878-84, f.p. 1903
   New Music Qtt.   ♯ *AmC.ML 4821*
   (*Italian Serenade*)   (♯ *Phi.A 01158L*)

SONGS
   SL—Spanisches Liederbuch.   1889-90
   IL—Italienisches Liederbuch.   1890-6
COLLECTIONS
   MÖRIKE LIEDER
       Abschied
       An eine Aeolsharfe
       Bei einer Trauung
       Fussreise
       Nimmersatte Liebe
       Peregrina I & II
       Selbstgeständnis
       Der Tambour
   GOETHE LIEDER
       Anakreons Grab
       Epiphanias
       Genialisch Treiben
       Harfenspieler Lieder I, II, III
       (Wer sich der Einsamkeit; An die Türen; Wer nie sein
        Brot)
   B. Boyce (B), R. Veyron-Lacroix (pf.)
               ♯ *LOL.OL 50026*

GOETHE LIEDER
   Anakreons Grab
   Cophtische Lieder I & II
   (Lasset Gelehrte . . . ; Geh! gehorche . . .)
   Erschaffen und Beleben;   Genialisch Treiben
   Harfenspieler Lieder, I, II, III
       Ob der Koran von Ewigkeit sei?;   Phänomen
   Alle gingen, Herz, zur Ruh' (S.L.)
   Fussreise (Mörike);   In der Frühe (Mörike)
   Lebewohl (Mörike)
   Verschwiegene Liebe (Eichendorff)
   Wer sein holdes Lieb verloren (Geibel)
   D. Fischer-Dieskau (B), G. Moore (pf.)
                   ♯ *G.ALP 1143*
                    (♯ *FALP 310*)

22 Songs from the Italienisches Liederbuch   [Nos.]
   Auch kleine Dinge   [1]
   Mir ward gesagt   [2]
   Wer rief dich denn   [6]
   Du denkst mit einem Fädchen   [10]
   Wie lange schon war immer mein Verlangen [11]
   Nein, junger Herr   [12]
   Mein Liebster ist so klein   [15]
   Ihr jungen Leute   [16]
   Wir haben beide lange Zeit geschwiegen [19]
   Mein Liebster singt [20]
   Man sagt mir, deine Mutter woll' es nicht [21]
   Mein Liebster hat zu Tisch mich geladen [25]
   Du sagst mir, dass ich keine Fürstin sei [28]
   Wohl kenn ich euren Stand   [29]
   Was soll der Zorn mein Schatz [32]
   Wenn du, mein Liebster, steigst zum Himmel auf [36]
   Gesegnet sei das Grün   [39]
   O wär dein Haus durchsichtig   [40]
   Heut' Nacht erhob ich mich   [41]
   Schweig' einmal still   [43]
   Verschling' der Abgrund   [45]
   Ich hab' in Penna   [46]
   I. Seefried (S), E. Werba (pf.) ♯ HP.DGM 18192
   (*Brahms on* ♯ *AmD.DL 9743*)

16 Songs from the Italienisches Liederbuch
   Gesegnet sei, durch den die Welt entstund [4]
   Selig ihr Blinden [5]
   Der Mond hat eine schwere Klag' erhoben [7]
   Nun lass uns Frieden schliessen   [8]
   Hoffärtig seid ihr, schönes Kind   [13]
   Geselle, woll'n wir uns in Kutten hüll'n [14]
   Und willst du deinen Liebsten sterben sehen [17]
   Heb' auf dein blondes Haupt   [18]
   Ein Ständchen Euch zu bringen [22]
   Was für ein Lied soll dir gesungen werden [23]
   Sterb' ich, so hüllt in Blumen meine Glieder [33]
   Und steht ihr früh am Morgen auf [34]
   Benedeit die sel'ge Mutter [35]
   Wie viele Zeit verlor' ich, dich zu lieben [37]
   Heut' Nacht erhob ich mich   [41]
   Nicht länger kann ich singen   [42]
   ☆ D. Fischer-Dieskau (B), H. Klust (pf.)
                 ♯ HP.DGM 18005
                 (♯ Eta. 820015)
   Abschied (Mörike)
   An die Geliebte (Mörike)
   An eine Aeolsharfe (Mörike)
   Anakreons Grab (Goethe)
   Auf einer Wanderung (Mörike)
   Fussreise (Mörike)
   Der Gärtner (Mörike)
   Gesang Weylas (Mörike)
   Gesegnet sei, durch den die Welt entstund (I.L.)
   Der Musikant (Eichendorff)
   Der Rattenfänger (Goethe)
   Über Nacht (Sturm)
   Und steht ihr früh am Morgen auf (I.L.)
   Verborgenheit (Mörike)
   ☆ A. Poell (Bs), F. Holetschek (pf.)   ♯ Nix.WLP 5048

   Cophtisches Lieder I & II (Goethe)
   Geselle, woll'n wir uns in Kutten hüll'n (I.L.)
   Grenzen der Menschheit (Goethe)
   Harfenspieler Lieder, I, II, III (Goethe)
   Michelangelo Lieder, I, II, III   1897
       (Wohl denk ich oft; Alles endet, was entstehet;
             Fühlt meine Seele)
   Prometheus (Goethe)
   H. Hotter (B), G. Moore (pf.)   ♯ C.CX 1162
                    (♯ Angel. 35057)
   An den Schlaf (Mörike)
   Begegnung (Mörike)
   Denk' es, o Seele (Mörike)
   Im Frühling (Mörike)
   In dem Schatten meiner Locken (S.L.)
   Mignon I, II, III (Goethe)
       (Heiss mich nicht reden; Nur wer die Sehnsucht
            kennt; So lasst mich . . .)
   Mögen alle bösen Zungen (S.L.)
   Wo find ich Trost (Mörike)
   D. v. Stein (A), H. Reutter (pf.)   ♯ *D.NLM 4561*

♯ = Long-playing, 33⅓ r.p.m.   ♭ = 45 r.p.m.   ♮ = Auto. couplings, 78 r.p.m.

Michelangelo Lieder, I, II, III
Der Freund (Eichendorff)
Der Musikant (Eichendorff)
Verschwiegene Liebe (Eichendorff)
Gesang Weylas (Mörike)
Storchenbotschaft (Mörike)
H. Rehfuss (B), H. W. v. Häusslein (pf.)
♯ **D.LW 5162**
(♯ Lon.LD 9182)

Fussreise (Mörike)
Gesang Weylas (Mörike)
Heimweh (Eichendorff: Wer in die Fremde)
In der Frühe (Mörike)
Lied eines Verliebten (Mörike)
Der Musikant (Eichendorff)
Nachtzauber (Eichendorff)
Der Tambour (Mörike)
Verschwiegene Liebe (Eichendorff)
☆ C. Calder (B), M. Carlay (pf.) (♯ Allo. 4045)

Liebesglück (Eichendorff)
Morgenstimmung (Reinick)
Die Nacht (Eichendorff)
Ob auch finstre Blicke glitten (S.L.)
M. Schloss (S), J. Brice (pf.)   ♯ **IRCC.L 7000**
(Franz, Schumann, R. Strauss)

Anakreons Grab (Goethe)
Gesang Weylas (Mörike)
Der Tambour (Mörike)
Verborgenheit (Mörike)
G. Hüsch (B), M. Gurlitt (pf.)   **JpV.SD 3091**
(omitting Der Tambour, & with Bach, Schubert, R. Strauss, on ♯ LS 2006)

Anakreons Grab (Goethe)
Schon streckt' ich aus im Bett (I.L.)
Ein Ständchen Euch zu bringen (I.L.)
H. Hotter (B), G. Moore (pf.)   **C.LB 142**

Ob der Koran von Ewigkeit sei? (Goethe)
Solang man nüchtern ist (Goethe)
Der Tambour (Mörike)
H. Hotter (B), G. Moore (pf.)   **C.LB 141**

Der Feuerreiter (Mörike)
Storchenbotschaft (Mörike)
Der Tambour (Mörike)
D. Fischer-Dieskau (B), G. Moore (pf.)
♭ **G.7ER 5044**
(Loewe: Erlkönig)
(Der Tambour, with Loewe on DA 5524:♭ 7PW 534;
Der Feuerreiter & Storchenbotschaft
on DB 11573: ♭ 7RW 533)

Die Bekehrte (Goethe)
Citronenfalter in April (Mörike)
Die Spröde (Goethe)
M. Dobbs (S), G. Moore (pf.)   ♯ **C.CX 1154**
(Schubert, Brahms, Fauré, Hahn, Chausson)
(♯ FCX 299: QCX 10097; Angel. 35094)

An eine Aeolsharfe (Mörike)
Begegnung (Mörike)
Das verlassene Mägdlein (Mörike)
I. Seefried (S), E. Werba (pf.)   ♯ **Pol. 19050**
(R. Strauss, Schubert, Brahms, etc.)   (♯ AmD.DL 9809)

Citronenfalter in April (Mörike)
Elfenlied (Mörike)
Mausfallen-Sprüchlein (Mörike)
E. Berger (S), M. Gurlitt (pf.) in **JpV.set JAS 272**
(♭ ES 8018)

Abschied (Mörike)
Er ist's (Mörike)
Verschwiegene Liebe (Eichendorff)
☆ H. Schlusnus (B) & pf.   ♯ **HP.DGM 18029**
(Brahms, Schubert, R. Strauss)

Abschied (Mörike)   ☐
M. Harrell (B), B. Smith (pf.) in ♯ **Rem. 199-140**
(below; Duparc, Massenet, Fauré, etc.)

Ach, des Knaben Augen (S.L.)
B. Troxell (S) & org.   in ♯ **Ply. 12-123**

Auch kleine Dinge (I.L.) ☐
R. Hayes (T), R. Boardman (pf.) in ♯ **A 440.12-3**

Auf eine Christblume I (Mörike)
E. Höngen (A), G. Moore (pf.) (2ss) **C.LB 140**

Denk es, o Seele (Mörike) ☐
I. Seefried (S), E. Werba (pf.)   **Pol. 62899**
(Nimmersatte Liebe)   (♭ Pol. 30010)

Er ist's (Mörike) ☐
— FOR PRACTICE: Vln. & pf. acc. (in ♯ VS.MHL 6000)

Ganymed (Goethe)
H. Krebs (T), R. Schlesier (pf.)   **Eta. 320162**
(Der Rattenfänger)   (o.n. 25-007)

(Der) Gärtner (Mörike) ☐
☆ A. Dermota (T), H. Dermota (pf.) (♭ D.VD 502)

Gesang Weylas (Mörike) ☐
M. Lawrence (S) & pf.   in ♯ **Cam.CAL 216**
(R. Strauss, Pfitzner, etc.)

Kennst du das Land? (Goethe) ("Mignon—Ballade")
☆ K. Thorborg (A), L. Rosenek (pf.) (in ♯ Vic.LCT 1115:
♭ set WCT 1115)

Mausfallen-Sprüchlein (Mörike) ☐
E. Schwarzkopf (S), G. Moore (pf.)   **C.LX 1577**
(½s—Wiegenlied im Sommer; & R. Strauss)
(also in ♯ CX 1044: FCX 182; Angel. 35023; perhaps n.v.)

(3) Michelangelo Lieder   ☐
D. Gramm (Bs), R. Cumming (pf.) in ♯ **ML. 7033**
(Cesti, Martini, Schubert, Bowles, etc.)

Morgenstimmung (Reinick)
S. Onegin (A)   V♯ **IRCC.L 7003**
(Massenet, Schubert, E. B. Onegin)

(Der) Musikant (Eichendorff) ☐
G. Pechner (B)   in ♯ **Roy. 1558**
H. Janssen (B), S. Leff (pf.)   in ♯ **Mur.P 110**
(followed by pf. acc. only)
☆ A. Dermota (T) (♭ D.VD 512)

Nimmersatte Liebe (Mörike) ☐
I. Seefried (S), E. Werba (pf.)   **Pol. 62899**
(Denk es, o Seele)   (♭ Pol. 30010)
☆ A. Dermota (T) (♭ D.VD 502)

Nun wandre, Maria (S.L.)
G. Pechner (B)   in ♯ **Roy. 1558**
R. Hayes (T), R. Boardman (pf.)
in ♯ **Van.VRS 7016**

Prometheus (Goethe) ☐
☸ H. Rehkemper (in ♯ Sca. 809*)

(Der) Rattenfänger (Goethe) ☐
H. Krebs (T), R. Schlesier (pf.)   **Eta. 320162**
(Ganymed)   (o.n. 25-007)

Schlafendes Jesuskind (Mörike)
B. Troxell (S) & org.   in ♯ **Ply. 12-123**
☆ I. Seefried (S), E. Werba (pf.) (in ♯ AmD.DL 7545)

Und willst du deinen Liebsten sterben sehen? (I.L.) ☐
M. Harrell (B), B. Smith (pf.) in ♯ **Rem. 199-140**
(above)

Verborgenheit (Mörike) ☐
J. Björling (T), F. Schauwecker (pf.) ♭ **G.ERC 1**
(Liszt & Sibelius)   (in ♯ ALP 1187; Vic.LM 1771:
♭ ERA 141; ♭ DV. 26045)
A. Konetzni (S), E. Werba (pf.)   **C.LV 20**
(Brahms: Mainacht)
— FOR PRACTICE: Vln. & pf. acc. (in ♯ VS.MHL 6000)

Verschwiegene Liebe (Eichendorff) ☐
☆ L. Slezak (T) (in ♯ Ete. 493)

Wiegenlied im Sommer (Reinick—Vom Berg . . .)
E. Schwarzkopf (S), G. Moore (pf.) **C.LX 1577**
(½s—Mausfallen-Sprüchlein & R. Strauss)
(in ♯ C.CX 1044: FCX 182; in ♯ Angel. 35023; perhaps n.v.)

WOLF-FERRARI, Ermanno (1876-1948)

OPERAS
(Le) DONNE CURIOSE 3 Acts 1903
Colei che adoro Bs.
☸ A. Pini-Corsi (SBDH.P 2*)

☆ = Re-issue of a recording to be found in previous volumes.

(I) GIOIELLI DELLA MADONNA, Op. 4
3 Acts   1911

Intermezzi, Acts II & III (Nos. 1 & 2 of Orch. Suite)
Württemberg State—Leitner   ♭ *Pol. 30037*
(*Schmidt: Notre Dame, Intermezzo*)   (& in ♯ *17001*)
(No. 2 is ☆; No. 1 also on *PV. 36102;*
                                  No. 2 also ♭ *Pol. 30027*)
Hamburg Philharmonia—H-J. Walther
                                  MSB. 78139
  ☆ Minneapolis Sym.—Ormandy (in ♯ *Cam.*CAL 119)
     Robin Hood Dell—Mitropoulos (♭ *AmC.A 1637*)
... **No. 2** only
  ☆ Philharmonia—Schüchter (in ♯ *P.PMD 1022;*
                                  ♭ *Od.BSOE 4006*)

(I) QUATTRO RUSTEGHI 4 Acts   1906
  (*Vier Grobiane: "School for Fathers"*)
COMPLETE RECORDING

Marina	A. Noni (S)
Lucieta	G. P. Labia (S)
Felice	E. Orell (S)
Margarita	A. Dubbini (M-S)
Filipeto	M. Carlin (T)
Lunardo	F. Corena (Bs)
Cancian	C. Dalamangas (Bs)
Count Riccardo	M. P. de Leon (T)

etc., Italian Radio Cho. & orch.—Simonetto
                                  ♯ *CCet.* set 1239
(6ss) [Intermezzo, Act II only, in ♯ *CCet.A* 50159]

Intermezzo, Act II
L.S.O.—Previtali   *G.C 4228*
(*Segreto di Susanna, Overture*)
  ☆ Philharmonia—Schüchter (in ♯ *P.PMD 1022;*
                                  ♭ *Od.BSOE 4006*)

Luceta xe un bel nome T
  ☆ F. Tagliavini (in ♯ *CCet.A* 50155)

(II) SEGRETO DI SUSANNA 1 Act   1909
COMPLETE RECORDINGS

Casts	Set A	Set B
Countess Susanna ...	E. Rizzieri (S)	E. Orell (S)
Count Gil	G. Valdengo (B)	M. Borriello (B)

Set A, with Italian Radio Orch.—Questa
                                  ♯ *CCet.* 1250

Set B, with Turin Sym. Orch.—Simonetto
                                  ♯ *HP.DGM* 18136
Overture   (♯ AmD.DL 9770)
L.S.O.—Previtali   *G.C 4228*
(*Quattro Rusteghi, Intermezzo*)   (in ♯ *BB.LBC* 1092)
Hamburg Philharmonia—H-J. Walther
                                  MSB. 78135
(*Meistersinger—Tanz der Lehrbuben*)
  ☆ Philharmonia—Fistoulari   in ♯ *P.PMC* 1031
  (*Rezniček, Nicolai, etc.*)
  ☆ Austrian Sym.—Gui (in ♯ *Rem.* 199-142; in ♯ *Ply.* 12-65)

Gioia, la nube leggera S
  ♮ C. Muzio (*IRCC.* 3134*)
     F. Alda (*AF.AGSB*) 16*

SONG: Rispetto, Op. 21, No. 1: Quando ti vidi
R. Ponselle (S), I. Chicagov (pf.)
                           in ♯ *Vic.LM* 1889
(*Donaudy, Tosti, Sadero, Lully, etc.*) (♯ *DV.L* 16493)

WOLFF, Albert (Louis) (b. 1884)

ITTO Film music
  ▽ S. Fillacier (S) & orch. (*G.K 7356/7*)

SONGS
Répit (Colette)
  S. Couderc (M-S), J. Allain (pf.)
J'ai chaud (Colette)
Sommeil (Colette)
  R. Doria (S), J. Allain (pf.) ♯ *FMer.MLP* 7073
  (*Damase & Poulenc*)

WOLKENSTEIN
  SEE: OSWALD VON WOLKENSTEIN

WOLPE, Stefan (b. 1902)

Passacaglia pf. 1934-8
  (from *Four Studies in Structure*)
  D. Tudor
Quartet tpt., sax., percussion & pf. 1950
  B. Nagel, A. Cohn, A. Howard, J. Maxin-Baron
Sonata vln. & pf. 1949
  F. Magnes & D. Tudor   ♯ *Eso.*ES 530
SONG: Frieden heisst Sieg (Ussowa)
  E. Busch (B) & Inst. Ens.   *Eta.* 10-99
  (*Shostakovich: Meeting on the Elbe, excpt.*)

WOOD, Charles (1866-1926)

ANTHEMS
Glory and honour and laud 1925
  St. George's Chapel Cho.—Harris *C.LX* 1613
  († *English Church Music IV*)

Hail, gladdening Light (Keble) Double cho. 1919
  St. Paul's Cath. Cho.—Dykes Bower
                               in ♯ *C.CX* 1237
  (*Bairstow, Wesley, Schütz, etc.*) (in ♯ *Angel.* 35139,
                                              set 3516)
CAROL ARRANGEMENT
Ding dong, merrily on high
  St. Paul's Cath. Cho.—Dykes Bower
                               in ♯ *C.CX* 1193
  (*Vaughan Williams, Sweelinck, etc.*)
                               (in ♯ *Angel.* 35138, in set 3516)
  Bach Cho.—Jacques   in ♯ *D.LK* 4085
  (also in ♯ *D.LF 1029*; ♯ *Lon.*LL 1095 & *LS 263*;
                                  ▽ *D.F 9513*)
  Nat. Presbyterian Chu. Cho.—Schaefer
                               in ♯ *McInt.MM* 107
  (*Christmas Candlelight Service*)
  St. Simon-the-Apostle Chu. Cho.—Lewis
                               in ♯ *Hall.J* 75

YARDUMIAN, Richard (b. 1917)

Armenian Suite orch. 1936-7, rev. 1954
Concerto, vln. & orch. 1949
Desolate City orch. 1943
Psalm 130 T & orch. 1947
  A. Brusilow (vln.), H. Zulick (T) & Philadelphia
  —Ormandy   ♯ *AmC.ML* 4991

YSAŸE, Eugène (1858-1931)

(4) SONATAS, Op. 27 vln. unacc.
No. 1, G minor
  G. Octors   ♯ *Gramo.GLP* 2510
  (*Vieuxtemps*)
No. 3, D minor
  D. Oistrakh (n.v.)   ♯ *CdM.LDA* 8075
  (*Khachaturian, Leclair, Tchaikovsky*)
  (*Beethoven & Leclair on ♯ Van.VRS 6024*)
  (*Brahms: Concerto on ♯ Csm.CRLP 150, ? d.v.*)
  R. Odnoposoff (*below*)   ♯ *CHS.CHS* 1175
No. 4, E minor
  R. Odnoposoff   ♯ *CHS.CHS* 1175
  (*above, Nin & Falla*)

ZANDONAI, Riccardo (1883-1944)

FRANCESCA DA RIMINI 4 Acts   1914
COMPLETE RECORDING
  ☆ Soloists, Italian Radio Cho. & orch.—Guarnieri
                                  (♯ *FSor.CS* 547/9)

♯ = Long-playing, 33⅓ r.p.m.   ♭ = 45 r.p.m.   ♮ = Auto. couplings, 78 r.p.m.

528

GIULIETTA E ROMEO 3 Acts 1922
Romeo's Ride (Cavalcata, Act III) orch.
☆ Covent Garden—Patanè (♭ *C.SED 5512: SEDQ 522*)

Sono la vostra sposa S
  M. L. Gemelli   *Cet.AT 0401*
  (*Vêpres Siciliennes—Mercè dilette amiche*)

Deh! Sorgi o luce in ciel T
  D. Cestari   **Cet.PE 212**
  (*Gomes: Lo Schiavo—Quando nascesti tu*)

Serenata medioevale vlc. & cha. orch. 1912
  L. W. Pratesi & Cha. Orch.—Fauré
                  ♯ *ArgOd.LDC 529*
  (*Saint-Saëns, Villa-Lobos, etc.*)

ZANGIUS, Nikolaus (*c.* 1570–*c.* 1619)

    SEE: † CHORAL SONGS (*c.* 1600)

ZANNETTI, Gasparo (fl. XVIIth Cent.)

(Li) SCOLARI before 1645
Dances (unspec.) orch.
  Naples Scarlatti—Lupi[1]   **♯ *Csm.CLPS 1045***
  (*Debussy & Saint-Saëns*)

ZELLER, Karl (1842-1898)

(Abridged listings only)
(Der) VOGELHÄNDLER Operetta, 1891
Vocal Selections
  A Schlemm, P. Anders, A. Rothenberger, W. Hofmann,
    F. Himmelmann, Cho. & orch.—Marszalek **PV. 58622**
                            (♭ *Pol. 20046*)
  (*Millöcker: Bettelstudent Selection on ♯ Pol. 45049*)

M. Cunitz, E. Loose, K. Terkal, etc.   **♯ *DT.TM 68008***
(*Millöcker: Bettelstudent Selection*)
        (♯ *D.LF 1517;* TV.VE 9030: ♭ *T.UX 4515*)
☆ W. A. Dotzer, M. Stelzer, A. Heusser, etc., Cho. &
    Vienna Sym. Orch.—Paulik (in ♯ *Phi.S 06014R*)

Schenkt man sich Rosen in Tirol S & T
  ☆ E. Sack & M. Wittrisch (♭ *T.UE 452222*)

Wie mein Ahn'l zwanzig Jahr
  P. Anders (T)   *Pol. 48927*
  (*Künneke: Vetter aus Dingsda, excpt.*)   (♭ *22031*)
  J. Patzak (T)   in ♯ *D.LX 3122*
  (also *Ome. 22291*)   (♯ *Lon.LS 862*)
  (*Gruber: Mei Muatterl . . . on D.F 43681:* ♭ *D 17681*)
  ☆ R. Tauber (in ♯ *ArgOd.LDM 7331*)

Selection from Zeller's works
  Vienna Radio—Schneider (in ♯ *Phi.S 05903R*)

ZELTER, Karl Friedrich (1758-1832)

SONGS
König in Thule (Goethe)
  E. Grümmer (S) & orch.   **Eta. 225029**
  (*Moussorgsky: Song of the Flea*)   (o.n. 20-161 & 25-006)

Wonne der Wehmuth (Goethe)
  B. Diamant (B), J. Newmark (fortepiano)
                        in ♯ *Hall.RS 6*
  († Musica Antica e Nuova)

ZIELENSKI, Mikolaj (Nicolas) (fl. XVIIth Cent.)

    SEE: † ANTHOLOGIE SONORE (♯ HS.AS 10)

ZIPOLI, Domenico (1688-1726)

    SEE: † OLD ITALIAN MASTERS

---

[1] Announced on this disc but not listed in the latest catalogue. The disc itself has not been checked.

ANTHOLOGIES

ARRANGED in alphabetical order of title, following the General Anthologies:—
L'ANTHOLOGIE SONORE
THE HISTORY OF MUSIC IN SOUND
MASTERPIECES OF MUSIC before 1750
ENGLISH CHURCH MUSIC

There are a few departures from strict alphabetical order to facilitate grouping of similar periods. Certain "Historical" re-issues are summarised under the heading VOCAL RE-ISSUES—including one instrumental disc.

L'ANTHOLOGIE SONORE

169: J. C. de CHAMBONNIÈRES (q.v.): Harpsichord Pieces
M. Charbonnier
[This appears to be the last 78 r.p.m. disc in this series]

V♯ 1802 LD: GERMAN RELIGIOUS MUSIC of the XVIth & XVIIth Centuries
M. PRAETORIUS: Beati omnes
HASSLER: Wenn mein Stündlein
SCHÜTZ: Selig sind die Toten
KRIEGER: Die Gerechten ...
☆ M. Meili (T) & Basle Cha. Cho.
—Sacher

V♯ 1803 LD: MACHAUT: Messe Notre Dame ("Sacre de Charles V")—excerpts
☆ Paraphonistes de St. Jean—de Van

V♯ 1804 LD: MONTEVERDI: Madrigals, q.v.
MARENZIO: Scendi dal Paradiso 5vv.
Ahi! dispietata morte 4vv.
L. Marenzio Ens.—Saraceni

V♯ 1805 LD: JANNEQUIN: Le Chant des Oyseaulx
☆ Chanterie de la Renaissance—Expert
JANNEQUIN: Au joly jeu
Ce moys de may
COSTELEY: Allons, gay bergères
Mignonne, allons voir
☆ Motet & Madrigal Cho.—Opienski

♯ 2505 LD: BEETHOVEN: Trio, C major, Op. 87 2 ob. & cor anglais
P. Pierlot (all 3 parts)
BEETHOVEN: Trio, B flat major, Op. 11 cl., vlc., pf.
J. Lancelot, R. Albin & R. Veyron-Lacroix

♯ 2506 LD: GLUCK: Orphée et Eurydice—Ballet
LULLY: Cadmus et Hermione—Chaconne
Phaeton—Overture & Entrée de danse
☆ Versailles Concerts Orch.—Cloëz
RAMEAU: Hippolyte et Aricie—Marche (Prologue)
Dardanus—Air en rondeau
Platée—Air vif; Menuet
Les Indes Galantes—Tambourin; Danse
☆ Orch.—Gerlin

♯ 2507 LD: MARAIS: Suites, Bk. III, No. 1 & Bk. IV, No. 5 orig. viol
R. Boulay (vla.) & L. Boulay (hpsi.)

♯ 2508 LD: MARAIS: Pièces en trio—Suites, D major, No. 3 & E Minor, No. 5 2 fls. or vlns. & continuo
F. Caratgé (fl.), R. Boulay (viol.), L. Boulay (hpsi.)

♯ 3004 LD: FRENCH DANCES, XVIIth Century ("Les 24 Violons du roy"; from Terpsichore 1612, & Cassel collection)
CAROUBEL: Bransles: gays doubles de Montirandé
de la VOYS: Allemande (à cinq)
DUMANOIR: Bransles: Grand
Gay à mener
Gavotte
de la HAYE: Sarabande
MAZUEL: 2 Courantes; Allemande
PRAETORIUS: Gaillarde avec diminution
Courante; Sarabande;
Les Passepieds de Bretaigne
BRUSLARD: Bransles: Grand; Gay, à mener, double; Gavotte;
Sarabande; Bourrée
LAZARIN: Allemande
L. ROSSI: Les pleurs d'Orphée ayant perdu sa femme (continued)

ANON: Französich Liedt
Sarabande de S. Altesse de Hesse (1650)
Sarabande du Roy
Courante; Ballet des Inconstans
Str. Orch.—Raugel

♯ 3005 LD: J. S. BACH: Concerto, C major (BWV 1060)
TELEMANN: Suite, A minor, q.v.
C. P. E. BACH: Sinfonia, C major, q.v.
Augsburg Cha. Orch.—Deyle

♯ 3006 LD: A. de BERTRAND: Je meurs, hélas(Ronsard)
Vivons, mignarde (J. Grévin)
Beauté qui sans pareille
Hola, Caron! (O. de Magny)
Certes mon oeil (Ronsard)
COSTELEY: La Prise du Havre (6 chansons)
GOUDIMEL: Ps. 1: Qui au conseil des malins
Ps. 55: O Dieu, la gloire qui t'est due
Ps. 68: Que Dieu se montre
Ps. 130: Du fond de ma pensée
CLAUDE LE JEUNE: Te Deum 6 vv.
Paris Traditional Singers—M. Honegger

♯ 3007 LD: J. C. BACH: Symphony, Op. 6, No. 6 ...
Andante
LOCATELLI: Concerto Grosso, Op. 1, No. 9
PERGOLESI: Concertino No. 2
VIVALDI: Concerto Grosso, Op. 3, No. 11
Augsburg Cha. Orch.—Deyle

♯ 3008 LD: CORELLI: Sonatas, Op. 5, Nos. 1 & 3
TARTINI: Sonata, G minor, Op. 1, No. 10
VERACINI: Sonata, E minor, Op. 1, No. 6
F. Zepparoni (vln.), R. Veyron-Lacroix (hpsi.)
[Recording of public concert of the Société de Musique d'Autrefois]

♯ 3009 LD: CAVALIERI: La Rappresentazione di Anima e di Corpo
CESTI: Serenata 1662
Y. Gouverné Vocal Ens. & Orch. —Chaillé

♯ 3010 LD: HAYDN: Trios, pf. vln. vlc.
No. 7, D major
No. 20, B flat major ... Andante cantabile
No. 27, C major
Salzburg Mozarteum Trio
[K. Neumüller (pf.), J. Schrocksnade (vln.), G. Weigl (vlc.).]

ANTHOLOGIE SONORE
HAYDN SOCIETY ISSUES

Space does not permit insertion of complete detailed contents of these ♯ re-issues here. If required, they can be found by reference to WERM and preceding supplements under the relative numbers in the Anthology sections. The majority are also entered in the composer lists.

VOLUME I: Set ♯ HS.AS-A

♯ HS.AS 1 GREGORIAN CHANT TO THE XIIIth CENTURY
(Including Gregorian Chant, Léonin, Perotin, Walther von der Vogelweide, Rumelant, Blondel de Nesles, Perrin d'Agincourt, Richard Coeur-de-Lion, Adam de la Halle, & Anon.)
[= AS. 18, 34, 65, 71, 99, 132]

♯ HS.AS 2 THE XIIIth & XIVth CENTURIES
(Including Vincenzo d'Arimini, Giovanni da Cascia, Matteo da Perugia, Landino, Pierre de Molins, Jacopo da Bologna, Ghirardello, & Anon.)
[= AS. 1, 16, 59, 63, 91]

♯ = Long-playing, 33⅓ r.p.m.   ♭ = 45 r.p.m.   ♮ = Auto. couplings, 78 r.p.m.

♯ HS.AS 3   THE XIVth & XVth CENTURIES (Machaut & Dufay)
　　　　　[= AS. 31/2, 35, 43, 67, 121]

♯ HS.AS 4   THE XVth CENTURY
　　　　　(Including Arnold de Lantins, Binchois, Grossin de Paris, Brasart, Pierre de la Rue, Isaac, Okeghem, Obrecht, Loyset Compère, & Anon.)
　　　　　[= AS. 3 (part), 27, 39, 43, 77, 80, 126]

♯ HS.AS 5   JOSQUIN des Prés & OTHER COMPOSERS OF THE LATE XVth & EARLY XVIth CENTURIES
　　　　　JOSQUIN des Prés: Mass (Hercules)
　　　　　　. . . Kyrie (☆ from AS. 73)
　　　　　　Miserere (☆ from AS. 107/8)
　　　　　　Stabat Mater (☆ from AS. 73)
　　　　　　Chansons—Se congié prends;
　　　　　　　Vive le roy (☆ from AS. 108)
　　　　　Paraphonistes de St. Jean; Inst. Ens.—Van
　　　　　OBRECHT: Ballade & Chanson de Nouvel an
　　　　　ISAAC: Chant de Pâques; Chanson tendre & Chant de l'adieu
　　　　　JOSQUIN des Prés: Chanson du soldat: Scaramella
　　　　　T. SUSATO: Chanson de Mai
　　　　　JOAN DE LATRE: Chanson à boire
　　　　　WILLAERT: Villotte; Villanesca & Madrigal
　　　　　SWEELINCK: Rozette
　　　　　Dutch Vocal Qtt.—Raugel
　　　　　[☆ from ♯ AS. 2501 LD]

VOLUME II: Set ♯ HS.AS-B

♯ HS.AS 6   FRENCH VOCAL MUSIC OF THE XVIth CENTURY
　　　　　(Including Jannequin, Costeley, Goudimel, Garnier, Berchem, Sermisy, Claude le Jeune, Mauduit, René, Gentian, Clemens non Papa (Jacques Clément), N. de la Grotte, Lassus & Anon.)
　　　　　[= AS. 7, 12, 15, 36 (part), 45, 104, 128]

♯ HS.AS 7   GERMAN VOCAL MUSIC OF THE XVth & XVIth CENTURIES
　　　　　(Including Finck, Senfl, Hassler, Praetorius, Schütz, Krieger)
　　　　　[= AS. 28, 51, 60, 72, 147]

♯ HS.AS 8   THE ITALIAN MADRIGAL AT THE END OF THE RENAISSANCE
　　　　　(Including Agazzari, Domenico, Marini, Marenzio & Banchieri [☆ of ♯ AS. 2502 LD] and Monteverdi & Marenzio)
　　　　　[as V♯ AS. 1604 LD, above]

♯ HS.AS 9   ITALIAN VOCAL MUSIC OF XVIth & XVIIth CENTURIES
　　　　　(Including Palestrina, Manzoli, Frescobaldi, Miniscalchi, Busca, Steffani, Gesualdo, Monteverdi (Il Combattimento . . ., etc.)
　　　　　[= AS. 21, 29, 47 (O crux ave & La cruda mia nemica only), 79, 120 (Gesualdo only), 141/3]

♯ HS.AS 10 XVIth CENTURY VOCAL MUSIC (Russia, Poland, Spain, England)
　　　　　(Including 7 Russian Orthodox liturgical chants [☆ of AS 139/40], Szamotulski (Waclaw of Szamotul), Gomolka, Zielenski, Milan, Vasquez, Fuenllana, Pisador, Taverner, R. Jones, Dowland, Morley)
　　　　　[= AS. 17, 53, 58, 97, 139/40]

VOLUME III: Set ♯ HS.AS-C
In preparation. The following available:—

♯ HS.AS 11 ORGAN MUSIC OF XVIth & XVIIth CENTURIES
　　　　　(Including Cabezon, Sancta Maria, Cabanilles, Gabrieli, Frescobaldi, Couperin, Grigny, Sweelinck, Pachelbel, Scheidt)
　　　　　[= AS. 69, 4, 75, 131, 10]

♯ HS.AS 12 BRASS & ORCHESTRAL MUSIC OF XVIth & XVIIth CENTURIES
　　　　　(Including Gabrieli, M. Franck, Schein, Pezel, Rosenmüller, J. C. F. Fischer)
　　　　　[= AS. 25, 57, 2, 52]

♯ HS.AS 13 INSTRUMENTAL & CHAMBER MUSIC OF XVIth & XVIIth CENTURIES
　　　　　(Including Byrd, Farnaby, Peerson, Purcell ("Golden" Sonata), Dall'Abaco (Sonata Op. 3, No. 2), Ortiz, Milan, Anon. Danceries (ed. Gervaise), Besard, Corbett, Visée)
　　　　　[= AS. 14, 22, 46, 40, 6, 36 (part), 89]

The following announced, but no details to hand:—

♯ HS.AS 14 ITALIAN HARPSICHORD MUSIC OF XVIIth & XVIIIth CENTURIES

♯ HS.AS 15 FRENCH HARPSICHORD MUSIC OF XVIIth & XVIIIth CENTURIES

VOLUME IV: Set ♯ HS.AS-D
In preparation. The following available:—

♯ HS.AS 19 THE FLUTE AT THE COURTS OF FRIEDRICH II & LOUIS XV
　　　　　QUANTZ: Sonata, G major, Op. 1, No. 6 fl. & hpsi.
　　　　　HASSE: Sonata, D minor, Op. 1, No. 11 fl. & hpsi.
　　　　　FRIEDRICH II: Sonata No. 2, C minor fl. & hpsi.
　　　　　NAUDOT: Sonata, B minor, Op. 4, No. 1 2 fls. unacc.
　　　　　CHÉDEVILLE: Sonata, C minor, Op. 8, No. 3 2 fls. unacc.
　　　　　BOISMORTIER: Concerto, A minor, Op. 15, No. 2 5 fls. unacc.
　　　　　J-P. Rampal (fl.—all parts) & R. Veyron-Lacroix (hpsi.)
　　　　　[☆ of ♯ AS. 3002 LD]

The following announced, but no details to hand:—

♯ HS.AS 16 CHAMBER MUSIC OF MARAIS, COUPERIN & RAMEAU

♯ HS.AS 17 FRENCH XVIIIth CENTURY CHAMBER MUSIC, I

♯ HS.AS 18 FRENCH XVIIIth CENTURY CHAMBER MUSIC, II

♯ HS.AS 20 XVIIth & XVIIIth CENTURY CLAVICHORD & ORGAN MUSIC

VOLUME VII: Set ♯ HS.AS-G
In preparation. The following available:

♯ HS.AS 31 J. S. BACH: Concerto, C major (2 clav. & orch.) (BWV 1061)
　　　　　R. Gerlin, M. Charbonnier (hpsi.) & Str. Orch.—Sachs
　　　　　A. VIVALDI: Concerto, D major, Op. 3, No. 9 (vln. & orch.)
　　　　　J. Fournier & Str. Orch. & hpsi.
　　　　　J. S. BACH: Transcription of the above
　　　　　R. Gerlin (hpsi.) (☆ of ♯ AS. 2503 LD)

♯ HS.AS 33 MOZART: Divertimento, K131; Les Petits Riens (q.v.) (☆ of ♯ AS. 3001 LD)

♯ HS.AS 34 MOZART: MOTETS & OFFERTORIES, q.v.
　　　　　Soloists, Cho. & Orch.—Raugel
　　　　　(☆ of ♯ AS. 2504 LD)

♯ HS.AS 35 As ♯ AS. 3005 LD, supra
The following announced, but details not to hand:
♯ HS.AS 32 THE CLASSICAL CONCERTO

VOLUME VIII: Set ♯ HS.AS-H
♯ HS.AS 36 As ♯ AS. 3004 LD, supra
♯ HS.AS 37 As ♯ AS. 2507 LD, supra
♯ HS.AS 38 As ♯ AS. 2508 LD, supra
♯ HS.AS 39 As ♯ AS. 3007 LD, supra
♯ HS.AS 40 As ♯ AS. 3008 LD, supra
♯ HS.AS 41 FRENCH MASTERS OF THE RENAISSANCE
　　　　　As ♯ AS. 3006 LD, supra

THE HISTORY OF MUSIC IN SOUND
(ed. Prof. G. Abraham)
VOL. I
ANCIENT & ORIENTAL MUSIC—"in preparation"

VOL. II
EARLY MEDIEVAL MUSIC UP TO 1300
(ed. Dom A. Hughes)
(also ♯ Vic. set LM 6015, 4ss)

G.HMS 10 BYZANTINE MUSIC
　　　　　Anastaseos imera; Doxology; O quando in cruce
　　　　　Ote to stavro; Veni, redemptor gentium
　　　　　Brompton Oratory Choir—Washington

G.HMS 11 PRE-GREGORIAN & GREGORIAN MUSIC
　　　　　Pater noster; In pace, in idipsum
　　　　　Lumen ad revelationem: Nunc dimittis;
　　　　　Sursum corda, Preface, Sanctus
　　　　　Brompton Oratory Choir—Washington

G.HMS 12 GREGORIAN MUSIC
　　　　　Protector noster; Domine, in virtute tua
　　　　　Domine, non secundum; Sancti Spiritus assit
　　　　　Nashdom Abbey Choir—Hughes

G.HMS 13 GREGORIAN MUSIC & LITURGICAL DRAMA
　　　　　Exsultet orbis gaudiis; Kyrie 'Altissime'
　　　　　Quem quaeritis in sepulchro? (Xth cent.)
　　　　　Daniel: Lament (XIIth cent.)
　　　　　Brompton Oratory Choir—Washington

☆ = Re issue of a recording to be found in previous volumes.

G.HMS 14   MEDIAEVAL SONGS
ANON: O admirabile Veneris ydolum
B. de VENTADORN: Quant vei l'aloete mover
G. BRULÉ: Je ne puis pas si loing fuir
ANON: Au tans d'aoust
ANON: Quant je voi yver retorner
   F. Fuller (B)
A. de la HALLE: Bergeronnete
ANON: Tuit cil qui sunt enamourat
THIBAUT de NAVARRE: Tuit mi desir
GUIOT de DIJON: Chanterai por mon coraige
   Pro Musica Antiqua Ens.—Cape

G.HMS 15   MEDIAEVAL SONGS
ANON: Worldes blis ne last no throwe
MEISSEN: Ey ich sach in dem trone
ANON: Quen â Virgen ben servir
   Como poden per sas culpas
   O divina Virgo, flore
   Plangiamo quel crudel basciare
   F. Fuller (B)

G.HMS 16   EARLY POLYPHONY
Sit gloria Domini; Alleluia, surrexit Christus;
Regi regum glorioso
   Brompton Oratory Choir—Washington
Rex immense; Congaudeant catholici (Spanish)
   Bodley Singers—Hughes

G.HMS 17   EARLY POLYPHONY, etc.
Verbum Patris humanatur; Orientis partibus;
Sumer is icumen in   (Norman & English)
   Bodley Singers—Hughes
(4) Dance-tunes[1] Rec., viol, cor ang., tabor
   C. Dolmetsch, N. Dolmetsch, D. Bridger,
   A. Taylor

G.HMS 18   ENGLISH POLYPHONY
(3) English dance-tunes[2] Rec., viol., cor ang.,
   tabor
   C. Dolmetsch, N. Dolmetsch, D. Bridger,
   A. Taylor
Veri floris sub figura
   Brompton Oratory Choir—Washington
Foweles in the frith; Ex semine Abrahae[3]
Mariam sanctificans; Beata viscera
   Bodley Singers—Rose

G.HMS 19   FRENCH & ENGLISH POLYPHONY
O Maria, virgo Davidica; Puellare gremium;
Triumphat hodie
   Bodley Singers—Rose
Marionette douce; Rosa fragrans; Alleluia psallat
   Brompton Oratory Choir—Washington

VOL. III

ARS NOVA AND THE RENAISSANCE
(ed. Dom A. Hughes)
(also ♯ Vic. set LM 6016, 4ss)

G.HMS 20   A. de la HALLE: Tant con je vivrai
J. de LESCUREL: A vous, douce debonaire
ANON: Le Moulin de Paris; Se je chant' mains[4]
   Pro Musica Antiqua Ens.—Cape

G.HMS 21   G. de MACHAUT: Ma fin est mon commence-
   ment
   L. Hughes (T), C. Roberts (T) & Ens.—Rose
Mass Notre Dame—Benedictus (ed. Stevens)
   Brompton Oratory Choir—Washington
G. de CASCIA: Nel mezzo a sei paon
   Pro Musica Antiqua Ens.—Cape

G.HMS 22   F. LANDINI: Amar si li alti tuo gentil costumi
MAESTRO PIERO: Cavalcando con un giovine
   accorto
   Pro Musica Antiqua Ens.—Cape
ANON: Angelus ad virginem
   Deo gratias, Anglia
   Brompton Oratory Choir—Washington

G.HMS 23   ANON: Now wel may we merthis make
   Tappster, drinker, fill another ale
   Schola Polyphonica—Washington
ANON: Credo   (XIVth Cent.)
BYTTERING: Nesciens mater virgo
   Bodley Singers—Rose

G.HMS 24   J. DUNSTABLE: Veni, Sancte Spiritus
   Pro Musica Antiqua Ens.—Cape

G.HMS 25   J. CICONIA: O rosa bella   (Giustiniani)
J. DUNSTABLE (?): O rosa bella
   A. Deller (C-T) & viols
G. DUFAY: Ave, regina coelorum
   Schola Polyphonica—Washington

G.HMS 26   G. BINCHOIS: Filles à marier
G. DUFAY: Pour l'amour de ma douce amye
   Pro Musica Antiqua Ens.—Cape
J. OKEGHEM: Mass 'Fors seulement'—Kyrie
   Renaissance Singers—Howard

G.HMS 27   J. OBRECHT: Si oblitus fuero tui   (1½ss)
P. de la RUE: Requiem Mass—Introit   (½s)
   Schola Polyphonica—Washington

G.HMS 28   JOSQUIN des Prés: El grillo e buon cantore
   (1505)
   Je ne me puis tenir d'aimer
   Pro Musica Antiqua Ens.—Cape
   Mass 'L'homme armé'
   —Sanctus   (part)
   Tribulatio et angustia (Motet)
   Schola Polyphonica—Washington

G.HMS 29   R. DAVY: Passion—Timuerunt valde
ANON: Mass 'Custodi nos'—Gloria
   Bodley Singers—Rose
R. FAYRFAX: Magnificat 'Regali'—Verse 1 &
   Gloria
   Renaissance Singers—Howard

G.HMS 30   J. TAVERNER: Mass 'Gloria tibi, Trinitas'—
   Benedictus
   Schola Polyphonica—Washington
K. PAUMANN: Mit ganczem Willen
H. BUCHNER: Es gieng ein Mann
J. REDFORD: O Lux, on the faburden
   S. Jeans (org.)

G.HMS 31   H. ISAAC: Chanson; La la hö hö;
   Innsbruck, ich muss dich lassen
   Basle Schola Cantorum Viol Ens.
Fr. de la TORRE: Alta (La Spagna)
L. COMPÈRE: Nous sommes de l'ordre de Saint
   Babouin
RUBINUS: Der Bauern Schwanz
   Instrumental Ensemble

VOL. IV

THE AGE OF HUMANISM
(ed. Prof. J. A. Westrup)
(Also ♯ Vic. set LM 6029, 4ss)

G.HMS 32   A. DÉMOPHON: A che son hormai conducto
   (1507)
L. MARENZIO: Scendi dal paradiso, Venere
   (1584)
L. LUZZASCHI: Quivi, sospiri, pianti   (Dante)
   (1576)
   London Chamber Singers—Bernard

G.HMS 33   J. WILBYE: Ye that do live in pleasures plenty
   (1609)
T. GREAVES: Come away, sweet love, and play
   thee   (1604)
T. WEELKES: O Care, thou wilt dispatch me
   (1600)
T. MORLEY: Ho! who comes here all along
   (1594)
   Golden Age Singers

G.HMS 34   G. COSTELEY: Allons au vert bocage   (1570)
C. de SERMISY: Tant que vivray en âge
   florissant   (1528)
PASSEREAU: Il est bel et bon, commère (1534)
   Pro Musica Antiqua Ens.—Cape
T. L. da VICTORIA: O Domine Jesu Christe
   Montserrat Monastery Choir—Pujol

G.HMS 35   P. de MONTE: Mass 'Benedicta es'—Benedictus
   & Agnus Dei II
G. P. da PALESTRINA: Mass 'Aeterna Christi
   munera'—Sanctus; Missa brevis—Agnus Dei II
   Brompton Oratory Choir—Washington

G.HMS 36   O. de LASSUS: Scio enim quod Redemptor meus
   vivit
   Mass 'Puisque j'ay perdu'—
   Benedictus
J. HANDL: Mirabile mysterium (1586) org. acc.
   Brompton Oratory Choir—Washington

G.HMS 37   T. TALLIS: Adesto nunc propitius
W. BYRD: Haec dies quam fecit Dominus
T. MORLEY: Agnus Dei   (1597)
   St. Paul's Cath. Choir—Dykes Bower

G.HMS 38   O. GIBBONS: Behold, thou hast made my days
   A. Hepworth (T), Hampstead Chu. Cho. &
   Str.—Westrup
M. PRAETORIUS: Wie schön leuchtet der
   Morgenstern   (1619)
   London Chamber Singers & Orch.—
   Bernard

G.HMS 39   G. GABRIELI: In ecclesiis benedicite Domino
   (2ss)
   Soloists, chorus & orch.—Goldsbrough

---

[1] From *Rosae nodum reserat, Fraude ceca desolato,* & *Perpetuo nomine* (Wolfenbüttel MS 677).
[2] Stantipes, ductia, stantipes.   [3] Really part of *Perotin: Alleluia Nativitas,* with a new text.
[4] As 2-pt. canon, ed. Besseler.

G.HMS 40 C. de SERMISY: Vivray-je toujours en soucy? (1528)
L. MILAN: Toda mi vada os amé (1535)
F. Fuller (B), D. Poulton (lute & vihuela)
T. MORLEY: Thyrsis and Milla arm in arm together (1600)
J. DOWLAND: Sleep, wayward thoughts (1597)
R. Soames (T), D. Poulton (lute)

G.HMS 41 A. WILLAERT: Ricercar No. 7 (1549)
P. PEUERL: Suite No. 3—Padouan & Intrada (1611)
O. GIBBONS: Three-part Fantasia No. 3 (1610)
G. COPERARIO: Four-part Fantasia
Basle Schola Cantorum Viol Ens.

G.HMS 42 ANON: My Lady Carey's Dompe
J. BULL: Dr. Bull's my selfe (FVB 189)
G. FARNABY: His humour (FVB 196)
O. GIBBONS: An Allmaine (Cosyn 78) "The King's Juell"
M. Hodsdon (virginals)
G. FRESCOBALDI: Capriccio sopra un soggetto (Bk. I, 1626)
T. Dart (hpsi.)

G.HMS 43 A. GABRIELI: Ricercar arioso No. 1 (1605)
J. P. SWEELINCK: Variations on 'Ach Gott, vom Himmel sieh' darein' (No. 34, Seiffert edn.)
S. Jeans (org. of Marienkirche, Lemgo)

G.HMS 44 C. MONTEVERDI: Orfeo—Excerpt from Act IV (1½ss)
A. Mandikian (S), R. Lewis (T), Cho. & orch.—Westrup
S. LANDI: La Morte d'Orfeo (1619)—
Bevi, bevi securo l'onda (½s)
N. Walker (Bs), hpsi & vlc.

VOL. V
OPERA AND CHURCH MUSIC, 1630-1750
(ed. Prof. J. A. Westrup)
(also ♯ Vic. set LM 6030, 4ss)

G.HMS 45 P. F. CAVALLI: L'Egisto (1637)—Musici della selva
V. de los Angeles (S), R. Lewis (T)
M. A. CESTI: Il Pomo d'Oro (1667)—E dove t'aggiri
A. Mandikian (S)

G.HMS 46 A. STRADELLA: Floridoro (c. 1675)—Stelle ingrate, che sarà?
M. Ritchie (S), D. Bond (S)
A. SCARLATTI: Tito Sempronio Gracco—Idolo mio, ti chiamo
M. Ritchie (S), D. Bond, N. Evans (M-S), A. Young (T)

G.HMS 47 G. F. HANDEL: Giulio Cesare—V'adoro, pupille
V. de los Angeles (S), R. Lewis (T)
N. LOGROSCINO: Io non songo bona bona
G. Ripley (A)

G.HMS 48 J. B. LULLY: Alceste—Scène infernale
A. Mandikian (S), L. Lovano (Bs) & cho.
J. P. RAMEAU: Dardanus—O jour affreux
A. Mandikian (S)

G.HMS 49 J. BLOW: Venus and Adonis—Lesson Scene
N. Evans (M-S), M. Studholme (S) & cho.
R. KEISER: Octavia[1] (1705)—Ach! Nero ist nicht Nero mehr!
S. Joynt (Bs)

G.HMS 50 G. CARISSIMI: Jonas—Justus es, Domine
W. Herbert (T)
B. MARCELLO: Le Quattro Stagioni—Dalle cime dell'Alpi
N. Walker (Bs)

G.HMS 51 J. P. RAMEAU: Quam dilecta—Cor meum et caro mea
A. SCARLATTI: Est dies trophaei—Miraculis in coelo
London Chamber Singers & Orch.—Bernard

G.HMS 52 P. HUMFREY: Hear, O heavens
M. GREENE: O clap your hands together
St. Paul's Cath. Choir—Dykes Bower

G.HMS 53 H. SCHÜTZ: Saul, Saul, was verfolgst du mich?
DIE SIEBEN WORTE—Darnach als Jesus wusste
Vocal Ens., org. & orch.—Goldsbrough

G.HMS 54 J. CHRISTOPH BACH: Ich lasse dich nicht
Chorus & organ—Westrup
J. S. BACH: Mass, F major—Kyrie
Chorus & Orch.—Goldsbrough

G.HMS 55 J. S. BACH: Johannes-Passion—Nos. 26-31
E. Greene (T), D. Franklin (Bs), S. Joynt (Bs)
W. Parsons (Bs), Cho., Orch. & org.—Westrup

G.HMS 56 D. BUXTEHUDE: Ich halte es dafür—Du gibest mir Ruh
I. Wolf (S), S. Joynt (Bs)
J. S. BACH: Cantata No. 50, Nun ist das Heil
Cho. & orch.—Goldsbrough

VOL. VI
The GROWTH OF INSTRUMENTAL MUSIC, 1630-1750
(ed. Prof. J. A. Westrup)
(also ♯ Vic. set LM 6031, 4ss)

G.HMS 57 H. PURCELL: What shall be done—Nos. 1, 2, 3
Soloists, London Cha. Singers & orch—Bernard
G. F. HANDEL: Susanna—How long, O Lord?
Chorus & Orch.—Goldsbrough

G.HMS 58 L. ROSSI: Del silentio—Occhi belli
W. Brown (T)
H. PURCELL: The fatal hour comes on apace
J. Alexander (S)

G.HMS 59 P. H. ERLEBACH: Meine Seufzer, meine Klagen (1697)
I. Wolf (S) & Inst. Ens.
J. S. BACH: W. T. C. No. 16, G minor
D. Swainson (clavichord)

G.HMS 60 J. C. de CHAMBONNIÈRES: Sarabande, Drollerie, Allemande, Volte
D. SCARLATTI: Sonata, B flat major L. 498
A. van der Wiele (hpsi.)

G.HMS 61 J. PACHELBEL: Chorale-Prelude, Durch Adams Fall (C 20)
J. S. BACH: Chorale-Prelude, Durch Adams Fall (BWV 637)
D. BUXTEHUDE: Chorale-Prelude, In dulci jubilo (II-2-17)
J. S. BACH: Chorale-Prelude, In dulci jubilo (BWV 608)
G. Jones (Steinkirchen Organ)

G.HMS 62 N. le BÈGUE: Dialogue, G minor
A. RAISON: Trio en passecaille, G minor
J. F. DANDRIEU: Basse et dessus de trompette, D major
H. Roget (Organ of St. Merry, Paris)
H. J. F. von BIBER: Sonata No. 4, D major—3 movts. (1681)
W. Roberts (vln.), G. Jones (hpsi.)

G.HMS 63 J. M. LECLAIR: Sonata, Op. 2, No. 5, G major
J. Pougnet (vln.), A. Goldsbrough (hpsi.) & gamba

G.HMS 64 G. B. VITALI: Sonata, Op. 2, No. 3, E minor
J. LEGRENZI: Sonata, Op. 2, No. ?, D minor ('La Cornara')
J. JENKINS: Fancy, F minor
Basil Lam Ensemble

G.HMS 65 A. CORELLI: Sonata, F minor, Op. 3, No. 9
A. Goldsbrough Ensemble

G.HMS 66 G. F. HANDEL: Sonata, F major, Op. 2, No. 5
Basil Lam Ensemble

G.HMS 67 H. PURCELL: The Indian Queen—Trumpet Overture
G. P. TELEMANN: Suite, E minor—Air
Goldsbrough Orch.—Goldsbrough

G.HMS 68 A. VIVALDI: Concerto, B flat major, P. 406
L. Brain (ob.), W. Roberts (vln.) & orch.—Goldsbrough

VOL. VII
(The) SYMPHONIC OUTLOOK, 1745-1790
(ed. Dr. E. Wellesz)

[This list is included for reference, from advance information. As the discs are not available at the time of going to press, certain identifications have not been possible, and entries have not been carried into the body of the work.]

G.HMS 69 C. W. von GLUCK: Iphigénie en Aulide, excerpts
L. Lovano, B. Demigny, Cho. & orch.—Désormière

G.HMS 70 W. A. MOZART: Die Entführung—Quartet, Act II
J. Vyvyan, M. Studholme, R. Lewis, A. Young

G.HMS 71 K. D. von DITTERSDORF: Doktor und Apotheker—Verliebte brauchen keine Zeugen
G. Catley (S)
A. E. M. GRÉTRY: Richard Coeur-de-Lion—Si l'univers entier m'oublie
R. Amade (C-T)

---

[1] Original title: Die römische Unruhe.

G.HMS 72 W. A. MOZART: La Clemenza di Tito—Se all'impero
   A. Young (T)
   D. CIMAROSA: Il Matrimonio segreto—Io ti lascio
   G. Catley & A. Young

G.HMS 73 J. M. HAYDN: Prope est ut veniat
   W. A. MOZART: Litaniae Lauretanae, K. 195—Agnus Dei
   E. Suddaby (S), Chorus & L.S.O.—Woodgate

G.HMS 74 W. BOYCE: Symphony No. 8, D minor
   New London Orch.—Désormière

G.HMS 75 J. W. A. STAMITZ: Symphony, E flat major
   L.P.O.—Boult

G.HMS 76 F. J. HAYDN: Symphony No. 31, D major—2 movts.
   Orch.—Westrup

G.HMS 77 C. P. E. BACH: Symphony, F major (unspec.)
   L.P.O.—Boult

G.HMS 78 M. G. MONN: Cello Concerto, G minor—1st movt.
   W. Pleeth & L.P.O.—Boult
   F. J. HAYDN: Minuets (unspec.)
   L.P.O.—Boult

G.HMS 79 J. C. BACH: Piano Concerto, A major—1st movt.
   R. Collet & L.P.O.—Boult

G.HMS 80 W. A. MOZART: Divertimento, E flat major, K289—2 movts.
   Wind Ensemble

G.HMS 81 F. J. HAYDN: Quartet (unspec.)
   F. J. HAYDN: Piano Trio No. 26, F sharp minor—2nd movt.
   E. Rubbra, E. Gruenberg, W. Pleeth
   C. P. E. BACH: Fantasia, C minor
   D. Swainson (clavi)

MASTERPIECES OF MUSIC BEFORE 1750
♯ HS. set HSL-B

(6ss) (also HS set I, with book)   (♯ HSL 2071/3)

HSL 2071 GREGORIAN CHANT TO THE XVIth CENTURY
   GREGORIAN CHANT:
      Laus Deo Patri Antiphon
      Psalm 113—Laudate pueri
      Vidimus stellam Alleluia
      Victimae Paschali Sequence
   Schola Gregoriana, Copenhagen—Lewkovitch
   ANON. (XIIth-XIIIth cent.): Or la truix
   N. von REUENTHAL: Willekommen Mayenschein DTÖ. XXXVII
   H. Nørgaard (Bs)
   ANON. ORGANA:
      Rex coeli, Domine (IXth cent.)
      Agnus Dei (XIIth cent.)
      Benedicamus Domino (XIIth cent.)
   Schola Gregoriana, Copenhagen—Lewkovich
   PEROTIN: Alleluya (Nativitas)—organum
   E. Thorborg (T), E. Sørensen (T), Copenhagen Univ. Male Cho.—Møller
   ANON. (XIIIth. Cent.): En non diu! Quant voi;
      Eius in Oriente—Organum triplum
   E. Thorborg (T), E. Sørensen (T), H. Deckert (gamba)
      De castitatis thalamo—conductus
   Copenhagen Univ. Female Cho.—Møller
   ANON. (XIIIth Cent.): Estampie MS., B.M.
   C. Thodberg (rec.), H. E. Deckert (gamba)
   MACHAUT: Mass "Notre Dame"—Agnus Dei I
   Copenhagen Boys' & Men's Cho.—Møller, & org.
   LANDINI: Chi più le vuol sapere Ballata
   N. Brincker (T), H. E. Deckert (gamba)
   DUFAY: Mass 'Se la face ay pale'—Kyrie I
   Copenhagen Boys' & Men's Cho.—Møller
   BINCHOIS: Adieu m'amour et ma maistresse
   D. Schou (A), C. Thodberg (rec.) & gambas
   OKEGHEM: Missa prolationum—Sanctus (1st section)
   OBRECHT: Parce, Domine Motet
   JOSQUIN des Prés: Ave Maria
   Copenhagen Boys' & Men's Cho.—Møller
   CRÉQUILLON: Pour ung plaisir Chanson
   Copenhagen Univ. Cho.—Møller
   Idem — ARR. HPSI. A. GABRIELI
   F. Viderø (hpsi.)
   ANON. (c. 1550): Der Prinzen-Tanz; Proportz
   T. Nielsen (lute)

HSL 2072 THE XVIth & XVIIth CENTURIES
   LASSUS: Tristis est anima mea Motet
   PALESTRINA: Mass 'Veni Sponsa Christi'—Agnus Dei I
   BYRD: Ego sum panis vivus Motet
   Copenhagen Boys' & Men's Cho.—Møller
   ANON. (XVIIth Cent.): Canzona per l'epistola
   F. Viderø (org.)
   MARENZIO: S'io parto, i' moro Madrigal
   BENNET: Thyrsis, sleepest thou? Madrigal
   Danish State Radio Madrigal Cho.—Wöldike
   FARNABY: Loth to depart Variations, Virginals (FVB 230)
   F. Viderø (hôpsi.)
   CACCINI: Dovrò dunque morire 1601
   V. Garde (M-S), T. Nielsen (lute)
   MONTEVERDI: ORFEO—Tu sei morta
   N. Brincker (T), T. Nielsen (lute), M. Wöldike (org.)
   CARISSIMI: JUDICIUM SALOMONIS—Afferte gladium
   E. Simonsen (S), V. Garde (M-S), H. Nørgaard (Bs), org. & vlc.
   SCHÜTZ: O Herr, hilf Cantata
   E. Brems (S), V. Garde (M-S), A. Schiøtz (T), 2 vlns, org. & vlc.
   FRESCOBALDI: Ricercar dopo il Credo
   F. Viderø (org.)
   FROBERGER: Suite, E minor
   F. Viderø (clavichord)
   LULLY: ARMIDE—Overture
   Danish Radio Cha. Orch.—Wöldike

HSL 2073 THE XVIIth & XVIIIth CENTURIES
   PACHELBEL: Toccata, E minor
   F. Viderø (org.)
   PURCELL: A new ground
   F. Viderø (hpsi.)
   CORELLI: Sonata, E minor, Op. 3, No. 7
   2 vlns. & cont.
   L. Hansen, C. Senderovitz, M. Wöldike (org.)
   V. Norup (vlc.)
   F. COUPERIN: La Galante
   F. Viderø (hpsi.)
   RAMEAU: CASTOR ET POLLUX—Séjour de l'éternelle paix
   N. Brincker (T)
   D. SCARLATTI: Sonata, C minor L 352
   F. Viderø (hpsi.)
   HANDEL: Concerto Grosso, C major (B & H No. 7) Oboes, str. & cont.
   ... 1st movt. only
   Danish Radio Cha. Orch.—Wöldike
   RINALDO—Al valor del mio brando . . .
      Cara sposa
   E. Berge (S), E. Brems (M-S), & Danish Radio Cha.—Wöldike
   SOLOMON: Draw the tear from hopeless love
   Danish Radio Cho. & Cha. Orch.—Wöldike
   J. S. BACH: CANTATA No. 4—Nos. 5 & 8
   Danish Radio Cho. & Cha. Orch.—Wöldike
   CHORALE PRELUDE, Christ lag' in Todesbanden BWV 625 (OB 27)
   F. Viderø (org.)
   MATTHAEUS-PASSION—Nos. 68/9, Ach Golgotha
   E. Brems (M-S)
   KUNST DER FUGE, No. 3
   F. Viderø (org.)

NOTE: Extracts from this Anthology are reissued in France as part of † HISTOIRE DE LA MUSIQUE VOCALE . . ., q.v.

ENGLISH CHURCH MUSIC

VOL. III

C.LX 1563   TALLIS: Te Deum laudamus (2ss)
   King's College Cho.—Ord

C.LB 132   BYRD: Laudibus in sanctis (2ss)
   New College Cho.—Andrews

C.LX 1564   DERING: Factum est silentium
   King's College Cho.—Ord
   MUNDY: O Lord, the Maker of all thing
   FARRANT: Hide not Thou thy face
   St. George's Chapel Cho.—Harris

C.LB 133   TALLIS: Salvator mundi, salva nos
   Canterbury Cath. Cho.—Knight
   REDFORD: Rejoice in the Lord alway
   York Minster Cho.—Jackson

C.LX 1565   CHILD: Sing we merrily
   York Minster Cho.—Jackson
   BLOW: O Lord God of my salvation
   St. Paul's Cath. Cho.—Dykes Bower

C.LX 1566   HUMFREY: O give thanks unto the Lord (2ss)
   Westminster Abbey Cho.—McKie

♯ = Long-playing, 33⅓ r.p.m.   ♭ = 45 r.p.m.   ♮ = Auto. couplings, 78 r.p.m.

C.LX 1567 GREENE: O clap your hands together
Canterbury Cath. Cho.—Knight
WALMISLEY: Magnificat, D minor
Westminster Abbey Cho.—McKie

C.LX 1568/9 S. S. WESLEY: The Wilderness (3ss)
St. Paul's Cathedral Cho.—Bower
OUSELEY: O Saviour of the world
WALFORD DAVIES: Blessed are the pure in heart
York Minster Cho.—Jackson

C.LX 1570 STANFORD: The Lord is my shepherd (2ss)
Canterbury Cath. Cho.—Knight

C.LX 1571 ANDREWS: Ah, see the fair chivalry come
New College Cho.—Andrews
ARMSTRONG: Christ whose glory fills the skies
St. George's Chapel Cho.—Harris

C.LX 1572 HOWELLS: Magnificat Collegium Regale
King's College Cho.—Ord
VAUGHAN-WILLIAMS: Come, Holy Spirit, most blessed Lord
St. George's Chapel Cho.—Harris

VOL. IV

C.LX 1604 MORLEY: Nolo mortem peccatoris
St. Paul's Cath. Cho.—Dykes Bower
TAVERNER: Christe Jesu, pastor bone
BYRD: Senex puerum portabat
King's College Cho.—Ord

C.LX 1605 BYRD: Exsurge, quare obdormis, Domine?
Westminster Abbey Cho.—McKie
BYRD: Justorum animae
BATTEN: Deliver us, O Lord our God
King's College Cho.—Ord

C.LX 1606 KIRBYE: Vox in Rama audita est
Westminster Abbey Cho.—McKie
PHILIPS: Ascendit Deus 1612
FARRANT: Call to remembrance, O Lord
Canterbury Cath. Cho.—Knight

C.LX 1607 BLOW: Magnificat, G major
PURCELL: O Lord God of hosts
Westminster Abbey Cho.—McKie

C.LX 1608 BOYCE: O where shall wisdom be found? (2ss)
York Minster Cho.—Jackson

C.LX 1609 BATTISHILL: O Lord, look down from heaven 1765
Canterbury Cath. Cho. —Knight
S. S. WESLEY: Cast me not away from Thy presence
King's College Cho.—Ord

C.LX 1610/1 PARRY: Hear my words, ye people (4ss)
St. Paul's Cath. Cho.—Dykes Bower

C.LX 1612 HARWOOD: O how glorious is the kingdom (2ss)
St. George's Chapel Cho.—Harris

C.LX 1613 WOOD: Glory and honour and laud
MOERAN: Jubilate Deo, E flat major
St. George's Chapel Cho.—Harris

C.LB 147 BULLOCK: Give us the wings of faith
York Minster Cho.—Jackson
GOSS: If we believe that Jesus died
Westminster Abbey Cho.—McKie

AIRS-À-BOIRE

(with *Poèmes sur le vin*, spoken by A. Reybaz)
ANON. (XVth Cent.): Gentils gallans
(Bayeux MS) Bevons sans comère
Bon vin je ne te puis laisser
DUFAY: Adieu ces bon vins de Lannoys
ANON. (XIIIth Cent.): Chanson bachique on *Letabundus* (extracts)
CLEMENS non Papa: Venes mes serfs 1553
MOULINIÉ: Buvons amis, l'ange passe
Amis, environs nous
Je puis dire sans vanité
(*Ballet de Mademoiselle*, 1635)
BACILLY: Mes chers amis tour à tour
Ah! que l'on est misérable (récit)
G. MICHEL: Devez-vous pas au moindre signe 1641 duet
ANON. (XVIIth Cent.): Quand Iris prend plaisir *l*
Puisque Bacchus *l*
A. de ROSIER: Le vin, le vin 1638 duet
A. Doniat (B), A. Vessières (Bs), M. Rollin (lute)
‡ *BàM.LD 019*
[Items marked *l* are lute only; the dates are those of the published collections.]

"(The) AMERICAN CLASSIC ORGAN"

This disc (♯ ASK. 1) is intended to demonstrate the tone colours of the organs of the Aeolian-Skinner Co. (Boston, Mass., U.S.A.). It contains 46 short excerpts from organ works, anonymously recorded. Composers represented include Alain, Arne, Bach, Brahms, Dandrieu, Debussy, Franck, Handel, Gigout, Peeters, Purcell, Sowerby, H. Willan, etc.

AMERICAN MUSIC

VOCAL MUSIC IN COLONIAL AMERICA
(The Moravians)
J. DENCKE: Ich will singen von einem Könige 1767
Freuet euch, ihr Töchter 1767
S. PETER: O Anblick, der mirs Herze bricht (Gregor)
J. F. PETER: Leite mich in deiner Wahrheit 1770
Der Herr ist in seinem heiligen Tempel 1786
ANTES: Go, congregation, go! (Gregor)
J. HERBST: Ich gehe einher in der Kraft des Herrn
G. G. MÜLLER: Mein Heiland geht ins Leiden
J. F. PETER: Ich will mit euch einen ewigen Bund machen 1782 *k*
Die Tage deines Leidens sollen ein Ende haben 1782 *k*
D. M. MICHAEL: Ich bin in meinem Geiste (Zinzendorf) *g*.
M. Noster (S) & Cha. Orch.—T. Johnson ♯NRI. 2017
[Sung in *English* to translations by Carleton Sprague Smith, T. J. Kelley (*k*) & H. Goehlich (*g*)]

AMERICAN ORGAN MUSIC
BINGHAM: Rhythmic Trumpet
HAINES: Promenade, Air & Toccata
EDMUNDSON: Gargoyles
SOWERBY: Fantasy for flute stops
Requiescat in pace
SIMONDS: Prelude on "Iam sol recedit igneus"
C. Crozier ♯ Ken. 2555
[Organ of First Baptist Church, Longview, Texas.]

ARIE ANTICHE & GERMAN LIEDER

FALCONIERI: Vezzosette e care pupillette
HANDEL: ALCINA—Ah mio cor
PAISIELLO: I ZINGARI IN FIERA—Chi vuol la zingarella
CACCINI: Amarilli mia bella
A. SCARLATTI: LA DONNA ANCORA È FEDELE—Se Florindo è fedele
MONTEVERDI: ARIANNA—Lasciatemi morire
CESTI: I CASTI AMORI D'ORONTEA—Intorno all' idol mio
A. SCARLATTI: L'HONESTÀ NEGLI AMORI—Già il sole del Gange
SCHUMANN: Widmung; Die Lotosblume; In der Fremde I
SCHUBERT: Der Musensohn; Du bist die Ruh'; Erlkönig
I. Kolassi (M-S), J. Bonneau (pf.) ♯ Lon.LL 747
(♯ D.FAT 173160)

"BAROQUE" ORGAN MUSIC

F. COUPERIN (1631-1701): Qui tollis peccata mundi
BUXTEHUDE: Prelude & Fugue, F sharp minor
SWEELINCK: Toccata, A major
A. van NOORDT: 2 Variations on Psalm 116
REGER: Prelude, D minor, Op. 65, No. 7
DISTLER: Chaconne (Partita) on Nun komm, der Heiden Heiland, Op. 8, No. 1
P. Kee ♯ G.DLP 1053
[Organ of St. Laurens, Alkmaar]

BAROQUE ORGAN MUSIC

VOL. I
ANON: Allein Gott in der Hoh'
◇SWEELINCK: Variations on 'Mein junges Leben hat ein End'
◇FROBERGER: Toccata & Fugue, A minor
◇STEIGLEDER: Ricercare No. 12, C major
◇PACHELBEL: Partita on 'Was Gott tut, das ist wohlgetan'
☆ W. Supper
LÜBECK: Prelude & Fugue, E major
E. Hölderlin ♯ Ren.X 53
[All are ☆ except the Froberger]

VOL. II
◇BUXTEHUDE: Toccata & Fugue, F major
◇J. G. WALTHER: Partita on 'Jesu, meine Freude'
◇SIMON: Prelude & Fugue, B flat major
◇PACHELBEL: Fantasia, G minor
◇BRUHNS: Prelude & Fugue, No. 3, E minor
☆ W. Supper
LÜBECK: Prelude & Fugue, C minor
☆ E. Hölderlin ♯ Ren.X 54
[☆ ♯ Cpt. set MC 20029, 4ss, contains the items marked ◇ above, plus J. S. BACH: Clavier Fantasia, A minor, BWV 904. This set also contains, according to catalogue, Decius: Choral. It has not been possible to check, but this is probably *Allein Gott in der Höh'*, above.]

☆ = Re-issue of a recording to be found in previous volumes.

(La) BIBLE DES NOËLS

N. MARTIN: Venez oury la trompette 1555
N. SABOLY: Sant Jousé m'a dit
G. BAROZAI (Bernard de la Monnoye): Hai mon Dieu
1700
ANON. NOËLS: D'ou viens-tu, bergère?
Réveillez-vous, pastoureaux
Complainte de Marie-Madeleine
O vous bourgeois de Reims
Krippenwiegenlied
Peh trouz zou ar en doar
Là où tu cours donc si vite
Nadalou
Mon petit Jesus, bonjour
Vocal & Inst. Ens.—Blanchard ♯ Cpt.MC 20107
Note: There is a similar collection (ed. Guilbert) sung by
G. Touraine (S), with I. Aïtoff (pf.), on ♭ Lum.LD 1-503.

CANZONE SCORDATE

ARR. Dørumsgaard
VOL. I
HELDER: Der Herr ist mein getreuer Hirt (Psalm 23)
ANON. (ed. CORNER): Ein neues andächtiges Kindelwiegen
BÖHM: Bringet meinen Herrn zur Ruh
VETTER: Liebster Gott, wann werd' ich sterben?
C. P. E. BACH: Jesus in Gethsemane
Weihnachtslied
Über die Finsternis
PERI: O miei giorni fugaci
RONTANI: Or ch'io non seguo più
CALESTANI: Ferma, Dorinda mia
QUAGLIATI: Apra il sua verde seno
CACCINI: Occh' immortali
FALCONIERI: Donn' ingrata
d'INDIA: Cara mia cetr' andiamo
A. SCARLATTI: FLAVIO—Chi vuole innamorarsi
Cara e dolce
O dolcissima speranza
(Il) POMPEO—Toglietemi . . .
Bellezza che s'ama
G. Souzay (B), J. Bonneau (pf.) ♯ D.LXT 2835
(♯ Lon.LL 731; D.FAT 173072)

VOL. II
C. M. BELLMANN: Appear, O God of Night (Träd fram,
du Nattens Gud)
Empty your glass (Drick ur ditt-glas)
Ulla, my Ulla (Ulla, min Ulla)
Listen, ye sons of Orpheus (Hör, I
Orfejs drängar)
How are you feeling, Mollberg?
(Tjänare Mollberg)
Weep, Father Berg (Gråt, Fader Berg)
Rest by this fountain (Vila vid denna
källa)
Hush, brothers, Bacchus sleeps
(Tys, bröder, Bacchus har sommat)
Butterflies at Haga (Fjäriln vingad
syns på Haga)
A. Schiøtz (B), J. Bonneau (pf.)
DOWLAND: 7 Ayres (q.v.)
R. Lewis (T), J. Bonneau (pf.) ♯ LI.TW 91067
(♯ D.FAT 173102)

CARILLON PIECES

M. v. d. GHEYN:[1] Preludium III
Preludium V
Minuetto
Prélude Coucou
Fugue, C major
ANON:[2] Marche d'hartop
Hasselts Meiliedeken
The Carillon of Dunkirk
FIOCCO:[2] Andante
SCHEPERS:[2] Allegro
W. de FESCH:[2] Tempo di Gavotta & double
BAUSTETTER:[2] Menuet & Suitte
Staf Nees (Carillon of Malines Cathedral) ♯Pol.13017

CHACONNE & PASSACAGLIA

CHAMBONNIÈRES: Chaconne, G major
L. COUPERIN: Chaconnes, D minor, F major (Nos. 55 & 80)
N. le BÈGUE: Chaconne Grave, G major
L. ROSSI: Passacaglia, A minor
J. CABANILLES: Pasacalles No. 1 (Op. omn. Vol. II, p. 40)
GEORG MUFFAT: Passacaglia, G minor (Apparatus
Musicoorganisticus, 1690)
PACHELBEL: Ciacona, F minor (D.T.B. II-1, No. 19)
BUXTEHUDE: Ciacona, E minor (S.I, No. 3)
N. Pierrónt (org.) ♯ Lum.LD 2-104
[St.-Merry organ]

CHANSONS & MOTETS

LASSUS: Mon coeur se recommande à vous
ARCADELT: Nous voyons que les hommes
REGNARD: Petite nymfe folâtre
LASSUS: Bonjour, mon coeur
DEBUSSY: 3 Chansons de Charles d'Orléans
PRÉGER: 4 Motets
PALESTRINA: Mass 'O admirabile commercium'
. . . Benedictus
MOZART: Ave verum corpus, K 618
ALLEGRI: Miserere mei, Deus
Harvard Glee Club & Radcliffe Cho. Soc.—
—Woodworth ♯ Camb.CRS 202
[D. Pinkham, org.]

CHANSONS DE FRANCE
(XVIth & XVIIth Centuries)

ANON: Les Anneaux de Marianson
Ils sont bien pelez
Suis-je belle? (Deschamps) 1536
La Jeune Religieuse 1575
M. Pifteau (M-S), P-M. Verger (pf.) ∇♯ BàM.LD 010
[ed. P-M. Verger]

CHANSONS FROM THE MUSIC BOOKS of
Margaret of Austria c. 1517

(MS. Brussels; ed. Ch. v. d. Borren & S. Cape)
ANON: Belle pour l'amour de vous 4 vv. ⊗
Triste suis 3 insts. ⊗
Il me fait mal 3 vv. ⊗
Entrée suis en pensée 4 insts. ⊗
Anima mea liquefacta est 4 vv. ⊗
P. de la RUE: Pourquoy non 4 vv. ⊗
Autant en emporte le vent 4 insts.
A. BRUMEL (?): Vray Dieu! Qui me confortera 4 vv.
ISAAC: Et qui la dira 4 vv.
Pro Musica Antiqua Ens.—Cape ♯ HP.APM 14032
(Susato) [Items marked ⊗ also on PV. 5407]

CHANSONS HISTORIQUES FRANÇAISES
(de Jeanne d'Arc à la Révolution)

ANON: Orléans, Bois-Jeancy (b)
Jeanne devant Paris (p)
Réveillez-vous Piccars (p)
Chanson nouvelle . . . sur la bataille de Marignan (m)
Chanson de Marie Stuart: En mon triste et doux
chant
Mignonne, allons voir si la rose . . . (c)
Le Convoi du duc de Guise
Vive l'imprimerie (c)
ed. ARBEAU: Pavane: Belle qui tient ma vie
Bransle: Vive Henri IV (Orchésographie,
1588)
GUÉDRON: Sus, sus bergers (a)
ANON: Chanson à danser sur la naissance de Louis XIV MS.
Siège de Fontarabie MS.
Les Alleluyas sur les barricades MS.
La Chasse donnée a Mazarin (b)
J'aime mieux ma mie, o gué! MS.
Y avoit la du Maine
Aux plaines de Fontenoy 1745
Pauvre Jacques (attrib. Marie Antoinette)
Ça ira (Chanson nouvelle du 14 juillet 1790)
La Carmagnole (La Gamelle patriotique)
Paris Univ. Lecturers' Cho.—Cornet ♯ BàM.LD 07
[M. Rollin (lute)]

Items marked MS. are from manuscript sources, mainly
in the Bibliothèque nationale, Paris; marked (b) from La
Clef des Chansonniers ed. J. B. C. Bellard, 1717; (a) from
Airs de Cour ed. P. Bellard, 1615-28; marked (p) are XVth
Cent. airs ed. Gaston Paris; (m) from Manuscrit de
Bayeux, XVth Cent.; (c) from Le receuil des plus belles . . .
chansons . . . of J. Chardavoine, 1576. All pieces are
taken from J. SEMPLE: La France qui chante (Bourrelier,
Paris, 1945 & 1953). Vive Henri IV is attributed to
Caurroy.

CHANSONS POÉTIQUES

ANON: Cruelle départie (Trésor harmonique, 1606)
ANON, ed. ATTAIGNANT: Le beau Robert 1530
MACHAUT: Douce dame jolie
TRAD.: Voici venir le joli mai
A Bordeaux
Un beau matin
and modern Chansons by Marcy, Trenet, etc.
J. Douai (T) & self J. Liebrard (guit.) ♯ BàM.LD 306
["Recital No. 1"]
For "Recital No. 2" (♯ BàM.LD 312) see: Thibaut,
Séverac.

---

[1] From Piéces de Carillon, 1785; MS. Brussels Conservatoire Library.
[2] From J. de Gruytters, Beyaert-boek of Antwerp, 1746; MS., Antwerp Conservatoire Library.

CHORAL MASTERPIECES FROM THE RUSSIAN LITURGY

ARCHANGELSKY: Hear my prayer
    Out of the depths
GRETCHANINOFF: Cherubic Hymn
    Nunc dimittis
IVANOV: Bless the Lord, O my soul
TCHESNOKOFF: Salvation is created
KOPYLOFF: Hear my prayer
RACHMANINOFF: To thee, O Lord
KASTALSKY: O gladsome light
BORTNIANSKY: Divine praise
    All Saints Church Male Cho.—Self   ♯ CEd.CE 1022
    (*Eng*)

CHORAL MUSIC OF THE XIIIth TO THE XVIth CENTURIES

ANON: Laude[1]—De la crudel morte
    Alleluia
    Dimmi, dolce Maria
    Giù per la mala vita
    O cor soave
VICTORIA:[2] O vos omnes
    Tenebrae factae sunt
PALESTRINA: Ave de coelis[2]
    Hodie Christus natus est[2]
    Magnificat quarti toni[2]
    Improperia—Popule meus[1]
    Hymn—Pange, lingua, gloriosi[1]
    Quartetto Polifonico   ♯ D.LXT 2945
                   (♯ Lon.LL 995)

CHORAL SONGS (*c.* 1600)

FRIDERICI: Wir lieben sehr im Herzen
ZANGIUS: Der Kölner Markt
DEMANTIUS: Mägdlein, wollt ihr nicht mit mir spazieren gahn?
WIDMANN: Schneiderlied
ANON: Ich sag ade; Presulem sanctissimum
    Berlin Motet Cho.—Arndt   ♭ *Pol.* 37006

CHRISTMAS ORGAN MUSIC

J. S. BACH: CHORALE-PRELUDES
    Vom Himmel hoch (BWV 606—OB)
    In dulci jubilo (BWV 608—OB)
    Lobt Gott, ihr Christen, allzugleich
       (BWV 609—OB)
    Pastorale, F major (BWV 590)
    Vom Himmel hoch
       (Canonische Veränderungen—BWV 769)
BÖHM: Chorale Variations: Gelobet seist du, Jesu Christ
J. G. WALTHER: Chorale Variations: Lobt Gott, ihr Christen, allzugleich
BUXTEHUDE: Wie schön leuchtet der Morgenstern
J. S. BACH: Fantasia, G major (BWV 572)
    ☆ F. Heitmann   ♯ DT.LGX 66009

(Les) CLAVECINISTES ESPAGNOLS ET PORTUGAIS

AVONDANO: Sonatas: D major; G major
PEREZ: Sonata, D major
ALBERO: Sonatas: G minor; D minor (from *30 Sonatas para clavicordio*)
SANTOS: Sonata, A major
BACHIXA: Sonata, D major (from MS., *Miscellanea*)
SILVA: Sonata, B flat major
A. SCARLATTI: Toccata No. 7, Fugue, & Partitas on "La Follia"
    R. Gerlin   ♯ LOL.OL 50032
               (♯ OL.LD 88)

(Les) CLAVECINISTES FRANÇAIS

D'ANGLEBERT: Allemande; Gavotte; Menuet, G major; Chaconne, D major
CHAMBONNIÈRES: Allemande (La Rare); Courante; Sarabande
F. COUPERIN: Les petits moulins à vent; Les Roseaux
L. COUPERIN: Chaconne, G minor (122)
DANDRIEU: La Ramage; Les Amours; L'Hymen
    (*Le Concert des Oiseaux*, Nos. 1, 2, 3)
DAQUIN: Musette et Tambourin; Les Bergères
RAMEAU: L'Entretien des Muses
    I. Nef (hpsi.)   ♯ LOL.OL 50028
               (♯ OL.LD 64)

(Les) CLAVECINISTES ITALIENS ET ALLEMANDS

DURANTE: Toccatas: D minor; A minor
Della CIAJA: Toccata, G major
GRECO: Balletto di Mantova (Variations)
B. MARCELLO: Sonata, C minor
F. T. RICHTER: Toccata, D minor (Suite No. 1)
    ᠎ Sarabande, D minor (Suite No. 2)
FROBERGER: Variations on 'Die Mayerin'
PACHELBEL: Fantasia, C major
KUHNAU: Partita, F major (1689) . . . Gigue luthée
HANDEL: "Suite"—Capriccio (7 Pieces, No. 3);
    Aylesford Pieces: 43, Allemande; 65, Minuet; 37, Aria
    R. Gerlin (hpsi.)   ♯ LOL.OL 50043
               (♯ OL.LD 67)

(The) CORONATION OF HER MAJESTY QUEEN ELIZABETH II, 2 June 1953

C. H. H. PARRY: I was glad   1056
H. HOWELLS: Behold, O God our defender
W. H. HARRIS: Let my prayer come up
R. VAUGHAN WILLIAMS: Mass, G minor—Creed & Sanctus
E. BULLOCK (arr.): Come, Holy Ghost
G. F. HANDEL: Zadok the Priest   1057
G. DYSON: Be strong and of a good courage
J. REDFORD (?): Rejoice in the Lord alway
H. WILLAN: O Lord our Governor
S. S. WESLEY: Thou wilt keep him in perfect peace
R. VAUGHAN WILLIAMS (arr.): The Old 100th   1058
    O taste and see
C. V. STANFORD: Gloria in Excelsis (from Op. 128)
O. GIBBONS: Great King of Gods—Amen
W. T. WALTON: Te Deum laudamus (1953)
G. JACOB (arr.): God save the Queen
    Coronation Chorus & Orch.—McKie
    (6ss)   ♯ G.ALP 1056/8

I was glad also on DB 21581
Zadok the Priest also on DB 21583
Be Strong *and* God save the Queen also on DB 21584
Excerpts on ♯ *BLP 1020*
Highlights on ♯ Vic.LBC 1063; ♭ *set WBC* 1033

DANCERIES ET BALLETS

♭ *Pat.ED 42* DANCERIES DE LA RENAISSANCE
    ANON (ed. ATTAIGNANT): Basse-dance "La Volunté"; Tourdion; Bransles: Simple; double
    GERVAISE: Gaillarde, Allemande
        Bransles: Gay, Couran, de Bourgogne, de Champaigne, de Poitou
    DU TERTRE: Bransle d'écosse
    ARBEAU: Belle qui tiens ma vie (Pavane)[3]
    T & insts. (all for 4 recorders & tabor)
♭ *Pat.ED 43* AIRS DE BALLET, XVIIth CENTURY
    ANON (ed. PRAETORIUS): Ballet de coqs
        Ballet des Grenouilles (*Terpsichore*, 1612) 5 recorders
    BATAILLE: Ballet de la délivrance, with recit. (1610)
    L. de BEAULIEU & MAÎTRE SALMON: Ballet comique de la reine 1582
     . . . Deîtez qui libres d'ennui
     . . . Chant des quatres vertus: Dieu que les filles
     . . . Chants des satyres I & II
     . . . Chanson de Mercure: Je ouis de tous les Dieux
     . . . Ballet: La Clochette de Circé
    Paris Ancient Inst. Group—Cotte
    [Y. Tessier (T)]

DOWLAND & HIS CONTEMPORARIES

AYRES
R. JONES: Go to bed, sweet muse (Book III) 1608
ROSSETER: When Laura smiles 1601
BARTLETT: What thing is love 1606
ATTEY: Sweet was the song (Book I) 1622
    On a time (Book I) 1622
ANON: Have you seen but a white lily grow (Jonson) 1614
    F. Fuller (B), J. de Azpiazu (lute)
ANON. LUTE MUSIC
    Greensleeves (from tablature of 1594)
    Heartes ease (MS, Cambridge)
    J. de Azpiazu (guitar)   ♯ EMS. 11
    (*Dowland*)

---

[1] ARR. Terni.   [2] ARR. Casimiri.
[3] From *Orchésographie*; used by Warlock in his *Capriol Suite, q.v.*

EIGHTEENTH CENTURY HARP MUSIC

C. P. E. BACH: Sonata, G major W.139
BEETHOVEN: 6 Variations on a Swiss song G.183
P. J. MEYER: Sonata, G minor, Op. 3, No. 6 *c.* 1780
F. A. RÖSSLER: Sonata, E flat major, Op. 2, No. 2[1] *c.* 1780
J. B. KRUMPHOLZ: Concerto, G minor, Op. 7, No. 5 . . .
   Andante con variazioni
   N. Zabaleta   ♯ Eso.ES 524

ELIZABETHAN & JACOBEAN MUSIC

DOWLAND: Can she excuse my wrongs?
         If my complaints could passions move Book I, 1597
         From silent night Book IV, 1612
         My Lady Hunsdon's Puffe lute
MORLEY: Air 3 viols (*Plain & easy introduction:* 1952 edn. p. 98)
BARTLETT: Of all the birds that I do know 1606
R. JOHNSON: Alman[2] FVB 147 hpsi.
JENKINS: Pavane (4 viols)
       Fancy, C major 4 viols MS, British Museum
CAMPIAN: I care not for these ladies 1601
PARSONS: Pandolpho (from a play)
G. FARNABY: Up tails all Variations FVB 242 (hpsi.)
   A. Deller (C-T), D. Dupré (lute), G. Leonhardt (hpsi.)
    & Consort of Viols   ♯ Van.BG 539
               (♯ Ama.AVRS 6001)

ELIZABETHAN KEYBOARD MUSIC

ANON: A Toye (FVB. 263); Coranto (FVB. 201)
MORLEY: Fantasia (FVB. 124)
PEERSON: The Primrose (FVB. 271)
       The Fall of the leafe (FVB. 272)
R. JOHNSON, ed. G. FARNABY: Pavan (FVB. 39)
R. FARNABY: Fayne would I wed (FVB. 197)
BULL: Pavan and Galliard (FVB. 34 & 38)
    In Nomine (FVB. 37)
    C. Koenig (hpsi.)   ♯ EMS. 236

ELIZABETHAN LOVE SONGS & HARPSI-CHORD PIECES

ROSSETER: When Laura smiles
J. BULL: Galiarda (Parthenia 14)
R. JONES: Go to bed, sweet muse
       Sweet Kate
R. JOHNSON: Alman (FVB. 146)
GIBBONS: The Lord of Salisbury: Pavan (Parthenia 18)
PILKINGTON: Underneath a cypress tree
ANON: The King's Morisco (FVB. 247)
DOWLAND: Weep you no more, sad fountains
       Sorrow, sorrow, stay
       Now, O now, I needs must part
       Away with these self-loving lads
R. FARNABY: Fayne would I wed (FVB. 197)
ANON: Drink to me only with thine eyes
       Have you seen but a white lily grow
PEERSON: The fall of the leafe (FVB. 272)
       The Primrose (FVB. 271)
G. FARNABY: Tower Hill (FVB. 245)
ANON. (Earle's MS.): Why dost thou turn away
G. FARNABY: His dreame (FVB. 194)
ANON: A Toye (FVB. 263)
    H. Cuénod (T), C. J. Chiasson (hpsi.) ♯ Nix.LLP 8037
                 (♯ Lyr.LL 37)

(AN) ELIZABETHAN SONGBAG FOR YOUNG PEOPLE

VOCAL
ANON: Hey boy, ho boy
       Well rung, Tom boy
       Come, Robin
       New oysters, new oysters Rounds
R. JONES: In Sherwood lived stout Robin Hood Ayre
    (Bk. IV—*A Musical dream*, 1609)
MORLEY: About the maypole new Ballett, 5 vv.
    (Bk. I, 1595)
BYRD: Hey, ho, to the green wood Round (MS., Brit. Museum)
RAVENSCROFT: There were three ravens
       It was a frog lived in the well
         (*Melismata*, 1611)
       Willy, prithee go to bed (*Deuteromelia*, 1609)
CAMPIAN: Jack & Joan they think no ill Ayre
PILKINGTON: Rest, sweet nymphs 4 vv. (1605)
       The messenger of the delightful spring
        Madrigal, 4 vv. (Set I, 1613)
J. HILTON Jr.: Come, let us all a-maying go
    (from *Catch as catch can*, 1652)
BARTLETT: Whither runneth my sweetheart? Ayre, 2 vv. (1606)
PEERSON: Now, Robin, laugh and sing Ayre (Bk. I) (1620)

[1] Originally for Harp, Hpsi. or Piano, with Vln.
[2] Set by G. Farnaby.

INSTRUMENTAL
J. BULL: Dr. Bull's my selfe (FVB. 189) Virginals
G. FARNABY: His dreame (FVB. 194) Virginals
J. BULL: The Duke of Brunswick's toye (Cosyn 38). Virginals
MORLEY: La Sampogna—Fancy 1595 2 recorders
    N. Y. Pro Musica Antiqua—Greenberg ♯ Eso.ESJ 6
    [Primavera Singers, B. Winogron (virginals), B. Krainis & E. Kyburg (recorders)]

(8) ENGLISH MADRIGALS

MORLEY: My bonnie lass she smileth
       April is in my mistress' face
       Fire, fire, my heart
GIBBONS: The silver swan
WEELKES: As Vesta was from Latmos hill descending
FARMER: Fair Phyllis I saw
DOWLAND: Weep you no more, sad fountains
RAVENSCROFT: Willy, prithee go to bed

MUSIC OF THE PILGRIMS

(9) Songs from the Ainsworth Psalter—Psalms 108, 3, 136, 15, 21, 24, 23, 34, 100
    New England Cons. Alumni Cho., J. Pease (B & Narr.)
   —de Varon   ♯ HS.HSL 2068
    [with reading from Bradford: *Of Plimouth Plantation*]

ENGLISH MEDIEVAL CAROLS

(Refs.: MB—*Musica Britannica*, Vol. IV—ed. D. Stevens
       HA—*Historical Anthology of Music*, ed. Davison & Apel
       Reese—*Music in the Middle Ages*, 1940)

ANON: Nowell sing we (MB. 16) 2 vv. with fauxbourdon
       Ave Maria (MB. 36) 1, 2, 3 vv.
       Gloria: Et in terra pax (HA. 57b)
       Alleluia (HA. 57a) Motet, 3 vv.
       Lullay lullow (MB. 1) 2 vv.
       What tidings bringest thou? (MB. 11) 2 vv. with fauxbourdon
       Marvel not, Joseph (MB. 81) 2 & 3 vv.
       Alma Redemptoris Mater (MB. 23) 1 & 2 vv.
       Make we joy now in this fest (MB. 26) 2 vv.
       Nowell, Nowell: Tidings true (MB. 4a) 1 v.
       Hail Mary, full of grace (MB. 2) 3 vv.
       Ave rex angelorum (MB. 52) 3 vv.
       Tibi laus, tibi gloria (MB. 44) 2 vv.)
       Nova, nova (MB. 51a)
DUNSTABLE: Sancta Maria (HA. 62; DTÖ VII) Motet, 3 vv.
L. POWER: Beata progenies (Reese, p. 413) Motet, 3 vv.
    Primavera Singers—Greenberg   ♯ Eso.ES 521

EVENING OF ELIZABETHAN VERSE & MUSIC

WEELKES: Tan ta ra cries Mars 3 vv. 1608
R. JONES: Sweet, if you like & love me still (Davison) Bk. 3 1608
       Sweet Kate, of late Bk. 4 1609
       Though your strangeness (Campian) Bk. 4
WILBYE: Flora gave me fairest flowers 5 vv. 1598
       Sweet honey-sucking bees 5 vv. 1609
FERRABOSCO: Come my Celia (B. Jonson) 1609
       So leave off this last lamenting kiss (Donne)
MORLEY: I saw my lady weeping 1600
KIRBYE: Up then Melpomene (Spenser) 1597
DOWLAND: In darkness let me dwell (*Musical Banquet*, 1610)
O. GIBBONS: What is our life (Raleigh) 5 vv. 1612.
J. WARD: Upon a bank with roses (Drayton) 5 vv. 1613
TOMKINS: When David heard that Absalom was slain 5 vv. 1622
    Pro Musica Antiqua (N.Y.)—Greenberg
                 ♯ AmC.ML 5051
    [with poems read by W. H. Auden]

FESTIVAL OF LESSONS & CAROLS

(As sung on Christmas Eve in King's College Chapel, Cambridge)

H. J. GAUNTLETT: Once in Royal David's City
BACH: Weihnachts-Oratorium, excpt.
ANON: Flos de radice Jesse
CORNELIUS: Die Könige (ARR. Atkins)
CAROLS & HYMNS: Ding, dong, ding (Swedish)
        God rest you merry, Gentlemen (English)
        In dulci jubilo (German)
        Hail Blessed Virgin Mary (Italian)
        A Virgin most pure (English)
        While Shepherds watched (English hymn)
        The Shepherd's cradle song (German)
        The Infant King (Basque)
        O come, all ye faithful
with Prayers & Lessons
    Kings Coll. Cho.—Ord   ♯ Argo.RG 39
    [H. McLean, org.]   (♯ West.WN 18105)

FIVE CENTURIES OF CHORAL MUSIC

ROSSELLI: Adoramus te, Christe
PALESTRINA: Alma Redemptoris Mater
TALLIS: If ye love me   Anthem
SCHÜTKY: Emitte Spiritum tuum
MELCHIOR FRANCK: Jesu, deine Seel'   Chorale[1]
J. S. BACH: Komm', süsser Tod (Eng)
        Cantata No. 22—excpt. (Eng)
        Cantata No. 147—excpt. (Eng)
C. FRANCK: Panis angelicus (Eng, as O Lord most holy)
GOUNOD: Jerusalem
TITCOMB: I will not leave you comfortless
SELF: Hymn of praise
    All Saints' Church Male Cho.—Self   ♯ CEd.CE 1023
    [A. Nicholson (Tr)]

FLEMISH CHORAL MUSIC

LASSUS: O la, o che bon eccho!
    Matona, mia cara (Landsknechtständchen) (in Flemish)
JOSQUIN des Prés: Milles regretz
J. van BELLE: In't Groene
ANON., XVIth cent.: Fiamengo   guitar
C. de RORE: Gagliarda   guitar
ANON., XVIth cent.: Maria die soude naer Bethlehem gaen
    Het was een maghet uutvercoren
TRAD.: Ic sag Caecilia Komen
CLEMENS non Papa: Ic seg adieu
MEULEMANS: Amoureus Liedekijn (Jules Frère) 1919
    Pop. Ring Dances — ARR. Meulemans
TINEL: Fantasia
MEULEMANS: Hymne an de Schoonheid
    (C.S.A. v. Scheltema)
    Ghent Oratorio Soc.—M. de Pauw   ♯ Eso.ES 514
    [M. Demasse (guitar)]   (♯ Cpt.MC 20017)

FOUR CENTURIES OF POLISH MUSIC

WACLAW OF SZAMOTUL: Children's Evening prayer (c. 1556) (a)
GOMOLKA: Psalm 136—By the waters of Babylon (a)
    Psalm 95—Let us applaud (1580) (b)
JARZEBSKI: Concerto a tre, Nova casa (1627)
    3 vlns & cont. (c)
SZARZYNSKI: Sonata, D major   2 vlns & org. (1706) (d)
MIELCZEWSKI: Cantata, Deus in nomine tuo (Psalm 53, 1659) Bs, 2 vlns., bsn. & hpsi. ("Concerto") (e, f)
JANIEWICZ: Trios, 2 vlns & vlc . . . No. 1, Allegro moderato & Allegro; No. 2, Andante
— ARR. A. Panufnik as Divertimento (f) ♯ Van.VRS 6017

(a) Poznan State Phil. Men's & Boys' Cho.—Stuligrosz
(b) Wroclaw Polish Radio Cho.—Kajdasz
(c) Polish Radio Soloists—Kolaczkowski
d) Z. Lednicki & I. Iwanow (vlns.), F. Raczkowski (org.)
(e) P. Matthen (Bs)
(f) N.Y. Coll. Musicum—Janiewicz

FRENCH BAROQUE ORGAN MUSIC

BALBATRE: Noëls—Joseph est bien marié &
        Mes bonnes gens
    Variations, D minor (Suite No. 1)
CLÉRAMBAULT: Suite No. 1, D minor—
    5. Basse et dessus de trompette
    7. Dialogue sur les grands jeux   1710
F. COUPERIN: Messe pour les paroisses—Benedictus;
    Élévation; Cromorne en taille
DANDRIEU: Musette, A major
DAQUIN: Noëls—Nos. 1, 3, 9, 10, 12
DU MAGE: Grand jeu   1708
JULLIEN: Dialogue & Basse de trompette
LE BÈGUE: Prelude & Fugue on the Kyrie: Cunctipotens Genitor
    Offertory on 'O filii et filiae'
    Noëls—Laissez paistre vos bêtes;
        Pour l'amour de Marie
        Puer nobis nascitur
LOEILLET: Suite No. 2, A major—Air & Giga (orig. hpsi.)
MARCHAND: Tierce en taille
RAISON: Offertory—Vive le roy des Parisiens (1687)
SIRET: Sarabande c. 1720
    C. Watters (4ss)   ♯ CEd. set 1008
    [organ of St. John's, West Hertford, Conn.]

FRENCH CHANSONS

VOL. I: LA FLEUR DES CHANSONS D'AMOUR

LOYSET COMPÈRE: Vous me faites mourir d'envie
ANON. ed. ATTAIGNANT: Ung petit coup (Bk. III, 1536)
SERMISY: Tant que vivray (Marot) 1529 (b)
ANON. ed. ATTAIGNANT: Destre amoureux   1529 (b)
ANON. ed BALLARD: Frétillarde amoureuse pucette 1606
MACHAUT: Plus dure qu'un dyamant (a)
G. MUREAU: Grâce attendant (Jardin de Plaisance, 1501) (c)
ANON., XVth Cent.: Mort, j'appelle (Villon) MS, Dijon (b)
LOYSET COMPÈRE: Le grant désir
ANON., XVth Cent.: J'ay prins amours MS, Dijon; & Wolfenbüttel Song book (c)
JANNEQUIN: Ce sont gallans (Attaignant, Bk. III, 1536)
BATAILLE: Un jour que ma rebelle (Airs de cour, 1608-18) (b)
ANON., ed ATTAIGNANT: Et gentil Mareschal! (Bk. III, 1536)
CRÉQUILLON: Puisque malheur me tient (Hortus musarum, 1553) (c)
COSTELEY: Hélas! que de mal j'endure 1570
BOESSET: Cruel tyran de mes désirs (Airs de cour, 1624) (c)

VOL. II: CHANSONS POLYPHONIQUES FRANÇAISES

ANON., XIVth Cent.: Or sus vous dormés trop (Virelay) (a)
BORLET: Ma trédol rosignol (Virelay)
CLAUDE le Jeune: Quand la terre . . ., 1606)
JANNEQUIN & CLAUDE: Le chant de l'alouette (Or sus) (Le Printemps, 1603)
JOSQUIN des Prés: Bergerette savoysienne   1501
PASSEREAU: Je ne seray jamais bergère (Attaignant; Bk. III, 1536)
BATAILLE: Ma bergère non légère (trs. P. Warlock) (c)
JANNEQUIN: Le Chant des oyseaulx—Réveillez-vous (Attaignant, Bk. II, 1540)
CLEMENS non Papa: Aymer est ma vie (Hortus musarum, 1553) (b)
JANNEQUIN: Or, viens ça (Attaignant, Bk. III, 1536)
BATAILLE: Ma belle, je vous prie (Airs de cour, 1611) (b)
ANON., ed. PETRUCCI: Ne l'oseray-je dire (Harmonice musices . . ., 1501)
ADRIEN LE ROY: Has tu point veu (Airs de cour, 1571) (c)
BATAILLE: Foux, taisez vous (trs. P. Warlock) (b)
ANON., ed. ATTAIGNANT: Pourquoi voulés vous cousturier (Bk. III, 1536)
PASSEREAU: Pourquoy donc . . . (Attaignant, Bk. III, 1536)
    R. Blanchard Vocal Ens.; J. Archimbaud (C–T, marked a), J. Dutey (B, b), A. Doniat (B, c), M. Clary (guit.); fl., ob. d'amore or cor anglais, & 2 bsns.
         ♯ Phi.N 00993/4R

FRENCH MADRIGALS

JOSQUIN des Prés: Ave Maria ø
JANNEQUIN: Ce moys de May ø
ANON: Belle qui tiens ma vie ø
LASSUS: Quand mon mary vient de dehors
MAUDUIT: Vous me tuez si doucement
COSTELEY: Allons, gay gay gay bergères
    Je voy des glissantes eaux ø
    Mignonne, allons voir si la roze ø
CLAUDE le Jeune: Qu'est devenu ce bel œil
    Voicy du gay printemps
    Paris Vocal Ens.—Jouve   V♯ Sel.LLA 1079[2]
    [those marked ø also in ♯ LT.MEL 94007; ♭ T.UV 116; V♯ Sel. 190.C.002]

---

[1] Sung to: Father, thy Holy Spirit send.   [2] This no. announced but not issued; later re-used (see Durante, etc.)

FRENCH MASTERS OF THE HARPSICHORD

SEE: Les clavecinistes français, *above*

FRENCH RENAISSANCE MUSIC

JOSQUIN des Prés: Milles regretz de vous abandonner
JANNEQUIN: Ce moys de May
        Le Chant des Oyseaulx—Réveillez-vous
CLAUDE le Jeune: Hélas, mon Dieu (*Meslanges,*
          Bk. II, 1612)
        Revecy venir du printans
        Tu ne l'entends pas, c'est latin
LASSUS: Bon jour, mon cœur
        Quand mon mary vient de dehors
ANON. (ed. ATTAIGNANT): À déclarer mon affection
    1529
COSTELEY: Noblesse gît au cœur 1570
        Mignonne, allons voir si la roze
SERMISY: Hau, hau, hau, le boys
        Au joly boys 1529
MAUDUIT: Vous me tuez si doucement (Baïf)
BONNET: Francion vint l'autre jour
    Vocal & Inst. Ensemble—Boulanger ♯ B.AXTL 1048
         (♯ D.FAT 263102; AmD.DL 9629)

FRENCH SACRED MUSIC (XVth-XVIIth Cent.)

G. v. WEERBECKE: Virgo Maria
GOUDIMEL: Psalm CXXXIII (Th. de Bèze)
BOUZIGNAC: Jubilate Deo
Du CAURROY: Missa pro defunctis—Requiem
    Petits Chanteurs de la Renaissance—Noyre & Pagot
                     V♯ *Éra.LDE 1009*
                     (in ♯ HS.HS 9007)
    [Except first item, also in † Histoire de la Musique
    vocale, *q.v.*]

FRENCH TROUBADOUR SONGS

R. de VAQUIERAS: Estampie (Kalenda maya)
J. RUDEL: No sap chantar
        Lan can li jorn
BLONDEL de NESLES: A l'entrée d'esté
GACE BRULÉ: Cil qui d'amor
MARCABRU: Pax in nomine
        Pastourelle: L'autrier jost . . .
THIBAUT de NAVARRE: O Dame!
GUIRAUT RIQUIER: Aisi com es sobronrada
ANON. ? : Un sirventes
CHARDON de REIMS: Chanson de croisade
GAUTIER de COINCY: Ma vièle
BERNART de VENTADORN: Can vei l'alauzeta mover
ANON.?: Quant hom es en autrui poder
GUIRAUT de BORNELH: Reis Glorios
    Y. Tessier (T), M. Clary (lute) [♯ Elek.EKL 31

GABRIELI & CONTEMPORARIES

SEE BELOW: MOTETS OF THE VENETIAN SCHOOL III

(A) GARLAND FOR THE QUEEN 1953

BLISS: Aubade (Reed)
A. BAX: What is it like to be young and fair (C. Bax)
TIPPETT: Dance, clarion air (Fry)
VAUGHAN WILLIAMS: Silence and music (Wood)
BERKELEY: Spring at this hour (Dehn)
IRELAND: The Hills (Kirkup)
HOWELLS: Inheritance (De la Mare)
FINZI: White flowering days (Blunden)
RAWSTHORNE: Canzonet (MacNeice)
RUBBRA: Salutation (Hassall)
    Cambridge Univ. Madrigal Soc. & Golden Age
      Singers—Ord ♯ C.CX 1063
    [M. Field-Hyde & E. Suddaby (SS)]

GERMAN MASTERS OF THE
HARPSICHORD

SEE: Les Clavecinistes italiens et allemands, *above*

[1] Labelled No. 12.

GERMAN SONGS (ed. Dørumsgaard)

SCHEMELLI: Ich lass dich nicht 1727
FREYLINGHAUSEN: Es ist vollbracht 1714
CRÜGER: Auf, auf mein Herz mit Freude (Gerhardt)
    1694
BÖHM: Geh' ein, mein Lieb, in deine Kammer
    (Elmenhorst) 1700
C. P. E. BACH: Die Gute Gottes
    (*q.v.*)   Busslied
               Passionslied
               Preis sei dem Gotte
J. S. BACH: Vergiss mein nicht
    (*q.v.*)   O finstre Nacht
               Liebster Herr Jesu
               Komm', süsser Tod
               Dir, dir, Jehova
J. W. FRANCK: Wie seh' ich dich, mein Jesu, bluten
               Sei nur still
               Auf, auf, zu Gottes Lob (all, Elmenhorst)
               1685
    K. Flagstad (S), G. Moore (pf.) ♯ Vic.LHMV 1070

GLOGAUER LIEDERBUCH

(Songs & Inst. Pieces, *c.* 1480)
(The spelling has been somewhat modernised
Christ, der ist erstanden
Probitate eminentem (insts.)
Du Lenze gut
O plasmator (insts.)
Elselein, liebstes Elselein
Ich bins erfreut
Der Pfauen Schwanz (insts.)
Seh hin mein Herz
Die Katzen phfote (insts.)
Al fol
    E. J. Gerstein (S), F. Brückner-Rüggeberg (T), &
    Inst. Ens.   ♯ *HP.AP 13030*

GOLDEN AGE OF BRASS

(All items are ed. R. King)
G. GABRIELI: Canzona septimi toni, No. I
A. BONELLI: Toccata (*Ricercari e canzoni, Bk. I*, 1602)
G. B. BUONAMENTE: Sonata, D minor (Dorian)(*Sonate e
    canzoni, Bk. VI*, 1636)
J. ADSON: 2 Ayres for Cornetts & Sagbutts
    (*Courtly Masquing Ayres*, 1611)
M. LOCKE: Pavan-Almand; Ayre (*Musick for the King's
    Sagbutts and cornetts*, 1661)
PURCELL: March (Dirge) & Canzona (for funeral of
    Queen Mary, 1694)
PEZEL: Hora Decima . . . Sonata No. 2
ANON: Sonata (*Bänkelsängerlieder, c.* 1684)
J. G. REICHE: Sonatas 18 & 19, G ma. & G mi.
    (*24 Neue Quatricinia*, 1696)
PEZEL: Fünfstimmigte blasende Musik
    . . . 13, Bal ("Intrada"); 63, Sarabande; 62, Bal.
J. S. BACH: Kunst der Fuge . . . Contrapunctus I
    Brass Ens.—R. Voisin   ♯ Uni.UN 1003

GUITAR MUSIC OF SPAIN

ALBENIZ: Asturias (S.E.5) (Leyenda)
        Orientale, Op. 232, No. 2
        Sevillañas (S.E.3)
FALLA: El Amor Brujo . . . Nos. 9 & 12
SEGOVIA: Anecdote No. 2 (from *5 Anecdotes*, 1948)
        Neblina
MORENO TORROBA: Serenata burlesca
SOR: Study A major, Op. 6, No. 6 [1]
TARREGA: Capricho arabe
        Tremolo (Recuerdos de la Alhambra)
TURINA: Homenaje a Tárrega, Op. 69 (Soleares; Garrotin)
    L. Almeida   ♯ DCap.CTL 7089
               (♯ Cap.P 8295)

GUITAR RECITAL I

CASTELNUOVO-TEDESCO: Tarantella
GRANADOS: La Maja de Goya
VILLA-LOBOS: Étude No. 1
PONCE: Valse
MORENO TORROBA: Fandanguillo & Nocturne
BACH: Prelude & Fugue, E flat major BWV 998
    Suite No. 3, unacc. vlc.: Courante
    Sonata No. 1, unacc. vln.: Fugue
    Sonata No. 2, unacc. vln.: Bourrée & Doubles
    C. Aubin   ♯ Eko.LG 1

GUITAR RECITAL II

F. CAMPION: Suite, B minor (Prelude: Gavotte: Gigue)
Suite, F minor (Prelude; Minuet; Les
soupirs; Les délices)
R. JOHNSON: Alman
J. GAULTIER: Sarabande
J. BITTNER: Suite, G minor 1682
(Prelude; Allemande; Sarabande; Passacaille)
S. L. WEISS: Sonata No. 2, D minor
... Prelude; Allemande; Courante; Bourrée
C. Aubin   ‡ Cpt.MC 20111

HEART OF THE PIANO CONCERTO

EXCERPTS from:
BACH: Concerto, D minor
BEETHOVEN: Concerto No. 3, C minor, Op. 37
GERSHWIN: Rhapsody in Blue
GRIEG: Concerto, A minor, Op. 16
MOZART: Concerto, D minor, K 466
RACHMANINOFF: Concerto No. 2, C minor, Op. 18
SCHUMANN: Concerto, A minor, Op. 54
TCHAIKOVSKY: Concerto No. 1, B flat minor, Op. 23
☆ Boston Pops—Fiedler (‡ Cam.CAL 113)
[J. M. Sanromá (pf.)]

HEART OF THE SYMPHONY

EXCERPTS from:
BEETHOVEN: Symphony No. 5, C minor, Op. 67
BRAHMS: Symphony No. 1, C minor, Op. 68
DVOŘÁK: Symphony No. 5, E minor, Op. 95
FRANCK: Symphony, D minor
RIMSKY-KORSAKOV: Scheherazade
SCHUBERT: Symphony No. 8, B minor
TCHAIKOVSKY: Symphony No. 4, F minor, Op. 36
Symphony No. 5, E minor, Op. 64
☆ Boston Prom.—Fiedler   ‡ G.CLP 1015
(♭ Vic. set ERB 23, 4ss)   (‡ Cam.CAL 112)
(These two anthologies are not fully cross-indexed under
composers)

HISTOIRE DE LA MUSIQUE VOCALE

(Du Grégorien à 1750)

GREGORIAN CHANT: Laus Deo Patri (Antiphon)
Psalm 113—Laudate pueri
Vidimus stellam (Alleluia)
Victimae Paschali (Sequence)
ANON. (XII-XIIIth Cent.): Or la truix
N. v. REUENTHAL: Willekommen Mayenschein
(Minnelied)
ANON. ORGANA: Res coeli Domine
Agnus Dei
Benedicamus Domino
PEROTIN: Alleluya (Nativitas) Organum
ANON. (XIIIth Cent.): En non diu! (Motet); De castitatis
thalamo (Conductus)
MACHAUT: Mass "Notre Dame"—Agnus Dei I
LANDINI: Chi più le vuol sapere (Ballata)
BINCHOIS: Adieu m'amour et ma maistresse
DUFAY: Mass 'Se la face ay pale'—Kyrie I
OKEGHEM: Missa prolationum—Sanctus (1st section)
OBRECHT: Parce, Domine Motet
JOSQUIN des Prés: Ave Maria
CRÉQUILLON: Pour ung plaisir Chanson
φ JANNEQUIN: Ce sont gallans
φ SERMISY: Hau le boys
LASSUS: Tristis est anima mea Motet
PALESTRINA: Mass 'Veni sponsa Christi'—Agnus Dei I
φ VICTORIA: Ave Maria
αφ GOUDIMEL: Psalm CXXXIII
BYRD: Ego sum panis vivus Motet
MARENZIO: S'io parto, i' moro Madrigal
BENNET: Thyrsis, sleepest thou? Madrigal
αφ BOUZIGNAC: Jubilate Deo
αφ CAURROY: Missa pro defunctis—Requiem
CACCINI: Dovró dunque morire
MONTEVERDI: ORFEO—Tu sei morta
CARISSIMI: Judicium Salomonis . . . Afferte gladium
SCHÜTZ: O Herr, hilf
RAMEAU: Castor et Pollux . . . Séjour de l'éternelle paix
HANDEL: Rinaldo: excerpts
Solomon . . . Draw the tear from hopeless love
J. S. BACH: Matthaeus-Passion Nos. 68/9
Cantata No. 4—Nos. 5 & 8
Petits Chanteurs de la Renaissance—M. Noyre &
J. Pagot,
Soloists & Danish Radio Ens.—Wöldike, etc.
o.n. ‡ CND. 4/5; now ‡ Era.LDE 3018/9
[All the above, except items marked φ, are from
† MASTERPIECES OF MUSIC BEFORE 1750, q.v. for
details; items marked α, also in † FRENCH SACRED
MUSIC]

HISTORY OF THE DANCE I

ALLEMANDES & MINUETS
ANON. (XVIIth Cent.): Alman, G minor
PURCELL: Suite, G minor—Almand
F. COUPERIN: Allemande (I)
FROBERGER: Suite, C major—Allemande DTÖ VI-i,
No. 12
KRIEGER: Partita No. 5, A major—Allemande
LÜBECK: Suite, G minor—Allemande 1728
MUFFAT: Suite, B flat major—Allemande
HANDEL: Suite No. 3, D minor—Allemande
J. S. BACH: Partita No. 5, G major—Allemande
RAMEAU: Minuets, G major & minor (Suite 5)
J. B. LOEILLET: Suite, G minor—Minuet
PURCELL: Minuet, D minor (Musick's Handmaid)
D. SCARLATTI: Sonata, D minor, L 106 . . . Minuet
FUX: Minuet No. 2 DTÖ. LXXXV
MUFFAT: Suite, B flat major—Minuets I & II
HANDEL: Suite No. 10—Minuet & 2 Varns.
HAYDN: Sonata No. 36—Minuet & Trio (p)
BEETHOVEN: Sonata F minor, Op. 2, No. 1—Minuet &
Trio (p)
SCHUBERT: Minuet "No. 11" (D 41-12) (p)
E. Heiller (hpsi., & pf.—marked p.)   ‡ Uni.LP 1010

HYMNS OF PRAISE & OTHER SELECTIONS

HYMN: Iste confessor (Plainsong)
BACH: Cantata 140, No. 7: Gloria sei dir Gesungen
O Ewigkeit, du Donnerwort (Chorale)
FARRANT: Call to remembrance, O Lord
JOSQUIN des Prés: Ave verum corpus
HANDL: Repleti sunt omnes (Motet, DTÖ. XV-64)
HASSLER: Cantate Domino (Motet, DDT. XXIV/V-6)
BILLINGS: Wake every breath (from New England Psalm
Singer, c. 1771)
ANON. ARR. Noss: O God, to rescue me (from Bay Psalm
Book, 1640)
ANON. ARR. Noss: Glorious things (from Southern Harmony,
1835)
GRETCHANINOFF: Liturgy, Op. 29—Credo; Nunc
dimittis
TCHESNOKOV: Salvation belongeth to our God
RACHMANINOFF: Glory be to God, Op. 37, No. 7
V. THOMSON: Psalms 123 & 136
STARK: Psalm 8
Yale University Divinity School Cho.—Borden
‡ Over.LP 2
[All items arc arr. male voices where originally for
mixed choir]

ITALIAN AIRS

VIVALDI: Un certo non so che
CALDARA: Come raggio del sol
PERGOLESI: FRATE 'INNAMORATO—D'ogni pena . . .
ANON: Laude: Gloria in cielo
Magdalena, degna da laudere
De la crudel morte de Christo
("La Passione", Nos. 2, 4 & 7)
MARTINI IL TEDESCO: Plaisir d'amour
A. SCARLATTI: L'HONESTÀ NEGLI AMORI, aria
GASPARINI: Caro laccio dolce nodo (from Cantata, Op. 1,
No. 2)
SARRI: Sen core l'agnelletta
G. M. BONONCINI: Deh più a me non v'ascondete
CARISSIMI: Piangete, ohimé, piangete
DURANTE: Danza, danza
M. Laszlo (S), F. Holetschek (pf.)   ‡ Nix.WLP 5375
(‡ West.WL 5375)

ITALIAN CLASSIC SONGS

CALDARA: Selve amiche
DURANTE: Vergin, tutto amor
CESTI: I CASTI AMORI D'ORONTEA—Intorno all' idol
mio
A. SCARLATTI: L'HONESTÀ NEGLI AMORI—Già il
sole del Gange
IL POMPEO—O cessate di piagarmi
MONTEVERDI: ARIANNA—Lasciatemi morire
GIORDANI: Caro mio ben
G. BONONCINI: GRISELDA—Per la gloria d'adorarvi
HANDEL: ATALANTA—Care selve
FASOLO: Cangia, cangia, tue voglie
CARISSIMI: Vittoria, vittoria, mio core
BASSANI: La Serenata . . . Posate, dormite
☆ B. Gigli (T) & orch.   ‡ G.ALP 1174
(‡ FALP 340: QALP 10073)

☆ = Re-issue of a recording to be found in previous volumes.

ITALIAN SONGS OF THE XVIth & XVIIth CENTURIES

M. da GAGLIANO: Valli profonde
P. FIORENTINO: Fantasia   lute
FRESCOBALDI: Se l'aura spira
WILLAERT: Con lagrime e con sospir
        Fuggi, fuggi, cuor mio
ANON: Veneziana   lute
CARISSIMI: Sventura, cuor mio
A. SCARLATTI: Cara e dolce
   ☆ H. Cuénod (T), H. Leeb (lute)   ♯ Nix.WLP 5059
   (*Milan & Mudarra*)

ITALIAN SONGS OF THE XVIIth & XVIIIth CENTURIES

MONTEVERDI: Partenza amorosa
    ARIANNA—Lasciatemi morire
A. SCARLATTI: Tutto acceso a quai rai
G. CACCINI: Amarilli, mia bella
G. CARISSIMI: Vittoria, vittoria mio core
B. MARCELLO: Quella fiamma che m'accende
G. B. BASSANI: Fuor dalle placid'onde
    La Serenata—Posate, dormite
(attrib.) PERGOLESI: Se tu m'ami
M-A. CESTI: ORONTEA—Intorno all'idol mio
A. CAMPRA: Fêtes Vénitiennes—Chanson du papillon
   ☆ M. Laszlo (S), F. Holetschek (pf.)
                 ♯ Nix.WLP 5119

ITALIAN MASTERS OF THE HARPSICHORD
SEE: Les clavecinistes italiens et allemands, *above*

LISTENER'S DIGEST
(condensed recordings; not fully cross-indexed)

BEETHOVEN: Symphony No. 5
   Hallé—Barbirolli
BEETHOVEN: Pf. Sonata, No. 14
    Pf. Sonata, No. 8
   A. Dorfmann
TCHAIKOVSKY: Capriccio Italien
    Ouverture solennelle, 1812
   Boston Pops.—Fiedler
FRANCK: Symphony, D minor
   San Francisco Sym.—Monteux
GRIEG: Concerto, A minor, Op. 16, pf. & orch.
   A. Rubinstein & Victor Sym.—Dorati
BEETHOVEN: Concerto No. 5, E flat major, Op. 73
   A. Schnabel & Chicago Sym.—Stock
BRAHMS: Symphony No. 1
   Hollywood Bowl Sym.—Stokowski
DVOŘÁK: Symphony No. 5
   Sym. Orch.—Stokowski
RIMSKY-KORSAKOV: Scheherazade
   Philharmonia—Stokowski [M. Parikian, vln.]
TCHAIKOVSKY: Nutcracker Suite
   N.B.C. Sym.—Toscanini   ♭ *Vic. set SPD 1*
   (20ss)   (♭ *FV.A 85201/10*)

LOUISVILLE ORCHESTRA

The First (1954-5) Subscription Series is entered in detail under the individual composers, but for convenience a summary is given here. The numbers quoted are "release" numbers; apparently the discs are actually numbered ♯ 545-1, 545-2 and so on.

1. Creston, Villa Lobos, H. Stevens
2. Cowell, Tcherepnin, Wagenaar
3. Mennin, Riegger, Toch
4. Hovhaness, Castelnuovo-Tedesco, Surinach
5. Ibert, G. Read, Luening & Ussachevsky
6. P. Glanville-Hicks (The Transposed Heads)
7. Persichetti, R. Sanders, B. Blacher
8. Dallapiccola, Moncayo, U. Kav, Milhaud
9. G. von Einem, K. Rathaus, G. Perle
10. Ginastera, Bergsma, Sauguet, R. Ward
11. Malipiero, Rieti, E. Bacon
12. Mohaupt (Double Trouble)

The 1956 Subscription Series was announced too late for details to be inserted under the composer listings; this will be for Supplement IV. The following is a summary of the prospectus:

546-1. ROSENBERG: Louisville Concerto
       CHOU WEN-CHUNG: And the fallen petals
       GUARNIERI: Suite IV Centenario
546-2. TANSMAN: Capriccio
       F. BOROWSKI: The Mirror
       I. DAHL: The Tower of St. Barbara
546-3. KRENEK: Eleven Transparencies
       R. CAAMAÑO: Magnificat, Op. 20
546-4. ANTHEIL: The Wish (Opera)
546-5. J. ORREGO SALAS: Serenata Concertante, Op. 42
       H. SHAPERO: Credo for Orchestra
       R. MUCZYNSKI: Piano Concerto No. 1
546-6. H. BADINGS: Louisville Symphony
       B. WEBER: Prelude & Passacaglia
       L. SOWERBY: All on a Summer's Day

LUTE MUSIC OF THE XVIth & XVIIth CENTURIES

J. DALZA: Pavana alla Ferrarese (Bk. IV, 1508)
      (Pavana; Saltarello; Piva)
P. ATTAIGNANT: Basse-danse: Patience (1529)
      (Basse-danse; Recoupe; Tourdion)
H. NEUSIEDLER: Ein gut Preambel (1536)
      Preambel (1536)
      Der Bethler Tantz; Hupff auff (1540)
      Der Juden Tantz; Hupff auff (1544)
MUDARRA: Pavana I   ⎱(*From 3 Libros de Música*
     Galliarda   *en Cifra,* 1546)
     Fantasia X   ⎰
J. GORZANIS: La Dura Partita (1561)
      (Pass'e mezzo; Padoana)
A. FRANCISQUE: Branle simple   ⎱(from *Le*
     Branle gay   *Trésor*
     Branle double de Poitou ⎰*d'Orphée,*
     Gavotte   1600)
C. NEGRI: Catena d'Amore   ⎱
     Villancico—Pava iglia ⎰(from *Le Gratie*
     Spagnoletto   *d'Amore,* 1602)
DOWLAND: Pavan—Semper Dowland, Semper dolens
    Galliard—The King of Denmark
    (from *Lachrymae,* 1604)
    Allemande Englessa (from *Linzer Lautenbuch, c.* 1610)
D. GAULTIER: Allemande—Echo
    Courante—La Consolation
    (from *La Rhétorique des Dieuz,* 1652)
    Gigue—Le Tocsin
    (from *Livre de Tablature . . .,* 1672)
  M. Podolsky (lute)   ♯ Per.SPL 577
              (♯ Cpt.MC 20052)

LUTENIST SONGS

CAMPIAN: Never weather-beaten sail
    Most sweet and pleasing are thy ways
    Author of Light
    To Music bent   (all Bk. I, 1613)
FRANCESCO da Milano: Fantasia   lute solo
ANON (*c.* 1615): Miserere my maker
   A. Deller (C-T), D. Dupré (lute)   ♯ LOL.OL 50102
   (*Buxtehude*)

MADRIGALS AND CACCIE
[From the Codex of Antonio Squarcialupi (d. 1475)]

LANDINI: Caro Signor   3 vv.
JACOPO da BOLOGNA: Fenice fu e vissi   2 vv.
LANDINI: Nessun ponga speranza   3 vv.
CASCIA: Nascoso el viso stava   2 vv.
LANDINI: Cosi pensoso (Pescha)   2 vv.
    El mie dolce sospir   3 vv.
GHIRARDELLO da FIRENZE: Tosto che l'alba   3 vv.
LANDINI: Gran tinant' agli occhi   3 vv.
   Pro Musica Antiqua—Cape   ♯ HP.APM 14019
   (*Dufay*) [4 voices & inst. ens.]   (♯ AmD.ARC 3003)
   [The Landini pieces also on ♭ Pol. 37003]

MADRIGALS & MOTETS

VICTORIA: Missa Dominicalis . . . Kyrie
MORLEY: Agnus Dei
TALLIS: Audivi vocem de coelo
HASSLER: Cantate Domino
CLEMENS non Papa: Adoramus te
R. THOMPSON: Felices ter et amplius   (Horace)
PALESTRINA: Super flumina Babylonis
COSTELEY: Je vois de glissantes eaux
    Lautrier priay de danser
MAUDUIT: En paradis je me pense voir
CERTON: La, la, la, je ne l'ose dire
WEELKES: Hark, all ye lovely saints
H. LICHFILD: I always loved to call my lady Rose
MORLEY: My bonny lass she smileth
FOLKSONGS
ARR. HOLST: Abroad as I was walking
ARR. VAUGHAN WILLIAMS: The Turtle dove W. Imig
   (B)
ARR. V. THOMSON: Ps. XXIII: My Shepherd will supply
   my need
ARR. NILES: I wonder as I wander
   Stanford Univ. Cho.—Schmidt   ♯ ML. 7022

MANUSCRIT DE BAYEUX
[Marked (*a*) are ARR. M. Frémiot; (*b*) ARR. S. Nigg]

CHANSONS, XVth Century
Le Roi Anglais; A la duchée de Normandie (*a*)
Ils ont menty . . .; Quand je voye renouveler . . .;   (*b*)
Et cuidez-vous que je me joue (*a*)
Virelai sur la mort d'Olivier Basselin (*b*)
   G. Sandri & Y. le Marc' Hadour (B), S. Cotelle (hp.),
   Inst. Ens.   V♯ *CdM.LDYA 8065*

♯ = Long-playing, 33⅓ r.p.m.   ♭ = 45 r.p.m.   ♮ = Auto. couplings, 78 r.p.m.

MASTERS OF EARLY ENGLISH KEYBOARD MUSIC

VOLUME I

ORGAN (Bureau org. by Snetzler, *c.* 1760)
ANON. (XIVth. Cent.): Estampie: Retroue (or Petrone)
    (Robertsbridge MS., Brit. Mus.)
ANON. (*c.* 1420): Oxford Offertory: Felix namque
    (Bodleian MS.)
T. PRESTON (?): Upon la mi re (British Museum MS.)
WHITE: Ut re mi (Christ Church, Oxford, MS.)
BLITHEMAN: Eterne rerum conditor III (Mulliner 51)
TALLIS: Natus est nobis (Mulliner 9)
O. GIBBONS: Fancy, A minor

HARPSICHORD
NEWMAN: A Pavyon (Mulliner 116)
J. BULL: Galiarda, D minor (Parthenia 14)
    Corant: 'The Prince's' (British Museum, MS)
O. GIBBONS: Pavan & Galliard: 'The Lord of Salisbury'
    (Parthenia 18, 19)

CLAVICHORD
ANON. (XVIth Cent.): La bounette; La doune cella;
    La shy myse (Mulliner 13-15)
ANON. (XVIIth Cent.): Allemande fitt for the Manicorde
    (MS., T. Dart Collection)
CROFT: Suite, C minor . . . Sarabande (Brit. Mus. MS.)

HARPSICHORD
R. JOHNSON: Alman (E. Rogers book, 46; Glyn 3)
E. HOOPER: Alman (FVB 222)
G. FARNABY: His Humor (FVB 196)
J. CLARKE: The Prince of Denmark's March (*Ayres*, 1700)
BLOW: 2 Corants (Egerton MS., Brit. Museum)
ROSEINGRAVE: Fugue, G minor (*Voluntaries & Fugues*,
    c. 1730)
T. A. ARNE: Sonata No. 1, F major . . . Allegro *c.* 1743
    Thurston Dart   ♯ LOL.OL 50075
    [All texts revised Dart, for this record]

VOLUME II
BYRD & TOMKINS: COLLECTIONS, *q.v.*
    Thurston Dart (hpsi. & org.)   ♯ LOL.OL 50076

MONUMENTA ITALICAE MUSICAE

TROUVÈRES & LAUDE
J. RUDEL: Can lo rieus de la fontayna
    Lan can li jorn
MARCABRU: Dire vos vuelh ses duptansa
B. de VENTADORN: Can vei l'alauzeta mover
PEIROL: Mainta jen me mal razona
VIDAL: Anc no mori per amor
    Be'm pac d'ivern e d'estieu
R. de VAQUEIRAS: Estampie (Kalenda maya)
JACOPONE da TODI: Troppo perde'l tempo
GARZO: Altissima luce
ANON. LAUDE: Sia laudato San Francesco
    Salve, Salve, Virgo pia
    San Domenico beato
    Spiritu Sancto
C. Carbi (M-S), R. Monterosso (hpsi.)
         ♯ Phi.A 00773R

[All ed. Monterosso; Trouvères from MS., Bibliotheque Nationale, Paris; Laude from MS. at Cortona and Laudario Magliabechiano II-1-122.]

SEE ALSO: Clementi; & Vivaldi, Op. 8, for further issues in this series.

MORE CATCHES & GLEES OF THE RESTORATION

W. LAWES: The Wise men (*Musical Banquet*, iii, 1651)
ELLIS: My lady and her maid (*idem.*)
BOYCE: 'Mongst other roses
HILTON, J. Jr.: There was three cooks (*Catch as catch
    can*, 1658)
BLOW: I'll tell my mother 1678
    Ring the bells 1701
TURNER: At the song of my Lady's lace
J. ECCLES: Hark Harry (*Joyful Cuckoldom*, 1695)
    Young Anthony's peeping
H. HALL: Tom making a manteau[1]
    Glee Singers—Bath   ♯ Allo. 3046
    (Purcell)

MOTETS OF THE XVth & XVIth CENTURIES

DUFAY: Gloria ad modum tubae
JOSQUIN des Prés: Ave verum
P. de la RUE: O salutaris hostia
PALESTRINA: Super flumina Babylonis
VICTORIA: Tantum ergo
PALESTRINA: Tu es Petrus
BYRD: Confirma hoc, Deus
    Beata viscera
ROSSELLI (ROUSSEL): Adoramus te
VICTORIA: Vere languores nostros
PALESTRINA: Sicut cervus
LOTTI: Crucifixus   8 vv.
PALESTRINA: Haec dies quam fecit Dominus
BYRD: Haec dies quam fecit Dominus
AICHINGER: Regina coeli
    Welch Chorale—J. B. Welch   ♯ Lyr.LL 52

MOTETS OF THE VENETIAN SCHOOL

VOL. I
A. GABRIELI: Cantate Domino
    Bonum est confiteri Domino
    O sacrum convivium
    Egredimini et videte
    Mass 'Pater, peccavi'—Sanctus &
        Benedictus
G. GABRIELI: Sancta Maria
NASCO: Tristis est anima mea
    O salutaris hostia
    Lamentations of Jeremiah—Lesson I
MERULO: Sancta et justi
ASOLA: Adoramus te, Domine Jesu Christe
    Treviso Cath. Cho.—d'Alessi ♯ E. & AmVox.PL 8030
         (♯ BàM.LD 010)[2]

VOL. II
ASOLA: Cantabant sancti
    Hoc signum crucis
    Surge, amica mea   3 vv.
    Introduxit me Rex   3 vv.
    Omnes de Saba
    Surrexit Pastor bonus
CROCE: Benedicam Dominum
    Beati eritis
    Ego sum pauper
    Exaltabo te, Domine
    Cantate Domino
WILLAERT: Ego dormivi
PORTA: Virtute magna; Repleti quidem
RUFFO: Adoramus te, Christe
VECCHI: Salutis humanae sator
NASCO: Migravit Judas (Lamentatio)
INGEGNERI: O Domine Jesu Christe
    Treviso Cath. Cho.—d'Alessi ♯ E. & AmVox.PL 8610
    [All for 4 vv. except where marked]

"VOL. III": 'A. GABRIELI & CONTEMPORARIES'
A. GABRIELI: In decachordo psalterio
    Sacerdos et pontifex
    Filiae Jerusalem
    Maria Magdalena
    Cor meum conturbatum est   5 vv.
    Annuntiate inter gentes   5 vv.
ASOLA: Lapidaverunt Stephanum
    Te gloriosus Apostolorum chorus
    Ave, rex noster   3 vv.
    Cum autem venisset
    Surge propera   3 vv.
    O altitudo divitiarum
    Tu es Petrus
NASCO: Facti sunt hostes (Lamentatio III)
    Ave Maria
PORTA: Praeparate corda vestra Domino
VIADANA: O sacrum convivium
    Treviso Cath. Cho.—d'Alessi ♯ E. & AmVox.PL 8790
    [All for 4 vv. except where marked]

MOTETS ON LUTHER TEXTS (XVIth & XVIIth Centuries)

Nun komm' der Heiden Heiland
Set by B. RESINARIUS, J. WALTHER, ECCARD,
    SCHEIN
Ein' feste Burg
Set by J. WALTHER, CALVISIUS, H. L. HASSLER,
    PRAETORIUS, SCHEIDT
Aus tiefer Not
Set by HASSLER, M. le MAISTRE
Vater unser im Himmelreich
Set by GUMPELTZHAIMER, HASSLER,
    PRAETORIUS
    Netherlands Madrigal & Motet Cho.—Voorberg
         ♯ Phi.N 00692 R

---

[1] Attrib. Purcell. *Pleasant Musical Companion Bk. II, Supplement.*
[2] Announced but never issued; the number re-used (see † CHANSONS DE FRANCE).

MUSIC FOR BRASS

A. HOLBORNE: Honie-suckle
    Wanton
    Night Watch (ed. King)
MONTEVERDI: ORFEO—Ritornelli, Sinfonia, Moresca
    Questi vaghi—Sinfonia
    Tempro la cetra—Sinfonia
SCHEIN: Banchetto Musicale . . . Intrada & Paduana
PEZEL: Fünff-stimmigte blasende Musik Brass Quintet
   ... 29, Bal; 64, Gigue; 84, Sarabande
   Hora decima Brass Quintet
   ... Sonata No. 3
BANCHIERI: 2 Fantasias[1] Brass Quintet
   Music Hall Brass Ens.   # Mono. 817

MUSIC FROM THE MIDDLE AGES TO THE RENAISSANCE

ANON. (XIIIth Cent.): Agniaus dous ed. P. Aubry (S. unacc.)
    Bele Doëtte ed. Beck
    Chanson d'amour (attrib. Béatrice de Die) ed. Gérold
    Sovent me fait souspirer ed. Rockseth (Motet profane) (i)
    Danse anglaise MS. Bodleian Lib. Oxford (i)
ANON. (XVth Cent.): Saltarello MS. Brit. Museum; ed. Moser (i)
MACHAUT: Rondeau 3 vv. (B & H. No. 2)
OKEGHEM: Les desleaulx ont la saison MS. Dijon ed. Droz & Thibault
DUFAY: Ce moys de May
    La Belle se siet
ANON. (XVIth Cent.): Pavane 1545 ed. Rollin lute
TROMBONCINO: Come harò donque ardire Madrigal (Michelangelo) ed. Einstein
J. CARMEN: Der Ratten Schwanz (Berliner Liederbuch) ed. R. Eitner (i)
    M. Rollin Ensemble   # LI.W 91116
    (Soprano, recorder, viol, lute)   (# D.FS 123632)
    [Items marked (i) are instrumental only.]

MUSIC IN SHAKESPEARE'S TIME

J. MUNDY: Robin (FVB. 15) Virginals
ANON: 2 Canaries (Straloch MS., 1603) Lute
    Willow Song (Lute MS., 1615) S & Lute
O. GIBBONS: Whoope, doe me no harme (Varns.) Virginals
DOWLAND: Semper Dowland, semper dolens (Pavan) Lute
CAMPIAN: The Peaceful Western wind (1601) S & lute
ANON: Mrs. Winter's Jumpp Lute
DOWLAND: Wilt thou, unkind S & Lute
ANON: Heart's Ease (MS., Cambridge) Lute
R. JONES: Farewell, dear love (1600) S & Lute
ARR. F. CUTTING: Greensleeves Lute
BYRD: O Mistress mine (Divisions) (FVB. 66) Virginals
ANON: Suite of Corantos (MS., Folger library)
    Heigh ho, for a husband S & Lute
    (John Gamble's Commonplace book, 1657, ARR. Bloch)
    S. Bloch (S, & lute & virginals)   # CHS.CHS 1225

MUSIC OF THE CHURCH

ROSA: Selve, voi che le speranza
BERCHEM: O Jesu Christe
CASCIOLINI: Panis angelicus
    O esca viatorum
LASSUS: Missa brevis—Sanctus & Benedictus
ANON. (XIth Cent.): Ave Maria
M. HAYDN: Adoro Te
MENEGALI: Jesu, Salvator mundi
    N.Y. Blessed Sacrament Qtt. & C. Sparks (org.)
                        # Bib.CL 221

MUSIC OF THE BAROQUE ERA

WECKMANN: Toccata, E minor
PACHELBEL: Aria Sebaldina & Variations, F mi. (c)
G. BÖHM: Praeludium, Fuga, Postludium, G mi. (Bk. I, No. 6)
RATHGEBER: 4 Pastorellas, Op. 22 (Musikalischer Zeitvertrieb, 1743)
J. C. F. FISCHER: Prelude & Chaconne, G major (c) (Suite 8, Musikalisches Blumenbüschlein, 1698)
SCHEIDT: Variations on the Canto Belgica—Ach, du feiner Reiter (Tablatura Nova)
    E. Bodky (hpsi., or, marked c, clavichord)
                        # Uni.LP 1002

MUSIC OF THE MIDDLE AGES

NIEDHART von REUENTHAL: Mei hat wunniklich
    Der Mei hat mennik herze
    So schönen wir den Anger nie gesahen
ANON. (XIIIth Cent.): Spielmannstanz insts.
WITZLAW von RÜGEN: We ich han gedacht
    Loybere risen
WALTHER von der VOGELWEIDE:
    Nu alerst lebe ich mir werde (Palästina Lied)
OSWALD von WOLKENSTEIN: Der May mit lieber Zal (after Vaillant)
ANON. (XIIIth Cent.): La quarte Estampie Royale
RAIMBAUT de VAQUEIRAS: Kalenda maya
BERNARD de VENTADORN: Lancan vei la folha
ADAM de la HALLE: Dieu soit en cheste maison
ANON. (c. 1147): Chevalier mult estes guariz[2]
ANON. (XIVth Cent.): Saltarello insts.
    Lamento de Tristano insts.
    E. Metzger-Ulrich (S), O. Pingel (T), Krefeld Collegium Musicum—R. Haas   # E. & AmVox.PL 8110
                        (# BàM.LD 08)

MUSIC OF THE RENAISSANCE

DUFAY: Veni creator spiritus (S & T)
    O Flos florum (S); Se la face ay pale (S & T)
BINCHOIS: De plus en plus (S)
ANON. (Glogauer Liederbuch, c. 1480):
    Der neue Bauernschwanz (I)
    Ich bins erfreut aus rotem Mund (T)
    Ich sach's einsmals dem lichten Morgenstern (T)
ANON. (Locheimer Liederbuch, 1455-1560): Ein Vroulein edel von Naturen (S)
    Der Walt hat sich entlaubet (T)
ANON. (Peter Schöffers Liederbuch, 1513): Ich kam vor Liebes Fensterlein (S & T)
ANON: Saltarello (I)
LANDINI: Gran piant' agli occhi (S & T)
TROMBONCINO: Non val aqua (Frottola, I)
ANON., c. 1500: Canto delle vedove—Perche ciascum difender (S & T)
F. PEÑALOSA: A tierras ajenas (i)
F. de la TORRE: O cuam dulce (T)
    Aire de danza (I)
ESCOBAR: Corazun triste (T)
    E. Metzger-Ulrich (S), O. Pingel (T), Krefeld Coll. Musicum—R. Haas # E. & AmVox.PL 8120
    [Items marked (I) above are inst. only]

MUSICA ANTICA E NUOVA

TELEMANN: Trio Sonata, E major fl., vln., cont. (pf. & vlc.)
    Duet: Die rechte Stimmung S, B & forte pf.
J. PAPINEAU-COUTURE: Eglogues (Baillargeon) (1. Printemps; 2. Regards; 3. L'Ombre) A., fl. & pf.
D. GABRIELLI: Flavio Cuniberto—Aria. T, vlc. & cont.
O. v. WOLKENSTEIN: Der May mit lieber Zal (Minnelied) A & vla.
ZELTER: Wonne der Wehmut (Goethe) B & cont.
    Vocal & Inst. Ens.—Bizony   # Hall.RS 6

MUSICAL ORGAN CLOCK ("c. 1787")[3]

STERKEL: Concerto
ANON: Waltz
    Andante & Allegro
    Ecossaise
"MOZART": Veilchenstrauss
    Vergiss mein nicht (K.Anh.246: by L. Schneider)
    Theme & Variations
HAYDN: Creation—In native worth (ARR.)
LISZT (?): Allegro
POLLEDRO: Allegro
    Clock, Hübner Collection, Vienna # Van.VRS 7020

---

[1] From Fantasie overo Canzoni . . . a 4 voci, 1603.
[2] Listed as included in French issue, but not in the American or English.
[3] It is suggested that the roll played here is much later than this, perhaps even as late as 1830. Notes suggest that the item attributed to Liszt may be by Anton Liste.

MUSICIENS DE LA COUR DE BOURGOGNE
VOLUME I
BINCHOIS (attrib.): Mass (MS., Brussels)[1]
  Cho.—Eeckhout
SECULAR & INSTRUMENTAL PIECES
ISAAC: La Martinella (Canzona) Insts.
CREQUILLON: Quand me souvient T & insts.
TOURNHOUT: En regardant ... T & bsn.
ANON. (Glogauer Liederbuch, etc.): 4 Inst. pieces
OKEGHEM; Ma Maitresse T & insts.
H. FINCK: O schönes Weib T & insts.
  B. De Pauw (T), R. Graindorge (cor ang.), C. Pirnay
  & L. Pecheny (bsns.)   ♯ LOL.OL 50104
                                (♯ OL.LD 80)
VOLUME II
MOTETS
P. de la RUE: Salve Regina
BINCHOIS: Virgo prefulgens
         Kyrie feriale
JOSQUIN des Prés: Quam pulchra es
JEAN DE CASTRO: Jubilate
BRUMEL: Mater Patris et Filia
LOYSET COMPÈRE: O vos omnes
ANON: Virgo gloriosissima
     Vitrum nostrum gloriosum
  Cho. —Eeckhout
INSTRUMENTAL PIECES
CLEMENS non Papa: Die Winter is verganghen
MORLEY: Though Philomela lost her love (Canzonet, 1593)
LOYSET COMPERE: Garissez moi
SCHEIN: Der kühle Maien
JOSQUIN des Prés: Si je perdu mon amy
BRUMEL: Vray Dieu d'amour
DUFAY: Mon chier amy
ANON: La plus grant chière de jamais
     Fantasie
     Fontaine à vous dire le voir
GASTOLDI: Musica a due voci
  Chapelle de Bourgogne Recorder Trio   ♯ OL.LD 81

(La) MUSIQUE DE LA GRANDE ÉCURIE
A. PHILIDOR: Ordonnance de la compagnie des Cannoniers
            de La Rochelle 1703
            Marche des Boulonnais
            Marche des pompes funèbres 1711
LULLY: Marche des Régiments du Roy 1670
      Marche royale
      Marche des forçats des galères turcs
DANDRIEU: Fanfares de Chantilly
F. COUPERIN: Marche du Régiment de Champagne
CORRETTE: Marche des Gardes françaises
       Marche des Gardes suisses
       Marche du Maréchal de Saxe
BARONVILLE: Ordonnance des Dragons du Roy
  Paris Collegium Musicum—Douatte ♯ Cpt.MC 20102

(La) MUSIQUE ET LA POÉSIE FRANÇAISE
(Middle Ages and Renaissance)
(Titles in light type are diction only)
ANON. (XIIIth Cent.): La quarte estampie royale I
ANON: Le Combat de Raynouard et d'Agrapart
B. de VENTADORN: La douza votz
ANON. (XIIIth Cent.): Conductus I
RUTEBEUF: Le Mariage de Rutebeuf
THIBAUT DE NAVARRE: En chantant veuil c
C. MUSET: Surprise suis d'une amourette l
ANON. (XIIIth Cent.): Quand je vois l'hiver retourner
             (Muset) c
        Hoquet I (MS., Montpellier)
G. FAIDIT: Planh ur la mort de Richard Cœur de Lion
  T, unacc.
ANON. (XIIIth Cent.): Motet I (Bamberg MS.)
FROISSART: Mon cœur s'ébat en oudourant la rose l
J. de LESCUREL: À vous, douce débonnaire Rondeau
MACHAUT: Ne cuidez pas que le cœur me deuille
MACHAUT: Je suis aussi com cil qui est ravi I
C. DE PISAN: Seulette suis ...
BINCHOIS: De plus en plus I
Ch. d'ORLÉANS: Dieu qu'il la fait bon regarder
P. M. VERGER: Puis ça, puis là (Ch. d'Orléans) Cho.
A. GRÉBAN: Ja Dieu ne plaise (from Le vrai mystere de la Passion)
ANON. (XVth Cent.): Mort, j'appelle de ta rigueur (Villon)
VILLON: Ballade des dames du temps jadis
DEBUSSY: Ballade que fit Villon à la requeste de sa mère
  pour prier Notre-Dame B & pf.
LASSUS: Qui dort icy? (Marot) 4 vv.
SERMISY: Secourez-moi (Marot) T & lute
MAROT: Plus ne suis ce que j'ai été
RAVEL: D'Anne, jouant de l'épinette (Marot) T & pf.
RONSARD: Marie, levez-vous

JANNEQUIN: Petite nymphe folâtre (Ronsard)
RAVEL: Ronsard à son âme T & pf.
ANON: Fantasia lute (MS., Louvain, 1545)
MAUDUIT: Vous me tuez si doucement (Baïf) 3 vv.
L. LABBÉ: Tant que mes yeux
ANON: Languir m'y faut lute 1545
JANNEQUIN: Laissez cela
  M. Rollin (S), Y. Tessier (T), B. Demigny (B), Rollin
  Trio & Cho. Sine nomine, etc.   ♯ CND. 9
  ARR. AND ED. P. Maillard Verger. Items marked I are
  instrumental only; marked c are from the Chan-
  sonnier Cangé; marked l are spoken to lute accom-
  paniment, improvised on contemporary themes.

MUSIQUES À LA CHAPELLE DU ROI
MOTETS
DUMONT de THIERS: O tu qui es
MINORET: Qui tribulant me
M-A. CHARPENTIER: Salve regina
           O vos omnes
           Lauda Sion
LALANDE: Deus in adjutorium ... Adjutor meus
COUPERIN: Ostende nobis
CAMPRA: Beati omnes—motet for solo voice
BERNIER: O triumphantes Jerusalem 1703
GERVAIS: O sacrum convivium
BLANCHARD: Magnificat ... Et misericordia ejus
  M. Casadesus Ens.   ♯ Plé.P 3083
  [M. Dupré (org.), L. Lavaillotte (fl.), J. Giraudeau (T)]
                       (♯ West.WN 18167)

OLD ENGLISH MASTERS
BYRD: The Bells (FVB. 69)
BULL: Fantasy on a Flemish Folk Song—Laet ons met
     herten reyne
     Vexilla Regis
PHILIPS: Trio
     Fantasy
PURCELL: Suite 5, C major—Prelude; & Annex: Cebell;
     March
CROFT: Voluntary
GREENE: Introduction & Trumpet Tune
STANLEY: Suite, D major
  F. Peeters   ♯ Per.SPL 578
  [Org. of St. Jans, Gouda, 1732-6] (♯ Cpt.MC 20049)

OLD ITALIAN MASTERS
(References: T—Torchi, L'Arte musicale
         R—Ritter, Geschichte des Orgelspiels)
A. GABRIELI: Canzon Arioso 1596
attrib. PALESTRINA: Ricercare primi toni (R II-6/7)
G. BRIGNOLI: Canzona francese c. 1607 (R II-16/17)
G. CAVAZZONI: Easter Hymn: Ad coenam agni providi
  1542 (T III-29)
G. GUAMI: Canzona francese: La Guamina (R II-6/7)
G. GABRIELI: Ricercare c. 1600 (R II-18-19)
FRESCOBALDI: Fiori musicali 1635
  ... Nos. 3, 4, 10, 17, 31
attrib. FRESCOBALDI: Fugue, G minor[2]
ZIPOLI: Pastorale, C major (T III-393/5)
G. MARTINI: Sonata No. 7, E minor 1741
  ... 1st movt., Prelude & Fugue, only
  F. Peeters (org.)   ♯ Nix.PLP 586
      (♯ Per.PLP 586; ♯ Cpt.MC 20048)

OLD NETHERLANDS MASTERS
CORNET: Fantasia in the 8th tone
DUFAY: Alma redemptoris mater
ISAAC: Herr Gott, lass dich erbarmen
JOSQUIN des Prés: Canzona
KERCKHOVEN: Prelude & Fugue, D major
MONTE: Canzona
OBRECHT: Ein fröhlich Wesen
OKEGHEM: Fuga trium vocum
SWEELINCK: Fantasia in Echo-style
WILLAERT: Ricercare
  ☆ F. Peeters (♯ Cpt.MC 20069)

OLD FRENCH AIRS
LOUIS XIII: Chanson (trs. Mersenne; 1636)
P. GUÉDRON: Cette Anne si belle (1615)
ANON: Tambourin (1732) (ARR. Tiersot)
A. BOESSET: Me veux-tu mourir? (c. 1620) (ARR.
     Tailleferre)
     Cachez, beaux yeux (1615)
ANON: Ma bergère non légère (ed. Bataille: 1613)
     Noël Auxois (XVIIth Cent.)
     Brezairola (Berceuse)[3]
     Malurous qu'o une fenno (Bourrée)[3]
  G. Souzay (B), J. Bonneau (pf.)   ♯ D.LW 5091
                     (♯ Lon.LD 9109)

---

[1] Van der Borren, Mass No. 2. The attribution to Binchois dates from XVIIIth Cent. and it is suggested that this is an error for BUSNOIS.
[2] From Clementi's Selection of Practical Harmony.
[3] ARR. Cantaloube; from Chants de l'Auvergne.

OLD ITALIAN AIRS

A. SCARLATTI: Su, venite a consiglio
LOTTI: Pur dicesti
DURANTE: Vergin, tutto amor
BASSANI: Posate, dormite
CALDARA: Sebben, crudele
CESTI: I CASTI AMORI D'ORONTEA—Aria
GIORDANI: Caro mio ben
A. SCARLATTI: Sento nel core
GLUCK: PARIDE ED ELENA—Aria
GASPARINI: Lascia d'amarti per non penar
LEGRENZI: ETEOCLE E POLINICE (1675)—Che fiero costume
Attrib. PERGOLESI: Nina
CARISSIMI: Vittoria, mio core!
    G. Prandelli (T), D. Marzollo (pf.) ♯ AmVox.PL 7930

OLD ITALIAN SONGS & AIRS

VIVALDI: Un certo non so che
CARISSIMI: Piangete, ohimé
HANDEL: RINALDO—Aria
CAVALLI: SERSE (1654)—Affe, mi fate ridere
PERGOLESI: Se tu m'ami
PAISIELLO: LA MOLINARA—Aria
MONTEVERDI: ARIANNA—Lasciatemi morire
CALDARA: Come raggio
CHERUBINI: DÉMOPHON—Aria
A. SCARLATTI: Il PIRRO È DEMETRIO—Aria
MARCELLO: Quella fiamma
PAISIELLO: I ZINGARI IN FIERA—Aria
    F. Barbieri (M-S), D. Marzollo (pf.) ♯ AmVox.PL 7980

OLD SPANISH KEYBOARD MUSIC

SEE SPANISH KEYBOARD MUSIC, *infra*

ORGAN MUSIC BY MODERN COMPOSERS

BARTÓK: En bateau
BRITTEN: Prelude & Fugue on a theme by Vittoria (*sic*)
COPLAND: Episode
COWELL: Processional
HINDEMITH: Sonata No. 2
MESSIAEN: Le Banquet céleste
MILHAUD: Pastorale
THOMSON: Pastorale on a Christmas plainsong
VAUGHAN WILLIAMS: Prelude on the Welsh hymn "Hyfrydol"
    R. Ellsasser   ♯ MGM.E 3064

ORGAN MUSIC FROM SWEELINCK TO HINDEMITH

SWEELINCK: Toccata, A minor
BYRD: Fortune (Variations) FVB. 65
PURCELL: Chaconne, F major
HANFF: Chorale Prelude—Ach Gott, vom Himmel sich darein
BÖHM: Chorale Variations—Wer nur den lieben Gott lässt walten
MICHEELSEN: Prelude & Fugue, D major
J. S. BACH: Prelude & Fugue, A minor (BWV 543)
    Toccata & Fugue, D minor (BWV 565)
PEPPING: Chorale Preludes—
    O Haupt voll Blut und Wunden
    Erschienen ist der herrliche Tag
    Heut' singt die liebe Christenheit
HINDEMITH: Sonata No. 1
    ☆ F. Heitmann   ♯ DT.LGX 66037/8
    (4ss) [Org. of St. Paul's, Berlin]

ORGAN RECITAL

FARNAM: Toccata on 'O Filii et Filiae'
KARG-ELERT: Herr Jesu Christ, dich zu uns wend, Op. 78, No. 9 1912
DUPRÉ: In dulci jubilo, Op. 28, No. 41
VIERNE: Carillon de Westminster, Op. 54, No. 6
MULET: Carillon-Sortie, D major
ALAIN: Litanies, Op. 79
BRAHMS: Chorale Prelude, Op. 122, No. 5
WIDOR: Symphony No. 5—Toccata
    A. Hamme   ♯ SRS.H 1

PARISIAN SONGS OF XVIth CENTURY

C. de SERMISY: Las, je m'y plains
    Dictes sans peur
PASSEREAU: Pourquoi donc ne fringuerons nous
    Sur la rousée
JANNEQUIN: L'amour, la mort et la vie
    Il estoit une fillette
    Ma peine n'est pas grande
CERTON: Que n'est-elle auprès de moi
HESDIN: Plaindre l'ennui de la peine
GARDANE: O doulx regard
SANDRIN: Amour si haut
NICOLAS de la GROTTE: Quand je te veux reconter
C. de RORE: Tout ce qu'on peut en elle voir
COSTELEY: En ce beau moys
GOUDIMEL: Amour me tue
BONI: Rossignol, mon mignon
BONNET: Mon père et ma mère
CLAUDE le Jeune: Rossignol mon mignon
    Fière cruelle
    Prince, la France te veut
ANON: Frétillarde amoureuse pucette
    Vocal Ens.—F. Lamy   ♯ LOL.OL 50027
    (♯ OL.LD 76)

POLYPHONIC MASTERS OF THE XVIth CENTURY

PALESTRINA: O vos omnes
INGEGNERI: Ecce quomodo moritur
LASSUS: In pace, in idipsum dormiam
JOSQUIN des Prés: Ave vera virginitas
    Mass, 'Ave maris stella'—Kyrie[1]
PALESTRINA: Laudate Dominum
ANDREAS: Jubilate Deo
VIADANA: Cantate Domino
    ☆Gregorian Institute Cho.—Vitry ♯ GIOA.PM-LP 1

POLYPHONIC MOTETS OF THE XVIth CENTURY

P. de la RUE: O salutaris hostia (cond. Pagot)
LASSUS: Nos qui sumus in hoc mundo (cond. Noyre)
PALESTRINA: Ego sum panis vivus (cond. Noyre)
MORALES: Puer natus est (cond. Pagot)
MARENZIO: O rex gloriae (cond. Noyre)
    Petits Chanteurs de la Renaissance V♯ Era.LDE 1001
    (in ♯ HS.HS 9007)

POLYPHONIE SACRÉE EN FRANCE (XIth to XXth CENTURY)

ANON. (XIIIth Cent.): Iste confessor
    Prophéties de la Sibylle
    Haec est clara dies
    Concordi laetitia
    Rex virginum
    Gaude, felix Francia
LOYSET COMPÈRE: Royne du ciel
A. de FEVIN: Mass, 'Mente tota'—Agnus Dei
CLAUDE le Jeune: Psalm 35
SAMSON: Mass, 'Amor a longe'
RUDEL: Amor de lonh
    Dijon Cath. Choir & Inst. Ens.—Samson ♯ SM. 33-05

PORTUGUESE KEYBOARD MUSIC

(Refs. are to *Old Portuguese Keyboard Music* ed. Kastner), pub. Schott
VOLUME I
SEIXAS: Sonata, A minor (Vol. II, No. 11)
    Toccata, E minor (Vol. I, No. 11—with Minuet)
    Sonata, B flat major (Vol. I, No. 12)
JACINTO: Toccata, D minor (Vol. I, No. 2)
CARVALHO: Toccata, G minor (Vol. I, No. 16)
    F. Blumenthal (pf.)   ♯ D.LXT 2805
    (*Spanish Keyboard Music*)   (♯ Lon.LL 769)

VOLUME II
ANON: Toccata, C major (Vol. I, No. 15)
SEIXAS: Fuga, A minor (Vol. II, No. 15)
    Sonata, C major (Vol. II, No. 8)
    Minuet, A minor (Vol. I, No. 4a)
    Toccata, D minor (Vol. I, No. 14)
    Minuet, F minor (Vol. I, No. 6a)
    Sonata, C minor (Vol. I, No. 9)
    Toccata, G minor (Vol. I, No. 10—with Giga & Minuet)
    F. Blumenthal (pf.)   ♯ D.LXT 5218
    (*Spanish Keyboard Music*)   (♯ Lon.LL 1194)

---

[1] The original 78 r.p.m. issue also contained *Agnus Dei* but this is not listed for the ♯ re-issue.

RECORDED LESSONS IN THE ART OF SONG INTERPRETATION

by Lotte Lehmann (S) & pupils   ‡ *Campbell. 1/24*
[The illustrations listed below are not cross-indexed under composers]

1   R. STRAUSS: Heimkehr, Op. 15, No. 5
            Cäcilie, Op. 27, No. 2
2   ROSENKAVALIER—Marschallin's Monologue
     SCHUMANN: Dichterliebe—No. 7
3   TORELLI: Tu lo sai
     DEBUSSY: Chansons de Bilitis—No. 1
     WOLF: Gesang Weylas
4   SCHUBERT: Im Abendroth D. 799
     BEETHOVEN: Der Kuss, Op. 128
     MOZART: Männer suchen stets zu naschen, K433
5   DEBUSSY: Les cloches
     MOZART: Das Veilchen, K476
6   MARX: Hat dich die Liebe berührt
     WOLF: Anakreons Grab
7   SCHUMANN: Waldesgespräch, Op. 39, No. 3
     R. STRAUSS: Heimliche Aufforderung, Op. 27, No. 3
8   CASTELNUOVO-TEDESCO: Recuerdo
     CHAUSSON: Chanson d'amour
     MOZART: Die Verschweigung, K518
9   PUCCINI: BOHÈME—Si, mi chiamano Mimi
     WOLF: Zur Ruh!   Zur Ruh!
     ARNOLD: Hist! Hist!
10   R. STRAUSS: Zueignung, Op. 10, No. 1
     TRAD. FRENCH: Maman, dites-moi . . .
11   MARX: Ein junger Dichter denkt an der Geliebte
     BANTOCK: Feast of Lanterns
     WOLF: In dem Schatten meiner Locken
12   Über Nacht
     SCHUMANN: Der Nussbaum, Op. 25, No. 3
13   MASSENET: HÉRODIADE—Il est doux, il est bon
     WAGNER: LOHENGRIN—In fernem Land
14   BRAHMS: Nicht mehr zu dir zu gehen, Op. 32, No. 2
     W. WATTS: Stresa
15   SCHUMANN: Dichterliebe, Op. 48—Nos. 1, 2, 3
     BRAHMS: Die Nachtigall   (VK.2)
16   WOLF: Die heisse schwüle Sommernacht
     SCHUBERT: Aufenthalt D.957-5
17   DEBUSSY: Chanson de Bilitis—No. 3
            Mandoline
     PALADILHE: Psyché
18   FOURDRAIN: Carnaval
     R. STRAUSS: ROSENKAVALIER—Duet
19   SCHUBERT: Fischerweise D.881
     BRAHMS: Das Mädchen spricht, Op. 107, No. 3
     WAGNER: Träume
20   R. STRAUSS: Wiegenlied, Op. 41, No. 1
            Ruhe meine Seele, Op. 27, No. 1
21   VERDI: OTELLO—Credo
     WOLF: Auf einer Wanderung
     HAHN: D'une prison
22   WOLF: Du denkst mit einem Fädchen
     WAGNER: DIE WALKÜRE—Du bist der Lenz
     BRAHMS: Immer leiser wird mein Schlummer, Op. 105, No. 2
     R. STRAUSS: Die Nacht, Op. 10, No. 3
23   PUCCINI: BOHÈME—Che gelida manina
     BARBER: A nun takes the veil, Op. 13, No. 1
     SCHUBERT: Die Krähe D.911-15
24   SCHUBERT: Der Jüngling an der Quelle D.300
     BRAHMS: Unbewegte laue Luft, Op. 57, No. 8
     Concluding remarks by L. Lehmann

RECORDER & HARPSICHORD RECITAL "No. 3"

TELEMANN: Sonata No. 2, G major (Partita)
SENALLIÉ: Sonata, G minor, Book I, No. 5   1710
ANON: Greensleeves to a ground
PEPUSCH: Sonata No. 4, F major
N. MATTEIS: Prelude, D major   *c.* 1670
ANON: Allemande & Corrente, G minor (recorder, unacc.)
CAIX d'HERVELOIS: Suite, G major, Op. 6, No. 3
     ... Prelude; La Tubeuf
HANDEL: Sonata, C major, Op. 1, No. 7
W. LAWES: Courtly Masquing Ayres: Alemain; Corant; Saraband; Jigg (ARR. Dolmetsch)
     C. Dolmetsch & J. Saxby   ‡ D.LXT 2943
                                   (‡ Lon.LL 1026)

NOTE.   Recitals 1 & 2 are entered in WERM and Supp. I, respectively, under the individual contents. For convenience, they are summarised here:

RECITAL 1:   ‡ *D.LM 4518; Lon.LS 24*
COSYNS: The Goldfinch
FARNABY: Woodycock; Tower Hill
MUNDY: Robin
COUPERIN: Le Rossignol en amour
ANON: Heartes ease; The King's Morisco
HANDEL: Sonata, A minor, Op. 1, No. 4
D. PURCELL: Divisions on a ground

RECITAL 2:   ‡ *D.LM 4535; Lon.LS 278*
TELEMANN: Sonata No. 1, D minor
ANON: Fortune my foe; Nobody's Jigg; Spagnoletta; Coranto
CORELLI: Sonata, D minor, Op. 5, No. 12 (La Follia)
LOEILLET: Sonata, C minor, Op. 3, No. 5
     ... Largo & Poco allegro, only

RECORDER MUSIC OF SIX CENTURIES

NIEDHARDT von REUENTHAL: Tanzlied
ANON (XIIIth Cent.): Stantipes; Saltarello
MACHAUT: Mes espris   Ballade 3 vv.
LANDINI: Gran piant' agli occhi   Ballata 3 vv.
JOSQUIN des Prés: Si je perdu mon amy   3 vv.
SUSATO: Suite of Dances   (*Musyck Boexken*, 1551)
ANON: Three Italian Villanellas
PRAETORIUS: Two German Dances: Umzung; Springtanz
WILLAERT: Ricercare No. 10   (Apel No. 115)
BASSANO: Fantasia a tre   1585
LASSUS: Three Fantasias
BYRD: Fantasia   3 vv.
MORLEY: Fantasias: Il Grillo; Il Lamento (from *Canzonets to 2 voices*, 1595)
DIOMEDE: Chromatic Fantasia
O. GIBBONS: Two Fantasias
     Musicians' Workshop Recorder Consort
                                     ‡ CEd.CE 1018

RENAISSANCE & BAROQUE LUTE & GUITAR MUSIC

R. de VISÉE: Suite, D major & minor
NEUSIEDLER: Preambul   1536
MILAN: Pavan: 'La Belle Francescina'
WAISSEL: Phantasia
Graf v. LOGI: Partita, A minor
WEISS: Sonata No. 2, D minor . . . Prelude; Minuet; Sarabande; Minuet
DOWLAND: Galliards—Captain Digorie Piper
            The King of Denmark
            (*Lachrymae*)
     K. Scheit (guitar)   ‡ Van.BG 548

RENAISSANCE MUSIC (Choral)

DUFAY: Kyrie eleison
JOSQUIN des Prés: Tu solus
LASSUS: Adoramus te, Christe
JOSQUIN des Prés: Ave Maria
MORLEY: Agnus Dei
VICTORIA: Ave Maria
PALESTRINA: Assumpta est Maria
BERCHEM: O Jesu Christe
LASSUS: Salve Regina
MOUTON: Jocundare, Jerusalem
MORLEY: Eheu, sustulerunt Dominum
            Domine, fac mecum
VICTORIA: O vos omnes
LASSUS: Resonet in laudibus
     N.Y. Primavera Singers—Greenberg   ‡ Per.SPL 597
                                   (‡ Cpt.MC 20077)

RENAISSANCE MUSIC FOR THE LUTE

LUTE ONLY
ANON. (ed. ATTAIGNANT): Pavane; Tous mes amys
                        La Roque
     (ed. NEUSIEDLER): Preambul
WAISSEL: Polish Dance
ANON. (Straloch MS.): Scotch canaries
DOWLAND: Lachrymae Pavan
FIORENTINO: Fantasia
NIGRINO: Passamezzo in Discant

VOICE & LUTE
ANON. (ed. ATTAIGNANT): Ces fâcheux sotz
            Il me suffit de tout mes maulx
            Tant que vivray
R. JONES: Go to bed, sweet muse
NEUSIEDLER: Freundlicher Gruss
TROMBONCINO: Ben che amor
M. CARA: Io non compro
ROSSETER: When Laura smiles
     S. Bloch (mainly ☆)   ‡ *Allo. 4043*

☆ = Re-issue of a recording to be found in previous volumes.

SACRED & SECULAR SONGS FROM THE RENAISSANCE

OKEGHEM: Mass 'Sine Nomine'—Kyrie & Gloria (a)
DUFAY: In festis beatae Mariae Virginis
OBRECHT: Parce, Domine (a)
JOSQUIN des Prés: Ave Maria (a)
DASCANIO: Il Grillo
OBRECHT: La Tortorella
SCHUYT: O leyda gratiosa (a)
SWEELINCK: Madonna, con quest' occhi (a)
TOLLIUS: Della veloce sona (a)
LASSUS: Matona, mia cara (a)
    Netherlands Cha. Cho.—de Nobel ‡ Phi.N 00678R
    (2ss)
    (marked a with Palestrina on ‡ Epic.LC 3045)

SCANDINAVIAN SONGS
(renamed Songs of Norway)

TRAD.: Shepherd's Song from Hallingdal[1]
KJERULF: Synnove's Song
    She is sweet
O. BULL: The Herdgirl's Sunday
GRIEG: To Norway, Op. 58, No. 2
    And I will take a sweetheart, Op. 60, No. 5
    Return to Rundarne, Op. 33, No. 9
    I love thee, Op. 5, No. 3
    A Dream, Op. 48, No. 6
NEUPERT: Sing me home
BACKER-GRONDAHL: The Linden, Op. 23, No. 1
            East Wind[1], Op. 56, No. 2
            At Eventide, Op. 42, No. 7
ALNAES: I sat by the sea
LIE: Snow
LAMMERS: Silver
SVENDSEN: Kom, Karina, Op. 24, No. 3
    (Venetian Serenade)
JOHANSEN: Mother sings
SINDING: There cried a bird, Op. 18, No. 5
    Sylvelin, Op. 55, No. 1
    Faith, Op. 13, No. 4[1]
    We will have our land, Op. 38, No. 1
    C. Hague (T), G. Steele (pf.) ‡ ML. 7034

SEGOVIA, THE ART OF

ANON. (XVIth Cent.): Six pieces (trs. from lute tablature
    by O. Chilesotti; ARR. Segovia)
PONCE: Sonata No. 3, D minor
    Valse
    Mazurka (Homage to Tárrega)
BACH: Vln. Sonata, G minor . . . Fugue
CASTELNUOVO-TEDESCO: Tonadilla on the name of
    A. Segovia
GOMEZ CRESPO: Homage to Aguirre
LAURO: Dance from Venezuela
J. CASSADÓ: Sardana, D minor
    A. Segovia (guitar) ‡ AmD.DL 9795
    (‡ D.UAT 273594)

SEGOVIA CONCERT

MILAN: Fantasia (vihuela) 1536
R. de VISÉE: Suite, D major & minor
SOR: Variations on a theme of Mozart
HANDEL: Allegretto grazioso
    Gavotte (Aylesford pieces Nos. 3, 4, 6)
BACH: Vlc. Suite No. 3—Courante
    Vln. Sonata 2—Bourrée
M. GIULIANI: Sonata
FALLA: Homenaje
VILLA-LOBOS: Étude No. 7, E major
    ☆ A. Segovia (‡ D.UAT 273142)

SEGOVIA (AN EVENING WITH . . .)

FRESCOBALDI: Aria detta la Frescobalda; Corrente No. 1
    (Bk. 3)
CASTELNUOVO-TEDESCO: Capriccio diabolico
M. PONCE: Six Preludes, Op. posth.
RAMEAU: Platée—Menuet
TANSMAN: Cavatina—Suite 1951
MORENO TORROBA: Nocturno
    A. Segovia ‡ B.AXTL 1070
    (‡ AmD.DL 9733; SpC.CCL 35015;
                  AFest.CFR 10-729)

SEGOVIA (AN EVENING WITH . . . II)

BACH: Prelude, C minor (BWV 999)
    Sonata, E major, unacc. vln—Gavotte
    Sonata, D minor, unacc. vln—Chaconne
    Suite 3, unacc. vlc.—Bourrée I ("Loure")
SOR: Minuet, D major, Op. 11, No. 5
    Andantino, Op. 24, No. 1
    Sonata, C major, Op. 22 . . . Minuet
MENDELSSOHN: Str. Qtt. Op. 12 . . . Canzonetta
VILLA-LOBOS: Prelude No. 4, E minor
RODRIGO: Sarabanda lejana
    A. Segovia ‡ B.AXTL 1069
    (‡ AmD.DL 9751)

SEGOVIA PLAYS[2]

L. COUPERIN: Passacaglia, G minor [99]
S. L. WEISS: Suite, A minor . . . Prelude & Allemande
HAYDN: Symphony No. 96 . . . Minuet
GRIEG: Melody, A minor, Op. 47, No. 3
PONCE: Mexican Folk Song No. 3: La Valentine
    Thème varié et finale, E minor
MORENO TORROBA: Serenata burlesca
C. P. E. BACH: Siciliana, D minor
C. FRANCK: Preludio; Allegretto (from L'Organiste)
AGUIRRE: Canción
PEDRELL: Guitarreo
MALATS: Serenata
    A. Segovia (guitar) ‡ AmD.DL 9734
    (‡ D.UAT 273573)

SEGOVIA PROGRAM(ME)

MILAN: Pavana No. 1
HANDEL: Sarabande (Aylesford No. 15, excerpts, ARR.)
    Minuet (Aylesford Nos. 28 & 18 alternating)
GLUCK: Orphée: Ballet, No. 29
BACH: Vln. Sonata No. 1—Sicilienne
    Lute Suite, E minor—Bourrée
SOR: Sonata, C major, Op. 25—Minuet
CHOPIN: Prelude, A major
SCHUMANN: Romanze—Flutenreicher Ebro
PAGANINI, ARR. PONCE: Andantino variato
BRAHMS: Waltz, Op. 39, No. 2
MORENO TORROBA: Madronos
VILLA-LOBOS: Prelude No. 1, E minor
    ☆ A. Segovia ‡ B.AXTL 1060

SEGOVIA RECITAL

MUDARRA: Romanesca 1546
WEISS: Suite, A minor—Prelude, Ballet, Gigue
BACH: Vlc. Suite No. 1, G major—Prelude
    Vlc. Suite No. 6, D major—Gavottes
SOR: Allegro (from Sonata, Op. 25)
MENDELSSOHN: Song without words, Op. 19, No. 6
SCHUBERT: Pf. Sonata, Op. 78—Minuet
MORENO TORROBA: Sonatina (Allegretto, Andante,
    Allegro)
ALBENIZ: Asturias (Leyenda) S.E.5
    ☆ A. Segovia—(‡ D.UAT 273141)

SEVEN CENTURIES OF SACRED MUSIC

☆ Y. Tinayre (T) ‡ AmD.DL 9653/4
    (4ss) (set DX 120)
‡ DL 9653 ANON. (XIIIth Cent.): Agniaus douz
    LÉONIN: Organum—Deum time
             Organum—Haec dies
    PÉROTIN: Conductus—Beata viscera
    ANON. (XIIIth Cent.): Ave, gloriosa Mater
        Salvatoris (attrib. Franco)
    ANON. (XIVth Cent.): Sancto Lorenzo, martyr
        d'amore
    PAUMANN: Allmächtiger Gott (Benedicite)
    DUFAY: Alma Redemptoris Mater
        Vergine bella
    ATTEY: Sweet was the song (Ayres, Vol. I)
    ANON. (XIVth Cent.): Ave Mater
    ANON. (XIIIth Cent.): Melisma—Ille
    BENET: Pleni sunt coeli
    F. della TORRE: Adoramos te, Señor
    GOMBERT: In Festis B.V.M.
    SCHÜTZ: Herr, unser Herrscher (Psalm 8)

---

[1] These titles have disappeared from later lists, though in the original announcements.
[2] These detailed contents, taken from Notes, were received too late for the full identifications to be inserted in the Composer listings in all cases.

SEVEN CENTURIES OF SACRED MUSIC (*continued*)

♯ DL 9654
GOMBERT: Confitemini Domino
J. S. BACH: Mass, A major—Qui tollis
H. ALBERT: Ach, lasst uns Gott
HAMMERSCHMIDT: Sei nun wieder zufrieden
J. W. FRANCK: Jesus neigt sein Haupt
J. S. BACH: Cantata No. 85—aria
H. ALBERT: Auf! mein Geist
F. COUPERIN: Ostende Domine
MOZART: Mass, C major, K 66—aria
    Litany, K243—aria
    Vespers, K339—Laudate Dominum
    Regina Coeli, K108—aria
PERGOLESI: Laudate Pueri—A solis ortu
HANDEL: Messiah—Nos. 29 & 30

SEVENTEENTH CENTURY ORGAN MUSIC

M. PRAETORIUS: Hymns: A solis ortus cardine
    Alvus tumescit virginis
C. ERBACH: Ricercare IX toni (Sopra le fughe *Io son ferito lasso* e *Vestiva i coll*)
FRESCOBALDI: Toccata prima (Bk. I)
T. MERULA: Sonata chromatica (Torchi, *L'arte musicale*, III)
FROBERGER: Toccata, No. 11, E minor
J. K. KERLL: Passacaglia No. 18
    Toccata cromatica No. 4, con durezze e ligature (DDT.Bay.II-ii)
S. A. SCHERER: Toccata 1664 (Guilmant *Archives*, VIII-98)
  G. Leonhardt   **♯ Van.BG 529**
  [organ of Stiftskirche, Klosterneuberg]

SHAKESPEARE SONGS & LUTE SOLOS

LUTE SOLOS
VAUTOR: Almaine
DOWLAND: Tarleton's riserrection
    Fantasia (Curwen No. 15)
    Toy—The Shoemaker's wife
CUTTING: Walsingham Variations

SONGS
MORLEY: It was a lover & his lass (As You Like It)
    O mistress mine (Twelfth Night)
ANON.: Sing willow, willow, willow (Othello)
WILSON: Take, O take those lips away (Measure for Measure)
R. JOHNSON: Where the bee sucks
    Full fathom five (The Tempest)
ANON: Callino castore me! (King Henry V)
    Peg-a-Ramsay (Twelfth Night)
    Greensleeves (Merry Wives of Windsor)
  A. Deller (C-T), D. Dupré (lute) **♯ G.ALP 1265**

SHAKESPEARE SONGS, VOL. III[1]

R. JONES: Farewell dear love 1600 (quoted in *As you like it*)
R. JOHNSON: Where the bee sucks (pub. 1660) (*The Tempest*)
PURCELL: Flout 'em and scout 'em (*The Tempest*)
J. VERNON: When that I was and a little tiny boy (*Twelfth Night*)
J. BANNISTER: Come unto these yellow sands (*The Tempest*)
R. JOHNSON: Full fathom five (*The Tempest*)
L. RICHMOND: Tell me, where is fancy bred? (*Merchant of Venice*)
ARNE: While you here do snoring lie (*The Tempest*)
    Hymen's song (*As you like it*)
J. HILTON Jnr.: What shall he have (*As You Like It*)
  L. Chelsi (B), pf. & lute **♯ MTR.MLO 1015**

XVIth & XVIIth CENTURY SONGS

FRENCH
P. ATTAIGNANT (ed.): Tant que vivrai
J-B. BESARD: Beaux yeux; En quelque lieu
    La voilà la nacelle
P. CERTON: Psalm 130
T. CRÉQUILLON: Quand me souvient
A. le ROY: Psalm 50
R. de VISÉE: Suite, D minor (lute solo)

ENGLISH
J. BARTLETT: What thing is love
    When from my love
    A pretty duck there was
J. DOWLAND: Flow my tears
    I saw my lady weep
    Fantasia (lute solo)
T. MORLEY: It was a lover and his lass
F. PILKINGTON: Rest, sweet nymphs
  ☆ H. Cuénod (T), H. Leeb (lute) **♯ Nix.WLP 5085**
  [The French side also on **V♯** *Sel.LAP 1021*]

SONATAS OF THE XVIIth & XVIIIth CENTURIES

KUHNAU: Sonata quarta, C minor (*Frische Clavierfrüchte*, 1692)
PASQUINI: Suonata di primo tuono (Torchi, Vol. III)
D. SCARLATTI: Sonata, F major (L. 384)
P. D. PARADIES: Sonata No. 10, D major c. 1744 (pub. 1754)
C. P. E. BACH: Sonata, C minor (W 65-31)
HAYDN: Sonata No. 34 (2), E minor
  D. Handman (pf.) **♯ LOL.OL 50078**

(THE) SONGS OF ENGLAND

PURCELL: Nymphs and shepherds φ
    Fairest isle φ
Arr. WHITTAKER: Bobby Shaftoe
Arr. VAUGHAN WILLIAMS: I will give my love an apple φ
MORLEY: Now is the month of maying φ
Arr. BRITTEN: Sweet Polly Oliver
Arr. GRAINGER: The Sprig of thyme
HEAD: Foxgloves (Hardy)
HOPKINS: A melancholy song (D. Kilham Roberts)
HORN: Cherry ripe (Herrick)
ANON., ARR. DOLMETSCH: Lye still my deare
ARNE: Where the bee sucks φ
    O Ravishing delight φ
VAUGHAN WILLIAMS: The new ghost (Shove)
HOWELLS: Gavotte (Newbolt)
QUILTER: Love's philosophy, Op. 3, No. 1 (Shelley)
  J. Vyvyan (S), E. Lush (pf.) **♯ D.LXT 2797**
          (**♯** Lon.LL 806)
  [Items marked φ also on **♯** *D.LW 5102; Lon.LD 9113*]

SONGS OF THE RENAISSANCE
(Germany—Austria)

LASSUS: Ich weiss nur ein Meidlein
    Wohl kommt der May 1583
HASSLER: Nun fanget an . . .
    Jungfrau, dein schön Gestalt
    Tantzen und Springen
SENFL: Das Geläut' zu Speyer
    Ach Elslein, liebes Elslein
SCANDELLI: Ein Hennlein weiss
M. FRANCK: Ich habs gewagt
H. FINCK: Ach herzigs Herz
L. LEMLIN: Der Gutzgauch
C. OTHMAYER: Es steht ein Lind
M. PRAETORIUS: Wach auf, mit heller Stimm
L. LECHNER: Gott b'hüte dich
ECCARD: Hans und Grete
VULPIUS: Hinunter est der Sonnenschein
FRIDERICI: Wir lieben sehr im Herzen
    Einstmals das Kind Kupido
  Vienna Academy Cho.—Gillesberger **♯ SPA. 55**

SPANISH GUITAR MUSIC

M. PONCE: Sonata meridional
J. GOMEZ CRESPO: Norteña
MORENO TORROBA: Suite Castellana
    ... Arada & Fandanguillo
TURINA: Fandanguillo
  ☆ A. Segovia   **♯ AmC.ML 473**
  (*Castelnuovo-Tedesco: Concerto*)

SPANISH KEYBOARD MUSIC

(refs. to the Nin collections: Vol. I, 16 Sonatas; Vol. II, 17 Sonatas & Pieces; pub. Eschig)

SOLER: Sonata, C sharp minor φ (N.I—No. 2)
    Sonata, D major   φ (N.I—No. 5)
ANGLÈS: Aria, D minor   φ (N.II—No. 9) c. 1770
M. ALBENIZ: Sonata, D major φ (N.I—No. 13) c. 1790
CANTALLOS: Sonata, C minor φ (N.I—No. 14) c. 1795
  F. Blumenthal (pf.) (Vol. I) **♯ D.LXT 2805**
           (**♯** Lon.LL 769)
  (*Portuguese Keyboard Music*)
  (Items marked φ also on **♯** *Lon.LD 9150*)

ANGLÈS: Adagietto, B flat major (N.II—No. 7)
    Fugatto, B flat major (N.II—No. 10)
SOLER: Sonata, G minor   (N.I—No. 11)
FERRER: Sonata, D major (N.I—No. 16) c. 1814
FREIXANET: Sonata, A major (N.II—No. 5)
  F. Blumenthal (pf.) (Vol. II) **♯ D.LXT 5218**
           (**♯** Lon.LL 1194)
  (*Portuguese Keyboard Music*)

(*continued on next page*)

---

[1] Vol. II (**♯** MTR.MLO 1010) is listed in Supp. II under individual titles : *see* Arne, J. C. Smith.

SPANISH KEYBOARD MUSIC (*continued*)

CABEZON: Diferencias—El Canto del caballero	
CASANOVAS: Sonata, F major	(N.II—No. 6) c. 1770
M. ALBENIZ: Sonata, D major	(N.I—No. 13) c. 1790
ANGLÈS: Aria, D minor	(N.II—No. 9) c. 1770
J. GALLES: Sonata, F minor	(N.II—No. 17) c.1800
FREIXANET: Sonata, A major	(N.II—No. 5)
V. RODRIGUEZ: Sonata, F major	(N.II—No. 1) 1744
SOLER: Sonatas—D major	(N.I—No. 5)
G minor	(*ibid.* No. 8)
D minor	(*ibid.* No. 4)
F sharp minor	(*ibid.* No. 6)
F sharp major	(*ibid.* No. 12)
J. Falgarona (pf.)	♯ AmVox.PL 8340

M. ALBENIZ: Sonata, D major	(N.I—No. 13) c. 1770
ANGLÈS: Adagietto, B flat major	(N.II—No. 7) c. 1770
Sonata, F major	(N.II—No. 8)
Aria, D minor	(N.II—No. 9) c. 1770
CASANOVAS: Sonata, F major	(N.II—No. 6) c. 1770
J. GALLES: Sonatas: F minor	(N.II—No. 17) c. 1800
C minor	(N.II—No. 13) c.1800
FREIXANET: Sonata, A major	(N.II—No. 5)
F. RODRIGUEZ: Rondo, B flat major (N.II—No. 11)	
	c. 1795
CANTALLOS: Sonata, C minor	(N.I—No. 14) c. 1810
B. SERRANO: Sonata, B flat major	(N.I—No. 15) c. 1810
H. FERNANDEZ: Sonata, C minor	
F. Valenti (hpsi.)	♯ Nix.WLP 5312
	(♯ West.WL 5312)

SOLER: (*q.v.*) SONATAS: C sharp minor, G minor,	
D major, F sharp minor, F sharp major	
ANGLÈS: Aria, D minor (Nin II-9) c. 1770	
CANTALLOS: Sonata, C minor (Nin I-14) c. 1795	
M. ALBENIZ: Sonata, D major (Nin I-13) c. 1790	
☆ H. Boschi (pf.)	V♯ CdM.LDY 8081

SPANISH & PORTUGUESE MASTERS OF THE HARPSICHORD

SEE: Les clavecinistes espagnols et portugais, *above*

SPANISH MUSIC OF XVIth-XXth CENTURIES

MILAN: 2 Pavanes
SANZ: Folía (unspec.)
SOR: 2 Menuets & Rondo
TARREGA: Alborada
    Tremolo Study
I. ALBENIZ: Asturias (Leyenda)
    Malagueña, Op. 71, No. 6
GRANADOS: Danza espanola, No. 10
FALLA: Homenaje, pour le tombeau de Debussy
TURINA: Fandanguillo
ESPLA: 2 Levantines
MORENO TORROBA: Melodia
RODRIGO: En los trigales
    N. Yepes (guitar)   ♯ D.LXT 2974
        (♯ FST 153076; Lon.LL 1042)

SPANISH MUSIC FROM THE COURT OF FERDINAND & ISABELLA (c. 1500)

[Numbers refer to items in Angles: *La Música en la Corte de los Reyes Catholicos*]

ANON.: Calabaza, no sé, buen amor [251] insts.
    Pase el agua, ma julieta dama [363] 3 viols & minstrel's hp.
    Dios te salva [86] F. Mertens (T), 4 vv. & insts.
    Desciende al valle, Niña [206] M. Ceuppens (S) & lute
J. del ENCINA: Ninguno cierre las puertas [167] 4 vv.
    Ay triste [293] 3 vv.
    Un sañosa porfia [126] L. Devos (T), 4 vv., lute
    Gasajemonos de hucia [165] 4 vv.
    Fata la parte [421] insts.
    Triste España [83] L. Devos, 4 vv., insts.
    Caldero y llave, Madona [249] insts.
    Hermitaño quiero ser [313] 2 vv., insts.
    Hoy comanos y bebamos 4 vv., insts.
G. MUÑOZ: Pues bien para esta [389] 4 vv.
VILCHES: Ya cantan los gallos [155] J. Deroubaix (A), insts.
J. PONCE: De la Resurreccion 4 vv.
A. de RIBERA: Por unos puertes [107] minstrel's harp
LUCHAS: A la caza [330] 4 vv.
    Pro Musica Antiqua—Cape   ♯ EMS. 219
        (♯ BàM.LD 026)

SPANISH RENAISSANCE MUSIC

VASQUEZ: Zagaleje
MORALES: Inter vestibulum
CABEZON: Canción
GUERRERO: Villanesca
MORATA: Endécha
LASERNA: El cordero perdido
VICTORIA: Officium defunctorum
    Pamplona Cho.—Morondo   ♯ Sel.LPG 8738

SPANISH TONADILLAS

LASERNA: Tiranilla del Tripili
    El cordero perido
ANON: Jacara
ESTEVE: Tirana del Zarandillo
FERRER: El remedo del Gato
    Pamplona Cha. Cho.—Morondo V♯ Sel.LAP 1078[1]
        (in ♯ West.WL 5350)

SPANISH SONGS

FALLA: Canciones populares españolas
MOMPOU: Combat del somni (Janés) (3 songs)
PITTALUGA: Romanza de Solita
TURINA: Farruca
    Canto a Sevilla . . . La Giralda
OBRADORS: Corazon porque pasais
    El majo celoso
    Con amores, la mi madre
    2 Cantares populares
    El Vito
MONTSALVATGE: Canciones negras:
    Nana para dormir a un negrito; Canto negro
    N. Merriman (M-S), G. Moore (pf.)   ♯ C.CX 1243
        (♯ FCX 392; Angel. 35208)

SYMPHONIES IN BRIEF

[For contents, see WERM Supp. I, p. 860]
    ☆ Col. Sym.—O'Connell (♯ AmC.RL 3108)

(THE) TRIUMPHS OF ORIANA   Madrigals 1601

COMPLETE RECORDING
D. NORCOME: With angel's face and brightness
J. MUNDY: Lightly she whipped
E. GIBBONS: Long live fair Oriana
J. BENNET: All creatures now are merry-minded
J. HILTON: Fair Oriana, beauty's queen
G. MARSON: The nymphs and shepherds danced
R. CARLTON: Calm was the air
J. HOLMES: Thus Bonny-boots the birthday celebrated
R. NICHOLSON: Sing, shepherds all
T. TOMKINS: The fauns and satyrs tripping
M. CAVENDISH: Come, gentle swains
W. COBBOLD: With wreaths of rose and laurel
T. MORLEY: Arise, awake, awake
J. FARMER: Fair nymph, I heard one telling
J. WILBYE: The lady Oriana
T. HUNT: Hark! did ye ever hear
T. WEELKES: As Vesta was from Latmos hill
J. MILTON: Fair Orian in the morn
E. GIBBONS: Round about her charret
G. KIRBYE: With angel's face and brightness
R. JONES: Fair Oriana, seeming to wink at folly
J. LISLEY: Fair Cytherea presents her doves
T. MORLEY: Hard by a crystal fountain
E. JOHNSON: Come, blessed bird
    Randolph Singers—Randolph   ♯ Nix.WLP 6212-1/2
    (3ss—*below*)   (♯ West. set WAL 212)

OTHER ORIANA MADRIGALS[2]
T. BATESON: Hark! hear you not (XXI)
    When Oriana walked to take the air (XXI)[3]
G. CROCE: Hard by a crystal fountain[4]
M. EAST: Hence, stars! too dim of light (XXXII)[3]
T. GREAVES: Long have the shepherds sung this song (XXXVI)
    Sweet nymphs that trip along (XXXVI)
F. PILKINGTON: When Oriana walked to take the air (XXV)
T. VAUTOR: Shepherds and nymphs that trooping (XXXIV)
    Randolph Singers—Randolph   ♯ Nix.WLP 6212-2
    (*above*, s. 3)   (in ♯ West. set WAL 212)

---

[1] Apparently the *Sel.* disc was never on sale, as the no. has been re-used (see Mozart: Divertimenti).
[2] The roman figures refer to volumes of *The English Madrigal School*.
[3] These madrigals arrived too late for inclusion in the original series.
[4] Originally *Ove tra l'herb'e i fiori*, from *Il Trionfo di Dori* (1592); translated thus in *Musica Transalpina* (1597)

TYROLESE XVIIIth CENTURY ORCHESTRAL MUSIC

FALK: Partita, D major *c.* 1770
SYLVA: Symphony, D major 1775
HAINDL: Symphony, G major 1765
MADLSEDER: Symphony, D major 1770
PALUSELLI: Divertimento, F major, oboe & orch. 1790
    F. Wächter (ob.) & Vienna Orch.—Adler ♯ SPA. 52

VIEUX NOËLS DE FRANCE

DANDRIEU: Où s'en vont ces gays bergers
BALBÂTRE: Noël bourguignon
DORNEL: Je me suis levé
DAQUIN: Noëls: No. 1, D minor; No. 8, G major
    N. Pierront   **V♯** *Lum.LD 1-105*
    [St.-Merry Organ]

VOCAL RE-ISSUES (Summary)

"HISTORIC" & ACOUSTIC "Recital" Recordings
    [Including one instrumental disc]
        (*Some items are electric*)

Discs containing collections of items from individual works will be found under:
BELLINI (Norma), BOITO (Nerone), DONIZETTI (Favorita), GLUCK, GOUNOD (Faust), HANDEL (Opera & Oratorio), LEONCAVALLO, MASCAGNI, VERDI (Ballo), WAGNER (Götterdämmerung), etc.

♯ **ABCD. 1**   "Little-known Operas by Great Composers"
        (Bohème (Leoncavallo), Manru, Don César de Bazan, Nerone, Maria di Rudenz, Maria di Rohan, Esclaramonde, Alessandro Stradella)

♯ *AudA.LP 0079* "Musicians of the Past" (Instrumental Acoustic re-issue)
        Violinists: J. Joachim, F. Drdla, P. Sarasate (playing Brahms, Bruch, Sarasate & Bach)

♯ **AudR.LPA 2340** Galvany, Marchesi, Caruso, Patti, McCormack, Fremstad, Plançon
        (Barbiere, Zauberflöte, Dido, Huguenots, Tosca, Aida, Walküre, Le Cid, & songs)

♯ **CEd. set 7002** F. de Lucia Operatic Recital
    (4ss)   (Barbiere, A. Lecouvreur, Iris, Fedora, Mignon, Elisir d'amore, Sonnambula, Bohème, Don Pasquale, Faust, Manon Lescaut, Pêcheurs de Perles, Mefistofele, Guarany, Rigoletto, Carmen, Pagliacci, Traviata, & 2 Neapolitan Songs)

♯ **CEd.CE 7010** H. Roswaenge Operatic Recital (*Ger*)
        (Vêpres siciliennes, Huguenots, Turandot, Postillon de Longjumeau, Aida, Madama Butterfly, Traviata, Don Giovanni, Carmen, Trovatore)

☆ ♯ *Cum.CE 185* J. McCormack Operatic Recital
        (Carmen, Favorita, Tosca, Cavalleria, Aida, Rigoletto)

☆ ♯ **Cum.CE 186** Lilli Lehman Operatic Recital
        (Entführung, Don Giovanni, Traviata, Joshua, Norma, Robert le Diable)

☆ ♯ **Cum.CE 187** R. Tauber Operatic Recital
        (Bohème, Butterfly, Mignon, Bartered Bride, Aida, Traviata, Rosenkavalier)

☆ ♯ **Cum.CE 188** Mozart Operatic Arias
        (D'Andrade, Renaud, Slezak, Ivogün, Sammarco, etc.)

♯ **Ete. 492** Famous Italian Tenors
        (Luisa Miller, Don Pasquale, Otello, Don Carlos, Fedora, Nerone, Paride ed Elena, Puritani, Rigoletto)

♯ **Ete. 493** L. Slezak Song Recital
        (Schubert, Schumann, R. Strauss, Wolf)

♯ **Ete. 494** Great Operatic Finales
        (Carmen, Tote Stadt, Tosca, Huguenots, Otello, Thaïs)

♯ *Ete. 496* J. McCormack Recital " No. 2 "
        (Carmen; & Songs)

♯ **Ete. 498** J. Schwarz Operatic Recital
        (Zar und Zimmermann, Guillaume Tell, The Demon, Rheingold, Rigoletto, & Songs)

♯ **Ete. 499** L. Slezak Wagner Arias
        (Lohengrin, Meistersinger, Tannhäuser)

♯ **Ete. 701** R. Tauber Operatic Recital No. 2
        (Eugene Oniegin, Kienzl: Die Kuhreigen, Walküre, Paganini, Rigoletto; & Weingartner: Liebesfeier)

♯ **Ete. 702** Lilli Lehmann Operatic Recital
        (Don Giovanni, Cosi, Figaro, Traviata, Huguenots, Walküre; Schubert & Beethoven songs)

♯ **Ete. 703** Verdi Tenor Arias
        (Otello, Rigoletto, Traviata, Trovatore, Ballo, Requiem)

♯ **Ete. 704** Nerone "Highlights", *q.v.*

♯ **Ete. 705** G. Zenatello Operatic Recital
        (Otello, Pagliacci, Bohème, Manon Lescaut, Traviata)

♯ **Ete. 706** Norma "Highlights", *q.v.*

♯ **Ete. 707** Rossini Opera Recital
        (G. Ritter-Ciampi, M. Battistini, L. Slezak, A. Didur, etc.)

♯ **Ete. 708** Famous French Tenors
        (C. Vezzani, S. Rayner, P. Franz, Escalais, Campagnola, C. Friant) (most are electric)

♯ **Ete. 709** M. Battistini Recital
        (Otello, Africaine, Trovatore, Tannhäuser, Damnation de Faust, Hamlet & Tosti Songs)

♯ **Ete. 710** A. Pertile Operatic Recital
        (Pagliacci, Adriana Lecouvreur, Mefistofele, Trovatore, Butterfly, Manon Lescaut, Turandot, Lohengrin; & Denza: Song)

♯ **Ete. 711** G. Anselmi Operatic Recital
        (Luisa Miller, Mefistofele, Favorita, Manon, Fedora, Marcella, Serse, Manon)

♯ **Ete. 712** R. Tauber Operatic Recital
        (Pagliacci, Turandot, Tosca, Tiefland, Meistersinger)

♯ **Ete. 714** Spanish Tenors
♯ **Ete. 715** F. de Lucia Recital
        (Contents data not to hand)

♯ *FRP. 1* Battistini, Escalais, Lilli Lehmann, de Luca, Bassi, McCormack, Kurz, Muzio, Schipa, Arnoldson, Butt, O'Sullivan
        (Otello, Robert le Diable, Traviata, Falstaff, Siberia, Rigoletto, Ballo, Gianni Schicchi, Tosca, Manon, Lucrezia Borgia)

♯ *FRP. 2* Renaud, Martinelli, Ponselle, Didur, Campanari, Slezak, Mardones, Nordica
        (Favorita, Bohème, Trovatore, Freischütz, Carmen, Faust, Huguenots, Hunyadi Lászlo)

♯ *FRP. 3* Pertile, Fremstad, Belhomme, Bressler-Gianoli, Scotti, Ancona, Tetrazzini, Sammarco, Caruso, Plançon, Raisa, Stracciari
        (Trovatore, Walküre, Philémon et Baucis, Carmen, Don Giovanni, Huguenots, Sonnambula, Favorita, Vepres siciliennes)

♯ *G.FKLP 7001* E. Caruso recital "No. 1"
  (*QKLP 501*) (Serse, Largo; Massenet: Élégie; Kahn: Ave Maria; Sullivan: The lost chord; & O sole mio, Because, For you alone, Sei morta. . . .)

♯ *G.FJLP 5009* E. Caruso recital "No. 2"
  (*QJLP 105*) (Elisir d'amore, Gioconda, Africaine, Bohème, Juive, Aida, Rigoletto, Carmen, Pagliacci, Pêcheurs de Perles)

♯ *G.FJLP 5004* "Golden Age of the Metropolitan Opera"
  QJLP 104; —Bori, Calvé, Caruso, Farrar, Galli-Curci, Journet, Ponselle, Ruffo, Schipa, Tetrazzini, Chaliapin Rethberg, McCormack
  Vic.LCT 1006) (Bohème, Carmen, Rigoletto, Tosca, Louise, Huguenots, Ernani, A. Chénier, Don Giovanni, Sonnambula, Barbiere, Aida)

♯ *G.FJLP 5010* "Famous Operatic Duets"—Bori, McCormack, Caruso, Ruffo, Scotti, Farrar, Ponselle, Telva, Gigli, Martinelli
  (♯ QJLP 101;
  Vic.LCT 1004) (Bohème, Otello, Forza, Faust, Norma, Gioconda, Aida)

(*continued on next page*)

☆ = Re-issue of a recording to be found in previous volumes.

VOCAL RE-ISSUES (Summary) (*continued*)

♯ **G.FJLP 5035** **Vanni-Marcoux Operatic Recital**[1]
(Don Carlos, Hamlet, Cléopatre, Boris, Jongleur de Notre-Dame, Mignon, Louise, Don Quichotte, & Laparra: Habanera)

♯ **G.QALP 10089** **T. Dal Monte Operatic Recital**[1]
(Linda di Chamounix, Don Pasquale, Mignon, Traviata, Norma, etc.)

♯ **HRS. 3001** **V. Maurel** (Falstaff & Songs); **R. Storchio** (Linda di Chamounix, Don Pasquale, Fra Diavolo)

♯ **HRS. 3002** **L. Nicoletti-Korman, G. Borgatti & Mme. Moga-Georgescu**
(Don Carlos, Macbeth, Otello, Walküre, Zauberflöte, Marina, Barbiere)

♯ **HRS. 3003** **G. Forst, L. Demuth, H. Winkelmann, H. Jadlowker**
(Mignon, Tiefland, Wintermärchen, Trovatore, Idomeneo, Cosi, Paride ed Elena)

♯ **HRS. 3004** **G. Kaschmann, E. Carelli, G. B. de Negri, F. Toresella, G. Gravina**
(Medici, Don Carlos, Siberia, Norma, Otello, Puritani, Robert le Diable)

♯ **HRS. 3005** **A. Bassi & T. Ruffo**
(Manon Lescaut, Panizza: Aurora, Pagliacci, Fedora, Don Carlos, Trovatore, Traviata)

♯ **HRS. 3006** **E. Schmedes, S. Kurz & H. Schlusnus**
(Iphigénie en Tauride, Dalibor, Otello, Evangelimann, Walküre, Rigoletto, Zauberflöte, Trovatore)

♯ **HRS. 3007** **E. Burzio & A. Pertile**
(Favorita, Gioconda, Nerone, Iris)

♯ **HRS. 3008** **E. Albani, E. Calvé, H. Albers, E. Clément**
(Serse, Contes d'Hoffmann, Favorita, Manon, Leroux: Le Chemineau; & Songs)

♯ **IRCC.L 7006**[2] **"Echoes of the Golden Age of Opera"**
(Fille du Régiment, Traviata, Pagliacci, Huguenots, Tristan, Lohengrin, Walküre, Siegfried, Faust, Africaine)

☆ ♯ **LI.TWV 91053**[3] **"The Duse of Song", Vol. II (C. Muzio)**
(Ernani, Trovatore, Mefistofele, Mme. Sans-Gêne, Pagliacci, Bianca e Fernando, Guillaume Tell, Butterfly, Tosca)

♯ **Od.ODX 115** **N. Vallin Operatic Recital**
(Manon, Werther, Hérodiade)

♯ **Od.ODX 126** **C. Vezzani Operatic Recital**
(Richard Coeur-de-Lion, Werther, Manon, Otello, Maître Pathelin, Pardon de Ploërmel, Africaine, Carmen, La Juive, Pagliacci, Mireille; Gounod & Schubert)

♯ **Od.ODX 127** **A. Pertile Operatic Recital**
(Pagliacci, Nerone, Ballo, Gioconda, Bohème, Tosca, Iris, Rigoletto, & Songs)

♯ **Od.ODX 135** **A. Pernet Operatic Recital**
(Barbiere, Lakmé, Philémon et Baucis, Faust, Mireille, Contes d'Hoffmann, Manon, Don Quichotte, Boris)

♯ **Od.ODX 136** **M. Villabella Operatic Recital**[1]
(Dame blanche, Lakmé, Roi d'Ys, Grisélidis, Jongleur de Notre-Dame, Contes d'Hoffmann, Barbiere, & Messager: Basoche & Fortunio)

♯ **Od.ODX 138** **C. Supervia Operatic Recital**[1]
(Barbiere, Italiana, Cenerentola)

♯ **Pat.PCX 5006** **A. Endrèze Operatic Recital**
(Tannhäuser, Sigurd, Roi Arthus, Favorita, Guillaume Tell, Faust, & Magnard: Guercoeur)

♯ **Roc.R 1** **Kurz, Santley, Herzog, Litvinnem, Marconi, Chaliapin**
(Figaro, Robert le Diable, Samson et Dalila, Lucia)

♯ **Roy. 1555** **J. McCormack Recital**
(Rigoletto, Tosca, Aida, Bohème, Favorita, Carmen, Pagliacci, Cavalleria Rusticana; & Songs)

♯ **SBDH.GL 1** **"Great Tenors of the Golden Age"**
(Macbeth, Lodoletta, Puritani, Faust, G. Tell, Trovatore, A. Chénier, Contes d'Hoffmann, Otello, Africaine, Puritani, Zaza, Duca d'Alba)

♯ **SBDH.LLP 3** **J. Mardones Recital**
(Salvator Rosa, Nabucco, Étoile du Nord, Faust, La Juive, Carmen, Mefistofele, Barbiere)

♯ **SBDH.LLP 4** **F. Chaliapin Recital**
(Lucrezia Borgia, Norma, Ernani, Robert le Diable, Faust, Mefistofele, Barbiere, Lakmé)

♯ **SBDH.LLP 5** **B. Gigli Recital**
(Faust, Mefistofele, Gioconda, Bohème, Amico Fritz, Favorita, Pecheurs de Perles)

♯ **SBDH.LLP 6** **P. Plançon Recital**
(Le Caïd, Étoile du Nord, Zauberflöte, Le Châlet, Pardon de Ploërmel, & Songs)

♯ **SBDH.LLP 7** **T. Ruffo Recital**
(Patrie, The Demon, Cristoforo Colombo, Gioconda, Africaine, Ernani, Siberia)

♯ **SBDH.LLP 8** **G. Zenatello Recital**
(Guarany, Faust, Siberia, Andrea Chénier, Mefistofele, Traviata, Pagliacci, Forza)

♯ **SBDH.LPG 4** **G. Martinelli Recital**
(Trovatore, Ernani, Ballo, Traviata, Don Carlos, Aida, Bohème, E. Oniegin, G. Tell, Faust, Carmen, Africaine, Martha)

♯ **SBDH.LPG 5** **M. Journet Recital**
(Robert le Diable, Lakmé, Zauberflöte, Cléopatre, Nerone, Sonnambula, Le Châlet, Don Carlos, Philémon et Baucis, Puritani, Lucia, Favorita, Damnation de Faust)

♯ **SBDH.PL 1** **"Eight Famous Basses of the Past"**
(Lakmé, Mefistofele; Flégier: Le Cor (Plançon); Favorita, La Juive, Huguenots, Nabucco, Fidelio)

♯ **Sca. 801** **F. Chaliapin Operatic Arias**
(P. Igor, Sadko, The Demon, Life for the Tsar, Faust, Lucrezia Borgia, Sonnambula, Norma, Ernani, Mefistofele)

♯ **Sca. 802** **R. Stracciari Operatic Recital**
(Africaine, Favorita, Pagliacci, Barbiere, Ernani, Don Carlos, Due Foscari, Ballo, Rigoletto, Trovatore, Vêpres siciliennes)

♯ **Sca. 803** **R. Ponselle Operatic Recital**
(Manon Lescaut, Guillaume Tell, Norma, Trovatore, Tosca, Butterfly, Bohème, Forza, Aida, Gioconda, Maritana)

♯ **Sca. 804** **E. Destinn Operatic Recital**
(Freischütz, Cavalleria, Aida, Robert le Diable, Tosca, Pagliacci, Fliegende Holländer, Russalka; & Songs)

♯ **Sca. 805** **T. Schipa Recital**
(Traviata, Don Pasquale, Tosca, Sonnambula, Pagliacci, Cavalleria Rusticana, Barbiere, Falstaff, Zaza, Bohème, Rigoletto)

♯ **Sca. 806** **M. Barrientos (S) & H. Lazaro (T)**
(Trovatore, Puritani, Pagliacci, Rigoletto, Tosca, Sonnambula, Fra Diavolo, Traviata; & Songs)

♯ **Sca. 807** **F. Chaliapin Recital**
(Songs by Massenet, Rubinstein, Tchaikovsky, etc.)

♯ **Sca. 808** **R. Raisa & G. Russ Operatic Recitals**
(Mefistofele, Butterfly, Otello, Forza, Cavalleria, Aida, Norma, Don Carlos, Traviata, Fedora)

♯ **Sca. 809** **H. Rehkemper Recital**
(Figaro, Zauberflöte, Rigoletto, Ballo in Maschera, Trovatore; & Songs by Schubert, Schumann & Wolf)

♯ **Sca. 810** **J. Mardones Operatic Recital**
(Huguenots, Robert le Diable, Simone Boccanegra, Ernani, La Juive, Salvator Rosa, Bohème, Mefistofele, Faust, Barbiere; & Rossini: Stabat Mater)

[1] Most are electrical recordings.
[2] From Mapleson cylinders.
[3] From Edison & Pathé hill & dale recordings. Withdrawn almost immediately after issue.

VOCAL RE-ISSUES (Summary) (*continued*)

‡ Sca. 811   **A. Bonci Operatic Recital**
(Puritani, Elisir d'Amore, Favorita, Rigoletto, Martha, Paride ed Elena, Lucia, A. Chénier, Don Pasquale, Bohème)

‡ Sca. 812   **T. Ruffo & G. de Luca Recitals**
(Hamlet, Traviata, Faust, Zaza, Barbiere, Don Carlos, Chatterton, Bohème, Don Pasquale, Rigoletto, Figaro, Favorita, Linda di Chamounix)

‡ Sca. 813   **C. Boninsegna Recital**
(Aida, Ernani, Semiramide, Gioconda, Manon Lescaut, Norma, Trovatore, Ballo in Maschera, Cavalleria Rusticana, A. Chénier & Africaine)

‡ Sca. 814   **F. de Lucia Recital**
(Barbiere, Don Pasquale, Pagliacci, Mignon, Pêcheurs de Perles, Traviata, Manon, Cav. Rusticana, Elisir d'Amore, Luisa Miller, Huguenots)

‡ Sca. 815   **M. Ivogün Recital**
(Traviata, Barbiere, Don Pasquale, Lucia, Huguenots; & Songs)

‡ Sca. 816   **G. Anselmi Recital**
(Don Pasquale, Favorita, Luisa Miller, Mignon, Manon Lescaut, Bohème, Gioconda, Manon, Pagliacci, Lucia, Manon)

‡ Sca. 817   **S. Kurz Recital**
(Königin von Saba, Ballo in Maschera, Étoile du Nord, Lakmé, Mignon, Zauberflöte, Ernani, Don Pasquale, Jolie Fille de Perth, Pardon de Ploërmel, Jocelyn; & Songs)

‡ Sca. 818   **G. Zenatello Recital**
(Ballo in Maschera, Gioconda, Mefistofele, Aïda, Guarany, Pagliacci, Otello, & Franchetti: Figlia de Joris)

‡ Sca. 819   [1] **S. Onegin Recital**
(Rinaldo, Prophete, Orphée et Eurydice, Gioconda, Rheingold, Tristan, Carmen, Samson et Dalila; & Songs)

‡ Sca. 820.   **E. Gerhardt Recital**—announced for this number, but not issued. See footnote[1]

‡ Sca. 821   [1] **E. Clément Recital**
(Barbiere, Roméo et Juliette, Manon, Lakmé, Cavalleria & Songs)

‡ Sca. 822   **R. Mayr & V. Maurel Recital**
(Domino Noir, Eugen Oniegin, Don Giovanni, Fidelio, Fliegende Holländer, Lohengrin, Siegfried, Otello, Falstaff & Songs)

‡ Vic. set LCT 6701   **50 Years of Great Operatic Singing**
(10ss)
1900-1910   Trovatore, Ballo, Don Carlos, Don Giovanni, Norma, Semiramide, Hamlet, Bohème, Favorita, Don Pasquale, Damnation de Faust, Hérodiade, Lustige Witwe, Carmen, Manon, Pagliacci.

1910-1920   Carmen, Macbeth, Manon, Aida, Puritani, Traviata, Bohème, Joseph, Manon Lescaut, Tosca, Gioconda, Reine de Saba.

1920-1930   Africaine, Chénier, Carmen, Fliegende Holländer, Guillaume Tell, Forza, Don Quichotte, Hamlet, Don Carlos, Prince Igor, Barbiere.

1930-1940   Don Giovanni, Figaro, Walküre, Oberon, Rosenkavalier, Lakmé, Ballo, Simone Boccanegra, Trovatore, Ernani, Chénier.

1940-1950   Louise, Damnation de Faust, Alceste, Contes d'Hoffmann; Grétry: Tableau Parlant; Trovatore, Norma, Traviata, Turandot, Porgy & Bess, Figaro, The Kiss, Lucia

[As we go to press, this set is announced as ‡ G.CSLP 500/41 10ss; it has not been possible to insert this no. under individua, titles.]

WELSH RECORDED MUSIC

We have no news of continued activity by the Society of the above name (see WERM & Supp. II) but the following issues continue the tradition, and are listed here although not strictly within our field.

‡ *Dely.EC 3133*   **Welsh Folk Songs** — ARR. O. Ellis
Nursery Songs: The little bird's song
The little boy's song
A shoeing song
The little old lady
Folk Songs: Oxen Song; Lisa Lân
Penillion: The Gypsy (Crwys)
Rabbits (Hoosen)
A sunset poem (D. Thomas)
Morte d'Arthur (T. Gwynn Jones)
O. ELLIS: Folk Song Suite vlc. & hp.
1. David of the white rock
2. A Welsh Carol
3. The cuckoo
4. Hunting the hare
5. Sweet Maiden
D. Ffrangcon Thomas (vlc.), O. Ellis (voice & hp.)

‡ *Dely.EC 3134*   **8 Favourite Welsh Airs** — ARR. T. & ORCH. Ellis
1. All through the night
2. Over the stone
3. Watching the wheat
4. The old minstrel
5. The Dove
6. In the Vale of Clwyd
7. Farewell to Wales
8. If it were summer ever
B. Powell & Orch. of Wales str.
—Ffrangcon Thomas

‡ *EFL.FP 835*   **Welsh Folk Songs**
Meredydd Evans (T)

YALE UNIVERSITY
VOL. I
MONTEVERDI: Lagrime d'amanti al sepolcro dell' amata 1614
WEELKES: O care, thou wilt despatch me (& Hence care, thou art too cruel) 5 vv. 1600
A sparrow-hawk proud 6 vv. 1600
GESUALDO: Dolcissima mia vita (Book V) 5 vv. 1611
Io pur respiro (Book VI) 5 vv. 1611
J. S. BACH: Motet: Singet dem Herrn ein neues Lied
Yale Univ. Music School Cho.—Hindemith
‡ Over.LP 4

VOL. II
PEROTIN-le-Grand: Alleluya (nativitas)
DUFAY: Mass 'Ave Regina cælorum'—Kyrie, only
PALESTRINA: Mass 'Sine Nomine'—Credo, only
LASSUS: Lagrime di San Pietro:
... No. 7, Ogni occhio del Signor
... No. 17, Ah, quanti gia felici
Im Lant zu Wirtemberg
HANDL: Mirabile mysterium (*Opus musicum*, 1586)
G. GABRIELI[2]: Nunc dimittis 3 five-vv. chos.
Virtute magna 2 six-vv. chos.
Yale Univ. Music School Cho.—Hindemith
‡ Over.LP 5

---

[1] In the 1956 Catalogue, received just as we go to press, the Onegin recital is given the number 821, the Clément is 819, and 820 is a recital by J. McCormack.
[2] Trs. Hindemith from Vienna MS.

APPENDIX I

PRE-RECORDED TAPES

A Summary of such information as is available of the tapes listed in December 1955, arranged under makes and numbers. The bulk of this list is also available in disc form and fuller details of artists and works will be found in the body of this or previous volumes.

No.	Composer	Title	Artist	Speed inches per sec.	No. of tracks
AMERITAPE (U.S.A.)					
101	PROKOFIEV	Pf. Sonata No. 2	E. Gilels	7½	1 or 2
	SHOSTAKOVICH	Preludes & Fugues, Op. 89	Shostakovich		
102	SCRIABIN	Concerto, pf. & orch.	Feinberg	..	..
	GLIER	Romance, vln. & orch.	Oistrakh		
103	TCHAIKOVSKY	Str. Qtt. No. 1	Oistrakh Qtt.	..	..
104	MIASKOVSKY	Str. Qtt. No. 13	Beethoven Qtt.	..	..
	GLAZOUNOV	Melody, Op. 20 No. 1	M. Rostropovich		
AUDIOSPHERE* (U.S.A.)					
701	SCHUBERT	Symphony No. 8		7½	1 or 2
	SIBELIUS	Finlandia			
702	WAGNER	Tannhäuser Overture		..	..
		Fl. Holländer Overture			
703	MOUSSORGSKY	Night on the Bare Mountain		..	..
	BORODIN	Prince Igor—Dances			
	SIBELIUS	Valse triste			
704	DEBUSSY	Prélude à l'après-midi . . .		..	..
	SCHUMANN	Manfred Overture			
	GLINKA	Kamarinskaya			
705	ROSSINI	Guillaume Tell, Overture		..	..
	BRAHMS	Akademisches Fest-Ouvertüre			
	MASSENET	Scenes alsaciennes, excerpt			
		all the above	Florence—Gui		
708	DUKAS	L'Apprenti sorcier	Gui	..	..
	PFITZNER	Kleine Sinfonie, Op. 44	Rapf		
		[Above also as Stereophonic tapes, nos. 701BN, etc.]			
Aud. 1	SIBELIUS	Finlandia; Valse triste		..	2
	GRIEG	Peer Gynt Suite 1			
	WAGNER	Overtures			
Aud. 2	DEBUSSY	Prélude à l'après-midi . . .		..	..
	DUKAS	L'Apprenti sorcier			
	BORODIN	Prince Igor, Dances			
	ROSSINI	Guillaume Tell, Overture			
Aud. 3	SCHUMANN	Manfred Overture		..	..
	BRAHMS	Akademisches Fest-Ouv.			
	SCHUBERT	Sym. No. 8			
		all these by	Florence—Gui		
	PFITZNER	Kleine Sinfonie	K. Rapf		
Aud. 8	J. S. BACH	Toccata & Fugue, D mi.		..	..
		Passacaglia, C minor			
	C. FRANCK	Choral No. 3			
	MENDELSSOHN	Sonata No. 2	K. Rapf (org.)		
		[Bach & Mendelssohn items also stereophonic, 711/2BN]			
A. V. TAPES (U.S.A.)					
306 (also 1502)	GRANADOS	Goyescas	F. Valenzi	3¾ or 7½	1 or 2
307 (& 1503)	J. STRAUSS II	Waltzes	Austrian—Wöss	..	..
308 (& 1504)	RIMSKY-K.	Golden Cockerel Suite	Singer	..	..
	DEBUSSY	L'Après-midi . . .	Moreau		
607 (& 1505)	C. FRANCK	Chorals Nos. 2 & 3		..	..
	BRAHMS	Ch.—Prel., O wie selig. . . .	R. Owen (org.)		
1001	GOUNOD	Faust, Ballet excerpts	Anon. orch.	..	..
	TCHAIKOVSKY	Nutcracker Suite			
1002	SCHUBERT	Symphony No. 9	Wöss	..	..
	DELIBES	Coppélia, excerpts	Schönherr		

No.	Composer	Title	Artist	Speed inches per sec.	No. of tracks
A. V. TAPES (U.S.A.)—*continued*					
1003	TCHAIKOVSKY	Romeo & Juliet	Wöss	3¾ or	1 or 2
	RACH-MANINOFF	Pf. Concerto No. 2	Karrer	7½	
	CHOPIN	Études, Op. 25, Nos. 1-3	Jenner		
1004	J. STRAUSS	Overtures, etc.	Schönherr, Günther	..	..
1005	BRAHMS	Symphony No. 4	Wöss	..	..
	HAYDN	Symphony No. 88	P. Walter		
1006	MOZART	Sinfonia Concertante, K 297b	Wöss	..	..
		Symphony No. 41	Wöss		
1007	DVOŘÁK	Symphony No. 5	Singer	..	..
	MOZART	Symphony No. 35	Wolf		
1008	TCHAIKOVSKY	Symphony No. 5	Wöss	..	..
	RIMSKY-K.	Capriccio espagnol	Mehlich		
1009	GRIEG	Pf. Concerto, A minor	Karrer	..	..
	SCHUBERT	Symphony No. 6	Wöss		
1010	BEETHOVEN	Symphony No. 4	Singer	..	..
	MOZART	Symphony No. 28	P. Walter		
		Cassation, unspec.			
1011	BEETHOVEN	Egmont, Coriolan Ovs.	Wolf	..	..
		Pf. Concerto No. 5	Karrer		
1012	TCHAIKOVSKY	The Tempest	Wöss	..	..
	BEETHOVEN	Symphony No. 6	Wöss		
1013	BRAHMS	Symphony No. 2	Wolf	..	..
	MENDELSSOHN	Ruy Blas Overture	Singer		
	ROSSINI	Guillaume Tell, Ov.	Wöss		
1014	MOZART	Pf. Concerto, K 466	Weidlich	..	..
	SCHUBERT	Symphony No. 4	Wöss		
1015	TCHAIKOVSKY	Vln. Concerto	Auclair	..	..
		1812 Overture	Singer		
	LISZT	Les Préludes	Singer		
1016	BEETHOVEN	Symphony No. 7	Wöss	..	..
	PAGANINI	Vln. Concerto No. 1	Gitlis		
1017	BEETHOVEN	Pf. Sonatas 30, 31	Demus	..	..
	CHOPIN	Impromptu No. 4			
		Polonaise No. 6			
		Scherzo No. 3	A. Jenner		
1018	MENDELSSOHN	Fair Melusina Ov.	Austrian Sym.	..	..
	BRAHMS	Symphony No. 1			
	BEETHOVEN	Namensfeier Ov.			
1019	MOUSSORGSKY	Pictures from an Exhibition	S. Biro (pf.)	..	..
	IPP.-IVANOFF	Caucasian Sketches	Wöss		
	SARASATE	Romanza andaluza	I. Gitlis, H. Berg.		
1020	MOZART	Serenade No. 13	Weidlich	..	..
		Pf. Concerto, K 491	Biro		
		Thamos, Entractes	Günther		
1021	HAYDN	Symphony No. 104	Annovazzi	..	..
	MOZART	Pf. Concerto, K 488	Kilenyi		
1022	HAYDN	Vlc. Concerto, D major	Cassadó	..	..
	MOZART	Sym. 33; Figaro Ov.	Heger		
1023	MENDELSSOHN	Midsummer Night's Dream, excerpts	Austrian Sym.	..	..
	SCHUBERT	Symphony No. 5	Paulmüller		
1024	TCHAIKOVSKY	Pf. Concerto No. 1	Schwartmann	..	..
	HAYDN	Symphony No. 7	Austrian Sym.		
1025	VERDI	Requiem Mass, excerpts	Koslik	..	..
1028	BEETHOVEN	Symphony No. 2	H-J. Walther	..	..
	WEBER	Oberon Overture			
	RESPIGHI	Pini di Roma			
1029	J. S. BACH	Suite No. 3	H-J. Walther	..	..
	HAYDN	Pf. Concerto, C major			
	CORELLI	Suite for Strings			
1030	SIBELIUS	Origin of Fire, etc.	Johnson	..	..
	DVOŘÁK	Symphony No. 4			
	[Sibelius also on 1508; Dvořák on 1507]				
1031	CLEMENTI	Sonata, G major		..	..
	LISZT	Paganini Étude No. 3			
	MOZART	Variations, K.Anh. 209b			
	SCHUMANN	Carnaval	S. Bianca (pf.)		

No.	Composer	Title	Artist	Speed inches per sec.	No. of tracks
A. V. TAPES (U.S.A.)—*continued*					
1511	A. BLOCH PROKOFIEV	Pf. Concerto Symphony No. 1	Bianca H-J. Walther	3¾ or 7½	1 or 2
1512	DELIBES BIZET	Sylvia, Suite Carmen, Suite	H-J. Walther	..	..
1513	SAINT-SAËNS TOCH	Carnaval des animaux Pinocchio Overture	H-J. Walther	..	..
1514	ELGAR SIEGMEISTER	Wand of Youth Suite 1 Ozark set	H-J. Walther	..	..
1516	BIZET SCHUMANN	Jeux d'enfants Kinderszenen	Bianca & Takajian (pfs.)	..	..
1517	BRAHMS DVOŘÁK MOUSSORGSKY SMETANA	Hungarian Dance No. 6 Slav. Dances Nos. 1, 3, 10 Gopak Bartered Bride—Dances	H-J. Walther	..	..
1518	GARDINER E. COATES POWELL	Shepherd Fennel's Dance London Suite In old Virginia	H-J. Walther	..	..
1519	KILPINEN, etc.	Part-Songs	Helsinki Cho.	..	..
5008	MOZART HANDEL	Les Petits Riens Serenade 13, excerpt Don Giovanni—Minuet Water & Fireworks Music Serse—Largo	H-J. Walther	..	..
5009	SCHUBERT PIERNÉ LIADOV MacDOWELL	Marche militaire Cydalise—Marche Marche des petits soldats Enchanted Lake Musical box Russian Dance No. 4 From Uncle Remus Of Br'er Rabbit	H-J. Walther	..	..
5010	SCHUMANN RAVEL	Kinderszenen Ma Mère l'oye	S. Bianca	..	..
5012	BOCCHERINI SKILTON GUION DUBENSKY	Quintet, E ma.—Minuet War Dance of the Cheyennes Turkey in the straw Gossips, etc.	H-J. Walther	..	..
5013	TCHAIKOVSKY	Nutcracker Suite Str. Qtt.—Andante cantabile	H-J. Walther Bartels Ens.	..	..
5014	J. STRAUSS E. GERMAN QUILTER	An der s. b. Donau Nell Gwyn suite Children's Overture	H-J. Walther	..	..
5015	GRIEG	Peer Gynt Suite, etc.	H-J. Walther	..	..
5016	MENDELSSOHN	Midsummer Night's Dream, excerpts	H-J. Walther	..	..
5017	DEBUSSY SAINT-SAËNS HALVORSEN	Children's Corner Phaeton Entry of the Boyars	H-J. Walther	..	..
5018	ROSSINI D. SCARLATTI CHOPIN	Guillaume Tell, Ov. Sonatas, L 413, 499 Polonaise No. 6 Prelude No. 15	H-J. Walther H. Unruh (hpsi.) S. Bianca	..	..
5019	J. S. BACH TOCH HUMPERDINCK	Suite No. 3 Minuets Weihnachtsoratorium, Nos. 5, 9 Pinocchio Overture Hansel & Gretel Ov.	H-J. Walther H. Unruh Bach Fest. Cho. H-J. Walther	..	..
5020	GLUCK HAYDN	Orphée, Nos. 28, 29, 30 Sym. 94—Andante Toy Symphony Str. Qtt. Op. 76-3, 2nd movt.	H-J. Walther Bartels Ens.	..	..
5021	VERDI RIMSKY-K. WAGNER	Aida—March Sadko—Chant hindoue Tsar Saltan—Bumble bee Snow Maiden—Dance of Tumblers Walküre—Ride & Feuerzauber	H-J. Walther	..	..
BERKSHIRE (U.S.A.)					
B2101	BEETHOVEN	Pf. Concerto No. 5	A. Biondi & Marseilles Phil.—Mandel	7½	2
B2102	BRAHMS	Symphony No. 4	Cremona Sym.—Curci	..	..

No.	Composer	Title	Artist	Speed inches per sec.	No. of tracks

BERKSHIRE (U.S.A.)—continued

No.	Composer	Title	Artist	Speed inches per sec.	No. of tracks
B2103	BRAHMS	Vln. Concerto	E. Gastaldi & Monaco Sym.—Gillet	7½	2
B2104	BEETHOVEN	Syms. 1 & 4	Marseilles—Mandel	..	..
B2105	SCHUBERT	Symphony No. 9	Oberammergau Sym.—Schwertfeger	..	..
B2106	GOUNOD BIZET MASSENET	Faust Ballet L'Arlésienne Suite Thais—Ballet	.. .. ..	..	..
B2107	TCHAIKOVSKY	Symphony No. 6		..	..
B2108	ROSSINI VERDI DONIZETTI	G. Tell & Barbiere Ovs. Aida & Forza Ovs. Figlia del R. & Don Pasquale Ovs.	San Remo Op.—Trucchi	..	..
B2109	CHABRIER J. STRAUSS ST. SAENS LISZT	Espana Fledermaus Ov. Danse macabre Hung. Rhapsody No. 1, etc.	Cremona Sym.—Curci	..	..
B2110	KHACHA- TURIAN PROKOFIEV BORODIN	Vlc. Concerto Love for 3 Oranges, Suite Prince Igor—Dances	Kazach & Strasbourg Sym.—Renair	..	..
B2111	J. STRAUSS & HELLMESBERGER—Waltzes		Fr. Light—Melou	..	..
B2112	J. STRAUSS, MILLÖCKER, etc.—Selections		..	..	..
B8001	BEETHOVEN	Pf. Concerto No. 1 Syms. 1 & 4	A. Biondi Marseilles Phil.—Mandel	3¾	2
B8002	J. S. BACH HAYDN	Concertos, 3 & 4 claviers Trumpet Concerto Horn Concerto, D major Symphonies 6, 7, 8	Heiller Wobitsch Koch Litschauer	..	..
B8003	As B2106 & 2109, above			..	..
B8006	As B2111 & 2112, above			..	..
B9001	MOZART	Don Giovanni, complete	Swarowsky	..	..
BH1001	..	.. (3 reels)	..	7½	2
BH1002	HAYDN	Die Schöpfung, complete (2 reels)	Krauss	..	..
BH1003	BACH HAYDN	Concertos, 3 & 4 claviers Trumpet Concerto Horn Concerto, D major	Heiller Wobitsch Koch	..	..
BH1004	HAYDN	Symphonies 6, 7, 8	Litschauer	..	..
BH1005	MOZART	Serenade No. 9, K 320	Sternberg	..	..
BH1006	MOZART	Don Giovanni, arias	Swarowsky	..	..
PM101	GERSHWIN	Pf. Concerto; Rhapsody in Blue	S. Bianca, H-J. Walther	..	..

BLUEBIRD (U.S.A.) (See also VICTOR, below)

No.	Composer	Title	Artist	Speed inches per sec.	No. of tracks
TB4	TCHAIKOVSKY	Swan Lake excerpts	Irving	7½	2

BOSTON (U.S.A.)

No.	Composer	Title	Artist	Speed inches per sec.	No. of tracks
BO7-1	BACH, FIOCCO, MOZART, BRÉVAL, HAYDN		Grumiaux (vln.), Mayes (vlc.)	7½	2
BO7-2	BRITTEN CHAVEZ FARBERMAN	Serenade Toccata Evolution	Lloyd Members Boston Sym.	..	..

COLUMBIA (G.B.)

No.	Composer	Title	Artist	Speed inches per sec.	No. of tracks
CAT251	BRAHMS	Symphony No. 1	Karajan	7½	2
CAT252	TCHAIKOVSKY	Sleeping Beauty & Swan Lake excerpts	Karajan	..	..
CAT253	RACH- MANINOFF	Concerto 2, & Preludes	G. Anda	..	..
CAT254	MENDELSSOHN	Midsummer Night's Dream	Kletzki	..	..
CAT255	SIBELIUS	Sym. 5, & Finlandia	Karajan	..	..
CAT256	BORODIN IPP.-IVANOFF	Symphony No. 2 Caucasian Sketches	Kletzki	..	..
CAT257	DEBUSSY RAVEL	La Mer Rapsodie espagnole	Karajan	..	..

No.	Composer	Title	Artist	Speed inches per sec.	No. of tracks
COLUMBIA (G.B.)—*continued*					
CAT258	DEBUSSY RAVEL SATIE WEBER	Prélude à l'après-midi . . . Daphnis et Chloë, Suite 2 Parade Aufforderung zum Tanz	Markevitch	7½	2
CAT259	TCHAIKOVSKY DELIBES	Pf. Concerto No. 1 Coppélia—Valse lente	Anda	..	..
CAT260	BRAHMS	Vln. Concerto	Martzy	..	..
CAT261	OPERATIC RECITAL (Rigoletto, Favorita, etc.)		Gedda	..	..
CAT262/3	LEHAR	Lustige Witwe, Complete	Schwarzkopf, etc.	..	..
CAT264	BERLIOZ	Symphonie fantastique	Karajan	..	..
CAT265	ST. SAENS BRITTEN	Carnaval des animaux Young person's guide . . .	Markevitch	..	..
CAT266/7	PUCCINI	Tosca, complete	Sabata	..	..
CAT268	Opera INTERMEZZI (Carmen, Thaïs, etc.)		Karajan	..	..
CAT269	BEETHOVEN	Symphony No. 6	Karajan	..	..
CAT270	MOZART	Four Horn Concertos	D. Brain	..	..
CAT271	R. STRAUSS	Arabella—excerpts	Schwarzkopf	..	..
CAT272	BRAHMS	Str. Qtt. No. 3	Italian Qtt.	..	..
CAT273	TCHAIKOVSKY	Symphony No. 4	Karajan	..	..
CAT274	MOZART	Pf. Concertos, K 466, 503	Gieseking	..	..
CAT275	BRUCH PROKOFIEV	Vln. Concerto No. 1 Vln. Concerto No. 1	Oistrakh	..	..
CAT276/7	HUMPERDINCK	Hänsel & Gretel, complete	Schwarzkopf, etc.	..	..
CBT551	MENDELSSOHN	Symphony No. 4	Beecham	..	..
CBT552	SCHUMANN	Pf. Concerto	Gieseking	..	..
CBT553	SIBELIUS	Vln. Concerto	Oistrakh	..	..
CBT554	R. STRAUSS	Capriccio—Final scene 4 Letzte Lieder	Schwarzkopf	..	..
CCT651	DVOŘÁK	Symphony No. 5	Galliera	..	..
CCT652	RIMSKY-K.	Golden Cockerel Suite Tsar Saltan Suite	Dobrowen	..	..
CCT653	DVOŘÁK	Symphony No. 4 Scherzo capriccioso	Sawallisch	..	..
CCT654	ELGAR	In the South Sea Pictures	Weldon Ripley	..	..
CDT851	RESPIGHI	Boutique fantasque	Galliera	..	..
Stereophonic tapes					
BTA101/2	SIBELIUS	Symphony No. 2	Kletzki	7½	2
BTA103	MOZART	Songs—Vol. 1	Schwarzkopf	..	..
BTC501	BACH	Cantata No. 6	Jacques	..	..
CONCERTAPES (U.S.A.) Stereophonic only: same titles as WEBCOR, *q.v.*					
CONNOISSEUR (U.S.A.)					
D100/1 (2 reels)	VERDI	Un Ballo in Maschera, complete	Leibowitz	7½	2
D102	MENDELSSOHN	Symphony No. 1 Pf. Concerto No. 2	v. Hoogstraten Balsam	..	..
D103	MOZART	Symphonies 19, 24 Clemenza, Schauspieldirektor Ovs. Pf. Concerto, K 175	Lund, Michael Gimpel	..	..
D104	BOCCHERINI MOZART CORELLI VIVALDI	Vlc. Concerto Horn Concerto K 447, ARR. Sonata, D ma. vlc. & pf. Concerto Op. 3 No. 9, ARR.	Starker	..	..
D105	CHOPIN	Pf. Concertos Nos. 1 & 2	Musulin	..	..
D106	RAVEL	Septet; & Recital	E. Vito (hp.), etc.	..	..

No.	Composer	Title	Artist	Speed inches per sec.	No. of tracks
ESOTERIC* (U.S.A.)					
ES5-1	—	English Mediæval Carols	N.Y. Pro Musica Antiqua	7½	1 or 2
ES5-2	GABRIELI	Canzonas	N.Y. Brass Ens.	..	..
ES5-3	—	XVIIIth Cent. Harp Music	Zabaleta	..	..
ES5-7	TAILLEFERRE, etc.	Harp Recital	Zabaleta	..	2
ES5-8	PURCELL	Songs	Oberlin	..	1 or 2
ES7-9D	ROUSSEL	Festin de l'araignée Le Marchand de sable. . . .	Leibowitz	..	..
	POULENC	Le Bal masqué	Fendler		
HIS MASTER'S VOICE (G.B.)					
HTA1	BEETHOVEN	Pf. Concertos 2 & 4	Solomon	7½	2
HTA2	MENDELSSOHN BEETHOVEN	Vln. Concerto Romances	Menuhin	..	..
HTA3	TCHAIKOVSKY	Symphony No. 6	Cantelli	..	..
HTA4	DVOŘÁK	Symphony No. 4	Kubelik	..	..
HTA5	BEETHOVEN	Symphony No. 6	Furtwängler	..	..
HTA6	SCHUBERT	Symphony No. 9	Barbirolli	..	..
HTA7	HAYDN MOZART	Symphony No. 60 Symphony No. 38	Gui	..	..
HTA8	BEETHOVEN	Vln. Concerto	Menuhin	..	..
HTA9/10	VERDI	Il Trovatore, Complete	Björling, etc.	..	..
HTA11	TURINA	Canto a Sevilla	de los Angeles	..	..
HTA12	BEETHOVEN	Symphony No. 5	Furtwängler	..	..
HTA13	FALLA	La Vida Breve	de los Angeles	..	..
HTA14	BUSONI	Arlecchino	Glyndebourne Co.	..	..
HTA15	VIVALDI	Concertos, Op. 8 Nos. 1-4	Fasano	..	..
HTA16	WAGNER LISZT	Lohengrin, Tannhäuser Preludes Les Préludes	Furtwängler	..	..
HTA17	ELGAR	Enigma Variations Wand of Youth Suite 1	Boult	..	..
HTA18	SCHUMANN	Carnaval; Études symphoniques	Cortot	..	..
HTA19	OPERATIC RECITAL (Ernani, Otello, Bohème, etc.)		de los Angeles	..	..
HTA20	BEETHOVEN	Symphony No. 4	Furtwängler	..	..
HTB401	SCHUMANN	Symphony No. 4	Cantelli	..	..
HTB402	BEETHOVEN	Pf. Concerto No. 3	Fischer	..	..
HTB403	R. STRAUSS	Don Juan; Till	Furtwängler	..	..
HTB404	RIMSKY-K. CHABRIER DEBUSSY	Capriccio espagnol España Prélude à l'après-midi . . .	Barbirolli	..	..
HTB405	ELGAR	Vlc. Concerto	Tortelier	..	..
HTB406	MOUSSORGSKY	Pictures from an Exhibition	Kubelik	..	..
HTB407	SCHUMANN	Liederkreis	Fischer-Dieskau	..	..
HTC601	SCHUBERT	Symphonies Nos. 4 & 5	H. Blech	..	..
HTC602	SCHUMANN CHOPIN	Carnaval (ORCH.) Les Sylphides	Irving	..	..
HTC604	GRIEG RACH-MANINOFF	Pf. Concerto Pf. Concerto No. 1	Lympany	..	..
HTC606	TCHAIKOVSKY	Swan Lake, excerpts	Irving	..	..
HTC607	SCHUMANN GRIEG	Pf. Concerto Pf. Concerto	Moiseiwitsch	..	..
HTC608	RACH-MANINOFF MENDELSSOHN	Pf. Concerto No. 2 Capriccio brillant	Lympany	..	..

No.	Composer	Title	Artist	Speed inches per sec.	No. of tracks
H.M.V. (G.B.)—*continued*					
HTC609	WEBER LISZT SCHUBERT	Euryanthe Overture Les Préludes Symphony No. 8	Schwarz	7½	2
HTD804	OFFENBACH	Gaîté parisienne	Susskind	..	..
HTD806	WEBER HÉROLD TCHAIKOVSKY	Oberon Overture Zampa Overture 1812 Overture	Malko	..	..
Stereophonic Tapes SAT1000/1	DVOŘÁK	Vlc. Concerto	Tortelier	7½	2
SAT1002	BIZET	Jeux d'enfants (ORCH.)	Gui	..	..
SAT1003/4 1006/7	MOZART	Nozze di Figaro—Acts 1 & 2, excerpts	Glyndebourne (4 tapes)	..	..
SBT1250	—	"Homage to Pavlova"	Kurtz	..	..
SCT1500	TCHAIKOVSKY	Nutcracker Suite	Malko	..	..
SDT1750	PROKOFIEV	Symphony No. 1	Malko	..	..
HI-FI (U.S.A.)		All discs are also available on tape, with similar nos.		7½ & 15	2 & 1
LYRICHORD (U.S.A.) LY5-2	CHOPIN	Impromptus; Berceuse; Tarantella	Balogh	7½	2
LY5-3	—	Elizabethan Love Songs Harpsichord Recital	Cuénod Chiasson	..	..
LY5-5D	J. S. BACH	Cantatas 65 & 106	Wagner Cho.	..	..
MUSIC TAPE SOCIETY (U.S.A.) n.d.	MOZART VAINBERG PROKOFIEV SHOSTAKOVICH	Vln. Concerto 7, K 271a Moldavian Rhapsody Stone Flower Ballet Ballet Suites 1-3	Oistrakh .. Samosud Stassevitch	n.d.	n.d.
MUSIKON (U.S.A.) 506	MEDTNER LISZT RACH- MANINOFF	Primavera, Op. 39, No. 2 Étude, D flat major Prelude, Op. 32, No. 12, etc.	A. Mundy	3¾ or 7½	1 or 2
507	RAVEL MEDTNER ARENSKY	Sonatina Fairy Tale, Op. 34, No. 2 Prelude, A minor, etc.	A. Mundy	..	..
601	GRIEG	Pf. Concerto	G. Johannesen	..	..
602	TARTINI VITALI	Sonata, G minor Chaconne	Odnoposoff	..	..
604	BEETHOVEN	Symphony No. 5	Ackermann	..	..
MUSITAPES (U.S.A.) C200	MASCAGNI	(or TEMPOTAPES) Cavalleria Rusticana, excpts.	Unspec. cast	7½	2
C202	VERDI	Aida, excpts.	..	..	..
OCEANIC (U.S.A.) OC7-4	CORELLI GLUCK HANDEL	Oboe Concerto Flute Concerto Oboe Concerto "No. 4" Org. Concertos 13, 14	Pierlot Rampal Kamesch Leonhardt	7½	2
OC7-5	BEETHOVEN HAYDN BIZET	Wellingtons Sieg König Stephan Overture Toy Symphony Symphony No. 1	Leibowitz	..	..
OMEGATAPE (U.S.A.) 5001	TCHAIKOVSKY	Nutcracker Suite	London Pro Musica —S. Burton	7½	2
5002	TCHAIKOVSKY	Serenade, Op. 48	Vicars	..	..
5007	MOZART	Pf. Concerto, K 467	Fiorentino	..	..

No.	Composer	Title	Artist	Speed inches per sec.	No. of tracks
OMEGATAPE (U.S.A.)—*continued*					
6001	MOZART	Divertimenti K 136-8	Vicars	7½	2
6002	BEETHOVEN	Pf. Concerto No. 3	Vitebsky	..	..
6005	LISZT	Malédiction Angélus (A. de P.) (ORCH.) Am Grabe R. Wagners	I. Kohler & orch. —Vicars Kohler	..	..
6006	J. S. BACH	Clavier Concertos, D mi., F ma.	J. Saxby (hpsi.) & London Mozart Ens. —Vicars	..	..
6007	MOZART	Serenade No. 13, K 525 Divertimento, K 247 (or Dances)	London Mozart Ens. —Vicars	..	..
6008	TCHAIKOVSKY	Elegy. str. orch. The Tempest	Fekete	..	..
6010	BEETHOVEN	Pf. Sonata Nos. 8, 14	Vitebsky	..	..
7001	RACH- MANINOFF	Pf. Concerto No. 1	S. Fiorentino & C. A. Sym.—Vicars	..	..
7005	KODÁLY PROKOFIEV	A Summer Evening Summer Day Suite	Vicars	..	..
7006	MENDELSSOHN	Vln. Concerto	J. Pougnet & Orch. —Vicars	..	..
7007	TCHAIKOVSKY	Ov. on Danish Nat. Hymn, Op. 15 Ov. to Ostrovsky's The Storm, Op. 76	Orch.—Vicars	..	..
3001	RIMSKY-K.	Scheherazade	Haefner	..	..
SONOTAPE (U.S.A.) Stereophonic only					
SW1001	BEETHOVEN	Symphony No. 5	Scherchen	7½	2
SW1002	TCHAIKOVSKY	1812 Overture Romeo & Juliet Overture	Scherchen	..	..
SW1003	RACH- MANINOFF	Pf. Concerto No. 2	Farnadi	..	..
SW1004	WALTON	Belshazzar's Feast	Boult, Noble	..	..
SW1005	HONEGGER MOSSOLOV REVUELTAS CHABRIER	Pacific 231 Steel Foundry Sensemayá España	Scherchen Quadri	..	..
SW1006	BRAHMS	Symphony No. 2	Boult	..	..
SW1007	SHOSTAKOVICH	Symphony No. 1	Mitchell	..	..
SW1008	BEETHOVEN	Trio, Op. 97 Pf. Sonatas Nos. 8, 13	Fournier, Janigro, Skoda Badura-Skoda	..	..
SW1010	J. STRAUSS	Waltzes, Polkas, etc.	Deutschmeister Band	..	..
SW1011	J. S. BACH	Toccatas, D mi., E ma., F ma.	Weinrich	..	..
SW5001	HOLST	The Planets	Boult	..	..
TAPE OF THE MONTH (U.S.A.)					
B507s	BEETHOVEN MOZART	Deutsche Tänze Deutsche Tänze	Leibowitz	7½	2
B509s	BARAB	A Child's Garden of Verses	Oberlin	..	..
TEFIFON (Italy)					
TA/K4001	MOZART	Serenade 13 Deutsche Tänze K 600, Nos. 1, 2, 3, 5; K 602, No. 3	Berlin Charlottenburg —Blech	n.d.	n.d.
TA/K4002	MOZART	Serenade No. 9, K 320	..		
TA/K4004	BIZET	Carmen, Preludes; Arlésienne Suite 2	..		
TA/K4005	CORELLI	Concerto Grosso, Op. 6 No. 8	Vienna Sym.—Moralt		
TA/S4006	SCHUMANN MENDELSSOHN	Kinderszenen Songs without words (unspec.)	W. Stech (pf.)		
TA/K4007	SCHUMANN SCHUBERT	Papillons Moment musical, Op. 94, No. 3 Impromptu, Op. 142, No. 3	G. Puchelt		

No.	Composer	Title	Artist	Speed inches per sec.	No. of tracks
TEFIFON (Italy)—*continued*					
TA/K4009	WAGNER	Meistersinger, Tannhäuser Ovs.	Berlin Charlottenburg —Blech	n.d.	n.d.
TA/K4010	MOZART	Horn Quintet, K 407	Freiberg & Stross Qtt.		
TA/K4013	VERDI	Aida—Prelude & March Forza Overture	Berlin Charlottenburg —Blech		
TA/K4014	LISZT HOFMANN	Polonaise No. 2 Hungarian Rhapsody No. 12 Kaleidoscope	S. Cherkassky		
TA/K4015	BEETHOVEN	Sonata 8; Andante favori	H. E. Riebensahm		
TA/K4016	WEBER	Cl. Quintet, B♭ ma., Op. 34	L. Wlach, Stross Qtt.		
TA/K4017	MENDELSSOHN	Midsummer Night's Dream, excerpts	Cho. & Vienna Sym.— Krauss		
TA/K4018	SCHUBERT	Symphony No. 4	Vienna Sym.—Sacher		
TA/K4019	SCHUBERT	Octet, Op. 166	Stross Qtt. & Members Vienna Phil.		
TC/K4020	BEETHOVEN	Septet, Op. 20	Stross Qtt. & Members Vienna Phil.		
TA/K4021	MOZART	Pf. Qtt., K 478	Riebensahm, Stross Qtt.		
TA/K4022	RAVEL	Str. Qtt., F major	Amsterdam Qtt.		
TC/K4023	BEETHOVEN	Pf. Sonata No. 26	Riebensahm		
TA/K4024	BEETHOVEN	Rondo a capriccio, Op. 129 Variations on 'Bei Männern' Varns. on 'Ich bin der Schneider Kakadu', Op. 121a	Riebensahm R. Metzmacher & do. Stross Trio		
TA/K4025	BEETHOVEN	Pf. Sonatas 14, 25	Riebensahm		
TA/K4026	BEETHOVEN	Fantasia, Op. 80, pf. cho. orch.	Krauss		
TA/K4027	BERLIOZ	Harold in Italy	Breitenbach, Moralt		
TC/K4028	WAGNER	Tannhäuser, Act III	Elmendorff		
TD/K4030	MOZART	Serenade No. 7, K 250	Krauss		
TC/K4031	BEETHOVEN	Symphony No. 6	Klemperer		
TC/K4032	HAYDN	Mass, "Theresien"	Krauss		
TD/K4033	HINDEMITH	Requiem	Hindemith		
TA/K4034	J. STRAUSS	Polkas & Waltzes	Paulik		
TB/K4035	BEETHOVEN	Str. Qtt. No. 12, Op. 127	Amsterdam Qtt.		
TA/K4036	SCHÜTZ	Motets: Das ist wahr; Der Engel sprach; Also hat Gott; Selig sind die Toten; & Io moro	Vienna Academy Cho.		
TA/K4037	MOZART	Cl. Quintet, K 581	Wlach, Stross Qtt.		
TB/K4038	SCHUMANN	Pf. Concerto	Novães		
TB/K4039	BEETHOVEN	Pf. Concerto No. 3	Kraus		
TB/K4040	MOZART	Pf. Concerto, K 537	Kraus		
TB/K4041	GERSHWIN	Rhapsody in Blue American in Paris	Rivkin Dixon		
TC/K4042	BRUCKNER	Symphony No. 4	Klemperer		
TB/K4043	BEETHOVEN	Symphony No. 5	Klemperer		
TC/K4044	DVOŘÁK	Symphony No. 5	Horenstein		
TA/K4045	SCHUBERT J. HERBECK K. HEISLER	Zur Namensfeier des Herrn Andreas Ziller, D.83 Trinklied—Freunde, sammelt . . . D. 75 10 Deutsche Tänze 7 Deutsche Tänze	L. Hoppe (Bs) & Vienna Acad. Cho. Vienna Acad. Orch. —Grossmann		
TA/K4046	CHOPIN	Ballade No. 4; Mazurka 6; Polonaise, Op. 22	Vienna Pro Musica Orch. —Reinhardt		
TA/K4048	J. STRAUSS	Waltzes	E. Roon (S)		
TA/K4049	SCHUMANN SCHUBERT	Fantasia, Op. 131, vln. & orch. Motets	Stücki Kmentt & cho.		

No.	Composer	Title	Artist	Speed inches per sec.	No. of tracks
TEFIFON (Italy)—*continued*					
TA/K4050	J. STRAUSS	Waltzes	E. Roon (S)	n.d.	n.d.
TA/K4051	J. STRAUSS	Der lustige Krieg, Highlights	Cho. & Vienna St. Phil.—Pauspertl		
TB/K4056	CHOPIN	Piano recital	A. Mozzati		
TB/K4057	SCHUBERT C. FRANCK	Sonatina, Op. 137 No. 1 Vln. Sonata	C. Ferraresi & A. Beltrami		
TB/K4058	CHOPIN MENDELSSOHN SCHUMANN	Bolero, Op. 19; Mazurkas 2, 6, 19 Scherzo, E minor, Op. 16 Arabeske, Op. 18	A. Mozzati		
TB/K4060	TCHAIKOVSKY	Serenade, Op. 48	Orch.—Schuster		
TC/K4061	PUCCINI	Tosca, Highlights	Guarnieri		
TA/S2034	LEHAR	Lustige Witwe, selection	O. Gerdes Orch.		
VICTOR (U.S.A.)					
BC 1	TCHAIKOVSKY	Aurora's Wedding	Stokowski	7½	2
DC 2	TCHAIKOVSKY	Symphony No. 5	Stokowski	..	..
BC 3	R. STRAUSS	Don Quixote	Münch	..	..
BC 4	BEETHOVEN	Pf. Concerto No. 5	Horowitz	..	..
CC 6	BRAHMS	Pf. Concerto No. 2	Rubinstein	..	..
BC 7	DVOŘÁK	Symphony No. 5	Toscanini	..	..
CC 8	BRAHMS	Symphony No. 1	Toscanini	..	..
BC 9	C. FRANCK	Symphony [also BB.TB 1]	Leinsdorf	..	..
DC 10	GRIEG MENDELSSOHN	Pf. Concerto Pf. Concerto No. 1	Dorfmann [both also BB.TB 2]	..	..
BC 11	GERSHWIN GROFÉ	Rhapsody in Blue Grand Canyon—excerpts	Winterhalter [both also BB.TB 3]	..	..
DC 12	TCHAIKOVSKY	Swan Lake, excerpts	Irving	..	..
CC 13	CHOPIN ARNOLD	Les Sylphides English Dances	Irving	..	..
DC 14	OFFENBACH MEYERBEER	Gaîté parisienne Les Patineurs	Fiedler	..	..
CC 15	BRAHMS	Pf. Concerto No. 1	Rubinstein	..	..
CC 16	MOUSSORGSKY C. FRANCK	Pictures at an Exhibition Psyche et Éros	Toscanini	..	..
Stereophonic tapes ECS 1/ ECSD 1	R. STRAUSS	Also sprach Zarathustra	Reiner	7½	2
FCS 2/ FCSD 2	R. STRAUSS	Ein Heldenleben	Reiner	..	..
ECS 3/ ECSD 3	LIEBERMANN R. STRAUSS	Jazz Concerto Don Juan	Reiner	..	..
ECS 4/ ECSD 4	BRAHMS	Vln. Concerto	Heifetz, Reiner	..	..
WEB* (U.S.A.) 120P	PIANO RECITAL	(Bach, Beethoven, Chopin, etc.)	D. A. Mandell	7½	2
WEBCOR (U.S.A.) 2922-3	—	Recital (Haydn, Borodin, etc.)	Fine Arts Qtt.	7½	2
2922-4	DITTERSDORF TURINA WOLF	Str. Qtt., E flat major Oración del Torero Italienische Serenade	Fine Arts Qtt.	..	..
2923-1	DEBUSSY HAYDN GRANADOS RAVEL LISZT	Str. Qtt., Op. 10 Str. Qtt., Op. 76-2—Andante La Maja y el ruiseñor Alborada del Gracioso Sonetto del Petrarca (unspec.) Mephisto Waltz	Fine Arts Qtt. R. McDowell (pf.)	..	..

No.	Composer	Title	Artist	Speed inches per sec.	No. of tracks
WEBCOR (U.S.A.)—*continued*					
2923-2	DVOŘÁK	Str. Qtt., Op. 96	Fine Arts Qtt.	7½	2
	HAYDN	Str. Qtt., Op. 64-5—Adagio			
	BARTÓK	Rumanian Dances (unspec.)	L. Sorkin (vln.)		
	FALLA	Jota; etc.			
	BLOCH	Nigun; etc.	G. Sopkin (vlc.)		
2923-3	VIVALDI	Concerto grosso (unspec.)	Webcor Symphonette	..	..
	MOZART	Serenade No. 13			
	TCHAIKOVSKY	Serenade, Op. 48			
2923-4	HAYDN	Str. Qtt., Op. 3 No. 5	Fine Arts Qtt.	..	..
	MOZART	Str. Qtt. K 387			
2923-5	BOCCHERINI	Cello Quintet (unspec.)	Fine Arts Quintet	..	..
	SCHUBERT	Str. Qtt. Op. 125 No. 1	Fine Arts Qtt.		
	MENDELSSOHN	Octet	Fine Arts Ensemble		

NOTE. This list is not complete; there are other companies, particularly in U.S.A., issuing tapes, but either the musical interest is problematic, or data is lacking. For our next Supplement, where it is hoped to incorporate tapes into the body of the work, readers are asked to co-operate in sending all data possible, to enable full identifications of contents to be made.

Makes marked * in the above list are stated to supply other speeds and tracks, usually to special order.

APPENDIX II
CHRISTOPHORUS RECORDS

Just as we go to press, we learn of the existence of this series of records in Germany. Rather than defer them until our next Supplement, a condensed summary of the most interesting issues is given here. It has not been possible to give full identifications, nor to enter any of them under the composer entries.

T and *TG* series are 10-inch and 12-inch 78 r.p.m. normal discs.
TV and *TGV* series are 10-inch and 12-inch 78 r.p.m. "variable-microgroove" long playing discs.
Records with numbers between 70100 and 70200 are recordings made by Telefunken from 1934 to 1941. The others are modern recordings.

T 70115/8   Gregorian Chant
     Düsseldorf Singers & Cologne Cho. School

T 70119   PEROSI: Oremus pro Pontifice
T 70120   PEROSI: Tu es Petrus
T 70122   PEROSI: O sacrum convivium
     Sixtine Chapel Cho. (each with speech & music descriptive of Rome)

T 71500   J. G. WALTHER: Ch.-Prel.—Wachet auf!
     J. S. BACH: Ch. Prel.—Vom Himmel hoch (Fughetta) BWV. 701
     A. Ehret (hpsi.)
     DISTLER: Den geboren hat ein' Magd 4 vv.
     St. Blasien College Boys' Cho.

T 71503   PEPUSCH: Sonata, F major Alto recorder & cont.
     V. Noack & A. Ehret (hpsi.)

TV 71516   HANDEL: Organ Concerto, B flat major, Op. 4 No. 2
     Freiburg i. Br. Catholic Youth Ens.

TGV 71529   STAMITZ: Concerto No. 2, A major, Vlc. & orch.
     Freiburg i. Br. Hochschule Students' Ens.

TV 71534   TELEMANN: Trio-Sonata, B flat major
     V. Ehret-Noack (rec.), A. Ehret (hpsi.), B. Hummel (vlc.), E. Ehret ("Spinett").

TGV 71535   J. C. F. BACH (1732-1795): Sonata, D major
     V. Ehret-Noack (fl.), A. Ehret (hpsi.), B. Hummel (vlc.)

TGV 71540   J. S. BACH: W. T. C., Prels. & Fugues B flat major & G minor (unspec.)
     A. Ehret (hpsi.)

TV 71542   LOEILLET: Sonata, G major [I-3] fl. & cont.
     V. Ehret-Noack, A. Ehret (hpsi.), B. Hummel (vlc.)

TV 71550   HANDEL: Oboe Concerto No. 3, G minor
     Freiburg i. Br. Music Circle

T 71509   SCHÜTZ: So fahr' ich hin 5 vv. (MC. 11)
     Neuss Schütz Singers
     SCHÜTZ: Johannes-Passion—O hilf, Christe
     Düsseldorf St. Gregor Singers

T 71510   SCHÜTZ: Also hat Gott die Welt geliebt 5 vv. (MC. 12)
     OKEGHEM: Alma redemptoris Mater Motet 4 vv.

T 71511   SCHÜTZ: Verleih uns Frieden gnädiglich 5 vv. (MC. 4)
     LECHNER: O Tod, du bist ein' bittre Gallen 5 vv.
     Neuss Schütz Singers

T 71532   VICTORIA: O quam gloriosum 4 vv.
     MARENZIO: Super omnia ligna 4 vv.
     Düsseldorf St. Gregor Singers

T 71533   LASSUS: Surrexit pastor bonus 5 vv.
     JOSQUIN des Prés: Tu pauperum refugium 4 vv.

TGV 71543/4   JOSQUIN des Prés: Mass, 'Pange lingua' (4ss)
T 71545   SCHÜTZ: Matthäus-Passion—Ehre sei dir, Christe
     Herr, auf dich traue ich 5 vv. (MC. 9)

T 71546   LASSUS: Exaudi Deus Motet 4 vv.
     J. S. BACH: O Ewigkeit, du Donnerwort Choral

T 71547   REGER: Der Mensch lebt und besteht, Op. 138, No. 1 8 vv.
     L. WEBER: Lasst die Wurzel . . .
     Palestrina Singers

T 71531   AICHINGER: Maria uns tröst Motet 5 vv.
     JOSQUIN des Prés: In pace . . . Motet 3 vv.
     Neuss Schütz Singers

T 71501   BUXTEHUDE: In dulci jubilo U.52 3 vv. cho., vln. & hpsi.
     St. Blasien College Boys' Cho., Freiburg Hochschule Inst. Ens.

T 71505   ISAAC: Innsbruck, ich muss dich lassen
     VULPIUS: Die beste Zeit im Jahr ist mein
T 71506   M. FRANCK: Kommt, ihr' G'spielen
     OTHMAYER: Es ist kein Jäger; Est ist ein Schnee . . .
     Düsseldorf St. Gregor Singers

T 71507   VULPIUS: Hinunter ist der Sonne Schein 4 vv.
     HASSLER: Tantzen und Springen 4 vv.
     Chilean Folksong
     Santiago (Chile) Singers

T 71512   B. RÖVENSTRUNKT (b. 1290): Ich fahr' dahin (*Locheimer Liederbuch*)
     SCANDELLI: Schein uns, du liebe Sonne (*Frankfurter Liederbuch*)
     Neuss Schütz Singers

In addition to the above, there are numerous recordings of Hymns, Carols, Folksongs, and the like; and Speech and Educational discs.